Peterson's Two-Year Colleges

2011

About Peterson's

To succeed on your lifelong educational journey, you will need accurate, dependable, and practical tools and resources. That is why Peterson's is everywhere education happens. Because whenever and however you need education content delivered, you can rely on Peterson's to provide the information, know-how, and guidance to help you reach your goals. Tools to match the right students with the right school. It's here. Personalized resources and expert guidance. It's here. Comprehensive and dependable education content—delivered whenever and however you need it. It's all here.

For more information, contact Peterson's, 2000 Lenox Drive, Lawrenceville, NJ 08648; 800-338-3282 Ext. 54229.

Previous editions published as *Peterson's Annual Guide to Undergraduate Study,* © 1970, 1971, 1972, 1973, 1974, 1975, 1976, 1977, 1978, 1979, 1980, 1981, 1982, and as *Peterson's Guide to Two-Year Colleges,* © 1983, 1984, 1985, 1986, 1987, 1988, 1989, 1990, 1991, 1992, 1993, 1994, 1995, 1996, 1997, 1998, 1999, 2000, 2001, 2002, 2003, 2004, 2005, 2006, 2007, 2008, 2009

Stephen Clemente, Managing Director, Publishing and Institutional Research; Bernadette Webster, Director of Publishing; Jill C. Schwartz, Editor; Ward Brigham, Research Project Manager; Cathleen Fee, Research Associate; Phyllis Johnson, Programmer; Ray Golaszewski, Publishing Operations Manager; Linda M. Williams, Composition Manager; Karen Mount, Danielle Vreeland, Shannon White, Client Relations Representatives

ISSN 0894-9328
ISBN-13: 978-0-7689-2835-8
ISBN-10: 0-7689-2835-4

Printed in the United States of America

10 9 8 7 6 5 4 3 2 1 12 11 10

Forty-first Edition

By producing this book on recycled paper (40% post consumer waste) 220 trees were saved.

Contents

A Note from the Peterson's Editors v

THE COLLEGE ADMISSIONS PROCESS: AN OVERVIEW

What You Need to Know About Two-Year Colleges 3

Surviving Standardized Tests 5

Who's Paying for This? Financial Aid Basics 9

Frequently Asked Questions About Transferring 12

Returning to School: Advice for Adult Students 15

What International Students Need to Know About Admission to U.S. Colleges and Universities 19

Community Colleges and the New Green Economy 23

How to Use This Guide 27

QUICK-REFERENCE CHART

Two-Year Colleges At-a-Glance 37

PROFILES OF TWO-YEAR COLLEGES

U.S. and U.S. Territories 55

International 393

COLLEGE CLOSE-UPS

Featured Schools 396

APPENDIX

2009–10 Changes in Institutions 476

INDEXES

Associate Degree Programs at Two-Year Colleges 482

Associate Degree Programs at Four-Year Colleges 532

Alphabetical Listing of Two-Year Colleges 548

A Note from the Peterson's Editors

For more than 40 years, Peterson's has given students and parents the most comprehensive, up-to-date information on undergraduate institutions in the United States. Peterson's researches the data published in *Peterson's Two-Year Colleges* each year. The information is furnished by the colleges and is accurate at the time of publishing.

This guide also features advice and tips on the college search and selection process, such as how to decide if a two-year college is right for you, how to approach transferring between colleges, and what's in store for adults returning to college. If you seem to be getting more, not less, anxious about choosing and getting into the right college, *Peterson's Two-Year Colleges* provides just the right help, giving you the information you need to make important college decisions and ace the admission process.

Opportunities abound for students, and this guide can help you find what you want in a number of ways:

- "What You Need to Know About Two-Year Colleges" outlines the basic features and advantages of two-year colleges. "Surviving Standardized Tests" gives an overview of the common examinations students take prior to attending college. "Who's Paying for This? Financial Aid Basics" provides guidelines for financing your college education. "Frequently Asked Questions About Transferring" takes a look at the two-year college scene from the perspective of a student who is looking toward the day when he or she may pursue additional education at a four-year institution. "Returning to School: Advice for Adult Students" is an analysis of the pros and cons (mostly pros) of returning to college after already having begun a professional career. "What International Students Need to Know About Admission to U.S. Colleges and Universities" is an article written particularly for students overseas who are considering a U.S. college education. "Community Colleges and the New Green Economy" offers two insightful essays by Mary F. T. Spilde, President, Lane Community College and James DeHaven, V.P. of Economic and Business Development, Kalamazoo Valley Community College. Finally, "How to Use This Guide" gives details on the data in this guide: what terms mean and why they're here.

- If you already have specifics in mind, such as a particular institution or major, turn to the easy-to-use **Quick-Reference Chart** or **Indexes**. You can look up a particular feature—location and programs offered—or use the alphabetical index and immediately find the colleges that meet your criteria.

- For information about particular colleges, turn to the **Profiles of Two-Year Colleges** section. Here, our comprehensive college descriptions are arranged alphabetically by state. They provide a complete picture of need-to-know information about every accredited two-year college—from admission to graduation, including expenses, financial aid, majors, and campus safety. All the information you need to apply is placed together at the conclusion of each college **Profile.** In addition, two-page narrative descriptions, which appear as **College Close-Ups**, are paid for and written by college officials and offer great detail about each college. They are edited to provide a consistent format across entries for your ease of comparison.

Join the college search conversation on Facebook® and Twitter™ at www.facebook.com/find.colleges and www.twitter.com/find_colleges. Peterson's is committed to providing you with the most comprehensive and reliable directories to help you unlock opportunities and realize your educational aspirations.

Peterson's publishes a full line of books—education exploration, test prep, financial aid, and career preparation. Peterson's publications can be found at high school guidance offices, college libraries and career centers, and your local bookstore and library. Peterson's books are now also available as eBooks.

We welcome any comments or suggestions you may have about this publication. Your feedback will help us make educational dreams possible for you—and others like you.

Colleges will be pleased to know that Peterson's helped you in your selection. Admissions staff members are more than happy to answer questions, address specific problems and help in any way they can. The editors at Peterson's wish you great success in your college search.

The College Admissions Process:

AN OVERVIEW

What You Need to Know About Two-Year Colleges

David R. Pierce

Two-year colleges—better known as community colleges—are often called "the people's colleges." With their open-door policies (admission is open to individuals with a high school diploma or its equivalent), community colleges provide access to higher education for millions of Americans who might otherwise be excluded from higher education. Community college students are diverse and of all ages, races, and economic backgrounds. While many community college students enroll full-time, an equally large number attend on a part-time basis so they can fulfill employment and family commitments as they advance their education.

Community colleges can also be referred to as either technical or junior colleges, and they may either be under public or independent control. What unites two-year colleges is that they are regionally accredited, postsecondary institutions, whose highest credential awarded is the associate degree. With few exceptions, community colleges offer a comprehensive curriculum, which includes transfer, technical, and continuing education programs.

IMPORTANT FACTORS IN A COMMUNITY COLLEGE EDUCATION

The student who attends a community college can count on receiving high-quality instruction in a supportive learning community. This setting frees the student to pursue his or her own goals, nurture special talents, explore new fields of learning, and develop the capacity for lifelong learning.

From the student's perspective, four characteristics capture the essence of community colleges:

1. They are community-based institutions that work in close partnership with high schools, community groups, and employers in extending high-quality programs at convenient times and places.

2. Community colleges are cost effective. Annual tuition and fees at public community colleges average approximately half those at public four-year colleges and less than 15 percent of private four-year institutions. In addition, since most community colleges are generally close to their students' homes, these students can also save a significant amount of money on the room, board, and transportation expenses traditionally associated with a college education.

3. They provide a caring environment, with faculty members who are expert instructors, known for excellent teaching and meeting students at the point of their individual needs, regardless of age, sex, race, current job status, or previous academic preparation. Community colleges join a strong curriculum with a broad range of counseling and career services that are intended to assist students in making the most of their educational opportunities.

4. Many offer comprehensive programs, including transfer curricula in such liberal arts programs as chemistry, psychology, and business management, that lead directly to a baccalaureate degree and career programs that prepare students for employment or assist those already employed in upgrading their skills. For those students who need to strengthen their academic skills, community colleges also offer a wide range of developmental programs in mathematics, languages, and learning skills, designed to prepare the student for success in college studies.

GETTING TO KNOW YOUR TWO-YEAR COLLEGE

The first step in determining the quality of a community college is to check the status of its accreditation. Once you have established that a community college is appropriately accredited, find out as much as you can about the programs and services it has to offer. Much of that information can be found in materials the college provides. However, the best way to learn about a college is to visit in person.

During a campus visit, be prepared to ask a lot of questions. Talk to students, faculty members, administrators, and counselors about the college and its programs, particularly those in which you have a special interest. Ask about available certificates and associate degrees. Don't be shy. Do what you can to dig below the surface. Ask college officials about the transfer rate to four-year colleges. If a college emphasizes student services, find out what particular assistance is offered, such as educational or career guidance. Colleges are eager to provide you with the information you need to make informed decisions.

COMMUNITY COLLEGES CAN SAVE YOU MONEY

If you are able to live at home while you attend college, you will certainly save money on room and board, but it does cost something to commute. Many two-year colleges offer you instruction in your own home through online learning programs or through home study courses that can save both time and money. Look into all the options, and be sure to add up all the costs of attending various colleges before deciding which is best for you.

FINANCIAL AID

Many students who attend community colleges are eligible for a range of financial aid programs, including Federal Pell Grants, Perkins and Stafford Loans, state aid, and on-campus jobs. Your high school counselor or the financial aid officer at a community college will also be able to help you. It is in your interest to apply for financial aid months in advance of the date you intend to start your college program, so find out early what assistance is available to you. While many community colleges are able to help students who make a last-minute decision to attend college, either through short-term loans or emergency grants, if you are considering entering college and think you might need financial aid, it is best to find out as much as you can as early as you can.

WORKING AND GOING TO SCHOOL

Many two-year college students maintain full-time or part-time employment while they earn their degrees. Over the years, a steadily growing number of students have chosen to attend community colleges while they fulfill family and employment responsibilities. To enable these students to balance the demands of home, work, and school, most community colleges offer classes at night and on weekends.

For the full-time student, the usual length of time it takes to obtain an associate degree is two years. However, your length of study will depend on the course load you take: the fewer credits you earn each term, the longer it will take you to earn a degree. To assist you in moving more quickly toward earning your degree, many community colleges now award credit through examination or for equivalent knowledge gained through relevant life experiences. Be certain to find out the credit options that are available to you at the college in which you are interested. You may discover that it will take less time to earn a degree than you first thought.

PREPARATION FOR TRANSFER

Studies have repeatedly shown that students who first attend a community college and then transfer to a four-year college or university do at least as well academically as the students who entered the four-year institutions as freshmen. Most community colleges have agreements with nearby four-year institutions to make transfer of credits easier. If you are thinking of transferring, be sure to meet with a counselor or faculty adviser before choosing your courses. You will want to map out a course of study with transfer in mind. Make sure you also find out the credit-transfer requirements of the four-year institution you might want to attend.

ATTENDING A TWO-YEAR COLLEGE IN ANOTHER REGION

Although many community colleges serve a specific county or district, they are committed (to the extent of their ability) to the goal of equal educational opportunity without regard to economic status, race, creed, color, sex, or national origin. Independent two-year colleges recruit from a much broader geographical area—throughout the United States and, increasingly, around the world.

Although some community colleges do provide on-campus housing for their students, most do not. However, even if on-campus housing is not available, most colleges do have housing referral services.

NEW CAREER OPPORTUNITIES

Community colleges realize that many entering students are not sure about the field in which they want to focus their studies or the career they would like to pursue. Often, students discover fields and careers they never knew existed. Community colleges have the resources to help students identify areas of career interest and to set challenging occupational goals.

Once a career goal is set, you can be confident that a community college will provide job-relevant, technical education. About half of the students who take courses for credit at community colleges do so to prepare for employment or to acquire or upgrade skills for their current job. Especially helpful in charting a career path is the assistance of a counselor or a faculty adviser, who can discuss job opportunities in your chosen field and help you map out your course of study.

In addition, since community colleges have close ties to their communities, they are in constant contact with leaders in business, industry, organized labor, and public life. Community colleges work with these individuals and their organizations to prepare students for direct entry into the world of work. For example, some community colleges have established partnerships with local businesses and industries to provide specialized training programs. Some also provide the academic portion of apprenticeship training, while others offer extensive job-shadowing and cooperative education opportunities. Be sure to examine all of the career-preparation opportunities offered by the community colleges in which you are interested.

David R. Pierce is the former President of the American Association of Community Colleges.

Surviving Standardized Tests

WHAT ARE STANDARDIZED TESTS?

Colleges and universities in the United States use tests to help evaluate applicants' readiness for admission or to place them in appropriate courses. The tests that are most frequently used by colleges are the ACT of American College Testing, Inc., and the College Board's SAT. In addition, the Educational Testing Service (ETS) offers the TOEFL test, which evaluates the English-language proficiency of nonnative speakers. The tests are offered at designated testing centers located at high schools and colleges throughout the United States and U.S. territories and at testing centers in various countries throughout the world.

Upon request, special accommodations for students with documented visual, hearing, physical, or learning disabilities are available. Examples of special accommodations include tests in Braille or large print and such aids as a reader, recorder, magnifying glass, or sign language interpreter. Additional testing time may be allowed in some instances. Contact the appropriate testing program or your guidance counselor for details on how to request special accommodations.

THE ACT

The ACT is a standardized college entrance examination that measures knowledge and skills in English, mathematics, reading, and science reasoning and the application of these skills to future academic tasks. The ACT consists of four multiple-choice tests.

Test 1: English

- 75 questions, 45 minutes
- Usage and mechanics
- Rhetorical skills

Test 2: Mathematics

- 60 questions, 60 minutes
- Pre-algebra
- Elementary algebra
- Intermediate algebra
- Coordinate geometry
- Plane geometry
- Trigonometry

Test 3: Reading

- 40 questions, 35 minutes
- Prose fiction
- Humanities
- Social studies
- Natural sciences

Test 4: Science

- 40 questions, 35 minutes
- Data representation
- Research summary
- Conflicting viewpoints

Each section is scored from 1 to 36 and is scaled for slight variations in difficulty. Students are not penalized for incorrect responses. The composite score is the average of the four scaled scores. There is also a 30-minute Writing Test that is an optional component of the ACT.

To prepare for the ACT, ask your guidance counselor for a free guidebook called *Preparing for the ACT.* Besides providing general test-preparation information and additional test-taking strategies, this guidebook describes the content and format of the four ACT subject area tests, summarizes test administration procedures followed at ACT test centers, and includes a practice test. Peterson's publishes *The Real ACT Prep Guide* that includes three official ACT tests.

THE SAT

The SAT measures developed verbal and mathematical reasoning abilities as they relate to successful performance in college. It is intended to supplement the secondary school record and other information about the student in assessing readiness for college. There is one unscored, experimental section on the exam, which is used for equating and/or pretesting purposes and can cover either the mathematics or verbal subject area.

DON'T FORGET TO . . .

- Take the SAT or ACT before application deadlines.
- Note that test registration deadlines precede test dates by about six weeks.
- Register to take the TOEFL test if English is not your native language and you are planning on studying at a North American college.
- Practice your test-taking skills with Peterson's Master the SAT, Peterson's Ultimate ACT Tool Kit, The Real ACT Prep Guide (published by Peterson's), Peterson's Master TOEFL Reading Skills, Peterson's Master TOEFL Vocabulary, and Peterson's Master TOEFL Writing Skills.
- Contact the College Board or American College Testing, Inc., in advance if you need special accommodations when taking tests.

Critical Reading

- 67 questions, 70 minutes
- Sentence completion
- Passage-based reading

Mathematics

- 54 questions, 70 minutes
- Multiple-choice
- Student-produced response (grid-ins)

Writing

- 49 questions plus essay, 60 minutes
- Identifying sentence errors
- Improving paragraphs
- Improving sentences
- Essay

Students receive one point for each correct response and lose a fraction of a point for each incorrect response (except for student-produced responses). These points are totaled to produce the raw scores, which are then scaled to equalize the scores for slight variations in difficulty for various editions of the test. The critical reading, writing, and mathematics scaled scores range from 200–800 per section. The total scaled score range is from 600–2400.

SAT SUBJECT TESTS

Subject Tests are required by some institutions for admission and/or placement in freshman-level courses. Each Subject Test measures one's knowledge of a specific subject and the ability to apply that knowledge. Students should check with each institution for its specific requirements. In general, students are required to take three Subject Tests (one English, one mathematics, and one of their choice).

Subject Tests are given in the following areas: biology, chemistry, Chinese, French, German, Italian, Japanese, Korean, Latin, literature, mathematics, modern Hebrew, physics, Spanish, U.S. history, and world history. These tests are 1 hour long and are primarily multiple-choice tests. Three Subject Tests may be taken on one test date.

Scored like the SAT, students gain a point for each correct answer and lose a fraction of a point for each incorrect answer. The raw scores are then converted to scaled scores that range from 200 to 800.

THE TOEFL INTERNET-BASED TEST (IBT)

The Test of English as a Foreign Language Internet-Based Test (TOEFL iBT) is designed to help assess a student's grasp of English if it is not the student's first language. Performance on the TOEFL test may help interpret scores on the verbal sections of the SAT. The test consists of four integrated sections: speaking, listening, reading, and writing. The TOEFL iBT emphasizes integrated skills. The paper-based versions of the TOEFL will continue to be administered in certain countries until the Internet-based version is fully administered by Educational Testing Service (ETS). For further information, visit www.toefl.org.

WHAT OTHER TESTS SHOULD I KNOW ABOUT?

The AP Program

This program allows high school students to try college-level work and build valuable skills and study habits in the process. Subject matter is explored in more depth in AP courses than in other high school classes. A qualifying score on an AP test—which varies from school to school—can earn you college credit or advanced placement. Getting qualifying grades on enough exams can even earn you a full year's credit and sophomore standing at more than 1,500 higher-education institutions. There are currently thirty-seven AP courses in twenty-two different subject areas, including art history, biology, and computer science. Speak to your guidance counselor for information about your school's offerings.

College-Level Examination Program (CLEP)

The CLEP enables students to earn college credit for what they already know, whether it was learned in school, through independent study, or through other experiences outside of the classroom. Approximately 2,900 colleges and universities now award credit for qualifying scores on one or more of the thirty-four CLEP exams. The exams, which are 90 minutes in length and are primarily multiple choice, are administered at participating colleges and universities. For more information, check out the Web site at www.collegeboard. com/clep.

DSST Exams

Previously known as DANTES Subject Standardized Tests, the DSST is a nationally accepted prior learning assessment program that enables individuals to earn college credit for knowledge they have acquired outside of the traditional university classroom. Whether you are an adult learner, a college student, or a member of the armed forces, experience gained through independent reading, work-related tasks, life experiences, or military training may provide you with the skills and qualifications needed to pass a DSST exam and receive college credit for any of the thirty-eight test subjects. Disciplines include business, humanities, mathematics, physical science, and more.

Nearly 2,000 accredited and respected colleges and universities across the nation award undergraduate credit for passing scores on DSST exams. The American Council of Education (ACE) suggests that colleges award 3 credit hours for passing scores on most DSST exams. With the DSST program, individuals can shave months off the time it takes to earn a degree.

It's important to know which universities offer DSST credit. In all likelihood, a college in your area awards credit for DSST exams, but find out before taking an exam by contacting the school directly. Second, review the list of exams on the DSST Web site at www.getcollegecredit.com to determine which tests are most relevant to the degree you are seeking and to your base of knowledge. Schedule an appointment with your college adviser to determine which exams best fit your degree program and which college courses the DSST exams can replace. Advisers should also be able to tell you the minimum score required on the DSST exam to receive university credit.

You can find DSST testing locations in community colleges and universities across the country. Go online to www.getcollegecredit.com to find a location near you. Keep in mind that some universities and colleges only administer DSST exams to enrolled students. DSST testing is available to men and women in the armed services at over 500 military installations around the world.

WHAT CAN I DO TO PREPARE FOR THESE TESTS?

Know what to expect. Get familiar with how the tests are structured, how much time is allowed, and the directions for each type of question. Get plenty of rest the night before the test and eat breakfast that morning.

There are a variety of products, from books to software to videos, available to help you prepare for most standardized tests. Find the learning style that suits you best. As for which products to buy, there are two major categories—those created by the test makers and those created by private companies. The best approach is to talk to someone who has been through the process and find out which product or products he or she recommends.

Some students report significant increases in scores after participating in coaching programs. Longer-term programs (40 hours) seem to raise scores more than short-term programs (20 hours), but beyond 40 hours, score gains are minor. Math scores appear to benefit more from coaching than verbal scores.

Resources

There are a variety of ways to prepare for standardized tests—find a method that fits your schedule and your budget. But you should definitely prepare. Far too many students walk into these tests cold, either because they find standardized tests frightening or annoying or they just haven't found the time to study. The key is that these exams are standardized. That means these tests are largely the same from administration to administration; they always test the same concepts. They have to, or else you couldn't compare the scores of people who took the tests on different dates. The numbers or words may change, but the underlying content doesn't.

So how do you prepare? At the very least, you should review relevant material, such as math formulas and commonly used vocabulary words, and know the directions for each question type or test section. You should take at least one practice test and review your mistakes so you don't make them again on the test day. Beyond that, you know best how much preparation you need. You'll also find lots of material in libraries or bookstores to help you: books and software from the test-makers and from other publishers (including Peterson's) or live courses that range from national test-preparation companies to teachers at your high school who offer classes.

TOP 10 WAYS NOT TO TAKE THE TEST

10. Cramming the night before the test.
9. Not becoming familiar with the directions before you take the test.
8. Not becoming familiar with the format of the test before you take it.
7. Not knowing how the test is graded.
6. Spending too much time on any one question.
5. Not checking spelling, grammar, and sentence structure in essays.
4. Second-guessing yourself.
3. Writing a one-paragraph essay.
2. Forgetting to take a deep breath to keep from—
1. Losing It!

Who's Paying for This? Financial Aid Basics

A college education can be expensive—costing more than $150,000 for four years at some of the higher priced private colleges and universities. Even at the lower cost state colleges and universities, the cost of a four-year education can approach $60,000. Determining how you and your family will come up with the necessary funds to pay for your education requires planning, perseverance, and learning as much as you can about the options that are available to you. But before you get discouraged, College Board statistics show that 56 percent of full-time students attend four-year public and private colleges with tuition and fees less than $9000, while 9 percent attend colleges that have tuition and fees more than $33,000. College costs tend to be less in the western states and higher in New England.

Paying for college should not be looked at as a four-year financial commitment. For many families, paying the total cost of a student's college education out of current income and savings is usually not realistic. For families that have planned ahead and have financial savings established for higher education, the burden is a lot easier. But for most, meeting the cost of college requires the pooling of current income and assets and investing in longer-term loan options. These family resources, together with financial assistance from state, federal, and institutional sources, enable millions of students each year to attend the institution of their choice.

FINANCIAL AID PROGRAMS

There are three types of financial aid:

1. Gift-aid—Scholarships and grants are funds that do not have to be repaid.
2. Loans—Loans must be repaid, usually after graduation; the amount you have to pay back is the total you've borrowed plus any accrued interest. This is considered a source of self-help aid.
3. Student employment—Student employment is a job arranged for you by the financial aid office. This is another source of self-help aid.

The federal government has four major grant programs—the Federal Pell Grant, the Federal Supplemental Educational Opportunity Grant, Academic Competitiveness Grants (ACG), and SMART grants. ACG and SMART grants are limited to students who qualify for a Pell grant and are awarded to a select group of students. Overall, these grants are targeted to low-to-moderate income families with significant financial need. The federal government also sponsors a student employment program called the Federal Work-Study Program, which offers jobs both on and off campus, and several loan programs, including those for students and for parents of undergraduate students.

There are two types of student loan programs: subsidized and unsubsidized. The subsidized Federal Direct Loan and the Federal Perkins Loan are need-based, government-subsidized loans. Students who borrow through these programs do not have to pay interest on the loan until after they graduate or leave school. The unsubsidized Federal Direct Loan and the Federal Direct PLUS Loan Program are not based on need, and borrowers are responsible for the interest while the student is in school. These loans are administered by different methods. Once you choose your college, the financial aid office will guide you through this process.

After you've submitted your financial aid application and you've been accepted for admission, each college will send you a letter describing your financial aid award. Most award letters show estimated college costs, how much you and your family are expected to contribute, and the amount and types of aid you have been awarded. Most students are awarded aid from a combination of sources and programs. Hence, your award is often called a financial aid "package."

SOURCES OF FINANCIAL AID

Millions of students and families apply for financial aid each year. Financial aid from all sources exceeds $143 billion per year. The largest single source of aid is the federal government, which will award more than $100 billion this year.

The next largest source of financial aid is found in the college and university community. Most of this aid is awarded to students who have a demonstrated need based on the Federal Methodology. Some institutions use a different formula, the Institutional Methodology (IM), to award their own funds in conjunction with other forms of aid. Institutional aid may be either need-based or non-need based. Aid that is not based on need is usually awarded for a student's academic performance (merit awards), specific talents or abilities, or to attract the type of students a college seeks to enroll.

Another source of financial aid is from state government. All states offer grant and/or scholarship aid, most of which is need-based. However, more and more states are offering substantial merit-based aid programs. Most state programs award aid only to students attending college in their home state.

Other sources of financial aid include:

- Private agencies
- Foundations
- Corporations
- Clubs
- Fraternal and service organizations
- Civic associations
- Unions
- Religious groups that award grants, scholarships, and low-interest loans
- Employers that provide tuition reimbursement benefits for employees and their children

More information about these different sources of aid is available from high school guidance offices, public libraries, college financial aid offices, directly from the sponsoring organizations, and on the Web at www.petersons.com and www.finaid.org.

HOW NEED-BASED FINANCIAL AID IS AWARDED

When you apply for aid, your family's financial situation is analyzed using a government-approved formula called the Federal Methodology. This formula looks at five items:

Demographic information of the family
Income of the parents
Assets of the parents
Income of the student
Assets of the student

This analysis determines the amount you and your family are expected to contribute toward your college expenses, called your Expected Family Contribution or EFC. If the EFC is equal to or more than the cost of attendance at a particular college, then you do not demonstrate financial need. However, even if you don't have financial need, you may still qualify for aid, as there are grants, scholarships, and loan programs that are not need-based.

If the cost of your education is greater than your EFC, then you do demonstrate financial need and qualify for assistance. The amount of your financial need that can be met varies from school to school. Some are able to meet your full need, while others can only cover a certain percentage of need. Here's the formula:

Cost of Attendance
− Expected Family Contribution
= Financial Need

The EFC remains constant, but your need will vary according to the costs of attendance at a particular college. In general, the higher the tuition and fees at a particular college, the higher the cost of attendance will be. Expenses for books and supplies, room and board, transportation, and other miscellaneous items are included in the overall cost of attendance. It is important to remember that you do not have to be "needy" to qualify for financial aid. Many middle and upper-middle income families qualify for need-based financial aid.

APPLYING FOR FINANCIAL AID

Every student must complete the Free Application for Federal Student Aid (FAFSA) to be considered for financial aid. The FAFSA is available from your high school guidance office, many public libraries, colleges in your area, or directly from the U.S. Department of Education.

Students are encouraged to apply for federal student aid on the Web. The electronic version of the FAFSA can be accessed at www.fafsa.ed.gov. Both the student and at least one parent must apply for a federal PIN at http://www.pin.ed.gov. The PIN serves as your electronic signature when applying for aid on the Web.

To award their own funds, some colleges require an additional application, the Financial Aid PROFILE® form. The PROFILE asks supplemental questions that some colleges and awarding agencies feel provide a more accurate assessment of the family's ability to pay for college. It is up to the college to decide whether it will use only the FAFSA or both the FAFSA and the PROFILE. PROFILE applications are available from the high school guidance office and on the Web. Both the paper application and the Web site list those colleges and programs that require the PROFILE application.

If Every College You're Applying to for Fall 2011 Requires the FAFSA

. . . then it's pretty simple: Complete the FAFSA after January 1, 2011, being certain to send it in before any college-imposed deadlines. (You are not permitted to send in the 2011–12 FAFSA before January 1, 2011.) Most college FAFSA application deadlines are in February or early March. It is easier if you have all your financial records for the previous year available, but if that is not possible, you are strongly encouraged to use estimated figures.

After you send in your FAFSA, either with the paper application or electronically, you'll receive a Student Aid Report (SAR) that includes all of the information you reported and shows your EFC. If you provided an e-mail address, the SAR is sent to you electronically; otherwise, you will receive a paper copy in the mail. Be sure to review the SAR, checking to see if the information you reported is accurately represented. If you used estimated numbers to complete the FAFSA, you may have to resubmit the SAR with any corrections to the data. The college(s) you have designated on the FAFSA will receive the information you reported and will use that data to make their decision. In many instances, the colleges to which you've applied will ask you to send copies of your and your parents' federal income tax returns for 2010, plus any other documents needed to verify the information you reported.

If a College Requires the PROFILE

Step 1: Register for the Financial Aid PROFILE in the fall of your senior year in high school. You can apply for the PROFILE online at http://profileonline.collegeboard.com/prf/index.jsp. Registration information with a list of the colleges that require the PROFILE is available in most high school guidance offices. There is a fee for using the Financial Aid PROFILE application ($25 for the first college and $16 for each additional college). You must pay for the service by credit card when you register. If you do not have a credit card, you will be billed. A limited number of fee waivers are automatically granted to first-time applicants based on the financial information provided on the PROFILE.

Step 2: Fill out your customized Financial Aid PROFILE. Once you register, your application will be immediately available online and will have questions which all students must complete, questions which must be completed by the student's parents (unless the student is independent and the colleges or programs selected do not require parental information), and *may* have supplemental questions needed by one or more of your schools or programs. If required, those will be found in Section Q of the application.

In addition to the PROFILE Application you complete online, you may also be required to complete a Business/Farm Supplement via traditional paper format. Completion of this form is not a part of the online process. If this form is required, instructions on how to download and print the supplemental form are provided. If your biological or adoptive parents are separated or divorced and your colleges and programs require it, your noncustodial parent may be asked to complete the Noncustodial PROFILE.

Once you complete and submit your PROFILE Application, it will be processed and sent directly to your requested colleges and programs.

IF YOU DON'T QUALIFY FOR NEED-BASED AID

If you are not eligible for need-based aid, you can still find ways to lessen your burden.

Here are some suggestions:

- Search for merit scholarships. You can start at the initial stages of your application process. College merit awards are increasingly important as more and more colleges award these to students they especially want to attract. As a result, applying to a college at which your qualifications put you at the top of the entering class may give you a larger merit award. Another source of aid to look for is private scholarships that are given for special skills and talents. Additional information can be found at www.petersons.com/finaid and at www.finaid.org.
- Seek employment during the summer and the academic year. The student employment office at your college can help you locate a school-year job. Many colleges and local businesses have vacancies remaining after they have hired students who are receiving Federal Work-Study Program financial aid.
- Borrow through the unsubsidized Federal Direct Loan program. This is generally available to all students. The terms and conditions are similar to the subsidized loans. The biggest difference is that the borrower is responsible for the interest while still in college, although the government permits students to delay paying the interest right away and add the accrued interest to the total amount owed. You must file the FAFSA to be considered.
- After you've secured what you can through scholarships, working, and borrowing, you and your parents will be expected to meet your share of the college bill (the Expected Family Contribution). Many colleges offer monthly payment plans that spread the cost over the academic year. If the monthly payments are too high, parents can borrow through the Federal Direct PLUS Loan Program, through one of the many private education loan programs available, or through home equity loans and lines of credit. Families seeking assistance in financing college expenses should inquire at the financial aid office about what programs are available at the college. Some families seek the advice of professional financial advisers and tax consultants.

Frequently Asked Questions About Transferring

Muriel M. Shishkoff

Among the students attending two-year colleges are a large number who began their higher education knowing they would eventually transfer to a four-year school to obtain their bachelor's degree. There are many reasons why students go this route. Upon graduating from high school, some simply do not have definite career goals. Although they don't want to put their education on hold, they prefer not to pay exorbitant amounts in tuition while trying to "find themselves." As the cost of a university education escalates—even in public institutions—the option of spending the freshman and sophomore years at a two-year college looks attractive to many students. Others attend a two-year college because they are unable to meet the initial entrance standards—a specified grade point average (GPA), standardized test scores, or knowledge of specific academic subjects—required by the four-year school of their choice. Many such students praise the community college system for giving them the chance to be, academically speaking, "born again." In addition, students from other countries often find that they can adapt more easily to language and cultural changes at a two-year school before transferring to a larger, more diverse four-year college.

If your plan is to attend a two-year college with the ultimate goal of transferring to a four-year school, you will be pleased to know that the increased importance of the community college route to a bachelor's degree is recognized by all segments of higher education. As a result, many two-year schools have revised their course outlines and established new courses in order to comply with the programs and curricular offerings of the universities. Institutional improvements to make transferring easier have also proliferated at both the two- and four-year levels. The generous transfer policies of the Pennsylvania, New York, and Florida state university systems, among others, reflect this attitude; these systems accept *all* credits from students who have graduated from accredited community colleges.

If you are interested in moving from a two-year college to a four-year school, the sooner you make up your mind that you are going to make the switch, the better position you will be in to transfer successfully (that is, without having wasted valuable time and credits). The ideal point at which to make such a decision is **before** you register for classes at your two-year school; a counselor can help you plan your course work with an eye toward fulfilling the requirements needed for your major course of study.

Naturally, it is not always possible to plan your transferring strategy that far in advance, but keep in mind that the key to a successful transfer is **preparation,** and preparation takes time—time to think through your objectives and time to plan the right classes to take.

As students face the prospect of transferring from a two-year to a four-year school, many thoughts and concerns about this complicated and often frustrating process race through their minds. Here are answers to the questions that are most frequently asked by transferring students.

Q Does every college and university accept transfer students?

A Most four-year institutions accept transfer students, but some do so more enthusiastically than others. Graduating from a community college is an advantage at, for example, Arizona State University and the University of Massachusetts Boston; both accept more community college transfer students than traditional freshmen. At the State University of New York at Albany, graduates of two-year transfer programs within the State University of New York System are given priority for upper-division (i.e., junior- and senior-level) vacancies.

Schools offering undergraduate work at the upper division only are especially receptive to transfer applications. On the other hand, some schools accept only a few transfer students; others refuse entrance to sophomores or those in their final year. Princeton University requires an "excellent academic record and particularly compelling reasons to transfer." Check the catalogs of several colleges for their transfer requirements before you make your final choice.

Q Do students who go directly from high school to a four-year college do better academically than transfer students from community colleges?

A On the contrary: some institutions report that transfers from two-year schools who persevere until graduation do *better* than those who started as freshmen in a four-year college.

Q Why is it so important that my two-year college be accredited?

A Four-year colleges and universities accept transfer credits only from schools formally recognized by a regional, national, or professional educational agency. This accreditation signifies that an institution or program of study meets or exceeds a minimum level of educational quality necessary for meeting stated educational objectives.

Q After enrolling at a four-year school, may I still make up necessary courses at a community college?

A Some institutions restrict credit after transfer to their own facilities. Others allow students to take a limited number of transfer courses after matriculation, depending on the subject matter. A few provide opportunities for cross-registration or dual enrollment, which means taking classes on more than one campus.

Q What do I need to do to transfer?

A First, send for your high school and college transcripts. Having chosen the school you wish to transfer to, check its admission requirements against your transcripts. If you find that you are admissible, file an application as early as possible before the deadline. Part of the process will be asking your former schools to send official transcripts to the admission office, i.e., not the copies you used in determining your admissibility.

Plan your transfer program with the head of your new department as soon as you have decided to transfer. Determine the recommended general education pattern and necessary preparation for your major. At your present school, take the courses you will need to meet transfer requirements for the new school.

Q What qualifies me for admission as a transfer student?

A Admission requirements for most four-year institutions vary. Depending on the reputation or popularity of the school and program you wish to enter, requirements may be quite selective and competitive. Usually, you will need to show satisfactory test scores, an academic record up to a certain standard, and completion of specific subject matter.

Transfer students can be eligible to enter a four-year school in a number of ways: by having been eligible for admission directly upon graduation from high school, by making up shortcomings in grades (or in subject matter not covered in high school) at a community college, or by satisfactory completion of necessary courses or credit hours at another postsecondary institution. Ordinarily, students coming from a community college or from another four-year institution must meet or exceed the receiving institution's standards for freshmen and show appropriate college-level course work taken since high school. Students who did not graduate from high school can present proof of proficiency through results on the General Educational Development (GED) test.

Q Are exceptions ever made for students who don't meet all the requirements for transfer?

A Extenuating circumstances, such as disability, low family income, refugee or veteran status, or athletic talent, may permit the special enrollment of students who would not otherwise be eligible but who demonstrate the potential for academic success. Consult the appropriate office—the Educational Opportunity Program, the disabled students' office, the athletic department, or the academic dean—to see whether an exception can be made in your case.

Q How far in advance do I need to apply for transfer?

A Some schools have a rolling admission policy, which means that they process transfer applications as they are received, all year long. With other schools, you must apply during the priority filing period, which can be up to a year before you wish to enter. Check the date with the admission office at your prospective campus.

Q Is it possible to transfer courses from several different institutions?

A Institutions ordinarily accept the courses that they consider transferable, regardless of the number of accredited schools involved. However, there is the danger of exceeding the maximum number of credit hours that can be transferred from all other schools or earned through credit by examination, extension courses, or correspondence courses. The limit placed on transfer credits varies from school to school, so read the catalog carefully to avoid taking courses you won't be able to use. To avoid duplicating courses, keep attendance at different campuses to a minimum.

Q What is involved in transferring from a semester system to a quarter or trimester system?

A In the semester system, the academic calendar is divided into two equal parts. The quarter system is more aptly named trimester, since the academic calendar is divided into three equal terms (not counting a summer session). To convert semester units into quarter units or credit hours, simply multiply the semester units by one and a half. Conversely, multiply quarter units by two thirds to come up with semester units. If you are used to a semester system of fifteen- to sixteen-week courses, the ten-week courses of the quarter system may seem to fly by.

Q Why might a course be approved for transfer credit by one four-year school but not by another?

A The beauty of postsecondary education in the United States lies in its variety. Entrance policies and graduation requirements are designed to reflect and serve each institution's mission. Because institutional policies vary so widely, schools may interpret the subject matter of a course from quite different points of view. Given that the granting of transfer credit indicates that a course is viewed as being, in effect, parallel to one offered by the receiving institution, it is easy to see how this might be the case at one university and not another.

Q Must I take a foreign language to transfer?

A Foreign language proficiency is often required for admission to a four-year institution; such proficiency also often figures in certain majors or in the general education pattern. Often, two or three years of a single language in high school will do the trick. Find out if scores received on Advanced Placement (AP) examinations, placement examinations given by the foreign language department, or SAT Subject Tests will be accepted in lieu of college course work.

Q Will the school to which I'm transferring accept pass/no pass, pass/fail, or credit/no credit grades in lieu of letter grades?

A Usually, a limit is placed on the number of these courses you can transfer, and there may be other restrictions as well. If you want to use other-than-letter grades for the fulfillment of general education requirements or lower-division (freshman and sophomore) preparation for the major, check with the receiving institution.

Q Which is more important for transfer—my grade point average or my course completion pattern?

A Some schools believe that your past grades indicate academic potential and overshadow prior preparation for a specific degree program. Others require completion of certain introductory courses before transfer to prepare you for upper-division work in your major. In any case, appropriate course selection will cut down the time to graduation and increase your chances of making a successful transfer.

Q What happens to my credits if I change majors?

A If you change majors after admission, your transferable course credit should remain fairly intact. However, because you may need extra or different preparation for your new major, some of the courses you've taken may now be useful only as electives. The need for additional lower-level preparation may mean you're staying longer at your new school than you originally planned. On the other hand, you may already have taken courses that count toward your new major as part of the university's general education pattern.

Returning to School: Advice for Adult Students

Sandra Cook, Ph.D.

Assistant Vice President for Academic Affairs, Enrollment Services, San Diego State University

Many adults think for a long time about returning to school without taking any action. One purpose of this article is to help the "thinkers" finally make some decisions by examining what is keeping them from action. Another purpose is to describe not only some of the difficulties and obstacles that adult students may face when returning to school but also tactics for coping with them.

If you have been thinking about going back to college, and believing that you are the only person your age contemplating college, you should know that approximately 7 million adult students are currently enrolled in higher education institutions. This number represents 50 percent of total higher education enrollments. The majority of adult students are enrolled at two-year colleges.

There are many reasons why adult students choose to attend a two-year college. Studies have shown that the three most important criteria that adult students consider when choosing a college are location, cost, and availability of the major or program desired. Most two-year colleges are public institutions that serve a geographic district, making them readily accessible to the community. Costs at most two-year colleges are far less than at other types of higher education institutions. For many students who plan to pursue a bachelor's degree, completing their first two years of college at a community college is an affordable means to that end. If you are interested in an academic program that will transfer to a four-year institution, most two-year colleges offer the "general education" courses that comprise most freshman and sophomore years. If you are interested in a vocational or technical program, two-year colleges excel in providing this type of training.

SETTING THE STAGE

There are three different "stages" in the process of adults returning to school. The first stage is uncertainty. Do I really want to go back to school? What will my friends or family think? Can I compete with those 18-year-old whiz kids? Am I too old? The second stage is choice. Once the decision to return has been made, you must choose where you will attend. There are many criteria to use in making this decision. The third stage is support. You have just added another role to your already-too-busy life. There are, however, strategies that will help you accomplish your goals—perhaps not without struggle, but with grace and humor nonetheless. Let's look at each of these stages.

UNCERTAINTY

Why are you thinking about returning to school? Is it to:

- fulfill a dream that had to be delayed?
- become more educationally well-rounded?
- fill an intellectual void in your life?

These reasons focus on *personal growth.*

If you are returning to school to:

- meet people and make friends
- attain and enjoy higher social status and prestige among friends, relatives, and associates
- understand/study a cultural heritage
- have a medium in which to exchange ideas

you are interested in *social and cultural opportunities.*

If you are like most adult students, you want to:

- qualify for a new occupation
- enter or reenter the job market
- increase earnings potential
- qualify for a more challenging position in the same field of work

You are seeking *career growth.*

Understanding the reasons why you want to go back to school is an important step in setting your educational goals and will help you to establish some criteria for selecting a college. However, don't delay your decision because you have not been able to clearly define your motives. Many times, these aren't clear until you have already begun the process, and they may change as you move through your college experience.

Assuming you agree that additional education will benefit you, what is it that keeps you from returning to school? You may have a litany of excuses running through your mind:

- I don't have time.
- I can't afford it.
- I'm too old to learn.
- My friends will think I'm crazy.
- Teachers and students will be younger than I.
- My family can't survive without me to take care of them every minute.
- I'll be X years old when I finish.
- I'm afraid.
- I don't know what to expect.

And that is just what these are—excuses. You can make school, like anything else in your life, a priority or not. If you really want to return, you can. The more you understand your motivation for returning to school and the more you understand what excuses are keeping you from taking action, the easier your task will be.

If you think you don't have time: The best way to decide how attending class and studying can fit into your schedule is to keep track of what you do with your time each day for several weeks. Completing a standard time-management grid (each day is plotted out by the half hour) is helpful for visualizing how your time is spent. For each 3-credit-hour class you take, you will need to find 3 hours for class plus 6 to 9 hours for reading-studying-library time. This study time should be spaced evenly throughout the week, not loaded up on one day. It is not possible to learn or retain the material that way. When you examine your grid, see where there are activities that could be replaced with school and study time. You may decide to give up your bowling league or some time in front of the TV. Try not to give up sleeping, and don't cut out every moment of free time. Here are some suggestions that have come from adults who have returned to school:

- Enroll in a time-management workshop. It helps you rethink how you use your time.
- Don't think you have to take more than one course at a time. You may eventually want to work up to taking more, but consider starting with one. (It is more than you are taking now!)
- If you have a family, start assigning to them those household chores that you usually do—and don't redo what they do.
- Use your lunch hour or commuting time for reading.

If you think you cannot afford it: As mentioned earlier, two-year colleges are extremely affordable. If you cannot afford the tuition, look into the various financial aid options. Most federal and state funds are available to full- and part-time students. Loans are also available. While many people prefer not to accumulate a debt for school, these same people will think nothing of taking out a loan to buy a car. After five or six years, which is the better investment? Adult students who work should look into whether their company has a tuition-reimbursement policy. There are also private scholarships, available through foundations, service organizations, and clubs, that are focused on adult learners. Your public library, the Web, and a college financial aid adviser are three excellent sources for reference materials regarding financial aid.

If you think you are too old to learn: This is pure myth. A number of studies have shown that adult learners perform as well as, or better than, traditional-age students.

If you are afraid your friends will think you're crazy: Who cares? Maybe they will, maybe they won't. Usually, they will admire your courage and be just a little jealous of your ambition (although they'll never tell you that). Follow your dreams, not theirs.

If you are concerned because the teachers or students will be younger than you: Don't be. The age differences that may be apparent in other settings evaporate in the classroom. If anything, an adult in the classroom strikes fear into the hearts of some 18-year-olds because adults have been known to be prepared, ask questions, be truly motivated, and be there to learn!

If you think your family will have a difficult time surviving while you are in school: If you have done everything for them up to now, they might struggle. Consider this an opportunity to help them become independent and self-sufficient. Your family can only make you feel guilty if you let them. You are not abandoning them; you are becoming an educational role model. When you are happy and working toward your goals, everyone benefits. Admittedly, it sometimes takes time for them to realize this. For single parents, there are schools that offer support groups, child care, and cooperative babysitting.

If you're appalled at the thought of being X years old when you graduate in Y years: How old will you be in Y years if you don't go back to school?

If you are afraid or don't know what to expect: Know that these are natural feelings when one encounters any new situation. Adult students find that their fears usually dissipate once they begin classes. Fear of trying is usually the biggest roadblock to the reentry process.

No doubt you have dreamed up a few more reasons for not making the decision to return to school. Keep in mind that what you are doing is making up excuses, and you are using these excuses to release you from the obligation to make a decision about your life. The thought of returning to college can be scary. Anytime anyone ventures into unknown territory, there is a risk, but taking risks is a necessary component of personal and professional growth. It is your life, and you alone are responsible for making the decisions that determine its course. Education is an investment in your future.

CHOICE

Once you have decided to go back to school, your next task is to decide where to go. If your educational goals are well defined (e.g., you want to pursue a degree in order to change careers), then your task is a bit easier. But even if your educational goals are still evolving, do not defer your return. Many students who enter higher education with a specific major in mind change that major at least once.

Most students who attend a public two-year college choose the community college in the district in which they live. This is generally the closest and least expensive option if the school offers the programs you want. If you are planning to begin your education at a two-year college and then transfer to a four-year school, there are distinct advantages to choosing your four-year school early. Many community and four-year colleges have "articulation" agreements that designate what credits from the two-year school will transfer to the four-year college and how. Some four-year institutions accept an associate degree as equivalent to the freshman and sophomore years, regardless of the courses you have taken. Some four-year schools accept two-year college work only on a course-by-course basis. If you can identify which school you will transfer to, you can know in advance exactly how your two-year credits will apply, preventing an unexpected loss of credit or time.

Each institution of higher education is distinctive. Your goal in choosing a college is to come up with the best student-institution fit—matching your needs with the offerings and characteristics of the school. The first step in choosing a college is to determine what criteria are most important to you in attaining your educational goals. Location, cost, and program availability are the three main factors that influence an adult student's college choice. In considering location, don't forget that some colleges have conveniently located branch campuses. In considering cost, remember to explore your financial aid options before ruling out an institution because of its tuition. Program availability should include not only the major in which you are interested, but also whether or not classes in that major are available when you can take them.

Some additional considerations beyond location, cost, and programs are:

- Does the school have a commitment to adult students and offer appropriate services, such as child care, tutoring, and advising?
- Are classes offered at times when you can take them?
- Are there academic options for adults, such as credit for life or work experience, credit by examination (including CLEP), credit for military service, or accelerated programs?
- Is the faculty sensitive to the needs of adult learners?

Once you determine which criteria are vital in your choice of an institution, you can begin to narrow your choices. There are myriad ways for you to locate the information you desire. Many newspapers publish a "School Guide" several times a year in which colleges and universities advertise to an adult student market. In addition, schools themselves publish catalogs, class schedules, and promotional materials that contain much of the information you need, and they are yours for the asking. Many colleges sponsor information sessions and open houses that allow you to visit the campus and ask questions. An appointment with an adviser is a good way to assess the fit between you and the institution. Be sure to bring your questions with you to your interview.

SUPPORT

Once you have made the decision to return to school and have chosen the institution that best meets your needs, take some additional steps to ensure your success during your crucial first semester. Take advantage of institutional support and build some social support systems of your own. Here are some ways of doing just that:

- Plan to participate in any orientation programs. These serve the threefold purpose of providing you with a great deal of important information, familiarizing you with the campus and its facilities, and giving you the opportunity to meet and begin networking with other students.
- Take steps to deal with any academic weaknesses. Take mathematics and writing placement tests if you have reason to believe you may need some extra help in these areas. It is not uncommon for adult students to need a math refresher course or a program to help alleviate math anxiety. Ignoring a weakness won't make it go away.
- Look into adult reentry programs. Many institutions offer adults workshops focusing on ways to improve study skills, textbook reading, test-taking, and time-management skills.
- Build new support networks by joining an adult student organization, making a point of meeting other adult students through workshops, or actively seeking out a "study buddy" in each class—that invaluable friend who shares and understands your experience.
- Incorporate your new status as "student" into your family life. Doing your homework with your children at a designated "homework time" is a valuable family activity and reinforces the importance of education.

- Make sure you take a reasonable course load in your first semester. It is far better to have some extra time on your hands and to succeed magnificently than to spend the entire semester on the brink of a breakdown. Also, whenever possible, try to focus your first courses not only on requirements, but also on areas of personal interest.
- Faculty members, advisers, and student affairs personnel are there to help you during difficult times—let them assist you as often as necessary.

After completing your first semester, you will probably look back in wonder at why you thought going back to school was so imposing. Certainly, it's not without its occasional exasperations. But, as with life, keeping things in perspective and maintaining your sense of humor make the difference between just coping and succeeding brilliantly.

What International Students Need to Know About Admission to U.S. Colleges and Universities

Kitty M. Villa

There are two principles to remember about admission to a university in the United States. First, applying is almost never a one-time request for admission but an ongoing process that may involve several exchanges of information between applicant and institution. "Admission process" or "application process" means that a "yes" or "no" is usually not immediate, and requests for additional information are to be expected. To successfully manage this process, you must be prepared to send additional information when requested and then wait for replies. You need a thoughtful balance of persistence to communicate regularly and effectively with your selected universities and patience to endure what can be a very long process.

The second principle involves a marketplace analogy. The most successful applicants are alert to opportunities to create a positive impression that sets them apart from other applicants. They are able to market themselves to their target institution. Institutions are also trying to attract the highest-quality student that they can. The admissions process presents you with the opportunity to analyze your strengths and weaknesses as a student and to look for ways to present yourself in the most marketable manner.

FIRST STEP—SELECTING INSTITUTIONS

With thousands of institutions of higher education in the United States, how do you begin to narrow your choices down to the institutions that are best for you? There are many factors to consider, and you must ultimately decide which factors are most important to you.

Location

You may spend several years studying in the United States. Do you prefer an urban or rural campus? Large or small metropolitan area? If you need to live on campus, will you be unhappy at a university where most students commute from off-campus housing? How do you feel about extremely hot summers or cold winters? Eliminating institutions that do not match your preferences in terms of location will narrow your choices.

Recommendations from Friends, Professors, or Others

There are valid academic reasons to consider the recommendations of people who know you well and have firsthand knowledge about particular institutions. Friends and contacts may be able to provide you with "inside information" about the campus or its academic programs to which published sources have no access. You should carefully balance anecdotal information with your own research and your own impressions. However, current and former students, professors, and others may provide excellent information during the application process.

Your Own Academic and Career Goals

Consideration of your academic goals is more complex than it may seem at first glance. All institutions do not offer the same academic programs. The application form usually provides a definitive listing of the academic programs offered by an institution. A course catalog describes the degree program and all the courses offered. In addition to printed sources, there is a tremendous amount of institutional information available on the Web. Program descriptions, even course descriptions and course syllabi, are often available to peruse online.

You may be interested in the rankings of either the university or of a program of study. Keep in mind, however, that rankings usually assume that quality is quantifiable. Rankings are usually based on presumptions about how data relate to quality and are likely to be unproven. It is important to carefully consider the source and the criteria of any ranking information before believing and acting upon it.

Your Own Educational Background

You may be concerned about the interpretation of your educational credentials, since your country's degree nomenclature and the grading scale may differ from those in the United States. Universities use reference books about the educational systems of other countries to help them understand specific educational credentials. Generally, these credentials are interpreted by each institution; there is not a single interpretation that applies to every institution. The lack of uniformity is good news for most students, since it means that students from a wide variety of educational backgrounds can find a U.S. university that is appropriate to their needs.

To choose an appropriate institution, you can and should do an informal self-evaluation of your educational background. This self-analysis involves three important questions:

1. How Many Years of Study Have You Completed?

Completion of secondary school with at least twelve total years of education usually qualifies students to apply for undergraduate (bachelor's) degree programs. Completion of a university degree program that involves at least sixteen years of total education qualifies one to apply for admission to graduate (master's) degree programs in the United States.

2. Does the Education That You Have Completed in Your Country Provide Access to Further Study in the United States?

Consider the kind of institution where you completed your previous studies. If educational opportunities in your country are limited, it may be necessary to investigate many U.S. institutions and programs in order to find a match.

3. Are Your Previous Marks or Grades Excellent, Average, or Poor?

Your educational record influences your choice of U.S. institutions. If your grades are average or poor, it may be advisable to apply to several institutions with minimally difficult or noncompetitive entrance levels.

YOU are one of the best sources of information about the level and quality of your previous studies. Awareness of your educational assets and liabilities will serve you well throughout the application process.

SECOND STEP—PLANNING AND ASSEMBLING THE APPLICATION

Planning and assembling a university application can be compared to the construction of a building. First, you must start with a solid foundation, which is the application form itself. The application, often available online as well as in paper form, usually contains a wealth of useful information, such as deadlines, fees, and degree programs available at that institution. To build a solid application, it is best to begin well in advance of the application deadline.

How to Obtain the Application Form

Application forms and links to institutional Web sites may also be available at a U.S. educational advising center associated with the American Embassy or Consulate in your country. These centers are excellent resources for international students and provide information about standardized test administration, scholarships, and other matters to students who are interested in studying in the United States. Your local U.S. Embassy or Consulate can guide you to the nearest educational advising center.

What Are the Key Components of a Complete Application?

Institutional requirements vary, but the standard components of a complete application include the following:

- Transcript
- Required standardized examination scores
- Evidence of financial support
- Letters of recommendation
- Application fee

Transcript

A complete academic record or transcript includes all courses completed, grades earned, and degrees awarded. Most universities require an official transcript to be sent directly from the school or university. In many other countries, however, the practice is to issue official transcripts and degree certificates directly to the student. If you have only one official copy of your transcript, it may be a challenge to get additional certified copies that are acceptable to U.S. universities. Some institutions will issue additional official copies for application purposes.

If your institution does not provide this service, you may have to seek an alternate source of certification. As a last resort, you may send a photocopy of your official transcript, explain that you have only one original, and ask the university for advice on how to deal with this situation.

Required Standardized Examination Scores

Arranging to take standardized examinations and earning the required scores seem to cause the most anxiety for international students.

The university application form usually indicates which examinations are required. The standardized examination required most often for undergraduate admission is the Test of English as a Foreign Language (TOEFL). Institutions may also require the SAT of undergraduate applicants. These standardized examinations are administered by the Educational Testing Service (ETS).

These examinations are offered in almost every country of the world. It is advisable to begin planning for standardized examinations at least six months prior to the application deadline of your desired institutions. Test centers fill up quickly, so it is important to register as soon as possible. Information about the examinations is available at U.S. educational advising centers associated with embassies or consulates.

FOR MORE INFORMATION

Questions about test formats, locations, dates, and registration may be addressed to:

ETS Corporate Headquarters
Rosedale Road
Princeton, New Jersey 08541
Web sites: http://www.ets.org
http://www.toefl.org
Phone: 609-921-9000
Fax: 609-734-5410

Most universities require that the original test scores, not a student copy, be sent directly by the testing service. When you register for the test, be sure to indicate that the testing service should send the test scores directly to the universities.

You should begin your application process before you receive your test scores. Delaying submission of your application until the test scores arrive may cause you to miss deadlines and negatively affect the outcome of your application. If you want to know your scores in order to assess your chances of admission to an institution with rigorous admission standards, you should take the tests early.

Many universities in the United States set minimum required scores on the TOEFL or other standardized examinations. Test scores are an important factor, but most institutions also look at a number of other factors in their consideration of a candidate for admission.

Evidence of Financial Support

Evidence of financial support is required to issue immigration documents to admitted students. This is part of a complete application package but usually plays no role in determining admission. Most institutions make admissions decisions without regard to the source and amount of financial support.

Letters of Recommendation

Most institutions require one or more letters of recommendation. The best letters are written by former professors, employers, or others who can comment on your academic achievements or professional potential.

Some universities provide a special form for the letters of recommendation. If possible, use the forms provided. If you are applying to a large number of universities, however, or if your recommenders are not available to complete several forms, it may be necessary for you to duplicate a general recommendation letter.

Application Fee

Most universities also require an application fee, ranging from $25 to $100, which must be paid to initiate consideration of the application.

Completing the Application Form

Whether sent by mail or electronically, the application form must be neat and thoroughly filled out. Although parts of the application may not seem to apply to you or your situation, do your best to answer all the questions.

Remember that this is a process. You provide information, and your proposed university then may request clarification and further information. If you have questions, it is better to initiate the entire process by submitting the application form rather than asking questions before you apply. The university will be better able to respond to you after it has your application. Always complete as much as you can. Do not permit uncertainty about the completion of the application form to cause unnecessary delays.

THIRD STEP—DISTINGUISH YOUR APPLICATION

To distinguish your application—to market yourself successfully—is ultimately the most important part of the application process. As you select your prospective universities, begin to analyze your strengths and weaknesses as a prospective student. As you complete your application, you should strive to create a positive impression and set yourself apart from other applicants, to highlight your assets and bring these qualities to the attention of the appropriate university administrators and professors. Applying early is a very easy way to distinguish your application.

Deadline or Guideline?

The application deadline is the last date that an application for a given semester will be accepted. Often, the application will specify that all required documents and information be submitted before the deadline date. To meet the deadlines, start the application process early. This also gives you more time to take—and perhaps retake and improve—the required standardized tests.

Admissions deliberations may take several weeks or months. In the meantime, most institutions accept additional information, including improved test scores, after the posted deadline.

Even if your application is initially rejected, you may be able to provide additional information to change the decision. You can request reconsideration based on additional information, such as improved test scores, strong letters of recommendation, or information about your class rank. Applying early allows more time to improve your application. Also, some students may decide not to accept their offers of admission, leaving room for offers to students on a waiting list. Reconsideration of the admission decisions can occur well beyond the application deadline.

Think of the deadline as a guideline rather than an impermeable barrier. Many factors—the strength of the application, your research interests, the number of spaces available at the proposed institution—can override the enforcement of an application deadline. So, if you lack a test score or transcript by the official deadline, you may still be able to apply and be accepted.

Statement of Purpose

The statement of purpose is your first and perhaps best opportunity to present yourself as an excellent candidate for admission. Whether or not a personal history essay or statement of purpose is required, always include a carefully written statement of purpose with your applications. A compelling statement of purpose does not have to be lengthy, but it should include some basic components:

- Part One—Introduce yourself and describe your educational background. This is your opportunity to describe any facet of your educational experience that you wish to emphasize. Perhaps you attended a highly ranked secondary school or university in your home country. Mention the name and any noteworthy characteristics of the secondary school or university from which you graduated. Explain the grading scale used at your university. Do not forget to mention your rank in your graduating class and any honors you may have received. This is not the time to be modest.
- Part Two—Describe your current academic and career interests and goals. Think about how these will fit into those of the institution to which you are applying, and mention the reasons why you have selected that particular institution.
- Part Three—Describe your long-term goals. When you finish your program of study, what do you plan to do next? If you already have a job offer or a career plan, describe it. Give some thought to how you'll demonstrate that studying in the United States will ultimately benefit others.

Use Personal Contacts When Possible

Appropriate and judicious use of your own network of contacts can be very helpful. Friends, former professors, former students of your selected institutions, and others may be willing to advise you during the application process and provide you with introductions to key administrators or professors. If suggested, you may wish to contact certain professors or administrators by mail, telephone, or e-mail. A personal visit to discuss your interest in the institution may be appropriate. Whatever your choice of communication, try to make the encounter pleasant and personal. Your goal is to make a positive impression, not to rush the admission decision.

There is no single right way to be admitted to U.S. universities. The same characteristics that make the educational choice in the United States so difficult—the number of institutions and the variety of programs of study—are the same attributes that allow so many international students to find the institution that's right for them.

Kitty M. Villa is the former Assistant Director, International Office, at the University of Texas at Austin.

Community Colleges and the New Green Economy

Community colleges are a focal point for state and national efforts to create a "green" economy and workforce. As the U.S. economy transforms itself into a green economy, community colleges are leading the way—filling the need for educated technicians whose skills can cross industry lines as well as the need for technicians who are able to learn new skills as technologies evolve. Community colleges are at the heart of the Obama administration's recovery strategy, with $12 billion allocated over the next decade. And with the support of local business partners, as well as state governments, America's community colleges are rising to meet the demands of the new green economy.

In this section, you can read about the green programs at Lane Community College in Eugene, Oregon, and the role it and other community colleges are playing in creating a workforce for the green economy. You can also read a first-hand account of the new Wind Turbine Training Program at Kalamazoo Valley Community College in Kalamazoo, Michigan—a program that has more applicants than spaces and one whose students are being hired BEFORE they even graduate. It's clear that there are exciting "green" happenings at community colleges throughout the United States.

THE ROLE OF COMMUNITY COLLEGES IN CREATING A WORKFORCE FOR THE GREEN ECONOMY

By Mary F.T. Spilde, President, Lane Community College

Community colleges are expected to play a leadership role in educating and training the workforce for the green economy. Due to close connections with local and regional labor markets, colleges assure a steady supply of skilled workers by developing and adapting programs to respond to the needs of business and industry. Further, instead of waiting for employers to create job openings, many colleges are actively engaged in local economic development to help educate potential employers to grow their green business opportunities and to participate in the creation of the green economy.

As the green movement emerges there has been confusion about what constitutes a green job. It is now clear that many of the green jobs span several economic sectors such as renewable energy, construction, manufacturing, transportation and agriculture. It is predicted that there will be many middle skill jobs requiring more than a high school diploma but less than a bachelor's degree. This is precisely the unique role that community colleges play. Community colleges develop training programs, including pre-apprenticeship, that ladder the curriculum to take lower skilled workers through a relevant and sequenced course of study that provides a clear pathway to career track jobs. As noted in *Going Green: The Vital Role of Community Colleges in Building a Sustainable Future and Green Workforce,* community colleges are strategically positioned to work with employers to redefine skills and competencies needed by the green workforce and to create the framework for new and expanded green career pathways.

While there will be new occupations such as solar and wind technologists, the majority of the jobs will be in the energy management sector—retrofitting the built environment. For example, President Obama called for retrofitting more than 75 percent of federal buildings and more than 2 million homes to make them more energy-efficient. The second major area for growth will be the "greening" of existing jobs as they evolve to incorporate green practices. Both will require new knowledge, skills and abilities. For community colleges, this means developing new programs that meet newly created industry standards and adapting existing programs and courses to integrate green skills. The key is to create a new talent pool of environmentally conscious, highly skilled workers.

These two areas show remarkable promise for education and training leading to high wage/high demand jobs:

- Efficiency and energy management: There is a need for auditors and energy efficiency experts to retrofit existing buildings. Consider how much built environment we have in this country, and it's not difficult to see that this is where the vast amount of jobs are now and will be in the future.
- Greening of existing jobs: There are few currently available jobs that environmental sustainability will not impact. Whether it is jobs in construction, such as plumbers, electricians, heating and cooling technicians, painters, and building supervisors, or chefs, farmers, custodians, architects, automotive technicians and interior designers, all will need to understand how to lessen their impact on the environment.

Lane Community College offers a variety of degree and certificate programs to prepare students to enter the energy efficiency fields. Lane has offered an Energy Management program since the late 1980s—before it was hip to be green! Students in this program learn to apply basic principles of physics and analysis techniques to the description and measurement of energy in today's building systems, with the goal of evaluating and recommending alternative energy solutions that will result in greater energy efficiency and energy cost savings. Students gain a working understanding of energy systems in today's built environment and the tools to analyze and quantify energy efficiency efforts. The program began with an emphasis in residential energy efficiency/solar energy systems and has evolved to include commercial energy efficiency and renewable energy system installation technology.

The Renewable Energy Technician program is offered as a second-year option within the Energy Management program. Course work prepares students for employment designing and installing solar electric and domestic hot water systems. Renewable Energy students, along with Energy Management students, take a first-year curriculum in commercial energy efficiency giving them a solid background that includes residential energy efficiency, HVAC systems, lighting, and physics and math. In the second year, Renewable Energy students diverge from the Energy Management curriculum and take course work that starts with two courses in electricity fundamentals and one course in energy economics. In the following terms, students learn to design, install, and develop a thorough understanding of photovoltaics and domestic hot water systems.

Recent additions to Lane's offerings are Sustainability Coordinator and Water Conservation Technician degrees. Both programs were added to meet workforce demand.

Lane graduates find employment in a wide variety of disciplines and may work as facility managers, energy auditors, energy program coordinators, or control system specialists, for such diverse employers as engineering firms, public and private utilities, energy equipment companies, and departments of energy and as sustainability leaders within public and private sector organizations.

Lane Community College also provides continuing education for working professionals. The Sustainable Building Advisor (SBA) Certificate Program is a nine-month, specialized training program for working professionals. Graduate are able to advise employers or clients on strategies and tools for implementing sustainable building practices. Benefits from participating in the SBA program often include saving long-term building operating costs; improving the environmental, social, and economic viability of the region; and reducing environmental impacts and owner liability—not to mention the chance to improve one's job skills in a rapidly growing field.

The Building Operators Certificate is a professional development program created by The Northwest Energy Efficiency Council. It is offered through the Northwest Energy Education Institute at Lane. The certificate is designed for operations and maintenance staff working in public or private commercial buildings. It certifies individuals in energy and resource-efficient operation of building systems at two levels: Level I–Building System Maintenance and Level II–Equipment Troubleshooting and Maintenance.

Lane Community College constantly scans the environment to assess workforce needs and develop programs that provide highly skilled employees. Lane, like most colleges, publishes information in its catalog on workforce demand and wages so that students can make informed decisions about program choice.

Green jobs will be a large part of a healthy economy. Opportunities will abound for those who take advantage of programs with a proven record of connecting with employers and successfully educating students to meet high skills standards.

ESTABLISHING A WORLD-CLASS WIND TURBINE TECHNICIAN ACADEMY

By James DeHaven, Vice President of Economic & Business Development, Kalamazoo Valley Community College

When Kalamazoo Valley Community College (KVCC) decided it wanted to become involved in the training of utility-grade technicians for wind-energy jobs, early on the choice was made to avoid another "me too" training course.

Our program here in Southwest Michigan, 30 miles from Lake Michigan, had to meet industry needs and industry standards.

It was also obvious from the start that the utility-grade or large wind industry had not yet adopted any uniform training standards in the United States.

Of course, these would come, but why should the college wait when European standards were solidly established and working well in Germany, France, Denmark and Great Britain?

As a result, in 2009, KVCC launched its Wind Turbine Technician Academy, the first of its kind in the United States. The noncredit academy runs 8 hours a day, five days a week, for twenty-six weeks of intense training in electricity, mechanics, wind dynamics, safety, and climbing. The college developed this program rather quickly—in eight months—to fast-track individuals into this emerging field.

KVCC based its program on the training standards forged by the Bildungszentrum fur Erneuerebare Energien (BZEE)—the Renewable Energy Education Center.

Located in Husum, Germany, and founded in 2000, the BZEE was created and supported by major wind-turbine manufacturers, component makers, and enterprises that provide operation and maintenance services.

As wind-energy production increased throughout Europe, the need for high-quality, industry-driven, international standards emerged. The BZEE has become the leading trainer for wind-turbine technicians across Europe and now in Asia.

With the exception of one college in Canada, the standards are not yet available in North America. When Kalamazoo Valley realized it could be the first college or university in the United States to offer this training program—that was enough motivation to move forward.

For the College to become certified by the BZEE, it needed to hire and send an electrical instructor and a mechanical instructor to Germany for six weeks of "train the trainer." The instructors not only had to excel in their respective fields, they also needed to be able to climb the skyscraper towers supporting megawatt-class turbines—a unique combination of skills to possess. Truly, individuals who fit this job description don't walk through the door everyday—but we found them! Amazingly, we found a top mechanical instructor who was a part-time fireman and comfortable with tall ladder rescues and a skilled electrical instructor who used to teach rappelling off the Rockies to the Marine Corps.

In addition to employing new instructors, the College needed a working utility-grade nacelle that could fit in its training lab that would be located in the KVCC Michigan Technical Education Center. So one of the instructors traveled to Denmark and purchased a 300-kilowatt turbine.

Once their own training was behind them and the turbine was on its way from the North Sea, the instructors quickly turned to crafting the curriculum necessary for our graduates to earn both an academy certificate from KVCC and a certification from the BZEE.

Promoting the innovative program to qualified potential students across the country was the next step. News releases were published throughout Michigan, and they were also picked up on the Internet. Rather quickly, KVCC found itself with more than 500 requests for applications for a program built for 16 students.

Acceptance into the academy includes a medical release, a climbing test, reading and math tests, relevant work experience, and, finally, an interview. Students in the academy's pioneer class, which graduated in spring 2010, ranged in age from their late teens to early 50s. They hailed from throughout Michigan, Indiana, Ohio, and Illinois as well as from Puerto Rico and Great Britain.

The students brought with them degrees in marketing, law, business, science, and architecture, as well as entrepreneurial experiences in several businesses, knowledge of other languages, military service, extensive travel, and electrical, computer, artistic, and technical/mechanical skills.

Kalamazoo Valley's academy has provided some high-value work experiences for the students in the form of two collaborations with industry that has allowed them to maintain and/or repair actual utility-grade turbines, including those at the 2.5 megawatt size. This hands-on experience will add to the attractiveness of the graduates in the market place. Potential employers were recently invited to an open house where they could see the lab and meet members of this pioneer class.

The College's Turbine Technician Academy has also attracted a federal grant for $550,000 to expand its program through additional equipment purchases. The plan is to erect our own climbing tower. Climbing is a vital part of any valid program, and yet wind farms cannot afford to shut turbines down just for climb-training.

When the students are asked what best distinguishes the Kalamazoo Valley program, their answers point to the experienced instructors and the working lab, which is constantly changing to offer the best training experiences to the wind students.

Industry continues to tell us that community colleges need to offer fast-track training programs of this caliber if the nation is to reach the U.S. Department of Energy's goal of 20 percent renewable energy by 2030. This would require more than 1,500 new technicians each year.

With that in mind, KVCC plans to host several BZEE orientation programs for other community colleges in order to encourage them to consider adopting the European training standards and start their own programs.

Meanwhile, applications are continuing to stream in from across the country for the next Wind Turbine Technician Academy program at Kalamazoo Valley Community College.

(A video about the program is available at www.mteckvcc.com/windtechacademy.html.)

How to Use This Guide

Peterson's Two-Year Colleges 2011 contains a wealth of information for anyone interested in colleges offering associate degrees. This section details the criteria that institutions must meet to be included in this guide and provides information about research procedures used by Peterson's.

QUICK-REFERENCE CHART

The **Quick-Reference Chart** is a geographically arranged table that lists colleges by name and city within the state, territory, or country in which they are located. Areas listed include the United States and its territories and other countries; the institutions in these countries are included because they are accredited by recognized U.S. accrediting bodies (see **Criteria for Inclusion** section).

The At-a-Glance chart contains basic information that enables you to compare institutions quickly according to broad characteristics such as enrollment, application requirements, financial aid availability, and numbers of sports and majors offered. A dagger (†) after the institution's name indicates that an institution has an entry in the **College Close-Ups** section.

Column 1: Degrees Awarded

C = *college transfer associate degree:* the degree awarded after a "university-parallel" program, equivalent to the first two years of a bachelor's degree.

T = *terminal associate degree:* the degree resulting from a one- to three-year program providing training for a specific occupation.

B = *bachelor's degree (baccalaureate):* the degree resulting from a liberal arts, science, professional, or preprofessional program normally lasting four years, although in some cases an accelerated program can be completed in three years.

M = *master's degree:* the first graduate (postbaccalaureate) degree in the liberal arts and sciences and certain professional fields, usually requiring one to two years of full-time study.

Column 2: Institutional Control

Private institutions are designated as one of the following:

Ind = *independent* (nonprofit)

I-R = *independent-religious:* nonprofit; sponsored by or affiliated with a particular religious group or having a nondenominational or interdenominational religious orientation.

Prop = *proprietary* (profit-making)

Public institutions are designated by the source of funding, as follows:

Fed = *federal*

St = *state*

Comm = *commonwealth* (Puerto Rico)

Terr = *territory* (U.S. territories)

Cou = *county*

Dist = *district:* an administrative unit of public education, often having boundaries different from units of local government.

City = *city*

St-L = *state and local:* local may refer to county, district, or city.

St-R = *state-related:* funded primarily by the state but administratively autonomous.

Column 3: Student Body

M = *men only* (100% of student body)

PM = *coed, primarily men*

W = *women only* (100% of student body)

PW = *coed, primarily women*

M/W = *coeducational*

Column 4: Undergraduate Enrollment

The figure shown represents the number of full-time and part-time students enrolled in undergraduate degree programs as of fall 2009.

Columns 5–7: Enrollment Percentages

Figures are shown for the percentages of the fall 2009 undergraduate enrollment made up of students attending part-time (column 5) and students 25 years of age or older (column 6). Also listed is the percentage of students in the last graduating class who completed a college-transfer associate program and went directly on to four-year colleges (column 7).

For columns 8 through 15, the following letter codes are used: Y = yes; N = no; R = recommended; S = for some.

Columns 8–10: Admission Policies

The information in these columns shows whether the college has an open admission policy (column 8) whereby virtually all applicants are accepted without regard to standardized test scores, grade average, or class rank; whether a high school equivalency certificate is accepted in place of a high school diploma for admission consideration (column 9); and whether a high school transcript (column 10) is required as part of the application process. In column 10, the combination of the codes R and S indicates that a high school transcript is recommended for all applicants (R) or required for some (S).

Columns 11–12: Financial Aid

These columns show which colleges offer the following types of financial aid: need-based aid (column 11) and part-time jobs (column 12), including those offered through the federal government's Federal Work-Study program.

Columns 13–15: Services and Facilities

These columns show which colleges offer the following: career counseling (column 13) on either an individual or group basis, job placement services (column 14) for individual students, and college-owned or -operated housing facilities (column 16) for noncommuting students.

Column 16: Sports

This figure indicates the number of sports that a college offers at the intramural and/or intercollegiate levels.

Column 17: Majors

This figure indicates the number of major fields of study in which a college offers degree programs.

PROFILES OF TWO-YEAR COLLEGES AND SPECIAL MESSAGES

The **Profiles of Two-Year Colleges** contain basic data in capsule form for quick review and comparison. The following outline of the **Profile** format shows the section headings and the items that each section covers. Any item that does not apply to a particular college or for which no information was supplied is omitted from that college's **Profile.**

Bulleted Highlights

The bulleted highlights section features important information, including the institution's Web site, for quick reference and comparison. The number of possible bulleted highlights that an ideal **Profile** would have if all questions were answered in a timely manner follow. However, not every institution provides all of the information necessary to fill out every bulleted line. In such instances, the line will not appear.

First Bullet

Institutional control: Private institutions are designated as independent (nonprofit), proprietary (profit-making), or independent, with a specific religious denomination or affiliation. Nondenominational or interdenominational religious orientation is possible and would be indicated.

Public institutions are designated by the source of funding. Designations include federal, state, province, commonwealth (Puerto Rico), territory (U.S. territories), county, district (an administrative unit of public education, often having boundaries different from units of local government), city, state and local (local may refer to county, district, or city), or state-related (funded primarily by the state but administratively autonomous).

Religious affiliation is also noted here.

Institutional type: Each institution is classified as one of the following:

Primarily two-year college: Awards baccalaureate degrees, but the vast majority of students are enrolled in two-year programs.

Four-year college: Awards baccalaureate degrees; may also award associate degrees; does not award graduate (postbaccalaureate) degrees.

Five-year college: Awards a five-year baccalaureate in a professional field such as architecture or pharmacy; does not award graduate degrees.

Upper-level institution: Awards baccalaureate degrees, but entering students must have at least two years of previous college-level credit; may also offer graduate degrees.

Comprehensive institution: Awards baccalaureate degrees; may also award associate degrees; offers graduate degree programs, primarily at the master's, specialist's, or professional level, although one or two doctoral programs may be offered.

University: Offers four years of undergraduate work plus graduate degrees through the doctorate in more than two academic or professional fields.

Founding date: If the year an institution was chartered differs from the year when instruction actually began, the earlier date is given.

System or administrative affiliation: Any coordinate institutions or system affiliations are indicated. An institution that has separate colleges or campuses for men and women but shares facilities and courses is termed a coordinate institution. A formal administrative grouping of institutions, either private or public, of which the college is a part, or the name of a single institution with which the college is administratively affiliated, is a system.

Second Bullet

Setting: Schools are designated as urban (located within a major city), suburban (a residential area within commuting distance of a major city), small-town (a small but compactly settled area not within commuting distance of a major city), or rural (a remote and sparsely populated area). The phrase *easy access to . . .* indicates that the campus is within an hour's drive of the nearest major metropolitan area that has a population greater than 500,000.

Third Bullet

Endowment: The total dollar value of funds and/or property donated to the institution or the multicampus educational system of which the institution is a part.

Fourth Bullet

Student body: An institution is coed (coeducational—admits men and women), primarily (80 percent or more) women, primarily men, women only, or men only. A few schools are designated as undergraduate: women only; graduate: coed or undergraduate: men only; graduate: coed.

Undergraduate students: Represents the number of full-time and part-time students enrolled in undergraduate degree programs as of fall 2009. The percentage of full-time undergraduates and the percentages of men and women are given.

Special Messages

These messages have been written by those colleges that chose to supplement their **Profile** data with additional, timely, important information.

Category Overviews

Undergraduates

For fall 2009, the number of full- and part-time undergraduate students is listed. This list provides the number of states and U.S. territories, including the District of Columbia and Puerto Rico (or, for Canadian institutions, provinces and territories), and other countries from which undergraduates come. Percentages are given of undergraduates who are from out of state; Native American, African American, and Asian American or Pacific Islander; international students; transfer students; and living on campus.

Retention: The percentage of freshmen (or, for upper-level institutions, entering students) who returned the following year for the fall term.

Freshmen

Admission: Figures are given for the number of students who applied for fall 2009 admission, the number of those who were admitted, and the number who enrolled. Freshman statistics include the average high school GPA; the percentage of freshmen who took the SAT and received critical reading, writing, and math scores above 500, above 600, and above 700; as well as the percentage of freshmen taking the ACT who received a composite score of 18 or higher.

Faculty

Total: The total number of faculty members; the percentage of full-time faculty members as of fall 2009; and the percentage of full-time faculty members who hold doctoral/first professional/terminal degrees.

Student-faculty ratio: The school's estimate of the ratio of matriculated undergraduate students to faculty members teaching undergraduate courses.

Majors

This section lists the major fields of study offered by the college.

Academics

Calendar: Most colleges indicate one of the following: 4-1-4, 4-4-1, or a similar arrangement (two terms of equal length plus an abbreviated winter or spring term, with the numbers referring to months); semesters; trimesters; quarters; 3-3 (three courses for each of three terms); modular (the academic year is divided into small blocks of time; courses of varying lengths are assembled according to individual programs); or standard year (for most Canadian institutions).

Degrees: This names the full range of levels of certificates, diplomas, and degrees, including prebaccalaureate, graduate, and professional, that are offered by this institution:

> ***Associate degree:*** Normally requires at least two but fewer than four years of full-time college work or its equivalent.
>
> ***Bachelor's degree (baccalaureate):*** Requires at least four years but not more than five years of full-time college-level work or its equivalent. This includes all bachelor's degrees in which the normal four years of work are completed in three years and bachelor's degrees conferred in a five-year cooperative (work-study plan) program. A cooperative plan provides for alternate class attendance and employment in business, industry, or government. This allows students to combine actual work experience with their college studies.
>
> ***Master's degree:*** Requires the successful completion of a program of study of at least the full-time equivalent of one but not more than two years of work beyond the bachelor's degree.
>
> ***Doctoral degree (doctorate):*** The highest degree in graduate study. The doctoral degree classification includes

Doctor of Education, Doctor of Juridical Science, Doctor of Public Health, and the Doctor of Philosophy in any nonprofessional field.

First professional degree: The first postbaccalaureate degree in one of the following fields: chiropractic (DC, DCM), dentistry (DDS, DMD), medicine (MD), optometry (OD), osteopathic medicine (DO), rabbinical and Talmudic studies (MHL, Rav), pharmacy (BPharm, PharmD), podiatry (PodD, DP, DPM), veterinary medicine (DVM), law (JD), or divinity/ministry (BD, MDiv).

First professional certificate (postdegree): Requires completion of an organized program of study after completion of the first professional degree. Examples are refresher courses or additional units of study in a specialty or subspecialty.

Post-master's certificate: Requires completion of an organized program of study of 24 credit hours beyond the master's degree but does not meet the requirements of academic degrees at the doctoral level.

Special study options: Details are next given here on study options available at each college:

Accelerated degree program: Students may earn a bachelor's degree in three academic years.

Academic remediation for entering students: Instructional courses designed for students deficient in the general competencies necessary for a regular postsecondary curriculum and educational setting.

Adult/continuing education programs: Courses offered for nontraditional students who are currently working or are returning to formal education.

Advanced placement: Credit toward a degree awarded for acceptable scores on College Board Advanced Placement (AP) tests.

Cooperative (co-op) education programs: Formal arrangements with off-campus employers allowing students to combine work and study in order to gain degree-related experience, usually extending the time required to complete a degree.

Distance learning: For-credit courses that can be accessed off-campus via cable television, the Internet, satellite, videotape, correspondence course, or other media.

Double major: A program of study in which a student concurrently completes the requirements of two majors.

English as a second language (ESL): A course of study designed specifically for students whose native language is not English.

External degree programs: A program of study in which students earn credits toward a degree through a combination of independent study, college courses, proficiency examinations, and personal experience. External degree programs require minimal or no classroom attendance.

Freshmen honors college: A separate academic program for talented freshmen.

Honors programs: Any special program for very able students offering the opportunity for educational enrichment, independent study, acceleration, or some combination of these.

Independent study: Academic work, usually undertaken outside the regular classroom structure, chosen or designed by the student with departmental approval and instructor supervision.

Internships: Any short-term, supervised work experience usually related to a student's major field, for which the student earns academic credit. The work can be full- or part-time, on or off-campus, paid or unpaid.

Off-campus study: A formal arrangement with one or more domestic institutions under which students may take courses at the other institution(s) for credit.

Part-time degree program: Students may earn a degree through part-time enrollment in regular session (daytime) classes or evening, weekend, or summer classes.

Self-designed major: Program of study based on individual interests, designed by the student with the assistance of an adviser.

Services for LD students: Special help for learning-disabled students with resolvable difficulties, such as dyslexia.

Study abroad: An arrangement by which a student completes part of the academic program studying in another country. A college may operate a campus abroad or it may have a cooperative agreement with other U.S. institutions or institutions in other countries.

Summer session for credit: Summer courses through which students may make up degree work or accelerate their program.

Tutorials: Undergraduates can arrange for special in-depth academic assignments (not for remediation) working with faculty members one-on-one or in small groups.

ROTC: Army, Naval, or Air Force Reserve Officers' Training Corps programs offered either on campus, at a branch campus [designated by a (b)], or at a cooperating host institution [designated by (c)].

Unusual degree programs: Nontraditional programs such as a 3-2 degree program, in which three years of liberal arts study is followed by two years of study in a professional field at another institution (or in a professional division of the same institution), resulting in two bachelor's degrees or a bachelor's and a master's degree.

Student Life

Housing options: The institution's policy about whether students are permitted to live off-campus or are required to live on campus for a specified period; whether freshmen-only, coed, single-sex, cooperative, and disabled student housing options are available; whether campus housing is leased by the school and/or provided by a third party; whether freshman applicants are given priority for college housing. The phrase *college housing not available* indicates that no college-owned or -operated housing facilities are provided for undergraduates and that noncommuting students must arrange for their own accommodations.

Activities and organizations: Lists information on drama-theater groups, choral groups, marching bands, student-run campus newspapers, student-run radio stations, and social organizations (sororities, fraternities, eating clubs, etc.) and how many are represented on campus.

Campus security: Campus safety measures including 24-hour emergency response devices (telephones and alarms) and patrols by trained security personnel, student patrols, late-night transport-escort service, and controlled dormitory access (key, security card, etc.).

Student services: Information provided indicates services offered to students by the college, such as legal services, health clinics, personal-psychological counseling, and women's centers.

Athletics

Membership in one or more of the following athletic associations is indicated by initials.

NCAA: National Collegiate Athletic Association

NAIA: National Association of Intercollegiate Athletics

NCCAA: National Christian College Athletic Association

NSCAA: National Small College Athletic Association

NJCAA: National Junior College Athletic Association

CIS: Canadian Interuniversity Sports

The overall NCAA division in which all or most intercollegiate teams compete is designated by a roman numeral I, II, or III. All teams that do not compete in this division are listed as exceptions.

Sports offered by the college are divided into two groups: intercollegiate (**M** or **W** following the name of each sport indicates that it is offered for men or women) and intramural. An s in parentheses following an **M** or **W** for an intercollegiate sport indicates that athletic scholarships (or grants-in-aid) are offered for men or women in that sport, and a c indicates a club team as opposed to a varsity team.

Standardized Tests

The most commonly required standardized tests are the ACT, SAT, and SAT Subject Tests. These and other standardized tests may be used for selective admission, as a basis for counseling or course placement, or for both purposes. This section notes if a test is used for admission or placement and whether it is required, required for some, or recommended.

In addition to the ACT and SAT, the following standardized entrance and placement examinations are referred to by their initials:

ABLE: Adult Basic Learning Examination

ACT ASSET: ACT Assessment of Skills for Successful Entry and Transfer

ACT PEP: ACT Proficiency Examination Program

CAT: California Achievement Tests

CELT: Comprehensive English Language Test

CPAt: Career Programs Assessment

CPT: Computerized Placement Test

DAT: Differential Aptitude Test

LSAT: Law School Admission Test

MAPS: Multiple Assessment Program Service

MCAT: Medical College Admission Test

MMPI: Minnesota Multiphasic Personality Inventory

OAT: Optometry Admission Test

PAA: Prueba de Aptitude Académica (Spanish-language version of the SAT)

PCAT: Pharmacy College Admission Test

PSAT/NMSQT: Preliminary SAT National Merit Scholarship Qualifying Test

SCAT: Scholastic College Aptitude Test

SRA: Scientific Research Association (administers verbal, arithmetical, and achievement tests)

TABE: Test of Adult Basic Education

TASP: Texas Academic Skills Program

TOEFL: Test of English as a Foreign Language (for international students whose native language is not English)

WPCT: Washington Pre-College Test

Costs

Costs are given for the 2010–11 academic year or for the 2009–10 academic year if 2010–11 figures were not yet available. Annual expenses may be expressed as a comprehensive fee (including full-time tuition, mandatory fees, and college room and board) or as separate figures for full-time tuition, fees, room and board, or room only. For public institutions where tuition differs according to residence, separate figures are given for area or state residents and for nonresidents. Part-time tuition is expressed in terms of a per-unit rate (per credit, per semester hour, etc.) as specified by the institution.

The tuition structure at some institutions is complex in that freshmen and sophomores may be charged a different rate from that for juniors and seniors, a professional or vocational division may have a different fee structure from the liberal arts division of the same institution, or part-time tuition may be prorated on a sliding scale according to the number of credit hours taken. Tuition and fees may vary according to academic program, campus/location, class time (day, evening, weekend), course/credit load, course level, degree level, reciprocity agreements, and student level. Room and board charges are reported as an average for one academic year and may vary according to the board plan selected, campus/location, type of housing facility, or student level. If no college-owned or -operated housing facilities are offered, the phrase *college housing not available* will appear in the Housing section of the Student Life paragraph.

Tuition payment plans that may be offered to undergraduates include tuition prepayment, installment payments, and deferred payment. A tuition prepayment plan gives a student the option of locking in the current tuition rate for the entire term of enrollment by paying the full amount in advance rather than year by year. Colleges that offer such a prepayment plan may also help the student to arrange financing.

The availability of full or partial undergraduate tuition waivers to minority students, children of alumni, employees or their children, adult students, and senior citizens may be listed.

Financial Aid

The number of Federal Work Study and/or part-time jobs and average earnings are listed. Financial aid deadlines are given as well.

Applying

Application and admission options include the following:

Early admission: Highly qualified students may matriculate before graduating from high school.

Early action plan: An admission plan that allows students to apply and be notified of an admission decision well in advance of the regular notification dates. If accepted, the candidate is not committed to enroll; students may reply to the offer under the college's regular reply policy.

Early decision plan: A plan that permits students to apply and be notified of an admission decision (and financial aid offer, if applicable) well in advance of the regular notification date. Applicants agree to accept an offer of admission and to withdraw their applications from other colleges. Candidates who are not accepted under early decision are automatically considered with the regular applicant pool, without prejudice.

Deferred entrance: The practice of permitting accepted students to postpone enrollment, usually for a period of one academic term or year.

Application fee: The fee required with an application is noted. This is typically nonrefundable, although under certain specified conditions it may be waived or returned.

Requirements: Other application requirements are grouped into three categories: required for all, required for some, and recommended. They may include an essay, standardized test scores, a high school transcript, a minimum high school grade point average (expressed as a number on a scale of 0 to 4.0, where 4.0 equals A, 3.0 equals B, etc.), letters of recommendation, an interview on campus or with local alumni, and, for certain types of schools or programs, special requirements such as a musical audition or an art portfolio.

Application deadlines and notification dates: Admission application deadlines and dates for notification of acceptance or rejection are given either as specific dates or as **rolling** and **continuous.** Rolling means that applications are processed as they are received, and qualified students are accepted as long as there are openings. Continuous means that applicants are notified of acceptance or rejection as applications are processed up until the date indicated or the actual beginning of classes. The application deadline and the notification date for transfers are given if they differ from the dates for freshmen. Early decision and early action application deadlines and notification dates are also indicated when relevant.

Admissions Contact

The name, title, and telephone number of the person to contact for application information are given at the end of the Profile. The admission office address is listed in most cases. Toll-free phone numbers may also be included. The admission office fax number and e-mail address, if available, are listed, provided the school wanted them printed for use by prospective students.

Additional Information

Each college that has a **College Close-Up** in the guide will have a cross-reference appended to the Profile, referring you directly to that **College Close-Up.**

COLLEGE CLOSE-UPS

These narrative descriptions provide an inside look at certain colleges and universities, shifting the focus to a variety of other factors, some of them intangible, that should also be considered. The descriptions provide a wealth of statistics that are crucial components in the college decision-making equation—components such as tuition, financial aid, and major fields of study. Prepared exclusively by college officials, the descriptions are designed to help give students a better sense of the individuality of each institution, in terms that include campus environment, student activities, and lifestyle. Such quality-of-life intangibles can be the deciding factors in the college selection process. The absence of any college or university does not constitute an editorial decision on the part of Peterson's. In essence, these descriptions are an open forum for colleges and universities, on a voluntary basis, to communicate their particular message to prospective college students. The colleges included have paid a fee to Peterson's to provide this information. The **College Close-Ups** are edited to provide a consistent format across entries for your ease of comparison.

INDEXES

Associate Degree Programs at Two- and Four-Year Colleges

These indexes present hundreds of undergraduate fields of study that are currently offered most widely according to the colleges' responses on *Peterson's Annual Survey of Undergraduate Institutions*. The majors appear in alphabetical order, each followed by an alphabetical list of the schools that offer an associate-level program in that field. Liberal Arts and Studies indicates a general program with no specified major. The terms used for the majors are those of the U.S. Department of Education Classification of Instructional Programs (CIPs). Many institutions, however, use different terms. Readers should refer to the **College Close-Up** in this book for the school's exact terminology. In addition, although the term "major" is used in this guide, some colleges may use other terms, such as "concentration," "program of study," or "field."

DATA COLLECTION PROCEDURES

The data contained in the **Profiles of Two-Year Colleges** and **Indexes** were researched in spring 2010 through *Peterson's Annual Survey of Undergraduate Institutions.* Questionnaires were sent to the more than 1,800 colleges that meet the outlined inclusion criteria. All data included in this edition have been submitted by officials (usually admission and financial aid officers, registrars, or institutional research personnel) at the colleges themselves. All usable information received in time for publication has been included. The omission of any particular item from the **Profiles of Two-Year Colleges** and **Indexes** listing signifies either that the item is not applicable to that institution or that data were not available. Because of the comprehensive editorial review that takes place in our offices and because all material comes directly from college officials, Peterson's has every reason to believe that the information presented in this guide is accurate at the time of printing. However, students should check with a specific college or university at the time of application to verify such figures as tuition and fees, which may have changed since the publication of this volume.

CRITERIA FOR INCLUSION IN THIS BOOK

Peterson's Two-Year Colleges 2011 covers accredited institutions in the United States, U.S. territories, and other countries that award the associate degree as their most popular undergraduate offering (a few also offer bachelor's, master's, or doctoral degrees). The term two-year college is the commonly used designation for institutions that grant the associate degree, since two years is the normal duration of the traditional associate degree program. However, some programs may be completed in one year, others require three years, and, of course, part-time programs may take a considerably longer period. Therefore, "two-year college" should be understood as a conventional term that accurately describes most of the institutions included in this guide but which should not be taken literally in all cases. Also included are some non-degree-granting institutions, usually branch campuses of a multicampus system, which offer the equivalent of the first two years of a bachelor's degree, transferable to a bachelor's degree–granting institution.

To be included in this guide, an institution must have full accreditation or be a candidate for accreditation (preaccreditation) status by an institutional or specialized accrediting body recognized by the U.S. Department of Education or the Council for Higher Education Accreditation (CHEA). Institutional accrediting bodies, which review each institution as a whole, include the six regional associations of schools and colleges (Middle States, New England, North Central, Northwest, Southern, and Western), each of which is responsible for a specified portion of the United States and its territories. Other institutional accrediting bodies are national in scope and accredit specific kinds of institutions (e.g., Bible colleges, independent colleges, and rabbinical and Talmudic schools). Program registration by the New York State Board of Regents is considered to be the equivalent of institutional accreditation, since the board requires that all programs offered by an institution meet its standards before recognition is granted. This guide also includes institutions outside the United States that are accredited by these U.S. accrediting bodies. There are recognized specialized or professional accrediting bodies in more than forty different fields, each of which is authorized to accredit institutions or specific programs in its particular field. For specialized institutions that offer programs in one field only, we designate this to be the equivalent of institutional accreditation. A full explanation of the accrediting process and complete information on recognized, institutional (regional and national), and specialized accrediting bodies can be found online at www.chea.org or at www.ed.gov//admins/finaid/accred/index.html.

Quick-Reference Chart

Two-Year Colleges At-a-Glance

This chart includes the names and locations of accredited two-year colleges in the United States and U.S. territories and shows institutions' responses to the *Peterson's Annual Survey of Undergraduate Institutions.* If an institution submitted incomplete data, one or more columns opposite the institution's name is blank. A dagger after the school name indicates that the institution has one or more entries in the *College Close-Ups* section. If a school does not appear, it did not report any of the information.

Y—Yes; N—No; R—Recommended; S—For Some

Institution	Location	**Degrees Awarded** College Transfer Associate (C), Terminal Associate (T), Bachelor's (B), Master's (M)	**Institutional Control** County, District, City, State and Local, State-Related Federal, State Commonwealth, Territory, Independent, Independent-Religious, Proprietary	**Student Body** Men, Primarily Men, Women, Primarily Women, Coed	Undergraduate Enrollment	Percent Attending Part-Time	Percent 25 Years of Age or Older	Percent of Grads Going on to Four-Year Colleges	Open Admissions	High School Equivalency Certificate Accepted	High School Transcript Required	Need-Based Aid Available	Part-Time Jobs Available	Career Counseling Available	Job Placement Services Available	College Housing Available	Number of Sports Offered	Number of Majors Offered
UNITED STATES																		
Alabama																		
Alabama Southern Community College	Monroeville	C,T	St	M/W	1,244													
Bevill State Community College	Sumiton	C,T	St	M/W	4,556	44	37		Y	Y	Y	Y	Y	Y	Y	Y	8	13
Enterprise State Community College	Enterprise	C,T	St	M/W	2,189													
Gadsden State Community College	Gadsden	C,T	St	M/W	5,803	42	22	19	Y	Y	Y	Y	Y	Y	Y	Y	6	25
George Corley Wallace State Community College	Selma	C,T	St	M/W	1,781													
H. Councill Trenholm State Technical College	Montgomery	T	St	M/W	1,587		48		Y	Y	Y	Y	Y	Y	Y	N		20
Herzing College	Birmingham	C,T,B	Prop	M/W	371													
ITT Technical Institute	Bessemer	T,B	Prop	M/W						Y		Y	Y			N		16
ITT Technical Institute	Madison	T,B	Prop	M/W														11
ITT Technical Institute	Mobile	T,B	Prop	M/W														11
Jefferson Davis Community College	Brewton	C,T	St	M/W	1,257													
Jefferson State Community College	Birmingham	C,T	St	M/W	8,548	62	39		Y	Y	S	Y	Y	Y	Y	N	4	25
J. F. Drake State Technical College	Huntsville	T	St	M/W	1,258	40	57		Y	Y	Y		Y	Y	Y	N		7
Lawson State Community College	Birmingham	C,T	St	M/W	4,353		18		Y	Y	Y	Y	Y	Y	Y	Y	10	31
Lurleen B. Wallace Community College	Andalusia	C	St	M/W	1,791	39	37		Y	Y	Y	Y	Y	Y		N	3	12
Northwest-Shoals Community College	Muscle Shoals	C	St	M/W	4,537	47	30		Y	Y	Y	Y	Y	Y	Y	Y	7	19
Reid State Technical College	Evergreen	T	St	M/W	610	40	13		Y		Y	Y	Y	Y	Y	N		2
Southern Union State Community College	Wadley	C,T	St	M/W	4,971		23		Y	Y	Y	Y	Y			Y		20
Alaska																		
Charter College	Anchorage	C,T,B	Prop	M/W	516													
University of Alaska Anchorage, Kenai Peninsula College	Soldotna	C,T,B	St	M/W	2,230				Y	Y	Y	Y	Y			N		9
University of Alaska Anchorage, Matanuska-Susitna College	Palmer	C,T	St	M/W	1,782		45		Y	Y	Y	Y	Y	Y		N		9
American Samoa																		
American Samoa Community College	Pago Pago	C,T	Terr	M/W	1,767													
Arizona																		
Apollo College–Phoenix	Phoenix	C,T	Prop	PW	3,166													
Apollo College–Tri-City, Inc.	Mesa	C,T	Prop	M/W														
Apollo College–Westside, Inc.	Phoenix	C,T	Prop	M/W														
Arizona Automotive Institute	Glendale	T	Prop	M/W	582													
Arizona Western College	Yuma	C,T	St-L	M/W	7,984	67			Y			Y	Y	Y	Y	Y	7	43
Brown Mackie College–Phoenix†	Phoenix	T,B	Prop	M/W														10
Brown Mackie College–Tucson†	Tucson	C,T,B	Prop	M/W														15
Central Arizona College	Coolidge	C,T	Pub	M/W	7,913	62	13		Y			Y	Y	Y	Y	Y	6	34
Coconino Community College	Flagstaff	C,T	St	M/W	3,751	78												
Eastern Arizona College	Thatcher	C,T	St-L	M/W	7,241	68	36	15	Y		R	Y	Y	Y	Y	Y	10	50
Estrella Mountain Community College	Avondale	C,T	St-L	M/W	6,358	74		0	Y			Y	Y	Y		N		2
Glendale Community College	Glendale	C,T	St-L	M/W	20,154	65	37		Y		S	Y	Y	Y	Y	Y	11	52
High-Tech Institute	Phoenix	T,B	Prop	M/W	5,742													
ITT Technical Institute	Phoenix	T,B	Prop	M/W						Y		Y	Y			N		12
ITT Technical Institute	Tucson	T,B	Prop	M/W					N	Y		Y	Y			N		13
Kaplan College, Phoenix Campus	Phoenix	T	Prop	M/W						Y								2
Lamson College	Tempe	C,T	Prop	M/W	349		55		N	Y	Y	Y	Y	Y	Y	N		2
Mohave Community College	Kingman	C,T	St	M/W	6,702	71	56		Y			Y	Y	Y	Y	N		34
Northland Pioneer College	Holbrook	C,T	St-L	M/W	4,636	80	67		Y			Y	Y	Y		N		57
Paradise Valley Community College	Phoenix	C,T	St-L	M/W	9,951				Y			Y	Y	Y	Y	N	7	31
Phoenix College	Phoenix	C,T	Cou	M/W	12,164				Y			Y	Y	Y	Y	N	12	39
Pima Community College	Tucson	C,T	St-L	M/W	35,880	67	42	50	Y			Y	Y	Y	Y	N	16	54
Pima Medical Institute	Mesa	T	Prop	M/W	958													
Pima Medical Institute	Tucson	T	Prop	M/W	900													
Rio Salado College	Tempe	C,T	St-L	M/W	20,865		43		Y			Y	Y	Y	Y	N		15
Scottsdale Community College	Scottsdale	C,T	St-L	M/W	10,923	66	26		Y			Y	Y	Y		N	14	25
Scottsdale Culinary Institute	Scottsdale	T,B	Prop	M/W	1,275													
Tohono O'odham Community College	Sells	C,T	Pub	M/W	254	90	74		Y	Y	Y			Y		N		6
Yavapai College	Prescott	C,T	St-L	M/W	8,276	77	70		Y	Y	Y	Y	Y	Y	Y	Y	5	25
Arkansas																		
Arkansas State University–Beebe	Beebe	C,T	St	M/W	4,491	42	32		Y	Y	Y	Y	Y	Y	Y	Y	12	17
Arkansas State University–Mountain Home	Mountain Home	T	St	M/W	1,232	38	38		Y	Y	Y	Y	Y	Y		N		10
Black River Technical College	Pocahontas	C,T	St	M/W	1,933													
Cossatot Community College of the University of Arkansas	De Queen	C,T	St	M/W	1,426		39		Y	Y	R	Y	Y	Y	Y	N		11
Crowley's Ridge College	Paragould	C,T	I-R	M/W	168													

This chart includes the names and locations of accredited two-year colleges in the United States and U.S. territories and shows institutions' responses to the *Peterson's Annual Survey of Undergraduate Institutions.* If an institution submitted incomplete data, one or more columns opposite the institution's name is blank. A dagger after the school name indicates that the institution has one or more entries in the *College Close-Ups* section. If a school does not appear, it did not report any of the information.

Y—Yes; N—No; R—Recommended; S—For Some

		Degrees Awarded College Transfer Associate (C), Terminal Associate (T), Bachelor's (B), Master's (M)	**Institutional Control** County, District, City, State and Local, State-Related; Independent, Independent-Religious, Proprietary, Federal, State, Commonwealth, Territory	**Student Body** Men, Primarily Men, Women, Primarily Women, Coed	Undergraduate Enrollment	Percent Attending Part-Time	Percent 25 Years of Age or Older	Percent of Grads Going on to Four-Year Colleges	Open Admissions	High School Equivalency Certificate Accepted	High School Transcript Required	Need-Based Aid Available	Part-Time Jobs Available	Career Counseling Available	Job Placement Services Available	College Housing Available	Number of Sports Offered	Number of Majors Offered
ITT Technical Institute	Little Rock	T,B	Prop	M/W						Y		Y	Y			N		12
North Arkansas College	Harrison	C,T	St-L	M/W	2,429	39	44		Y	Y	S	Y	Y	Y	Y	N	11	15
NorthWest Arkansas Community College	Bentonville	C,T	St-L	M/W	8,006	62	47		Y	Y	Y	Y	Y	Y	Y	N	6	24
Ouachita Technical College	Malvern	C,T	St	M/W	1,610	62			Y	Y	Y	Y	Y	Y	Y	N		16
Phillips Community College of the University of Arkansas	Helena	C,T	St-L	M/W	2,337													
Pulaski Technical College	North Little Rock	C,T	St	M/W	10,255	53	60		Y	Y	Y	Y	Y	Y	Y	N		19
Rich Mountain Community College	Mena	C,T	St-L	M/W	1,004													
Southern Arkansas University Tech	Camden	C,T	St	M/W	1,817	68												
University of Arkansas Community College at Morrilton	Morrilton	C,T	St	M/W	2,421	33	36		Y	Y	Y	Y	Y	Y	Y	N	5	16
California																		
Allan Hancock College	Santa Maria	C,T	St-L	M/W	10,387	71			Y			Y	Y	Y	Y	N	10	50
American Academy of Dramatic Arts	Hollywood	C	Ind	M/W	180		10		N	Y	Y	Y	Y	Y		N		1
American River College	Sacramento	C,T	Dist	M/W	33,821													
Antelope Valley College	Lancaster	C,T	St-L	M/W	15,108	68	32		Y		Y	Y	Y	Y	Y	N	12	45
Bakersfield College	Bakersfield	C,T	St-L	M/W	15,001		50		Y			Y	Y	Y	Y	N	11	77
Berkeley City College	Berkeley	C,T	St-L	M/W	7,300		65		Y		R	Y	Y	Y				21
Butte College	Oroville	C,T	Dist	M/W	12,228													
California Culinary Academy	San Francisco	T	Prop	M/W	997													
Cambridge Career College	Yuba City	T	Prop	PW	162		49			Y	Y					N		2
Cerro Coso Community College	Ridgecrest	C,T	St	M/W	4,577													
Chabot College	Hayward	C,T	St	M/W	13,229													
Coastline Community College	Fountain Valley	C	St-L	M/W	9,316													
College of the Canyons	Santa Clarita	C,T	St-L	M/W	23,416		32		Y		R	Y	Y	Y	Y	N	11	54
College of the Sequoias	Visalia	C,T	St-L	M/W	13,449	62												
Copper Mountain College	Joshua Tree	C,T	St	M/W	1,673													
Cuyamaca College	El Cajon	C,T	St	M/W	7,706	79			Y	Y		Y	Y	Y	Y	N	7	33
Deep Springs College	Deep Springs	C	Ind	M	24		0	100	N	Y	Y					Y	12	1
Diablo Valley College	Pleasant Hill	C,T	St-L	M/W	22,567		38		Y		R	Y	Y	Y	Y	N	10	8
East Los Angeles College	Monterey Park	C,T	St-L	M/W	30,149	71	31		N		R	Y	Y	Y	Y	N	10	59
Empire College	Santa Rosa	T	Prop	M/W	900													
Fashion Careers College	San Diego	C,T	Prop	PW	91		34		N	Y	Y	Y	Y	Y	Y	N		2
FIDM/The Fashion Institute of Design & Merchandising, Los Angeles Campus†	Los Angeles	C,T,B	Prop	M/W	4,562		25	59	N	Y	Y	Y	Y	Y	Y	Y		10
FIDM/The Fashion Institute of Design & Merchandising, San Diego Campus	San Diego	C,T	Prop	PW	287		12		N	Y	Y		Y	Y	Y	Y		7
FIDM/The Fashion Institute of Design & Merchandising, San Francisco Campus	San Francisco	C,T	Prop	M/W	921		7		N	Y	Y		Y	Y	Y	N		8
Folsom Lake College	Folsom	C,T	St	M/W	9,352						R					N		21
Golden West College	Huntington Beach	C,T	St-L	M/W	13,226		44		Y	Y	R	Y	Y	Y	Y	N	9	31
ITT Technical Institute	Anaheim	T,B	Prop	M/W					N	Y		Y	Y			N		11
ITT Technical Institute	Lathrop	T,B	Prop	M/W						Y		Y	Y			N		13
ITT Technical Institute	Oxnard	C,T,B	Prop	M/W						Y		Y	Y			N		11
ITT Technical Institute	Rancho Cordova	T,B	Prop	M/W					N	Y		Y	Y			N		13
ITT Technical Institute	San Bernardino	T,B	Prop	M/W						Y		Y	Y			N		14
ITT Technical Institute	San Diego	T,B	Prop	M/W					N	Y		Y	Y			N		13
ITT Technical Institute	San Dimas	T,B	Prop	M/W					N	Y		Y	Y			N		14
ITT Technical Institute	Sylmar	T,B	Prop	M/W					N	Y		Y	Y			N		13
ITT Technical Institute	Torrance	T,B	Prop	M/W					N	Y		Y	Y			N		15
Kaplan College, Bakersfield Campus	Bakersfield	T	Prop	M/W						Y								
Kaplan College, Chula Vista Campus	Chula Vista		Prop	M/W						Y								
Kaplan College, Fresno Campus	Clovis		Prop	M/W						Y								
Kaplan College, Modesto Campus	Salida	T	Prop	PW						Y								2
Kaplan College, Palm Springs Campus	Palm Springs	T	Prop	M/W						Y								
Kaplan College, Panorama City Campus	Panorama City	T	Prop	M/W						Y								4
Kaplan College, Riverside Campus	Riverside	T	Prop	M/W						Y								
Kaplan College, Sacramento Campus	Sacramento	C,T	Prop	M/W						Y								3
Kaplan College, San Diego Campus	San Diego	T	Prop	M/W						Y			Y					1
Kaplan College, Stockton Campus	Stockton	T	Prop	M/W						Y								
Kaplan College, Vista Campus	Vista	T	Prop	M/W						Y								
Los Angeles Harbor College	Wilmington	C,T	St-L	M/W	10,083	72	35		Y			Y	Y	Y	Y	N	6	23
Los Angeles Valley College	Van Nuys	C,T	St-L	M/W	17,264													
Mendocino College	Ukiah	C,T	St-L	M/W	4,767	74	65	25	Y		Y	Y	Y	Y	Y	N	7	34
Merritt College	Oakland	C,T	St-L	M/W	6,944													
Modesto Junior College	Modesto	C,T	St-L	M/W	19,307	64												
Mt. San Antonio College	Walnut	C,T	Dist	M/W	30,026	67												
Mt. San Jacinto College	San Jacinto	C,T	St-L	M/W	17,583	64	38		Y		R	Y	Y	Y	Y	N	8	33
National Polytechnic College of Science	Wilmington	C	Prop	PM	397													
Orange Coast College	Costa Mesa	C,T	St-L	M/W	24,742	60	32		Y			Y	Y	Y	Y	N	14	100
Palomar College	San Marcos	C	St-L	M/W	27,222													
Pasadena City College	Pasadena	C,T	St-L	M/W	27,000		43		Y				Y	Y	Y	N	11	111
Pima Medical Institute	Chula Vista	T	Prop	M/W	813													
Platt College	Cerritos	C,T	Prop	M/W	320													
Platt College	Huntington Beach	C,B	Prop	M/W	50													
Platt College	Ontario	C,T,B	Prop	M/W	604													
Platt College–Los Angeles	Alhambra	C,T	Prop	M/W	116													
Reedley College	Reedley	C,T	St-L	M/W	11,782	62	39		Y	Y	Y	Y	Y	Y	Y	Y	9	39
San Diego City College	San Diego	C	St-L	M/W	19,309				Y		S	Y	Y	Y		N	16	68
San Diego Golf Academy	Vista	C,T	Prop	M/W	230													

This chart includes the names and locations of accredited two-year colleges in the United States and U.S. territories and shows institutions' responses to the *Peterson's Annual Survey of Undergraduate Institutions.* If an institution submitted incomplete data, one or more columns opposite the institution's name is blank. A dagger after the school name indicates that the institution has one or more entries in the *College Close-Ups* section. If a school does not appear, it did not report any of the information.

Y—Yes; N—No; R—Recommended; S—For Some

Institution	Location	**Degrees Awarded** College Transfer Associate (C), Terminal Associate (T), Bachelor's (B), Master's (M)	**Institutional Control** Independent, Independent-Religious, Proprietary, Federal, State, Commonwealth, Territory, County, District, City, State and Local, State-Related	**Student Body** Men, Primarily Men, Women, Primarily Women, Coed	Undergraduate Enrollment	Percent Attending Part-Time	Percent 25 Years of Age or Older	Percent of Grads Going on to Four-Year Colleges	Open Admissions	High School Equivalency Certificate Accepted	High School Transcript Required	Need-Based Aid Available	Part-Time Jobs Available	Career Counseling Available	Job Placement Services Available	College Housing Available	Number of Sports Offered	Number of Majors Offered
San Diego Mesa College	San Diego	C	St-L	M/W	24,250		51		Y			Y	Y	Y	Y	N	19	55
San Diego Miramar College	San Diego	C	St-L	M/W	10,650													
San Joaquin Delta College	Stockton	C,T	Dist	M/W	20,190													
San Joaquin Valley College	Bakersfield	T	Prop	M/W	542													
San Joaquin Valley College–Online	Visalia	T	Prop	M/W	887													
San Jose City College	San Jose	C,T	Dist	M/W	9,805													
Santa Monica College	Santa Monica	C,T	St-L	M/W	28,958													
Santa Rosa Junior College	Santa Rosa	C,T	St-L	M/W	25,319		54		Y			Y	Y	Y	Y	N	15	57
School of Urban Missions	Oakland	T,B	I-R	M/W	139	4				Y								1
Sierra College	Rocklin	C,T	St	M/W	19,416	72	32		Y			Y	Y	Y	Y	Y	13	61
Solano Community College	Fairfield	C,T	St-L	M/W	12,027													
Victor Valley College	Victorville	C,T	St	M/W			37		Y			Y	Y	Y	Y	N	12	41
WyoTech	Fremont	T	Prop	M/W	1,926									Y	Y	N		2
Colorado																		
Bel–Rea Institute of Animal Technology	Denver	T	Prop	M/W	644													
CollegeAmerica–Fort Collins	Fort Collins	T,B	Prop	M/W	116													
Colorado Northwestern Community College	Rangely	C,T	St	M/W	1,430													
Colorado School of Trades	Lakewood	T	Prop	M/W	125			4		Y	Y	Y						1
Denver Academy of Court Reporting	Westminster	T	Prop	M/W	150													
Denver Automotive and Diesel College	Denver	T	Prop	PM	863													
Front Range Community College	Westminster	C,T	St	M/W	18,713	63	41		Y			Y	Y	Y	Y	N		32
Institute of Business & Medical Careers	Fort Collins	T	Priv	M/W	302		20		Y	Y	Y	Y	Y	Y	Y	N		9
IntelliTec College	Colorado Springs	T	Prop	M/W	587													
IntelliTec Medical Institute	Colorado Springs	T	Prop	PW	434													
ITT Technical Institute	Aurora	T,B	Prop	M/W														8
ITT Technical Institute	Thornton	T,B	Prop	M/W					N	Y		Y	Y			N		12
Kaplan College, Denver Campus	Thornton	T	Prop	M/W						Y								3
Morgan Community College	Fort Morgan	C,T	St	M/W	1,643	70												
Northeastern Junior College	Sterling	C,T	St	M/W	2,698	66	28		Y		Y	Y	Y	Y	Y	Y	15	59
Otero Junior College	La Junta	C,T	St	M/W	1,660	48	25		Y	Y	R	Y	Y	Y	Y	Y	6	24
Pikes Peak Community College	Colorado Springs	C,T	St	M/W	13,572		45		Y		S	Y	Y	Y	Y	N		29
Pima Medical Institute	Denver	T	Prop	M/W	922													
Platt College	Aurora	T,B	Prop	M/W	134													
Pueblo Community College	Pueblo	C,T	St	M/W	6,528	58	57		Y	Y		Y	Y	Y	Y	N		33
Red Rocks Community College	Lakewood	C,T	St	M/W	9,105	66	51		Y			Y	Y	Y	Y	N	1	37
Redstone College–Denver	Broomfield	T	Prop	M/W	590					Y		Y	Y					2
Remington College–Colorado Springs Campus	Colorado Springs	C,T,B	Prop	M/W														
Connecticut																		
Gateway Community College	New Haven	C,T	St	M/W	6,847	64	39		Y	Y	Y	Y	Y	Y	Y	N	4	34
Goodwin College	East Hartford	C,T,B	Prop	M/W	2,083	75	62		Y	Y	Y	Y	Y	Y	Y	N		18
Housatonic Community College	Bridgeport	C,T	St	M/W	5,609				Y	Y	Y	Y	Y	Y	Y	N		24
Manchester Community College	Manchester	C,T	St	M/W	7,366	53	31		Y	Y	Y	Y	Y	Y	Y	N	4	31
Middlesex Community College	Middletown	C,T	St	M/W	2,914		38		Y	Y	Y	Y	Y	Y	Y	N		24
Northwestern Connecticut Community College	Winsted	C,T	St	M/W	1,711	65	34		Y	Y		Y	Y	Y	Y	N		35
Three Rivers Community College	Norwich	C,T	St	M/W	4,561		48	41	Y	Y	R	Y	Y	Y	Y	N	1	39
Tunxis Community College	Farmington	C,T	St	M/W	4,496	58	38		Y	Y	Y		Y	Y	Y	N		23
Delaware																		
Delaware Technical & Community College, Jack F. Owens Campus	Georgetown	C,T	St	M/W	4,787	50			Y		S	Y	Y	Y	Y	N	4	51
Delaware Technical & Community College, Stanton/ Wilmington Campus	Newark	C,T	St	M/W	7,488	56			Y		S	Y	Y	Y	Y	N	5	64
Delaware Technical & Community College, Terry Campus	Dover	C,T	St	M/W	3,406	53			Y		S	Y	Y	Y	Y	N	3	43
Florida																		
ATI Career Training Center	Fort Lauderdale	T	Prop	M/W	312													
ATI College of Health	Miami	C,T	Prop	M/W	1,191													
Brevard Community College	Cocoa	C,T	St	M/W	15,607	61												
Brown Mackie College–Miami†	Miami	T,B	Prop	M/W														8
Central Florida Institute	Palm Harbor	T	Prop	M/W	545													
Chipola College	Marianna	C,T,B	St	M/W	2,341	52	39		Y	Y	Y	Y	Y	Y	Y	N	4	19
Daytona State College	Daytona Beach	C,T,B	St	M/W	17,779	55	44	64	Y	Y	Y	Y	Y	Y	Y	N	12	49
Edison State College	Fort Myers	C,T,B	St-L	M/W	13,007	65												
Florida Career College	Miami	T	Prop	M/W	3,952													
Florida Keys Community College	Key West	C,T	St	M/W	1,012													
Florida State College at Jacksonville	Jacksonville	C,T,B	St	M/W	25,903	69												
Florida Technical College	Jacksonville	T	Prop	M/W	185													
Florida Technical College	Orlando	T	Prop	M/W	1,355													
Gulf Coast Community College	Panama City	C,T	St	M/W	5,758													
Herzing College	Winter Park	T,B	Prop	M/W	209													
Hillsborough Community College	Tampa	C,T	St	M/W	26,964	58	33		Y	Y	Y	Y	Y	Y	Y	Y	5	41
Indian River State College	Fort Pierce	C,T,B	St	M/W	17,110	65	45	84	Y	Y	Y	Y	Y	Y	Y	N	7	92
ITT Technical Institute	Fort Lauderdale	T,B	Prop	M/W					N	Y		Y	Y			N		16
ITT Technical Institute	Fort Myers	T,B	Prop	M/W														9
ITT Technical Institute	Jacksonville	T,B	Prop	M/W					N	Y		Y	Y			N		14
ITT Technical Institute	Lake Mary	T,B	Prop	M/W						Y		Y	Y			N		17

This chart includes the names and locations of accredited two-year colleges in the United States and U.S. territories and shows institutions' responses to the *Peterson's Annual Survey of Undergraduate Institutions.* If an institution submitted incomplete data, one or more columns opposite the institution's name is blank. A dagger after the school name indicates that the institution has one or more entries in the *College Close-Ups* section. If a school does not appear, it did not report any of the information.

Y—Yes; N—No; R—Recommended; S—For Some

		Degrees Awarded College Transfer Associate (C), Terminal Associate (T), Bachelor's (B), Master's (M)	**Institutional Control** Independent, Independent-Religious, Proprietary, Federal, State, Commonwealth, Territory, County, District, City, State and Local, State-Related	**Student Body** Men, Primarily Men, Women, Primarily Women, Coed	Undergraduate Enrollment	Percent Attending Part-Time	Percent 25 Years of Age or Older	Percent of Grads Going on to Four-Year Colleges	Open Admissions	High School Equivalency Certificate Accepted	High School Transcript Required	Need-Based Aid Available	Part-Time Jobs Available	Career Counseling Available	Job Placement Services Available	College Housing Available	Number of Sports Offered	Number of Majors Offered
ITT Technical Institute	Miami	T,B	Prop	M/W						Y		Y	Y			N		16
ITT Technical Institute	Pinellas Park	T,B	Prop	M/W														12
ITT Technical Institute	Tallahassee	T,B	Prop	M/W														10
ITT Technical Institute	Tampa	T,B	Prop	M/W					N	Y		Y	Y			N		17
Kaplan College, Pembroke Pines	Pembroke Pines		Prop	M/W						Y								
Key College	Dania	C,T	Prop	PW	100													
Lake-Sumter Community College	Leesburg	C	St-L	M/W	4,500	66	31		Y	Y	Y	Y	Y	Y	Y	N	6	12
Lincoln College of Technology	West Palm Beach	C,T,B	Prop	M/W	1,521													
Miami Dade College†	Miami	C,T,B	St-L	M/W	57,222	62	32		Y	Y	Y	Y	Y	Y	Y	N	8	141
Northwest Florida State College	Niceville	C,T,B	St-L	M/W	10,317		43		Y	Y	Y	Y	Y	Y	Y	N	4	55
Palm Beach State College	Lake Worth	C,T,B	St	M/W	28,587	62	37		Y	Y		Y	Y	Y	Y	N	9	67
Pasco-Hernando Community College	New Port Richey	C,T	St	M/W	11,969		35		Y	Y	Y	Y	Y	Y		N	5	19
Pensacola Junior College	Pensacola	C,T	St	M/W	11,598	58	38		Y	Y	Y	Y	Y	Y	Y	N	16	37
Polk State College	Winter Haven	C,T,B	St	M/W	9,437	65	35		Y	Y	Y	Y	Y	Y	Y	N	7	22
Rasmussen College Ocala	Ocala	T,B	Prop	PW	507													
Rasmussen College Pasco County	Holiday	T,B	Prop	M/W	453													
Seminole State College of Florida	Sanford	C,T	St-L	M/W	16,449	57	58		Y	Y	Y	Y	Y	Y	Y	N	3	50
State College of Florida Manatee-Sarasota	Bradenton	C,T,B	St	M/W	11,232	52	39		Y	Y	Y	Y	Y	Y	Y	N	5	96
Tallahassee Community College	Tallahassee	C,T	St-L	M/W	14,526	48	23		Y	Y	Y	Y	Y	Y	Y	N	6	30
Georgia																		
Albany Technical College	Albany	T	St	M/W	3,962	36	62		Y	Y	Y					N		17
Altamaha Technical College	Jesup	T	St	M/W	1,551	59	53		Y	Y	Y					N		9
Andrew College	Cuthbert	C	I-R	M/W														
Athens Technical College	Athens	T	St	M/W	5,167	59	49		Y	Y	Y	Y	Y			N		27
Atlanta Technical College	Atlanta	T	St	M/W	4,740	49	63		Y	Y	Y					N		11
Augusta Technical College	Augusta	T	St	M/W	5,028	52	56		Y	Y	Y	Y	Y			N		24
Bainbridge College	Bainbridge	C,T	St	M/W	3,545		54			Y	S	Y	Y	Y	Y	N	2	34
Brown Mackie College–Atlanta†	Atlanta	T	Prop	M/W														10
Central Georgia Technical College	Macon	T	St	M/W	6,950	44	60		Y	Y	Y	Y	Y			N		27
Chattahoochee Technical College	Marietta	T	St	M/W	11,391	53	50		Y	Y	Y	Y	Y			N		22
Columbus Technical College	Columbus	T	St	M/W	4,172	57	53		Y	Y	Y	Y	Y			N		24
Darton College	Albany	C,T	St	M/W	5,854	51	50		Y	Y	Y	Y	Y	Y	Y	Y	13	72
DeKalb Technical College	Clarkston	T	St	M/W	4,742	58	67		Y	Y	Y	Y	Y			N		27
East Central Technical College	Fitzgerald	T	St	M/W	1,761	46	57		Y	Y	Y					N		5
Emory University, Oxford College	Oxford	C,T,B	I-R	M/W	756		0	97	N	N	Y	Y	Y	Y		Y	9	1
Flint River Technical College	Thomaston	T	St	M/W	959	42	61		Y	Y	Y					N		10
Gainesville State College	Oakwood	C,T,B	St	M/W	8,801	31	16		N	Y	Y	Y	Y	Y	Y	N	6	35
Georgia Highlands College	Rome	C,T	St	M/W	5,246	39	27		N	Y	Y	Y	Y	Y		N	12	40
Georgia Military College	Milledgeville	C,T	St-L	M/W	5,724	30	37		N	Y	Y	Y	Y	Y		Y	9	27
Georgia Northwestern Technical College	Rome	T	St	M/W	5,994	49	58		Y	Y	Y					N		13
Georgia Perimeter College	Decatur	C,T	St	M/W	24,549	53	34		N	Y	Y	Y	Y	Y	Y	N	5	8
Griffin Technical College	Griffin	T	St	M/W	5,185	51	55		Y	Y	Y	Y						23
Gupton-Jones College of Funeral Service	Decatur	T	Ind	M/W	149													
Gwinnett Technical College	Lawrenceville	T	St	M/W	6,649	54	5		Y	Y	Y	Y	Y			N		27
Heart of Georgia Technical College	Dublin	T	St	M/W	1,815	55	49		Y	Y	Y					N		9
ITT Technical Institute	Atlanta	T,B	Prop	M/W														7
ITT Technical Institute	Duluth	T,B	Prop	M/W					N	Y		Y				N		10
ITT Technical Institute	Kennesaw	T,B	Prop	M/W														10
Lanier Technical College	Oakwood	T	St	M/W	4,115	60	59		Y	Y	Y					N		21
Middle Georgia College	Cochran	C,T,B	St	M/W	3,614	28	21		N	Y	Y	Y	Y	Y	Y	Y	10	18
Middle Georgia Technical College	Warner Robbins	T	St	M/W	3,543	38	55		Y	Y	Y	Y	Y			N		11
Moultrie Technical College	Moultrie	T	St	M/W	2,407	47	50		Y	Y	Y					N		10
North Georgia Technical College	Clarkesville	T	St	M/W	2,865	37	50		Y	Y	Y					Y		10
Ogeechee Technical College	Statesboro	T	St	M/W	2,419	49	47		Y	Y	Y					N		24
Okefenokee Technical College	Waycross	T	St	M/W	1,734	61	53		Y	Y	Y					N		11
Sandersville Technical College	Sandersville	T	St	M/W	1,116	65	50		Y	Y	Y					N		5
Savannah Technical College	Savannah	T	St	M/W	5,483	56	51		Y	Y	Y	Y				N		16
Southeastern Technical College	Vidalia	T	St	M/W	1,972	54	50		Y	Y	Y					N		13
South Georgia College	Douglas	C,T	St	M/W	2,000	26	22		N	Y	Y	Y	Y			Y	10	40
South Georgia Technical College	Americus	T	St	M/W	2,562	38	47		Y	Y	Y					Y		15
Southwest Georgia Technical College	Thomasville	T	St	M/W	1,721	60	52		Y	Y	Y	Y	Y			N		11
Valdosta Technical College	Valdosta	T	St	M/W	3,585	48	53		Y	Y	Y					N		15
Waycross College	Waycross	C,T	St	M/W	1,118		38			Y	Y	Y	Y			N	2	3
West Georgia Technical College	Waco	T	St	M/W	7,313	61	50		Y	Y	Y	Y	Y			N		17
Hawaii																		
Hawaii Community College	Hilo	C,T	St	M/W	2,603													
Hawaii Tokai International College	Honolulu	C,T	Ind	M/W	60	2		90	N	Y	Y	Y				Y		3
Honolulu Community College	Honolulu	C,T	St	M/W	4,218	65			Y			Y	Y	Y	Y	N		22
Kauai Community College	Lihue	C	St	M/W	1,345				Y		R,S	Y	Y	Y	Y	N	3	11
Leeward Community College	Pearl City	C,T	St	M/W	7,484		27	42	Y	Y	S	Y	Y	Y	Y	N	4	12
Maui Community College	Kahului	C,T	St	M/W	3,254	61												
Remington College–Honolulu Campus	Honolulu	C,T,B	Prop	M/W														
Idaho																		
Apollo College–Boise	Boise	C,T	Prop	M/W	600													
Brown Mackie College–Boise†	Boise	T,B	Prop	M/W														12

This chart includes the names and locations of accredited two-year colleges in the United States and U.S. territories and shows institutions' responses to the *Peterson's Annual Survey of Undergraduate Institutions.* If an institution submitted incomplete data, one or more columns opposite the institution's name is blank. A dagger after the school name indicates that the institution has one or more entries in the *College Close-Ups* section. If a school does not appear, it did not report any of the information.

Y—Yes; N—No; R—Recommended; S—For Some

		Degrees Awarded: College Transfer Associate (C), Terminal Associate (T), Bachelor's (B), Master's (M)	Institutional Control: Independent, Independent-Religious, Proprietary, Federal, State, Commonwealth, Territory, County, District, City, State and Local, State-Related	Student Body: Men, Primarily Men, Women, Primarily Women, Coed	Undergraduate Enrollment	Percent Attending Part-Time	Percent 25 Years of Age or Older	Percent of Grads Going on to Four-Year Colleges	Open Admissions	High School Equivalency Certificate Accepted	High School Transcript Required	Need-Based Aid Available	Part-Time Jobs Available	Career Counseling Available	Job Placement Services Available	College Housing Available	Number of Sports Offered	Number of Majors Offered
Eastern Idaho Technical College	Idaho Falls	T	St	M/W	766													
ITT Technical Institute	Boise	T,B	Prop	M/W					N	Y		Y	Y			N		16
North Idaho College	Coeur d'Alene	C,T	St-L	M/W	4,323	40	10		N		S	Y	Y	Y	Y	Y	18	68
Illinois																		
Black Hawk College	Moline	C,T	St-L	M/W	6,267	57	40	69	Y		R	Y	Y	Y	Y	N	6	50
Brown Mackie College–Quad Cities†	Moline	T	Prop	M/W														3
Carl Sandburg College	Galesburg	C,T	St-L	M/W	2,693													
City Colleges of Chicago, Malcolm X College	Chicago	C,T	St-L	M/W	6,031	58	60	29	Y	Y	Y	Y	Y	Y	Y	N	3	26
City Colleges of Chicago, Richard J. Daley College	Chicago	C,T	St-L	M/W	9,711	64	53		Y	Y	Y	Y	Y	Y	Y	N	2	15
College of DuPage	Glen Ellyn	C,T	St-L	M/W	27,083	61			Y			Y	Y	Y	Y	N	16	84
College of Lake County	Grayslake	C,T	Dist	M/W	18,092		40		Y		S	Y	Y	Y	Y	N	9	40
Danville Area Community College	Danville	C,T	St-L	M/W	3,584	59			Y	Y	Y	Y	Y	Y	Y	N	8	28
Elgin Community College	Elgin	C,T	St-L	M/W	9,821	63	40		Y		S		Y	Y	Y	N	8	43
Fox College	Bedford Park	T	Priv	M/W	345											N		9
Gem City College	Quincy	T	Prop	M/W	67													
Heartland Community College	Normal	C,T	St-L	M/W	4,667													
Highland Community College	Freeport	C,T	St-L	M/W	2,455	48	38		Y	Y	S	Y	Y	Y		N	5	53
Illinois Eastern Community Colleges, Frontier Community College	Fairfield	C,T	St-L	M/W	2,009	84	57		Y	Y	Y	Y	Y	Y	Y	N		9
Illinois Eastern Community Colleges, Lincoln Trail College	Robinson	C,T	St-L	M/W	1,231	54	50		Y	Y	Y	Y	Y	Y	Y	N	4	13
Illinois Eastern Community Colleges, Olney Central College	Olney	C,T	St-L	M/W	1,627	43	41		Y	Y	Y	Y	Y	Y	Y	N	4	15
Illinois Eastern Community Colleges, Wabash Valley College	Mount Carmel	C,T	St-L	M/W	4,810	82	55		Y	Y	Y	Y	Y	Y	Y	N	6	18
Illinois Valley Community College	Oglesby	C,T	Dist	M/W	4,529	54	35		Y		Y	Y	Y	Y	Y	N	6	46
ITT Technical Institute	Burr Ridge	T,B	Prop	M/W						Y		Y	Y			N		9
ITT Technical Institute	Mount Prospect	T,B	Prop	M/W					N	Y		Y	Y			N		9
ITT Technical Institute	Orland Park	T,B	Prop	M/W						Y		Y	Y			N		8
John Wood Community College	Quincy	C,T	Dist	M/W	2,403	49	35		Y	Y	Y	Y	Y	Y	Y	N	5	33
Kankakee Community College	Kankakee	C,T	St-L	M/W	4,027	54			Y	Y	Y	Y	Y	Y	Y	N	5	40
Kaskaskia College	Centralia	C,T	St-L	M/W	5,337	55	45		Y	Y	Y	Y	Y	Y		N	8	25
Kishwaukee College	Malta	C,T	St-L	M/W	4,466													
Lewis and Clark Community College	Godfrey	C,T	Dist	M/W	8,179				Y		R	Y	Y	Y	Y	N	7	28
Lincoln Land Community College	Springfield	C,T	Dist	M/W	7,677	57	37	35	Y		R	Y	Y	Y	Y	N	6	29
McHenry County College	Crystal Lake	C,T	St-L	M/W	5,274													
Moraine Valley Community College	Palos Hills	C,T	St-L	M/W	17,774	56	30	89	Y	Y	Y	Y	Y	Y	Y	N	9	35
Northwestern College	Rosemont	C,T	Prop	M/W	1,762		61		N	Y	Y	Y	Y	Y	Y	N		15
Oakton Community College	Des Plaines	C,T	Dist	M/W	10,805													
Rend Lake College	Ina	C,T	St	M/W	5,871		47		Y	Y	Y	Y	Y	Y	Y	N	8	28
Rock Valley College	Rockford	C,T	Dist	M/W	8,145	57												
Sauk Valley Community College	Dixon	C,T	Dist	M/W	2,393	54												
Shawnee Community College	Ullin	C,T	St-L	M/W	3,190	70	54		Y	Y	Y	Y	Y	Y	Y	Y	7	23
Solex College	Wheeling	T	Prop	M/W						Y	Y							1
South Suburban College	South Holland	C,T	St-L	M/W	7,279		52		Y	Y	Y	Y	Y	Y		N	5	23
Triton College	River Grove	C,T	St	M/W	15,658	75	40		Y	Y	Y	Y	Y	Y	Y	N	6	69
Vet Tech Institute at Fox College	Tinley Park	T	Priv	M/W	185											N		1
Indiana																		
Aviation Institute of Maintenance–Indianapolis	Indianapolis	T	Prop	M/W	205													
Brown Mackie College–Fort Wayne†	Fort Wayne	T,B	Prop	M/W														15
Brown Mackie College–Indianapolis†	Indianapolis	T,B	Prop	M/W														7
Brown Mackie College–Merrillville†	Merrillville	T,B	Prop	M/W														12
Brown Mackie College–Michigan City†	Michigan City	C,T,B	Prop	M/W														13
Brown Mackie College–South Bend†	South Bend	C,T,B	Prop	PW														14
Harrison College	Anderson	T	Prop	M/W	225				N	Y	Y			Y	Y			10
Harrison College	Columbus	T	Prop	M/W	270				N	Y	Y	Y	Y	Y	Y	N		8
Harrison College	Elkhart	T,B	Prop	M/W	192					Y	Y							8
Harrison College	Evansville	T,B	Prop	M/W	212				N	Y	Y	Y	Y	Y	Y			11
Harrison College	Fort Wayne	T,B	Prop	M/W	561				N	Y	Y	Y	Y	Y	Y	N		11
Harrison College	Indianapolis	T,B	Prop	M/W	1,889				N	Y	Y	Y	Y	Y	Y	N		17
Harrison College	Indianapolis	T	Prop	M/W	247						Y			Y	Y	N		2
Harrison College	Indianapolis	T	Prop	PW	458				N	Y	Y			Y	Y	N		7
Harrison College	Lafayette	T,B	Prop	M/W	272				N	Y	Y	Y	Y	Y	Y	N		9
Harrison College	Muncie	T,B	Prop	PW	201				N	Y	Y	Y	Y	Y	Y	N		15
Harrison College	Terre Haute	T,B	Prop	M/W	257				N	Y	Y			Y	Y			11
International Business College	Indianapolis	T	Priv	M/W	406					Y		Y				Y		11
ITT Technical Institute	Fort Wayne	T,B	Prop	M/W					N	Y		Y	Y			N		18
ITT Technical Institute	Indianapolis	T,B	Prop	M/W					N	Y		Y	Y			N		22
ITT Technical Institute	Merrillville	T,B	Prop	M/W														8
ITT Technical Institute	Newburgh	T,B	Prop	M/W					N	Y		Y	Y			N		15
Ivy Tech Community College–Bloomington	Bloomington	C,T	St	M/W	4,720	53	42		Y		Y	Y	Y	Y	Y			27
Ivy Tech Community College–Central Indiana	Indianapolis	C,T	St	M/W	21,501	67	46		Y		Y	Y	Y	Y	Y	N	6	42
Ivy Tech Community College–Columbus	Columbus	C,T	St	M/W	4,944	61	49		Y		Y	Y	Y	Y	Y	N		32
Ivy Tech Community College–East Central	Muncie	C,T	St	M/W	8,579	53	49		Y		Y	Y	Y	Y	Y	N		38
Ivy Tech Community College–Kokomo	Kokomo	C,T	St	M/W	5,434	58	60		Y		Y	Y	Y	Y	Y	N		31
Ivy Tech Community College–Lafayette	Lafayette	C,T	St	M/W	8,305	55	29		Y		Y	Y	Y	Y	Y	N		42
Ivy Tech Community College–North Central	South Bend	C,T	St	M/W	8,665	68	59		Y		Y	Y	Y	Y	Y	N		42
Ivy Tech Community College–Northeast	Fort Wayne	C,T	St	M/W	11,497	59	51		Y		Y	Y	Y	Y	Y	N		39

This chart includes the names and locations of accredited two-year colleges in the United States and U.S. territories and shows institutions' responses to the *Peterson's Annual Survey of Undergraduate Institutions.* If an institution submitted incomplete data, one or more columns opposite the institution's name is blank. A dagger after the school name indicates that the institution has one or more entries in the *College Close-Ups* section. If a school does not appear, it did not report any of the information.

Y—Yes; N—No; R—Recommended; S—For Some

Institution	City	Degrees Awarded: College Transfer Associate (C), Terminal Associate (T), Bachelor's (B), Master's (M)	Institutional Control: Independent, Independent-Religious, Proprietary, Federal, State, Commonwealth, Territory, County, District, City, State and Local, State-Related	Student Body: Men, Primarily Men, Women, Primarily Women, Coed	Undergraduate Enrollment	Percent Attending Part-Time	Percent 25 Years of Age or Older	Percent of Grads Going on to Four-Year Colleges	Open Admissions	High School Equivalency Certificate Accepted	High School Transcript Required	Need-Based Aid Available	Part-Time Jobs Available	Career Counseling Available	Job Placement Services Available	College Housing Available	Number of Sports Offered	Number of Majors Offered
Ivy Tech Community College–Northwest	Gary	C,T	St	M/W	9,301	62	52		Y		Y	Y	Y	Y	Y	N		42
Ivy Tech Community College–Richmond	Richmond	C,T	St	M/W	3,785	64	62		Y		Y	Y	Y	Y	Y	N	1	30
Ivy Tech Community College–Southeast	Madison	C,T	St	M/W	3,080	61	47		Y		Y	Y	Y	Y	Y	N		18
Ivy Tech Community College–Southern Indiana	Sellersburg	C,T	St	M/W	4,843	62	52		Y		Y	Y	Y	Y	Y	N		31
Ivy Tech Community College–Southwest	Evansville	C,T	St	M/W	6,501	63	48		Y		Y	Y	Y	Y	Y	N		42
Ivy Tech Community College–Wabash Valley	Terre Haute	C,T	St	M/W	6,646	58	50		Y		Y	Y	Y	Y	Y	N	2	44
Kaplan College, Hammond Campus	Hammond	T	Prop	M/W						Y		Y						3
Kaplan College, Merrillville Campus	Merrillville	T	Prop	M/W						Y								10
Kaplan College, Northwest Indianapolis Campus	Indianapolis	T	Prop	PW						Y		Y						2
Lincoln Technical Institute	Indianapolis	T	Prop	M/W	1,650													
Vet Tech Institute at International Business College	Fort Wayne	T	Priv	M/W	147											Y		1
Vet Tech Institute at International Business College	Indianapolis	T	Priv	M/W	83											Y		1
Vincennes University Jasper Campus	Jasper	C,T,B	St	M/W	915		50		Y	Y	Y	Y	Y	Y		N		25
Iowa																		
Clinton Community College	Clinton	C,T	St-L	M/W	1,240	54												
Des Moines Area Community College	Ankeny	C,T	St-L	M/W	22,324	60	41		Y		S	Y	Y	Y	Y	Y	8	50
Ellsworth Community College	Iowa Falls	C,T	St-L	M/W	916													
Hawkeye Community College	Waterloo	C,T	St-L	M/W	6,321	50	22		Y	Y	Y	Y	Y	Y	Y	N	7	32
Indian Hills Community College	Ottumwa	C,T	St-L	M/W	4,174													
Iowa Lakes Community College	Estherville	C,T	St-L	M/W	3,169	42	20		Y	Y	Y	Y	Y	Y	Y	Y	17	188
Iowa Western Community College	Council Bluffs	C,T	Dist	M/W	5,300													
ITT Technical Institute	Cedar Rapids	T,B	Prop	M/W														7
ITT Technical Institute	Clive	T,B	Prop	M/W														7
Kaplan University, Cedar Falls	Cedar Falls	C,T,B	Prop	M/W						Y								
Kaplan University, Cedar Rapids	Cedar Rapids	C,T,B	Prop	M/W						Y		Y	Y					7
Kaplan University, Council Bluffs	Council Bluffs	C,T,B	Prop	M/W						Y						N		
Kaplan University, Des Moines	Urbandale	C,T,B	Prop	M/W						Y								
Kirkwood Community College	Cedar Rapids	C,T	St-L	M/W	17,841		35		Y		Y	Y	Y	Y	Y	N	10	64
Marshalltown Community College	Marshalltown	C,T	Dist	M/W	1,701													
Muscatine Community College	Muscatine	C,T	St	M/W	1,624	63												
Northeast Iowa Community College	Calmar	C,T	St-L	M/W	5,389		38	50	Y		R	Y	Y	Y	Y	N	9	29
North Iowa Area Community College	Mason City	C	St-L	M/W	3,729	47	23		Y	Y		Y	Y	Y	Y	Y	10	38
St. Luke's College	Sioux City	T	Ind	M/W	179	25	36		N	Y	Y	Y	Y	Y	Y	N		3
Scott Community College	Bettendorf	C,T	St-L	M/W	4,111	50												
Southeastern Community College	West Burlington	C	St-L	M/W	3,754	44	36		Y			Y	Y	Y		Y	6	29
Southwestern Community College	Creston	C,T	St	M/W	1,680	50	29		Y	Y	Y	Y	Y	Y	Y	Y	4	14
Kansas																		
Allen Community College	Iola	C,T	St-L	M/W	2,776	58	35		Y	Y	Y	Y	Y	Y	Y	Y	12	69
Barton County Community College	Great Bend	C,T	St-L	M/W	4,723	78	46		Y	Y	R	Y	Y	Y	Y	Y	14	102
Brown Mackie College–Kansas City†	Lenexa	T	Prop	M/W														12
Brown Mackie College–Salina†	Salina	C,T	Prop	M/W														13
Cloud County Community College	Concordia	C,T	St-L	M/W	2,728													
Colby Community College	Colby	C,T	St-L	M/W	1,565	52	12		Y	Y	Y	Y	Y	Y	Y	Y	10	20
Cowley County Community College and Area Vocational–Technical School	Arkansas City	C,T	St-L	M/W	4,014	50	38		Y	Y	Y	Y	Y	Y		Y	10	44
Donnelly College	Kansas City	C,T,B	I-R	M/W	661	56	65		Y	Y	R	Y	Y	Y	Y	Y		1
Fort Scott Community College	Fort Scott	C,T	St-L	M/W	1,696													
Garden City Community College	Garden City	C,T	Cou	M/W	1,996													
Highland Community College	Highland	C,T	St-L	M/W	2,810													
Hutchinson Community College and Area Vocational School	Hutchinson	C,T	St-L	M/W	5,453	56	40	60	Y	Y	R	Y	Y	Y	Y	Y	14	43
Johnson County Community College	Overland Park	C,T	St-L	M/W	18,897													
Manhattan Area Technical College	Manhattan	T	St-L	M/W	473	27	32			Y	R,S			Y		N		12
Northeast Kansas Technical Center of Highland Community College	Atchison		St	M/W	364													
Seward County Community College	Liberal	C,T	St-L	M/W	1,656													
Kentucky																		
Beckfield College	Florence	T,B	Prop	M/W	605													
Big Sandy Community and Technical College	Prestonsburg	C,T	St	M/W	4,856													
Bowling Green Technical College	Bowling Green	T	St	M/W	4,953													
Brown Mackie College–Hopkinsville†	Hopkinsville	C,T	Prop	M/W														10
Brown Mackie College–Louisville†	Louisville	T,B	Prop	M/W														16
Brown Mackie College–Northern Kentucky†	Fort Mitchell	C,T	Prop	M/W														12
Daymar College	Louisville	T	Prop	M/W	321													
Daymar College	Owensboro	C	Prop	M/W	257													
Gateway Community and Technical College	Covington	C	St	M/W	4,206		50		Y	Y	Y			Y		N		15
Hazard Community and Technical College	Hazard	C,T	St	M/W	4,714	62	43		Y	Y	Y	Y	Y					10
Henderson Community College	Henderson	C,T	St	M/W	1,984													
Hopkinsville Community College	Hopkinsville	C,T	St	M/W	3,753	53	53		Y	Y	R	Y	Y	Y	Y	N	5	20
ITT Technical Institute	Louisville	T,B	Prop	M/W						Y		Y	Y			N		14
Maysville Community and Technical College	Maysville	C,T	St	M/W	3,630													
Maysville Community and Technical College	Morehead	T	St	M/W														
Owensboro Community and Technical College	Owensboro	C,T	St	M/W	6,328	66	27		Y	Y	Y	Y	Y	Y	Y			20
Somerset Community College	Somerset	C,T	St	M/W	8,201		45		Y	Y	Y	Y	Y			N		18
Southeast Kentucky Community and Technical College	Cumberland	C,T	St	M/W	4,959	61	35	50	Y	Y	Y	Y	Y	Y	Y	N	5	14

This chart includes the names and locations of accredited two-year colleges in the United States and U.S. territories and shows institutions' responses to the *Peterson's Annual Survey of Undergraduate Institutions.* If an institution submitted incomplete data, one or more columns opposite the institution's name is blank. A dagger after the school name indicates that the institution has one or more entries in the *College Close-Ups* section. If a school does not appear, it did not report any of the information.

Y—Yes; N—No; R—Recommended; S—For Some

Institution	Location	**Degrees Awarded** College Transfer Associate (C), Terminal Associate (T), Bachelor's (B), Master's (M)	**Institutional Control** Independent, Independent-Religious, Proprietary, Federal, State, Commonwealth, Territory, County, District, City, State and Local, State-Related	**Student Body** Men, Primarily Men, Women, Primarily Women, Coed	Undergraduate Enrollment	Percent Attending Part-Time	Percent 25 Years of Age or Older	Percent of Grads Going on to Four-Year Colleges	Open Admissions	High School Equivalency Certificate Accepted	High School Transcript Required	Need-Based Aid Available	Part-Time Jobs Available	Career Counseling Available	Job Placement Services Available	College Housing Available	Number of Sports Offered	Number of Majors Offered
Spencerian College	Louisville	T	Prop	M/W	1,282	27			Y	Y	Y	Y		Y	Y	Y		12
Sullivan College of Technology and Design	Louisville	T,B	Prop	M/W	662	38	44	0	N	Y	Y	Y		Y	Y	Y	1	43
West Kentucky Community and Technical College	Paducah	C,T	St	M/W	3,511	41	43		Y	Y	S	Y	Y	Y	Y	N	4	14
Louisiana																		
Baton Rouge Community College	Baton Rouge	C,T	St	M/W	7,031													
Blue Cliff College–Lafayette	Lafayette	T	Prop	M/W	116													
Blue Cliff College–Shreveport	Shreveport	T	Prop	M/W	237		58			Y	S			Y	Y	N		3
Bossier Parish Community College	Bossier City	C,T	St	M/W	4,986													
Cameron College	New Orleans	T	Prop	M/W	9													
Delta College of Arts and Technology	Baton Rouge	T	Rrop	PW	137													
Elaine P. Nunez Community College	Chalmette	C,T	St	M/W	1,834	60	47		Y		S	Y	Y	Y	Y	N	4	22
Herzing College	Kenner	C,T,B	Prop	M/W	166													
ITI Technical College	Baton Rouge	T	Prop	PM	393		46		Y		Y			Y	Y	N		7
ITT Technical Institute	Baton Rouge		Prop	M/W														12
ITT Technical Institute	St. Rose	T,B	Prop	M/W						Y		Y	Y			N		15
Louisiana Technical College	Baton Rouge	C	St	M/W	13,414	46					Y					N		28
Louisiana Technical College–Florida Parishes Campus	Greensburg	T	St	M/W	618													
MedVance Institute	Baton Rouge	T	Prop	M/W	327													
River Parishes Community College	Sorrento	C	St	M/W	1,163													
Maine																		
Central Maine Medical Center College of Nursing and Health Professions	Lewiston	T	Ind	M/W	157	85	77		N	Y	Y	Y				Y		2
Eastern Maine Community College	Bangor	C,T	St	M/W	1,923													
Kaplan University	Lewiston	T	Prop	M/W						Y								
Kaplan University	South Portland	T	Prop	M/W						Y		Y	Y					9
Kennebec Valley Community College	Fairfield	C,T	St	M/W	2,298	68	43		Y	Y	Y	Y	Y	Y	Y	N	7	30
Southern Maine Community College	South Portland	C,T	St	M/W	6,261	52	37		N	Y		Y	Y	Y	Y	Y	7	58
York County Community College	Wells	C,T	St	M/W	1,444				Y	Y	Y	Y	Y	Y	Y	N	5	11
Maryland																		
Allegany College of Maryland	Cumberland	C,T	St-L	M/W	4,913				Y	Y	Y	Y	Y	Y	Y	Y	6	26
Anne Arundel Community College	Arnold	C,T	St-L	M/W	16,741	64	37		Y			Y	Y	Y	Y	N	8	68
Carroll Community College	Westminster	C,T	St-L	M/W	3,913	56	28		Y		Y	Y	Y	Y	Y	N	4	27
Cecil College	North East	C	Cou	M/W	2,388	63	33		Y	Y	Y	Y	Y	Y	Y	N	7	37
College of Southern Maryland	La Plata	C,T	St-L	M/W	8,810	59	34		Y		R	Y	Y	Y	Y	N	7	33
The Community College of Baltimore County	Baltimore	C,T	Cou	M/W	23,584	64				Y	Y			Y		N	7	87
Frederick Community College	Frederick	C,T	St-L	M/W	6,233	62	50		Y			Y	Y	Y	Y	N	6	43
Hagerstown Community College	Hagerstown	C,T	St-L	M/W	4,002	66												
Harford Community College	Bel Air	C,T	St-L	M/W	6,656	55	32	92	Y			Y	Y	Y		N	12	39
Howard Community College	Columbia	C,T	St-L	M/W	8,777				Y		S	Y	Y	Y	Y	N	7	54
ITT Technical Institute	Owings Mills	T,B	Prop	M/W														10
Kaplan University, Hagerstown Campus	Hagerstown	T,B	Prop	M/W						Y		Y	Y					13
Montgomery College	Rockville	C,T	St-L	M/W	26,147	60	32	60	Y		R	Y	Y	Y	Y	N	11	43
TESST College of Technology	Baltimore	T	Prop	M/W						Y								3
TESST College of Technology	Beltsville	T	Prop	M/W						Y								3
TESST College of Technology	Towson	T	Prop	M/W														
Wor-Wic Community College	Salisbury	C,T	St-L	M/W	4,045	68	45		Y		R		Y	Y		N		20
Massachusetts																		
Benjamin Franklin Institute of Technology	Boston	C,T,B	Ind	M/W	536	22												
Berkshire Community College	Pittsfield	C,T	St	M/W	2,275	56	36		Y	Y	Y	Y	Y	Y	Y	N		19
Bunker Hill Community College	Boston	C,T	St	M/W	11,009	66	45		Y	Y	Y	Y	Y	Y	Y	N	7	40
Dean College	Franklin	C,T,B	Ind	M/W	1,106	12	0		N	Y	Y	Y	Y	Y	Y	Y	11	13
FINE Mortuary College, LLC	Norwood	T	Prop	M/W	73													
Greenfield Community College	Greenfield	C,T	St	M/W	2,546	59	47	42	Y	Y	S	Y	Y	Y	Y	N		30
Holyoke Community College	Holyoke	C,T	St	M/W	7,469	47	13		Y		Y	Y	Y	Y	Y	N	7	22
ITT Technical Institute	Norwood	T,B	Prop	M/W					N	Y		Y	Y			N		7
ITT Technical Institute	Woburn	T,B	Prop	M/W						Y		Y	Y			N		9
Labouré College	Boston	C,T	I-R	M/W	548													
Massasoit Community College	Brockton	C,T	St	M/W	7,941	54	38		Y	Y		Y	Y	Y	Y	N	4	35
Middlesex Community College	Bedford	C,T	St	M/W	8,124													
Mount Wachusett Community College	Gardner	C,T	St	M/W	4,761	58	45		Y	Y	Y	Y	Y	Y	Y	N	8	28
North Shore Community College	Danvers	C,T	St	M/W	7,224	57												
Quinsigamond Community College	Worcester	C,T	St	M/W	8,349	51	35	53	Y	Y	Y	Y	Y	Y	Y	N	4	46
Springfield Technical Community College	Springfield	C,T	St	M/W	6,782	56	38		Y	Y	Y	Y	Y	Y	Y	N	9	64
Michigan																		
Alpena Community College	Alpena	C,T	St-L	M/W	2,098		40		Y		Y	Y	Y	Y	Y	Y	7	29
Bay de Noc Community College	Escanaba	C,T	Cou	M/W	2,414	42												
Bay Mills Community College	Brimley	C	Dist	M/W	427													
Delta College	University Center	C,T	Dist	M/W	10,899	59	35	32	Y		R	Y	Y	Y	Y	N	8	67
Glen Oaks Community College	Centreville	C,T	St-L	M/W	1,383													
Gogebic Community College	Ironwood	C,T	St-L	M/W	975													
Grand Rapids Community College	Grand Rapids	C,T	Dist	M/W	16,942	55	33		Y	Y	Y	Y	Y	Y	Y	N	14	30
ITT Technical Institute	Canton	T,B	Prop	M/W						Y		Y	Y			N		17
ITT Technical Institute	Swartz Creek	C	Prop	M/W														16

This chart includes the names and locations of accredited two-year colleges in the United States and U.S. territories and shows institutions' responses to the *Peterson's Annual Survey of Undergraduate Institutions.* If an institution submitted incomplete data, one or more columns opposite the institution's name is blank. A dagger after the school name indicates that the institution has one or more entries in the *College Close-Ups* section. If a school does not appear, it did not report any of the information.

Y—Yes; N—No; R—Recommended; S—For Some

Institution	Location	Degrees Awarded: College Transfer Associate (C), Terminal Associate (T), Bachelor's (B), Master's (M)	Institutional Control: Independent, Independent-Religious, Proprietary, Federal, State, Commonwealth, Territory, County, District, City, State and Local, State-Related	Student Body: Men, Primarily Men, Women, Primarily Women, Coed	Undergraduate Enrollment	Percent Attending Part-Time	Percent 25 Years of Age or Older	Percent of Grads Going on to Four-Year Colleges	Open Admissions	High School Equivalency Certificate Accepted	High School Transcript Required	Need-Based Aid Available	Part-Time Jobs Available	Career Counseling Available	Job Placement Services Available	College Housing Available	Number of Sports Offered	Number of Majors Offered
ITT Technical Institute	Troy	T,B	Prop	M/W						Y		Y	Y			N		16
ITT Technical Institute	Wyoming	T,B	Prop	M/W					N	Y		Y	Y			N		16
Jackson Community College	Jackson	C,T	Cou	M/W	6,173	57	42		Y	Y		Y	Y		Y	Y	8	26
Kalamazoo Valley Community College	Kalamazoo	C,T	St-L	M/W	11,113		37		Y	Y	Y	Y	Y	Y	Y	N	6	34
Kellogg Community College	Battle Creek	C,T	St-L	M/W	5,976	66	46		Y		S	Y	Y	Y	Y	N	5	40
Kirtland Community College	Roscommon	C,T	Dist	M/W	1,972	53	45		Y	Y		Y	Y	Y	Y	N	3	31
Lake Michigan College	Benton Harbor	C,T	Dist	M/W	4,697	66	38		Y		Y	Y	Y	Y	Y	N	4	61
Lansing Community College	Lansing	C,T	St-L	M/W	21,123	63	40		Y		S	Y	Y	Y	Y	N	9	103
Macomb Community College	Warren	C,T	Dist	M/W	24,376	61	45		Y			Y	Y	Y	Y	N	11	72
Montcalm Community College	Sidney	C,T	St-L	M/W	2,328	60	60		Y	Y	R	Y	Y	Y	Y	N	1	23
Muskegon Community College	Muskegon	C,T	St-L	M/W	5,148				Y	Y	Y	Y	Y	Y	Y	N	8	44
Oakland Community College	Bloomfield Hills	C,T	St-L	M/W	28,042	64	47	9	Y		R	Y	Y	Y	Y	N	8	84
Southwestern Michigan College	Dowagiac	C,T	St-L	M/W	2,970	51	42		Y	Y	Y	Y	Y			Y	8	20
West Shore Community College	Scottville	C,T	Dist	M/W	1,553	58	39		Y		Y	Y	Y	Y	Y	N	8	14
Minnesota																		
Alexandria Technical College	Alexandria	C,T	St	M/W	2,205		28		Y	Y	Y	Y	Y	Y	Y	N	7	55
Anoka-Ramsey Community College	Coon Rapids	C,T	St	M/W	7,530		31		Y	Y	S	Y	Y	Y	Y	N	10	21
Anoka-Ramsey Community College, Cambridge Campus	Cambridge	C,T	St	M/W	2,636		39		Y	Y	S	Y	Y	Y	Y	N	7	20
Anoka Technical College	Anoka	C,T	St	M/W	2,141													
Argosy University, Twin Cities†	Eagan	T,B,M	Prop	M/W						Y								21
Central Lakes College	Brainerd	C,T	St	M/W	4,010		31		Y	Y	Y	Y	Y	Y	Y	N	8	30
Century College	White Bear Lake	C,T	St	M/W	10,469	53	39		Y	Y	Y	Y	Y	Y		N	6	50
Dakota County Technical College	Rosemount	C,T	St	M/W	2,864													
Duluth Business University	Duluth	T	Prop	PW	296													
Hennepin Technical College	Brooklyn Park	C,T	St	M/W	13,832		51		Y	Y	R	Y	Y	Y	Y	N		18
Inver Hills Community College	Inver Grove Heights	C,T	St	M/W	6,215	59	43		Y	Y	R,S	Y	Y	Y	Y	N	9	23
Itasca Community College	Grand Rapids	C,T	St	M/W	1,130		24		Y	Y	Y	Y	Y	Y	Y	Y	8	30
ITT Technical Institute	Eden Prairie	T,B	Prop	M/W														13
Leech Lake Tribal College	Cass Lake	C,T	Pub	M/W	243	22	20		Y	Y	Y			Y	Y	N		4
Mesabi Range Community and Technical College	Virginia	C,T	St	M/W	1,467		37		Y	Y	Y	Y	Y	Y	Y	Y	13	16
Minneapolis Business College	Roseville	T	Priv	PW	373											Y		9
Minneapolis Community and Technical College	Minneapolis	C,T	St	M/W					Y	Y	Y	Y	Y	Y	Y	N	1	43
Minnesota State College–Southeast Technical	Winona	C,T	St	M/W	2,529	40	50		Y	Y	Y	Y	Y	Y	Y	Y		34
Minnesota State Community and Technical College	Fergus Falls	C,T	St	M/W	6,732	49	38	75	Y	Y	Y	Y	Y	Y	Y	Y	14	55
Minnesota West Community and Technical College	Pipestone	C,T	St	M/W	2,863	44	43		Y	Y	Y	Y	Y	Y	Y	N	8	8
North Hennepin Community College	Brooklyn Park	C,T	St	M/W	7,444	60	44		Y	Y	R	Y	Y	Y	Y	N	14	28
Northland Community and Technical College–Thief River Falls	Thief River Falls	C,T	St	M/W	4,243	52			Y	Y	Y	Y	Y	Y	Y	N	10	56
Northwest Technical College	Bemidji	T	St	M/W	1,603	63	45		Y	Y	Y	Y	Y	Y		Y		14
Northwest Technical Institute	Eagan	C,T	Prop	M/W	72		4		Y	Y	Y	Y		Y	Y	N		2
Pine Technical College	Pine City	C,T	St	M/W	812	64												
Rasmussen College Eagan	Eagan	T,B	Prop	PW	537													
Rasmussen College St. Cloud	St. Cloud	C,T,B	Prop	PW	743													
Rochester Community and Technical College	Rochester	C,T,B	St	M/W	5,898													
St. Cloud Technical College	St. Cloud	C,T	St	M/W	3,949	37	19		Y	Y	Y	Y	Y	Y	Y	N	4	36
Saint Paul College–A Community & Technical College	St. Paul	C,T	St-R	M/W	5,928	59	54		Y	Y	S	Y	Y	Y	Y	N		37
Mississippi																		
Antonelli College	Hattiesburg	C	Prop	M/W	354													10
Antonelli College	Jackson	C,T	Prop	M/W	240		67		Y			Y	Y			N		10
East Central Community College	Decatur	C,T	St-L	M/W	2,281													
East Mississippi Community College	Scooba	C,T	St-L	M/W	4,012													
Hinds Community College	Raymond	C,T	St-L	M/W	9,941													
Holmes Community College	Goodman	C,T	St-L	M/W	5,107													
Meridian Community College	Meridian	C,T	St-L	M/W	3,614		30		Y	Y	Y	Y	Y	Y	Y	Y	12	21
Northeast Mississippi Community College	Booneville	C,T	St	M/W	3,339													
Southwest Mississippi Community College	Summit	C,T	St-L	M/W	2,119	14	30		Y	Y	Y	Y	Y	Y	Y	Y	7	50
Missouri																		
Brown Mackie College–St. Louis†	Fenton	T,B	Prop	M/W														11
Cottey College	Nevada	C	Ind	W	331													
Crowder College	Neosho	C,T	St-L	M/W	4,482		12		Y	Y	Y	Y	Y	Y	Y	Y	3	35
East Central College	Union	C,T	Dist	M/W	4,203	49			Y	Y	Y	Y	Y	Y	Y	N	3	33
ITT Technical Institute	Arnold	T,B	Prop	M/W						Y		Y	Y			N		16
ITT Technical Institute	Earth City	T,B	Prop	M/W					N	Y		Y	Y			N		15
ITT Technical Institute	Kansas City	T,B	Prop	M/W														11
Jefferson College	Hillsboro	C,T	St	M/W	5,788	45	25		Y	Y	Y	Y	Y	Y	Y	Y	6	
Linn State Technical College	Linn	T	St	PM	1,142	16	16		Y	Y	Y	Y	Y	Y	Y	Y	9	22
Metro Business College	Cape Girardeau	T,B	Prop	M/W	396													
Metropolitan Community College–Blue River	Independence	C,T	St-L	M/W	3,131	53	34		Y	Y		Y	Y	Y	Y	N	1	9
Metropolitan Community College–Business & Technology Campus	Kansas City	C,T	St-L	M/W	707	67				Y				Y	Y	N		43
Metropolitan Community College–Longview	Lee's Summit	C,T	St-L	M/W	6,292	54	36		Y	Y		Y	Y	Y	Y	N	5	25
Metropolitan Community College–Maple Woods	Kansas City	C,T	St-L	M/W	4,880	56	29		Y	Y		Y	Y	Y	Y	N	4	19
Metropolitan Community College–Penn Valley	Kansas City	C,T	St-L	M/W	4,656	67	55		Y	Y	Y	Y	Y	Y	Y	N	1	31
Mineral Area College	Park Hills	C,T	Dist	M/W	3,061													
Missouri College	St. Louis	T,B	Prop	PW	508													

This chart includes the names and locations of accredited two-year colleges in the United States and U.S. territories and shows institutions' responses to the *Peterson's Annual Survey of Undergraduate Institutions.* If an institution submitted incomplete data, one or more columns opposite the institution's name is blank. A dagger after the school name indicates that the institution has one or more entries in the *College Close-Ups* section. If a school does not appear, it did not report any of the information.

Y—Yes; N—No; R—Recommended; S—For Some

Institution	Location	**Degrees Awarded** College Transfer Associate (C), Terminal Associate (T), Bachelor's (B), Master's (M)	**Institutional Control** County, District, City, State and Local, State-Related, Federal, State, Commonwealth, Territory, Independent, Independent-Religious, Proprietary	**Student Body** Men, Primarily Men, Women, Primarily Women, Coed	Undergraduate Enrollment	Percent Attending Part-Time	Percent 25 Years of Age or Older	Percent of Grads Going on to Four-Year Colleges	Open Admissions	High School Equivalency Certificate Accepted	High School Transcript Required	Need-Based Aid Available	Part-Time Jobs Available	Career Counseling Available	Job Placement Services Available	College Housing Available	Number of Sports Offered	Number of Majors Offered
Missouri State University–West Plains	West Plains	C,T	St	M/W	2,162	42	37		Y	Y	S	Y	Y	Y	Y	Y	2	22
Pinnacle Career Institute	Kansas City	C	Prop	M/W	437													
Ranken Technical College	St. Louis	C,T,B	Ind	PM	1,743													
Saint Charles Community College	Cottleville	C,T	St	M/W	7,814	48	29		Y	Y	R,S	Y	Y	Y	Y	N	3	55
Sanford-Brown College	Fenton	T,B	Prop	M/W	659													
Sanford-Brown College	Hazelwood	C,T	Prop	M/W	428													
Sanford-Brown College	St. Peters	C,T	Prop	M/W	557													
State Fair Community College	Sedalia	C,T	Dist	M/W	4,263	42	39		Y	Y	Y	Y	Y	Y	Y	Y	1	29
Three Rivers Community College	Poplar Bluff	C,T	St-L	M/W	3,185	39	44		Y	Y	Y	Y	Y	Y	Y	Y	4	24
Vet Tech Institute at Hickey College	St. Louis	T	Priv	M/W	125											Y		1
Montana																		
Blackfeet Community College	Browning	C,T	Ind	M/W	471													
Dawson Community College	Glendive	C,T	St-L	M/W	446													
Flathead Valley Community College	Kalispell	C,T	St-L	M/W	2,501	43	49	45	Y	Y	Y	Y	Y	Y	Y	N	9	27
Fort Peck Community College	Poplar	C,T	Dist	M/W	422													
Miles Community College	Miles City	C,T	St-L	M/W	506													
Montana State University–Great Falls College of Technology	Great Falls	C,T	St	M/W	2,451	63	32	0	Y	Y	Y	Y	Y	Y		N		33
The University of Montana–Helena College of Technology	Helena	C,T	St	M/W	1,380	47	41		Y	Y	S	Y	Y	Y	Y	N	2	16
Nebraska																		
Central Community College–Columbus Campus	Columbus	C,T	St-L	M/W	2,601	82	41		Y	Y	Y	Y	Y	Y	Y	Y	6	25
Central Community College–Grand Island Campus	Grand Island	C,T	St-L	M/W	3,263	86	50		Y	Y	Y	Y	Y	Y	Y	Y	4	24
Central Community College–Hastings Campus	Hastings	C,T	St-L	M/W	2,858	62	42		Y	Y	Y	Y	Y	Y	Y	Y	6	39
Creative Center	Omaha	T,B	Prop	M/W						Y	Y			Y	Y	N		3
ITT Technical Institute	Omaha	T,B	Prop	M/W					N	Y		Y				N		13
Kaplan University, Lincoln	Lincoln	C,T,B	Prop	M/W						Y		Y	Y					8
Kaplan University, Omaha	Omaha	C,T,B	Prop	M/W						Y			Y					8
Little Priest Tribal College	Winnebago	C,T	Ind	M/W	120													
Metropolitan Community College	Omaha	C,T	St-L	M/W	17,003	58	44		Y		R	Y	Y	Y	Y	Y		33
Mid-Plains Community College	North Platte	C,T	Dist	M/W	2,765	61	.40		Y	Y	Y			Y		Y	5	18
Nebraska College of Technical Agriculture	Curtis	C,T	St	M/W	425	42	0.02		Y	Y	Y	Y	Y	Y	Y	Y	4	4
Northeast Community College	Norfolk	C,T	St-L	M/W	5,205	56	62	50	Y		R,S	Y	Y	Y	Y	Y	8	96
Nevada																		
Career College of Northern Nevada	Sparks	T	Prop	M/W	363		70		Y	Y	Y	Y	Y	Y	Y	N		6
Everest College	Henderson	T	Prop	M/W	639													
ITT Technical Institute	Henderson	T,B	Prop	M/W						Y		Y	Y			N		15
Pima Medical Institute	Las Vegas	T	Prop	M/W	820													
New Hampshire																		
Hesser College, Concord	Concord	C,T,B	Prop	M/W														
Hesser College, Manchester†	Manchester	C,T,B	Prop	M/W						Y		Y	Y					13
Hesser College, Nashua	Nashua	C,T,B	Prop	M/W														
Hesser College, Portsmouth	Portsmouth	C,T,B	Prop	M/W						Y								
Hesser College, Salem	Salem	C,T,B	Prop	M/W						Y								
White Mountains Community College	Berlin	C,T	St	M/W	985	61			N	Y	Y	Y	Y	Y		N	4	16
New Jersey																		
Brookdale Community College	Lincroft	C,T	Cou	M/W	14,025													
Burlington County College	Pemberton	C,T	Cou	M/W	9,693	44	31		Y	Y	Y	Y	Y	Y	Y	N	6	58
Camden County College	Blackwood	C,T	St-L	M/W	15,670	46	39		Y	Y	S	Y	Y	Y	Y	N	5	40
County College of Morris	Randolph	C,T	Cou	M/W	8,738				Y		Y	Y	Y			N	12	30
Cumberland County College	Vineland	C,T	St-L	M/W	4,014		37		Y	Y	Y	Y	Y	Y	Y	N	6	20
Essex County College	Newark	C,T	Cou	M/W	13,314	41	49		Y		Y	Y	Y	Y	Y	N	6	48
Hudson County Community College	Jersey City	C,T	St-L	M/W	7,019													
Mercer County Community College	Trenton	C,T	St-L	M/W	9,621	55	39		Y		Y	Y	Y	Y	Y	N	9	51
Ocean County College	Toms River	C,T	Cou	M/W	10,415	43	20		Y		S	Y	Y	Y		N	11	32
Raritan Valley Community College	Branchburg	C,T	Cou	M/W	7,888	48	30		Y	Y	Y	Y	Y	Y	Y	N	5	62
Union County College	Cranford	C,T	St-L	M/W	12,751	50	39		Y	Y	Y	Y	Y	Y	Y	N	6	35
New Mexico																		
Brown Mackie College–Albuquerque†	Albuquerque	T,B	Prop	M/W														12
Central New Mexico Community College	Albuquerque	C,T	St	M/W	27,938	68	52		Y			Y	Y	Y	Y	N		43
Clovis Community College	Clovis	C,T	St	M/W	3,706	84	51		Y	Y	Y	Y	Y	Y	Y	N	5	36
Doña Ana Branch Community College	Las Cruces	C,T	St-L	M/W	7,803	67												
Institute of American Indian Arts	Santa Fe	C,B	Fed	M/W	231													
ITT Technical Institute	Albuquerque	T,B	Prop	M/W					N	Y		Y	Y			N		16
Luna Community College	Las Vegas	C,T	St	M/W	1,789	70	25		Y	Y	Y	Y	Y	Y	Y	N		17
Mesalands Community College	Tucumcari	C,T	St	M/W	635													
New Mexico State University–Alamogordo	Alamogordo	C,T	St	M/W	3,237	75												
New Mexico State University–Carlsbad	Carlsbad	C,T	St	M/W	1,998	71	28		Y	Y	S	Y	Y	Y	Y	N		25
New Mexico State University–Grants	Grants	C,T	St	M/W	798													
Northern New Mexico College	Española	C,T,B	St	M/W	2,272													
Pima Medical Institute	Albuquerque	T	Prop	M/W	716													

This chart includes the names and locations of accredited two-year colleges in the United States and U.S. territories and shows institutions' responses to the *Peterson's Annual Survey of Undergraduate Institutions.* If an institution submitted incomplete data, one or more columns opposite the institution's name is blank. A dagger after the school name indicates that the institution has one or more entries in the *College Close-Ups* section. If a school does not appear, it did not report any of the information.

Y—Yes; N—No; R—Recommended; S—For Some

		College Transfer Associate (C), Terminal Associate (T), Bachelor's (B), Master's (M) **Degrees Awarded**	County, District, City, State and Local, State-Related, Federal, State, Commonwealth, Territory, Independent, Independent-Religious, Proprietary, **Institutional Control**	Men, Primarily Men, Women, Primarily Women, Coed **Student Body**	Undergraduate Enrollment	Percent Attending Part-Time	Percent 25 Years of Age or Older	Percent of Grads Going on to Four-Year Colleges	Open Admissions	High School Equivalency Certificate Accepted	High School Transcript Required	Need-Based Aid Available	Part-Time Jobs Available	Career Counseling Available	Job Placement Services Available	College Housing Available	Number of Sports Offered	Number of Majors Offered
San Juan College	Farmington	C,T	St	M/W	8,990	66	57		Y	Y	Y	Y	Y	Y	Y	N	16	67
Southwestern Indian Polytechnic Institute	Albuquerque	C,T	Fed	M/W	635	21	35		N	Y	Y	Y	Y			Y	3	15
New York																		
Adirondack Community College	Queensbury	C,T	St-L	M/W	3,408													
American Academy of Dramatic Arts	New York	T	Ind	M/W	228		7		N	Y	Y	Y	Y	Y	Y	N		1
The Art Institute of New York City†	New York	C,T	Prop	M/W														5
ASA Institute, The College of Advanced Technology	Brooklyn	T	Prop	M/W	3,033													
Bronx Community College of the City University of New York	Bronx	C,T	St-L	M/W	10,131	41	35		Y	Y	Y		Y	Y	Y		6	27
Broome Community College	Binghamton	C,T	St-L	M/W	6,877	32	29		Y	Y	Y	Y	Y	Y	Y	N	10	35
Bryant & Stratton College - Albany Campus	Albany	T	Prop	M/W	470	25	51		N	Y	Y	Y	Y	Y	Y	N		11
Bryant & Stratton College - Amherst Campus	Clarence	T,B	Prop	M/W	474	42	56		N		Y	Y	Y	Y	Y	N		16
Bryant & Stratton College - Buffalo Campus	Buffalo	T,B	Prop	M/W	693	32	46		N		Y	Y	Y	Y	Y	N		14
Bryant & Stratton College - Greece Campus	Rochester	T	Prop	M/W	279	31	73		N	Y	Y	Y	Y	Y	Y	N	1	13
Bryant & Stratton College - Henrietta Campus	Rochester	T	Prop	M/W	407	29	47		N	Y	Y	Y	Y	Y	Y	N	1	18
Bryant & Stratton College - North Campus	Liverpool	T	Prop	M/W	497	33	52		Y	Y	Y	Y	Y	Y	Y	N		12
Bryant & Stratton College - Southtowns Campus	Orchard Park	T,B	Prop	M/W	1,206	45	49		N		Y	Y	Y	Y	Y	N		13
Bryant & Stratton College - Syracuse Campus	Syracuse	T	Prop	M/W	715	31	48	2	N	Y	Y	Y	Y	Y	Y	Y	1	9
Cayuga County Community College	Auburn	C,T	St-L	M/W	4,050													
Corning Community College	Corning	C,T	St-L	M/W	5,671	55	38		Y	Y	Y	Y	Y	Y		N	11	45
Crouse Hospital School of Nursing	Syracuse	C,T	Ind	PW	285		52		N	Y	Y	Y		Y	Y	Y		1
Erie Community College	Buffalo	C,T	St-L	M/W	3,599	26	41		Y	Y	Y	Y	Y	Y	Y	N	14	18
Erie Community College, North Campus	Williamsville	C,T	St-L	M/W	6,741	33	31		Y	Y	Y	Y	Y	Y	Y	N	14	25
Erie Community College, South Campus	Orchard Park	C,T	St-L	M/W	4,483	38	21		Y	Y	Y	Y	Y	Y	Y	N	14	22
Everest Institute	Rochester	T	Prop	M/W	1,150		59		N		Y	Y	Y			N		8
Fashion Institute of Technology†	New York	C,T,B,M	St-L	PW	10,207	30	26		N	Y	Y	Y	Y	Y	Y	Y	7	21
Finger Lakes Community College	Canandaigua	C,T	St-L	M/W	6,699	44	29		Y	Y	Y	Y	Y	Y	Y	N	9	53
Fiorello H. LaGuardia Community College of the City University of New York	Long Island City	C,T	St-L	M/W	16,963	45	35	51	Y	Y	Y	Y	Y	Y	Y	N	8	42
Fulton-Montgomery Community College	Johnstown	C,T	St-L	M/W	2,732	35	25		Y		Y	Y	Y	Y	Y	Y	7	44
Genesee Community College	Batavia	C,T	St-L	M/W	7,208	52	33		Y	Y	Y	Y	Y	Y	Y	Y	12	36
Herkimer County Community College	Herkimer	C,T	St-L	M/W	3,328													
Island Drafting and Technical Institute	Amityville	C,T	Prop	M/W	131		45	0	Y	Y	R	Y		Y	Y	N		8
ITT Technical Institute	Albany	T	Prop	M/W						Y		Y	Y			N		6
ITT Technical Institute	Getzville	T	Prop	M/W					N	Y		Y	Y			N		6
ITT Technical Institute	Liverpool	T	Prop	M/W						Y		Y	Y			N		6
Jamestown Business College	Jamestown	T,B	Prop	M/W	329	5	53		N	Y	Y	Y		Y	Y	N	10	7
Jamestown Community College	Jamestown	C,T	St-L	M/W	3,931	29	29	36	Y	Y	Y	Y	Y	Y	Y	Y	13	35
Jefferson Community College	Watertown	C,T	St-L	M/W	3,314	39	34		N	Y	Y	Y	Y	Y	Y	N	6	23
Kingsborough Community College of the City University of New York	Brooklyn	C,T	St-L	M/W	17,793	42	27		Y	Y	Y	Y	Y	Y	Y	N	7	38
Long Island Business Institute	Commack	C	Prop	PW	653	37	60	0		Y	Y			Y	Y	N		4
Mildred Elley School	Albany	C,T	Prop	M/W	396													
Mohawk Valley Community College†	Utica	C,T	St-L	M/W	6,701	34	31		Y		Y	Y	Y	Y	Y	Y	15	50
Nassau Community College	Garden City	C,T	St-L	M/W	21,952	33	23		Y	Y	Y	Y	Y	Y	Y	N	19	55
Niagara County Community College	Sanborn	C,T	St-L	M/W	7,279	36	27		Y	Y	Y	Y	Y	Y	Y	Y	14	38
Olean Business Institute	Olean	T	Prop	M/W	87		66			Y	Y	Y		Y	Y	N		7
Phillips Beth Israel School of Nursing	New York	C,T	Ind	M/W	256	90	65		N	Y	Y	Y		Y		N		2
Plaza College	Jackson Heights	C,T,B	Prop	M/W	776		56		N	Y		Y		Y	Y	N		5
Rockland Community College	Suffern	C,T	St-L	M/W	6,984	38			Y	Y	Y	Y	Y	Y	Y	N	11	41
St. Elizabeth College of Nursing	Utica	T	Ind	M/W	239	34	52		Y	Y	Y					N		1
St. Joseph's College of Nursing	Syracuse	T	I-R	M/W	293		51			Y	Y	Y		Y	Y	Y		1
Schenectady County Community College	Schenectady	C,T	St-L	M/W														
State University of New York College of Technology at Alfred	Alfred	C,T,B	St	M/W	3,539	10	14		N	Y	Y	Y	Y	Y	Y	Y	20	53
Suffolk County Community College	Selden	C,T	St-L	M/W	24,560		33		Y	Y	Y	Y	Y	Y	Y	N	12	45
Tompkins Cortland Community College	Dryden	C,T	St-L	M/W	3,699	22	29		Y	Y	Y	Y	Y	Y	Y	Y	22	34
Ulster County Community College	Stone Ridge	C,T	St-L	M/W	3,540	50	23	59	Y	Y	Y	Y	Y	Y	Y	N	7	26
Westchester Community College	Valhalla	C,T	St-L	M/W	14,147	45	35		Y	Y	Y	Y	Y	Y	Y	N	11	45
Wood Tobe–Coburn School	New York	T	Priv	PW	305				N	Y		Y				N		9
North Carolina																		
Alamance Community College	Graham	C,T	St	M/W	5,483	50	44		Y	Y	Y	Y	Y	Y	Y	N	4	28
Beaufort County Community College	Washington	C,T	St	M/W	1,923		58		Y	Y	S	Y	Y	Y	Y	N		18
Bladen Community College	Dublin	C,T	St-L	M/W	1,736		62		Y	Y	Y	Y	Y	Y	Y	N		15
Blue Ridge Community College	Flat Rock	C	St-L	M/W	2,488	69	38		Y	Y	Y	Y	Y	Y	Y	N	2	36
Cape Fear Community College	Wilmington	C,T	St	M/W	8,989	56	37		Y	Y	S	Y	Y	Y	Y	N	7	34
Carolinas College of Health Sciences	Charlotte	T	Ind	M/W	510	80	34		N	Y	Y	Y	Y	Y	Y	Y		3
Carteret Community College	Morehead City	C,T	St	M/W	1,872	57	53		Y	Y	Y	Y	Y	Y	Y	N		17
Catawba Valley Community College	Hickory	C,T	St-L	M/W	5,528	61	47		Y	Y	Y	Y	Y	Y	Y	N	3	42
Central Carolina Community College	Sanford	C,T	St-L	M/W	5,411		50		Y	Y	Y	Y	Y	Y	Y	N	5	29
Central Piedmont Community College	Charlotte	C,T	St-L	M/W	19,364	61	47		Y	Y	Y	Y	Y	Y	Y	N	1	69
Craven Community College	New Bern	C,T	St	M/W	3,032													
Durham Technical Community College	Durham	C,T	St	M/W	5,170													
Edgecombe Community College	Tarboro	C,T	St-L	M/W	1,687													
Fayetteville Technical Community College	Fayetteville	C,T	St	M/W	11,203	69	53	11	Y	Y	S	Y	Y	Y		N	5	53
Guilford Technical Community College	Jamestown	C,T	St-L	M/W	13,532	27	43		Y	Y	Y	Y	Y	Y		N	3	54
Halifax Community College	Weldon	C,T	St-L	M/W	1,142													

This chart includes the names and locations of accredited two-year colleges in the United States and U.S. territories and shows institutions' responses to the *Peterson's Annual Survey of Undergraduate Institutions*. If an institution submitted incomplete data, one or more columns opposite the institution's name is blank. A dagger after the school name indicates that the institution has one or more entries in the *College Close-Ups* section. If a school does not appear, it did not report any of the information.

Y—Yes; N—No; R—Recommended; S—For Some

Institution	Location	**Degrees Awarded** College Transfer Associate (C), Terminal Associate (T), Bachelor's (B), Master's (M)	**Institutional Control** County, District, City, State and Local, State-Related; Federal, State Commonwealth, Territory; Independent, Independent-Religious, Proprietary	**Student Body** Men, Primarily Men, Women, Primarily Women, Coed	Undergraduate Enrollment	Percent Attending Part-Time	Percent 25 Years of Age or Older	Percent of Grads Going on to Four-Year Colleges	Open Admissions	High School Equivalency Certificate Accepted	High School Transcript Required	Need-Based Aid Available	Part-Time Jobs Available	Career Counseling Available	Job Placement Services Available	College Housing Available	Number of Sports Offered	Number of Majors Offered
Haywood Community College	Clyde	C,T	St-L	M/W	2,127													
ITT Technical Institute	Charlotte	T,B	Prop	M/W														7
ITT Technical Institute	High Point	T,B	Prop	M/W														6
ITT Technical Institute	Morrisville	T,B	Prop	M/W														6
James Sprunt Community College	Kenansville	C,T	St	M/W	1,534	53	51	1	Y	Y	Y	Y	Y	Y	Y	N	2	13
Johnston Community College	Smithfield	C,T	St	M/W	4,410	48	40		Y	Y	Y	Y	Y	Y	Y	N	4	23
Mayland Community College	Spruce Pine	C,T	St-L	M/W	1,472													
McDowell Technical Community College	Marion	C,T	St	M/W	1,134													
Mitchell Community College	Statesville	C,T	St	M/W	2,687													
Montgomery Community College	Troy	C,T	St	M/W	1,039	67	50		Y	Y	Y	Y	Y	Y	Y	N		10
Nash Community College	Rocky Mount	C,T	St	M/W	2,916													
Piedmont Community College	Roxboro	C,T	St	M/W	2,874	56	47		Y	Y	S	Y	Y	Y	Y	N	1	24
Pitt Community College	Greenville	C,T	St-L	M/W	7,076	46												
Randolph Community College	Asheboro	C,T	St	M/W	3,047	55	48	50	Y	Y	Y	Y	Y			N		38
Roanoke-Chowan Community College	Ahoskie	C,T	St	M/W	384													
Rockingham Community College	Wentworth	C,T	St	M/W	2,636	56	41		Y	Y		Y	Y	Y	Y	N	10	10
Rowan-Cabarrus Community College	Salisbury	C,T	St	M/W	5,158													
Sandhills Community College	Pinehurst	C,T	St	M/W	4,200				Y	Y	Y	Y	Y	Y	Y	N	3	46
Stanly Community College	Albemarle	C,T	St	M/W	3,200		48		Y	Y	Y	Y	Y	Y	Y	N	2	31
Tri-County Community College	Murphy	C,T	St	M/W	1,353		65		Y	Y	Y	Y	Y	Y	Y	N		11
Wayne Community College	Goldsboro	C,T	St-L	M/W	3,585	44	33		Y	Y	Y	Y	Y	Y	Y	N	10	27
Wilson Community College	Wilson	C,T	St	M/W	2,119	54	54		Y	Y	Y	Y	Y	Y	Y	N		18
North Dakota																		
Dakota College at Bottineau	Bottineau	C,T	St	M/W	748	53	36		Y	Y	Y	Y	Y	Y	Y	Y	9	68
Lake Region State College	Devils Lake	C,T	St	M/W	1,702	71	21		Y	Y	Y	Y	Y	Y	Y	Y	7	38
Ohio																		
Antonelli College	Cincinnati	T	Prop	M/W	377		55		Y	Y	Y	Y	Y	Y	Y	N		8
The Art Institute of Ohio–Cincinnati	Cincinnati	C,T,B	Prop	M/W														10
ATS Institute of Technology	Highland Heights	C,T	Prop	M/W	353				Y	Y	Y							1
Belmont Technical College	St. Clairsville	T	St	M/W	1,742													
Bowling Green State University–Firelands College	Huron	C,T,B	St	M/W	2,454	45			Y	Y	Y	Y	Y	Y	Y	N		28
Bradford School	Columbus	C,T	Priv	PW	575				N	Y		Y				Y		11
Brown Mackie College–Akron†	Akron	T	Prop	M/W														14
Brown Mackie College–Cincinnati†	Cincinnati	T	Prop	M/W														17
Brown Mackie College–Findlay†	Findlay	T	Prop	M/W														12
Brown Mackie College–North Canton†	Canton	T	Prop	M/W														11
Bryant & Stratton College	Eastlake	C,T,B	Prop	M/W	762	36	63		N	Y	Y	Y	Y	Y	Y	N		14
Bryant & Stratton College	Parma	C,T,B	Prop	M/W	528	45	34		N	Y	Y	Y	Y	Y	Y	N		13
Central Ohio Technical College	Newark	T	St	M/W	4,350	49	76	17	Y	Y	Y	Y	Y	Y	Y	N	8	24
Cincinnati State Technical and Community College	Cincinnati	C,T	St	M/W	10,165	60	49		Y	Y	Y	Y	Y	Y	Y	N	4	65
Cleveland Institute of Electronics	Cleveland	T	Prop	PM	2,146	100	85		Y	Y	Y			Y		N		3
Columbus Culinary Institute at Bradford School	Columbus	T	Priv	M/W	245											Y		1
Columbus State Community College	Columbus	C,T	St	M/W	23,057													
Cuyahoga Community College	Cleveland	C,T	St-L	M/W	30,325	60	50		Y		S	Y	Y	Y	Y	N	8	32
Davis College	Toledo	T	Prop	M/W	527	61	56		N	Y	Y	Y	Y	Y	Y	Y		19
Edison State Community College	Piqua	C,T	St	M/W	3,457		54	59	Y	Y	Y		Y	Y	Y	N	2	50
ETI Technical College of Niles	Niles	T	Prop	M/W	421		45	24		Y	Y	Y		Y	Y	N		11
Fortis College	Centerville	C,T	Prop	M/W	533													
Fortis College–Ravenna	Ravenna	T	Ind	M/W	482													
Harrison College	Grove City	T	Prop	M/W						Y	Y							9
Hondros College	Westerville	C,T	Prop	M/W	255													
International College of Broadcasting	Dayton	C,T	Priv	M/W	84													
ITT Technical Institute	Akron	T	Prop	M/W														4
ITT Technical Institute	Columbus	T	Prop	M/W														7
ITT Technical Institute	Dayton	T	Prop	M/W					N	Y		Y	Y			N		9
ITT Technical Institute	Hilliard	T	Prop	M/W														8
ITT Technical Institute	Maumee	T	Prop	M/W														7
ITT Technical Institute	Norwood	C	Prop	M/W					N	Y		Y	Y			N		11
ITT Technical Institute	Strongsville	T	Prop	M/W					N	Y		Y	Y			N		11
ITT Technical Institute	Warrensville Heights	T	Prop	M/W														9
ITT Technical Institute	Youngstown	T	Prop	M/W					N	Y		Y	Y			N		10
James A. Rhodes State College	Lima	C,T	St	M/W	3,385													
Kaplan College, Cincinnati Campus	Cincinnati	T	Prop	M/W						Y								
Kaplan College, Columbus Campus	Columbus	T	Prop	M/W						Y								
Kaplan College, Dayton Campus	Dayton	T	Prop	M/W						Y		Y	Y					4
Kent State University at Ashtabula	Ashtabula	C,T,B	St	M/W	2,187	47	55		Y	Y		Y	Y	Y	Y	N		20
Kent State University at East Liverpool	East Liverpool	C,T	St	M/W	1,235	43	47		Y	Y	Y	Y	Y	Y	Y	N		10
Kent State University at Geauga	Burton	C,T	St	M/W	1,866	40	44			Y	Y	Y	Y	Y	Y	N		11
Kent State University at Salem	Salem	C,T,B	St	M/W	1,577	28	41		Y	Y	S	Y	Y	Y	Y	N	5	9
Kent State University at Trumbull	Warren	C,T,B	St	M/W	2,607	37	45		Y	Y	Y	Y	Y	Y	Y	N		19
Kent State University at Tuscarawas	New Philadelphia	C,B	St	M/W	2,384	40	44		Y	Y	Y	Y	Y	Y	Y	N	2	17
Lakeland Community College	Kirtland	C,T	St-L	M/W	9,406	56			Y	Y	Y	Y	Y	Y	Y	N	6	39
Marion Technical College	Marion	T	St	M/W	2,659	49	51		Y	Y	Y	Y	Y	Y	Y	N	14	23
Miami–Jacobs College	Dayton	T	Prop	M/W	811													
North Central State College	Mansfield	T	St	M/W	3,148													
Northwest State Community College	Archbold	C,T	St	M/W	2,944													
Ohio Business College	Lorain	T	Prop	PW	231													

This chart includes the names and locations of accredited two-year colleges in the United States and U.S. territories and shows institutions' responses to the *Peterson's Annual Survey of Undergraduate Institutions.* If an institution submitted incomplete data, one or more columns opposite the institution's name is blank. A dagger after the school name indicates that the institution has one or more entries in the *College Close-Ups* section. If a school does not appear, it did not report any of the information.

Y—Yes; N—No; R—Recommended; S—For Some

Institution	Location	Degrees Awarded: College Transfer Associate (C), Terminal Associate (T), Bachelor's (B), Master's (M)	Institutional Control: Independent (Ind), Independent-Religious, Proprietary, Federal, State, Commonwealth, Territory, County, District, City, State and Local, State-Related	Student Body: Men, Primarily Men, Women, Primarily Women, Coed	Undergraduate Enrollment	Percent Attending Part-Time	Percent 25 Years of Age or Older	Percent of Grads Going on to Four-Year Colleges	Open Admissions	High School Equivalency Certificate Accepted	High School Transcript Required	Need-Based Aid Available	Part-Time Jobs Available	Career Counseling Available	Job Placement Services Available	College Housing Available	Number of Sports Offered	Number of Majors Offered
The Ohio State University Agricultural Technical Institute	Wooster	C,T	St	M/W	747		10		Y	Y	Y		Y	Y	Y	Y	5	35
Ohio Valley College of Technology	East Liverpool	T	Prop	M/W	147	10												
Owens Community College	Toledo	C,T	St	M/W	23,561	61	48		Y			Y	Y	Y	Y	N	11	50
Professional Skills Institute	Toledo	T	Prop	M/W	292													
Southern State Community College	Hillsboro	C,T	St	M/W	3,363	38		21	Y	Y	R	Y	Y	Y	Y	N	5	17
Stark State College of Technology	North Canton	C,T	St-L	M/W	12,483		49		Y	Y	Y	Y	Y	Y	Y	N		49
Terra State Community College	Fremont	C,T	St	M/W	3,152	54	50		Y	Y	Y	Y	Y	Y	Y	N	6	67
University of Cincinnati Clermont College	Batavia	C,T	St	M/W	3,713	36	38		Y	Y	Y	Y	Y	Y	Y	N	5	32
Vet Tech Institute at Bradford School	Columbus	T	Priv	M/W	177											Y		1
Virginia Marti College of Art and Design	Lakewood	T	Prop	M/W	271		26		N	Y	Y		Y			N		5
Oklahoma																		
Brown Mackie College–Tulsa†	Tulsa	T,B	Prop	M/W														11
Clary Sage College	Tulsa	T	Prop	M/W	118		42		Y	Y	Y			Y	Y			
Community Care College	Tulsa	T	Prop	M/W	286		60		Y	Y	Y			Y	Y	N		11
Connors State College	Warner	C,T	St	M/W	2,250													
Eastern Oklahoma State College	Wilburton	C,T	St	M/W	1,772													
ITT Technical Institute	Tulsa	T,B	Prop	M/W														12
Murray State College	Tishomingo	C,T	St	M/W	2,497				Y	Y	Y	Y	Y	Y	Y	Y	3	31
Oklahoma City Community College	Oklahoma City	C,T	St	M/W	14,159	60	42		Y		Y	Y	Y	Y	Y	N	7	47
Oklahoma State University, Oklahoma City	Oklahoma City	C,T,B	St	M/W	7,179		51		Y	Y	Y	Y	Y	Y	Y	N		46
Oklahoma Technical College	Tulsa	T	Prop	M/W					Y	Y	Y			Y	Y			4
Seminole State College	Seminole	C,T	St	M/W	2,534		47		Y		Y	Y	Y	Y	Y	Y	5	18
Spartan College of Aeronautics and Technology	Tulsa	T,B	Prop	M	1,438		30			Y	Y	Y	Y			Y		5
Oregon																		
Blue Mountain Community College	Pendleton	C,T	St-L	M/W	1,782													
Central Oregon Community College	Bend	C,T	Dist	M/W	6,261	54	49		Y	Y		Y	Y	Y	Y	Y	11	56
Clackamas Community College	Oregon City	C,T	Dist	M/W	8,144	61	45		Y			Y	Y	Y	Y	N	10	39
Columbia Gorge Community College	The Dalles	C,T	St	M/W	920													
ITT Technical Institute	Portland	T,B	Prop	M/W						Y		Y	Y			N		17
Lane Community College	Eugene	C,T	St-L	M/W	8,618													
Linn-Benton Community College	Albany	C,T	St-L	M/W	6,539	46			Y		S	Y	Y	Y	Y	N	5	59
Oregon Coast Community College	Newport	C,T	Pub	M/W	652	73	56	75	Y					Y		N		4
Portland Community College	Portland	C,T	St-L	M/W	24,353													
Rogue Community College	Grants Pass	C,T	St-L	M/W	5,441	54	51		Y			Y	Y	Y	Y	N	4	27
Umpqua Community College	Roseburg	C,T	St-L	M/W	2,586	47		51	Y		R	Y	Y	Y	Y	N	2	53
Pennsylvania																		
The Art Institute of York–Pennsylvania	York	T,B	Prop	M/W														5
Bradford School	Pittsburgh	T	Priv	M/W	567							Y				Y		11
Bucks County Community College	Newtown	C,T	Cou	M/W	11,009	53	34	49	Y	Y	Y	Y	Y	Y	Y	N	8	53
Career Training Academy	Pittsburgh	T	Prop	M/W	85		55	0		Y	Y							3
CHI Institute, Broomall Campus	Broomall	T	Prop	M/W						Y		Y	Y					3
CHI Institute, Franklin Mills Campus	Philadelphia	C,T	Prop	M/W						Y		Y	Y					3
Community College of Allegheny County	Pittsburgh	C,T	Cou	M/W	20,520	58	35		Y	Y	R	Y	Y	Y	Y	N	15	115
Community College of Philadelphia	Philadelphia	C,T	St-L	M/W	34,854		53	79	Y	Y	S		Y	Y	Y	N	9	40
Consolidated School of Business	Lancaster	T	Prop	M/W	182	2	59		Y	Y	Y	Y		Y	Y	N		6
Dean Institute of Technology	Pittsburgh	T	Prop	M/W	132													
Delaware County Community College	Media	C,T	St-L	M/W	12,237	55	56	72	Y	Y	Y	Y	Y	Y	Y	N	9	57
Douglas Education Center	Monessen	C,T	Prop	M/W	354		34		Y	Y	Y	Y	Y	Y	Y			9
DuBois Business College	DuBois	T	Prop	PW	233													
Fortis Institute	Forty Fort	C,T	Prop	M/W	402													
Harcum College	Bryn Mawr	C,T	Ind	PW	1,154				N	Y	Y	Y	Y	Y	Y	Y	4	27
Harrisburg Area Community College	Harrisburg	C,T	St-L	M/W	22,529	61	58	43	Y		S	Y	Y	Y	Y	N	5	87
Hussian School of Art	Philadelphia	C,T	Prop	PM	136													
ITT Technical Institute	Bensalem	T	Prop	M/W					N	Y		Y	Y			N		4
ITT Technical Institute	Dunmore	T	Prop	M/W														4
ITT Technical Institute	Harrisburg	T	Prop	M/W														5
ITT Technical Institute	King of Prussia	T	Prop	M/W														4
ITT Technical Institute	Pittsburgh	T	Prop	M/W					N			Y	Y			N		6
ITT Technical Institute	Tarentum	T	Prop	M/W					N	Y		Y	Y			N		7
Kaplan Career Institute, Harrisburg	Harrisburg	T	Prop	M/W						Y		Y	Y					7
Kaplan Career Institute, ICM Campus	Pittsburgh	C,T	Prop	M/W						Y		Y	Y					8
Keystone Technical Institute	Harrisburg	C,T	Prop	PW	207													
Lackawanna College	Scranton	C,T	Ind	M/W	1,387	28	28		Y	Y	Y	Y	Y	Y	Y	Y	9	32
Lansdale School of Business	North Wales	C,T	Prop	M/W	372													
Lehigh Carbon Community College	Schnecksville	C,T	St-L	M/W	8,127	58	40	38	Y		S	Y	Y	Y	Y	N	13	66
Lincoln Technical Institute	Allentown	T	Prop	M/W	539													
Lincoln Technical Institute	Philadelphia	T	Prop	PM	499													
McCann School of Business & Technology	Pottsville	C,T	Prop	M/W	1,657													
Montgomery County Community College	Blue Bell	C,T	Cou	M/W	13,310	53	37	68	Y	Y	Y	Y	Y	Y	Y	N	13	54
New Castle School of Trades	Pulaski	C	Ind	PM	441													
Newport Business Institute	Williamsport	T	Prop	PW	124		69		N	Y	Y	Y		Y	Y	N		4
Northampton Community College	Bethlehem	C,T	St-L	M/W	11,218	52	37	72	Y	Y	R,S	Y	Y	Y	Y	Y	10	60
Orleans Technical Institute	Philadelphia	C,T	Prop	M/W	567													
Penn Commercial Business and Technical School	Washington	C,T	Prop	M/W	435													
Pennco Tech	Bristol	C,T	Prop	M/W	400	39												

This chart includes the names and locations of accredited two-year colleges in the United States and U.S. territories and shows institutions' responses to the *Peterson's Annual Survey of Undergraduate Institutions.* If an institution submitted incomplete data, one or more columns opposite the institution's name is blank. A dagger after the school name indicates that the institution has one or more entries in the *College Close-Ups* section. If a school does not appear, it did not report any of the information.

Y—Yes; N—No; R—Recommended; S—For Some

Institution	Location	**Degrees Awarded** College Transfer Associate (C), Terminal Associate (T), Bachelor's (B), Master's (M)	**Institutional Control** Independent, Independent-Religious, Proprietary, Federal, State, Commonwealth, Territory, County, District, City, State and Local, State-Related	**Student Body** Men, Primarily Men, Women, Primarily Women, Coed	Undergraduate Enrollment	Percent Attending Part-Time	Percent 25 Years of Age or Older	Percent of Grads Going on to Four-Year Colleges	Open Admissions	High School Equivalency Certificate Accepted	High School Transcript Required	Need-Based Aid Available	Part-Time Jobs Available	Career Counseling Available	Job Placement Services Available	College Housing Available	Number of Sports Offered	Number of Majors Offered
Penn State Beaver	Monaca	C,T,B,M	St-R	M/W	851	23	9		N	Y	Y	Y	Y	Y	Y	Y	10	118
Penn State Brandywine	Media	C,T,B	St-R	M/W	1,607	14	11		N	Y	Y	Y	Y	Y	Y	N	10	120
Penn State DuBois	DuBois	C,T,B,M	St-R	M/W	937	19	30		N	Y	Y	Y	Y	Y	Y	N	7	127
Penn State Fayette, The Eberly Campus	Uniontown	C,T,B	St-R	M/W	1,095	26	31		N	Y	Y	Y	Y	Y	Y	N	11	124
Penn State Greater Allegheny	McKeesport	C,T,B,M	St-R	M/W	750	14	7		N	Y	Y	Y	Y	Y	Y	Y	12	119
Penn State Hazleton	Hazleton	C,T,B,M	St-R	M/W	1,245	4	5		N	Y	Y	Y	Y	Y	Y	Y	8	125
Penn State Lehigh Valley	Fogelsville	C,T,B	St-R	M/W	824	26	13		N	Y	Y	Y	Y	Y	Y	N	13	119
Penn State Mont Alto	Mont Alto	C,T,B	St-R	M/W	1,174	25	21		N	Y	Y	Y	Y	Y	Y	Y	10	120
Penn State New Kensington	New Kensington	C,T,B,M	St-R	M/W	819	25	23		N	Y	Y	Y	Y	Y	Y	N	13	124
Penn State Schuylkill	Schuylkill Haven	C,T,B	St-R	M/W	1,007	15	12		N	Y	Y	Y	Y	Y	Y	Y	8	124
Penn State Shenango	Sharon	C,T,B	St-R	M/W	816	40	49		N	Y	Y	Y	Y	Y	Y	N	7	124
Penn State Wilkes-Barre	Lehman	C,T,B	St-R	M/W	672	14	12		N	Y	Y	Y	Y	Y	Y	N	11	122
Penn State Worthington Scranton	Dunmore	C,T,B	St-R	M/W	1,388	22	21		N	Y	Y	Y	Y	Y	Y	N	10	119
Penn State York	York	C,T,B,M	St-R	M/W	1,439	32	25		N	Y	Y	Y	Y	Y	Y	N		126
Pennsylvania College of Technology†	Williamsport	C,T,B	St-R	M/W	6,409	15	18		Y	Y	Y	Y	Y	Y	Y	Y	18	114
Pennsylvania Culinary Institute	Pittsburgh	T	Prop	M/W	996													
Pennsylvania Highlands Community College	Johnstown	C,T	St-L	M/W	1,768		45		Y			Y	Y	Y	Y	N		23
Pennsylvania Institute of Technology	Media	C,T	Ind	M/W	1,046	12	35			Y	Y	Y	Y	Y	Y	N	1	10
Pennsylvania School of Business	Allentown	C,T	Priv	M/W	401													
Pittsburgh Institute of Mortuary Science, Incorporated	Pittsburgh	C,T	Ind	M/W	193	56	53		Y	Y	Y	Y		Y	Y	N		1
Pittsburgh Technical Institute	Oakdale	T	Prop	M/W	2,073													
The Restaurant School at Walnut Hill College	Philadelphia	T,B	Prop	M/W	509		13		Y	Y	Y	Y				Y		4
Sanford-Brown Institute–Pittsburgh	Pittsburgh	T	Prop	M/W	472													
Triangle Tech–Greensburg School	Greensburg	T	Prop	PM	260		45	1	N	Y	Y	Y	Y	Y	Y	N		8
Triangle Tech Inc–Bethlehem	Bethlehem	T	Prop	PM	140		34	2	Y	Y	Y			Y	Y	N		2
Triangle Tech, Inc.–DuBois School	DuBois	T	Prop	PM	331		48	1	N	Y	Y	Y		Y	Y	N		4
Triangle Tech, Inc.–Erie School	Erie	C,T	Prop	PM	176		65		N	Y	Y	Y	Y	Y	Y	N		4
Triangle Tech, Inc.–Sunbury School	Sunbury	T	Prop	M/W	170		39	0		Y	Y					N		3
University of Pittsburgh at Titusville	Titusville	C,B	St-R	M/W	544	14	15		N	Y	Y	Y	Y	Y	Y	Y	11	8
Vet Tech Institute	Pittsburgh	T	Priv	M/W	338					Y		Y				Y		1
Westmoreland County Community College	Youngwood	C,T	Cou	M/W	7,089	49	43		Y			Y	Y	Y	Y	N	10	45
Puerto Rico																		
Huertas Junior College	Caguas	T	Prop	M/W	1,777													
Humacao Community College	Humacao	T	Ind	M/W	777													
Ramírez College of Business and Technology	San Juan	C,T	Prop	M/W	460													
Rhode Island																		
Community College of Rhode Island	Warwick	C,T	St	M/W	17,760	62	34		Y	Y		Y	Y	Y	Y	N	10	54
South Carolina																		
Brown Mackie College–Greenville†	Greenville	T,B	Prop	M/W														10
Central Carolina Technical College	Sumter	C,T	St	M/W	4,137	65	50		Y	Y	Y	Y	Y	Y	Y	N		17
Denmark Technical College	Denmark	C,T	St	M/W	1,105	19	30		Y	Y	Y	Y	Y	Y	Y	Y	6	8
Forrest Junior College	Anderson	C,T	Prop	M/W	94	40	60			Y	Y	Y	Y	Y	Y	N		10
ITT Technical Institute	Columbia	T,B	Prop	M/W														10
ITT Technical Institute	Greenville	T,B	Prop	M/W					N	Y		Y	Y			N		12
Midlands Technical College	Columbia	C,T	St-L	M/W	11,890		41		Y		R	Y	Y	Y	Y	N	7	46
Miller-Motte Technical College	Charleston	T	Prop	M/W	764		57		Y	Y	Y			Y	Y	N		7
Orangeburg-Calhoun Technical College	Orangeburg	C,T	St-L	M/W	3,219	52	38		Y	Y	Y	Y	Y	Y	Y	N		16
Spartanburg Community College	Spartanburg	C,T	St	M/W	5,713		46		Y	Y	Y	Y	Y	Y	Y	N		25
Spartanburg Methodist College	Spartanburg	C,T	I-R	M/W	808	4	2	82	N	Y	Y	Y	Y	Y	Y	Y	12	3
Trident Technical College	Charleston	C,T	St-L	M/W	14,834	54	44		Y	Y	S	Y	Y	Y	Y	N		39
University of South Carolina Lancaster	Lancaster	C,T	St	M/W	1,593		13		Y	Y	Y	Y	Y			N	4	4
University of South Carolina Salkehatchie	Allendale	C,T	St	M/W	965		25			Y	Y	Y	Y			N	5	1
South Dakota																		
Kilian Community College	Sioux Falls	C,T	Ind	M/W	336	81	60		Y	Y	Y	Y	Y	Y		N		8
Lake Area Technical Institute	Watertown	T	St	M/W	1,090													
Mitchell Technical Institute	Mitchell	C,T	St	M/W	1,003		22		Y	Y	Y	Y	Y	Y	Y	Y	5	36
Sisseton-Wahpeton Community College	Sisseton	C,T	Fed	M/W	237	24	42		Y	Y	Y	Y	Y	Y	Y	Y		12
Southeast Technical Institute	Sioux Falls	T	St	M/W	2,489	21	27		N	Y	Y	Y	Y	Y	Y	Y	3	49
Tennessee																		
Chattanooga College–Medical, Dental and Technical Careers	Chattanooga	C	Prop	M/W	147													
Chattanooga State Community College	Chattanooga	C,T	St	M/W	9,431		41		Y	Y	R,S	Y	Y	Y	Y	N	3	41
Cleveland State Community College	Cleveland	C,T	St	M/W	3,615	44	38	53	Y	Y	Y	Y	Y	Y	Y	N	8	12
Columbia State Community College	Columbia	C,T	St	M/W	4,633													
Daymar Institute	Nashville	C,T	Prop	M/W	286													
ITT Technical Institute	Chattanooga	T,B	Prop	M/W														9
ITT Technical Institute	Cordova	T,B	Prop	M/W					N	Y		Y	Y			N		14
ITT Technical Institute	Johnson City	T,B	Prop	M/W														7
ITT Technical Institute	Knoxville	T,B	Prop	M/W					N	Y		Y	Y			N		14
ITT Technical Institute	Nashville	T,B	Prop	M/W					N	Y		Y	Y			N		17
Jackson State Community College	Jackson	C,T	St	M/W	5,109		37	80	Y	Y	S	Y	Y	Y	Y		3	16
Kaplan Career Institute, Nashville Campus	Nashville	T	Prop	M/W						Y								2
MedVance Institute	Cookeville	T	Prop	PW	283													

This chart includes the names and locations of accredited two-year colleges in the United States and U.S. territories and shows institutions' responses to the *Peterson's Annual Survey of Undergraduate Institutions*. If an institution submitted incomplete data, one or more columns opposite the institution's name is blank. A dagger after the school name indicates that the institution has one or more entries in the *College Close-Ups* section. If a school does not appear, it did not report any of the information.

Y—Yes; N—No; R—Recommended; S—For Some

College	Location	**Degrees Awarded** College Transfer Associate (C), Terminal Associate (T), Bachelor's (B), Master's (M)	**Institutional Control** Independent, Independent-Religious, Proprietary, Federal, State, Commonwealth, Territory, County, District, City, State and Local, State-Related	**Student Body** Men, Primarily Men, Women, Primarily Women, Coed	Undergraduate Enrollment	Percent Attending Part-Time	Percent 25 Years of Age or Older	Percent of Grads Going on to Four-Year Colleges	Open Admissions	High School Equivalency Certificate Accepted	High School Transcript Required	Need-Based Aid Available	Part-Time Jobs Available	Career Counseling Available	Job Placement Services Available	College Housing Available	Number of Sports Offered	Number of Majors Offered
Nashville State Technical Community College	Nashville	C,T	St	M/W	7,077	64												
Northeast State Technical Community College	Blountville	C,T	St	M/W	5,470	46												
Volunteer State Community College	Gallatin	C,T	St	M/W	8,430	48	35		Y	Y	Y	Y	Y	Y	Y	N	3	20
Walters State Community College	Morristown	C,T	St	M/W	6,853	48			Y	Y	Y	Y	Y	Y	Y	N	4	12
Texas																		
Alvin Community College	Alvin	C,T	St-L	M/W	4,400	70	35		Y	Y	S	Y	Y	Y	Y	Y	3	33
Amarillo College	Amarillo	C,T	St-L	M/W	11,289		39		Y		Y	Y	Y	Y	Y	N	5	83
ATI Technical Training Center	Dallas		Prop	M/W	568													
Austin Community College	Austin	C,T	St-L	M/W	40,248		41		Y	Y	Y	Y	Y	Y		N	5	93
Central Texas College	Killeen	C,T	St-L	M/W	24,498	83	61		Y	Y	Y	Y	Y	Y	Y	Y	10	49
Clarendon College	Clarendon	C,T	St-L	M/W	1,114	67	29		Y	Y	Y	Y	Y	Y		Y	6	42
College of the Mainland	Texas City	C,T	St-L	M/W	3,561	69												
Collin County Community College District	McKinney	C,T	St-L	M/W	24,872	61	32		Y	Y	Y	Y	Y	Y	Y		3	49
Commonwealth Institute of Funeral Service	Houston	T	Ind	M/W	122		52		N	Y	Y	Y		Y	Y	Y		1
Computer Career Center	El Paso	C,T	Prop	M/W	351													
Court Reporting Institute of Dallas	Dallas	C,T	Prop	PW	1,018													
Del Mar College	Corpus Christi	C,T	St-L	M/W	12,007		38		Y	Y	Y	Y	Y	Y	Y	N	10	102
Eastfield College	Mesquite	C,T	St-L	M/W	11,944	74	37		Y	Y	R	Y	Y	Y	Y	N	8	35
El Centro College	Dallas	C,T	Cou	M/W	8,513	80	51		Y	Y	S	Y	Y	Y	Y	N		37
El Paso Community College	El Paso	C,T	Cou	M/W	28,168	61	30		Y	Y		Y	Y	Y	Y	N	10	65
Frank Phillips College	Borger	C,T	St-L	M/W	1,248	53												
Galveston College	Galveston	C,T	St-L	M/W	2,230	62												
Hallmark College of Technology	San Antonio	T,B	Prop	M/W	294													
Hallmark Institute of Aeronautics	San Antonio	T	Priv	M/W	218		54			Y	Y	Y		Y	Y	N		2
Hill College of the Hill Junior College District	Hillsboro	C,T	Dist	M/W	3,556													
Houston Community College System	Houston	C,T	St-L	M/W	54,942	69	33		Y		S	Y	Y	Y	Y	N		61
Howard College	Big Spring	C,T	St-L	M/W	4,103	60	29	100	Y	Y	Y	Y	Y	Y	Y	Y	8	69
ITT Technical Institute	Arlington	T,B	Prop	M/W					N	Y		Y	Y			N		9
ITT Technical Institute	Austin	T,B	Prop	M/W						Y		Y	Y			N		11
ITT Technical Institute	DeSoto	T,B	Prop	M/W														7
ITT Technical Institute	Houston	T,B	Prop	M/W					N	Y		Y	Y			N		8
ITT Technical Institute	Houston	T,B	Prop	M/W					N	Y		Y	Y			N		7
ITT Technical Institute	Richardson	T	Prop	M/W						Y		Y	Y			N		11
ITT Technical Institute	San Antonio	T	Prop	M/W					N	Y		Y	Y			N		9
ITT Technical Institute	Webster	T,B	Prop	M/W					N	Y		Y	Y			N		8
Kaplan College, Arlington	Arlington		Prop	M/W						Y								
Kaplan College, Dallas	Dallas	T	Prop	M/W						Y								
KD Studio	Dallas	T	Prop	M/W	102		18		Y	Y	Y	Y		Y		N		2
Kilgore College	Kilgore	C,T	St-L	M/W	6,375	53	30		Y	Y	Y	Y	Y	Y	Y	Y	6	72
Lonestar College–Cy-Fair	Cypress	C,T	St-L	M/W	15,175	72	32		Y	Y				Y		N		55
Lonestar College–Kingwood	Kingwood	C,T	St-L	M/W	9,293	75	39		Y	Y		Y	Y	Y		N	1	48
Lonestar College–Montgomery	Conroe	C,T	St-L	M/W	10,962	72	36		Y	Y		Y	Y	Y	Y	N		60
Lonestar College–North Harris	Houston	C,T	St-L	M/W	13,549	80	39		Y	Y		Y	Y	Y	Y		15	61
Lonestar College–Tomball	Tomball	C,T	St-L	M/W	9,865	78	33		Y	Y		Y	Y	Y	Y	N		38
Lon Morris College	Jacksonville	C,T	I-R	M/W	815	8	3			Y	Y	Y	Y	Y		Y	11	41
North Central Texas College	Gainesville	C,T	St-L	M/W	9,156		33		Y	Y	Y	Y	Y	Y		Y	15	42
Northeast Texas Community College	Mount Pleasant	C,T	St-L	M/W	1,010													
North Lake College	Irving	C,T	Cou	M/W	10,174	69	38	30	Y	Y	R	Y	Y	Y	Y		5	15
Odessa College	Odessa	C,T	St-L	M/W	5,132		41		Y	Y		Y	Y	Y	Y	Y	11	55
Panola College	Carthage	C,T	St-L	M/W	2,124	55	30		Y	Y	R,S	Y	Y	Y	Y	Y	7	8
Paris Junior College	Paris	C,T	St-L	M/W	5,580	53	31		Y	Y	Y	Y	Y	Y	Y	Y	9	24
St. Philip's College	San Antonio	C,T	Dist	M/W	11,008	69	51		Y	Y	Y	Y	Y	Y	Y	N	5	64
San Jacinto College District	Pasadena	C,T	St-L	M/W	27,011	64	31		Y	Y	Y			Y	Y	N	13	91
South Plains College	Levelland	C,T	St-L	M/W	10,028	53	39		Y	Y	Y	Y	Y	Y	Y	Y	11	59
Tarrant County College District	Fort Worth	C,T	Cou	M/W	39,596	66	38		Y			Y	Y	Y	Y	N	6	43
Temple College	Temple	C,T	Dist	M/W	5,659	60	38	44	Y	Y	R,S	Y	Y	Y	Y	Y	5	20
Trinity Valley Community College	Athens	C,T	St-L	M/W	6,738	60	35		Y	Y	Y	Y	Y	Y	Y	Y	6	54
Vet Tech Institute of Houston	Houston	T	Priv	M/W	136											N		1
Victoria College	Victoria	C,T	Cou	M/W	4,054	66	33		Y	Y	Y	Y	Y	Y	Y	N	2	16
Wade College	Dallas	C,T	Prop	PW	238		31		Y	Y	Y	Y		Y	Y	Y		4
Westwood College–Houston South Campus	Houston	T,B	Prop	M/W														7
Utah																		
ITT Technical Institute	Murray	T,B	Prop	M/W					N	Y		Y	Y			N		16
LDS Business College	Salt Lake City	C,T	I-R	M/W	1,588	23	31		Y	Y	Y	Y		Y	Y	N		20
Salt Lake Community College	Salt Lake City	C,T	St	M/W	32,831	71	35		Y			Y	Y	Y	Y	N	6	69
Snow College	Ephraim	C,T	St	M/W	4,368	39	13		Y	Y	Y	Y	Y	Y		Y	14	55
Vermont																		
Community College of Vermont	Montpelier	C,T	St	M/W	6,299	80	50	50	Y	Y		Y	Y	Y		N		26
Landmark College†	Putney	C,T	Ind	M/W	498		4		N	Y	Y	Y	Y			Y	13	4
Virginia																		
Bryant & Stratton College - Richmond Campus	Richmond	T,B	Prop	M/W	572	51	84		N	Y	Y		Y	Y	Y	N		13
Bryant & Stratton College - Virginia Beach	Virginia Beach	T,B	Prop	M/W	595	55	64		Y	Y	Y	Y	Y	Y	Y	N		14
Dabney S. Lancaster Community College	Clifton Forge	C,T	St	M/W	1,453		59		Y	Y		Y	Y	Y	Y	N	9	17
Eastern Shore Community College	Melfa	C,T	St	M/W	1,332				Y	Y	Y	Y	Y	Y	Y	N		9

This chart includes the names and locations of accredited two-year colleges in the United States and U.S. territories and shows institutions' responses to the *Peterson's Annual Survey of Undergraduate Institutions.* If an institution submitted incomplete data, one or more columns opposite the institution's name is blank. A dagger after the school name indicates that the institution has one or more entries in the *College Close-Ups* section. If a school does not appear, it did not report any of the information.

Y—Yes; N—No; R—Recommended; S—For Some

Institution	Location	Degrees Awarded: College Transfer Associate (C), Terminal Associate (T), Bachelor's (B), Master's (M)	Institutional Control: Independent, Independent-Religious, Proprietary, Federal, State, Commonwealth, Territory, County, District, City, State and Local, State-Related	Student Body: Men, Primarily Men, Women, Primarily Women, Coed	Undergraduate Enrollment	Percent Attending Part-Time	Percent 25 Years of Age or Older	Percent of Grads Going on to Four-Year Colleges	Open Admissions	High School Equivalency Certificate Accepted	High School Transcript Required	Need-Based Aid Available	Part-Time Jobs Available	Career Counseling Available	Job Placement Services Available	College Housing Available	Number of Sports Offered	Number of Majors Offered
Germanna Community College	Locust Grove	C,T	St	M/W	7,035	67	28		Y		S	Y	Y	Y		N	3	9
ITT Technical Institute	Chantilly	T,B	Prop	M/W						Y		Y	Y			N		15
ITT Technical Institute	Norfolk	T,B	Prop	M/W					N	Y		Y	Y			N		17
ITT Technical Institute	Richmond	T,B	Prop	M/W						Y		Y	Y			N		16
ITT Technical Institute	Salem	T,B	Prop	M/W														8
ITT Technical Institute	Springfield	T,B	Prop	M/W					N	Y		Y	Y			N		16
John Tyler Community College	Chester	C,T	St	M/W	9,692	71	43		Y		R	Y	Y	Y	Y	N		12
J. Sargeant Reynolds Community College	Richmond	C,T	St	M/W	12,740		41		Y	Y	Y	Y	Y	Y	Y	N		26
Mountain Empire Community College	Big Stone Gap	C,T	St	M/W	3,383		32	59	Y	Y	Y	Y	Y	Y	Y	N	3	24
Northern Virginia Community College	Annandale	C,T	St	M/W	41,266													
Patrick Henry Community College	Martinsville	C,T	St	M/W	3,501		60		Y	Y	Y	Y	Y	Y	Y	N	8	15
Rappahannock Community College	Glenns	C,T	St-R	M/W	3,406	75	36		Y			Y	Y	Y	Y	N	4	9
Richard Bland College of The College of William and Mary	Petersburg	C	St	M/W	1,634	36												
Southside Virginia Community College	Alberta	C,T	St	M/W	4,686	71	46		Y	Y	Y	Y	Y	Y	Y	N	7	15
Southwest Virginia Community College	Richlands	C,T	St	M/W	3,855	57	39		Y	Y	Y	Y	Y	Y	Y	N	3	27
Thomas Nelson Community College	Hampton	C,T	St	M/W	10,606				Y		R	Y	Y	Y	Y		2	31
Tidewater Community College	Norfolk	C,T	St	M/W	30,447		45		Y			Y	Y	Y	Y	N	5	26
Washington																		
Apollo College	Spokane	T	Prop	M/W														
The Art Institute of Seattle†	Seattle	T,B	Prop	M/W														13
Bates Technical College	Tacoma	T	St	M/W	5,463													
Bellevue College	Bellevue	C,T,B	St	M/W	12,305													
Cascadia Community College	Bothell	C,T	St	M/W	3,250	55	24		Y							N		3
Clark College	Vancouver	C,T	St	M/W	12,646	51	27	57	Y		S	Y	Y	Y	Y	N	8	37
Clover Park Technical College	Lakewood	T	St	M/W	9,829													
Everett Community College	Everett	C,T	St	M/W	7,562	51	32		Y		R	Y	Y	Y	Y	N	12	53
Grays Harbor College	Aberdeen	C,T	St	M/W	2,330	49												
Green River Community College	Auburn	C,T	St	M/W	9,114	45	29		Y	Y	S	Y	Y	Y	Y		10	30
Highline Community College	Des Moines	C,T	St	M/W	6,725	45	51		Y			Y	Y	Y	Y	N	7	47
ITT Technical Institute	Everett	T,B	Prop	M/W														15
ITT Technical Institute	Seattle	T,B	Prop	M/W						Y		Y	Y			N		15
ITT Technical Institute	Spokane Valley	T,B	Prop	M/W					N	Y		Y	Y			N		13
Lake Washington Technical College	Kirkland	C,T	St	M/W	3,996													
Lower Columbia College	Longview	C,T	St	M/W	4,245	53	37	25	Y		R	Y	Y	Y		N	3	22
Olympic College	Bremerton	C,T,B	St	M/W	7,536	48	22		Y		S	Y	Y	Y	Y	N	7	60
Peninsula College	Port Angeles	C,T,B	St	M/W	3,776													
Pima Medical Institute	Seattle	T	Prop	M/W	357													
South Puget Sound Community College	Olympia	C,T	St	M/W	5,617	46	48	49	Y			Y	Y	Y	Y	N	3	23
Wenatchee Valley College	Wenatchee	C,T	St-L	M/W	3,504	40												
West Virginia																		
Blue Ridge Community and Technical College	Martinsburg	C,T	St	M/W	3,422	73	25		Y	Y	Y							15
Community & Technical College at West Virginia University Institute of Technology	Montgomery	T	Cou	M/W	760													
Huntington Junior College	Huntington	T	Prop	M/W	745													
ITT Technical Institute	Huntington	T	Prop	M/W														7
Mountain State College	Parkersburg	T	Prop	M/W	166		55		N	Y		Y	Y	Y	Y	N		7
Mountwest Community & Technical College†	Huntington	T	Cou	M/W	2,534	45												
New River Community and Technical College	Beckley	C,T	Cou	M/W	2,232													
Potomac State College of West Virginia University	Keyser	C,T,B	St	M/W	1,810	26	12		Y	Y	Y	Y	Y	Y		Y	7	53
West Virginia Northern Community College	Wheeling	C,T	St	M/W	3,150	50	49		Y	Y	S	Y	Y	Y	Y	N	4	10
Wisconsin																		
Blackhawk Technical College	Janesville	C,T	Dist	M/W	2,283													
Bryant & Stratton College	Milwaukee	T,B	Prop	M/W	828	44			N	Y	Y	Y	Y	Y	Y	N		12
Fox Valley Technical College	Appleton	C,T	St-L	M/W	10,244	70	47		Y	Y	Y	Y	Y	Y	Y	N	8	35
ITT Technical Institute	Green Bay	T,B	Prop	M/W						Y		Y	Y			N		15
ITT Technical Institute	Greenfield	T,B	Prop	M/W						Y		Y	Y			N		15
ITT Technical Institute	Madison	T,B	Prop	M/W														10
Lac Courte Oreilles Ojibwa Community College	Hayward	C,T	Fed	M/W	561	39	63		Y	Y	Y	Y	Y	Y	Y	N	4	20
Milwaukee Area Technical College	Milwaukee	C,T	Dist	M/W	20,215	65	55		Y	Y	Y	Y	Y	Y	Y	N	9	80
Moraine Park Technical College	Fond du Lac	C,T	Dist	M/W	8,466	80	62		Y	Y	Y	Y		Y	Y	N		59
Nicolet Area Technical College	Rhinelander	C,T	St-L	M/W	1,600		64		Y	Y	Y	Y	Y	Y	Y	N	6	21
Northcentral Technical College	Wausau	C,T	Dist	M/W	3,729													
Northeast Wisconsin Technical College	Green Bay	T	St-L	M/W	8,105													
Southwest Wisconsin Technical College	Fennimore	T	St-L	M/W	3,409	75	40		Y		Y	Y	Y	Y	Y	Y	3	20
University of Wisconsin–Fond du Lac	Fond du Lac	C	St	M/W	779	35	18		N	Y	Y	Y	Y	Y		N	6	1
University of Wisconsin–Fox Valley	Menasha	C,T	St	M/W	1,747	44	19		N	Y	Y	Y	Y	Y		N	6	1
University of Wisconsin–Richland	Richland Center	C	St	M/W	495	33	18			Y	Y	Y	Y	Y		Y	9	2
University of Wisconsin–Waukesha	Waukesha	C	St	M/W	2,087	44	30		N	Y	Y	Y	Y	Y	Y	N	9	1
Waukesha County Technical College	Pewaukee	T	St-L	M/W	7,606	72	48		Y		Y	Y	Y	Y		N		34
Wisconsin Indianhead Technical College	Shell Lake	T	Dist	M/W	4,118	58	58									N		21
Wyoming																		
Casper College	Casper	C,T	St-L	M/W	4,478	54	23	40	Y	Y	Y	Y	Y	Y	Y	Y	11	93
Central Wyoming College	Riverton	C,T	St-L	M/W	2,158	57	42	47	Y		R	Y	Y	Y	Y	Y	15	62

This chart includes the names and locations of accredited two-year colleges in the United States and U.S. territories and shows institutions' responses to the *Peterson's Annual Survey of Undergraduate Institutions*. If an institution submitted incomplete data, one or more columns opposite the institution's name is blank. A dagger after the school name indicates that the institution has one or more entries in the *College Close-Ups* section. If a school does not appear, it did not report any of the information.

Y—Yes; N—No; R—Recommended; S—For Some

		Degrees Awarded College Transfer Associate (C), Terminal Associate (T), Bachelor's (B), Master's (M)	**Institutional Control** County, District City, State and Local State-Related Federal, State, Commonwealth, Territory, Independent, Independent-Religious, Proprietary	**Student Body** Men, Primarily Men, Women, Primarily Women, Coed	Undergraduate Enrollment	Percent Attending Part-Time	Percent 25 Years of Age or Older	Percent of Grads Going on to Four-Year Colleges	Open Admissions	High School Equivalency Certificate Accepted	High School Transcript Required	Need-Based Aid Available	Part-Time Jobs Available	Career Counseling Available	Job Placement Services Available	College Housing Available	Number of Sports Offered	Number of Majors Offered
Eastern Wyoming College	Torrington	C,T	St-L	M/W	1,391	55			Y	Y	R	Y	Y	Y	Y	Y		49
Laramie County Community College	Cheyenne	C,T	St	M/W	4,905	57	42	61	Y	Y	S	Y	Y	Y	Y	Y	11	70
Northwest College	Powell	C,T	St-L	M/W	2,099	36	28	47	Y	Y	Y	Y	Y	Y		Y	10	66
Sheridan College	Sheridan	C,T	St-L	M/W	3,930	64	39		Y	Y	R,S	Y	Y	Y	Y	Y	9	46
Western Wyoming Community College	Rock Springs	C,T	St-L	M/W	4,120	70			Y	Y	Y	Y	Y	Y	Y	Y	15	84
CANADA																		
Alberta																		
Southern Alberta Institute of Technology	Calgary	T,B	Prov	M/W	7,672	9			N	Y	Y					Y	7	5

Profiles of Two-Year Colleges

U.S. AND U.S. TERRITORIES

ALABAMA

ALABAMA SOUTHERN COMMUNITY COLLEGE

Monroeville, Alabama **www.ascc.edu/**

- **State-supported** 2-year, founded 1965, part of Alabama College System
- **Rural** 80-acre campus
- **Coed**

Academics *Calendar:* semesters. *Degree:* certificates and associate. *Special study options:* academic remediation for entering students, adult/continuing education programs, advanced placement credit, honors programs, part-time degree program, summer session for credit.

Student Life *Campus security:* 24-hour patrols.

Athletics Member NJCAA.

Applying *Options:* early admission. *Required:* high school transcript.

Director of Admissions Ms. Jana S. Horton, Registrar, Alabama Southern Community College, PO Box 2000, Monroeville, AL 36461. *Phone:* 251-575-3156 Ext. 252. *E-mail:* jhorton@ascc.edu.

BEVILL STATE COMMUNITY COLLEGE

Sumiton, Alabama **www.bscc.edu/**

- **State-supported** 2-year, founded 1969, part of Alabama College System
- **Rural** 245-acre campus with easy access to Birmingham
- **Endowment** $142,934
- **Coed,** 4,556 undergraduate students, 56% full-time, 63% women, 37% men

Undergraduates 2,544 full-time, 2,012 part-time.

Freshmen *Admission:* 1,184 enrolled.

Faculty *Total:* 329, 35% full-time, 10% with terminal degrees.

Majors Administrative assistant and secretarial science; child-care and support services management; computer and information sciences; drafting and design technology; electrician; emergency medical technology (EMT paramedic); general studies; heating, air conditioning and refrigeration technology; industrial electronics technology; legal assistant/paralegal; liberal arts and sciences/liberal studies; nursing (registered nurse training); tool and die technology.

Academics *Calendar:* semesters. *Degree:* certificates and associate. *Special study options:* academic remediation for entering students, adult/continuing education programs, advanced placement credit, cooperative education, honors programs, off-campus study, part-time degree program, services for LD students, summer session for credit.

Library 31,690 titles, 192 serial subscriptions, an OPAC, a Web page.

Student Life *Housing Options:* coed. Campus housing is university owned. *Activities and Organizations:* choral group, Student Government Association, Campus Ministries, Circle K, Outdoors men Club, Students Against Destructive Decisions. *Campus security:* 24-hour emergency response devices.

Athletics Member NJCAA. *Intercollegiate sports:* baseball M(s), basketball M(s), cross-country running W(s), softball W(s), track and field W. *Intramural sports:* basketball M/W, football M, softball M/W, table tennis M/W, volleyball M/W.

Costs (2010–11) *One-time required fee:* $40. *Tuition:* state resident $2720 full-time, $85 per credit hour part-time; nonresident $5440 full-time, $170 per credit hour part-time. Full-time tuition and fees vary according to course load. Part-time tuition and fees vary according to course load. *Required fees:* $638 full-time, $11 per credit hour part-time, $15 per semester part-time. *Room and board:* $1850; room only: $1185. Room and board charges vary according to housing facility and location.

Financial Aid Of all full-time matriculated undergraduates who enrolled in 2008, 88 Federal Work-Study jobs (averaging $1807).

Applying *Options:* electronic application, early admission, deferred entrance. *Required:* high school transcript. *Application deadlines:* rolling (freshmen), rolling (transfers).

Freshman Application Contact Bevill State Community College, PO Box 800, Sumiton, AL 35148. *Phone:* 205-932-3221 Ext. 5101.

BISHOP STATE COMMUNITY COLLEGE

Mobile, Alabama **www.bscc.cc.al.us/**

Freshman Application Contact Dr. Terry Hazzard, Dean of Students, Bishop State Community College, 351 North Broad Street, Mobile, AL 36603-5898. *Phone:* 251-405-7089. *Fax:* 251-438-5403. *E-mail:* info@bishop.edu.

CALHOUN COMMUNITY COLLEGE

Decatur, Alabama **www.calhoun.edu/**

Freshman Application Contact Ms. Patricia Landers, Admissions Receptionist, Calhoun Community College, PO Box 2216, 6250 Highway 31 North, Decatur, AL 35609-2216. *Phone:* 256-306-2593. *Toll-free phone:* 800-626-3628 Ext. 2594. *Fax:* 256-306-2941. *E-mail:* pml@calhoun.edu.

CENTRAL ALABAMA COMMUNITY COLLEGE

Alexander City, Alabama **www.cacc.edu/**

Freshman Application Contact Ms. Donna Whaley, Central Alabama Community College, PO Box 699, Alexander City, AL 35011-0699. *Phone:* 256-234-6346 Ext. 6232. *Toll-free phone:* 800-643-2657 Ext. 6232.

CHATTAHOOCHEE VALLEY COMMUNITY COLLEGE

Phenix City, Alabama **www.cv.edu/**

Freshman Application Contact Ms. Rita Cherry, Admissions Clerk, Chattahoochee Valley Community College, PO Box 1000, Phenix City, AL 36869. *Phone:* 334-291-4995. *Toll-free phone:* 800-842-2822. *Fax:* 334-291-4994. *E-mail:* information@cv.edu.

COMMUNITY COLLEGE OF THE AIR FORCE

Maxwell Air Force Base, Alabama **www.au.af.mil/au/ccaf/**

Freshman Application Contact C.M. Sgt. Robert McAlexander, Director of Admissions/Registrar, Community College of the Air Force, 130 West Maxwell Boulevard, Building 836, Maxwell Air Force Base, Maxwell AFB, AL 36112-6613. *Phone:* 334-953-6436. *Fax:* 334-953-8211. *E-mail:* ronald.hall@maxwell.af.mil.

ENTERPRISE STATE COMMUNITY COLLEGE

Enterprise, Alabama **www.eocc.edu/**

- **State-supported** 2-year, founded 1965, part of Alabama College System
- **Small-town** 100-acre campus
- **Coed**

Academics *Calendar:* semesters. *Degree:* certificates and associate. *Special study options:* academic remediation for entering students, adult/continuing education programs, advanced placement credit, English as a second language, honors programs, internships, part-time degree program, services for LD students, summer session for credit.

Student Life *Campus security:* security personnel.

Athletics Member NJCAA.

Financial Aid Of all full-time matriculated undergraduates who enrolled in 2008, 99 Federal Work-Study jobs (averaging $2000).

Enterprise State Community College (continued)

Applying *Options:* early admission, deferred entrance. *Required:* high school transcript.

Director of Admissions Mr. Gary Deas, Associate Dean of Students/Registrar, Enterprise State Community College, PO Box 1300, Enterprise, AL 36331. *Phone:* 334-347-2623 Ext. 2233. *E-mail:* gdeas@eocc.edu.

GADSDEN STATE COMMUNITY COLLEGE

Gadsden, Alabama **www.gadsdenstate.edu/**

- **State-supported** 2-year, founded 1965, part of Alabama Community College System
- **Small-town** 275-acre campus with easy access to Birmingham
- **Endowment** $2.5 million
- **Coed,** 5,803 undergraduate students, 58% full-time, 61% women, 39% men

Undergraduates 3,354 full-time, 2,449 part-time. Students come from 16 states and territories, 46 other countries, 4% are from out of state, 20% African American, 0.5% Asian American or Pacific Islander, 2% Hispanic American, 0.4% Native American, 2% international, 5% transferred in, 2% live on campus. *Retention:* 57% of 2008 full-time freshmen returned.

Freshmen *Admission:* 1,539 enrolled.

Faculty *Total:* 346, 43% full-time. *Student/faculty ratio:* 17:1.

Majors Accounting technology and bookkeeping; administrative assistant and secretarial science; child-care and support services management; civil engineering technology; clinical/medical laboratory technology; communication and journalism related; computer and information sciences; court reporting; criminal justice/police science; drafting and design technology; electrical, electronic and communications engineering technology; emergency medical technology (EMT paramedic); general studies; heating, air conditioning and refrigeration technology; industrial mechanics and maintenance technology; legal assistant/paralegal; liberal arts and sciences/liberal studies; manufacturing technology; mechanical engineering/mechanical technology; medical radiologic technology; nursing (registered nurse training); sales, distribution and marketing; substance abuse/addiction counseling; telecommunications technology; tool and die technology.

Academics *Calendar:* semesters. *Degree:* certificates and associate. *Special study options:* academic remediation for entering students, adult/continuing education programs, advanced placement credit, cooperative education, distance learning, English as a second language, external degree program, honors programs, internships, part-time degree program, services for LD students, study abroad, summer session for credit. *ROTC:* Army (b).

Library Meadows Library with 109,568 titles, 234 serial subscriptions, 12,030 audiovisual materials, an OPAC, a Web page.

Student Life *Housing Options:* coed. Campus housing is university owned. *Activities and Organizations:* drama/theater group, choral group, National Society of Leadership and Success, Student Government Association, Circle K, Phi Beta Kappa, International Club. *Campus security:* 24-hour patrols. *Student services:* personal/psychological counseling.

Athletics Member NJCAA. *Intercollegiate sports:* baseball M(s), basketball M(s)/W(s), cross-country running W(s), softball W(s), tennis M(s), volleyball W(s).

Costs (2010–11) *Tuition:* state resident $3240 full-time, $90 per credit hour part-time; nonresident $6300 full-time, $175 per credit hour part-time. Full-time tuition and fees vary according to reciprocity agreements. Part-time tuition and fees vary according to reciprocity agreements. *Required fees:* $684 full-time, $19 per credit hour part-time. *Room and board:* $3200. *Waivers:* minority students, adult students, senior citizens, and employees or children of employees.

Applying *Options:* early admission, deferred entrance. *Required:* high school transcript. *Application deadlines:* rolling (freshmen), rolling (transfers).

Freshman Application Contact Dr. Teresa Rhea, Admissions and Records, Gadsden State Community College, Admissions, Allen Hall, PO Box 227, Gadsden, AL 35902-0227. *Phone:* 256-549-8210. *Toll-free phone:* 800-226-5563. *Fax:* 256-549-8205. *E-mail:* info@gadsdenstate.edu.

GEORGE CORLEY WALLACE STATE COMMUNITY COLLEGE

Selma, Alabama **www.wccs.edu/**

- **State-supported** 2-year, founded 1966, part of Alabama College System
- **Small-town** campus
- **Coed**

Academics *Calendar:* semesters. *Degree:* certificates, diplomas, and associate. *Special study options:* academic remediation for entering students, adult/continuing education programs, advanced placement credit, independent study, part-time degree program, services for LD students, summer session for credit.

Student Life *Campus security:* 24-hour patrols.

Athletics Member NJCAA.

Costs (2009–10) *Tuition:* state resident $1704 full-time, $71 per credit hour part-time; nonresident $3408 full-time, $142 per credit hour part-time. Part-time tuition and fees vary according to course load. *Required fees:* $456 full-time, $19 per credit hour part-time.

Financial Aid Of all full-time matriculated undergraduates who enrolled in 2008, 50 Federal Work-Study jobs (averaging $3000).

Applying *Options:* early admission, deferred entrance.

Director of Admissions Ms. Sunette Newman, Registrar, George Corley Wallace State Community College, 3000 Earl Goodwin Parkway, Selma, AL 36702-2530. *Phone:* 334-876-9305.

GEORGE C. WALLACE COMMUNITY COLLEGE

Dothan, Alabama **www.wallace.edu/**

Freshman Application Contact Dr. Brenda Barnes, Assistant Dean of Student Affairs, George C. Wallace Community College, 1141 Wallace Drive, Dothan, AL 36303-9234. *Phone:* 334-983-3521 Ext. 2470. *Toll-free phone:* 800-543-2426. *Fax:* 334-983-3600. *E-mail:* bbarnes@wallace.edu.

H. COUNCILL TRENHOLM STATE TECHNICAL COLLEGE

Montgomery, Alabama **www.trenholmstate.edu/**

- **State-supported** 2-year, founded 1962, part of Alabama Department of Postsecondary Education
- **Urban** 81-acre campus
- **Coed,** 1,587 undergraduate students

Undergraduates Students come from 2 states and territories, 1% are from out of state, 63% African American, 0.8% Asian American or Pacific Islander, 0.8% Hispanic American, 0.8% Native American. *Retention:* 54% of 2008 full-time freshmen returned.

Freshmen *Admission:* 1,048 applied, 572 admitted.

Faculty *Total:* 147, 50% full-time, 3% with terminal degrees. *Student/faculty ratio:* 10:1.

Majors Accounting technology and bookkeeping; administrative assistant and secretarial science; autobody/collision and repair technology; automotive engineering technology; child-care and support services management; computer and information sciences; culinary arts; dental assisting; diagnostic medical sonography and ultrasound technology; drafting and design technology; electrician; emergency medical technology (EMT paramedic); graphic and printing equipment operation/production; heating, air conditioning and refrigeration technology; industrial electronics technology; industrial mechanics and maintenance technology; machine tool technology; medical/clinical assistant; occupational therapist assistant; radiologic technology/science.

Academics *Calendar:* semesters. *Degree:* certificates, diplomas, and associate. *Special study options:* academic remediation for entering students, adult/continuing education programs, advanced placement credit, cooperative education, distance learning, external degree program, independent study, internships, part-time degree program, services for LD students, summer session for credit.

Library Trenholm State Learning Resources plus 1 other with 40,004 titles, 9,762 serial subscriptions, 863 audiovisual materials, an OPAC, a Web page.

Student Life *Housing:* college housing not available. *Activities and Organizations:* student-run newspaper, Student Government Association, College Ambassadors, Photography Club, Skills USA - VICA, Student Leadership Academy. *Campus security:* 24-hour emergency response devices and patrols, late-night transport/escort service. *Student services:* personal/psychological counseling.

Standardized Tests *Required for some:* ACT (for admission).

Costs (2010–11) *Tuition:* state resident $2550 full-time, $85 per credit hour part-time; nonresident $5100 full-time, $170 per credit hour part-time. *Required fees:* $570 full-time, $19 per credit hour part-time. *Waivers:* senior citizens and employees or children of employees.

Applying *Options:* early admission. *Required:* high school transcript. *Application deadlines:* rolling (freshmen), rolling (out-of-state freshmen), rolling (transfers).

Freshman Application Contact Mrs. Tennie McBryde, Registrar, H. Councill Trenholm State Technical College, 1225 Air Base Boulevard, Montgomery, AL 36108. *Phone:* 334-420-4306. *Fax:* 334-420-4201. *E-mail:* tmcbryde@trenholmstate.edu.

HERZING COLLEGE

Birmingham, Alabama **www.herzing.edu/birmingham/**

- **Proprietary** primarily 2-year, founded 1965, part of Herzing Institutes, Inc.
- **Urban** 4-acre campus
- **Coed**

Academics *Calendar:* semesters. *Degrees:* diplomas, associate, and bachelor's. *Special study options:* adult/continuing education programs, advanced placement credit, cooperative education, external degree program, internships, student-designed majors, summer session for credit.

Student Life *Campus security:* 24-hour emergency response devices, late-night transport/escort service, security guard.

Applying *Options:* early admission, deferred entrance.

Director of Admissions Ms. Tess Anderson, Admissions Coordinator, Herzing College, 280 West Valley Avenue, Birmingham, AL 35209. *Phone:* 205-916-2800. *E-mail:* admiss@bhm.herzing.edu.

ITT TECHNICAL INSTITUTE

Bessemer, Alabama **www.itt-tech.edu/**

- **Proprietary** primarily 2-year, founded 1994, part of ITT Educational Services, Inc.
- **Suburban** campus
- **Coed**

Majors Animation, interactive technology, video graphics and special effects; business administration and management; CAD/CADD drafting/design technology; computer and information systems security; computer engineering technology; computer software and media applications related; computer software engineering; computer software technology; construction management; criminal justice/law enforcement administration; design and visual communications; electrical, electronic and communications engineering technology; legal assistant/paralegal; system, networking, and LAN/WAN management; web/multimedia management and webmaster; web page, digital/multimedia and information resources design.

Academics *Calendar:* quarters. *Degrees:* associate and bachelor's.

Student Life *Housing:* college housing not available. *Campus security:* 24-hour emergency response devices.

Freshman Application Contact Director of Recruitment, ITT Technical Institute, 6270 Park South Drive, Bessemer, AL 35022. *Phone:* 205-497-5700. *Toll-free phone:* 800-488-7033.

ITT TECHNICAL INSTITUTE

Madison, Alabama **www.itt-tech.edu/**

- **Proprietary** primarily 2-year, part of ITT Educational Services, Inc.
- **Coed**

Majors CAD/CADD drafting/design technology; computer and information systems security; computer engineering technology; computer software engineering; computer software technology; construction management; criminal justice/law enforcement administration; design and visual communications; electrical, electronic and communications engineering technology; legal assistant/paralegal; system, networking, and LAN/WAN management.

Academics *Degrees:* associate and bachelor's.

Freshman Application Contact Director of Recruitment, ITT Technical Institute, 9238 Madison Boulevard, Suite 500, Madison, AL 35758. *Phone:* 256-542-2900. *Toll-free phone:* 877-210-4900.

ITT TECHNICAL INSTITUTE

Mobile, Alabama **www.itt-tech.edu/**

- **Proprietary** primarily 2-year, part of ITT Educational Services, Inc.
- **Coed**

Majors CAD/CADD drafting/design technology; computer and information systems security; computer engineering technology; computer software engineering; computer software technology; construction management; criminal justice/law enforcement administration; design and visual communications; electrical, electronic and communications engineering technology; legal assistant/paralegal; system, networking, and LAN/WAN management.

Academics *Degrees:* associate and bachelor's.

Freshman Application Contact Director of Recruitment, ITT Technical Institute, Office Mall South, 3100 Cottage Hill Road, Building 3, Mobile, AL 36606. *Phone:* 251-472-4760. *Toll-free phone:* 877-327-1013.

JAMES H. FAULKNER STATE COMMUNITY COLLEGE

Bay Minette, Alabama **www.faulknerstate.edu/**

Freshman Application Contact Ms. Carmelita Mikkelsen, Director of Admissions and High School Relations, James H. Faulkner State Community College, 1900 Highway 31 South, Bay Minette, AL 36507. *Phone:* 251-580-2213. *Toll-free phone:* 800-231-3752 Ext. 2111. *Fax:* 251-580-2285. *E-mail:* cmikkelsen@faulknerstate.edu.

JEFFERSON DAVIS COMMUNITY COLLEGE

Brewton, Alabama **www.jdcc.edu/**

- **State-supported** 2-year, founded 1965
- **Small-town** 100-acre campus
- **Coed**

Academics *Calendar:* semesters. *Degree:* certificates and associate. *Special study options:* academic remediation for entering students, adult/continuing education programs, advanced placement credit, honors programs, part-time degree program, services for LD students, summer session for credit.

Athletics Member NJCAA.

Financial Aid Of all full-time matriculated undergraduates who enrolled in 2008, 50 Federal Work-Study jobs (averaging $2700).

Applying *Options:* early admission. *Required:* high school transcript.

Director of Admissions Ms. Robin Sessions, Registrar, Jefferson Davis Community College, PO Box 958, Brewton, AL 36427. *Phone:* 251-867-4832.

JEFFERSON STATE COMMUNITY COLLEGE

Birmingham, Alabama **www.jeffstateonline.com/**

- **State-supported** 2-year, founded 1965, part of Alabama Community College System
- **Suburban** 234-acre campus
- **Coed,** 8,548 undergraduate students, 38% full-time, 60% women, 40% men

Undergraduates 3,270 full-time, 5,278 part-time. Students come from 31 states and territories, 71 other countries, 2% are from out of state, 18% African American, 2% Asian American or Pacific Islander, 2% Hispanic American, 0.3% Native American, 0.9% international, 9% transferred in.

Freshmen *Admission:* 1,538 enrolled.

Faculty *Total:* 441, 33% full-time, 16% with terminal degrees. *Student/faculty ratio:* 20:1.

Majors Accounting technology and bookkeeping; administrative assistant and secretarial science; agricultural business and management; banking and financial support services; business/commerce; child-care and support services management; clinical/medical laboratory technology; computer and information sciences; construction engineering technology; criminal justice/police science; emergency medical technology (EMT paramedic); engineering technology; fire services administration; funeral service and mortuary science; general studies; hospitality administration; liberal arts and sciences/liberal studies; manufacturing technology; medical radiologic technology; nursing (licensed practical/vocational nurse training); nursing (registered nurse training); physical therapist assistant; radio and television broadcasting technology; robotics technology; veterinary/animal health technology.

Academics *Calendar:* semesters. *Degree:* certificates and associate. *Special study options:* academic remediation for entering students, adult/continuing

Jefferson State Community College (continued)

education programs, advanced placement credit, distance learning, honors programs, independent study, internships, part-time degree program, services for LD students, summer session for credit. *ROTC:* Army (c), Air Force (c).

Library Jefferson State Libraries plus 3 others with 150,000 titles, 334 serial subscriptions, 3,349 audiovisual materials, an OPAC, a Web page.

Student Life *Housing:* college housing not available. *Activities and Organizations:* drama/theater group, student-run newspaper, radio station, choral group, Student Government Association, Phi Theta Kappa, Baptist Campus Ministries, Jefferson State Ambassadors, Students in Free Enterprise (SIFE). *Campus security:* 24-hour patrols.

Athletics Member NJCAA. *Intercollegiate sports:* baseball M(s), softball W(s). *Intramural sports:* basketball M/W, football M/W.

Costs (2010–11) *Tuition:* state resident $3480 full-time, $116 per semester hour part-time; nonresident $6030 full-time, $201 per semester hour part-time. Full-time tuition and fees vary according to course load. Part-time tuition and fees vary according to course load. *Waivers:* senior citizens and employees or children of employees.

Financial Aid Of all full-time matriculated undergraduates who enrolled in 2008, 189 Federal Work-Study jobs (averaging $1926).

Applying *Options:* electronic application, early admission, deferred entrance. *Required for some:* high school transcript. *Application deadline:* rolling (freshmen). *Notification:* continuous (freshmen), continuous (transfers).

Freshman Application Contact Mrs. Lillian Owens, Director of Admissions and Retention, Jefferson State Community College, 2601 Carson Road, Birmingham, AL 35215-3098. *Phone:* 205-853-1200 Ext. 7990. *Toll-free phone:* 800-239-5900. *Fax:* 205-856-6070. *E-mail:* lowens@jeffstateonline.com.

J. F. Drake State Technical College

Huntsville, Alabama **www.drakestate.edu/**

- **State-supported** 2-year, founded 1961, part of Alabama Department of Postsecondary Education
- **Urban** 6-acre campus
- **Coed,** 1,258 undergraduate students, 60% full-time, 55% women, 45% men

Undergraduates 754 full-time, 504 part-time. Students come from 1 other state, 4% are from out of state, 63% African American, 2% Asian American or Pacific Islander, 1% Hispanic American, 0.6% Native American, 0.4% international, 23% transferred in.

Freshmen *Admission:* 1,010 applied, 699 admitted, 347 enrolled.

Faculty *Total:* 72, 35% full-time, 7% with terminal degrees. *Student/faculty ratio:* 17:1.

Majors Accounting; administrative assistant and secretarial science; commercial and advertising art; drafting and design technology; electrical, electronic and communications engineering technology; information science/studies; machine tool technology.

Academics *Calendar:* semesters. *Degree:* certificates, diplomas, and associate. *Special study options:* academic remediation for entering students, cooperative education, internships, part-time degree program, services for LD students.

Library S.C. O'Neal Library Technology Center.

Student Life *Housing:* college housing not available. *Activities and Organizations:* Phi Beta Lambda, VICA (Vocational Industrial Clubs of America). *Campus security:* 24-hour patrols.

Costs (2009–10) *Tuition:* state resident $2160 full-time, $72 per credit hour part-time; nonresident $4320 full-time, $144 per credit hour part-time. *Required fees:* $135 full-time, $18 per credit hour part-time. *Waivers:* employees or children of employees.

Applying *Options:* electronic application, deferred entrance. *Required:* high school transcript. *Application deadline:* rolling (freshmen).

Freshman Application Contact Mrs. Monica Sudeall, Registrar, J. F. Drake State Technical College, 3421 Meridian Street, Huntsville, AL 35811. *Phone:* 256-539-8161. *Toll-free phone:* 888-413-7253. *Fax:* 256-551-3142. *E-mail:* sudeall@drakestate.edu.

Lawson State Community College

Birmingham, Alabama **www.lawsonstate.edu/**

- **State-supported** 2-year, founded 1949, part of Alabama Community College System
- **Urban** 30-acre campus
- **Coed,** 4,353 undergraduate students, 58% full-time, 63% women, 37% men

Undergraduates 2,542 full-time, 1,811 part-time. 1% are from out of state, 81% African American, 0.4% Asian American or Pacific Islander, 0.9% Hispanic American, 0.1% Native American, 0.1% international, 1% live on campus. *Retention:* 54% of 2008 full-time freshmen returned.

Freshmen *Admission:* 1,637 applied, 1,354 admitted.

Faculty *Total:* 218, 43% full-time. *Student/faculty ratio:* 17:1.

Majors Accounting; administrative assistant and secretarial science; biology/biological sciences; business administration and management; business teacher education; chemistry; clinical laboratory science/medical technology; computer and information sciences related; criminal justice/law enforcement administration; criminal justice/police science; dietetics; drafting and design technology; electrical, electronic and communications engineering technology; English; health and physical education; history; information science/studies; legal administrative assistant/secretary; liberal arts and sciences/liberal studies; mathematics; music; nursing (registered nurse training); physical sciences; physical therapy; political science and government; pre-engineering; pre-law studies; psychology; social sciences; social work; sociology.

Academics *Calendar:* semesters. *Degree:* certificates and associate. *Special study options:* academic remediation for entering students, adult/continuing education programs, cooperative education, distance learning, freshman honors college, honors programs, internships, part-time degree program, services for LD students, summer session for credit.

Library Lawson State Library with 69,249 titles, 257 serial subscriptions, an OPAC.

Student Life *Housing Options:* coed. Campus housing is university owned. *Activities and Organizations:* choral group, Student Government Association, Phi Theta Kappa, Kappa Beta Delta Honor Society, Phi Beta Lambda, Social Work Club. *Campus security:* 24-hour emergency response devices and patrols, student patrols. *Student services:* personal/psychological counseling.

Athletics Member NJCAA. *Intercollegiate sports:* basketball M/W, cross-country running M(s), equestrian sports M, volleyball W(s). *Intramural sports:* basketball M/W, softball M/W, swimming and diving M/W, table tennis M/W, tennis M/W, track and field M/W, volleyball W, weight lifting M.

Costs (2010–11) *Tuition:* state resident $2850 full-time; nonresident $5700 full-time. *Room and board:* Room and board charges vary according to board plan. *Payment plan:* installment. *Waivers:* senior citizens and employees or children of employees.

Financial Aid Of all full-time matriculated undergraduates who enrolled in 2008, 91 Federal Work-Study jobs (averaging $3000).

Applying *Options:* electronic application, early admission, deferred entrance. *Required:* high school transcript. *Application deadlines:* rolling (freshmen), rolling (transfers). *Notification:* continuous (freshmen), continuous (transfers).

Freshman Application Contact Mr. Jeff Shelley, Director of Admissions and Records, Lawson State Community College, 3060 Wilson Road, SW, Birmingham, AL 35221-1798. *Phone:* 205-929-6361. *Fax:* 205-923-7106. *E-mail:* jshelley@lawsonstate.edu.

Lurleen B. Wallace Community College

Andalusia, Alabama **www.lbwcc.edu/**

- **State-supported** 2-year, founded 1969, part of Alabama College System
- **Small-town** 200-acre campus
- **Endowment** $1.2 million
- **Coed,** 1,791 undergraduate students, 61% full-time, 63% women, 37% men

Undergraduates 1,088 full-time, 703 part-time. Students come from 9 states and territories, 3 other countries, 11% are from out of state, 21% African American, 0.4% Asian American or Pacific Islander, 1% Hispanic American, 0.4% Native American, 0.1% international, 18% transferred in.

Freshmen *Admission:* 403 enrolled.

Faculty *Total:* 110, 46% full-time, 5% with terminal degrees. *Student/faculty ratio:* 16:1.

Majors Accounting technology and bookkeeping; administrative assistant and secretarial science; child-care and support services management; computer and information sciences; drafting and design technology; electrician; emergency medical technology (EMT paramedic); forestry technology; general studies; industrial electronics technology; liberal arts and sciences/liberal studies; nursing (registered nurse training).

Academics *Calendar:* semesters. *Degree:* certificates, diplomas, and associate. *Special study options:* academic remediation for entering students, advanced placement credit, cooperative education, distance learning, double majors, English as a second language, external degree program, independent study, off-campus study, part-time degree program, services for LD students, summer session for credit.

Library Lurleen B. Wallace Library plus 2 others with 40,004 titles, 40 serial subscriptions, 2,249 audiovisual materials, a Web page.

Student Life *Housing:* college housing not available. *Activities and Organizations:* drama/theater group, choral group, Christian Student Ministries, Civitan, Mu Alpha Theta, Phi Theta Kappa, Student Government Association. *Student services:* personal/psychological counseling.

Athletics Member NJCAA. *Intercollegiate sports:* baseball M(s), basketball M(s)/W(s), softball W(s).

Costs (2010–11) *Tuition:* state resident $3270 full-time, $109 per credit hour part-time; nonresident $5820 full-time, $194 per credit hour part-time. Full-time tuition and fees vary according to course load. Part-time tuition and fees vary according to course load. *Waivers:* senior citizens and employees or children of employees.

Financial Aid Of all full-time matriculated undergraduates who enrolled in 2008, 70 Federal Work-Study jobs.

Applying *Required:* high school transcript. *Application deadlines:* rolling (freshmen), rolling (transfers). *Notification:* continuous until 9/15 (freshmen), continuous until 9/15 (transfers).

Freshman Application Contact Lurleen B. Wallace Community College, PO Box 1418, Andalusia, AL 36420. *Phone:* 334-881-2273.

MARION MILITARY INSTITUTE

Marion, Alabama **www.marionmilitary.org/**

Director of Admissions Director of Admissions, Marion Military Institute, 1101 Washington Street, Marion, AL 36756. *Phone:* 800-664-1842 Ext. 306. *Toll-free phone:* 800-664-1842 Ext. 307.

NORTHEAST ALABAMA COMMUNITY COLLEGE

Rainsville, Alabama **www.nacc.edu/**

Freshman Application Contact Northeast Alabama Community College, PO Box 159, Rainsville, AL 35986. *Phone:* 256-228-6001 Ext. 325.

NORTHWEST-SHOALS COMMUNITY COLLEGE

Muscle Shoals, Alabama **www.nwscc.edu/**

- **State-supported** 2-year, founded 1963, part of Alabama Department of Postsecondary Education
- **Small-town** 210-acre campus
- **Coed,** 4,537 undergraduate students, 53% full-time, 58% women, 42% men

Undergraduates 2,414 full-time, 2,123 part-time. Students come from 12 states and territories, 3 other countries, 2% are from out of state, 11% African American, 0.8% Asian American or Pacific Islander, 2% Hispanic American, 0.9% Native American, 4% transferred in, 2% live on campus.

Freshmen *Admission:* 3,250 applied, 3,250 admitted, 1,103 enrolled.

Faculty *Total:* 239, 38% full-time, 5% with terminal degrees. *Student/faculty ratio:* 22:1.

Majors Accounting; administrative assistant and secretarial science; child development; computer and information sciences; computer programming; computer science; criminal justice/law enforcement administration; criminal justice/police science; drafting and design technology; electrical, electronic and communications engineering technology; general studies; industrial electronics technology; industrial mechanics and maintenance technology; information science/studies; liberal arts and sciences/liberal studies; multi/interdisciplinary studies related; nursing (registered nurse training); water quality and wastewater treatment management and recycling technology; welding technology.

Academics *Calendar:* semesters. *Degree:* certificates, diplomas, and associate. *Special study options:* academic remediation for entering students, accelerated degree program, adult/continuing education programs, advanced placement credit, cooperative education, distance learning, honors programs, independent study, part-time degree program, services for LD students, summer session for credit.

Library Larry W. McCoy Learning Resource Center and James Glasgow Library with 69,048 titles, 202 serial subscriptions, 6,836 audiovisual materials, an OPAC.

Student Life *Housing Options:* coed. Campus housing is university owned. *Activities and Organizations:* choral group, Student Government Association, Science Club, Phi Theta Kappa, Baptist Campus Ministry, Northwest-Shoals Singers. *Campus security:* 24-hour emergency response devices and patrols. *Student services:* personal/psychological counseling.

Athletics Member NJCAA. *Intercollegiate sports:* baseball M(s), basketball M(s)/W(s), cheerleading M(s)/W(s), softball W(s), volleyball W(s). *Intramural sports:* basketball M/W, softball M/W, table tennis M/W, tennis M/W, volleyball M/W.

Standardized Tests *Required:* COMPASS Placement Test for English and Math (for admission).

Costs (2010–11) *Tuition:* state resident $2550 full-time, $85 per credit hour part-time; nonresident $5100 full-time, $170 per credit hour part-time. Full-time tuition and fees vary according to program. Part-time tuition and fees vary according to program. *Required fees:* $765 full-time, $25 per credit hour part-time. *Room and board:* room only: $1800. *Waivers:* minority students, senior citizens, and employees or children of employees.

Financial Aid Of all full-time matriculated undergraduates who enrolled in 2009, 42 Federal Work-Study jobs (averaging $2784). *Financial aid deadline:* 6/1.

Applying *Options:* electronic application. *Required:* high school transcript. *Application deadlines:* rolling (freshmen), rolling (transfers). *Notification:* continuous (transfers).

Freshman Application Contact Dr. Karen Berryhill, Vice President of Student Development Services, Northwest-Shoals Community College, PO Box 2545, Muscle Shoals, AL 35662. *Phone:* 256-331-5261. *Toll-free phone:* 800-645-8967. *Fax:* 256-331-5366. *E-mail:* berryk@nwscc.edu.

PRINCE INSTITUTE OF PROFESSIONAL STUDIES

Montgomery, Alabama **www.princeinstitute.edu/**

Freshman Application Contact Ms. Sherry Hill, Director of Admissions, Prince Institute of Professional Studies, 7735 Atlanta Highway, Montgomery, AL 36117. *Phone:* 334-271-1670. *Toll-free phone:* 877-853-5569. *Fax:* 334-271-1671. *E-mail:* admissions@princeinstitute.edu.

REID STATE TECHNICAL COLLEGE

Evergreen, Alabama **www.rstc.edu/**

- **State-supported** 2-year, founded 1966, part of Alabama College System
- **Rural** 26-acre campus
- **Coed,** 610 undergraduate students, 60% full-time, 68% women, 32% men

Undergraduates 365 full-time, 245 part-time. Students come from 2 states and territories, 1% are from out of state.

Freshmen *Admission:* 242 applied, 242 admitted, 106 enrolled.

Faculty *Total:* 36, 69% full-time, 17% with terminal degrees. *Student/faculty ratio:* 12:1.

Majors Administrative assistant and secretarial science; electrical, electronic and communications engineering technology.

Academics *Calendar:* semesters. *Degree:* certificates, diplomas, and associate. *Special study options:* academic remediation for entering students, adult/continuing education programs, double majors, independent study, internships, part-time degree program, services for LD students, summer session for credit.

Library Edith A. Gray Library with 3,800 titles, 17,236 serial subscriptions, 360 audiovisual materials, a Web page.

Student Life *Housing:* college housing not available. *Activities and Organizations:* student-run newspaper, Student Government Association, Skills USA. *Campus security:* 24-hour emergency response devices, day and evening security guard. *Student services:* personal/psychological counseling.

Costs (2009–10) *Tuition:* state resident $2592 full-time; nonresident $5184 full-time. *Required fees:* $648 full-time. *Waivers:* senior citizens and employees or children of employees.

Financial Aid Of all full-time matriculated undergraduates who enrolled in 2008, 35 Federal Work-Study jobs (averaging $1500).

Applying *Options:* early admission. *Required:* high school transcript. *Application deadlines:* rolling (freshmen), rolling (transfers).

Freshman Application Contact Dr. Alesia Stuart, Public Relations/Marketing, Reid State Technical College, PO Box 588, Intersection of I-95 and Highway 83, Evergreen, AL 36401-0588. *Phone:* 251-578-1313 Ext. 108.

REMINGTON COLLEGE–MOBILE CAMPUS

Mobile, Alabama **www.remingtoncollege.edu/**

Freshman Application Contact Remington College–Mobile Campus, 828 Downtowner Loop West, Mobile, AL 36609. *Phone:* 251-343-8200. *Toll-free phone:* 800-866-0850.

SHELTON STATE COMMUNITY COLLEGE

Tuscaloosa, Alabama **www.sheltonstate.edu/**

Freshman Application Contact Ms. Loretta Jones, Assistant to the Dean of Students, Shelton State Community College, Shelton State Community College, 9500 Old Greensboro Road, Tuscaloosa, AL 35405. *Phone:* 205-391-2236. *Fax:* 205-391-3910.

SNEAD STATE COMMUNITY COLLEGE

Boaz, Alabama **www.snead.edu/**

Freshman Application Contact Dr. Greg Chapman, Director of Instruction, Snead State Community College, PO Box 734, Boaz, AL 35957-0734. *Phone:* 256-840-4111. *Fax:* 256-593-7180. *E-mail:* gchapman@snead.edu.

SOUTHERN UNION STATE COMMUNITY COLLEGE

Wadley, Alabama **www.suscc.cc.al.us/**

- **State-supported** 2-year, founded 1922, part of Alabama College System
- **Rural** campus
- **Coed,** 4,971 undergraduate students

Undergraduates 12% are from out of state. *Retention:* 58% of 2008 full-time freshmen returned.

Faculty *Student/faculty ratio:* 25:1.

Majors Administrative assistant and secretarial science; autobody/collision and repair technology; automobile/automotive mechanics technology; business/commerce; child-care and support services management; computer and information sciences; cosmetology; electrical, electronic and communications engineering technology; emergency medical technology (EMT paramedic); general studies; health information/medical records technology; heating, air conditioning, ventilation and refrigeration maintenance technology; industrial electronics technology; industrial mechanics and maintenance technology; liberal arts and sciences/liberal studies; machine shop technology; medical radiologic technology; multi/interdisciplinary studies related; nursing (registered nurse training); welding technology.

Academics *Calendar:* semesters. *Degree:* certificates, diplomas, and associate. *Special study options:* academic remediation for entering students, adult/continuing education programs, advanced placement credit, distance learning, part-time degree program, summer session for credit. *ROTC:* Air Force (c).

Library McClintock-Ensminger Library.

Student Life *Housing Options:* coed. *Campus security:* 24-hour patrols, controlled dormitory access.

Athletics Member NJCAA.

Costs (2009–10) *Tuition:* state resident $3120 full-time, $104 per credit hour part-time; nonresident $5670 full-time, $189 per credit hour part-time.

Financial Aid Of all full-time matriculated undergraduates who enrolled in 2008, 120 Federal Work-Study jobs (averaging $1000). 30 state and other part-time jobs (averaging $800).

Applying *Options:* early admission, deferred entrance. *Required:* high school transcript. *Application deadlines:* rolling (freshmen), rolling (transfers). *Notification:* continuous (freshmen), continuous (transfers).

Freshman Application Contact Admissions Office, Southern Union State Community College, PO Box 1000, Roberts Street, Wadley, AL 36276. *Phone:* 256-395-5157. *E-mail:* info@suscc.edu.

WALLACE STATE COMMUNITY COLLEGE

Hanceville, Alabama **www.wallacestate.edu/**

Director of Admissions Ms. Linda Sperling, Director of Admissions, Wallace State Community College, PO Box 2000, 801 Main Street, Hanceville, AL 35077-2000. *Phone:* 256-352-8278. *Toll-free phone:* 866-350-9722.

ALASKA

CHARTER COLLEGE

Anchorage, Alaska **www.chartercollege.edu/**

- **Proprietary** primarily 2-year, founded 1985
- **Urban** campus
- **Coed**

Faculty *Student/faculty ratio:* 15:1.

Academics *Calendar:* quarters. *Degrees:* certificates, associate, and bachelor's. *Special study options:* adult/continuing education programs, internships, part-time degree program, summer session for credit.

Student Life *Campus security:* 24-hour emergency response devices.

Applying *Application fee:* $20. *Required:* high school transcript, interview.

Director of Admissions Ms. Lily Sirianni, Vice President, Charter College, 2221 East Northern Lights Boulevard, Suite 120, Anchorage, AK 99508-4157. *Phone:* 907-277-1000. *Toll-free phone:* 800-279-1008.

ILISAGVIK COLLEGE

Barrow, Alaska **www.ilisagvik.cc/**

Freshman Application Contact Ms. Beverly Patkotak Grinage, President, Ilisagvik College, UIC/Narl, Barrow, AK 99723. *Phone:* 907-852-1820. *Toll-free phone:* 800-478-7337. *Fax:* 907-852-1821. *E-mail:* beverly.grinage@ilisagvik.cc.

UNIVERSITY OF ALASKA ANCHORAGE, KENAI PENINSULA COLLEGE

Soldotna, Alaska **www.kpc.alaska.edu/**

- **State-supported** primarily 2-year, founded 1964, part of University of Alaska System
- **Rural** 360-acre campus
- **Coed,** 2,230 undergraduate students

Majors Business administration and management; digital communication and media/multimedia; early childhood education; elementary education; emergency medical technology (EMT paramedic); human services; liberal arts and sciences/liberal studies; occupational safety and health technology; psychology.

Academics *Calendar:* semesters. *Degrees:* certificates, associate, and bachelor's. *Special study options:* academic remediation for entering students, adult/continuing education programs, advanced placement credit, cooperative education, English as a second language, part-time degree program, services for LD students.

Library Kenai Peninsula College Library.

Student Life *Housing:* college housing not available. *Campus security:* 24-hour emergency response devices. *Student services:* health clinic.

Costs (2009–10) *Tuition:* state resident $141 per credit hour part-time; nonresident $141 per credit hour part-time. *Payment plan:* installment.

Financial Aid Of all full-time matriculated undergraduates who enrolled in 2008, 50 Federal Work-Study jobs (averaging $3000). 50 state and other part-time jobs (averaging $3000).

Applying *Options:* electronic application. *Application fee:* $40. *Required:* high school transcript, ACT, SAT or Accuplacer scores. *Application deadlines:* rolling (freshmen), rolling (transfers).

Freshman Application Contact Ms. Shelly Love Blatchford, Admission and Registration Coordinator, University of Alaska Anchorage, Kenai Peninsula College, 156 College Road, Soldotna, AK 99669-9798. *Phone:* 907-262-0311. *Toll-free phone:* 877-262-0330.

UNIVERSITY OF ALASKA ANCHORAGE, KODIAK COLLEGE

Kodiak, Alaska www.koc.alaska.edu/

Director of Admissions Jennifer Myrick, Registrar, University of Alaska Anchorage, Kodiak College, 117 Benny Benson Drive, Kodiak, AK 99615. *Phone:* 907-486-1235. *Toll-free phone:* 800-486-7660. *Fax:* 907-486-1264. *E-mail:* jmyrick@kodiak.alaska.edu.

UNIVERSITY OF ALASKA ANCHORAGE, MATANUSKA-SUSITNA COLLEGE

Palmer, Alaska www.matsu.alaska.edu/

- **State-supported** 2-year, founded 1958, part of University of Alaska System
- **Small-town** 950-acre campus with easy access to Anchorage
- **Coed,** 1,782 undergraduate students, 25% full-time, 38% women, 62% men

Undergraduates 452 full-time, 1,330 part-time. 1% African American, 3% Asian American or Pacific Islander, 3% Hispanic American, 7% Native American. *Retention:* 55% of 2008 full-time freshmen returned.

Faculty *Total:* 116, 22% full-time. *Student/faculty ratio:* 16:1.

Majors Accounting; administrative assistant and secretarial science; architectural engineering technology; business administration and management; electrical, electronic and communications engineering technology; emergency medical technology (EMT paramedic); heating, air conditioning, ventilation and refrigeration maintenance technology; human services; liberal arts and sciences/liberal studies.

Academics *Calendar:* semesters. *Degree:* certificates and associate. *Special study options:* academic remediation for entering students, adult/continuing education programs, advanced placement credit, cooperative education, distance learning, double majors, independent study, internships, off-campus study, part-time degree program, summer session for credit.

Library Al Okeson Library with 50,000 titles, 280 serial subscriptions, 1,840 audiovisual materials, an OPAC, a Web page.

Student Life *Housing:* college housing not available. *Activities and Organizations:* student-run newspaper, choral group, student government, Math Club, Phi Theta Kappa, Basketball, Students for Christ. *Campus security:* 24-hour patrols.

Costs (2010–11) *Tuition:* state resident $147 per semester hour part-time; nonresident $500 per semester hour part-time. Full-time tuition and fees vary according to course level and course load. Part-time tuition and fees vary according to course level and course load. *Required fees:* $8 per semester hour part-time, $10 per term part-time. *Payment plan:* installment. *Waivers:* children of alumni, senior citizens, and employees or children of employees.

Financial Aid Of all full-time matriculated undergraduates who enrolled in 2008, 8 Federal Work-Study jobs (averaging $3000).

Applying *Options:* electronic application. *Application fee:* $40. *Required:* high school transcript.

Freshman Application Contact Ms. Sandra Gravley, Student Services Director, University of Alaska Anchorage, Matanuska-Susitna College, PO Box 2889, Palmer, AK 99645-2889. *Phone:* 907-745-9712. *Fax:* 907-745-9747. *E-mail:* info@matsu.alaska.edu.

UNIVERSITY OF ALASKA, PRINCE WILLIAM SOUND COMMUNITY COLLEGE

Valdez, Alaska www.pwscc.edu/

Freshman Application Contact Mr. Nathan J. Platt, Director of Student Services, University of Alaska, Prince William Sound Community College, PO Box 97, Valdez, AK 99686-0097. *Phone:* 907-834-1631. *Toll-free phone:* 800-478-8800 Ext. 1600. *E-mail:* studentservices@pwscc.edu.

UNIVERSITY OF ALASKA SOUTHEAST, KETCHIKAN CAMPUS

Ketchikan, Alaska www.ketch.alaska.edu/

Freshman Application Contact Admissions Office, University of Alaska Southeast, Ketchikan Campus, 2600 7th Avenue, Ketchikan, AK 99901-5798. *Phone:* 907-225-6177. *Toll-free phone:* 888-550-6177. *Fax:* 907-225-3895. *E-mail:* ketch.info@uas.alaska.edu.

UNIVERSITY OF ALASKA SOUTHEAST, SITKA CAMPUS

Sitka, Alaska www.uas.alaska.edu/

Freshman Application Contact Cynthia Rogers, Coordinator of Admissions, University of Alaska Southeast, Sitka Campus, 1332 Seward Avenue, Sitka, AK 99835-9418. *Phone:* 907-747-7705. *Toll-free phone:* 800-478-6653. *Fax:* 907-747-7793. *E-mail:* cynthia.rogers@uas.alaska.edu.

AMERICAN SAMOA

AMERICAN SAMOA COMMUNITY COLLEGE

Pago Pago, American Samoa www.amsamoa.edu/

- **Territory-supported** 2-year, founded 1969
- **Rural** 20-acre campus
- **Coed**

Academics *Calendar:* semesters. *Degree:* certificates and associate. *Special study options:* academic remediation for entering students, adult/continuing education programs, off-campus study, part-time degree program, summer session for credit.

Applying *Options:* deferred entrance.

Director of Admissions Sifagatogo Tuitasi, Admissions, American Samoa Community College, PO Box 2609, Pago Pago, AS 96799. *Phone:* 684-699-1141. *E-mail:* admissions@amsamoa.edu.

ARIZONA

APOLLO COLLEGE–PHOENIX

Phoenix, Arizona www.apollocollege.edu/

- **Proprietary** 2-year, founded 1976, part of Apollo Colleges, Inc.
- **Urban** campus
- **Coed, primarily women**

Academics *Calendar:* continuous. *Degree:* certificates, diplomas, and associate. *Special study options:* academic remediation for entering students.

Applying *Application fee:* $75. *Required:* high school transcript. *Required for some:* essay or personal statement, interview.

Director of Admissions Admissions Director, Apollo College–Phoenix, 2701 West Bethany Home Road, Phoenix, AZ 85051. *Phone:* 602-324-5505. *Toll-free phone:* 800-36-TRAIN.

APOLLO COLLEGE–TRI-CITY, INC.

Mesa, Arizona www.apollocollege.com/

- **Proprietary** 2-year, founded 1977, part of Apollo Colleges, Inc.
- **Suburban** campus
- **Coed**

Academics *Calendar:* semesters. *Degree:* diplomas and associate.

Student Life *Campus security:* 24-hour emergency response devices, late-night transport/escort service.

Standardized Tests *Required:* Wonderlic aptitude test (for admission).

Applying *Required:* essay or personal statement, high school transcript. *Required for some:* interview.

Apollo College–Tri-City, Inc. (continued)

Director of Admissions Valentina Colmone, Campus Director, Apollo College–Tri-City, Inc., 630 West Southern Avenue, Mesa, AZ 85210-5004. *Phone:* 480-212-1600. *Toll-free phone:* 800-36-TRAIN. *E-mail:* vcolmone@apollocollege.edu.

APOLLO COLLEGE–TUCSON, INC.

Tucson, Arizona **www.apollocollege.com/**

Director of Admissions Mr. Dennis C. Wilson, Executive Director, Apollo College–Tucson, Inc., 3550 North Oracle Road, Tucson, AZ 85705-3227. *Phone:* 520-888-5885. *Toll-free phone:* 800-36-TRAIN. *Fax:* 520-887-3005. *E-mail:* dwilson@apollo.edu.

APOLLO COLLEGE–WESTSIDE, INC.

Phoenix, Arizona **www.apollocollege.com/**

- **Proprietary** 2-year, part of Apollo Colleges, Inc.
- **Urban** campus
- **Coed**

Academics *Calendar:* semesters. *Degree:* associate.

Student Life *Campus security:* 24-hour emergency response devices, late-night transport/escort service.

Standardized Tests *Required:* Wonderlic aptitude test (for admission).

Applying *Required:* essay or personal statement, high school transcript. *Required for some:* interview.

Director of Admissions Admissions, Apollo College–Westside, Inc., 2701 West Bethany Home Road, Phoenix, AZ 85017. *Phone:* 602-433-1222. *Toll-free phone:* 800-36-TRAIN. *Fax:* 602-433-1222. *E-mail:* cnestor@apollocollege.com.

ARIZONA AUTOMOTIVE INSTITUTE

Glendale, Arizona **www.aai.edu/**

- **Proprietary** 2-year
- **Coed**

Academics *Degree:* diplomas and associate.

Applying *Application fee:* $100. *Required:* high school transcript.

Director of Admissions Director of Admissions, Arizona Automotive Institute, 6829 North 46th Avenue, Glendale, AZ 85301-3597. *Phone:* 623-934-7273 Ext. 211. *Fax:* 623-937-5000. *E-mail:* info@azautoinst.com.

ARIZONA COLLEGE OF ALLIED HEALTH

Glendale, Arizona **www.arizonacollege.edu/**

Freshman Application Contact Admissions Department, Arizona College of Allied Health, 4425 West Olive Avenue, Suite 300, Glendale, AZ 85302. *E-mail:* lhicks@arizonacollege.edu.

ARIZONA WESTERN COLLEGE

Yuma, Arizona **www.azwestern.edu/**

- **State and locally supported** 2-year, founded 1962, part of Arizona State Community College System
- **Rural** 640-acre campus
- **Endowment** $1.5 million
- **Coed,** 7,984 undergraduate students, 33% full-time, 58% women, 42% men

Undergraduates 2,672 full-time, 5,312 part-time. 3% African American, 2% Asian American or Pacific Islander, 56% Hispanic American, 2% Native American, 10% international, 3% live on campus.

Freshmen *Admission:* 1,874 enrolled.

Faculty *Student/faculty ratio:* 20:1.

Majors Administrative assistant and secretarial science; agricultural business and management; agriculture; art; automobile/automotive mechanics technology; biological and physical sciences; biology/biological sciences; broadcast journalism; business administration and management; chemistry; computer science; criminal justice/law enforcement administration; criminal justice/police science; developmental and child psychology; drafting and design technology; dramatic/theater arts; education; electrical, electronic and communications engineering technology; engineering technology; English; environmental studies; family and consumer economics related; fire science; geology/earth science; health professions related; heating, air conditioning, ventilation and refrigeration maintenance technology; hospitality administration; hospitality administration related; human services; information science/studies; marketing/marketing management; massage therapy; mathematics; music; nursing (licensed practical/vocational nurse training); nursing (registered nurse training); physical education teaching and coaching; physics; radiologic technology/science; social sciences; Spanish; water quality and wastewater treatment management and recycling technology; welding technology.

Academics *Calendar:* semesters. *Degree:* certificates and associate. *Special study options:* academic remediation for entering students, adult/continuing education programs, advanced placement credit, cooperative education, distance learning, English as a second language, honors programs, independent study, part-time degree program, summer session for credit.

Library Arizona Western College Library with 94,116 titles, 402 serial subscriptions, 4,486 audiovisual materials, an OPAC, a Web page.

Student Life *Housing Options:* coed. Campus housing is university owned. *Activities and Organizations:* drama/theater group, student-run newspaper, radio and television station, choral group, Student Government Association, Spirit Squad, Dance Team, Students in Free Enterprise (SIFE), International Students Team. *Campus security:* 24-hour emergency response devices and patrols, student patrols, late-night transport/escort service. *Student services:* health clinic, personal/psychological counseling.

Athletics Member NJCAA. *Intercollegiate sports:* baseball M(s), basketball M(s)/W(s), football M(s), soccer M(s), softball W(s), volleyball W(s). *Intramural sports:* cheerleading M(c)/W(c).

Standardized Tests *Required for some:* SAT or ACT (for admission).

Costs (2009–10) *Tuition:* state resident $1440 full-time, $60 per credit hour part-time; nonresident $6000 full-time, $66 per credit hour part-time. Full-time tuition and fees vary according to course load and program. Part-time tuition and fees vary according to course load and program. *Room and board:* $5140; room only: $1990. Room and board charges vary according to board plan and housing facility. *Payment plan:* installment. *Waivers:* senior citizens and employees or children of employees.

Financial Aid Of all full-time matriculated undergraduates who enrolled in 2008, 350 Federal Work-Study jobs (averaging $1500). 100 state and other part-time jobs (averaging $1800).

Applying *Options:* electronic application, early admission, deferred entrance. *Application deadlines:* rolling (freshmen), rolling (transfers).

Freshman Application Contact Amy Pignatore, Director of Admissions/Registrar, Arizona Western College, PO Box 929, Yuma, AZ 85366. *Phone:* 928-317-7600. *Toll-free phone:* 888-293-0392. *Fax:* 928-344-7712. *E-mail:* amy.pignatore@azwestern.edu.

BROWN MACKIE COLLEGE–PHOENIX

Phoenix, Arizona **www.brownmackie.edu/phoenix/**

- **Proprietary** primarily 2-year, part of Education Management Corporation
- **Coed**

Majors Accounting technology and bookkeeping; business administration and management; criminal justice/law enforcement administration; health services administration; information technology; legal assistant/paralegal; legal studies; medical/clinical assistant; occupational therapist assistant; surgical technology.

Academics *Degrees:* diplomas, associate, and bachelor's.

Costs (2009–10) *Tuition:* Tuition varies by program. Students should contact Brown Mackie College for tuition information.

Freshman Application Contact Brown Mackie College–Phoenix, 13430 North Black Canyon Highway, Suite 190, Phoenix, AZ 85029. *Phone:* 602-337-3044. *Toll-free phone:* 866-824-4793.

►See page 438 for the College Close-Up.

BROWN MACKIE COLLEGE–TUCSON

Tucson, Arizona **www.brownmackie.edu/tucson/**

- **Proprietary** primarily 2-year, founded 1972, part of Education Management Corporation
- **Suburban** campus
- **Coed**

Majors Accounting; accounting technology and bookkeeping; athletic training; biomedical technology; business administration and management; computer and information systems security; criminal justice/law enforcement administration; early childhood education; health/health-care administration; information technology; legal assistant/paralegal; legal studies; medical/clinical assistant; occupational therapist assistant; surgical technology.
Academics *Degrees:* diplomas, associate, and bachelor's.
Costs (2009–10) *Tuition:* Tuition varies by program. Students should contact Brown Mackie College for tuition information.
Freshman Application Contact Brown Mackie College–Tucson, 4585 East Speedway Boulevard, Suite 204, Tucson, AZ 85712. *Phone:* 520-319-3300.

▶See page 448 for the College Close-Up.

THE BRYMAN SCHOOL OF ARIZONA

Phoenix, Arizona **www.brymanschool.edu/**

Freshman Application Contact Admissions Office, The Bryman School of Arizona, 2250 West Peoria Avenue, Phoenix, AZ 85029. *Phone:* 602-274-4300. *Toll-free phone:* 800-729-4819. *Fax:* 602-248-9087.

CENTRAL ARIZONA COLLEGE

Coolidge, Arizona **www.centralaz.edu/**

- **Public** 2-year, founded 1961
- **Rural** 850-acre campus with easy access to Phoenix
- **Coed,** 7,913 undergraduate students, 38% full-time, 61% women, 39% men

Undergraduates 2,976 full-time, 4,937 part-time. Students come from 4 other countries, 7% African American, 2% Asian American or Pacific Islander, 27% Hispanic American, 5% Native American, 0.3% international, 17% live on campus.
Freshmen *Admission:* 1,726 enrolled.
Faculty *Total:* 210, 45% full-time. *Student/faculty ratio:* 14:1.
Majors Accounting; administrative assistant and secretarial science; agricultural business and management; agricultural mechanics and equipment technology; agriculture; automobile/automotive mechanics technology; business/commerce; child development; civil engineering technology; clinical nutrition; computer and information sciences; computer science; construction/heavy equipment/earthmoving equipment operation; corrections; corrections and criminal justice related; criminal justice/law enforcement administration; diesel mechanics technology; dietetics; elementary education; emergency medical technology (EMT paramedic); fire protection related; general studies; health aide; hotel/motel administration; industrial technology; kindergarten/preschool education; legal administrative assistant/secretary; liberal arts and sciences/liberal studies; manufacturing engineering; massage therapy; medical administrative assistant and medical secretary; medical transcription; nursing (licensed practical/vocational nurse training); nursing (registered nurse training).
Academics *Calendar:* semesters. *Degree:* certificates and associate. *Special study options:* academic remediation for entering students, adult/continuing education programs, distance learning, honors programs, independent study, internships, part-time degree program, services for LD students, student-designed majors, study abroad, summer session for credit.
Library Learning Resource Center with 77,709 titles, 16,306 serial subscriptions, 4,784 audiovisual materials, an OPAC, a Web page.
Student Life *Housing Options:* coed, men-only, women-only. Campus housing is university owned. *Activities and Organizations:* drama/theater group, student-run newspaper, choral group. *Campus security:* 24-hour emergency response devices and patrols, late-night transport/escort service. *Student services:* personal/psychological counseling.
Athletics Member NJCAA. *Intercollegiate sports:* baseball M(s), basketball M(s)/W(s), cross-country running M(s)/W(s), equestrian sports M(s)/W(s), softball W(s), track and field M(s)/W(s).
Costs (2010–11) *Tuition:* state resident $1560 full-time, $65 per credit hour part-time; nonresident $6936 full-time, $130 per credit hour part-time. Full-time tuition and fees vary according to course level, course load, program, reciprocity agreements, and student level. Part-time tuition and fees vary according to course level, course load, program, and student level. *Room and board:* $4612. Room and board charges vary according to housing facility and location. *Payment plan:* installment. *Waivers:* employees or children of employees.
Financial Aid Of all full-time matriculated undergraduates who enrolled in 2008, 68 Federal Work-Study jobs (averaging $1310).
Applying *Options:* electronic application, early admission, deferred entrance. *Application deadlines:* rolling (freshmen), rolling (transfers). *Notification:* continuous (freshmen), continuous (transfers).
Freshman Application Contact Dr. James Moore, Dean of Records and Admissions, Central Arizona College, 8470 North Overfield Road, Coolidge, AZ 85228. *Phone:* 520-494-5261. *Toll-free phone:* 800-237-9814. *Fax:* 520-426-5083. *E-mail:* james.moore@centralaz.edu.

CHANDLER-GILBERT COMMUNITY COLLEGE

Chandler, Arizona **www.cgc.maricopa.edu/**

Director of Admissions Ms. Irene Pearl, Supervisor of Admissions and Records, Chandler-Gilbert Community College, 2626 East Pecos Road, Chandler, AZ 85225-2479. *Phone:* 480-732-7307.

COCHISE COLLEGE

Sierra Vista, Arizona **www.cochise.edu/**

Freshman Application Contact Ms. Debbie Quick, Director of Admissions and Records, Cochise College, 901 North Columbo, Sierra Vista, AZ 85635-2317. *Phone:* 520-515-5412. *Toll-free phone:* 800-593-9567. *Fax:* 520-515-4006. *E-mail:* quickd@cochise.edu.

COCONINO COMMUNITY COLLEGE

Flagstaff, Arizona **www.coconino.edu/**

- **State-supported** 2-year, founded 1991
- **Small-town** 5-acre campus
- **Endowment** $264,023
- **Coed**

Undergraduates 840 full-time, 2,911 part-time. Students come from 10 states and territories, 3% are from out of state, 9% transferred in.
Faculty *Student/faculty ratio:* 14:1.
Academics *Calendar:* semesters. *Degree:* certificates and associate. *Special study options:* academic remediation for entering students, adult/continuing education programs, distance learning, honors programs, independent study, internships, part-time degree program, study abroad, summer session for credit. *ROTC:* Army (b), Air Force (b).
Student Life *Campus security:* 24-hour emergency response devices, student patrols, late-night transport/escort service, Security patrols while campuses are open. Electronic access throughout the campuses with security cards.
Costs (2009–10) *Tuition:* state resident $1800 full-time, $75 per credit hour part-time; nonresident $6000 full-time, $250 per credit hour part-time.
Financial Aid Of all full-time matriculated undergraduates who enrolled in 2008, 25 Federal Work-Study jobs (averaging $4000).
Applying *Options:* electronic application.
Freshman Application Contact Miss Veronica Hipolito, Director of Student Services, Coconino Community College, 2800 South Lone Tree Road, Flagstaff, AZ 86001. *Phone:* 928-226-4334 Ext. 4334. *Toll-free phone:* 800-350-7122. *Fax:* 928-226-4114. *E-mail:* veronica.hipolito@coconino.edu.

COLLEGEAMERICA–FLAGSTAFF

Flagstaff, Arizona **www.collegeamerica.com/**

Freshman Application Contact Admissions Office, CollegeAmerica–Flagstaff, 5200 East Cortland Boulevard, Suite A-19, Flagstaff, AZ 86004. *Phone:* 928-526-0763 Ext. 1402. *Toll-free phone:* 800-622-2894. *Fax:* 928-526-3468.

DINÉ COLLEGE

Tsaile, Arizona **www.dinecollege.edu/**

Freshman Application Contact Mrs. Louise Litzin, Registrar, Diné College, PO Box 67, Tsaile, AZ 86556. *Phone:* 928-724-6633. *Fax:* 928-724-3349. *E-mail:* louise@dinecollege.edu.

Eastern Arizona College

Thatcher, Arizona **www.eac.edu/**

- **State and locally supported** 2-year, founded 1888, part of Arizona State Community College System
- **Small-town** campus
- **Endowment** $2.8 million
- **Coed,** 7,241 undergraduate students, 32% full-time, 56% women, 44% men

Undergraduates 2,285 full-time, 4,956 part-time. Students come from 31 states and territories, 23 other countries, 5% are from out of state, 3% African American, 1% Asian American or Pacific Islander, 21% Hispanic American, 9% Native American, 0.7% international, 1% transferred in, 5% live on campus. *Retention:* 54% of 2008 full-time freshmen returned.

Freshmen *Admission:* 2,926 applied, 2,926 admitted, 1,463 enrolled.

Faculty *Total:* 359, 26% full-time, 5% with terminal degrees. *Student/faculty ratio:* 22:1.

Majors Agribusiness; agriculture; anthropology; art; art teacher education; automobile/automotive mechanics technology; biology/biological sciences; business administration and management; business, management, and marketing related; business operations support and secretarial services related; business teacher education; chemistry; child-care provision; civil engineering technology; commercial and advertising art; corrections; criminal justice/law enforcement administration; criminal justice/police science; data entry/microcomputer applications; drafting and design technology; dramatic/theater arts; elementary education; emergency medical technology (EMT paramedic); English; entrepreneurship; foreign languages and literatures; forestry; geology/earth science; health and physical education; health/medical preparatory programs related; history; information science/studies; liberal arts and sciences/liberal studies; machine shop technology; management information systems and services related; mathematics; mining technology; music; nursing (registered nurse training); physics; political science and government; pre-law studies; premedical studies; pre-pharmacy studies; psychology; secondary education; sociology; technology/industrial arts teacher education; welding technology; wildlife biology.

Academics *Calendar:* semesters. *Degree:* certificates and associate. *Special study options:* academic remediation for entering students, adult/continuing education programs, advanced placement credit, cooperative education, distance learning, double majors, independent study, internships, part-time degree program, services for LD students, study abroad, summer session for credit.

Library Alumni Library with an OPAC, a Web page.

Student Life *Housing Options:* men-only, women-only. Campus housing is university owned. *Activities and Organizations:* drama/theater group, choral group, marching band, Latter-Day Saints Student Association, Criminal Justice Student Association, Multicultural Council, Phi Theta Kappa, Mark Allen Dorm Club. *Campus security:* 24-hour emergency response devices, late-night transport/escort service, controlled dormitory access, 20-hour patrols by trained security personnel. *Student services:* personal/psychological counseling.

Athletics Member NJCAA. *Intercollegiate sports:* baseball M(s), basketball M(s)/W(s), football M(s), golf M/W, softball W(s), volleyball W(s). *Intramural sports:* basketball M/W, racquetball M/W, swimming and diving M/W, table tennis M/W, tennis M/W, volleyball M/W.

Costs (2009–10) *Tuition:* state resident $1520 full-time, $85 per credit hour part-time; nonresident $8120 full-time, $140 per credit hour part-time. *Room and board:* $5075; room only: $2690. Room and board charges vary according to board plan and housing facility. *Waivers:* senior citizens and employees or children of employees.

Financial Aid Of all full-time matriculated undergraduates who enrolled in 2008, 202 Federal Work-Study jobs (averaging $1800). 158 state and other part-time jobs (averaging $1800).

Applying *Options:* electronic application, early admission, deferred entrance. *Recommended:* high school transcript. *Application deadlines:* rolling (freshmen), rolling (transfers). *Notification:* continuous (freshmen).

Freshman Application Contact Dr. Gary Sorenson, Director of Recruitment, Eastern Arizona College, 615 North Stadium Avenue, Thatcher, AZ 85552-0769. *Phone:* 928-426-8354. *Toll-free phone:* 800-678-3808. *Fax:* 928-428-8354. *E-mail:* admissions@eac.edu.

Estrella Mountain Community College

Avondale, Arizona **www.emc.maricopa.edu/**

- **State and locally supported** 2-year, founded 1992, part of Maricopa County Community College District System
- **Urban** campus with easy access to Phoenix
- **Coed,** 6,358 undergraduate students, 26% full-time, 63% women, 37% men

Undergraduates 1,631 full-time, 4,727 part-time. 8% African American, 4% Asian American or Pacific Islander, 35% Hispanic American, 1% Native American, 0.7% international.

Freshmen *Admission:* 920 applied, 920 admitted, 920 enrolled.

Faculty *Total:* 356, 20% full-time. *Student/faculty ratio:* 22:1.

Majors General studies; liberal arts and sciences/liberal studies.

Academics *Calendar:* semesters. *Degree:* certificates and associate. *Special study options:* academic remediation for entering students, adult/continuing education programs, advanced placement credit, cooperative education, distance learning, English as a second language, honors programs, independent study, part-time degree program, services for LD students, summer session for credit. *ROTC:* Air Force (c).

Library Estrella Mountain Library with 57,000 titles, 50 serial subscriptions, 3,000 audiovisual materials, an OPAC, a Web page.

Student Life *Housing:* college housing not available. *Activities and Organizations:* Phi Theta Kappa, Men Of Color Association (M.O.C.A.), Movimiento Estudiantil Chicano de Aztlan (M.E.Ch.A), Savings and Investment Club. *Campus security:* 24-hour emergency response devices and patrols, late-night transport/escort service. *Student services:* personal/psychological counseling.

Costs (2010–11) *Tuition:* area resident $1704 full-time, $71 per credit hour part-time; state resident $7488 full-time, $312 per credit hour part-time; nonresident $7488 full-time, $312 per credit hour part-time. *Required fees:* $30 full-time, $15 per term part-time. *Payment plan:* installment. *Waivers:* employees or children of employees.

Financial Aid Of all full-time matriculated undergraduates who enrolled in 2009, 45 Federal Work-Study jobs (averaging $3000).

Applying *Options:* electronic application.

Freshman Application Contact Estrella Mountain Community College, 3000 North Dysart Road, Avondale, AZ 85392. *Phone:* 623-935-8812.

Everest College

Phoenix, Arizona **www.everest.edu/**

Freshman Application Contact Mr. Jim Askins, Director of Admissions, Everest College, 10400 North 25th Avenue, Suite 190, Phoenix, AZ 85021. *Phone:* 602-942-4141. *Fax:* 602-943-0960. *E-mail:* jaskins@cci.edu.

GateWay Community College

Phoenix, Arizona **www.gwc.maricopa.edu/**

Freshman Application Contact Ms. Cathy Gibson, Director of Admissions and Records, GateWay Community College, 108 North 40th Street, Phoenix, AZ 85034. *Phone:* 602-286-8052. *Fax:* 602-286-8200. *E-mail:* cathy.gibson@gwmail.maricopa.edu.

Glendale Community College

Glendale, Arizona **www.gc.maricopa.edu/**

- **State and locally supported** 2-year, founded 1965, part of Maricopa County Community College District System
- **Suburban** 222-acre campus with easy access to Phoenix
- **Endowment** $1.0 million
- **Coed,** 20,154 undergraduate students, 35% full-time, 54% women, 46% men

Undergraduates 7,131 full-time, 13,023 part-time. Students come from 51 states and territories, 93 other countries, 5% are from out of state, 6% African American, 4% Asian American or Pacific Islander, 24% Hispanic American, 2% Native American. *Retention:* 56% of 2008 full-time freshmen returned.

Freshmen *Admission:* 4,733 enrolled.

Faculty *Total:* 1,042, 22% full-time. *Student/faculty ratio:* 22:1.

Majors Accounting; accounting and computer science; accounting technology and bookkeeping; administrative assistant and secretarial science; adult development and aging; architectural drafting and CAD/CADD; automobile/automotive mechanics technology; behavioral sciences; biotechnology; business automation/technology/data entry; business/commerce; CAD/CADD drafting/design technology; child-care and support services management; cinematography and film/video production; commercial and advertising art; computer and information sciences; computer and information systems security; computer graphics; computer systems analysis; computer systems networking and telecommunications; criminal justice/police science; criminal justice/safety; data entry/microcomputer applications; early childhood education; educational leadership and administration; emergency medical technology (EMT paramedic); energy management and systems technology; entrepreneurship; family and community services; fire science; foods, nutrition, and wellness; graphic design; human development and family studies related; interior design; kinesiology and exercise science; marketing/marketing management; mental and social health services and allied professions related; music; music management and merchandising; nursing (licensed practical/vocational nurse training); nursing (registered nurse training); office management; public relations/image management; radio and television broadcasting technology; real estate; recording arts technology; security and loss prevention; security and protective services related; system, networking, and LAN/WAN management; trade and industrial teacher education; truck and bus driver/commercial vehicle operation; web page, digital/multimedia and information resources design.

Academics *Calendar:* semesters. *Degree:* certificates and associate. *Special study options:* academic remediation for entering students, adult/continuing education programs, advanced placement credit, cooperative education, distance learning, double majors, English as a second language, freshman honors college, honors programs, internships, off-campus study, part-time degree program, services for LD students, study abroad, summer session for credit. *ROTC:* Army (c), Air Force (c).

Library Library/Media Center plus 1 other with 97,768 titles, 30,094 serial subscriptions, 6,032 audiovisual materials, an OPAC, a Web page.

Student Life *Activities and Organizations:* drama/theater group, student-run newspaper, choral group, marching band, Phi Theta Kappa, M.E.Ch.A. (Movimiento Estudiantil Chicano de Aztlan), Associated Student Government, Biotechnology Club, Compass. *Campus security:* 24-hour patrols, student patrols, late-night transport/escort service. *Student services:* personal/psychological counseling, legal services.

Athletics Member NJCAA. *Intercollegiate sports:* baseball M(s), basketball M(s)/W(s), cross-country running M(s)/W(s), football M(s), golf M(s), soccer M(s)/W(s), softball W(s), tennis M(s)/W(s), track and field M(s)/W(s), volleyball W(s). *Intramural sports:* golf M, racquetball M/W, softball W, tennis M/W, volleyball W.

Costs (2010–11) *Tuition:* state resident $1704 full-time, $71 per semester hour part-time; nonresident $7488 full-time, $312 per semester hour part-time. Full-time tuition and fees vary according to program and reciprocity agreements. Part-time tuition and fees vary according to course load, program, and reciprocity agreements. *Required fees:* $30 full-time, $15 per term part-time. *Room and board:* $8352. *Payment plan:* installment. *Waivers:* employees or children of employees.

Financial Aid Of all full-time matriculated undergraduates who enrolled in 2008, 350 Federal Work-Study jobs (averaging $1700).

Applying *Options:* electronic application. *Required for some:* high school transcript. *Notification:* continuous until 8/21 (freshmen), continuous until 8/21 (transfers).

Freshman Application Contact Ms. Mary Blackwell, Dean of Enrollment Services, Glendale Community College, 6000 West Olive Avenue, Glendale, AZ 85302. *Phone:* 623-435-3305. *Fax:* 623-845-3303. *E-mail:* info@gc.maricopa.edu.

HIGH-TECH INSTITUTE

Phoenix, Arizona **www.high-techinstitute.com/**

- **Proprietary** primarily 2-year, founded 1982
- **Urban** 4-acre campus
- **Coed**

Academics *Calendar:* semesters. *Degrees:* diplomas, associate, and bachelor's.

Financial Aid Of all full-time matriculated undergraduates who enrolled in 2008, 29 Federal Work-Study jobs (averaging $2500).

Applying *Application fee:* $50. *Required:* high school transcript.

Freshman Application Contact Mr. Glen Husband, Vice President of Admissions, High-Tech Institute, 1515 East Indian School Road, Phoenix, AZ 85014-4901. *Phone:* 602-279-9700.

ITT TECHNICAL INSTITUTE

Phoenix, Arizona **www.itt-tech.edu/**

- **Proprietary** primarily 2-year, founded 1972, part of ITT Educational Services, Inc.
- **Urban** campus
- **Coed**

Majors CAD/CADD drafting/design technology; computer and information systems security; computer engineering technology; computer software engineering; computer software technology; construction management; criminal justice/law enforcement administration; design and visual communications; electrical, electronic and communications engineering technology; legal assistant/paralegal; nursing (registered nurse training); system, networking, and LAN/WAN management.

Academics *Calendar:* quarters. *Degrees:* associate and bachelor's.

Student Life *Housing:* college housing not available.

Financial Aid Of all full-time matriculated undergraduates who enrolled in 2008, 10 Federal Work-Study jobs (averaging $4000).

Freshman Application Contact Director of Recruitment, ITT Technical Institute, 10220 North 25th Avenue, Suite 100, Phoenix, AZ 85021. *Phone:* 602-749-7900. *Toll-free phone:* 877-221-1132.

ITT TECHNICAL INSTITUTE

Tucson, Arizona **www.itt-tech.edu/**

- **Proprietary** primarily 2-year, founded 1984, part of ITT Educational Services, Inc.
- **Urban** campus
- **Coed**

Majors Animation, interactive technology, video graphics and special effects; CAD/CADD drafting/design technology; computer and information systems security; computer software engineering; computer software technology; construction management; criminal justice/law enforcement administration; design and visual communications; electrical, electronic and communications engineering technology; legal assistant/paralegal; system, networking, and LAN/WAN management; web/multimedia management and webmaster; web page, digital/multimedia and information resources design.

Academics *Calendar:* quarters. *Degrees:* associate and bachelor's.

Student Life *Housing:* college housing not available.

Freshman Application Contact Director of Recruitment, ITT Technical Institute, 1455 West River Road, Tucson, AZ 85704. *Phone:* 520-408-7488. *Toll-free phone:* 800-870-9730.

KAPLAN COLLEGE, PHOENIX CAMPUS

Phoenix, Arizona **www.kc-phoenix.com/**

- **Proprietary** 2-year, founded 1972
- **Coed**

Majors Respiratory care therapy; veterinary/animal health technology.

Academics *Calendar:* continuous. *Degree:* diplomas and associate.

Freshman Application Contact Kaplan College, Phoenix Campus, 13610 North Black Canyon Highway, Suite 104, Phoenix, AZ 85029. *Phone:* 602-548-1955. *Toll-free phone:* 877-548-1955.

LAMSON COLLEGE

Tempe, Arizona **www.lamsoncollege.com/**

- **Proprietary** 2-year, founded 1889, part of National Career Education, Inc.
- **Urban** campus with easy access to Phoenix
- **Coed,** 349 undergraduate students

Majors Business administration and management; legal assistant/paralegal.

Academics *Calendar:* quarters. *Degree:* diplomas and associate. *Special study options:* academic remediation for entering students, adult/continuing education programs, English as a second language, internships, summer session for credit.

Library 4,400 titles, 18 serial subscriptions.

Student Life *Housing:* college housing not available. *Campus security:* 24-hour patrols.

Standardized Tests *Required:* Wonderlic (for admission).

Applying *Application fee:* $25. *Required:* high school transcript, interview. *Application deadline:* rolling (freshmen). *Notification:* continuous (freshmen).

Freshman Application Contact Lamson College, 875 West Elliot Road, Suite 206, Tempe, AZ 85284. *Phone:* 480-898-7000. *Toll-free phone:* 800-898-7017.

MESA COMMUNITY COLLEGE

Mesa, Arizona www.mc.maricopa.edu/

Freshman Application Contact Ms. Kathleen Perales, Manager, Recruitment, Mesa Community College, 1833 West Southern Avenue, Mesa, AZ 85202-4866. *Phone:* 480-461-7751. *Fax:* 480-654-7379. *E-mail:* admissions@mc.maricopa.edu.

MOHAVE COMMUNITY COLLEGE

Kingman, Arizona www.mohave.edu/

- **State-supported** 2-year, founded 1971
- **Small-town** 160-acre campus
- **Coed,** 6,702 undergraduate students, 29% full-time, 63% women, 37% men

Undergraduates 1,922 full-time, 4,780 part-time. Students come from 12 states and territories, 4% are from out of state, 1% African American, 2% Asian American or Pacific Islander, 13% Hispanic American, 2% Native American.

Freshmen *Admission:* 1,348 enrolled.

Faculty *Total:* 410, 16% full-time, 8% with terminal degrees. *Student/faculty ratio:* 19:1.

Majors Accounting; art; automobile/automotive mechanics technology; building/construction finishing, management, and inspection related; business administration and management; computer and information sciences related; computer programming (specific applications); computer science; criminal justice/police science; culinary arts; dental assisting; dental hygiene; drafting and design technology; education; emergency medical technology (EMT paramedic); English; fire science; heating, air conditioning, ventilation and refrigeration maintenance technology; history; information technology; legal assistant/paralegal; liberal arts and sciences/liberal studies; mathematics; medical/clinical assistant; nursing (registered nurse training); personal and culinary services related; pharmacy technician; physical therapist assistant; psychology; sociology; substance abuse/addiction counseling; surgical technology; truck and bus driver/commercial vehicle operation; welding technology.

Academics *Calendar:* semesters. *Degree:* certificates and associate. *Special study options:* academic remediation for entering students, adult/continuing education programs, cooperative education, distance learning, English as a second language, independent study, part-time degree program, summer session for credit.

Library Mohave Community College Library with 45,849 titles, 476 serial subscriptions, an OPAC, a Web page.

Student Life *Housing:* college housing not available. *Activities and Organizations:* Art Club, Phi Theta Kappa, Computer Club (MC4), Science Club, student government. *Campus security:* late-night transport/escort service.

Costs (2010–11) *Tuition:* state resident $2070 full-time, $69 per credit hour part-time; nonresident $5910 full-time, $197 per credit hour part-time. Full-time tuition and fees vary according to program. Part-time tuition and fees vary according to program. *Required fees:* $180 full-time, $6 per credit part-time. *Payment plans:* installment, deferred payment. *Waivers:* employees or children of employees.

Applying *Options:* early admission, deferred entrance. *Application deadlines:* rolling (freshmen), rolling (transfers). *Notification:* continuous (freshmen), continuous (transfers).

Freshman Application Contact Ms. Jann Woods, Dean of Student Services, Mohave Community College, 1971 Jagerson Avenue, Kingman, AZ 86401. *Phone:* 928-757-0803. *Toll-free phone:* 888-664-2832. *Fax:* 928-757-0808. *E-mail:* jwoods@mohave.edu.

NORTHLAND PIONEER COLLEGE

Holbrook, Arizona www.npc.edu/

- **State and locally supported** 2-year, founded 1974, part of Arizona State Community College System
- **Rural** 50-acre campus
- **Coed,** 4,636 undergraduate students, 20% full-time, 66% women, 34% men

Undergraduates 946 full-time, 3,690 part-time. Students come from 17 states and territories, 3 other countries, 1% African American, 0.7% Asian American or Pacific Islander, 7% Hispanic American, 36% Native American, 0.9% transferred in.

Freshmen *Admission:* 335 enrolled.

Faculty *Total:* 226, 32% full-time. *Student/faculty ratio:* 17:1.

Majors Accounting technology and bookkeeping; administrative assistant and secretarial science; agriculture; apparel and textiles; biological and physical sciences; building/property maintenance and management; business administration and management; business and personal/financial services marketing; business automation/technology/data entry; business/commerce; carpentry; child-care and support services management; child-care provision; child development; computer and information sciences; computer graphics; computer installation and repair technology; computer systems networking and telecommunications; corrections; cosmetology; court reporting; data modeling/warehousing and database administration; drafting and design technology; early childhood education; electrical, electronic and communications engineering technology; electrician; elementary education; emergency medical technology (EMT paramedic); entrepreneurial and small business related; fire science; general studies; health information/medical records administration; industrial mechanics and maintenance technology; industrial technology; information science/studies; kindergarten/preschool education; legal administrative assistant/secretary; legal assistant/paralegal; legal professions and studies related; liberal arts and sciences/liberal studies; library assistant; management information systems; management information systems and services related; massage therapy; medical transcription; museum studies; nursing (licensed practical/vocational nurse training); nursing (registered nurse training); parks, recreation and leisure facilities management; photography; restaurant, culinary, and catering management; small business administration; special education (early childhood); teacher assistant/aide; teaching assistants/aides related; turf and turfgrass management; welding technology.

Academics *Calendar:* semesters. *Degree:* certificates and associate. *Special study options:* advanced placement credit, cooperative education, distance learning, double majors, English as a second language, freshman honors college, honors programs, independent study, internships, part-time degree program, services for LD students, summer session for credit.

Library Northland Pioneer College Library with 60,000 titles, 240 serial subscriptions, an OPAC.

Student Life *Housing:* college housing not available. *Activities and Organizations:* drama/theater group, choral group. *Campus security:* evening security.

Costs (2010–11) *Tuition:* state resident $1248 full-time, $52 per credit hour part-time; nonresident $6000 full-time, $85 per credit hour part-time. *Required fees:* $35 full-time, $35 per term part-time. *Payment plans:* installment, deferred payment. *Waivers:* senior citizens and employees or children of employees.

Financial Aid Of all full-time matriculated undergraduates who enrolled in 2008, 80 Federal Work-Study jobs (averaging $4000).

Applying *Options:* early admission. *Application deadline:* rolling (freshmen). *Notification:* continuous (transfers).

Freshman Application Contact Ms. Suzette Willis, Coordinator of Admissions, Northland Pioneer College, PO Box 610, Holbrook, AZ 86025-0610. *Phone:* 928-536-6271. *Toll-free phone:* 800-266-7845. *Fax:* 928-536-6212.

PARADISE VALLEY COMMUNITY COLLEGE

Phoenix, Arizona www.pvc.maricopa.edu/

- **State and locally supported** 2-year, founded 1985, part of Maricopa County Community College District System
- **Urban** campus
- **Coed,** 9,951 undergraduate students, 31% full-time, 57% women, 43% men

Undergraduates 3,043 full-time, 6,908 part-time. 4% are from out of state, 3% African American, 4% Asian American or Pacific Islander, 10% Hispanic American, 2% Native American.

Faculty *Total:* 542, 18% full-time.

Majors Accounting; accounting technology and bookkeeping; administrative assistant and secretarial science; business administration and management; business automation/technology/data entry; business/commerce; commercial and advertising art; computer installation and repair technology; computer programming (vendor/product certification); computer systems networking and telecommunications; computer typography and composition equipment operation; criminal justice/safety; early childhood education; elementary education; emergency medical technology (EMT paramedic); fine/studio arts; fire science; general studies; international business/trade/commerce; journalism; kinesiology and exercise science; liberal arts and sciences/liberal studies; music management and merchandising; natural sciences; nursing assistant/aide and patient care assistant; nursing (registered nurse training); occupational safety and health technology; physical sciences; recording arts technology; visual and performing arts; web page, digital/multimedia and information resources design.

Academics *Calendar:* semesters. *Degree:* certificates and associate. *Special study options:* academic remediation for entering students, accelerated degree program, adult/continuing education programs, advanced placement credit, cooperative education, distance learning, English as a second language, honors programs, independent study, internships, off-campus study, part-time degree program, services for LD students, study abroad, summer session for credit. *ROTC:* Army (c).

Library Paradise Valley Community College Library plus 1 other with an OPAC, a Web page.

Student Life *Housing:* college housing not available. *Activities and Organizations:* drama/theater group, student-run newspaper, choral group, Phi Theta Kappa, International Student Club, Recreational Outing Club, AWARE, Student Christian Association, national fraternities. *Campus security:* 24-hour emergency response devices and patrols, late-night transport/escort service. *Student services:* personal/psychological counseling.

Athletics Member NJCAA. *Intercollegiate sports:* baseball M, cross-country running M/W, golf M/W, soccer M/W, softball W, tennis M/W, track and field M/W.

Costs (2010–11) *Tuition:* state resident $2130 full-time, $71 per credit hour part-time; nonresident $9360 full-time, $312 per credit hour part-time. *Payment plan:* deferred payment. *Waivers:* senior citizens and employees or children of employees.

Financial Aid Of all full-time matriculated undergraduates who enrolled in 2008, 50 Federal Work-Study jobs (averaging $2500).

Applying *Options:* early admission. *Application deadlines:* rolling (freshmen), rolling (transfers).

Freshman Application Contact Paradise Valley Community College, 18401 North 32nd Street, Phoenix, AZ 85032. *Phone:* 602-787-7020. *E-mail:* donna.simon@pvmail.maricopa.edu.

THE PARALEGAL INSTITUTE, INC.

Phoenix, Arizona **www.theparalegalinstitute.com/**

Freshman Application Contact Patricia Yancy, Director of Admissions, The Paralegal Institute, Inc., 2933 West Indian School Road, Drawer 11408, Phoenix, AZ 85061-1408. *Phone:* 602-212-0501. *Toll-free phone:* 800-354-1254. *Fax:* 602-212-0502. *E-mail:* paralegalinst@mindspring.com.

PHOENIX COLLEGE

Phoenix, Arizona **www.pc.maricopa.edu/**

- **County-supported** 2-year, founded 1920, part of Maricopa County Community College District System
- **Urban** 52-acre campus
- **Coed,** 12,164 undergraduate students, 25% full-time, 62% women, 38% men

Undergraduates 3,054 full-time, 9,110 part-time. 10% African American, 3% Asian American or Pacific Islander, 33% Hispanic American, 4% Native American, 0.6% international.

Faculty *Total:* 714, 21% full-time. *Student/faculty ratio:* 17:1.

Majors Accounting; administrative assistant and secretarial science; architectural engineering technology; art; behavioral sciences; business administration and management; civil engineering technology; clinical laboratory science/medical technology; clinical/medical laboratory technology; computer and information sciences; computer graphics; construction engineering technology; corrections; criminal justice/police science; criminal justice/safety; data processing and data processing technology; dental hygiene; drafting and design technology; drafting/design engineering technologies related; emergency medical technology (EMT paramedic); family and consumer sciences/human sciences; fashion/apparel design; finance; fire science; health information/medical records administration; information science/studies; interior design; legal administrative assistant/secretary; legal assistant/paralegal; liberal arts and sciences/liberal studies; management science; marketing/marketing management; mass communication/media; medical administrative assistant and medical secretary; medical/clinical assistant; nursing (registered nurse training); real estate; special products marketing; tourism and travel services management.

Academics *Calendar:* semesters. *Degree:* certificates, diplomas, and associate. *Special study options:* academic remediation for entering students, adult/continuing education programs, advanced placement credit, cooperative education, distance learning, English as a second language, freshman honors college, honors programs, independent study, internships, off-campus study, part-time degree program, services for LD students, study abroad, summer session for credit. *ROTC:* Army (c), Navy (c), Air Force (c).

Library Fannin Library with 83,000 titles, 394 serial subscriptions.

Student Life *Housing:* college housing not available. *Activities and Organizations:* drama/theater group, student-run radio station, choral group, Black Student Union, NASA (Native American Club), International Club, MECHA (Mexican Club), ALE (Asociacion Latina Estudiantil). *Campus security:* 24-hour emergency response devices, student patrols, late-night transport/escort service. *Student services:* personal/psychological counseling.

Athletics Member NJCAA. *Intercollegiate sports:* baseball M(s), basketball M(s)/W(s), cross-country running M(s)/W(s), football M(s), golf M(s)/W(s), soccer M/W, softball W(s), tennis M(s)/W(s), track and field M(s)/W(s), volleyball W(s). *Intramural sports:* skiing (cross-country) M(c)/W(c), skiing (downhill) M(c)/W(c).

Costs (2010–11) *Tuition:* area resident $1704 full-time, $71 per credit hour part-time; state resident $6432 full-time, $268 per credit hour part-time; nonresident $6864 full-time, $286 per credit hour part-time. Full-time tuition and fees vary according to location, program, and reciprocity agreements. Part-time tuition and fees vary according to course load, location, program, and reciprocity agreements. *Required fees:* $30 full-time, $15 per term part-time. *Payment plan:* installment. *Waivers:* employees or children of employees.

Financial Aid Of all full-time matriculated undergraduates who enrolled in 2008, 220 Federal Work-Study jobs (averaging $4800).

Applying *Options:* early admission, deferred entrance. *Application deadlines:* rolling (freshmen), rolling (out-of-state freshmen), rolling (transfers). *Notification:* continuous (freshmen), continuous (out-of-state freshmen), continuous (transfers).

Freshman Application Contact Ms. Kathleen French, Director of Admissions, Registration and Records, Phoenix College, Phoenix, AZ 85013. *Phone:* 602-285-7503. *Fax:* 602-285-7813. *E-mail:* kathy.french@pcmail.maricopa.edu.

PIMA COMMUNITY COLLEGE

Tucson, Arizona **www.pima.edu/**

- **State and locally supported** 2-year, founded 1966
- **Urban** 483-acre campus with easy access to Tucson, Arizona
- **Endowment** $3.8 million
- **Coed,** 35,880 undergraduate students, 33% full-time, 55% women, 45% men

Undergraduates 11,708 full-time, 24,172 part-time. Students come from 35 states and territories, 73 other countries, 6% are from out of state, 4% African American, 3% Asian American or Pacific Islander, 29% Hispanic American, 3% Native American, 1% international, 12% transferred in. *Retention:* 65% of 2008 full-time freshmen returned.

Freshmen *Admission:* 6,619 enrolled.

Faculty *Total:* 1,553, 21% full-time. *Student/faculty ratio:* 21:1.

Majors Accounting; administrative assistant and secretarial science; aircraft powerplant technology; American Indian/Native American studies; animation, interactive technology, video graphics and special effects; anthropology; architectural drafting and CAD/CADD; automobile/automotive mechanics technology; building/property maintenance and management; business administration and management; clinical/medical laboratory science and allied professions related; clinical/medical laboratory technology; clinical/medical social work; computer systems analysis; computer systems networking and telecommunications; criminal justice/police science; criminal justice/safety; dental hygiene; dental laboratory technology; design and visual communications; early childhood education; electrical, electronic and communications engineering technology; elementary education; emergency medical technology (EMT paramedic); environmental engineering technology; fire science; general studies; health and medical administrative services related; histologic technician; hospitality administration; industrial electronics technology; industrial production technologies related; industrial technology; language interpretation and translation; legal assistant/paralegal; liberal arts and sciences/liberal studies; logistics and materials management; machine shop technology; massage therapy; medical radiologic technology; music; nursing (registered nurse training); pharmacy technician; political science and government; radio and television; radiologic technology/science; respiratory care therapy; restaurant, culinary, and catering management; security and protective services related; sign language interpretation and translation; sociology; veterinary/animal health technology; visual and performing arts; welding technology.

Academics *Calendar:* semesters. *Degrees:* certificates, associate, and post-bachelor's certificates. *Special study options:* academic remediation for entering students, accelerated degree program, adult/continuing education programs, advanced placement credit, cooperative education, distance learning, double majors, English as a second language, honors programs, independent study, internships, part-time degree program, services for LD students, student-designed majors, summer session for credit. *ROTC:* Army (b), Navy (b), Air Force (b).

Library Pima College Library with 333,719 titles, 900 serial subscriptions, 23,314 audiovisual materials, an OPAC, a Web page.

Student Life *Housing:* college housing not available. *Activities and Organizations:* drama/theater group, student-run newspaper, choral group, Phi Theta Kappa, Student Government. *Campus security:* 24-hour emergency response devices and patrols, late-night transport/escort service. *Student services:* health clinic, personal/psychological counseling, women's center.

Pima Community College (continued)

Athletics Member NJCAA. *Intercollegiate sports:* baseball M(s), basketball M(s)/W(s), cheerleading W, cross-country running M(s)/W(s), football M(s), golf M(s)/W(s), soccer M(s)/W(s), softball W(s), tennis M(s)/W(s), track and field M(s)/W(s), volleyball W(s). *Intramural sports:* badminton M/W, basketball M/W, cross-country running M/W, equestrian sports M(c)/W(c), football M, golf M/W, ice hockey M(c), racquetball M/W, tennis M/W, track and field M/W, volleyball M/W, wrestling M(c).

Costs (2010–11) *Tuition:* state resident $1284 full-time, $54 per credit hour part-time; nonresident $6456 full-time, $90 per credit hour part-time. *Required fees:* $128 full-time, $5 per credit hour part-time, $10 per term part-time. *Payment plans:* installment, deferred payment. *Waivers:* employees or children of employees.

Applying *Options:* electronic application. *Application deadlines:* rolling (freshmen), rolling (transfers).

Freshman Application Contact Michael Tulino, Director of Admissions and Registrar, Pima Community College, 4905B East Broadway Boulevard, Tucson, AZ 85709-1120. *Phone:* 520-206-4640. *Fax:* 520-206-4790. *E-mail:* mtulino@pima.edu.

PIMA MEDICAL INSTITUTE

Mesa, Arizona **www.pmi.edu/**

- **Proprietary** 2-year, founded 1985, part of Vocational Training Institutes, Inc.
- **Urban** campus
- **Coed**

Academics *Calendar:* modular. *Degree:* certificates and associate.

Standardized Tests *Required:* Wonderlic aptitude test (for admission).

Applying *Required:* interview. *Required for some:* high school transcript.

Freshman Application Contact Admissions Office, Pima Medical Institute, Pima Medical Institute, 957 South Dobson Road, Mesa, AZ 85202. *Phone:* 480-644-0267 Ext. 225. *Toll-free phone:* 888-898-9048.

PIMA MEDICAL INSTITUTE

Tucson, Arizona **www.pmi.edu/**

- **Proprietary** 2-year, founded 1972, part of Vocational Training Institutes, Inc.
- **Urban** campus
- **Coed**

Academics *Calendar:* modular. *Degree:* certificates and associate. *Special study options:* academic remediation for entering students, accelerated degree program, adult/continuing education programs, cooperative education, internships.

Standardized Tests *Required:* Wonderlic Scholastic Level Exam (for admission).

Applying *Options:* early admission. *Required:* interview. *Required for some:* high school transcript.

Freshman Application Contact Admissions Office, Pima Medical Institute, Pima Medical Institute, 3350 East Grant Road, Tucson, AZ 85716-2800. *Phone:* 520-326-1600 Ext. 5112. *Toll-free phone:* 888-898-9048.

THE REFRIGERATION SCHOOL

Phoenix, Arizona **www.refrigerationschool.com/**

Freshman Application Contact Ms. Heather Haskell, The Refrigeration School, 4210 East Washington Street, Phoenix, AZ 85034-1816. *Phone:* 602-275-7133. *Fax:* 602-267-4811. *E-mail:* heather@rsiaz.edu.

RIO SALADO COLLEGE

Tempe, Arizona **www.rio.maricopa.edu/**

- **State and locally supported** 2-year, founded 1978, part of Maricopa County Community College District System
- **Urban** campus
- **Coed,** 20,865 undergraduate students

Undergraduates Students come from 44 states and territories, 38 other countries, 4% are from out of state, 7% African American, 4% Asian American or Pacific Islander, 13% Hispanic American, 2% Native American.

Faculty *Total:* 1,004. *Student/faculty ratio:* 25:1.

Majors Business administration and management; computer and information sciences and support services related; computer and information sciences related; computer programming related; computer science; consumer services and advocacy; data entry/microcomputer applications; dental hygiene; information science/studies; information technology; public administration; substance abuse/addiction counseling; system administration; web/multimedia management and webmaster; web page, digital/multimedia and information resources design.

Academics *Calendar:* semesters. *Degree:* certificates and associate. *Special study options:* academic remediation for entering students, accelerated degree program, adult/continuing education programs, advanced placement credit, cooperative education, distance learning, double majors, English as a second language, external degree program, honors programs, independent study, internships, part-time degree program, services for LD students, summer session for credit.

Library Rio Salado Library and Information Center with 16,000 titles, 125 serial subscriptions, 8,000 audiovisual materials, an OPAC, a Web page.

Student Life *Housing:* college housing not available. *Campus security:* 24-hour emergency response devices, late-night transport/escort service. *Student services:* personal/psychological counseling.

Costs (2009–10) *Tuition:* area resident $1704 full-time, $71 per credit hour part-time; state resident $7488 full-time, $312 per credit hour part-time; nonresident $7488 full-time, $312 per credit hour part-time. Full-time tuition and fees vary according to course load, program, and reciprocity agreements. Part-time tuition and fees vary according to course load and reciprocity agreements. *Required fees:* $30 full-time, $15 per term part-time. *Payment plans:* installment, deferred payment.

Applying *Options:* electronic application, early admission, deferred entrance. *Application deadlines:* rolling (freshmen), rolling (transfers).

Freshman Application Contact Laurel Redman, Director Instruction Support Services and Student Development, Rio Salado College, 2323 West 14th Street, Tempe, AZ 85281-6950. *Phone:* 480-517-8563. *Toll-free phone:* 800-729-1197. *Fax:* 480-517-8199. *E-mail:* admission@riomail.maricopa.edu.

SCOTTSDALE COMMUNITY COLLEGE

Scottsdale, Arizona **www.scottsdalecc.edu/**

- **State and locally supported** 2-year, founded 1969, part of Maricopa County Community College District System
- **Urban** 160-acre campus with easy access to Phoenix
- **Coed,** 10,923 undergraduate students, 34% full-time, 53% women, 47% men

Undergraduates 3,698 full-time, 7,225 part-time. Students come from 47 states and territories, 70 other countries, 2% are from out of state, 3% African American, 3% Asian American or Pacific Islander, 10% Hispanic American, 5% Native American, 2% international, 15% transferred in. *Retention:* 55% of 2008 full-time freshmen returned.

Freshmen *Admission:* 1,785 applied, 1,785 admitted.

Faculty *Total:* 636, 26% full-time, 13% with terminal degrees. *Student/faculty ratio:* 19:1.

Majors Accounting; administrative assistant and secretarial science; business administration and management; criminal justice/law enforcement administration; culinary arts; dramatic/theater arts; electrical, electronic and communications engineering technology; emergency medical technology (EMT paramedic); environmental design/architecture; equestrian studies; fashion merchandising; finance; fire science; hospitality administration; hotel/motel administration; information science/studies; interior design; kindergarten/preschool education; mathematics; medical administrative assistant and medical secretary; nursing (registered nurse training); photography; public administration; real estate; special products marketing.

Academics *Calendar:* semesters. *Degree:* certificates, diplomas, and associate. *Special study options:* academic remediation for entering students, adult/continuing education programs, advanced placement credit, cooperative education, English as a second language, honors programs, internships, off-campus study, part-time degree program, services for LD students, study abroad, summer session for credit.

Library Scottsdale Community College Library with an OPAC, a Web page.

Student Life *Housing:* college housing not available. *Activities and Organizations:* drama/theater group, student-run newspaper, radio station, choral group, Student Leadership Forum, International Community Club, Phi Theta Kappa, Music Industry Club, SCC ASID-Interior Design group. *Campus security:* 24-hour emergency response devices and patrols, student patrols, late-night transport/escort service, 24-hour automatic surveillance cameras. *Student services:* personal/psychological counseling.

Athletics Member NCAA, NJCAA. All NCAA Division II. *Intercollegiate sports:* baseball M, basketball M/W, cross-country running M/W, football M, golf M/W, soccer M/W, softball W, tennis M/W, track and field M/W, volleyball W. *Intramural sports:* archery M/W, badminton M/W, basketball M/W, bowling M/W, racquetball M/W, track and field M/W, volleyball M/W.

Costs (2010–11) *Tuition:* area resident $2130 full-time, $71 per credit hour part-time; state resident $9360 full-time, $96 per credit hour part-time; nonresident $9360 full-time, $96 per credit hour part-time. *Required fees:* $30 full-time, $15 per term part-time. *Payment plan:* deferred payment. *Waivers:* employees or children of employees.

Financial Aid Of all full-time matriculated undergraduates who enrolled in 2008, 75 Federal Work-Study jobs (averaging $2000). *Financial aid deadline:* 7/15.

Applying *Options:* electronic application, early admission. *Application deadline:* rolling (freshmen). *Notification:* continuous (freshmen).

Freshman Application Contact Ms. Fran Watkins, Director of Admissions and Records, Scottsdale Community College, 9000 East Chaparral Road, Scottsdale, AZ 85256. *Phone:* 480-423-6133. *Fax:* 480-423-6200. *E-mail:* fran.watkins@sccmail.maricopa.edu.

Scottsdale Culinary Institute

Scottsdale, Arizona **www.scichefs.com/**

- **Proprietary** primarily 2-year, founded 1986
- **Coed**

Academics *Calendar:* semesters. *Degrees:* certificates, associate, and bachelor's.

Applying *Application fee:* $50.

Director of Admissions Scottsdale Culinary Institute, 8100 East Camelback Road, Suite 1001, Scottsdale, AZ 85251-3940. *Toll-free phone:* 800-848-2433.

Sessions College for Professional Design

Tempe, Arizona **www.sessions.edu/**

Admissions Office Contact Sessions College for Professional Design, 398 South MIll Avenue, Suite 300, Tempe, AZ 85281.

South Mountain Community College

Phoenix, Arizona **www.smc.maricopa.edu/**

Director of Admissions Dean of Enrollment Services, South Mountain Community College, 7050 South 24th Street, Phoenix, AZ 85042. *Phone:* 602-243-8120.

Southwest Institute of Healing Arts

Tempe, Arizona **www.swiha.org/**

Director of Admissions Katie Yearous, Student Advisor, Southwest Institute of Healing Arts, 1100 East Apache Boulevard, Tempe, AZ 85281. *Phone:* 480-994-9244. *Toll-free phone:* 888-504-9106. *E-mail:* joannl@swiha.net.

Tohono O'odham Community College

Sells, Arizona **www.tocc.cc.az.us/**

- **Public** 2-year, founded 1998
- **Rural** 10-acre campus
- **Endowment** $138,720
- **Coed,** 254 undergraduate students, 10% full-time, 59% women, 41% men

Undergraduates 25 full-time, 229 part-time. Students come from 1 other state, 0.4% African American, 1% Asian American or Pacific Islander, 5% Hispanic American, 88% Native American. *Retention:* 100% of 2008 full-time freshmen returned.

Freshmen *Admission:* 15 enrolled.

Faculty *Total:* 28, 61% full-time, 7% with terminal degrees. *Student/faculty ratio:* 4:1.

Majors Business administration and management; child development; computer systems analysis; early childhood education; human services; liberal arts and sciences/liberal studies.

Academics *Calendar:* semesters. *Degree:* certificates, diplomas, and associate. *Special study options:* academic remediation for entering students, adult/continuing education programs, cooperative education, distance learning, double majors, part-time degree program, services for LD students, summer session for credit.

Library Tohono O'odham Community College Library plus 2 others with 7,886 titles, 80 serial subscriptions, 1,398 audiovisual materials, an OPAC, a Web page.

Student Life *Housing:* college housing not available. *Student services:* personal/psychological counseling.

Costs (2009–10) *Tuition:* state resident $1008 full-time, $42 per credit hour part-time; nonresident $5064 full-time, $72 per credit hour part-time.

Applying *Application fee:* $25. *Required:* high school transcript. *Application deadlines:* rolling (freshmen), rolling (transfers). *Notification:* continuous (freshmen), continuous (transfers).

Freshman Application Contact Admissions, Tohono O'odham Community College, PO Box 3129, Sells, AZ 85634. *Phone:* 520-383-8401. *E-mail:* info@tocc.cc.az.us.

Universal Technical Institute

Avondale, Arizona **www.uticorp.com/**

Freshman Application Contact Director of Admission, Universal Technical Institute, 10695 West Pierce Street, Avondale, AZ 85323. *Phone:* 623-245-4600. *Toll-free phone:* 800-859-1202. *Fax:* 623-245-4601.

Yavapai College

Prescott, Arizona **www.yc.edu/**

- **State and locally supported** 2-year, founded 1966, part of Arizona State Community College System
- **Small-town** 100-acre campus
- **Coed,** 8,276 undergraduate students, 23% full-time, 59% women, 41% men

Undergraduates 1,917 full-time, 6,359 part-time. Students come from 30 states and territories, 18% are from out of state, 1% African American, 1% Asian American or Pacific Islander, 10% Hispanic American, 3% Native American, 0.2% international, 5% live on campus.

Freshmen *Admission:* 1,098 enrolled.

Faculty *Total:* 404, 28% full-time. *Student/faculty ratio:* 15:1.

Majors Accounting; administrative assistant and secretarial science; agribusiness; agricultural business and management; agriculture; aquaculture; architectural drafting and CAD/CADD; automobile/automotive mechanics technology; business administration and management; commercial and advertising art; construction engineering technology; criminal justice/police science; education related; equestrian studies; film/cinema studies; fine arts related; fire science; graphic design; gunsmithing; horse husbandry/equine science and management; information science/studies; legal administrative assistant/secretary; legal assistant/paralegal; liberal arts and sciences/liberal studies; nursing (registered nurse training).

Academics *Calendar:* semesters. *Degree:* certificates and associate. *Special study options:* academic remediation for entering students, adult/continuing education programs, advanced placement credit, cooperative education, distance learning, English as a second language, honors programs, independent study, internships, off-campus study, part-time degree program, services for LD students, summer session for credit. *ROTC:* Army (c), Air Force (c).

Library Yavapai College Library with 81,144 titles, 1,091 serial subscriptions, an OPAC, a Web page.

Student Life *Housing Options:* coed. Campus housing is university owned. *Activities and Organizations:* drama/theater group, student-run newspaper, choral group, Re-Entry Club, Student Nurses Association, Native American Club, International Club, VICA (Vocational Industrial Clubs of America). *Campus security:* 24-hour emergency response devices and patrols, student patrols, late-night transport/escort service, controlled dormitory access. *Student services:* health clinic, personal/psychological counseling, women's center.

Yavapai College (continued)

Athletics Member NJCAA. *Intercollegiate sports:* baseball M(s), basketball M(s)/W(s), soccer M(s), softball W(s), volleyball W(s).

Costs (2010–11) *Tuition:* state resident $1488 full-time; nonresident $8158 full-time. *Room and board:* $5020.

Financial Aid Of all full-time matriculated undergraduates who enrolled in 2008, 100 Federal Work-Study jobs (averaging $2000).

Applying *Options:* early admission, deferred entrance. *Required:* high school transcript. *Required for some:* essay or personal statement. *Application deadlines:* rolling (freshmen), rolling (transfers).

Freshman Application Contact Mrs. Sheila Jarrell, Admissions, Registration, and Records Manager, Yavapai College, 1100 East Sheldon Street, Prescott, AZ 86301-3297. *Phone:* 928-776-2107. *Toll-free phone:* 800-922-6787. *Fax:* 520-776-2151. *E-mail:* registration@yc.edu.

ARKANSAS

Arkansas Northeastern College

Blytheville, Arkansas **www.anc.edu/**

Freshman Application Contact Mrs. Leslie Wells, Admissions Counselor, Arkansas Northeastern College, PO Box 1109, Blytheville, AR 72316. *Phone:* 870-762-1020 Ext. 1118. *Fax:* 870-763-1654. *E-mail:* lwells@anc.edu.

Arkansas State University–Beebe

Beebe, Arkansas **www.asub.edu/**

- **State-supported** 2-year, founded 1927, part of Arkansas State University System
- **Small-town** 320-acre campus with easy access to Memphis
- **Coed,** 4,491 undergraduate students, 58% full-time, 59% women, 41% men

Undergraduates 2,601 full-time, 1,890 part-time. Students come from 20 states and territories, 1% are from out of state, 5% African American, 0.8% Asian American or Pacific Islander, 3% Hispanic American, 0.6% Native American, 0.4% international, 6% transferred in, 12% live on campus. *Retention:* 64% of 2008 full-time freshmen returned.

Freshmen *Admission:* 3,451 applied, 1,866 admitted, 1,047 enrolled. *Average high school GPA:* 2.75.

Faculty *Total:* 97, 65% full-time, 22% with terminal degrees. *Student/faculty ratio:* 30:1.

Majors Agriculture; animal sciences; business administration and management; clinical/medical laboratory technology; computer programming (vendor/product certification); computer systems networking and telecommunications; computer technology/computer systems technology; drafting and design technology; electrical, electronic and communications engineering technology; general studies; health/medical preparatory programs related; industrial mechanics and maintenance technology; information technology; liberal arts and sciences/liberal studies; nursing (registered nurse training); quality control technology; vehicle maintenance and repair technologies related.

Academics *Calendar:* semesters. *Degree:* certificates and associate. *Special study options:* academic remediation for entering students, adult/continuing education programs, advanced placement credit, distance learning, honors programs, part-time degree program, summer session for credit. *ROTC:* Army (b).

Library Abington Library with 90,000 titles, 500 serial subscriptions, 10 audiovisual materials.

Student Life *Housing Options:* men-only, women-only. Campus housing is university owned. *Activities and Organizations:* drama/theater group, choral group, Student Arkansas Education Association, Art Club, Agri Club, Social Science Club, Leadership Council. *Campus security:* 24-hour emergency response devices and patrols. *Student services:* personal/psychological counseling.

Athletics *Intramural sports:* archery M/W, badminton M/W, basketball M/W, football M/W, golf M/W, racquetball M/W, softball M/W, squash M/W, table tennis M/W, tennis M/W, track and field M/W, volleyball M/W.

Financial Aid Of all full-time matriculated undergraduates who enrolled in 2008, 16 Federal Work-Study jobs (averaging $1800). 112 state and other part-time jobs (averaging $750).

Applying *Options:* electronic application, deferred entrance. *Required:* high school transcript. *Application deadline:* rolling (freshmen). *Notification:* continuous (freshmen).

Freshman Application Contact Mr. Ronald Hudson, Coordinator of Student Recruitment, Arkansas State University–Beebe, PO Box 1000, Beebe, AR 72012-1000. *Phone:* 501-882-8860. *Toll-free phone:* 800-632-9985. *E-mail:* rdhudson@asub.edu.

Arkansas State University–Mountain Home

Mountain Home, Arkansas **www.asumh.edu/**

- **State-supported** 2-year, founded 2000, part of Arkansas State University System
- **Small-town** 136-acre campus
- **Endowment** $3.3 million
- **Coed,** 1,232 undergraduate students, 62% full-time, 60% women, 40% men

Undergraduates 765 full-time, 467 part-time. Students come from 22 states and territories, 1 other country, 0.1% are from out of state, 0.6% African American, 0.9% Asian American or Pacific Islander, 1% Hispanic American, 2% Native American, 12% transferred in. *Retention:* 46% of 2008 full-time freshmen returned.

Freshmen *Admission:* 651 applied, 531 admitted, 294 enrolled. *Average high school GPA:* 2.44.

Faculty *Total:* 72, 60% full-time, 22% with terminal degrees. *Student/faculty ratio:* 22:1.

Majors Business automation/technology/data entry; criminal justice/law enforcement administration; criminal justice/safety; emergency medical technology (EMT paramedic); forensic science and technology; funeral service and mortuary science; information science/studies; liberal arts and sciences/liberal studies; middle school education; respiratory care therapy.

Academics *Calendar:* semesters. *Degree:* certificates and associate. *Special study options:* academic remediation for entering students, advanced placement credit, cooperative education, distance learning, independent study, part-time degree program, services for LD students, summer session for credit. *ROTC:* Army (b).

Library Norma Wood Library with 33,573 titles, 15,360 serial subscriptions, 2,212 audiovisual materials, an OPAC, a Web page.

Student Life *Housing:* college housing not available. *Activities and Organizations:* Phi Theta Kappa, Circle K, Criminal Justice Club, Mortuary Science Club, Student Ambassadors. *Campus security:* during operation hours security is present and available as needed.

Standardized Tests *Recommended:* SAT or ACT (for admission), COMPASS, ASSET.

Costs (2010–11) *Tuition:* state resident $2310 full-time, $77 per credit hour part-time; nonresident $3960 full-time, $132 per credit hour part-time. Full-time tuition and fees vary according to course load. Part-time tuition and fees vary according to course load. *Required fees:* $450 full-time, $77 per credit hour part-time, $450 per credit hour part-time. *Room and board:* Room and board charges vary according to housing facility. *Payment plan:* installment. *Waivers:* children of alumni, senior citizens, and employees or children of employees.

Applying *Options:* electronic application. *Required:* high school transcript. *Recommended:* placement scores, GED scores accepted. *Notification:* continuous (freshmen).

Freshman Application Contact Mr. Scott Raney, Director of Student Services, Arkansas State University–Mountain Home, 1600 South College Street, Mountain Home, AR 72653. *Phone:* 870-508-6168. *Fax:* 870-508-6287. *E-mail:* araney@asumh.edu.

Arkansas State University–Newport

Newport, Arkansas **www.asun.edu/**

Director of Admissions Ms. Tara Byrd, Registrar, Director of Admissions, Arkansas State University–Newport, 7648 Victory Boulevard, Newport, AR 72112. *Phone:* 870-512-7800. *Toll-free phone:* 800-976-1676.

Black River Technical College

Pocahontas, Arkansas **www.blackrivertech.edu/**

- **State-supported** 2-year, founded 1972
- **Small-town** 55-acre campus
- **Coed**

Academics *Calendar:* semesters. *Degree:* associate. *Special study options:* academic remediation for entering students, cooperative education, honors programs, internships, part-time degree program, services for LD students, student-designed majors, summer session for credit.

Student Life *Campus security:* night patrol.

Standardized Tests *Required for some:* ACT, ACT ASSET, or SAT.

Costs (2009–10) *Tuition:* state resident $1680 full-time, $70 per credit hour part-time; nonresident $4368 full-time, $182 per credit hour part-time. Full-time tuition and fees vary according to course load. Part-time tuition and fees vary according to course load. *Required fees:* $72 full-time, $3 per credit hour part-time.

Applying *Required for some:* high school transcript, interview.

Director of Admissions Director of Admissions, Black River Technical College, 1410 Highway 304 East, Pocahontas, AR 72455. *Phone:* 870-892-4565. *Toll-free phone:* 800-919-3086.

Cossatot Community College of the University of Arkansas

De Queen, Arkansas **www.cccua.edu/**

- **State-supported** 2-year, founded 1991, part of University of Arkansas System
- **Rural** 30-acre campus
- **Endowment** $108,167
- **Coed,** 1,426 undergraduate students

Undergraduates Students come from 4 states and territories, 2% are from out of state, 12% African American, 0.6% Asian American or Pacific Islander, 12% Hispanic American, 1% Native American.

Faculty *Total:* 74, 46% full-time, 3% with terminal degrees. *Student/faculty ratio:* 12:1.

Majors Automobile/automotive mechanics technology; business administration and management; criminal justice/law enforcement administration; early childhood education; forensic science and technology; general studies; liberal arts and sciences/liberal studies; management information systems; medical/clinical assistant; middle school education; multi/interdisciplinary studies related.

Academics *Calendar:* semesters. *Degree:* certificates and associate. *Special study options:* academic remediation for entering students, accelerated degree program, adult/continuing education programs, advanced placement credit, cooperative education, distance learning, double majors, independent study, internships, off-campus study, part-time degree program, services for LD students, summer session for credit.

Library Kimbell Library.

Student Life *Housing:* college housing not available. *Activities and Organizations:* student-run newspaper, Students 4 Students, Phi Theta Kappa, ALPNA, VICA (Vocational Industrial Clubs of America), Journalism Club. *Student services:* personal/psychological counseling.

Costs (2010–11) *Tuition:* area resident $1440 full-time, $48 per credit hour part-time; state resident $1740 full-time, $58 per credit hour part-time; nonresident $4500 full-time, $150 per credit hour part-time. Full-time tuition and fees vary according to course load and program. Part-time tuition and fees vary according to course load and program. *Required fees:* $280 full-time, $5 per credit hour part-time, $65 per credit hour part-time. *Payment plan:* installment. *Waivers:* senior citizens and employees or children of employees.

Financial Aid Of all full-time matriculated undergraduates who enrolled in 2008, 14 Federal Work-Study jobs (averaging $2700).

Applying *Options:* electronic application. *Recommended:* high school transcript.

Freshman Application Contact Cossatot Community College of the University of Arkansas, PO Box 960, DeQueen, AR 71832. *Phone:* 870-584-4471. *Toll-free phone:* 800-844-4471.

Crowley's Ridge College

Paragould, Arkansas **www.crowleysridgecollege.edu/**

- **Independent** 2-year, founded 1964, affiliated with Church of Christ
- **Small-town** 112-acre campus
- **Coed**

Academics *Calendar:* semesters. *Degree:* associate. *Special study options:* academic remediation for entering students, double majors, honors programs, independent study, part-time degree program, summer session for credit.

Financial Aid Of all full-time matriculated undergraduates who enrolled in 2008, 78 Federal Work-Study jobs (averaging $500).

Applying *Options:* electronic application. *Required:* high school transcript, recommendation form filled out by high school. *Required for some:* interview.

Freshman Application Contact Amanda Drake, Director of Admissions, Crowley's Ridge College, 100 College Drive, Paragould, AR 72450. *Phone:* 870-236-6901. *Toll-free phone:* 800-264-1096. *Fax:* 870-236-7748. *E-mail:* njoneshi@crc.pioneer.paragould.ar.us.

East Arkansas Community College

Forrest City, Arkansas **www.eacc.edu/**

Freshman Application Contact Ms. DeAnna Adams, Director of Enrollment Management/Institutional Research, East Arkansas Community College, 1700 Newcastle Road, Forrest City, AR 72335-2204. *Phone:* 870-633-4480. *Toll-free phone:* 877-797-3222. *Fax:* 870-633-3840. *E-mail:* dadams@eacc.edu.

ITT Technical Institute

Little Rock, Arkansas **www.itt-tech.edu/**

- **Proprietary** primarily 2-year, founded 1993, part of ITT Educational Services, Inc.
- **Urban** campus
- **Coed**

Majors Animation, interactive technology, video graphics and special effects; CAD/CADD drafting/design technology; computer and information systems security; computer engineering technology; computer software and media applications related; computer software engineering; construction management; criminal justice/law enforcement administration; design and visual communications; electrical, electronic and communications engineering technology; system, networking, and LAN/WAN management; web page, digital/multimedia and information resources design.

Academics *Calendar:* quarters. *Degrees:* associate and bachelor's.

Student Life *Housing:* college housing not available.

Freshman Application Contact Director of Recruitment, ITT Technical Institute, 4520 South University Avenue, Little Rock, AR 72204-9925. *Phone:* 501-565-5550. *Toll-free phone:* 800-359-4429.

Mid-South Community College

West Memphis, Arkansas **www.midsouthcc.edu/**

Freshman Application Contact Jeremy Reece, Director of Admissions, Mid-South Community College, 2000 West Broadway, West Memphis, AR 72301. *Phone:* 870-733-6786. *Fax:* 870-733-6719. *E-mail:* jreece@midsouthcc.edu.

National Park Community College

Hot Springs, Arkansas **www.npcc.edu/**

Director of Admissions Dr. Allen B. Moody, Director of Institutional Services/Registrar, National Park Community College, 101 College Drive, Hot Springs, AR 71913. *Phone:* 501-760-4222. *Toll-free phone:* 800-760-1825. *E-mail:* bmoody@npcc.edu.

North Arkansas College

Harrison, Arkansas **www.northark.edu/**

- **State and locally supported** 2-year, founded 1974
- **Small-town** 40-acre campus
- **Coed,** 2,429 undergraduate students, 61% full-time, 60% women, 40% men
- 100% of applicants were admitted

Undergraduates 1,491 full-time, 938 part-time. Students come from 1 other country, 2% are from out of state, 0.6% African American, 0.6% Asian American or Pacific Islander, 2% Hispanic American, 1% Native American, 0.2% international, 10% transferred in. *Retention:* 50% of 2008 full-time freshmen returned.

North Arkansas College (continued)

Freshmen *Admission:* 927 applied, 927 admitted, 578 enrolled. *Average high school GPA:* 2.93. *Test scores:* ACT scores over 18: 79%; ACT scores over 24: 19%.

Faculty *Total:* 139, 4% with terminal degrees. *Student/faculty ratio:* 19:1.

Majors Biomedical technology; business/commerce; clinical/medical laboratory technology; computer and information sciences; criminal justice/law enforcement administration; education (multiple levels); electrical, electronic and communications engineering technology; emergency medical technology (EMT paramedic); forensic science and technology; general studies; liberal arts and sciences/liberal studies; medical radiologic technology; multi/interdisciplinary studies related; nursing (registered nurse training); surgical technology.

Academics *Calendar:* semesters. *Degree:* certificates and associate. *Special study options:* academic remediation for entering students, adult/continuing education programs, advanced placement credit, distance learning, freshman honors college, honors programs, independent study, internships, part-time degree program, services for LD students, summer session for credit.

Library North Arkansas College Library plus 1 other with 28,751 titles, 219 serial subscriptions, 1,235 audiovisual materials, an OPAC, a Web page.

Student Life *Housing:* college housing not available. *Activities and Organizations:* drama/theater group, Phi Beta Lambda, Phi Theta Kappa, Student Nurses Association, VICA (Vocational Industrial Clubs of America), Baptist Student Union. *Campus security:* 24-hour emergency response devices. *Student services:* personal/psychological counseling.

Athletics Member NJCAA. *Intercollegiate sports:* baseball M, basketball M(s)/W(s), softball W. *Intramural sports:* archery M/W, badminton M/W, baseball M/W, football M/W, golf M/W, racquetball M/W, softball W, table tennis M/W, tennis M/W, volleyball M/W.

Costs (2010–11) *Tuition:* area resident $1770 full-time, $59 per credit hour part-time; state resident $2430 full-time, $82 per credit hour part-time; nonresident $4560 full-time, $152 per credit hour part-time. Full-time tuition and fees vary according to course load. Part-time tuition and fees vary according to course load. *Required fees:* $150 full-time, $5 per credit hour part-time. *Payment plan:* installment. *Waivers:* senior citizens and employees or children of employees.

Applying *Options:* deferred entrance. *Required for some:* high school transcript. *Application deadlines:* rolling (freshmen), rolling (out-of-state freshmen), rolling (transfers). *Notification:* continuous (freshmen), continuous (out-of-state freshmen), continuous (transfers).

Freshman Application Contact Mrs. Charla Jennings, Director of Admissions, North Arkansas College, 1515 Pioneer Drive, Harrison, AR 72601. *Phone:* 870-391-3221. *Toll-free phone:* 800-679-6622. *Fax:* 870-391-3339. *E-mail:* charlam@northark.edu.

NorthWest Arkansas Community College

Bentonville, Arkansas **www.nwacc.edu/**

- **State and locally supported** 2-year, founded 1989
- **Urban** 77-acre campus
- **Coed,** 8,006 undergraduate students, 38% full-time, 58% women, 42% men
- 100% of applicants were admitted

Undergraduates 3,034 full-time, 4,972 part-time. Students come from 21 states and territories, 2% are from out of state, 13% transferred in. *Retention:* 57% of 2008 full-time freshmen returned.

Freshmen *Admission:* 2,625 applied, 2,625 admitted, 1,275 enrolled. *Average high school GPA:* 2.8. *Test scores:* ACT scores over 18: 74%; ACT scores over 24: 17%; ACT scores over 30: 1%.

Faculty *Total:* 449, 27% full-time, 14% with terminal degrees. *Student/faculty ratio:* 20:1.

Majors Accounting; administrative assistant and secretarial science; business administration and management; commercial and advertising art; computer programming; criminal justice/law enforcement administration; criminal justice/safety; culinary arts; data processing and data processing technology; drafting and design technology; early childhood education; education; electrical, electronic and communications engineering technology; emergency medical technology (EMT paramedic); environmental science; finance; fire services administration; legal assistant/paralegal; liberal arts and sciences/liberal studies; nursing (registered nurse training); occupational safety and health technology; physical therapy; respiratory care therapy; security and protective services related.

Academics *Calendar:* semesters. *Degree:* certificates and associate. *Special study options:* academic remediation for entering students, accelerated degree program, adult/continuing education programs, advanced placement credit, cooperative education, distance learning, double majors, English as a second language, honors programs, independent study, internships, part-time degree program, services for LD students, student-designed majors, summer session for credit. *ROTC:* Army (c), Air Force (c).

Library Library Resource Center plus 1 other with 15,500 titles, 159 serial subscriptions, an OPAC, a Web page.

Student Life *Housing:* college housing not available. *Activities and Organizations:* drama/theater group, student-run newspaper, choral group, Student Advisory Activity Council, Gamma Beta Phi, Phi Beta Lambda, Student Nurses Association, Students in Free Enterprise (SIFE). *Campus security:* 24-hour emergency response devices and patrols. *Student services:* personal/psychological counseling.

Athletics *Intramural sports:* basketball M(c)/W(c), bowling M(c)/W(c), golf M(c), soccer M(c)/W(c), softball M(c)/W(c), volleyball W(c).

Costs (2010–11) *Tuition:* area resident $1980 full-time, $66 per credit hour part-time; state resident $3090 full-time, $103 per credit hour part-time; nonresident $4350 full-time, $145 per credit hour part-time. *Required fees:* $512 full-time, $14 per credit hour part-time, $50 per term part-time. *Payment plan:* installment. *Waivers:* senior citizens and employees or children of employees.

Applying *Options:* electronic application. *Application fee:* $10. *Required:* high school transcript. *Application deadline:* rolling (freshmen). *Notification:* continuous (freshmen).

Freshman Application Contact NorthWest Arkansas Community College, One College Drive, Bentonville, AR 72712. *Phone:* 479-636-9222. *Toll-free phone:* 800-995-6922. *Fax:* 479-619-4116. *E-mail:* admissions@nwacc.edu.

Ouachita Technical College

Malvern, Arkansas **www.otcweb.edu/**

- **State-supported** 2-year, founded 1972
- **Small-town** 11-acre campus
- **Coed,** 1,610 undergraduate students, 38% full-time, 57% women, 43% men

Undergraduates 605 full-time, 1,005 part-time. 12% African American, 0.9% Asian American or Pacific Islander, 1% Hispanic American, 0.6% Native American, 0.3% international.

Freshmen *Admission:* 170 enrolled. *Test scores:* ACT scores over 18: 62%; ACT scores over 24: 9%.

Faculty *Total:* 99, 33% full-time, 12% with terminal degrees. *Student/faculty ratio:* 16:1.

Majors Accounting; administrative assistant and secretarial science; automobile/automotive mechanics technology; business administration and management; child-care and support services management; computer and information sciences; industrial arts; industrial technology; legal administrative assistant/secretary; legal assistant/paralegal; liberal arts and sciences/liberal studies; machine tool technology; management information systems; marketing/marketing management; medical administrative assistant and medical secretary; nursing (licensed practical/vocational nurse training).

Academics *Calendar:* semesters. *Degree:* certificates and associate. *Special study options:* academic remediation for entering students, accelerated degree program, advanced placement credit, cooperative education, distance learning, double majors, independent study, internships, part-time degree program, services for LD students, summer session for credit.

Library Ouachita Technical College Library/Learning Resource Center with 8,000 titles, 100 serial subscriptions, 1,200 audiovisual materials, an OPAC, a Web page.

Student Life *Housing:* college housing not available. *Campus security:* 24-hour patrols. *Student services:* personal/psychological counseling.

Standardized Tests *Recommended:* SAT or ACT (for admission), ACT COMPASS or ASSET.

Financial Aid Of all full-time matriculated undergraduates who enrolled in 2008, 18 Federal Work-Study jobs (averaging $2400).

Applying *Options:* electronic application, early admission, deferred entrance. *Required:* high school transcript. *Application deadlines:* rolling (freshmen), rolling (transfers).

Freshman Application Contact Kathy Lazenby, Counselor, Ouachita Technical College, One College Circle, Malvern, AR 72104. *Phone:* 501-337-5000 Ext. 1103. *Toll-free phone:* 800-337-0266. *Fax:* 501-337-9382. *E-mail:* vkesterson@otcweb.edu.

Ozarka College

Melbourne, Arkansas **www.ozarka.edu/**

Freshman Application Contact Ms. Zeda Wilkerson, Director of Admissions, Ozarka College, PO Box 12, 218 College Drive, Melbourne, AR 72556. *Phone:* 870-368-7371 Ext. 2028. *Toll-free phone:* 800-821-4335. *E-mail:* zwilkerson@ozarka.edu.

Phillips Community College of the University of Arkansas

Helena, Arkansas **www.pccua.edu/**

- **State and locally supported** 2-year, founded 1965, part of University of Arkansas System
- **Small-town** 80-acre campus with easy access to Memphis
- **Coed**

Academics *Calendar:* semesters. *Degree:* certificates and associate. *Special study options:* academic remediation for entering students, adult/continuing education programs, advanced placement credit, part-time degree program, services for LD students, summer session for credit.

Student Life *Campus security:* 24-hour patrols.

Costs (2009–10) *Tuition:* area resident $1650 full-time, $55 per semester hour part-time; state resident $2300 full-time, $64 per semester hour part-time; nonresident $3060 full-time, $102 per semester hour part-time. Full-time tuition and fees vary according to course load. Part-time tuition and fees vary according to course load. *Required fees:* $400 full-time, $12 per semester hour part-time, $10 per term part-time.

Applying *Options:* early admission.

Director of Admissions Mr. Lynn Boone, Registrar, Phillips Community College of the University of Arkansas, PO Box 785, Helena, AR 72342-0785. *Phone:* 870-338-6474.

Pulaski Technical College

North Little Rock, Arkansas **www.pulaskitech.edu/**

- **State-supported** 2-year, founded 1945
- **Urban** 40-acre campus with easy access to Little Rock
- **Coed,** 10,255 undergraduate students, 47% full-time, 66% women, 34% men

Undergraduates 4,856 full-time, 5,399 part-time. Students come from 5 states and territories, 1% are from out of state, 51% African American, 1% Asian American or Pacific Islander, 3% Hispanic American, 0.5% Native American, 0.1% international, 6% transferred in.

Freshmen *Admission:* 3,193 applied, 3,193 admitted, 1,478 enrolled. *Average high school GPA:* 2.47.

Faculty *Total:* 473, 32% full-time, 7% with terminal degrees. *Student/faculty ratio:* 25:1.

Majors Administrative assistant and secretarial science; aircraft powerplant technology; airline pilot and flight crew; business operations support and secretarial services related; child development; computer technology/computer systems technology; construction trades related; culinary arts; drafting and design technology; electromechanical technology; environmental engineering technology; heating, air conditioning, ventilation and refrigeration maintenance technology; hospitality administration; industrial technology; liberal arts and sciences/liberal studies; management information systems; military technologies; occupational therapist assistant; respiratory care therapy.

Academics *Calendar:* semesters. *Degree:* certificates and associate. *Special study options:* academic remediation for entering students, advanced placement credit, distance learning, part-time degree program, services for LD students, summer session for credit.

Library Ottenheimer Library with 35,406 titles, 276 serial subscriptions, 1,994 audiovisual materials, an OPAC, a Web page.

Student Life *Housing:* college housing not available. *Activities and Organizations:* drama/theater group, choral group. *Campus security:* certified law enforcement personnel 7 am to 11 pm.

Costs (2010–11) *Tuition:* state resident $1968 full-time, $82 per credit hour part-time; nonresident $3240 full-time, $135 per credit hour part-time. Full-time tuition and fees vary according to course load. *Required fees:* $290 full-time, $10 per credit hour part-time, $25 per term part-time. *Payment plan:* deferred payment. *Waivers:* senior citizens and employees or children of employees.

Applying *Options:* electronic application. *Required:* high school transcript. *Application deadline:* rolling (freshmen).

Freshman Application Contact Mr. Clark Atkins, Director of Admissions, Pulaski Technical College, 3000 West Scenic Drive, North Little Rock, AR 72118. *Phone:* 501-812-2734. *Fax:* 501-812-2316. *E-mail:* catkins@pulaskitech.edu.

Remington College–Little Rock Campus

Little Rock, Arkansas **www.remingtoncollege.edu/**

Director of Admissions Brian Maggio, Director of Recruitment, Remington College–Little Rock Campus, 19 Remington Drive, Little Rock, AR 72204. *Phone:* 501-312-0007. *Fax:* 501-225-3819. *E-mail:* brian.maggio@remingtoncollege.edu.

Rich Mountain Community College

Mena, Arkansas **www.rmcc.edu/**

- **State and locally supported** 2-year, founded 1983
- **Small-town** 40-acre campus
- **Coed**

Academics *Calendar:* semesters. *Degree:* certificates and associate. *Special study options:* academic remediation for entering students, adult/continuing education programs, advanced placement credit, distance learning, double majors, English as a second language, part-time degree program, services for LD students, summer session for credit.

Student Life *Campus security:* administrator on night duty.

Financial Aid Of all full-time matriculated undergraduates who enrolled in 2008, 12 Federal Work-Study jobs (averaging $1500).

Applying *Options:* early admission. *Required:* high school transcript.

Director of Admissions Dr. Steve Rook, Dean of Students, Rich Mountain Community College, 1100 College Drive, Mena, AR 71953. *Phone:* 479-394-7622 Ext. 1400.

South Arkansas Community College

El Dorado, Arkansas **www.southark.edu/**

Freshman Application Contact Mr. Dean Inman, Director of Enrollment Services, South Arkansas Community College, PO Box 7010, El Dorado, AR 71731-7010. *Phone:* 870-864-7142. *Toll-free phone:* 800-955-2289 Ext. 142. *Fax:* 870-864-7109. *E-mail:* dinman@southark.edu.

Southeast Arkansas College

Pine Bluff, Arkansas **www.seark.edu/**

Freshman Application Contact Ms. Barbara Dunn, Coordinator of Admissions and Enrollment Management, Southeast Arkansas College, 1900 Hazel Street, Pine Bluff, AR 71603. *Phone:* 870-543-5957. *Toll-free phone:* 888-SEARK TC. *Fax:* 870-543-5956. *E-mail:* bdunn@seark.edu.

Southern Arkansas University Tech

Camden, Arkansas **www.sautech.edu/**

- **State-supported** 2-year, founded 1967, part of Southern Arkansas University
- **Rural** 96-acre campus
- **Endowment** $403,394
- **Coed**
- 100% of applicants were admitted

Undergraduates 589 full-time, 1,228 part-time. Students come from 12 states and territories, 8 other countries, 10% are from out of state, 30% African American, 0.7% Asian American or Pacific Islander, 1% Hispanic American, 0.6% Native American, 0.8% international, 16% transferred in, 2% live on campus.

Faculty *Student/faculty ratio:* 19:1.

Academics *Calendar:* semesters. *Degree:* certificates and associate. *Special study options:* academic remediation for entering students, adult/continuing education programs, advanced placement credit, distance learning, double majors,

Southern Arkansas University Tech (continued)

external degree program, honors programs, independent study, internships, off-campus study, part-time degree program, services for LD students, summer session for credit.

Student Life *Campus security:* 24-hour emergency response devices and patrols.

Costs (2009–10) *Tuition:* state resident $2550 full-time, $85 per credit hour part-time; nonresident $3870 full-time, $129 per credit hour part-time. Full-time tuition and fees vary according to course load and program. Part-time tuition and fees vary according to course load and program. *Required fees:* $1000 full-time, $21 per credit hour part-time. *Room and board:* $4875; room only: $3000. Room and board charges vary according to housing facility.

Applying *Options:* electronic application, deferred entrance. *Required:* high school transcript.

Freshman Application Contact Mrs. Beverly Ellis, Admissions Analyst, Southern Arkansas University Tech, PO Box 3499, East Camden, AR 71711. *Phone:* 870-574-4558. *Fax:* 870-574-4478. *E-mail:* bellis@sautech.edu.

University of Arkansas Community College at Batesville

Batesville, Arkansas **www.uaccb.edu/**

Freshman Application Contact Ms. Sharon Gage, Admissions Coordinator, University of Arkansas Community College at Batesville, PO Box 3350, Batesville, AR 72503. *Phone:* 870-612-2042. *Toll-free phone:* 800-508-7878. *Fax:* 870-612-2129. *E-mail:* sgage@uaccb.edu.

University of Arkansas Community College at Hope

Hope, Arkansas **www.uacch.edu/**

Freshman Application Contact University of Arkansas Community College at Hope, PO Box 140, Hope, AR 71802. *Phone:* 870-772-8174.

University of Arkansas Community College at Morrilton

Morrilton, Arkansas **www.uaccm.edu/**

- **State-supported** 2-year, founded 1961, part of University of Arkansas System
- **Rural** 70-acre campus
- **Coed,** 2,421 undergraduate students, 67% full-time, 58% women, 42% men

Undergraduates 1,625 full-time, 796 part-time. Students come from 2 states and territories, 9% African American, 1% Asian American or Pacific Islander, 4% Hispanic American, 4% Native American, 13% transferred in. *Retention:* 53% of 2008 full-time freshmen returned.

Freshmen *Admission:* 1,425 applied, 1,053 admitted, 765 enrolled. *Average high school GPA:* 2.88. *Test scores:* ACT scores over 18: 75%; ACT scores over 24: 19%.

Faculty *Total:* 100, 59% full-time, 7% with terminal degrees. *Student/faculty ratio:* 19:1.

Majors Autobody/collision and repair technology; automobile/automotive mechanics technology; business/commerce; child development; commercial and advertising art; computer technology/computer systems technology; criminal justice/law enforcement administration; drafting and design technology; education (multiple levels); forensic science and technology; general studies; heating, air conditioning, ventilation and refrigeration maintenance technology; liberal arts and sciences/liberal studies; nursing (registered nurse training); petroleum technology; survey technology.

Academics *Calendar:* semesters. *Degree:* certificates and associate. *Special study options:* academic remediation for entering students, advanced placement credit, distance learning, double majors, internships, part-time degree program, services for LD students, summer session for credit.

Library E. Allen Gordon Library with 24,981 titles, 71 serial subscriptions, 2,011 audiovisual materials, an OPAC, a Web page.

Student Life *Housing:* college housing not available. *Activities and Organizations:* drama/theater group, choral group, Student Government Association, Phi Beta Lambda, Student Practical Nurses Organization, Computer Information Systems Club, Early Childhood Development Organization. *Campus security:* 24-hour emergency response devices, Campus Alert System. *Student services:* personal/psychological counseling.

Athletics Member NJCAA. *Intramural sports:* basketball M/W, football M/W, table tennis M/W, ultimate Frisbee M/W, volleyball M/W.

Costs (2010–11) *Tuition:* area resident $2100 full-time, $70 per credit hour part-time; state resident $2310 full-time, $77 per credit hour part-time; nonresident $3360 full-time, $112 per credit hour part-time. Full-time tuition and fees vary according to course load. Part-time tuition and fees vary according to course load. *Required fees:* $540 full-time, $17 per credit hour part-time, $15 per term part-time. *Payment plan:* installment. *Waivers:* senior citizens and employees or children of employees.

Financial Aid Of all full-time matriculated undergraduates who enrolled in 2008, 20 Federal Work-Study jobs (averaging $1000). *Financial aid deadline:* 7/23.

Applying *Options:* electronic application, early admission, deferred entrance. *Required:* high school transcript. *Required for some:* immunization records and prior college transcript(s). *Application deadlines:* rolling (freshmen), rolling (transfers). *Notification:* continuous (freshmen), continuous (transfers).

Freshman Application Contact Ms. Rachel Mullins, Coordinator of Recruitment, University of Arkansas Community College at Morrilton, One Bruce Street, Morrilton, AR 72110. *Phone:* 501-977-2174. *Toll-free phone:* 800-264-1094. *Fax:* 501-977-2123. *E-mail:* mullins@uaccm.edu.

CALIFORNIA

Allan Hancock College

Santa Maria, California **www.hancockcollege.edu/**

- **State and locally supported** 2-year, founded 1920
- **Small-town** 120-acre campus
- **Endowment** $1.1 million
- **Coed,** 10,387 undergraduate students, 29% full-time, 55% women, 45% men

Undergraduates 2,996 full-time, 7,391 part-time. Students come from 27 states and territories, 12 other countries, 4% African American, 3% Asian American or Pacific Islander, 33% Hispanic American, 1% Native American, 0.1% international.

Freshmen *Admission:* 715 enrolled.

Faculty *Total:* 594, 26% full-time. *Student/faculty ratio:* 17:1.

Majors Accounting; administrative assistant and secretarial science; aerospace, aeronautical and astronautical engineering; agribusiness; applied art; architectural engineering technology; art; automobile/automotive mechanics technology; biology/biological sciences; business administration and management; chemistry; civil engineering technology; commercial and advertising art; computer engineering technology; computer science; cosmetology; criminal justice/police science; dance; dental assisting; dietetics; electrical, electronic and communications engineering technology; engineering; engineering technology; English; environmental engineering technology; family and consumer economics related; fashion/apparel design; film/cinema studies; fire science; heavy equipment maintenance technology; human services; information science/studies; interior design; international relations and affairs; kindergarten/preschool education; legal administrative assistant/secretary; liberal arts and sciences/liberal studies; machine tool technology; medical/clinical assistant; music; nursing (licensed practical/vocational nurse training); nursing (registered nurse training); parks, recreation and leisure; photography; physical education teaching and coaching; physical therapy; physics; social sciences; Spanish; welding technology.

Academics *Calendar:* semesters. *Degree:* certificates and associate. *Special study options:* adult/continuing education programs, advanced placement credit, cooperative education, distance learning, English as a second language, part-time degree program, services for LD students, study abroad, summer session for credit.

Library Learning Resources Center with 47,370 titles, 397 serial subscriptions, 2,463 audiovisual materials, an OPAC, a Web page.

Student Life *Housing:* college housing not available. *Activities and Organizations:* drama/theater group, student-run newspaper, choral group, MECHA, AHC Student Club, Club Med (medical), Hancock Christian Fellowship, VICA (Vocational Industrial Clubs of America). *Campus security:* 24-hour emergency response devices and patrols, student patrols, late-night transport/escort service. *Student services:* health clinic, personal/psychological counseling, legal services.

Athletics *Intercollegiate sports:* baseball M, basketball M/W, cross-country running M/W, football M, golf M, soccer M/W, softball W, tennis M/W, track and field M/W, volleyball W.

Costs (2009–10) *Tuition:* state resident $0 full-time; nonresident $4560 full-time, $190 per unit part-time. Full-time tuition and fees vary according to course load. Part-time tuition and fees vary according to course load. *Required fees:* $673 full-time, $26 per unit part-time.

Financial Aid Of all full-time matriculated undergraduates who enrolled in 2008, 250 Federal Work-Study jobs (averaging $3000).

Applying *Options:* electronic application. *Application deadlines:* rolling (freshmen), rolling (transfers). *Notification:* continuous (freshmen), continuous (transfers).

Freshman Application Contact Ms. Adela Esquivel Swinson, Director of Admissions and Records, Allan Hancock College, 800 South College Drive, Santa Maria, CA 93454-6399. *Phone:* 805-922-6966 Ext. 3272. *Toll-free phone:* 866-342-5242. *Fax:* 805-922-3477.

AMERICAN ACADEMY OF DRAMATIC ARTS

Hollywood, California **www.aada.org/**

- **Independent** 2-year, founded 1974
- **Suburban** 4-acre campus with easy access to Los Angeles
- **Endowment** $1.7 million
- **Coed,** 180 undergraduate students, 100% full-time, 54% women, 46% men

Undergraduates 180 full-time. Students come from 25 states and territories, 10 other countries, 32% are from out of state, 7% African American, 1% Asian American or Pacific Islander, 9% Hispanic American, 0.6% Native American, 22% international.

Freshmen *Admission:* 397 applied, 75 admitted, 75 enrolled.

Faculty *Total:* 30, 27% full-time. *Student/faculty ratio:* 12:1.

Majors Dramatic/theater arts.

Academics *Calendar:* continuous. *Degree:* certificates, diplomas, and associate. *Special study options:* internships.

Library Bryn Morgan Library with 7,700 titles, 24 serial subscriptions, 320 audiovisual materials.

Student Life *Housing:* college housing not available. *Campus security:* 24-hour emergency response devices, 8-hour patrols by trained security personnel.

Costs (2010–11) *Tuition:* $28,620 full-time. *Required fees:* $600 full-time. *Payment plan:* installment.

Financial Aid Of all full-time matriculated undergraduates who enrolled in 2008, 15 Federal Work-Study jobs (averaging $2000).

Applying *Options:* deferred entrance. *Application fee:* $50. *Required:* essay or personal statement, high school transcript, 2 letters of recommendation, interview, audition. *Recommended:* minimum 2 GPA. *Application deadlines:* rolling (freshmen), rolling (transfers). *Notification:* continuous (freshmen), continuous (transfers).

Freshman Application Contact American Academy of Dramatic Arts, 1336 North LaBrea Avenue, Hollywood, CA 90028. *Phone:* 323-464-2777. *Toll-free phone:* 800-222-2867.

AMERICAN CAREER COLLEGE

Anaheim, California **www.americancareer.com/**

Admissions Office Contact American Career College, 1200 North Magnolia Avenue, Anaheim, CA 92801. *Toll-free phone:* 888-844-6522.

AMERICAN CAREER COLLEGE

Los Angeles, California **www.americancareer.com/**

Admissions Office Contact American Career College, 4021 Rosewood Avenue, Los Angeles, CA 90004-2932. *Toll-free phone:* 888-844-6522.

AMERICAN CAREER COLLEGE

Ontario, California **www.americancareer.com/**

Admissions Office Contact American Career College, 3130 East Sedona Court, Ontario, CA 91764. *Toll-free phone:* 888-844-6522.

AMERICAN RIVER COLLEGE

Sacramento, California **www.arc.losrios.edu/**

- **District-supported** 2-year, founded 1955, part of Los Rios Community College District System
- **Suburban** 153-acre campus
- **Coed**

Academics *Calendar:* semesters. *Degree:* certificates and associate. *Special study options:* academic remediation for entering students, adult/continuing education programs, advanced placement credit, cooperative education, English as a second language, part-time degree program, services for LD students, summer session for credit.

Student Life *Campus security:* 24-hour emergency response devices and patrols, student patrols, late-night transport/escort service.

Financial Aid Of all full-time matriculated undergraduates who enrolled in 2008, 300 Federal Work-Study jobs (averaging $1500). 100 state and other part-time jobs (averaging $2000).

Applying *Options:* early admission, deferred entrance.

Freshman Application Contact American River College, 4700 College Oak Drive, Sacramento, CA 95841-4286. *Phone:* 916-484-8171.

ANTELOPE VALLEY COLLEGE

Lancaster, California **www.avc.edu/**

- **State and locally supported** 2-year, founded 1929, part of California Community College System
- **Suburban** 135-acre campus with easy access to Los Angeles
- **Endowment** $299,569
- **Coed,** 15,108 undergraduate students, 32% full-time, 60% women, 40% men

Undergraduates 4,802 full-time, 10,306 part-time. Students come from 7 states and territories, 1% are from out of state, 20% African American, 5% Asian American or Pacific Islander, 31% Hispanic American, 1% Native American, 0.2% international, 16% transferred in. *Retention:* 68% of 2008 full-time freshmen returned.

Freshmen *Admission:* 2,830 applied, 2,830 admitted, 2,830 enrolled.

Faculty *Total:* 618, 32% full-time. *Student/faculty ratio:* 45:1.

Majors Administrative assistant and secretarial science; aircraft powerplant technology; airframe mechanics and aircraft maintenance technology; apparel and textiles; autobody/collision and repair technology; automobile/automotive mechanics technology; avionics maintenance technology; biology/biological sciences; business administration and management; business/commerce; child-care and support services management; child development; cinematography and film/video production; computer and information sciences; computer graphics; computer programming; construction engineering technology; corrections; criminal justice/law enforcement administration; criminal justice/police science; data processing and data processing technology; drafting and design technology; electrical, electronic and communications engineering technology; engineering; engineering technology; family and consumer sciences/home economics teacher education; fiber, textile and weaving arts; fire protection and safety technology; foods, nutrition, and wellness; health and physical education; heating, air conditioning, ventilation and refrigeration maintenance technology; interior design; liberal arts and sciences/liberal studies; marketing/marketing management; mathematics; medical administrative assistant and medical secretary; music; nursing (registered nurse training); ornamental horticulture; photography; physical sciences; real estate; teacher assistant/aide; welding technology; work and family studies.

Academics *Calendar:* semesters. *Degree:* certificates and associate. *Special study options:* academic remediation for entering students, adult/continuing education programs, advanced placement credit, cooperative education, distance learning, English as a second language, honors programs, independent study, part-time degree program, services for LD students, student-designed majors, summer session for credit. *ROTC:* Air Force (c).

Library Antelope Valley College Library with 43,000 titles, 175 serial subscriptions, an OPAC.

Antelope Valley College (continued)

Student Life *Housing:* college housing not available. *Activities and Organizations:* drama/theater group, student-run newspaper, choral group. *Campus security:* 24-hour emergency response devices and patrols, late-night transport/escort service. *Student services:* personal/psychological counseling.

Athletics *Intercollegiate sports:* baseball M, basketball M/W, cross-country running M/W, football M, soccer W, softball W, tennis W, track and field M/W, volleyball W. *Intramural sports:* basketball M/W, golf M/W, swimming and diving M/W, tennis M/W, volleyball M/W, weight lifting M/W.

Costs (2009–10) *Tuition:* state resident $0 full-time; nonresident $4710 full-time, $157 per unit part-time. Full-time tuition and fees vary according to course load. Part-time tuition and fees vary according to course load. *Required fees:* $780 full-time, $26 per unit part-time.

Applying *Options:* electronic application, early admission. *Required:* high school transcript. *Recommended:* assessment. *Application deadlines:* rolling (freshmen), rolling (transfers). *Notification:* continuous (freshmen), continuous (transfers).

Freshman Application Contact Welcome Center, Antelope Valley College, 3041 West Avenue K, Lancaster, CA 93536-5426. *Phone:* 661-722-6331.

Applied Professional Training, Inc.

Carlsbad, California **www.aptc.edu/**

Admissions Office Contact Applied Professional Training, Inc., 5751 Palmer Way, Suite D, PO Box 131717, Carlsbad, CA 92013.

Aviation & Electronic Schools of America

Colfax, California **www.aesa.com/**

Admissions Office Contact Aviation & Electronic Schools of America, P.O. Box 1810, 111 South Railroad Street, Colfax, CA 95713. *Toll-free phone:* 800-345-2742.

Bakersfield College

Bakersfield, California **www.bakersfieldcollege.edu/**

- **State and locally supported** 2-year, founded 1913, part of California Community College System
- **Urban** 175-acre campus
- **Coed,** 15,001 undergraduate students

Majors Accounting; administrative assistant and secretarial science; agricultural business and management; agriculture; animal sciences; anthropology; architectural engineering technology; art; art teacher education; automobile/automotive mechanics technology; biology/biological sciences; broadcast journalism; business administration and management; carpentry; chemistry; child development; computer science; corrections; cosmetology; criminal justice/law enforcement administration; criminal justice/police science; culinary arts; data processing and data processing technology; dental hygiene; developmental and child psychology; dietetics; drafting and design technology; dramatic/theater arts; economics; electrical, electronic and communications engineering technology; emergency medical technology (EMT paramedic); engineering; English; environmental engineering technology; family and consumer economics related; finance; fire science; foods, nutrition, and wellness; forestry; French; geography; geology/earth science; German; history; horticultural science; hotel/motel administration; human services; industrial arts; industrial radiologic technology; industrial technology; information science/studies; interior design; journalism; legal administrative assistant/secretary; liberal arts and sciences/liberal studies; machine tool technology; marketing/marketing management; mathematics; music; nursing (registered nurse training); ornamental horticulture; parks, recreation and leisure; petroleum technology; philosophy; photography; physical education teaching and coaching; physics; pipefitting and sprinkler fitting; political science and government; psychology; real estate; sociology; Spanish; speech and rhetoric; survey technology; welding technology; wood science and wood products/pulp and paper technology.

Academics *Calendar:* semesters. *Degree:* associate. *Special study options:* academic remediation for entering students, accelerated degree program, adult/continuing education programs, advanced placement credit, cooperative education, English as a second language, internships, part-time degree program, services for LD students, summer session for credit.

Library Grace Van Dyke Bird Library with 93,500 titles, 298 serial subscriptions, an OPAC, a Web page.

Student Life *Housing:* college housing not available. *Activities and Organizations:* drama/theater group, student-run newspaper, radio station, choral group. *Campus security:* 24-hour patrols, late-night transport/escort service. *Student services:* health clinic, women's center.

Athletics *Intercollegiate sports:* baseball M, basketball M/W, cross-country running M/W, football M, golf M, soccer W, softball W, tennis M/W, track and field M/W, volleyball W, wrestling M.

Financial Aid Of all full-time matriculated undergraduates who enrolled in 2008, 300 Federal Work-Study jobs (averaging $2500). 15 state and other part-time jobs (averaging $2500).

Applying *Application deadline:* rolling (freshmen).

Freshman Application Contact Bakersfield College, 1801 Panorama Drive, Bakersfield, CA 93305-1299. *Phone:* 661-395-4301.

Barstow College

Barstow, California **www.barstow.edu/**

Director of Admissions Mr. Don Low, Interim Vice President, Barstow College, 2700 Barstow Road, Barstow, CA 92311-6699.

Berkeley City College

Berkeley, California **www.berkeleycitycollege.edu/**

- **State and locally supported** 2-year, founded 1974, part of California Community College System, administratively affiliated with Peralta Community College District
- **Urban** campus with easy access to San Francisco
- **Coed,** 7,300 undergraduate students

Undergraduates 1% are from out of state.

Freshmen *Admission:* 6,245 applied, 6,245 admitted.

Faculty *Total:* 180, 27% full-time. *Student/faculty ratio:* 35:1.

Majors Accounting; art; biology/biotechnology laboratory technician; business administration and management; business/commerce; computer and information sciences; computer and information sciences related; computer and information systems security; computer graphics; computer software and media applications related; creative writing; data entry/microcomputer applications related; English; English composition; fine/studio arts; general studies; liberal arts and sciences/liberal studies; medical administrative assistant and medical secretary; office management; Spanish; web page, digital/multimedia and information resources design.

Academics *Calendar:* semesters. *Degree:* certificates and associate. *Special study options:* academic remediation for entering students, adult/continuing education programs, cooperative education, distance learning, double majors, English as a second language, independent study, internships, off-campus study, part-time degree program, services for LD students, student-designed majors, study abroad, summer session for credit.

Library Susan A. Duncan Library plus 1 other with an OPAC, a Web page.

Student Life *Activities and Organizations:* drama/theater group, student-run newspaper, choral group. *Campus security:* 24-hour patrols. *Student services:* personal/psychological counseling.

Costs (2010–11) *Tuition:* state resident $0 full-time; nonresident $5880 full-time, $196 per unit part-time. Full-time tuition and fees vary according to course load. Part-time tuition and fees vary according to course load. *Required fees:* $780 full-time, $26 per unit part-time. *Waivers:* minority students, children of alumni, adult students, senior citizens, and employees or children of employees.

Financial Aid Of all full-time matriculated undergraduates who enrolled in 2008, 34 Federal Work-Study jobs (averaging $3000).

Applying *Options:* electronic application, early admission, deferred entrance. *Recommended:* high school transcript. *Application deadlines:* rolling (freshmen), rolling (out-of-state freshmen), rolling (transfers). *Notification:* continuous (freshmen), continuous (out-of-state freshmen), continuous (transfers).

Freshman Application Contact Dr. May Kuang-chi Chen, Vice President of Student Services, Berkeley City College, 2020 Milvia Street, Berkeley, CA 94704. *Phone:* 510-981-2820. *Fax:* 510-841-7333. *E-mail:* mrivas@peralta.edu.

Bryan College

Gold River, California **www.bryancollege.edu/**

Freshman Application Contact Admissions Office, Bryan College, 2317 Gold Meadow Way, Gold River, CA 95670-4443. *Phone:* 916-649-2400. *Toll-free phone:* 866-649-2400.

Butte College

Oroville, California www.butte.edu/

- **District-supported** 2-year, founded 1966, part of California Community College System
- **Rural** 900-acre campus
- **Coed**

Academics *Calendar:* semesters. *Degree:* certificates and associate. *Special study options:* academic remediation for entering students, accelerated degree program, adult/continuing education programs, advanced placement credit, cooperative education, English as a second language, honors programs, internships, part-time degree program, services for LD students, study abroad, summer session for credit.

Student Life *Campus security:* 24-hour emergency response devices and patrols, student patrols.

Costs (2009–10) *Tuition:* state resident $0 full-time; nonresident $4560 full-time, $190 per unit part-time. Full-time tuition and fees vary according to course level, course load, and program. Part-time tuition and fees vary according to course level, course load, and program. *Required fees:* $804 full-time, $26 per unit part-time, $90 per term part-time. *Payment plans:* installment, deferred payment.

Applying *Options:* early admission, deferred entrance. *Required for some:* high school transcript.

Freshman Application Contact Ms. Nancy Jenson, Registrar, Butte College, 3536 Butte Campus Drive, Oroville, CA 95965. *Phone:* 530-895-2361.

Cabrillo College

Aptos, California www.cabrillo.edu/

Freshman Application Contact Ms. Esperanza Nee, Interim Director of Admissions and Records, Cabrillo College, 6500 Soquel Drive, Aptos, CA 95003. *Phone:* 831-479-6213. *Fax:* 831-479-5782. *E-mail:* esnee@cabrillo.edu.

California Culinary Academy

San Francisco, California www.baychef.com/

- **Proprietary** 2-year, founded 1977
- **Urban** campus
- **Coed**

Academics *Calendar:* continuous. *Degree:* certificates and associate. *Special study options:* cooperative education, services for LD students.

Student Life *Campus security:* 24-hour emergency response devices and patrols, controlled dormitory access.

Financial Aid Of all full-time matriculated undergraduates who enrolled in 2008, 45 Federal Work-Study jobs (averaging $3000).

Applying *Options:* electronic application. *Application fee:* $65. *Required:* high school transcript, interview.

Director of Admissions Ms. Nancy Seyfert, Vice President of Admissions, California Culinary Academy, 625 Polk Street, San Francisco, CA 94102-3368. *Phone:* 800-229-2433 Ext. 275. *Toll-free phone:* 800-229-2433 (in-state); 800-BAYCHEF (out-of-state).

California School of Culinary Arts

Pasadena, California www.csca.edu/

Director of Admissions Admissions Office, California School of Culinary Arts, 521 East Green Street, Pasadena, CA 91101.

Cambridge Career College

Yuba City, California cambridge.edu/

- **Proprietary** 2-year
- **Suburban** campus with easy access to Sacramento
- **Coed, primarily women,** 162 undergraduate students, 100% full-time, 91% women, 9% men

Undergraduates 162 full-time. *Retention:* 89% of 2008 full-time freshmen returned.

Freshmen *Admission:* 147 applied, 162 enrolled.

Majors Accounting; accounting and business/management.

Academics *Degree:* certificates and associate.

Student Life *Housing:* college housing not available.

Applying *Application fee:* $100. *Required:* high school transcript, interview.

Freshman Application Contact Admissions Office, Cambridge Career College, 990-A Klamath Lane, Yuba City, CA 95993. *Phone:* 530-674-9199. *Fax:* 530-671-7319.

Cañada College

Redwood City, California www.canadacollege.net/

Freshman Application Contact Cañada College, 4200 Farm Hill Boulevard, Redwood City, CA 94061. *Phone:* 650-306-3118.

Cerritos College

Norwalk, California www.cerritos.edu/

Director of Admissions Ms. Stephanie Murguia, Director of Admissions and Records, Cerritos College, 11110 Alondra Boulevard, Norwalk, CA 90650-6298. *Phone:* 562-860-2451. *E-mail:* smurguia@cerritos.edu.

Cerro Coso Community College

Ridgecrest, California www.cerrocoso.edu/

- **State-supported** 2-year, founded 1973, part of Kern Community College District System
- **Small-town** 320-acre campus
- **Coed**

Academics *Calendar:* semesters. *Degree:* certificates and associate. *Special study options:* academic remediation for entering students, adult/continuing education programs, cooperative education, distance learning, English as a second language, honors programs, part-time degree program, services for LD students, summer session for credit.

Student Life *Campus security:* patrols by trained security personnel.

Financial Aid Of all full-time matriculated undergraduates who enrolled in 2008, 150 Federal Work-Study jobs (averaging $2000).

Applying *Options:* early admission. *Recommended:* high school transcript.

Freshman Application Contact Mrs. Heather Ootash, Counseling/Matriculation Coordinator, Cerro Coso Community College, 3000 College Heights Boulevard, Ridgecrest, CA 93555. *Phone:* 760-384-6291. *Fax:* 760-375-4776. *E-mail:* hostash@cerrocoso.edu.

Chabot College

Hayward, California www.chabotcollege.edu/

- **State-supported** 2-year, founded 1961, part of California Community College System
- **Suburban** 245-acre campus with easy access to San Francisco
- **Coed**

Academics *Calendar:* semesters. *Degree:* certificates and associate. *Special study options:* academic remediation for entering students, adult/continuing education programs, advanced placement credit, distance learning, double majors, English as a second language, internships, off-campus study, part-time degree program, services for LD students, student-designed majors, study abroad, summer session for credit. *ROTC:* Army (c), Air Force (c).

Student Life *Campus security:* 24-hour emergency response devices, late-night transport/escort service.

Financial Aid Of all full-time matriculated undergraduates who enrolled in 2008, 75 Federal Work-Study jobs (averaging $3000).

Applying *Options:* electronic application. *Required:* high school transcript.

Director of Admissions Ms. Judy Young, Director of Admissions and Records, Chabot College, 25555 Hesperian Boulevard, Hayward, CA 94545. *Phone:* 510-723-6700.

CHAFFEY COLLEGE

Rancho Cucamonga, California **www.chaffey.edu/**

Director of Admissions Ms. Cecilia Carerra, Director of Admissions, Registration, and Records, Chaffey College, 5885 Haven Avenue, Rancho Cucamonga, CA 91737-3002. *Phone:* 909-941-2631. *Fax:* 909-466-2820.

CITRUS COLLEGE

Glendora, California **www.citruscollege.edu/**

Freshman Application Contact Admissions and Records, Citrus College, 1000 West Foothill Boulevard, Glendora, CA 91741-1899. *Phone:* 626-914-8511. *Fax:* 626-914-8613. *E-mail:* admissions@citruscollege.edu.

CITY COLLEGE OF SAN FRANCISCO

San Francisco, California **www.ccsf.edu/**

Freshman Application Contact Ms. Mary Lou Leyba-Frank, Dean of Admissions and Records, City College of San Francisco, 50 Phelan Avenue, San Francisco, CA 94112-1821. *Phone:* 415-239-3860. *Fax:* 415-239-3936. *E-mail:* mleyba@ccsf.edu.

COASTLINE COMMUNITY COLLEGE

Fountain Valley, California **coastline.cccd.edu/**

- **State and locally supported** 2-year, founded 1976, part of Coast Community College District System
- **Urban** campus with easy access to Los Angeles
- **Coed**

Academics *Calendar:* semesters. *Degree:* certificates and associate. *Special study options:* academic remediation for entering students, adult/continuing education programs, advanced placement credit, cooperative education, distance learning, English as a second language, external degree program, internships, part-time degree program, services for LD students, summer session for credit.

Student Life *Campus security:* 24-hour emergency response devices.

Financial Aid Of all full-time matriculated undergraduates who enrolled in 2008, 20 Federal Work-Study jobs (averaging $4500).

Applying *Options:* early admission. *Recommended:* high school transcript.

Freshman Application Contact Jennifer McDonald, Director of Admissions and Records, Coastline Community College, 11460 Warner Avenue, Fountain Valley, CA 92708. *Phone:* 714-241-6163.

COLEMAN UNIVERSITY

San Marcos, California **www.coleman.edu/**

Director of Admissions Senior Admissions Officer, Coleman University, 1284 West San Marcos Boulevard, San Marcos, CA 92078. *Phone:* 760-747-3990. *Fax:* 760-752-9808.

COLLEGE OF ALAMEDA

Alameda, California **www.peralta.cc.ca.us/**

Freshman Application Contact Ms. Barbara Simmons, District Admissions Officer, College of Alameda, 555 Ralph Appezzato Memorial Parkway, Alameda, CA 94501-2109. *Phone:* 510-466-7370. *E-mail:* hperdue@peralta.cc.ca.us.

COLLEGE OF MARIN

Kentfield, California **www.marin.edu/**

Freshman Application Contact Ms. Gina Longo, Administrative Assistant to the Dean of Enrollment Services, College of Marin, 835 College Avenue, Kentfield, CA 94904. *Phone:* 415-485-9417. *Fax:* 415-460-0773. *E-mail:* gina.longo@marin.edu.

COLLEGE OF SAN MATEO

San Mateo, California **www.collegeofsanmateo.edu/**

Director of Admissions Mr. Henry Villareal, Dean of Admissions and Records, College of San Mateo, 1700 West Hillsdale Boulevard, San Mateo, CA 94402-3784. *Phone:* 650-574-6594. *E-mail:* csmadmission@smcccd.cc.ca.us.

COLLEGE OF THE CANYONS

Santa Clarita, California **www.canyons.edu/**

- **State and locally supported** 2-year, founded 1969, part of California Community College System
- **Suburban** 224-acre campus with easy access to Los Angeles
- **Coed;** 23,416 undergraduate students

Undergraduates 4% are from out of state, 6% African American, 10% Asian American or Pacific Islander, 27% Hispanic American, 0.6% Native American, 0.6% international. *Retention:* 64% of 2008 full-time freshmen returned.

Faculty *Total:* 617, 27% full-time. *Student/faculty ratio:* 36:1.

Majors Accounting; administrative assistant and secretarial science; animation, interactive technology, video graphics and special effects; architectural drafting and CAD/CADD; art; athletic training; automobile/automotive mechanics technology; biology/biological sciences; building/construction site management; business administration and management; child development; cinematography and film/video production; computer science; computer systems networking and telecommunications; criminal justice/law enforcement administration; digital communication and media/multimedia; dramatic/theater arts; engineering; English; fire science; French; graphic design; health and physical education; hospitality administration; hotel/motel administration; humanities; interior design; intermedia/multimedia; journalism; landscaping and groundskeeping; legal assistant/paralegal; liberal arts and sciences/liberal studies; library assistant; manufacturing technology; mathematics; multi/interdisciplinary studies related; music; nursing (registered nurse training); parks, recreation and leisure; photography; psychology; radio and television; real estate; restaurant, culinary, and catering management; sales, distribution and marketing; sign language interpretation and translation; small business administration; social sciences; sociology; Spanish; special education (early childhood); survey technology; water quality and wastewater treatment management and recycling technology; welding technology.

Academics *Calendar:* semesters. *Degree:* certificates and associate. *Special study options:* academic remediation for entering students, adult/continuing education programs, advanced placement credit, cooperative education, distance learning, double majors, English as a second language, honors programs, independent study, internships, off-campus study, part-time degree program, services for LD students, study abroad, summer session for credit.

Library College of the Canyons Library with 57,433 titles, 150 serial subscriptions, 9,109 audiovisual materials, an OPAC, a Web page.

Student Life *Housing:* college housing not available. *Activities and Organizations:* drama/theater group, choral group, Phi Theta Kappa, National Student Nurses Association, Future Educators Club, COC Ice Hockey Club, Grace on Campus. *Campus security:* 24-hour emergency response devices, late-night transport/escort service. *Student services:* health clinic, personal/psychological counseling.

Athletics *Intercollegiate sports:* baseball M, basketball M/W, cross-country running M/W, football M, golf M/W, ice hockey M(c), soccer M/W, softball W, swimming and diving M/W, track and field M/W, volleyball W.

Costs (2010–11) *Tuition:* state resident $0 full-time; nonresident $5142 full-time, $180 per unit part-time. *Required fees:* $774 full-time, $26 per unit part-time.

Applying *Options:* electronic application, early admission. *Recommended:* high school transcript. *Application deadlines:* rolling (freshmen), rolling (transfers). *Notification:* continuous (freshmen), continuous (transfers).

Freshman Application Contact Ms. Jasmine Ruys, Director, Admissions and Records and Online Services, College of the Canyons, 26455 Rockwell Canyon Road, Santa Clara, CA 91355. *Phone:* 661-362-3280. *Toll-free phone:* 888-206-7827. *Fax:* 661-254-7996. *E-mail:* jasmine.ruys@canyons.edu.

College of the Desert

Palm Desert, California **desert.cc.ca.us/**

Freshman Application Contact Ms. Kathi Westerfield, Registrar, College of the Desert, 43-500 Monterey Avenue, Palm Desert, CA 92260-9305. *Phone:* 760-773-2519.

►**See Display below.**

College of the Redwoods

Eureka, California **www.redwoods.edu/**

Freshman Application Contact Kathy Goodlive, Director of Enrollment Management, College of the Redwoods, 7351 Tompkins Hill Road, Eureka, CA 95501-9300. *Phone:* 707-476-4168. *Toll-free phone:* 800-641-0400.

College of the Sequoias

Visalia, California **www.cos.edu/**

- **State and locally supported** 2-year, founded 1925, part of California Community College System
- **Small-town** 215-acre campus with easy access to Fresno
- **Endowment** $3.0 million
- **Coed**

Undergraduates 5,147 full-time, 8,302 part-time. Students come from 15 states and territories, 6 other countries, 0.1% are from out of state, 4% African American, 4% Asian American or Pacific Islander, 47% Hispanic American, 1% Native American, 0.1% international, 53% transferred in.

Faculty *Student/faculty ratio:* 27:1.

Academics *Calendar:* semesters. *Degree:* certificates and associate. *Special study options:* academic remediation for entering students, accelerated degree program, adult/continuing education programs, advanced placement credit, cooperative education, distance learning, double majors, English as a second language, freshman honors college, honors programs, internships, off-campus study, part-time degree program, services for LD students, study abroad, summer session for credit. *ROTC:* Air Force (c).

Student Life *Campus security:* 24-hour emergency response devices and patrols, student patrols, late-night transport/escort service, 18 hour patrols by trained security personnel.

Athletics Member NJCAA.

Costs (2009–10) *Tuition:* state resident $0 full-time; nonresident $5352 full-time, $223 per unit part-time. Full-time tuition and fees vary according to course load. Part-time tuition and fees vary according to course load. *Required fees:* $658 full-time, $26 per unit part-time, $34 per term part-time.

Applying *Required:* high school transcript.

Freshman Application Contact Ms. Lisa Hott, Director for Admissions, College of the Sequoias, 915 South Mooney Boulevard, Visalia, CA 93277-2234. *Phone:* 559-737-4844. *Fax:* 559-737-4820.

College of the Siskiyous

Weed, California **www.siskiyous.edu/**

Freshman Application Contact Ms. Christina Bruck, Recruitment and Outreach Coordinator, College of the Siskiyous, 800 College Avenue, Weed, CA 96094. *Phone:* 530-938-5847. *Toll-free phone:* 888-397-4339 Ext. 5847.

Columbia College

Sonora, California **www.gocolumbia.org/**

Freshman Application Contact Dr. Kathleen Smith, Director Student Success/ Matriculation, Columbia College, Columbia College, 11600 Columbia College Drive, Sonora, CA 95370. *Phone:* 209-588-5234. *Fax:* 209-588-5337. *E-mail:* smithk@yosemite.edu.

Community Christian College

Redlands, California www.cccollege.edu/

Freshman Application Contact Ruth Pena, Admissions Counselor, Community Christian College, 251 Tennessee Street, Redlands, CA 92373. *Phone:* 909-335-8863.

Concorde Career College

Garden Grove, California www.concorde.edu/

Freshman Application Contact Admissions Office, Concorde Career College, 12951 Euclid Street, Suite 101, Garden Grove, CA 92840-9201.

Concorde Career Institute

North Hollywood, California www.concordecareercolleges.com/

Freshman Application Contact Admissions Office, Concorde Career Institute, 12412 Victory Boulevard, North Hollywood, CA 91606.

Contra Costa College

San Pablo, California www.contracosta.edu/

Freshman Application Contact Ken Blustajn, Admissions and Records Manager, Contra Costa College, 2600 Mission Bell Drive, San Pablo, CA 94806-3195. *Phone:* 510-235-7800.

Copper Mountain College

Joshua Tree, California www.cmccd.edu/

- **State-supported** 2-year, founded 1966
- **Coed**

Academics *Calendar:* semesters. *Degree:* certificates and associate.

Freshman Application Contact Dr. Laraine Turk, Associate Dean of Student Services, Copper Mountain College, 6162 Rotary Way, Joshua Tree, CA 92252. *Phone:* 760-366-5290.

Cosumnes River College

Sacramento, California www.crc.losrios.edu/

Freshman Application Contact Ms. Dianna L. Moore, Supervisor of Admissions Records, Cosumnes River College, 8401 Center Parkway, Sacramento, CA 95823-5799. *Phone:* 916-688-7423.

Crafton Hills College

Yucaipa, California www.craftonhills.edu/

Director of Admissions Mr. Joe Caabrales, Director of Admissions, Crafton Hills College, 11711 Sand Canyon Road, Yucaipa, CA 92399. *Phone:* 909-389-3355.

Crimson Technical College

Inglewood, California www.crimsontechnicalcollege.com/

Freshman Application Contact Admissions Office, Crimson Technical College, 8911 Aviation Boulevard, Inglewood, CA 90301. *Phone:* 866-451-0818. *Toll-free phone:* 866-451-0818.

Cuesta College

San Luis Obispo, California www.cuesta.edu/

Freshman Application Contact Ms. Juileta Siu, Admissions Clerk, Cuesta College, PO Box 8106, Highway 1, San Luis Obispo, CA 93403-8106. *Phone:* 805-546-3140. *E-mail:* jsiu@cuesta.edu.

Cuyamaca College

El Cajon, California www.cuyamaca.net/

- **State-supported** 2-year, founded 1978, part of Grossmont-Cuyamaca Community College District
- **Suburban** 165-acre campus with easy access to San Diego
- **Coed,** 7,706 undergraduate students, 21% full-time, 56% women, 44% men

Undergraduates 1,636 full-time, 6,070 part-time. Students come from 8 other countries, 7% African American, 7% Asian American or Pacific Islander, 22% Hispanic American, 1% Native American, 0.4% international.

Freshmen *Admission:* 1,789 enrolled.

Faculty *Total:* 645, 13% full-time, 3% with terminal degrees.

Majors Accounting; accounting technology and bookkeeping; automobile/automotive mechanics technology; biological and physical sciences; business administration and management; business/commerce; chemistry; child development; commercial and advertising art; drafting and design technology; drafting/design engineering technologies related; drawing; elementary education; English; entrepreneurship; environmental engineering technology; general studies; history; information science/studies; landscaping and groundskeeping; legal assistant/paralegal; liberal arts and sciences/liberal studies; occupational safety and health technology; office management; ornamental horticulture; painting; physics; plant nursery management; real estate; special products marketing; speech and rhetoric; survey technology; turf and turfgrass management.

Academics *Calendar:* semesters. *Degree:* certificates, diplomas, and associate. *Special study options:* academic remediation for entering students, adult/continuing education programs, advanced placement credit, cooperative education, distance learning, double majors, English as a second language, honors programs, internships, off-campus study, part-time degree program, services for LD students, student-designed majors, study abroad, summer session for credit. *ROTC:* Army (c), Air Force (c).

Library Library plus 1 other with 81,304 titles, 72 serial subscriptions, 2,068 audiovisual materials, an OPAC, a Web page.

Student Life *Housing:* college housing not available. *Activities and Organizations:* drama/theater group, student-run newspaper. *Campus security:* 24-hour emergency response devices and patrols, late-night transport/escort service. *Student services:* health clinic, personal/psychological counseling.

Athletics *Intercollegiate sports:* basketball M/W, cross-country running M/W, golf M, soccer M/W, tennis W, track and field M/W, volleyball W.

Costs (2009–10) *Tuition:* state resident $0 full-time; nonresident $5700 full-time, $190 per unit part-time. Full-time tuition and fees vary according to course load. Part-time tuition and fees vary according to course load. *Required fees:* $820 full-time, $26 per unit part-time, $20 per term part-time. *Payment plan:* deferred payment. *Waivers:* employees or children of employees.

Financial Aid Of all full-time matriculated undergraduates who enrolled in 2008, 42 Federal Work-Study jobs (averaging $2700). 51 state and other part-time jobs (averaging $1100).

Applying *Options:* electronic application, early admission. *Application deadlines:* rolling (freshmen), rolling (transfers).

Freshman Application Contact Ms. Susan Topham, Dean of Admissions and Records, Cuyamaca College, 900 Rancho San Diego Parkway, El Cajon, CA 92019-4304. *Phone:* 619-660-4302. *Fax:* 619-660-4575. *E-mail:* susan.topham@gcccd.edu.

Cypress College

Cypress, California www.cypress.cc.ca.us/

Director of Admissions Mr. David Wassenaar, Dean of Admissions and Records, Cypress College, 9200 Valley View, Cypress, CA 90630. *Phone:* 714-484-7435. *E-mail:* dwassenaar@cypresscollege.edu.

DE ANZA COLLEGE

Cupertino, California www.deanza.fhda.edu/

Director of Admissions Ms. Kathleen Moberg, Director of Records and Admissions, De Anza College, 21250 Stevens Creek Boulevard, Cupertino, CA 95014. *Phone:* 408-864-8292. *E-mail:* webregda@mercury.fhda.edu.

DEEP SPRINGS COLLEGE

Deep Springs, California www.deepsprings.edu/

- **Independent** 2-year, founded 1917
- **Rural** 3000-acre campus
- **Endowment** $10.6 million
- **Men only,** 24 undergraduate students, 100% full-time

Undergraduates 24 full-time. Students come from 13 states and territories, 1 other country, 80% are from out of state, 8% African American, 4% Asian American or Pacific Islander, 4% international, 100% live on campus. *Retention:* 92% of 2008 full-time freshmen returned.

Freshmen *Admission:* 144 applied, 12 admitted, 24 enrolled. *Average high school GPA:* 3.87. *Test scores:* SAT verbal scores over 500: 100%; SAT math scores over 500: 100%; SAT writing scores over 500: 100%; SAT verbal scores over 600: 100%; SAT math scores over 600: 95%; SAT writing scores over 600: 100%; SAT verbal scores over 700: 95%; SAT math scores over 700: 80%; SAT writing scores over 700: 60%.

Faculty *Total:* 7, 57% full-time, 71% with terminal degrees. *Student/faculty ratio:* 4:1.

Majors Liberal arts and sciences/liberal studies.

Academics *Calendar:* 6 seven-week terms. *Degree:* associate. *Special study options:* accelerated degree program, cooperative education, freshman honors college, honors programs, independent study, internships, student-designed majors, summer session for credit.

Library Mossner Library of Deep Springs with 20,000 titles, 60 serial subscriptions, an OPAC, a Web page.

Student Life *Housing:* on-campus residence required through sophomore year. *Options:* men-only. Campus housing is university owned. Freshman campus housing is guaranteed. *Activities and Organizations:* drama/theater group, choral group, Student Self-Government, Labor Program, Applications Committee, Review Committee, Curriculum Committee. *Student services:* personal/psychological counseling, legal services.

Athletics *Intramural sports:* basketball M, cross-country running M, equestrian sports M, football M, riflery M, rock climbing M, soccer M, swimming and diving M, table tennis M, ultimate Frisbee M, water polo M, weight lifting M.

Standardized Tests *Required:* SAT and SAT Subject Tests or ACT (for admission).

Costs (2009–10) *Tuition:* All students receive full scholarship covering tuition, room, and board valued at $52,000.

Applying *Required:* essay or personal statement, high school transcript, interview. *Application deadlines:* 11/15 (freshmen), 11/15 (transfers). *Notification:* 4/15 (freshmen), 4/15 (transfers).

Freshman Application Contact David Neidorf, President, Deep Springs College, HC 72, Box 45001, Dyer, NV 89010-9803. *Phone:* 760-872-2000. *Fax:* 760-872-4466. *E-mail:* apcom@deepsprings.edu.

DIABLO VALLEY COLLEGE

Pleasant Hill, California www.dvc.edu/

- **State and locally supported** 2-year, founded 1949, part of Contra Costa Community College District
- **Suburban** 100-acre campus with easy access to San Francisco
- **Coed,** 22,567 undergraduate students, 33% full-time, 52% women, 48% men

Undergraduates 7,340 full-time, 15,227 part-time. Students come from 16 states and territories, 68 other countries, 0.2% are from out of state, 5% African American, 15% Asian American or Pacific Islander, 12% Hispanic American, 0.6% Native American. *Retention:* 61% of 2008 full-time freshmen returned.

Faculty *Total:* 805, 32% full-time. *Student/faculty ratio:* 17:1.

Majors Atmospheric sciences and meteorology; electrical/electronics equipment installation and repair; English; geography; humanities; liberal arts and sciences/liberal studies; political science and government; psychology.

Academics *Calendar:* semesters. *Degree:* certificates and associate. *Special study options:* academic remediation for entering students, adult/continuing education programs, advanced placement credit, cooperative education, part-time degree program, services for LD students, student-designed majors, study abroad, summer session for credit. *ROTC:* Air Force (c).

Library Diablo Valley College Library with 88,286 titles, 298 serial subscriptions.

Student Life *Housing:* college housing not available. *Activities and Organizations:* drama/theater group, student-run newspaper, choral group. *Campus security:* 24-hour emergency response devices and patrols, student patrols. *Student services:* women's center.

Athletics *Intercollegiate sports:* basketball M/W, cross-country running M/W, football M, soccer W, softball W, swimming and diving M/W, tennis M/W, track and field M/W, volleyball W, water polo M/W.

Costs (2010–11) *Tuition:* state resident $0 full-time; nonresident $4440 full-time, $185 per unit part-time. *Required fees:* $634 full-time, $26 per unit part-time.

Financial Aid Of all full-time matriculated undergraduates who enrolled in 2008, 67 Federal Work-Study jobs (averaging $3000). *Financial aid deadline:* 5/23.

Applying *Options:* early admission. *Recommended:* high school transcript. *Application deadlines:* 8/15 (freshmen), rolling (transfers).

Freshman Application Contact Ileana Dorn, Director of Admissions and Records, Diablo Valley College, 321 Golf Club Road, Pleasant Hill, CA 94523-1529. *Phone:* 925-685-1230 Ext. 2330. *Fax:* 925-609-8085. *E-mail:* idorn@dvc.edu.

EAST LOS ANGELES COLLEGE

Monterey Park, California www.elac.edu/

- **State and locally supported** 2-year, founded 1945, part of Los Angeles Community College District System
- **Urban** 84-acre campus with easy access to Los Angeles
- **Coed,** 30,149 undergraduate students, 29% full-time, 60% women, 40% men

Undergraduates 8,640 full-time, 21,509 part-time. Students come from 15 states and territories, 1% are from out of state, 2% African American, 10% Asian American or Pacific Islander, 48% Hispanic American, 0.5% Native American, 9% international.

Freshmen *Admission:* 2,485 enrolled.

Faculty *Total:* 1,028, 21% full-time. *Student/faculty ratio:* 44:1.

Majors Accounting; administrative assistant and secretarial science; anthropology; architectural engineering technology; art; Asian studies; automobile/automotive mechanics technology; biology/biological sciences; business administration and management; chemistry; child development; civil engineering technology; computer engineering technology; computer programming; counselor education/school counseling and guidance; criminal justice/law enforcement administration; criminal justice/police science; data processing and data processing technology; developmental and child psychology; drafting and design technology; dramatic/theater arts; electrical, electronic and communications engineering technology; emergency medical technology (EMT paramedic); engineering; English; environmental studies; family and consumer sciences/human sciences; finance; fire science; French; geography; geology/earth science; health information/medical records administration; Hispanic American, Puerto Rican, and Mexican American/Chicano studies; history; Japanese; journalism; legal administrative assistant/secretary; liberal arts and sciences/liberal studies; marketing/marketing management; mathematics; medical administrative assistant and medical secretary; medical/clinical assistant; music; nursing (registered nurse training); philosophy; photography; physical education teaching and coaching; political science and government; pre-engineering; psychology; public administration; real estate; respiratory care therapy; social work; sociology; Spanish; speech and rhetoric; trade and industrial teacher education.

Academics *Calendar:* semesters. *Degree:* certificates and associate. *Special study options:* academic remediation for entering students, accelerated degree program, adult/continuing education programs, advanced placement credit, cooperative education, distance learning, double majors, English as a second language, freshman honors college, honors programs, independent study, off-campus study, part-time degree program, services for LD students, student-designed majors, study abroad, summer session for credit.

Library ELAC Helen Miller Bailey Library plus 2 others with 102,000 titles, 228 serial subscriptions, an OPAC, a Web page.

Student Life *Housing:* college housing not available. *Activities and Organizations:* drama/theater group, student-run newspaper, choral group, marching band, Administration of Justice, American Society of Engineers and Architects, Society of Hispanic Professional Engineers, MENTE, Asian Student Intercultural Association (A.S.I.A) and the International Student Club, Chicano/Community for Creative Medicine, Science Associations, Advocates and Educators for Young Children, Child Development Club. *Campus security:* 24-hour emergency response devices and patrols, late-night transport/escort service, Los Angeles County Sheriff Sub-station. *Student services:* health clinic, personal/psychological counseling.

East Los Angeles College (continued)

Athletics *Intercollegiate sports:* baseball M, basketball M/W, cheerleading W, cross-country running M/W, football M, soccer M/W, softball W, track and field M/W, volleyball W, wrestling M.

Standardized Tests *Required:* mathematics and English placement tests, international students require TOEFL score of 450, CBT score 133, IBT score 45 or highe (for admission).

Costs (2010–11) *Tuition:* state resident $0 full-time; nonresident $5790 full-time, $193 per unit part-time. No tuition increase for student's term of enrollment. *Required fees:* $780 full-time, $26 per unit part-time.

Financial Aid Of all full-time matriculated undergraduates who enrolled in 2008, 189 Federal Work-Study jobs (averaging $3000).

Applying *Options:* electronic application, early admission. *Recommended:* high school transcript, English and mathematics placement test. *Application deadline:* rolling (freshmen). *Notification:* continuous until 9/2 (freshmen).

Freshman Application Contact Mr. Jeremy Allred, Associate Dean of Admissions, East Los Angeles College, 1301 Avenida Cesar Chavez, Monterey Park, CA 91754-6001. *Phone:* 323-265-8801. *Fax:* 323-265-8688. *E-mail:* allredjp@elac.edu.

El Camino College

Torrance, California www.elcamino.edu/

Director of Admissions Mr. William Mulrooney, Director of Admissions, El Camino College, 16007 Crenshaw Boulevard, Torrence, CA 90506. *Phone:* 310-660-3418. *Toll-free phone:* 866-ELCAMINO. *Fax:* 310-660-6779. *E-mail:* wmulrooney@elcamino.edu.

Empire College

Santa Rosa, California www.empcol.com/

- **Proprietary** 2-year, founded 1961
- **Suburban** campus with easy access to San Francisco
- **Coed**

Academics *Calendar:* continuous. *Degree:* certificates, diplomas, and associate. *Special study options:* double majors.

Student Life *Campus security:* 24-hour emergency response devices.

Standardized Tests *Required:* Wonderlic aptitude test (for admission).

Financial Aid Of all full-time matriculated undergraduates who enrolled in 2008, 15 Federal Work-Study jobs (averaging $1500).

Applying *Application fee:* $75. *Required:* high school transcript, interview. *Required for some:* essay or personal statement.

Freshman Application Contact Ms. Dahnja Barker, Admissions Officer, Empire College, 3035 Cleveland Avenue, Santa Rosa, CA 95403. *Phone:* 707-546-4000.

Everest College

City of Industry, California www.everest.edu/

Freshman Application Contact Admissions Office, Everest College, 12801 Crossroads Parkway South, City of Industry, CA 91746-1023. *Phone:* 562-908-2500. *Toll-free phone:* 888-741-4270. *Fax:* 562-908-7656.

Everest College

Ontario, California www.everest.edu/campus/ontario/

Freshman Application Contact Admissions Office, Everest College, 1819 South Excise Avenue, Ontario, CA 91761.

Everest College

Rancho Cucamonga, California www.everest-college.com/

Admissions Office Contact Everest College, 9616 Archibald Avenue, Suite 100, Rancho Cucamonga, CA 91730.

Everest Institute

Long Beach, California www.everest.edu/

Admissions Office Contact Everest Institute, 2161 Technology Place, Long Beach, CA 90810.

Evergreen Valley College

San Jose, California www.evc.edu/

Freshman Application Contact Ms. Cindy Tayag, Admissions and Records, Evergreen Valley College, 3095 Yerba Buena Road, San Jose, CA 95135-1598. *Phone:* 408-274-7900 Ext. 6443. *Fax:* 408-223-9351.

Fashion Careers College

San Diego, California www.fashioncareerscollege.com/

- **Proprietary** 2-year, founded 1979
- **Urban** campus with easy access to San Diego
- **Coed, primarily women,** 91 undergraduate students, 100% full-time, 88% women, 12% men

Undergraduates 91 full-time. Students come from 18 states and territories, 2 other countries, 20% are from out of state.

Freshmen *Admission:* 28 enrolled.

Faculty *Total:* 9, 11% full-time.

Majors Fashion/apparel design; fashion merchandising.

Academics *Calendar:* quarters. *Degree:* certificates and associate. *Special study options:* adult/continuing education programs, cooperative education, double majors, internships.

Library Fashion Careers of California Library with 800 titles, 14 serial subscriptions, 175 audiovisual materials.

Student Life *Housing:* college housing not available. *Campus security:* 24-hour emergency response devices.

Standardized Tests *Required:* Wonderlic aptitude test (for admission).

Costs (2010–11) *Tuition:* $19,900 full-time. Full-time tuition and fees vary according to class time, course load, degree level, and program. *Required fees:* $525 full-time. *Payment plan:* installment.

Financial Aid Of all full-time matriculated undergraduates who enrolled in 2008, 10 Federal Work-Study jobs (averaging $1760).

Applying *Options:* electronic application. *Application fee:* $25. *Required:* essay or personal statement, high school transcript, interview. *Application deadlines:* rolling (freshmen), rolling (out-of-state freshmen), rolling (transfers). *Notification:* continuous (freshmen), continuous (out-of-state freshmen), continuous (transfers).

Freshman Application Contact Ms. Ronny Catarcio, Admissions Advisory, Fashion Careers College, 1923 Morena Boulevard, San Diego, CA 92110. *Phone:* 619-275-4700 Ext. 328. *Toll-free phone:* 888-FCCC999. *Fax:* 619-275-0635. *E-mail:* ronny@fashioncareerscollege.com.

Feather River College

Quincy, California www.frc.edu/

Freshman Application Contact Ms. Karen Sue Hayden, Registrar, Feather River College, 570 Golden Eagle Avenue, Quincy, CA 95971. *Phone:* 530-283-0202 Ext. 285. *Toll-free phone:* 800-442-9799 Ext. 286. *Fax:* 530-283-9961. *E-mail:* info@frc.edu.

FIDM/The Fashion Institute of Design & Merchandising, Los Angeles Campus

Los Angeles, California www.fidm.edu/

- **Proprietary** primarily 2-year, founded 1969, part of The Fashion Institute of Design and Merehandising/FIDM
- **Urban** campus
- **Coed,** 4,562 undergraduate students, 88% full-time, 90% women, 10% men

Undergraduates 4,013 full-time, 549 part-time. Students come from 41 states and territories, 9 other countries, 38% are from out of state, 5% African American, 13% Asian American or Pacific Islander, 20% Hispanic American, 0.7% Native American, 8% international. *Retention:* 69% of 2008 full-time freshmen returned.

Freshmen *Admission:* 2,887 applied, 2,044 admitted. *Average high school GPA:* 2.75.

Faculty *Total:* 317, 21% full-time. *Student/faculty ratio:* 17:1.

Majors Apparel and accessories marketing; apparel and textiles; business administration and management; commercial and advertising art; consumer merchandising/retailing management; design and visual communications; fashion/apparel design; fashion merchandising; interior design; metal and jewelry arts.

Academics *Calendar:* quarters. *Degrees:* associate and bachelor's (also includes Orange County Campus). *Special study options:* academic remediation for entering students, adult/continuing education programs, advanced placement credit, cooperative education, distance learning, English as a second language, independent study, internships, part-time degree program, services for LD students, study abroad, summer session for credit.

Library FIDM Los Angeles Campus Library with 24,564 titles, 280 serial subscriptions, 5,298 audiovisual materials, an OPAC.

Student Life *Activities and Organizations:* student-run newspaper, ASID (student chapter), Design Council, Phi Theta Kappa Honor Society, Student Council, MODE. *Campus security:* 24-hour emergency response devices and patrols, late-night transport/escort service. *Student services:* personal/psychological counseling.

Standardized Tests *Recommended:* SAT or ACT (for admission).

Costs (2009–10) *Tuition:* Full-time tuition and fees vary according to program. Part-time tuition and fees vary according to program. No tuition increase for student's term of enrollment. *Room and board:* room only: $3250. *Payment plans:* tuition prepayment, installment. *Waivers:* employees or children of employees.

Financial Aid Of all full-time matriculated undergraduates who enrolled in 2008, 88 Federal Work-Study jobs (averaging $2935).

Applying *Options:* electronic application, deferred entrance. *Application fee:* $225. *Required:* essay or personal statement, high school transcript, minimum 2 GPA, 3 letters of recommendation, interview, major-determined project. *Application deadlines:* rolling (freshmen), rolling (out-of-state freshmen), rolling (transfers).

Freshman Application Contact Ms. Susan Aronson, Director of Admissions, FIDM/The Fashion Institute of Design & Merchandising, Los Angeles Campus, FIDM LA, 919 South Grand Avenue, Los Angeles, CA 90015. *Phone:* 213-624-1201. *Toll-free phone:* 800-624-1200. *Fax:* 213-624-4799. *E-mail:* saronson@fidm.com.

▶**See page 454 for the College Close-Up.**

FIDM/The Fashion Institute of Design & Merchandising, Orange County Campus

Irvine, California **www.fidm.com/**

Freshman Application Contact Admissions, FIDM/The Fashion Institute of Design & Merchandising, Orange County Campus, 17590 Gillette Avenue, Irvine, CA 92614. *Phone:* 949-851-6200. *Toll-free phone:* 888-974-3436. *Fax:* 949-851-6808.

FIDM/The Fashion Institute of Design & Merchandising, San Diego Campus

San Diego, California **www.fidm.com/**

- **Proprietary** 2-year, founded 1985, part of The Fashion Institute of Design and Merchandising/FIDM San Diego
- **Urban** campus
- **Coed, primarily women,** 287 undergraduate students, 91% full-time, 93% women, 7% men

Undergraduates 262 full-time, 25 part-time. Students come from 41 states and territories, 9 other countries, 18% are from out of state, 3% African American, 9% Asian American or Pacific Islander, 25% Hispanic American, 1% Native American, 2% international. *Retention:* 73% of 2008 full-time freshmen returned.

Freshmen *Admission:* 215 applied, 127 admitted. *Average high school GPA:* 2.75. *Test scores:* ACT scores over 18: 100%; ACT scores over 24: 40%; ACT scores over 30: 10%.

Faculty *Total:* 19, 16% full-time. *Student/faculty ratio:* 18:1.

Majors Apparel and accessories marketing; commercial and advertising art; consumer merchandising/retailing management; design and visual communications; fashion/apparel design; fashion merchandising; interior design.

Academics *Calendar:* quarters. *Degree:* associate. *Special study options:* academic remediation for entering students, adult/continuing education programs, advanced placement credit, cooperative education, distance learning, English as a second language, independent study, internships, part-time degree program, services for LD students, study abroad, summer session for credit.

Library FIDM San Diego Campus Library with 4,777 titles, 143 serial subscriptions, 1,808 audiovisual materials, an OPAC.

Student Life *Activities and Organizations:* Student Council, Phi Theta Kappa. *Campus security:* 24-hour emergency response devices and patrols. *Student services:* personal/psychological counseling.

Standardized Tests *Recommended:* SAT or ACT (for admission).

Costs (2009–10) *Tuition:* Full-time tuition and fees vary according to program. Part-time tuition and fees vary according to program. No tuition increase for student's term of enrollment. *Room and board:* room only: $3250. *Payment plans:* tuition prepayment, installment. *Waivers:* employees or children of employees.

Applying *Options:* electronic application, deferred entrance. *Application fee:* $225. *Required:* essay or personal statement, high school transcript, minimum 2 GPA, 3 letters of recommendation, interview, major-determined project. *Application deadlines:* rolling (freshmen), rolling (out-of-state freshmen), rolling (transfers).

Freshman Application Contact Ms. Susan Aronson, Director of Admissions, FIDM/The Fashion Institute of Design & Merchandising, San Diego Campus, FIDM San Diego, 1010 2nd Avenue, San Diego, CA 92101. *Phone:* 213-624-1200 Ext. 5400. *Toll-free phone:* 800-243-3436. *Fax:* 619-232-4322. *E-mail:* info@fidm.com.

FIDM/The Fashion Institute of Design & Merchandising, San Francisco Campus

San Francisco, California **www.fidm.edu/**

- **Proprietary** 2-year, founded 1973, part of The Fashion Institute of Design and Merchandising/FIDM
- **Urban** campus
- **Coed,** 921 undergraduate students

Undergraduates Students come from 41 states and territories, 8% are from out of state, 5% African American, 19% Asian American or Pacific Islander, 20% Hispanic American, 0.3% Native American, 3% international. *Retention:* 67% of 2008 full-time freshmen returned.

Freshmen *Admission:* 345 applied, 210 admitted. *Average high school GPA:* 2.75. *Test scores:* ACT scores over 18: 100%; ACT scores over 24: 40%; ACT scores over 30: 10%.

Faculty *Total:* 73, 12% full-time. *Student/faculty ratio:* 16:1.

Majors Apparel and accessories marketing; apparel and textiles; commercial and advertising art; consumer merchandising/retailing management; design and visual communications; fashion/apparel design; fashion merchandising; interior design.

Academics *Calendar:* quarters. *Degree:* associate. *Special study options:* academic remediation for entering students, adult/continuing education programs, advanced placement credit, cooperative education, distance learning, English as a second language, honors programs, independent study, internships, off-campus study, part-time degree program, services for LD students, study abroad, summer session for credit.

Library FIDM San Francisco Library with 6,928 titles, 281 serial subscriptions, 2,287 audiovisual materials, an OPAC.

Student Life *Housing:* college housing not available. *Activities and Organizations:* ASID (student chapter), Student Council, Premiere Marketing Group, Phi Theta Kappa. *Campus security:* 24-hour emergency response devices and patrols. *Student services:* personal/psychological counseling.

Standardized Tests *Recommended:* SAT or ACT (for admission).

Applying *Options:* electronic application, deferred entrance. *Application fee:* $225. *Required:* essay or personal statement, high school transcript, 3 letters of recommendation, interview, major-determined project. *Application deadlines:* rolling (freshmen), rolling (out-of-state freshmen), rolling (transfers).

Freshman Application Contact Ms. Susan Aronson, Director of Admissions, FIDM/The Fashion Institute of Design & Merchandising, San Francisco Cam-

FIDM/The Fashion Institute of Design & Merchandising, San Francisco Campus (continued)

pus, 55 Stockton Street, San Francisco, CA 94108. *Phone:* 213-624-1201. *Toll-free phone:* 800-711-7175. *Fax:* 415-296-7299. *E-mail:* info@fidm.com.

FOLSOM LAKE COLLEGE

Folsom, California **www.flc.losrios.edu/**

- **State-supported** 2-year, founded 2004, part of Los Rios Community College District System
- **Suburban** campus with easy access to Sacramento
- **Coed,** 9,352 undergraduate students

Faculty *Total:* 295, 37% full-time. *Student/faculty ratio:* 32:1.
Majors Accounting; art; biology/biological sciences; business administration and management; communication and journalism related; computer and information sciences; criminal justice/law enforcement administration; early childhood education; education; English; finance; geology/earth science; human services; interdisciplinary studies; liberal arts and sciences/liberal studies; marketing/marketing management; mathematics; physical sciences related; psychology; real estate; social sciences.
Academics *Degree:* certificates, diplomas, and associate. *Special study options:* academic remediation for entering students, advanced placement credit, cooperative education, distance learning, English as a second language, independent study, internships, services for LD students, study abroad, summer session for credit.
Library Library with 26,100 titles, 62 serial subscriptions, 5 audiovisual materials, an OPAC, a Web page.
Student Life *Housing:* college housing not available. *Activities and Organizations:* drama/theater group, choral group. *Campus security:* 24-hour emergency response devices and patrols, late-night transport/escort service. *Student services:* health clinic, personal/psychological counseling.
Costs (2010–11) *Tuition:* state resident $0 full-time; nonresident $4560 full-time, $190 per unit part-time. *Required fees:* $624 full-time, $26 per unit part-time. *Payment plan:* installment.
Applying *Options:* electronic application. *Recommended:* high school transcript. *Application deadlines:* rolling (freshmen), rolling (transfers).
Freshman Application Contact Admissions Office, Folsom Lake College, 10 College Parkway, Folsom, CA 95630. *Phone:* 916-608-6500.

FOOTHILL COLLEGE

Los Altos Hills, California **www.foothill.edu/**

Freshman Application Contact Ms. Penny Johnson, Dean, Counseling and Student Services, Foothill College, Admissions and Records, 12345 El Monte Road, Los Altos Hills, CA 94022. *Phone:* 650-949-7326. *Fax:* 650-949-7375.

FRESNO CITY COLLEGE

Fresno, California **www.fresnocitycollege.edu/**

Freshman Application Contact Ms. Stephanie Pauhi, Office Assistant, Fresno City College, 1101 East University Avenue, Fresno, CA 93741. *Phone:* 559-442-8225. *Toll-free phone:* 866-245-3276.

FULLERTON COLLEGE

Fullerton, California **www.fullcoll.edu/**

Director of Admissions Mr. Peter Fong, Dean of Admissions and Records, Fullerton College, 321 East Chapman Avenue, Fullerton, CA 92832-2095. *Phone:* 714-992-7582.

GAVILAN COLLEGE

Gilroy, California **www.gavilan.edu/**

Freshman Application Contact Ms. Joy Parker, Director of Admissions, Gavilan College, 5055 Santa Teresa Boulevard, Gilroy, CA 95020. *Phone:* 408-848-4735. *Fax:* 408-846-4940.

GLENDALE COMMUNITY COLLEGE

Glendale, California **www.glendale.edu/**

Freshman Application Contact Ms. Sharon Combs, Dean, Admissions, and Records, Glendale Community College, 1500 North Verdugo Road, Glendale, CA 91208. *Phone:* 818-551-5115. *Fax:* 818-551-5255. *E-mail:* scombs@glendale.edu.

GOLDEN WEST COLLEGE

Huntington Beach, California **www.gwc.cccd.edu/**

- **State and locally supported** 2-year, founded 1966, part of Coast Community College District System
- **Suburban** 122-acre campus with easy access to Los Angeles
- **Endowment** $880,684
- **Coed,** 13,226 undergraduate students, 32% full-time, 54% women, 46% men

Undergraduates 4,291 full-time, 8,935 part-time. Students come from 28 other countries.
Faculty *Total:* 410, 40% full-time. *Student/faculty ratio:* 34:1.
Majors Accounting; administrative assistant and secretarial science; architectural engineering technology; art; automobile/automotive mechanics technology; biological and physical sciences; biology/biological sciences; business administration and management; commercial and advertising art; consumer merchandising/retailing management; cosmetology; criminal justice/law enforcement administration; criminal justice/police science; drafting and design technology; electrical, electronic and communications engineering technology; engineering technology; graphic and printing equipment operation/production; humanities; journalism; legal administrative assistant/secretary; liberal arts and sciences/liberal studies; marketing/marketing management; mathematics; music; natural sciences; nursing (registered nurse training); ornamental horticulture; physical sciences; radio and television; real estate; sign language interpretation and translation.
Academics *Calendar:* semesters (summer session). *Degree:* certificates and associate. *Special study options:* academic remediation for entering students, adult/continuing education programs, advanced placement credit, cooperative education, distance learning, English as a second language, external degree program, honors programs, independent study, internships, part-time degree program, services for LD students, student-designed majors, study abroad, summer session for credit. *ROTC:* Air Force (c).
Library Golden West College Library plus 1 other with 95,000 titles, 410 serial subscriptions, an OPAC, a Web page.
Student Life *Housing:* college housing not available. *Activities and Organizations:* drama/theater group, student-run newspaper, choral group. *Campus security:* 24-hour emergency response devices and patrols, late-night transport/escort service. *Student services:* health clinic, personal/psychological counseling, legal services.
Athletics Member NJCAA. *Intercollegiate sports:* baseball M, cross-country running M/W, football M, soccer M/W, softball W, swimming and diving M/W, track and field M/W, volleyball M/W, water polo M/W.
Costs (2009–10) *Tuition:* state resident $0 full-time; nonresident $4940 full-time, $190 per unit part-time. *Required fees:* $800 full-time, $26 per unit part-time, $30 per term part-time.
Applying *Options:* early admission. *Required for some:* essay or personal statement. *Recommended:* high school transcript. *Application deadlines:* rolling (freshmen), rolling (transfers). *Notification:* continuous (freshmen), continuous (transfers).
Freshman Application Contact Golden West College, 15744 Golden West Street, PO Box 2748, Huntington Beach, CA 92647. *Phone:* 714-892-7711 Ext. 58196.

GROSSMONT COLLEGE

El Cajon, California **www.grossmont.edu/**

Freshman Application Contact Ms. Sharon Clark, Registrar, Grossmont College, 8800 Grossmont College Drive, El Cajon, CA 92020-1799. *Phone:* 619-644-7170.

HARTNELL COLLEGE

Salinas, California **www.hartnell.edu/**

Director of Admissions Ms. Mary Dominguez, Director of Admissions, Hartnell College, 156 Homestead Avenue, Salinas, CA 93901-1697. *Phone:* 831-755-6711.

Heald College–Concord

Concord, California **www.heald.edu/**

Freshman Application Contact Keith Woodman, Director of Admissions, Heald College–Concord, 5130 Commercial Circle, Concord, CA 94520. *Phone:* 925-288-5800. *Toll-free phone:* 800-755-3550. *Fax:* 925-288-5896. *E-mail:* kwoodman@heald.edu.

Heald College–Fresno

Fresno, California **www.heald.edu/**

Freshman Application Contact Ms. Tina Mathis, Director of Admissions, Heald College–Fresno, 255 West Bullard Avenue, Fresno, CA 93704-1706. *Phone:* 559-438-4222. *Toll-free phone:* 800-755-3550. *E-mail:* tmathis@heald.edu.

Heald College–Hayward

Hayward, California **www.heald.edu/**

Freshman Application Contact Mrs. Barbara Gordon, Director of Admissions, Heald College–Hayward, 25500 Industrial Boulevard, Hayward, CA 94545. *Phone:* 510-783-2100. *Toll-free phone:* 800-755-3550. *Fax:* 510-783-3287. *E-mail:* bgordon@heald.edu.

Heald College–Rancho Cordova

Rancho Cordova, California **www.heald.edu/**

Freshman Application Contact Director of Admissions, Heald College–Rancho Cordova, 2910 Prospect Park Drive, Rancho Cordova, CA 95670-6005. *Phone:* 916-638-1616. *Toll-free phone:* 800-755-3550. *Fax:* 916-853-8282. *E-mail:* info@heald.edu.

Heald College–Roseville

Roseville, California **www.heald.edu/**

Freshman Application Contact Kristi Culpepper, Director of Admissions, Heald College–Roseville, 7 Sierra Gate Plaza, Roseville, CA 95678. *Phone:* 916-789-8600. *Toll-free phone:* 800-755-3550. *E-mail:* kculpepp@heald.edu.

Heald College–Salinas

Salinas, California **www.heald.edu/**

Freshman Application Contact Mr. Jason Ferguson, Director of Admissions, Heald College–Salinas, 1450 North Main Street, Salinas, CA 93906. *Phone:* 831-443-1700. *Toll-free phone:* 800-755-3550. *Fax:* 831-443-1050. *E-mail:* jferguso@heald.edu.

Heald College–San Francisco

San Francisco, California **www.heald.edu/**

Freshman Application Contact Ms. Jennifer Dunckel, Director of Admissions, Heald College–San Francisco, 350 Mission Street, San Francisco, CA 94105. *Phone:* 415-808-3000. *Toll-free phone:* 800-755-3550. *Fax:* 415-808-3003. *E-mail:* jennifer_dunckel@heald.edu.

Heald College–San Jose

Milpitas, California **www.heald.edu/**

Freshman Application Contact Clarence Hardiman, Director of Admissions, Heald College–San Jose, 341 Great Mall Parkway, Milpitas, CA 95035. *Phone:* 408-934-4900. *Toll-free phone:* 800-755-3550. *Fax:* 408-934-7777. *E-mail:* chardima@heald.edu.

Heald College–Stockton

Stockton, California **www.heald.edu/**

Freshman Application Contact Director of Admissions, Heald College–Stockton, 1605 East March Lane, Stockton, CA 95210. *Phone:* 209-473-5200. *Toll-free phone:* 800-755-3550. *Fax:* 209-477-2739. *E-mail:* info@heald.edu.

High-Tech Institute

Sacramento, California **www.high-techinstitute.com/**

Freshman Application Contact Admissions Office, High-Tech Institute, 9738 Lincoln Village Drive, Suite 100, Sacramento, CA 95827. *Phone:* 916-929-9700. *Toll-free phone:* 800-322-4128.

Imperial Valley College

Imperial, California **www.imperial.cc.ca.us/**

Director of Admissions Dawn Chun, Associate Dean of Admissions and Records, Imperial Valley College, 380 East Aten Road, PO Box 158, Imperial, CA 92251. *Phone:* 760-352-8320 Ext. 200.

Irvine Valley College

Irvine, California **www.ivc.edu/**

Director of Admissions Mr. John Edwards, Director of Admissions, Records and Enrollment Services, Irvine Valley College, 5500 Irvine Center Drive, Irvine, CA 92618. *Phone:* 949-451-5416.

ITT Technical Institute

Anaheim, California **www.itt-tech.edu/**

- **Proprietary** primarily 2-year, founded 1982, part of ITT Educational Services, Inc.
- **Suburban** campus
- **Coed**

Majors Animation, interactive technology, video graphics and special effects; business administration and management; CAD/CADD drafting/design technology; computer systems networking and telecommunications; construction management; criminal justice/law enforcement administration; design and visual communications; electrical, electronic and communications engineering technology; health information/medical records technology; legal assistant/paralegal; system, networking, and LAN/WAN management.

Academics *Calendar:* quarters. *Degrees:* associate and bachelor's.

Student Life *Housing:* college housing not available.

Financial Aid Of all full-time matriculated undergraduates who enrolled in 2008, 20 Federal Work-Study jobs (averaging $5000).

Freshman Application Contact Director of Recruitment, ITT Technical Institute, 525 North Muller Avenue, Anaheim, CA 92801. *Phone:* 714-535-3700. *Fax:* 714-535-1802.

ITT Technical Institute

Lathrop, California www.itt-tech.edu/

- **Proprietary** primarily 2-year, founded 1997, part of ITT Educational Services, Inc.
- **Coed**

Majors Animation, interactive technology, video graphics and special effects; business administration and management; CAD/CADD drafting/design technology; computer and information systems security; computer engineering technology; computer systems networking and telecommunications; construction management; criminal justice/law enforcement administration; design and visual communications; electrical, electronic and communications engineering technology; legal assistant/paralegal; system, networking, and LAN/WAN management; web page, digital/multimedia and information resources design.

Academics *Calendar:* quarters. *Degrees:* associate and bachelor's.

Student Life *Housing:* college housing not available.

Freshman Application Contact Director of Recruitment, ITT Technical Institute, 16916 South Harlan Road, Lathrop, CA 95330. *Phone:* 209-858-0077. *Toll-free phone:* 800-346-1786.

ITT Technical Institute

Oxnard, California www.itt-tech.edu/

- **Proprietary** primarily 2-year, founded 1993, part of ITT Educational Services, Inc.
- **Urban** campus
- **Coed**

Majors Animation, interactive technology, video graphics and special effects; CAD/CADD drafting/design technology; computer and information systems security; computer engineering technology; construction management; criminal justice/law enforcement administration; design and visual communications; electrical, electronic and communications engineering technology; health information/medical records technology; legal assistant/paralegal; system, networking, and LAN/WAN management.

Academics *Calendar:* quarters. *Degrees:* associate and bachelor's.

Student Life *Housing:* college housing not available.

Freshman Application Contact Director of Recruitment, ITT Technical Institute, 2051 Solar Drive, Building B, Oxnard, CA 93036. *Phone:* 805-988-0143. *Toll-free phone:* 800-530-1582.

ITT Technical Institute

Rancho Cordova, California www.itt-tech.edu/

- **Proprietary** primarily 2-year, founded 1954, part of ITT Educational Services, Inc.
- **Urban** campus
- **Coed**

Majors Animation, interactive technology, video graphics and special effects; business administration and management; CAD/CADD drafting/design technology; computer and information systems security; computer engineering technology; computer systems networking and telecommunications; construction management; criminal justice/law enforcement administration; design and visual communications; electrical, electronic and communications engineering technology; legal assistant/paralegal; system, networking, and LAN/WAN management; web page, digital/multimedia and information resources design.

Academics *Calendar:* quarters. *Degrees:* associate and bachelor's.

Student Life *Housing:* college housing not available.

Freshman Application Contact Director of Recruitment, ITT Technical Institute, 10863 Gold Center Drive, Rancho Cordova, CA 95670-6034. *Phone:* 916-851-3900. *Toll-free phone:* 800-488-8466.

ITT Technical Institute

San Bernardino, California www.itt-tech.edu/

- **Proprietary** primarily 2-year, founded 1987, part of ITT Educational Services, Inc.
- **Urban** campus
- **Coed**

Majors Animation, interactive technology, video graphics and special effects; business administration and management; CAD/CADD drafting/design technology; computer and information systems security; computer engineering technology; computer software and media applications related; construction management; criminal justice/law enforcement administration; design and visual communications; electrical, electronic and communications engineering technology; health information/medical records technology; legal assistant/paralegal; system, networking, and LAN/WAN management; web page, digital/multimedia and information resources design.

Academics *Calendar:* quarters. *Degrees:* associate and bachelor's.

Student Life *Housing:* college housing not available.

Freshman Application Contact Director of Recruitment, ITT Technical Institute, 670 East Carnegie Drive, San Bernardino, CA 92408. *Phone:* 909-806-4600. *Toll-free phone:* 800-888-3801.

ITT Technical Institute

San Diego, California www.itt-tech.edu/

- **Proprietary** primarily 2-year, founded 1981, part of ITT Educational Services, Inc.
- **Suburban** campus
- **Coed**

Majors Animation, interactive technology, video graphics and special effects; business administration and management; CAD/CADD drafting/design technology; computer and information systems security; computer engineering technology; computer software engineering; construction management; criminal justice/law enforcement administration; design and visual communications; electrical, electronic and communications engineering technology; legal assistant/paralegal; system, networking, and LAN/WAN management; web page, digital/multimedia and information resources design.

Academics *Calendar:* quarters. *Degrees:* associate and bachelor's.

Student Life *Housing:* college housing not available.

Freshman Application Contact Director of Recruitment, ITT Technical Institute, 9680 Granite Ridge Drive, San Diego, CA 92123. *Phone:* 858-571-8500. *Toll-free phone:* 800-883-0380.

ITT Technical Institute

San Dimas, California www.itt-tech.edu/

- **Proprietary** primarily 2-year, founded 1982, part of ITT Educational Services, Inc.
- **Suburban** campus
- **Coed**

Majors Animation, interactive technology, video graphics and special effects; business administration and management; CAD/CADD drafting/design technology; computer and information systems security; computer engineering technology; construction management; criminal justice/law enforcement administration; design and visual communications; electrical, electronic and communications engineering technology; health information/medical records technology; industrial technology; legal assistant/paralegal; system, networking, and LAN/WAN management; web page, digital/multimedia and information resources design.

Academics *Calendar:* quarters. *Degrees:* associate and bachelor's.

Student Life *Housing:* college housing not available.

Financial Aid Of all full-time matriculated undergraduates who enrolled in 2008, 20 Federal Work-Study jobs (averaging $4500).

Freshman Application Contact Director of Recruitment, ITT Technical Institute, 650 West Cienega Avenue, San Dimas, CA 91773. *Phone:* 909-971-2300. *Toll-free phone:* 800-414-6522.

ITT Technical Institute

Sylmar, California www.itt-tech.edu/

- **Proprietary** primarily 2-year, founded 1982, part of ITT Educational Services, Inc.
- **Urban** campus
- **Coed**

Majors Animation, interactive technology, video graphics and special effects; business administration and management; CAD/CADD drafting/design technology; computer and information systems security; computer engineering technology; construction management; criminal justice/law enforcement administration; design and visual communications; electrical, electronic and communications engineering technology; health information/medical records technology; legal assistant/paralegal; system, networking, and LAN/WAN management; web page, digital/multimedia and information resources design.

Academics *Calendar:* quarters. *Degrees:* associate and bachelor's.

Student Life *Housing:* college housing not available.

Freshman Application Contact Director of Recruitment, ITT Technical Institute, 12669 Encinitas Avenue, Sylmar, CA 91342. *Phone:* 818-364-5151. *Toll-free phone:* 800-363-2086.

ITT Technical Institute

Torrance, California **www.itt-tech.edu/**

- **Proprietary** primarily 2-year, founded 1987, part of ITT Educational Services, Inc.
- **Urban** campus
- **Coed**

Majors Animation, interactive technology, video graphics and special effects; business administration and management; CAD/CADD drafting/design technology; computer and information systems security; computer engineering technology; computer software engineering; computer systems networking and telecommunications; construction management; criminal justice/law enforcement administration; design and visual communications; electrical, electronic and communications engineering technology; health information/medical records technology; legal assistant/paralegal; system, networking, and LAN/WAN management; web page, digital/multimedia and information resources design.

Academics *Calendar:* quarters. *Degrees:* associate and bachelor's.

Student Life *Housing:* college housing not available.

Financial Aid Of all full-time matriculated undergraduates who enrolled in 2008, 6 Federal Work-Study jobs (averaging $4000).

Freshman Application Contact Director of Recruitment, ITT Technical Institute, 20050 South Vermont Avenue, Torrance, CA 90502. *Phone:* 310-380-1555.

Kaplan College, Bakersfield Campus

Bakersfield, California **www.kc-bakersfield.com/**

- **Proprietary** 2-year
- **Coed**

Academics *Degree:* certificates, diplomas, and associate.

Freshman Application Contact Kaplan College, Bakersfield Campus, 1914 Wible Road, Bakersfield, CA 93304. *Phone:* 661-836-6300.

Kaplan College, Chula Vista Campus

Chula Vista, California **www.kc-chulavista.com/**

- **Proprietary** 2-year
- **Coed**

Freshman Application Contact Kaplan College, Chula Vista Campus, 555 Broadway, Chula Vista, CA 91910. *Phone:* 877-473-3052. *Toll-free phone:* 887-473-3052.

Kaplan College, Fresno Campus

Clovis, California **www.kc-fresno.com/**

- **Proprietary** 2-year
- **Coed**

Freshman Application Contact Kaplan College, Fresno Campus, 44 Shaw Avenue, Rodeo Plaza Shopping Center, Clovis, CA 93612. *Phone:* 559-325-5100. *Toll-free phone:* 800-526-0256.

Kaplan College, Modesto Campus

Salida, California **www.kc-modesto.com/**

- **Proprietary** 2-year
- **Coed, primarily women**

Majors Criminal justice/safety; respiratory therapy technician.

Academics *Calendar:* semesters. *Degree:* diplomas and associate.

Freshman Application Contact Kaplan College, Modesto Campus, 5172 Kiernan Court, Salida, CA 95368. *Phone:* 209-543-7000. *Toll-free phone:* 800-526-0256.

Kaplan College, Palm Springs Campus

Palm Springs, California **www.kc-palmsprings.com/**

- **Proprietary** 2-year
- **Coed**

Academics *Degree:* diplomas and associate.

Freshman Application Contact Kaplan College, Palm Springs Campus, 2475 East Tahquitz Canyon Way, Palm Springs, CA 92262. *Phone:* 760-778-3540.

Kaplan College, Panorama City Campus

Panorama City, California **www.kc-panoramacity.com/**

- **Proprietary** 2-year, founded 1996
- **Coed**

Majors Business administration, management and operations related; computer and information sciences related; court reporting; legal assistant/paralegal.

Academics *Degree:* diplomas and associate.

Freshman Application Contact Kaplan College, Panorama City Campus, 14355 Roscoe Boulevard, Panorama City, PA 91402. *Phone:* 818-672-3005. *Toll-free phone:* 800-526-0256.

Kaplan College, Riverside Campus

Riverside, California **www.kc-riverside.com/**

- **Proprietary** 2-year
- **Coed**

Academics *Degree:* diplomas and associate.

Freshman Application Contact Kaplan College, Riverside Campus, 4040 Vine Street, Riverside, CA 92507. *Phone:* 951-276-1704.

Kaplan College, Sacramento Campus

Sacramento, California **www.kc-sacramento.com/**

- **Proprietary** 2-year
- **Coed**

Majors Corrections; interior design; legal assistant/paralegal.

Academics *Calendar:* semesters. *Degree:* diplomas and associate.

Freshman Application Contact Kaplan College, Sacramento Campus, 4330 Watt Avenue, Suite 400, Sacramento, CA 95821. *Phone:* 916-649-8168. *Toll-free phone:* 800-526-0256.

KAPLAN COLLEGE, SAN DIEGO CAMPUS

San Diego, California **www.kc-sandiego.com/**

- **Proprietary** 2-year, founded 1976
- **Urban** campus
- **Coed**

Majors Nursing (registered nurse training).

Academics *Calendar:* semesters. *Degrees:* certificates, diplomas, and associate (also includes Vista campus).

Freshman Application Contact Kaplan College, San Diego Campus, 9055 Balboa Avenue, San Diego, CA 92123. *Phone:* 858-279-4500. *Toll-free phone:* 800-526-0256.

KAPLAN COLLEGE, STOCKTON CAMPUS

Stockton, California **www.kc-stockton.com/**

- **Proprietary** 2-year
- **Coed**

Academics *Degree:* diplomas and associate.

Freshman Application Contact Kaplan College, Stockton Campus, 722 West March Lane, Stockton, CA 95207. *Phone:* 209-954-4208.

KAPLAN COLLEGE, VISTA CAMPUS

Vista, California **www.kc-vista.com/**

- **Proprietary** 2-year
- **Coed**

Academics *Degree:* diplomas and associate.

Freshman Application Contact Kaplan College, Vista Campus, 2022 University Drive, Vista, CA 92083. *Phone:* 760-630-1555.

LAKE TAHOE COMMUNITY COLLEGE

South Lake Tahoe, California **www.ltcc.edu/**

Freshman Application Contact Office of Admissions and Records, Lake Tahoe Community College, One College Drive, South Lake Tahoe, CA 96150-4524. *Phone:* 530-541-4660 Ext. 211. *Fax:* 530-541-7852. *E-mail:* admissions@ltcc.edu.

LANEY COLLEGE

Oakland, California **www.peralta.cc.ca.us/**

Freshman Application Contact Mrs. Barbara Simmons, District Admissions Officer, Laney College, 900 Fallon Street, Oakland, CA 94607-4893. *Phone:* 510-466-7369.

LAS POSITAS COLLEGE

Livermore, California **www.laspositascollege.edu/**

Director of Admissions Mrs. Sylvia R. Rodriguez, Director of Admissions and Records, Las Positas College, 3033 Collier Canyon Road, Livermore, CA 94551-7650. *Phone:* 925-373-4942.

LASSEN COMMUNITY COLLEGE DISTRICT

Susanville, California **www.lassencollege.edu/**

Freshman Application Contact Mr. Chris J. Alberico, Registrar, Lassen Community College District, Highway 139, PO Box 3000, Susanville, CA 96130. *Phone:* 530-257-6181.

LONG BEACH CITY COLLEGE

Long Beach, California **www.lbcc.edu/**

Director of Admissions Mr. Ross Miyashiro, Dean of Admissions and Records, Long Beach City College, 4901 East Carson Boulevard, Long Beach, CA 90808. *Phone:* 562-938-4130.

►See Display on page 89.

LOS ANGELES CITY COLLEGE

Los Angeles, California **www.lacitycollege.edu/**

Freshman Application Contact Elaine Geismar, Director of Student Assistance Center, Los Angeles City College, 855 North Vermont Avenue, Los Angeles, CA 90029. *Phone:* 323-953-4340.

LOS ANGELES COUNTY COLLEGE OF NURSING AND ALLIED HEALTH

Los Angeles, California **www.dhs.co.la.ca.us/wps/portal/collegeofnursing/**

Freshman Application Contact Admissions Office, Los Angeles County College of Nursing and Allied Health, 1237 North Mission Road, Los Angeles, CA 90033. *Phone:* 323-226-4911.

LOS ANGELES HARBOR COLLEGE

Wilmington, California **www.lahc.edu/**

- **State and locally supported** 2-year, founded 1949, part of Los Angeles Community College District System
- **Suburban** 80-acre campus with easy access to Los Angeles
- **Coed,** 10,083 undergraduate students, 28% full-time, 61% women, 39% men

Undergraduates 2,872 full-time, 7,211 part-time. Students come from 14 states and territories, 15 other countries, 14% African American, 18% Asian American or Pacific Islander, 43% Hispanic American, 0.5% Native American, 1% international.

Freshmen *Admission:* 1,511 enrolled. *Average high school GPA:* 2.5.

Faculty *Total:* 270, 41% full-time. *Student/faculty ratio:* 40:1.

Majors Accounting; administrative assistant and secretarial science; architectural engineering technology; automobile/automotive mechanics technology; biology/biological sciences; business administration and management; computer engineering technology; criminal justice/police science; data processing and data processing technology; developmental and child psychology; drafting and design technology; electrical, electronic and communications engineering technology; electromechanical technology; engineering technology; fire science; information science/studies; legal administrative assistant/secretary; liberal arts and sciences/liberal studies; medical administrative assistant and medical secretary; nursing (registered nurse training); physics; pre-engineering; real estate.

Academics *Calendar:* semesters. *Degree:* certificates and associate. *Special study options:* academic remediation for entering students, accelerated degree program, adult/continuing education programs, advanced placement credit, cooperative education, distance learning, double majors, English as a second language, freshman honors college, honors programs, independent study, off-campus study, part-time degree program, services for LD students, study abroad, summer session for credit.

Library Harbor College Library with 110,433 titles, 31 serial subscriptions, 77 audiovisual materials, an OPAC, a Web page.

Student Life *Housing:* college housing not available. *Activities and Organizations:* drama/theater group, student-run newspaper, television station, choral group, Alpha Gamma Sigma, EOP&S, Creando Un Nuevo Futuro, Psychology Club, Honors Transfer Program. *Campus security:* 24-hour emergency response devices and patrols, late-night transport/escort service. *Student services:* health clinic, personal/psychological counseling, legal services.

Athletics *Intercollegiate sports:* baseball M, basketball M, football M, soccer M/W, softball W, volleyball W.

Costs (2010–11) *Tuition:* state resident $0 full-time; nonresident $4512 full-time, $188 per unit part-time. *Required fees:* $646 full-time, $26 per unit part-time, $11 per term part-time.

Financial Aid Of all full-time matriculated undergraduates who enrolled in 2008, 100 Federal Work-Study jobs (averaging $1800).

Study in Long Beach, California

American Language and Cultural Institute (ALCI)

A year-round intensive English program offered in 9-week sessions, providing students the opportunity to acquire and improve English language skills through combinations of in-class instruction and explorations of American culture.

Why ALCI?

- Small class size (5-15 students)
- Personalized attention to overcome your particular linguistic challenge
- Gradual adaptation into American culture and college life
- Highly qualified & caring faculty
- No TOEFL or English exam requirement
- Open admission every three months
- Affordable tuition cost
- Smooth transfer to regular college upon completion

LONG BEACH
CITY COLLEGE

Long Beach City College

International Student Programs

College Profile

LBCC is a public, co-educational, comprehensive two-year institution offering wide range of university transfer programs, associate degrees, technical and vocational certificates, as well as English language training. Founded in 1927 and accredited by the Western Association of Schools and Colleges, the college operates on two campuses which have gone through major building expansions, renovation, and modernization to provide students with the most advanced academic and professional technology. A culturally diverse college, LBCC welcomes international students from around the globe who desire to grow, serve and succeed in their academic and professional life.

Our Location

LBCC is located in sunny Southern California, in the city of Long Beach, a modern urban center on the shore of the Pacific Ocean, with easy access to Los Angeles and minutes from the beautiful California beaches. The city of Long Beach has vibrant and active atmosphere with major sporting, cultural, musical and entertainment events throughout the year.

Key Fields of Study

Accounting • Administration of Justice • Aviation Technology
Business Administration • Computer Information System • Culinary Arts
Engineering • Fashion Design • Film/Radio/TV • Marketing
Music Production • Nursing

Complete list of majors available at ***http://osca.lbcc.edu/curriculumguides.cfm***

Why Study at LBCC?

- Low tuition cost
- State-of-the-art science & media labs and classrooms
- #1 transfers to California State University, Long Beach and other California universities
- Over 100 programs and majors to choose from
- Excellent student support services
- Dedicated professional counselors for immigration and academic issues
- Active International Student Club

Long Beach City College
International Student Programs
4901 East Carson Street - B9 • Long Beach, CA 90808
(562) 938-4745 • Fax (562) 938-4747
international@LBCC.edu • http://intl.LBCC.edu

Los Angeles Harbor College (continued)

Applying *Options:* electronic application, early admission, deferred entrance. *Application deadlines:* 9/3 (freshmen), 9/3 (out-of-state freshmen), 9/3 (transfers).

Freshman Application Contact Los Angeles Harbor College, 1111 Figueroa Place, Wilmington, CA 90744-2397. *Phone:* 310-233-4091.

Los Angeles Mission College

Sylmar, California **www.lamission.edu/**

Freshman Application Contact Ms. Angela Merrill, Admissions Supervisor, Los Angeles Mission College, 13356 Eldridge Avenue, Sylmar, CA 91342-3245. *Phone:* 818-364-7658.

Los Angeles Pierce College

Woodland Hills, California **www.lapc.cc.ca.us/**

Director of Admissions Ms. Shelley L. Gerstl, Dean of Admissions and Records, Los Angeles Pierce College, 6201 Winnetka Avenue, Woodland Hills, CA 91371-0001. *Phone:* 818-719-6448.

Los Angeles Southwest College

Los Angeles, California **www.lasc.edu/**

Director of Admissions Dan W. Walden, Dean of Academic Affairs, Los Angeles Southwest College, 1600 West Imperial Highway, Los Angeles, CA 90047-4810. *Phone:* 323-242-5511.

Los Angeles Trade-Technical College

Los Angeles, California **www.lattc.edu/**

Director of Admissions Dr. Raul Cardoza, Los Angeles Trade-Technical College, 400 West Washington Boulevard, Los Angeles, CA 90015. *Phone:* 213-763-5301. *E-mail:* CardozaRJ@lattc.edu.

Los Angeles Valley College

Van Nuys, California **www.lavc.cc.ca.us/**

- **State and locally supported** 2-year, founded 1949, part of Los Angeles Community College District System
- **Suburban** 105-acre campus
- **Coed**

Academics *Calendar:* semesters. *Degree:* certificates and associate. *Special study options:* academic remediation for entering students, adult/continuing education programs, cooperative education, distance learning, double majors, English as a second language, honors programs, independent study, internships, part-time degree program, services for LD students, student-designed majors, summer session for credit.

Student Life *Campus security:* 24-hour emergency response devices and patrols, student patrols, late-night transport/escort service.

Athletics Member NJCAA.

Financial Aid Of all full-time matriculated undergraduates who enrolled in 2008, 65 Federal Work-Study jobs (averaging $4000).

Applying *Options:* electronic application, early admission. *Recommended:* high school transcript.

Director of Admissions Mr. Florentino Manzano, Associate Dean, Los Angeles Valley College, 5800 Fulton Avenue, Valley Glen, CA 91401. *Phone:* 818-947-2353. *E-mail:* manzanf@lavc.edu.

Los Medanos College

Pittsburg, California **www.losmedanos.net/**

Freshman Application Contact Ms. Gail Newman, Director of Admissions and Records, Los Medanos College, 2700 East Leland Road, Pittsburg, CA 94565-5197. *Phone:* 925-439-2181 Ext. 7500.

Mendocino College

Ukiah, California **www.mendocino.edu/**

- **State and locally supported** 2-year, founded 1973, part of California Community College System
- **Rural** 127-acre campus
- **Coed,** 4,767 undergraduate students, 26% full-time, 63% women, 37% men

Undergraduates 1,247 full-time, 3,520 part-time. Students come from 16 states and territories, 2 other countries, 1% African American, 2% Asian American or Pacific Islander, 13% Hispanic American, 4% Native American, 3% international, 0.2% transferred in. *Retention:* 80% of 2008 full-time freshmen returned.

Freshmen *Admission:* 1,033 applied, 1,033 admitted, 521 enrolled.

Faculty *Total:* 305, 16% full-time, 3% with terminal degrees. *Student/faculty ratio:* 12:1.

Majors Accounting; administrative assistant and secretarial science; agriculture; art; automobile/automotive mechanics technology; biology/biological sciences; business administration and management; chemistry; child development; criminal justice/law enforcement administration; criminal justice/police science; data processing and data processing technology; developmental and child psychology; dramatic/theater arts; English; fiber, textile and weaving arts; finance; French; health professions related; human services; information science/studies; kindergarten/preschool education; liberal arts and sciences/liberal studies; mathematics; music; ornamental horticulture; physical education teaching and coaching; physical sciences; psychology; real estate; social sciences; Spanish; speech and rhetoric; substance abuse/addiction counseling.

Academics *Calendar:* semesters. *Degree:* certificates and associate. *Special study options:* academic remediation for entering students, adult/continuing education programs, advanced placement credit, cooperative education, distance learning, English as a second language, honors programs, independent study, internships, part-time degree program, services for LD students, summer session for credit.

Library Lowery Library with 27,441 titles, 275 serial subscriptions, a Web page.

Student Life *Housing:* college housing not available. *Activities and Organizations:* drama/theater group, student-run newspaper, radio station, choral group. *Campus security:* late-night transport/escort service, security patrols 6 pm to 10 pm.

Athletics Member NJCAA. *Intercollegiate sports:* baseball M, basketball M/W, football M, soccer W, volleyball W. *Intramural sports:* table tennis M/W, tennis M/W.

Costs (2010–11) *Tuition:* state resident $0 full-time; nonresident $5700 full-time, $190 per unit part-time. Full-time tuition and fees vary according to course load. Part-time tuition and fees vary according to course load. *Required fees:* $780 full-time, $26 per unit part-time.

Financial Aid *Financial aid deadline:* 5/20.

Applying *Options:* electronic application, early admission, deferred entrance. *Required:* high school transcript. *Application deadlines:* rolling (freshmen), rolling (transfers). *Notification:* continuous (freshmen), continuous (transfers).

Freshman Application Contact Mendocino College, 1000 Hensley Creek Road, Ukiah, CA 95482-0300. *Phone:* 707-468-3103.

Merced College

Merced, California **www.mccd.edu/**

Freshman Application Contact Ms. Cherie Davis, Associate Registrar, Merced College, 3600 M Street, Merced, CA 95348-2898. *Phone:* 209-384-6188. *Fax:* 209-384-6339.

Merritt College

Oakland, California **www.merritt.edu/**

- **State and locally supported** 2-year, founded 1953, part of Peralta Community College District System
- **Urban** 130-acre campus with easy access to San Francisco
- **Coed**

Academics *Calendar:* semesters. *Degree:* certificates and associate. *Special study options:* academic remediation for entering students, adult/continuing education programs, cooperative education, English as a second language, off-campus study, part-time degree program, services for LD students, summer session for credit.

Applying *Options:* early admission, deferred entrance.

Freshman Application Contact Ms. Barbara Simmons, District Admissions Officer, Merritt College, 12500 Campus Drive, Oakland, CA 94619-3196. *Phone:* 510-466-7369. *E-mail:* hperdue@peralta.cc.ca.us.

MiraCosta College

Oceanside, California **www.miracosta.edu/**

Freshman Application Contact Admissions and Records Assistant, MiraCosta College, One Barnard Drive, Oceanside, CA 92056. *Phone:* 760-795-6620. *Toll-free phone:* 888-201-8480.

Mission College

Santa Clara, California **www.missioncollege.org/**

Director of Admissions Daniel Sanidad, Dean of Student Services, Mission College, 3000 Mission College Boulevard, Santa Clara, CA 95054-1897. *Phone:* 408-855-5139.

Modesto Junior College

Modesto, California **www.mjc.edu/**

- **State and locally supported** 2-year, founded 1921, part of Yosemite Community College District System
- **Urban** 229-acre campus
- **Coed**

Undergraduates 6,874 full-time, 12,433 part-time. 3% African American, 7% Asian American or Pacific Islander, 28% Hispanic American, 1% Native American, 0.2% international, 4% transferred in. *Retention:* 73% of 2008 full-time freshmen returned.

Faculty *Student/faculty ratio:* 29:1.

Academics *Calendar:* semesters. *Degree:* certificates and associate. *Special study options:* academic remediation for entering students, adult/continuing education programs, advanced placement credit, cooperative education, distance learning, English as a second language, honors programs, independent study, part-time degree program, services for LD students, study abroad, summer session for credit.

Student Life *Campus security:* 24-hour emergency response devices and patrols, late-night transport/escort service.

Costs (2009–10) *Tuition:* state resident $0 full-time; nonresident $4868 full-time, $190 per unit part-time. *Required fees:* $722 full-time, $26 per unit part-time, $74 per year part-time.

Financial Aid Of all full-time matriculated undergraduates who enrolled in 2008, 152 Federal Work-Study jobs (averaging $2732). 62 state and other part-time jobs (averaging $1655).

Applying *Options:* electronic application. *Recommended:* high school transcript.

Freshman Application Contact Ms. Susie Agostini, Dean of Matriculation, Admissions, and Records, Modesto Junior College, 435 College Avenue, Modesto, CA 95350. *Phone:* 209-575-6470. *Fax:* 209-575-6859. *E-mail:* mjcadmissions@mail.yosemite.cc.ca.us.

Monterey Peninsula College

Monterey, California **www.mpc.edu/**

Director of Admissions Ms. Vera Coleman, Registrar, Monterey Peninsula College, 980 Fremont Street, Monterey, CA 93940. *Phone:* 831-646-4007. *E-mail:* vcoleman@mpc.edu.

Moorpark College

Moorpark, California **www.moorpark.cc.ca.us/**

Freshman Application Contact Ms. Katherine Colborn, Registrar, Moorpark College, 7075 Campus Road, Moorpark, CA 93021-2899. *Phone:* 805-378-1415.

Mt. San Antonio College

Walnut, California **www.mtsac.edu/**

- **District-supported** 2-year, founded 1946, part of California Community College System
- **Suburban** 421-acre campus with easy access to Los Angeles
- **Coed**

Undergraduates 9,827 full-time, 20,199 part-time. Students come from 51 states and territories, 6% African American, 24% Asian American or Pacific Islander, 45% Hispanic American, 0.5% Native American, 1% international.

Faculty *Student/faculty ratio:* 23:1.

Academics *Calendar:* semesters. *Degree:* certificates, diplomas, and associate. *Special study options:* academic remediation for entering students, adult/continuing education programs, advanced placement credit, cooperative education, distance learning, double majors, English as a second language, honors programs, independent study, part-time degree program, services for LD students, study abroad, summer session for credit. *ROTC:* Army (b), Air Force (b).

Student Life *Campus security:* 24-hour emergency response devices and patrols, late-night transport/escort service.

Costs (2009–10) *Tuition:* state resident $0 full-time; nonresident $4560 full-time. Full-time tuition and fees vary according to course load and program. Part-time tuition and fees vary according to course load and program. *Required fees:* $658 full-time.

Applying *Options:* electronic application, early admission, deferred entrance. *Required for some:* high school transcript.

Freshman Application Contact Dr. George Bradshaw, Dean of Enrollment Management, Mt. San Antonio College, 1100 North Grand Avenue, Walnut, CA 91789. *Phone:* 909-594-5611 Ext. 4505. *Toll-free phone:* 800-672-2463 Ext. 4415.

Mt. San Jacinto College

San Jacinto, California **www.msjc.edu/**

- **State and locally supported** 2-year, founded 1963, part of California Community College System
- **Suburban** 180-acre campus with easy access to San Diego
- **Coed,** 17,583 undergraduate students, 36% full-time, 59% women, 41% men

Undergraduates 6,356 full-time, 11,227 part-time. 8% African American, 7% Asian American or Pacific Islander, 30% Hispanic American, 1% Native American.

Majors Administrative assistant and secretarial science; adult development and aging; art; automobile/automotive mechanics technology; biological and physical sciences; business administration and management; child development; criminal justice/police science; dance; design and visual communications; diagnostic medical sonography and ultrasound technology; digital communication and media/multimedia; drafting and design technology; dramatic/theater arts; fire science; geography related; health and physical education; humanities; information technology; legal assistant/paralegal; liberal arts and sciences/liberal studies; mathematics; medical/clinical assistant; music; music management and merchandising; nursing (registered nurse training); photography; real estate; social sciences; substance abuse/addiction counseling; turf and turfgrass management; visual and performing arts; water quality and wastewater treatment management and recycling technology.

Academics *Calendar:* semesters. *Degree:* certificates, diplomas, and associate. *Special study options:* academic remediation for entering students, adult/continuing education programs, advanced placement credit, distance learning, double majors, English as a second language, honors programs, off-campus study, part-time degree program, services for LD students, study abroad, summer session for credit.

Library Milo P. Johnson Library plus 1 other with 28,000 titles, 330 serial subscriptions.

Student Life *Housing:* college housing not available. *Activities and Organizations:* drama/theater group. *Campus security:* part-time trained security personnel. *Student services:* personal/psychological counseling.

Athletics *Intercollegiate sports:* baseball M, basketball M/W, football M, golf M, soccer W, softball W, tennis M/W, volleyball W.

Financial Aid Of all full-time matriculated undergraduates who enrolled in 2008, 109 Federal Work-Study jobs (averaging $1114). 125 state and other part-time jobs (averaging $1000).

Applying *Options:* early admission. *Recommended:* high school transcript. *Application deadlines:* rolling (freshmen), rolling (transfers).

Freshman Application Contact Loomis, Mt. San Jacinto College, 1499 North State Street, San Jacinto, CA 92583-2399. *Phone:* 951-639-5212. *Toll-free phone:* 800-624-5561 Ext. 1410.

MTI College of Business & Technology

Sacramento, California **www.mticollege.com/**

Freshman Application Contact Ms. Marije Miller, Director of Admissions, MTI College of Business & Technology, 5221 Madison Avenue, Sacramento, CA 95841. *Phone:* 916-339-1500. *Fax:* 916-339-0305. *E-mail:* mmiller@mticollege.edu.

Napa Valley College

Napa, California **www.napavalley.edu/**

Director of Admissions Mr. Oscar De Haro, Vice President of Student Services, Napa Valley College, 2277 Napa-Vallejo Highway, Napa, CA 94558-6236. *Phone:* 707-253-3000. *E-mail:* odeharo@napavalley.edu.

National Polytechnic College of Science

Wilmington, California **www.natpoly.edu/**

- **Proprietary** 2-year
- **Suburban** 5-acre campus with easy access to Los Angeles
- **Coed, primarily men**

Academics *Calendar:* continuous. *Degree:* certificates and associate. *Special study options:* advanced placement credit, cooperative education, double majors, internships, off-campus study.

Student Life *Campus security:* 24-hour emergency response devices.

Financial Aid Of all full-time matriculated undergraduates who enrolled in 2008, 22 Federal Work-Study jobs (averaging $4000).

Applying *Options:* electronic application, deferred entrance. *Application fee:* $60. *Required:* essay or personal statement, high school transcript, interview, physical examination.

Director of Admissions Tony Rodriquez, Director of Admissions, National Polytechnic College of Science, 272 South Fries Avenue, Wilmington, CA 90744-6399. *Phone:* 310-834-2501 Ext. 237. *Toll-free phone:* 800-432-DIVE Ext. 237.

New York Film Academy

Los Angeles, California **www.nyfa.com/**

Freshman Application Contact Admissions Office, New York Film Academy, 3801 Barham Boulevard, Los Angeles, CA 90068. *Phone:* 818-733-2600. *Fax:* 818-733-4074. *E-mail:* studios@nyfa.edu.

Ohlone College

Fremont, California **www.ohlone.edu/**

Freshman Application Contact Christopher Williamson, Director of Admissions and Records, Ohlone College, 43600 Mission Boulevard, Fremont, CA 94539-5884. *Phone:* 510-659-6518. *Fax:* 510-659-7321. *E-mail:* cwilliamson@ohlone.edu.

Orange Coast College

Costa Mesa, California **www.orangecoastcollege.com/**

- **State and locally supported** 2-year, founded 1947, part of Coast Community College District System
- **Suburban** 162-acre campus with easy access to Los Angeles
- **Endowment** $10.0 million
- **Coed,** 24,742 undergraduate students, 40% full-time, 49% women, 51% men

Undergraduates 9,776 full-time, 14,966 part-time. Students come from 52 states and territories, 74 other countries, 3% are from out of state, 2% African American, 24% Asian American or Pacific Islander, 19% Hispanic American, 0.7% Native American, 3% international, 8% transferred in. *Retention:* 79% of 2008 full-time freshmen returned.

Freshmen *Admission:* 5,255 enrolled.

Faculty *Total:* 781, 37% full-time. *Student/faculty ratio:* 33:1.

Majors Accounting; administrative assistant and secretarial science; aeronautics/aviation/aerospace science and technology; airline pilot and flight crew; anthropology; architectural engineering technology; art; athletic training; avionics maintenance technology; behavioral sciences; biology/biological sciences; building/home/construction inspection; business administration and management; cardiovascular technology; chemistry; child-care and support services management; child-care provision; cinematography and film/video production; clinical laboratory science/medical technology; commercial and advertising art; communications technology; computer engineering technology; computer graphics; computer programming; computer programming (specific applications); computer typography and composition equipment operation; construction engineering technology; culinary arts; dance; data entry/microcomputer applications related; data processing and data processing technology; dental hygiene; dietetics; drafting and design technology; dramatic/theater arts; economics; electrical and power transmission installation; electrical, electronic and communications engineering technology; electrical/electronics equipment installation and repair; emergency medical technology (EMT paramedic); engineering; English; family and consumer economics related; family and consumer sciences/human sciences; fashion merchandising; film/cinema studies; food science; foods, nutrition, and wellness; food technology and processing; French; geography; geology/earth science; German; health professions related; heating, air conditioning, ventilation and refrigeration maintenance technology; history; horticultural science; hotel/motel administration; housing and human environments; human development and family studies; humanities; industrial design; industrial radiologic technology; information science/studies; interior design; journalism; kindergarten/preschool education; kinesiology and exercise science; legal administrative assistant/secretary; liberal arts and sciences/liberal studies; machine shop technology; machine tool technology; marine technology; marketing/marketing management; mass communication/media; mathematics; medical administrative assistant and medical secretary; medical/clinical assistant; music; musical instrument fabrication and repair; music management and merchandising; natural sciences; nuclear medical technology; ornamental horticulture; philosophy; photography; physical education teaching and coaching; physics; political science and government; religious studies; respiratory care therapy; restaurant, culinary, and catering management; retailing; selling skills and sales; social sciences; sociology; Spanish; special products marketing; welding technology; word processing.

Academics *Calendar:* semesters plus summer session. *Degree:* certificates and associate. *Special study options:* academic remediation for entering students, adult/continuing education programs, advanced placement credit, cooperative education, distance learning, double majors, English as a second language, external degree program, freshman honors college, honors programs, internships, off-campus study, part-time degree program, services for LD students, student-designed majors, study abroad, summer session for credit. *ROTC:* Army (c), Air Force (c).

Library Library with 112,018 titles, 271 serial subscriptions, 3,843 audiovisual materials, an OPAC, a Web page.

Student Life *Housing:* college housing not available. *Activities and Organizations:* drama/theater group, student-run newspaper, choral group, Vietnamese Student Association, International Club, Adventurist Souls, Muslim Student Association. *Campus security:* 24-hour emergency response devices and patrols, student patrols, late-night transport/escort service. *Student services:* health clinic, personal/psychological counseling, legal services.

Athletics *Intercollegiate sports:* baseball M, basketball M/W, bowling M(c)/W(c), crew M/W, cross-country running M/W, football M, golf M/W, soccer M/W, softball W, swimming and diving M/W, tennis M/W, track and field M/W, volleyball W, water polo M/W.

Costs (2010–11) *Tuition:* state resident $0 full-time; nonresident $5700 full-time, $190 per unit part-time. *Required fees:* $902 full-time, $26 per unit part-time.

Financial Aid Of all full-time matriculated undergraduates who enrolled in 2008, 108 Federal Work-Study jobs (averaging $3000). *Financial aid deadline:* 5/28.

Applying *Options:* electronic application. *Application deadlines:* rolling (freshmen), rolling (transfers). *Notification:* continuous (freshmen), continuous (transfers).

Freshman Application Contact Ms. Kristin Clark, Dean of Enrollment Services, Orange Coast College, 2701 Fairview Road, Costa Mesa, CA 92626. *Phone:* 714-432-5788. *Fax:* 714-432-5072. *E-mail:* kclark@occ.cccd.edu.

Oxnard College

Oxnard, California **www.oxnardcollege.edu/**

Freshman Application Contact Ms. Susan Cabral, Registrar, Oxnard College, 4000 South Rose Avenue, Oxnard, CA 93033-6699. *Phone:* 805-986-5843. *Fax:* 805-986-5943. *E-mail:* scabral@vcccd.edu.

Palomar College

San Marcos, California **www.palomar.edu/**

- **State and locally supported** 2-year, founded 1946, part of California Community College System
- **Suburban** 156-acre campus with easy access to San Diego
- **Coed**

Academics *Calendar:* semesters. *Degree:* certificates and associate. *Special study options:* academic remediation for entering students, advanced placement credit, cooperative education, distance learning, English as a second language, internships, part-time degree program, services for LD students, study abroad, summer session for credit.

Student Life *Campus security:* 24-hour patrols, student patrols, late-night transport/escort service.

Applying *Options:* electronic application.

Freshman Application Contact Mr. Herman Lee, Director of Enrollment Services, Palomar College, 1140 West Mission Road, San Marcos, CA 92069-1487. *Phone:* 760-744-1150 Ext. 2171. *Fax:* 760-744-2932. *E-mail:* admissions@palomar.edu.

Palo Verde College

Blythe, California **www.paloverde.edu/**

Freshman Application Contact Ms. Pat Koester, Vice President of Student Services, Palo Verde College, 1 College Drive, Blythe, CA 92225. *Phone:* 760-921-5409. *Fax:* 760-921-3608.

Pasadena City College

Pasadena, California **www.pasadena.edu/**

- **State and locally supported** 2-year, founded 1924, part of California Community College System
- **Urban** 55-acre campus with easy access to Los Angeles
- **Coed,** 29,000 undergraduate students, 93% full-time, 52% women, 41% men

Undergraduates 27,000 full-time.

Faculty *Total:* 1,325, 32% full-time. *Student/faculty ratio:* 20:1.

Majors Accounting; accounting technology and bookkeeping; administrative assistant and secretarial science; African American/Black studies; animation, interactive technology, video graphics and special effects; anthropology; architecture; art; art history, criticism and conservation; Asian American studies; audiology and speech-language pathology; automobile/automotive mechanics technology; biochemistry; bioethics/medical ethics; biological and physical sciences; biology/biological sciences; broadcast journalism; building/home/construction inspection; business administration and management; business automation/technology/data entry; chemical engineering; chemistry; child development; cinematography and film/video production; civil engineering; classics and languages, literatures and linguistics; communication/speech communication and rhetoric; computer/information technology services administration related; computer science; computer technology/computer systems technology; construction trades; cosmetology; cosmetology, barber/styling, and nail instruction; criminal justice/law enforcement administration; dance; data entry/microcomputer applications related; dental assisting; dental hygiene; dental laboratory technology; desktop publishing and digital imaging design; dietetics; digital communication and media/multimedia; drafting and design technology;

Pasadena City College (continued)

dramatic/theater arts; economics; electrical and electronic engineering technologies related; electrical, electronics and communications engineering; engineering technology; entrepreneurship; environmental science; European studies; fashion/apparel design; fashion merchandising; financial planning and services; fire protection and safety technology; food service and dining room management; graphic and printing equipment operation/production; graphic design; Hispanic American, Puerto Rican, and Mexican American/Chicano studies; history; hospitality administration; hotel/motel administration; humanities; industrial electronics technology; international business/trade/commerce; international/global studies; international relations and affairs; journalism; Latin American studies; legal assistant/paralegal; legal studies; liberal arts and sciences/liberal studies; library science related; machine shop technology; management science; marketing/marketing management; mathematics; mechanical engineering; medical/clinical assistant; medical insurance/medical billing; medical office assistant; music; nursing (licensed practical/vocational nurse training); nursing (registered nurse training); occupational therapy; philosophy; photography; photojournalism; physical education teaching and coaching; physical therapy; physician assistant; physics; platemaking/imaging; political science and government related; pre-dentistry studies; premedical studies; pre-pharmacy studies; pre-veterinary studies; psychology; public policy analysis; radio and television; radio and television broadcasting technology; radiologic technology/science; religious studies; retailing; sociology; Spanish; theater design and technology; tourism promotion; urban studies/affairs; welding technology.

Academics *Calendar:* semesters. *Degree:* certificates and associate. *Special study options:* academic remediation for entering students, adult/continuing education programs, advanced placement credit, English as a second language, honors programs, part-time degree program, services for LD students, student-designed majors, study abroad, summer session for credit.

Library Pasadena City College Library plus 1 other with 120,000 titles, 350 serial subscriptions, an OPAC.

Student Life *Housing:* college housing not available. *Campus security:* 24-hour emergency response devices and patrols, late-night transport/escort service, cadet patrols. *Student services:* health clinic, personal/psychological counseling.

Athletics *Intercollegiate sports:* baseball M, basketball M/W, cross-country running M/W, football M, soccer M/W, softball W, swimming and diving M/W, tennis M/W, track and field M/W, volleyball W, water polo M.

Costs (2009–10) *Tuition:* nonresident $190 per unit part-time. Full-time tuition and fees vary according to course load. Part-time tuition and fees vary according to course load. *Required fees:* $26 per unit part-time, $14 per term part-time. *Room and board:* Room and board charges vary according to housing facility.

Applying *Application deadlines:* rolling (freshmen), rolling (transfers). *Notification:* continuous (freshmen), continuous (transfers).

Freshman Application Contact Pasadena City College, 1570 East Colorado Boulevard, Pasadena, CA 91106. *Phone:* 626-585-7805. *Fax:* 626-585-7915.

PIMA MEDICAL INSTITUTE

Chula Vista, California **www.pmi.edu/**

- **Proprietary** 2-year, founded 1998, administratively affiliated with Vocational Training Institutes, Inc.
- **Urban** campus
- **Coed**

Academics *Calendar:* modular. *Degree:* certificates and associate. *Special study options:* cooperative education, internships.

Standardized Tests *Required:* Wonderlic Scholastic Level Exam (for admission).

Applying *Required:* high school transcript, interview.

Freshman Application Contact Admissions Office, Pima Medical Institute, Pima Medical Institute, 780 Bay Boulevard, Suite 101, Chula Vista, CA 91910. *Phone:* 619-425-3200. *Toll-free phone:* 888-898-9048.

PLATT COLLEGE

Cerritos, California **www.platt.edu/**

- **Proprietary** 2-year, founded 1879
- **Urban** campus with easy access to Los Angeles
- **Coed**

Faculty *Student/faculty ratio:* 12:1.

Academics *Calendar:* continuous. *Degree:* certificates, diplomas, and associate.

Standardized Tests *Required:* Wonderlic aptitude test (for admission).

Freshman Application Contact Ms. Ilene Holt, Dean of Student Services, Platt College, 10900 East 183rd Street, Suite 290, Cerritos, CA 90703-5342. *Phone:* 562-809-5100. *Toll-free phone:* 800-807-5288.

PLATT COLLEGE

Huntington Beach, California **www.plattcollege.edu/**

- **Proprietary** primarily 2-year, founded 1985
- **Urban** campus
- **Coed**

Academics *Calendar:* continuous. *Degrees:* certificates, diplomas, associate, and bachelor's. *Special study options:* accelerated degree program, adult/continuing education programs, summer session for credit.

Student Life *Campus security:* 24-hour emergency response devices.

Standardized Tests *Required:* CPAt (for admission).

Applying *Application fee:* $75. *Required:* essay or personal statement, high school transcript, interview.

Director of Admissions Ms. Lisa Rhodes, President, Platt College, 3901 MacArthur Boulevard, Suite 101, Newport Beach, CA 92660. *Phone:* 949-833-2300 Ext. 222. *Toll-free phone:* 888-866-6697 Ext. 230.

PLATT COLLEGE

Ontario, California **www.plattcollege.edu/**

- **Proprietary** primarily 2-year
- **Coed**

Academics *Calendar:* continuous. *Degrees:* certificates, diplomas, associate, and bachelor's. *Special study options:* academic remediation for entering students, accelerated degree program, honors programs, independent study, internships, summer session for credit.

Standardized Tests *Required:* CPAt (for admission).

Applying *Application fee:* $75. *Required:* essay or personal statement, interview.

Director of Admissions Ms. Jennifer Abandonato, Director of Admissions, Platt College, 3700 Inland Empire Boulevard, Ontario, CA 91764. *Phone:* 909-941-9410. *Toll-free phone:* 888-866-6697.

PLATT COLLEGE–LOS ANGELES

Alhambra, California **www.plattcollege.edu/**

- **Proprietary** 2-year, founded 1987
- **Suburban** campus
- **Coed**

Academics *Calendar:* continuous. *Degree:* certificates, diplomas, and associate. *Special study options:* academic remediation for entering students, accelerated degree program, internships, summer session for credit.

Student Life *Campus security:* parking lot security.

Standardized Tests *Required:* CPAt (for admission).

Applying *Application fee:* $75. *Required:* interview. *Required for some:* essay or personal statement.

Director of Admissions Mr. Detroit Whiteside, Director of Admissions, Platt College–Los Angeles, 7470 North Figueroa Street, Los Angeles, CA 90041-1717. *Phone:* 323-258-8050. *Toll-free phone:* 888-866-6697.

PORTERVILLE COLLEGE

Porterville, California **www.pc.cc.ca.us/**

Director of Admissions Ms. Judy Pope, Director of Admissions and Records/Registrar, Porterville College, 100 East College Avenue, Porterville, CA 93257-6058. *Phone:* 559-791-2222.

Professional Golfers Career College

Temecula, California www.golfcollege.edu/

Freshman Application Contact Mr. Mark Bland, Director of Admissions, Professional Golfers Career College, PO Box 892319, 261 Ynez Road, Temecula, CA 92589-2319. *Phone:* 951-719-2994. *Toll-free phone:* 800-877-4380. *Fax:* 951-719-1643. *E-mail:* Mark@golfcollege.edu.

Reedley College

Reedley, California www.reedleycollege.edu/

- **State and locally supported** 2-year, founded 1926, part of State Center Community College District System
- **Rural** 350-acre campus
- **Coed,** 11,782 undergraduate students, 38% full-time, 61% women, 39% men

Undergraduates 4,423 full-time, 7,359 part-time. Students come from 15 states and territories, 1% are from out of state.

Freshmen *Admission:* 1,224 applied, 1,224 admitted, 1,089 enrolled. *Average high school GPA:* 2.5.

Faculty *Total:* 534, 34% full-time. *Student/faculty ratio:* 14:1.

Majors Accounting; administrative assistant and secretarial science; agricultural business and management; agricultural mechanization related; agriculture; animal sciences; art; automobile/automotive mechanics technology; avionics maintenance technology; biology/biological sciences; business/commerce; child-care and support services management; commercial and advertising art; computer and information sciences; corrections and criminal justice related; criminal justice/police science; dental assisting; English; entrepreneurship; fine arts related; foreign languages and literatures; general studies; health and physical education; horticultural science; hospitality administration; information science/studies; liberal arts and sciences/liberal studies; machine tool technology; management science; mathematics; music performance; natural resources management; office occupations and clerical services; physical sciences; plant sciences; precision metal working related; social sciences; voice and opera; welding technology.

Academics *Calendar:* semesters. *Degree:* certificates, diplomas, and associate. *Special study options:* academic remediation for entering students, adult/continuing education programs, advanced placement credit, cooperative education, distance learning, English as a second language, freshman honors college, honors programs, independent study, part-time degree program, services for LD students, study abroad, summer session for credit. *ROTC:* Air Force (c).

Library Reedley College Library with 36,000 titles, 217 serial subscriptions, an OPAC.

Student Life *Housing Options:* coed. Campus housing is university owned. *Activities and Organizations:* drama/theater group, student-run newspaper, choral group. *Campus security:* 24-hour emergency response devices, late-night transport/escort service, 24-hour on-campus police dispatcher. *Student services:* personal/psychological counseling.

Athletics *Intercollegiate sports:* baseball M, basketball M/W, football M, golf M, softball W, tennis M/W, track and field M/W, volleyball W. *Intramural sports:* basketball M/W, football M/W, swimming and diving M/W, tennis M/W, track and field M/W, volleyball M/W.

Costs (2010–11) *Tuition:* state resident $0 full-time; nonresident $5700 full-time. *Required fees:* $1496 full-time. *Room and board:* $2502; room only: $1402.

Applying *Required:* high school transcript. *Application deadlines:* rolling (freshmen), rolling (transfers). *Notification:* continuous until 8/1 (freshmen), continuous until 8/1 (transfers).

Freshman Application Contact Admissions and Records Office, Reedley College, 995 North Reed Avenue, Reedley, CA 93654. *Phone:* 559-638-0323. *Fax:* 559-637-2523.

Rio Hondo College

Whittier, California www.rh.cc.ca.us/

Director of Admissions Ms. Judy G. Pearson, Director of Admissions and Records, Rio Hondo College, 3600 Workman Mill Road, Whittier, CA 90601-1699. *Phone:* 562-692-0921 Ext. 3153.

Riverside Community College District

Riverside, California www.rcc.edu/

Freshman Application Contact Ms. Lorraine Anderson, District Dean of Admissions and Records, Riverside Community College District, 4800 Magnolia Avenue, Riverside, CA 92506. *Phone:* 951-222-8600. *Fax:* 951-222-8037. *E-mail:* admissions@rcc.edu.

Sacramento City College

Sacramento, California www.scc.losrios.edu/

Director of Admissions Mr. Sam T. Sandusky, Dean, Student Services, Sacramento City College, 3835 Freeport Boulevard, Sacramento, CA 95822-1386. *Phone:* 916-558-2438.

Saddleback College

Mission Viejo, California www.saddleback.cc.ca.us/

Freshman Application Contact Admissions Office, Saddleback College, 28000 Marguerite Parkway, Mission Viejo, CA 92692. *Phone:* 949-582-4555. *Fax:* 949-347-8315. *E-mail:* earaiza@saddleback.edu.

Sage College

Moreno Valley, California www.sagecollege.edu/

Admissions Office Contact Sage College, 12125 Day Street, Building L, Moreno Valley, CA 92557-6720. *Toll-free phone:* 888-781-2727.

The Salvation Army College for Officer Training at Crestmont

Rancho Palos Verdes, California www.crestmont.edu/

Freshman Application Contact Capt. Kevin Jackson, Director of Curriculum, The Salvation Army College for Officer Training at Crestmont, 30840 Hawthorne Boulevard, Rancho Palos Verdes, CA 90275. *Phone:* 310-544-6442. *Fax:* 310-265-6520.

San Bernardino Valley College

San Bernardino, California www.valleycollege.edu/

Director of Admissions Ms. Helena Johnson, Director of Admissions and Records, San Bernardino Valley College, 701 South Mount Vernon Avenue, San Bernardino, CA 92410-2748. *Phone:* 909-384-4401.

San Diego City College

San Diego, California www.sdcity.edu/

- **State and locally supported** 2-year, founded 1914, part of San Diego Community College District System
- **Urban** 56-acre campus with easy access to San Diego and Tijuana
- **Coed,** 19,309 undergraduate students

Undergraduates 15% African American, 11% Asian American or Pacific Islander, 34% Hispanic American, 1% Native American.

Faculty *Total:* 485, 33% full-time, 26% with terminal degrees. *Student/faculty ratio:* 35:1.

Majors Accounting; administrative assistant and secretarial science; African American/Black studies; anthropology; art; artificial intelligence and robotics; automobile/automotive mechanics technology; behavioral sciences; biology/biological sciences; business administration and management; carpentry; commercial and advertising art; computer engineering technology; consumer services

San Diego City College (continued)

and advocacy; cosmetology; court reporting; data processing and data processing technology; developmental and child psychology; drafting and design technology; dramatic/theater arts; electrical, electronic and communications engineering technology; emergency medical technology (EMT paramedic); engineering technology; English; environmental engineering technology; fashion merchandising; finance; graphic and printing equipment operation/production; Hispanic American, Puerto Rican, and Mexican American/Chicano studies; hospitality administration; industrial arts; industrial technology; insurance; interior design; journalism; labor and industrial relations; Latin American studies; legal administrative assistant/secretary; legal assistant/paralegal; liberal arts and sciences/liberal studies; machine tool technology; marketing/marketing management; mathematics; modern languages; music; nursing (licensed practical/vocational nurse training); nursing (registered nurse training); occupational safety and health technology; parks, recreation and leisure; photography; physical education teaching and coaching; physical sciences; political science and government; postal management; pre-engineering; psychology; radio and television; real estate; social sciences; social work; sociology; special products marketing; speech and rhetoric; teacher assistant/aide; telecommunications technology; tourism and travel services management; transportation and materials moving related; welding technology.

Academics *Calendar:* semesters. *Degree:* certificates and associate. *Special study options:* academic remediation for entering students, adult/continuing education programs, cooperative education, distance learning, English as a second language, external degree program, honors programs, independent study, off-campus study, part-time degree program, services for LD students, student-designed majors, summer session for credit. *ROTC:* Air Force (c).

Library San Diego City College Library with 73,000 titles, 337 serial subscriptions, an OPAC.

Student Life *Housing:* college housing not available. *Activities and Organizations:* drama/theater group, student-run newspaper, radio station, choral group, Alpha Gamma Sigma, Association of United Latin American Students, MECHA, Afrikan Student Union, Student Nurses Association. *Campus security:* 24-hour emergency response devices and patrols, late-night transport/escort service. *Student services:* health clinic, personal/psychological counseling.

Athletics Member NJCAA. *Intercollegiate sports:* baseball M, basketball M/W, cross-country running M/W, football M, golf M/W, soccer M/W, softball W, tennis M/W, track and field M/W, volleyball M/W. *Intramural sports:* archery M/W, badminton M/W, baseball M, basketball M/W, bowling M/W, racquetball M/W, soccer M/W, softball W, swimming and diving M/W, tennis M/W, track and field M/W, volleyball M/W, weight lifting M/W.

Costs (2010–11) *Tuition:* state resident $0 full-time; nonresident $5700 full-time, $190 per unit part-time. *Required fees:* $780 full-time. *Room and board:* Room and board charges vary according to location. *Payment plan:* deferred payment.

Financial Aid Of all full-time matriculated undergraduates who enrolled in 2009, 79 Federal Work-Study jobs (averaging $3669). 27 state and other part-time jobs (averaging $1399).

Applying *Options:* electronic application. *Required for some:* high school transcript. *Application deadlines:* rolling (freshmen), rolling (transfers).

Freshman Application Contact Ms. Lou Humphries, Registrar/Supervisor of Admissions, Records and Veterans, San Diego City College, 1313 Twelfth Avenue, San Diego, CA 92101-4787. *Phone:* 619-388-3474. *Fax:* 619-388-3505. *E-mail:* lhumphri@sdccd.edu.

SAN DIEGO GOLF ACADEMY

Vista, California **www.sdgagolf.com/**

- **Proprietary** 2-year, founded 1974
- **Coed**

Academics *Calendar:* semesters. *Degree:* associate.

Applying *Application fee:* $50.

Director of Admissions Ms. Deborah Wells, Admissions Coordinator, San Diego Golf Academy, 1910 Shadowridge Drive, Suite 111, Vista, CA 92083. *Phone:* 760-414-1501. *Toll-free phone:* 800-342-7342. *E-mail:* sdga@sdgagolf.com.

SAN DIEGO MESA COLLEGE

San Diego, California **www.sdmesa.edu/**

- **State and locally supported** 2-year, founded 1964, part of San Diego Community College District
- **Suburban** 104-acre campus
- **Coed,** 24,252 undergraduate students, 100% full-time, 53% women, 47% men

Undergraduates 24,250 full-time. 7% African American, 20% Asian American or Pacific Islander, 21% Hispanic American, 0.8% Native American.

Freshmen *Admission:* 2,303 applied, 2,303 admitted.

Faculty *Total:* 840, 34% full-time.

Majors Accounting; administrative assistant and secretarial science; African American/Black studies; architectural engineering technology; architecture; art; biology/biological sciences; business administration and management; chemistry; child-care provision; clinical/medical laboratory technology; computer and information sciences; computer programming related; computer programming (specific applications); computer science; computer software and media applications related; construction engineering technology; data entry/microcomputer applications related; dental assisting; engineering; English; fashion/apparel design; fashion merchandising; foods and nutrition related; foods, nutrition, and wellness; French; geography; health information/medical records administration; Hispanic American, Puerto Rican, and Mexican American/Chicano studies; hospitality and recreation marketing; hotel/motel administration; industrial radiologic technology; interior design; intermedia/multimedia; landscape architecture; legal administrative assistant/secretary; liberal arts and sciences/liberal studies; marketing/marketing management; marketing research; mathematics; medical/clinical assistant; music; physical education teaching and coaching; physical sciences; physical therapist assistant; physics; psychology; real estate; social sciences; sociology; Spanish; speech and rhetoric; tourism and travel services management; tourism and travel services marketing; veterinary/animal health technology.

Academics *Calendar:* semesters. *Degree:* certificates, diplomas, and associate. *Special study options:* academic remediation for entering students, adult/continuing education programs, English as a second language, external degree program, honors programs, independent study, part-time degree program, services for LD students, summer session for credit.

Library 84,353 titles, 657 serial subscriptions.

Student Life *Housing:* college housing not available. *Activities and Organizations:* drama/theater group, student-run newspaper, choral group, Alpha Gamma Sigma, Black Students Association, MECHA, Gay and Lesbian Student Group, Vietnamese Student Association. *Campus security:* 24-hour emergency response devices and patrols, late-night transport/escort service. *Student services:* health clinic, personal/psychological counseling.

Athletics *Intercollegiate sports:* baseball M, basketball M/W, cross-country running M/W, football M, soccer M/W, softball W, swimming and diving M/W, tennis M/W, track and field M/W, volleyball M/W, water polo M/W. *Intramural sports:* badminton M/W, basketball M/W, bowling M/W, fencing M/W, football M, golf M/W, gymnastics M/W, racquetball M/W, skiing (downhill) M, soccer M/W, softball M/W, swimming and diving M/W, tennis M/W, volleyball M/W, weight lifting M/W.

Financial Aid Of all full-time matriculated undergraduates who enrolled in 2008, 115 Federal Work-Study jobs (averaging $5000). *Financial aid deadline:* 6/30.

Applying *Options:* electronic application, early admission. *Application deadline:* rolling (freshmen). *Notification:* continuous (freshmen).

Freshman Application Contact Ms. Cheri Sawyer, Admissions Supervisor, San Diego Mesa College, 7250 Mesa College Drive, San Diego, CA 92111. *Phone:* 619-388-2686. *Fax:* 619-388-2960. *E-mail:* csawyer@sdccd.edu.

SAN DIEGO MIRAMAR COLLEGE

San Diego, California **www.sdmiramar.edu/**

- **State and locally supported** 2-year, founded 1969, part of San Diego Community College District System
- **Suburban** 120-acre campus
- **Coed**

Academics *Calendar:* semesters. *Degree:* associate. *Special study options:* academic remediation for entering students, accelerated degree program, adult/continuing education programs, advanced placement credit, cooperative education, distance learning, double majors, English as a second language, honors programs, independent study, part-time degree program, services for LD students, student-designed majors, study abroad, summer session for credit.

Student Life *Campus security:* 24-hour emergency response devices and patrols.

Financial Aid Of all full-time matriculated undergraduates who enrolled in 2008, 39 Federal Work-Study jobs (averaging $1500).

Applying *Options:* electronic application.

Freshman Application Contact Ms. Dana Andras, Admissions Supervisor, San Diego Miramar College, 10440 Black Mountain Road, San Diego, CA 92126-2999. *Phone:* 619-536-7854. *E-mail:* dmaxwell@sdccd.cc.ca.us.

SAN JOAQUIN DELTA COLLEGE

Stockton, California **www.deltacollege.edu/**

- **District-supported** 2-year, founded 1935, part of California Community College System
- **Urban** 165-acre campus with easy access to Sacramento
- **Coed**

Undergraduates Students come from 20 states and territories, 0.2% are from out of state, 11% African American, 20% Asian American or Pacific Islander, 28% Hispanic American, 1% Native American, 0.4% international. *Retention:* 72% of 2008 full-time freshmen returned.

Faculty *Student/faculty ratio:* 31:1.

Academics *Calendar:* semesters. *Degree:* certificates and associate. *Special study options:* academic remediation for entering students, adult/continuing education programs, advanced placement credit, cooperative education, distance learning, English as a second language, honors programs, independent study, part-time degree program, services for LD students, summer session for credit.

Student Life *Campus security:* 24-hour emergency response devices and patrols, late-night transport/escort service.

Athletics Member NJCAA.

Costs (2009–10) *Tuition:* nonresident $190 per unit part-time. Full-time tuition and fees vary according to course load. Part-time tuition and fees vary according to course load. *Required fees:* $26 per unit part-time, $1 per term part-time.

Financial Aid Of all full-time matriculated undergraduates who enrolled in 2008, 315 Federal Work-Study jobs (averaging $3100). 210 state and other part-time jobs (averaging $1172).

Applying *Options:* electronic application, early admission.

Freshman Application Contact Ms. Catherine Mooney, Registrar, San Joaquin Delta College, 5151 Pacific Avenue, Stockton, CA 95207. *Phone:* 209-954-5635. *Fax:* 209-954-5769. *E-mail:* admissions@deltacollege.edu.

SAN JOAQUIN VALLEY COLLEGE

Bakersfield, California **www.sjvc.edu/**

- **Proprietary** 2-year, founded 1977, part of San Joaquin Valley College
- **Coed**

Undergraduates 541 full-time. Students come from 6 states and territories, 2 other countries, 1% are from out of state, 6% African American, 4% Asian American or Pacific Islander, 45% Hispanic American, 2% Native American, 8% international.

Faculty *Student/faculty ratio:* 12:1.

Academics *Degree:* associate.

Applying *Required for some:* essay or personal statement, interview.

Freshman Application Contact Enrollment Services Director, San Joaquin Valley College, 201 New Stine Road, #200, Bakersfield, CA 93309. *Phone:* 661-834-0126. *Toll-free phone:* 866-544-7898. *Fax:* 661-834-8124. *E-mail:* admissions@sjvc.edu.

SAN JOAQUIN VALLEY COLLEGE

Visalia, California **www.sjvc.edu/**

Freshman Application Contact Enrollment Services Director, San Joaquin Valley College, 8400 West Mineral King Avenue, Visalia, CA 93291. *Phone:* 559-651-2500. *Fax:* 559-734-9048. *E-mail:* admissions@sjvc.edu.

SAN JOAQUIN VALLEY COLLEGE–FRESNO AVIATION CAMPUS

Fresno, California **www.sjvc.edu/**

Freshman Application Contact Enrollment Services Coordinator, San Joaquin Valley College–Fresno Aviation Campus, 4985 East Anderson Avenue, Fresno, CA 93727. *Phone:* 559-453-0123. *Fax:* 599-453-0133. *E-mail:* admissions@sjvc.edu.

SAN JOAQUIN VALLEY COLLEGE–ONLINE

Visalia, California **www.sjvconline.edu/**

- **Proprietary** 2-year, part of San Joaquin Valley College
- **Suburban** campus with easy access to Fresno
- **Coed**

Undergraduates 887 full-time. Students come from 14 states and territories, 31% are from out of state. *Retention:* 77% of 2008 full-time freshmen returned.

Faculty *Student/faculty ratio:* 21:1.

Academics *Degree:* certificates and associate.

Applying *Options:* electronic application. *Required for some:* essay or personal statement, interview.

Freshman Application Contact Enrollment Services Director, San Joaquin Valley College–Online, 3808 West Caldwell Avenue, Suite A, Visalia, CA 93277. *E-mail:* admissions@sjvc.edu.

SAN JOSE CITY COLLEGE

San Jose, California **www.sjcc.edu/**

- **District-supported** 2-year, founded 1921, part of San Jose/Evergreen Community College District System
- **Urban** 58-acre campus
- **Coed**

Academics *Calendar:* semesters. *Degree:* associate. *Special study options:* academic remediation for entering students, adult/continuing education programs, advanced placement credit, cooperative education, English as a second language, part-time degree program, services for LD students, student-designed majors, summer session for credit. *ROTC:* Army (c), Air Force (c).

Financial Aid Of all full-time matriculated undergraduates who enrolled in 2008, 105 Federal Work-Study jobs (averaging $2500).

Applying *Options:* early admission, deferred entrance.

Freshman Application Contact Mr. Carlo Santos, Director of Admissions/Registrar, San Jose City College, 2100 Moorpark Avenue, San Jose, CA 95128-2799. *Phone:* 408-288-3707. *Fax:* 408-298-1935.

SANTA ANA COLLEGE

Santa Ana, California **www.sac.edu/**

Freshman Application Contact Mrs. Christie Steward, Admissions Clerk, Santa Ana College, 1530 West 17th Street, Santa Ana, CA 92704. *Phone:* 714-564-6053.

SANTA BARBARA CITY COLLEGE

Santa Barbara, California **www.sbcc.edu/**

Freshman Application Contact Ms. Allison Curtis, Director of Admissions and Records, Santa Barbara City College, 721 Cliff Drive, Santa Barbara, CA 93109. *Phone:* 805-965-0581 Ext. 2352. *Fax:* 805-962-0497. *E-mail:* admissions@sbcc.edu.

SANTA MONICA COLLEGE

Santa Monica, California **www.smc.edu/**

- **State and locally supported** 2-year, founded 1929, part of California Community College System
- **Urban** 40-acre campus with easy access to Los Angeles
- **Coed**

Academics *Calendar:* semester plus optional winter and summer terms. *Degree:* certificates and associate. *Special study options:* academic remediation for entering students, adult/continuing education programs, advanced placement credit, cooperative education, distance learning, English as a second language, honors programs, independent study, internships, part-time degree program, services for LD students, study abroad, summer session for credit. *ROTC:* Army (c).

Santa Monica College (continued)

Student Life *Campus security:* 24-hour emergency response devices and patrols, student patrols, late-night transport/escort service.

Financial Aid Of all full-time matriculated undergraduates who enrolled in 2008, 450 Federal Work-Study jobs (averaging $3000).

Applying *Options:* early admission. *Required:* high school transcript.

Director of Admissions Ms. Teresita Rodriguez, Dean of Enrollment Services, Santa Monica College, 1900 Pico Boulevard, Santa Monica, CA 90405-1628. *Phone:* 310-434-4774.

SANTA ROSA JUNIOR COLLEGE

Santa Rosa, California **www.santarosa.edu/**

- **State and locally supported** 2-year, founded 1918, part of California Community College System
- **Urban** 93-acre campus with easy access to San Francisco
- **Endowment** $16.8 million
- **Coed,** 25,319 undergraduate students, 35% full-time, 56% women, 44% men

Undergraduates 8,801 full-time, 16,518 part-time. 2% are from out of state, 2% African American, 4% Asian American or Pacific Islander, 14% Hispanic American, 0.9% Native American.

Freshmen *Admission:* 13,326 applied, 13,326 admitted.

Faculty *Total:* 1,421, 21% full-time, 10% with terminal degrees. *Student/faculty ratio:* 22:1.

Majors Agricultural business and management; agricultural mechanization; agriculture; animal sciences; anthropology; architecture; architecture related; art; art history, criticism and conservation; automobile/automotive mechanics technology; behavioral sciences; biology/biological sciences; business administration and management; chemistry; child development; civil engineering; computer science; criminal justice/law enforcement administration; culinary arts; dance; dental hygiene; diesel mechanics technology; dramatic/theater arts; economics; electrical, electronic and communications engineering technology; emergency medical technology (EMT paramedic); English; environmental studies; ethnic, cultural minority, and gender studies related; fashion and fabric consulting; fashion/apparel design; fashion merchandising; fire science; floriculture/floristry management; graphic design; health and physical education related; history; horse husbandry/equine science and management; humanities; human services; interior design; landscape architecture; Latin American studies; mathematics; natural resources/conservation; natural resources management and policy; nursing (licensed practical/vocational nurse training); nursing (registered nurse training); philosophy; physics; political science and government; precision production trades; pre-pharmacy studies; psychology; social sciences; surveying engineering; women's studies.

Academics *Calendar:* semesters. *Degree:* certificates and associate. *Special study options:* academic remediation for entering students, adult/continuing education programs, advanced placement credit, cooperative education, distance learning, English as a second language, independent study, internships, off-campus study, part-time degree program, services for LD students, study abroad, summer session for credit.

Library Plover Library with 127,394 titles, 390 serial subscriptions, 14,450 audiovisual materials, an OPAC, a Web page.

Student Life *Housing:* college housing not available. *Activities and Organizations:* drama/theater group, student-run newspaper, choral group, AG Ambassadors, MECHA, Alpha Gamma Sigma, Phi Theta Kappa, Puente. *Campus security:* 24-hour emergency response devices and patrols. *Student services:* health clinic, personal/psychological counseling.

Athletics Member NJCAA. *Intercollegiate sports:* baseball M, basketball M/W, cross-country running M/W, football M, golf M, ice hockey M(c), rugby M(c), soccer M/W, softball W, swimming and diving M/W, tennis M/W, track and field M/W, volleyball W, water polo M/W, wrestling M.

Costs (2010–11) *One-time required fee:* $34. *Tuition:* state resident $0 full-time; nonresident $4392 full-time, $183 per unit part-time. *Required fees:* $624 full-time, $26 per unit part-time. *Payment plans:* installment, deferred payment.

Financial Aid Of all full-time matriculated undergraduates who enrolled in 2008, 130 Federal Work-Study jobs (averaging $2700).

Applying *Options:* electronic application, early admission. *Application deadlines:* rolling (freshmen), rolling (out-of-state freshmen), rolling (transfers). *Notification:* continuous (freshmen), continuous (out-of-state freshmen), continuous (transfers).

Freshman Application Contact Ms. Diane Traversi, Director of Enrollment Services, Santa Rosa Junior College, 1501 Mendocino Avenue, Santa Rosa, CA 95401. *Phone:* 707-527-4510. *Fax:* 707-527-4798. *E-mail:* admininfo@santarosa.edu.

SANTIAGO CANYON COLLEGE

Orange, California **www.sccollege.edu/**

Freshman Application Contact Denise Pennock, Admissions and Records, Santiago Canyon College, 8045 East Chapman, Orange, CA 92669. *Phone:* 714-564-4000.

SCHOOL OF URBAN MISSIONS

Oakland, California **www.sum.edu/**

- **Independent interdenominational** primarily 2-year, founded 1991
- **Coed,** 139 undergraduate students, 96% full-time, 43% women, 57% men
- 59% of applicants were admitted

Undergraduates 133 full-time, 6 part-time. 32% African American, 16% Asian American or Pacific Islander, 22% Hispanic American, 45% transferred in.

Freshmen *Admission:* 111 applied, 65 admitted, 42 enrolled.

Faculty *Total:* 22, 18% full-time, 23% with terminal degrees. *Student/faculty ratio:* 11:1.

Majors Biblical studies.

Academics *Calendar:* trimesters. *Degrees:* associate and bachelor's. *Special study options:* distance learning.

Student Life *Housing Options:* men-only, women-only.

Applying *Options:* deferred entrance. *Application fee:* $25. *Required:* essay or personal statement, 2 letters of recommendation, interview, pastoral recommendation. *Application deadlines:* rolling (freshmen), rolling (transfers). *Notification:* continuous (freshmen), continuous (transfers).

Freshman Application Contact Admissions, School of Urban Missions, PO Box 53344, New Orleans, LA 70153. *Phone:* 510-567-6174. *Toll-free phone:* 800-385-6364. *Fax:* 510-568-1024.

SHASTA COLLEGE

Redding, California **www.shastacollege.edu/**

Director of Admissions Dr. Kevin O'Rorke, Dean of Enrollment Services, Shasta College, PO Box 496006, 11555 Old Oregon Trail, Redding, CA 96049-6006. *Phone:* 530-242-7669.

SIERRA COLLEGE

Rocklin, California **www.sierracollege.edu/**

- **State-supported** 2-year, founded 1936, part of California Community College System
- **Suburban** 327-acre campus with easy access to Sacramento
- **Coed,** 19,416 undergraduate students, 28% full-time, 57% women, 43% men

Undergraduates 5,355 full-time, 14,061 part-time. 1% are from out of state, 2% African American, 2% Asian American or Pacific Islander, 8% Hispanic American, 2% Native American, 1% international, 4% transferred in, 1% live on campus.

Freshmen *Admission:* 24,000 applied, 24,000 admitted, 2,112 enrolled.

Faculty *Total:* 870, 18% full-time. *Student/faculty ratio:* 25:1.

Majors Accounting; administrative assistant and secretarial science; agriculture; American Sign Language (ASL); animal/livestock husbandry and production; apparel and textile manufacturing; apparel and textile marketing management; applied horticulture; architectural drafting and CAD/CADD; art; automobile/automotive mechanics technology; biological and physical sciences; biology/biological sciences; business administration and management; business/commerce; cabinetmaking and millwork; chemistry; child development; commercial photography; computer and information sciences and support services related; computer installation and repair technology; computer programming; computer systems networking and telecommunications; construction trades; corrections; criminal justice/police science; data entry/microcomputer applications; digital communication and media/multimedia; electrical/electronics equipment installation and repair; engineering; English; equestrian studies; fire science; forestry; general studies; geology/earth science; graphic design; hazardous materials management and waste technology; health and physical education; industrial electronics technology; information technology; liberal arts and sciences/liberal studies; manufacturing technology; mathematics; mechanical drafting and CAD/

CADD; music; nursing (licensed practical/vocational nurse training); nursing (registered nurse training); parks, recreation and leisure; philosophy; physics; psychology; real estate; sales, distribution and marketing; small business administration; social sciences; speech and rhetoric; system administration; visual and performing arts; web page, digital/multimedia and information resources design; women's studies.

Academics *Calendar:* semesters. *Degree:* certificates and associate. *Special study options:* academic remediation for entering students, accelerated degree program, advanced placement credit, distance learning, double majors, English as a second language, honors programs, independent study, internships, off-campus study, part-time degree program, services for LD students, study abroad, summer session for credit.

Library Leary Resource Center plus 1 other with 69,879 titles, 189 serial subscriptions, an OPAC, a Web page.

Student Life *Housing Options:* coed. Campus housing is university owned. *Activities and Organizations:* drama/theater group, student-run newspaper, choral group, Drama Club, student government, Art Club, band, Aggie Club. *Campus security:* 24-hour emergency response devices and patrols, late-night transport/escort service. *Student services:* health clinic, personal/psychological counseling.

Athletics *Intercollegiate sports:* baseball M, basketball M/W, football M, golf M/W, soccer W, softball W, swimming and diving M/W, tennis M/W, volleyball W, water polo M/W, wrestling M. *Intramural sports:* archery M/W, badminton M/W, basketball M/W, tennis M/W, volleyball M/W.

Costs (2010–11) *Tuition:* state resident $0 full-time; nonresident $5320 full-time, $190 per unit part-time. Full-time tuition and fees vary according to course load. Part-time tuition and fees vary according to course load. *Required fees:* $772 full-time, $26 per unit part-time, $22 per term part-time. *Room and board:* $6700.

Financial Aid Of all full-time matriculated undergraduates who enrolled in 2008, 150 Federal Work-Study jobs (averaging $2340).

Applying *Options:* electronic application, early admission. *Application deadline:* rolling (freshmen). *Notification:* continuous (freshmen), continuous (transfers).

Freshman Application Contact Sierra College, 5000 Rocklin Road, Rocklin, CA 93677-3397. *Phone:* 916-660-7341.

SKYLINE COLLEGE

San Bruno, California **skylinecollege.net/**

Freshman Application Contact Terry Stats, Admissions Office, Skyline College, 3300 College Drive, San Bruno, CA 94066-1698. *Phone:* 650-738-4251. *E-mail:* stats@smccd.net.

SOLANO COMMUNITY COLLEGE

Fairfield, California **www.solano.edu/**

- **State and locally supported** 2-year, founded 1945, part of California Community College System
- **Rural** 192-acre campus with easy access to Sacramento and San Francisco
- **Coed**

Undergraduates Students come from 43 states and territories, 6 other countries, 1% are from out of state, 15% African American, 18% Asian American or Pacific Islander, 14% Hispanic American, 1% Native American, 0.2% international.

Faculty *Student/faculty ratio:* 27:1.

Academics *Calendar:* semesters. *Degree:* certificates, diplomas, and associate. *Special study options:* academic remediation for entering students, adult/continuing education programs, advanced placement credit, cooperative education, distance learning, double majors, English as a second language, honors programs, independent study, off-campus study, part-time degree program, services for LD students, study abroad, summer session for credit.

Student Life *Campus security:* 24-hour patrols, student patrols, late-night transport/escort service.

Costs (2009–10) *Tuition:* state resident $0 full-time; nonresident $4584 full-time, $191 per unit part-time. Full-time tuition and fees vary according to course load. Part-time tuition and fees vary according to course load. *Required fees:* $660 full-time, $26 per unit part-time, $13 per term part-time.

Financial Aid Of all full-time matriculated undergraduates who enrolled in 2008, 125 Federal Work-Study jobs (averaging $2000). 30 state and other part-time jobs (averaging $2000).

Applying *Options:* electronic application, early admission, deferred entrance.

Freshman Application Contact Solano Community College, 4000 Suisun Valley Road, Fairfield, CA 94534. *Phone:* 707-864-7000 Ext. 4313.

SOUTH COAST COLLEGE

Orange, California **www.southcoastcollege.com/**

Director of Admissions South Coast College, 2011 West Chapman Avenue, Orange, CA 92868. *Toll-free phone:* 800-337-8366.

SOUTHWESTERN COLLEGE

Chula Vista, California **www.swc.edu/**

Freshman Application Contact Director of Admissions and Records, Southwestern College, 900 Otay Lakes Road, Chula Vista, CA 91910. *Phone:* 619-421-6700 Ext. 5215. *Fax:* 619-482-6489.

STANBRIDGE COLLEGE

Irvine, California **www.stanbridge.edu/**

Admissions Office Contact Stanbridge College, 2041 Business Center Drive, Irvine, CA 92612.

TAFT COLLEGE

Taft, California **www.taftcollege.edu/**

Freshman Application Contact Harold Russell III, Director of Financial Aid and Admissions, Taft College, 29 Emmons Park Drive, Taft, CA 93268. *Phone:* 661-763-7763. *Fax:* 661-763-7758. *E-mail:* hrussell@taft.org.

VENTURA COLLEGE

Ventura, California **www.venturacollege.edu/**

Freshman Application Contact Ms. Susan Bricker, Registrar, Ventura College, 4667 Telegraph Road, Ventura, CA 93003-3899. *Phone:* 805-654-6456. *Fax:* 805-654-6357. *E-mail:* sbricker@vcccd.net.

VICTOR VALLEY COLLEGE

Victorville, California **www.vvc.edu/**

- **State-supported** 2-year, founded 1961, part of California Community College System
- **Small-town** 253-acre campus with easy access to Los Angeles
- **Coed,** 6,437 students

Undergraduates 2% are from out of state, 13% African American, 3% Asian American or Pacific Islander, 27% Hispanic American, 1% Native American. *Retention:* 63% of 2008 full-time freshmen returned.

Faculty *Total:* 574, 23% full-time. *Student/faculty ratio:* 28:1.

Majors Administrative assistant and secretarial science; agricultural teacher education; art; automobile/automotive mechanics technology; biological and physical sciences; biology/biological sciences; building/construction finishing, management, and inspection related; business administration and management; business/commerce; child-care and support services management; child development; computer and information sciences; computer programming (specific applications); computer science; construction engineering technology; criminal justice/police science; dramatic/theater arts; electrical, electronic and communications engineering technology; fire protection and safety technology; fire science; food technology and processing; horticultural science; humanities; information science/studies; kindergarten/preschool education; liberal arts and sciences/liberal studies; management information systems; mathematics; music; natural sciences; nursing (registered nurse training); ornamental horticulture; physical sciences; real estate; respiratory care therapy; science technologies related; social sciences; teacher assistant/aide; trade and industrial teacher education; vehicle maintenance and repair technologies related; welding technology.

Victor Valley College (continued)

Academics *Calendar:* semesters. *Degree:* certificates, diplomas, and associate. *Special study options:* academic remediation for entering students, accelerated degree program, advanced placement credit, cooperative education, distance learning, double majors, English as a second language, honors programs, independent study, internships, off-campus study, part-time degree program, services for LD students, study abroad, summer session for credit.

Library Learning Resource Center with an OPAC, a Web page.

Student Life *Housing:* college housing not available. *Activities and Organizations:* drama/theater group, student-run newspaper, choral group, Black Student Union, Drama Club, rugby, Phi Theta Kappa. *Campus security:* 24-hour emergency response devices and patrols, late-night transport/escort service, part-time trained security personnel. *Student services:* health clinic, personal/psychological counseling.

Athletics Member NCAA, NJCAA. *Intercollegiate sports:* baseball M, basketball M/W, cross-country running M/W, football M, golf M, soccer M/W, softball W, tennis M/W, track and field M/W, volleyball W, wrestling M. *Intramural sports:* rock climbing M/W.

Costs (2009–10) *Tuition:* state resident $0 full-time; nonresident $4560 full-time, $190 per unit part-time. *Required fees:* $624 full-time, $26 per unit part-time. *Payment plan:* installment.

Financial Aid *Average need-based loan:* $6168. *Average need-based gift aid:* $3707.

Applying *Application deadline:* rolling (freshmen). *Notification:* continuous (freshmen).

Freshman Application Contact Ms. Greta Moon, Director of Admissions and Records (Interim), Victor Valley College, 18422 Bear Valley Road, Victorville, CA 92392. *Phone:* 760-245-4271. *Fax:* 760-843-7707. *E-mail:* moong@vvc.edu.

Western Career College

Emeryville, California www.westerncollege.edu/

Freshman Application Contact Admissions Office, Western Career College, 1400 65th Street, Suite 200, Emeryville, CA 94608. *Phone:* 510-601-0133. *Toll-free phone:* 800-750-5627. *Fax:* 510-623-9822.

Western Career College

Fremont, California www.westerncollege.edu/

Director of Admissions Mr. Anton Croos, Admissions Director, Western Career College, 41350 Christy Street, Fremont, CA 94538. *Phone:* 510-623-9966 Ext. 212. *Toll-free phone:* 800-750-5627.

Western Career College

Pleasant Hill, California www.westerncollege.edu/

Admissions Office Contact Western Career College, 380 Civic Drive, Suite 300, Pleasant Hill, CA 94523. *Toll-free phone:* 888-203-9947.

Western Career College

Sacramento, California www.westerncollege.edu/

Admissions Office Contact Western Career College, 8909 Folsom Boulevard, Sacramento, CA 95826. *Toll-free phone:* 888-203-9947.

Western Career College

San Jose, California www.westerncollege.edu/

Director of Admissions Admissions Director, Western Career College, 6201 San Ignacio Avenue, San Jose, CA 95119. *Phone:* 408-360-0840. *Toll-free phone:* 800-750-5627.

Western Career College

San Leandro, California www.westerncollege.edu/

Admissions Office Contact Western Career College, 15555 E. 14th Street, Suite 500, San Leandro, CA 94578. *Toll-free phone:* 888-203-9947.

Western Career College

Walnut Creek, California www.westerncollege.edu/

Freshman Application Contact Admissions Director, Western Career College, 2157 Country Hills Drive, Antioch, CA 94598. *Phone:* 925-522-7777. *Toll-free phone:* 888-203-9947.

West Hills Community College

Coalinga, California www.westhillscollege.com/

Freshman Application Contact Sandra Dagnino, West Hills Community College, 300 Cherry Lane, Coalinga, CA 93210-1399. *Phone:* 559-934-3203. *Toll-free phone:* 800-266-1114. *Fax:* 559-934-2830. *E-mail:* sandradagnino@westhillscollege.com.

West Los Angeles College

Culver City, California www.lacolleges.net/

Director of Admissions Mr. Len Isaksen, Director of Admissions, West Los Angeles College, 9000 Overland Avenue, Culver City, CA 90230-3519. *Phone:* 310-287-4255.

West Valley College

Saratoga, California www.westvalley.edu/

Freshman Application Contact Ms. Barbara Ogilive, Supervisor, Admissions and Records, West Valley College, 14000 Fruitvale Avenue, Saratoga, CA 95070-5698. *Phone:* 408-741-4630. *E-mail:* barbara_ogilvie@westvalley.edu.

Woodland Community College

Woodland, California www.yccd.edu/woodland/

Admissions Office Contact Woodland Community College, 2300 East Gibson Road, Woodland, CA 95776.

WyoTech

Fremont, California www.wyotech.edu/

- **Proprietary** 2-year, founded 1966, administratively affiliated with Corinthian Colleges, Inc.
- **Urban** campus
- **Coed,** 1,926 undergraduate students, 100% full-time, 6% women, 94% men
- 84% of applicants were admitted

Undergraduates 1,926 full-time. 16% African American, 15% Asian American or Pacific Islander, 36% Hispanic American, 0.4% Native American, 0.1% international.

Freshmen *Admission:* 209 applied, 176 admitted.

Faculty *Total:* 108, 89% full-time. *Student/faculty ratio:* 25:1.

Majors Automobile/automotive mechanics technology; automotive engineering technology.

Academics *Calendar:* continuous. *Degree:* certificates, diplomas, and associate. *Special study options:* academic remediation for entering students.

Library Learning Resource Center with 1,000 audiovisual materials.

Student Life *Housing:* college housing not available. *Campus security:* security personnel.
Standardized Tests *Required:* CPAT or ATB Entrance Exam (for admission).
Applying *Required:* successful completion of school's admission requirements as outlined in catalog.
Freshman Application Contact Admissions Department, WyoTech, 200 Whitney Place, Fremont, CA 94539-7663. *Phone:* 510-580-3507. *Toll-free phone:* 800-248-8585. *Fax:* 510-490-8599.

WYOTECH

West Sacramento, California **www.wyotech.com/**

Freshman Application Contact Admissions Office, WyoTech, 980 Riverside Parkway, West Sacramento, CA 95605-1507. *Phone:* 916-376-8888. *Toll-free phone:* 888-577-7559. *Fax:* 916-617-2059.

YUBA COLLEGE

Marysville, California **www.yccd.edu/**

Director of Admissions Dr. David Farrell, Dean of Student Development, Yuba College, 2088 North Beale Road, Marysville, CA 95901. *Phone:* 530-741-6705.

COLORADO

AIMS COMMUNITY COLLEGE

Greeley, Colorado **www.aims.edu/**

Freshman Application Contact Ms. Susie Gallardo, Admissions Technician, Aims Community College, Box 69, 5401 West 20th Street, Greeley, CO 80632-0069. *Phone:* 970-330-8008 Ext. 6624. *E-mail:* wgreen@chiron.aims.edu.

ANTHEM COLLEGE AURORA

Aurora, Colorado **www.anthem.edu/locations/anthem-college-aurora/**

Director of Admissions Admissions Office, Anthem College Aurora, 350 Blackhawk Street, Aurora, CO 80011. *Toll-free phone:* 800-322-4132.

ARAPAHOE COMMUNITY COLLEGE

Littleton, Colorado **www.arapahoe.edu/**

Freshman Application Contact Emily Dovi, Admissions Specialist, Arapahoe Community College, 5900 South Santa Fe Drive, PO Box 9002, Littleton, CO 80160-9002. *Phone:* 303-797-5622. *Fax:* 303-797-5970. *E-mail:* hfukaye@arapahoe.edu.

BEL–REA INSTITUTE OF ANIMAL TECHNOLOGY

Denver, Colorado **www.bel-rea.com/**

- **Proprietary** 2-year, founded 1971
- **Suburban** 4-acre campus
- **Coed**

Academics *Calendar:* quarters. *Degree:* associate. *Special study options:* academic remediation for entering students, internships.
Applying *Required:* high school transcript, minimum 2.5 GPA. *Recommended:* interview.
Director of Admissions Ms. Paulette Kaufman, Director, Bel–Rea Institute of Animal Technology, 1681 South Dayton Street, Denver, CO 80247. *Phone:* 303-751-8700. *Toll-free phone:* 800-950-8001. *E-mail:* admissions@bel-rea.com.

BOULDER COLLEGE OF MASSAGE THERAPY

Boulder, Colorado **www.bcmt.org/**

Freshman Application Contact Admissions Office, Boulder College of Massage Therapy, 6255 Longbow Drive, Boulder, CO 80301-3295. *Toll-free phone:* 800-442-5131.

COLLEGEAMERICA–COLORADO SPRINGS

Colorado Springs, Colorado **www.collegeamerica.edu/**

Freshman Application Contact Admissions Office, CollegeAmerica–Colorado Springs, 3645 Citadel Drive South, Colorado Springs, CO 80909.

COLLEGEAMERICA–DENVER

Denver, Colorado **www.collegeamerica.com/**

Freshman Application Contact Admissions Office, CollegeAmerica–Denver, 1385 South Colorado Boulevard, Denver, CO 80222. *Phone:* 303-691-9756. *Toll-free phone:* 800-97-SKILLS.

COLLEGEAMERICA–FORT COLLINS

Fort Collins, Colorado **www.collegeamerica.edu/**

- **Proprietary** primarily 2-year, founded 1962
- **Suburban** campus
- **Coed**

Academics *Calendar:* continuous. *Degrees:* associate and bachelor's. *Special study options:* independent study, internships.
Applying *Required:* essay or personal statement, high school transcript, interview. *Recommended:* minimum 2.0 GPA.
Director of Admissions Ms. Anna DiTorrice-Mull, Director of Admissions, CollegeAmerica–Fort Collins, 4601 South Mason Street, Fort Collins, CO 80525. *Phone:* 970-223-6060 Ext. 8002. *Toll-free phone:* 800-97-SKILLS.

COLORADO MOUNTAIN COLLEGE

Glenwood Springs, Colorado **www.coloradomtn.edu/**

Freshman Application Contact Vicky Butler, Admissions Assistant, Colorado Mountain College, PO Box 10001, Department PG, Glenwood Springs, CO 81601. *Phone:* 970-947-8276. *Toll-free phone:* 800-621-8559. *E-mail:* joinus@coloradomtn.edu.

COLORADO MOUNTAIN COLLEGE, ALPINE CAMPUS

Steamboat Springs, Colorado **www.coloradomtn.edu/**

Freshman Application Contact Ms. Janice Bell, Admissions Assistant, Colorado Mountain College, Alpine Campus, PO Box 10001, Department PG, Glenwood Springs, CO 81602. *Phone:* 970-870-4417 Ext. 4417. *Toll-free phone:* 800-621-8559. *E-mail:* joinus@coloradomtn.edu.

Colorado Mountain College, Timberline Campus

Leadville, Colorado **www.coloradomtn.edu/**

Freshman Application Contact Ms. Mary Laing, Admissions Assistant, Colorado Mountain College, Timberline Campus, PO Box 10001, Department PG, Glenwood Springs, CO 81602. *Phone:* 719-486-4292. *Toll-free phone:* 800-621-8559. *E-mail:* joinus@coloradomtn.edu.

Colorado Northwestern Community College

Rangely, Colorado **www.cncc.edu/**

- **State-supported** 2-year, founded 1962, part of Colorado Community College and Occupational Education System
- **Rural** 150-acre campus
- **Coed**

Academics *Calendar:* semesters. *Degree:* certificates and associate. *Special study options:* academic remediation for entering students, adult/continuing education programs, advanced placement credit, distance learning, double majors, independent study, internships, part-time degree program, services for LD students, student-designed majors, summer session for credit.

Student Life *Campus security:* student patrols, late-night transport/escort service.

Costs (2009–10) *Tuition:* state resident $2649 full-time, $88 per credit hour part-time; nonresident $5450 full-time, $182 per credit hour part-time. Full-time tuition and fees vary according to program. Part-time tuition and fees vary according to course load, program, and reciprocity agreements. *Required fees:* $249 full-time, $8 per credit hour part-time, $11 per term part-time. *Room and board:* $5868; room only: $2306. Room and board charges vary according to board plan and housing facility.

Financial Aid Of all full-time matriculated undergraduates who enrolled in 2009, 358 applied for aid, 285 were judged to have need.

Applying *Options:* early admission, deferred entrance. *Required:* high school transcript. *Required for some:* essay or personal statement, 3 letters of recommendation, interview.

Director of Admissions Mr. Gene Bilodeau, Registrar, Colorado Northwestern Community College, 500 Kennedy Drive, Rangely, CO 81648. *Phone:* 970-824-1103. *Toll-free phone:* 970-675-3221 Ext. 218 (in-state); 800-562-1105 Ext. 218 (out-of-state). *E-mail:* gene.bilodeau@cncc.edu.

Colorado School of Healing Arts

Lakewood, Colorado **www.csha.net/**

Freshman Application Contact Ms. Chris Smith, Colorado School of Healing Arts, 7655 West Mississippi Avenue, Suite 100, Lakewood, CO 80226. *Phone:* 303-986-2320. *Toll-free phone:* 800-233-7114. *Fax:* 303-980-6594.

Colorado School of Trades

Lakewood, Colorado **www.schooloftrades.com/**

- **Proprietary** 2-year, founded 1947
- **Suburban** campus
- **Coed,** 125 undergraduate students, 100% full-time, 2% women, 98% men
- 87% of applicants were admitted

Undergraduates 125 full-time. 88% are from out of state.

Freshmen *Admission:* 174 applied, 152 admitted, 20 enrolled.

Faculty *Total:* 10. *Student/faculty ratio:* 12:1.

Majors Gunsmithing.

Academics *Degree:* associate.

Applying *Application fee:* $25. *Required:* essay or personal statement, high school transcript, interview.

Freshman Application Contact Colorado School of Trades, 1575 Hoyt Street, Lakewood, CO 80215-2996. *Toll-free phone:* 800-234-4594.

Community College of Aurora

Aurora, Colorado **www.ccaurora.edu/**

Freshman Application Contact Ms. Connie Simpson, Director of Registrations, Records, and Admission, Community College of Aurora, 16000 East CentreTech Parkway, Aurora, CO 80011-9036. *Phone:* 303-360-4700.

Community College of Denver

Denver, Colorado **www.ccd.edu/**

Freshman Application Contact Mr. Michael Rusk, Dean of Students, Community College of Denver, PO Box 173363, 1111 West Colfax Avenue, Denver, CO 80217-3363. *Phone:* 303-556-6325. *Fax:* 303-556-2431. *E-mail:* enrollment_services@ccd.edu.

Denver Academy of Court Reporting

Westminster, Colorado **www.denveracademy.edu/**

- **Proprietary** 2-year, founded 1975
- **Urban** campus
- **Coed**

Academics *Calendar:* quarters. *Degree:* associate. *Special study options:* adult/continuing education programs, double majors, external degree program, internships, part-time degree program.

Student Life *Campus security:* 24-hour emergency response devices, late-night transport/escort service.

Applying *Application fee:* $150. *Required:* high school transcript. *Recommended:* interview.

Director of Admissions Mr. Howard Brookner, Director of Admissions, Denver Academy of Court Reporting, 7290 Samuel Drive, Suite 200, Denver, CO 80221-2792. *Phone:* 303-427-5292 Ext. 14. *Toll-free phone:* 800-574-2087.

Denver Automotive and Diesel College

Denver, Colorado **www.dadc.com/**

- **Proprietary** 2-year, founded 1963
- **Urban** campus
- **Coed, primarily men**

Academics *Calendar:* 8 six-week terms. *Degree:* diplomas and associate. *Special study options:* services for LD students, summer session for credit.

Student Life *Campus security:* 24-hour emergency response devices and patrols.

Applying *Application fee:* $150.

Director of Admissions Jennifer Hash, Assistant Director of Admissions, Denver Automotive and Diesel College, 460 South Lipan Street, Denver, CO 80223-2025. *Phone:* 800-347-3232 Ext. 43032. *Toll-free phone:* 800-347-3232.

Everest College

Aurora, Colorado **www.everest.edu/**

Freshman Application Contact Everest College, 14280 East Jewell Avenue, Suite 100, Aurora, CO 80012. *Phone:* 303-745-6244.

Everest College

Colorado Springs, Colorado **www.everest.edu/**

Director of Admissions Director of Admissions, Everest College, 1815 Jet Wing Drive, Colorado Springs, CO 80916. *Phone:* 719-630-6580. *Toll-free phone:* 888-741-4271. *Fax:* 719-638-6818.

Everest College

Denver, Colorado **www.everest.edu/**

Freshman Application Contact Admissions Office, Everest College, 9065 Grant Street, Denver, CO 80229-4339. *Phone:* 303-457-2757. *Fax:* 303-457-4030.

Front Range Community College

Westminster, Colorado **frcc.cc.co.us/**

- **State-supported** 2-year, founded 1968, part of Community Colleges of Colorado System
- **Suburban** 90-acre campus with easy access to Denver
- **Endowment** $247,433
- **Coed,** 18,713 undergraduate students, 37% full-time, 57% women, 43% men

Undergraduates 6,905 full-time, 11,808 part-time. Students come from 44 states and territories, 9 other countries, 2% are from out of state, 2% African American, 4% Asian American or Pacific Islander, 12% Hispanic American, 1% Native American, 1% international, 3% transferred in. *Retention:* 59% of 2008 full-time freshmen returned.

Freshmen *Admission:* 3,741 enrolled.

Faculty *Total:* 1,067, 19% full-time. *Student/faculty ratio:* 22:1.

Majors Accounting technology and bookkeeping; animal health; animation, interactive technology, video graphics and special effects; applied horticulture; architectural engineering technology; automobile/automotive mechanics technology; CAD/CADD drafting/design technology; child-care and support services management; dietitian assistant; early childhood education; electrical, electronic and communications engineering technology; emergency medical technology (EMT paramedic); general studies; health information/medical records technology; heating, air conditioning and refrigeration technology; hospitality administration; interior design; legal assistant/paralegal; liberal arts and sciences and humanities related; liberal arts and sciences/liberal studies; machine shop technology; management information systems; manufacturing technology; masonry; medical office assistant; nursing (registered nurse training); office management; science technologies related; sign language interpretation and translation; veterinary/animal health technology; welding technology; wildlife and wildlands science and management.

Academics *Calendar:* semesters. *Degree:* certificates and associate. *Special study options:* academic remediation for entering students, advanced placement credit, cooperative education, distance learning, double majors, English as a second language, freshman honors college, honors programs, independent study, internships, off-campus study, part-time degree program, services for LD students, student-designed majors, study abroad, summer session for credit. *ROTC:* Army (c), Air Force (c).

Library College Hill Library with an OPAC, a Web page.

Student Life *Housing:* college housing not available. *Activities and Organizations:* drama/theater group, student-run newspaper, Student Government Association, Student Colorado Registry of Interpreters for the Deaf, Students in Free Enterprise (SIFE), Gay Straight Alliance, Recycling Club. *Campus security:* 24-hour patrols, late-night transport/escort service. *Student services:* personal/psychological counseling.

Costs (2010–11) *Tuition:* state resident $2649 full-time; nonresident $11,817 full-time. Full-time tuition and fees vary according to location. Part-time tuition and fees vary according to location. *Required fees:* $244 full-time. *Waivers:* employees or children of employees.

Financial Aid Of all full-time matriculated undergraduates who enrolled in 2008, 165 Federal Work-Study jobs (averaging $1316). 277 state and other part-time jobs (averaging $1635).

Applying *Options:* electronic application, early admission, deferred entrance. *Application deadlines:* rolling (freshmen), rolling (out-of-state freshmen), rolling (transfers). *Notification:* continuous (freshmen), continuous (out-of-state freshmen), continuous (transfers).

Freshman Application Contact Ms. Yolanda Espinoza, Registrar, Front Range Community College, 3645 West 112th Avenue, Westminster, CO 80031. *Phone:* 303-404-5000. *Fax:* 303-439-2614. *E-mail:* yolanda.espinoza@frontrange.edu.

Heritage College

Denver, Colorado **www.heritage-education.com/**

Freshman Application Contact Admissions Office, Heritage College, 12 Lakeside Lane, Denver, CO 80212.

Institute of Business & Medical Careers

Fort Collins, Colorado **www.ibmc.edu/**

- **Private** 2-year, founded 1987, administratively affiliated with Institute of Business and Medical Careers- Greeley, Colorado and Cheyenne, Wyoming
- **Suburban** campus with easy access to Denver
- **Coed,** 302 undergraduate students, 100% full-time, 89% women, 11% men
- 100% of applicants were admitted

Undergraduates 302 full-time. Students come from 1 other state, 2% are from out of state, 1% African American, 6% Asian American or Pacific Islander, 22% Hispanic American, 0.3% Native American. *Retention:* 69% of 2008 full-time freshmen returned.

Freshmen *Admission:* 366 applied, 366 admitted, 302 enrolled.

Faculty *Total:* 34, 32% full-time. *Student/faculty ratio:* 14:1.

Majors Accounting technology and bookkeeping; business administration and management; legal administrative assistant/secretary; legal assistant/paralegal; massage therapy; medical administrative assistant and medical secretary; medical/clinical assistant; office occupations and clerical services; pharmacy technician.

Academics *Calendar:* continuous. *Degree:* certificates, diplomas, and associate. *Special study options:* accelerated degree program, cooperative education, honors programs, internships.

Student Life *Housing:* college housing not available. *Activities and Organizations:* student-run newspaper, Alpha Beta Kappa.

Costs (2010–11) *Tuition:* $10,800 full-time, $300 per credit hour part-time. Full-time tuition and fees vary according to course load and program. Part-time tuition and fees vary according to course load and program. No tuition increase for student's term of enrollment. *Payment plans:* tuition prepayment, installment. *Waivers:* employees or children of employees.

Financial Aid Of all full-time matriculated undergraduates who enrolled in 2008, 823 applied for aid, 778 were judged to have need, 660 had their need fully met. *Average percent of need met:* 70%. *Average financial aid package:* $6531. *Average need-based loan:* $3500. *Average need-based gift aid:* $2815.

Applying *Application fee:* $75. *Required:* high school transcript, interview. *Application deadline:* rolling (freshmen).

Freshman Application Contact Mr. Kevin McNeil, Regional Director of Admissions, Institute of Business & Medical Careers, 1609 Oakridge Drive, Fort Collins, CO 80525. *Phone:* 970-223-2669 Ext. 1105. *Toll-free phone:* 800-495-2669. *E-mail:* kmcneil@ibmc.edu.

IntelliTec College

Colorado Springs, Colorado **www.intelliteccollege.edu/**

- **Proprietary** 2-year, founded 1965, part of Technical Trades Institute, Inc.
- **Urban** 2-acre campus with easy access to Denver
- **Coed**

Academics *Calendar:* 6-week terms. *Degree:* certificates, diplomas, and associate. *Special study options:* advanced placement credit, double majors.

Student Life *Campus security:* 24-hour emergency response devices.

Financial Aid Of all full-time matriculated undergraduates who enrolled in 2008, 10 Federal Work-Study jobs (averaging $6500).

Applying *Application fee:* $30. *Required:* high school transcript, interview.

Director of Admissions Director of Admissions, IntelliTec College, 2315 East Pikes Peak Avenue, Colorado Springs, CO 80909-6030. *Phone:* 719-632-7626. *Toll-free phone:* 800-748-2282.

IntelliTec College

Grand Junction, Colorado **www.intelliteccollege.edu/**

Freshman Application Contact Admissions, IntelliTec College, 772 Horizon Drive, Grand Junction, CO 81506. *Phone:* 970-245-8101. *Fax:* 970-243-8074.

IntelliTec Medical Institute

Colorado Springs, Colorado **www.intelliteccollege.edu/**

- **Proprietary** 2-year, founded 1966
- **Suburban** campus
- **Coed, primarily women**

IntelliTec Medical Institute (continued)

Academics *Calendar:* clock hours. *Degree:* diplomas and associate. *Special study options:* advanced placement credit, cooperative education, independent study, internships, part-time degree program, services for LD students.

Financial Aid Of all full-time matriculated undergraduates who enrolled in 2008, 10 Federal Work-Study jobs (averaging $4000).

Applying *Options:* electronic application. *Required:* high school transcript, interview.

Director of Admissions Michelle Squibb, Admissions Representative, IntelliTec Medical Institute, 2345 North Academy Boulevard, Colorado Springs, CO 80909. *Phone:* 719-596-7400.

ITT Technical Institute

Aurora, Colorado **www.itt-tech.edu/**

- **Proprietary** primarily 2-year
- **Coed**

Majors CAD/CADD drafting/design technology; computer and information systems security; computer engineering technology; criminal justice/law enforcement administration; design and visual communications; electrical, electronic and communications engineering technology; legal assistant/paralegal; system, networking, and LAN/WAN management.

Academics *Degrees:* associate and bachelor's.

Freshman Application Contact ITT Technical Institute, 12500 East Iliff Avenue, Suite 100, Aurora, CO 80014. *Phone:* 303-695-6317.

ITT Technical Institute

Thornton, Colorado **www.itt-tech.edu/**

- **Proprietary** primarily 2-year, founded 1984, part of ITT Educational Services, Inc.
- **Suburban** campus
- **Coed**

Majors CAD/CADD drafting/design technology; computer and information systems security; computer software engineering; computer software technology; construction management; criminal justice/law enforcement administration; design and visual communications; electrical, electronic and communications engineering technology; legal assistant/paralegal; system, networking, and LAN/WAN management; web/multimedia management and webmaster; web page, digital/multimedia and information resources design.

Academics *Calendar:* quarters. *Degrees:* associate and bachelor's.

Student Life *Housing:* college housing not available.

Freshman Application Contact Director of Recruitment, ITT Technical Institute, 500 East 84th Avenue, Suite B12, Thornton, CO 80229. *Phone:* 303-288-4488. *Toll-free phone:* 800-395-4488.

Kaplan College, Denver Campus

Thornton, Colorado **www.kc-denver.com/**

- **Proprietary** 2-year, founded 1977
- **Coed**

Majors Business administration and management; criminal justice/safety; legal assistant/paralegal.

Academics *Calendar:* continuous. *Degree:* certificates, diplomas, and associate.

Freshman Application Contact Kaplan College, Denver Campus, 500 East 84th Avenue, Suite W-200, Thornton, CO 80229. *Phone:* 303-295-0550.

Lamar Community College

Lamar, Colorado **www.lamarcc.edu/**

Freshman Application Contact Director of Admissions, Lamar Community College, 2401 South Main Street, Lamar, CO 81052-3999. *Phone:* 719-336-1590. *Toll-free phone:* 800-968-6920. *E-mail:* admissions@lamarcc.edu.

Morgan Community College

Fort Morgan, Colorado **www.morgancc.edu/**

- **State-supported** 2-year, founded 1967, part of Colorado Community College and Occupational Education System
- **Small-town** 20-acre campus with easy access to Denver
- **Coed**

Undergraduates 501 full-time, 1,142 part-time. Students come from 5 states and territories, 4% are from out of state, 1% African American, 0.6% Asian American or Pacific Islander, 17% Hispanic American, 0.7% Native American, 0.6% international, 2% transferred in. *Retention:* 41% of 2008 full-time freshmen returned.

Faculty *Student/faculty ratio:* 11:1.

Academics *Calendar:* semesters. *Degree:* certificates and associate. *Special study options:* academic remediation for entering students, adult/continuing education programs, advanced placement credit, distance learning, double majors, internships, part-time degree program, services for LD students, summer session for credit.

Financial Aid Of all full-time matriculated undergraduates who enrolled in 2008, 20 Federal Work-Study jobs (averaging $1700). 50 state and other part-time jobs (averaging $2000).

Applying *Options:* electronic application, early admission, deferred entrance. *Recommended:* high school transcript.

Freshman Application Contact Ms. Kim Maxwell, Morgan Community College, Student Services, 17800 Road 20, Fort Morgan, CO 80701. *Phone:* 970-542-3111. *Toll-free phone:* 800-622-0216. *Fax:* 970-867-6608. *E-mail:* kim.maxwell@morgancc.edu.

Northeastern Junior College

Sterling, Colorado **www.njc.edu/**

- **State-supported** 2-year, founded 1941, part of Colorado Community College and Occupational Education System
- **Small-town** 65-acre campus
- **Endowment** $5.4 million
- **Coed,** 2,698 undergraduate students, 34% full-time, 62% women, 38% men

Undergraduates 910 full-time, 1,788 part-time. Students come from 21 states and territories, 8 other countries, 6% are from out of state, 3% African American, 0.6% Asian American or Pacific Islander, 7% Hispanic American, 0.7% Native American, 0.9% international, 2% transferred in, 44% live on campus. *Retention:* 56% of 2008 full-time freshmen returned.

Freshmen *Admission:* 1,247 applied, 1,247 admitted, 456 enrolled. *Average high school GPA:* 3.33.

Faculty *Total:* 115, 46% full-time, 0.9% with terminal degrees. *Student/faculty ratio:* 36:1.

Majors Accounting; agricultural business and management; agricultural economics; agricultural mechanization; agricultural teacher education; agriculture; agronomy and crop science; anatomy; animal sciences; applied mathematics; art; art teacher education; automobile/automotive mechanics technology; biological and physical sciences; biology/biological sciences; business administration and management; business teacher education; child development; clinical laboratory science/medical technology; computer engineering technology; computer science; corrections; cosmetology; criminal justice/police science; dramatic/theater arts; drawing; economics; education; elementary education; emergency medical technology (EMT paramedic); English; equestrian studies; family and consumer sciences/human sciences; farm and ranch management; fashion merchandising; fine/studio arts; health professions related; history; humanities; journalism; kindergarten/preschool education; legal administrative assistant/secretary; liberal arts and sciences/liberal studies; marketing/marketing management; mathematics; medical administrative assistant and medical secretary; music; music teacher education; natural sciences; nursing (licensed practical/vocational nurse training); nursing (registered nurse training); physical education teaching and coaching; physical sciences; pre-engineering; psychology; social sciences; social work; trade and industrial teacher education; zoology/animal biology.

Academics *Calendar:* semesters. *Degree:* certificates and associate. *Special study options:* academic remediation for entering students, accelerated degree program, adult/continuing education programs, advanced placement credit, cooperative education, distance learning, double majors, English as a second language, honors programs, independent study, internships, part-time degree program, services for LD students, summer session for credit.

Library Monahan Library with 29,549 titles, 245 serial subscriptions, 3,542 audiovisual materials, an OPAC, a Web page.

Student Life *Housing:* on-campus residence required for freshman year. *Options:* coed, women-only. Campus housing is university owned. Freshman campus housing is guaranteed. *Activities and Organizations:* drama/theater group, student-run newspaper, choral group, Associated Student Government, Post Secondary Agriculture (PAS), Creative Inferno, Students in Free Enterprise (SIFE), Crossroads. *Campus security:* 24-hour emergency response devices, late-night transport/escort service, controlled dormitory access. *Student services:* health clinic, personal/psychological counseling.

Athletics Member NCAA, NJCAA. All NCAA Division I. *Intercollegiate sports:* baseball M(s), basketball M(s)/W(s), equestrian sports M(s)/W(s), volleyball W(s). *Intramural sports:* badminton M/W, baseball M/W, basketball M/W, bowling M/W, cheerleading M/W, football M, golf M/W, racquetball M/W, soccer M/W, softball M/W, tennis M/W, ultimate Frisbee M/W, volleyball M/W, weight lifting M/W.

Costs (2010–11) *Tuition:* state resident $2310 full-time, $96 per credit hour part-time; nonresident $8242 full-time, $343 per credit hour part-time. Full-time tuition and fees vary according to course load. Part-time tuition and fees vary according to course load. *Required fees:* $574 full-time, $10 per semester hour part-time, $11 per semester part-time. *Room and board:* $5654; room only: $2580. Room and board charges vary according to board plan and housing facility. *Payment plan:* installment. *Waivers:* senior citizens and employees or children of employees.

Applying *Options:* electronic application, early admission, deferred entrance. *Required:* high school transcript. *Application deadline:* rolling (out-of-state freshmen). *Notification:* continuous until 8/1 (freshmen), continuous (out-of-state freshmen), continuous until 8/1 (transfers).

Freshman Application Contact Andy Long, Director of Admissions, Northeastern Junior College, 100 College Avenue, Sterling, CO 80751. *Phone:* 970-521-7000. *Toll-free phone:* 800-626-4637. *E-mail:* andy.long@njc.edu.

OTERO JUNIOR COLLEGE

La Junta, Colorado **www.ojc.edu/**

- **State-supported** 2-year, founded 1941, part of Colorado Community College and Occupational Education System
- **Rural** 50-acre campus
- **Coed,** 1,660 undergraduate students, 52% full-time, 61% women, 39% men

Undergraduates 870 full-time, 790 part-time. 3% African American, 1% Asian American or Pacific Islander, 29% Hispanic American, 1% Native American, 2% international, 17% live on campus.

Freshmen *Admission:* 318 enrolled.

Faculty *Total:* 75, 44% full-time.

Majors Administrative assistant and secretarial science; agricultural business and management; automobile/automotive mechanics technology; biological and physical sciences; biology/biological sciences; business administration and management; child development; comparative literature; data processing and data processing technology; dramatic/theater arts; elementary education; history; humanities; kindergarten/preschool education; legal administrative assistant/secretary; liberal arts and sciences/liberal studies; mathematics; medical administrative assistant and medical secretary; modern languages; nursing (registered nurse training); political science and government; pre-engineering; psychology; social sciences.

Academics *Calendar:* semesters. *Degree:* certificates and associate. *Special study options:* academic remediation for entering students, adult/continuing education programs, advanced placement credit, distance learning, external degree program, internships, part-time degree program, summer session for credit.

Library Wheeler Library with 36,701 titles, 183 serial subscriptions, an OPAC.

Student Life *Housing:* on-campus residence required for freshman year. *Options:* men-only, women-only. Campus housing is university owned. *Activities and Organizations:* drama/theater group, student-run newspaper, choral group. *Campus security:* 24-hour patrols, late-night transport/escort service. *Student services:* personal/psychological counseling.

Athletics Member NJCAA. *Intercollegiate sports:* baseball M(s), basketball M(s)/W(s), golf M(s)/W(s), soccer M(s), softball W(s), volleyball W(s). *Intramural sports:* basketball M, volleyball M/W.

Costs (2010–11) *Tuition:* state resident $2310 full-time; nonresident $4578 full-time. *Required fees:* $206 full-time. *Room and board:* $5354.

Financial Aid Of all full-time matriculated undergraduates who enrolled in 2008, 30 Federal Work-Study jobs (averaging $2000). 100 state and other part-time jobs (averaging $2000).

Applying *Options:* electronic application, early admission. *Recommended:* high school transcript. *Notification:* continuous (freshmen), continuous (transfers).

Freshman Application Contact Mr. Jeff Paolucci, Vice President for Student Services, Otero Junior College, 1802 Colorado Avenue, La Junta, CO 81050-3415. *Phone:* 719-384-6833. *Fax:* 719-384-6933. *E-mail:* jan.schiro@ojc.edu.

PIKES PEAK COMMUNITY COLLEGE

Colorado Springs, Colorado **www.ppcc.edu/**

- **State-supported** 2-year, founded 1968, part of Colorado Community College and Occupational Education System
- **Urban** 287-acre campus with easy access to Denver
- **Coed,** 13,572 undergraduate students

Majors Accounting technology and bookkeeping; animation, interactive technology, video graphics and special effects; architectural engineering technology; autobody/collision and repair technology; automobile/automotive mechanics technology; building/construction finishing, management, and inspection related; business administration and management; CAD/CADD drafting/design technology; child development; cooking and related culinary arts; criminal justice/law enforcement administration; dental assisting; educational/instructional media design; electrical, electronic and communications engineering technology; emergency medical technology (EMT paramedic); fire protection and safety technology; general studies; interior design; legal assistant/paralegal; liberal arts and sciences/liberal studies; management information systems; medical office management; natural resources management and policy; nursing (registered nurse training); psychiatric/mental health services technology; radio and television broadcasting technology; security and protective services related; sign language interpretation and translation; welding technology.

Academics *Calendar:* semesters. *Degree:* certificates and associate. *Special study options:* academic remediation for entering students, adult/continuing education programs, advanced placement credit, cooperative education, distance learning, double majors, English as a second language, independent study, internships, part-time degree program, services for LD students, summer session for credit. *ROTC:* Army (c).

Library PPCC Library plus 1 other with 34,332 titles, 311 serial subscriptions, 3,832 audiovisual materials, an OPAC.

Student Life *Housing:* college housing not available. *Activities and Organizations:* drama/theater group, student-run newspaper. *Campus security:* 24-hour emergency response devices and patrols, late-night transport/escort service. *Student services:* women's center.

Financial Aid Of all full-time matriculated undergraduates who enrolled in 2008, 168 Federal Work-Study jobs (averaging $1225). 327 state and other part-time jobs (averaging $1791).

Applying *Required for some:* high school transcript. *Application deadlines:* rolling (freshmen), rolling (transfers).

Freshman Application Contact Pikes Peak Community College, 5675 South Academy Boulevard, Colorado Springs, CO 80906-5498. *Phone:* 719-540-7041. *Toll-free phone:* 866-411-7722.

PIMA MEDICAL INSTITUTE

Denver, Colorado **www.pmi.edu/**

- **Proprietary** 2-year, founded 1988, part of Vocational Training Institutes, Inc.
- **Urban** campus
- **Coed**

Academics *Calendar:* modular. *Degree:* certificates and associate. *Special study options:* academic remediation for entering students, cooperative education, internships.

Standardized Tests *Required:* Wonderlic Scholastic Level Exam (for admission).

Applying *Required:* interview. *Required for some:* high school transcript.

Freshman Application Contact Admissions Office, Pima Medical Institute, Pima Medical Institute, 1701 West 72nd Avenue, Suite 130, Denver, CO 80221. *Phone:* 303-426-1800. *Toll-free phone:* 888-898-9048.

PLATT COLLEGE

Aurora, Colorado **www.plattcolorado.edu/**

- **Proprietary** primarily 2-year, founded 1986
- **Suburban** campus
- **Coed**

Academics *Calendar:* continuous. *Degrees:* diplomas, associate, and bachelor's. *Special study options:* academic remediation for entering students, advanced placement credit.

Applying *Application fee:* $75. *Required:* high school transcript, interview.

Freshman Application Contact Admissions Office, Platt College, 3100 South Parker Road, Suite 200, Aurora, CO 80014-3141. *Phone:* 303-369-5151.

PUEBLO COMMUNITY COLLEGE

Pueblo, Colorado **www.pueblocc.edu/**

- **State-supported** 2-year, founded 1933, part of Colorado Community College System
- **Urban** 35-acre campus
- **Endowment** $490,871
- **Coed,** 6,528 undergraduate students, 42% full-time, 60% women, 40% men

Undergraduates 2,772 full-time, 3,756 part-time. Students come from 32 states and territories, 4 other countries, 2% are from out of state, 7% transferred in.

Freshmen *Admission:* 2,524 applied, 2,524 admitted, 1,414 enrolled.

Faculty *Total:* 439, 23% full-time. *Student/faculty ratio:* 19:1.

Majors Accounting technology and bookkeeping; animation, interactive technology, video graphics and special effects; autobody/collision and repair technology; automobile/automotive mechanics technology; business administration and management; child development; communications technology; computer/information technology services administration related; cosmetology; criminal justice/law enforcement administration; dental assisting; dental hygiene; diagnostic medical sonography and ultrasound technology; electrical, electronic and communications engineering technology; emergency medical technology (EMT paramedic); energy management and systems technology; engineering technology; fire science; general studies; hair styling and hair design; hospitality and recreation marketing; liberal arts and sciences and humanities related; liberal arts and sciences/liberal studies; library assistant; machine shop technology; nursing (registered nurse training); occupational therapist assistant; physical therapist assistant; radiologic technology/science; respiratory care therapy; science technologies related; web page, digital/multimedia and information resources design; welding technology.

Academics *Calendar:* semesters. *Degree:* certificates and associate. *Special study options:* academic remediation for entering students, accelerated degree program, advanced placement credit, cooperative education, distance learning, double majors, English as a second language, honors programs, independent study, internships, part-time degree program, services for LD students, summer session for credit.

Library The Library @ PCC with 38,956 titles, 8,031 serial subscriptions, 16,892 audiovisual materials, an OPAC.

Student Life *Housing:* college housing not available. *Activities and Organizations:* drama/theater group, choral group, Phi Theta Kappa, Welding Club, Culinary Arts Club, Performing Arts Club, Art Club. *Campus security:* 24-hour emergency response devices, late-night transport/escort service. *Student services:* personal/psychological counseling.

Costs (2009–10) *One-time required fee:* $10. *Tuition:* state resident $2700 full-time, $173 per credit part-time; nonresident $11,525 full-time, $375 per credit part-time. Full-time tuition and fees vary according to location and program. Part-time tuition and fees vary according to location and program. *Required fees:* $271 full-time, $9 per course part-time, $63 per term part-time. *Payment plan:* installment. *Waivers:* senior citizens.

Financial Aid Of all full-time matriculated undergraduates who enrolled in 2008, 1,548 applied for aid, 1,480 were judged to have need, 53 had their need fully met. 150 Federal Work-Study jobs (averaging $3750). 150 state and other part-time jobs (averaging $3750). In 2008, 68 non-need-based awards were made. *Average percent of need met:* 70%. *Average financial aid package:* $4550. *Average need-based loan:* $3245. *Average need-based gift aid:* $2800. *Average non-need-based aid:* $1200. *Average indebtedness upon graduation:* $15,000.

Applying *Options:* electronic application, early admission, deferred entrance. *Application deadlines:* rolling (freshmen), rolling (out-of-state freshmen), rolling (transfers). *Notification:* continuous until 9/1 (freshmen), continuous until 9/1 (out-of-state freshmen), continuous until 9/1 (transfers).

Freshman Application Contact Ms. Barbara Benedict, Assistant Director of Admissions and Records, Pueblo Community College, 900 West Orman Avenue, Pueblo, CO 81004. *Phone:* 719-549-3039. *Toll-free phone:* 800-642-6017. *Fax:* 719-549-3012.

RED ROCKS COMMUNITY COLLEGE

Lakewood, Colorado **www.rrcc.edu/**

- **State-supported** 2-year, founded 1969, part of Colorado Community College and Occupational Education System
- **Urban** 120-acre campus with easy access to Denver
- **Coed,** 9,105 undergraduate students, 34% full-time, 49% women, 51% men

Undergraduates 3,058 full-time, 6,047 part-time. Students come from 35 states and territories, 13 other countries, 4% are from out of state, 2% African American, 3% Asian American or Pacific Islander, 12% Hispanic American, 2% Native American, 9% transferred in. *Retention:* 41% of 2008 full-time freshmen returned.

Freshmen *Admission:* 4,080 applied, 4,080 admitted, 1,858 enrolled.

Faculty *Total:* 508, 16% full-time, 16% with terminal degrees. *Student/faculty ratio:* 23:1.

Majors Animation, interactive technology, video graphics and special effects; art; biology/biological sciences; biotechnology; business administration and management; chemistry; cinematography and film/video production; communication disorders; communication/speech communication and rhetoric; computer science; criminal justice/law enforcement administration; dramatic/theater arts; economics; elementary education; engineering; English; French; general studies; geology/earth science; German; graphic design; history; humanities; kindergarten/preschool education; liberal arts and sciences/liberal studies; mass communication/media; mathematics; music performance; parks, recreation and leisure; philosophy; physical education teaching and coaching; physics; political science and government; psychology; secondary education; sociology; Spanish.

Academics *Calendar:* semesters. *Degree:* certificates and associate. *Special study options:* academic remediation for entering students, adult/continuing education programs, cooperative education, English as a second language, honors programs, off-campus study, part-time degree program, services for LD students, study abroad, summer session for credit.

Library Marvin Buckels Library with 40,909 titles, 140 serial subscriptions, 4,117 audiovisual materials, an OPAC, a Web page.

Student Life *Housing:* college housing not available. *Activities and Organizations:* drama/theater group. *Campus security:* 24-hour emergency response devices and patrols. *Student services:* personal/psychological counseling.

Athletics *Intramural sports:* volleyball M/W.

Costs (2009–10) *Tuition:* state resident $2649 full-time, $88 per credit hour part-time; nonresident $11,817 full-time, $394 per credit hour part-time. Full-time tuition and fees vary according to program and reciprocity agreements. Part-time tuition and fees vary according to program and reciprocity agreements. *Required fees:* $298 full-time, $9 per credit hour part-time, $11 per term part-time. *Payment plans:* installment, deferred payment. *Waivers:* employees or children of employees.

Financial Aid Of all full-time matriculated undergraduates who enrolled in 2008, 21 Federal Work-Study jobs (averaging $5000). 95 state and other part-time jobs (averaging $5000).

Applying *Options:* electronic application, early admission. *Application deadlines:* rolling (freshmen), rolling (out-of-state freshmen), rolling (transfers). *Notification:* continuous (freshmen), continuous (out-of-state freshmen), continuous (transfers).

Freshman Application Contact Admissions Office, Red Rocks Community College, 13300 West 6th Avenue Box 5, Lakewood, CO 80228-1255. *Phone:* 303-914-6360. *Fax:* 303-914-6919. *E-mail:* admissions@rrcc.edu.

REDSTONE COLLEGE–DENVER

Broomfield, Colorado **www.redstone.edu/**

- **Proprietary** 2-year, founded 1965
- **Coed,** 590 undergraduate students

Faculty *Total:* 48.

Majors Avionics maintenance technology; construction management.

Academics *Calendar:* continuous. *Degree:* certificates, diplomas, and associate.

Financial Aid Of all full-time matriculated undergraduates who enrolled in 2008, 20 Federal Work-Study jobs.

Freshman Application Contact Redstone College–Denver, 10851 West 120th Avenue, Broomfield, CO 80021. *Phone:* 303-466-7383. *Toll-free phone:* 877-801-1025.

REMINGTON COLLEGE–COLORADO SPRINGS CAMPUS

Colorado Springs, Colorado **www.remingtoncollege.edu/**

- **Proprietary** primarily 2-year
- **Urban** 3-acre campus
- **Coed**

Academics *Calendar:* quarters. *Degrees:* diplomas, associate, and bachelor's.

Student Life *Campus security:* 24-hour emergency response devices, late-night transport/escort service.

Freshman Application Contact Remington College–Colorado Springs Campus, 6050 Erin Park Drive, #250, Colorado Springs, CO 80918. *Phone:* 719-532-1234 Ext. 202.

TRINIDAD STATE JUNIOR COLLEGE

Trinidad, Colorado **www.trinidadstate.edu/**

Freshman Application Contact Dr. Sandra Veltri, Vice President of Student/Academic Affairs, Trinidad State Junior College, 600 Prospect, Trinidad, CO 81082-2396. *Phone:* 719-846-5559. *Toll-free phone:* 800-621-8752. *Fax:* 719-846-5620. *E-mail:* sandy.veltri@trinidadstate.edu.

CONNECTICUT

ASNUNTUCK COMMUNITY COLLEGE

Enfield, Connecticut **www.acc.commnet.edu/**

Freshman Application Contact Ms. Donna Shaw, Director of Admissions, Asnuntuck Community College, 170 Elm Street, Enfield, CT 06082-3800. *Phone:* 860-253-3018. *Toll-free phone:* 800-501-3967. *Fax:* 860-253-3014. *E-mail:* dshaw@acc.commnet.edu.

CAPITAL COMMUNITY COLLEGE

Hartford, Connecticut **www.ccc.commnet.edu/**

Freshman Application Contact Ms. Jackie Phillips, Director of the Welcome and Advising Center, Capital Community College, 950 Main Street, Hartford, CT 06103. *Phone:* 860-906-5078. *Toll-free phone:* 800-894-6126. *E-mail:* mballj-davis@ccc.commnet.edu.

GATEWAY COMMUNITY COLLEGE

New Haven, Connecticut **www.gwcc.commnet.edu/**

- **State-supported** 2-year, founded 1992, part of Connecticut Community–Technical College System
- **Urban** 5-acre campus with easy access to New York City
- **Coed,** 6,847 undergraduate students, 36% full-time, 60% women, 40% men

Undergraduates 2,474 full-time, 4,373 part-time. 22% African American, 3% Asian American or Pacific Islander, 14% Hispanic American, 0.3% Native American, 2% international.

Freshmen *Admission:* 3,773 applied, 3,763 admitted, 1,431 enrolled.

Faculty *Total:* 407, 21% full-time, 4% with terminal degrees. *Student/faculty ratio:* 9:1.

Majors Accounting; automobile/automotive mechanics technology; avionics maintenance technology; biomedical technology; business administration and management; computer and information sciences related; computer engineering related; computer engineering technology; computer graphics; computer typography and composition equipment operation; consumer merchandising/retailing management; data entry/microcomputer applications; data processing and data processing technology; dietetics; electrical, electronic and communications engineering technology; engineering technology; fashion merchandising; fire science; gerontology; hotel/motel administration; human services; industrial radiologic technology; industrial technology; kindergarten/preschool education; legal administrative assistant/secretary; liberal arts and sciences/liberal studies; mechanical engineering/mechanical technology; medical administrative assistant and medical secretary; mental health/rehabilitation; nuclear medical technology; nursing (registered nurse training); special products marketing; substance abuse/addiction counseling; word processing.

Academics *Calendar:* semesters. *Degree:* certificates and associate. *Special study options:* academic remediation for entering students, adult/continuing education programs, advanced placement credit, distance learning, English as a second language, external degree program, independent study, internships, off-campus study, part-time degree program, services for LD students, summer session for credit.

Library Gateway Community College Library plus 2 others with 45,409 titles, 226 serial subscriptions, 3,063 audiovisual materials, an OPAC, a Web page.

Student Life *Housing:* college housing not available. *Activities and Organizations:* student-run newspaper. *Campus security:* late-night transport/escort service. *Student services:* personal/psychological counseling, women's center.

Athletics Member NJCAA. *Intercollegiate sports:* baseball M, basketball M/W, soccer M, softball W.

Costs (2010–11) *Tuition:* state resident $3024 full-time, $126 per credit part-time; nonresident $9072 full-time, $378 per credit part-time. *Required fees:* $382 full-time. *Payment plan:* installment. *Waivers:* senior citizens and employees or children of employees.

Financial Aid Of all full-time matriculated undergraduates who enrolled in 2009, 85 Federal Work-Study jobs (averaging $5000).

Applying *Options:* early admission, deferred entrance. *Application fee:* $20. *Required:* high school transcript. *Required for some:* essay or personal statement, interview. *Notification:* continuous until 9/1 (freshmen), continuous until 9/1 (transfers).

Freshman Application Contact Ms. Kim Shea, Director of Admissions, Gateway Community College, 60 Sargent Drive, New Haven, CT 06511. *Phone:* 203-789-7043. *Toll-free phone:* 800-390-7723. *Fax:* 203-285-2018. *E-mail:* gateway_ctc@commnet.edu.

GOODWIN COLLEGE

East Hartford, Connecticut **www.goodwin.edu/**

- **Proprietary** primarily 2-year, founded 1999
- **Urban** campus with easy access to Hartford
- **Coed,** 2,083 undergraduate students, 25% full-time, 85% women, 15% men

Undergraduates 523 full-time, 1,560 part-time. 1% are from out of state, 27% African American, 2% Asian American or Pacific Islander, 18% Hispanic American, 0.2% Native American, 17% transferred in. *Retention:* 54% of 2008 full-time freshmen returned.

Freshmen *Admission:* 871 applied, 871 admitted, 387 enrolled.

Faculty *Total:* 179, 25% full-time, 18% with terminal degrees. *Student/faculty ratio:* 12:1.

Majors Accounting technology and bookkeeping; business administration and management; business/commerce; computer and information sciences; early childhood education; emergency medical technology (EMT paramedic); entrepreneurship; histologic technician; human services; liberal arts and sciences/liberal studies; medical administrative assistant and medical secretary; medical/clinical assistant; medical insurance coding; medical insurance/medical billing; nursing (registered nurse training); respiratory care therapy; security and protective services related; teacher assistant/aide.

Academics *Calendar:* semesters. *Degrees:* certificates, associate, and bachelor's. *Special study options:* academic remediation for entering students, adult/continuing education programs, advanced placement credit, distance learning, double majors, English as a second language, internships, off-campus study, part-time degree program, services for LD students, summer session for credit.

Library Goodwin College Library with an OPAC.

Student Life *Housing:* college housing not available. *Activities and Organizations:* Student Council, Multicultural Club. *Campus security:* evening security patrolman.

Costs (2009–10) *Tuition:* $15,920 full-time, $530 per credit hour part-time. Full-time tuition and fees vary according to course load and program. Part-time tuition and fees vary according to course load and program. *Required fees:* $500 full-time. *Payment plan:* installment. *Waivers:* employees or children of employees.

Financial Aid Of all full-time matriculated undergraduates who enrolled in 2009, 508 applied for aid, 506 were judged to have need. *Average percent of need met:* 31%. *Average financial aid package:* $9109. *Average need-based loan:* $3567. *Average need-based gift aid:* $4876.

Applying *Options:* electronic application, early decision, early action, deferred entrance. *Application fee:* $50. *Required:* essay or personal statement, high school transcript, minimum 2 GPA, medical exam. *Recommended:* 2 letters of recommendation, interview. *Application deadlines:* rolling (freshmen), rolling (transfers). *Notification:* continuous (freshmen), continuous (transfers).

Freshman Application Contact Mr. Nicholas Lantino, Director of High School Admissions, Goodwin College, 745 Burnside Avenue, East Hartford, CT 06108. *Phone:* 860-528-4111 Ext. 6765. *Toll-free phone:* 800-889-3282. *Fax:* 860-291-8285. *E-mail:* nlantino@goodwin.edu.

HOUSATONIC COMMUNITY COLLEGE

Bridgeport, Connecticut **www.hctc.commnet.edu/**

- **State-supported** 2-year, founded 1965, part of Connecticut Community–Technical College System
- **Urban** 4-acre campus with easy access to New York City
- **Coed,** 5,609 undergraduate students

Faculty *Total:* 391, 18% full-time. *Student/faculty ratio:* 14:1.

Majors Accounting; administrative assistant and secretarial science; art; avionics maintenance technology; business administration and management; child development; clinical/medical laboratory technology; commercial and advertising art; computer typography and composition equipment operation; criminal justice/law enforcement administration; data processing and data processing technology; environmental studies; humanities; human services; journalism; liberal arts and sciences/liberal studies; mathematics; mental health/rehabilitation; nursing (registered nurse training); physical therapy; pre-engineering; public administration; social sciences; substance abuse/addiction counseling.

Academics *Calendar:* semesters. *Degree:* certificates and associate. *Special study options:* academic remediation for entering students, adult/continuing education programs, advanced placement credit, cooperative education, distance learning, double majors, English as a second language, honors programs, independent study, internships, part-time degree program, services for LD students, summer session for credit. *ROTC:* Army (c). *Unusual degree programs:* nursing with Bridgeport Hospital.

Library Housatonic Community College Library with 30,000 titles, 300 serial subscriptions, an OPAC, a Web page.

Student Life *Housing:* college housing not available. *Activities and Organizations:* drama/theater group, student-run newspaper, Student Senate, Association of Latin American Students, Community Action Network, Drama Club. *Campus security:* 24-hour emergency response devices, late-night transport/escort service. *Student services:* health clinic, personal/psychological counseling, women's center.

Financial Aid Of all full-time matriculated undergraduates who enrolled in 2008, 70 Federal Work-Study jobs (averaging $2850).

Applying *Options:* electronic application, deferred entrance. *Application fee:* $20. *Required:* high school transcript. *Required for some:* interview. *Application deadlines:* rolling (freshmen), rolling (transfers). *Notification:* continuous (freshmen), continuous (transfers).

Freshman Application Contact Ms. Delores Y. Curtis, Director of Admissions, Housatonic Community College, 900 Lafayette Boulevard, Bridgeport, CT 06604-4704. *Phone:* 203-332-5102.

LINCOLN COLLEGE OF NEW ENGLAND

Suffield, Connecticut **www.clemenscollege.edu/**

Freshman Application Contact Mrs. Jolie Swanson, Director of Admissions, Lincoln College of New England, 1760 Mapleton Avenue, Suffield, CT 06078. *Phone:* 860-668-3515 Ext. 126. *Toll-free phone:* 800-955-0809. *Fax:* 860-668-7369. *E-mail:* admissions@ichm.edu.

MANCHESTER COMMUNITY COLLEGE

Manchester, Connecticut **www.mcc.commnet.edu/**

- **State-supported** 2-year, founded 1963, part of Connecticut Community–Technical College System
- **Small-town** 160-acre campus with easy access to Hartford
- **Coed,** 7,366 undergraduate students, 47% full-time, 52% women, 48% men

Undergraduates 3,430 full-time, 3,936 part-time. 13% African American, 3% Asian American or Pacific Islander, 13% Hispanic American, 0.2% Native American, 0.6% international, 12% transferred in. *Retention:* 58% of 2008 full-time freshmen returned.

Freshmen *Admission:* 2,997 applied, 2,980 admitted, 1,745 enrolled.

Majors Accounting; administrative assistant and secretarial science; business administration and management; clinical/medical laboratory technology; commercial and advertising art; communication/speech communication and rhetoric; criminal justice/law enforcement administration; dramatic/theater arts; engineering science; fine/studio arts; general studies; hotel/motel administration; human services; industrial engineering; industrial technology; information science/studies; journalism; kindergarten/preschool education; legal administrative assistant/secretary; legal assistant/paralegal; liberal arts and sciences/liberal studies; management information systems; marketing/marketing management; medical administrative assistant and medical secretary; music; occupational therapist assistant; physical therapist assistant; respiratory care therapy; social work; surgical technology; teacher assistant/aide.

Academics *Calendar:* semesters. *Degree:* certificates and associate. *Special study options:* academic remediation for entering students, adult/continuing education programs, cooperative education, distance learning, double majors, English as a second language, independent study, internships, off-campus study, part-time degree program, services for LD students, student-designed majors, summer session for credit.

Student Life *Housing:* college housing not available. *Activities and Organizations:* drama/theater group, student-run newspaper, choral group. *Student services:* women's center.

Athletics Member NJCAA. *Intercollegiate sports:* baseball M, basketball M/W, soccer M/W, softball W.

Costs (2009–10) *Tuition:* state resident $3200 full-time, $118 per credit hour part-time; nonresident $9560 full-time, $354 per credit hour part-time. *Payment plan:* installment. *Waivers:* senior citizens and employees or children of employees.

Financial Aid Of all full-time matriculated undergraduates who enrolled in 2008, 80 Federal Work-Study jobs (averaging $2000). 45 state and other part-time jobs (averaging $2000).

Applying *Options:* electronic application. *Application fee:* $20. *Required:* high school transcript. *Application deadlines:* rolling (freshmen), rolling (transfers). *Notification:* continuous (freshmen), continuous (transfers).

Freshman Application Contact Mr. Peter Harris, Director of Admissions, Manchester Community College, PO Box 1046, MS #12, Manchester, CT 06045-1046. *Phone:* 860-512-3210. *Fax:* 860-512-3221.

MIDDLESEX COMMUNITY COLLEGE

Middletown, Connecticut **www.mxcc.commnet.edu/**

- **State-supported** 2-year, founded 1966, part of Connecticut Community–Technical College System
- **Suburban** 38-acre campus with easy access to Hartford
- **Endowment** $341,678
- **Coed,** 2,914 undergraduate students, 42% full-time, 59% women, 41% men

Undergraduates 1,222 full-time, 1,692 part-time. Students come from 6 states and territories, 8 other countries, 1% are from out of state, 9% African American, 2% Asian American or Pacific Islander, 14% Hispanic American, 0.1% Native American, 0.3% international. *Retention:* 45% of 2008 full-time freshmen returned.

Freshmen *Admission:* 942 applied, 917 admitted.

Faculty *Total:* 179, 23% full-time, 16% with terminal degrees. *Student/faculty ratio:* 20:1.

Majors Accounting; administrative assistant and secretarial science; biological and physical sciences; biology/biotechnology laboratory technician; broadcast journalism; business administration and management; commercial and advertising art; computer programming; engineering science; engineering technology; environmental studies; fine/studio arts; human services; industrial radiologic technology; intermedia/multimedia; legal administrative assistant/secretary; liberal arts and sciences/liberal studies; marketing/marketing management; mass communication/media; medical administrative assistant and medical secretary; mental health/rehabilitation; ophthalmic laboratory technology; pre-engineering; substance abuse/addiction counseling.

Academics *Calendar:* semesters. *Degree:* certificates and associate. *Special study options:* academic remediation for entering students, adult/continuing education programs, advanced placement credit, cooperative education, distance learning, double majors, English as a second language, honors programs, independent study, internships, off-campus study, part-time degree program, services for LD students, summer session for credit.

Library Jean Burr Smith Library with 70,265 titles, 26,025 serial subscriptions, 4,364 audiovisual materials, an OPAC, a Web page.

Student Life *Housing:* college housing not available. *Activities and Organizations:* drama/theater group, student-run newspaper, Phi Theta Kappa, Human Services Association, Peace and Justice Club, Poetry Club, International Student Club. *Campus security:* 24-hour emergency response devices and patrols.

Costs (2010–11) *Tuition:* state resident $3024 full-time, $126 per credit hour part-time; nonresident $9796 full-time, $378 per credit hour part-time. Full-time tuition and fees vary according to course load, degree level, program, and reciprocity agreements. Part-time tuition and fees vary according to course load, degree level, program, and reciprocity agreements. *Required fees:* $382 full-time. *Payment plan:* installment. *Waivers:* employees or children of employees.

Financial Aid Of all full-time matriculated undergraduates who enrolled in 2008, 50 Federal Work-Study jobs (averaging $5000). 2 state and other part-time jobs (averaging $5000).

Applying *Options:* electronic application, early admission, deferred entrance. *Application fee:* $20. *Required:* high school transcript, CPT. *Application deadlines:* rolling (freshmen), rolling (transfers).

Freshman Application Contact Mensimah Shabazz, Director of Admissions, Middlesex Community College, 100 Training Hill Road, Middletown, CT 06457-4889. *Phone:* 860-343-5742. *Fax:* 860-344-3055. *E-mail:* mshabazz@mxcc.commnet.edu.

NAUGATUCK VALLEY COMMUNITY COLLEGE

Waterbury, Connecticut **www.nvcc.commnet.edu/**

Freshman Application Contact Ms. Lucretia Sveda, Director of Enrollment Services, Naugatuck Valley Community College, Waterbury, CT 06708. *Phone:* 203-575-8016. *Fax:* 203-596-8766. *E-mail:* lsveda@nvcc.commnet.edu.

NORTHWESTERN CONNECTICUT COMMUNITY COLLEGE

Winsted, Connecticut **www.nwcc.commnet.edu/**

- **State-supported** 2-year, founded 1965, part of Connecticut Community–Technical College System
- **Small-town** 5-acre campus with easy access to Hartford
- **Coed,** 1,711 undergraduate students, 35% full-time, 68% women, 32% men

Undergraduates 591 full-time, 1,120 part-time. Students come from 5 states and territories, 1% are from out of state, 2% African American, 1% Asian American or Pacific Islander, 5% Hispanic American, 0.2% Native American, 8% transferred in. *Retention:* 63% of 2008 full-time freshmen returned.

Freshmen *Admission:* 312 enrolled.

Majors Accounting; administrative assistant and secretarial science; art; behavioral sciences; biology/biological sciences; business administration and management; child development; commercial and advertising art; communications technology; computer engineering technology; computer graphics; computer programming; computer science; criminal justice/law enforcement administration; criminal justice/police science; electrical, electronic and communications engineering technology; engineering; English; health professions related; human services; information science/studies; kindergarten/preschool education; legal assistant/paralegal; liberal arts and sciences/liberal studies; mathematics; medical/clinical assistant; parks, recreation and leisure; parks, recreation and leisure facilities management; physical sciences; pre-engineering; sign language interpretation and translation; social sciences; substance abuse/addiction counseling; therapeutic recreation; veterinary/animal health technology.

Academics *Calendar:* semesters. *Degree:* certificates and associate. *Special study options:* academic remediation for entering students, adult/continuing education programs, advanced placement credit, cooperative education, distance learning, double majors, English as a second language, independent study, internships, part-time degree program, services for LD students, summer session for credit.

Library Northwestern Connecticut Community–Technical College Learning Center with 37,666 titles, 267 serial subscriptions, 1,599 audiovisual materials, an OPAC.

Student Life *Housing:* college housing not available. *Activities and Organizations:* student-run newspaper, Ski Club, Student Senate, Deaf Club, Recreation Club, Early Childhood Educational Club. *Campus security:* evening security patrols.

Costs (2009–10) *Tuition:* state resident $2832 full-time, $118 per credit hour part-time; nonresident $8496 full-time, $354 per credit hour part-time. Full-time tuition and fees vary according to reciprocity agreements. Part-time tuition and fees vary according to course load and reciprocity agreements. *Required fees:* $368 full-time, $64 per credit hour part-time. *Waivers:* senior citizens and employees or children of employees.

Financial Aid Of all full-time matriculated undergraduates who enrolled in 2008, 75 Federal Work-Study jobs (averaging $2000). 15 state and other part-time jobs (averaging $1500).

Applying *Options:* deferred entrance. *Application fee:* $20. *Application deadlines:* rolling (freshmen), rolling (transfers). *Notification:* continuous (freshmen), continuous (transfers).

Freshman Application Contact Admissions Office, Northwestern Connecticut Community College, Park Place East, Winsted, CT 06098. *Phone:* 860-738-6330. *Fax:* 860-738-6437. *E-mail:* admissions@nwcc.commnet.edu.

NORWALK COMMUNITY COLLEGE

Norwalk, Connecticut **www.ncc.commnet.edu/**

Freshman Application Contact Mr. Curtis Antrum, Admissions Counselor, Norwalk Community College, 188 Richards Avenue, Norwalk, CT 06854-1655. *Phone:* 203-857-7060. *Toll-free phone:* 888-462-6282. *Fax:* 203-857-3335. *E-mail:* admissions@commnet.edu.

QUINEBAUG VALLEY COMMUNITY COLLEGE

Danielson, Connecticut **www.qvcc.commnet.edu/**

Freshman Application Contact Dr. Toni Moumouris, Director of Admissions, Quinebaug Valley Community College, 742 Upper Maple Street, Danielson, CT 06239. *Phone:* 860-774-1130 Ext. 318. *Fax:* 860-774-7768. *E-mail:* qu_isd@commnet.edu.

ST. VINCENT'S COLLEGE

Bridgeport, Connecticut **www.stvincentscollege.edu/**

Freshman Application Contact Mr. Joseph Marrone, Director of Admissions and Recruitment Marketing, St. Vincent's College, 2800 Main Street, Bridgeport, CT 06606-4292. *Phone:* 203-576-5515. *Toll-free phone:* 800-873-1013. *Fax:* 203-576-5893. *E-mail:* jmarrone@stvincentscollege.edu.

THREE RIVERS COMMUNITY COLLEGE

Norwich, Connecticut **www.trcc.commnet.edu/**

- **State-supported** 2-year, founded 1963, part of Connecticut Community–Technical College System
- **Small-town** 40-acre campus with easy access to Hartford
- **Endowment** $3.5 million
- **Coed,** 4,561 undergraduate students

Undergraduates Students come from 12 other countries, 1% are from out of state, 7% African American, 4% Asian American or Pacific Islander, 11% Hispanic American, 0.7% Native American, 0.3% international. *Retention:* 11% of 2008 full-time freshmen returned.

Freshmen *Admission:* 1,597 applied, 1,559 admitted.

Faculty *Total:* 240, 3% with terminal degrees. *Student/faculty ratio:* 20:1.

Majors Accounting; administrative assistant and secretarial science; architectural engineering technology; avionics maintenance technology; business administration and management; civil engineering technology; computer engineering technology; computer programming; consumer merchandising/retailing management; corrections; criminal justice/law enforcement administration; data processing and data processing technology; drafting and design technology; dramatic/theater arts; electrical, electronic and communications engineering technology; engineering; engineering science; engineering technology; environmental engineering technology; fire science; hospitality administration; hotel/motel administration; human services; hydrology and water resources science; industrial technology; kindergarten/preschool education; laser and optical technology; legal administrative assistant/secretary; liberal arts and sciences/liberal studies; marketing/marketing management; mechanical engineering/mechanical technology; nuclear/nuclear power technology; nursing (registered nurse training); pre-engineering; public administration; special products marketing; substance abuse/addiction counseling; technical and business writing; tourism and travel services management.

Academics *Calendar:* semesters. *Degrees:* certificates and associate (engineering technology programs are offered on the Thames Valley Campus; liberal arts, transfer and career programs are offered on the Mohegan Campus). *Special study options:* academic remediation for entering students, adult/continuing education programs, advanced placement credit, cooperative education, distance learning, double majors, English as a second language, external degree program, independent study, internships, part-time degree program, student-designed majors, study abroad, summer session for credit.

Library Three Rivers Community College Learning Resource Center plus 1 other with 48,000 titles, 221 serial subscriptions, 6,000 audiovisual materials, an OPAC.

Student Life *Housing:* college housing not available. *Activities and Organizations:* drama/theater group, student-run newspaper, Student Senate/Student Government Association, Theater Guild, Student Volunteers "TRUE", national

Three Rivers Community College (continued)

fraternities. *Campus security:* 24-hour emergency response devices, late-night transport/escort service, 14 hour patrols by trained security personnel. *Student services:* personal/psychological counseling.

Athletics *Intramural sports:* golf M(c)/W(c).

Standardized Tests *Recommended:* SAT (for admission).

Costs (2010–11) *Tuition:* state resident $3200 full-time, $118 per credit hour part-time; nonresident $9560 full-time, $354 per credit hour part-time. *Required fees:* $368 full-time, $64 per credit hour part-time, $182 per credit hour part-time. *Payment plan:* installment. *Waivers:* senior citizens and employees or children of employees.

Financial Aid Of all full-time matriculated undergraduates who enrolled in 2008, 40 Federal Work-Study jobs (averaging $3000). 80 state and other part-time jobs (averaging $3000).

Applying *Options:* electronic application, early admission, deferred entrance. *Application fee:* $20. *Required for some:* minimum 3 GPA. *Recommended:* high school transcript. *Application deadlines:* rolling (freshmen), rolling (transfers). *Notification:* continuous (freshmen), continuous (transfers).

Freshman Application Contact Ms. Aida Garcia, Admissions and Recruitment Counselor, Three Rivers Community College, Mahan Drive, Norwich, CT 06360. *Phone:* 860-383-5260. *Fax:* 860-885-1684. *E-mail:* admissions@trcc.commnet.edu.

TUNXIS COMMUNITY COLLEGE

Farmington, Connecticut **www.tunxis.commnet.edu/**

- **State-supported** 2-year, founded 1969, part of Connecticut Community–Technical College System
- **Suburban** 12-acre campus with easy access to Hartford
- **Coed,** 4,496 undergraduate students, 42% full-time, 59% women, 41% men

Undergraduates 1,874 full-time, 2,622 part-time. Students come from 6 states and territories, 2% are from out of state, 5% African American, 3% Asian American or Pacific Islander, 11% Hispanic American, 0.2% Native American, 3% international. *Retention:* 59% of 2008 full-time freshmen returned.

Freshmen *Admission:* 846 enrolled.

Faculty *Total:* 239, 28% full-time, 12% with terminal degrees. *Student/faculty ratio:* 19:1.

Majors Accounting; administrative assistant and secretarial science; applied art; art; business administration and management; commercial and advertising art; corrections; criminal justice/law enforcement administration; data processing and data processing technology; dental hygiene; engineering; engineering technology; fashion merchandising; forensic science and technology; human services; information science/studies; kindergarten/preschool education; legal administrative assistant/secretary; liberal arts and sciences/liberal studies; marketing/marketing management; medical administrative assistant and medical secretary; physical therapy; substance abuse/addiction counseling.

Academics *Calendar:* semesters. *Degree:* certificates and associate. *Special study options:* academic remediation for entering students, adult/continuing education programs, cooperative education, distance learning, double majors, English as a second language, honors programs, independent study, internships, part-time degree program, services for LD students, summer session for credit.

Library Tunxis Community College Library with 33,866 titles, 285 serial subscriptions, an OPAC.

Student Life *Housing:* college housing not available. *Activities and Organizations:* drama/theater group, student-run newspaper, Phi Theta Kappa, Student American Dental Hygiene Association (SADHA), Human Services Club, student newspaper, Criminal Justice Club. *Campus security:* 24-hour emergency response devices.

Costs (2010–11) *Tuition:* state resident $3024 full-time, $126 per credit hour part-time; nonresident $9072 full-time, $189 per credit hour part-time. *Required fees:* $382 full-time. *Payment plan:* installment. *Waivers:* senior citizens and employees or children of employees.

Applying *Options:* deferred entrance. *Application fee:* $20. *Required:* high school transcript. *Application deadlines:* rolling (freshmen), rolling (transfers).

Freshman Application Contact Mr. Peter McCluskey, Director of Admissions, Tunxis Community College, 271 Scott Swamp Road, Farmington, CT 06032. *Phone:* 860-255-3550. *Fax:* 860-255-3559. *E-mail:* pmccluskey@txcc.commnet.edu.

DELAWARE

DELAWARE COLLEGE OF ART AND DESIGN

Wilmington, Delaware **www.dcad.edu/**

Freshman Application Contact Ms. Allison Gullo, Delaware College of Art and Design, 600 North Market Street, Wilmington, DE 19801. *Phone:* 302-622-8867 Ext. 111. *Fax:* 302-622-8870. *E-mail:* agullo@dcad.edu.

DELAWARE TECHNICAL & COMMUNITY COLLEGE, JACK F. OWENS CAMPUS

Georgetown, Delaware **www.dtcc.edu/**

- **State-supported** 2-year, founded 1967, part of Delaware Technical and Community College System
- **Small-town** 120-acre campus
- **Coed,** 4,787 undergraduate students, 50% full-time, 65% women, 35% men

Undergraduates 2,382 full-time, 2,405 part-time. 16% African American, 2% Asian American or Pacific Islander, 4% Hispanic American, 0.3% Native American, 3% international. *Retention:* 58% of 2008 full-time freshmen returned.

Freshmen *Admission:* 785 enrolled.

Faculty *Total:* 354, 33% full-time. *Student/faculty ratio:* 16:1.

Majors Accounting; aeronautical/aerospace engineering technology; agricultural business and management; agricultural production; applied horticulture; architectural engineering technology; automobile/automotive mechanics technology; biology/biological sciences; biology/biotechnology laboratory technician; business automation/technology/data entry; business/commerce; civil engineering technology; clinical/medical laboratory assistant; computer and information sciences; computer technology/computer systems technology; construction management; criminal justice/law enforcement administration; criminal justice/police science; customer service support/call center/teleservice operation; diagnostic medical sonography and ultrasound technology; drafting and design technology; early childhood education; e-commerce; education (multiple levels); electrical, electronic and communications engineering technology; elementary education; emergency medical technology (EMT paramedic); entrepreneurship; heating, air conditioning, ventilation and refrigeration maintenance technology; human services; kindergarten/preschool education; legal administrative assistant/secretary; management information systems; marketing/marketing management; mathematics teacher education; mechanical drafting and CAD/CADD; medical/clinical assistant; middle school education; nuclear engineering technology; nursing (licensed practical/vocational nurse training); nursing (registered nurse training); occupational therapist assistant; office management; physical therapist assistant; poultry science; radiologic technology/science; respiratory therapy technician; survey technology; turf and turfgrass management; veterinary/animal health technology; water quality and wastewater treatment management and recycling technology.

Academics *Calendar:* semesters. *Degree:* certificates, diplomas, and associate. *Special study options:* academic remediation for entering students, advanced placement credit, cooperative education, distance learning, double majors, English as a second language, internships, part-time degree program, services for LD students, study abroad, summer session for credit.

Library Stephen J. Betze Library with 62,663 titles, 514 serial subscriptions, an OPAC, a Web page.

Student Life *Housing:* college housing not available. *Activities and Organizations:* student-run radio station. *Campus security:* 24-hour emergency response devices, late-night transport/escort service.

Athletics Member NJCAA. *Intercollegiate sports:* baseball M(s), golf M, softball W(s). *Intramural sports:* football M/W.

Costs (2009–10) *Tuition:* state resident $2472 full-time, $103 per credit hour part-time; nonresident $6180 full-time, $258 per credit hour part-time. *Required fees:* $516 full-time, $7 per credit hour part-time, $25 per term part-time. *Payment plan:* deferred payment. *Waivers:* senior citizens and employees or children of employees.

Financial Aid Of all full-time matriculated undergraduates who enrolled in 2008, 250 Federal Work-Study jobs (averaging $2000).

Applying *Options:* electronic application, early admission, deferred entrance. *Application fee:* $10. *Required for some:* high school transcript. *Application deadlines:* rolling (freshmen), rolling (transfers). *Notification:* continuous (freshmen), continuous (transfers).

Freshman Application Contact Ms. Claire McDonald, Admissions Counselor, Delaware Technical & Community College, Jack F. Owens Campus, PO Box 610, Georgetown, DE 19947. *Phone:* 302-856-5400. *Fax:* 302-856-9461.

DELAWARE TECHNICAL & COMMUNITY COLLEGE, STANTON/WILMINGTON CAMPUS

Newark, Delaware **www.dtcc.edu/**

- **State-supported** 2-year, founded 1968, part of Delaware Technical and Community College System
- **Coed,** 7,488 undergraduate students, 44% full-time, 59% women, 41% men

Undergraduates 3,290 full-time, 4,198 part-time. 23% African American, 4% Asian American or Pacific Islander, 7% Hispanic American, 0.2% Native American, 2% international. *Retention:* 59% of 2008 full-time freshmen returned.

Freshmen *Admission:* 1,438 enrolled.

Faculty *Total:* 524, 34% full-time. *Student/faculty ratio:* 16:1.

Majors Accounting; agricultural business and management; architectural engineering technology; automobile/automotive mechanics technology; banking and financial support services; biology/biological sciences; biology/biotechnology laboratory technician; business administration and management; business automation/technology/data entry; business/commerce; CAD/CADD drafting/design technology; cardiovascular technology; chemical technology; civil drafting and CAD/CADD; computer and information sciences; computer engineering technology; computer systems networking and telecommunications; construction management; criminal justice/law enforcement administration; criminal justice/police science; culinary arts; customer service management; customer service support/call center/teleservice operation; dental hygiene; diagnostic medical sonography and ultrasound technology; drafting and design technology; early childhood education; education (multiple levels); electrical, electronic and communications engineering technology; electrocardiograph technology; elementary education; emergency care attendant (EMT ambulance); emergency medical technology (EMT paramedic); engineering/industrial management; fire protection and safety technology; fire science; fire services administration; heating, air conditioning and refrigeration technology; histologic technology/histotechnologist; hotel/motel administration; human services; kindergarten/preschool education; kinesiology and exercise science; management information systems; management science; manufacturing technology; marketing/marketing management; mathematics teacher education; mechanical engineering/mechanical technology; medical/clinical assistant; middle school education; nuclear engineering technology; nuclear medical technology; nursing (registered nurse training); occupational therapist assistant; office management; operations research; physical therapist assistant; radiologic technology/science; respiratory therapy technician; restaurant, culinary, and catering management; science technologies related; substance abuse/addiction counseling; survey technology.

Academics *Calendar:* semesters. *Degree:* certificates, diplomas, and associate. *Special study options:* academic remediation for entering students, advanced placement credit, cooperative education, distance learning, double majors, English as a second language, internships, part-time degree program, services for LD students, study abroad, summer session for credit. *ROTC:* Air Force (c).

Library Stanton Campus Library and John Eugene Derrickson Memorial Library with 74,259 titles, 793 serial subscriptions, an OPAC, a Web page.

Student Life *Housing:* college housing not available. *Campus security:* 24-hour emergency response devices, late-night transport/escort service. *Student services:* personal/psychological counseling, women's center.

Athletics Member NJCAA. *Intercollegiate sports:* basketball M(s)/W(s), soccer M(s), softball W(s). *Intramural sports:* basketball M/W, football M/W, softball W, volleyball M/W.

Costs (2009–10) *Tuition:* state resident $2472 full-time, $103 per credit hour part-time; nonresident $6180 full-time, $258 per credit hour part-time. *Required fees:* $516 full-time, $7 per credit hour part-time, $25 per term part-time. *Payment plan:* deferred payment. *Waivers:* senior citizens and employees or children of employees.

Applying *Options:* electronic application, early admission, deferred entrance. *Application fee:* $10. *Required for some:* high school transcript. *Application deadlines:* rolling (freshmen), rolling (transfers). *Notification:* continuous (freshmen), continuous (transfers).

Freshman Application Contact Ms. Rebecca Bailey, Admissions Coordinator, Wilmington, Delaware Technical & Community College, Stanton/Wilmington Campus, 333 Shipley Street, Wilmington, DE 19713. *Phone:* 302-571-5343. *Fax:* 302-577-2548.

DELAWARE TECHNICAL & COMMUNITY COLLEGE, TERRY CAMPUS

Dover, Delaware **www.dtcc.edu/terry/**

- **State-supported** 2-year, founded 1972, part of Delaware Technical and Community College System
- **Small-town** 70-acre campus with easy access to Philadelphia
- **Coed,** 3,406 undergraduate students, 47% full-time, 66% women, 34% men

Undergraduates 1,607 full-time, 1,799 part-time. 28% African American, 3% Asian American or Pacific Islander, 4% Hispanic American, 0.5% Native American, 2% international. *Retention:* 60% of 2008 full-time freshmen returned.

Freshmen *Admission:* 687 enrolled.

Faculty *Total:* 244, 33% full-time. *Student/faculty ratio:* 16:1.

Majors Accounting; agricultural business and management; architectural engineering technology; bilingual and multilingual education; biomedical technology; business administration and management; business automation/technology/data entry; business/commerce; civil engineering technology; commercial and advertising art; computer and information sciences; computer engineering technology; computer systems networking and telecommunications; computer technology/computer systems technology; construction management; criminal justice/law enforcement administration; criminal justice/police science; culinary arts; digital communication and media/multimedia; drafting and design technology; early childhood education; e-commerce; education (multiple levels); electrical, electronic and communications engineering technology; electromechanical technology; elementary education; emergency medical technology (EMT paramedic); entrepreneurship; hotel/motel administration; human resources management; human services; interior design; kindergarten/preschool education; legal administrative assistant/secretary; management information systems; marketing/marketing management; mathematics teacher education; medical/clinical assistant; middle school education; nursing (registered nurse training); office management; photography; substance abuse/addiction counseling.

Academics *Calendar:* semesters. *Degree:* certificates, diplomas, and associate. *Special study options:* academic remediation for entering students, advanced placement credit, cooperative education, distance learning, double majors, English as a second language, internships, part-time degree program, services for LD students, study abroad, summer session for credit.

Library 15,327 titles, 245 serial subscriptions, an OPAC.

Student Life *Housing:* college housing not available. *Activities and Organizations:* marching band. *Campus security:* 24-hour emergency response devices, late-night transport/escort service.

Athletics Member NJCAA. *Intercollegiate sports:* lacrosse M(s), soccer M(s)/W(s), softball W(s).

Costs (2009–10) *Tuition:* state resident $2472 full-time, $103 per credit hour part-time; nonresident $6180 full-time, $258 per credit hour part-time. *Required fees:* $516 full-time, $7 per credit hour part-time, $25 per term part-time. *Payment plan:* deferred payment. *Waivers:* senior citizens and employees or children of employees.

Financial Aid Of all full-time matriculated undergraduates who enrolled in 2008, 50 Federal Work-Study jobs (averaging $1500).

Applying *Options:* electronic application, early admission, deferred entrance. *Application fee:* $10. *Required for some:* high school transcript. *Application deadlines:* rolling (freshmen), rolling (transfers). *Notification:* continuous (freshmen), continuous (transfers).

Freshman Application Contact Mrs. Maria Harris, Admissions Officer, Delaware Technical & Community College, Terry Campus, 100 Campus Drive, Dover, DE 19904. *Phone:* 302-857-1020. *Fax:* 302-857-1296. *E-mail:* mharris@outland.dtcc.edu.

FLORIDA

ANGLEY COLLEGE

Deland, Florida **www.angley.edu/**

Freshman Application Contact Admissions Office, Angley College, 230 North Woodland Boulevard, Suite 310, Deland, FL 32720. *Phone:* 386-740-1215 Ext. 125. *Toll-free phone:* 866-639-1215. *E-mail:* admissions@angley.edu.

ATI Career Training Center

Fort Lauderdale, Florida www.aticareertraining.com/

- **Proprietary** 2-year
- **Suburban** campus
- **Coed**
- 100% of applicants were admitted

Academics *Calendar:* quarters. *Degree:* associate.

Applying *Application fee:* $100.

Director of Admissions Director of Admissions, ATI Career Training Center, 2880 NW 62nd Street, Fort Lauderdale, FL 33309-9731. *Phone:* 954-973-4760.

ATI Career Training Center

Oakland Park, Florida www.aticareertraining.edu/

Freshman Application Contact Admissions Office, ATI Career Training Center, 3501 Northwest 9th Avenue, Oakland Park, FL 33309. *Phone:* 954-563-5899.

ATI College of Health

Miami, Florida www.aticareertraining.edu/

- **Proprietary** 2-year, founded 1976, part of ATI Enterprises, Inc. of Florida
- **Urban** 1-acre campus
- **Coed**

Academics *Calendar:* semesters. *Degree:* associate. *Special study options:* academic remediation for entering students.

Applying *Application fee:* $100. *Required:* high school transcript, interview.

Director of Admissions Admissions, ATI College of Health, 1395 NW 167th Street, Suite 200, Miami, FL 33169-5742. *Phone:* 305-628-1000. *Fax:* 305-628-1461. *E-mail:* admissions@atienterprises.edu.

Brevard Community College

Cocoa, Florida www.brevardcc.edu/

- **State-supported** 2-year, founded 1960, part of Florida Community College System
- **Suburban** 100-acre campus with easy access to Orlando
- **Coed**

Undergraduates 6,125 full-time, 9,482 part-time. Students come from 42 states and territories, 67 other countries, 11% African American, 3% Asian American or Pacific Islander, 8% Hispanic American, 0.8% Native American, 0.9% international.

Faculty *Student/faculty ratio:* 19:1.

Academics *Calendar:* semesters. *Degree:* certificates and associate. *Special study options:* academic remediation for entering students, accelerated degree program, adult/continuing education programs, advanced placement credit, cooperative education, distance learning, double majors, English as a second language, external degree program, honors programs, independent study, internships, part-time degree program, services for LD students, study abroad, summer session for credit. *ROTC:* Army (b), Air Force (b).

Student Life *Campus security:* 24-hour emergency response devices and patrols.

Athletics Member NJCAA.

Costs (2009–10) *Tuition:* state resident $1622 full-time; nonresident $6484 full-time. *Required fees:* $526 full-time. *Payment plans:* tuition prepayment, installment, deferred payment.

Financial Aid Of all full-time matriculated undergraduates who enrolled in 2008, 200 Federal Work-Study jobs (averaging $2244). 200 state and other part-time jobs (averaging $2000).

Applying *Options:* electronic application, early admission. *Application fee:* $30. *Required:* high school transcript.

Freshman Application Contact Ms. Stephanie Burnette, Registrar, Brevard Community College, 1519 Clearlake Road, Cocoa, FL 32922-6597. *Phone:* 321-433-7271. *Fax:* 321-433-7172. *E-mail:* cocoaadmissions@brevardcc.edu.

Broward College

Fort Lauderdale, Florida www.broward.edu/

Freshman Application Contact Willie J. Alexander, Associate Vice President for Student Affairs/College Registrar, Broward College, 225 East Las Olas Boulevard, Fort Lauderdale, FL 33301-2298. *Phone:* 954-201-7471. *Fax:* 954-201-7466.

Brown Mackie College–Miami

Miami, Florida www.brownmackie.edu/miami/

- **Proprietary** primarily 2-year, part of Education Management Corporation
- **Coed**

Majors Accounting technology and bookkeeping; business administration and management; criminal justice/law enforcement administration; early childhood education; health/health-care administration; information technology; legal assistant/paralegal; medical/clinical assistant.

Academics *Degrees:* diplomas, associate, and bachelor's.

Costs (2009–10) *Tuition:* Tuition varies by program. Students should contact Brown Mackie College for tuition information.

Freshman Application Contact Brown Mackie College–Miami, 1501 Biscayne Boulevard, Miami, FL 33132. *Phone:* 305-341-6600. *Toll-free phone:* 866-505-0335.

▶See page 430 for the College Close-Up.

Central Florida Community College

Ocala, Florida www.cf.edu/

Freshman Application Contact Ms. Christy Jones, Registrar, Central Florida Community College, PO Box 1388, 3001 SW College Road, Ocala, FL 34474-1388. *Phone:* 352-237-2111 Ext. 1398. *Fax:* 352-873-5882. *E-mail:* jonesch@cf.edu.

Central Florida Institute

Palm Harbor, Florida www.cfinstitute.com/

- **Proprietary** 2-year, founded 1997
- **Urban** campus
- **Coed**

Academics *Calendar:* continuous. *Degree:* certificates, diplomas, and associate.

Applying *Application fee:* $50.

Director of Admissions Carol Bruno, Director of Admissions, Central Florida Institute, 60522 US Highway 19 North, Suite 200, Palm Harbor, FL 34684. *Phone:* 727-786-4707.

Centura Institute

Orlando, Florida www.centurainstitute.edu/

Admissions Office Contact Centura Institute, 6359 Edgewater Drive, Orlando, FL 32810.

Chipola College

Marianna, Florida www.chipola.edu/

- **State-supported** primarily 2-year, founded 1947
- **Rural** 105-acre campus
- **Coed,** 2,341 undergraduate students, 48% full-time, 61% women, 39% men

Undergraduates 1,112 full-time, 1,229 part-time. Students come from 11 states and territories, 3 other countries, 6% are from out of state, 17% African American, 1% Asian American or Pacific Islander, 2% Hispanic American, 0.7% Native American, 5% transferred in.

Freshmen *Admission:* 852 applied, 668 admitted, 462 enrolled. *Average high school GPA:* 2.5. *Test scores:* SAT verbal scores over 500: 16%; SAT math scores over 500: 36%; ACT scores over 18: 81%; SAT verbal scores over 600: 4%; SAT math scores over 600: 12%; ACT scores over 24: 25%; ACT scores over 30: 3%.

Faculty *Total:* 69, 78% full-time, 12% with terminal degrees. *Student/faculty ratio:* 24:1.

Majors Accounting; agriculture; agronomy and crop science; art; biological and physical sciences; business administration and management; clinical laboratory science/medical technology; computer and information sciences related; computer science; education; finance; liberal arts and sciences/liberal studies; mass communication/media; mathematics teacher education; nursing (registered nurse training); pre-engineering; science teacher education; secondary education; social work.

Academics *Calendar:* semesters. *Degrees:* certificates, associate, and bachelor's. *Special study options:* academic remediation for entering students, adult/continuing education programs, advanced placement credit, distance learning, honors programs, independent study, part-time degree program, services for LD students, summer session for credit.

Library Chipola Library with 37,740 titles, 226 serial subscriptions.

Student Life *Housing:* college housing not available. *Activities and Organizations:* drama/theater group, student-run newspaper, choral group, Drama/Theater Group. *Campus security:* night security personnel.

Athletics Member NJCAA. *Intercollegiate sports:* baseball M(s), basketball M(s)/W(s), softball W(s).

Costs (2010–11) *Tuition:* state resident $2550 full-time, $85 per semester hour part-time; nonresident $7314 full-time, $244 per credit hour part-time. Full-time tuition and fees vary according to degree level. Part-time tuition and fees vary according to degree level. *Waivers:* employees or children of employees.

Applying *Options:* early admission. *Required:* high school transcript. *Application deadlines:* rolling (freshmen), rolling (transfers). *Notification:* continuous (freshmen), continuous (transfers).

Freshman Application Contact Mrs. Kathy L. Rehberg, Registrar, Chipola College, Marianna, FL 32446. *Phone:* 850-718-2233. *Fax:* 850-718-2287. *E-mail:* rehbergk@chipola.edu.

City College

Casselberry, Florida — **www.citycollegeorlando.edu/**

Director of Admissions Ms. Kimberly Bowden, Director of Admissions, City College, 853 Semoran Boulevard, Suite 200, Casselberry, FL 32707-5342. *Phone:* 352-335-4000. *Fax:* 352-335-4303. *E-mail:* kbowden@citycollege.edu.

City College

Fort Lauderdale, Florida — **www.citycollege.edu/**

Freshman Application Contact Admissions Office, City College, 2000 West Commercial Boulevard, Suite 200, Fort Lauderdale, FL 33309. *Phone:* 954-492-5353.

City College

Gainesville, Florida — **www.citycollege.edu/**

Freshman Application Contact Admissions Office, City College, 2400 S.W. 13th Street, Gainesville, FL 32608.

City College

Miami, Florida — **www.citycollege.edu/**

Freshman Application Contact Admissions Office, City College, 9300 South Dadeland Boulevard, Suite PH, Miami, FL 33156. *Phone:* 305-666-9242. *Fax:* 305-666-9243.

College of Business and Technology

Miami, Florida — **www.cbt.edu/**

Freshman Application Contact Ms. Ivis Delgado, Admissions Representative, College of Business and Technology, 8991 Southwest 107 Avenue, Suite 200, Miami, FL 33176. *Phone:* 305-273-4499 Ext. 2204. *Fax:* 305-485-4411. *E-mail:* admissions@cbt.edu.

Daytona State College

Daytona Beach, Florida — **www.daytonastate.edu/**

- **State-supported** primarily 2-year, founded 1958, part of Florida Community College System
- **Suburban** 100-acre campus with easy access to Orlando
- **Coed,** 17,779 undergraduate students, 45% full-time, 61% women, 39% men

Undergraduates 8,083 full-time, 9,696 part-time. Students come from 51 states and territories, 52 other countries, 7% are from out of state, 16% African American, 2% Asian American or Pacific Islander, 9% Hispanic American, 0.5% Native American, 0.3% international, 3% transferred in. *Retention:* 74% of 2008 full-time freshmen returned.

Freshmen *Admission:* 2,654 applied, 2,654 admitted, 2,654 enrolled.

Faculty *Total:* 979, 32% full-time, 15% with terminal degrees. *Student/faculty ratio:* 19:1.

Majors Accounting; administrative assistant and secretarial science; architectural engineering technology; automobile/automotive mechanics technology; biology teacher education; business administration and management; child development; communications technology; computer and information sciences related; computer engineering related; computer graphics; computer/information technology services administration related; computer programming; computer programming (specific applications); computer science; computer systems networking and telecommunications; criminal justice/law enforcement administration; criminal justice/police science; culinary arts; dental hygiene; drafting and design technology; electrical, electronic and communications engineering technology; elementary education; emergency medical technology (EMT paramedic); fire science; health information/medical records administration; hospitality administration; hotel/motel administration; human services; industrial radiologic technology; industrial technology; information technology; interior design; kindergarten/preschool education; legal assistant/paralegal; machine shop technology; mathematics teacher education; medical administrative assistant and medical secretary; nursing (registered nurse training); occupational therapist assistant; photographic and film/video technology; physical therapy; plastics engineering technology; radio and television; respiratory care therapy; robotics technology; secondary education; special education (early childhood); tourism and travel services management.

Academics *Calendar:* semesters. *Degrees:* certificates, diplomas, associate, bachelor's, and postbachelor's certificates. *Special study options:* academic remediation for entering students, adult/continuing education programs, advanced placement credit, cooperative education, distance learning, double majors, English as a second language, external degree program, freshman honors college, honors programs, independent study, internships, part-time degree program, services for LD students, study abroad, summer session for credit. *ROTC:* Army (c), Air Force (c).

Library Mary Karl Memorial Library plus 1 other with 91,000 titles, 700 serial subscriptions, 5,000 audiovisual materials, an OPAC, a Web page.

Student Life *Housing:* college housing not available. *Activities and Organizations:* drama/theater group, student-run newspaper, choral group, Florida Student Nursing Association, Phi Theta Kappa, Mu Rho Chapter, Student Government Association, Campus Crusade for Christ, Student Paralegal Association. *Campus security:* 24-hour emergency response devices and patrols, late-night transport/escort service. *Student services:* personal/psychological counseling, women's center.

Athletics Member NJCAA. *Intercollegiate sports:* baseball M(s), basketball M(s)/W(s), golf W(s), softball W(s), swimming and diving M(s)/W(s). *Intramural sports:* basketball M/W, cheerleading M/W, football M/W, golf M/W, racquetball M/W, soccer M/W, table tennis M/W, tennis M/W, volleyball M/W.

Costs (2009–10) *One-time required fee:* $20. *Tuition:* state resident $2253 full-time, $94 per credit hour part-time; nonresident $8098 full-time, $337 per credit hour part-time. Full-time tuition and fees vary according to course load, degree level, and program. Part-time tuition and fees vary according to course load, degree level, and program. *Required fees:* $60 full-time, $30 per term part-time. *Payment plan:* installment. *Waivers:* employees or children of employees.

Financial Aid Of all full-time matriculated undergraduates who enrolled in 2008, 193 Federal Work-Study jobs (averaging $1542).

Daytona State College (continued)

Applying *Options:* electronic application, early admission, deferred entrance. *Required:* high school transcript. *Application deadlines:* rolling (freshmen), rolling (transfers). *Notification:* continuous (freshmen), continuous (transfers).

Freshman Application Contact Mrs. Karen Sanders, Director of Admissions and Recruitment, Daytona State College, PO Box 2811, Daytona Beach, FL 32120-2811. *Phone:* 386-506-3050. *E-mail:* sanderk@daytonastate.edu.

EDISON STATE COLLEGE

Fort Myers, Florida **www.edison.edu/**

- **State and locally supported** primarily 2-year, founded 1962, part of Florida Community College System
- **Urban** 80-acre campus
- **Coed**

Undergraduates 4,570 full-time, 8,437 part-time. Students come from 1 other state, 36 other countries, 10% African American, 2% Asian American or Pacific Islander, 17% Hispanic American, 0.3% Native American, 2% international, 7% transferred in. *Retention:* 52% of 2008 full-time freshmen returned.

Academics *Calendar:* semesters. *Degrees:* certificates, diplomas, associate, and bachelor's. *Special study options:* academic remediation for entering students, accelerated degree program, adult/continuing education programs, advanced placement credit, cooperative education, distance learning, English as a second language, honors programs, independent study, internships, part-time degree program, services for LD students, summer session for credit.

Student Life *Campus security:* 24-hour emergency response devices and patrols, student patrols, late-night transport/escort service.

Standardized Tests *Recommended:* SAT or ACT (for admission).

Applying *Options:* electronic application, early admission, deferred entrance. *Application fee:* $30. *Required:* high school transcript.

Freshman Application Contact Ms. Pat Armstrong, Admissions Specialist, Edison State College, PO Box 60210, Fort Myers, FL 33906-6210. *Phone:* 239-489-9360 Ext. 1360. *Toll-free phone:* 800-749-2ECC. *E-mail:* registrar@edison.edu.

EVEREST INSTITUTE

Fort Lauderdale, Florida **www.everest.edu/**

Freshman Application Contact Admissions Office, Everest Institute, 1040 Bayview Drive, Fort Lauderdale, FL 33304. *Phone:* 954-630-0066. *Toll-free phone:* 888-741-4270.

EVEREST INSTITUTE

Hialeah, Florida **www.everest.edu/**

Director of Admissions Mr. Daniel Alonso, Director of Admissions, Everest Institute, 4410 West 16th Avenue, Suite 52, Hialeah, FL 33012. *Phone:* 305-558-9500. *Toll-free phone:* 888-741-4270. *Fax:* 305-558-4419. *E-mail:* dalonso@cci.edu.

EVEREST INSTITUTE

Miami, Florida **www.everest.edu/**

Director of Admissions Director of Admissions, Everest Institute, 111 Northwest 183rd Street, Second Floor, Miami, FL 33169. *Phone:* 305-949-9500.

EVEREST INSTITUTE

Miami, Florida **www.everest.edu/**

Freshman Application Contact Director of Admissions, Everest Institute, 9020 Southwest 137th Avenue, Miami, FL 33186. *Phone:* 305-386-9900. *Fax:* 305-388-1740.

EVEREST UNIVERSITY

Orange Park, Florida **www.everest.edu/**

Freshman Application Contact Admissions Office, Everest University, 805 Wells Road, Orange Park, FL 32073.

FLORIDA CAREER COLLEGE

Miami, Florida **www.careercollege.edu/**

- **Proprietary** 2-year, founded 1982
- **Urban** campus
- **Coed**

Academics *Calendar:* quarters. *Degree:* certificates, diplomas, and associate. *Special study options:* academic remediation for entering students, independent study, part-time degree program, summer session for credit.

Student Life *Campus security:* 24-hour emergency response devices.

Applying *Options:* deferred entrance. *Application fee:* $100. *Required:* high school transcript, interview.

Director of Admissions Mr. David Knobel, President, Florida Career College, 1321 Southwest 107 Avenue, Miami, FL 33174. *Phone:* 305-553-6065.

FLORIDA COLLEGE OF NATURAL HEALTH

Bradenton, Florida **www.fcnh.com/**

Freshman Application Contact Admissions Office, Florida College of Natural Health, 616 67th Street Circle East, Bradenton, FL 34208. *Phone:* 941-954-8999. *Toll-free phone:* 800-966-7117.

FLORIDA COLLEGE OF NATURAL HEALTH

Maitland, Florida **www.fcnh.com/**

Freshman Application Contact Admissions Office, Florida College of Natural Health, 2600 Lake Lucien Drive, Suite 140, Maitland, FL 32751. *Phone:* 407-261-0319. *Toll-free phone:* 800-393-7337.

FLORIDA COLLEGE OF NATURAL HEALTH

Miami, Florida **www.fcnh.com/**

Director of Admissions Ms. Lissette Vidal, Admissions Coordinator, Florida College of Natural Health, 7925 Northwest 12th Street, Suite 201, Miami, FL 33126. *Phone:* 305-597-9599. *Toll-free phone:* 800-599-9599. *Fax:* 305-597-9110. *E-mail:* miami@fcnh.com.

FLORIDA COLLEGE OF NATURAL HEALTH

Pompano Beach, Florida **www.fcnh.com/**

Freshman Application Contact Admissions Office, Florida College of Natural Health, 2001 West Sample Road, Suite 100, Pompano Beach, FL 33064. *Phone:* 954-975-6400. *Toll-free phone:* 800-541-9299.

Florida Keys Community College

Key West, Florida www.fkcc.edu/

- **State-supported** 2-year, founded 1965, part of Florida Community College System
- **Small-town** 20-acre campus
- **Coed**

Academics *Calendar:* trimesters. *Degree:* certificates and associate. *Special study options:* academic remediation for entering students, adult/continuing education programs, advanced placement credit, cooperative education, distance learning, double majors, English as a second language, independent study, internships, part-time degree program, services for LD students, student-designed majors, summer session for credit.

Student Life *Campus security:* 24-hour patrols.

Financial Aid Of all full-time matriculated undergraduates who enrolled in 2008, 30 Federal Work-Study jobs (averaging $2000).

Applying *Options:* early admission, deferred entrance. *Application fee:* $20. *Required for some:* high school transcript.

Director of Admissions Ms. Cheryl A. Malsheimer, Director of Admissions and Records, Florida Keys Community College, 5901 College Road, Key West, FL 33040. *Phone:* 305-296-9081 Ext. 201.

The Florida School of Midwifery

Gainseville, Florida www.midwiferyschool.org/

Freshman Application Contact Admissions Office, The Florida School of Midwifery, PO Box 5505, Gainseville, FL 32627-5505. *Phone:* 352-338-0766. *Fax:* 352-338-2013. *E-mail:* info@midwiferyschool.org.

Florida State College at Jacksonville

Jacksonville, Florida www.fscj.edu/

- **State-supported** primarily 2-year, founded 1963, part of Florida Community College System
- **Urban** 656-acre campus
- **Endowment** $28.8 million
- **Coed**

Undergraduates 8,080 full-time, 17,823 part-time. Students come from 16 states and territories, 91 other countries, 20% are from out of state, 34% transferred in. *Retention:* 60% of 2008 full-time freshmen returned.

Faculty *Student/faculty ratio:* 22:1.

Academics *Calendar:* semesters. *Degrees:* certificates, diplomas, associate, and bachelor's. *Special study options:* academic remediation for entering students, accelerated degree program, adult/continuing education programs, advanced placement credit, cooperative education, distance learning, double majors, English as a second language, honors programs, independent study, internships, off-campus study, part-time degree program, services for LD students, study abroad, summer session for credit. *ROTC:* Navy (c).

Student Life *Campus security:* 24-hour emergency response devices and patrols, student patrols, late-night transport/escort service.

Athletics Member NJCAA.

Costs (2009–10) *Tuition:* state resident $2044 full-time, $85 per credit hour part-time; nonresident $7797 full-time, $325 per credit hour part-time. Full-time tuition and fees vary according to degree level and program. Part-time tuition and fees vary according to degree level and program. *Required fees:* $525 full-time.

Applying *Options:* electronic application, early admission, deferred entrance. *Application fee:* $15. *Required:* high school transcript.

Freshman Application Contact Mr. Peter Biegel, District Executive Director for Student Success and Services, Florida State College at Jacksonville, 501 West State Street, Jacksonville, FL 32202. *Phone:* 904-632-3131. *Fax:* 904-632-5105. *E-mail:* admissions@fccj.edu.

Florida Technical College

Auburndale, Florida www.flatech.edu/

Director of Admissions Mr. Charles Owens, Admissions Office, Florida Technical College, 298 Havendale Boulevard, Auburndale, FL 33823. *Phone:* 863-967-8822.

Florida Technical College

DeLand, Florida www.flatech.edu/

Freshman Application Contact Mr. Bill Atkinson, Director, Florida Technical College, 1450 South Woodland Boulevard, 3rd Floor, DeLand, FL 32720. *Phone:* 386-734-3303. *Fax:* 386-734-5150.

Florida Technical College

Jacksonville, Florida www.flatech.edu/

- **Proprietary** 2-year, founded 1982
- **Coed**

Academics *Calendar:* quarters. *Degree:* diplomas and associate.

Applying *Application fee:* $25.

Director of Admissions Mr. Bryan Gulebiam, Director of Admissions, Florida Technical College, 8711 Lone Star Road, Jacksonville, FL 32211. *Phone:* 407-678-5600.

Florida Technical College

Orlando, Florida www.flatech.edu/

- **Proprietary** 2-year, founded 1982, part of Fore Front Education, Inc.
- **Urban** 1-acre campus
- **Coed**

Academics *Calendar:* quarters. *Degree:* certificates, diplomas, and associate. *Special study options:* accelerated degree program, advanced placement credit, distance learning, double majors, external degree program, independent study.

Applying *Application fee:* $25. *Required:* high school transcript, interview. *Recommended:* essay or personal statement.

Director of Admissions Ms. Jeanette E. Muschlitz, Director of Admissions, Florida Technical College, 1819 North Semoran Boulevard, Orlando, FL 32807-3546. *Phone:* 407-678-5600.

Fortis College

Winter Park, Florida www.fortis.edu/

Freshman Application Contact Admissions Office, Fortis College, 1573 West Fairbanks Avenue, Suite 100, Winter Park, FL 32789. *Toll-free phone:* 800-442-7610.

Gulf Coast College

Tampa, Florida gulfcoastcollege.edu/

Director of Admissions Gulf Coast College, 3910 US Hwy 301 North, Suite 200, Tampa, FL 33619. *Toll-free phone:* 888-729-7247.

Gulf Coast Community College

Panama City, Florida www.gulfcoast.edu/

- **State-supported** 2-year, founded 1957
- **Suburban** 80-acre campus
- **Coed**

Academics *Calendar:* semesters. *Degree:* certificates and associate. *Special study options:* academic remediation for entering students, accelerated degree program, adult/continuing education programs, advanced placement credit, cooperative education, distance learning, double majors, English as a second language, external degree program, honors programs, independent study, off-campus study, part-time degree program, services for LD students, summer session for credit.

Student Life *Campus security:* patrols by trained security personnel during campus hours.

Athletics Member NJCAA.

Gulf Coast Community College (continued)

Financial Aid Of all full-time matriculated undergraduates who enrolled in 2008, 145 Federal Work-Study jobs (averaging $3200). 60 state and other part-time jobs (averaging $2600).

Applying *Options:* electronic application, early admission, deferred entrance. *Required:* high school transcript.

Freshman Application Contact Mrs. Jackie Kuczenski, Administrative Secretary of Admissions, Gulf Coast Community College, 5230 West Highway 98, Panama City, FL 32401. *Phone:* 850-769-1551 Ext. 4892. *Toll-free phone:* 800-311-3628. *Fax:* 850-913-3308.

HERZING COLLEGE

Winter Park, Florida **www.herzing.edu/**

- **Proprietary** primarily 2-year, founded 1989
- **Coed**

Academics *Calendar:* semesters. *Degrees:* certificates, diplomas, associate, and bachelor's.

Director of Admissions Tessie Uranga, Director of Admissions, Herzing College, 1595 South Semoran Boulevard, Suite 1501, Winter Park, FL 32792. *Phone:* 407-478-0500. *Fax:* 407-380-0269.

HIGH-TECH INSTITUTE

Orlando, Florida **www.high-techinstitute.com/**

Freshman Application Contact Admissions Office, High-Tech Institute, 3710 Maguire Boulevard, Orlando, FL 32803. *Toll-free phone:* 866-326-1985.

HILLSBOROUGH COMMUNITY COLLEGE

Tampa, Florida **www.hccfl.edu/**

- **State-supported** 2-year, founded 1968, part of Florida Community College System
- **Urban** campus
- **Coed,** 26,964 undergraduate students, 42% full-time, 58% women, 42% men

Undergraduates 11,277 full-time, 15,687 part-time. Students come from 39 states and territories, 120 other countries, 0.8% are from out of state, 19% African American, 4% Asian American or Pacific Islander, 23% Hispanic American, 0.4% Native American, 3% international, 12% transferred in.

Freshmen *Admission:* 7,816 applied, 7,816 admitted, 4,513 enrolled.

Faculty *Total:* 1,285, 22% full-time, 13% with terminal degrees.

Majors Accounting technology and bookkeeping; aquaculture; architectural engineering technology; biomedical technology; biotechnology; building/construction site management; business administration and management; child-care and support services management; cinematography and film/video production; computer/information technology services administration related; computer programming (specific applications); computer systems analysis; computer technology/computer systems technology; criminal justice/law enforcement administration; dental hygiene; diagnostic medical sonography and ultrasound technology; dietitian assistant; electrical, electronic and communications engineering technology; emergency medical technology (EMT paramedic); engineering technology; environmental control technologies related; executive assistant/executive secretary; fire protection and safety technology; hospitality administration; landscaping and groundskeeping; legal assistant/paralegal; liberal arts and sciences/liberal studies; management information systems; management information systems and services related; medical radiologic technology; nuclear medical technology; nursing (registered nurse training); operations management; opticianry; optometric technician; psychiatric/mental health services technology; respiratory care therapy; restaurant, culinary, and catering management; restaurant/food services management; special education (hearing impaired); veterinary/animal health technology.

Academics *Calendar:* semesters. *Degree:* certificates and associate. *Special study options:* academic remediation for entering students, adult/continuing education programs, advanced placement credit, cooperative education, distance learning, English as a second language, honors programs, off-campus study, part-time degree program, services for LD students, summer session for credit. *ROTC:* Army (c), Air Force (c).

Library Main Library plus 4 others with 170,615 titles, 1,283 serial subscriptions, 50,000 audiovisual materials, an OPAC, a Web page.

Student Life *Housing Options:* Campus housing is provided by a third party. *Activities and Organizations:* drama/theater group, student-run newspaper, radio station, choral group, Student Government Association, Student Nursing Association, Phi Theta Kappa, International Students, Radiography Club. *Campus security:* 24-hour emergency response devices and patrols, late-night transport/escort service. *Student services:* personal/psychological counseling.

Athletics Member NJCAA. *Intercollegiate sports:* baseball M(s), basketball M(s)/W(s), softball W(s), tennis W(s), volleyball W(s).

Standardized Tests *Required:* Florida College Placement Test (CPT) (for admission).

Costs (2009–10) *Tuition:* state resident $2097 full-time, $88 per credit hour part-time; nonresident $7640 full-time, $318 per credit hour part-time. *Payment plan:* installment. *Waivers:* senior citizens and employees or children of employees.

Applying *Options:* electronic application, early admission. *Application fee:* $20. *Required:* high school transcript. *Notification:* continuous (freshmen), continuous (out-of-state freshmen), continuous (transfers).

Freshman Application Contact Mr. Edwin Olmo, Enrollment and Student Success Officer, Hillsborough Community College, PO Box 31127, Tampa, FL 33631-3127. *Phone:* 813-253-7032. *E-mail:* eolmo2@hccfl.edu.

INDIAN RIVER STATE COLLEGE

Fort Pierce, Florida **www.ircc.edu/**

- **State-supported** primarily 2-year, founded 1960, part of Florida Community College System
- **Small-town** 133-acre campus
- **Coed,** 17,110 undergraduate students, 35% full-time, 61% women, 39% men

Undergraduates 5,966 full-time, 11,144 part-time. Students come from 31 states and territories, 105 other countries, 15% are from out of state, 16% African American, 2% Asian American or Pacific Islander, 12% Hispanic American, 0.4% Native American, 1% international, 12% transferred in.

Freshmen *Admission:* 2,472 enrolled. *Average high school GPA:* 2.84.

Faculty *Total:* 843, 24% full-time, 14% with terminal degrees. *Student/faculty ratio:* 24:1.

Majors Accounting; administrative assistant and secretarial science; agricultural business and management; airline pilot and flight crew; anthropology; apparel and textiles; architectural drafting and CAD/CADD; art teacher education; automobile/automotive mechanics technology; banking and financial support services; biology/biological sciences; biology teacher education; business administration and management; carpentry; chemistry; child development; civil engineering technology; clinical/medical laboratory technology; computer engineering technology; computer programming; computer science; computer typography and composition equipment operation; consumer merchandising/retailing management; corrections; cosmetology; criminal justice/law enforcement administration; criminal justice/police science; criminal justice/safety; culinary arts; dental hygiene; drafting and design technology; dramatic/theater arts; economics; education; electrical, electronic and communications engineering technology; emergency medical technology (EMT paramedic); engineering; engineering technology; English; family and consumer sciences/human sciences; fashion merchandising; finance; fire science; foods, nutrition, and wellness; forestry; French; health/health-care administration; health information/medical records administration; heating, air conditioning, ventilation and refrigeration maintenance technology; history; hotel/motel administration; humanities; human services; hydrology and water resources science; industrial radiologic technology; information science/studies; interior design; journalism; kindergarten/preschool education; language interpretation and translation; legal assistant/paralegal; liberal arts and sciences/liberal studies; library science; marine science/merchant marine officer; marketing/marketing management; mathematics; mathematics teacher education; medical administrative assistant and medical secretary; music; nursing (licensed practical/vocational nurse training); nursing (registered nurse training); organizational behavior; pharmacy; philosophy; physical education teaching and coaching; physical therapist assistant; physical therapy; physics; political science and government; pre-engineering; psychology; respiratory care therapy; science teacher education; social sciences; social work; sociology; Spanish; special education; special products marketing; speech and rhetoric; survey technology; teacher assistant/aide.

Academics *Calendar:* semesters. *Degrees:* certificates, diplomas, associate, and bachelor's. *Special study options:* academic remediation for entering students, adult/continuing education programs, advanced placement credit, distance learning, English as a second language, independent study, part-time degree program, services for LD students, summer session for credit.

Library Charles S. Miley Learning Resource Center with 88,397 titles, 198 serial subscriptions, 3,094 audiovisual materials, an OPAC, a Web page.

Student Life *Housing:* college housing not available. *Activities and Organizations:* drama/theater group, choral group. *Campus security:* 24-hour emergency response devices and patrols. *Student services:* health clinic, personal/psychological counseling, women's center.

Athletics Member NJCAA. *Intercollegiate sports:* baseball M(s), basketball M(s)/W(s), softball W(s), swimming and diving M(s)/W(s), volleyball W(s). *Intramural sports:* basketball M/W, racquetball M/W, soccer M, volleyball M/W.

Financial Aid Of all full-time matriculated undergraduates who enrolled in 2008, 130 Federal Work-Study jobs (averaging $1500).

Applying *Options:* early admission, deferred entrance. *Required:* high school transcript. *Application deadlines:* rolling (freshmen), rolling (transfers). *Notification:* continuous (freshmen), continuous (transfers).

Freshman Application Contact Mr. Steven Payne, Dean of Educational Services, Indian River State College, 3209 Virginia Avenue, Fort Pierce, FL 34981-5596. *Phone:* 772-462-7805. *E-mail:* spayne@ircc.edu.

ITT TECHNICAL INSTITUTE

Fort Lauderdale, Florida — www.itt-tech.edu/

- **Proprietary** primarily 2-year, founded 1991, part of ITT Educational Services, Inc.
- **Suburban** campus
- **Coed**

Majors Animation, interactive technology, video graphics and special effects; CAD/CADD drafting/design technology; computer and information systems security; computer engineering technology; computer software and media applications related; computer software engineering; computer software technology; construction management; criminal justice/law enforcement administration; design and visual communications; electrical, electronic and communications engineering technology; health information/medical records technology; legal assistant/paralegal; system, networking, and LAN/WAN management; web/multimedia management and webmaster; web page, digital/multimedia and information resources design.

Academics *Calendar:* quarters. *Degrees:* associate and bachelor's.

Student Life *Housing:* college housing not available.

Freshman Application Contact Director of Recruitment, ITT Technical Institute, 3401 South University Drive, Fort Lauderdale, FL 33328. *Phone:* 954-476-9300. *Toll-free phone:* 800-488-7797.

ITT TECHNICAL INSTITUTE

Fort Myers, Florida — www.itt-tech.edu/

- **Proprietary** primarily 2-year
- **Coed**

Majors CAD/CADD drafting/design technology; computer and information systems security; computer engineering technology; computer software and media applications related; construction management; criminal justice/law enforcement administration; electrical, electronic and communications engineering technology; system, networking, and LAN/WAN management; web/multimedia management and webmaster.

Academics *Degrees:* associate and bachelor's.

Freshman Application Contact Director of Recruitment, ITT Technical Institute, 13500 Powers Court, Suite 100, Fort Myers, FL 33912. *Phone:* 239-603-8700. *Toll-free phone:* 877-485-5313.

ITT TECHNICAL INSTITUTE

Jacksonville, Florida — www.itt-tech.edu/

- **Proprietary** primarily 2-year, founded 1991, part of ITT Educational Services, Inc.
- **Urban** campus
- **Coed**

Majors CAD/CADD drafting/design technology; computer and information systems security; computer engineering technology; computer software and media applications related; computer software engineering; computer software technology; construction management; criminal justice/law enforcement administration; design and visual communications; electrical, electronic and communications engineering technology; legal assistant/paralegal; system, networking, and LAN/WAN management; web/multimedia management and webmaster; web page, digital/multimedia and information resources design.

Academics *Calendar:* quarters. *Degrees:* associate and bachelor's.

Student Life *Housing:* college housing not available.

Financial Aid Of all full-time matriculated undergraduates who enrolled in 2008, 5 Federal Work-Study jobs.

Freshman Application Contact Director of Recruitment, ITT Technical Institute, 6600-10 Youngerman Circle, Jacksonville, FL 32244. *Phone:* 904-573-9100. *Toll-free phone:* 800-318-1264.

ITT TECHNICAL INSTITUTE

Lake Mary, Florida — www.itt-tech.edu/

- **Proprietary** primarily 2-year, founded 1989, part of ITT Educational Services, Inc.
- **Suburban** campus
- **Coed**

Majors Animation, interactive technology, video graphics and special effects; CAD/CADD drafting/design technology; computer and information systems security; computer engineering technology; computer software and media applications related; computer software engineering; computer software technology; computer systems networking and telecommunications; construction management; criminal justice/law enforcement administration; design and visual communications; electrical, electronic and communications engineering technology; health information/medical records technology; legal assistant/paralegal; system, networking, and LAN/WAN management; web/multimedia management and webmaster; web page, digital/multimedia and information resources design.

Academics *Calendar:* quarters. *Degrees:* associate and bachelor's.

Student Life *Housing:* college housing not available.

Freshman Application Contact Director of Recruitment, ITT Technical Institute, 1400 International Pkwy South, Lake Mary, FL 32746. *Phone:* 407-660-2900. *Toll-free phone:* 866-489-8441. *Fax:* 407-660-2566.

ITT TECHNICAL INSTITUTE

Miami, Florida — www.itt-tech.edu/

- **Proprietary** primarily 2-year, founded 1996, part of ITT Educational Services, Inc.
- **Coed**

Majors Accounting technology and bookkeeping; business administration and management; CAD/CADD drafting/design technology; computer and information systems security; computer engineering technology; computer software and media applications related; computer software engineering; construction management; criminal justice/law enforcement administration; design and visual communications; electrical, electronic and communications engineering technology; health information/medical records technology; legal assistant/paralegal; system, networking, and LAN/WAN management; web/multimedia management and webmaster; web page, digital/multimedia and information resources design.

Academics *Calendar:* quarters. *Degrees:* associate and bachelor's.

Student Life *Housing:* college housing not available.

Freshman Application Contact Director of Recruitment, ITT Technical Institute, 7955 NW 12th Street, Suite 119, Miami, FL 33126. *Phone:* 305-477-3080.

ITT TECHNICAL INSTITUTE

Pinellas Park, Florida — www.itt-tech.edu/

- **Proprietary** primarily 2-year, part of ITT Educational Services, Inc.
- **Coed**

Majors CAD/CADD drafting/design technology; computer and information systems security; computer engineering technology; computer software and media applications related; computer software engineering; computer software technology; construction management; criminal justice/law enforcement administration; design and visual communications; legal assistant/paralegal; system, networking, and LAN/WAN management; web/multimedia management and webmaster.

Academics *Degrees:* associate and bachelor's.

Freshman Application Contact Director of Recruitment, ITT Technical Institute, 3491 Gandy Boulevard, Suite 101, Pinellas Park, FL 33781-2658. *Phone:* 727-209-4700. *Toll-free phone:* 866-488-5084.

ITT Technical Institute
Tallahassee, Florida www.itt-tech.edu/

- **Proprietary** primarily 2-year
- **Coed**

Majors CAD/CADD drafting/design technology; computer and information systems security; computer engineering technology; computer software and media applications related; construction management; criminal justice/law enforcement administration; design and visual communications; electrical, electronic and communications engineering technology; system, networking, and LAN/WAN management; web/multimedia management and webmaster.

Academics *Degrees:* associate and bachelor's.

Freshman Application Contact Director of Recruitment, ITT Technical Institute, 2639 North Monroe Street, Tallahassee, FL 32303. *Phone:* 850-422-6300. *Toll-free phone:* 877-230-3559.

ITT Technical Institute
Tampa, Florida www.itt-tech.edu/

- **Proprietary** primarily 2-year, founded 1981, part of ITT Educational Services, Inc.
- **Suburban** campus
- **Coed**

Majors Animation, interactive technology, video graphics and special effects; CAD/CADD drafting/design technology; computer and information systems security; computer engineering technology; computer software and media applications related; computer software engineering; computer software technology; construction management; criminal justice/law enforcement administration; design and visual communications; electrical, electronic and communications engineering technology; health information/medical records technology; legal assistant/paralegal; nursing (registered nurse training); system, networking, and LAN/WAN management; web/multimedia management and webmaster; web page, digital/multimedia and information resources design.

Academics *Calendar:* quarters. *Degrees:* associate and bachelor's.

Student Life *Housing:* college housing not available.

Freshman Application Contact Director of Recruitment, ITT Technical Institute, 4809 Memorial Highway, Tampa, FL 33634. *Phone:* 813-885-2244. *Toll-free phone:* 800-825-2831.

Kaplan College, Pembroke Pines
Pembroke Pines, Florida www.kc-pembrokepines.com/

- **Proprietary** 2-year
- **Coed**

Freshman Application Contact Kaplan College, Pembroke Pines, 10131 Pines Boulevard, Pembroke Pines, FL 33026. *Phone:* 954-885-3500.

Keiser Career College–Greenacres
Greenacres, Florida www.keisercareer.edu/kcc2009/ga_campus.htm

Freshman Application Contact Admissions Office, Keiser Career College–Greenacres, 6812 Forest Hill Boulevard, Suite D-1, Greenacres, FL 33413.

Key College
Dania, Florida www.keycollege.edu/

- **Proprietary** 2-year, founded 1881
- **Suburban** campus with easy access to Miami
- **Coed, primarily women**

Academics *Calendar:* quarters. *Degree:* certificates, diplomas, and associate. *Special study options:* adult/continuing education programs, advanced placement credit, double majors, external degree program, honors programs, internships.

Student Life *Campus security:* 24-hour emergency response devices.

Standardized Tests *Required for some:* CPAt, SAT, or ACT.

Applying *Options:* electronic application, deferred entrance. *Application fee:* $35. *Required:* high school transcript, interview.

Director of Admissions Mr. Ronald H. Dooley, President and Director of Admissions, Key College, 5225 West Broward Boulevard, Ft. Lauderdale, FL 33317. *Phone:* 954-581-2223 Ext. 23. *Toll-free phone:* 800-581-8292.

Lake City Community College
Lake City, Florida www.lakecitycc.edu/

Freshman Application Contact Lake City Community College, Route 19, Box 1030, Lake City, FL 32025-8703. *Fax:* 386-755-1521. *E-mail:* admissions@mail.lakecity.cc.fl.us.

Lake-Sumter Community College
Leesburg, Florida www.lscc.edu/

- **State and locally supported** 2-year, founded 1962, part of Florida Community College System
- **Suburban** 112-acre campus with easy access to Orlando
- **Endowment** $3.9 million
- **Coed,** 4,500 undergraduate students, 34% full-time, 64% women, 36% men

Undergraduates 1,513 full-time, 2,987 part-time. Students come from 2 states and territories, 1% are from out of state, 9% African American, 2% Asian American or Pacific Islander, 8% Hispanic American, 0.5% Native American, 0.5% international, 9% transferred in.

Freshmen *Admission:* 1,246 applied, 1,246 admitted, 981 enrolled.

Faculty *Total:* 337, 22% full-time, 16% with terminal degrees. *Student/faculty ratio:* 15:1.

Majors Business administration and management; child-care provision; commercial and advertising art; computer and information sciences related; computer science; criminal justice/law enforcement administration; emergency medical technology (EMT paramedic); fire science; health information/medical records administration; liberal arts and sciences/liberal studies; nursing (registered nurse training); office management.

Academics *Calendar:* semesters. *Degree:* certificates, diplomas, and associate. *Special study options:* academic remediation for entering students, adult/continuing education programs, advanced placement credit, cooperative education, distance learning, double majors, independent study, off-campus study, part-time degree program, services for LD students, summer session for credit.

Library Lake-Sumter Community College Library with 82,908 titles, 144 serial subscriptions, 1,296 audiovisual materials, an OPAC, a Web page.

Student Life *Housing:* college housing not available. *Activities and Organizations:* drama/theater group, student-run newspaper, choral group, Phi Theta Kappa, Student Government Association, Theatre Arts Society, Nursing Student's Association, Safire. *Campus security:* 24-hour emergency response devices.

Athletics Member NJCAA. *Intercollegiate sports:* baseball M(s), softball W(s), volleyball W(s). *Intramural sports:* basketball M/W, golf M/W, softball W, table tennis M/W, volleyball W.

Costs (2009–10) *Tuition:* state resident $2556 full-time, $85 per credit hour part-time; nonresident $9627 full-time, $321 per credit hour part-time. Full-time tuition and fees vary according to course load. Part-time tuition and fees vary according to course load. *Payment plan:* installment. *Waivers:* employees or children of employees.

Financial Aid Of all full-time matriculated undergraduates who enrolled in 2009, 420 applied for aid, 420 were judged to have need. 39 Federal Work-Study jobs (averaging $1701). In 2009, 95 non-need-based awards were made. *Average financial aid package:* $3166. *Average need-based gift aid:* $1912. *Average non-need-based aid:* $770.

Applying *Options:* electronic application. *Application fee:* $25. *Required:* high school transcript. *Application deadlines:* rolling (freshmen), rolling (transfers). *Notification:* continuous (freshmen), continuous (transfers).

Freshman Application Contact Ms. Bonnie Yanick, Enrollment Specialist, Lake-Sumter Community College, 9501 US Highway 441, Leesburg, FL 34788-8751. *Phone:* 352-365-3561. *Fax:* 352-365-3553. *E-mail:* admissinquiry@lscc.edu.

LE CORDON BLEU COLLEGE OF CULINARY ARTS, MIAMI

Miramar, Florida **www.miamiculinary.com/**

Freshman Application Contact Admissions Office, Le Cordon Bleu College of Culinary Arts, Miami, 3221 Enterprise Way, Miramar, FL 33025. *Phone:* 954-628-4000. *Toll-free phone:* 888-569-3222.

LINCOLN COLLEGE OF TECHNOLOGY

West Palm Beach, Florida **www.lincolnedu.com/**

- **Proprietary** primarily 2-year, founded 1983
- **Urban** 7-acre campus with easy access to Miami
- **Coed**

Academics *Calendar:* quarters. *Degrees:* certificates, diplomas, associate, and bachelor's. *Special study options:* academic remediation for entering students, internships.

Applying *Options:* early admission. *Application fee:* $25. *Required:* high school transcript.

Director of Admissions Mr. Kevin Cassidy, Director of Admissions, Lincoln College of Technology, 1126 53rd Court, West Palm Beach, FL 33407-2384. *Phone:* 561-842-8324 Ext. 117. *Toll-free phone:* 800-826-9986. *Fax:* 561-842-9503.

MEDVANCE INSTITUTE

Atlantis, Florida **www.medvance.edu/**

Director of Admissions Campus Director, MedVance Institute, 170 JFK Drive, Atlantis, FL 33462. *Phone:* 561-304-3466. *Toll-free phone:* 877-606-3382. *Fax:* 561-304-3471.

MIAMI DADE COLLEGE

Miami, Florida **www.mdc.edu/**

- **State and locally supported** primarily 2-year, founded 1960, part of Florida Community College System
- **Urban** campus
- **Endowment** $167.4 million
- **Coed,** 57,222 undergraduate students, 38% full-time, 60% women, 40% men

Undergraduates 21,768 full-time, 35,454 part-time. Students come from 39 states and territories, 179 other countries, 1% are from out of state, 18% African American, 1% Asian American or Pacific Islander, 67% Hispanic American, 0.1% Native American, 3% international, 2% transferred in.

Freshmen *Admission:* 11,743 enrolled.

Faculty *Total:* 2,210, 30% full-time, 19% with terminal degrees. *Student/faculty ratio:* 30:1.

Majors Accounting technology and bookkeeping; administrative assistant and secretarial science; aeronautics/aviation/aerospace science and technology; agriculture; airline pilot and flight crew; air traffic control; American studies; anthropology; architectural drafting and CAD/CADD; architectural engineering technology; art; Asian studies; audiology and speech-language pathology; aviation/airway management; behavioral sciences; biology/biological sciences; biology teacher education; biomedical technology; biotechnology; business administration and management; business administration, management and operations related; chemistry; chemistry teacher education; child development; cinematography and film/video production; civil engineering technology; clinical/medical laboratory technology; commercial and advertising art; comparative literature; computer engineering technology; computer graphics; computer programming; computer science; computer software technology; computer technology/computer systems technology; construction engineering technology; cooking and related culinary arts; court reporting; criminal justice/law enforcement administration; criminal justice/police science; dance; data processing and data processing technology; dental hygiene; diagnostic medical sonography and ultrasound technology; dietetics; dietetic technician; drafting and design technology; dramatic/theater arts; economics; education; education related; electrical and electronic engineering technologies related; electrical, electronic and communications engineering technology; elementary education; emergency medical technology (EMT paramedic); engineering; engineering related; engineering technology; English; environmental engineering technology; finance; fire science; food science; forestry; French; funeral service and mortuary science; general studies; geology/earth science; German; health information/medical records administration; health/medical preparatory programs related; health professions related; health services/allied health/health sciences; heating, air conditioning and refrigeration technology; heating, air conditioning, ventilation and refrigeration maintenance technology; histologic technician; history; horticultural science; hospitality administration; humanities; human services; industrial technology; information science/studies; interior design; international relations and affairs; Italian; journalism; kindergarten/preschool education; landscaping and groundskeeping; Latin American studies; legal administrative assistant/secretary; legal assistant/paralegal; management information systems; marketing/marketing management; mass communication/media; mathematics; mathematics teacher education; medical/clinical assistant; middle school education; music; music performance; music teacher education; natural sciences; nonprofit management; nuclear medical technology; nursing (registered nurse training); ophthalmic technology; ornamental horticulture; parks, recreation and leisure; philosophy; photographic and film/video technology; photography; physical education teaching and coaching; physical sciences; physical therapist assistant; physics; physics teacher education; plant nursery management; political science and government; Portuguese; pre-engineering; psychology; public administration; radio and television; radio and television broadcasting technology; radiologic technology/science; recording arts technology; respiratory care therapy; respiratory therapy technician; science teacher education; security and protective services related; sign language interpretation and translation; social sciences; social work; sociology; Spanish; special education; substance abuse/addiction counseling; teacher assistant/aide; telecommunications technology; tourism and travel services management.

Academics *Calendar:* 16-16-6-6. *Degrees:* certificates, associate, and bachelor's. *Special study options:* academic remediation for entering students, adult/continuing education programs, advanced placement credit, cooperative education, distance learning, English as a second language, freshman honors college, honors programs, independent study, internships, part-time degree program, services for LD students, study abroad, summer session for credit. *ROTC:* Army (c), Air Force (c).

Library Main Library plus 8 others with 363,432 titles, 3,824 serial subscriptions, 30,991 audiovisual materials, an OPAC, a Web page.

Student Life *Housing:* college housing not available. *Activities and Organizations:* drama/theater group, student-run newspaper, radio and television station, choral group, national fraternities. *Campus security:* 24-hour patrols. *Student services:* personal/psychological counseling.

Athletics Member NJCAA. *Intercollegiate sports:* baseball M(s), basketball M(s)/W(s), softball W(s), volleyball W(s). *Intramural sports:* basketball M/W, racquetball M/W, soccer M/W, softball M/W, tennis M/W, volleyball M/W, weight lifting M/W.

Costs (2010–11) *One-time required fee:* $20. *Tuition:* state resident $2028 full-time, $68 per credit hour part-time; nonresident $8116 full-time, $271 per credit hour part-time. Full-time tuition and fees vary according to course load. Part-time tuition and fees vary according to course load. *Required fees:* $558 full-time, $19 per credit hour part-time. *Waivers:* employees or children of employees.

Financial Aid Of all full-time matriculated undergraduates who enrolled in 2008, 800 Federal Work-Study jobs (averaging $5000). 125 state and other part-time jobs (averaging $5000).

Applying *Options:* electronic application, early admission. *Application fee:* $20. *Required:* high school transcript. *Application deadlines:* rolling (freshmen), rolling (transfers). *Notification:* continuous (freshmen), continuous (transfers).

Freshman Application Contact Ms. Dulce Beltran, College Registrar, Miami Dade College, 11011 SW 104th Street, Miami, FL 33176. *Phone:* 305-237-2103. *Fax:* 305-237-2964. *E-mail:* dbeltran@mdc.edu.

▶**See page 462 for the College Close-Up.**

NORTH FLORIDA COMMUNITY COLLEGE

Madison, Florida **www.nfcc.edu/**

Freshman Application Contact Mr. Bobby Scott, North Florida Community College, 325 Northwest Turner Davis Drive, Madison, FL 32340. *Phone:* 850-973-9450. *Fax:* 850-973-1697.

NORTHWEST FLORIDA STATE COLLEGE

Niceville, Florida **www.nwfstatecollege.edu/**

- **State and locally supported** primarily 2-year, founded 1963, part of Florida Community College System
- **Small-town** 264-acre campus
- **Endowment** $28.6 million
- **Coed,** 10,317 undergraduate students

Northwest Florida State College (continued)

Undergraduates Students come from 18 states and territories, 10% African American.

Faculty *Total:* 283, 33% full-time. *Student/faculty ratio:* 15:1.

Majors Accounting; administrative assistant and secretarial science; art; atmospheric sciences and meteorology; automobile/automotive mechanics technology; avionics maintenance technology; biological and physical sciences; biology/biological sciences; business administration and management; chemistry; child development; clinical laboratory science/medical technology; commercial and advertising art; computer engineering related; computer programming; computer programming (specific applications); computer science; computer systems networking and telecommunications; construction engineering technology; criminal justice/law enforcement administration; criminal justice/police science; data entry/microcomputer applications; dietetics; divinity/ministry; drafting and design technology; education; electrical, electronic and communications engineering technology; elementary education; engineering; family and consumer sciences/home economics teacher education; fashion merchandising; finance; foods, nutrition, and wellness; heating, air conditioning, ventilation and refrigeration maintenance technology; hotel/motel administration; humanities; human resources management; information technology; interior design; kindergarten/preschool education; legal assistant/paralegal; legal studies; liberal arts and sciences/liberal studies; mathematics; modern languages; music; nursing (registered nurse training); physical education teaching and coaching; physics; purchasing, procurement/acquisitions and contracts management; real estate; social sciences; social work; welding technology; word processing.

Academics *Calendar:* semesters plus summer sessions. *Degrees:* certificates, associate, and bachelor's. *Special study options:* academic remediation for entering students, accelerated degree program, adult/continuing education programs, advanced placement credit, distance learning, English as a second language, independent study, part-time degree program, services for LD students, summer session for credit. *ROTC:* Army (b).

Library Northwest Florida State College Learning Resources Center with 106,383 titles, 480 serial subscriptions, 10,219 audiovisual materials, an OPAC, a Web page.

Student Life *Housing:* college housing not available. *Activities and Organizations:* drama/theater group, choral group. *Campus security:* 24-hour patrols. *Student services:* health clinic.

Athletics Member NJCAA. *Intercollegiate sports:* baseball M(s), basketball M(s)/W(s), softball W(s). *Intramural sports:* baseball M, basketball M/W, soccer M(c)/W(c), softball W.

Standardized Tests *Required for some:* ACT, SAT I, ACT ASSET, MAPS, or Florida College Entry Placement Test are used for placement not admission.

Costs (2010–11) *Tuition:* state resident $2272 full-time, $76 per credit hour part-time; nonresident $9198 full-time, $307 per credit hour part-time. Full-time tuition and fees vary according to course load, degree level, and reciprocity agreements. Part-time tuition and fees vary according to course load, degree level, and reciprocity agreements. *Payment plans:* tuition prepayment, installment, deferred payment. *Waivers:* employees or children of employees.

Financial Aid Of all full-time matriculated undergraduates who enrolled in 2008, 81 Federal Work-Study jobs (averaging $1500). 11 state and other part-time jobs (averaging $1460).

Applying *Options:* electronic application. *Required:* high school transcript. *Application deadlines:* rolling (freshmen), rolling (transfers). *Notification:* continuous (freshmen), continuous (transfers).

Freshman Application Contact Ms. Christine Bishop, Registrar/Division Director Enrollment Services, Northwest Florida State College, 100 College Boulevard, Niceville, FL 32578. *Phone:* 850-729-5373. *Fax:* 850-729-5323. *E-mail:* registrar@nwfsc.edu.

ORLANDO CULINARY ACADEMY

Orlando, Florida **www.orlandoculinary.com/**

Admissions Office Contact Orlando Culinary Academy, 8511 Commodity Circle, Suite 100, Orlando, FL 32819. *Toll-free phone:* 888-793-3222.

PALM BEACH STATE COLLEGE

Lake Worth, Florida **www.palmbeachstate.edu/**

- **State-supported** primarily 2-year, founded 1933, part of Florida State College System
- **Urban** 150-acre campus with easy access to West Palm Beach
- **Endowment** $14.4 million
- **Coed,** 28,587 undergraduate students, 38% full-time, 57% women, 43% men

Undergraduates 10,725 full-time, 17,862 part-time. Students come from 49 states and territories, 138 other countries, 5% are from out of state, 24% African American, 3% Asian American or Pacific Islander, 19% Hispanic American, 0.4% Native American, 2% international, 4% transferred in.

Freshmen *Admission:* 4,399 applied, 4,399 admitted, 4,399 enrolled.

Faculty *Total:* 1,356, 20% full-time, 13% with terminal degrees. *Student/faculty ratio:* 21:1.

Majors Accounting; administrative assistant and secretarial science; airline pilot and flight crew; apparel and textiles; art; art history, criticism and conservation; biology/biological sciences; botany/plant biology; building/construction finishing, management, and inspection related; business administration and management; ceramic arts and ceramics; chemistry; commercial and advertising art; comparative literature; computer and information sciences and support services related; computer programming; computer programming (specific applications); computer science; criminal justice/law enforcement administration; criminal justice/police science; data processing and data processing technology; dental hygiene; drafting and design technology; dramatic/theater arts; economics; education; electrical, electronic and communications engineering technology; elementary education; English; family and consumer sciences/human sciences; fashion/apparel design; fashion merchandising; finance; fire science; foods, nutrition, and wellness; health teacher education; history; hotel/motel administration; industrial radiologic technology; interior design; journalism; kindergarten/preschool education; legal administrative assistant/secretary; liberal arts and sciences/liberal studies; marketing/marketing management; mass communication/media; mathematics; music; nursing (registered nurse training); occupational therapy; philosophy; photography; physical education teaching and coaching; physical sciences; physical therapy; political science and government; pre-engineering; psychology; religious studies; social sciences; social work; special products marketing; survey technology; system administration; web page, digital/multimedia and information resources design; word processing; zoology/animal biology.

Academics *Calendar:* semesters. *Degrees:* certificates, associate, and bachelor's. *Special study options:* academic remediation for entering students, adult/continuing education programs, advanced placement credit, cooperative education, distance learning, double majors, English as a second language, freshman honors college, honors programs, independent study, internships, off-campus study, part-time degree program, services for LD students, student-designed majors, study abroad, summer session for credit.

Library Harold C. Manor Library plus 3 others with 151,000 titles, 1,474 serial subscriptions, an OPAC, a Web page.

Student Life *Housing:* college housing not available. *Activities and Organizations:* drama/theater group, student-run newspaper, choral group, student government, Phi Theta Kappa, Students for International Understanding, Black Student Union, Drama Club, national fraternities. *Campus security:* 24-hour emergency response devices and patrols. *Student services:* health clinic, women's center.

Athletics Member NJCAA. *Intercollegiate sports:* baseball M(s), basketball M(s)/W(s), softball W(s), volleyball M(s)/W(s). *Intramural sports:* basketball M/W, bowling M/W, football M/W, racquetball M/W, soccer M, tennis M/W, volleyball M/W.

Costs (2009–10) *One-time required fee:* $20. *Tuition:* state resident $1980 full-time, $83 per credit hour part-time; nonresident $7185 full-time, $299 per credit hour part-time. Full-time tuition and fees vary according to course level, course load, and student level. Part-time tuition and fees vary according to course level, course load, and student level. *Required fees:* $10 full-time, $10 per term part-time. *Room and board:* Room and board charges vary according to location. *Waivers:* employees or children of employees.

Applying *Options:* electronic application, early admission, deferred entrance. *Application fee:* $20. *Notification:* continuous until 8/20 (freshmen), continuous until 8/20 (transfers).

Freshman Application Contact Ms. Anne Guiler, Coordinator of Distance Learning, Palm Beach State College, 4200 Congress Avenue, Lake Worth, FL 33461. *Phone:* 561-868-3032. *Fax:* 561-868-3584. *E-mail:* enrollmt@palmbeachstate.edu.

PASCO-HERNANDO COMMUNITY COLLEGE

New Port Richey, Florida **www.phcc.edu/**

- **State-supported** 2-year, founded 1972, part of Florida Community College System
- **Suburban** 142-acre campus with easy access to Tampa
- **Endowment** $20.3 million
- **Coed,** 11,969 undergraduate students

Undergraduates 1% are from out of state, 5% African American, 2% Asian American or Pacific Islander, 8% Hispanic American, 0.5% Native American.

Faculty *Total:* 396, 28% full-time. *Student/faculty ratio:* 26:1.

Majors Business administration and management; computer programming related; computer programming (specific applications); computer systems networking and telecommunications; computer technology/computer systems technology; criminal justice/law enforcement administration; dental hygiene; drafting and design technology; e-commerce; emergency medical technology (EMT paramedic); human services; information technology; legal assistant/paralegal; liberal arts and sciences/liberal studies; marketing/marketing management; nursing (registered nurse training); physical therapist assistant; radiologic technology/science; web page, digital/multimedia and information resources design.

Academics *Calendar:* semesters. *Degree:* certificates, diplomas, and associate. *Special study options:* academic remediation for entering students, accelerated degree program, adult/continuing education programs, advanced placement credit, cooperative education, distance learning, double majors, honors programs, independent study, internships, off-campus study, part-time degree program, services for LD students, study abroad, summer session for credit. *ROTC:* Army (c).

Library Alric Pottberg Library plus 2 others with 4,016 audiovisual materials, an OPAC, a Web page.

Student Life *Housing:* college housing not available. *Activities and Organizations:* drama/theater group, choral group, Student Government Association, Phi Theta Kappa, Phi Beta Lambda, Human Services, PHCC Cares. *Campus security:* 24-hour patrols. *Student services:* personal/psychological counseling.

Athletics *Intercollegiate sports:* baseball M(s), basketball M(s), cross-country running W(s), softball W(s), volleyball W(s).

Standardized Tests *Recommended:* SAT and SAT Subject Tests or ACT (for admission), CPT.

Costs (2010–11) *Tuition:* state resident $2438 full-time, $81 per credit part-time; nonresident $9272 full-time, $309 per credit part-time. *Payment plans:* installment, deferred payment.

Financial Aid Of all full-time matriculated undergraduates who enrolled in 2008, 83 Federal Work-Study jobs (averaging $3201).

Applying *Options:* electronic application. *Application fee:* $25. *Required:* high school transcript. *Application deadlines:* rolling (freshmen), rolling (transfers). *Notification:* continuous (freshmen), continuous (transfers).

Freshman Application Contact Ms. Debra Bullard, Director of Admissions and Student Records, Pasco-Hernando Community College, 10230 Ridge Road, New Port Richey, FL 34654-5199. *Phone:* 727-816-3261. *Fax:* 727-816-3389. *E-mail:* bullard@phcc.edu.

PENSACOLA JUNIOR COLLEGE

Pensacola, Florida **www.pjc.edu/**

- **State-supported** 2-year, founded 1948, part of Florida Community College System
- **Urban** 160-acre campus
- **Coed,** 11,598 undergraduate students, 42% full-time, 61% women, 39% men

Undergraduates 4,901 full-time, 6,697 part-time. 1% are from out of state, 15% African American, 4% Asian American or Pacific Islander, 5% Hispanic American, 2% Native American, 0.5% international, 5% transferred in.

Freshmen *Admission:* 1,938 enrolled.

Majors Accounting technology and bookkeeping; animal sciences related; automobile/automotive mechanics technology; business administration and management; child-care provision; cinematography and film/video production; civil engineering technology; commercial and advertising art; computer and information sciences related; computer programming (specific applications); computer systems analysis; construction engineering technology; criminal justice/law enforcement administration; dental hygiene; diagnostic medical sonography and ultrasound technology; dietetics; drafting and design technology; education; electrical, electronic and communications engineering technology; emergency medical technology (EMT paramedic); executive assistant/executive secretary; fire protection and safety technology; forestry technology; health/health-care administration; health information/medical records administration; hospitality administration; landscaping and groundskeeping; legal assistant/paralegal; liberal arts and sciences/liberal studies; management information systems and services related; manufacturing technology; medical radiologic technology; nursing (registered nurse training); operations management; photographic and film/video technology; physical therapist assistant; restaurant, culinary, and catering management.

Academics *Calendar:* semesters. *Degree:* certificates, diplomas, and associate. *Special study options:* academic remediation for entering students, adult/continuing education programs, advanced placement credit, cooperative education, distance learning, double majors, external degree program, honors programs, independent study, part-time degree program, services for LD students, summer session for credit. *ROTC:* Army (b).

Library Learning Resource Center plus 2 others.

Student Life *Housing:* college housing not available. *Activities and Organizations:* drama/theater group, student-run newspaper, choral group. *Campus security:* 24-hour emergency response devices and patrols, student patrols, late-night transport/escort service. *Student services:* health clinic, personal/psychological counseling.

Athletics Member NJCAA. *Intercollegiate sports:* baseball M(s), basketball M(s)/W(s), softball W(s), volleyball W. *Intramural sports:* archery M/W, badminton M/W, basketball M/W, bowling M/W, cross-country running M/W, gymnastics M/W, racquetball M/W, sailing M/W, swimming and diving M/W, tennis M/W, track and field M/W, volleyball M/W, weight lifting M/W, wrestling M.

Costs (2009–10) *Tuition:* state resident $3026 full-time, $84 per semester hour part-time; nonresident $11,412 full-time, $317 per semester hour part-time. *Waivers:* senior citizens and employees or children of employees.

Financial Aid Of all full-time matriculated undergraduates who enrolled in 2008, 120 Federal Work-Study jobs (averaging $3000).

Applying *Options:* early admission. *Application fee:* $30. *Required:* high school transcript. *Notification:* continuous until 8/30 (freshmen), continuous until 8/30 (transfers).

Freshman Application Contact Ms. Martha Caughey, Registrar, Pensacola Junior College, 1000 College Boulevard, Pensacola, FL 32504-8998. *Phone:* 850-484-1600. *Fax:* 850-484-1829.

POLK STATE COLLEGE

Winter Haven, Florida **www.polk.edu/**

- **State-supported** primarily 2-year, founded 1964, part of Florida Community College System
- **Suburban** 98-acre campus with easy access to Orlando and Tampa
- **Endowment** $12.0 million
- **Coed,** 9,437 undergraduate students, 35% full-time, 63% women, 37% men

Undergraduates 3,262 full-time, 6,175 part-time. Students come from 18 states and territories, 63 other countries, 1% are from out of state, 16% African American, 3% Asian American or Pacific Islander, 13% Hispanic American, 0.3% Native American, 0.9% international, 4% transferred in.

Freshmen *Admission:* 1,479 enrolled.

Faculty *Total:* 510, 30% full-time, 6% with terminal degrees. *Student/faculty ratio:* 19:1.

Majors Accounting technology and bookkeeping; business administration and management; cardiovascular technology; child development; corrections; criminal justice/law enforcement administration; data processing and data processing technology; diagnostic medical sonography and ultrasound technology; emergency medical technology (EMT paramedic); finance; fire science; health information/medical records administration; information science/studies; liberal arts and sciences/liberal studies; marketing/marketing management; medical administrative assistant and medical secretary; nursing (registered nurse training); occupational therapist assistant; physical therapist assistant; pre-engineering; radiologic technology/science; respiratory care therapy.

Academics *Calendar:* semesters 16-16-6-6. *Degrees:* certificates, associate, and bachelor's. *Special study options:* academic remediation for entering students, accelerated degree program, adult/continuing education programs, advanced placement credit, cooperative education, distance learning, double majors, English as a second language, honors programs, independent study, off-campus study, part-time degree program, services for LD students, student-designed majors, study abroad, summer session for credit. *ROTC:* Army (c).

Library Polk State College Library with 151,274 titles, 249 serial subscriptions, 4,998 audiovisual materials, an OPAC, a Web page.

Student Life *Housing:* college housing not available. *Activities and Organizations:* drama/theater group, choral group. *Campus security:* 24-hour emergency response devices and patrols. *Student services:* personal/psychological counseling.

Athletics Member NJCAA. *Intercollegiate sports:* baseball M(s), basketball M(s), soccer W(s), softball W(s), volleyball W(s). *Intramural sports:* basketball M/W, bowling M/W, football M/W, volleyball M/W.

Costs (2009–10) *Tuition:* state resident $2585 full-time, $86 per credit hour part-time; nonresident $9596 full-time, $320 per credit hour part-time. Full-time tuition and fees vary according to course load and degree level. Part-time tuition and fees vary according to course load and degree level. *Waivers:* employees or children of employees.

Financial Aid Of all full-time matriculated undergraduates who enrolled in 2008, 16 Federal Work-Study jobs (averaging $400).

Applying *Options:* electronic application, early admission, deferred entrance. *Application fee:* $20. *Required:* high school transcript. *Application deadlines:* rolling (freshmen), rolling (transfers). *Notification:* continuous (freshmen), continuous (transfers).

Freshman Application Contact Polk State College, 999 Avenue H, Northeast, Winter Haven, FL 33881. *Phone:* 863-297-1010 Ext. 5016.

Rasmussen College Fort Myers

Fort Myers, Florida www.rasmussen.edu/

Director of Admissions Admissions Director, Rasmussen College Fort Myers, 9160 Forum Corporate Parkway, Suite 100, Fort Myers, FL 33905. *Phone:* 239-477-2100. *Toll-free phone:* 866-344-0229. *Fax:* 239-477-2101.

Rasmussen College Ocala

Ocala, Florida www.rasmussen.edu/

- **Proprietary** primarily 2-year, founded 1984
- **Suburban** 3-acre campus with easy access to Orlando
- **Coed, primarily women**

Academics *Calendar:* quarters. *Degrees:* diplomas, associate, and bachelor's. *Special study options:* academic remediation for entering students, adult/continuing education programs, part-time degree program, summer session for credit.

Student Life *Campus security:* 24-hour emergency response devices, late-night transport/escort service.

Costs (2009–10) *Tuition:* $365 per credit part-time. Part-time tuition and fees vary according to program.

Applying *Options:* deferred entrance. *Application fee:* $60. *Required:* high school transcript, minimum 2.0 GPA, interview.

Freshman Application Contact Admissions Office, Rasmussen College Ocala, 2221 Southwest 19th Avenue Road, Ocala, FL 34471. *Phone:* 352-629-1941. *Toll-free phone:* 877-593-2783.

Rasmussen College Pasco County

Holiday, Florida www.rasmussen.edu/

- **Proprietary** primarily 2-year
- **Coed**

Academics *Degrees:* diplomas, associate, and bachelor's.

Standardized Tests *Required:* Wonderlic aptitude test (for admission).

Costs (2009–10) *Tuition:* $365 per credit part-time. Part-time tuition and fees vary according to course level and program.

Financial Aid Of all full-time matriculated undergraduates who enrolled in 2008, 6 Federal Work-Study jobs.

Applying *Application fee:* $60. *Required:* high school transcript, minimum 2.0 GPA, interview. *Required for some:* essay or personal statement.

Director of Admissions Ms. Claire L. Walker, Senior Admissions Representative, Rasmussen College Pasco County, 2127 Grand Boulevard, Holiday, FL 34690. *Phone:* 727-942-0069. *Toll-free phone:* 888-729-7247.

Remington College–Largo Campus

Largo, Florida www.remingtoncollege.edu/

Director of Admissions Kathy McCabe, Director of Recruitment, Remington College–Largo Campus, 8550 Ulmerton Road, Largo, FL 33771. *Phone:* 727-532-1999. *Toll-free phone:* 888-900-2343. *Fax:* 727-530-7710. *E-mail:* kathy.mccabe@remingtoncollege.edu.

Remington College–Tampa Campus

Tampa, Florida www.remingtoncollege.edu/

Freshman Application Contact Remington College–Tampa Campus, 2410 East Busch Boulevard, Tampa, FL 33612. *Phone:* 813-932-0701. *Toll-free phone:* 800-992-4850.

St. Johns River Community College

Palatka, Florida www.sjrcc.cc.fl.us/

Director of Admissions Mr. O'Neal Williams, Dean of Admissions and Records, St. Johns River Community College, 5001 Saint Johns Avenue, Palatka, FL 32177-3897. *Phone:* 386-312-4032. *Fax:* 386-312-4289.

Sanford-Brown Institute

Fort Lauderdale, Florida www.sbftlauderdale.com/

Director of Admissions Scott Nelowet, Sanford-Brown Institute, 1201 West Cypress Creek Road, Ft. Lauderdale, FL 33309. *Phone:* 904-363-6221. *Fax:* 904-363-6824. *E-mail:* snelowet@sbjacksonville.com.

Sanford-Brown Institute

Jacksonville, Florida www.sbjacksonville.com/

Freshman Application Contact Denise Neal, Assistant Director of Admissions, Sanford-Brown Institute, 10255 Fortune Parkway, Suite 501, Jacksonville, FL 32256. *Phone:* 904-380-2912. *Fax:* 904-363-6824. *E-mail:* dneal@sbjacksonville.com.

Sanford-Brown Institute

Tampa, Florida www.sbtampa.com/

Admissions Office Contact Sanford-Brown Institute, 5701 East Hillsborough Avenue, Tampa, FL 33610. *Toll-free phone:* 888-450-0333.

Seminole State College of Florida

Sanford, Florida www.seminolestate.edu/

- **State and locally supported** 2-year, founded 1966
- **Small-town** 200-acre campus with easy access to Orlando
- **Endowment** $6.5 million
- **Coed,** 16,449 undergraduate students, 43% full-time, 58% women, 42% men

Undergraduates 7,019 full-time, 9,430 part-time. Students come from 96 other countries, 4% are from out of state, 16% African American, 3% Asian American or Pacific Islander, 17% Hispanic American, 0.5% Native American, 3% international, 6% transferred in. *Retention:* 60% of 2008 full-time freshmen returned.

Freshmen *Admission:* 7,437 applied, 7,437 admitted, 2,822 enrolled.

Faculty *Total:* 723, 29% full-time, 13% with terminal degrees. *Student/faculty ratio:* 27:1.

Majors Accounting; administrative assistant and secretarial science; architectural engineering technology; automobile/automotive mechanics technology; banking and financial support services; building/construction finishing, management, and inspection related; business administration and management; child development; civil engineering technology; computer and information sciences and support services related; computer and information sciences related; computer and information systems security; computer engineering related; computer engineering technology; computer graphics; computer hardware engineering; computer/information technology services administration related; computer programming; computer programming related; computer programming (specific applications); computer programming (vendor/product certification); computer software and media applications related; computer software engineering; computer systems networking and telecommunications; construction engineering technology; criminal justice/law enforcement administration; data entry/microcomputer applications; data entry/microcomputer applications related; data modeling/warehousing and database administration; data processing and data processing technology; drafting and design technology; electrical, electronic and communications engineering technology; emergency medical technology (EMT paramedic); finance; fire science; industrial technology; information science/studies; information technology; interior design; legal assistant/paralegal; liberal arts and sciences/liberal studies; marketing/marketing management; nursing (registered nurse training); physical therapy; respiratory care therapy; system administration; telecommunications technology; web/multimedia management and webmaster; web page, digital/multimedia and information resources design; word processing.

Academics *Calendar:* semesters. *Degree:* certificates, diplomas, and associate. *Special study options:* academic remediation for entering students, accelerated degree program, adult/continuing education programs, advanced placement credit, cooperative education, distance learning, double majors, English as a second language, external degree program, honors programs, independent study, internships, part-time degree program, services for LD students, study abroad, summer session for credit. *ROTC:* Army (b).

Library Seminole State College Library - SLM plus 5 others with 93,296 titles, 413 serial subscriptions, 5,848 audiovisual materials, an OPAC, a Web page.

Student Life *Housing:* college housing not available. *Activities and Organizations:* drama/theater group, student-run newspaper, choral group, Phi Beta Lambda, Phi Theta Kappa, Student Government Association, Sigma Phi Gamma, Hispanic Student Association. *Campus security:* 24-hour emergency response devices and patrols. *Student services:* personal/psychological counseling.

Athletics Member NJCAA. *Intercollegiate sports:* baseball M(s), golf W(s), softball W(s).

Standardized Tests *Required:* CPT (for admission). *Recommended:* ACT (for admission).

Costs (2010–11) *Tuition:* state resident $2028 full-time, $91 per credit hour part-time; nonresident $8116 full-time, $327 per credit hour part-time. *Required fees:* $24 per credit hour part-time. *Payment plan:* deferred payment. *Waivers:* senior citizens and employees or children of employees.

Applying *Options:* early admission, deferred entrance. *Required:* high school transcript, minimum 2 GPA. *Application deadlines:* rolling (freshmen), rolling (transfers). *Notification:* continuous (freshmen), continuous (transfers).

Freshman Application Contact Ms. Pamela Mennechey, Director of Admissions, Seminole State College of Florida, 100 Weldon Boulevard, Sanford, FL 32773-6199. *Phone:* 407-708-2050. *Fax:* 407-708-2395. *E-mail:* admissions@scc-fl.edu.

SOUTH FLORIDA COMMUNITY COLLEGE

Avon Park, Florida **www.sfcc.cc.fl.us/**

Director of Admissions Ms. Annie Alexander-Harvey, Dean of Student Services, South Florida Community College, 600 West College Drive, Avon Park, FL 33825-9356. *Phone:* 863-453-6661 Ext. 7107.

SOUTHWEST FLORIDA COLLEGE

Tampa, Florida **www.swfc.edu/**

Director of Admissions Admissions, Southwest Florida College, 3910 Riga Boulevard, Tampa, FL 33619. *Phone:* 813-630-4401. *Toll-free phone:* 877-907-2456.

STATE COLLEGE OF FLORIDA MANATEE-SARASOTA

Bradenton, Florida **www.scf.edu/**

- **State-supported** primarily 2-year, founded 1957, part of Florida Community College System
- **Suburban** 100-acre campus with easy access to Tampa-St. Petersburg
- **Coed,** 11,232 undergraduate students, 48% full-time, 62% women, 38% men

Undergraduates 5,419 full-time, 5,813 part-time. Students come from 29 states and territories, 43 other countries, 2% are from out of state, 12% African American, 2% Asian American or Pacific Islander, 10% Hispanic American, 0.4% Native American, 1% international, 5% transferred in. *Retention:* 63% of 2008 full-time freshmen returned.

Freshmen *Admission:* 2,845 applied, 2,845 admitted, 1,843 enrolled. *Test scores:* SAT verbal scores over 500: 41%; SAT math scores over 500: 37%; SAT writing scores over 500: 42%; ACT scores over 18: 54%; SAT verbal scores over 600: 7%; SAT math scores over 600: 5%; SAT writing scores over 600: 7%; ACT scores over 24: 17%; SAT math scores over 700: 1%; ACT scores over 30: 2%.

Faculty *Total:* 524, 32% full-time.

Majors Accounting; administrative assistant and secretarial science; advertising; African American/Black studies; American government and politics; American studies; art; art history, criticism and conservation; Asian studies; astronomy; biology/biological sciences; biology teacher education; business administration and management; business/commerce; business/managerial economics; chemistry; chemistry teacher education; child development; civil engineering technology; commercial and advertising art; community health services counseling; computer and information sciences; computer and information sciences related; computer engineering technology; computer graphics; computer programming; computer programming related; construction engineering technology; criminal justice/safety; dietetics; drafting and design technology; dramatic/theater arts; economics; electrical, electronic and communications engineering technology; engineering; English; English/language arts teacher education; European studies (Central and Eastern); family and consumer sciences/home economics teacher education; finance; fine/studio arts; fire science; foreign language teacher education; French; German; health/health-care administration; health teacher education; history; hospital and health-care facilities administration; humanities; information science/studies; jazz/jazz studies; Jewish/Judaic studies; journalism; kindergarten/preschool education; Latin American studies; legal assistant/paralegal; liberal arts and sciences/liberal studies; mass communication/media; mathematics teacher education; medical radiologic technology; music; music performance; music teacher education; music theory and composition; nursing (registered nurse training); occupational therapist assistant; occupational therapy; philosophy; physical education teaching and coaching; physical therapist assistant; physical therapy; physician assistant; physics; physics teacher education; pre-pharmacy studies; psychology; public administration; radio and television; radio and television broadcasting technology; radiologic technology/science; religious studies; respiratory care therapy; Russian studies; science teacher education; social psychology; social sciences; social studies teacher education; social work; Spanish; speech and rhetoric; statistics; technology/industrial arts teacher education; trade and industrial teacher education; vocational rehabilitation counseling; women's studies.

Academics *Calendar:* semesters. *Degrees:* certificates, associate, and bachelor's. *Special study options:* academic remediation for entering students, advanced placement credit, cooperative education, distance learning, English as a second language, honors programs, independent study, part-time degree program, services for LD students, summer session for credit.

Library Sara Harlee Library plus 1 other with 65,386 titles, 378 serial subscriptions, an OPAC, a Web page.

Student Life *Housing:* college housing not available. *Activities and Organizations:* drama/theater group, student-run newspaper, choral group, Student Government Association, Phi Theta Kappa, American Chemical Society Student Affiliate, Campus Ministry, Medical Community Club. *Campus security:* 24-hour emergency response devices and patrols, late-night transport/escort service.

Athletics Member NJCAA. *Intercollegiate sports:* baseball M(s), basketball M(s), softball W(s), volleyball W(s). *Intramural sports:* basketball M/W, softball M/W, volleyball M/W, weight lifting M/W.

Costs (2009–10) *Tuition:* state resident $2636 full-time, $88 per credit hour part-time; nonresident $9942 full-time, $331 per credit hour part-time. *Required fees:* $40 full-time. *Payment plan:* deferred payment. *Waivers:* employees or children of employees.

Financial Aid Of all full-time matriculated undergraduates who enrolled in 2008, 82 Federal Work-Study jobs (averaging $2800). *Financial aid deadline:* 8/15.

Applying *Options:* early admission. *Required:* high school transcript. *Notification:* continuous (freshmen), continuous (transfers).

Freshman Application Contact Ms. MariLynn Lewy, AVP, Student Services, State College of Florida Manatee-Sarasota, PO Box 1849, Bradenton, FL 34206. *Phone:* 941-752-5384. *Fax:* 941-727-6380. *E-mail:* lewym@scf.edu.

TALLAHASSEE COMMUNITY COLLEGE

Tallahassee, Florida **www.tcc.fl.edu/**

- **State and locally supported** 2-year, founded 1966, part of Florida Community College System
- **Suburban** 258-acre campus
- **Endowment** $6.3 million
- **Coed,** 14,526 undergraduate students, 52% full-time, 56% women, 44% men

Undergraduates 7,553 full-time, 6,973 part-time. Students come from 37 states and territories, 61 other countries, 7% are from out of state, 34% African American, 2% Asian American or Pacific Islander, 7% Hispanic American, 0.4% Native American, 0.8% international, 26% transferred in. *Retention:* 61% of 2008 full-time freshmen returned.

Freshmen *Admission:* 3,328 applied, 3,328 admitted, 3,328 enrolled.

Faculty *Total:* 842, 22% full-time, 16% with terminal degrees. *Student/faculty ratio:* 25:1.

Majors Accounting technology and bookkeeping; administrative assistant and secretarial science; business administration and management; civil engineering technology; computer and information sciences; computer graphics; computer

Tallahassee Community College (continued)

programming; computer programming (specific applications); computer systems networking and telecommunications; construction engineering technology; criminal justice/law enforcement administration; data processing and data processing technology; dental hygiene; emergency medical technology (EMT paramedic); engineering; film/cinema studies; finance; health information/medical records technology; kindergarten/preschool education; legal administrative assistant/secretary; legal assistant/paralegal; liberal arts and sciences/liberal studies; management information systems; marketing/marketing management; nursing (registered nurse training); parks, recreation and leisure; public administration; respiratory care therapy; system administration; word processing.

Academics *Calendar:* semesters. *Degree:* certificates and associate. *Special study options:* academic remediation for entering students, accelerated degree program, adult/continuing education programs, advanced placement credit, distance learning, English as a second language, external degree program, honors programs, independent study, off-campus study, part-time degree program, services for LD students, study abroad, summer session for credit. *ROTC:* Army (c), Navy (c), Air Force (c).

Library Tallahassee Community College Library with 120,152 titles, 13,000 serial subscriptions, 6,508 audiovisual materials, an OPAC.

Student Life *Housing:* college housing not available. *Activities and Organizations:* drama/theater group, student-run newspaper, choral group, Student Government Association, International Student Organization, Phi Theta Kappa, Model United Nations, Honors Council. *Campus security:* 24-hour emergency response devices and patrols, late-night transport/escort service. *Student services:* personal/psychological counseling.

Athletics Member NJCAA. *Intercollegiate sports:* baseball M(s), basketball M(s)/W(s), softball W(s). *Intramural sports:* basketball M/W, football M/W, soccer M/W, softball M/W, volleyball M/W.

Costs (2010–11) *Tuition:* state resident $2232 full-time, $86 per credit hour part-time; nonresident $7887 full-time, $303 per credit hour part-time. Full-time tuition and fees vary according to course load. Part-time tuition and fees vary according to course load. *Payment plan:* installment. *Waivers:* employees or children of employees.

Financial Aid Of all full-time matriculated undergraduates who enrolled in 2008, 226 Federal Work-Study jobs (averaging $2000).

Applying *Options:* electronic application, early admission, deferred entrance. *Required:* high school transcript.

Freshman Application Contact Student Success Center, Tallahassee Community College, 444 Appleyard Drive, Tallahassee, FL 32304-2895. *Phone:* 850-201-8555. *E-mail:* admissions@tcc.fl.edu.

VALENCIA COMMUNITY COLLEGE

Orlando, Florida **www.valencia.cc.fl.us/**

Freshman Application Contact Dr. Renee Simpson, Assistant Vice President of Admissions and Records, Valencia Community College, PO Box 3028, Orlando, FL 32802-3028. *Phone:* 407-582-1511. *Fax:* 407-582-1866. *E-mail:* rsimpson@valenciacc.edu.

GEORGIA

ALBANY TECHNICAL COLLEGE

Albany, Georgia **www.albanytech.edu/**

- **State-supported** 2-year, founded 1961, part of Technical College System of Georgia
- **Coed,** 3,962 undergraduate students, 64% full-time, 58% women, 42% men

Undergraduates 2,526 full-time, 1,436 part-time. 73% African American, 0.4% Asian American or Pacific Islander, 0.4% Hispanic American, 0.4% Native American. *Retention:* 59% of 2008 full-time freshmen returned.

Freshmen *Admission:* 841 enrolled.

Majors Accounting; adult development and aging; child development; computer and information sciences; corrections and criminal justice related; culinary arts; drafting and design technology; electrical and electronic engineering technologies related; forestry technology; hotel/motel administration; human development and family studies related; industrial technology; manufacturing technology; marketing/marketing management; medical radiologic technology; pharmacy technician; tourism and travel services management.

Academics *Calendar:* quarters. *Degree:* certificates, diplomas, and associate. *Special study options:* distance learning.

Library Albany Technical College Library and Media Center.

Student Life *Housing:* college housing not available.

Applying *Options:* early admission. *Application fee:* $15. *Required:* high school transcript.

Freshman Application Contact Albany Technical College, 1704 South Slappey Boulevard, Albany, GA 31701. *Phone:* 229-430-3520.

ALTAMAHA TECHNICAL COLLEGE

Jesup, Georgia **www.altamahatech.edu/**

- **State-supported** 2-year, part of Technical College System of Georgia
- **Coed,** 1,551 undergraduate students, 41% full-time, 48% women, 52% men

Undergraduates 641 full-time, 910 part-time. 0.5% are from out of state, 31% African American, 0.5% Asian American or Pacific Islander, 0.8% Hispanic American, 1% Native American. *Retention:* 64% of 2008 full-time freshmen returned.

Freshmen *Admission:* 407 enrolled.

Majors Administrative assistant and secretarial science; child development; computer programming; computer systems networking and telecommunications; criminal justice/safety; information science/studies; machine tool technology; manufacturing technology; marketing/marketing management.

Academics *Calendar:* quarters. *Degree:* certificates, diplomas, and associate. *Special study options:* distance learning.

Student Life *Housing:* college housing not available.

Applying *Options:* early admission. *Application fee:* $15. *Required:* high school transcript.

Freshman Application Contact Altamaha Technical College, 1777 West Cherry Street, Jesup, GA 31545. *Phone:* 912-427-5821.

ANDREW COLLEGE

Cuthbert, Georgia **www.andrewcollege.edu/**

- **Independent United Methodist** 2-year, founded 1854
- **Rural** 40-acre campus
- **Coed**

Undergraduates Students come from 13 other countries, 40% African American, 0.7% Asian American or Pacific Islander, 3% Hispanic American, 8% international.

Faculty *Student/faculty ratio:* 12:1.

Academics *Calendar:* semesters. *Degree:* certificates and associate. *Special study options:* academic remediation for entering students, advanced placement credit, English as a second language, honors programs, part-time degree program, services for LD students, summer session for credit.

Student Life *Campus security:* 24-hour patrols, controlled dormitory access, campus police.

Athletics Member NJCAA.

Standardized Tests *Required:* SAT or ACT (for admission).

Costs (2009–10) *Comprehensive fee:* $18,584 includes full-time tuition ($11,415) and room and board ($7169).

Financial Aid Of all full-time matriculated undergraduates who enrolled in 2008, 72 Federal Work-Study jobs (averaging $772).

Applying *Options:* electronic application, early admission, deferred entrance. *Application fee:* $20. *Required:* high school transcript. *Required for some:* essay or personal statement, 1 letter of recommendation, interview. *Recommended:* minimum 2 GPA.

Freshman Application Contact Ms. Bridget Kurkowski, Director of Admission, Andrew College, 413 College Street, Cuthbert, GA 39840. *Phone:* 229-732-5986. *Toll-free phone:* 800-664-9250. *Fax:* 229-732-2176. *E-mail:* admissions@andrewcollege.edu.

ATHENS TECHNICAL COLLEGE

Athens, Georgia **www.athenstech.edu/**

- **State-supported** 2-year, founded 1958, part of Technical College System of Georgia
- **Suburban** 41-acre campus with easy access to Atlanta
- **Coed,** 5,167 undergraduate students, 41% full-time, 65% women, 35% men

Undergraduates 2,099 full-time, 3,068 part-time. 0.4% are from out of state, 23% African American, 6% Asian American or Pacific Islander, 3% Hispanic American, 0.3% Native American. *Retention:* 52% of 2008 full-time freshmen returned.

Freshmen *Admission:* 793 enrolled.

Majors Accounting; administrative assistant and secretarial science; biology/biotechnology laboratory technician; child development; clinical laboratory science/medical technology; communications technology; computer programming; computer systems networking and telecommunications; criminal justice/law enforcement administration; dental assisting; dental hygiene; diagnostic medical sonography and ultrasound technology; electrical, electronic and communications engineering technology; emergency medical technology (EMT paramedic); hotel/motel administration; information science/studies; legal assistant/paralegal; logistics and materials management; marketing/marketing management; medical radiologic technology; nursing (licensed practical/vocational nurse training); nursing (registered nurse training); physical therapy; respiratory care therapy; surgical technology; tourism and travel services management; veterinary/animal health technology.

Academics *Calendar:* quarters. *Degree:* certificates, diplomas, and associate. *Special study options:* distance learning, summer session for credit.

Student Life *Housing:* college housing not available.

Financial Aid Of all full-time matriculated undergraduates who enrolled in 2008, 34 Federal Work-Study jobs (averaging $3090).

Applying *Options:* early admission. *Application fee:* $20. *Required:* high school transcript.

Freshman Application Contact Athens Technical College, 800 US Highway 29 North, Athens, GA 30601-1500. *Phone:* 706-355-5008.

Atlanta Metropolitan College

Atlanta, Georgia **www.atlm.edu/**

Freshman Application Contact Ms. Audrey Reid, Director, Office of Admissions, Atlanta Metropolitan College, 1630 Metropolitan Parkway, SW, Atlanta, GA 30310-4498. *Phone:* 404-756-4004. *Fax:* 404-756-4407. *E-mail:* admissions@atlm.edu.

Atlanta Technical College

Atlanta, Georgia **www.atlantatech.org/**

- **State-supported** 2-year, founded 1945, part of Technical College System of Georgia
- **Coed,** 4,740 undergraduate students, 51% full-time, 58% women, 42% men

Undergraduates 2,395 full-time, 2,345 part-time. 93% African American, 1% Asian American or Pacific Islander, 0.9% Hispanic American, 0.2% Native American. *Retention:* 56% of 2008 full-time freshmen returned.

Freshmen *Admission:* 1,033 enrolled.

Majors Accounting; child development; computer programming; culinary arts; dental hygiene; health information/medical records technology; hotel/motel administration; information technology; legal assistant/paralegal; marketing/marketing management; tourism and travel services management.

Academics *Calendar:* quarters. *Degree:* certificates, diplomas, and associate. *Special study options:* distance learning, study abroad.

Student Life *Housing:* college housing not available.

Applying *Options:* early admission. *Application fee:* $20. *Required:* high school transcript.

Freshman Application Contact Atlanta Technical College, 1560 Metropolitan Parkway SW, Atlanta, GA 30310-4446. *Phone:* 404-225-4455.

Augusta Technical College

Augusta, Georgia **www.augustatech.edu/**

- **State-supported** 2-year, founded 1961, part of Technical College System of Georgia
- **Urban** 70-acre campus
- **Coed,** 5,028 undergraduate students, 48% full-time, 62% women, 38% men

Undergraduates 2,398 full-time, 2,630 part-time. 3% are from out of state, 52% African American, 2% Asian American or Pacific Islander, 2% Hispanic American, 0.3% Native American, 0.1% international. *Retention:* 52% of 2008 full-time freshmen returned.

Freshmen *Admission:* 802 enrolled.

Majors Accounting; administrative assistant and secretarial science; biotechnology; business administration and management; cardiovascular technology; child development; computer programming; computer systems networking and telecommunications; criminal justice/safety; culinary arts; e-commerce; electrical, electronic and communications engineering technology; emergency medical technology (EMT paramedic); fire science; information science/studies; marketing/marketing management; mechanical engineering/mechanical technology; medical radiologic technology; occupational therapist assistant; parks, recreation and leisure facilities management; pharmacy technician; respiratory care therapy; respiratory therapy technician; surgical technology.

Academics *Calendar:* quarters. *Degree:* certificates, diplomas, and associate. *Special study options:* distance learning, study abroad.

Library Information Technology Center.

Student Life *Housing:* college housing not available.

Applying *Options:* early admission. *Application fee:* $20. *Required:* high school transcript.

Freshman Application Contact Augusta Technical College, 3200 Augusta Tech Drive, Augusta, GA 30906. *Phone:* 706-771-4150.

Bainbridge College

Bainbridge, Georgia **www.bainbridge.edu/**

- **State-supported** 2-year, founded 1972, part of University System of Georgia
- **Small-town** 160-acre campus
- **Coed,** 3,545 undergraduate students, 49% full-time, 70% women, 30% men

Undergraduates 1,745 full-time, 1,800 part-time. Students come from 3 states and territories, 1% are from out of state, 55% African American, 2% Asian American or Pacific Islander, 0.8% Hispanic American, 0.1% Native American.

Freshmen *Admission:* 1,902 applied, 1,526 admitted.

Faculty *Total:* 169, 42% full-time, 20% with terminal degrees.

Majors Accounting; administrative assistant and secretarial science; agriculture; art; automobile/automotive mechanics technology; biology/biological sciences; business administration and management; business teacher education; chemistry; criminal justice/law enforcement administration; data processing and data processing technology; drafting and design technology; dramatic/theater arts; education; electrical, electronic and communications engineering technology; elementary education; English; family and consumer sciences/human sciences; forestry; health teacher education; history; information science/studies; journalism; kindergarten/preschool education; liberal arts and sciences/liberal studies; marketing/marketing management; mathematics; nursing (licensed practical/vocational nurse training); nursing (registered nurse training); political science and government; psychology; sociology; speech and rhetoric; welding technology.

Academics *Calendar:* semesters. *Degree:* certificates and associate. *Special study options:* academic remediation for entering students, adult/continuing education programs, advanced placement credit, distance learning, double majors, independent study, part-time degree program, services for LD students, study abroad, summer session for credit.

Library Bainbridge College Library with 40,950 titles, 102 serial subscriptions, 2,572 audiovisual materials, an OPAC.

Student Life *Housing:* college housing not available. *Activities and Organizations:* drama/theater group, Phi Theta Kappa, Alpha Beta Gamma, Drama Club, Sigma Kappa Delta, Student Government Association. *Campus security:* 24-hour patrols.

Athletics *Intramural sports:* table tennis M/W, volleyball M/W.

Standardized Tests *Required for some:* SAT or ACT (for admission), ACT COMPASS.

Costs (2009–10) *Tuition:* state resident $1838 full-time, $77 per credit hour part-time; nonresident $7340 full-time, $306 per credit hour part-time. Full-time tuition and fees vary according to course load. Part-time tuition and fees vary according to course load. No tuition increase for student's term of enrollment. *Required fees:* $488 full-time. *Waivers:* senior citizens.

Applying *Options:* electronic application, early admission. *Required for some:* high school transcript, minimum 1.8 GPA, 3 letters of recommendation, interview, immunizations/waivers, medical records and criminal. *Notification:* continuous (freshmen), continuous (transfers).

Freshman Application Contact Mrs. Connie Snyder, Director of Admissions and Records, Bainbridge College, 2500 East Shotwell Street, Bainbridge, GA 39819. *Phone:* 229-248-2504. *Fax:* 229-248-2525. *E-mail:* csnyder@bainbridge.edu.

BROWN MACKIE COLLEGE–ATLANTA

Atlanta, Georgia **www.brownmackie.edu/atlanta/**

- **Proprietary** 2-year, part of Education Management Corporation
- **Urban** campus
- **Coed**

Majors Accounting technology and bookkeeping; business administration and management; criminal justice/law enforcement administration; early childhood education; health/health-care administration; legal assistant/paralegal; medical/clinical assistant; occupational therapist assistant; pharmacy technician; surgical technology.

Academics *Degree:* diplomas and associate.

Costs (2009–10) *Tuition:* Tuition varies by program. Students should contact Brown Mackie College for tuition information.

Freshman Application Contact Brown Mackie College–Atlanta, 4370 Peachtree Road, NE, Atlanta, GA 30319. *Phone:* 404-799-4500.

►**See page 408 for the College Close-Up.**

CENTRAL GEORGIA TECHNICAL COLLEGE

Macon, Georgia **www.centralgatech.edu/**

- **State-supported** 2-year, founded 1966, part of Technical College System of Georgia
- **Suburban** campus
- **Coed,** 6,950 undergraduate students, 56% full-time, 67% women, 33% men

Undergraduates 3,913 full-time, 3,037 part-time. 61% African American, 0.9% Asian American or Pacific Islander, 0.4% Hispanic American, 0.4% Native American, 0.1% international. *Retention:* 50% of 2008 full-time freshmen returned.

Freshmen *Admission:* 1,402 enrolled.

Majors Accounting; administrative assistant and secretarial science; adult development and aging; banking and financial support services; business administration and management; cabinetmaking and millwork; cardiovascular technology; carpentry; child-care and support services management; child development; clinical/medical laboratory technology; computer programming; computer systems networking and telecommunications; criminal justice/safety; dental hygiene; drafting and design technology; e-commerce; electrical, electronic and communications engineering technology; hotel/motel administration; industrial technology; information science/studies; legal assistant/paralegal; marketing/marketing management; medical radiologic technology; tourism and travel services management; veterinary/animal health technology; web page, digital/multimedia and information resources design.

Academics *Calendar:* quarters. *Degree:* certificates, diplomas, and associate. *Special study options:* distance learning.

Student Life *Housing:* college housing not available.

Financial Aid Of all full-time matriculated undergraduates who enrolled in 2008, 175 Federal Work-Study jobs (averaging $2000). *Financial aid deadline:* 9/1.

Applying *Options:* early admission. *Application fee:* $15. *Required:* high school transcript.

Freshman Application Contact Central Georgia Technical College, 3300 Macon Tech Drive, Macon, GA 31206. *Phone:* 478-757-3408.

CHATTAHOOCHEE TECHNICAL COLLEGE

Marietta, Georgia **www.chattahoocheetech.edu/**

- **State-supported** 2-year, founded 1961, part of Technical College System of Georgia
- **Suburban** campus with easy access to Atlanta
- **Coed,** 11,391 undergraduate students, 47% full-time, 59% women, 41% men

Undergraduates 5,335 full-time, 6,056 part-time. 0.1% are from out of state, 31% African American, 2% Asian American or Pacific Islander, 3% Hispanic American, 0.4% Native American, 1% international. *Retention:* 53% of 2008 full-time freshmen returned.

Freshmen *Admission:* 7,801 enrolled.

Majors Accounting; administrative assistant and secretarial science; automobile/automotive mechanics technology; biomedical technology; business administration and management; child development; civil engineering technology; computer and information systems security; computer programming; computer systems networking and telecommunications; criminal justice/safety; culinary arts; drafting and design technology; electrical, electronic and communications engineering technology; fire science; horticultural science; information science/studies; logistics and materials management; marketing/marketing management; medical radiologic technology; parks, recreation and leisure facilities management; web page, digital/multimedia and information resources design.

Academics *Calendar:* quarters. *Degree:* certificates, diplomas, and associate. *Special study options:* distance learning.

Student Life *Housing:* college housing not available.

Financial Aid Of all full-time matriculated undergraduates who enrolled in 2008, 40 Federal Work-Study jobs (averaging $2500).

Applying *Options:* early admission. *Application fee:* $15. *Required:* high school transcript.

Freshman Application Contact Chattahoochee Technical College, 980 South Cobb Drive, Marietta, GA 30060-3398. *Phone:* 770-528-4581.

COLUMBUS TECHNICAL COLLEGE

Columbus, Georgia **www.columbustech.edu/**

- **State-supported** 2-year, founded 1961, part of Technical College System of Georgia
- **Urban** campus with easy access to Atlanta
- **Coed,** 4,172 undergraduate students, 43% full-time, 68% women, 32% men

Undergraduates 1,791 full-time, 2,381 part-time. 12% are from out of state, 46% African American, 2% Asian American or Pacific Islander, 3% Hispanic American, 0.6% Native American. *Retention:* 52% of 2008 full-time freshmen returned.

Freshmen *Admission:* 855 enrolled.

Majors Accounting; administrative assistant and secretarial science; automobile/automotive mechanics technology; child development; computer engineering related; computer systems networking and telecommunications; dental hygiene; diagnostic medical sonography and ultrasound technology; drafting and design technology; electrical, electronic and communications engineering technology; emergency medical technology (EMT paramedic); health information/medical records technology; horticultural science; industrial technology; information science/studies; machine tool technology; mechanical engineering/mechanical technology; medical office management; medical radiologic technology; nursing (registered nurse training); pharmacy technician; respiratory therapy technician; surgical technology; web page, digital/multimedia and information resources design.

Academics *Calendar:* quarters. *Degree:* certificates, diplomas, and associate. *Special study options:* distance learning.

Library Columbus Technical College Library.

Student Life *Housing:* college housing not available.

Financial Aid Of all full-time matriculated undergraduates who enrolled in 2008, 6 Federal Work-Study jobs (averaging $2000).

Applying *Options:* early admission. *Application fee:* $25. *Required:* high school transcript.

Freshman Application Contact Columbus Technical College, 928 Manchester Expressway, Columbus, GA 31904-6572. *Phone:* 706-649-1901.

DARTON COLLEGE

Albany, Georgia **www.darton.edu/**

- **State-supported** 2-year, founded 1965, part of University System of Georgia
- **Urban** 185-acre campus
- **Endowment** $908,201
- **Coed,** 5,854 undergraduate students, 49% full-time, 69% women, 31% men

Undergraduates 2,874 full-time, 2,980 part-time. Students come from 32 states and territories, 46 other countries, 7% are from out of state, 43% African American, 1% Asian American or Pacific Islander, 2% Hispanic American, 0.2% Native American, 1% international, 14% transferred in. *Retention:* 51% of 2008 full-time freshmen returned.

Freshmen *Admission:* 1,464 enrolled. *Average high school GPA:* 2.73. *Test scores:* SAT math scores over 500: 33%; SAT writing scores over 500: 34%; SAT math scores over 600: 5%; SAT writing scores over 600: 7%; SAT writing scores over 700: 1%.

Faculty *Total:* 271, 44% full-time. *Student/faculty ratio:* 21:1.

Majors Accounting; administrative assistant and secretarial science; agriculture; anthropology; art; art teacher education; biological and biomedical sciences related; biology/biological sciences; business administration and management; business teacher education; cardiovascular technology; chemistry; clinical laboratory science/medical technology; computer and information sciences; computer and information sciences and support services related; computer installation and repair technology; computer science; criminal justice/law enforcement administration; dance; dental hygiene; diagnostic medical sonography and ultrasound technology; drama and dance teacher education; dramatic/theater arts; economics; emergency medical technology (EMT paramedic); engineering technology; English; English/language arts teacher education; environmental studies; foreign languages and literatures; forensic science and technology; forestry; general studies; geography; health and physical education; health information/medical records administration; health information/medical records technology; health/medical preparatory programs related; histologic technician; history; history teacher education; journalism; mathematics; mathematics teacher education; medical insurance coding; middle school education; music; music teacher education; nuclear medical technology; nursing (licensed practical/vocational nurse training); nursing (registered nurse training); occupational therapist assistant; office occupations and clerical services; philosophy; physical therapist assistant; physics; political science and government; pre-dentistry studies; pre-engineering; pre-law studies; premedical studies; pre-pharmacy studies; pre-veterinary studies; psychology; respiratory care therapy; science teacher education; social work; sociology; special education; speech and rhetoric; speech teacher education; trade and industrial teacher education.

Academics *Calendar:* semesters. *Degrees:* certificates, associate, and post-bachelor's certificates. *Special study options:* academic remediation for entering students, accelerated degree program, adult/continuing education programs, advanced placement credit, cooperative education, distance learning, double majors, English as a second language, honors programs, independent study, part-time degree program, services for LD students, student-designed majors, study abroad, summer session for credit. *ROTC:* Army (c).

Library Weatherbee Learning Resources Center with 67,507 titles, an OPAC, a Web page.

Student Life *Housing Options:* coed. Campus housing is university owned. *Activities and Organizations:* drama/theater group, choral group. *Campus security:* 24-hour emergency response devices and patrols, student patrols, late-night transport/escort service. *Student services:* personal/psychological counseling.

Athletics Member NJCAA. *Intercollegiate sports:* baseball M(s), basketball W(s), cross-country running M(s)/W(s), golf M(s), soccer M(s)/W(s), softball W(s), swimming and diving M(s)/W(s), wrestling M. *Intramural sports:* badminton M/W, basketball M/W, bowling M/W, football M, racquetball M/W, volleyball M/W.

Standardized Tests *Required for some:* SAT or ACT (for admission), SAT Subject Tests (for admission). *Recommended:* SAT or ACT (for admission), SAT Subject Tests (for admission).

Costs (2009–10) *Tuition:* state resident $1848 full-time, $77 per credit hour part-time; nonresident $7344 full-time, $306 per credit hour part-time. $2,298 if 15 credits/semester in-state; $7,340 if 15 credits/semester out-of-state. *Required fees:* $694 full-time, $253 per term part-time. *Room and board:* room only: $5040. Room and board charges vary according to board plan. *Waivers:* senior citizens and employees or children of employees.

Financial Aid Of all full-time matriculated undergraduates who enrolled in 2008, 60 Federal Work-Study jobs.

Applying *Options:* electronic application. *Application fee:* $20. *Required:* high school transcript, minimum 1.8 GPA, proof of immunization. *Notification:* continuous until 7/27 (freshmen), continuous until 7/27 (transfers).

Freshman Application Contact Darton College, 2400 Gillionville Road, Albany, GA 31707. *Phone:* 229-430-6740.

DeKalb Technical College

Clarkston, Georgia **www.dekalbtech.edu/**

- **State-supported** 2-year, founded 1961, part of Technical College System of Georgia
- **Suburban** 17-acre campus with easy access to Atlanta
- **Coed,** 4,742 undergraduate students, 42% full-time, 62% women, 38% men

Undergraduates 1,971 full-time, 2,771 part-time. 0.2% are from out of state, 75% African American, 3% Asian American or Pacific Islander, 0.6% Hispanic American, 0.5% Native American. *Retention:* 53% of 2008 full-time freshmen returned.

Freshmen *Admission:* 942 enrolled.

Majors Accounting; administrative assistant and secretarial science; automobile/automotive mechanics technology; business/commerce; clinical/medical laboratory technology; computer engineering technology; computer programming; computer systems networking and telecommunications; criminal justice/safety; drafting and design technology; electrical, electronic and communications engineering technology; electromechanical technology; engineering technology; heating, air conditioning and refrigeration technology; industrial technology; information science/studies; instrumentation technology; legal administrative assistant/secretary; legal assistant/paralegal; machine tool technology; marketing/marketing management; medical/clinical assistant; operations management; ophthalmic laboratory technology; opticianry; surgical technology; telecommunications technology.

Academics *Calendar:* quarters. *Degree:* certificates, diplomas, and associate. *Special study options:* distance learning.

Student Life *Housing:* college housing not available.

Financial Aid Of all full-time matriculated undergraduates who enrolled in 2008, 50 Federal Work-Study jobs (averaging $4000).

Applying *Options:* early admission. *Application fee:* $25. *Required:* high school transcript.

Freshman Application Contact DeKalb Technical College, 495 North Indian Creek Drive, Clarkston, GA 30021-2397. *Phone:* 404-297-9522.

East Central Technical College

Fitzgerald, Georgia **www.eastcentraltech.edu/**

- **State-supported** 2-year, founded 1968, part of Technical College System of Georgia
- **Rural** 30-acre campus
- **Coed,** 1,761 undergraduate students, 54% full-time, 63% women, 37% men

Undergraduates 952 full-time, 809 part-time. 40% African American, 0.3% Asian American or Pacific Islander, 1% Hispanic American, 0.2% Native American. *Retention:* 57% of 2008 full-time freshmen returned.

Freshmen *Admission:* 468 enrolled.

Majors Administrative assistant and secretarial science; child development; computer systems networking and telecommunications; criminal justice/safety; information science/studies.

Academics *Calendar:* quarters. *Degree:* certificates, diplomas, and associate. *Special study options:* distance learning.

Student Life *Housing:* college housing not available.

Applying *Options:* early admission. *Application fee:* $15. *Required:* high school transcript.

Freshman Application Contact East Central Technical College, 667 Perry House Road, Fitzgerald, GA 31750. *Phone:* 229-468-2225.

East Georgia College

Swainsboro, Georgia **www.ega.edu/**

Freshman Application Contact Ms. Linda Connelly, Office Coordinator, East Georgia College, 131 College Circle, Swainsboro, GA 30401. *Phone:* 478-289-2019.

Emory University, Oxford College

Oxford, Georgia **oxford.emory.edu/**

- **Independent Methodist** primarily 2-year, founded 1836, administratively affiliated with Emory University
- **Small-town** 150-acre campus with easy access to Atlanta
- **Endowment** $26.0 million
- **Coed,** 756 undergraduate students, 100% full-time, 55% women, 45% men

Undergraduates 755 full-time, 1 part-time. Students come from 36 states and territories, 16 other countries, 62% are from out of state, 15% African American, 27% Asian American or Pacific Islander, 6% Hispanic American, 0.3% Native American, 6% international, 95% live on campus. *Retention:* 89% of 2008 full-time freshmen returned.

Freshmen *Admission:* 389 enrolled. *Average high school GPA:* 3.56. *Test scores:* SAT verbal scores over 500: 98%; SAT writing scores over 500: 99%; ACT scores over 18: 99%; SAT verbal scores over 600: 67%; SAT writing scores over 600: 75%; ACT scores over 24: 72%; SAT verbal scores over 700: 21%; SAT writing scores over 700: 24%; ACT scores over 30: 13%.

Faculty *Total:* 71, 80% full-time, 73% with terminal degrees. *Student/faculty ratio:* 10:1.

Majors Liberal arts and sciences/liberal studies.

Emory University, Oxford College (continued)

Academics *Calendar:* semesters. *Degrees:* associate and bachelor's. *Special study options:* advanced placement credit, double majors, independent study, internships, off-campus study, services for LD students, study abroad, summer session for credit. *Unusual degree programs:* 3-2 engineering with Georgia Institute of Technology.

Library Hoke O'Kelly Library with 92,681 titles, 167 serial subscriptions, 1,352 audiovisual materials, an OPAC, a Web page.

Student Life *Housing:* on-campus residence required through sophomore year. *Options:* coed, women-only, disabled students. Campus housing is university owned. Freshman campus housing is guaranteed. *Activities and Organizations:* drama/theater group, student-run newspaper, choral group, Residence Hall Association, intramurals/junior varsity sports, Student Government Association, Student Admissions Association, Volunteer Oxford. *Campus security:* 24-hour emergency response devices and patrols, student patrols, late-night transport/escort service, controlled dormitory access. *Student services:* health clinic, personal/psychological counseling.

Athletics Member NJCAA. *Intercollegiate sports:* basketball M, soccer W, tennis M/W. *Intramural sports:* badminton M/W, baseball M(c), basketball M/W, football M, soccer M/W, swimming and diving M/W, tennis M/W, ultimate Frisbee M/W, volleyball M/W.

Standardized Tests *Required:* SAT or ACT (for admission). *Required for some:* SAT Subject Tests (for admission).

Costs (2010–11) *Comprehensive fee:* $42,734 includes full-time tuition ($32,800), mandatory fees ($462), and room and board ($9472). Full-time tuition and fees vary according to course load. Part-time tuition: $1000 per credit hour. Part-time tuition and fees vary according to course load. *Room and board:* Room and board charges vary according to board plan. *Payment plan:* installment. *Waivers:* employees or children of employees.

Financial Aid Of all full-time matriculated undergraduates who enrolled in 2008, 225 Federal Work-Study jobs (averaging $1600).

Applying *Options:* electronic application, early admission, early action, deferred entrance. *Application fee:* $50. *Required:* essay or personal statement, high school transcript, 1 letter of recommendation, SAT or ACT scores. *Required for some:* interview. *Recommended:* minimum 3 GPA, 2 letters of recommendation. *Application deadlines:* 1/15 (freshmen), rolling (transfers), 11/1 (early action). *Notification:* continuous until 4/1 (freshmen), continuous (transfers), 12/15 (early action).

Freshman Application Contact Emory University, Oxford College, 100 Hamill Street, PO Box 1418, Oxford, GA 30054. *Phone:* 770-784-8328. *Toll-free phone:* 800-723-8328.

EVEREST INSTITUTE

Atlanta, Georgia **www.everest.edu/**

Freshman Application Contact Admissions Office, Everest Institute, 2460 Wesley Chapel Road, Suite 100, Decatur, GA 30035. *Phone:* 404-327-8787. *Toll-free phone:* 888-741-4270.

FLINT RIVER TECHNICAL COLLEGE

Thomaston, Georgia **www.flintrivertech.edu/**

- **State-supported** 2-year, founded 1961, part of Technical College System of Georgia
- **Coed,** 959 undergraduate students, 58% full-time, 70% women, 30% men

Undergraduates 554 full-time, 405 part-time. 47% African American, 0.4% Hispanic American, 0.1% Native American. *Retention:* 55% of 2008 full-time freshmen returned.

Freshmen *Admission:* 240 enrolled.

Majors Accounting; administrative assistant and secretarial science; child development; computer and information systems security; computer systems networking and telecommunications; criminal justice/safety; electrical, electronic and communications engineering technology; information science/studies; manufacturing technology; web page, digital/multimedia and information resources design.

Academics *Calendar:* quarters. *Degree:* certificates, diplomas, and associate. *Special study options:* distance learning.

Student Life *Housing:* college housing not available.

Applying *Options:* early admission. *Application fee:* $15. *Required:* high school transcript.

Freshman Application Contact Flint River Technical College, 1533 US Highway 19 South, Thomaston, GA 30286-4752. *Phone:* 706-646-6148. *Toll-free phone:* 800-752-9681.

GAINESVILLE STATE COLLEGE

Oakwood, Georgia **www.gsc.edu/**

- **State-supported** primarily 2-year, founded 1964, part of University System of Georgia
- **Small-town** 220-acre campus with easy access to Atlanta
- **Coed,** 8,801 undergraduate students, 69% full-time, 54% women, 46% men

Undergraduates 6,068 full-time, 2,733 part-time. Students come from 17 states and territories, 72 other countries, 1% are from out of state, 5% African American, 3% Asian American or Pacific Islander, 8% Hispanic American, 0.5% Native American, 1% international, 7% transferred in.

Freshmen *Admission:* 6,657 applied, 5,540 admitted, 2,457 enrolled. *Average high school GPA:* 2.9.

Faculty *Total:* 401, 49% full-time. *Student/faculty ratio:* 26:1.

Majors Anthropology; biology/biological sciences; business administration and management; chemistry; computer science; criminal justice/law enforcement administration; dramatic/theater arts; early childhood education; elementary education; engineering technology; English; environmental design/architecture; foreign languages and literatures; forestry; general studies; geography; geology/earth science; history; information technology; journalism; kinesiology and exercise science; mass communication/media; mathematics; middle school education; music; physics; political science and government; premedical studies; prenursing studies; pre-pharmacy studies; psychology; secondary education; social work; sociology; sport and fitness administration/management.

Academics *Calendar:* semesters. *Degrees:* associate and bachelor's. *Special study options:* academic remediation for entering students, adult/continuing education programs, advanced placement credit, distance learning, double majors, English as a second language, honors programs, internships, off-campus study, part-time degree program, services for LD students, study abroad, summer session for credit. *ROTC:* Army (c), Air Force (c).

Library John Harrison Hosch Library with 70,000 titles, 398 serial subscriptions, an OPAC, a Web page.

Student Life *Housing:* college housing not available. *Activities and Organizations:* drama/theater group, student-run newspaper, choral group, Students in Free Enterprise (SIFE), Politically Incorrect Club, Student Government Association, Latino Student Association, Campus Activities Board. *Campus security:* 24-hour emergency response devices and patrols. *Student services:* personal/psychological counseling.

Athletics *Intramural sports:* basketball M/W, bowling M/W, football M/W, softball M/W, tennis M/W, volleyball M/W.

Standardized Tests *Recommended:* SAT or ACT (for admission).

Costs (2010–11) *Tuition:* state resident $2016 full-time, $84 per credit hour part-time; nonresident $7992 full-time, $333 per credit hour part-time. *Required fees:* $554 full-time, $484 per year part-time. *Waivers:* senior citizens.

Applying *Options:* electronic application, early admission. *Application fee:* $35. *Required:* high school transcript.

Freshman Application Contact Mr. Mack Palmour, Director of Admissions, Gainesville State College, PO Box 1358, Gainesville, GA 30503. *Phone:* 678-717-3641. *Fax:* 678-717-3751. *E-mail:* admissions@gsc.edu.

GEORGIA HIGHLANDS COLLEGE

Rome, Georgia **www.highlands.edu/**

- **State-supported** 2-year, founded 1970, part of University System of Georgia
- **Suburban** 226-acre campus with easy access to Atlanta
- **Endowment** $1.1 million
- **Coed,** 5,246 undergraduate students, 61% full-time, 63% women, 37% men

Undergraduates 3,184 full-time, 2,062 part-time. Students come from 46 states and territories, 45 other countries, 7% are from out of state, 11% African American, 2% Asian American or Pacific Islander, 5% Hispanic American, 0.4% Native American, 0.5% international, 6% transferred in. *Retention:* 58% of 2008 full-time freshmen returned.

Freshmen *Admission:* 2,081 applied, 1,616 admitted, 1,439 enrolled. *Average high school GPA:* 2.7.

Faculty *Total:* 214, 54% full-time, 33% with terminal degrees. *Student/faculty ratio:* 25:1.

Majors Accounting; agriculture; art; automobile/automotive mechanics technology; biological and physical sciences; business administration and management; clinical laboratory science/medical technology; computer programming; criminal justice/police science; criminal justice/safety; dental hygiene; economics; electrical, electronic and communications engineering technology; emergency medical technology (EMT paramedic); English; foreign languages and literatures; forestry; geology/earth science; history; horticultural science; hotel/motel administration; human services; information science/studies; journalism; kindergarten/preschool education; legal assistant/paralegal; liberal arts and sciences/liberal studies; marketing/marketing management; nursing (registered nurse training); occupational therapy; philosophy; physical therapist assistant; physical therapy; physician assistant; political science and government; psychology; radiologic technology/science; respiratory care therapy; secondary education; sociology.

Academics *Calendar:* semesters. *Degree:* diplomas and associate. *Special study options:* academic remediation for entering students, advanced placement credit, cooperative education, distance learning, double majors, honors programs, independent study, part-time degree program, services for LD students, study abroad, summer session for credit.

Library Georgia Highlands Library plus 2 others with 68,346 titles, 248 serial subscriptions, 7,383 audiovisual materials, an OPAC, a Web page.

Student Life *Housing:* college housing not available. *Activities and Organizations:* student-run newspaper, Highlands Association of Nursing Students, Green Highlands, Black Awareness Society, Political Science Association, Phi Theta Kappa. *Campus security:* 24-hour patrols, emergency phone/email alert system. *Student services:* personal/psychological counseling.

Athletics *Intramural sports:* basketball M/W, bowling M/W, football M/W, golf M/W, sailing M/W, soccer M/W, softball M/W, table tennis M/W, tennis M/W, ultimate Frisbee M/W, volleyball M/W, weight lifting M/W.

Costs (2010–11) *Tuition:* state resident $1848 full-time, $77 per credit hour part-time; nonresident $7344 full-time, $306 per credit hour part-time. Part-time tuition and fees vary according to course load. *Required fees:* $434 full-time, $217 per term part-time, $217 per term part-time. *Waivers:* senior citizens.

Financial Aid Of all full-time matriculated undergraduates who enrolled in 2008, 50 Federal Work-Study jobs (averaging $3500).

Applying *Options:* electronic application, deferred entrance. *Application fee:* $20. *Required:* high school transcript, minimum 2 GPA. *Required for some:* minimum 2.2 GPA. *Application deadlines:* rolling (freshmen), rolling (out-of-state freshmen), rolling (transfers). *Notification:* continuous (freshmen), continuous (out-of-state freshmen), continuous (transfers).

Freshman Application Contact Mr. Todd Jones, Director of Admissions, Georgia Highlands College, 3175 Cedartown Highway, Rome, GA 30162. *Phone:* 706-295-6339. *Toll-free phone:* 800-332-2406. *Fax:* 706-295-6610. *E-mail:* tjones@highlands.edu.

Georgia Military College

Milledgeville, Georgia — www.gmc.cc.ga.us/

- **State and locally supported** 2-year, founded 1879
- **Small-town** 40-acre campus
- **Coed,** 5,724 undergraduate students, 70% full-time, 62% women, 38% men

Undergraduates 4,035 full-time, 1,689 part-time. Students come from 39 states and territories, 5% are from out of state, 41% African American, 2% Asian American or Pacific Islander, 3% Hispanic American, 0.4% Native American, 36% transferred in.

Freshmen *Admission:* 1,389 applied, 1,389 admitted, 1,389 enrolled.

Faculty *Total:* 231, 35% full-time, 3% with terminal degrees. *Student/faculty ratio:* 20:1.

Majors Army ROTC/military science; biological and physical sciences; biology/biological sciences; business administration and management; criminal justice/law enforcement administration; early childhood education; education; engineering; fire science; general studies; health services/allied health/health sciences; history; human development and family studies; information technology; international relations and affairs; kindergarten/preschool education; legal assistant/paralegal; liberal arts and sciences/liberal studies; logistics and materials management; mass communication/media; nuclear/nuclear power technology; pre-engineering; prenursing studies; psychology; public health education and promotion; security and protective services related; social sciences.

Academics *Calendar:* quarters. *Degree:* associate. *Special study options:* academic remediation for entering students, advanced placement credit, cooperative education, distance learning, double majors, external degree program, independent study, off-campus study, part-time degree program, summer session for credit. *ROTC:* Army (b).

Library Sibley-Cone Library with 57,000 titles, 27,500 serial subscriptions, 1,700 audiovisual materials, an OPAC, a Web page.

Student Life *Housing:* on-campus residence required through sophomore year. *Options:* coed. Campus housing is university owned. *Activities and Organizations:* student-run newspaper, choral group. *Campus security:* 24-hour emergency response devices and patrols. *Student services:* health clinic.

Athletics *Intercollegiate sports:* football M(s), riflery M(s)/W(s). *Intramural sports:* basketball M, cross-country running M/W, football M, golf M, soccer M/W, tennis M/W, track and field M/W, volleyball M/W.

Standardized Tests *Required for some:* SAT or ACT (for admission). *Recommended:* SAT or ACT (for admission).

Costs (2009–10) *One-time required fee:* $900. *Tuition:* state resident $12,510 full-time, $105 per quarter hour part-time. Part-time tuition and fees vary according to course load. *Required fees:* $652 full-time. *Room and board:* $5835. *Waivers:* senior citizens.

Financial Aid Of all full-time matriculated undergraduates who enrolled in 2008, 50 Federal Work-Study jobs (averaging $1421).

Applying *Options:* electronic application, early admission, deferred entrance. *Application fee:* $35. *Required:* high school transcript. *Application deadlines:* rolling (freshmen), rolling (transfers).

Freshman Application Contact Georgia Military College, 201 East Greene Street, Milledgeville, GA 31061-3398. *Phone:* 478-387-4948. *Toll-free phone:* 800-342-0413.

Georgia Northwestern Technical College

Rome, Georgia — www.gntc.edu/

- **State-supported** 2-year, founded 1962, part of Technical College System of Georgia
- **Coed,** 5,994 undergraduate students, 51% full-time, 61% women, 39% men

Undergraduates 3,053 full-time, 2,941 part-time. 1% are from out of state, 9% African American, 0.6% Asian American or Pacific Islander, 2% Hispanic American, 0.4% Native American. *Retention:* 44% of 2008 full-time freshmen returned.

Freshmen *Admission:* 3,825 enrolled.

Majors Accounting; child development; computer programming; criminal justice/safety; environmental engineering technology; fire science; information science/studies; legal assistant/paralegal; marketing/marketing management; medical office management; respiratory therapy technician; surgical technology; web page, digital/multimedia and information resources design.

Academics *Calendar:* quarters. *Degree:* certificates, diplomas, and associate. *Special study options:* distance learning.

Student Life *Housing:* college housing not available.

Applying *Options:* early admission. *Application fee:* $15. *Required:* high school transcript.

Freshman Application Contact Georgia Northwestern Technical College, One Maurice Culberson Drive, Rome, GA 30161. *Phone:* 706-295-6933.

Georgia Perimeter College

Decatur, Georgia — www.gpc.edu/

- **State-supported** 2-year, founded 1964, part of University System of Georgia
- **Suburban** 100-acre campus with easy access to Atlanta
- **Coed,** 24,549 undergraduate students, 47% full-time, 61% women, 39% men

Undergraduates 11,522 full-time, 13,027 part-time. 10% are from out of state, 43% African American, 8% Asian American or Pacific Islander, 6% Hispanic American, 0.3% Native American, 4% international, 5% transferred in.

Freshmen *Admission:* 9,475 applied, 5,603 admitted, 4,773 enrolled.

Faculty *Total:* 914, 38% full-time, 30% with terminal degrees. *Student/faculty ratio:* 24:1.

Majors Clinical/medical laboratory technology; dental hygiene; fire protection and safety technology; liberal arts and sciences/liberal studies; library assistant; medical/clinical assistant; nursing (registered nurse training); sign language interpretation and translation.

Academics *Calendar:* semesters. *Degree:* certificates and associate. *Special study options:* academic remediation for entering students, adult/continuing education programs, advanced placement credit, distance learning, English as a second language, honors programs, part-time degree program, services for LD students, study abroad, summer session for credit. *ROTC:* Army (c).

Library Georgia Perimeter College Library with 369,969 titles, 2,032 serial subscriptions, 15,500 audiovisual materials, an OPAC.

Student Life *Housing:* college housing not available. *Activities and Organizations:* drama/theater group, student-run newspaper, choral group. *Campus security:* 24-hour emergency response devices and patrols, late-night transport/escort service. *Student services:* personal/psychological counseling.

Athletics Member NJCAA. *Intercollegiate sports:* baseball M(s), basketball M(s)/W(s), soccer M(s)/W(s), softball W(s), tennis W(s).

Georgia Perimeter College (continued)

Standardized Tests *Recommended:* SAT or ACT (for admission).

Costs (2009–10) *Tuition:* state resident $2298 full-time, $77 per credit hour part-time; nonresident $9176 full-time, $306 per credit hour part-time. Full-time tuition and fees vary according to course load. Part-time tuition and fees vary according to course load. *Required fees:* $544 full-time, $272 per term part-time. *Waivers:* senior citizens.

Financial Aid Of all full-time matriculated undergraduates who enrolled in 2008, 218 Federal Work-Study jobs (averaging $3000).

Applying *Options:* electronic application, early admission. *Application fee:* $20. *Required:* high school transcript. *Notification:* continuous (freshmen), continuous (transfers).

Freshman Application Contact Georgia Perimeter College, 555 North Indian Creek Drive, Clarkston, GA 30021-2396. *Phone:* 678-891-3250. *Toll-free phone:* 888-696-2780.

GORDON COLLEGE

Barnesville, Georgia **www.gdn.edu/**

Freshman Application Contact Gordon College, 419 College Drive, Barnesville, GA 30204. *Phone:* 770-358-5023. *Toll-free phone:* 800-282-6504. *Fax:* 770-358-3031. *E-mail:* gordon@gdn.edu.

GRIFFIN TECHNICAL COLLEGE

Griffin, Georgia **www.griffintech.edu/**

- **State-supported** 2-year, founded 1965, part of Technical College System of Georgia
- **Small-town** 10-acre campus with easy access to Atlanta
- **Coed,** 5,185 undergraduate students, 49% full-time, 66% women, 34% men

Undergraduates 2,546 full-time, 2,639 part-time. 39% African American, 1% Asian American or Pacific Islander, 0.8% Hispanic American, 0.2% Native American. *Retention:* 56% of 2008 full-time freshmen returned.

Freshmen *Admission:* 1,075 enrolled.

Majors Accounting; administrative assistant and secretarial science; automobile/automotive mechanics technology; business administration and management; child development; computer and information systems security; computer programming; computer systems networking and telecommunications; criminal justice/safety; drafting and design technology; electrical, electronic and communications engineering technology; emergency medical technology (EMT paramedic); heating, air conditioning and refrigeration technology; horticultural science; industrial technology; legal assistant/paralegal; manufacturing technology; marketing/marketing management; medical radiologic technology; pharmacy technician; respiratory therapy technician; surgical technology; web page, digital/multimedia and information resources design.

Academics *Calendar:* quarters. *Degree:* certificates, diplomas, and associate. *Special study options:* distance learning.

Library Griffin Technical College Library.

Applying *Options:* early admission. *Application fee:* $26. *Required:* high school transcript.

Freshman Application Contact Griffin Technical College, 501 Varsity Road, Griffin, GA 30223-2042. *Phone:* 770-229-3409.

GUPTON-JONES COLLEGE OF FUNERAL SERVICE

Decatur, Georgia **www.gupton-jones.edu/**

- **Independent** 2-year, founded 1920, part of Pierce Mortuary Colleges, Inc.
- **Suburban** 3-acre campus with easy access to Atlanta
- **Coed**

Academics *Calendar:* quarters. *Degree:* associate. *Special study options:* academic remediation for entering students, distance learning, summer session for credit.

Applying *Options:* electronic application. *Application fee:* $50. *Required:* high school transcript, health certificate. *Recommended:* minimum 3.0 GPA.

Freshman Application Contact Ms. Beverly Wheaton, Registrar, Gupton-Jones College of Funeral Service, 5141 Snapfinger Woods Drive, Decatur, GA 30035. *Phone:* 770-593-2257. *Toll-free phone:* 800-848-5352.

GWINNETT TECHNICAL COLLEGE

Lawrenceville, Georgia **www.gwinnetttech.edu/**

- **State-supported** 2-year, founded 1984, part of Technical College System of Georgia
- **Suburban** 93-acre campus with easy access to Atlanta
- **Coed,** 6,649 undergraduate students, 46% full-time, 58% women, 42% men

Undergraduates 3,066 full-time, 3,583 part-time. 0.3% are from out of state, 31% African American, 7% Asian American or Pacific Islander, 7% Hispanic American, 0.3% Native American. *Retention:* 52% of 2008 full-time freshmen returned.

Freshmen *Admission:* 1,078 enrolled.

Majors Accounting; administrative assistant and secretarial science; automobile/automotive mechanics technology; building/construction finishing, management, and inspection related; business administration and management; computer programming; computer science; computer systems networking and telecommunications; drafting and design technology; electrical, electronic and communications engineering technology; emergency medical technology (EMT paramedic); horticultural science; hotel/motel administration; information science/studies; interior design; machine tool technology; management information systems; marketing/marketing management; medical/clinical assistant; medical radiologic technology; ornamental horticulture; photography; physical therapist assistant; physical therapy; respiratory care therapy; tourism and travel services management; veterinary/animal health technology.

Academics *Calendar:* quarters. *Degree:* certificates, diplomas, and associate. *Special study options:* distance learning.

Library Gwinnett Technical Institute Media Center.

Student Life *Housing:* college housing not available.

Financial Aid Of all full-time matriculated undergraduates who enrolled in 2008, 20 Federal Work-Study jobs (averaging $2100).

Applying *Options:* early admission. *Application fee:* $20. *Required:* high school transcript.

Freshman Application Contact Gwinnett Technical College, PO Box 1505, 5150 Sugarloaf Parkway, Lawrenceville, GA 30043-5702. *Phone:* 678-762-7580 Ext. 434.

HEART OF GEORGIA TECHNICAL COLLEGE

Dublin, Georgia **www.heartofgatech.edu/**

- **State-supported** 2-year, founded 1984, part of Technical College System of Georgia
- **Small-town** campus with easy access to Atlanta
- **Coed,** 1,815 undergraduate students, 45% full-time, 59% women, 41% men

Undergraduates 811 full-time, 1,004 part-time. 44% African American, 0.1% Asian American or Pacific Islander, 0.5% Hispanic American, 0.4% Native American. *Retention:* 62% of 2008 full-time freshmen returned.

Freshmen *Admission:* 355 enrolled.

Majors Business, management, and marketing related; child development; criminal justice/safety; electrical, electronic and communications engineering technology; health information/medical records technology; machine tool technology; marketing/marketing management; medical radiologic technology; respiratory therapy technician.

Academics *Calendar:* quarters. *Degree:* certificates, diplomas, and associate. *Special study options:* distance learning.

Student Life *Housing:* college housing not available.

Applying *Options:* early admission. *Application fee:* $15. *Required:* high school transcript.

Freshman Application Contact Heart of Georgia Technical College, 560 Pinehill Road, Dublin, GA 31021. *Phone:* 478-274-7837.

HIGH-TECH INSTITUTE

Marietta, Georgia **www.high-techinstitute.com/**

Director of Admissions Frank Webster, Office Manager, High-Tech Institute, 1090 Northchase Parkway, Suite 150, Marietta, GA 30067. *Phone:* 770-988-9877. *Toll-free phone:* 800-987-0110. *Fax:* 770-988-8824. *E-mail:* ckusema@hightechschools.com.

Interactive College of Technology

Chamblee, Georgia **www.ict-ils.edu/**

Freshman Application Contact Ms. Nicole Caruso, Associate Dean of Admissions, Interactive College of Technology, 5303 New Peachtree Road, Chamblee, GA 30341. *Phone:* 770-216-2960. *Toll-free phone:* 800-550-3475. *Fax:* 770-216-2989.

ITT Technical Institute

Atlanta, Georgia **www.itt-tech.edu/**

- **Proprietary** primarily 2-year, part of ITT Educational Services, Inc.
- **Coed**

Majors CAD/CADD drafting/design technology; computer and information systems security; computer engineering technology; criminal justice/law enforcement administration; design and visual communications; electrical, electronic and communications engineering technology; system, networking, and LAN/WAN management.

Academics *Degrees:* associate and bachelor's.

Freshman Application Contact Director of Recruitment, ITT Technical Institute, Two Crown Center 1745 Phoenix Boulevard, Suite 100, Atlanta, GA 30349. *Phone:* 770-909-4606. *Toll-free phone:* 877-488-6102.

ITT Technical Institute

Duluth, Georgia **www.itt-tech.edu/**

- **Proprietary** primarily 2-year, founded 2003, part of ITT Educational Services, Inc.
- **Coed**

Majors Animation, interactive technology, video graphics and special effects; CAD/CADD drafting/design technology; computer and information systems security; computer engineering technology; construction management; criminal justice/law enforcement administration; design and visual communications; electrical, electronic and communications engineering technology; system, networking, and LAN/WAN management; web page, digital/multimedia and information resources design.

Academics *Calendar:* quarters. *Degrees:* associate and bachelor's.

Student Life *Housing:* college housing not available.

Freshman Application Contact Director of Recruitment, ITT Technical Institute, 10700 Abbotts Bridge Road, Suite 190, Duluth, GA 30097. *Phone:* 678-957-8510. *Toll-free phone:* 866-489-8818.

ITT Technical Institute

Kennesaw, Georgia **www.itt-tech.edu/**

- **Proprietary** primarily 2-year, founded 2004, part of ITT Educational Services, Inc.
- **Coed**

Majors Animation, interactive technology, video graphics and special effects; CAD/CADD drafting/design technology; computer and information systems security; computer engineering technology; construction management; criminal justice/law enforcement administration; design and visual communications; electrical, electronic and communications engineering technology; system, networking, and LAN/WAN management; web page, digital/multimedia and information resources design.

Academics *Calendar:* quarters. *Degrees:* associate and bachelor's.

Freshman Application Contact Director of Recruitment, ITT Technical Institute, 1000 Cobb Place Boulevard NW, Kennesaw, GA 30144. *Phone:* 770-426-2300. *Toll-free phone:* 877-231-6415.

Lanier Technical College

Oakwood, Georgia **www.laniertech.edu/**

- **State-supported** 2-year, founded 1964, part of Technical College System of Georgia
- **Coed,** 4,115 undergraduate students, 40% full-time, 63% women, 37% men

Undergraduates 1,646 full-time, 2,469 part-time. 11% African American, 2% Asian American or Pacific Islander, 5% Hispanic American, 0.5% Native American. *Retention:* 59% of 2008 full-time freshmen returned.

Freshmen *Admission:* 1,010 enrolled.

Majors Accounting; administrative assistant and secretarial science; banking and financial support services; child development; computer and information systems security; computer programming; computer science; computer systems networking and telecommunications; criminal justice/safety; drafting and design technology; electrical, electronic and communications engineering technology; fire science; health professions related; industrial technology; information science/studies; interior design; marketing/marketing management; medical radiologic technology; occupational safety and health technology; surgical technology; web page, digital/multimedia and information resources design.

Academics *Calendar:* quarters. *Degree:* certificates, diplomas, and associate. *Special study options:* distance learning.

Student Life *Housing:* college housing not available.

Applying *Options:* early admission. *Application fee:* $15. *Required:* high school transcript.

Freshman Application Contact Lanier Technical College, 2990 Landrum Education Drive, Oakwood, GA 30566. *Phone:* 770-531-6332.

Le Cordon Bleu College of Culinary Arts, Atlanta

Tucker, Georgia **www.atlantaculinary.com/**

Freshman Application Contact Admissions Office, Le Cordon Bleu College of Culinary Arts, Atlanta, 1957 Lakeside Parkway, Tucker, GA 30084. *Toll-free phone:* 888-549-8222.

Middle Georgia College

Cochran, Georgia **www.mgc.edu/**

- **State-supported** primarily 2-year, founded 1884, part of University System of Georgia
- **Small-town** 165-acre campus
- **Endowment** $847,031
- **Coed,** 3,614 undergraduate students, 72% full-time, 54% women, 46% men

Undergraduates 2,586 full-time, 1,028 part-time. Students come from 36 states and territories, 31 other countries, 4% are from out of state, 40% African American, 1% Asian American or Pacific Islander, 2% Hispanic American, 0.3% Native American, 0.9% international, 7% transferred in, 35% live on campus. *Retention:* 63% of 2008 full-time freshmen returned.

Freshmen *Admission:* 2,188 applied, 1,938 admitted, 1,226 enrolled. *Average high school GPA:* 2.68. *Test scores:* SAT verbal scores over 500: 39%; SAT math scores over 500: 33%; ACT scores over 18: 42%; SAT verbal scores over 600: 10%; SAT math scores over 600: 9%; ACT scores over 24: 9%; SAT verbal scores over 700: 1%; SAT math scores over 700: 1%; ACT scores over 30: 2%.

Faculty *Total:* 170, 68% full-time. *Student/faculty ratio:* 22:1.

Majors Air traffic control; aviation/airway management; business administration and management; computer and information sciences related; computer engineering related; computer/information technology services administration related; computer science; criminal justice/police science; data processing and data processing technology; fashion merchandising; information science/studies; liberal arts and sciences/liberal studies; logistics and materials management; nursing (registered nurse training); occupational therapist assistant; physical therapist assistant; public administration; survey technology.

Academics *Calendar:* semesters. *Degrees:* certificates, associate, and bachelor's. *Special study options:* academic remediation for entering students, accelerated degree program, advanced placement credit, cooperative education, distance learning, double majors, honors programs, internships, part-time degree program, student-designed majors, study abroad, summer session for credit.

Library Roberts Memorial Library with 105,568 titles, 220 serial subscriptions, 1,000 audiovisual materials, an OPAC, a Web page.

Student Life *Housing:* on-campus residence required through sophomore year. *Options:* coed, men-only, women-only. Campus housing is university owned. Freshman campus housing is guaranteed. *Activities and Organizations:* drama/theater group, choral group, marching band, Baptist Student Union, Student Government Association, MGC Ambassadors, Encore Productions, United Voices of Praise. *Campus security:* 24-hour emergency response devices and patrols, late-night transport/escort service, controlled dormitory access, patrols by police officers. *Student services:* health clinic, personal/psychological counseling.

Middle Georgia College (continued)

Athletics Member NJCAA. *Intercollegiate sports:* baseball M(s), basketball M(s)/W(s), soccer M(s)/W(s), softball W(s). *Intramural sports:* badminton M/W, basketball M/W, football M/W, golf M/W, softball M/W, swimming and diving M/W, tennis M/W, volleyball M/W.

Standardized Tests *Required for some:* SAT or ACT (for admission). *Recommended:* SAT or ACT (for admission).

Costs (2009–10) *Tuition:* state resident $2494 full-time, $84 per credit hour part-time; nonresident $9976 full-time, $333 per credit hour part-time. Full-time tuition and fees vary according to course load and program. Part-time tuition and fees vary according to course load and program. No tuition increase for student's term of enrollment. *Required fees:* $474 full-time. *Room and board:* $6800. Room and board charges vary according to board plan and housing facility.

Financial Aid Of all full-time matriculated undergraduates who enrolled in 2008, 91 Federal Work-Study jobs (averaging $692).

Applying *Options:* electronic application, early admission, deferred entrance. *Application fee:* $20. *Required:* high school transcript, minimum 2 GPA. *Required for some:* essay or personal statement, minimum 3.5 GPA, 3 letters of recommendation, interview. *Application deadlines:* rolling (freshmen), rolling (transfers). *Notification:* continuous (freshmen), continuous (transfers).

Freshman Application Contact Ms. Jennifer Brannon, Director of Admissions, Middle Georgia College, 1100 2nd Street, SE, Cochran, GA 31014. *Phone:* 478-934-3103. *Fax:* 478-934-3403. *E-mail:* admissions@mgc.edu.

MIDDLE GEORGIA TECHNICAL COLLEGE

Warner Robbins, Georgia **www.middlegatech.edu/**

- **State-supported** 2-year, founded 1973, part of Technical College System of Georgia
- **Coed,** 3,543 undergraduate students, 62% full-time, 56% women, 44% men

Undergraduates 2,199 full-time, 1,344 part-time. 2% are from out of state, 38% African American, 1% Asian American or Pacific Islander, 0.4% Hispanic American, 0.3% Native American. *Retention:* 55% of 2008 full-time freshmen returned.

Freshmen *Admission:* 1,157 enrolled.

Majors Accounting; administrative assistant and secretarial science; airframe mechanics and aircraft maintenance technology; child development; computer systems networking and telecommunications; dental hygiene; drafting and design technology; information science/studies; marketing/marketing management; medical radiologic technology; web page, digital/multimedia and information resources design.

Academics *Calendar:* quarters. *Degree:* certificates, diplomas, and associate. *Special study options:* distance learning.

Student Life *Housing:* college housing not available.

Applying *Options:* early admission. *Application fee:* $15. *Required:* high school transcript.

Freshman Application Contact Middle Georgia Technical College, 80 Cohen Walker Drive, Warner Robins, GA 31088. *Phone:* 478-988-6850. *Toll-free phone:* 800-474-1031.

MOULTRIE TECHNICAL COLLEGE

Moultrie, Georgia **www.moultrietech.edu/**

- **State-supported** 2-year, founded 1964, part of Technical College System of Georgia
- **Coed,** 2,407 undergraduate students, 53% full-time, 61% women, 39% men

Undergraduates 1,286 full-time, 1,121 part-time. 34% African American, 0.3% Asian American or Pacific Islander, 3% Hispanic American, 0.2% Native American. *Retention:* 53% of 2008 full-time freshmen returned.

Freshmen *Admission:* 483 enrolled.

Majors Accounting; administrative assistant and secretarial science; child development; civil engineering technology; computer systems networking and telecommunications; criminal justice/safety; electrical, electronic and communications engineering technology; information science/studies; marketing/marketing management; web page, digital/multimedia and information resources design.

Academics *Calendar:* quarters. *Degree:* certificates, diplomas, and associate. *Special study options:* distance learning.

Student Life *Housing:* college housing not available.

Applying *Options:* early admission. *Application fee:* $15. *Required:* high school transcript.

Freshman Application Contact Moultrie Technical College, 800 Veterans Parkway North, Moultrie, GA 31788. *Phone:* 229-217-4144.

NORTH GEORGIA TECHNICAL COLLEGE

Clarkesville, Georgia **www.northgatech.edu/**

- **State-supported** 2-year, founded 1943, part of Technical College System of Georgia
- **Coed,** 2,865 undergraduate students, 63% full-time, 58% women, 42% men

Undergraduates 1,814 full-time, 1,051 part-time. 1% are from out of state, 7% African American, 0.8% Asian American or Pacific Islander, 1% Hispanic American, 0.5% Native American, 0.1% international. *Retention:* 60% of 2008 full-time freshmen returned.

Freshmen *Admission:* 819 enrolled.

Majors Administrative assistant and secretarial science; computer systems networking and telecommunications; criminal justice/safety; culinary arts; heating, air conditioning and refrigeration technology; horticultural science; industrial technology; parks, recreation and leisure facilities management; turf and turfgrass management; web page, digital/multimedia and information resources design.

Academics *Calendar:* quarters. *Degree:* certificates, diplomas, and associate. *Special study options:* distance learning.

Student Life *Housing Options:* coed. Campus housing is university owned.

Applying *Options:* early admission. *Application fee:* $15. *Required:* high school transcript.

Freshman Application Contact North Georgia Technical College, PO Box 65, 1500 Georgia Highway 197, Clarkesville, GA 30523. *Phone:* 706-754-7724.

OGEECHEE TECHNICAL COLLEGE

Statesboro, Georgia **www.ogeecheetech.edu/**

- **State-supported** 2-year, founded 1989, part of Technical College System of Georgia
- **Small-town** campus
- **Coed,** 2,419 undergraduate students, 51% full-time, 64% women, 36% men

Undergraduates 1,242 full-time, 1,177 part-time. 33% African American, 0.7% Asian American or Pacific Islander, 0.6% Hispanic American, 0.1% Native American. *Retention:* 56% of 2008 full-time freshmen returned.

Freshmen *Admission:* 456 enrolled.

Majors Accounting; administrative assistant and secretarial science; agribusiness; automobile/automotive mechanics technology; banking and financial support services; child development; computer systems networking and telecommunications; construction trades; culinary arts; dental hygiene; forestry technology; funeral service and mortuary science; health information/medical records technology; hotel/motel administration; information science/studies; interior design; legal assistant/paralegal; marketing/marketing management; opticianry; tourism and travel services management; veterinary/animal health technology; water quality and wastewater treatment management and recycling technology; wildlife and wildlands science and management; wood science and wood products/pulp and paper technology.

Academics *Calendar:* quarters. *Degree:* certificates, diplomas, and associate. *Special study options:* distance learning.

Student Life *Housing:* college housing not available.

Applying *Options:* early admission. *Application fee:* $20. *Required:* high school transcript.

Freshman Application Contact Ogeechee Technical College, One Joe Kennedy Boulevard, Statesboro, GA 30458. *Phone:* 912-871-1600. *Toll-free phone:* 800-646-1316.

OKEFENOKEE TECHNICAL COLLEGE

Waycross, Georgia **www.okefenokeetech.edu/**

- **State-supported** 2-year, part of Technical College System of Georgia
- **Small-town** campus
- **Coed,** 1,734 undergraduate students, 39% full-time, 64% women, 36% men

Undergraduates 684 full-time, 1,050 part-time. 25% African American, 0.6% Asian American or Pacific Islander, 2% Hispanic American, 0.4% Native American. *Retention:* 50% of 2008 full-time freshmen returned.

Freshmen *Admission:* 476 enrolled.

Majors Administrative assistant and secretarial science; child development; clinical/medical laboratory technology; computer systems networking and telecommunications; computer technology/computer systems technology; criminal justice/police science; forestry technology; information science/studies; occupational safety and health technology; respiratory therapy technician; surgical technology.

Academics *Calendar:* quarters. *Degree:* certificates, diplomas, and associate. *Special study options:* distance learning.

Student Life *Housing:* college housing not available.

Applying *Options:* early admission. *Application fee:* $20. *Required:* high school transcript.

Freshman Application Contact Okefenokee Technical College, 1701 Carswell Avenue, Waycross, GA 31503. *Phone:* 912-338-5251.

SANDERSVILLE TECHNICAL COLLEGE

Sandersville, Georgia **www.sandersvilletech.edu/**

- **State-supported** 2-year, part of Technical College System of Georgia
- **Coed,** 1,116 undergraduate students, 35% full-time, 58% women, 42% men

Undergraduates 389 full-time, 727 part-time. 66% African American, 0.3% Asian American or Pacific Islander, 0.1% Hispanic American. *Retention:* 65% of 2008 full-time freshmen returned.

Freshmen *Admission:* 269 enrolled.

Majors Accounting; administrative assistant and secretarial science; child development; computer systems networking and telecommunications; information science/studies.

Academics *Calendar:* quarters. *Degree:* certificates, diplomas, and associate. *Special study options:* distance learning.

Student Life *Housing:* college housing not available.

Applying *Options:* early admission. *Application fee:* $15. *Required:* high school transcript.

Freshman Application Contact Sandersville Technical College, 1189 Deepstep Road, Sandersville, GA 31082. *Phone:* 478-553-2065.

SAVANNAH RIVER COLLEGE

Augusta, Georgia **www.savannahrivercollege.edu/**

Admissions Office Contact Savannah River College, 2528 Center West Parkway, Augusta, GA 30909.

SAVANNAH TECHNICAL COLLEGE

Savannah, Georgia **www.savannahtech.edu/**

- **State-supported** 2-year, founded 1929, part of Technical College System of Georgia
- **Urban** 15-acre campus
- **Coed,** 5,483 undergraduate students, 44% full-time, 66% women, 34% men

Undergraduates 2,430 full-time, 3,053 part-time. 0.7% are from out of state, 51% African American, 4% Asian American or Pacific Islander, 3% Hispanic American, 0.3% Native American, 1% international. *Retention:* 52% of 2008 full-time freshmen returned.

Freshmen *Admission:* 1,160 enrolled.

Majors Accounting; administrative assistant and secretarial science; automobile/automotive mechanics technology; child development; computer systems networking and telecommunications; criminal justice/safety; culinary arts; electrical, electronic and communications engineering technology; fire science; heating, air conditioning and refrigeration technology; hotel/motel administration; industrial technology; information technology; marketing/marketing management; surgical technology; tourism and travel services management.

Academics *Calendar:* quarters. *Degree:* certificates, diplomas, and associate. *Special study options:* distance learning.

Student Life *Housing:* college housing not available.

Applying *Options:* early admission. *Application fee:* $20. *Required:* high school transcript.

Freshman Application Contact Savannah Technical College, 5717 White Bluff Road, Savannah, GA 31405-5594. *Phone:* 912-443-5511. *Toll-free phone:* 800-769-6362.

SOUTHEASTERN TECHNICAL COLLEGE

Vidalia, Georgia **www.southeasterntech.edu/**

- **State-supported** 2-year, founded 1989, part of Technical College System of Georgia
- **Coed,** 1,972 undergraduate students, 46% full-time, 73% women, 27% men

Undergraduates 899 full-time, 1,073 part-time. 34% African American, 0.2% Asian American or Pacific Islander, 2% Hispanic American, 0.2% Native American. *Retention:* 47% of 2008 full-time freshmen returned.

Freshmen *Admission:* 1,067 enrolled.

Majors Accounting; administrative assistant and secretarial science; child development; computer systems networking and telecommunications; criminal justice/safety; dental hygiene; design and visual communications; electrical, electronic and communications engineering technology; information science/studies; marketing/marketing management; medical radiologic technology; respiratory therapy technician; web page, digital/multimedia and information resources design.

Academics *Calendar:* quarters. *Degree:* certificates, diplomas, and associate. *Special study options:* distance learning.

Student Life *Housing:* college housing not available.

Applying *Options:* early admission. *Application fee:* $15. *Required:* high school transcript.

Freshman Application Contact Southeastern Technical College, 3001 East First Street, Vidalia, GA 30474. *Phone:* 912-538-3121.

SOUTH GEORGIA COLLEGE

Douglas, Georgia **www.sgc.edu/**

- **State-supported** 2-year, founded 1906, part of University System of Georgia
- **Small-town** 250-acre campus
- **Endowment** $153,798
- **Coed,** 2,000 undergraduate students, 74% full-time, 63% women, 37% men

Undergraduates 1,487 full-time, 513 part-time. Students come from 13 states and territories, 2% are from out of state, 35% African American, 0.9% Asian American or Pacific Islander, 3% Hispanic American, 0.3% Native American, 0.6% international, 6% transferred in.

Freshmen *Admission:* 789 enrolled. *Average high school GPA:* 2.8. *Test scores:* SAT math scores over 500: 22%; ACT scores over 18: 41%; SAT math scores over 600: 4%; ACT scores over 24: 6%.

Faculty *Total:* 100, 42% full-time, 20% with terminal degrees. *Student/faculty ratio:* 27:1.

Majors Accounting; administrative assistant and secretarial science; agricultural business and management; agricultural teacher education; agriculture; animal sciences; applied mathematics; biological and physical sciences; biology/biological sciences; business administration and management; business/managerial economics; business teacher education; chemistry; computer and information sciences; computer programming; computer science; creative writing; criminal justice/law enforcement administration; criminology; dramatic/theater arts; economics; education; elementary education; English; finance; French; German; health teacher education; history; humanities; information science/studies; journalism; kindergarten/preschool education; kinesiology and exercise science; liberal arts and sciences/liberal studies; mass communication/media; mathematics; middle school education; nursing (registered nurse training); parks, recreation and leisure.

Academics *Calendar:* semesters. *Degree:* certificates and associate. *Special study options:* academic remediation for entering students, adult/continuing education programs, advanced placement credit, part-time degree program, services for LD students, study abroad, summer session for credit.

Library William S. Smith Library with an OPAC, a Web page.

Student Life *Housing:* on-campus residence required for freshman year. *Options:* Campus housing is university owned. *Activities and Organizations:* drama/theater group, student-run newspaper. *Campus security:* 24-hour emergency response devices and patrols, controlled dormitory access.

South Georgia College (continued)

Athletics Member NJCAA. *Intercollegiate sports:* baseball M(s), soccer M, softball W(s). *Intramural sports:* basketball M/W, cross-country running M/W, football M, golf M/W, soccer M, swimming and diving M/W, tennis M/W, volleyball M/W.

Costs (2010–11) *Tuition:* state resident $2298 full-time, $77 per credit hour part-time; nonresident $9176 full-time, $306 per credit hour part-time. *Required fees:* $540 full-time, $540 per term part-time. *Room and board:* $7600; room only: $4250. Room and board charges vary according to board plan and housing facility.

Applying *Options:* electronic application, early admission, deferred entrance. *Application fee:* $20. *Required:* high school transcript. *Application deadlines:* rolling (freshmen), rolling (transfers). *Notification:* continuous (freshmen), continuous (transfers).

Freshman Application Contact South Georgia College, 100 West College Park Drive, Douglas, GA 31533-5098. *Phone:* 912-260-4419. *Toll-free phone:* 800-342-6364.

South Georgia Technical College

Americus, Georgia **www.southgatech.edu/**

- **State-supported** 2-year, founded 1948, part of Technical College System of Georgia
- **Coed,** 2,562 undergraduate students, 62% full-time, 50% women, 50% men

Undergraduates 1,597 full-time, 965 part-time. 1% are from out of state, 60% African American, 0.2% Asian American or Pacific Islander, 0.5% Hispanic American, 0.1% Native American. *Retention:* 51% of 2008 full-time freshmen returned.

Freshmen *Admission:* 781 enrolled.

Majors Accounting; administrative assistant and secretarial science; child development; computer systems networking and telecommunications; criminal justice/safety; culinary arts; drafting and design technology; electrical, electronic and communications engineering technology; heating, air conditioning and refrigeration technology; horticultural science; industrial technology; information science/studies; legal assistant/paralegal; manufacturing technology; marketing/marketing management.

Academics *Calendar:* quarters. *Degree:* certificates, diplomas, and associate. *Special study options:* distance learning.

Student Life *Housing Options:* men-only, women-only. Campus housing is university owned.

Applying *Options:* early admission. *Application fee:* $20. *Required:* high school transcript.

Freshman Application Contact South Georgia Technical College, 900 South Georgia Tech Parkway, Americus, GA 31709-8104. *Phone:* 229-931-2299.

Southwest Georgia Technical College

Thomasville, Georgia **www.southwestgatech.edu/**

- **State-supported** 2-year, founded 1963, part of Technical College System of Georgia
- **Coed,** 1,721 undergraduate students, 40% full-time, 67% women, 33% men

Undergraduates 689 full-time, 1,032 part-time. 1% are from out of state, 36% African American, 0.8% Asian American or Pacific Islander, 1% Hispanic American, 0.4% Native American. *Retention:* 52% of 2008 full-time freshmen returned.

Freshmen *Admission:* 282 enrolled.

Majors Accounting; administrative assistant and secretarial science; agricultural mechanization; child development; computer systems networking and telecommunications; criminal justice/safety; information science/studies; medical radiologic technology; nursing (registered nurse training); respiratory care therapy; surgical technology.

Academics *Calendar:* quarters. *Degree:* certificates, diplomas, and associate. *Special study options:* distance learning.

Student Life *Housing:* college housing not available.

Applying *Options:* electronic application, early admission. *Application fee:* $20. *Required:* high school transcript.

Freshman Application Contact Southwest Georgia Technical College, 15689 US Highway 19 N, Thomasville, GA 31792. *Phone:* 229-225-5089.

Valdosta Technical College

Valdosta, Georgia **www.valdostatech.edu/**

- **State-supported** 2-year, founded 1963, part of Technical College System of Georgia
- **Suburban** 18-acre campus
- **Coed,** 3,585 undergraduate students, 52% full-time, 64% women, 36% men

Undergraduates 1,875 full-time, 1,710 part-time. 2% are from out of state, 38% African American, 0.8% Asian American or Pacific Islander, 0.9% Hispanic American, 0.7% Native American. *Retention:* 56% of 2008 full-time freshmen returned.

Freshmen *Admission:* 785 enrolled.

Majors Accounting; administrative assistant and secretarial science; banking and financial support services; child development; computer and information systems security; computer programming; computer systems networking and telecommunications; criminal justice/safety; drafting and design technology; e-commerce; fire science; machine tool technology; marketing/marketing management; medical radiologic technology; web page, digital/multimedia and information resources design.

Academics *Calendar:* quarters. *Degree:* certificates, diplomas, and associate. *Special study options:* distance learning.

Student Life *Housing:* college housing not available.

Applying *Options:* early admission. *Application fee:* $15. *Required:* high school transcript.

Freshman Application Contact Valdosta Technical College, Student Customer Services, PO Box 928, 4089 Valtech Road, Valdosta, GA 31602. *Phone:* 229-259-5195.

Waycross College

Waycross, Georgia **www.waycross.edu/**

- **State-supported** 2-year, founded 1976, part of University System of Georgia
- **Small-town** 150-acre campus
- **Coed,** 1,118 undergraduate students

Undergraduates 3% are from out of state. *Retention:* 58% of 2008 full-time freshmen returned.

Freshmen *Admission:* 1,118 applied, 1,118 admitted.

Faculty *Student/faculty ratio:* 19:1.

Majors Health professions related; liberal arts and sciences/liberal studies; precision production related.

Academics *Calendar:* semesters. *Degree:* certificates and associate. *Special study options:* academic remediation for entering students, adult/continuing education programs, advanced placement credit, distance learning, off-campus study, part-time degree program, study abroad, summer session for credit.

Library Waycross College Library.

Student Life *Housing:* college housing not available. *Campus security:* late-night transport/escort service, security guards.

Athletics Member NJCAA. *Intercollegiate sports:* basketball M(s), softball W(s).

Standardized Tests *Recommended:* SAT or ACT (for admission).

Costs (2009–10) *Tuition:* state resident $2298 full-time, $77 per hour part-time; nonresident $9176 full-time, $306 per hour part-time. Full-time tuition and fees vary according to course load. Part-time tuition and fees vary according to course load. *Required fees:* $140 full-time, $6 per hour part-time, $77 per term part-time. *Waivers:* senior citizens.

Financial Aid Of all full-time matriculated undergraduates who enrolled in 2008, 20 Federal Work-Study jobs (averaging $2000).

Applying *Options:* electronic application, early admission, deferred entrance. *Application fee:* $20. *Required:* high school transcript. *Application deadlines:* rolling (freshmen), rolling (transfers). *Notification:* continuous (freshmen), continuous (transfers).

Freshman Application Contact Waycross College, 2001 South Georgia Parkway, Waycross, GA 31503. *Phone:* 912-449-7600.

West Georgia Technical College

Waco, Georgia **www.westgatech.edu/**

- **State-supported** 2-year, founded 1966, part of Technical College System of Georgia
- **Coed,** 7,313 undergraduate students, 39% full-time, 68% women, 32% men

Undergraduates 2,833 full-time, 4,480 part-time. 2% are from out of state, 28% African American, 0.9% Asian American or Pacific Islander, 2% Hispanic American, 0.4% Native American, 0.1% international. *Retention:* 44% of 2008 full-time freshmen returned.
Freshmen *Admission:* 4,399 enrolled.
Majors Accounting; administrative assistant and secretarial science; automobile/automotive mechanics technology; child development; computer systems networking and telecommunications; criminal justice/safety; electrical, electronic and communications engineering technology; fire science; health information/medical records technology; industrial technology; information science/studies; marketing/marketing management; medical radiologic technology; pharmacy technician; plastics engineering technology; social work; web page, digital/multimedia and information resources design.
Academics *Calendar:* quarters. *Degree:* certificates, diplomas, and associate. *Special study options:* distance learning.
Student Life *Housing:* college housing not available.
Financial Aid Of all full-time matriculated undergraduates who enrolled in 2008, 68 Federal Work-Study jobs (averaging $800).
Applying *Options:* early admission. *Application fee:* $25. *Required:* high school transcript.
Freshman Application Contact West Georgia Technical College, 303 Fort Drive, LaGrange, GA 30240. *Phone:* 770-537-5719.

GUAM

Guam Community College

Barrigada, Guam **www.guamcc.net/**

Freshman Application Contact Mr. Patrick L. Clymer, Registrar, Guam Community College, PO Box 23069, Sesame Street, Barrigada, GU 96921, Guam. *Phone:* 671-735-5531. *Fax:* 671-735-5531. *E-mail:* pclymer@guamcc.edu.

HAWAII

Hawaii Community College

Hilo, Hawaii **www.hawcc.hawaii.edu/**

- **State-supported** 2-year, founded 1954, part of University of Hawaii System
- **Small-town** campus
- **Coed**

Academics *Calendar:* semesters. *Degree:* certificates, diplomas, and associate. *Special study options:* advanced placement credit, cooperative education, English as a second language, honors programs, part-time degree program, services for LD students, summer session for credit.
Student Life *Campus security:* 24-hour patrols.
Applying *Options:* early admission. *Application fee:* $25.
Director of Admissions Mrs. Tammy M. Tanaka, Admissions Specialist, Hawaii Community College, 200 West Kawili Street, Hilo, HI 96720-4091. *Phone:* 808-974-7661.

Hawaii Tokai International College

Honolulu, Hawaii **www.hawaiitokai.edu/**

- **Independent** 2-year, founded 1992, part of Tokai University Educational System (Japan)
- **Urban** campus
- **Coed,** 60 undergraduate students, 98% full-time, 52% women, 48% men

Undergraduates 59 full-time, 1 part-time. Students come from 2 states and territories, 2 other countries, 18% Asian American or Pacific Islander, 82% international, 60% live on campus. *Retention:* 88% of 2008 full-time freshmen returned.
Freshmen *Admission:* 9 applied, 9 admitted, 9 enrolled. *Average high school GPA:* 3.
Faculty *Total:* 17, 35% full-time, 35% with terminal degrees. *Student/faculty ratio:* 4:1.
Majors Japanese; Japanese studies; liberal arts and sciences/liberal studies.
Academics *Calendar:* quarters. *Degree:* certificates, diplomas, and associate. *Special study options:* English as a second language, part-time degree program, study abroad, summer session for credit.
Library The Learning Center with 7,000 titles, 35 serial subscriptions, 500 audiovisual materials, an OPAC.
Student Life *Housing:* on-campus residence required for freshman year. *Options:* coed. Campus housing is university owned. Freshman campus housing is guaranteed. *Activities and Organizations:* Running Club, Kendo Club, Music Club, Baseball Club, Phi Beta Kappa. *Campus security:* 24-hour patrols. *Student services:* personal/psychological counseling.
Costs (2010–11) *Comprehensive fee:* $22,840 includes full-time tuition ($13,400), mandatory fees ($560), and room and board ($8880). Full-time tuition and fees vary according to course load and program. Part-time tuition: $400 per credit hour. Part-time tuition and fees vary according to course load and program. *Required fees:* $140 per term part-time. *Room and board:* college room only: $6000. Room and board charges vary according to board plan. *Waivers:* employees or children of employees.
Applying *Options:* deferred entrance. *Application fee:* $50. *Required:* essay or personal statement, high school transcript, minimum 2.5 GPA. *Required for some:* interview, TOEFL score of 450 PBT for international students. *Recommended:* 1 letter of recommendation. *Application deadlines:* rolling (freshmen), rolling (out-of-state freshmen), rolling (transfers). *Notification:* continuous (freshmen), continuous (out-of-state freshmen), continuous (transfers).
Freshman Application Contact Ms. Morna Dexter, Director, Student Services, Hawaii Tokai International College, 2241 Kapiolani Boulevard, Honolulu, HI 96826. *Phone:* 808-983-4187. *Fax:* 808-983-4173. *E-mail:* studentservices@tokai.edu.

Heald College–Honolulu

Honolulu, Hawaii **www.heald.edu/**

Freshman Application Contact Wendy Nishimura, Director of Admissions, Heald College–Honolulu, 1500 Kapiolani Boulevard, Suite 201, Honolulu, HI 96814. *Phone:* 808-955-1500. *Toll-free phone:* 800-755-3550. *Fax:* 808-955-6964. *E-mail:* wnishimu@heald.edu.

Honolulu Community College

Honolulu, Hawaii **www.honolulu.hawaii.edu/**

- **State-supported** 2-year, founded 1920, part of University of Hawaii System
- **Urban** 20-acre campus
- **Coed,** 4,218 undergraduate students, 35% full-time, 46% women, 54% men

Undergraduates 1,481 full-time, 2,737 part-time. Students come from 27 states and territories, 15 other countries, 2% are from out of state, 1% African American, 83% Asian American or Pacific Islander, 2% Hispanic American, 0.4% Native American, 1% international, 21% transferred in. *Retention:* 53% of 2008 full-time freshmen returned.
Freshmen *Admission:* 779 enrolled.
Faculty *Total:* 198, 63% full-time. *Student/faculty ratio:* 16:1.
Majors Architectural engineering technology; automobile/automotive mechanics technology; avionics maintenance technology; carpentry; commercial and advertising art; community organization and advocacy; cosmetology; criminal justice/police science; drafting and design technology; electrical, electronic and communications engineering technology; engineering technology; fashion/apparel design; fire science; food technology and processing; heating, air conditioning, ventilation and refrigeration maintenance technology; human services; industrial arts; kindergarten/preschool education; liberal arts and sciences/liberal studies; marine technology; occupational safety and health technology; welding technology.
Academics *Calendar:* semesters. *Degree:* certificates and associate. *Special study options:* academic remediation for entering students, accelerated degree program, advanced placement credit, cooperative education, distance learning,

Honolulu Community College (continued)

English as a second language, internships, part-time degree program, services for LD students, student-designed majors, summer session for credit. *ROTC:* Army (c), Air Force (c).

Library Honolulu Community College Library with 54,902 titles, 1,280 serial subscriptions, 858 audiovisual materials, an OPAC, a Web page.

Student Life *Housing:* college housing not available. *Activities and Organizations:* student-run newspaper, Phi Theta Kappa, Hui ʻOiwi, Fashion Society. *Campus security:* 24-hour emergency response devices. *Student services:* health clinic, personal/psychological counseling.

Standardized Tests *Required for some:* TOEFL required for international applicants.

Costs (2010–11) *Tuition:* state resident $2142 full-time, $88 per credit hour part-time; nonresident $6774 full-time, $281 per credit hour part-time. Full-time tuition and fees vary according to course load. Part-time tuition and fees vary according to course load. *Required fees:* $1 per credit hour part-time, $10 per credit hour part-time. *Payment plan:* installment. *Waivers:* employees or children of employees.

Financial Aid Of all full-time matriculated undergraduates who enrolled in 2008, 30 Federal Work-Study jobs (averaging $1600).

Applying *Options:* early admission. *Application deadlines:* 8/15 (freshmen), 8/15 (transfers). *Notification:* continuous until 8/15 (freshmen), continuous until 8/15 (transfers).

Freshman Application Contact Admissions Office, Honolulu Community College, 874 Dillingham Boulevard, Honolulu, HI 96817. *Phone:* 808-845-9129. *E-mail:* admission@hccadb.hcc.hawaii.edu.

KAPIOLANI COMMUNITY COLLEGE

Honolulu, Hawaii **www.kcc.hawaii.edu/**

Freshman Application Contact Ms. Jerilynn Lorenzo, Registrar, Kapiolani Community College, 4303 Diamond Head Road, Honolulu, HI 96816-4421. *Phone:* 808-734-9555. *E-mail:* kapinfo@hawaii.edu.

KAUAI COMMUNITY COLLEGE

Lihue, Hawaii **kauai.hawaii.edu/**

- **State-supported** 2-year, founded 1965, part of University of Hawaii System
- **Small-town** 100-acre campus
- **Coed,** 1,345 undergraduate students

Majors Accounting; administrative assistant and secretarial science; autobody/collision and repair technology; automobile/automotive mechanics technology; carpentry; culinary arts; electrical, electronic and communications engineering technology; hospitality administration; kindergarten/preschool education; liberal arts and sciences/liberal studies; nursing (registered nurse training).

Academics *Calendar:* semesters. *Degree:* certificates and associate. *Special study options:* accelerated degree program, advanced placement credit, cooperative education, distance learning, English as a second language, internships, part-time degree program, services for LD students, summer session for credit.

Library S. W. Wilcox II Learning Resource Center plus 1 other with 51,875 titles, 165 serial subscriptions, 1,248 audiovisual materials, an OPAC, a Web page.

Student Life *Housing:* college housing not available. *Activities and Organizations:* student-run newspaper, choral group, Food Service Club, Hui O Hana Poʻokela (Hoper Club), Nursing Club, Phi Theta Kappa, Pamantasan Club. *Campus security:* student patrols, 6-hour evening patrols by trained security personnel. *Student services:* health clinic, personal/psychological counseling.

Athletics *Intramural sports:* basketball M/W, golf M/W, tennis M/W.

Financial Aid Of all full-time matriculated undergraduates who enrolled in 2008, 10 Federal Work-Study jobs (averaging $3000). 30 state and other part-time jobs (averaging $3000).

Applying *Options:* early admission. *Required for some:* high school transcript. *Recommended:* high school transcript. *Application deadlines:* 8/1 (freshmen), 8/1 (transfers). *Notification:* continuous until 8/1 (freshmen), continuous until 8/1 (transfers).

Freshman Application Contact Mr. Leighton Oride, Admissions Officer and Registrar, Kauai Community College, 3-1901 Kaumualii Highway, Lihue, HI 96766. *Phone:* 808-245-8225. *Fax:* 808-245-8297. *E-mail:* arkauai@hawaii.edu.

LEEWARD COMMUNITY COLLEGE

Pearl City, Hawaii **www.lcc.hawaii.edu/**

- **State-supported** 2-year, founded 1968, part of University of Hawaii System
- **Suburban** 49-acre campus with easy access to Honolulu
- **Coed,** 7,484 undergraduate students

Undergraduates Students come from 50 states and territories, 44 other countries, 10% are from out of state, 2% African American, 79% Asian American or Pacific Islander, 3% Hispanic American, 0.4% Native American, 0.2% international.

Freshmen *Average high school GPA:* 3.03.

Faculty *Total:* 236, 76% full-time.

Majors Accounting; administrative assistant and secretarial science; automobile/automotive mechanics technology; business administration and management; commercial and advertising art; computer science; consumer merchandising/retailing management; drafting and design technology; food technology and processing; human services; liberal arts and sciences/liberal studies; parks, recreation and leisure.

Academics *Calendar:* semesters. *Degree:* certificates and associate. *Special study options:* academic remediation for entering students, adult/continuing education programs, advanced placement credit, cooperative education, distance learning, English as a second language, honors programs, independent study, internships, off-campus study, part-time degree program, services for LD students, summer session for credit. *ROTC:* Army (b), Air Force (c).

Library 62,000 titles, 358 serial subscriptions, 1,009 audiovisual materials, an OPAC, a Web page.

Student Life *Housing:* college housing not available. *Activities and Organizations:* drama/theater group, student-run newspaper, choral group. *Campus security:* 24-hour patrols, late-night transport/escort service. *Student services:* health clinic, personal/psychological counseling.

Athletics *Intramural sports:* basketball M/W, bowling M/W, tennis M/W, volleyball M/W.

Financial Aid Of all full-time matriculated undergraduates who enrolled in 2008, 34 Federal Work-Study jobs (averaging $2000).

Applying *Options:* early admission. *Application fee:* $25. *Required for some:* high school transcript. *Application deadlines:* 8/1 (freshmen), 8/1 (transfers). *Notification:* continuous until 8/5 (freshmen), continuous until 8/5 (transfers).

Freshman Application Contact Ms. Anna Donald, Office Assistant, Leeward Community College, 96-045 Ala Ike, Pearl City, HI 96782-3393. *Phone:* 808-455-0642.

MAUI COMMUNITY COLLEGE

Kahului, Hawaii **mauicc.hawaii.edu/**

- **State-supported** 2-year, founded 1967, part of University of Hawaii System
- **Rural** 77-acre campus
- **Coed**

Undergraduates 1,258 full-time, 1,996 part-time. Students come from 15 other countries, 1% live on campus.

Academics *Calendar:* semesters. *Degree:* certificates and associate. *Special study options:* academic remediation for entering students, adult/continuing education programs, cooperative education, English as a second language, external degree program, part-time degree program, services for LD students, summer session for credit.

Student Life *Campus security:* 24-hour emergency response devices and patrols.

Costs (2009–10) *Tuition:* state resident $1896 full-time, $79 per credit part-time; nonresident $9600 full-time, $400 per credit part-time. *Required fees:* $126 full-time, $5 per credit part-time, $12 per term part-time. *Room and board:* $10,043; room only: $6111.

Financial Aid Of all full-time matriculated undergraduates who enrolled in 2008, 40 Federal Work-Study jobs (averaging $4000).

Applying *Options:* electronic application, early admission. *Application fee:* $25. *Required for some:* high school transcript.

Freshman Application Contact Mr. Stephen Kameda, Director of Admissions and Records, Maui Community College, 310 Kaahumanu Avenue, Kahului, HI 96732. *Phone:* 808-984-3267. *Toll-free phone:* 800-479-6692. *Fax:* 808-242-9618. *E-mail:* kameda@hawaii.edu.

REMINGTON COLLEGE–HONOLULU CAMPUS

Honolulu, Hawaii **www.remingtoncollege.edu/**

- **Proprietary** primarily 2-year
- **Coed**

Academics *Degrees:* diplomas, associate, and bachelor's.

Director of Admissions Louis LaMair, Director of Recruitment, Remington College–Honolulu Campus, 1111 Bishop Street, Suite 400, Honolulu, HI 96813. *Phone:* 808-942-1000. *Fax:* 808-533-3064. *E-mail:* louis.lamair@remingtoncollege.edu.

WINDWARD COMMUNITY COLLEGE

Kaneohe, Hawaii **www.wcc.hawaii.edu/**

Director of Admissions Geri Imai, Registrar, Windward Community College, 45-720 Keaahala Road, Kaneohe, HI 96744. *Phone:* 808-235-7430. *E-mail:* gerii@hawaii.edu.

IDAHO

APOLLO COLLEGE–BOISE

Boise, Idaho **www.apollocollege.edu/**

- **Proprietary** 2-year, founded 1980, administratively affiliated with U.S. Education Corporation
- **Coed**

Academics *Calendar:* semesters. *Degree:* certificates, diplomas, and associate.

Student Life *Campus security:* 24-hour patrols.

Standardized Tests *Required:* Wonderlic aptitude test (for admission).

Applying *Application fee:* $100. *Required:* high school transcript, 3 letters of recommendation, interview. *Required for some:* essay or personal statement.

Director of Admissions Director of Admissions, Apollo College–Boise, 1200 North Liberty, Boise, ID 83704. *Phone:* 208-377-8080 Ext. 35. *Toll-free phone:* 800-473-4365.

BRIGHAM YOUNG UNIVERSITY–IDAHO

Rexburg, Idaho **www.byui.edu/**

Freshman Application Contact Mr. Steven Davis, Assistant Director of Admissions, Brigham Young University–Idaho, 120 Kimball, Rexburg, ID 83460-1615. *Phone:* 208-356-1026. *E-mail:* daviss@byui.edu.

BROWN MACKIE COLLEGE–BOISE

Boise, Idaho **www.brownmackie.edu/boise/**

- **Proprietary** primarily 2-year
- **Coed**

Majors Accounting technology and bookkeeping; business administration and management; criminal justice/law enforcement administration; health/health-care administration; information technology; legal assistant/paralegal; legal studies; medical/clinical assistant; occupational therapist assistant; office management; surgical technology; veterinary/animal health technology.

Academics *Degrees:* diplomas, associate, and bachelor's.

Costs (2009–10) *Tuition:* Tuition varies by program. Students should contact Brown Mackie College for tuition information.

Freshman Application Contact Brown Mackie College–Boise, 9050 West Overland Road, Suite 100, Boise, ID 83709. *Phone:* 208-321-8800.

▶**See page 410 for the College Close-Up.**

COLLEGE OF SOUTHERN IDAHO

Twin Falls, Idaho **www.csi.edu/**

Freshman Application Contact Director of Admissions, Registration, and Records, College of Southern Idaho, PO Box 1238, 315 Falls Avenue, Twin Falls, ID 83303. *Phone:* 208-732-6232. *Toll-free phone:* 800-680-0274. *Fax:* 208-736-3014.

EASTERN IDAHO TECHNICAL COLLEGE

Idaho Falls, Idaho **www.eitc.edu/**

- **State-supported** 2-year, founded 1970
- **Small-town** 40-acre campus
- **Endowment** $1.4 million
- **Coed**

Undergraduates 296 full-time, 470 part-time. Students come from 5 states and territories, 0.8% African American, 0.5% Asian American or Pacific Islander, 7% Hispanic American, 0.8% Native American, 0.3% international.

Faculty *Student/faculty ratio:* 11:1.

Academics *Calendar:* semesters. *Degree:* certificates and associate. *Special study options:* academic remediation for entering students, adult/continuing education programs, distance learning, English as a second language, part-time degree program, services for LD students, summer session for credit.

Student Life *Campus security:* 24-hour patrols.

Costs (2009–10) *Tuition:* state resident $1750 full-time, $84 per credit part-time; nonresident $6414 full-time, $168 per credit part-time. *Required fees:* $130 full-time, $15 per term part-time.

Financial Aid Of all full-time matriculated undergraduates who enrolled in 2008, 37 Federal Work-Study jobs (averaging $1176). 11 state and other part-time jobs (averaging $1619).

Applying *Options:* deferred entrance. *Application fee:* $10. *Required:* high school transcript, interview, COMPASS. *Required for some:* essay or personal statement.

Freshman Application Contact Dr. Steve Albiston, Dean of Students, Eastern Idaho Technical College, 1600 South 25th East, Idaho Falls, ID 83404. *Phone:* 208-524-3000 Ext. 3366. *Toll-free phone:* 800-662-0261 Ext. 3371. *Fax:* 208-525-7026. *E-mail:* steven.albiston@my.eitc.edu.

ITT TECHNICAL INSTITUTE

Boise, Idaho **www.itt-tech.edu/**

- **Proprietary** primarily 2-year, founded 1906, part of ITT Educational Services, Inc.
- **Urban** campus
- **Coed**

Majors Animation, interactive technology, video graphics and special effects; business administration and management; CAD/CADD drafting/design technology; computer and information systems security; computer engineering technology; computer software engineering; construction management; criminal justice/law enforcement administration; design and visual communications; electrical, electronic and communications engineering technology; health information/medical records technology; legal assistant/paralegal; nursing (registered nurse training); system, networking, and LAN/WAN management; web/multimedia management and webmaster; web page, digital/multimedia and information resources design.

Academics *Calendar:* quarters. *Degrees:* associate and bachelor's.

Student Life *Housing:* college housing not available.

Financial Aid Of all full-time matriculated undergraduates who enrolled in 2008, 9 Federal Work-Study jobs (averaging $5500).

Freshman Application Contact Director of Recruitment, ITT Technical Institute, 12302 West Explorer Drive, Boise, ID 83713-1529. *Phone:* 208-322-8844. *Toll-free phone:* 800-666-4888. *Fax:* 208-322-0173.

NORTH IDAHO COLLEGE

Coeur d'Alene, Idaho **www.nic.edu/**

- **State and locally supported** 2-year, founded 1933
- **Small-town** 42-acre campus
- **Coed,** 4,323 undergraduate students, 60% full-time, 62% women, 38% men

North Idaho College (continued)

Undergraduates 2,575 full-time, 1,748 part-time. 0.8% African American, 2% Asian American or Pacific Islander, 3% Hispanic American, 2% Native American, 7% transferred in.

Freshmen *Admission:* 1,047 enrolled.

Faculty *Total:* 307, 50% full-time, 8% with terminal degrees. *Student/faculty ratio:* 17:1.

Majors Administrative assistant and secretarial science; agriculture; American Indian/Native American studies; anthropology; art; astronomy; athletic training; automobile/automotive mechanics technology; biological and physical sciences; biology/biological sciences; botany/plant biology; business administration and management; business teacher education; carpentry; chemistry; clinical laboratory science/medical technology; commercial and advertising art; computer and information sciences and support services related; computer and information sciences related; computer programming; computer science; criminal justice/law enforcement administration; criminal justice/police science; culinary arts; developmental and child psychology; drafting and design technology; dramatic/theater arts; education; electrical, electronic and communications engineering technology; elementary education; engineering; English; environmental health; fishing and fisheries sciences and management; forestry; French; geology/earth science; German; health/health-care administration; heating, air conditioning, ventilation and refrigeration maintenance technology; heavy equipment maintenance technology; history; hospitality administration; human services; journalism; legal administrative assistant/secretary; legal assistant/paralegal; liberal arts and sciences/liberal studies; machine tool technology; marine technology; mass communication/media; mathematics; medical administrative assistant and medical secretary; music; music teacher education; nursing (licensed practical/vocational nurse training); nursing (registered nurse training); physical sciences; physics; political science and government; psychology; social sciences; sociology; Spanish; welding technology; wildlife and wildlands science and management; wildlife biology; zoology/animal biology.

Academics *Calendar:* semesters. *Degree:* certificates and associate. *Special study options:* academic remediation for entering students, adult/continuing education programs, advanced placement credit, cooperative education, distance learning, English as a second language, independent study, internships, off-campus study, part-time degree program, services for LD students, summer session for credit. *ROTC:* Army (b).

Library Molstead Library Computer Center with 60,893 titles, 751 serial subscriptions, an OPAC, a Web page.

Student Life *Housing Options:* coed. Campus housing is university owned. *Activities and Organizations:* drama/theater group, student-run newspaper, choral group, Ski Club, Fusion, Baptist student ministries, Journalism Club, Phi Theta Kappa. *Campus security:* 24-hour emergency response devices and patrols, late-night transport/escort service. *Student services:* health clinic, personal/psychological counseling, women's center, legal services.

Athletics Member NJCAA. *Intercollegiate sports:* basketball M(s)/W(s), cheerleading M(s)/W(s), soccer M(s)/W(s), softball W(s), volleyball W(s), wrestling M(s). *Intramural sports:* basketball M/W, bowling M/W, cheerleading M/W, crew M(c)/W(c), cross-country running M(c)/W(c), football M/W, golf M/W, racquetball M/W, sailing M(c)/W(c), skiing (cross-country) M(c)/W(c), skiing (downhill) M(c)/W(c), soccer M(c)/W(c), softball M/W, table tennis M/W, tennis M/W, track and field M(c)/W(c), volleyball M/W.

Costs (2009–10) *Tuition:* area resident $1464 full-time, $83 per credit part-time; state resident $2464 full-time, $124 per credit part-time; nonresident $6016 full-time, $273 per credit part-time. *Required fees:* $1050 full-time, $1050 per term part-time. *Room and board:* $5750.

Financial Aid Of all full-time matriculated undergraduates who enrolled in 2008, 142 Federal Work-Study jobs (averaging $1425). 106 state and other part-time jobs (averaging $1327).

Applying *Options:* electronic application, early admission, deferred entrance. *Application fee:* $25. *Required for some:* essay or personal statement, high school transcript, county residency certificate.

Freshman Application Contact North Idaho College, 1000 West Garden Avenue, Coeur d'Alene, ID 83814-2199. *Phone:* 208-769-3303. *Toll-free phone:* 877-404-4536 Ext. 3311. *E-mail:* admit@nic.edu.

ILLINOIS

Black Hawk College

Moline, Illinois www.bhc.edu/

- **State and locally supported** 2-year, founded 1946, part of Black Hawk College District System
- **Urban** 161-acre campus
- **Coed,** 6,267 undergraduate students, 43% full-time, 60% women, 40% men

Undergraduates 2,715 full-time, 3,552 part-time. Students come from 14 states and territories, 9 other countries, 6% are from out of state, 9% African American, 2% Asian American or Pacific Islander, 10% Hispanic American, 0.4% Native American, 0.3% international, 3% transferred in.

Freshmen *Admission:* 732 applied, 732 admitted, 590 enrolled. *Test scores:* ACT scores over 18: 52%; ACT scores over 24: 10%.

Faculty *Total:* 329, 41% full-time, 11% with terminal degrees. *Student/faculty ratio:* 19:1.

Majors Accounting; accounting technology and bookkeeping; administrative assistant and secretarial science; agricultural business and management; agricultural mechanics and equipment technology; agricultural production; applied horticulture; autobody/collision and repair technology; automobile/automotive mechanics technology; banking and financial support services; business automation/technology/data entry; carpentry; child-care provision; child development; computer programming; concrete finishing; criminal justice/law enforcement administration; criminal justice/police science; crop production; culinary arts; design and visual communications; diesel mechanics technology; early childhood education; electrician; electroneurodiagnostic/electroencephalographic technology; emergency medical technology (EMT paramedic); environmental engineering technology; equestrian studies; finance; general studies; health information/medical records administration; health information/medical records technology; heating, air conditioning, ventilation and refrigeration maintenance technology; horse husbandry/equine science and management; horticultural science; interior design; legal administrative assistant/secretary; legal assistant/paralegal; manufacturing technology; mathematics teacher education; nursing (registered nurse training); physical therapist assistant; pipefitting and sprinkler fitting; radiologic technology/science; retailing; sign language interpretation and translation; small business administration; special education; technical and business writing; web/multimedia management and webmaster.

Academics *Calendar:* semesters. *Degree:* certificates and associate. *Special study options:* academic remediation for entering students, accelerated degree program, adult/continuing education programs, advanced placement credit, cooperative education, distance learning, English as a second language, independent study, internships, off-campus study, part-time degree program, services for LD students, study abroad, summer session for credit.

Library Quad City Campus Library plus 1 other with 59,840 titles, 612 serial subscriptions, 140 audiovisual materials, an OPAC, a Web page.

Student Life *Housing:* college housing not available. *Activities and Organizations:* drama/theater group, student-run newspaper, television station, choral group. *Campus security:* 24-hour patrols. *Student services:* personal/psychological counseling.

Athletics Member NJCAA. *Intercollegiate sports:* baseball M(s), basketball M(s)/W(s), golf M(s), softball W(s), volleyball W(s). *Intramural sports:* soccer M.

Financial Aid Of all full-time matriculated undergraduates who enrolled in 2008, 157 Federal Work-Study jobs (averaging $1437). 176 state and other part-time jobs (averaging $1023).

Applying *Options:* electronic application, early admission, deferred entrance. *Recommended:* high school transcript. *Application deadline:* rolling (freshmen). *Notification:* continuous (freshmen).

Freshman Application Contact Ms. Vashti Berry, College Recruiter, Black Hawk College, 6600 34th Avenue, Moline, IL 61265. *Phone:* 309-796-5341. *E-mail:* berryv@bhc.edu.

Brown Mackie College–Quad Cities

Moline, Illinois www.brownmackie.edu/quad-cities/

- **Proprietary** 2-year, part of Education Management Corporation
- **Coed**

Majors Accounting technology and bookkeeping; business administration and management; medical/clinical assistant.

Academics *Degree:* diplomas and associate.

Costs (2009–10) *Tuition:* Tuition varies by program. Students should contact Brown Mackie College for tuition information.

Freshman Application Contact Brown Mackie College–Quad Cities, 1527 47th Avenue, Moline, IL 61265-7062. *Phone:* 309-762-2100.

►See page 440 for the College Close-Up.

Carl Sandburg College

Galesburg, Illinois www.sandburg.edu/

- **State and locally supported** 2-year, founded 1967, part of Illinois Community College Board
- **Small-town** 105-acre campus
- **Coed**

Academics *Calendar:* semesters. *Degree:* certificates and associate. *Special study options:* academic remediation for entering students, adult/continuing education programs, advanced placement credit, cooperative education, English as a second language, internships, part-time degree program, services for LD students, student-designed majors, summer session for credit. *ROTC:* Army (c).

Student Life *Campus security:* 24-hour emergency response devices and patrols.

Athletics Member NJCAA.

Financial Aid Of all full-time matriculated undergraduates who enrolled in 2008, 80 Federal Work-Study jobs (averaging $3000).

Applying *Options:* early admission, deferred entrance. *Required:* high school transcript.

Director of Admissions Ms. Carol Kreider, Dean of Student Support Services, Carl Sandburg College, 2400 Tom L. Wilson Boulevard, Galesburg, IL 61401-9576. *Phone:* 309-341-5234.

City Colleges of Chicago, Harold Washington College

Chicago, Illinois **hwashington.ccc.edu/**

Director of Admissions Mr. Terry Pendleton, Admissions Coordinator, City Colleges of Chicago, Harold Washington College, 30 East Lake Street, Chicago, IL 60601. *Phone:* 312-553-6006.

City Colleges of Chicago, Harry S. Truman College

Chicago, Illinois **www.trumancollege.cc/**

Director of Admissions Mrs. Kelly O'Malley, Assistant Dean, Student Services, City Colleges of Chicago, Harry S. Truman College, 1145 West Wilson Avenue, Chicago, IL 60640-5616. *Phone:* 773-907-4720.

City Colleges of Chicago, Kennedy-King College

Chicago, Illinois **kennedyking.ccc.edu/**

Freshman Application Contact Ms. Joyce Collins, Clerical Supervisor for Admissions and Records, City Colleges of Chicago, Kennedy-King College, 6800 South Wentworth Avenue, Chicago, IL 60621. *Phone:* 773-602-5000 Ext. 5055.

City Colleges of Chicago, Malcolm X College

Chicago, Illinois **malcolmx.ccc.edu/**

- **State and locally supported** 2-year, founded 1911, part of City Colleges of Chicago
- **Urban** 20-acre campus
- **Coed,** 6,031 undergraduate students, 42% full-time, 66% women, 34% men

Undergraduates 2,522 full-time, 3,509 part-time. 57% African American, 4% Asian American or Pacific Islander, 30% Hispanic American, 0.4% Native American.

Freshmen *Admission:* 784 enrolled.

Faculty *Total:* 240, 31% full-time. *Student/faculty ratio:* 25:1.

Majors Accounting; administrative assistant and secretarial science; art; child-care provision; clinical/medical laboratory technology; computer programming (specific applications); dietitian assistant; elementary education; emergency medical technology (EMT paramedic); funeral service and mortuary science; general studies; hospital and health-care facilities administration; liberal arts and sciences/liberal studies; medical/clinical assistant; medical radiologic technology; music; nursing (registered nurse training); physical education teaching and coaching; physician assistant; premedical studies; pre-pharmacy studies; respiratory care therapy; restaurant, culinary, and catering management; secondary education; surgical technology; teacher assistant/aide.

Academics *Calendar:* semesters. *Degree:* certificates and associate. *Special study options:* academic remediation for entering students, adult/continuing education programs, advanced placement credit, cooperative education, distance learning, English as a second language, part-time degree program, services for LD students, summer session for credit.

Library The Carter G. Woodson Library with 50,000 titles, 250 serial subscriptions, an OPAC, a Web page.

Student Life *Housing:* college housing not available. *Activities and Organizations:* student-run newspaper, Student Government Association, Phi Theta Kappa, Phi Beta Lambda, Chess Club, Latino Leadership Council. *Campus security:* 24-hour emergency response devices and patrols. *Student services:* personal/psychological counseling.

Athletics Member NJCAA. *Intercollegiate sports:* basketball M/W, cross-country running M. *Intramural sports:* basketball M/W, weight lifting M/W.

Costs (2010–11) *Tuition:* area resident $2370 full-time, $79 per credit hour part-time; state resident $7775 full-time, $259 per credit hour part-time; nonresident $9257 full-time, $309 per credit hour part-time. Full-time tuition and fees vary according to program. Part-time tuition and fees vary according to program. *Required fees:* $350 full-time. *Payment plan:* installment. *Waivers:* employees or children of employees.

Financial Aid Of all full-time matriculated undergraduates who enrolled in 2008, 200 Federal Work-Study jobs (averaging $2500).

Applying *Options:* electronic application. *Required:* high school transcript, minimum 2 GPA. *Required for some:* essay or personal statement, interview. *Application deadlines:* rolling (freshmen), rolling (transfers). *Notification:* continuous (freshmen).

Freshman Application Contact Ms. Kimberly Hollingsworth, Dean of Student Services, City Colleges of Chicago, Malcolm X College, 1900 West Van Buren Street, Chicago, IL 60612. *Phone:* 312-850-7120. *Fax:* 312-850-7119. *E-mail:* khollingsworth@ccc.edu.

City Colleges of Chicago, Olive-Harvey College

Chicago, Illinois **oliveharvey.ccc.edu/**

Freshman Application Contact Michelle Adams, Assistant Dean of Student Services, City Colleges of Chicago, Olive-Harvey College, 10001 South Woodlawn, Chicago, IL 60628-1696. *Phone:* 773-291-6349. *Fax:* 773-291-6304. *E-mail:* OH_admissions@ccc.edu.

City Colleges of Chicago, Richard J. Daley College

Chicago, Illinois **daley.ccc.edu/**

- **State and locally supported** 2-year, founded 1960, part of City Colleges of Chicago
- **Urban** 25-acre campus
- **Coed,** 9,711 undergraduate students, 36% full-time, 60% women, 40% men

Undergraduates 3,507 full-time, 6,204 part-time. Students come from 2 states and territories. *Retention:* 52% of 2008 full-time freshmen returned.

Freshmen *Admission:* 837 applied, 837 admitted, 837 enrolled.

Faculty *Total:* 162, 35% full-time, 28% with terminal degrees. *Student/faculty ratio:* 44:1.

Majors Accounting; architectural engineering technology; business administration and management; child development; clinical laboratory science/medical technology; criminal justice/police science; electrical, electronic and communications engineering technology; horticultural science; humanities; liberal arts and sciences/liberal studies; marketing/marketing management; medical administrative assistant and medical secretary; nursing (registered nurse training); pre-engineering; transportation and materials moving related.

Academics *Calendar:* semesters. *Degree:* certificates and associate. *Special study options:* academic remediation for entering students, adult/continuing education programs, advanced placement credit, distance learning, English as a second language, honors programs, off-campus study, part-time degree program, services for LD students, study abroad, summer session for credit. *ROTC:* Air Force (c).

Library Learning Resource Center plus 1 other with 53,201 titles, 275 serial subscriptions, an OPAC, a Web page.

Student Life *Housing:* college housing not available. *Activities and Organizations:* drama/theater group, Latin Student Organization, Student Government Association, African-American Culture Club. *Campus security:* 24-hour emergency response devices and patrols.

City Colleges of Chicago, Richard J. Daley College (continued)

Athletics Member NJCAA. *Intercollegiate sports:* basketball M/W, soccer M/W.

Costs (2010–11) *Tuition:* area resident $2370 full-time; state resident $7775 full-time; nonresident $9257 full-time. Full-time tuition and fees vary according to course load. Part-time tuition and fees vary according to course load. *Required fees:* $350 full-time. *Payment plans:* installment, deferred payment. *Waivers:* senior citizens and employees or children of employees.

Financial Aid Of all full-time matriculated undergraduates who enrolled in 2008, 250 Federal Work-Study jobs (averaging $2500).

Applying *Options:* early admission, deferred entrance. *Required:* high school transcript. *Required for some:* essay or personal statement. *Recommended:* interview. *Application deadlines:* rolling (freshmen), rolling (transfers).

Freshman Application Contact City Colleges of Chicago, Richard J. Daley College, 7500 South Pulaski Road, Chicago, IL 60652-1242. *Phone:* 773-838-7606.

CITY COLLEGES OF CHICAGO, WILBUR WRIGHT COLLEGE

Chicago, Illinois **wright.ccc.edu/**

Freshman Application Contact Ms. Amy Aiello, Assistant Dean of Student Services, City Colleges of Chicago, Wilbur Wright College, 4300 North Narragansett, Chicago, IL 60634. *Phone:* 773-481-8207. *Fax:* 773-481-8185. *E-mail:* aaiello@ccc.edu.

COLLEGE OF DUPAGE

Glen Ellyn, Illinois **www.cod.edu/**

- **State and locally supported** 2-year, founded 1967
- **Suburban** 297-acre campus with easy access to Chicago
- **Coed,** 27,083 undergraduate students, 39% full-time, 54% women, 46% men

Undergraduates 10,591 full-time, 16,492 part-time. Students come from 11 states and territories, 6% African American, 10% Asian American or Pacific Islander, 12% Hispanic American, 0.3% Native American, 0.4% international, 3% transferred in. *Retention:* 66% of 2008 full-time freshmen returned.

Freshmen *Admission:* 2,866 enrolled.

Faculty *Total:* 1,134, 24% full-time, 25% with terminal degrees. *Student/faculty ratio:* 24:1.

Majors Accounting; administrative assistant and secretarial science; automobile/automotive mechanics technology; baking and pastry arts; biological and physical sciences; building/property maintenance and management; business administration and management; child-care and support services management; child-care provision; child development; cinematography and film/video production; commercial and advertising art; communications systems installation and repair technology; communications technology; computer installation and repair technology; computer programming (specific applications); computer typography and composition equipment operation; corrections; criminal justice/law enforcement administration; criminal justice/police science; culinary arts; data entry/microcomputer applications related; dental hygiene; design and visual communications; desktop publishing and digital imaging design; drafting and design technology; drafting/design engineering technologies related; electrical, electronic and communications engineering technology; electrical/electronics equipment installation and repair; electromechanical technology; emergency medical technology (EMT paramedic); engineering; fashion and fabric consulting; fashion/apparel design; fashion merchandising; fire science; graphic and printing equipment operation/production; health/health-care administration; health information/medical records administration; health information/medical records technology; heating, air conditioning, ventilation and refrigeration maintenance technology; hospital and health-care facilities administration; hospitality administration; hotel/motel administration; human services; industrial electronics technology; industrial technology; interior design; landscaping and groundskeeping; legal administrative assistant/secretary; liberal arts and sciences/liberal studies; library assistant; library science; machine tool technology; manufacturing technology; marketing/marketing management; massage therapy; medical radiologic technology; merchandising; nuclear medical technology; nursing (registered nurse training); occupational therapist assistant; occupational therapy; office management; ornamental horticulture; photography; physical therapist assistant; plastics engineering technology; precision production trades; real estate; respiratory care therapy; restaurant, culinary, and catering management; retailing; robotics technology; sales, distribution and marketing; selling skills and sales; speech-language pathology; substance abuse/addiction counseling; surgical technology; tourism and travel services management; tourism and travel services marketing; tourism promotion; transportation and materials moving related; welding technology.

Academics *Calendar:* semesters. *Degree:* certificates and associate. *Special study options:* academic remediation for entering students, accelerated degree program, adult/continuing education programs, advanced placement credit, cooperative education, distance learning, double majors, English as a second language, external degree program, honors programs, independent study, internships, off-campus study, part-time degree program, services for LD students, student-designed majors, study abroad, summer session for credit.

Library College of DuPage Library with 203,300 titles, 6,005 serial subscriptions, an OPAC, a Web page.

Student Life *Housing:* college housing not available. *Activities and Organizations:* drama/theater group, student-run newspaper, choral group, Latino Ethnic Awareness Association, The Christian Group, Phi Theta Kappa, International Students Organization, Muslim Student Association. *Campus security:* 24-hour emergency response devices and patrols, student patrols, late-night transport/escort service. *Student services:* health clinic, personal/psychological counseling.

Athletics Member NJCAA. *Intercollegiate sports:* baseball M, basketball M/W, cheerleading M/W, cross-country running M/W, football M, golf M, soccer M/W, softball W, swimming and diving M/W, tennis M/W, track and field M/W, volleyball W. *Intramural sports:* basketball M/W, bowling M/W, golf M/W, ice hockey M(c), racquetball M/W, soccer M/W, softball M/W, swimming and diving M/W, tennis M/W, volleyball M/W, weight lifting M/W.

Costs (2010–11) *Tuition:* area resident $3870 full-time, $129 per credit hour part-time; state resident $9480 full-time, $316 per credit hour part-time; nonresident $11,580 full-time, $386 per credit hour part-time. *Waivers:* employees or children of employees.

Financial Aid Of all full-time matriculated undergraduates who enrolled in 2008, 424 Federal Work-Study jobs (averaging $4135).

Applying *Options:* early admission, deferred entrance. *Application fee:* $20. *Application deadlines:* rolling (freshmen), rolling (transfers). *Notification:* continuous (freshmen), continuous (transfers).

Freshman Application Contact Amy Hauenstein, Coordinator of Admission Services, College of DuPage, SRC 2046, 425 Fawell Boulevard, Glen Ellyn, IL 60137-6599. *Phone:* 630-942-2442. *Fax:* 630-790-2686. *E-mail:* hauenstein@cod.edu.

COLLEGE OF LAKE COUNTY

Grayslake, Illinois **www.clcillinois.edu/**

- **District-supported** 2-year, founded 1967, part of Illinois Community College Board
- **Suburban** 226-acre campus with easy access to Chicago and Milwaukee
- **Coed,** 18,092 undergraduate students

Undergraduates Students come from 18 states and territories, 31 other countries, 1% are from out of state, 8% African American, 6% Asian American or Pacific Islander, 18% Hispanic American, 0.2% Native American, 9% international.

Freshmen *Admission:* 2,401 applied, 2,401 admitted.

Faculty *Total:* 963, 21% full-time, 12% with terminal degrees. *Student/faculty ratio:* 19:1.

Majors Accounting technology and bookkeeping; administrative assistant and secretarial science; architectural drafting and CAD/CADD; art; automobile/automotive mechanics technology; biological and physical sciences; business administration and management; business automation/technology/data entry; chemical technology; child-care provision; civil engineering technology; computer installation and repair technology; computer programming (specific applications); computer systems networking and telecommunications; construction engineering technology; criminal justice/police science; dental hygiene; electrical, electronic and communications engineering technology; electrician; engineering; fire protection and safety technology; heating, air conditioning, ventilation and refrigeration maintenance technology; industrial mechanics and maintenance technology; landscaping and groundskeeping; liberal arts and sciences/liberal studies; machine shop technology; mechanical engineering/mechanical technology; medical office management; medical radiologic technology; music; music teacher education; natural resources management and policy; nursing (registered nurse training); ornamental horticulture; restaurant, culinary, and catering management; selling skills and sales; social work; substance abuse/addiction counseling; technical and business writing; turf and turfgrass management.

Academics *Calendar:* semesters. *Degree:* certificates and associate. *Special study options:* academic remediation for entering students, adult/continuing education programs, advanced placement credit, cooperative education, distance learning, double majors, English as a second language, honors programs, independent study, internships, off-campus study, part-time degree program, services for LD students, student-designed majors, study abroad, summer session for credit.

Library College of Lake County Library plus 1 other with 106,842 titles, 766 serial subscriptions, an OPAC, a Web page.

Student Life *Housing:* college housing not available. *Activities and Organizations:* drama/theater group, student-run newspaper, radio station, choral group, Latino Alliance, Asian Student Alliance, Pride Alliance, Black Student Union, International Club. *Campus security:* 24-hour emergency response devices and patrols, late-night transport/escort service. *Student services:* health clinic, personal/psychological counseling, women's center.

Athletics Member NJCAA. *Intercollegiate sports:* baseball M(s), basketball M(s)/W(s), cross-country running M(s)/W(s), golf M(s), soccer M(s)/W(s), softball W(s), tennis M(s)/W(s), volleyball W(s). *Intramural sports:* cheerleading W, golf M/W.

Costs (2010–11) *Tuition:* area resident $1944 full-time, $81 per credit hour part-time; state resident $4944 full-time, $206 per credit hour part-time; nonresident $6648 full-time, $277 per credit hour part-time. *Required fees:* $336 full-time, $14 per credit hour part-time. *Payment plan:* installment. *Waivers:* senior citizens and employees or children of employees.

Financial Aid Of all full-time matriculated undergraduates who enrolled in 2008, 98 Federal Work-Study jobs (averaging $1311).

Applying *Options:* electronic application, early admission, deferred entrance. *Required for some:* high school transcript, interview. *Application deadlines:* rolling (freshmen), rolling (transfers). *Notification:* continuous (freshmen), continuous (transfers).

Freshman Application Contact Director, Student Recruitment, College of Lake County, 19351 West Washington Street, Grayslake, IL 60030-1198. *Phone:* 847-543-2383. *Fax:* 847-543-3061.

THE COLLEGE OF OFFICE TECHNOLOGY

Chicago, Illinois **www.cotedu.com/**

Director of Admissions Mr. William Bolton, Director of Admissions, The College of Office Technology, 1520 West Division Street, Chicago, IL 60622. *Phone:* 773-278-0042. *Toll-free phone:* 800-953-6161. *E-mail:* bbolton@cotedu.com.

DANVILLE AREA COMMUNITY COLLEGE

Danville, Illinois **www.dacc.cc.il.us/**

- **State and locally supported** 2-year, founded 1946, part of Illinois Community College Board
- **Small-town** 50-acre campus
- **Coed,** 3,584 undergraduate students, 41% full-time, 59% women, 41% men

Undergraduates 1,486 full-time, 2,098 part-time. 8% are from out of state, 12% African American, 0.9% Asian American or Pacific Islander, 2% Hispanic American, 0.1% Native American, 4% transferred in.

Freshmen *Admission:* 1,054 enrolled.

Faculty *Total:* 151, 34% full-time. *Student/faculty ratio:* 26:1.

Majors Accounting technology and bookkeeping; agricultural business and management; automobile/automotive mechanics technology; business automation/technology/data entry; CAD/CADD drafting/design technology; child-care provision; computer programming; computer programming (specific applications); computer systems networking and telecommunications; corrections; criminal justice/police science; engineering; executive assistant/executive secretary; fire science; floriculture/floristry management; general studies; health information/medical records technology; industrial electronics technology; industrial mechanics and maintenance technology; juvenile corrections; landscaping and groundskeeping; manufacturing technology; mechanical engineering/mechanical technology; medical administrative assistant and medical secretary; nursing (registered nurse training); radiologic technology/science; teacher assistant/aide; turf and turfgrass management.

Academics *Calendar:* semesters. *Degree:* certificates and associate. *Special study options:* academic remediation for entering students, adult/continuing education programs, advanced placement credit, cooperative education, distance learning, double majors, English as a second language, independent study, internships, part-time degree program, services for LD students, summer session for credit.

Library Learning Resources Center with 50,000 titles, 2,487 audiovisual materials, an OPAC.

Student Life *Housing:* college housing not available. *Activities and Organizations:* choral group. *Campus security:* 24-hour patrols. *Student services:* personal/psychological counseling.

Athletics Member NJCAA. *Intercollegiate sports:* baseball M(s), basketball M(s)/W(s), cross-country running M(s)/W(s), golf M(s), soccer M(s), softball W(s), volleyball W(s).

Costs (2010–11) *Tuition:* area resident $2670 full-time, $89 per credit hour part-time; state resident $5250 full-time, $175 per credit hour part-time; nonresident $5250 full-time, $175 per credit hour part-time. Full-time tuition and fees vary according to program. Part-time tuition and fees vary according to program. *Required fees:* $360 full-time, $12 per credit hour part-time. *Payment plan:* installment. *Waivers:* senior citizens and employees or children of employees.

Financial Aid Of all full-time matriculated undergraduates who enrolled in 2008, 60 Federal Work-Study jobs (averaging $2500). 113 state and other part-time jobs (averaging $4500).

Applying *Options:* early admission, deferred entrance. *Required:* high school transcript. *Application deadlines:* rolling (freshmen), rolling (transfers).

Freshman Application Contact Danville Area Community College, 2000 East Main Street, Danville, IL 61832-5199. *Phone:* 217-443-8800.

ELGIN COMMUNITY COLLEGE

Elgin, Illinois **www.elgin.edu/**

- **State and locally supported** 2-year, founded 1949, part of Illinois Community College Board
- **Suburban** 145-acre campus with easy access to Chicago
- **Endowment** $1.6 million
- **Coed,** 9,821 undergraduate students, 37% full-time, 56% women, 44% men

Undergraduates 3,624 full-time, 6,197 part-time. Students come from 2 states and territories, 2 other countries, 6% African American, 8% Asian American or Pacific Islander, 19% Hispanic American, 0.2% Native American, 0.2% international, 5% transferred in. *Retention:* 67% of 2008 full-time freshmen returned.

Freshmen *Admission:* 1,039 admitted, 1,039 enrolled.

Faculty *Total:* 499, 25% full-time. *Student/faculty ratio:* 23:1.

Majors Accounting; administrative assistant and secretarial science; animation, interactive technology, video graphics and special effects; automobile/automotive mechanics technology; baking and pastry arts; biological and physical sciences; business administration and management; CAD/CADD drafting/design technology; child-care provision; clinical/medical laboratory technology; computer systems networking and telecommunications; criminal justice/police science; culinary arts; data entry/microcomputer applications; design and visual communications; electrical, electronic and communications engineering technology; emergency medical technology (EMT paramedic); engineering; entrepreneurship; executive assistant/executive secretary; fine/studio arts; fire science; general studies; graphic design; heating, air conditioning, ventilation and refrigeration maintenance technology; hotel/motel administration; kinesiology and exercise science; legal administrative assistant/secretary; legal assistant/paralegal; liberal arts and sciences/liberal studies; machine tool technology; manufacturing technology; marketing/marketing management; medical transcription; music; nursing (registered nurse training); physical therapist assistant; radiologic technology/science; restaurant, culinary, and catering management; retailing; social work; web page, digital/multimedia and information resources design; welding technology.

Academics *Calendar:* semesters. *Degree:* certificates, diplomas, and associate. *Special study options:* academic remediation for entering students, accelerated degree program, adult/continuing education programs, advanced placement credit, cooperative education, distance learning, double majors, English as a second language, honors programs, independent study, internships, off-campus study, part-time degree program, services for LD students, student-designed majors, study abroad, summer session for credit.

Library Renner Learning Resource Center with 71,561 titles, 450 serial subscriptions, an OPAC, a Web page.

Student Life *Housing:* college housing not available. *Activities and Organizations:* drama/theater group, student-run newspaper, choral group, Phi Theta Kappa, United Students of All Cultures, Organization of Latin American Students, Black Student Association, Office Administration Student Association. *Campus security:* 24-hour patrols. *Student services:* personal/psychological counseling, legal services.

Athletics Member NJCAA. *Intercollegiate sports:* baseball M(s), basketball M(s)/W(s), cross-country running M(s)/W(s), golf M(s), soccer M(s)/W(s), softball W(s), tennis M(s)/W(s), volleyball W(s).

Costs (2009–10) *Tuition:* area resident $2730 full-time, $91 per credit hour part-time; state resident $10,742 full-time, $358 per credit hour part-time; nonresident $13,280 full-time, $443 per credit hour part-time. Full-time tuition and fees vary according to program. Part-time tuition and fees vary according to program. *Required fees:* $10 full-time. *Payment plan:* installment. *Waivers:* senior citizens.

Applying *Options:* electronic application, early admission. *Required for some:* high school transcript. *Application deadlines:* rolling (freshmen), rolling (transfers). *Notification:* continuous (freshmen), continuous (transfers).

Elgin Community College (continued)

Freshman Application Contact Admissions, Recruitment, and Student Life, Elgin Community College, 1700 Spartan Drive, Elgin, IL 60123. *Phone:* 847-214-7414. *E-mail:* admissions@elgin.edu.

FOX COLLEGE

Bedford Park, Illinois **www.foxcollege.edu/**

- **Private** 2-year, founded 1932
- **Suburban** campus
- **Coed,** 345 undergraduate students
- 62% of applicants were admitted

Freshmen *Admission:* 745 applied, 462 admitted.

Majors Accounting and business/management; administrative assistant and secretarial science; business administration and management; graphic design; medical/clinical assistant; physical therapist assistant; retailing; tourism and travel services management; veterinary/animal health technology.

Academics *Degree:* diplomas and associate. *Special study options:* accelerated degree program, internships.

Student Life *Housing:* college housing not available.

Freshman Application Contact Admissions Office, Fox College, 6640 South Cicero, Bedford Park, IL 60638. *Phone:* 708-444-4500.

GEM CITY COLLEGE

Quincy, Illinois **www.gemcitycollege.com/**

- **Proprietary** 2-year, founded 1870
- **Small-town** campus
- **Coed**

Academics *Calendar:* quarters. *Degree:* diplomas and associate. *Special study options:* academic remediation for entering students, adult/continuing education programs, internships, part-time degree program, summer session for credit.

Applying *Options:* early admission, deferred entrance. *Application fee:* $50.

Director of Admissions Admissions Director, Gem City College, PO Box 179, Quincy, IL 62306-0179. *Phone:* 217-222-0391.

HARPER COLLEGE

Palatine, Illinois **www.harpercollege.edu/**

Freshman Application Contact Admissions Office, Harper College, 1200 West Algonquin Road, Palatine, IL 60067. *Phone:* 847-925-6700. *Fax:* 847-925-6044. *E-mail:* admissions@harpercollege.edu.

HEARTLAND COMMUNITY COLLEGE

Normal, Illinois **www.heartland.edu/**

- **State and locally supported** 2-year, founded 1990, part of Illinois Community College Board
- **Urban** campus
- **Coed**

Undergraduates Students come from 5 states and territories, 2 other countries, 1% are from out of state. *Retention:* 55% of 2008 full-time freshmen returned.

Faculty *Student/faculty ratio:* 19:1.

Academics *Calendar:* semesters. *Degree:* certificates and associate. *Special study options:* academic remediation for entering students, adult/continuing education programs, advanced placement credit, cooperative education, distance learning, double majors, English as a second language, honors programs, independent study, internships, part-time degree program, services for LD students, study abroad, summer session for credit. *ROTC:* Army (c).

Student Life *Campus security:* 24-hour emergency response devices and patrols.

Athletics Member NJCAA.

Costs (2009–10) *Tuition:* area resident $2640 full-time, $88 per semester hour part-time; state resident $5280 full-time, $176 per semester hour part-time; nonresident $7920 full-time, $264 per semester hour part-time. Full-time tuition and fees vary according to reciprocity agreements. Part-time tuition and fees vary according to reciprocity agreements. *Required fees:* $210 full-time, $7 per semester hour part-time.

Financial Aid Of all full-time matriculated undergraduates who enrolled in 2008, 65 Federal Work-Study jobs (averaging $1500).

Applying *Options:* electronic application. *Recommended:* high school transcript.

Freshman Application Contact Ms. Candace Brownlee, Director of Student Recruitment, Heartland Community College, 1500 West Raab Road, Normal, IL 61761. *Phone:* 309-268-8041. *Fax:* 309-268-7992. *E-mail:* candace.brownlee@heartland.edu.

HIGHLAND COMMUNITY COLLEGE

Freeport, Illinois **www.highland.edu/**

- **State and locally supported** 2-year, founded 1962, part of Illinois Community College Board
- **Rural** 240-acre campus
- **Endowment** $3.8 million
- **Coed,** 2,455 undergraduate students, 52% full-time, 63% women, 37% men

Undergraduates 1,269 full-time, 1,186 part-time. Students come from 13 states and territories, 3 other countries, 3% are from out of state, 10% African American, 0.7% Asian American or Pacific Islander, 2% Hispanic American, 0.8% Native American, 4% transferred in.

Freshmen *Admission:* 665 applied, 665 admitted, 495 enrolled. *Test scores:* ACT scores over 18: 72%; ACT scores over 24: 22%; ACT scores over 30: 1%.

Faculty *Total:* 161, 29% full-time, 7% with terminal degrees. *Student/faculty ratio:* 20:1.

Majors Accounting; administrative assistant and secretarial science; agricultural business and management; agricultural mechanization; art; autobody/collision and repair technology; automobile/automotive mechanics technology; biological and physical sciences; business administration and management; chemistry; child-care and support services management; child-care provision; child development; commercial and advertising art; computer and information sciences and support services related; computer and information sciences related; computer programming (specific applications); computer science; data processing and data processing technology; drafting and design technology; dramatic/theater arts; education; electrical, electronic and communications engineering technology; engineering; engineering science; engineering technology; general studies; geology/earth science; graphic design; health information/medical records technology; heavy equipment maintenance technology; history; human services; information technology; kindergarten/preschool education; liberal arts and sciences/liberal studies; marketing/marketing management; mathematics; mathematics teacher education; mechanical engineering/mechanical technology; medical/clinical assistant; music teacher education; nursing (registered nurse training); physical sciences; physics; political science and government; pre-engineering; psychology; sociology; special education; speech teacher education; teacher assistant/aide; web page, digital/multimedia and information resources design.

Academics *Calendar:* semesters. *Degree:* certificates and associate. *Special study options:* academic remediation for entering students, adult/continuing education programs, advanced placement credit, cooperative education, distance learning, English as a second language, external degree program, honors programs, independent study, internships, part-time degree program, services for LD students, student-designed majors, summer session for credit.

Library Clarence Mitchell Libarary with 1.7 million titles, 71 serial subscriptions, 6,843 audiovisual materials, an OPAC, a Web page.

Student Life *Housing:* college housing not available. *Activities and Organizations:* drama/theater group, student-run newspaper, choral group, Phi Theta Kappa, Royal Scots, Prairie Wind, intramurals, Collegiate Choir. *Campus security:* 24-hour emergency response devices and patrols. *Student services:* personal/psychological counseling.

Athletics Member NJCAA. *Intercollegiate sports:* baseball M(s), basketball M(s)/W(s), golf M(s)/W(s), softball W(s), volleyball W(s). *Intramural sports:* basketball M/W, volleyball M/W.

Financial Aid Of all full-time matriculated undergraduates who enrolled in 2009, 721 applied for aid, 616 were judged to have need, 2 had their need fully met. 45 Federal Work-Study jobs (averaging $1791). In 2009, 62 non-need-based awards were made. *Average percent of need met:* 33%. *Average financial aid package:* $4987. *Average need-based loan:* $2803. *Average need-based gift aid:* $4200. *Average non-need-based aid:* $2800.

Applying *Options:* electronic application, early admission, deferred entrance. *Required for some:* high school transcript. *Application deadlines:* rolling (freshmen), rolling (transfers).

Freshman Application Contact Mr. Jeremy Bradt, Director, Enrollment and Records, Highland Community College, 2998 West Pearl City Road, Freeport, IL 61032. *Phone:* 815-235-6121 Ext. 3486. *Fax:* 815-235-6130. *E-mail:* jeremy.bradt@highland.edu.

Illinois Central College

East Peoria, Illinois **www.icc.edu/**

Freshman Application Contact Mr. John Avendano, Vice President of Academic Affairs and Student Development, Illinois Central College, One College Drive, East Peoria, IL 61635-0001. *Phone:* 309-694-5784. *Toll-free phone:* 800-422-2293. *Fax:* 309-694-5450. *E-mail:* info@icc.edu.

Illinois Eastern Community Colleges, Frontier Community College

Fairfield, Illinois **www.iecc.edu/fcc/**

- **State and locally supported** 2-year, founded 1976, part of Illinois Eastern Community College System
- **Rural** 8-acre campus
- **Coed,** 2,009 undergraduate students, 16% full-time, 59% women, 41% men

Undergraduates 330 full-time, 1,679 part-time. 0.4% African American, 0.4% Asian American or Pacific Islander, 0.4% Hispanic American, 0.2% Native American.

Freshmen *Admission:* 48 enrolled.

Faculty *Total:* 205, 3% full-time.

Majors Administrative assistant and secretarial science; automobile/automotive mechanics technology; biological and physical sciences; business automation/technology/data entry; corrections; general studies; liberal arts and sciences/liberal studies; nursing (registered nurse training); quality control technology.

Academics *Calendar:* semesters. *Degree:* certificates and associate. *Special study options:* academic remediation for entering students, adult/continuing education programs, advanced placement credit, cooperative education, distance learning, double majors, English as a second language, external degree program, independent study, part-time degree program, services for LD students, student-designed majors, summer session for credit.

Library 19,875 titles, 30,249 serial subscriptions, 2,646 audiovisual materials.

Student Life *Housing:* college housing not available.

Costs (2010–11) *One-time required fee:* $10. *Tuition:* area resident $2272 full-time, $71 per semester hour part-time; state resident $6341 full-time, $198 per semester hour part-time; nonresident $7969 full-time, $249 per semester hour part-time. *Required fees:* $170 full-time, $5 per semester hour part-time, $5 per term part-time. *Waivers:* senior citizens and employees or children of employees.

Applying *Options:* early admission, deferred entrance. *Application fee:* $10. *Required:* high school transcript. *Application deadlines:* rolling (freshmen), rolling (transfers). *Notification:* continuous (freshmen), continuous (transfers).

Freshman Application Contact Ms. Mary Atkins, Coordinator of Registration and Records, Illinois Eastern Community Colleges, Frontier Community College, 2 Frontier Drive, Fairfield, IL 62837. *Phone:* 618-842-3711 Ext. 4111. *Fax:* 618-842-6340. *E-mail:* atkinsm@iecc.edu.

Illinois Eastern Community Colleges, Lincoln Trail College

Robinson, Illinois **www.iecc.edu/ltc/**

- **State and locally supported** 2-year, founded 1969, part of Illinois Eastern Community College System
- **Rural** 120-acre campus
- **Coed,** 1,231 undergraduate students, 46% full-time, 49% women, 51% men

Undergraduates 564 full-time, 667 part-time. 1% are from out of state, 13% African American, 1% Asian American or Pacific Islander, 3% Hispanic American, 0.3% Native American.

Freshmen *Admission:* 182 enrolled.

Faculty *Total:* 92, 23% full-time.

Majors Biological and physical sciences; building/property maintenance and management; business automation/technology/data entry; corrections; culinary arts; general studies; health information/medical records administration; liberal arts and sciences/liberal studies; mechanical engineering/mechanical technology; music; quality control technology; teacher assistant/aide; telecommunications technology.

Academics *Calendar:* semesters. *Degree:* certificates and associate. *Special study options:* academic remediation for entering students, adult/continuing education programs, advanced placement credit, cooperative education, distance learning, double majors, English as a second language, external degree program, independent study, internships, part-time degree program, services for LD students, student-designed majors, summer session for credit.

Library Eagleton Learning Resource Center with 16,240 titles, 30,337 serial subscriptions, 743 audiovisual materials.

Student Life *Housing:* college housing not available. *Activities and Organizations:* drama/theater group, choral group, national fraternities.

Athletics Member NJCAA. *Intercollegiate sports:* baseball M(s), basketball M(s)/W(s), softball W(s), volleyball W(s). *Intramural sports:* baseball M, basketball M, softball W, volleyball M/W.

Costs (2010–11) *One-time required fee:* $10. *Tuition:* area resident $2272 full-time, $71 per semester hour part-time; state resident $6341 full-time, $198 per semester hour part-time; nonresident $7969 full-time, $249 per semester hour part-time. *Required fees:* $170 full-time, $5 per semester hour part-time, $5 per term part-time. *Waivers:* senior citizens and employees or children of employees.

Applying *Options:* early admission, deferred entrance. *Application fee:* $10. *Required:* high school transcript. *Application deadlines:* rolling (freshmen), rolling (transfers). *Notification:* continuous (freshmen), continuous (transfers).

Freshman Application Contact Ms. Becky Mikeworth, Director of Admissions, Illinois Eastern Community Colleges, Lincoln Trail College, 11220 State Highway 1, Robinson, IL 62454. *Phone:* 618-544-8657 Ext. 1137. *Fax:* 618-544-7423. *E-mail:* mikeworthb@iecc.edu.

Illinois Eastern Community Colleges, Olney Central College

Olney, Illinois **www.iecc.edu/occ/**

- **State and locally supported** 2-year, founded 1962, part of Illinois Eastern Community College System
- **Rural** 128-acre campus
- **Coed,** 1,627 undergraduate students, 57% full-time, 63% women, 37% men

Undergraduates 924 full-time, 703 part-time. 1% African American, 1% Asian American or Pacific Islander, 0.5% Hispanic American, 0.1% Native American.

Freshmen *Admission:* 117 enrolled.

Faculty *Total:* 125, 39% full-time.

Majors Accounting; administrative assistant and secretarial science; autobody/collision and repair technology; automobile/automotive mechanics technology; biological and physical sciences; business automation/technology/data entry; corrections; criminal justice/police science; general studies; industrial mechanics and maintenance technology; liberal arts and sciences/liberal studies; medical administrative assistant and medical secretary; medical radiologic technology; music; nursing (registered nurse training).

Academics *Calendar:* semesters. *Degree:* certificates and associate. *Special study options:* academic remediation for entering students, adult/continuing education programs, advanced placement credit, cooperative education, distance learning, double majors, English as a second language, external degree program, independent study, internships, part-time degree program, services for LD students, student-designed majors, summer session for credit.

Library Anderson Learning Resources Center with 22,652 titles, 37,707 serial subscriptions, 1,069 audiovisual materials.

Student Life *Housing:* college housing not available. *Activities and Organizations:* drama/theater group, student-run newspaper, choral group.

Athletics Member NJCAA. *Intercollegiate sports:* baseball M(s), basketball M(s)/W(s), softball W(s), volleyball W(s). *Intramural sports:* baseball M, basketball M/W, softball W.

Costs (2010–11) *One-time required fee:* $10. *Tuition:* area resident $2272 full-time, $71 per semester hour part-time; state resident $6341 full-time, $198 per semester hour part-time; nonresident $7969 full-time, $249 per semester hour part-time. *Required fees:* $170 full-time, $5 per semester hour part-time, $5 per term part-time. *Waivers:* senior citizens and employees or children of employees.

Applying *Options:* early admission, deferred entrance. *Application fee:* $10. *Required:* high school transcript. *Application deadlines:* rolling (freshmen), rolling (transfers). *Notification:* continuous (freshmen), continuous (transfers).

Freshman Application Contact Ms. Chris Webber, Assistant Dean for Student Services, Illinois Eastern Community Colleges, Olney Central College, 305 North West Street, Olney, IL 62450. *Phone:* 618-395-7777 Ext. 2005. *Fax:* 618-392-5212. *E-mail:* webberc@iecc.edu.

Illinois Eastern Community Colleges, Wabash Valley College

Mount Carmel, Illinois **www.iecc.edu/wvc/**

- **State and locally supported** 2-year, founded 1960, part of Illinois Eastern Community College System
- **Rural** 40-acre campus
- **Coed,** 4,810 undergraduate students, 18% full-time, 46% women, 54% men

Undergraduates 868 full-time, 3,942 part-time. 4% are from out of state, 2% African American, 1% Asian American or Pacific Islander, 1% Hispanic American, 0.1% Native American.

Freshmen *Admission:* 136 enrolled.

Faculty *Total:* 150, 26% full-time.

Majors Administrative assistant and secretarial science; agricultural business and management; agricultural production; biological and physical sciences; business administration and management; business automation/technology/data entry; child development; corrections; diesel mechanics technology; electrical, electronic and communications engineering technology; general studies; industrial technology; liberal arts and sciences/liberal studies; machine shop technology; manufacturing technology; mining technology; radio and television; social work.

Academics *Calendar:* semesters. *Degree:* certificates and associate. *Special study options:* academic remediation for entering students, adult/continuing education programs, advanced placement credit, cooperative education, distance learning, double majors, English as a second language, external degree program, independent study, internships, part-time degree program, services for LD students, student-designed majors, summer session for credit.

Library Bauer Media Center with 32,237 titles, 25,296 serial subscriptions, 1,422 audiovisual materials.

Student Life *Housing:* college housing not available. *Activities and Organizations:* drama/theater group, student-run newspaper, radio and television station, choral group.

Athletics Member NJCAA. *Intercollegiate sports:* baseball M(s), basketball M(s)/W(s), softball W(s), tennis M, volleyball W(s). *Intramural sports:* baseball M, basketball M/W, cross-country running M/W, softball W, volleyball M/W.

Costs (2010–11) *One-time required fee:* $10. *Tuition:* area resident $2272 full-time, $71 per semester hour part-time; state resident $6341 full-time, $198 per semester hour part-time; nonresident $7969 full-time, $249 per semester hour part-time. *Required fees:* $170 full-time, $5 per semester hour part-time, $5 per term part-time. *Waivers:* senior citizens and employees or children of employees.

Applying *Options:* early admission, deferred entrance. *Application fee:* $10. *Required:* high school transcript. *Application deadlines:* rolling (freshmen), rolling (transfers). *Notification:* continuous (freshmen), continuous (transfers).

Freshman Application Contact Mrs. Diana Spear, Assistant Dean for Student Services, Illinois Eastern Community Colleges, Wabash Valley College, 2200 College Drive, Mt. Carmel, IL 62863. *Phone:* 618-262-8641 Ext. 3101. *Fax:* 618-262-8641. *E-mail:* speard@iecc.edu.

Illinois Valley Community College

Oglesby, Illinois **www.ivcc.edu/**

- **District-supported** 2-year, founded 1924, part of Illinois Community College Board
- **Rural** 410-acre campus with easy access to Chicago
- **Endowment** $3.2 million
- **Coed,** 4,529 undergraduate students, 46% full-time, 58% women, 42% men

Undergraduates 2,082 full-time, 2,447 part-time. Students come from 3 states and territories, 0.1% are from out of state, 3% African American, 1% Asian American or Pacific Islander, 7% Hispanic American, 0.4% Native American, 36% transferred in. *Retention:* 62% of 2008 full-time freshmen returned.

Freshmen *Admission:* 360 enrolled.

Faculty *Total:* 242, 37% full-time.

Majors Accounting; administrative assistant and secretarial science; agricultural business and management; agriculture; automobile/automotive mechanics technology; biological and physical sciences; business administration and management; business automation/technology/data entry; CAD/CADD drafting/design technology; carpentry; child-care provision; child development; computer programming; computer systems networking and telecommunications; corrections; criminal justice/law enforcement administration; criminal justice/police science; data processing and data processing technology; drafting and design technology; drafting/design engineering technologies related; early childhood education; education; electrical, electronic and communications engineering technology; electrician; elementary education; engineering; English; floriculture/floristry management; forensic science and technology; general studies; graphic design; industrial technology; information technology; journalism; juvenile corrections; landscaping and groundskeeping; liberal arts and sciences/liberal studies; marketing/marketing management; massage therapy; mechanical engineering/mechanical technology; nursing (registered nurse training); pre-engineering; selling skills and sales; social work; system administration; teacher assistant/aide.

Academics *Calendar:* semesters. *Degree:* certificates and associate. *Special study options:* academic remediation for entering students, adult/continuing education programs, advanced placement credit, distance learning, English as a second language, honors programs, independent study, internships, off-campus study, part-time degree program, services for LD students, student-designed majors, study abroad, summer session for credit.

Library Jacobs Library with 58,248 titles, 415 serial subscriptions.

Student Life *Housing:* college housing not available. *Activities and Organizations:* drama/theater group, student-run newspaper, choral group. *Campus security:* 24-hour patrols. *Student services:* personal/psychological counseling.

Athletics *Intercollegiate sports:* baseball M, basketball M/W, golf M, softball W, tennis M/W. *Intramural sports:* basketball M, volleyball W.

Standardized Tests *Recommended:* ACT (for admission).

Costs (2010–11) *Tuition:* area resident $2188 full-time, $68 per credit hour part-time; state resident $7879 full-time, $246 per credit hour part-time; nonresident $8943 full-time, $279 per credit hour part-time. *Required fees:* $2434 full-time, $7 per credit hour part-time. *Payment plan:* deferred payment. *Waivers:* senior citizens and employees or children of employees.

Financial Aid Of all full-time matriculated undergraduates who enrolled in 2008, 81 Federal Work-Study jobs (averaging $955).

Applying *Options:* electronic application, early admission, deferred entrance. *Required:* high school transcript. *Application deadlines:* rolling (freshmen), rolling (transfers). *Notification:* continuous (freshmen), continuous (transfers).

Freshman Application Contact Ms. Tracy Morris, Director of Admissions and Records, Illinois Valley Community College, 815 North Orlando Smith Avenue Oglesby, Oglesby, IL 61348. *Phone:* 815-224-0437. *Fax:* 815-224-3033. *E-mail:* tracy_morris@ivcc.edu.

ITT Technical Institute

Burr Ridge, Illinois **www.itt-tech.edu/**

- **Proprietary** primarily 2-year, founded 1998, part of ITT Educational Services, Inc.
- **Coed**

Majors CAD/CADD drafting/design technology; computer and information systems security; computer engineering technology; construction management; criminal justice/law enforcement administration; design and visual communications; electrical, electronic and communications engineering technology; system, networking, and LAN/WAN management; web page, digital/multimedia and information resources design.

Academics *Calendar:* quarters. *Degrees:* associate and bachelor's.

Student Life *Housing:* college housing not available.

Freshman Application Contact Director of Recruitment, ITT Technical Institute, 7040 High Grove Boulevard, Burr Ridge, IL 60527. *Phone:* 630-455-6470. *Toll-free phone:* 877-488-0001.

ITT Technical Institute

Mount Prospect, Illinois **www.itt-tech.edu/**

- **Proprietary** primarily 2-year, founded 1986, part of ITT Educational Services, Inc.
- **Suburban** campus
- **Coed**

Majors Animation, interactive technology, video graphics and special effects; CAD/CADD drafting/design technology; computer and information systems security; construction management; criminal justice/law enforcement administration; design and visual communications; electrical, electronic and communications engineering technology; system, networking, and LAN/WAN management; web page, digital/multimedia and information resources design.

Academics *Calendar:* quarters. *Degrees:* associate and bachelor's.

Student Life *Housing:* college housing not available.

Freshman Application Contact Director of Recruitment, ITT Technical Institute, 1401 Feehanville Drive, Mount Prospect, IL 60056. *Phone:* 847-375-8800.

ITT Technical Institute

Orland Park, Illinois **www.itt-tech.edu/**

- **Proprietary** primarily 2-year, founded 1993, part of ITT Educational Services, Inc.
- **Suburban** campus
- **Coed**

Majors CAD/CADD drafting/design technology; computer engineering technology; construction management; criminal justice/law enforcement administration; design and visual communications; electrical, electronic and communications engineering technology; system, networking, and LAN/WAN management; web page, digital/multimedia and information resources design.

Academics *Calendar:* quarters. *Degrees:* associate and bachelor's.

Student Life *Housing:* college housing not available.

Financial Aid Of all full-time matriculated undergraduates who enrolled in 2008, 6 Federal Work-Study jobs (averaging $4000).

Freshman Application Contact Director of Recruitment, ITT Technical Institute, 11551 184th Place, Orland Park, IL 60467. *Phone:* 708-326-3200.

John A. Logan College

Carterville, Illinois **www.jalc.edu/**

Director of Admissions Mr. Terry Crain, Dean of Student Services, John A. Logan College, 700 Logan College Road, Carterville, IL 62918-9900. *Phone:* 618-985-3741 Ext. 8382. *Fax:* 618-985-4433. *E-mail:* terrycrain@jalc.edu.

John Wood Community College

Quincy, Illinois **www.jwcc.edu/**

- **District-supported** 2-year, founded 1974, part of Illinois Community College Board
- **Small-town** campus
- **Coed,** 2,403 undergraduate students, 51% full-time, 62% women, 38% men

Undergraduates 1,216 full-time, 1,187 part-time. Students come from 13 states and territories, 5 other countries, 8% are from out of state, 3% African American, 2% Asian American or Pacific Islander, 0.8% Hispanic American, 0.4% Native American, 0.2% international, 9% transferred in. *Retention:* 61% of 2008 full-time freshmen returned.

Freshmen *Admission:* 630 enrolled. *Test scores:* ACT scores over 18: 62%; ACT scores over 24: 8%.

Faculty *Total:* 230, 23% full-time, 5% with terminal degrees. *Student/faculty ratio:* 14:1.

Majors Accounting; accounting technology and bookkeeping; administrative assistant and secretarial science; agricultural business and management; agricultural production; animal/livestock husbandry and production; applied horticulture; biological and physical sciences; business administration and management; business/commerce; clinical/medical laboratory technology; criminal justice/police science; early childhood education; electrical, electronic and communications engineering technology; electrician; emergency medical technology (EMT paramedic); executive assistant/executive secretary; fire protection and safety technology; general studies; health and physical education; hotel/motel administration; industrial electronics technology; industrial mechanics and maintenance technology; legal administrative assistant/secretary; liberal arts and sciences/liberal studies; mechanical drafting and CAD/CADD; medical administrative assistant and medical secretary; medical radiologic technology; nursing (registered nurse training); psychology; restaurant, culinary, and catering management; sales, distribution and marketing; sociology.

Academics *Calendar:* semesters. *Degree:* certificates and associate. *Special study options:* academic remediation for entering students, adult/continuing education programs, advanced placement credit, cooperative education, distance learning, English as a second language, external degree program, independent study, internships, off-campus study, part-time degree program, services for LD students, student-designed majors, study abroad, summer session for credit.

Library 18,000 titles, 160 serial subscriptions, an OPAC, a Web page.

Student Life *Housing:* college housing not available. *Activities and Organizations:* choral group. *Campus security:* 24-hour emergency response devices, late-night transport/escort service.

Athletics Member NJCAA. *Intercollegiate sports:* baseball M(s), basketball M(s)/W(s), golf M(s), softball W(s), volleyball W(s). *Intramural sports:* basketball M/W, volleyball M/W.

Standardized Tests *Recommended:* ACT (for admission).

Costs (2009–10) *Tuition:* area resident $2910 full-time, $97 per credit hour part-time; state resident $5910 full-time, $197 per credit hour part-time; nonresident $5910 full-time, $197 per credit hour part-time. Full-time tuition and fees vary according to reciprocity agreements. Part-time tuition and fees vary according to reciprocity agreements. *Required fees:* $300 full-time, $10 per credit hour part-time. *Payment plan:* installment. *Waivers:* employees or children of employees.

Financial Aid Of all full-time matriculated undergraduates who enrolled in 2008, 360 Federal Work-Study jobs (averaging $364).

Applying *Options:* early admission. *Required:* high school transcript. *Application deadlines:* rolling (freshmen), rolling (transfers). *Notification:* continuous (freshmen), continuous (transfers).

Freshman Application Contact Mr. Lee Wibbell, Director of Admissions, John Wood Community College, 1301 South 48th Street, Quincy, IL 62305-8736. *Phone:* 217-641-4339. *Fax:* 217-224-4208. *E-mail:* admissions@jwcc.edu.

Joliet Junior College

Joliet, Illinois **www.jjc.edu/**

Freshman Application Contact Ms. Jennifer Kloberdanz, Dean of Admissions and Financial Aid, Joliet Junior College, 1215 Houbolt Road, Joliet, IL 60431. *Phone:* 815-280-2493. *Fax:* 815-280-6740. *E-mail:* admission@jjc.edu.

Kankakee Community College

Kankakee, Illinois **www.kcc.edu/**

- **State and locally supported** 2-year, founded 1966, part of Illinois Community College Board
- **Small-town** 178-acre campus with easy access to Chicago
- **Endowment** $2.9 million
- **Coed,** 4,027 undergraduate students, 46% full-time, 62% women, 38% men

Undergraduates 1,835 full-time, 2,192 part-time. Students come from 9 other countries, 15% African American, 2% Asian American or Pacific Islander, 6% Hispanic American, 0.5% Native American, 0.1% international, 46% transferred in. *Retention:* 63% of 2008 full-time freshmen returned.

Freshmen *Admission:* 376 enrolled.

Faculty *Total:* 174, 37% full-time, 6% with terminal degrees. *Student/faculty ratio:* 20:1.

Majors Accounting; administrative assistant and secretarial science; agriculture; applied horticulture; automobile/automotive mechanics technology; avionics maintenance technology; biological and physical sciences; business/commerce; business, management, and marketing related; child development; clinical/medical laboratory technology; construction management; criminal justice/law enforcement administration; drafting and design technology; electrical, electronic and communications engineering technology; elementary education; emergency medical technology (EMT paramedic); engineering; fine/studio arts; general studies; graphic design; heating, air conditioning, ventilation and refrigeration maintenance technology; horticultural science; industrial radiologic technology; information science/studies; legal assistant/paralegal; machine tool technology; marketing/marketing management; mathematics teacher education; medical office assistant; nursing (registered nurse training); physical therapist assistant; psychology; radiologic technology/science; respiratory care therapy; secondary education; special education; teacher assistant/aide; visual and performing arts related; welding technology.

Academics *Calendar:* semesters. *Degrees:* certificates, diplomas, and associate (also offers continuing education program with significant enrollment not reflected in profile). *Special study options:* academic remediation for entering students, advanced placement credit, distance learning, English as a second language, honors programs, independent study, internships, off-campus study, part-time degree program, services for LD students, student-designed majors, study abroad, summer session for credit. *ROTC:* Army (c).

Library Kankakee Community College Learning Resource Center with 42,861 titles, 140 serial subscriptions, 4,475 audiovisual materials, an OPAC, a Web page.

Student Life *Housing:* college housing not available. *Activities and Organizations:* drama/theater group, student-run radio station, Student Advisory Council, Brother to Brother, Phi Theta Kappa, Political Science Involved, Rotaract. *Campus security:* 24-hour patrols, late-night transport/escort service.

Athletics Member NJCAA. *Intercollegiate sports:* baseball M(s), basketball M(s)/W(s), soccer M, softball W(s), volleyball W(s). *Intramural sports:* basketball M.

Kankakee Community College (continued)

Costs (2010–11) *Tuition:* area resident $2970 full-time; state resident $5125 full-time; nonresident $12,355 full-time. *Required fees:* $300 full-time. *Payment plan:* installment. *Waivers:* senior citizens and employees or children of employees.

Financial Aid Of all full-time matriculated undergraduates who enrolled in 2008, 70 Federal Work-Study jobs (averaging $1100). *Financial aid deadline:* 10/1.

Applying *Options:* electronic application, early admission. *Required:* high school transcript. *Application deadlines:* rolling (freshmen), rolling (transfers). *Notification:* continuous (freshmen), continuous (transfers).

Freshman Application Contact Ms. Michelle Driscoll, Kankakee Community College, Box 888, Kankakee, IL 60901. *Phone:* 815-802-8520. *Fax:* 815-802-8521. *E-mail:* mdriscoll@kcc.edu.

KASKASKIA COLLEGE

Centralia, Illinois **www.kaskaskia.edu/**

- **State and locally supported** 2-year, founded 1966, part of Illinois Community College Board
- **Rural** 195-acre campus with easy access to St. Louis
- **Endowment** $2.1 million
- **Coed,** 5,337 undergraduate students, 45% full-time, 61% women, 39% men

Undergraduates 2,425 full-time, 2,912 part-time. Students come from 18 states and territories, 4 other countries, 1% are from out of state, 6% African American, 0.9% Asian American or Pacific Islander, 1% Hispanic American, 0.5% Native American, 0.5% international, 30% transferred in.

Freshmen *Admission:* 797 applied, 797 admitted, 797 enrolled.

Faculty *Total:* 237, 32% full-time, 5% with terminal degrees. *Student/faculty ratio:* 23:1.

Majors Accounting; architectural drafting and CAD/CADD; autobody/collision and repair technology; automobile/automotive mechanics technology; biological and physical sciences; business automation/technology/data entry; business/commerce; carpentry; child-care provision; criminal justice/law enforcement administration; culinary arts; electrical, electronic and communications engineering technology; emergency medical technology (EMT paramedic); executive assistant/executive secretary; general studies; industrial mechanics and maintenance technology; juvenile corrections; liberal arts and sciences/liberal studies; mathematics teacher education; nursing (registered nurse training); physical therapist assistant; radiologic technology/science; respiratory care therapy; teacher assistant/aide; veterinary/animal health technology.

Academics *Calendar:* semesters. *Degree:* certificates and associate. *Special study options:* academic remediation for entering students, accelerated degree program, adult/continuing education programs, cooperative education, distance learning, double majors, English as a second language, honors programs, independent study, internships, off-campus study, part-time degree program, services for LD students, study abroad, summer session for credit.

Library Kaskaskia College Library with 21,096 titles, 97 serial subscriptions, 932 audiovisual materials, an OPAC, a Web page.

Student Life *Housing:* college housing not available. *Activities and Organizations:* drama/theater group, student-run newspaper, choral group, Phi Theta Kappa, Administration of Justice, Student Radiology Club, Cosmetology Club, Vocal Music Club. *Campus security:* 24-hour emergency response devices and patrols, late-night transport/escort service. *Student services:* personal/psychological counseling.

Athletics Member NJCAA. *Intercollegiate sports:* baseball M(s), basketball M(s)/W(s), cheerleading M(s)/W(s), golf M(s)/W(s), soccer M(s)/W(s), softball W(s), tennis M(s), volleyball W(s).

Standardized Tests *Recommended:* ACT (for admission).

Costs (2009–10) *Tuition:* area resident $2240 full-time, $70 per credit hour part-time; state resident $4320 full-time, $135 per credit hour part-time; nonresident $9920 full-time, $310 per credit hour part-time. Full-time tuition and fees vary according to location and program. Part-time tuition and fees vary according to location and program. *Required fees:* $352 full-time, $11 per credit hour part-time. *Payment plan:* installment. *Waivers:* senior citizens and employees or children of employees.

Applying *Options:* early admission, deferred entrance. *Required:* high school transcript. *Required for some:* interview. *Application deadlines:* rolling (freshmen), rolling (transfers). *Notification:* continuous (freshmen), continuous (transfers).

Freshman Application Contact Jan Ripperda, Manager of Records & Registration, Kaskaskia College, 27210 College Road, Centralia, IL 62801. *Phone:* 618-545-3041. *Toll-free phone:* 800-642-0859. *Fax:* 618-532-1990. *E-mail:* jripperda@kaskaskia.edu.

KISHWAUKEE COLLEGE

Malta, Illinois **www.kishwaukeecollege.edu/**

- **State and locally supported** 2-year, founded 1967, part of Illinois Community College Board
- **Rural** 120-acre campus with easy access to Chicago
- **Coed**

Academics *Calendar:* semesters. *Degree:* certificates and associate. *Special study options:* academic remediation for entering students, adult/continuing education programs, advanced placement credit, cooperative education, distance learning, double majors, English as a second language, external degree program, independent study, internships, off-campus study, part-time degree program, services for LD students, study abroad, summer session for credit.

Student Life *Campus security:* 24-hour patrols.

Athletics Member NJCAA.

Costs (2009–10) *Tuition:* area resident $2250 full-time, $75 per credit hour part-time; state resident $8070 full-time, $269 per credit hour part-time; nonresident $9330 full-time, $311 per credit hour part-time. Full-time tuition and fees vary according to program and reciprocity agreements. Part-time tuition and fees vary according to program and reciprocity agreements. *Required fees:* $300 full-time, $8 per credit hour part-time, $6 per course part-time. *Payment plans:* installment, deferred payment.

Financial Aid Of all full-time matriculated undergraduates who enrolled in 2008, 75 Federal Work-Study jobs (averaging $1245). 76 state and other part-time jobs (averaging $918).

Applying *Options:* early admission, deferred entrance. *Required:* high school transcript, transcripts from all other colleges or universities previously attended. *Required for some:* minimum 2.0 GPA. *Recommended:* minimum 2.0 GPA.

Freshman Application Contact Ms. Sally Misciasci, Admission Analyst, Kishwaukee College, 21193 Malta Road, Malta, IL 60150-9699. *Phone:* 815-825-2086 Ext. 400.

LAKE LAND COLLEGE

Mattoon, Illinois **www.lakelandcollege.edu/**

Freshman Application Contact Mr. Jon VanDyke, Dean of Admission Services, Lake Land College, Mattoon, IL 61938-9366. *Phone:* 217-234-5378. *Toll-free phone:* 800-252-4121. *E-mail:* admissions@lakeland.cc.il.us.

LE CORDON BLEU COLLEGE OF CULINARY ARTS IN CHICAGO

Chicago, Illinois **www.chefs.edu/chicago/**

Freshman Application Contact Mr. Matthew Verratti, Vice President of Admissions and Marketing, Le Cordon Bleu College of Culinary Arts in Chicago, 361 West Chestnut, Chicago, IL 60610. *Phone:* 312-873-2064. *Toll-free phone:* 877-828-7772. *Fax:* 312-798-2903. *E-mail:* mverratti@chicnet.org.

LEWIS AND CLARK COMMUNITY COLLEGE

Godfrey, Illinois **www.lc.edu/**

- **District-supported** 2-year, founded 1970, part of Illinois Community College Board
- **Small-town** 275-acre campus with easy access to St. Louis
- **Coed,** 8,179 undergraduate students

Undergraduates 7% African American, 0.6% Asian American or Pacific Islander, 1% Hispanic American, 0.3% Native American.

Majors Accounting; administrative assistant and secretarial science; art; automobile/automotive mechanics technology; biological and physical sciences; business administration and management; CAD/CADD drafting/design technology; child-care provision; computer graphics; computer programming; computer systems networking and telecommunications; criminal justice/law enforcement administration; dental hygiene; engineering; fire science; general studies; kinesiology and exercise science; legal administrative assistant/secretary; legal assistant/paralegal; liberal arts and sciences/liberal studies; library assistant; manufacturing technology; massage therapy; medical administrative assistant and medical secretary; nursing (registered nurse training); occupational therapist assistant; radio and television; web page, digital/multimedia and information resources design.

Academics *Calendar:* semesters. *Degree:* certificates and associate. *Special study options:* academic remediation for entering students, adult/continuing education programs, advanced placement credit, cooperative education, distance learning, double majors, English as a second language, independent study, internships, off-campus study, part-time degree program, services for LD students, summer session for credit. *ROTC:* Army (b).

Library Reid Memorial Library with 47,000 titles, 3,500 serial subscriptions, 1,700 audiovisual materials, an OPAC, a Web page.

Student Life *Housing:* college housing not available. *Activities and Organizations:* student-run newspaper, radio station, choral group. *Campus security:* 24-hour emergency response devices and patrols. *Student services:* health clinic, personal/psychological counseling.

Athletics Member NJCAA. *Intercollegiate sports:* baseball M, basketball M/W(s), golf M, soccer M(s)/W, softball W, tennis M(s)/W(s), volleyball W(s).

Applying *Options:* early admission, deferred entrance. *Required for some:* interview. *Recommended:* high school transcript. *Application deadlines:* rolling (freshmen), rolling (transfers). *Notification:* continuous (freshmen), continuous (transfers).

Freshman Application Contact Lewis and Clark Community College, Enrollment Center, 5800 Godfrey Road, Godfrey, IL 62035. *Phone:* 618-468-5100. *Toll-free phone:* 800-500-LCCC.

LINCOLN COLLEGE

Lincoln, Illinois **www.lincolncollege.edu/**

Director of Admissions Mr. Tony Schilling, Director of Admissions, Lincoln College, 300 Keokuk Street, Lincoln, IL 62656-1699. *Toll-free phone:* 800-569-0556.

LINCOLN LAND COMMUNITY COLLEGE

Springfield, Illinois **www.llcc.edu/**

- **District-supported** 2-year, founded 1967, part of Illinois Community College Board
- **Suburban** 441-acre campus with easy access to St. Louis
- **Endowment** $2.7 million
- **Coed,** 7,677 undergraduate students, 43% full-time, 59% women, 41% men

Undergraduates 3,264 full-time, 4,413 part-time. Students come from 9 states and territories, 1% are from out of state, 7% African American, 1% Asian American or Pacific Islander, 1% Hispanic American, 0.3% Native American, 0.1% international, 2% transferred in. *Retention:* 45% of 2008 full-time freshmen returned.

Freshmen *Admission:* 836 enrolled. *Average high school GPA:* 2.87. *Test scores:* ACT scores over 18: 65%; ACT scores over 24: 15%; ACT scores over 30: 1%.

Faculty *Total:* 345, 36% full-time, 33% with terminal degrees. *Student/faculty ratio:* 17:1.

Majors Administrative assistant and secretarial science; agricultural production; architectural drafting and CAD/CADD; art; automobile/automotive mechanics technology; biological and physical sciences; business administration and management; business automation/technology/data entry; child-care provision; child development; comparative literature; computer programming (specific applications); computer systems networking and telecommunications; criminal justice/police science; electrical, electronic and communications engineering technology; fire protection and safety technology; general studies; hotel/motel administration; landscaping and groundskeeping; legal administrative assistant/secretary; liberal arts and sciences/liberal studies; medical radiologic technology; music; nursing (registered nurse training); occupational therapist assistant; physical therapist assistant; pre-engineering; respiratory care therapy; selling skills and sales.

Academics *Calendar:* semesters. *Degree:* certificates and associate. *Special study options:* academic remediation for entering students, accelerated degree program, adult/continuing education programs, advanced placement credit, distance learning, English as a second language, external degree program, honors programs, independent study, internships, off-campus study, part-time degree program, services for LD students, study abroad, summer session for credit.

Library Learning Resource Center with 65,000 titles, 10,000 serial subscriptions, an OPAC, a Web page.

Student Life *Housing:* college housing not available. *Activities and Organizations:* drama/theater group, student-run newspaper, choral group, Student Senate, Phi Theta Kappa, Model Illinois Government, student newspaper, Madrigals. *Campus security:* 24-hour emergency response devices and patrols, late-night transport/escort service. *Student services:* health clinic, personal/psychological counseling.

Athletics Member NJCAA. *Intercollegiate sports:* baseball M(s), basketball M(s)/W(s), soccer M(s), softball W(s), volleyball W(s). *Intramural sports:* basketball M/W, cheerleading W, volleyball W.

Costs (2010–11) *Tuition:* area resident $2370 full-time, $79 per credit hour part-time; state resident $4740 full-time, $158 per credit hour part-time; nonresident $7110 full-time, $237 per credit hour part-time. *Required fees:* $330 full-time, $11 per credit hour part-time. *Payment plans:* installment, deferred payment. *Waivers:* senior citizens and employees or children of employees.

Applying *Options:* electronic application, early admission, deferred entrance. *Recommended:* high school transcript. *Application deadlines:* rolling (freshmen), rolling (transfers). *Notification:* continuous (freshmen), continuous (transfers).

Freshman Application Contact Mr. Ron Gregoire, Executive Director of Admissions and Records, Lincoln Land Community College, 5250 Shepherd Road, PO Box 19256, Springfield, IL 62794-9256. *Phone:* 217-786-2243. *Toll-free phone:* 800-727-4161 Ext. 298. *Fax:* 217-786-2492. *E-mail:* ron.gregoire@llcc.edu.

MACCORMAC COLLEGE

Chicago, Illinois **www.maccormac.edu/**

Director of Admissions Mr. David Grassi, Director of Admissions, MacCormac College, 506 South Wabash Avenue, Chicago, IL 60605-1667. *Phone:* 312-922-1884 Ext. 102.

MCHENRY COUNTY COLLEGE

Crystal Lake, Illinois **www.mchenry.edu/**

- **State and locally supported** 2-year, founded 1967, part of Illinois Community College Board
- **Suburban** 109-acre campus with easy access to Chicago
- **Coed**

Academics *Calendar:* semesters. *Degree:* certificates and associate. *Special study options:* academic remediation for entering students, accelerated degree program, adult/continuing education programs, advanced placement credit, cooperative education, distance learning, English as a second language, honors programs, independent study, internships, part-time degree program, services for LD students, study abroad, summer session for credit.

Student Life *Campus security:* 24-hour emergency response devices and patrols, late-night transport/escort service.

Athletics Member NJCAA.

Financial Aid Of all full-time matriculated undergraduates who enrolled in 2008, 200 Federal Work-Study jobs (averaging $3700). 130 state and other part-time jobs (averaging $2000).

Applying *Options:* early admission, deferred entrance. *Application fee:* $15. *Required:* high school transcript.

Freshman Application Contact Fran Duwaldt, Coordinator of Admissions, McHenry County College, 8900 US Highway 14, Crystal Lake, IL 60012. *Phone:* 815-479-7620. *E-mail:* admissions@mchenry.edu.

MORAINE VALLEY COMMUNITY COLLEGE

Palos Hills, Illinois **www.morainevalley.edu/**

- **State and locally supported** 2-year, founded 1967, part of Illinois Community College Board
- **Suburban** 294-acre campus with easy access to Chicago
- **Endowment** $13.6 million
- **Coed,** 17,774 undergraduate students, 44% full-time, 54% women, 46% men

Undergraduates 7,761 full-time, 10,013 part-time. Students come from 7 states and territories, 42 other countries, 10% African American, 2% Asian American or Pacific Islander, 14% Hispanic American, 0.2% Native American, 2% international, 4% transferred in. *Retention:* 66% of 2008 full-time freshmen returned.

Freshmen *Admission:* 4,798 applied, 4,798 admitted, 1,850 enrolled.

Faculty *Total:* 763, 24% full-time, 9% with terminal degrees. *Student/faculty ratio:* 30:1.

Moraine Valley Community College (continued)

Majors Administrative assistant and secretarial science; automobile/automotive mechanics technology; biological and physical sciences; business administration and management; business/commerce; child-care provision; computer and information systems security; criminal justice/police science; fire science; graphic design; health aides/attendants/orderlies related; health information/medical records technology; heating, air conditioning, ventilation and refrigeration maintenance technology; human resources management; industrial electronics technology; instrumentation technology; liberal arts and sciences/liberal studies; management information systems; mathematics teacher education; mechanical engineering/mechanical technology; nursing (registered nurse training); parks, recreation and leisure facilities management; radiologic technology/science; respiratory care therapy; restaurant, culinary, and catering management; retailing; science teacher education; small business administration; special education; substance abuse/addiction counseling; system, networking, and LAN/WAN management; teacher assistant/aide; tourism and travel services management; visual and performing arts; web/multimedia management and webmaster.

Academics *Calendar:* semesters. *Degree:* certificates and associate. *Special study options:* academic remediation for entering students, accelerated degree program, adult/continuing education programs, advanced placement credit, cooperative education, distance learning, double majors, English as a second language, honors programs, independent study, internships, off-campus study, part-time degree program, services for LD students, study abroad, summer session for credit.

Library Library with 71,069 titles, 414 serial subscriptions, 14,623 audiovisual materials, an OPAC, a Web page.

Student Life *Housing:* college housing not available. *Activities and Organizations:* drama/theater group, student-run newspaper, choral group, student newspaper, Speech Team, Alliance of Latin American Students, Phi Theta Kappa, Arab Student Union. *Campus security:* 24-hour emergency response devices and patrols, late-night transport/escort service, safety and security programs. *Student services:* personal/psychological counseling, women's center.

Athletics Member NJCAA. *Intercollegiate sports:* baseball M(s), basketball M(s)/W(s), cross-country running M(s)/W(s), golf M(s), soccer M(s)/W(s), softball W, tennis M(s)/W(s), volleyball W(s). *Intramural sports:* badminton M/W, basketball M/W, softball W, volleyball W.

Costs (2010–11) *Tuition:* area resident $2610 full-time, $87 per credit hour part-time; state resident $6960 full-time, $232 per credit hour part-time; nonresident $8160 full-time, $272 per credit hour part-time. *Required fees:* $156 full-time, $5 per credit hour part-time, $3 per credit hour part-time. *Payment plan:* installment. *Waivers:* senior citizens and employees or children of employees.

Financial Aid Of all full-time matriculated undergraduates who enrolled in 2008, 84 Federal Work-Study jobs (averaging $2500). 260 state and other part-time jobs (averaging $2200).

Applying *Options:* electronic application, early admission, deferred entrance. *Required:* high school transcript. *Application deadlines:* rolling (freshmen), rolling (transfers). *Notification:* continuous (freshmen), continuous (transfers).

Freshman Application Contact Ms. Claudia Roselli, Director, Admissions and Recruitment, Moraine Valley Community College, 9000 West College Parkway, Palos Hills, IL 60465-0937. *Phone:* 708-974-5357. *Fax:* 708-974-0681. *E-mail:* roselli@morainevalley.edu.

MORRISON INSTITUTE OF TECHNOLOGY

Morrison, Illinois **www.morrison.tec.il.us/**

Freshman Application Contact Mrs. Tammy Pruis, Admission Secretary, Morrison Institute of Technology, 701 Portland Avenue, Morrison, IL 61270. *Phone:* 815-772-7218. *Fax:* 815-772-7584. *E-mail:* admissions@morrison.tec.il.us.

MORTON COLLEGE

Cicero, Illinois **www.morton.edu/**

Director of Admissions Roslyn Castro, Director of Admissions, Morton College, 3801 South Central Avenue, Cicero, IL 60804. *Phone:* 708-656-8000 Ext. 400.

NORTHWESTERN COLLEGE

Rosemont, Illinois **www.northwesterncollege.edu/**

- **Proprietary** 2-year, founded 1902
- **Urban** 3-acre campus
- **Coed,** 1,762 undergraduate students, 40% full-time, 79% women, 21% men

Undergraduates 706 full-time, 1,056 part-time. 41% African American, 2% Asian American or Pacific Islander, 33% Hispanic American, 0.3% Native American.

Freshmen *Admission:* 981 applied.

Majors Accounting technology and bookkeeping; administrative assistant and secretarial science; business administration and management; computer and information sciences and support services related; computer and information systems security; computer programming; computer software and media applications related; criminal justice/law enforcement administration; desktop publishing and digital imaging design; health information/medical records technology; legal assistant/paralegal; management information systems; massage therapy; medical/clinical assistant; web page, digital/multimedia and information resources design.

Academics *Calendar:* quarters. *Degrees:* certificates and associate (profile includes branch campuses in Bridgeview and Naperville, IL). *Special study options:* academic remediation for entering students, cooperative education, double majors, honors programs, independent study, internships, part-time degree program, summer session for credit.

Library Edward G. Schumacher Memorial Library with 2,000 titles, 20 serial subscriptions.

Student Life *Housing:* college housing not available.

Standardized Tests *Required:* SAT or ACT (for admission).

Costs (2009–10) *Tuition:* $410 per credit hour part-time.

Applying *Application fee:* $25. *Required:* high school transcript. *Application deadline:* rolling (freshmen).

Freshman Application Contact Northwestern College, 4839 North Milwaukee Avenue, Chicago, IL 60630. *Phone:* 773-481-3730. *Toll-free phone:* 800-396-5613.

OAKTON COMMUNITY COLLEGE

Des Plaines, Illinois **www.oakton.edu/**

- **District-supported** 2-year, founded 1969, part of Illinois Community College Board
- **Suburban** 193-acre campus with easy access to Chicago
- **Coed**

Academics *Calendar:* semesters. *Degree:* certificates and associate. *Special study options:* academic remediation for entering students, adult/continuing education programs, advanced placement credit, distance learning, English as a second language, honors programs, independent study, part-time degree program, services for LD students, study abroad, summer session for credit.

Student Life *Campus security:* 24-hour emergency response devices and patrols, student patrols, late-night transport/escort service.

Athletics Member NJCAA.

Applying *Application fee:* $25. *Required for some:* interview. *Recommended:* high school transcript.

Freshman Application Contact Mr. Dale Cohen, Admissions Specialist, Oakton Community College, 1600 East Golf Road, Des Plaines, IL 60016. *Phone:* 847-635-1703. *Fax:* 847-635-1890. *E-mail:* dcohen@oakton.edu.

PARKLAND COLLEGE

Champaign, Illinois **www.parkland.edu/**

Freshman Application Contact Admissions Representative, Parkland College, 2400 West Bradley Avenue, Champaign, IL 61821-1899. *Phone:* 217-351-2482. *Toll-free phone:* 800-346-8089. *Fax:* 217-351-2640. *E-mail:* mhenry@parkland.edu.

PRAIRIE STATE COLLEGE

Chicago Heights, Illinois **www.prairiestate.edu/**

Freshman Application Contact Ms. Marietta Turner, Director, Admissions, Enrollment and Career Development Services, Prairie State College, 202 South Halsted Street, Chicago Heights, IL 60411. *Phone:* 708-709-3542. *E-mail:* webmaster@prairiestate.edu.

RASMUSSEN COLLEGE AURORA

Aurora, Illinois **www.rasmussen.edu/**

Admissions Office Contact Rasmussen College Aurora, 2363 Sequoia Drive, Aurora, IL 60506. *Toll-free phone:* 877-888-4110.

RASMUSSEN COLLEGE ROCKFORD, ILLINOIS

Rockford, Illinois **www.rasmussen.edu/**

Admissions Office Contact Rasmussen College Rockford, Illinois, 6000 East State Street, Fourth Floor, Rockford, IL 61108-2513. *Toll-free phone:* 877-533-5825.

REND LAKE COLLEGE

Ina, Illinois **www.rlc.edu/**

- **State-supported** 2-year, founded 1967, part of Illinois Community College Board
- **Rural** 350-acre campus
- **Coed,** 5,871 undergraduate students

Majors Agricultural mechanics and equipment technology; agricultural mechanization; agricultural production; applied horticulture; architectural drafting and CAD/CADD; automobile/automotive mechanics technology; biological and physical sciences; child-care provision; clinical/medical laboratory technology; computer technology/computer systems technology; criminal justice/police science; culinary arts; drafting and design technology; e-commerce; electrical, electronic and communications engineering technology; electrician; emergency medical technology (EMT paramedic); engineering; fine/studio arts; graphic design; health information/medical records technology; heavy equipment maintenance technology; industrial mechanics and maintenance technology; liberal arts and sciences/liberal studies; medical staff services technology; occupational therapist assistant; plant sciences; special education.

Academics *Calendar:* semesters. *Degree:* certificates and associate. *Special study options:* academic remediation for entering students, adult/continuing education programs, advanced placement credit, cooperative education, distance learning, honors programs, independent study, internships, off-campus study, part-time degree program, services for LD students, summer session for credit.

Library Learning Resource Center with 35,426 titles, 265 serial subscriptions, 3,770 audiovisual materials, an OPAC, a Web page.

Student Life *Housing:* college housing not available. *Activities and Organizations:* drama/theater group, student-run newspaper, choral group. *Campus security:* 24-hour emergency response devices and patrols, late-night transport/escort service.

Athletics Member NJCAA. *Intercollegiate sports:* baseball M(s), basketball M(s)/W(s), cross-country running M(s), golf M(s)/W(s), softball W(s), tennis W(s), track and field M/W, volleyball W(s).

Financial Aid Of all full-time matriculated undergraduates who enrolled in 2008, 133 Federal Work-Study jobs (averaging $1000). 174 state and other part-time jobs (averaging $940).

Applying *Options:* electronic application, deferred entrance. *Required:* high school transcript.

Freshman Application Contact Mr. Jason Swann, Recruiter, Rend Lake College, 468 North Ken Gray Parkway, Ina, IL 62846-9801. *Phone:* 618-437-5321 Ext. 1265. *Toll-free phone:* 800-369-5321. *Fax:* 618-437-5677. *E-mail:* swannj@rlc.edu.

RICHLAND COMMUNITY COLLEGE

Decatur, Illinois **www.richland.edu/**

Freshman Application Contact Ms. JoAnn Wirey, Director of Admissions and Records, Richland Community College, One College Park, Decatur, IL 62521. *Phone:* 217-875-7200 Ext. 284. *Fax:* 217-875-7783. *E-mail:* jwirey@richland.edu.

ROCKFORD BUSINESS COLLEGE

Rockford, Illinois **www.rbcsuccess.com/**

Director of Admissions Ms. Barbara Holliman, Director of Admissions, Rockford Business College, 730 North Church Street, Rockford, IL 61103. *Phone:* 815-965-8616 Ext. 16.

ROCK VALLEY COLLEGE

Rockford, Illinois **www.rockvalleycollege.edu/**

- **District-supported** 2-year, founded 1964, part of Illinois Community College Board
- **Suburban** 217-acre campus with easy access to Chicago
- **Coed**

Undergraduates 3,508 full-time, 4,637 part-time. Students come from 2 states and territories, 3 other countries, 1% are from out of state, 9% African American, 3% Asian American or Pacific Islander, 6% Hispanic American, 0.4% Native American, 0.3% international.

Faculty *Student/faculty ratio:* 25:1.

Academics *Calendar:* semesters. *Degree:* certificates and associate. *Special study options:* academic remediation for entering students, adult/continuing education programs, advanced placement credit, cooperative education, distance learning, English as a second language, honors programs, independent study, internships, part-time degree program, services for LD students, student-designed majors, study abroad, summer session for credit.

Student Life *Campus security:* 24-hour emergency response devices and patrols, late-night transport/escort service.

Athletics Member NJCAA.

Costs (2009–10) *Tuition:* area resident $1980 full-time, $66 per credit hour part-time; state resident $8430 full-time, $281 per credit hour part-time; nonresident $13,320 full-time, $444 per credit hour part-time. Full-time tuition and fees vary according to course load. Part-time tuition and fees vary according to course load. *Required fees:* $302 full-time, $8 per credit hour part-time, $55 per term part-time. *Payment plans:* installment, deferred payment.

Financial Aid Of all full-time matriculated undergraduates who enrolled in 2008, 120 Federal Work-Study jobs (averaging $1800).

Applying *Required:* high school transcript.

Freshman Application Contact Rock Valley College, 3301 North Mulford Road, Rockford, IL 61114-5699. *Phone:* 815-921-4283. *Toll-free phone:* 800-973-7821.

SAUK VALLEY COMMUNITY COLLEGE

Dixon, Illinois **www.svcc.edu/**

- **District-supported** 2-year, founded 1965, part of Illinois Community College Board
- **Rural** 165-acre campus
- **Coed**

Undergraduates 1,092 full-time, 1,301 part-time. 3% African American, 2% Asian American or Pacific Islander, 9% Hispanic American, 0.2% Native American.

Faculty *Student/faculty ratio:* 11:1.

Academics *Calendar:* semesters. *Degree:* certificates and associate. *Special study options:* academic remediation for entering students, accelerated degree program, adult/continuing education programs, cooperative education, distance learning, English as a second language, honors programs, independent study, internships, off-campus study, part-time degree program, services for LD students, student-designed majors, summer session for credit.

Student Life *Campus security:* 24-hour emergency response devices and patrols, late-night transport/escort service.

Athletics Member NJCAA.

Standardized Tests *Recommended:* ACT (for admission).

Costs (2009–10) *Tuition:* area resident $2848 full-time, $89 per credit hour part-time; state resident $8000 full-time, $250 per credit hour part-time; nonresident $9152 full-time, $286 per credit hour part-time. *Room and board:* room only: $4131. Room and board charges vary according to housing facility.

Financial Aid Of all full-time matriculated undergraduates who enrolled in 2008, 781 applied for aid, 680 were judged to have need, 25 had their need fully met. *Average percent of need met:* 46. *Average financial aid package:* $4394. *Average need-based loan:* $2187. *Average need-based gift aid:* $4316.

Sauk Valley Community College (continued)

Applying *Options:* electronic application, early admission, deferred entrance. *Recommended:* high school transcript.

Freshman Application Contact Sauk Valley Community College, 173 Illinois Route 2, Dixon, IL 61021. *Phone:* 815-288-5511 Ext. 378.

SHAWNEE COMMUNITY COLLEGE

Ullin, Illinois **www.shawneecc.edu/**

- **State and locally supported** 2-year, founded 1967, part of Illinois Community College Board
- **Rural** 163-acre campus
- **Coed,** 3,190 undergraduate students, 30% full-time, 55% women, 45% men

Undergraduates 942 full-time, 2,248 part-time. Students come from 6 states and territories, 2 other countries, 4% are from out of state, 22% African American, 0.7% Asian American or Pacific Islander, 1% Hispanic American, 0.6% Native American, 0.1% international.

Freshmen *Admission:* 392 enrolled.

Faculty *Total:* 212, 20% full-time, 4% with terminal degrees. *Student/faculty ratio:* 20:1.

Majors Accounting; administrative assistant and secretarial science; agricultural business and management; agriculture; agronomy and crop science; animal sciences; automobile/automotive mechanics technology; biological and physical sciences; business administration and management; child development; cosmetology; criminal justice/police science; electrical, electronic and communications engineering technology; horticultural science; human services; information science/studies; legal administrative assistant/secretary; liberal arts and sciences/liberal studies; medical administrative assistant and medical secretary; nursing (registered nurse training); social work; welding technology; wildlife and wildlands science and management.

Academics *Calendar:* semesters. *Degree:* certificates and associate. *Special study options:* academic remediation for entering students, accelerated degree program, adult/continuing education programs, advanced placement credit, distance learning, double majors, English as a second language, external degree program, independent study, internships, off-campus study, part-time degree program, services for LD students, summer session for credit.

Library Shawnee Community College Library with 46,313 titles, 148 serial subscriptions, 1,842 audiovisual materials, an OPAC, a Web page.

Student Life *Activities and Organizations:* drama/theater group, student-run newspaper, choral group, Phi Theta Kappa, Phi Beta Lambda, Music Club, Student Senate, Future Teachers Organization. *Campus security:* 24-hour patrols. *Student services:* personal/psychological counseling.

Athletics Member NJCAA. *Intercollegiate sports:* baseball M(s), basketball M(s)/W(s), cheerleading M(s)/W(s), golf M(s)/W(s), softball W(s), volleyball W(s). *Intramural sports:* weight lifting M/W.

Standardized Tests *Required for some:* ACT (for admission). *Recommended:* ACT (for admission).

Costs (2010–11) *Tuition:* area resident $2610 full-time, $87 per credit hour part-time; state resident $3930 full-time, $131 per credit hour part-time; nonresident $4350 full-time, $145 per credit hour part-time. Full-time tuition and fees vary according to program and reciprocity agreements. Part-time tuition and fees vary according to program and reciprocity agreements. *Payment plan:* installment. *Waivers:* senior citizens and employees or children of employees.

Financial Aid Of all full-time matriculated undergraduates who enrolled in 2008, 60 Federal Work-Study jobs (averaging $2000). 50 state and other part-time jobs (averaging $2000).

Applying *Options:* electronic application, early admission, deferred entrance. *Required:* high school transcript. *Application deadlines:* rolling (freshmen), rolling (transfers). *Notification:* continuous (freshmen), continuous (transfers).

Freshman Application Contact Mrs. Erin King, Recruiter/Advisor, Shawnee Community College, 8364 Shawnee College Road, Ullin, IL 62992. *Phone:* 618-634-3200. *Toll-free phone:* 800-481-2242. *Fax:* 618-634-3300. *E-mail:* erink@shawneecc.edu.

SOLEX COLLEGE

Wheeling, Illinois **www.solex.edu/**

- **Proprietary** 2-year, administratively affiliated with The School of Massage Therapy at SOLEX
- **Suburban** campus with easy access to Chicago
- **Coed**

Majors Accounting.

Academics *Degree:* certificates and associate. *Special study options:* adult/continuing education programs, English as a second language, internships, off-campus study, part-time degree program, summer session for credit.

Student Life *Housing Options:* Campus housing is provided by a third party.

Standardized Tests *Required:* SAT or ACT (for admission).

Applying *Options:* electronic application. *Application fee:* $150. *Required:* high school transcript.

Freshman Application Contact Solex College, 350 East Dundee Road, Wheeling, IL 60090.

SOUTHEASTERN ILLINOIS COLLEGE

Harrisburg, Illinois **www.sic.edu/**

Freshman Application Contact Dr. David Nudo, Director of Counseling, Southeastern Illinois College, 3575 College Road, Harrisburg, IL 62946-4925. *Phone:* 618-252-5400 Ext. 2430. *Toll-free phone:* 866-338-2742.

SOUTH SUBURBAN COLLEGE

South Holland, Illinois **www.ssc.edu/**

- **State and locally supported** 2-year, founded 1927, part of Illinois Community College Board
- **Suburban** campus with easy access to Chicago
- **Coed,** 7,279 undergraduate students, 33% full-time, 72% women, 28% men

Undergraduates 2,428 full-time, 4,851 part-time. 6% are from out of state, 69% African American, 1% Asian American or Pacific Islander, 9% Hispanic American, 0.4% Native American, 0.2% international. *Retention:* 58% of 2008 full-time freshmen returned.

Faculty *Total:* 337, 36% full-time. *Student/faculty ratio:* 22:1.

Majors Accounting; accounting technology and bookkeeping; architectural drafting and CAD/CADD; biological and physical sciences; building/home/construction inspection; CAD/CADD drafting/design technology; child-care provision; construction engineering technology; court reporting; criminal justice/safety; electrical, electronic and communications engineering technology; executive assistant/executive secretary; fine/studio arts; information technology; kinesiology and exercise science; legal assistant/paralegal; liberal arts and sciences/liberal studies; nursing administration; occupational therapist assistant; office management; radiologic technology/science; small business administration; social work.

Academics *Calendar:* semesters. *Degree:* certificates and associate. *Special study options:* academic remediation for entering students, adult/continuing education programs, advanced placement credit, cooperative education, distance learning, English as a second language, honors programs, off-campus study, part-time degree program, services for LD students, study abroad, summer session for credit.

Library South Suburban College Library with an OPAC, a Web page.

Student Life *Housing:* college housing not available. *Activities and Organizations:* drama/theater group, choral group. *Campus security:* 24-hour emergency response devices and patrols.

Athletics Member NJCAA. *Intercollegiate sports:* baseball M, basketball M/W, soccer M/W, softball W, volleyball W.

Costs (2009–10) *Tuition:* area resident $2700 full-time, $90 per credit hour part-time; state resident $8040 full-time, $268 per credit hour part-time; nonresident $9690 full-time, $325 per credit hour part-time. *Required fees:* $413 full-time, $14 per credit hour part-time.

Financial Aid Of all full-time matriculated undergraduates who enrolled in 2008, 121 Federal Work-Study jobs (averaging $1750).

Applying *Options:* early admission, deferred entrance. *Required:* high school transcript. *Recommended:* minimum 2 GPA. *Application deadlines:* rolling (freshmen), rolling (transfers). *Notification:* continuous (freshmen), continuous (transfers).

Freshman Application Contact Admissions, South Suburban College, 15800 South State Street, South Holland, IL 60473-1270. *Phone:* 708-596-2000 Ext. 2330. *Fax:* 708-225-5823. *E-mail:* admissionsquestions@southsuburbancollege.edu.

SOUTHWESTERN ILLINOIS COLLEGE

Belleville, Illinois **www.southwestern.cc.il.us/**

Freshman Application Contact Mike Leiker, Director of Admissions, Southwestern Illinois College, 2500 Carlyle Road, Belleville, IL 62221-5899. *Phone:* 618-235-2700 Ext. 5400. *Toll-free phone:* 800-222-5131. *Fax:* 618-277-0631.

Spoon River College

Canton, Illinois www.spoonrivercollege.net/

Freshman Application Contact Ms. Missy Wilkinson, Director of Admissions and Records, Spoon River College, 23235 North County 22, Canton, IL 61520-9801. *Phone:* 309-649-6305. *Toll-free phone:* 800-334-7337. *Fax:* 309-649-6235. *E-mail:* info@spoonrivercollege.edu.

Springfield College in Illinois

Springfield, Illinois www.sci.edu/

Freshman Application Contact Kevin Hinkle, Associate Director of Admissions, Springfield College in Illinois, 1500 North Fifth Street, Springfield, IL 62702. *Phone:* 217-525-1420 Ext. 321. *Toll-free phone:* 800-635-7289. *Fax:* 217-525-1497. *E-mail:* khinkle@sci.edu.

Taylor Business Institute

Chicago, Illinois www.tbiil.edu/

Director of Admissions Mr. Rashed Jahangir, Taylor Business Institute, 318 West Adams, Chicago, IL 60007.

Triton College

River Grove, Illinois www.triton.cc.il.us/

- **State-supported** 2-year, founded 1964, part of Illinois Community College Board
- **Suburban** 100-acre campus with easy access to Chicago
- **Coed,** 15,658 undergraduate students, 25% full-time, 55% women, 45% men

Undergraduates 3,893 full-time, 11,765 part-time. 17% African American, 4% Asian American or Pacific Islander, 29% Hispanic American, 0.2% Native American, 0.4% international. *Retention:* 56% of 2008 full-time freshmen returned.

Freshmen *Admission:* 2,230 enrolled.

Faculty *Total:* 644, 19% full-time, 13% with terminal degrees. *Student/faculty ratio:* 24:1.

Majors Accounting; anthropology; architectural drafting and CAD/CADD; art; automobile/automotive mechanics technology; biological and physical sciences; biology/biological sciences; business administration and management; CAD/CADD drafting/design technology; chemistry; child-care provision; communication/speech communication and rhetoric; computer and information sciences; computer science; computer systems networking and telecommunications; construction management; criminal justice/law enforcement administration; culinary arts; design and visual communications; diagnostic medical sonography and ultrasound technology; early childhood education; economics; education; educational/instructional media design; emergency medical technology (EMT paramedic); English; financial planning and services; fine/studio arts; fire science; French; geography; geology/earth science; health and physical education; heating, air conditioning, ventilation and refrigeration maintenance technology; history; home furnishings and equipment installation; hotel/motel administration; human resources management; information science/studies; intercultural/multicultural and diversity studies; international business/trade/commerce; Italian; liberal arts and sciences/liberal studies; mathematics; mathematics teacher education; mechanical engineering/mechanical technology; mechanic and repair technologies related; multi/interdisciplinary studies related; music; music related; nuclear medical technology; nursing (registered nurse training); ophthalmic technology; ornamental horticulture; philosophy; physics; political science and government; psychology; radiologic technology/science; respiratory care therapy; restaurant/food services management; selling skills and sales; sociology; Spanish; speech and rhetoric; substance abuse/addiction counseling; survey technology; welding technology; women's studies.

Academics *Calendar:* semesters. *Degree:* certificates and associate. *Special study options:* academic remediation for entering students, adult/continuing education programs, advanced placement credit, cooperative education, distance learning, English as a second language, freshman honors college, honors programs, internships, part-time degree program, student-designed majors, summer session for credit.

Library Learning Resource Center with 70,859 titles, 1,247 serial subscriptions.

Student Life *Housing:* college housing not available. *Activities and Organizations:* drama/theater group, student-run newspaper, radio station, choral group, student government, Program Board. *Campus security:* 24-hour emergency response devices and patrols. *Student services:* health clinic, personal/psychological counseling.

Athletics Member NJCAA. *Intercollegiate sports:* baseball M, basketball M/W, soccer M, softball W, volleyball W, wrestling M.

Financial Aid Of all full-time matriculated undergraduates who enrolled in 2008, 250 Federal Work-Study jobs (averaging $2000).

Applying *Options:* deferred entrance. *Application fee:* $10. *Required:* high school transcript. *Application deadlines:* rolling (freshmen), rolling (transfers).

Freshman Application Contact Ms. Mary-Rita Moore, Dean of Admissions, Triton College, 2000 Fifth Avenue, River Grove, IL 60171. *Phone:* 708-456-0300 Ext. 3679. *Toll-free phone:* 800-942-7404. *Fax:* 708-583-3162. *E-mail:* mpatrice@triton.edu.

Vet Tech Institute at Fox College

Tinley Park, Illinois www.vettechinstitute.edu/camp_fox.php

- **Private** 2-year, founded 2006
- **Suburban** campus
- **Coed,** 185 undergraduate students
- 61% of applicants were admitted

Freshmen *Admission:* 343 applied, 208 admitted.

Majors Veterinary/animal health technology.

Academics *Degree:* associate. *Special study options:* accelerated degree program, internships.

Student Life *Housing:* college housing not available.

Freshman Application Contact Admissions Office, Vet Tech Institute at Fox College, 18020 South Oak Park Avenue, Tinley Park, IL 60477. *Phone:* 888-884-3694.

Waubonsee Community College

Sugar Grove, Illinois www.waubonsee.edu/

Freshman Application Contact Recruitment and Retention Office, Waubonsee Community College, Route 47 at Waubonsee Drive, Sugar Grove, IL 60554. *Phone:* 630-466-7900 Ext. 5756. *Fax:* 630-466-4964. *E-mail:* recruitment@waubonsee.edu.

Worsham College of Mortuary Science

Wheeling, Illinois www.worshamcollege.com/

Director of Admissions President, Worsham College of Mortuary Science, 495 Northgate Parkway, Wheeling, IL 60090-2646. *Phone:* 847-808-8444.

INDIANA

Ancilla College

Donaldson, Indiana www.ancilla.edu/

Freshman Application Contact Erin Alonzo, Director of Admissions, Ancilla College, 9601 Union Road, Donaldson, IN 46513. *Phone:* 574-936-8898 Ext. 330. *Toll-free phone:* 866-262-4552 Ext. 350. *Fax:* 574-935-1773. *E-mail:* admissions@ancilla.edu.

Aviation Institute of Maintenance–Indianapolis

Indianapolis, Indiana **www.aviationmaintenance.edu/**

- **Proprietary** 2-year, founded 1992
- **Coed**

Academics *Calendar:* semesters. *Degree:* associate.
Applying *Application fee:* $25.
Freshman Application Contact Admissions Office, Aviation Institute of Maintenance–Indianapolis, 7251 West McCarty Street, Indianapolis, IN 46241. *Toll-free phone:* 888-349-5387.

Brown Mackie College–Fort Wayne

Fort Wayne, Indiana **www.brownmackie.edu/fortwayne/**

- **Proprietary** primarily 2-year, part of Education Management Corporation
- **Coed**

Majors Accounting technology and bookkeeping; athletic training; biomedical technology; business administration and management; computer software technology; criminal justice/law enforcement administration; dietetic technician; health/health-care administration; legal assistant/paralegal; legal studies; medical/clinical assistant; occupational therapist assistant; office management; physical therapist assistant; surgical technology.
Academics *Calendar:* quarters. *Degrees:* certificates, diplomas, associate, and bachelor's.
Costs (2009–10) *Tuition:* Tuition varies by program. Students should contact Brown Mackie College for tuition information.
Freshman Application Contact Brown Mackie College–Fort Wayne, 3000 East Coliseum Boulevard, Fort Wayne, IN 46805. *Phone:* 260-484-4400. *Toll-free phone:* 866-433-2289.

►See page 416 for the College Close-Up.

Brown Mackie College–Indianapolis

Indianapolis, Indiana **www.brownmackie.edu/indianapolis/**

- **Proprietary** primarily 2-year, part of Education Management Corporation
- **Coed**

Majors Business administration and management; criminal justice/law enforcement administration; health/health-care administration; legal assistant/paralegal; legal studies; medical/clinical assistant; occupational therapist assistant.
Academics *Degrees:* certificates, diplomas, associate, and bachelor's.
Costs (2009–10) *Tuition:* Tuition varies by program. Students should contact Brown Mackie College for tuition information.
Freshman Application Contact Brown Mackie College–Indianapolis, 1200 North Meridian Street, Suite 100, Indianapolis, IN 46204. *Phone:* 317-554-8301. *Toll-free phone:* 866-255-0279.

►See page 422 for the College Close-Up.

Brown Mackie College–Merrillville

Merrillville, Indiana **www.brownmackie.edu/merrillville/**

- **Proprietary** primarily 2-year, founded 1890, part of Education Management Corporation
- **Small-town** campus
- **Coed**

Majors Accounting technology and bookkeeping; business administration and management; computer software technology; criminal justice/law enforcement administration; gerontology; health/health-care administration; legal assistant/paralegal; legal studies; medical/clinical assistant; medical office management; occupational therapist assistant; surgical technology.
Academics *Calendar:* quarters. *Degrees:* certificates, diplomas, associate, and bachelor's.
Costs (2009–10) *Tuition:* Tuition varies by program. Students should contact Brown Mackie College for tuition information.
Freshman Application Contact Brown Mackie College–Merrillville, 1000 East 80th Place, Suite 101N, Merrillville, IN 46410. *Phone:* 219-769-3321. *Toll-free phone:* 800-258-3321.

►See page 428 for the College Close-Up.

Brown Mackie College–Michigan City

Michigan City, Indiana **www.brownmackie.edu/michigancity/**

- **Proprietary** primarily 2-year, part of Education Management Corporation
- **Rural** campus
- **Coed**

Majors Accounting technology and bookkeeping; business administration and management; computer software technology; criminal justice/law enforcement administration; early childhood education; health/health-care administration; legal assistant/paralegal; legal studies; massage therapy; medical/clinical assistant; medical office management; surgical technology; veterinary/animal health technology.
Academics *Calendar:* quarters. *Degrees:* certificates, diplomas, associate, and bachelor's.
Costs (2009–10) *Tuition:* Tuition varies by program. Students should contact Brown Mackie College for tuition information.
Freshman Application Contact Brown Mackie College–Michigan City, 325 East US Highway 20, Michigan City, IN 46360. *Phone:* 219-877-3100. *Toll-free phone:* 800-519-2416.

►See page 432 for the College Close-Up.

Brown Mackie College–South Bend

South Bend, Indiana **www.brownmackie.edu/southbend/**

- **Proprietary** primarily 2-year, founded 1882, part of Education Management Corporation
- **Urban** campus
- **Coed, primarily women**

Majors Accounting technology and bookkeeping; business administration and management; computer software technology; criminal justice/law enforcement administration; early childhood education; health/health-care administration; information technology; legal assistant/paralegal; legal studies; massage therapy; medical/clinical assistant; occupational therapist assistant; physical therapist assistant; veterinary/animal health technology.
Academics *Calendar:* quarters. *Degrees:* certificates, associate, and bachelor's.
Costs (2009–10) *Tuition:* Tuition varies by program. Students should contact Brown Mackie College for tuition information.
Freshman Application Contact Brown Mackie College–South Bend, 1030 East Jefferson Boulevard, South Bend, IN 46617. *Phone:* 574-237-0774. *Toll-free phone:* 800-743-2447.

►See page 446 for the College Close-Up.

College of Court Reporting

Hobart, Indiana **www.ccredu.com/**

Freshman Application Contact Ms. Nicky Rodriquez, Director of Admissions, College of Court Reporting, 111 West Tenth Street, Suite 111, Hobart, IN 46342. *Phone:* 219-942-1459 Ext. 226. *Toll-free phone:* 866-294-3974. *Fax:* 219-942-1631. *E-mail:* nrodriquez@ccredu.com.

Harrison College

Anderson, Indiana **www.harrison.edu/**

- **Proprietary** 2-year, founded 1902
- **Small-town** campus
- **Coed,** 225 undergraduate students

Faculty *Student/faculty ratio:* 16:1.
Majors Accounting; administrative assistant and secretarial science; banking and financial support services; business administration and management; criminal justice/law enforcement administration; health information/medical records technology; human resources management; marketing/marketing management; medical/clinical assistant; medical insurance coding.
Academics *Calendar:* quarters. *Degree:* certificates, diplomas, and associate. *Special study options:* adult/continuing education programs, cooperative education, distance learning, double majors, independent study, internships, part-time degree program.
Standardized Tests *Required:* Wonderlic Scholastic Level Exam (SLE) (for admission).
Costs (2009–10) *Tuition:* Tuition cost varies by program. Prospective students should contact the school for current tuition costs.
Applying *Options:* electronic application, early admission. *Application fee:* $50. *Required:* high school transcript, interview. *Application deadlines:* rolling (freshmen), rolling (transfers). *Notification:* continuous (freshmen), continuous (transfers).
Freshman Application Contact Mr. Kynan Simison, Director of Admissions, Harrison College, 140 East 53rd Street, Anderson, IN 46013. *Phone:* 765-644-7514. *Toll-free phone:* 888-544-4422. *Fax:* 765-664-5724. *E-mail:* kynan.simison@harrison.edu.

HARRISON COLLEGE

Columbus, Indiana **www.harrison.edu/**

- **Proprietary** 2-year
- **Rural** campus
- **Coed,** 270 undergraduate students

Faculty *Student/faculty ratio:* 15:1.
Majors Accounting; administrative assistant and secretarial science; banking and financial support services; business administration and management; health information/medical records technology; marketing/marketing management; medical/clinical assistant; medical insurance coding.
Academics *Calendar:* quarters. *Degree:* certificates, diplomas, and associate. *Special study options:* adult/continuing education programs, cooperative education, distance learning, double majors, independent study, internships, part-time degree program.
Library Main Library plus 1 other.
Student Life *Housing:* college housing not available.
Standardized Tests *Required:* Wonderlic Scholastic Level Exam (SLE) (for admission).
Costs (2009–10) *Tuition:* Tuition cost varies by program. Prospective students should contact the school for current tuition costs.
Applying *Options:* electronic application. *Application fee:* $50. *Required:* high school transcript, interview. *Application deadlines:* rolling (freshmen), rolling (out-of-state freshmen), rolling (transfers). *Notification:* continuous (freshmen), continuous (out-of-state freshmen), continuous (transfers).
Freshman Application Contact Ms. Gina Pate, Director of Admissions, Harrison College, 2222 Poshard Drive, Columbus, IN 47203. *Phone:* 812-379-9000. *Toll-free phone:* 888-544-4422. *Fax:* 812-375-0414. *E-mail:* gina.pate@harrison.edu.

HARRISON COLLEGE

Elkhart, Indiana **www.harrison.edu/**

- **Proprietary** primarily 2-year
- **Coed,** 192 undergraduate students

Faculty *Student/faculty ratio:* 25:1.
Majors Accounting; administrative assistant and secretarial science; business administration and management; criminal justice/law enforcement administration; finance; marketing/marketing management; medical/clinical assistant; medical insurance/medical billing.
Academics *Calendar:* quarters. *Degrees:* certificates, diplomas, associate, and bachelor's.
Standardized Tests *Required:* Wonderlic Scholastic Level Exam (SLE) (for admission).
Costs (2009–10) *Tuition:* Tuition cost varies by program. Prospective students should contact the school for current tuition costs.
Applying *Application fee:* $50. *Required:* high school transcript, interview. *Application deadlines:* rolling (freshmen), rolling (transfers). *Notification:* continuous (freshmen), continuous (transfers).
Freshman Application Contact Matt Brady, Director of Admissions, Harrison College, 56075 Parkway Avenue, Elkhart, IN 46516. *Phone:* 574-522-0397. *Toll-free phone:* 888-544-4422. *E-mail:* matt.brady@harrison.edu.

HARRISON COLLEGE

Evansville, Indiana **www.harrison.edu/**

- **Proprietary** primarily 2-year
- **Urban** campus
- **Coed,** 212 undergraduate students

Faculty *Total:* 19. *Student/faculty ratio:* 15:1.
Majors Accounting; administrative assistant and secretarial science; business administration and management; criminal justice/safety; finance; health/health-care administration; information technology; marketing/marketing management; medical/clinical assistant; medical insurance coding; medical insurance/medical billing.
Academics *Calendar:* quarters. *Degrees:* certificates, diplomas, associate, and bachelor's. *Special study options:* adult/continuing education programs, cooperative education, distance learning, double majors, independent study, internships, part-time degree program.
Library Main Library plus 1 other.
Standardized Tests *Required:* Wonderlic Scholastic Level Exam (SLE) (for admission).
Costs (2009–10) *Tuition:* Tuition cost varies by program. Prospective students should contact the school for current tuition costs.
Applying *Options:* electronic application. *Application fee:* $50. *Required:* high school transcript, interview. *Application deadlines:* rolling (freshmen), rolling (transfers). *Notification:* continuous (freshmen), continuous (transfers).
Freshman Application Contact Mr. Bryan Barber, Harrison College, 4601 Theater Drive, Evansville, IN 47715. *Phone:* 812-476-6000. *Toll-free phone:* 888-544-4422. *Fax:* 812-471-8576. *E-mail:* bryan.barber@harrison.edu.

HARRISON COLLEGE

Fort Wayne, Indiana **www.harrison.edu/**

- **Proprietary** primarily 2-year
- **Urban** campus
- **Coed,** 561 undergraduate students

Faculty *Student/faculty ratio:* 15:1.
Majors Accounting; administrative assistant and secretarial science; business administration and management; criminal justice/safety; finance; health/health-care administration; information technology; marketing/marketing management; medical/clinical assistant; medical insurance/medical billing; surgical technology.
Academics *Calendar:* quarters. *Degrees:* certificates, diplomas, associate, and bachelor's. *Special study options:* adult/continuing education programs, cooperative education, distance learning, double majors, independent study, internships, part-time degree program.
Library Main Library plus 1 other.
Student Life *Housing:* college housing not available.
Standardized Tests *Required:* Wonderlic Scholastic Level Exam (SLE) (for admission).
Costs (2009–10) *Tuition:* Tuition cost varies by program. Prospective students should contact the school for current tuition costs.
Applying *Options:* electronic application. *Application fee:* $50. *Required:* high school transcript, interview. *Application deadlines:* rolling (freshmen), rolling (transfers). *Notification:* continuous (freshmen), continuous (transfers).
Freshman Application Contact Mr. Matt Wallace, Associate Director of Admissions, Harrison College, 6413 North Clinton Street, Fort Wayne, IN 46825. *Phone:* 260-471-7667. *Toll-free phone:* 888-544-4422. *Fax:* 260-471-6918. *E-mail:* matt.wallace@harrison.edu.

HARRISON COLLEGE

Indianapolis, Indiana **www.harrison.edu/**

- **Proprietary** primarily 2-year, founded 1902
- **Urban** 1-acre campus
- **Coed,** 1,889 undergraduate students

Faculty *Student/faculty ratio:* 16:1.

Harrison College (continued)

Majors Accounting; administrative assistant and secretarial science; baking and pastry arts; business administration and management; computer systems networking and telecommunications; computer technology/computer systems technology; criminal justice/safety; culinary arts; fashion merchandising; finance; health/health-care administration; hotel/motel administration; human resources management; information technology; management information systems and services related; marketing/marketing management; medical/clinical assistant.

Academics *Calendar:* quarters. *Degrees:* certificates, diplomas, associate, and bachelor's. *Special study options:* adult/continuing education programs, cooperative education, distance learning, double majors, internships, part-time degree program, summer session for credit.

Student Life *Housing:* college housing not available. *Activities and Organizations:* Student Advisory Board, Student Ambassadors, Phi Beta Lambda. *Campus security:* 24-hour patrols.

Standardized Tests *Required:* Wonderlic Scholastic Level Exam (SLE) (for admission).

Costs (2009–10) *Tuition:* Tuition cost varies by program. Prospective students should contact the school for current tuition costs.

Applying *Options:* electronic application. *Application fee:* $50. *Required:* high school transcript, interview. *Application deadlines:* rolling (freshmen), rolling (transfers). *Notification:* continuous (freshmen), continuous (transfers).

Freshman Application Contact Mr. Ted Lukomski, Director of Admissions, Harrison College, 550 East Washington Street, Indianapolis, IN 46204. *Phone:* 317-264-5656. *Toll-free phone:* 888-544-4422. *Fax:* 317-264-5650. *E-mail:* ted.lukomski@ibcschools.edu.

HARRISON COLLEGE

Indianapolis, Indiana **www.harrison.edu/**

- **Proprietary** 2-year
- **Urban** campus
- **Coed,** 247 undergraduate students

Faculty *Total:* 14. *Student/faculty ratio:* 15:1.

Majors Computer and information sciences; veterinary/animal health technology.

Academics *Calendar:* quarters. *Degree:* certificates, diplomas, and associate. *Special study options:* adult/continuing education programs.

Student Life *Housing:* college housing not available.

Standardized Tests *Required:* Wonderlic Scholastic Level Exam (for admission).

Costs (2009–10) *Tuition:* Tuition cost varies by program. Prospective students should contact the school for current tuition costs.

Applying *Application fee:* $50. *Required:* high school transcript, interview. *Application deadlines:* rolling (freshmen), rolling (out-of-state freshmen), rolling (transfers). *Notification:* continuous (freshmen), continuous (out-of-state freshmen), continuous (transfers).

Freshman Application Contact Mr. Matt Stein, Director of Admissions, Harrison College, 6300 Technology Center Drive, Indianapolis, IN 46278. *Phone:* 317-873-6500. *Toll-free phone:* 888-544-4422. *Fax:* 317-733-6266. *E-mail:* matthew.stein@harrison.edu.

HARRISON COLLEGE

Indianapolis, Indiana **www.harrison.edu/**

- **Proprietary** 2-year
- **Urban** campus
- **Coed, primarily women,** 458 undergraduate students

Faculty *Total:* 35. *Student/faculty ratio:* 15:1.

Majors Clinical laboratory science/medical technology; health information/medical records technology; massage therapy; medical/clinical assistant; medical insurance coding; nursing (registered nurse training); surgical technology.

Academics *Calendar:* quarters. *Degree:* certificates, diplomas, and associate. *Special study options:* adult/continuing education programs, cooperative education, distance learning, double majors, independent study, internships, part-time degree program.

Student Life *Housing:* college housing not available.

Standardized Tests *Required:* Wonderlic Scholastic Level Exam (SLE) for Associate Degree in Nursing- TEAS Exam (for admission).

Costs (2009–10) *Tuition:* Tuition cost varies by program. Prospective students should contact the school for current tuition costs.

Applying *Options:* electronic application. *Application fee:* $50. *Required:* high school transcript, interview. *Application deadlines:* rolling (freshmen), rolling (transfers). *Notification:* continuous (freshmen), continuous (transfers).

Freshman Application Contact Jan Carter, Director of Admissions, Harrison College, 8150 Brookville Road, Indianapolis, IN 46239. *Phone:* 317-375-8000. *Toll-free phone:* 888-544-4422. *Fax:* 317-351-1871. *E-mail:* jan.carter@harrison.edu.

HARRISON COLLEGE

Lafayette, Indiana **www.harrison.edu/**

- **Proprietary** primarily 2-year
- **Small-town** campus
- **Coed,** 272 undergraduate students

Faculty *Student/faculty ratio:* 15:1.

Majors Accounting; administrative assistant and secretarial science; banking and financial support services; business administration and management; health information/medical records technology; human resources management; marketing/marketing management; medical/clinical assistant; medical insurance coding.

Academics *Calendar:* quarters. *Degrees:* certificates, diplomas, associate, and bachelor's. *Special study options:* adult/continuing education programs, cooperative education, distance learning, double majors, independent study, internships, part-time degree program.

Library Main Library plus 1 other.

Student Life *Housing:* college housing not available.

Standardized Tests *Required:* Wonderlic Scholastic Level Exam (SLE) (for admission).

Costs (2009–10) *Tuition:* Tuition cost varies by program. Prospective students should contact the school for current tuition costs.

Applying *Options:* electronic application. *Application fee:* $50. *Required:* high school transcript, interview. *Application deadlines:* rolling (freshmen), rolling (out-of-state freshmen), rolling (transfers). *Notification:* continuous (freshmen), continuous (out-of-state freshmen), continuous (transfers).

Freshman Application Contact Ms. Stacy Golleher, Associate Director of Admissions, Harrison College, 2 Executive Drive, Lafayette, IN 47905. *Phone:* 765-447-9550. *Toll-free phone:* 888-544-4422. *Fax:* 765-447-0868. *E-mail:* stacy.golleher@harrison.edu.

HARRISON COLLEGE

Muncie, Indiana **www.harrison.edu/**

- **Proprietary** primarily 2-year
- **Small-town** campus
- **Coed, primarily women,** 201 undergraduate students

Faculty *Student/faculty ratio:* 16:1.

Majors Accounting; administrative assistant and secretarial science; business administration and management; business administration, management and operations related; computer and information sciences and support services related; computer technology/computer systems technology; criminal justice/safety; finance; health/health-care administration; health information/medical records technology; human resources management; information technology; management information systems and services related; marketing/marketing management; medical/clinical assistant.

Academics *Calendar:* quarters. *Degrees:* certificates, diplomas, associate, and bachelor's. *Special study options:* adult/continuing education programs, cooperative education, distance learning, double majors, independent study, part-time degree program.

Library Main Library plus 1 other.

Student Life *Housing:* college housing not available. *Activities and Organizations:* Phi Beta Lambda.

Standardized Tests *Required:* Wonderlic Scholastic Level Exam (SLE) (for admission).

Costs (2009–10) *Tuition:* Tuition cost varies by program. Prospective students should contact the school for current tuition costs.

Applying *Options:* electronic application. *Application fee:* $50. *Required:* high school transcript, interview. *Application deadlines:* rolling (freshmen), rolling (transfers). *Notification:* continuous (freshmen), continuous (transfers).

Freshman Application Contact Mr. Jeremy Linder, Associate Director of Admissions, Harrison College, 411 West Riggin Road, Muncie, IN 47303. *Phone:* 765-288-8681. *Toll-free phone:* 888-544-4422. *Fax:* 765-288-8797. *E-mail:* Jeremy.linder@harrison.edu.

HARRISON COLLEGE

Terre Haute, Indiana www.harrison.edu/

- **Proprietary** primarily 2-year, founded 1902
- **Small-town** campus
- **Coed,** 257 undergraduate students

Faculty *Student/faculty ratio:* 15:1.

Majors Accounting; administrative assistant and secretarial science; business administration and management; business administration, management and operations related; finance; health/health-care administration; human resources management; information technology; marketing/marketing management; medical/clinical assistant; medical insurance/medical billing.

Academics *Calendar:* quarters. *Degrees:* certificates, diplomas, associate, and bachelor's. *Special study options:* adult/continuing education programs, cooperative education, distance learning, double majors, independent study, internships, part-time degree program.

Standardized Tests *Required:* Wonderlic Scholastic Level Exam (SLE) (for admission).

Costs (2009–10) *Tuition:* Tuition cost varies by program. Prospective students should contact the school for current tuition costs.

Applying *Options:* electronic application. *Application fee:* $50. *Required:* high school transcript, interview, Wonderlic Scholastic Level Exam. *Application deadlines:* rolling (freshmen), rolling (transfers). *Notification:* continuous (freshmen), continuous (transfers).

Freshman Application Contact Sarah Stultz, Associate Director of Admissions, Harrison College, 3175 South Third Place, Terre Haute, IN 47802. *Phone:* 812-877-2100. *Toll-free phone:* 888-544-4422. *Fax:* 812-877-4440. *E-mail:* sarah.stultz@harrison.edu.

INTERNATIONAL BUSINESS COLLEGE

Indianapolis, Indiana www.ibcindianapolis.edu/

- **Private** 2-year, founded 1889
- **Suburban** campus
- **Coed,** 406 undergraduate students
- 77% of applicants were admitted

Freshmen *Admission:* 951 applied, 731 admitted.

Majors Accounting and business/management; business administration and management; computer programming; dental assisting; graphic design; legal administrative assistant/secretary; legal assistant/paralegal; medical/clinical assistant; system, networking, and LAN/WAN management; tourism and travel services management; veterinary/animal health technology.

Academics *Calendar:* semesters. *Degree:* diplomas and associate. *Special study options:* accelerated degree program, internships.

Freshman Application Contact Admissions Office, International Business College, 7205 Shadeland Station, Indianapolis, IN 46256. *Phone:* 317-813-2300. *Toll-free phone:* 800-589-6500.

ITT TECHNICAL INSTITUTE

Fort Wayne, Indiana www.itt-tech.edu/

- **Proprietary** primarily 2-year, founded 1967, part of ITT Educational Services, Inc.
- **Coed**

Majors Animation, interactive technology, video graphics and special effects; business administration and management; CAD/CADD drafting/design technology; computer and information systems security; computer engineering technology; computer software and media applications related; computer software engineering; computer software technology; computer systems networking and telecommunications; construction management; criminal justice/law enforcement administration; design and visual communications; electrical, electronic and communications engineering technology; industrial technology; legal assistant/paralegal; nursing (registered nurse training); system, networking, and LAN/WAN management; web page, digital/multimedia and information resources design.

Academics *Calendar:* quarters. *Degrees:* associate and bachelor's.

Student Life *Housing:* college housing not available.

Freshman Application Contact Director of Recruitment, ITT Technical Institute, 2810 Dupont Commerce Court, Fort Wayne, IN 46825. *Phone:* 260-497-6200. *Toll-free phone:* 800-866-4488. *Fax:* 260-497-6299.

ITT TECHNICAL INSTITUTE

Indianapolis, Indiana www.itt-tech.edu/

- **Proprietary** founded 1966, part of ITT Educational Services, Inc.
- **Suburban** campus
- **Coed**

Majors Accounting technology and bookkeeping; animation, interactive technology, video graphics and special effects; business administration and management; CAD/CADD drafting/design technology; computer and information sciences; computer and information systems security; computer engineering technology; computer software and media applications related; computer software engineering; computer software technology; construction management; construction trades; criminal justice/law enforcement administration; design and visual communications; electrical, electronic and communications engineering technology; health information/medical records technology; industrial technology; legal assistant/paralegal; nursing (registered nurse training); system, networking, and LAN/WAN management; web/multimedia management and webmaster; web page, digital/multimedia and information resources design.

Academics *Calendar:* quarters. *Degrees:* diplomas, associate, and bachelor's.

Student Life *Housing:* college housing not available.

Freshman Application Contact Director of Recruitment, ITT Technical Institute, 9511 Angola Court, Indianapolis, IN 46268. *Phone:* 317-875-8640. *Toll-free phone:* 800-937-4488.

ITT TECHNICAL INSTITUTE

Merrillville, Indiana www.itt-tech.edu/

- **Proprietary** primarily 2-year
- **Coed**

Majors CAD/CADD drafting/design technology; computer and information systems security; computer engineering technology; construction management; criminal justice/law enforcement administration; electrical, electronic and communications engineering technology; legal assistant/paralegal; system, networking, and LAN/WAN management.

Academics *Degrees:* associate and bachelor's.

Freshman Application Contact Director of Recruitment, ITT Technical Institute, 8488 Georgia Street, Merrillville, IN 46410. *Phone:* 219-738-6100. *Toll-free phone:* 877-418-8134.

ITT TECHNICAL INSTITUTE

Newburgh, Indiana www.itt-tech.edu/

- **Proprietary** primarily 2-year, founded 1966, part of ITT Educational Services, Inc.
- **Coed**

Majors Animation, interactive technology, video graphics and special effects; CAD/CADD drafting/design technology; computer and information systems security; computer engineering technology; computer software and media applications related; computer software engineering; computer software technology; construction management; criminal justice/law enforcement administration; design and visual communications; industrial technology; legal assistant/paralegal; nursing (registered nurse training); system, networking, and LAN/WAN management; web page, digital/multimedia and information resources design.

Academics *Calendar:* quarters. *Degrees:* associate and bachelor's.

Student Life *Housing:* college housing not available.

Freshman Application Contact Director of Recruitment, ITT Technical Institute, 10999 Stahl Road, Newburgh, IN 47630. *Phone:* 812-858-1600. *Toll-free phone:* 800-832-4488.

IVY TECH COMMUNITY COLLEGE–BLOOMINGTON

Bloomington, Indiana www.ivytech.edu/

- **State-supported** 2-year, founded 2001, part of Ivy Tech Community College System
- **Coed,** 4,720 undergraduate students, 47% full-time, 59% women, 41% men

Ivy Tech Community College–Bloomington (continued)

Undergraduates 2,237 full-time, 2,483 part-time. 1% are from out of state, 3% African American, 0.9% Asian American or Pacific Islander, 1% Hispanic American, 0.2% Native American, 1% international, 5% transferred in.

Freshmen *Admission:* 2,141 applied, 2,141 admitted, 1,332 enrolled.

Faculty *Total:* 326, 17% full-time.

Majors Accounting technology and bookkeeping; building/property maintenance and management; business administration and management; business automation/technology/data entry; cabinetmaking and millwork; child-care and support services management; computer and information sciences; criminal justice/safety; early childhood education; electrical, electronic and communications engineering technology; electrician; emergency medical technology (EMT paramedic); executive assistant/executive secretary; general studies; heating, air conditioning, ventilation and refrigeration maintenance technology; human services; industrial technology; legal assistant/paralegal; liberal arts and sciences/liberal studies; library assistant; machine tool technology; mechanic and repair technologies related; mechanics and repair; nursing (registered nurse training); pipefitting and sprinkler fitting; psychiatric/mental health services technology; tool and die technology.

Academics *Calendar:* semesters. *Degree:* certificates and associate. *Special study options:* academic remediation for entering students, adult/continuing education programs, advanced placement credit, distance learning, external degree program, internships, part-time degree program, services for LD students, summer session for credit.

Library 5,516 titles, 97 serial subscriptions, 1,281 audiovisual materials, an OPAC, a Web page.

Student Life *Activities and Organizations:* student government, Phi Theta Kappa. *Campus security:* late-night transport/escort service.

Costs (2010–11) *Tuition:* state resident $105 per credit hour part-time; nonresident $221 per credit hour part-time. *Required fees:* $60 per term part-time.

Financial Aid Of all full-time matriculated undergraduates who enrolled in 2008, 51 Federal Work-Study jobs (averaging $3259).

Applying *Options:* electronic application, deferred entrance. *Required:* high school transcript. *Required for some:* interview. *Application deadlines:* rolling (freshmen), rolling (transfers). *Notification:* continuous (freshmen), continuous (transfers).

Freshman Application Contact Mr. Neil Frederick, Assistant Director of Admissions, Ivy Tech Community College–Bloomington, 200 Daniels Way, Bloomington, IN 47404-1511. *Phone:* 812-330-6026. *Fax:* 812-332-8147. *E-mail:* nfrederi@ivytech.edu.

IVY TECH COMMUNITY COLLEGE–CENTRAL INDIANA

Indianapolis, Indiana **www.ivytech.edu/**

- **State-supported** 2-year, founded 1963, part of Ivy Tech Community College System
- **Urban** 10-acre campus
- **Coed,** 21,501 undergraduate students, 33% full-time, 58% women, 42% men

Undergraduates 7,053 full-time, 14,448 part-time. 1% are from out of state, 25% African American, 2% Asian American or Pacific Islander, 4% Hispanic American, 0.4% Native American, 7% transferred in.

Freshmen *Admission:* 4,598 enrolled.

Faculty *Total:* 705, 22% full-time.

Majors Accounting technology and bookkeeping; automobile/automotive mechanics technology; biotechnology; building/property maintenance and management; business administration and management; business automation/technology/data entry; cabinetmaking and millwork; carpentry; child-care and support services management; child development; computer and information sciences; criminal justice/safety; design and visual communications; drafting and design technology; early childhood education; electrical, electronic and communications engineering technology; electrician; executive assistant/executive secretary; general studies; heating, air conditioning, ventilation and refrigeration maintenance technology; hospitality administration related; human services; industrial production technologies related; industrial technology; legal assistant/paralegal; liberal arts and sciences/liberal studies; machine shop technology; machine tool technology; masonry; mechanics and repair; medical/clinical assistant; medical radiologic technology; nursing (registered nurse training); occupational safety and health technology; occupational therapist assistant; painting and wall covering; pipefitting and sprinkler fitting; psychiatric/mental health services technology; respiratory care therapy; sheet metal technology; surgical technology; tool and die technology.

Academics *Calendar:* semesters. *Degree:* certificates and associate. *Special study options:* academic remediation for entering students, adult/continuing education programs, advanced placement credit, cooperative education, distance learning, English as a second language, internships, off-campus study, part-time degree program, services for LD students, summer session for credit.

Library 20,247 titles, 138 serial subscriptions, 2,135 audiovisual materials, an OPAC, a Web page.

Student Life *Housing:* college housing not available. *Activities and Organizations:* student-run newspaper, student government, Phi Theta Kappa, Human Services Club, Administrative Office Assistants Club, Radiology Club. *Campus security:* 24-hour emergency response devices and patrols, late-night transport/escort service. *Student services:* personal/psychological counseling.

Athletics *Intramural sports:* baseball M, basketball M/W, cheerleading W, golf M/W, softball W, volleyball M/W.

Costs (2010–11) *Tuition:* state resident $105 per credit hour part-time; nonresident $221 per credit hour part-time. *Required fees:* $60 per term part-time.

Financial Aid Of all full-time matriculated undergraduates who enrolled in 2008, 92 Federal Work-Study jobs (averaging $3766).

Applying *Options:* electronic application, early admission, deferred entrance. *Required:* high school transcript. *Required for some:* interview. *Application deadlines:* rolling (freshmen), rolling (transfers). *Notification:* continuous (freshmen), continuous (transfers).

Freshman Application Contact Ms. Tracy Funk, Director of Admissions, Ivy Tech Community College–Central Indiana, One West 26th Street, Indianapolis, IN 46208-4777. *Phone:* 317-921-4371. *Toll-free phone:* 888-IVYLINE. *Fax:* 317-917-5919. *E-mail:* tfunk@ivytech.edu.

IVY TECH COMMUNITY COLLEGE–COLUMBUS

Columbus, Indiana **www.ivytech.edu/**

- **State-supported** 2-year, founded 1963, part of Ivy Tech Community College System
- **Small-town** campus with easy access to Indianapolis
- **Coed,** 4,944 undergraduate students, 39% full-time, 69% women, 31% men

Undergraduates 1,940 full-time, 3,004 part-time. 2% African American, 0.7% Asian American or Pacific Islander, 1% Hispanic American, 0.4% Native American, 6% transferred in.

Freshmen *Admission:* 1,116 enrolled.

Faculty *Total:* 259, 19% full-time.

Majors Accounting technology and bookkeeping; automobile/automotive mechanics technology; building/property maintenance and management; business administration and management; business automation/technology/data entry; cabinetmaking and millwork; child-care and support services management; computer and information sciences; design and visual communications; drafting and design technology; early childhood education; electrical and power transmission installation; electrical, electronic and communications engineering technology; executive assistant/executive secretary; general studies; heating, air conditioning, ventilation and refrigeration maintenance technology; human services; industrial technology; legal assistant/paralegal; liberal arts and sciences/liberal studies; library assistant; machine tool technology; masonry; mechanic and repair technologies related; mechanics and repair; medical/clinical assistant; medical radiologic technology; pipefitting and sprinkler fitting; psychiatric/mental health services technology; robotics technology; surgical technology; tool and die technology.

Academics *Calendar:* semesters. *Degree:* certificates and associate. *Special study options:* academic remediation for entering students, adult/continuing education programs, advanced placement credit, distance learning, internships, part-time degree program, services for LD students, summer session for credit.

Library 7,855 titles, 13,382 serial subscriptions, 989 audiovisual materials, an OPAC, a Web page.

Student Life *Housing:* college housing not available. *Activities and Organizations:* student government, Phi Theta Kappa, LPN Club. *Campus security:* late-night transport/escort service, trained evening security personnel, escort service.

Costs (2010–11) *Tuition:* state resident $105 per credit hour part-time; nonresident $221 per credit hour part-time. *Required fees:* $60 per term part-time.

Financial Aid Of all full-time matriculated undergraduates who enrolled in 2008, 26 Federal Work-Study jobs (averaging $1694).

Applying *Options:* electronic application, early admission, deferred entrance. *Required:* high school transcript. *Required for some:* interview. *Application deadlines:* rolling (freshmen), rolling (transfers). *Notification:* continuous (freshmen), continuous (transfers).

Freshman Application Contact Mr. Neil Bagadiong, Assistant Director of Student Affairs, Ivy Tech Community College–Columbus, 4475 Central Avenue, Columbus, IN 47203-1868. *Phone:* 812-374-5129. *Toll-free phone:* 800-922-4838. *Fax:* 812-372-0331. *E-mail:* nbagadio@ivytech.edu.

Ivy Tech Community College–East Central

Muncie, Indiana **www.ivytech.edu/**

- **State-supported** 2-year, founded 1968, part of Ivy Tech Community College System
- **Suburban** 15-acre campus with easy access to Indianapolis
- **Coed,** 8,579 undergraduate students, 47% full-time, 64% women, 36% men

Undergraduates 4,069 full-time, 4,510 part-time. 7% African American, 0.4% Asian American or Pacific Islander, 1% Hispanic American, 0.4% Native American, 5% transferred in.

Freshmen *Admission:* 2,099 enrolled.

Faculty *Total:* 486, 19% full-time.

Majors Accounting technology and bookkeeping; automobile/automotive mechanics technology; building/property maintenance and management; business administration and management; business automation/technology/data entry; cabinetmaking and millwork; carpentry; child-care and support services management; computer and information sciences; construction trades; construction trades related; criminal justice/safety; early childhood education; electrical, electronic and communications engineering technology; electrician; executive assistant/executive secretary; general studies; heating, air conditioning, ventilation and refrigeration maintenance technology; hospitality administration; hospitality administration related; human services; industrial mechanics and maintenance technology; industrial production technologies related; industrial technology; legal assistant/paralegal; liberal arts and sciences/liberal studies; library assistant; machine tool technology; masonry; medical/clinical assistant; medical radiologic technology; nursing (registered nurse training); painting and wall covering; physical therapist assistant; pipefitting and sprinkler fitting; psychiatric/mental health services technology; surgical technology; tool and die technology.

Academics *Calendar:* semesters. *Degree:* certificates and associate. *Special study options:* academic remediation for entering students, adult/continuing education programs, advanced placement credit, distance learning, internships, part-time degree program, services for LD students.

Library 5,779 titles, 145 serial subscriptions, 6,266 audiovisual materials, an OPAC, a Web page.

Student Life *Housing:* college housing not available. *Activities and Organizations:* Business Professionals of America, Skills USA - VICA, student government, Phi Theta Kappa, Human Services Club.

Costs (2010–11) *Tuition:* state resident $105 per credit hour part-time; nonresident $231 per credit hour part-time. *Required fees:* $60 per term part-time.

Financial Aid Of all full-time matriculated undergraduates who enrolled in 2008, 65 Federal Work-Study jobs (averaging $2666).

Applying *Options:* electronic application, early admission, deferred entrance. *Required:* high school transcript. *Required for some:* interview. *Application deadlines:* rolling (freshmen), rolling (transfers). *Notification:* continuous (freshmen), continuous (transfers).

Freshman Application Contact Ms. Mary Lewellen, Ivy Tech Community College–East Central, 4301 South Cowan Road, Muncie, IN 47302-9448. *Phone:* 765-289-2291 Ext. 391. *Toll-free phone:* 800-589-8324. *Fax:* 765-289-2292. *E-mail:* mlewelle@ivytech.edu.

Ivy Tech Community College–Kokomo

Kokomo, Indiana **www.ivytech.edu/**

- **State-supported** 2-year, founded 1968, part of Ivy Tech Community College System
- **Small-town** 20-acre campus with easy access to Indianapolis
- **Coed,** 5,434 undergraduate students, 42% full-time, 65% women, 35% men

Undergraduates 2,265 full-time, 3,169 part-time. 6% African American, 0.4% Asian American or Pacific Islander, 2% Hispanic American, 0.7% Native American, 4% transferred in.

Freshmen *Admission:* 997 enrolled.

Faculty *Total:* 320, 21% full-time.

Majors Accounting technology and bookkeeping; automobile/automotive mechanics technology; building/property maintenance and management; business administration and management; business automation/technology/data entry; cabinetmaking and millwork; child-care and support services management; computer and information sciences; construction trades related; criminal justice/safety; drafting and design technology; early childhood education; electrical, electronic and communications engineering technology; electrician; emergency medical technology (EMT paramedic); executive assistant/executive secretary; general studies; heating, air conditioning, ventilation and refrigeration maintenance technology; human services; industrial technology; legal assistant/paralegal; liberal arts and sciences/liberal studies; library assistant; machine tool technology; mechanic and repair technologies related; mechanics and repair; medical/clinical assistant; pipefitting and sprinkler fitting; psychiatric/mental health services technology; surgical technology; tool and die technology.

Academics *Calendar:* semesters. *Degree:* certificates and associate. *Special study options:* academic remediation for entering students, adult/continuing education programs, advanced placement credit, distance learning, internships, part-time degree program, services for LD students, summer session for credit.

Library 5,177 titles, 99 serial subscriptions, 772 audiovisual materials, an OPAC, a Web page.

Student Life *Housing:* college housing not available. *Activities and Organizations:* student-run newspaper, student government, Collegiate Secretaries International, Licensed Practical Nursing Club, Phi Theta Kappa. *Campus security:* 24-hour emergency response devices, late-night transport/escort service. *Student services:* personal/psychological counseling.

Costs (2010–11) *Tuition:* state resident $105 per credit hour part-time; nonresident $221 per credit hour part-time. *Required fees:* $60 per term part-time.

Financial Aid Of all full-time matriculated undergraduates who enrolled in 2008, 45 Federal Work-Study jobs (averaging $1829).

Applying *Options:* electronic application, early admission. *Required:* high school transcript. *Required for some:* interview. *Application deadlines:* rolling (freshmen), rolling (transfers). *Notification:* continuous (freshmen), continuous (transfers).

Freshman Application Contact Ms. Suzanne Dillman, Director of Admissions, Ivy Tech Community College–Kokomo, 1815 East Morgan Street, Kokomo, IN 46903-1373. *Phone:* 765-459-0561 Ext. 318. *Toll-free phone:* 800-459-0561. *Fax:* 765-454-5111. *E-mail:* sdillman@ivytech.edu.

Ivy Tech Community College–Lafayette

Lafayette, Indiana **www.ivytech.edu/**

- **State-supported** 2-year, founded 1968, part of Ivy Tech Community College System
- **Suburban** campus with easy access to Indianapolis
- **Coed,** 8,305 undergraduate students, 45% full-time, 53% women, 47% men

Undergraduates 3,768 full-time, 4,537 part-time. 4% African American, 1% Asian American or Pacific Islander, 4% Hispanic American, 0.6% Native American, 6% transferred in.

Freshmen *Admission:* 1,784 enrolled.

Faculty *Total:* 376, 23% full-time.

Majors Accounting; accounting technology and bookkeeping; automobile/automotive mechanics technology; biotechnology; building/property maintenance and management; business administration and management; business automation/technology/data entry; cabinetmaking and millwork; carpentry; child-care and support services management; computer and information sciences; drafting and design technology; early childhood education; electrical, electronic and communications engineering technology; electrician; executive assistant/executive secretary; general studies; heating, air conditioning, ventilation and refrigeration maintenance technology; human services; industrial production technologies related; industrial technology; ironworking; legal assistant/paralegal; liberal arts and sciences/liberal studies; library assistant; lineworker; machine tool technology; masonry; mechanic and repair technologies related; mechanics and repair; medical/clinical assistant; nursing (registered nurse training); painting and wall covering; pipefitting and sprinkler fitting; psychiatric/mental health services technology; quality control and safety technologies related; quality control technology; respiratory care therapy; robotics technology; sheet metal technology; surgical technology; tool and die technology.

Academics *Calendar:* semesters. *Degree:* certificates and associate. *Special study options:* academic remediation for entering students, advanced placement credit, distance learning, internships, part-time degree program, services for LD students, summer session for credit.

Library 8,043 titles, 200 serial subscriptions, 2,234 audiovisual materials, an OPAC, a Web page.

Student Life *Housing:* college housing not available. *Activities and Organizations:* student-run newspaper, student government, Phi Theta Kappa, LPN Club, Accounting Club, Student Computer Technology Association. *Student services:* personal/psychological counseling.

Costs (2010–11) *Tuition:* state resident $105 per credit hour part-time; nonresident $221 per credit hour part-time. *Required fees:* $60 per term part-time.

Financial Aid Of all full-time matriculated undergraduates who enrolled in 2008, 65 Federal Work-Study jobs (averaging $2222). 1 state and other part-time job (averaging $2436).

Ivy Tech Community College–Lafayette (continued)

Applying *Options:* electronic application. *Required:* high school transcript. *Required for some:* interview. *Application deadlines:* rolling (freshmen), rolling (transfers). *Notification:* continuous (freshmen), continuous (transfers).

Freshman Application Contact Ms. Judy Doppelfeld, Director of Admissions, Ivy Tech Community College–Lafayette, 3101 South Creagy Lane, PO Box 6299, Lafayette, IN 47903. *Phone:* 765-269-5116. *Toll-free phone:* 800-669-4882. *Fax:* 765-772-9293. *E-mail:* jdopplef@ivytech.edu.

Ivy Tech Community College–North Central

South Bend, Indiana **www.ivytech.edu/**

- **State-supported** 2-year, founded 1968, part of Ivy Tech Community College System
- **Suburban** 4-acre campus
- **Coed,** 8,665 undergraduate students, 32% full-time, 59% women, 41% men

Undergraduates 2,765 full-time, 5,900 part-time. 2% are from out of state, 15% African American, 1% Asian American or Pacific Islander, 5% Hispanic American, 0.4% Native American, 6% transferred in.

Freshmen *Admission:* 1,684 enrolled.

Faculty *Total:* 370, 22% full-time.

Majors Accounting technology and bookkeeping; automobile/automotive mechanics technology; biotechnology; building/property maintenance and management; business administration and management; business automation/technology/data entry; cabinetmaking and millwork; carpentry; child-care and support services management; clinical/medical laboratory technology; computer and information sciences; criminal justice/safety; design and visual communications; early childhood education; educational/instructional media design; electrical, electronic and communications engineering technology; electrician; emergency medical technology (EMT paramedic); executive assistant/executive secretary; general studies; heating, air conditioning, ventilation and refrigeration maintenance technology; hospitality administration; human services; industrial production technologies related; industrial technology; interior design; ironworking; legal assistant/paralegal; liberal arts and sciences/liberal studies; library assistant; machine tool technology; masonry; mechanic and repair technologies related; mechanics and repair; medical/clinical assistant; nursing (registered nurse training); painting and wall covering; pipefitting and sprinkler fitting; robotics technology; sheet metal technology; telecommunications technology; tool and die technology.

Academics *Calendar:* semesters. *Degree:* certificates and associate. *Special study options:* academic remediation for entering students, adult/continuing education programs, advanced placement credit, distance learning, English as a second language, internships, off-campus study, part-time degree program, services for LD students, summer session for credit.

Library 6,246 titles, 90 serial subscriptions, 689 audiovisual materials, an OPAC, a Web page.

Student Life *Housing:* college housing not available. *Activities and Organizations:* Phi Theta Kappa, student government, LPN Club. *Campus security:* 24-hour emergency response devices and patrols, late-night transport/escort service, security during open hours. *Student services:* personal/psychological counseling, women's center.

Costs (2010–11) *Tuition:* state resident $105 per credit hour part-time; nonresident $221 per credit hour part-time. *Required fees:* $60 per term part-time.

Financial Aid Of all full-time matriculated undergraduates who enrolled in 2008, 100 Federal Work-Study jobs (averaging $1538).

Applying *Options:* electronic application, early admission, deferred entrance. *Required:* high school transcript. *Required for some:* interview. *Application deadlines:* rolling (freshmen), rolling (transfers). *Notification:* continuous (freshmen), continuous (transfers).

Freshman Application Contact Ms. Pam Decker, Director of Admissions, Ivy Tech Community College–North Central, 220 Dean Johnson Boulevard, South Bend, IN 46601-3415. *Phone:* 574-289-7001. *Fax:* 574-236-7177. *E-mail:* pdecker@ivytech.edu.

Ivy Tech Community College–Northeast

Fort Wayne, Indiana **www.ivytech.edu/**

- **State-supported** 2-year, founded 1969, part of Ivy Tech Community College System
- **Urban** 22-acre campus
- **Coed,** 11,497 undergraduate students, 41% full-time, 59% women, 41% men

Undergraduates 4,771 full-time, 6,726 part-time. 3% are from out of state, 15% African American, 2% Asian American or Pacific Islander, 4% Hispanic American, 0.6% Native American, 6% transferred in.

Freshmen *Admission:* 2,453 enrolled.

Faculty *Total:* 496, 23% full-time.

Majors Accounting technology and bookkeeping; automobile/automotive mechanics technology; building/property maintenance and management; business administration and management; business automation/technology/data entry; cabinetmaking and millwork; child-care and support services management; computer and information sciences; construction trades; construction trades related; drafting and design technology; early childhood education; electrical, electronic and communications engineering technology; electrician; executive assistant/executive secretary; general studies; heating, air conditioning, ventilation and refrigeration maintenance technology; hospitality administration; hospitality administration related; human services; industrial production technologies related; industrial technology; ironworking; legal assistant/paralegal; liberal arts and sciences/liberal studies; library assistant; machine tool technology; masonry; massage therapy; mechanics and repair; medical/clinical assistant; occupational safety and health technology; painting and wall covering; pipefitting and sprinkler fitting; psychiatric/mental health services technology; respiratory care therapy; robotics technology; sheet metal technology; tool and die technology.

Academics *Calendar:* semesters. *Degree:* certificates and associate. *Special study options:* adult/continuing education programs, advanced placement credit, distance learning, English as a second language, internships, part-time degree program, services for LD students, summer session for credit.

Library 18,389 titles, 110 serial subscriptions, 3,397 audiovisual materials, an OPAC, a Web page.

Student Life *Housing:* college housing not available. *Activities and Organizations:* student-run newspaper, student government, LPN Club, Phi Theta Kappa. *Campus security:* 24-hour emergency response devices and patrols, late-night transport/escort service.

Costs (2010–11) *Tuition:* state resident $105 per credit hour part-time; nonresident $221 per credit hour part-time. *Required fees:* $60 per term part-time.

Financial Aid Of all full-time matriculated undergraduates who enrolled in 2008, 40 Federal Work-Study jobs (averaging $4041).

Applying *Options:* early admission. *Required:* high school transcript. *Required for some:* interview. *Application deadlines:* rolling (freshmen), rolling (transfers). *Notification:* continuous (freshmen), continuous (transfers).

Freshman Application Contact Mr. Steve Scheer, Director of Admissions, Ivy Tech Community College–Northeast, 3800 North Anthony Boulevard, Ft. Wayne, IN 46805-1489. *Phone:* 260-480-4221. *Toll-free phone:* 800-859-4882. *Fax:* 260-480-2053. *E-mail:* sscheer@ivytech.edu.

Ivy Tech Community College–Northwest

Gary, Indiana **www.ivytech.edu/**

- **State-supported** 2-year, founded 1963, part of Ivy Tech Community College System
- **Urban** 13-acre campus with easy access to Chicago
- **Coed,** 9,301 undergraduate students, 38% full-time, 61% women, 39% men

Undergraduates 3,518 full-time, 5,783 part-time. 25% African American, 0.6% Asian American or Pacific Islander, 10% Hispanic American, 0.3% Native American, 8% transferred in. *Retention:* 53% of 2008 full-time freshmen returned.

Freshmen *Admission:* 2,189 enrolled.

Faculty *Total:* 383, 28% full-time.

Majors Accounting technology and bookkeeping; automobile/automotive mechanics technology; building/construction finishing, management, and inspection related; building/property maintenance and management; business administration and management; business automation/technology/data entry; cabinetmaking and millwork; carpentry; child-care and support services management; computer and information sciences; construction trades; criminal justice/safety; drafting and design technology; early childhood education; electrical, electronic and communications engineering technology; electrician; executive assistant/executive secretary; funeral service and mortuary science; general studies; heating, air conditioning, ventilation and refrigeration maintenance technology; hospitality administration; human services; industrial technology; ironworking; legal assistant/paralegal; liberal arts and sciences/liberal studies; library assistant; machine tool technology; masonry; mechanic and repair technologies related; mechanics and repair; medical/clinical assistant; nursing (registered nurse training); occupational safety and health technology; painting and wall covering; pipefitting and sprinkler fitting; psychiatric/mental health services technology; respiratory care therapy; sheet metal technology; surgical technology; telecommunications technology; tool and die technology.

Academics *Calendar:* semesters. *Degree:* certificates and associate. *Special study options:* academic remediation for entering students, adult/continuing education programs, advanced placement credit, distance learning, internships, part-time degree program, services for LD students, summer session for credit.

Library 13,805 titles, 160 serial subscriptions, 4,295 audiovisual materials, an OPAC, a Web page.

Student Life *Housing:* college housing not available. *Activities and Organizations:* Phi Theta Kappa, LPN Club, Computer Club, student government, Business Club. *Campus security:* 24-hour emergency response devices, late-night transport/escort service.

Costs (2010–11) *Tuition:* state resident $105 per credit hour part-time; nonresident $221 per credit hour part-time. *Required fees:* $60 per term part-time.

Financial Aid Of all full-time matriculated undergraduates who enrolled in 2008, 74 Federal Work-Study jobs (averaging $2131).

Applying *Options:* electronic application, deferred entrance. *Required:* high school transcript. *Required for some:* interview. *Application deadlines:* rolling (freshmen), rolling (transfers). *Notification:* continuous (freshmen), continuous (transfers).

Freshman Application Contact Ms. Twilla Lewis, Associate Dean of Student Affairs, Ivy Tech Community College–Northwest, 1440 East 35th Avenue, Gary, IN 46409-1499. *Phone:* 219-981-1111 Ext. 2273. *Toll-free phone:* 800-843-4882. *Fax:* 219-981-4415. *E-mail:* tlewis@ivytech.edu.

Ivy Tech Community College–Richmond

Richmond, Indiana **www.ivytech.edu/richmond/**

- **State-supported** 2-year, founded 1963, part of Ivy Tech Community College System
- **Small-town** 23-acre campus with easy access to Indianapolis
- **Coed,** 3,785 undergraduate students, 36% full-time, 67% women, 33% men

Undergraduates 1,347 full-time, 2,438 part-time. 7% are from out of state, 4% African American, 0.3% Asian American or Pacific Islander, 1% Hispanic American, 0.5% Native American, 5% transferred in.

Freshmen *Admission:* 692 enrolled.

Faculty *Total:* 171, 20% full-time.

Majors Accounting technology and bookkeeping; automobile/automotive mechanics technology; building/property maintenance and management; business administration and management; business automation/technology/data entry; cabinetmaking and millwork; child-care and support services management; computer and information sciences; construction trades; construction trades related; early childhood education; electrical, electronic and communications engineering technology; electrician; executive assistant/executive secretary; general studies; heating, air conditioning, ventilation and refrigeration maintenance technology; human services; industrial production technologies related; industrial technology; legal assistant/paralegal; liberal arts and sciences/liberal studies; library assistant; machine tool technology; mechanics and repair; medical/clinical assistant; nursing (registered nurse training); pipefitting and sprinkler fitting; psychiatric/mental health services technology; robotics technology; tool and die technology.

Academics *Calendar:* semesters. *Degree:* certificates and associate. *Special study options:* academic remediation for entering students, adult/continuing education programs, advanced placement credit, distance learning, independent study, internships, off-campus study, part-time degree program, services for LD students, summer session for credit.

Student Life *Housing:* college housing not available. *Activities and Organizations:* student-run newspaper, student government, Phi Theta Kappa, LPN Club, CATS 2000, Business Professionals of America. *Campus security:* 24-hour emergency response devices, late-night transport/escort service. *Student services:* personal/psychological counseling.

Athletics *Intramural sports:* softball M/W.

Costs (2010–11) *Tuition:* state resident $105 per credit hour part-time; nonresident $221 per credit hour part-time. *Required fees:* $60 per term part-time.

Financial Aid Of all full-time matriculated undergraduates who enrolled in 2008, 14 Federal Work-Study jobs (averaging $3106). 1 state and other part-time job (averaging $3380).

Applying *Options:* electronic application, early admission. *Required:* high school transcript. *Required for some:* interview. *Application deadlines:* rolling (freshmen), rolling (transfers). *Notification:* continuous (freshmen), continuous (transfers).

Freshman Application Contact Mr. Jeff Plasterer, Director of Admissions, Ivy Tech Community College–Richmond, 2325 Chester Boulevard, Richmond, IN 47374-1298. *Phone:* 765-966-2656 Ext. 1212. *Toll-free phone:* 800-659-4562. *Fax:* 765-962-8741. *E-mail:* jplaster@ivytech.edu.

Ivy Tech Community College–Southeast

Madison, Indiana **www.ivytech.edu/**

- **State-supported** 2-year, founded 1963, part of Ivy Tech Community College System
- **Small-town** 5-acre campus with easy access to Louisville
- **Coed,** 3,080 undergraduate students, 39% full-time, 70% women, 30% men

Undergraduates 1,213 full-time, 1,867 part-time. 4% are from out of state, 0.8% African American, 0.4% Asian American or Pacific Islander, 0.6% Hispanic American, 0.3% Native American, 5% transferred in.

Freshmen *Admission:* 554 enrolled.

Faculty *Total:* 175, 23% full-time.

Majors Accounting technology and bookkeeping; business administration and management; business automation/technology/data entry; child-care and support services management; computer and information sciences; early childhood education; electrical, electronic and communications engineering technology; executive assistant/executive secretary; general studies; human services; industrial technology; legal assistant/paralegal; liberal arts and sciences/liberal studies; library assistant; medical/clinical assistant; nursing (licensed practical/vocational nurse training); nursing (registered nurse training); psychiatric/mental health services technology.

Academics *Calendar:* semesters. *Degree:* certificates and associate. *Special study options:* academic remediation for entering students, advanced placement credit, distance learning, internships, part-time degree program, services for LD students, summer session for credit.

Library 9,027 titles, 14,299 serial subscriptions, 1,341 audiovisual materials, an OPAC, a Web page.

Student Life *Housing:* college housing not available. *Activities and Organizations:* student government, Phi Theta Kappa, LPN Club. *Campus security:* 24-hour emergency response devices.

Costs (2010–11) *Tuition:* state resident $105 per credit hour part-time; nonresident $221 per credit hour part-time. *Required fees:* $60 per term part-time.

Financial Aid Of all full-time matriculated undergraduates who enrolled in 2008, 26 Federal Work-Study jobs (averaging $1696).

Applying *Options:* electronic application. *Required:* high school transcript. *Required for some:* interview. *Application deadlines:* rolling (freshmen), rolling (transfers). *Notification:* continuous (freshmen), continuous (transfers).

Freshman Application Contact Ms. Cindy Hutcherson, Assistant Director of Admission/Career Counselor, Ivy Tech Community College–Southeast, 590 Ivy Tech Drive, Madison, IN 47250-1881. *Phone:* 812-265-2580 Ext. 4142. *Toll-free phone:* 800-403-2190. *Fax:* 812-265-4028. *E-mail:* chutcher@ivytech.edu.

Ivy Tech Community College–Southern Indiana

Sellersburg, Indiana **www.ivytech.edu/**

- **State-supported** 2-year, founded 1968, part of Ivy Tech Community College System
- **Small-town** 63-acre campus with easy access to Louisville
- **Coed,** 4,843 undergraduate students, 38% full-time, 55% women, 45% men

Undergraduates 1,861 full-time, 2,982 part-time. 9% are from out of state, 6% African American, 0.6% Asian American or Pacific Islander, 1% Hispanic American, 0.4% Native American, 7% transferred in.

Freshmen *Admission:* 1,278 enrolled.

Faculty *Total:* 196, 26% full-time.

Majors Accounting technology and bookkeeping; automobile/automotive mechanics technology; building/property maintenance and management; business administration and management; business automation/technology/data entry; cabinetmaking and millwork; carpentry; child-care and support services management; computer and information sciences; design and visual communications; early childhood education; electrical, electronic and communications engineering technology; electrician; executive assistant/executive secretary; general studies; heating, air conditioning, ventilation and refrigeration maintenance technology; human services; industrial technology; legal assistant/paralegal; liberal arts and sciences/liberal studies; library assistant; machine tool technology; masonry; mechanics and repair; medical/clinical assistant; nursing (registered nurse training); pipefitting and sprinkler fitting; psychiatric/mental health services technology; respiratory care therapy; sheet metal technology; tool and die technology.

Ivy Tech Community College–Southern Indiana (continued)

Academics *Calendar:* semesters. *Degree:* certificates and associate. *Special study options:* academic remediation for entering students, adult/continuing education programs, advanced placement credit, cooperative education, distance learning, internships, part-time degree program, services for LD students, summer session for credit.

Library 7,634 titles, 66 serial subscriptions, 648 audiovisual materials, an OPAC, a Web page.

Student Life *Housing:* college housing not available. *Activities and Organizations:* Phi Theta Kappa, Practical Nursing Club, Medical Assistant Club, Accounting Club, student government. *Campus security:* late-night transport/escort service.

Costs (2010–11) *Tuition:* state resident $105 per credit hour part-time; nonresident $221 per credit hour part-time. *Required fees:* $60 per term part-time.

Financial Aid Of all full-time matriculated undergraduates who enrolled in 2008, 20 Federal Work-Study jobs (averaging $5007). 1 state and other part-time job (averaging $6080).

Applying *Options:* electronic application, early admission, deferred entrance. *Required:* high school transcript. *Required for some:* interview. *Application deadlines:* rolling (freshmen), rolling (transfers). *Notification:* continuous (freshmen), continuous (transfers).

Freshman Application Contact Ms. Mindy Steinberg, Director of Admissions, Ivy Tech Community College–Southern Indiana, 8204 Highway 311, Sellersburg, IN 47172-1897. *Phone:* 812-246-3301. *Toll-free phone:* 800-321-9021. *Fax:* 812-246-9905. *E-mail:* msteinbe@ivytech.edu.

Ivy Tech Community College–Southwest

Evansville, Indiana **www.ivytech.edu/**

- **State-supported** 2-year, founded 1963, part of Ivy Tech Community College System
- **Suburban** 15-acre campus
- **Coed,** 6,501 undergraduate students, 37% full-time, 55% women, 45% men

Undergraduates 2,402 full-time, 4,099 part-time. 3% are from out of state, 9% African American, 0.7% Asian American or Pacific Islander, 0.9% Hispanic American, 0.3% Native American, 7% transferred in.

Freshmen *Admission:* 1,361 enrolled.

Faculty *Total:* 328, 24% full-time.

Majors Accounting technology and bookkeeping; automobile/automotive mechanics technology; boilermaking; building/property maintenance and management; business administration and management; business automation/technology/data entry; cabinetmaking and millwork; carpentry; child-care and support services management; computer and information sciences; construction/heavy equipment/earthmoving equipment operation; criminal justice/safety; design and visual communications; early childhood education; electrical, electronic and communications engineering technology; electrician; emergency medical technology (EMT paramedic); executive assistant/executive secretary; general studies; graphic design; heating, air conditioning, ventilation and refrigeration maintenance technology; human services; industrial production technologies related; industrial technology; interior design; ironworking; legal assistant/paralegal; liberal arts and sciences/liberal studies; library assistant; machine tool technology; masonry; mechanic and repair technologies related; mechanics and repair; medical/clinical assistant; nursing (registered nurse training); painting and wall covering; pipefitting and sprinkler fitting; psychiatric/mental health services technology; robotics technology; sheet metal technology; surgical technology; tool and die technology.

Academics *Calendar:* semesters. *Degree:* certificates and associate. *Special study options:* academic remediation for entering students, advanced placement credit, cooperative education, distance learning, independent study, internships, part-time degree program, services for LD students, summer session for credit.

Library 7,082 titles, 107 serial subscriptions, 1,755 audiovisual materials, an OPAC, a Web page.

Student Life *Housing:* college housing not available. *Activities and Organizations:* student government, Phi Theta Kappa, LPN Club, National Association of Industrial Technology, Design Club. *Campus security:* late-night transport/escort service.

Costs (2010–11) *Tuition:* state resident $105 per credit hour part-time; nonresident $221 per credit hour part-time. *Required fees:* $60 per term part-time.

Financial Aid Of all full-time matriculated undergraduates who enrolled in 2008, 65 Federal Work-Study jobs (averaging $2264).

Applying *Options:* electronic application, early admission, deferred entrance. *Required:* high school transcript. *Required for some:* interview. *Application deadlines:* rolling (freshmen), rolling (transfers). *Notification:* continuous (freshmen), continuous (transfers).

Freshman Application Contact Ms. Denise Johnson-Kincade, Director of Admissions, Ivy Tech Community College–Southwest, 3501 First Avenue, Evansville, IN 47710-3398. *Phone:* 812-429-1430. *Fax:* 812-429-9878. *E-mail:* ajohnson@ivytech.edu.

Ivy Tech Community College–Wabash Valley

Terre Haute, Indiana **www.ivytech.edu/**

- **State-supported** 2-year, founded 1966, part of Ivy Tech Community College System
- **Suburban** 55-acre campus with easy access to Indianapolis
- **Coed,** 6,646 undergraduate students, 42% full-time, 59% women, 41% men

Undergraduates 2,784 full-time, 3,862 part-time. 4% are from out of state, 4% African American, 0.5% Asian American or Pacific Islander, 0.8% Hispanic American, 0.4% Native American, 6% transferred in.

Freshmen *Admission:* 1,113 enrolled.

Faculty *Total:* 285, 29% full-time.

Majors Accounting technology and bookkeeping; airframe mechanics and aircraft maintenance technology; allied health diagnostic, intervention, and treatment professions related; automobile/automotive mechanics technology; building/property maintenance and management; business administration and management; cabinetmaking and millwork; carpentry; child-care and support services management; clinical/medical laboratory technology; computer and information sciences; construction/heavy equipment/earthmoving equipment operation; criminal justice/safety; design and visual communications; early childhood education; electrical, electronic and communications engineering technology; electrician; emergency medical technology (EMT paramedic); executive assistant/executive secretary; general studies; heating, air conditioning, ventilation and refrigeration maintenance technology; human services; industrial production technologies related; industrial technology; ironworking; legal assistant/paralegal; liberal arts and sciences/liberal studies; library assistant; machine tool technology; masonry; mechanics and repair; medical/clinical assistant; medical radiologic technology; nursing (registered nurse training); occupational safety and health technology; office management; painting and wall covering; pipefitting and sprinkler fitting; psychiatric/mental health services technology; quality control and safety technologies related; robotics technology; sheet metal technology; surgical technology; tool and die technology.

Academics *Calendar:* semesters. *Degree:* certificates and associate. *Special study options:* academic remediation for entering students, adult/continuing education programs, advanced placement credit, distance learning, internships, part-time degree program, services for LD students, summer session for credit.

Library 4,403 titles, 77 serial subscriptions, 406 audiovisual materials, an OPAC, a Web page.

Student Life *Housing:* college housing not available. *Activities and Organizations:* student government, Phi Theta Kappa, LPN Club, National Association of Industrial Technology. *Campus security:* 24-hour emergency response devices. *Student services:* personal/psychological counseling, women's center.

Athletics *Intramural sports:* basketball M/W, volleyball M/W.

Costs (2010–11) *Tuition:* state resident $105 per credit hour part-time; nonresident $221 per credit hour part-time. *Required fees:* $60 per term part-time.

Financial Aid Of all full-time matriculated undergraduates who enrolled in 2008, 51 Federal Work-Study jobs (averaging $2110). 1 state and other part-time job (averaging $2963).

Applying *Options:* electronic application, early admission, deferred entrance. *Required:* high school transcript. *Required for some:* interview. *Application deadlines:* rolling (freshmen), rolling (transfers). *Notification:* continuous (freshmen), continuous (transfers).

Freshman Application Contact Mr. Michael Fisher, Director of Admissions, Ivy Tech Community College–Wabash Valley, 7999 U.S. Highway 41 South, Terre Haute, IN 47802-4898. *Phone:* 812-298-2300. *Toll-free phone:* 800-377-4882. *Fax:* 812-298-2291. *E-mail:* mfisher@ivytech.edu.

Kaplan College, Hammond Campus

Hammond, Indiana **www.kc-hammond.com/**

- **Proprietary** 2-year, founded 1962
- **Suburban** campus
- **Coed**

Majors Data processing and data processing technology; medical administrative assistant and medical secretary; medical/clinical assistant.

Academics *Calendar:* quarters. *Degree:* certificates, diplomas, and associate.

Freshman Application Contact Kaplan College, Hammond Campus, 7833 Indianapolis Boulevard, Hammond, IN 46324. *Phone:* 219-844-0100.

KAPLAN COLLEGE, MERRILLVILLE CAMPUS

Merrillville, Indiana **www.kc-merrillville.com/**

- **Proprietary** 2-year, founded 1968
- **Coed**

Majors Accounting; computer programming; computer systems networking and telecommunications; computer technology/computer systems technology; data processing and data processing technology; legal administrative assistant/secretary; massage therapy; medical/clinical assistant; medical reception; web page, digital/multimedia and information resources design.

Academics *Degree:* certificates, diplomas, and associate.

Freshman Application Contact Kaplan College, Merrillville Campus, 3803 East Lincoln Highway, Merrillville, IN 46410. *Phone:* 219-947-8400.

KAPLAN COLLEGE, NORTHWEST INDIANAPOLIS CAMPUS

Indianapolis, Indiana **www.kc-indy.com/**

- **Proprietary** 2-year
- **Coed, primarily women**

Majors Computer programming (specific applications); computer software and media applications related.

Academics *Degree:* diplomas and associate.

Freshman Application Contact Kaplan College, Northwest Indianapolis Campus, 7302 Woodland Drive, Indianapolis, IN 46217. *Phone:* 317-299-6001. *Toll-free phone:* 800-849-4995.

LINCOLN TECHNICAL INSTITUTE

Indianapolis, Indiana **www.lincolnedu.com/**

- **Proprietary** 2-year, founded 1946, part of Lincoln Technical Institute, Inc
- **Urban** campus
- **Coed**

Academics *Calendar:* modular. *Degree:* certificates and associate. *Special study options:* summer session for credit.

Applying *Required:* high school transcript, interview.

Director of Admissions Ms. Cindy Ryan, Director of Admissions, Lincoln Technical Institute, 1201 Stadium Drive, Indianapolis, IN 46202-2194. *Phone:* 317-632-5553. *Toll-free phone:* 800-554-4465.

MID-AMERICA COLLEGE OF FUNERAL SERVICE

Jeffersonville, Indiana **www.mid-america.edu/**

Freshman Application Contact Mr. Richard Nelson, Dean of Students, Mid-America College of Funeral Service, 3111 Hamburg Pike, Jeffersonville, IN 47130-9630. *Phone:* 812-288-8878. *Toll-free phone:* 800-221-6158. *Fax:* 812-288-5942. *E-mail:* macfs@mindspring.com.

VET TECH INSTITUTE AT INTERNATIONAL BUSINESS COLLEGE

Fort Wayne, Indiana **www.vettechinstitute.edu/**

- **Private** 2-year, founded 2005
- **Suburban** campus
- **Coed,** 147 undergraduate students
- 51% of applicants were admitted

Freshmen *Admission:* 283 applied, 143 admitted.

Majors Veterinary/animal health technology.

Academics *Degree:* associate. *Special study options:* accelerated degree program, internships.

Freshman Application Contact Admissions Office, Vet Tech Institute at International Business College, 5699 Coventry Lane, Fort Wayne, IN 46804. *Phone:* 800-589-6363. *Toll-free phone:* 800-589-6363.

VET TECH INSTITUTE AT INTERNATIONAL BUSINESS COLLEGE

Indianapolis, Indiana **www.vettechinstitute.edu/**

- **Private** 2-year, founded 2007
- **Suburban** campus
- **Coed,** 83 undergraduate students
- 55% of applicants were admitted

Freshmen *Admission:* 336 applied, 184 admitted.

Majors Veterinary/animal health technology.

Academics *Degree:* associate. *Special study options:* accelerated degree program, internships.

Freshman Application Contact Admissions Office, Vet Tech Institute at International Business College, 7205 Shadeland Station, Indianapolis, IN 46256. *Phone:* 800-589-6500. *Toll-free phone:* 800-589-6500.

VINCENNES UNIVERSITY

Vincennes, Indiana **www.vinu.edu/**

Director of Admissions Christian Blome, Director of Admissions, Vincennes University, 1002 North First Street, Vincennes, IN 47591. *Phone:* 800-742-9198. *Toll-free phone:* 800-742-9198. *E-mail:* cblome@vinu.edu.

VINCENNES UNIVERSITY JASPER CAMPUS

Jasper, Indiana **vujc.vinu.edu/**

- **State-supported** primarily 2-year, founded 1970, part of Vincennes University
- **Small-town** 120-acre campus
- **Coed,** 915 undergraduate students

Undergraduates Students come from 1 other state, 1 other country, 0.5% African American, 0.4% Asian American or Pacific Islander, 3% Hispanic American, 0.3% Native American.

Faculty *Total:* 51, 39% full-time. *Student/faculty ratio:* 16:1.

Majors Accounting; administrative assistant and secretarial science; behavioral sciences; business administration and management; business teacher education; computer programming; computer programming related; computer systems networking and telecommunications; criminal justice/police science; drafting and design technology; education; education (multiple levels); elementary education; finance; furniture design and manufacturing; industrial technology; legal administrative assistant/secretary; liberal arts and sciences/liberal studies; management information systems; medical administrative assistant and medical secretary; psychology; social sciences; social work; sociology; word processing.

Academics *Calendar:* semesters. *Degrees:* certificates, associate, and bachelor's. *Special study options:* academic remediation for entering students, adult/continuing education programs, advanced placement credit, distance learning, part-time degree program, summer session for credit.

Library Vincennes University Jasper Library with 14,000 titles, 180 serial subscriptions, an OPAC.

Student Life *Housing:* college housing not available. *Activities and Organizations:* student-run newspaper. *Student services:* personal/psychological counseling.

Financial Aid Of all full-time matriculated undergraduates who enrolled in 2008, 3 Federal Work-Study jobs (averaging $3200).

Applying *Application fee:* $20. *Required:* high school transcript. *Application deadlines:* rolling (freshmen), rolling (transfers).

Freshman Application Contact Ms. Louann Gilbert, Director, Vincennes University Jasper Campus, 850 College Avenue, Jasper, IN 47546. *Phone:* 812-482-3030. *Toll-free phone:* 800-809-VUJC. *Fax:* 812-481-5960. *E-mail:* lagilbert@vinu.edu.

IOWA

CLINTON COMMUNITY COLLEGE

Clinton, Iowa **www.eicc.edu/ccc/**

- **State and locally supported** 2-year, founded 1946, part of Eastern Iowa Community College District
- **Small-town** 20-acre campus
- **Coed**

Undergraduates 571 full-time, 669 part-time. Students come from 8 states and territories, 5 other countries, 8% are from out of state. *Retention:* 58% of 2008 full-time freshmen returned.

Faculty *Student/faculty ratio:* 23:1.

Academics *Calendar:* semesters. *Degree:* certificates, diplomas, and associate. *Special study options:* academic remediation for entering students, adult/continuing education programs, advanced placement credit, cooperative education, distance learning, double majors, English as a second language, independent study, internships, part-time degree program, services for LD students, student-designed majors, study abroad, summer session for credit.

Student Life *Campus security:* 24-hour emergency response devices.

Athletics Member NJCAA.

Costs (2009–10) *Tuition:* state resident $2688 full-time, $112 per credit hour part-time; nonresident $4032 full-time, $168 per credit hour part-time. Full-time tuition and fees vary according to class time, program, and reciprocity agreements. Part-time tuition and fees vary according to class time, program, and reciprocity agreements.

Financial Aid Of all full-time matriculated undergraduates who enrolled in 2008, 33 Federal Work-Study jobs (averaging $3000). 4 state and other part-time jobs (averaging $3000).

Applying *Options:* electronic application, early admission, deferred entrance.

Freshman Application Contact Mr. Gary Mohr, Executive Director of Enrollment Management and Marketing, Clinton Community College, 1000 Lincoln Boulevard, Clinton, IA 52732-6299. *Phone:* 563-336-3322. *Fax:* 563-336-3350. *E-mail:* gmohr@eicc.edu.

DES MOINES AREA COMMUNITY COLLEGE

Ankeny, Iowa **www.dmacc.edu/**

- **State and locally supported** 2-year, founded 1966, part of Iowa Area Community Colleges System
- **Small-town** 362-acre campus
- **Endowment** $11.1 million
- **Coed,** 22,324 undergraduate students, 40% full-time, 55% women, 45% men

Undergraduates 8,947 full-time, 13,377 part-time. Students come from 43 states and territories, 69 other countries, 8% African American, 3% Asian American or Pacific Islander, 4% Hispanic American, 0.7% Native American, 1% international. *Retention:* 58% of 2008 full-time freshmen returned.

Freshmen *Admission:* 5,183 enrolled.

Faculty *Total:* 326, 99% full-time. *Student/faculty ratio:* 33:1.

Majors Accounting; accounting and business/management; accounting technology and bookkeeping; agricultural/farm supplies retailing and wholesaling; apparel and accessories marketing; applied horticulture/horticultural business services related; architectural drafting and CAD/CADD; autobody/collision and repair technology; automobile/automotive mechanics technology; biomedical technology; business administration and management; child-care provision; civil engineering technology; clinical/medical laboratory technology; commercial and advertising art; communications systems installation and repair technology; computer and information sciences and support services related; computer engineering technology; computer programming (specific applications); criminal justice/law enforcement administration; culinary arts; dental hygiene; desktop publishing and digital imaging design; diesel mechanics technology; electrical, electronic and communications engineering technology; fire protection and safety technology; funeral service and mortuary science; health/health-care administration; heating, air conditioning, ventilation and refrigeration maintenance technology; hospitality administration; industrial electronics technology; industrial mechanics and maintenance technology; information technology; language interpretation and translation; legal assistant/paralegal; liberal arts and sciences/liberal studies; machine tool technology; marketing/marketing management; mechanical drafting and CAD/CADD; medical administrative assistant and medical secretary; medical/clinical assistant; nursing (licensed practical/vocational nurse training); nursing (registered nurse training); office management; respiratory care therapy; sales, distribution and marketing; sport and fitness administration/management; surveying engineering; tool and die technology; veterinary/animal health technology.

Academics *Calendar:* semesters. *Degrees:* certificates, diplomas, and associate (profile also includes information from the Boone, Carroll, Des Moines, and Newton campuses). *Special study options:* academic remediation for entering students, adult/continuing education programs, advanced placement credit, cooperative education, distance learning, English as a second language, honors programs, off-campus study, part-time degree program, services for LD students, student-designed majors, summer session for credit.

Library DMACC District Library plus 4 others with 62,986 titles, 3,784 serial subscriptions, 7,224 audiovisual materials, an OPAC, a Web page.

Student Life *Housing Options:* coed. Campus housing is university owned. *Activities and Organizations:* drama/theater group, student-run newspaper, choral group, Agri-Business Club, Horticulture Club, Hospitality Arts Club, Iowa Delta Epsilon Chi, Dental Hygienist Club. *Campus security:* 24-hour emergency response devices and patrols, late-night transport/escort service. *Student services:* health clinic, personal/psychological counseling.

Athletics Member NJCAA. *Intercollegiate sports:* baseball M(s), basketball M(s)/W(s), cross-country running W(s), golf M(s)/W(s), volleyball W(s). *Intramural sports:* badminton M/W, basketball M/W, football M/W, golf M/W, soccer M/W, volleyball M/W.

Standardized Tests *Required for some:* SAT or ACT (for admission), ACT COMPASS.

Costs (2009–10) *Tuition:* state resident $3450 full-time, $115 per credit hour part-time; nonresident $6900 full-time, $230 per credit hour part-time. Full-time tuition and fees vary according to course load and reciprocity agreements. Part-time tuition and fees vary according to course load and reciprocity agreements. *Room and board:* Room and board charges vary according to location. *Payment plan:* installment. *Waivers:* senior citizens and employees or children of employees.

Financial Aid Of all full-time matriculated undergraduates who enrolled in 2008, 377 Federal Work-Study jobs (averaging $1055).

Applying *Options:* electronic application, early admission, deferred entrance. *Required for some:* high school transcript, interview. *Application deadlines:* rolling (freshmen), rolling (transfers).

Freshman Application Contact Mr. Michael Lentsch, Director of Enrollment Management, Des Moines Area Community College, Building 1, 2006 South Ankeny Boulevard, Ankeny, IA 50021. *Phone:* 515-964-6216. *Toll-free phone:* 800-362-2127. *Fax:* 515-964-6391. *E-mail:* mjleutsch@dmacc.edu.

ELLSWORTH COMMUNITY COLLEGE

Iowa Falls, Iowa **www.iavalley.cc.ia.us/ecc/**

- **State and locally supported** 2-year, founded 1890, part of Iowa Valley Community College District System
- **Small-town** 10-acre campus
- **Coed**

Academics *Calendar:* semesters. *Degree:* diplomas and associate. *Special study options:* academic remediation for entering students, adult/continuing education programs, advanced placement credit, cooperative education, distance learning, honors programs, internships, part-time degree program, services for LD students, student-designed majors, summer session for credit.

Student Life *Campus security:* 24-hour emergency response devices and patrols.

Athletics Member NJCAA.

Financial Aid Of all full-time matriculated undergraduates who enrolled in 2008, 95 Federal Work-Study jobs (averaging $1200). 40 state and other part-time jobs (averaging $1200).

Applying *Options:* electronic application, early admission, deferred entrance. *Required:* high school transcript.

Director of Admissions Mrs. Nancy Walters, Registrar, Ellsworth Community College, 1100 College Avenue, Iowa Falls, IA 50126-1199. *Phone:* 641-648-4611. *Toll-free phone:* 800-ECC-9235.

HAWKEYE COMMUNITY COLLEGE

Waterloo, Iowa **www.hawkeyecollege.edu/**

- **State and locally supported** 2-year, founded 1966
- **Rural** 320-acre campus
- **Endowment** $872,006
- **Coed,** 6,321 undergraduate students, 50% full-time, 54% women, 46% men

Undergraduates 3,189 full-time, 3,132 part-time. Students come from 7 states and territories, 6 other countries, 1% are from out of state, 9% African American, 1% Asian American or Pacific Islander, 2% Hispanic American, 0.5% Native American, 0.6% international, 16% transferred in. *Retention:* 57% of 2008 full-time freshmen returned.

Freshmen *Admission:* 2,608 applied, 1,737 admitted, 1,672 enrolled. *Test scores:* ACT scores over 18: 50%; ACT scores over 24: 12%; ACT scores over 30: 2%.

Faculty *Total:* 296, 39% full-time, 8% with terminal degrees. *Student/faculty ratio:* 24:1.

Majors Accounting; agricultural/farm supplies retailing and wholesaling; agricultural power machinery operation; animal/livestock husbandry and production; applied horticulture; architectural drafting and CAD/CADD; autobody/collision and repair technology; automobile/automotive mechanics technology; child-care provision; civil engineering technology; clinical/medical laboratory technology; commercial photography; computer and information sciences; computer systems networking and telecommunications; criminal justice/police science; dental hygiene; diesel mechanics technology; electrical, electronic and communications engineering technology; executive assistant/executive secretary; graphic communications; interior design; liberal arts and sciences/liberal studies; machine tool technology; manufacturing technology; medical administrative assistant and medical secretary; multi/interdisciplinary studies related; natural resources management and policy; nursing (registered nurse training); respiratory care therapy; sales, distribution and marketing; tool and die technology; web page, digital/multimedia and information resources design.

Academics *Calendar:* semesters. *Degree:* certificates, diplomas, and associate. *Special study options:* academic remediation for entering students, adult/continuing education programs, advanced placement credit, cooperative education, distance learning, English as a second language, external degree program, part-time degree program, services for LD students, study abroad, summer session for credit. *ROTC:* Army (c).

Library Hawkeye Community College Library with 94,295 titles, 327 serial subscriptions, 2,757 audiovisual materials, an OPAC, a Web page.

Student Life *Housing:* college housing not available. *Activities and Organizations:* Student Senate, Phi Theta Kappa, Student Ambassadors, All Ag/Horticulture, IAAP. *Campus security:* 24-hour patrols. *Student services:* health clinic, personal/psychological counseling, women's center.

Athletics *Intramural sports:* basketball M/W, bowling M/W, cross-country running M/W, golf M/W, soccer M/W, softball M/W, volleyball M/W.

Standardized Tests *Required for some:* ACT (for admission).

Costs (2009–10) *Tuition:* state resident $3630 full-time, $121 per credit hour part-time; nonresident $4380 full-time, $146 per credit hour part-time. Full-time tuition and fees vary according to course load and program. Part-time tuition and fees vary according to course load and program. *Required fees:* $210 full-time, $7 per credit hour part-time. *Payment plans:* installment, deferred payment. *Waivers:* employees or children of employees.

Applying *Options:* electronic application, deferred entrance. *Required:* high school transcript. *Application deadlines:* rolling (freshmen), rolling (out-of-state freshmen), rolling (transfers). *Notification:* continuous (freshmen), continuous (out-of-state freshmen), continuous (transfers).

Freshman Application Contact Ms. Holly Grimm-See, Associate Director, Admissions & Recruitment, Hawkeye Community College, PO Box 8015, Waterloo, IA 50704-8015. *Phone:* 319-296-4277. *Toll-free phone:* 800-670-4769. *Fax:* 319-296-2505. *E-mail:* hgrimm-see@hawkeyecollege.edu.

Indian Hills Community College

Ottumwa, Iowa **www.ihcc.cc.ia.us/**

- **State and locally supported** 2-year, founded 1966, part of Iowa Area Community Colleges System
- **Small-town** 400-acre campus
- **Coed**

Academics *Calendar:* quarters. *Degree:* certificates, diplomas, and associate. *Special study options:* academic remediation for entering students, adult/continuing education programs, cooperative education, English as a second language, honors programs, internships, part-time degree program, services for LD students, student-designed majors, summer session for credit.

Student Life *Campus security:* 24-hour emergency response devices and patrols.

Athletics Member NJCAA.

Financial Aid Of all full-time matriculated undergraduates who enrolled in 2008, 123 Federal Work-Study jobs (averaging $742). 62 state and other part-time jobs (averaging $823).

Applying *Options:* early admission. *Required for some:* high school transcript.

Freshman Application Contact Mrs. Jane Sapp, Admissions Officer, Indian Hills Community College, 525 Grandview Avenue, Building #1, Ottumwa, IA 52501-1398. *Phone:* 641-683-5155. *Toll-free phone:* 800-726-2585.

Iowa Central Community College

Fort Dodge, Iowa **www.iccc.cc.ia.us/**

Freshman Application Contact Mrs. Deb Bahis, Coordinator of Admissions, Iowa Central Community College, 330 Avenue M, Ft. Dodge, IA 50501. *Phone:* 515-576-0099 Ext. 2402. *Toll-free phone:* 800-362-2793. *Fax:* 515-576-7724. *E-mail:* bahls@iowacentral.com.

Iowa Lakes Community College

Estherville, Iowa **www.iowalakes.edu/**

- **State and locally supported** 2-year, founded 1967, part of Iowa Community College System
- **Small-town** 20-acre campus
- **Endowment** $1.7 million
- **Coed,** 3,169 undergraduate students, 58% full-time, 55% women, 45% men

Undergraduates 1,839 full-time, 1,330 part-time. Students come from 34 states and territories, 7 other countries, 35% live on campus. *Retention:* 59% of 2008 full-time freshmen returned.

Freshmen *Admission:* 1,450 applied, 1,388 admitted, 842 enrolled.

Faculty *Total:* 129, 68% full-time. *Student/faculty ratio:* 24:1.

Majors Accounting; accounting technology and bookkeeping; administrative assistant and secretarial science; agribusiness; agricultural business and management; agricultural business and management related; agricultural business technology; agricultural economics; agricultural/farm supplies retailing and wholesaling; agricultural mechanics and equipment technology; agricultural mechanization; agricultural power machinery operation; agricultural production; agricultural production related; agricultural teacher education; agriculture; agronomy and crop science; airline pilot and flight crew; animal/livestock husbandry and production; animal sciences; applied art; art; art history, criticism and conservation; art teacher education; astronomy; athletic training; autobody/collision and repair technology; automobile/automotive mechanics technology; aviation/airway management; behavioral sciences; biological and physical sciences; biology/biological sciences; botany/plant biology; broadcast journalism; business administration and management; business automation/technology/data entry; business machine repair; business teacher education; carpentry; ceramic arts and ceramics; chemistry; child-care provision; child development; chiropractic assistant; commercial and advertising art; communication and journalism related; comparative literature; computer and information sciences related; computer graphics; computer/information technology services administration related; computer programming; computer science; computer software technology; computer systems networking and telecommunications; construction engineering technology; construction management; construction trades; consumer merchandising/retailing management; cooking and related culinary arts; corrections; criminal justice/law enforcement administration; criminal justice/police science; crop production; culinary arts related; data entry/microcomputer applications; data processing and data processing technology; desktop publishing and digital imaging design; developmental and child psychology; drawing; early childhood education; ecology; economics; education; elementary education; emergency care attendant (EMT ambulance); energy management and systems technology; engineering; English; environmental design/architecture; environmental education; environmental engineering technology; environmental studies; family and consumer sciences/human sciences; farm and ranch management; fashion merchandising; finance; fine/studio arts; fishing and fisheries sciences and management; flight instruction; food preparation; foods and nutrition related; food service and dining room management; foreign languages and literatures; forestry; general studies; geology/earth science; graphic and printing equipment operation/production; graphic communications; graphic design; health and physical education; health/health-care administration; history; hospitality administration; hotel/motel administration; humanities; human resources management and services related; hydrology and water resources science; information technology; institutional food workers; jazz/jazz studies; journalism; kindergarten/preschool education; landscaping and groundskeeping; legal administrative assistant/secretary; legal assistant/paralegal; legal studies; liberal arts and sciences and humanities related; liberal arts and sciences/liberal studies; marine maintenance and ship repair technology; marketing/marketing management; massage therapy; mass communication/media; mathematics; medical administrative assistant and medical secretary; medical/clinical assistant; medical office assistant; medical office computer specialist; medical reception; medical transcription; merchandising, sales, and marketing operations related (general); motorcycle maintenance and repair technology; music; music teacher education; natural resources/conservation; natural sciences; nursing (registered nurse training); office management; office occupations and clerical services; parks, recreation and leisure; pharmacy; philosophy; photography; physical education teaching and coaching; physical sciences; piano and organ; political science and government; pre-dentistry studies; pre-engineering; pre-law studies; premedical studies;

Iowa Lakes Community College (continued)

prenursing studies; pre-pharmacy studies; pre-veterinary studies; printing press operation; psychology; radio and television; radio and television broadcasting technology; real estate; receptionist; rehabilitation therapy; restaurant, culinary, and catering management; restaurant/food services management; retailing; sales, distribution and marketing; science teacher education; selling skills and sales; small business administration; small engine mechanics and repair technology; social sciences; social work; sociology; soil science and agronomy; Spanish; speech and rhetoric; sport and fitness administration/management; surgical technology; system administration; system, networking, and LAN/WAN management; technology/industrial arts teacher education; trade and industrial teacher education; turf and turfgrass management; voice and opera; water, wetlands, and marine resources management; welding technology; wildlife and wildlands science and management; wildlife biology; wind/percussion instruments; word processing.

Academics *Calendar:* semesters. *Degree:* certificates, diplomas, and associate. *Special study options:* academic remediation for entering students, accelerated degree program, adult/continuing education programs, advanced placement credit, cooperative education, distance learning, English as a second language, external degree program, honors programs, independent study, internships, part-time degree program, services for LD students, summer session for credit.

Library Iowa Lakes Community College Library plus 2 others with 42,867 titles, 5,975 serial subscriptions, 6,623 audiovisual materials, an OPAC.

Student Life *Housing Options:* coed, disabled students. Campus housing is university owned. Freshman campus housing is guaranteed. *Activities and Organizations:* drama/theater group, student-run newspaper, radio and television station, choral group, music, Criminal Justice, nursing clubs, Environmental Studies, Business. *Campus security:* 24-hour emergency response devices, student patrols.

Athletics Member NJCAA. *Intercollegiate sports:* baseball M(s), basketball M(s)/W(s), cross-country running M(s)/W(s), golf M(s)/W(s), soccer M(s)/W(s), softball W(s), volleyball W(s), wrestling M(s). *Intramural sports:* basketball M/W, football M/W, golf M/W, racquetball M/W, skiing (cross-country) M/W, skiing (downhill) M/W, soccer M/W, softball M/W, swimming and diving M/W, table tennis M/W, tennis M/W, ultimate Frisbee M/W, volleyball M/W, weight lifting M/W, wrestling M.

Costs (2009–10) *Tuition:* state resident $4363 full-time, $128 per credit hour part-time; nonresident $4423 full-time, $130 per credit hour part-time. Full-time tuition and fees vary according to course load, program, and reciprocity agreements. Part-time tuition and fees vary according to course load, program, and reciprocity agreements. *Required fees:* $556 full-time, $17 per credit hour part-time, $17 per credit hour part-time. *Room and board:* $4800. Room and board charges vary according to housing facility and location. *Payment plan:* installment. *Waivers:* children of alumni and employees or children of employees.

Financial Aid Of all full-time matriculated undergraduates who enrolled in 2008, 210 Federal Work-Study jobs (averaging $800).

Applying *Options:* electronic application. *Required:* high school transcript. *Required for some:* interview. *Application deadlines:* rolling (freshmen), rolling (out-of-state freshmen), rolling (transfers).

Freshman Application Contact Ms. Anne Stansbury Johnson, Assistant Director, Admissions, Iowa Lakes Community College, 3200 College Drive, Emmetsburg, IA 50536. *Phone:* 712-852-5254. *Toll-free phone:* 800-521-5054. *Fax:* 712-852-2152. *E-mail:* info@iowalakes.edu.

IOWA WESTERN COMMUNITY COLLEGE

Council Bluffs, Iowa **www.iwcc.edu/**

- **District-supported** 2-year, founded 1966, part of Iowa Department of Education Division of Community Colleges
- **Suburban** 282-acre campus with easy access to Omaha
- **Coed**

Academics *Calendar:* semesters. *Degree:* certificates, diplomas, and associate. *Special study options:* academic remediation for entering students, adult/continuing education programs, cooperative education, distance learning, English as a second language, independent study, internships, part-time degree program, services for LD students, summer session for credit. *ROTC:* Army (c), Air Force (c).

Student Life *Campus security:* 24-hour patrols, late-night transport/escort service.

Athletics Member NJCAA.

Applying *Options:* early admission, deferred entrance. *Required:* high school transcript.

Freshman Application Contact Ms. Tori Christie, Director of Admissions, Iowa Western Community College, 2700 College Road, Box 4-C, Council Bluffs, IA 51502. *Phone:* 712-325-3288. *Toll-free phone:* 800-432-5852. *E-mail:* admissions@iwcc.edu.

ITT TECHNICAL INSTITUTE

Cedar Rapids, Iowa **www.itt-tech.edu/**

- **Proprietary** primarily 2-year
- **Coed**

Majors CAD/CADD drafting/design technology; computer and information systems security; computer engineering technology; construction management; electrical, electronic and communications engineering technology; legal assistant/paralegal; system, networking, and LAN/WAN management.

Academics *Degrees:* associate and bachelor's.

Freshman Application Contact ITT Technical Institute, 3735 Queen Court SW, Cedar Rapids, IA 52404. *Phone:* 319-297-3400. *Toll-free phone:* 877-320-4625.

ITT TECHNICAL INSTITUTE

Clive, Iowa **www.itt-tech.edu/**

- **Proprietary** primarily 2-year, part of ITT Educational Services, Inc.
- **Coed**

Majors CAD/CADD drafting/design technology; computer and information systems security; computer engineering technology; construction management; criminal justice/law enforcement administration; electrical, electronic and communications engineering technology; system, networking, and LAN/WAN management.

Academics *Degrees:* associate and bachelor's.

Freshman Application Contact Director of Recruitment, ITT Technical Institute, 1860 Northwest 118th Street, Suite 110, Clive, IA 50325. *Phone:* 515-327-5500. *Toll-free phone:* 877-526-7312.

KAPLAN UNIVERSITY, CEDAR FALLS

Cedar Falls, Iowa **www.cedarfalls.kaplanuniversity.edu/**

- **Proprietary** primarily 2-year, founded 2000
- **Coed**

Academics *Calendar:* quarters. *Degrees:* certificates, diplomas, associate, and bachelor's.

Applying *Application deadline:* rolling (freshmen).

Freshman Application Contact Kaplan University, Cedar Falls, 7009 Nordic Drive, Cedar Falls, IA 50613. *Phone:* 319-277-0220. *Toll-free phone:* 800-728-1220.

KAPLAN UNIVERSITY, CEDAR RAPIDS

Cedar Rapids, Iowa **www.cedarrapids.kaplanuniversity.edu/**

- **Proprietary** primarily 2-year, founded 1900, administratively affiliated with Kaplan University - branch of the Davenport Campus
- **Suburban** campus
- **Coed**

Majors Accounting; business administration and management; computer and information sciences related; criminal justice/law enforcement administration; information technology; interdisciplinary studies; medical/clinical assistant.

Academics *Calendar:* quarters. *Degrees:* certificates, diplomas, associate, and bachelor's (branch locations in Des Moines, Mason City, and Cedar Falls with significant enrollment not reflected in profile).

Financial Aid Of all full-time matriculated undergraduates who enrolled in 2008, 10 Federal Work-Study jobs (averaging $889). 3 state and other part-time jobs (averaging $1885).

Freshman Application Contact Kaplan University, Cedar Rapids, 3165 Edgewood Parkway, SW, Cedar Rapids, IA 52404. *Phone:* 319-363-0481. *Toll-free phone:* 800-728-0481.

KAPLAN UNIVERSITY, COUNCIL BLUFFS

Council Bluffs, Iowa **www.councilbluffs.kaplanuniversity.edu/**

- **Proprietary** primarily 2-year, founded 2004
- **Coed**

Academics *Degrees:* certificates, associate, and bachelor's.
Student Life *Housing:* college housing not available.
Standardized Tests *Required:* Wonderlic aptitude test (for admission).
Freshman Application Contact Kaplan University, Council Bluffs, 1751 Madison Avenue, Council Bluffs, IA 51503. *Phone:* 712-328-4212. *Toll-free phone:* 800-518-4212.

KAPLAN UNIVERSITY, DES MOINES

Urbandale, Iowa **www.desmoines.kaplanuniversity.edu/**

- **Proprietary** primarily 2-year
- **Coed**

Academics *Degrees:* certificates, diplomas, associate, and bachelor's.
Freshman Application Contact Kaplan University, Des Moines, 4655 121st Street, Urbandale, IA 50323. *Phone:* 515-727-2100.

KIRKWOOD COMMUNITY COLLEGE

Cedar Rapids, Iowa **www.kirkwood.cc.ia.us/**

- **State and locally supported** 2-year, founded 1966, part of Iowa Department of Education Division of Community Colleges
- **Suburban** 630-acre campus
- **Endowment** $16.0 million
- **Coed,** 17,841 undergraduate students, 54% full-time, 52% women, 48% men

Undergraduates 9,715 full-time, 8,126 part-time. Students come from 37 states and territories, 94 other countries, 3% are from out of state, 5% African American, 1% Asian American or Pacific Islander, 2% Hispanic American, 0.6% Native American, 1% international.
Faculty *Total:* 968, 30% full-time. *Student/faculty ratio:* 24:1.
Majors Accounting; administrative assistant and secretarial science; agricultural business and management; agricultural/farm supplies retailing and wholesaling; agricultural power machinery operation; agricultural production; agriculture; apparel and accessories marketing; applied horticulture/horticultural business services related; architectural drafting and CAD/CADD; automobile/automotive mechanics technology; biotechnology; business administration and management; child-care provision; community organization and advocacy; computer and information sciences and support services related; computer/information technology services administration related; computer programming (specific applications); construction trades; corrections; criminal justice/police science; culinary arts; dental assisting; dental hygiene; dental laboratory technology; diesel mechanics technology; education; electrical, electronic and communications engineering technology; electroneurodiagnostic/electroencephalographic technology; emergency medical technology (EMT paramedic); finance; fire protection and safety technology; fire science; graphic communications; health information/medical records technology; horse husbandry/equine science and management; hospitality administration; industrial electronics technology; landscaping and groundskeeping; legal assistant/paralegal; liberal arts and sciences/liberal studies; machine tool technology; marketing/marketing management; mechanical drafting and CAD/CADD; medical/clinical assistant; natural resources/conservation; nursing (registered nurse training); occupational therapist assistant; physical therapist assistant; radio and television broadcasting technology; respiratory care therapy; restaurant, culinary, and catering management; sheet metal technology; sign language interpretation and translation; social work related; surgical technology; surveying engineering; system administration; telecommunications technology; turf and turfgrass management; veterinary/animal health technology; water quality and wastewater treatment management and recycling technology; web page, digital/multimedia and information resources design; welding technology.
Academics *Calendar:* semesters. *Degree:* certificates, diplomas, and associate. *Special study options:* academic remediation for entering students, accelerated degree program, adult/continuing education programs, advanced placement credit, cooperative education, distance learning, English as a second language, external degree program, honors programs, independent study, internships, off-campus study, part-time degree program, services for LD students, student-designed majors, summer session for credit.
Library Library with 60,622 titles, 565 serial subscriptions, an OPAC.
Student Life *Housing:* college housing not available. *Activities and Organizations:* drama/theater group, student-run newspaper, choral group. *Campus security:* 24-hour emergency response devices and patrols. *Student services:* health clinic, personal/psychological counseling, legal services.
Athletics Member NJCAA. *Intercollegiate sports:* baseball M(s), basketball M(s)/W(s), golf M(s), soccer M/W, softball W(s), volleyball W(s). *Intramural sports:* basketball M/W, football M/W, golf M/W, racquetball M/W, soccer M/W, softball W, tennis M/W, volleyball M/W, weight lifting M/W.
Costs (2009–10) *Tuition:* state resident $2664 full-time, $111 per credit hour part-time; nonresident $3264 full-time, $136 per credit hour part-time. *Waivers:* employees or children of employees.
Applying *Options:* electronic application, early admission. *Required:* high school transcript. *Application deadlines:* rolling (freshmen), rolling (transfers). *Notification:* continuous (freshmen), continuous (transfers).
Freshman Application Contact Kirkwood Community College, PO Box 2068, Cedar Rapids, IA 52406-2068. *Phone:* 319-398-5517. *Toll-free phone:* 800-332-2055.

MARSHALLTOWN COMMUNITY COLLEGE

Marshalltown, Iowa **www.marshalltowncommunitycollege.com/**

- **District-supported** 2-year, founded 1927, part of Iowa Valley Community College District System
- **Small-town** 200-acre campus
- **Coed**

Academics *Calendar:* semesters. *Degree:* certificates, diplomas, and associate. *Special study options:* academic remediation for entering students, adult/continuing education programs, advanced placement credit, cooperative education, distance learning, English as a second language, freshman honors college, honors programs, independent study, internships, part-time degree program, services for LD students, student-designed majors, study abroad, summer session for credit. *ROTC:* Air Force (c).
Athletics Member NJCAA.
Standardized Tests *Required:* ACT COMPASS (for admission). *Recommended:* ACT (for admission).
Financial Aid Of all full-time matriculated undergraduates who enrolled in 2008, 28 Federal Work-Study jobs (averaging $1800).
Applying *Options:* electronic application, early admission. *Required:* high school transcript. *Required for some:* interview.
Freshman Application Contact Ms. Deana Inman, Director of Admissions, Marshalltown Community College, 3700 South Center Street, Marshalltown, IA 50158. *Phone:* 641-752-7106. *Toll-free phone:* 866-622-4748. *Fax:* 641-752-8149.

MUSCATINE COMMUNITY COLLEGE

Muscatine, Iowa **www.eicc.edu/**

- **State-supported** 2-year, founded 1929, part of Eastern Iowa Community College District
- **Small-town** 25-acre campus
- **Coed**

Undergraduates 608 full-time, 1,016 part-time. Students come from 6 states and territories, 8 other countries, 3% are from out of state, 4% live on campus. *Retention:* 55% of 2008 full-time freshmen returned.
Academics *Calendar:* semesters. *Degree:* diplomas and associate. *Special study options:* academic remediation for entering students, adult/continuing education programs, advanced placement credit, cooperative education, distance learning, double majors, English as a second language, honors programs, independent study, internships, off-campus study, part-time degree program, services for LD students, student-designed majors, study abroad, summer session for credit.
Student Life *Campus security:* 24-hour emergency response devices.
Athletics Member NJCAA.
Costs (2009–10) *Tuition:* state resident $2688 full-time, $112 per credit hour part-time; nonresident $4032 full-time, $168 per credit hour part-time. Full-time tuition and fees vary according to class time, program, and reciprocity agreements. Part-time tuition and fees vary according to class time, program, and reciprocity agreements. *Room and board:* room only: $3780.
Financial Aid Of all full-time matriculated undergraduates who enrolled in 2008, 33 Federal Work-Study jobs (averaging $3000). 4 state and other part-time jobs (averaging $3000).
Applying *Options:* electronic application.
Freshman Application Contact Gary Mohr, Executive Director of Enrollment Management and Marketing, Muscatine Community College, 152 Colorado Street, Muscatine, IA 52761-5396. *Phone:* 563-336-3322. *Toll-free phone:* 800-351-4669. *Fax:* 563-336-3350. *E-mail:* gmohr@eicc.edu.

NORTHEAST IOWA COMMUNITY COLLEGE

Calmar, Iowa **www.nicc.edu/**

- **State and locally supported** 2-year, founded 1966, part of Iowa Area Community Colleges System
- **Rural** 210-acre campus
- **Endowment** $558,880
- **Coed,** 5,389 undergraduate students, 48% full-time, 60% women, 40% men

Undergraduates 2,564 full-time, 2,825 part-time. Students come from 16 states and territories, 5 other countries, 13% are from out of state, 2% African American, 0.1% Asian American or Pacific Islander, 1% Hispanic American, 0.2% Native American, 0.2% international. *Retention:* 60% of 2008 full-time freshmen returned.

Freshmen *Admission:* 1,648 applied, 1,227 admitted. *Average high school GPA:* 2.65.

Faculty *Total:* 281, 41% full-time, 3% with terminal degrees. *Student/faculty ratio:* 18:1.

Majors Accounting; administrative assistant and secretarial science; agribusiness; agricultural and food products processing; agricultural power machinery operation; agricultural production; automobile/automotive mechanics technology; business administration and management; business automation/technology/data entry; clinical/medical laboratory technology; computer programming (specific applications); construction trades; cosmetology; crop production; dairy husbandry and production; desktop publishing and digital imaging design; electrical, electronic and communications engineering technology; electrician; emergency medical technology (EMT paramedic); fire science; health information/medical records technology; liberal arts and sciences/liberal studies; massage therapy; nursing (registered nurse training); plumbing technology; radiologic technology/science; respiratory care therapy; sales, distribution and marketing; social work.

Academics *Calendar:* semesters. *Degree:* certificates, diplomas, and associate. *Special study options:* academic remediation for entering students, adult/continuing education programs, advanced placement credit, cooperative education, distance learning, double majors, English as a second language, honors programs, independent study, internships, off-campus study, part-time degree program, services for LD students, student-designed majors, study abroad, summer session for credit.

Library Wilder Resource Center plus 1 other with 21,337 titles, 294 serial subscriptions, 4,813 audiovisual materials, an OPAC.

Student Life *Housing:* college housing not available. *Activities and Organizations:* student-run newspaper, national fraternities, national sororities. *Campus security:* security personnel on weeknights. *Student services:* personal/psychological counseling.

Athletics *Intramural sports:* basketball M/W, bowling M/W, football M/W, golf M/W, skiing (downhill) M/W, swimming and diving M/W, table tennis M/W, tennis M/W, volleyball M/W.

Costs (2010–11) *Tuition:* state resident $4352 full-time, $136 per credit hour part-time; nonresident $4352 full-time, $136 per credit hour part-time. *Required fees:* $416 full-time, $13 per credit hour part-time. *Payment plan:* installment. *Waivers:* senior citizens and employees or children of employees.

Financial Aid Of all full-time matriculated undergraduates who enrolled in 2008, 154 Federal Work-Study jobs (averaging $1248). 45 state and other part-time jobs (averaging $980).

Applying *Options:* electronic application. *Recommended:* high school transcript. *Application deadlines:* rolling (freshmen), rolling (out-of-state freshmen), rolling (transfers). *Notification:* continuous (freshmen), continuous (out-of-state freshmen), continuous (transfers).

Freshman Application Contact Ms. Martha Keune, Admissions Representative, Northeast Iowa Community College, PO Box 400, Calmar, IA 52132. *Phone:* 563-562-3263 Ext. 307. *Toll-free phone:* 800-728-CALMAR. *Fax:* 563-562-4369. *E-mail:* keunem@nicc.edu.

NORTH IOWA AREA COMMUNITY COLLEGE

Mason City, Iowa **www.niacc.edu/**

- **State and locally supported** 2-year, founded 1918, part of Iowa Community Colleges System
- **Rural** 320-acre campus
- **Coed,** 3,729 undergraduate students, 53% full-time, 54% women, 46% men

Undergraduates 1,990 full-time, 1,739 part-time. 23% are from out of state, 2% African American, 1% Asian American or Pacific Islander, 3% Hispanic American, 0.4% Native American, 0.8% international.

Freshmen *Admission:* 894 enrolled.

Faculty *Total:* 256, 33% full-time, 7% with terminal degrees.

Majors Accounting; accounting technology and bookkeeping; administrative assistant and secretarial science; agricultural production; automobile/automotive mechanics technology; business administration and management; carpentry; clinical/medical laboratory technology; criminal justice/police science; criminology; early childhood education; education; electrical, electronic and communications engineering technology; emergency medical technology (EMT paramedic); entrepreneurship; family and consumer sciences/human sciences; fire services administration; funeral service and mortuary science; geography; heating, air conditioning, ventilation and refrigeration maintenance technology; industrial electronics technology; liberal arts and sciences/liberal studies; machine shop technology; machine tool technology; medical/clinical assistant; nursing assistant/aide and patient care assistant; nursing (licensed practical/vocational nurse training); nursing (registered nurse training); physical education teaching and coaching; physical therapist assistant; political science and government; secondary education; social sciences; sociology; sport and fitness administration/management; system administration; tool and die technology; welding technology.

Academics *Calendar:* semesters. *Degree:* certificates, diplomas, and associate. *Special study options:* academic remediation for entering students, advanced placement credit, cooperative education, distance learning, English as a second language, external degree program, honors programs, internships, part-time degree program, services for LD students, student-designed majors, study abroad, summer session for credit.

Library North Iowa Area Community College Library with 29,540 titles, 413 serial subscriptions, 7,773 audiovisual materials, an OPAC, a Web page.

Student Life *Housing:* on-campus residence required for freshman year. *Options:* coed. Campus housing is university owned. *Activities and Organizations:* student-run newspaper, choral group, Student Senate, school newspaper, intramurals, choral groups, band/orchestra. *Campus security:* 24-hour emergency response devices, controlled dormitory access. *Student services:* health clinic, personal/psychological counseling.

Athletics Member NJCAA. *Intercollegiate sports:* baseball M(s), basketball M(s)/W(s), cross-country running M(s)/W(s), golf M(s)/W(s), soccer M(s), softball W(s), track and field M(s)/W(s), volleyball W(s), wrestling M(s). *Intramural sports:* basketball M/W, cheerleading W, volleyball M/W.

Costs (2009–10) *Tuition:* state resident $3292 full-time, $109 per semester hour part-time; nonresident $4939 full-time, $164 per semester hour part-time. Full-time tuition and fees vary according to course load. Part-time tuition and fees vary according to course load. *Required fees:* $398 full-time, $13 per semester hour part-time. *Room and board:* $4806. Room and board charges vary according to housing facility. *Payment plan:* installment. *Waivers:* senior citizens and employees or children of employees.

Financial Aid Of all full-time matriculated undergraduates who enrolled in 2008, 125 Federal Work-Study jobs (averaging $2000). 4 state and other part-time jobs (averaging $2000).

Applying *Options:* electronic application. *Application deadlines:* rolling (freshmen), rolling (transfers). *Notification:* continuous (freshmen), continuous (transfers).

Freshman Application Contact Ms. Rachel McGuire, Director of Admissions, North Iowa Area Community College, 500 College Drive, Mason City, IA 50401. *Phone:* 641-422-4104. *Toll-free phone:* 888-GO NIACC Ext. 4245. *Fax:* 641-422-4385. *E-mail:* request@niacc.edu.

NORTHWEST IOWA COMMUNITY COLLEGE

Sheldon, Iowa **www.nwicc.edu/**

Director of Admissions Ms. Lisa Story, Director of Enrollment Management, Northwest Iowa Community College, 603 West Park Street, Sheldon, IA 51201-1046. *Phone:* 712-324-5061 Ext. 115. *Toll-free phone:* 800-352-4907. *E-mail:* lstory@nwicc.edu.

ST. LUKE'S COLLEGE

Sioux City, Iowa **stlukescollege.edu/**

- **Independent** 2-year, founded 1967, part of St. Luke's Regional Medical Center
- **Rural** 3-acre campus with easy access to Omaha
- **Endowment** $1.1 million
- **Coed,** 179 undergraduate students, 75% full-time, 87% women, 13% men

Undergraduates 135 full-time, 44 part-time. Students come from 15 states and territories, 47% are from out of state, 1% African American, 1% Asian American or Pacific Islander, 5% Hispanic American, 0.6% Native American, 22% transferred in. *Retention:* 100% of 2008 full-time freshmen returned.
Freshmen *Admission:* 216 applied, 104 admitted, 5 enrolled. *Average high school GPA:* 3.32.
Faculty *Total:* 32, 59% full-time, 13% with terminal degrees. *Student/faculty ratio:* 8:1.
Majors Nursing (registered nurse training); radiologic technology/science; respiratory care therapy.
Academics *Calendar:* semesters. *Degree:* certificates and associate. *Special study options:* advanced placement credit, cooperative education, part-time degree program, summer session for credit.
Library St. Luke's Library with 2,724 titles, 73 serial subscriptions, 45 audiovisual materials, an OPAC, a Web page.
Student Life *Housing:* college housing not available. *Campus security:* 24-hour emergency response devices and patrols, late-night transport/escort service. *Student services:* health clinic, personal/psychological counseling.
Standardized Tests *Required:* SAT or ACT (for admission).
Costs (2010–11) *Tuition:* $14,580 full-time, $405 per credit hour part-time. Full-time tuition and fees vary according to course load, degree level, and program. Part-time tuition and fees vary according to course load and degree level. *Required fees:* $920 full-time. *Room only:* Room and board charges vary according to board plan. *Payment plans:* installment, deferred payment. *Waivers:* employees or children of employees.
Financial Aid Of all full-time matriculated undergraduates who enrolled in 2008, 14 Federal Work-Study jobs (averaging $960). 1 state and other part-time job (averaging $186).
Applying *Options:* electronic application. *Application fee:* $50. *Required:* essay or personal statement, high school transcript, minimum 2.5 GPA, interview. *Notification:* continuous (transfers).
Freshman Application Contact Ms. Sherry McCarthy, Admissions Coordinator, St. Luke's College, 2720 Stone Park Boulevard, Sioux City, IA 51104. *Phone:* 712-279-3149. *Toll-free phone:* 800-352-4660 Ext. 3149. *Fax:* 712-233-8017. *E-mail:* mccartsj@stlukes.org.

SCOTT COMMUNITY COLLEGE

Bettendorf, Iowa **www.eicc.edu/scc/**

- **State and locally supported** 2-year, founded 1966, part of Eastern Iowa Community College District
- **Urban** campus
- **Coed**

Undergraduates 2,059 full-time, 2,052 part-time. Students come from 26 states and territories, 23 other countries, 9% are from out of state, 9% African American, 2% Asian American or Pacific Islander, 5% Hispanic American, 1% Native American, 1% international, 1% transferred in. *Retention:* 48% of 2008 full-time freshmen returned.
Faculty *Student/faculty ratio:* 20:1.
Academics *Calendar:* semesters. *Degree:* certificates, diplomas, and associate. *Special study options:* academic remediation for entering students, adult/continuing education programs, advanced placement credit, cooperative education, distance learning, double majors, English as a second language, honors programs, independent study, internships, off-campus study, part-time degree program, services for LD students, student-designed majors, study abroad, summer session for credit.
Student Life *Campus security:* 24-hour emergency response devices.
Athletics Member NJCAA.
Costs (2009–10) *Tuition:* state resident $2688 full-time, $112 per credit hour part-time; nonresident $4032 full-time, $168 per credit hour part-time.
Financial Aid Of all full-time matriculated undergraduates who enrolled in 2008, 59 Federal Work-Study jobs (averaging $3000). 12 state and other part-time jobs (averaging $3000).
Applying *Options:* electronic application.
Freshman Application Contact Mr. Gary Mohr, Executive Director of Enrollment Management and Marketing, Scott Community College, 500 Belmont Road, Bettendorf, IA 52722-6804. *Phone:* 563-336-3322. *Toll-free phone:* 800-895-0811. *Fax:* 563-336-3350. *E-mail:* gmohr@eicc.edu.

SOUTHEASTERN COMMUNITY COLLEGE

West Burlington, Iowa **www.secc.cc.ia.us/**

- **State and locally supported** 2-year, founded 1968, part of Iowa Department of Education Division of Community Colleges
- **Small-town** 160-acre campus
- **Coed,** 3,754 undergraduate students, 56% full-time, 61% women, 39% men

Undergraduates 2,087 full-time, 1,667 part-time. 15% are from out of state, 2% African American, 0.5% Asian American or Pacific Islander, 1% Hispanic American, 0.2% Native American, 0.5% international, 2% live on campus.
Freshmen *Admission:* 538 enrolled.
Majors Accounting; administrative assistant and secretarial science; agricultural business and management; agronomy and crop science; artificial intelligence and robotics; automobile/automotive mechanics technology; biomedical technology; business administration and management; child development; computer programming; construction engineering technology; cosmetology; criminal justice/law enforcement administration; drafting and design technology; electrical, electronic and communications engineering technology; emergency medical technology (EMT paramedic); engineering related; industrial radiologic technology; information science/studies; liberal arts and sciences/liberal studies; machine tool technology; mechanical engineering/mechanical technology; medical/clinical assistant; nursing (licensed practical/vocational nurse training); nursing (registered nurse training); respiratory care therapy; substance abuse/addiction counseling; trade and industrial teacher education; welding technology.
Academics *Calendar:* semesters. *Degree:* certificates, diplomas, and associate. *Special study options:* academic remediation for entering students, adult/continuing education programs, advanced placement credit, cooperative education, distance learning, English as a second language, independent study, internships, part-time degree program, services for LD students, student-designed majors, summer session for credit.
Library Yohe Memorial Library.
Student Life *Housing Options:* coed, men-only, disabled students. Campus housing is university owned. *Activities and Organizations:* drama/theater group, student-run newspaper, choral group, Student Senate, Criminal Justice Club, Art Club, Science Club. *Campus security:* controlled dormitory access, night patrols by trained security personnel.
Athletics Member NJCAA. *Intercollegiate sports:* baseball M(s), basketball M(s), softball W(s), volleyball W(s). *Intramural sports:* basketball M, bowling M/W, softball M/W, volleyball M/W, weight lifting M/W.
Costs (2009–10) *Tuition:* state resident $3450 full-time, $115 per credit hour part-time; nonresident $3600 full-time, $120 per credit hour part-time. *Room and board:* $3856.
Financial Aid Of all full-time matriculated undergraduates who enrolled in 2008, 1,572 applied for aid, 1,127 were judged to have need. In 2008, 68 non-need-based awards were made. *Average financial aid package:* $6701. *Average need-based loan:* $3013. *Average need-based gift aid:* $3623. *Average non-need-based aid:* $1154.
Applying *Options:* early admission, deferred entrance. *Application deadlines:* rolling (freshmen), rolling (transfers). *Notification:* continuous (freshmen).
Freshman Application Contact Ms. Stacy White, Admissions, Southeastern Community College, 1500 West Agency Street, PO Box 180, West Burlington, IA 52655-0180. *Phone:* 319-752-2731 Ext. 8137. *Toll-free phone:* 866-722-4692. *E-mail:* admoff@scciowa.edu.

SOUTHWESTERN COMMUNITY COLLEGE

Creston, Iowa **www.swcciowa.edu/**

- **State-supported** 2-year, founded 1966, part of Iowa Department of Education Division of Community Colleges
- **Rural** 420-acre campus
- **Coed,** 1,680 undergraduate students, 50% full-time, 64% women, 36% men

Undergraduates 839 full-time, 841 part-time. Students come from 21 states and territories, 2 other countries, 5% are from out of state, 1% African American, 1% Asian American or Pacific Islander, 3% Hispanic American, 0.5% Native American, 0.4% international, 6% transferred in, 3% live on campus. *Retention:* 57% of 2008 full-time freshmen returned.
Freshmen *Admission:* 219 enrolled. *Average high school GPA:* 2.96.
Faculty *Total:* 123, 35% full-time, 2% with terminal degrees. *Student/faculty ratio:* 13:1.
Majors Accounting technology and bookkeeping; agribusiness; autobody/collision and repair technology; automobile/automotive mechanics technology; business administration and management; carpentry; civil drafting and CAD/CADD; computer systems networking and telecommunications; liberal arts and sciences/liberal studies; library science; medical transcription; music; nursing (registered nurse training); web page, digital/multimedia and information resources design.
Academics *Calendar:* semesters. *Degree:* certificates, diplomas, and associate. *Special study options:* academic remediation for entering students, adult/continuing education programs, advanced placement credit, distance learning, double majors, part-time degree program, summer session for credit.
Library Learning Resources Center with 20,500 titles.
Student Life *Housing Options:* men-only, women-only. Campus housing is university owned. *Activities and Organizations:* choral group. *Campus security:*

Southwestern Community College (continued)

24-hour emergency response devices and patrols, controlled dormitory access. *Student services:* personal/psychological counseling.

Athletics Member NJCAA. *Intercollegiate sports:* baseball M(s), basketball M(s)/W(s). *Intramural sports:* basketball M/W, football M, volleyball M/W.

Standardized Tests *Required for some:* SAT or ACT (for admission), ACT COMPASS.

Costs (2010–11) *Tuition:* state resident $4096 full-time; nonresident $4635 full-time. *Room and board:* $4900. Room and board charges vary according to housing facility. *Payment plan:* installment. *Waivers:* employees or children of employees.

Financial Aid Of all full-time matriculated undergraduates who enrolled in 2008, 84 Federal Work-Study jobs (averaging $1075). 42 state and other part-time jobs (averaging $1080).

Applying *Options:* electronic application, early admission. *Required:* high school transcript. *Application deadlines:* 9/5 (freshmen), 9/5 (transfers). *Notification:* continuous (freshmen), continuous (transfers).

Freshman Application Contact Ms. Lisa Carstens, Admissions Coordinator, Southwestern Community College, 1501 West Townline Street, Creston, IA 50801. *Phone:* 641-782-7081 Ext. 453. *Toll-free phone:* 800-247-4023. *Fax:* 641-782-3312. *E-mail:* carstens@swcciowa.edu.

VATTEROTT COLLEGE

Des Moines, Iowa **www.vatterott-college.edu/**

Freshman Application Contact Mr. Henry Franken, Co-Director, Vatterott College, 6100 Thornton Avenue, Suite 290, Des Moines, IA 50321. *Phone:* 515-309-9000. *Toll-free phone:* 800-353-7264. *Fax:* 515-309-0366.

WESTERN IOWA TECH COMMUNITY COLLEGE

Sioux City, Iowa **www.witcc.edu/**

Freshman Application Contact Lora Vanderzwaag, Director of Admissions, Western Iowa Tech Community College, 4647 Stone Avenue, Sioux City, IA 51102-5199. *Phone:* 712-274-6400. *Toll-free phone:* 800-352-4649 Ext. 6403. *Fax:* 712-274-6441.

KANSAS

ALLEN COMMUNITY COLLEGE

Iola, Kansas **www.allencc.edu/**

- **State and locally supported** 2-year, founded 1923, part of Kansas State Board of Regents
- **Small-town** 88-acre campus
- **Coed,** 2,776 undergraduate students, 42% full-time, 62% women, 38% men

Undergraduates 1,164 full-time, 1,612 part-time. Students come from 20 states and territories, 8 other countries, 9% are from out of state. *Retention:* 56% of 2008 full-time freshmen returned.

Freshmen *Admission:* 655 enrolled. *Average high school GPA:* 2.97.

Faculty *Total:* 155, 23% full-time. *Student/faculty ratio:* 17:1.

Majors Accounting; administrative assistant and secretarial science; agricultural production; architecture; art; athletic training; banking and financial support services; biology/biological sciences; business administration and management; business/commerce; business teacher education; chemistry; child development; computer science; computer systems networking and telecommunications; criminal justice/law enforcement administration; data processing and data processing technology; drafting and design technology; dramatic/theater arts; economics; electrical, electronic and communications engineering technology; electrical, electronics and communications engineering; elementary education; emergency medical technology (EMT paramedic); engineering; engineering technology; English composition; equestrian studies; family and consumer sciences/human sciences; farm and ranch management; forestry; funeral service and mortuary science; general studies; geography; health aide; health and physical education; history; home health aide/home attendant; hospital and health-care facilities administration; humanities; industrial arts; industrial technology; information science/studies; journalism; language interpretation and translation; library science; mathematics; music; nuclear/nuclear power technology; nursing assistant/aide and patient care assistant; parks, recreation and leisure facilities management; philosophy; physical therapy; physics; political science and government; postal management; pre-dentistry studies; pre-law studies; premedical studies; pre-pharmacy studies; pre-veterinary studies; psychology; religious studies; secondary education; social work; sociology; speech and rhetoric; technology/industrial arts teacher education; wood science and wood products/pulp and paper technology.

Academics *Calendar:* semesters. *Degree:* certificates and associate. *Special study options:* academic remediation for entering students, adult/continuing education programs, cooperative education, distance learning, English as a second language, independent study, internships, part-time degree program, services for LD students, student-designed majors, summer session for credit.

Library Learning Resource Center with 49,416 titles, 159 serial subscriptions, an OPAC.

Student Life *Housing Options:* coed, men-only, women-only. Campus housing is university owned. *Activities and Organizations:* drama/theater group, choral group, intramurals, Student Senate, Biology Club, Theatre, Phi Theta Kappa. *Student services:* personal/psychological counseling.

Athletics Member NJCAA. *Intercollegiate sports:* baseball M(s), basketball M(s)/W(s), cheerleading M(s)/W(s), cross-country running M(s)/W(s), golf M(s), soccer M(s)/W(s), softball W(s), track and field M(s)/W(s), volleyball W(s). *Intramural sports:* basketball M/W, football M/W, soccer M/W, softball M/W, table tennis M/W, tennis M/W, volleyball M/W.

Costs (2010–11) *Tuition:* state resident $1410 full-time, $47 per credit hour part-time; nonresident $1410 full-time, $47 per credit hour part-time. Full-time tuition and fees vary according to course load. Part-time tuition and fees vary according to course load. *Required fees:* $540 full-time, $18 per credit hour part-time. *Room and board:* $4300; room only: $3600. Room and board charges vary according to housing facility. *Waivers:* employees or children of employees.

Financial Aid Of all full-time matriculated undergraduates who enrolled in 2008, 510 applied for aid, 411 were judged to have need, 384 had their need fully met. 40 Federal Work-Study jobs (averaging $2600). 112 state and other part-time jobs (averaging $2600). In 2008, 22 non-need-based awards were made. *Average percent of need met:* 80%. *Average financial aid package:* $4738. *Average need-based loan:* $2482. *Average need-based gift aid:* $3257. *Average non-need-based aid:* $1241.

Applying *Options:* electronic application, early admission, deferred entrance. *Required:* high school transcript. *Notification:* continuous (freshmen), continuous (transfers).

Freshman Application Contact Mr. Randall Weber, Dean of Student Affairs, Allen Community College, 1801 North Cottonwood, Iola, KS 66749. *Phone:* 620-365-5116 Ext. 213. *Fax:* 620-365-7406. *E-mail:* weber@allencc.edu.

BARTON COUNTY COMMUNITY COLLEGE

Great Bend, Kansas **www.bartonccc.edu/**

- **State and locally supported** 2-year, founded 1969, part of Kansas Board of Regents
- **Rural** 140-acre campus
- **Endowment** $5.5 million
- **Coed,** 4,723 undergraduate students, 22% full-time, 44% women, 56% men

Undergraduates 1,028 full-time, 3,695 part-time. Students come from 49 states and territories, 23 other countries, 7% are from out of state, 4% transferred in, 8% live on campus.

Freshmen *Admission:* 395 enrolled. *Average high school GPA:* 3.03. *Test scores:* ACT scores over 18: 72%; ACT scores over 24: 17%; ACT scores over 30: 1%.

Faculty *Total:* 196, 35% full-time, 3% with terminal degrees. *Student/faculty ratio:* 23:1.

Majors Accounting; administrative assistant and secretarial science; agricultural business and management; agriculture; anthropology; architecture; art; athletic training; automobile/automotive mechanics technology; banking and financial support services; biology/biological sciences; business administration and management; chemistry; child-care and support services management; chiropractic assistant; clinical/medical laboratory technology; communication/speech communication and rhetoric; computer/information technology services administration related; computer programming (specific applications); computer science; computer systems networking and telecommunications; corrections; criminal justice/police science; crop production; cytotechnology; dance; dental hygiene; dietitian assistant; dramatic/theater arts; early childhood education; economics; elementary education; emergency care attendant (EMT ambulance);

emergency medical technology (EMT paramedic); engineering technology; English; financial planning and services; fire science; forestry; funeral service and mortuary science; general studies; geology/earth science; graphic design; hazardous materials management and waste technology; health aides/attendants/orderlies related; health and medical administrative services related; health information/medical records administration; history; home health aide/home attendant; human resources management; human resources management and services related; industrial production technologies related; information science/studies; journalism; kinesiology and exercise science; liberal arts and sciences/liberal studies; livestock management; logistics and materials management; marketing/marketing management; mathematics; medical administrative assistant and medical secretary; medical/clinical assistant; medical insurance coding; medical office assistant; medical transcription; medication aide; military studies; military technologies; modern languages; music; nursing assistant/aide and patient care assistant; nursing (licensed practical/vocational nurse training); nursing (registered nurse training); occupational therapy; optometric technician; pharmacy; pharmacy technician; philosophy; phlebotomy; physical education teaching and coaching; physical sciences; physical therapist assistant; physical therapy; physician assistant; physics; political science and government; pre-dentistry studies; pre-engineering; pre-law studies; premedical studies; pre-veterinary studies; psychology; public administration; radiologic technology/science; religious studies; respiratory care therapy; secondary education; security and protective services related; social work; sociology; sport and fitness administration/management; wildlife and wildlands science and management.

Academics *Calendar:* semesters. *Degree:* certificates and associate. *Special study options:* academic remediation for entering students, accelerated degree program, adult/continuing education programs, advanced placement credit, cooperative education, distance learning, double majors, English as a second language, external degree program, honors programs, independent study, internships, part-time degree program, services for LD students, summer session for credit.

Library Barton County Community College Library with 49,204 titles, 12,306 serial subscriptions, 1,389 audiovisual materials, an OPAC, a Web page.

Student Life *Housing Options:* coed, disabled students. Campus housing is university owned. Freshman campus housing is guaranteed. *Activities and Organizations:* drama/theater group, student-run newspaper, choral group, Danceline, Business Professionals, Psychology Club, Agriculture Club, Cougarettes. *Campus security:* 24-hour emergency response devices and patrols. *Student services:* health clinic, personal/psychological counseling.

Athletics Member NJCAA. *Intercollegiate sports:* baseball M(s), basketball M(s)/W(s), cheerleading M(s)/W(s), cross-country running M(s)/W(s), golf M(s)/W(s), soccer M(s)/W(s), softball W(s), tennis M(s)/W(s), track and field M(s)/W(s), volleyball W(s). *Intramural sports:* basketball M/W, bowling M/W, football M/W, golf M/W, softball M/W, swimming and diving M/W, table tennis M/W, tennis M/W, track and field M/W, volleyball M/W.

Costs (2009–10) *Tuition:* state resident $1470 full-time, $49 per credit hour part-time; nonresident $2100 full-time, $70 per credit hour part-time. Full-time tuition and fees vary according to course load. Part-time tuition and fees vary according to course load. *Required fees:* $750 full-time, $25 per credit hour part-time. *Room and board:* $4342. Room and board charges vary according to board plan. *Payment plans:* installment, deferred payment. *Waivers:* senior citizens and employees or children of employees.

Financial Aid Of all full-time matriculated undergraduates who enrolled in 2008, 102 Federal Work-Study jobs (averaging $2400).

Applying *Options:* electronic application, early admission. *Recommended:* high school transcript. *Application deadlines:* rolling (freshmen), rolling (transfers).

Freshman Application Contact Mr. Todd Moore, Director of Admissions and Promotions, Barton County Community College, 245 Northeast 30th Road, Great Bend, KS 67530. *Phone:* 620-792-9241. *Toll-free phone:* 800-722-6842. *Fax:* 620-786-1160. *E-mail:* admissions@bartonccc.edu.

Brown Mackie College–Kansas City

Lenexa, Kansas www.brownmackie.edu/kansascity/

- **Proprietary** 2-year, founded 1892, part of Education Management Corporation
- **Suburban** campus
- **Coed**

Majors Accounting technology and bookkeeping; athletic training; business administration and management; CAD/CADD drafting/design technology; criminal justice/law enforcement administration; health/health-care administration; legal assistant/paralegal; medical/clinical assistant; nursing (licensed practical/vocational nurse training); occupational therapist assistant; office management; veterinary/animal health technology.

Academics *Calendar:* quarters. *Degree:* certificates, diplomas, and associate.

Costs (2009–10) *Tuition:* Tuition varies by program. Students should contact Brown Mackie College for tuition information.

Freshman Application Contact Brown Mackie College–Kansas City, 9705 Lenexa Drive, Lenexa, KS 66215. *Phone:* 913-768-1900. *Toll-free phone:* 800-635-9101.

▶See page 424 for the College Close-Up.

Brown Mackie College–Salina

Salina, Kansas www.brownmackie.edu/salina/

- **Proprietary** 2-year, founded 1892, part of Education Management Corporation
- **Small-town** campus
- **Coed**

Majors Accounting technology and bookkeeping; athletic training; business administration and management; CAD/CADD drafting/design technology; computer systems networking and telecommunications; criminal justice/law enforcement administration; general studies; health/health-care administration; legal assistant/paralegal; medical/clinical assistant; nursing (licensed practical/vocational nurse training); occupational therapist assistant; office management.

Academics *Calendar:* modular. *Degree:* certificates, diplomas, and associate.

Costs (2009–10) *Tuition:* Tuition varies by program. Students should contact Brown Mackie College for tuition information.

Freshman Application Contact Brown Mackie College–Salina, 2106 South 9th Street, Salina, KS 67404. *Phone:* 785-825-5422. *Toll-free phone:* 800-365-0433.

▶See page 444 for the College Close-Up.

Butler Community College

El Dorado, Kansas www.butlercc.edu/

Freshman Application Contact Mr. Glenn Lygrisse, Interim Director of Enrollment Management, Butler Community College, 901 South Haverhill Road, El Dorado, KS 67042. *Phone:* 316-321-2222. *Fax:* 316-322-3109. *E-mail:* admissions@butlercc.edu.

Cloud County Community College

Concordia, Kansas www.cloud.edu/

- **State and locally supported** 2-year, founded 1965, part of Kansas Community College System
- **Rural** 35-acre campus
- **Coed**

Academics *Calendar:* semesters. *Degree:* certificates, diplomas, and associate. *Special study options:* academic remediation for entering students, adult/continuing education programs, advanced placement credit, cooperative education, internships, part-time degree program, services for LD students, summer session for credit.

Student Life *Campus security:* 24-hour emergency response devices.

Athletics Member NJCAA.

Financial Aid Of all full-time matriculated undergraduates who enrolled in 2008, 122 Federal Work-Study jobs (averaging $800).

Applying *Options:* early admission, deferred entrance. *Required:* high school transcript.

Director of Admissions Kim Reynolds, Director of Admissions, Cloud County Community College, 2221 Campus Drive, PO Box 1002, Concordia, KS 66901-1002. *Phone:* 785-243-1435 Ext. 214. *Toll-free phone:* 800-729-5101.

Coffeyville Community College

Coffeyville, Kansas www.coffeyville.edu/

Freshman Application Contact Ms. Kelli Baur, Administrative Assistant to the Executive Vice President, Coffeyville Community College, 400 West 11th, Coffeyville, KS 67337. *Phone:* 620-252-7700. *E-mail:* kellib@coffeyville.edu.

COLBY COMMUNITY COLLEGE

Colby, Kansas www.colbycc.edu/

- **State and locally supported** 2-year, founded 1964, part of Kansas State Board of Education
- **Small-town** 80-acre campus
- **Endowment** $3.4 million
- **Coed,** 1,565 undergraduate students, 48% full-time, 62% women, 38% men

Undergraduates 759 full-time, 806 part-time. Students come from 15 states and territories, 5 other countries, 30% are from out of state, 3% African American, 1% Asian American or Pacific Islander, 3% Hispanic American, 0.8% Native American, 3% international, 6% transferred in, 30% live on campus.

Freshmen *Admission:* 622 applied, 622 admitted, 230 enrolled. *Average high school GPA:* 2.96. *Test scores:* ACT scores over 18: 67%; ACT scores over 24: 12%; ACT scores over 30: 2%.

Faculty *Total:* 153, 38% full-time, 11% with terminal degrees. *Student/faculty ratio:* 11:1.

Majors Administrative assistant and secretarial science; agribusiness; agricultural business and management; agricultural teacher education; agronomy and crop science; broadcast journalism; business administration and management; child-care and support services management; child development; computer and information sciences; computer and information sciences related; criminal justice/law enforcement administration; dental hygiene; farm and ranch management; horse husbandry/equine science and management; nursing (licensed practical/vocational nurse training); nursing (registered nurse training); physical therapist assistant; radio and television; veterinary/animal health technology.

Academics *Calendar:* semesters. *Degree:* certificates, diplomas, and associate. *Special study options:* academic remediation for entering students, adult/continuing education programs, advanced placement credit, cooperative education, distance learning, double majors, honors programs, internships, part-time degree program, services for LD students, student-designed majors, summer session for credit.

Library Davis Library with 34,000 titles, 463 serial subscriptions, 600 audiovisual materials, an OPAC.

Student Life *Housing:* on-campus residence required for freshman year. *Options:* coed, men-only, women-only. Campus housing is university owned. *Activities and Organizations:* drama/theater group, student-run newspaper, radio and television station, choral group, KSNEA, Physical Therapist Assistants Club, Block and Bridle, SVTA, COPNS. *Campus security:* 24-hour emergency response devices and patrols. *Student services:* health clinic, personal/psychological counseling.

Athletics Member NJCAA. *Intercollegiate sports:* baseball M(s), basketball M(s)/W(s), cheerleading M(s)/W(s), cross-country running M(s)/W(s), equestrian sports M/W, golf M(s)/W(s), softball W(s), track and field M(s)/W(s), volleyball W(s), wrestling M(s). *Intramural sports:* basketball M/W, softball M/W, volleyball M/W.

Standardized Tests *Recommended:* SAT or ACT (for admission).

Costs (2010–11) *Tuition:* state resident $1664 full-time, $52 per credit hour part-time; nonresident $3104 full-time, $97 per credit hour part-time. Full-time tuition and fees vary according to course load and program. Part-time tuition and fees vary according to course load and program. *Required fees:* $1152 full-time, $36 per credit hour part-time. *Room and board:* $4690. Room and board charges vary according to housing facility. *Payment plan:* installment. *Waivers:* senior citizens and employees or children of employees.

Financial Aid Of all full-time matriculated undergraduates who enrolled in 2008, 95 Federal Work-Study jobs (averaging $1500). 30 state and other part-time jobs (averaging $2000).

Applying *Options:* electronic application, early admission, deferred entrance. *Required:* high school transcript. *Required for some:* interview. *Application deadlines:* rolling (freshmen), rolling (out-of-state freshmen), rolling (transfers). *Notification:* continuous (freshmen), continuous (out-of-state freshmen), continuous (transfers).

Freshman Application Contact Ms. Nikol Nolan, Admissions Director, Colby Community College, 1255 South Range, Colby, KS 67701-4099. *Phone:* 785-462-3984 Ext. 5496. *Toll-free phone:* 888-634-9350 Ext. 690. *Fax:* 785-460-4691. *E-mail:* admissions@colbycc.edu.

COWLEY COUNTY COMMUNITY COLLEGE AND AREA VOCATIONAL–TECHNICAL SCHOOL

Arkansas City, Kansas www.cowley.cc.ks.us/

- **State and locally supported** 2-year, founded 1922, part of Kansas State Board of Education
- **Small-town** 19-acre campus
- **Endowment** $2.9 million
- **Coed,** 4,014 undergraduate students, 50% full-time, 60% women, 40% men

Undergraduates 2,019 full-time, 1,995 part-time. 6% are from out of state, 8% African American, 3% Asian American or Pacific Islander, 5% Hispanic American, 1% Native American, 0.1% international, 10% live on campus.

Freshmen *Admission:* 598 applied, 598 admitted, 598 enrolled. *Average high school GPA:* 2.79. *Test scores:* ACT scores over 18: 75%; ACT scores over 24: 21%; ACT scores over 30: 1%.

Faculty *Total:* 199, 24% full-time. *Student/faculty ratio:* 27:1.

Majors Accounting; administrative assistant and secretarial science; agriculture; art; automobile/automotive mechanics technology; biology/biological sciences; business administration and management; chemistry; child-care and support services management; child development; computer and information sciences; computer and information systems security; computer graphics; computer programming (specific applications); computer science; cosmetology; criminal justice/law enforcement administration; criminal justice/police science; dietetics and clinical nutrition services related; drafting and design technology; dramatic/theater arts; education; electromechanical and instrumentation and maintenance technologies related; elementary education; emergency medical technology (EMT paramedic); engineering technology; entrepreneurship; forensic science and technology; hotel/motel administration; industrial radiologic technology; journalism; legal administrative assistant/secretary; liberal arts and sciences/liberal studies; machine tool technology; marketing/marketing management; medical insurance coding; medical transcription; music; physical anthropology; pre-engineering; religious studies; social work; technology/industrial arts teacher education; welding technology.

Academics *Calendar:* semesters. *Degree:* certificates, diplomas, and associate. *Special study options:* academic remediation for entering students, accelerated degree program, adult/continuing education programs, advanced placement credit, cooperative education, distance learning, external degree program, independent study, off-campus study, part-time degree program, services for LD students, summer session for credit.

Library Renn Memorial Library with 30,000 titles, 15,000 serial subscriptions, 700 audiovisual materials, an OPAC, a Web page.

Student Life *Housing Options:* coed, men-only, women-only. Campus housing is university owned. *Activities and Organizations:* drama/theater group, student-run newspaper, choral group, Academic Civic Engagement through Services (ACES), Peers Advocating for Wellness (PAWS), Phi Theta Kappa, Student Government Association, Phi Beta Lambda. *Campus security:* 24-hour emergency response devices and patrols, late-night transport/escort service, controlled dormitory access, residence hall entrances are locked at night. *Student services:* health clinic, personal/psychological counseling.

Athletics Member NJCAA. *Intercollegiate sports:* baseball M(s), basketball M(s)/W(s), cross-country running M(s)/W(s), soccer M(s)/W(s), softball W(s), tennis M(s)/W(s), track and field M(s)/W(s), volleyball W(s). *Intramural sports:* basketball M/W, bowling M/W, football M, softball M/W, tennis M/W, volleyball M/W.

Standardized Tests *Recommended:* ACT (for admission).

Costs (2009–10) *Tuition:* area resident $1440 full-time, $45 per credit hour part-time; state resident $1760 full-time, $55 per credit hour part-time; nonresident $3328 full-time, $104 per credit hour part-time. *Required fees:* $690 full-time, $23 per credit hour part-time. *Room and board:* $4375. Room and board charges vary according to board plan. *Payment plan:* installment. *Waivers:* employees or children of employees.

Financial Aid Of all full-time matriculated undergraduates who enrolled in 2008, 50 Federal Work-Study jobs (averaging $1500). 75 state and other part-time jobs (averaging $2000).

Applying *Options:* electronic application, early admission. *Required:* high school transcript. *Application deadlines:* rolling (freshmen), rolling (transfers).

Freshman Application Contact Mr. Ben Schears, Executive Director of Enrollment and Outreach Services, Cowley County Community College and Area Vocational–Technical School, 125 South Second, PO Box 1147, Arkansas City, KS 67005-1147. *Phone:* 620-441-5368. *Toll-free phone:* 800-593-CCCC. *Fax:* 620-441-5350. *E-mail:* admissions@cowley.edu.

DODGE CITY COMMUNITY COLLEGE

Dodge City, Kansas **www.dc3.edu/**

Director of Admissions Mrs. Tammy Tabor, Director of Admissions, Placement, Testing and Student Services Marketing, Dodge City Community College, 2501 North 14th Street, Dodge City, KS 67801-2399. *Phone:* 620-225-1321. *Toll-free phone:* 800-742-9519. *E-mail:* admin@dc3.edu.

DONNELLY COLLEGE

Kansas City, Kansas **www.donnelly.edu/**

- **Independent Roman Catholic** primarily 2-year, founded 1949
- **Urban** 4-acre campus
- **Coed,** 661 undergraduate students, 44% full-time, 75% women, 25% men

Undergraduates 291 full-time, 370 part-time. Students come from 2 states and territories, 42 other countries, 15% are from out of state, 48% African American, 5% Asian American or Pacific Islander, 26% Hispanic American, 0.8% Native American, 7% international, 2% transferred in, 2% live on campus. *Retention:* 48% of 2008 full-time freshmen returned.

Freshmen *Admission:* 93 enrolled.

Faculty *Total:* 48, 31% full-time, 13% with terminal degrees. *Student/faculty ratio:* 16:1.

Majors Liberal arts and sciences/liberal studies.

Academics *Calendar:* semesters. *Degrees:* certificates, associate, and bachelor's. *Special study options:* academic remediation for entering students, advanced placement credit, distance learning, double majors, English as a second language, external degree program, independent study, internships, part-time degree program, services for LD students, summer session for credit.

Library Trant Memorial Library with 33,752 titles, 114 serial subscriptions, 1,020 audiovisual materials, an OPAC, a Web page.

Student Life *Housing Options:* men-only, women-only. Campus housing is university owned and is provided by a third party. *Activities and Organizations:* Organization of Student Leadership, Student Ambassadors, Healthy Student Task Force, Men's Soccer Club, Women's Soccer Club. *Campus security:* 24-hour emergency response devices. *Student services:* personal/psychological counseling.

Applying *Options:* electronic application, early admission, deferred entrance. *Recommended:* high school transcript. *Application deadlines:* rolling (freshmen), rolling (transfers).

Freshman Application Contact Mr. Edward Marquez, Director of Admissions, Donnelly College, 608 North 18th Street, Kansas City, KS 66102. *Phone:* 913-621-8713. *Fax:* 913-621-8719. *E-mail:* admissions@donnelly.edu.

FLINT HILLS TECHNICAL COLLEGE

Emporia, Kansas **www.fhtc.net/**

Freshman Application Contact Admissions Office, Flint Hills Technical College, 3301 West 18th Avenue, Emporia, KS 66801. *Phone:* 620-341-1325. *Toll-free phone:* 800-711-6947.

FORT SCOTT COMMUNITY COLLEGE

Fort Scott, Kansas **www.fortscott.edu/**

- **State and locally supported** 2-year, founded 1919
- **Small-town** 147-acre campus
- **Coed**

Academics *Calendar:* semesters. *Degree:* certificates and associate. *Special study options:* academic remediation for entering students, adult/continuing education programs, advanced placement credit, cooperative education, distance learning, English as a second language, external degree program, independent study, internships, part-time degree program, services for LD students, student-designed majors, study abroad, summer session for credit. *ROTC:* Army (c).

Student Life *Campus security:* controlled dormitory access, evening security from 9 pm to 6 am.

Athletics Member NJCAA.

Costs (2009–10) *Tuition:* state resident $1776 full-time, $74 per credit hour part-time; nonresident $3120 full-time, $130 per credit hour part-time. Full-time tuition and fees vary according to course load. Part-time tuition and fees vary according to course load. *Room and board:* $4600. Room and board charges vary according to housing facility.

Applying *Options:* early admission, deferred entrance.

Director of Admissions Mrs. Mert Barrows, Director of Admissions, Fort Scott Community College, 2108 South Horton, Fort Scott, KS 66701. *Phone:* 620-223-2700 Ext. 353. *Toll-free phone:* 800-874-3722.

GARDEN CITY COMMUNITY COLLEGE

Garden City, Kansas **www.gcccks.edu/**

- **County-supported** 2-year, founded 1919, part of Kansas Board of Regents
- **Rural** 63-acre campus
- **Coed**

Academics *Calendar:* semesters. *Degree:* certificates and associate. *Special study options:* academic remediation for entering students, adult/continuing education programs, advanced placement credit, distance learning, English as a second language, external degree program, part-time degree program, services for LD students, student-designed majors, summer session for credit.

Student Life *Campus security:* 24-hour emergency response devices and patrols, student patrols, late-night transport/escort service, controlled dormitory access.

Athletics Member NJCAA.

Standardized Tests *Required:* ACT COMPASS (for admission). *Recommended:* ACT (for admission).

Financial Aid Of all full-time matriculated undergraduates who enrolled in 2008, 90 Federal Work-Study jobs (averaging $1000). 100 state and other part-time jobs (averaging $900).

Applying *Required:* high school transcript.

Freshman Application Contact Office of Admissions, Garden City Community College, 801 Campus Drive, Garden City, KS 67846. *Phone:* 620-276-9531. *Fax:* 620-276-9650. *E-mail:* admissions@gcccks.edu.

HESSTON COLLEGE

Hesston, Kansas **www.hesston.edu/**

Freshman Application Contact Joel Kauffman, Vice President of Admissions, Hesston College, Box 3000, Hesston, KS 67062. *Phone:* 620-327-8222. *Toll-free phone:* 800-995-2757. *Fax:* 620-327-8300. *E-mail:* admissions@hesston.edu.

HIGHLAND COMMUNITY COLLEGE

Highland, Kansas **www.highlandcc.edu/**

- **State and locally supported** 2-year, founded 1858, part of Kansas Community College System
- **Rural** 20-acre campus
- **Coed**

Academics *Calendar:* semesters. *Degree:* certificates and associate. *Special study options:* academic remediation for entering students, adult/continuing education programs, advanced placement credit, cooperative education, internships, off-campus study, part-time degree program, services for LD students, student-designed majors, summer session for credit. *ROTC:* Army (c).

Athletics Member NJCAA.

Financial Aid Of all full-time matriculated undergraduates who enrolled in 2008, 75 Federal Work-Study jobs (averaging $1200). 25 state and other part-time jobs (averaging $1000).

Applying *Options:* early admission. *Required:* high school transcript.

Director of Admissions Ms. Cheryl Rasmussen, Vice President of Student Services, Highland Community College, 606 West Main Street, Highland, KS 66035-4165. *Phone:* 785-442-6020. *Fax:* 785-442-6106.

HUTCHINSON COMMUNITY COLLEGE AND AREA VOCATIONAL SCHOOL

Hutchinson, Kansas **www.hutchcc.edu/**

- **State and locally supported** 2-year, founded 1928, part of Kansas Board of Regents
- **Small-town** 47-acre campus
- **Coed,** 5,453 undergraduate students, 44% full-time, 58% women, 42% men

Hutchinson Community College and Area Vocational School (continued)

Undergraduates 2,415 full-time, 3,038 part-time. Students come from 41 states and territories, 5 other countries, 6% are from out of state, 6% African American, 0.6% Asian American or Pacific Islander, 6% Hispanic American, 1% Native American, 0.5% international, 8% transferred in, 7% live on campus. *Retention:* 64% of 2008 full-time freshmen returned.

Freshmen *Admission:* 1,184 enrolled. *Average high school GPA:* 2.85.

Faculty *Total:* 347, 33% full-time, 6% with terminal degrees. *Student/faculty ratio:* 18:1.

Majors Administrative assistant and secretarial science; agricultural mechanization; agriculture; autobody/collision and repair technology; automobile/automotive mechanics technology; biology/biological sciences; biotechnology; business and personal/financial services marketing; business/commerce; carpentry; child-care and support services management; communication/speech communication and rhetoric; communications technology; computer and information sciences; computer systems analysis; criminal justice/police science; drafting and design technology; education; educational/instructional media design; electrical/electronics equipment installation and repair; emergency medical technology (EMT paramedic); engineering; English; family and consumer sciences/human sciences; farm and ranch management; fire science; foreign languages and literatures; health information/medical records technology; legal assistant/paralegal; liberal arts and sciences/liberal studies; machine tool technology; manufacturing technology; mathematics; medical radiologic technology; nursing (registered nurse training); physical sciences; physical therapist assistant; psychology; respiratory care therapy; retailing; social sciences; visual and performing arts; welding technology.

Academics *Calendar:* semesters. *Degree:* certificates and associate. *Special study options:* academic remediation for entering students, adult/continuing education programs, advanced placement credit, cooperative education, distance learning, double majors, English as a second language, honors programs, independent study, internships, part-time degree program, services for LD students, student-designed majors, summer session for credit. *ROTC:* Army (c).

Library John F. Kennedy Library plus 1 other with 42,500 titles, 245 serial subscriptions, 3,150 audiovisual materials, an OPAC, a Web page.

Student Life *Housing Options:* men-only, women-only. Campus housing is university owned. *Activities and Organizations:* drama/theater group, student-run newspaper, choral group. *Campus security:* 24-hour emergency response devices and patrols, student patrols, late-night transport/escort service, controlled dormitory access. *Student services:* health clinic, personal/psychological counseling.

Athletics Member NJCAA. *Intercollegiate sports:* baseball M(s), basketball M(s)/W(s), cheerleading M(s)/W(s), cross-country running M(s)/W(s), football M(s), golf M(s), soccer W(s), softball W(s), track and field M(s)/W(s), volleyball W(s). *Intramural sports:* badminton M/W, basketball M/W, bowling M/W, football M/W, racquetball M/W, soccer M/W, tennis M/W, track and field M/W, volleyball M/W.

Costs (2009–10) *Tuition:* state resident $1920 full-time, $60 per credit hour part-time; nonresident $3008 full-time, $94 per credit hour part-time. *Required fees:* $512 full-time, $16 per credit hour part-time. *Room and board:* $4816. Room and board charges vary according to board plan. *Payment plan:* installment.

Applying *Options:* electronic application, early admission, deferred entrance. *Required for some:* interview. *Recommended:* high school transcript. *Application deadlines:* rolling (freshmen), rolling (transfers).

Freshman Application Contact Mr. Corbin Strobel, Director of Admissions, Hutchinson Community College and Area Vocational School, 1300 North Plum, Hutchinson, KS 67501. *Phone:* 620-665-3536. *Toll-free phone:* 800-289-3501 Ext. 3536. *Fax:* 620-665-3301. *E-mail:* strobelc@hutchcc.edu.

INDEPENDENCE COMMUNITY COLLEGE

Independence, Kansas **www.indycc.edu/**

Freshman Application Contact Ms. Sally A. Ciufulescu, Director of Admissions, Independence Community College, PO Box 708, Independence, KS 67301. *Phone:* 620-332-5400. *Toll-free phone:* 800-842-6063. *Fax:* 620-331-0946. *E-mail:* sciufulescu@indycc.edu.

JOHNSON COUNTY COMMUNITY COLLEGE

Overland Park, Kansas **www.johnco.cc.ks.us/**

- **State and locally supported** 2-year, founded 1967, part of Kansas State Board of Education
- **Suburban** 220-acre campus with easy access to Kansas City
- **Coed**

Academics *Calendar:* semesters. *Degree:* certificates and associate. *Special study options:* academic remediation for entering students, adult/continuing education programs, advanced placement credit, cooperative education, distance learning, double majors, English as a second language, honors programs, independent study, internships, off-campus study, part-time degree program, services for LD students, student-designed majors, summer session for credit.

Student Life *Campus security:* 24-hour emergency response devices and patrols, late-night transport/escort service.

Athletics Member NJCAA.

Financial Aid Of all full-time matriculated undergraduates who enrolled in 2008, 85 Federal Work-Study jobs (averaging $4000).

Applying *Options:* early admission. *Required for some:* high school transcript.

Director of Admissions Dr. Charles J. Carlsen, President, Johnson County Community College, 12345 College Park Boulevard, Overland Park, KS 66210. *Phone:* 913-469-8500 Ext. 3806.

KANSAS CITY KANSAS COMMUNITY COLLEGE

Kansas City, Kansas **www.kckcc.edu/**

Freshman Application Contact Dr. Denise McDowell, Dean of Enrollment Management/Registrar, Kansas City Kansas Community College, 7250 State Avenue, Kansas City, KS 66112. *Phone:* 913-288-7694. *Fax:* 913-288-7648. *E-mail:* dmcdowell@kckcc.edu.

LABETTE COMMUNITY COLLEGE

Parsons, Kansas **www.labette.edu/**

Freshman Application Contact Ms. Tammy Fuentez, Director of Admission, Labette Community College, 200 South 14th Street, Parsons, KS 67357. *Phone:* 620-421-6700. *Toll-free phone:* 888-522-3883. *Fax:* 620-421-0180.

MANHATTAN AREA TECHNICAL COLLEGE

Manhattan, Kansas **www.matc.net/**

- **State and locally supported** 2-year, founded 1965
- **Suburban** 19-acre campus
- **Coed,** 473 undergraduate students, 73% full-time, 48% women, 52% men

Undergraduates 343 full-time, 130 part-time. 5% African American, 2% Asian American or Pacific Islander, 3% Hispanic American, 0.6% Native American, 23% transferred in.

Freshmen *Admission:* 126 admitted, 100 enrolled.

Faculty *Total:* 35, 77% full-time. *Student/faculty ratio:* 11:1.

Majors Autobody/collision and repair technology; automobile/automotive mechanics technology; building/construction finishing, management, and inspection related; computer systems networking and telecommunications; computer technology/computer systems technology; drafting and design technology; electrical and power transmission installation related; heating, air conditioning and refrigeration technology; management information systems; nursing (licensed practical/vocational nurse training); nursing (registered nurse training); welding technology.

Academics *Calendar:* semesters. *Degree:* certificates, diplomas, and associate.

Library Matc Library with an OPAC.

Student Life *Housing:* college housing not available.

Applying *Application fee:* $40. *Required for some:* high school transcript. *Recommended:* high school transcript.

Freshman Application Contact Mr. Rick Smith, Coordinator of Admissions and Recruitment, Manhattan Area Technical College, 3136 Dickens Avenue, Manhattan, KS 66503. *Phone:* 785-587-2800 Ext. 104. *Toll-free phone:* 800-352-7575. *Fax:* 913-587-2804.

NATIONAL AMERICAN UNIVERSITY

Overland Park, Kansas **www.national.edu/**

Freshman Application Contact Admissions Office, National American University, 10310 Mastin, Overland Park, KS 66212.

NEOSHO COUNTY COMMUNITY COLLEGE

Chanute, Kansas **www.neosho.edu/**

Freshman Application Contact Ms. Lisa Last, Dean of Student Development, Neosho County Community College, 800 West 14th Street, Chanute, KS 66720-2699. *Phone:* 620-431-2820 Ext. 213. *Toll-free phone:* 800-729-6222. *Fax:* 620-431-0082. *E-mail:* llast@neosho.edu.

NORTH CENTRAL KANSAS TECHNICAL COLLEGE

Beloit, Kansas **www.ncktc.edu/**

Freshman Application Contact Ms. Judy Heidrick, Director of Admissions, North Central Kansas Technical College, PO Box 507, 3033 US Highway 24, Beloit, KS 67420. *Toll-free phone:* 800-658-4655. *E-mail:* jheidrick@ncktc.tec.ks.us.

NORTHEAST KANSAS TECHNICAL CENTER OF HIGHLAND COMMUNITY COLLEGE

Atchison, Kansas **www.nektc.net/**

- **State-supported** 2-year, founded 1965
- **Coed**

Academics *Calendar:* semesters.

Applying *Application fee:* $25.

Admissions Office Contact Northeast Kansas Technical Center of Highland Community College, 1501 West Riley Street, Atchison, KS 66002. *Toll-free phone:* 800-567-4890.

NORTHWEST KANSAS TECHNICAL COLLEGE

Goodland, Kansas **www.nwktc.org/**

Admissions Office Contact Northwest Kansas Technical College, PO Box 668, 1209 Harrison Street, Goodland, KS 67735. *Toll-free phone:* 800-316-4127.

PRATT COMMUNITY COLLEGE

Pratt, Kansas **www.prattcc.edu/**

Freshman Application Contact Ms. Theresa Ziehr, Student Services, Pratt Community College, 348 Northeast State Road 61, Pratt, KS 67124. *Phone:* 620-450-2217. *Toll-free phone:* 800-794-3091. *Fax:* 620-672-5288. *E-mail:* theresaz@prattcc.edu.

SEWARD COUNTY COMMUNITY COLLEGE

Liberal, Kansas **www.sccc.edu/**

- **State and locally supported** 2-year, founded 1969, part of Kansas State Board of Regents
- **Rural** 120-acre campus
- **Coed**

Academics *Calendar:* semesters. *Degree:* certificates, diplomas, and associate. *Special study options:* academic remediation for entering students, adult/continuing education programs, cooperative education, distance learning, English as a second language, external degree program, internships, part-time degree program, student-designed majors, summer session for credit.

Student Life *Campus security:* 24-hour patrols, late-night transport/escort service.

Athletics Member NJCAA.

Financial Aid Of all full-time matriculated undergraduates who enrolled in 2008, 60 Federal Work-Study jobs (averaging $1854). 168 state and other part-time jobs (averaging $1854).

Applying *Options:* early admission, deferred entrance. *Required:* high school transcript. *Required for some:* minimum 2.0 GPA, 1 letter of recommendation, interview.

Director of Admissions Dr. Gerald Harris, Dean of Student Services, Seward County Community College, PO Box 1137, Liberal, KS 67905-1137. *Phone:* 620-624-1951 Ext. 617. *Toll-free phone:* 800-373-9951 Ext. 710.

WICHITA AREA TECHNICAL COLLEGE

Wichita, Kansas **www.wichitatech.com/**

Freshman Application Contact Ms. Jessica Ross, Dean, Enrollment Management, Wichita Area Technical College, 301 South Grove Street, Wichita, KS 67211. *Phone:* 316-677-9400. *Fax:* 316-677-9555. *E-mail:* info@watc.edu.

KENTUCKY

ASHLAND COMMUNITY AND TECHNICAL COLLEGE

Ashland, Kentucky **www.ashland.kctcs.edu/**

Freshman Application Contact Mrs. Willie G. McCullough, Dean of Student Affairs, Ashland Community and Technical College, 1400 College Drive, Ashland, KY 41101. *Phone:* 606-326-2114. *Toll-free phone:* 800-370-7191. *E-mail:* willie.mccullough@kctcs.net.

ATA CAREER EDUCATION

Louisville, Kentucky **www.atai.com/**

Freshman Application Contact Admissions Office, ATA Career Education, 10180 Linn Station Road, Suite A200, Louisville, KY 40223. *Phone:* 502-371-8330. *Fax:* 502-371-8598.

BECKFIELD COLLEGE

Florence, Kentucky **www.beckfield.edu/**

- **Proprietary** primarily 2-year, founded 1984
- **Suburban** campus
- **Coed**

Academics *Calendar:* quarters. *Degrees:* certificates, diplomas, associate, and bachelor's.

Applying *Application fee:* $150.

Beckfield College (continued)

Freshman Application Contact Mrs. Leah Boerger, Director of Admissions, Beckfield College, 16 Spiral Drive, Florence, KY 41042. *Phone:* 859-371-9393. *E-mail:* lboerger@beckfield.edu.

BIG SANDY COMMUNITY AND TECHNICAL COLLEGE

Prestonsburg, Kentucky **www.bigsandy.kctcs.edu/**

- **State-supported** 2-year, founded 1964, part of Kentucky Community and Technical College System
- **Rural** 50-acre campus
- **Coed**

Academics *Calendar:* semesters. *Degree:* associate. *Special study options:* academic remediation for entering students, adult/continuing education programs, advanced placement credit, cooperative education, distance learning, independent study, off-campus study, part-time degree program, services for LD students, summer session for credit.

Student Life *Campus security:* 24-hour emergency response devices.

Costs (2009–10) *Tuition:* state resident $3750 full-time, $125 per credit hour part-time; nonresident $12,750 full-time, $425 per credit hour part-time.

Financial Aid Of all full-time matriculated undergraduates who enrolled in 2008, 112 Federal Work-Study jobs (averaging $1749).

Applying *Options:* early admission, deferred entrance. *Required:* high school transcript.

Director of Admissions Jimmy Wright, Director of Admissions, Big Sandy Community and Technical College, One Bert T. Combs Drive, Prestonsburg, KY 41653-1815. *Phone:* 606-886-3863. *Toll-free phone:* 888-641-4132. *E-mail:* jimmy.wright@kctcs.edu.

BLUEGRASS COMMUNITY AND TECHNICAL COLLEGE

Lexington, Kentucky **www.bluegrass.kctcs.edu/**

Freshman Application Contact Mrs. Shelbie Hugle, Director of Admission Services, Bluegrass Community and Technical College, 200 Oswald Building, Cooper Drive, Lexington, KY 40506-0235. *Phone:* 859-246-6216. *Toll-free phone:* 866-744-4872 Ext. 5111. *E-mail:* shelbie.hugle@kctcs.edu.

BOWLING GREEN TECHNICAL COLLEGE

Bowling Green, Kentucky **www.bowlinggreen.kctcs.edu/**

- **State-supported** 2-year, founded 1938
- **Coed**

Academics *Calendar:* semesters. *Degree:* associate.

Director of Admissions Mark Garrett, Chief Student Affairs Officer, Bowling Green Technical College, 1845 Loop Drive, Bowling Green, KY 42101. *Phone:* 270-901-1114. *Toll-free phone:* 800-790.0990.

BROWN MACKIE COLLEGE–HOPKINSVILLE

Hopkinsville, Kentucky **www.brownmackie.edu/Hopkinsville/**

- **Proprietary** 2-year, part of Education Management Corporation
- **Small-town** campus
- **Coed**

Majors Accounting technology and bookkeeping; business administration and management; computer programming; computer programming (specific applications); computer software technology; criminal justice/law enforcement administration; legal assistant/paralegal; medical/clinical assistant; medical office management; occupational therapist assistant.

Academics *Calendar:* quarters. *Degree:* diplomas and associate.

Costs (2009–10) *Tuition:* Tuition varies by program. Students should contact Brown Mackie College for tuition information.

Freshman Application Contact Brown Mackie College–Hopkinsville, 4001 Fort Campbell Boulevard, Hopkinsville, KY 42240. *Phone:* 270-886-1302. *Toll-free phone:* 800-359-4753.

▶See page 420 for the College Close-Up.

BROWN MACKIE COLLEGE–LOUISVILLE

Louisville, Kentucky **www.brownmackie.edu/louisville/**

- **Proprietary** primarily 2-year, founded 1972, part of Education Management Corporation
- **Suburban** campus
- **Coed**

Majors Accounting technology and bookkeeping; biomedical technology; business administration and management; computer systems networking and telecommunications; criminal justice/law enforcement administration; early childhood education; electrical, electronic and communications engineering technology; graphic design; health/health-care administration; legal assistant/paralegal; legal studies; medical/clinical assistant; occupational therapist assistant; pharmacy technician; surgical technology; veterinary/animal health technology.

Academics *Calendar:* quarters. *Degrees:* certificates, diplomas, associate, and bachelor's.

Costs (2009–10) *Tuition:* Tuition varies by program. Students should contact Brown Mackie College for tuition information.

Freshman Application Contact Brown Mackie College–Louisville, 3605 Fern Valley Road, Louisville, KY 40219. *Phone:* 502-968-7191. *Toll-free phone:* 800-999-7387.

▶See page 426 for the College Close-Up.

BROWN MACKIE COLLEGE–NORTHERN KENTUCKY

Fort Mitchell, Kentucky **www.brownmackie.edu/northernkentucky/**

- **Proprietary** 2-year, founded 1927, part of Education Management Corporation
- **Suburban** campus
- **Coed**

Majors Accounting technology and bookkeeping; business administration and management; CAD/CADD drafting/design technology; computer software technology; criminal justice/law enforcement administration; health/health-care administration; information technology; legal assistant/paralegal; medical/clinical assistant; occupational therapist assistant; pharmacy technician; surgical technology.

Academics *Calendar:* quarters. *Degree:* certificates, diplomas, and associate.

Costs (2009–10) *Tuition:* Tuition varies by program. Students should contact Brown Mackie College for tuition information.

Freshman Application Contact Brown Mackie College–Northern Kentucky, 309 Buttermilk Pike, Fort Mitchell, KY 41017. *Phone:* 859-341-5627. *Toll-free phone:* 800-888-1445.

▶See page 436 for the College Close-Up.

DAYMAR COLLEGE

Bellevue, Kentucky **www.daymarcollege.edu/**

Freshman Application Contact Director of Admissions, Daymar College, 119 Fairfield Avenue, Bellevue, KY 41073. *Phone:* 859-291-0800. *Toll-free phone:* 877-258-7796. *Fax:* 859-491-7500.

DAYMAR COLLEGE

Bowling Green, Kentucky **www.draughons.edu/**

Freshman Application Contact Mrs. Traci Henderson, Admissions Director, Daymar College, 2421 Fitzgerald Industrial Drive, Bowling Green, KY 42101. *Phone:* 270-843-6750.

DAYMAR COLLEGE

Louisville, Kentucky **www.daymarcollege.edu/**

- **Proprietary** 2-year, founded 2001
- **Coed**

Academics *Calendar:* quarters. *Degree:* diplomas and associate.

Applying *Required:* high school transcript, interview.

Director of Admissions Mr. Patrick Carney, Director of Admissions, Daymar College, 4400 Breckenridge Lane, Suite 415, Louisville, KY 40218.

DAYMAR COLLEGE

Owensboro, Kentucky **www.daymarcollege.edu/**

- **Proprietary** 2-year, founded 1963
- **Small-town** 1-acre campus
- **Coed**

Academics *Calendar:* quarters. *Degree:* certificates, diplomas, and associate. *Special study options:* academic remediation for entering students, accelerated degree program, adult/continuing education programs, advanced placement credit, cooperative education, double majors, independent study, internships, part-time degree program, summer session for credit.

Student Life *Campus security:* 24-hour emergency response devices.

Standardized Tests *Required:* Wonderlic aptitude test (for admission). *Required for some:* SAT or ACT (for admission).

Financial Aid Of all full-time matriculated undergraduates who enrolled in 2008, 12 Federal Work-Study jobs (averaging $6500).

Applying *Options:* deferred entrance. *Application fee:* $150. *Required:* high school transcript, interview.

Freshman Application Contact Ms. Vickie McDougal, Director of Admissions, Daymar College, 3361 Buckland Square, PO Box 22150, Owensboro, KY 42303. *Phone:* 270-926-4040. *Toll-free phone:* 800-960-4090. *Fax:* 270-685-4090. *E-mail:* info@daymarcollege.edu.

DAYMAR COLLEGE

Paducah, Kentucky **www.daymarcollege.edu/**

Freshman Application Contact Senior Director of Admissions, Daymar College, 509 South 30th Street, Paducah, KY 42001. *Phone:* 270-444-9950. *Toll-free phone:* 877-258-7796.

ELIZABETHTOWN COMMUNITY AND TECHNICAL COLLEGE

Elizabethtown, Kentucky **www.elizabethtown.kctcs.edu/**

Freshman Application Contact Elizabethtown Community and Technical College, 600 College Street Road, Elizabethtown, KY 42701. *Phone:* 270-706-8800. *Toll-free phone:* 877-246-2322.

GATEWAY COMMUNITY AND TECHNICAL COLLEGE

Covington, Kentucky **www.gateway.kctcs.edu/**

- **State-supported** 2-year, founded 1961, part of Kentucky Community and Technical College System
- **Suburban** campus with easy access to Cincinnati
- **Coed,** 4,206 undergraduate students, 35% full-time, 57% women, 43% men

Undergraduates 1,477 full-time, 2,729 part-time. 9% African American, 0.9% Asian American or Pacific Islander, 1% Hispanic American, 0.4% Native American.

Freshmen *Average high school GPA:* 2.55.

Faculty *Total:* 242, 34% full-time. *Student/faculty ratio:* 18:1.

Majors Accounting technology and bookkeeping; business administration and management; CAD/CADD drafting/design technology; carpentry; criminal justice/law enforcement administration; early childhood education; engineering technology; fire science; general studies; health professions related; industrial technology; information technology; manufacturing technology; nursing (registered nurse training); office occupations and clerical services.

Academics *Calendar:* semesters. *Degree:* certificates, diplomas, and associate. *Special study options:* academic remediation for entering students, cooperative education, distance learning, internships, part-time degree program, services for LD students, summer session for credit.

Library Main Library plus 3 others.

Student Life *Housing:* college housing not available. *Activities and Organizations:* Multi-Cultural Student Organization, Student Government Association, Speech Team, American Criminal Justice Association, Phi Theta Kappa. *Student services:* personal/psychological counseling.

Standardized Tests *Required:* ACT or ACT COMPASS (for admission).

Costs (2009–10) *Tuition:* state resident $3750 full-time, $125 per credit hour part-time; nonresident $12,750 full-time, $425 per credit hour part-time. Full-time tuition and fees vary according to course load. Part-time tuition and fees vary according to course load. *Payment plan:* installment. *Waivers:* senior citizens and employees or children of employees.

Applying *Options:* electronic application, early admission. *Required:* high school transcript. *Application deadlines:* rolling (freshmen), rolling (out-of-state freshmen), rolling (transfers), rolling (early action). *Early decision deadline:* rolling (for plan 1), rolling (for plan 2). *Notification:* continuous (freshmen), continuous (out-of-state freshmen), continuous (transfers), rolling (early decision plan 1), rolling (early decision plan 2), rolling (early action).

Freshman Application Contact Gateway Community and Technical College, 1025 Amsterdam Road, Covington, KY 41011. *Phone:* 859-442-4176. *E-mail:* andre.washington@kctcs.edu.

HAZARD COMMUNITY AND TECHNICAL COLLEGE

Hazard, Kentucky **www.hazard.kctcs.edu/**

- **State-supported** 2-year, founded 1968, part of Kentucky Community and Technical College System
- **Rural** 34-acre campus
- **Coed,** 4,714 undergraduate students, 38% full-time, 47% women, 53% men

Undergraduates 1,806 full-time, 2,908 part-time. 2% are from out of state.

Freshmen *Admission:* 539 enrolled. *Average high school GPA:* 2.98. *Test scores:* ACT scores over 18: 55%; ACT scores over 24: 6%.

Faculty *Total:* 170, 47% full-time, 8% with terminal degrees. *Student/faculty ratio:* 25:1.

Majors Business administration and management; child-care provision; computer and information sciences; crafts, folk art and artisanry; liberal arts and sciences/liberal studies; medical administrative assistant and medical secretary; medical radiologic technology; multi/interdisciplinary studies related; nursing (registered nurse training); physical therapist assistant.

Academics *Calendar:* semesters. *Degree:* certificates, diplomas, and associate. *Special study options:* cooperative education, distance learning, honors programs, independent study.

Costs (2009–10) *Tuition:* state resident $3000 full-time, $125 per credit hour part-time; nonresident $10,200 full-time, $425 per credit hour part-time. *Payment plans:* installment, deferred payment. *Waivers:* senior citizens and employees or children of employees.

Applying *Options:* early admission. *Required:* high school transcript. *Application deadlines:* rolling (freshmen), rolling (transfers). *Notification:* continuous (freshmen), continuous (transfers).

Freshman Application Contact Director of Admissions, Hazard Community and Technical College, 1 Community College Drive, Hazard, KY 41701-2403. *Phone:* 606-487-3102. *Toll-free phone:* 800-246-7521.

HENDERSON COMMUNITY COLLEGE

Henderson, Kentucky **www.henderson.kctcs.edu/**

- **State-supported** 2-year, founded 1963, part of Kentucky Community and Technical College System
- **Small-town** 120-acre campus
- **Coed**

Undergraduates 7% African American, 0.3% Asian American or Pacific Islander, 1% Hispanic American, 0.5% Native American. *Retention:* 57% of 2008 full-time freshmen returned.

Henderson Community College (continued)

Academics *Calendar:* semesters. *Degree:* associate. *Special study options:* academic remediation for entering students, accelerated degree program, adult/continuing education programs, advanced placement credit, cooperative education, distance learning, double majors, English as a second language, external degree program, independent study, internships, off-campus study, part-time degree program, summer session for credit.

Student Life *Campus security:* 24-hour emergency response devices.

Applying *Required:* high school transcript. *Required for some:* essay or personal statement, interview.

Freshman Application Contact Ms. Teresa Hamiton, Admissions Counselor, Henderson Community College, 2660 South Green Street, Henderson, KY 42420-4623. *Phone:* 270-827-1867 Ext. 354.

HOPKINSVILLE COMMUNITY COLLEGE

Hopkinsville, Kentucky **hopkinsville.kctcs.edu/**

- **State-supported** 2-year, founded 1965, part of Kentucky Community and Technical College System
- **Small-town** 69-acre campus with easy access to Nashville
- **Coed,** 3,753 undergraduate students, 47% full-time, 68% women, 32% men

Undergraduates 1,771 full-time, 1,982 part-time. Students come from 7 states and territories, 31% are from out of state, 25% African American, 2% Asian American or Pacific Islander, 5% Hispanic American, 0.5% Native American, 8% transferred in. *Retention:* 55% of 2008 full-time freshmen returned.

Freshmen *Admission:* 1,119 applied, 1,119 admitted, 675 enrolled. *Average high school GPA:* 2.59.

Faculty *Total:* 163, 40% full-time. *Student/faculty ratio:* 25:1.

Majors Administrative assistant and secretarial science; agricultural production; animal/livestock husbandry and production; business administration and management; child-care and support services management; child-care provision; computer and information sciences; criminal justice/law enforcement administration; criminal justice/police science; early childhood education; electrical, electronic and communications engineering technology; engineering technology; executive assistant/executive secretary; human services; industrial technology; liberal arts and sciences/liberal studies; multi/interdisciplinary studies related; nursing (registered nurse training); social work; teacher assistant/aide.

Academics *Calendar:* semesters. *Degree:* certificates, diplomas, and associate. *Special study options:* academic remediation for entering students, advanced placement credit, cooperative education, distance learning, honors programs, independent study, part-time degree program, services for LD students, summer session for credit.

Library Learning Resource Center with an OPAC, a Web page.

Student Life *Housing:* college housing not available. *Activities and Organizations:* student-run newspaper, Ag Tech, Amateur Radio, Ballroom Dance, Baptist Campus Ministries, Black Men United. *Campus security:* 24-hour emergency response devices, late-night transport/escort service, security provided by trained security personnel during hours of normal operation.

Athletics *Intramural sports:* basketball M, football M, golf M, table tennis M/W, volleyball M/W.

Costs (2009–10) *Tuition:* state resident $3250 full-time, $125 per credit hour part-time; nonresident $11,050 full-time, $425 per credit hour part-time. *Payment plan:* installment. *Waivers:* senior citizens and employees or children of employees.

Financial Aid Of all full-time matriculated undergraduates who enrolled in 2008, 30 Federal Work-Study jobs (averaging $1500). *Financial aid deadline:* 6/30.

Applying *Options:* electronic application, deferred entrance. *Recommended:* high school transcript. *Application deadlines:* rolling (freshmen), rolling (out-of-state freshmen), rolling (transfers). *Notification:* continuous (freshmen), continuous (out-of-state freshmen), continuous (transfers).

Freshman Application Contact Ms. Janet Level, Student Records, Hopkinsville Community College, North Drive, PO Box 2100, Hopkinsville, KY 42241-2100. *Phone:* 270-707-3918. *Fax:* 270-7073973. *E-mail:* janet.level@kctcs.edu.

ITT TECHNICAL INSTITUTE

Louisville, Kentucky **www.itt-tech.edu/**

- **Proprietary** primarily 2-year, founded 1993, part of ITT Educational Services, Inc.
- **Suburban** campus
- **Coed**

Majors Animation, interactive technology, video graphics and special effects; CAD/CADD drafting/design technology; computer and information systems security; computer engineering technology; computer software and media applications related; computer software engineering; computer software technology; construction management; criminal justice/law enforcement administration; design and visual communications; electrical, electronic and communications engineering technology; legal assistant/paralegal; system, networking, and LAN/WAN management; web page, digital/multimedia and information resources design.

Academics *Calendar:* quarters. *Degrees:* associate and bachelor's.

Student Life *Housing:* college housing not available.

Freshman Application Contact Director of Recruitment, ITT Technical Institute, 10509 Timberwood Circle, Louisville, KY 40223. *Phone:* 502-327-7424. *Toll-free phone:* 888-790-7427.

JEFFERSON COMMUNITY AND TECHNICAL COLLEGE

Louisville, Kentucky **www.jctc.kctcs.edu/**

Freshman Application Contact Ms. Melanie Vaughan-Cooke, Admissions Coordinator, Jefferson Community and Technical College, 109 East Broadway, Louisville, KY 40202. *Phone:* 502-213-4000. *Fax:* 502-213-2540.

MADISONVILLE COMMUNITY COLLEGE

Madisonville, Kentucky **www.madcc.kctcs.edu/**

Director of Admissions Mr. Jay Parent, Registrar, Madisonville Community College, 2000 College Drive, Madisonville, KY 42431. *Phone:* 270-821-2250.

MAYSVILLE COMMUNITY AND TECHNICAL COLLEGE

Maysville, Kentucky **www.maycc.kctcs.net/**

- **State-supported** 2-year, founded 1967, part of Kentucky Community and Technical College System
- **Rural** 12-acre campus
- **Coed**

Academics *Calendar:* semesters. *Degree:* certificates, diplomas, and associate. *Special study options:* academic remediation for entering students, adult/continuing education programs, advanced placement credit, cooperative education, distance learning, English as a second language, external degree program, honors programs, independent study, internships, off-campus study, part-time degree program, services for LD students, summer session for credit.

Student Life *Campus security:* student patrols, evening parking lot security.

Financial Aid Of all full-time matriculated undergraduates who enrolled in 2008, 30 Federal Work-Study jobs (averaging $1960).

Applying *Options:* early admission. *Required:* high school transcript.

Director of Admissions Ms. Patee Massie, Registrar, Maysville Community and Technical College, 1755 US 68, Maysville, KY 41056. *Phone:* 606-759-7141. *Fax:* 606-759-5818. *E-mail:* ccsmayrg@ukcc.uky.edu.

MAYSVILLE COMMUNITY AND TECHNICAL COLLEGE

Morehead, Kentucky **www.maysville.kctcs.edu/**

- **State-supported** 2-year, founded 1984
- **Coed**

Academics *Calendar:* semesters. *Degree:* certificates, diplomas, and associate.

Director of Admissions Patee Massie, Registrar, Maysville Community and Technical College, 609 Viking Drive, Morehead, KY 40351. *Phone:* 606-759-7141 Ext. 66184.

NATIONAL COLLEGE

Danville, Kentucky **www.national-college.edu/**

Director of Admissions James McGuire, Campus Director, National College, 115 East Lexington Avenue, Danville, KY 40422. *Phone:* 859-236-6991. *Toll-free phone:* 800-664-1886.

NATIONAL COLLEGE

Florence, Kentucky **www.national-college.edu/**

Director of Admissions Mr. Terry Kovacs, Campus Director, National College, 7627 Ewing Boulevard, Florence, KY 41042. *Phone:* 859-525-6510. *Toll-free phone:* 800-664-1886.

NATIONAL COLLEGE

Lexington, Kentucky **www.national-college.edu/**

Director of Admissions Kim Thomasson, Campus Director, National College, 2376 Sir Barton Way, Lexington, KY 40509. *Phone:* 859-253-0621. *Toll-free phone:* 800-664-1886.

NATIONAL COLLEGE

Louisville, Kentucky **www.national-college.edu/**

Director of Admissions Vincent C. Tinebra, Campus Director, National College, 3950 Dixie Highway, Louisville, KY 40216. *Phone:* 502-447-7634. *Toll-free phone:* 800-664-1886.

NATIONAL COLLEGE

Pikeville, Kentucky **www.national-college.edu/**

Director of Admissions Tammy Riley, Campus Director, National College, 50 National College Boulevard, Pikeville, KY 41501. *Phone:* 606-478-7200. *Toll-free phone:* 800-664-1886.

NATIONAL COLLEGE

Richmond, Kentucky **www.national-college.edu/**

Director of Admissions Ms. Keeley Gadd, Campus Director, National College, 125 South Killarney Lane, Richmond, KY 40475. *Phone:* 859-623-8956. *Toll-free phone:* 800-664-1886.

OWENSBORO COMMUNITY AND TECHNICAL COLLEGE

Owensboro, Kentucky **www.octc.kctcs.edu/**

- **State-supported** 2-year, founded 1986, part of Kentucky Community and Technical College System
- **Suburban** 102-acre campus
- **Coed,** 6,328 undergraduate students, 34% full-time, 55% women, 45% men

Undergraduates 2,136 full-time, 4,192 part-time. Students come from 3 states and territories, 2% are from out of state, 5% African American, 0.4% Asian American or Pacific Islander, 0.9% Hispanic American, 0.3% Native American. *Retention:* 57% of 2008 full-time freshmen returned.

Freshmen *Admission:* 703 enrolled.

Faculty *Total:* 207, 50% full-time, 11% with terminal degrees. *Student/faculty ratio:* 26:1.

Majors Agriculture; business administration and management; computer and information sciences; computer/information technology services administration related; criminal justice/police science; data entry/microcomputer applications; diagnostic medical sonography and ultrasound technology; electrical, electronic and communications engineering technology; executive assistant/executive secretary; fire science; human services; information technology; kindergarten/preschool education; liberal arts and sciences/liberal studies; medical radiologic technology; nursing (registered nurse training); precision production trades; social work; system administration; word processing.

Academics *Calendar:* semesters. *Degree:* certificates, diplomas, and associate. *Special study options:* academic remediation for entering students, adult/continuing education programs, advanced placement credit, cooperative education, distance learning, double majors, English as a second language, external degree program, honors programs, independent study, off-campus study, part-time degree program, services for LD students, student-designed majors, study abroad.

Library Learning Resource Center with 25,600 titles, 24,614 serial subscriptions, an OPAC, a Web page.

Student Life *Activities and Organizations:* drama/theater group, student-run newspaper, radio and television station, choral group, Student Government Association, Psychology Club, Nursing Club. *Campus security:* 24-hour emergency response devices, late-night transport/escort service.

Standardized Tests *Recommended:* SAT or ACT (for admission).

Costs (2009–10) *Tuition:* state resident $3750 full-time, $125 per credit hour part-time; nonresident $12,750 full-time, $425 per credit hour part-time. Full-time tuition and fees vary according to location and reciprocity agreements. Part-time tuition and fees vary according to location and reciprocity agreements. *Payment plan:* installment. *Waivers:* senior citizens and employees or children of employees.

Financial Aid *Financial aid deadline:* 4/1.

Applying *Options:* electronic application. *Required:* high school transcript. *Application deadlines:* rolling (freshmen), rolling (transfers). *Notification:* continuous (freshmen), continuous (transfers).

Freshman Application Contact Ms. Barbara Tipmore, Admissions Counselor, Owensboro Community and Technical College, 4800 New Hartford Road, Owensboro, KY 42303. *Phone:* 270-686-4530. *Toll-free phone:* 866-755-6282. *E-mail:* barb.tipmore@kctcs.edu.

ST. CATHARINE COLLEGE

St. Catharine, Kentucky **www.sccky.edu/**

Director of Admissions Ms. Amy C. Carrico, Director of Admissions, St. Catharine College, 2735 Bardstown Road, St. Catharine, KY 40061. *Phone:* 859-336-5082. *Toll-free phone:* 800-599-2000 Ext. 1227.

SOMERSET COMMUNITY COLLEGE

Somerset, Kentucky **www.somerset.kctcs.edu/**

- **State-supported** 2-year, founded 1965, part of Kentucky Community and Technical College System
- **Small-town** 70-acre campus
- **Coed,** 8,201 undergraduate students

Undergraduates *Retention:* 59% of 2008 full-time freshmen returned.

Faculty *Student/faculty ratio:* 23:1.

Majors Aircraft powerplant technology; business administration and management; child care provider; clinical/medical laboratory assistant; computer and information sciences; criminal justice/law enforcement administration; engineering technology; executive assistant/executive secretary; industrial mechanics and maintenance technology; liberal arts and sciences/liberal studies; medical administrative assistant and medical secretary; medical radiologic technology; multi/interdisciplinary studies related; nursing (registered nurse training); physical therapist assistant; respiratory care therapy; surgical technology; teacher assistant/aide.

Academics *Calendar:* semesters. *Degree:* certificates, diplomas, and associate. *Special study options:* academic remediation for entering students, adult/continuing education programs, advanced placement credit, distance learning, part-time degree program, summer session for credit.

Library Somerset Community College Library.

Student Life *Housing:* college housing not available.

Applying *Options:* electronic application, early admission. *Required:* high school transcript. *Application deadlines:* 8/14 (freshmen), 8/14 (transfers). *Notification:* continuous (freshmen), continuous (transfers).

Freshman Application Contact Director of Admission, Somerset Community College, 808 Monticello Street, Somerset, KY 42501. *Phone:* 606-451-6630. *Toll-free phone:* 877-629-9722. *E-mail:* somerset-admissions@kctcs.edu.

SOUTHEAST KENTUCKY COMMUNITY AND TECHNICAL COLLEGE

Cumberland, Kentucky **www.soucc.kctcs.net/**

- **State-supported** 2-year, founded 1960, part of Kentucky Community and Technical College System
- **Rural** 150-acre campus
- **Coed,** 4,959 undergraduate students, 39% full-time, 49% women, 51% men

Undergraduates 1,943 full-time, 3,016 part-time. Students come from 10 states and territories, 1 other country, 5% are from out of state, 2% African American, 0.2% Asian American or Pacific Islander, 0.5% Hispanic American, 0.7% Native American, 1% transferred in. *Retention:* 65% of 2008 full-time freshmen returned.

Freshmen *Admission:* 650 applied, 639 admitted, 427 enrolled. *Average high school GPA:* 3. *Test scores:* ACT scores over 18: 57%; ACT scores over 24: 12%; ACT scores over 30: 2%.

Faculty *Total:* 214, 50% full-time, 7% with terminal degrees. *Student/faculty ratio:* 19:1.

Majors Administrative assistant and secretarial science; business administration and management; clinical/medical laboratory technology; computer engineering technology; computer/information technology services administration related; criminal justice/police science; data processing and data processing technology; information technology; liberal arts and sciences/liberal studies; management information systems; medical radiologic technology; nursing (registered nurse training); physical therapist assistant; respiratory care therapy.

Academics *Calendar:* semesters. *Degree:* certificates, diplomas, and associate. *Special study options:* academic remediation for entering students, accelerated degree program, adult/continuing education programs, advanced placement credit, distance learning, independent study, part-time degree program, study abroad, summer session for credit.

Library Gertrude Dale Library plus 4 others with 25,921 titles, 200 serial subscriptions, 924 audiovisual materials, an OPAC, a Web page.

Student Life *Housing:* college housing not available. *Activities and Organizations:* drama/theater group, student-run newspaper, choral group, Professional Business Leaders, Student Government Association, Phi Theta Kappa, Black Student Union, Nursing Club.

Athletics *Intramural sports:* basketball M/W, football M/W, golf M/W, table tennis M/W, volleyball M/W.

Standardized Tests *Recommended:* ACT (for admission).

Costs (2010–11) *Tuition:* state resident $3900 full-time, $130 per credit hour part-time; nonresident $13,000 full-time, $430 per credit hour part-time. Full-time tuition and fees vary according to reciprocity agreements. Part-time tuition and fees vary according to reciprocity agreements. *Required fees:* $144 full-time. *Payment plan:* installment. *Waivers:* senior citizens and employees or children of employees.

Financial Aid Of all full-time matriculated undergraduates who enrolled in 2008, 90 Federal Work-Study jobs (averaging $635).

Applying *Required:* high school transcript. *Notification:* continuous until 9/3 (freshmen), continuous until 9/3 (transfers).

Freshman Application Contact Southeast Kentucky Community and Technical College, 700 College Road, Cumberland, KY 40823. *Phone:* 606-589-2145 Ext. 13018. *Toll-free phone:* 888-274-SECC Ext. 2108.

SOUTHWESTERN COLLEGE OF BUSINESS

Florence, Kentucky **www.swcollege.net/**

Freshman Application Contact Director of Admission, Southwestern College of Business, 8095 Connector Drive, Florence, KY 41042. *Phone:* 859-282-9999.

SPENCERIAN COLLEGE

Louisville, Kentucky **www.spencerian.edu/**

- **Proprietary** 2-year, founded 1892, administratively affiliated with The Sullivan University System
- **Urban** 10-acre campus
- **Coed,** 1,282 undergraduate students, 73% full-time, 86% women, 14% men

Undergraduates 939 full-time, 343 part-time. 14% African American, 0.8% Asian American or Pacific Islander, 0.6% Hispanic American, 0.5% Native American, 0.1% international. *Retention:* 73% of 2008 full-time freshmen returned.

Freshmen *Admission:* 444 admitted, 444 enrolled.

Faculty *Total:* 130, 38% full-time, 5% with terminal degrees. *Student/faculty ratio:* 13:1.

Majors Accounting; accounting and business/management; business administration and management; cardiovascular technology; clinical laboratory science/medical technology; massage therapy; medical insurance/medical billing; medical office management; medical radiologic technology; nursing (registered nurse training); radiologic technology/science; surgical technology.

Academics *Calendar:* quarters. *Degree:* certificates, diplomas, and associate. *Special study options:* accelerated degree program, distance learning, independent study, internships, off-campus study, part-time degree program, services for LD students, summer session for credit.

Library Spencerian College Learning Resource Center with 1,650 titles, 31,000 serial subscriptions, 277 audiovisual materials, an OPAC, a Web page.

Student Life *Housing Options:* coed. Campus housing is leased by the school and is provided by a third party. *Activities and Organizations:* Student Activities Board. *Campus security:* 24-hour emergency response devices, late-night transport/escort service. *Student services:* personal/psychological counseling.

Costs (2009–10) *Tuition:* $14,580 full-time, $245 per credit hour part-time. Full-time tuition and fees vary according to program. Part-time tuition and fees vary according to program. No tuition increase for student's term of enrollment. *Required fees:* $2070 full-time, $50 per course part-time. *Room only:* $4950. *Payment plan:* installment. *Waivers:* employees or children of employees.

Applying *Application fee:* $100. *Required:* high school transcript, interview. *Required for some:* essay or personal statement. *Notification:* continuous (freshmen), continuous (out-of-state freshmen), continuous (transfers).

Freshman Application Contact Spencerian College, 4627 Dixie Highway, Louisville, KY 40299. *Phone:* 502-447-1000 Ext. 7808. *Toll-free phone:* 800-264-1799.

SPENCERIAN COLLEGE–LEXINGTON

Lexington, Kentucky **www.spencerian.edu/**

Freshman Application Contact Spencerian College–Lexington, 2355 Harrodsburg Road, Lexington, KY 40504. *Phone:* 859-223-9608 Ext. 5430. *Toll-free phone:* 800-456-3253.

SULLIVAN COLLEGE OF TECHNOLOGY AND DESIGN

Louisville, Kentucky **www.louisvilletech.com/**

- **Proprietary** primarily 2-year, founded 1961, part of The Sullivan University System, Inc.
- **Suburban** 10-acre campus with easy access to Louisville
- **Coed,** 662 undergraduate students, 62% full-time, 34% women, 66% men

Undergraduates 413 full-time, 249 part-time. Students come from 7 states and territories, 13% are from out of state, 17% African American, 1% Asian American or Pacific Islander, 0.2% Hispanic American, 0.5% Native American, 3% transferred in. *Retention:* 76% of 2008 full-time freshmen returned.

Freshmen *Admission:* 187 enrolled.

Faculty *Total:* 72, 43% full-time. *Student/faculty ratio:* 14:1.

Majors Animation, interactive technology, video graphics and special effects; architectural drafting and CAD/CADD; architectural engineering technology; architecture related; artificial intelligence and robotics; CAD/CADD drafting/design technology; computer and information sciences; computer and information sciences and support services related; computer and information systems security; computer engineering technology; computer graphics; computer hardware engineering; computer hardware technology; computer installation and repair technology; computer programming (vendor/product certification); computer systems networking and telecommunications; computer technology/computer systems technology; desktop publishing and digital imaging design; digital communication and media/multimedia; drafting and design technology; drafting/design engineering technologies related; electrical and electronic engineering technologies related; electrical, electronic and communications engineering technology; electrical/electronics equipment installation and repair; electrical/electronics maintenance and repair technology related; electromechanical and instrumentation and maintenance technologies related; engineering technologies related; engineering technology; graphic and printing equipment operation/production; graphic communications; graphic communications related; graphic design; heating, air conditioning and refrigeration technology; housing and human environments; industrial electronics technology; industrial mechanics and maintenance technology; information technology; interior design; mechanical drafting and CAD/CADD; mechanical engineering/mechanical technology; robotics technology; system administration; web page, digital/multimedia and information resources design.

Academics *Calendar:* quarters. *Degrees:* certificates, diplomas, associate, and bachelor's. *Special study options:* academic remediation for entering students, accelerated degree program, adult/continuing education programs, cooperative education, distance learning, double majors, independent study, internships, part-time degree program, services for LD students, summer session for credit.

Library Sullivan College of Technology and Design Library with 2,332 titles, 59 serial subscriptions, 337 audiovisual materials, an OPAC, a Web page.

Student Life *Housing Options:* men-only, women-only. Campus housing is leased by the school. Freshman campus housing is guaranteed. *Activities and Organizations:* ASID, IIDA, ADDA, Robotics International, Skills USA. *Campus security:* late-night transport/escort service, telephone alarm device during hours school is open.

Athletics *Intramural sports:* basketball M.

Standardized Tests *Required:* the college uses the Career Performance Assessment Test (CPAt) for its entrance examination. It will accept ACT or SAT scores in place of CPAt results. (for admission). *Recommended:* SAT or ACT (for admission).

Costs (2009–10) *One-time required fee:* $100. *Tuition:* $15,570 full-time, $395 per credit hour part-time. Full-time tuition and fees vary according to course load and program. Part-time tuition and fees vary according to course load and program. No tuition increase for student's term of enrollment. *Required fees:* $540 full-time, $50 per course part-time. *Room only:* $4950. *Payment plan:* installment. *Waivers:* employees or children of employees.

Applying *Options:* deferred entrance. *Application fee:* $100. *Required:* high school transcript, interview. *Recommended:* minimum 2 GPA. *Application deadlines:* rolling (freshmen), rolling (out-of-state freshmen), rolling (transfers). *Notification:* continuous (freshmen), continuous (out-of-state freshmen), continuous (transfers).

Freshman Application Contact Mr. Aamer Z. Chauhdri, Director of Admissions, Sullivan College of Technology and Design, 3901 Atkinson Square Drive, Louisville, KY 40218. *Phone:* 502-456-6509 Ext. 8220. *Toll-free phone:* 800-884-6528. *Fax:* 502-456-2341. *E-mail:* achauhdri@sctd.edu.

WEST KENTUCKY COMMUNITY AND TECHNICAL COLLEGE

Paducah, Kentucky **www.westkentucky.kctcs.edu/**

- **State-supported** 2-year, founded 1932, part of Kentucky Community and Technical College System
- **Small-town** 117-acre campus
- **Coed,** 3,511 undergraduate students, 59% full-time, 64% women, 36% men

Undergraduates 2,072 full-time, 1,439 part-time. Students come from 14 states and territories, 1 other country, 5% are from out of state, 6% African American, 0.8% Asian American or Pacific Islander, 1% Hispanic American, 0.2% Native American. *Retention:* 64% of 2008 full-time freshmen returned.

Freshmen *Admission:* 762 enrolled. *Test scores:* ACT scores over 18: 91%; ACT scores over 24: 37%; ACT scores over 30: 7%.

Faculty *Total:* 369, 36% full-time. *Student/faculty ratio:* 17:1.

Majors Accounting; business administration and management; computer and information sciences; court reporting; criminal justice/law enforcement administration; culinary arts; diagnostic medical sonography and ultrasound technology; electrician; fire science; machine shop technology; nursing (registered nurse training); physical therapist assistant; respiratory care therapy; surgical technology.

Academics *Calendar:* semesters. *Degree:* certificates, diplomas, and associate. *Special study options:* academic remediation for entering students, adult/continuing education programs, cooperative education, distance learning, English as a second language, honors programs, independent study, internships, part-time degree program, study abroad.

Library WKCTC Matheson Library with 74,676 titles, 155 serial subscriptions, 5,043 audiovisual materials, an OPAC, a Web page.

Student Life *Housing:* college housing not available. *Activities and Organizations:* drama/theater group, choral group. *Campus security:* late-night transport/escort service, 14-hour patrols by trained security personnel.

Athletics *Intramural sports:* basketball M/W, golf M/W, soccer M/W, volleyball M/W.

Costs (2009–10) *Tuition:* state resident $3750 full-time, $125 per credit hour part-time; nonresident $12,750 full-time, $425 per credit hour part-time. *Waivers:* senior citizens and employees or children of employees.

Financial Aid Of all full-time matriculated undergraduates who enrolled in 2008, 50 Federal Work-Study jobs (averaging $1650).

Applying *Options:* early admission. *Required for some:* high school transcript. *Application deadlines:* rolling (freshmen), rolling (transfers).

Freshman Application Contact Mr. Jerry Anderson, Admissions Counselor, West Kentucky Community and Technical College, 4810 Alben Barkley Drive, PO Box 7380, Paducah, KY 42002-7380. *Phone:* 270-554-3266. *E-mail:* jerry.anderson@kctcs.edu.

LOUISIANA

BATON ROUGE COMMUNITY COLLEGE

Baton Rouge, Louisiana **www.brcc.cc.la.us/**

- **State-supported** 2-year, founded 1995
- **Coed**

Academics *Calendar:* semesters. *Degree:* associate.

Athletics Member NJCAA.

Applying *Application fee:* $7.

Director of Admissions Nancy Clay, Interim Executive Director for Enrollment Services, Baton Rouge Community College, 5310 Florida Boulevard, Baton Rouge, LA 70806. *Phone:* 225-216-8700. *Toll-free phone:* 800-601-4558.

BATON ROUGE SCHOOL OF COMPUTERS

Baton Rouge, Louisiana **www.brsc.edu/**

Freshman Application Contact Brenda Boss, Baton Rouge School of Computers, 10425 Plaza Americana, Baton Rouge, LA 70816-8188. *Phone:* 225-923-2524. *Fax:* 225-923-2979. *E-mail:* admissions@brsc.net.

BLUE CLIFF COLLEGE–LAFAYETTE

Lafayette, Louisiana **www.bluecliffcollege.com/**

- **Proprietary** 2-year
- **Coed**

Academics *Degree:* certificates and associate.

Applying *Application fee:* $25.

Freshman Application Contact Admissions Office, Blue Cliff College–Lafayette, 100 Asma Boulevard, Suite 350, Lafayette, LA 70508-3862. *Toll-free phone:* 800-514-2609.

BLUE CLIFF COLLEGE–SHREVEPORT

Shreveport, Louisiana **www.bluecliffcollege.com/**

- **Proprietary** 2-year
- **Urban** campus
- **Coed,** 237 undergraduate students

Faculty *Total:* 21, 90% full-time. *Student/faculty ratio:* 12:1.

Majors Criminal justice/law enforcement administration; massage therapy; medical administrative assistant and medical secretary.

Academics *Degree:* certificates and associate. *Special study options:* part-time degree program, summer session for credit.

Library an OPAC, a Web page.

Student Life *Housing:* college housing not available. *Student services:* personal/psychological counseling, legal services.

Applying *Required:* interview. *Required for some:* high school transcript.

Freshman Application Contact Blue Cliff College–Shreveport, 200 North Thomas Drive, Suite A, Shreveport, LA 71107. *Toll-free phone:* 800-516-6597.

Bossier Parish Community College

Bossier City, Louisiana **www.bpcc.edu/**

- **State-supported** 2-year, founded 1967, part of Louisiana Community and Technical College System
- **Urban** 64-acre campus
- **Coed**

Academics *Calendar:* semesters. *Degree:* certificates, diplomas, and associate. *Special study options:* academic remediation for entering students, adult/continuing education programs, advanced placement credit, distance learning, double majors, part-time degree program, services for LD students, summer session for credit.

Student Life *Campus security:* student patrols.

Athletics Member NJCAA.

Financial Aid Of all full-time matriculated undergraduates who enrolled in 2008, 53 Federal Work-Study jobs.

Applying *Options:* early admission. *Application fee:* $15. *Required:* high school transcript.

Freshman Application Contact Ms. Ann Jampole, Director of Admissions, Bossier Parish Community College, 2719 Airline Drive North, Bossier City, LA 71111-5801. *Phone:* 318-678-6166. *Fax:* 318-742-8664.

Camelot College

Baton Rouge, Louisiana **www.camelotcollege.com/**

Freshman Application Contact Camelot College, 2618 Wooddale Boulevard, Suite A, Baton Rouge, LA 70805. *Phone:* 225-928-3005. *Toll-free phone:* 800-470-3320.

Cameron College

New Orleans, Louisiana **www.cameroncollege.com/**

- **Proprietary** 2-year, founded 1981
- **Coed**

Academics *Degree:* associate.

Applying *Application fee:* $100.

Admissions Office Contact Cameron College, 2740 Canal Street, New Orleans, LA 70119.

Career Technical College

Monroe, Louisiana **www.careertc.edu/**

Freshman Application Contact Admissions Office, Career Technical College, 2319 Louisville Avenue, Monroe, LA 71201. *Toll-free phone:* 800-234-6766.

Delgado Community College

New Orleans, Louisiana **www.dcc.edu/**

Freshman Application Contact Ms. Gwen Boute, Director of Admissions, Delgado Community College, 615 City Park Avenue, New Orleans, LA 70119. *Phone:* 504-671-5010. *Fax:* 504-483-1895. *E-mail:* enroll@dcc.edu.

Delta College of Arts and Technology

Baton Rouge, Louisiana **www.deltacollege.com/**

- **Proprietary** 2-year
- **Urban** 3-acre campus
- **Coed, primarily women**

Academics *Calendar:* continuous (for most programs). *Degree:* certificates, diplomas, and associate.

Applying *Application fee:* $100.

Freshman Application Contact Ms. Beulah Laverghe-Brown, Admissions Director, Delta College of Arts and Technology, 7380 Exchange Place, Baton Rouge, LA 70806. *Phone:* 225-928-7770. *Fax:* 225-927-9096. *E-mail:* bbrown@deltacollege.com.

Delta School of Business & Technology

Lake Charles, Louisiana **www.deltatech.edu/**

Director of Admissions Mr. Gary J. Holt, President, Delta School of Business & Technology, 517 Broad Street, Lake Charles, LA 70601. *Phone:* 337-439-5765. *Toll-free phone:* 800-259-5627. *Fax:* 337-436-5151. *E-mail:* gholt@deltatech.edu.

Elaine P. Nunez Community College

Chalmette, Louisiana **www.nunez.edu/**

- **State-supported** 2-year, founded 1992, part of Louisiana Community and Technical College System
- **Suburban** 20-acre campus with easy access to New Orleans
- **Endowment** $412,188
- **Coed,** 1,834 undergraduate students, 40% full-time, 64% women, 36% men

Undergraduates 729 full-time, 1,105 part-time. Students come from 4 states and territories, 0.3% are from out of state, 38% African American, 1% Asian American or Pacific Islander, 2% Hispanic American, 1% Native American, 10% transferred in. *Retention:* 49% of 2008 full-time freshmen returned.

Freshmen *Admission:* 219 enrolled.

Faculty *Total:* 67, 60% full-time, 4% with terminal degrees. *Student/faculty ratio:* 22:1.

Majors Administrative assistant and secretarial science; business/commerce; carpentry; child-care provision; computer and information sciences and support services related; computer engineering technology; culinary arts; education; electrical, electronic and communications engineering technology; emergency medical technology (EMT paramedic); general studies; health information/medical records administration; heating, air conditioning, ventilation and refrigeration maintenance technology; industrial technology; information science/studies; kindergarten/preschool education; legal assistant/paralegal; liberal arts and sciences and humanities related; liberal arts and sciences/liberal studies; medical office management; nursing assistant/aide and patient care assistant; welding technology.

Academics *Calendar:* semesters. *Degree:* certificates, diplomas, and associate. *Special study options:* academic remediation for entering students, adult/continuing education programs, advanced placement credit, cooperative education, distance learning, double majors, English as a second language, independent study, internships, off-campus study, part-time degree program, services for LD students, student-designed majors, summer session for credit.

Library Nunez Community College Library with 68,000 titles, 2,500 serial subscriptions, 750 audiovisual materials, an OPAC, a Web page.

Student Life *Housing:* college housing not available. *Activities and Organizations:* drama/theater group, student-run newspaper, Nunez Environmental Team, national fraternities. *Campus security:* 24-hour emergency response devices, late-night transport/escort service, security cameras. *Student services:* personal/psychological counseling.

Athletics *Intramural sports:* basketball M, football M/W, softball M/W, volleyball M/W.

Costs (2009–10) *Tuition:* state resident $1582 full-time; nonresident $4102 full-time. Part-time tuition and fees vary according to course load. *Required fees:* $368 full-time. *Payment plan:* installment. *Waivers:* senior citizens and employees or children of employees.

Financial Aid Of all full-time matriculated undergraduates who enrolled in 2008, 70 Federal Work-Study jobs (averaging $1452).

Applying *Options:* deferred entrance. *Application fee:* $10. *Required for some:* high school transcript. *Application deadlines:* rolling (freshmen), rolling (transfers).

Freshman Application Contact Mrs. Becky Maillet, Elaine P. Nunez Community College, 3710 Paris Road, Chalmette, LA 70043. *Phone:* 504-278-6477. *E-mail:* bmaillet@nunez.edu.

Gretna Career College

Gretna, Louisiana **www.gretnacareercollege.com/**

Freshman Application Contact Admissions Office, Gretna Career College, 1415 Whitney Avenue, Gretna, LA 70053.

Herzing College

Kenner, Louisiana **www.herzing.edu/**

- **Proprietary** primarily 2-year, founded 1996
- **Coed**

Academics *Calendar:* semesters. *Degrees:* diplomas, associate, and bachelor's.

Director of Admissions Genny Bordelon, Director of Admissions, Herzing College, 2500 Williams Boulevard, Kenner, LA 70062. *Phone:* 504-733-0074. *Fax:* 504-733-0020.

ITI Technical College

Baton Rouge, Louisiana **www.iticollege.edu/**

- **Proprietary** 2-year, founded 1973
- **Suburban** 10-acre campus
- **Coed, primarily men,** 393 undergraduate students, 100% full-time, 18% women, 82% men

Undergraduates 393 full-time. Students come from 3 states and territories, 1% are from out of state, 33% African American, 0.9% Asian American or Pacific Islander, 1% Hispanic American. *Retention:* 72% of 2008 full-time freshmen returned.

Freshmen *Admission:* 435 applied, 371 admitted, 75 enrolled.

Faculty *Total:* 51, 47% full-time, 49% with terminal degrees. *Student/faculty ratio:* 15:1.

Majors Chemical technology; computer technology/computer systems technology; drafting and design technology; electrical, electronic and communications engineering technology; information technology; instrumentation technology; office occupations and clerical services.

Academics *Calendar:* continuous. *Degree:* certificates and associate.

Student Life *Housing:* college housing not available.

Costs (2009–10) *Tuition:* Tuition and fees vary depending upon program; please contact school directly for costs.

Applying *Required:* high school transcript, interview.

Freshman Application Contact Marcia Stevens, ITI Technical College, 13944 Airline Highway, Baton Rouge, LA 70817. *Phone:* 225-752-4230 Ext. 261. *Toll-free phone:* 800-467-4484. *Fax:* 225-756-0903. *E-mail:* mstevens@iticollege.edu.

ITT Technical Institute

Baton Rouge, Louisiana **www.itt-tech.edu/**

- **Proprietary** 2-year
- **Coed**

Majors CAD/CADD drafting/design technology; computer and information systems security; computer engineering technology; computer software and media applications related; computer software engineering; computer software technology; criminal justice/law enforcement administration; design and visual communications; electrical, electronic and communications engineering technology; legal assistant/paralegal; system, networking, and LAN/WAN management; web/multimedia management and webmaster.

Freshman Application Contact Director of Recruitment, ITT Technical Institute, 14141 Airline Highway, Building 3, Suite K, Baton Rouge, LA 70817. *Phone:* 225-754-5800. *Toll-free phone:* 800-295-8485.

ITT Technical Institute

St. Rose, Louisiana **www.itt-tech.edu/**

- **Proprietary** primarily 2-year, founded 1998, part of ITT Educational Services, Inc.
- **Coed**

Majors Animation, interactive technology, video graphics and special effects; CAD/CADD drafting/design technology; computer and information systems security; computer engineering technology; computer software and media applications related; computer software engineering; computer software technology; construction management; criminal justice/law enforcement administration; design and visual communications; electrical, electronic and communications engineering technology; legal assistant/paralegal; system, networking, and LAN/WAN management; web/multimedia management and webmaster; web page, digital/multimedia and information resources design.

Academics *Calendar:* quarters. *Degrees:* associate and bachelor's.

Student Life *Housing:* college housing not available.

Freshman Application Contact Director of Recruitment, ITT Technical Institute, 140 James Drive East, Saint Rose, LA 70087. *Phone:* 504-463-0338. *Toll-free phone:* 866-463-0338.

Louisiana State University at Alexandria

Alexandria, Louisiana **www.lsua.edu/**

Freshman Application Contact Ms. Shelly Kieffer, Recruiter/Admissions Counselor, Louisiana State University at Alexandria, 8100 Highway 71 South, Alexandria, LA 71302-9121. *Phone:* 318-473-6508. *Toll-free phone:* 888-473-6417. *Fax:* 318-473-6418. *E-mail:* skieffer@isua.edu.

Louisiana State University at Eunice

Eunice, Louisiana **www.lsue.edu/**

Freshman Application Contact Ms. Gracie Guillory, Director of Financial Aid, Louisiana State University at Eunice, PO Box 1129, Eunice, LA 70535-1129. *Phone:* 337-550-1282. *Toll-free phone:* 888-367-5783.

Louisiana Technical College

Baton Rouge, Louisiana **region2.ltc.edu/**

- **State-supported** 2-year, founded 1930, part of Louisiana Community and Technical College System
- **Urban** campus
- **Endowment** $286,936
- **Coed,** 13,414 undergraduate students, 54% full-time, 48% women, 52% men

Undergraduates 7,264 full-time, 6,150 part-time. 1% are from out of state, 37% African American, 0.9% Asian American or Pacific Islander, 1% Hispanic American, 0.7% Native American.

Freshmen *Admission:* 2,094 applied, 2,094 admitted, 2,094 enrolled.

Faculty *Total:* 1,353, 58% full-time. *Student/faculty ratio:* 10:1.

Majors Accounting technology and bookkeeping; administrative assistant and secretarial science; aircraft powerplant technology; automobile/automotive mechanics technology; child-care provision; clinical/medical laboratory assistant; communications systems installation and repair technology; computer installation and repair technology; computer programming (specific applications); computer systems analysis; computer systems networking and telecommunications; criminal justice/safety; culinary arts; data processing and data processing technology; desktop publishing and digital imaging design; drafting and design technology; forestry technology; hotel/motel administration; industrial electronics technology; industrial production technologies related; instrumentation technology; precision systems maintenance and repair technologies related; printing press operation; respiratory therapy technician; surgical technology; survey technology; system administration; technical teacher education.

Academics *Degree:* certificates, diplomas, and associate.

Student Life *Housing:* college housing not available.

Standardized Tests *Required:* Compass (for admission).

Applying *Application fee:* $5. *Required:* high school transcript.

Freshman Application Contact Ms. Amber Aguillard, Admissions Officer, Louisiana Technical College, 3250 North Acadian Thruway, E, Baton Rouge, LA 70805. *Phone:* 225-359-9263. *Toll-free phone:* 800-351-7611. *Fax:* 225-359-9354. *E-mail:* aaguillard@ltc.edu.

Louisiana Technical College–Florida Parishes Campus

Greensburg, Louisiana **www.ltc.edu/**

- **State-supported** 2-year, part of Louisiana Community and Technical College System
- **Coed**

Academics *Calendar:* semesters. *Degree:* certificates, diplomas, and associate. *Special study options:* academic remediation for entering students, adult/continuing education programs, advanced placement credit, cooperative education, distance learning, internships, services for LD students.

Student Life *Campus security:* 24-hour emergency response devices.

Costs (2009–10) *Tuition:* state resident $630 full-time, $26 per credit hour part-time; nonresident $1260 full-time, $53 per credit hour part-time. Full-time tuition and fees vary according to course load. Part-time tuition and fees vary according to course load. *Required fees:* $374 full-time, $14 per credit hour part-time, $25 per term part-time.

Applying *Options:* early action. *Application fee:* $5. *Required:* high school transcript. *Required for some:* essay or personal statement, interview.

Director of Admissions Mrs. Sharon G. Hornsby, Campus Dean, Louisiana Technical College–Florida Parishes Campus, Student Services, PO Box 1300, 100 College Street, Greensburg, LA 70441. *Phone:* 225-222-4251. *Toll-free phone:* 800-827-9750.

Louisiana Technical College–Northeast Louisiana Campus

Winnsboro, Louisiana **www.ltc.edu/**

Director of Admissions Admissions Office, Louisiana Technical College–Northeast Louisiana Campus, 1710 Warren Street, Winnsboro, LA 71295. *Phone:* 318-435-2163. *Toll-free phone:* 800-320-6133.

Louisiana Technical College–Young Memorial Campus

Morgan City, Louisiana **www.ltc.edu/**

Director of Admissions Ms. Melanie Henry, Admissions Office, Louisiana Technical College–Young Memorial Campus, PO Drawer 2148, 900 Youngs Road, Morgan City, LA 70381. *Phone:* 504-380-2436. *Fax:* 504-380-2440.

MedVance Institute

Baton Rouge, Louisiana **www.medvance.org/**

- **Proprietary** 2-year, founded 1970
- **Urban** 4-acre campus
- **Coed**

Academics *Calendar:* quarters. *Degree:* diplomas and associate. *Special study options:* internships.

Standardized Tests *Required:* Wonderlic aptitude test (for admission).

Applying *Application fee:* $25. *Required:* high school transcript, interview. *Recommended:* minimum 2.0 GPA, 2 letters of recommendation.

Director of Admissions Ms. Sheri Kirley, Associate Director of Admissions, MedVance Institute, 4173 Government Street, Baton Rouge, LA 70806. *Phone:* 225-248-1015.

Remington College–Baton Rouge Campus

Baton Rouge, Louisiana **www.remingtoncollege.edu/**

Director of Admissions Monica Butler-Johnson, Director of Recruitment, Remington College–Baton Rouge Campus, 10551 Coursey Boulevard, Baton Rouge, LA 70816. *Phone:* 225-236-3200. *Fax:* 225-922-3250. *E-mail:* monica.johnson@remingtoncollege.edu.

Remington College–Lafayette Campus

Lafayette, Louisiana **www.remingtoncollege.edu/**

Freshman Application Contact Remington College–Lafayette Campus, 303 Rue Louis XIV, Lafayette, LA 70508. *Phone:* 337-981-4010. *Toll-free phone:* 800-736-2687.

Remington College–Shreveport

Shreveport, Louisiana **www.remingtoncollege.edu/shreveport/**

Freshman Application Contact Marc Wright, Remington College–Shreveport, 2106 Bert Kouns Industrial Loop, Shreveport, LA 71118. *Phone:* 318-671-4000.

River Parishes Community College

Sorrento, Louisiana **www.rpcc.edu/**

- **State-supported** 2-year, founded 1997
- **Coed**

Academics *Calendar:* semesters. *Degree:* certificates, diplomas, and associate.

Applying *Application fee:* $10.

Director of Admissions Ms. Allison Dauzat, Dean of Students and Enrollment Management, River Parishes Community College, PO Box 310, 7384 John LeBlanc Boulevard, Sorrento, LA 70778. *Phone:* 225-675-8270. *Fax:* 225-675-5478. *E-mail:* adauzat@rpcc.cc.la.us.

Southern University at Shreveport

Shreveport, Louisiana **www.susla.edu/**

Freshman Application Contact Ms. Juanita Johnson, Acting Admissions Records Technician, Southern University at Shreveport, 3050 Martin Luther King, Jr. Drive, Shreveport, LA 71107. *Phone:* 318-674-3342. *Toll-free phone:* 800-458-1472 Ext. 342.

MAINE

Beal College

Bangor, Maine **www.bealcollege.edu/**

Freshman Application Contact Ms. Susan Palmer, Admissions Assistant, Beal College, 629 Main Street, Bangor, ME 04401. *Phone:* 207-947-4591. *Toll-free phone:* 800-660-7351. *Fax:* 207-947-0208.

Central Maine Community College

Auburn, Maine **www.cmcc.edu/**

Freshman Application Contact Ms. Joan Nichols, Administrative Assistant, Admissions Department, Central Maine Community College, 1250 Turner Street, Auburn, ME 04210-6498. *Phone:* 207-755-5273. *Toll-free phone:* 800-891-2002. *Fax:* 207-755-5493. *E-mail:* jnichols@cmcc.edu.

Central Maine Medical Center College of Nursing and Health Professions

Lewiston, Maine www.cmmcson.edu/

- **Independent** 2-year, founded 1891
- **Urban** campus
- **Coed,** 157 undergraduate students, 15% full-time, 88% women, 12% men

Undergraduates 23 full-time, 134 part-time. Students come from 2 states and territories, 1% are from out of state, 1% Asian American or Pacific Islander, 2% Hispanic American, 6% live on campus.

Freshmen *Admission:* 3 enrolled.

Faculty *Total:* 19, 79% full-time, 5% with terminal degrees. *Student/faculty ratio:* 12:1.

Majors Nursing (registered nurse training); radiologic technology/science.

Academics *Calendar:* semesters. *Degree:* associate. *Special study options:* advanced placement credit, off-campus study, services for LD students, summer session for credit.

Library Gerrish True Health Sciences Library plus 1 other with 1,975 titles, 339 serial subscriptions, an OPAC, a Web page.

Student Life *Housing Options:* coed. Campus housing is university owned. *Activities and Organizations:* Student Communication Council, student government, Student Nurses Association. *Campus security:* 24-hour emergency response devices and patrols, late-night transport/escort service, controlled dormitory access. *Student services:* health clinic, personal/psychological counseling.

Standardized Tests *Required:* SAT or ACT (for admission).

Costs (2010–11) *Tuition:* $7140 full-time, $210 per credit hour part-time. *Required fees:* $1430 full-time. *Room only:* $1900. Room and board charges vary according to housing facility.

Applying *Options:* electronic application. *Application fee:* $40. *Required:* essay or personal statement, high school transcript, entrance exam; SAT/ACT or 12 college credits.

Freshman Application Contact Ms. Dagmar Jenison, Assistant Registrar, Central Maine Medical Center College of Nursing and Health Professions, 70 Middle Street, Lewiston, ME 04240-0305. *Phone:* 207-795-2843. *Fax:* 207-795-2849. *E-mail:* jenisod@cmhc.org.

Eastern Maine Community College

Bangor, Maine www.emcc.edu/

- **State-supported** 2-year, founded 1966, part of Maine Community College System
- **Small-town** 72-acre campus
- **Coed**

Academics *Calendar:* semesters. *Degree:* certificates, diplomas, and associate. *Special study options:* academic remediation for entering students, adult/continuing education programs, advanced placement credit, part-time degree program, summer session for credit.

Student Life *Campus security:* late-night transport/escort service, controlled dormitory access.

Standardized Tests *Required:* ACCUPLACER (for admission). *Required for some:* SAT (for admission).

Financial Aid Of all full-time matriculated undergraduates who enrolled in 2008, 100 Federal Work-Study jobs (averaging $1000).

Applying *Options:* deferred entrance. *Application fee:* $20. *Required:* essay or personal statement, high school transcript. *Required for some:* interview. *Recommended:* minimum 2.0 GPA.

Freshman Application Contact Mr. W. Gregory Swett, Director of Admissions, Eastern Maine Community College, 354 Hogan Road, Bangor, ME 04401. *Phone:* 207-974-4680. *Toll-free phone:* 800-286-9357. *Fax:* 207-974-4683. *E-mail:* admissions@emcc.edu.

Kaplan University

Lewiston, Maine www.kaplanuniversity.edu/

- **Proprietary** 2-year
- **Coed**

Academics *Degree:* certificates and associate.

Freshman Application Contact Kaplan University, 475 Lisbon Street, Lewiston, ME 04240. *Phone:* 207-333-3300.

Kaplan University

South Portland, Maine www.kaplanuniversity.edu/

- **Proprietary** 2-year, founded 1966
- **Urban** campus
- **Coed**

Majors Accounting; administrative assistant and secretarial science; business administration and management; child-care and support services management; criminal justice/law enforcement administration; legal assistant/paralegal; management information systems; medical/clinical assistant; tourism and travel services management.

Academics *Calendar:* modular. *Degree:* certificates and associate.

Financial Aid Of all full-time matriculated undergraduates who enrolled in 2008, 25 Federal Work-Study jobs (averaging $3000).

Freshman Application Contact Kaplan University, 265 Western Avenue, South Portland, ME 04106. *Phone:* 207-774-6126. *Toll-free phone:* 800-639-3110 Ext. 240 (in-state); 800-639-3110 Ext. 242 (out-of-state).

Kennebec Valley Community College

Fairfield, Maine www.kvcc.me.edu/

- **State-supported** 2-year, founded 1970, part of Maine Community College System
- **Small-town** 61-acre campus
- **Endowment** $246,029
- **Coed,** 2,298 undergraduate students, 32% full-time, 67% women, 33% men

Undergraduates 730 full-time, 1,568 part-time. Students come from 3 states and territories, 1% are from out of state, 0.7% African American, 0.9% Asian American or Pacific Islander, 1% Hispanic American, 0.9% Native American, 9% transferred in.

Freshmen *Admission:* 481 applied, 345 admitted, 313 enrolled.

Faculty *Total:* 201, 21% full-time.

Majors Accounting technology and bookkeeping; biology/biotechnology laboratory technician; child development; diagnostic medical sonography and ultrasound technology; drafting/design engineering technologies related; electrical, electronic and communications engineering technology; electrical/electronics maintenance and repair technology related; electrician; emergency medical technology (EMT paramedic); executive assistant/executive secretary; health information/medical records technology; industrial mechanics and maintenance technology; legal administrative assistant/secretary; liberal arts and sciences and humanities related; liberal arts and sciences/liberal studies; lineworker; machine tool technology; management information systems; marketing/marketing management; massage therapy; medical administrative assistant and medical secretary; medical/clinical assistant; mental and social health services and allied professions related; nursing (registered nurse training); occupational therapist assistant; physical therapist assistant; radiologic technology/science; respiratory care therapy; teacher assistant/aide; wood science and wood products/pulp and paper technology.

Academics *Calendar:* semesters. *Degree:* certificates, diplomas, and associate. *Special study options:* academic remediation for entering students, accelerated degree program, adult/continuing education programs, advanced placement credit, distance learning, external degree program, independent study, internships, part-time degree program, services for LD students, summer session for credit.

Library Lunder Library with 17,454 titles, 144 serial subscriptions, 2,955 audiovisual materials, an OPAC, a Web page.

Student Life *Housing:* college housing not available. *Activities and Organizations:* choral group, Campus Activities Board, Respiratory Therapy (RT) Club, Physical Therapist Assistant (PTA) Club, Student Senate, Phi Theta Kappa. *Campus security:* evening security patrol. *Student services:* personal/psychological counseling.

Athletics *Intercollegiate sports:* ice hockey M/W. *Intramural sports:* basketball M/W, bowling M/W, golf M/W, soccer M/W, softball M/W, volleyball M/W.

Standardized Tests *Required for some:* HESI nursing exam, HOBET for Allied Health programs, ACCUPLACER. *Recommended:* SAT or ACT (for admission).

Costs (2009–10) *Tuition:* state resident $2520 full-time, $84 per credit hour part-time; nonresident $5040 full-time, $168 per credit hour part-time. *Required fees:* $756 full-time.

Kennebec Valley Community College (continued)

Financial Aid Of all full-time matriculated undergraduates who enrolled in 2008, 34 Federal Work-Study jobs (averaging $1207).

Applying *Options:* electronic application, deferred entrance. *Application fee:* $20. *Required:* essay or personal statement, high school transcript. *Required for some:* interview. *Application deadlines:* rolling (freshmen), rolling (transfers). *Notification:* continuous (freshmen), continuous (transfers).

Freshman Application Contact Mr. Jim Bourgoin, Director of Admissions, Kennebec Valley Community College, 92 Western Avenue, Fairfield, ME 04937-1367. *Phone:* 207-453-5035. *Toll-free phone:* 800-528-5882 Ext. 5035. *Fax:* 207-453-5011. *E-mail:* admissions@kvcc.me.edu.

Northern Maine Community College

Presque Isle, Maine **www.nmcc.edu/**

Freshman Application Contact Ms. Nancy Gagnon, Admissions Secretary, Northern Maine Community College, 33 Edgemont Drive, Presque Isle, ME 04769-2016. *Phone:* 207-768-2785. *Toll-free phone:* 800-535-6682. *Fax:* 207-768-2848. *E-mail:* ngagnon@nmcc.edu.

Southern Maine Community College

South Portland, Maine **www.smccme.edu/**

- **State-supported** 2-year, founded 1946, part of Maine Community College System
- **Small-town** 80-acre campus
- **Coed,** 6,261 undergraduate students, 48% full-time, 49% women, 51% men

Undergraduates 2,993 full-time, 3,268 part-time. Students come from 28 states and territories, 58 other countries, 4% are from out of state, 4% African American, 2% Asian American or Pacific Islander, 1% Hispanic American, 1% Native American, 0.7% international, 10% transferred in, 5% live on campus. *Retention:* 49% of 2008 full-time freshmen returned.

Freshmen *Admission:* 1,393 enrolled.

Faculty *Total:* 415, 26% full-time. *Student/faculty ratio:* 19:1.

Majors Agronomy and crop science; applied horticulture; architectural drafting and CAD/CADD; architectural engineering technology; automobile/automotive mechanics technology; biotechnology; botany/plant biology; business administration and management; business machine repair; cardiovascular technology; carpentry; child development; cinematography and film/video production; communications technology; computer engineering technology; construction engineering technology; construction trades; criminal justice/law enforcement administration; criminal justice/police science; culinary arts; dietetics; dietetic technician; digital communication and media/multimedia; drafting and design technology; early childhood education; electrical, electronic and communications engineering technology; emergency medical technology (EMT paramedic); engineering related; engineering technologies related; environmental engineering technology; fire science; food technology and processing; general studies; heating, air conditioning, ventilation and refrigeration maintenance technology; horticultural science; hospitality administration; hotel/motel administration; industrial radiologic technology; information science/studies; kindergarten/preschool education; landscaping and groundskeeping; liberal arts and sciences and humanities related; liberal arts and sciences/liberal studies; machine tool technology; management information systems; marine biology and biological oceanography; medical/clinical assistant; medical radiologic technology; mental and social health services and allied professions related; nursing (licensed practical/vocational nurse training); nursing (registered nurse training); oceanography (chemical and physical); pipefitting and sprinkler fitting; plumbing technology; radiologic technology/science; respiratory care therapy; special products marketing; surgical technology.

Academics *Calendar:* semesters. *Degree:* certificates, diplomas, and associate. *Special study options:* academic remediation for entering students, advanced placement credit, distance learning, double majors, English as a second language, honors programs, internships, off-campus study, part-time degree program, services for LD students, study abroad, summer session for credit.

Library Southern Maine Community College Library with 18,500 titles, 300 serial subscriptions, an OPAC, a Web page.

Student Life *Housing Options:* coed. Campus housing is university owned. *Activities and Organizations:* student-run newspaper, choral group, Student Senate. *Campus security:* 24-hour emergency response devices and patrols, student patrols, late-night transport/escort service, controlled dormitory access. *Student services:* personal/psychological counseling.

Athletics *Intercollegiate sports:* baseball M, basketball M, golf M/W, soccer M/W, softball W, volleyball M/W. *Intramural sports:* basketball M/W, football M/W, golf M/W, soccer M/W, volleyball M/W.

Standardized Tests *Recommended:* SAT or ACT (for admission), AccuPlacer.

Costs (2010–11) *Tuition:* state resident $2520 full-time, $84 per credit hour part-time; nonresident $5040 full-time, $168 per credit hour part-time. *Required fees:* $845 full-time, $19 per credit hour part-time, $25 per term part-time. *Room and board:* $8212; room only: $5212. *Payment plan:* installment. *Waivers:* senior citizens and employees or children of employees.

Financial Aid Of all full-time matriculated undergraduates who enrolled in 2008, 130 Federal Work-Study jobs (averaging $1500).

Applying *Options:* electronic application. *Application fee:* $20. *Required:* high school transcript or proof of high school graduation. *Application deadlines:* rolling (freshmen), rolling (out-of-state freshmen), rolling (transfers). *Notification:* continuous (freshmen), continuous (out-of-state freshmen), continuous (transfers).

Freshman Application Contact Staci Grasky, Associate Dean for Enrollment Services, Southern Maine Community College, Admissions, 2 Fort Road, South Portland, ME 04106. *Phone:* 207-741-5515. *Toll-free phone:* 877-282-2182. *Fax:* 207-741-5760. *E-mail:* sgrasky@smccme.edu.

Washington County Community College

Calais, Maine **www.wccc.me.edu/**

Director of Admissions Mr. Kent Lyons, Admissions Counselor, Washington County Community College, One College Drive, Calais, ME 04619. *Phone:* 207-454-1000. *Toll-free phone:* 800-210-6932 Ext. 41049.

York County Community College

Wells, Maine **www.yccc.edu/**

- **State-supported** 2-year, founded 1994, part of Maine Community College System
- **Small-town** 84-acre campus with easy access to Boston
- **Coed,** 1,444 undergraduate students

Undergraduates Students come from 3 states and territories, 3 other countries, 2% are from out of state.

Freshmen *Admission:* 1,021 applied, 760 admitted.

Faculty *Total:* 77, 22% full-time, 5% with terminal degrees. *Student/faculty ratio:* 15:1.

Majors Accounting; business administration and management; computer/information technology services administration related; computer systems networking and telecommunications; criminal justice/law enforcement administration; criminal justice/safety; culinary arts; drafting and design technology; general studies; kindergarten/preschool education; web page, digital/multimedia and information resources design.

Academics *Calendar:* semesters. *Degree:* certificates and associate. *Special study options:* academic remediation for entering students, accelerated degree program, adult/continuing education programs, advanced placement credit, cooperative education, distance learning, internships, part-time degree program, services for LD students, summer session for credit.

Library Library and Learning Resource Center plus 1 other with 4,000 titles, 75 serial subscriptions, an OPAC, a Web page.

Student Life *Housing:* college housing not available. *Activities and Organizations:* student-run newspaper, Student Senate, The Voice Student Newspaper, Phi Theta Kappa, Gaming Club, Diversity Club. *Campus security:* 24-hour emergency response devices, late-night transport/escort service.

Athletics *Intercollegiate sports:* golf M(c). *Intramural sports:* basketball M/W, football M/W, ice hockey M/W, ultimate Frisbee M/W.

Costs (2009–10) *Tuition:* state resident $84 per credit hour part-time; nonresident $168 per credit hour part-time. Full-time tuition and fees vary according to course load and program. Part-time tuition and fees vary according to course load and program. *Payment plan:* installment. *Waivers:* minority students and employees or children of employees.

Financial Aid Of all full-time matriculated undergraduates who enrolled in 2009, 418 applied for aid, 326 were judged to have need, 22 had their need fully met. 25 Federal Work-Study jobs (averaging $1200). In 2009, 7 non-need-based awards were made. *Average percent of need met:* 52%. *Average financial aid package:* $5700. *Average need-based loan:* $2650. *Average need-based gift aid:* $4658. *Average non-need-based aid:* $928.

Applying *Options:* electronic application. *Application fee:* $20. *Required:* high school transcript, interview. *Application deadlines:* rolling (freshmen), rolling (transfers).

Freshman Application Contact York County Community College, 112 College Drive, Wells, ME 04090. *Phone:* 207-646-9282 Ext. 311. *Toll-free phone:* 800-580-3820.

MARYLAND

ALLEGANY COLLEGE OF MARYLAND

Cumberland, Maryland **www.allegany.edu/**

- **State and locally supported** 2-year, founded 1961, part of Maryland State Community Colleges System
- **Small-town** 311-acre campus
- **Coed,** 4,913 undergraduate students

Undergraduates 7% African American, 0.5% Asian American or Pacific Islander, 0.4% Hispanic American, 0.5% Native American, 7% live on campus.

Faculty *Total:* 232, 49% full-time, 10% with terminal degrees. *Student/faculty ratio:* 16:1.

Majors Accounting technology and bookkeeping; administrative assistant and secretarial science; automobile/automotive mechanics technology; business administration and management; clinical/medical laboratory assistant; clinical/medical laboratory technology; communications technology; computer engineering technology; cosmetology and personal grooming arts related; criminal justice/police science; culinary arts; dental hygiene; forest/forest resources management; health professions related; hospitality administration; legal assistant/paralegal; liberal arts and sciences/liberal studies; management information systems; marketing/marketing management; medical radiologic technology; nursing (registered nurse training); occupational therapist assistant; occupational therapy; physical therapist assistant; psychiatric/mental health services technology; respiratory care therapy.

Academics *Calendar:* semesters. *Degree:* certificates and associate. *Special study options:* academic remediation for entering students, adult/continuing education programs, advanced placement credit, distance learning, double majors, English as a second language, honors programs, independent study, internships, part-time degree program, summer session for credit. *ROTC:* Army (c).

Library Allegany College of Maryland Library with 86,636 titles, 313 serial subscriptions, an OPAC, a Web page.

Student Life *Housing Options:* Campus housing is provided by a third party. *Activities and Organizations:* choral group, SAHDA, Honors Club, EMT Club, Forestry Club. *Campus security:* 24-hour emergency response devices and patrols, late-night transport/escort service. *Student services:* personal/psychological counseling, women's center.

Athletics Member NJCAA. *Intercollegiate sports:* baseball M, basketball M/W, soccer M/W, softball W, tennis M/W, volleyball W.

Standardized Tests *Required for some:* ACT (for admission).

Costs (2009–10) *Tuition:* area resident $3234 full-time; state resident $5714 full-time; nonresident $6824 full-time. Full-time tuition and fees vary according to course load and location. Part-time tuition and fees vary according to course load and location. *Required fees:* $194 full-time. *Room and board:* $8000; room only: $6000. Room and board charges vary according to housing facility. *Waivers:* employees or children of employees.

Financial Aid Of all full-time matriculated undergraduates who enrolled in 2008, 198 Federal Work-Study jobs (averaging $1352).

Applying *Options:* electronic application, early admission. *Required:* high school transcript. *Application deadlines:* rolling (freshmen), rolling (transfers). *Notification:* continuous (transfers).

Freshman Application Contact Ms. Cathy Nolan, Director of Admissions and Registration, Allegany College of Maryland, 12401 Willowbrook Road, SE, Cumberland, MD 21502. *Phone:* 301-784-5000 Ext. 5202. *Fax:* 301-784-5220. *E-mail:* cnolan@allegany.edu.

ANNE ARUNDEL COMMUNITY COLLEGE

Arnold, Maryland **www.aacc.edu/**

- **State and locally supported** 2-year, founded 1961
- **Suburban** 230-acre campus with easy access to Baltimore and Washington, DC
- **Coed,** 16,741 undergraduate students, 36% full-time, 61% women, 39% men

Undergraduates 5,957 full-time, 10,784 part-time. Students come from 19 states and territories, 16% African American, 4% Asian American or Pacific Islander, 3% Hispanic American, 0.6% Native American. *Retention:* 58% of 2008 full-time freshmen returned.

Freshmen *Admission:* 3,064 enrolled.

Faculty *Total:* 1,016, 26% full-time, 11% with terminal degrees. *Student/faculty ratio:* 18:1.

Majors Accounting; administrative assistant and secretarial science; American studies; applied art; architectural engineering technology; art; astronomy; behavioral sciences; biological and physical sciences; biology/biological sciences; botany/plant biology; broadcast journalism; business administration and management; business/managerial economics; chemistry; cinematography and film/video production; clinical laboratory science/medical technology; communications technology; computer and information sciences and support services related; computer and information sciences related; computer engineering technology; computer programming; computer science; consumer merchandising/retailing management; corrections; criminal justice/law enforcement administration; criminal justice/police science; data entry/microcomputer applications; data processing and data processing technology; economics; education; electrical, electronic and communications engineering technology; elementary education; emergency medical technology (EMT paramedic); engineering technology; English; environmental studies; European studies; food technology and processing; health teacher education; horticultural science; hotel/motel administration; humanities; human services; industrial radiologic technology; industrial technology; information science/studies; kindergarten/preschool education; landscape architecture; legal assistant/paralegal; liberal arts and sciences/liberal studies; marine science/merchant marine officer; marketing/marketing management; mass communication/media; mathematics; mechanical engineering/mechanical technology; medical/clinical assistant; mental health/rehabilitation; music; nursing (registered nurse training); photography; physical education teaching and coaching; public administration; public policy analysis; real estate; social sciences; system administration; telecommunications technology.

Academics *Calendar:* semesters. *Degree:* certificates and associate. *Special study options:* academic remediation for entering students, accelerated degree program, adult/continuing education programs, advanced placement credit, cooperative education, distance learning, English as a second language, freshman honors college, honors programs, independent study, internships, part-time degree program, services for LD students, summer session for credit. *ROTC:* Army (c), Air Force (c).

Library Andrew G. Truxal Library with 144,694 titles, 403 serial subscriptions, 8,060 audiovisual materials, an OPAC, a Web page.

Student Life *Housing:* college housing not available. *Activities and Organizations:* drama/theater group, student-run newspaper, choral group, Drama Club, Student Association, Black Student Union, International Student Association, Chemistry Club. *Campus security:* 24-hour emergency response devices and patrols, student patrols, late-night transport/escort service. *Student services:* health clinic, personal/psychological counseling.

Athletics Member NJCAA. *Intercollegiate sports:* baseball M(s), basketball M/W, cross-country running M(s)/W(s), golf M, lacrosse M(s)/W(s), soccer M(s)/W(s), softball W(s), volleyball W.

Costs (2010–11) *Tuition:* area resident $2640 full-time, $88 per credit hour part-time; state resident $5070 full-time, $169 per credit hour part-time; nonresident $8970 full-time, $299 per credit hour part-time. Full-time tuition and fees vary according to course load. Part-time tuition and fees vary according to course load. *Required fees:* $370 full-time, $11 per credit hour part-time, $20 per term part-time. *Payment plan:* installment. *Waivers:* senior citizens and employees or children of employees.

Financial Aid Of all full-time matriculated undergraduates who enrolled in 2008, 104 Federal Work-Study jobs (averaging $1900). 55 state and other part-time jobs (averaging $1740).

Applying *Options:* early admission, deferred entrance. *Application deadlines:* rolling (freshmen), rolling (transfers).

Freshman Application Contact Mr. Thomas McGinn, Director of Enrollment Development and Admissions, Anne Arundel Community College, 101 College Parkway, Arnold, MD 21012-1895. *Phone:* 410-777-2240. *Fax:* 410-777-2246. *E-mail:* 4info@aacc.edu.

BALTIMORE CITY COMMUNITY COLLEGE

Baltimore, Maryland **www.bccc.state.md.us/**

Freshman Application Contact Mrs. Scheherazade Forman, Admissions Coordinator, Baltimore City Community College, 2901 Liberty Heights Avenue, Baltimore, MD 21215. *Phone:* 410-462-8300. *Toll-free phone:* 888-203-1261 Ext. 8300. *E-mail:* sforman@bccc.edu.

BALTIMORE INTERNATIONAL COLLEGE

Baltimore, Maryland **www.bic.edu/**

Freshman Application Contact Ms. Kristin Ciarlo, Director of Admissions, Baltimore International College, Commerce Exchange, 17 Commerce Street, Baltimore, MD 21202-3230. *Phone:* 410-752-4710 Ext. 239. *Toll-free phone:* 800-624-9926 Ext. 120. *Fax:* 410-752-3730. *E-mail:* admissions@bic.edu.

CARROLL COMMUNITY COLLEGE

Westminster, Maryland **www.carrollcc.edu/**

- **State and locally supported** 2-year, founded 1993, part of Maryland Higher Education Commission
- **Suburban** 80-acre campus with easy access to Baltimore
- **Endowment** $2.3 million
- **Coed,** 3,913 undergraduate students, 44% full-time, 61% women, 39% men

Undergraduates 1,730 full-time, 2,183 part-time. Students come from 6 states and territories, 4 other countries, 2% are from out of state, 3% African American, 1% Asian American or Pacific Islander, 2% Hispanic American, 0.4% Native American, 0.2% international, 9% transferred in.

Freshmen *Admission:* 989 applied, 989 admitted, 989 enrolled.

Faculty *Total:* 288, 24% full-time, 3% with terminal degrees. *Student/faculty ratio:* 17:1.

Majors Accounting; administrative assistant and secretarial science; architectural drafting and CAD/CADD; art; business administration and management; child-care and support services management; commercial and advertising art; computer and information sciences; computer graphics; criminal justice/police science; education (multiple levels); emergency care attendant (EMT ambulance); forensic science and technology; general studies; health information/medical records technology; health professions related; human services; kindergarten/preschool education; kinesiology and exercise science; legal studies; liberal arts and sciences/liberal studies; management information systems; music; nursing (registered nurse training); physical therapist assistant; psychology; theater design and technology.

Academics *Calendar:* semesters plus winter session. *Degree:* certificates and associate. *Special study options:* academic remediation for entering students, advanced placement credit, distance learning, English as a second language, honors programs, independent study, internships, part-time degree program, services for LD students, summer session for credit.

Library Random House Learning Resources Center with 68,038 titles, 215 serial subscriptions, 2,712 audiovisual materials, an OPAC, a Web page.

Student Life *Housing:* college housing not available. *Activities and Organizations:* drama/theater group, choral group, Student Government Organization, Carroll Community Chorus, Campus Activities Board, Green Team, Academic Communities: Creativity, Education, Great Ideas, Health and Wellness and more. *Campus security:* 24-hour emergency response devices, late-night transport/escort service.

Athletics *Intramural sports:* baseball M/W, rugby M, soccer M/W, volleyball M/W.

Costs (2010–11) *Tuition:* area resident $3565 full-time, $119 per credit hour part-time; state resident $5158 full-time, $172 per credit hour part-time; nonresident $7246 full-time, $242 per credit hour part-time. *Payment plan:* deferred payment. *Waivers:* senior citizens and employees or children of employees.

Financial Aid Of all full-time matriculated undergraduates who enrolled in 2008, 17 Federal Work-Study jobs (averaging $1487).

Applying *Options:* early admission. *Required:* high school transcript. *Application deadlines:* rolling (freshmen), rolling (transfers). *Notification:* continuous (freshmen), continuous (transfers).

Freshman Application Contact Ms. Candace Edwards, Coordinator of Admissions, Carroll Community College, 1601 Washington Road, Westminster, MD 21157. *Phone:* 410-386-8430. *Toll-free phone:* 888-221-9748. *Fax:* 410-386-8446. *E-mail:* cedwards@carrollcc.edu.

CECIL COLLEGE

North East, Maryland **www.cecil.edu/**

- **County-supported** 2-year, founded 1968
- **Small-town** 105-acre campus with easy access to Baltimore
- **Endowment** $3.3 million
- **Coed,** 2,388 undergraduate students, 37% full-time, 62% women, 38% men

Undergraduates 874 full-time, 1,514 part-time. Students come from 11 states and territories, 14 other countries, 10% are from out of state, 7% African American, 1% Asian American or Pacific Islander, 2% Hispanic American, 0.5% Native American, 0.5% international, 0.2% transferred in.

Freshmen *Admission:* 521 applied, 521 admitted, 484 enrolled.

Faculty *Total:* 226, 21% full-time, 6% with terminal degrees. *Student/faculty ratio:* 13:1.

Majors Accounting technology and bookkeeping; biology/biological sciences; business administration and management; business administration, management and operations related; business/commerce; business/corporate communications; child-care and support services management; commercial photography; computer and information sciences; computer programming; computer programming (specific applications); criminal justice/police science; data processing and data processing technology; education; elementary education; emergency medical technology (EMT paramedic); fire science; general studies; graphic design; health services/allied health/health sciences; horse husbandry/equine science and management; information science/studies; information technology; kindergarten/preschool education; liberal arts and sciences/liberal studies; logistics and materials management; management information systems; marketing/marketing management; mathematics; nursing (registered nurse training); photography; physical sciences; physics; public relations/image management; transportation and materials moving related; transportation management; web page, digital/multimedia and information resources design.

Academics *Calendar:* semesters. *Degree:* certificates and associate. *Special study options:* academic remediation for entering students, accelerated degree program, adult/continuing education programs, advanced placement credit, cooperative education, distance learning, double majors, English as a second language, independent study, internships, off-campus study, part-time degree program, services for LD students, summer session for credit.

Library Cecil County Veteran's Memorial Library with 38,105 titles, 222 serial subscriptions, 1,217 audiovisual materials, an OPAC, a Web page.

Student Life *Housing:* college housing not available. *Activities and Organizations:* drama/theater group, student-run newspaper, student government, Non-traditional Student Organization, Student Nurses Association, national fraternities. *Campus security:* 24-hour emergency response devices, late-night transport/escort service. *Student services:* personal/psychological counseling, women's center.

Athletics Member NJCAA. *Intercollegiate sports:* baseball M(s), basketball M(s)/W(s), cheerleading W, soccer W(s), softball W(s), tennis W(s), volleyball W(s).

Costs (2010–11) *Tuition:* area resident $2550 full-time, $85 per credit hour part-time; state resident $5250 full-time, $175 per credit hour part-time; nonresident $6600 full-time, $220 per credit hour part-time. *Required fees:* $362 full-time. *Payment plan:* deferred payment. *Waivers:* senior citizens and employees or children of employees.

Applying *Options:* electronic application, early admission, deferred entrance. *Required:* high school transcript. *Application deadlines:* rolling (freshmen), rolling (out-of-state freshmen), rolling (transfers). *Notification:* continuous (freshmen), continuous (out-of-state freshmen), continuous (transfers).

Freshman Application Contact Dr. Diane Lane, Cecil College, One Seahawk Drive, North East, MD 21901. *Phone:* 410-287-1002. *Fax:* 410-287-1001. *E-mail:* dlane@cecil.edu.

CHESAPEAKE COLLEGE

Wye Mills, Maryland **www.chesapeake.edu/**

Freshman Application Contact Ms. Kathy Petrichenko, Dean of Recruitment, Chesapeake College, PO Box 8, Wye Mills, MD 21679. *Phone:* 410-822-5400 Ext. 287. *E-mail:* kpetrichenko@chesapeake.edu.

COLLEGE OF SOUTHERN MARYLAND

La Plata, Maryland **www.csmd.edu/**

- **State and locally supported** 2-year, founded 1958
- **Rural** 175-acre campus with easy access to Washington, DC
- **Coed,** 8,810 undergraduate students, 41% full-time, 63% women, 37% men

Undergraduates 3,595 full-time, 5,215 part-time. 22% African American, 4% Asian American or Pacific Islander, 3% Hispanic American, 0.6% Native American, 0.1% international, 4% transferred in.

Freshmen *Admission:* 1,519 applied, 1,519 admitted, 1,519 enrolled.

Faculty *Total:* 572, 22% full-time, 11% with terminal degrees.

Majors Accounting; accounting technology and bookkeeping; building/construction finishing, management, and inspection related; business administration and management; business/commerce; child-care and support services management; clinical/medical laboratory technology; computer and information sciences; computer programming; criminal justice/law enforcement administration; early childhood education; education; electrician; elementary education; emergency medical technology (EMT paramedic); engineering; engineering technologies related; environmental engineering technology; fire protection and safety technology; fire science; health and physical education related; hospitality administration; information technology; legal assistant/paralegal; liberal arts and sciences and humanities related; liberal arts and sciences/liberal studies; lineworker; massage therapy; mental and social health services and allied professions related; multi/interdisciplinary studies related; nursing (licensed practical/vocational nurse training); nursing (registered nurse training); physical therapist assistant.

Academics *Calendar:* semesters. *Degree:* certificates and associate. *Special study options:* academic remediation for entering students, accelerated degree program, adult/continuing education programs, advanced placement credit, cooperative education, distance learning, honors programs, internships, part-time degree program, services for LD students, study abroad, summer session for credit.

Library College of Southern Maryland Library with 44,896 titles, 166 serial subscriptions, an OPAC, a Web page.

Student Life *Housing:* college housing not available. *Activities and Organizations:* drama/theater group, student-run newspaper, television station, choral group, Spanish Club, Nursing Student Association, Science Club, Black Student Union, BACCHUS. *Campus security:* 24-hour emergency response devices and patrols. *Student services:* personal/psychological counseling, women's center.

Athletics Member NJCAA. *Intercollegiate sports:* baseball M, basketball M/W, golf M, soccer M/W, softball W, tennis M, volleyball W.

Costs (2009–10) *Tuition:* area resident $3690 full-time, $100 per credit hour part-time; state resident $6420 full-time, $174 per credit hour part-time; nonresident $8303 full-time, $225 per credit hour part-time. *Payment plan:* deferred payment. *Waivers:* senior citizens and employees or children of employees.

Financial Aid Of all full-time matriculated undergraduates who enrolled in 2008, 25 Federal Work-Study jobs (averaging $1200).

Applying *Options:* electronic application, early admission, deferred entrance. *Recommended:* high school transcript. *Application deadlines:* rolling (freshmen), rolling (transfers). *Notification:* continuous (freshmen), continuous (transfers).

Freshman Application Contact Information Center Coordinator, College of Southern Maryland, PO Box 910, La Plata, MD 20646-0910. *Phone:* 301-934-7520 Ext. 7765. *Toll-free phone:* 800-933-9177. *Fax:* 301-934-7698. *E-mail:* info@csmd.edu.

THE COMMUNITY COLLEGE OF BALTIMORE COUNTY

Baltimore, Maryland **www.ccbcmd.edu/**

- **County-supported** 2-year, founded 1957
- **Suburban** 350-acre campus
- **Coed,** 23,584 undergraduate students, 36% full-time, 63% women, 37% men

Undergraduates 8,558 full-time, 15,026 part-time. 34% African American, 4% Asian American or Pacific Islander, 3% Hispanic American, 0.4% Native American, 2% international.

Freshmen *Admission:* 4,387 enrolled.

Faculty *Total:* 1,248, 32% full-time, 8% with terminal degrees.

Majors Accounting technology and bookkeeping; administrative assistant and secretarial science; aeronautics/aviation/aerospace science and technology; applied horticulture; architectural drafting and CAD/CADD; autobody/collision and repair technology; automobile/automotive mechanics technology; banking and financial support services; biological and physical sciences; building/construction finishing, management, and inspection related; building/construction site management; building/home/construction inspection; business administration and management; business administration, management and operations related; business/commerce; chemistry teacher education; child-care and support services management; child-care provision; civil engineering technology; clinical/medical laboratory technology; commercial and advertising art; commercial photography; computer and information sciences; computer systems networking and telecommunications; computer technology/computer systems technology; court reporting; criminal justice/police science; dental hygiene; diagnostic medical sonography and ultrasound technology; diesel mechanics technology; drafting and design technology; early childhood education; education; electrical, electronic and communications engineering technology; elementary education; emergency medical technology (EMT paramedic); engineering; engineering technologies related; environmental engineering technology; fire protection and safety technology; funeral service and mortuary science; geography; graphic and printing equipment operation/production; health and medical administrative services related; health information/medical records technology; heating, air conditioning, ventilation and refrigeration maintenance technology; hotel/motel administration; human resources management; hydraulics and fluid power technology; industrial technology; instrumentation technology; labor and industrial relations; legal assistant/paralegal; liberal arts and sciences and humanities related; liberal arts and sciences/liberal studies; management information systems; mathematics teacher education; mechanical engineering/mechanical technology; medical administrative assistant and medical secretary; medical/clinical assistant; medical informatics; medical radiologic technology; merchandising, sales, and marketing operations related (general); multi/interdisciplinary studies related; nursing (registered nurse training); occupational safety and health technology; occupational therapy; parks, recreation and leisure; physician assistant; physics teacher education; plant sciences; psychiatric/mental health services technology; public administration; quality control technology; radio and television broadcasting technology; real estate; respiratory care therapy; restaurant, culinary, and catering management; sales, distribution and marketing; science technologies related; sign language interpretation and translation; Spanish language teacher education; special education; substance abuse/addiction counseling; veterinary/animal health technology; visual and performing arts; water quality and wastewater treatment management and recycling technology.

Academics *Calendar:* semesters. *Degree:* certificates and associate. *Special study options:* academic remediation for entering students, advanced placement credit, cooperative education, distance learning, English as a second language, honors programs, independent study, internships, off-campus study, services for LD students, study abroad, summer session for credit.

Student Life *Housing:* college housing not available. *Campus security:* 24-hour emergency response devices and patrols, late-night transport/escort service.

Athletics Member NJCAA. *Intercollegiate sports:* baseball M, basketball M/W, lacrosse M/W, soccer M/W, softball W, track and field W, volleyball W.

Standardized Tests *Recommended:* SAT or ACT (for admission).

Costs (2009–10) *Tuition:* area resident $2700 full-time; state resident $5490 full-time; nonresident $8220 full-time. *Required fees:* $402 full-time. *Payment plan:* installment. *Waivers:* employees or children of employees.

Applying *Required:* high school transcript. *Application deadlines:* rolling (freshmen), rolling (out-of-state freshmen), rolling (transfers).

Freshman Application Contact Ms. Diane Drake, Director of Admissions, The Community College of Baltimore County, 7201 Rossville Boulevard, Baltimore, MD 21228. *Phone:* 443-840-4392. *E-mail:* ddrake@ccbcmd.edu.

FREDERICK COMMUNITY COLLEGE

Frederick, Maryland **www.frederick.edu/**

- **State and locally supported** 2-year, founded 1957
- **Small-town** 125-acre campus with easy access to Baltimore and Washington, DC
- **Endowment** $4.0 million
- **Coed,** 6,233 undergraduate students, 38% full-time, 59% women, 41% men

Undergraduates 2,359 full-time, 3,874 part-time. 1% are from out of state, 11% African American, 4% Asian American or Pacific Islander, 6% Hispanic American, 0.6% Native American.

Freshmen *Admission:* 1,573 admitted, 1,573 enrolled.

Faculty *Total:* 522, 19% full-time. *Student/faculty ratio:* 12:1.

Majors Accounting; art; biology/biological sciences; building/construction finishing, management, and inspection related; business administration and management; chemistry; child development; computer engineering technology; computer science; criminal justice/law enforcement administration; data processing and data processing technology; drafting and design technology; education; electrical, electronic and communications engineering technology; elementary education; emergency medical technology (EMT paramedic); engineering; English; finance; fire science; general studies; human services; information technology; international business/trade/commerce; kindergarten/preschool education; legal administrative assistant/secretary; legal assistant/paralegal; liberal arts and sciences/liberal studies; marketing/marketing management; mass communication/media; mathematics; mathematics teacher education; medical administrative assistant and medical secretary; music teacher education; nuclear medical technology; nursing (registered nurse training); physical education teaching and coaching; physical sciences; political science and government; psychology; respiratory care therapy; Spanish language teacher education; surgical technology.

Academics *Calendar:* semesters. *Degree:* certificates and associate. *Special study options:* academic remediation for entering students, adult/continuing education programs, advanced placement credit, cooperative education, distance learning, English as a second language, freshman honors college, honors programs, independent study, internships, off-campus study, part-time degree program, services for LD students, study abroad, summer session for credit. *ROTC:* Army (c).

Library FCC Library with 40,000 titles, 5,150 serial subscriptions, an OPAC, a Web page.

Frederick Community College (continued)

Student Life *Housing:* college housing not available. *Activities and Organizations:* drama/theater group, student-run newspaper. *Campus security:* 24-hour emergency response devices and patrols, late-night transport/escort service. *Student services:* personal/psychological counseling, women's center.

Athletics Member NJCAA. *Intercollegiate sports:* baseball M, basketball M/W, golf M/W, soccer M/W, softball W, volleyball W.

Costs (2010–11) *Tuition:* area resident $3000 full-time; state resident $6400 full-time; nonresident $8600 full-time. *Required fees:* $400 full-time. *Payment plan:* deferred payment. *Waivers:* senior citizens and employees or children of employees.

Financial Aid Of all full-time matriculated undergraduates who enrolled in 2008, 25 Federal Work-Study jobs (averaging $1368). 14 state and other part-time jobs (averaging $2715).

Applying *Options:* electronic application. *Notification:* continuous (freshmen), continuous (transfers).

Freshman Application Contact Ms. Lisa A. Freel, Director of Recruitment and Outreach, Frederick Community College, Welcome and Registration Center, 7932 Opossumtown Pike, Frederick, MD 21702. *Phone:* 301-846-2468. *Fax:* 301-624-2799. *E-mail:* admissions@frederick.edu.

GARRETT COLLEGE

McHenry, Maryland **www.garrettcollege.edu/**

Freshman Application Contact Connie Meyers, Coordinator of Student Assistance Center, Garrett College, 687 Mosser Road, McHenry, MD 21541. *Phone:* 301-387-3044. *Fax:* 301-387-3038. *E-mail:* admissions@garrettcollege.edu.

HAGERSTOWN COMMUNITY COLLEGE

Hagerstown, Maryland **www.hagerstowncc.edu/**

- **State and locally supported** 2-year, founded 1946
- **Suburban** 319-acre campus with easy access to Baltimore and Washington, DC
- **Coed**

Undergraduates 1,342 full-time, 2,660 part-time. Students come from 9 states and territories, 17% are from out of state, 10% African American, 2% Asian American or Pacific Islander, 3% Hispanic American, 0.5% Native American, 6% transferred in. *Retention:* 61% of 2008 full-time freshmen returned.

Faculty *Student/faculty ratio:* 18:1.

Academics *Calendar:* semesters. *Degree:* certificates and associate. *Special study options:* academic remediation for entering students, accelerated degree program, adult/continuing education programs, advanced placement credit, cooperative education, distance learning, English as a second language, honors programs, independent study, internships, off-campus study, part-time degree program, services for LD students, student-designed majors, summer session for credit.

Student Life *Campus security:* 24-hour patrols.

Athletics Member NJCAA.

Costs (2009–10) *Tuition:* area resident $2940 full-time, $98 per credit hour part-time; state resident $4590 full-time, $153 per credit hour part-time; nonresident $6060 full-time, $202 per credit hour part-time. *Required fees:* $330 full-time, $8 per credit hour part-time, $20 per term part-time.

Financial Aid Of all full-time matriculated undergraduates who enrolled in 2008, 27 Federal Work-Study jobs (averaging $2955).

Applying *Options:* electronic application, early admission, deferred entrance. *Required for some:* high school transcript, selective admissions for RN, LPN, EMT, and radiography programs.

Freshman Application Contact Dr. Daniel Bock, Assistant Director, Admissions, Records and Registration, Hagerstown Community College, 11400 Robinwood Drive, Hagerstown, MD 21742-6590. *Phone:* 301-790-2800 Ext. 335. *Fax:* 301-791-9165. *E-mail:* bockd@hagerstowncc.edu.

HARFORD COMMUNITY COLLEGE

Bel Air, Maryland **www.harford.edu/**

- **State and locally supported** 2-year, founded 1957
- **Small-town** 331-acre campus with easy access to Baltimore
- **Coed,** 6,656 undergraduate students, 45% full-time, 61% women, 39% men

Undergraduates 2,973 full-time, 3,683 part-time. 14% African American, 3% Asian American or Pacific Islander, 3% Hispanic American, 0.4% Native American, 0.8% international.

Freshmen *Admission:* 1,409 enrolled.

Faculty *Total:* 379, 27% full-time, 7% with terminal degrees. *Student/faculty ratio:* 20:1.

Majors Accounting; accounting technology and bookkeeping; administrative assistant and secretarial science; applied horticulture; business administration and management; business/commerce; CAD/CADD drafting/design technology; chemistry teacher education; child-care and support services management; commercial photography; communications technologies and support services related; computer and information sciences; computer and information systems security; computer programming (specific applications); criminal justice/police science; design and visual communications; early childhood education; education; electroneurodiagnostic/electroencephalographic technology; elementary education; engineering; engineering technologies related; environmental engineering technology; interior design; legal assistant/paralegal; legal studies; liberal arts and sciences and humanities related; liberal arts and sciences/liberal studies; massage therapy; mathematics teacher education; medical/clinical assistant; multi/interdisciplinary studies related; nursing (registered nurse training); psychiatric/mental health services technology; science technologies related; security and loss prevention; substance abuse/addiction counseling; theater design and technology; visual and performing arts.

Academics *Calendar:* semesters. *Degree:* certificates, diplomas, and associate. *Special study options:* academic remediation for entering students, adult/continuing education programs, advanced placement credit, cooperative education, distance learning, double majors, English as a second language, independent study, internships, part-time degree program, services for LD students, student-designed majors, summer session for credit.

Library Harford Community College Library with 80,777 titles, 18,142 serial subscriptions, 4,919 audiovisual materials, an OPAC, a Web page.

Student Life *Housing:* college housing not available. *Activities and Organizations:* drama/theater group, student-run newspaper, radio station, choral group, Student Association, Paralegal Club, Multi-National Students Association, Student Nurses Association, Gamers Guild. *Campus security:* 24-hour patrols, late-night transport/escort service. *Student services:* personal/psychological counseling.

Athletics Member NJCAA. *Intercollegiate sports:* baseball M(s), basketball M(s)/W(s), cheerleading M(c)/W(c), cross-country running M(c)/W(c), golf M(s), lacrosse M(s)/W(s), soccer M(s)/W(s), softball W(s), tennis M(s)/W(s), volleyball W(s). *Intramural sports:* badminton M/W, basketball M/W, soccer M/W, softball M/W, table tennis M/W, volleyball M/W.

Costs (2010–11) *Tuition:* area resident $2310 full-time, $77 per credit hour part-time; state resident $4620 full-time, $154 per credit hour part-time; nonresident $6930 full-time, $231 per credit hour part-time. *Required fees:* $300 full-time. *Waivers:* senior citizens and employees or children of employees.

Financial Aid Of all full-time matriculated undergraduates who enrolled in 2008, 55 Federal Work-Study jobs (averaging $1800).

Applying *Options:* electronic application. *Application deadlines:* rolling (freshmen), rolling (transfers). *Notification:* continuous (transfers).

Freshman Application Contact Ms. Donna Strasavich, Enrollment Specialist, Harford Community College, 401 Thomas Run Road, Bel Air, MD 21015-1698. *Phone:* 443-412-2311. *Fax:* 443-412-2169. *E-mail:* sendinfo@harford.edu.

HOWARD COMMUNITY COLLEGE

Columbia, Maryland **www.howardcc.edu/**

- **State and locally supported** 2-year, founded 1966
- **Suburban** 122-acre campus with easy access to Baltimore and Washington, DC
- **Coed,** 8,777 undergraduate students, 39% full-time, 57% women, 43% men

Undergraduates 3,443 full-time, 5,334 part-time. 25% African American, 12% Asian American or Pacific Islander, 5% Hispanic American, 0.6% Native American. *Retention:* 64% of 2008 full-time freshmen returned.

Faculty *Total:* 627, 24% full-time. *Student/faculty ratio:* 19:1.

Majors Accounting; administrative assistant and secretarial science; applied art; architecture; art; biological and physical sciences; biomedical technology; biotechnology; business administration and management; cardiovascular technology; child development; clinical laboratory science/medical technology; computer and information sciences related; computer graphics; computer/information technology services administration related; computer science; computer systems networking and telecommunications; consumer merchandising/retailing management; criminal justice/law enforcement administration; data entry/microcomputer applications; dramatic/theater arts; electrical, electronic and communications engineering technology; elementary education; emergency medical technology (EMT paramedic); engineering; environmental studies; fashion merchandising; financial planning and services; general studies; health teacher education; information science/studies; information technology; kindergarten/preschool education; legal administrative assistant/secretary; liberal arts and sciences/liberal studies; medical administrative assistant and medical secretary; music; nuclear medical technology; nursing (licensed practical/vocational nurse training); nursing (registered nurse training); office management; photography; physical sciences; pre-dentistry studies; premedical studies; pre-pharmacy studies; pre-veterinary studies; psychology; secondary education; social sciences; sport and fitness administration/management; substance abuse/addiction counseling; telecommunications technology; theater design and technology.

Academics *Calendar:* semesters. *Degree:* certificates and associate. *Special study options:* academic remediation for entering students, adult/continuing education programs, advanced placement credit, cooperative education, distance learning, double majors, English as a second language, external degree program, freshman honors college, honors programs, off-campus study, part-time degree program, services for LD students, study abroad, summer session for credit.

Library Howard Community College Library with 45,707 titles, 39,910 serial subscriptions, 2,636 audiovisual materials, an OPAC, a Web page.

Student Life *Housing:* college housing not available. *Activities and Organizations:* drama/theater group, student-run newspaper, choral group, Phi Theta Kappa, Nursing Club, Black Leadership Organization, student newspaper, Student Government Association. *Campus security:* 24-hour emergency response devices and patrols, late-night transport/escort service. *Student services:* personal/psychological counseling.

Athletics Member NJCAA. *Intercollegiate sports:* basketball M/W, cross-country running M/W, lacrosse M/W, soccer M/W, track and field M/W, volleyball W. *Intramural sports:* basketball M/W, lacrosse M, softball W.

Standardized Tests *Required for some:* SAT or ACT (for admission).

Costs (2009–10) *Tuition:* area resident $3420 full-time, $114 per credit hour part-time; state resident $5910 full-time, $197 per credit hour part-time; nonresident $7260 full-time, $242 per credit hour part-time. *Required fees:* $572 full-time, $19 per credit hour part-time. *Payment plan:* installment. *Waivers:* senior citizens and employees or children of employees.

Applying *Options:* electronic application, early admission, deferred entrance. *Application fee:* $25. *Required for some:* essay or personal statement, high school transcript, 2 letters of recommendation. *Application deadlines:* rolling (freshmen), rolling (out-of-state freshmen), rolling (transfers). *Notification:* continuous (freshmen), continuous (out-of-state freshmen), continuous (transfers).

Freshman Application Contact Ms. Christy Thomson, Assistant Director of Admissions, Howard Community College, 10901 Little Patuxent Parkway, Columbia, MD 21044-3197. *Phone:* 410-772-4856. *Fax:* 410-772-4589. *E-mail:* hsinfo@howardcc.edu.

ITT Technical Institute

Owings Mills, Maryland **www.itt-tech.edu/**

- **Proprietary** primarily 2-year, founded 2005
- **Coed**

Majors Animation, interactive technology, video graphics and special effects; CAD/CADD drafting/design technology; computer and information systems security; computer engineering technology; computer software and media applications related; computer systems networking and telecommunications; construction management; electrical, electronic and communications engineering technology; system, networking, and LAN/WAN management; web page, digital/multimedia and information resources design.

Academics *Calendar:* quarters. *Degrees:* associate and bachelor's.

Freshman Application Contact Director of Recruitment, ITT Technical Institute, 11301 Red Run Boulevard, Owings Mills, MD 21117. *Phone:* 443-394-7115. *Toll-free phone:* 877-411-6782.

Kaplan University, Hagerstown Campus

Hagerstown, Maryland **www.ku-hagerstown.com/**

- **Proprietary** primarily 2-year, founded 1938, administratively affiliated with Kaplan Higher Education
- **Small-town** 8-acre campus
- **Coed**

Undergraduates 3% live on campus.

Majors Accounting; administrative assistant and secretarial science; business administration and management; computer and information systems security; criminal justice/law enforcement administration; data processing and data processing technology; health information/medical records administration; information science/studies; legal administrative assistant/secretary; legal assistant/paralegal; marketing/marketing management; medical administrative assistant and medical secretary; medical/clinical assistant.

Academics *Calendar:* quarters. *Degrees:* certificates, diplomas, associate, and bachelor's.

Financial Aid Of all full-time matriculated undergraduates who enrolled in 2008, 21 Federal Work-Study jobs (averaging $1343).

Freshman Application Contact Kaplan University, Hagerstown Campus, 18618 Crestwood Drive, Hagerstown, MD 21742-2797. *Phone:* 301-739-2680 Ext. 217. *Toll-free phone:* 800-422-2670.

Montgomery College

Rockville, Maryland **www.montgomerycollege.edu/**

- **State and locally supported** 2-year, founded 1946, part of Maryland Higher Education Commission
- **Suburban** 333-acre campus with easy access to Washington, DC
- **Endowment** $14.8 million
- **Coed,** 26,147 undergraduate students, 40% full-time, 54% women, 46% men

Undergraduates 10,379 full-time, 15,768 part-time. Students come from 30 states and territories, 174 other countries, 4% are from out of state, 26% African American, 13% Asian American or Pacific Islander, 11% Hispanic American, 0.2% Native American, 8% international, 6% transferred in.

Freshmen *Admission:* 10,220 applied, 10,220 admitted, 3,868 enrolled.

Faculty *Total:* 1,280, 40% full-time, 28% with terminal degrees. *Student/faculty ratio:* 20:1.

Majors Accounting technology and bookkeeping; animation, interactive technology, video graphics and special effects; applied horticulture; architectural drafting and CAD/CADD; art; automobile/automotive mechanics technology; biology/biotechnology laboratory technician; building/construction finishing, management, and inspection related; business/commerce; chemistry teacher education; child-care provision; commercial and advertising art; commercial photography; communication/speech communication and rhetoric; communications technologies and support services related; computer and information sciences; computer and information systems security; computer technology/computer systems technology; criminal justice/police science; data entry/microcomputer applications; diagnostic medical sonography and ultrasound technology; early childhood education; elementary education; engineering; English/language arts teacher education; fire protection and safety technology; geography; graphic and printing equipment operation/production; health information/medical records technology; hotel/motel administration; interior design; legal assistant/paralegal; liberal arts and sciences and humanities related; liberal arts and sciences/liberal studies; management information systems and services related; mathematics teacher education; medical radiologic technology; physical therapist assistant; physics teacher education; psychiatric/mental health services technology; sign language interpretation and translation; Spanish language teacher education; surgical technology.

Academics *Calendar:* semesters. *Degree:* certificates and associate. *Special study options:* academic remediation for entering students, accelerated degree program, adult/continuing education programs, advanced placement credit, cooperative education, distance learning, double majors, English as a second language, external degree program, honors programs, independent study, internships, off-campus study, part-time degree program, services for LD students, study abroad, summer session for credit.

Library Montgomery College Libraries plus 1 other with 286,116 titles, 20,977 serial subscriptions, 32,484 audiovisual materials, an OPAC, a Web page.

Student Life *Housing:* college housing not available. *Activities and Organizations:* drama/theater group, student-run newspaper, radio station, choral group. *Campus security:* 24-hour emergency response devices and patrols, late-night transport/escort service. *Student services:* personal/psychological counseling, women's center.

Athletics Member NJCAA. *Intercollegiate sports:* baseball M, basketball M, cross-country running M/W, golf M, lacrosse M, soccer M/W, softball W, tennis M/W, track and field M/W, volleyball M/W. *Intramural sports:* baseball M, basketball M/W, bowling M/W, cross-country running M/W, golf M/W, lacrosse M, soccer M/W, softball W, tennis M/W, track and field M/W, volleyball M/W.

Costs (2010–11) *One-time required fee:* $25. *Tuition:* area resident $3210 full-time, $107 per credit hour part-time; state resident $6570 full-time, $219 per credit hour part-time; nonresident $8970 full-time, $299 per credit hour part-time. *Required fees:* $1062 full-time, $64 per credit hour part-time. *Payment plans:* installment, deferred payment. *Waivers:* senior citizens and employees or children of employees.

Financial Aid Of all full-time matriculated undergraduates who enrolled in 2008, 216 Federal Work-Study jobs (averaging $3050). 250 state and other part-time jobs (averaging $2000).

Montgomery College (continued)

Applying *Options:* electronic application, early admission, deferred entrance. *Application fee:* $25. *Recommended:* high school transcript, interview. *Application deadlines:* rolling (freshmen), rolling (transfers). *Notification:* continuous (freshmen), continuous (transfers).

Freshman Application Contact Montgomery College, 51 Mannakee Street, Rockville, MD 20850. *Phone:* 240-567-5034.

PRINCE GEORGE'S COMMUNITY COLLEGE

Largo, Maryland **www.pgcc.edu/**

Freshman Application Contact Ms. Vera Bagley, Director of Admissions and Records, Prince George's Community College, 301 Largo Road, Largo, MD 20774-2199. *Phone:* 301-322-0801. *Fax:* 301-322-0119. *E-mail:* enrollmentservices@pgcc.edu.

TESST COLLEGE OF TECHNOLOGY

Baltimore, Maryland **www.tesst.com/**

- **Proprietary** 2-year, founded 1956
- **Coed**

Majors Computer systems networking and telecommunications; criminal justice/law enforcement administration; electrical, electronic and communications engineering technology.

Academics *Calendar:* quarters. *Degree:* certificates and associate.

Freshman Application Contact TESST College of Technology, 1520 South Caton Avenue, Baltimore, MD 21227-1063. *Phone:* 410-644-6400. *Toll-free phone:* 800-833-0209.

TESST COLLEGE OF TECHNOLOGY

Beltsville, Maryland **www.tesst.com/**

- **Proprietary** 2-year, founded 1967
- **Coed**

Majors Computer systems networking and telecommunications; criminal justice/police science; electrical, electronic and communications engineering technology.

Academics *Calendar:* quarters. *Degree:* certificates and associate.

Applying *Application fee:* $20.

Freshman Application Contact TESST College of Technology, 4600 Powder Mill Road, Beltsville, MD 20705. *Phone:* 301-937-8448. *Toll-free phone:* 800-833-0209.

TESST COLLEGE OF TECHNOLOGY

Towson, Maryland **www.tesst.com/**

- **Proprietary** 2-year, founded 1992
- **Coed**

Academics *Calendar:* quarters. *Degree:* certificates and associate.

Freshman Application Contact TESST College of Technology, 803 Glen Eagles Court, Towson, MD 21286. *Phone:* 410-296-5350. *Toll-free phone:* 800-48-TESST.

WOR-WIC COMMUNITY COLLEGE

Salisbury, Maryland **www.worwic.edu/**

- **State and locally supported** 2-year, founded 1976
- **Small-town** 202-acre campus
- **Endowment** $5.5 million
- **Coed,** 4,045 undergraduate students, 32% full-time, 65% women, 35% men

Undergraduates 1,290 full-time, 2,755 part-time. Students come from 11 states and territories, 2% are from out of state, 26% African American, 1% Asian American or Pacific Islander, 2% Hispanic American, 0.6% Native American, 7% transferred in.

Freshmen *Admission:* 1,005 applied, 1,005 admitted, 901 enrolled.

Faculty *Total:* 181, 38% full-time, 15% with terminal degrees. *Student/faculty ratio:* 21:1.

Majors Accounting technology and bookkeeping; administrative assistant and secretarial science; biological and physical sciences; business administration and management; business/commerce; child-care and support services management; computer and information sciences; computer systems analysis; criminal justice/police science; early childhood education; education; electrical, electronic and communications engineering technology; elementary education; emergency medical technology (EMT paramedic); engineering technologies related; hospitality administration; liberal arts and sciences and humanities related; medical radiologic technology; nursing (registered nurse training); substance abuse/addiction counseling.

Academics *Calendar:* semesters. *Degree:* certificates and associate. *Special study options:* academic remediation for entering students, accelerated degree program, adult/continuing education programs, advanced placement credit, distance learning, double majors, English as a second language, honors programs, independent study, internships, part-time degree program, services for LD students, summer session for credit.

Library Patricia M. Hazel Media Center plus 2 others with 44 serial subscriptions, 272 audiovisual materials, a Web page.

Student Life *Housing:* college housing not available. *Activities and Organizations:* drama/theater group, student-run newspaper, choral group, Student Government Association, Arts Club, Hotel-Motel-Restaurant Student Organization, Phi Beta Lambda, Nursing Student Organization. *Campus security:* 24-hour emergency response devices, late-night transport/escort service, patrols by trained security personnel 9 am to midnight. *Student services:* personal/psychological counseling.

Standardized Tests *Required for some:* ACT (for admission).

Costs (2010–11) *Tuition:* area resident $2670 full-time, $89 per credit hour part-time; state resident $5910 full-time, $197 per credit hour part-time; nonresident $7290 full-time, $243 per credit hour part-time. *Required fees:* $228 full-time, $7 per credit hour part-time, $15 per term part-time. *Payment plan:* installment. *Waivers:* senior citizens and employees or children of employees.

Applying *Options:* early admission. *Recommended:* high school transcript. *Application deadlines:* rolling (freshmen), rolling (transfers).

Freshman Application Contact Mr. Richard Webster, Director of Admissions, Wor-Wic Community College, 32000 Campus Drive, Salisbury, MD 21804. *Phone:* 410-334-2895. *Fax:* 410-334-2954. *E-mail:* admissions@worwic.edu.

MASSACHUSETTS

BAY STATE COLLEGE

Boston, Massachusetts **www.baystate.edu/**

Freshman Application Contact Kim Olds, Director of Admissions, Bay State College, 122 Commonwealth Avenue, Boston, MA 02116. *Phone:* 617-217-9115. *Toll-free phone:* 800-81-LEARN. *Fax:* 617-536-1735. *E-mail:* admissions@baystate.edu.

▶**See page 402 for the College Close-Up.**

BENJAMIN FRANKLIN INSTITUTE OF TECHNOLOGY

Boston, Massachusetts **www.bfit.edu/**

- **Independent** primarily 2-year, founded 1908
- **Urban** 3-acre campus
- **Coed**

Undergraduates 416 full-time, 120 part-time. Students come from 7 states and territories, 5% are from out of state, 18% African American, 8% Asian American or Pacific Islander, 7% Hispanic American, 0.6% Native American, 7% transferred in, 11% live on campus.

Faculty *Student/faculty ratio:* 12:1.

Academics *Calendar:* semesters. *Degrees:* certificates, associate, and bachelor's. *Special study options:* academic remediation for entering students, adult/continuing education programs, advanced placement credit, cooperative education, English as a second language, internships, off-campus study, part-time degree program, services for LD students, summer session for credit.

Student Life *Campus security:* 24-hour emergency response devices.

Athletics Member NJCAA.

Costs (2009–10) *Comprehensive fee:* $23,884 includes full-time tuition ($13,950), mandatory fees ($334), and room and board ($9600). Full-time tuition and fees vary according to course load, degree level, and program. Part-time tuition: $581 per credit. Part-time tuition and fees vary according to course load, degree level, and program. *Required fees:* $581 per credit hour part-time. *Room and board:* Room and board charges vary according to housing facility.

Applying *Options:* electronic application, deferred entrance. *Application fee:* $25. *Required:* high school transcript. *Recommended:* essay or personal statement, minimum 2 GPA, interview.

Freshman Application Contact Ms. Brittainy Johnson, Associate Director of Admissions, Benjamin Franklin Institute of Technology, 41 Berkeley Street, Boston, MA 02116-6296. *Phone:* 617-423-4630 Ext. 122. *Fax:* 617-482-3706. *E-mail:* bjohnson@bfit.edu.

BERKSHIRE COMMUNITY COLLEGE

Pittsfield, Massachusetts **www.berkshirecc.edu/**

- **State-supported** 2-year, founded 1960, part of Massachusetts Public Higher Education System
- **Rural** 100-acre campus
- **Endowment** $4.4 million
- **Coed,** 2,275 undergraduate students, 44% full-time, 62% women, 38% men

Undergraduates 996 full-time, 1,279 part-time. Students come from 4 states and territories, 21 other countries, 4% are from out of state, 6% African American, 2% Asian American or Pacific Islander, 4% Hispanic American, 0.2% Native American, 2% international, 6% transferred in.

Freshmen *Admission:* 497 applied, 497 admitted, 497 enrolled.

Faculty *Total:* 175, 31% full-time, 78% with terminal degrees. *Student/faculty ratio:* 15:1.

Majors Business administration and management; business automation/technology/data entry; business/commerce; community organization and advocacy; computer and information sciences; criminal justice/safety; electrical, electronic and communications engineering technology; engineering; environmental studies; fire science; health professions related; hospitality administration; human services; international/global studies; liberal arts and sciences/liberal studies; nursing (registered nurse training); physical therapist assistant; respiratory care therapy; visual and performing arts.

Academics *Calendar:* semesters. *Degree:* certificates and associate. *Special study options:* academic remediation for entering students, accelerated degree program, adult/continuing education programs, advanced placement credit, cooperative education, distance learning, double majors, English as a second language, honors programs, independent study, internships, off-campus study, part-time degree program, services for LD students, summer session for credit.

Library Jonathan Edwards Library plus 1 other with 77,497 titles, 273 serial subscriptions, 13,304 audiovisual materials, an OPAC, a Web page.

Student Life *Housing:* college housing not available. *Activities and Organizations:* drama/theater group, student-run newspaper, choral group, Mass PIRG, Student Nurse Organization, Student Senate, Diversity Club, LPN Organization. *Campus security:* 24-hour emergency response devices and patrols, late-night transport/escort service. *Student services:* personal/psychological counseling.

Athletics Member NJCAA.

Costs (2009–10) *One-time required fee:* $10. *Tuition:* state resident $624 full-time, $26 per credit part-time; nonresident $6720 full-time, $280 per credit part-time. Full-time tuition and fees vary according to reciprocity agreements. Part-time tuition and fees vary according to reciprocity agreements. *Required fees:* $3120 full-time, $130 per credit part-time. *Payment plan:* installment.

Financial Aid Of all full-time matriculated undergraduates who enrolled in 2008, 80 Federal Work-Study jobs (averaging $1600).

Applying *Options:* deferred entrance. *Application fee:* $10. *Required:* high school transcript. *Recommended:* interview. *Application deadlines:* rolling (freshmen), rolling (transfers). *Notification:* continuous (freshmen), continuous (transfers).

Freshman Application Contact Ms. Tina Schettini, Enrollment Services, Berkshire Community College, 1350 West Street, Pittsfield, MA 01201-5786. *Phone:* 413-236-1635. *Toll-free phone:* 800-816-1233 Ext. 242. *Fax:* 413-496-9511. *E-mail:* tschetti@berkshirecc.edu.

BRISTOL COMMUNITY COLLEGE

Fall River, Massachusetts **www.bristolcc.edu/**

Freshman Application Contact Mr. Rodney Clark, Director of Admissions, Bristol Community College, 777 Elsbree Street, Hudnall Administration Building, Fall River, MA 02720. *Phone:* 508-678-2811 Ext. 2177. *Fax:* 508-730-3265. *E-mail:* rodney.clark@bristolcc.edu.

BUNKER HILL COMMUNITY COLLEGE

Boston, Massachusetts **www.bhcc.mass.edu/**

- **State-supported** 2-year, founded 1973
- **Urban** 21-acre campus
- **Endowment** $1.6 million
- **Coed,** 11,009 undergraduate students, 34% full-time, 58% women, 42% men

Undergraduates 3,767 full-time, 7,242 part-time. Students come from 78 other countries, 20% African American, 9% Asian American or Pacific Islander, 17% Hispanic American, 0.4% Native American, 5% international, 7% transferred in.

Freshmen *Admission:* 4,033 applied, 3,443 admitted, 3,045 enrolled.

Faculty *Total:* 578, 23% full-time. *Student/faculty ratio:* 19:1.

Majors Accounting; art; biology/biological sciences; business administration and management; cardiovascular technology; chemistry; communication/speech communication and rhetoric; computer and information sciences and support services related; computer programming; computer programming (specific applications); computer science; computer systems networking and telecommunications; criminal justice/law enforcement administration; culinary arts; data entry/microcomputer applications; design and visual communications; dramatic/theater arts; early childhood education; education; electrical/electronics maintenance and repair technology related; English; finance; fire protection and safety technology; general studies; health information/medical records administration; history; hospitality administration; hotel/motel administration; human services; international business/trade/commerce; mass communication/media; mathematics; medical radiologic technology; nursing (registered nurse training); operations management; physics; psychology; sociology; tourism and travel services management; web page, digital/multimedia and information resources design.

Academics *Calendar:* semesters. *Degree:* certificates and associate. *Special study options:* academic remediation for entering students, advanced placement credit, cooperative education, distance learning, English as a second language, external degree program, honors programs, independent study, internships, part-time degree program, services for LD students, study abroad, summer session for credit.

Library Bunker Hill Community College Library with 66,777 titles, 284 serial subscriptions, 3,788 audiovisual materials, an OPAC, a Web page.

Student Life *Housing:* college housing not available. *Activities and Organizations:* drama/theater group, student-run radio station, choral group, Alpha Kappa Mu Honor Society, Asian-Pacific Students Association, African Students Club, Latinos Unidos Club, Haitian Students Club. *Campus security:* 24-hour emergency response devices and patrols, late-night transport/escort service. *Student services:* health clinic, personal/psychological counseling.

Athletics Member NJCAA. *Intercollegiate sports:* baseball M, basketball M/W, golf M/W, soccer M/W, softball W. *Intramural sports:* basketball M/W, table tennis M/W, tennis M/W.

Costs (2009–10) *Tuition:* state resident $576 full-time, $24 per credit part-time; nonresident $5520 full-time, $230 per credit part-time. Full-time tuition and fees vary according to course load. Part-time tuition and fees vary according to course load. *Required fees:* $2448 full-time, $97 per credit part-time. *Payment plan:* installment. *Waivers:* minority students, senior citizens, and employees or children of employees.

Financial Aid Of all full-time matriculated undergraduates who enrolled in 2008, 147 Federal Work-Study jobs (averaging $1902).

Applying *Options:* deferred entrance. *Application fee:* $10. *Required:* high school transcript. *Application deadlines:* rolling (freshmen), rolling (transfers). *Notification:* continuous (freshmen), continuous (transfers).

Freshman Application Contact Mr. David Gomes, Director of Admissions, Bunker Hill Community College, BHCC Enrollment Services Center, 250 New Rutherford Avenue, Boston, MA 02129. *Phone:* 617-228-2346. *Fax:* 617-228-2082.

CAPE COD COMMUNITY COLLEGE

West Barnstable, Massachusetts **www.capecod.edu/**

Freshman Application Contact Ms. Susan Kline-Symington, Director of Admissions, Cape Cod Community College, 2240 Lyanough Road, West

Cape Cod Community College (continued)

Barnstable, MA 02668-1599. *Phone:* 508-362-2131. *Toll-free phone:* 877-846-3672. *Fax:* 508-375-4089. *E-mail:* admiss@capecod.edu.

DEAN COLLEGE

Franklin, Massachusetts **www.dean.edu/**

- **Independent** primarily 2-year, founded 1865
- **Small-town** 100-acre campus with easy access to Boston and Providence
- **Endowment** $22.8 million
- **Coed,** 1,106 undergraduate students, 88% full-time, 48% women, 52% men

Undergraduates 975 full-time, 131 part-time. Students come from 23 states and territories, 131 other countries, 48% are from out of state, 7% African American, 1% Asian American or Pacific Islander, 3% Hispanic American, 0.6% Native American, 10% international, 4% transferred in, 88% live on campus. *Retention:* 62% of 2008 full-time freshmen returned.

Freshmen *Admission:* 1,910 applied, 1,398 admitted, 551 enrolled. *Average high school GPA:* 2.2. *Test scores:* SAT verbal scores over 500: 24%; SAT math scores over 500: 23%; ACT scores over 18: 48%; SAT verbal scores over 600: 4%; SAT math scores over 600: 4%; ACT scores over 24: 7%.

Faculty *Total:* 112, 29% full-time, 20% with terminal degrees. *Student/faculty ratio:* 19:1.

Majors Arts management; athletic training; business administration and management; communication/speech communication and rhetoric; criminal justice/law enforcement administration; criminal justice/police science; dance; dramatic/theater arts; early childhood education; liberal arts and sciences/liberal studies; mathematics and computer science; physical education teaching and coaching; sport and fitness administration/management.

Academics *Calendar:* semesters. *Degrees:* certificates, associate, and bachelor's. *Special study options:* academic remediation for entering students, accelerated degree program, adult/continuing education programs, advanced placement credit, English as a second language, freshman honors college, honors programs, independent study, internships, off-campus study, part-time degree program, services for LD students, student-designed majors, summer session for credit.

Library E. Ross Anderson Library with 45,565 titles, 174 serial subscriptions, 1,203 audiovisual materials.

Student Life *Housing:* on-campus residence required through sophomore year. *Options:* coed, women-only, disabled students. Campus housing is university owned. Freshman campus housing is guaranteed. *Activities and Organizations:* drama/theater group, student-run radio station, choral group, Emerging Leaders, College Success Staff, Student Ambassadors, student government, Phi Theta Kappa. *Campus security:* 24-hour emergency response devices and patrols, late-night transport/escort service, controlled dormitory access. *Student services:* health clinic, personal/psychological counseling.

Athletics Member NJCAA. *Intercollegiate sports:* baseball M(s), basketball M(s)/W(s), football M(s), golf M, lacrosse M(s)/W(s), soccer M(s)/W(s), softball W(s), volleyball W(s). *Intramural sports:* basketball M, football M, golf M, lacrosse M, skiing (cross-country) M/W, skiing (downhill) M/W, tennis M/W, volleyball M/W.

Standardized Tests *Required:* SAT or ACT (for admission).

Costs (2010–11) *Comprehensive fee:* $41,582 includes full-time tuition ($29,140) and room and board ($12,442). Part-time tuition: $780 per course. *Room and board:* college room only: $7868.

Applying *Options:* electronic application, deferred entrance. *Application fee:* $35. *Required:* essay or personal statement, high school transcript. *Recommended:* minimum 2 GPA, interview. *Application deadlines:* rolling (freshmen), rolling (transfers). *Notification:* continuous (freshmen), continuous (transfers).

Freshman Application Contact Mr. James Fowler, Dean College, 99 Main Street, Franklin, MA 02038. *Phone:* 508-541-1547. *Toll-free phone:* 877-TRY-DEAN. *Fax:* 508-541-8726. *E-mail:* jfowler@dean.edu.

FINE MORTUARY COLLEGE, LLC

Norwood, Massachusetts **www.fine-ne.com/**

- **Proprietary** 2-year, founded 1996
- **Suburban** campus
- **Coed**

Faculty *Student/faculty ratio:* 5:1.

Academics *Calendar:* continuous. *Degree:* associate. *Special study options:* academic remediation for entering students, distance learning, internships, off-campus study, summer session for credit.

Standardized Tests *Required:* CPAt (for admission).

Applying *Application fee:* $55. *Required:* essay or personal statement, high school transcript. *Recommended:* interview.

Freshman Application Contact Dean Marsha Wise, Admissions Office, FINE Mortuary College, LLC, 150 Kerry Place, Norwood, MA 02062. *Phone:* 781-762-1211. *Fax:* 781-762-7177. *E-mail:* mwise@fine-ne.com.

GREENFIELD COMMUNITY COLLEGE

Greenfield, Massachusetts **www.gcc.mass.edu/**

- **State-supported** 2-year, founded 1962, part of Commonwealth of Massachusetts Department of Higher Education
- **Small-town** 120-acre campus
- **Coed,** 2,546 undergraduate students, 41% full-time, 59% women, 41% men

Undergraduates 1,045 full-time, 1,501 part-time. Students come from 5 states and territories, 7 other countries, 5% are from out of state, 3% African American, 3% Asian American or Pacific Islander, 3% Hispanic American, 0.6% Native American, 9% transferred in. *Retention:* 59% of 2008 full-time freshmen returned.

Freshmen *Admission:* 798 applied, 798 admitted, 519 enrolled.

Faculty *Total:* 191, 31% full-time.

Majors Accounting; administrative assistant and secretarial science; American studies; art; behavioral sciences; biological and physical sciences; business administration and management; commercial and advertising art; computer programming; criminal justice/law enforcement administration; education; engineering science; family and consumer sciences/human sciences; fire science; food science; humanities; human services; industrial technology; information science/studies; kindergarten/preschool education; liberal arts and sciences/liberal studies; marketing/marketing management; mass communication/media; mathematics; natural resources/conservation related; natural resources management and policy; nursing (registered nurse training); parks, recreation and leisure; photography; pre-engineering.

Academics *Calendar:* semesters. *Degree:* certificates and associate. *Special study options:* academic remediation for entering students, adult/continuing education programs, advanced placement credit, cooperative education, distance learning, double majors, English as a second language, honors programs, independent study, internships, part-time degree program, services for LD students, summer session for credit.

Library Greenfield Community College Library with 52,690 titles, 356 serial subscriptions, a Web page.

Student Life *Housing:* college housing not available. *Activities and Organizations:* drama/theater group, choral group. *Campus security:* 24-hour emergency response devices and patrols, late-night transport/escort service. *Student services:* health clinic, personal/psychological counseling, women's center.

Standardized Tests *Required for some:* Psychological Corporation Practical Nursing Entrance Examination.

Applying *Options:* electronic application. *Application fee:* $10. *Required for some:* high school transcript, interview. *Application deadlines:* rolling (freshmen), rolling (transfers).

Freshman Application Contact Mr. Herbert Hentz, Assistant Director of Admission, Greenfield Community College, 1 College Drive, Greenfield, MA 01301-9739. *Phone:* 413-775-1000. *Fax:* 413-773-5129. *E-mail:* admission@gcc.mass.edu.

HOLYOKE COMMUNITY COLLEGE

Holyoke, Massachusetts **www.hcc.mass.edu/**

- **State-supported** 2-year, founded 1946, part of Massachusetts Public Higher Education System
- **Small-town** 135-acre campus
- **Endowment** $5.9 million
- **Coed,** 7,469 undergraduate students, 53% full-time, 61% women, 39% men

Undergraduates 3,969 full-time, 3,500 part-time. Students come from 5 states and territories, 1% are from out of state, 6% African American, 2% Asian American or Pacific Islander, 18% Hispanic American, 0.5% Native American, 0.5% international, 7% transferred in.

Freshmen *Admission:* 1,933 admitted, 1,933 enrolled.

Faculty *Total:* 481, 27% full-time, 18% with terminal degrees. *Student/faculty ratio:* 21:1.

Majors Accounting technology and bookkeeping; administrative assistant and secretarial science; art; business administration and management; child-care and support services management; computer programming (specific applications);

criminal justice/safety; engineering; environmental control technologies related; geography; health and physical education; hospitality administration related; liberal arts and sciences and humanities related; liberal arts and sciences/liberal studies; medical radiologic technology; music; nursing (registered nurse training); opticianry; retailing; social work; sport and fitness administration/management; veterinary/animal health technology.

Academics *Calendar:* semesters. *Degree:* certificates and associate. *Special study options:* academic remediation for entering students, adult/continuing education programs, advanced placement credit, cooperative education, distance learning, double majors, English as a second language, external degree program, honors programs, independent study, internships, off-campus study, part-time degree program, services for LD students, student-designed majors, study abroad, summer session for credit. *ROTC:* Army (c), Air Force (c).

Library Elaine Marieb Library with 88,149 titles, 29,599 serial subscriptions, 9,327 audiovisual materials, an OPAC, a Web page.

Student Life *Housing:* college housing not available. *Activities and Organizations:* drama/theater group, student-run newspaper, radio station, Drama Club, Japanese Anime Club, Student Senate, LISA Club, STRIVE. *Campus security:* 24-hour emergency response devices and patrols, late-night transport/escort service. *Student services:* health clinic, personal/psychological counseling, women's center.

Athletics Member NJCAA. *Intercollegiate sports:* baseball M, basketball M/W, golf M/W, skiing (downhill) M(c)/W(c), soccer M/W, softball W, volleyball W.

Costs (2009–10) *Tuition:* state resident $576 full-time, $121 per credit part-time; nonresident $5520 full-time, $327 per credit part-time. Full-time tuition and fees vary according to course load. Part-time tuition and fees vary according to course load. *Required fees:* $2496 full-time, $84 per term part-time. *Payment plan:* installment. *Waivers:* senior citizens and employees or children of employees.

Applying *Options:* early admission, deferred entrance. *Required:* high school transcript. *Recommended:* interview. *Application deadlines:* rolling (freshmen), rolling (transfers). *Notification:* continuous (freshmen), continuous (transfers).

Freshman Application Contact Ms. Marcia Rosbury-Henne, Director of Admissions and Transfer Affairs, Holyoke Community College, Holyoke Community College, Holyoke, MA 01040. *Phone:* 413-552-2000. *Toll-free phone:* 888-530-8855. *Fax:* 413-552-2045. *E-mail:* admissions@hcc.edu.

ITT Technical Institute

Norwood, Massachusetts **www.itt-tech.edu/**

- **Proprietary** primarily 2-year, founded 1990, part of ITT Educational Services, Inc.
- **Suburban** campus
- **Coed**

Majors Animation, interactive technology, video graphics and special effects; CAD/CADD drafting/design technology; computer and information systems security; electrical, electronic and communications engineering technology; system, networking, and LAN/WAN management; web/multimedia management and webmaster; web page, digital/multimedia and information resources design.

Academics *Calendar:* quarters. *Degrees:* associate and bachelor's.

Student Life *Housing:* college housing not available.

Freshman Application Contact Director of Recruitment, ITT Technical Institute, 333 Providence Highway, Norwood, MA 02062. *Phone:* 781-278-7200. *Toll-free phone:* 800-879-8324.

ITT Technical Institute

Woburn, Massachusetts **www.itt-tech.edu/**

- **Proprietary** primarily 2-year, founded 2000, part of ITT Educational Services, Inc.
- **Coed**

Majors Animation, interactive technology, video graphics and special effects; CAD/CADD drafting/design technology; computer and information systems security; computer engineering technology; computer software and media applications related; electrical, electronic and communications engineering technology; system, networking, and LAN/WAN management; web/multimedia management and webmaster; web page, digital/multimedia and information resources design.

Academics *Calendar:* quarters. *Degrees:* associate and bachelor's.

Student Life *Housing:* college housing not available.

Freshman Application Contact Director of Recruitment, ITT Technical Institute, 10 Forbes Road, Woburn, MA 01801. *Phone:* 781-937-8324. *Toll-free phone:* 800-430-5097.

Labouré College

Boston, Massachusetts **www.laboure.edu/**

- **Independent Roman Catholic** 2-year, founded 1971
- **Urban** campus
- **Coed**

Academics *Calendar:* semesters. *Degree:* certificates and associate. *Special study options:* academic remediation for entering students, accelerated degree program, adult/continuing education programs, independent study, part-time degree program, services for LD students, summer session for credit.

Student Life *Campus security:* 24-hour emergency response devices.

Financial Aid Of all full-time matriculated undergraduates who enrolled in 2008, 18 Federal Work-Study jobs (averaging $1000).

Applying *Options:* deferred entrance. *Application fee:* $25. *Required:* high school transcript.

Director of Admissions Ms. Gina M. Morrissette, Director of Admissions, Labouré College, 2120 Dorchester Avenue, Boston, MA 02124. *Phone:* 617-296-8300.

Marian Court College

Swampscott, Massachusetts **www.mariancourt.edu/**

Director of Admissions Mrs. Lisa Emerson Parker, Associate Director of Admissions, Marian Court College, 35 Little's Point Road, Swampscott, MA 01907-2840. *Phone:* 781-595-6768 Ext. 239. *Fax:* 781-595-3536. *E-mail:* lparker@mariancourt.edu.

Massachusetts Bay Community College

Wellesley Hills, Massachusetts **www.massbay.edu/**

Freshman Application Contact Ms. Donna Raposa, Director of Admissions, Massachusetts Bay Community College, 50 Oakland Street, Wellesley Hills, MA 02481. *Phone:* 781-239-2500. *Fax:* 781-239-1047. *E-mail:* info@massbay.edu.

Massasoit Community College

Brockton, Massachusetts **www.massasoit.mass.edu/**

- **State-supported** 2-year, founded 1966
- **Suburban** 100-acre campus with easy access to Boston
- **Coed**, 7,941 undergraduate students, 46% full time, 56% women, 44% men

Undergraduates 3,631 full-time, 4,310 part-time. Students come from 13 states and territories, 6 other countries, 1% are from out of state, 20% African American, 2% Asian American or Pacific Islander, 4% Hispanic American, 0.4% Native American, 0.4% international, 6% transferred in.

Freshmen *Admission:* 1,662 enrolled.

Faculty *Total:* 503, 24% full-time.

Majors Accounting; accounting and finance; administrative assistant and secretarial science; architectural engineering technology; business administration and management; business administration, management and operations related; business automation/technology/data entry; child-care and support services management; child-care provision; computer and information sciences; computer and information sciences and support services related; computer and information sciences related; computer programming; criminal justice/police science; culinary arts; dental assisting; diesel mechanics technology; dramatic/theater arts; electrical, electronic and communications engineering technology; fine/studio arts; fire science; graphic design; heating, air conditioning and refrigeration technology; hospitality administration; human services; liberal arts and sciences/liberal studies; mass communication/media; medical/clinical assistant; nursing (registered nurse training); office management; office occupations and clerical services; radiologic technology/science; respiratory care therapy; teacher assistant/aide; telecommunications technology.

Academics *Calendar:* semesters. *Degree:* certificates and associate. *Special study options:* academic remediation for entering students, accelerated degree program, adult/continuing education programs, cooperative education, distance learning, English as a second language, independent study, internships, off-campus study, part-time degree program, services for LD students, summer session for credit.

Massasoit Community College (continued)

Library 75,000 titles, 396 serial subscriptions, a Web page.

Student Life *Housing:* college housing not available. *Activities and Organizations:* drama/theater group, student-run newspaper, radio station, Drama Club, student newspaper, Phi Theta Kappa, International Student Association, Student Senate. *Campus security:* 24-hour patrols. *Student services:* health clinic, personal/psychological counseling, women's center.

Athletics Member NJCAA. *Intercollegiate sports:* baseball M, basketball M(s)/W, soccer M(s)/W, softball W(s).

Costs (2009–10) *Tuition:* state resident $576 full-time, $24 per credit hour part-time; nonresident $5520 full-time, $230 per credit hour part-time. Full-time tuition and fees vary according to program. Part-time tuition and fees vary according to program. *Required fees:* $2712 full-time, $113 per credit hour part-time. *Payment plans:* installment, deferred payment. *Waivers:* senior citizens and employees or children of employees.

Financial Aid Of all full-time matriculated undergraduates who enrolled in 2008, 45 Federal Work-Study jobs (averaging $3200).

Applying *Application deadlines:* rolling (freshmen), rolling (transfers). *Notification:* continuous (freshmen), continuous (transfers).

Freshman Application Contact Michelle Hughes, Director of Admissions, Massasoit Community College, 1 Massasoit Boulevard, Brockton, MA 02302-3996. *Phone:* 508-588-9100. *Toll-free phone:* 800-CAREERS.

MIDDLESEX COMMUNITY COLLEGE

Bedford, Massachusetts **www.middlesex.mass.edu/**

- **State-supported** 2-year, founded 1970, part of Massachusetts Public Higher Education System
- **Suburban** 200-acre campus with easy access to Boston
- **Coed**

Academics *Calendar:* semesters. *Degree:* certificates and associate. *Special study options:* academic remediation for entering students, accelerated degree program, adult/continuing education programs, advanced placement credit, cooperative education, distance learning, English as a second language, honors programs, independent study, internships, off-campus study, part-time degree program, services for LD students, study abroad, summer session for credit. *ROTC:* Air Force (c).

Student Life *Campus security:* 24-hour emergency response devices and patrols.

Standardized Tests *Required for some:* CPT.

Financial Aid Of all full-time matriculated undergraduates who enrolled in 2008, 68 Federal Work-Study jobs (averaging $2200).

Applying *Options:* electronic application, early admission. *Required for some:* essay or personal statement, high school transcript, 3 letters of recommendation, interview.

Director of Admissions Ms. Laurie Dimitrov, Director, Admissions and Recruitment, Middlesex Community College, 33 Kearney Square, Lowell, MA 01852. *Phone:* 978-656-3207. *Toll-free phone:* 800-818-3434. *E-mail:* orellanad@middlesex.cc.ma.us.

MOUNT WACHUSETT COMMUNITY COLLEGE

Gardner, Massachusetts **www.mwcc.mass.edu/**

- **State-supported** 2-year, founded 1963, part of Massachusetts Public Higher Education System
- **Small-town** 270-acre campus with easy access to Boston
- **Endowment** $3.9 million
- **Coed,** 4,761 undergraduate students, 42% full-time, 65% women, 35% men

Undergraduates 1,987 full-time, 2,774 part-time. Students come from 12 states and territories, 21 other countries, 5% are from out of state, 6% transferred in. *Retention:* 56% of 2008 full-time freshmen returned.

Freshmen *Admission:* 2,074 applied, 2,071 admitted, 1,073 enrolled.

Faculty *Total:* 211, 35% full-time. *Student/faculty ratio:* 24:1.

Majors Allied health and medical assisting services related; alternative and complementary medical support services related; art; automobile/automotive mechanics technology; biotechnology; child-care and support services management; child development; clinical/medical laboratory technology; computer and information sciences; computer graphics; computer technology/computer systems technology; corrections; criminal justice/law enforcement administration; criminal justice/safety; dental hygiene; environmental studies; fire protection and safety technology; general studies; human services; legal assistant/paralegal; liberal arts and sciences/liberal studies; medical/clinical assistant; nursing (registered nurse training); physical therapist assistant; plastics engineering technology; psychiatric/mental health services technology; radio and television broadcasting technology; web page, digital/multimedia and information resources design.

Academics *Calendar:* semesters. *Degree:* certificates and associate. *Special study options:* academic remediation for entering students, accelerated degree program, adult/continuing education programs, advanced placement credit, cooperative education, distance learning, double majors, English as a second language, honors programs, independent study, internships, part-time degree program, services for LD students, study abroad, summer session for credit.

Library LaChance Library with 53,763 titles, 2,495 audiovisual materials, an OPAC, a Web page.

Student Life *Housing:* college housing not available. *Activities and Organizations:* drama/theater group, student-run newspaper, choral group, Art Club, Dental Hygienist Club, International Club, Student Government Association, Student Nurses Association. *Campus security:* 24-hour emergency response devices and patrols. *Student services:* health clinic, personal/psychological counseling.

Athletics *Intramural sports:* badminton M/W, basketball M/W, football M/W, soccer M/W, softball M/W, table tennis M/W, volleyball M/W, water polo M/W.

Standardized Tests *Required for some:* SAT (for admission). *Recommended:* SAT (for admission), ACT (for admission), SAT or ACT (for admission), SAT and SAT Subject Tests or ACT (for admission), SAT Subject Tests (for admission).

Costs (2010–11) *Tuition:* state resident $600 full-time, $25 per credit hour part-time; nonresident $5520 full-time, $230 per credit hour part-time. Full-time tuition and fees vary according to program and reciprocity agreements. Part-time tuition and fees vary according to program and reciprocity agreements. *Required fees:* $3510 full-time, $140 per credit hour part-time, $75 per term part-time. *Payment plan:* installment. *Waivers:* senior citizens and employees or children of employees.

Financial Aid Of all full-time matriculated undergraduates who enrolled in 2008, 47 Federal Work-Study jobs (averaging $2228).

Applying *Options:* electronic application, early admission. *Application fee:* $10. *Required:* high school transcript. *Required for some:* 2 letters of recommendation. *Recommended:* interview. *Application deadlines:* rolling (freshmen), rolling (transfers). *Notification:* continuous (freshmen), continuous (transfers).

Freshman Application Contact Mr. John D. Walsh, Director of Admissions, Mount Wachusett Community College, 444 Green Street, Gardner, MA 01440-1000. *Phone:* 978-632-6600 Ext. 110. *Fax:* 978-630-9554. *E-mail:* admissions@mwcc.mass.edu.

NORTHERN ESSEX COMMUNITY COLLEGE

Haverhill, Massachusetts **www.necc.mass.edu/**

Freshman Application Contact Ms. Nora Sheridan, Director of Admissions, Northern Essex Community College, 100 Elliott Street, Haverhill, MA 01830. *Phone:* 978-556-3616. *Toll-free phone:* 800-NECC-123. *Fax:* 978-556-3155.

NORTH SHORE COMMUNITY COLLEGE

Danvers, Massachusetts **www.northshore.edu/**

- **State-supported** 2-year, founded 1965
- **Suburban** campus with easy access to Boston
- **Endowment** $5.2 million
- **Coed**

Undergraduates 3,120 full-time, 4,104 part-time. Students come from 9 states and territories, 8 other countries, 2% are from out of state, 8% African American, 4% Asian American or Pacific Islander, 14% Hispanic American, 0.4% Native American, 0.2% international, 9% transferred in.

Faculty *Student/faculty ratio:* 17:1.

Academics *Calendar:* semesters. *Degree:* certificates and associate. *Special study options:* academic remediation for entering students, accelerated degree program, adult/continuing education programs, advanced placement credit, cooperative education, distance learning, English as a second language, honors programs, independent study, internships, part-time degree program, services for LD students, summer session for credit.

Student Life *Campus security:* 24-hour emergency response devices and patrols, late-night transport/escort service.

Costs (2009–10) *Tuition:* state resident $600 full-time, $25 per credit part-time; nonresident $6168 full-time, $257 per credit part-time. *Required fees:* $2688 full-time, $112 per credit part-time.

Financial Aid Of all full-time matriculated undergraduates who enrolled in 2009, 1,658 applied for aid, 1,438 were judged to have need, 23 had their need fully met. 123 Federal Work-Study jobs (averaging $1359). In 2009, 11. *Average percent of need met:* 18. *Average financial aid package:* $6856. *Average need-based loan:* $1639. *Average need-based gift aid:* $2522. *Average non-need-based aid:* $614.

Applying *Options:* electronic application, early admission. *Required for some:* high school transcript, interview.

Freshman Application Contact Dr. Joanne Light, Dean of Enrollment Services, North Shore Community College, PO Box 3340, Danvers, MA 01923. *Phone:* 978-762-4000 Ext. 4337. *Fax:* 978-762-4015. *E-mail:* info@northshore.edu.

QUINCY COLLEGE

Quincy, Massachusetts **www.quincycollege.edu/**

Freshman Application Contact Paula Smith, Dean Enrollment Services, Quincy College, 34 Coddington Street, Quincy, MA 02169. *Phone:* 617-984-1700. *Toll-free phone:* 800-698-1700. *Fax:* 617-984-1779. *E-mail:* psmith@quincycollege.edu.

QUINSIGAMOND COMMUNITY COLLEGE

Worcester, Massachusetts **www.qcc.edu/**

- **State-supported** 2-year, founded 1963, part of Massachusetts System of Higher Education
- **Urban** 57-acre campus with easy access to Boston
- **Endowment** $365,447
- **Coed,** 8,349 undergraduate students, 49% full-time, 56% women, 44% men

Undergraduates 4,089 full-time, 4,260 part-time. Students come from 10 states and territories, 32 other countries, 1% are from out of state, 7% transferred in. *Retention:* 58% of 2008 full-time freshmen returned.

Freshmen *Admission:* 3,599 applied, 3,599 admitted, 2,052 enrolled.

Faculty *Total:* 514, 24% full-time, 21% with terminal degrees. *Student/faculty ratio:* 22:1.

Majors Accounting; administrative assistant and secretarial science; alternative and complementary medicine related; art; automobile/automotive mechanics technology; business administration and management; business/commerce; civil engineering technology; commercial and advertising art; community organization and advocacy; computer engineering technology; computer graphics; computer programming; computer programming (specific applications); computer systems analysis; computer technology/computer systems technology; consumer merchandising/retailing management; criminal justice/law enforcement administration; criminal justice/police science; data processing and data processing technology; dental hygiene; dental services and allied professions related; electrical, electronic and communications engineering technology; electromechanical technology; emergency medical technology (EMT paramedic); executive assistant/executive secretary; fire science; fire services administration; general studies; hospitality administration; hotel/motel administration; human services; information science/studies; kindergarten/preschool education; liberal arts and sciences/liberal studies; manufacturing technology; medical office assistant; medical radiologic technology; nursing (registered nurse training); occupational therapist assistant; occupational therapy; respiratory care therapy; restaurant/food services management; telecommunications technology; tourism and travel services management; web page, digital/multimedia and information resources design.

Academics *Calendar:* semesters. *Degree:* certificates and associate. *Special study options:* academic remediation for entering students, accelerated degree program, adult/continuing education programs, advanced placement credit, cooperative education, distance learning, double majors, English as a second language, honors programs, independent study, internships, off-campus study, part-time degree program, services for LD students, summer session for credit. *ROTC:* Army (c).

Library Quinsigamond Library with 60,000 titles, 280 serial subscriptions, 2,800 audiovisual materials, an OPAC, a Web page.

Student Life *Housing:* college housing not available. *Activities and Organizations:* drama/theater group, student-run newspaper, Phi Theta Kappa, academic-related clubs, Student Senate, Chess Club, Oasis (Older than Average Students in School). *Campus security:* 24-hour emergency response devices and patrols, late-night transport/escort service. *Student services:* personal/psychological counseling.

Athletics Member NJCAA. *Intercollegiate sports:* basketball M/W, softball W. *Intramural sports:* basketball M/W, soccer M/W, volleyball M/W.

Costs (2010–11) *Tuition:* state resident $24 per credit part-time; nonresident $230 per credit part-time. Full-time tuition and fees vary according to course load and program. Part-time tuition and fees vary according to course load and program. *Payment plan:* installment. *Waivers:* senior citizens and employees or children of employees.

Applying *Options:* electronic application. *Application fee:* $20. *Required:* high school transcript. *Required for some:* interview. *Application deadlines:* rolling (freshmen), rolling (out-of-state freshmen), rolling (transfers). *Notification:* continuous (freshmen), continuous (out-of-state freshmen), continuous (transfers).

Freshman Application Contact Quinsigamond Community College, 670 West Boylston Street, Worcester, MA 01606-2092. *Phone:* 508-854-4260.

ROXBURY COMMUNITY COLLEGE

Roxbury Crossing, Massachusetts **www.rcc.mass.edu/**

Director of Admissions Mr. Milton Samuels, Director/Admissions, Roxbury Community College, 1234 Columbus Avenue, Roxbury Crossing, MA 02120-3400. *Phone:* 617-541-5310.

SPRINGFIELD TECHNICAL COMMUNITY COLLEGE

Springfield, Massachusetts **www.stcc.edu/**

- **State-supported** 2-year, founded 1967
- **Urban** 34-acre campus
- **Coed,** 6,782 undergraduate students, 44% full-time, 57% women, 43% men

Undergraduates 2,952 full-time, 3,830 part-time. Students come from 10 states and territories, 3% are from out of state, 16% African American, 2% Asian American or Pacific Islander, 19% Hispanic American, 0.6% Native American, 0.7% international.

Freshmen *Admission:* 3,255 applied, 2,717 admitted, 1,460 enrolled.

Faculty *Total:* 426, 36% full-time. *Student/faculty ratio:* 17:1.

Majors Accounting; administrative assistant and secretarial science; animation, interactive technology, video graphics and special effects; architectural engineering technology; automotive engineering technology; biology/biological sciences; biotechnology; building/construction finishing, management, and inspection related; business administration and management; business/commerce; chemistry; civil engineering technology; clinical/medical laboratory technology; commercial and advertising art; commercial photography; communications technologies and support services related; computer and information systems security; computer engineering technology; computer programming (specific applications); computer science; cosmetology; criminal justice/police science; data processing and data processing technology; dental hygiene; diagnostic medical sonography and ultrasound technology; early childhood education; electrical and electronic engineering technologies related; electrical, electronic and communications engineering technology; electromechanical technology; elementary education; engineering; entrepreneurship; finance; fine/studio arts; fire science; general studies; graphic design; heating, air conditioning and refrigeration technology; landscaping and groundskeeping; laser and optical technology; liberal arts and sciences/liberal studies; marketing/marketing management; massage therapy; mathematics; mechanical engineering/mechanical technology; medical administrative assistant and medical secretary; medical/clinical assistant; medical insurance coding; medical radiologic technology; nuclear medical technology; nursing (registered nurse training); occupational therapist assistant; physical therapist assistant; physics; radio and television broadcasting technology; recording arts technology; rehabilitation and therapeutic professions related; respiratory care therapy; secondary education; sport and fitness administration/management; surgical technology; system administration; telecommunications technology; web page, digital/multimedia and information resources design.

Academics *Calendar:* semesters. *Degree:* certificates and associate. *Special study options:* academic remediation for entering students, adult/continuing education programs, advanced placement credit, cooperative education, distance learning, English as a second language, honors programs, independent study, internships, off-campus study, part-time degree program, services for LD students, summer session for credit.

Library Springfield Technical Community College Library with 59,369 titles, 298 serial subscriptions, 14,921 audiovisual materials, an OPAC, a Web page.

Student Life *Housing:* college housing not available. *Activities and Organizations:* Phi Theta Kappa, Landscape Design Club, Dental Hygiene Club, Clinical Lab Science Club, Physical Therapist Assistant Club. *Campus security:* 24-hour emergency response devices and patrols, late-night transport/escort service. *Student services:* health clinic, personal/psychological counseling.

Springfield Technical Community College (continued)

Athletics Member NJCAA. *Intercollegiate sports:* basketball M/W, golf M, lacrosse W, soccer M/W, wrestling M. *Intramural sports:* basketball M/W, cross-country running M/W, golf M/W, skiing (cross-country) M/W, volleyball M/W, weight lifting M/W.

Standardized Tests *Required for some:* SAT (for admission).

Costs (2009–10) *Tuition:* state resident $750 full-time, $25 per credit part-time; nonresident $7260 full-time, $242 per credit part-time. Full-time tuition and fees vary according to reciprocity agreements. Part-time tuition and fees vary according to reciprocity agreements. No tuition increase for student's term of enrollment. *Required fees:* $3186 full-time, $99 per credit part-time, $108 per term part-time. *Payment plan:* installment. *Waivers:* senior citizens and employees or children of employees.

Financial Aid Of all full-time matriculated undergraduates who enrolled in 2008, 124 Federal Work-Study jobs (averaging $2400).

Applying *Options:* electronic application. *Application fee:* $10. *Required:* high school transcript. *Required for some:* interview. *Application deadlines:* rolling (freshmen), rolling (transfers).

Freshman Application Contact Mr. Ray Blair, Springfield Technical Community College, One Armory Square, Springfield, MA 01105. *Phone:* 413-781-7822 Ext. 4868. *E-mail:* rblair@stcc.edu.

URBAN COLLEGE OF BOSTON

Boston, Massachusetts **www.urbancollegeofboston.org/**

Director of Admissions Dr. Henry J. Johnson, Director of Enrollment Services/Registrar, Urban College of Boston, 178 Tremont Street, Boston, MA 02111-1093. *Phone:* 617-348-6353.

MICHIGAN

ALPENA COMMUNITY COLLEGE

Alpena, Michigan **www.alpenacc.edu/**

- **State and locally supported** 2-year, founded 1952
- **Small-town** 700-acre campus
- **Endowment** $3.3 million
- **Coed,** 2,098 undergraduate students

Undergraduates Students come from 4 states and territories, 2% live on campus. *Retention:* 55% of 2008 full-time freshmen returned.

Freshmen *Admission:* 1,163 applied, 1,163 admitted. *Average high school GPA:* 2.67.

Faculty *Total:* 125, 41% full-time, 2% with terminal degrees. *Student/faculty ratio:* 17:1.

Majors Accounting; administrative assistant and secretarial science; automobile/automotive mechanics technology; biology/biological sciences; business administration and management; business automation/technology/data entry; chemical engineering; chemistry; computer and information sciences; computer/information technology services administration related; computer systems networking and telecommunications; corrections; criminal justice/police science; data processing and data processing technology; drafting and design technology; elementary education; English; general studies; information science/studies; liberal arts and sciences/liberal studies; manufacturing technology; mathematics; medical office assistant; nursing (licensed practical/vocational nurse training); nursing (registered nurse training); office management; operations management; pre-engineering; secondary education.

Academics *Calendar:* semesters. *Degree:* certificates and associate. *Special study options:* academic remediation for entering students, advanced placement credit, distance learning, double majors, internships, part-time degree program, services for LD students, summer session for credit.

Library Stephen Fletcher Library with 29,000 titles, 183 serial subscriptions, an OPAC, a Web page.

Student Life *Housing Options:* coed, men-only, women-only. Campus housing is provided by a third party. *Activities and Organizations:* drama/theater group, student-run newspaper, choral group, Nursing Association, Student Senate, Phi Theta Kappa, Lumberjack Newspaper, Law Enforcement Club. *Campus security:* 24-hour emergency response devices. *Student services:* personal/psychological counseling, women's center.

Athletics Member NJCAA. *Intercollegiate sports:* basketball M(s)/W(s), golf M, softball W(s), volleyball W(s). *Intramural sports:* basketball M/W, bowling M/W, football M, soccer M, softball M/W, volleyball M/W.

Costs (2010–11) *Tuition:* area resident $2760 full-time, $92 per contact hour part-time; state resident $4140 full-time, $138 per contact hour part-time; nonresident $4740 full-time, $184 per contact hour part-time. *Required fees:* $500 full-time, $16 per contact hour part-time. *Room and board:* room only: $3000. *Waivers:* senior citizens and employees or children of employees.

Financial Aid Of all full-time matriculated undergraduates who enrolled in 2008, 80 Federal Work-Study jobs (averaging $1200). 20 state and other part-time jobs (averaging $800).

Applying *Options:* electronic application, early admission, deferred entrance. *Required:* high school transcript. *Application deadlines:* rolling (freshmen), rolling (transfers). *Notification:* continuous (freshmen), continuous (transfers).

Freshman Application Contact Mr. Mike Kollien, Director of Admissions, Alpena Community College, 665 Johnson Street, Alpena, MI 49707-1495. *Phone:* 989-358-7339. *Toll-free phone:* 888-468-6222. *Fax:* 989-358-7540. *E-mail:* kollienm@alpenacc.edu.

BAY DE NOC COMMUNITY COLLEGE

Escanaba, Michigan **www.baydenoc.cc.mi.us/**

- **County-supported** 2-year, founded 1963, part of Michigan Department of Education
- **Rural** 150-acre campus
- **Endowment** $8.3 million
- **Coed**

Undergraduates 1,400 full-time, 1,014 part-time. Students come from 3 states and territories, 6% are from out of state, 0.4% African American, 0.6% Asian American or Pacific Islander, 0.7% Hispanic American, 4% Native American, 19% transferred in, 4% live on campus. *Retention:* 56% of 2008 full-time freshmen returned.

Faculty *Student/faculty ratio:* 20:1.

Academics *Calendar:* semesters. *Degree:* certificates and associate. *Special study options:* academic remediation for entering students, adult/continuing education programs, advanced placement credit, cooperative education, distance learning, double majors, internships, part-time degree program, summer session for credit.

Student Life *Campus security:* Resident Assistants in Housing.

Costs (2009–10) *One-time required fee:* $25. *Tuition:* area resident $2475 full-time, $83 per contact hour part-time; state resident $4125 full-time, $138 per contact hour part-time; nonresident $5235 full-time, $175 per contact hour part-time. Full-time tuition and fees vary according to course load, location, and reciprocity agreements. Part-time tuition and fees vary according to course load, location, and reciprocity agreements. *Required fees:* $330 full-time, $11 per contact hour part-time. *Room and board:* room only: $2800. Room and board charges vary according to housing facility.

Applying *Options:* electronic application, early admission. *Application fee:* $25. *Required:* high school transcript.

Freshman Application Contact Bay de Noc Community College, Student Center, 2001 North Lincoln Road, Escanaba, MI 49829-2511. *Phone:* 906-786-5802 Ext. 1276. *Toll-free phone:* 800-221-2001 Ext. 1276.

BAY MILLS COMMUNITY COLLEGE

Brimley, Michigan **www.bmcc.edu/**

- **District-supported** 2-year, founded 1984
- **Rural** campus
- **Coed**

Academics *Calendar:* semesters. *Degree:* certificates, diplomas, and associate. *Special study options:* academic remediation for entering students, internships, part-time degree program.

Student Life *Campus security:* 24-hour emergency response devices.

Financial Aid Of all full-time matriculated undergraduates who enrolled in 2008, 7 Federal Work-Study jobs (averaging $2466). 6 state and other part-time jobs (averaging $2634).

Applying *Options:* early admission. *Required:* high school transcript.

Freshman Application Contact Ms. Elaine Lehre, Admissions Officer, Bay Mills Community College, 12214 West Lakeshore Drive, Brimley, MI 49715. *Phone:* 906-248-3354. *Toll-free phone:* 800-844-BMCC. *Fax:* 906-248-3351.

DELTA COLLEGE

University Center, Michigan **www.delta.edu/**

- **District-supported** 2-year, founded 1961
- **Rural** 640-acre campus
- **Endowment** $12.0 million
- **Coed,** 10,899 undergraduate students, 41% full-time, 55% women, 45% men

Undergraduates 4,499 full-time, 6,400 part-time. Students come from 2 states and territories, 22 other countries, 8% African American, 0.6% Asian American or Pacific Islander, 4% Hispanic American, 0.5% Native American, 0.5% international, 4% transferred in.

Freshmen *Admission:* 3,344 applied, 3,344 admitted, 1,726 enrolled.

Faculty *Total:* 527, 40% full-time. *Student/faculty ratio:* 20:1.

Majors Accounting; administrative assistant and secretarial science; architectural engineering technology; art; automobile/automotive mechanics technology; avionics maintenance technology; building/construction finishing, management, and inspection related; business administration and management; carpentry; chemical engineering; child development; computer and information systems security; computer science; construction engineering technology; construction trades; consumer merchandising/retailing management; corrections; cosmetology; criminal justice/law enforcement administration; criminal justice/police science; dental assisting; dental hygiene; diagnostic medical sonography and ultrasound technology; drafting and design technology; drafting/design engineering technologies related; electrician; emergency medical technology (EMT paramedic); engineering technology; entrepreneurship; environmental engineering technology; executive assistant/executive secretary; fire science; heating, air conditioning and refrigeration technology; heating, air conditioning, ventilation and refrigeration maintenance technology; industrial arts; industrial radiologic technology; information technology; interior design; legal administrative assistant/secretary; legal assistant/paralegal; liberal arts and sciences/liberal studies; machine tool technology; marketing/marketing management; mechanical engineering/mechanical technology; mechanic and repair technologies related; medical administrative assistant and medical secretary; medical/clinical assistant; merchandising; nursing (licensed practical/vocational nurse training); nursing (registered nurse training); office management; office occupations and clerical services; physical therapist assistant; physician assistant; pipefitting and sprinkler fitting; psychology; public health education and promotion; radio and television broadcasting technology; radiologic technology/science; respiratory care therapy; security and loss prevention; surgical technology; tool and die technology; water quality and wastewater treatment management and recycling technology; web/multimedia management and webmaster; web page, digital/multimedia and information resources design; welding technology.

Academics *Calendar:* semesters. *Degree:* certificates and associate. *Special study options:* academic remediation for entering students, adult/continuing education programs, advanced placement credit, cooperative education, distance learning, double majors, external degree program, freshman honors college, honors programs, independent study, internships, off-campus study, part-time degree program, services for LD students, student-designed majors, study abroad, summer session for credit.

Library Library Learning Information Center with 110,985 titles, 267 serial subscriptions, 4,500 audiovisual materials, an OPAC, a Web page.

Student Life *Housing:* college housing not available. *Activities and Organizations:* student-run newspaper, intramural activities, Student Senate, Phi Theta Kappa, Inter-Varsity Christian Fellowship, DECA. *Campus security:* 24-hour emergency response devices and patrols, student patrols, late-night transport/escort service. *Student services:* personal/psychological counseling.

Athletics Member NJCAA. *Intercollegiate sports:* basketball M(s)/W(s), soccer M(s), softball W(s), volleyball W(s). *Intramural sports:* baseball M(c), basketball M/W, bowling M(c)/W(c), football M, golf M(c), soccer W(c), volleyball M/W.

Costs (2010–11) *Tuition:* area resident $1968 full-time, $82 per credit hour part-time; state resident $2976 full-time, $124 per credit hour part-time; nonresident $4320 full-time, $180 per credit hour part-time. Full-time tuition and fees vary according to course load. Part-time tuition and fees vary according to course load. *Required fees:* $360 full-time, $30 per term part-time. *Payment plan:* installment. *Waivers:* senior citizens and employees or children of employees.

Financial Aid Of all full-time matriculated undergraduates who enrolled in 2008, 115 Federal Work-Study jobs (averaging $2307). 67 state and other part-time jobs (averaging $2214).

Applying *Options:* electronic application, early admission, deferred entrance. *Application fee:* $20. *Required for some:* essay or personal statement. *Recommended:* high school transcript. *Application deadlines:* rolling (freshmen), rolling (transfers).

Freshman Application Contact Mr. Gary Brasseur, Associate Director of Admissions, Delta College, 1961 Delta Road, University Center, MI 48710. *Phone:* 989-686-9590. *Toll-free phone:* 800-285-1705. *Fax:* 989-667-2202. *E-mail:* admit@delta.edu.

GLEN OAKS COMMUNITY COLLEGE

Centreville, Michigan **www.glenoaks.edu/**

- **State and locally supported** 2-year, founded 1965, part of Michigan Department of Career Development
- **Rural** 300-acre campus
- **Coed**

Academics *Calendar:* semesters. *Degree:* certificates and associate. *Special study options:* academic remediation for entering students, adult/continuing education programs, advanced placement credit, distance learning, internships, part-time degree program, services for LD students, summer session for credit.

Student Life *Campus security:* 24-hour emergency response devices.

Athletics Member NJCAA.

Financial Aid Of all full-time matriculated undergraduates who enrolled in 2008, 70 Federal Work-Study jobs (averaging $1100). 38 state and other part-time jobs (averaging $1200).

Applying *Required:* high school transcript.

Freshman Application Contact Ms. Beverly M. Andrews, Director of Admissions/Registrar, Glen Oaks Community College, 62249 Shimmel Road, Centreville, MI 49032-9719. *Phone:* 269-467-9945 Ext. 248. *Toll-free phone:* 888-994-7818.

GOGEBIC COMMUNITY COLLEGE

Ironwood, Michigan **www.gogebic.edu/**

- **State and locally supported** 2-year, founded 1932, part of Michigan Department of Education
- **Small-town** 195-acre campus
- **Coed**

Academics *Calendar:* semesters. *Degree:* certificates and associate. *Special study options:* academic remediation for entering students, adult/continuing education programs, advanced placement credit, cooperative education, distance learning, honors programs, internships, part-time degree program, services for LD students, summer session for credit.

Athletics Member NJCAA.

Financial Aid Of all full-time matriculated undergraduates who enrolled in 2008, 75 Federal Work-Study jobs (averaging $1800). 50 state and other part-time jobs (averaging $1800).

Applying *Options:* electronic application, early admission, deferred entrance. *Application fee:* $10. *Required:* high school transcript.

Freshman Application Contact Ms. Jeanne Graham, Director of Admissions, Gogebic Community College, E-4946 Jackson Road, Ironwood, MI 49938. *Phone:* 906-932-4231 Ext. 306. *Toll-free phone:* 800-682-5910 Ext. 207. *Fax:* 906-932-2339. *E-mail:* jeanneg@gogebic.edu.

GRAND RAPIDS COMMUNITY COLLEGE

Grand Rapids, Michigan **www.grcc.edu/**

- **District-supported** 2-year, founded 1914, part of Michigan Department of Education
- **Urban** 35-acre campus
- **Endowment** $20.3 million
- **Coed,** 16,942 undergraduate students, 45% full-time, 52% women, 48% men

Undergraduates 7,546 full-time, 9,396 part-time. Students come from 6 states and territories, 20 other countries, 1% are from out of state, 13% African American, 3% Asian American or Pacific Islander, 7% Hispanic American, 1% Native American, 0.3% international, 37% transferred in.

Freshmen *Admission:* 9,137 applied, 7,217 admitted, 4,028 enrolled. *Average high school GPA:* 2.78.

Faculty *Total:* 847, 32% full-time, 8% with terminal degrees. *Student/faculty ratio:* 23:1.

Majors Administrative assistant and secretarial science; architectural engineering technology; art; automobile/automotive mechanics technology; business administration and management; computer engineering technology; computer programming; computer science; corrections; criminal justice/law enforcement administration; criminal justice/police science; culinary arts; dental hygiene; drafting and design technology; electrical, electronic and communications engineering technology; fashion merchandising; forestry; geology/earth science; heating, air conditioning, ventilation and refrigeration maintenance technology; industrial technology; legal administrative assistant/secretary; liberal arts and sciences/liberal studies; mass communication/media; medical administrative

Grand Rapids Community College (continued)

assistant and medical secretary; music; nursing (licensed practical/vocational nurse training); nursing (registered nurse training); plastics engineering technology; quality control technology; welding technology.

Academics *Calendar:* semesters. *Degree:* certificates and associate. *Special study options:* academic remediation for entering students, adult/continuing education programs, advanced placement credit, cooperative education, distance learning, English as a second language, honors programs, independent study, off-campus study, part-time degree program, services for LD students, study abroad, summer session for credit.

Library Arthur Andrews Memorial Library plus 1 other with 170,884 titles, 22,110 serial subscriptions, 2,824 audiovisual materials, an OPAC, a Web page.

Student Life *Housing:* college housing not available. *Activities and Organizations:* drama/theater group, student-run newspaper, choral group, Student Congress, Phi Theta Kappa, Hispanic Student Organization, Asian Student Organization, Service Learning Advisory Board, national fraternities, national sororities. *Campus security:* 24-hour emergency response devices, late-night transport/escort service. *Student services:* personal/psychological counseling.

Athletics Member NJCAA. *Intercollegiate sports:* baseball M, basketball M(s)/W(s), football M(s), golf M(s), softball W(s), swimming and diving M(s)/W(s), tennis M(s)/W(s), track and field M(s), volleyball W(s), wrestling M(s). *Intramural sports:* badminton M/W, basketball M/W, skiing (cross-country) M/W, skiing (downhill) M/W, soccer M/W, swimming and diving M/W, tennis M/W, volleyball M/W.

Standardized Tests *Required for some:* ACT ASSET. *Recommended:* SAT or ACT (for admission).

Costs (2010–11) *Tuition:* area resident $2535 full-time; state resident $5430 full-time; nonresident $8040 full-time. *Required fees:* $220 full-time. *Payment plan:* installment. *Waivers:* employees or children of employees.

Financial Aid Of all full-time matriculated undergraduates who enrolled in 2008, 6,142 applied for aid, 4,896 were judged to have need, 1,012 had their need fully met. In 2008, 96 non-need-based awards were made. *Average financial aid package:* $4850. *Average need-based loan:* $2764. *Average need-based gift aid:* $3984. *Average non-need-based aid:* $1051.

Applying *Options:* early admission, deferred entrance. *Application fee:* $20. *Required:* high school transcript. *Notification:* continuous (freshmen), continuous (transfers).

Freshman Application Contact Ms. Diane Patrick, Director of Admissions, Grand Rapids Community College, 143 Bostwick Avenue, NE, Grand Rapids, MI 49503-3201. *Phone:* 616-234-4100. *Fax:* 616-234-4005. *E-mail:* dpatrick@grcc.edu.

HENRY FORD COMMUNITY COLLEGE

Dearborn, Michigan **www.hfcc.edu/**

Freshman Application Contact Henry Ford Community College, 5101 Evergreen Road, Dearborn, MI 48128-1495. *Phone:* 313-845-9600.

ITT TECHNICAL INSTITUTE

Canton, Michigan **www.itt-tech.edu/**

- **Proprietary** primarily 2-year, founded 2002, part of ITT Educational Services, Inc.
- **Coed**

Majors Animation, interactive technology, video graphics and special effects; business administration and management; CAD/CADD drafting/design technology; computer and information systems security; computer engineering technology; computer software and media applications related; computer software engineering; computer software technology; construction management; criminal justice/law enforcement administration; design and visual communications; electrical, electronic and communications engineering technology; legal assistant/paralegal; nursing (registered nurse training); system, networking, and LAN/WAN management; web/multimedia management and webmaster; web page, digital/multimedia and information resources design.

Academics *Calendar:* quarters. *Degrees:* associate and bachelor's.

Student Life *Housing:* college housing not available.

Freshman Application Contact Director of Recruitment, ITT Technical Institute, 1905 South Haggerty Road, Canton, MI 48188-2025. *Phone:* 784-397-7800. *Toll-free phone:* 800-247-4477.

ITT TECHNICAL INSTITUTE

Swartz Creek, Michigan **www.itt-tech.edu/**

- **Proprietary** 2-year, founded 2005, part of ITT Educational Services, Inc.
- **Coed**

Majors Animation, interactive technology, video graphics and special effects; business administration and management; CAD/CADD drafting/design technology; computer and information systems security; computer engineering technology; computer software and media applications related; computer software engineering; computer software technology; construction management; criminal justice/law enforcement administration; design and visual communications; electrical, electronic and communications engineering technology; legal assistant/paralegal; system, networking, and LAN/WAN management; web/multimedia management and webmaster; web page, digital/multimedia and information resources design.

Academics *Calendar:* quarters. *Degree:* associate.

Freshman Application Contact Director of Recruitment, ITT Technical Institute, 6359 Miller Road, Swartz Creek, MI 48473. *Phone:* 810-628-2500. *Toll-free phone:* 800-514-6564.

ITT TECHNICAL INSTITUTE

Troy, Michigan **www.itt-tech.edu/**

- **Proprietary** primarily 2-year, founded 1987, part of ITT Educational Services, Inc.
- **Coed**

Majors Animation, interactive technology, video graphics and special effects; business administration and management; CAD/CADD drafting/design technology; computer and information systems security; computer engineering technology; computer software and media applications related; computer software engineering; computer software technology; construction management; criminal justice/law enforcement administration; design and visual communications; electrical, electronic and communications engineering technology; legal assistant/paralegal; system, networking, and LAN/WAN management; web/multimedia management and webmaster; web page, digital/multimedia and information resources design.

Academics *Calendar:* quarters. *Degrees:* associate and bachelor's.

Student Life *Housing:* college housing not available.

Freshman Application Contact Director of Recruitment, ITT Technical Institute, 1522 East Big Beaver Road, Troy, MI 48083-1905. *Phone:* 248-524-1800. *Toll-free phone:* 800-832-6817. *Fax:* 248-524-1965.

ITT TECHNICAL INSTITUTE

Wyoming, Michigan **www.itt-tech.edu/**

- **Proprietary** primarily 2-year, part of ITT Educational Services, Inc.
- **Coed**

Majors Animation, interactive technology, video graphics and special effects; business administration and management; CAD/CADD drafting/design technology; computer and information systems security; computer engineering technology; computer software and media applications related; computer software engineering; computer software technology; construction management; criminal justice/law enforcement administration; design and visual communications; electrical, electronic and communications engineering technology; legal assistant/paralegal; system, networking, and LAN/WAN management; web/multimedia management and webmaster; web page, digital/multimedia and information resources design.

Academics *Calendar:* quarters. *Degrees:* associate and bachelor's.

Student Life *Housing:* college housing not available.

Freshman Application Contact Director of Recruitment, ITT Technical Institute, 4020 Sparks Drive SE, Grand Rapids, MI 49546. *Phone:* 616-406-1200. *Toll-free phone:* 800-632-4676.

JACKSON COMMUNITY COLLEGE

Jackson, Michigan **www.jccmi.edu/**

- **County-supported** 2-year, founded 1928
- **Suburban** 580-acre campus with easy access to Detroit
- **Endowment** $10.7 million
- **Coed,** 6,173 undergraduate students, 43% full-time, 63% women, 37% men

Undergraduates 2,673 full-time, 3,500 part-time. 1% are from out of state, 5% African American, 1% Asian American or Pacific Islander, 3% Hispanic American, 1% Native American, 0.3% international. *Retention:* 62% of 2008 full-time freshmen returned.

Freshmen *Admission:* 1,262 enrolled. *Average high school GPA:* 2.26. *Test scores:* ACT scores over 18: 75%; ACT scores over 24: 18%; ACT scores over 30: 1%.

Faculty *Total:* 392, 23% full-time, 3% with terminal degrees. *Student/faculty ratio:* 20:1.

Majors Accounting and finance; administrative assistant and secretarial science; airline pilot and flight crew; automobile/automotive mechanics technology; business administration and management; computer and information sciences and support services related; construction trades related; corrections; criminal justice/law enforcement administration; data processing and data processing technology; diagnostic medical sonography and ultrasound technology; early childhood education; electrical, electronic and communications engineering technology; emergency medical technology (EMT paramedic); executive assistant/executive secretary; general studies; graphic design; heating, air conditioning and refrigeration technology; liberal arts and sciences/liberal studies; marketing/marketing management; medical/clinical assistant; medical insurance/medical billing; medical radiologic technology; medical transcription; nursing (licensed practical/vocational nurse training); nursing (registered nurse training).

Academics *Calendar:* semesters. *Degree:* certificates and associate. *Special study options:* academic remediation for entering students, accelerated degree program, adult/continuing education programs, advanced placement credit, cooperative education, distance learning, English as a second language, external degree program, independent study, internships, part-time degree program, services for LD students, summer session for credit. *ROTC:* Army (c).

Library Atkinson Learning Resources Center plus 1 other with 67,000 titles, 300 serial subscriptions, 2,000 audiovisual materials, an OPAC, a Web page.

Student Life *Housing Options:* coed, disabled students. Campus housing is university owned. *Activities and Organizations:* drama/theater group, choral group, Drama Club, Men of Merit, Sisters of Strength, ABIG (Alternative Break Interest Group), Phi Theta Kappa. *Campus security:* 24-hour emergency response devices and patrols, student patrols, late-night transport/escort service, controlled dormitory access. *Student services:* personal/psychological counseling.

Athletics Member NJCAA. *Intercollegiate sports:* baseball M(s), basketball M(s)/W(s), cross-country running M(s)/W(s), golf M(s)/W(s), ice hockey M(c), soccer M(s)/W(s), softball W(s), volleyball W(s).

Standardized Tests *Recommended:* SAT and SAT Subject Tests or ACT (for admission).

Costs (2009–10) *Tuition:* area resident $2172 full-time, $91 per contact hour part-time; state resident $3048 full-time, $127 per contact hour part-time; nonresident $4368 full-time, $182 per contact hour part-time. Full-time tuition and fees vary according to course load. Part-time tuition and fees vary according to course load. *Required fees:* $612 full-time, $26 per contact hour part-time. *Room and board:* room only: $5900. *Payment plan:* deferred payment. *Waivers:* senior citizens and employees or children of employees.

Financial Aid Of all full-time matriculated undergraduates who enrolled in 2008, 60 Federal Work-Study jobs (averaging $1304). 19 state and other part-time jobs (averaging $1192).

Applying *Options:* electronic application, early admission. *Application deadlines:* rolling (freshmen), rolling (transfers). *Notification:* continuous (freshmen), continuous (transfers).

Freshman Application Contact Ms. Julie Hand, Assistant Dean of Enrollment Services, Jackson Community College, 2111 Emmons Road, Jackson, MI 49201. *Phone:* 517-796-8425. *Toll-free phone:* 888-522-7344. *Fax:* 517-796-8631. *E-mail:* admissions@jccmi.edu.

KALAMAZOO VALLEY COMMUNITY COLLEGE

Kalamazoo, Michigan **www.kvcc.edu/**

- **State and locally supported** 2-year, founded 1966
- **Suburban** 187-acre campus
- **Coed,** 11,113 undergraduate students

Undergraduates 1% are from out of state, 14% African American, 2% Asian American or Pacific Islander, 4% Hispanic American, 0.8% Native American, 0.5% international.

Majors Accounting technology and bookkeeping; animation, interactive technology, video graphics and special effects; automobile/automotive mechanics technology; business administration and management; CAD/CADD drafting/design technology; chemical technology; computer programming; computer systems analysis; criminal justice/police science; dental hygiene; e-commerce; electrical, electronic and communications engineering technology; elementary education; emergency medical technology (EMT paramedic); engineering; engineering technology; executive assistant/executive secretary; fire science; general studies; graphic design; heating, air conditioning and refrigeration technology; illustration; international/global studies; liberal arts and sciences/liberal studies; machine tool technology; marketing/marketing management; mechanical engineering/mechanical technology; mechanics and repair; nursing (registered nurse training); respiratory care therapy; surgical technology; web/multimedia management and webmaster; web page, digital/multimedia and information resources design; welding technology.

Academics *Calendar:* semesters. *Degree:* certificates and associate. *Special study options:* academic remediation for entering students, advanced placement credit, cooperative education, distance learning, English as a second language, honors programs, independent study, internships, off-campus study, part-time degree program, services for LD students, student-designed majors, summer session for credit. *ROTC:* Army (c).

Library Kalamazoo Valley Community College Library with 88,791 titles, 420 serial subscriptions, an OPAC, a Web page.

Student Life *Housing:* college housing not available. *Activities and Organizations:* choral group. *Campus security:* 24-hour emergency response devices and patrols. *Student services:* personal/psychological counseling.

Athletics Member NJCAA. *Intercollegiate sports:* baseball M(s), basketball M(s)/W(s), golf M, softball W(s), tennis W(s), volleyball W(s). *Intramural sports:* basketball M/W.

Standardized Tests *Required:* ACT (for admission).

Financial Aid Of all full-time matriculated undergraduates who enrolled in 2009, 61 Federal Work-Study jobs (averaging $2254).

Applying *Required:* high school transcript. *Application deadlines:* rolling (freshmen), rolling (transfers). *Notification:* continuous (freshmen), continuous (transfers).

Freshman Application Contact Kalamazoo Valley Community College, PO Box 4070, Kalamazoo, MI 49003-4070. *Phone:* 269-488-4207.

KELLOGG COMMUNITY COLLEGE

Battle Creek, Michigan **www.kellogg.edu/**

- **State and locally supported** 2-year, founded 1956, part of Michigan Department of Education
- **Urban** 120-acre campus
- **Coed,** 5,976 undergraduate students, 34% full-time, 65% women, 35% men

Undergraduates 2,053 full-time, 3,923 part-time.

Freshmen *Admission:* 2,623 applied, 2,623 admitted, 1,052 enrolled.

Faculty *Total:* 385, 24% full-time, 3% with terminal degrees. *Student/faculty ratio:* 23:1.

Majors Accounting; administrative assistant and secretarial science; business administration and management; chemical technology; clinical/medical laboratory technology; computer engineering technology; computer graphics; computer programming; computer programming (specific applications); computer software and media applications related; corrections; criminal justice/police science; criminal justice/safety; data entry/microcomputer applications related; dental hygiene; drafting and design technology; elementary education; emergency medical technology (EMT paramedic); engineering; executive assistant/executive secretary; fire protection and safety technology; general studies; heating, air conditioning, ventilation and refrigeration maintenance technology; human services; industrial technology; legal administrative assistant/secretary; legal assistant/paralegal; liberal arts and sciences/liberal studies; machine tool technology; medical administrative assistant and medical secretary; medical radiologic technology; nursing (licensed practical/vocational nurse training); nursing (registered nurse training); physical therapist assistant; pipefitting and sprinkler fitting; plastics engineering technology; sheet metal technology; social work; welding technology; word processing.

Academics *Calendar:* semesters. *Degree:* certificates and associate. *Special study options:* academic remediation for entering students, accelerated degree program, adult/continuing education programs, advanced placement credit, cooperative education, distance learning, double majors, English as a second language, freshman honors college, honors programs, independent study, internships, off-campus study, part-time degree program, services for LD students, summer session for credit.

Library Emory W. Morris Learning Resource Center with 42,131 titles, 172 serial subscriptions, an OPAC, a Web page.

Student Life *Housing:* college housing not available. *Activities and Organizations:* drama/theater group, student-run newspaper, choral group, Tech Club, Phi Theta Kappa, Student Nurses Association, Crude Arts Club, Art League. *Campus security:* 24-hour emergency response devices and patrols, late-night transport/escort service.

Athletics Member NJCAA. *Intercollegiate sports:* baseball M(s), basketball M(s)/W(s), soccer M, softball W(s), volleyball W(s).

Standardized Tests *Required for some:* ACT (for admission), SAT or ACT (for admission).

Kellogg Community College (continued)

Costs (2010–11) *Tuition:* area resident $2295 full-time, $79 per credit hour part-time; state resident $3720 full-time, $124 per credit hour part-time; nonresident $5325 full-time, $178 per credit hour part-time. *Required fees:* $210 full-time, $7 per credit hour part-time. *Payment plan:* installment. *Waivers:* senior citizens and employees or children of employees.

Financial Aid Of all full-time matriculated undergraduates who enrolled in 2008, 41 Federal Work-Study jobs (averaging $2251). 43 state and other part-time jobs (averaging $2058).

Applying *Options:* electronic application, early admission. *Required for some:* high school transcript, minimum 2 GPA. *Application deadlines:* rolling (freshmen), rolling (transfers). *Notification:* continuous (freshmen), continuous (transfers).

Freshman Application Contact Ms. Denise Newman, Director of Enrollment Services, Kellogg Community College, 450 North Avenue, Battle Creek, MI 49017. *Phone:* 269-965-3931 Ext. 2620. *Fax:* 269-965-4133. *E-mail:* harriss@kellogg.edu.

Keweenaw Bay Ojibwa Community College

Baraga, Michigan **www.kbocc.org/**

Admissions Office Contact Keweenaw Bay Ojibwa Community College, 111 Beartown Road, Baraga, MI 49908.

Kirtland Community College

Roscommon, Michigan **www.kirtland.edu/**

- **District-supported** 2-year, founded 1966, part of Michigan Department of Energy, Labor and Economic Growth - Community Colleges Service Unit
- **Rural** 180-acre campus
- **Coed,** 1,972 undergraduate students, 47% full-time, 60% women, 40% men

Undergraduates 925 full-time, 1,047 part-time. Students come from 3 states and territories, 1 other country, 1% African American, 0.5% Asian American or Pacific Islander, 1% Hispanic American, 1% Native American, 0.2% international.

Freshmen *Admission:* 364 enrolled. *Test scores:* ACT scores over 18: 46%; ACT scores over 24: 8%; ACT scores over 30: 1%.

Faculty *Total:* 139, 27% full-time. *Student/faculty ratio:* 19:1.

Majors Administrative assistant and secretarial science; art; automobile/automotive mechanics technology; biological and physical sciences; business administration and management; cardiovascular technology; carpentry; corrections; cosmetology; creative writing; criminal justice/law enforcement administration; drafting and design technology; education (multiple levels); electrical, electronic and communications engineering technology; fire services administration; general studies; graphic design; heating, air conditioning, ventilation and refrigeration maintenance technology; industrial design; industrial technology; information science/studies; legal administrative assistant/secretary; liberal arts and sciences/liberal studies; management information systems; massage therapy; medical administrative assistant and medical secretary; nursing (licensed practical/vocational nurse training); nursing (registered nurse training); small engine mechanics and repair technology; surgical technology; welding technology.

Academics *Calendar:* semesters. *Degree:* certificates and associate. *Special study options:* academic remediation for entering students, adult/continuing education programs, advanced placement credit, cooperative education, distance learning, English as a second language, honors programs, independent study, internships, part-time degree program, summer session for credit.

Library Kirtland Community College Library with 35,000 titles, 317 serial subscriptions, an OPAC.

Student Life *Housing:* college housing not available. *Activities and Organizations:* student-run newspaper. *Campus security:* student patrols, late-night transport/escort service, campus warning siren, uniformed armed police officers. *Student services:* personal/psychological counseling.

Athletics Member NJCAA. *Intercollegiate sports:* basketball M(s)/W(s), cross-country running M(s)/W(s), golf M(s)/W(s).

Standardized Tests *Recommended:* ACT (for admission).

Costs (2010–11) *Tuition:* area resident $2402 full-time, $81 per contact hour part-time; state resident $4402 full-time, $149 per contact hour part-time; nonresident $5440 full-time, $184 per contact hour part-time. *Required fees:* $270 full-time, $8 per contact hour part-time. *Payment plan:* installment. *Waivers:* minority students, senior citizens, and employees or children of employees.

Financial Aid Of all full-time matriculated undergraduates who enrolled in 2008, 50 Federal Work-Study jobs (averaging $1253). 28 state and other part-time jobs (averaging $1647).

Applying *Options:* electronic application. *Application deadlines:* rolling (freshmen), rolling (transfers). *Notification:* continuous until 8/22 (freshmen), continuous until 8/22 (transfers).

Freshman Application Contact Ms. Luann Mabarak, Registrar, Kirtland Community College, 10775 North St. Helen Road, Roscommon, MI 48653-9699. *Phone:* 989-275-5000 Ext. 291. *Fax:* 989-275-6789. *E-mail:* registrar@kirtland.edu.

Lake Michigan College

Benton Harbor, Michigan **www.lakemichigancollege.edu/**

- **District-supported** 2-year, founded 1946, part of Michigan Department of Education
- **Small-town** 260-acre campus
- **Endowment** $8.9 million
- **Coed,** 4,697 undergraduate students, 34% full-time, 59% women, 41% men

Undergraduates 1,616 full-time, 3,081 part-time. Students come from 9 states and territories, 48 other countries, 2% are from out of state, 18% African American, 1% Asian American or Pacific Islander, 4% Hispanic American, 1% Native American, 0.1% international, 6% transferred in. *Retention:* 58% of 2008 full-time freshmen returned.

Freshmen *Admission:* 898 enrolled. *Average high school GPA:* 2.72.

Faculty *Total:* 331, 16% full-time. *Student/faculty ratio:* 18:1.

Majors Accounting; administrative assistant and secretarial science; art; athletic training; biology/biological sciences; business administration and management; chemistry; computer and information sciences; corrections; criminal justice/law enforcement administration; dental assisting; diagnostic medical sonography and ultrasound technology; drafting and design technology; dramatic/theater arts; early childhood education; elementary education; emergency medical technology (EMT paramedic); English; environmental science; foreign languages and literatures; general studies; geography; geology/earth science; graphic design; health and physical education; health professions related; history; hospitality administration; humanities; industrial technology; legal administrative assistant/secretary; liberal arts and sciences/liberal studies; machine tool technology; manufacturing engineering; marketing/marketing management; mass communication/media; mathematics; medical administrative assistant and medical secretary; medical radiologic technology; mortuary science and embalming; music; nuclear/nuclear power technology; nursing (registered nurse training); philosophy; physical sciences; physical therapy; physician assistant; physics; political science and government; precision production related; pre-dentistry studies; pre-engineering; pre-law studies; premedical studies; pre-pharmacy studies; pre-veterinary studies; psychology; radiologic technology/science; secondary education; social work; sociology.

Academics *Calendar:* semesters. *Degree:* certificates and associate. *Special study options:* academic remediation for entering students, adult/continuing education programs, cooperative education, distance learning, honors programs, independent study, part-time degree program, services for LD students, student-designed majors, summer session for credit.

Library William Hessel Library with 93,803 titles, 15,750 serial subscriptions, 3,627 audiovisual materials, an OPAC, a Web page.

Student Life *Housing:* college housing not available. *Activities and Organizations:* drama/theater group, choral group, Soccer Club, Phi Theta Kappa, Gamers Guild, Student Nursing Association, Drama Club. *Campus security:* 24-hour emergency response devices.

Athletics Member NJCAA. *Intercollegiate sports:* baseball M(s), basketball M(s)/W(s), softball W(s), volleyball W(s).

Costs (2010–11) *Tuition:* area resident $3105 full-time, $73 per contact hour part-time; state resident $4170 full-time, $102 per credit part-time; nonresident $5190 full-time, $142 per contact hour part-time. *Payment plan:* installment. *Waivers:* senior citizens and employees or children of employees.

Applying *Options:* electronic application. *Required:* high school transcript. *Required for some:* interview. *Application deadlines:* rolling (freshmen), rolling (transfers). *Notification:* continuous (freshmen), continuous (transfers).

Freshman Application Contact Sara Skinner, Assistant Registrar, Lake Michigan College, 2755 East Napier, Benton Harbor, MI 49022-1899. *Phone:* 616-927-8100 Ext. 5268. *Toll-free phone:* 800-252-1LMC. *E-mail:* skinner@lakemichigancollege.edu.

Lansing Community College

Lansing, Michigan **www.lcc.edu/**

- **State and locally supported** 2-year, founded 1957, part of Michigan Department of Education
- **Urban** 28-acre campus
- **Endowment** $5.2 million
- **Coed,** 21,123 undergraduate students, 37% full-time, 55% women, 45% men

Undergraduates 7,815 full-time, 13,308 part-time. Students come from 18 states and territories, 27 other countries, 1% are from out of state, 11% African American, 2% Asian American or Pacific Islander, 4% Hispanic American, 0.8% Native American, 0.9% international.

Freshmen *Admission:* 4,015 enrolled.

Faculty *Total:* 1,920, 13% full-time. *Student/faculty ratio:* 14:1.

Majors Accounting; administrative assistant and secretarial science; airline pilot and flight crew; architectural engineering technology; art; automobile/automotive mechanics technology; avionics maintenance technology; biological and physical sciences; biology/biological sciences; biology/biotechnology laboratory technician; broadcast journalism; business administration and management; carpentry; chemical engineering; chemistry; child development; cinematography and film/video production; civil engineering technology; clinical laboratory science/medical technology; commercial and advertising art; computer engineering technology; computer graphics; computer programming; computer typography and composition equipment operation; construction engineering technology; consumer merchandising/retailing management; corrections; court reporting; criminal justice/law enforcement administration; criminal justice/police science; dance; dental hygiene; developmental and child psychology; diagnostic medical sonography and ultrasound technology; drafting and design technology; drafting/design engineering technologies related; dramatic/theater arts; education; electrical, electronic and communications engineering technology; electromechanical technology; elementary education; emergency medical technology (EMT paramedic); engineering; engineering technology; English; film/cinema studies; finance; fine/studio arts; fire science; geography; geology/earth science; gerontology; heating, air conditioning, ventilation and refrigeration maintenance technology; heavy equipment maintenance technology; horticultural science; hospitality administration; hotel/motel administration; human resources management; human services; industrial technology; information science/studies; international business/trade/commerce; journalism; kindergarten/preschool education; labor and industrial relations; landscape architecture; legal administrative assistant/secretary; legal assistant/paralegal; liberal arts and sciences/liberal studies; machine tool technology; management information systems; marketing/marketing management; mass communication/media; mathematics; mechanical engineering/mechanical technology; medical/clinical assistant; medical radiologic technology; music; nursing (licensed practical/vocational nurse training); nursing (registered nurse training); philosophy; photography; physical education teaching and coaching; pre-engineering; public administration; public relations/image management; quality control technology; radio and television; real estate; religious studies; respiratory care therapy; sign language interpretation and translation; social work; special products marketing; speech and rhetoric; surgical technology; survey technology; teacher assistant/aide; telecommunications technology; tourism and travel services management; veterinary/animal health technology; voice and opera; welding technology.

Academics *Calendar:* semesters. *Degree:* certificates and associate. *Special study options:* academic remediation for entering students, adult/continuing education programs, advanced placement credit, cooperative education, distance learning, double majors, English as a second language, external degree program, honors programs, independent study, internships, part-time degree program, services for LD students, study abroad, summer session for credit. *ROTC:* Army (c), Air Force (c).

Library Abel Sykes Technology and Learning Center plus 1 other with 98,125 titles, 600 serial subscriptions, an OPAC, a Web page.

Student Life *Housing:* college housing not available. *Activities and Organizations:* drama/theater group, student-run newspaper, radio station, choral group, Student Marketing, Legal Assistants Club, Student Nursing Club, Phi Theta Kappa, Student Advising Club, national fraternities, national sororities. *Campus security:* 24-hour emergency response devices and patrols, student patrols, late-night transport/escort service. *Student services:* personal/psychological counseling, women's center.

Athletics Member NJCAA. *Intercollegiate sports:* basketball M(s)/W(s), cross-country running M(s)/W(s), golf M(s), track and field M(s)/W(s), volleyball W(s). *Intramural sports:* baseball M, basketball M/W, cross-country running M/W, ice hockey M, soccer M/W, softball W, track and field M/W, volleyball W.

Costs (2009–10) *One-time required fee:* $35. *Tuition:* area resident $2190 full-time, $73 per contact hour part-time; state resident $4020 full-time, $134 per contact hour part-time; nonresident $6030 full-time, $201 per contact hour part-time. *Required fees:* $50 full-time, $35 per term part-time.

Financial Aid Of all full-time matriculated undergraduates who enrolled in 2008, 125 Federal Work-Study jobs (averaging $2636). 122 state and other part-time jobs (averaging $2563).

Applying *Options:* electronic application, early admission, deferred entrance. *Required for some:* essay or personal statement, high school transcript, 2 letters of recommendation, interview. *Application deadlines:* rolling (freshmen), rolling (transfers).

Freshman Application Contact Ms. Tammy Grossbauer, Director of Admissions/Registrar, Lansing Community College, PO Box 40010, Lansing, MI 48901-7210. *Phone:* 517-483-9886. *Toll-free phone:* 800-644-4LCC. *Fax:* 517-483-1170. *E-mail:* grossbt@lcc.edu.

Macomb Community College

Warren, Michigan **www.macomb.edu/**

- **District-supported** 2-year, founded 1954, part of Michigan Public Community College System
- **Suburban** 384-acre campus with easy access to Detroit
- **Endowment** $12.3 million
- **Coed,** 24,376 undergraduate students, 39% full-time, 52% women, 48% men

Undergraduates 9,599 full-time, 14,777 part-time. Students come from 5 states and territories, 7% African American, 3% Asian American or Pacific Islander, 2% Hispanic American, 0.5% Native American, 0.7% international. *Retention:* 75% of 2008 full-time freshmen returned.

Freshmen *Admission:* 1,479 enrolled.

Faculty *Total:* 1,115, 21% full-time, 10% with terminal degrees. *Student/faculty ratio:* 28:1.

Majors Accounting; administrative assistant and secretarial science; agriculture; architectural drafting and CAD/CADD; automobile/automotive mechanics technology; automotive engineering technology; biology/biological sciences; business administration and management; business automation/technology/data entry; business/commerce; cabinetmaking and millwork; chemistry; child-care and support services management; civil engineering technology; commercial and advertising art; communication/speech communication and rhetoric; computer programming; computer programming (specific applications); construction engineering technology; criminal justice/law enforcement administration; criminal justice/police science; culinary arts; drafting and design technology; drafting/design engineering technologies related; electrical, electronic and communications engineering technology; electrical/electronics equipment installation and repair; electromechanical technology; emergency medical technology (EMT paramedic); energy management and systems technology; engineering related; finance; fire protection and safety technology; forensic science and technology; general studies; graphic and printing equipment operation/production; heating, air conditioning and refrigeration technology; heating, air conditioning, ventilation and refrigeration maintenance technology; industrial mechanics and maintenance technology; industrial technology; international/global studies; legal assistant/paralegal; legal studies; liberal arts and sciences/liberal studies; machine tool technology; manufacturing technology; marketing/marketing management; mathematics; mechanical drafting and CAD/CADD; mechanical engineering/mechanical technology; mechanic and repair technologies related; medical/clinical assistant; mental health/rehabilitation; metallurgical technology; music performance; nursing (registered nurse training); occupational therapist assistant; operations management; physical therapist assistant; plastics engineering technology; plumbing technology; pre-engineering; quality control and safety technologies related; quality control technology; respiratory care therapy; robotics technology; sheet metal technology; social psychology; surgical technology; survey technology; tool and die technology; veterinary/animal health technology; welding technology.

Academics *Calendar:* semesters. *Degree:* certificates and associate. *Special study options:* academic remediation for entering students, adult/continuing education programs, advanced placement credit, cooperative education, English as a second language, honors programs, internships, off-campus study, part-time degree program, services for LD students, student-designed majors, summer session for credit.

Library Library of South Campus, Library of Center Campus with 159,226 titles, 4,240 serial subscriptions, an OPAC.

Student Life *Housing:* college housing not available. *Activities and Organizations:* drama/theater group, Phi Beta Kappa, Adventure Unlimited, Alpha Rho Rho, SADD. *Campus security:* 24-hour emergency response devices and patrols, late-night transport/escort service, security phones in parking lots, surveillance cameras. *Student services:* health clinic, personal/psychological counseling.

Athletics Member NJCAA. *Intercollegiate sports:* baseball M(s), basketball M(s), cross-country running M(s)/W(s), soccer M(s), softball W(s), track and field M(s)/W(s), volleyball W(s). *Intramural sports:* baseball M, basketball M, bowling M/W, cross-country running M/W, football M/W, skiing (cross-country) M/W, skiing (downhill) M/W, volleyball M/W.

Costs (2009–10) *Tuition:* area resident $2232 full-time, $72 per credit hour part-time; state resident $3410 full-time, $110 per credit hour part-time; nonresident $4433 full-time, $143 per credit hour part-time. Full-time tuition and fees

Macomb Community College (continued)

vary according to course load. Part-time tuition and fees vary according to course load. *Required fees:* $40 full-time, $20 part-time. *Waivers:* senior citizens and employees or children of employees.

Applying *Options:* early admission, deferred entrance. *Application deadlines:* rolling (freshmen), rolling (transfers).

Freshman Application Contact Mr. Brian Bouwman, Coordinator of Admissions and Transfer Credit, Macomb Community College, G312, 14500 East 12 Mile Road, Warren, MI 48088-3896. *Phone:* 586-445-7246. *Toll-free phone:* 866-622-6624. *Fax:* 586-445-7140. *E-mail:* stevensr@macomb.edu.

MID MICHIGAN COMMUNITY COLLEGE

Harrison, Michigan **www.midmich.edu/**

Freshman Application Contact Tena Diamond, Admissions Specialist, Mid Michigan Community College, 1375 South Clare Avenue, Harrison, MI 48625. *Phone:* 989-386-6661. *E-mail:* apply@midmich.edu.

MONROE COUNTY COMMUNITY COLLEGE

Monroe, Michigan **www.monroeccc.edu/**

Freshman Application Contact Mr. Mark V. Hall, Director of Admissions and Guidance Services, Monroe County Community College, 155 South Raisinville Road, Monroe, MI 48161-9047. *Phone:* 734-384-4261. *Toll-free phone:* 877-YES MCCC. *Fax:* 734-242-9711. *E-mail:* mhall@monroeccc.edu.

MONTCALM COMMUNITY COLLEGE

Sidney, Michigan **www.montcalm.edu/**

- **State and locally supported** 2-year, founded 1965, part of Michigan Department of Education
- **Rural** 240-acre campus with easy access to Grand Rapids
- **Endowment** $4.2 million
- **Coed,** 2,328 undergraduate students, 40% full-time, 66% women, 34% men

Undergraduates 937 full-time, 1,391 part-time. 0.1% African American, 0.1% Asian American or Pacific Islander, 0.8% Hispanic American, 0.4% Native American.

Freshmen *Admission:* 856 applied, 856 admitted, 340 enrolled. *Average high school GPA:* 2.28. *Test scores:* ACT scores over 18: 74%; ACT scores over 24: 15%.

Faculty *Total:* 179, 19% full-time, 7% with terminal degrees. *Student/faculty ratio:* 21:1.

Majors Accounting; administrative assistant and secretarial science; business administration and management; child-care and support services management; child-care provision; computer installation and repair technology; corrections; cosmetology; criminal justice/law enforcement administration; data processing and data processing technology; drafting and design technology; electrical, electronic and communications engineering technology; emergency medical technology (EMT paramedic); entrepreneurship; executive assistant/executive secretary; general studies; industrial technology; liberal arts and sciences/liberal studies; management information systems; medical administrative assistant and medical secretary; medical radiologic technology; nursing (registered nurse training); teacher assistant/aide.

Academics *Calendar:* semesters. *Degree:* certificates and associate. *Special study options:* academic remediation for entering students, adult/continuing education programs, advanced placement credit, cooperative education, distance learning, double majors, independent study, internships, off-campus study, part-time degree program, services for LD students, summer session for credit.

Library Montcalm Community College Library with 29,848 titles, 3,670 serial subscriptions, an OPAC, a Web page.

Student Life *Housing:* college housing not available. *Activities and Organizations:* drama/theater group, student-run newspaper, choral group, Nursing Club, Native American Club, Phi Theta Kappa, Business Club, Judo Club. *Student services:* personal/psychological counseling.

Athletics *Intramural sports:* volleyball M/W.

Costs (2009–10) *Tuition:* area resident $2310 full-time, $77 per credit hour part-time; state resident $3990 full-time, $133 per credit hour part-time; nonresident $5850 full-time, $195 per credit hour part-time. Full-time tuition and fees vary according to course load. Part-time tuition and fees vary according to course load. *Required fees:* $195 full-time, $7 per credit hour part-time. *Payment plan:* installment. *Waivers:* senior citizens and employees or children of employees.

Financial Aid Of all full-time matriculated undergraduates who enrolled in 2008, 57 Federal Work-Study jobs (averaging $2000).

Applying *Options:* electronic application, early admission, deferred entrance. *Recommended:* high school transcript. *Application deadlines:* rolling (freshmen), rolling (transfers). *Notification:* continuous (freshmen), continuous (transfers).

Freshman Application Contact Ms. Debra Alexander, Director of Admissions, Montcalm Community College, 2800 College Drive, Sidney, MI 48885. *Phone:* 989-328-1276. *Toll-free phone:* 877-328-2111. *E-mail:* admissions@montcalm.edu.

MOTT COMMUNITY COLLEGE

Flint, Michigan **www.mcc.edu/**

Freshman Application Contact Ms. Delores Deen, Executive Dean of Student Services, Mott Community College, 1401 East Court Street, Flint, MI 48503. *Phone:* 810-762-0315. *Toll-free phone:* 800-852-8614. *Fax:* 810-232-9442.

MUSKEGON COMMUNITY COLLEGE

Muskegon, Michigan **www.muskegoncc.edu/**

- **State and locally supported** 2-year, founded 1926, part of Michigan Department of Education
- **Small-town** 112-acre campus with easy access to Grand Rapids
- **Coed,** 5,148 undergraduate students

Faculty *Total:* 150, 67% full-time. *Student/faculty ratio:* 20:1.

Majors Accounting; administrative assistant and secretarial science; advertising; anthropology; applied art; applied mathematics; art; art history, criticism and conservation; art teacher education; automobile/automotive mechanics technology; biology/biotechnology laboratory technician; biomedical technology; business administration and management; business machine repair; chemical engineering; child development; commercial and advertising art; criminal justice/law enforcement administration; data processing and data processing technology; developmental and child psychology; drafting and design technology; economics; education; electrical, electronic and communications engineering technology; electromechanical technology; elementary education; engineering technology; finance; hospitality administration; hospitality and recreation marketing; hotel/motel administration; industrial arts; industrial technology; information science/studies; legal administrative assistant/secretary; liberal arts and sciences/liberal studies; machine tool technology; marketing/marketing management; medical administrative assistant and medical secretary; nursing (registered nurse training); parks, recreation and leisure; special products marketing; transportation and materials moving related; welding technology.

Academics *Calendar:* semesters. *Degree:* associate. *Special study options:* academic remediation for entering students, adult/continuing education programs, cooperative education, honors programs, part-time degree program, student-designed majors, summer session for credit.

Library Hendrik Meijer and Technology Center with 48,597 titles, 450 serial subscriptions.

Student Life *Housing:* college housing not available. *Activities and Organizations:* drama/theater group, student-run newspaper, choral group, Respiratory Therapy, Hispanic Student Organization, Black Student Alliance, International Club, Rotaract. *Campus security:* 24-hour emergency response devices, on-campus security officer. *Student services:* personal/psychological counseling.

Athletics Member NJCAA. *Intercollegiate sports:* baseball M, basketball M(s)/W(s), golf M/W, softball W, tennis M/W, volleyball W(s), wrestling M. *Intramural sports:* basketball M/W, skiing (downhill) M(c)/W(c).

Costs (2010–11) *Tuition:* $72 per credit hour part-time; state resident $119 per credit hour part-time; nonresident $162 per credit hour part-time. *Payment plan:* deferred payment.

Financial Aid Of all full-time matriculated undergraduates who enrolled in 2008, 250 Federal Work-Study jobs (averaging $2500). 50 state and other part-time jobs (averaging $2500).

Applying *Options:* electronic application, early admission, deferred entrance. *Required:* high school transcript. *Application deadlines:* rolling (freshmen), rolling (transfers). *Notification:* continuous (freshmen), continuous (transfers).

Freshman Application Contact Ms. Darlene Peklar, Enrollment Generalist, Muskegon Community College, 221 South Quarterline Road, Muskegon, MI 49442-1493. *Phone:* 231-773-9131 Ext. 366.

North Central Michigan College

Petoskey, Michigan **www.ncmich.edu/**

Director of Admissions Ms. Julieanne Tobin, Director of Enrollment Management, North Central Michigan College, 1515 Howard Street, Petoskey, MI 49770-8717. *Phone:* 231-439-6511. *Toll-free phone:* 888-298-6605. *E-mail:* jtobin@ncmich.edu.

Northwestern Michigan College

Traverse City, Michigan **www.nmc.edu/**

Freshman Application Contact Mr. James Bensley, Coordinator of Admissions, Northwestern Michigan College, 1701 East Front Street, Traverse City, MI 49686. *Phone:* 231-995-1034. *Toll-free phone:* 800-748-0566. *Fax:* 616-955-1339. *E-mail:* welcome@nmc.edu.

Oakland Community College

Bloomfield Hills, Michigan **www.oaklandcc.edu/**

- **State and locally supported** 2-year, founded 1964
- **Suburban** 540-acre campus with easy access to Detroit
- **Endowment** $809,825
- **Coed,** 28,042 undergraduate students, 36% full-time, 57% women, 43% men

Undergraduates 10,032 full-time, 18,010 part-time. Students come from 11 states and territories, 66 other countries, 0.1% are from out of state, 19% African American, 2% Asian American or Pacific Islander, 2% Hispanic American, 0.5% Native American, 7% international. *Retention:* 57% of 2008 full-time freshmen returned.

Freshmen *Admission:* 7,904 applied, 7,904 admitted, 4,649 enrolled.

Faculty *Total:* 1,058, 23% full-time. *Student/faculty ratio:* 27:1.

Majors Accounting and business/management; accounting technology and bookkeeping; architectural engineering technology; business administration and management; business automation/technology/data entry; carpentry; ceramic arts and ceramics; child-care and support services management; community health services counseling; computer and information sciences and support services related; computer and information systems security; computer hardware technology; computer/information technology services administration related; computer programming; computer systems analysis; computer technology/computer systems technology; construction management; corrections; cosmetology; court reporting; criminalistics and criminal science; criminal justice/police science; culinary arts; data processing and data processing technology; dental hygiene; diagnostic medical sonography and ultrasound technology; drafting and design technology; dramatic/theater arts; electrical, electronic and communications engineering technology; electrician; electromechanical technology; emergency medical technology (EMT paramedic); engineering; entrepreneurship; fire science; general studies; graphic design; health/health-care administration; health professions related; heating, air conditioning and refrigeration technology; histologic technology/histotechnologist; hotel/motel administration; industrial technology; information technology; interior design; international business/trade/commerce; kinesiology and exercise science; landscape architecture; landscaping and groundskeeping; legal assistant/paralegal; liberal arts and sciences/liberal studies; library assistant; machine tool technology; manufacturing technology; massage therapy; mechanical drafting and CAD/CADD; mechanics and repair; medical/clinical assistant; medical radiologic technology; medical transcription; medium/heavy vehicle and truck technology; music performance; music theory and composition; nuclear medical technology; nursing (registered nurse training); occupational therapist assistant; pharmacy technician; photographic and film/video technology; photography; pipefitting and sprinkler fitting; precision metal working related; radio and television broadcasting technology; respiratory care therapy; restaurant/food services management; robotics technology; salon/beauty salon management; sheet metal technology; sign language interpretation and translation; surgical technology; tool and die technology; veterinary/animal health technology; voice and opera; welding technology; woodworking related.

Academics *Calendar:* semesters. *Degree:* certificates and associate. *Special study options:* academic remediation for entering students, adult/continuing education programs, advanced placement credit, cooperative education, distance learning, English as a second language, internships, off-campus study, part-time degree program, services for LD students, study abroad, summer session for credit.

Library Main Library plus 5 others with 276,969 titles, 2,054 serial subscriptions, 12,793 audiovisual materials, an OPAC, a Web page.

Student Life *Housing:* college housing not available. *Activities and Organizations:* drama/theater group, choral group, Phi Theta Kappa, International Student Organization, organizations related to student majors, Gamers, student government. *Campus security:* 24-hour emergency response devices, late-night transport/escort service. *Student services:* personal/psychological counseling, women's center.

Athletics Member NJCAA. *Intercollegiate sports:* basketball M(s)/W(s), cross-country running M(s)/W(s), golf M(s), soccer M(c), softball W(s), tennis W(s), track and field M(s)(c)/W(s)(c), volleyball W(s).

Costs (2010–11) *Tuition:* area resident $1803 full-time, $60 per credit hour part-time; state resident $3051 full-time, $102 per credit hour part-time; nonresident $4281 full-time, $143 per credit hour part-time. Full-time tuition and fees vary according to course load. Part-time tuition and fees vary according to course load. *Required fees:* $70 full-time, $35 per term part-time. *Waivers:* senior citizens and employees or children of employees.

Financial Aid Of all full-time matriculated undergraduates who enrolled in 2008, 135 Federal Work-Study jobs (averaging $2800). 70 state and other part-time jobs (averaging $2800).

Applying *Options:* deferred entrance. *Recommended:* high school transcript, interview. *Application deadlines:* rolling (freshmen), rolling (transfers). *Notification:* continuous (freshmen), continuous (transfers).

Freshman Application Contact Dr. Maurice McCall, Registrar and Director of Enrollment Services, Oakland Community College, METC Building, 2900 Featherstone Road, Auburn Hills, MI 48304-2845. *Phone:* 248-341-2186. *Fax:* 248-341-2099. *E-mail:* mhmccall@oaklandcc.edu.

Saginaw Chippewa Tribal College

Mount Pleasant, Michigan **www.sagchip.org/tribalcollege/**

Freshman Application Contact Ms. Tracy Reed, Admissions Officer/Registrar/Financial Aid, Saginaw Chippewa Tribal College, 2274 Enterprise Drive, Mount Pleasant, MI 48858. *Phone:* 989-775-4123. *Fax:* 989-775-4528. *E-mail:* treed@sagchip.org.

St. Clair County Community College

Port Huron, Michigan **www.sc4.edu/**

Director of Admissions Mr. Pete Lacey, Director of Admissions and Records, St. Clair County Community College, 323 Erie Street, PO Box 5015, PO Box 5015, Port Huron, MI 48061-5015. *Phone:* 810-989-5552. *Toll-free phone:* 800-553-2427.

Schoolcraft College

Livonia, Michigan **www.schoolcraft.edu/**

Freshman Application Contact Ms. Cheryl Hagen, Dean of Student Services, Schoolcraft College, 18600 Hagerty Road, Livonia, MI 48152-2696. *Phone:* 734-462-4426. *Fax:* 734-462-4553. *E-mail:* admissions@schoolcraft.edu.

Southwestern Michigan College

Dowagiac, Michigan **www.swmich.edu/**

- **State and locally supported** 2-year, founded 1964
- **Rural** 240-acre campus
- **Coed,** 2,970 undergraduate students, 49% full-time, 62% women, 38% men

Undergraduates 1,458 full-time, 1,512 part-time. Students come from 3 states and territories, 18 other countries, 7% are from out of state, 8% African American, 0.8% Asian American or Pacific Islander, 3% Hispanic American, 1% Native American, 2% international, 41% transferred in, 5% live on campus. *Retention:* 62% of 2008 full-time freshmen returned.

Freshmen *Admission:* 659 applied, 659 admitted, 659 enrolled.

Faculty *Total:* 154, 34% full-time, 12% with terminal degrees. *Student/faculty ratio:* 23:1.

Majors Accounting technology and bookkeeping; automobile/automotive mechanics technology; business administration and management; computer programming; computer systems networking and telecommunications; drafting and design technology; early childhood education; electrical, electronic and

Southwestern Michigan College (continued)

communications engineering technology; emergency medical technology (EMT paramedic); executive assistant/executive secretary; graphic and printing equipment operation/production; health information/medical records technology; industrial mechanics and maintenance technology; industrial production technologies related; liberal arts and sciences/liberal studies; medical/clinical assistant; nursing (registered nurse training); precision systems maintenance and repair technologies related; social work; teacher assistant/aide.

Academics *Calendar:* semesters. *Degree:* certificates and associate. *Special study options:* academic remediation for entering students, accelerated degree program, adult/continuing education programs, advanced placement credit, cooperative education, distance learning, double majors, English as a second language, independent study, internships, part-time degree program, services for LD students, student-designed majors, summer session for credit.

Library Fred L. Mathews Library plus 1 other with 36,149 titles, 6,174 serial subscriptions, 2,171 audiovisual materials, an OPAC, a Web page.

Student Life *Housing Options:* coed. Campus housing is university owned. *Activities and Organizations:* drama/theater group, choral group, Phi Theta Kappa, Business Professionals of America, Chi Alpha, Dionysis Drama Club, Green Club. *Campus security:* 24-hour emergency response devices, controlled dormitory access, day and evening police patrols.

Athletics *Intramural sports:* basketball M/W, football M/W, golf M/W, racquetball M/W, rock climbing M/W, soccer M/W, volleyball M/W, wrestling M.

Costs (2009–10) *Tuition:* area resident $2648 full-time, $88 per credit hour part-time; state resident $3383 full-time, $113 per credit hour part-time; nonresident $3668 full-time, $122 per credit hour part-time. *Required fees:* $810 full-time, $27 per credit hour part-time. *Room and board:* $7160; room only: $5000. *Payment plan:* installment. *Waivers:* employees or children of employees.

Financial Aid Of all full-time matriculated undergraduates who enrolled in 2008, 125 Federal Work-Study jobs (averaging $1000). 75 state and other part-time jobs (averaging $1000).

Applying *Options:* electronic application, deferred entrance. *Required:* high school transcript. *Required for some:* interview. *Application deadlines:* rolling (freshmen), rolling (transfers). *Notification:* continuous until 9/10 (freshmen), continuous until 9/10 (transfers).

Freshman Application Contact Dr. Margaret Hay, Dean of Students and Academic Support, Southwestern Michigan College, 58900 Cherry Grove Road, Dowagiac, MI 49047. *Phone:* 269-782-1000 Ext. 1306. *Toll-free phone:* 800-456-8675. *Fax:* 269-782-1331. *E-mail:* mhay@swmich.edu.

WASHTENAW COMMUNITY COLLEGE

Ann Arbor, Michigan **www.wccnet.edu/**

Freshman Application Contact Washtenaw Community College, 4800 East Huron River Drive, PO Box D-1, Ann Arbor, MI 48106. *Phone:* 734-973-3315.

WAYNE COUNTY COMMUNITY COLLEGE DISTRICT

Detroit, Michigan **www.wcccd.edu/**

Freshman Application Contact Office of Enrollment Management and Student Services, Wayne County Community College District, 801 West Fort Street, Detroit, MI 48226-2539. *Phone:* 313-496-2634. *E-mail:* caafjh@wccc.edu.

WEST SHORE COMMUNITY COLLEGE

Scottville, Michigan **www.westshore.edu/**

- **District-supported** 2-year, founded 1967, part of Michigan Department of Education
- **Rural** 375-acre campus
- **Coed,** 1,553 undergraduate students, 42% full-time, 62% women, 38% men

Undergraduates 658 full-time, 895 part-time. Students come from 1 other state, 1% African American, 0.7% Asian American or Pacific Islander, 4% Hispanic American, 2% Native American, 3% transferred in.

Freshmen *Admission:* 245 applied, 245 admitted, 245 enrolled.

Faculty *Total:* 100, 28% full-time.

Majors Accounting; corrections; criminal justice/police science; data entry/microcomputer applications related; data processing and data processing technology; electrical, electronic and communications engineering technology; emergency medical technology (EMT paramedic); information technology; liberal arts and sciences/liberal studies; machine tool technology; marketing/marketing management; nursing (licensed practical/vocational nurse training); nursing (registered nurse training); welding technology.

Academics *Calendar:* semesters. *Degree:* certificates and associate. *Special study options:* academic remediation for entering students, adult/continuing education programs, advanced placement credit, cooperative education, distance learning, independent study, internships, off-campus study, part-time degree program, services for LD students, student-designed majors, summer session for credit.

Library West Shore Library plus 1 other with 2,500 titles, 150 serial subscriptions, 1,100 audiovisual materials, an OPAC, a Web page.

Student Life *Housing:* college housing not available. *Activities and Organizations:* drama/theater group, student-run newspaper, choral group, Art Club, Student Senate, Phi Theta Kappa, Science Club, Law Enforcement Club. *Campus security:* 24-hour emergency response devices and patrols. *Student services:* personal/psychological counseling.

Athletics *Intramural sports:* basketball M/W, football M/W, racquetball M/W, softball M/W, swimming and diving M/W, table tennis M/W, volleyball M/W, weight lifting M/W.

Financial Aid Of all full-time matriculated undergraduates who enrolled in 2008, 80 Federal Work-Study jobs (averaging $3000). 40 state and other part-time jobs (averaging $3000).

Applying *Options:* early admission, deferred entrance. *Application fee:* $15. *Required:* high school transcript. *Application deadlines:* rolling (freshmen), rolling (transfers). *Notification:* continuous (freshmen), continuous (transfers).

Freshman Application Contact Wendy Fought, Director of Admissions, West Shore Community College, PO Box 277, 3000 North Stiles Road, Scottville, MI 49454-0277. *Phone:* 231-843-5503. *Fax:* 231-845-3944. *E-mail:* admissions@westshore.edu.

MICRONESIA

COLLEGE OF MICRONESIA–FSM

Kolonia Pohnpei, Federated States of Micronesia, Micronesia **www.comfsm.fm/**

Director of Admissions Mr. Wilson J. Kalio, Coordinator of Admissions and Records, College of Micronesia–FSM, PO Box 159, Kolonia Pohnpei, FM 96941-0159, Micronesia. *Phone:* 691-320-2480 Ext. 6200.

MINNESOTA

ALEXANDRIA TECHNICAL COLLEGE

Alexandria, Minnesota **www.alextech.edu/**

- **State-supported** 2-year, founded 1961, part of Minnesota State Colleges and Universities System
- **Small-town** 106-acre campus
- **Coed,** 2,205 undergraduate students, 71% full-time, 47% women, 53% men

Undergraduates 1,562 full-time, 643 part-time. Students come from 19 states and territories, 4% are from out of state, 0.8% African American, 0.8% Asian American or Pacific Islander, 0.7% Hispanic American, 0.8% Native American.

Freshmen *Admission:* 1,941 applied, 1,308 admitted.

Faculty *Total:* 103, 70% full-time. *Student/faculty ratio:* 20:1.

Majors Accounting; administrative assistant and secretarial science; banking and financial support services; business administration and management; carpentry; cartography; child-care and support services management; child-care provision; clinical/medical laboratory technology; commercial and advertising art; computer and information sciences; computer and information systems security; computer programming; computer systems networking and telecommunications; computer technology/computer systems technology; criminal justice/police science; customer service management; diesel mechanics technology; energy management and systems technology; farm and ranch management; fashion merchandising; general studies; health and physical education; hospitality administration; human resources development; human services; hydraulics and fluid power technology; industrial mechanics and maintenance technology; industrial technology; interior design; legal administrative assistant/secretary; legal assistant/paralegal; machine tool technology; manufacturing technology; marine maintenance and ship repair technology; marketing/marketing management; masonry; mechanical drafting and CAD/CADD; medical administrative assistant and medical secretary; medical insurance coding; medical reception; medical transcription; nursing assistant/aide and patient care assistant; nursing (licensed practical/vocational nurse training); nursing (registered nurse training); office management; office occupations and clerical services; operations management; phlebotomy; receptionist; selling skills and sales; small engine mechanics and repair technology; truck and bus driver/commercial vehicle operation; web page, digital/multimedia and information resources design; welding technology.

Academics *Calendar:* semesters. *Degree:* certificates, diplomas, and associate. *Special study options:* academic remediation for entering students, advanced placement credit, distance learning, double majors, independent study, internships, part-time degree program, services for LD students, student-designed majors, summer session for credit.

Library Learning Resource Center with 13,378 titles, 110 serial subscriptions, 1,655 audiovisual materials, an OPAC, a Web page.

Student Life *Housing:* college housing not available. *Activities and Organizations:* Skills USA, Business Professionals of America, Delta Epsilon Chi, Student Senate, Phi Theta Kappa. *Campus security:* student patrols, late-night transport/escort service, security cameras inside and outside. *Student services:* personal/psychological counseling.

Athletics *Intramural sports:* basketball M/W, football M/W, golf M/W, ice hockey M, skiing (downhill) M/W, softball M/W, volleyball M/W.

Costs (2009–10) *Tuition:* state resident $5278 full-time, $139 per credit part-time; nonresident $5278 full-time, $139 per credit part-time. *Required fees:* $563 full-time, $17 per credit hour part-time. *Payment plan:* installment. *Waivers:* senior citizens and employees or children of employees.

Financial Aid Of all full-time matriculated undergraduates who enrolled in 2008, 94 Federal Work-Study jobs (averaging $1871).

Applying *Options:* electronic application, early admission, deferred entrance. *Application fee:* $20. *Required:* high school transcript, interview. *Required for some:* contact admissions for more information. *Application deadlines:* rolling (freshmen), rolling (out-of-state freshmen), rolling (transfers). *Notification:* continuous (freshmen), continuous (out-of-state freshmen), continuous (transfers).

Freshman Application Contact Janet Dropik, Admissions Receptionist, Alexandria Technical College, 1601 Jefferson Street, Alexandria, MN 56308. *Phone:* 320-762-4520. *Toll-free phone:* 888-234-1222. *Fax:* 320-762-4603. *E-mail:* admissionsrep@alextech.edu.

Anoka-Ramsey Community College

Coon Rapids, Minnesota **www.anokaramsey.edu/**

- **State-supported** 2-year, founded 1965, part of Minnesota State Colleges and Universities System
- **Suburban** 100-acre campus with easy access to Minneapolis-St. Paul
- **Coed,** 7,530 undergraduate students

Undergraduates 2% are from out of state, 8% African American, 4% Asian American or Pacific Islander, 2% Hispanic American, 1% Native American, 0.2% international. *Retention:* 50% of 2008 full-time freshmen returned.

Freshmen *Admission:* 3,314 applied, 3,046 admitted.

Faculty *Total:* 250, 36% full-time. *Student/faculty ratio:* 30:1.

Majors Accounting; accounting technology and bookkeeping; alternative and complementary medical support services related; biology/biological sciences; biology/biotechnology laboratory technician; business administration and management; business/commerce; computer science; computer systems networking and telecommunications; dramatic/theater arts; engineering; environmental science; fine/studio arts; human resources management; liberal arts and sciences/liberal studies; marketing/marketing management; multi/interdisciplinary studies related; music; nursing (registered nurse training); physical therapist assistant; public health education and promotion.

Academics *Calendar:* semesters. *Degree:* certificates and associate. *Special study options:* academic remediation for entering students, accelerated degree program, advanced placement credit, cooperative education, distance learning, honors programs, independent study, internships, off-campus study, part-time degree program, services for LD students, study abroad, summer session for credit. *ROTC:* Air Force (c).

Library Coon Rapids Campus Library with 41,522 titles, 202 serial subscriptions, 1,517 audiovisual materials, an OPAC, a Web page.

Student Life *Housing:* college housing not available. *Activities and Organizations:* drama/theater group, student-run newspaper, choral group, student government, Phi Theta Kappa, Multicultural Club, CRU (Campus Christian group), Salmagundi (student newspaper). *Campus security:* 24-hour emergency response devices, late-night transport/escort service. *Student services:* personal/psychological counseling.

Athletics Member NJCAA. *Intercollegiate sports:* baseball M, basketball M/W, soccer M/W, softball W, volleyball W. *Intramural sports:* basketball M/W, bowling M/W, football M/W, golf M/W, ice hockey M/W, soccer M/W, softball M/W, tennis M/W, volleyball M/W.

Costs (2009–10) *Tuition:* state resident $3704 full-time, $123 per credit part-time; nonresident $3704 full-time, $123 per credit part-time. Full-time tuition and fees vary according to course load and program. Part-time tuition and fees vary according to course load and program. *Required fees:* $504 full-time, $17 per credit part-time. *Payment plans:* installment, deferred payment. *Waivers:* senior citizens and employees or children of employees.

Financial Aid Of all full-time matriculated undergraduates who enrolled in 2008, 111 Federal Work-Study jobs (averaging $4000). 151 state and other part-time jobs (averaging $4000).

Applying *Options:* electronic application, early admission, deferred entrance. *Application fee:* $20. *Required for some:* high school transcript. *Application deadlines:* rolling (freshmen), rolling (out-of-state freshmen), rolling (transfers). *Notification:* continuous (freshmen), continuous (out-of-state freshmen), continuous (transfers).

Freshman Application Contact Admissions Department, Anoka-Ramsey Community College, 11200 Mississippi Boulevard NW, Coon Rapids, MN 55433. *Phone:* 763-433-1300. *Fax:* 763-433-1521. *E-mail:* admissions@anokaramsey.edu.

Anoka-Ramsey Community College, Cambridge Campus

Cambridge, Minnesota **www.anokaramsey.edu/**

- **State-supported** 2-year, founded 1965, part of Minnesota State Colleges and Universities System
- **Small-town** campus
- **Coed,** 2,636 undergraduate students, 44% full-time, 66% women, 34% men

Undergraduates 1,150 full-time, 1,486 part-time. 2% are from out of state, 2% African American, 0.9% Asian American or Pacific Islander, 1% Hispanic American, 1% Native American, 0.2% international. *Retention:* 59% of 2008 full-time freshmen returned.

Freshmen *Admission:* 741 applied, 679 admitted.

Faculty *Total:* 59, 44% full-time. *Student/faculty ratio:* 31:1.

Majors Accounting; accounting technology and bookkeeping; alternative and complementary medical support services related; biology/biological sciences; biology/biotechnology laboratory technician; business administration and management; business/commerce; computer science; computer systems networking and telecommunications; dramatic/theater arts; engineering; environmental science; fine/studio arts; human resources management; liberal arts and sciences/liberal studies; marketing/marketing management; multi/interdisciplinary studies related; music; nursing (registered nurse training); public health education and promotion.

Academics *Calendar:* semesters. *Degree:* certificates and associate. *Special study options:* academic remediation for entering students, accelerated degree program, advanced placement credit, cooperative education, distance learning, honors programs, independent study, internships, off-campus study, part-time degree program, services for LD students, study abroad, summer session for credit. *ROTC:* Air Force (c).

Library Cambridge Campus Library with 15,739 titles, 99 serial subscriptions, 1,561 audiovisual materials, an OPAC, a Web page.

Student Life *Housing:* college housing not available. *Activities and Organizations:* drama/theater group, student-run newspaper, choral group. *Campus security:* 24-hour emergency response devices, late-night transport/escort service. *Student services:* personal/psychological counseling.

Athletics Member NJCAA. *Intercollegiate sports:* baseball M, basketball M/W, soccer M/W, softball W, volleyball W. *Intramural sports:* bowling M/W, golf M/W, volleyball M/W.

Costs (2009–10) *Tuition:* state resident $3704 full-time, $123 per credit part-time; nonresident $3704 full-time, $123 per credit part-time. Full-time tuition and fees vary according to course load and program. Part-time tuition and fees vary according to course load and program. *Required fees:* $504 full-time, $17 per credit part-time. *Payment plans:* installment, deferred payment. *Waivers:* senior citizens and employees or children of employees.

Applying *Options:* electronic application, early admission, deferred entrance. *Application fee:* $20. *Required for some:* high school transcript. *Application deadlines:* rolling (freshmen), rolling (out-of-state freshmen), rolling (transfers). *Notification:* continuous (freshmen), continuous (out-of-state freshmen), continuous (transfers).

Anoka-Ramsey Community College, Cambridge Campus (continued)

Freshman Application Contact Admissions Department, Anoka-Ramsey Community College, Cambridge Campus, 300 Polk Street South, Cambridge, MN 55008. *Phone:* 763-433-1300. *Fax:* 763-433-1841. *E-mail:* admissions@anokaramsey.edu.

ANOKA TECHNICAL COLLEGE

Anoka, Minnesota **www.anokatech.edu/**

- **State-supported** 2-year, founded 1967, part of Minnesota State Colleges and Universities System
- **Small-town** campus with easy access to Minneapolis-St. Paul
- **Coed**

Academics *Calendar:* semesters. *Degree:* certificates, diplomas, and associate. *Special study options:* academic remediation for entering students, advanced placement credit, cooperative education, distance learning, double majors, English as a second language, internships, part-time degree program, services for LD students.

Student Life *Campus security:* late-night transport/escort service.

Applying *Options:* electronic application, deferred entrance. *Application fee:* $20. *Required:* high school transcript. *Required for some:* interview.

Director of Admissions Mr. Robert Hoenie, Director of Admissions, Anoka Technical College, 1355 West Highway 10, Anoka, MN 55303. *Phone:* 763-576-4746. *E-mail:* info@anokatech.edu.

ARGOSY UNIVERSITY, TWIN CITIES

Eagan, Minnesota **www.argosy.edu/twincities**

- **Proprietary** university, founded 1961, part of Education Management Corporation
- **Suburban** campus
- **Coed**

Majors Accounting; business administration and management; clinical/medical laboratory technology; criminal justice/law enforcement administration; dental hygiene; diagnostic medical sonography and ultrasound technology; electrocardiograph technology; finance; health/health-care administration; histologic technology/histotechnologist; human resources management; international business/trade/commerce; liberal arts and sciences/liberal studies; marketing/marketing management; medical/clinical assistant; medical radiologic technology; organizational behavior; psychology; radiologic technology/science; substance abuse/addiction counseling; veterinary/animal health technology.

Academics *Calendar:* semesters. *Degrees:* associate, bachelor's, master's, and post-master's certificates.

Costs (2009–10) *Tuition:* Tuition varies by program. Students should contact Argosy University for tuition information.

Freshman Application Contact Argosy University, Twin Cities, 1515 Central Parkway, Eagan, MN 55121. *Phone:* 651-846-2882. *Toll-free phone:* 888-844-2004.

▸**See page 396 for the College Close-Up.**

BROWN COLLEGE

Mendota Heights, Minnesota **www.browncollege.edu/**

Freshman Application Contact Mr. Mark Fredrichs, Registrar, Brown College, 1440 Northland Drive, Mendota Heights, MN 55120. *Phone:* 651-905-3400. *Toll-free phone:* 800-6BROWN6. *Fax:* 651-905-3550.

CENTRAL LAKES COLLEGE

Brainerd, Minnesota **www.clcmn.edu/**

- **State-supported** 2-year, founded 1938, part of Minnesota State Colleges and Universities System
- **Small-town** campus
- **Endowment** $3.4 million
- **Coed,** 4,010 undergraduate students, 58% full-time, 57% women, 43% men

Undergraduates 2,313 full-time, 1,697 part-time. Students come from 11 states and territories, 0.3% are from out of state, 1% African American, 0.8% Asian American or Pacific Islander, 0.6% Hispanic American, 2% Native American.

Faculty *Total:* 149, 58% full-time. *Student/faculty ratio:* 17:1.

Majors Accounting; administrative assistant and secretarial science; applied horticulture; business administration and management; child-care and support services management; commercial and advertising art; computer systems networking and telecommunications; computer technology/computer systems technology; conservation biology; criminalistics and criminal science; criminal justice/police science; criminal justice/safety; developmental and child psychology; diesel mechanics technology; engineering; horticultural science; industrial electronics technology; industrial engineering; kindergarten/preschool education; legal administrative assistant/secretary; liberal arts and sciences/liberal studies; machine tool technology; marketing/marketing management; mechanical drafting and CAD/CADD; medical administrative assistant and medical secretary; natural resources/conservation; nursing (registered nurse training); photographic and film/video technology; robotics technology; welding technology.

Academics *Calendar:* semesters. *Degree:* certificates, diplomas, and associate. *Special study options:* academic remediation for entering students, advanced placement credit, distance learning, English as a second language, external degree program, independent study, internships, off-campus study, part-time degree program, services for LD students, summer session for credit.

Library Learning Resource Center with 16,052 titles, 286 serial subscriptions, an OPAC, a Web page.

Student Life *Housing:* college housing not available. *Activities and Organizations:* drama/theater group, student-run newspaper, choral group. *Campus security:* 24-hour emergency response devices, student patrols, late-night transport/escort service.

Athletics Member NJCAA. *Intercollegiate sports:* baseball M, basketball M/W, football M, golf M/W, softball W, volleyball W. *Intramural sports:* basketball M/W, bowling M/W, football M, golf M/W, softball M/W, tennis M/W, volleyball M/W.

Costs (2009–10) *Tuition:* state resident $4382 full-time, $137 per credit part-time; nonresident $4382 full-time, $137 per credit part-time. Full-time tuition and fees vary according to course load and program. Part-time tuition and fees vary according to course load and program. *Required fees:* $637 full-time, $20 per credit part-time. *Payment plan:* installment. *Waivers:* senior citizens and employees or children of employees.

Applying *Options:* electronic application, deferred entrance. *Application fee:* $20. *Required:* high school transcript. *Application deadlines:* rolling (freshmen), rolling (transfers).

Freshman Application Contact Ms. Rose Tretter, Central Lakes College, 501 West College Drive, Brainerd, MN 56401-3904. *Phone:* 218-855-8036. *Toll-free phone:* 800-933-0346 Ext. 2586. *Fax:* 218-855-8220. *E-mail:* cdaniels@clcmn.edu.

CENTURY COLLEGE

White Bear Lake, Minnesota **www.century.edu/**

- **State-supported** 2-year, founded 1970, part of Minnesota State Colleges and Universities System
- **Suburban** 150-acre campus with easy access to Minneapolis-St. Paul
- **Coed,** 10,469 undergraduate students, 47% full-time, 55% women, 45% men

Undergraduates 4,937 full-time, 5,532 part-time. Students come from 41 states and territories, 52 other countries, 7% are from out of state, 11% African American, 14% Asian American or Pacific Islander, 3% Hispanic American, 1% Native American, 1% international, 35% transferred in.

Freshmen *Admission:* 3,730 applied, 3,730 admitted, 1,979 enrolled.

Faculty *Total:* 366, 50% full-time. *Student/faculty ratio:* 28:1.

Majors Accounting; accounting technology and bookkeeping; administrative assistant and secretarial science; autobody/collision and repair technology; automobile/automotive mechanics technology; building/property maintenance and management; business administration and management; CAD/CADD drafting/design technology; computer and information sciences; computer and information systems security; computer science; computer systems networking and telecommunications; computer technology/computer systems technology; cosmetology; criminalistics and criminal science; criminal justice/police science; criminal justice/safety; dental assisting; dental hygiene; digital communication and media/multimedia; education (multiple levels); emergency medical technology (EMT paramedic); energy management and systems technology; engineering; greenhouse management; heating, air conditioning, ventilation and refrigeration maintenance technology; horticultural science; human services; interior design; international/global studies; landscaping and groundskeeping; language interpretation and translation; liberal arts and sciences/liberal studies; marketing/

marketing management; medical administrative assistant and medical secretary; medical/clinical assistant; music; nail technician and manicurist; nursing assistant/aide and patient care assistant; nursing (registered nurse training); office occupations and clerical services; orthotics/prosthetics; radiologic technology/science; security and protective services related; solar energy technology; sport and fitness administration/management; substance abuse/addiction counseling; system administration; teacher assistant/aide; women's studies.

Academics *Calendar:* semesters. *Degree:* certificates, diplomas, and associate. *Special study options:* academic remediation for entering students, adult/continuing education programs, advanced placement credit, distance learning, double majors, English as a second language, honors programs, internships, part-time degree program, services for LD students, study abroad, summer session for credit. *ROTC:* Air Force (c).

Library Century College Library with 67,214 titles, 338 serial subscriptions, 5,221 audiovisual materials, an OPAC, a Web page.

Student Life *Housing:* college housing not available. *Activities and Organizations:* drama/theater group, student-run newspaper, choral group, Student Senate, Planning Activities Committee, Asian Student Association, Phi Theta Kappa, Intramurals. *Campus security:* late-night transport/escort service, day patrols. *Student services:* personal/psychological counseling.

Athletics Member NJCAA. *Intercollegiate sports:* golf M/W, soccer M/W. *Intramural sports:* badminton M/W, basketball M/W, golf M/W, soccer M/W, softball M/W, volleyball M/W.

Costs (2009–10) *Tuition:* state resident $4162 full-time, $139 per credit hour part-time; nonresident $4162 full-time, $139 per credit hour part-time. Full-time tuition and fees vary according to program. Part-time tuition and fees vary according to program. *Required fees:* $527 full-time, $18 per credit hour part-time. *Payment plan:* installment. *Waivers:* senior citizens and employees or children of employees.

Financial Aid Of all full-time matriculated undergraduates who enrolled in 2008, 81 Federal Work-Study jobs (averaging $2763). 85 state and other part-time jobs (averaging $2646).

Applying *Options:* electronic application, deferred entrance. *Application fee:* $20. *Required:* high school transcript. *Application deadlines:* rolling (freshmen), rolling (transfers).

Freshman Application Contact Ms. Christine Paulos, Admissions Director, Century College, 3300 Century Avenue North, White Bear Lake, MN 55110. *Phone:* 651-779-2619. *Toll-free phone:* 800-228-1978. *Fax:* 651-773-1796. *E-mail:* admissions@century.edu.

DAKOTA COUNTY TECHNICAL COLLEGE

Rosemount, Minnesota **www.dctc.edu/**

- **State-supported** 2-year, founded 1970, part of Minnesota State Colleges and Universities System
- **Suburban** 100-acre campus with easy access to Minneapolis-St. Paul
- **Coed**

Academics *Calendar:* semesters. *Degree:* certificates, diplomas, and associate. *Special study options:* academic remediation for entering students, cooperative education, distance learning, double majors, English as a second language, independent study, internships, part-time degree program, services for LD students, summer session for credit.

Student Life *Campus security:* 24-hour emergency response devices, late-night transport/escort service.

Athletics Member NJCAA.

Costs (2009–10) *Tuition:* state resident $5084 full-time, $149 per credit part-time; nonresident $8920 full-time, $297 per credit part-time. Full-time tuition and fees vary according to program and reciprocity agreements. Part-time tuition and fees vary according to program and reciprocity agreements. *Required fees:* $624 full-time, $21 per credit part-time. *Payment plans:* installment, deferred payment.

Financial Aid Of all full-time matriculated undergraduates who enrolled in 2008, 49 Federal Work-Study jobs (averaging $1680). 125 state and other part-time jobs (averaging $1731).

Applying *Options:* electronic application. *Application fee:* $20. *Required for some:* high school transcript. *Recommended:* interview.

Freshman Application Contact Mr. Patrick Lair, Admissions Director, Dakota County Technical College, 1300 145th Street East, Rosemount, MN 55068. *Phone:* 651-423-8399. *Toll-free phone:* 877-YES-DCTC Ext. 302 (in-state); 877-YES-DCTC (out-of-state). *Fax:* 651-423-8775. *E-mail:* admissions@dctc.mnscu.edu.

DULUTH BUSINESS UNIVERSITY

Duluth, Minnesota **www.dbumn.edu/**

- **Proprietary** 2-year, founded 1891
- **Urban** campus
- **Coed, primarily women**

Academics *Calendar:* quarters. *Degree:* diplomas and associate.

Applying *Application fee:* $35.

Freshman Application Contact Mr. Mark Traux, Director of Admissions, Duluth Business University, 4724 Mike Colalillo Drive, Duluth, MN 55807. *Phone:* 218-722-4000. *Toll-free phone:* 800-777-8406. *Fax:* 218-628-2127. *E-mail:* markt@dbumn.edu.

DUNWOODY COLLEGE OF TECHNOLOGY

Minneapolis, Minnesota **www.dunwoody.edu/**

Freshman Application Contact Shaun Manning, Director of Admissions, Dunwoody College of Technology, 818 Dunwoody Boulevard, Minneapolis, MN 55403. *Phone:* 612-374-5800 Ext. 8110. *Toll-free phone:* 800-292-4625. *E-mail:* smanning@dunwoody.edu.

FOND DU LAC TRIBAL AND COMMUNITY COLLEGE

Cloquet, Minnesota **www.fdltcc.edu/**

Freshman Application Contact Ms. Nancy Gordon, Admissions Representative, Fond du Lac Tribal and Community College, 2101 14th Street, Cloquet, MN 55720. *Phone:* 218-879-0808. *Toll-free phone:* 800-657-3712. *E-mail:* darla@asab.fdl.cc.mn.us.

HENNEPIN TECHNICAL COLLEGE

Brooklyn Park, Minnesota **www.hennepintech.edu/**

- **State-supported** 2-year, founded 1972, part of Minnesota State Colleges and Universities System
- **Suburban** 100-acre campus with easy access to Minneapolis-St. Paul
- **Coed,** 13,832 undergraduate students

Freshmen *Admission:* 7,690 applied, 7,690 admitted.

Faculty *Total:* 172. *Student/faculty ratio:* 25:1.

Majors Architectural drafting and CAD/CADD; automobile/automotive mechanics technology; carpentry; child development; computer programming; computer systems networking and telecommunications; dental assisting; desktop publishing and digital imaging design; drafting/design engineering technologies related; electrical, electronic and communications engineering technology; fire science; hydraulics and fluid power technology; legal administrative assistant/secretary; machine tool technology; medical administrative assistant and medical secretary; photography; plastics engineering technology; publishing.

Academics *Calendar:* semesters. *Degree:* certificates, diplomas, and associate. *Special study options:* academic remediation for entering students, adult/continuing education programs, advanced placement credit, cooperative education, distance learning, double majors, English as a second language, honors programs, independent study, internships, services for LD students, student-designed majors, summer session for credit.

Library Main Library plus 1 other.

Student Life *Housing:* college housing not available. *Activities and Organizations:* Student Senate, Pangea, Images, Skills USA. *Campus security:* late-night transport/escort service, security service. *Student services:* personal/psychological counseling.

Costs (2010–11) *Tuition:* state resident $157 per credit part-time; nonresident $157 per credit part-time. *Payment plan:* installment. *Waivers:* senior citizens.

Financial Aid Of all full-time matriculated undergraduates who enrolled in 2008, 72 Federal Work-Study jobs (averaging $3000).

Applying *Options:* electronic application. *Application fee:* $20. *Recommended:* high school transcript. *Application deadlines:* rolling (freshmen), rolling (transfers). *Notification:* continuous (freshmen), continuous (transfers).

Freshman Application Contact Hennepin Technical College, 9000 Brooklyn Boulevard, Brooklyn Park, MN 55445. *Phone:* 763-488-2415. *Toll-free phone:* 800-345-4655.

Herzing College

Minneapolis, Minnesota **www.herzing.edu/**

Freshman Application Contact Ms. Shelly Larson, Director of Admissions, Herzing College, 5700 West Broadway, Minneapolis, MN 55428. *Phone:* 763-231-3155. *Toll-free phone:* 800-878-DRAW. *Fax:* 763-535-9205. *E-mail:* info@mpls.herzing.edu.

Hibbing Community College

Hibbing, Minnesota **www.hcc.mnscu.edu/**

Freshman Application Contact Ms. Shelly Corradi, Admissions, Hibbing Community College, 1515 East 25th Street, Hibbing, MN 55746. *Phone:* 218-262-7207. *Toll-free phone:* 800-224-4HCC. *Fax:* 218-262-6717. *E-mail:* admissions@hibbing.edu.

High-Tech Institute

St. Louis Park, Minnesota **www.high-techinstitute.com/**

Freshman Application Contact Admissions Office, High-Tech Institute, 5100 Gamble Drive, St. Louis Park, MN 55416. *Toll-free phone:* 888-324-9700.

Inver Hills Community College

Inver Grove Heights, Minnesota **www.inverhills.edu/**

- **State-supported** 2-year, founded 1969, part of Minnesota State Colleges and Universities System
- **Suburban** 100-acre campus with easy access to Minneapolis-St. Paul
- **Coed,** 6,215 undergraduate students, 41% full-time, 60% women, 40% men

Undergraduates 2,541 full-time, 3,674 part-time. Students come from 33 states and territories, 1 other country, 4% are from out of state, 10% African American, 6% Asian American or Pacific Islander, 4% Hispanic American, 0.9% Native American, 0.6% international, 13% transferred in. *Retention:* 59% of 2008 full-time freshmen returned.

Freshmen *Admission:* 3,252 applied, 2,626 admitted, 931 enrolled.

Faculty *Total:* 235, 43% full-time. *Student/faculty ratio:* 24:1.

Majors Accounting; biology/biological sciences; building/construction finishing, management, and inspection related; building/home/construction inspection; business administration and management; computer and information sciences and support services related; computer programming (specific applications); computer programming (vendor/product certification); computer systems networking and telecommunications; criminal justice/police science; criminal justice/safety; education; emergency medical technology (EMT paramedic); fine/studio arts; health/health-care administration; human services; legal administrative assistant/secretary; legal assistant/paralegal; liberal arts and sciences/liberal studies; medical administrative assistant and medical secretary; nursing (registered nurse training); physical education teaching and coaching; system administration.

Academics *Calendar:* semesters. *Degree:* certificates and associate. *Special study options:* academic remediation for entering students, advanced placement credit, cooperative education, English as a second language, external degree program, honors programs, independent study, internships, off-campus study, part-time degree program, services for LD students, summer session for credit.

Library 42,073 titles, 300 serial subscriptions, an OPAC, a Web page.

Student Life *Housing:* college housing not available. *Activities and Organizations:* drama/theater group, choral group, VIBE, Student Senate, Health Service Student Association, Phi Theta Kappa, Nursing Club. *Campus security:* late-night transport/escort service, evening police patrol. *Student services:* health clinic, personal/psychological counseling.

Athletics *Intramural sports:* basketball M/W, football M/W, golf M/W, ice hockey M/W, skiing (cross-country) M/W, soccer M/W, tennis M/W, volleyball M/W, weight lifting M/W.

Costs (2009–10) *Tuition:* state resident $3459 full-time, $144 per credit hour part-time; nonresident $3459 full-time, $144 per credit hour part-time. Full-time tuition and fees vary according to course load, location, program, and reciprocity agreements. Part-time tuition and fees vary according to course load, location, program, and reciprocity agreements. *Required fees:* $390 full-time, $16 per credit part-time. *Payment plan:* installment. *Waivers:* senior citizens and employees or children of employees.

Financial Aid Of all full-time matriculated undergraduates who enrolled in 2009, 3,600 applied for aid, 3,250 were judged to have need. 175 Federal Work-Study jobs (averaging $2300). 153 state and other part-time jobs (averaging $2300). *Average percent of need met:* 48%. *Average financial aid package:* $4300. *Average need-based loan:* $4200. *Average need-based gift aid:* $3800.

Applying *Options:* electronic application. *Application fee:* $20. *Required for some:* high school transcript. *Recommended:* high school transcript. *Application deadline:* rolling (transfers). *Notification:* continuous (freshmen), continuous (transfers).

Freshman Application Contact Mr. Casey Carmody, Admissions Representative, Inver Hills Community College, 2500 East 80th Street, Inver Grove Heights, MN 55076-3224. *Phone:* 651-450-3589. *Fax:* 651-450-3677. *E-mail:* admissions@inverhills.edu.

Itasca Community College

Grand Rapids, Minnesota **www.itascacc.edu/**

- **State-supported** 2-year, founded 1922, part of Minnesota State Colleges and Universities System
- **Rural** 24-acre campus
- **Endowment** $3.9 million
- **Coed,** 1,130 undergraduate students, 78% full-time, 48% women, 52% men

Undergraduates 879 full-time, 251 part-time. Students come from 2 other countries, 4% are from out of state, 2% African American, 0.7% Asian American or Pacific Islander, 0.4% Hispanic American, 4% Native American, 2% international, 10% live on campus. *Retention:* 53% of 2008 full-time freshmen returned.

Freshmen *Admission:* 602 applied, 602 admitted.

Faculty *Total:* 77, 56% full-time, 1% with terminal degrees. *Student/faculty ratio:* 15:1.

Majors Accounting; American Indian/Native American studies; business administration and management; chemical engineering; civil engineering; computer engineering; computer engineering related; education; education (multiple levels); engineering; engineering related; engineering science; engineering technology; environmental studies; fishing and fisheries sciences and management; forestry; forestry technology; general studies; geography; human services; liberal arts and sciences/liberal studies; mechanical engineering; natural resources/conservation; natural resources management and policy; nuclear engineering; nursing (licensed practical/vocational nurse training); pre-engineering; psychology; special education (early childhood); wildlife and wildlands science and management.

Academics *Calendar:* semesters. *Degree:* certificates, diplomas, and associate. *Special study options:* academic remediation for entering students, adult/continuing education programs, advanced placement credit, cooperative education, double majors, independent study, internships, off-campus study, part-time degree program, services for LD students, study abroad, summer session for credit.

Library Itasca Community College Library with 28,790 titles, 280 serial subscriptions, an OPAC, a Web page.

Student Life *Housing Options:* coed. Campus housing is university owned. *Activities and Organizations:* Student Association, Circle K, Student Ambassadors, Minority Student Club, Psychology Club. *Campus security:* student patrols, late-night transport/escort service, controlled dormitory access, evening patrols by trained security personnel. *Student services:* personal/psychological counseling.

Athletics Member NJCAA. *Intercollegiate sports:* baseball M, basketball M/W, football M, softball W, volleyball W, wrestling M. *Intramural sports:* basketball M, bowling M/W, softball M/W, table tennis M/W, volleyball M/W.

Costs (2010–11) *Tuition:* state resident $4282 full-time, $143 per credit part-time; nonresident $5459 full-time, $182 per credit part-time. Full-time tuition and fees vary according to course load and program. Part-time tuition and fees vary according to program. *Required fees:* $572 full-time, $19 per credit part-time. *Room and board:* Room and board charges vary according to board plan and housing facility. *Payment plan:* installment. *Waivers:* senior citizens and employees or children of employees.

Applying *Options:* electronic application. *Application fee:* $20. *Required:* high school transcript. *Required for some:* 3 letters of recommendation. *Notification:* continuous (freshmen), continuous (transfers).

Freshman Application Contact Ms. Candace Perry, Director of Enrollment Services, Itasca Community College, 1851 East Highway 169, Grand Rapids, MN 55744. *Phone:* 218-322-2340. *Toll-free phone:* 800-996-6422 Ext. 4464. *Fax:* 218-327-4350. *E-mail:* iccinfo@itascacc.edu.

ITT Technical Institute

Eden Prairie, Minnesota **www.itt-tech.edu/**

- **Proprietary** primarily 2-year, founded 2003, part of ITT Educational Services, Inc.
- **Coed**

Majors Animation, interactive technology, video graphics and special effects; CAD/CADD drafting/design technology; computer and information systems security; computer engineering technology; computer software and media applications related; computer software engineering; computer software technology; criminal justice/law enforcement administration; design and visual communications; electrical, electronic and communications engineering technology; legal assistant/paralegal; system, networking, and LAN/WAN management; web page, digital/multimedia and information resources design.

Academics *Calendar:* quarters. *Degrees:* associate and bachelor's.

Freshman Application Contact Director of Recruitment, ITT Technical Institute, 8911 Columbine Road, Eden Prairie, MN 55347. *Phone:* 952-914-5300. *Toll-free phone:* 888-488-9646.

Lake Superior College

Duluth, Minnesota **www.lsc.edu/**

Freshman Application Contact Ms. Melissa Leno, Director of Admissions, Lake Superior College, 2101 Trinity Road, Duluth, MN 55811. *Phone:* 218-723-4895. *Toll-free phone:* 800-432-2884. *Fax:* 218-733-5945. *E-mail:* enroll@lsc.edu.

Le Cordon Bleu College of Culinary Arts

Saint Paul, Minnesota **www.twincitiesculinary.com/**

Freshman Application Contact Admissions Office, Le Cordon Bleu College of Culinary Arts, 1315 Mendota Heights Road, Saint Paul, MN 55120. *Phone:* 651-675-4700. *Toll-free phone:* 888-348-5222.

Leech Lake Tribal College

Cass Lake, Minnesota **www.lltc.edu/**

- **Public** 2-year, founded 1992
- **Rural** campus
- **Coed,** 243 undergraduate students, 78% full-time, 53% women, 47% men

Undergraduates 190 full-time, 53 part-time. Students come from 1 other state, 91% Native American.

Freshmen *Admission:* 78 enrolled.

Faculty *Total:* 28, 32% full-time, 4% with terminal degrees. *Student/faculty ratio:* 16:1.

Majors Business administration, management and operations related; early childhood education; foods, nutrition, and wellness; liberal arts and sciences/liberal studies.

Academics *Calendar:* semesters. *Degree:* certificates, diplomas, and associate. *Special study options:* academic remediation for entering students, advanced placement credit, double majors, independent study, internships, part-time degree program, services for LD students, summer session for credit.

Library Agindaasoowigamig.

Student Life *Housing:* college housing not available. *Student services:* personal/psychological counseling.

Costs (2010–11) *Tuition:* $4200 full-time. *Required fees:* $230 full-time. *Payment plans:* installment, deferred payment. *Waivers:* senior citizens and employees or children of employees.

Applying *Application fee:* $15. *Required:* high school transcript. *Notification:* continuous until 8/22 (freshmen).

Freshman Application Contact Ms. Shelly Braford, Recruiter, Leech Lake Tribal College, 6945 Littlewolf Road NW, PO Box180, Cass Lake, MN 56633. *Phone:* 218-335-4200 Ext. 4270. *Fax:* 218-335-4217. *E-mail:* shelly.braford@lltc.edu.

Mesabi Range Community and Technical College

Virginia, Minnesota **www.mesabirange.edu/**

- **State-supported** 2-year, founded 1918, part of Minnesota State Colleges and Universities System
- **Small-town** 30-acre campus
- **Coed,** 1,467 undergraduate students

Undergraduates Students come from 6 states and territories, 2 other countries, 4% are from out of state, 4% African American, 0.3% Asian American or Pacific Islander, 0.4% Hispanic American, 3% Native American, 10% live on campus.

Faculty *Total:* 89. *Student/faculty ratio:* 24:1.

Majors Administrative assistant and secretarial science; business/commerce; computer graphics; computer/information technology services administration related; computer programming related; computer programming (specific applications); computer software and media applications related; computer systems networking and telecommunications; electrical/electronics equipment installation and repair; human services; information technology; instrumentation technology; liberal arts and sciences/liberal studies; pre-engineering; substance abuse/addiction counseling; web page, digital/multimedia and information resources design.

Academics *Calendar:* semesters. *Degree:* certificates, diplomas, and associate. *Special study options:* academic remediation for entering students, adult/continuing education programs, advanced placement credit, cooperative education, independent study, internships, off-campus study, part-time degree program, services for LD students, student-designed majors, study abroad, summer session for credit.

Library Mesabi Library with 23,000 titles, 167 serial subscriptions.

Student Life *Housing Options:* coed. Campus housing is provided by a third party. *Activities and Organizations:* drama/theater group, student-run newspaper, choral group, Student Senate, Human Services Club, Native American Club, Student Life Club, Black Awareness Club. *Campus security:* late-night transport/escort service. *Student services:* personal/psychological counseling.

Athletics Member NJCAA. *Intercollegiate sports:* baseball M, basketball M/W, football M, softball W, volleyball W. *Intramural sports:* badminton M/W, basketball M/W, bowling M/W, field hockey M/W, football M/W, golf M/W, ice hockey M/W, skiing (cross-country) M/W, skiing (downhill) M/W, tennis M/W, volleyball M/W.

Costs (2010–11) *Tuition:* state resident $4630 full-time, $136 per credit hour part-time; nonresident $5630 full-time, $173 per credit hour part-time. *Required fees:* $19 per credit hour part-time. *Room and board:* room only: $3776. *Payment plan:* installment. *Waivers:* senior citizens.

Financial Aid Of all full-time matriculated undergraduates who enrolled in 2008, 117 Federal Work-Study jobs (averaging $1610). 77 state and other part-time jobs (averaging $1470).

Applying *Options:* early admission, deferred entrance. *Application fee:* $20. *Required:* high school transcript. *Application deadlines:* rolling (freshmen), rolling (transfers). *Notification:* continuous (freshmen), continuous (transfers).

Freshman Application Contact Ms. Brenda Kochevar, Enrollment Services Director, Mesabi Range Community and Technical College, 1001 Chestnut Street West, Virginia, MN 55792. *Phone:* 218-749-0314. *Toll-free phone:* 800-657-3860. *Fax:* 218-749-0318. *E-mail:* b.kochevar@mr.mnscu.edu.

Minneapolis Business College

Roseville, Minnesota **www.minneapolisbusinesscollege.edu/**

- **Private** 2-year, founded 1874
- **Suburban** campus with easy access to Minneapolis-St. Paul
- **Coed, primarily women,** 373 undergraduate students
- 89% of applicants were admitted

Freshmen *Admission:* 741 applied, 658 admitted.

Majors Accounting and business/management; business administration and management; computer programming; graphic design; legal administrative assistant/secretary; legal assistant/paralegal; medical/clinical assistant; system, networking, and LAN/WAN management; tourism and travel services management.

Academics *Degree:* diplomas and associate. *Special study options:* accelerated degree program, internships.

Freshman Application Contact Admissions Office, Minneapolis Business College, 1711 West County Road B, Roseville, MN 55113. *Phone:* 651-636-7406. *Toll-free phone:* 800-279-5200.

Minneapolis Community and Technical College

Minneapolis, Minnesota **www.mctc.mnscu.edu/**

- **State-supported** 2-year, founded 1965, part of Minnesota State Colleges and Universities System
- **Urban** 22-acre campus
- **Coed**

Majors Accounting technology and bookkeeping; administrative assistant and secretarial science; aircraft powerplant technology; airframe mechanics and aircraft maintenance technology; air traffic control; allied health diagnostic, intervention, and treatment professions related; biology/biological sciences; biotechnology; business administration and management; business automation/technology/data entry; cabinetmaking and millwork; chemistry; child-care and support services management; cinematography and film/video production; commercial photography; computer and information systems security; computer programming; computer systems networking and telecommunications; criminal justice/police science; criminal justice/safety; culinary arts; dental assisting; design and visual communications; digital communication and media/multimedia; dramatic/theater arts; education (multiple levels); electroneurodiagnostic/electroencephalographic technology; fine/studio arts; heating, air conditioning, ventilation and refrigeration maintenance technology; homeopathic medicine; human services; liberal arts and sciences/liberal studies; library assistant; mathematics; nursing (registered nurse training); parks, recreation and leisure; photographic and film/video technology; playwriting and screenwriting; public administration; recording arts technology; substance abuse/addiction counseling; watchmaking and jewelrymaking; web page, digital/multimedia and information resources design.

Academics *Calendar:* semesters. *Degree:* certificates, diplomas, and associate. *Special study options:* academic remediation for entering students, adult/continuing education programs, advanced placement credit, distance learning, English as a second language, honors programs, independent study, internships, off-campus study, part-time degree program, services for LD students, student-designed majors, study abroad, summer session for credit.

Library Minneapolis Community and Technical College Library with 65,865 titles, 600 serial subscriptions, an OPAC.

Student Life *Housing:* college housing not available. *Activities and Organizations:* drama/theater group, student-run newspaper, choral group, Student Senate, College Choirs, Muslin Student Association, Science Club, Phi Theta Kappa. *Campus security:* 24-hour emergency response devices, late-night transport/escort service. *Student services:* health clinic, personal/psychological counseling, women's center.

Athletics Member NJCAA. *Intercollegiate sports:* basketball M/W.

Costs (2009–10) *Tuition:* state resident $4223 full-time, $141 per credit hour part-time; nonresident $4223 full-time, $141 per credit hour part-time. Full-time tuition and fees vary according to program and reciprocity agreements. Part-time tuition and fees vary according to program and reciprocity agreements. Tuition costs reflect general education courses. Online, Nursing, Filmmaking, Video and Digital Arts, Screenwriting, Sound Arts, Law Enforcement, and Air Traffic Control programs all have different per credit rate. *Required fees:* $662 full-time, $22 per credit hour part-time. *Payment plan:* installment. *Waivers:* senior citizens and employees or children of employees.

Financial Aid Of all full-time matriculated undergraduates who enrolled in 2008, 188 Federal Work-Study jobs (averaging $5000). 190 state and other part-time jobs (averaging $5000).

Applying *Options:* electronic application, early admission, deferred entrance. *Application fee:* $20. *Required:* high school transcript. *Application deadlines:* rolling (freshmen), rolling (transfers). *Notification:* continuous (freshmen), continuous (transfers).

Freshman Application Contact Minneapolis Community and Technical College, 1501 Hennepin Avenue, Minneapolis, MN 55403. *Phone:* 612-659-6200. *Toll-free phone:* 800-247-0911. *E-mail:* admissions.office@minneapolis.edu.

Minnesota School of Business–Brooklyn Center

Brooklyn Center, Minnesota **www.msbcollege.edu/**

Freshman Application Contact Mr. Bruce Christman, Director of Admissions, Minnesota School of Business–Brooklyn Center, 5910 Shingle Creek Parkway, Brooklyn Center, MN 55430. *Phone:* 763-585-7777. *Fax:* 763-566-7030.

Minnesota School of Business–Plymouth

Minneapolis, Minnesota **www.msbcollege.edu/**

Freshman Application Contact Minnesota School of Business–Plymouth, 1455 County Road 101 North, Plymouth, MN 55447. *Phone:* 763-476-2000. *Fax:* 763-476-1000.

Minnesota School of Business–Richfield

Richfield, Minnesota **www.msbcollege.edu/**

Freshman Application Contact Ms. Patricia Murray, Director of Admissions, Minnesota School of Business–Richfield, 1401 West 76th Street, Richfield, MN 55430. *Phone:* 612-861-2000 Ext. 720. *Toll-free phone:* 800-752-4223. *Fax:* 612-861-5548. *E-mail:* pmurray@msbcollege.com.

Minnesota School of Business–St. Cloud

Waite Park, Minnesota **www.msbcollege.edu/**

Freshman Application Contact Ms. Candi Janssen, Director of Admissions, Minnesota School of Business–St. Cloud, 1201 2nd Street S, Waite Park, MN 56387. *Phone:* 320-257-2000. *Toll-free phone:* 866-403-3333. *Fax:* 320-257-0131. *E-mail:* cjanssen@msbcollege.edu.

Minnesota School of Business–Shakopee

Shakopee, Minnesota **www.msbcollege.edu/**

Freshman Application Contact Ms. Gretchen Seifert, Director of Admissions, Minnesota School of Business–Shakopee, 1200 Shakopee Town Square, Shakopee, MN 55379. *Phone:* 952-516-7015. *Toll-free phone:* 866-766-1200. *Fax:* 952-345-1201.

Minnesota State College–Southeast Technical

Winona, Minnesota **www.southeastmn.edu/**

- **State-supported** 2-year, founded 1992, part of Minnesota State Colleges and Universities System
- **Small-town** 132-acre campus with easy access to Minneapolis-St. Paul
- **Coed,** 2,529 undergraduate students, 60% full-time, 60% women, 40% men

Undergraduates 1,524 full-time, 1,005 part-time. Students come from 24 states and territories, 27 other countries, 26% are from out of state, 4% African American, 2% Asian American or Pacific Islander, 2% Hispanic American, 1% Native American, 0.3% international, 16% transferred in. *Retention:* 42% of 2008 full-time freshmen returned.

Freshmen *Admission:* 475 enrolled.

Faculty *Total:* 96, 59% full-time, 48% with terminal degrees. *Student/faculty ratio:* 19:1.

Majors Accounting; accounting technology and bookkeeping; administrative assistant and secretarial science; automobile/automotive mechanics technology; avionics maintenance technology; business administration and management; business machine repair; carpentry; child development; computer engineering technology; computer programming; computer systems networking and telecommunications; computer typography and composition equipment operation; consumer merchandising/retailing management; cosmetology; drafting and design technology; drafting/design engineering technologies related; electrical, electronic and communications engineering technology; emergency medical technology (EMT paramedic); heating, air conditioning, ventilation and refrigeration maintenance technology; industrial technology; kindergarten/preschool education; legal administrative assistant/secretary; machine tool technology; marketing/marketing management; medical administrative assistant and medical secretary; musical instrument fabrication and repair; nursing (licensed practical/vocational nurse training); nursing (registered nurse training); retailing; selling skills and sales; violin, viola, guitar and other stringed instruments; web page, digital/multimedia and information resources design; welding technology.

Academics *Calendar:* semesters. *Degree:* certificates, diplomas, and associate. *Special study options:* academic remediation for entering students, distance learning, part-time degree program, services for LD students, student-designed majors, summer session for credit.

Library Learning Resource Center with an OPAC, a Web page.

Student Life *Activities and Organizations:* Student Senate, Business Professionals of America, Skills USA, Delta Epsilon Chi (DEX). *Campus security:* 24-hour emergency response devices, late-night transport/escort service.

Costs (2010–11) *Tuition:* state resident $5076 full-time, $152 per credit hour part-time; nonresident $5076 full-time, $152 per credit hour part-time. *Required fees:* $417 full-time. *Room and board:* $6412. *Payment plan:* installment. *Waivers:* senior citizens and employees or children of employees.

Financial Aid Of all full-time matriculated undergraduates who enrolled in 2008, 65 Federal Work-Study jobs (averaging $2500). 65 state and other part-time jobs (averaging $2500).

Applying *Options:* electronic application. *Application fee:* $20. *Required:* high school transcript. *Application deadlines:* rolling (freshmen), rolling (out-of-state freshmen), rolling (transfers). *Notification:* continuous (freshmen), continuous (out-of-state freshmen), continuous (transfers).

Freshman Application Contact Admissions - SE Technical, Minnesota State College–Southeast Technical, PO Box 409, Winona, MN 55987. *Phone:* 877-853-8324. *Toll-free phone:* 800-372-8164. *E-mail:* enrollmentservices@southeastmn.edu.

Minnesota State Community and Technical College

Fergus Falls, Minnesota www.minnesota.edu/

- **State-supported** 2-year, founded 1960, part of Minnesota State Colleges and Universities System
- **Rural** campus
- **Coed,** 6,732 undergraduate students, 51% full-time, 58% women, 42% men

Undergraduates 3,462 full-time, 3,270 part-time. 3% African American, 1% Asian American or Pacific Islander, 2% Hispanic American, 2% Native American, 9% transferred in, 2% live on campus. *Retention:* 48% of 2008 full-time freshmen returned.

Freshmen *Admission:* 1,205 enrolled.

Faculty *Total:* 324, 54% full-time, 2% with terminal degrees. *Student/faculty ratio:* 18:1.

Majors Accounting; administrative assistant and secretarial science; architectural drafting and CAD/CADD; autobody/collision and repair technology; automotive engineering technology; biology/biological sciences; building/construction site management; business administration and management; business automation/technology/data entry; carpentry; civil engineering technology; clinical/medical laboratory assistant; clinical/medical laboratory technology; computer and information systems security; computer engineering technology; computer programming; computer systems networking and telecommunications; computer technology/computer systems technology; corrections; cosmetology; criminal justice/safety; dental assisting; dental hygiene; diesel mechanics technology; electrical and electronic engineering technologies related; electrical, electronic and communications engineering technology; environmental studies; fashion merchandising; financial planning and services; fire services administration; forensic science and technology; graphic design; health information/medical records technology; heating, air conditioning and refrigeration technology; human resources management; kindergarten/preschool education; legal administrative assistant/secretary; legal assistant/paralegal; liberal arts and sciences/liberal studies; lineworker; manufacturing technology; marine maintenance and ship repair technology; marketing/marketing management; mechanical drafting and CAD/CADD; medical administrative assistant and medical secretary; merchandising, sales, and marketing operations related (general); music; nursing (licensed practical/vocational nurse training); nursing (registered nurse training); pharmacy technician; plumbing technology; pre-engineering; radiologic technology/science; telecommunications technology; web page, digital/multimedia and information resources design.

Academics *Calendar:* semesters. *Degree:* certificates, diplomas, and associate. *Special study options:* academic remediation for entering students, advanced placement credit, cooperative education, distance learning, double majors, English as a second language, freshman honors college, honors programs, independent study, internships, off-campus study, part-time degree program, services for LD students, study abroad, summer session for credit.

Library Minnesota State Community and Technical College - Fergus Falls Library plus 3 others with 63,721 titles, 256 serial subscriptions, 4,977 audiovisual materials, an OPAC.

Student Life *Housing Options:* coed. Campus housing is university owned. *Activities and Organizations:* drama/theater group, choral group, Student Senate, Students In Free Enterprise (SIFE), Phi Theta Kappa, Business Professionals of America, Skills USA - VICA. *Campus security:* 24-hour emergency response devices, late-night transport/escort service, security for special events. *Student services:* personal/psychological counseling, women's center.

Athletics Member NJCAA. *Intercollegiate sports:* baseball M, basketball M/W, football M, golf M/W, softball W, volleyball W. *Intramural sports:* badminton M/W, basketball M, bowling M/W, football M/W, golf M/W, skiing (cross-country) M/W, skiing (downhill) M/W, soccer M/W, softball M/W, table tennis M/W, tennis M/W, volleyball M/W, weight lifting M/W.

Costs (2009–10) *Tuition:* state resident $4310 full-time, $144 per credit part-time; nonresident $4310 full-time, $144 per credit part-time. Full-time tuition and fees vary according to location and program. Part-time tuition and fees vary according to location and program. *Required fees:* $651 full-time, $22 per credit part-time. *Room and board:* room only: $3100. Room and board charges vary according to board plan and housing facility. *Waivers:* senior citizens and employees or children of employees.

Financial Aid Of all full-time matriculated undergraduates who enrolled in 2008, 80 Federal Work-Study jobs (averaging $1900). 80 state and other part-time jobs (averaging $1900).

Applying *Options:* electronic application, early admission, deferred entrance. *Application fee:* $20. *Required:* high school transcript. *Application deadlines:* rolling (freshmen), rolling (transfers). *Notification:* continuous (freshmen), continuous (transfers).

Freshman Application Contact Ms. Carrie Brimhall, Dean of Enrollment Management, Minnesota State Community and Technical College, 1414 College Way, Fergus Falls, MN 56537-1009. *Phone:* 218-736-1528. *Toll-free phone:* 888-MY-MSCTC. *Fax:* 218-736-1510. *E-mail:* carrie.brimhall@minnesota.edu.

Minnesota West Community and Technical College

Pipestone, Minnesota www.mnwest.edu/

- **State-supported** 2-year, founded 1967, part of Minnesota State Colleges and Universities System
- **Rural** campus
- **Coed,** 2,863 undergraduate students, 56% full-time, 55% women, 45% men

Undergraduates 1,600 full-time, 1,263 part-time. Students come from 25 states and territories, 3 other countries, 11% are from out of state, 3% African American, 2% Asian American or Pacific Islander, 4% Hispanic American, 0.9% Native American, 5% transferred in. *Retention:* 63% of 2008 full-time freshmen returned.

Freshmen *Admission:* 2,568 applied, 1,818 admitted, 504 enrolled. *Average high school GPA:* 2.58.

Faculty *Total:* 208, 43% full-time. *Student/faculty ratio:* 13:1.

Majors Accounting; administrative assistant and secretarial science; clinical/medical laboratory technology; heating, air conditioning, ventilation and refrigeration maintenance technology; liberal arts and sciences/liberal studies; medical administrative assistant and medical secretary; medical/clinical assistant; plumbing technology.

Academics *Calendar:* semesters. *Degrees:* certificates, diplomas, and associate (profile contains information from Canby, Granite Falls, Jackson, and Worthington campuses). *Special study options:* academic remediation for entering students, advanced placement credit, cooperative education, distance learning, double majors, external degree program, honors programs, independent study, internships, part-time degree program, services for LD students, summer session for credit.

Library Library and Academic Resource Center plus 4 others with 46,057 titles, 313 serial subscriptions, 4,632 audiovisual materials, an OPAC.

Student Life *Housing:* college housing not available. *Activities and Organizations:* choral group.

Athletics Member NJCAA. *Intercollegiate sports:* baseball M, basketball M/W, cheerleading M/W, football M, golf M/W, softball W, volleyball W, wrestling M. *Intramural sports:* softball M/W, volleyball M/W.

Costs (2009–10) *Tuition:* state resident $4761 full-time, $149 per credit hour part-time; nonresident $4761 full-time, $149 per credit hour part-time. Full-time tuition and fees vary according to reciprocity agreements. Part-time tuition and fees vary according to reciprocity agreements. *Required fees:* $507 full-time, $16 per credit hour part-time. *Payment plan:* installment. *Waivers:* senior citizens and employees or children of employees.

Applying *Options:* electronic application. *Application fee:* $20. *Required:* high school transcript. *Application deadlines:* rolling (freshmen), rolling (transfers).

Minnesota West Community and Technical College (continued)

Freshman Application Contact Ms. Crystal Strouth, College Registrar, Minnesota West Community and Technical College, 1314 North Hiawatha Avenue, Pipestone, MN 56164. *Phone:* 507-372-3451. *Toll-free phone:* 800-658-2330. *Fax:* 507-372-5803. *E-mail:* crystal.strouth@mnwest.edu.

National American University

Bloomington, Minnesota **www.national.edu/**

Freshman Application Contact Ms. Jennifer Michaelson, Admissions Assistant, National American University, 321 Kansas City Street, Rapid City, SD 57201. *Phone:* 605-394-4827. *Toll-free phone:* 800-209-0490. *E-mail:* jmichaelson@national.edu.

National American University

Brooklyn Center, Minnesota **www.national.edu/**

Freshman Application Contact Admissions Office, National American University, 6120 Earle Brown Drive, Suite 100, Brooklyn Center, MN 55430.

Normandale Community College

Bloomington, Minnesota **www.normandale.edu/**

Freshman Application Contact Admissions Office, Normandale Community College, 9700 France Avenue South, Bloomington, MN 55431. *Phone:* 952-487-8201. *Toll-free phone:* 866-880-8740. *Fax:* 952-487-8230. *E-mail:* information@normandale.edu.

North Hennepin Community College

Brooklyn Park, Minnesota **www.nhcc.edu/**

- **State-supported** 2-year, founded 1966, part of Minnesota State Colleges and Universities System
- **Suburban** 80-acre campus
- **Endowment** $693,764
- **Coed,** 7,444 undergraduate students, 40% full-time, 58% women, 42% men

Undergraduates 2,984 full-time, 4,460 part-time. Students come from 16 states and territories, 64 other countries, 0.5% are from out of state, 18% African American, 11% Asian American or Pacific Islander, 2% Hispanic American, 0.9% Native American, 1% international, 39% transferred in. *Retention:* 56% of 2008 full-time freshmen returned.

Freshmen *Admission:* 1,486 enrolled.

Faculty *Total:* 248, 42% full-time. *Student/faculty ratio:* 29:1.

Majors Accounting; biology/biological sciences; building/construction site management; building/home/construction inspection; business administration and management; chemistry; clinical/medical laboratory technology; computer science; construction management; criminal justice/law enforcement administration; criminal justice/police science; criminal justice/safety; engineering; finance; fine/studio arts; graphic design; histologic technology/histotechnologist; history; legal assistant/paralegal; liberal arts and sciences/liberal studies; management information systems; marketing/marketing management; mathematics; multi/interdisciplinary studies related; nursing (registered nurse training); physical education teaching and coaching; pre-engineering; small business administration.

Academics *Calendar:* semesters. *Degree:* certificates and associate. *Special study options:* academic remediation for entering students, accelerated degree program, adult/continuing education programs, advanced placement credit, distance learning, double majors, English as a second language, external degree program, honors programs, independent study, internships, off-campus study, part-time degree program, services for LD students, student-designed majors, study abroad, summer session for credit. *ROTC:* Army (c), Navy (c), Air Force (c).

Library Learning Resource Center with 46,636 titles, 8,000 serial subscriptions, 2,385 audiovisual materials, an OPAC, a Web page.

Student Life *Housing:* college housing not available. *Activities and Organizations:* drama/theater group, choral group, Muslim Student Association, African Student Association, Game Club, Hispanic Student Association, Student Nurses Association. *Campus security:* 24-hour emergency response devices, student patrols, late-night transport/escort service. *Student services:* personal/psychological counseling.

Athletics *Intramural sports:* badminton M/W, basketball M/W, bowling M/W, cross-country running M/W, football M/W, golf M/W, ice hockey M/W, rock climbing M/W, soccer M/W, softball M/W, table tennis M/W, tennis M/W, volleyball M/W, weight lifting M/W.

Costs (2009–10) *Tuition:* state resident $3451 full-time, $144 per credit hour part-time; nonresident $3451 full-time, $144 per credit hour part-time. Full-time tuition and fees vary according to course load, location, and program. Part-time tuition and fees vary according to course load, location, and program. *Required fees:* $348 full-time, $15 per credit hour part-time. *Payment plan:* installment. *Waivers:* senior citizens and employees or children of employees.

Financial Aid Of all full-time matriculated undergraduates who enrolled in 2008, 100 Federal Work-Study jobs (averaging $6000). 100 state and other part-time jobs (averaging $6000).

Applying *Options:* electronic application, early admission, deferred entrance. *Application fee:* $20. *Recommended:* high school transcript. *Application deadlines:* rolling (freshmen), rolling (transfers). *Notification:* continuous (freshmen), continuous (transfers).

Freshman Application Contact Ms. Jennifer Lambrecht, Director of Campus Outreach, North Hennepin Community College, 7411 85th Avenue North, Brooklyn Park, MN 55445-2231. *Phone:* 763-424-0702. *Fax:* 763-424-0929. *E-mail:* jlsummer@nhcc.edu.

Northland Community and Technical College–Thief River Falls

Thief River Falls, Minnesota **www.northlandcollege.edu/**

- **State-supported** 2-year, founded 1965, part of Minnesota State Colleges and Universities System
- **Small-town** campus
- **Coed,** 4,243 undergraduate students, 48% full-time, 56% women, 44% men

Undergraduates 2,038 full-time, 2,205 part-time. Students come from 33 states and territories, 6 other countries, 34% are from out of state, 6% African American, 1% Asian American or Pacific Islander, 3% Hispanic American, 3% Native American, 0.6% international, 11% transferred in.

Freshmen *Admission:* 1,926 applied, 1,926 admitted, 644 enrolled.

Faculty *Total:* 246, 50% full-time. *Student/faculty ratio:* 21:1.

Majors Accounting; administrative assistant and secretarial science; aeronautics/aviation/aerospace science and technology; architectural engineering technology; autobody/collision and repair technology; automobile/automotive mechanics technology; aviation/airway management; avionics maintenance technology; business administration and management; cardiovascular technology; carpentry; child-care provision; child development; computer and information sciences and support services related; computer and information sciences related; computer graphics; computer science; computer software and media applications related; consumer merchandising/retailing management; cosmetology; criminal justice/law enforcement administration; criminal justice/police science; criminology; data entry/microcomputer applications; data entry/microcomputer applications related; data modeling/warehousing and database administration; drafting and design technology; electrical, electronic and communications engineering technology; emergency medical technology (EMT paramedic); entrepreneurship; farm and ranch management; fire protection and safety technology; heating, air conditioning, ventilation and refrigeration maintenance technology; industrial electronics technology; information technology; legal administrative assistant/secretary; liberal arts and sciences/liberal studies; manufacturing technology; marketing/marketing management; massage therapy; mass communication/media; medical administrative assistant and medical secretary; nursing (licensed practical/vocational nurse training); nursing (registered nurse training); occupational therapist assistant; pharmacy technician; physical therapist assistant; plumbing technology; radiologic technology/science; respiratory care therapy; surgical technology; system administration; web/multimedia management and webmaster; web page, digital/multimedia and information resources design; welding technology; word processing.

Academics *Calendar:* semesters. *Degree:* certificates, diplomas, and associate. *Special study options:* academic remediation for entering students, adult/continuing education programs, advanced placement credit, distance learning, double majors, internships, off-campus study, part-time degree program, services for LD students, summer session for credit.

Library Northland Comm & Tech College Library.

Student Life *Housing:* college housing not available. *Activities and Organizations:* student-run newspaper, radio station, choral group, Law Enforcement Club, All-Nations Club, Environmental Club, PAMA, VICA (Vocational Industrial Clubs of America). *Campus security:* student patrols, late-night transport/escort service. *Student services:* personal/psychological counseling, women's center.

Athletics Member NJCAA. *Intercollegiate sports:* baseball M, basketball M/W, football M, softball W, volleyball W. *Intramural sports:* basketball M/W, bowling M/W, golf M/W, soccer M/W, softball M/W, tennis M/W, volleyball M/W, weight lifting M/W.

Costs (2010–11) *Tuition:* state resident $4422 full-time, $147 per credit hour part-time; nonresident $4422 full-time, $147 per credit hour part-time. Full-time tuition and fees vary according to course load, location, program, and reciprocity agreements. Part-time tuition and fees vary according to course load, location, program, and reciprocity agreements. *Required fees:* $522 full-time, $17 per credit hour part-time. *Payment plan:* installment. *Waivers:* senior citizens and employees or children of employees.

Financial Aid Of all full-time matriculated undergraduates who enrolled in 2008, 75 Federal Work-Study jobs (averaging $2500). 40 state and other part-time jobs (averaging $2500).

Applying *Options:* electronic application, early admission, deferred entrance. *Application fee:* $20. *Required:* high school transcript. *Notification:* continuous (freshmen), continuous (out-of-state freshmen), continuous (transfers).

Freshman Application Contact Mr. Eugene Klinke, Director of Enrollment Management and Multicultural Services, Northland Community and Technical College–Thief River Falls, 1101 Highway #1 East, Thief River Falls, MN 56701. *Phone:* 218-683-8554. *Toll-free phone:* 800-959-6282. *Fax:* 218-683-8980. *E-mail:* eugene.klinke@northlandcollege.edu.

NORTHWEST TECHNICAL COLLEGE

Bemidji, Minnesota **www.ntcmn.edu/**

- **State-supported** 2-year, founded 1993, part of Minnesota State Colleges and Universities System, administratively affiliated with Bemidji State University
- **Small-town** campus
- **Coed,** 1,603 undergraduate students, 37% full-time, 67% women, 33% men

Undergraduates 590 full-time, 1,013 part-time. Students come from 20 states and territories, 2 other countries, 4% are from out of state, 2% African American, 2% Asian American or Pacific Islander, 1% Hispanic American, 10% Native American, 0.2% international, 23% transferred in.

Freshmen *Admission:* 237 applied, 237 admitted, 231 enrolled.

Faculty *Total:* 63, 43% full-time. *Student/faculty ratio:* 24:1.

Majors Accounting; administrative assistant and secretarial science; automobile/automotive mechanics technology; business administration and management; child-care and support services management; engine machinist; industrial technology; landscaping and groundskeeping; liberal arts and sciences/liberal studies; manufacturing technology; medical administrative assistant and medical secretary; nursing (licensed practical/vocational nurse training); nursing (registered nurse training); sales, distribution and marketing.

Academics *Calendar:* semesters. *Degree:* certificates, diplomas, and associate. *Special study options:* academic remediation for entering students, advanced placement credit, cooperative education, distance learning, double majors, external degree program, independent study, internships, off-campus study, part-time degree program, services for LD students, student-designed majors, summer session for credit.

Library Northwest Technical College Learning Enrichment Center with an OPAC.

Student Life *Housing Options:* coed. Campus housing is provided by a third party. *Activities and Organizations:* campus government, Phi Theta Kappa. *Campus security:* student patrols, late-night transport/escort service. *Student services:* health clinic, personal/psychological counseling.

Costs (2009–10) *Tuition:* state resident $4616 full-time, $154 per credit hour part-time; nonresident $4616 full-time, $154 per credit hour part-time. Full-time tuition and fees vary according to course load, program, and reciprocity agreements. Part-time tuition and fees vary according to course load, program, and reciprocity agreements. *Required fees:* $296 full-time, $10 per credit hour part-time. *Room and board:* $6240; room only: $3940. Room and board charges vary according to board plan. *Payment plan:* installment. *Waivers:* senior citizens and employees or children of employees.

Financial Aid Of all full-time matriculated undergraduates who enrolled in 2008, 20 Federal Work-Study jobs (averaging $1500). 10 state and other part-time jobs (averaging $1500).

Applying *Options:* electronic application. *Application fee:* $20. *Required:* high school transcript. *Application deadlines:* rolling (freshmen), rolling (out-of-state freshmen), rolling (transfers). *Notification:* continuous (freshmen), continuous (out-of-state freshmen), continuous (transfers).

Freshman Application Contact Miss Kari Kantack, Diversity and Enrollment Representative, Northwest Technical College, 905 Grant Avenue, SE, Bemidji, MN 56601. *Phone:* 218-333-6645. *Toll-free phone:* 800-942-8324. *Fax:* 218-333-6694. *E-mail:* kari.kantack@ntcmn.edu.

NORTHWEST TECHNICAL INSTITUTE

Eagan, Minnesota **www.nti.edu/**

- **Proprietary** 2-year, founded 1957
- **Suburban** 2-acre campus with easy access to Minneapolis-St. Paul
- **Coed,** 72 undergraduate students

Majors Architectural drafting and CAD/CADD; CAD/CADD drafting/design technology.

Academics *Calendar:* semesters. *Degree:* associate. *Special study options:* honors programs, independent study.

Library 565 titles, 4 serial subscriptions.

Student Life *Housing:* college housing not available. *Campus security:* 24-hour emergency response devices and patrols, late-night transport/escort service.

Costs (2009–10) *Tuition:* $15,850 full-time. No tuition increase for student's term of enrollment. *Payment plans:* tuition prepayment, installment.

Applying *Application fee:* $25. *Required:* high school transcript, interview. *Application deadlines:* rolling (freshmen), rolling (transfers). *Notification:* continuous (freshmen), continuous (transfers).

Freshman Application Contact Northwest Technical Institute, 11995 Singletree Lane, Eden Prairie, MN 55344-5351. *Phone:* 952-944-0080 Ext. 103. *Toll-free phone:* 800-443-4223.

PINE TECHNICAL COLLEGE

Pine City, Minnesota **www.pinetech.edu/**

- **State-supported** 2-year, founded 1965, part of Minnesota State Colleges and Universities System
- **Small-town** 6-acre campus with easy access to Minneapolis-St. Paul
- **Coed**

Undergraduates 296 full-time, 516 part-time. Students come from 5 states and territories, 10% are from out of state, 11% transferred in.

Faculty *Student/faculty ratio:* 18:1.

Academics *Calendar:* semesters. *Degree:* certificates, diplomas, and associate. *Special study options:* academic remediation for entering students, advanced placement credit, distance learning, double majors, independent study, internships, part-time degree program, services for LD students, summer session for credit.

Student Life *Campus security:* late-night transport/escort service.

Costs (2009–10) *One-time required fee:* $20. *Tuition:* state resident $4005 full-time; nonresident $8010 full-time. *Required fees:* $486 full-time.

Financial Aid Of all full-time matriculated undergraduates who enrolled in 2008, 6 Federal Work-Study jobs (averaging $2000). 10 state and other part-time jobs.

Applying *Options:* early admission. *Application fee:* $20. *Required:* high school transcript.

Freshman Application Contact Pine Technical College, 900 Fourth Street, SE, Pine City, MN 55063. *Phone:* 320-629-5100. *Toll-free phone:* 800-521-7463.

RAINY RIVER COMMUNITY COLLEGE

International Falls, Minnesota **www.rrcc.mnscu.edu/**

Freshman Application Contact Ms. Berta Hagen, Registrar, Rainy River Community College, 1501 Highway 71, International Falls, MN 56649. *Phone:* 218-285-2207. *Toll-free phone:* 800-456-3996. *Fax:* 218-285-2239. *E-mail:* hagen_b@rrcc.mnscu.edu.

RASMUSSEN COLLEGE BROOKLYN PARK

Brooklyn Park, Minnesota **www.rasmussen.edu/**

Admissions Office Contact Rasmussen College Brooklyn Park, 8301 93rd Avenue North, Brooklyn Park, MN 55445-1512. *Toll-free phone:* 877-495-4500.

RASMUSSEN COLLEGE EAGAN

Eagan, Minnesota www.rasmussen.edu/

- **Proprietary** primarily 2-year, founded 1904, part of Rasmussen College System
- **Suburban** 10-acre campus with easy access to Minneapolis-St. Paul
- **Coed, primarily women**

Faculty *Student/faculty ratio:* 12:1.
Academics *Calendar:* quarters. *Degrees:* certificates, diplomas, associate, and bachelor's. *Special study options:* academic remediation for entering students, adult/continuing education programs, internships, part-time degree program.
Student Life *Campus security:* safety and security programs.
Standardized Tests *Required:* ACT COMPASS (for admission).
Costs (2009–10) *Tuition:* $420 per credit part-time. Part-time tuition and fees vary according to course level, course load, and program.
Applying *Application fee:* $60. *Required:* high school transcript, minimum 2.0 GPA, interview.
Director of Admissions Ms. Jacinda Miller, Admissions Coordinator, Rasmussen College Eagan, 3500 Federal Drive, Eagan, MN 55122-1346. *Phone:* 651-687-9000. *Toll-free phone:* 800-852-6367.

RASMUSSEN COLLEGE EDEN PRAIRIE

Eden Prairie, Minnesota www.rasmussen.edu/

Freshman Application Contact Mr. Jeff Hagy, Director of Admissions, Rasmussen College Eden Prairie, 7905 Golden Triangle Drive, Suite 100, Eden Prairie, MN 55344. *Phone:* 952-545-2000. *Toll-free phone:* 800-852-0929.

RASMUSSEN COLLEGE LAKE ELMO/WOODBURY

Lake Elmo, Minnesota www.rasmussen.edu/

Admissions Office Contact Rasmussen College Lake Elmo/Woodbury, 8565 Eagle Point Circle, Lake Elmo, MN 55042. *Toll-free phone:* 888-813-2358.

RASMUSSEN COLLEGE MANKATO

Mankato, Minnesota www.rasmussen.edu/

Freshman Application Contact Ms. Kathy Clifford, Director of Admissions, Rasmussen College Mankato, 501 Holly Lane, Mankato, MN 56001-6803. *Phone:* 507-625-6556. *Toll-free phone:* 800-657-6767. *Fax:* 507-625-6557. *E-mail:* rascoll@ic.mankato.mn.us.

RASMUSSEN COLLEGE MOORHEAD

Moorhead, Minnesota www.rasmussen.edu/

Admissions Office Contact Rasmussen College Moorhead, 1250 29th Avenue South, Moorhead, MN 56560. *Toll-free phone:* 866-562-2758.

RASMUSSEN COLLEGE ST. CLOUD

St. Cloud, Minnesota www.rasmussen.edu/

- **Proprietary** primarily 2-year, founded 1904, part of Rasmussen College System
- **Urban** campus with easy access to Minneapolis-St. Paul
- **Coed, primarily women**

Academics *Calendar:* quarters. *Degrees:* certificates, diplomas, associate, and bachelor's. *Special study options:* academic remediation for entering students, adult/continuing education programs, distance learning, double majors, internships, part-time degree program, summer session for credit.
Standardized Tests *Required:* ACT COMPASS (for admission).
Costs (2009–10) *Tuition:* $420 per credit part-time. Part-time tuition and fees vary according to course load and program.
Financial Aid Of all full-time matriculated undergraduates who enrolled in 2008, 34 Federal Work-Study jobs (averaging $866). 51 state and other part-time jobs (averaging $700).
Applying *Options:* electronic application, early admission, deferred entrance. *Application fee:* $60. *Required:* high school transcript, minimum 2.0 GPA, interview.
Freshman Application Contact Ms. Andrea Peters, Director of Admissions, Rasmussen College St. Cloud, 226 Park Avenue South, St. Cloud, MN 56301. *Phone:* 320-251-5600. *Toll-free phone:* 800-852-0460. *Fax:* 320-251-3702. *E-mail:* admstc@rasmussen.edu.

RIDGEWATER COLLEGE

Willmar, Minnesota www.ridgewater.edu/

Freshman Application Contact Ms. Linda Barron, Admissions Assistant, Ridgewater College, PO Box 1097, Willmar, MN 56201-1097. *Phone:* 320-222-5976. *Toll-free phone:* 800-722-1151 Ext. 2906. *E-mail:* linda.barron@ridgewater.edu.

RIVERLAND COMMUNITY COLLEGE

Austin, Minnesota www.riverland.edu/

Freshman Application Contact Ms. Renee Njos, Admission Secretary, Riverland Community College, 1900 8th Avenue NW, Austin, MN 55912. *Phone:* 507-433-0820. *Toll-free phone:* 800-247-5039. *Fax:* 507-433-0515. *E-mail:* admissions@riverland.edu.

ROCHESTER COMMUNITY AND TECHNICAL COLLEGE

Rochester, Minnesota www.rctc.edu/

- **State-supported** primarily 2-year, founded 1915, part of Minnesota State Colleges and Universities System
- **Small-town** 460-acre campus
- **Coed**

Academics *Calendar:* semesters. *Degrees:* certificates, diplomas, associate, and bachelor's (also offers 13 programs that lead to a bachelor's degree with Winona State University or University of Minnesota). *Special study options:* academic remediation for entering students, advanced placement credit, distance learning, English as a second language, honors programs, independent study, internships, off-campus study, part-time degree program, services for LD students, summer session for credit.
Student Life *Campus security:* student patrols, late-night transport/escort service.
Athletics Member NJCAA.
Financial Aid Of all full-time matriculated undergraduates who enrolled in 2008, 500 Federal Work-Study jobs (averaging $3000). 300 state and other part-time jobs (averaging $3000).
Applying *Options:* early admission. *Application fee:* $20. *Required:* high school transcript.
Director of Admissions Mr. Troy Tynsky, Director of Admissions, Rochester Community and Technical College, 851 30th Avenue, SE, Rochester, MN 55904-4999. *Phone:* 507-280-3509.

ST. CLOUD TECHNICAL COLLEGE

St. Cloud, Minnesota www.sctc.edu/

- **State-supported** 2-year, founded 1948, part of Minnesota State Colleges and Universities System
- **Urban** 35-acre campus with easy access to Minneapolis-St. Paul
- **Coed,** 3,949 undergraduate students, 63% full-time, 50% women, 50% men

Undergraduates 2,484 full-time, 1,465 part-time. Students come from 19 states and territories, 3 other countries, 2% are from out of state, 3% African American, 1% Asian American or Pacific Islander, 1% Hispanic American, 1% Native American, 0.2% international, 43% transferred in.

Freshmen *Admission:* 1,860 applied, 1,695 admitted, 927 enrolled. *Average high school GPA:* 3.16.

Faculty *Total:* 184, 64% full-time, 2% with terminal degrees.

Majors Accounting; advertising; architectural drafting and CAD/CADD; autobody/collision and repair technology; automobile/automotive mechanics technology; banking and financial support services; business administration and management; cardiovascular technology; carpentry; child-care and support services management; civil engineering technology; computer programming; computer programming (specific applications); computer systems networking and telecommunications; dental assisting; dental hygiene; diagnostic medical sonography and ultrasound technology; electrical and power transmission installation; electrical, electronic and communications engineering technology; emergency medical technology (EMT paramedic); executive assistant/executive secretary; health information/medical records technology; heating, air conditioning, ventilation and refrigeration maintenance technology; instrumentation technology; legal administrative assistant/secretary; machine tool technology; mechanical drafting and CAD/CADD; medium/heavy vehicle and truck technology; nursing (licensed practical/vocational nurse training); plumbing technology; sales, distribution and marketing; surgical technology; teacher assistant/aide; water quality and wastewater treatment management and recycling technology; web page, digital/multimedia and information resources design; welding technology.

Academics *Calendar:* semesters. *Degree:* certificates, diplomas, and associate. *Special study options:* academic remediation for entering students, adult/continuing education programs, advanced placement credit, cooperative education, distance learning, English as a second language, independent study, internships, part-time degree program, services for LD students, summer session for credit.

Library Learning Resource Center plus 1 other with 10,000 titles, 600 serial subscriptions, an OPAC, a Web page.

Student Life *Housing:* college housing not available. *Activities and Organizations:* drama/theater group, student-run newspaper, Student Senate, Distributive Education Club of America, Business Professionals of America, Child and Adult Care Education, Central Minnesota Builders Association. *Campus security:* late-night transport/escort service. *Student services:* personal/psychological counseling, women's center.

Athletics Member NJCAA. *Intercollegiate sports:* baseball M, basketball M/W, softball W, volleyball W. *Intramural sports:* volleyball M/W.

Costs (2009–10) *Tuition:* state resident $4219 full-time, $141 per credit part-time; nonresident $4219 full-time, $141 per credit part-time. Full-time tuition and fees vary according to course load and program. Part-time tuition and fees vary according to course load and program. *Required fees:* $518 full-time, $17 per credit part-time. *Payment plan:* installment. *Waivers:* senior citizens and employees or children of employees.

Financial Aid Of all full-time matriculated undergraduates who enrolled in 2008, 38 Federal Work-Study jobs (averaging $4000). 38 state and other part-time jobs (averaging $4000).

Applying *Options:* electronic application, early admission, deferred entrance. *Application fee:* $20. *Required:* high school transcript. *Required for some:* essay or personal statement, interview. *Application deadlines:* rolling (freshmen), rolling (transfers). *Notification:* continuous until 8/1 (freshmen), continuous until 8/1 (transfers).

Freshman Application Contact Ms. Jodi Elness, Admissions Office, St. Cloud Technical College, 1540 Northway Drive, St. Cloud, MN 56303. *Phone:* 320-308-5089. *Toll-free phone:* 800-222-1009. *Fax:* 320-308-5981. *E-mail:* jelness@sctc.edu.

SAINT PAUL COLLEGE–A COMMUNITY & TECHNICAL COLLEGE

St. Paul, Minnesota **www.saintpaul.edu/**

- **State-related** 2-year, founded 1919, part of Minnesota State Colleges and Universities System
- **Urban** campus
- **Coed,** 5,928 undergraduate students, 41% full-time, 52% women, 48% men

Undergraduates 2,454 full-time, 3,474 part-time. 8% are from out of state, 36% African American, 11% Asian American or Pacific Islander, 3% Hispanic American, 0.8% Native American, 0.3% international, 13% transferred in.

Freshmen *Admission:* 4,454 applied, 4,454 admitted, 1,214 enrolled.

Faculty *Total:* 316, 34% full-time, 33% with terminal degrees. *Student/faculty ratio:* 18:1.

Majors Accounting; administrative assistant and secretarial science; aesthetician/esthetician and skin care; animation, interactive technology, video graphics and special effects; athletic training; autobody/collision and repair technology; automobile/automotive mechanics technology; biomedical technology; building/construction site management; business administration and management; chemical technology; child-care and support services management; clinical/medical laboratory technology; computer graphics; computer programming; computer science; computer systems networking and telecommunications; cosmetology; culinary arts; electrical, electronic and communications engineering technology; entrepreneurship; health information/medical records technology; hospitality administration; human resources management; industrial technology; international marketing; liberal arts and sciences/liberal studies; logistics and materials management; management information systems; manufacturing technology; massage therapy; medical office assistant; nursing (licensed practical/vocational nurse training); office management; respiratory care therapy; sign language interpretation and translation; survey technology.

Academics *Calendar:* semesters. *Degree:* certificates, diplomas, and associate. *Special study options:* academic remediation for entering students, adult/continuing education programs, distance learning, English as a second language, honors programs, internships, off-campus study, part-time degree program, summer session for credit.

Library Saint Paul College Library with 12,000 titles, 110 serial subscriptions, an OPAC, a Web page.

Student Life *Housing:* college housing not available. *Activities and Organizations:* Student Senate. *Campus security:* late-night transport/escort service. *Student services:* personal/psychological counseling, women's center.

Standardized Tests *Required:* ACCUPLACER (for admission).

Financial Aid Of all full-time matriculated undergraduates who enrolled in 2008, 48 Federal Work-Study jobs (averaging $2500). 94 state and other part-time jobs (averaging $2500).

Applying *Options:* electronic application, early admission. *Application fee:* $20. *Required for some:* high school transcript, interview. *Application deadline:* rolling (freshmen).

Freshman Application Contact Ms. Sarah Carrico, Saint Paul College–A Community & Technical College, 235 Marshall Avenue, Saint Paul, MN 55102. *Phone:* 651-846-1424. *Toll-free phone:* 800-227-6029. *Fax:* 651-846-1703. *E-mail:* admissions@saintpaul.edu.

SOUTH CENTRAL COLLEGE

North Mankato, Minnesota **southcentral.edu/**

Freshman Application Contact Ms. Beverly Herda, Director of Admissions, South Central College, 1920 Lee Boulevard, North Mankato, MN 56003. *Phone:* 507-389-7334. *Fax:* 507-388-9951.

VERMILION COMMUNITY COLLEGE

Ely, Minnesota **www.vcc.edu/**

Freshman Application Contact Mr. Todd Heiman, Director of Enrollment Services, Vermilion Community College, 1900 East Camp Street, Ely, MN 55731-1996. *Phone:* 218-365-7224. *Toll-free phone:* 800-657-3608.

MISSISSIPPI

ANTONELLI COLLEGE

Hattiesburg, Mississippi **antonellicollege.edu/**

- **Proprietary** 2-year
- **Coed,** 354 undergraduate students

Majors Accounting technology and bookkeeping; administrative assistant and secretarial science; allied health and medical assisting services related; business automation/technology/data entry; information technology; interior design; legal administrative assistant/secretary; massage therapy; medical insurance coding; medical transcription.

Academics *Calendar:* quarters. *Degree:* certificates and associate.

Applying *Application fee:* $75.

Freshman Application Contact Mrs. Karen Gautreau, Director, Antonelli College, 1500 North 31st Avenue, Hattiesburg, MS 39401. *Phone:* 601-583-4100. *Fax:* 601-583-0839. *E-mail:* admissionsh@antonellicollege.edu.

Antonelli College

Jackson, Mississippi www.antonellicollege.edu/

- **Proprietary** 2-year
- **Coed,** 240 undergraduate students

Majors Accounting technology and bookkeeping; business automation/technology/data entry; commercial and advertising art; computer systems networking and telecommunications; interior design; legal assistant/paralegal; massage therapy; medical/clinical assistant; medical insurance coding; medical transcription.

Academics *Calendar:* quarters. *Degree:* diplomas and associate.

Student Life *Housing:* college housing not available.

Applying *Application fee:* $75.

Freshman Application Contact Antonelli College, 2323 Lakeland Drive, Jackson, MS 39232. *Phone:* 601-362-9991.

Coahoma Community College

Clarksdale, Mississippi www.ccc.cc.ms.us/

Freshman Application Contact Mrs. Wanda Holmes, Director of Admissions and Records, Coahoma Community College, Route 1, PO Box 616, Clarksdale, MS 38614-9799. *Phone:* 662-621-4205. *Toll-free phone:* 800-844-1222.

Copiah-Lincoln Community College

Wesson, Mississippi www.colin.edu/

Freshman Application Contact Julia Parker, Director of Distance Learning, Copiah-Lincoln Community College, PO Box 371, Wesson, MS 39191-0457. *Phone:* 601-643-8619. *Fax:* 601-643-8222. *E-mail:* julia.parker@colin.edu.

Copiah-Lincoln Community College–Natchez Campus

Natchez, Mississippi www.colin.edu/

Freshman Application Contact Copiah-Lincoln Community College–Natchez Campus, 11 Co-Lin Circle, Natchez, MS 39120. *Phone:* 601-442-9111 Ext. 224.

East Central Community College

Decatur, Mississippi www.eccc.cc.ms.us/

- **State and locally supported** 2-year, founded 1928, part of Mississippi State Board for Community and Junior Colleges
- **Rural** 200-acre campus
- **Coed**

Academics *Calendar:* semesters. *Degree:* certificates and associate. *Special study options:* academic remediation for entering students, adult/continuing education programs, advanced placement credit, honors programs, part-time degree program, services for LD students, summer session for credit.

Student Life *Campus security:* 24-hour patrols.

Athletics Member NJCAA.

Financial Aid Of all full-time matriculated undergraduates who enrolled in 2008, 90 Federal Work-Study jobs (averaging $850). 38 state and other part-time jobs (averaging $1020).

Applying *Options:* early admission. *Required:* high school transcript.

Director of Admissions Ms. Donna Luke, Director of Admissions, Records, and Research, East Central Community College, PO Box 129, Decatur, MS 39327-0129. *Phone:* 601-635-2111 Ext. 206. *Toll-free phone:* 877-462-3222.

East Mississippi Community College

Scooba, Mississippi www.eastms.edu/

- **State and locally supported** 2-year, founded 1927, part of Mississippi State Board for Community and Junior Colleges
- **Rural** 25-acre campus
- **Coed**

Academics *Calendar:* semesters. *Degree:* certificates and associate. *Special study options:* academic remediation for entering students, adult/continuing education programs, advanced placement credit, cooperative education, distance learning, double majors, honors programs, part-time degree program, services for LD students, summer session for credit.

Student Life *Campus security:* 24-hour emergency response devices and patrols.

Athletics Member NJCAA.

Financial Aid Of all full-time matriculated undergraduates who enrolled in 2008, 200 Federal Work-Study jobs (averaging $1200).

Applying *Options:* electronic application, deferred entrance. *Required:* high school transcript.

Director of Admissions Ms. Melinda Sciple, Admissions Officer, East Mississippi Community College, PO Box 158, Scooba, MS 39358-0158. *Phone:* 662-476-5041.

Hinds Community College

Raymond, Mississippi www.hindscc.edu/

- **State and locally supported** 2-year, founded 1917, part of Mississippi State Board for Community and Junior Colleges
- **Small-town** 671-acre campus
- **Coed**

Academics *Calendar:* semesters. *Degrees:* certificates, diplomas, and associate (reported data includes Raymond, Jackson Academic and Technical Center, Jackson Nursing-Allied Health Center, Rankin, Utica, and Vicksburg campus locations). *Special study options:* academic remediation for entering students, accelerated degree program, adult/continuing education programs, advanced placement credit, cooperative education, distance learning, double majors, freshman honors college, honors programs, independent study, part-time degree program, services for LD students, summer session for credit. *ROTC:* Army (c).

Student Life *Campus security:* 24-hour emergency response devices and patrols, controlled dormitory access.

Athletics Member NJCAA.

Standardized Tests *Required for some:* SAT and SAT Subject Tests or ACT (for admission).

Financial Aid Of all full-time matriculated undergraduates who enrolled in 2008, 300 Federal Work-Study jobs (averaging $1250). 200 state and other part-time jobs (averaging $1000).

Applying *Options:* early admission. *Required:* high school transcript.

Director of Admissions Ms. Ginger Turner, Director of Admissions and Records, Hinds Community College, PO Box 1100, Raymond, MS 39154-1100. *Phone:* 601-857-3280. *Toll-free phone:* 800-HINDSCC. *Fax:* 601-857-3539.

Holmes Community College

Goodman, Mississippi www.holmescc.edu/

- **State and locally supported** 2-year, founded 1928, part of Mississippi State Board for Community and Junior Colleges
- **Small-town** 196-acre campus
- **Coed**

Academics *Calendar:* semesters. *Degree:* certificates and associate. *Special study options:* academic remediation for entering students, adult/continuing education programs, advanced placement credit, cooperative education, distance learning, services for LD students, summer session for credit.

Student Life *Campus security:* 24-hour emergency response devices and patrols.

Athletics Member NJCAA.

Costs (2009–10) *Tuition:* state resident $1300 full-time, $75 per semester hour part-time; nonresident $3250 full-time, $85 per semester hour part-time. Full-time tuition and fees vary according to course load. Part-time tuition and fees vary according to course load. *Required fees:* $360 full-time, $12 per semester hour part-time. *Room and board:* $2180. Room and board charges vary according to housing facility.

Financial Aid Of all full-time matriculated undergraduates who enrolled in 2008, 160 Federal Work-Study jobs (averaging $700).

Applying *Options:* early admission. *Required:* high school transcript.

Director of Admissions Dr. Lynn Wright, Dean of Admissions and Records, Holmes Community College, PO Box 369, Goodman, MS 39079-0369. *Phone:* 601-472-2312 Ext. 1023.

ITAWAMBA COMMUNITY COLLEGE

Fulton, Mississippi **www.icc.cc.ms.us/**

Freshman Application Contact Mr. Larry Boggs, Director of Student Recruitment and Scholarships, Itawamba Community College, 602 West Hill Street, Fulton, MS 38843. *Phone:* 601-862-8252. *E-mail:* laboggs@iccms.edu.

JONES COUNTY JUNIOR COLLEGE

Ellisville, Mississippi **www.jcjc.edu/**

Director of Admissions Mrs. Dianne Speed, Director of Admissions and Records, Jones County Junior College, 900 South Court Street, Ellisville, MS 39437. *Phone:* 601-477-4025.

MERIDIAN COMMUNITY COLLEGE

Meridian, Mississippi **www.meridiancc.edu/**

- **State and locally supported** 2-year, founded 1937, part of Mississippi State Board for Community and Junior Colleges
- **Small-town** 62-acre campus
- **Endowment** $6.3 million
- **Coed,** 3,614 undergraduate students, 73% full-time, 69% women, 31% men

Undergraduates 2,651 full-time, 963 part-time. Students come from 16 states and territories, 3% are from out of state, 42% African American, 0.5% Asian American or Pacific Islander, 0.7% Hispanic American, 1% Native American, 0.4% international, 12% live on campus. *Retention:* 51% of 2008 full-time freshmen returned.

Freshmen *Admission:* 1,214 admitted.

Faculty *Total:* 209, 74% full-time, 4% with terminal degrees. *Student/faculty ratio:* 18:1.

Majors Administrative assistant and secretarial science; athletic training; broadcast journalism; clinical/medical laboratory technology; computer engineering technology; computer graphics; dental hygiene; drafting and design technology; electrical, electronic and communications engineering technology; emergency medical technology (EMT paramedic); fire science; health information/medical records administration; horticultural science; hotel/motel administration; machine tool technology; marketing/marketing management; medical radiologic technology; nursing (registered nurse training); physical therapy; respiratory care therapy; telecommunications technology.

Academics *Calendar:* semesters. *Degree:* certificates and associate. *Special study options:* academic remediation for entering students, adult/continuing education programs, advanced placement credit, cooperative education, distance learning, English as a second language, external degree program, independent study, part-time degree program, services for LD students, summer session for credit.

Library L. O. Todd Library with 50,000 titles, 600 serial subscriptions.

Student Life *Housing Options:* coed, men-only, women-only. Campus housing is university owned and leased by the school. *Activities and Organizations:* drama/theater group, student-run newspaper, radio station, choral group, Phi Theta Kappa, VICA (Vocational Industrial Clubs of America), Health Occupations Students of America, Organization of Student Nurses, Distributive Education Clubs of America. *Campus security:* 24-hour patrols, student patrols. *Student services:* health clinic, personal/psychological counseling.

Athletics Member NJCAA. *Intercollegiate sports:* baseball M(s), basketball M(s)/W(s), cheerleading W(s), cross-country running M(s)/W(s), golf M(s), soccer M(s), softball W(s), tennis M(s)/W(s), track and field M(s)/W(s). *Intramural sports:* basketball M/W, bowling M/W, cross-country running M/W, swimming and diving M/W, tennis M/W, volleyball M/W.

Standardized Tests *Required:* (for admission). *Recommended:* ACT (for admission).

Costs (2009–10) *Tuition:* state resident $1600 full-time, $90 per semester hour part-time; nonresident $2980 full-time, $147 per semester hour part-time. Full-time tuition and fees vary according to course load and program. Part-time tuition and fees vary according to course load and program. *Required fees:* $160 full-time, $25 per credit hour part-time. *Room and board:* $3050. Room and board charges vary according to board plan. *Payment plan:* installment. *Waivers:* employees or children of employees.

Financial Aid Of all full-time matriculated undergraduates who enrolled in 2008, 100 Federal Work-Study jobs (averaging $2100).

Applying *Options:* early admission. *Required:* high school transcript, minimum 2 GPA. *Required for some:* essay or personal statement. *Application deadlines:* rolling (freshmen), rolling (transfers).

Freshman Application Contact Ms. Angela Payne, Director of Admissions, Meridian Community College, 910 Highway 19 North, Meridian, MS 39307. *Phone:* 601-484-8357. *Toll-free phone:* 800-622-8731. *E-mail:* apayne@meridiancc.edu.

MISSISSIPPI DELTA COMMUNITY COLLEGE

Moorhead, Mississippi **www.msdelta.edu/**

Director of Admissions Mr. Joseph F. Ray Jr., Vice President of Admissions, Mississippi Delta Community College, PO Box 668, Highway 3 and Cherry Street, Moorhead, MS 38761-0668. *Phone:* 662-246-6308.

MISSISSIPPI GULF COAST COMMUNITY COLLEGE

Perkinston, Mississippi **www.mgccc.edu/**

Freshman Application Contact Mr. Ladd Taylor, Director of Admissions, Mississippi Gulf Coast Community College, PO Box 548, Perkinston, MS 39573. *Phone:* 601-928-6264. *Fax:* 601-928-6299. *E-mail:* ladd.taylor@mgccc.edu.

NORTHEAST MISSISSIPPI COMMUNITY COLLEGE

Booneville, Mississippi **www.nemcc.edu/**

- **State-supported** 2-year, founded 1948, part of Mississippi State Board for Community and Junior Colleges
- **Small-town** 100-acre campus
- **Coed**

Academics *Calendar:* semesters. *Degree:* certificates and associate. *Special study options:* academic remediation for entering students, adult/continuing education programs, advanced placement credit, cooperative education, part-time degree program, services for LD students, student-designed majors, summer session for credit.

Student Life *Campus security:* 24-hour patrols, student patrols, controlled dormitory access.

Athletics Member NJCAA.

Standardized Tests *Required for some:* SAT or ACT (for admission).

Applying *Options:* early admission.

Freshman Application Contact Office of Enrollment Services, Northeast Mississippi Community College, 101 Cunningham Boulevard, Booneville, MS 38829. *Phone:* 662-720-7239. *Toll-free phone:* 800-555-2154. *E-mail:* admitme@nemcc.edu.

NORTHWEST MISSISSIPPI COMMUNITY COLLEGE

Senatobia, Mississippi **www.northwestms.edu/**

Director of Admissions Ms. Deanna Ferguson, Director of Admissions and Recruiting, Northwest Mississippi Community College, 4975 Highway 51 North, Senatobia, MS 38668-1701. *Phone:* 662-562-3222.

Pearl River Community College

Poplarville, Mississippi www.prcc.edu/

Freshman Application Contact Mr. J. Dow Ford, Director of Admissions, Pearl River Community College, 101 Highway 11 North, Poplarville, MS 39470. *Phone:* 601-403-1000. *Toll-free phone:* 877-772-2338. *E-mail:* dford@prcc.edu.

Southwest Mississippi Community College

Summit, Mississippi www.smcc.cc.ms.us/

- **State and locally supported** 2-year, founded 1918, part of Mississippi State Board for Community and Junior Colleges
- **Rural** 701-acre campus
- **Coed,** 2,119 undergraduate students, 86% full-time, 65% women, 35% men

Undergraduates 1,822 full-time, 297 part-time. Students come from 8 states and territories, 5 other countries, 10% are from out of state, 43% African American, 0.6% Asian American or Pacific Islander, 0.5% Hispanic American, 0.3% Native American, 0.2% international, 64% transferred in, 35% live on campus. *Retention:* 65% of 2008 full-time freshmen returned.

Freshmen *Admission:* 555 enrolled.

Faculty *Total:* 90, 79% full-time. *Student/faculty ratio:* 24:1.

Majors Accounting; administrative assistant and secretarial science; advertising; automobile/automotive mechanics technology; biological and physical sciences; biology/biological sciences; business administration and management; business teacher education; carpentry; chemistry; computer programming related; computer science; computer systems networking and telecommunications; construction engineering technology; cosmetology; diesel mechanics technology; early childhood education; education; electrical, electronic and communications engineering technology; elementary education; emergency medical technology (EMT paramedic); engineering; English; fashion merchandising; finance; health information/medical records technology; health professions related; heating, air conditioning, ventilation and refrigeration maintenance technology; history; humanities; information technology; legal administrative assistant/secretary; liberal arts and sciences/liberal studies; marketing/marketing management; massage therapy; medical insurance/medical billing; music; music teacher education; nursing assistant/aide and patient care assistant; nursing (licensed practical/vocational nurse training); nursing (registered nurse training); occupational safety and health technology; petroleum technology; physical education teaching and coaching; physical sciences; social sciences; system administration; web/multimedia management and webmaster; welding technology; well drilling.

Academics *Calendar:* semesters. *Degree:* certificates and associate. *Special study options:* academic remediation for entering students, adult/continuing education programs, advanced placement credit, distance learning, part-time degree program, summer session for credit.

Library Library Learning Resources Center (LLRC) with 34,000 titles, 150 serial subscriptions, an OPAC.

Student Life *Housing Options:* men-only, women-only. Campus housing is university owned. *Activities and Organizations:* student-run newspaper, choral group, marching band. *Campus security:* 24-hour patrols.

Athletics Member NJCAA. *Intercollegiate sports:* baseball M(s), basketball M(s)/W(s), football M(s), soccer M(s)/W(s), softball W(s), tennis M(s)/W(s), track and field M(s)/W(s). *Intramural sports:* basketball M/W.

Costs (2009–10) *Tuition:* state resident $1700 full-time, $85 per credit hour part-time; nonresident $4400 full-time, $180 per credit hour part-time. Full-time tuition and fees vary according to class time., Part-time tuition and fees vary according to class time and course load. *Required fees:* $100 full-time, $50 per term part-time. *Room and board:* $2530; room only: $1130. Room and board charges vary according to board plan. *Payment plan:* deferred payment. *Waivers:* senior citizens.

Financial Aid Of all full-time matriculated undergraduates who enrolled in 2008, 85 Federal Work-Study jobs (averaging $698). 6 state and other part-time jobs (averaging $550).

Applying *Required:* high school transcript.

Freshman Application Contact Mr. Matthew Calhoun, Vice President of Admissions and Records, Southwest Mississippi Community College, 1156 College Drive, Summit, MS 39666. *Phone:* 601-276-2001. *Fax:* 601-276-3888. *E-mail:* mattc@smcc.edu.

Virginia College at Jackson

Jackson, Mississippi www.vc.edu/

Director of Admissions Director of Admissions, Virginia College at Jackson, Interstate 55 North, Jackson, MS 39211. *Phone:* 601-977-0960. *Toll-free phone:* 866-623-6765.

MISSOURI

Allied College

Maryland Heights, Missouri www.hightechinstitute.edu/

Freshman Application Contact Admissions Office, Allied College, 13723 Riverport Drive, Maryland Heights, MO 63043. *Phone:* 314-595-3400. *Toll-free phone:* 866-501-1291.

American College of Technology

Saint Joseph, Missouri www.acot.edu/

Admissions Office Contact American College of Technology, 2921 North Belt Highway, Saint Joseph, MO 64506.

Aviation Institute of Maintenance–Kansas City

Kansas City, Missouri www.aviationmaintenance.edu/aviation-kansascity.asp

Freshman Application Contact Kansas City School Director, Aviation Institute of Maintenance–Kansas City, 3130 Terrace Street, Kansas City, MO 64111. *Phone:* 816-753-9920. *Toll-free phone:* 877-538-5627. *Fax:* 816-753.-9941. *E-mail:* directoramk@tidetech.com.

Brown Mackie College–St. Louis

Fenton, Missouri www.brownmackie.edu/st-louis/

- **Proprietary** primarily 2-year
- **Coed**

Majors Accounting technology and bookkeeping; business administration and management; criminal justice/law enforcement administration; health/health-care administration; information technology; legal assistant/paralegal; legal studies; medical/clinical assistant; office management; pharmacy technician; surgical technology.

Academics *Degrees:* diplomas, associate, and bachelor's.

Freshman Application Contact Brown Mackie College–St. Louis, #2 Soccer Park Road, Fenton, MO 63026. *Phone:* 636-651-3290.

▶**See page 442 for the College Close-Up.**

Concorde Career Institute

Kansas City, Missouri www.concordecareercolleges.com/

Freshman Application Contact Admissions Office, Concorde Career Institute, 3239 Broadway, Kansas City, MO 64111.

Cottey College

Nevada, Missouri www.cottey.edu/

- **Independent** 2-year, founded 1884
- **Small-town** 51-acre campus
- **Endowment** $95,497
- **Women only**

Undergraduates 331 full-time. Students come from 40 states and territories, 21 other countries, 80% are from out of state, 5% African American, 2% Asian American or Pacific Islander, 5% Hispanic American, 3% Native American, 9% international, 0.6% transferred in, 98% live on campus. *Retention:* 78% of 2008 full-time freshmen returned.

Faculty *Student/faculty ratio:* 9:1.

Academics *Calendar:* semesters. *Degree:* associate. *Special study options:* advanced placement credit, distance learning, independent study, internships, part-time degree program, services for LD students, study abroad.

Student Life *Campus security:* 24-hour emergency response devices and patrols, late-night transport/escort service, controlled dormitory access.

Athletics Member NAIA, NJCAA.

Standardized Tests *Required:* SAT or ACT (for admission).

Costs (2009–10) *Comprehensive fee:* $20,300 includes full-time tuition ($13,800), mandatory fees ($700), and room and board ($5800). Part-time tuition: $150 per credit hour. *Required fees:* $11 per credit hour part-time.

Financial Aid Of all full-time matriculated undergraduates who enrolled in 2009, 243 applied for aid, 207 were judged to have need, 68 had their need fully met. 27 Federal Work-Study jobs (averaging $1893). 162 state and other part-time jobs (averaging $1833). In 2009, 101. *Average percent of need met:* 88. *Average financial aid package:* $15,443. *Average need-based loan:* $2791. *Average need-based gift aid:* $12,573. *Average non-need-based aid:* $7914. *Average indebtedness upon graduation:* $8709.

Applying *Options:* electronic application, early admission, deferred entrance. *Application fee:* $20. *Required:* essay or personal statement, high school transcript, 1 letter of recommendation. *Recommended:* minimum 2.6 GPA, interview.

Freshman Application Contact Ms. Judi Steege, Director of Admission, Cottey College, 1000 West Austin Boulevard, Nevada, MO 64772. *Phone:* 417-667-8181. *Toll-free phone:* 888-526-8839. *Fax:* 417-667-8103. *E-mail:* enrollmgt@cottey.edu.

Crowder College

Neosho, Missouri www.crowder.edu/

- **State and locally supported** 2-year, founded 1963, part of Missouri Coordinating Board for Higher Education
- **Rural** 608-acre campus
- **Coed,** 4,482 undergraduate students, 47% full-time, 63% women, 37% men

Undergraduates 2,111 full-time, 2,371 part-time. Students come from 19 states and territories, 23 other countries, 4% are from out of state, 1% African American, 2% Asian American or Pacific Islander, 5% Hispanic American, 2% Native American, 0.6% international, 10% live on campus.

Freshmen *Admission:* 1,169 applied, 1,169 admitted.

Faculty *Total:* 304, 22% full-time. *Student/faculty ratio:* 19:1.

Majors Administrative assistant and secretarial science; agribusiness; agriculture; art; biology/biological sciences; business administration and management; business automation/technology/data entry; computer systems networking and telecommunications; construction engineering technology; drafting and design technology; dramatic/theater arts; education; electrical, electronic and communications engineering technology; elementary education; environmental engineering technology; environmental health; executive assistant/executive secretary; farm and ranch management; fire science; general studies; industrial technology; legal administrative assistant/secretary; liberal arts and sciences/liberal studies; mass communication/media; mathematics; mathematics and computer science; medical administrative assistant and medical secretary; music; nursing (registered nurse training); physical education teaching and coaching; physical sciences; poultry science; pre-engineering; psychology; public relations/image management.

Academics *Calendar:* semesters. *Degree:* certificates and associate. *Special study options:* academic remediation for entering students, adult/continuing education programs, advanced placement credit, cooperative education, English as a second language, freshman honors college, honors programs, independent study, part-time degree program, student-designed majors, study abroad, summer session for credit.

Library Crowder College Learning Resources Center with 37,452 titles, 163 serial subscriptions, an OPAC, a Web page.

Student Life *Housing Options:* men-only, women-only. Campus housing is university owned. *Activities and Organizations:* drama/theater group, student-run newspaper, choral group, Phi Theta Kappa, Students in Free Enterprise (SIFE), Baptist Student Union, Student Senate, Student Ambassadors. *Campus security:* 24-hour patrols. *Student services:* personal/psychological counseling.

Athletics Member NJCAA. *Intercollegiate sports:* baseball M(s), basketball W(s), soccer M(s).

Costs (2009–10) *Tuition:* area resident $2040 full-time, $68 per credit hour part-time; state resident $2850 full-time, $95 per credit hour part-time; nonresident $3690 full-time, $123 per credit hour part-time. *Required fees:* $340 full-time. *Room and board:* $3870. *Payment plan:* installment. *Waivers:* senior citizens and employees or children of employees.

Financial Aid Of all full-time matriculated undergraduates who enrolled in 2008, 150 Federal Work-Study jobs (averaging $1000).

Applying *Application fee:* $25. *Required:* high school transcript. *Application deadlines:* rolling (freshmen), rolling (transfers). *Notification:* continuous (freshmen).

Freshman Application Contact Mr. Jim Riggs, Admissions Coordinator, Crowder College, 601 Laclede Avenue, Neosho, MO 64850. *Phone:* 417-451-3223 Ext. 5466. *Toll-free phone:* 866-238-7788. *Fax:* 417-455-5731. *E-mail:* jriggs@crowder.edu.

Culinary Institute of St. Louis at Hickey College

St. Louis, Missouri ci-stl.com/

Freshman Application Contact Admissions Office, Culinary Institute of St. Louis at Hickey College, 940 West Port Plaza, St. Louis, MO 63146. *Phone:* 314-434-2212.

East Central College

Union, Missouri www.eastcentral.edu/

- **District-supported** 2-year, founded 1959
- **Rural** 207-acre campus with easy access to St. Louis
- **Endowment** $2.5 million
- **Coed,** 4,203 undergraduate students, 51% full-time, 59% women, 41% men

Undergraduates 2,137 full-time, 2,066 part-time. Students come from 6 states and territories, 2 other countries, 1% African American, 0.5% Asian American or Pacific Islander, 1% Hispanic American, 0.4% Native American. *Retention:* 61% of 2008 full-time freshmen returned.

Freshmen *Admission:* 940 admitted, 940 enrolled. *Test scores:* ACT scores over 18: 78%; ACT scores over 24: 21%; ACT scores over 30: 1%.

Faculty *Total:* 241, 30% full-time, 7% with terminal degrees. *Student/faculty ratio:* 22:1.

Majors Accounting technology and bookkeeping; automobile/automotive mechanics technology; biology/biotechnology laboratory technician; business, management, and marketing related; business operations support and secretarial services related; child-care and support services management; commercial and advertising art; communications technologies and support services related; computer systems networking and telecommunications; construction trades; construction trades related; criminal justice/police science; culinary arts; drafting and design technology; education; education related; emergency medical technology (EMT paramedic); engineering; fire science; general studies; heating, air conditioning, ventilation and refrigeration maintenance technology; heavy/industrial equipment maintenance technologies related; legal administrative assistant/secretary; machine tool technology; manufacturing technology; medical administrative assistant and medical secretary; medical radiologic technology; nursing (registered nurse training); occupational therapist assistant; radiologic technology/science; respiratory care therapy; teacher assistant/aide; welding technology.

Academics *Calendar:* semesters. *Degree:* certificates and associate. *Special study options:* academic remediation for entering students, adult/continuing education programs, advanced placement credit, distance learning, English as a second language, honors programs, independent study, internships, off-campus study, part-time degree program, services for LD students, study abroad, summer session for credit.

Library East Central College Library with an OPAC, a Web page.

Student Life *Housing:* college housing not available. *Activities and Organizations:* drama/theater group, student-run newspaper, choral group, ECC Student Senate, Phi Theta Kappa, Student Nurses Assoc, Sigma Alpha Pi, S-MSTA. *Campus security:* 24-hour emergency response devices, late-night transport/escort service. *Student services:* personal/psychological counseling.

East Central College (continued)

Athletics Member NJCAA. *Intercollegiate sports:* soccer M(s), softball W(s), volleyball W(s).

Costs (2010–11) *Tuition:* area resident $1464 full-time, $61 per credit hour part-time; state resident $2088 full-time, $87 per credit hour part-time; nonresident $3144 full-time, $131 per credit hour part-time. Full-time tuition and fees vary according to program. Part-time tuition and fees vary according to program. *Required fees:* $240 full-time, $10 per credit hour part-time. *Payment plans:* installment, deferred payment. *Waivers:* senior citizens and employees or children of employees.

Financial Aid Of all full-time matriculated undergraduates who enrolled in 2008, 35 Federal Work-Study jobs (averaging $1500). 35 state and other part-time jobs (averaging $1500).

Applying *Options:* early admission, deferred entrance. *Required:* high school transcript. *Application deadlines:* rolling (freshmen), rolling (transfers).

Freshman Application Contact Miss Megen Poynter, Admissions Coordinator, East Central College, 1964 Prairie Dell Road, Union, MO 63084. *Phone:* 636-584-6564. *Fax:* 636-584-7347. *E-mail:* poynterm@eastcentral.edu.

EVEREST COLLEGE

Springfield, Missouri **www.everest.edu/campus/springfield/**

Freshman Application Contact Admissions Office, Everest College, 1010 West Sunshine Street, Springfield, MO 65807. *Phone:* 417-864-7220. *Fax:* 417-864-5697.

HERITAGE COLLEGE

Kansas City, Missouri **www.heritage-education.com/**

Freshman Application Contact Admissions Office, Heritage College, 1200 East 104th Street, Suite 300, Kansas City, MO 64131. *Phone:* 816-942-5474. *Toll-free phone:* 888-334-7339. *E-mail:* info@heritage-education.com.

HIGH-TECH INSTITUTE

Kansas City, Missouri **www.high-techinstitute.com/**

Freshman Application Contact Admissions Office, High-Tech Institute, 9001 State Line Road, Kansas City, MO 64114. *Phone:* 816-444-4300. *Toll-free phone:* 866-296-2110. *Fax:* 816-444-4494.

IHM HEALTH STUDIES CENTER

St. Louis, Missouri **www.ihmhealthstudies.com/**

Freshman Application Contact Admissions Director, IHM Health Studies Center, 2500 Abbott Place, St. Louis, MO 63143. *Phone:* 314-768-1234. *Fax:* 314-768-1595. *E-mail:* info@ihmhealthstudies.edu.

ITT TECHNICAL INSTITUTE

Arnold, Missouri **www.itt-tech.edu/**

- **Proprietary** primarily 2-year, founded 1997, part of ITT Educational Services, Inc.
- **Coed**

Majors Animation, interactive technology, video graphics and special effects; business administration and management; CAD/CADD drafting/design technology; computer and information systems security; computer engineering technology; computer software and media applications related; computer software engineering; computer software technology; construction management; criminal justice/law enforcement administration; design and visual communications; electrical, electronic and communications engineering technology; legal assistant/paralegal; system, networking, and LAN/WAN management; web/multimedia management and webmaster; web page, digital/multimedia and information resources design.

Academics *Calendar:* quarters. *Degrees:* associate and bachelor's.

Student Life *Housing:* college housing not available.

Freshman Application Contact Director of Recruitment, ITT Technical Institute, 1930 Meyer Drury Drive, Arnold, MO 63010. *Phone:* 636 464 6600. *Toll-free phone:* 888-488-1082.

ITT TECHNICAL INSTITUTE

Earth City, Missouri **www.itt-tech.edu/**

- **Proprietary** primarily 2-year, founded 1936, part of ITT Educational Services, Inc.
- **Suburban** campus
- **Coed**

Majors Animation, interactive technology, video graphics and special effects; CAD/CADD drafting/design technology; computer and information systems security; computer engineering technology; computer software and media applications related; computer software engineering; computer software technology; construction management; criminal justice/law enforcement administration; design and visual communications; electrical, electronic and communications engineering technology; legal assistant/paralegal; nursing (registered nurse training); system, networking, and LAN/WAN management; web page, digital/multimedia and information resources design.

Academics *Calendar:* quarters. *Degrees:* associate and bachelor's.

Student Life *Housing:* college housing not available.

Freshman Application Contact Director of Recruitment, ITT Technical Institute, 3640 Corporate Trail Drive, Earth City, MO 63045. *Phone:* 314-298-7800. *Toll-free phone:* 800-235-5488.

ITT TECHNICAL INSTITUTE

Kansas City, Missouri **www.itt-tech.edu/**

- **Proprietary** primarily 2-year, founded 2004, part of ITT Educational Services, Inc.
- **Coed**

Majors CAD/CADD drafting/design technology; computer and information systems security; computer engineering technology; computer software engineering; computer software technology; construction management; criminal justice/law enforcement administration; design and visual communications; electrical, electronic and communications engineering technology; legal assistant/paralegal; system, networking, and LAN/WAN management.

Academics *Calendar:* quarters. *Degrees:* associate and bachelor's.

Freshman Application Contact Director of Recruitment, ITT Technical Institute, 9150 East 41st Terrace, Kansas City, MO 64133. *Phone:* 816-276-1400. *Toll-free phone:* 877-488-1442.

JEFFERSON COLLEGE

Hillsboro, Missouri **www.jeffco.edu/**

- **State-supported** 2-year, founded 1963
- **Rural** 480-acre campus with easy access to St. Louis
- **Coed,** 5,788 undergraduate students, 55% full-time, 58% women, 42% men

Undergraduates 3,179 full-time, 2,609 part-time. 2% African American, 0.6% Asian American or Pacific Islander, 0.6% Hispanic American, 0.7% Native American, 0.4% international.

Freshmen *Admission:* 1,469 enrolled.

Faculty *Total:* 287, 33% full-time, 10% with terminal degrees.

Academics *Calendar:* semesters. *Degree:* certificates, diplomas, and associate. *Special study options:* academic remediation for entering students, adult/continuing education programs, advanced placement credit, distance learning, English as a second language, freshman honors college, honors programs, internships, off-campus study, part-time degree program, services for LD students, summer session for credit.

Library Jefferson College Library plus 1 other with 70,402 titles, 242 serial subscriptions, 5,085 audiovisual materials, an OPAC, a Web page.

Student Life *Housing Options:* coed. Campus housing is university owned. *Activities and Organizations:* drama/theater group, student-run newspaper, television station, choral group, Student Senate, Nursing associations, Baptist Student Unit, Phi Beta Lambda, Phi Theta Kappa, national sororities. *Campus security:* 24-hour patrols. *Student services:* personal/psychological counseling.

Athletics Member NJCAA. *Intercollegiate sports:* baseball M(s), basketball W(s), cheerleading M(s)/W(s), soccer M(s), softball W(s), volleyball W(s).

Costs (2009–10) *Tuition:* area resident $2550 full-time, $85 per credit hour part-time; state resident $3840 full-time, $128 per credit hour part-time; nonresident $5100 full-time, $170 per credit hour part-time. Full-time tuition and fees vary according to program. Part-time tuition and fees vary according to program. *Room and board:* Room and board charges vary according to housing facility. *Waivers:* senior citizens and employees or children of employees.

Financial Aid Of all full-time matriculated undergraduates who enrolled in 2008, 2,050 applied for aid, 1,428 were judged to have need, 61 had their need fully met. 84 Federal Work-Study jobs (averaging $1133). 194 state and other part-time jobs (averaging $1444). In 2008, 196 non-need-based awards were made. *Average percent of need met:* 55%. *Average financial aid package:* $4465. *Average need-based loan:* $2977. *Average need-based gift aid:* $2139. *Average non-need-based aid:* $1578.

Applying *Options:* electronic application, early admission. *Application fee:* $25. *Required:* high school transcript. *Application deadlines:* rolling (freshmen), rolling (transfers).

Freshman Application Contact Ms. Julie Fraser, Director of Admissions and Financial Aid, Jefferson College, 1000 Viking Drive, Hillsboro, MO 63050. *Phone:* 636-797-3000. *Fax:* 636-789-5103. *E-mail:* admissions@jeffco.edu.

LINN STATE TECHNICAL COLLEGE

Linn, Missouri **www.linnstate.edu/**

- **State-supported** 2-year, founded 1961
- **Rural** 249-acre campus
- **Endowment** $91,731
- **Coed, primarily men,** 1,142 undergraduate students, 84% full-time, 10% women, 90% men
- 57% of applicants were admitted

Undergraduates 961 full-time, 181 part-time. Students come from 3 states and territories, 3% are from out of state, 1% African American, 0.2% Asian American or Pacific Islander, 1% Hispanic American, 0.5% Native American, 8% transferred in, 15% live on campus. *Retention:* 73% of 2008 full-time freshmen returned.

Freshmen *Admission:* 1,295 applied, 734 admitted, 492 enrolled. *Average high school GPA:* 2.9. *Test scores:* ACT scores over 18: 69%; ACT scores over 24: 13%.

Faculty *Total:* 84, 98% full-time. *Student/faculty ratio:* 13:1.

Majors Aircraft powerplant technology; airframe mechanics and aircraft maintenance technology; autobody/collision and repair technology; automobile/automotive mechanics technology; civil engineering technology; computer programming; computer systems networking and telecommunications; drafting and design technology; electrical, electronic and communications engineering technology; electrical/electronics equipment installation and repair; electrician; heating, air conditioning, ventilation and refrigeration maintenance technology; heavy equipment maintenance technology; lineworker; machine tool technology; management information systems; manufacturing technology; medium/heavy vehicle and truck technology; motorcycle maintenance and repair technology; nuclear/nuclear power technology; physical therapist assistant; turf and turfgrass management.

Academics *Calendar:* semesters. *Degree:* certificates and associate. *Special study options:* academic remediation for entering students, accelerated degree program, adult/continuing education programs, advanced placement credit, cooperative education, distance learning, double majors, independent study, internships, off-campus study, part-time degree program, services for LD students, summer session for credit. *ROTC:* Army (c).

Library Linn State Technical College Library with 14,984 titles, 126 serial subscriptions, 1,931 audiovisual materials, an OPAC, a Web page.

Student Life *Housing Options:* coed, men-only, women-only, disabled students. Campus housing is university owned. *Activities and Organizations:* Skills USA, Phi Theta Kappa, Student Government Association, Aviation Club, Electricity Club. *Campus security:* 24-hour emergency response devices, student patrols, controlled dormitory access, indoor and outdoor surveillance cameras. *Student services:* personal/psychological counseling.

Athletics *Intramural sports:* archery M/W, basketball M/W, bowling M/W, football M/W, golf M/W, riflery M/W, softball M/W, table tennis M/W, volleyball M/W.

Standardized Tests *Required:* COMPASS (for admission). *Required for some:* ACT (for admission).

Costs (2010–11) *Tuition:* state resident $4380 full-time, $146 per credit hour part-time; nonresident $8760 full-time, $292 per credit hour part-time. *Required fees:* $990 full-time, $33 per credit hour part-time. *Room and board:* $4120; room only: $3120. Room and board charges vary according to board plan. *Payment plan:* installment. *Waivers:* employees or children of employees.

Financial Aid Of all full-time matriculated undergraduates who enrolled in 2008, 70 Federal Work-Study jobs (averaging $769).

Applying *Options:* electronic application. *Required:* high school transcript. *Required for some:* essay or personal statement, interview, some require high school attendance, mechanical test. *Application deadlines:* rolling (freshmen), rolling (out-of-state freshmen), rolling (transfers). *Notification:* continuous (freshmen), continuous (out-of-state freshmen), continuous (transfers).

Freshman Application Contact Linn State Technical College, One Technology Drive, Linn, MO 65051. *Phone:* 573-897-5196. *Toll-free phone:* 800-743-TECH.

METRO BUSINESS COLLEGE

Cape Girardeau, Missouri **www.metrobusinesscollege.edu/**

- **Proprietary** primarily 2-year
- **Coed**

Academics *Calendar:* quarters. *Degrees:* certificates, diplomas, associate, and bachelor's.

Applying *Application fee:* $25.

Director of Admissions Ms. Kyla Evans, Admissions Director, Metro Business College, 1732 North Kingshighway, Cape Girardeau, MO 63701. *Phone:* 573-334-9181. *Fax:* 573-334-0617.

METRO BUSINESS COLLEGE

Jefferson City, Missouri **www.metrobusinesscollege.edu/**

Freshman Application Contact Ms. Cheri Chockley, Campus Director, Metro Business College, 1407 Southwest Boulevard, Jefferson City, MO 65109. *Phone:* 573-635-6600. *Toll-free phone:* 800-467-0786. *Fax:* 573-635-6999. *E-mail:* cheri@metrobusinesscollege.edu.

METRO BUSINESS COLLEGE

Rolla, Missouri **www.metrobusinesscollege.edu/**

Freshman Application Contact Admissions Office, Metro Business College, 1202 East Highway 72, Rolla, MO 65401. *Phone:* 573-364-8464. *Toll-free phone:* 888-43-METRO. *E-mail:* inforolla@metrobusinesscollege.edu.

METROPOLITAN COMMUNITY COLLEGE–BLUE RIVER

Independence, Missouri **www.mcckc.edu/**

- **State and locally supported** 2-year, founded 1997, part of Metropolitan Community Colleges System
- **Suburban** campus with easy access to Kansas City
- **Endowment** $3.0 million
- **Coed,** 3,131 undergraduate students, 47% full-time, 60% women, 40% men

Undergraduates 1,481 full-time, 1,650 part-time. Students come from 2 states and territories, 4% African American, 0.7% Asian American or Pacific Islander, 5% Hispanic American, 0.6% Native American, 8% transferred in. *Retention:* 58% of 2008 full-time freshmen returned.

Freshmen *Admission:* 776 applied, 776 admitted, 776 enrolled.

Faculty *Total:* 390, 11% full-time, 4% with terminal degrees. *Student/faculty ratio:* 13:1.

Majors Accounting technology and bookkeeping; administrative assistant and secretarial science; business administration and management; computer and information sciences related; computer science; criminal justice/police science; fire science; information science/studies; liberal arts and sciences/liberal studies.

Academics *Calendar:* semesters. *Degree:* certificates and associate. *Special study options:* academic remediation for entering students, accelerated degree program, adult/continuing education programs, advanced placement credit, cooperative education, distance learning, English as a second language, honors programs, independent study, internships, off-campus study, part-time degree program, study abroad.

Library Blue River Community College Library with 10,312 titles, 66 serial subscriptions, an OPAC, a Web page.

Student Life *Housing:* college housing not available. *Activities and Organizations:* choral group. *Campus security:* 24-hour emergency response devices and patrols.

Metropolitan Community College–Blue River (continued)

Athletics Member NJCAA. *Intercollegiate sports:* soccer M/W.

Costs (2010–11) *Tuition:* area resident $2310 full-time, $77 per credit hour part-time; state resident $4230 full-time, $141 per credit hour part-time; nonresident $5700 full-time, $190 per credit hour part-time. *Required fees:* $150 full-time, $5 per credit hour part-time. *Payment plan:* installment. *Waivers:* senior citizens and employees or children of employees.

Applying *Options:* early admission, deferred entrance. *Application deadlines:* rolling (freshmen), rolling (transfers).

Freshman Application Contact Dr. Jon Burke, Dean of Student Development, Metropolitan Community College–Blue River, 20301 East 78 Highway, Independence, MO 64057. *Phone:* 816-604-6118. *Fax:* 816-655-6014.

METROPOLITAN COMMUNITY COLLEGE–BUSINESS & TECHNOLOGY CAMPUS

Kansas City, Missouri **www.mcckc.edu/**

- **State and locally supported** 2-year, founded 1995, part of Metropolitan Community Colleges System
- **Urban** 23-acre campus
- **Endowment** $3.0 million
- **Coed,** 707 undergraduate students, 33% full-time, 15% women, 85% men
- 100% of applicants were admitted

Undergraduates 232 full-time, 475 part-time. Students come from 2 states and territories, 3% are from out of state, 12% African American, 0.6% Asian American or Pacific Islander, 5% Hispanic American, 0.8% Native American, 3% transferred in. *Retention:* 38% of 2008 full-time freshmen returned.

Freshmen *Admission:* 135 applied, 135 admitted, 135 enrolled.

Faculty *Total:* 146, 9% full-time. *Student/faculty ratio:* 7:1.

Majors Accounting; accounting technology and bookkeeping; artificial intelligence and robotics; building/construction site management; business administration and management; business/commerce; carpentry; computer and information sciences; computer and information sciences and support services related; computer and information sciences related; computer and information systems security; computer graphics; computer/information technology services administration related; computer programming; computer programming related; computer programming (specific applications); computer programming (vendor/product certification); computer science; computer software and media applications related; computer systems analysis; computer systems networking and telecommunications; data entry/microcomputer applications; data entry/microcomputer applications related; data modeling/warehousing and database administration; data processing and data processing technology; drafting and design technology; electrical, electronic and communications engineering technology; engineering; engineering-related technologies; environmental engineering technology; glazier; information science/studies; information technology; liberal arts and sciences/liberal studies; machine shop technology; management information systems and services related; masonry; quality control technology; system administration; system, networking, and LAN/WAN management; web/multimedia management and webmaster; web page, digital/multimedia and information resources design; word processing.

Academics *Calendar:* semesters. *Degree:* certificates and associate.

Library Learning Resource Center/Library with an OPAC.

Student Life *Housing:* college housing not available. *Campus security:* 24-hour patrols, late-night transport/escort service.

Costs (2010–11) *Tuition:* area resident $2310 full-time; state resident $4230 full-time; nonresident $5700 full-time. *Required fees:* $150 full-time. *Payment plan:* installment. *Waivers:* senior citizens and employees or children of employees.

Applying *Application deadlines:* rolling (freshmen), rolling (transfers).

Freshman Application Contact Mr. Tom Wheeler, Dean of Instruction, Metropolitan Community College–Business & Technology Campus, 1775 Universal Avenue, Kansas City, MO 64120. *Phone:* 816-604-1090. *Toll-free phone:* 800-841-7158.

METROPOLITAN COMMUNITY COLLEGE–LONGVIEW

Lee's Summit, Missouri **www.mcckc.edu/**

- **State and locally supported** 2-year, founded 1969, part of Metropolitan Community Colleges System
- **Suburban** 147-acre campus with easy access to Kansas City
- **Endowment** $3.0 million
- **Coed,** 6,292 undergraduate students, 46% full-time, 57% women, 43% men

Undergraduates 2,917 full-time, 3,375 part-time. Students come from 2 states and territories, 1% are from out of state, 15% African American, 1% Asian American or Pacific Islander, 5% Hispanic American, 0.6% Native American, 5% transferred in. *Retention:* 52% of 2008 full-time freshmen returned.

Freshmen *Admission:* 1,441 applied, 1,441 admitted, 1,441 enrolled.

Faculty *Total:* 435, 20% full-time, 6% with terminal degrees. *Student/faculty ratio:* 21:1.

Majors Accounting; administrative assistant and secretarial science; agricultural mechanization; automobile/automotive mechanics technology; biological and physical sciences; biology/biological sciences; business administration and management; chemistry; computer and information sciences related; computer programming; computer science; computer typography and composition equipment operation; corrections; criminal justice/law enforcement administration; criminal justice/police science; data processing and data processing technology; engineering; heavy equipment maintenance technology; human services; legal administrative assistant/secretary; liberal arts and sciences/liberal studies; marketing/marketing management; medical administrative assistant and medical secretary; postal management; pre-engineering.

Academics *Calendar:* semesters. *Degree:* certificates and associate. *Special study options:* academic remediation for entering students, accelerated degree program, adult/continuing education programs, advanced placement credit, cooperative education, distance learning, English as a second language, honors programs, independent study, internships, off-campus study, part-time degree program, study abroad.

Library Longview Community College Library with 56,266 titles, 288 serial subscriptions, an OPAC, a Web page.

Student Life *Housing:* college housing not available. *Activities and Organizations:* drama/theater group, student-run newspaper, choral group, student newspaper, student government, Phi Theta Kappa, Longview Mighty Voices Choir, Longview Broadcasting Network, national fraternities. *Campus security:* 24-hour patrols. *Student services:* personal/psychological counseling.

Athletics Member NJCAA. *Intercollegiate sports:* baseball M(s), cross-country running W(s), volleyball W(s). *Intramural sports:* basketball M/W, swimming and diving M/W, volleyball M/W.

Costs (2010–11) *Tuition:* area resident $2310 full-time, $77 per credit hour part-time; state resident $4230 full-time, $141 per credit hour part-time; nonresident $5700 full-time, $190 per credit hour part-time. *Required fees:* $150 full-time, $5 per credit hour part-time. *Payment plan:* installment. *Waivers:* senior citizens and employees or children of employees.

Applying *Options:* early admission, deferred entrance. *Application deadlines:* rolling (freshmen), rolling (transfers).

Freshman Application Contact Ms. Janet Cline, Dean of Student Development, Metropolitan Community College–Longview, 500 Southwest Longview Road, Lee's Summit, MO 64081-2105. *Phone:* 816-604-2249. *Fax:* 816-672-2040. *E-mail:* janet.cline@mcckc.edu.

METROPOLITAN COMMUNITY COLLEGE–MAPLE WOODS

Kansas City, Missouri **www.mcckc.edu/**

- **State and locally supported** 2-year, founded 1969, part of Metropolitan Community Colleges System
- **Suburban** 205-acre campus
- **Endowment** $3.0 million
- **Coed,** 4,880 undergraduate students, 44% full-time, 58% women, 42% men

Undergraduates 2,138 full-time, 2,742 part-time. Students come from 3 states and territories, 1 other country, 5% African American, 3% Asian American or Pacific Islander, 6% Hispanic American, 0.3% Native American, 7% transferred in. *Retention:* 52% of 2008 full-time freshmen returned.

Freshmen *Admission:* 1,135 applied, 1,135 admitted, 1,135 enrolled.

Faculty *Total:* 323, 16% full-time, 6% with terminal degrees. *Student/faculty ratio:* 19:1.

Majors Accounting; administrative assistant and secretarial science; avionics maintenance technology; biological and physical sciences; biology/biological sciences; business administration and management; chemistry; computer and information sciences related; computer programming; computer science; criminal justice/law enforcement administration; criminal justice/police science; data processing and data processing technology; legal administrative assistant/secretary; liberal arts and sciences/liberal studies; marketing/marketing management; medical administrative assistant and medical secretary; pre-engineering; veterinary/animal health technology.

Academics *Calendar:* semesters. *Degree:* certificates and associate. *Special study options:* academic remediation for entering students, accelerated degree program, adult/continuing education programs, advanced placement credit, cooperative education, distance learning, English as a second language, honors programs, internships, off-campus study, part-time degree program, services for LD students, summer session for credit.

Library Maple Woods Community College Library with 32,906 titles, 250 serial subscriptions, an OPAC.

Student Life *Housing:* college housing not available. *Activities and Organizations:* drama/theater group, student-run newspaper, choral group, Student Activities Council, Art Club, Friends of All Cultures, Phi Theta Kappa, Engineering Club, national fraternities. *Campus security:* 24-hour patrols, late-night transport/escort service. *Student services:* personal/psychological counseling.

Athletics Member NJCAA. *Intercollegiate sports:* baseball M(s), soccer M/W, softball W(s). *Intramural sports:* softball M/W, volleyball M/W.

Costs (2010–11) *Tuition:* area resident $2310 full-time, $77 per credit hour part-time; state resident $4230 full-time, $141 per credit hour part-time; nonresident $5700 full-time, $190 per credit hour part-time. *Required fees:* $150 full-time, $5 per credit hour part-time. *Payment plan:* installment. *Waivers:* senior citizens and employees or children of employees.

Applying *Options:* early admission, deferred entrance. *Application deadlines:* rolling (freshmen), rolling (transfers). *Notification:* continuous (freshmen), continuous (transfers).

Freshman Application Contact Ms. Shelli Allen, Dean of Student Development and Enrollment Management, Metropolitan Community College–Maple Woods, 2601 Northeast Barry Road, Kansas City, MO 64156-1299. *Phone:* 816-604-3175. *Fax:* 816-437-3351.

METROPOLITAN COMMUNITY COLLEGE–PENN VALLEY

Kansas City, Missouri **www.mcckc.edu/**

- **State and locally supported** 2-year, founded 1969, part of Metropolitan Community Colleges System
- **Urban** 25-acre campus
- **Endowment** $3.0 million
- **Coed,** 4,656 undergraduate students, 33% full-time, 70% women, 30% men

Undergraduates 1,541 full-time, 3,115 part-time. Students come from 4 states and territories, 47 other countries, 2% are from out of state, 37% African American, 5% Asian American or Pacific Islander, 8% Hispanic American, 0.4% Native American, 14% transferred in. *Retention:* 45% of 2008 full-time freshmen returned.

Freshmen *Admission:* 921 applied, 921 admitted, 921 enrolled.

Faculty *Total:* 432, 24% full-time, 5% with terminal degrees. *Student/faculty ratio:* 12:1.

Majors Accounting; administrative assistant and secretarial science; biological and physical sciences; biology/biological sciences; business administration and management; chemistry; child-care provision; commercial and advertising art; computer and information sciences related; computer science; corrections; criminal justice/law enforcement administration; criminal justice/police science; data processing and data processing technology; emergency medical technology (EMT paramedic); engineering; family and consumer sciences/human sciences; fashion/apparel design; fashion merchandising; health information/medical records administration; kindergarten/preschool education; legal administrative assistant/secretary; legal assistant/paralegal; liberal arts and sciences/liberal studies; marketing/marketing management; medical administrative assistant and medical secretary; nursing (registered nurse training); occupational therapy; physical therapy; respiratory care therapy; special products marketing.

Academics *Calendar:* semesters. *Degree:* certificates and associate. *Special study options:* academic remediation for entering students, accelerated degree program, adult/continuing education programs, advanced placement credit, cooperative education, distance learning, English as a second language, honors programs, independent study, internships, off-campus study, part-time degree program, study abroad.

Library Penn Valley Community College Library with 91,428 titles, 89,242 serial subscriptions, an OPAC.

Student Life *Housing:* college housing not available. *Activities and Organizations:* drama/theater group, student-run newspaper, choral group, Black Student Association, Los Americanos, Phi Theta Kappa, Fashion Club, national fraternities. *Campus security:* 24-hour patrols. *Student services:* personal/psychological counseling.

Athletics Member NJCAA. *Intercollegiate sports:* basketball M(s)/W(s).

Costs (2010–11) *Tuition:* area resident $2310 full-time, $77 per credit hour part-time; state resident $4230 full-time, $141 per credit hour part-time; nonresident $5700 full-time, $190 per credit hour part-time. *Required fees:* $150 full-time, $5 per credit hour part-time. *Payment plan:* installment. *Waivers:* senior citizens and employees or children of employees.

Applying *Options:* early admission. *Required:* high school transcript. *Application deadlines:* rolling (freshmen), rolling (transfers).

Freshman Application Contact Ms. Lisa Minis, Dean of Student Services, Metropolitan Community College–Penn Valley, 3201 Southwest Trafficway, Kansas City, MO 64111. *Phone:* 816-604-4101. *Fax:* 816-759-4478.

MIDWEST INSTITUTE

Earth City, Missouri **www.midwestinstitute.com/**

Freshman Application Contact Admissions Office, Midwest Institute, 4260 Shoreline Drive, Earth City, MO 63045. *Phone:* 314-344-4440. *Toll-free phone:* 800-695-5550. *Fax:* 314-344-0494.

MIDWEST INSTITUTE

Kirkwood, Missouri **www.midwestinstitute.com/**

Freshman Application Contact Admissions Office, Midwest Institute, 10910 Manchester Road, Kirkwood, MO 63122.

MINERAL AREA COLLEGE

Park Hills, Missouri **www.mineralarea.edu/**

- **District-supported** 2-year, founded 1922, part of Missouri Coordinating Board for Higher Education
- **Rural** 240-acre campus with easy access to St. Louis
- **Coed**

Academics *Calendar:* semesters. *Degree:* certificates and associate. *Special study options:* academic remediation for entering students, advanced placement credit, distance learning, honors programs, internships, off-campus study, part-time degree program, services for LD students, summer session for credit.

Student Life *Campus security:* 24-hour patrols.

Athletics Member NJCAA.

Financial Aid Of all full-time matriculated undergraduates who enrolled in 2008, 65 Federal Work-Study jobs (averaging $3708).

Applying *Options:* electronic application, early admission. *Application fee:* $15. *Required:* high school transcript.

Freshman Application Contact Linda Huffman, Registrar, Mineral Area College, PO Box 1000, Park Hills, MO 63601-1000. *Phone:* 573-518-2130. *Fax:* 573-518-2166. *E-mail:* lhuffman@mineralarea.edu.

MISSOURI COLLEGE

St. Louis, Missouri **www.mocollege.com/**

- **Proprietary** primarily 2-year, founded 1963
- **Coed, primarily women**

Academics *Degrees:* diplomas, associate, and bachelor's.

Financial Aid Of all full-time matriculated undergraduates who enrolled in 2008, 12 Federal Work-Study jobs (averaging $1000).

Applying *Application fee:* $35. *Required:* essay or personal statement, interview.

Director of Admissions Mr. Doug Brinker, Admissions Director, Missouri College, 10121 Manchester Road, St. Louis, MO 63122-1583. *Phone:* 314-821-7700. *Fax:* 314-821-0891.

MISSOURI STATE UNIVERSITY–WEST PLAINS

West Plains, Missouri **wp.missouristate.edu/**

- **State-supported** 2-year, founded 1963, part of Missouri State University
- **Small-town** 20-acre campus
- **Endowment** $1.8 million
- **Coed,** 2,162 undergraduate students, 58% full-time, 59% women, 41% men

Undergraduates 1,260 full-time, 902 part-time. Students come from 26 states and territories, 6 other countries, 3% are from out of state, 1% African American,

Missouri State University–West Plains (continued)

0.7% Asian American or Pacific Islander, 2% Hispanic American, 1% Native American, 0.4% international, 2% transferred in, 6% live on campus. *Retention:* 56% of 2008 full-time freshmen returned.

Freshmen *Admission:* 696 applied, 696 admitted, 489 enrolled. *Average high school GPA:* 3.11. *Test scores:* ACT scores over 18: 60%; ACT scores over 24: 15%.

Faculty *Total:* 111, 30% full-time. *Student/faculty ratio:* 26:1.

Majors Accounting; agriculture; business administration and management; business/commerce; child-care and support services management; computer and information sciences related; computer graphics; computer programming (specific applications); criminal justice/law enforcement administration; criminal justice/police science; engineering; entrepreneurship; fire science; food science; general studies; horticultural science; industrial technology; information technology; legal assistant/paralegal; management information systems and services related; nursing (registered nurse training); respiratory therapy technician.

Academics *Calendar:* semesters. *Degree:* certificates and associate. *Special study options:* academic remediation for entering students, advanced placement credit, cooperative education, distance learning, honors programs, internships, off-campus study, part-time degree program, services for LD students, study abroad, summer session for credit.

Library Garnett Library with 50,717 titles, 142 serial subscriptions, 1,236 audiovisual materials, an OPAC, a Web page.

Student Life *Housing Options:* men-only, women-only. Campus housing is university owned. *Activities and Organizations:* Student Government Association, Chi Alpha, Adult Students in Higher Education, Lambda Lambda Lambda, Programming Board. *Campus security:* late-night transport/escort service, access only with key. *Student services:* health clinic, personal/psychological counseling.

Athletics Member NJCAA. *Intercollegiate sports:* basketball M(s), volleyball W(s).

Costs (2010–11) *Tuition:* state resident $102 per credit hour part-time; nonresident $204 per credit hour part-time. Full-time tuition and fees vary according to course load, location, and program. Part-time tuition and fees vary according to course load and location. *Room and board:* Room and board charges vary according to board plan. *Payment plan:* deferred payment. *Waivers:* senior citizens and employees or children of employees.

Financial Aid Of all full-time matriculated undergraduates who enrolled in 2008, 63 Federal Work-Study jobs (averaging $2000).

Applying *Options:* electronic application. *Application fee:* $15. *Required for some:* high school transcript. *Notification:* continuous (freshmen), continuous (out-of-state freshmen), continuous (transfers).

Freshman Application Contact Ms. Melissa Jett, Coordinator of Admissions, Missouri State University–West Plains, 128 Garfield, West Plains, MO 65775. *Phone:* 417-255-7955. *Fax:* 417-255-7959. *E-mail:* melissajett@missouristate.edu.

Moberly Area Community College

Moberly, Missouri www.macc.edu/

Freshman Application Contact Dr. James Grant, Dean of Student Services, Moberly Area Community College, 101 College Avenue, Moberly, MO 65270-1304. *Phone:* 660-263-4110 Ext. 235. *Toll-free phone:* 800-622-2070 Ext. 270. *Fax:* 660-263-2406. *E-mail:* info@macc.edu.

North Central Missouri College

Trenton, Missouri www.ncmissouri.edu/

Freshman Application Contact Megan Goodin, Admissions Assistant, North Central Missouri College, 1301 Main Street, Trenton, MO 64683. *Phone:* 660-359-3948 Ext. 1410. *Toll-free phone:* 800-880-6180 Ext. 401. *E-mail:* megoodin@mail.ncmissouri.edu.

Ozarks Technical Community College

Springfield, Missouri www.otc.edu/

Director of Admissions Mr. Jeff Jochems, Dean of Student Development, Ozarks Technical Community College, PO Box 5958, 1001 East Chestnut Expressway, Springfield, MO 65801. *Phone:* 417-895-7136.

Pinnacle Career Institute

Kansas City, Missouri www.pcitraining.edu/

- **Proprietary** 2-year, founded 1953
- **Coed**

Academics *Degree:* certificates and associate.

Applying *Application fee:* $50.

Director of Admissions Ms. Ruth Matous, Director of Admissions, Pinnacle Career Institute, 1001 East 101st Terrace, Suite 325, Kansas City, MO 64131. *Phone:* 816-331-5700 Ext. 212. *Toll-free phone:* 800-614-0900.

Ranken Technical College

St. Louis, Missouri www.ranken.edu/

- **Independent** primarily 2-year, founded 1907
- **Urban** 10-acre campus
- **Coed, primarily men**

Academics *Calendar:* semesters. *Degrees:* certificates, associate, and bachelor's. *Special study options:* academic remediation for entering students, adult/continuing education programs, advanced placement credit, cooperative education, distance learning, independent study, internships, part-time degree program, services for LD students, summer session for credit.

Student Life *Campus security:* 24-hour emergency response devices and patrols.

Costs (2009–10) *Comprehensive fee:* $20,418 includes full-time tuition ($12,348), mandatory fees ($570), and room and board ($7500). Full-time tuition and fees vary according to class time, course load, degree level, and program. Part-time tuition: $4944 per year. Part-time tuition and fees vary according to class time, course load, and program. *Room and board:* college room only: $5120. Room and board charges vary according to board plan.

Financial Aid Of all full-time matriculated undergraduates who enrolled in 2008, 30 Federal Work-Study jobs (averaging $2000).

Applying *Options:* electronic application. *Application fee:* $25. *Required:* essay or personal statement, high school transcript, interview.

Director of Admissions Ms. Elizabeth Keserauskis, Director of Admissions, Ranken Technical College, 4431 Finney Avenue, St. Louis, MO 63113. *Phone:* 314-371-0233 Ext. 4811. *Toll-free phone:* 866-4RANKEN.

Saint Charles Community College

Cottleville, Missouri www.stchas.edu/

- **State-supported** 2-year, founded 1986, part of Missouri Coordinating Board for Higher Education
- **Suburban** 234-acre campus with easy access to St. Louis
- **Coed,** 7,814 undergraduate students, 52% full-time, 58% women, 42% men

Undergraduates 4,067 full-time, 3,747 part-time. Students come from 7 states and territories, 20 other countries, 5% African American, 2% Asian American or Pacific Islander, 2% Hispanic American, 0.4% Native American, 1% international, 5% transferred in. *Retention:* 64% of 2008 full-time freshmen returned.

Freshmen *Admission:* 1,956 applied, 1,956 admitted, 1,884 enrolled.

Faculty *Total:* 445, 21% full-time, 18% with terminal degrees. *Student/faculty ratio:* 24:1.

Majors Accounting; accounting technology and bookkeeping; administrative assistant and secretarial science; biology/biological sciences; business administration and management; chemistry; child-care and support services management; child development; civil engineering; computer and information sciences and support services related; computer programming; computer programming related; computer programming (specific applications); computer science; computer systems networking and telecommunications; criminal justice/law enforcement administration; drafting and design technology; dramatic/theater arts; economics; education; education (specific subject areas) related; emergency medical technology (EMT paramedic); engineering; English; fire science; foreign languages and literatures; French; general studies; health information/medical records administration; health information/medical records technology; history; industrial technology; liberal arts and sciences/liberal studies; marketing/marketing management; massage therapy; mathematics; mechanical engineering; medical transcription; music history, literature, and theory; nursing (licensed practical/vocational nurse training); nursing (registered nurse training); occupational therapist assistant; occupational therapy; office management; philosophy; political science and government; precision production related; pre-engineering;

psychology; social work; sociology; Spanish; speech and rhetoric; teacher assistant/aide; web/multimedia management and webmaster.

Academics *Calendar:* semesters. *Degree:* certificates and associate. *Special study options:* academic remediation for entering students, adult/continuing education programs, advanced placement credit, cooperative education, distance learning, double majors, English as a second language, independent study, internships, part-time degree program, services for LD students, study abroad, summer session for credit.

Library Learning Resource Center with 93,332 titles, 262 serial subscriptions, 8,008 audiovisual materials, an OPAC, a Web page.

Student Life *Housing:* college housing not available. *Activities and Organizations:* drama/theater group, student-run newspaper, choral group, Phi Theta Kappa, Student Nurse Organization, Student Ambassadors, SAGE, Roller Hockey. *Campus security:* 24-hour emergency response devices and patrols, late-night transport/escort service, campus police officers on duty during normal operating hours. *Student services:* personal/psychological counseling.

Athletics Member NJCAA. *Intercollegiate sports:* baseball M(s), soccer M(s)/W(s), softball W(s).

Costs (2010–11) *Tuition:* area resident $1920 full-time, $80 per credit hour part-time; state resident $2832 full-time, $118 per credit hour part-time; nonresident $4200 full-time, $175 per credit hour part-time. *Payment plan:* installment. *Waivers:* senior citizens and employees or children of employees.

Applying *Options:* electronic application, early admission, deferred entrance. *Required for some:* high school transcript. *Recommended:* high school transcript. *Application deadlines:* rolling (freshmen), rolling (transfers). *Notification:* continuous (freshmen), continuous (transfers).

Freshman Application Contact Ms. Kathy Brockgreitens-Gober, Director of Admissions/Registrar/Financial Assistance, Saint Charles Community College, 4601 Mid Rivers Mall Drive, St. Peters, MO 63376-0975. *Phone:* 636-922-8229. *Fax:* 636-922-8236. *E-mail:* regist@stchas.edu.

St. Louis College of Health Careers

St. Louis, Missouri **www.slchc.com/**

Freshman Application Contact Admissions Office, St. Louis College of Health Careers, 909 South Taylor Avenue, St. Louis, MO 63110-1511. *Phone:* 314-652-0300. *Toll-free phone:* 866-529-7380. *Fax:* 314-652-4825.

St. Louis Community College at Florissant Valley

St. Louis, Missouri **www.stlcc.edu/**

Freshman Application Contact Ms. Brenda Davenport, Manager of Admissions and Registration, St. Louis Community College at Florissant Valley, 3400 Pershall Road, St. Louis, MO 63135-1499. *Phone:* 314-513-4248. *Fax:* 314-513-4724.

St. Louis Community College at Forest Park

St. Louis, Missouri **www.stlcc.edu/**

Freshman Application Contact Director of Admissions, St. Louis Community College at Forest Park, 5600 Oakland Avenue, St. Louis, MO 63110. *Phone:* 314-644-9129. *Fax:* 314-644-9375. *E-mail:* fp_admissions@stlcc.edu.

St. Louis Community College at Meramec

Kirkwood, Missouri **www.stlcc.edu/**

Freshman Application Contact Director of Admissions, St. Louis Community College at Meramec, 11333 Big Bend Boulevard, Kirkwood, MO 63122-5720. *Phone:* 314-984-7601. *Fax:* 314-984-7051. *E-mail:* mc-admissions@stlcc.edu.

Sanford-Brown College

Fenton, Missouri **www.sanford-brown.edu/**

- **Proprietary** primarily 2-year, founded 1868
- **Suburban** 6-acre campus with easy access to St. Louis
- **Coed**

Academics *Calendar:* quarters. *Degrees:* certificates, diplomas, associate, and bachelor's. *Special study options:* adult/continuing education programs, independent study, internships, services for LD students.

Student Life *Campus security:* late-night transport/escort service, trained security personnel from 7:30 pm to 10:30 pm.

Standardized Tests *Required:* CPAt (for admission).

Applying *Options:* deferred entrance. *Application fee:* $25. *Required:* high school transcript, interview.

Director of Admissions Ms. Judy Wilga, Director of Admissions, Sanford-Brown College, 1203 Smizer Mill Road, Fenton, MO 63026. *Phone:* 636-349-4900 Ext. 102. *Toll-free phone:* 800-456-7222. *Fax:* 636-349-9170.

Sanford-Brown College

Hazelwood, Missouri **www.sanford-brown.edu/**

- **Proprietary** 2-year, founded 1868
- 1-acre campus with easy access to St. Louis
- **Coed**

Academics *Calendar:* quarters. *Degree:* diplomas and associate. *Special study options:* academic remediation for entering students, adult/continuing education programs, internships, part-time degree program, services for LD students.

Student Life *Campus security:* 24-hour emergency response devices and patrols.

Applying *Options:* deferred entrance. *Application fee:* $25. *Required:* high school transcript, interview.

Director of Admissions Sherri Bremer, Director of Admissions, Sanford-Brown College, 75 Village Square, Hazelwood, MO 63042. *Phone:* 314-731-5200 Ext. 201.

Sanford-Brown College

St. Peters, Missouri **www.sanford-brown.edu/**

- **Proprietary** 2-year, founded 1868
- **Suburban** 2-acre campus with easy access to St. Louis
- **Coed**

Academics *Calendar:* quarters. *Degree:* diplomas and associate. *Special study options:* academic remediation for entering students, adult/continuing education programs, cooperative education, internships, part-time degree program, services for LD students, summer session for credit.

Student Life *Campus security:* 24-hour emergency response devices.

Standardized Tests *Required for some:* Thurston Mental Alertness Test.

Applying *Options:* deferred entrance. *Application fee:* $25. *Required:* high school transcript, interview.

Director of Admissions Karl J. Petersen, Executive Director, Sanford-Brown College, 100 Richmond Center Boulevard, St. Peters, MO 63376. *Phone:* 636-949-2620. *Toll-free phone:* 888-793-2433. *Fax:* 636-949-5081. *E-mail:* karl.peterson@wix.net.

Southeast Missouri Hospital College of Nursing and Health Sciences

Cape Girardeau, Missouri **www.southeastmissourihospital.com/college/**

Director of Admissions Tonya L. Buttry, President, Southeast Missouri Hospital College of Nursing and Health Sciences, 2001 William Street, Cape Girardeau, MO 63701. *Phone:* 534-334-6825. *E-mail:* tbuttry@sehosp.org.

State Fair Community College

Sedalia, Missouri **www.sfccmo.edu/**

- **District-supported** 2-year, founded 1966, part of Missouri Coordinating Board for Higher Education
- **Small-town** 128-acre campus
- **Endowment** $6.5 million
- **Coed,** 4,263 undergraduate students, 58% full-time, 63% women, 37% men

Undergraduates 2,455 full-time, 1,808 part-time. Students come from 19 states and territories, 1% are from out of state, 5% African American, 1% Asian American or Pacific Islander, 2% Hispanic American, 0.7% Native American, 5% transferred in, 3% live on campus. *Retention:* 61% of 2008 full-time freshmen returned.

Freshmen *Admission:* 1,160 admitted, 1,160 enrolled.

Faculty *Total:* 302, 22% full-time. *Student/faculty ratio:* 21:1.

Majors Accounting; accounting and computer science; agribusiness; applied horticulture; automobile/automotive mechanics technology; building/construction site management; business administration and management; CAD/CADD drafting/design technology; child-care and support services management; computer programming (specific applications); computer systems networking and telecommunications; criminal justice/police science; dental hygiene; education (specific subject areas) related; health information/medical records technology; liberal arts and sciences/liberal studies; machine tool technology; manufacturing technology; marine maintenance and ship repair technology; mechanic and repair technologies related; medical administrative assistant and medical secretary; nursing (registered nurse training); occupational therapist assistant; physical therapist assistant; radiologic technology/science; special products marketing; teacher assistant/aide; technical teacher education; web page, digital/multimedia and information resources design.

Academics *Calendar:* semesters. *Degree:* certificates and associate. *Special study options:* academic remediation for entering students, adult/continuing education programs, advanced placement credit, distance learning, English as a second language, internships, off-campus study, part-time degree program, services for LD students, summer session for credit. *ROTC:* Army (b).

Library Donald C. Proctor Library with 41,258 titles, 10,227 serial subscriptions, 1,633 audiovisual materials, an OPAC, a Web page.

Student Life *Housing Options:* coed. Campus housing is university owned. *Activities and Organizations:* drama/theater group, choral group. *Campus security:* controlled dormitory access, security during evening class hours.

Athletics Member NJCAA. *Intercollegiate sports:* basketball M(s)/W(s).

Costs (2010–11) *Tuition:* area resident $2040 full-time, $68 per credit hour part-time; state resident $2880 full-time, $96 per credit hour part-time; nonresident $4560 full-time, $152 per credit hour part-time. Full-time tuition and fees vary according to location and program. Part-time tuition and fees vary according to location and program. *Required fees:* $540 full-time, $18 per credit hour part-time. *Room and board:* $4350. *Payment plan:* installment. *Waivers:* senior citizens and employees or children of employees.

Financial Aid Of all full-time matriculated undergraduates who enrolled in 2009, 85 Federal Work-Study jobs (averaging $1616).

Applying *Options:* electronic application. *Application fee:* $25. *Required:* high school transcript. *Application deadlines:* rolling (freshmen), rolling (transfers).

Freshman Application Contact State Fair Community College, 3201 West 16th, Sedalia, MO 65301. *Phone:* 660-596-7221. *Toll-free phone:* 877-311-7322 Ext. 217 (in-state); 877-311-7322 (out-of-state).

Three Rivers Community College

Poplar Bluff, Missouri **www.trcc.edu/**

- **State and locally supported** 2-year, founded 1966, part of Missouri Coordinating Board for Higher Education
- **Rural** 70-acre campus
- **Endowment** $678,633
- **Coed,** 3,185 undergraduate students, 61% full-time, 67% women, 33% men

Undergraduates 1,942 full-time, 1,243 part-time. Students come from 13 states and territories, 4% are from out of state, 7% African American, 0.4% Asian American or Pacific Islander, 1% Hispanic American, 0.6% Native American, 0.1% transferred in, 5% live on campus.

Freshmen *Admission:* 691 applied, 691 admitted, 691 enrolled.

Faculty *Total:* 189, 32% full-time, 7% with terminal degrees. *Student/faculty ratio:* 23:1.

Majors Accounting; administrative assistant and secretarial science; agricultural business and management; agricultural mechanization; business administration and management; clinical/medical laboratory technology; computer and information sciences and support services related; computer and information sciences related; computer engineering technology; construction engineering technology; criminal justice/law enforcement administration; criminal justice/police science; data entry/microcomputer applications; data entry/microcomputer applications related; education; elementary education; engineering technology; industrial technology; information technology; liberal arts and sciences/liberal studies; marketing/marketing management; music; nursing (registered nurse training); word processing.

Academics *Calendar:* semesters. *Degree:* certificates and associate. *Special study options:* academic remediation for entering students, accelerated degree program, adult/continuing education programs, advanced placement credit, distance learning, double majors, English as a second language, external degree program, honors programs, independent study, internships, part-time degree program, services for LD students, summer session for credit.

Library Rutland Library with 33,289 titles, 177 serial subscriptions, 1,200 audiovisual materials, an OPAC, a Web page.

Student Life *Housing Options:* coed. Campus housing is university owned. *Activities and Organizations:* Marketing Management Association, Phi Theta Kappa, Phi Beta Lambda, Alpha Beta Gamma, TRCC Aggies. *Campus security:* 24-hour patrols.

Athletics Member NJCAA. *Intercollegiate sports:* baseball M(s), basketball M(s)/W(s), cheerleading M(s)/W(s), softball W(s).

Costs (2009–10) *Tuition:* area resident $2010 full-time, $67 per credit hour part-time; state resident $3210 full-time, $107 per credit hour part-time; nonresident $4020 full-time, $134 per credit hour part-time. *Required fees:* $605 full-time, $14 per credit hour part-time. *Room and board:* room only: $3324. *Payment plan:* installment. *Waivers:* senior citizens and employees or children of employees.

Applying *Options:* early admission. *Application fee:* $20. *Required:* high school transcript.

Freshman Application Contact Ms. Marcia Fields, Director of Admissions and Recruiting, Three Rivers Community College, 2080 Three Rivers Boulevard, Poplar Bluff, MO 63901. *Phone:* 573-840-9675. *Toll-free phone:* 877-TRY-TRCC Ext. 605 (in-state); 877-TRY-TRCC (out-of-state). *E-mail:* trytrcc@trcc.edu.

Vatterott College

Kansas City, Missouri **www.vatterott-college.edu/**

Admissions Office Contact Vatterott College, 8955 East 38th Terrace, Kansas City, MO 64129. *Toll-free phone:* 866-314-6454.

Vatterott College

O'Fallon, Missouri **www.vatterott-college.edu/**

Director of Admissions Gertrude Bogan-Jones, Director of Admissions, Vatterott College, 927 East Terra Lane, O'Fallon, MO 63366. *Phone:* 636-978-7488. *Toll-free phone:* 888-766-3601. *Fax:* 636-978-5121. *E-mail:* ofallon@vatterott-college.edu.

Vatterott College

St. Ann, Missouri **www.vatterott-college.edu/**

Director of Admissions Ann Farajallah, Director of Admissions, Vatterott College, 3925 Industrial Drive, St. Ann, MO 63074-1807. *Phone:* 314-264-1020. *Toll-free phone:* 866-314-6454.

Vatterott College

St. Joseph, Missouri **www.vatterott-college.edu/**

Director of Admissions Director of Admissions, Vatterott College, 3131 Frederick Avenue, St. Joseph, MO 64506. *Phone:* 816-364-5399. *Toll-free phone:* 800-282-5327. *Fax:* 816-364-1593.

VATTEROTT COLLEGE

Sunset Hills, Missouri **www.vatterott-college.edu/**

Director of Admissions Director of Admission, Vatterott College, 12970 Maurer Industrial Drive, St. Louis, MO 63127. *Phone:* 314-843-4200. *Fax:* 314-843-1709.

VATTEROTT COLLEGE

Springfield, Missouri **www.vatterott-college.edu/**

Freshman Application Contact Mr. Scott Lester, Director of Admissions, Vatterott College, 3850 South Campbell, Springfield, MO 65807. *Phone:* 417-831-8116. *Toll-free phone:* 800-766-5829. *Fax:* 417-831-5099. *E-mail:* springfield@vatterott-college.edu.

VET TECH INSTITUTE AT HICKEY COLLEGE

St. Louis, Missouri **www.vettechinstitute.edu/**

- **Private** 2-year, founded 2007
- **Suburban** campus
- **Coed,** 125 undergraduate students
- 55% of applicants were admitted

Freshmen *Admission:* 502 applied, 275 admitted.
Majors Veterinary/animal health technology.
Academics *Degree:* associate. *Special study options:* accelerated degree program, internships.
Freshman Application Contact Admissions Office, Vet Tech Institute at Hickey College, 2780 North Lindbergh Boulevard, St. Louis, MO 63114. *Phone:* 888-884-1459.

WENTWORTH MILITARY ACADEMY AND COLLEGE

Lexington, Missouri **www.wma1880.org/**

Freshman Application Contact Dr. Roger Hamilton, Vice President for Academic Affairs, Wentworth Military Academy and College, 1880 Washington Avenue, Lexington, MO 64067. *Phone:* 660-259-2221. *Fax:* 660-259-2677. *E-mail:* admissions@wma1880.org.

MONTANA

BLACKFEET COMMUNITY COLLEGE

Browning, Montana **www.bfcc.org/**

- **Independent** 2-year, founded 1974
- **Small-town** 5-acre campus
- **Coed**

Academics *Calendar:* semesters. *Degree:* certificates, diplomas, and associate. *Special study options:* academic remediation for entering students, adult/continuing education programs, off-campus study, part-time degree program.
Student Life *Campus security:* 16 hour patrols by security personnel.
Costs (2009–10) *Tuition:* $1650 full-time, $75 per credit hour part-time. Full-time tuition and fees vary according to course load. Part-time tuition and fees vary according to course load. *Required fees:* $350 full-time, $75 per credit hour part-time, $100 per term part-time.
Financial Aid Of all full-time matriculated undergraduates who enrolled in 2008, 10 Federal Work-Study jobs (averaging $2316). *Financial aid deadline:* 6/30.
Applying *Options:* early admission. *Application fee:* $15. *Required:* high school transcript, immunization with second MMR; certificate of Indian blood.
Freshman Application Contact Ms. Deana M. McNabb, Registrar and Admissions Officer, Blackfeet Community College, PO Box 819, Browning, MT 59417. *Phone:* 406-338-5421. *Toll-free phone:* 800-549-7457. *Fax:* 406-338-3272.

CHIEF DULL KNIFE COLLEGE

Lame Deer, Montana **www.cdkc.edu/**

Director of Admissions Mr. William L. Wertman, Registrar and Director of Admissions, Chief Dull Knife College, PO Box 98, 1 College Drive, Lame Deer, MT 59043-0098. *Phone:* 406-477-6215.

DAWSON COMMUNITY COLLEGE

Glendive, Montana **www.dawson.edu/**

- **State and locally supported** 2-year, founded 1940, part of Montana University System
- **Rural** 300-acre campus
- **Endowment** $344,944
- **Coed**

Academics *Calendar:* semesters. *Degree:* certificates and associate. *Special study options:* academic remediation for entering students, adult/continuing education programs, independent study, internships, part-time degree program, services for LD students, summer session for credit.
Student Life *Campus security:* 24-hour emergency response devices.
Athletics Member NJCAA.
Costs (2009–10) *Tuition:* area resident $1566 full-time, $52 per credit part-time; state resident $2673 full-time, $89 per credit part-time; nonresident $7329 full-time, $244 per credit part-time. *Required fees:* $1170 full-time, $39 per credit part-time. *Room and board:* $3300. *Payment plans:* installment, deferred payment.
Financial Aid Of all full-time matriculated undergraduates who enrolled in 2008, 45 Federal Work-Study jobs (averaging $1500). 17 state and other part-time jobs (averaging $1500).
Applying *Options:* deferred entrance. *Application fee:* $30. *Required:* high school transcript.
Director of Admissions Jolene Myers, Director of Admissions and Financial Aid, Dawson Community College, Box 421, Glendive, MT 59330-0421. *Phone:* 406-377-3396 Ext. 410. *Toll-free phone:* 800-821-8320.

FLATHEAD VALLEY COMMUNITY COLLEGE

Kalispell, Montana **www.fvcc.edu/**

- **State and locally supported** 2-year, founded 1967, part of Montana University System
- **Small-town** 209-acre campus
- **Endowment** $2.5 million
- **Coed,** 2,501 undergraduate students, 57% full-time, 57% women, 43% men

Undergraduates 1,430 full-time, 1,071 part-time. Students come from 34 states and territories, 4 other countries, 4% are from out of state, 0.4% African American, 1% Asian American or Pacific Islander, 2% Hispanic American, 3% Native American, 0.1% international, 7% transferred in. *Retention:* 56% of 2008 full-time freshmen returned.
Freshmen *Admission:* 407 enrolled. *Average high school GPA:* 2.86.
Faculty *Total:* 204, 21% full-time, 9% with terminal degrees. *Student/faculty ratio:* 18:1.
Majors Accounting; administrative assistant and secretarial science; business administration and management; carpentry; child-care and support services management; computer engineering technology; computer/information technology services administration related; criminal justice/law enforcement administration; culinary arts; electrician; emergency medical technology (EMT paramedic); graphic design; hospitality and recreation marketing; human services; liberal arts and sciences/liberal studies; medical administrative assistant and medical secretary; medical/clinical assistant; medical radiologic technology; metal and jewelry arts; nursing (licensed practical/vocational nurse training); small business administration; substance abuse/addiction counseling; surgical

Flathead Valley Community College (continued)

technology; survey technology; web/multimedia management and webmaster; wildlife and wildlands science and management; word processing.

Academics *Calendar:* semesters. *Degree:* certificates and associate. *Special study options:* academic remediation for entering students, adult/continuing education programs, advanced placement credit, cooperative education, distance learning, double majors, English as a second language, honors programs, independent study, internships, part-time degree program, services for LD students, study abroad, summer session for credit.

Library Flathead Valley Community College Library with 35,000 titles, 125 serial subscriptions, 514 audiovisual materials, an OPAC, a Web page.

Student Life *Housing:* college housing not available. *Activities and Organizations:* drama/theater group, student-run newspaper, choral group, Forestry Club, Pi-Ta Club. *Student services:* personal/psychological counseling.

Athletics *Intercollegiate sports:* cross-country running M(s)/W(s), soccer M(s)/W(s). *Intramural sports:* basketball M/W, football M/W, golf M/W, softball M/W, table tennis M/W, ultimate Frisbee M/W, volleyball M/W.

Costs (2009–10) *Tuition:* area resident $2604 full-time, $93 per credit part-time; state resident $3976 full-time, $142 per credit part-time; nonresident $9744 full-time, $348 per credit part-time. Part-time tuition and fees vary according to course load. *Required fees:* $892 full-time, $32 per credit part-time. *Payment plan:* deferred payment. *Waivers:* senior citizens and employees or children of employees.

Applying *Options:* early admission, deferred entrance. *Application fee:* $15. *Required:* high school transcript. *Application deadlines:* rolling (freshmen), rolling (transfers).

Freshman Application Contact Ms. Marlene C. Stoltz, Admissions/Graduation Coordinator, Flathead Valley Community College, 777 Grandview Avenue, Kalispell, MT 59901-2622. *Phone:* 406-756-3846. *Toll-free phone:* 800-313-3822. *E-mail:* mstoltz@fvcc.cc.mt.us.

Fort Belknap College

Harlem, Montana **www.fbcc.edu/**

Director of Admissions Ms. Dixie Brockie, Registrar and Admissions Officer, Fort Belknap College, PO Box 159, Harlem, MT 59526-0159. *Phone:* 406-353-2607 Ext. 233. *Fax:* 406-353-2898.

Fort Peck Community College

Poplar, Montana **www.fpcc.edu/**

- **District-supported** 2-year, founded 1978
- **Small-town** campus
- **Coed**

Academics *Calendar:* semesters. *Degree:* certificates and associate. *Special study options:* off-campus study, part-time degree program, summer session for credit.

Applying *Options:* electronic application, early admission. *Application fee:* $15.

Director of Admissions Mr. Robert McAnally, Vice President for Student Services, Fort Peck Community College, PO Box 398, Poplar, MT 59255-0398. *Phone:* 406-768-6329.

Little Big Horn College

Crow Agency, Montana **www.lbhc.cc.mt.us/**

Freshman Application Contact Ms. Ann Bullis, Dean of Student Services, Little Big Horn College, Box 370, 1 Forest Lane, Crow Agency, MT 59022-0370. *Phone:* 406-638-2228 Ext. 50.

Miles Community College

Miles City, Montana **www.milescc.edu/**

- **State and locally supported** 2-year, founded 1939, part of Montana University System
- **Small-town** 8-acre campus
- **Coed**

Academics *Calendar:* semesters. *Degree:* certificates and associate. *Special study options:* academic remediation for entering students, accelerated degree program, adult/continuing education programs, advanced placement credit, cooperative education, distance learning, double majors, English as a second language, independent study, internships, off-campus study, part-time degree program, services for LD students, summer session for credit.

Student Life *Campus security:* 24-hour emergency response devices.

Athletics Member NJCAA.

Costs (2009–10) *Tuition:* area resident $2130 full-time, $71 per credit part-time; state resident $3000 full-time, $100 per credit part-time; nonresident $5790 full-time, $193 per credit part-time. Full-time tuition and fees vary according to reciprocity agreements. Part-time tuition and fees vary according to reciprocity agreements. *Required fees:* $1290 full-time, $43 per credit part-time. *Room and board:* $4200; room only: $2250. Room and board charges vary according to board plan, housing facility, and location. *Payment plans:* installment, deferred payment.

Financial Aid Of all full-time matriculated undergraduates who enrolled in 2008, 25 Federal Work-Study jobs (averaging $1400). 22 state and other part-time jobs (averaging $1300).

Applying *Options:* early admission, deferred entrance. *Application fee:* $30. *Required:* high school transcript.

Director of Admissions Ms. Laura J. Pierce, Chief Student Services Officer, Miles Community College, 2715 Dickinson, Miles City, MT 59301-4799. *Phone:* 406-874-6159. *Toll-free phone:* 800-541-9281.

Montana State University–Great Falls College of Technology

Great Falls, Montana **www.msugf.edu/**

- **State-supported** 2-year, founded 1969, part of Montana University System
- **Small-town** 40-acre campus
- **Endowment** $11,300
- **Coed,** 2,451 undergraduate students, 37% full-time, 65% women, 35% men

Undergraduates 907 full-time, 1,544 part-time. Students come from 29 states and territories, 2% are from out of state, 2% African American, 1% Asian American or Pacific Islander, 3% Hispanic American, 7% Native American, 8% transferred in. *Retention:* 57% of 2008 full-time freshmen returned.

Freshmen *Admission:* 400 applied, 394 admitted, 282 enrolled. *Average high school GPA:* 2.74.

Faculty *Total:* 142, 32% full-time.

Majors Accounting; accounting technology and bookkeeping; aeronautics/aviation/aerospace science and technology; airline pilot and flight crew; autobody/collision and repair technology; business administration and management; carpentry; computer systems networking and telecommunications; dental assisting; dental hygiene; drafting and design technology; education; emergency medical technology (EMT paramedic); fire science; graphic design; health information/medical records administration; health information/medical records technology; information technology; interior design; liberal arts and sciences and humanities related; medical/clinical assistant; medical insurance/medical billing; medical radiologic technology; medical transcription; nursing (licensed practical/vocational nurse training); physical therapist assistant; radiologic technology/science; respiratory care therapy; security and protective services related; surgical technology; system administration; web page, digital/multimedia and information resources design; welding technology.

Academics *Calendar:* semesters. *Degree:* certificates and associate. *Special study options:* academic remediation for entering students, advanced placement credit, distance learning, double majors, English as a second language, independent study, internships, off-campus study, part-time degree program, services for LD students, summer session for credit.

Library Weaver Library with 8,783 titles, 100 serial subscriptions, 1,043 audiovisual materials, an OPAC, a Web page.

Student Life *Housing:* college housing not available. *Activities and Organizations:* drama/theater group, The Associated Students of Montana State University - Great Falls (ASMSUGF), Thesperadoes. *Campus security:* 24-hour emergency response devices.

Costs (2010–11) *Tuition:* state resident $2496 full-time, $104 per credit hour part-time; nonresident $8748 full-time, $364 per credit hour part-time. Full-time tuition and fees vary according to course load and program. Part-time tuition and fees vary according to course load and program. *Required fees:* $529 full-time, $67 per credit hour part-time. *Payment plan:* deferred payment. *Waivers:* minority students, senior citizens, and employees or children of employees.

Financial Aid Of all full-time matriculated undergraduates who enrolled in 2008, 48 Federal Work-Study jobs (averaging $2000). 13 state and other part-time jobs (averaging $2000).

Applying *Options:* early admission. *Application fee:* $30. *Required:* high school transcript, proof of immunization. *Application deadlines:* rolling (freshmen), rolling (out-of-state freshmen), rolling (transfers).

Freshman Application Contact Ms. Dana Freshly, Admissions, Montana State University–Great Falls College of Technology, 2100 16th Avenue South, Great Falls, MT 59405. *Phone:* 406-771-4300. *Toll-free phone:* 800-446-2698. *Fax:* 406-771-4329. *E-mail:* dfreshly@msugf.edu.

SALISH KOOTENAI COLLEGE

Pablo, Montana **www.skc.edu/**

Freshman Application Contact Ms. Jackie Moran, Admissions Officer, Salish Kootenai College, 52000 Highway 93, PO Box 70, Pablo, MT 59855. *Phone:* 406-275-4866. *Fax:* 406-275-4810. *E-mail:* jackie_moran@skc.edu.

STONE CHILD COLLEGE

Box Elder, Montana **www.stonechild.edu/**

Director of Admissions Mr. Ted Whitford, Director of Admissions/Registrar, Stone Child College, RR1, Box 1082, Box Elder, MT 59521. *Phone:* 406-395-4313 Ext. 110. *E-mail:* uanet337@quest.ocsc.montana.edu.

THE UNIVERSITY OF MONTANA–HELENA COLLEGE OF TECHNOLOGY

Helena, Montana **www.umhelena.edu/**

- **State-supported** 2-year, founded 1939, part of Montana University System
- **Small-town** campus
- **Coed,** 1,380 undergraduate students, 53% full-time, 54% women, 46% men

Undergraduates 732 full-time, 648 part-time. Students come from 14 states and territories, 1% are from out of state, 0.4% African American, 0.7% Asian American or Pacific Islander, 2% Hispanic American, 5% Native American, 11% transferred in.

Freshmen *Admission:* 481 applied, 354 admitted, 344 enrolled.

Faculty *Total:* 90, 61% full-time. *Student/faculty ratio:* 14:1.

Majors Accounting technology and bookkeeping; airframe mechanics and aircraft maintenance technology; automobile/automotive mechanics technology; business automation/technology/data entry; carpentry; computer programming; diesel mechanics technology; executive assistant/executive secretary; fire science; general studies; legal administrative assistant/secretary; machine tool technology; medical administrative assistant and medical secretary; nursing (licensed practical/vocational nurse training); office occupations and clerical services; welding technology.

Academics *Calendar:* semesters. *Degree:* certificates and associate. *Special study options:* academic remediation for entering students, adult/continuing education programs, distance learning, part-time degree program, services for LD students, summer session for credit.

Library UM-Helena Library with 60,281 titles, 30,903 serial subscriptions, 3,337 audiovisual materials, an OPAC, a Web page.

Student Life *Housing:* college housing not available. *Activities and Organizations:* Student Senate, Circle K. *Student services:* personal/psychological counseling.

Athletics *Intramural sports:* basketball M/W, volleyball M/W.

Costs (2010–11) *Tuition:* state resident $3041 full-time, $98 per credit hour part-time; nonresident $8066 full-time. Full-time tuition and fees vary according to course load and reciprocity agreements. Part-time tuition and fees vary according to course load and reciprocity agreements. *Payment plan:* installment. *Waivers:* minority students, senior citizens, and employees or children of employees.

Financial Aid Of all full-time matriculated undergraduates who enrolled in 2008, 445 applied for aid, 334 were judged to have need. 42 Federal Work-Study jobs (averaging $1549). 22 state and other part-time jobs (averaging $1476). In 2008, 37 non-need-based awards were made. *Average financial aid package:* $6368. *Average need-based loan:* $3428. *Average need-based gift aid:* $3111. *Average non-need-based aid:* $1769. *Average indebtedness upon graduation:* $14,068.

Applying *Options:* electronic application, early admission, deferred entrance. *Application fee:* $30. *Required for some:* high school transcript. *Application deadlines:* rolling (freshmen), rolling (transfers).

Freshman Application Contact Mr. Kendall May, Admissions Representative/Recruiter, The University of Montana–Helena College of Technology, 1115 North Roberts Street, Helena, MT 59601. *Phone:* 406-444-5436. *Toll-free phone:* 800-241-4882. *E-mail:* kendall.may@umhelena.edu.

NEBRASKA

CENTRAL COMMUNITY COLLEGE–COLUMBUS CAMPUS

Columbus, Nebraska **www.cccneb.edu/**

- **State and locally supported** 2-year, founded 1968, part of Central Community College
- **Small-town** 90-acre campus
- **Coed,** 2,601 undergraduate students, 18% full-time, 62% women, 38% men

Undergraduates 481 full-time, 2,120 part-time. Students come from 36 states and territories, 17 other countries, 4% are from out of state, 1% African American, 0.5% Asian American or Pacific Islander, 9% Hispanic American, 0.4% Native American, 5% transferred in, 17% live on campus.

Freshmen *Admission:* 328 enrolled.

Faculty *Total:* 88, 45% full-time, 8% with terminal degrees.

Majors Accounting; administrative assistant and secretarial science; agricultural business and management; automobile/automotive mechanics technology; business administration and management; child-care and support services management; commercial and advertising art; computer and information sciences; computer programming (specific applications); criminal justice/safety; drafting and design technology; electrical, electronic and communications engineering technology; electromechanical technology; hospital and health-care facilities administration; industrial technology; information technology; liberal arts and sciences/liberal studies; machine tool technology; marketing/marketing management; medical/clinical assistant; nursing (licensed practical/vocational nurse training); quality control technology; system administration; web/multimedia management and webmaster; welding technology.

Academics *Calendar:* semesters plus six-week summer session. *Degree:* certificates, diplomas, and associate. *Special study options:* academic remediation for entering students, accelerated degree program, adult/continuing education programs, advanced placement credit, cooperative education, distance learning, English as a second language, external degree program, independent study, internships, off-campus study, part-time degree program, services for LD students, student-designed majors, summer session for credit.

Library Learning Resources Center with 22,000 titles, 118 serial subscriptions, an OPAC.

Student Life *Housing Options:* coed. Campus housing is university owned. *Activities and Organizations:* drama/theater group, choral group, Phi Theta Kappa, Drama Club, Art Club, Cantari, Chorale. *Campus security:* 24-hour emergency response devices and patrols, controlled dormitory access, night security. *Student services:* personal/psychological counseling, women's center.

Athletics Member NJCAA. *Intercollegiate sports:* basketball M(s), golf M(s), softball W(s), volleyball W(s). *Intramural sports:* basketball M/W, football M, softball M/W, table tennis M/W, volleyball M/W.

Costs (2010–11) *Tuition:* state resident $1776 full-time, $74 per credit part-time; nonresident $2664 full-time, $111 per credit part-time. *Required fees:* $168 full-time, $7 per credit part-time. *Room and board:* $5120. Room and board charges vary according to board plan. *Payment plan:* deferred payment. *Waivers:* employees or children of employees.

Applying *Options:* electronic application, early admission. *Required:* high school transcript. *Required for some:* 3 letters of recommendation, interview. *Application deadlines:* rolling (freshmen), rolling (transfers). *Notification:* continuous (freshmen), continuous (transfers).

Freshman Application Contact Ms. Mary Young, Admissions/Recruiting Coordinator, Central Community College–Columbus Campus, PO Box 1027, Columbus, NE 68602-1027. *Phone:* 402-562-1296. *Toll-free phone:* 800-642-1083. *Fax:* 402-562-1201. *E-mail:* myoung@cccneb.edu.

CENTRAL COMMUNITY COLLEGE–GRAND ISLAND CAMPUS

Grand Island, Nebraska **www.cccneb.edu/**

- **State and locally supported** 2-year, founded 1976, part of Central Community College
- **Small-town** 64-acre campus
- **Coed,** 3,263 undergraduate students, 14% full-time, 67% women, 33% men

Central Community College–Grand Island Campus (continued)

Undergraduates 456 full-time, 2,807 part-time. Students come from 36 states and territories, 17 other countries, 4% are from out of state, 2% African American, 1% Asian American or Pacific Islander, 10% Hispanic American, 0.6% Native American, 3% transferred in, 10% live on campus.

Freshmen *Admission:* 414 enrolled.

Faculty *Total:* 112, 41% full-time, 7% with terminal degrees. *Student/faculty ratio:* 15:1.

Majors Accounting; administrative assistant and secretarial science; automobile/automotive mechanics technology; business administration and management; child development; clinical/medical social work; computer and information sciences; computer programming (specific applications); criminal justice/safety; data processing and data processing technology; drafting and design technology; electrical, electronic and communications engineering technology; heating, air conditioning, ventilation and refrigeration maintenance technology; hospital and health-care facilities administration; industrial technology; information technology; legal assistant/paralegal; liberal arts and sciences/liberal studies; medical/clinical assistant; nursing (licensed practical/vocational nurse training); nursing (registered nurse training); system administration; web/multimedia management and webmaster; welding technology.

Academics *Calendar:* semesters plus six-week summer session. *Degree:* certificates, diplomas, and associate. *Special study options:* academic remediation for entering students, accelerated degree program, adult/continuing education programs, advanced placement credit, cooperative education, distance learning, English as a second language, external degree program, independent study, internships, off-campus study, part-time degree program, services for LD students, student-designed majors, summer session for credit.

Library Central Community College–Grand Island Campus Library with 5,700 titles, 94 serial subscriptions, an OPAC, a Web page.

Student Life *Housing Options:* coed. Campus housing is provided by a third party. Freshman applicants given priority for college housing. *Activities and Organizations:* Mid-Nebraska Users of Computers, Student Activities Organization, intramurals, TRIO, Phi Theta Kappa. *Student services:* personal/psychological counseling.

Athletics *Intramural sports:* bowling M/W, softball M/W, table tennis M/W, volleyball M/W.

Costs (2010–11) *Tuition:* state resident $1776 full-time, $74 per credit part-time; nonresident $2664 full-time, $111 per credit part-time. *Required fees:* $168 full-time. *Payment plan:* deferred payment. *Waivers:* employees or children of employees.

Applying *Options:* electronic application, early admission. *Required:* high school transcript. *Required for some:* 3 letters of recommendation, interview. *Application deadlines:* rolling (freshmen), rolling (transfers). *Notification:* continuous (freshmen), continuous (transfers).

Freshman Application Contact Michelle Svoboda, Admissions Director, Central Community College–Grand Island Campus, PO Box 4903, Grand Island, NE 68802-4903. *Phone:* 308-398-7406 Ext. 406. *Toll-free phone:* 800-652-9177. *Fax:* 308-398-7398. *E-mail:* msvoboda@cccneb.edu.

Central Community College–Hastings Campus

Hastings, Nebraska **www.cccneb.edu/**

- **State and locally supported** 2-year, founded 1966, part of Central Community College
- **Small-town** 600-acre campus
- **Coed,** 2,858 undergraduate students, 38% full-time, 56% women, 44% men

Undergraduates 1,083 full-time, 1,775 part-time. Students come from 36 states and territories, 17 other countries, 4% are from out of state, 0.8% African American, 1% Asian American or Pacific Islander, 6% Hispanic American, 0.5% Native American, 6% transferred in, 26% live on campus.

Freshmen *Admission:* 599 enrolled.

Faculty *Total:* 91, 69% full-time, 9% with terminal degrees.

Majors Accounting; administrative assistant and secretarial science; agricultural business and management; applied horticulture; autobody/collision and repair technology; automobile/automotive mechanics technology; business administration and management; child-care and support services management; child development; clinical/medical social work; commercial and advertising art; computer and information sciences; computer programming (specific applications); construction engineering technology; criminal justice/safety; dental assisting; dental hygiene; diesel mechanics technology; drafting and design technology; electrical, electronic and communications engineering technology; graphic and printing equipment operation/production; health information/medical records technology; heating, air conditioning, ventilation and refrigeration maintenance technology; hospital and health-care facilities administration; hospitality administration; hotel/motel administration; industrial technology; information technology; liberal arts and sciences/liberal studies; machine tool technology; mass communication/media; medical administrative assistant and medical secretary; medical/clinical assistant; radio and television broadcasting technology; system administration; vehicle and vehicle parts and accessories marketing; vehicle/petroleum products marketing; web/multimedia management and webmaster; welding technology.

Academics *Calendar:* semesters plus six-week summer session. *Degree:* certificates, diplomas, and associate. *Special study options:* academic remediation for entering students, accelerated degree program, adult/continuing education programs, advanced placement credit, cooperative education, distance learning, English as a second language, external degree program, independent study, internships, off-campus study, part-time degree program, services for LD students, student-designed majors, summer session for credit.

Library Nuckolls Library with 4,025 titles, 52 serial subscriptions, an OPAC.

Student Life *Housing Options:* coed, men-only, women-only. Campus housing is university owned. *Activities and Organizations:* student-run radio station, Student Senate, Central Dormitory Council, Judicial Board, Seeds and Soils, Young Farmers and Ranchers. *Campus security:* 24-hour emergency response devices and patrols, controlled dormitory access. *Student services:* personal/psychological counseling, women's center.

Athletics *Intramural sports:* basketball M/W, bowling M/W, golf M/W, softball M/W, volleyball M/W, weight lifting M/W.

Costs (2010–11) *Tuition:* state resident $1776 full-time, $74 per credit hour part-time; nonresident $2664 full-time, $111 per credit hour part-time. *Required fees:* $168 full-time, $7 per credit hour part-time. *Room and board:* $5120. Room and board charges vary according to board plan. *Payment plan:* deferred payment. *Waivers:* employees or children of employees.

Financial Aid Of all full-time matriculated undergraduates who enrolled in 2008, 70 Federal Work-Study jobs (averaging $1200). 12 state and other part-time jobs (averaging $1250).

Applying *Options:* electronic application, early admission. *Required:* high school transcript. *Required for some:* 3 letters of recommendation, interview. *Application deadlines:* rolling (freshmen), rolling (transfers). *Notification:* continuous (freshmen), continuous (transfers).

Freshman Application Contact Mr. Robert Glenn, Admissions and Recruiting Director, Central Community College–Hastings Campus, PO Box 1024, East Highway 6, Hastings, NE 68902-1024. *Phone:* 402-461-2428. *Toll-free phone:* 800-742-7872. *E-mail:* rglenn@ccneb.edu.

Creative Center

Omaha, Nebraska **www.creativecenter.edu/**

- **Proprietary** primarily 2-year, founded 1993
- **Urban** 1-acre campus
- **Coed**

Faculty *Total:* 17. *Student/faculty ratio:* 26:1.

Majors Computer graphics; design and visual communications; illustration.

Academics *Calendar:* semesters. *Degrees:* associate and bachelor's. *Special study options:* distance learning, part-time degree program, services for LD students.

Library Student Library plus 1 other.

Student Life *Housing:* college housing not available.

Applying *Application fee:* $100. *Required:* essay or personal statement, high school transcript, 1 letter of recommendation, interview, portfolio.

Freshman Application Contact Admissions and Placement Coordinator, Creative Center, 10850 Emmet Street, Omaha, NE 68164. *Phone:* 402-898-1000. *Toll-free phone:* 888-898-1789. *Fax:* 402-898-1301. *E-mail:* admission@creativecenter.edu.

ITT Technical Institute

Omaha, Nebraska **www.itt-tech.edu/**

- **Proprietary** primarily 2-year, founded 1991, part of ITT Educational Services, Inc.
- **Urban** campus
- **Coed**

Majors Animation, interactive technology, video graphics and special effects; CAD/CADD drafting/design technology; computer and information systems security; computer engineering technology; computer software and media applications related; computer systems networking and telecommunications; construction management; criminal justice/law enforcement administration; design and visual communications; electrical, electronic and communications engineering technology; nursing (registered nurse training); system, networking, and LAN/WAN management; web page, digital/multimedia and information resources design.

Academics *Calendar:* quarters. *Degrees:* associate and bachelor's.

Student Life *Housing:* college housing not available.

Freshman Application Contact Director of Recruitment, ITT Technical Institute, 9814 M Street, Omaha, NE 68127. *Phone:* 402-331-2900. *Toll-free phone:* 800-677-9260.

KAPLAN UNIVERSITY, LINCOLN

Lincoln, Nebraska **www.lincoln.kaplanuniversity.edu/**

- **Proprietary** primarily 2-year, founded 1884
- **Urban** campus
- **Coed**

Majors Accounting; business administration and management; computer and information sciences; criminal justice/law enforcement administration; information technology; interdisciplinary studies; legal assistant/paralegal; medical/clinical assistant.

Academics *Calendar:* quarters. *Degrees:* certificates, diplomas, associate, and bachelor's.

Freshman Application Contact Kaplan University, Lincoln, 1821 K Street, Lincoln, NE 68508. *Phone:* 402-474-5315.

KAPLAN UNIVERSITY, OMAHA

Omaha, Nebraska **www.omaha.kaplanuniversity.edu/**

- **Proprietary** primarily 2-year, founded 1891
- **Urban** campus
- **Coed**

Majors Accounting; business administration and management; computer and information sciences; criminal justice/law enforcement administration; information technology; interdisciplinary studies; legal assistant/paralegal; medical/clinical assistant.

Academics *Calendar:* quarters. *Degrees:* certificates, diplomas, associate, and bachelor's.

Freshman Application Contact Kaplan University, Omaha, 5425 North 103rd Street, Omaha, NE 68134. *Phone:* 402-572-8500. *Toll-free phone:* 800-642-1456.

LITTLE PRIEST TRIBAL COLLEGE

Winnebago, Nebraska **www.lptc.bia.edu/**

- **Independent** 2-year, founded 1996
- **Rural** campus
- **Coed**

Academics *Degree:* certificates, diplomas, and associate.

Costs (2009–10) *Tuition:* $2400 full-time, $80 per credit hour part-time. *Required fees:* $575 full-time, $19 per credit hour part-time, $10 per term part-time.

Financial Aid Of all full-time matriculated undergraduates who enrolled in 2008, 8 Federal Work-Study jobs (averaging $750).

Applying *Application fee:* $10.

Director of Admissions Ms. Karen Kemling, Director of Admissions and Records, Little Priest Tribal College, PO Box 270, Winnebago, NE 68071. *Phone:* 402-878-2380.

METROPOLITAN COMMUNITY COLLEGE

Omaha, Nebraska **www.mccneb.edu/**

- **State and locally supported** 2-year, founded 1974, part of Nebraska Coordinating Commission for Postsecondary Education
- **Urban** 172-acre campus
- **Endowment** $1.4 million
- **Coed,** 17,003 undergraduate students, 42% full-time, 57% women, 43% men

Undergraduates 7,095 full-time, 9,908 part-time. Students come from 31 states and territories, 3% are from out of state, 13% African American, 3% Asian American or Pacific Islander, 6% Hispanic American, 0.9% Native American, 2% international, 17% transferred in. *Retention:* 50% of 2008 full-time freshmen returned.

Freshmen *Admission:* 4,141 applied, 4,141 admitted, 1,663 enrolled.

Faculty *Total:* 877, 23% full-time, 6% with terminal degrees. *Student/faculty ratio:* 16:1.

Majors Accounting; administrative assistant and secretarial science; architectural engineering technology; automobile/automotive mechanics technology; business administration and management; child development; civil engineering technology; commercial and advertising art; computer programming; construction engineering technology; criminal justice/police science; culinary arts; drafting and design technology; electrical, electronic and communications engineering technology; graphic and printing equipment operation/production; heating, air conditioning, ventilation and refrigeration maintenance technology; heavy equipment maintenance technology; human services; interior design; kindergarten/preschool education; legal administrative assistant/secretary; legal assistant/paralegal; legal studies; liberal arts and sciences/liberal studies; mental health/rehabilitation; nursing (licensed practical/vocational nurse training); nursing (registered nurse training); ornamental horticulture; photography; pre-engineering; respiratory care therapy; surgical technology; welding technology.

Academics *Calendar:* quarters. *Degree:* certificates, diplomas, and associate. *Special study options:* academic remediation for entering students, adult/continuing education programs, advanced placement credit, cooperative education, distance learning, English as a second language, independent study, internships, part-time degree program, services for LD students, summer session for credit. *ROTC:* Army (c).

Library Metropolitan Community College plus 2 others with 43,788 titles, 453 serial subscriptions, 8,008 audiovisual materials, an OPAC, a Web page.

Student Life *Housing Options:* coed, men-only, women-only, disabled students. Campus housing is university owned. *Campus security:* 24-hour emergency response devices and patrols, late-night transport/escort service, controlled dormitory access, security on duty 9 pm to 6 am. *Student services:* personal/psychological counseling.

Costs (2010–11) *Tuition:* state resident $2115 full-time, $47 per credit hour part-time; nonresident $3173 full-time, $71 per credit hour part-time. Full-time tuition and fees vary according to course load. Part-time tuition and fees vary according to course load. *Required fees:* $225 full-time, $5 per credit hour part-time. *Room and board:* $4740. *Payment plan:* deferred payment. *Waivers:* senior citizens and employees or children of employees.

Financial Aid Of all full-time matriculated undergraduates who enrolled in 2008, 180 Federal Work-Study jobs (averaging $1339).

Applying *Options:* early admission. *Recommended:* high school transcript. *Application deadlines:* rolling (freshmen), rolling (transfers). *Notification:* continuous (freshmen), continuous (transfers).

Freshman Application Contact Ms. Maria Vazquez, Associate Vice President for Student Affairs, Metropolitan Community College, PO Box 3777, Omaha, NE 69103-0777. *Phone:* 402-457-2430. *Toll-free phone:* 800-228-9553. *Fax:* 402-457-2238. *E-mail:* mvazquez@mccneb.edu.

MID-PLAINS COMMUNITY COLLEGE

North Platte, Nebraska **www.mpcc.edu/**

- **District-supported** 2-year, founded 1973
- **Small-town** campus
- **Endowment** $1.7 million
- **Coed,** 2,765 undergraduate students, 39% full-time, 58% women, 42% men

Undergraduates 1,086 full-time, 1,679 part-time. Students come from 23 states and territories, 3 other countries, 20% are from out of state, 2% African American, 0.5% Asian American or Pacific Islander, 4% Hispanic American, 0.5% Native American, 0.2% international, 8% live on campus. *Retention:* 34% of 2008 full-time freshmen returned.

Freshmen *Admission:* 512 applied, 512 admitted, 416 enrolled. *Test scores:* ACT scores over 18: 75%; ACT scores over 24: 19%; ACT scores over 30: 2%.

Faculty *Total:* 313, 21% full-time, 2% with terminal degrees. *Student/faculty ratio:* 9:1.

Majors Administrative assistant and secretarial science; autobody/collision and repair technology; automobile/automotive mechanics technology; building/construction finishing, management, and inspection related; business administration and management; clinical/medical laboratory technology; commercial and advertising art; computer and information sciences; construction engineering technology; dental assisting; diesel mechanics technology; fire science; heating, air conditioning, ventilation and refrigeration maintenance technology; liberal arts and sciences/liberal studies; nursing (licensed practical/vocational nurse training); nursing (registered nurse training); transportation and materials moving related; welding technology.

Mid-Plains Community College (continued)

Academics *Calendar:* semesters. *Degree:* certificates, diplomas, and associate. *Special study options:* academic remediation for entering students, adult/continuing education programs, advanced placement credit, cooperative education, distance learning, external degree program, independent study, internships, part-time degree program, summer session for credit.

Library McDonald-Belton L R C plus 1 other with 65,352 titles, 4,697 serial subscriptions, 3,455 audiovisual materials, an OPAC, a Web page.

Student Life *Housing Options:* coed, disabled students. Campus housing is university owned. *Activities and Organizations:* drama/theater group, student-run newspaper, choral group, Student Senate, Phi Theta Kappa, Phi Beta Lambda, Intercollegiate Athletics, MPCC Student Nurses Association. *Campus security:* controlled dormitory access, patrols by trained security personnel.

Athletics Member NJCAA. *Intercollegiate sports:* baseball M(s), basketball M(s)/W(s), golf M(s), softball W(s), volleyball W(s). *Intramural sports:* baseball M, basketball M/W, softball W, volleyball W.

Standardized Tests *Required for some:* COMPASS. *Recommended:* ACT (for admission).

Costs (2009–10) *Tuition:* state resident $2010 full-time, $67 per credit hour part-time; nonresident $2610 full-time, $87 per credit hour part-time. *Required fees:* $420 full-time, $14 per credit hour part-time. *Room and board:* $4900. Room and board charges vary according to board plan, housing facility, and location. *Waivers:* senior citizens and employees or children of employees.

Applying *Options:* electronic application. *Required:* high school transcript. *Required for some:* interview. *Application deadlines:* rolling (freshmen), rolling (transfers). *Notification:* continuous (freshmen), continuous (transfers).

Freshman Application Contact Ms. Sherry Mihel, Advisor, Mid-Plains Community College, 1101 Halligan Drive, North Platte, NE 69101. *Phone:* 308-535-3710. *Toll-free phone:* 800-658-4308 (in-state); 800-658-4348 (out-of-state). *E-mail:* mihels@mpcc.edu.

Myotherapy Institute

Lincoln, Nebraska **www.myotherapy.edu/**

Freshman Application Contact Admissions Office, Myotherapy Institute, 6020 South 58th Street, Lincoln, NE 68516. *Phone:* 402-421-7410. *Toll-free phone:* 800-896-3363.

Nebraska College of Technical Agriculture

Curtis, Nebraska **www.ncta.unl.edu/**

- **State-supported** 2-year, founded 1965, part of University of Nebraska System, administratively affiliated with Institute of Agriculture and Natural Resources - University of Nebraska
- **Rural** 634-acre campus
- **Coed,** 425 undergraduate students, 58% full-time, 51% women, 49% men

Undergraduates 246 full-time, 179 part-time. Students come from 10 states and territories, 1% Hispanic American, 45% live on campus. *Retention:* 64% of 2008 full-time freshmen returned.

Freshmen *Admission:* 312 enrolled. *Average high school GPA:* 2.5.

Faculty *Total:* 21, 62% full-time, 14% with terminal degrees. *Student/faculty ratio:* 13:1.

Majors Agricultural business and management; agricultural production; applied horticulture; veterinary/animal health technology.

Academics *Calendar:* 8-week modular system. *Degree:* certificates and associate. *Special study options:* academic remediation for entering students, adult/continuing education programs, distance learning, double majors, external degree program, independent study, internships, part-time degree program, study abroad.

Library Nebraska College of Technical Agriculture Library with 6,000 titles, 230 serial subscriptions, an OPAC, a Web page.

Student Life *Housing:* on-campus residence required for freshman year. *Options:* men-only, women-only. Campus housing is university owned. Freshman campus housing is guaranteed. *Activities and Organizations:* student-run newspaper, Aggie Livestock Association, Student Technicians Veterinary Medicine Association, Business Club, Phi Theta Kappa, Rodeo Club. *Campus security:* 24-hour emergency response devices, controlled dormitory access, night security. *Student services:* health clinic, personal/psychological counseling.

Athletics *Intercollegiate sports:* basketball M/W, golf M. *Intramural sports:* basketball M/W, golf M/W, softball M/W, volleyball M/W.

Standardized Tests *Required:* ACT (for admission).

Costs (2010–11) *Tuition:* state resident $3015 full-time; nonresident $6023 full-time. *Required fees:* $628 full-time. *Room and board:* $4580; room only: $2100. Room and board charges vary according to board plan.

Applying *Options:* early admission. *Application fee:* $25. *Required:* high school transcript. *Recommended:* interview. *Application deadline:* rolling (freshmen).

Freshman Application Contact Kevin Martin, Assistant Admissions Coordinator, Nebraska College of Technical Agriculture, RR3, Box 23A, Curtis, NE 69025-9205. *Phone:* 308-367-4124. *Toll-free phone:* 800-3CURTIS.

Nebraska Indian Community College

Macy, Nebraska **www.thenicc.edu/**

Director of Admissions Ms. Theresa Henry, Admission Counselor, Nebraska Indian Community College, 2451 Saint Mary's Avenue, Omaha, NE 68105. *Phone:* 402-837-5078. *Toll-free phone:* 888-843-6432 Ext. 14.

Northeast Community College

Norfolk, Nebraska **www.northeast.edu/**

- **State and locally supported** 2-year, founded 1973, part of Nebraska Coordinating Commission for Postsecondary Education
- **Small-town** 205-acre campus
- **Coed,** 5,205 undergraduate students, 44% full-time, 46% women, 54% men

Undergraduates 2,268 full-time, 2,937 part-time. Students come from 30 states and territories, 30 other countries, 8% are from out of state, 1% African American, 0.4% Asian American or Pacific Islander, 5% Hispanic American, 0.5% Native American, 3% international, 22% transferred in, 16% live on campus. *Retention:* 68% of 2008 full-time freshmen returned.

Freshmen *Admission:* 1,241 applied, 968 enrolled.

Faculty *Total:* 362, 31% full-time. *Student/faculty ratio:* 16:1.

Majors Accounting; administrative assistant and secretarial science; agribusiness; agricultural mechanics and equipment technology; agricultural mechanization; agriculture; agriculture and agriculture operations related; agronomy and crop science; animal sciences; applied horticulture; applied horticulture/horticultural business services related; architectural drafting and CAD/CADD; art; autobody/collision and repair technology; automobile/automotive mechanics technology; banking and financial support services; biological and biomedical sciences related; biology/biological sciences; building/construction finishing, management, and inspection related; business administration and management; business operations support and secretarial services related; chemistry; computer and information sciences; computer and information sciences and support services related; computer programming; computer programming (specific applications); computer science; corrections; criminal justice/police science; crop production; culinary arts; dairy science; diesel mechanics technology; dramatic/theater arts; early childhood education; education; electrician; electromechanical technology; elementary education; emergency medical technology (EMT paramedic); energy management and systems technology; engineering; English; entrepreneurship; farm and ranch management; finance and financial management services related; food service systems administration; general studies; graphic design; health aide; health and medical administrative services related; health and physical education; health/medical preparatory programs related; heating, air conditioning, ventilation and refrigeration maintenance technology; industrial mechanics and maintenance technology; international business/trade/commerce; journalism; legal administrative assistant/secretary; liberal arts and sciences/liberal studies; library assistant; lineworker; livestock management; marketing/marketing management; mass communication/media; mathematics; medical administrative assistant and medical secretary; medical insurance coding; medical radiologic technology; medium/heavy vehicle and truck technology; merchandising; music management and merchandising; music performance; music teacher education; nursing (licensed practical/vocational nurse training); nursing (registered nurse training); office management; office occupations and clerical services; physical therapist assistant; physics; pre-dentistry studies; pre-engineering; pre-law studies; premedical studies; prenursing studies; pre-pharmacy studies; pre-veterinary studies; psychology; radio and television broadcasting technology; real estate; recording arts technology; secondary education; social sciences; speech and rhetoric; surgical technology; veterinary/animal health technology; welding technology.

Academics *Calendar:* semesters. *Degree:* certificates, diplomas, and associate. *Special study options:* academic remediation for entering students, adult/continuing education programs, advanced placement credit, cooperative education,

distance learning, double majors, English as a second language, internships, off-campus study, part-time degree program, services for LD students, summer session for credit.

Library Library Resource Center plus 1 other with 64,122 titles, 194 serial subscriptions, 1,074 audiovisual materials, an OPAC, a Web page.

Student Life *Housing Options:* disabled students. Campus housing is university owned. *Activities and Organizations:* drama/theater group, student-run newspaper, radio and television station, choral group, Phi Theta Kappa, Campus Crusade for Christ, Student Nurses Association, Electricians Club, Utility Line Club. *Campus security:* 24-hour patrols, controlled dormitory access. *Student services:* personal/psychological counseling.

Athletics Member NJCAA. *Intercollegiate sports:* basketball M(s)/W(s), cheerleading W(s). *Intramural sports:* basketball M/W, bowling M/W, football M/W, soccer M/W, softball M/W, table tennis M/W, volleyball M/W.

Costs (2009–10) *Tuition:* state resident $2010 full-time; nonresident $2513 full-time. *Required fees:* $420 full-time. *Room and board:* $4980; room only: $2820. Room and board charges vary according to board plan and housing facility. *Waivers:* employees or children of employees.

Financial Aid Of all full-time matriculated undergraduates who enrolled in 2008, 1,508 applied for aid, 1,187 were judged to have need, 229 had their need fully met. In 2008, 45 non-need-based awards were made. *Average percent of need met:* 62%. *Average financial aid package:* $5641. *Average need-based loan:* $2901. *Average need-based gift aid:* $3462. *Average non-need-based aid:* $1100. *Average indebtedness upon graduation:* $9766.

Applying *Options:* electronic application, early admission. *Required for some:* high school transcript, minimum 2 GPA, 3 letters of recommendation, interview. *Recommended:* high school transcript. *Application deadlines:* rolling (freshmen), rolling (out-of-state freshmen), rolling (transfers). *Notification:* continuous (freshmen), continuous (out-of-state freshmen), continuous (transfers).

Freshman Application Contact Maureen Baker, Dean of Students, Northeast Community College, PO Box 469, Norfolk, NE 68702-0469. *Phone:* 402-844-7258. *Toll-free phone:* 800-348-9033 Ext. 7260. *Fax:* 402-844-7403. *E-mail:* admission@northeast.edu.

Southeast Community College, Beatrice Campus

Beatrice, Nebraska **www.southeast.edu/**

Freshman Application Contact Admissions Office, Southeast Community College, Beatrice Campus, 4771 West Scott Road, Beatrice, NE 68310. *Phone:* 402-228-3468. *Toll-free phone:* 800-233-5027. *Fax:* 402-228-2218.

Southeast Community College, Lincoln Campus

Lincoln, Nebraska **www.southeast.edu/**

Freshman Application Contact Admissions Office, Southeast Community College, Lincoln Campus, 8800 "O" Street, Lincoln, NE 68520. *Phone:* 402-471-3333. *Toll-free phone:* 800-642-4075. *Fax:* 402-437-2404.

Southeast Community College, Milford Campus

Milford, Nebraska **www.southeast.edu/**

Freshman Application Contact Admissions Office, Southeast Community College, Milford Campus, 600 State Street, Milford, NE 68405. *Phone:* 402-761-2131. *Toll-free phone:* 800-933-7223. *Fax:* 402-761-2324.

Vatterott College

Omaha, Nebraska **www.vatterott-college.edu/**

Freshman Application Contact Admissions Office, Vatterott College, 5318 South 136th Street, Omaha, NE 68137. *Phone:* 402-891-9411. *Fax:* 402-891-9413.

Western Nebraska Community College

Sidney, Nebraska **www.wncc.net/**

Director of Admissions Mr. Troy Archuleta, Admissions and Recruitment Director, Western Nebraska Community College, 371 College Drive, Sidney, NE 69162. *Phone:* 308-635-6015. *Toll-free phone:* 800-222-9682 (in-state); 800-348-4435 (out-of-state). *E-mail:* rhovey@wncc.net.

NEVADA

Career College of Northern Nevada

Sparks, Nevada **www.ccnn.edu/**

- **Proprietary** 2-year, founded 1984
- **Urban** 1-acre campus
- **Coed,** 363 undergraduate students, 100% full-time, 69% women, 31% men

Undergraduates 363 full-time. Students come from 3 states and territories, 2 other countries, 3% are from out of state, 5% African American, 5% Asian American or Pacific Islander, 18% Hispanic American, 6% Native American. *Retention:* 51% of 2008 full-time freshmen returned.

Freshmen *Admission:* 419 applied, 419 admitted.

Faculty *Total:* 23, 48% full-time, 17% with terminal degrees. *Student/faculty ratio:* 20:1.

Majors Business administration and management; computer and information sciences; data processing and data processing technology; electrical, electronic and communications engineering technology; management information systems; medical/clinical assistant.

Academics *Calendar:* quarters six-week terms. *Degree:* diplomas and associate. *Special study options:* academic remediation for entering students, accelerated degree program, cooperative education, double majors, internships, summer session for credit.

Library 380 titles, 7 serial subscriptions.

Student Life *Housing:* college housing not available. *Activities and Organizations:* student-run newspaper. *Campus security:* 24-hour emergency response devices.

Financial Aid Of all full-time matriculated undergraduates who enrolled in 2008, 6 Federal Work-Study jobs (averaging $3000).

Applying *Application fee:* $25. *Required:* essay or personal statement, high school transcript, interview. *Application deadlines:* rolling (freshmen), rolling (transfers). *Notification:* continuous (freshmen), continuous (transfers).

Freshman Application Contact Ms. Laura Goldhammer, Director of Admissions, Career College of Northern Nevada, 1195-A Corporate Boulevard, Reno, NV 89502. *Phone:* 775-856-2266 Ext. 11. *Fax:* 775-856-0935. *E-mail:* lgoldhammer@ccnn4u.com.

College of Southern Nevada

North Las Vegas, Nevada **www.csn.edu/**

Director of Admissions Mr. Arlie J. Stops, Associate Vice President for Admissions and Records, College of Southern Nevada, 3200 East Cheyenne Avenue, North Las Vegas, NV 89030-4296. *Phone:* 702-651-4060. *Toll-free phone:* 800-492-5728. *E-mail:* stops@ccmail.ccsn.nevada.edu.

Everest College

Henderson, Nevada **www.everest.edu/campus/henderson/**

- **Proprietary** 2-year
- **Coed**

Academics *Degree:* associate.

Everest College (continued)

Admissions Office Contact Everest College, 170 North Stephanie Street, 1st Floor, Henderson, NV 89074.

GREAT BASIN COLLEGE

Elko, Nevada **www.gbcnv.edu/**

Freshman Application Contact Ms. Julie Byrnes, Director of Enrollment Management, Great Basin College, 1500 College Parkway, Elko, NV 89801-3348. *Phone:* 775-753-2271. *Fax:* 775-753-2311. *E-mail:* stdsvc@gbcnv.edu.

HIGH-TECH INSTITUTE

Las Vegas, Nevada **www.high-techinstitute.com/**

Freshman Application Contact Admissions Office, High-Tech Institute, 2320 South Rancho Drive, Las Vegas, NV 89102. *Phone:* 702-385-6700. *Toll-free phone:* 866-385-6700.

ITT TECHNICAL INSTITUTE

Henderson, Nevada **www.itt-tech.edu/**

- **Proprietary** primarily 2-year, founded 1997, part of ITT Educational Services, Inc.
- **Coed**

Majors Animation, interactive technology, video graphics and special effects; business administration and management; CAD/CADD drafting/design technology; computer and information systems security; computer engineering technology; computer software and media applications related; computer software engineering; computer software technology; construction management; criminal justice/law enforcement administration; design and visual communications; electrical, electronic and communications engineering technology; system, networking, and LAN/WAN management; web/multimedia management and webmaster; web page, digital/multimedia and information resources design.

Academics *Degrees:* associate and bachelor's.

Student Life *Housing:* college housing not available.

Financial Aid Of all full-time matriculated undergraduates who enrolled in 2008, 6 Federal Work-Study jobs (averaging $5000).

Freshman Application Contact Director of Recruitment, ITT Technical Institute, 168 North Gibson Road, Henderson, NV 89014. *Phone:* 702-558-5404. *Toll-free phone:* 800-488-8459.

KAPLAN COLLEGE–LAS VEGAS CAMPUS

Las Vegas, Nevada **las-vegas.kaplancollege.com/**

Freshman Application Contact Admissions Office, Kaplan College–Las Vegas Campus, 3315 Spring Mountain Road, Las Vegas, NV 89102. *Toll-free phone:* 888-727-7863.

LE CORDON BLEU COLLEGE OF CULINARY ARTS, LAS VEGAS

Las Vegas, Nevada **www.vegasculinary.com/**

Freshman Application Contact Admissions Office, Le Cordon Bleu College of Culinary Arts, Las Vegas, 1451 Center Crossing Road, Las Vegas, NV 89144. *Toll-free phone:* 888-551-8222.

PIMA MEDICAL INSTITUTE

Las Vegas, Nevada **www.pmi.edu/**

- **Proprietary** 2-year, founded 2003, part of Vocational Training Institutes, Inc.
- **Urban** campus
- **Coed**

Academics *Calendar:* modular. *Degree:* associate. *Special study options:* advanced placement credit, internships.

Standardized Tests *Required:* Wonderlic Scholastic Level Exam (for admission).

Applying *Required:* interview. *Required for some:* essay or personal statement, high school transcript.

Freshman Application Contact Admissions Office, Pima Medical Institute, Pima Medical Institute, 3333 East Flamingo Road, Las Vegas, NV 89121. *Phone:* 702-458-9650 Ext. 202. *Toll-free phone:* 800-477-PIMA.

TRUCKEE MEADOWS COMMUNITY COLLEGE

Reno, Nevada **www.tmcc.edu/**

Director of Admissions Mr. Dave Harbeck, Director of Admissions and Records, Truckee Meadows Community College, Mail Station #15, 7000 Dandini Boulevard, MS RDMT 319, Reno, NV 89512-3901. *Phone:* 775-674-7623. *Fax:* 775-673-7028. *E-mail:* dharbeck@tmcc.edu.

WESTERN NEVADA COLLEGE

Carson City, Nevada **www.wnc.edu/**

Freshman Application Contact Admissions and Records, Western Nevada College, 2201 West College Parkway, Carson City, NV 89703-7399. *Phone:* 775-445-2377. *Fax:* 775-445-3147. *E-mail:* wncc_aro@wncc.edu.

NEW HAMPSHIRE

GREAT BAY COMMUNITY COLLEGE

Portsmouth, New Hampshire **www.greatbay.edu/**

Admissions Office Contact Great Bay Community College, 320 Corporate Drive, Portsmouth, NH 03801. *Toll-free phone:* 800-522.1194.

HESSER COLLEGE, CONCORD

Concord, New Hampshire **www.concord.hesser.edu/**

- **Proprietary** primarily 2-year
- **Coed**

Academics *Degrees:* certificates, diplomas, associate, and bachelor's.

Freshman Application Contact Hesser College, Concord, 25 Hall Street, Suite 104, Concord, NH 03301. *Phone:* 603-225-9200.

HESSER COLLEGE, MANCHESTER

Manchester, New Hampshire **www.manchester.hesser.edu/**

- **Proprietary** primarily 2-year, founded 1900
- **Urban** campus
- **Coed**

Majors Accounting; business administration and management; communication/speech communication and rhetoric; criminal justice/law enforcement administration; early childhood education; graphic design; interior design; legal assistant/paralegal; liberal arts and sciences/liberal studies; medical/clinical assistant; physical therapist assistant; psychology; radio and television.

Academics *Calendar:* semesters. *Degrees:* certificates, diplomas, associate, and bachelor's.

Financial Aid Of all full-time matriculated undergraduates who enrolled in 2008, 700 Federal Work-Study jobs (averaging $1000).

Freshman Application Contact Hesser College, Manchester, 3 Sundial Avenue, Manchester, NH 03103. *Phone:* 603-668-6660.

►See page 456 for the College Close-Up.

HESSER COLLEGE, NASHUA

Nashua, New Hampshire **www.nashua.hesser.edu/**

- **Proprietary** primarily 2-year
- **Coed**

Academics *Degrees:* certificates, diplomas, associate, and bachelor's.
Freshman Application Contact Hesser College, Nashua, 410 Amherst Street, Nashua, NH 03063. *Phone:* 603-883-0404.

HESSER COLLEGE, PORTSMOUTH

Portsmouth, New Hampshire **www.portsmouth.hesser.edu/**

- **Proprietary** primarily 2-year
- **Coed**

Academics *Degrees:* certificates, diplomas, associate, and bachelor's.
Freshman Application Contact Hesser College, Portsmouth, 170 Commerce Way, Portsmouth, NH 03801. *Phone:* 603-436-5300.

HESSER COLLEGE, SALEM

Salem, New Hampshire **www.salem.hesser.edu/**

- **Proprietary** primarily 2-year
- **Coed**

Academics *Degrees:* certificates, diplomas, associate, and bachelor's.
Freshman Application Contact Hesser College, Salem, 11 Manor Parkway, Salem, NH 03079. *Phone:* 603-898-3480.

LAKES REGION COMMUNITY COLLEGE

Laconia, New Hampshire **www.lrcc.edu/**

Admissions Office Contact Lakes Region Community College, 379 Belmont Road, Laconia, NH 03246. *Toll-free phone:* 800-357-2992.

MANCHESTER COMMUNITY COLLEGE

Manchester, New Hampshire **www.manchester.nhctc.edu/**

Freshman Application Contact Ms. Jacquie Poirier, Coordinator of Admissions, Manchester Community College, 1066 Front Street, Manchester, NH 03102-8518. *Phone:* 603-668-6706 Ext. 283. *E-mail:* jpoirier@nhctc.edu.

NASHUA COMMUNITY COLLEGE

Nashua, New Hampshire **www.nashuacc.edu/**

Freshman Application Contact Ms. Patricia Goodman, Vice President of Student Services, Nashua Community College, 505 Amherst Street, Nashua, NH 03063. *Phone:* 603-882-6923. *Fax:* 603-882-8690. *E-mail:* nashua@nhctc.edu.

NEW HAMPSHIRE TECHNICAL INSTITUTE

Concord, New Hampshire **www.nhti.edu/**

Freshman Application Contact Mr. Francis P. Meyer, Director of Admissions, New Hampshire Technical Institute, 11 Institute Drive, Concord, NH 03301-7412. *Phone:* 603-271-7131. *Toll-free phone:* 800-247-0179. *E-mail:* fmeyer@nhctc.edu.

NHTI, CONCORD'S COMMUNITY COLLEGE

Concord, New Hampshire **www.nhti.edu/**

Admissions Office Contact NHTI, Concord's Community College, 31 College Drive, Concord, NH 03301.

RIVER VALLEY COMMUNITY COLLEGE

Claremont, New Hampshire **www.rivervalley.edu/**

Admissions Office Contact River Valley Community College, 1 College Drive, Claremont, NH 03743. *Toll-free phone:* 800-837-0658.

WHITE MOUNTAINS COMMUNITY COLLEGE

Berlin, New Hampshire **www.wmcc.edu/**

- **State-supported** 2-year, founded 1966, part of Community College System of New Hampshire
- **Rural** 325-acre campus
- **Coed,** 985 undergraduate students, 39% full-time, 65% women, 35% men

Undergraduates 381 full-time, 604 part-time. Students come from 4 states and territories, 4% are from out of state, 0.6% African American, 0.6% Asian American or Pacific Islander, 0.8% Hispanic American, 0.5% Native American.
Freshmen *Admission:* 206 enrolled.
Faculty *Total:* 253, 11% full-time, 0.4% with terminal degrees.
Majors Accounting; administrative assistant and secretarial science; automobile/automotive mechanics technology; business administration and management; cartography; computer and information sciences; computer engineering technology; culinary arts; diesel mechanics technology; environmental studies; general studies; human services; kindergarten/preschool education; liberal arts and sciences/liberal studies; nursing (registered nurse training); survey technology.
Academics *Calendar:* semesters. *Degree:* certificates, diplomas, and associate. *Special study options:* academic remediation for entering students, adult/continuing education programs, advanced placement credit, distance learning, double majors, external degree program, independent study, internships, part-time degree program, services for LD students, summer session for credit.
Library Fortier Library with 18,000 titles, 85 serial subscriptions, 350 audiovisual materials, an OPAC.
Student Life *Housing:* college housing not available. *Activities and Organizations:* Student Senate.
Athletics *Intercollegiate sports:* basketball M/W, ice hockey M/W, soccer M/W. *Intramural sports:* basketball M/W, ice hockey M/W, skiing (cross-country) M/W.
Standardized Tests *Required:* Accuplacer Placement Test (for admission).
Costs (2010–11) *Tuition:* state resident $5490 full-time, $183 per credit part-time; nonresident $12,540 full-time, $418 per credit part-time. *Required fees:* $510 full-time, $17 per credit part-time. *Payment plan:* deferred payment. *Waivers:* senior citizens and employees or children of employees.
Applying *Options:* electronic application. *Application fee:* $10. *Required:* high school transcript, placement test. *Required for some:* essay or personal statement. *Application deadlines:* rolling (freshmen), rolling (transfers). *Notification:* continuous (freshmen), continuous (transfers).
Freshman Application Contact Ms. Jamie Rivard, Program Assistant, White Mountains Community College, 2020 Riverside Drive, Berlin, NH 03570-3717. *Phone:* 603-752-1113 Ext. 3000. *Toll-free phone:* 800-445-4525. *Fax:* 603-752-6335. *E-mail:* jrivard@ccsnh.edu.

NEW JERSEY

ASSUMPTION COLLEGE FOR SISTERS

Mendham, New Jersey **www.acs350.org/**

Freshman Application Contact Sr. Gerardine Tantsits, Academic Dean/Registrar, Assumption College for Sisters, 350 Bernardsville Road, Mendham, NJ 07945-2923. *Phone:* 973-543-6528 Ext. 228. *Fax:* 973-543-1738. *E-mail:* srgeraldine@scceat.org.

ATLANTIC CAPE COMMUNITY COLLEGE

Mays Landing, New Jersey **www.atlantic.edu/**

Freshman Application Contact Mrs. Linda McLeod, Assistant Director, Admissions and College Recruitment, Atlantic Cape Community College, 5100 Black Horse Pike, Mays Landing, NJ 08330-2699. *Phone:* 609-343-5000 Ext. 5009. *Toll-free phone:* 800-645-CHIEF. *Fax:* 609-343-4921. *E-mail:* accadmit@atlantic.edu.

BERGEN COMMUNITY COLLEGE

Paramus, New Jersey **www.bergen.edu/**

Freshman Application Contact Director of Admissions and Recruitment, Bergen Community College, 400 Paramus Road, Paramus, NJ 07652-1595. *Phone:* 201-447-7193. *Fax:* 201-670-7973. *E-mail:* admsoffice@bergen.edu.

BERKELEY COLLEGE

Woodland Park, New Jersey **www.berkeleycollege.edu/**

Freshman Application Contact Mr. David Bertone, Senior Director of Enrollment, Berkeley College, 44 Rifle Camp Road, West Paterson, NJ 07424. *Phone:* 973-278-5400. *Toll-free phone:* 800-446-5400. *Fax:* 973-328-9141. *E-mail:* info@berkeleycollege.edu.

BROOKDALE COMMUNITY COLLEGE

Lincroft, New Jersey **www.brookdalecc.edu/**

- **County-supported** 2-year, founded 1967, part of New Jersey Commission on Higher Education
- **Small-town** 221-acre campus with easy access to New York City
- **Coed**

Academics *Calendar:* semesters plus 1 ten-week and 2 six-week summer terms. *Degree:* certificates and associate. *Special study options:* academic remediation for entering students, adult/continuing education programs, advanced placement credit, cooperative education, distance learning, English as a second language, honors programs, independent study, internships, part-time degree program, services for LD students, study abroad, summer session for credit. *ROTC:* Army (c), Air Force (c).

Student Life *Campus security:* 24-hour emergency response devices and patrols.

Athletics Member NJCAA.

Applying *Options:* early admission, deferred entrance. *Application fee:* $25. *Required:* high school transcript.

Director of Admissions Ms. Kim Toomey, Registrar, Brookdale Community College, 765 Newman Springs Road, Lincroft, NJ 07738. *Phone:* 732-224-2268.

BURLINGTON COUNTY COLLEGE

Pemberton, New Jersey **www.bcc.edu/**

- **County-supported** 2-year, founded 1966
- **Suburban** 225-acre campus with easy access to Philadelphia
- **Coed,** 9,693 undergraduate students, 56% full-time, 58% women, 42% men

Undergraduates 5,445 full-time, 4,248 part-time. Students come from 7 states and territories, 1% are from out of state, 20% African American, 4% Asian American or Pacific Islander, 7% Hispanic American, 0.4% Native American, 1% international, 3% transferred in.

Freshmen *Admission:* 4,182 applied, 4,182 admitted, 2,349 enrolled.

Faculty *Total:* 591, 9% full-time. *Student/faculty ratio:* 30:1.

Majors Accounting; agribusiness; American Sign Language (ASL); animation, interactive technology, video graphics and special effects; art; automotive engineering technology; biological and physical sciences; biology/biological sciences; biotechnology; business administration and management; chemical engineering; chemistry; commercial and advertising art; communication disorders sciences and services related; computer graphics; computer science; construction engineering technology; criminal justice/police science; dental hygiene; drafting and design technology; dramatic/theater arts; education; electrical, electronic and communications engineering technology; engineering; engineering technologies related; English; environmental science; fashion/apparel design; fire science; food service systems administration; geological and earth sciences/geosciences related; graphic and printing equipment operation/production; graphic design; health information/medical records technology; health services/allied health/health sciences; history; hospitality administration; human services; information technology; international/global studies; journalism; legal assistant/paralegal; liberal arts and sciences/liberal studies; management information systems; mathematics; medical radiologic technology; music; nursing (registered nurse training); philosophy; physics; psychology; respiratory care therapy; restaurant/food services management; retailing; sales, distribution and marketing; sign language interpretation and translation; social sciences; sociology.

Academics *Calendar:* semesters plus 2 summer terms. *Degree:* certificates and associate. *Special study options:* academic remediation for entering students, adult/continuing education programs, advanced placement credit, cooperative education, distance learning, double majors, English as a second language, honors programs, independent study, internships, part-time degree program, services for LD students, summer session for credit.

Library Burlington County College Library plus 1 other with 92,400 titles, 1,750 serial subscriptions, an OPAC, a Web page.

Student Life *Housing:* college housing not available. *Activities and Organizations:* drama/theater group, student-run radio station, choral group, Student Government Association, Phi Theta Kappa, Creative Writing Guild. *Campus security:* 24-hour emergency response devices and patrols, late-night transport/escort service, electronic entrances to buildings and rooms, surveillance cameras. *Student services:* health clinic, personal/psychological counseling.

Athletics Member NJCAA. *Intercollegiate sports:* baseball M, basketball M/W, golf M/W, soccer M/W, softball W. *Intramural sports:* archery M.

Costs (2010–11) *Tuition:* area resident $2760 full-time, $92 per credit part-time; state resident $3240 full-time, $108 per credit part-time; nonresident $5190 full-time, $173 per credit part-time. Full-time tuition and fees vary according to course load. Part-time tuition and fees vary according to course load. *Required fees:* $855 full-time, $29 per credit part-time.

Financial Aid Of all full-time matriculated undergraduates who enrolled in 2008, 100 Federal Work-Study jobs (averaging $1200). 100 state and other part-time jobs (averaging $2000).

Applying *Options:* electronic application, early admission, deferred entrance. *Application fee:* $20. *Required:* high school transcript. *Application deadlines:* rolling (freshmen), rolling (transfers). *Notification:* continuous (freshmen), continuous (transfers).

Freshman Application Contact Burlington County College, 601 Pemberton-Browns Mills Road, Pemberton, NJ 08068-1599. *Phone:* 609-894-9311 Ext. 1200.

CAMDEN COUNTY COLLEGE

Blackwood, New Jersey **www.camdencc.edu/**

- **State and locally supported** 2-year, founded 1967, part of New Jersey Commission on Higher Education
- **Suburban** 320-acre campus with easy access to Philadelphia
- **Coed,** 15,670 undergraduate students, 54% full-time, 61% women, 39% men

Undergraduates 8,529 full-time, 7,141 part-time. Students come from 9 states and territories, 22% African American, 6% Asian American or Pacific Islander, 9% Hispanic American, 0.4% Native American. *Retention:* 67% of 2008 full-time freshmen returned.

Freshmen *Admission:* 7,889 applied, 2,203 enrolled.

Faculty *Total:* 729, 19% full-time.

Majors Accounting and business/management; administrative assistant and secretarial science; automotive engineering technology; banking and financial support services; biology/biotechnology laboratory technician; business administration and management; cinematography and film/video production; clinical/medical laboratory technology; criminal justice/law enforcement administration; data entry/microcomputer applications related; dental assisting; dental hygiene; desktop publishing and digital imaging design; dietetics; drafting and design technology; education; electrical, electronic and communications engineering technology; electromechanical technology; emergency medical technology (EMT paramedic); engineering science; fine/studio arts; fire protection and safety technology; health information/medical records administration; health services/allied health/health sciences; industrial production technologies related; laser and optical technology; legal assistant/paralegal; liberal arts and sciences/liberal studies; management information systems; marketing/marketing management; massage therapy; mechanical engineering/mechanical technology; nursing (registered nurse training); opticianry; real estate; sign language interpretation and translation; social work; sport and fitness administration/management; substance abuse/addiction counseling; veterinary/animal health technology.

Academics *Calendar:* semesters. *Degree:* certificates and associate. *Special study options:* academic remediation for entering students, adult/continuing

education programs, cooperative education, distance learning, double majors, English as a second language, external degree program, freshman honors college, honors programs, independent study, internships, off-campus study, part-time degree program, services for LD students, study abroad, summer session for credit.

Library Learning Resource Center with 91,366 titles, 449 serial subscriptions, 2,038 audiovisual materials, an OPAC.

Student Life *Housing:* college housing not available. *Activities and Organizations:* drama/theater group, student-run radio station, choral group. *Campus security:* 24-hour emergency response devices.

Athletics Member NJCAA. *Intercollegiate sports:* baseball M, basketball M/W, golf M, soccer M/W, softball W. *Intramural sports:* baseball M, basketball M/W, soccer M/W, softball W.

Costs (2010–11) *Tuition:* $93 per credit part-time; state resident $97 per credit part-time; nonresident $97 per credit part-time. *Required fees:* $27 per credit part-time, $3 per term part-time.

Financial Aid Of all full-time matriculated undergraduates who enrolled in 2008, 117 Federal Work-Study jobs (averaging $1126).

Applying *Options:* early admission. *Required for some:* high school transcript. *Application deadlines:* rolling (freshmen), rolling (transfers).

Freshman Application Contact Donald Delaney, Outreach Coordinator, School and Community Academic Programs, Camden County College, PO Box 200, College Drive, Blackwood, NJ 08012-0200. *Phone:* 856-227-7200 Ext. 4371. *Toll-free phone:* 888-228-2466. *Fax:* 856-374-4916. *E-mail:* ddelaney@camdencc.edu.

COUNTY COLLEGE OF MORRIS

Randolph, New Jersey **www.ccm.edu/**

- **County-supported** 2-year, founded 1966, part of New Jersey Commission on Higher Education
- **Suburban** 218-acre campus with easy access to New York City
- **Coed,** 8,738 undergraduate students, 58% full-time, 49% women, 51% men

Undergraduates 5,076 full-time, 3,662 part-time.

Majors Administrative assistant and secretarial science; agricultural business and management; airline pilot and flight crew; biology/biotechnology laboratory technician; business administration and management; business, management, and marketing related; chemical technology; criminal justice/police science; design and applied arts related; electrical, electronic and communications engineering technology; engineering science; fine/studio arts; fire protection and safety technology; graphic design; hospitality and recreation marketing; kindergarten/preschool education; kinesiology and exercise science; liberal arts and sciences/liberal studies; management information systems; mechanical engineering/mechanical technology; multi/interdisciplinary studies related; music; nursing (registered nurse training); photography; public administration; radiologic technology/science; respiratory care therapy; telecommunications technology; veterinary/animal health technology; web page, digital/multimedia and information resources design.

Academics *Calendar:* semesters. *Degree:* certificates and associate.

Student Life *Housing:* college housing not available.

Athletics Member NJCAA. *Intercollegiate sports:* baseball M(s), basketball M(s)/W(s), golf M, ice hockey M(s), soccer M/W, softball W(s), tennis M. *Intramural sports:* badminton M/W, basketball M/W, football M, soccer W, softball W, tennis M/W, volleyball M/W, weight lifting M/W, wrestling M/W.

Costs (2010–11) *Tuition:* area resident $3300 full-time, $110 per credit part-time; state resident $6600 full-time, $220 per credit part-time; nonresident $9330 full-time, $311 per credit part-time. *Required fees:* $645 full-time, $17 per credit part-time, $15 per course part-time. *Waivers:* senior citizens.

Financial Aid Of all full-time matriculated undergraduates who enrolled in 2008, 588 Federal Work-Study jobs (averaging $1947).

Applying *Application fee:* $30. *Required:* high school transcript. *Notification:* continuous (freshmen), continuous (transfers).

Freshman Application Contact County College of Morris, 214 Center Grove Road, Randolph, NJ 07869-2086. *Phone:* 973-328-5100. *Toll-free phone:* 888-226-8001.

CUMBERLAND COUNTY COLLEGE

Vineland, New Jersey **www.cccnj.edu/**

- **State and locally supported** 2-year, founded 1963, part of New Jersey Commission on Higher Education
- **Small-town** 100-acre campus with easy access to Philadelphia
- **Coed,** 4,014 undergraduate students, 59% full-time, 65% women, 35% men

Undergraduates 2,365 full-time, 1,649 part-time. 21% African American, 2% Asian American or Pacific Islander, 20% Hispanic American, 2% Native American.

Faculty *Total:* 290, 16% full-time. *Student/faculty ratio:* 14:1.

Majors Accounting; administrative assistant and secretarial science; aeronautical/aerospace engineering technology; building/construction finishing, management, and inspection related; business administration and management; computer and information sciences; computer systems networking and telecommunications; criminal justice/police science; education; fine/studio arts; health and medical administrative services related; horticultural science; industrial technology; legal assistant/paralegal; liberal arts and sciences/liberal studies; medical radiologic technology; nursing (registered nurse training); ornamental horticulture; respiratory care therapy; social work.

Academics *Calendar:* semesters. *Degree:* certificates and associate. *Special study options:* academic remediation for entering students, advanced placement credit, cooperative education, distance learning, double majors, English as a second language, honors programs, part-time degree program, services for LD students, summer session for credit.

Library Cumberland County College Library with 51,000 titles, 213 serial subscriptions, 480 audiovisual materials, an OPAC, a Web page.

Student Life *Housing:* college housing not available. *Activities and Organizations:* drama/theater group, student-run newspaper, choral group. *Campus security:* 24-hour emergency response devices, late-night transport/escort service. *Student services:* personal/psychological counseling.

Athletics Member NJCAA. *Intercollegiate sports:* baseball M, basketball M/W, softball W, track and field M. *Intramural sports:* fencing M/W, soccer M.

Costs (2010–11) *Tuition:* area resident $2970 full-time, $99 per credit hour part-time; state resident $5940 full-time, $188 per credit hour part-time; nonresident $11,880 full-time, $376 per credit hour part-time. *Required fees:* $870 full-time, $29 per credit hour part-time. *Payment plan:* installment. *Waivers:* employees or children of employees.

Financial Aid Of all full-time matriculated undergraduates who enrolled in 2008, 100 Federal Work-Study jobs (averaging $500). 100 state and other part-time jobs (averaging $600).

Applying *Options:* electronic application, early admission, deferred entrance. *Application fee:* $25. *Required:* high school transcript. *Application deadlines:* rolling (freshmen), rolling (transfers). *Notification:* continuous (freshmen), continuous (transfers).

Freshman Application Contact Ms. Anne Daly-Eimer, Director of Admissions and Registration, Cumberland County College, College Drive, Vineland, NJ 08362-1500. *Phone:* 856-691-8986.

ESSEX COUNTY COLLEGE

Newark, New Jersey **www.essex.edu/**

- **County-supported** 2-year, founded 1966, part of New Jersey Commission on Higher Education
- **Urban** 22-acre campus with easy access to New York City
- **Coed,** 13,314 undergraduate students, 59% full-time, 59% women, 41% men

Undergraduates 7,915 full-time, 5,399 part-time. Students come from 9 states and territories, 69 other countries, 1% are from out of state, 50% African American, 4% Asian American or Pacific Islander, 22% Hispanic American, 0.2% Native American, 5% international, 2% transferred in. *Retention:* 55% of 2008 full-time freshmen returned.

Freshmen *Admission:* 7,948 applied, 7,948 admitted, 3,122 enrolled.

Faculty *Total:* 601, 20% full-time. *Student/faculty ratio:* 29:1.

Majors Accounting; accounting technology and bookkeeping; administrative assistant and secretarial science; architectural engineering technology; art; biology/biological sciences; business administration and management; business teacher education; chemical technology; chemistry; civil engineering technology; communications technology; computer programming; computer programming (specific applications); computer science; criminal justice/law enforcement administration; criminal justice/police science; data processing and data processing technology; dental assisting; dental hygiene; electrical, electronic and communications engineering technology; elementary education; emergency medical technology (EMT paramedic); fire science; health/health-care administration; health professions related; hotel/motel administration; human services; industrial production technologies related; information science/studies; kindergarten/preschool education; legal assistant/paralegal; legal professions and studies related; liberal arts and sciences/liberal studies; mathematics; medical administrative assistant and medical secretary; medical radiologic technology; music; nursing (registered nurse training); opticianry; physical education teaching and coaching; physical therapist assistant; physical therapy; pre-engineering; respiratory care therapy; secondary education; social sciences; social work.

Academics *Calendar:* semesters. *Degree:* certificates and associate. *Special study options:* academic remediation for entering students, accelerated degree program, adult/continuing education programs, advanced placement credit,

Essex County College (continued)

cooperative education, distance learning, double majors, English as a second language, independent study, internships, off-campus study, part-time degree program, services for LD students, summer session for credit. *ROTC:* Army (c).

Library Martin Luther King, Jr. Library with 91,000 titles, 639 serial subscriptions, an OPAC, a Web page.

Student Life *Housing:* college housing not available. *Activities and Organizations:* drama/theater group, student-run newspaper, choral group, Fashion Entertainment Board, Phi Theta Kappa, Latin Student Union, DECA, Black Student Association. *Campus security:* 24-hour emergency response devices and patrols. *Student services:* personal/psychological counseling, women's center.

Athletics Member NJCAA. *Intercollegiate sports:* basketball M(s)/W(s), cross-country running M(s)/W(s), soccer M, track and field M/W. *Intramural sports:* table tennis M, weight lifting M.

Costs (2009–10) *Tuition:* area resident $3105 full-time, $104 per credit hour part-time; state resident $6210 full-time, $207 per credit hour part-time; nonresident $6210 full-time, $207 per credit hour part-time. *Required fees:* $915 full-time, $33 per credit hour part-time. *Payment plan:* deferred payment. *Waivers:* employees or children of employees.

Financial Aid Of all full-time matriculated undergraduates who enrolled in 2008, 250 Federal Work-Study jobs (averaging $2880).

Applying *Options:* electronic application, deferred entrance. *Application fee:* $25. *Required:* high school transcript. *Application deadline:* rolling (transfers). *Notification:* continuous (freshmen), continuous (out-of-state freshmen), continuous (transfers).

Freshman Application Contact Ms. Marva Mack, Director of Admissions, Essex County College, 303 University Avenue, Newark, NJ 07102. *Phone:* 973-877-3119. *Fax:* 973-623-6449.

GLOUCESTER COUNTY COLLEGE

Sewell, New Jersey **www.gccnj.edu/**

Freshman Application Contact Ms. Judy Apkinson, Admissions Supervisor, Gloucester County College, 1400 Tanyard Road, Sewell, NJ 08080. *Phone:* 856-468-5000. *E-mail:* japkinso@gccnj.edu.

HUDSON COUNTY COMMUNITY COLLEGE

Jersey City, New Jersey **www.hccc.edu/**

- **State and locally supported** 2-year, founded 1974, part of New Jersey Commission on Higher Education
- **Urban** campus with easy access to New York City
- **Coed**

Academics *Calendar:* semesters. *Degree:* diplomas and associate. *Special study options:* academic remediation for entering students, adult/continuing education programs, advanced placement credit, double majors, English as a second language, honors programs, independent study, internships, part-time degree program, services for LD students, summer session for credit.

Student Life *Campus security:* 24-hour emergency response devices.

Costs (2009–10) *Tuition:* area resident $2887 full-time, $96 per credit part-time; state resident $5775 full-time, $193 per credit part-time; nonresident $8662 full-time, $289 per credit part-time. Full-time tuition and fees vary according to course load. Part-time tuition and fees vary according to course load. *Required fees:* $1162 full-time, $39 per credit part-time, $20 per term part-time.

Financial Aid Of all full-time matriculated undergraduates who enrolled in 2008, 102 Federal Work-Study jobs (averaging $3000).

Applying *Application fee:* $15. *Required:* high school transcript.

Director of Admissions Mr. Robert Martin, Assistant Dean of Admissions, Hudson County Community College, 162 Sip Avenue, Jersey City, NJ 07306. *Phone:* 201-714-2115. *Fax:* 201-714-2136. *E-mail:* martin@hccc.edu.

MERCER COUNTY COMMUNITY COLLEGE

Trenton, New Jersey **www.mccc.edu/**

- **State and locally supported** 2-year, founded 1966
- **Suburban** 292-acre campus with easy access to New York City and Philadelphia
- **Coed,** 9,621 undergraduate students, 45% full-time, 55% women, 45% men

Undergraduates 4,372 full-time, 5,249 part-time. Students come from 5 states and territories, 91 other countries, 7% are from out of state, 24% African American, 5% Asian American or Pacific Islander, 12% Hispanic American, 0.1% Native American, 5% international, 3% transferred in. *Retention:* 68% of 2008 full-time freshmen returned.

Freshmen *Admission:* 2,282 applied, 2,282 admitted, 2,282 enrolled.

Faculty *Total:* 583, 22% full-time. *Student/faculty ratio:* 22:1.

Majors Accounting; administrative assistant and secretarial science; airline flight attendant; airline pilot and flight crew; architectural engineering technology; art; art history, criticism and conservation; automotive engineering technology; aviation/airway management; biology/biological sciences; biology/biotechnology laboratory technician; business administration and management; ceramic arts and ceramics; chemistry; civil engineering technology; clinical/medical laboratory technology; commercial and advertising art; community organization and advocacy; computer graphics; computer science; computer systems networking and telecommunications; corrections; criminal justice/police science; culinary arts; dance; dramatic/theater arts; electrical, electronic and communications engineering technology; engineering science; fire science; funeral service and mortuary science; health professions related; heating, air conditioning and refrigeration technology; hotel/motel administration; humanities; legal assistant/paralegal; liberal arts and sciences/liberal studies; management information systems; mass communication/media; mathematics; medical radiologic technology; music; nursing (registered nurse training); ornamental horticulture; photography; physical therapist assistant; physics; plant sciences; radio and television broadcasting technology; respiratory care therapy; sculpture; teacher assistant/aide.

Academics *Calendar:* semesters. *Degree:* certificates and associate. *Special study options:* academic remediation for entering students, accelerated degree program, adult/continuing education programs, advanced placement credit, cooperative education, distance learning, double majors, English as a second language, external degree program, independent study, internships, part-time degree program, services for LD students, student-designed majors, summer session for credit. *ROTC:* Army (c), Air Force (c).

Library Mercer County Community College Library plus 1 other with 57,317 titles, 8,934 audiovisual materials, an OPAC, a Web page.

Student Life *Housing:* college housing not available. *Activities and Organizations:* drama/theater group, student-run newspaper, radio station, choral group, Student Government Association, student radio station, African-American Student Organization, Student Activities Board, Phi Theta Kappa. *Campus security:* 24-hour emergency response devices and patrols. *Student services:* personal/psychological counseling.

Athletics Member NJCAA. *Intercollegiate sports:* baseball M, basketball M(s)/W(s), golf M/W, soccer M(s)/W(s), softball W, tennis M/W, track and field M/W. *Intramural sports:* basketball M/W, skiing (downhill) M/W, softball M/W, volleyball M/W.

Costs (2009–10) *Tuition:* area resident $2316 full-time, $119 per credit hour part-time; state resident $3276 full-time, $159 per credit hour part-time; nonresident $5196 full-time, $239 per credit hour part-time. *Required fees:* $540 full-time, $23 per credit hour part-time. *Payment plan:* installment. *Waivers:* senior citizens and employees or children of employees.

Financial Aid Of all full-time matriculated undergraduates who enrolled in 2008, 100 Federal Work-Study jobs (averaging $1500). 12 state and other part-time jobs (averaging $1500).

Applying *Options:* electronic application, deferred entrance. *Required:* high school transcript. *Recommended:* interview. *Application deadlines:* rolling (freshmen), rolling (transfers). *Notification:* continuous (freshmen), continuous (transfers).

Freshman Application Contact Dr. L. Campbell, Dean for Student and Academic Services, Mercer County Community College, 1200 Old Trenton Road, PO Box B, Trenton, NJ 08690-1004. *Phone:* 609-586-4800 Ext. 3222. *Toll-free phone:* 800-392-MCCC. *Fax:* 609-586-6944. *E-mail:* admiss@mccc.edu.

MIDDLESEX COUNTY COLLEGE

Edison, New Jersey **www.middlesexcc.edu/**

Director of Admissions Mr. Peter W. Rice, Director of Admissions and Recruitment, Middlesex County College, 2600 Woodbridge Avenue, PO Box 3050, Edison, NJ 08818-3050. *Phone:* 732-906-4243.

OCEAN COUNTY COLLEGE

Toms River, New Jersey **www.ocean.edu/**

- **County-supported** 2-year, founded 1964, part of New Jersey Commission on Higher Education
- **Small-town** 275-acre campus with easy access to Philadelphia
- **Coed,** 10,415 undergraduate students, 57% full-time, 58% women, 42% men

Undergraduates 5,907 full-time, 4,508 part-time. Students come from 13 states and territories, 6 other countries, 4% African American, 3% Asian American or Pacific Islander, 7% Hispanic American, 0.2% Native American, 2% transferred in. *Retention:* 74% of 2008 full-time freshmen returned.

Freshmen *Admission:* 2,917 enrolled.

Faculty *Total:* 525, 22% full-time. *Student/faculty ratio:* 30:1.

Majors Accounting; administrative assistant and secretarial science; allied health and medical assisting services related; broadcast journalism; business administration and management; business/commerce; child-care and support services management; civil engineering technology; clinical/medical laboratory technology; commercial and advertising art; communications technologies and support services related; communications technology; computer and information sciences; computer programming; construction engineering technology; criminal justice/police science; electrical, electronic and communications engineering technology; engineering; environmental science; fire protection and safety technology; general studies; health professions related; information science/studies; journalism; legal assistant/paralegal; liberal arts and sciences/liberal studies; medical/clinical assistant; nursing (registered nurse training); real estate; sign language interpretation and translation; social work; teacher assistant/aide.

Academics *Calendar:* semesters. *Degree:* certificates, diplomas, and associate. *Special study options:* academic remediation for entering students, accelerated degree program, adult/continuing education programs, advanced placement credit, cooperative education, distance learning, English as a second language, freshman honors college, honors programs, independent study, internships, part-time degree program, services for LD students, study abroad, summer session for credit.

Library Ocean County College Library with 74,215 titles, 428 serial subscriptions, 2,308 audiovisual materials, an OPAC, a Web page.

Student Life *Housing:* college housing not available. *Activities and Organizations:* drama/theater group, student-run newspaper, radio and television station, choral group, Phi Theta Kappa, ASOCC - Student Government, Student Nurses Organization, NJ STARS Club, Phi Beta Lambda. *Campus security:* 24-hour emergency response devices and patrols, late-night transport/escort service. *Student services:* personal/psychological counseling.

Athletics Member NJCAA. *Intercollegiate sports:* baseball M, basketball M/W, cross-country running M/W, golf M/W, soccer M/W, softball W, swimming and diving M/W, tennis M/W. *Intramural sports:* basketball M/W, cheerleading M(c)/W(c), sailing M(c)/W(c), soccer M/W, volleyball M/W.

Costs (2010–11) *Tuition:* area resident $2256 full-time, $94 per credit part-time; state resident $3072 full-time, $128 per credit part-time; nonresident $4990 full-time, $208 per credit part-time. Full-time tuition and fees vary according to program. Part-time tuition and fees vary according to program. *Required fees:* $890 full-time, $28 per credit part-time, $20 per term part-time. *Payment plan:* installment. *Waivers:* senior citizens and employees or children of employees.

Financial Aid Of all full-time matriculated undergraduates who enrolled in 2008, 76 Federal Work-Study jobs (averaging $1300). 45 state and other part-time jobs (averaging $850).

Applying *Options:* electronic application, early admission, deferred entrance. *Application fee:* $20. *Required for some:* high school transcript. *Application deadlines:* rolling (freshmen), rolling (transfers). *Notification:* continuous (freshmen), continuous (transfers).

Freshman Application Contact Ocean County College, College Drive, PO Box 2001, Toms River, NJ 08754-2001. *Phone:* 732-255-0304 Ext. 2423.

PASSAIC COUNTY COMMUNITY COLLEGE

Paterson, New Jersey **www.pccc.cc.nj.us/**

Freshman Application Contact Mr. Patrick Noonan, Director of Admissions, Passaic County Community College, One College Boulevard, Paterson, NJ 07505. *Phone:* 973-684-6304.

RARITAN VALLEY COMMUNITY COLLEGE

Branchburg, New Jersey **www.raritanval.edu/**

- **County-supported** 2-year, founded 1965
- **Small-town** 225-acre campus with easy access to New York City and Philadelphia
- **Endowment** $594,415
- **Coed,** 7,888 undergraduate students, 52% full-time, 54% women, 46% men

Undergraduates 4,086 full-time, 3,802 part-time. Students come from 20 states and territories, 0.1% are from out of state, 9% African American, 5% Asian American or Pacific Islander, 12% Hispanic American, 0.4% Native American, 3% international, 8% transferred in.

Freshmen *Admission:* 1,595 enrolled.

Faculty *Total:* 458, 25% full-time. *Student/faculty ratio:* 23:1.

Majors Accounting; accounting related; accounting technology and bookkeeping; administrative assistant and secretarial science; animation, interactive technology, video graphics and special effects; automotive engineering technology; biotechnology; business administration and management; business/commerce; chemical technology; child-care provision; cinematography and film/video production; communication and media related; computer and information sciences and support services related; computer programming (vendor/product certification); computer systems networking and telecommunications; construction engineering technology; corrections; corrections and criminal justice related; criminal justice/law enforcement administration; criminal justice/police science; dance; data processing and data processing technology; dental assisting; dental hygiene; design and applied arts related; diesel mechanics technology; digital communication and media/multimedia; education (multiple levels); engineering science; engineering technologies related; English; financial planning and services; fine/studio arts; health and physical education; health information/medical records technology; health services/allied health/health sciences; heating, air conditioning and refrigeration technology; hospitality administration related; information technology; interior design; international business/trade/commerce; kindergarten/preschool education; kinesiology and exercise science; legal assistant/paralegal; liberal arts and sciences/liberal studies; lineworker; management information systems; manufacturing technology; marketing/marketing management; medical/clinical assistant; multi/interdisciplinary studies related; music; nursing (registered nurse training); opticianry; optometric technician; respiratory care therapy; restaurant, culinary, and catering management; small business administration; teaching assistants/aides related; theater design and technology; web page, digital/multimedia and information resources design.

Academics *Calendar:* semesters. *Degree:* certificates and associate. *Special study options:* academic remediation for entering students, adult/continuing education programs, advanced placement credit, cooperative education, distance learning, double majors, English as a second language, honors programs, independent study, internships, off-campus study, part-time degree program, services for LD students, summer session for credit. *ROTC:* Army (c), Air Force (c).

Library Evelyn S. Field Library with 69,634 titles, 23,874 serial subscriptions, 2,049 audiovisual materials, an OPAC, a Web page.

Student Life *Housing:* college housing not available. *Activities and Organizations:* drama/theater group, student-run newspaper, choral group, Phi Theta Kappa, Club Unity, Student Nurses Association, Social Justice Club, Orgullo Latino. *Campus security:* 24-hour emergency response devices and patrols, late-night transport/escort service, 24-hour outdoor and indoor surveillance cameras. *Student services:* personal/psychological counseling.

Athletics Member NJCAA. *Intercollegiate sports:* baseball M, basketball M/W, soccer M, softball W. *Intramural sports:* golf M/W.

Costs (2009–10) *Tuition:* state resident $106 per credit part-time; nonresident $106 per credit part-time. Full-time tuition and fees vary according to course load. Part-time tuition and fees vary according to course load. *Required fees:* $22 per credit part-time, $80 part-time. *Payment plan:* installment. *Waivers:* senior citizens and employees or children of employees.

Financial Aid Of all full-time matriculated undergraduates who enrolled in 2008, 12 Federal Work-Study jobs (averaging $2500).

Applying *Options:* electronic application, early admission. *Application fee:* $25. *Required:* high school transcript. *Application deadlines:* rolling (freshmen), rolling (transfers).

Freshman Application Contact Mr. Daniel Palubniak, Registrar, Enrollment Services, Raritan Valley Community College, PO Box 3300, Somerville, NJ 08876-1265. *Phone:* 908-526-1200 Ext. 8206. *Fax:* 908-704-3442. *E-mail:* dpalubni@raritanval.edu.

SALEM COMMUNITY COLLEGE

Carneys Point, New Jersey **www.salemcc.org/**

Freshman Application Contact Dr. Reva Curry, Vice President of Student Services, Salem Community College, 460 Hollywood Avenue, Carneys Point, NJ 08069. *Phone:* 856-351-2707. *Fax:* 856-299-9193. *E-mail:* info@salemcc.edu.

SUSSEX COUNTY COMMUNITY COLLEGE

Newton, New Jersey **www.sussex.edu/**

Freshman Application Contact Mr. James Donohue, Director of Admissions and Registrar, Sussex County Community College, 1 College Hill, Newton, NJ 07860. *Phone:* 973-300-2219. *Fax:* 973-579-5226. *E-mail:* jdonohue@sussex.edu.

UNION COUNTY COLLEGE

Cranford, New Jersey **www.ucc.edu/**

- **State and locally supported** 2-year, founded 1933, part of New Jersey Commission on Higher Education
- **Urban** 48-acre campus with easy access to New York City
- **Endowment** $8.7 million
- **Coed,** 12,751 undergraduate students, 50% full-time, 62% women, 38% men

Undergraduates 6,338 full-time, 6,413 part-time. Students come from 9 states and territories, 77 other countries, 3% are from out of state, 17% African American, 3% Asian American or Pacific Islander, 21% Hispanic American, 0.7% Native American, 2% international, 6% transferred in. *Retention:* 54% of 2008 full-time freshmen returned.

Freshmen *Admission:* 7,335 applied, 6,169 admitted, 2,764 enrolled.

Faculty *Total:* 461, 39% full-time, 22% with terminal degrees. *Student/faculty ratio:* 30:1.

Majors Accounting technology and bookkeeping; administrative assistant and secretarial science; allied health diagnostic, intervention, and treatment professions related; animation, interactive technology, video graphics and special effects; business administration and management; business and personal/financial services marketing; business/commerce; chemistry; civil engineering technology; computer and information sciences and support services related; computer science; criminal justice/police science; customer service support/call center/teleservice operation; dental hygiene; diagnostic medical sonography and ultrasound technology; electromechanical technology; engineering; fire protection and safety technology; hotel/motel administration; information science/studies; language interpretation and translation; legal assistant/paralegal; liberal arts and sciences/liberal studies; management information systems; manufacturing technology; marketing/marketing management; mechanical engineering/mechanical technology; medical radiologic technology; nuclear medical technology; nursing (licensed practical/vocational nurse training); nursing (registered nurse training); physical therapist assistant; rehabilitation and therapeutic professions related; respiratory care therapy; sign language interpretation and translation.

Academics *Calendar:* semesters. *Degree:* certificates, diplomas, and associate. *Special study options:* academic remediation for entering students, accelerated degree program, adult/continuing education programs, advanced placement credit, distance learning, English as a second language, honors programs, independent study, internships, off-campus study, part-time degree program, services for LD students, student-designed majors, summer session for credit. *ROTC:* Air Force (c).

Library MacKay Library plus 2 others with 137,731 titles, 20,938 serial subscriptions, 3,610 audiovisual materials, an OPAC, a Web page.

Student Life *Housing:* college housing not available. *Activities and Organizations:* drama/theater group, student-run newspaper, radio and television station, SIGN, Business Management Club, Art Society, La Sociedad Hispanica de UCC, Architecture Club. *Campus security:* 24-hour emergency response devices and patrols, late-night transport/escort service. *Student services:* personal/psychological counseling.

Athletics Member NJCAA. *Intercollegiate sports:* baseball M, basketball M/W(s), golf M/W, soccer M, volleyball W. *Intramural sports:* cheerleading W.

Costs (2010–11) *Tuition:* area resident $2400 full-time, $100 per credit part-time; state resident $4800 full-time, $200 per credit part-time; nonresident $4800 full-time, $200 per credit part-time. Full-time tuition and fees vary according to course load. Part-time tuition and fees vary according to course load. *Required fees:* $810 full-time, $27 per credit part-time. *Payment plan:* deferred payment. *Waivers:* senior citizens and employees or children of employees.

Financial Aid Of all full-time matriculated undergraduates who enrolled in 2008, 150 Federal Work-Study jobs (averaging $1700).

Applying *Options:* electronic application, early admission, deferred entrance. *Application fee:* $35. *Required:* high school transcript. *Required for some:* interview. *Application deadlines:* rolling (freshmen), rolling (transfers). *Notification:* continuous (freshmen), continuous (transfers).

Freshman Application Contact Ms. Jo Ann Davis-Wayne, Director of Admissions, Records, and Registration, Union County College, 1033 Springfield Avenue, Cranford, NJ 07016. *Phone:* 908-709-7127. *Fax:* 908-709-7125. *E-mail:* Davis@ucc.edu.

WARREN COUNTY COMMUNITY COLLEGE

Washington, New Jersey **www.warren.edu/**

Freshman Application Contact Admissions Advisor, Warren County Community College, 475 Route 57 West, Washington, NJ 07882-9605. *Phone:* 908-835-2300.

NEW MEXICO

BROWN MACKIE COLLEGE–ALBUQUERQUE

Albuquerque, New Mexico **www.brownmackie.edu/**

- **Proprietary** primarily 2-year
- **Coed**

Majors Accounting technology and bookkeeping; architectural drafting and CAD/CADD; business administration and management; criminal justice/law enforcement administration; health/health-care administration; information technology; legal assistant/paralegal; legal studies; medical/clinical assistant; occupational therapist assistant; pharmacy technician; veterinary/animal health technology.

Academics *Degrees:* associate and bachelor's.

Freshman Application Contact Brown Mackie College–Albuquerque, 10500 Cooper Avenue NE, Albuquerque, NM 87123. *Phone:* 505-559-5200. *Toll-free phone:* 877-271-3488.

►See page 406 for the College Close-Up.

CENTRAL NEW MEXICO COMMUNITY COLLEGE

Albuquerque, New Mexico **www.cnm.edu/**

- **State-supported** 2-year, founded 1965
- **Urban** 60-acre campus
- **Endowment** $1.1 million
- **Coed,** 27,938 undergraduate students, 32% full-time, 56% women, 44% men

Undergraduates 8,980 full-time, 18,958 part-time. Students come from 11 states and territories, 1 other country, 14% are from out of state, 4% African American, 2% Asian American or Pacific Islander, 41% Hispanic American, 8% Native American, 0.8% international, 5% transferred in. *Retention:* 49% of 2008 full-time freshmen returned.

Freshmen *Admission:* 8,700 applied, 8,700 admitted, 4,022 enrolled.

Faculty *Total:* 1,098, 30% full-time. *Student/faculty ratio:* 26:1.

Majors Accounting; administrative assistant and secretarial science; agriculture; architectural drafting and CAD/CADD; art; automotive engineering technology; banking and financial support services; biotechnology; building/construction finishing, management, and inspection related; business administration and management; child-care and support services management; clinical/medical laboratory technology; computer systems analysis; construction trades related; cosmetology; criminal justice/safety; culinary arts; data processing and data processing technology; diagnostic medical sonography and ultrasound technology; electrical, electronic and communications engineering technology; electrical/electronics drafting and CAD/CADD; elementary education; engineering; environmental/environmental health engineering; executive assistant/executive secretary; fire protection and safety technology; general studies; health information/medical records administration; hospitality administration; information science/studies; international business/trade/commerce; laser and optical technology; legal assistant/paralegal; liberal arts and sciences/liberal studies; manufacturing technology; medical radiologic technology; nursing (registered nurse training); parks, recreation and leisure; respiratory care therapy; survey technology; technology/industrial arts teacher education; vehicle maintenance and repair technologies related; veterinary/animal health technology.

Academics *Calendar:* trimesters. *Degree:* certificates and associate. *Special study options:* academic remediation for entering students, adult/continuing education programs, advanced placement credit, cooperative education, distance learning, double majors, English as a second language, internships, part-time degree program, services for LD students, summer session for credit. *ROTC:* Army (c), Navy (c), Air Force (c).

Library Main Campus Library plus 1 other with 75,167 titles, 622 serial subscriptions, an OPAC, a Web page.

Student Life *Housing:* college housing not available. *Activities and Organizations:* student-run newspaper, Skills USA, Native American Student Club, ESL Club, GED Club, Artworks. *Campus security:* 24-hour emergency response devices and patrols, late-night transport/escort service. *Student services:* health clinic, personal/psychological counseling.

Costs (2010–11) *Tuition:* area resident $1476 full-time, $41 per credit hour part-time; state resident $1836 full-time, $51 per credit hour part-time; nonresident $7200 full-time, $200 per credit hour part-time. Full-time tuition and fees vary according to course load. Part-time tuition and fees vary according to course load. *Required fees:* $120 full-time, $43 per term part-time. *Payment plan:* installment. *Waivers:* senior citizens.

Financial Aid Of all full-time matriculated undergraduates who enrolled in 2008, 175 Federal Work-Study jobs (averaging $6000). 225 state and other part-time jobs (averaging $6000).

Applying *Options:* electronic application. *Application deadlines:* rolling (freshmen), rolling (out-of-state freshmen), rolling (transfers). *Notification:* continuous (freshmen), continuous (out-of-state freshmen), continuous (transfers).

Freshman Application Contact Ms. Jane Campbell, Director, Enrollment Services, Central New Mexico Community College, 900 University, SE, Albuquerque, NM 87106-4096. *Phone:* 505-224-3160. *Fax:* 505-224-3237.

Clovis Community College

Clovis, New Mexico **www.clovis.edu/**

- **State-supported** 2-year, founded 1990
- **Small-town** 25-acre campus
- **Endowment** $812,000
- **Coed,** 3,706 undergraduate students, 16% full-time, 64% women, 36% men

Undergraduates 582 full-time, 3,124 part-time. Students come from 50 states and territories, 12% are from out of state, 5% African American, 2% Asian American or Pacific Islander, 27% Hispanic American, 0.7% Native American, 5% transferred in. *Retention:* 33% of 2008 full-time freshmen returned.

Freshmen *Admission:* 192 applied, 192 admitted, 192 enrolled.

Faculty *Total:* 175, 27% full-time, 10% with terminal degrees. *Student/faculty ratio:* 15:1.

Majors Accounting; administrative assistant and secretarial science; automobile/automotive mechanics technology; bilingual and multilingual education; business administration and management; business automation/technology/data entry; commercial and advertising art; computer and information sciences; computer typography and composition equipment operation; corrections; cosmetology; criminal justice/police science; electromechanical technology; executive assistant/executive secretary; finance; fine/studio arts; health and physical education; heating, air conditioning, ventilation and refrigeration maintenance technology; legal administrative assistant/secretary; legal assistant/paralegal; liberal arts and sciences/liberal studies; library assistant; management information systems; mathematics; medical administrative assistant and medical secretary; medical office assistant; medical radiologic technology; nail technician and manicurist; nursing (registered nurse training); physical sciences; psychology; sign language interpretation and translation; teacher assistant/aide; technical and business writing; web/multimedia management and webmaster; web page, digital/multimedia and information resources design.

Academics *Calendar:* semesters. *Degree:* certificates and associate. *Special study options:* academic remediation for entering students, adult/continuing education programs, advanced placement credit, cooperative education, distance learning, double majors, English as a second language, independent study, internships, part-time degree program, services for LD students, summer session for credit.

Library Clovis Community College Library and Learning Resources Center with 52,000 titles, 370 serial subscriptions, an OPAC.

Student Life *Housing:* college housing not available. *Activities and Organizations:* drama/theater group, choral group, Student Senate, Student Nursing Association, Black Advisory Council, Hispanic Advisory Council, student ambassadors. *Campus security:* student patrols, late-night transport/escort service. *Student services:* personal/psychological counseling.

Athletics *Intramural sports:* basketball M/W, cross-country running M/W, racquetball M/W, tennis M/W, volleyball M/W.

Costs (2009–10) *Tuition:* $30 per credit hour part-time; state resident $32 per credit hour part-time; nonresident $65 per credit hour part-time. Full-time tuition and fees vary according to course load and program. Part-time tuition and fees vary according to course load and program. *Required fees:* $20 per term part-time. *Payment plan:* installment. *Waivers:* senior citizens and employees or children of employees.

Applying *Required:* high school transcript. *Required for some:* interview. *Application deadlines:* rolling (freshmen), rolling (transfers). *Notification:* continuous (freshmen), continuous (transfers).

Freshman Application Contact Ms. Rosie Corrie, Director of Admissions and Records/Registrar, Clovis Community College, 417 Schepps Boulevard, Clovis, NM 88101-8381. *Phone:* 575-769-4962. *Fax:* 575-769-4190. *E-mail:* admissions@clovis.edu.

Doña Ana Branch Community College

Las Cruces, New Mexico **dabcc-www.nmsu.edu/**

- **State and locally supported** 2-year, founded 1973, part of New Mexico State University System
- **Urban** 15-acre campus with easy access to El Paso
- **Coed**

Undergraduates 2,552 full-time, 5,251 part-time. 2% African American, 0.8% Asian American or Pacific Islander, 59% Hispanic American, 3% Native American, 7% international, 2% transferred in. *Retention:* 85% of 2008 full-time freshmen returned.

Faculty *Student/faculty ratio:* 21:1.

Academics *Calendar:* semesters. *Degree:* certificates and associate. *Special study options:* academic remediation for entering students, adult/continuing education programs, advanced placement credit, cooperative education, English as a second language, freshman honors college, honors programs, internships, part-time degree program, services for LD students, summer session for credit. *ROTC:* Army (c), Air Force (c).

Student Life *Campus security:* 24-hour emergency response devices and patrols, late-night transport/escort service, controlled dormitory access.

Standardized Tests *Recommended:* ACT, ACT ASSET, or ACT COMPASS.

Costs (2009–10) *Tuition:* area resident $1272 full-time, $53 per credit hour part-time; state resident $1512 full-time, $63 per credit hour part-time; nonresident $3984 full-time, $166 per credit hour part-time. Full-time tuition and fees vary according to course load and program. Part-time tuition and fees vary according to course load and program. *Room and board:* $8924; room only: $5739. Room and board charges vary according to board plan and housing facility.

Financial Aid Of all full-time matriculated undergraduates who enrolled in 2008, 15 Federal Work-Study jobs (averaging $2800). 106 state and other part-time jobs (averaging $2800). *Financial aid deadline:* 6/30.

Applying *Options:* electronic application, deferred entrance. *Application fee:* $15. *Required:* high school transcript.

Freshman Application Contact Mrs. Ricci Montes, Admissions Advisor, Doña Ana Branch Community College, MSC-3DA, Box 30001, Las Cruces, NM 88003-8001. *Phone:* 575-527-7683. *Toll-free phone:* 800-903-7503. *Fax:* 575-527-7515.

Eastern New Mexico University–Roswell

Roswell, New Mexico **www.enmu.edu/**

Freshman Application Contact Mr. James Mares, Assistant Director, Eastern New Mexico University–Roswell, PO Box 6000, Roswell, NM 88202-6000. *Phone:* 505-624-7149. *Toll-free phone:* 800-243-6687.

Institute of American Indian Arts

Santa Fe, New Mexico **www.iaia.edu/**

- **Federally supported** primarily 2-year, founded 1962
- **Urban** 120-acre campus
- **Coed**

Academics *Calendar:* semesters. *Degrees:* associate and bachelor's. *Special study options:* academic remediation for entering students, internships, off-campus study.

Student Life *Campus security:* 24-hour patrols, late-night transport/escort service.

Financial Aid Of all full-time matriculated undergraduates who enrolled in 2008, 293 applied for aid, 209 were judged to have need, 87 had their need fully met. 17 Federal Work-Study jobs (averaging $605). 16 state and other part-time jobs (averaging $649). In 2008, 84. *Average financial aid package:* $4434. *Average need-based loan:* $1950. *Average need-based gift aid:* $2050. *Average non-need-based aid:* $1500. *Average indebtedness upon graduation:* $2000.

Applying *Options:* deferred entrance. *Application fee:* $5. *Required:* high school transcript, minimum 2.0 GPA, 3 letters of recommendation. *Recommended:* interview.

Director of Admissions Myra Garro, Manager of Enrollment and Admissions, Institute of American Indian Arts, 83 Avan Nu Po Road, Santa Fe, NM 87508. *Phone:* 505-424-2328.

ITT Technical Institute

Albuquerque, New Mexico www.itt-tech.edu/

- **Proprietary** primarily 2-year, founded 1989, part of ITT Educational Services, Inc.
- **Coed**

Majors Business administration and management; CAD/CADD drafting/design technology; computer and information systems security; computer engineering technology; computer software and media applications related; computer software engineering; construction management; criminal justice/law enforcement administration; design and visual communications; electrical, electronic and communications engineering technology; health information/medical records technology; legal assistant/paralegal; nursing (registered nurse training); system, networking, and LAN/WAN management; web/multimedia management and webmaster; web page, digital/multimedia and information resources design.

Academics *Calendar:* quarters. *Degrees:* associate and bachelor's.

Student Life *Housing:* college housing not available.

Freshman Application Contact Director of Recruitment, ITT Technical Institute, 5100 Masthead Street NE, Albuquerque, NM 87109. *Phone:* 505-828-1114. *Toll-free phone:* 800-636-1114.

Luna Community College

Las Vegas, New Mexico www.luna.edu/

- **State-supported** 2-year
- **Small-town** 25-acre campus
- **Coed,** 1,789 undergraduate students, 30% full-time, 56% women, 44% men

Undergraduates 544 full-time, 1,245 part-time. Students come from 6 states and territories, 1% are from out of state, 1% transferred in. *Retention:* 38% of 2008 full-time freshmen returned.

Freshmen *Admission:* 229 enrolled.

Majors Accounting; administrative assistant and secretarial science; autobody/collision and repair technology; business administration and management; computer programming (vendor/product certification); criminal justice/safety; culinary arts; dental assisting; drafting and design technology; education; electrical, electronic and communications engineering technology; general studies; industrial arts; kindergarten/preschool education; liberal arts and sciences/liberal studies; nursing (registered nurse training); office management.

Academics *Calendar:* semesters. *Degree:* certificates, diplomas, and associate. *Special study options:* academic remediation for entering students, cooperative education, distance learning, honors programs, independent study, part-time degree program.

Library Samuel F. Vigil Learning Resource Center plus 1 other with 37,343 titles, 178 serial subscriptions, 5,000 audiovisual materials, an OPAC.

Student Life *Housing:* college housing not available.

Applying *Options:* electronic application. *Required:* high school transcript.

Freshman Application Contact Ms. Henrietta Griego, Director of Admissions, Recruitment, and Retention, Luna Community College, 366 Luna Drive, Las Vegas, NM 87701. *Phone:* 505-454-2020. *Toll-free phone:* 800-588-7232 Ext. 1202. *Fax:* 505-454-2588. *E-mail:* hgriego@luna.cc.nm.us.

Mesalands Community College

Tucumcari, New Mexico www.mesalands.edu/

- **State-supported** 2-year, founded 1979
- **Small-town** campus
- **Coed**

Academics *Calendar:* semesters. *Degree:* certificates and associate.

Student Life *Campus security:* 24-hour emergency response devices.

Applying *Required:* high school transcript.

Director of Admissions Mr. Ken Brashear, Director of Enrollment Management, Mesalands Community College, 911 South Tenth Street, Tucumcari, NM 88401. *Phone:* 505-461-4413.

National American University

Rio Rancho, New Mexico www.national.edu/

Freshman Application Contact Admissions Office, National American University, 1601 Rio Rancho, Suite 200, Rio Rancho, NM 87124.

Navajo Technical College

Crownpoint, New Mexico www.navajotech.edu/

Director of Admissions Director of Admission, Navajo Technical College, PO Box 849, Crownpoint, NM 87313. *Phone:* 505-786-4100.

New Mexico Junior College

Hobbs, New Mexico www.nmjc.edu/

Director of Admissions Mr. Robert Bensing, Dean of Enrollment Management, New Mexico Junior College, 5317 Lovington Highway, Hobbs, NM 88240-9123. *Phone:* 505-392-5092. *Toll-free phone:* 800-657-6260.

New Mexico Military Institute

Roswell, New Mexico www.nmmi.edu/

Freshman Application Contact New Mexico Military Institute, 101 West College Boulevard, Roswell, NM 88201-5173. *Phone:* 505-624-8050. *Toll-free phone:* 800-421-5376. *Fax:* 505-624-8058. *E-mail:* admissions@nmmi.edu.

New Mexico State University–Alamogordo

Alamogordo, New Mexico alamo.nmsu.edu/

- **State-supported** 2-year, founded 1958, part of New Mexico State University System
- **Small-town** 540-acre campus
- **Coed**

Undergraduates 801 full-time, 2,436 part-time. Students come from 30 states and territories, 9% are from out of state, 4% African American, 2% Asian American or Pacific Islander, 33% Hispanic American, 4% Native American, 3% international, 6% transferred in. *Retention:* 51% of 2008 full-time freshmen returned.

Faculty *Student/faculty ratio:* 29:1.

Academics *Calendar:* semesters. *Degree:* certificates and associate. *Special study options:* academic remediation for entering students, adult/continuing education programs, advanced placement credit, distance learning, honors programs, independent study, internships, off-campus study, part-time degree program, services for LD students, study abroad, summer session for credit.

Student Life *Campus security:* 24-hour emergency response devices.

Costs (2009–10) *Tuition:* area resident $1512 full-time, $63 per credit hour part-time; state resident $1728 full-time, $72 per credit hour part-time; nonresident $4176 full-time, $174 per credit hour part-time. *Required fees:* $48 full-time, $2 per credit hour part-time. *Payment plans:* installment, deferred payment.

Financial Aid Of all full-time matriculated undergraduates who enrolled in 2008, 10 Federal Work-Study jobs (averaging $3300). 60 state and other part-time jobs (averaging $3300). *Financial aid deadline:* 5/1.

Applying *Options:* electronic application, early admission, deferred entrance. *Application fee:* $15. *Required:* high school transcript, minimum 2 GPA.

Freshman Application Contact Ms. Kathy Fuller, Coordinator of Admissions and Records, New Mexico State University–Alamogordo, 2400 North Scenic Drive, Alamogordo, NM 88311-0477. *Phone:* 505-439-3700. *E-mail:* advisor@nmsua.nmsu.edu.

New Mexico State University–Carlsbad

Carlsbad, New Mexico www.cavern.nmsu.edu/

- **State-supported** 2-year, founded 1950, part of New Mexico State University System
- **Small-town** 40-acre campus
- **Coed,** 1,998 undergraduate students, 29% full-time, 64% women, 36% men

Undergraduates 583 full-time, 1,415 part-time. Students come from 20 states and territories, 0.6% are from out of state, 2% African American, 1% Asian American or Pacific Islander, 46% Hispanic American, 2% Native American, 0.3% international, 5% transferred in. *Retention:* 41% of 2008 full-time freshmen returned.

Freshmen *Admission:* 306 applied, 306 admitted, 287 enrolled. *Average high school GPA:* 2.75. *Test scores:* ACT scores over 18: 43%; ACT scores over 24: 2%.

Faculty *Total:* 91, 45% full-time.

Majors Accounting; administrative assistant and secretarial science; architectural drafting and CAD/CADD; area, ethnic, cultural, and gender studies related; building/property maintenance and management; business/commerce; carpentry; criminal justice/law enforcement administration; criminal justice/safety; digital communication and media/multimedia; early childhood education; education; electrical, electronic and communications engineering technology; engineering; general studies; heating, air conditioning and refrigeration technology; human services; industrial electronics technology; medical transcription; multi/interdisciplinary studies related; nursing (registered nurse training); office occupations and clerical services; teacher assistant/aide; welding technology; word processing.

Academics *Calendar:* semesters. *Degree:* certificates, diplomas, and associate. *Special study options:* academic remediation for entering students, adult/continuing education programs, advanced placement credit, cooperative education, distance learning, double majors, English as a second language, honors programs, independent study, internships, part-time degree program, services for LD students, student-designed majors, summer session for credit.

Library Library/Media Center with 25,890 titles, 194 serial subscriptions, 1,632 audiovisual materials, an OPAC, a Web page.

Student Life *Housing:* college housing not available. *Activities and Organizations:* Student Nurses Association, Alpha Sigma Phi Criminal Justice Association, Phi Theta Kappa International Honors Society, Associated Students Student Government Association. *Campus security:* 24-hour emergency response devices, late-night transport/escort service. *Student services:* health clinic, personal/psychological counseling.

Costs (2009–10) *One-time required fee:* $15. *Tuition:* area resident $864 full-time, $36 per credit hour part-time; state resident $1320 full-time, $55 per credit hour part-time; nonresident $2712 full-time, $113 per credit hour part-time. *Required fees:* $100 full-time. *Payment plan:* installment. *Waivers:* senior citizens and employees or children of employees.

Financial Aid Of all full-time matriculated undergraduates who enrolled in 2008, 5 Federal Work-Study jobs (averaging $2300). 29 state and other part-time jobs (averaging $3000).

Applying *Options:* electronic application, early admission. *Application fee:* $20. *Required for some:* high school transcript. *Application deadlines:* rolling (freshmen), rolling (out-of-state freshmen), rolling (transfers). *Notification:* continuous (freshmen), continuous (out-of-state freshmen), continuous (transfers).

Freshman Application Contact Ms. Everal Shannon, Records Specialist, New Mexico State University–Carlsbad, 1500 University Drive, Carlsbad, NM 88220-3509. *Phone:* 575-234-9222. *Fax:* 575-885-4951. *E-mail:* eshannon@nmsu.edu.

NEW MEXICO STATE UNIVERSITY–GRANTS

Grants, New Mexico grants.nmsu.edu/

- **State-supported** 2-year, founded 1968, part of New Mexico State University System
- **Small-town** campus
- **Coed**

Academics *Calendar:* semesters. *Degree:* certificates and associate. *Special study options:* part-time degree program, summer session for credit.

Standardized Tests *Required:* CPT (for admission).

Financial Aid Of all full-time matriculated undergraduates who enrolled in 2008, 3 Federal Work-Study jobs (averaging $1800). 6 state and other part-time jobs (averaging $1500).

Applying *Options:* early admission. *Application fee:* $15. *Required:* high school transcript.

Director of Admissions Ms. Irene Lutz, Campus Student Services Officer, New Mexico State University–Grants, 1500 3rd Street, Grants, NM 87020-2025. *Phone:* 505-287-7981.

NORTHERN NEW MEXICO COLLEGE

Española, New Mexico www.nnmc.edu/

- **State-supported** primarily 2-year, founded 1909
- **Rural** 35-acre campus
- **Endowment** $829,791
- **Coed**

Undergraduates Students come from 5 states and territories, 1% are from out of state, 1% live on campus.

Academics *Calendar:* semesters. *Degrees:* certificates, associate, bachelor's, and postbachelor's certificates. *Special study options:* academic remediation for entering students, advanced placement credit, distance learning, part-time degree program, services for LD students, summer session for credit.

Student Life *Campus security:* 24-hour emergency response devices and patrols.

Financial Aid Of all full-time matriculated undergraduates who enrolled in 2008, 150 Federal Work-Study jobs (averaging $3000). 140 state and other part-time jobs (averaging $3000).

Applying *Options:* early admission, deferred entrance. *Required:* high school transcript.

Freshman Application Contact Mr. Mike L. Costello, Registrar, Northern New Mexico College, 921 Paseo de Oñate, Española, NM 87532. *Phone:* 505-747-2193. *Fax:* 505-747-2191. *E-mail:* dms@nnmc.edu.

PIMA MEDICAL INSTITUTE

Albuquerque, New Mexico www.pmi.edu/

- **Proprietary** 2-year, founded 1985, part of Vocational Training Institutes, Inc.
- **Urban** campus
- **Coed**

Academics *Calendar:* modular. *Degree:* certificates and associate. *Special study options:* academic remediation for entering students, cooperative education, internships, services for LD students.

Standardized Tests *Required:* Wonderlic Scholastic Level Exam (for admission).

Financial Aid Of all full-time matriculated undergraduates who enrolled in 2008, 6 Federal Work-Study jobs.

Applying *Options:* early admission. *Required:* interview. *Required for some:* high school transcript.

Freshman Application Contact Admissions Office, Pima Medical Institute, 2201 San Pedro NE, Building 3, Suite 100, Albuquerque, NM 87110. *Phone:* 505-881-1234. *Toll-free phone:* 888-898-9048. *Fax:* 505-881-5329.

SAN JUAN COLLEGE

Farmington, New Mexico www.sanjuancollege.edu/

- **State-supported** 2-year, founded 1958, part of New Mexico Higher Education Department
- **Small-town** 698-acre campus
- **Endowment** $9.4 million
- **Coed,** 8,990 undergraduate students, 34% full-time, 46% women, 54% men

Undergraduates 3,028 full-time, 5,962 part-time. Students come from 50 states and territories, 20 other countries, 17% are from out of state, 1% African American, 0.8% Asian American or Pacific Islander, 13% Hispanic American, 31% Native American, 0.2% international, 6% transferred in.

Freshmen *Admission:* 1,190 applied, 1,190 admitted, 1,078 enrolled.

Faculty *Total:* 449, 32% full-time. *Student/faculty ratio:* 24:1.

Majors Accounting technology and bookkeeping; administrative assistant and secretarial science; agricultural business and management; airline pilot and flight crew; autobody/collision and repair technology; automobile/automotive mechanics technology; banking and financial support services; biology/biological sciences; business administration and management; carpentry; chemistry; childcare provision; clinical/medical laboratory technology; commercial and advertising art; communication/speech communication and rhetoric; computer science; cosmetology; criminal justice/police science; criminal justice/safety; data processing and data processing technology; dental hygiene; diesel mechanics technology; drafting and design technology; dramatic/theater arts; education; electrical and electronic engineering technologies related; elementary education; emergency medical technology (EMT paramedic); engineering; English; fire protection and safety technology; fire science; foreign languages and literatures;

San Juan College (continued)

general studies; geology/earth science; health and physical education; health information/medical records technology; history; human services; industrial mechanics and maintenance technology; industrial technology; information science/studies; instrumentation technology; kindergarten/preschool education; legal assistant/paralegal; liberal arts and sciences/liberal studies; machine shop technology; mathematics; nursing (registered nurse training); occupational safety and health technology; parks, recreation and leisure; philosophy; physical sciences; physical therapist assistant; physics; premedical studies; psychology; public administration; respiratory care therapy; secondary education; social work; solar energy technology; special education; surgical technology; survey technology; veterinary/animal health technology; welding technology.

Academics *Calendar:* semesters. *Degree:* certificates, diplomas, and associate. *Special study options:* academic remediation for entering students, adult/continuing education programs, advanced placement credit, cooperative education, distance learning, English as a second language, honors programs, independent study, internships, part-time degree program, services for LD students, summer session for credit.

Library San Juan College Library with 81,116 titles, 6,677 serial subscriptions, 2,415 audiovisual materials, an OPAC, a Web page.

Student Life *Housing:* college housing not available. *Activities and Organizations:* drama/theater group, student-run newspaper, radio station, choral group, national fraternities, national sororities. *Campus security:* 24-hour emergency response devices and patrols, late-night transport/escort service. *Student services:* personal/psychological counseling.

Athletics *Intramural sports:* archery M/W, badminton M/W, basketball M/W, bowling M/W, cross-country running M/W, football M/W, golf M/W, racquetball M/W, rock climbing M/W, skiing (cross-country) M/W, skiing (downhill) M/W, soccer M/W, softball M/W, table tennis M/W, tennis M/W, volleyball M/W.

Costs (2010–11) *Tuition:* state resident $1110 full-time, $37 per credit hour part-time; nonresident $2730 full-time, $91 per credit hour part-time. Full-time tuition and fees vary according to reciprocity agreements. *Required fees:* $180 full-time, $6 per credit hour part-time. *Payment plans:* tuition prepayment, installment. *Waivers:* senior citizens and employees or children of employees.

Financial Aid Of all full-time matriculated undergraduates who enrolled in 2008, 150 Federal Work-Study jobs (averaging $2500). 175 state and other part-time jobs (averaging $2500).

Applying *Options:* electronic application, early admission, deferred entrance. *Required:* high school transcript. *Application deadlines:* rolling (freshmen), rolling (transfers). *Notification:* continuous (freshmen), continuous (transfers).

Freshman Application Contact Skylar Maston, Admissions Specialist, San Juan College, 4601 College Boulevard, Farmington, NM 87402. *Phone:* 505-566-3300. *E-mail:* mastons@sanjuancollege.edu.

SANTA FE COMMUNITY COLLEGE

Santa Fe, New Mexico **www.sfccnm.edu/**

Freshman Application Contact Ms. Rebecca Estrada, Admissions Counselor, Santa Fe Community College, 6401 Richards Avenue, Santa Fe, NM 87505. *Phone:* 505-428-1604. *Fax:* 505-428-1468. *E-mail:* restrada@sfccnm.edu.

SOUTHWESTERN INDIAN POLYTECHNIC INSTITUTE

Albuquerque, New Mexico **www.sipi.bia.edu/**

- **Federally supported** 2-year, founded 1971
- **Suburban** 144-acre campus
- **Coed,** 635 undergraduate students, 79% full-time, 54% women, 46% men

Undergraduates 502 full-time, 133 part-time. Students come from 33 states and territories, 60% live on campus.

Freshmen *Admission:* 262 enrolled. *Average high school GPA:* 2.11.

Faculty *Total:* 48, 35% full-time. *Student/faculty ratio:* 15:1.

Majors Accounting technology and bookkeeping; business administration and management; business automation/technology/data entry; business/commerce; cartography; data processing and data processing technology; early childhood education; engineering; instrumentation technology; liberal arts and sciences/liberal studies; management information systems and services related; manufacturing technology; natural resources and conservation related; opticianry; system, networking, and LAN/WAN management.

Academics *Calendar:* trimesters. *Degree:* certificates and associate. *Special study options:* academic remediation for entering students, advanced placement credit, cooperative education, distance learning, double majors, internships, part-time degree program, services for LD students, summer session for credit.

Library 26,000 titles, 120 serial subscriptions.

Student Life *Housing Options:* men-only, women-only. Campus housing is university owned. *Activities and Organizations:* Dance club, Student Senate, Book club, Natural Resources, Pow-wow club. *Campus security:* 24-hour emergency response devices and patrols, late-night transport/escort service. *Student services:* health clinic, personal/psychological counseling.

Athletics *Intramural sports:* basketball M/W, softball M/W, volleyball M/W.

Costs (2010–11) *Tuition:* state resident $675 full-time; nonresident $675 full-time. Part-time tuition and fees vary according to course load. Students attending SIPI are required to be registered member of federally recognized Indian Tribes. *Required fees:* $150 per term part-time. *Room and board:* $165. *Payment plan:* deferred payment.

Financial Aid Of all full-time matriculated undergraduates who enrolled in 2008, 25 Federal Work-Study jobs (averaging $300). 37 state and other part-time jobs (averaging $400). *Financial aid deadline:* 10/1.

Applying *Required:* high school transcript, Certificate of Indian Blood. *Application deadlines:* 7/30 (freshmen), 7/30 (out-of-state freshmen), 7/30 (transfers). *Early decision deadline:* 7/30. *Notification:* continuous (freshmen).

Freshman Application Contact Southwestern Indian Polytechnic Institute, 9169 Coors, NW, Box 10146, Albuquerque, NM 87120-3103. *Phone:* 505-346-2324. *Toll-free phone:* 800-586-7474.

UNIVERSITY OF NEW MEXICO–GALLUP

Gallup, New Mexico **www.gallup.unm.edu/**

Director of Admissions Ms. Pearl A. Morris, Admissions Representative, University of New Mexico–Gallup, 200 College Road, Gallup, NM 87301-5603. *Phone:* 505-863-7576.

UNIVERSITY OF NEW MEXICO–LOS ALAMOS BRANCH

Los Alamos, New Mexico **www.la.unm.edu/**

Director of Admissions Ms. Anna Mae Apodaca, Associate Campus Director for Student Services, University of New Mexico–Los Alamos Branch, 4000 University Drive, Los Alamos, NM 87544-2233. *Phone:* 505-661-4692. *Toll-free phone:* 800-894-5919. *E-mail:* aapodaca@la.unm.edu.

UNIVERSITY OF NEW MEXICO–TAOS

Taos, New Mexico **taos.unm.edu/**

Admissions Office Contact University of New Mexico–Taos, 115 Civic Plaza Drive, Taos, NM 87571.

UNIVERSITY OF NEW MEXICO–VALENCIA CAMPUS

Los Lunas, New Mexico **www.unm.edu/~unmvc/**

Director of Admissions Ms. Lucy Sanchez, Registrar, University of New Mexico–Valencia Campus, 280 La Entrada, Los Lunas, NM 87031-7633. *Phone:* 505-925-8580.

NEW YORK

ADIRONDACK COMMUNITY COLLEGE

Queensbury, New York **www.sunyacc.edu/**

- **State and locally supported** 2-year, founded 1960, part of State University of New York System
- **Small-town** 141-acre campus
- **Coed**

Academics *Calendar:* semesters. *Degree:* certificates and associate. *Special study options:* academic remediation for entering students, accelerated degree program, adult/continuing education programs, advanced placement credit, cooperative education, double majors, external degree program, independent study, internships, part-time degree program, services for LD students, study abroad, summer session for credit.

Student Life *Campus security:* late-night transport/escort service, patrols by trained security personnel 8 am to 10 pm.

Athletics Member NJCAA.

Costs (2009–10) *Tuition:* state resident $3256 full-time, $136 per credit hour part-time; nonresident $6512 full-time, $272 per credit hour part-time. Full-time tuition and fees vary according to course load. Part-time tuition and fees vary according to course load. *Required fees:* $254 full-time, $9 per credit hour part-time.

Financial Aid Of all full-time matriculated undergraduates who enrolled in 2008, 98 Federal Work-Study jobs (averaging $462).

Applying *Application fee:* $40.

Freshman Application Contact Office of Admissions, Adirondack Community College, 640 Bay Road, Queensbury, NY 12804. *Phone:* 518-743-2264. *Fax:* 518-743-2200.

American Academy McAllister Institute of Funeral Service

New York, New York **www.funeraleducation.org/**

Freshman Application Contact Mr. Norman Provost, Registrar, American Academy McAllister Institute of Funeral Service, 619 West 54th Street, New York, NY 10019-3602. *Phone:* 212-757-1190. *Toll-free phone:* 866-932-2264.

American Academy of Dramatic Arts

New York, New York **www.aada.org/**

- **Independent** 2-year, founded 1884
- **Urban** campus
- **Endowment** $4.6 million
- **Coed,** 228 undergraduate students, 100% full-time, 62% women, 38% men

Undergraduates 228 full-time. Students come from 33 states and territories, 19 other countries, 87% are from out of state, 6% African American, 0.9% Asian American or Pacific Islander, 7% Hispanic American, 24% international.

Freshmen *Admission:* 243 applied, 126 admitted, 61 enrolled. *Average high school GPA:* 2.88.

Faculty *Total:* 26, 27% full-time, 15% with terminal degrees. *Student/faculty ratio:* 14:1.

Majors Dramatic/theater arts.

Academics *Calendar:* continuous. *Degree:* certificates and associate.

Library Academy/CBS Library with 7,467 titles, 24 serial subscriptions, 570 audiovisual materials.

Student Life *Housing:* college housing not available. *Campus security:* 24-hour emergency response devices, trained security guard during hours of operation.

Costs (2010–11) *Tuition:* $28,620 full-time. *Required fees:* $600 full-time. *Payment plan:* installment. *Waivers:* employees or children of employees.

Financial Aid Of all full-time matriculated undergraduates who enrolled in 2009, 200 applied for aid, 130 were judged to have need. In 2009, 40 non-need-based awards were made. *Average percent of need met:* 70%. *Average financial aid package:* $15,400. *Average need-based loan:* $4500. *Average need-based gift aid:* $6000. *Average non-need-based aid:* $7000. *Average indebtedness upon graduation:* $20,000. *Financial aid deadline:* 5/15.

Applying *Options:* deferred entrance. *Application fee:* $50. *Required:* essay or personal statement, high school transcript, minimum 2 GPA, 2 letters of recommendation, interview, audition. *Application deadlines:* rolling (freshmen), rolling (transfers). *Notification:* continuous (freshmen), continuous (transfers).

Freshman Application Contact Ms. Karen Higginbotham, Director of Admissions, American Academy of Dramatic Arts, 120 Madison Avenue, New York, NY 10016. *Phone:* 212-686-9244 Ext. 315. *Toll-free phone:* 800-463-8990. *Fax:* 212-696-1284. *E-mail:* admissions-ny@aada.org.

The Art Institute of New York City

New York, New York **www.artinstitutes.edu/newyork/**

- **Proprietary** 2-year, founded 1980, part of Education Management Corporation
- **Urban** campus
- **Coed**

Majors Cinematography and film/video production; fashion/apparel design; graphic design; interior design; web page, digital/multimedia and information resources design.

Academics *Calendar:* quarters. *Degree:* certificates, diplomas, and associate.

Costs (2009–10) *Tuition:* Tuition cost varies by program. Prospective students should contact the school for current tuition costs. Other charges include a starting kit for all first-quarter students. Kits vary in price, depending on the program of study.

Freshman Application Contact The Art Institute of New York City, 75 Varick Street, 16th Floor, New York, NY 10013-1917. *Phone:* 212-226-5500. *Toll-free phone:* 800-654-2433.

▶**See page 398 for the College Close-Up.**

ASA Institute, The College of Advanced Technology

Brooklyn, New York **www.asa.edu/**

- **Proprietary** 2-year, founded 1985
- **Coed**

Academics *Calendar:* semesters. *Degree:* certificates and associate.

Applying *Application fee:* $25. *Required:* high school transcript.

Freshman Application Contact Admissions Office, ASA Institute, The College of Advanced Technology, 151 Lawrence Street, Brooklyn, NY 11201. *Phone:* 718-522-9073.

Berkeley College–New York City Campus

New York, New York **www.berkeleycollege.edu/**

Freshman Application Contact Ms. Linda Pinsky, Associate Vice President, Enrollment, Berkeley College–New York City Campus, 3 East 43rd Street, New York, NY 10017. *Phone:* 212-986-4343 Ext. 4117. *Toll-free phone:* 800-446-5400. *Fax:* 212-818-1079. *E-mail:* info@berkeleycollege.edu.

Berkeley College–Westchester Campus

White Plains, New York **www.berkeleycollege.edu/**

Freshman Application Contact Mr. John Wool, Assistant Director of Admissions, Berkeley College–Westchester Campus, 99 Church Street, White Plains, NY 10601. *Phone:* 914-694-1122 Ext. 3110. *Toll-free phone:* 800-446-5400. *Fax:* 914-328-9469. *E-mail:* info@berkeleycollege.edu.

Borough of Manhattan Community College of the City University of New York

New York, New York **www.bmcc.cuny.edu/**

Freshman Application Contact Mr. Eugenio Barrios, Director of Admissions, Borough of Manhattan Community College of the City University of New York, 199 Chambers Street, Room S-300, New York, NY 10007. *Phone:* 212-220-1265. *Fax:* 212-220-2366. *E-mail:* admissions@bmcc.cuny.edu.

BRAMSON ORT COLLEGE

Forest Hills, New York www.bramsonort.edu/

Freshman Application Contact Admissions Office, Bramson ORT College, 69-30 Austin Street, Forest Hills, NY 11375-4239. *Phone:* 718-261-5800. *Fax:* 718-575-5119. *E-mail:* admission@bramsonort.edu.

BRONX COMMUNITY COLLEGE OF THE CITY UNIVERSITY OF NEW YORK

Bronx, New York www.bcc.cuny.edu/

- **State and locally supported** 2-year, founded 1959, part of City University of New York System
- **Urban** 50-acre campus with easy access to New York City
- **Endowment** $469,572
- **Coed,** 10,131 undergraduate students, 59% full-time, 61% women, 39% men

Undergraduates 6,013 full-time, 4,118 part-time. Students come from 119 other countries, 8% are from out of state, 35% African American, 3% Asian American or Pacific Islander, 59% Hispanic American, 0.2% Native American, 10% transferred in. *Retention:* 65% of 2008 full-time freshmen returned.

Freshmen *Admission:* 2,056 enrolled.

Faculty *Total:* 363, 72% full-time. *Student/faculty ratio:* 28:1.

Majors Accounting; administrative assistant and secretarial science; African American/Black studies; art; biology/biological sciences; business administration and management; business teacher education; chemistry; child development; clinical/medical laboratory technology; computer science; data processing and data processing technology; electrical, electronic and communications engineering technology; history; human services; international relations and affairs; legal assistant/paralegal; liberal arts and sciences/liberal studies; marketing/marketing management; mathematics; medical administrative assistant and medical secretary; music; nuclear medical technology; nursing (registered nurse training); ornamental horticulture; pre-engineering; psychology.

Academics *Calendar:* semesters. *Degree:* certificates and associate. *Special study options:* academic remediation for entering students, accelerated degree program, adult/continuing education programs, advanced placement credit, cooperative education, distance learning, double majors, English as a second language, honors programs, independent study, internships, off-campus study, part-time degree program, services for LD students, study abroad, summer session for credit.

Library Library & Gerald S. Lieblich Learning Resources Center with 75,000 titles, 800 serial subscriptions, 4,501 audiovisual materials, an OPAC, a Web page.

Student Life *Activities and Organizations:* drama/theater group, student-run newspaper, choral group, Muslim Students Association, Top Models Club, Anime/Manga Gaming Club, Business Club, Media Technology and Film Society. *Campus security:* 24-hour emergency response devices and patrols, late-night transport/escort service, a free shuttle bus service provides evening students with transportation from campus to several subway and bus lines between 5pm-11pm. *Student services:* health clinic, personal/psychological counseling.

Athletics Member NJCAA. *Intercollegiate sports:* baseball M, basketball M, cross-country running M/W, soccer M, track and field M/W, volleyball W. *Intramural sports:* basketball M, soccer M, volleyball M/W.

Standardized Tests *Recommended:* SAT or ACT (for admission).

Costs (2010–11) *Tuition:* state resident $3150 full-time, $135 per credit hour part-time; nonresident $5040 full-time, $210 per credit hour part-time. Full-time tuition and fees vary according to course load. Part-time tuition and fees vary according to course load. *Required fees:* $354 full-time. *Payment plan:* deferred payment. *Waivers:* employees or children of employees.

Applying *Options:* early admission. *Application fee:* $65. *Required:* high school transcript, copy of accredited high school diploma or GED scores.

Freshman Application Contact Ms. Alba N. Cancetty, Admissions Officer, Bronx Community College of the City University of New York, University Avenue and West 181st Street, Bronx, NY 10453. *Phone:* 718-289-5888. *E-mail:* admission@bcc.cuny.edu.

BROOME COMMUNITY COLLEGE

Binghamton, New York www.sunybroome.edu/

- **State and locally supported** 2-year, founded 1946, part of State University of New York System
- **Suburban** 223-acre campus
- **Endowment** $1.3 million
- **Coed,** 6,877 undergraduate students, 68% full-time, 55% women, 45% men

Undergraduates 4,655 full-time, 2,222 part-time. Students come from 26 states and territories, 43 other countries, 1% are from out of state, 5% African American, 2% Asian American or Pacific Islander, 2% Hispanic American, 1% Native American, 3% international, 6% transferred in.

Freshmen *Admission:* 1,487 enrolled.

Faculty *Total:* 406, 35% full-time.

Majors Accounting technology and bookkeeping; business administration and management; child-care and support services management; civil engineering technology; clinical/medical laboratory technology; communication/speech communication and rhetoric; communications systems installation and repair technology; computer and information sciences; computer engineering technology; corrections; criminal justice/police science; data processing and data processing technology; dental hygiene; electrical, electronic and communications engineering technology; emergency medical technology (EMT paramedic); engineering science; executive assistant/executive secretary; financial planning and services; fire science; health information/medical records technology; hotel/motel administration; industrial production technologies related; information science/studies; international finance; legal assistant/paralegal; liberal arts and sciences/liberal studies; mechanical engineering/mechanical technology; medical/clinical assistant; medical radiologic technology; mental and social health services and allied professions related; merchandising, sales, and marketing operations related (general); nursing (registered nurse training); physical therapist assistant; quality control technology; substance abuse/addiction counseling.

Academics *Calendar:* semesters. *Degree:* certificates and associate. *Special study options:* academic remediation for entering students, adult/continuing education programs, advanced placement credit, distance learning, English as a second language, external degree program, honors programs, independent study, internships, off-campus study, part-time degree program, services for LD students, student-designed majors, study abroad, summer session for credit.

Library Cecil C. Tyrrell Learning Resources Center with an OPAC, a Web page.

Student Life *Housing:* college housing not available. *Activities and Organizations:* student-run newspaper, choral group, Broome Early Childhood Organization, Differentially Disabled Student Association, Ecology Club, Phi Theta Kappa, Criminal Justice Club. *Campus security:* 24-hour emergency response devices and patrols. *Student services:* health clinic, personal/psychological counseling.

Athletics Member NJCAA. *Intercollegiate sports:* baseball M, basketball M/W, cross-country running M/W, golf M, ice hockey M, lacrosse M, soccer M/W, softball W, tennis M/W, volleyball W. *Intramural sports:* basketball M/W, volleyball M/W.

Costs (2009–10) *One-time required fee:* $70. *Tuition:* state resident $3276 full-time, $137 per credit hour part-time; nonresident $6552 full-time, $274 per credit hour part-time. Full-time tuition and fees vary according to course load. Part-time tuition and fees vary according to course load. *Required fees:* $325 full-time, $7 per credit hour part-time, $228 per year part-time. *Waivers:* senior citizens and employees or children of employees.

Financial Aid Of all full-time matriculated undergraduates who enrolled in 2008, 186 Federal Work-Study jobs (averaging $1140).

Applying *Options:* electronic application, early admission. *Required:* high school transcript. *Required for some:* interview. *Application deadlines:* rolling (freshmen), rolling (transfers). *Notification:* continuous (freshmen), continuous (transfers).

Freshman Application Contact Ms. Jenae Norris, Director of Admissions, Broome Community College, PO Box 1017, Upper Front Street, Binghamton, NY 13902. *Phone:* 607-778-5001. *Fax:* 607-778-5394. *E-mail:* admissions@sunybroome.edu.

BRYANT & STRATTON COLLEGE - ALBANY CAMPUS

Albany, New York www.bryantstratton.edu/

- **Proprietary** 2-year, founded 1857, part of Bryant and Stratton College, Inc.
- **Suburban** campus
- **Coed,** 470 undergraduate students, 75% full-time, 78% women, 22% men

Undergraduates 354 full-time, 116 part-time. Students come from 1 other state, 48% African American, 2% Asian American or Pacific Islander, 7% Hispanic American, 1% Native American. *Retention:* 45% of 2008 full-time freshmen returned.

Freshmen *Admission:* 109 enrolled.

Faculty *Total:* 45, 27% full-time, 22% with terminal degrees.

Majors Accounting; administrative assistant and secretarial science; business/commerce; computer and information systems security; criminal justice/law enforcement administration; human resources management and services related; information technology; legal assistant/paralegal; medical administrative assistant and medical secretary; medical/clinical assistant; system, networking, and LAN/WAN management.

Academics *Calendar:* semesters. *Degree:* associate. *Special study options:* academic remediation for entering students, distance learning, double majors, independent study, internships, part-time degree program, services for LD students, summer session for credit.

Library Library with 3,500 titles, 5 serial subscriptions, 136 audiovisual materials, an OPAC, a Web page.

Student Life *Housing:* college housing not available. *Activities and Organizations:* student-run newspaper. *Campus security:* 24-hour emergency response devices.

Standardized Tests *Required:* CPAt, ACCUPLACER (for admission). *Recommended:* SAT or ACT (for admission).

Financial Aid Of all full-time matriculated undergraduates who enrolled in 2008, 41 Federal Work-Study jobs (averaging $1343).

Applying *Options:* deferred entrance. *Required:* high school transcript, interview, entrance and placement evaluations. *Application deadlines:* rolling (freshmen), rolling (transfers).

Freshman Application Contact Mr. Robert Ferrell, Director of Admissions, Bryant & Stratton College - Albany Campus, 1259 Central Avenue, Albany, NY 12205. *Phone:* 518-437-1802 Ext. 205. *Fax:* 518-437-1048.

BRYANT & STRATTON COLLEGE - AMHERST CAMPUS

Clarence, New York **www.bryantstratton.edu/**

- **Proprietary** primarily 2-year, founded 1977
- **Suburban** 5-acre campus with easy access to Buffalo
- **Coed,** 474 undergraduate students, 58% full-time, 75% women, 25% men

Undergraduates 277 full-time, 197 part-time. Students come from 1 other state, 19% African American, 1% Asian American or Pacific Islander, 3% Hispanic American, 1% Native American, 9% transferred in.

Freshmen *Admission:* 108 enrolled.

Faculty *Total:* 67, 13% full-time.

Majors Accounting; administrative assistant and secretarial science; business administration and management; business administration, management and operations related; business/commerce; commercial and advertising art; computer and information sciences; computer and information systems security; design and visual communications; graphic design; human resources management; human resources management and services related; information technology; legal assistant/paralegal; medical administrative assistant and medical secretary; system, networking, and LAN/WAN management.

Academics *Calendar:* trimesters. *Degrees:* associate and bachelor's. *Special study options:* academic remediation for entering students, adult/continuing education programs, advanced placement credit, distance learning, internships, part-time degree program, services for LD students, summer session for credit.

Library Library Resource Center with 4,500 titles, 25 serial subscriptions, 150 audiovisual materials, an OPAC, a Web page.

Student Life *Housing:* college housing not available. *Activities and Organizations:* Phi Beta Lambda, Student Government Association, Information Technology Club, Ambassadors Club, National Technical Honor Society.

Standardized Tests *Required:* TABE, CPAt or ACCUPLACER (for admission). *Recommended:* SAT or ACT (for admission).

Applying *Options:* electronic application, early admission. *Required:* high school transcript, interview, entrance evaluation and placement evaluation. *Required for some:* essay or personal statement. *Application deadlines:* rolling (freshmen), rolling (transfers).

Freshman Application Contact Mr. Brian K. Dioguardi, Director of Admissions, Bryant & Stratton College - Amherst Campus, 40 Hazelwood Drive, Amherst, NY 14228. *Phone:* 716-691-0012. *Fax:* 716-691-0012. *E-mail:* bkdioguardi@bryantstratton.edu.

BRYANT & STRATTON COLLEGE - BUFFALO CAMPUS

Buffalo, New York **www.bryantstratton.edu/**

- **Proprietary** primarily 2-year, founded 1854
- **Urban** campus
- **Coed,** 693 undergraduate students, 68% full-time, 76% women, 24% men
- 75% of applicants were admitted

Undergraduates 473 full-time, 220 part-time. Students come from 1 other state, 56% African American, 9% Hispanic American, 0.7% Native American, 7% transferred in.

Freshmen *Admission:* 305 applied, 229 admitted, 225 enrolled.

Faculty *Total:* 53, 21% full-time.

Majors Accounting; administrative assistant and secretarial science; business administration and management; business administration, management and operations related; business/commerce; computer and information sciences; computer and information systems security; criminal justice/law enforcement administration; human resources management; human resources management and services related; information technology; medical administrative assistant and medical secretary; medical/clinical assistant; system, networking, and LAN/WAN management.

Academics *Calendar:* trimesters. *Degrees:* associate and bachelor's. *Special study options:* academic remediation for entering students, adult/continuing education programs, advanced placement credit, distance learning, internships, part-time degree program, services for LD students, summer session for credit.

Library Library Resource Center plus 2 others with 30,000 titles, 28,217 serial subscriptions, 252 audiovisual materials, an OPAC.

Student Life *Housing:* college housing not available. *Activities and Organizations:* Medical Assisting Club, Criminal Justice Club, SHRM, National Technical Honor Society, Phi Beta Lambda.

Standardized Tests *Required:* TABE, CPAt or ACCUPLACER (for admission). *Recommended:* SAT or ACT (for admission).

Applying *Options:* electronic application, early admission. *Required:* high school transcript, interview, entrance and placement evaluation. *Required for some:* essay or personal statement. *Application deadlines:* rolling (freshmen), rolling (transfers).

Freshman Application Contact Mr. Philip J. Struebel, Director of Admissions, Bryant & Stratton College - Buffalo Campus, 465 Main Street, Suite 400, Buffalo, NY 14203-1713. *Phone:* 716-884-9120. *Fax:* 716-884-0091. *E-mail:* pjstruebel@bryantstratton.edu.

BRYANT & STRATTON COLLEGE - GREECE CAMPUS

Rochester, New York **www.bryantstratton.edu/**

- **Proprietary** 2-year, founded 1973, part of Bryant and Stratton College, Inc.
- **Suburban** campus
- **Coed,** 279 undergraduate students, 69% full-time, 83% women, 17% men

Undergraduates 192 full-time, 87 part-time. Students come from 1 other state, 33% African American, 0.7% Asian American or Pacific Islander, 14% Hispanic American, 0.7% Native American, 4% transferred in.

Freshmen *Admission:* 83 enrolled.

Faculty *Total:* 49, 18% full-time, 4% with terminal degrees. *Student/faculty ratio:* 10:1.

Majors Accounting; administrative assistant and secretarial science; business administration, management and operations related; business/commerce; computer and information sciences; computer and information systems security; criminal justice/law enforcement administration; human resources management; human resources management and services related; information technology; medical administrative assistant and medical secretary; medical/clinical assistant; system, networking, and LAN/WAN management.

Academics *Calendar:* semesters. *Degree:* associate. *Special study options:* academic remediation for entering students, adult/continuing education programs, advanced placement credit, distance learning, independent study, internships, part-time degree program, services for LD students, summer session for credit.

Library Greece Campus Library with 2,824 titles, 28 serial subscriptions, 104 audiovisual materials, an OPAC.

Bryant & Stratton College - Greece Campus (continued)

Student Life *Housing:* college housing not available. *Activities and Organizations:* BASSA, Student Ambassadors, Criminal Justice Club. *Campus security:* 24-hour emergency response devices, late-night transport/escort service.

Athletics *Intramural sports:* bowling M/W.

Standardized Tests *Required:* CPAt (for admission). *Recommended:* SAT or ACT (for admission).

Costs (2009–10) *Tuition:* $14,670 full-time, $489 per credit hour part-time. *Required fees:* $35 full-time, $35 per degree program part-time.

Financial Aid Of all full-time matriculated undergraduates who enrolled in 2008, 40 Federal Work-Study jobs (averaging $600).

Applying *Options:* electronic application, deferred entrance. *Required:* high school transcript, interview, entrance evaluation and placement evaluation. *Application deadlines:* rolling (freshmen), rolling (transfers).

Freshman Application Contact Bryant & Stratton College - Greece Campus, 1225 Jefferson Road, Henrietta Campus, Rochester, NY 14623. *Phone:* 585-720-0660.

BRYANT & STRATTON COLLEGE - HENRIETTA CAMPUS

Rochester, New York **www.bryantstratton.edu/**

- **Proprietary** 2-year, founded 1985, part of Bryant and Stratton College, Inc.
- **Urban** 1-acre campus
- **Coed,** 407 undergraduate students, 71% full-time, 78% women, 22% men

Undergraduates 288 full-time, 119 part-time. Students come from 1 other state, 38% African American, 0.7% Asian American or Pacific Islander, 7% Hispanic American, 0.2% Native American, 7% transferred in.

Freshmen *Admission:* 181 applied, 142 admitted, 140 enrolled.

Faculty *Total:* 64, 27% full-time, 11% with terminal degrees. *Student/faculty ratio:* 10:1.

Majors Accounting; administrative assistant and secretarial science; business administration and management; business administration, management and operations related; business/commerce; commercial and advertising art; computer and information sciences; computer and information systems security; criminal justice/law enforcement administration; design and visual communications; graphic design; human resources management; human resources management and services related; information technology; legal assistant/paralegal; medical administrative assistant and medical secretary; medical/clinical assistant; system, networking, and LAN/WAN management.

Academics *Calendar:* semesters. *Degree:* associate. *Special study options:* academic remediation for entering students, adult/continuing education programs, advanced placement credit, distance learning, independent study, internships, part-time degree program, services for LD students, summer session for credit.

Library Henrietta Campus Library with 4,056 titles, 43 serial subscriptions, 72 audiovisual materials, an OPAC.

Student Life *Housing:* college housing not available. *Activities and Organizations:* BASSA, Student Ambassadors, Paralegal Club, Graphic Design Club. *Campus security:* late-night transport/escort service.

Athletics *Intramural sports:* bowling M/W.

Standardized Tests *Required:* CPAt (for admission). *Recommended:* SAT or ACT (for admission).

Costs (2009–10) *Tuition:* $14,670 full-time, $489 per credit hour part-time. *Required fees:* $35 full-time, $35 per degree program part-time.

Financial Aid Of all full-time matriculated undergraduates who enrolled in 2008, 44 Federal Work-Study jobs (averaging $630).

Applying *Options:* electronic application, deferred entrance. *Required:* high school transcript, interview, entrance evaluation and placement evaluation. *Recommended:* minimum 2 GPA. *Application deadlines:* rolling (freshmen), rolling (transfers).

Freshman Application Contact Bryant & Stratton College - Henrietta Campus, 150 Bellwood Drive, Greece Campus, Rochester, NY 14606. *Phone:* 585-292-5627 Ext. 101.

BRYANT & STRATTON COLLEGE - NORTH CAMPUS

Liverpool, New York **www.bryantstratton.edu/**

- **Proprietary** 2-year, founded 1983, part of Bryant and Stratton Business Institute, Inc.
- **Suburban** 1-acre campus with easy access to Syracuse
- **Coed,** 497 undergraduate students, 67% full-time, 73% women, 27% men

Undergraduates 333 full-time, 164 part-time. 5% African American, 0.4% Asian American or Pacific Islander, 2% Hispanic American, 0.6% Native American.

Freshmen *Admission:* 188 enrolled.

Faculty *Total:* 57, 28% full-time, 2% with terminal degrees. *Student/faculty ratio:* 9:1.

Majors Accounting; administrative assistant and secretarial science; business administration and management; computer and information systems security; graphic design; human resources management; information technology; legal assistant/paralegal; medical administrative assistant and medical secretary; medical/clinical assistant; system, networking, and LAN/WAN management; web page, digital/multimedia and information resources design.

Academics *Calendar:* semesters. *Degree:* diplomas and associate. *Special study options:* academic remediation for entering students, adult/continuing education programs, advanced placement credit, cooperative education, distance learning, double majors, independent study, internships, part-time degree program, services for LD students, summer session for credit.

Library Resource Center plus 1 other with 1,936 titles, 13 serial subscriptions, 85 audiovisual materials, an OPAC.

Student Life *Housing:* college housing not available. *Activities and Organizations:* national fraternities. *Campus security:* 24-hour emergency response devices. *Student services:* personal/psychological counseling.

Standardized Tests *Required:* TABE, CPAt (for admission).

Applying *Options:* deferred entrance. *Application fee:* $25. *Required:* high school transcript, interview, entrance evaluation and placement evaluation. *Recommended:* minimum 2 GPA. *Application deadlines:* rolling (freshmen), rolling (transfers). *Notification:* continuous (freshmen), continuous (transfers).

Freshman Application Contact Ms. Heather Macnik, Director of Admissions, Bryant & Stratton College - North Campus, 8687 Carling Road, Liverpool, NY 13090-1315. *Phone:* 315-652-6500.

BRYANT & STRATTON COLLEGE - SOUTHTOWNS CAMPUS

Orchard Park, New York **www.bryantstratton.edu/**

- **Proprietary** primarily 2-year, founded 1989
- **Suburban** campus with easy access to Buffalo
- **Coed,** 1,206 undergraduate students, 55% full-time, 79% women, 21% men

Undergraduates 663 full-time, 543 part-time. Students come from 27 states and territories, 1 other country, 60% are from out of state, 20% African American, 0.7% Asian American or Pacific Islander, 3% Hispanic American, 0.5% Native American, 11% transferred in.

Freshmen *Admission:* 325 enrolled.

Faculty *Total:* 75, 31% full-time.

Majors Accounting; administrative assistant and secretarial science; business administration and management; business administration, management and operations related; business/commerce; computer and information sciences; court reporting; criminal justice/law enforcement administration; human resources management; human resources management and services related; information technology; medical administrative assistant and medical secretary; medical/clinical assistant.

Academics *Calendar:* trimesters. *Degrees:* associate and bachelor's. *Special study options:* academic remediation for entering students, adult/continuing education programs, advanced placement credit, distance learning, internships, part-time degree program, services for LD students, summer session for credit.

Library Library Resource Center with 1,402 titles, 42 serial subscriptions, 128 audiovisual materials, an OPAC, a Web page.

Student Life *Housing:* college housing not available. *Activities and Organizations:* Accounting/Business Club, Administrative Professionals Club, Phi Beta Lambda, National Technical Honor Society, student newsletter.

Standardized Tests *Required:* TABE, CPAt or ACCUPLACER (for admission). *Recommended:* SAT or ACT (for admission).

Applying *Options:* electronic application, early admission. *Required:* high school transcript, interview, entrance and placement evaluations. *Required for some:* essay or personal statement. *Application deadlines:* rolling (freshmen), rolling (transfers).

Freshman Application Contact Bryant & Stratton College - Southtowns Campus, Sterling Park, 200 Redtail, Orchard Park, NY 14127. *Phone:* 716-677-9500.

BRYANT & STRATTON COLLEGE - SYRACUSE CAMPUS

Syracuse, New York **www.bryantstratton.edu/**

- **Proprietary** 2-year, founded 1854, part of Bryant and Stratton Business Institute, Inc.
- **Urban** 1-acre campus
- **Coed,** 715 undergraduate students, 69% full-time, 75% women, 25% men

Undergraduates 494 full-time, 221 part-time. Students come from 2 states and territories, 2 other countries, 1% are from out of state, 34% African American, 0.7% Asian American or Pacific Islander, 12% Hispanic American, 2% Native American, 1% international, 6% transferred in, 12% live on campus. *Retention:* 38% of 2008 full-time freshmen returned.

Freshmen *Admission:* 254 applied, 240 admitted, 234 enrolled.

Faculty *Total:* 55, 38% full-time, 4% with terminal degrees. *Student/faculty ratio:* 13:1.

Majors Accounting; administrative assistant and secretarial science; business/commerce; hotel/motel administration; human resources management and services related; information technology; medical administrative assistant and medical secretary; medical/clinical assistant; tourism and travel services management.

Academics *Calendar:* semesters. *Degree:* associate. *Special study options:* academic remediation for entering students, cooperative education, distance learning, double majors, internships, part-time degree program, services for LD students, summer session for credit.

Library Bryant and Stratton, Syracuse Campus Library with 1,325 titles, 40 serial subscriptions, 40 audiovisual materials.

Student Life *Housing Options:* coed, disabled students. Campus housing is university owned. *Activities and Organizations:* student-run newspaper, Management Club, Travel Club, Medical Club, Computer Club, Veterans Club. *Campus security:* 24-hour emergency response devices and patrols, controlled dormitory access.

Athletics Member NJCAA. *Intercollegiate sports:* soccer M(s)/W(s).

Standardized Tests *Required:* CPAt (for admission). *Recommended:* SAT or ACT (for admission).

Applying *Required:* high school transcript, interview, entrance, placement evaluations. *Application deadlines:* rolling (freshmen), rolling (transfers).

Freshman Application Contact Ms. Dawn Rajkowski, Director of High School Enrollments, Bryant & Stratton College - Syracuse Campus, 953 James Street, Syracuse, NY 13203-2502. *Phone:* 315-472-6603 Ext. 248. *Fax:* 315-474-4383.

BUSINESS INFORMATICS CENTER, INC.

Valley Stream, New York **www.thecollegeforbusiness.com/**

Freshman Application Contact Admissions Office, Business Informatics Center, Inc., 134 South Central Avenue, Valley Stream, NY 11580-5431.

CAYUGA COUNTY COMMUNITY COLLEGE

Auburn, New York **www.cayuga-cc.edu/**

- **State and locally supported** 2-year, founded 1953, part of State University of New York System
- **Small-town** 50-acre campus with easy access to Rochester and Syracuse
- **Coed**

Academics *Calendar:* semesters. *Degree:* certificates and associate. *Special study options:* academic remediation for entering students, accelerated degree program, adult/continuing education programs, advanced placement credit, distance learning, double majors, honors programs, independent study, internships, part-time degree program, services for LD students, study abroad, summer session for credit.

Student Life *Campus security:* security from 8 am to 9 pm.

Athletics Member NJCAA.

Financial Aid Of all full-time matriculated undergraduates who enrolled in 2008, 150 Federal Work-Study jobs (averaging $2000). 200 state and other part-time jobs (averaging $1000).

Applying *Options:* electronic application, deferred entrance. *Required:* high school transcript. *Required for some:* interview.

Director of Admissions Mr. Bruce M. Blodgett, Director of Admissions, Cayuga County Community College, 197 Franklin Street, Auburn, NY 13021-3099. *Phone:* 315-255-1743 Ext. 2244.

CLINTON COMMUNITY COLLEGE

Plattsburgh, New York **clintoncc.suny.edu/**

Director of Admissions Mrs. Karen L. Burnam, Director of Admissions and Financial Aid, Clinton Community College, 136 Clinton Point Drive, Plattsburgh, NY 12901. *Phone:* 518-562-4170. *Toll-free phone:* 800-552-1160.

COCHRAN SCHOOL OF NURSING

Yonkers, New York **www.cochranschoolofnursing.us/**

Freshman Application Contact Cochran School of Nursing, 967 North Broadway, Yonkers, NY 10701. *Phone:* 914-964-4606.

THE COLLEGE OF WESTCHESTER

White Plains, New York **www.cw.edu/**

Freshman Application Contact Mr. Dale T. Smith, Vice President, The College of Westchester, 325 Central Avenue, PO Box 710, White Plains, NY 10602. *Phone:* 914-948-4442 Ext. 311. *Toll-free phone:* 800-333-4924 Ext. 318. *Fax:* 914-948-5441. *E-mail:* admissions@cw.edu.

COLUMBIA-GREENE COMMUNITY COLLEGE

Hudson, New York **www.sunycgcc.edu/**

Freshman Application Contact Admissions Counselors, Columbia-Greene Community College, 4400 Route 23, Hudson, NY 12534-0327. *Phone:* 518-828-4181 Ext. 5513. *E-mail:* info@mycommunitycollege.com.

CORNING COMMUNITY COLLEGE

Corning, New York **www.corning-cc.edu/**

- **State and locally supported** 2-year, founded 1956, part of State University of New York System
- **Rural** 404-acre campus
- **Endowment** $2.7 million
- **Coed,** 5,671 undergraduate students, 45% full-time, 55% women, 45% men

Undergraduates 2,558 full-time, 3,113 part-time. Students come from 9 states and territories, 18 other countries, 5% are from out of state, 3% African American, 0.7% Asian American or Pacific Islander, 1% Hispanic American, 0.3% Native American, 0.1% international, 4% transferred in. *Retention:* 59% of 2008 full-time freshmen returned.

Freshmen *Admission:* 1,093 enrolled.

Faculty *Total:* 264, 37% full-time, 12% with terminal degrees. *Student/faculty ratio:* 26:1.

Majors Accounting; administrative assistant and secretarial science; autobody/collision and repair technology; automobile/automotive mechanics technology; automotive engineering technology; biological and physical sciences; business administration and management; chemical technology; child-care provision; computer and information sciences; computer and information sciences related; computer graphics; computer/information technology services administration related; computer programming; computer programming related; computer science; computer systems networking and telecommunications; computer technology/computer systems technology; corrections and criminal justice related;

Corning Community College (continued)

criminal justice/law enforcement administration; drafting and design technology; education related; electrical, electronic and communications engineering technology; elementary education; emergency medical technology (EMT paramedic); fine/studio arts; fire science; general studies; health and physical education; hospitality administration related; humanities; human services; industrial technology; information technology; liberal arts and sciences/liberal studies; machine shop technology; machine tool technology; mathematics; mechanical engineering/mechanical technology; nursing (registered nurse training); optical sciences; pre-engineering; social sciences; substance abuse/addiction counseling; word processing.

Academics *Calendar:* semesters. *Degree:* certificates and associate. *Special study options:* academic remediation for entering students, accelerated degree program, adult/continuing education programs, advanced placement credit, cooperative education, distance learning, double majors, honors programs, independent study, internships, off-campus study, part-time degree program, services for LD students, student-designed majors, study abroad, summer session for credit. *ROTC:* Army (c), Navy (c), Air Force (c).

Library Arthur A. Houghton, Jr. Library with 53,438 titles, 24,350 serial subscriptions, 755 audiovisual materials, an OPAC, a Web page.

Student Life *Housing:* college housing not available. *Activities and Organizations:* drama/theater group, student-run newspaper, radio station, choral group, Student Association, WCEB radio station, Muse of Fire theatre group, Activities Programming Committee, Nursing Society. *Campus security:* 24-hour emergency response devices and patrols, late-night transport/escort service. *Student services:* health clinic, personal/psychological counseling.

Athletics Member NJCAA. *Intercollegiate sports:* baseball M, basketball M/W, golf M/W, soccer M/W, softball W, volleyball W. *Intramural sports:* badminton M/W, basketball M/W, bowling M/W, cross-country running M/W, golf M/W, soccer M/W, softball M/W, table tennis M/W, volleyball M/W, weight lifting M/W.

Costs (2010–11) *Tuition:* state resident $3570 full-time, $149 per credit part-time; nonresident $7140 full-time, $298 per credit part-time. *Required fees:* $408 full-time, $8 per credit part-time. *Payment plan:* installment. *Waivers:* senior citizens and employees or children of employees.

Financial Aid Of all full-time matriculated undergraduates who enrolled in 2008, 264 Federal Work-Study jobs (averaging $1128).

Applying *Options:* electronic application, early admission. *Application fee:* $25. *Required:* high school transcript. *Required for some:* interview. *Application deadlines:* rolling (freshmen), rolling (transfers). *Notification:* continuous (freshmen), continuous (transfers).

Freshman Application Contact Corning Community College, 1 Academic Drive, Corning, NY 14830. *Phone:* 607-962-9427. *Toll-free phone:* 800-358-7171 Ext. 220.

CROUSE HOSPITAL SCHOOL OF NURSING

Syracuse, New York **www.crouse.org/nursing/**

- **Independent** 2-year, founded 1913
- **Urban** campus
- **Coed, primarily women,** 285 undergraduate students

Undergraduates Students come from 2 states and territories, 1% are from out of state.

Freshmen *Admission:* 253 applied.

Majors Nursing (registered nurse training).

Academics *Calendar:* semesters. *Degree:* associate. *Special study options:* academic remediation for entering students, advanced placement credit, part-time degree program, services for LD students.

Library Crouse Hospital Library with 5,000 titles, 913 serial subscriptions, 250 audiovisual materials, an OPAC, a Web page.

Student Life *Housing Options:* women-only. Campus housing is university owned. *Activities and Organizations:* NSNA. *Campus security:* 24-hour emergency response devices and patrols, late-night transport/escort service, controlled dormitory access. *Student services:* health clinic, personal/psychological counseling.

Standardized Tests *Required for some:* SAT or ACT (for admission). *Recommended:* SAT or ACT (for admission).

Costs (2010–11) *Tuition:* $8136 full-time, $245 per credit hour part-time. Full-time tuition and fees vary according to course load. Part-time tuition and fees vary according to course load. *Required fees:* $850 full-time, $990 per term part-time. *Room only:* $3500. *Waivers:* employees or children of employees.

Financial Aid Of all full-time matriculated undergraduates who enrolled in 2008, 121 applied for aid, 121 were judged to have need. *Average percent of need met:* 66%. *Average financial aid package:* $4677. *Average need-based loan:* $3324. *Average need-based gift aid:* $2141. *Average indebtedness upon graduation:* $2896.

Applying *Options:* deferred entrance. *Application fee:* $30. *Required:* high school transcript, minimum 2.5 GPA, 2 letters of recommendation.

Freshman Application Contact Ms. Amy Graham, Enrollment Management Supervisor, Crouse Hospital School of Nursing, 736 Irving Avenue, Syracuse, NY 13210. *Phone:* 315-470-7481. *Fax:* 315-470-7925. *E-mail:* amygraham@crouse.org.

DOROTHEA HOPFER SCHOOL OF NURSING AT THE MOUNT VERNON HOSPITAL

Mount Vernon, New York **www.ssmc.org/**

Director of Admissions Office of Admissions, Dorothea Hopfer School of Nursing at The Mount Vernon Hospital, 53 Valentine Street, Mount Vernon, NY 10550. *Phone:* 914-664-8000.

DUTCHESS COMMUNITY COLLEGE

Poughkeepsie, New York **www.sunydutchess.edu/**

Director of Admissions Ms. Rita Banner, Director of Admissions, Dutchess Community College, 53 Pendell Road, Poughkeepsie, NY 12601. *Phone:* 845-431-8010. *Toll-free phone:* 800-763-3933. *E-mail:* banner@sunydutchess.edu.

ELLIS HOSPITAL SCHOOL OF NURSING

Schenectady, New York **www.ehson.org/**

Freshman Application Contact Mary Lee Pollard, Director of School, Ellis Hospital School of Nursing, 1101 Nott Street, Schenectady, NY 12308. *Phone:* 518-243-4471. *Fax:* 518-243-4470.

ELMIRA BUSINESS INSTITUTE

Elmira, New York **www.ebi-college.com/**

Freshman Application Contact Ms. Lisa Roan, Admissions Director, Elmira Business Institute, 303 North Main Street, Langdon Plaza, Elmira, NY 14901. *Phone:* 607-733-7178. *Toll-free phone:* 800-843-1812. *E-mail:* lroan@ebi-college.com.

ERIE COMMUNITY COLLEGE

Buffalo, New York **www.ecc.edu/**

- **State and locally supported** 2-year, founded 1971, part of State University of New York System
- **Urban** 1-acre campus
- **Coed,** 3,599 undergraduate students, 74% full-time, 61% women, 39% men

Undergraduates 2,646 full-time, 953 part-time. Students come from 18 states and territories, 2 other countries, 1% are from out of state, 43% African American, 2% Asian American or Pacific Islander, 9% Hispanic American, 1% Native American, 0.2% international, 3% transferred in.

Freshmen *Admission:* 846 enrolled.

Faculty *Total:* 373, 24% full-time. *Student/faculty ratio:* 18:1.

Majors Administrative assistant and secretarial science; building/property maintenance and management; business administration and management; child-care and support services management; community health services counseling; criminal justice/law enforcement administration; criminal justice/police science; culinary arts; fire protection related; humanities; information technology; legal assistant/paralegal; liberal arts and sciences/liberal studies; medical radiologic technology; nursing (registered nurse training); office management; physical education teaching and coaching; substance abuse/addiction counseling.

Academics *Calendar:* semesters. *Degree:* certificates, diplomas, and associate. *Special study options:* academic remediation for entering students, adult/

continuing education programs, advanced placement credit, cooperative education, distance learning, double majors, English as a second language, honors programs, independent study, internships, part-time degree program, services for LD students, student-designed majors, study abroad, summer session for credit. *ROTC:* Army (c).

Library Leon E. Butler Library with 26,269 titles, 152 serial subscriptions, 1,571 audiovisual materials, an OPAC, a Web page.

Student Life *Housing:* college housing not available. *Activities and Organizations:* drama/theater group, student-run newspaper, radio station, choral group. *Campus security:* 24-hour emergency response devices and patrols, late-night transport/escort service. *Student services:* health clinic, personal/psychological counseling, women's center.

Athletics Member NJCAA. *Intercollegiate sports:* baseball M, basketball M/W, bowling M/W, cheerleading W, cross-country running M/W, football M, golf M/W, ice hockey M, lacrosse W, soccer M/W, softball W, swimming and diving M/W, track and field M/W, volleyball W.

Costs (2009–10) *One-time required fee:* $50. *Tuition:* area resident $3300 full-time, $138 per credit hour part-time; state resident $6600 full-time, $276 per credit hour part-time; nonresident $6600 full-time, $276 per credit hour part-time. *Required fees:* $340 full-time, $5 per credit hour part-time, $50 per term part-time. *Payment plan:* installment. *Waivers:* senior citizens and employees or children of employees.

Applying *Options:* electronic application. *Application fee:* $25. *Required:* high school transcript. *Required for some:* interview. *Application deadlines:* rolling (freshmen), rolling (transfers). *Notification:* continuous (freshmen), continuous (transfers).

Freshman Application Contact Erie Community College, 121 Ellicott Street, Buffalo, NY 14203-2698. *Phone:* 716-851-1155. *Fax:* 716-270-2821.

Erie Community College, North Campus

Williamsville, New York **www.ecc.edu/**

- **State and locally supported** 2-year, founded 1946, part of State University of New York System
- **Suburban** 120-acre campus with easy access to Buffalo
- **Coed,** 6,741 undergraduate students, 67% full-time, 48% women, 52% men

Undergraduates 4,502 full-time, 2,239 part-time. Students come from 25 states and territories, 17 other countries, 0.6% are from out of state, 13% African American, 3% Asian American or Pacific Islander, 3% Hispanic American, 0.9% Native American, 1% international, 5% transferred in.

Freshmen *Admission:* 1,356 enrolled.

Faculty *Total:* 564, 30% full-time. *Student/faculty ratio:* 18:1.

Majors Business administration and management; civil engineering technology; clinical/medical laboratory technology; computer and information sciences; construction management; criminal justice/police science; culinary arts; dental hygiene; dietitian assistant; electrical, electronic and communications engineering technology; engineering; health information/medical records technology; humanities; industrial technology; information technology; liberal arts and sciences/liberal studies; mechanical engineering/mechanical technology; medical office management; nursing (registered nurse training); occupational therapist assistant; office management; opticianry; physical education teaching and coaching; respiratory care therapy; restaurant, culinary, and catering management.

Academics *Calendar:* semesters plus summer sessions, winter intersession. *Degree:* certificates, diplomas, and associate. *Special study options:* academic remediation for entering students, adult/continuing education programs, advanced placement credit, cooperative education, distance learning, double majors, English as a second language, honors programs, independent study, internships, part-time degree program, services for LD students, student-designed majors, study abroad, summer session for credit. *ROTC:* Army (c).

Library Richard R. Dry Memorial Library with 54,438 titles, 245 serial subscriptions, 4,989 audiovisual materials, an OPAC, a Web page.

Student Life *Housing:* college housing not available. *Activities and Organizations:* drama/theater group, student-run newspaper, radio station, choral group. *Campus security:* 24-hour emergency response devices and patrols, late-night transport/escort service. *Student services:* health clinic, personal/psychological counseling, women's center.

Athletics Member NJCAA. *Intercollegiate sports:* baseball M, basketball M/W, bowling M/W, cheerleading W, cross-country running M/W, football M, golf M/W, ice hockey M, lacrosse W, soccer M/W, softball W, swimming and diving M/W, track and field M/W, volleyball W.

Costs (2009–10) *One-time required fee:* $50. *Tuition:* area resident $3300 full-time, $138 per credit hour part-time; state resident $6600 full-time, $276 per credit hour part-time; nonresident $6600 full-time, $276 per credit hour part-time. *Required fees:* $340 full-time, $5 per credit hour part-time, $50 per term part-time. *Payment plan:* installment. *Waivers:* senior citizens and employees or children of employees.

Applying *Options:* electronic application. *Application fee:* $25. *Required:* high school transcript. *Required for some:* interview. *Application deadlines:* rolling (freshmen), rolling (transfers). *Notification:* continuous (freshmen), continuous (transfers).

Freshman Application Contact Erie Community College, North Campus, 6205 Main Street, Williamsville, NY 14221-7095. *Phone:* 716-851-1455. *Fax:* 716-270-2961.

Erie Community College, South Campus

Orchard Park, New York **www.ecc.edu/**

- **State and locally supported** 2-year, founded 1974, part of State University of New York System
- **Suburban** 110-acre campus with easy access to Buffalo
- **Coed,** 4,483 undergraduate students, 62% full-time, 44% women, 56% men

Undergraduates 2,801 full-time, 1,682 part-time. Students come from 19 states and territories, 4 other countries, 2% are from out of state, 6% African American, 0.8% Asian American or Pacific Islander, 3% Hispanic American, 1% Native American, 0.1% international, 4% transferred in.

Freshmen *Admission:* 986 enrolled.

Faculty *Total:* 541, 20% full-time. *Student/faculty ratio:* 18:1.

Majors Architectural engineering technology; autobody/collision and repair technology; automobile/automotive mechanics technology; business administration and management; CAD/CADD drafting/design technology; communication/speech communication and rhetoric; communications systems installation and repair technology; computer technology/computer systems technology; criminal justice/police science; dental laboratory technology; emergency medical technology (EMT paramedic); fire services administration; graphic and printing equipment operation/production; humanities; industrial technology; information technology; liberal arts and sciences/liberal studies; office management; parks, recreation and leisure facilities management; physical education teaching and coaching; public administration and social service professions related; telecommunications technology.

Academics *Calendar:* semesters plus summer sessions, winter intersession. *Degree:* certificates, diplomas, and associate. *Special study options:* academic remediation for entering students, adult/continuing education programs, advanced placement credit, cooperative education, distance learning, double majors, English as a second language, honors programs, independent study, internships, part-time degree program, services for LD students, student-designed majors, study abroad, summer session for credit. *ROTC:* Army (c).

Library 45,501 titles, 190 serial subscriptions, 2,212 audiovisual materials, an OPAC, a Web page.

Student Life *Housing:* college housing not available. *Activities and Organizations:* drama/theater group, student-run newspaper, radio station, choral group. *Campus security:* 24-hour emergency response devices and patrols, late-night transport/escort service. *Student services:* health clinic, personal/psychological counseling, women's center.

Athletics Member NJCAA. *Intercollegiate sports:* baseball M, basketball M/W, bowling M/W, cheerleading W, cross-country running M/W, football M, golf M/W, ice hockey M, lacrosse W, soccer M/W, softball W, swimming and diving M/W, track and field M/W, volleyball W.

Costs (2009–10) *One-time required fee:* $50. *Tuition:* area resident $3300 full-time, $138 per credit hour part-time; state resident $6600 full-time, $276 per credit hour part-time; nonresident $6600 full-time, $276 per credit hour part-time. *Required fees:* $340 full-time, $5 per credit hour part-time, $50 per term part-time. *Payment plan:* installment. *Waivers:* senior citizens and employees or children of employees.

Applying *Options:* electronic application. *Application fee:* $25. *Required:* high school transcript. *Required for some:* interview. *Application deadlines:* rolling (freshmen), rolling (transfers). *Notification:* continuous (freshmen), continuous (transfers).

Freshman Application Contact Erie Community College, South Campus, 4041 Southwestern Boulevard, Orchard Park, NY 14127-2199. *Phone:* 716-851-1655. *Fax:* 716-851-1687.

Eugenio María de Hostos Community College of the City University of New York

Bronx, New York **www.hostos.cuny.edu/**

Freshman Application Contact Mr. Roland Velez, Director of Admissions, Eugenio María de Hostos Community College of the City University of New York, 120 149th Street, Room D-210, Bronx, NY 10451. *Phone:* 718-518-4406. *Fax:* 718-518-4256. *E-mail:* admissions2@hostos.cuny.edu.

Everest Institute

Rochester, New York **www.everest.edu/campus/rochester/**

- **Proprietary** 2-year, founded 1863, part of Corinthian Colleges, Inc.
- **Suburban** 2-acre campus
- **Coed,** 1,150 undergraduate students

Undergraduates *Retention:* 64% of 2008 full-time freshmen returned.

Faculty *Student/faculty ratio:* 16:1.

Majors Accounting technology and bookkeeping; administrative assistant and secretarial science; allied health and medical assisting services related; business administration and management; corrections and criminal justice related; data processing and data processing technology; legal assistant/paralegal; medical insurance coding.

Academics *Calendar:* quarters. *Degree:* certificates, diplomas, and associate. *Special study options:* adult/continuing education programs, advanced placement credit, cooperative education, distance learning, part-time degree program, summer session for credit.

Library Betty Cronk Memorial Library.

Student Life *Housing:* college housing not available.

Standardized Tests *Required for some:* CPAt for those with High School Diploma or GED. Compass or Asset for applicants without a High School Diploma or GED.

Applying *Options:* early admission, deferred entrance. *Required:* high school transcript, interview. *Application deadlines:* rolling (freshmen), rolling (out-of-state freshmen), rolling (transfers). *Notification:* continuous (freshmen), continuous (out-of-state freshmen), continuous (transfers).

Freshman Application Contact Deanna Pfluke, Director of Admissions, Everest Institute, 1630 Portland Avenue, Rochester, NY 14621. *Phone:* 585-266-0430. *Fax:* 585-266-8243.

Fashion Institute of Technology

New York, New York **www.fitnyc.edu/**

- **State and locally supported** comprehensive, founded 1944, part of State University of New York System
- **Urban** 5-acre campus
- **Endowment** $29.3 million
- **Coed, primarily women,** 10,207 undergraduate students, 70% full-time, 84% women, 16% men

Undergraduates 7,163 full-time, 3,044 part-time. Students come from 46 states and territories, 73 other countries, 29% are from out of state, 6% African American, 7% Asian American or Pacific Islander, 9% Hispanic American, 0.1% Native American, 11% international, 8% transferred in, 25% live on campus. *Retention:* 86% of 2008 full-time freshmen returned.

Freshmen *Admission:* 3,973 applied, 1,605 admitted, 1,068 enrolled. *Average high school GPA:* 3.3.

Faculty *Total:* 1,007, 25% full-time. *Student/faculty ratio:* 17:1.

Majors Advertising; animation, interactive technology, video graphics and special effects; apparel and textile manufacturing; apparel and textiles; art history, criticism and conservation; arts management; commercial and advertising art; commercial photography; fashion/apparel design; fashion merchandising; fashion modeling; fine/studio arts; graphic design; illustration; industrial design; interior design; international marketing; marketing research; merchandising, sales, and marketing operations related (specialized); metal and jewelry arts; special products marketing.

Academics *Calendar:* semesters. *Degrees:* certificates, associate, bachelor's, and master's. *Special study options:* academic remediation for entering students, adult/continuing education programs, advanced placement credit, distance learning, English as a second language, honors programs, internships, part-time degree program, services for LD students, study abroad, summer session for credit.

Library Gladys Marcus Library.

Student Life *Housing Options:* coed, women-only. Campus housing is university owned and is provided by a third party. Freshman applicants given priority for college housing. *Activities and Organizations:* drama/theater group, student-run newspaper, radio and television station, choral group, FITSA/Student Government, Merchandising Society/Style Shop, Delta Epilson Chi: Promoting Leadership in Marketing, Merchandising, and Advertising, PRSSA: Public Relations Student Society of America, Student Ambassadors. *Campus security:* 24-hour emergency response devices and patrols, late-night transport/escort service, controlled dormitory access. *Student services:* health clinic, personal/psychological counseling.

Athletics Member NJCAA. *Intercollegiate sports:* basketball M, cheerleading W, cross-country running M/W, swimming and diving M/W, table tennis M/W, tennis W, volleyball W. *Intramural sports:* basketball M/W, table tennis M/W, tennis M/W, volleyball M/W.

Costs (2009–10) *Tuition:* state resident $5168 full-time, $215 per credit hour part-time; nonresident $12,604 full-time, $525 per credit hour part-time. Full-time tuition and fees vary according to degree level. Part-time tuition and fees vary according to degree level. *Required fees:* $450 full-time, $70 per year part-time. *Room and board:* $11,248. Room and board charges vary according to board plan and housing facility. *Payment plan:* installment. *Waivers:* employees or children of employees.

Financial Aid Of all full-time matriculated undergraduates who enrolled in 2009, 4,507 applied for aid, 3,509 were judged to have need, 468 had their need fully met. In 2009, 170 non-need-based awards were made. *Average percent of need met:* 66%. *Average financial aid package:* $11,288. *Average need-based loan:* $4292. *Average need-based gift aid:* $5327. *Average non-need-based aid:* $1641. *Average indebtedness upon graduation:* $24,554.

Applying *Options:* electronic application. *Application fee:* $40. *Required:* essay or personal statement, high school transcript. *Required for some:* portfolio for art and design programs. *Notification:* continuous (freshmen), continuous (transfers).

Freshman Application Contact Ms. Yamiley Saintvil, Director of Admissions, Fashion Institute of Technology, Seventh Avenue at 27th Street, New York, NY 10001-5992. *Phone:* 212-217-3760. *Toll-free phone:* 800-GOTOFIT. *Fax:* 212-217-3761. *E-mail:* fitinfo@fitnyc.edu.

▶**See page 452 for the College Close-Up.**

Finger Lakes Community College

Canandaigua, New York **www.flcc.edu/**

- **State and locally supported** 2-year, founded 1965, part of State University of New York System
- **Small-town** 300-acre campus with easy access to Rochester
- **Coed,** 6,699 undergraduate students, 56% full-time, 56% women, 44% men

Undergraduates 3,750 full-time, 2,949 part-time. Students come from 12 states and territories, 2 other countries, 0.3% are from out of state, 7% African American, 0.6% Asian American or Pacific Islander, 3% Hispanic American, 0.6% Native American, 4% transferred in.

Freshmen *Admission:* 4,517 applied, 3,646 admitted, 1,694 enrolled.

Faculty *Total:* 342, 33% full-time. *Student/faculty ratio:* 20:1.

Majors Accounting; administrative assistant and secretarial science; animation, interactive technology, video graphics and special effects; architectural engineering technology; biological and physical sciences; biology/biological sciences; biology/biotechnology laboratory technician; broadcast journalism; business administration and management; chemistry; commercial and advertising art; computer and information sciences; computer science; criminal justice/law enforcement administration; criminal justice/police science; data processing and data processing technology; digital communication and media/multimedia; drafting and design technology; dramatic/theater arts; early childhood education; e-commerce; emergency medical technology (EMT paramedic); engineering science; environmental studies; fine/studio arts; fishing and fisheries sciences and management; hotel/motel administration; humanities; human services; kindergarten/preschool education; legal assistant/paralegal; liberal arts and sciences/liberal studies; marketing/marketing management; mass communication/media; mathematics; mechanical engineering/mechanical technology; music; natural resources/conservation; natural resources management; natural resources management and policy; nursing (registered nurse training); ornamental horticulture; parks, recreation and leisure facilities management; physical education teaching and coaching; physics; political science and government; pre-engineering; psychology; recording arts technology; social sciences; sociology; substance abuse/addiction counseling; tourism and travel services management.

Academics *Calendar:* semesters. *Degree:* certificates and associate. *Special study options:* academic remediation for entering students, advanced placement credit, distance learning, English as a second language, honors programs, internships, off-campus study, part-time degree program, services for LD students, summer session for credit. *ROTC:* Army (c).

Library Charles Meder Library with 75,610 titles, 464 serial subscriptions, 6,954 audiovisual materials, an OPAC.

Student Life *Housing:* college housing not available. *Options:* Campus housing is provided by a third party. *Activities and Organizations:* drama/theater group, student-run radio station, choral group. *Campus security:* 24-hour emergency response devices and patrols, late-night transport/escort service. *Student services:* health clinic, personal/psychological counseling, legal services.

Athletics Member NJCAA. *Intercollegiate sports:* baseball M, basketball M/W, cross-country running M/W, lacrosse M, soccer M/W, softball W, track and field M/W, volleyball W. *Intramural sports:* basketball M/W, tennis M/W, volleyball M/W.

Costs (2009–10) *Tuition:* state resident $3296 full-time, $126 per credit hour part-time; nonresident $6592 full-time, $252 per credit hour part-time. Full-time tuition and fees vary according to course load. Part-time tuition and fees vary according to course load. *Required fees:* $410 full-time, $12 per credit hour part-time. *Payment plan:* installment.

Financial Aid Of all full-time matriculated undergraduates who enrolled in 2008, 200 Federal Work-Study jobs (averaging $2200). 100 state and other part-time jobs (averaging $2200).

Applying *Options:* electronic application, early admission, deferred entrance. *Required:* high school transcript. *Recommended:* interview. *Application deadlines:* rolling (freshmen), rolling (transfers). *Notification:* continuous (freshmen), continuous (transfers).

Freshman Application Contact Ms. Bonnie B. Ritts, Director of Admissions, Finger Lakes Community College, 4355 Lake Shore Drive, Canandaigua, NY 14424-8395. *Phone:* 585-394-3500 Ext. 7278. *Fax:* 585-394-5005. *E-mail:* admissions@flcc.edu.

Fiorello H. LaGuardia Community College of the City University of New York

Long Island City, New York **www.lagcc.cuny.edu/**

- **State and locally supported** 2-year, founded 1970, part of City University of New York System
- **Urban** 6-acre campus
- **Endowment** $1.7 million
- **Coed,** 16,963 undergraduate students, 55% full-time, 60% women, 40% men

Undergraduates 9,324 full-time, 7,639 part-time. Students come from 13 states and territories, 152 other countries, 0.3% are from out of state, 12% African American, 12% Asian American or Pacific Islander, 25% Hispanic American, 0.2% Native American, 15% international, 9% transferred in.

Freshmen *Admission:* 6,025 applied, 6,025 admitted, 2,930 enrolled. *Average high school GPA:* 1.9.

Faculty *Total:* 1,045, 29% full-time, 22% with terminal degrees. *Student/faculty ratio:* 26:1.

Majors Accounting; accounting technology and bookkeeping; administrative assistant and secretarial science; adult development and aging; business administration and management; civil engineering; commercial photography; communication/speech communication and rhetoric; computer and information sciences and support services related; computer engineering technology; computer installation and repair technology; computer programming; computer science; data entry/microcomputer applications; dietetics; dietetic technician; electrical, electronics and communications engineering; emergency medical technology (EMT paramedic); engineering science; funeral service and mortuary science; gerontology; human services; information science/studies; legal administrative assistant/secretary; legal assistant/paralegal; liberal arts and sciences/liberal studies; mechanical engineering; mental health/rehabilitation; nursing (licensed practical/vocational nurse training); nursing (registered nurse training); occupational therapist assistant; occupational therapy; photographic and film/video technology; physical therapist assistant; physical therapy; psychiatric/mental health services technology; restaurant/food services management; Spanish; teacher assistant/aide; tourism and travel services management; veterinary/animal health technology; visual and performing arts.

Academics *Calendar:* enhanced semester. *Degree:* certificates and associate. *Special study options:* academic remediation for entering students, accelerated degree program, adult/continuing education programs, advanced placement credit, cooperative education, distance learning, double majors, English as a second language, honors programs, independent study, internships, off-campus study, part-time degree program, services for LD students, student-designed majors, study abroad, summer session for credit.

Library Fiorello H. LaGuardia Community College Library Media Resources Center plus 1 other with 211,914 titles, 522 serial subscriptions, 3,176 audiovisual materials, an OPAC, a Web page.

Student Life *Housing:* college housing not available. *Activities and Organizations:* drama/theater group, student-run newspaper, radio station, Bangladesh Student Association, Christian Club, Chinese Club, Web Radio, Black Student Union. *Campus security:* 24-hour emergency response devices and patrols, late-night transport/escort service. *Student services:* health clinic, personal/psychological counseling, women's center, legal services.

Athletics *Intramural sports:* basketball M/W, bowling M/W, football M, soccer M/W, softball M/W, swimming and diving M/W, table tennis M/W, volleyball M/W.

Costs (2010–11) *Tuition:* state resident $3150 full-time, $135 per credit hour part-time; nonresident $5040 full-time, $210 per credit hour part-time. *Required fees:* $342 full-time, $86 per term part-time. *Payment plans:* installment, deferred payment. *Waivers:* senior citizens and employees or children of employees.

Financial Aid Of all full-time matriculated undergraduates who enrolled in 2008, 1,425 Federal Work-Study jobs (averaging $1194).

Applying *Options:* electronic application, early admission, deferred entrance. *Application fee:* $65. *Required:* high school transcript. *Application deadlines:* rolling (freshmen), rolling (transfers). *Notification:* continuous (freshmen), continuous (transfers).

Freshman Application Contact Ms. LaVora Desvigne, Director of Admissions, Fiorello H. LaGuardia Community College of the City University of New York, RM-147, 31-10 Thomson Avenue, Long Island City, NY 11101. *Phone:* 718-482-5114. *Fax:* 718-482-5112. *E-mail:* admissions@lagcc.cuny.edu.

Fulton-Montgomery Community College

Johnstown, New York **www.fmcc.suny.edu/**

- **State and locally supported** 2-year, founded 1964, part of State University of New York System
- **Rural** 195-acre campus
- **Endowment** $1.3 million
- **Coed,** 2,732 undergraduate students, 65% full-time, 57% women, 43% men

Undergraduates 1,784 full-time, 948 part-time. Students come from 6 states and territories, 18 other countries, 5% are from out of state, 7% African American, 0.9% Asian American or Pacific Islander, 7% Hispanic American, 0.3% Native American, 4% international, 3% transferred in. *Retention:* 56% of 2008 full-time freshmen returned.

Freshmen *Admission:* 767 enrolled.

Faculty *Total:* 140, 38% full-time. *Student/faculty ratio:* 24:1.

Majors Accounting; administrative assistant and secretarial science; art; automobile/automotive mechanics technology; behavioral sciences; biological and physical sciences; biology/biological sciences; business administration and management; carpentry; commercial and advertising art; computer engineering technology; computer science; computer typography and composition equipment operation; construction engineering technology; criminal justice/law enforcement administration; data processing and data processing technology; developmental and child psychology; dramatic/theater arts; electrical, electronic and communications engineering technology; elementary education; engineering science; English; environmental studies; finance; fine/studio arts; graphic and printing equipment operation/production; health teacher education; history; humanities; human services; information science/studies; kindergarten/preschool education; legal administrative assistant/secretary; liberal arts and sciences/liberal studies; mass communication/media; mathematics; medical administrative assistant and medical secretary; natural resources/conservation; nursing (registered nurse training); physical education teaching and coaching; physical sciences; psychology; social sciences; teacher assistant/aide.

Academics *Calendar:* semesters plus winter session. *Degree:* certificates and associate. *Special study options:* academic remediation for entering students, accelerated degree program, adult/continuing education programs, advanced placement credit, cooperative education, distance learning, double majors, English as a second language, external degree program, honors programs, independent study, internships, off-campus study, part-time degree program, services for LD students, student-designed majors, study abroad, summer session for credit.

Library Evans Library with 51,642 titles, 139 serial subscriptions, 1,536 audiovisual materials, an OPAC, a Web page.

Student Life *Housing Options:* Campus housing is provided by a third party. *Activities and Organizations:* drama/theater group, student-run newspaper, choral group. *Campus security:* weekend and night security. *Student services:* personal/psychological counseling.

Athletics Member NJCAA. *Intercollegiate sports:* baseball M, basketball M/W, soccer M/W, softball W, volleyball W. *Intramural sports:* baseball M, basketball M/W, skiing (cross-country) M(c)/W(c), skiing (downhill) M(c)/W(c), volleyball M/W.

Fulton-Montgomery Community College (continued)

Costs (2010–11) *Tuition:* state resident $3194 full-time, $133 per credit hour part-time; nonresident $6388 full-time, $266 per credit hour part-time. Part-time tuition and fees vary according to course load. *Required fees:* $534 full-time. *Room and board:* $8290; room only: $5660. *Payment plans:* installment, deferred payment. *Waivers:* senior citizens and employees or children of employees.

Financial Aid Of all full-time matriculated undergraduates who enrolled in 2008, 87 Federal Work-Study jobs (averaging $1500).

Applying *Options:* electronic application, early admission, deferred entrance. *Required:* high school transcript. *Application deadlines:* 9/10 (freshmen), 9/10 (transfers). *Notification:* continuous (freshmen), continuous (transfers).

Freshman Application Contact Fulton-Montgomery Community College, 2805 State Highway 67, Johnstown, NY 12095-3790. *Phone:* 518-762-4651 Ext. 8301.

GAMLA COLLEGE

Brooklyn, New York

Admissions Office Contact Gamla College, 1213 Elm Avenue, Brooklyn, NY 11230.

GENESEE COMMUNITY COLLEGE

Batavia, New York www.genesee.edu/

- **State and locally supported** 2-year, founded 1966, part of State University of New York System
- **Small-town** 256-acre campus with easy access to Buffalo and Rochester
- **Endowment** $1.9 million
- **Coed,** 7,208 undergraduate students, 48% full-time, 63% women, 37% men

Undergraduates 3,452 full-time, 3,756 part-time. Students come from 18 states and territories, 27 other countries, 2% are from out of state, 7% African American, 1% Asian American or Pacific Islander, 2% Hispanic American, 0.8% Native American, 2% international, 6% transferred in.

Freshmen *Admission:* 1,175 enrolled.

Faculty *Total:* 316, 24% full-time. *Student/faculty ratio:* 18:1.

Majors Accounting; administrative assistant and secretarial science; business administration and management; clinical/medical laboratory technology; computer and information sciences related; computer engineering technology; computer graphics; computer software and media applications related; criminal justice/law enforcement administration; criminology; drafting and design technology; dramatic/theater arts; education; electrical, electronic and communications engineering technology; elementary education; engineering science; fashion merchandising; gerontology; health professions related; hotel/motel administration; human services; information science/studies; kindergarten/preschool education; legal assistant/paralegal; liberal arts and sciences/liberal studies; marketing/marketing management; mass communication/media; mathematics; nursing (registered nurse training); physical education teaching and coaching; physical therapy; psychology; respiratory care therapy; substance abuse/addiction counseling; system administration; tourism and travel services management.

Academics *Calendar:* semesters. *Degree:* certificates and associate. *Special study options:* academic remediation for entering students, adult/continuing education programs, advanced placement credit, cooperative education, distance learning, double majors, honors programs, independent study, internships, part-time degree program, services for LD students, summer session for credit.

Library Alfred C. O'Connell Library with 80,000 titles, 332 serial subscriptions, an OPAC, a Web page.

Student Life *Housing Options:* disabled students. Campus housing is university owned. *Activities and Organizations:* drama/theater group, student-run newspaper, radio station, choral group, Student Government Association, Phi Theta Kappa, DECA, Student Activities Council, Forum Players. *Campus security:* 24-hour emergency response devices and patrols, student patrols, late-night transport/escort service. *Student services:* health clinic, personal/psychological counseling.

Athletics Member NJCAA. *Intercollegiate sports:* baseball M, basketball M(s)/W(s), cross-country running M/W, golf M/W, lacrosse M, soccer M/W, softball W, swimming and diving M/W, volleyball M/W(s). *Intramural sports:* badminton M/W, basketball M/W, soccer M/W, swimming and diving M/W, tennis M/W, track and field M/W, volleyball M/W.

Standardized Tests *Recommended:* ACT (for admission).

Costs (2010–11) *Tuition:* state resident $3720 full-time, $140 per credit hour part-time; nonresident $4320 full-time, $160 per credit hour part-time. Full-time tuition and fees vary according to course load. Part-time tuition and fees vary according to course load. *Required fees:* $320 full-time, $24 per credit hour part-time. *Room and board:* room only: $5300. Room and board charges vary according to board plan and housing facility. *Payment plan:* installment. *Waivers:* senior citizens and employees or children of employees.

Financial Aid Of all full-time matriculated undergraduates who enrolled in 2008, 2,755 applied for aid, 2,300 were judged to have need, 874 had their need fully met. 147 Federal Work-Study jobs (averaging $1102). 59 state and other part-time jobs (averaging $1831). In 2008, 36 non-need-based awards were made. *Average percent of need met:* 65%. *Average financial aid package:* $4210. *Average need-based loan:* $3275. *Average need-based gift aid:* $2675. *Average non-need-based aid:* $1675. *Average indebtedness upon graduation:* $7950.

Applying *Options:* electronic application. *Required:* high school transcript. *Required for some:* 1 letter of recommendation. *Application deadlines:* rolling (freshmen), rolling (out-of-state freshmen), rolling (transfers). *Notification:* continuous (freshmen), continuous (out-of-state freshmen), continuous (transfers).

Freshman Application Contact Mrs. Tanya Lane-Martin, Director of Admissions, Genesee Community College, 1 College Road, Batavia, NY 14020. *Phone:* 585-343-0055 Ext. 6413. *Toll-free phone:* 800-CALL GCC. *Fax:* 585-345-6892. *E-mail:* tmlanemartin@genesee.edu.

HELENE FULD COLLEGE OF NURSING OF NORTH GENERAL HOSPITAL

New York, New York www.helenefuld.edu/

Freshman Application Contact Mrs. Gladys Pineda, Student Services, Helene Fuld College of Nursing of North General Hospital, 1879 Madison Avenue, New York, NY 10035. *Phone:* 212-423-2768.

HERKIMER COUNTY COMMUNITY COLLEGE

Herkimer, New York www.herkimer.edu/

- **State and locally supported** 2-year, founded 1966, part of State University of New York System
- **Small-town** 500-acre campus with easy access to Syracuse
- **Coed**

Academics *Calendar:* semesters. *Degree:* certificates and associate. *Special study options:* academic remediation for entering students, adult/continuing education programs, advanced placement credit, English as a second language, honors programs, internships, part-time degree program, services for LD students, summer session for credit.

Student Life *Campus security:* 24-hour emergency response devices and patrols.

Athletics Member NJCAA.

Financial Aid Of all full-time matriculated undergraduates who enrolled in 2008, 150 Federal Work-Study jobs (averaging $700).

Applying *Options:* early admission. *Required:* high school transcript.

Director of Admissions Mr. Scott J. Hughes, Associate Dean for Enrollment Management, Herkimer County Community College, Herkimer, NY 13350. *Phone:* 315-866-0300 Ext. 278. *Toll-free phone:* 888-464-4222 Ext. 8278.

HUDSON VALLEY COMMUNITY COLLEGE

Troy, New York www.hvcc.edu/

Freshman Application Contact Ms. MaryClaire Bauer, Director of Admissions, Hudson Valley Community College, 80 Vandenburgh Avenue, Troy, NY 12180-6096. *Phone:* 518-629-4603. *E-mail:* panzajul@hvcc.edu.

INSTITUTE OF DESIGN AND CONSTRUCTION

Brooklyn, New York www.idcbrooklyn.org/

Director of Admissions Mr. Kevin Giannetti, Director of Admissions, Institute of Design and Construction, 141 Willoughby Street, Brooklyn, NY 11201-5317. *Phone:* 718-855-3661.

ISLAND DRAFTING AND TECHNICAL INSTITUTE

Amityville, New York **www.idti.edu/**

- **Proprietary** 2-year, founded 1957
- **Suburban** campus with easy access to New York City
- **Coed,** 131 undergraduate students, 100% full-time, 24% women, 76% men

Undergraduates 131 full-time. Students come from 1 other state, 11% African American, 2% Asian American or Pacific Islander, 21% Hispanic American.

Freshmen *Admission:* 57 applied, 53 admitted, 45 enrolled. *Average high school GPA:* 2.5.

Faculty *Total:* 10, 50% full-time. *Student/faculty ratio:* 15:1.

Majors Architectural drafting and CAD/CADD; computer and information sciences and support services related; computer and information systems security; computer systems networking and telecommunications; computer technology/computer systems technology; electrical, electronic and communications engineering technology; mechanical drafting and CAD/CADD; system administration.

Academics *Calendar:* semesters. *Degree:* certificates, diplomas, and associate. *Special study options:* accelerated degree program, adult/continuing education programs, summer session for credit.

Student Life *Housing:* college housing not available.

Costs (2009–10) *Tuition:* $14,250 full-time, $475 per credit hour part-time. No tuition increase for student's term of enrollment. *Required fees:* $350 full-time. *Payment plan:* installment.

Applying *Options:* early admission. *Application fee:* $25. *Required:* interview. *Recommended:* high school transcript. *Notification:* continuous (freshmen).

Freshman Application Contact Jaimie Laudicina, Director of Enrollment Services, Island Drafting and Technical Institute, 128 Broadway, Amityville, NY 11701. *Phone:* 631-691-8733. *Fax:* 631-691-8738. *E-mail:* info@idti.edu.

ITT TECHNICAL INSTITUTE

Albany, New York **www.itt-tech.edu/**

- **Proprietary** 2-year, founded 1998, part of ITT Educational Services, Inc.
- **Coed**

Majors CAD/CADD drafting/design technology; computer engineering technology; computer software and media applications related; system, networking, and LAN/WAN management; web/multimedia management and webmaster; web page, digital/multimedia and information resources design.

Academics *Calendar:* quarters. *Degree:* associate.

Student Life *Housing:* college housing not available.

Freshman Application Contact Director of Recruitment, ITT Technical Institute, 13 Airline Drive, Albany, NY 12205. *Phone:* 518-452-9300. *Toll-free phone:* 800-489-1191.

ITT TECHNICAL INSTITUTE

Getzville, New York **www.itt-tech.edu/**

- **Proprietary** 2-year, part of ITT Educational Services, Inc.
- **Coed**

Majors CAD/CADD drafting/design technology; computer engineering technology; computer software and media applications related; system, networking, and LAN/WAN management; web/multimedia management and webmaster; web page, digital/multimedia and information resources design.

Academics *Degree:* associate.

Student Life *Housing:* college housing not available.

Freshman Application Contact Director of Recruitment, ITT Technical Institute, 2295 Millersport Highway, PO Box 327, Getzville, NY 14068. *Phone:* 716-689-2200. *Toll-free phone:* 800-469-7593.

ITT TECHNICAL INSTITUTE

Liverpool, New York **www.itt-tech.edu/**

- **Proprietary** 2-year, founded 1998, part of ITT Educational Services, Inc.
- **Coed**

Majors CAD/CADD drafting/design technology; computer engineering technology; computer software and media applications related; system, networking, and LAN/WAN management; web/multimedia management and webmaster; web page, digital/multimedia and information resources design.

Academics *Calendar:* semesters. *Degree:* associate.

Student Life *Housing:* college housing not available.

Freshman Application Contact Director of Recruitment, ITT Technical Institute, 235 Greenfield Parkway, Liverpool, NY 13088-0011. *Phone:* 315-461-8000. *Toll-free phone:* 877-488-0011.

JAMESTOWN BUSINESS COLLEGE

Jamestown, New York **www.jbcny.org/**

- **Proprietary** primarily 2-year, founded 1886
- **Small-town** 1-acre campus
- **Coed,** 329 undergraduate students, 95% full-time, 74% women, 26% men

Undergraduates 311 full-time, 18 part-time. Students come from 2 states and territories, 9% are from out of state, 2% African American, 0.9% Asian American or Pacific Islander, 5% Hispanic American, 2% Native American, 16% transferred in.

Freshmen *Admission:* 118 applied, 107 admitted, 90 enrolled.

Faculty *Total:* 22, 36% full-time. *Student/faculty ratio:* 25:1.

Majors Accounting; administrative assistant and secretarial science; business administration and management; computer and information sciences; legal administrative assistant/secretary; marketing/marketing management; medical administrative assistant and medical secretary.

Academics *Calendar:* quarters. *Degrees:* certificates, associate, and bachelor's. *Special study options:* academic remediation for entering students, advanced placement credit, double majors, internships, part-time degree program, summer session for credit.

Library James Prendergast Library with 279,270 titles, 372 serial subscriptions, an OPAC, a Web page.

Student Life *Housing:* college housing not available. *Campus security:* 24-hour emergency response devices.

Athletics *Intramural sports:* basketball M(c)/W(c), bowling M(c)/W(c), racquetball M(c)/W(c), skiing (cross-country) M(c)/W(c), skiing (downhill) M(c)/W(c), softball M(c)/W(c), swimming and diving M(c)/W(c), table tennis M(c)/W(c), volleyball M(c)/W(c), weight lifting M(c)/W(c).

Costs (2010–11) *One-time required fee:* $25. *Tuition:* $10,200 full-time, $283 per credit hour part-time. *Required fees:* $900 full-time, $150 per term part-time.

Applying *Application fee:* $25. *Required:* essay or personal statement, high school transcript, interview. *Application deadlines:* rolling (freshmen), rolling (transfers).

Freshman Application Contact Mrs. Brenda Salemme, Director of Admissions and Placement, Jamestown Business College, 7 Fairmount Avenue, Jamestown, NY 14701. *Phone:* 716-664-5100. *Fax:* 716-664-3144. *E-mail:* admissions@jbcny.org.

JAMESTOWN COMMUNITY COLLEGE

Jamestown, New York **www.sunyjcc.edu/**

- **State and locally supported** 2-year, founded 1950, part of State University of New York System
- **Small-town** 107-acre campus
- **Endowment** $6.4 million
- **Coed,** 3,931 undergraduate students, 71% full-time, 57% women, 43% men

Undergraduates 2,807 full-time, 1,124 part-time. Students come from 13 states and territories, 9% are from out of state, 3% African American, 0.8% Asian American or Pacific Islander, 3% Hispanic American, 2% Native American, 0.4% international, 6% transferred in.

Freshmen *Admission:* 1,819 applied, 1,654 admitted, 1,288 enrolled. *Average high school GPA:* 3.03.

Faculty *Total:* 378, 21% full-time, 7% with terminal degrees. *Student/faculty ratio:* 18:1.

Majors Accounting; airline pilot and flight crew; business administration and management; clinical/medical laboratory technology; communication/speech communication and rhetoric; computer and information sciences; computer and information sciences related; computer and information systems security; computer engineering technology; computer science; criminal justice/police science; criminal justice/safety; early childhood education; electrical, electronic and communications engineering technology; elementary and middle school administration/

Jamestown Community College (continued)

principalship; engineering; fine/studio arts; fire science; forestry; health and physical education; humanities; human services; information technology; liberal arts and sciences and humanities related; liberal arts and sciences/liberal studies; mathematics; mechanical engineering/mechanical technology; medical office assistant; music; nursing (registered nurse training); occupational therapist assistant; office occupations and clerical services; physical sciences; social sciences; welding technology.

Academics *Calendar:* semesters. *Degree:* certificates and associate. *Special study options:* academic remediation for entering students, adult/continuing education programs, advanced placement credit, cooperative education, distance learning, honors programs, independent study, internships, off-campus study, part-time degree program, services for LD students, study abroad, summer session for credit.

Library Hultquist Library with 66,808 titles, 370 serial subscriptions, an OPAC, a Web page.

Student Life *Housing Options:* coed. Campus housing is university owned. *Activities and Organizations:* drama/theater group, student-run radio station, choral group, Nursing Club, Inter-Varsity Christian Fellowship, Earth Awareness, Adult Student Network, Student Senate. *Student services:* health clinic, personal/psychological counseling.

Athletics Member NJCAA. *Intercollegiate sports:* baseball M, basketball M/W, cheerleading W, cross-country running M/W, golf M, soccer M/W, softball W, swimming and diving M/W, volleyball W, wrestling M. *Intramural sports:* basketball M/W, bowling M/W, softball M/W, table tennis M/W, tennis M/W, volleyball M/W.

Costs (2009–10) *Tuition:* state resident $3640 full-time, $151 per credit hour part-time; nonresident $7280 full-time, $272 per credit hour part-time. Full-time tuition and fees vary according to course load and program. Part-time tuition and fees vary according to course load and program. *Required fees:* $500 full-time. *Room and board:* $7850. Room and board charges vary according to board plan.

Financial Aid Of all full-time matriculated undergraduates who enrolled in 2008, 85 Federal Work-Study jobs (averaging $1500). 85 state and other part-time jobs (averaging $1300).

Applying *Options:* electronic application, deferred entrance. *Required:* high school transcript. *Required for some:* standardized test scores used for placement. *Application deadlines:* rolling (freshmen), rolling (out-of-state freshmen), rolling (transfers). *Notification:* continuous (freshmen), continuous (out-of-state freshmen), continuous (transfers).

Freshman Application Contact Ms. Wendy Present, Director of Admissions and Recruitment, Jamestown Community College, 525 Falconer Street, PO Box 20, Jamestown, NY 14702-0020. *Phone:* 716-338-1001. *Toll-free phone:* 800-388-8557. *Fax:* 716-338-1450. *E-mail:* admissions@mail.sunyjcc.edu.

Jefferson Community College

Watertown, New York **www.sunyjefferson.edu/**

- **State and locally supported** 2-year, founded 1961, part of State University of New York System
- **Small-town** 90-acre campus with easy access to Syracuse
- **Coed,** 3,314 undergraduate students, 61% full-time, 62% women, 38% men

Undergraduates 2,024 full-time, 1,290 part-time. Students come from 9 states and territories, 3 other countries.

Freshmen *Admission:* 869 enrolled.

Faculty *Total:* 191, 40% full-time, 13% with terminal degrees. *Student/faculty ratio:* 18:1.

Majors Accounting; accounting technology and bookkeeping; animal/livestock husbandry and production; business administration and management; child-care and support services management; child development; computer and information sciences; computer and information sciences and support services related; computer/information technology services administration related; computer science; criminal justice/law enforcement administration; early childhood education; emergency medical technology (EMT paramedic); engineering science; fire protection and safety technology; forestry technology; hospitality administration; humanities; human services; legal assistant/paralegal; mathematics; nursing (registered nurse training); office management.

Academics *Calendar:* semesters. *Degree:* certificates and associate. *Special study options:* academic remediation for entering students, advanced placement credit, cooperative education, distance learning, double majors, honors programs, independent study, internships, part-time degree program, services for LD students, student-designed majors, summer session for credit.

Library Melvil Dewey Library with 68,664 titles, 233 serial subscriptions, 4,756 audiovisual materials, an OPAC, a Web page.

Student Life *Housing:* college housing not available. *Activities and Organizations:* student-run newspaper, Phi Theta Kappa, Dionysian Players, Military Loved One's Club, student-run newspaper, choral group. *Campus security:* 24-hour emergency response devices and patrols. *Student services:* health clinic, personal/psychological counseling.

Athletics Member NJCAA. *Intercollegiate sports:* baseball M, basketball M/W, lacrosse M/W, soccer M/W, softball W, volleyball W.

Standardized Tests *Recommended:* SAT or ACT (for admission).

Costs (2009–10) *Tuition:* state resident $3312 full-time, $138 per credit hour part-time; nonresident $5160 full-time, $215 per credit hour part-time. Full-time tuition and fees vary according to course load and reciprocity agreements. Part-time tuition and fees vary according to course load and reciprocity agreements. *Required fees:* $382 full-time, $15 per credit hour part-time. *Payment plan:* installment. *Waivers:* senior citizens and employees or children of employees.

Financial Aid Of all full-time matriculated undergraduates who enrolled in 2009, 1,748 applied for aid. 98 Federal Work-Study jobs (averaging $1093).

Applying *Options:* electronic application, early admission, deferred entrance. *Required:* high school transcript. *Required for some:* interview. *Application deadline:* rolling (transfers). *Notification:* continuous (freshmen), continuous (transfers).

Freshman Application Contact Ms. Rosanne N. Weir, Director of Admissions, Jefferson Community College, 1220 Coffeen Street, Watertown, NY 13601. *Phone:* 315-786-2277. *Fax:* 315-786-2459. *E-mail:* admissions@sunyjefferson.edu.

Kingsborough Community College of the City University of New York

Brooklyn, New York **www.kbcc.cuny.edu/**

- **State and locally supported** 2-year, founded 1963, part of City University of New York System
- **Urban** 72-acre campus with easy access to New York City
- **Coed,** 17,793 undergraduate students, 58% full-time, 56% women, 44% men

Undergraduates 10,382 full-time, 7,411 part-time. Students come from 10 states and territories, 136 other countries, 1% are from out of state, 34% African American, 11% Asian American or Pacific Islander, 15% Hispanic American, 0.2% Native American, 5% international, 11% transferred in. *Retention:* 69% of 2008 full-time freshmen returned.

Freshmen *Admission:* 2,965 enrolled. *Average high school GPA:* 2.7.

Faculty *Total:* 858, 36% full-time, 34% with terminal degrees. *Student/faculty ratio:* 23:1.

Majors Accounting; administrative assistant and secretarial science; applied art; art; biology/biological sciences; broadcast journalism; business administration and management; chemistry; commercial and advertising art; community health services counseling; computer and information sciences; computer science; data processing and data processing technology; dramatic/theater arts; early childhood education; education; elementary education; engineering science; fashion merchandising; health and physical education related; human services; journalism; labor and industrial relations; liberal arts and sciences/liberal studies; marine technology; marketing/marketing management; mathematics; mental health/rehabilitation; music; nursing (registered nurse training); parks, recreation and leisure; physical therapist assistant; physical therapy; physics; psychiatric/mental health services technology; sport and fitness administration/management; teacher assistant/aide; tourism and travel services management.

Academics *Calendar:* semesters. *Degree:* associate. *Special study options:* academic remediation for entering students, adult/continuing education programs, advanced placement credit, distance learning, English as a second language, honors programs, independent study, internships, off-campus study, part-time degree program, services for LD students, summer session for credit.

Library Robert J. Kibbee Library with 185,912 titles, 458 serial subscriptions, an OPAC.

Student Life *Housing:* college housing not available. *Activities and Organizations:* drama/theater group, student-run newspaper, radio station, choral group, Peer Advisors, Caribbean Club, DECA. *Campus security:* 24-hour emergency response devices and patrols. *Student services:* health clinic, personal/psychological counseling, women's center.

Athletics Member NJCAA. *Intercollegiate sports:* baseball M, basketball M/W, soccer M, softball W, tennis M/W, track and field M/W, volleyball W. *Intramural sports:* baseball M, basketball M/W, soccer M, softball W, tennis M/W, track and field M/W, volleyball W.

Costs (2010–11) *Tuition:* state resident $3150 full-time; nonresident $6300 full-time. *Payment plan:* installment. *Waivers:* senior citizens.

Applying *Application fee:* $65. *Required:* high school transcript. *Application deadline:* rolling (transfers).

Freshman Application Contact Mr. Robert Ingenito, Director of Admissions Information Center, Kingsborough Community College of the City University of New York, 2001 Oriental Boulevard, Brooklyn, NY 11235. *Phone:* 718-368-4600. *Fax:* 718-368-5356. *E-mail:* info@kbcc.cuny.edu.

Long Island Business Institute

Commack, New York **www.libi.edu/**

- **Proprietary** 2-year, founded 1968, administratively affiliated with Long Island Business Institute in Flushing, NY
- **Urban** campus with easy access to New York City
- **Coed, primarily women,** 653 undergraduate students, 63% full-time, 78% women, 22% men

Undergraduates 412 full-time, 241 part-time. Students come from 2 states and territories, 10 other countries, 10% African American, 38% Asian American or Pacific Islander, 19% Hispanic American, 0.2% Native American, 2% international, 3% transferred in.

Freshmen *Admission:* 251 applied, 203 admitted, 153 enrolled.

Faculty *Total:* 94, 24% full-time, 2% with terminal degrees. *Student/faculty ratio:* 15:1.

Majors Accounting; business administration and management; court reporting; medical office management.

Academics *Calendar:* semesters. *Degrees:* certificates, diplomas, and associate (information provided for Commack and Flushing campuses). *Special study options:* academic remediation for entering students, adult/continuing education programs, advanced placement credit, cooperative education, English as a second language, honors programs, independent study, internships, part-time degree program, summer session for credit.

Library Commack Branch Campus Library, Flushing Main Campus Library with 4,400 titles, 69 serial subscriptions, 799 audiovisual materials, an OPAC, a Web page.

Student Life *Housing:* college housing not available. *Activities and Organizations:* Small Business Club, Web Design Club, Investment Club, Court Reporting Alumni Association. *Campus security:* 24-hour emergency response devices.

Standardized Tests *Required:* ASSET; CELSA (for admission).

Costs (2009–10) *Tuition:* $11,250 full-time, $375 per credit hour part-time. *Required fees:* $700 full-time. *Payment plans:* installment, deferred payment.

Applying *Application fee:* $50. *Required:* essay or personal statement, high school transcript, interview. *Application deadlines:* rolling (freshmen), rolling (transfers).

Freshman Application Contact Mr. Robert Nazar, Director of Admissions, Long Island Business Institute, 6500 Jericho Turnpike, Commack, NY 11725. *Phone:* 718-939-5100. *Fax:* 718-939-9235. *E-mail:* rnazar@libi.edu.

Long Island College Hospital School of Nursing

Brooklyn, New York **www.futurenurselich.org/**

Freshman Application Contact Ms. Barbara Evans, Admissions Assistant, Long Island College Hospital School of Nursing, 350 Henry Street, 7th Floor, Brooklyn, NY 11201. *Phone:* 718-780-1071. *Fax:* 718-780-1936. *E-mail:* bevans@chpnet.org.

Memorial Hospital School of Nursing

Albany, New York **www.nehealth.com/son/**

Freshman Application Contact Admissions Office, Memorial Hospital School of Nursing, 600 Northern Boulevard, Albany, NY 12204.

Mildred Elley School

Albany, New York **www.mildred-elley.edu/**

- **Proprietary** 2-year, founded 1917
- **Suburban** campus
- **Coed**

Academics *Degree:* certificates, diplomas, and associate.

Standardized Tests *Required:* CPAt (for admission).

Applying *Application fee:* $25.

Director of Admissions Mr. Michael Cahalan, Enrollment Manager, Mildred Elley School, 800 New Loudon Road, Suite 5120, Latham, NY 12110. *Phone:* 518-786-3171 Ext. 227. *Toll-free phone:* 800-622-6327.

Mohawk Valley Community College

Utica, New York **www.mvcc.edu/**

- **State and locally supported** 2-year, founded 1946, part of State University of New York System
- **Suburban** 80-acre campus
- **Endowment** $3.2 million
- **Coed,** 6,701 undergraduate students, 66% full-time, 55% women, 45% men

Undergraduates 4,403 full-time, 2,298 part-time. Students come from 11 states and territories, 18 other countries, 7% African American, 2% Asian American or Pacific Islander, 4% Hispanic American, 0.6% Native American, 1% international, 5% transferred in, 9% live on campus.

Freshmen *Admission:* 4,678 applied, 3,773 admitted, 1,688 enrolled. *Average high school GPA:* 2.7.

Faculty *Total:* 356, 38% full-time. *Student/faculty ratio:* 23:1.

Majors Accounting technology and bookkeeping; administrative assistant and secretarial science; advertising; airframe mechanics and aircraft maintenance technology; art; banking and financial support services; building/property maintenance and management; business administration and management; chemical technology; civil engineering technology; commercial and advertising art; commercial photography; communications systems installation and repair technology; community organization and advocacy; computer and information sciences; computer and information sciences and support services related; computer programming; criminal justice/law enforcement administration; design and applied arts related; drafting and design technology; dramatic/theater arts; electrical and electronic engineering technologies related; electrical, electronic and communications engineering technology; electrical/electronics maintenance and repair technology related; elementary education; emergency medical technology (EMT paramedic); engineering; entrepreneurship; fire services administration; food service systems administration; heating, air conditioning and refrigeration technology; hotel/motel administration; humanities; industrial production technologies related; liberal arts and sciences and humanities related; liberal arts and sciences/liberal studies; management information systems and services related; mechanical engineering/mechanical technology; medical/clinical assistant; medical radiologic technology; nursing (registered nurse training); nutrition sciences; parks, recreation and leisure facilities management; public administration; respiratory care therapy; restaurant, culinary, and catering management; secondary education; sign language interpretation and translation; substance abuse/addiction counseling; survey technology.

Academics *Calendar:* semesters. *Degree:* certificates and associate. *Special study options:* academic remediation for entering students, advanced placement credit, distance learning, double majors, English as a second language, honors programs, independent study, internships, off-campus study, part-time degree program, services for LD students, student-designed majors, summer session for credit. *ROTC:* Army (c).

Library Mohawk Valley Community College Library plus 1 other with 98,317 titles, 29,313 serial subscriptions, 7,933 audiovisual materials, an OPAC, a Web page.

Student Life *Housing Options:* coed, men-only, women-only, disabled students. Campus housing is university owned and is provided by a third party. Freshman applicants given priority for college housing. *Activities and Organizations:* drama/theater group, student-run newspaper, choral group, Black Student Union, Veterans Club, Phi Theta Kappa, International Club, Kidz 'n Coaches. *Campus security:* 24-hour emergency response devices and patrols, late-night transport/escort service, controlled dormitory access. *Student services:* health clinic, personal/psychological counseling.

Athletics Member NJCAA. *Intercollegiate sports:* baseball M, basketball M/W, bowling M/W, cross-country running M/W, golf M/W, ice hockey M, lacrosse M, soccer M/W, softball W, tennis M/W, track and field M/W, volleyball W. *Intramural sports:* basketball M/W, football M/W, racquetball M/W, soccer M/W, softball M/W, tennis M/W, volleyball M/W, weight lifting M/W.

Costs (2009–10) *Tuition:* state resident $3350 full-time, $120 per credit hour part-time; nonresident $6700 full-time, $240 per credit hour part-time. *Required fees:* $424 full-time, $5 per credit hour part-time, $35 part-time. *Room and board:* $7500; room only: $4550. *Payment plan:* installment. *Waivers:* senior citizens and employees or children of employees.

Financial Aid Of all full-time matriculated undergraduates who enrolled in 2008, 229 Federal Work-Study jobs (averaging $1750).

Mohawk Valley Community College (continued)

Applying *Options:* electronic application, early decision, deferred entrance. *Required:* high school transcript. *Application deadlines:* rolling (freshmen), rolling (transfers).

Freshman Application Contact Mrs. Sandra Fiebiger, Data Processing Clerk, Admissions, Mohawk Valley Community College, 1101 Sherman Drive, Utica, NY 13501. *Phone:* 315-792-5640. *Toll-free phone:* 800-SEE-MVCC. *Fax:* 315-792-5527. *E-mail:* sfiebiger@mvcc.edu.

▶See page 464 for the College Close-Up.

Monroe Community College

Rochester, New York **www.monroecc.edu/**

Freshman Application Contact Mr. Andrew Freeman, Director of Admissions, Monroe Community College, 1000 East Henrietta Road, Rochester, NY 14623-5780. *Phone:* 585-292-2231. *Fax:* 585-292-3860. *E-mail:* admissions@monroecc.edu.

Nassau Community College

Garden City, New York **www.ncc.edu/**

- **State and locally supported** 2-year, founded 1959, part of State University of New York System
- **Suburban** 225-acre campus with easy access to New York City
- **Coed,** 21,952 undergraduate students, 67% full-time, 52% women, 48% men

Undergraduates 14,702 full-time, 7,250 part-time. Students come from 19 states and territories, 69 other countries, 0.3% are from out of state, 20% African American, 7% Asian American or Pacific Islander, 16% Hispanic American, 0.3% Native American, 2% international, 7% transferred in. *Retention:* 32% of 2008 full-time freshmen returned.

Freshmen *Admission:* 5,542 enrolled. *Average high school GPA:* 2.51.

Faculty *Total:* 1,489, 37% full-time, 27% with terminal degrees. *Student/faculty ratio:* 18:1.

Majors Accounting; accounting technology and bookkeeping; administrative assistant and secretarial science; African American/Black studies; art; business administration and management; civil engineering technology; clinical/medical laboratory technology; commercial and advertising art; communication/speech communication and rhetoric; computer and information sciences; computer and information sciences related; computer graphics; computer science; computer systems networking and telecommunications; criminal justice/law enforcement administration; criminal justice/safety; dance; data processing and data processing technology; design and visual communications; dramatic/theater arts; engineering; entrepreneurship; fashion/apparel design; fashion merchandising; funeral service and mortuary science; general studies; health professions related; hotel/motel administration; instrumentation technology; insurance; interior design; kindergarten/preschool education; legal administrative assistant/secretary; legal assistant/paralegal; liberal arts and sciences/liberal studies; management information systems; marketing/marketing management; mass communication/media; mathematics; medical administrative assistant and medical secretary; medical radiologic technology; music performance; nursing (registered nurse training); photography; physical therapist assistant; real estate; rehabilitation therapy; respiratory care therapy; retailing; security and loss prevention; surgical technology; theater design and technology; transportation and materials moving related; visual and performing arts.

Academics *Calendar:* semesters. *Degree:* certificates and associate. *Special study options:* academic remediation for entering students, adult/continuing education programs, advanced placement credit, cooperative education, distance learning, English as a second language, honors programs, internships, off-campus study, part-time degree program, services for LD students, summer session for credit.

Library A. Holly Patterson Library with 186,782 titles, 401 serial subscriptions, 18,903 audiovisual materials, an OPAC, a Web page.

Student Life *Housing:* college housing not available. *Activities and Organizations:* drama/theater group, student-run newspaper, radio station, choral group, Muslim Student Association, Make a Difference Club, Interact Club, Political Science Club, Investment Club. *Campus security:* 24-hour emergency response devices and patrols, late-night transport/escort service. *Student services:* personal/psychological counseling, women's center.

Athletics Member NJCAA. *Intercollegiate sports:* baseball M, basketball M/W, bowling M/W, cheerleading M/W, cross-country running M/W, equestrian sports M/W, football M, golf M/W, lacrosse M/W, soccer M/W, softball W, tennis M/W, track and field M/W, volleyball W, wrestling M. *Intramural sports:* badminton M/W, baseball M, basketball M/W, racquetball M/W, soccer M/W, softball M/W, swimming and diving M/W, table tennis M/W, tennis M/W, volleyball M/W.

Standardized Tests *Recommended:* SAT or ACT (for admission).

Financial Aid Of all full-time matriculated undergraduates who enrolled in 2008, 400 Federal Work-Study jobs (averaging $3000).

Applying *Options:* electronic application, deferred entrance. *Application fee:* $40. *Required:* high school transcript. *Required for some:* minimum 3 GPA, interview. *Recommended:* minimum 2 GPA. *Notification:* continuous (freshmen), continuous (transfers).

Freshman Application Contact Mr. Craig Wright, Vice President of Enrollment Management, Nassau Community College, One Education Drive, Garden City, NY 11530. *Phone:* 516-572-7345. *E-mail:* admissions@sunynassau.edu.

New York Career Institute

New York, New York **www.nyci.com/**

Freshman Application Contact Ms. Cindy McMahon, Director of Admissions, New York Career Institute, 11 Park Place- 4th Floor, New York, NY 10007. *Phone:* 212-962-0002 Ext. 101. *Fax:* 212-385-7574. *E-mail:* cmcmahon@nyci.edu.

New York College of Health Professions

Syosset, New York **www.nycollege.edu/**

Director of Admissions Ms. Mary Rodas, Associate Director of Admissions, New York College of Health Professions, 6801 Jericho Turnpike, Syosset, NY 11791. *Toll-free phone:* 800-922-7337 Ext. 351. *E-mail:* rdodas@nycollege.edu.

Niagara County Community College

Sanborn, New York **www.niagaracc.suny.edu/**

- **State and locally supported** 2-year, founded 1962, part of State University of New York System
- **Rural** 287-acre campus with easy access to Buffalo
- **Endowment** $2.3 million
- **Coed,** 7,279 undergraduate students, 64% full-time, 57% women, 43% men

Undergraduates 4,647 full-time, 2,632 part-time. Students come from 16 states and territories, 5 other countries, 1% are from out of state, 9% African American, 1% Asian American or Pacific Islander, 0.2% Hispanic American, 2% Native American, 0.1% international, 4% transferred in.

Freshmen *Admission:* 2,003 applied, 2,003 admitted, 1,933 enrolled. *Average high school GPA:* 2.48.

Faculty *Total:* 409, 28% full-time, 13% with terminal degrees. *Student/faculty ratio:* 17:1.

Majors Accounting; administrative assistant and secretarial science; animal sciences; biological and physical sciences; business administration and management; chemical technology; computer science; consumer merchandising/retailing management; criminal justice/law enforcement administration; culinary arts; design and applied arts related; drafting and design technology; drafting/design engineering technologies related; dramatic/theater arts; electrical, electronic and communications engineering technology; electroneurodiagnostic/electroencephalographic technology; fine/studio arts; general studies; hospitality administration; humanities; human services; information science/studies; liberal arts and sciences/liberal studies; mass communication/media; mathematics; medical/clinical assistant; music; natural resources/conservation; nursing (registered nurse training); occupational health and industrial hygiene; parks, recreation and leisure; physical education teaching and coaching; physical therapist assistant; radiologic technology/science; social sciences; sport and fitness administration/management; surgical technology; web page, digital/multimedia and information resources design.

Academics *Calendar:* semesters. *Degree:* certificates and associate. *Special study options:* academic remediation for entering students, adult/continuing education programs, advanced placement credit, cooperative education, double majors, honors programs, independent study, internships, off-campus study, part-time degree program, services for LD students, student-designed majors, study abroad, summer session for credit. *ROTC:* Army (c).

Library Henrietta G. Lewis Library with 94,782 titles, 399 serial subscriptions, 5,471 audiovisual materials, an OPAC, a Web page.

Student Life *Activities and Organizations:* drama/theater group, student-run newspaper, radio station, choral group, student radio station, Student Nurses

Association, Phi Theta Kappa, Alpha Beta Gamma, Physical Education Club. *Campus security:* student patrols, late-night transport/escort service, emergency telephones. *Student services:* health clinic, personal/psychological counseling.

Athletics Member NJCAA. *Intercollegiate sports:* baseball M, basketball M(s)/W, golf M/W, lacrosse M/W, soccer M/W, softball W, volleyball W, wrestling M(s). *Intramural sports:* basketball M/W, bowling M/W, cheerleading W, football M/W, racquetball M/W, skiing (cross-country) M(c)/W(c), table tennis M/W, volleyball M/W.

Costs (2009–10) *Tuition:* state resident $3408 full-time, $142 per credit hour part-time; nonresident $6816 full-time, $284 per credit hour part-time. Full-time tuition and fees vary according to course load and program. Part-time tuition and fees vary according to course load and program. *Required fees:* $342 full-time, $84 per term part-time. *Room and board:* room only: $4900. *Payment plan:* installment. *Waivers:* senior citizens and employees or children of employees.

Financial Aid Of all full-time matriculated undergraduates who enrolled in 2009, 3,190 applied for aid, 3,190 were judged to have need. 249 Federal Work-Study jobs (averaging $1851). 62 state and other part-time jobs (averaging $799). *Average financial aid package:* $2158. *Average need-based loan:* $2517. *Average need-based gift aid:* $1644.

Applying *Options:* electronic application, early admission. *Required:* high school transcript. *Required for some:* minimum 2 GPA. *Notification:* continuous until 8/31 (freshmen), continuous until 8/31 (transfers).

Freshman Application Contact Ms. Kathy Saunders, Director of Enrollment Services, Niagara County Community College, 3111 Saunders Settlement Road, Sanborn, NY 14132. *Phone:* 716-614-6200. *Fax:* 716-614-6820. *E-mail:* admissions@niagaracc.suny.edu.

North Country Community College

Saranac Lake, New York www.nccc.edu/

Freshman Application Contact Enrollment Management Assistant, North Country Community College, 23 Santanoni Avenue, PO Box 89, Saranac Lake, NY 12983-0089. *Phone:* 518-891-2915 Ext. 686. *Toll-free phone:* 888-TRY-NCCC Ext. 233. *Fax:* 518-891-0898. *E-mail:* info@nccc.edu.

Olean Business Institute

Olean, New York www.obi.edu/

- **Proprietary** 2-year, founded 1961
- **Small-town** campus
- **Coed,** 87 undergraduate students

Majors Accounting; administrative assistant and secretarial science; business administration and management; computer and information sciences; computer and information sciences and support services related; legal assistant/paralegal; medical/clinical assistant.

Academics *Calendar:* semesters. *Degree:* diplomas and associate. *Special study options:* double majors, internships, part-time degree program, summer session for credit.

Library 1,800 titles, 25 serial subscriptions, an OPAC.

Student Life *Housing:* college housing not available. *Campus security:* 24-hour emergency response devices, late-night transport/escort service. *Student services:* personal/psychological counseling.

Financial Aid Of all full-time matriculated undergraduates who enrolled in 2008, 24 applied for aid, 24 were judged to have need. *Average percent of need met:* 56%. *Average financial aid package:* $6840. *Average need-based loan:* $2716. *Average need-based gift aid:* $5487. *Average indebtedness upon graduation:* $4044.

Applying *Application fee:* $25. *Required:* high school transcript. *Required for some:* essay or personal statement, interview. *Notification:* continuous until 9/1 (freshmen), continuous until 9/1 (transfers).

Freshman Application Contact Olean Business Institute, 301 North Union Street, Olean, NY 14760-2691. *Phone:* 716-372-7978.

Onondaga Community College

Syracuse, New York www.sunyocc.edu/

Freshman Application Contact Mrs. Katherine Perry, Director of Admissions, Onondaga Community College, 4941 Onondaga Road, Syracuse, NY 13215. *Phone:* 315-488-2602. *Fax:* 315-488-2107. *E-mail:* admissions@sunyocc.edu.

Orange County Community College

Middletown, New York www.orange.cc.ny.us/

Freshman Application Contact Ms. Margot St. Lawrence, Director of Admissions, Orange County Community College, 115 South Street, Middletown, NY 10940. *Phone:* 845-341-4030. *Fax:* 845-343-1228. *E-mail:* admssns@sunyorange.edu.

Phillips Beth Israel School of Nursing

New York, New York www.futurenursebi.org/

- **Independent** 2-year, founded 1904
- **Urban** campus
- **Endowment** $1.2 million
- **Coed,** 256 undergraduate students, 10% full-time, 81% women, 19% men

Undergraduates 26 full-time, 230 part-time. Students come from 9 states and territories, 6 other countries, 15% are from out of state, 16% African American, 16% Asian American or Pacific Islander, 10% Hispanic American, 2% international, 50% transferred in.

Freshmen *Admission:* 90 applied, 15 admitted, 10 enrolled. *Average high school GPA:* 2.9. *Test scores:* SAT verbal scores over 500: 100%; SAT math scores over 500: 100%.

Faculty *Total:* 25, 40% full-time, 32% with terminal degrees. *Student/faculty ratio:* 10:1.

Majors Health professions related; nursing (registered nurse training).

Academics *Calendar:* semesters. *Degree:* associate. *Special study options:* academic remediation for entering students, advanced placement credit, cooperative education, distance learning, honors programs, off-campus study, part-time degree program, services for LD students, summer session for credit.

Library Phillips Health Science Library with 12,000 titles, 950 serial subscriptions, an OPAC.

Student Life *Housing:* college housing not available. *Activities and Organizations:* student-run newspaper, choral group, Student Government Organization, National Student Nurses Association. *Campus security:* 24-hour emergency response devices. *Student services:* health clinic, personal/psychological counseling.

Standardized Tests *Required:* nursing exam (for admission). *Recommended:* SAT (for admission).

Costs (2010–11) *Tuition:* $15,580 full-time, $380 per credit part-time. Full-time tuition and fees vary according to course load. Part-time tuition and fees vary according to course load. *Required fees:* $2590 full-time. *Payment plan:* installment. *Waivers:* employees or children of employees.

Financial Aid *Financial aid deadline:* 6/1.

Applying *Options:* deferred entrance. *Application fee:* $50. *Required:* essay or personal statement, high school transcript, minimum 2.5 GPA, 2 letters of recommendation, interview, entrance exam. *Notification:* continuous (freshmen), continuous (transfers).

Freshman Application Contact Mrs. Bernice Pass-Stern, Assistant Dean, Phillips Beth Israel School of Nursing, 310 East 22nd Street, 9th Floor, New York, NY 10010-5702. *Phone:* 212-614-6176. *Fax:* 212-614-6109. *E-mail:* bstern@bethisraelny.org.

Plaza College

Jackson Heights, New York www.plazacollege.edu/

- **Proprietary** primarily 2-year, founded 1916
- **Urban** campus with easy access to New York City
- **Coed,** 776 undergraduate students

Freshmen *Admission:* 1,138 applied.

Majors Accounting technology and bookkeeping; administrative assistant and secretarial science; allied health and medical assisting services related; business administration and management; health information/medical records technology.

Academics *Calendar:* semesters. *Degrees:* associate and bachelor's. *Special study options:* academic remediation for entering students, English as a second language, internships, services for LD students, summer session for credit.

Student Life *Housing:* college housing not available. *Campus security:* 24-hour emergency response devices.

Plaza College (continued)

Standardized Tests *Required:* CPAt (for admission).

Costs (2010–11) *One-time required fee:* $100. *Tuition:* $9900 full-time. Full-time tuition and fees vary according to program. Part-time tuition and fees vary according to course load and program. *Required fees:* $1450 full-time. *Payment plan:* installment. *Waivers:* employees or children of employees.

Applying *Options:* electronic application. *Application fee:* $100. *Required:* essay or personal statement, interview, placement test. *Application deadlines:* rolling (freshmen), rolling (transfers).

Freshman Application Contact Dean Rose Ann Black, Dean of Administration, Plaza College, 7409 37th Avenue, Jackson Heights, NY 11372-6300. *Phone:* 718-779-1430. *Toll-free phone:* 877-752-9233. *E-mail:* info@plazacollege.edu.

Queensborough Community College of the City University of New York

Bayside, New York www.qcc.cuny.edu/

Freshman Application Contact Ms. Ann Tullio, Director of Registration, Queensborough Community College of the City University of New York, 222-05 56th Avenue, Bayside, NY 11364. *Phone:* 718-631-6307. *Fax:* 718-281-5189.

Rockland Community College

Suffern, New York www.sunyrockland.edu/

- **State and locally supported** 2-year, founded 1959, part of State University of New York System
- **Suburban** 150-acre campus with easy access to New York City
- **Coed,** 6,984 undergraduate students, 62% full-time, 55% women, 45% men

Undergraduates 4,314 full-time, 2,670 part-time. 2% are from out of state, 21% African American, 6% Asian American or Pacific Islander, 14% Hispanic American, 0.3% Native American, 3% international, 7% transferred in. *Retention:* 69% of 2008 full-time freshmen returned.

Freshmen *Admission:* 1,422 enrolled.

Majors Accounting; administrative assistant and secretarial science; advertising; applied art; art; automobile/automotive mechanics technology; biological and physical sciences; business administration and management; commercial and advertising art; computer and information sciences related; computer graphics; computer/information technology services administration related; computer programming; computer programming related; computer programming (specific applications); computer systems networking and telecommunications; criminal justice/law enforcement administration; culinary arts; data processing and data processing technology; developmental and child psychology; dietetics; drafting and design technology; dramatic/theater arts; electrical, electronic and communications engineering technology; emergency medical technology (EMT paramedic); finance; fine/studio arts; fire science; health information/medical records administration; hospitality administration; human services; liberal arts and sciences/liberal studies; marketing/marketing management; mass communication/media; mathematics; nursing (registered nurse training); occupational therapy; photography; respiratory care therapy; system administration; tourism and travel services management.

Academics *Calendar:* semesters. *Degree:* certificates and associate. *Special study options:* academic remediation for entering students, adult/continuing education programs, advanced placement credit, cooperative education, distance learning, double majors, English as a second language, honors programs, independent study, internships, part-time degree program, services for LD students, student-designed majors, study abroad, summer session for credit.

Library Rockland Community College Library with an OPAC.

Student Life *Housing:* college housing not available. *Activities and Organizations:* drama/theater group, student-run newspaper, television station, choral group. *Campus security:* 24-hour emergency response devices and patrols, student patrols, late-night transport/escort service. *Student services:* personal/psychological counseling, legal services.

Athletics Member NJCAA. *Intercollegiate sports:* baseball M(s), basketball M/W, bowling M/W, golf M(s), soccer M/W, softball W, tennis M/W, volleyball W. *Intramural sports:* basketball M/W, bowling M/W, field hockey M/W, football M/W, golf M, racquetball M/W, soccer M/W, softball M/W, tennis M/W, volleyball M/W.

Financial Aid Of all full-time matriculated undergraduates who enrolled in 2008, 69 Federal Work-Study jobs (averaging $2208).

Applying *Options:* early admission, deferred entrance. *Required:* high school transcript. *Application deadlines:* rolling (freshmen), rolling (transfers).

Freshman Application Contact Rockland Community College, 145 College Road, Suffern, NY 10901-3699. *Phone:* 845-574-4237. *Toll-free phone:* 800-722-7666.

St. Elizabeth College of Nursing

Utica, New York www.secon.edu/

- **Independent** 2-year, founded 1904, administratively affiliated with St. Elizabeth Medical Center
- **Small-town** campus with easy access to Syracuse
- **Coed,** 239 undergraduate students, 66% full-time, 86% women, 14% men
- 45% of applicants were admitted

Undergraduates 157 full-time, 82 part-time. Students come from 5 states and territories, 4 other countries, 2% are from out of state, 0.8% African American, 2% Asian American or Pacific Islander, 0.4% Hispanic American, 0.4% Native American, 4% international, 42% transferred in. *Retention:* 56% of 2008 full-time freshmen returned.

Freshmen *Admission:* 55 applied, 25 admitted, 19 enrolled. *Test scores:* SAT verbal scores over 500: 47%; SAT math scores over 500: 29%; ACT scores over 18: 100%.

Faculty *Total:* 21, 81% full-time. *Student/faculty ratio:* 10:1.

Majors Nursing (registered nurse training).

Academics *Calendar:* semesters. *Degree:* associate. *Special study options:* accelerated degree program, distance learning, off-campus study, part-time degree program, services for LD students, summer session for credit.

Student Life *Housing:* college housing not available. *Campus security:* 24-hour patrols. *Student services:* health clinic, personal/psychological counseling.

Standardized Tests *Recommended:* SAT or ACT (for admission).

Costs (2010–11) *Tuition:* $11,530 full-time, $325 per credit hour part-time. Full-time tuition and fees vary according to course load, program, and student level. Part-time tuition and fees vary according to course load, program, and student level. *Required fees:* $950 full-time, $475 per term part-time. *Payment plan:* installment. *Waivers:* employees or children of employees.

Applying *Application fee:* $65. *Required:* essay or personal statement, high school transcript, 2 letters of recommendation. *Recommended:* minimum 2.5 GPA. *Application deadline:* rolling (freshmen). *Notification:* continuous (freshmen).

Freshman Application Contact St. Elizabeth College of Nursing, 2215 Genesee Street, Utica, NY 13501. *Phone:* 315-798-8253.

St. Joseph's College of Nursing

Syracuse, New York www.sjhsyr.org/nursing/

- **Independent religious** 2-year, founded 1898
- **Urban** campus
- **Coed,** 293 undergraduate students

Undergraduates Students come from 2 states and territories, 3% African American, 1% Asian American or Pacific Islander, 2% Hispanic American, 2% Native American, 25% live on campus.

Freshmen *Admission:* 42 applied, 23 admitted. *Average high school GPA:* 3. *Test scores:* SAT verbal scores over 500: 56%; SAT math scores over 500: 50%; ACT scores over 18: 100%; ACT scores over 24: 1%.

Faculty *Total:* 29, 55% full-time. *Student/faculty ratio:* 9:1.

Majors Nursing (registered nurse training).

Academics *Calendar:* semesters. *Degree:* associate. *Special study options:* academic remediation for entering students, adult/continuing education programs, advanced placement credit, cooperative education, internships, part-time degree program, services for LD students.

Library St. Joseph's Hospital Health Center School of Nursing Library with 4,500 titles, 230 serial subscriptions, 500 audiovisual materials, an OPAC.

Student Life *Housing Options:* coed. Campus housing is university owned. Freshman applicants given priority for college housing. *Activities and Organizations:* New York State Student Nurse's Association, Syracuse Area Black Nurses Association, Student Body Organization. *Campus security:* 24-hour patrols. *Student services:* health clinic, personal/psychological counseling, legal services.

Standardized Tests *Required:* SAT or ACT (for admission).

Costs (2010–11) *Tuition:* $330 per credit hour part-time. Full-time tuition and fees vary according to course load. Part-time tuition and fees vary according to course load. *Payment plan:* installment. *Waivers:* employees or children of employees.

Applying *Options:* deferred entrance. *Application fee:* $50. *Required:* essay or personal statement, high school transcript, minimum 3 GPA, 2 letters of recommendation, interview.

Freshman Application Contact Ms. Rhonda Reader, Assistant Dean for Admissions, St. Joseph's College of Nursing, 206 Prospect Avenue, Syracuse, NY 13203. *Phone:* 315-448-5040. *Fax:* 315-448-5745. *E-mail:* collegeofnursing@sjhsyr.org.

St. Paul's School of Nursing

Flushing, New York **www.stpaulsschoolofnursing.com/**

Director of Admissions Nancy Wolinski, Chairperson of Admissions, St. Paul's School of Nursing, 30-50 Whitestone Expressway, Suite 400, Flushing, NY 11354. *Phone:* 718-357-0500 Ext. 131. *E-mail:* nwolinski@svcmcny.org.

Samaritan Hospital School of Nursing

Troy, New York **www.nehealth.com/**

Director of Admissions Ms. Jennifer Marrone, Student Services Coordinator, Samaritan Hospital School of Nursing, 2215 Burdett Avenue, Troy, NY 12180. *Phone:* 518-271-3734. *Fax:* 518-271-3303. *E-mail:* marronej@nehealth.com.

Schenectady County Community College

Schenectady, New York **www.sunysccc.edu/**

- **State and locally supported** 2-year, founded 1969, part of State University of New York System
- **Urban** 50-acre campus
- **Coed**

Academics *Calendar:* semesters. *Degree:* certificates and associate. *Special study options:* academic remediation for entering students, adult/continuing education programs, advanced placement credit, distance learning, double majors, English as a second language, honors programs, internships, off-campus study, part-time degree program, services for LD students, summer session for credit.

Student Life *Campus security:* 24-hour emergency response devices and patrols, late-night transport/escort service.

Athletics Member NJCAA.

Financial Aid Of all full-time matriculated undergraduates who enrolled in 2008, 50 Federal Work-Study jobs (averaging $2400).

Applying *Options:* electronic application, early admission, deferred entrance. *Required:* high school transcript.

Freshman Application Contact Mr. David Sampson, Director of Admissions, Schenectady County Community College, 78 Washington Avenue, Schenectady, NY 12305. *Phone:* 518-381-1370. *E-mail:* sampsodg@gw.sunysccc.edu.

Simmons Institute of Funeral Service

Syracuse, New York **www.simmonsinstitute.com/**

Freshman Application Contact Ms. Vera Wightman, Director of Admissions, Simmons Institute of Funeral Service, 1828 South Avenue, Syracuse, NY 13207. *Phone:* 315-475-5142. *Toll-free phone:* 800-727-3536. *Fax:* 315-475-3817. *E-mail:* admissions@simmonsinstitute.com.

State University of New York College of Environmental Science & Forestry, Ranger School

Wanakena, New York **www.esf.edu/**

Freshman Application Contact Ms. Susan Sanford, Director of Admissions, State University of New York College of Environmental Science & Forestry, Ranger School, Bray 106, Syracuse, NY 13210-2779. *Phone:* 315-470-6600. *Toll-free phone:* 800-777-7373. *Fax:* 315-470-6933. *E-mail:* esfinfo@esf.edu.

►**See page 470 for the College Close-Up.**

State University of New York College of Technology at Alfred

Alfred, New York **www.alfredstate.edu/**

- **State-supported** primarily 2-year, founded 1908, part of The State University of New York System
- **Rural** 1084-acre campus
- **Coed,** 3,539 undergraduate students, 90% full-time, 38% women, 62% men

Undergraduates 3,184 full-time, 355 part-time. Students come from 33 states and territories, 10 other countries, 6% are from out of state, 9% African American, 3% Asian American or Pacific Islander, 4% Hispanic American, 0.2% Native American, 8% transferred in, 67% live on campus.

Freshmen *Admission:* 5,699 applied, 3,483 admitted, 1,286 enrolled. *Average high school GPA:* 2.8.

Faculty *Total:* 201, 79% full-time. *Student/faculty ratio:* 18:1.

Majors Accounting; agricultural business and management; agriculture; animal sciences; animation, interactive technology, video graphics and special effects; architectural engineering technology; autobody/collision and repair technology; automobile/automotive mechanics technology; baking and pastry arts; biological and physical sciences; business administration and management; CAD/CADD drafting/design technology; carpentry; computer hardware engineering; computer/information technology services administration related; computer installation and repair technology; computer science; computer systems networking and telecommunications; construction engineering technology; court reporting; culinary arts; drafting and design technology; drafting/design engineering technologies related; electrical, electronics and communications engineering; electrical/electronics equipment installation and repair; electromechanical technology; engineering science; entrepreneurship; environmental studies; finance; forensic science and technology; health information/medical records administration; heating, air conditioning and refrigeration technology; heating, air conditioning, ventilation and refrigeration maintenance technology; heavy equipment maintenance technology; heavy/industrial equipment maintenance technologies related; humanities; human services; information technology; interior design; liberal arts and sciences/liberal studies; machine tool technology; marketing/marketing management; masonry; mechanical engineering/mechanical technology; nursing (registered nurse training); robotics technology; social sciences; sport and fitness administration/management; surveying engineering; veterinary/animal health technology; web/multimedia management and webmaster; welding technology.

Academics *Calendar:* semesters. *Degrees:* certificates, associate, and bachelor's. *Special study options:* academic remediation for entering students, adult/continuing education programs, advanced placement credit, cooperative education, distance learning, double majors, English as a second language, honors programs, independent study, internships, off-campus study, part-time degree program, services for LD students, student-designed majors, study abroad, summer session for credit. *ROTC:* Army (c).

Library Walter C. Hinkle Memorial Library plus 1 other with 64,151 titles, 79,605 serial subscriptions, 4,055 audiovisual materials, an OPAC, a Web page.

Student Life *Housing Options:* coed, men-only, women-only, disabled students. Campus housing is university owned. Freshman campus housing is guaranteed. *Activities and Organizations:* drama/theater group, student-run newspaper, radio station, choral group, Outdoor Recreation Club, International Club, intramural sports, Sustainability Club, Student Senate, national fraternities, national sororities. *Campus security:* 24-hour emergency response devices and patrols, late-night transport/escort service, controlled dormitory access, residence hall entrance guards. *Student services:* health clinic, personal/psychological counseling.

Athletics Member NJCAA. *Intercollegiate sports:* baseball M, basketball M/W, cross-country running M/W, football M, lacrosse M, soccer M/W, softball W, swimming and diving M/W, track and field M/W, volleyball W, wrestling M. *Intramural sports:* basketball M/W, equestrian sports W(c), fencing M/W,

State University of New York College of Technology at Alfred (continued)

football M/W, golf M/W, ice hockey M(c), rock climbing M/W, skiing (downhill) M/W, soccer M/W, softball M/W, tennis M/W, ultimate Frisbee M/W, volleyball M/W, water polo M/W.

Standardized Tests *Required for some:* SAT or ACT (for admission). *Recommended:* SAT or ACT (for admission).

Costs (2010–11) *Tuition:* $207 per credit hour part-time; state resident $4970 full-time; nonresident $8750 full-time, $365 per credit hour part-time. Full-time tuition and fees vary according to degree level. Part-time tuition and fees vary according to degree level. *Required fees:* $1192 full-time. *Room and board:* $9190. Room and board charges vary according to board plan and housing facility. *Payment plan:* installment. *Waivers:* senior citizens and employees or children of employees.

Financial Aid Of all full-time matriculated undergraduates who enrolled in 2009, 2,875 applied for aid, 2,531 were judged to have need, 75 had their need fully met. In 2009, 191 non-need-based awards were made. *Average percent of need met:* 64%. *Average financial aid package:* $12,452. *Average need-based loan:* $7987. *Average need-based gift aid:* $5248. *Average non-need-based aid:* $4982. *Average indebtedness upon graduation:* $25,987.

Applying *Options:* electronic application. *Application fee:* $40. *Required:* high school transcript, minimum 2 GPA. *Recommended:* essay or personal statement, interview. *Application deadlines:* rolling (freshmen), rolling (out-of-state freshmen), rolling (transfers). *Notification:* continuous (freshmen), continuous (out-of-state freshmen), continuous (transfers).

Freshman Application Contact Mrs. Deborah Goodrich, Associate Vice President for Enrollment Management, State University of New York College of Technology at Alfred, Huntington Administration Building, 10 Upper College Drive, Alfred, NY 14802. *Phone:* 607-587-4215. *Toll-free phone:* 800-4-ALFRED. *Fax:* 607-587-4299. *E-mail:* admissions@alfredstate.edu.

SUFFOLK COUNTY COMMUNITY COLLEGE

Selden, New York **www.sunysuffolk.edu/**

- **State and locally supported** 2-year, founded 1959, part of State University of New York System
- **Small-town** 500-acre campus with easy access to New York City
- **Coed,** 24,560 undergraduate students, 50% full-time, 55% women, 45% men

Undergraduates 12,200 full-time, 12,360 part-time. Students come from 14 states and territories, 1% are from out of state, 7% African American, 3% Asian American or Pacific Islander, 15% Hispanic American, 0.3% Native American, 0.9% international.

Freshmen *Average high school GPA:* 2.5. *Test scores:* SAT verbal scores over 500: 36%; SAT math scores over 500: 38%; ACT scores over 18: 30%; SAT verbal scores over 600: 8%; SAT math scores over 600: 8%; ACT scores over 24: 4%; SAT verbal scores over 700: 1%.

Faculty *Total:* 1,162, 27% full-time. *Student/faculty ratio:* 18:1.

Majors Accounting; art; automobile/automotive mechanics technology; biological and physical sciences; biology/biological sciences; business administration and management; chemistry; child development; civil engineering technology; communications systems installation and repair technology; computer and information sciences and support services related; computer programming; computer science; construction engineering technology; consumer merchandising/retailing management; criminal justice/law enforcement administration; criminal justice/police science; culinary arts; data processing and data processing technology; dietetics; drafting and design technology; dramatic/theater arts; electrical, electronic and communications engineering technology; engineering; engineering science; English; humanities; human services; information science/studies; information technology; interior design; journalism; kindergarten/preschool education; legal assistant/paralegal; liberal arts and sciences/liberal studies; marketing/marketing management; mathematics; music; nursing (registered nurse training); photographic and film/video technology; physical therapy; sign language interpretation and translation; social sciences; substance abuse/addiction counseling; women's studies.

Academics *Calendar:* semesters. *Degree:* certificates, diplomas, and associate. *Special study options:* academic remediation for entering students, adult/continuing education programs, advanced placement credit, cooperative education, distance learning, English as a second language, freshman honors college, honors programs, independent study, internships, off-campus study, part-time degree program, services for LD students, study abroad, summer session for credit. *ROTC:* Army (c).

Library 659 serial subscriptions, an OPAC, a Web page.

Student Life *Housing:* college housing not available. *Activities and Organizations:* drama/theater group, student-run newspaper, choral group. *Campus security:* 24-hour emergency response devices and patrols. *Student services:* personal/psychological counseling.

Athletics Member NJCAA. *Intercollegiate sports:* baseball M, basketball M/W, bowling M/W, cross-country running M/W, golf M/W, lacrosse M, soccer M, softball W, swimming and diving M/W, tennis M/W, track and field M/W, volleyball W.

Costs (2010–11) *Tuition:* area resident $4196 full-time, $158 per credit hour part-time; state resident $8392 full-time, $316 per credit hour part-time; nonresident $8392 full-time, $316 per credit hour part-time. *Payment plan:* installment.

Financial Aid Of all full-time matriculated undergraduates who enrolled in 2008, 109 Federal Work-Study jobs (averaging $1377).

Applying *Options:* electronic application, deferred entrance. *Application fee:* $35. *Required:* high school transcript. *Required for some:* interview. *Application deadlines:* rolling (freshmen), rolling (transfers). *Notification:* continuous (freshmen), continuous (transfers).

Freshman Application Contact Suffolk County Community College, 533 College Road, Selden, NY 11784-2899. *Phone:* 631-451-4000.

SULLIVAN COUNTY COMMUNITY COLLEGE

Loch Sheldrake, New York **www.sullivan.suny.edu/**

Freshman Application Contact Ms. Sari Rosenheck, Director of Admissions and Registration Services, Sullivan County Community College, 112 College Road, Loch Sheldrake, NY 12759. *Phone:* 845-434-5750 Ext. 4200. *Toll-free phone:* 800-577-5243. *Fax:* 845-434-4806. *E-mail:* sarir@sullivan.suny.edu.

TAYLOR BUSINESS INSTITUTE

New York, New York **www.tbiglobal.com/**

Freshman Application Contact Mr. Christopher Carbowell, Director of Admissions, Taylor Business Institute, 23 West 17th Street, 7th floor, New York, NY 10011. *Phone:* 212-229-1963. *Fax:* 212-229-2187.

TCI–THE COLLEGE OF TECHNOLOGY

New York, New York **www.tciedu.com/**

Freshman Application Contact Director of Admission, TCI–The College of Technology, 320 West 31st Street, New York, NY 10001-2705. *Phone:* 212-594-4000. *Toll-free phone:* 800-878-8246. *E-mail:* admissions@tcicollege.edu.

TOMPKINS CORTLAND COMMUNITY COLLEGE

Dryden, New York **www.TC3.edu/**

- **State and locally supported** 2-year, founded 1968, part of State University of New York System
- **Rural** 250-acre campus with easy access to Syracuse
- **Endowment** $7.3 million
- **Coed,** 3,699 undergraduate students, 78% full-time, 55% women, 45% men

Undergraduates 2,874 full-time, 825 part-time. Students come from 26 states and territories, 44 other countries, 1% are from out of state, 8% African American, 1% Asian American or Pacific Islander, 4% Hispanic American, 0.5% Native American, 3% international, 10% transferred in, 22% live on campus.

Freshmen *Admission:* 4,866 applied, 1,064 enrolled. *Average high school GPA:* 2.4.

Faculty *Total:* 312, 24% full-time, 21% with terminal degrees. *Student/faculty ratio:* 19:1.

Majors Accounting technology and bookkeeping; administrative assistant and secretarial science; biotechnology; business administration and management; business, management, and marketing related; child-care and support services management; commercial and advertising art; communication/speech communication and rhetoric; community organization and advocacy; computer and information sciences; computer and information sciences and support services related; construction trades related; creative writing; criminal justice/law enforcement administration; early childhood education; electrical, electronic and communications engineering technology; engineering; forensic science and technology; hotel/motel administration; humanities; information science/studies; international business/trade/commerce; kindergarten/preschool education; legal assistant/

paralegal; liberal arts and sciences/liberal studies; natural resources/conservation; nursing (registered nurse training); parks, recreation and leisure facilities management; parks, recreation, and leisure related; photography; radio and television broadcasting technology; sport and fitness administration/management; substance abuse/addiction counseling; web/multimedia management and webmaster.

Academics *Calendar:* semesters. *Degree:* certificates and associate. *Special study options:* academic remediation for entering students, adult/continuing education programs, advanced placement credit, cooperative education, distance learning, double majors, English as a second language, honors programs, independent study, internships, off-campus study, part-time degree program, services for LD students, study abroad, summer session for credit.

Library Gerald A. Barry Memorial Library plus 1 other with 51,700 titles, 291 serial subscriptions, 2,118 audiovisual materials, an OPAC, a Web page.

Student Life *Housing Options:* coed. Campus housing is provided by a third party. *Activities and Organizations:* drama/theater group, College Entertainment Board, Sport Management Club, Nursing Club, Media Club, Writer's Guild. *Campus security:* 24-hour patrols, late-night transport/escort service, controlled dormitory access, armed peace officers. *Student services:* health clinic, personal/psychological counseling.

Athletics Member NJCAA. *Intercollegiate sports:* baseball M, basketball M/W, golf M/W, lacrosse M, soccer M/W, softball W, volleyball W. *Intramural sports:* archery M/W, badminton M/W, basketball M/W, bowling M/W, football M/W, golf M/W, lacrosse M/W, racquetball M/W, skiing (cross-country) M/W, skiing (downhill) M/W, soccer M/W, softball M/W, squash M/W, swimming and diving M/W, table tennis M/W, tennis M/W, ultimate Frisbee M/W, volleyball M/W, water polo M/W, weight lifting M/W, wrestling M/W.

Costs (2009–10) *Tuition:* state resident $3580 full-time, $135 per credit hour part-time; nonresident $7460 full-time, $280 per credit hour part-time. Part-time tuition and fees vary according to course load. *Required fees:* $626 full-time, $35 per credit hour part-time. *Room and board:* $7500. Room and board charges vary according to board plan and housing facility. *Payment plans:* installment, deferred payment. *Waivers:* employees or children of employees.

Financial Aid Of all full-time matriculated undergraduates who enrolled in 2008, 150 Federal Work-Study jobs (averaging $1000). 150 state and other part-time jobs (averaging $1000).

Applying *Options:* electronic application, early admission, deferred entrance. *Application fee:* $15. *Required:* high school transcript. *Required for some:* essay or personal statement, interview. *Application deadlines:* rolling (freshmen), rolling (out-of-state freshmen), rolling (transfers). *Notification:* continuous (freshmen), continuous (out-of-state freshmen), continuous (transfers).

Freshman Application Contact Mr. Sandy Drumluk, Director of Admissions, Tompkins Cortland Community College, 170 North Street, PO Box 139, Dryden, NY 13053-0139. *Phone:* 607-844-8211. *Toll-free phone:* 888-567-8211. *Fax:* 607-844-6538. *E-mail:* admissions@tc3.edu.

Trocaire College

Buffalo, New York **www.trocaire.edu/**

Freshman Application Contact Mrs. Theresa Horner, Director of Records, Trocaire College, 360 Choate Avenue, Buffalo, NY 14220. *Phone:* 716-827-2459. *Fax:* 716-828-6107. *E-mail:* info@trocaire.edu.

Ulster County Community College

Stone Ridge, New York **www.sunyulster.edu/**

- **State and locally supported** 2-year, founded 1961, part of State University of New York System
- **Rural** 165-acre campus
- **Endowment** $4.9 million
- **Coed,** 3,540 undergraduate students, 50% full-time, 59% women, 41% men

Undergraduates 1,759 full-time, 1,781 part-time. Students come from 10 states and territories, 8 other countries, 6% African American, 1% Asian American or Pacific Islander, 8% Hispanic American, 0.7% Native American, 0.4% international, 6% transferred in.

Freshmen *Admission:* 618 applied, 618 admitted, 618 enrolled.

Faculty *Total:* 189, 35% full-time. *Student/faculty ratio:* 19:1.

Majors Accounting technology and bookkeeping; biology teacher education; business administration and management; chemistry teacher education; commercial and advertising art; communication/speech communication and rhetoric; community organization and advocacy; computer and information sciences; computer and information sciences and support services related; criminal justice/law enforcement administration; drafting/design engineering technologies related; dramatic/theater arts; engineering; kindergarten/preschool education; liberal arts and sciences/liberal studies; management information systems and services related; mathematics teacher education; natural resources/conservation; nursing (registered nurse training); parks, recreation and leisure facilities management; public administration and social service professions related; science teacher education; social studies teacher education; Spanish language teacher education; veterinary/animal health technology; visual and performing arts.

Academics *Calendar:* semesters. *Degree:* certificates, diplomas, and associate. *Special study options:* academic remediation for entering students, adult/continuing education programs, advanced placement credit, cooperative education, distance learning, double majors, English as a second language, honors programs, independent study, internships, off-campus study, part-time degree program, services for LD students, student-designed majors, study abroad, summer session for credit.

Library McDonald Dewitt Library with 86,597 titles, 202 serial subscriptions, 4,828 audiovisual materials, an OPAC, a Web page.

Student Life *Housing:* college housing not available. *Activities and Organizations:* drama/theater group, choral group, Vet Tech, Biology Club, Nursing Club, Business Club, Visual Arts Club. *Campus security:* 24-hour emergency response devices and patrols. *Student services:* personal/psychological counseling.

Athletics Member NJCAA. *Intercollegiate sports:* baseball M, basketball M/W, golf M, soccer M, softball W, tennis M, volleyball W.

Costs (2009–10) *Tuition:* state resident $3620 full-time, $135 per credit part-time; nonresident $7240 full-time, $270 per credit part-time. *Required fees:* $500 full-time, $45 per course part-time, $22 part-time.

Financial Aid Of all full-time matriculated undergraduates who enrolled in 2008, 125 Federal Work-Study jobs (averaging $1000).

Applying *Options:* electronic application, early admission, deferred entrance. *Required:* high school transcript. *Application deadlines:* rolling (freshmen), rolling (transfers). *Notification:* continuous (freshmen), continuous (transfers).

Freshman Application Contact Admissions Office, Ulster County Community College, Cottekill Road, Stone Ridge, NY. *Phone:* 845-687-5022. *Toll-free phone:* 800-724-0833. *E-mail:* admissionsoffice@sunyulster.edu.

Utica School of Commerce

Utica, New York **www.uscny.edu/**

Freshman Application Contact Senior Admissions Coordinator, Utica School of Commerce, 201 Bleecker Street, Utica, NY 13501. *Phone:* 315-733-2300. *Toll-free phone:* 800-321-4USC. *Fax:* 315-733-9281.

Westchester Community College

Valhalla, New York **www.sunywcc.edu/**

- **State and locally supported** 2-year, founded 1946, part of State University of New York System
- **Suburban** 218-acre campus with easy access to New York City
- **Coed,** 14,147 undergraduate students, 55% full-time, 55% women, 45% men

Undergraduates 7,789 full-time, 6,358 part-time. Students come from 12 states and territories, 57 other countries, 0.5% are from out of state, 20% African American, 5% Asian American or Pacific Islander, 22% Hispanic American, 0.8% Native American, 2% international, 9% transferred in.

Freshmen *Admission:* 8,886 applied, 8,886 admitted, 2,834 enrolled.

Faculty *Total:* 479, 35% full-time. *Student/faculty ratio:* 18:1.

Majors Accounting; administrative assistant and secretarial science; applied art; business administration and management; chemical engineering; child-care provision; child development; civil engineering technology; clinical laboratory science/medical technology; clinical/medical laboratory technology; community organization and advocacy; computer and information sciences; computer and information sciences and support services related; computer and information sciences related; computer and information systems security; computer science; computer systems networking and telecommunications; consumer merchandising/retailing management; corrections; culinary arts; dance; data processing and data processing technology; dietetics; education (multiple levels); electrical, electronic and communications engineering technology; emergency medical technology (EMT paramedic); engineering science; engineering technology; film/video and photographic arts related; finance; fine/studio arts; food technology and processing; humanities; information science/studies; international business/trade/commerce; legal assistant/paralegal; liberal arts and sciences/liberal studies; marketing/marketing management; mass communication/media; mechanical engineering/mechanical technology; nursing (registered nurse training); public administration; respiratory care therapy; social sciences; substance abuse/addiction counseling.

Academics *Calendar:* semesters. *Degree:* certificates and associate. *Special study options:* academic remediation for entering students, adult/continuing education programs, cooperative education, distance learning, double majors,

Westchester Community College (continued)

English as a second language, honors programs, independent study, internships, off-campus study, part-time degree program, services for LD students, student-designed majors, study abroad, summer session for credit.

Library Harold L. Drimmer Library plus 1 other with 190,772 titles, 452 serial subscriptions, 6,857 audiovisual materials, an OPAC, a Web page.

Student Life *Housing:* college housing not available. *Activities and Organizations:* drama/theater group, student-run newspaper, radio station, choral group, Deca Fashion Retail, Future Educators, Respiratory Club, Black Student Union, Diversity Action. *Campus security:* 24-hour emergency response devices and patrols, late-night transport/escort service. *Student services:* health clinic, personal/psychological counseling, women's center.

Athletics Member NJCAA. *Intercollegiate sports:* baseball M, basketball M/W, bowling M/W, golf M, soccer M, softball W, volleyball W. *Intramural sports:* badminton M/W, basketball M/W, softball M/W, swimming and diving M/W, tennis M/W, volleyball M/W, weight lifting M/W.

Costs (2010–11) *Tuition:* state resident $3650 full-time, $153 per credit part-time; nonresident $9126 full-time, $383 per credit part-time. *Required fees:* $363 full-time, $83 per term part-time.

Financial Aid Of all full-time matriculated undergraduates who enrolled in 2008, 200 Federal Work-Study jobs (averaging $1000).

Applying *Options:* early admission. *Application fee:* $25. *Required:* high school transcript. *Recommended:* interview. *Application deadlines:* rolling (freshmen), rolling (transfers). *Notification:* continuous until 2/2 (freshmen), continuous (transfers).

Freshman Application Contact Ms. Gloria Leon, Director of Admissions, Westchester Community College, 75 Grasslands Road, Administration Building, Valhalla, NY 10595-1698. *Phone:* 914-606-6735. *Fax:* 914-606-6540. *E-mail:* admissions@sunywcc.edu.

WOOD TOBE–COBURN SCHOOL

New York, New York **www.woodtobecoburn.edu/**

- **Private** 2-year, founded 1879, part of Bradford Schools, Inc.
- **Urban** campus
- **Coed, primarily women,** 305 undergraduate students
- 84% of applicants were admitted

Freshmen *Admission:* 836 applied, 702 admitted.

Majors Accounting and business/management; business administration and management; computer programming; fashion/apparel design; fashion merchandising; graphic design; medical/clinical assistant; system, networking, and LAN/WAN management; tourism and travel services management.

Academics *Calendar:* semesters. *Degree:* diplomas and associate. *Special study options:* accelerated degree program, internships.

Student Life *Housing:* college housing not available.

Freshman Application Contact Admissions Office, Wood Tobe–Coburn School, 8 East 40th Street, New York, NY 10016. *Phone:* 212-686-9040. *Toll-free phone:* 800-394-9663.

NORTH CAROLINA

ALAMANCE COMMUNITY COLLEGE

Graham, North Carolina **www.alamancecc.edu/**

- **State-supported** 2-year, founded 1959, part of North Carolina Community College System
- **Small-town** 48-acre campus
- **Endowment** $2.9 million
- **Coed,** 5,483 undergraduate students, 50% full-time, 65% women, 35% men

Undergraduates 2,717 full-time, 2,766 part-time. Students come from 6 states and territories, 1% are from out of state, 23% African American, 2% Asian American or Pacific Islander, 3% Hispanic American, 0.9% Native American, 18% transferred in.

Freshmen *Admission:* 699 applied, 699 admitted, 699 enrolled. *Average high school GPA:* 2.

Faculty *Total:* 386, 26% full-time, 3% with terminal degrees. *Student/faculty ratio:* 12:1.

Majors Accounting technology and bookkeeping; animal sciences; applied horticulture; automobile/automotive mechanics technology; banking and financial support services; biotechnology; business administration and management; carpentry; clinical/medical laboratory technology; commercial and advertising art; criminal justice/safety; culinary arts; electrical, electronic and communications engineering technology; executive assistant/executive secretary; heating, air conditioning and refrigeration technology; information science/studies; kindergarten/preschool education; legal administrative assistant/secretary; liberal arts and sciences/liberal studies; machine tool technology; mechanical engineering/mechanical technology; medical administrative assistant and medical secretary; medical/clinical assistant; nursing (registered nurse training); office occupations and clerical services; retailing; teacher assistant/aide; welding technology.

Academics *Calendar:* semesters. *Degree:* certificates, diplomas, and associate. *Special study options:* academic remediation for entering students, adult/continuing education programs, cooperative education, distance learning, double majors, English as a second language, independent study, off-campus study, part-time degree program, services for LD students, summer session for credit.

Library Learning Resources Center with 22,114 titles, 185 serial subscriptions, an OPAC, a Web page.

Student Life *Housing:* college housing not available. *Campus security:* 24-hour emergency response devices and patrols, student patrols, late-night transport/escort service. *Student services:* personal/psychological counseling.

Athletics *Intramural sports:* basketball M/W, bowling M/W, tennis M/W, volleyball M/W.

Costs (2009–10) *Tuition:* state resident $1600 full-time, $50 per credit hour part-time; nonresident $7720 full-time, $241 per credit hour part-time. Full-time tuition and fees vary according to course load. Part-time tuition and fees vary according to course load. *Required fees:* $30 full-time, $5 per term part-time. *Waivers:* senior citizens.

Financial Aid Of all full-time matriculated undergraduates who enrolled in 2009, 4,000 applied for aid, 3,500 were judged to have need. *Average percent of need met:* 30%. *Average financial aid package:* $4500. *Average need-based gift aid:* $4500.

Applying *Options:* electronic application. *Required:* high school transcript. *Application deadlines:* rolling (freshmen), rolling (transfers). *Notification:* continuous (freshmen), continuous (transfers).

Freshman Application Contact Ms. Elizabeth Brehler, Director for Enrollment Management, Alamance Community College, Jimmy Kerr Road, Graham, NC 27253-8000. *Phone:* 336-506-4120. *Fax:* 336-506-4264. *E-mail:* brehlere@alamancecc.edu.

ASHEVILLE-BUNCOMBE TECHNICAL COMMUNITY COLLEGE

Asheville, North Carolina **www.abtech.edu/**

Freshman Application Contact Ms. Lisa Bush, Director, Admissions, Asheville-Buncombe Technical Community College, 340 Victoria Road, Asheville, NC 28801. *Phone:* 828-254-1921 Ext. 202. *E-mail:* lbush@abtech.edu.

BEAUFORT COUNTY COMMUNITY COLLEGE

Washington, North Carolina **www.beaufortccc.edu/**

- **State-supported** 2-year, founded 1967, part of North Carolina Community College System
- **Rural** 67-acre campus
- **Coed,** 1,923 undergraduate students

Undergraduates 1% are from out of state, 35% African American, 0.1% Asian American or Pacific Islander, 2% Hispanic American, 0.3% Native American.

Freshmen *Admission:* 1,048 applied, 1,048 admitted.

Majors Accounting; administrative assistant and secretarial science; automobile/automotive mechanics technology; business administration and management; clinical/medical laboratory technology; computer programming; criminal justice/law enforcement administration; criminal justice/police science; drafting and design technology; electrical, electronic and communications engineering technology; heavy equipment maintenance technology; information science/studies; kindergarten/preschool education; liberal arts and sciences/liberal studies; mechanical engineering/mechanical technology; medical office management; nursing (registered nurse training); welding technology.

Academics *Calendar:* semesters. *Degree:* certificates, diplomas, and associate. *Special study options:* academic remediation for entering students, advanced placement credit, cooperative education, distance learning, English as a second language, off-campus study, part-time degree program, services for LD students, summer session for credit.

Library Beaufort Community College Library with 25,734 titles, 214 serial subscriptions, an OPAC, a Web page.

Student Life *Housing:* college housing not available. *Activities and Organizations:* Student Government Association, Gamma Beta Phi, BECANS-Nursing, Hope Club-Human Services. *Campus security:* 24-hour emergency response devices and patrols, late-night transport/escort service. *Student services:* personal/psychological counseling.

Standardized Tests *Required:* Accuplacer, Compass, Asset (for admission). *Recommended:* SAT or ACT (for admission).

Costs (2009–10) *Tuition:* state resident $1600 full-time, $50 per credit hour part-time; nonresident $7722 full-time, $241 per credit hour part-time. Part-time tuition and fees vary according to course load. *Required fees:* $64 full-time, $2 per credit hour part-time. *Waivers:* senior citizens and employees or children of employees.

Applying *Options:* electronic application. *Required for some:* high school transcript. *Application deadlines:* rolling (freshmen), rolling (out-of-state freshmen), rolling (transfers). *Notification:* continuous (freshmen), continuous (out-of-state freshmen), continuous (transfers).

Freshman Application Contact Mr. Gary Burbage, Director of Admissions, Beaufort County Community College, PO Box 1069, 5337 US Highway 264 East, Washington, NC 27889-1069. *Phone:* 252-940-6233. *Fax:* 252-940-6393. *E-mail:* garyb@beaufortccc.edu.

BLADEN COMMUNITY COLLEGE

Dublin, North Carolina **www.bladen.cc.nc.us/**

- **State and locally supported** 2-year, founded 1967, part of North Carolina Community College System
- **Rural** 45-acre campus
- **Endowment** $72,151
- **Coed,** 1,736 undergraduate students

Undergraduates Students come from 3 states and territories, 43% African American, 0.1% Asian American or Pacific Islander, 1% Hispanic American, 15% Native American. *Retention:* 35% of 2008 full-time freshmen returned.

Freshmen *Average high school GPA:* 2.6.

Faculty *Total:* 85, 41% full-time, 5% with terminal degrees.

Majors Administrative assistant and secretarial science; biotechnology; business administration and management; child-care provision; computer programming; computer programming (specific applications); cosmetology; criminal justice/police science; electrical, electronic and communications engineering technology; general studies; industrial technology; information technology; liberal arts and sciences/liberal studies; nursing (registered nurse training); welding technology.

Academics *Calendar:* semesters. *Degree:* certificates, diplomas, and associate. *Special study options:* academic remediation for entering students, adult/continuing education programs, advanced placement credit, distance learning, double majors, independent study, part-time degree program, services for LD students, summer session for credit.

Library Learning Resource Center with 19,881 titles, 52 serial subscriptions, 2,364 audiovisual materials, an OPAC, a Web page.

Student Life *Housing:* college housing not available. *Activities and Organizations:* Student Government Association, National Honors English Society, History Club, Criminal Justice Club, Bladen Community College Gospel Choir. *Campus security:* 14-hour patrols. *Student services:* personal/psychological counseling.

Standardized Tests *Required:* ACT COMPASS (for admission). *Recommended:* SAT or ACT (for admission).

Costs (2010–11) *Tuition:* state resident $1200 full-time; nonresident $5791 full-time. Full-time tuition and fees vary according to course load. Part-time tuition and fees vary according to course load. *Required fees:* $83 full-time. *Waivers:* senior citizens.

Financial Aid Of all full-time matriculated undergraduates who enrolled in 2008, 30 Federal Work-Study jobs (averaging $1200).

Applying *Options:* electronic application, deferred entrance. *Required:* high school transcript. *Notification:* continuous until 8/15 (freshmen), continuous until 8/15 (transfers).

Freshman Application Contact Ms. Andrea Fisher, Enrollment Specialist, Bladen Community College, PO Box 266, Dublin, NC 28332. *Phone:* 910-879-5593. *Fax:* 910-879-5564. *E-mail:* acarterfisher@bladencc.edu.

BLUE RIDGE COMMUNITY COLLEGE

Flat Rock, North Carolina **www.blueridge.edu/**

- **State and locally supported** 2-year, founded 1969, part of North Carolina Community College System
- **Small-town** 109-acre campus
- **Coed,** 2,488 undergraduate students, 31% full-time, 57% women, 43% men

Undergraduates 766 full-time, 1,722 part-time. Students come from 6 states and territories, 1% are from out of state, 4% African American, 0.9% Asian American or Pacific Islander, 5% Hispanic American, 0.4% Native American.

Freshmen *Admission:* 350 enrolled.

Majors Agricultural business technology; applied horticulture; automobile/automotive mechanics technology; business administration and management; child-care and support services management; computer and information sciences and support services related; computer programming; computer programming related; computer systems analysis; cosmetology; early childhood education; electrical, electronic and communications engineering technology; electromechanical technology; environmental science; executive assistant/executive secretary; general studies; heavy/industrial equipment maintenance technologies related; humanities; information science/studies; information technology; liberal arts and sciences/liberal studies; machine tool technology; marketing/marketing management; mechanical engineering/mechanical technology; mechanical engineering technologies related; nursing (registered nurse training); retailing; sign language interpretation and translation; special education (early childhood); surgical technology; system, networking, and LAN/WAN management; teacher assistant/aide; tourism and travel services management; tourism promotion; water quality and wastewater treatment management and recycling technology; welding technology.

Academics *Calendar:* semesters. *Degree:* certificates, diplomas, and associate. *Special study options:* academic remediation for entering students, adult/continuing education programs, advanced placement credit, cooperative education, distance learning, double majors, English as a second language, internships, part-time degree program, services for LD students, summer session for credit.

Library Blue Ridge Community College Library plus 1 other with 47,655 titles, 3,875 serial subscriptions, 1,692 audiovisual materials, an OPAC.

Student Life *Housing:* college housing not available. *Activities and Organizations:* drama/theater group, student-run newspaper. *Campus security:* sheriff's deputy during class hours. *Student services:* personal/psychological counseling.

Athletics Member NJCAA. *Intercollegiate sports:* baseball M, volleyball W.

Financial Aid Of all full-time matriculated undergraduates who enrolled in 2008, 35 Federal Work-Study jobs (averaging $1920). 34 state and other part-time jobs (averaging $1920).

Applying *Options:* early admission. *Required:* high school transcript. *Application deadlines:* rolling (freshmen), rolling (transfers). *Notification:* continuous (freshmen), continuous (transfers).

Freshman Application Contact Blue Ridge Community College, 180 West Campus Drive, Flat Rock, NC 28731. *Phone:* 828-694-1810.

BRUNSWICK COMMUNITY COLLEGE

Supply, North Carolina **www.brunswickcc.edu/**

Freshman Application Contact Ms. Julie Olsen, Admissions Counselor, Brunswick Community College, PO Box 30, Supply, NC 28462. *Phone:* 910-755-7324. *Toll-free phone:* 800-754-1050 Ext. 324. *Fax:* 910-754-9609. *E-mail:* olsenj@brunswickcc.edu.

CALDWELL COMMUNITY COLLEGE AND TECHNICAL INSTITUTE

Hudson, North Carolina **www.cccti.edu/**

Freshman Application Contact Carolyn Woodard, Director of Enrollment Management Services, Caldwell Community College and Technical Institute, 2855 Hickory Boulevard, Hudson, NC 28638. *Phone:* 828-726-2703. *Fax:* 828-726-2709. *E-mail:* cwoodard@cccti.edu.

Cape Fear Community College

Wilmington, North Carolina **www.cfcc.edu/**

- **State-supported** 2-year, founded 1959, part of North Carolina Community College System
- **Urban** 150-acre campus
- **Endowment** $3.6 million
- **Coed,** 8,989 undergraduate students, 44% full-time, 54% women, 46% men

Undergraduates 3,984 full-time, 5,005 part-time. Students come from 42 states and territories, 9% are from out of state, 15% African American, 1% Asian American or Pacific Islander, 3% Hispanic American, 0.8% Native American, 0.2% international, 29% transferred in. *Retention:* 64% of 2008 full-time freshmen returned.

Freshmen *Admission:* 1,612 enrolled.

Faculty *Total:* 495, 52% full-time, 6% with terminal degrees. *Student/faculty ratio:* 15:1.

Majors Accounting technology and bookkeeping; architectural engineering technology; automobile/automotive mechanics technology; building/property maintenance and management; business administration and management; chemical technology; cinematography and film/video production; computer systems networking and telecommunications; computer technology/computer systems technology; criminal justice/police science; culinary arts; dental hygiene; diagnostic medical sonography and ultrasound technology; early childhood education; electrical, electronic and communications engineering technology; electrical/electronics equipment installation and repair; electromechanical and instrumentation and maintenance technologies related; executive assistant/executive secretary; hotel/motel administration; instrumentation technology; interior design; landscaping and groundskeeping; legal assistant/paralegal; liberal arts and sciences/liberal studies; machine shop technology; marine maintenance and ship repair technology; marine technology; mechanical engineering/mechanical technology; medical office management; medical radiologic technology; nuclear/nuclear power technology; nursing (registered nurse training); occupational therapist assistant; surgical technology.

Academics *Calendar:* semesters. *Degree:* certificates, diplomas, and associate. *Special study options:* academic remediation for entering students, adult/continuing education programs, advanced placement credit, cooperative education, distance learning, double majors, English as a second language, independent study, off-campus study, part-time degree program, services for LD students, summer session for credit.

Library Cape Fear Community College Library with 47,352 titles, 581 serial subscriptions, 7,175 audiovisual materials, an OPAC, a Web page.

Student Life *Housing:* college housing not available. *Activities and Organizations:* student-run newspaper, choral group, Nursing Club, Dental Hygiene Club, Pineapple Guild, Phi Theta Kappa, Occupational Therapy. *Campus security:* 24-hour emergency response devices and patrols, late-night transport/escort service, armed police officer. *Student services:* personal/psychological counseling.

Athletics Member NJCAA. *Intercollegiate sports:* basketball M, cheerleading M/W, golf M/W, soccer M/W, volleyball M/W. *Intramural sports:* softball M/W, tennis M/W.

Costs (2009–10) *Tuition:* state resident $1600 full-time, $50 per credit part-time; nonresident $7722 full-time, $241 per credit part-time. Full-time tuition and fees vary according to course load. Part-time tuition and fees vary according to course load. *Required fees:* $137 full-time. *Payment plan:* deferred payment. *Waivers:* senior citizens and employees or children of employees.

Financial Aid Of all full-time matriculated undergraduates who enrolled in 2009, 92 Federal Work-Study jobs (averaging $2389).

Applying *Options:* electronic application, early admission. *Required for some:* high school transcript, interview, placement testing. *Application deadlines:* 8/15 (freshmen), rolling (transfers). *Notification:* continuous (freshmen), continuous (transfers).

Freshman Application Contact Ms. Linda Kasyan, Director of Enrollment Management, Cape Fear Community College, 411 North Front Street, Wilmington, NC 28401-3993. *Phone:* 910-362-7054. *Toll-free phone:* 910-362-7557. *Fax:* 910-362-7080. *E-mail:* admissions@cfcc.edu.

Carolinas College of Health Sciences

Charlotte, North Carolina **www.carolinascollege.edu/**

- **Independent** 2-year, founded 1990
- **Urban** 3-acre campus with easy access to Charlotte
- **Endowment** $1.4 million
- **Coed,** 510 undergraduate students, 20% full-time, 88% women, 12% men

Undergraduates 101 full-time, 409 part-time. Students come from 2 states and territories, 8% are from out of state, 9% African American, 1% Asian American or Pacific Islander, 3% Hispanic American, 0.8% Native American, 30% transferred in.

Freshmen *Admission:* 801 applied, 202 admitted, 8 enrolled. *Average high school GPA:* 3.35.

Faculty *Total:* 71, 37% full-time. *Student/faculty ratio:* 7:1.

Majors Medical radiologic technology; nursing (registered nurse training); radiologic technology/science.

Academics *Calendar:* semesters. *Degree:* certificates, diplomas, and associate. *Special study options:* advanced placement credit, distance learning, independent study, services for LD students, summer session for credit.

Library AHEC Library with 9,810 titles, 503 serial subscriptions, an OPAC, a Web page.

Student Life *Housing Options:* Campus housing is provided by a third party. *Campus security:* 24-hour emergency response devices and patrols, late-night transport/escort service. *Student services:* health clinic, personal/psychological counseling.

Standardized Tests *Required for some:* SAT or ACT (for admission).

Costs (2010–11) *Tuition:* $7848 full-time, $218 per credit hour part-time. Full-time tuition and fees vary according to course load and program. Part-time tuition and fees vary according to course load and program. *Required fees:* $215 full-time, $110 per term part-time. *Waivers:* employees or children of employees.

Financial Aid Of all full-time matriculated undergraduates who enrolled in 2008, 5 Federal Work-Study jobs (averaging $5500).

Applying *Options:* electronic application. *Application fee:* $50. *Required:* high school transcript. *Required for some:* minimum 2.5 GPA, interview, SAT or ACT scores. *Recommended:* minimum 2.5 GPA.

Freshman Application Contact Ms. Nicki Sabourin, Admissions Representative, Carolinas College of Health Sciences, PO Box 32861, Charlotte, NC 28232-2861. *Phone:* 704-355-5043. *Fax:* 704-355-9336. *E-mail:* cchsinformation@carolinashealthcare.org.

Carteret Community College

Morehead City, North Carolina **www.carteret.edu/**

- **State-supported** 2-year, founded 1963, part of North Carolina Community College System
- **Small-town** 25-acre campus
- **Coed,** 1,872 undergraduate students, 43% full-time, 69% women, 31% men

Undergraduates 804 full-time, 1,068 part-time. Students come from 27 states and territories, 2 other countries, 10% African American, 1% Asian American or Pacific Islander, 3% Hispanic American, 0.3% Native American, 8% transferred in. *Retention:* 52% of 2008 full-time freshmen returned.

Freshmen *Admission:* 2,156 applied, 1,970 admitted, 304 enrolled.

Faculty *Total:* 253, 26% full-time, 7% with terminal degrees. *Student/faculty ratio:* 9:1.

Majors Administrative assistant and secretarial science; business administration and management; computer engineering technology; computer software and media applications related; computer systems networking and telecommunications; criminal justice/law enforcement administration; industrial radiologic technology; information technology; interior design; legal administrative assistant/secretary; legal assistant/paralegal; liberal arts and sciences/liberal studies; medical/clinical assistant; nursing (licensed practical/vocational nurse training); photography; respiratory care therapy; teacher assistant/aide.

Academics *Calendar:* semesters. *Degree:* certificates, diplomas, and associate. *Special study options:* academic remediation for entering students, adult/continuing education programs, cooperative education, distance learning, double majors, internships, part-time degree program, services for LD students, summer session for credit.

Library Michael J. Smith Learning Resource Center with 22,000 titles, 168 serial subscriptions, an OPAC, a Web page.

Student Life *Housing:* college housing not available. *Activities and Organizations:* drama/theater group, student-run newspaper, Student Government Association, Medical Assisting Club, Respiratory Therapy Club, Radiography Club, Chess Club. *Campus security:* late-night transport/escort service, security service from 7 am until 11:30 pm.

Standardized Tests *Recommended:* SAT or ACT (for admission).

Costs (2010–11) *Tuition:* state resident $1628 full-time, $50 per credit hour part-time; nonresident $5854 full-time, $241 per credit hour part-time. Full-time tuition and fees vary according to course load and program. *Required fees:* $51 full-time, $19 per term part-time. *Waivers:* senior citizens and employees or children of employees.

Applying *Options:* electronic application. *Required:* high school transcript. *Required for some:* interview. *Application deadlines:* rolling (freshmen), rolling (out-of-state freshmen), rolling (transfers). *Notification:* continuous (freshmen), continuous (out-of-state freshmen), continuous (transfers).

Freshman Application Contact Ms. Margie Ward, Admissions Officer, Carteret Community College, 3505 Arendell Street, Morehead City, NC 28557-2989. *Phone:* 252-222-6155. *Fax:* 252-222-6265. *E-mail:* admissions@carteret.edu.

CATAWBA VALLEY COMMUNITY COLLEGE

Hickory, North Carolina **www.cvcc.cc.nc.us/**

- **State and locally supported** 2-year, founded 1960, part of North Carolina Community College System
- **Small-town** 50-acre campus with easy access to Charlotte
- **Endowment** $843,694
- **Coed,** 5,528 undergraduate students, 39% full-time, 58% women, 42% men

Undergraduates 2,135 full-time, 3,393 part-time. Students come from 9 states and territories, 1% are from out of state, 8% African American, 8% Asian American or Pacific Islander, 11% Hispanic American, 1% Native American, 0.1% international, 26% transferred in.

Freshmen *Admission:* 1,626 applied, 1,622 admitted, 1,134 enrolled. *Average high school GPA:* 2.89.

Faculty *Total:* 483, 30% full-time. *Student/faculty ratio:* 11:1.

Majors Accounting technology and bookkeeping; allied health diagnostic, intervention, and treatment professions related; applied horticulture; architectural engineering technology; automobile/automotive mechanics technology; banking and financial support services; business administration and management; commercial and advertising art; computer engineering technology; computer programming; computer systems networking and telecommunications; corrections and criminal justice related; criminal justice/safety; customer service management; dental hygiene; e-commerce; electrical, electronic and communications engineering technology; electromechanical and instrumentation and maintenance technologies related; emergency medical technology (EMT paramedic); fire protection and safety technology; forensic science and technology; funeral service and mortuary science; furniture design and manufacturing; general studies; health information/medical records technology; health services/allied health/health sciences; industrial engineering; information technology; legal assistant/paralegal; liberal arts and sciences/liberal studies; mechanical engineering/mechanical technology; medical office management; medical radiologic technology; nursing (registered nurse training); office management; operations management; photographic and film/video technology; real estate; respiratory care therapy; speech-language pathology; teacher assistant/aide; turf and turfgrass management.

Academics *Calendar:* semesters. *Degree:* certificates, diplomas, and associate. *Special study options:* academic remediation for entering students, adult/continuing education programs, advanced placement credit, cooperative education, distance learning, double majors, English as a second language, independent study, part-time degree program, services for LD students, student-designed majors, summer session for credit.

Library Learning Resource Center with 25,000 titles, 610 serial subscriptions, 700 audiovisual materials, an OPAC, a Web page.

Student Life *Housing:* college housing not available. *Activities and Organizations:* choral group, NCANS (Nursing), Phi Theta Kappa, Catawba Valley Outing Club, Respiratory Care Club, Rotaract. *Campus security:* 24-hour patrols. *Student services:* personal/psychological counseling.

Athletics Member NJCAA. *Intercollegiate sports:* baseball M, basketball M/W, volleyball W.

Costs (2010–11) *Tuition:* state resident $1600 full-time, $50 per credit hour part-time; nonresident $7723 full-time, $241 per credit hour part-time. Part-time tuition and fees vary according to course load. *Required fees:* $87 full-time, $44 per term part-time. *Payment plan:* installment. *Waivers:* senior citizens and employees or children of employees.

Applying *Options:* electronic application, early admission, deferred entrance. *Required:* high school transcript. *Application deadlines:* rolling (freshmen), rolling (out-of-state freshmen), rolling (transfers). *Notification:* continuous (freshmen), continuous (out-of-state freshmen), continuous (transfers).

Freshman Application Contact Catawba Valley Community College, 2550 Highway 70 SE, Hickory, NC 28602-9699. *Phone:* 828-327-7000 Ext. 4618.

CENTRAL CAROLINA COMMUNITY COLLEGE

Sanford, North Carolina **www.cccc.edu/**

- **State and locally supported** 2-year, founded 1962, part of North Carolina Community College System
- **Small-town** 41-acre campus
- **Endowment** $2.0 million
- **Coed,** 5,411 undergraduate students, 100% full-time, 64% women, 36% men

Undergraduates 5,411 full-time. Students come from 36 states and territories, 6% are from out of state.

Faculty *Total:* 500, 70% full-time. *Student/faculty ratio:* 10:1.

Majors Accounting; administrative assistant and secretarial science; automobile/automotive mechanics technology; business administration and management; computer/information technology services administration related; computer programming; computer programming (specific applications); computer systems networking and telecommunications; criminal justice/law enforcement administration; drafting and design technology; electrical, electronic and communications engineering technology; information science/studies; information technology; instrumentation technology; kindergarten/preschool education; laser and optical technology; legal administrative assistant/secretary; legal assistant/paralegal; liberal arts and sciences/liberal studies; marketing/marketing management; medical administrative assistant and medical secretary; medical/clinical assistant; nursing (registered nurse training); operations management; quality control technology; radio and television; social work; telecommunications technology; veterinary/animal health technology.

Academics *Calendar:* semesters. *Degree:* certificates, diplomas, and associate. *Special study options:* academic remediation for entering students, adult/continuing education programs, advanced placement credit, distance learning, double majors, English as a second language, independent study, internships, part-time degree program, services for LD students, summer session for credit.

Library Library/Learning Resources Center plus 2 others with 50,479 titles, 240 serial subscriptions, 5,946 audiovisual materials, an OPAC, a Web page.

Student Life *Housing:* college housing not available. *Activities and Organizations:* student-run radio station. *Campus security:* 24-hour emergency response devices and patrols, student patrols, patrols by trained security personnel during operating hours. *Student services:* personal/psychological counseling.

Athletics Member NJCAA. *Intercollegiate sports:* basketball M/W, golf M/W, softball W, volleyball W. *Intramural sports:* bowling M/W, golf M/W, softball W, volleyball W.

Costs (2009–10) *Tuition:* state resident $1594 full-time; nonresident $7329 full-time. Full-time tuition and fees vary according to course load. Part-time tuition and fees vary according to course load. *Payment plan:* installment. *Waivers:* senior citizens.

Financial Aid Of all full-time matriculated undergraduates who enrolled in 2008, 70 Federal Work-Study jobs (averaging $1361). *Financial aid deadline:* 5/4.

Applying *Options:* electronic application, early admission, deferred entrance. *Required:* high school transcript. *Application deadlines:* rolling (freshmen), rolling (transfers). *Notification:* continuous (freshmen), continuous (transfers).

Freshman Application Contact Ms. Michelle Wheeler, Registrar, Central Carolina Community College, 1105 Kelly Drive, Sanford, NC 27330. *Phone:* 919-718-7239. *Toll-free phone:* 800-682-8353 Ext. 7300. *Fax:* 919-718-7380.

CENTRAL PIEDMONT COMMUNITY COLLEGE

Charlotte, North Carolina **www.cpcc.edu/**

- **State and locally supported** 2-year, founded 1963, part of North Carolina Community College System
- **Urban** 37-acre campus
- **Endowment** $16.7 million
- **Coed,** 19,364 undergraduate students, 39% full-time, 56% women, 44% men

Undergraduates 7,630 full-time, 11,734 part-time. Students come from 13 states and territories, 117 other countries, 3% are from out of state, 31% African American, 3% Asian American or Pacific Islander, 5% Hispanic American, 0.4% Native American, 9% international, 11% transferred in.

Freshmen *Admission:* 2,243 applied, 2,243 admitted, 2,243 enrolled.

Faculty *Total:* 1,741, 19% full-time. *Student/faculty ratio:* 24:1.

Majors Accounting; administrative assistant and secretarial science; advertising; applied art; architectural engineering technology; art; automobile/automotive

Central Piedmont Community College (continued)

mechanics technology; biology/biological sciences; business administration and management; business machine repair; child development; civil engineering technology; clinical laboratory science/medical technology; clinical/medical laboratory technology; commercial and advertising art; computer engineering technology; computer programming; computer programming (specific applications); computer science; consumer merchandising/retailing management; criminal justice/law enforcement administration; criminal justice/police science; culinary arts; dance; data processing and data processing technology; dental hygiene; drafting and design technology; electrical, electronic and communications engineering technology; electromechanical technology; engineering technology; environmental engineering technology; fashion merchandising; finance; fire science; food science; food technology and processing; graphic and printing equipment operation/production; health/health-care administration; health information/medical records administration; horticultural science; hospitality administration; hotel/motel administration; human services; industrial technology; insurance; interior design; kindergarten/preschool education; legal administrative assistant/secretary; legal assistant/paralegal; liberal arts and sciences/liberal studies; machine tool technology; marketing/marketing management; mechanical engineering/mechanical technology; medical administrative assistant and medical secretary; medical/clinical assistant; music; nursing (licensed practical/vocational nurse training); nursing (registered nurse training); physical therapy; postal management; real estate; respiratory care therapy; sign language interpretation and translation; social work; special products marketing; survey technology; tourism and travel services management; transportation and materials moving related; welding technology.

Academics *Calendar:* semesters. *Degree:* certificates, diplomas, and associate. *Special study options:* academic remediation for entering students, accelerated degree program, advanced placement credit, cooperative education, distance learning, English as a second language, honors programs, off-campus study, part-time degree program, services for LD students, student-designed majors, summer session for credit.

Library Hagemeyer Learning Center plus 5 others with 102,649 titles, 750 serial subscriptions, 17,802 audiovisual materials, an OPAC, a Web page.

Student Life *Housing:* college housing not available. *Activities and Organizations:* drama/theater group, student-run newspaper, choral group, Phi Theta Kappa, Black Students Organization, Students for Environmental Sanity, Sierra Club, Nursing Club. *Campus security:* 24-hour emergency response devices and patrols. *Student services:* personal/psychological counseling, women's center.

Athletics Member NJCAA. *Intramural sports:* soccer M/W.

Costs (2009–10) *Tuition:* state resident $1500 full-time, $50 per semester hour part-time; nonresident $7722 full-time, $241 per semester hour part-time. *Required fees:* $218 full-time, $1 per credit hour part-time, $60 per term part-time. *Payment plan:* installment. *Waivers:* senior citizens and employees or children of employees.

Financial Aid Of all full-time matriculated undergraduates who enrolled in 2008, 99 Federal Work-Study jobs (averaging $2988).

Applying *Required:* high school transcript. *Application deadlines:* rolling (freshmen), rolling (out-of-state freshmen), rolling (transfers). *Notification:* continuous (freshmen), continuous (out-of-state freshmen), continuous (transfers).

Freshman Application Contact Ms. Linda McComb, Associate Dean, Central Piedmont Community College, PO Box 35009, Charlotte, NC 28235-5009. *Phone:* 704-330-6784. *Fax:* 704-330-6136.

CLEVELAND COMMUNITY COLLEGE

Shelby, North Carolina www.clevelandcommunitycollege.edu/

Freshman Application Contact Mr. Alan Price, Dean of Enrollment Management, Cleveland Community College, 137 South Post Road, Shelby, NC 28152. *Phone:* 704-484-4073. *Fax:* 704-484-5305. *E-mail:* price@cleveland.cc.nc.us.

COASTAL CAROLINA COMMUNITY COLLEGE

Jacksonville, North Carolina **www.coastalcarolina.edu/**

Freshman Application Contact Ms. Heather Calihan, Counseling Coordinator, Coastal Carolina Community College, 444 Western Boulevard, Jacksonville, NC 28546. *Phone:* 910-938-6241. *Fax:* 910-455-2767. *E-mail:* calihanh@coastal.cc.nc.us.

COLLEGE OF THE ALBEMARLE

Elizabeth City, North Carolina **www.albemarle.edu/**

Freshman Application Contact Mr. Kenny Krentz, Director of Admissions and International Students, College of The Albemarle, PO Box 2327, 1208 North Road Street, Elizabeth City, NC 27909-2327. *Phone:* 252-335-0821. *Fax:* 252-335-2011. *E-mail:* kkrentz@albemarle.edu.

CRAVEN COMMUNITY COLLEGE

New Bern, North Carolina **www.craven.cc.nc.us/**

- **State-supported** 2-year, founded 1965, part of North Carolina Community College System
- **Suburban** 100-acre campus
- **Coed**

Academics *Calendar:* semesters. *Degree:* certificates, diplomas, and associate. *Special study options:* academic remediation for entering students, adult/continuing education programs, advanced placement credit, cooperative education, distance learning, double majors, independent study, internships, part-time degree program, services for LD students, student-designed majors, summer session for credit.

Student Life *Campus security:* 24-hour patrols.

Costs (2009–10) *Tuition:* state resident $1600 full-time, $50 per credit hour part-time; nonresident $7722 full-time, $242 per credit hour part-time. Full-time tuition and fees vary according to course load. Part-time tuition and fees vary according to course load. *Required fees:* $60 full-time.

Financial Aid Of all full-time matriculated undergraduates who enrolled in 2008, 41 Federal Work-Study jobs (averaging $1898).

Applying *Required:* high school transcript, interview.

Freshman Application Contact Ms. Millicent Fulford, Recruiter, Craven Community College, 800 College Court, New Bern, NC 28562-4984. *Phone:* 252-638-7232.

DAVIDSON COUNTY COMMUNITY COLLEGE

Lexington, North Carolina **www.davidsonccc.edu/**

Freshman Application Contact Davidson County Community College, PO Box 1287, Lexington, NC 27293-1287. *Phone:* 336-249-8186 Ext. 6715. *Fax:* 336-224-0240. *E-mail:* admissions@davidsonccc.edu.

DURHAM TECHNICAL COMMUNITY COLLEGE

Durham, North Carolina **www.durhamtech.edu/**

- **State-supported** 2-year, founded 1961, part of North Carolina Community College System
- **Urban** campus
- **Coed**

Academics *Calendar:* semesters. *Degree:* certificates, diplomas, and associate. *Special study options:* academic remediation for entering students, accelerated degree program, adult/continuing education programs, advanced placement credit, cooperative education, distance learning, English as a second language, internships, off-campus study, part-time degree program, services for LD students, student-designed majors, summer session for credit.

Student Life *Campus security:* 24-hour patrols, late-night transport/escort service.

Financial Aid Of all full-time matriculated undergraduates who enrolled in 2008, 35 Federal Work-Study jobs (averaging $2000).

Applying *Options:* deferred entrance. *Required:* high school transcript. *Recommended:* interview.

Director of Admissions Ms. Penny Augustine, Director of Admissions and Testing, Durham Technical Community College, 1637 Lawson Street, Durham, NC 27703. *Phone:* 919-686-3619.

ECPI TECHNICAL COLLEGE

Raleigh, North Carolina **www.ecpi.edu/**

Freshman Application Contact Ms. Susan Wells, Campus President, ECPI Technical College, 4101 Doie Cope Road, Raleigh, NC 27613. *Phone:* 919-571-0057. *Toll-free phone:* 800-986-1200. *Fax:* 919-571-0780. *E-mail:* swells@ecpi.edu.

EDGECOMBE COMMUNITY COLLEGE

Tarboro, North Carolina **www.edgecombe.edu/**

- **State and locally supported** 2-year, founded 1968, part of North Carolina Community College System
- **Small-town** 90-acre campus
- **Coed**

Academics *Calendar:* semesters. *Degree:* certificates, diplomas, and associate. *Special study options:* academic remediation for entering students, adult/continuing education programs, advanced placement credit, cooperative education, distance learning, double majors, English as a second language, independent study, off-campus study, part-time degree program, services for LD students, summer session for credit.

Financial Aid Of all full-time matriculated undergraduates who enrolled in 2008, 45 Federal Work-Study jobs (averaging $800).

Applying *Options:* electronic application. *Required:* high school transcript, minimum 2.0 GPA.

Freshman Application Contact Ms. Jackie Heath, Admissions Officer, Edgecombe Community College, 2009 West Wilson Street, Tarboro, NC 27886. *Phone:* 252-823-5166 Ext. 254.

FAYETTEVILLE TECHNICAL COMMUNITY COLLEGE

Fayetteville, North Carolina **www.faytechcc.edu/**

- **State-supported** 2-year, founded 1961, part of North Carolina Community College System
- **Suburban** 267-acre campus with easy access to Raleigh
- **Endowment** $14,543
- **Coed,** 11,203 undergraduate students, 31% full-time, 70% women, 30% men

Undergraduates 3,496 full-time, 7,707 part-time. Students come from 32 states and territories, 2% are from out of state, 45% African American, 2% Asian American or Pacific Islander, 7% Hispanic American, 3% Native American, 0.3% international, 19% transferred in.

Freshmen *Admission:* 6,686 applied, 6,686 admitted, 2,321 enrolled. *Average high school GPA:* 2.44.

Faculty *Total:* 772, 39% full-time. *Student/faculty ratio:* 13:1.

Majors Accounting; applied horticulture; architectural engineering technology; automobile/automotive mechanics technology; banking and financial support services; biology/biotechnology laboratory technician; building/construction finishing, management, and inspection related; business administration and management; business administration, management and operations related; civil engineering technology; commercial and advertising art; computer and information systems security; computer programming; corrections and criminal justice related; criminal justice/safety; culinary arts; dental hygiene; early childhood education; e-commerce; electrical, electronic and communications engineering technology; electrician; elementary education; emergency medical technology (EMT paramedic); fire protection and safety technology; fire protection related; forensic science and technology; funeral service and mortuary science; health information/medical records technology; heating, air conditioning, ventilation and refrigeration maintenance technology; hotel/motel administration; human resources management; information science/studies; information technology; language interpretation and translation; legal assistant/paralegal; liberal arts and sciences and humanities related; liberal arts and sciences/liberal studies; machine shop technology; marketing/marketing management; medical office management; nuclear medical technology; nursing (registered nurse training); office management; operations management; physical therapist assistant; public administration; radiologic technology/science; respiratory care therapy; special education; speech-language pathology; surgical technology; survey technology; system, networking, and LAN/WAN management.

Academics *Calendar:* semesters. *Degree:* certificates, diplomas, and associate. *Special study options:* academic remediation for entering students, adult/continuing education programs, advanced placement credit, cooperative education, distance learning, double majors, English as a second language, independent study, internships, off-campus study, part-time degree program, services for LD students, student-designed majors, summer session for credit.

Library Paul H. Thompson Library plus 1 other with 68,604 titles, 359 serial subscriptions, 7,416 audiovisual materials, an OPAC, a Web page.

Student Life *Housing:* college housing not available. *Activities and Organizations:* Criminal Justice Association, Early Childhood Club, Phi Beta Lambda, Student Nurses Club, Data Processing Management Association. *Campus security:* 24-hour emergency response devices and patrols, late-night transport/escort service. *Student services:* personal/psychological counseling.

Athletics *Intramural sports:* basketball M/W, bowling M/W, softball M/W, table tennis M/W, volleyball M/W.

Standardized Tests *Required:* Accuplacer is required. The College will accept ACT and SAT scores in lieu of Accuplacer if the scores are no more than 5 years old and they meet the minimum scores for each section of the SAT/ACT. ASSET and COMPASS scores are also accepted if they are no more than 3 years old. (for admission).

Costs (2010–11) *One-time required fee:* $25. *Tuition:* state resident $1600 full-time, $50 per credit hour part-time; nonresident $7722 full-time, $242 per credit hour part-time. Full-time tuition and fees vary according to course load. Part-time tuition and fees vary according to course load. *Required fees:* $60 full-time, $30 per term part-time. *Waivers:* senior citizens and employees or children of employees.

Financial Aid Of all full-time matriculated undergraduates who enrolled in 2008, 75 Federal Work-Study jobs (averaging $2000). *Financial aid deadline:* 6/1.

Applying *Options:* electronic application. *Required for some:* essay or personal statement, high school transcript, interview. *Application deadlines:* rolling (freshmen), rolling (transfers). *Notification:* continuous (freshmen), continuous (transfers).

Freshman Application Contact Dr. Vincent Castano, Director of Admissions, Fayetteville Technical Community College, PO Box 35236, Fayetteville, NC 28303. *Phone:* 910-678-8473. *Fax:* 910-678-0085. *E-mail:* castanov@faytechcc.edu.

FORSYTH TECHNICAL COMMUNITY COLLEGE

Winston-Salem, North Carolina **www.forsythtech.edu/**

Freshman Application Contact Ms. Patrice Mitchell, Dean of Enrollment Services, Forsyth Technical Community College, 2100 Silas Creek Parkway, Winston-Salem, NC 27103-5197. *Phone:* 336-734-7331. *Fax:* 336-761-2098. *E-mail:* admissions@forsythtech.edu.

GASTON COLLEGE

Dallas, North Carolina **www.gaston.edu/**

Freshman Application Contact Ms. Alice D. Hopper, Admissions Specialist, Gaston College, 201 Highway 321 South, Dallas, NC 28034. *Phone:* 704-922-6214. *Fax:* 704-922-6443.

GUILFORD TECHNICAL COMMUNITY COLLEGE

Jamestown, North Carolina **www.gtcc.edu/**

- **State and locally supported** 2-year, founded 1958, part of North Carolina Community College System
- **Suburban** 158-acre campus
- **Endowment** $2.7 million
- **Coed,** 13,532 undergraduate students, 73% full-time, 55% women, 45% men

Undergraduates 9,930 full-time, 3,602 part-time. Students come from 22 states and territories, 100 other countries, 0.7% are from out of state, 41% African American, 3% Asian American or Pacific Islander, 4% Hispanic American, 0.7% Native American, 0.7% international, 29% transferred in. *Retention:* 58% of 2008 full-time freshmen returned.

Freshmen *Admission:* 11,390 applied, 6,890 admitted, 3,405 enrolled. *Average high school GPA:* 2.39.

Faculty *Total:* 1,020, 29% full-time, 6% with terminal degrees. *Student/faculty ratio:* 21:1.

Majors Accounting technology and bookkeeping; agricultural power machinery operation; airline pilot and flight crew; architectural engineering technology; automobile/automotive mechanics technology; avionics maintenance technology; biology/biotechnology laboratory technician; building/property maintenance and management; business administration and management; chemical technology; civil engineering technology; commercial and advertising art; computer programming; computer systems analysis; computer systems networking and telecommunications; cosmetology; criminal justice/safety; culinary arts; dental hygiene; early childhood education; education related; electrical, electronic and communications engineering technology; electrician; electromechanical technology; emergency medical technology (EMT paramedic); fire protection

Guilford Technical Community College (continued)

and safety technology; general studies; heating, air conditioning, ventilation and refrigeration maintenance technology; hotel/motel administration; human resources management; industrial production technologies related; information science/studies; information technology; legal assistant/paralegal; liberal arts and sciences and humanities related; liberal arts and sciences/liberal studies; logistics and materials management; machine shop technology; mechanical engineering/mechanical technology; medical/clinical assistant; medical office management; nursing (registered nurse training); office management; pharmacy technician; physical therapist assistant; psychiatric/mental health services technology; recording arts technology; substance abuse/addiction counseling; surgical technology; survey technology; system, networking, and LAN/WAN management; telecommunications technology; turf and turfgrass management; vehicle maintenance and repair technologies related.

Academics *Calendar:* semesters. *Degree:* certificates, diplomas, and associate. *Special study options:* academic remediation for entering students, adult/continuing education programs, advanced placement credit, cooperative education, distance learning, double majors, English as a second language, external degree program, independent study, internships, off-campus study, part-time degree program, services for LD students, student-designed majors, summer session for credit. *ROTC:* Army (c), Air Force (c).

Library M. W. Bell Library plus 2 others with 117,599 titles, 390 serial subscriptions, 8,461 audiovisual materials, an OPAC, a Web page.

Student Life *Housing:* college housing not available. *Activities and Organizations:* drama/theater group, International Students Association, Steppin' N Style, Surgical Technology, Rotaract, Fellowship of Christian Athletes. *Campus security:* 24-hour emergency response devices and patrols, late-night transport/escort service. *Student services:* personal/psychological counseling.

Athletics Member NJCAA. *Intercollegiate sports:* baseball M(s), basketball M(s)/W(s), volleyball W(s).

Costs (2010–11) *Tuition:* state resident $1600 full-time, $50 per credit hour part-time; nonresident $7722 full-time, $241 per credit hour part-time. Full-time tuition and fees vary according to course load and program. Part-time tuition and fees vary according to course load and program. *Required fees:* $173 full-time, $45 per term part-time. *Payment plan:* deferred payment. *Waivers:* senior citizens and employees or children of employees.

Financial Aid Of all full-time matriculated undergraduates who enrolled in 2008, 91 Federal Work-Study jobs (averaging $2994).

Applying *Options:* electronic application, early admission, deferred entrance. *Required:* high school transcript. *Required for some:* interview. *Application deadlines:* rolling (freshmen), rolling (transfers). *Notification:* continuous (freshmen), continuous (transfers).

Freshman Application Contact Guilford Technical Community College, PO Box 309, Jamestown, NC 27282. *Phone:* 336-334-4822 Ext. 2901.

HALIFAX COMMUNITY COLLEGE

Weldon, North Carolina **www.hcc.cc.nc.us/**

- **State and locally supported** 2-year, founded 1967, part of North Carolina Community College System
- **Rural** 109-acre campus
- **Coed**

Academics *Calendar:* semesters. *Degree:* certificates, diplomas, and associate. *Special study options:* academic remediation for entering students, adult/continuing education programs, cooperative education, part-time degree program, summer session for credit.

Student Life *Campus security:* 12-hour patrols by trained security personnel.

Applying *Options:* deferred entrance. *Required:* high school transcript.

Director of Admissions Mrs. Scottie Dickens, Director of Admissions, Halifax Community College, PO Drawer 809, Weldon, NC 27890-0809. *Phone:* 252-536-7220.

HAYWOOD COMMUNITY COLLEGE

Clyde, North Carolina **www.haywood.edu/**

- **State and locally supported** 2-year, founded 1964, part of North Carolina Community College System
- **Rural** 85-acre campus
- **Coed**

Academics *Calendar:* semesters. *Degree:* certificates, diplomas, and associate. *Special study options:* academic remediation for entering students, adult/continuing education programs, advanced placement credit, cooperative education, distance learning, double majors, English as a second language, independent study, internships, part-time degree program, services for LD students.

Student Life *Campus security:* 24-hour patrols.

Financial Aid Of all full-time matriculated undergraduates who enrolled in 2008, 41 Federal Work-Study jobs (averaging $857).

Applying *Required:* high school transcript. *Required for some:* interview.

Director of Admissions Ms. Debbie Rowland, Coordinator of Admissions, Haywood Community College, 185 Freedlander Drive, Clyde, NC 28721-9453. *Phone:* 828-627-4505.

ISOTHERMAL COMMUNITY COLLEGE

Spindale, North Carolina **www.isothermal.edu/**

Freshman Application Contact Ms. Vickie Searcy, Enrollment Management Office, Isothermal Community College, PO Box 804, Spindale, NC 28160-0804. *Phone:* 828-286-3636 Ext. 251. *Fax:* 828-286-8109. *E-mail:* vsearcy@isothermal.edu.

ITT TECHNICAL INSTITUTE

Charlotte, North Carolina **www.itt-tech.edu/**

- **Proprietary** primarily 2-year
- **Coed**

Majors Computer and information systems security; computer engineering technology; construction management; criminal justice/law enforcement administration; electrical, electronic and communications engineering technology; system, networking, and LAN/WAN management; web page, digital/multimedia and information resources design.

Academics *Degrees:* associate and bachelor's.

Freshman Application Contact Director of Recruitment, ITT Technical Institute, 4135 South Stream Boulevard, Suite 200, Charlotte, NC 28217. *Phone:* 704-423-3100. *Toll-free phone:* 800-488-0173.

ITT TECHNICAL INSTITUTE

High Point, North Carolina **www.itt-tech.edu/**

- **Proprietary** primarily 2-year, founded 2007, part of ITT Educational Services, Inc.
- **Coed**

Majors Computer and information systems security; computer engineering technology; construction management; criminal justice/law enforcement administration; electrical, electronic and communications engineering technology; system, networking, and LAN/WAN management.

Academics *Calendar:* quarters. *Degrees:* associate and bachelor's.

Freshman Application Contact Director of Recruitment, ITT Technical Institute, 4050 Piedmont Parkway, Suite 110, High Point, NC 27265. *Phone:* 336-819-5900. *Toll-free phone:* 877-536-5231.

ITT TECHNICAL INSTITUTE

Morrisville, North Carolina **www.itt-tech.edu/**

- **Proprietary** primarily 2-year, part of ITT Educational Services, Inc.
- **Coed**

Majors Computer and information systems security; computer engineering technology; construction management; criminal justice/law enforcement administration; electrical, electronic and communications engineering technology; system, networking, and LAN/WAN management.

Academics *Degrees:* associate and bachelor's.

Freshman Application Contact Director of Recruitment, ITT Technical Institute, 3200 Gateway Centre Boulevard, Suite 105, Morrisville, NC 27560. *Phone:* 919-463-5800. *Toll-free phone:* 877-203-5533.

JAMES SPRUNT COMMUNITY COLLEGE

Kenansville, North Carolina **www.jamessprunt.com/**

- **State-supported** 2-year, founded 1964, part of North Carolina Community College System
- **Rural** 51-acre campus
- **Endowment** $1.1 million
- **Coed,** 1,534 undergraduate students, 47% full-time, 69% women, 31% men

Undergraduates 724 full-time, 810 part-time. Students come from 1 other state, 20% transferred in.

Freshmen *Admission:* 433 applied, 266 admitted, 266 enrolled.

Faculty *Total:* 143, 43% full-time, 3% with terminal degrees.

Majors Accounting; administrative assistant and secretarial science; agribusiness; animal sciences; business administration and management; commercial and advertising art; computer systems analysis; cosmetology; criminal justice/police science; kindergarten/preschool education; liberal arts and sciences/liberal studies; medical/clinical assistant; nursing (registered nurse training).

Academics *Calendar:* semesters. *Degree:* certificates, diplomas, and associate. *Special study options:* academic remediation for entering students, accelerated degree program, advanced placement credit, cooperative education, distance learning, double majors, English as a second language, independent study, internships, part-time degree program, services for LD students, summer session for credit.

Library James Sprunt Community College Library with 27,471 titles, 134 serial subscriptions, 487 audiovisual materials, an OPAC.

Student Life *Housing:* college housing not available. *Activities and Organizations:* student-run newspaper, Student Nurses Association, Art Club, Alumni Association, National Technical-Vocational Honor Society, Phi Theta Kappa, national sororities. *Campus security:* day, evening and Saturday trained security personnel. *Student services:* personal/psychological counseling.

Athletics *Intercollegiate sports:* softball M/W, volleyball M/W.

Costs (2010–11) *Tuition:* state resident $1600 full-time, $50 per semester hour part-time; nonresident $7722 full-time, $241 per semester hour part-time. Full-time tuition and fees vary according to course load. Part-time tuition and fees vary according to course load. *Required fees:* $70 full-time, $35 per term part-time. *Waivers:* senior citizens and employees or children of employees.

Financial Aid Of all full-time matriculated undergraduates who enrolled in 2008, 35 Federal Work-Study jobs (averaging $1057).

Applying *Options:* electronic application. *Required:* high school transcript. *Application deadlines:* rolling (freshmen), rolling (transfers). *Notification:* continuous (freshmen), continuous (transfers).

Freshman Application Contact Ms. Lea Grady, Admissions Specialist, James Sprunt Community College, Highway 11 South, 133 James Sprunt Drive, Kenansville, NC 28349. *Phone:* 910-296-6078. *Fax:* 910-296-1222. *E-mail:* lgrady@jamessprunt.edu.

JOHNSTON COMMUNITY COLLEGE

Smithfield, North Carolina **www.johnston.cc.nc.us/**

- **State-supported** 2-year, founded 1969, part of North Carolina Community College System
- **Rural** 100-acre campus
- **Coed,** 4,410 undergraduate students, 52% full-time, 63% women, 37% men

Undergraduates 2,283 full-time, 2,127 part-time. 21% African American, 0.7% Asian American or Pacific Islander, 5% Hispanic American, 0.7% Native American.

Freshmen *Admission:* 1,028 enrolled.

Faculty *Total:* 385, 37% full-time. *Student/faculty ratio:* 14:1.

Majors Accounting; accounting technology and bookkeeping; administrative assistant and secretarial science; business administration and management; commercial and advertising art; computer programming; criminal justice/police science; diesel mechanics technology; early childhood education; electrical, electronic and communications engineering technology; heating, air conditioning, ventilation and refrigeration maintenance technology; kindergarten/preschool education; landscaping and groundskeeping; legal assistant/paralegal; liberal arts and sciences/liberal studies; machine shop technology; machine tool technology; medical administrative assistant and medical secretary; medical/clinical assistant; medical office management; medical radiologic technology; nursing (registered nurse training); office management.

Academics *Calendar:* semesters. *Degree:* certificates, diplomas, and associate. *Special study options:* academic remediation for entering students, adult/continuing education programs, advanced placement credit, cooperative education, distance learning, double majors, honors programs, independent study, part-time degree program, services for LD students, summer session for credit.

Library Johnston Community College Library plus 1 other with 33,094 titles, 197 serial subscriptions, an OPAC, a Web page.

Student Life *Housing:* college housing not available. *Activities and Organizations:* choral group. *Campus security:* 24-hour patrols. *Student services:* personal/psychological counseling.

Athletics Member NJCAA. *Intercollegiate sports:* golf M/W, softball M/W, volleyball M/W. *Intramural sports:* basketball M/W.

Standardized Tests *Required:* ACCUPLACER (for admission). *Recommended:* SAT or ACT (for admission).

Costs (2010–11) *Tuition:* state resident $1600 full-time, $50 per credit hour part-time; nonresident $7722 full-time, $241 per credit hour part-time. Full-time tuition and fees vary according to course load. Part-time tuition and fees vary according to course load. *Required fees:* $97 full-time. *Waivers:* senior citizens and employees or children of employees.

Financial Aid Of all full-time matriculated undergraduates who enrolled in 2008, 35 Federal Work-Study jobs (averaging $1853).

Applying *Options:* electronic application. *Required:* high school transcript, interview. *Application deadlines:* rolling (freshmen), rolling (transfers). *Notification:* continuous (freshmen), continuous (transfers).

Freshman Application Contact Dr. Pamela J. Harrell, Vice President of Student Services, Johnston Community College, PO Box 2350, Smithfield, NC 27577-2350. *Phone:* 919-209-2048. *Fax:* 919-989-7862. *E-mail:* pjharrell@johnstoncc.edu.

KING'S COLLEGE

Charlotte, North Carolina **www.kingscollegecharlotte.edu/**

Freshman Application Contact Admissions Office, King's College, 322 Lamar Avenue, Charlotte, NC 28204-2436. *Phone:* 704-372-0266. *Toll-free phone:* 800-768-2255.

LENOIR COMMUNITY COLLEGE

Kinston, North Carolina **www.lenoircc.edu/**

Freshman Application Contact Ms. Tammy Buck, Director of Enrollment Management, Lenoir Community College, PO Box 188, Kinston, NC 28502-0188. *Phone:* 252-527-6223 Ext. 309. *Fax:* 252-526-5112. *E-mail:* tbuck@lenoircc.edu.

LOUISBURG COLLEGE

Louisburg, North Carolina **www.louisburg.edu/**

Freshman Application Contact Mr. Jim Schlimmer, Vice President for Enrollment Management, Louisburg College, 501 North Main Street, Louisburg, NC 27549-2399. *Phone:* 919-497-3233. *Toll-free phone:* 800-775-0208. *Fax:* 919-496-1788. *E-mail:* admissions@louisburg.edu.

MARTIN COMMUNITY COLLEGE

Williamston, North Carolina **www.martin.cc.nc.us/**

Director of Admissions Ms. Sonya C. Atkinson, Registrar and Admissions Officer, Martin Community College, 1161 Kehukee Park Road, Williamston, NC 27892. *Phone:* 252-792-1521 Ext. 243.

MAYLAND COMMUNITY COLLEGE

Spruce Pine, North Carolina **www.mayland.edu/**

- **State and locally supported** 2-year, founded 1971, part of North Carolina Community College System
- **Rural** 38-acre campus
- **Coed**

Academics *Calendar:* semesters. *Degree:* certificates, diplomas, and associate. *Special study options:* academic remediation for entering students, adult/continuing education programs, advanced placement credit, cooperative education,

Mayland Community College (continued)
distance learning, double majors, independent study, internships, part-time degree program, services for LD students, summer session for credit.
Athletics Member NJCAA.
Standardized Tests *Required for some:* CPT required for all for placement, required for admission to nursing program.
Financial Aid Of all full-time matriculated undergraduates who enrolled in 2009, 16 Federal Work-Study jobs (averaging $1800).
Applying *Options:* electronic application, deferred entrance. *Required:* high school transcript.
Director of Admissions Ms. Cathy Morrison, Director of Admissions, Mayland Community College, PO Box 547, Spruce Pine, NC 28777. *Phone:* 828-765-7351 Ext. 224.

McDowell Technical Community College

Marion, North Carolina **www.mcdowelltech.edu/**

- **State-supported** 2-year, founded 1964, part of North Carolina Community College System
- **Rural** 31-acre campus
- **Coed**

Academics *Calendar:* semesters. *Degree:* certificates, diplomas, and associate. *Special study options:* academic remediation for entering students, accelerated degree program, adult/continuing education programs, cooperative education, distance learning, English as a second language, independent study, part-time degree program, services for LD students, summer session for credit.
Student Life *Campus security:* 24-hour emergency response devices.
Costs (2009–10) *Tuition:* state resident $1600 full-time, $50 per credit hour part-time; nonresident $7722 full-time, $242 per credit hour part-time. *Required fees:* $50 full-time, $1 per credit hour part-time, $5 per term part-time.
Financial Aid Of all full-time matriculated undergraduates who enrolled in 2008, 15 Federal Work-Study jobs (averaging $1900).
Applying *Options:* early admission, deferred entrance. *Required for some:* high school transcript.
Freshman Application Contact Mr. Rick L. Wilson, Director of Admissions, McDowell Technical Community College, 54 College Drive, Marion, NC 28752-9724. *Phone:* 828-652-0632. *Fax:* 828-652-1014. *E-mail:* rickw@mcdowelltech.edu.

Mitchell Community College

Statesville, North Carolina **www.mitchell.cc.nc.us/**

- **State-supported** 2-year, founded 1852, part of North Carolina Community College System
- **Small-town** 8-acre campus with easy access to Charlotte
- **Coed**

Academics *Calendar:* semesters. *Degree:* certificates, diplomas, and associate. *Special study options:* academic remediation for entering students, adult/continuing education programs, advanced placement credit, distance learning, English as a second language, part-time degree program, services for LD students, summer session for credit. *ROTC:* Army (c).
Student Life *Campus security:* day and evening security guards.
Financial Aid Of all full-time matriculated undergraduates who enrolled in 2008, 30 Federal Work-Study jobs.
Applying *Required:* high school transcript.
Freshman Application Contact Mr. Doug Rhoney, Counselor, Mitchell Community College, 500 West Broad, Statesville, NC 28677-5293. *Phone:* 704-878-3280.

Montgomery Community College

Troy, North Carolina **www.montgomery.edu/**

- **State-supported** 2-year, founded 1967, part of North Carolina Community College System
- **Rural** 159-acre campus
- **Coed,** 1,039 undergraduate students, 33% full-time, 66% women, 34% men

Undergraduates 346 full-time, 693 part-time. 16% African American, 2% Asian American or Pacific Islander, 3% Hispanic American, 1% Native American, 0.4% international.
Freshmen *Admission:* 187 enrolled.
Faculty *Total:* 76, 47% full-time.
Majors Accounting; administrative assistant and secretarial science; business administration and management; ceramic arts and ceramics; child-care and support services management; criminal justice/police science; forestry technology; liberal arts and sciences/liberal studies; management information systems; medical/clinical assistant.
Academics *Calendar:* semesters. *Degree:* certificates, diplomas, and associate. *Special study options:* academic remediation for entering students, advanced placement credit, cooperative education, distance learning, English as a second language, part-time degree program, services for LD students, summer session for credit.
Library 19,850 titles, 100 serial subscriptions, 1,430 audiovisual materials, an OPAC.
Student Life *Housing:* college housing not available. *Activities and Organizations:* Student Government Association, Nursing Club, Gunsmithing Society, Medical Assisting Club, Forestry Club. *Student services:* personal/psychological counseling.
Costs (2009–10) *Tuition:* state resident $1600 full-time, $50 per credit hour part-time; nonresident $7722 full-time, $241 per credit hour part-time. Full-time tuition and fees vary according to course load. Part-time tuition and fees vary according to course load. *Required fees:* $65 full-time, $33 per term part-time. *Payment plan:* deferred payment. *Waivers:* senior citizens and employees or children of employees.
Financial Aid Of all full-time matriculated undergraduates who enrolled in 2008, 24 Federal Work-Study jobs (averaging $500).
Applying *Options:* early admission, deferred entrance. *Required:* high school transcript. *Application deadlines:* rolling (freshmen), rolling (transfers). *Notification:* continuous (freshmen), continuous (transfers).
Freshman Application Contact Montgomery Community College, 1011 Page Street, Troy, NC 27371. *Phone:* 910-576-6222 Ext. 240. *Toll-free phone:* 800-839-6222.

Nash Community College

Rocky Mount, North Carolina **www.nash.cc.nc.us/**

- **State-supported** 2-year, founded 1967, part of North Carolina Community College System
- **Rural** 69-acre campus
- **Coed**

Academics *Calendar:* semesters. *Degree:* certificates, diplomas, and associate. *Special study options:* academic remediation for entering students, adult/continuing education programs, advanced placement credit, distance learning, double majors, English as a second language, independent study, part-time degree program, services for LD students, summer session for credit.
Student Life *Campus security:* 24-hour emergency response devices, late-night transport/escort service.
Standardized Tests *Required for some:* SAT or ACT (for admission), SAT and SAT Subject Tests or ACT (for admission), ACT ASSET or ACT COMPASS.
Applying *Options:* deferred entrance. *Required:* high school transcript. *Recommended:* interview.
Freshman Application Contact Ms. Dorothy Gardner, Admissions Officer, Nash Community College, 522 North Old Carriage Road, Rocky Mount, NC 27804. *Phone:* 252-451-8300. *E-mail:* dgardner@nashcc.edu.

Pamlico Community College

Grantsboro, North Carolina **www.pamlico.cc.nc.us/**

Director of Admissions Mr. Floyd H. Hardison, Admissions Counselor, Pamlico Community College, PO Box 185, Grantsboro, NC 28529-0185. *Phone:* 252-249-1851 Ext. 28.

Piedmont Community College

Roxboro, North Carolina **www.piedmont.cc.nc.us/**

- **State-supported** 2-year, founded 1970, part of North Carolina Community College System
- **Small-town** 178-acre campus
- **Coed,** 2,874 undergraduate students, 44% full-time, 56% women, 44% men

Undergraduates 1,251 full-time, 1,623 part-time. Students come from 3 states and territories, 4 other countries, 41% African American, 0.5% Asian American or Pacific Islander, 2% Hispanic American, 0.8% Native American.

Freshmen *Admission:* 502 enrolled.

Majors Accounting; building/property maintenance and management; business administration and management; child-care and support services management; cinematography and film/video production; clinical/medical social work; computer programming (specific applications); computer systems networking and telecommunications; criminal justice/law enforcement administration; e-commerce; electrical and power transmission installation; electrician; electromechanical and instrumentation and maintenance technologies related; elementary education; general studies; graphic communications; health professions related; industrial technology; information technology; liberal arts and sciences and humanities related; liberal arts and sciences/liberal studies; medical administrative assistant and medical secretary; nursing (registered nurse training); office management.

Academics *Calendar:* semesters. *Degree:* certificates, diplomas, and associate. *Special study options:* academic remediation for entering students, adult/continuing education programs, advanced placement credit, cooperative education, English as a second language, off-campus study, part-time degree program, summer session for credit.

Library Learning Resource Center with 24,166 titles, 278 serial subscriptions.

Student Life *Housing:* college housing not available. *Campus security:* security guard during certain evening and weekend hours. *Student services:* personal/psychological counseling.

Athletics *Intramural sports:* volleyball M/W.

Costs (2009–10) *Tuition:* state resident $1549 full-time, $51 per credit hour part-time; nonresident $7288 full-time, $241 per credit hour part-time. *Required fees:* $49 full-time, $21 per term part-time. *Payment plan:* installment.

Financial Aid Of all full-time matriculated undergraduates who enrolled in 2008, 30 Federal Work-Study jobs (averaging $1500).

Applying *Options:* electronic application, early admission, deferred entrance. *Required for some:* high school transcript. *Application deadlines:* rolling (freshmen), rolling (transfers). *Notification:* continuous until 9/29 (freshmen), continuous until 9/29 (transfers).

Freshman Application Contact Piedmont Community College, PO Box 1197, 1715 College Drive, Roxboro, NC 27573. *Phone:* 336-599-1181 Ext. 219.

PITT COMMUNITY COLLEGE

Greenville, North Carolina **www.pittcc.edu/**

- **State and locally supported** 2-year, founded 1961, part of North Carolina Community College System
- **Small-town** 172-acre campus
- **Coed**

Undergraduates 3,822 full-time, 3,254 part-time. 33% African American, 0.8% Asian American or Pacific Islander, 2% Hispanic American, 0.4% Native American, 0.8% international.

Academics *Calendar:* semesters. *Degree:* certificates, diplomas, and associate. *Special study options:* academic remediation for entering students, adult/continuing education programs, advanced placement credit, cooperative education, distance learning, double majors, English as a second language, external degree program, independent study, internships, part-time degree program, services for LD students, summer session for credit. *ROTC:* Army (b).

Student Life *Campus security:* 24-hour patrols, student patrols, late-night transport/escort service.

Athletics Member NJCAA.

Costs (2009–10) *Tuition:* state resident $1600 full-time, $50 per credit hour part-time; nonresident $7722 full-time, $241 per credit hour part-time. Part-time tuition and fees vary according to course level. *Required fees:* $86 full-time, $43 per term part-time.

Financial Aid Of all full-time matriculated undergraduates who enrolled in 2008, 79 Federal Work-Study jobs (averaging $1772).

Applying *Options:* electronic application, deferred entrance. *Required:* high school transcript.

Freshman Application Contact Ms. Bev Webster, Interim Coordinator of Counseling, Pitt Community College, PO Drawer 7007, 1986 Pitt Tech Road, Greenville, NC 27835-7007. *Phone:* 252-493-7217. *Fax:* 252-321-4612. *E-mail:* pittadm@pcc.pitt.cc.nc.us.

RANDOLPH COMMUNITY COLLEGE

Asheboro, North Carolina **www.randolph.edu/**

- **State-supported** 2-year, founded 1962, part of North Carolina Community College System
- **Small-town** 35-acre campus
- **Endowment** $7.2 million
- **Coed,** 3,047 undergraduate students, 45% full-time, 64% women, 36% men

Undergraduates 1,366 full-time, 1,681 part-time. Students come from 2 states and territories, 16 other countries, 1% are from out of state, 10% African American, 1% Asian American or Pacific Islander, 5% Hispanic American, 0.8% Native American, 0.8% transferred in. *Retention:* 65% of 2008 full-time freshmen returned.

Freshmen *Admission:* 2,213 applied, 2,213 admitted, 381 enrolled. *Average high school GPA:* 2.8.

Faculty *Total:* 315, 19% full-time. *Student/faculty ratio:* 13:1.

Majors Accounting; accounting technology and bookkeeping; administrative assistant and secretarial science; automobile/automotive mechanics technology; biology/biotechnology laboratory technician; business administration and management; commercial and advertising art; commercial photography; computer systems networking and telecommunications; cosmetology; criminal justice/police science; criminal justice/safety; early childhood education; electrical and electronic engineering technologies related; electrician; electromechanical and instrumentation and maintenance technologies related; entrepreneurship; funeral service and mortuary science; health information/medical records technology; industrial electronics technology; industrial engineering; industrial technology; information technology; interior design; liberal arts and sciences and humanities related; liberal arts and sciences/liberal studies; logistics and materials management; machine shop technology; machine tool technology; medical office management; nursing (registered nurse training); office management; photographic and film/video technology; photography; photojournalism; physical therapist assistant; prenursing studies; radiologic technology/science.

Academics *Calendar:* semesters. *Degree:* certificates, diplomas, and associate. *Special study options:* academic remediation for entering students, adult/continuing education programs, advanced placement credit, cooperative education, distance learning, double majors, English as a second language, independent study, internships, off-campus study, part-time degree program, services for LD students, summer session for credit.

Library R. Alton Cox Learning Resources Center with 41,000 titles, 200 serial subscriptions, 5,500 audiovisual materials, an OPAC, a Web page.

Student Life *Housing:* college housing not available. *Activities and Organizations:* Student Government Association, Phi Theta Kappa, Student Nurse Association, Phi Beta Lambda, Common Threads. *Campus security:* 24-hour emergency response devices, security officer during open hours. *Student services:* personal/psychological counseling.

Costs (2010–11) *Tuition:* state resident $1600 full-time, $50 per credit hour part-time; nonresident $7722 full-time, $241 per credit hour part-time. *Required fees:* $88 full-time, $3 per credit hour part-time. *Payment plan:* installment. *Waivers:* senior citizens.

Applying *Options:* electronic application, deferred entrance. *Required:* high school transcript. *Application deadlines:* rolling (freshmen), rolling (transfers). *Notification:* continuous (freshmen), continuous (transfers).

Freshman Application Contact Ms. Brandi F. Hagerman, Director of Enrollment Management/Registrar, Randolph Community College, PO Box 1009, Asheboro, NC 27204-1009. *Phone:* 336-633-0213. *Fax:* 336-629-9547. *E-mail:* bhagerman@randolph.edu.

RICHMOND COMMUNITY COLLEGE

Hamlet, North Carolina **www.richmondcc.edu/**

Freshman Application Contact Ms. Wanda Watts, Director of Admissions/Registrar, Richmond Community College, PO Box 1189, Hamlet, NC 28345. *Phone:* 910-582-7113. *Fax:* 910-582-7102.

ROANOKE-CHOWAN COMMUNITY COLLEGE

Ahoskie, North Carolina **www.roanokechowan.edu/**

- **State-supported** 2-year, founded 1967, part of North Carolina Community College System
- **Rural** 39-acre campus
- **Coed**

Roanoke-Chowan Community College (continued)

Academics *Calendar:* semesters. *Degree:* certificates, diplomas, and associate. *Special study options:* academic remediation for entering students, adult/continuing education programs, cooperative education, distance learning, part-time degree program, summer session for credit.

Financial Aid Of all full-time matriculated undergraduates who enrolled in 2008, 50 Federal Work-Study jobs (averaging $1120).

Applying *Options:* early admission. *Required for some:* interview.

Director of Admissions Miss Sandra Copeland, Director, Counseling Services, Roanoke-Chowan Community College, 109 Community College Road, Ahoskie, NC 27910. *Phone:* 252-862-1225.

ROBESON COMMUNITY COLLEGE

Lumberton, North Carolina **www.robeson.cc.nc.us/**

Freshman Application Contact Ms. Judy Revels, Director of Admissions, Robeson Community College, PO Box 1420, 5160 Fayetteville Road, Lumberton, NC 28359. *Phone:* 910-618-5680 Ext. 251.

ROCKINGHAM COMMUNITY COLLEGE

Wentworth, North Carolina **www.rcc.cc.nc.us/**

- **State-supported** 2-year, founded 1964, part of North Carolina Community College System
- **Rural** 257-acre campus
- **Coed,** 2,636 undergraduate students, 44% full-time, 62% women, 38% men

Undergraduates 1,160 full-time, 1,476 part-time. Students come from 3 states and territories, 2 other countries, 1% are from out of state, 24% African American, 1% Asian American or Pacific Islander, 2% Hispanic American, 0.4% Native American, 18% transferred in.

Freshmen *Admission:* 569 enrolled.

Faculty *Total:* 111, 59% full-time, 5% with terminal degrees. *Student/faculty ratio:* 18:1.

Majors Accounting; administrative assistant and secretarial science; business administration and management; criminal justice/police science; electromechanical technology; human resources management; liberal arts and sciences/liberal studies; medical administrative assistant and medical secretary; nursing (registered nurse training); respiratory care therapy.

Academics *Calendar:* semesters. *Degree:* certificates, diplomas, and associate. *Special study options:* academic remediation for entering students, adult/continuing education programs, advanced placement credit, cooperative education, part-time degree program, student-designed majors, summer session for credit.

Library Gerald B. James Library with 43,044 titles, 374 serial subscriptions, 3,990 audiovisual materials, an OPAC, a Web page.

Student Life *Housing:* college housing not available. *Activities and Organizations:* student-run newspaper, Phi Theta Kappa, International Studies Club, Students in Free Enterprise (SIFE), Student Government Association, Environmental Club. *Student services:* personal/psychological counseling.

Athletics Member NJCAA. *Intercollegiate sports:* baseball M, basketball M, golf M/W, softball W, volleyball W. *Intramural sports:* archery M/W, badminton M/W, cheerleading W, table tennis M/W, tennis M/W, volleyball M/W.

Costs (2009–10) *Tuition:* state resident $1600 full-time, $50 per credit hour part-time; nonresident $7722 full-time, $241 per credit hour part-time. Full-time tuition and fees vary according to course load. Part-time tuition and fees vary according to course load. *Required fees:* $96 full-time. *Payment plan:* installment.

Financial Aid Of all full-time matriculated undergraduates who enrolled in 2008, 37 Federal Work-Study jobs (averaging $2300).

Applying *Options:* early admission, deferred entrance. *Application deadlines:* rolling (freshmen), rolling (transfers). *Notification:* continuous (freshmen), continuous (transfers).

Freshman Application Contact Mrs. Leigh Tysor, Director of Enrollment Services, Rockingham Community College, PO Box 38, Wentworth, NC 27375-0038. *Phone:* 336-342-4261 Ext. 2114. *Fax:* 336-342-1809. *E-mail:* admissions@rockinghamcc.edu.

ROWAN-CABARRUS COMMUNITY COLLEGE

Salisbury, North Carolina **www.rowancabarrus.edu/**

- **State-supported** 2-year, founded 1963, part of North Carolina Community College System
- **Small-town** 100-acre campus
- **Coed**

Academics *Calendar:* semesters. *Degree:* diplomas and associate. *Special study options:* academic remediation for entering students, adult/continuing education programs, advanced placement credit, cooperative education, distance learning, English as a second language, internships, part-time degree program, services for LD students, summer session for credit.

Student Life *Campus security:* on-campus security during operating hours.

Applying *Required:* high school transcript.

Freshman Application Contact Mrs. Gail Cummins, Director of Admissions and Recruitment, Rowan-Cabarrus Community College, PO Box 1595, Salisbury, NC 28145. *Phone:* 704-637-0760. *Fax:* 704-633-6804.

SAMPSON COMMUNITY COLLEGE

Clinton, North Carolina **www.sampsoncc.edu/**

Director of Admissions Mr. William R. Jordan, Director of Admissions, Sampson Community College, PO Box 318, 1801 Sunset Avenue, Highway 24 West, Clinton, NC 28329. *Phone:* 910-592-8084 Ext. 2022.

SANDHILLS COMMUNITY COLLEGE

Pinehurst, North Carolina **www.sandhills.edu/**

- **State-supported** 2-year, founded 1963, part of North Carolina Community College System
- **Small-town** 240-acre campus
- **Endowment** $4.1 million
- **Coed,** 4,200 undergraduate students

Faculty *Total:* 178, 66% full-time. *Student/faculty ratio:* 18:1.

Majors Accounting; administrative assistant and secretarial science; architectural engineering technology; art; art teacher education; automobile/automotive mechanics technology; biological and physical sciences; business administration and management; business, management, and marketing related; child development; civil engineering technology; clinical/medical laboratory technology; computer engineering related; computer engineering technology; computer/information technology services administration related; computer programming; computer programming (specific applications); cosmetology; criminal justice/law enforcement administration; criminal justice/police science; culinary arts; fine/studio arts; gerontology; hotel/motel administration; human services; information science/studies; kindergarten/preschool education; landscaping and groundskeeping; liberal arts and sciences/liberal studies; mathematics; medical administrative assistant and medical secretary; mental health/rehabilitation; music; music teacher education; nursing assistant/aide and patient care assistant; nursing (licensed practical/vocational nurse training); nursing (registered nurse training); pre-engineering; radiologic technology/science; respiratory care therapy; science teacher education; substance abuse/addiction counseling; surgical technology; survey technology; turf and turfgrass management; web/multimedia management and webmaster.

Academics *Calendar:* semesters. *Degree:* certificates, diplomas, and associate. *Special study options:* academic remediation for entering students, advanced placement credit, cooperative education, distance learning, double majors, English as a second language, independent study, internships, off-campus study, part-time degree program, services for LD students, summer session for credit.

Library Boyd Library with 76,080 titles, 286 serial subscriptions, 2,317 audiovisual materials, an OPAC, a Web page.

Student Life *Housing:* college housing not available. *Activities and Organizations:* drama/theater group, student-run newspaper, choral group, marching band, Student Government Association, Minority Male Mentoring, Video and Gaming. *Campus security:* 24-hour emergency response devices, security on duty until 12 am. *Student services:* personal/psychological counseling.

Athletics Member NJCAA. *Intercollegiate sports:* basketball M, golf M/W, volleyball W.

Financial Aid Of all full-time matriculated undergraduates who enrolled in 2008, 59 Federal Work-Study jobs (averaging $1750).

Applying *Options:* electronic application, deferred entrance. *Required:* high school transcript. *Application deadlines:* rolling (freshmen), rolling (transfers). *Notification:* continuous (freshmen), continuous (transfers).

Freshman Application Contact Mr. Isai Robledo, Recruiter, Sandhills Community College, 3395 Airport Road, Pinehurst, NC 28374. *Phone:* 910-695-3738. *Toll-free phone:* 800-338-3944. *E-mail:* robledoi@sandhills.edu.

SCHOOL OF COMMUNICATION ARTS

Raleigh, North Carolina **www.higherdigital.com/**

Freshman Application Contact Wayne Moseley, Admissions, School of Communication Arts, 3000 Wakefield Crossing Drive, Raleigh, NC 27614. *Phone:* 919-488-5912. *Toll-free phone:* 800-288-7442. *Fax:* 919-488-8490. *E-mail:* wmoseley@hdigi.com.

SOUTH COLLEGE–ASHEVILLE

Asheville, North Carolina **www.southcollegenc.com/**

Freshman Application Contact Director of Admissions, South College–Asheville, 1567 Patton Avenue, Asheville, NC 28806. *Phone:* 828-277-5521. *Fax:* 828-277-6151.

SOUTHEASTERN COMMUNITY COLLEGE

Whiteville, North Carolina **www.sccnc.edu/**

Freshman Application Contact Ms. Sylvia Tart, Registrar, Southeastern Community College, PO Box 151, Whiteville, NC 28472. *Phone:* 910-642-7141 Ext. 249. *Fax:* 910-642-5658. *E-mail:* start@sccnc.edu.

SOUTH PIEDMONT COMMUNITY COLLEGE

Polkton, North Carolina **www.spcc.edu/**

Freshman Application Contact Ms. Jeania Martin, Admissions Coordinator, South Piedmont Community College, PO Box 126, Polkton, NC 28135. *Phone:* 704-272-7635. *Toll-free phone:* 800-766-0319. *E-mail:* abaucom@vnet.net.

SOUTHWESTERN COMMUNITY COLLEGE

Sylva, North Carolina **www.southwesterncc.edu/**

Freshman Application Contact Mr. Delos Monteith, Institutional Research and Planning Officer, Southwestern Community College, 447 College Drive, Sylva, NC 28779. *Phone:* 828-586-4091 Ext. 236. *Toll-free phone:* 800-447-4091. *Fax:* 828-586-3129. *E-mail:* delos@southwesterncc.edu.

STANLY COMMUNITY COLLEGE

Albemarle, North Carolina **www.stanly.edu/**

- **State-supported** 2-year, founded 1971, part of North Carolina Community College System
- **Small-town** 150-acre campus with easy access to Charlotte
- **Coed,** 3,200 undergraduate students

Undergraduates Students come from 13 states and territories, 3 other countries, 3% are from out of state.

Freshmen *Admission:* 642 applied, 642 admitted.

Faculty *Total:* 106, 50% full-time. *Student/faculty ratio:* 9:1.

Majors Accounting technology and bookkeeping; autobody/collision and repair technology; biomedical technology; business administration and management; child-care and support services management; computer and information sciences and support services related; computer hardware engineering; computer/information technology services administration related; computer programming related; computer programming (specific applications); computer systems networking and telecommunications; computer technology/computer systems technology; cosmetology; criminal justice/police science; electrical, electronic and communications engineering technology; executive assistant/executive secretary; human services; industrial technology; information science/studies; legal administrative assistant/secretary; mechanical drafting and CAD/CADD; medical administrative assistant and medical secretary; medical/clinical assistant; nursing (registered nurse training); occupational therapist assistant; physical therapist assistant; respiratory care therapy; system administration; web/multimedia management and webmaster; web page, digital/multimedia and information resources design; word processing.

Academics *Calendar:* semesters. *Degree:* certificates, diplomas, and associate. *Special study options:* academic remediation for entering students, adult/continuing education programs, advanced placement credit, cooperative education, distance learning, double majors, English as a second language, independent study, internships, part-time degree program, services for LD students, study abroad, summer session for credit.

Library 23,966 titles, 200 serial subscriptions, 2,500 audiovisual materials, an OPAC, a Web page.

Student Life *Housing:* college housing not available. *Activities and Organizations:* student-run newspaper, television station. *Campus security:* 24-hour emergency response devices and patrols, late-night transport/escort service. *Student services:* personal/psychological counseling.

Athletics *Intercollegiate sports:* baseball M(s), softball W(s).

Financial Aid Of all full-time matriculated undergraduates who enrolled in 2008, 20 Federal Work-Study jobs (averaging $1800).

Applying *Options:* electronic application, early admission, deferred entrance. *Required:* high school transcript. *Application deadlines:* rolling (freshmen), rolling (transfers). *Notification:* continuous (freshmen), continuous (transfers).

Freshman Application Contact Mrs. Denise B. Ross, Associate Dean, Admissions, Stanly Community College, 141 College Drive, Albemarle, NC 28001. *Phone:* 704-982-0121 Ext. 264. *Fax:* 704-982-0255. *E-mail:* dross7926@stanly.edu.

SURRY COMMUNITY COLLEGE

Dobson, North Carolina **www.surry.cc.nc.us/**

Freshman Application Contact Renita Hazelwood, Director of Admissions, Surry Community College, PO Box 304, Dobson, NC 27017-0304. *Phone:* 336-386-3392. *Fax:* 336-386-3690. *E-mail:* hazelwoodr@surry.edu.

TRI-COUNTY COMMUNITY COLLEGE

Murphy, North Carolina **www.tricountycc.edu/**

- **State-supported** 2-year, founded 1964, part of North Carolina Community College System
- **Rural** 40-acre campus
- **Coed,** 1,353 undergraduate students

Undergraduates 0.7% African American, 1% Hispanic American, 2% Native American.

Freshmen *Average high school GPA:* 2.9.

Faculty *Total:* 80, 58% full-time, 5% with terminal degrees. *Student/faculty ratio:* 21:1.

Majors Accounting; automobile/automotive mechanics technology; business administration and management; early childhood education; electrical, electronic and communications engineering technology; engine machinist; information technology; liberal arts and sciences/liberal studies; medical/clinical assistant; nursing (registered nurse training); welding technology.

Academics *Calendar:* semesters. *Degree:* certificates, diplomas, and associate. *Special study options:* academic remediation for entering students, adult/continuing education programs, distance learning, double majors, internships, part-time degree program, study abroad, summer session for credit.

Library 16,224 titles, 306 serial subscriptions.

Student Life *Housing:* college housing not available. *Student services:* personal/psychological counseling.

Costs (2010–11) *Tuition:* state resident $1200 full-time; nonresident $5791 full-time. *Required fees:* $29 full-time. *Waivers:* senior citizens.

Financial Aid Of all full-time matriculated undergraduates who enrolled in 2008, 11 Federal Work-Study jobs.

Applying *Required:* high school transcript. *Application deadlines:* rolling (freshmen), rolling (transfers). *Notification:* continuous (freshmen), continuous (transfers).

Freshman Application Contact Dr. Jason Chambers, Director of Student Services and Admissions, Tri-County Community College, 21 Campus Circle, Murphy, NC 28906-7919. *Phone:* 828-837-6810. *Fax:* 828-837-3266. *E-mail:* jchambers@tricountycc.edu.

Vance-Granville Community College

Henderson, North Carolina **www.vgcc.cc.nc.us/**

Freshman Application Contact Ms. Kathy Kutl, Admissions Officer, Vance-Granville Community College, PO Box 917, State Road 1126, Henderson, NC 27536. *Phone:* 252-492-2061 Ext. 3265. *Fax:* 252-430-0460.

Wake Technical Community College

Raleigh, North Carolina **www.waketech.edu/**

Director of Admissions Ms. Susan Bloomfield, Director of Admissions, Wake Technical Community College, 9101 Fayetteville Road, Raleigh, NC 27603-5696. *Phone:* 919-866-5452. *E-mail:* srbloomfield@waketech.edu.

Wayne Community College

Goldsboro, North Carolina **www.waynecc.edu/**

- **State and locally supported** 2-year, founded 1957, part of North Carolina Community College System
- **Small-town** 125-acre campus
- **Endowment** $92,210
- **Coed,** 3,585 undergraduate students, 56% full-time, 65% women, 35% men

Undergraduates 2,008 full-time, 1,577 part-time. Students come from 47 states and territories, 16% are from out of state, 30% African American, 2% Asian American or Pacific Islander, 4% Hispanic American, 0.5% Native American, 0.1% international, 19% transferred in.

Freshmen *Admission:* 1,919 applied, 1,069 admitted, 748 enrolled.

Faculty *Total:* 302, 41% full-time, 2% with terminal degrees. *Student/faculty ratio:* 20:1.

Majors Accounting technology and bookkeeping; agribusiness; agricultural production; automobile/automotive mechanics technology; avionics maintenance technology; biological and physical sciences; business administration and management; clinical/medical social work; computer systems analysis; criminal justice/police science; dental hygiene; electrical, electronic and communications engineering technology; electromechanical technology; executive assistant/executive secretary; forestry technology; liberal arts and sciences/liberal studies; machine tool technology; mechanical engineering/mechanical technology; medical administrative assistant and medical secretary; medical/clinical assistant; medical office management; nursing (registered nurse training); poultry science; psychiatric/mental health services technology; rehabilitation therapy; retailing; turf and turfgrass management.

Academics *Calendar:* semesters. *Degree:* certificates, diplomas, and associate. *Special study options:* academic remediation for entering students, adult/continuing education programs, advanced placement credit, cooperative education, distance learning, double majors, English as a second language, external degree program, honors programs, part-time degree program, services for LD students, summer session for credit.

Library Wayne Community College Library with 35,000 titles, 114 serial subscriptions, 15,000 audiovisual materials, an OPAC, a Web page.

Student Life *Housing:* college housing not available. *Activities and Organizations:* student-run newspaper, choral group, Student Government Association, Phi Beta Lambda, Phi Theta Kappa, Criminal Justice, International, national fraternities. *Campus security:* 24-hour emergency response devices and patrols, student patrols. *Student services:* health clinic, personal/psychological counseling.

Athletics *Intramural sports:* basketball M/W, bowling M/W, football M/W, golf M/W, soccer M/W, softball M/W, table tennis M/W, tennis M/W, volleyball M/W, weight lifting M/W.

Costs (2010–11) *Tuition:* state resident $1600 full-time, $50 per credit hour part-time; nonresident $7722 full-time, $241 per credit hour part-time. *Waivers:* senior citizens and employees or children of employees.

Financial Aid Of all full-time matriculated undergraduates who enrolled in 2008, 100 Federal Work-Study jobs (averaging $2000).

Applying *Options:* electronic application, deferred entrance. *Required:* high school transcript, interview. *Application deadlines:* rolling (freshmen), rolling (transfers). *Notification:* continuous (freshmen), continuous (transfers).

Freshman Application Contact Ms. Jennifer Parker, Associate/Director of Admissions and Records, Wayne Community College, PO Box 8002, Goldsboro, NC 27533-8002. *Phone:* 919-735-5151 Ext. 6721. *Fax:* 919-736-9425. *E-mail:* jbparker@waynecc.edu.

Western Piedmont Community College

Morganton, North Carolina **www.wpcc.edu/**

Freshman Application Contact Susan Williams, Director of Admissions, Western Piedmont Community College, 1001 Burkemont Avenue, Morganton, NC 28655-4511. *Phone:* 828-438-6051. *Fax:* 828-438-6065. *E-mail:* swilliams@wpcc.edu.

Wilkes Community College

Wilkesboro, North Carolina **www.wilkescc.edu/**

Freshman Application Contact Mr. Mac Warren, Director of Admissions, Wilkes Community College, PO Box 120, Wilkesboro, NC 28697. *Phone:* 336-838-6141. *Fax:* 336-838-6547. *E-mail:* mac.warren@wilkescc.edu.

Wilson Community College

Wilson, North Carolina **www.wilsoncc.edu/**

- **State-supported** 2-year, founded 1958, part of North Carolina Community College System
- **Small-town** 35-acre campus
- **Endowment** $837,828
- **Coed,** 2,119 undergraduate students, 46% full-time, 68% women, 32% men

Undergraduates 984 full-time, 1,135 part-time. Students come from 2 states and territories, 47% African American, 0.7% Asian American or Pacific Islander, 3% Hispanic American, 0.3% Native American, 15% transferred in.

Freshmen *Admission:* 363 enrolled.

Faculty *Total:* 104, 49% full-time, 3% with terminal degrees. *Student/faculty ratio:* 20:1.

Majors Accounting; administrative assistant and secretarial science; business administration and management; computer programming; criminal justice/law enforcement administration; electrical, electronic and communications engineering technology; fire science; general studies; industrial technology; information science/studies; kindergarten/preschool education; language interpretation and translation; legal assistant/paralegal; liberal arts and sciences/liberal studies; mechanical engineering/mechanical technology; nursing (registered nurse training); sign language interpretation and translation; tool and die technology.

Academics *Calendar:* semesters. *Degree:* certificates, diplomas, and associate. *Special study options:* academic remediation for entering students, advanced placement credit, cooperative education, distance learning, double majors, English as a second language, independent study, internships, part-time degree program, services for LD students, summer session for credit.

Library 38,466 titles, an OPAC.

Student Life *Housing:* college housing not available. *Campus security:* 11-hour patrols by trained security personnel.

Costs (2009–10) *Tuition:* state resident $1600 full-time, $50 per credit hour part-time; nonresident $7722 full-time, $241 per credit hour part-time. *Required fees:* $87 full-time, $1 per credit hour part-time, $22 per term part-time.

Financial Aid Of all full-time matriculated undergraduates who enrolled in 2008, 65 Federal Work-Study jobs (averaging $1500).

Applying *Options:* electronic application, deferred entrance. *Required:* high school transcript. *Application deadlines:* rolling (freshmen), rolling (transfers). *Notification:* continuous (freshmen), continuous (transfers).

Freshman Application Contact Mrs. Maegan Williams, Admissions Technician, Wilson Community College, PO Box 4305, Wilson, NC 27893-0305. *Phone:* 252-246-1275. *Fax:* 252-243-7148. *E-mail:* mwilliams@wilsoncc.edu.

NORTH DAKOTA

Bismarck State College

Bismarck, North Dakota **www.bismarckstate.edu/**

Freshman Application Contact Ms. Karla Gabriel, Dean of Admissions and Enrollment Services, Bismarck State College, PO Box 5587, Bismarck, ND

58506-5587. *Phone:* 701-224-5426. *Toll-free phone:* 800-445-5073 Ext. 45429 (in-state); 800-445-5073 (out-of-state). *Fax:* 701-224-5643. *E-mail:* karla.gabriel@bsc.nodak.edu.

CANKDESKA CIKANA COMMUNITY COLLEGE

Fort Totten, North Dakota **www.littlehoop.edu/**

Director of Admissions Mr. Ermen Brown Jr., Registrar, Cankdeska Cikana Community College, PO Box 269, Fort Totten, ND 58335. *Phone:* 701-766-1342.

DAKOTA COLLEGE AT BOTTINEAU

Bottineau, North Dakota **www.dakotacollege.edu/**

- **State-supported** 2-year, founded 1906, part of North Dakota University System
- **Rural** 35-acre campus
- **Endowment** $1.0 million
- **Coed,** 748 undergraduate students, 47% full-time, 53% women, 47% men

Undergraduates 348 full-time, 400 part-time. Students come from 29 states and territories, 2 other countries, 11% are from out of state, 3% African American, 0.9% Asian American or Pacific Islander, 1% Hispanic American, 5% Native American, 2% international.

Freshmen *Admission:* 171 enrolled.

Faculty *Total:* 76, 33% full-time, 7% with terminal degrees. *Student/faculty ratio:* 17:1.

Majors Accounting; accounting technology and bookkeeping; administrative assistant and secretarial science; adult development and aging; advertising; agriculture; applied horticulture; applied horticulture/horticultural business services related; biology/biological sciences; business administration and management; business automation/technology/data entry; chemistry; child-care and support services management; child-care provision; computer and information sciences; computer and information sciences and support services related; computer technology/computer systems technology; education; entrepreneurial and small business related; environmental engineering technology; executive assistant/executive secretary; fishing and fisheries sciences and management; floriculture/floristry management; general studies; greenhouse management; health and physical education; health services/allied health/health sciences; history; horticultural science; hospitality and recreation marketing; humanities; information science/studies; information technology; landscaping and groundskeeping; liberal arts and sciences and humanities related; liberal arts and sciences/liberal studies; marketing/marketing management; marketing related; mathematics; medical administrative assistant and medical secretary; medical/clinical assistant; medical insurance coding; medical office assistant; medical transcription; natural resources/conservation; nursing (licensed practical/vocational nurse training); nursing (registered nurse training); office management; office occupations and clerical services; ornamental horticulture; parks, recreation and leisure; parks, recreation and leisure facilities management; parks, recreation, and leisure related; physical sciences; physical sciences related; premedical studies; prenursing studies; pre-veterinary studies; psychology; receptionist; science technologies related; social sciences; system administration; teacher assistant/aide; turf and turfgrass management; urban forestry; wildlife and wildlands science and management; zoology/animal biology.

Academics *Calendar:* semesters. *Degree:* certificates, diplomas, and associate. *Special study options:* academic remediation for entering students, advanced placement credit, cooperative education, distance learning, double majors, internships, off-campus study, part-time degree program, services for LD students, summer session for credit.

Library Dakota College at Bottineau Library plus 1 other with 46,294 titles, 174 serial subscriptions, an OPAC, a Web page.

Student Life *Housing:* on-campus residence required through sophomore year. *Options:* men-only, women-only. Campus housing is university owned. Freshman campus housing is guaranteed. *Activities and Organizations:* drama/theater group, student-run newspaper, choral group, Student Senate, Wildlife Club/Horticulture Club, Snowboarding Club, Phi Theta Kappa, Delta Epsilon Chi. *Campus security:* controlled dormitory access. *Student services:* health clinic, personal/psychological counseling.

Athletics Member NJCAA. *Intercollegiate sports:* baseball M(s), basketball M(s)/W(s), football M(s), ice hockey M(s), softball W(s), volleyball W(s). *Intramural sports:* archery M/W, badminton M/W, basketball M/W, skiing (downhill) M/W, volleyball M/W.

Standardized Tests *Required:* ACT (for admission).

Costs (2009–10) *Tuition:* state resident $3837 full-time; nonresident $5397 full-time. Full-time tuition and fees vary according to location and reciprocity agreements. Part-time tuition and fees vary according to course load, location, and reciprocity agreements. *Required fees:* $183 per credit hour part-time. *Room and board:* $4328. Room and board charges vary according to gender, housing facility, and location. *Waivers:* minority students.

Financial Aid Of all full-time matriculated undergraduates who enrolled in 2008, 50 Federal Work-Study jobs (averaging $1100).

Applying *Options:* electronic application, early admission, deferred entrance. *Application fee:* $35. *Required:* high school transcript, ACT, immunization records. *Required for some:* ACT, immunization records. *Application deadlines:* rolling (freshmen), rolling (out-of-state freshmen), rolling (transfers).

Freshman Application Contact Mrs. Jancy Brisson, Admissions Counselor, Dakota College at Bottineau, 105 Simrall Boulevard, Bottineau, ND 58318. *Phone:* 701-228-5494. *Toll-free phone:* 800-542-6866. *Fax:* 701-228-5499. *E-mail:* jancy.brisson@dakotacollege.edu.

FORT BERTHOLD COMMUNITY COLLEGE

New Town, North Dakota **www.fbcc.bia.edu/**

Freshman Application Contact Twila Aulaumea, Registrar/Admissions Director, Fort Berthold Community College, PO Box 490, 220 8th Avenue North, New Town, ND 58763-0490. *Phone:* 701-627-4738 Ext. 286. *Fax:* 701-627-3609. *E-mail:* taulau@fbcc.bia.edu.

LAKE REGION STATE COLLEGE

Devils Lake, North Dakota **www.lrsc.edu/**

- **State-supported** 2-year, founded 1941, part of North Dakota University System
- **Small-town** 120-acre campus
- **Coed,** 1,702 undergraduate students, 29% full-time, 54% women, 46% men

Undergraduates 490 full-time, 1,212 part-time. Students come from 28 states and territories, 10 other countries, 10% are from out of state, 4% African American, 2% Asian American or Pacific Islander, 2% Hispanic American, 5% Native American, 3% international, 5% transferred in, 30% live on campus.

Freshmen *Admission:* 233 applied, 230 admitted, 219 enrolled.

Faculty *Total:* 141, 25% full-time, 12% with terminal degrees. *Student/faculty ratio:* 13:1.

Majors Accounting; accounting technology and bookkeeping; administrative assistant and secretarial science; agricultural business and management; automobile/automotive mechanics technology; avionics maintenance technology; business administration and management; child-care and support services management; child-care provision; computer and information sciences; computer programming (specific applications); computer programming (vendor/product certification); computer science; computer systems networking and telecommunications; criminal justice/police science; diesel mechanics technology; electrical and electronic engineering technologies related; electrical, electronics and communications engineering; electrical/electronics equipment installation and repair; executive assistant/executive secretary; fashion merchandising; information technology; legal administrative assistant/secretary; legal assistant/paralegal; liberal arts and sciences/liberal studies; management information systems; marketing research; medical administrative assistant and medical secretary; nursing assistant/aide and patient care assistant; nursing (licensed practical/vocational nurse training); office management; office occupations and clerical services; pathologist assistant; sales, distribution and marketing; sign language interpretation and translation; small business administration; teacher assistant/aide; technical teacher education.

Academics *Calendar:* semesters. *Degree:* certificates, diplomas, and associate. *Special study options:* academic remediation for entering students, adult/continuing education programs, cooperative education, distance learning, double majors, English as a second language, freshman honors college, honors programs, internships, part-time degree program, summer session for credit.

Library Paul Hoghaug Library with 60,000 titles, 200 serial subscriptions, 2,000 audiovisual materials, an OPAC.

Student Life *Housing Options:* men-only, women-only. Campus housing is university owned. *Activities and Organizations:* drama/theater group, DECA, drama, SOTA (Students Other than Average), Student Senate, Computer Club. *Campus security:* 24-hour emergency response devices, controlled dormitory access. *Student services:* personal/psychological counseling.

Athletics Member NJCAA. *Intercollegiate sports:* basketball M(s)/W(s). *Intramural sports:* basketball M/W, football M/W, golf M/W, ice hockey M/W, softball M/W, table tennis M/W, volleyball M/W.

Lake Region State College (continued)

Standardized Tests *Required:* SAT or ACT (for admission), COMPASS (for admission).

Costs (2010–11) *Tuition:* state resident $3065 full-time, $128 per credit hour part-time; nonresident $3065 full-time, $128 per credit hour part-time. *Room and board:* $5230; room only: $1820. Room and board charges vary according to board plan and housing facility. *Payment plan:* installment. *Waivers:* minority students.

Financial Aid Of all full-time matriculated undergraduates who enrolled in 2008, 300 applied for aid, 249 were judged to have need, 37 had their need fully met. 40 Federal Work-Study jobs (averaging $1600). In 2008, 184 non-need-based awards were made. *Average percent of need met:* 70%. *Average financial aid package:* $6936. *Average need-based loan:* $3353. *Average need-based gift aid:* $3682. *Average non-need-based aid:* $651. *Average indebtedness upon graduation:* $9392.

Applying *Options:* electronic application. *Application fee:* $35. *Required:* high school transcript, immunizations, transcripts. *Required for some:* interview. *Application deadlines:* rolling (freshmen), rolling (transfers). *Notification:* continuous (freshmen), continuous (transfers).

Freshman Application Contact Ms. Diane Knodel, Administrative Assistant, Admissions Office, Lake Region State College, 1801 College Drive North, Devils Lake, ND 58301. *Phone:* 701-662-1514. *Toll-free phone:* 800-443-1313 Ext. 514. *Fax:* 701-662-1581. *E-mail:* diane.knodel@lrsc.edu.

North Dakota State College of Science

Wahpeton, North Dakota **www.ndscs.nodak.edu/**

Freshman Application Contact Ms. Karen Reilly, Director of Enrollment Services, North Dakota State College of Science, 800 North 6th Street, Wahpeton, ND 58076. *Phone:* 701-671-2189. *Toll-free phone:* 800-342-4325 Ext. 2202. *Fax:* 701-671-2332.

Rasmussen College Bismarck

Bismarck, North Dakota **www.rasmussen.edu/**

Admissions Office Contact Rasmussen College Bismarck, 1701 East Century Avenue, Bismarck, ND 58503. *Toll-free phone:* 877-530-9600.

Rasmussen College Fargo

Fargo, North Dakota **www.rasmussen.edu/**

Freshman Application Contact Ms. Elizabeth Largent, Director, Rasmussen College Fargo, 4012 19th Avenue, SW, Fargo, ND 58103. *Phone:* 701-277-3889. *Toll-free phone:* 800-817-0009. *Fax:* 701-277-5604.

Sitting Bull College

Fort Yates, North Dakota **www.sittingbull.edu/**

Director of Admissions Ms. Melody Silk, Director of Registration and Admissions, Sitting Bull College, 1341 92nd Street, Fort Yates, ND 58538-9701. *Phone:* 701-854-3864. *Fax:* 701-854-3403. *E-mail:* melodys@sbcl.edu.

Turtle Mountain Community College

Belcourt, North Dakota **www.turtle-mountain.cc.nd.us/**

Director of Admissions Ms. Joni LaFontaine, Admissions/Records Officer, Turtle Mountain Community College, Box 340, Belcourt, ND 58316-0340. *Phone:* 701-477-5605 Ext. 217. *E-mail:* jlafontaine@tm.edu.

United Tribes Technical College

Bismarck, North Dakota **www.uttc.edu/**

Freshman Application Contact Ms. Vivian Gillette, Director of Admissions, United Tribes Technical College, 3315 University Drive, Bismarck, ND 58504. *Phone:* 701-255-3285 Ext. 1334. *Fax:* 701-530-0640. *E-mail:* vgillette@uttc.edu.

Williston State College

Williston, North Dakota **www.wsc.nodak.edu/**

Freshman Application Contact Ms. Jan Solem, Director for Admission and Records, Williston State College, PO Box 1326, Williston, ND 58802-1326. *Phone:* 701-774-4554. *Toll-free phone:* 888-863-9455. *Fax:* 701-774-4211. *E-mail:* wsc.admission@wsc.nodak.edu.

NORTHERN MARIANA ISLANDS

Northern Marianas College

Saipan, Northern Mariana Islands **www.nmcnet.edu/**

Freshman Application Contact Ms. Leilani M. Basa-Alam, Admission Specialist, Northern Marianas College, PO Box 501250, Saipan, MP 96950-1250. *Phone:* 670-234-3690 Ext. 1539. *Fax:* 670-235-4967. *E-mail:* leilanib@nmcnet.edu.

OHIO

Academy of Court Reporting

Akron, Ohio **www.acr.edu/**

Freshman Application Contact Admissions, Academy of Court Reporting, 2930 West Market Street, Akron, OH 44333. *Phone:* 330-867-4030. *Toll-free phone:* 866-323-0540. *Fax:* 330-867-3432. *E-mail:* careeradvocate@miamijacobs.edu.

Academy of Court Reporting

Cleveland, Ohio **www.acr.edu/**

Freshman Application Contact Ms. Sheila Woods, Director of Admissions, Academy of Court Reporting, 2044 Euclid Avenue, Cleveland, OH 44115. *Phone:* 216-861-3222. *Fax:* 216-861-4517. *E-mail:* admissionaocr@hotmail.com.

Antonelli College

Cincinnati, Ohio **www.antonellicollege.edu/**

- **Proprietary** 2-year, founded 1947
- **Urban** campus
- **Coed,** 377 undergraduate students

Majors Accounting and business/management; commercial and advertising art; computer and information sciences; computer systems networking and telecommunications; graphic design; interior design; photography; web/multimedia management and webmaster.

Academics *Calendar:* quarters. *Degree:* diplomas and associate. *Special study options:* honors programs, internships, part-time degree program, summer session for credit.
Library Main Library plus 1 other with 2,000 titles, 30 serial subscriptions.
Student Life *Housing:* college housing not available. *Campus security:* 24-hour emergency response devices, security personnel while classes are in session. *Student services:* personal/psychological counseling.
Applying *Options:* early admission, deferred entrance. *Application fee:* $100. *Required:* high school transcript, interview. *Required for some:* art portfolio. *Application deadlines:* rolling (freshmen), rolling (transfers). *Notification:* continuous (transfers).
Freshman Application Contact Antonelli College, 124 East Seventh Street, Cincinnati, OH 45202. *Phone:* 513-241-4338. *Toll-free phone:* 800-505-4338.

THE ART INSTITUTE OF CINCINNATI

Cincinnati, Ohio **www.theartinstituteofcincinnati.com/**

Director of Admissions Director of Admissions, The Art Institute of Cincinnati, 1171 East Kemper Road, Cincinnati, OH 45246. *Phone:* 513-751-1206. *Fax:* 513-751-1209.

THE ART INSTITUTE OF OHIO–CINCINNATI

Cincinnati, Ohio **www.artinstitutes.edu/cincinnati/**

- **Proprietary** primarily 2-year, part of Education Management Corporation
- **Urban** campus
- **Coed**

Majors Advertising; animation, interactive technology, video graphics and special effects; cinematography and film/video production; culinary arts; design and visual communications; fashion merchandising; graphic design; interior design; restaurant, culinary, and catering management; web page, digital/multimedia and information resources design.
Academics *Calendar:* continuous. *Degrees:* diplomas, associate, and bachelor's.
Costs (2009–10) *Tuition:* Tuition cost varies by program. Prospective students should contact the school for current tuition costs. Other charges include a starting kit for all first-quarter students. Kits vary in price, depending on the program of study.
Freshman Application Contact The Art Institute of Ohio–Cincinnati, 1011 Glendale-Milford Road, Cincinnati, OH 45215-1107. *Phone:* 513-833-2400. *Toll-free phone:* 866-613-5184.

ATS INSTITUTE OF TECHNOLOGY

Highland Heights, Ohio **www.atsinstitute.edu/**

- **Proprietary** 2-year
- **Suburban** campus with easy access to Cleveland
- **Coed,** 353 undergraduate students

Majors Nursing (licensed practical/vocational nurse training).
Academics *Degree:* diplomas and associate. *Special study options:* academic remediation for entering students, accelerated degree program, English as a second language, external degree program, part-time degree program. *Unusual degree programs:* nursing.
Library ATS Library plus 1 other.
Standardized Tests *Required:* Entrance exam called PSB(Psychological Service Bureau) is required for all entering students except for those applying for Bridge program. (for admission).
Costs (2010–11) *Tuition:* $497 per credit hour part-time. Full-time tuition and fees vary according to course load, degree level, and program. Part-time tuition and fees vary according to course load and program. *Payment plan:* installment.
Applying *Application fee:* $30. *Required:* high school transcript, minimum 2.5 GPA, interview, complete background check and physical evaluation. *Required for some:* essay or personal statement.
Freshman Application Contact Admissions Office, ATS Institute of Technology, 230 Alpha Park Drive, Highland Heights, OH 44143. *Phone:* 440-449-1700 Ext. 103. *E-mail:* info@atsinstitute.com.

BELMONT TECHNICAL COLLEGE

St. Clairsville, Ohio **www.btc.edu/**

- **State-supported** 2-year, founded 1971, part of Ohio Board of Regents
- **Rural** 55-acre campus
- **Coed**

Academics *Calendar:* quarters. *Degree:* diplomas and associate. *Special study options:* academic remediation for entering students, distance learning, independent study, part-time degree program, summer session for credit.
Financial Aid Of all full-time matriculated undergraduates who enrolled in 2008, 15 Federal Work-Study jobs (averaging $4500).
Applying *Options:* early admission.
Director of Admissions Michael Sterling, Director of Recruitment, Belmont Technical College, 120 Fox Shannon Place, St. Clairsville, OH 43950-9735. *Phone:* 740-695-9500 Ext. 1563. *Toll-free phone:* 800-423-1188. *E-mail:* msterling@btc.edu.

BOWLING GREEN STATE UNIVERSITY–FIRELANDS COLLEGE

Huron, Ohio **www.firelands.bgsu.edu/**

- **State-supported** primarily 2-year, founded 1968, part of Bowling Green State University System
- **Rural** 216-acre campus with easy access to Cleveland and Toledo
- **Endowment** $2.0 million
- **Coed,** 2,454 undergraduate students, 55% full-time, 65% women, 35% men

Undergraduates 1,352 full-time, 1,102 part-time. Students come from 4 states and territories, 10% African American, 0.3% Asian American or Pacific Islander, 4% Hispanic American, 0.7% Native American, 0.4% international, 6% transferred in.
Freshmen *Admission:* 498 enrolled.
Faculty *Total:* 144, 35% full-time. *Student/faculty ratio:* 18:1.
Majors Accounting technology and bookkeeping; biological and physical sciences; business operations support and secretarial services related; communications technologies and support services related; computer and information sciences and support services related; computer engineering technology; computer programming; computer systems networking and telecommunications; criminal justice/safety; design and visual communications; drafting/design engineering technologies related; education; electrical, electronic and communications engineering technology; engineering technologies related; family and community services; health information/medical records administration; health professions related; humanities; human services; industrial technology; interdisciplinary studies; kindergarten/preschool education; liberal arts and sciences/liberal studies; nursing (registered nurse training); operations management; pre-engineering; respiratory care therapy; social sciences.
Academics *Calendar:* semesters. *Degrees:* certificates, associate, and bachelor's (also offers some upper-level and graduate courses). *Special study options:* academic remediation for entering students, adult/continuing education programs, advanced placement credit, distance learning, double majors, independent study, internships, part-time degree program, services for LD students, student-designed majors, summer session for credit. *ROTC:* Army (c), Air Force (c).
Library BGSU Firelands College Library with 61,019 titles, 224 serial subscriptions, 2,163 audiovisual materials, an OPAC, a Web page.
Student Life *Housing:* college housing not available. *Activities and Organizations:* drama/theater group, History Club, Science and Environment Club, Speech Activities Organization - Theatre, Visual Communication Technology Organization, intramurals. *Campus security:* 24-hour emergency response devices, late-night transport/escort service, patrols by trained security personnel.
Costs (2009–10) *Tuition:* state resident $4022 full-time, $2352 per year part-time; nonresident $11,300 full-time, $6012 per year part-time. Full-time tuition and fees vary according to course load and location. Part-time tuition and fees vary according to course load and location. *Required fees:* $206 full-time, $136 per year part-time. *Payment plans:* tuition prepayment, installment. *Waivers:* employees or children of employees.
Applying *Options:* electronic application, early admission, deferred entrance. *Application fee:* $40. *Required:* high school transcript. *Notification:* continuous (freshmen), continuous (transfers).
Freshman Application Contact Debralee Divers, Director of Admissions and Financial Aid, Bowling Green State University–Firelands College, One University Drive, Huron, OH 44839. *Phone:* 419-433-5560. *Toll-free phone:* 800-322-4787. *Fax:* 419-372-0604. *E-mail:* divers@bgsu.edu.

BRADFORD SCHOOL

Columbus, Ohio **www.bradfordschoolcolumbus.edu/**

- **Private** 2-year, founded 1911
- **Suburban** campus
- **Coed, primarily women,** 575 undergraduate students
- 54% of applicants were admitted

Freshmen *Admission:* 2,085 applied, 1,127 admitted.
Majors Accounting and business/management; business administration and management; computer programming; culinary arts; graphic design; legal administrative assistant/secretary; legal assistant/paralegal; medical/clinical assistant; system, networking, and LAN/WAN management; tourism and travel services management; veterinary/animal health technology.
Academics *Calendar:* semesters. *Degree:* diplomas and associate. *Special study options:* accelerated degree program, independent study.
Freshman Application Contact Admissions Office, Bradford School, 2469 Stelzer Road, Columbus, OH 43219. *Phone:* 614-416-6200. *Toll-free phone:* 800-678-7981.

BROWN MACKIE COLLEGE–AKRON

Akron, Ohio **www.brownmackie.edu/akron/**

- **Proprietary** 2-year, founded 1968, part of Education Management Corporation
- **Suburban** campus
- **Coed**

Majors Accounting technology and bookkeeping; business administration and management; criminal justice/law enforcement administration; data modeling/warehousing and database administration; early childhood education; health/health-care administration; information technology; legal assistant/paralegal; medical/clinical assistant; occupational therapist assistant; office management; pharmacy technician; surgical technology; veterinary/animal health technology.
Academics *Calendar:* quarters. *Degree:* certificates, diplomas, and associate.
Costs (2009–10) *Tuition:* Tuition varies by program. Students should contact Brown Mackie College for tuition information.
Freshman Application Contact Brown Mackie College–Akron, 755 White Pond Drive, Suite 101, Akron, OH 44320. *Phone:* 330-869-3600.

▶**See page 404 for the College Close-Up.**

BROWN MACKIE COLLEGE–CINCINNATI

Cincinnati, Ohio **www.brownmackie.edu/cincinnati/**

- **Proprietary** 2-year, founded 1927, part of Education Management Corporation
- **Suburban** campus
- **Coed**

Majors Accounting technology and bookkeeping; audiovisual communications technologies related; biomedical technology; business administration and management; computer systems networking and telecommunications; criminal justice/law enforcement administration; data modeling/warehousing and database administration; early childhood education; electrical, electronic and communications engineering technology; health/health-care administration; information technology; legal assistant/paralegal; medical/clinical assistant; office management; pharmacy technician; surgical technology; veterinary/animal health technology.
Academics *Calendar:* quarters. *Degree:* certificates, diplomas, and associate.
Costs (2009–10) *Tuition:* Tuition varies by program. Students should contact Brown Mackie College for tuition information.
Freshman Application Contact Brown Mackie College–Cincinnati, 1011 Glendale-Milford Road, Cincinnati, OH 45215. *Phone:* 513-771-2424. *Toll-free phone:* 800-888-1445.

▶**See page 412 for the College Close-Up.**

BROWN MACKIE COLLEGE–FINDLAY

Findlay, Ohio **www.brownmackie.edu/findlay/**

- **Proprietary** 2-year, founded 1929, part of Education Management Corporation
- **Rural** campus
- **Coed**

Majors Accounting technology and bookkeeping; business administration and management; criminal justice/law enforcement administration; early childhood education; health/health-care administration; legal assistant/paralegal; medical/clinical assistant; occupational therapist assistant; office management; pharmacy technician; surgical technology; veterinary/animal health technology.
Academics *Calendar:* continuous. *Degree:* diplomas and associate.
Costs (2009–10) *Tuition:* Tuition varies by program. Students should contact Brown Mackie College for tuition information.
Freshman Application Contact Brown Mackie College–Findlay, 1700 Fostoria Avenue, Suite 100, Findlay, OH 45840. *Phone:* 419-423-2211. *Toll-free phone:* 800-842-3687.

▶**See page 414 for the College Close-Up.**

BROWN MACKIE COLLEGE–NORTH CANTON

Canton, Ohio **www.brownmackie.edu/northcanton/**

- **Proprietary** 2-year, founded 1929, part of Education Management Corporation
- **Suburban** campus
- **Coed**

Majors Accounting technology and bookkeeping; business administration and management; CAD/CADD drafting/design technology; computer systems networking and telecommunications; criminal justice/law enforcement administration; health/health-care administration; legal assistant/paralegal; medical/clinical assistant; pharmacy technician; surgical technology; veterinary/animal health technology.
Academics *Calendar:* quarters. *Degree:* diplomas and associate.
Costs (2009–10) *Tuition:* Tuition varies by program. Students should contact Brown Mackie College for tuition information.
Freshman Application Contact Brown Mackie College–North Canton, 4300 Munson Street NW, Canton, OH 44718-3674. *Phone:* 330-494-1214.

▶**See page 434 for the College Close-Up.**

BRYANT & STRATTON COLLEGE

Eastlake, Ohio **www.bryantstratton.edu/**

- **Proprietary** primarily 2-year, founded 1987, part of Bryant and Stratton College, Inc.
- **Suburban** campus with easy access to Cleveland
- **Coed,** 762 undergraduate students, 64% full-time, 88% women, 12% men

Undergraduates 490 full-time, 272 part-time. Students come from 1 other state, 58% African American, 2% Hispanic American, 0.3% Native American, 1% transferred in. *Retention:* 28% of 2008 full-time freshmen returned.
Freshmen *Admission:* 312 applied, 378 enrolled.
Faculty *Total:* 63, 38% full-time, 13% with terminal degrees. *Student/faculty ratio:* 12:1.
Majors Accounting; administrative assistant and secretarial science; business administration and management; computer and information systems security; data processing and data processing technology; electrical and electronic engineering technologies related; electrical, electronic and communications engineering technology; human resources management; information technology; legal assistant/paralegal; medical administrative assistant and medical secretary; medical/clinical assistant; nursing (registered nurse training); system, networking, and LAN/WAN management.
Academics *Calendar:* semesters. *Degrees:* associate and bachelor's. *Special study options:* academic remediation for entering students, advanced placement credit, distance learning, independent study, internships, part-time degree program, summer session for credit.
Library Main Library plus 1 other with 1,500 titles, 19 serial subscriptions, an OPAC.
Student Life *Housing:* college housing not available. *Activities and Organizations:* student-run newspaper, Criminal Justice Club, Rotaract, Medical Assisting Club, International Association of Administrative Professionals (IAAP), Student Senate. *Campus security:* 24-hour emergency response devices, late-night transport/escort service.
Standardized Tests *Required:* CPAt (for admission). *Recommended:* SAT or ACT (for admission).
Financial Aid Of all full-time matriculated undergraduates who enrolled in 2008, 12 Federal Work-Study jobs (averaging $2800).

Applying *Options:* deferred entrance. *Application fee:* $35. *Required:* high school transcript, interview, entrance evaluation and placement evaluation. *Required for some:* essay or personal statement. *Recommended:* minimum 2 GPA. *Application deadlines:* rolling (freshmen), rolling (transfers).

Freshman Application Contact Ms. Melanie Pettit, Director of Admissions, Bryant & Stratton College, 27557 Chardon Road, Willoughby Hills, OH 44092. *Phone:* 440-510-1112.

BRYANT & STRATTON COLLEGE

Parma, Ohio **www.bryantstratton.edu/**

- **Proprietary** primarily 2-year, founded 1981, part of Bryant and Stratton College, Inc.
- **Suburban** 4-acre campus with easy access to Cleveland
- **Coed,** 528 undergraduate students, 55% full-time, 81% women, 19% men

Undergraduates 288 full-time, 240 part-time. Students come from 1 other state, 24% African American, 1% Asian American or Pacific Islander, 16% Hispanic American, 0.6% Native American. *Retention:* 60% of 2008 full-time freshmen returned.

Freshmen *Admission:* 189 enrolled.

Faculty *Total:* 57, 28% full-time. *Student/faculty ratio:* 12:1.

Majors Accounting; administrative assistant and secretarial science; business administration and management; business/commerce; computer and information systems security; criminal justice/law enforcement administration; human resources management and services related; information technology; legal administrative assistant/secretary; medical administrative assistant and medical secretary; medical/clinical assistant; nursing (registered nurse training); system, networking, and LAN/WAN management.

Academics *Calendar:* semesters. *Degrees:* associate and bachelor's. *Special study options:* academic remediation for entering students, cooperative education, distance learning, double majors, independent study, internships, part-time degree program, summer session for credit.

Library Main Library plus 1 other with 1,500 titles, 20 serial subscriptions, an OPAC.

Student Life *Housing:* college housing not available. *Activities and Organizations:* SHRM, Student Services Club, Sigma Psi Phi - Lambda Alpha Epsilon, Student Nursing Club, Medical Administrative Assistant Club. *Campus security:* 24-hour emergency response devices.

Standardized Tests *Required:* CPAt (for admission). *Recommended:* SAT or ACT (for admission).

Applying *Options:* deferred entrance. *Required:* high school transcript, interview, entrance evaluation and placement evaluation. *Application deadlines:* rolling (freshmen), rolling (transfers).

Freshman Application Contact Bryant & Stratton College, 12955 Snow Road, Parma, OH 44130. *Phone:* 216-265-3151. *Toll-free phone:* 800-327-3151.

CENTRAL OHIO TECHNICAL COLLEGE

Newark, Ohio **www.cotc.edu/**

- **State-supported** 2-year, founded 1971, part of Ohio Board of Regents
- **Small-town** 155-acre campus with easy access to Columbus
- **Endowment** $1.7 million
- **Coed,** 4,350 undergraduate students, 51% full-time, 72% women, 28% men

Undergraduates 2,213 full-time, 2,137 part-time. Students come from 3 states and territories, 1% are from out of state, 7% African American, 0.9% Asian American or Pacific Islander, 1% Hispanic American, 0.6% Native American, 6% transferred in. *Retention:* 51% of 2008 full-time freshmen returned.

Freshmen *Admission:* 1,578 applied, 1,578 admitted, 828 enrolled.

Faculty *Total:* 331, 18% full-time, 12% with terminal degrees. *Student/faculty ratio:* 22:1.

Majors Accounting; business administration and management; computer programming; criminal justice/law enforcement administration; criminal justice/police science; culinary arts; data processing and data processing technology; desktop publishing and digital imaging design; diagnostic medical sonography and ultrasound technology; drafting and design technology; electrical, electronic and communications engineering technology; electromechanical technology; emergency medical technology (EMT paramedic); entrepreneurship; fire science; forensic science and technology; human services; kindergarten/preschool education; liberal arts and sciences/liberal studies; manufacturing technology; medical radiologic technology; nursing (licensed practical/vocational nurse training); nursing (registered nurse training); surgical technology.

Academics *Calendar:* quarters. *Degree:* certificates and associate. *Special study options:* academic remediation for entering students, accelerated degree program, adult/continuing education programs, advanced placement credit, cooperative education, distance learning, double majors, English as a second language, internships, off-campus study, part-time degree program, services for LD students, summer session for credit.

Library Newark Campus Library with 45,000 titles, 500 serial subscriptions, an OPAC, a Web page.

Student Life *Housing:* college housing not available. *Activities and Organizations:* drama/theater group, choral group, Student Nurses Organization, Phi Theta Kappa, Forensic Science Club, Campus Chorus, Student Senate. *Campus security:* 24-hour emergency response devices and patrols, student patrols, late-night transport/escort service. *Student services:* personal/psychological counseling.

Athletics *Intercollegiate sports:* baseball M, basketball M/W, softball W, volleyball M/W. *Intramural sports:* baseball M, basketball M/W, cheerleading M/W, football M, skiing (downhill) M/W, softball W, volleyball M/W, weight lifting M/W.

Costs (2010–11) *Tuition:* state resident $3726 full-time, $104 per credit hour part-time; nonresident $6426 full-time, $179 per credit hour part-time. *Payment plan:* installment. *Waivers:* senior citizens and employees or children of employees.

Financial Aid Of all full-time matriculated undergraduates who enrolled in 2008, 43 Federal Work-Study jobs (averaging $4000).

Applying *Options:* electronic application, early admission, deferred entrance. *Application fee:* $20. *Required:* high school transcript. *Application deadlines:* rolling (freshmen), rolling (transfers).

Freshman Application Contact Mr. John K. Merrin, Admissions Representative, Central Ohio Technical College, 1179 University Drive, Newark, OH 43055-1767. *Phone:* 740-366-9222. *Toll-free phone:* 800-9NEWARK. *Fax:* 740-366-5047. *E-mail:* jmerrin@cotc.edu.

CHATFIELD COLLEGE

St. Martin, Ohio **www.chatfield.edu/**

Freshman Application Contact Ms. Anna Jones, Director of Admissions, Chatfield College, St. Martin, OH 45118. *Phone:* 513-875-3344. *Fax:* 513-875-3912. *E-mail:* chatfield@chatfield.edu.

THE CHRIST COLLEGE OF NURSING AND HEALTH SCIENCES

Cincinnati, Ohio **www.thechristcollege.edu/**

Admissions Office Contact The Christ College of Nursing and Health Sciences, 2139 Auburn Avenue, Cincinnati, OH 45219.

CINCINNATI STATE TECHNICAL AND COMMUNITY COLLEGE

Cincinnati, Ohio **www.cincinnatistate.edu/**

- **State-supported** 2-year, founded 1966, part of Ohio Board of Regents
- **Urban** 46-acre campus
- **Endowment** $2.2 million
- **Coed,** 10,165 undergraduate students, 40% full-time, 54% women, 46% men

Undergraduates 4,065 full-time, 6,100 part-time. Students come from 8 states and territories, 76 other countries, 10% are from out of state, 25% African American, 0.9% Asian American or Pacific Islander, 1% Hispanic American, 0.5% Native American, 3% international, 4% transferred in. *Retention:* 52% of 2008 full-time freshmen returned.

Freshmen *Admission:* 1,659 enrolled.

Faculty *Total:* 617, 28% full-time. *Student/faculty ratio:* 15:1.

Majors Accounting; administrative assistant and secretarial science; aeronautical/aerospace engineering technology; allied health and medical assisting services related; applied horticulture/horticultural business services related; architectural engineering technology; automotive engineering technology; biomedical technology; business administration and management; business, management, and marketing related; chemical technology; child-care provision; cinematography and film/video production; civil engineering technology; clinical/medical labo-

Cincinnati State Technical and Community College (continued)

ratory technology; commercial and advertising art; computer and information sciences; computer engineering technology; computer programming; computer programming (specific applications); criminal justice/police science; culinary arts; diagnostic medical sonography and ultrasound technology; dietetics; electrical and electronic engineering technologies related; electrical, electronic and communications engineering technology; electromechanical technology; emergency medical technology (EMT paramedic); entrepreneurship; environmental engineering technology; executive assistant/executive secretary; fire science; general studies; health information/medical records technology; health professions related; heating, air conditioning and refrigeration technology; hotel/motel administration; information science/studies; international business/trade/commerce; landscaping and groundskeeping; laser and optical technology; liberal arts and sciences/liberal studies; management information systems; marketing/marketing management; mechanical engineering/mechanical technology; mechanic and repair technologies related; medical/clinical assistant; nursing (registered nurse training); nursing related; occupational therapist assistant; office management; parks, recreation, and leisure related; plastics engineering technology; purchasing, procurement/acquisitions and contracts management; real estate; respiratory care therapy; restaurant, culinary, and catering management; science technologies related; security and loss prevention; sign language interpretation and translation; surgical technology; survey technology; technical and business writing; telecommunications technology; turf and turfgrass management.

Academics *Calendar:* 5 ten-week terms. *Degree:* certificates and associate. *Special study options:* academic remediation for entering students, advanced placement credit, cooperative education, distance learning, double majors, English as a second language, honors programs, independent study, internships, off-campus study, part-time degree program, services for LD students, student-designed majors, summer session for credit.

Library Johnnie Mae Berry Library with 39,802 titles, 309 serial subscriptions, 3,570 audiovisual materials, an OPAC, a Web page.

Student Life *Housing:* college housing not available. *Activities and Organizations:* drama/theater group, student government, Nursing Student Association, Phi Theta Kappa, American Society of Civil Engineers, Students in Free Enterprise (SIFE). *Campus security:* 24-hour emergency response devices and patrols, late-night transport/escort service. *Student services:* personal/psychological counseling.

Athletics Member NJCAA. *Intercollegiate sports:* basketball M/W, golf M/W, soccer M/W. *Intramural sports:* cheerleading W.

Costs (2010–11) *One-time required fee:* $10. *Tuition:* state resident $4675 full-time, $83 per credit hour part-time; nonresident $9350 full-time, $166 per credit hour part-time. *Required fees:* $258 full-time, $6 per credit hour part-time, $31 per term part-time.

Financial Aid Of all full-time matriculated undergraduates who enrolled in 2008, 100 Federal Work-Study jobs (averaging $3500).

Applying *Options:* electronic application. *Required:* high school transcript. *Application deadlines:* rolling (freshmen), rolling (transfers). *Notification:* continuous (freshmen).

Freshman Application Contact Ms. Gabriele Boeckermann, Director of Admission, Cincinnati State Technical and Community College, 3520 Central Parkway, Cincinnati, OH 45223-2690. *Phone:* 513-569-1550. *Fax:* 513-569-1562. *E-mail:* adm@cincinnatistate.edu.

Clark State Community College

Springfield, Ohio — **www.clarkstate.edu/**

Freshman Application Contact Admissions Office, Clark State Community College, PO Box 570, Springfield, OH 45501-0570. *Phone:* 937-328-3858. *Fax:* 937-328-6133. *E-mail:* admissions@clarkstate.edu.

Cleveland Institute of Electronics

Cleveland, Ohio — **www.cie-wc.edu/**

- **Proprietary** 2-year, founded 1934
- **Coed, primarily men,** 2,146 undergraduate students, 7% women, 93% men

Undergraduates 2,146 part-time. Students come from 52 states and territories, 70 other countries, 97% are from out of state, 10% African American, 0.7% Asian American or Pacific Islander, 5% Hispanic American, 3% Native American.

Freshmen *Admission:* 193 enrolled.

Faculty *Total:* 8, 50% full-time.

Majors Computer/information technology services administration related; computer software engineering; electrical, electronic and communications engineering technology.

Academics *Calendar:* continuous. *Degrees:* diplomas and associate (offers only external degree programs conducted through home study). *Special study options:* accelerated degree program, adult/continuing education programs, distance learning, external degree program, independent study, part-time degree program.

Library 5,000 titles, 38 serial subscriptions.

Student Life *Housing:* college housing not available.

Costs (2010–11) *Tuition:* $1885 per term part-time. No tuition increase for student's term of enrollment. *Payment plans:* tuition prepayment, installment.

Applying *Options:* electronic application, early admission. *Required:* high school transcript. *Application deadlines:* rolling (freshmen), rolling (out-of-state freshmen), rolling (transfers). *Notification:* continuous (freshmen), continuous (out-of-state freshmen), continuous (transfers).

Freshman Application Contact Mr. Scott Katzenmeyer, Registrar, Cleveland Institute of Electronics, 1776 East 17th Street, Cleveland, OH 44114. *Phone:* 216-781-9400. *Toll-free phone:* 800-243-6446. *Fax:* 216-781-0331. *E-mail:* instruct@cie-wc.edu.

Columbus Culinary Institute at Bradford School

Columbus, Ohio — **www.columbusculinary.com/**

- **Private** 2-year, founded 2006
- **Suburban** campus
- **Coed,** 245 undergraduate students
- 55% of applicants were admitted

Freshmen *Admission:* 1,001 applied, 550 admitted.

Majors Culinary arts.

Academics *Calendar:* semesters. *Degree:* associate.

Freshman Application Contact Admissions Office, Columbus Culinary Institute at Bradford School, 2435 Stelzer Road, Columbus, OH 43219. *Phone:* 614-944-4200. *Toll-free phone:* 800-678-7981.

Columbus State Community College

Columbus, Ohio — **www.cscc.edu/**

- **State-supported** 2-year, founded 1963, part of Ohio Board of Regents
- **Urban** 75-acre campus
- **Coed**

Academics *Calendar:* quarters. *Degree:* certificates and associate. *Special study options:* academic remediation for entering students, adult/continuing education programs, advanced placement credit, cooperative education, distance learning, English as a second language, honors programs, internships, off-campus study, part-time degree program, services for LD students, student-designed majors, summer session for credit. *ROTC:* Army (b), Air Force (c).

Student Life *Campus security:* 24-hour emergency response devices and patrols, late-night transport/escort service.

Athletics Member NJCAA.

Financial Aid Of all full-time matriculated undergraduates who enrolled in 2008, 133 Federal Work-Study jobs (averaging $1500).

Applying *Options:* early admission, deferred entrance. *Application fee:* $50. *Recommended:* high school transcript.

Freshman Application Contact Ms. Tari Blaney, Director of Admissions, Columbus State Community College, 550 East Spring Street, Madison Hall, Columbus, OH 43215. *Phone:* 614-287-2669. *Toll-free phone:* 800-621-6407 Ext. 2669. *Fax:* 614-287-6019. *E-mail:* tblaney@cscc.edu.

Cuyahoga Community College

Cleveland, Ohio — **www.tri-c.edu/**

- **State and locally supported** 2-year, founded 1963
- **Urban** campus
- **Endowment** $22.5 million
- **Coed,** 30,325 undergraduate students, 40% full-time, 62% women, 38% men

Undergraduates 12,120 full-time, 18,205 part-time. Students come from 32 states and territories, 27 other countries, 1% are from out of state, 32% African American, 2% Asian American or Pacific Islander, 4% Hispanic American, 0.6% Native American, 2% international, 4% transferred in. *Retention:* 48% of 2008 full-time freshmen returned.

Freshmen *Admission:* 7,076 applied, 7,076 admitted, 3,033 enrolled.

Faculty *Total:* 1,608, 21% full-time, 11% with terminal degrees. *Student/faculty ratio:* 18:1.

Majors Accounting; administrative assistant and secretarial science; automobile/automotive mechanics technology; avionics maintenance technology; business administration and management; clinical laboratory science/medical technology; commercial and advertising art; computer engineering technology; computer typography and composition equipment operation; court reporting; criminal justice/police science; engineering technology; finance; fire science; industrial radiologic technology; kindergarten/preschool education; legal assistant/paralegal; liberal arts and sciences/liberal studies; marketing/marketing management; merchandising; nursing (registered nurse training); opticianry; photography; physician assistant; quality control and safety technologies related; real estate; respiratory care therapy; restaurant, culinary, and catering management; sales, distribution and marketing; selling skills and sales; surgical technology; veterinary/animal health technology.

Academics *Calendar:* semesters. *Degree:* certificates and associate. *Special study options:* adult/continuing education programs, advanced placement credit, cooperative education, distance learning, English as a second language, external degree program, independent study, part-time degree program, services for LD students, summer session for credit.

Library Metro Library plus 3 others with 177,767 titles, 1,135 serial subscriptions, an OPAC, a Web page.

Student Life *Housing:* college housing not available. *Activities and Organizations:* drama/theater group, student-run newspaper, choral group, Student Senate, Student Nursing Organization, Business Focus, Phi Theta Kappa. *Campus security:* 24-hour emergency response devices and patrols, late-night transport/escort service. *Student services:* health clinic, personal/psychological counseling.

Athletics Member NJCAA. *Intercollegiate sports:* baseball M(s), basketball M(s), cross-country running M(s)/W(s), soccer M(s), softball W(s). *Intramural sports:* basketball M, tennis M/W, track and field M/W, volleyball M/W.

Costs (2010–11) *Tuition:* area resident $2537 full-time, $85 per credit hour part-time; state resident $3354 full-time, $112 per credit hour part-time; nonresident $6868 full-time, $229 per credit hour part-time. *Payment plans:* installment, deferred payment.

Financial Aid Of all full-time matriculated undergraduates who enrolled in 2008, 802 Federal Work-Study jobs (averaging $3300).

Applying *Options:* early admission, deferred entrance. *Required for some:* high school transcript. *Application deadlines:* rolling (freshmen), rolling (transfers). *Notification:* continuous (freshmen), continuous (transfers).

Freshman Application Contact Mr. Kevin McDaniel, Director of Admissions and Records, Cuyahoga Community College, 2900 Community College Avenue, Cleveland, OH 44115. *Phone:* 216-987-4030. *Toll-free phone:* 800-954-8742. *Fax:* 216-696-2567.

DAVIS COLLEGE

Toledo, Ohio **daviscollege.edu/**

- **Proprietary** 2-year, founded 1858
- **Urban** 1-acre campus with easy access to Detroit
- **Coed,** 527 undergraduate students, 39% full-time, 86% women, 14% men

Undergraduates 207 full-time, 320 part-time. Students come from 2 states and territories, 3% are from out of state, 42% African American, 2% Hispanic American, 16% transferred in.

Freshmen *Admission:* 81 applied, 81 admitted, 68 enrolled.

Faculty *Total:* 33, 45% full-time. *Student/faculty ratio:* 15:1.

Majors Accounting; accounting related; administrative assistant and secretarial science; business administration and management; commercial and advertising art; computer systems networking and telecommunications; data processing and data processing technology; early childhood education; fashion merchandising; graphic design; information technology; insurance; interior design; marketing/marketing management; marketing related; medical administrative assistant and medical secretary; medical/clinical assistant; system administration; web page, digital/multimedia and information resources design.

Academics *Calendar:* quarters. *Degree:* diplomas and associate. *Special study options:* academic remediation for entering students, adult/continuing education programs, advanced placement credit, distance learning, internships, part-time degree program, summer session for credit.

Library Davis College Resource Center with 3,400 titles, 107 serial subscriptions, 191 audiovisual materials, an OPAC.

Student Life *Activities and Organizations:* Student Advisory Board. *Campus security:* 24-hour emergency response devices, security cameras for parking lot. *Student services:* personal/psychological counseling.

Standardized Tests *Required:* CPAt (for admission).

Costs (2010–11) *Comprehensive fee:* $18,021 includes full-time tuition ($8748), mandatory fees ($480), and room and board ($8793). Part-time tuition: $243 per credit hour. *Payment plan:* installment. *Waivers:* employees or children of employees.

Financial Aid Of all full-time matriculated undergraduates who enrolled in 2008, 10 Federal Work-Study jobs (averaging $3500).

Applying *Options:* electronic application, early admission, deferred entrance. *Application fee:* $30. *Required:* high school transcript, interview. *Application deadlines:* rolling (freshmen), rolling (transfers). *Notification:* continuous (freshmen), continuous (transfers).

Freshman Application Contact Ms. Dana Stern, Davis College, 4747 Monroe Street, Toledo, OH 43623-4307. *Phone:* 419-473-2700. *Toll-free phone:* 800-477-7021. *Fax:* 419-473-2472. *E-mail:* dstern@daviscollege.edu.

DAYMAR COLLEGE

Chillicothe, Ohio **www.daymarcollege.edu/**

Freshman Application Contact Admissions Office, Daymar College, 1410 Industrial Drive, Chillicothe, OH 45601. *Phone:* 740-774-6300. *Toll-free phone:* 877-258-7796. *Fax:* 740-774-6317.

DAYMAR COLLEGE

Jackson, Ohio **www.daymarcollege.edu/**

Director of Admissions Mr. Todd A. Riegel, Director of Education, Daymar College, 504 McCarty Lane, Jackson, OH 45640. *Phone:* 740-286-1554. *Fax:* 740-286-4476. *E-mail:* todd_sbc@yahoo.com.

DAYMAR COLLEGE

Lancaster, Ohio **www.daymarcollege.edu/**

Director of Admissions Mr. Ray Predmore, Director, Daymar College, 1522 Sheridan Drive, Lancaster, OH 43130-1303. *Phone:* 740-687-6126. *Fax:* 740-687-0431. *E-mail:* rp_sbc@yahoo.com.

DAYMAR COLLEGE

New Boston, Ohio **www.daymarcollege.edu/**

Admissions Office Contact Daymar College, 3879 Rhodes Avenue, New Boston, OH 45662.

EASTERN GATEWAY COMMUNITY COLLEGE

Steubenville, Ohio **www.easterngatewaycc.com/**

Freshman Application Contact Ms. Kristen Taylor, Director of Admissions, Eastern Gateway Community College, 4000 Sunset Boulevard, Steubenville, OH 43952. *Phone:* 740-264-5591. *Toll-free phone:* 800-68-COLLEGE Ext. 142. *Fax:* 740-266-2944. *E-mail:* cmascellino@jcc.edu.

EDISON STATE COMMUNITY COLLEGE

Piqua, Ohio **www.edisonohio.edu/**

- **State-supported** 2-year, founded 1973, part of Ohio Board of Regents
- **Small-town** 130-acre campus with easy access to Cincinnati and Dayton
- **Endowment** $1.5 million
- **Coed,** 3,457 undergraduate students, 39% full-time, 64% women, 36% men

Edison State Community College (continued)

Undergraduates 1,357 full-time, 2,100 part-time. Students come from 4 states and territories, 3 other countries, 1% are from out of state, 2% African American, 0.8% Asian American or Pacific Islander, 0.7% Hispanic American, 0.3% Native American, 0.1% international. *Retention:* 56% of 2008 full-time freshmen returned.

Freshmen *Admission:* 670 applied, 670 admitted. *Average high school GPA:* 2.93. *Test scores:* ACT scores over 18: 75%; ACT scores over 24: 10%.

Faculty *Total:* 211, 25% full-time, 9% with terminal degrees. *Student/faculty ratio:* 19:1.

Majors Accounting; administrative assistant and secretarial science; advertising; art; business administration and management; child development; clinical/medical laboratory technology; commercial and advertising art; communication/speech communication and rhetoric; computer and information sciences; computer and information systems security; computer engineering technology; computer graphics; computer programming; computer science; computer systems networking and telecommunications; computer technology/computer systems technology; criminal justice/police science; data processing and data processing technology; design and visual communications; drafting and design technology; dramatic/theater arts; education; electrical, electronic and communications engineering technology; electromechanical technology; engineering technology; executive assistant/executive secretary; health information/medical records administration; human resources management; human services; industrial technology; information technology; kindergarten/preschool education; legal administrative assistant/secretary; legal assistant/paralegal; legal studies; liberal arts and sciences/liberal studies; logistics and materials management; marketing/marketing management; mechanical drafting and CAD/CADD; mechanical engineering/mechanical technology; medical administrative assistant and medical secretary; medium/heavy vehicle and truck technology; nursing (registered nurse training); physical therapist assistant; pre-engineering; real estate; sales, distribution and marketing; social work; welding technology.

Academics *Calendar:* semesters. *Degree:* certificates and associate. *Special study options:* academic remediation for entering students, accelerated degree program, adult/continuing education programs, advanced placement credit, distance learning, double majors, English as a second language, honors programs, independent study, internships, off-campus study, part-time degree program, services for LD students, student-designed majors, summer session for credit.

Library Edison Community College Library with 29,851 titles, 542 serial subscriptions, 2,424 audiovisual materials, an OPAC, a Web page.

Student Life *Housing:* college housing not available. *Activities and Organizations:* drama/theater group, Campus Crusade for Christ, Student Ambassadors, Edison Stagelight Players, Writers Club, Edison Photo Society. *Campus security:* late-night transport/escort service, 18-hour patrols by trained security personnel. *Student services:* health clinic, personal/psychological counseling.

Athletics Member NJCAA. *Intercollegiate sports:* basketball M(s)/W(s), volleyball W(s).

Standardized Tests *Required:* ACT ASSET, ACT COMPASS (for admission).

Costs (2010–11) *Tuition:* state resident $3570 full-time, $119 per credit hour part-time; nonresident $6660 full-time, $222 per credit hour part-time. Full-time tuition and fees vary according to course load, program, and reciprocity agreements. Part-time tuition and fees vary according to course load, program, and reciprocity agreements. *Required fees:* $15 full-time. *Payment plans:* installment, deferred payment. *Waivers:* senior citizens and employees or children of employees.

Financial Aid Of all full-time matriculated undergraduates who enrolled in 2008, 42 Federal Work-Study jobs (averaging $3000).

Applying *Options:* electronic application. *Application fee:* $20. *Required:* high school transcript. *Application deadlines:* rolling (freshmen), rolling (transfers).

Freshman Application Contact Edison State Community College, 1973 Edison Drive, Piqua, OH 45356. *Phone:* 937-778-7852. *Toll-free phone:* 800-922-3722.

ETI Technical College of Niles

Niles, Ohio **www.eti-college.com/**

- **Proprietary** 2-year, founded 1989
- **Small-town** campus with easy access to Cleveland and Pittsburgh
- **Coed,** 421 undergraduate students

Undergraduates Students come from 2 states and territories, 10% are from out of state, 22% African American, 1% Hispanic American.

Freshmen *Admission:* 25 applied, 25 admitted. *Average high school GPA:* 2.6.

Faculty *Total:* 19, 32% full-time. *Student/faculty ratio:* 22:1.

Majors Computer/information technology services administration related; computer programming (specific applications); computer programming (vendor/product certification); computer software and media applications related; computer software engineering; data entry/microcomputer applications; data entry/microcomputer applications related; electrical, electronic and communications engineering technology; legal assistant/paralegal; medical/clinical assistant; word processing.

Academics *Calendar:* semesters. *Degree:* diplomas and associate. *Special study options:* academic remediation for entering students, adult/continuing education programs, advanced placement credit, part-time degree program, services for LD students.

Library Main Library plus 3 others with a Web page.

Student Life *Housing:* college housing not available. *Activities and Organizations:* student-run newspaper, student government. *Campus security:* 24-hour emergency response devices. *Student services:* personal/psychological counseling.

Standardized Tests *Recommended:* SAT (for admission), ACT (for admission).

Costs (2010–11) *Tuition:* $7715 full-time, $261 per credit hour part-time. Full-time tuition and fees vary according to course load and program. Part-time tuition and fees vary according to course load and program. *Required fees:* $375 full-time, $150 per term part-time. *Payment plan:* installment. *Waivers:* employees or children of employees.

Applying *Options:* early admission, deferred entrance. *Application fee:* $50. *Required:* high school transcript, interview. *Application deadlines:* rolling (freshmen), rolling (transfers). *Notification:* continuous (freshmen), continuous (transfers).

Freshman Application Contact Ms. Diane Marsteller, Director of Admissions, ETI Technical College of Niles, 2076 Youngstown-Warren Road, Niles, OH 44446-4398. *Phone:* 330-652-9919. *Fax:* 330-652-4399.

Everest Institute

Cuyahoga Falls, Ohio **www.everest.edu/**

Freshman Application Contact Admissions Office, Everest Institute, 2545 Bailey Road, Cuyahoga Falls, OH 44221. *Toll-free phone:* 888-519-4689.

Fortis College

Centerville, Ohio **www.retstechcenter.com/**

- **Proprietary** 2-year, founded 1953
- **Suburban** 4-acre campus with easy access to Dayton
- **Endowment** $893
- **Coed**

Undergraduates 533 full-time. Students come from 2 states and territories, 1% are from out of state, 0.9% transferred in.

Faculty *Student/faculty ratio:* 18:1.

Academics *Calendar:* semesters. *Degree:* diplomas and associate. *Special study options:* advanced placement credit, internships, summer session for credit.

Student Life *Campus security:* 24-hour emergency response devices.

Costs (2009–10) *Tuition:* $9721 full-time. Full-time tuition and fees vary according to class time, course load, degree level, and program. *Required fees:* $598 full-time.

Applying *Options:* early admission, deferred entrance. *Application fee:* $100. *Required:* high school transcript, interview.

Freshman Application Contact Fortis College, 555 East Alex Bell Road, Centerville, OH 45459-2712. *Phone:* 937-433-3410. *Toll-free phone:* 800-837-7387.

Fortis College–Ravenna

Ravenna, Ohio **www.fortis.edu/**

- **Independent** 2-year
- **Coed**

Academics *Degree:* certificates and associate.

Applying *Application fee:* $60.

Freshman Application Contact Admissions Office, Fortis College–Ravenna, 653 Enterprise Parkway, Ravenna, OH 44266. *Toll-free phone:* 800-794-2856.

Gallipolis Career College

Gallipolis, Ohio www.gallipoliscareercollege.com/

Freshman Application Contact Mr. Jack Henson, Director of Admissions, Gallipolis Career College, 1176 Jackson Pike, Suite 312, Gallipolis, OH 45631. *Phone:* 740-446-4367. *Toll-free phone:* 800-214-0452. *Fax:* 740-446-4124. *E-mail:* admissions@gallipoliscareercollege.com.

Good Samaritan College of Nursing and Health Science

Cincinnati, Ohio www.gscollege.edu/

Admissions Office Contact Good Samaritan College of Nursing and Health Science, 375 Dixmyth Avenue, Cincinnati, OH 45220.

Harrison College

Grove City, Ohio www.harrison.edu/

- **Proprietary** 2-year
- **Coed**

Majors Accounting; administrative assistant and secretarial science; business administration and management; criminal justice/law enforcement administration; finance; human resources management; marketing/marketing management; medical/clinical assistant; medical insurance/medical billing.

Academics *Calendar:* quarters. *Degree:* associate.

Library Main Library plus 1 other.

Standardized Tests *Required:* Wonderlic Scholastic Level Exam (SLE) (for admission).

Costs (2009–10) *Tuition:* Tuition cost varies by program. Prospective students should contact the school for current tuition costs.

Applying *Application fee:* $50. *Required:* high school transcript, interview. *Application deadlines:* rolling (freshmen), rolling (transfers). *Notification:* continuous (freshmen), continuous (transfers).

Freshman Application Contact Mark Jones, Harrison College, 3880 Jackpot Road, Grove City, OH 43123. *Phone:* 614-539-8800. *Toll-free phone:* 888-544-4422. *E-mail:* mark.jones@harrison.edu.

Hocking College

Nelsonville, Ohio www.hocking.edu/

Director of Admissions Ms. Lyn Hull, Director of Admissions, Hocking College, 3301 Hocking Parkway, Nelsonville, OH 45764-9588. *Phone:* 740-753-3591 Ext. 2803. *Toll-free phone:* 877-462-5464. *E-mail:* hull_lyn@hocking.edu.

Hondros College

Westerville, Ohio www.hondroscollege.com/

- **Proprietary** 2-year, founded 1981
- **Coed**

Academics *Calendar:* quarters. *Degree:* certificates and associate.

Student Life *Campus security:* 24-hour emergency response devices.

Applying *Application fee:* $25.

Director of Admissions Ms. Carol Thomas, Operations Manager, Hondros College, 4140 Executive Parkway, Westerville, OH 43081. *Phone:* 614-508-7244. *Toll-free phone:* 800-783-0095.

International College of Broadcasting

Dayton, Ohio www.icbcollege.com/

- **Private** 2-year, founded 1968
- **Urban** 1-acre campus
- **Coed**

Academics *Calendar:* semesters. *Degree:* diplomas and associate.

Applying *Application fee:* $100.

Director of Admissions Mr. Aan McIntosh, Director of Admissions, International College of Broadcasting, 6 South Smithville Road, Dayton, OH 45431. *Phone:* 937-258-8251. *Fax:* 937-258-8714.

ITT Technical Institute

Akron, Ohio www.itt-tech.edu/

- **Proprietary** 2-year
- **Coed**

Majors CAD/CADD drafting/design technology; computer engineering technology; legal assistant/paralegal; system, networking, and LAN/WAN management.

Academics *Degree:* associate.

Freshman Application Contact ITT Technical Institute, 3428 West Market Street, Akron, OH 44333. *Phone:* 330-865-8600. *Toll-free phone:* 877-818-0154.

ITT Technical Institute

Columbus, Ohio www.itt-tech.edu/

- **Proprietary** 2-year, part of ITT Educational Services, Inc.
- **Coed**

Majors CAD/CADD drafting/design technology; computer engineering technology; computer software technology; criminal justice/law enforcement administration; design and visual communications; legal assistant/paralegal; system, networking, and LAN/WAN management.

Academics *Calendar:* quarters. *Degree:* associate.

Freshman Application Contact Director or Recruitment, ITT Technical Institute, 4717 Hilton Corporate Drive, Columbus, OH 43232. *Phone:* 614-868-2000.

ITT Technical Institute

Dayton, Ohio www.itt-tech.edu/

- **Proprietary** 2-year, founded 1935, part of ITT Educational Services, Inc.
- **Suburban** campus
- **Coed**

Majors Business administration and management; CAD/CADD drafting/design technology; computer engineering technology; computer software and media applications related; criminal justice/law enforcement administration; design and visual communications; legal assistant/paralegal; system, networking, and LAN/WAN management; web page, digital/multimedia and information resources design.

Academics *Calendar:* quarters. *Degree:* associate.

Student Life *Housing:* college housing not available.

Freshman Application Contact Director of Recruitment, ITT Technical Institute, 3325 Stop 8 Road, Dayton, OH 45414. *Phone:* 937-264-7700. *Toll-free phone:* 800-568-3241.

ITT Technical Institute

Hilliard, Ohio www.itt-tech.edu/

- **Proprietary** 2-year, founded 2003, part of ITT Educational Services, Inc.
- **Coed**

Majors CAD/CADD drafting/design technology; computer engineering technology; computer software technology; criminal justice/law enforcement administration; design and visual communications; legal assistant/paralegal; system, networking, and LAN/WAN management; web page, digital/multimedia and information resources design.

Academics *Calendar:* quarters. *Degree:* associate.

Freshman Application Contact Director of Recruitment, ITT Technical Institute, 3781 Park Mill Run Drive, Hilliard, OH 43026. *Phone:* 614-771-4888. *Toll-free phone:* 888-483-4888.

ITT Technical Institute

Maumee, Ohio **www.itt-tech.edu/**

- **Proprietary** 2-year
- **Coed**

Majors Business administration and management; CAD/CADD drafting/design technology; computer engineering technology; criminal justice/law enforcement administration; design and visual communications; legal assistant/paralegal; system, networking, and LAN/WAN management.

Academics *Degree:* associate.

Freshman Application Contact Director of Recruitment, ITT Technical Institute, 1656 Henthorne Boulevard, Suite B, Maumee, OH 43537. *Phone:* 419-861-6500. *Toll-free phone:* 877-205-4639.

ITT Technical Institute

Norwood, Ohio **www.itt-tech.edu/**

- **Proprietary** 2-year, founded 1995, part of ITT Educational Services, Inc.
- **Coed**

Majors Accounting technology and bookkeeping; business administration and management; CAD/CADD drafting/design technology; computer engineering technology; computer software and media applications related; criminal justice/law enforcement administration; design and visual communications; legal assistant/paralegal; system, networking, and LAN/WAN management; web/multimedia management and webmaster; web page, digital/multimedia and information resources design.

Academics *Calendar:* quarters. *Degree:* associate.

Student Life *Housing:* college housing not available.

Freshman Application Contact Director of Recruitment, ITT Technical Institute, 4750 Wesley Avenue, Norwood, OH 45212. *Phone:* 513-531-8300. *Toll-free phone:* 800-314-8324.

ITT Technical Institute

Strongsville, Ohio **www.itt-tech.edu/**

- **Proprietary** 2-year, founded 1994, part of ITT Educational Services, Inc.
- **Coed**

Majors Accounting technology and bookkeeping; business administration and management; CAD/CADD drafting/design technology; computer engineering technology; computer software and media applications related; criminal justice/law enforcement administration; design and visual communications; legal assistant/paralegal; system, networking, and LAN/WAN management; web/multimedia management and webmaster; web page, digital/multimedia and information resources design.

Academics *Calendar:* quarters. *Degree:* associate.

Student Life *Housing:* college housing not available.

Freshman Application Contact Director of Recruitment, ITT Technical Institute, 14955 Sprague Road, Strongsville, OH 44136. *Phone:* 440-234-9091. *Toll-free phone:* 800-331-1488.

ITT Technical Institute

Warrensville Heights, Ohio **www.itt-tech.edu/**

- **Proprietary** 2-year, founded 2005
- **Coed**

Majors Business administration and management; CAD/CADD drafting/design technology; computer engineering technology; computer software technology; criminal justice/law enforcement administration; design and visual communications; legal assistant/paralegal; system, networking, and LAN/WAN management; web page, digital/multimedia and information resources design.

Academics *Calendar:* quarters. *Degree:* associate.

Freshman Application Contact Director of Recruitment, ITT Technical Institute, 4700 Richmond Road, Warrensville Heights, OH 44128. *Phone:* 216-896-6500. *Toll-free phone:* 800-741-3494.

ITT Technical Institute

Youngstown, Ohio **www.itt-tech.edu/**

- **Proprietary** 2-year, founded 1967, part of ITT Educational Services, Inc.
- **Suburban** campus
- **Coed**

Majors Business administration and management; CAD/CADD drafting/design technology; computer engineering technology; computer software and media applications related; criminal justice/law enforcement administration; design and visual communications; legal assistant/paralegal; system, networking, and LAN/WAN management; web/multimedia management and webmaster; web page, digital/multimedia and information resources design.

Academics *Calendar:* quarters. *Degree:* associate.

Student Life *Housing:* college housing not available.

Financial Aid Of all full-time matriculated undergraduates who enrolled in 2008, 5 Federal Work-Study jobs (averaging $3979).

Freshman Application Contact Director of Recruitment, ITT Technical Institute, 1030 North Meridian Road, Youngstown, OH 44509. *Phone:* 330-270-1600. *Toll-free phone:* 800-832-5001.

James A. Rhodes State College

Lima, Ohio **www.rhodesstate.edu/**

- **State-supported** 2-year, founded 1971
- **Rural** 565-acre campus
- **Coed**

Academics *Calendar:* quarters. *Degree:* certificates and associate. *Special study options:* academic remediation for entering students, adult/continuing education programs, advanced placement credit, cooperative education, distance learning, independent study, internships, off-campus study, part-time degree program, services for LD students, student-designed majors, summer session for credit.

Student Life *Campus security:* student patrols, late-night transport/escort service.

Costs (2009–10) *One-time required fee:* $25. *Tuition:* state resident $4154 full-time, $92 per credit hour part-time; nonresident $8307 full-time, $185 per credit hour part-time. Full-time tuition and fees vary according to program. Part-time tuition and fees vary according to program. *Required fees:* $75 full-time, $25 per term part-time. *Payment plans:* installment, deferred payment.

Financial Aid Of all full-time matriculated undergraduates who enrolled in 2008, 110 Federal Work-Study jobs (averaging $1000).

Applying *Options:* early admission, deferred entrance. *Application fee:* $25. *Required:* high school transcript.

Freshman Application Contact Mr. Scot Lingrell, Director, Student Advising and Development, James A. Rhodes State College, 4240 Campus Drive, Lima, OH 45804-3597. *Phone:* 419-995-8050. *E-mail:* peterl@ltc.tec.oh.us.

Kaplan College, Cincinnati Campus

Cincinnati, Ohio **www.kc-cincy.com/**

- **Proprietary** 2-year
- **Coed**

Academics *Degree:* diplomas and associate.

Freshman Application Contact Kaplan College, Cincinnati Campus, 801 Linn Street, Cincinnati, OH 45203. *Phone:* 513-421-9900.

Kaplan College, Columbus Campus

Columbus, Ohio **www.kc-columbus.com/**

- **Proprietary** 2-year
- **Coed**

Academics *Degree:* diplomas and associate.

Freshman Application Contact Kaplan College, Columbus Campus, 2745 Winchester Pike, Columbus, OH 43232. *Phone:* 614-456-4600.

Kaplan College, Dayton Campus

Dayton, Ohio www.kc-dayton.com/

- **Proprietary** 2-year, founded 1971
- **Urban** campus
- **Coed**

Majors Criminal justice/law enforcement administration; graphic design; medical office management; photography.

Academics *Calendar:* quarters. *Degree:* diplomas and associate.

Freshman Application Contact Kaplan College, Dayton Campus, 2800 East River Road, Dayton, OH 45439. *Phone:* 937-294-6155. *Toll-free phone:* 800-932-9698.

Kent State University at Ashtabula

Ashtabula, Ohio www.ashtabula.kent.edu/

- **State-supported** primarily 2-year, founded 1958, part of Kent State University System
- **Small-town** 120-acre campus with easy access to Cleveland
- **Coed,** 2,187 undergraduate students, 53% full-time, 64% women, 36% men

Undergraduates 1,161 full-time, 1,026 part-time. 2% are from out of state, 9% African American, 0.7% Asian American or Pacific Islander, 3% Hispanic American, 0.4% Native American, 9% transferred in. *Retention:* 67% of 2008 full-time freshmen returned.

Freshmen *Admission:* 713 applied, 563 admitted, 436 enrolled. *Average high school GPA:* 2.55.

Faculty *Total:* 107, 46% full-time. *Student/faculty ratio:* 22:1.

Majors Accounting; administrative assistant and secretarial science; business administration and management; computer engineering technology; criminal justice/police science; electrical, electronic and communications engineering technology; engineering technology; environmental studies; finance; human services; industrial technology; kindergarten/preschool education; legal administrative assistant/secretary; liberal arts and sciences/liberal studies; marketing/marketing management; materials science; mechanical engineering/mechanical technology; nursing (registered nurse training); physical therapy; real estate.

Academics *Calendar:* semesters. *Degrees:* certificates, associate, and bachelor's (also offers some upper-level and graduate courses). *Special study options:* academic remediation for entering students, advanced placement credit, freshman honors college, honors programs, internships, part-time degree program, student-designed majors, summer session for credit. *ROTC:* Army (c).

Library 51,884 titles, 225 serial subscriptions.

Student Life *Housing:* college housing not available. *Activities and Organizations:* drama/theater group, student-run newspaper, student government, student newspaper, Student Nurses Association. *Campus security:* 24-hour emergency response devices.

Standardized Tests *Required for some:* SAT or ACT (for admission). *Recommended:* SAT or ACT (for admission).

Costs (2009–10) *Tuition:* state resident $4938 full-time, $225 per credit hour part-time; nonresident $12,630 full-time, $575 per credit hour part-time. Full-time tuition and fees vary according to course level and course load. Part-time tuition and fees vary according to course level and course load. *Payment plans:* installment, deferred payment. *Waivers:* senior citizens and employees or children of employees.

Financial Aid Of all full-time matriculated undergraduates who enrolled in 2009, 867 applied for aid, 809 were judged to have need, 166 had their need fully met. In 2009, 11 non-need-based awards were made. *Average percent of need met:* 46%. *Average financial aid package:* $7717. *Average need-based loan:* $3720. *Average need-based gift aid:* $5172. *Average non-need-based aid:* $1673.

Applying *Options:* early admission, deferred entrance. *Application fee:* $30. *Application deadlines:* 8/1 (freshmen), 7/15 (out-of-state freshmen), 7/15 (transfers). *Notification:* continuous until 8/1 (freshmen), continuous until 7/15 (out-of-state freshmen), continuous until 7/15 (transfers).

Freshman Application Contact Kent State University at Ashtabula, 3300 Lake Road West, Ashtabula, OH 44004-2299. *Phone:* 440-964-4217.

Kent State University at East Liverpool

East Liverpool, Ohio www.kenteliv.kent.edu/

- **State-supported** 2-year, founded 1967, part of Kent State University System
- **Small-town** 4-acre campus with easy access to Pittsburgh
- **Coed,** 1,235 undergraduate students, 57% full-time, 72% women, 28% men

Undergraduates 706 full-time, 529 part-time. Students come from 3 states and territories, 6% are from out of state, 4% African American, 0.5% Asian American or Pacific Islander, 0.5% Hispanic American, 0.3% Native American.

Freshmen *Admission:* 253 applied, 193 admitted, 144 enrolled. *Average high school GPA:* 2.81.

Faculty *Total:* 66, 39% full-time. *Student/faculty ratio:* 22:1.

Majors Accounting; business administration and management; computer and information sciences related; computer engineering technology; criminal justice/law enforcement administration; legal administrative assistant/secretary; liberal arts and sciences/liberal studies; nursing (registered nurse training); occupational therapy; physical therapy.

Academics *Calendar:* semesters. *Degrees:* certificates and associate (also offers some upper-level and graduate courses). *Special study options:* academic remediation for entering students, accelerated degree program, adult/continuing education programs, advanced placement credit, distance learning, internships, part-time degree program, services for LD students, student-designed majors, summer session for credit. *ROTC:* Navy (c), Air Force (c).

Library Blair Memorial Library with 31,320 titles, 135 serial subscriptions, an OPAC, a Web page.

Student Life *Housing:* college housing not available. *Activities and Organizations:* student-run newspaper, Student Senate, Student Nurses Association, Alpha Beta Gamma, Occupational Therapist Assistant Club, Physical Therapist Assistant Club. *Campus security:* student patrols, late-night transport/escort service.

Standardized Tests *Required for some:* SAT (for admission). *Recommended:* SAT (for admission).

Financial Aid Of all full-time matriculated undergraduates who enrolled in 2009, 430 applied for aid, 396 were judged to have need, 77 had their need fully met. In 2009, 3 non-need-based awards were made. *Average percent of need met:* 43%. *Average financial aid package:* $7517. *Average need-based loan:* $3558. *Average need-based gift aid:* $5414. *Average non-need-based aid:* $1782.

Applying *Options:* early admission, deferred entrance. *Application fee:* $30. *Required:* high school transcript. *Application deadlines:* rolling (freshmen), rolling (transfers). *Notification:* continuous until 9/1 (freshmen), continuous until 9/1 (transfers).

Freshman Application Contact Mr. Anthony M. Underwood, Director of Enrollment Management and Student Services, Kent State University at East Liverpool, 400 East Fourth Street, East Liverpool, OH 43920. *Phone:* 330-382—7414. *E-mail:* admissions@eliv.kent.edu.

Kent State University at Geauga

Burton, Ohio www.geauga.kent.edu/

- **State-supported** founded 1964, part of Kent State University System
- **Rural** 87-acre campus with easy access to Cleveland
- **Coed,** 1,866 undergraduate students, 60% full-time, 63% women, 37% men

Undergraduates 1,116 full-time, 750 part-time. Students come from 10 states and territories, 4 other countries, 1% are from out of state, 8% African American, 1% Asian American or Pacific Islander, 1% Hispanic American, 0.7% Native American, 0.1% international, 8% transferred in. *Retention:* 72% of 2008 full-time freshmen returned.

Freshmen *Admission:* 222 enrolled. *Average high school GPA:* 2.55.

Faculty *Total:* 93, 27% full-time. *Student/faculty ratio:* 29:1.

Majors Accounting technology and bookkeeping; applied horticulture; business administration and management; emergency medical technology (EMT paramedic); general studies; industrial technology; information technology; liberal arts and sciences/liberal studies; nursing science; physical sciences; science technologies related.

Academics *Calendar:* semesters. *Degree:* certificates and associate. *Special study options:* academic remediation for entering students, adult/continuing education programs, advanced placement credit, distance learning, double majors, independent study, internships, part-time degree program, services for LD students, student-designed majors, summer session for credit. *ROTC:* Army (c), Air Force (c).

Kent State University at Geauga (continued)

Library Kent State University Library with 8,300 titles, 6,600 serial subscriptions, an OPAC, a Web page.

Student Life *Housing:* college housing not available. *Activities and Organizations:* student-run newspaper. *Campus security:* 24-hour emergency response devices.

Standardized Tests *Required for some:* SAT or ACT (for admission). *Recommended:* SAT or ACT (for admission).

Financial Aid Of all full-time matriculated undergraduates who enrolled in 2009, 479 applied for aid, 419 were judged to have need, 113 had their need fully met. In 2009, 7 non-need-based awards were made. *Average percent of need met:* 40%. *Average financial aid package:* $1753. *Average need-based loan:* $3615. *Average need-based gift aid:* $4798. *Average non-need-based aid:* $1170.

Applying *Options:* deferred entrance. *Application fee:* $30. *Required:* high school transcript. *Application deadlines:* rolling (freshmen), rolling (transfers). *Notification:* continuous (freshmen), continuous (transfers).

Freshman Application Contact Thomas Hoiles, Kent State University at Geauga, 14111 Claridon-Troy Road, Burton, OH 44021. *Phone:* 440-834-4187. *Fax:* 440-834-8846. *E-mail:* thoiles@kent.edu.

KENT STATE UNIVERSITY AT SALEM

Salem, Ohio **www.salem.kent.edu/**

- **State-supported** primarily 2-year, founded 1966, part of Kent State University System
- **Rural** 98-acre campus
- **Coed,** 1,577 undergraduate students, 72% full-time, 69% women, 31% men

Undergraduates 1,132 full-time, 445 part-time. 1% are from out of state, 2% African American, 0.6% Asian American or Pacific Islander, 0.5% Hispanic American, 0.5% Native American, 9% transferred in. *Retention:* 70% of 2008 full-time freshmen returned.

Freshmen *Admission:* 486 applied, 301 admitted, 295 enrolled. *Average high school GPA:* 2.71.

Faculty *Total:* 99, 41% full-time. *Student/faculty ratio:* 21:1.

Majors Administrative assistant and secretarial science; allied health diagnostic, intervention, and treatment professions related; applied horticulture; business/commerce; computer programming (specific applications); education; industrial technology; liberal arts and sciences/liberal studies; medical radiologic technology.

Academics *Calendar:* semesters. *Degrees:* associate and bachelor's (also offers some upper-level and graduate courses). *Special study options:* academic remediation for entering students, adult/continuing education programs, advanced placement credit, distance learning, freshman honors college, honors programs, internships, part-time degree program, services for LD students, summer session for credit. *ROTC:* Army (c), Air Force (c).

Library 19,000 titles, 163 serial subscriptions, 158 audiovisual materials, an OPAC, a Web page.

Student Life *Housing:* college housing not available. *Activities and Organizations:* drama/theater group. *Campus security:* 24-hour emergency response devices, late-night transport/escort service. *Student services:* personal/psychological counseling, women's center.

Athletics *Intramural sports:* basketball M/W, skiing (downhill) M/W, table tennis M/W, tennis M/W, volleyball M/W.

Standardized Tests *Required for some:* SAT or ACT (for admission). *Recommended:* SAT or ACT (for admission).

Financial Aid Of all full-time matriculated undergraduates who enrolled in 2009, 809 applied for aid, 737 were judged to have need, 159 had their need fully met. In 2009, 4 non-need-based awards were made. *Average percent of need met:* 42%. *Average financial aid package:* $7227. *Average need-based loan:* $3570. *Average need-based gift aid:* $5132. *Average non-need-based aid:* $688. *Average indebtedness upon graduation:* $23,058.

Applying *Options:* early admission, deferred entrance. *Application fee:* $30. *Required:* high school transcript. *Required for some:* essay or personal statement. *Application deadlines:* rolling (freshmen), rolling (transfers).

Freshman Application Contact Mrs. Judy Heisler, Admissions Secretary, Kent State University at Salem, 2491 State Route 45 South, Salem, OH 44460-9412. *Phone:* 330-332-0361 Ext. 74201. *E-mail:* ask-us@salem.kent.edu.

KENT STATE UNIVERSITY AT TRUMBULL

Warren, Ohio **www.trumbull.kent.edu/**

- **State-supported** primarily 2-year, founded 1954, part of Kent State University System
- **Suburban** 200-acre campus with easy access to Cleveland
- **Coed,** 2,607 undergraduate students, 63% full-time, 62% women, 38% men

Undergraduates 1,637 full-time, 970 part-time. Students come from 4 states and territories, 6 other countries, 13% African American, 0.6% Asian American or Pacific Islander, 1% Hispanic American, 0.6% Native American, 0.2% international, 4% transferred in. *Retention:* 66% of 2008 full-time freshmen returned.

Freshmen *Admission:* 618 applied, 488 admitted, 415 enrolled. *Average high school GPA:* 2.66. *Test scores:* SAT verbal scores over 500: 57%; SAT math scores over 500: 29%; ACT scores over 18: 64%; SAT verbal scores over 600: 14%; SAT math scores over 600: 14%; ACT scores over 24: 10%.

Faculty *Total:* 114, 51% full-time. *Student/faculty ratio:* 25:1.

Majors Accounting technology and bookkeeping; automobile/automotive mechanics technology; business administration and management; communication/speech communication and rhetoric; computer engineering technology; computer/information technology services administration related; computer technology/computer systems technology; criminal justice/safety; electrical, electronic and communications engineering technology; English; environmental engineering technology; general studies; industrial technology; legal assistant/paralegal; liberal arts and sciences/liberal studies; manufacturing engineering; mechanical engineering/mechanical technology; nursing science; systems engineering.

Academics *Calendar:* semesters. *Degrees:* certificates, associate, and bachelor's (also offers some upper-level and graduate courses). *Special study options:* academic remediation for entering students, adult/continuing education programs, advanced placement credit, cooperative education, distance learning, freshman honors college, honors programs, independent study, internships, part-time degree program, services for LD students, student-designed majors, summer session for credit. *ROTC:* Army (c), Air Force (c).

Library Trumbull Campus Library with 65,951 titles, 759 serial subscriptions, an OPAC, a Web page.

Student Life *Housing:* college housing not available. *Activities and Organizations:* drama/theater group, National Student Nurses Association, Spot On Improv Group, Amnesty International, Campus Crusade for Christ. *Campus security:* 24-hour emergency response devices, late-night transport/escort service, patrols by trained security personnel during open hours. *Student services:* personal/psychological counseling.

Standardized Tests *Required for some:* SAT or ACT (for admission). *Recommended:* SAT or ACT (for admission).

Financial Aid Of all full-time matriculated undergraduates who enrolled in 2009, 1,133 applied for aid, 1,047 were judged to have need, 237 had their need fully met. In 2009, 6 non-need-based awards were made. *Average percent of need met:* 46%. *Average financial aid package:* $7726. *Average need-based loan:* $3617. *Average need-based gift aid:* $5432. *Average non-need-based aid:* $1417.

Applying *Options:* deferred entrance. *Application fee:* $30. *Required:* high school transcript. *Application deadlines:* rolling (freshmen), rolling (transfers). *Notification:* continuous until 8/30 (freshmen), continuous until 8/30 (transfers).

Freshman Application Contact Kent State University at Trumbull, 4314 Mahoning Avenue, NW, Warren, OH 44483-1998. *Phone:* 330-675-8935.

KENT STATE UNIVERSITY AT TUSCARAWAS

New Philadelphia, Ohio **www.tusc.kent.edu/**

- **State-supported** primarily 2-year, founded 1962, part of Kent State University System
- **Small-town** 172-acre campus with easy access to Cleveland
- **Endowment** $1.6 million
- **Coed,** 2,384 undergraduate students, 60% full-time, 61% women, 39% men

Undergraduates 1,424 full-time, 960 part-time. 1% are from out of state, 2% African American, 0.5% Asian American or Pacific Islander, 0.6% Hispanic American, 0.4% Native American, 0.1% international, 7% transferred in. *Retention:* 70% of 2008 full-time freshmen returned.

Freshmen *Admission:* 722 applied, 594 admitted, 461 enrolled. *Average high school GPA:* 2.7.

Faculty *Total:* 116, 42% full-time. *Student/faculty ratio:* 24:1.

Majors Accounting; administrative assistant and secretarial science; animation, interactive technology, video graphics and special effects; business administration and management; communications technology; computer engineering technology; criminal justice/police science; early childhood education; electrical, electronic and communications engineering technology; engineering technology; environmental studies; industrial technology; liberal arts and sciences/liberal studies; mechanical engineering/mechanical technology; nursing (registered nurse training); plastics engineering technology; veterinary/animal health technology.

Academics *Calendar:* semesters. *Degrees:* certificates, associate, and bachelor's (also offers some upper-level and graduate courses). *Special study options:* academic remediation for entering students, accelerated degree program, adult/continuing education programs, advanced placement credit, distance learning, double majors, freshman honors college, honors programs, independent study, internships, part-time degree program, services for LD students, student-designed majors, study abroad, summer session for credit. *ROTC:* Army (c), Air Force (c).

Library Tuscarawas Campus Library with 63,880 titles, 208 serial subscriptions, 1,179 audiovisual materials, an OPAC, a Web page.

Student Life *Housing:* college housing not available. *Activities and Organizations:* choral group, Society of Mechanical Engineers, IEEE, Imagineers, Criminal Justice Club, Salt and Light.

Athletics *Intramural sports:* basketball M/W, volleyball M/W.

Standardized Tests *Required for some:* SAT or ACT (for admission). *Recommended:* SAT or ACT (for admission).

Costs (2010–11) *Tuition:* state resident $4938 full-time, $225 per credit hour part-time; nonresident $12,630 full-time, $575 per credit hour part-time. Full-time tuition and fees vary according to course level, location, and program. Part-time tuition and fees vary according to course level, location, and program. *Payment plans:* installment, deferred payment. *Waivers:* employees or children of employees.

Financial Aid Of all full-time matriculated undergraduates who enrolled in 2009, 1,050 applied for aid, 961 were judged to have need, 135 had their need fully met. In 2009, 14 non-need-based awards were made. *Average percent of need met:* 46%. *Average financial aid package:* $7450. *Average need-based loan:* $3485. *Average need-based gift aid:* $5189. *Average non-need-based aid:* $1468.

Applying *Options:* electronic application, early admission, deferred entrance. *Application fee:* $30. *Required:* high school transcript. *Application deadlines:* 9/1 (freshmen), 9/1 (transfers). *Notification:* continuous (freshmen), continuous (transfers).

Freshman Application Contact Mrs. Laurie R. Donley, Director of Enrollment Management and Student Services, Kent State University at Tuscarawas, 330 University Drive NE, New Philadelphia, OH 44663-9403. *Phone:* 330-339-3391 Ext. 47425. *Fax:* 330-339-3321. *E-mail:* ldonley@kent.edu.

LAKELAND COMMUNITY COLLEGE

Kirtland, Ohio **www.lakeland.cc.oh.us/**

- **State and locally supported** 2-year, founded 1967, part of Ohio Board of Regents
- **Suburban** 380-acre campus with easy access to Cleveland
- **Endowment** $354,142
- **Coed,** 9,406 undergraduate students, 44% full-time, 59% women, 41% men

Undergraduates 4,151 full-time, 5,255 part-time. 14% African American, 1% Asian American or Pacific Islander, 2% Hispanic American, 0.3% Native American, 0.5% international, 4% transferred in.

Freshmen *Admission:* 1,569 enrolled.

Faculty *Total:* 630, 19% full-time. *Student/faculty ratio:* 20:1.

Majors Accounting; administrative assistant and secretarial science; biotechnology; business administration and management; child-care provision; civil engineering technology; clinical/medical laboratory technology; commercial and advertising art; computer engineering technology; computer programming (specific applications); computer systems analysis; computer systems networking and telecommunications; computer technology/computer systems technology; corrections; criminal justice/police science; dental hygiene; electrical, electronic and communications engineering technology; energy management and systems technology; fire protection and safety technology; health professions related; hospitality administration; instrumentation technology; legal assistant/paralegal; liberal arts and sciences/liberal studies; management information systems; marketing/marketing management; mechanical engineering/mechanical technology; medical radiologic technology; nuclear medical technology; nursing (registered nurse training); ophthalmic technology; quality control technology; respiratory care therapy; restaurant, culinary, and catering management; security and protective services related; sign language interpretation and translation; social work; surgical technology; tourism and travel services management.

Academics *Calendar:* semesters. *Degree:* certificates and associate. *Special study options:* academic remediation for entering students, adult/continuing education programs, advanced placement credit, cooperative education, distance learning, English as a second language, external degree program, independent study, internships, off-campus study, part-time degree program, services for LD students, study abroad, summer session for credit.

Library Lakeland Community College Library with 65,814 titles, 248 serial subscriptions, 4,212 audiovisual materials, an OPAC, a Web page.

Student Life *Housing:* college housing not available. *Activities and Organizations:* drama/theater group, student-run newspaper, radio station, choral group, Campus Activities Board, Lakeland Student Government, Lakeland Signers, Thousand Shoes Skat Dance Team, Gamer's Guild. *Campus security:* 24-hour emergency response devices and patrols, student patrols, late-night transport/escort service. *Student services:* health clinic, personal/psychological counseling, women's center.

Athletics Member NJCAA. *Intercollegiate sports:* baseball M(s), basketball M(s)/W(s), golf M(s), soccer M(s), softball W(s), volleyball W(s).

Costs (2010–11) *Tuition:* area resident $2888 full-time, $96 per credit hour part-time; state resident $3537 full-time, $118 per credit hour part-time; nonresident $7569 full-time, $252 per credit hour part-time. Full-time tuition and fees vary according to course load. Part-time tuition and fees vary according to course load. *Required fees:* $14 per term part-time. *Payment plan:* installment. *Waivers:* senior citizens and employees or children of employees.

Financial Aid Of all full-time matriculated undergraduates who enrolled in 2008, 71 Federal Work-Study jobs (averaging $2500). 166 state and other part-time jobs (averaging $1700).

Applying *Options:* electronic application, early admission, deferred entrance. *Application fee:* $15. *Required:* high school transcript. *Notification:* continuous until 9/1 (freshmen), continuous until 9/1 (transfers).

Freshman Application Contact Lakeland Community College, 7700 Clocktower Drive, Kirtland, OH 44094. *Phone:* 440-525-7230. *Toll-free phone:* 800-589-8520.

LORAIN COUNTY COMMUNITY COLLEGE

Elyria, Ohio **www.lorainccc.edu/**

Director of Admissions Ms. Thalia Fountain, Interim Director of Enrollment Services, Lorain County Community College, 1005 Abbe Road, North, Elyria, OH 44035. *Phone:* 440-366-7683. *Toll-free phone:* 800-995-5222 Ext. 4032. *Fax:* 440-366-4150.

MARION TECHNICAL COLLEGE

Marion, Ohio **www.mtc.edu/**

- **State-supported** 2-year, founded 1971, part of Ohio Board of Regents
- **Small-town** 180-acre campus with easy access to Columbus
- **Coed,** 2,659 undergraduate students, 51% full-time, 60% women, 40% men

Undergraduates 1,369 full-time, 1,290 part-time. *Retention:* 45% of 2008 full-time freshmen returned.

Freshmen *Admission:* 641 enrolled.

Faculty *Total:* 185, 19% full-time. *Student/faculty ratio:* 18:1.

Majors Accounting; administrative assistant and secretarial science; business administration and management; clinical/medical laboratory technology; computer programming (vendor/product certification); computer software and media applications related; computer systems networking and telecommunications; drafting and design technology; electrical, electronic and communications engineering technology; engineering technology; finance; human services; industrial technology; information technology; legal assistant/paralegal; marketing/marketing management; mechanical engineering/mechanical technology; medical administrative assistant and medical secretary; nursing (registered nurse training); physical therapist assistant; radiologic technology/science; social work; telecommunications technology.

Academics *Calendar:* quarters. *Degree:* certificates and associate. *Special study options:* academic remediation for entering students, accelerated degree program, adult/continuing education programs, advanced placement credit, cooperative education, distance learning, double majors, independent study, internships, off-campus study, part-time degree program, services for LD students, student-designed majors, summer session for credit.

Library Marion Campus Library with 52,000 titles, 251 serial subscriptions, 1,582 audiovisual materials, an OPAC, a Web page.

Student Life *Housing:* college housing not available. *Activities and Organizations:* drama/theater group, choral group, outdoor pursuits, Young Republicans,

Marion Technical College (continued)

Environmental Group, Economics and Business Club, Psychology Club. *Student services:* personal/psychological counseling.

Athletics *Intercollegiate sports:* basketball M/W, golf M/W, rugby M, softball W, volleyball W. *Intramural sports:* badminton M/W, basketball M/W, bowling M/W, football M, golf M, racquetball M/W, rock climbing M/W, rugby M/W, skiing (cross-country) M/W, skiing (downhill) M/W, soccer M/W, table tennis M/W, volleyball M/W.

Standardized Tests *Required:* COMPASS or ACT (for admission). *Required for some:* ACT (for admission).

Costs (2009–10) *Tuition:* state resident $3636 full-time, $101 per credit hour part-time; nonresident $5544 full-time, $154 per credit hour part-time. *Required fees:* $150 full-time.

Financial Aid Of all full-time matriculated undergraduates who enrolled in 2008, 28 Federal Work-Study jobs (averaging $1200). 45 state and other part-time jobs (averaging $1000).

Applying *Options:* electronic application, early admission, deferred entrance. *Application fee:* $20. *Required:* high school transcript. *Required for some:* minimum 2.5 GPA. *Recommended:* interview. *Application deadlines:* rolling (freshmen), rolling (out-of-state freshmen), rolling (transfers). *Notification:* continuous (freshmen), continuous (out-of-state freshmen), continuous (transfers).

Freshman Application Contact Mr. Joel Liles, Dean of Enrollment Services, Marion Technical College, 1467 Mount Vernon Avenue, Marion, OH 43302. *Phone:* 740-389-4636 Ext. 249. *Fax:* 740-389-6136. *E-mail:* enroll@mtc.edu.

MIAMI–JACOBS COLLEGE

Dayton, Ohio **www.miamijacobs.edu/**

- **Proprietary** 2-year, founded 1860
- **Small-town** campus
- **Coed**

Academics *Calendar:* quarters. *Degree:* certificates, diplomas, and associate. *Special study options:* academic remediation for entering students, distance learning, honors programs, internships, off-campus study, part-time degree program, summer session for credit.

Student Life *Campus security:* late-night transport/escort service.

Standardized Tests *Required:* Wonderlic aptitude test (for admission). *Required for some:* ACT (for admission). *Recommended:* SAT or ACT (for admission).

Applying *Options:* early admission, deferred entrance. *Application fee:* $20. *Required:* essay or personal statement, high school transcript, interview.

Director of Admissions Mary Percell, Vice President of Information Services, Miami–Jacobs College, 110 North Patterson Street, PO Box 1433, Dayton, OH 45402. *Phone:* 937-461-5174 Ext. 118.

MIAMI UNIVERSITY–MIDDLETOWN CAMPUS

Middletown, Ohio **www.mid.muohio.edu/**

Freshman Application Contact Diane Cantonwine, Assistant Director of Admission and Financial Aid, Miami University–Middletown Campus, 4200 East University Boulevard, Middletown, OH 45042. *Phone:* 513-727-3346. *Toll-free phone:* 866-426-4643. *Fax:* 513-727-3223. *E-mail:* cantondm@muohio.edu.

NORTH CENTRAL STATE COLLEGE

Mansfield, Ohio **www.ncstatecollege.edu/**

- **State-supported** 2-year, founded 1961, part of Ohio Board of Regents
- **Suburban** 600-acre campus with easy access to Cleveland and Columbus
- **Coed**

Academics *Calendar:* quarters. *Degree:* certificates and associate. *Special study options:* academic remediation for entering students, adult/continuing education programs, advanced placement credit, distance learning, independent study, internships, part-time degree program, services for LD students, student-designed majors, summer session for credit.

Student Life *Campus security:* 24-hour emergency response devices and patrols, late-night transport/escort service.

Applying *Options:* early admission, deferred entrance. *Required for some:* high school transcript.

Freshman Application Contact Ms. Nikia L. Fletcher, Director of Admissions, North Central State College, PO Box 698, Mansfield, OH 44901-0698. *Phone:* 419-755-4813. *Toll-free phone:* 888-755-4899. *E-mail:* nfletcher@ncstatecollege.edu.

NORTHWEST STATE COMMUNITY COLLEGE

Archbold, Ohio **www.northweststate.edu/**

- **State-supported** 2-year, founded 1968, part of Ohio Board of Regents
- **Rural** 80-acre campus with easy access to Toledo
- **Coed**

Academics *Calendar:* semesters. *Degree:* certificates and associate. *Special study options:* academic remediation for entering students, adult/continuing education programs, advanced placement credit, cooperative education, distance learning, double majors, external degree program, independent study, internships, off-campus study, part-time degree program, services for LD students, student-designed majors, summer session for credit.

Student Life *Campus security:* security patrols.

Costs (2009–10) *Tuition:* state resident $3930 full-time, $131 per credit part-time; nonresident $7680 full-time, $256 per credit part-time. Full-time tuition and fees vary according to course load. Part-time tuition and fees vary according to course load. *Required fees:* $60 full-time, $30 per term part-time. *Payment plans:* installment, deferred payment.

Financial Aid Of all full-time matriculated undergraduates who enrolled in 2008, 43 Federal Work-Study jobs (averaging $1077).

Applying *Options:* electronic application, early admission, deferred entrance. *Application fee:* $20. *Required:* high school transcript.

Director of Admissions Mr. Jeffrey Ferezan, Dean of Student Success and Advocacy Center, Northwest State Community College, 22600 State Route 34, Archbold, OH 43502-9542. *Phone:* 419-267-1213.

OHIO BUSINESS COLLEGE

Lorain, Ohio **www.ohiobusinesscollege.com/**

- **Proprietary** 2-year, founded 1903, part of Tri State Educational Systems
- **Coed, primarily women**

Academics *Calendar:* quarters. *Degree:* diplomas and associate. *Special study options:* academic remediation for entering students, accelerated degree program, adult/continuing education programs, advanced placement credit, double majors, external degree program, independent study, internships, part-time degree program, summer session for credit.

Applying *Options:* electronic application. *Application fee:* $25. *Required:* high school transcript, interview.

Director of Admissions Mr. Jim Unger, Admissions Director, Ohio Business College, 1907 North Ridge Road, Lorain, OH 44055. *Toll-free phone:* 888-514-3126.

OHIO BUSINESS COLLEGE

Sandusky, Ohio **www.ohiobusinesscollege.com/**

Freshman Application Contact Rohnda Pickering, Student Services Coordinator, Ohio Business College, 5202 Timber Commons Drive, Sandusky, OH 44870. *Phone:* 419-627-8345. *Toll-free phone:* 888-627-8345. *Fax:* 419-627-1958. *E-mail:* rpickering@ohiobusinesscollege.edu.

OHIO COLLEGE OF MASSOTHERAPY

Akron, Ohio **www.ocm.edu/**

Director of Admissions Mr. John Atkins, Director of Admissions and Marketing, Ohio College of Massotherapy, 225 Heritage Woods Drive, Akron, OH 44321. *Phone:* 330-665-1084 Ext. 11. *Toll-free phone:* 888-888-4325. *E-mail:* johna@ocm.edu.

THE OHIO STATE UNIVERSITY AGRICULTURAL TECHNICAL INSTITUTE

Wooster, Ohio **www.ati.osu.edu/**

- **State-supported** 2-year, founded 1971, part of Ohio State University
- **Small-town** campus with easy access to Cleveland and Columbus
- **Endowment** $2.2 million
- **Coed,** 747 undergraduate students, 100% full-time, 35% women, 65% men

Undergraduates 747 full-time. Students come from 13 states and territories, 2 other countries, 2% are from out of state, 0.9% African American, 0.4% Hispanic American, 0.7% Native American, 0.4% international, 7% transferred in. *Retention:* 68% of 2008 full-time freshmen returned.

Freshmen *Admission:* 533 applied, 506 admitted, 348 enrolled. *Test scores:* ACT scores over 18: 57%; ACT scores over 24: 11%.

Faculty *Total:* 70, 47% full-time, 33% with terminal degrees. *Student/faculty ratio:* 16:1.

Majors Agribusiness; agricultural business and management; agricultural business technology; agricultural communication/journalism; agricultural economics; agricultural mechanization; agricultural power machinery operation; agricultural teacher education; agronomy and crop science; animal/livestock husbandry and production; animal sciences; biology/biotechnology laboratory technician; building/construction site management; clinical/medical laboratory technology; construction engineering technology; construction management; crop production; dairy husbandry and production; dairy science; environmental science; equestrian studies; floriculture/floristry management; greenhouse management; heavy equipment maintenance technology; horse husbandry/equine science and management; horticultural science; hydraulics and fluid power technology; industrial technology; landscaping and groundskeeping; livestock management; natural resources management; natural resources management and policy; plant nursery management; soil science and agronomy; turf and turfgrass management.

Academics *Calendar:* quarters. *Degree:* certificates, diplomas, and associate. *Special study options:* academic remediation for entering students, accelerated degree program, adult/continuing education programs, advanced placement credit, cooperative education, distance learning, double majors, independent study, internships, part-time degree program, services for LD students, student-designed majors, study abroad, summer session for credit. *ROTC:* Army (c), Navy (c), Air Force (c).

Library Agricultural Technical Institute Library with 9,000 titles, 260 serial subscriptions, 100 audiovisual materials, an OPAC, a Web page.

Student Life *Housing:* on-campus residence required for freshman year. *Options:* coed. Campus housing is university owned. *Activities and Organizations:* Hoof-n-Hide Club, Horticulture Club, Campus Crusade for Christ, Phi Theta Kappa, Artist de Fleur Club. *Campus security:* 24-hour emergency response devices and patrols, controlled dormitory access. *Student services:* health clinic, personal/psychological counseling.

Athletics *Intramural sports:* basketball M/W, football M/W, racquetball M/W, softball M/W, volleyball M/W.

Standardized Tests *Required for some:* SAT or ACT (for admission).

Costs (2010–11) *Tuition:* state resident $5859 full-time; nonresident $19,431 full-time. Full-time tuition and fees vary according to course load. Part-time tuition and fees vary according to course load. *Room and board:* $6765; room only: $5655. Room and board charges vary according to board plan. *Payment plan:* installment. *Waivers:* employees or children of employees.

Applying *Options:* electronic application. *Application fee:* $40. *Required:* high school transcript. *Notification:* continuous (freshmen).

Freshman Application Contact Ms. Sarah Elvey, Admissions Counselor, The Ohio State University Agricultural Technical Institute, 1328 Dover Road, Wooster, OH 44691. *Phone:* 330-287-1228. *Toll-free phone:* 800-647-8283 Ext. 1327. *Fax:* 330-287-1333. *E-mail:* elvey.3@osu.edu.

OHIO TECHNICAL COLLEGE

Cleveland, Ohio **www.ohiotechnicalcollege.com/**

Director of Admissions Mr. Marc Brenner, President, Ohio Technical College, 1374 East 51st Street, Cleveland, OH 44103. *Phone:* 216-881-1700. *Toll-free phone:* 800-322-7000. *Fax:* 216-881-9145. *E-mail:* ohioauto@aol.com.

OHIO VALLEY COLLEGE OF TECHNOLOGY

East Liverpool, Ohio **www.ovct.edu/**

- **Proprietary** 2-year, founded 1886
- **Small-town** campus with easy access to Pittsburgh
- **Coed**

Undergraduates 132 full-time, 15 part-time. 7% are from out of state, 3% African American, 0.7% Hispanic American.

Faculty *Student/faculty ratio:* 18:1.

Academics *Calendar:* semesters. *Degree:* associate. *Special study options:* internships, part-time degree program, summer session for credit.

Standardized Tests *Required:* COMPASS (for admission).

Applying *Required:* high school transcript, interview.

Freshman Application Contact Mr. Scott S. Rogers, Director, Ohio Valley College of Technology, PO Box 7000, East Liverpool, OH 43920. *Phone:* 330-385-1070. *Toll-free phone:* 877-777-8451.

OWENS COMMUNITY COLLEGE

Toledo, Ohio **www.owens.edu/**

- **State-supported** 2-year, founded 1966
- **Suburban** 100-acre campus
- **Endowment** $1.0 million
- **Coed,** 23,561 undergraduate students, 39% full-time, 47% women, 53% men

Undergraduates 9,100 full-time, 14,461 part-time. Students come from 21 states and territories, 35 other countries, 3% are from out of state, 13% African American, 1% Asian American or Pacific Islander, 4% Hispanic American, 0.5% Native American, 0.7% international, 0.5% transferred in. *Retention:* 54% of 2008 full-time freshmen returned.

Freshmen *Admission:* 13,791 applied, 13,791 admitted, 3,057 enrolled. *Average high school GPA:* 2.51. *Test scores:* SAT verbal scores over 500: 34%; SAT math scores over 500: 35%; SAT writing scores over 500: 24%; ACT scores over 18: 59%; SAT verbal scores over 600: 10%; SAT math scores over 600: 10%; SAT writing scores over 600: 5%; ACT scores over 24: 9%; SAT math scores over 700: 5%.

Faculty *Total:* 1,684, 12% full-time, 8% with terminal degrees. *Student/faculty ratio:* 20:1.

Majors Accounting technology and bookkeeping; agricultural business and management; agricultural mechanization; architectural drafting and CAD/CADD; architectural engineering technology; automotive engineering technology; biomedical technology; business/commerce; commercial and advertising art; communications technology; computer engineering technology; computer programming (specific applications); corrections; criminal justice/law enforcement administration; criminal justice/police science; dental hygiene; diagnostic medical sonography and ultrasound technology; dietetics; early childhood education; education; electrical, electronic and communications engineering technology; electromechanical technology; environmental engineering technology; executive assistant/executive secretary; fire protection and safety technology; food technology and processing; general studies; health/health-care administration; health information/medical records technology; industrial technology; information technology; landscaping and groundskeeping; manufacturing technology; massage therapy; mechanical engineering/mechanical technology; medical/health management and clinical assistant; medical radiologic technology; nuclear medical technology; nursing (licensed practical/vocational nurse training); nursing (registered nurse training); occupational therapist assistant; operations management; physical therapist assistant; public administration; quality control technology; restaurant/food services management; sales, distribution and marketing; surgical technology; survey technology; welding technology.

Academics *Calendar:* semesters. *Degree:* certificates and associate. *Special study options:* academic remediation for entering students, accelerated degree program, adult/continuing education programs, advanced placement credit, cooperative education, distance learning, double majors, English as a second language, external degree program, freshman honors college, honors programs, independent study, internships, part-time degree program, services for LD students, summer session for credit. *ROTC:* Army (c), Air Force (c).

Library Owens Community College Library plus 1 other with 55,708 titles, 9,271 serial subscriptions, 7,982 audiovisual materials, an OPAC, a Web page.

Student Life *Housing:* college housing not available. *Activities and Organizations:* drama/theater group, student-run newspaper, choral group, student government, Black Student Union, Gay-Straight Alliance, International Student Union, Red Cross Club. *Campus security:* 24-hour emergency response devices and patrols, student patrols.

Owens Community College (continued)

Athletics Member NJCAA. *Intercollegiate sports:* baseball M, basketball M(s)/W(s), soccer M, softball W, volleyball W. *Intramural sports:* basketball M/W, bowling M/W, football M/W, golf M/W, softball M/W, table tennis M/W, tennis M/W, volleyball M/W, weight lifting M/W.

Costs (2010–11) *Tuition:* state resident $2683 full-time, $128 per credit hour part-time; nonresident $5366 full-time, $255 per credit hour part-time. Full-time tuition and fees vary according to reciprocity agreements. Part-time tuition and fees vary according to reciprocity agreements. *Required fees:* $432 full-time. *Payment plans:* installment, deferred payment. *Waivers:* senior citizens and employees or children of employees.

Applying *Options:* electronic application, early admission. *Required for some:* minimum 2 GPA. *Application deadlines:* rolling (freshmen), rolling (transfers). *Notification:* continuous (freshmen), continuous (transfers).

Freshman Application Contact Ms. Jennifer Irelan, Director, Enrollment Services, Owens Community College, PO Box 1000, Toledo, OH 43699. *Phone:* 567-661-7225. *Toll-free phone:* 800-GO-OWENS. *E-mail:* jennifer_irelan@owens.edu.

Professional Skills Institute

Toledo, Ohio **www.proskills.com/**

- **Proprietary** 2-year, founded 1984
- **Urban** 2-acre campus with easy access to Detroit
- **Coed**

Academics *Calendar:* quarters. *Degree:* certificates, diplomas, and associate. *Special study options:* internships, off-campus study, part-time degree program, services for LD students.

Student Life *Campus security:* 24-hour emergency response devices, camera, alarm system.

Standardized Tests *Required:* Wonderlic aptitude test (for admission).

Applying *Application fee:* $25. *Required:* high school transcript, minimum 2.0 GPA, interview.

Director of Admissions Ms. Hope Finch, Director of Marketing, Professional Skills Institute, 20 Arco Drive, Toledo, OH 43607. *Phone:* 419-531-9610.

Remington College–Cleveland Campus

Cleveland, Ohio **www.remingtoncollege.edu/**

Director of Admissions Director of Recruitment, Remington College–Cleveland Campus, 14445 Broadway Avenue, Cleveland, OH 44125-1957. *Phone:* 216-475-7520. *Fax:* 216-475-6055.

Remington College–Cleveland West Campus

North Olmstead, Ohio **www.remingtoncollege.edu/**

Freshman Application Contact Remington College–Cleveland West Campus, 26350 Brookpark Road, North Olmstead, OH 44070. *Phone:* 440-777-2560.

Rosedale Bible College

Irwin, Ohio **www.rosedalebible.org/**

Director of Admissions Mr. John Showalter, Director of Enrollment Services, Rosedale Bible College, 2270 Rosedale Road, Irwin, OH 43029-9501. *Phone:* 740-857-1311. *Fax:* 740-857-1577. *E-mail:* pweber@rosedale.edu.

School of Advertising Art

Kettering, Ohio **www.saacollege.com/**

Freshman Application Contact Mr. Nathan Summers, Secretary, School of Advertising Art, 1725 East David Road, Kettering, OH 45440. *Phone:* 937-294-0592. *Toll-free phone:* 877-300-9866. *Fax:* 937-294-5869. *E-mail:* nathan@saacollege.com.

Sinclair Community College

Dayton, Ohio **www.sinclair.edu/**

Freshman Application Contact Ms. Sara Smith, Director and Systems Manager, Outreach Services, Sinclair Community College, 444 West Third Street, Dayton, OH 45402-1460. *Phone:* 937-512-3060. *Toll-free phone:* 800-315-3000. *Fax:* 937-512-2393. *E-mail:* ssmith@sinclair.edu.

Southern State Community College

Hillsboro, Ohio **www.sscc.edu/**

- **State-supported** 2-year, founded 1975
- **Rural** 60-acre campus
- **Endowment** $1.6 million
- **Coed,** 3,363 undergraduate students, 62% full-time, 70% women, 30% men

Undergraduates 2,084 full-time, 1,279 part-time. 2% African American, 0.9% Asian American or Pacific Islander, 0.4% Hispanic American, 0.4% Native American.

Freshmen *Admission:* 1,167 applied, 1,167 admitted, 739 enrolled.

Faculty *Total:* 178, 33% full-time, 12% with terminal degrees. *Student/faculty ratio:* 26:1.

Majors Accounting technology and bookkeeping; agricultural production; business/commerce; computer programming (specific applications); computer technology/computer systems technology; corrections; criminal justice/law enforcement administration; drafting and design technology; emergency medical technology (EMT paramedic); executive assistant/executive secretary; human services; kindergarten/preschool education; liberal arts and sciences/liberal studies; medical/clinical assistant; nursing (registered nurse training); real estate; respiratory care therapy.

Academics *Calendar:* quarters. *Degree:* certificates and associate. *Special study options:* academic remediation for entering students, advanced placement credit, cooperative education, distance learning, double majors, independent study, internships, off-campus study, part-time degree program, services for LD students, student-designed majors, summer session for credit.

Library Learning Resources Center plus 3 others with 50,550 titles, 2,850 serial subscriptions, 9,525 audiovisual materials, an OPAC, a Web page.

Student Life *Housing:* college housing not available. *Activities and Organizations:* drama/theater group, choral group, Student Government Association, Drama Club.

Athletics *Intercollegiate sports:* baseball M(c), basketball M(s)/W(s), soccer M(s), softball W(s), volleyball W(s).

Costs (2009–10) *Tuition:* state resident $3390 full-time, $87 per quarter hour part-time; nonresident $6528 full-time, $168 per quarter hour part-time. Full-time tuition and fees vary according to course load. Part-time tuition and fees vary according to course load. *Payment plan:* deferred payment. *Waivers:* senior citizens and employees or children of employees.

Applying *Options:* early admission, deferred entrance. *Recommended:* high school transcript. *Application deadlines:* rolling (freshmen), rolling (transfers). *Notification:* continuous (freshmen), continuous (transfers).

Freshman Application Contact Ms. Wendy Johnson, Director of Admissions, Southern State Community College, 100 Hobart Drive, Hillsboro, OH 45133. *Phone:* 937-393-3431 Ext. 2720. *Toll-free phone:* 800-628-7722. *Fax:* 937-393-6682. *E-mail:* wjohnson@sscc.edu.

Southwestern College of Business

Cincinnati, Ohio **www.swcollege.net/**

Freshman Application Contact Director of Admission, Southwestern College of Business, 149 Northland Boulevard, Cincinnati, OH 45246-1122. *Phone:* 513-874-0432. *Fax:* 513-874-1330.

Southwestern College of Business

Cincinnati, Ohio **www.swcollege.net/**

Freshman Application Contact Admissions Director, Southwestern College of Business, 632 Vine Street, Suite 200, Cincinnati, OH 45202-4304. *Phone:* 513-421-3212. *Fax:* 513-421-8325.

Southwestern College of Business

Dayton, Ohio www.swcollege.net/

Director of Admissions William Furlong, Director of Admissions, Southwestern College of Business, 111 West First Street, Dayton, OH 45402-3003. *Phone:* 937-224-0061.

Southwestern College of Business

Franklin, Ohio www.swcollege.net/

Freshman Application Contact Admissions Director, Southwestern College of Business, 201 East Second Street, Franklin, OH 45005. *Phone:* 937-746-6633. *Fax:* 937-746-6754.

Stark State College of Technology

North Canton, Ohio www.starkstate.edu/

- **State and locally supported** 2-year, founded 1970, part of Ohio Board of Regents
- **Suburban** 34-acre campus with easy access to Cleveland
- **Endowment** $1.7 million
- **Coed,** 12,483 undergraduate students

Undergraduates Students come from 23 states and territories, 0.5% are from out of state.

Freshmen *Admission:* 1,865 admitted. *Test scores:* ACT scores over 18: 64%; ACT scores over 24: 14%; ACT scores over 30: 1%.

Faculty *Total:* 719, 21% full-time. *Student/faculty ratio:* 17:1.

Majors Accounting; administrative assistant and secretarial science; architectural engineering technology; automobile/automotive mechanics technology; biomedical technology; business administration and management; child development; civil engineering technology; clinical/medical laboratory technology; computer and information sciences and support services related; computer and information sciences related; computer engineering related; computer hardware engineering; computer/information technology services administration related; computer programming; computer programming related; computer programming (specific applications); computer programming (vendor/product certification); computer software and media applications related; computer software engineering; computer systems networking and telecommunications; consumer merchandising/retailing management; court reporting; data entry/microcomputer applications; data entry/microcomputer applications related; dental hygiene; drafting and design technology; environmental studies; finance; fire science; food technology and processing; health information/medical records administration; human services; industrial technology; information technology; international business/trade/commerce; legal administrative assistant/secretary; marketing/marketing management; mechanical engineering/mechanical technology; medical/clinical assistant; nursing (registered nurse training); occupational therapy; operations management; physical therapy; respiratory care therapy; survey technology; web/multimedia management and webmaster; web page, digital/multimedia and information resources design; word processing.

Academics *Calendar:* semesters. *Degree:* certificates and associate. *Special study options:* academic remediation for entering students, adult/continuing education programs, distance learning, external degree program, independent study, off-campus study, part-time degree program, services for LD students, student-designed majors, summer session for credit.

Library Learning Resource Center with 81,962 titles, 231 serial subscriptions, an OPAC.

Student Life *Housing:* college housing not available. *Activities and Organizations:* student-run newspaper, Phi Theta Kappa, Business Student Club, Institute of Management Accountants, Stark State College Association of Medical Assistants, Student Health Information Management Association. *Campus security:* 24-hour emergency response devices, late-night transport/escort service. *Student services:* personal/psychological counseling.

Standardized Tests *Recommended:* SAT or ACT (for admission).

Costs (2009–10) *Tuition:* state resident $3810 full-time, $127 per credit hour part-time; nonresident $5610 full-time, $187 per credit hour part-time. *Payment plan:* installment. *Waivers:* senior citizens and employees or children of employees.

Financial Aid Of all full-time matriculated undergraduates who enrolled in 2008, 194 Federal Work-Study jobs (averaging $2383).

Applying *Options:* electronic application, early admission, deferred entrance. *Application fee:* $65. *Required:* high school transcript. *Application deadlines:* rolling (freshmen), rolling (transfers).

Freshman Application Contact Mr. Wallace Hoffer, Dean of Student Services, Stark State College of Technology, 6200 Frank Road, NW, Canton, OH 44720. *Phone:* 330-966-5450. *Toll-free phone:* 800-797-8275. *Fax:* 330-497-6313. *E-mail:* info@starkstate.edu.

Stautzenberger College

Maumee, Ohio www.stautzen.com/

Director of Admissions Ms. Karen Fitzgerald, Director of Admissions and Marketing, Stautzenberger College, 1796 Indian Wood Circle, Maumee, OH 43537. *Phone:* 419-866-0261. *Toll-free phone:* 800-552-5099. *Fax:* 419-867-9821. *E-mail:* klfitzgerald@stautzenberger.com.

Terra State Community College

Fremont, Ohio www.terra.edu/

- **State-supported** 2-year, founded 1968, part of Ohio Board of Regents
- **Small-town** 100-acre campus with easy access to Toledo
- **Coed,** 3,152 undergraduate students, 46% full-time, 55% women, 45% men

Undergraduates 1,459 full-time, 1,693 part-time. Students come from 4 states and territories, 2 other countries, 0.3% are from out of state, 5% African American, 0.4% Asian American or Pacific Islander, 7% Hispanic American, 0.5% Native American, 0.1% international, 20% transferred in. *Retention:* 39% of 2008 full-time freshmen returned.

Freshmen *Admission:* 2,428 enrolled.

Faculty *Total:* 204, 20% full-time. *Student/faculty ratio:* 21:1.

Majors Accounting; agricultural business and management; animation, interactive technology, video graphics and special effects; architectural engineering technology; art history, criticism and conservation; automotive engineering technology; banking and financial support services; biological and physical sciences; biology/biological sciences; business administration and management; business/commerce; chemistry; commercial and advertising art; computer and information sciences; computer programming; computer systems networking and telecommunications; criminal justice/police science; data processing and data processing technology; desktop publishing and digital imaging design; economics; education; electrical and electronic engineering technologies related; electrical, electronic and communications engineering technology; engineering; English; executive assistant/executive secretary; fine/studio arts; general studies; health/health-care administration; health information/medical records administration; health information/medical records technology; health professions related; heating, air conditioning and refrigeration technology; history; hospitality administration; humanities; kindergarten/preschool education; language interpretation and translation; liberal arts and sciences/liberal studies; manufacturing technology; marketing/marketing management; mathematics; mechanical engineering/mechanical technology; mechanical engineering technologies related; medical administrative assistant and medical secretary; medical/clinical assistant; medical/health management and clinical assistant; medical insurance coding; medical office assistant; music; music management and merchandising; music performance; music related; nuclear/nuclear power technology; nursing (registered nurse training); operations management; physics; plastics engineering technology; psychology; real estate; robotics technology; sheet metal technology; social sciences; social work; teaching assistants/aides related; web page, digital/multimedia and information resources design; welding technology.

Academics *Calendar:* semesters. *Degree:* certificates, diplomas, and associate. *Special study options:* academic remediation for entering students, adult/continuing education programs, advanced placement credit, cooperative education, distance learning, double majors, independent study, internships, off-campus study, part-time degree program, services for LD students, student-designed majors, summer session for credit.

Library Learning Resource Center with 22,675 titles, 383 serial subscriptions, an OPAC, a Web page.

Student Life *Housing:* college housing not available. *Activities and Organizations:* choral group, Phi Theta Kappa, Student Activities Club, Society of Plastic Engineers, Koinonia, Student Senate. *Campus security:* 24-hour emergency response devices. *Student services:* personal/psychological counseling, legal services.

Athletics *Intramural sports:* basketball M/W, bowling M/W, football M, golf M/W, table tennis M/W, volleyball M/W.

Terra State Community College (continued)

Costs (2010–11) *Tuition:* state resident $2769 full-time, $115 per semester hour part-time; nonresident $4523 full-time, $188 per semester hour part-time. Full-time tuition and fees vary according to course load. Part-time tuition and fees vary according to course load. *Required fees:* $307 full-time, $13 per semester hour part-time. *Payment plan:* installment. *Waivers:* senior citizens and employees or children of employees.

Financial Aid Of all full-time matriculated undergraduates who enrolled in 2008, 57 Federal Work-Study jobs (averaging $1450).

Applying *Options:* electronic application, early admission, deferred entrance. *Required:* high school transcript. *Application deadlines:* rolling (freshmen), rolling (transfers).

Freshman Application Contact Mr. Heath Martin, Director of Admissions and Enrollment Services, Terra State Community College, 2830 Napoleon Road, Fremont, OH 43420. *Phone:* 419-559-2350. *Toll-free phone:* 800-334-3886. *Fax:* 419-559-2352. *E-mail:* hmartin01@terra.edu.

TRUMBULL BUSINESS COLLEGE

Warren, Ohio **www.tbc-trumbullbusiness.com/**

Director of Admissions Admissions Office, Trumbull Business College, 3200 Ridge Road, Warren, OH 44484. *Phone:* 330-369-6792. *E-mail:* admissions@tbc-trumbullbusiness.com.

THE UNIVERSITY OF AKRON–WAYNE COLLEGE

Orrville, Ohio **www.wayne.uakron.edu/**

Freshman Application Contact Ms. Alicia Broadus, Student Services Counselor, The University of Akron–Wayne College, 1901 Smucker Road, Orrville, OH 44667. *Phone:* 800-221-8308 Ext. 8901. *Toll-free phone:* 800-221-8308 Ext. 8900. *Fax:* 330-684-8989. *E-mail:* wayneadmissions@uakron.edu.

UNIVERSITY OF CINCINNATI CLERMONT COLLEGE

Batavia, Ohio **www.ucclermont.edu/**

- **State-supported** 2-year, founded 1972, part of University of Cincinnati System
- **Rural** 91-acre campus with easy access to Cincinnati
- **Endowment** $338,141
- **Coed,** 3,713 undergraduate students, 64% full-time, 59% women, 41% men

Undergraduates 2,391 full-time, 1,322 part-time. Students come from 16 states and territories, 21% are from out of state, 3% African American, 0.8% Asian American or Pacific Islander, 1% Hispanic American, 0.5% Native American, 0.5% international.

Freshmen *Admission:* 1,454 applied, 1,143 admitted, 888 enrolled.

Faculty *Total:* 336, 23% full-time. *Student/faculty ratio:* 20:1.

Majors Accounting; aeronautics/aviation/aerospace science and technology; biology/biological sciences; business administration and management; business/commerce; chemistry; computer and information sciences; computer technology/computer systems technology; computer typography and composition equipment operation; criminal justice/safety; data processing and data processing technology; elementary education; emergency medical technology (EMT paramedic); general studies; kindergarten/preschool education; legal assistant/paralegal; liberal arts and sciences/liberal studies; middle school education; multi/interdisciplinary studies related; organizational behavior; physical therapist assistant; pre-law studies; pre-pharmacy studies; psychology; respiratory care therapy; science technologies related; secondary education; social sciences; social work; special education; surgical technology; urban studies/affairs.

Academics *Calendar:* quarters. *Degrees:* certificates, associate, and post-bachelor's certificates. *Special study options:* academic remediation for entering students, adult/continuing education programs, advanced placement credit, cooperative education, distance learning, double majors, honors programs, independent study, internships, off-campus study, part-time degree program, services for LD students, student-designed majors, study abroad, summer session for credit. *ROTC:* Air Force (c).

Library UC Clermont College Library with 3.7 million titles, 80,890 serial subscriptions, 1,143 audiovisual materials, an OPAC, a Web page.

Student Life *Housing:* college housing not available. *Activities and Organizations:* drama/theater group, student-run newspaper, Active Minds, Art Collaborative, Education Club, Tribunal. *Campus security:* 24-hour emergency response devices, Implementing 24-hour patrols by trained security personnel in spring or summer 2010. *Student services:* personal/psychological counseling.

Athletics *Intercollegiate sports:* baseball M, basketball M/W, golf M, softball W, volleyball W.

Costs (2009–10) *Tuition:* state resident $3861 full-time, $107 per credit hour part-time; nonresident $10,713 full-time, $297 per credit hour part-time. Full-time tuition and fees vary according to course load, program, and reciprocity agreements. Part-time tuition and fees vary according to course load, program, and reciprocity agreements. *Required fees:* $681 full-time, $20 per credit hour part-time. *Payment plan:* installment. *Waivers:* senior citizens and employees or children of employees.

Applying *Options:* electronic application, deferred entrance. *Application fee:* $50. *Required:* high school transcript. *Application deadlines:* rolling (freshmen), rolling (transfers). *Notification:* continuous (freshmen), continuous (transfers).

Freshman Application Contact Mrs. Jamie Adkins, Records Management Officer, University of Cincinnati Clermont College, 4200 Clermont College Drive, Batavia, OH 45103-1785. *Phone:* 513-732-5294. *Fax:* 513-732-5303. *E-mail:* jamie.adkins@uc.edu.

UNIVERSITY OF CINCINNATI RAYMOND WALTERS COLLEGE

Cincinnati, Ohio **www.rwc.uc.edu/**

Freshman Application Contact Leigh Schlegal, Admission Counselor, University of Cincinnati Raymond Walters College, 9555 Plainfield Road, Cincinnati, OH 45236-1007. *Phone:* 513-745-5783. *Fax:* 513-745-5768.

UNIVERSITY OF NORTHWESTERN OHIO

Lima, Ohio **www.unoh.edu/**

Freshman Application Contact Mr. Dan Klopp, Vice President for Enrollment Management, University of Northwestern Ohio, 1441 North Cable Road, Lima, OH 45805-1498. *Phone:* 419-227-3141. *Fax:* 419-229-6926. *E-mail:* klopp_d@unoh.edu.

VATTEROTT COLLEGE

Broadview Heights, Ohio **www.vatterott-college.edu/**

Director of Admissions Mr. Jack Chalk, Director of Admissions, Vatterott College, 5025 East Royalton Road, Broadview Heights, OH 44147. *Phone:* 440-526-1660. *Toll-free phone:* 866-314-6454.

VET TECH INSTITUTE AT BRADFORD SCHOOL

Columbus, Ohio **www.vettechinstitute.edu/**

- **Private** 2-year, founded 2005
- **Suburban** campus
- **Coed,** 177 undergraduate students
- 36% of applicants were admitted

Freshmen *Admission:* 541 applied, 197 admitted.

Majors Veterinary/animal health technology.

Academics *Degree:* associate. *Special study options:* accelerated degree program, internships.

Freshman Application Contact Admissions Office, Vet Tech Institute at Bradford School, 2469 Stelzer Road, Columbus, OH 43219. *Phone:* 800-678-7981. *Toll-free phone:* 800-678-7981.

Virginia Marti College of Art and Design

Lakewood, Ohio **www.vmcad.edu/**

- **Proprietary** 2-year, founded 1966
- **Urban** campus with easy access to Cleveland
- **Coed,** 271 undergraduate students

Undergraduates *Retention:* 62% of 2008 full-time freshmen returned.
Freshmen *Admission:* 88 applied.
Faculty *Student/faculty ratio:* 12:1.
Majors Commercial and advertising art; digital communication and media/multimedia; fashion/apparel design; fashion merchandising; interior design.
Academics *Calendar:* quarters. *Degree:* certificates and associate. *Special study options:* academic remediation for entering students, adult/continuing education programs, internships, part-time degree program, summer session for credit.
Student Life *Housing:* college housing not available. *Campus security:* 24-hour emergency response devices.
Standardized Tests *Required:* CAPS (for admission).
Applying *Options:* electronic application, early admission, deferred entrance. *Application fee:* $50. *Required:* essay or personal statement, high school transcript, minimum 2 GPA, 1 letter of recommendation, interview. *Required for some:* Entrance Evaluation Test. *Application deadlines:* rolling (freshmen), rolling (transfers).
Freshman Application Contact Virginia Marti College of Art and Design, 11724 Detroit Avenue, PO Box 580, Lakewood, OH 44107-3002. *Phone:* 216-221-8584 Ext. 106.

Washington State Community College

Marietta, Ohio **www.wscc.edu/**

Freshman Application Contact Ms. Rebecca Peroni, Director of Admissions, Washington State Community College, 710 Colegate Drive, Marietta, OH 45750-9225. *Phone:* 740-374-8716. *Fax:* 740-376-0257. *E-mail:* rperoni@wscc.edu.

Wright State University, Lake Campus

Celina, Ohio **www.wright.edu/lake/**

Freshman Application Contact Sandra Gilbert, Student Services Officer, Wright State University, Lake Campus, 7600 State Route 703, Celina, OH 45822-2921. *Phone:* 419-586-0324. *Toll-free phone:* 800-237-1477. *Fax:* 419-586-0358.

Zane State College

Zanesville, Ohio **www.zanestate.edu/**

Director of Admissions Mr. Paul Young, Director of Admissions, Zane State College, 1555 Newark Road, Zanesville, OH 43701-2626. *Phone:* 740-454-2501 Ext. 1225. *Toll-free phone:* 800-686-8324 Ext. 1225.

OKLAHOMA

Brown Mackie College–Tulsa

Tulsa, Oklahoma **www.brownmackie.edu/tulsa/**

- **Proprietary** primarily 2-year
- **Coed**

Majors Accounting technology and bookkeeping; business administration and management; criminal justice/law enforcement administration; health services administration; information technology; legal assistant/paralegal; legal studies; medical/clinical assistant; occupational therapist assistant; office management; surgical technology.
Academics *Degrees:* diplomas, associate, and bachelor's.
Costs (2009–10) *Tuition:* Tuition varies by program. Students should contact Brown Mackie College for tuition information.
Freshman Application Contact Brown Mackie College–Tulsa, 4608 South Garnett, Suite 110, Tulsa, OK 74146. *Phone:* 918-628-3700. *Toll-free phone:* 888-794-8411.

▶See page 450 for the College Close-Up.

Carl Albert State College

Poteau, Oklahoma **www.carlalbert.edu/**

Freshman Application Contact Dawn Webster, Admission Clerk, Carl Albert State College, 1507 South McKenna Street, Poteau, OK 74953. *Phone:* 918-647-1300. *Fax:* 918-647-1306. *E-mail:* dwebster@carlalbert.edu.

Clary Sage College

Tulsa, Oklahoma **www.clarysagecollege.com/**

- **Proprietary** 2-year, part of Dental Directions, Inc.
- **Urban** 6-acre campus
- **Coed,** 118 undergraduate students, 100% full-time, 97% women, 3% men

Undergraduates 118 full-time. Students come from 2 states and territories.
Faculty *Total:* 15, 87% full-time. *Student/faculty ratio:* 15:1.
Academics *Degree:* certificates, diplomas, and associate. *Special study options:* distance learning, honors programs, internships.
Student Life *Campus security:* security guard during hours of operation.
Costs (2009–10) *Tuition:* $9733 full-time. Full-time tuition and fees vary according to program. Part-time tuition and fees vary according to program. *Required fees:* $2000 full-time. *Payment plan:* tuition prepayment. *Waivers:* employees or children of employees.
Applying *Options:* electronic application, deferred entrance. *Application fee:* $100. *Required:* essay or personal statement, high school transcript, interview. *Application deadlines:* rolling (freshmen), rolling (out-of-state freshmen), rolling (transfers).
Freshman Application Contact Ms. Teresa Knox, Chief Executive Officer, Clary Sage College, 3131 South Sheridan, Tulsa, OK 74145. *Phone:* 918-610-0027. *E-mail:* tknox@clarysagecollege.com.

Community Care College

Tulsa, Oklahoma **www.communitycarecollege.edu/**

- **Proprietary** 2-year, founded 1995, part of Dental Directions, Inc.
- **Urban** 6-acre campus
- **Coed,** 286 undergraduate students, 100% full-time, 90% women, 10% men

Undergraduates 286 full-time. Students come from 9 states and territories, 2% are from out of state, 19% African American, 2% Asian American or Pacific Islander, 5% Hispanic American, 3% Native American.
Faculty *Total:* 26, 100% full-time. *Student/faculty ratio:* 20:1.
Majors Business administration, management and operations related; dental assisting; early childhood education; health and physical education; health/health-care administration; massage therapy; medical/clinical assistant; medical insurance coding; pharmacy technician; surgical technology; veterinary/animal health technology.
Academics *Calendar:* continuous. *Degree:* diplomas and associate. *Special study options:* adult/continuing education programs, distance learning, internships, part-time degree program.
Student Life *Housing:* college housing not available. *Student services:* personal/psychological counseling.
Costs (2009–10) *Tuition:* $15,000 full-time. Full-time tuition and fees vary according to course load, degree level, and program. No tuition increase for student's term of enrollment. *Required fees:* $1900 full-time. *Payment plan:* installment. *Waivers:* employees or children of employees.

Community Care College (continued)

Applying *Options:* electronic application. *Application fee:* $100. *Required:* high school transcript, interview. *Required for some:* essay or personal statement. *Application deadlines:* rolling (freshmen), rolling (out-of-state freshmen). *Notification:* continuous (freshmen), continuous (out-of-state freshmen).

Freshman Application Contact Ms. Teresa Knox, Chief Executive Officer, Community Care College, 4242 South Sheridan, Tulsa, OK 74145. *Phone:* 918-610-0027. *Fax:* 918-610-0029. *E-mail:* tknox@communitycarecollege.com.

CONNORS STATE COLLEGE

Warner, Oklahoma **www.connorsstate.edu/**

- **State-supported** 2-year, founded 1908, part of Oklahoma State Regents for Higher Education
- **Rural** 1658-acre campus
- **Coed**

Academics *Calendar:* semesters. *Degree:* certificates, diplomas, and associate. *Special study options:* academic remediation for entering students, accelerated degree program, adult/continuing education programs, advanced placement credit, internships, part-time degree program, summer session for credit.

Student Life *Campus security:* late-night transport/escort service, trained security personnel.

Athletics Member NJCAA.

Financial Aid Of all full-time matriculated undergraduates who enrolled in 2008, 100 Federal Work-Study jobs (averaging $800).

Applying *Options:* early admission, deferred entrance. *Required for some:* high school transcript.

Freshman Application Contact Ms. Sonya Baker, Registrar, Connors State College, Route 1 Box 1000 College Road, Warner, OK 74469. *Phone:* 918-463-6233.

EASTERN OKLAHOMA STATE COLLEGE

Wilburton, Oklahoma **www.eosc.edu/**

- **State-supported** 2-year, founded 1908, part of Oklahoma State Regents for Higher Education
- **Rural** 4000-acre campus
- **Coed**

Academics *Calendar:* semesters. *Degree:* certificates and associate. *Special study options:* academic remediation for entering students, adult/continuing education programs, advanced placement credit, cooperative education, double majors, honors programs, internships, off-campus study, part-time degree program, summer session for credit.

Athletics Member NJCAA.

Financial Aid Of all full-time matriculated undergraduates who enrolled in 2008, 111 Federal Work-Study jobs (averaging $825). 125 state and other part-time jobs (averaging $721).

Applying *Options:* early admission, deferred entrance. *Application fee:* $10. *Required:* high school transcript.

Freshman Application Contact Ms. Leah McLaughlin, Director of Admissions, Eastern Oklahoma State College, 1301 West Main, Wilburton, OK 74578-4999. *Phone:* 918-465-1811. *Fax:* 918-465-2431. *E-mail:* lmiller@eosc.edu.

HERITAGE COLLEGE

Oklahoma City, Oklahoma **www.heritage-education.com/campus_oklahoma.htm**

Freshman Application Contact Admissions Office, Heritage College, 7100 I-35 Services Road, Suite 7118, Oklahoma City, OK 73149. *Phone:* 405-631-3399. *Toll-free phone:* 888-334-7339. *E-mail:* info@heritage-education.com.

ITT TECHNICAL INSTITUTE

Tulsa, Oklahoma **www.itt-tech.edu/**

- **Proprietary** primarily 2-year, founded 2005
- **Coed**

Majors CAD/CADD drafting/design technology; computer and information systems security; computer engineering technology; computer software engineering; computer software technology; construction management; criminal justice/law enforcement administration; design and visual communications; electrical, electronic and communications engineering technology; legal assistant/paralegal; nursing (registered nurse training); system, networking, and LAN/WAN management.

Academics *Calendar:* quarters. *Degrees:* associate and bachelor's.

Freshman Application Contact Director of Recruitment, ITT Technical Institute, 4943 South 78th East Avenue, Tulsa, OK 74145. *Phone:* 918-615-3900. *Toll-free phone:* 800-514-6535.

MURRAY STATE COLLEGE

Tishomingo, Oklahoma **www.mscok.edu/**

- **State-supported** 2-year, founded 1908, part of Oklahoma State Regents for Higher Education
- **Rural** 120-acre campus
- **Coed,** 2,497 undergraduate students, 52% full-time, 67% women, 33% men

Undergraduates 1,291 full-time, 1,206 part-time. Students come from 20 states and territories, 13 other countries, 3% are from out of state, 6% African American, 0.8% Asian American or Pacific Islander, 5% Hispanic American, 21% Native American, 0.2% international, 6% live on campus.

Faculty *Total:* 73, 59% full-time. *Student/faculty ratio:* 27:1.

Majors Administrative assistant and secretarial science; agricultural teacher education; agriculture; animal sciences; art; biological and physical sciences; business administration and management; business teacher education; chemistry; child development; computer science; drafting and design technology; electrical, electronic and communications engineering technology; elementary education; engineering; engineering technology; English; equestrian studies; health professions related; history; information science/studies; liberal arts and sciences/liberal studies; mathematics; metallurgical technology; natural resources/conservation; nursing (registered nurse training); physical education teaching and coaching; physical therapy; pre-engineering; veterinary/animal health technology; wildlife and wildlands science and management.

Academics *Calendar:* semesters. *Degree:* associate. *Special study options:* academic remediation for entering students, advanced placement credit, distance learning, honors programs, internships, part-time degree program, services for LD students, summer session for credit.

Library Murray State College Library plus 1 other with 20,000 titles, 160 serial subscriptions.

Student Life *Housing Options:* coed. Campus housing is university owned. *Activities and Organizations:* drama/theater group, choral group. *Campus security:* 24-hour patrols. *Student services:* personal/psychological counseling.

Athletics Member NJCAA. *Intercollegiate sports:* baseball M, basketball M(s)/W(s), softball W(s). *Intramural sports:* basketball M/W.

Standardized Tests *Required:* SAT or ACT (for admission).

Financial Aid Of all full-time matriculated undergraduates who enrolled in 2008, 68 Federal Work-Study jobs (averaging $3354). 20 state and other part-time jobs (averaging $2516).

Applying *Options:* electronic application, early admission. *Required:* high school transcript. *Application deadlines:* rolling (freshmen), rolling (transfers). *Notification:* continuous (freshmen), continuous (transfers).

Freshman Application Contact Murray State College, One Murray Campus, Tishomingo, OK 73460. *Phone:* 580-371-2371.

NORTHEASTERN OKLAHOMA AGRICULTURAL AND MECHANICAL COLLEGE

Miami, Oklahoma **www.neo.edu/**

Freshman Application Contact Amy Ishmael, Vice President for Enrollment Management, Northeastern Oklahoma Agricultural and Mechanical College, PO Box 3842, 200 I Street NE, Miami, OK 74354. *Phone:* 918-540-6212. *Toll-free phone:* 800-464-6636. *Fax:* 918-540-6946. *E-mail:* neoadmission@neo.edu.

NORTHERN OKLAHOMA COLLEGE

Tonkawa, Oklahoma **www.north-ok.edu/**

Freshman Application Contact Ms. Sheri Snyder, Director of College Relations, Northern Oklahoma College, PO Box 310, Tonkawa, OK 74653. *Phone:* 580-628-6290. *Toll-free phone:* 800-429-5715.

OKLAHOMA CITY COMMUNITY COLLEGE

Oklahoma City, Oklahoma **www.occc.edu/**

- **State-supported** 2-year, founded 1969, part of Oklahoma State Regents for Higher Education
- **Urban** 143-acre campus
- **Endowment** $301,575
- **Coed,** 14,159 undergraduate students, 40% full-time, 57% women, 43% men

Undergraduates 5,705 full-time, 8,454 part-time. Students come from 20 states and territories, 44 other countries, 4% are from out of state, 10% African American, 4% Asian American or Pacific Islander, 8% Hispanic American, 6% Native American, 5% international.

Freshmen *Admission:* 2,698 enrolled. *Test scores:* ACT scores over 18: 70%; ACT scores over 24: 16%.

Faculty *Total:* 540, 27% full-time, 10% with terminal degrees. *Student/faculty ratio:* 26:1.

Majors Accounting; airframe mechanics and aircraft maintenance technology; American government and politics; applied art; area studies related; art; automobile/automotive mechanics technology; avionics maintenance technology; biology/biological sciences; biomedical technology; biotechnology; broadcast journalism; business administration and management; chemistry; child development; commercial and advertising art; comparative literature; computer engineering technology; computer science; design and visual communications; drafting and design technology; dramatic/theater arts; electrical, electronic and communications engineering technology; emergency medical technology (EMT paramedic); finance; fine/studio arts; foreign languages and literatures; health information/medical records administration; history; humanities; insurance; liberal arts and sciences/liberal studies; mass communication/media; mathematics; modern languages; music; nursing (registered nurse training); occupational therapy; philosophy; physical therapy; physics; political science and government; pre-engineering; psychology; respiratory care therapy; sociology; surgical technology.

Academics *Calendar:* semesters. *Degree:* certificates and associate. *Special study options:* academic remediation for entering students, accelerated degree program, advanced placement credit, cooperative education, distance learning, double majors, English as a second language, honors programs, independent study, part-time degree program, services for LD students, student-designed majors, summer session for credit.

Library Keith Leftwich Memorial Library with 93,808 titles, 557 serial subscriptions, 9,189 audiovisual materials, an OPAC, a Web page.

Student Life *Housing:* college housing not available. *Activities and Organizations:* drama/theater group, student-run newspaper, choral group, Health Professions Association, Black Student Association, Nursing Student Association, Hispanic Organization Promoting Education (H.O.P.E), Phi Theta Kappa (Honorary). *Campus security:* 24-hour emergency response devices and patrols, late-night transport/escort service. *Student services:* personal/psychological counseling.

Athletics *Intramural sports:* basketball M/W, bowling M/W, football M/W, rock climbing M/W, soccer M(c)/W(c), volleyball M/W, weight lifting M/W.

Costs (2010–11) *One-time required fee:* $25. *Tuition:* state resident $1454 full-time, $61 per credit hour part-time; nonresident $4814 full-time, $201 per credit hour part-time. Full-time tuition and fees vary according to class time and course level. Part time tuition and fees vary according to class time and course level. *Required fees:* $562 full-time, $23 per credit hour part-time. *Payment plan:* installment. *Waivers:* senior citizens and employees or children of employees.

Financial Aid Of all full-time matriculated undergraduates who enrolled in 2008, 4,223 applied for aid, 1,689 were judged to have need, 1,351 had their need fully met. 309 Federal Work-Study jobs (averaging $4800). 242 state and other part-time jobs (averaging $2537). In 2008, 514 non-need-based awards were made. *Average percent of need met:* 60%. *Average financial aid package:* $3187. *Average need-based loan:* $2444. *Average need-based gift aid:* $1368. *Average non-need-based aid:* $563.

Applying *Options:* electronic application. *Application fee:* $25. *Required:* high school transcript. *Required for some:* ACT. *Application deadlines:* rolling (freshmen), rolling (out-of-state freshmen), rolling (transfers). *Notification:* continuous (freshmen), continuous (out-of-state freshmen), continuous (transfers).

Freshman Application Contact Mr. Jon Horinek, Director of Admissions and Recruitment, Oklahoma City Community College, 7777 South May Avenue, Oklahoma City, OK 73159. *Phone:* 405-682-7515. *Fax:* 405-682-7521. *E-mail:* jhorinek@occc.edu.

OKLAHOMA STATE UNIVERSITY INSTITUTE OF TECHNOLOGY

Okmulgee, Oklahoma **www.osuit.edu/**

Freshman Application Contact Mary Graves, Director, Admissions, Oklahoma State University Institute of Technology, 1801 East Fourth Street, Okmulgee, OK 74447-3901. *Phone:* 918-293-5298. *Toll-free phone:* 800-722-4471. *Fax:* 918-293-4643. *E-mail:* mary.r.graves@okstate.edu.

OKLAHOMA STATE UNIVERSITY, OKLAHOMA CITY

Oklahoma City, Oklahoma **www.osuokc.edu/**

- **State-supported** primarily 2-year, founded 1961, part of Oklahoma State University
- **Urban** 80-acre campus
- **Coed,** 7,179 undergraduate students

Undergraduates Students come from 9 states and territories, 8 other countries, 1% are from out of state. *Retention:* 36% of 2008 full-time freshmen returned.

Freshmen *Admission:* 1,177 applied, 1,177 admitted.

Faculty *Total:* 340, 24% full-time. *Student/faculty ratio:* 20:1.

Majors Accounting; American Sign Language (ASL); architectural engineering technology; art; building/home/construction inspection; business administration and management; civil engineering technology; construction engineering technology; construction management; construction trades; criminal justice/police science; drafting and design technology; early childhood education; economics; electrical and power transmission installation; electrical, electronic and communications engineering technology; electrocardiograph technology; emergency medical technology (EMT paramedic); engineering technology; fire protection and safety technology; fire science; general studies; health/health-care administration; history; horticultural science; humanities; human services; illustration; information science/studies; information technology; language interpretation and translation; nursing (registered nurse training); occupational safety and health technology; physics; pre-engineering; prenursing studies; psychology; public administration and social service professions related; radiologic technology/science; sign language interpretation and translation; substance abuse/addiction counseling; survey technology; technical and business writing; turf and turfgrass management; veterinary/animal health technology; web page, digital/multimedia and information resources design.

Academics *Calendar:* semesters. *Degrees:* certificates, associate, and bachelor's. *Special study options:* academic remediation for entering students, advanced placement credit, cooperative education, distance learning, double majors, honors programs, independent study, part-time degree program, services for LD students, study abroad, summer session for credit.

Library Oklahoma State University-Oklahoma City Campus Library with 11,973 titles, 265 serial subscriptions, an OPAC, a Web page.

Student Life *Housing:* college housing not available. *Activities and Organizations:* Phi Theta Kappa, Deaf/Hearing Social Club, American Criminal Justice Association, Horticulture Club, Vet-Tech Club. *Campus security:* 24-hour patrols, late-night transport/escort service.

Costs (2010–11) *Tuition:* state resident $2889 full-time, $96 per credit hour part-time; nonresident $7749 full-time, $258 per credit hour part-time. Full-time tuition and fees vary according to course level, degree level, and program. Part-time tuition and fees vary according to course level, degree level, and program. No tuition increase for student's term of enrollment. *Required fees:* $30 full-time, $11 per credit hour part-time. *Payment plan:* installment. *Waivers:* senior citizens and employees or children of employees.

Applying *Options:* electronic application, early admission. *Required:* high school transcript. *Application deadlines:* rolling (freshmen), rolling (transfers). *Notification:* continuous (freshmen), continuous (transfers).

Freshman Application Contact Kyle Williams, Director, Enrollment Management, Oklahoma State University, Oklahoma City, 900 North Portland Avenue, Oklahoma City, OK 73107. *Phone:* 405-945-9152. *E-mail:* wilkylw@osuokc.edu.

OKLAHOMA TECHNICAL COLLEGE

Tulsa, Oklahoma **www.oklahomatechnicalcollege.com/**

- **Proprietary** 2-year, part of Dental Directions, Inc.
- **Urban** 9-acre campus
- **Coed**

Oklahoma Technical College (continued)

Faculty *Total:* 6, 100% full-time. *Student/faculty ratio:* 13:1.
Majors Automobile/automotive mechanics technology; barbering; diesel mechanics technology; welding technology.
Academics *Degree:* certificates, diplomas, and associate. *Special study options:* distance learning, internships.
Costs (2009–10) *Tuition:* $14,000 full-time. Full-time tuition and fees vary according to program. Part-time tuition and fees vary according to program. *Payment plans:* tuition prepayment, installment. *Waivers:* employees or children of employees.
Applying *Options:* electronic application. *Required:* high school transcript, interview. *Required for some:* essay or personal statement. *Application deadlines:* rolling (freshmen), rolling (out-of-state freshmen), rolling (transfers).
Freshman Application Contact Ms. Teresa Knox, Chief Executive Officer, Oklahoma Technical College, 4444 South Sheridan, Tulsa, OK 74145. *Phone:* 918-610-0027. *E-mail:* tknox@communitycarecollege.com.

Platt College

Moore, Oklahoma plattcollege.org/campuses/moore-campus/

Admissions Office Contact Platt College, 201 North Eastern Avenue, Moore, OK 73160.

Platt College

Oklahoma City, Oklahoma www.plattcollege.org/

Director of Admissions Ms. Jane Nowlin, Director, Platt College, 309 South Ann Arbor Avenue, Oklahoma City, OK 73128. *Phone:* 405-946-7799. *Fax:* 405-943-2150. *E-mail:* janen@plattcollege.org.

Platt College

Tulsa, Oklahoma www.plattcollege.org/

Director of Admissions Mrs. Susan Rone, Director, Platt College, 3801 South Sheridan Road, Tulsa, OK 74145-111. *Phone:* 918-663-9000. *Fax:* 918-622-1240. *E-mail:* susanr@plattcollege.org.

Redlands Community College

El Reno, Oklahoma www.redlandscc.edu/

Director of Admissions Ms. Tricia Hobson, Director, Enrollment Management, Redlands Community College, 1300 South Country Club Road, El Reno, OK 73036. *Phone:* 405-262-2552 Ext. 1263. *Toll-free phone:* 866-415-6367. *Fax:* 405-422-1239. *E-mail:* hobsont@redlandscc.edu.

Rose State College

Midwest City, Oklahoma www.rose.edu/

Freshman Application Contact Ms. Mechelle Aitson-Roessler, Registrar and Director of Admissions, Rose State College, 6420 Southeast 15th Street, Midwest City, OK 73110-2799. *Phone:* 405-733-7308. *Toll-free phone:* 866-621-0987. *Fax:* 405-736-0203. *E-mail:* maitson@ms.rose.cc.ok.us.

Seminole State College

Seminole, Oklahoma www.ssc.cc.ok.us/

- **State-supported** 2-year, founded 1931, part of Oklahoma State Regents for Higher Education
- **Small-town** 40-acre campus with easy access to Oklahoma City
- **Coed,** 2,534 undergraduate students

Undergraduates Students come from 13 states and territories, 5 other countries, 2% are from out of state, 8% live on campus.
Freshmen *Test scores:* ACT scores over 18: 56%; ACT scores over 24: 6%.
Faculty *Total:* 101, 46% full-time, 4% with terminal degrees. *Student/faculty ratio:* 25:1.
Majors Accounting; administrative assistant and secretarial science; art; behavioral sciences; biology/biological sciences; business administration and management; clinical/medical laboratory technology; computer science; criminal justice/police science; elementary education; English; liberal arts and sciences/liberal studies; mathematics; nursing (registered nurse training); physical education teaching and coaching; physical sciences; pre-engineering; social sciences.
Academics *Calendar:* semesters. *Degree:* diplomas and associate. *Special study options:* academic remediation for entering students, accelerated degree program, adult/continuing education programs, advanced placement credit, cooperative education, distance learning, honors programs, independent study, off-campus study, part-time degree program, services for LD students, summer session for credit.
Library Boren Library with 27,507 titles, 200 serial subscriptions, an OPAC.
Student Life *Housing Options:* coed. Campus housing is university owned. *Activities and Organizations:* student-run newspaper, choral group, Student Government Association, Native American Student Association, Psi Beta Honor Society, Student Nurses Association, Phi Theta Kappa. *Campus security:* 24-hour patrols, student patrols, late-night transport/escort service, controlled dormitory access. *Student services:* personal/psychological counseling.
Athletics Member NJCAA. *Intercollegiate sports:* baseball M(s), basketball M(s)/W(s), golf M(s)/W(s), softball W(s), volleyball W(s).
Standardized Tests *Recommended:* ACT (for admission).
Applying *Options:* early admission, deferred entrance. *Application fee:* $15. *Required:* high school transcript. *Application deadlines:* rolling (freshmen), rolling (transfers). *Notification:* continuous (freshmen), continuous (transfers).
Freshman Application Contact Mr. Chris Lindley, Director of Enrollment Management, Seminole State College, PO Box 351, 2701 Boren Boulevard, Seminole, OK 74818-0351. *Phone:* 405-382-9272. *Fax:* 405-382-9524. *E-mail:* lindley_c@ssc.cc.ok.us.

Southwestern Oklahoma State University at Sayre

Sayre, Oklahoma www.swosu.edu/sayre/

Freshman Application Contact Ms. Kim Seymour, Registrar, Southwestern Oklahoma State University at Sayre, 409 East Mississippi Street, Sayre, OK 73662-1236. *Phone:* 580-928-5533 Ext. 101. *Fax:* 580-928-1140. *E-mail:* kim.seymour@swosu.edu.

Spartan College of Aeronautics and Technology

Tulsa, Oklahoma www.spartan.edu/

- **Proprietary** primarily 2-year, founded 1928
- **Urban** 26-acre campus
- **Men only,** 1,438 undergraduate students, 100% full-time

Undergraduates 1,438 full-time. 76% are from out of state, 0.2% transferred in. *Retention:* 66% of 2008 full-time freshmen returned.
Freshmen *Admission:* 844 applied, 380 enrolled.
Faculty *Student/faculty ratio:* 14:1.
Majors Aeronautical/aerospace engineering technology; airline pilot and flight crew; instrumentation technology; quality control technology; telecommunications technology.
Academics *Calendar:* calendar terms. *Degrees:* certificates, diplomas, associate, and bachelor's. *Special study options:* cooperative education, honors programs, independent study.
Financial Aid Of all full-time matriculated undergraduates who enrolled in 2008, 23 Federal Work-Study jobs (averaging $4341).
Applying *Application fee:* $100. *Required:* high school transcript. *Recommended:* interview. *Application deadlines:* rolling (freshmen), rolling (transfers).
Freshman Application Contact Mr. Mark Fowler, Vice President of Student Records and Finance, Spartan College of Aeronautics and Technology, 8820 East Pine Street, PO Box 582833, Tulsa, OK 74158-2833. *Phone:* 918-836-6886. *Toll-free phone:* 800-331-1204 (in-state); 800-331-124 (out-of-state).

Tulsa Community College

Tulsa, Oklahoma www.tulsacc.edu/

Freshman Application Contact Ms. Leanne Brewer, Director of Admissions and Records, Tulsa Community College, 6111 East Skelly Drive, Tulsa, OK 74135. *Phone:* 918-595-7811. *Fax:* 918-595-7910. *E-mail:* lbrewer@tulsacc.edu.

TULSA WELDING SCHOOL

Tulsa, Oklahoma **www.weldingschool.com/**

Freshman Application Contact Mrs. Debbie Renee Burke, Vice President/ Executive Director, Tulsa Welding School, 2545 East 11th Street, Tulsa, OK 74104. *Phone:* 918-587-6789 Ext. 2258. *Toll-free phone:* 800-WELD-PRO. *Fax:* 918-295-6812. *E-mail:* dburke@twsweld.com.

VATTEROTT COLLEGE

Oklahoma City, Oklahoma **www.vatterott-college.edu/**

Freshman Application Contact Mr. Mark Hybers, Director of Admissions, Vatterott College, 4629 Northwest 23rd Street, Oklahoma City, OK 73127. *Phone:* 405-945-0088 Ext. 4416. *Toll-free phone:* 888-948-0088. *Fax:* 405-945-0788. *E-mail:* mark.hybers@vatterott-college.edu.

VATTEROTT COLLEGE

Tulsa, Oklahoma **www.vatterott-college.edu/**

Freshman Application Contact Mr. Terry Queeno, Campus Director, Vatterott College, 555 South Memorial Drive, Tulsa, OK 74112. *Phone:* 918-836-6656. *Toll-free phone:* 888-857-4016. *Fax:* 918-836-9698. *E-mail:* tulsa@vatterott-college.edu.

WESTERN OKLAHOMA STATE COLLEGE

Altus, Oklahoma **www.wosc.edu/**

Freshman Application Contact Dr. Larry W. Paxton, Director of Academic Services, Western Oklahoma State College, 2801 North Main Street, Altus, OK 73521-1397. *Phone:* 580-477-7720. *Fax:* 580-477-7723. *E-mail:* larry.paxton@wosc.edu.

OREGON

AMERICAN COLLEGE OF HEALTHCARE SCIENCES

Portland, Oregon **www.achs.edu/**

Freshman Application Contact ACHS Admissions, American College of Healthcare Sciences, 5940 Southwest Hood Avenue, Portland, OR 97239-3719. *Phone:* 503-244-0726. *Toll-free phone:* 800-487-8839. *Fax:* 503-244-0727. *E-mail:* admissions@achs.edu.

APOLLO COLLEGE–PORTLAND

Portland, Oregon **www.apollocollege.edu/**

Freshman Application Contact Admissions Office, Apollo College–Portland, 2600 SE 98th Avenue, Portland, OR 97266. *Phone:* 503-761-6100. *Toll-free phone:* 877-205-1458.

BLUE MOUNTAIN COMMUNITY COLLEGE

Pendleton, Oregon **www.bluecc.edu/**

- **State and locally supported** 2-year, founded 1962
- **Rural** 170-acre campus
- **Coed**

Academics *Calendar:* quarters. *Degree:* certificates and associate. *Special study options:* academic remediation for entering students, adult/continuing education programs, advanced placement credit, cooperative education, distance learning, English as a second language, part-time degree program, services for LD students, summer session for credit.

Athletics Member NJCAA.

Costs (2009–10) *Tuition:* state resident $3235 full-time, $68 per credit hour part-time; nonresident $9705 full-time, $204 per credit hour part-time. Full-time tuition and fees vary according to course load, program, and reciprocity agreements. Part-time tuition and fees vary according to course load, program, and reciprocity agreements. *Required fees:* $175 full-time, $4 per credit hour part-time, $18 per term part-time.

Financial Aid Of all full-time matriculated undergraduates who enrolled in 2008, 60 Federal Work-Study jobs (averaging $1800). 100 state and other part-time jobs (averaging $1200).

Applying *Options:* electronic application. *Required:* high school transcript.

Director of Admissions Ms. Theresa Bosworth, Director of Admissions, Blue Mountain Community College, PO Box 100, Pendleton, OR 97801. *Phone:* 541-278-5774. *E-mail:* tbosworth@bluecc.edu.

CENTRAL OREGON COMMUNITY COLLEGE

Bend, Oregon **www.cocc.edu/**

- **District-supported** 2-year, founded 1949, part of Oregon Community College Association
- **Small-town** 193-acre campus
- **Endowment** $10.0 million
- **Coed,** 6,261 undergraduate students, 46% full-time, 55% women, 45% men

Undergraduates 2,876 full-time, 3,385 part-time. Students come from 10 states and territories, 5% are from out of state, 0.6% African American, 2% Asian American or Pacific Islander, 5% Hispanic American, 2% Native American, 10% transferred in, 1% live on campus. *Retention:* 45% of 2008 full-time freshmen returned.

Freshmen *Admission:* 1,713 applied, 1,713 admitted, 1,044 enrolled.

Faculty *Total:* 241, 41% full-time. *Student/faculty ratio:* 27:1.

Majors Accounting; administrative assistant and secretarial science; airline pilot and flight crew; art; automobile/automotive mechanics technology; biological and physical sciences; biology/biological sciences; business administration and management; CAD/CADD drafting/design technology; child-care and support services management; communication/speech communication and rhetoric; computer and information sciences related; computer science; computer systems networking and telecommunications; cooking and related culinary arts; customer service management; dental assisting; dietetics; drafting and design technology; early childhood education; education; electrical, electronic and communications engineering technology; emergency medical technology (EMT paramedic); engineering; fire science; fishing and fisheries sciences and management; foreign languages and literatures; forestry; forestry technology; health and physical education; health information/medical records technology; hotel/motel administration; humanities; industrial technology; kinesiology and exercise science; liberal arts and sciences/liberal studies; management information systems; manufacturing technology; marketing/marketing management; massage therapy; mathematics; medical/clinical assistant; natural resources/conservation; nursing (licensed practical/vocational nurse training); nursing (registered nurse training); physical sciences; physical therapy; polymer/plastics engineering; pre-law studies; premedical studies; pre-pharmacy studies; radiologic technology/science; retailing; social sciences; sport and fitness administration/management; substance abuse/addiction counseling.

Academics *Calendar:* quarters. *Degree:* certificates and associate. *Special study options:* academic remediation for entering students, cooperative education, distance learning, double majors, English as a second language, independent study, internships, part-time degree program, student-designed majors, study abroad, summer session for credit. *ROTC:* Army (b).

Library COCC Library plus 1 other with 76,421 titles, 329 serial subscriptions, 3,570 audiovisual materials, an OPAC, a Web page.

Student Life *Housing Options:* coed. Campus housing is university owned. *Activities and Organizations:* drama/theater group, student-run newspaper, choral group, club sports, student newspaper, Criminal Justice Club, Aviation Club. *Campus security:* 24-hour emergency response devices and patrols, late-night transport/escort service. *Student services:* personal/psychological counseling.

Athletics *Intercollegiate sports:* golf M/W. *Intramural sports:* baseball M, basketball M/W, cross-country running M/W, football M, skiing (cross-country) M/W, skiing (downhill) M/W, soccer M/W, track and field M/W, volleyball M/W, weight lifting M/W.

Central Oregon Community College (continued)

Costs (2009–10) *Tuition:* area resident $2970 full-time; state resident $4095 full-time; nonresident $8370 full-time. *Required fees:* $123 full-time. *Room and board:* $7326. *Waivers:* employees or children of employees.

Financial Aid Of all full-time matriculated undergraduates who enrolled in 2008, 725 Federal Work-Study jobs (averaging $2130).

Applying *Options:* electronic application. *Application fee:* $25. *Application deadlines:* rolling (freshmen), rolling (transfers). *Notification:* continuous (freshmen), continuous (transfers).

Freshman Application Contact Central Oregon Community College, 2600 Northwest College Way, Bend, OR 97701-5998. *Phone:* 541-383-7500.

Chemeketa Community College

Salem, Oregon **www.chemeketa.edu/**

Freshman Application Contact Enrollment Center, Chemeketa Community College, 4000 Lancaster Drive, NE, Salem, OR 97305-7070. *Phone:* 503-399-5001. *Fax:* 503-399-3918. *E-mail:* registrar@chemeketa.edu.

Clackamas Community College

Oregon City, Oregon **www.clackamas.edu/**

- **District-supported** 2-year, founded 1966
- **Suburban** 175-acre campus with easy access to Portland
- **Endowment** $9.7 million
- **Coed,** 8,144 undergraduate students, 39% full-time, 53% women, 47% men

Undergraduates 3,205 full-time, 4,939 part-time. Students come from 21 states and territories, 16 other countries, 1% are from out of state, 2% African American, 4% Asian American or Pacific Islander, 9% Hispanic American, 1% Native American, 0.2% international, 41% transferred in. *Retention:* 91% of 2008 full-time freshmen returned.

Freshmen *Admission:* 2,117 enrolled.

Faculty *Total:* 577, 26% full-time, 3% with terminal degrees. *Student/faculty ratio:* 14:1.

Majors Accounting; administrative assistant and secretarial science; applied horticulture; architectural drafting and CAD/CADD; autobody/collision and repair technology; automobile/automotive mechanics technology; CAD/CADD drafting/design technology; child-care and support services management; community organization and advocacy; computer programming (specific applications); computer systems networking and telecommunications; computer technology/computer systems technology; construction trades; corrections; criminal justice/police science; digital communication and media/multimedia; drafting and design technology; electrical and power transmission installation; electrical, electronic and communications engineering technology; emergency medical technology (EMT paramedic); fire science; general studies; industrial engineering; industrial technology; landscaping and groundskeeping; liberal arts and sciences/liberal studies; machine tool technology; manufacturing technology; marketing/marketing management; nursing (registered nurse training); office management; operations management; ornamental horticulture; retailing; social work; survey technology; water quality and wastewater treatment management and recycling technology; web/multimedia management and webmaster; welding technology.

Academics *Calendar:* quarters. *Degree:* certificates, diplomas, and associate. *Special study options:* academic remediation for entering students, accelerated degree program, adult/continuing education programs, advanced placement credit, cooperative education, distance learning, double majors, English as a second language, honors programs, independent study, internships, part-time degree program, services for LD students, study abroad, summer session for credit.

Library Dye Learning Resource Center plus 1 other with 41,263 titles, 274 serial subscriptions, 1,141 audiovisual materials, an OPAC, a Web page.

Student Life *Housing:* college housing not available. *Activities and Organizations:* drama/theater group, student-run newspaper, choral group, Ski Club, Spanish Club, Phi Theta Kappa, Horticulture Club, Speech Club, national fraternities. *Campus security:* 24-hour emergency response devices and patrols, student patrols, late-night transport/escort service. *Student services:* personal/psychological counseling, women's center.

Athletics Member NJCAA. *Intercollegiate sports:* baseball M(s), basketball M(s)/W(s), cross-country running M(s)/W(s), soccer W, softball W(s), track and field M(s)/W(s), volleyball W(s), wrestling M(s). *Intramural sports:* basketball M/W, soccer W, squash W, tennis M/W.

Costs (2010–11) *Tuition:* state resident $3465 full-time; nonresident $9585 full-time. *Required fees:* $225 full-time.

Financial Aid Of all full-time matriculated undergraduates who enrolled in 2008, 115 Federal Work-Study jobs (averaging $1330).

Applying *Options:* early admission. *Application deadlines:* rolling (freshmen), rolling (transfers).

Freshman Application Contact Ms. Tara Sprehe, Registrar, Clackamas Community College, 19600 South Molalla Avenue, Oregon City, OR 97045. *Phone:* 503-657-6958 Ext. 2742. *Fax:* 503-650-6654. *E-mail:* pattyw@clackamas.edu.

Clatsop Community College

Astoria, Oregon **www.clatsopcc.edu/**

Freshman Application Contact Ms. Kristen Lee, Director, Enrollment Services, Clatsop Community College, 1653 Jerome, Astoria, OR 97103-3698. *Phone:* 503-338-2326. *Toll-free phone:* 866-252-8767. *Fax:* 503-325-5738. *E-mail:* admissions@clatsopcc.edu.

Columbia Gorge Community College

The Dalles, Oregon **www.cgcc.cc.or.us/**

- **State-supported** 2-year, founded 1977
- **Coed**

Academics *Calendar:* quarters. *Degree:* certificates, diplomas, and associate.

Costs (2009–10) *Tuition:* state resident $2240 full-time, $70 per credit hour part-time.

Director of Admissions Ms. Karen Carter, Chief Student Services Officer, Columbia Gorge Community College, 400 East Scenic Drive, The Dalles, OR 97058. *Phone:* 541-506-6011. *E-mail:* kcarter@cgcc.cc.or.us.

Everest College

Portland, Oregon **www.everest.edu/**

Freshman Application Contact Ms. Melanie Zea, Everest College, 425 Southwest Washington Street, Portland, OR 97204. *Phone:* 503-222-3225. *Fax:* 503-228-6926. *E-mail:* mzea@cci.edu.

Heald College–Portland

Portland, Oregon **www.heald.edu/**

Freshman Application Contact Director of Admissions, Heald College–Portland, 625 Southwest Broadway, 4th Floor, Portland, OR 97205. *Phone:* 503-229-0492. *Toll-free phone:* 800-755-3550. *Fax:* 503-229-0498. *E-mail:* info@heald.edu.

ITT Technical Institute

Portland, Oregon **www.itt-tech.edu/**

- **Proprietary** primarily 2-year, founded 1971, part of ITT Educational Services, Inc.
- **Urban** campus
- **Coed**

Majors Animation, interactive technology, video graphics and special effects; CAD/CADD drafting/design technology; computer and information systems security; computer engineering technology; computer software and media applications related; computer software engineering; computer software technology; computer systems networking and telecommunications; construction management; criminal justice/law enforcement administration; design and visual communications; electrical, electronic and communications engineering technology; industrial technology; legal assistant/paralegal; system, networking, and LAN/WAN management; web/multimedia management and webmaster; web page, digital/multimedia and information resources design.

Academics *Calendar:* quarters. *Degrees:* associate and bachelor's.

Student Life *Housing:* college housing not available.

Financial Aid Of all full-time matriculated undergraduates who enrolled in 2008, 15 Federal Work-Study jobs (averaging $5000).

Freshman Application Contact Director of Recruitment, ITT Technical Institute, 6035 Northeast 78th Court, Portland, OR 97218. *Phone:* 503-255-6500. *Toll-free phone:* 800-234-5488.

KLAMATH COMMUNITY COLLEGE

Klamath Falls, Oregon **www.klamathcc.edu/**

Freshman Application Contact Admissions Office, Klamath Community College, 7390 South 6th Street, Klamath Falls, OR 97603. *Phone:* 541-882-3521.

LANE COMMUNITY COLLEGE

Eugene, Oregon **www.lanecc.edu/**

- **State and locally supported** 2-year, founded 1964
- **Suburban** 240-acre campus
- **Coed**

Academics *Calendar:* quarters. *Degree:* certificates and associate. *Special study options:* academic remediation for entering students, adult/continuing education programs, advanced placement credit, English as a second language, internships, part-time degree program, services for LD students, summer session for credit.

Student Life *Campus security:* 24-hour emergency response devices and patrols, student patrols, late-night transport/escort service.

Financial Aid Of all full-time matriculated undergraduates who enrolled in 2008, 400 Federal Work-Study jobs (averaging $3600).

Applying *Options:* early admission.

Director of Admissions Ms. Helen Garrett, Director of Admissions/Registrar, Lane Community College, 4000 East 30th Avenue, Eugene, OR 97405-0640. *Phone:* 541-747-4501 Ext. 2686.

LINN-BENTON COMMUNITY COLLEGE

Albany, Oregon **www.linnbenton.edu/**

- **State and locally supported** 2-year, founded 1966
- **Small-town** 104-acre campus
- **Coed,** 6,539 undergraduate students, 54% full-time, 51% women, 49% men

Undergraduates 3,551 full-time, 2,988 part-time. 1% African American, 3% Asian American or Pacific Islander, 5% Hispanic American, 1% Native American, 0.1% international.

Freshmen *Admission:* 2,448 enrolled.

Faculty *Total:* 513, 32% full-time.

Majors Accounting; administrative assistant and secretarial science; agricultural business and management; agricultural teacher education; agriculture; animal sciences; art; automobile/automotive mechanics technology; biological and physical sciences; biology/biological sciences; business administration and management; chemistry; child-care and support services management; civil engineering technology; commercial and advertising art; computer and information sciences; computer and information sciences and support services related; computer programming (specific applications); criminal justice/police science; criminal justice/safety; culinary arts; culinary arts related; dairy husbandry and production; desktop publishing and digital imaging design; diesel mechanics technology; drafting and design technology; dramatic/theater arts; economics; education; elementary education; engineering; English; family and consumer sciences/human sciences; foreign languages and literatures; graphic communications related; horse husbandry/equine science and management; horticultural science; industrial technology; juvenile corrections; legal administrative assistant/secretary; liberal arts and sciences/liberal studies; machine tool technology; mathematics; medical administrative assistant and medical secretary; medical/clinical assistant; metallurgical technology; multi/interdisciplinary studies related; nursing (registered nurse training); physical education teaching and coaching; physical sciences; physics; pre-engineering; restaurant, culinary, and catering management; speech and rhetoric; system administration; teacher assistant/aide; technical and business writing; water quality and wastewater treatment management and recycling technology; welding technology.

Academics *Calendar:* quarters. *Degree:* certificates and associate. *Special study options:* academic remediation for entering students, adult/continuing education programs, advanced placement credit, cooperative education, distance learning, English as a second language, independent study, internships, part-time degree program, services for LD students, student-designed majors, study abroad, summer session for credit. *ROTC:* Army (c), Air Force (c).

Library Linn-Benton Community College Library with 42,561 titles, 91 serial subscriptions, 8,758 audiovisual materials, an OPAC, a Web page.

Student Life *Housing:* college housing not available. *Activities and Organizations:* drama/theater group, student-run newspaper, choral group, EBOP Club, Multicultural Club, Campus Family Co-op, Horticulture Club, Collegiate Secretary Club. *Campus security:* 24-hour emergency response devices and patrols, student patrols, late-night transport/escort service. *Student services:* personal/psychological counseling.

Athletics *Intercollegiate sports:* baseball M(s), basketball M(s)/W(s), volleyball W(s). *Intramural sports:* basketball M/W, tennis M/W, ultimate Frisbee M/W, volleyball M/W.

Costs (2010–11) *Tuition:* state resident $3092 full-time; nonresident $7637 full-time. *Required fees:* $238 full-time.

Financial Aid Of all full-time matriculated undergraduates who enrolled in 2008, 290 Federal Work-Study jobs (averaging $1800).

Applying *Options:* deferred entrance. *Application fee:* $30. *Required for some:* high school transcript. *Application deadlines:* rolling (freshmen), rolling (transfers).

Freshman Application Contact Ms. Christine Baker, Outreach Coordinator, Linn-Benton Community College, 6500 Pacific Boulevard, SW, Albany, OR 97321. *Phone:* 541-917-4813. *Fax:* 541-917-4838. *E-mail:* admissions@linnbenton.edu.

MT. HOOD COMMUNITY COLLEGE

Gresham, Oregon **www.mhcc.cc.or.us/**

Director of Admissions Dr. Craig Kolins, Associate Vice President of Enrollment Services, Mt. Hood Community College, 26000 Southeast Stark Street, Gresham, OR 97030-3300. *Phone:* 503-491-7265.

OREGON COAST COMMUNITY COLLEGE

Newport, Oregon **www.occc.cc.or.us/**

- **Public** 2-year, founded 1987, administratively affiliated with Chemeketa Community College
- **Small-town** 24-acre campus
- **Coed,** 652 undergraduate students, 27% full-time, 66% women, 34% men

Undergraduates 178 full-time, 474 part-time. Students come from 10 states and territories, 2% are from out of state, 1% African American, 4% Asian American or Pacific Islander, 5% Hispanic American, 4% Native American, 30% transferred in.

Freshmen *Admission:* 135 enrolled.

Faculty *Total:* 50, 16% full-time, 28% with terminal degrees. *Student/faculty ratio:* 15:1.

Majors General studies; liberal arts and sciences/liberal studies; marine biology and biological oceanography; nursing (registered nurse training).

Academics *Calendar:* quarters. *Degree:* certificates and associate. *Special study options:* academic remediation for entering students, cooperative education, distance learning, English as a second language, honors programs, internships, part-time degree program, services for LD students, summer session for credit.

Library Oregon Coast Community College Library with 10,455 titles, 50 serial subscriptions, 1,537 audiovisual materials, an OPAC, a Web page.

Student Life *Housing:* college housing not available.

Standardized Tests *Required for some:* Nursing Entrance Exam.

Costs (2009–10) *Tuition:* state resident $2664 full-time, $74 per credit part-time; nonresident $6192 full-time, $172 per credit part-time. Full-time tuition and fees vary according to program. Part-time tuition and fees vary according to program. *Required fees:* $110 full-time, $11 per course part-time. *Payment plan:* deferred payment. *Waivers:* employees or children of employees.

Freshman Application Contact Student Services, Oregon Coast Community College, 332 Southwest Coast Highway, Newport, OR 97365. *Phone:* 541-265-2283. *Fax:* 541-265-3820. *E-mail:* webinfo@occc.cc.or.us.

PORTLAND COMMUNITY COLLEGE

Portland, Oregon **www.pcc.edu/**

- **State and locally supported** 2-year, founded 1961
- **Urban** 400-acre campus
- **Coed**

Portland Community College (continued)

Academics *Calendar:* quarters. *Degree:* certificates, diplomas, and associate. *Special study options:* academic remediation for entering students, adult/continuing education programs, advanced placement credit, cooperative education, distance learning, double majors, English as a second language, external degree program, independent study, internships, off-campus study, part-time degree program, services for LD students, study abroad, summer session for credit.

Student Life *Campus security:* 24-hour emergency response devices and patrols, late-night transport/escort service.

Athletics Member NJCAA.

Applying *Options:* electronic application. *Application fee:* $25.

Freshman Application Contact PCC Admissions and Registration Office, Portland Community College, PO Box 19000, Portland, OR 97280. *Phone:* 503-977-8888.

Rogue Community College

Grants Pass, Oregon **www.roguecc.edu/**

- **State and locally supported** 2-year, founded 1970
- **Rural** 84-acre campus
- **Coed,** 5,441 undergraduate students, 46% full-time, 55% women, 45% men

Undergraduates 2,490 full-time, 2,951 part-time. Students come from 18 states and territories, 4 other countries, 1% are from out of state, 1% African American, 2% Asian American or Pacific Islander, 8% Hispanic American, 2% Native American, 0.1% international, 62% transferred in.

Freshmen *Admission:* 968 enrolled.

Faculty *Total:* 338, 23% full-time. *Student/faculty ratio:* 21:1.

Majors Automobile/automotive mechanics technology; business administration and management; business/commerce; child-care and support services management; child development; computer software technology; construction engineering technology; construction management; construction trades; criminal justice/law enforcement administration; criminal justice/police science; diesel mechanics technology; electrical and power transmission installation; electrical, electronic and communications engineering technology; emergency medical technology (EMT paramedic); fire protection and safety technology; fire science; general studies; human development and family studies; industrial technology; liberal arts and sciences/liberal studies; manufacturing technology; mechanics and repair; medical office computer specialist; nursing (registered nurse training); social work; welding technology.

Academics *Calendar:* quarters. *Degree:* certificates, diplomas, and associate. *Special study options:* academic remediation for entering students, adult/continuing education programs, advanced placement credit, cooperative education, distance learning, double majors, English as a second language, independent study, internships, part-time degree program, services for LD students, study abroad, summer session for credit.

Library Rogue Community College Library with 33,000 titles, 275 serial subscriptions, an OPAC.

Student Life *Housing:* college housing not available. *Activities and Organizations:* drama/theater group, student-run newspaper, choral group. *Campus security:* 24-hour emergency response devices and patrols, late-night transport/escort service. *Student services:* personal/psychological counseling, women's center.

Athletics *Intramural sports:* basketball M/W, soccer M/W, tennis M/W, volleyball M/W.

Costs (2009–10) *Tuition:* state resident $2628 full-time, $73 per credit hour part-time; nonresident $3204 full-time, $89 per credit hour part-time. *Required fees:* $330 full-time, $110 per term part-time. *Payment plan:* installment. *Waivers:* employees or children of employees.

Financial Aid Of all full-time matriculated undergraduates who enrolled in 2008, 1,137 applied for aid, 933 were judged to have need, 150 had their need fully met. 87 Federal Work-Study jobs (averaging $1508). In 2008, 118 non-need-based awards were made. *Average percent of need met:* 63%. *Average financial aid package:* $7512. *Average need-based loan:* $1210. *Average need-based gift aid:* $1088. *Average non-need-based aid:* $569.

Applying *Options:* electronic application, early admission. *Application deadlines:* rolling (freshmen), rolling (out-of-state freshmen), rolling (transfers).

Freshman Application Contact Ms. Claudia Sullivan, Director of Enrollment Services, Rogue Community College, 3345 Redwood Highway, Grants Pass, OR 97527-9298. *Phone:* 541-956-7176. *Fax:* 541-471-3585. *E-mail:* csullivan@roguecc.edu.

Southwestern Oregon Community College

Coos Bay, Oregon **www.socc.edu/**

Freshman Application Contact Miss Lela Wells, Southwestern Oregon Community College, Student First Stop, 1988 Newmark Avenue, Coos Bay, OR 97420. *Phone:* 541-888-7611. *Toll-free phone:* 800-962-2838. *E-mail:* lwells@socc.edu.

Tillamook Bay Community College

Tillamook, Oregon **www.tbcc.cc.or.us/**

Freshman Application Contact Lori Gates, Tillamook Bay Community College, 4301 Third Street, Tillamook, OR 97141. *Phone:* 503-842-8222. *Fax:* 503-842-2214. *E-mail:* gates@tillamookbay.cc.

Treasure Valley Community College

Ontario, Oregon **www.tvcc.cc.or.us/**

Freshman Application Contact Ms. Candace Bell, Office of Admissions and Student Services, Treasure Valley Community College, 650 College Boulevard, Ontario, OR 97914. *Phone:* 541-881-8822 Ext. 239. *Fax:* 541-881-2721. *E-mail:* clbell@tvcc.cc.

Umpqua Community College

Roseburg, Oregon **www.umpqua.edu/**

- **State and locally supported** 2-year, founded 1964
- **Rural** 100-acre campus
- **Endowment** $6.1 million
- **Coed,** 2,586 undergraduate students, 53% full-time, 59% women, 41% men

Undergraduates 1,376 full-time, 1,210 part-time. Students come from 4 states and territories, 4 other countries, 0.8% African American, 0.9% Asian American or Pacific Islander, 4% Hispanic American, 2% Native American, 0.1% international, 60% transferred in.

Freshmen *Admission:* 501 applied, 501 admitted, 403 enrolled.

Faculty *Total:* 171, 36% full-time. *Student/faculty ratio:* 23:1.

Majors Accounting; administrative assistant and secretarial science; agriculture; anthropology; art; art history, criticism and conservation; art teacher education; automobile/automotive mechanics technology; behavioral sciences; biological and physical sciences; biology/biological sciences; business administration and management; chemistry; child development; civil engineering technology; computer engineering technology; computer science; cosmetology; criminal justice/law enforcement administration; desktop publishing and digital imaging design; dramatic/theater arts; economics; education; electrical, electronic and communications engineering technology; elementary education; emergency medical technology (EMT paramedic); engineering; English; fire science; forestry; health teacher education; history; humanities; human resources management; journalism; kindergarten/preschool education; legal administrative assistant/secretary; liberal arts and sciences/liberal studies; marketing/marketing management; mathematics; medical administrative assistant and medical secretary; music; music teacher education; natural sciences; nursing (registered nurse training); physical education teaching and coaching; physical sciences; political science and government; pre-engineering; psychology; social sciences; social work; sociology.

Academics *Calendar:* quarters. *Degree:* certificates and associate. *Special study options:* academic remediation for entering students, accelerated degree program, adult/continuing education programs, advanced placement credit, cooperative education, distance learning, English as a second language, honors programs, independent study, internships, part-time degree program, services for LD students, study abroad, summer session for credit.

Library Umpqua Community College Library with 41,000 titles, 350 serial subscriptions, an OPAC, a Web page.

Student Life *Housing:* college housing not available. *Activities and Organizations:* drama/theater group, student-run newspaper, choral group, Phi Theta Kappa, Computer Club, Phi Beta Lambda, Nursing Club, Umpqua Accounting

Associates. *Campus security:* 24-hour emergency response devices and patrols. *Student services:* personal/psychological counseling.

Athletics *Intercollegiate sports:* basketball M(s)/W(s), volleyball W(s). *Intramural sports:* basketball M/W.

Costs (2010–11) *Tuition:* state resident $3585 full-time, $65 per credit hour part-time; nonresident $8865 full-time, $192 per credit hour part-time. *Required fees:* $300 full-time, $7 per credit hour part-time, $15 per term part-time. *Waivers:* employees or children of employees.

Financial Aid Of all full-time matriculated undergraduates who enrolled in 2008, 120 Federal Work-Study jobs (averaging $3000).

Applying *Options:* early admission, deferred entrance. *Application fee:* $25. *Recommended:* high school transcript. *Application deadlines:* rolling (freshmen), rolling (transfers).

Freshman Application Contact Mr. Ted Swagerty, Recruiter, Umpqua Community College, PO Box 967, 1140 College Road, Roseburg, OR 97470. *Phone:* 541-440-4600 Ext. 7661. *Fax:* 541-440-4612. *E-mail:* Ted.Swagerty@umpqua.edu.

Western Culinary Institute

Portland, Oregon **www.wci.edu/**

Admissions Office Contact Western Culinary Institute, 921 SW Morrison Street Suite 400, Portland, OR 97205. *Toll-free phone:* 888-891-6222.

PENNSYLVANIA

Antonelli Institute

Erdenheim, Pennsylvania **www.antonelli.edu/**

Freshman Application Contact Mr. Anthony Detore, Director of Admissions, Antonelli Institute, 300 Montgomery Avenue, Erdenheim, PA 19038. *Phone:* 215-836-2222. *Toll-free phone:* 800-722-7871. *Fax:* 215-836-2794.

The Art Institute of York–Pennsylvania

York, Pennsylvania **www.artinstitutes.edu/york/**

- **Proprietary** primarily 2-year, founded 1952, part of Education Management Corporation
- **Suburban** campus
- **Coed**

Majors Animation, interactive technology, video graphics and special effects; consumer merchandising/retailing management; graphic design; interior design; web page, digital/multimedia and information resources design.

Academics *Calendar:* quarters. *Degrees:* associate and bachelor's.

Costs (2009–10) *Tuition:* Tuition cost varies by program. Prospective students should contact the school for current tuition costs. Other charges include a starting kit for all first-quarter students. Kits vary in price, depending on the program of study.

Freshman Application Contact The Art Institute of York–Pennsylvania, 1409 Williams Road, York, PA 17402-9012. *Phone:* 717-755-2300. *Toll-free phone:* 800-864-7725.

Berks Technical Institute

Wyomissing, Pennsylvania **www.berkstech.com/**

Freshman Application Contact Mr. Allan Brussolo, Academic Dean, Berks Technical Institute, 2205 Ridgewood Road, Wyomissing, PA 19610-1168. *Phone:* 610-372-1722. *Toll-free phone:* 800-284-4672 (in-state); 800-821-4662 (out-of-state). *Fax:* 610-376-4684. *E-mail:* abrussolo@berks.edu.

Bidwell Training Center

Pittsburgh, Pennsylvania **www.bidwell-training.org/**

Freshman Application Contact Admissions Office, Bidwell Training Center, 1815 Metropolitan Street, Pittsburgh, PA 15233. *E-mail:* admissions@mcg-btc.org.

Bradford School

Pittsburgh, Pennsylvania **www.bradfordpittsburgh.edu/**

- **Private** 2-year, founded 1968
- **Urban** campus
- **Coed,** 567 undergraduate students
- 86% of applicants were admitted

Freshmen *Admission:* 1,032 applied, 887 admitted.

Majors Accounting and business/management; business administration and management; computer programming; dental assisting; graphic design; legal administrative assistant/secretary; legal assistant/paralegal; medical/clinical assistant; merchandising; system, networking, and LAN/WAN management; tourism and travel services management.

Academics *Degree:* diplomas and associate. *Special study options:* accelerated degree program, independent study.

Freshman Application Contact Admissions Office, Bradford School, 125 West Station Square Drive, Suite 129, Pittsburgh, PA 15219. *Phone:* 412-391-6710. *Toll-free phone:* 800-391-6810.

Bucks County Community College

Newtown, Pennsylvania **www.bucks.edu/**

- **County-supported** 2-year, founded 1964
- **Suburban** 200-acre campus with easy access to Philadelphia
- **Endowment** $3.3 million
- **Coed,** 11,009 undergraduate students, 47% full-time, 57% women, 43% men

Undergraduates 5,209 full-time, 5,800 part-time. Students come from 11 states and territories, 35 other countries, 0.5% are from out of state, 5% African American, 2% Asian American or Pacific Islander, 3% Hispanic American, 0.4% Native American, 0.5% international, 74% transferred in. *Retention:* 61% of 2008 full-time freshmen returned.

Freshmen *Admission:* 3,174 enrolled.

Faculty *Total:* 637, 26% full-time. *Student/faculty ratio:* 22:1.

Majors Accounting; American studies; art; biology/biological sciences; business administration and management; chemistry; cinematography and film/video production; commercial and advertising art; computer and information sciences; computer and information sciences related; computer engineering technology; computer/information technology services administration related; computer programming; computer programming related; computer programming (specific applications); computer science; consumer merchandising/retailing management; corrections; criminal justice/law enforcement administration; criminal justice/police science; culinary arts; data processing and data processing technology; dramatic/theater arts; education; engineering; environmental studies; health professions related; health teacher education; historic preservation and conservation; hospitality administration; hotel/motel administration; humanities; information science/studies; information technology; journalism; kindergarten/preschool education; legal assistant/paralegal; liberal arts and sciences/liberal studies; marketing/marketing management; mass communication/media; mathematics; medical/clinical assistant; music; nursing (registered nurse training); physical education teaching and coaching; psychology; radio and television; social sciences; social work; sport and fitness administration/management; teacher assistant/aide; visual and performing arts; woodworking.

Academics *Calendar:* semesters. *Degree:* certificates and associate. *Special study options:* academic remediation for entering students, adult/continuing education programs, advanced placement credit, cooperative education, distance learning, English as a second language, external degree program, independent study, internships, part-time degree program, services for LD students, student-designed majors, summer session for credit.

Library Bucks County Community College Library with 155,779 titles, 515 serial subscriptions, an OPAC, a Web page.

Student Life *Housing:* college housing not available. *Activities and Organizations:* drama/theater group, student-run newspaper, television station, choral group, Phi Theta Kappa, Students in Free Enterprise (SIFE), student council, The Centurion (student newspaper). *Campus security:* 24-hour emergency response

Bucks County Community College (continued)

devices and patrols, late-night transport/escort service. *Student services:* personal/psychological counseling, women's center.

Athletics Member NJCAA. *Intercollegiate sports:* baseball M, basketball M, equestrian sports M/W, golf M/W, soccer M/W, tennis M/W, volleyball W. *Intramural sports:* basketball M/W, soccer M/W, softball M/W, tennis M/W, volleyball W.

Costs (2009–10) *Tuition:* area resident $2970 full-time, $99 per credit hour part-time; state resident $5940 full-time, $198 per credit hour part-time; nonresident $8910 full-time, $297 per credit hour part-time. Full-time tuition and fees vary according to course load and reciprocity agreements. Part-time tuition and fees vary according to course load and reciprocity agreements. *Required fees:* $824 full-time. *Payment plans:* installment, deferred payment. *Waivers:* senior citizens and employees or children of employees.

Financial Aid Of all full-time matriculated undergraduates who enrolled in 2008, 129 Federal Work-Study jobs (averaging $2345).

Applying *Options:* electronic application, early admission. *Required:* high school transcript. *Required for some:* essay or personal statement, interview.

Freshman Application Contact Ms. Marlene Barlow, Director of Admissions, Bucks County Community College, 275 Swamp Road, Newtown, PA 18940. *Phone:* 215-968-8137. *Fax:* 215-968-8110. *E-mail:* wilsona@bucks.edu.

BUTLER COUNTY COMMUNITY COLLEGE

Butler, Pennsylvania **www.bc3.edu/**

Freshman Application Contact Ms. Patricia Bajuszik, Director of Admissions, Butler County Community College, 107 College Drive, Butler, PA 16003-1203. *Phone:* 724-287-8711 Ext. 344. *Toll-free phone:* 888-826-2829. *Fax:* 724-287-4961. *E-mail:* pattie.bajoszik@bc3.edu.

CAMBRIA-ROWE BUSINESS COLLEGE

Indiana, Pennsylvania **www.crbc.net/**

Freshman Application Contact Mrs. Stacey Bell-Leger, Representative at Indiana Campus, Cambria-Rowe Business College, 422 South 13th Street, Indiana, PA 15701. *Phone:* 724-483-0222. *Fax:* 724-463-7246. *E-mail:* sbell-leger@crbc.net.

CAMBRIA-ROWE BUSINESS COLLEGE

Johnstown, Pennsylvania **www.crbc.net/**

Freshman Application Contact Mrs. Amanda Artim, Director of Admissions, Cambria-Rowe Business College, 221 Central Avenue, Johnstown, PA 15902-2494. *Phone:* 814-536-5168. *Fax:* 814-536-5160. *E-mail:* admissions@crbc.net.

CAREER TRAINING ACADEMY

Monroeville, Pennsylvania **www.careerta.edu/**

Freshman Application Contact Career Training Academy, 4314 Old William Penn Highway, Suite 103, Monroeville, PA 15146. *Phone:* 412-372-3900.

CAREER TRAINING ACADEMY

New Kensington, Pennsylvania **www.careerta.com/**

Freshman Application Contact Career Training Academy, 950 Fifth Avenue, New Kensington, PA 15068. *Phone:* 724-337-1000.

CAREER TRAINING ACADEMY

Pittsburgh, Pennsylvania **www.careerta.edu/**

- **Proprietary** 2-year
- **Suburban** campus with easy access to Pittsburgh
- **Coed,** 85 undergraduate students, 100% full-time, 93% women, 7% men

Undergraduates 85 full-time. Students come from 2 states and territories, 12% African American, 1% Asian American or Pacific Islander, 1% Hispanic American.

Freshmen *Admission:* 9 enrolled.

Faculty *Total:* 11, 73% full-time, 9% with terminal degrees. *Student/faculty ratio:* 11:1.

Majors Massage therapy; medical/clinical assistant; medical insurance coding.

Academics *Calendar:* continuous. *Degree:* diplomas and associate. *Special study options:* academic remediation for entering students, advanced placement credit, internships.

Applying *Application fee:* $30. *Required:* essay or personal statement, high school transcript, interview. *Application deadlines:* rolling (freshmen), rolling (out-of-state freshmen).

Freshman Application Contact Jamie Vignone, Career Training Academy, 1500 Northway Mall, Suite 200, Pittsburgh, PA 15237. *Phone:* 412-367-4000. *Fax:* 412-369-7223. *E-mail:* admission3@careerta.edu.

CHI INSTITUTE, BROOMALL CAMPUS

Broomall, Pennsylvania **www.chitraining.com/**

- **Proprietary** 2-year, founded 1958
- **Small-town** campus
- **Coed**

Majors Computer and information sciences and support services related; computer programming; medical/clinical assistant.

Academics *Calendar:* quarters. *Degree:* diplomas and associate.

Freshman Application Contact CHI Institute, Broomall Campus, 1991 Sproul Road, Suite 42, Broomall, PA 19008. *Phone:* 610-353-3300.

CHI INSTITUTE, FRANKLIN MILLS CAMPUS

Philadelphia, Pennsylvania **www.chitraining.com/**

- **Proprietary** 2-year, founded 1981
- **Suburban** campus
- **Coed**

Majors Computer engineering technology; criminal justice/law enforcement administration; graphic design.

Academics *Calendar:* quarters. *Degree:* certificates, diplomas, and associate.

Financial Aid Of all full-time matriculated undergraduates who enrolled in 2008, 30 Federal Work-Study jobs (averaging $2050).

Freshman Application Contact CHI Institute, Franklin Mills Campus, 520 Street Road, Southampton, PA 18966. *Phone:* 215-612-6600. *Toll-free phone:* 800-336-7696.

COMMONWEALTH TECHNICAL INSTITUTE

Johnstown, Pennsylvania **www.hgac.org/**

Freshman Application Contact Ms. Rebecca Halza, Admissions Supervisor, Commonwealth Technical Institute, 727 Goucher Street, Johnstown, PA 15905-3092. *Phone:* 814-255-8200. *Toll-free phone:* 800-762-4211 Ext. 8237. *Fax:* 814-255-8283. *E-mail:* rhalza@state.pa.us.

COMMUNITY COLLEGE OF ALLEGHENY COUNTY

Pittsburgh, Pennsylvania **www.ccac.edu/**

- **County-supported** 2-year, founded 1966
- **Urban** 242-acre campus
- **Coed,** 20,520 undergraduate students, 42% full-time, 57% women, 43% men

Undergraduates 8,525 full-time, 11,995 part-time. 1% are from out of state, 15% African American, 1% Asian American or Pacific Islander, 0.7% Hispanic American, 0.5% Native American, 0.5% international.

Freshmen *Admission:* 4,830 enrolled.

Faculty *Total:* 1,625, 17% full-time. *Student/faculty ratio:* 17:1.

Majors Accounting technology and bookkeeping; administrative assistant and secretarial science; airline pilot and flight crew; applied horticulture; architectural drafting and CAD/CADD; art; athletic training; automotive engineering technology; aviation/airway management; banking and financial support services; biology/biological sciences; building/property maintenance and management; business administration and management; business automation/technology/data entry; business machine repair; carpentry; chemical technology; chemistry; child-care provision; child development; civil drafting and CAD/CADD; civil engineering technology; clinical/medical laboratory technology; commercial and advertising art; communications technologies and support services related; community health services counseling; computer engineering technology; computer systems networking and telecommunications; computer technology/computer systems technology; construction engineering technology; construction trades related; corrections; cosmetology and personal grooming arts related; court reporting; criminal justice/police science; culinary arts; diagnostic medical sonography and ultrasound technology; dietitian assistant; drafting and design technology; drafting/design engineering technologies related; dramatic/theater arts; education (specific levels and methods) related; education (specific subject areas) related; electrical, electronic and communications engineering technology; electroneurodiagnostic/electroencephalographic technology; energy management and systems technology; engineering technologies related; English; entrepreneurship; environmental engineering technology; fire protection and safety technology; food service systems administration; foreign languages and literatures; general studies; greenhouse management; health and physical education; health information/medical records technology; health professions related; health unit coordinator/ward clerk; heating, air conditioning, ventilation and refrigeration maintenance technology; hotel/motel administration; housing and human environments related; human development and family studies related; humanities; human resources management; industrial technology; insurance; journalism; landscaping and groundskeeping; legal administrative assistant/secretary; legal assistant/paralegal; liberal arts and sciences/liberal studies; machine shop technology; management information systems; marketing/marketing management; mathematics; mechanical drafting and CAD/CADD; medical administrative assistant and medical secretary; medical/clinical assistant; medical radiologic technology; music; nuclear medical technology; nursing assistant/aide and patient care assistant; nursing (licensed practical/vocational nurse training); nursing (registered nurse training); occupational therapist assistant; office management; ornamental horticulture; perioperative/operating room and surgical nursing; pharmacy technician; physical therapist assistant; physics; plant nursery management; psychiatric/mental health services technology; psychology; quality control technology; real estate; respiratory care therapy; restaurant, culinary, and catering management; retailing; robotics technology; science technologies related; sheet metal technology; sign language interpretation and translation; social sciences; social work; sociology; solar energy technology; substance abuse/addiction counseling; surgical technology; therapeutic recreation; tourism promotion; turf and turfgrass management; visual and performing arts related; welding technology.

Academics *Calendar:* semesters. *Degree:* certificates, diplomas, and associate. *Special study options:* academic remediation for entering students, advanced placement credit, cooperative education, distance learning, English as a second language, independent study, internships, off-campus study, part-time degree program, services for LD students, summer session for credit.

Library Community College of Allegheny County Library with an OPAC, a Web page.

Student Life *Housing:* college housing not available. *Activities and Organizations:* drama/theater group, student-run newspaper, Phi Theta Kappa. *Campus security:* 24-hour emergency response devices and patrols, late-night transport/escort service. *Student services:* health clinic, personal/psychological counseling, women's center.

Athletics Member NJCAA. *Intercollegiate sports:* baseball M, basketball M/W, bowling M/W, golf M/W, ice hockey M, softball W, table tennis M/W, tennis M/W, volleyball W. *Intramural sports:* badminton M/W, basketball M/W, bowling M/W, cross-country running M/W, football M, golf M/W, lacrosse M, racquetball M/W, softball M/W, table tennis M/W, tennis M/W, volleyball M/W, weight lifting M/W.

Applying *Recommended:* high school transcript. *Application deadlines:* rolling (freshmen), rolling (transfers). *Notification:* continuous (freshmen), continuous (transfers).

Freshman Application Contact Admissions, Community College of Allegheny County, 800 Allegheny Avenue, Pittsburgh, PA 15233. *Phone:* 412-237-2511.

Community College of Beaver County

Monaca, Pennsylvania www.ccbc.edu/

Freshman Application Contact Mr. Michael Macon, Vice President for Enrollment Management, Community College of Beaver County, One Campus Drive, Monaca, PA 15061-2588. *Phone:* 724-775-8561. *Toll-free phone:* 800-335-0222. *Fax:* 724-775-4055. *E-mail:* mike.macon@ccbc.edu.

Community College of Philadelphia

Philadelphia, Pennsylvania www.ccp.edu/

- **State and locally supported** 2-year, founded 1964
- **Urban** 14-acre campus
- **Coed,** 34,854 undergraduate students

Undergraduates Students come from 50 other countries.

Faculty *Total:* 1,083, 38% full-time.

Majors Accounting; architectural engineering technology; art; automobile/automotive mechanics technology; business administration and management; chemical technology; clinical/medical laboratory technology; computer science; construction engineering technology; criminal justice/law enforcement administration; culinary arts; dental hygiene; drafting and design technology; education; engineering; engineering technology; facilities planning and management; finance; fire science; forensic science and technology; health information/medical records administration; health professions related; hotel/motel administration; human services; industrial radiologic technology; international business/trade/commerce; kindergarten/preschool education; legal assistant/paralegal; liberal arts and sciences/liberal studies; marketing/marketing management; medical administrative assistant and medical secretary; medical/clinical assistant; mental health/rehabilitation; music; nursing (registered nurse training); photography; pre-engineering; recording arts technology; respiratory care therapy; sign language interpretation and translation.

Academics *Calendar:* semesters. *Degree:* certificates, diplomas, and associate. *Special study options:* academic remediation for entering students, accelerated degree program, adult/continuing education programs, advanced placement credit, cooperative education, distance learning, English as a second language, external degree program, honors programs, independent study, internships, off-campus study, part-time degree program, services for LD students, student-designed majors, study abroad, summer session for credit. *ROTC:* Army (c).

Library Main Campus Library plus 2 others with 110,000 titles, 420 serial subscriptions, an OPAC, a Web page.

Student Life *Housing:* college housing not available. *Activities and Organizations:* drama/theater group, student-run newspaper, choral group, Philadelphia L.E.A.D.S., Phi Theta Kappa, Student Government Association, Vanguard Student Newspaper, Fundraising Club. *Campus security:* 24-hour emergency response devices and patrols, phone/alert systems in classrooms/buildings. *Student services:* personal/psychological counseling, women's center.

Athletics *Intercollegiate sports:* baseball M, basketball M/W, cheerleading W, cross-country running M/W, soccer M, softball W, tennis M/W, track and field M/W, volleyball M/W. *Intramural sports:* basketball M/W, soccer M/W, tennis M/W, track and field M/W, volleyball M/W.

Costs (2010–11) *Tuition:* area resident $4410 full-time; state resident $8160 full-time; nonresident $11,910 full-time. *Payment plan:* installment. *Waivers:* senior citizens and employees or children of employees.

Applying *Options:* electronic application, early admission, deferred entrance. *Application fee:* $20. *Required for some:* high school transcript, allied health and nursing programs have specific entry requirements. *Application deadlines:* rolling (freshmen), rolling (transfers). *Notification:* continuous (freshmen), continuous (transfers).

Freshman Application Contact Community College of Philadelphia, 1700 Spring Garden Street, Philadelphia, PA 19130-3991. *Phone:* 215-751-8010.

Consolidated School of Business

Lancaster, Pennsylvania www.csb.edu/

- **Proprietary** 2-year, founded 1986
- **Suburban** 4-acre campus with easy access to Philadelphia
- **Coed,** 182 undergraduate students, 98% full-time, 86% women, 14% men

Undergraduates 179 full-time, 3 part-time. Students come from 2 states and territories, 1% are from out of state, 14% African American, 0.5% Asian American or Pacific Islander, 26% Hispanic American.

Freshmen *Admission:* 182 enrolled. *Average high school GPA:* 2.6.

Faculty *Total:* 25, 96% full-time. *Student/faculty ratio:* 15:1.

Majors Accounting; business administration and management; health/health-care administration; legal administrative assistant/secretary; medical administrative assistant and medical secretary; office management.

Consolidated School of Business (continued)

Academics *Calendar:* continuous. *Degree:* diplomas and associate. *Special study options:* accelerated degree program, honors programs, independent study, internships, part-time degree program, services for LD students, student-designed majors.

Library Main Library plus 1 other.

Student Life *Housing:* college housing not available. *Activities and Organizations:* Community Service Club.

Costs (2010–11) *Tuition:* $26,500 full-time, $350 per credit hour part-time. Full-time tuition and fees vary according to course load and program. Part-time tuition and fees vary according to course load and program. No tuition increase for student's term of enrollment. *Required fees:* $3750 full-time. *Payment plans:* installment, deferred payment.

Applying *Options:* electronic application. *Required:* high school transcript, interview. *Application deadlines:* rolling (freshmen), rolling (transfers).

Freshman Application Contact Ms. Libby Paul, Admissions Representative, Consolidated School of Business, 2124 Ambassador Circle, Lancaster, PA 17603. *Phone:* 717-394-6211. *Toll-free phone:* 800-541-8298. *Fax:* 717-394-6213. *E-mail:* lpaul@csb.edu.

CONSOLIDATED SCHOOL OF BUSINESS

York, Pennsylvania **www.csb.edu/**

Freshman Application Contact Ms. Sandra Swanger, Admissions Representative, Consolidated School of Business, 1605 Clugston Road, York, PA 17404. *Phone:* 717-764-9550. *Toll-free phone:* 800-520-0691. *Fax:* 717-764-9469. *E-mail:* sswanger@csb.edu.

DEAN INSTITUTE OF TECHNOLOGY

Pittsburgh, Pennsylvania **home.earthlink.net/~deantech/**

- **Proprietary** 2-year, founded 1947
- **Urban** 2-acre campus
- **Coed**

Academics *Calendar:* quarters. *Degree:* diplomas and associate. *Special study options:* part-time degree program.

Student Life *Campus security:* 24-hour emergency response devices.

Applying *Options:* early admission, deferred entrance. *Application fee:* $50.

Director of Admissions Mr. Richard D. Ali, Admissions Director, Dean Institute of Technology, 1501 West Liberty Avenue, Pittsburgh, PA 15226-1103. *Phone:* 412-531-4433.

DELAWARE COUNTY COMMUNITY COLLEGE

Media, Pennsylvania **www.dccc.edu/**

- **State and locally supported** 2-year, founded 1967
- **Suburban** 123-acre campus with easy access to Philadelphia
- **Endowment** $3.8 million
- **Coed,** 12,237 undergraduate students, 45% full-time, 56% women, 44% men

Undergraduates 5,557 full-time, 6,680 part-time. Students come from 9 states and territories, 53 other countries, 1% are from out of state, 19% African American, 4% Asian American or Pacific Islander, 2% Hispanic American, 0.1% Native American, 2% international, 9% transferred in. *Retention:* 61% of 2008 full-time freshmen returned.

Freshmen *Admission:* 4,818 applied, 4,818 admitted, 2,867 enrolled.

Faculty *Total:* 802, 18% full-time. *Student/faculty ratio:* 24:1.

Majors Accounting technology and bookkeeping; animation, interactive technology, video graphics and special effects; anthropology; architectural engineering technology; automobile/automotive mechanics technology; biological and physical sciences; biomedical technology; building/property maintenance and management; business administration and management; CAD/CADD drafting/design technology; commercial and advertising art; communication and journalism related; communication/speech communication and rhetoric; computer and information sciences; computer programming (specific applications); computer systems networking and telecommunications; computer technology/computer systems technology; construction management; criminal justice/police science; data entry/microcomputer applications; early childhood education; e-commerce; education (multiple levels); electrical and power transmission installation; electrical, electronic and communications engineering technology; emergency medical technology (EMT paramedic); engineering; entrepreneurship; fine/studio arts; fire protection and safety technology; general studies; health services/allied health/health sciences; health unit management/ward supervision; heating, air conditioning and refrigeration technology; heating, air conditioning, ventilation and refrigeration maintenance technology; hotel/motel administration; human services; industrial mechanics and maintenance technology; journalism; legal assistant/paralegal; liberal arts and sciences/liberal studies; machine tool technology; management information systems; mechanical engineering/mechanical technology; medical/clinical assistant; nursing (registered nurse training); office management; psychology; respiratory care therapy; retailing; robotics technology; science technologies related; sociology; surgical technology; telecommunications technology; web/multimedia management and webmaster; web page, digital/multimedia and information resources design.

Academics *Calendar:* semesters. *Degree:* certificates and associate. *Special study options:* academic remediation for entering students, adult/continuing education programs, advanced placement credit, cooperative education, distance learning, double majors, English as a second language, independent study, internships, part-time degree program, services for LD students, student-designed majors, summer session for credit.

Library Delaware County Community College Library with 55,779 titles, 249 serial subscriptions, 2,863 audiovisual materials, an OPAC, a Web page.

Student Life *Housing:* college housing not available. *Activities and Organizations:* drama/theater group, student-run newspaper, radio station, Business Society, Phi Theta Kappa, Student Government Association, Campus Bible Fellowship, Engineering Club. *Campus security:* 24-hour emergency response devices and patrols, late-night transport/escort service. *Student services:* health clinic, personal/psychological counseling.

Athletics Member NJCAA. *Intercollegiate sports:* baseball M, basketball M/W, golf M/W, soccer M, softball W, tennis M/W, volleyball W. *Intramural sports:* basketball M/W, lacrosse M(c), rugby W, volleyball W.

Costs (2010–11) *One-time required fee:* $50. *Tuition:* area resident $2232 full-time, $93 per credit hour part-time; state resident $4464 full-time, $186 per credit hour part-time; nonresident $6696 full-time, $279 per credit hour part-time. Full-time tuition and fees vary according to course load. Part-time tuition and fees vary according to course load. *Required fees:* $928 full-time, $37 per credit hour part-time, $20 per term part-time. *Payment plan:* installment. *Waivers:* senior citizens and employees or children of employees.

Financial Aid Of all full-time matriculated undergraduates who enrolled in 2008, 95 Federal Work-Study jobs (averaging $900).

Applying *Options:* early admission. *Application fee:* $25. *Required:* high school transcript. *Application deadlines:* rolling (freshmen), rolling (out-of-state freshmen), rolling (transfers). *Notification:* continuous (freshmen), continuous (out-of-state freshmen), continuous (transfers).

Freshman Application Contact Ms. Hope Diehl, Director of Admissions and Enrollment Services, Delaware County Community College, Admissions Office, 901 South Media Line Road, Media, PA 19063-1094. *Phone:* 610-359-5050. *Toll-free phone:* 800-872-1102 (in-state); 800-543-0146 (out-of-state). *Fax:* 610-723-1530. *E-mail:* admiss@dccc.edu.

DOUGLAS EDUCATION CENTER

Monessen, Pennsylvania **www.dec.edu/**

- **Proprietary** 2-year, founded 1904
- **Small-town** campus with easy access to Pittsburgh
- **Coed,** 354 undergraduate students, 100% full-time, 60% women, 40% men

Undergraduates 354 full-time. Students come from 49 states and territories, 2 other countries, 43% are from out of state, 6% African American, 1% Asian American or Pacific Islander, 4% Hispanic American, 0.6% Native American, 0.6% international, 11% transferred in. *Retention:* 84% of 2008 full-time freshmen returned.

Freshmen *Admission:* 231 enrolled.

Faculty *Total:* 15. *Student/faculty ratio:* 10:1.

Majors Art; business administration and management; cosmetology; design and visual communications; film/cinema studies; graphic design; illustration; medical/clinical assistant; medical office management.

Academics *Degree:* certificates, diplomas, and associate.

Library Douglas Education Center Library / Learning Resource Center plus 2 others with 126 serial subscriptions, 587 audiovisual materials, an OPAC.

Standardized Tests *Required:* Wonderlic aptitude test (for admission).

Financial Aid Of all full-time matriculated undergraduates who enrolled in 2008, 5 Federal Work-Study jobs (averaging $2500).

Applying *Application fee:* $50. *Required:* high school transcript, interview. *Application deadline:* rolling (freshmen). *Notification:* continuous (freshmen).

Freshman Application Contact Sherry Lee Walters, Director of Enrollment Services, Douglas Education Center, 130 Seventh Street, Monessen, PA 15062. *Phone:* 724-684-3684 Ext. 2181.

DuBois Business College

DuBois, Pennsylvania **www.dbcollege.com/**

- **Proprietary** 2-year, founded 1885
- **Rural** 4-acre campus
- **Coed, primarily women**

Academics *Calendar:* quarters. *Degree:* diplomas and associate. *Special study options:* academic remediation for entering students, accelerated degree program, double majors, part-time degree program, summer session for credit.
Student Life *Campus security:* late-night transport/escort service, controlled dormitory access.
Applying *Options:* electronic application, deferred entrance. *Application fee:* $25. *Required:* high school transcript, interview.
Director of Admissions Mrs. Lisa Doty, Director of Admissions, DuBois Business College, 1 Beaver Drive, DuBois, PA 15801-2401. *Phone:* 814-371-6920. *Toll-free phone:* 800-692-6213. *Fax:* 814-371-3947. *E-mail:* dotylj@dbcollege.com.

Erie Business Center, Main

Erie, Pennsylvania **www.eriebc.edu/**

Freshman Application Contact Ms. Rose Mello, Academic Administrator, Erie Business Center, Main, 220 West Ninth Street, Erie, PA 16501-1392. *Phone:* 814-456-7504 Ext. 102. *Toll-free phone:* 800-352-3743. *Fax:* 814-456-4882. *E-mail:* mellor@eriebc.com.

Erie Business Center, South

New Castle, Pennsylvania **www.eriebc.edu/**

Freshman Application Contact Erie Business Center, South, 170 Cascade Galleria, New Castle, PA 16101-3950. *Phone:* 724-658-9066. *Toll-free phone:* 800-722-6227. *E-mail:* admissions@eriebcs.com.

Erie Institute of Technology

Erie, Pennsylvania **www.erieit.edu/**

Freshman Application Contact Erie Institute of Technology, 940 Millcreek Mall, Erie, PA 16565. *Phone:* 814-868-9900. *Toll-free phone:* 866-868-3743.

Everest Institute

Pittsburgh, Pennsylvania **www.everest.edu/**

Director of Admissions Director of Admissions, Everest Institute, 100 Forbes Avenue, Suite 1200, Pittsburgh, PA 15222. *Phone:* 412-261-4520. *Toll-free phone:* 888-279-3314. *Fax:* 412-261-4546.

Fortis Institute

Forty Fort, Pennsylvania **www.fortis.edu/**

- **Proprietary** 2-year, founded 1984
- **Coed**

Academics *Degree:* diplomas and associate.
Applying *Application fee:* $50.
Freshman Application Contact Admissions Office, Fortis Institute, 166 Slocum Street, Forty Fort, PA 18704. *Phone:* 570-288-8400.

Harcum College

Bryn Mawr, Pennsylvania **www.harcum.edu/**

- **Independent** 2-year, founded 1915
- **Suburban** 12-acre campus with easy access to Philadelphia
- **Coed, primarily women,** 1,154 undergraduate students

Undergraduates 39% African American, 3% Asian American or Pacific Islander, 7% Hispanic American, 0.3% Native American, 1% international, 20% live on campus. *Retention:* 64% of 2008 full-time freshmen returned.
Freshmen *Admission:* 485 applied, 314 admitted. *Average high school GPA:* 2.5.
Faculty *Total:* 190, 19% full-time. *Student/faculty ratio:* 12:1.
Majors Allied health diagnostic, intervention, and treatment professions related; animal sciences; business administration and management; child-care provision; clinical/medical laboratory technology; consumer merchandising/retailing management; criminal justice/law enforcement administration; dental assisting; dental hygiene; electroneurodiagnostic/electroencephalographic technology; entrepreneurship; fashion/apparel design; fashion merchandising; general studies; health professions related; histologic technology/histotechnologist; human services; interior design; international business/trade/commerce; legal studies; medical radiologic technology; nursing (registered nurse training); occupational therapist assistant; physical therapist assistant; prenursing studies; sport and fitness administration/management; veterinary/animal health technology.
Academics *Calendar:* semesters. *Degree:* certificates and associate. *Special study options:* academic remediation for entering students, accelerated degree program, adult/continuing education programs, advanced placement credit, distance learning, English as a second language, honors programs, independent study, internships, off-campus study, part-time degree program, services for LD students, summer session for credit.
Library Harcum College Library with 39,994 titles, 298 serial subscriptions, 1,905 audiovisual materials, an OPAC, a Web page.
Student Life *Housing Options:* coed. Campus housing is university owned. Freshman campus housing is guaranteed. *Activities and Organizations:* OATS (Organization for Animal Tech Students), Student Association of Dental Hygienist of America, Student Nurses Association, Dental Assisting Club, HAECY (Organization for Early Childhood Development). *Campus security:* 24-hour emergency response devices and patrols, late-night transport/escort service, controlled dormitory access. *Student services:* health clinic, personal/psychological counseling.
Athletics Member NJCAA. *Intercollegiate sports:* basketball M(s)/W(s), track and field M(s)/W(s), volleyball W(s). *Intramural sports:* cheerleading W.
Standardized Tests *Recommended:* SAT or ACT (for admission).
Financial Aid Of all full-time matriculated undergraduates who enrolled in 2009, 703 applied for aid, 675 were judged to have need, 17 had their need fully met. 160 Federal Work-Study jobs (averaging $1500). *Average percent of need met:* 51%. *Average financial aid package:* $13,662. *Average need-based loan:* $3876. *Average need-based gift aid:* $10,390. *Average indebtedness upon graduation:* $17,641. *Financial aid deadline:* 5/1.
Applying *Options:* electronic application, deferred entrance. *Application fee:* $50. *Required:* high school transcript, minimum 2 GPA. *Required for some:* 1 letter of recommendation, interview. *Recommended:* essay or personal statement. *Application deadlines:* rolling (freshmen), rolling (transfers). *Notification:* continuous (freshmen), continuous (transfers).
Freshman Application Contact Office of Enrollment Management, Harcum College, 750 Montgomery Avenue, Melville Hall, Bryn Mawr, PA 19010-3476. *Phone:* 610-526-6050. *Toll-free phone:* 800-345-2600. *E-mail:* enroll@harcum.edu.

Harrisburg Area Community College

Harrisburg, Pennsylvania **www.hacc.edu/**

- **State and locally supported** 2-year, founded 1964
- **Urban** 212-acre campus
- **Endowment** $24.9 million
- **Coed,** 22,529 undergraduate students, 39% full-time, 64% women, 36% men

Undergraduates 8,838 full-time, 13,691 part-time. Students come from 10 states and territories, 58 other countries, 1% are from out of state, 9% African American, 3% Asian American or Pacific Islander, 8% Hispanic American, 0.4% Native American, 2% international, 8% transferred in.
Freshmen *Admission:* 11,121 applied, 10,793 admitted, 2,245 enrolled.
Faculty *Total:* 1,168, 30% full-time, 5% with terminal degrees. *Student/faculty ratio:* 21:1.

Harrisburg Area Community College (continued)

Majors Accounting and business/management; accounting technology and bookkeeping; administrative assistant and secretarial science; agribusiness; architectural engineering technology; architecture; art; automobile/automotive mechanics technology; banking and financial support services; biology/biological sciences; building/home/construction inspection; business administration and management; business/commerce; cardiovascular technology; chemistry; civil engineering technology; clinical/medical laboratory technology; computer and information sciences; computer and information systems security; computer installation and repair technology; computer science; computer systems networking and telecommunications; construction engineering technology; construction trades; court reporting; crafts, folk art and artisanry; criminalistics and criminal science; criminal justice/law enforcement administration; criminal justice/police science; culinary arts; dental hygiene; design and visual communications; diagnostic medical sonography and ultrasound technology; dietetics; dietetics and clinical nutrition services related; dramatic/theater arts; early childhood education; electrical, electronic and communications engineering technology; electrician; elementary education; emergency medical technology (EMT paramedic); engineering; engineering technologies related; environmental science; environmental studies; fire science; food service systems administration; general studies; graphic design; health/health-care administration; health information/ medical records technology; health services administration; heating, air conditioning, ventilation and refrigeration maintenance technology; hospitality administration; hotel/motel administration; human services; industrial mechanics and maintenance technology; information technology; international relations and affairs; landscaping and groundskeeping; legal assistant/paralegal; lineworker; management information systems and services related; mass communication/ media; mathematics; mechanical engineering/mechanical technology; medical/ clinical assistant; music; music management and merchandising; nuclear medical technology; nursing (registered nurse training); photography; physical sciences; psychology; radiologic technology/science; real estate; respiratory care therapy; restaurant/food services management; sales, distribution and marketing; secondary education; small business administration; social sciences; social work; tourism and travel services management; visual and performing arts; web page, digital/multimedia and information resources design; woodworking related.

Academics *Calendar:* semesters. *Degree:* certificates, diplomas, and associate. *Special study options:* academic remediation for entering students, adult/ continuing education programs, advanced placement credit, distance learning, double majors, English as a second language, honors programs, independent study, internships, part-time degree program, services for LD students, student-designed majors, study abroad, summer session for credit. *ROTC:* Army (b).

Library McCormick Library with 174,523 titles, 701 serial subscriptions, 8,003 audiovisual materials, an OPAC, a Web page.

Student Life *Housing:* college housing not available. *Activities and Organizations:* drama/theater group, student-run newspaper, Student Government Association, Phi Theta Kappa, African American Student Association, Mosiaco Club, Fourth Estate. *Campus security:* 24-hour emergency response devices and patrols, late-night transport/escort service.

Athletics *Intercollegiate sports:* basketball M/W, soccer M, tennis M/W. *Intramural sports:* basketball M/W, soccer M/W, swimming and diving M/W, tennis M/W, volleyball M/W.

Costs (2009–10) *One-time required fee:* $35. *Tuition:* area resident $2955 full-time, $99 per credit hour part-time; state resident $5460 full-time, $182 per credit hour part-time; nonresident $8265 full-time, $276 per credit hour part-time. Full-time tuition and fees vary according to program. Part-time tuition and fees vary according to program. *Required fees:* $525 full-time, $18 per credit hour part-time. *Payment plan:* installment. *Waivers:* employees or children of employees.

Applying *Options:* electronic application, early admission, deferred entrance. *Application fee:* $35. *Required for some:* high school transcript, 1 letter of recommendation, interview. *Application deadlines:* rolling (freshmen), rolling (transfers).

Freshman Application Contact Mrs. Vanita L. Cowan, Administrative Clerk, Admissions, Harrisburg Area Community College, 1 HACC Drive, Harrisburg, PA 17110. *Phone:* 717-780-2406. *Toll-free phone:* 800-ABC-HACC. *Fax:* 717-231-7674. *E-mail:* admit@hacc.edu.

HUSSIAN SCHOOL OF ART

Philadelphia, Pennsylvania **www.hussianart.edu/**

- **Proprietary** 2-year, founded 1946
- **Urban** 1-acre campus
- **Coed, primarily men**

Undergraduates 136 full-time. Students come from 4 states and territories, 20% are from out of state, 17% African American, 1% Asian American or Pacific Islander, 7% Hispanic American. *Retention:* 65% of 2008 full-time freshmen returned.

Academics *Calendar:* semesters. *Degree:* associate. *Special study options:* independent study, internships.

Student Life *Campus security:* security guard during open hours.

Costs (2009–10) *Tuition:* $12,000 full-time. *Required fees:* $550 full-time.

Applying *Options:* electronic application, deferred entrance. *Application fee:* $25. *Required:* high school transcript, interview, art portfolio.

Freshman Application Contact Ms. Lynne Wartman, Director of Admissions, Hussian School of Art, 1118 Market Street, Philadelphia, PA 19107. *Phone:* 215-574-9600 Ext. 201. *Fax:* 215-574-9800. *E-mail:* lwartman@ hussianart.edu.

ITT TECHNICAL INSTITUTE

Bensalem, Pennsylvania **www.itt-tech.edu/**

- **Proprietary** 2-year, founded 2000, part of ITT Educational Services, Inc.
- **Coed**

Majors CAD/CADD drafting/design technology; computer engineering technology; system, networking, and LAN/WAN management; web page, digital/ multimedia and information resources design.

Academics *Calendar:* quarters. *Degree:* diplomas and associate.

Student Life *Housing:* college housing not available.

Freshman Application Contact Director of Recruitment, ITT Technical Institute, 3330 Tillman Drive, Bensalem, PA 19020. *Phone:* 215-244-8871. *Toll-free phone:* 866-488-8324.

ITT TECHNICAL INSTITUTE

Dunmore, Pennsylvania **www.itt-tech.edu/**

- **Proprietary** 2-year, part of ITT Educational Services, Inc.
- **Coed**

Majors CAD/CADD drafting/design technology; computer engineering technology; criminal justice/law enforcement administration; system, networking, and LAN/WAN management.

Academics *Calendar:* quarters. *Degree:* diplomas and associate.

Freshman Application Contact ITT Technical Institute, 1000 Meade Street, Dunmore, PA 18512. *Phone:* 570-330-0600. *Toll-free phone:* 800-774-9791.

ITT TECHNICAL INSTITUTE

Harrisburg, Pennsylvania **www.itt-tech.edu/**

- **Proprietary** 2-year, part of ITT Educational Services, Inc.
- **Coed**

Majors CAD/CADD drafting/design technology; computer engineering technology; computer software and media applications related; system, networking, and LAN/WAN management; web page, digital/multimedia and information resources design.

Academics *Degree:* diplomas and associate.

Freshman Application Contact Director of Recruitment, ITT Technical Institute, 449 Eisenhower Boulevard, Suite 100, Harrisburg, PA 17111. *Phone:* 717-565-1700. *Toll-free phone:* 800-847-4756.

ITT TECHNICAL INSTITUTE

King of Prussia, Pennsylvania **www.itt-tech.edu/**

- **Proprietary** 2-year, founded 2002, part of ITT Educational Services, Inc.
- **Coed**

Majors CAD/CADD drafting/design technology; criminal justice/law enforcement administration; system, networking, and LAN/WAN management; web page, digital/multimedia and information resources design.

Academics *Calendar:* quarters. *Degree:* diplomas and associate.

Freshman Application Contact Director of Recruitment, ITT Technical Institute, 760 Moore Road, King of Prussia, PA 19046. *Phone:* 610-491-8004. *Toll-free phone:* 866-902-8324.

ITT Technical Institute

Pittsburgh, Pennsylvania www.itt-tech.edu/

- **Proprietary** 2-year, part of ITT Educational Services, Inc.
- **Coed**

Majors CAD/CADD drafting/design technology; computer engineering technology; computer software and media applications related; criminal justice/law enforcement administration; system, networking, and LAN/WAN management; web page, digital/multimedia and information resources design.

Academics *Calendar:* quarters. *Degree:* diplomas and associate.

Student Life *Housing:* college housing not available.

Freshman Application Contact Director of Recruitment, ITT Technical Institute, 10 Parkway Center, Pittsburgh, PA 15220-3801. *Phone:* 412-937-9150. *Toll-free phone:* 800-353-8324.

ITT Technical Institute

Tarentum, Pennsylvania www.itt-tech.edu/

- **Proprietary** 2-year, part of ITT Educational Services, Inc.
- **Coed**

Majors CAD/CADD drafting/design technology; computer engineering technology; computer software and media applications related; criminal justice/law enforcement administration; system, networking, and LAN/WAN management; web/multimedia management and webmaster; web page, digital/multimedia and information resources design.

Academics *Calendar:* quarters. *Degree:* diplomas and associate.

Student Life *Housing:* college housing not available.

Freshman Application Contact Director of Recruitment, ITT Technical Institute, 105 Mall Boulevard, Suite 200 E, Monroeville, PA 15146. *Phone:* 724-274-1400. *Toll-free phone:* 800-488-0121.

JNA Institute of Culinary Arts

Philadelphia, Pennsylvania www.culinaryarts.com/

Freshman Application Contact Admissions Office, JNA Institute of Culinary Arts, 1212 South Broad Street, Philadelphia, PA 19146.

Johnson College

Scranton, Pennsylvania www.johnson.edu/

Freshman Application Contact Ms. Melissa Ide, Director of Enrollment Management, Johnson College, 3427 North Main Avenue, Scranton, PA 18508. *Phone:* 570-702-8910. *Toll-free phone:* 800-2-WE-WORK Ext. 125. *Fax:* 570-348-2181. *E-mail:* admit@johnson.edu.

Kaplan Career Institute, Harrisburg

Harrisburg, Pennsylvania www.kci-Harrisburg.com/

- **Proprietary** 2-year, founded 1918
- **Suburban** campus
- **Coed**

Majors Accounting; business administration and management; corrections and criminal justice related; digital communication and media/multimedia; drafting and design technology; medical/clinical assistant; system, networking, and LAN/WAN management.

Academics *Calendar:* quarters. *Degree:* certificates, diplomas, and associate.

Freshman Application Contact Kaplan Career Institute, Harrisburg, 5650 Derry Street, Harrisburg, PA 17111. *Phone:* 717-558-1300. *Toll-free phone:* 800-431-1995.

Kaplan Career Institute, ICM Campus

Pittsburgh, Pennsylvania www.kci-pittsburgh.com/

- **Proprietary** 2-year, founded 1963
- **Urban** campus
- **Coed**

Majors Accounting; business administration and management; criminal justice/law enforcement administration; data modeling/warehousing and database administration; fashion merchandising; legal administrative assistant/secretary; medical administrative assistant and medical secretary; occupational therapy.

Academics *Calendar:* continuous. *Degree:* diplomas and associate.

Freshman Application Contact Kaplan Career Institute, ICM Campus, 10 Wood Street, Pittsburgh, PA 15222. *Phone:* 412-261-2647. *Toll-free phone:* 800-441-5222.

Keystone Technical Institute

Harrisburg, Pennsylvania www.acadcampus.com/

- **Proprietary** 2-year, founded 1980
- **Suburban** 8-acre campus
- **Coed, primarily women**

Academics *Calendar:* continuous. *Degree:* diplomas and associate. *Special study options:* advanced placement credit, internships.

Financial Aid Of all full-time matriculated undergraduates who enrolled in 2008, 25 Federal Work-Study jobs (averaging $6000).

Applying *Application fee:* $20. *Required:* high school transcript, interview.

Freshman Application Contact Tom Bogush, Director of Admissions, Keystone Technical Institute, 2301 Academy Drive, Harrisburg, PA 17112. *Phone:* 717-545-4747. *Toll-free phone:* 800-400-3322. *Fax:* 717-901-9090. *E-mail:* info@acadcampus.com.

Lackawanna College

Scranton, Pennsylvania www.lackawanna.edu/

- **Independent** 2-year, founded 1894
- **Urban** 4-acre campus
- **Endowment** $1.9 million
- **Coed,** 1,387 undergraduate students, 72% full-time, 52% women, 48% men

Undergraduates 999 full-time, 388 part-time. Students come from 13 states and territories, 10% are from out of state, 15% African American, 1% Asian American or Pacific Islander, 6% Hispanic American, 0.4% Native American, 10% transferred in, 17% live on campus. *Retention:* 34% of 2008 full-time freshmen returned.

Freshmen *Admission:* 809 applied, 521 admitted, 395 enrolled. *Test scores:* SAT verbal scores over 500: 19%; SAT math scores over 500: 23%; SAT writing scores over 500: 15%; SAT verbal scores over 600: 2%; SAT math scores over 600: 3%; SAT writing scores over 600: 1%.

Faculty *Total:* 215, 15% full-time, 4% with terminal degrees. *Student/faculty ratio:* 13:1.

Majors Accounting; accounting technology and bookkeeping; administrative assistant and secretarial science; banking and financial support services; biology/biological sciences; biotechnology; business administration and management; business administration, management and operations related; business/commerce; cardiopulmonary technology; communication/speech communication and rhetoric; communications technology; computer and information sciences; criminal justice/safety; diagnostic medical sonography and ultrasound technology; early childhood education; education; emergency medical technology (EMT paramedic); environmental studies; general studies; humanities; human services; industrial electronics technology; industrial technology; legal assistant/paralegal; liberal arts and sciences/liberal studies; management information systems; mass communication/media; medical administrative assistant and medical secretary; mental health/rehabilitation; petroleum technology; surgical technology.

Academics *Calendar:* semesters. *Degree:* certificates, diplomas, and associate. *Special study options:* academic remediation for entering students, adult/continuing education programs, cooperative education, double majors, English as a second language, internships, part-time degree program, services for LD students, summer session for credit. *ROTC:* Army (c), Air Force (c).

Library Seeley Memorial Library with 17,068 titles, 52 serial subscriptions, 1,120 audiovisual materials, an OPAC, a Web page.

Lackawanna College (continued)

Student Life *Housing:* on-campus residence required through sophomore year. *Options:* coed, men-only. Campus housing is university owned. *Activities and Organizations:* drama/theater group, student-run newspaper, choral group, student government, Student/Alumni Association, United Cultures Leadership Association, Green Falcons: Sustainability Action Group, Sonography Club. *Campus security:* 24-hour emergency response devices and patrols, late-night transport/escort service, controlled dormitory access, patrols by college liaison staff.

Athletics Member NJCAA. *Intercollegiate sports:* baseball M(s), basketball M(s)/W(s), cheerleading W(s), cross-country running M(s)/W(s), football M(s), golf M(s)/W(s), soccer W(s), softball W(s), volleyball W(s).

Standardized Tests *Recommended:* SAT (for admission), ACT (for admission), SAT or ACT (for admission).

Costs (2010–11) *Comprehensive fee:* $18,160 includes full-time tuition ($11,000), mandatory fees ($160), and room and board ($7000). Full-time tuition and fees vary according to course load. Part-time tuition: $370 per credit hour. Part-time tuition and fees vary according to course load. *Required fees:* $55 per term part-time. *Payment plans:* installment, deferred payment. *Waivers:* employees or children of employees.

Financial Aid Of all full-time matriculated undergraduates who enrolled in 2008, 92 Federal Work-Study jobs (averaging $1100).

Applying *Options:* electronic application, early admission, deferred entrance. *Application fee:* $30. *Required:* high school transcript, interview. *Application deadlines:* rolling (freshmen), rolling (out-of-state freshmen), rolling (transfers).

Freshman Application Contact Ms. Stacey Muchal, Associate Director of Admissions, Lackawanna College, 501 Vine Street, Scranton, PA 18509. *Phone:* 570-961-7868. *Toll-free phone:* 877-346-3552. *Fax:* 570-961-7843. *E-mail:* muchals@lackawanna.edu.

LANCASTER GENERAL COLLEGE OF NURSING & HEALTH SCIENCES

Lancaster, Pennsylvania www.lancastergeneralcollege.edu/content/

Freshman Application Contact Admissions Office, Lancaster General College of Nursing & Health Sciences, 410 North Lime Street, Lancaster, PA 17602.

LANSDALE SCHOOL OF BUSINESS

North Wales, Pennsylvania www.lsbonline.com/

- **Proprietary** 2-year, founded 1918
- **Suburban** campus with easy access to Philadelphia
- **Coed**

Academics *Calendar:* semesters. *Degree:* certificates, diplomas, and associate. *Special study options:* accelerated degree program, adult/continuing education programs, double majors, honors programs, independent study, internships, off-campus study, part-time degree program, summer session for credit.

Applying *Application fee:* $30. *Required:* high school transcript, interview.

Director of Admissions Ms. Marianne H. Johnson, Director of Admissions, Lansdale School of Business, 201 Church Road, North Wales, PA 19454-4148. *Phone:* 215-699-5700 Ext. 112. *Fax:* 215-699-8770. *E-mail:* mjohnson@lsb.edu.

LAUREL BUSINESS INSTITUTE

Uniontown, Pennsylvania www.laurel.edu/

Freshman Application Contact Mrs. Lisa Dolan, Laurel Business Institute, 11-15 Penn Street, PO Box 877, Uniontown, PA 15401. *Phone:* 724-439-4900 Ext. 158. *Fax:* 724-439-3607. *E-mail:* ldolan@laurel.edu.

LAUREL TECHNICAL INSTITUTE

Meadville, Pennsylvania www.laurel.edu/lti/

Freshman Application Contact Ms. Cheryl Mever, Admissions Officer, Laurel Technical Institute, 628 Arch Street, Suite B105, Meadville, PA 16335. *Phone:* 814-724-0700. *Fax:* 814-724-2777. *E-mail:* info@biop.edu.

LAUREL TECHNICAL INSTITUTE

Sharon, Pennsylvania www.laurel.edu/lti/

Freshman Application Contact Irene Lewis, Laurel Technical Institute, 335 Boyd Drive, Sharon, PA 16146. *Phone:* 724-983-0700. *Toll-free phone:* 800-289-2069. *Fax:* 724-983-8355. *E-mail:* info@biop.edu.

LEHIGH CARBON COMMUNITY COLLEGE

Schnecksville, Pennsylvania www.lccc.edu/

- **State and locally supported** 2-year, founded 1967
- **Suburban** 254-acre campus with easy access to Philadelphia
- **Endowment** $1.9 million
- **Coed,** 8,127 undergraduate students, 42% full-time, 62% women, 38% men

Undergraduates 3,421 full-time, 4,706 part-time. Students come from 9 states and territories, 39 other countries, 2% are from out of state, 6% African American, 2% Asian American or Pacific Islander, 14% Hispanic American, 0.2% Native American, 0.4% international, 56% transferred in. *Retention:* 57% of 2008 full-time freshmen returned.

Freshmen *Admission:* 4,513 applied, 4,511 admitted, 2,227 enrolled.

Faculty *Total:* 488, 22% full-time, 4% with terminal degrees. *Student/faculty ratio:* 18:1.

Majors Accounting technology and bookkeeping; airline pilot and flight crew; air transportation related; animation, interactive technology, video graphics and special effects; art; biology/biological sciences; biotechnology; business administration and management; chemical technology; commercial and advertising art; communication/speech communication and rhetoric; computer and information systems security; computer engineering technology; computer programming; computer systems analysis; computer systems networking and telecommunications; construction engineering technology; construction management; criminal justice/law enforcement administration; criminal justice/safety; culinary arts related; drafting and design technology; drafting/design engineering technologies related; early childhood education; education; electrical, electronic and communications engineering technology; engineering; executive assistant/executive secretary; fashion/apparel design; general studies; health information/medical records technology; heating, air conditioning, ventilation and refrigeration maintenance technology; horticultural science; hotel/motel administration; humanities; human resources management; human services; industrial electronics technology; information science/studies; interior design; legal administrative assistant/secretary; legal assistant/paralegal; liberal arts and sciences/liberal studies; logistics and materials management; manufacturing technology; mathematics; mechanical engineering; mechanical engineering/mechanical technology; medical/clinical assistant; Montessori teacher education; nursing (licensed practical/vocational nurse training); nursing (registered nurse training); occupational therapist assistant; operations management; physical sciences; physical therapist assistant; psychology; recording arts technology; resort management; restaurant/food services management; social sciences; special education; sport and fitness administration/management; teacher assistant/aide; veterinary/animal health technology; web page, digital/multimedia and information resources design.

Academics *Calendar:* semesters. *Degree:* certificates, diplomas, and associate. *Special study options:* academic remediation for entering students, adult/continuing education programs, advanced placement credit, cooperative education, distance learning, English as a second language, external degree program, honors programs, independent study, internships, part-time degree program, services for LD students, summer session for credit. *ROTC:* Army (c).

Library Rothrock Library with 88,426 titles, 339 serial subscriptions, 5,496 audiovisual materials, an OPAC, a Web page.

Student Life *Housing:* college housing not available. *Activities and Organizations:* drama/theater group, student-run radio station, choral group, Phi Theta Kappa, STEP Student Association, Students in Free Enterprise (SIFE), Student Government Association, WXLV 90.3FM- college radio station. *Campus security:* 24-hour emergency response devices and patrols. *Student services:* personal/psychological counseling.

Athletics *Intercollegiate sports:* baseball M, basketball M/W, golf M/W, soccer M, softball W, volleyball W. *Intramural sports:* baseball M, basketball M/W, bowling M/W, field hockey W, football M/W, golf M/W, racquetball M/W, soccer M/W, softball M/W, table tennis M/W, tennis M/W, track and field M, volleyball M/W.

Standardized Tests *Required for some:* TEAS (for those applying to Nursing Program).

Costs (2010–11) *Tuition:* area resident $2640 full-time, $88 per credit part-time; state resident $5550 full-time, $185 per credit part-time; nonresident $8460 full-time, $282 per credit part-time. *Required fees:* $480 full-time, $16 per credit part-time. *Payment plan:* installment. *Waivers:* senior citizens and employees or children of employees.

Applying *Options:* electronic application. *Application fee:* $30. *Required for some:* essay or personal statement, high school transcript, interview. *Application deadlines:* rolling (freshmen), rolling (out-of-state freshmen), rolling (transfers). *Notification:* continuous (freshmen), continuous (out-of-state freshmen), continuous (transfers).

Freshman Application Contact Ms. Mary Theresa Taglang, Associate Dean of Admissions and Strategic Outreach, Lehigh Carbon Community College, 4525 Education Park Drive, Schnecksville, PA 18078-2598. *Phone:* 610-799-1575. *Fax:* 610-799-1527. *E-mail:* tellme@lccc.edu.

LINCOLN TECHNICAL INSTITUTE

Allentown, Pennsylvania **www.lincolnedu.com/**

- **Proprietary** 2-year, founded 1949, part of Lincoln Technical Institute, Inc
- **Suburban** 10-acre campus with easy access to Philadelphia
- **Coed**

Academics *Calendar:* semesters. *Degree:* diplomas and associate. *Special study options:* summer session for credit.

Financial Aid Of all full-time matriculated undergraduates who enrolled in 2008, 5 Federal Work-Study jobs.

Applying *Options:* early admission. *Application fee:* $25. *Required:* high school transcript, interview.

Freshman Application Contact Admissions Office, Lincoln Technical Institute, 5151 Tilghman Street, Allentown, PA 18104-3298. *Phone:* 610-398-5301.

LINCOLN TECHNICAL INSTITUTE

Philadelphia, Pennsylvania **www.lincolnedu.com/**

- **Proprietary** 2-year, founded 1946, part of Lincoln Technical Institute, Inc
- **Suburban** 3-acre campus
- **Coed, primarily men**

Academics *Calendar:* modular. *Degree:* associate. *Special study options:* adult/continuing education programs, cooperative education, part-time degree program.

Student Life *Campus security:* 16-hour patrols by trained security personnel.

Applying *Options:* deferred entrance. *Application fee:* $25. *Required:* high school transcript, minimum 2.0 GPA, interview.

Director of Admissions Mr. James Kuntz, Executive Director, Lincoln Technical Institute, 9191 Torresdale Avenue, Philadelphia, PA 19136-1595. *Phone:* 215-335-0800. *Toll-free phone:* 800-238-8381. *Fax:* 215-335-1443. *E-mail:* jkuntz@lincolntech.com.

LINCOLN TECHNICAL INSTITUTE

Plymouth Meeting, Pennsylvania **www.lincolnedu.com/**

Freshman Application Contact Admissions Office, Lincoln Technical Institute, 1 Plymouth Meeting, #300, Plymouth Meeting, PA 19462.

LUZERNE COUNTY COMMUNITY COLLEGE

Nanticoke, Pennsylvania **www.luzerne.edu/**

Freshman Application Contact Mr. Francis Curry, Director of Admissions, Luzerne County Community College, 1333 South Prospect Street, Nanticoke, PA 18634. *Phone:* 570-740-0337. *Toll-free phone:* 800-377-5222 Ext. 337. *Fax:* 570-740-0238. *E-mail:* admissions@luzerne.edu.

MANOR COLLEGE

Jenkintown, Pennsylvania **www.manor.edu/**

Director of Admissions Ms. I. Jerry Czenstuch, Vice President of Enrollment Management, Manor College, 700 Fox Chase Road, Jenkintown, PA 19046. *Phone:* 215-884-2216. *E-mail:* ftadmiss@manor.edu.

▶**See page 460 for the College Close-Up.**

MCCANN SCHOOL OF BUSINESS & TECHNOLOGY

Pottsville, Pennsylvania **www.mccannschool.com/**

- **Proprietary** 2-year, founded 1897
- **Small-town** campus
- **Coed**

Academics *Calendar:* quarters. *Degree:* certificates, diplomas, and associate. *Special study options:* advanced placement credit, double majors, independent study, internships, part-time degree program, summer session for credit.

Standardized Tests *Required:* Wonderlic aptitude test (for admission).

Applying *Options:* electronic application. *Application fee:* $40. *Required:* high school transcript, minimum 2.0 GPA, interview.

Freshman Application Contact Ms. Linda Walinsky, Director, Pottsville Campus, McCann School of Business & Technology, 2650 Woodglen Road, Pottsville, PA 17901. *Phone:* 570-622-7622. *Toll-free phone:* 888-622-2664. *Fax:* 570-622-7770.

MERCYHURST NORTH EAST

North East, Pennsylvania **northeast.mercyhurst.edu/**

Director of Admissions Travis Lindahl, Director of Admissions, Mercyhurst North East, 16 West Division Street, North East, PA 16428. *Phone:* 814-725-6217. *Toll-free phone:* 866-846-6042. *Fax:* 814-725-6251. *E-mail:* neadmiss@mercyhurst.edu.

METROPOLITAN CAREER CENTER

Philadelphia, Pennsylvania **www.careersinit.org/**

Freshman Application Contact Admissions Office, Metropolitan Career Center, 100 South Broad Street, Suite 830, Philadelphia, PA 19110. *Phone:* 215-568-7861.

MONTGOMERY COUNTY COMMUNITY COLLEGE

Blue Bell, Pennsylvania **www.mc3.edu/**

- **County-supported** 2-year, founded 1964
- **Suburban** 186-acre campus with easy access to Philadelphia
- **Coed,** 13,310 undergraduate students, 47% full-time, 57% women, 43% men

Undergraduates 6,288 full-time, 7,022 part-time. Students come from 13 states and territories, 91 other countries, 0.2% are from out of state, 12% African American, 6% Asian American or Pacific Islander, 4% Hispanic American, 0.3% Native American, 2% international, 4% transferred in. *Retention:* 61% of 2008 full-time freshmen returned.

Freshmen *Admission:* 7,653 applied, 7,653 admitted, 4,530 enrolled.

Faculty *Total:* 754, 26% full-time. *Student/faculty ratio:* 23:1.

Majors Accounting; accounting technology and bookkeeping; administrative assistant and secretarial science; architectural drafting and CAD/CADD; art; automotive engineering technology; baking and pastry arts; biology/biological sciences; biotechnology; business administration and management; business/commerce; business/corporate communications; CAD/CADD drafting/design technology; child-care and support services management; clinical/medical laboratory technology; commercial and advertising art; communication/speech communication and rhetoric; communications technologies and support services related; computer and information sciences; computer programming; computer

Montgomery County Community College (continued)

systems networking and telecommunications; criminal justice/police science; culinary arts; dental hygiene; electrical, electronic and communications engineering technology; electromechanical technology; elementary education; engineering science; engineering technologies related; environmental science; fire protection and safety technology; hospitality and recreation marketing; humanities; information science/studies; liberal arts and sciences/liberal studies; management information systems and services related; mathematics; mechanical drafting and CAD/CADD; mechanical engineering/mechanical technology; medical/clinical assistant; medical radiologic technology; nursing (registered nurse training); physical education teaching and coaching; physical sciences; psychiatric/mental health services technology; radio, television, and digital communication related; real estate; recording arts technology; sales, distribution and marketing; secondary education; social sciences; surgical technology; teacher assistant/aide; tourism and travel services marketing.

Academics *Calendar:* semesters. *Degree:* certificates and associate. *Special study options:* academic remediation for entering students, accelerated degree program, adult/continuing education programs, advanced placement credit, cooperative education, distance learning, English as a second language, honors programs, independent study, internships, part-time degree program, services for LD students, student-designed majors, study abroad, summer session for credit.

Library The Brendlinger Library/Branch Library Pottstown Campus plus 1 other with 92,850 titles, 16,280 audiovisual materials, an OPAC, a Web page.

Student Life *Housing:* college housing not available. *Activities and Organizations:* drama/theater group, student-run newspaper, radio and television station, choral group, student government, Thrive (Christian Fellowship), radio station, Drama Club, African - American Student League. *Campus security:* 24-hour emergency response devices and patrols, late-night transport/escort service, bicycle patrol. *Student services:* health clinic, personal/psychological counseling.

Athletics Member NJCAA. *Intercollegiate sports:* baseball M, basketball M/W, soccer M/W, softball W. *Intramural sports:* badminton M/W, basketball M/W, bowling M/W, cross-country running M/W, football M, racquetball M/W, soccer M/W, table tennis M/W, tennis M/W, volleyball M/W, weight lifting M/W.

Costs (2009–10) *Tuition:* area resident $2700 full-time, $90 per credit hour part-time; state resident $5700 full-time, $180 per credit hour part-time; nonresident $8700 full-time, $270 per credit hour part-time. *Required fees:* $570 full-time, $19 per credit hour part-time. *Payment plan:* deferred payment. *Waivers:* senior citizens and employees or children of employees.

Financial Aid Of all full-time matriculated undergraduates who enrolled in 2008, 60 Federal Work-Study jobs (averaging $2500).

Applying *Options:* electronic application, early admission, deferred entrance. *Application fee:* $25. *Required:* high school transcript. *Required for some:* interview. *Application deadline:* rolling (transfers). *Notification:* continuous (freshmen), continuous (transfers).

Freshman Application Contact Ms. Penny Sawyer, Director of Admissions and Recruitment, Montgomery County Community College, Office of Admissions and Records, Blue Bell, PA 19422. *Phone:* 215-641-6551. *Fax:* 215-619-7188. *E-mail:* admrec@admin.mc3.edu.

New Castle School of Trades

Pulaski, Pennsylvania www.ncstrades.com/

- **Independent** 2-year, founded 1945, part of Educational Enterprises Incorporated
- **Rural** 20-acre campus with easy access to Cleveland
- **Coed, primarily men**
- 100% of applicants were admitted

Academics *Calendar:* quarters. *Degree:* diplomas and associate.

Student Life *Campus security:* 24-hour emergency response devices.

Standardized Tests *Required:* Wonderlic aptitude test (for admission).

Applying *Application fee:* $25. *Required:* high school transcript, interview. *Required for some:* essay or personal statement.

Freshman Application Contact Mr. James Catheline, Admissions Director, New Castle School of Trades, RD 1, Route 422, Pulaski, PA 16143. *Phone:* 724-964-8811. *Toll-free phone:* 800-837-8299 Ext. 12.

Newport Business Institute

Lower Burrell, Pennsylvania www.nbi.edu/

Freshman Application Contact Ms. Melissa Beck, Admissions Coordinator, Newport Business Institute, Lower Burrell, PA 15068. *Phone:* 724-339-7542. *Toll-free phone:* 800-752-7695. *Fax:* 724-339-2950.

Newport Business Institute

Williamsport, Pennsylvania www.nbi.edu/

- **Proprietary** 2-year, founded 1955
- **Small-town** campus
- **Coed, primarily women,** 124 undergraduate students, 100% full-time, 97% women, 3% men

Undergraduates 124 full-time. 19% African American, 0.8% Hispanic American, 10% transferred in. *Retention:* 59% of 2008 full-time freshmen returned.

Freshmen *Admission:* 46 applied, 46 admitted, 46 enrolled.

Faculty *Total:* 15, 40% full-time. *Student/faculty ratio:* 14:1.

Majors Administrative assistant and secretarial science; business administration and management; legal administrative assistant/secretary; medical administrative assistant and medical secretary.

Academics *Calendar:* quarters. *Degree:* associate. *Special study options:* distance learning, internships, part-time degree program, summer session for credit.

Student Life *Housing:* college housing not available. *Activities and Organizations:* Student Council.

Financial Aid *Financial aid deadline:* 8/1.

Applying *Options:* electronic application, deferred entrance. *Application fee:* $25. *Required:* high school transcript, interview. *Application deadlines:* rolling (freshmen), rolling (transfers).

Freshman Application Contact Mr. David Andrus, Admissions Representative, Newport Business Institute, 941 West Third Street, Williamsport, PA 17701. *Phone:* 570-326-2869. *Toll-free phone:* 800-962-6971. *Fax:* 570-326-2136. *E-mail:* admissions_NBI@suscom.net.

Northampton Community College

Bethlehem, Pennsylvania www.northampton.edu/

- **State and locally supported** 2-year, founded 1967
- **Suburban** 165-acre campus with easy access to Philadelphia
- **Endowment** $19.8 million
- **Coed,** 11,218 undergraduate students, 48% full-time, 60% women, 40% men

Undergraduates 5,427 full-time, 5,791 part-time. Students come from 28 states and territories, 40 other countries, 2% are from out of state, 9% African American, 2% Asian American or Pacific Islander, 12% Hispanic American, 0.5% Native American, 1% international, 9% transferred in, 2% live on campus.

Freshmen *Admission:* 4,613 applied, 4,613 admitted, 2,614 enrolled.

Faculty *Total:* 688, 18% full-time, 22% with terminal degrees. *Student/faculty ratio:* 24:1.

Majors Accounting technology and bookkeeping; acting; administrative assistant and secretarial science; architectural engineering technology; athletic training; automobile/automotive mechanics technology; biology/biological sciences; biotechnology; business administration and management; business/commerce; CAD/CADD drafting/design technology; chemical technology; chemistry; communication/speech communication and rhetoric; computer and information systems security; computer installation and repair technology; computer programming; computer science; computer systems networking and telecommunications; construction management; criminal justice/safety; culinary arts; dental hygiene; diagnostic medical sonography and ultrasound technology; early childhood education; electrical, electronic and communications engineering technology; electrician; electromechanical technology; engineering; fine/studio arts; fire science; fire services administration; funeral service and mortuary science; general studies; graphic design; heating, air conditioning, ventilation and refrigeration maintenance technology; hotel/motel administration; industrial electronics technology; interior design; journalism; legal administrative assistant/secretary; legal assistant/paralegal; liberal arts and sciences and humanities related; liberal arts and sciences/liberal studies; marketing/marketing management; mathematics; medical administrative assistant and medical secretary; middle school education; nursing (registered nurse training); physics; quality control technology; radio and television broadcasting technology; radiologic technology/science; restaurant/food services management; social work; sport and fitness administration/management; surgical technology; teacher assistant/aide; veterinary/animal health technology; web page, digital/multimedia and information resources design.

Academics *Calendar:* semesters. *Degree:* certificates, diplomas, and associate. *Special study options:* academic remediation for entering students, adult/continuing education programs, advanced placement credit, distance learning, English as a second language, honors programs, independent study, internships, off-campus study, part-time degree program, services for LD students, student-designed majors, study abroad, summer session for credit.

Library Paul & Harriett Mack Library with 90,642 titles, 302 serial subscriptions, 5,274 audiovisual materials, an OPAC, a Web page.

Student Life *Housing Options:* coed. Campus housing is university owned. *Activities and Organizations:* drama/theater group, student-run newspaper, radio station, choral group, Phi Theta Kappa, Student Senate, Acta Non Verba, Dental Hygiene Club, Hispanic American Cultural Club. *Campus security:* 24-hour emergency response devices and patrols, controlled dormitory access. *Student services:* health clinic, personal/psychological counseling.

Athletics Member NJCAA. *Intercollegiate sports:* baseball M, basketball M/W, golf M/W, soccer M, softball W, tennis M/W, volleyball M(c)/W. *Intramural sports:* basketball M/W, bowling M(c)/W(c), cheerleading M(c)/W(c), soccer M/W, volleyball M/W, wrestling M(c).

Costs (2009–10) *Tuition:* area resident $2310 full-time, $77 per credit hour part-time; state resident $4620 full-time, $154 per credit hour part-time; nonresident $6930 full-time, $231 per credit hour part-time. Full-time tuition and fees vary according to course load. Part-time tuition and fees vary according to course load. *Required fees:* $870 full-time, $29 per credit hour part-time. *Room and board:* $6862; room only: $3944. Room and board charges vary according to board plan and housing facility. *Payment plan:* installment. *Waivers:* senior citizens and employees or children of employees.

Financial Aid Of all full-time matriculated undergraduates who enrolled in 2009, 2,060 applied for aid, 1,545 were judged to have need, 587 had their need fully met. 250 Federal Work-Study jobs (averaging $1120). 100 state and other part-time jobs (averaging $1600). In 2009, 400 non-need-based awards were made. *Average percent of need met:* 80%. *Average financial aid package:* $3744. *Average need-based loan:* $3100. *Average need-based gift aid:* $1100. *Average non-need-based aid:* $1000.

Applying *Options:* electronic application, deferred entrance. *Application fee:* $25. *Required for some:* high school transcript, minimum 2.5 GPA, interview, interview required: rad, veterinary, and surgical technologies. *Recommended:* high school transcript. *Application deadlines:* rolling (freshmen), rolling (out-of-state freshmen), rolling (transfers). *Notification:* continuous (freshmen), continuous (out-of-state freshmen), continuous (transfers).

Freshman Application Contact Mr. James McCarthy, Director of Admissions, Northampton Community College, 3835 Green Pond Road, Bethlehem, PA 18020-7599. *Phone:* 610-861-5506. *Fax:* 610-861-5551. *E-mail:* jrmccarthy@northampton.edu.

NORTH CENTRAL INDUSTRIAL TECHNICAL EDUCATION CENTER

Ridgway, Pennsylvania **www.ncitec.edu/**

Director of Admissions Lugene Inzana, Director, North Central Industrial Technical Education Center, 653 Montmorenci Avenue, Ridgway, PA 15853. *Phone:* 814-772-1012. *Toll-free phone:* 800-242-5872. *Fax:* 814-772-1554. *E-mail:* linzana@ncentral.com.

OAKBRIDGE ACADEMY OF ARTS

Lower Burrell, Pennsylvania **www.akvalley.com/oakbridge/**

Freshman Application Contact Ms. Melissa Beck, Admissions Representative, Oakbridge Academy of Arts, 1250 Greensburg Road, Lower Burrell, PA 15068. *Phone:* 724-335-5336. *Toll-free phone:* 800-734-5601. *Fax:* 724-335-3367.

ORLEANS TECHNICAL INSTITUTE

Philadelphia, Pennsylvania **www.orleanstech.edu/**

- **Proprietary** 2-year
- **Urban** campus
- **Coed**

Academics *Calendar:* trimesters. *Degree:* associate. *Special study options:* academic remediation for entering students, internships, part-time degree program, summer session for credit.

Standardized Tests *Required:* CPAt (for admission).

Financial Aid Of all full-time matriculated undergraduates who enrolled in 2008, 5 Federal Work-Study jobs (averaging $4800). *Financial aid deadline:* 8/1.

Applying *Application fee:* $100. *Required:* high school transcript, interview.

Director of Admissions Mr. Gary Bello, Admissions Representative, Orleans Technical Institute, 1845 Walnut Street, 7th Floor, Philadelphia, PA 19103. *Phone:* 215-854-1853.

PACE INSTITUTE

Reading, Pennsylvania **www.paceinstitute.com/**

Director of Admissions Mr. Ed Levandowski, Director of Enrollment Management, Pace Institute, 606 Court Street, Reading, PA 19601. *Phone:* 610-375-1212. *Fax:* 610-375-1924.

PENN COMMERCIAL BUSINESS AND TECHNICAL SCHOOL

Washington, Pennsylvania **www.penncommercial.net/**

- **Proprietary** 2-year, founded 1929
- **Small-town** 1-acre campus with easy access to Pittsburgh
- **Coed**

Academics *Calendar:* quarters. *Degree:* certificates, diplomas, and associate. *Special study options:* academic remediation for entering students, part-time degree program, summer session for credit.

Financial Aid *Financial aid deadline:* 8/1.

Applying *Options:* early admission, deferred entrance. *Application fee:* $100. *Required:* high school transcript.

Director of Admissions Mr. Michael John Joyce, Director of Admissions, Penn Commercial Business and Technical School, 242 Oak Spring Road, Washington, PA 15301. *Phone:* 724-222-5330 Ext. 1. *E-mail:* mjoyce@penncommercial.com.

PENNCO TECH

Bristol, Pennsylvania **www.penncotech.com/**

- **Proprietary** 2-year, founded 1961, part of Pennco Institutes, Inc.
- **Suburban** 7-acre campus with easy access to Philadelphia
- **Coed**

Undergraduates 245 full-time, 155 part-time. Students come from 3 states and territories, 5% are from out of state, 1% transferred in, 2% live on campus.

Faculty *Student/faculty ratio:* 14:1.

Academics *Calendar:* modular. *Degree:* certificates, diplomas, and associate. *Special study options:* academic remediation for entering students, adult/continuing education programs, advanced placement credit, double majors.

Student Life *Campus security:* 24-hour emergency response devices, controlled dormitory access.

Standardized Tests *Required for some:* SAT and SAT Subject Tests or ACT (for admission), IBM Aptitude Test.

Applying *Application fee:* $100. *Required:* interview. *Required for some:* essay or personal statement.

Freshman Application Contact Pennco Tech, 3815 Otter Street, Bristol, PA 19007-3696. *Phone:* 215-785-0111.

PENN FOSTER CAREER SCHOOL

Scranton, Pennsylvania **www.pennfoster.edu/**

Freshman Application Contact Ms. Connie Dempsey, Director of Compliance and Academic Affairs, Penn Foster Career School, 925 Oak Street, Scranton, PA 18515. *Phone:* 570-342-7701 Ext. 4692. *Toll-free phone:* 800-233-4191.

PENN STATE BEAVER

Monaca, Pennsylvania **www.br.psu.edu/**

- **State-related** primarily 2-year, founded 1964, part of Pennsylvania State University
- **Small-town** 91-acre campus with easy access to Pittsburgh
- **Coed,** 851 undergraduate students, 77% full-time, 45% women, 55% men

Undergraduates 658 full-time, 193 part-time. 7% are from out of state, 8% African American, 3% Asian American or Pacific Islander, 3% Hispanic American, 0.2% international, 4% transferred in, 21% live on campus. *Retention:* 69% of 2008 full-time freshmen returned.

Penn State Beaver (continued)

Freshmen *Admission:* 761 applied, 708 admitted, 250 enrolled. *Average high school GPA:* 2.91. *Test scores:* SAT verbal scores over 500: 38%; SAT math scores over 500: 49%; SAT writing scores over 500: 30%; SAT verbal scores over 600: 4%; SAT math scores over 600: 12%; SAT writing scores over 600: 4%.

Faculty *Total:* 58, 57% full-time, 45% with terminal degrees. *Student/faculty ratio:* 18:1.

Majors Accounting; acting; actuarial science; adult and continuing education administration; advertising; aerospace, aeronautical and astronautical engineering; African American/Black studies; agribusiness; agricultural and extension education; agricultural/biological engineering and bioengineering; agricultural business and management related; agricultural mechanization; agriculture; agronomy and crop science; animal sciences; animal sciences related; anthropology; applied economics; archeology; architectural engineering; art; art history, criticism and conservation; art teacher education; Asian studies (East); astronomy; atmospheric sciences and meteorology; biochemistry; biological and biomedical sciences related; biological and physical sciences; biology/biological sciences; biology/biotechnology laboratory technician; biomedical/medical engineering; business administration and management; business/commerce; business/managerial economics; chemical engineering; chemistry; civil engineering; classics and languages, literatures and linguistics; communication and journalism related; communication disorders; communication/speech communication and rhetoric; comparative literature; computer and information sciences; computer engineering; criminal justice/law enforcement administration; economics; electrical, electronics and communications engineering; elementary education; engineering science; English; environmental/environmental health engineering; film/cinema studies; finance; food science; foreign language teacher education; forestry technology; forest sciences and biology; French; geography; geological and earth sciences/geosciences related; geology/earth science; German; graphic design; health/health-care administration; history; horticultural science; hospitality administration related; human development and family studies; human nutrition; industrial engineering; information science/studies; international relations and affairs; Italian; Japanese; Jewish/Judaic studies; journalism; kinesiology and exercise science; labor and industrial relations; landscaping and groundskeeping; Latin American studies; liberal arts and sciences/liberal studies; logistics and materials management; management information systems; marketing/marketing management; materials science; mathematics; mechanical engineering; medical microbiology and bacteriology; medieval and Renaissance studies; mining and mineral engineering; music; natural resources and conservation related; natural resources/conservation; nuclear engineering; nursing (registered nurse training); organizational behavior; parks, recreation and leisure facilities management; petroleum engineering; philosophy; physics; political science and government; premedical studies; psychology; rehabilitation and therapeutic professions related; religious studies; Russian; secondary education; sociology; soil science and agronomy; Spanish; special education; statistics; theater design and technology; toxicology; turf and turfgrass management; visual and performing arts; women's studies.

Academics *Calendar:* semesters. *Degrees:* associate, bachelor's, and master's. *Special study options:* academic remediation for entering students, adult/continuing education programs, advanced placement credit, distance learning, double majors, English as a second language, honors programs, independent study, internships, services for LD students, study abroad, summer session for credit.

Student Life *Housing Options:* coed. Campus housing is university owned. Freshman campus housing is guaranteed. *Activities and Organizations:* drama/theater group, student-run newspaper, radio station. *Campus security:* 24-hour patrols, controlled dormitory access. *Student services:* health clinic, personal/psychological counseling.

Athletics Member NJCAA. *Intercollegiate sports:* baseball M, basketball M, softball M/W, volleyball W. *Intramural sports:* basketball M/W, cheerleading M(c)/W(c), cross-country running M/W, football M, golf M/W, soccer M/W, softball M/W, table tennis M/W.

Standardized Tests *Required:* SAT or ACT (for admission).

Costs (2009–10) *Tuition:* state resident $11,442 full-time, $463 per credit hour part-time; nonresident $17,460 full-time, $728 per credit hour part-time. Full-time tuition and fees vary according to course level, location, and program. Part-time tuition and fees vary according to course level, location, and program. *Required fees:* $808 full-time. *Room and board:* $8170; room only: $4430. Room and board charges vary according to board plan, housing facility, and location.

Financial Aid Of all full-time matriculated undergraduates who enrolled in 2008, 590 applied for aid, 479 were judged to have need, 36 had their need fully met. In 2008, 40 non-need-based awards were made. *Average percent of need met:* 65%. *Average financial aid package:* $8543. *Average need-based loan:* $3743. *Average need-based gift aid:* $5248. *Average non-need-based aid:* $2056. *Average indebtedness upon graduation:* $28,680.

Applying *Options:* electronic application, early admission, deferred entrance. *Application fee:* $50. *Required:* high school transcript. *Required for some:* interview. *Recommended:* essay or personal statement. *Application deadlines:* rolling (freshmen), rolling (transfers). *Notification:* continuous (freshmen), continuous (transfers).

Freshman Application Contact Penn State Beaver, 100 University Drive, Suite 113, Monaca, PA 15061-2799. *Phone:* 814-865-5471.

PENN STATE BRANDYWINE

Media, Pennsylvania **www.brandywine.psu.edu/**

- **State-related** primarily 2-year, founded 1966, part of Pennsylvania State University
- **Small-town** 87-acre campus with easy access to Philadelphia
- **Coed,** 1,607 undergraduate students, 86% full-time, 42% women, 58% men

Undergraduates 1,383 full-time, 224 part-time. 4% are from out of state, 12% African American, 7% Asian American or Pacific Islander, 3% Hispanic American, 0.1% Native American, 0.2% international, 4% transferred in. *Retention:* 71% of 2008 full-time freshmen returned.

Freshmen *Admission:* 1,277 applied, 1,089 admitted, 397 enrolled. *Average high school GPA:* 2.96. *Test scores:* SAT verbal scores over 500: 38%; SAT math scores over 500: 43%; SAT writing scores over 500: 38%; SAT verbal scores over 600: 10%; SAT math scores over 600: 12%; SAT writing scores over 600: 7%; SAT verbal scores over 700: 2%; SAT math scores over 700: 1%; SAT writing scores over 700: 1%.

Faculty *Total:* 133, 44% full-time, 41% with terminal degrees. *Student/faculty ratio:* 17:1.

Majors Accounting; acting; actuarial science; adult and continuing education administration; advertising; aerospace, aeronautical and astronautical engineering; African American/Black studies; agribusiness; agricultural and extension education; agricultural/biological engineering and bioengineering; agricultural business and management related; agricultural mechanization; agriculture; agronomy and crop science; American studies; animal sciences; animal sciences related; anthropology; applied economics; archeology; architectural engineering; art; art history, criticism and conservation; art teacher education; Asian studies (East); astronomy; atmospheric sciences and meteorology; biochemistry; biological and biomedical sciences related; biological and physical sciences; biology/biological sciences; biology/biotechnology laboratory technician; biomedical/medical engineering; business administration and management; business/commerce; business/managerial economics; chemical engineering; chemistry; civil engineering; classics and languages, literatures and linguistics; communication and journalism related; communication disorders; communication/speech communication and rhetoric; comparative literature; computer and information sciences; computer engineering; criminal justice/law enforcement administration; economics; electrical, electronic and communications engineering technology; electrical, electronics and communications engineering; elementary education; engineering science; English; environmental/environmental health engineering; film/cinema studies; finance; food science; foreign language teacher education; forestry technology; forest sciences and biology; French; geography; geological and earth sciences/geosciences related; geology/earth science; German; graphic design; health/health-care administration; history; horticultural science; hospitality administration related; human development and family studies; human nutrition; industrial engineering; information science/studies; international relations and affairs; Italian; Japanese; Jewish/Judaic studies; journalism; kinesiology and exercise science; labor and industrial relations; landscape architecture; landscaping and groundskeeping; Latin American studies; liberal arts and sciences/liberal studies; logistics and materials management; management information systems; marketing/marketing management; materials science; mathematics; mechanical engineering; medical microbiology and bacteriology; medieval and Renaissance studies; mining and mineral engineering; music; natural resources and conservation related; natural resources/conservation; nuclear engineering; nursing (registered nurse training); organizational behavior; parks, recreation and leisure facilities management; petroleum engineering; philosophy; physics; political science and government; premedical studies; psychology; rehabilitation and therapeutic professions related; religious studies; Russian; secondary education; sociology; soil science and agronomy; Spanish; special education; statistics; theater design and technology; turf and turfgrass management; visual and performing arts; women's studies.

Academics *Calendar:* semesters. *Degrees:* certificates, associate, bachelor's, and postbachelor's certificates. *Special study options:* academic remediation for entering students, adult/continuing education programs, advanced placement credit, distance learning, double majors, English as a second language, honors programs, independent study, internships, services for LD students, study abroad, summer session for credit. *ROTC:* Army (c), Air Force (c).

Student Life *Housing:* college housing not available. *Activities and Organizations:* student-run newspaper, choral group. *Campus security:* late-night transport/escort service, part-time trained security personnel. *Student services:* health clinic, personal/psychological counseling, women's center.

Athletics Member NJCAA. *Intercollegiate sports:* baseball M, basketball M/W, soccer M/W, tennis M/W, volleyball W. *Intramural sports:* basketball M/W, cheerleading M(c)/W(c), golf M/W, ice hockey M(c)/W(c), lacrosse M/W, soccer M/W, softball W(c), tennis M/W, volleyball M(c)/W.

Standardized Tests *Required:* SAT or ACT (for admission).

Costs (2009–10) *Tuition:* state resident $11,442 full-time, $463 per credit hour part-time; nonresident $17,460 full-time, $728 per credit hour part-time. Full-time tuition and fees vary according to course level, location, program, and student level. Part-time tuition and fees vary according to course level, course load, location, program, and student level. *Required fees:* $708 full-time.

Financial Aid Of all full-time matriculated undergraduates who enrolled in 2008, 991 applied for aid, 741 were judged to have need, 50 had their need fully met. In 2008, 123 non-need-based awards were made. *Average percent of need met:* 65%. *Average financial aid package:* $8490. *Average need-based loan:* $3741. *Average need-based gift aid:* $5689. *Average non-need-based aid:* $2435. *Average indebtedness upon graduation:* $28,680.

Applying *Options:* electronic application, early admission, deferred entrance. *Application fee:* $50. *Required:* high school transcript. *Required for some:* interview. *Recommended:* essay or personal statement. *Application deadlines:* rolling (freshmen), rolling (transfers). *Notification:* continuous (freshmen), continuous (transfers).

Freshman Application Contact Penn State Brandywine, 25 Yearsley Mill Road, Media, PA 19063-5596. *Phone:* 814-865-5471.

PENN STATE DUBOIS

DuBois, Pennsylvania **www.ds.psu.edu/**

- **State-related** primarily 2-year, founded 1935, part of Pennsylvania State University
- **Small-town** 20-acre campus
- **Coed,** 937 undergraduate students, 81% full-time, 49% women, 51% men

Undergraduates 763 full-time, 174 part-time. 1% are from out of state, 0.9% African American, 0.7% Asian American or Pacific Islander, 2% Hispanic American, 0.4% Native American, 0.3% international, 4% transferred in. *Retention:* 74% of 2008 full-time freshmen returned.

Freshmen *Admission:* 550 applied, 505 admitted, 243 enrolled. *Average high school GPA:* 2.83. *Test scores:* SAT math scores over 500: 37%; SAT writing scores over 500: 22%; SAT math scores over 600: 10%; SAT writing scores over 600: 4%; SAT math scores over 700: 2%.

Faculty *Total:* 94, 49% full-time, 43% with terminal degrees. *Student/faculty ratio:* 13:1.

Majors Accounting; acting; actuarial science; adult and continuing education administration; advertising; aerospace, aeronautical and astronautical engineering; African American/Black studies; agribusiness; agricultural and extension education; agricultural/biological engineering and bioengineering; agricultural business and management related; agricultural mechanization; agriculture; agronomy and crop science; animal sciences; animal sciences related; anthropology; applied economics; archeology; architectural engineering; art; art history, criticism and conservation; art teacher education; Asian studies (East); astronomy; atmospheric sciences and meteorology; biochemistry; biological and biomedical sciences related; biological and physical sciences; biology/biological sciences; biology/biotechnology laboratory technician; biomedical/medical engineering; biomedical technology; business administration and management; business/commerce; business/managerial economics; chemical engineering; chemistry; civil engineering; classics and languages, literatures and linguistics; clinical/medical laboratory technology; communication and journalism related; communication disorders; communication/speech communication and rhetoric; comparative literature; computer and information sciences; computer engineering; criminal justice/law enforcement administration; economics; electrical, electronic and communications engineering technology; electrical, electronics and communications engineering; elementary education; engineering science; English; environmental/environmental health engineering; film/cinema studies; finance; food science; foreign language teacher education; forestry technology; forest sciences and biology; French; geography; geological and earth sciences/geosciences related; geology/earth science; German; graphic design; health/health-care administration; history; horticultural science; hospitality administration related; human development and family studies; human nutrition; industrial engineering; information science/studies; international business/trade/commerce; international relations and affairs; Italian; Japanese; Jewish/Judaic studies; journalism; kinesiology and exercise science; labor and industrial relations; landscaping and groundskeeping; Latin American studies; liberal arts and sciences/liberal studies; management information systems; marketing/marketing management; materials science; mathematics; mechanical engineering; mechanical engineering/mechanical technology; medical microbiology and bacteriology; medieval and Renaissance studies; metallurgical technology; mining and mineral engineering; music; natural resources and conservation related; natural resources/conservation; nuclear engineering; nursing (registered nurse training); occupational therapist assistant; organizational behavior; parks, recreation and leisure facilities management; petroleum engineering; philosophy; physical therapist assistant; physics; political science and government; premedical studies; psychology; rehabilitation and therapeutic professions related; religious studies; Russian; secondary education; sociology; soil science and agronomy; Spanish; special education; statistics; telecommunications technology; theater design and technology; toxicology; turf and turfgrass management; visual and performing arts; wildlife and wildlands science and management; women's studies.

Academics *Calendar:* semesters. *Degrees:* associate, bachelor's, and master's. *Special study options:* academic remediation for entering students, accelerated degree program, adult/continuing education programs, advanced placement credit, distance learning, double majors, honors programs, independent study, internships, services for LD students, student-designed majors, study abroad, summer session for credit.

Student Life *Housing:* college housing not available. *Activities and Organizations:* drama/theater group, student-run newspaper, choral group. *Student services:* health clinic, personal/psychological counseling, women's center.

Athletics Member NJCAA. *Intercollegiate sports:* basketball M, cross-country running M/W, golf M/W, volleyball W. *Intramural sports:* basketball M/W, football M, soccer M/W, table tennis M/W, volleyball M/W.

Standardized Tests *Required:* SAT or ACT (for admission).

Costs (2009–10) *Tuition:* state resident $11,442 full-time, $463 per credit hour part-time; nonresident $17,460 full-time, $728 per credit hour part-time. Full-time tuition and fees vary according to course level, location, program, and student level. Part-time tuition and fees vary according to course level, course load, location, program, and student level. *Required fees:* $688 full-time.

Financial Aid Of all full-time matriculated undergraduates who enrolled in 2008, 608 applied for aid, 545 were judged to have need, 36 had their need fully met. In 2008, 13 non-need-based awards were made. *Average percent of need met:* 68%. *Average financial aid package:* $10,240. *Average need-based loan:* $3877. *Average need-based gift aid:* $6082. *Average non-need-based aid:* $1721. *Average indebtedness upon graduation:* $28,680.

Applying *Options:* electronic application, early admission, deferred entrance. *Application fee:* $50. *Required:* high school transcript. *Required for some:* interview. *Recommended:* essay or personal statement. *Application deadlines:* rolling (freshmen), rolling (transfers). *Notification:* continuous (freshmen), continuous (transfers).

Freshman Application Contact Penn State DuBois, Enrollment Services House, DuBois, PA 15801-3199. *Phone:* 814-865-5471. *Toll-free phone:* 800-346-7627.

PENN STATE FAYETTE, THE EBERLY CAMPUS

Uniontown, Pennsylvania **www.fe.psu.edu/**

- **State-related** primarily 2-year, founded 1934, part of Pennsylvania State University
- **Small-town** 92-acre campus
- **Coed,** 1,095 undergraduate students, 74% full-time, 55% women, 45% men

Undergraduates 807 full-time, 288 part-time. 2% are from out of state, 5% African American, 0.3% Asian American or Pacific Islander, 0.7% Hispanic American, 0.3% Native American, 0.9% international, 4% transferred in. *Retention:* 78% of 2008 full-time freshmen returned.

Freshmen *Admission:* 574 applied, 531 admitted, 233 enrolled. *Average high school GPA:* 3. *Test scores:* SAT math scores over 500: 41%; SAT writing scores over 500: 26%; SAT math scores over 600: 10%; SAT writing scores over 600: 4%; SAT math scores over 700: 1%.

Faculty *Total:* 94, 57% full-time, 40% with terminal degrees. *Student/faculty ratio:* 13:1.

Majors Accounting; acting; actuarial science; adult and continuing education administration; advertising; aerospace, aeronautical and astronautical engineering; African American/Black studies; agribusiness; agricultural and extension education; agricultural/biological engineering and bioengineering; agricultural business and management related; agricultural mechanization; agriculture; agronomy and crop science; animal sciences; animal sciences related; anthropology; applied economics; archeology; architectural engineering; architectural engineering technology; art; art history, criticism and conservation; art teacher education; Asian studies (East); astronomy; atmospheric sciences and meteorology; biochemistry; biological and biomedical sciences related; biological and physical sciences; biology/biological sciences; biology/biotechnology laboratory technician; biomedical/medical engineering; biomedical technology; business administration and management; business/commerce; business/managerial economics; chemical engineering; chemistry; civil engineering; classics and languages, literatures and linguistics; communication and journalism related; communication disorders; communication/speech communication and rhetoric; comparative literature; computer and information sciences; computer engineering; criminal justice/law enforcement administration; criminal justice/safety; economics; electrical, electronic and communications engineering technology; electrical, electronics and communications engineering; elementary education; engineering science; English; environmental/environmental health engineering; film/cinema studies; finance; food science; foreign language teacher education; forestry technology; forest sciences and biology; French; geography; geological and earth sciences/geosciences related; geology/earth science; German; graphic design; health/health-care administration; history; horticultural science; hospitality administration related; human development and family studies; human

Penn State Fayette, The Eberly Campus (continued)

nutrition; industrial engineering; information science/studies; international relations and affairs; Italian; Japanese; Jewish/Judaic studies; journalism; kinesiology and exercise science; labor and industrial relations; landscaping and groundskeeping; Latin American studies; liberal arts and sciences/liberal studies; logistics and materials management; management information systems; manufacturing engineering; marketing/marketing management; materials science; mathematics; mechanical engineering; medical microbiology and bacteriology; medieval and Renaissance studies; metallurgical technology; mining and mineral engineering; natural resources and conservation related; natural resources/conservation; nuclear engineering; nursing (registered nurse training); organizational behavior; parks, recreation and leisure facilities management; petroleum engineering; philosophy; physics; political science and government; premedical studies; psychology; rehabilitation and therapeutic professions related; religious studies; Russian; secondary education; sociology; soil science and agronomy; Spanish; special education; statistics; telecommunications technology; theater design and technology; toxicology; turf and turfgrass management; visual and performing arts; women's studies.

Academics *Calendar:* semesters. *Degrees:* certificates, associate, and bachelor's. *Special study options:* academic remediation for entering students, accelerated degree program, adult/continuing education programs, advanced placement credit, distance learning, double majors, honors programs, independent study, internships, services for LD students, student-designed majors, study abroad, summer session for credit.

Student Life *Housing:* college housing not available. *Activities and Organizations:* drama/theater group. *Campus security:* student patrols, 8-hour patrols by trained security personnel. *Student services:* health clinic, personal/psychological counseling.

Athletics Member NJCAA. *Intercollegiate sports:* baseball M, basketball M, softball W, volleyball W. *Intramural sports:* badminton M/W, basketball M/W, cheerleading M(c)/W(c), equestrian sports M(c)/W(c), football M/W, golf M(c)/W(c), softball M/W, tennis M/W, volleyball M/W, weight lifting M/W.

Standardized Tests *Required:* SAT or ACT (for admission).

Costs (2009–10) *Tuition:* state resident $11,442 full-time, $463 per credit hour part-time; nonresident $17,460 full-time, $728 per credit hour part-time. Full-time tuition and fees vary according to course level, location, program, and student level. Part-time tuition and fees vary according to course level, course load, location, program, and student level. *Required fees:* $708 full-time.

Financial Aid Of all full-time matriculated undergraduates who enrolled in 2008, 689 applied for aid, 614 were judged to have need, 53 had their need fully met. In 2008, 26 non-need-based awards were made. *Average percent of need met:* 68%. *Average financial aid package:* $9610. *Average need-based loan:* $3863. *Average need-based gift aid:* $5852. *Average non-need-based aid:* $2068. *Average indebtedness upon graduation:* $28,680.

Applying *Options:* electronic application, early admission, deferred entrance. *Application fee:* $50. *Required:* high school transcript. *Required for some:* interview. *Recommended:* essay or personal statement. *Application deadlines:* rolling (freshmen), rolling (transfers). *Notification:* continuous (freshmen), continuous (transfers).

Freshman Application Contact Penn State Fayette, The Eberly Campus, PO Box 519, Route 119 North, 108 Williams Building, Uniontown, PA 15401-0519. *Phone:* 814-865-5471. *Toll-free phone:* 877-568-4130.

PENN STATE GREATER ALLEGHENY

McKeesport, Pennsylvania **www.mk.psu.edu/**

- **State-related** primarily 2-year, founded 1947, part of Pennsylvania State University
- **Small-town** 40-acre campus with easy access to Pittsburgh
- **Coed,** 750 undergraduate students, 86% full-time, 44% women, 56% men

Undergraduates 645 full-time, 105 part-time. 12% are from out of state, 25% African American, 4% Asian American or Pacific Islander, 3% Hispanic American, 0.3% Native American, 3% international, 4% transferred in, 28% live on campus. *Retention:* 71% of 2008 full-time freshmen returned.

Freshmen *Admission:* 710 applied, 611 admitted, 262 enrolled. *Average high school GPA:* 2.85. *Test scores:* SAT verbal scores over 500: 34%; SAT math scores over 500: 40%; SAT writing scores over 500: 31%; SAT verbal scores over 600: 7%; SAT math scores over 600: 12%; SAT writing scores over 600: 5%; SAT verbal scores over 700: 1%; SAT math scores over 700: 2%; SAT writing scores over 700: 1%.

Faculty *Total:* 61, 59% full-time, 49% with terminal degrees. *Student/faculty ratio:* 15:1.

Majors Accounting; acting; actuarial science; adult and continuing education administration; advertising; aerospace, aeronautical and astronautical engineering; African American/Black studies; agribusiness; agricultural and extension education; agricultural/biological engineering and bioengineering; agricultural business and management related; agricultural mechanization; agriculture; agronomy and crop science; animal sciences; animal sciences related; anthropology; applied economics; archeology; architectural engineering; art; art history, criticism and conservation; art teacher education; Asian studies (East); astronomy; atmospheric sciences and meteorology; biochemistry; biological and biomedical sciences related; biological and physical sciences; biology/biological sciences; biology/biotechnology laboratory technician; biomedical/medical engineering; business administration and management; business/commerce; business/managerial economics; chemical engineering; chemistry; civil engineering; classics and languages, literatures and linguistics; communication and journalism related; communication disorders; communication/speech communication and rhetoric; comparative literature; computer and information sciences; computer engineering; criminal justice/law enforcement administration; economics; electrical, electronics and communications engineering; elementary education; engineering science; English; environmental/environmental health engineering; film/cinema studies; finance; food science; foreign language teacher education; forestry technology; forest sciences and biology; French; geography; geological and earth sciences/geosciences related; geology/earth science; German; graphic design; health/health-care administration; history; horticultural science; hospitality administration related; human development and family studies; human nutrition; industrial engineering; information science/studies; international relations and affairs; Italian; Japanese; Jewish/Judaic studies; journalism; kinesiology and exercise science; labor and industrial relations; landscaping and groundskeeping; Latin American studies; liberal arts and sciences/liberal studies; logistics and materials management; management information systems; manufacturing engineering; marketing/marketing management; materials science; mathematics; mechanical engineering; medical microbiology and bacteriology; medieval and Renaissance studies; mining and mineral engineering; music; natural resources and conservation related; natural resources/conservation; nuclear engineering; nursing (registered nurse training); organizational behavior; parks, recreation and leisure facilities management; petroleum engineering; philosophy; physics; political science and government; premedical studies; psychology; rehabilitation and therapeutic professions related; religious studies; Russian; secondary education; sociology; soil science and agronomy; Spanish; special education; statistics; theater design and technology; toxicology; turf and turfgrass management; visual and performing arts; women's studies.

Academics *Calendar:* semesters. *Degrees:* certificates, associate, bachelor's, and master's. *Special study options:* academic remediation for entering students, adult/continuing education programs, advanced placement credit, distance learning, double majors, English as a second language, honors programs, independent study, internships, services for LD students, student-designed majors, study abroad, summer session for credit.

Student Life *Housing Options:* coed, disabled students. Campus housing is university owned. Freshman campus housing is guaranteed. *Activities and Organizations:* drama/theater group, student-run newspaper, radio and television station, choral group. *Campus security:* 24-hour patrols, controlled dormitory access. *Student services:* health clinic, personal/psychological counseling, women's center.

Athletics Member NJCAA. *Intercollegiate sports:* baseball M, basketball M, softball W, volleyball W. *Intramural sports:* basketball M/W, cheerleading M(c)/W(c), football M/W, ice hockey M(c), racquetball M/W, skiing (cross-country) M(c)/W(c), skiing (downhill) M(c)/W(c), soccer M(c)/W(c), softball M/W, tennis M/W, volleyball M/W.

Standardized Tests *Required:* SAT or ACT (for admission).

Costs (2009–10) *Tuition:* state resident $11,442 full-time, $463 per credit hour part-time; nonresident $17,460 full-time, $728 per credit hour part-time. Full-time tuition and fees vary according to course level, location, program, and student level. Part-time tuition and fees vary according to course level, course load, location, program, and student level. *Required fees:* $808 full-time. *Room and board:* $8170; room only: $4430. Room and board charges vary according to board plan, housing facility, and location.

Financial Aid Of all full-time matriculated undergraduates who enrolled in 2009, 522 applied for aid, 459 were judged to have need, 17 had their need fully met. 33 Federal Work-Study jobs (averaging $1869). In 2009, 44 non-need-based awards were made. *Average percent of need met:* 68%. *Average financial aid package:* $9931. *Average need-based loan:* $3806. *Average need-based gift aid:* $6158. *Average non-need-based aid:* $3266. *Average indebtedness upon graduation:* $28,680.

Applying *Options:* electronic application, early admission, deferred entrance. *Application fee:* $50. *Required:* high school transcript. *Required for some:* interview. *Recommended:* essay or personal statement. *Application deadlines:* rolling (freshmen), rolling (transfers). *Notification:* continuous (freshmen), continuous (transfers).

Freshman Application Contact Penn State Greater Allegheny, 101 Frable Building, 4000 University Drive, McKeesport, PA 15132-7698. *Phone:* 814-865-5471.

PENN STATE HAZLETON

Hazleton, Pennsylvania **www.hn.psu.edu/**

- **State-related** primarily 2-year, founded 1934, part of Pennsylvania State University
- **Small-town** 98-acre campus
- **Coed,** 1,245 undergraduate students, 96% full-time, 43% women, 57% men

Undergraduates 1,191 full-time, 54 part-time. 28% are from out of state, 11% African American, 4% Asian American or Pacific Islander, 13% Hispanic American, 0.1% Native American, 0.4% international, 3% transferred in, 38% live on campus. *Retention:* 79% of 2008 full-time freshmen returned.

Freshmen *Admission:* 1,514 applied, 1,391 admitted, 564 enrolled. *Average high school GPA:* 2.81. *Test scores:* SAT verbal scores over 500: 34%; SAT math scores over 500: 38%; SAT writing scores over 500: 29%; SAT verbal scores over 600: 4%; SAT math scores over 600: 11%; SAT writing scores over 600: 5%; SAT math scores over 700: 1%.

Faculty *Total:* 85, 64% full-time, 45% with terminal degrees. *Student/faculty ratio:* 19:1.

Majors Accounting; acting; actuarial science; adult and continuing education administration; advertising; aerospace, aeronautical and astronautical engineering; African American/Black studies; agribusiness; agricultural and extension education; agricultural/biological engineering and bioengineering; agricultural business and management related; agricultural mechanization; agriculture; agronomy and crop science; animal sciences; animal sciences related; anthropology; applied economics; archeology; architectural engineering; art; art history, criticism and conservation; art teacher education; Asian studies (East); astronomy; atmospheric sciences and meteorology; biochemistry; biological and biomedical sciences related; biological and physical sciences; biology/biological sciences; biology/biotechnology laboratory technician; biomedical/medical engineering; biomedical technology; business administration and management; business/commerce; business/managerial economics; chemical engineering; chemistry; civil engineering; classics and languages, literatures and linguistics; clinical/medical laboratory technology; communication and journalism related; communication disorders; communication/speech communication and rhetoric; comparative literature; computer and information sciences; computer engineering; criminal justice/law enforcement administration; economics; electrical, electronic and communications engineering technology; electrical, electronics and communications engineering; elementary education; engineering science; English; environmental/environmental health engineering; film/cinema studies; finance; food science; forestry technology; forest sciences and biology; French; geography; geological and earth sciences/geosciences related; geology/earth science; German; graphic design; health/health-care administration; history; horticultural science; hospitality administration related; human development and family studies; human nutrition; industrial engineering; information science/studies; international relations and affairs; Italian; Japanese; Jewish/Judaic studies; journalism; kinesiology and exercise science; labor and industrial relations; landscaping and groundskeeping; Latin American studies; liberal arts and sciences/liberal studies; logistics and materials management; management information systems; manufacturing engineering; marketing/marketing management; materials science; mathematics; mechanical engineering; mechanical engineering/mechanical technology; medical microbiology and bacteriology; medieval and Renaissance studies; metallurgical technology; mining and mineral engineering; music; natural resources and conservation related; natural resources/conservation; nuclear engineering; nursing (registered nurse training); organizational behavior; parks, recreation and leisure facilities management; petroleum engineering; philosophy; physical therapist assistant; physics; political science and government; premedical studies; psychology; rehabilitation and therapeutic professions related; religious studies; Russian; secondary education; sociology; soil science and agronomy; Spanish; special education; statistics; telecommunications technology; theater design and technology; toxicology; turf and turfgrass management; visual and performing arts; women's studies.

Academics *Calendar:* semesters. *Degrees:* associate, bachelor's, and master's. *Special study options:* academic remediation for entering students, accelerated degree program, adult/continuing education programs, advanced placement credit, distance learning, double majors, English as a second language, honors programs, independent study, internships, services for LD students, student-designed majors, study abroad, summer session for credit. *ROTC:* Army (b), Air Force (c).

Student Life *Housing Options:* coed. Campus housing is university owned. Freshman campus housing is guaranteed. *Activities and Organizations:* drama/theater group, student-run newspaper, radio station, choral group. *Campus security:* 24-hour patrols, late-night transport/escort service, controlled dormitory access. *Student services:* health clinic, personal/psychological counseling, women's center, legal services.

Athletics Member NJCAA. *Intercollegiate sports:* baseball M, basketball M/W, cheerleading M/W, soccer M, softball W(s), tennis M/W, volleyball M/W. *Intramural sports:* basketball M/W, skiing (downhill) M(c)/W(c), soccer M/W, volleyball M/W.

Standardized Tests *Required:* SAT or ACT (for admission).

Costs (2009–10) *Tuition:* state resident $11,442 full-time, $463 per credit hour part-time; nonresident $17,460 full-time, $728 per credit hour part-time. Full-time tuition and fees vary according to course level, location, program, and student level. Part-time tuition and fees vary according to course level, course load, location, program, and student level. *Required fees:* $758 full-time. *Room and board:* $8170; room only: $4430. Room and board charges vary according to board plan, housing facility, and location.

Financial Aid Of all full-time matriculated undergraduates who enrolled in 2008, 992 applied for aid, 835 were judged to have need, 39 had their need fully met. In 2008, 92 non-need-based awards were made. *Average percent of need met:* 62%. *Average financial aid package:* $8362. *Average need-based loan:* $3770. *Average need-based gift aid:* $5632. *Average non-need-based aid:* $2366. *Average indebtedness upon graduation:* $28,680.

Applying *Options:* electronic application, early admission, deferred entrance. *Application fee:* $50. *Required:* high school transcript. *Required for some:* interview. *Recommended:* essay or personal statement. *Application deadlines:* rolling (freshmen), rolling (transfers). *Notification:* continuous (freshmen), continuous (transfers).

Freshman Application Contact Penn State Hazleton, 110 Administration Building, 76 University Drive, Hazleton, PA 18202-1291. *Phone:* 814-865-5471. *Toll-free phone:* 800-279-8495.

PENN STATE LEHIGH VALLEY

Fogelsville, Pennsylvania **www.lv.psu.edu/**

- **State-related** primarily 2-year, founded 1912, part of Pennsylvania State University
- **Small-town** 42-acre campus
- **Coed,** 824 undergraduate students, 74% full-time, 44% women, 56% men

Undergraduates 612 full-time, 212 part-time. 3% are from out of state, 3% African American, 9% Asian American or Pacific Islander, 12% Hispanic American, 0.2% Native American, 0.6% international, 4% transferred in. *Retention:* 78% of 2008 full-time freshmen returned.

Freshmen *Admission:* 797 applied, 746 admitted, 227 enrolled. *Average high school GPA:* 2.81. *Test scores:* SAT verbal scores over 500: 37%; SAT math scores over 500: 40%; SAT writing scores over 500: 32%; SAT verbal scores over 600: 10%; SAT math scores over 600: 11%; SAT writing scores over 600: 7%; SAT verbal scores over 700: 1%; SAT math scores over 700: 1%.

Faculty *Total:* 95, 37% full-time, 40% with terminal degrees. *Student/faculty ratio:* 13:1.

Majors Accounting; acting; actuarial science; adult and continuing education administration; advertising; aerospace, aeronautical and astronautical engineering; African American/Black studies; agribusiness; agricultural and extension education; agricultural/biological engineering and bioengineering; agricultural business and management related; agricultural mechanization; agriculture; American studies; animal sciences; animal sciences related; anthropology; applied economics; archeology; architectural engineering; art; art history, criticism and conservation; art teacher education; Asian studies (East); astronomy; atmospheric sciences and meteorology; biochemistry; biological and biomedical sciences related; biological and physical sciences; biology/biological sciences; biology/biotechnology laboratory technician; biomedical/medical engineering; business/commerce; business/managerial economics; chemical engineering; chemistry; civil engineering; classics and languages, literatures and linguistics; communication and journalism related; communication disorders; communication/speech communication and rhetoric; comparative literature; computer and information sciences; computer engineering; criminal justice/law enforcement administration; economics; electrical, electronics and communications engineering; elementary education; engineering science; English; environmental/environmental health engineering; film/cinema studies; finance; food science; foreign languages and literatures; forestry technology; forest sciences and biology; French; geography; geological and earth sciences/geosciences related; geology/earth science; German; graphic design; health/health-care administration; history; horticultural science; hospitality administration related; human development and family studies; human nutrition; industrial engineering; information science/studies; international business/trade/commerce; international relations and affairs; Italian; Japanese; Jewish/Judaic studies; journalism; kinesiology and exercise science; labor and industrial relations; landscape architecture; landscaping and groundskeeping; Latin American studies; liberal arts and sciences/liberal studies; logistics and materials management; management information systems; management sciences and quantitative methods related; marketing/marketing management; materials science; mathematics; mechanical engineering; medical microbiology and bacteriology; medieval and Renaissance studies; mining and mineral engineering; natural resources and conservation related; natural resources/conservation; nuclear engineering; nursing (registered nurse training); organizational behavior; parks, recreation and leisure facilities management; petroleum engineering; philosophy; physics; political science and government; premedical studies; psychology; rehabilitation and therapeutic professions related; religious studies; Russian; secondary education; sociology;

Penn State Lehigh Valley (continued)

soil science and agronomy; Spanish; special education; statistics; technical and business writing; theater design and technology; turf and turfgrass management; visual and performing arts; women's studies.

Academics *Calendar:* semesters. *Degrees:* certificates, associate, and bachelor's. *Special study options:* academic remediation for entering students, accelerated degree program, adult/continuing education programs, advanced placement credit, cooperative education, distance learning, honors programs, independent study, internships, services for LD students, study abroad, summer session for credit. *ROTC:* Army (c).

Student Life *Housing:* college housing not available. *Activities and Organizations:* drama/theater group, student-run newspaper.

Athletics Member NJCAA. *Intercollegiate sports:* baseball M, basketball M/W, bowling M(c)/W(c), cheerleading M/W, cross-country running M/W, football M(c), golf M(c)/W(c), ice hockey M(c)/W(c), skiing (downhill) M(c)/W(c), soccer M(c)/W, tennis M/W, volleyball M(c)/W. *Intramural sports:* badminton M/W, basketball M/W, football M/W, golf M/W, soccer M/W, volleyball M/W.

Standardized Tests *Required:* SAT or ACT (for admission).

Costs (2009–10) *Tuition:* state resident $11,442 full-time, $463 per credit hour part-time; nonresident $17,460 full-time, $728 per credit hour part-time. Full-time tuition and fees vary according to course level, location, program, and student level. Part-time tuition and fees vary according to course level, course load, location, program, and student level. *Required fees:* $808 full-time.

Financial Aid Of all full-time matriculated undergraduates who enrolled in 2009, 477 applied for aid, 359 were judged to have need, 18 had their need fully met. 19 Federal Work-Study jobs (averaging $1907). In 2009, 32 non-need-based awards were made. *Average percent of need met:* 60%. *Average financial aid package:* $8078. *Average need-based loan:* $3968. *Average need-based gift aid:* $5355. *Average non-need-based aid:* $1940. *Average indebtedness upon graduation:* $28,680.

Applying *Options:* electronic application, early admission, deferred entrance. *Application fee:* $50. *Required:* high school transcript. *Application deadlines:* rolling (freshmen), rolling (transfers). *Notification:* continuous (freshmen), continuous (transfers).

Freshman Application Contact Penn State Lehigh Valley, 8380 Mohr Lane, Academic Building, Fogelsville, PA 18051-9999. *Phone:* 814-865-5471.

PENN STATE MONT ALTO

Mont Alto, Pennsylvania — www.ma.psu.edu/

- **State-related** primarily 2-year, founded 1929, part of Pennsylvania State University
- **Small-town** 64-acre campus
- **Coed,** 1,174 undergraduate students, 75% full-time, 57% women, 43% men

Undergraduates 885 full-time, 289 part-time. 18% are from out of state, 13% African American, 3% Asian American or Pacific Islander, 4% Hispanic American, 0.4% Native American, 0.2% international, 6% transferred in, 37% live on campus. *Retention:* 76% of 2008 full-time freshmen returned.

Freshmen *Admission:* 900 applied, 810 admitted, 426 enrolled. *Average high school GPA:* 2.93. *Test scores:* SAT verbal scores over 500: 36%; SAT math scores over 500: 45%; SAT writing scores over 500: 30%; SAT verbal scores over 600: 7%; SAT math scores over 600: 13%; SAT writing scores over 600: 3%; SAT verbal scores over 700: 1%.

Faculty *Total:* 117, 50% full-time, 35% with terminal degrees. *Student/faculty ratio:* 13:1.

Majors Accounting; acting; actuarial science; adult and continuing education administration; advertising; aerospace, aeronautical and astronautical engineering; African American/Black studies; agribusiness; agricultural and extension education; agricultural/biological engineering and bioengineering; agricultural business and management related; agricultural mechanization; agriculture; agronomy and crop science; animal sciences; animal sciences related; anthropology; applied economics; archeology; architectural engineering; art; art history, criticism and conservation; art teacher education; Asian studies (East); astronomy; atmospheric sciences and meteorology; biochemistry; biological and biomedical sciences related; biological and physical sciences; biology/biological sciences; biology/biotechnology laboratory technician; biomedical/medical engineering; business administration and management; business/commerce; business/managerial economics; chemical engineering; chemistry; civil engineering; classics and languages, literatures and linguistics; communication and journalism related; communication disorders; communication/speech communication and rhetoric; comparative literature; computer and information sciences; computer engineering; criminal justice/law enforcement administration; economics; electrical, electronics and communications engineering; elementary education; engineering science; English; environmental/environmental health engineering; film/cinema studies; finance; food science; foreign language teacher education; forestry technology; forest sciences and biology; French; geography; geological and earth sciences/geosciences related; geology/earth science; German; graphic design; health/health-care administration; history; horticultural science; hospitality administration related; human development and family studies; human nutrition; industrial engineering; information science/studies; international relations and affairs; Italian; Japanese; Jewish/Judaic studies; journalism; kinesiology and exercise science; labor and industrial relations; landscaping and groundskeeping; Latin American studies; liberal arts and sciences/liberal studies; management information systems; marketing/marketing management; materials science; mathematics; mechanical engineering; medical microbiology and bacteriology; medieval and Renaissance studies; mining and mineral engineering; music; natural resources and conservation related; natural resources/conservation; nuclear engineering; nursing (registered nurse training); occupational therapist assistant; occupational therapy; organizational behavior; parks, recreation and leisure facilities management; petroleum engineering; philosophy; physical therapist assistant; physics; political science and government; premedical studies; psychology; rehabilitation and therapeutic professions related; religious studies; Russian; secondary education; sociology; soil science and agronomy; Spanish; special education; statistics; theater design and technology; toxicology; turf and turfgrass management; visual and performing arts; women's studies.

Academics *Calendar:* semesters. *Degrees:* associate and bachelor's. *Special study options:* academic remediation for entering students, accelerated degree program, adult/continuing education programs, advanced placement credit, distance learning, double majors, honors programs, independent study, internships, services for LD students, study abroad, summer session for credit. *ROTC:* Army (c).

Student Life *Housing Options:* coed, disabled students. Campus housing is university owned. Freshman campus housing is guaranteed. *Activities and Organizations:* drama/theater group, student-run newspaper. *Campus security:* 24-hour patrols, controlled dormitory access. *Student services:* health clinic, women's center.

Athletics Member NJCAA. *Intercollegiate sports:* basketball M/W, cheerleading M/W, cross-country running M/W, golf M/W, soccer M/W, softball W, tennis M/W, volleyball W. *Intramural sports:* badminton M/W, basketball M/W, cheerleading M(c)/W(c), racquetball M/W, soccer M/W, softball W, volleyball M/W.

Standardized Tests *Required:* SAT or ACT (for admission).

Costs (2009–10) *Tuition:* state resident $11,442 full-time, $463 per credit hour part-time; nonresident $17,460 full-time, $728 per credit hour part-time. Full-time tuition and fees vary according to course level, location, program, and student level. Part-time tuition and fees vary according to course level, course load, location, program, and student level. *Required fees:* $808 full-time. *Room and board:* $8170; room only: $4430. Room and board charges vary according to board plan, housing facility, and location.

Financial Aid Of all full-time matriculated undergraduates who enrolled in 2008, 703 applied for aid, 575 were judged to have need, 42 had their need fully met. In 2008, 48 non-need-based awards were made. *Average percent of need met:* 65%. *Average financial aid package:* $8708. *Average need-based loan:* $3659. *Average need-based gift aid:* $5101. *Average non-need-based aid:* $2697. *Average indebtedness upon graduation:* $28,680.

Applying *Options:* electronic application, early admission, deferred entrance. *Application fee:* $50. *Required:* high school transcript. *Required for some:* interview. *Recommended:* essay or personal statement. *Application deadlines:* rolling (freshmen), rolling (transfers). *Notification:* continuous (freshmen), continuous (transfers).

Freshman Application Contact Penn State Mont Alto, 1 Campus Drive, Mont Alto, PA 17237-9703. *Phone:* 814-865-5471. *Toll-free phone:* 800-392-6173.

PENN STATE NEW KENSINGTON

New Kensington, Pennsylvania — www.nk.psu.edu/

- **State-related** primarily 2-year, founded 1958, part of Pennsylvania State University
- **Small-town** 71-acre campus with easy access to Pittsburgh
- **Coed,** 819 undergraduate students, 75% full-time, 40% women, 60% men

Undergraduates 617 full-time, 202 part-time. 1% are from out of state, 2% African American, 0.7% Asian American or Pacific Islander, 1% Hispanic American, 0.1% Native American, 0.3% international, 6% transferred in. *Retention:* 76% of 2008 full-time freshmen returned.

Freshmen *Admission:* 476 applied, 422 admitted, 184 enrolled. *Average high school GPA:* 2.87. *Test scores:* SAT verbal scores over 500: 36%; SAT math scores over 500: 51%; SAT writing scores over 500: 38%; SAT verbal scores over 600: 3%; SAT math scores over 600: 9%; SAT writing scores over 600: 7%.

Faculty *Total:* 74, 53% full-time, 43% with terminal degrees. *Student/faculty ratio:* 14:1.

Majors Accounting; acting; actuarial science; adult and continuing education administration; advertising; aerospace, aeronautical and astronautical engineering; African American/Black studies; agribusiness; agricultural and extension education; agricultural/biological engineering and bioengineering; agricultural business and management related; agricultural mechanization; agriculture; agronomy and crop science; animal sciences; animal sciences related; anthropology; applied economics; archeology; architectural engineering; art; art history, criticism and conservation; art teacher education; Asian studies (East); astronomy; atmospheric sciences and meteorology; biochemistry; biological and biomedical sciences related; biological and physical sciences; biology/biological sciences; biology/biotechnology laboratory technician; biomedical/medical engineering; biomedical technology; business administration and management; business/commerce; business/managerial economics; chemical engineering; chemistry; civil engineering; classics and languages, literatures and linguistics; communication and journalism related; communication disorders; communication/speech communication and rhetoric; comparative literature; computer and information sciences; computer engineering; computer engineering technology; criminal justice/law enforcement administration; economics; electrical, electronic and communications engineering technology; electrical, electronics and communications engineering; elementary education; engineering science; English; environmental/environmental health engineering; film/cinema studies; finance; food science; forestry technology; forest sciences and biology; French; geography; geological and earth sciences/geosciences related; geology/earth science; German; graphic design; health/health-care administration; history; horticultural science; hospitality administration related; human development and family studies; human nutrition; industrial engineering; information science/studies; international relations and affairs; Italian; Japanese; Jewish/Judaic studies; journalism; kinesiology and exercise science; labor and industrial relations; landscaping and groundskeeping; Latin American studies; liberal arts and sciences/liberal studies; logistics and materials management; management information systems; marketing/marketing management; materials science; mathematics; mechanical engineering; mechanical engineering/mechanical technology; medical microbiology and bacteriology; medical radiologic technology; medieval and Renaissance studies; metallurgical technology; mining and mineral engineering; music; natural resources and conservation related; natural resources/conservation; nuclear engineering; nursing (registered nurse training); organizational behavior; parks, recreation and leisure facilities management; petroleum engineering; philosophy; physics; political science and government; premedical studies; psychology; rehabilitation and therapeutic professions related; religious studies; Russian; secondary education; sociology; soil science and agronomy; Spanish; special education; statistics; telecommunications technology; theater design and technology; toxicology; turf and turfgrass management; visual and performing arts; women's studies.

Academics *Calendar:* semesters. *Degrees:* certificates, associate, bachelor's, and master's. *Special study options:* academic remediation for entering students, adult/continuing education programs, advanced placement credit, distance learning, double majors, external degree program, honors programs, independent study, internships, services for LD students, study abroad, summer session for credit. *ROTC:* Air Force (c).

Student Life *Housing:* college housing not available. *Activities and Organizations:* drama/theater group, student-run newspaper, choral group. *Campus security:* part-time trained security personnel. *Student services:* health clinic, women's center.

Athletics Member NJCAA. *Intercollegiate sports:* baseball M, basketball M/W, cheerleading M/W, golf M/W, softball W, volleyball W. *Intramural sports:* badminton M/W, basketball M/W, bowling M/W, cheerleading M(c)/W(c), football M/W, ice hockey M(c)/W(c), racquetball M/W, skiing (downhill) M(c)/W(c), soccer M/W, softball W, volleyball M/W.

Standardized Tests *Required:* SAT or ACT (for admission).

Costs (2009–10) *Tuition:* state resident $11,442 full-time, $463 per credit hour part-time; nonresident $17,460 full-time, $728 per credit hour part-time. Full-time tuition and fees vary according to course level, location, program, and student level. Part-time tuition and fees vary according to course level, course load, location, program, and student level. *Required fees:* $758 full-time.

Financial Aid Of all full-time matriculated undergraduates who enrolled in 2008, 503 applied for aid, 404 were judged to have need, 31 had their need fully met. In 2008, 35 non-need-based awards were made. *Average percent of need met:* 66%. *Average financial aid package:* $8530. *Average need-based loan:* $3907. *Average need-based gift aid:* $4999. *Average non-need-based aid:* $2443. *Average indebtedness upon graduation:* $28,680.

Applying *Options:* electronic application, early admission, deferred entrance. *Application fee:* $50. *Required:* high school transcript. *Required for some:* interview. *Recommended:* essay or personal statement. *Application deadlines:* rolling (freshmen), rolling (transfers). *Notification:* continuous (freshmen), continuous (transfers).

Freshman Application Contact Penn State New Kensington, 3550 7th Street Road, Route 780, New Kensington, PA 15068-1765. *Phone:* 814-865-5471. *Toll-free phone:* 888-968-7297.

PENN STATE SCHUYLKILL

Schuylkill Haven, Pennsylvania **www.sl.psu.edu/**

- **State-related** primarily 2-year, founded 1934, part of Pennsylvania State University
- **Small-town** 42-acre campus
- **Coed,** 1,007 undergraduate students, 85% full-time, 55% women, 45% men

Undergraduates 859 full-time, 148 part-time. 16% are from out of state, 29% African American, 2% Asian American or Pacific Islander, 5% Hispanic American, 0.2% Native American, 4% transferred in, 25% live on campus. *Retention:* 79% of 2008 full-time freshmen returned.

Freshmen *Admission:* 894 applied, 766 admitted, 348 enrolled. *Average high school GPA:* 2.74. *Test scores:* SAT verbal scores over 500: 20%; SAT math scores over 500: 21%; SAT writing scores over 500: 18%; SAT verbal scores over 600: 4%; SAT math scores over 600: 3%; SAT writing scores over 600: 2%; SAT verbal scores over 700: 1%.

Faculty *Total:* 77, 56% full-time, 48% with terminal degrees. *Student/faculty ratio:* 17:1.

Majors Accounting; acting; actuarial science; adult and continuing education administration; advertising; aerospace, aeronautical and astronautical engineering; African American/Black studies; agribusiness; agricultural and extension education; agricultural/biological engineering and bioengineering; agricultural business and management related; agricultural mechanization; agriculture; American studies; animal sciences; animal sciences related; anthropology; applied economics; archeology; architectural engineering; art; art history, criticism and conservation; art teacher education; Asian studies (East); astronomy; atmospheric sciences and meteorology; biochemistry; biological and biomedical sciences related; biological and physical sciences; biology/biological sciences; biology/biotechnology laboratory technician; biomedical/medical engineering; biomedical technology; business/commerce; business/managerial economics; chemical engineering; chemistry; civil engineering; classics and languages, literatures and linguistics; clinical/medical laboratory technology; communication and journalism related; communication disorders; communication/speech communication and rhetoric; comparative literature; computer and information sciences; computer engineering; criminal justice/law enforcement administration; criminal justice/safety; economics; electrical, electronic and communications engineering technology; electrical, electronics and communications engineering; elementary education; engineering science; English; environmental/environmental health engineering; film/cinema studies; finance; food science; forestry technology; forest sciences and biology; French; geography; geological and earth sciences/geosciences related; geology/earth science; German; graphic design; health/health-care administration; history; horticultural science; hospitality administration related; human development and family studies; human nutrition; industrial engineering; information science/studies; international business/trade/commerce; international relations and affairs; Italian; Japanese; Jewish/Judaic studies; journalism; kinesiology and exercise science; labor and industrial relations; landscape architecture; landscaping and groundskeeping; Latin American studies; liberal arts and sciences/liberal studies; logistics and materials management; management information systems; management sciences and quantitative methods related; marketing/marketing management; materials science; mathematics; mechanical engineering; medical microbiology and bacteriology; medical radiologic technology; medieval and Renaissance studies; metallurgical technology; mining and mineral engineering; natural resources and conservation related; natural resources/conservation; nuclear engineering; nursing (registered nurse training); organizational behavior; parks, recreation and leisure facilities management; petroleum engineering; philosophy; physics; political science and government; premedical studies; psychology; rehabilitation and therapeutic professions related; religious studies; Russian; secondary education; sociology; soil science and agronomy; Spanish; special education; statistics; telecommunications technology; theater design and technology; turf and turfgrass management; visual and performing arts; women's studies.

Academics *Calendar:* semesters. *Degrees:* certificates, associate, and bachelor's (bachelor's degree programs completed at the Harrisburg campus). *Special study options:* academic remediation for entering students, accelerated degree program, adult/continuing education programs, advanced placement credit, cooperative education, distance learning, double majors, honors programs, independent study, internships, services for LD students, student-designed majors, study abroad, summer session for credit.

Student Life *Housing Options:* disabled students. Campus housing is provided by a third party. Freshman campus housing is guaranteed. *Activities and Organizations:* drama/theater group, student-run newspaper, choral group. *Campus security:* 24-hour patrols, controlled dormitory access.

Athletics Member NJCAA. *Intercollegiate sports:* basketball M, cross-country running M/W, golf M, soccer M, softball W, volleyball W. *Intramural sports:* basketball M/W, football M, soccer M/W, softball M/W, table tennis M/W, volleyball M/W.

Standardized Tests *Required:* SAT or ACT (for admission).

Costs (2009–10) *Tuition:* state resident $11,442 full-time, $463 per credit hour part-time; nonresident $17,460 full-time, $728 per credit hour part-time. Full-

Penn State Schuylkill (continued)
time tuition and fees vary according to course level, location, program, and student level. Part-time tuition and fees vary according to course level, course load, location, program, and student level. *Required fees:* $708 full-time.

Financial Aid Of all full-time matriculated undergraduates who enrolled in 2008, 761 applied for aid, 680 were judged to have need, 32 had their need fully met. In 2008, 15 non-need-based awards were made. *Average percent of need met:* 68%. *Average financial aid package:* $10,359. *Average need-based loan:* $3761. *Average need-based gift aid:* $6246. *Average non-need-based aid:* $2641. *Average indebtedness upon graduation:* $28,680.

Applying *Options:* electronic application, early admission, deferred entrance. *Application fee:* $50. *Required:* high school transcript. *Application deadlines:* rolling (freshmen), rolling (transfers). *Notification:* continuous (freshmen), continuous (transfers).

Freshman Application Contact Penn State Schuylkill, 200 University Drive, A102 Administration Building, Schuylkill Haven, PA 17972-2208. *Phone:* 814-865-5471.

PENN STATE SHENANGO

Sharon, Pennsylvania **www.shenango.psu.edu/**

- **State-related** primarily 2-year, founded 1965, part of Pennsylvania State University
- **Small-town** 14-acre campus
- **Coed,** 816 undergraduate students, 60% full-time, 69% women, 31% men

Undergraduates 493 full-time, 323 part-time. 14% are from out of state, 7% African American, 0.8% Asian American or Pacific Islander, 2% Hispanic American, 0.2% Native American, 0.3% international, 7% transferred in. *Retention:* 57% of 2008 full-time freshmen returned.

Freshmen *Admission:* 273 applied, 211 admitted, 139 enrolled. *Average high school GPA:* 2.86. *Test scores:* SAT verbal scores over 500: 38%; SAT math scores over 500: 37%; SAT writing scores over 500: 16%; SAT verbal scores over 600: 4%; SAT math scores over 600: 7%; SAT writing scores over 600: 4%.

Faculty *Total:* 73, 42% full-time, 30% with terminal degrees. *Student/faculty ratio:* 13:1.

Majors Accounting; acting; actuarial science; adult and continuing education administration; advertising; aerospace, aeronautical and astronautical engineering; African American/Black studies; agribusiness; agricultural and extension education; agricultural/biological engineering and bioengineering; agricultural business and management related; agricultural mechanization; agriculture; agronomy and crop science; animal sciences; animal sciences related; anthropology; applied economics; archeology; architectural engineering; art; art history, criticism and conservation; art teacher education; Asian studies (East); astronomy; atmospheric sciences and meteorology; biochemistry; biological and biomedical sciences related; biological and physical sciences; biology/biological sciences; biology/biotechnology laboratory technician; biomedical/medical engineering; biomedical technology; business administration and management; business/commerce; business/managerial economics; chemical engineering; chemistry; civil engineering; classics and languages, literatures and linguistics; communication and journalism related; communication disorders; communication/speech communication and rhetoric; comparative literature; computer and information sciences; computer engineering; criminal justice/law enforcement administration; economics; electrical, electronic and communications engineering technology; electrical, electronics and communications engineering; elementary education; engineering science; English; environmental/environmental health engineering; film/cinema studies; finance; food science; foreign language teacher education; forestry technology; forest sciences and biology; French; geography; geological and earth sciences/geosciences related; geology/earth science; German; graphic design; health/health-care administration; history; horticultural science; hospitality administration related; human development and family studies; human nutrition; industrial engineering; information science/studies; international relations and affairs; Italian; Japanese; Jewish/Judaic studies; journalism; kinesiology and exercise science; labor and industrial relations; landscaping and groundskeeping; Latin American studies; liberal arts and sciences/liberal studies; logistics and materials management; management information systems; marketing/marketing management; materials science; mathematics; mechanical engineering; mechanical engineering/mechanical technology; medical microbiology and bacteriology; medieval and Renaissance studies; metallurgical technology; mining and mineral engineering; music; natural resources and conservation related; natural resources/conservation; nuclear engineering; nursing (registered nurse training); organizational behavior; parks, recreation and leisure facilities management; petroleum engineering; philosophy; physical therapist assistant; physics; political science and government; premedical studies; psychology; rehabilitation and therapeutic professions related; religious studies; Russian; secondary education; sociology; soil science and agronomy; Spanish; special education; statistics; telecommunications technology; theater design and technology; toxicology; turf and turfgrass management; visual and performing arts; women's studies.

Academics *Calendar:* semesters. *Degrees:* certificates, associate, and bachelor's. *Special study options:* academic remediation for entering students, accelerated degree program, adult/continuing education programs, advanced placement credit, distance learning, double majors, honors programs, independent study, internships, services for LD students, student-designed majors, study abroad, summer session for credit.

Student Life *Housing:* college housing not available. *Activities and Organizations:* choral group. *Campus security:* part-time trained security personnel. *Student services:* health clinic, women's center.

Athletics *Intramural sports:* basketball M(c)/W, bowling M/W, football M(c), golf M/W, softball M/W, tennis M/W, volleyball M/W.

Standardized Tests *Required:* SAT or ACT (for admission).

Costs (2009–10) *Tuition:* state resident $11,442 full-time, $463 per credit hour part-time; nonresident $17,460 full-time, $728 per credit hour part-time. Full-time tuition and fees vary according to course level, location, program, and student level. Part-time tuition and fees vary according to course level, course load, location, program, and student level. *Required fees:* $608 full-time.

Financial Aid Of all full-time matriculated undergraduates who enrolled in 2008, 437 applied for aid, 403 were judged to have need, 20 had their need fully met. In 2008, 21 non-need-based awards were made. *Average percent of need met:* 68%. *Average financial aid package:* $10,743. *Average need-based loan:* $3876. *Average need-based gift aid:* $6000. *Average non-need-based aid:* $2234. *Average indebtedness upon graduation:* $28,680.

Applying *Options:* electronic application, early admission, deferred entrance. *Application fee:* $50. *Required:* high school transcript. *Required for some:* interview. *Recommended:* essay or personal statement. *Application deadlines:* rolling (freshmen), rolling (transfers). *Notification:* continuous (freshmen), continuous (transfers).

Freshman Application Contact Penn State Shenango, 147 Shenango Avenue, Sharon, PA 16146-1597. *Phone:* 814-865-5471.

PENN STATE WILKES-BARRE

Lehman, Pennsylvania **www.wb.psu.edu/**

- **State-related** primarily 2-year, founded 1916, part of Pennsylvania State University
- **Rural** 156-acre campus
- **Coed,** 672 undergraduate students, 86% full-time, 31% women, 69% men

Undergraduates 578 full-time, 94 part-time. 5% are from out of state, 3% African American, 2% Asian American or Pacific Islander, 2% Hispanic American, 0.3% Native American, 4% transferred in. *Retention:* 73% of 2008 full-time freshmen returned.

Freshmen *Admission:* 609 applied, 554 admitted, 204 enrolled. *Average high school GPA:* 2.95. *Test scores:* SAT verbal scores over 500: 40%; SAT math scores over 500: 48%; SAT writing scores over 500: 28%; SAT verbal scores over 600: 5%; SAT math scores over 600: 15%; SAT writing scores over 600: 3%; SAT math scores over 700: 1%.

Faculty *Total:* 56, 64% full-time, 46% with terminal degrees. *Student/faculty ratio:* 15:1.

Majors Accounting; acting; actuarial science; adult and continuing education administration; advertising; aerospace, aeronautical and astronautical engineering; African American/Black studies; agribusiness; agricultural and extension education; agricultural/biological engineering and bioengineering; agricultural business and management related; agricultural mechanization; agriculture; agronomy and crop science; animal sciences; animal sciences related; anthropology; applied economics; archeology; architectural engineering; art; art history, criticism and conservation; art teacher education; astronomy; atmospheric sciences and meteorology; biochemistry; biological and biomedical sciences related; biological and physical sciences; biology/biological sciences; biology/biotechnology laboratory technician; biomedical/medical engineering; business administration and management; business/commerce; business/managerial economics; chemical engineering; chemistry; civil engineering; classics and languages, literatures and linguistics; communication and journalism related; communication disorders; communication/speech communication and rhetoric; comparative literature; computer and information sciences; computer engineering; criminal justice/law enforcement administration; criminal justice/safety; economics; electrical, electronic and communications engineering technology; electrical, electronics and communications engineering; elementary education; engineering science; English; environmental/environmental health engineering; film/cinema studies; finance; food science; forestry technology; forest sciences and biology; French; geography; geological and earth sciences/geosciences related; geology/earth science; German; graphic design; health/health-care administration; history; horticultural science; hospitality administration related; human development and family studies; human nutrition; industrial engineering; information science/studies; international relations and affairs; Italian; Japanese; Jewish/Judaic studies; journalism; kinesiology and exercise science; labor and industrial relations; landscape architecture; landscaping and groundskeeping;

Latin American studies; liberal arts and sciences/liberal studies; management information systems; manufacturing engineering; marketing/marketing management; materials science; mathematics; mechanical engineering; medical microbiology and bacteriology; medieval and Renaissance studies; metallurgical technology; mining and mineral engineering; music; natural resources and conservation related; natural resources/conservation; nuclear engineering; nursing (registered nurse training); organizational behavior; parks, recreation and leisure facilities management; petroleum engineering; philosophy; physics; political science and government; premedical studies; psychology; rehabilitation and therapeutic professions related; religious studies; Russian; secondary education; sociology; soil science and agronomy; Spanish; special education; statistics; survey technology; telecommunications technology; theater design and technology; toxicology; turf and turfgrass management; visual and performing arts; women's studies.

Academics *Calendar:* semesters. *Degrees:* certificates, associate, bachelor's, and postbachelor's certificates. *Special study options:* academic remediation for entering students, accelerated degree program, adult/continuing education programs, advanced placement credit, distance learning, double majors, honors programs, independent study, internships, services for LD students, student-designed majors, study abroad, summer session for credit. *ROTC:* Army (c), Air Force (c).

Student Life *Housing:* college housing not available. *Activities and Organizations:* student-run newspaper, radio station. *Campus security:* part-time trained security personnel. *Student services:* health clinic, personal/psychological counseling.

Athletics Member NJCAA. *Intercollegiate sports:* baseball M, basketball M, cross-country running M/W, golf M/W, soccer M/W, volleyball W. *Intramural sports:* basketball M/W, bowling M(c)/W(c), cheerleading M(c)/W(c), football M, racquetball M/W, softball W, volleyball M(c)/W.

Standardized Tests *Required:* SAT or ACT (for admission).

Costs (2009–10) *Tuition:* state resident $11,442 full-time, $463 per credit hour part-time; nonresident $17,460 full-time, $728 per credit hour part-time. Full-time tuition and fees vary according to course level, location, program, and student level. Part-time tuition and fees vary according to course level, course load, location, program, and student level. *Required fees:* $708 full-time.

Financial Aid Of all full-time matriculated undergraduates who enrolled in 2009, 430 applied for aid, 334 were judged to have need, 27 had their need fully met. 15 Federal Work-Study jobs (averaging $1750). In 2009, 38 non-need-based awards were made. *Average percent of need met:* 67%. *Average financial aid package:* $8787. *Average need-based loan:* $3806. *Average need-based gift aid:* $5573. *Average non-need-based aid:* $3006. *Average indebtedness upon graduation:* $28,680.

Applying *Options:* electronic application, early admission, deferred entrance. *Application fee:* $50. *Required:* high school transcript. *Required for some:* interview. *Recommended:* essay or personal statement. *Application deadlines:* rolling (freshmen), rolling (transfers). *Notification:* continuous (freshmen), continuous (transfers).

Freshman Application Contact Penn State Wilkes-Barre, PO Box PSU, Old Route 115, Lehman, PA 18627-9999. *Phone:* 814-865-5471. *Toll-free phone:* 800-966-6613.

PENN STATE WORTHINGTON SCRANTON

Dunmore, Pennsylvania **www.sn.psu.edu/**

- **State-related** primarily 2-year, founded 1923, part of Pennsylvania State University
- **Small-town** 43-acre campus
- **Coed,** 1,388 undergraduate students, 78% full-time, 51% women, 49% men

Undergraduates 1,084 full-time, 304 part-time. 1% are from out of state, 1% African American, 2% Asian American or Pacific Islander, 3% Hispanic American, 0.4% Native American, 4% transferred in. *Retention:* 74% of 2008 full-time freshmen returned.

Freshmen *Admission:* 915 applied, 812 admitted, 353 enrolled. *Average high school GPA:* 2.83. *Test scores:* SAT verbal scores over 500: 31%; SAT math scores over 500: 30%; SAT verbal scores over 600: 5%; SAT math scores over 600: 6%.

Faculty *Total:* 103, 55% full-time, 42% with terminal degrees. *Student/faculty ratio:* 16:1.

Majors Accounting; acting; actuarial science; adult and continuing education administration; advertising; aerospace, aeronautical and astronautical engineering; African American/Black studies; agribusiness; agricultural and extension education; agricultural/biological engineering and bioengineering; agricultural business and management related; agricultural mechanization; agriculture; agronomy and crop science; American studies; animal sciences; animal sciences related; anthropology; applied economics; archeology; architectural engineering; architectural engineering technology; art; art history, criticism and conservation; art teacher education; Asian studies (East); astronomy; atmospheric sciences and meteorology; biochemistry; biological and biomedical sciences related; biological and physical sciences; biology/biological sciences; biology/biotechnology laboratory technician; biomedical/medical engineering; business administration and management; business/commerce; business/managerial economics; chemical engineering; chemistry; civil engineering; classics and languages, literatures and linguistics; communication and journalism related; communication disorders; communication/speech communication and rhetoric; comparative literature; computer and information sciences; computer engineering; criminal justice/law enforcement administration; economics; electrical, electronic and communications engineering technology; electrical, electronics and communications engineering; elementary education; engineering science; English; environmental/environmental health engineering; film/cinema studies; finance; food science; foreign language teacher education; forestry technology; forest sciences and biology; French; geography; geological and earth sciences/geosciences related; geology/earth science; German; graphic design; health/health-care administration; history; horticultural science; hospitality administration related; human development and family studies; human nutrition; industrial engineering; information science/studies; international relations and affairs; Italian; Japanese; Jewish/Judaic studies; journalism; kinesiology and exercise science; labor and industrial relations; landscaping and groundskeeping; Latin American studies; liberal arts and sciences/liberal studies; management information systems; marketing/marketing management; materials science; mathematics; mechanical engineering; medical microbiology and bacteriology; medieval and Renaissance studies; mining and mineral engineering; music; natural resources and conservation related; natural resources/conservation; nuclear engineering; nursing (registered nurse training); organizational behavior; parks, recreation and leisure facilities management; petroleum engineering; philosophy; physics; political science and government; premedical studies; psychology; rehabilitation and therapeutic professions related; religious studies; Russian; secondary education; sociology; soil science and agronomy; Spanish; special education; statistics; theater design and technology; turf and turfgrass management; visual and performing arts; women's studies.

Academics *Calendar:* semesters. *Degrees:* associate and bachelor's. *Special study options:* academic remediation for entering students, accelerated degree program, adult/continuing education programs, advanced placement credit, cooperative education, distance learning, double majors, honors programs, independent study, internships, services for LD students, study abroad, summer session for credit. *ROTC:* Army (c), Air Force (c).

Student Life *Housing:* college housing not available. *Activities and Organizations:* drama/theater group, student-run newspaper, choral group. *Campus security:* part-time trained security personnel. *Student services:* health clinic, personal/psychological counseling, women's center.

Athletics Member NJCAA. *Intercollegiate sports:* baseball M, basketball M/W, cheerleading M/W, cross-country running M/W, soccer M, softball W, volleyball W. *Intramural sports:* basketball M/W, bowling M(c)/W(c), skiing (downhill) M(c)/W(c), soccer M/W, softball M/W, volleyball M/W(c), weight lifting M(c)/W(c).

Standardized Tests *Required:* SAT or ACT (for admission).

Costs (2009–10) *Tuition:* state resident $11,442 full-time, $463 per credit hour part-time; nonresident $17,460 full-time, $728 per credit hour part-time. Full-time tuition and fees vary according to course level, location, program, and student level. Part-time tuition and fees vary according to course level, course load, location, program, and student level. *Required fees:* $668 full-time.

Financial Aid Of all full-time matriculated undergraduates who enrolled in 2009, 909 applied for aid, 752 were judged to have need, 45 had their need fully met. 23 Federal Work-Study jobs (averaging $2020). In 2009, 65 non-need-based awards were made. *Average percent of need met:* 65%. *Average financial aid package:* $8297. *Average need-based loan:* $3833. *Average need-based gift aid:* $5158. *Average non-need-based aid:* $2358. *Average indebtedness upon graduation:* $28,680.

Applying *Options:* electronic application, early admission, deferred entrance. *Application fee:* $50. *Required:* high school transcript. *Required for some:* interview. *Recommended:* essay or personal statement. *Application deadlines:* rolling (freshmen), rolling (transfers). *Notification:* continuous (freshmen), continuous (transfers).

Freshman Application Contact Penn State Worthington Scranton, 120 Ridge View Drive, Dunmore, PA 18512-1699. *Phone:* 814-865-5471.

PENN STATE YORK

York, Pennsylvania **www.yk.psu.edu/**

- **State-related** primarily 2-year, founded 1926, part of Pennsylvania State University
- **Suburban** 53-acre campus
- **Coed,** 1,439 undergraduate students, 68% full-time, 46% women, 54% men

Penn State York (continued)

Undergraduates 973 full-time, 466 part-time. 7% are from out of state, 6% African American, 5% Asian American or Pacific Islander, 5% Hispanic American, 0.1% Native American, 2% international, 3% transferred in. *Retention:* 74% of 2008 full-time freshmen returned.

Freshmen *Admission:* 1,236 applied, 1,080 admitted, 313 enrolled. *Average high school GPA:* 2.91. *Test scores:* SAT verbal scores over 500: 39%; SAT math scores over 500: 49%; SAT writing scores over 500: 38%; SAT verbal scores over 600: 8%; SAT math scores over 600: 15%; SAT writing scores over 600: 6%; SAT math scores over 700: 2%.

Faculty *Total:* 108, 54% full-time, 46% with terminal degrees. *Student/faculty ratio:* 15:1.

Majors Accounting; acting; actuarial science; adult and continuing education administration; advertising; aerospace, aeronautical and astronautical engineering; African American/Black studies; agribusiness; agricultural and extension education; agricultural/biological engineering and bioengineering; agricultural business and management related; agricultural mechanization; agriculture; agronomy and crop science; American studies; animal sciences; animal sciences related; anthropology; applied economics; archeology; architectural engineering; art; art history, criticism and conservation; art teacher education; Asian studies (East); astronomy; atmospheric sciences and meteorology; biochemistry; biological and biomedical sciences related; biological and physical sciences; biology/biological sciences; biology/biotechnology laboratory technician; biomedical/medical engineering; biomedical technology; business administration and management; business/commerce; business/managerial economics; chemical engineering; chemistry; civil engineering; classics and languages, literatures and linguistics; communication and journalism related; communication disorders; communication/speech communication and rhetoric; comparative literature; computer and information sciences; computer engineering; criminal justice/law enforcement administration; economics; electrical, electronic and communications engineering technology; electrical, electronics and communications engineering; elementary education; engineering science; English; environmental/environmental health engineering; film/cinema studies; finance; food science; foreign language teacher education; forestry technology; forest sciences and biology; French; geography; geological and earth sciences/geosciences related; geology/earth science; German; graphic design; health/health-care administration; history; horticultural science; hospitality administration related; human development and family studies; human nutrition; industrial engineering; industrial technology; information science/studies; international relations and affairs; Italian; Japanese; Jewish/Judaic studies; journalism; kinesiology and exercise science; labor and industrial relations; landscaping and groundskeeping; Latin American studies; liberal arts and sciences/liberal studies; logistics and materials management; management information systems; manufacturing engineering; marketing/marketing management; materials science; mathematics; mechanical engineering; mechanical engineering/mechanical technology; medical microbiology and bacteriology; medieval and Renaissance studies; metallurgical technology; mining and mineral engineering; music; natural resources and conservation related; natural resources/conservation; nuclear engineering; nursing (registered nurse training); organizational behavior; parks, recreation and leisure facilities management; petroleum engineering; philosophy; physics; political science and government; premedical studies; psychology; rehabilitation and therapeutic professions related; religious studies; Russian; secondary education; sociology; soil science and agronomy; Spanish; special education; statistics; telecommunications technology; theater design and technology; toxicology; turf and turfgrass management; visual and performing arts; women's studies.

Academics *Calendar:* semesters. *Degrees:* certificates, associate, bachelor's, and master's (also offers up to 2 years of most bachelor's degree programs offered at University Park campus). *Special study options:* academic remediation for entering students, accelerated degree program, adult/continuing education programs, advanced placement credit, distance learning, double majors, English as a second language, honors programs, independent study, internships, services for LD students, student-designed majors, study abroad, summer session for credit.

Student Life *Housing:* college housing not available. *Activities and Organizations:* drama/theater group, student-run newspaper. *Campus security:* part-time trained security personnel. *Student services:* health clinic, personal/psychological counseling, women's center.

Athletics Member NJCAA.

Standardized Tests *Required:* SAT or ACT (for admission).

Costs (2009–10) *Tuition:* state resident $11,442 full-time, $463 per credit hour part-time; nonresident $17,460 full-time, $728 per credit hour part-time. Full-time tuition and fees vary according to course level, location, program, and student level. Part-time tuition and fees vary according to course level, course load, location, program, and student level. *Required fees:* $668 full-time.

Financial Aid Of all full-time matriculated undergraduates who enrolled in 2008, 711 applied for aid, 527 were judged to have need, 41 had their need fully met. In 2008, 70 non-need-based awards were made. *Average percent of need met:* 64%. *Average financial aid package:* $8225. *Average need-based loan:* $3701. *Average need-based gift aid:* $5388. *Average non-need-based aid:* $2964. *Average indebtedness upon graduation:* $28,680.

Applying *Options:* electronic application, early admission, deferred entrance. *Application fee:* $50. *Required:* high school transcript. *Required for some:* interview. *Recommended:* essay or personal statement. *Application deadlines:* rolling (freshmen), rolling (transfers). *Notification:* continuous (freshmen), continuous (transfers).

Freshman Application Contact Penn State York, 1031 Edgecomb Avenue, York, PA 17403-3398. *Phone:* 814-865-5471. *Toll-free phone:* 800-778-6227.

Pennsylvania College of Technology

Williamsport, Pennsylvania **www.pct.edu/**

- **State-related** 4-year, founded 1965, administratively affiliated with Pennsylvania State University
- **Small-town** 996-acre campus
- **Endowment** $378,763
- **Coed,** 6,409 undergraduate students, 85% full-time, 35% women, 65% men

Undergraduates 5,469 full-time, 940 part-time. Students come from 35 states and territories, 12 other countries, 10% are from out of state, 3% African American, 1% Asian American or Pacific Islander, 2% Hispanic American, 0.4% Native American, 0.3% international, 23% live on campus. *Retention:* 66% of 2008 full-time freshmen returned.

Freshmen *Admission:* 4,061 applied, 3,567 admitted, 1,389 enrolled.

Faculty *Total:* 484, 61% full-time. *Student/faculty ratio:* 18:1.

Majors Accounting; accounting technology and bookkeeping; administrative assistant and secretarial science; adult health nursing; aeronautical/aerospace engineering technology; aircraft powerplant technology; allied health diagnostic, intervention, and treatment professions related; applied art; applied horticulture; applied horticulture/horticultural business services related; architectural engineering technology; autobody/collision and repair technology; automotive engineering technology; baking and pastry arts; banking and financial support services; biology/biological sciences; biomedical technology; broadcast journalism; business administration and management; business administration, management and operations related; business automation/technology/data entry; cabinetmaking and millwork; cardiovascular technology; carpentry; child-care and support services management; child-care provision; computer and information sciences; computer and information sciences and support services related; computer and information systems security; computer engineering technologies related; computer/information technology services administration related; computer programming (specific applications); computer systems analysis; computer technology/computer systems technology; construction management; dental services and allied professions related; diesel mechanics technology; dietitian assistant; drafting and design technology; drafting/design engineering technologies related; early childhood education; education (specific subject areas) related; electrical and electronic engineering technologies related; electrical and power transmission installation related; electrical/electronics maintenance and repair technology related; electrician; emergency medical technology (EMT paramedic); energy management and systems technology; engineering science; engineering technologies related; entrepreneurial and small business related; environmental control technologies related; fine/studio arts; forestry technology; general studies; graphic design; health and medical administrative services related; health and physical education related; health information/medical records administration; health information/medical records technology; health professions related; health services/allied health/health sciences; heavy equipment maintenance technology; heavy/industrial equipment maintenance technologies related; hospitality administration; human resources management; industrial electronics technology; industrial mechanics and maintenance technology; information technology; institutional food workers; instrumentation technology; kinesiology and exercise science; landscaping and groundskeeping; laser and optical technology; legal assistant/paralegal; legal professions and studies related; legal studies; liberal arts and sciences and humanities related; liberal arts and sciences/liberal studies; machine shop technology; management information systems; management science; marketing/marketing management; masonry; mass communication/media; mechanical engineering/mechanical technology; mechanic and repair technologies related; medical administrative assistant and medical secretary; medical/clinical assistant; medical radiologic technology; mental and social health services and allied professions related; multi/interdisciplinary studies related; nursing (licensed practical/vocational nurse training); occupational therapist assistant; office occupations and clerical services; ornamental horticulture; physical sciences; plant nursery management; platemaking/imaging; plumbing technology; quality control technology; radiologic technology/science; robotics technology; solar energy technology; surgical technology; survey technology; system administration; technical and business writing; tool and die technology; tourism and travel services management; turf and turfgrass management; vehicle and vehicle parts and accessories marketing; vehicle maintenance and repair technologies related; web page, digital/multimedia and information resources design.

Academics *Calendar:* semesters. *Degrees:* certificates, associate, and bachelor's. *Special study options:* academic remediation for entering students, advanced-placement credit, cooperative education, distance learning, double majors, English as a second language, independent study, internships, off-campus study, part-time degree program, services for LD students, student-designed majors, summer session for credit. *ROTC:* Army (c).

Library Roger and Peggy Madigan Library plus 1 other with 127,995 titles, 30,883 serial subscriptions, 9,669 audiovisual materials, an OPAC, a Web page.

Student Life *Housing Options:* coed, disabled students. Campus housing is university owned. Freshman campus housing is guaranteed. *Activities and Organizations:* student-run radio station, Student Government Association, Residence Hall Association, Wildcats Event Board, Association of Computing Machinery, Campus Crusade for Christ, national fraternities, national sororities. *Campus security:* 24-hour emergency response devices and patrols, late-night transport/escort service, controlled dormitory access. *Student services:* health clinic, personal/psychological counseling.

Athletics *Intercollegiate sports:* archery M/W, baseball M, basketball M/W, bowling M/W, cross-country running M/W, golf M/W, soccer M/W, softball W, tennis M/W, volleyball M/W. *Intramural sports:* archery M/W, badminton M/W, basketball M/W, bowling M/W, football M/W, golf M/W, lacrosse M/W, racquetball M/W, soccer M/W, softball M/W, table tennis M/W, tennis M/W, ultimate Frisbee M/W, volleyball M/W, weight lifting M/W, wrestling M/W.

Standardized Tests *Required for some:* SAT (for admission).

Costs (2009–10) *Tuition:* state resident $10,500 full-time, $416 per credit hour part-time; nonresident $13,650 full-time, $521 per credit hour part-time. Full-time tuition and fees vary according to course load and program. Part-time tuition and fees vary according to course load and program. *Required fees:* $1980 full-time. *Room and board:* $8350; room only: $5350. Room and board charges vary according to board plan, housing facility, and location. *Payment plan:* deferred payment. *Waivers:* employees or children of employees.

Financial Aid Of all full-time matriculated undergraduates who enrolled in 2008, 6,510 applied for aid, 5,960 were judged to have need. 223 Federal Work-Study jobs (averaging $1364). 392 state and other part-time jobs (averaging $1659). *Average percent of need met:* 78%. *Average financial aid package:* $13,348. *Average need-based gift aid:* $2666.

Applying *Options:* electronic application, early admission, deferred entrance. *Application fee:* $50. *Required:* high school transcript. *Application deadline:* rolling (transfers).

Freshman Application Contact Mr. Dennis Correll, Associate Dean for Admissions/Financial Aid, Pennsylvania College of Technology, One College Avenue, DIF #119, Williamsport, PA 17701. *Phone:* 570-327-4761 Ext. 7337. *Toll-free phone:* 800-367-9222. *Fax:* 570-321-5551. *E-mail:* dcorrell@pct.edu.

▸**See page 468 for the College Close-Up.**

PENNSYLVANIA CULINARY INSTITUTE

Pittsburgh, Pennsylvania **www.paculinary.com/**

- **Proprietary** 2-year, founded 1986
- **Urban** campus
- **Coed**

Academics *Calendar:* semesters. *Degree:* associate. *Special study options:* academic remediation for entering students, double majors, internships, services for LD students.

Applying *Options:* electronic application. *Application fee:* $50. *Required:* high school transcript, interview. *Required for some:* entrance examination. *Recommended:* essay or personal statement.

Freshman Application Contact Ms. Juliette Mariani, Dean of Students, Pennsylvania Culinary Institute, 717 Liberty Avenue, Pittsburgh, PA 15222-3500. *Phone:* 412-566-2433. *Toll-free phone:* 800-432-2433. *Fax:* 412-566-2434.

PENNSYLVANIA HIGHLANDS COMMUNITY COLLEGE

Johnstown, Pennsylvania **www.pennhighlands.edu/**

- **State and locally supported** 2-year, founded 1994
- **Small-town** campus
- **Coed,** 1,768 undergraduate students, 52% full-time, 58% women, 42% men

Undergraduates 923 full-time, 845 part-time. Students come from 4 states and territories, 2% are from out of state, 5% African American, 0.2% Asian American or Pacific Islander, 1% Hispanic American, 0.1% Native American. *Retention:* 34% of 2008 full-time freshmen returned.

Faculty *Student/faculty ratio:* 13:1.

Majors Accounting; banking and financial support services; computer and information sciences; computer and information sciences and support services related; computer/information technology services administration related; computer programming; computer programming related; computer programming (specific applications); construction engineering technology; consumer merchandising/retailing management; court reporting; electrical, electronic and communications engineering technology; environmental engineering technology; general studies; geography; health/health-care administration; heating, air conditioning and refrigeration technology; hospitality administration; human services; industrial technology; liberal arts and sciences/liberal studies; system administration; web/multimedia management and webmaster.

Academics *Calendar:* semesters. *Degree:* certificates, diplomas, and associate. *Special study options:* academic remediation for entering students, adult/continuing education programs, advanced placement credit, cooperative education, distance learning, honors programs, independent study, internships, part-time degree program, services for LD students.

Library Pennsylvania Highlands Community College Main Library plus 1 other with an OPAC.

Student Life *Housing:* college housing not available.

Financial Aid Of all full-time matriculated undergraduates who enrolled in 2008, 25 Federal Work-Study jobs (averaging $2500).

Applying *Application fee:* $20.

Freshman Application Contact Mr. Jeff Maul, Admissions Officer, Pennsylvania Highlands Community College, PO Box 68, Johnstown, PA 15907. *Phone:* 814-262-6431. *E-mail:* jmaul@pennhighlands.edu.

PENNSYLVANIA INSTITUTE OF TECHNOLOGY

Media, Pennsylvania **www.pit.edu/**

- **Independent** 2-year, founded 1953
- **Small-town** 12-acre campus with easy access to Philadelphia
- **Coed,** 1,046 undergraduate students, 88% full-time, 75% women, 25% men

Undergraduates 923 full-time, 123 part-time. 48% African American, 2% Asian American or Pacific Islander, 4% Hispanic American, 0.3% Native American, 0.2% international. *Retention:* 45% of 2008 full-time freshmen returned.

Freshmen *Admission:* 526 enrolled.

Faculty *Total:* 86, 28% full-time. *Student/faculty ratio:* 22:1.

Majors Allied health and medical assisting services related; architectural engineering technology; business administration and management; electrical, electronic and communications engineering technology; engineering technology; mechanical engineering/mechanical technology; mechanical engineering technologies related; medical office management; office occupations and clerical services; web page, digital/multimedia and information resources design.

Academics *Calendar:* semesters. *Degree:* certificates and associate. *Special study options:* academic remediation for entering students, adult/continuing education programs, advanced placement credit, cooperative education, part-time degree program, summer session for credit.

Library Pennsylvania Institute of Technology Library/Learning Resource Center with 16,500 titles, 217 serial subscriptions, an OPAC, a Web page.

Student Life *Housing:* college housing not available. *Campus security:* 24-hour emergency response devices. *Student services:* personal/psychological counseling.

Athletics *Intramural sports:* basketball M/W.

Costs (2010–11) *Tuition:* $9900 full-time, $330 per credit part-time. Full-time tuition and fees vary according to course load, degree level, and program. Part-time tuition and fees vary according to course load, degree level, and program. *Required fees:* $900 full-time, $30 per credit part-time. *Payment plan:* installment. *Waivers:* employees or children of employees.

Financial Aid Of all full-time matriculated undergraduates who enrolled in 2008, 15 Federal Work-Study jobs (averaging $1025). *Financial aid deadline:* 8/1.

Applying *Options:* electronic application, deferred entrance. *Application fee:* $25. *Required:* high school transcript, interview. *Required for some:* 2 letters of recommendation. *Recommended:* essay or personal statement. *Notification:* continuous until 9/19 (freshmen), continuous until 9/19 (transfers).

Freshman Application Contact Ms. Angela Cassetta, Dean of Enrollment Management, Pennsylvania Institute of Technology, 800 Manchester Avenue, Media, PA 19063-4036. *Phone:* 610-892-1550 Ext. 1553. *Toll-free phone:* 800-422-0025. *Fax:* 610-892-1510. *E-mail:* info@pit.edu.

Pennsylvania School of Business

Allentown, Pennsylvania www.psb.edu/

- **Private** 2-year, founded 1978
- **Coed**

Academics *Degree:* certificates and associate.

Freshman Application Contact Mr. Bill Barber, Director, Pennsylvania School of Business, 406 West Hamilton Street, Allentown, PA 18101. *Phone:* 610-841-3333. *Fax:* 610-841-3334. *E-mail:* wbarber@pennschoolofbusiness.edu.

Pittsburgh Institute of Aeronautics

Pittsburgh, Pennsylvania www.pia.edu/

Freshman Application Contact Mr. Vincent J. Mezza, Director of Admissions, Pittsburgh Institute of Aeronautics, PO Box 10897, Pittsburgh, PA 15236. *Phone:* 412-346-2100. *Toll-free phone:* 800-444-1440. *Fax:* 412-466-5013. *E-mail:* admissions@pia.edu.

Pittsburgh Institute of Mortuary Science, Incorporated

Pittsburgh, Pennsylvania www.pims.edu/

- **Independent** 2-year, founded 1939
- **Urban** campus
- **Coed,** 193 undergraduate students, 44% full-time, 43% women, 57% men

Undergraduates 85 full-time, 108 part-time. Students come from 12 states and territories, 1 other country, 37% are from out of state, 10% African American, 1% Hispanic American, 0.5% Native American.

Freshmen *Admission:* 68 enrolled.

Faculty *Total:* 24, 8% full-time, 13% with terminal degrees. *Student/faculty ratio:* 13:1.

Majors Funeral service and mortuary science.

Academics *Calendar:* trimesters. *Degree:* diplomas and associate. *Special study options:* academic remediation for entering students, adult/continuing education programs, distance learning, part-time degree program, services for LD students.

Library William J. Musmanno Memorial Library with 2,547 titles, 48 serial subscriptions, 284 audiovisual materials, an OPAC, a Web page.

Student Life *Housing:* college housing not available. *Campus security:* 24-hour emergency response devices.

Costs (2009–10) *Tuition:* $9200 full-time, $265 per semester hour part-time. *Required fees:* $1700 full-time.

Applying *Options:* electronic application. *Application fee:* $40. *Required:* essay or personal statement, high school transcript, minimum 2 GPA, 2 letters of recommendation, interview, immunizations. *Application deadlines:* rolling (freshmen), rolling (transfers). *Notification:* continuous (freshmen), continuous (transfers).

Freshman Application Contact Ms. Karen Rocco, Registrar, Pittsburgh Institute of Mortuary Science, Incorporated, 5808 Baum Boulevard, Pittsburgh, PA 15206-3706. *Phone:* 412-362-8500 Ext. 105. *Toll-free phone:* 800-933-5808. *Fax:* 412-362-1684. *E-mail:* pims5808@aol.com.

Pittsburgh Technical Institute

Oakdale, Pennsylvania www.pti.edu/

- **Proprietary** 2-year, founded 1946
- **Suburban** 180-acre campus with easy access to Pittsburgh
- **Coed**
- 88% of applicants were admitted

Undergraduates 2,073 full-time. Students come from 20 states and territories, 3 other countries, 20% are from out of state, 40% live on campus.

Academics *Calendar:* quarters. *Degree:* certificates and associate. *Special study options:* academic remediation for entering students, adult/continuing education programs, distance learning, double majors, internships.

Student Life *Campus security:* 24-hour emergency response devices and patrols, controlled dormitory access.

Applying *Options:* electronic application, deferred entrance. *Required:* high school transcript, interview. *Required for some:* certain programs require a criminal background check; surgical technology requires a dexterity test; some programs require applicants to be in top 50-80% of class.

Freshman Application Contact Ms. Nancy Goodlin, Admissions Office Assistant, Pittsburgh Technical Institute, 1111 McKee Road, Oakdale, PA 15071. *Phone:* 412-809-5100. *Toll-free phone:* 800-784-9675. *Fax:* 412-809-5351. *E-mail:* goodlin.nancy@pti.edu.

The PJA School

Upper Darby, Pennsylvania www.pjaschool.com/

Director of Admissions Ms. Dina Gentile, Director, The PJA School, 7900 West Chester Pike, Upper Darby, PA 19082-1926. *Phone:* 610-789-6700. *Toll-free phone:* 800-RING-PJA. *Fax:* 610-789-5208. *E-mail:* dgentile@pjaschool.com.

Reading Area Community College

Reading, Pennsylvania www.racc.edu/

Director of Admissions Ms. Maria Mitchell, Associate Vice President of Enrollment Management and Student Services, Reading Area Community College, PO Box 1706, Reading, PA 19603-1706. *Phone:* 610-607-6224. *Toll-free phone:* 800-626-1665. *E-mail:* mmitchell@racc.edu.

The Restaurant School at Walnut Hill College

Philadelphia, Pennsylvania www.walnuthillcollege.edu/

- **Proprietary** primarily 2-year, founded 1974
- **Urban** 2-acre campus
- **Coed,** 509 undergraduate students

Undergraduates Students come from 2 other countries, 33% are from out of state. *Retention:* 64% of 2008 full-time freshmen returned.

Faculty *Student/faculty ratio:* 29:1.

Majors Baking and pastry arts; culinary arts; hotel/motel administration; restaurant/food services management.

Academics *Calendar:* quarters. *Degrees:* associate and bachelor's. *Special study options:* internships, part-time degree program.

Library Alumni Resource Center with a Web page.

Student Life *Housing Options:* coed.

Standardized Tests *Recommended:* SAT or ACT (for admission).

Applying *Options:* early admission, early decision, deferred entrance. *Application fee:* $50. *Required:* essay or personal statement, high school transcript, 2 letters of recommendation, interview. *Required for some:* entrance exam. *Recommended:* minimum 2 GPA. *Application deadline:* rolling (freshmen).

Freshman Application Contact Mr. Karl D. Becker, Director of Admissions, The Restaurant School at Walnut Hill College, 4207 Walnut Street, Philadelphia, PA 19104. *Phone:* 267-295-2373. *Toll-free phone:* 877-925-6884 Ext. 3011. *Fax:* 215-222-4219. *E-mail:* kbecker@walnuthillcollege.edu.

Rosedale Technical Institute

Pittsburgh, Pennsylvania www.rosedaletech.org/

Freshman Application Contact Ms. Debbie Bier, Director of Admissions, Rosedale Technical Institute, 215 Beecham Drive, Suite 2, Pitsburgh, PA 15205-9791. *Phone:* 412-521-6200. *Toll-free phone:* 800-521-6262. *Fax:* 412-521-2520. *E-mail:* admissions@rosedaletech.org.

SANFORD-BROWN INSTITUTE–MONROEVILLE

Pittsburgh, Pennsylvania **www.monroeville.sanfordbrown.edu/**

Director of Admissions Timothy Babyok, Director of Admission, Sanford-Brown Institute–Monroeville, Penn Center East, 777 Penn Center Boulevard, Building 7, Pittsburgh, PA 15235. *Phone:* 412-373-6400. *Toll-free phone:* 888-381-2433.

SANFORD-BROWN INSTITUTE–PITTSBURGH

Pittsburgh, Pennsylvania **www.sanfordbrown.edu/**

- **Proprietary** 2-year, founded 1980
- **Urban** campus
- **Coed**

Academics *Calendar:* continuous. *Degree:* associate. *Special study options:* academic remediation for entering students, accelerated degree program, adult/continuing education programs, advanced placement credit, cooperative education, English as a second language, internships, services for LD students.

Student Life *Campus security:* 24-hour emergency response devices, 14-hour security patrols Monday through Friday.

Standardized Tests *Recommended:* SAT or ACT (for admission), SAT Subject Tests (for admission).

Financial Aid Of all full-time matriculated undergraduates who enrolled in 2008, 25 Federal Work-Study jobs (averaging $1200).

Applying *Options:* electronic application, early admission, deferred entrance. *Application fee:* $25. *Required:* high school transcript, interview.

Director of Admissions Mr. Bruce E. Jones, Director of Admission, Sanford-Brown Institute–Pittsburgh, 421 Seventh Avenue, Pittsburgh, PA 15219. *Phone:* 412-281-7083 Ext. 114. *Toll-free phone:* 800-333-6607.

SOUTH HILLS SCHOOL OF BUSINESS & TECHNOLOGY

Altoona, Pennsylvania **www.southhills.edu/**

Freshman Application Contact Ms. Holly J. Emerick, Director of Admissions, South Hills School of Business & Technology, 508 58th Street, Altoona, PA 16602. *Phone:* 814-944-6134. *Fax:* 814-944-4684. *E-mail:* hemerick@southhills.edu.

SOUTH HILLS SCHOOL OF BUSINESS & TECHNOLOGY

State College, Pennsylvania **www.southhills.edu/**

Freshman Application Contact Ms. Diane M. Brown, Director of Admissions, South Hills School of Business & Technology, 480 Waupelani Drive, State College, PA 16801-4516. *Phone:* 814-234-7755 Ext. 2020. *Toll-free phone:* 888-282-7427 Ext. 2020. *Fax:* 814-234-0926. *E-mail:* admissions@southhills.edu.

THADDEUS STEVENS COLLEGE OF TECHNOLOGY

Lancaster, Pennsylvania **www.stevenscollege.edu/**

Director of Admissions Ms. Erin Kate Nelsen, Director of Enrollment, Thaddeus Stevens College of Technology, Enrollment Services, 750 East King Street, Lancaster, PA 17602-3198. *Phone:* 717-299-7772. *Toll-free phone:* 800-842-3832.

TRIANGLE TECH–GREENSBURG SCHOOL

Greensburg, Pennsylvania **www.triangle-tech.com/**

- **Proprietary** 2-year, founded 1944, part of Triangle Tech Group, Inc.
- **Small-town** 1-acre campus with easy access to Pittsburgh
- **Coed, primarily men,** 260 undergraduate students, 100% full-time, 2% women, 98% men

Undergraduates 260 full-time. Students come from 1 other state, 1% African American, 0.4% Asian American or Pacific Islander, 0.4% Native American.

Freshmen *Admission:* 247 applied, 247 admitted, 131 enrolled.

Faculty *Total:* 21, 100% full-time. *Student/faculty ratio:* 12:1.

Majors Carpentry; construction trades; drafting and design technology; electrical/electronics equipment installation and repair; electrical/electronics maintenance and repair technology related; heating, air conditioning and refrigeration technology; heating, air conditioning, ventilation and refrigeration maintenance technology; mechanical drafting and CAD/CADD.

Academics *Calendar:* semesters. *Degree:* diplomas and associate. *Special study options:* academic remediation for entering students, adult/continuing education programs, advanced placement credit, summer session for credit.

Library Triangle Tech Library plus 1 other with 550 titles, 15 serial subscriptions.

Student Life *Housing:* college housing not available. *Student services:* personal/psychological counseling.

Costs (2010–11) *Tuition:* $14,557 full-time. *Required fees:* $348 full-time. *Payment plan:* installment. *Waivers:* employees or children of employees.

Financial Aid Of all full-time matriculated undergraduates who enrolled in 2008, 5 Federal Work-Study jobs (averaging $2000).

Applying *Options:* deferred entrance. *Application fee:* $75. *Required:* high school transcript, interview. *Application deadlines:* rolling (freshmen), rolling (transfers).

Freshman Application Contact Mr. John Mazzarese, Vice President of Admissions, Triangle Tech–Greensburg School, 222 East Pittsburgh Street, Greensburg, PA 15601. *Phone:* 412-359-1000. *Toll-free phone:* 800-874-8324.

TRIANGLE TECH INC–BETHLEHEM

Bethlehem, Pennsylvania **www.triangle-tech.edu/**

- **Proprietary** 2-year
- **Urban** campus
- **Coed, primarily men,** 140 undergraduate students, 100% full-time, 4% women, 96% men

Undergraduates 140 full-time. Students come from 2 states and territories, 11% are from out of state, 13% African American, 6% Hispanic American, 4% transferred in.

Freshmen *Admission:* 109 applied, 108 admitted, 70 enrolled.

Faculty *Total:* 10, 80% full-time. *Student/faculty ratio:* 15:1.

Majors Carpentry; electrician.

Academics *Degree:* associate.

Library Main Library plus 1 other.

Student Life *Housing:* college housing not available.

Standardized Tests *Required:* Students are required to take the TABE test as an entrance exam. Admission is not dependent upon the test results. The test scores are used to measure student aptitude in reading and math to better assist in student advising and to evaluate tutorial help if necessary. (for admission).

Costs (2009–10) *Tuition:* Tuition and fees vary according to program.

Applying *Required:* high school transcript, interview, high school diploma or GED, tour of school.

Freshman Application Contact Triangle Tech Inc–Bethlehem, Lehigh Valley Industrial Park IV, 31 South Commerce Way, Bethlehem, PA 18017.

TRIANGLE TECH, INC.–DUBOIS SCHOOL

DuBois, Pennsylvania **www.triangle-tech.edu/**

- **Proprietary** 2-year, founded 1944, part of Triangle Tech Group, Inc.
- **Small-town** 5-acre campus
- **Coed, primarily men,** 331 undergraduate students, 100% full-time, 4% women, 96% men

Triangle Tech, Inc.–DuBois School (continued)

Undergraduates 331 full-time. Students come from 2 states and territories, 1% African American, 1% Hispanic American.
Freshmen *Admission:* 205 applied, 205 admitted, 186 enrolled. *Average high school GPA:* 2.
Faculty *Total:* 21, 100% full-time. *Student/faculty ratio:* 15:1.
Majors Carpentry; drafting and design technology; electrical, electronic and communications engineering technology; welding technology.
Academics *Calendar:* semesters. *Degree:* diplomas and associate. *Special study options:* academic remediation for entering students, advanced placement credit, off-campus study.
Library Library Resource Center with 1,200 titles, 15 serial subscriptions, 60 audiovisual materials.
Student Life *Housing:* college housing not available. *Activities and Organizations:* Student Council.
Costs (2010–11) *Tuition:* $13,864 full-time. *Required fees:* $447 full-time. *Payment plan:* installment. *Waivers:* employees or children of employees.
Applying *Options:* deferred entrance. *Required:* high school transcript, minimum 2 GPA, interview. *Application deadlines:* rolling (freshmen), rolling (transfers).
Freshman Application Contact Jason Vallozzi, Director of Admissions, Triangle Tech, Inc.–DuBois School, PO Box 551, DuBois, PA 15801. *Phone:* 412-359-1000. *Toll-free phone:* 800-874-8324. *Fax:* 814-371-9227. *E-mail:* info@triangle-tech.com.

TRIANGLE TECH, INC.–ERIE SCHOOL

Erie, Pennsylvania **www.triangle-tech.com/**

- **Proprietary** 2-year, founded 1976, part of Triangle Tech Group, Inc.
- **Urban** 1-acre campus
- **Coed, primarily men,** 176 undergraduate students, 100% full-time, 5% women, 95% men

Undergraduates 176 full-time. Students come from 3 states and territories, 10% are from out of state, 6% African American, 0.6% Asian American or Pacific Islander, 2% Hispanic American.
Freshmen *Admission:* 76 applied, 76 admitted, 72 enrolled.
Faculty *Total:* 16, 88% full-time. *Student/faculty ratio:* 12:1.
Majors Architectural drafting and CAD/CADD; carpentry; electrician; mechanical drafting and CAD/CADD.
Academics *Calendar:* semesters. *Degree:* associate. *Special study options:* academic remediation for entering students, advanced placement credit, services for LD students.
Library 1,000 titles, 15 serial subscriptions.
Student Life *Housing:* college housing not available. *Campus security:* 24-hour emergency response devices.
Financial Aid Of all full-time matriculated undergraduates who enrolled in 2008, 5 Federal Work-Study jobs (averaging $2000).
Applying *Options:* deferred entrance. *Application fee:* $75. *Required:* high school transcript, interview. *Application deadlines:* rolling (freshmen), rolling (transfers).
Freshman Application Contact Admissions Representative, Triangle Tech, Inc.–Erie School, 2000 Liberty Street, Erie, PA 16502. *Phone:* 814-453-6016. *Toll-free phone:* 800-874-8324 (in-state); 800-TRI-TECH (out-of-state).

TRIANGLE TECH, INC.–PITTSBURGH SCHOOL

Pittsburgh, Pennsylvania **www.triangle-tech.edu/**

Freshman Application Contact Director of Admissions, Triangle Tech, Inc.–Pittsburgh School, 1940 Perrysville Avenue, Pittsburgh, PA 15214. *Phone:* 412-359-1000. *Toll-free phone:* 800-874-8324. *Fax:* 412-359-1012. *E-mail:* info@triangle-tech.edu.

TRIANGLE TECH, INC.–SUNBURY SCHOOL

Sunbury, Pennsylvania **www.triangle-tech.edu/**

- **Proprietary** 2-year
- **Rural** 4-acre campus
- **Coed,** 170 undergraduate students, 100% full-time, 2% women, 98% men
- 100% of applicants were admitted

Undergraduates 170 full-time. Students come from 2 states and territories, 2% African American, 1% Hispanic American. *Retention:* 75% of 2008 full-time freshmen returned.
Freshmen *Admission:* 76 applied, 76 admitted, 94 enrolled.
Faculty *Total:* 15, 93% full-time. *Student/faculty ratio:* 12:1.
Majors Carpentry; electrician; welding technology.
Academics *Calendar:* semesters. *Degree:* associate. *Special study options:* advanced placement credit, cooperative education.
Library Main Library plus 1 other with 300 titles, 50 serial subscriptions, 25 audiovisual materials.
Student Life *Housing:* college housing not available.
Applying *Required:* high school transcript.
Freshman Application Contact Triangle Tech, Inc.–Sunbury School, RR #1, Box 51, Sunbury, PA 17801. *Phone:* 412-359-1000.

TRI-STATE BUSINESS INSTITUTE

Erie, Pennsylvania **www.tsbi.org/**

Director of Admissions Guy M. Euliano, President, Tri-State Business Institute, 5757 West 26th Street, Erie, PA 16506. *Phone:* 814-838-7673. *Fax:* 814-838-8642. *E-mail:* geuliano@tsbi.org.

UNIVERSITY OF PITTSBURGH AT TITUSVILLE

Titusville, Pennsylvania **www.upt.pitt.edu/**

- **State-related** primarily 2-year, founded 1963, part of University of Pittsburgh System
- **Small-town** 10-acre campus
- **Endowment** $850,000
- **Coed,** 544 undergraduate students, 86% full-time, 65% women, 35% men

Undergraduates 466 full-time, 78 part-time. Students come from 15 states and territories, 11% are from out of state, 20% African American, 2% Asian American or Pacific Islander, 2% Hispanic American, 0.7% Native American, 7% transferred in, 48% live on campus.
Freshmen *Admission:* 205 enrolled. *Average high school GPA:* 2.94. *Test scores:* SAT verbal scores over 500: 19%; SAT math scores over 500: 23%; SAT writing scores over 500: 19%; ACT scores over 18: 59%; SAT verbal scores over 600: 2%; SAT math scores over 600: 2%; SAT writing scores over 600: 2%; ACT scores over 24: 10%; SAT verbal scores over 700: 1%.
Majors Accounting; business/commerce; human services; liberal arts and sciences/liberal studies; management information systems; natural sciences; nursing (registered nurse training); physical therapist assistant.
Academics *Calendar:* semesters. *Degrees:* certificates, associate, and bachelor's. *Special study options:* academic remediation for entering students, advanced placement credit, distance learning, internships, part-time degree program, study abroad, summer session for credit.
Library Haskell Memorial Library with 49,256 titles, 126 serial subscriptions, an OPAC.
Student Life *Housing:* on-campus residence required through sophomore year. *Options:* coed, disabled students. Campus housing is university owned. Freshman campus housing is guaranteed. *Activities and Organizations:* drama/theater group, Phi Theta Kappa, Weight Club, SAB, Students in Free Enterprise (SIFE), Diversity Club. *Campus security:* 24-hour emergency response devices and patrols, controlled dormitory access. *Student services:* health clinic, personal/psychological counseling.
Athletics Member NJCAA. *Intercollegiate sports:* basketball M(s)/W(s). *Intramural sports:* badminton M/W, basketball M/W, bowling M/W, football M/W, golf M/W, racquetball M/W, softball M/W, table tennis M/W, tennis M/W, volleyball M/W, weight lifting M/W.
Standardized Tests *Required:* SAT or ACT (for admission). *Recommended:* SAT (for admission).
Costs (2009–10) *Tuition:* state resident $9700 full-time, $404 per credit part-time; nonresident $18,320 full-time, $763 per credit part-time. Full-time tuition and fees vary according to program. Part-time tuition and fees vary according to program. *Required fees:* $800 full-time, $113 per term part-time. *Room and board:* $8156. Room and board charges vary according to board plan. *Payment plan:* installment.
Financial Aid Of all full-time matriculated undergraduates who enrolled in 2009, 445 applied for aid, 426 were judged to have need, 15 had their need fully met. *Average percent of need met:* 84%. *Average financial aid package:* $17,138. *Average need-based loan:* $7905. *Average need-based gift aid:* $8156.

Applying *Options:* electronic application, early admission, deferred entrance. *Application fee:* $45. *Required:* high school transcript, minimum 2 GPA. *Required for some:* essay or personal statement, 1 letter of recommendation. *Recommended:* interview. *Application deadlines:* rolling (freshmen), rolling (transfers). *Notification:* continuous (freshmen).

Freshman Application Contact Mr. John R. Mumford, Executive Director of Enrollment Management, University of Pittsburgh at Titusville, PO Box 287, Titusville, PA 16354. *Phone:* 814-827-4409. *Toll-free phone:* 888-878-0462. *Fax:* 814-827-4519. *E-mail:* uptadm@pitt.edu.

VALLEY FORGE MILITARY COLLEGE

Wayne, Pennsylvania **www.vfmac.edu/**

Freshman Application Contact Maj. Greg Potts, Dean of Enrollment Management, Valley Forge Military College, 1001 Eagle Road, Wayne, PA 19087-3695. *Phone:* 610-989-1300. *Toll-free phone:* 800-234-8362. *Fax:* 610-688-1545. *E-mail:* admissions@vfmac.edu.

►**See page 472 for the College Close-Up.**

VET TECH INSTITUTE

Pittsburgh, Pennsylvania **www.vettechinstitute.edu/**

- **Private** 2-year, founded 1958
- **Urban** campus
- **Coed,** 338 undergraduate students
- 66% of applicants were admitted

Freshmen *Admission:* 520 applied, 341 admitted.

Majors Veterinary/animal health technology.

Academics *Calendar:* quarters. *Degree:* associate. *Special study options:* accelerated degree program, internships.

Freshman Application Contact Admissions Office, Vet Tech Institute, 125 7th Street, Pittsburgh, PA 15222-3400. *Phone:* 888-391-7021.

WESTMORELAND COUNTY COMMUNITY COLLEGE

Youngwood, Pennsylvania **www.wccc.edu/**

- **County-supported** 2-year, founded 1970
- **Rural** 85-acre campus with easy access to Pittsburgh
- **Endowment** $395,295
- **Coed,** 7,089 undergraduate students, 51% full-time, 63% women, 37% men

Undergraduates 3,608 full-time, 3,481 part-time. Students come from 6 states and territories, 0.1% are from out of state, 4% African American, 0.4% Asian American or Pacific Islander, 0.9% Hispanic American, 0.2% Native American, 24% transferred in. *Retention:* 63% of 2008 full-time freshmen returned.

Freshmen *Admission:* 2,941 applied, 2,941 admitted, 1,918 enrolled.

Faculty *Total:* 554, 16% full-time. *Student/faculty ratio:* 19:1.

Majors Accounting technology and bookkeeping; applied horticulture; architectural drafting and CAD/CADD; baking and pastry arts; banking and financial support services; biology/biotechnology laboratory technician; business administration and management; chemical technology; child-care provision; computer and information systems security; computer engineering technology; computer programming; computer systems networking and telecommunications; criminal justice/safety; culinary arts; dental hygiene; dietetic technician; early childhood education; electrical, electronic and communications engineering technology; executive assistant/executive secretary; fire protection and safety technology; fire science; floriculture/floristry management; health and medical administrative services related; heating, air conditioning, ventilation and refrigeration maintenance technology; human resources management; human services; industrial mechanics and maintenance technology; legal assistant/paralegal; liberal arts and sciences/liberal studies; machine shop technology; machine tool technology; manufacturing technology; marketing/marketing management; mechanical drafting and CAD/CADD; mechanical engineering/mechanical technology; nursing (registered nurse training); photographic and film/video technology; radiologic technology/science; real estate; restaurant, culinary, and catering management; tourism and travel services management; turf and turfgrass management; web page, digital/multimedia and information resources design; welding technology.

Academics *Calendar:* semesters. *Degree:* certificates, diplomas, and associate. *Special study options:* academic remediation for entering students, adult/

Westmoreland County Community College (continued)

continuing education programs, advanced placement credit, cooperative education, distance learning, double majors, English as a second language, honors programs, independent study, internships, off-campus study, part-time degree program, services for LD students, summer session for credit.

Library Westmoreland County Community College Library with 64,000 titles, 250 serial subscriptions, 3,500 audiovisual materials, an OPAC, a Web page.

Student Life *Housing:* college housing not available. *Activities and Organizations:* drama/theater group, choral group, Phi Theta Kappa, Sigma Alpha Pi Leadership Society, Criminal Justice Fraternity, Early Childhood Education Club, SADAA/SADHA. *Campus security:* 24-hour emergency response devices and patrols, late-night transport/escort service. *Student services:* personal/psychological counseling.

Athletics Member NJCAA. *Intercollegiate sports:* baseball M, basketball M/W, bowling M/W, cross-country running M/W, golf M/W, softball W, volleyball W. *Intramural sports:* basketball M/W, bowling M/W, golf M/W, skiing (downhill) M/W, table tennis M/W, volleyball M/W, weight lifting M/W.

Applying *Options:* electronic application, early admission. *Application fee:* $10. *Application deadlines:* rolling (freshmen), rolling (transfers). *Notification:* continuous (freshmen), continuous (transfers).

Freshman Application Contact Mr. Andrew Colosimo, Admissions Coordinator, Westmoreland County Community College, 400 Armbrust Road, Youngwood, PA 15697. *Phone:* 724-925-4064. *Toll-free phone:* 800-262-2103. *Fax:* 724-925-5802. *E-mail:* admission@wccc.edu.

The Williamson Free School of Mechanical Trades

Media, Pennsylvania **www.williamson.edu/**

Freshman Application Contact Mr. Jay Merillat, Dean of Enrollments, The Williamson Free School of Mechanical Trades, 106 South New Middletown Road, Media, PA 19063. *Phone:* 610-566-1776 Ext. 235. *E-mail:* jmerillat@williamson.edu.

WyoTech

Blairsville, Pennsylvania **www.wyotech.com/**

Freshman Application Contact Mr. Tim Smyers, WyoTech, 500 Innovation Drive, Blairsville, PA 15717. *Phone:* 724-459-2311. *Toll-free phone:* 800-822-8253. *Fax:* 724-459-6499. *E-mail:* tsmyers@wyotech.edu.

Yorktowne Business Institute

York, Pennsylvania **www.ybi.edu/**

Director of Admissions Director of Admissions, Yorktowne Business Institute, West Seventh Avenue, York, PA 17404. *Phone:* 717-846-5000. *Toll-free phone:* 800-840-1004.

YTI Career Institute–York

York, Pennsylvania **www.yti.edu/**

Freshman Application Contact YTI Career Institute–York, 1405 Williams Road, York, PA 17402. *Phone:* 717-757-1100 Ext. 318. *Toll-free phone:* 800-229-9675 (in-state); 800-227-9675 (out-of-state).

PUERTO RICO

Centro de Estudios Multidisciplinarios

Rio Piedras, Puerto Rico **www.cempr.edu/**

Director of Admissions Admissions Department, Centro de Estudios Multidisciplinarios, Calle 13 #1206, Ext. San Agustin, San Juan, PR 00926. *Phone:* 787-765-4210 Ext. 115.

Colegio Universitario de San Juan

San Juan, Puerto Rico **www.cunisanjuan.edu/**

Freshman Application Contact Mrs. Nilsa E. Rivera-Almenas, Director of Enrollment Management, Colegio Universitario de San Juan, 180 Jose R. Oliver Street, Tres Monjitas Industrial Park, San Juan, PR 00918. *Phone:* 787-250-7111. *Fax:* 787-250-7395.

Huertas Junior College

Caguas, Puerto Rico **www.huertas.edu/**

- **Proprietary** 2-year, founded 1945
- **Urban** 4-acre campus with easy access to San Juan
- **Coed**

Undergraduates 100% Hispanic American.

Academics *Calendar:* trimesters. *Degree:* certificates and associate. *Special study options:* academic remediation for entering students, English as a second language, internships, part-time degree program.

Student Life *Campus security:* 24-hour patrols.

Applying *Options:* deferred entrance. *Application fee:* $25. *Required for some:* minimum 2.0 GPA.

Director of Admissions Mrs. Barbara Hassim López, Director of Admissions, Huertas Junior College, PO Box 8429, Caguas, PR 00726. *Phone:* 787-743-1242. *Fax:* 787-743-0203. *E-mail:* huertas@huertas.org.

Humacao Community College

Humacao, Puerto Rico

- **Independent** 2-year
- **Coed**

Undergraduates 100% Hispanic American.

Academics *Calendar:* trimesters. *Degree:* certificates, diplomas, and associate. *Special study options:* academic remediation for entering students, English as a second language, internships, services for LD students.

Student Life *Campus security:* 24-hour emergency response devices and patrols.

Financial Aid Of all full-time matriculated undergraduates who enrolled in 2008, 64 Federal Work-Study jobs (averaging $546).

Applying *Options:* early admission. *Application fee:* $15. *Required:* high school transcript.

Director of Admissions Ms. Xiomara Sanchez, Director of Admissions, Humacao Community College, PO Box 9139, Humacao, PR 00792. *Phone:* 787-852-2525.

Instituto Comercial de Puerto Rico Junior College

San Juan, Puerto Rico **www.icprjc.edu/**

Freshman Application Contact Admissions Office, Instituto Comercial de Puerto Rico Junior College, PO Box 190304, San Juan, PR 00919-0304. *Phone:* 787-753-6335.

Puerto Rico Technical Junior College

San Juan, Puerto Rico

Director of Admissions Admissions Department, Puerto Rico Technical Junior College, 703 Ponce De Leon Avenue, Hato Rey, San Juan, PR 00917. *Phone:* 787-751-0628 Ext. 28.

Ramírez College of Business and Technology

San Juan, Puerto Rico **www.galeon.com/ramirezcollege/**

- **Proprietary** 2-year, founded 1922
- **Suburban** campus
- **Coed**

Undergraduates 100% Hispanic American.

Academics *Calendar:* trimesters. *Degree:* diplomas and associate. *Special study options:* academic remediation for entering students, adult/continuing education programs.

Student Life *Campus security:* private security service.

Applying *Application fee:* $25. *Required:* minimum 2.0 GPA, interview. *Required for some:* high school transcript.

Director of Admissions Mr. Arnaldo Castro, Director of Admissions, Ramírez College of Business and Technology, Avenue Ponce de Leon #70, San Juan, PR 00918. *Phone:* 787-763-3120. *E-mail:* ramirezcollege@prtc.net.

Universidad Central del Caribe

Bayamón, Puerto Rico **www.uccaribe.edu/**

Director of Admissions Admissions Department, Universidad Central del Caribe, PO Box 60-327, Bayamón, PR 00960-6032. *Phone:* 787-740-1611.

University of Puerto Rico at Carolina

Carolina, Puerto Rico **uprc.edu/**

Director of Admissions Ms. Celia Mendez, Admissions Officer, University of Puerto Rico at Carolina, PO Box 4800, Carolina, PR 00984-4800. *Phone:* 787-757-1485.

RHODE ISLAND

Community College of Rhode Island

Warwick, Rhode Island **www.ccri.edu/**

- **State-supported** 2-year, founded 1964
- **Suburban** 205-acre campus with easy access to Boston
- **Coed,** 17,760 undergraduate students, 38% full-time, 60% women, 40% men

Undergraduates 6,663 full-time, 11,097 part-time. Students come from 15 states and territories, 4% are from out of state, 8% African American, 3% Asian American or Pacific Islander, 13% Hispanic American, 0.6% Native American, 0.1% international.

Freshmen *Admission:* 7,785 applied, 7,726 admitted, 3,598 enrolled.

Faculty *Total:* 799, 41% full-time. *Student/faculty ratio:* 22:1.

Majors Accounting; administrative assistant and secretarial science; adult development and aging; art; banking and financial support services; biological and physical sciences; biotechnology; business administration and management; business/commerce; chemical technology; clinical/medical laboratory technology; computer and information sciences; computer engineering technology; computer hardware technology; computer programming; computer programming (specific applications); computer systems networking and telecommunications; criminal justice/police science; customer service management; dental hygiene; diagnostic medical sonography and ultrasound technology; dramatic/theater arts; early childhood education; electrical, electronic and communications engineering technology; engineering; fire science; general studies; histologic technician; jazz/jazz studies; kindergarten/preschool education; legal administrative assistant/secretary; legal assistant/paralegal; liberal arts and sciences/liberal studies; marketing/marketing management; massage therapy; mechanical engineering/mechanical technology; medical administrative assistant and medical secretary; mental health counseling; music; nursing (licensed practical/vocational nurse training); nursing (registered nurse training); occupational therapist assistant; opticianry; physical therapist assistant; radiologic technology/science; respiratory care therapy; social work; special education; substance abuse/addiction counseling; surveying engineering; telecommunications technology; theater design and technology; urban studies/affairs; web/multimedia management and webmaster.

Academics *Calendar:* semesters. *Degree:* certificates, diplomas, and associate. *Special study options:* academic remediation for entering students, adult/continuing education programs, advanced placement credit, cooperative education, distance learning, double majors, English as a second language, external degree program, honors programs, independent study, internships, off-campus study, part-time degree program, services for LD students, study abroad, summer session for credit. *ROTC:* Army (c).

Library Community College of Rhode Island Learning Resources Center plus 3 others with an OPAC, a Web page.

Student Life *Housing:* college housing not available. *Activities and Organizations:* drama/theater group, choral group, Distributive Education Clubs of America, Theater group - Players, Skills USA, Phi Theta Kappa, student government. *Campus security:* 24-hour emergency response devices and patrols. *Student services:* health clinic, personal/psychological counseling.

Athletics Member NJCAA. *Intercollegiate sports:* baseball M(s), basketball M(s)/W(s), cross-country running M/W, golf M/W, soccer M(s)/W(s), softball W(s), tennis M/W, track and field M/W, volleyball W(s). *Intramural sports:* basketball M/W, cross-country running M/W, volleyball M/W, water polo M/W.

Costs (2010–11) *Tuition:* state resident $3356 full-time, $153 per credit hour part-time; nonresident $9496 full-time, $454 per credit hour part-time. Part-time tuition and fees vary according to course load. *Required fees:* $11 per credit hour part-time, $17 per term part-time. *Payment plans:* installment, deferred payment. *Waivers:* senior citizens and employees or children of employees.

Financial Aid Of all full-time matriculated undergraduates who enrolled in 2008, 500 Federal Work-Study jobs (averaging $2500).

Applying *Options:* deferred entrance. *Application fee:* $20. *Application deadlines:* rolling (freshmen), rolling (transfers). *Notification:* continuous (freshmen).

Freshman Application Contact Community College of Rhode Island, 400 East Avenue, Warwick, RI 02886. *Phone:* 401-333-7490. *Fax:* 401-333-7122. *E-mail:* webadmission@ccri.edu.

New England Institute of Technology

Warwick, Rhode Island **www.neit.edu/**

Freshman Application Contact Mr. Michael Kwiatkowski, Director of Admissions, New England Institute of Technology, 2500 Post Road, Warwick, RI 02886-2266. *Phone:* 401-739-5000. *E-mail:* neit@ids.net.

SOUTH CAROLINA

Aiken Technical College

Aiken, South Carolina **www.aik.tec.sc.us/**

Freshman Application Contact Ms. Evelyn Pride Patterson, Director of Admissions and Records, Aiken Technical College, PO Drawer 696, Aiken, SC 29802-0696. *Phone:* 803-593-9231. *E-mail:* pridepae@atc.edu.

Brown Mackie College–Greenville

Greenville, South Carolina **www.brownmackie.edu/greenville/**

- **Proprietary** primarily 2-year
- **Coed**

Majors Accounting technology and bookkeeping; business administration and management; criminal justice/law enforcement administration; health/health-care administration; information technology; legal assistant/paralegal; legal studies; medical/clinical assistant; office management; surgical technology.

Academics *Degrees:* certificates, associate, and bachelor's.

Brown Mackie College–Greenville (continued)

Freshman Application Contact Brown Mackie College–Greenville, Two Liberty Square, 75 Beattie Place, Suite 100, Greenville, SC 29601. *Phone:* 864-239-5300. *Toll-free phone:* 877-479-8465.

►See page 418 for the College Close-Up.

CENTRAL CAROLINA TECHNICAL COLLEGE

Sumter, South Carolina **www.cctech.edu/**

- **State-supported** 2-year, founded 1963, part of South Carolina State Board for Technical and Comprehensive Education
- **Small-town** 70-acre campus
- **Endowment** $1.1 million
- **Coed,** 4,137 undergraduate students, 35% full-time, 69% women, 31% men

Undergraduates 1,438 full-time, 2,699 part-time. Students come from 4 states and territories, 1 other country, 1% are from out of state, 51% African American, 1% Asian American or Pacific Islander, 1% Hispanic American, 0.3% Native American, 7% transferred in.

Freshmen *Admission:* 809 enrolled.

Faculty *Total:* 228, 39% full-time. *Student/faculty ratio:* 19:1.

Majors Accounting; administrative assistant and secretarial science; business administration and management; child-care and support services management; civil engineering technology; criminal justice/safety; data processing and data processing technology; environmental control technologies related; industrial electronics technology; legal assistant/paralegal; liberal arts and sciences/liberal studies; mechanical drafting and CAD/CADD; multi/interdisciplinary studies related; natural resources management and policy; nursing (registered nurse training); sales, distribution and marketing; surgical technology.

Academics *Calendar:* semesters. *Degree:* certificates, diplomas, and associate. *Special study options:* academic remediation for entering students, adult/continuing education programs, advanced placement credit, cooperative education, distance learning, external degree program, independent study, internships, part-time degree program, services for LD students, summer session for credit.

Library Central Carolina Technical College Library with 20,356 titles, 245 serial subscriptions, an OPAC, a Web page.

Student Life *Housing:* college housing not available. *Activities and Organizations:* Creative Arts Society, Phi Theta Kappa, Computer Club, National Student Nurses Association (local chapter), Natural Resources Management Club. *Campus security:* 24-hour emergency response devices, security attendants for parking lots and halls during working hrs. Off-duty Sumter officers during peak hrs including outreach campuses. *Student services:* personal/psychological counseling.

Standardized Tests *Required:* COMPASS/ASSET (for admission). *Required for some:* SAT (for admission), ACT (for admission), SAT or ACT (for admission).

Costs (2009–10) *Tuition:* area resident $3300 full-time, $138 per credit hour part-time; state resident $3388 full-time, $162 per credit hour part-time; nonresident $5888 full-time, $245 per credit hour part-time. *Required fees:* $20 full-time. *Payment plan:* installment. *Waivers:* senior citizens and employees or children of employees.

Applying *Options:* electronic application. *Required:* high school transcript. *Application deadlines:* rolling (freshmen), rolling (transfers).

Freshman Application Contact Ms. Barbara Wright, Director of Admissions and Counseling, Central Carolina Technical College, 506 North Guignard Drive, Sumter, SC 29150. *Phone:* 803-778-6695. *Toll-free phone:* 800-221-8711 Ext. 455. *Fax:* 803-778-6696. *E-mail:* brackenlm@cctech.edu.

CLINTON JUNIOR COLLEGE

Rock Hill, South Carolina **www.clintonjuniorcollege.edu/**

Director of Admissions Dr. Janis Pen, President, Clinton Junior College, 1029 Crawford Road, Rock Hill, SC 29730. *Phone:* 803-327-7402. *Toll-free phone:* 877-837-9645. *Fax:* 803-327-3261. *E-mail:* ecopeland@clintonjrcollege.org.

DENMARK TECHNICAL COLLEGE

Denmark, South Carolina **www.denmarktech.edu/**

- **State-supported** 2-year, founded 1948, part of South Carolina State Board for Technical and Comprehensive Education
- **Rural** 53-acre campus
- **Coed,** 1,105 undergraduate students, 81% full-time, 60% women, 40% men

Undergraduates 896 full-time, 209 part-time. 6% are from out of state, 95% African American, 0.2% Asian American or Pacific Islander, 0.2% Hispanic American, 0.3% Native American, 0.1% international, 1% transferred in. *Retention:* 34% of 2008 full-time freshmen returned.

Freshmen *Admission:* 431 enrolled.

Faculty *Total:* 52, 63% full-time. *Student/faculty ratio:* 25:1.

Majors Administrative assistant and secretarial science; automobile/automotive mechanics technology; business administration and management; computer and information sciences; criminal justice/law enforcement administration; engineering technology; human services; kindergarten/preschool education.

Academics *Calendar:* semesters. *Degree:* certificates, diplomas, and associate. *Special study options:* academic remediation for entering students, adult/continuing education programs, advanced placement credit, cooperative education, distance learning, independent study, internships, off-campus study, part-time degree program, summer session for credit.

Library Denmark Technical College Learning Resources Center with 18,727 titles, 195 serial subscriptions, 801 audiovisual materials, an OPAC.

Student Life *Housing Options:* men-only, women-only. Campus housing is university owned. Freshman applicants given priority for college housing. *Activities and Organizations:* choral group, Student Government Association, DTC Choir, Atlectics, Phi Theta Kappa Internal Honor Society, Esquire Club (men & women). *Campus security:* 24-hour patrols. *Student services:* health clinic, personal/psychological counseling.

Athletics *Intercollegiate sports:* basketball M/W, cheerleading W. *Intramural sports:* baseball M, basketball M/W, softball W, tennis M/W, volleyball M/W.

Standardized Tests *Required:* ACT ASSET (for admission). *Recommended:* SAT or ACT (for admission).

Costs (2010–11) *Tuition:* state resident $6260 full-time, $95 per credit hour part-time; nonresident $8540 full-time, $190 per credit hour part-time. No tuition increase for student's term of enrollment. *Room and board:* $3566; room only: $1762. *Payment plan:* installment. *Waivers:* senior citizens.

Financial Aid Of all full-time matriculated undergraduates who enrolled in 2008, 250 Federal Work-Study jobs (averaging $2000).

Applying *Options:* early admission, deferred entrance. *Application fee:* $10. *Required:* high school transcript. *Application deadlines:* rolling (freshmen), rolling (transfers).

Freshman Application Contact Mrs. Tonya Thomas, Dean of Enrollment Management, Denmark Technical College, Solomon Blatt Boulevard, Box 327, Denmark, SC 29042-0327. *Phone:* 803-793-5182. *Fax:* 803-793-5942. *E-mail:* thomast@denmarktech.edu.

FLORENCE-DARLINGTON TECHNICAL COLLEGE

Florence, South Carolina **www.fdtc.edu/**

Director of Admissions Mr. Kevin Qualls, Director of Enrollment Services, Florence-Darlington Technical College, 2715 West Lucas Street, PO Box 100548, Florence, SC 29501-0548. *Phone:* 843-661-8153. *Toll-free phone:* 800-228-5745. *E-mail:* kirvenp@flo.tec.sc.us.

FORREST JUNIOR COLLEGE

Anderson, South Carolina **www.forrestcollege.edu/**

- **Proprietary** 2-year, founded 1946
- **Rural** 3-acre campus
- **Coed,** 94 undergraduate students, 60% full-time, 88% women, 12% men

Undergraduates 56 full-time, 38 part-time. Students come from 2 states and territories, 1% are from out of state, 36% African American, 10% transferred in.

Freshmen *Admission:* 34 applied, 24 admitted, 21 enrolled.

Faculty *Total:* 20, 10% full-time, 20% with terminal degrees. *Student/faculty ratio:* 5:1.

Majors Accounting; business administration and management; child-care and support services management; computer installation and repair technology; computer technology/computer systems technology; legal administrative assistant/secretary; legal assistant/paralegal; medical/clinical assistant; medical office management; office management.

Academics *Calendar:* quarters. *Degree:* certificates, diplomas, and associate. *Special study options:* advanced placement credit, cooperative education, distance learning, double majors, independent study, internships, part-time degree program, summer session for credit.

Library Forrest Junior College Library with 40,000 titles, 225 serial subscriptions, 2,200 audiovisual materials, an OPAC.

Student Life *Housing:* college housing not available. *Campus security:* 24-hour emergency response devices, late-night transport/escort service.

Standardized Tests *Required:* Gates-McGinnity (for admission).

Costs (2010–11) *Tuition:* $8820 full-time, $245 per credit hour part-time. *Required fees:* $150 full-time, $245 per credit hour part-time. *Payment plan:* deferred payment.

Financial Aid Of all full-time matriculated undergraduates who enrolled in 2008, 18 Federal Work-Study jobs (averaging $700).

Applying *Options:* electronic application, deferred entrance. *Application fee:* $50. *Required:* essay or personal statement, high school transcript, minimum 2 GPA, interview. *Recommended:* minimum 2.5 GPA. *Application deadlines:* rolling (freshmen), rolling (out-of-state freshmen), rolling (transfers). *Notification:* continuous (freshmen), continuous (out-of-state freshmen), continuous (transfers).

Freshman Application Contact Ms. Janie Turmon, Admissions and Placement Coordinator-Representative, Forrest Junior College, 601 East River Street, Anderson, SC 29624. *Phone:* 864-225-7653 Ext. 210. *Fax:* 864-261-7471. *E-mail:* janieturmon@forrestcollege.com.

GREENVILLE TECHNICAL COLLEGE

Greenville, South Carolina **www.greenvilletech.com/**

Director of Admissions Ms. Martha S. White, Director of Admissions, Greenville Technical College, PO Box 5616, Greenville, SC 29606-5616. *Phone:* 864-250-8109. *Toll-free phone:* 800-922-1183 (in-state); 800-723-0673 (out-of-state).

HORRY-GEORGETOWN TECHNICAL COLLEGE

Conway, South Carolina **www.hgtc.edu/**

Freshman Application Contact Mr. George Swindoll, Vice President for Enrollment Development and Registration, Horry-Georgetown Technical College, 2050 Highway 501 East, PO Box 261966, Conway, SC 29528-6066. *Phone:* 843-349-5277. *Fax:* 843-349-7501. *E-mail:* george.swindoll@hgtc.edu.

ITT TECHNICAL INSTITUTE

Columbia, South Carolina **www.itt-tech.edu/**

- **Proprietary** primarily 2-year, part of ITT Educational Services, Inc.
- **Coed**

Majors CAD/CADD drafting/design technology; computer and information systems security; computer engineering technology; computer software and media applications related; construction management; criminal justice/law enforcement administration; design and visual communications; system, networking, and LAN/WAN management; web/multimedia management and webmaster; web page, digital/multimedia and information resources design.

Academics *Degrees:* associate and bachelor's.

Freshman Application Contact Director of Recruitment, ITT Technical Institute, 720 Gracern Road, Suite 120, Columbia, SC 29210. *Phone:* 803-216-6000. *Toll-free phone:* 800-242-5158.

ITT TECHNICAL INSTITUTE

Greenville, South Carolina **www.itt-tech.edu/**

- **Proprietary** primarily 2-year, founded 1992, part of ITT Educational Services, Inc.
- **Coed**

Majors Animation, interactive technology, video graphics and special effects; CAD/CADD drafting/design technology; computer and information systems security; computer engineering technology; computer software and media applications related; construction management; criminal justice/law enforcement administration; design and visual communications; electrical, electronic and communications engineering technology; system, networking, and LAN/WAN management; web/multimedia management and webmaster; web page, digital/multimedia and information resources design.

Academics *Calendar:* quarters. *Degrees:* associate and bachelor's.

Student Life *Housing:* college housing not available.

Financial Aid Of all full-time matriculated undergraduates who enrolled in 2008, 3 Federal Work-Study jobs.

Freshman Application Contact Director of Recruitment, ITT Technical Institute, Six Independence Point, Greenville, SC 29615. *Phone:* 864-288-0777. *Toll-free phone:* 800-932-4488.

MIDLANDS TECHNICAL COLLEGE

Columbia, South Carolina **www.midlandstech.edu/**

- **State and locally supported** 2-year, founded 1974, part of South Carolina State Board for Technical and Comprehensive Education
- **Suburban** 113-acre campus
- **Endowment** $5.1 million
- **Coed,** 11,890 undergraduate students, 47% full-time, 62% women, 38% men

Undergraduates 5,564 full-time, 6,326 part-time. Students come from 30 states and territories, 3% are from out of state, 35% African American, 2% Asian American or Pacific Islander, 2% Hispanic American, 0.6% Native American, 0.1% international.

Freshmen *Admission:* 5,753 applied, 3,763 admitted.

Faculty *Total:* 733, 29% full-time, 12% with terminal degrees. *Student/faculty ratio:* 20:1.

Majors Accounting; administrative assistant and secretarial science; architectural engineering technology; automobile/automotive mechanics technology; business administration and management; business/commerce; child-care provision; civil engineering technology; clinical/medical laboratory technology; commercial and advertising art; computer and information sciences and support services related; computer installation and repair technology; computer systems networking and telecommunications; construction engineering technology; court reporting; criminal justice/safety; data processing and data processing technology; dental assisting; dental hygiene; electrical, electronic and communications engineering technology; engineering technology; gerontology; health information/medical records technology; health professions related; heating, air conditioning, ventilation and refrigeration maintenance technology; industrial electronics technology; industrial mechanics and maintenance technology; legal assistant/paralegal; liberal arts and sciences/liberal studies; mechanical drafting and CAD/CADD; mechanical engineering/mechanical technology; medical/clinical assistant; medical radiologic technology; multi/interdisciplinary studies related; nuclear medical technology; nursing (licensed practical/vocational nurse training); nursing (registered nurse training); occupational therapist assistant; pharmacy technician; physical therapist assistant; precision production related; precision production trades; respiratory care therapy; sales, distribution and marketing; surgical technology; youth services.

Academics *Calendar:* semesters. *Degree:* certificates, diplomas, and associate. *Special study options:* academic remediation for entering students, adult/continuing education programs, advanced placement credit, cooperative education, distance learning, double majors, English as a second language, internships, part-time degree program, services for LD students, student-designed majors, summer session for credit.

Library Midlands Technical College Library with 98,507 titles, 423 serial subscriptions, 2,114 audiovisual materials, an OPAC, a Web page.

Student Life *Housing:* college housing not available. *Activities and Organizations:* drama/theater group, student-run newspaper. *Campus security:* 24-hour emergency response devices and patrols, late-night transport/escort service.

Athletics *Intramural sports:* basketball M, bowling M/W, equestrian sports M/W, football M, softball M/W, ultimate Frisbee M/W, volleyball M/W.

Standardized Tests *Required for some:* ACT ASSET. *Recommended:* SAT or ACT (for admission).

Costs (2010–11) *One-time required fee:* $25. *Tuition:* area resident $3408 full-time, $142 per credit hour part-time; state resident $4272 full-time, $178 per credit hour part-time; nonresident $10,224 full-time, $426 per credit hour part-time. Full-time tuition and fees vary according to course load. Part-time tuition and fees vary according to course load. *Required fees:* $200 full-time, $100 per term part-time. *Payment plan:* installment. *Waivers:* employees or children of employees.

Financial Aid Of all full-time matriculated undergraduates who enrolled in 2008, 138 Federal Work-Study jobs (averaging $2496).

Applying *Options:* electronic application, early admission, deferred entrance. *Application fee:* $35. *Required for some:* interview. *Recommended:* high school transcript. *Application deadlines:* rolling (freshmen), rolling (transfers). *Notification:* continuous (freshmen), continuous (transfers).

Freshman Application Contact Ms. Sylvia Littlejohn, Director of Admissions, Midlands Technical College, PO Box 2408, Columbia, SC 29202. *Phone:* 803-738-8324. *Fax:* 803-790-7524. *E-mail:* admissions@midlandstech.edu.

MILLER-MOTTE TECHNICAL COLLEGE

Charleston, South Carolina **www.miller-motte.com/**

- **Proprietary** 2-year, founded 2000, part of Delta Career Education Corporation
- **Urban** campus
- **Coed,** 764 undergraduate students

Undergraduates 64% African American, 0.7% Asian American or Pacific Islander, 0.7% Hispanic American, 0.5% Native American.

Freshmen *Admission:* 352 applied.

Majors Business, management, and marketing related; computer and information sciences; criminal justice/law enforcement administration; legal assistant/paralegal; massage therapy; medical/clinical assistant; surgical technology.

Academics *Calendar:* quarters. *Degree:* certificates, diplomas, and associate. *Special study options:* distance learning, part-time degree program.

Student Life *Housing:* college housing not available.

Costs (2010–11) *Tuition:* $11,750 full-time. Full-time tuition and fees vary according to course load and program. Part-time tuition and fees vary according to course load and program. No tuition increase for student's term of enrollment. *Required fees:* $575 full-time. *Payment plan:* installment. *Waivers:* employees or children of employees.

Applying *Application fee:* $35. *Required:* high school transcript, interview, Admissions Assessment-Wonderlic.

Freshman Application Contact Ms. Elaine Cue, Campus President, Miller-Motte Technical College, 8085 Rivers Avenue, Suite E, Charleston, SC 29406. *Phone:* 843-574-0101. *Toll-free phone:* 877-617-4740. *Fax:* 843-266-3424. *E-mail:* juliasc@miller-mott.net.

NORTHEASTERN TECHNICAL COLLEGE

Cheraw, South Carolina **www.netc.edu/**

Freshman Application Contact Mrs. Mary K. Newton, Dean of Students, Northeastern Technical College, PO Drawer 1007, Cheraw, SC 29520-1007. *Phone:* 843-921-6935. *Fax:* 843-921-1476. *E-mail:* mpace@netc.edu.

ORANGEBURG-CALHOUN TECHNICAL COLLEGE

Orangeburg, South Carolina **www.octech.edu/**

- **State and locally supported** 2-year, founded 1968, part of State Board for Technical and Comprehensive Education, South Carolina
- **Small-town** 100-acre campus with easy access to Columbia
- **Coed,** 3,219 undergraduate students, 48% full-time, 67% women, 33% men

Undergraduates 1,538 full-time, 1,681 part-time. Students come from 11 states and territories, 1 other country, 58% African American, 0.4% Asian American or Pacific Islander, 0.6% Hispanic American, 0.3% Native American, 0.3% international.

Freshmen *Admission:* 606 enrolled.

Faculty *Total:* 163, 46% full-time. *Student/faculty ratio:* 20:1.

Majors Accounting; administrative assistant and secretarial science; automobile/automotive mechanics technology; business/commerce; clinical/medical laboratory technology; computer programming related; criminal justice/safety; electrical, electronic and communications engineering technology; instrumentation technology; kindergarten/preschool education; legal assistant/paralegal; liberal arts and sciences/liberal studies; machine tool technology; medical radiologic technology; nursing (registered nurse training); respiratory care therapy.

Academics *Calendar:* semesters. *Degree:* certificates, diplomas, and associate. *Special study options:* academic remediation for entering students, adult/continuing education programs, advanced placement credit, cooperative education, distance learning, independent study, internships, part-time degree program, services for LD students, student-designed majors, summer session for credit.

Library Gressette Learning Center plus 1 other with 43,500 titles, 143 serial subscriptions, 2,253 audiovisual materials, an OPAC.

Student Life *Housing:* college housing not available. *Campus security:* 24-hour emergency response devices and patrols. *Student services:* personal/psychological counseling.

Applying *Application fee:* $15. *Required:* high school transcript. *Required for some:* interview. *Application deadlines:* rolling (freshmen), rolling (transfers). *Notification:* continuous (freshmen), continuous (transfers).

Freshman Application Contact Mr. Dana Rickards, Director of Recruitment, Orangeburg-Calhoun Technical College, 3250 St. Matthews Road, Highway 601, Orangeburg, SC 29118. *Phone:* 803-535-1219. *Toll-free phone:* 800-813-6519.

PIEDMONT TECHNICAL COLLEGE

Greenwood, South Carolina **www.ptc.edu/**

Director of Admissions Mr. Steve Coleman, Director of Admissions, Piedmont Technical College, 620 North Emerald Road, PO Box 1467, Greenwood, SC 29648. *Phone:* 864-941-8603. *Toll-free phone:* 800-868-5528.

SPARTANBURG COMMUNITY COLLEGE

Spartanburg, South Carolina **www.sccsc.edu/**

- **State-supported** 2-year, founded 1961, part of South Carolina State Board for Technical and Comprehensive Education
- **Suburban** 104-acre campus
- **Endowment** $508,220
- **Coed,** 5,713 undergraduate students, 54% full-time, 63% women, 37% men

Undergraduates 3,076 full-time, 2,637 part-time. Students come from 10 states and territories, 5 other countries, 1% are from out of state, 27% African American, 3% Asian American or Pacific Islander, 2% Hispanic American, 0.2% Native American, 0.1% international. *Retention:* 57% of 2008 full-time freshmen returned.

Freshmen *Admission:* 3,946 applied, 2,237 admitted.

Faculty *Total:* 365, 30% full-time. *Student/faculty ratio:* 16:1.

Majors Accounting; administrative assistant and secretarial science; applied horticulture; automobile/automotive mechanics technology; business administration and management; clinical/medical laboratory technology; computer and information sciences; data processing and data processing technology; drafting and design technology; electrical, electronic and communications engineering technology; engineering technology; heating, air conditioning, ventilation and refrigeration maintenance technology; horticultural science; industrial electronics technology; liberal arts and sciences/liberal studies; machine tool technology; marketing/marketing management; mechanical drafting and CAD/CADD; mechanical engineering/mechanical technology; medical radiologic technology; multi/interdisciplinary studies related; nursing (registered nurse training); radiation protection/health physics technology; respiratory care therapy; sales, distribution and marketing.

Academics *Calendar:* semesters condensed semesters plus summer sessions. *Degree:* certificates, diplomas, and associate. *Special study options:* academic remediation for entering students, adult/continuing education programs, advanced placement credit, cooperative education, distance learning, English as a second language, part-time degree program, services for LD students, summer session for credit.

Library Spartanburg Community College Library with 40,078 titles, 295 serial subscriptions, an OPAC, a Web page.

Student Life *Housing:* college housing not available. *Activities and Organizations:* drama/theater group, student-run newspaper. *Campus security:* 24-hour emergency response devices and patrols. *Student services:* personal/psychological counseling, women's center.

Standardized Tests *Required for some:* SAT or ACT (for admission).

Costs (2010–11) *Tuition:* area resident $3434 full-time, $142 per credit hour part-time; state resident $4282 full-time, $177 per credit hour part-time; nonresident $7196 full-time, $299 per credit hour part-time. *Required fees:* $20 per term part-time. *Payment plan:* installment. *Waivers:* senior citizens.

Financial Aid Of all full-time matriculated undergraduates who enrolled in 2008, 82 Federal Work-Study jobs (averaging $2665).

Applying *Options:* early admission. *Required:* high school transcript, interview, high school diploma, GED or equivalent. *Application deadlines:* rolling (freshmen), rolling (transfers). *Notification:* continuous (freshmen), continuous (transfers).

Freshman Application Contact Kathy Jo Lancaster, Admissions Counselor, Spartanburg Community College, PO Box 4386, Spartanburg, SC 29305. *Phone:* 864-592-4815. *Toll-free phone:* 866-591-3700. *Fax:* 864-592-4564. *E-mail:* admissions@stcsc.edu.

Spartanburg Methodist College

Spartanburg, South Carolina www.smcsc.edu/

- **Independent Methodist** 2-year, founded 1911
- **Urban** 110-acre campus with easy access to Charlotte
- **Endowment** $14.2 million
- **Coed,** 808 undergraduate students, 96% full-time, 43% women, 57% men

Undergraduates 775 full-time, 33 part-time. Students come from 8 states and territories, 1 other country, 6% are from out of state, 28% African American, 1% Asian American or Pacific Islander, 5% Hispanic American, 0.1% Native American, 0.4% international, 4% transferred in, 68% live on campus.

Freshmen *Admission:* 1,202 applied, 847 admitted, 452 enrolled. *Average high school GPA:* 3.25. *Test scores:* SAT verbal scores over 500: 22%; SAT math scores over 500: 26%; SAT verbal scores over 600: 2%; SAT math scores over 600: 4%.

Faculty *Total:* 68, 47% full-time, 19% with terminal degrees. *Student/faculty ratio:* 18:1.

Majors Criminal justice/law enforcement administration; liberal arts and sciences/liberal studies; religious studies related.

Academics *Calendar:* semesters. *Degree:* associate. *Special study options:* academic remediation for entering students, advanced placement credit, English as a second language, honors programs, independent study, part-time degree program, services for LD students, summer session for credit.

Library Marie Blair Burgess Learning Resource Center with 75,000 titles, 5,000 serial subscriptions, 3,150 audiovisual materials, an OPAC, a Web page.

Student Life *Housing:* on-campus residence required through sophomore year. *Options:* coed, men-only, women-only. Campus housing is university owned. Freshman campus housing is guaranteed. *Activities and Organizations:* drama/theater group, student-run newspaper, choral group, College Christian Movement, Alpha Phi Omega, Campus Union, Fellowship of Christian Athletes, Kappa Sigma Alpha. *Campus security:* 24-hour emergency response devices and patrols, student patrols, late-night transport/escort service, controlled dormitory access. *Student services:* health clinic, personal/psychological counseling.

Athletics Member NJCAA. *Intercollegiate sports:* baseball M(s), basketball M(s)/W(s), cross-country running M(s)/W(s), golf M(s)/W(s), soccer M(s)/W(s), softball W(s), tennis M(s)/W(s), volleyball W(s), wrestling M(s). *Intramural sports:* basketball M/W, cheerleading M/W, football M/W, softball M/W, table tennis M/W, volleyball M/W.

Standardized Tests *Required:* SAT or ACT (for admission).

Costs (2010–11) *One-time required fee:* $150. *Comprehensive fee:* $20,363 includes full-time tuition ($12,723), mandatory fees ($225), and room and board ($7415). Part-time tuition: $334 per semester hour. *Payment plans:* installment, deferred payment. *Waivers:* employees or children of employees.

Financial Aid Of all full-time matriculated undergraduates who enrolled in 2008, 80 Federal Work-Study jobs (averaging $1600). 90 state and other part-time jobs (averaging $1600). *Financial aid deadline:* 8/30.

Applying *Options:* electronic application, deferred entrance. *Application fee:* $20. *Required:* essay or personal statement, high school transcript, minimum 2 GPA, rank in upper 75% of high school class. *Required for some:* interview. *Recommended:* interview. *Application deadlines:* rolling (freshmen), rolling (transfers). *Notification:* continuous (freshmen), continuous (transfers).

Freshman Application Contact Daniel L. Philbeck, Vice President for Enrollment Management, Spartanburg Methodist College, 1000 Powell Mill Road, Spartanburg, SC 29301-5899. *Phone:* 864-587-4223. *Toll-free phone:* 800-772-7286. *Fax:* 864-587-4355. *E-mail:* admiss@smcsc.edu.

Technical College of the Lowcountry

Beaufort, South Carolina www.tclonline.org/

Freshman Application Contact Rhonda Cole, Admissions Services Manager, Technical College of the Lowcountry, 921 Ribaut Road, PO Box 1288, Beaufort, SC 29901-1288. *Phone:* 843-525-8229. *Fax:* 843-525-8285. *E-mail:* rcole@tcl.edu.

Tri-County Technical College

Pendleton, South Carolina www.tctc.edu/

Director of Admissions Renae Frazier, Director, Recruitment and Admissions, Tri-County Technical College, PO Box 587, Highway 76, Pendleton, SC 29670-0587. *Phone:* 864-646-1550. *Fax:* 864-646-1890. *E-mail:* infocent@tctc.edu.

Trident Technical College

Charleston, South Carolina www.tridenttech.edu/

- **State and locally supported** 2-year, founded 1964, part of South Carolina State Board for Technical and Comprehensive Education
- **Urban** campus
- **Coed,** 14,834 undergraduate students, 46% full-time, 63% women, 37% men

Undergraduates 6,856 full-time, 7,978 part-time. 4% are from out of state, 29% African American, 2% Asian American or Pacific Islander, 3% Hispanic American, 0.4% Native American.

Freshmen *Admission:* 2,850 admitted, 2,850 enrolled.

Faculty *Total:* 699, 44% full-time. *Student/faculty ratio:* 20:1.

Majors Accounting; administrative assistant and secretarial science; airframe mechanics and aircraft maintenance technology; automobile/automotive mechanics technology; biological and physical sciences; business administration and management; child-care provision; civil engineering technology; clinical/medical laboratory technology; commercial and advertising art; computer engineering technology; computer graphics; computer/information technology services administration related; computer programming (specific applications); computer systems networking and telecommunications; criminal justice/law enforcement administration; culinary arts; dental hygiene; electrical, electronic and communications engineering technology; engineering technology; horticultural science; hotel/motel administration; human services; industrial technology; legal assistant/paralegal; legal studies; liberal arts and sciences/liberal studies; machine tool technology; marketing/marketing management; mechanical engineering/mechanical technology; medical administrative assistant and medical secretary; nursing (registered nurse training); occupational therapy; physical therapy; respiratory care therapy; telecommunications technology; veterinary/animal health technology; web/multimedia management and webmaster; web page, digital/multimedia and information resources design.

Academics *Calendar:* semesters. *Degree:* certificates, diplomas, and associate. *Special study options:* academic remediation for entering students, advanced placement credit, cooperative education, distance learning, double majors, English as a second language, part-time degree program, services for LD students, summer session for credit.

Library Learning Resources Center plus 3 others with 135,345 titles, 785 serial subscriptions, 12,486 audiovisual materials, an OPAC, a Web page.

Student Life *Housing:* college housing not available. *Activities and Organizations:* drama/theater group, student-run newspaper, radio station, Phi Theta Kappa, Lex Artis Paralegal Society, Hospitality and Culinary Student Association, Partnership for Change in Communities and Families, Society of Student Leaders. *Campus security:* 24-hour emergency response devices and patrols, late-night transport/escort service. *Student services:* personal/psychological counseling.

Costs (2010–11) *Tuition:* area resident $3450 full-time; state resident $3828 full-time; nonresident $6532 full-time. Full-time tuition and fees vary according to course load. Part-time tuition and fees vary according to course load. *Payment plan:* installment. *Waivers:* senior citizens and employees or children of employees.

Applying *Options:* electronic application, early admission. *Application fee:* $30. *Required for some:* high school transcript. *Notification:* continuous (freshmen), continuous (transfers).

Freshman Application Contact Ms. Clara Martin, Admissions Director, Trident Technical College, 7000 Rivers Avenue, Charleston, SC 29423-8067. *Phone:* 843-574-6626. *Fax:* 843-574-6109. *E-mail:* Clara.Martin@tridenttech.edu.

University of South Carolina Lancaster

Lancaster, South Carolina usclancaster.sc.edu/

- **State-supported** 2-year, founded 1959, part of University of South Carolina System
- **Small-town** 17-acre campus with easy access to Charlotte
- **Coed,** 1,593 undergraduate students, 50% full-time, 60% women, 40% men

Undergraduates 794 full-time, 799 part-time. Students come from 10 states and territories, 2 other countries, 1% are from out of state, 18% African American, 0.3% Asian American or Pacific Islander, 1% Hispanic American, 0.6% Native American.

Freshmen *Admission:* 557 applied, 555 admitted.

Faculty *Total:* 105, 60% full-time, 44% with terminal degrees. *Student/faculty ratio:* 14:1.

University of South Carolina Lancaster (continued)

Majors Business administration and management; criminal justice/law enforcement administration; liberal arts and sciences/liberal studies; nursing (registered nurse training).

Academics *Calendar:* semesters. *Degree:* associate. *Special study options:* academic remediation for entering students, advanced placement credit, distance learning, honors programs, independent study, internships, part-time degree program, services for LD students.

Library Medford Library with 82,000 titles, 150 serial subscriptions, an OPAC, a Web page.

Student Life *Housing:* college housing not available. *Activities and Organizations:* drama/theater group, student-run newspaper. *Student services:* personal/psychological counseling.

Athletics Member NJCAA. *Intercollegiate sports:* baseball M, golf M, soccer W, tennis M/W.

Standardized Tests *Required:* SAT or ACT (for admission).

Costs (2010–11) *One-time required fee:* $50. *Tuition:* state resident $5136 full-time, $214 per credit hour part-time; nonresident $12,912 full-time, $538 per credit hour part-time. Full-time tuition and fees vary according to student level. Part-time tuition and fees vary according to student level. *Required fees:* $462 full-time, $15 per credit hour part-time. *Payment plan:* deferred payment. *Waivers:* senior citizens.

Applying *Options:* electronic application, early admission. *Application fee:* $40. *Required:* high school transcript. *Application deadlines:* rolling (freshmen), rolling (out-of-state freshmen), rolling (transfers). *Notification:* continuous (freshmen), continuous (out-of-state freshmen), continuous (transfers).

Freshman Application Contact Susan Vinson, Admissions Counselor, University of South Carolina Lancaster, PO Box 889, Lancaster, SC 29721-0889. *Phone:* 803-313-7000. *Fax:* 803-313-7116. *E-mail:* vinsons@mailbox.sc.edu.

University of South Carolina Salkehatchie

Allendale, South Carolina uscsalkehatchie.sc.edu/

- **State-supported** 2-year, founded 1965, part of University of South Carolina System
- **Rural** 95-acre campus
- **Coed,** 965 undergraduate students

Undergraduates 6% are from out of state. *Retention:* 45% of 2008 full-time freshmen returned.

Freshmen *Admission:* 421 applied.

Faculty *Student/faculty ratio:* 16:1.

Majors Liberal arts and sciences/liberal studies.

Academics *Calendar:* semesters. *Degree:* associate. *Special study options:* academic remediation for entering students, adult/continuing education programs, advanced placement credit, distance learning, part-time degree program, summer session for credit.

Library Salkehatchie Learning Resource Center with an OPAC, a Web page.

Student Life *Housing:* college housing not available. *Campus security:* 24-hour emergency response devices.

Athletics Member NJCAA. *Intercollegiate sports:* baseball M, basketball M, soccer M/W, softball W, volleyball W.

Standardized Tests *Required:* SAT or ACT (for admission).

Applying *Options:* electronic application. *Application fee:* $40. *Required:* high school transcript, minimum 2 GPA, ACT or SAT scores. *Application deadlines:* rolling (freshmen), rolling (transfers).

Freshman Application Contact Ms. Carmen Brown, Admissions Coordinator, University of South Carolina Salkehatchie, PO Box 617, Allendale, SC 29810-0617. *Phone:* 803-584-3446. *Toll-free phone:* 800-922-5500. *Fax:* 803-584-3884. *E-mail:* cdbrown@mailbox.sc.edu.

University of South Carolina Sumter

Sumter, South Carolina www.uscsumter.edu/

Freshman Application Contact Mr. Keith Britton, Director of Admissions, University of South Carolina Sumter, 200 Miller Road, Sumter, SC 29150-2498. *Phone:* 803-938-3882. *Fax:* 803-938-3901. *E-mail:* kbritton@usc.sumter.edu.

University of South Carolina Union

Union, South Carolina uscunion.sc.edu/

Freshman Application Contact Mr. Terry Young, Director of Enrollment Services, University of South Carolina Union, PO Drawer 729, Union, SC 29379-0729. *Phone:* 864-429-8728. *E-mail:* tyoung@gwm.sc.edu.

Williamsburg Technical College

Kingstree, South Carolina www.wiltech.edu/

Freshman Application Contact Williamsburg Technical College, 601 Martin Luther King Jr Avenue, Kingstree, SC 29556-4197. *Phone:* 843-355-4162. *Toll-free phone:* 800-768-2021.

York Technical College

Rock Hill, South Carolina www.yorktech.com/

Freshman Application Contact Mr. Kenny Aldridge, Admissions Department Manager, York Technical College, 452 South Anderson Road, Rock Hill, SC 29730. *Phone:* 803-327-8008. *Toll-free phone:* 800-922-8324. *Fax:* 803-981-7237. *E-mail:* kaldridge@yorktech.com.

SOUTH DAKOTA

Kilian Community College

Sioux Falls, South Dakota www.kilian.edu/

- **Independent** 2-year, founded 1977
- **Urban** 2-acre campus
- **Coed,** 336 undergraduate students, 19% full-time, 71% women, 29% men

Undergraduates 64 full-time, 272 part-time. Students come from 3 states and territories, 6% are from out of state, 10% African American, 0.6% Asian American or Pacific Islander, 1% Hispanic American, 12% Native American, 11% transferred in.

Freshmen *Admission:* 65 enrolled.

Faculty *Total:* 32, 19% full-time, 13% with terminal degrees. *Student/faculty ratio:* 5:1.

Majors Accounting; business administration and management; counseling psychology; criminal justice/law enforcement administration; information technology; liberal arts and sciences/liberal studies; medical office management; social work.

Academics *Calendar:* trimesters. *Degree:* certificates and associate. *Special study options:* academic remediation for entering students, distance learning, double majors, English as a second language, independent study, off-campus study, part-time degree program, services for LD students, summer session for credit.

Library Sioux Falls Public Library with 78,000 titles, 395 serial subscriptions, an OPAC, a Web page.

Student Life *Housing:* college housing not available. *Activities and Organizations:* Phi Theta Kappa, Students in Free Enterprise (SIFE). *Campus security:* late-night transport/escort service. *Student services:* personal/psychological counseling.

Costs (2009–10) *Tuition:* $8820 full-time, $245 per credit hour part-time. *Required fees:* $255 full-time, $85 part-time. *Payment plan:* installment. *Waivers:* senior citizens and employees or children of employees.

Financial Aid Of all full-time matriculated undergraduates who enrolled in 2009, 15 Federal Work-Study jobs (averaging $35,510).

Applying *Options:* electronic application, deferred entrance. *Application fee:* $25. *Required:* high school transcript. *Application deadlines:* rolling (freshmen), rolling (out-of-state freshmen), rolling (transfers).

Freshman Application Contact Ms. Mary Klockman, Director of Admissions, Kilian Community College, 224 North Phillips Avenue, Sioux Falls, SD 57104-6014. *Phone:* 605-221-3100. *Toll-free phone:* 800-888-1147. *Fax:* 605-336-2606. *E-mail:* info@killian.edu.

LAKE AREA TECHNICAL INSTITUTE

Watertown, South Dakota **www.lakeareatech.edu/**

- **State-supported** 2-year, founded 1964
- **Small-town** 16-acre campus
- **Coed**

Academics *Calendar:* semesters. *Degree:* diplomas and associate. *Special study options:* academic remediation for entering students, internships, services for LD students.

Standardized Tests *Required:* ACT (for admission).

Costs (2009–10) *One-time required fee:* $20. *Tuition:* state resident $3024 full-time; nonresident $3024 full-time. Full-time tuition and fees vary according to program. *Required fees:* $1958 full-time.

Applying *Options:* electronic application. *Application fee:* $20. *Required:* high school transcript. *Required for some:* essay or personal statement, 3 letters of recommendation, interview.

Director of Admissions Ms. Debra Shephard, Assistant Director, Lake Area Technical Institute, 230 11th Street, NE, Watertown, SD 57201. *Phone:* 605-882-5284. *Toll-free phone:* 800-657-4344. *E-mail:* latiinfo@lati.tec.sd.us.

MITCHELL TECHNICAL INSTITUTE

Mitchell, South Dakota **www.mitchelltech.edu/**

- **State-supported** 2-year, founded 1968
- **Rural** 90-acre campus
- **Coed,** 1,003 undergraduate students, 88% full-time, 31% women, 69% men

Undergraduates 882 full-time, 121 part-time. Students come from 12 states and territories, 10% are from out of state, 0.6% African American, 0.7% Asian American or Pacific Islander, 0.4% Hispanic American, 2% Native American.

Freshmen *Admission:* 1,339 applied, 641 admitted.

Faculty *Total:* 61, 87% full-time. *Student/faculty ratio:* 16:1.

Majors Accounting; administrative assistant and secretarial science; agricultural business and management; agricultural production; appliance installation and repair technology; architectural drafting and CAD/CADD; carpentry; clinical/medical laboratory technology; communications technologies and support services related; computer and information sciences; computer and information sciences and support services related; computer/information technology services administration related; computer software and media applications related; computer systems networking and telecommunications; computer technology/computer systems technology; construction trades related; culinary arts; data entry/microcomputer applications; drafting and design technology; electrical and electronic engineering technologies related; electrical and power transmission installation; electrical, electronic and communications engineering technology; electrician; electromechanical technology; engineering technologies related; farm and ranch management; heating, air conditioning and refrigeration technology; heating, air conditioning, ventilation and refrigeration maintenance technology; industrial electronics technology; information science/studies; lineworker; medical administrative assistant and medical secretary; medical/clinical assistant; radiologic technology/science; system, networking, and LAN/WAN management; telecommunications technology.

Academics *Calendar:* semesters. *Degree:* diplomas and associate. *Special study options:* academic remediation for entering students, advanced placement credit, cooperative education, distance learning, internships, part-time degree program, services for LD students, summer session for credit.

Library Instructional Services Center with 100 serial subscriptions, an OPAC.

Student Life *Housing Options:* coed. Campus housing is provided by a third party. *Activities and Organizations:* Student Representative Board, Skills USA, Post-Secondary Agricultural Students, Rodeo Club, Technology Club. *Student services:* personal/psychological counseling.

Athletics *Intercollegiate sports:* equestrian sports M/W. *Intramural sports:* basketball M/W, riflery M/W, softball M/W, volleyball M/W.

Standardized Tests *Required for some:* Compass. *Recommended:* ACT (for admission).

Costs (2010–11) *Tuition:* state resident $3240 full-time, $90 per credit hour part-time; nonresident $3240 full-time, $90 per credit hour part-time. Full-time tuition and fees vary according to program. Part-time tuition and fees vary according to program. *Required fees:* $3000 full-time, $49 per credit hour part-time, $49 per credit hour part-time. *Waivers:* employees or children of employees.

Financial Aid Of all full-time matriculated undergraduates who enrolled in 2008, 52 Federal Work-Study jobs (averaging $1375).

Applying *Options:* electronic application. *Application fee:* $25. *Required:* high school transcript. *Required for some:* essay or personal statement, interview. *Recommended:* minimum 2 GPA. *Application deadlines:* rolling (freshmen), rolling (out-of-state freshmen), rolling (transfers). *Notification:* continuous (freshmen), continuous (out-of-state freshmen), continuous (transfers).

Freshman Application Contact Mr. Clayton Deuter, Director of Admissions, Mitchell Technical Institute, 821 North Capital, Mitchell, SD 57301. *Phone:* 605-995-3025. *Toll-free phone:* 800-952-0042. *Fax:* 605-996-3299. *E-mail:* clayton.deuter@mitchelltech.edu.

NATIONAL AMERICAN UNIVERSITY

Ellsworth AFB, South Dakota **www.national.edu/**

Freshman Application Contact Admissions Office, National American University, 1000 Ellsworth Street, Suite 2400B, Ellsworth AFB, SD 57706.

SISSETON-WAHPETON COMMUNITY COLLEGE

Sisseton, South Dakota **www.swc.tc/**

- **Federally supported** 2-year, founded 1979
- **Rural** 2-acre campus
- **Coed,** 237 undergraduate students, 76% full-time, 75% women, 25% men

Undergraduates 181 full-time, 56 part-time. 2% are from out of state, 0.4% African American, 0.4% Asian American or Pacific Islander, 0.4% Hispanic American, 81% Native American, 0.4% transferred in.

Freshmen *Admission:* 67 applied, 63 admitted, 63 enrolled.

Faculty *Total:* 30, 33% full-time, 33% with terminal degrees. *Student/faculty ratio:* 10:1.

Majors Accounting; American Indian/Native American studies; business administration and management; electrical, electronic and communications engineering technology; hospitality administration; information science/studies; kindergarten/preschool education; liberal arts and sciences/liberal studies; natural sciences; nursing (registered nurse training); nutrition sciences; substance abuse/addiction counseling.

Academics *Calendar:* semesters. *Degree:* certificates and associate. *Special study options:* academic remediation for entering students, adult/continuing education programs, cooperative education, double majors, internships, off-campus study, part-time degree program, summer session for credit.

Library Sisseton-Wahpeton Community College Library with 15,481 titles, 162 serial subscriptions, 885 audiovisual materials, an OPAC, a Web page.

Student Life *Activities and Organizations:* AIHEC, AISES, Student Senate, Student Nurses Association, AIBL. *Campus security:* 24-hour emergency response devices. *Student services:* personal/psychological counseling.

Standardized Tests *Required:* compass test (for admission).

Costs (2010–11) *Tuition:* state resident $3300 full-time, $110 per credit hour part-time; nonresident $3300 full-time, $110 per credit hour part-time. Full-time tuition and fees vary according to course load and program. Part-time tuition and fees vary according to course load and program. No tuition increase for student's term of enrollment. *Room and board:* $6000. *Payment plan:* installment. *Waivers:* senior citizens.

Financial Aid Of all full-time matriculated undergraduates who enrolled in 2008, 5 Federal Work-Study jobs (averaging $1200).

Applying *Required:* high school transcript. *Required for some:* CIB if an enrolled tribal member. *Recommended:* minimum 2 GPA, interview. *Application deadlines:* rolling (freshmen), rolling (transfers).

Freshman Application Contact Sisseton-Wahpeton Community College, Old Agency Box 689, Sisseton, SD 57262. *Phone:* 605-698-3966 Ext. 1180.

SOUTHEAST TECHNICAL INSTITUTE

Sioux Falls, South Dakota **www.southeasttech.edu/**

- **State-supported** 2-year, founded 1968
- **Urban** 169-acre campus
- **Endowment** $468,959
- **Coed,** 2,489 undergraduate students, 79% full-time, 45% women, 55% men

Southeast Technical Institute (continued)

Undergraduates 1,967 full-time, 522 part-time. Students come from 7 states and territories, 9% are from out of state, 2% African American, 1% Asian American or Pacific Islander, 1% Hispanic American, 3% Native American, 13% transferred in, 7% live on campus. *Retention:* 69% of 2008 full-time freshmen returned.

Freshmen *Admission:* 2,992 applied, 1,477 admitted, 734 enrolled. *Average high school GPA:* 2.73.

Faculty *Total:* 136, 59% full-time, 4% with terminal degrees. *Student/faculty ratio:* 16:1.

Majors Accounting; animation, interactive technology, video graphics and special effects; applied horticulture; architectural engineering technology; autobody/collision and repair technology; automobile/automotive mechanics technology; banking and financial support services; biomedical technology; building/construction finishing, management, and inspection related; business administration and management; cardiovascular technology; child-care and support services management; child-care provision; civil engineering technology; clinical/medical laboratory science and allied professions related; clinical/medical laboratory technology; commercial and advertising art; computer and information sciences and support services related; computer and information systems security; computer/information technology services administration related; computer installation and repair technology; computer programming; computer programming related; computer software engineering; computer systems networking and telecommunications; computer technology/computer systems technology; criminal justice/police science; desktop publishing and digital imaging design; diagnostic medical sonography and ultrasound technology; diesel mechanics technology; electrical, electronic and communications engineering technology; electrical/electronics equipment installation and repair; electromechanical technology; finance; health unit coordinator/ward clerk; heating, air conditioning, ventilation and refrigeration maintenance technology; horticultural science; industrial technology; machine shop technology; machine tool technology; marketing/marketing management; mechanical engineering/mechanical technology; merchandising, sales, and marketing operations related (general); nuclear medical technology; nursing (licensed practical/vocational nurse training); nursing related; office occupations and clerical services; surgical technology; turf and turfgrass management.

Academics *Calendar:* semesters. *Degree:* certificates, diplomas, and associate. *Special study options:* academic remediation for entering students, accelerated degree program, advanced placement credit, distance learning, double majors, independent study, internships, part-time degree program, services for LD students, summer session for credit.

Library Southeast Library with 10,643 titles, 158 serial subscriptions, an OPAC, a Web page.

Student Life *Housing Options:* coed. Campus housing is provided by a third party. *Activities and Organizations:* VICA (Vocational Industrial Clubs of America), American Landscape Contractors Association. *Campus security:* 24-hour emergency response devices and patrols, late-night transport/escort service. *Student services:* personal/psychological counseling.

Athletics *Intramural sports:* basketball M/W, bowling M/W, volleyball M/W.

Standardized Tests *Recommended:* ACT (for admission).

Costs (2009–10) *Tuition:* state resident $2520 full-time, $84 per credit hour part-time; nonresident $2520 full-time, $84 per credit hour part-time. *Required fees:* $1717 full-time, $57 per credit hour part-time. *Room and board:* room only: $4600. *Payment plan:* installment.

Financial Aid Of all full-time matriculated undergraduates who enrolled in 2008, 35 Federal Work-Study jobs (averaging $2550).

Applying *Options:* electronic application. *Required:* high school transcript, minimum 2.2 GPA. *Required for some:* interview, background check and drug testing. *Application deadlines:* rolling (freshmen), rolling (transfers). *Notification:* continuous (freshmen), continuous (transfers).

Freshman Application Contact Mr. Scott Dorman, Recruiter, Southeast Technical Institute, 2320 North Career Avenue, Sioux Falls, SD 57107. *Phone:* 605-367-4458. *Toll-free phone:* 800-247-0789. *Fax:* 605-367-8305. *E-mail:* scott.dorman@southeasttech.edu.

Western Dakota Technical Institute

Rapid City, South Dakota **www.westerndakotatech.org/**

Freshman Application Contact Jill Elder, Western Dakota Technical Institute, 800 Mickelson Drive, Rapid City, SD 57703. *Phone:* 605-718-2411. *Toll-free phone:* 800-544-8765. *Fax:* 605-394-2204. *E-mail:* jill.elder@wdt.edu.

TENNESSEE

Chattanooga College–Medical, Dental and Technical Careers

Chattanooga, Tennessee **www.ecpconline.com/**

- **Proprietary** 2-year
- **Coed**

Academics *Degree:* associate.

Applying *Application fee:* $75.

Director of Admissions Toney McFadden, Admission Director, Chattanooga College–Medical, Dental and Technical Careers, 3805 Brainerd Road, Chattanooga, TN 37411-3798. *Phone:* 423-624-0077. *Fax:* 423-624-1575.

Chattanooga State Community College

Chattanooga, Tennessee **www.chattanoogastate.edu/**

- **State-supported** 2-year, founded 1965, part of Tennessee Board of Regents
- **Urban** 100-acre campus
- **Endowment** $5.6 million
- **Coed,** 9,431 undergraduate students, 47% full-time, 59% women, 41% men

Undergraduates 4,412 full-time, 5,019 part-time. Students come from 30 states and territories, 11 other countries, 9% are from out of state, 17% African American, 1% Asian American or Pacific Islander, 2% Hispanic American, 0.3% Native American.

Freshmen *Admission:* 1,560 applied, 1,560 admitted. *Average high school GPA:* 2.66.

Faculty *Total:* 628, 34% full-time. *Student/faculty ratio:* 19:1.

Majors Accounting; accounting technology and bookkeeping; administrative assistant and secretarial science; business automation/technology/data entry; cardiovascular technology; child development; civil engineering technology; commercial and advertising art; community organization and advocacy; computer and information systems security; court reporting; dental assisting; dental hygiene; diagnostic medical sonography and ultrasound technology; drafting and design technology; education; electrical, electronic and communications engineering technology; electrician; engineering technology; environmental engineering technology; environmental health; finance; fire science; foods, nutrition, and wellness; general studies; health information/medical records technology; health/medical physics; industrial arts; industrial technology; legal administrative assistant/secretary; legal assistant/paralegal; management information systems; medical radiologic technology; nursing (registered nurse training); operations management; pharmacy technician; physical therapist assistant; radio and television; respiratory care therapy; veterinary/animal health technology; web page, digital/multimedia and information resources design.

Academics *Calendar:* semesters. *Degree:* certificates, diplomas, and associate. *Special study options:* academic remediation for entering students, accelerated degree program, adult/continuing education programs, advanced placement credit, cooperative education, distance learning, double majors, external degree program, honors programs, independent study, internships, part-time degree program, services for LD students, summer session for credit.

Library Augusta R. Kolwyck Library with 161,086 titles, 256 serial subscriptions, 3,680 audiovisual materials, an OPAC, a Web page.

Student Life *Housing:* college housing not available. *Activities and Organizations:* drama/theater group, student-run newspaper, choral group, Black Student Association, Adult Connections, Human Services Specialists, Student Government Association, Student Nurses Association. *Campus security:* 24-hour emergency response devices and patrols, late-night transport/escort service. *Student services:* personal/psychological counseling, women's center.

Athletics Member NJCAA. *Intercollegiate sports:* baseball M(s), basketball M(s)/W(s), softball W(s). *Intramural sports:* softball W.

Costs (2009–10) *Tuition:* state resident $2955 full-time, $111 per credit hour part-time; nonresident $11,331 full-time, $349 per credit hour part-time. *Required fees:* $291 full-time. *Payment plan:* deferred payment. *Waivers:* senior citizens and employees or children of employees.

Applying *Options:* electronic application, early admission, deferred entrance. *Application fee:* $15. *Required for some:* high school transcript, interview. *Recommended:* high school transcript. *Application deadlines:* rolling (freshmen), rolling (out-of-state freshmen), rolling (transfers). *Notification:* continuous (freshmen), continuous (out-of-state freshmen), continuous (transfers).

Freshman Application Contact Ms. Diane Norris, Director of Admissions, Chattanooga State Community College, 4501 Amnicola Highway, Chattanooga, TN 37406-1097. *Phone:* 423-697-4401 Ext. 3107. *Fax:* 423-697-4709. *E-mail:* diane.norris@chattanoogastate.edu.

CLEVELAND STATE COMMUNITY COLLEGE

Cleveland, Tennessee **www.clevelandstatecc.edu/**

- **State-supported** 2-year, founded 1967, part of Tennessee Board of Regents
- **Suburban** 83-acre campus
- **Endowment** $5.1 million
- **Coed,** 3,615 undergraduate students, 56% full-time, 61% women, 39% men

Undergraduates 2,032 full-time, 1,583 part-time. Students come from 2 other countries, 1% are from out of state, 6% African American, 1% Asian American or Pacific Islander, 2% Hispanic American, 0.4% Native American, 0.1% international, 6% transferred in.

Freshmen *Admission:* 748 enrolled. *Average high school GPA:* 3.12. *Test scores:* ACT scores over 18: 73%; ACT scores over 24: 11%.

Faculty *Total:* 187, 37% full-time, 12% with terminal degrees. *Student/faculty ratio:* 14:1.

Majors Administrative assistant and secretarial science; business administration and management; child development; community organization and advocacy; criminal justice/police science; general studies; industrial arts; industrial technology; kindergarten/preschool education; liberal arts and sciences/liberal studies; nursing (registered nurse training); public administration and social service professions related.

Academics *Calendar:* semesters. *Degree:* certificates and associate. *Special study options:* academic remediation for entering students, adult/continuing education programs, advanced placement credit, cooperative education, distance learning, double majors, external degree program, honors programs, independent study, internships, off-campus study, part-time degree program, services for LD students, summer session for credit.

Library Cleveland State Community College Library with 147,405 titles, 831 serial subscriptions, 9,142 audiovisual materials, an OPAC, a Web page.

Student Life *Housing:* college housing not available. *Activities and Organizations:* student-run newspaper, choral group, Human Services/Social Work, Computer Aided Design, Phi Theta Kappa, Student Nursing Association, Early Childhood Education. *Campus security:* 24-hour emergency response devices and patrols. *Student services:* personal/psychological counseling.

Athletics Member NJCAA. *Intercollegiate sports:* baseball M(s), basketball M(s)/W(s), softball W(s). *Intramural sports:* archery M/W, basketball M/W, bowling M/W, cheerleading M(c)/W(c), softball W, table tennis M/W, volleyball M/W.

Standardized Tests *Recommended:* SAT or ACT (for admission).

Costs (2009–10) *Tuition:* state resident $3039 full-time, $111 per credit hour part-time; nonresident $11,487 full-time, $460 per credit hour part-time. Full time tuition and fees vary according to course load. *Required fees:* $269 full-time, $14 per credit hour part-time. *Payment plan:* deferred payment. *Waivers:* senior citizens and employees or children of employees.

Financial Aid Of all full-time matriculated undergraduates who enrolled in 2008, 52 Federal Work-Study jobs (averaging $1025).

Applying *Options:* electronic application, early admission, deferred entrance. *Application fee:* $10. *Required:* high school transcript. *Application deadlines:* rolling (freshmen), rolling (transfers). *Notification:* continuous (freshmen), continuous (transfers).

Freshman Application Contact Ms. Midge Burnette, Director of Admissions and Records, Cleveland State Community College, 3535 Adkisson Drive, Cleveland, TN 37320-3570. *Phone:* 423-472-7141 Ext. 212. *Toll-free phone:* 800-604-2722. *Fax:* 423-478-6255. *E-mail:* mburnette@clevelandstatecc.edu.

COLUMBIA STATE COMMUNITY COLLEGE

Columbia, Tennessee **www.columbiastate.edu/**

- **State-supported** 2-year, founded 1966
- **Small-town** 179-acre campus with easy access to Nashville
- **Coed**

Academics *Calendar:* semesters. *Degree:* certificates and associate. *Special study options:* academic remediation for entering students, adult/continuing education programs, advanced placement credit, double majors, honors programs, part-time degree program, services for LD students, summer session for credit.

Student Life *Campus security:* 24-hour patrols.

Athletics Member NJCAA.

Costs (2009–10) *Tuition:* state resident $2664 full-time, $111 per semester hour part-time; nonresident $11,040 full-time, $460 per semester hour part-time. Full-time tuition and fees vary according to course load. Part-time tuition and fees vary according to course load. *Required fees:* $241 full-time, $10 per credit hour part-time, $8 per term part-time.

Financial Aid Of all full-time matriculated undergraduates who enrolled in 2008, 50 Federal Work-Study jobs (averaging $1680).

Applying *Options:* early admission. *Application fee:* $10. *Required:* high school transcript.

Freshman Application Contact Mr. Joey Scruggs, Coordinator of Recruitment, Columbia State Community College, PO Box 1315, Columbia, TN 38402-1315. *Phone:* 931-540-2540. *E-mail:* scruggs@coscc.cc.tn.us.

CONCORDE CAREER COLLEGE

Memphis, Tennessee **www.concordecareercolleges.com/**

Admissions Office Contact Concorde Career College, 5100 Poplar Avenue, Suite 132, Memphis, TN 38137.

DAYMAR INSTITUTE

Nashville, Tennessee **www.daymarinstitute.edu/**

- **Proprietary** 2-year, founded 1884
- **Suburban** 5-acre campus
- **Coed**

Academics *Calendar:* semesters. *Degree:* associate. *Special study options:* academic remediation for entering students, internships, part-time degree program, summer session for credit.

Student Life *Campus security:* 24-hour emergency response devices.

Financial Aid Of all full-time matriculated undergraduates who enrolled in 2008, 26 Federal Work-Study jobs (averaging $2975).

Applying *Options:* deferred entrance. *Required:* high school transcript.

Director of Admissions Admissions Office, Daymar Institute, 340 Plus Park, Nashville, TN 37217. *Phone:* 615-361-7555. *Fax:* 615-367-2736.

DYERSBURG STATE COMMUNITY COLLEGE

Dyersburg, Tennessee **www.dscc.edu/**

Freshman Application Contact Mr. Ron Coffman, Assistant Vice President for Academic Affairs, Dyersburg State Community College, 1510 Lake Road, Dyersburg, TN 38024. *Phone:* 731-286-3327. *Fax:* 731-286-3325. *E-mail:* gulett@dscc.edu.

FOUNTAINHEAD COLLEGE OF TECHNOLOGY

Knoxville, Tennessee **www.fountainheadcollege.edu/**

Freshman Application Contact Mr. Todd Hill, Director of Administration, Fountainhead College of Technology, 3203 Tazewell Pike, Knoxville, TN 37918-2530. *Phone:* 865-688-9422. *Toll-free phone:* 888 218 7335. *Fax:* 865-688-2419.

HIGH-TECH INSTITUTE

Memphis, Tennessee **www.high-techinstitute.com/**

Freshman Application Contact Admissions Office, High-Tech Institute, 5865 Shelby Oaks Circle, Suite 100, Memphis, TN 38134. *Toll-free phone:* 866-269-7251.

HIGH-TECH INSTITUTE

Nashville, Tennessee www.high-techinstitute.com/

Freshman Application Contact Admissions Office, High-Tech Institute, 560 Royal Parkway, Nashville, TN 37214. *Phone:* 615-902-9705. *Toll-free phone:* 888-616-6549.

ITT TECHNICAL INSTITUTE

Chattanooga, Tennessee www.itt-tech.edu/

- **Proprietary** primarily 2-year, part of ITT Educational Services, Inc.
- **Coed**

Majors CAD/CADD drafting/design technology; computer and information systems security; computer engineering technology; computer software engineering; construction management; criminal justice/law enforcement administration; design and visual communications; electrical, electronic and communications engineering technology; system, networking, and LAN/WAN management.

Academics *Degrees:* associate and bachelor's.

Freshman Application Contact Director of Recruitment, ITT Technical Institute, 5600 Brainerd Road, Suite G-1, Chattanooga, TN 37411. *Phone:* 423-510-6800. *Toll-free phone:* 877-474-8312.

ITT TECHNICAL INSTITUTE

Cordova, Tennessee www.itt-tech.edu/

- **Proprietary** primarily 2-year, founded 1994, part of ITT Educational Services, Inc.
- **Suburban** campus
- **Coed**

Majors Accounting technology and bookkeeping; animation, interactive technology, video graphics and special effects; business administration and management; CAD/CADD drafting/design technology; computer and information systems security; computer software engineering; computer systems networking and telecommunications; construction management; criminal justice/law enforcement administration; design and visual communications; electrical, electronic and communications engineering technology; legal assistant/paralegal; system, networking, and LAN/WAN management; web page, digital/multimedia and information resources design.

Academics *Calendar:* quarters. *Degrees:* associate and bachelor's.

Student Life *Housing:* college housing not available.

Freshman Application Contact Director of Recruitment, ITT Technical Institute, 7260 Goodlett Farms Parkway, Cordova, TN 38016. *Phone:* 901-381-0200. *Toll-free phone:* 866-444-5141.

ITT TECHNICAL INSTITUTE

Johnson City, Tennessee www.itt-tech.edu/

- **Proprietary** primarily 2-year
- **Coed**

Majors CAD/CADD drafting/design technology; computer and information systems security; computer engineering technology; construction management; electrical, electronic and communications engineering technology; legal assistant/paralegal; system, networking, and LAN/WAN management.

Academics *Degrees:* associate and bachelor's.

Freshman Application Contact ITT Technical Institute, 4721 Lake Park Drive, Suite 100, Johnson City, TN 37615. *Phone:* 423-952-4400. *Toll-free phone:* 877-301-9691.

ITT TECHNICAL INSTITUTE

Knoxville, Tennessee www.itt-tech.edu/

- **Proprietary** primarily 2-year, founded 1988, part of ITT Educational Services, Inc.
- **Suburban** campus
- **Coed**

Majors Animation, interactive technology, video graphics and special effects; CAD/CADD drafting/design technology; computer and information systems security; computer engineering technology; computer software and media applications related; computer software engineering; computer systems networking and telecommunications; construction management; criminal justice/law enforcement administration; design and visual communications; electrical, electronic and communications engineering technology; legal assistant/paralegal; system, networking, and LAN/WAN management; web page, digital/multimedia and information resources design.

Academics *Calendar:* quarters. *Degrees:* associate and bachelor's.

Student Life *Housing:* college housing not available.

Freshman Application Contact Director of Recruitment, ITT Technical Institute, 10208 Technology Drive, Knoxville, TN 37932. *Phone:* 865-671-2800. *Toll-free phone:* 800-671-2801.

ITT TECHNICAL INSTITUTE

Nashville, Tennessee www.itt-tech.edu/

- **Proprietary** primarily 2-year, founded 1984, part of ITT Educational Services, Inc.
- **Urban** campus
- **Coed**

Majors Accounting technology and bookkeeping; animation, interactive technology, video graphics and special effects; business administration and management; CAD/CADD drafting/design technology; computer and information systems security; computer engineering technology; computer software and media applications related; computer software engineering; computer software technology; computer systems networking and telecommunications; construction management; criminal justice/law enforcement administration; design and visual communications; electrical, electronic and communications engineering technology; legal assistant/paralegal; system, networking, and LAN/WAN management; web page, digital/multimedia and information resources design.

Academics *Calendar:* quarters. *Degrees:* associate and bachelor's.

Student Life *Housing:* college housing not available.

Freshman Application Contact Director of Recruitment, ITT Technical Institute, 2845 Elm Hill Pike, Nashville, TN 37214-3717. *Phone:* 615-889-8700. *Toll-free phone:* 800-331-8386.

JACKSON STATE COMMUNITY COLLEGE

Jackson, Tennessee www.jscc.edu/

- **State-supported** 2-year, founded 1967, part of Tennessee Board of Regents
- **Suburban** 97-acre campus with easy access to Memphis
- **Endowment** $800,579
- **Coed,** 5,109 undergraduate students

Undergraduates Students come from 7 states and territories, 3 other countries, 19% African American, 1% Asian American or Pacific Islander, 1% Native American, 0.1% international. *Retention:* 49% of 2008 full-time freshmen returned.

Faculty *Total:* 306, 32% full-time, 5% with terminal degrees. *Student/faculty ratio:* 21:1.

Majors Agriculture; business administration and management; child development; clinical/medical laboratory technology; computer science; education; general studies; industrial arts; industrial technology; liberal arts and sciences/liberal studies; management information systems; medical radiologic technology; nursing (registered nurse training); physical therapist assistant; respiratory care therapy; science technologies related.

Academics *Calendar:* semesters. *Degree:* certificates, diplomas, and associate. *Special study options:* academic remediation for entering students, adult/continuing education programs, advanced placement credit, cooperative education, distance learning, external degree program, honors programs, independent study, internships, off-campus study, part-time degree program, services for LD students, summer session for credit. *ROTC:* Army (b).

Library Jackson State Community College Library with 56,024 titles, 105 serial subscriptions, 2,128 audiovisual materials, an OPAC, a Web page.

Student Life *Activities and Organizations:* drama/theater group, choral group, Spanish Club, Philosophy Club, Nation Against Genocide, FFA/Agriculture Club, Biology Club. *Campus security:* 24-hour patrols, late-night transport/escort service, field camera surveillance. *Student services:* personal/psychological counseling.

Athletics Member NJCAA. *Intercollegiate sports:* baseball M(s), basketball M(s)/W(s), softball W(s).

Standardized Tests *Required:* SAT or ACT (for admission), COMPASS (for admission). *Recommended:* ACT (for admission).
Costs (2009–10) *One-time required fee:* $10. *Tuition:* state resident $2953 full-time, $111 per credit hour part-time; nonresident $11,184 full-time, $349 per credit hour part-time. Full-time tuition and fees vary according to course load. Part-time tuition and fees vary according to course load. *Required fees:* $253 full-time, $9 per credit hour part-time, $14 per term part-time. *Payment plan:* deferred payment. *Waivers:* senior citizens and employees or children of employees.
Financial Aid Of all full-time matriculated undergraduates who enrolled in 2008, 30 Federal Work-Study jobs (averaging $3000). 10 state and other part-time jobs (averaging $3000).
Applying *Options:* electronic application. *Application fee:* $10. *Required for some:* high school transcript. *Application deadlines:* 8/23 (freshmen), 8/23 (out-of-state freshmen), rolling (transfers). *Notification:* continuous (freshmen), continuous (out-of-state freshmen), continuous (transfers).
Freshman Application Contact Ms. Andrea Winchester, Director of Admissions, Jackson State Community College, 2046 North Parkway, Jackson, TN 38301. *Phone:* 731-425-8844 Ext. 484. *Toll-free phone:* 800-355-5722. *Fax:* 731-425-9559. *E-mail:* awinchester@jscc.edu.

JOHN A. GUPTON COLLEGE

Nashville, Tennessee **www.guptoncollege.edu/**

Director of Admissions Ms. Lisa Bolin, Registrar, John A. Gupton College, 1616 Church Street, Nashville, TN 37203. *Phone:* 615-327-3927.

KAPLAN CAREER INSTITUTE, NASHVILLE CAMPUS

Nashville, Tennessee **www.kci-nashville.com/**

- **Proprietary** 2-year, founded 1981
- **Coed**

Majors Criminal justice/law enforcement administration; legal assistant/paralegal.
Academics *Degree:* certificates, diplomas, and associate.
Freshman Application Contact Kaplan Career Institute, Nashville Campus, 750 Envious Lane, Nashville, TN 37217. *Phone:* 615-269-9900. *Toll-free phone:* 800-336-4457.

MEDVANCE INSTITUTE

Cookeville, Tennessee **www.medvance.edu/**

- **Proprietary** 2-year, founded 1970
- **Small-town** 4-acre campus
- **Coed, primarily women**

Academics *Calendar:* quarters. *Degree:* certificates, diplomas, and associate. *Special study options:* internships.
Standardized Tests *Required:* Wonderlic aptitude test (for admission).
Applying *Application fee:* $25. *Required:* high school transcript, interview. *Recommended:* minimum 2.0 GPA, 2 letters of recommendation.
Director of Admissions Ms. Sharon Mellott, Director of Admissions, MedVance Institute, 1065 East 10th Street, Cookeville, TN 38501-1907. *Phone:* 931-526-3660. *Toll-free phone:* 800-259-3659 (in-state); 800-256-9085 (out-of-state).

MID-AMERICA BAPTIST THEOLOGICAL SEMINARY

Cordova, Tennessee **www.mabts.edu/**

Freshman Application Contact Mr. Duffy Guyton, Director of Admissions, Mid-America Baptist Theological Seminary, PO Box 2350, 2095 Appling Road, Cordova, TN 38016. *Phone:* 901-751-8453 Ext. 3066. *Toll-free phone:* 800-968-4508. *Fax:* 901-751-8454. *E-mail:* info@mabts.edu.

MILLER-MOTTE TECHNICAL COLLEGE

Clarksville, Tennessee **www.miller-motte.com/**

Director of Admissions Ms. Lisa Teague, Director of Admissions, Miller-Motte Technical College, 1820 Business Park Drive, Clarksville, TN 37040. *Phone:* 800-558-0071. *E-mail:* lisateague@hotmail.com.

MOTLOW STATE COMMUNITY COLLEGE

Tullahoma, Tennessee **www.mscc.cc.tn.us/**

Freshman Application Contact Ms. Laura Monks, Assistant Director of Student Services, Motlow State Community College, PO Box 8500, Lynchburg, TN 37352. *Phone:* 931-393-1764. *Toll-free phone:* 800-654-4877. *Fax:* 931-393-1681. *E-mail:* lmonks@mscc.edu.

NASHVILLE AUTO DIESEL COLLEGE

Nashville, Tennessee **www.nadcedu.com/**

Freshman Application Contact Ms. Peggie Werrbach, Director of Admissions, Nashville Auto Diesel College, 1524 Gallatin Road, Nashville, TN 37206. *Phone:* 615-226-3990 Ext. 8465. *Toll-free phone:* 800-228-NADC. *Fax:* 615-262-8466. *E-mail:* wpruitt@nadcedu.com.

NASHVILLE STATE TECHNICAL COMMUNITY COLLEGE

Nashville, Tennessee **www.nscc.edu/**

- **State-supported** 2-year, founded 1970, part of Tennessee Board of Regents
- **Urban** 85-acre campus
- **Coed**

Undergraduates 2,556 full-time, 4,521 part-time. Students come from 36 states and territories, 55 other countries, 2% are from out of state, 25% African American, 2% Asian American or Pacific Islander, 2% Hispanic American, 0.4% Native American, 9% international, 3% transferred in.
Faculty *Student/faculty ratio:* 18:1.
Academics *Calendar:* semesters. *Degree:* certificates and associate. *Special study options:* academic remediation for entering students, adult/continuing education programs, advanced placement credit, cooperative education, distance learning, English as a second language, off-campus study, part-time degree program, services for LD students, summer session for credit.
Student Life *Campus security:* 24-hour emergency response devices and patrols, late-night transport/escort service.
Standardized Tests *Required:* SAT or ACT (for admission).
Costs (2009–10) *Tuition:* state resident $3510 full-time, $121 per credit hour part-time; nonresident $14,520 full-time, $470 per credit hour part-time. Part-time tuition and fees vary according to course load. *Required fees:* $225 full-time.
Financial Aid Of all full-time matriculated undergraduates who enrolled in 2009, 1,918 applied for aid, 1,559 were judged to have need, 233 had their need fully met. 247 Federal Work-Study jobs (averaging $3600). 79 state and other part-time jobs (averaging $2904). In 2009, 15. *Average percent of need met:* 52. *Average financial aid package:* $6421. *Average need-based loan:* $1341. *Average need-based gift aid:* $4420. *Average non-need-based aid:* $1885.
Applying *Options:* electronic application, deferred entrance. *Application fee:* $5. *Required:* high school transcript.
Freshman Application Contact Mr. Beth Mahan, Coordinator of Recruitment, Nashville State Technical Community College, 120 White Bridge Road, Nashville, TN 37209. *Phone:* 615-353-3214. *Toll-free phone:* 800-272-7363. *E-mail:* beth.mahan@nscc.edu.

NATIONAL COLLEGE

Bristol, Tennessee **www.national-college.edu/**

Freshman Application Contact National College, 1328 Highway 11 West, Bristol, TN 37620. *Phone:* 423-878-4440.

NATIONAL COLLEGE

Knoxville, Tennessee www.national-college.edu/

Director of Admissions Frank Alvey, Campus Director, National College, 8415 Kingston Pike, Knoxville, TN 37919. *Phone:* 865-539-2011. *Toll-free phone:* 800-664-1886. *Fax:* 865-539-2049.

NATIONAL COLLEGE

Nashville, Tennessee www.national-college.edu/

Director of Admissions Jerry Lafferty, Campus Director, National College, 3748 Nolensville Pike, Nashville, TN 37211. *Phone:* 615-333-3344. *Toll-free phone:* 800-664-1886.

NORTH CENTRAL INSTITUTE

Clarksville, Tennessee www.nci.edu/

Freshman Application Contact Mrs. Sheri Nash-Kutch, Dean of Student Services, North Central Institute, 168 Jack Miller Boulevard, Clarksville, TN 37042. *Phone:* 931-431-9700 Ext. 247. *Fax:* 931-431-9771. *E-mail:* admissions@nci.edu.

NORTHEAST STATE TECHNICAL COMMUNITY COLLEGE

Blountville, Tennessee www.northeaststate.edu/

- **State-supported** 2-year, founded 1966, part of Tennessee Board of Regents
- **Small-town** 100-acre campus
- **Endowment** $4.0 million
- **Coed**

Undergraduates 2,927 full-time, 2,543 part-time. Students come from 3 states and territories, 2 other countries, 3% are from out of state, 3% African American, 0.7% Asian American or Pacific Islander, 1% Hispanic American, 0.5% Native American, 5% transferred in. *Retention:* 58% of 2008 full-time freshmen returned.

Faculty *Student/faculty ratio:* 11:1.

Academics *Calendar:* semesters. *Degree:* certificates and associate. *Special study options:* academic remediation for entering students, advanced placement credit, cooperative education, distance learning, double majors, honors programs, part-time degree program, services for LD students, summer session for credit.

Student Life *Campus security:* 24-hour emergency response devices and patrols, late-night transport/escort service.

Financial Aid Of all full-time matriculated undergraduates who enrolled in 2008, 109 Federal Work-Study jobs (averaging $1318). 35 state and other part-time jobs.

Applying *Options:* electronic application. *Application fee:* $10. *Required:* high school transcript, minimum 2 GPA.

Freshman Application Contact Dr. Jon P. Harr, Vice President for Student Affairs, Northeast State Technical Community College, PO Box 246, Blountville, TN 37617. *Phone:* 423-323-0231. *Toll-free phone:* 800-836-7822. *Fax:* 423-323-0240. *E-mail:* jpharr@northeaststate.edu.

NOSSI COLLEGE OF ART

Goodlettsville, Tennessee www.nossi.com/

Freshman Application Contact Ms. Mary Alexander, Admissions Director, Nossi College of Art, 907 Rivergate Parkway, Goodlettsville, TN 37072. *Phone:* 615-851-1088. *Toll-free phone:* 877-860-1601. *E-mail:* admissions@nossi.com.

PELLISSIPPI STATE TECHNICAL COMMUNITY COLLEGE

Knoxville, Tennessee www.pstcc.edu/

Freshman Application Contact Ms. Leigh Anne Touzeau, Director of Admissions and Records, Pellissippi State Technical Community College, PO Box 22990, Knoxville, TN 37933-0990. *Phone:* 865-694-6681. *E-mail:* latouzeau@pstcc.cc.tn.us.

REMINGTON COLLEGE–MEMPHIS CAMPUS

Memphis, Tennessee www.remingtoncollege.edu/

Director of Admissions Randal Hayes, Director of Recruitment, Remington College–Memphis Campus, 2731 Nonconnah Boulevard, Memphis, TN 38132-2131. *Phone:* 901-345-1000. *Fax:* 901-396-8310. *E-mail:* randal.hayes@remingtoncollege.edu.

REMINGTON COLLEGE–NASHVILLE CAMPUS

Nashville, Tennessee www.remingtoncollege.edu/

Director of Admissions Mr. Frank Vivelo, Campus President, Remington College–Nashville Campus, 441 Donelson Pike, Suite 150, Nashville, TN 37214. *Phone:* 615-889-5520. *Fax:* 615-889-5528. *E-mail:* frank.vivelo@remingtoncollege.edu.

ROANE STATE COMMUNITY COLLEGE

Harriman, Tennessee www.roanestate.edu/

Freshman Application Contact Admissions Office, Roane State Community College, 276 Patton Lane, Harriman, TN 37748. *Phone:* 865-882-4523. *Toll-free phone:* 800-343-9104. *E-mail:* admissions@roanestate.edu.

SOUTHWEST TENNESSEE COMMUNITY COLLEGE

Memphis, Tennessee www.southwest.tn.edu/

Freshman Application Contact Ms. Cindy Meziere, Assistant Director of Recruiting, Southwest Tennessee Community College, PO Box 780, Memphis, TN 38103-0780. *Phone:* 901-333-4195. *Toll-free phone:* 877-717-STCC. *Fax:* 901-333-4473. *E-mail:* cmeziere@southwest.tn.edu.

VATTEROTT COLLEGE

Memphis, Tennessee www.vatterott-college.edu/

Admissions Office Contact Vatterott College, 2655 Dividend Drive, Memphis, TN 38132. *Toll-free phone:* 866-314-6454.

VOLUNTEER STATE COMMUNITY COLLEGE

Gallatin, Tennessee www.volstate.edu/

- **State-supported** 2-year, founded 1970, part of Tennessee Board of Regents
- **Small-town** 100-acre campus with easy access to Nashville
- **Endowment** $3.4 million
- **Coed,** 8,430 undergraduate students, 52% full-time, 63% women, 37% men

Undergraduates 4,348 full-time, 4,082 part-time. Students come from 9 states and territories, 12 other countries, 4% are from out of state, 10% African American, 1% Asian American or Pacific Islander, 2% Hispanic American, 0.4% Native American, 0.4% international, 11% transferred in.

Freshmen *Admission:* 2,337 applied, 2,337 admitted, 1,696 enrolled. *Average high school GPA:* 2.88.

Faculty *Total:* 397, 37% full-time, 6% with terminal degrees. *Student/faculty ratio:* 25:1.

Majors Business administration and management; child development; clinical/medical laboratory technology; community organization and advocacy; criminal justice/police science; education; fire science; general studies; health information/medical records technology; health professions related; health services/allied health/health sciences; histologic technician; industrial arts; legal assistant/paralegal; liberal arts and sciences/liberal studies; medical radiologic technology; ophthalmic technology; physical therapist assistant; respiratory care therapy; web page, digital/multimedia and information resources design.

Academics *Calendar:* semesters. *Degree:* certificates and associate. *Special study options:* academic remediation for entering students, accelerated degree program, adult/continuing education programs, advanced placement credit, distance learning, double majors, English as a second language, honors programs, independent study, part-time degree program, services for LD students, summer session for credit.

Library Thigpen Learning Resource Center with 53,000 titles, 275 serial subscriptions, an OPAC, a Web page.

Student Life *Housing:* college housing not available. *Activities and Organizations:* drama/theater group, student-run newspaper, radio station, choral group, Gamma Beta Phi, Returning Woman's Organization, Phi Theta Kappa, Student Government Association, The Settler. *Campus security:* 24-hour emergency response devices and patrols, late-night transport/escort service. *Student services:* health clinic, personal/psychological counseling.

Athletics Member NJCAA. *Intercollegiate sports:* baseball M(s), basketball M(s)/W(s), softball W(s). *Intramural sports:* basketball M/W.

Standardized Tests *Required for some:* SAT or ACT (for admission).

Costs (2009–10) *Tuition:* state resident $2664 full-time, $110 per credit hour part-time; nonresident $11,040 full-time, $460 per credit hour part-time. Full-time tuition and fees vary according to course load. Part-time tuition and fees vary according to course load. *Required fees:* $265 full-time, $9 per credit hour part-time, $18 per credit hour part-time. *Payment plan:* deferred payment. *Waivers:* senior citizens and employees or children of employees.

Financial Aid Of all full-time matriculated undergraduates who enrolled in 2008, 2,321 applied for aid, 1,690 were judged to have need, 116 had their need fully met. 18 Federal Work-Study jobs (averaging $1957). In 2008, 66 non-need-based awards were made. *Average percent of need met:* 48%. *Average financial aid package:* $5152. *Average need-based loan:* $2822. *Average need-based gift aid:* $3959. *Average non-need-based aid:* $1911.

Applying *Options:* electronic application, early admission, deferred entrance. *Application fee:* $10. *Required:* high school transcript. *Required for some:* essay or personal statement, minimum 2 GPA. *Notification:* continuous (freshmen), continuous (transfers).

Freshman Application Contact Mr. Tim Amyx, Director of Admissions, Volunteer State Community College, 1480 Nashville Pike, Gallatin, TN 37066-3188. *Phone:* 615-452-8600 Ext. 3614. *Toll-free phone:* 888-335-8722. *Fax:* 615-230-4875. *E-mail:* admissions@volstate.edu.

Walters State Community College

Morristown, Tennessee **www.ws.edu/**

- **State-supported** 2-year, founded 1970, part of Tennessee Board of Regents
- **Small-town** 100-acre campus
- **Endowment** $7.6 million
- **Coed,** 6,853 undergraduate students, 52% full-time, 62% women, 38% men

Undergraduates 3,591 full-time, 3,262 part-time. Students come from 11 states and territories, 9 other countries, 0.6% are from out of state, 3% African American, 1% Asian American or Pacific Islander, 2% Hispanic American, 0.3% Native American, 0.1% international, 5% transferred in. *Retention:* 58% of 2008 full-time freshmen returned.

Freshmen *Admission:* 2,515 applied, 2,515 admitted, 1,421 enrolled. *Average high school GPA:* 2.98. *Test scores:* SAT verbal scores over 500: 50%; SAT math scores over 500: 50%; ACT scores over 18: 55%; SAT verbal scores over 600: 20%; SAT math scores over 600: 20%; ACT scores over 24: 21%; SAT verbal scores over 700: 10%; SAT math scores over 700: 10%; ACT scores over 30: 1%.

Faculty *Total:* 388, 36% full-time, 19% with terminal degrees. *Student/faculty ratio:* 22:1.

Majors Administrative assistant and secretarial science; agricultural business and management; art; business administration and management; child development; computer and information sciences related; computer science; criminal justice/law enforcement administration; education; interdisciplinary studies; liberal arts and sciences/liberal studies; nursing (registered nurse training).

Academics *Calendar:* semesters. *Degree:* certificates and associate. *Special study options:* academic remediation for entering students, accelerated degree program, adult/continuing education programs, advanced placement credit, distance learning, freshman honors college, honors programs, part-time degree program, summer session for credit. *ROTC:* Army (c).

Library Walters State Library with 154,995 titles, 28,218 serial subscriptions, 6,393 audiovisual materials, an OPAC, a Web page.

Student Life *Housing:* college housing not available. *Activities and Organizations:* student-run newspaper, choral group. *Campus security:* 24-hour emergency response devices and patrols, late-night transport/escort service. *Student services:* health clinic.

Athletics Member NJCAA. *Intercollegiate sports:* baseball M(s), basketball M(s)/W(s), golf M(s), softball W(s). *Intramural sports:* baseball M, basketball M/W.

Standardized Tests *Required:* SAT or ACT (for admission).

Costs (2009–10) *Tuition:* state resident $2664 full-time, $111 per semester hour part-time; nonresident $11,400 full-time, $460 per semester hour part-time. *Required fees:* $269 full-time, $16 per semester hour part-time, $16 per semester part-time. *Waivers:* senior citizens and employees or children of employees.

Financial Aid Of all full-time matriculated undergraduates who enrolled in 2008, 60 Federal Work-Study jobs (averaging $2400).

Applying *Options:* early admission. *Application fee:* $10. *Required:* high school transcript. *Application deadlines:* rolling (freshmen), rolling (transfers). *Notification:* continuous (freshmen), continuous (transfers).

Freshman Application Contact Mr. Michael Campbell, Assistant Vice President for Student Affairs, Walters State Community College, 500 South Davy Crockett Parkway, Morristown, TN 37813-6899. *Phone:* 423-585-2682. *Toll-free phone:* 800-225-4770. *Fax:* 423-585-6876. *E-mail:* mike.campbell@ws.edu.

TEXAS

The Academy of Health Care Professions

Houston, Texas **www.academyofhealth.com/**

Freshman Application Contact Admissions Office, The Academy of Health Care Professions, 1900 North Loop West, Suite 100, Houston, TX 77018. *Phone:* 713-425-3100. *Toll-free phone:* 800-487-6728. *Fax:* 713-425-3192.

Alvin Community College

Alvin, Texas **www.alvincollege.edu/**

- **State and locally supported** 2-year, founded 1949
- **Suburban** 114-acre campus with easy access to Houston
- **Coed,** 4,400 undergraduate students, 30% full-time, 55% women, 45% men

Undergraduates 1,325 full-time, 3,075 part-time. 9% African American, 3% Asian American or Pacific Islander, 23% Hispanic American, 0.8% Native American.

Freshmen *Admission:* 706 enrolled.

Faculty *Total:* 262, 37% full-time. *Student/faculty ratio:* 17:1.

Majors Accounting; administrative assistant and secretarial science; aeronautics/aviation/aerospace science and technology; art; biology/biological sciences; business administration and management; chemical technology; child development; computer engineering technology; computer programming; corrections; court reporting; criminal justice/police science; drafting and design technology; dramatic/theater arts; electrical, electronic and communications engineering technology; emergency medical technology (EMT paramedic); legal administrative assistant/secretary; legal assistant/paralegal; legal studies; liberal arts and sciences/liberal studies; marketing/marketing management; mathematics; medical administrative assistant and medical secretary; mental health/rehabilitation; music; nursing (registered nurse training); physical education teaching and

Alvin Community College (continued)

coaching; physical sciences; radio and television; respiratory care therapy; substance abuse/addiction counseling; voice and opera.

Academics *Calendar:* semesters. *Degree:* certificates, diplomas, and associate. *Special study options:* academic remediation for entering students, accelerated degree program, adult/continuing education programs, advanced placement credit, distance learning, double majors, English as a second language, honors programs, independent study, internships, part-time degree program, services for LD students, student-designed majors, study abroad, summer session for credit.

Library Alvin Community College Library with an OPAC, a Web page.

Student Life *Campus security:* 24-hour patrols, late-night transport/escort service. *Student services:* personal/psychological counseling.

Athletics Member NJCAA. *Intercollegiate sports:* baseball M(s), softball W(s). *Intramural sports:* soccer M(c)/W(c).

Costs (2010–11) *Tuition:* area resident $960 full-time, $32 per credit hour part-time; state resident $1950 full-time, $65 per credit hour part-time; nonresident $3300 full-time, $110 per credit hour part-time. Full-time tuition and fees vary according to program. Part-time tuition and fees vary according to program. *Required fees:* $376 full-time. *Payment plan:* installment.

Financial Aid Of all full-time matriculated undergraduates who enrolled in 2008, 65 Federal Work-Study jobs (averaging $3300). 3 state and other part-time jobs (averaging $3000).

Applying *Options:* electronic application. *Required for some:* high school transcript. *Application deadlines:* rolling (freshmen), rolling (transfers).

Freshman Application Contact Alvin Community College, 3110 Mustang Road, Alvin, TX 77511. *Phone:* 281-756-3531.

AMARILLO COLLEGE

Amarillo, Texas **www.actx.edu/**

- **State and locally supported** 2-year, founded 1929
- **Urban** 1542-acre campus
- **Endowment** $23.6 million
- **Coed,** 11,289 undergraduate students, 32% full-time, 59% women, 41% men

Undergraduates 3,610 full-time, 7,679 part-time. 5% African American, 2% Asian American or Pacific Islander, 26% Hispanic American, 0.9% Native American. *Retention:* 78% of 2008 full-time freshmen returned.

Faculty *Total:* 428, 47% full-time, 8% with terminal degrees.

Majors Accounting; administrative assistant and secretarial science; airframe mechanics and aircraft maintenance technology; architectural engineering technology; art; automobile/automotive mechanics technology; behavioral sciences; biblical studies; biology/biological sciences; broadcast journalism; business administration and management; business teacher education; chemical technology; chemistry; child development; clinical laboratory science/medical technology; commercial and advertising art; computer engineering technology; computer programming; computer science; computer systems analysis; corrections; criminal justice/law enforcement administration; criminal justice/police science; dental hygiene; drafting and design technology; dramatic/theater arts; electrical, electronic and communications engineering technology; elementary education; emergency medical technology (EMT paramedic); engineering; English; environmental health; fine/studio arts; fire science; funeral service and mortuary science; general studies; geology/earth science; health information/medical records administration; heating, air conditioning, ventilation and refrigeration maintenance technology; heavy equipment maintenance technology; history; industrial radiologic technology; information science/studies; instrumentation technology; interior design; journalism; laser and optical technology; legal administrative assistant/secretary; liberal arts and sciences/liberal studies; machine tool technology; mass communication/media; mathematics; medical administrative assistant and medical secretary; modern languages; music; music teacher education; natural sciences; nuclear medical technology; nursing (licensed practical/vocational nurse training); nursing (registered nurse training); occupational therapy; photography; physical education teaching and coaching; physical sciences; physical therapy; physics; pre-engineering; pre-pharmacy studies; psychology; public relations/image management; radio and television; radiologic technology/science; real estate; religious studies; respiratory care therapy; social sciences; social work; speech and rhetoric; substance abuse/addiction counseling; telecommunications technology; tourism and travel services management; visual and performing arts.

Academics *Calendar:* semesters. *Degree:* certificates and associate. *Special study options:* academic remediation for entering students, adult/continuing education programs, advanced placement credit, cooperative education, distance learning, English as a second language, freshman honors college, honors programs, part-time degree program, services for LD students, summer session for credit.

Library Lynn Library Learning Center plus 2 others with 116,000 titles, 110 serial subscriptions, an OPAC, a Web page.

Student Life *Housing:* college housing not available. *Activities and Organizations:* drama/theater group, student-run newspaper, radio station, choral group, Student Government Association, College Republicans. *Campus security:* 24-hour patrols, late-night transport/escort service.

Athletics *Intramural sports:* basketball M/W, soccer M/W, softball M/W, tennis M/W, volleyball M/W.

Costs (2009–10) *Tuition:* area resident $1763 full-time, $76 per semester hour part-time; state resident $2273 full-time, $93 per semester hour part-time; nonresident $3353 full-time, $243 per semester hour part-time. Full-time tuition and fees vary according to course load. Part-time tuition and fees vary according to course load. *Payment plan:* installment. *Waivers:* senior citizens and employees or children of employees.

Financial Aid Of all full-time matriculated undergraduates who enrolled in 2008, 100 Federal Work-Study jobs (averaging $3000).

Applying *Options:* early admission, deferred entrance. *Required:* high school transcript. *Notification:* continuous (freshmen), continuous (transfers).

Freshman Application Contact Amarillo College, PO Box 447, Amarillo, TX 79178-0001. *Phone:* 806-371-5000. *Fax:* 806-371-5497. *E-mail:* askac@actx.edu.

ANGELINA COLLEGE

Lufkin, Texas **www.angelina.cc.tx.us/**

Freshman Application Contact Ms. Judith Cutting, Registrar/Enrollment Director, Angelina College, PO Box 1768, Lufkin, TX 75902-1768. *Phone:* 936-639-1301 Ext. 213.

ATI TECHNICAL TRAINING CENTER

Dallas, Texas **www.aticareertraining.edu/**

- **Proprietary** 2-year
- **Coed**

Academics *Calendar:* quarters. *Degree:* certificates.

Applying *Application fee:* $100.

Freshman Application Contact Admissions Office, ATI Technical Training Center, 6627 Maple Ave, Dallas, TX 75235. *Phone:* 214-352-2222.

AUSTIN COMMUNITY COLLEGE

Austin, Texas **www.austincc.edu/**

- **State and locally supported** 2-year, founded 1972
- **Urban** campus with easy access to Austin
- **Endowment** $1.7 million
- **Coed,** 40,248 undergraduate students, 27% full-time, 56% women, 44% men

Undergraduates 10,815 full-time, 29,433 part-time. 9% African American, 6% Asian American or Pacific Islander, 25% Hispanic American, 0.9% Native American, 1% international.

Faculty *Total:* 1,962, 28% full-time. *Student/faculty ratio:* 20:1.

Majors Accounting; accounting technology and bookkeeping; administrative assistant and secretarial science; animation, interactive technology, video graphics and special effects; anthropology; art; automobile/automotive mechanics technology; banking and financial support services; biology/biological sciences; biology/biotechnology laboratory technician; business administration and management; business/commerce; carpentry; cartography; chemistry; child development; Chinese; clinical/medical laboratory technology; commercial and advertising art; commercial photography; computer and information sciences; computer programming; computer systems networking and telecommunications; corrections; criminal justice/police science; culinary arts; dance; dental hygiene; diagnostic medical sonography and ultrasound technology; drafting and design technology; dramatic/theater arts; early childhood education; economics; electrical, electronic and communications engineering technology; emergency medical technology (EMT paramedic); engineering; English; English composition; environmental engineering technology; fire protection and safety technology; foreign languages and literatures; French; general studies; geography; geology/earth science; German; health and physical education; health information/medical records technology; health teacher education; heating, air conditioning and refrigeration technology; history; hospitality administration; human services; international business/trade/commerce; Japanese; Latin; legal assistant/paralegal; marketing/marketing management; mathematics; middle school education; music; music management and merchandising; nursing (registered nurse training); occupational therapist assistant; philosophy; physical sciences;

physical therapist assistant; physics; political science and government; pre-dentistry studies; premedical studies; pre-pharmacy studies; pre-veterinary studies; psychology; quality control technology; radio and television; radiologic technology/science; real estate; Russian; secondary education; sign language interpretation and translation; social work; sociology; Spanish; speech and rhetoric; substance abuse/addiction counseling; surgical technology; survey technology; technical and business writing; therapeutic recreation; tourism and travel services management; watchmaking and jewelrymaking; welding technology.

Academics *Calendar:* semesters. *Degree:* certificates and associate. *Special study options:* academic remediation for entering students, accelerated degree program, adult/continuing education programs, advanced placement credit, cooperative education, distance learning, English as a second language, honors programs, independent study, internships, part-time degree program, services for LD students, summer session for credit. *ROTC:* Army (c), Air Force (c).

Library Main Library plus 7 others with 172,938 titles, 45,233 serial subscriptions, 17,731 audiovisual materials, an OPAC, a Web page.

Student Life *Housing:* college housing not available. *Activities and Organizations:* student-run newspaper, Student Government Association, Physical Therapist Assistant Club, African Student Association, ASL Friends United. *Student services:* personal/psychological counseling.

Athletics *Intramural sports:* basketball M, bowling M/W, golf M/W, soccer M, volleyball W.

Costs (2009–10) *Tuition:* area resident $1170 full-time, $39 per credit hour part-time; state resident $3810 full-time, $127 per credit hour part-time; nonresident $8550 full-time, $285 per credit hour part-time. Full-time tuition and fees vary according to course load. Part-time tuition and fees vary according to course load. *Required fees:* $438 full-time, $15 per credit hour part-time. *Payment plan:* installment. *Waivers:* senior citizens and employees or children of employees.

Financial Aid Of all full-time matriculated undergraduates who enrolled in 2008, 296 Federal Work-Study jobs (averaging $2000). 12 state and other part-time jobs (averaging $2000).

Applying *Options:* electronic application. *Required:* high school transcript. *Application deadlines:* rolling (freshmen), rolling (transfers).

Freshman Application Contact Ms. Linda Kluck, Director, Admissions and Records, Austin Community College, 5930 Middle Fiskville Road, Austin, TX 78752-4390. *Phone:* 512-223-7503. *Fax:* 512-223-7665. *E-mail:* admission@austincc.edu.

BLINN COLLEGE

Brenham, Texas **www.blinn.edu/**

Freshman Application Contact Mrs. Stephanie Wehring, Coordinator, Recruitment and Admissions, Blinn College, 902 College Avenue, Brenham, TX 77833-4049. *Phone:* 979-830-4152. *Fax:* 979-830-4110. *E-mail:* recruit@blinn.edu.

BRAZOSPORT COLLEGE

Lake Jackson, Texas **www.brazosport.edu/**

Freshman Application Contact Ms. Patricia S. Leyendecker, Director of Admissions/Registrar, Brazosport College, 500 College Drive, Lake Jackson, TX 77566. *Phone:* 979-230-3217. *Fax:* 979-230-3376. *E-mail:* pleyende@brazosport.edu.

BROOKHAVEN COLLEGE

Farmers Branch, Texas **www.brookhavencollege.edu/**

Freshman Application Contact Marketing and Public Information Office, Brookhaven College, 3939 Valley View Lane, Farmers Branch, TX 75244-4997. *Phone:* 972-860-4883. *Fax:* 972-860-4886. *E-mail:* bhcinfo@dcccd.edu.

CEDAR VALLEY COLLEGE

Lancaster, Texas **www.cedarvalleycollege.edu/**

Freshman Application Contact Ms. Carolyn Ward, Director of Admissions/Registrar, Cedar Valley College, 3030 North Dallas Avenue, Lancaster, TX 75134-3799. *Phone:* 972-860-8201. *Fax:* 972-860-8207. *E-mail:* cboswell-ward@dcccd.edu.

CENTER FOR ADVANCED LEGAL STUDIES

Houston, Texas **www.paralegal.edu/**

Freshman Application Contact Mr. James Scheffer, Center for Advanced Legal Studies, 3910 Kirby Drive, Suite 200, Houston, TX 77098-4151. *Phone:* 713-529-2778. *Fax:* 713-523-2715. *E-mail:* james.scheffer@paralegal.edu.

CENTRAL TEXAS COLLEGE

Killeen, Texas **www.ctcd.edu/**

- **State and locally supported** 2-year, founded 1967
- **Suburban** 500-acre campus with easy access to Austin
- **Endowment** $3.5 million
- **Coed,** 24,498 undergraduate students, 17% full-time, 45% women, 55% men

Undergraduates 4,163 full-time, 20,335 part-time. Students come from 50 states and territories, 38 other countries, 19% are from out of state, 7% transferred in, 1% live on campus. *Retention:* 58% of 2008 full-time freshmen returned.

Freshmen *Admission:* 4,553 enrolled.

Faculty *Total:* 2,413, 10% full-time, 10% with terminal degrees. *Student/faculty ratio:* 11:1.

Majors Administrative assistant and secretarial science; agriculture; aircraft powerplant technology; airline pilot and flight crew; automobile/automotive mechanics technology; biology/biological sciences; business administration and management; chemistry; child-care and support services management; clinical/medical laboratory technology; commercial and advertising art; computer and information sciences; computer programming; computer programming related; computer programming (specific applications); computer programming (vendor/product certification); cosmetology; criminal justice/police science; criminal justice/safety; data processing and data processing technology; drafting and design technology; electrical, electronic and communications engineering technology; emergency medical technology (EMT paramedic); engineering; environmental studies; equestrian studies; farm and ranch management; geology/earth science; graphic and printing equipment operation/production; heating, air conditioning, ventilation and refrigeration maintenance technology; hotel/motel administration; interdisciplinary studies; journalism; legal assistant/paralegal; liberal arts and sciences/liberal studies; marketing/marketing management; mathematics; medical administrative assistant and medical secretary; medical radiologic technology; music; nursing (licensed practical/vocational nurse training); nursing (registered nurse training); office management; physical education teaching and coaching; public administration; radio and television; social sciences; substance abuse/addiction counseling; welding technology.

Academics *Calendar:* semesters. *Degree:* certificates and associate. *Special study options:* academic remediation for entering students, accelerated degree program, adult/continuing education programs, advanced placement credit, distance learning, English as a second language, external degree program, internships, part-time degree program, services for LD students, student-designed majors, summer session for credit. *ROTC:* Army (b).

Library Oveta Culp Hobby Memorial Library with 80,381 titles, 467 serial subscriptions, an OPAC, a Web page.

Student Life *Housing Options:* coed. Campus housing is university owned. *Activities and Organizations:* drama/theater group, student-run newspaper, International Student Association, We Can Do It Club, Students in Free Enterprise (SIFE), Student Nurses Association, NAACP, national fraternities. *Campus security:* 24-hour emergency response devices and patrols.

Athletics *Intramural sports:* badminton M/W, basketball M/W, bowling M/W, football M/W, golf M/W, soccer M/W, softball M/W, table tennis M/W, tennis M/W, volleyball M/W.

Costs (2009–10) *Tuition:* area resident $1200 full-time; state resident $1500 full-time; nonresident $3900 full-time. *Required fees:* $390 full-time. *Room and board:* $4550.

Financial Aid Of all full-time matriculated undergraduates who enrolled in 2008, 68 Federal Work-Study jobs (averaging $3658).

Applying *Options:* electronic application, early admission, deferred entrance. *Required:* high school transcript, minimum 2 GPA. *Application deadlines:* rolling (freshmen), rolling (transfers).

Freshman Application Contact Admissions Office, Central Texas College, PO Box 1800, Killeen, TX 76540-1800. *Phone:* 254-526-1696. *Toll-free phone:* 800-792-3348 Ext. 1696. *Fax:* 254-526-1545. *E-mail:* admrec@ctcd.edu.

Cisco College

Cisco, Texas **www.cisco.edu/**

Freshman Application Contact Mr. Olin O. Odom III, Dean of Admission/Registrar, Cisco College, 101 College Heights, Cisco, TX 76437-9321. *Phone:* 254-442-2567 Ext. 5130. *E-mail:* oodom@cjc.edu.

Clarendon College

Clarendon, Texas **www.clarendoncollege.edu/**

- **State and locally supported** 2-year, founded 1898
- **Rural** 109-acre campus
- **Endowment** $2.5 million
- **Coed,** 1,114 undergraduate students, 33% full-time, 48% women, 52% men

Undergraduates 371 full-time, 743 part-time. Students come from 14 states and territories, 2 other countries, 4% are from out of state, 7% African American, 1% Asian American or Pacific Islander, 20% Hispanic American, 1% Native American, 1% international, 21% live on campus.

Freshmen *Admission:* 498 applied, 498 admitted, 346 enrolled.

Faculty *Total:* 82, 41% full-time, 5% with terminal degrees. *Student/faculty ratio:* 18:1.

Majors Accounting; agribusiness; agricultural economics; agriculture; architecture; art; behavioral sciences; biology/biological sciences; business administration and management; chemistry; computer and information sciences; dramatic/theater arts; economics; education; elementary education; engineering; English; environmental science; farm and ranch management; finance; general studies; health services/allied health/health sciences; history; horse husbandry/equine science and management; kinesiology and exercise science; liberal arts and sciences/liberal studies; marketing/marketing management; mass communication/media; mathematics; music; nursing (registered nurse training); physical education teaching and coaching; physical therapy; pre-dentistry studies; pre-law studies; premedical studies; psychology; secondary education; social sciences; social work related; sociology; speech and rhetoric.

Academics *Calendar:* semesters. *Degree:* certificates and associate. *Special study options:* academic remediation for entering students, adult/continuing education programs, advanced placement credit, distance learning, double majors, English as a second language, independent study, part-time degree program, services for LD students, summer session for credit.

Library Vera Dial Dickey Library plus 1 other with 21,027 titles, 10,588 serial subscriptions, 448 audiovisual materials, an OPAC, a Web page.

Student Life *Housing:* on-campus residence required through sophomore year. *Options:* coed, men-only, women-only. Campus housing is university owned. *Activities and Organizations:* drama/theater group, choral group. *Campus security:* 8-hour patrols by trained security personnel, Emergency notification system through text messaging.

Athletics Member NJCAA. *Intercollegiate sports:* baseball M(s), basketball M(s)/W(s), cheerleading M(s)/W(s), cross-country running M(s)/W(s), softball W(s), volleyball W(s). *Intramural sports:* basketball M/W, volleyball M/W.

Costs (2010–11) *Tuition:* area resident $1140 full-time; state resident $1710 full-time, $38 per credit hour part-time; nonresident $2280 full-time, $57 per credit hour part-time. *Required fees:* $1230 full-time, $41 per credit hour part-time. *Room and board:* $3500; room only: $1200. *Payment plan:* installment. *Waivers:* senior citizens.

Financial Aid Of all full-time matriculated undergraduates who enrolled in 2008, 51 Federal Work-Study jobs (averaging $875). 6 state and other part-time jobs (averaging $450).

Applying *Options:* electronic application, early admission, deferred entrance. *Required:* high school transcript. *Required for some:* interview. *Application deadlines:* rolling (freshmen), rolling (transfers). *Notification:* continuous (freshmen), continuous (transfers).

Freshman Application Contact Ms. Martha Smith, Admissions Director, Clarendon College, PO Box 968, Clarendon, TX 79226-0968. *Phone:* 806-874-3571 Ext. 106. *Toll-free phone:* 800-687-9737. *Fax:* 806-874-3201. *E-mail:* martha.smith@clarendoncollege.edu.

Coastal Bend College

Beeville, Texas **www.cbc.cc.tx.us/**

Freshman Application Contact Ms. Alicia Ulloa, Director of Admissions/Registrar, Coastal Bend College, 3800 Charco Road, Beeville, TX 78102-2197. *Phone:* 361-354-2245. *Fax:* 361-354-2254. *E-mail:* register@coastalbend.edu.

College of the Mainland

Texas City, Texas **www.com.edu/**

- **State and locally supported** 2-year, founded 1967
- **Suburban** 120-acre campus with easy access to Houston
- **Endowment** $1.3 million
- **Coed**

Undergraduates 1,093 full-time, 2,468 part-time. Students come from 1 other state, 19% African American, 2% Asian American or Pacific Islander, 20% Hispanic American, 0.6% Native American, 0.1% international, 16% transferred in. *Retention:* 58% of 2008 full-time freshmen returned.

Faculty *Student/faculty ratio:* 14:1.

Academics *Calendar:* semesters. *Degree:* certificates, diplomas, and associate. *Special study options:* academic remediation for entering students, adult/continuing education programs, cooperative education, distance learning, English as a second language, honors programs, part-time degree program, services for LD students, summer session for credit.

Student Life *Campus security:* 24-hour emergency response devices and patrols, student patrols.

Standardized Tests *Recommended:* SAT or ACT (for admission).

Costs (2009–10) *Tuition:* area resident $792 full-time, $33 per credit hour part-time; state resident $1560 full-time, $65 per credit hour part-time; nonresident $2544 full-time, $106 per credit hour part-time. *Required fees:* $167 full-time.

Financial Aid Of all full-time matriculated undergraduates who enrolled in 2008, 93 Federal Work-Study jobs (averaging $1203). 88 state and other part-time jobs (averaging $1069).

Applying *Options:* electronic application, early admission, deferred entrance. *Required for some:* high school transcript.

Freshman Application Contact Ms. Kelly Musick, Registrar/Director of Admissions, College of the Mainland, 1200 Amburn Road, Texas City, TX 77591. *Phone:* 409-938-1211 Ext. 469. *Toll-free phone:* 888-258-8859 Ext. 264. *Fax:* 409-938-3126. *E-mail:* sem@com.edu.

Collin County Community College District

McKinney, Texas **www.collin.edu/**

- **State and locally supported** 2-year, founded 1985
- **Suburban** 333-acre campus with easy access to Dallas-Fort Worth
- **Endowment** $3.6 million
- **Coed,** 24,872 undergraduate students, 39% full-time, 57% women, 43% men

Undergraduates 9,675 full-time, 15,197 part-time. Students come from 46 states and territories, 101 other countries, 5% are from out of state, 10% African American, 9% Asian American or Pacific Islander, 13% Hispanic American, 0.7% Native American, 4% international, 11% transferred in. *Retention:* 65% of 2008 full-time freshmen returned.

Freshmen *Admission:* 4,634 enrolled.

Faculty *Total:* 1,018, 32% full-time, 23% with terminal degrees. *Student/faculty ratio:* 27:1.

Majors Administrative assistant and secretarial science; animation, interactive technology, video graphics and special effects; audio engineering; biology/biotechnology laboratory technician; business administration and management; business automation/technology/data entry; child-care provision; child development; commercial and advertising art; communication/speech communication and rhetoric; computer and information sciences; computer and information systems security; computer programming; computer systems networking and telecommunications; criminal justice/police science; culinary arts; dental hygiene; drafting and design technology; early childhood education; educational/instructional media design; electrical, electronic and communications engineering technology; electrical/electronics drafting and CAD/CADD; electrical/electronics equipment installation and repair; emergency medical technology (EMT paramedic); engineering technology; environmental engineering technology; fire protection and safety technology; fire science; general studies; health information/medical records technology; Hispanic American, Puerto Rican, and Mexican American/Chicano studies; hospitality administration; interior design; kindergarten/preschool education; legal assistant/paralegal; liberal arts and sciences/liberal studies; medical transcription; middle school education; music; music management and merchandising; nursing (registered nurse training); real estate; respiratory care therapy; sales, distribution and marketing; secondary education; sign language interpretation and translation; surgical technology; telecommunications technology; web page, digital/multimedia and information resources design.

Academics *Calendar:* semesters. *Degree:* certificates and associate. *Special study options:* academic remediation for entering students, adult/continuing education programs, advanced placement credit, cooperative education, distance learning, English as a second language, honors programs, internships, part-time degree program, services for LD students, summer session for credit. *ROTC:* Air Force (c).
Library Spring Creek Library, Preston Ridge Library, Central Park Library plus 3 others with 178,212 titles, 888 serial subscriptions, 32,095 audiovisual materials, an OPAC, a Web page.
Student Life *Activities and Organizations:* drama/theater group, choral group, student government, Phi Theta Kappa, Baptist Student Ministry, National Society of Leadership Success, Political Science Club. *Campus security:* 24-hour emergency response devices and patrols, late-night transport/escort service. *Student services:* personal/psychological counseling.
Athletics Member NJCAA. *Intercollegiate sports:* basketball M(s)/W(s), tennis M(s)/W(s), volleyball W(s).
Standardized Tests *Required:* THEA (for admission).
Costs (2010–11) *Tuition:* area resident $810 full-time, $27 per semester hour part-time; state resident $1575 full-time, $54 per semester hour part-time; nonresident $3225 full-time, $109 per semester hour part-time. *Required fees:* $255 full-time, $7 per semester hour part-time. *Payment plan:* installment. *Waivers:* senior citizens and employees or children of employees.
Financial Aid Of all full-time matriculated undergraduates who enrolled in 2008, 80 Federal Work-Study jobs (averaging $3490).
Applying *Options:* electronic application. *Required:* high school transcript. *Application deadlines:* rolling (freshmen), rolling (out-of-state freshmen), rolling (transfers). *Notification:* continuous (freshmen), continuous (out-of-state freshmen), continuous (transfers).
Freshman Application Contact Mr. Todd Fields, Registrar, Collin County Community College District, 2200 West University Drive, McKinney, TX 75070-8001. *Phone:* 972-881-5174. *Fax:* 972-881-5175. *E-mail:* tfields@collin.edu.

COMMONWEALTH INSTITUTE OF FUNERAL SERVICE

Houston, Texas **www.commonwealth.edu/**

- **Independent** 2-year, founded 1988
- **Urban** campus with easy access to Houston
- **Coed,** 122 undergraduate students

Freshmen *Admission:* 55 applied, 55 admitted.
Majors Funeral service and mortuary science.
Academics *Calendar:* quarters. *Degree:* certificates and associate. *Special study options:* adult/continuing education programs, external degree program.
Library Commonwealth Institute Library and York Learning Resource Center with 1,500 titles, 12 serial subscriptions.
Student Life *Campus security:* 24-hour emergency response devices, daytime trained security personnel.
Standardized Tests *Required for some:* Wonderlic aptitude test or THEA. *Recommended:* SAT or ACT (for admission).
Costs (2010–11) *One-time required fee:* $100. *Comprehensive fee:* $22,800 includes full-time tuition ($12,800), mandatory fees ($100), and room and board ($9900). Full-time tuition and fees vary according to course load and program. Part-time tuition and fees vary according to course load and program. *Payment plan:* installment.
Applying *Application fee:* $50. *Required:* high school transcript. *Application deadline:* rolling (freshmen). *Notification:* continuous (freshmen).
Freshman Application Contact Ms. Patricia Moreno, Registrar, Commonwealth Institute of Funeral Service, 415 Barren Springs Drive, Houston, TX 77090. *Phone:* 281-873-0262. *Toll-free phone:* 800-628-1580. *Fax:* 281-873-5232. *E-mail:* p.moreno@commonwealth.edu.

COMPUTER CAREER CENTER

El Paso, Texas **www.computercareercenter.com/**

- **Proprietary** 2-year, founded 1985
- **Urban** campus
- **Coed**

Academics *Calendar:* 8 six-week terms. *Degree:* certificates, diplomas, and associate.
Applying *Application fee:* $100.
Director of Admissions Ms. Sarah Hernandez, Registrar, Computer Career Center, 6101 Montana Avenue, El Paso, TX 79925. *Phone:* 915-779-8031.

COURT REPORTING INSTITUTE OF DALLAS

Dallas, Texas **www.crid.com/**

- **Proprietary** 2-year, founded 1978
- **Urban** campus
- **Coed, primarily women**

Academics *Calendar:* quarters. *Degree:* associate.
Student Life *Campus security:* 24-hour patrols, late-night transport/escort service.
Applying *Options:* early decision. *Application fee:* $100. *Required:* high school transcript, interview.
Director of Admissions Ms. Debra Smith-Armstrong, Director of Admissions, Court Reporting Institute of Dallas, 8585 North Stemmons, #200 North Tower, Dallas, TX 75247. *Phone:* 214-350-9722 Ext. 227. *Toll-free phone:* 800-880-9722.

COURT REPORTING INSTITUTE OF HOUSTON

Houston, Texas **www.crid.com/**

Freshman Application Contact Admissions Office, Court Reporting Institute of Houston, 13101 Northwest Freeway, Suite 100, Houston, TX 77040. *Phone:* 713-996-8300. *Toll-free phone:* 866-996-8300.

CULINARY INSTITUTE ALAIN & MARIE LENOTRE

Houston, Texas **www.ciaml.com/**

Freshman Application Contact Admissions Office, Culinary Institute Alain & Marie LeNotre, 7070 Allensby, Houston, TX 77022-4322.

DALLAS INSTITUTE OF FUNERAL SERVICE

Dallas, Texas **www.dallasinstitute.edu/**

Freshman Application Contact Terry Parrish, Director of Admissions, Dallas Institute of Funeral Service, 3909 South Buckner Boulevard, Dallas, TX 75227. *Phone:* 214-388-5466. *Toll-free phone:* 800-235-5444. *Fax:* 214-388-0316. *E-mail:* difs@dallasinstitute.edu.

DEL MAR COLLEGE

Corpus Christi, Texas **www.delmar.edu/**

- **State and locally supported** 2-year, founded 1935
- **Urban** 159-acre campus
- **Coed,** 12,007 undergraduate students, 31% full-time, 58% women, 42% men

Undergraduates 3,722 full-time, 8,285 part-time. Students come from 43 states and territories, 57 other countries, 1% are from out of state, 3% African American, 2% Asian American or Pacific Islander, 59% Hispanic American, 0.3% Native American.
Faculty *Total:* 560, 48% full-time. *Student/faculty ratio:* 18:1.
Majors Accounting; accounting technology and bookkeeping; administrative assistant and secretarial science; applied art; architectural engineering technology; art; art teacher education; automobile/automotive mechanics technology; biology/biological sciences; building/property maintenance and management; business administration and management; business/commerce; business machine repair; chemical technology; chemistry; child development; clinical laboratory science/medical technology; clinical/medical laboratory technology; community organization and advocacy; computer and information sciences and support services related; computer and information sciences related; computer programming; computer programming related; computer programming (specific applications); computer programming (vendor/product certification); computer science;

Del Mar College (continued)

computer systems networking and telecommunications; computer typography and composition equipment operation; consumer merchandising/retailing management; cosmetology; court reporting; criminal justice/law enforcement administration; criminal justice/police science; culinary arts; data entry/microcomputer applications; dental hygiene; diagnostic medical sonography and ultrasound technology; drafting and design technology; dramatic/theater arts; e-commerce; education; electrical, electronic and communications engineering technology; elementary education; emergency medical technology (EMT paramedic); English; finance; fine/studio arts; fire protection and safety technology; fire science; geography; geology/earth science; health information/medical records technology; health teacher education; heavy equipment maintenance technology; history; hotel/motel administration; industrial radiologic technology; information science/studies; information technology; interdisciplinary studies; journalism; kindergarten/preschool education; legal administrative assistant/secretary; legal studies; liberal arts and sciences/liberal studies; machine tool technology; management information systems; mathematics; medical administrative assistant and medical secretary; medical radiologic technology; mental health/rehabilitation; music; music teacher education; nuclear medical technology; nursing (registered nurse training); occupational safety and health technology; occupational therapist assistant; office occupations and clerical services; parks, recreation and leisure; physical education teaching and coaching; physics; political science and government; pre-engineering; psychology; public administration; public policy analysis; radio and television; real estate; respiratory care therapy; sign language interpretation and translation; social work; sociology; special products marketing; speech and rhetoric; system administration; trade and industrial teacher education; transportation management; voice and opera; web/multimedia management and webmaster; web page, digital/multimedia and information resources design; welding technology; word processing.

Academics *Calendar:* semesters. *Degree:* certificates and associate. *Special study options:* academic remediation for entering students, accelerated degree program, adult/continuing education programs, advanced placement credit, cooperative education, distance learning, double majors, English as a second language, freshman honors college, honors programs, internships, off-campus study, part-time degree program, services for LD students, summer session for credit. *ROTC:* Army (b).

Library White Library plus 1 other with 127,717 titles, 739 serial subscriptions, an OPAC, a Web page.

Student Life *Housing:* college housing not available. *Activities and Organizations:* drama/theater group, student-run newspaper, radio station, choral group, Phi Theta Kappa, Alpha Beta Gamma, Student Government Association. *Campus security:* 24-hour emergency response devices and patrols. *Student services:* personal/psychological counseling.

Athletics *Intramural sports:* badminton M/W, basketball M/W, bowling M/W, football M/W, golf M/W, racquetball M/W, tennis M/W, track and field M/W, volleyball M/W, weight lifting M/W.

Costs (2009–10) *Tuition:* $38 per credit hour part-time; state resident $88 per credit hour part-time; nonresident $125 per credit hour part-time. Full-time tuition and fees vary according to course load. Part-time tuition and fees vary according to course load. *Required fees:* $30 per credit hour part-time, $57 per term part-time. *Payment plan:* installment. *Waivers:* senior citizens and employees or children of employees.

Financial Aid Of all full-time matriculated undergraduates who enrolled in 2008, 259 Federal Work-Study jobs (averaging $960). 449 state and other part-time jobs (averaging $1082).

Applying *Options:* electronic application, early admission, deferred entrance. *Required:* high school transcript. *Application deadlines:* rolling (freshmen), rolling (transfers).

Freshman Application Contact Ms. Frances P. Jordan, Director of Admissions and Registrar, Del Mar College, 101 Baldwin Boulevard, Corpus Christi, TX 78404-3897. *Phone:* 361-698-1255. *Toll-free phone:* 800-652-3357. *Fax:* 361-698-1595. *E-mail:* fjordan@delmar.edu.

EASTFIELD COLLEGE

Mesquite, Texas **www.efc.dcccd.edu/**

- **State and locally supported** 2-year, founded 1970, part of Dallas County Community College District System
- **Suburban** 244-acre campus with easy access to Dallas-Fort Worth
- **Coed,** 11,944 undergraduate students, 26% full-time, 59% women, 41% men

Undergraduates 3,140 full-time, 8,804 part-time. Students come from 13 states and territories, 11 other countries, 0.5% are from out of state, 24% African American, 4% Asian American or Pacific Islander, 31% Hispanic American, 0.4% Native American, 0.3% international, 4% transferred in. *Retention:* 73% of 2008 full-time freshmen returned.

Freshmen *Admission:* 2,100 applied, 2,100 admitted, 1,496 enrolled.

Faculty *Total:* 397, 29% full-time. *Student/faculty ratio:* 29:1.

Majors Accounting; autobody/collision and repair technology; automobile/automotive mechanics technology; business administration and management; business/commerce; child-care and support services management; communication/speech communication and rhetoric; computer and information sciences related; computer engineering technology; computer hardware engineering; computer/information technology services administration related; computer programming; computer programming related; computer systems networking and telecommunications; criminal justice/safety; data entry/microcomputer applications; data processing and data processing technology; drafting and design technology; e-commerce; education; electrical, electronic and communications engineering technology; electrical/electronics drafting and CAD/CADD; executive assistant/executive secretary; graphic and printing equipment operation/production; heating, air conditioning, ventilation and refrigeration maintenance technology; legal administrative assistant/secretary; liberal arts and sciences/liberal studies; multi/interdisciplinary studies related; music; psychiatric/mental health services technology; sign language interpretation and translation; social work; substance abuse/addiction counseling; system administration; word processing.

Academics *Calendar:* semesters. *Degree:* certificates and associate. *Special study options:* academic remediation for entering students, adult/continuing education programs, advanced placement credit, cooperative education, distance learning, English as a second language, honors programs, part-time degree program, services for LD students, summer session for credit.

Library Eastfield College Learning Resource Center with 66,988 titles, 415 serial subscriptions, 2,620 audiovisual materials, an OPAC, a Web page.

Student Life *Housing:* college housing not available. *Activities and Organizations:* drama/theater group, student-run newspaper, choral group, LULAC, Rodeo Club, Phi Theta Kappa, Rising Star, Communications Club. *Campus security:* 24-hour emergency response devices and patrols. *Student services:* health clinic, personal/psychological counseling, women's center.

Athletics Member NJCAA. *Intercollegiate sports:* baseball M, basketball M, golf M, soccer W, tennis M/W, volleyball M/W. *Intramural sports:* basketball M, football M, softball M/W, volleyball M/W.

Costs (2009–10) *Tuition:* area resident $1230 full-time, $41 per credit part-time; state resident $2280 full-time, $76 per credit part-time; nonresident $3630 full-time, $121 per credit part-time. Full-time tuition and fees vary according to course load. Part-time tuition and fees vary according to course load. *Payment plan:* installment. *Waivers:* senior citizens.

Applying *Options:* early admission, deferred entrance. *Recommended:* high school transcript. *Application deadlines:* rolling (freshmen), rolling (transfers). *Notification:* continuous (freshmen), continuous (transfers).

Freshman Application Contact Ms. Glynis Miller, Director of Admissions/Registrar, Eastfield College, 3737 Motley Drive, Mesquite, TX 75150-2099. *Phone:* 972-860-7010. *Fax:* 972-860-8306. *E-mail:* efc@dcccd.edu.

EL CENTRO COLLEGE

Dallas, Texas **www.ecc.dcccd.edu/**

- **County-supported** 2-year, founded 1966, part of Dallas County Community College District System
- **Urban** 2-acre campus
- **Coed,** 8,513 undergraduate students, 20% full-time, 69% women, 31% men

Undergraduates 1,733 full-time, 6,780 part-time. Students come from 15 states and territories, 59 other countries, 1% are from out of state, 63% transferred in. *Retention:* 52% of 2008 full-time freshmen returned.

Freshmen *Admission:* 2,277 applied, 2,277 admitted, 1,128 enrolled.

Faculty *Total:* 460, 28% full-time, 10% with terminal degrees. *Student/faculty ratio:* 16:1.

Majors Accounting; apparel and accessories marketing; baking and pastry arts; biotechnology; business administration and management; business automation/technology/data entry; business/commerce; cardiovascular technology; clinical/medical laboratory technology; computer and information systems security; computer/information technology services administration related; computer programming; computer science; culinary arts; data processing and data processing technology; diagnostic medical sonography and ultrasound technology; emergency medical technology (EMT paramedic); executive assistant/executive secretary; fashion/apparel design; health information/medical records administration; information science/studies; interior design; legal administrative assistant/secretary; legal assistant/paralegal; medical/clinical assistant; medical radiologic technology; medical transcription; nursing (licensed practical/vocational nurse training); nursing (registered nurse training); office occupations and clerical services; peace studies and conflict resolution; radiologic technology/science; respiratory care therapy; special products marketing; surgical technology; teacher assistant/aide; web page, digital/multimedia and information resources design.

Academics *Calendar:* semesters. *Degree:* certificates and associate. *Special study options:* academic remediation for entering students, adult/continuing education programs, advanced placement credit, cooperative education, distance learning, double majors, English as a second language, freshman honors college, honors programs, internships, part-time degree program, services for LD students, summer session for credit. *ROTC:* Army (c).

Library El Centro College Library with 77,902 titles, 224 serial subscriptions, 585 audiovisual materials, an OPAC, a Web page.

Student Life *Housing:* college housing not available. *Activities and Organizations:* choral group, Phi Theta Kappa, student government, Paralegal Student Association, El Centro Computer Society, Conflict Resolution Society. *Campus security:* 24-hour emergency response devices and patrols, late-night transport/escort service. *Student services:* health clinic, personal/psychological counseling.

Costs (2010–11) *Tuition:* area resident $984 full-time, $41 per credit hour part-time; state resident $1824 full-time, $76 per credit hour part-time; nonresident $2904 full-time, $121 per credit hour part-time. Full-time tuition and fees vary according to class time and program. Part-time tuition and fees vary according to class time and program. *Payment plans:* installment, deferred payment. *Waivers:* senior citizens and employees or children of employees.

Applying *Options:* electronic application, early admission. *Required for some:* high school transcript, 1 letter of recommendation. *Application deadlines:* rolling (freshmen), rolling (transfers).

Freshman Application Contact Ms. Rebecca Garza, Director of Admissions and Registrar, El Centro College, 801 Main Street, Dallas, TX 75202. *Phone:* 214-860-2618. *Fax:* 214-860-2233. *E-mail:* rgarza@dcccd.edu.

El Paso Community College

El Paso, Texas **www.epcc.edu/**

- **County-supported** 2-year, founded 1969
- **Urban** campus
- **Coed,** 28,168 undergraduate students, 39% full-time, 58% women, 42% men

Undergraduates 10,943 full-time, 17,225 part-time. 2% African American, 0.8% Asian American or Pacific Islander, 87% Hispanic American, 0.3% Native American, 2% international.

Freshmen *Admission:* 5,583 enrolled.

Faculty *Total:* 1,411, 29% full-time, 3% with terminal degrees.

Majors Accounting; administrative assistant and secretarial science; adult development and aging; automobile/automotive mechanics technology; business administration and management; business automation/technology/data entry; business/commerce; child-care and support services management; child development; cinematography and film/video production; clinical/medical laboratory technology; commercial and advertising art; communication/speech communication and rhetoric; computer and information sciences; computer programming; corrections; corrections and criminal justice related; court reporting; criminal justice/police science; criminal justice/safety; culinary arts; dental assisting; dental hygiene; diagnostic medical sonography and ultrasound technology; dietetics; drafting and design technology; electrical, electronic and communications engineering technology; emergency medical technology (EMT paramedic); engineering; environmental engineering technology; fashion/apparel design; fire protection and safety technology; general studies; health information/medical records administration; heating, air conditioning, ventilation and refrigeration maintenance technology; hotel/motel administration; institutional food workers; interior design; international business/trade/commerce; kindergarten/preschool education; legal assistant/paralegal; liberal arts and sciences/liberal studies; machine tool technology; medical/clinical assistant; medical radiologic technology; middle school education; multi/interdisciplinary studies related; music; nursing (registered nurse training); opticianry; optometric technician; pharmacy technician; physical therapist assistant; plastics engineering technology; psychiatric/mental health services technology; radiologic technology/science; real estate; respiratory care therapy; security and protective services related; sign language interpretation and translation; social work; substance abuse/addiction counseling; surgical technology; system, networking, and LAN/WAN management; tourism and travel services management.

Academics *Calendar:* semesters. *Degree:* certificates and associate. *Special study options:* academic remediation for entering students, adult/continuing education programs, advanced placement credit, cooperative education, distance learning, English as a second language, external degree program, honors programs, internships, off-campus study, part-time degree program, services for LD students, summer session for credit. *ROTC:* Army (c).

Library El Paso Community College Learning Resource Center plus 4 others with 442,879 titles, 938 serial subscriptions, 12,035 audiovisual materials, an OPAC, a Web page.

Student Life *Housing:* college housing not available. *Activities and Organizations:* drama/theater group, student-run newspaper, radio and television station, choral group. *Campus security:* 24-hour patrols, late-night transport/escort service. *Student services:* personal/psychological counseling.

Athletics Member NJCAA. *Intercollegiate sports:* baseball M(s), softball W(s), track and field M/W. *Intramural sports:* basketball M/W, bowling M/W, cross-country running M/W, softball M/W, table tennis M/W, tennis M/W, volleyball M/W, weight lifting M/W.

Costs (2010–11) *Tuition:* state resident $1428 full-time, $60 per hour part-time; nonresident $1980 full-time, $83 per hour part-time. Full-time tuition and fees vary according to course load. Part-time tuition and fees vary according to course load. *Required fees:* $240 full-time. *Payment plan:* installment. *Waivers:* senior citizens and employees or children of employees.

Financial Aid Of all full-time matriculated undergraduates who enrolled in 2008, 750 Federal Work-Study jobs (averaging $1800). 50 state and other part-time jobs (averaging $1800).

Applying *Options:* early admission, deferred entrance. *Application fee:* $10.

Freshman Application Contact Daryle Hendry, Director of Admissions, El Paso Community College, PO Box 20500, El Paso, TX 79998-0500. *Phone:* 915-831-2580. *E-mail:* daryleh@epcc.edu.

Everest College

Arlington, Texas **www.everest.edu/**

Freshman Application Contact Admissions Office, Everest College, 2801 East Division Street, Suite 250, Arlington, TX 76011.

Everest College

Dallas, Texas **www.everest.edu/**

Freshman Application Contact Admissions Office, Everest College, 6080 North Central Expressway, Dallas, TX 75206.

Everest College

Fort Worth, Texas **www.everest.edu/**

Freshman Application Contact Admissions Office, Everest College, 5237 North Riverside Drive, Suite 100, Fort Worth, TX 76137.

Frank Phillips College

Borger, Texas **www.fpctx.edu/**

- **State and locally supported** 2-year, founded 1948
- **Small-town** 60-acre campus
- **Coed**

Undergraduates 585 full-time, 663 part-time. Students come from 15 states and territories, 6 other countries, 10% are from out of state, 20% live on campus. *Retention:* 52% of 2008 full-time freshmen returned.

Faculty *Student/faculty ratio:* 16:1.

Academics *Calendar:* semesters. *Degree:* certificates and associate. *Special study options:* academic remediation for entering students, accelerated degree program, adult/continuing education programs, advanced placement credit, cooperative education, distance learning, honors programs, internships, part-time degree program, services for LD students, summer session for credit.

Student Life *Campus security:* 24-hour emergency response devices and patrols, controlled dormitory access.

Athletics Member NJCAA.

Costs (2009–10) *Tuition:* area resident $768 full-time, $32 per hour part-time; state resident $1272 full-time, $53 per hour part-time; nonresident $1460 full-time, $60 per hour part-time. Part-time tuition and fees vary according to course load. *Required fees:* $1162 full-time, $44 per hour part-time, $53 per hour part-time. *Room and board:* $3950. Room and board charges vary according to housing facility.

Financial Aid Of all full-time matriculated undergraduates who enrolled in 2008, 24 Federal Work-Study jobs (averaging $5200). 6 state and other part-time jobs (averaging $4800). *Financial aid deadline:* 8/31.

Applying *Options:* electronic application, early admission, deferred entrance. *Required:* high school transcript.

Freshman Application Contact Ms. Beth Raper, Director of Enrollment Management, Frank Phillips College, Borger, TX 79008-5118. *Phone:* 806-457-4200 Ext. 740. *Toll-free phone:* 800-687-2056. *Fax:* 806-457-4225. *E-mail:* braper@fpctx.edu.

Galveston College

Galveston, Texas **www.gc.edu/**

- **State and locally supported** 2-year, founded 1967
- **Urban** 11-acre campus with easy access to Houston
- **Endowment** $3.4 million
- **Coed**

Undergraduates 851 full-time, 1,379 part-time. Students come from 26 states and territories, 2% are from out of state, 19% African American, 3% Asian American or Pacific Islander, 24% Hispanic American, 0.3% Native American, 1% international, 33% transferred in. *Retention:* 51% of 2008 full-time freshmen returned.

Faculty *Student/faculty ratio:* 11:1.

Academics *Calendar:* semesters. *Degree:* certificates and associate. *Special study options:* academic remediation for entering students, adult/continuing education programs, advanced placement credit, cooperative education, distance learning, internships, off-campus study, part-time degree program, services for LD students, summer session for credit.

Student Life *Campus security:* 24-hour emergency response devices and patrols, late-night transport/escort service.

Athletics Member NJCAA.

Costs (2009–10) *Tuition:* state resident $900 full-time, $30 per semester hour part-time; nonresident $1800 full-time, $60 per semester hour part-time. *Required fees:* $514 full-time, $13 per credit hour part-time, $62 per term part-time.

Financial Aid Of all full-time matriculated undergraduates who enrolled in 2008, 36 Federal Work-Study jobs (averaging $2000).

Applying *Required for some:* high school transcript.

Freshman Application Contact Galveston College, 4015 Avenue Q, Galveston, TX 77550. *Phone:* 409-944-1234.

Grayson County College

Denison, Texas **www.grayson.edu/**

Director of Admissions Dr. Debbie Plyler, Associate Vice President for Admissions, Records and Institutional Research, Grayson County College, 6101 Grayson Drive, Denison, TX 75020. *Phone:* 903-463-8727.

Hallmark College of Technology

San Antonio, Texas **www.hallmarkcollege.edu/**

- **Proprietary** primarily 2-year, founded 1969
- **Suburban** 3-acre campus
- **Coed**

Undergraduates 294 full-time. 9% African American, 3% Asian American or Pacific Islander, 59% Hispanic American, 0.3% Native American, 1% transferred in.

Faculty *Student/faculty ratio:* 10:1.

Academics *Calendar:* continuous. *Degrees:* certificates, associate, and bachelor's. *Special study options:* accelerated degree program, internships.

Student Life *Campus security:* 24-hour emergency response devices.

Standardized Tests *Required:* Wonderlic aptitude test (for admission).

Costs (2009–10) *One-time required fee:* $110. *Tuition:* $12,600 to $55,000 depending on program enrolled. Administrative fee $110.

Applying *Application fee:* $110. *Required:* high school transcript, interview, Wonderlic Assessment, tour. *Required for some:* essay or personal statement.

Freshman Application Contact Hallmark College of Technology, 10401 IH 10 West, San Antonio, TX 78230. *Phone:* 210-690-9000 Ext. 212. *Toll-free phone:* 800-880-6600.

Hallmark Institute of Aeronautics

San Antonio, Texas **www.hallmarkcollege.edu/programs-school-of-aeronautics.aspx/**

- **Private** 2-year, administratively affiliated with Hallmark College of Technology
- **Urban** 2-acre campus
- **Coed,** 218 undergraduate students, 100% full-time, 5% women, 95% men

Undergraduates 218 full-time. 11% African American, 3% Asian American or Pacific Islander, 52% Hispanic American, 1% Native American, 2% transferred in.

Freshmen *Admission:* 37 enrolled.

Faculty *Total:* 8. *Student/faculty ratio:* 17:1.

Majors Aircraft powerplant technology; airframe mechanics and aircraft maintenance technology.

Academics *Calendar:* continuous. *Degree:* diplomas and associate. *Special study options:* academic remediation for entering students.

Student Life *Housing:* college housing not available. *Activities and Organizations:* Alpha Beta Kappa. *Campus security:* 24-hour emergency response devices and patrols.

Applying *Application fee:* $110. *Required:* high school transcript, interview, assessment, tour, background check. *Application deadlines:* rolling (freshmen), rolling (transfers).

Freshman Application Contact Hallmark Institute of Aeronautics, 8901 Wetmore Road, San Antonio, TX 78216. *Phone:* 210-826-1000 Ext. 106. *Toll-free phone:* 888-656-9300.

Hill College of the Hill Junior College District

Hillsboro, Texas **www.hillcollege.edu/**

- **District-supported** 2-year, founded 1923
- **Small-town** 80-acre campus with easy access to Dallas-Fort Worth
- **Coed**

Academics *Calendar:* semesters. *Degree:* certificates and associate. *Special study options:* academic remediation for entering students, adult/continuing education programs, advanced placement credit, cooperative education, distance learning, double majors, English as a second language, honors programs, internships, part-time degree program, services for LD students, summer session for credit.

Student Life *Campus security:* late-night transport/escort service, controlled dormitory access, security officers.

Athletics Member NJCAA.

Financial Aid Of all full-time matriculated undergraduates who enrolled in 2008, 51 Federal Work-Study jobs (averaging $858). 20 state and other part-time jobs (averaging $230).

Applying *Options:* early admission, deferred entrance. *Required:* high school transcript.

Freshman Application Contact Ms. Diane Harvey, Director of Admissions/Registrar, Hill College of the Hill Junior College District, PO Box 619, Hillsboro, TX 76645-0619. *Phone:* 254-582-2555. *Fax:* 254-582-7591. *E-mail:* diharvey@hill-college.cc.tx.us.

Houston Community College System

Houston, Texas **www.hccs.edu/**

- **State and locally supported** 2-year, founded 1971
- **Urban** campus
- **Coed,** 54,942 undergraduate students, 31% full-time, 59% women, 41% men

Undergraduates 16,821 full-time, 38,121 part-time. 10% are from out of state, 25% African American, 10% Asian American or Pacific Islander, 29% Hispanic American, 0.2% Native American, 11% international, 5% transferred in. *Retention:* 63% of 2008 full-time freshmen returned.

Freshmen *Admission:* 10,124 enrolled.

Faculty *Total:* 2,952, 28% full-time, 13% with terminal degrees.

Majors Accounting; animation, interactive technology, video graphics and special effects; applied horticulture; automobile/automotive mechanics technology; banking and financial support services; biology/biotechnology laboratory technician; business administration and management; business automation/technology/data entry; business/corporate communications; cardiovascular technology; cartography; chemical technology; child development; cinematography and film/video production; clinical/medical laboratory science and allied professions related; clinical/medical laboratory technology; commercial photography; computer engineering technology; computer programming; computer programming (specific applications); computer systems networking and telecommunications; construction engineering technology; cosmetology; court reporting; criminal justice/police science; culinary arts; desktop publishing and digital imaging design; drafting and design technology; emergency medical technology (EMT paramedic); fashion/apparel design; fashion merchandising; fire protection and safety technology; graphic and printing equipment operation/production; health and physical education; health information/medical records technology; histologic technician; hotel/motel administration; instrumentation technology; interior design; international business/trade/commerce; legal assistant/paralegal; logistics and materials management; manufacturing technology; marketing/marketing management; music management and merchandising; music performance; music theory and composition; nuclear medical technology; nursing (registered nurse training); occupational therapist assistant; physical therapist assistant; psychiatric/mental health services technology; public administration; radio and television broadcasting technology; radiologic technology/science; real estate; respiratory care therapy; sign language interpretation and translation; system administration; tourism and travel services management; turf and turfgrass management.

Academics *Calendar:* semesters. *Degree:* certificates and associate. *Special study options:* academic remediation for entering students, adult/continuing education programs, advanced placement credit, cooperative education, distance learning, English as a second language, honors programs, independent study, internships, part-time degree program, services for LD students, study abroad, summer session for credit. *ROTC:* Army (c), Air Force (c).

Library an OPAC, a Web page.

Student Life *Housing:* college housing not available. *Activities and Organizations:* drama/theater group, student-run newspaper, television station, Phi Theta Kappa, Eastwood Student Association, Eagle's Club, Society of Hispanic Professional Engineers, International Student Association. *Campus security:* 24-hour emergency response devices and patrols, late-night transport/escort service. *Student services:* personal/psychological counseling.

Costs (2009–10) *Tuition:* area resident $1392 full-time, $58 per credit hour part-time; state resident $2688 full-time, $112 per credit hour part-time; nonresident $3168 full-time, $132 per credit hour part-time. Full-time tuition and fees vary according to course load. Part-time tuition and fees vary according to course load. *Required fees:* $6 per term part-time.

Applying *Required for some:* high school transcript, interview. *Application deadline:* rolling (freshmen). *Notification:* continuous (transfers).

Freshman Application Contact Ms. Mary Lemburg, Registrar, Houston Community College System, 3100 Main Street, PO Box 667517, Houston, TX 77266-7517. *Phone:* 713-718-8500. *Fax:* 713-718-2111.

HOWARD COLLEGE

Big Spring, Texas — www.howardcollege.edu/

- **State and locally supported** 2-year, founded 1945, part of Howard County Junior College District SystemHoward College at Big SpringHoward College at San AngeloHoward College at LamesaSouthwest Collegiate Institute for the Deaf
- **Small-town** 120-acre campus
- **Endowment** $1.2 million
- **Coed,** 4,103 undergraduate students, 40% full-time, 61% women, 39% men

Undergraduates 1,636 full-time, 2,467 part-time. 5% African American, 1% Asian American or Pacific Islander, 36% Hispanic American, 0.5% Native American, 8% live on campus. *Retention:* 54% of 2008 full-time freshmen returned.

Freshmen *Admission:* 506 enrolled.

Faculty *Total:* 243, 59% full-time, 3% with terminal degrees. *Student/faculty ratio:* 14:1.

Majors Accounting; administrative assistant and secretarial science; agriculture; art; automobile/automotive mechanics technology; behavioral sciences; biology/biological sciences; business administration and management; business/commerce; chemistry; chemistry teacher education; child development; communication/speech communication and rhetoric; computer and information sciences; computer and information sciences related; computer programming; computer science; cosmetology; criminal justice/law enforcement administration; criminal justice/police science; criminal justice/safety; dental hygiene; desktop publishing and digital imaging design; drafting and design technology; drama and dance teacher education; dramatic/theater arts; education; education related; elementary education; English; finance; foreign language teacher education; general studies; health and physical education; health information/medical records administration; health information/medical records technology; health occupations teacher education; history; history teacher education; industrial arts; industrial production technologies related; mathematics; mathematics teacher education; middle school education; music; music teacher education; nursing (licensed practical/vocational nurse training); nursing (registered nurse training); ornamental horticulture; physical education teaching and coaching; physics teacher education; psychology; radiologic technology/science; reading teacher education; respiratory care therapy; secondary education; sign language interpretation and translation; social sciences; social science teacher education; social studies teacher education; sociology; Spanish; special education; speech and rhetoric; speech teacher education; substance abuse/addiction counseling; technical teacher education; trade and industrial teacher education; web/multimedia management and webmaster.

Academics *Calendar:* semesters. *Degree:* certificates and associate. *Special study options:* academic remediation for entering students, adult/continuing education programs, advanced placement credit, cooperative education, distance learning, English as a second language, independent study, internships, part-time degree program, services for LD students, summer session for credit.

Library Howard College Library with 30,921 titles, 16,006 serial subscriptions, 1,710 audiovisual materials, an OPAC, a Web page.

Student Life *Housing:* on-campus residence required for freshman year. *Options:* coed, men-only, women-only. Campus housing is university owned. Freshman applicants given priority for college housing. *Activities and Organizations:* drama/theater group, choral group, Phi Theta Kappa, Student Government Association, Mexican-American Student Association, Baptist Student Ministries, Various departmental student organizations. *Campus security:* 24-hour emergency response devices and patrols. *Student services:* personal/psychological counseling.

Athletics Member NJCAA. *Intercollegiate sports:* baseball M(s), basketball M(s)/W(s), cheerleading M(s)/W(s), softball W(s). *Intramural sports:* basketball M/W, bowling M/W, football M/W, racquetball M/W, softball W, volleyball M/W.

Costs (2010–11) *Tuition:* area resident $1500 full-time, $40 per hour part-time; state resident $1920 full-time, $52 per hour part-time; nonresident $2620 full-time, $74 per hour part-time. Full-time tuition and fees vary according to course load and location. Part-time tuition and fees vary according to course load and location. *Required fees:* $212 full-time, $176 per term part-time. *Room and board:* $3984. Room and board charges vary according to housing facility and location. *Payment plans:* installment, deferred payment. *Waivers:* senior citizens and employees or children of employees.

Applying *Options:* electronic application, early admission. *Required:* high school transcript. *Application deadlines:* rolling (freshmen), rolling (transfers). *Notification:* continuous until 8/31 (freshmen), continuous until 8/31 (transfers).

Freshman Application Contact Ms. TaNeal Richardson, Assistant Registrar, Howard College, 1001 Birdwell Lane, Big Spring, TX 79720-3702. *Phone:* 432-264-5105. *Toll-free phone:* 866-HC-HAWKS. *Fax:* 432-264-5604. *E-mail:* trichardson@howardcollege.edu.

ITT TECHNICAL INSTITUTE

Arlington, Texas — www.itt-tech.edu/

- **Proprietary** primarily 2-year, founded 1982, part of ITT Educational Services, Inc.
- **Suburban** campus
- **Coed**

Majors CAD/CADD drafting/design technology; computer and information systems security; computer software and media applications related; computer software technology; construction management; drafting and design technology; electrical, electronic and communications engineering technology; legal assistant/paralegal; system, networking, and LAN/WAN management.

Academics *Calendar:* quarters. *Degrees:* associate and bachelor's.

Student Life *Housing:* college housing not available.

Freshman Application Contact Director of Recruitment, ITT Technical Institute, 551 Ryan Plaza Drive, Arlington, TX 76011. *Phone:* 817-794-5100. *Toll-free phone:* 888-288-4950. *Fax:* 817-275-8446.

ITT TECHNICAL INSTITUTE

Austin, Texas — www.itt-tech.edu/

- **Proprietary** primarily 2-year, founded 1985, part of ITT Educational Services, Inc.
- **Urban** campus
- **Coed**

Majors Accounting technology and bookkeeping; CAD/CADD drafting/design technology; computer and information systems security; computer engineering technology; computer software and media applications related; computer software technology; construction management; electrical, electronic and communications engineering technology; legal assistant/paralegal; system, networking, and LAN/WAN management; web page, digital/multimedia and information resources design.

Academics *Calendar:* quarters. *Degrees:* associate and bachelor's.

Student Life *Housing:* college housing not available.

Financial Aid Of all full-time matriculated undergraduates who enrolled in 2008, 1 Federal Work-Study job.

ITT Technical Institute (continued)

Freshman Application Contact Director of Recruitment, ITT Technical Institute, 6330 Highway 290 East, Suite 150, Austin, TX 78723. *Phone:* 512-467-6800. *Toll-free phone:* 800-431-0677. *Fax:* 512-467-6677.

ITT Technical Institute

DeSoto, Texas **www.itt-tech.edu/**

- **Proprietary** primarily 2-year
- **Coed**

Majors CAD/CADD drafting/design technology; computer and information systems security; computer engineering technology; construction management; electrical, electronic and communications engineering technology; legal assistant/paralegal; system, networking, and LAN/WAN management.

Academics *Degrees:* associate and bachelor's.

Freshman Application Contact ITT Technical Institute, 921 West Belt Line Road, Suite 181, DeSoto, TX 75115. *Phone:* 972-274-8600. *Toll-free phone:* 877-854-5728.

ITT Technical Institute

Houston, Texas **www.itt-tech.edu/**

- **Proprietary** primarily 2-year, founded 1985, part of ITT Educational Services, Inc.
- **Suburban** campus
- **Coed**

Majors CAD/CADD drafting/design technology; computer and information systems security; computer engineering technology; computer software technology; construction management; electrical, electronic and communications engineering technology; legal assistant/paralegal; system, networking, and LAN/WAN management.

Academics *Calendar:* quarters. *Degrees:* associate and bachelor's.

Student Life *Housing:* college housing not available.

Freshman Application Contact Director of Recruitment, ITT Technical Institute, 15651 North Freeway, Houston, TX 77090. *Phone:* 281-873-0512. *Toll-free phone:* 800-879-6486.

ITT Technical Institute

Houston, Texas **www.itt-tech.edu/**

- **Proprietary** primarily 2-year, founded 1983, part of ITT Educational Services, Inc.
- **Urban** campus
- **Coed**

Majors CAD/CADD drafting/design technology; computer and information systems security; computer software technology; construction management; electrical, electronic and communications engineering technology; legal assistant/paralegal; system, networking, and LAN/WAN management.

Academics *Calendar:* quarters. *Degrees:* associate and bachelor's.

Student Life *Housing:* college housing not available.

Freshman Application Contact Director of Recruitment, ITT Technical Institute, 2950 South Gessner, Houston, TX 77063. *Phone:* 713-952-2294. *Toll-free phone:* 800-235-4787.

ITT Technical Institute

Richardson, Texas **www.itt-tech.edu/**

- **Proprietary** 2-year, founded 1989, part of ITT Educational Services, Inc.
- **Suburban** campus
- **Coed**

Majors Accounting technology and bookkeeping; CAD/CADD drafting/design technology; computer and information systems security; computer engineering technology; computer software and media applications related; computer software technology; construction management; electrical, electronic and communications engineering technology; legal assistant/paralegal; system, networking, and LAN/WAN management; web page, digital/multimedia and information resources design.

Academics *Calendar:* quarters. *Degree:* associate.

Student Life *Housing:* college housing not available.

Financial Aid Of all full-time matriculated undergraduates who enrolled in 2008, 5 Federal Work-Study jobs (averaging $5000).

Freshman Application Contact Director of Recruitment, ITT Technical Institute, 2101 Waterview Parkway, Richardson, TX 75080. *Phone:* 972-690-9100. *Toll-free phone:* 888-488-5761.

ITT Technical Institute

San Antonio, Texas **www.itt-tech.edu/**

- **Proprietary** 2-year, founded 1988, part of ITT Educational Services, Inc.
- **Urban** campus
- **Coed**

Majors Accounting technology and bookkeeping; CAD/CADD drafting/design technology; computer and information systems security; computer software technology; construction management; electrical, electronic and communications engineering technology; legal assistant/paralegal; system, networking, and LAN/WAN management; web page, digital/multimedia and information resources design.

Academics *Calendar:* quarters. *Degree:* associate.

Student Life *Housing:* college housing not available.

Freshman Application Contact Director of Recruitment, ITT Technical Institute, 5700 Northwest Parkway, San Antonio, TX 78249-3303. *Phone:* 210-694-4612. *Toll-free phone:* 800-880-0570.

ITT Technical Institute

Webster, Texas **www.itt-tech.edu/**

- **Proprietary** primarily 2-year, founded 1995, part of ITT Educational Services, Inc.
- **Coed**

Majors CAD/CADD drafting/design technology; computer and information systems security; computer engineering technology; computer software technology; construction management; electrical, electronic and communications engineering technology; legal assistant/paralegal; system, networking, and LAN/WAN management.

Academics *Calendar:* quarters. *Degrees:* associate and bachelor's.

Student Life *Housing:* college housing not available.

Freshman Application Contact Director of Recruitment, ITT Technical Institute, 1001 Magnolia Avenue, Webster, TX 77598. *Phone:* 281-316-4700. *Toll-free phone:* 888-488-9347.

Jacksonville College

Jacksonville, Texas **www.jacksonville-college.edu/**

Freshman Application Contact Ms. Melissa Walles, Director of Admissions, Jacksonville College, 105 B.J. Albritton Drive, Jacksonville, TX 75766. *Phone:* 903-586-2518 Ext. 7134. *Toll-free phone:* 800-256-8522. *Fax:* 903-586-0743. *E-mail:* admissions@jacksonville-college.org.

Kaplan College, Arlington

Arlington, Texas **www.kc-arlington.com/**

- **Proprietary** 2-year
- **Coed**

Freshman Application Contact Kaplan College, Arlington, 2241 South Watson Road, Arlington, TX 76010. *Phone:* 866-249-2074. *Toll-free phone:* 866-249-2074.

KAPLAN COLLEGE, DALLAS

Dallas, Texas **www.kc-dallas.com/**

- **Proprietary** 2-year, founded 1987
- **Coed**

Academics *Degree:* diplomas and associate.

Freshman Application Contact Kaplan College, Dallas, 12005 Ford Road, Suite 100, Dallas, TX 75234. *Phone:* 972-385-1446. *Toll-free phone:* 800-525-1446.

KD STUDIO

Dallas, Texas **www.kdstudio.com/**

- **Proprietary** 2-year, founded 1979
- **Urban** campus
- **Coed,** 102 undergraduate students, 100% full-time, 49% women, 51% men

Undergraduates 102 full-time. Students come from 1 other state, 41% African American, 4% Asian American or Pacific Islander, 13% Hispanic American.

Freshmen *Admission:* 14 admitted, 14 enrolled.

Faculty *Total:* 21, 100% full-time. *Student/faculty ratio:* 5:1.

Majors Acting; music related.

Academics *Calendar:* semesters. *Degree:* associate. *Special study options:* cooperative education.

Library KD Studio Library with 800 titles, 15 serial subscriptions.

Student Life *Housing:* college housing not available. *Activities and Organizations:* drama/theater group, Student Council. *Campus security:* 24-hour emergency response devices and patrols.

Applying *Options:* deferred entrance. *Application fee:* $100. *Required:* essay or personal statement, high school transcript, interview, audition. *Application deadlines:* rolling (freshmen), rolling (transfers).

Freshman Application Contact Mr. T. A. Taylor, Director of Education, KD Studio, 2600 Stemmons Freeway, Suite 117, Dallas, TX 75207. *Phone:* 214-638-0484. *Fax:* 214-630-5140. *E-mail:* tataylor@kdstudio.com.

KILGORE COLLEGE

Kilgore, Texas **www.kilgore.edu/**

- **State and locally supported** 2-year, founded 1935
- **Small-town** 35-acre campus with easy access to Dallas-Fort Worth
- **Coed,** 6,375 undergraduate students, 47% full-time, 61% women, 39% men

Undergraduates 2,977 full-time, 3,398 part-time. Students come from 26 states and territories, 34 other countries, 1% are from out of state, 20% African American, 1% Asian American or Pacific Islander, 9% Hispanic American, 0.5% Native American, 2% international, 6% transferred in, 7% live on campus. *Retention:* 54% of 2008 full-time freshmen returned.

Freshmen *Admission:* 1,416 enrolled.

Faculty *Total:* 281, 49% full-time, 8% with terminal degrees. *Student/faculty ratio:* 22:1.

Majors Accounting technology and bookkeeping; aerospace, aeronautical and astronautical engineering; agriculture; architecture; art; autobody/collision and repair technology; automobile/automotive mechanics technology; biological and physical sciences; business administration and management; business/commerce; chemical engineering; chemistry; child-care and support services management; child-care provision; civil engineering; clinical/medical laboratory technology; commercial and advertising art; commercial photography; computer and information sciences; computer installation and repair technology; computer programming; computer systems networking and telecommunications; corrections; court reporting; criminal justice/law enforcement administration; dance; diesel mechanics technology; drafting and design technology; dramatic/theater arts; electrical, electronic and communications engineering technology; elementary education; emergency medical technology (EMT paramedic); English; executive assistant/executive secretary; fashion merchandising; forestry; general studies; geology/earth science; health teacher education; heating, air conditioning, ventilation and refrigeration maintenance technology; journalism; legal assistant/paralegal; management information systems; mathematics; mechanical engineering; medical radiologic technology; metallurgical technology; multi/interdisciplinary studies related; music; nursing (registered nurse training); occupational safety and health technology; occupational therapist assistant; operations management; petroleum engineering; physical education teaching and coaching; physical therapist assistant; physical therapy; physics; pre-dentistry studies; pre-law studies; premedical studies; pre-pharmacy studies; pre-veterinary studies; psychology; radiologic technology/science; religious studies; social sciences; speech and rhetoric; surgical technology; trade and industrial teacher education; web/multimedia management and webmaster; welding technology.

Academics *Calendar:* semesters. *Degree:* certificates and associate. *Special study options:* academic remediation for entering students, adult/continuing education programs, advanced placement credit, cooperative education, distance learning, English as a second language, internships, part-time degree program, services for LD students, student-designed majors, summer session for credit.

Library Randolph C. Watson Library plus 1 other with 65,000 titles, 6,679 serial subscriptions, 13,351 audiovisual materials, an OPAC, a Web page.

Student Life *Housing Options:* coed, men-only, women-only. Campus housing is university owned. *Activities and Organizations:* drama/theater group, student-run newspaper, choral group, marching band. *Campus security:* 24-hour emergency response devices and patrols. *Student services:* personal/psychological counseling.

Athletics Member NJCAA. *Intercollegiate sports:* basketball M(s)/W(s), cheerleading M(s)/W(s), football M(s). *Intramural sports:* basketball M/W, football M/W, racquetball M/W, tennis M/W, volleyball M/W.

Costs (2010–11) *Tuition:* area resident $552 full-time, $23 per semester hour part-time; state resident $1776 full-time, $74 per semester hour part-time; nonresident $2640 full-time, $110 per semester hour part-time. *Required fees:* $528 full-time, $22 per semester hour part-time. *Room and board:* $3980. *Payment plan:* installment. *Waivers:* senior citizens and employees or children of employees.

Financial Aid Of all full-time matriculated undergraduates who enrolled in 2008, 80 Federal Work-Study jobs (averaging $2500). *Financial aid deadline:* 6/1.

Applying *Options:* electronic application, early admission. *Required:* high school transcript. *Required for some:* interview. *Application deadlines:* rolling (freshmen), rolling (out-of-state freshmen), rolling (transfers).

Freshman Application Contact Ms. Jeanna Centers, Admissions Specialist, Kilgore College, 1100 Broadway, Kilgore, TX 75662. *Phone:* 903-983-8202. *Fax:* 903-983-8607. *E-mail:* register@kilgore.cc.tx.us.

LAMAR INSTITUTE OF TECHNOLOGY

Beaumont, Texas **www.lit.edu/**

Freshman Application Contact Admissions Office, Lamar Institute of Technology, 855 East Lavaca, Beaumont, TX 77705. *Phone:* 409-880-8354. *Toll-free phone:* 800-950-6989.

LAMAR STATE COLLEGE–ORANGE

Orange, Texas **www.lsco.edu/**

Freshman Application Contact Kerry Olson, Director of Admissions and Financial Aid, Lamar State College–Orange, 410 Front Street, Orange, TX 77632. *Phone:* 409-882-3362. *Fax:* 409-882-3374.

LAMAR STATE COLLEGE–PORT ARTHUR

Port Arthur, Texas **www.lamarpa.edu/**

Freshman Application Contact Ms. Connie Nicholas, Registrar, Lamar State College–Port Arthur, PO Box 310, Port Arthur, TX 77641-0310. *Phone:* 409-984-6165. *Toll-free phone:* 800-477-5872. *Fax:* 409-984-6025. *E-mail:* connie.nicholas@lamarpa.edu.

LAREDO COMMUNITY COLLEGE

Laredo, Texas **www.laredo.edu/**

Freshman Application Contact Ms. Josie Soliz, Admissions Records Supervisor, Laredo Community College, West End Washington Street, Laredo, TX 78040-4395. *Phone:* 956-721-5177. *Fax:* 956-721-5493.

Lee College

Baytown, Texas www.lee.edu/

Director of Admissions Ms. Becki Griffith, Registrar, Lee College, PO Box 818, Baytown, TX 77522-0818. *Phone:* 281-425-6399. *Toll-free phone:* 800-621-8724. *E-mail:* bgriffit@lee.edu.

Lonestar College–Cy-Fair

Cypress, Texas www.lonestar.edu/cyfair

- **State and locally supported** 2-year, founded 2002, part of Lone Star College System
- **Suburban** campus with easy access to Houston
- **Coed,** 15,175 undergraduate students, 28% full-time, 58% women, 42% men

Undergraduates 4,208 full-time, 10,967 part-time. Students come from 69 other countries, 1% are from out of state, 11% African American, 10% Asian American or Pacific Islander, 30% Hispanic American, 0.4% Native American, 1% international.

Freshmen *Admission:* 5,038 applied, 5,038 admitted, 5,038 enrolled.

Faculty *Total:* 1,793, 35% full-time, 13% with terminal degrees.

Majors Accounting; agricultural business and management; anthropology; architecture; art; biology/biological sciences; business administration and management; chemistry; communication/speech communication and rhetoric; computer and information sciences; computer science; criminal justice/law enforcement administration; dance; design and visual communications; diagnostic medical sonography and ultrasound technology; dramatic/theater arts; economics; education; electrical, electronic and communications engineering technology; emergency medical technology (EMT paramedic); engineering; English; finance; fire science; food science; foreign languages and literatures; geography; geology/earth science; health information/medical records technology; history; humanities; industrial technology; information technology; interdisciplinary studies; kinesiology and exercise science; language interpretation and translation; logistics and materials management; management science; marketing/marketing management; mathematics; medical radiologic technology; metallurgical technology; music; nursing (registered nurse training); office occupations and clerical services; philosophy; physics; political science and government; psychology; radiation protection/health physics technology; religious studies; social sciences; sociology; speech and rhetoric; welding technology.

Academics *Calendar:* semesters. *Degree:* certificates, diplomas, and associate. *Special study options:* academic remediation for entering students, accelerated degree program, adult/continuing education programs, advanced placement credit, cooperative education, distance learning, double majors, English as a second language, honors programs, independent study, internships, part-time degree program, services for LD students, study abroad, summer session for credit.

Library an OPAC, a Web page.

Student Life *Housing:* college housing not available. *Activities and Organizations:* drama/theater group, choral group. *Campus security:* 24-hour emergency response devices and patrols, late-night transport/escort service. *Student services:* personal/psychological counseling.

Costs (2009–10) *Tuition:* area resident $912 full-time, $38 per credit hour part-time; state resident $2592 full-time, $108 per credit hour part-time; nonresident $2952 full-time, $123 per credit hour part-time. Full-time tuition and fees vary according to course load. Part-time tuition and fees vary according to course load. *Required fees:* $288 full-time, $11 per credit hour part-time, $12 per term part-time. *Payment plan:* installment.

Applying *Options:* electronic application, early admission.

Freshman Application Contact Admissions Office, Lonestar College–Cy-Fair, 9191 Barker Cypress Road, Cypress, TX 77433-1383. *Phone:* 281-290-3200. *E-mail:* cfc.info@lonestar.edu.

Lonestar College–Kingwood

Kingwood, Texas www.lonestar.edu/kingwood/

- **State and locally supported** 2-year, founded 1984, part of Lone Star College System
- **Suburban** 264-acre campus with easy access to Houston
- **Coed,** 9,293 undergraduate students, 25% full-time, 64% women, 36% men

Undergraduates 2,364 full-time, 6,929 part-time. Students come from 39 other countries, 1% are from out of state, 12% African American, 4% Asian American or Pacific Islander, 19% Hispanic American, 0.5% Native American, 0.8% international.

Freshmen *Admission:* 2,759 applied, 2,759 admitted, 2,759 enrolled.

Faculty *Total:* 1,254, 40% full-time, 8% with terminal degrees.

Majors Accounting; administrative assistant and secretarial science; architecture; art; astronomy; biology/biological sciences; business administration and management; chemistry; computer and information sciences; computer engineering technology; computer graphics; computer science; computer typography and composition equipment operation; cosmetology; criminal justice/law enforcement administration; dental hygiene; design and visual communications; dramatic/theater arts; economics; education; engineering; English; facilities planning and management; finance; foreign languages and literatures; geography; geology/earth science; health information/medical records technology; history; humanities; information science/studies; interdisciplinary studies; interior design; kinesiology and exercise science; marketing/marketing management; mathematics; music; nursing (licensed practical/vocational nurse training); occupational therapy; philosophy; physics; political science and government; psychology; respiratory care therapy; social sciences; sociology; speech and rhetoric; visual and performing arts.

Academics *Calendar:* semesters. *Degree:* certificates and associate. *Special study options:* academic remediation for entering students, accelerated degree program, adult/continuing education programs, advanced placement credit, cooperative education, distance learning, double majors, English as a second language, honors programs, independent study, internships, part-time degree program, services for LD students, study abroad, summer session for credit.

Library Lone Star College-Kingwood Library with an OPAC, a Web page.

Student Life *Housing:* college housing not available. *Activities and Organizations:* drama/theater group, student-run television station, choral group. *Campus security:* 24-hour emergency response devices and patrols, late-night transport/escort service. *Student services:* personal/psychological counseling.

Athletics *Intramural sports:* baseball M.

Costs (2009–10) *One-time required fee:* $24. *Tuition:* area resident $1200 full-time; state resident $2880 full-time; nonresident $3240 full-time. Full-time tuition and fees vary according to program. Part-time tuition and fees vary according to program. *Required fees:* $528 full-time. *Payment plan:* installment.

Financial Aid Of all full-time matriculated undergraduates who enrolled in 2009, 28 Federal Work-Study jobs, 6 state and other part-time jobs. *Financial aid deadline:* 4/1.

Applying *Options:* electronic application, early admission. *Application deadlines:* rolling (freshmen), rolling (transfers).

Freshman Application Contact Admissions Office, Lonestar College–Kingwood, 20000 Kingwood Drive, Kingwood, TX 77339. *Phone:* 281-312-1525. *Fax:* 281-312-1477. *E-mail:* kingwoodadvising@lonestar.edu.

Lonestar College–Montgomery

Conroe, Texas www.lonestar.edu/montgomery/

- **State and locally supported** 2-year, founded 1995, part of Lone Star College System
- **Suburban** campus with easy access to Houston
- **Coed,** 10,962 undergraduate students, 28% full-time, 60% women, 40% men

Undergraduates 3,113 full-time, 7,849 part-time. Students come from 55 other countries, 2% are from out of state, 7% African American, 4% Asian American or Pacific Islander, 18% Hispanic American, 0.6% Native American, 0.8% international.

Freshmen *Admission:* 3,627 applied, 3,627 admitted, 3,627 enrolled.

Faculty *Total:* 1,322, 40% full-time, 12% with terminal degrees.

Majors Accounting and business/management; administrative assistant and secretarial science; animation, interactive technology, video graphics and special effects; anthropology; architecture; art; astronomy; audiovisual communications technologies related; automobile/automotive mechanics technology; biology/biological sciences; biology/biotechnology laboratory technician; business administration and management; CAD/CADD drafting/design technology; chemistry; computer and information systems security; computer programming; computer software technology; computer systems networking and telecommunications; criminal justice/law enforcement administration; design and visual communications; drafting/design engineering technologies related; dramatic/theater arts; economics; education; emergency medical technology (EMT paramedic); engineering; English; finance; fire science; foreign languages and literatures; geology/earth science; health information/medical records technology; heating, air conditioning, ventilation and refrigeration maintenance technology; history; humanities; human services; information technology; interdisciplinary studies; kinesiology and exercise science; land use planning and management; marketing/marketing management; mathematics; medical radiologic technology; music; nursing (registered nurse training); philosophy; physical therapist assistant;

physics; political science and government; psychology; radiation protection/health physics technology; religious studies; robotics technology; social work; sociology; speech and rhetoric; system, networking, and LAN/WAN management; web/multimedia management and webmaster; web page, digital/multimedia and information resources design; welding technology.

Academics *Calendar:* semesters. *Degree:* certificates and associate. *Special study options:* academic remediation for entering students, adult/continuing education programs, advanced placement credit, cooperative education, distance learning, double majors, English as a second language, honors programs, independent study, internships, part-time degree program, services for LD students, study abroad, summer session for credit.

Library Library/Learning Resources Center with an OPAC, a Web page.

Student Life *Housing:* college housing not available. *Activities and Organizations:* drama/theater group, student-run newspaper, choral group, Campus Crusade for Christ, Criminal Justice Club, Phi Theta Kappa, Latino-American Student Association, African-American Cultural Awareness. *Campus security:* 24-hour emergency response devices and patrols, late-night transport/escort service. *Student services:* personal/psychological counseling.

Costs (2009–10) *Tuition:* area resident $912 full-time, $38 per credit hour part-time; state resident $2592 full-time, $108 per credit hour part-time; nonresident $2952 full-time, $123 per credit hour part-time. Full-time tuition and fees vary according to course load. Part-time tuition and fees vary according to course load. *Required fees:* $288 full-time, $11 per credit hour part-time, $12 per term part-time. *Payment plan:* installment. *Waivers:* employees or children of employees.

Financial Aid Of all full-time matriculated undergraduates who enrolled in 2008, 25 Federal Work-Study jobs (averaging $2500). 4 state and other part-time jobs.

Applying *Options:* electronic application, early admission. *Application deadlines:* rolling (freshmen), rolling (transfers).

Freshman Application Contact Lonestar College–Montgomery, 3200 College Park Drive, Conroe, TX 77384. *Phone:* 936-273-7236.

LONESTAR COLLEGE–NORTH HARRIS

Houston, Texas **www.lonestar.edu/northharris/**

- **State and locally supported** 2-year, founded 1972, part of Lone Star College System
- **Suburban** campus with easy access to Houston
- **Coed,** 13,549 undergraduate students, 20% full-time, 61% women, 39% men

Undergraduates 2,714 full-time, 10,835 part-time. Students come from 50 other countries, 1% are from out of state, 24% African American, 7% Asian American or Pacific Islander, 34% Hispanic American, 0.3% Native American, 2% international.

Freshmen *Admission:* 4,193 applied, 4,193 admitted, 4,193 enrolled.

Faculty *Total:* 1,609, 46% full-time, 9% with terminal degrees.

Majors Accounting; administrative assistant and secretarial science; animation, interactive technology, video graphics and special effects; anthropology; architecture; art; automobile/automotive mechanics technology; aviation/airway management; biology/biological sciences; business administration and management; CAD/CADD drafting/design technology; chemistry; computer and information sciences; computer science; cosmetology; criminal justice/law enforcement administration; dance; design and visual communications; drafting and design technology; dramatic/theater arts; economics; education; electrical, electronic and communications engineering technology; emergency medical technology (EMT paramedic); engineering; English; finance; foreign languages and literatures; geography; geology/earth science; health information/medical records technology; heating, air conditioning, ventilation and refrigeration maintenance technology; history; hospitality administration; human services; information science/studies; interdisciplinary studies; journalism; kinesiology and exercise science; language interpretation and translation; legal administrative assistant/secretary; legal studies; liberal arts and sciences/liberal studies; management information systems; marketing/marketing management; mathematics; music; nursing (registered nurse training); pharmacy technician; philosophy; photography; physical education teaching and coaching; physics; political science and government; pre-engineering; psychology; religious studies; respiratory care therapy; sociology; speech and rhetoric; welding technology.

Academics *Calendar:* semesters. *Degree:* certificates and associate. *Special study options:* academic remediation for entering students, adult/continuing education programs, advanced placement credit, cooperative education, distance learning, double majors, English as a second language, honors programs, independent study, internships, part-time degree program, services for LD students, study abroad, summer session for credit.

Library an OPAC, a Web page.

Student Life *Activities and Organizations:* drama/theater group, student-run newspaper, choral group, Student Government Association, Phi Theta Kappa, Ambassadors, honors student organizations, Soccer Club. *Campus security:* 24-hour emergency response devices and patrols, late-night transport/escort service. *Student services:* personal/psychological counseling, women's center.

Athletics *Intramural sports:* badminton M/W, baseball M/W, basketball M/W, bowling M/W, football M/W, golf M/W, gymnastics M/W, racquetball M/W, soccer M/W, softball M/W, table tennis M/W, tennis M/W, track and field M/W, volleyball M/W, weight lifting M/W.

Costs (2009–10) *Tuition:* area resident $912 full-time, $38 per credit hour part-time; state resident $2592 full-time, $108 per credit hour part-time; nonresident $2952 full-time, $123 per credit hour part-time. Full-time tuition and fees vary according to course load. Part-time tuition and fees vary according to course load. *Required fees:* $11 per credit hour part-time, $12 per term part-time. *Payment plan:* installment. *Waivers:* employees or children of employees.

Applying *Options:* electronic application, early admission. *Application deadlines:* rolling (freshmen), rolling (transfers).

Freshman Application Contact Admissions Office, Lonestar College–North Harris, 2700 W.W. Thorne Drive, Houston, TX 77073. *Phone:* 281-618-5410. *E-mail:* nhcounselor@lonestar.edu.

LONESTAR COLLEGE–TOMBALL

Tomball, Texas **www.lonestar.edu/tomball/**

- **State and locally supported** 2-year, founded 1988, part of Lone Star College System
- **Suburban** campus with easy access to Houston
- **Coed,** 9,865 undergraduate students, 22% full-time, 59% women, 41% men

Undergraduates 2,137 full-time, 7,728 part-time. Students come from 44 other countries, 0.9% are from out of state, 10% African American, 8% Asian American or Pacific Islander, 20% Hispanic American, 0.5% Native American, 1% international.

Freshmen *Admission:* 3,098 applied, 3,098 admitted, 3,098 enrolled.

Faculty *Total:* 1,028, 46% full-time, 13% with terminal degrees.

Majors Accounting; administrative assistant and secretarial science; animation, interactive technology, video graphics and special effects; art; biology/biological sciences; chemistry; computer and information sciences; computer programming; computer science; criminal justice/law enforcement administration; dance; dramatic/theater arts; economics; education; engineering; English; finance; foreign languages and literatures; geography; geology/earth science; health information/medical records technology; history; humanities; interdisciplinary studies; kinesiology and exercise science; marketing/marketing management; mathematics; music; occupational therapy; pharmacy technician; philosophy; physics; political science and government; religious studies; sociology; speech and rhetoric; system, networking, and LAN/WAN management; veterinary/animal health technology.

Academics *Calendar:* semesters. *Degree:* certificates and associate. *Special study options:* academic remediation for entering students, adult/continuing education programs, advanced placement credit, cooperative education, distance learning, double majors, English as a second language, honors programs, independent study, internships, part-time degree program, services for LD students, study abroad, summer session for credit.

Library an OPAC, a Web page.

Student Life *Housing:* college housing not available. *Activities and Organizations:* drama/theater group, student-run newspaper, choral group, Phi Theta Kappa, Occupational Therapy OTA, Veterinary Technicians Student Organization, STARS, Student Nurses Association. *Campus security:* 24-hour emergency response devices and patrols, late-night transport/escort service, trained security personnel during open hours. *Student services:* personal/psychological counseling.

Costs (2009–10) *Tuition:* area resident $912 full-time, $38 per credit hour part-time; state resident $2592 full-time, $108 per credit hour part-time; nonresident $2952 full-time, $123 per credit hour part-time. Full-time tuition and fees vary according to class time and program. Part-time tuition and fees vary according to class time and program. *Required fees:* $288 full-time, $11 per credit hour part-time, $12 per term part-time. *Payment plans:* tuition prepayment, installment. *Waivers:* employees or children of employees.

Financial Aid Of all full-time matriculated undergraduates who enrolled in 2008, 34 Federal Work-Study jobs (averaging $3000).

Applying *Options:* electronic application, early admission. *Application deadlines:* rolling (freshmen), rolling (transfers).

Freshman Application Contact Admissions Office, Lonestar College–Tomball, 30555 Tomball Parkway, Tomball, TX 77375-4036. *Phone:* 281-351-3310. *E-mail:* tcinfo@lonestar.edu.

Lon Morris College

Jacksonville, Texas www.lonmorris.edu/

- **Independent United Methodist** 2-year, founded 1854
- **Small-town** 76-acre campus
- **Endowment** $20.1 million
- **Coed,** 815 undergraduate students, 92% full-time, 27% women, 73% men

Undergraduates 747 full-time, 68 part-time. Students come from 15 states and territories, 4% are from out of state, 43% African American, 0.4% Asian American or Pacific Islander, 12% Hispanic American, 0.6% Native American, 4% international, 2% transferred in, 76% live on campus. *Retention:* 53% of 2008 full-time freshmen returned.

Freshmen *Admission:* 613 enrolled. *Average high school GPA:* 3.2.

Faculty *Total:* 72, 58% full-time, 19% with terminal degrees. *Student/faculty ratio:* 15:1.

Majors Accounting; applied art; art; art history, criticism and conservation; art teacher education; biblical studies; biology/biological sciences; botany/plant biology; business administration and management; chemistry; computer science; dance; divinity/ministry; dramatic/theater arts; drawing; education; elementary education; English; fine/studio arts; history; humanities; liberal arts and sciences/liberal studies; mass communication/media; mathematics; modern languages; music; philosophy; physical education teaching and coaching; physics; piano and organ; political science and government; pre-engineering; psychology; religious education; religious studies; social sciences; sociology; Spanish; speech and rhetoric; theology; voice and opera.

Academics *Calendar:* semesters. *Degree:* associate. *Special study options:* academic remediation for entering students, advanced placement credit, distance learning, English as a second language, independent study, part-time degree program, services for LD students, study abroad, summer session for credit.

Library Henderson Library with 26,000 titles, 265 serial subscriptions, an OPAC, a Web page.

Student Life *Housing:* on-campus residence required through sophomore year. *Options:* men-only, women-only. Campus housing is university owned and leased by the school. *Activities and Organizations:* drama/theater group, choral group. *Campus security:* 24-hour emergency response devices and patrols, late-night transport/escort service, controlled dormitory access. *Student services:* personal/psychological counseling.

Athletics Member NJCAA. *Intercollegiate sports:* baseball M(s), basketball M(s)/W(s), cheerleading M(s)/W(s), cross-country running M(s)/W(s), football M(s), golf M(s)/W(s), soccer M(s)/W(s), softball W(s). *Intramural sports:* basketball M/W, cross-country running M/W, football M/W, softball W, tennis M/W, volleyball M, weight lifting M/W.

Standardized Tests *Recommended:* SAT (for admission), ACT (for admission), SAT or ACT (for admission).

Financial Aid Of all full-time matriculated undergraduates who enrolled in 2008, 63 Federal Work-Study jobs (averaging $1300). 9 state and other part-time jobs (averaging $2500).

Applying *Options:* electronic application, deferred entrance. *Application fee:* $35. *Required:* essay or personal statement, high school transcript. *Application deadlines:* rolling (freshmen), rolling (transfers).

Freshman Application Contact Mr. Rafael Gonzalez, Director of Enrollment Management, Lon Morris College, 800 College Avenue, Jacksonville, TX 75766. *Phone:* 903-589-4059. *Toll-free phone:* 800-259-5753.

McLennan Community College

Waco, Texas www.mclennan.edu/

Freshman Application Contact Dr. Vivian G. Jefferson, Director, Admissions and Recruitment, McLennan Community College, 1400 College Drive, Waco, TX 76708-1499. *Phone:* 254-299-8689. *Fax:* 254-299-8694. *E-mail:* vjefferson@mclennan.edu.

Mountain View College

Dallas, Texas www.mvc.dcccd.edu/

Freshman Application Contact Ms. Glenda Hall, Associate Dean of Student Support Services, Mountain View College, 4849 West Illinois Avenue, Dallas, TX 75211-6599. *Phone:* 214-860-8666. *Fax:* 214-860-8570. *E-mail:* ghall@dcccd.edu.

Navarro College

Corsicana, Texas www.navarrocollege.edu/

Freshman Application Contact David Edwards, Registrar, Navarro College, 3200 West 7th Avenue, Corsicana, TX 75110-4899. *Phone:* 903-875-7348. *Toll-free phone:* 800-NAVARRO (in-state); 800-628-2776 (out-of-state). *Fax:* 903-875-7353. *E-mail:* david.edwards@navarrocollege.edu.

North Central Texas College

Gainesville, Texas www.nctc.edu/

- **State and locally supported** 2-year, founded 1924
- **Suburban** 132-acre campus with easy access to Dallas-Fort Worth
- **Endowment** $4.3 million
- **Coed,** 9,156 undergraduate students

Undergraduates Students come from 14 states and territories, 21 other countries, 5% are from out of state, 8% African American, 2% Asian American or Pacific Islander, 13% Hispanic American, 0.8% Native American, 0.9% international, 1% live on campus. *Retention:* 68% of 2008 full-time freshmen returned.

Freshmen *Admission:* 1,964 applied, 1,964 admitted.

Faculty *Total:* 395, 31% full-time, 10% with terminal degrees. *Student/faculty ratio:* 25:1.

Majors Administrative assistant and secretarial science; agricultural mechanization; animal/livestock husbandry and production; automobile/automotive mechanics technology; biological and physical sciences; business administration and management; business and personal/financial services marketing; computer and information sciences and support services related; computer engineering technology; computer graphics; computer/information technology services administration related; computer programming; computer programming related; computer programming (specific applications); computer programming (vendor/product certification); computer science; criminal justice/law enforcement administration; criminal justice/police science; data processing and data processing technology; drafting and design technology; electrical, electronic and communications engineering technology; emergency medical technology (EMT paramedic); engineering technology; equestrian studies; farm and ranch management; health information/medical records administration; industrial mechanics and maintenance technology; information science/studies; legal administrative assistant/secretary; legal assistant/paralegal; liberal arts and sciences/liberal studies; machine shop technology; machine tool technology; merchandising; nursing (registered nurse training); occupational therapy; pre-engineering; real estate; retailing; sales, distribution and marketing; welding technology; word processing.

Academics *Calendar:* semesters. *Degree:* certificates, diplomas, and associate. *Special study options:* academic remediation for entering students, adult/continuing education programs, advanced placement credit, cooperative education, distance learning, internships, part-time degree program, services for LD students, summer session for credit. *ROTC:* Army (c).

Library North Central Texas College Library plus 1 other with 44,861 titles, 273 serial subscriptions, an OPAC.

Student Life *Housing Options:* coed. *Activities and Organizations:* drama/theater group, choral group, Student Nursing Association, Residence Hall Association, Cosmetology Student Association, Student Government Association - Gainesville, Gainesville Program Council. *Campus security:* late-night transport/escort service, controlled dormitory access, cameras added to campus. *Student services:* personal/psychological counseling.

Athletics Member NJCAA. *Intercollegiate sports:* baseball M(s), equestrian sports M(s)/W(s), tennis W(s), volleyball W(s). *Intramural sports:* archery M/W, basketball M/W, bowling M/W, field hockey M/W, football M/W, golf M/W, soccer M/W, softball M/W, swimming and diving M/W, table tennis M/W, tennis M/W, ultimate Frisbee M/W, volleyball M/W.

Costs (2010–11) *Tuition:* $36 per credit hour part-time; state resident $70 per credit hour part-time; nonresident $116 per credit hour part-time. *Required fees:* $10 per credit hour part-time. *Room and board:* Room and board charges vary according to housing facility. *Payment plans:* installment, deferred payment. *Waivers:* employees or children of employees.

Financial Aid Of all full-time matriculated undergraduates who enrolled in 2008, 108 Federal Work-Study jobs (averaging $1253). 29 state and other part-time jobs (averaging $392).

Applying *Options:* electronic application, early admission. *Required:* high school transcript. *Application deadlines:* rolling (freshmen), rolling (out-of-state freshmen), rolling (transfers).

Freshman Application Contact Melinda Carroll, Director of Admissions/Registrar, North Central Texas College, 1525 West California Street, Gainesville, TX 76240-4699. *Phone:* 940-668-7731. *Fax:* 940-668-7075. *E-mail:* mcarroll@nctc.edu.

Northeast Texas Community College

Mount Pleasant, Texas **www.ntcc.edu/**

- **State and locally supported** 2-year, founded 1985
- **Rural** 175-acre campus
- **Coed**

Academics *Calendar:* semesters. *Degree:* certificates and associate. *Special study options:* academic remediation for entering students, adult/continuing education programs, advanced placement credit, cooperative education, distance learning, English as a second language, independent study, part-time degree program, services for LD students, summer session for credit.

Student Life *Campus security:* 24-hour patrols.

Athletics Member NJCAA.

Financial Aid Of all full-time matriculated undergraduates who enrolled in 2008, 91 Federal Work-Study jobs (averaging $1600). 10 state and other part-time jobs (averaging $1600).

Applying *Options:* early admission. *Required:* high school transcript.

Freshman Application Contact Ms. Sherry Keys, Director of Admissions, Northeast Texas Community College, PO Box 1307, 1735 Farm to Market Road, Mount Pleasant, TX 75456-1307. *Phone:* 903-572-1911 Ext. 263.

North Lake College

Irving, Texas **www.northlakecollege.edu/**

- **County-supported** 2-year, founded 1977, part of Dallas County Community College District System
- **Suburban** 250-acre campus with easy access to Dallas-Fort Worth
- **Coed,** 10,174 undergraduate students, 31% full-time, 54% women, 46% men

Undergraduates 3,171 full-time, 7,003 part-time. Students come from 18 states and territories, 23 other countries, 9% are from out of state, 16% African American, 11% Asian American or Pacific Islander, 23% Hispanic American, 0.5% Native American, 8% international, 8% transferred in. *Retention:* 55% of 2008 full-time freshmen returned.

Freshmen *Admission:* 977 enrolled.

Faculty *Total:* 504, 19% full-time, 9% with terminal degrees. *Student/faculty ratio:* 21:1.

Majors Accounting; administrative assistant and secretarial science; business administration and management; carpentry; communications technology; computer programming; construction engineering technology; data processing and data processing technology; electrical, electronic and communications engineering technology; heating, air conditioning, ventilation and refrigeration maintenance technology; information science/studies; kinesiology and exercise science; legal administrative assistant/secretary; liberal arts and sciences/liberal studies; real estate.

Academics *Calendar:* semesters. *Degree:* certificates and associate. *Special study options:* academic remediation for entering students, accelerated degree program, adult/continuing education programs, advanced placement credit, cooperative education, distance learning, double majors, English as a second language, external degree program, independent study, internships, off-campus study, part-time degree program, services for LD students, study abroad, summer session for credit.

Library North Lake College Library plus 3 others with 35,000 titles, 400 serial subscriptions, 1,200 audiovisual materials, an OPAC, a Web page.

Student Life *Activities and Organizations:* drama/theater group, student-run newspaper, choral group. *Campus security:* 24-hour emergency response devices, student patrols, late-night transport/escort service. *Student services:* health clinic, personal/psychological counseling.

Athletics Member NJCAA. *Intercollegiate sports:* baseball M, basketball M, cheerleading W, swimming and diving M/W, volleyball W.

Costs (2010–11) *Tuition:* $41 per credit hour part-time; state resident $76 per credit hour part-time; nonresident $121 per credit hour part-time. *Payment plan:* installment. *Waivers:* senior citizens and employees or children of employees.

Applying *Options:* electronic application, early admission. *Recommended:* high school transcript. *Application deadlines:* rolling (freshmen), rolling (transfers). *Notification:* continuous (freshmen), continuous (transfers).

Freshman Application Contact Admissions/Registration Office (A405), North Lake College, 5001 North MacArthur Boulevard, Irving, TX 75038-3899. *Phone:* 972-273-3183.

Northwest Vista College

San Antonio, Texas **www.accd.edu/nvc/**

Freshman Application Contact Dr. Elaine Lang, Interim Director of Enrollment Management, Northwest Vista College, 3535 North Ellison Drive, San Antonio, TX 78251. *Phone:* 210-348-2016. *E-mail:* elang@accd.edu.

Odessa College

Odessa, Texas **www.odessa.edu/**

- **State and locally supported** 2-year, founded 1946
- **Urban** 87-acre campus
- **Endowment** $813,199
- **Coed,** 5,132 undergraduate students, 29% full-time, 60% women, 40% men

Undergraduates 1,475 full-time, 3,657 part-time. Students come from 20 states and territories, 2% are from out of state, 5% African American, 0.8% Asian American or Pacific Islander, 52% Hispanic American, 0.7% Native American, 0.3% international, 4% live on campus. *Retention:* 44% of 2008 full-time freshmen returned.

Freshmen *Admission:* 344 applied, 344 admitted.

Faculty *Total:* 236, 50% full-time, 6% with terminal degrees. *Student/faculty ratio:* 19:1.

Majors Accounting; administrative assistant and secretarial science; agriculture; applied art; art; athletic training; automobile/automotive mechanics technology; biology/biological sciences; business administration and management; chemistry; child development; clinical/medical laboratory technology; computer and information sciences; computer science; computer systems networking and telecommunications; construction engineering technology; cosmetology; criminal justice/law enforcement administration; criminal justice/police science; culinary arts; data processing and data processing technology; drafting and design technology; education; electrical, electronic and communications engineering technology; emergency medical technology (EMT paramedic); English; fire science; geology/earth science; hazardous materials management and waste technology; heating, air conditioning, ventilation and refrigeration maintenance technology; history; human services; industrial radiologic technology; information science/studies; kindergarten/preschool education; legal administrative assistant/secretary; liberal arts and sciences/liberal studies; machine tool technology; mathematics; modern languages; music; nursing (registered nurse training); photography; physical education teaching and coaching; physical therapy; physics; political science and government; pre-engineering; psychology; social sciences; sociology; speech and rhetoric; substance abuse/addiction counseling; teacher assistant/aide; welding technology.

Academics *Calendar:* semesters. *Degree:* certificates and associate. *Special study options:* academic remediation for entering students, adult/continuing education programs, advanced placement credit, cooperative education, distance learning, independent study, internships, part-time degree program, services for LD students, summer session for credit.

Library Murry H. Fly Learning Resources Center with 123,000 titles, 350 serial subscriptions, 6,800 audiovisual materials, an OPAC, a Web page.

Student Life *Housing Options:* coed. Campus housing is provided by a third party. *Activities and Organizations:* choral group, Baptist Student Union, Student Government Association, Rodeo Club, Physical Therapy Assistant Club, American Chemical Society. *Campus security:* 24-hour emergency response devices and patrols, late-night transport/escort service, controlled dormitory access. *Student services:* personal/psychological counseling.

Athletics Member NJCAA. *Intercollegiate sports:* baseball M(s), basketball M(s)/W(s), cross-country running M(s)/W(s), golf M(s), softball W(s). *Intramural sports:* basketball M/W, bowling M/W, football M, racquetball M/W, softball M/W, table tennis M/W, volleyball M/W, weight lifting M/W.

Costs (2010–11) *Tuition:* area resident $1740 full-time, $141 per course part-time; state resident $2340 full-time, $201 per course part-time; nonresident $3240 full-time, $411 per course part-time. *Required fees:* $33 per course part-time.

Financial Aid Of all full-time matriculated undergraduates who enrolled in 2008, 59 Federal Work-Study jobs (averaging $1527). 8 state and other part-time jobs (averaging $1904).

Applying *Options:* electronic application, early admission, deferred entrance. *Application deadlines:* rolling (freshmen), rolling (transfers). *Notification:* continuous (freshmen), continuous (transfers).

Freshman Application Contact Ms. Tracy Hilliard, Associate Director Admissions, Odessa College, 201 West University Avenue, Odessa, TX 79764-7127. *Phone:* 432-335-6816. *Fax:* 432-335-6303. *E-mail:* thilliard@odessa.edu.

Palo Alto College

San Antonio, Texas www.alamo.edu/pac/

Freshman Application Contact Ms. Rachel Montejano, Director of Enrollment Management, Palo Alto College, 1400 West Villaret Boulevard, San Antonio, TX 78224. *Phone:* 210-921-5279. *Fax:* 210-921-5310. *E-mail:* pacar@accd.edu.

Panola College

Carthage, Texas www.panola.edu/

- **State and locally supported** 2-year, founded 1947
- **Small-town** 35-acre campus
- **Endowment** $1.8 million
- **Coed,** 2,124 undergraduate students, 45% full-time, 67% women, 33% men

Undergraduates 949 full-time, 1,175 part-time. Students come from 16 states and territories, 9 other countries, 8% are from out of state, 20% African American, 0.9% Asian American or Pacific Islander, 6% Hispanic American, 0.4% Native American, 0.9% international, 11% transferred in, 9% live on campus. *Retention:* 43% of 2008 full-time freshmen returned.

Freshmen *Admission:* 383 enrolled.

Faculty *Total:* 122, 53% full-time. *Student/faculty ratio:* 16:1.

Majors Business automation/technology/data entry; general studies; health information/medical records technology; industrial technology; information science/studies; multi/interdisciplinary studies related; nursing (registered nurse training); occupational therapist assistant.

Academics *Calendar:* semesters. *Degree:* certificates and associate. *Special study options:* academic remediation for entering students, advanced placement credit, cooperative education, distance learning, English as a second language, part-time degree program, services for LD students, summer session for credit.

Library M. P. Baker Library with 81,337 titles, 347 serial subscriptions, 300 audiovisual materials, an OPAC, a Web page.

Student Life *Housing Options:* coed. Campus housing is university owned. *Activities and Organizations:* drama/theater group, student-run newspaper, choral group, Student Government Organization, Student Occupational Therapy Asst. Club, Baptist Student Union, Texas Nursing Student Association, Phi Theta Kappa. *Campus security:* controlled dormitory access.

Athletics Member NCAA, NJCAA. All NCAA Division I. *Intercollegiate sports:* baseball M(s), basketball M(s)/W(s), volleyball W(s). *Intramural sports:* basketball M/W, football M/W, racquetball M/W, table tennis M/W, volleyball M/W, weight lifting M/W.

Costs (2009–10) *Tuition:* $56 per credit hour part-time; state resident $87 per credit hour part-time; nonresident $113 per credit hour part-time. *Room and board:* Room and board charges vary according to housing facility. *Payment plan:* deferred payment. *Waivers:* employees or children of employees.

Applying *Options:* electronic application, early admission. *Required for some:* high school transcript. *Recommended:* high school transcript. *Application deadlines:* rolling (freshmen), rolling (transfers). *Notification:* continuous (freshmen), continuous (transfers).

Freshman Application Contact Mr. Jeremy Dorman, Registrar/Director of Admissions, Panola College, 1109 West Panola Street, Carthage, TX 75633-2397. *Phone:* 903-693-2009. *Fax:* 903-693-2031. *E-mail:* bsimpson@panola.edu.

Paris Junior College

Paris, Texas www.parisjc.edu/

- **State and locally supported** 2-year, founded 1924
- **Rural** 54-acre campus
- **Endowment** $9.5 million
- **Coed,** 5,580 undergraduate students, 47% full-time, 60% women, 40% men

Undergraduates 2,649 full-time, 2,931 part-time. Students come from 29 states and territories, 5 other countries, 3% are from out of state, 13% African American, 1% Asian American or Pacific Islander, 8% Hispanic American, 2% Native American, 50% transferred in, 4% live on campus. *Retention:* 53% of 2008 full-time freshmen returned.

Freshmen *Admission:* 1,373 applied, 1,373 admitted, 1,373 enrolled.

Faculty *Total:* 229, 43% full-time, 10% with terminal degrees. *Student/faculty ratio:* 25:1.

Majors Agricultural mechanization; art; biological and physical sciences; business administration and management; business teacher education; computer engineering technology; computer typography and composition equipment operation; cosmetology; drafting and design technology; education; electrical, electronic and communications engineering technology; elementary education; emergency medical technology (EMT paramedic); engineering; heating, air conditioning, ventilation and refrigeration maintenance technology; information science/studies; liberal arts and sciences/liberal studies; mathematics; medical insurance coding; metal and jewelry arts; nursing (registered nurse training); radiologic technology/science; surgical technology; welding technology.

Academics *Calendar:* semesters. *Degree:* certificates, diplomas, and associate. *Special study options:* academic remediation for entering students, adult/continuing education programs, advanced placement credit, cooperative education, distance learning, English as a second language, external degree program, part-time degree program, services for LD students, summer session for credit.

Library Mike Rheudasil Learning Center with 38,150 titles, 404 serial subscriptions, an OPAC.

Student Life *Housing Options:* men-only, women-only. Campus housing is university owned. *Activities and Organizations:* drama/theater group, student-run newspaper, choral group, Student Government Organization, Hispanic Club. *Campus security:* 24-hour emergency response devices and patrols, late-night transport/escort service. *Student services:* personal/psychological counseling.

Athletics Member NJCAA. *Intercollegiate sports:* baseball M(s), basketball M(s)/W(s), golf M(s), softball W(s), volleyball W(s). *Intramural sports:* badminton M/W, basketball M, football M, table tennis M/W, tennis M/W, volleyball M/W.

Costs (2010–11) *Tuition:* area resident $936 full-time, $39 per credit hour part-time; state resident $1680 full-time, $70 per credit hour part-time; nonresident $2664 full-time, $111 per credit hour part-time. Full-time tuition and fees vary according to course load. Part-time tuition and fees vary according to course load. *Required fees:* $228 full-time. *Room and board:* $3400. Room and board charges vary according to board plan. *Payment plan:* installment. *Waivers:* employees or children of employees.

Financial Aid Of all full-time matriculated undergraduates who enrolled in 2008, 60 Federal Work-Study jobs (averaging $3800).

Applying *Options:* electronic application, early admission. *Required:* high school transcript. *Application deadlines:* rolling (freshmen), rolling (transfers).

Freshman Application Contact Paris Junior College, 2400 Clarksville Street, Paris, TX 75460-6298. *Phone:* 903-782-0425. *Toll-free phone:* 800-232-5804.

Ranger College

Ranger, Texas www.ranger.cc.tx.us/

Freshman Application Contact Dr. Jim Davis, Dean of Students, Ranger College, 1100 College Circle, Ranger, TX 76470. *Phone:* 254-647-3234 Ext. 110.

Remington College–Dallas Campus

Garland, Texas www.remingtoncollege.edu/

Director of Admissions Ms. Shonda Wisenhunt, Remington College–Dallas Campus, 1800 Eastgate Drive, Garland, TX 75041-5513. *Phone:* 972-686-7878. *Fax:* 972-686-5116. *E-mail:* shonda.wisenhunt@remingtoncollege.edu.

Remington College–Fort Worth Campus

Fort Worth, Texas www.remingtoncollege.edu/

Director of Admissions Marcia Kline, Director of Recruitment, Remington College–Fort Worth Campus, 300 East Loop 820, Fort Worth, TX 76112. *Phone:* 817-451-0017. *Toll-free phone:* 800-336-6668. *Fax:* 817-496-1257. *E-mail:* marcia.kline@remingtoncollege.edu.

Remington College–Houston Campus

Houston, Texas www.remingtoncollege.edu/houston/

Director of Admissions Kevin Wilkinson, Director of Recruitment, Remington College–Houston Campus, 3110 Hayes Road, Suite 380, Houston, TX 77082. *Phone:* 281-899-1240. *Fax:* 281-597-8466. *E-mail:* kevin.wilkinson@remingtoncollege.edu.

Remington College–Houston Southeast

Webster, Texas www.remingtoncollege.edu/houstonsoutheast/

Director of Admissions Lori Minor, Director of Recruitment, Remington College–Houston Southeast, 20985 Interstate 45 South, Webster, TX 77598. *Phone:* 281-554-1700. *Fax:* 281-554-1765. *E-mail:* lori.minor@remingtoncollege.edu.

Remington College–North Houston Campus

Houston, Texas **www.remingtoncollege.edu/**

Director of Admissions Edmund Flores, Director of Recruitment, Remington College–North Houston Campus, 11310 Greens Crossing Boulevard, Suite 300, Houston, TX 77067. *Phone:* 281-885-4450. *Fax:* 281-875-9964. *E-mail:* edmund.flores@remingtoncollege.edu.

Richland College

Dallas, Texas **www.rlc.dcccd.edu/**

Freshman Application Contact Ms. Carol McKinney, Department Assistant, Richland College, 12800 Abrams Road, Dallas, TX 75243-2199. *Phone:* 972-238-6100.

St. Philip's College

San Antonio, Texas **www.alamo.edu/spc/**

- **District-supported** 2-year, founded 1898, part of Alamo Community College District System
- **Urban** 68-acre campus
- **Coed,** 11,008 undergraduate students, 31% full-time, 56% women, 44% men

Undergraduates 3,465 full-time, 7,543 part-time. Students come from 45 states and territories, 11 other countries, 1% are from out of state, 17% African American, 2% Asian American or Pacific Islander, 50% Hispanic American, 0.4% Native American, 0.1% international, 9% transferred in.

Freshmen *Admission:* 1,650 enrolled.

Faculty *Total:* 533, 44% full-time, 8% with terminal degrees. *Student/faculty ratio:* 18:1.

Majors Accounting; administrative assistant and secretarial science; aircraft powerplant technology; airframe mechanics and aircraft maintenance technology; art; autobody/collision and repair technology; automobile/automotive mechanics technology; biology/biological sciences; biomedical technology; building/construction finishing, management, and inspection related; business administration and management; CAD/CADD drafting/design technology; chemistry; clinical/medical laboratory technology; computer and information systems security; computer systems networking and telecommunications; computer technology/computer systems technology; construction engineering technology; criminal justice/law enforcement administration; culinary arts; data entry/microcomputer applications; diesel mechanics technology; dramatic/theater arts; dramatic/theater arts and stagecraft related; early childhood education; e-commerce; economics; education; electrical/electronics equipment installation and repair; electromechanical technology; English; environmental science; geology/earth science; health information/medical records technology; heating, air conditioning, ventilation and refrigeration maintenance technology; history; hotel/motel administration; kinesiology and exercise science; legal administrative assistant/secretary; liberal arts and sciences/liberal studies; mathematics; medical administrative assistant and medical secretary; medical radiologic technology; music; occupational therapist assistant; philosophy; physical therapist assistant; political science and government; pre-dentistry studies; pre-engineering; pre-law studies; premedical studies; prenursing studies; pre-pharmacy studies; psychology; respiratory care therapy; restaurant/food services management; social work; sociology; Spanish; speech and rhetoric; system, networking, and LAN/WAN management; teacher assistant/aide; welding technology.

Academics *Calendar:* semesters. *Degree:* certificates, diplomas, and associate. *Special study options:* academic remediation for entering students, adult/continuing education programs, advanced placement credit, cooperative education, distance learning, double majors, English as a second language, honors programs, independent study, internships, off-campus study, part-time degree program, services for LD students, study abroad, summer session for credit. *ROTC:* Army (c).

Library Learning Resource Center plus 1 other with 125,966 titles, 393 serial subscriptions, 11,622 audiovisual materials, an OPAC, a Web page.

Student Life *Housing:* college housing not available. *Activities and Organizations:* drama/theater group, student-run newspaper, choral group, Allied Health clubs, African-American Men on the Move, Culinary Arts Club. *Campus security:* 24-hour emergency response devices and patrols, late-night transport/escort service. *Student services:* health clinic, women's center.

Athletics *Intramural sports:* basketball M/W, cheerleading M/W, table tennis M/W, volleyball M/W, weight lifting M/W.

Costs (2009–10) *Tuition:* area resident $1605 full-time, $54 per semester hour part-time; state resident $3105 full-time, $104 per semester hour part-time; nonresident $6090 full-time, $204 per semester hour part-time. *Required fees:* $284 full-time, $142 part-time. *Payment plan:* installment. *Waivers:* senior citizens and employees or children of employees.

Applying *Options:* electronic application, early admission. *Required:* high school transcript. *Application deadlines:* rolling (freshmen), rolling (transfers). *Notification:* continuous (freshmen), continuous (transfers).

Freshman Application Contact Ms. Penelope Velasco, Associate Director, Residency and Reports, St. Philip's College, 1801 Martin Luther King Drive, San Antonio, TX 78203-2098. *Phone:* 210-486-2283. *Fax:* 210-486-2103. *E-mail:* pvelasco@alamo.edu.

San Antonio College

San Antonio, Texas **www.accd.edu/**

Director of Admissions Mr. J. Martin Ortega, Director of Admissions and Records, San Antonio College, 1300 San Pedro Avenue, San Antonio, TX 78212-4299. *Phone:* 210-733-2582. *Toll-free phone:* 800-944-7575.

San Jacinto College District

Pasadena, Texas **www.sanjac.edu/**

- **State and locally supported** 2-year, founded 1961
- **Suburban** 445-acre campus with easy access to Houston
- **Endowment** $2.2 million
- **Coed,** 27,011 undergraduate students, 36% full-time, 56% women, 44% men

Undergraduates 9,689 full-time, 17,322 part-time. Students come from 40 states and territories, 92 other countries, 4% are from out of state, 11% African American, 6% Asian American or Pacific Islander, 38% Hispanic American, 0.5% Native American, 3% international, 47% transferred in.

Freshmen *Admission:* 5,227 applied, 5,227 admitted, 5,202 enrolled.

Faculty *Total:* 1,133, 40% full-time, 12% with terminal degrees. *Student/faculty ratio:* 24:1.

Majors Accounting; administrative assistant and secretarial science; aerospace, aeronautical and astronautical engineering; airline pilot and flight crew; art; autobody/collision and repair technology; automobile/automotive mechanics technology; automotive engineering technology; biblical studies; biology/biological sciences; biotechnology; business administration and management; business automation/technology/data entry; business/commerce; chemical technology; chemistry; child development; clinical laboratory science/medical technology; clinical/medical laboratory technology; commercial and advertising art; communication/speech communication and rhetoric; computer and information sciences; computer and information systems security; computer programming; computer science; construction engineering technology; cosmetology; criminal justice/police science; culinary arts; diesel mechanics technology; dietitian assistant; drafting and design technology; dramatic/theater arts; education (multiple levels); electrical and power transmission installation; electrical, electronic and communications engineering technology; elementary education; emergency medical technology (EMT paramedic); engineering; engineering mechanics; English; environmental engineering technology; fashion merchandising; film/cinema studies; fire protection and safety technology; fire protection related; fire science; food preparation; food service systems administration; foreign languages and literatures; general studies; geology/earth science; graphic and printing equipment operation/production; health and physical education; health information/medical records technology; heating, air conditioning, ventilation and refrigeration maintenance technology; history; hospitality and recreation marketing; institutional food workers; instrumentation technology; interior design; international business/trade/commerce; journalism; legal assistant/paralegal; management information systems; mathematics; medical administrative assistant and medical secretary; medical/clinical assistant; medical radiologic technology; multi/interdisciplinary studies related; music; nursing (licensed practical/

San Jacinto College District (continued)

vocational nurse training); nursing (registered nurse training); occupational safety and health technology; optometric technician; philosophy; physical sciences; physical therapist assistant; physics; psychology; public administration; radiologic technology/science; real estate; respiratory care therapy; social sciences; sociology; speech and rhetoric; surgical technology; survey technology; system, networking, and LAN/WAN management; welding technology.

Academics *Calendar:* semesters. *Degree:* certificates and associate. *Special study options:* academic remediation for entering students, accelerated degree program, adult/continuing education programs, advanced placement credit, cooperative education, distance learning, double majors, English as a second language, honors programs, part-time degree program, services for LD students, student-designed majors, study abroad, summer session for credit. *ROTC:* Army (c), Air Force (c).

Library Lee Davis Library (C), Edwin E. Lehr (N), and Parker Williams (S) with 280,000 titles, 27,745 serial subscriptions, 1,000 audiovisual materials, an OPAC, a Web page.

Student Life *Housing:* college housing not available. *Activities and Organizations:* drama/theater group, student-run newspaper, choral group, Phi Theta Kappa, Nurses Association, Student Government Association, ABG Radiography, Texas Student Education Association. *Campus security:* 24-hour emergency response devices and patrols, late-night transport/escort service.

Athletics Member NJCAA. *Intercollegiate sports:* baseball M, basketball M(s), cheerleading M(s), golf M, soccer M/W, softball W, tennis M/W, volleyball W(s). *Intramural sports:* basketball M/W, bowling M/W, football M/W, racquetball M/W, table tennis M/W, volleyball M/W, weight lifting M/W.

Costs (2010–11) *Tuition:* area resident $1376 full-time, $33 per credit hour part-time; state resident $2176 full-time, $58 per credit hour part-time; nonresident $3776 full-time, $108 per credit hour part-time. Full-time tuition and fees vary according to course load. Part-time tuition and fees vary according to course load. *Required fees:* $260 full-time, $130 per term part-time. *Payment plan:* installment. *Waivers:* senior citizens.

Applying *Options:* electronic application, early admission. *Required:* high school transcript. *Required for some:* interview.

Freshman Application Contact San Jacinto College District, 4624 Fairmont Parkway, Pasadena, TX 77504-3323. *Phone:* 281-998-6150.

SOUTH PLAINS COLLEGE

Levelland, Texas **www.southplainscollege.edu/**

- **State and locally supported** 2-year, founded 1958
- **Small-town** 177-acre campus
- **Endowment** $3.0 million
- **Coed,** 10,028 undergraduate students, 47% full-time, 54% women, 46% men

Undergraduates 4,704 full-time, 5,324 part-time. Students come from 21 states and territories, 8 other countries, 4% are from out of state, 5% African American, 1% Asian American or Pacific Islander, 31% Hispanic American, 0.6% Native American, 0.7% international, 9% transferred in, 10% live on campus. *Retention:* 45% of 2008 full-time freshmen returned.

Freshmen *Admission:* 3,189 applied, 3,189 admitted, 1,496 enrolled.

Faculty *Total:* 454, 60% full-time. *Student/faculty ratio:* 20:1.

Majors Accounting; administrative assistant and secretarial science; advertising; agricultural economics; agriculture; agronomy and crop science; art; audio engineering; automobile/automotive mechanics technology; biological and physical sciences; biology/biological sciences; business administration and management; carpentry; chemistry; child development; commercial and advertising art; computer engineering technology; computer programming; computer science; consumer merchandising/retailing management; cosmetology; criminal justice/law enforcement administration; criminal justice/police science; data processing and data processing technology; developmental and child psychology; dietetics; drafting and design technology; education; electrical, electronic and communications engineering technology; engineering; fashion merchandising; fire science; health/health-care administration; health information/medical records administration; heating, air conditioning, ventilation and refrigeration maintenance technology; industrial radiologic technology; journalism; legal administrative assistant/secretary; liberal arts and sciences/liberal studies; machine tool technology; marketing/marketing management; mass communication/media; medical administrative assistant and medical secretary; mental health/rehabilitation; music; nursing (licensed practical/vocational nurse training); nursing (registered nurse training); petroleum technology; physical education teaching and coaching; physical therapy; postal management; pre-engineering; real estate; respiratory care therapy; social work; special products marketing; surgical technology; telecommunications technology; welding technology.

Academics *Calendar:* semesters. *Degree:* certificates and associate. *Special study options:* academic remediation for entering students, accelerated degree program, adult/continuing education programs, advanced placement credit, distance learning, double majors, internships, off-campus study, part-time degree program, services for LD students, study abroad, summer session for credit. *ROTC:* Army (c), Air Force (c).

Library South Plains College Library plus 1 other with 70,000 titles, 310 serial subscriptions, an OPAC.

Student Life *Housing:* on-campus residence required through sophomore year. *Options:* men-only, women-only. Campus housing is university owned. Freshman applicants given priority for college housing. *Activities and Organizations:* drama/theater group, student-run newspaper, radio and television station, choral group, student government, Phi Beta Kappa, Bleacher Bums, Law Enforcement Association. *Campus security:* 24-hour emergency response devices and patrols, controlled dormitory access. *Student services:* health clinic.

Athletics Member NJCAA. *Intercollegiate sports:* basketball M(s)/W(s), cross-country running M(s)/W(s), equestrian sports M(s)/W(s), track and field M(s)/W(s). *Intramural sports:* basketball M/W, cross-country running M/W, football M/W, golf M/W, racquetball M/W, softball M/W, table tennis M/W, tennis M/W, volleyball M/W.

Standardized Tests *Recommended:* ACT (for admission), SAT Subject Tests (for admission).

Costs (2010–11) *Tuition:* area resident $1484 full-time, $26 per credit hour part-time; state resident $2012 full-time, $48 per credit hour part-time; nonresident $2396 full-time, $64 per credit hour part-time. Full-time tuition and fees vary according to class time, course load, location, and program. Part-time tuition and fees vary according to class time, course load, location, and program. *Required fees:* $1142 full-time, $580 per credit hour part-time, $69 per term part-time. *Room and board:* $3100. Room and board charges vary according to housing facility. *Payment plan:* installment. *Waivers:* senior citizens.

Financial Aid Of all full-time matriculated undergraduates who enrolled in 2008, 80 Federal Work-Study jobs (averaging $2000). 22 state and other part-time jobs (averaging $2000).

Applying *Options:* electronic application, early admission. *Required:* high school transcript. *Application deadlines:* rolling (freshmen), rolling (transfers).

Freshman Application Contact Mrs. Andrea Rangel, Dean of Admissions and Records, South Plains College, 1401 College Avenue, Levelland, TX 78336. *Phone:* 806-894-9611 Ext. 2370. *Fax:* 806-897-3167. *E-mail:* arangel@southplainscollege.edu.

SOUTH TEXAS COLLEGE

McAllen, Texas **www.southtexascollege.edu/**

Freshman Application Contact Mr. Matthew Hebbard, Director of Enrollment Services and Registrar, South Texas College, 3201 West Pecan, McAllen, TX 78501. *Phone:* 956-872-2147. *Toll-free phone:* 800-742-7822. *E-mail:* mshebbar@southtexascollege.edu.

SOUTHWEST INSTITUTE OF TECHNOLOGY

Austin, Texas **www.swse.net/**

Freshman Application Contact Director of Admissions, Southwest Institute of Technology, 5424 Highway 290 West, Suite 200, Austin, TX 78735-8800. *Phone:* 512-892-2640. *Fax:* 512-892-1045.

SOUTHWEST TEXAS JUNIOR COLLEGE

Uvalde, Texas **www.swtjc.net/**

Director of Admissions Mr. Joe C. Barker, Dean of Admissions and Student Services, Southwest Texas Junior College, 2401 Garner Field Road, Uvalde, TX 78801. *Phone:* 830-278-4401 Ext. 7284.

TARRANT COUNTY COLLEGE DISTRICT

Fort Worth, Texas **www.tccd.edu/**

- **County-supported** 2-year, founded 1967
- **Urban** 667-acre campus
- **Endowment** $1.5 million
- **Coed,** 39,596 undergraduate students, 34% full-time, 59% women, 41% men

Undergraduates 13,623 full-time, 25,973 part-time. Students come from 37 states and territories.

Freshmen *Admission:* 9,119 enrolled.

Faculty *Total:* 1,756, 34% full-time. *Student/faculty ratio:* 23:1.

Majors Accounting; administrative assistant and secretarial science; architectural engineering technology; automobile/automotive mechanics technology; avionics maintenance technology; business administration and management; clinical laboratory science/medical technology; clinical/medical laboratory technology; computer programming; computer science; construction engineering technology; consumer merchandising/retailing management; criminal justice/law enforcement administration; dental hygiene; developmental and child psychology; dietetics; drafting and design technology; educational/instructional media design; electrical, electronic and communications engineering technology; electromechanical technology; emergency medical technology (EMT paramedic); fashion merchandising; fire science; food technology and processing; graphic and printing equipment operation/production; health information/medical records administration; heating, air conditioning, ventilation and refrigeration maintenance technology; horticultural science; industrial radiologic technology; legal assistant/paralegal; liberal arts and sciences/liberal studies; machine tool technology; marketing/marketing management; mechanical engineering/mechanical technology; mental health/rehabilitation; nursing (registered nurse training); physical therapy; postal management; quality control technology; respiratory care therapy; sign language interpretation and translation; surgical technology; welding technology.

Academics *Calendar:* semesters. *Degree:* certificates and associate. *Special study options:* academic remediation for entering students, adult/continuing education programs, advanced placement credit, distance learning, English as a second language, honors programs, part-time degree program, services for LD students, summer session for credit. *ROTC:* Army (c), Air Force (c).

Library 197,352 titles, 1,649 serial subscriptions, 18,833 audiovisual materials, an OPAC, a Web page.

Student Life *Housing:* college housing not available. *Activities and Organizations:* drama/theater group, student-run newspaper, choral group. *Campus security:* 24-hour emergency response devices and patrols. *Student services:* health clinic, personal/psychological counseling.

Athletics *Intramural sports:* football M, golf M, sailing M/W, table tennis M, tennis M/W, volleyball M/W.

Costs (2009–10) *Tuition:* area resident $1200 full-time, $50 per credit hour part-time; state resident $1752 full-time, $73 per credit hour part-time; nonresident $3960 full-time, $165 per credit hour part-time. *Payment plan:* installment.

Financial Aid Of all full-time matriculated undergraduates who enrolled in 2008, 372 Federal Work-Study jobs (averaging $1325). 39 state and other part-time jobs (averaging $927).

Applying *Options:* early admission. *Application deadlines:* rolling (freshmen), rolling (transfers).

Freshman Application Contact Dr. Billy Roessler, Director of Records and Reports, Tarrant County College District, 1500 Houston Street, Fort Worth, TX 76102-6599. *Phone:* 817-515-5026. *E-mail:* billy.roessler@tccd.edu.

TEMPLE COLLEGE

Temple, Texas **www.templejc.edu/**

- **District-supported** 2-year, founded 1926
- **Suburban** 106-acre campus with easy access to Austin
- **Endowment** $638,964
- **Coed,** 5,659 undergraduate students, 40% full-time, 66% women, 34% men

Undergraduates 2,250 full-time, 3,409 part-time. Students come from 30 states and territories, 9 other countries, 2% are from out of state, 19% African American, 2% Asian American or Pacific Islander, 19% Hispanic American, 1% Native American, 0.2% international, 7% transferred in.

Freshmen *Admission:* 782 applied, 782 admitted, 765 enrolled.

Faculty *Total:* 284, 44% full-time, 15% with terminal degrees. *Student/faculty ratio:* 19:1.

Majors Administrative assistant and secretarial science; art; biology/biotechnology laboratory technician; business administration and management; computer and information sciences; computer programming; computer science; criminal justice/law enforcement administration; criminal justice/police science; data processing and data processing technology; dental hygiene; diagnostic medical sonography and ultrasound technology; drafting and design technology; emergency medical technology (EMT paramedic); liberal arts and sciences/liberal studies; nursing (licensed practical/vocational nurse training); nursing (registered nurse training); respiratory care therapy; system, networking, and LAN/WAN management; web/multimedia management and webmaster.

Academics *Calendar:* semesters. *Degree:* certificates and associate. *Special study options:* academic remediation for entering students, adult/continuing education programs, advanced placement credit, cooperative education, distance learning, English as a second language, internships, off-campus study, part-time degree program, services for LD students, study abroad, summer session for credit.

Library Hubert Dawson Library with 58,907 titles, 271 serial subscriptions, 2,900 audiovisual materials, an OPAC, a Web page.

Student Life *Housing Options:* coed, disabled students. Campus housing is provided by a third party. *Activities and Organizations:* drama/theater group, choral group, Baptist Student Ministries, student government, Phi Theta Kappa, Delta Epsilon Chi, Nursing Student Organization. *Campus security:* 24-hour emergency response devices and patrols.

Athletics Member NJCAA. *Intercollegiate sports:* baseball M(s), basketball M(s)/W(s), softball W(s), tennis M(s)/W(s), volleyball W(s).

Standardized Tests *Required:* (for admission).

Costs (2009–10) *Tuition:* area resident $2250 full-time, $75 per semester hour part-time; state resident $3600 full-time, $120 per semester hour part-time; nonresident $5700 full-time, $310 per semester hour part-time. Allied health courses cost an additional $15 per semester hour. *Required fees:* $150 full-time, $24 per course part-time, $25 per term part-time. *Room and board:* $7309. *Payment plan:* installment. *Waivers:* senior citizens and employees or children of employees.

Applying *Options:* electronic application, early admission. *Required for some:* high school transcript. *Recommended:* high school transcript. *Application deadlines:* rolling (freshmen), rolling (transfers).

Freshman Application Contact Ms. Carey Rose, Director of Admissions and Records, Temple College, 2600 South First Street, Temple, TX 76504-7435. *Phone:* 254-298-8303. *Toll-free phone:* 800-460-4636. *E-mail:* carey.rose@templejc.edu.

TEXARKANA COLLEGE

Texarkana, Texas **www.texarkanacollege.edu/**

Freshman Application Contact Mr. Van Miller, Director of Admissions, Texarkana College, 2500 North Robison Road, Texarkana, TX 75599. *Phone:* 903-838-4541. *Fax:* 903-832-5030. *E-mail:* vmiller@texarkanacollege.edu.

TEXAS CULINARY ACADEMY

Austin, Texas **www.txca.com/**

Director of Admissions Paula Paulette, Vice President of Marketing and Admissions, Texas Culinary Academy, 11400 Burnet Road, Austin, TX 78758. *Phone:* 512-837-2665. *Toll-free phone:* 888-553-2433. *E-mail:* ppaulette@txca.com.

TEXAS SOUTHMOST COLLEGE

Brownsville, Texas **www.utb.edu/**

Freshman Application Contact New Student Relations, Texas Southmost College, 80 Fort Brown, Brownsville, TX 78520-4991. *Phone:* 956-882-8860. *Toll-free phone:* 877-882-8721. *Fax:* 956-882-8959.

TEXAS STATE TECHNICAL COLLEGE HARLINGEN

Harlingen, Texas **www.harlingen.tstc.edu/**

Director of Admissions Mrs. Blanca Guerra, Director of Admissions and Records, Texas State Technical College Harlingen, 1902 North Loop 499, Harlingen, TX 78550-3697. *Phone:* 956-364-4100. *Toll-free phone:* 800-852-8784. *Fax:* 956-364-5117. *E-mail:* blanca.guerra@harlingen.tstc.edu.

TEXAS STATE TECHNICAL COLLEGE–MARSHALL

Marshall, Texas **www.marshall.tstc.edu/**

Director of Admissions Pat Robbins, Registrar, Texas State Technical College–Marshall, 2650 East End Blvd. South, Marshall, TX 75671. *Phone:* 903-935-1010. *Toll-free phone:* 888-382-8782. *Fax:* 903-923-3282. *E-mail:* Pat.Robbins@marshall.tstc.edu.

TEXAS STATE TECHNICAL COLLEGE WACO

Waco, Texas **waco.tstc.edu/**

Freshman Application Contact Mr. Marcus Balch, Director, Recruiting Services, Texas State Technical College Waco, 3801 Campus Drive, Waco, TX 76705. *Phone:* 254-867-2026. *Toll-free phone:* 800-792-8784 Ext. 2362. *Fax:* 254-867-3827. *E-mail:* marcus.balch@tstc.edu.

TEXAS STATE TECHNICAL COLLEGE WEST TEXAS

Sweetwater, Texas **www.westtexas.tstc.edu/**

Freshman Application Contact Ms. Maria Aguirre-Acuna, Texas State Technical College West Texas, 300 College Drive, Sweetwater, TX 79556-4108. *Phone:* 325-235-7349. *Toll-free phone:* 800-592-8784.

TRINITY VALLEY COMMUNITY COLLEGE

Athens, Texas **www.tvcc.edu/**

- **State and locally supported** 2-year, founded 1946
- **Small-town** 65-acre campus with easy access to Dallas-Fort Worth
- **Endowment** $1.9 million
- **Coed,** 6,738 undergraduate students, 40% full-time, 60% women, 40% men

Undergraduates 2,688 full-time, 4,050 part-time. Students come from 48 states and territories, 1% are from out of state, 11% African American, 0.4% Asian American or Pacific Islander, 10% Hispanic American, 0.2% Native American, 0.5% international, 12% live on campus.

Freshmen *Admission:* 716 enrolled.

Faculty *Total:* 253, 55% full-time, 5% with terminal degrees. *Student/faculty ratio:* 22:1.

Majors Accounting; agricultural teacher education; animal sciences; art; automobile/automotive mechanics technology; biology/biological sciences; business administration and management; business teacher education; chemistry; child development; computer science; corrections; cosmetology; criminal justice/law enforcement administration; criminal justice/police science; dance; data processing and data processing technology; developmental and child psychology; drafting and design technology; dramatic/theater arts; education; elementary education; emergency medical technology (EMT paramedic); English; farm and ranch management; fashion merchandising; finance; geology/earth science; heating, air conditioning, ventilation and refrigeration maintenance technology; history; horticultural science; insurance; journalism; kindergarten/preschool education; legal administrative assistant/secretary; liberal arts and sciences/liberal studies; marketing/marketing management; mathematics; music; nursing (licensed practical/vocational nurse training); nursing (registered nurse training); physical education teaching and coaching; physical sciences; political science and government; pre-engineering; psychology; range science and management; real estate; religious studies; sociology; Spanish; speech and rhetoric; surgical technology; welding technology.

Academics *Calendar:* semesters. *Degree:* certificates, diplomas, and associate. *Special study options:* academic remediation for entering students, adult/continuing education programs, advanced placement credit, cooperative education, distance learning, honors programs, independent study, internships, part-time degree program, services for LD students, summer session for credit.

Library Ginger Murchison Learning Resource Center plus 3 others with 54,940 titles, 257 serial subscriptions, 1,954 audiovisual materials, an OPAC, a Web page.

Student Life *Housing Options:* men-only, women-only. Campus housing is university owned. *Activities and Organizations:* drama/theater group, student-run newspaper, choral group, marching band, Student Senate, Phi Theta Kappa, Delta Epsilon Chi. *Campus security:* 24-hour emergency response devices and patrols, controlled dormitory access. *Student services:* personal/psychological counseling.

Athletics Member NJCAA. *Intercollegiate sports:* basketball M(s)/W(s), cheerleading M(s)/W(s), football M(s), volleyball W(s). *Intramural sports:* baseball M/W, basketball M/W, football M, table tennis M/W, volleyball M/W.

Costs (2010–11) *Tuition:* area resident $1200 full-time; state resident $1800 full-time; nonresident $2400 full-time. *Room and board:* $3870. Room and board charges vary according to board plan. *Payment plan:* installment. *Waivers:* employees or children of employees.

Financial Aid Of all full-time matriculated undergraduates who enrolled in 2008, 80 Federal Work-Study jobs (averaging $1544). 40 state and other part-time jobs (averaging $1544).

Applying *Options:* early admission. *Required:* high school transcript. *Application deadlines:* rolling (freshmen), rolling (transfers). *Notification:* continuous (freshmen), continuous (transfers).

Freshman Application Contact Dr. Colette Hilliard, Dean of Enrollment Management and Registrar, Trinity Valley Community College, 100 Cardinal Drive, Athens, TX 75751. *Phone:* 903-675-6209 Ext. 209.

TYLER JUNIOR COLLEGE

Tyler, Texas **www.tjc.edu/**

Freshman Application Contact Ms. Janna Chancey, Director of Enrollment Management, Tyler Junior College, PO Box 9020, Tyler, TX 75711. *Phone:* 903-510-2396. *Toll-free phone:* 800-687-5680.

UNIVERSAL TECHNICAL INSTITUTE

Houston, Texas **www.uticorp.com/**

Director of Admissions Director of Admissions, Universal Technical Institute, 721 Lockhaven Drive, Houston, TX 77073-5598. *Phone:* 281-443-6262. *Toll-free phone:* 800-325-0354. *Fax:* 281-443-0610.

VERNON COLLEGE

Vernon, Texas **www.vernoncollege.edu/**

Director of Admissions Mr. Joe Hite, Dean of Admissions/Registrar, Vernon College, 4400 College Drive, Vernon, TX 76384-4092. *Phone:* 940-552-6291 Ext. 2204.

VET TECH INSTITUTE OF HOUSTON

Houston, Texas **www.vettechinstitute.edu/**

- **Private** 2-year, founded 1958
- **Suburban** campus
- **Coed,** 136 undergraduate students
- 57% of applicants were admitted

Freshmen *Admission:* 567 applied, 321 admitted.

Majors Veterinary/animal health technology.

Academics *Degree:* associate. *Special study options:* accelerated degree program, internships.

Student Life *Housing:* college housing not available.

Freshman Application Contact Admissions Office, Vet Tech Institute of Houston, 4669 Southwest Freeway, #300, Houston, TX 77027. *Phone:* 888-884-1468.

VICTORIA COLLEGE

Victoria, Texas **www.victoriacollege.edu/**

- **County-supported** 2-year, founded 1925
- **Urban** 80-acre campus
- **Endowment** $2.3 million
- **Coed,** 4,054 undergraduate students, 34% full-time, 65% women, 35% men

Undergraduates 1,362 full-time, 2,692 part-time. Students come from 12 states and territories, 15 other countries, 0.6% are from out of state, 6% African American, 1% Asian American or Pacific Islander, 34% Hispanic American, 0.2% Native American, 0.8% international, 66% transferred in.

Freshmen *Admission:* 748 admitted, 709 enrolled.

Faculty *Total:* 186, 53% full-time. *Student/faculty ratio:* 18:1.

Majors Accounting; administrative assistant and secretarial science; business administration and management; clinical/medical laboratory technology; computer programming; computer systems networking and telecommunications; criminal justice/police science; drafting and design technology; electrical, electronic and communications engineering technology; emergency medical technology (EMT paramedic); industrial technology; information science/studies; legal assistant/paralegal; liberal arts and sciences/liberal studies; nursing (registered nurse training); respiratory care therapy.

Academics *Calendar:* semesters. *Degree:* certificates and associate. *Special study options:* academic remediation for entering students, adult/continuing education programs, advanced placement credit, distance learning, part-time degree program, services for LD students, summer session for credit.

Library Victoria College Library with 150,000 titles, 1,500 serial subscriptions.

Student Life *Housing:* college housing not available. *Activities and Organizations:* drama/theater group, choral group, Student Senate. *Campus security:* 24-hour emergency response devices. *Student services:* personal/psychological counseling.

Athletics *Intramural sports:* basketball M, softball M.

Costs (2009–10) *Tuition:* area resident $1020 full-time, $34 per semester hour part-time; state resident $2370 full-time, $79 per semester hour part-time; nonresident $3000 full-time, $100 per semester hour part-time. Full-time tuition and fees vary according to course load and location. Part-time tuition and fees vary according to course load and location. *Required fees:* $1050 full-time, $35 per semester hour part-time. *Payment plan:* installment. *Waivers:* senior citizens and employees or children of employees.

Applying *Required:* high school transcript. *Application deadlines:* rolling (freshmen), rolling (transfers).

Freshman Application Contact Ms. Lavern Dentler, Registrar, Victoria College, 2200 East Red River, Victoria, TX 77901-4494. *Phone:* 361-573-3291. *Toll-free phone:* 877-843-4369. *Fax:* 361-582-2525. *E-mail:* registrar@victoriacollege.edu.

Virginia College at Austin

Austin, Texas www.vc.edu/

Admissions Office Contact Virginia College at Austin, 6301 East Highway 290, Austin, TX 78723. *Toll-free phone:* 866-314-6324.

Wade College

Dallas, Texas www.wadecollege.edu/

- **Proprietary** 2-year, founded 1965
- **Urban** 175-acre campus
- **Coed, primarily women,** 238 undergraduate students

Undergraduates 5% are from out of state. *Retention:* 49% of 2008 full-time freshmen returned.

Faculty *Total:* 18, 50% full-time, 11% with terminal degrees. *Student/faculty ratio:* 15:1.

Majors Fashion/apparel design; graphic design; interior design; merchandising, sales, and marketing operations related (specialized).

Academics *Calendar:* trimesters. *Degree:* associate. *Special study options:* academic remediation for entering students, advanced placement credit, double majors, part-time degree program, summer session for credit.

Library College Library with 4,782 titles, 109 serial subscriptions, 147 audiovisual materials, an OPAC.

Student Life *Housing Options:* coed, men-only, women-only. Campus housing is leased by the school. *Activities and Organizations:* Merchandising & Design Student Association. *Campus security:* 24-hour emergency response devices and patrols, late-night transport/escort service, controlled dormitory access.

Applying *Options:* electronic application. *Required:* high school transcript, interview. *Application deadlines:* rolling (freshmen), rolling (transfers).

Freshman Application Contact Wade College, INFOMart, 1950 Stemmons Freeway, Suite 2026, Box 562, Dallas, TX 75207. *Phone:* 214-637-3530. *Toll-free phone:* 800-624-4850.

Weatherford College

Weatherford, Texas www.wc.edu/

Freshman Application Contact Mr. Ralph Willingham, Director of Admissions, Weatherford College, 225 College Park Drive, Weatherford, TX 76086-5699. *Phone:* 817-598-6248. *Toll-free phone:* 800-287-5471 Ext. 248. *Fax:* 817-598-6205. *E-mail:* willingham@wc.edu.

Western Technical College

El Paso, Texas www.westerntech.edu/

Freshman Application Contact Laura Pena, Director of Admissions, Western Technical College, 9451 Diana Drive, El Paso, TX 79930-2610. *Phone:* 915-566-9621. *Toll-free phone:* 800-201-9232. *E-mail:* lpena@westerntech.edu.

Western Technical College

El Paso, Texas www.westerntech.edu/

Freshman Application Contact Mr. Bill Terrell, Chief Admissions Officer, Western Technical College, 9624 Plaza Circle, El Paso, TX 79927. *Phone:* 915-532-3737 Ext. 117. *Fax:* 915-532-6946. *E-mail:* bterrell@wtc-ep.edu.

Western Texas College

Snyder, Texas www.wtc.edu/

Director of Admissions Dr. Jim Clifton, Dean of Student Services, Western Texas College, 6200 College Avenue, Snyder, TX 79549-6105. *Phone:* 325-573-8511 Ext. 204. *Toll-free phone:* 888-GO-TO-WTC. *E-mail:* jclifton@wtc.cc.tx.us.

Westwood College–Houston South Campus

Houston, Texas www.westwood.edu/

- **Proprietary** primarily 2-year, founded 2003
- **Coed,** 478 students

Faculty *Total:* 54.

Majors Architectural drafting and CAD/CADD; construction management; design and visual communications; graphic design; information technology; legal assistant/paralegal; system, networking, and LAN/WAN management.

Academics *Calendar:* continuous. *Degrees:* diplomas, associate, and bachelor's.

Freshman Application Contact Westwood College–Houston South Campus, One Arena Place, 7322 Southwest Freeway, Houston, TX 77074. *Phone:* 713-777-4779. *Toll-free phone:* 800-281-2978.

Wharton County Junior College

Wharton, Texas www.wcjc.edu/

Freshman Application Contact Mr. Albert Barnes, Dean of Admissions and Registration, Wharton County Junior College, 911 Boling Highway, Wharton, TX 77488-3298. *Phone:* 979-532-6381. *E-mail:* albertb@wcjc.edu.

UTAH

College of Eastern Utah

Price, Utah www.ceu.edu/

Freshman Application Contact Mr. Todd Olsen, Director of Admissions and Scholarships, College of Eastern Utah, 451 East 400 North, Price, UT 84501. *Phone:* 435-613-5217. *Fax:* 435-613-5814. *E-mail:* todd.olsen@ceu.edu.

Everest College

West Valley City, Utah www.everest.edu/

Director of Admissions Director of Admissions, Everest College, 3280 West 3500 South, West Valley City, UT 84119. *Phone:* 801-840-4800. *Toll-free phone:* 888-741-4271. *Fax:* 801-969-0828.

ITT Technical Institute

Murray, Utah www.itt-tech.edu/

- **Proprietary** primarily 2-year, founded 1984, part of ITT Educational Services, Inc.
- **Suburban** campus
- **Coed**

Majors Animation, interactive technology, video graphics and special effects; CAD/CADD drafting/design technology; computer and information systems security; computer engineering technology; computer software and media applications related; computer software engineering; computer software technology; construction management; criminal justice/law enforcement administration; design and visual communications; electrical, electronic and communications engineering technology; graphic design; legal assistant/paralegal; system, networking, and LAN/WAN management; web/multimedia management and webmaster; web page, digital/multimedia and information resources design.

Academics *Calendar:* quarters. *Degrees:* associate and bachelor's.

Student Life *Housing:* college housing not available.

Freshman Application Contact Director of Recruitment, ITT Technical Institute, 920 West Levoy Drive, Murray, UT 84123. *Phone:* 801-263-3313. *Toll-free phone:* 800-365-2136.

LDS Business College

Salt Lake City, Utah www.ldsbc.edu/

- **Independent** 2-year, founded 1886, affiliated with The Church of Jesus Christ of Latter-day Saints, part of Latter-day Saints Church Educational System
- **Urban** 2-acre campus with easy access to Salt Lake City
- **Coed,** 1,588 undergraduate students, 77% full-time, 46% women, 54% men

Undergraduates 1,218 full-time, 370 part-time. Students come from 47 states and territories, 64 other countries, 48% are from out of state, 1% African American, 3% Asian American or Pacific Islander, 9% Hispanic American, 0.2% Native American, 17% international, 54% transferred in.

Freshmen *Admission:* 650 applied, 550 admitted, 429 enrolled.

Faculty *Total:* 100, 19% full-time, 3% with terminal degrees. *Student/faculty ratio:* 20:1.

Majors Accounting; accounting and business/management; accounting technology and bookkeeping; administrative assistant and secretarial science; business administration and management; computer and information sciences and support services related; entrepreneurship; executive assistant/executive secretary; general studies; health information/medical records administration; information technology; interior design; legal administrative assistant/secretary; liberal arts and sciences/liberal studies; medical administrative assistant and medical secretary; medical/clinical assistant; medical office assistant; medical transcription; system, networking, and LAN/WAN management; web page, digital/multimedia and information resources design.

Academics *Calendar:* semesters. *Degree:* certificates and associate. *Special study options:* academic remediation for entering students, adult/continuing education programs, advanced placement credit, internships, part-time degree program, services for LD students, summer session for credit. *ROTC:* Army (c), Air Force (c).

Library LDS Business College Library with 383,760 titles, 130 serial subscriptions, 1,055 audiovisual materials, an OPAC, a Web page.

Student Life *Housing:* college housing not available. *Activities and Organizations:* drama/theater group, choral group. *Campus security:* 24-hour emergency response devices and patrols.

Standardized Tests *Recommended:* SAT or ACT (for admission).

Costs (2010–11) *Tuition:* $2900 full-time, $121 per credit hour part-time. Full-time tuition and fees vary according to course load. Part-time tuition and fees vary according to course load. Students who are not members of the LDS Church pay $5,800 per year. *Payment plan:* deferred payment. *Waivers:* employees or children of employees.

Financial Aid *Average need-based gift aid:* $3797.

Applying *Options:* electronic application, deferred entrance. *Application fee:* $35. *Required:* essay or personal statement, high school transcript, interview. *Application deadlines:* rolling (freshmen), rolling (out-of-state freshmen), rolling (transfers). *Notification:* continuous (freshmen), continuous (out-of-state freshmen), continuous (transfers).

Freshman Application Contact Miss Dawn Fellows, Assistant Director of Admissions, LDS Business College, 411 East South Temple, Salt Lake City, UT 84111-1392. *Phone:* 801-524-8146. *Toll-free phone:* 800-999-5767. *Fax:* 801-524-1900. *E-mail:* DFellows@ldsbc.edu.

Provo College

Provo, Utah www.provocollege.edu/

Director of Admissions Mr. Gordon Peters, College Director, Provo College, 1450 West 820 North, Provo, UT 84601. *Phone:* 801-375-1861. *Toll-free phone:* 877- 777-5886. *Fax:* 801-375-9728. *E-mail:* gordonp@provocollege.org.

Salt Lake Community College

Salt Lake City, Utah www.slcc.edu/

- **State-supported** 2-year, founded 1948, part of Utah System of Higher Education
- **Urban** 114-acre campus with easy access to Salt Lake City
- **Endowment** $818,597
- **Coed,** 32,831 undergraduate students, 29% full-time, 51% women, 49% men

Undergraduates 9,566 full-time, 23,265 part-time. 2% African American, 5% Asian American or Pacific Islander, 9% Hispanic American, 1% Native American, 1% international, 4% transferred in.

Freshmen *Admission:* 5,147 applied, 5,147 admitted, 3,932 enrolled.

Faculty *Total:* 1,499, 22% full-time. *Student/faculty ratio:* 20:1.

Majors Accounting technology and bookkeeping; airline pilot and flight crew; architectural engineering technology; autobody/collision and repair technology; avionics maintenance technology; biology/biological sciences; biology/biotechnology laboratory technician; building/construction finishing, management, and inspection related; business administration and management; chemistry; clinical/medical laboratory technology; communication/speech communication and rhetoric; computer and information sciences; computer science; cosmetology; criminal justice/law enforcement administration; culinary arts; dental hygiene; design and visual communications; diesel mechanics technology; drafting and design technology; economics; electrical, electronic and communications engineering technology; engineering; engineering technology; English; entrepreneurship; environmental engineering technology; finance; general studies; geology/earth science; graphic design; health professions related; heating, air conditioning, ventilation and refrigeration maintenance technology; history; human development and family studies; humanities; industrial radiologic technology; information science/studies; information technology; instrumentation technology; international/global studies; international relations and affairs; kinesiology and exercise science; legal assistant/paralegal; marketing/marketing management; mass communication/media; medical/clinical assistant; medical radiologic technology; music; nursing (registered nurse training); occupational therapist assistant; photographic and film/video technology; physical sciences; physical therapist assistant; physics; political science and government; psychology; public health related; quality control technology; radio and television broadcasting technology; sign language interpretation and translation; social work; sociology; sport and fitness administration/management; survey technology; teacher assistant/aide; telecommunications technology; welding technology.

Academics *Calendar:* semesters. *Degree:* certificates, diplomas, and associate. *Special study options:* academic remediation for entering students, advanced placement credit, cooperative education, distance learning, double majors, English as a second language, internships, part-time degree program, services for LD students, student-designed majors, study abroad, summer session for credit. *ROTC:* Army (c), Air Force (c).

Library Markosian Library plus 2 others with 152,537 titles, 21,736 serial subscriptions, 20,645 audiovisual materials, an OPAC, a Web page.

Student Life *Housing:* college housing not available. *Activities and Organizations:* drama/theater group, student-run newspaper, radio and television station, choral group, marching band. *Campus security:* 24-hour emergency response devices and patrols, late-night transport/escort service. *Student services:* health clinic, personal/psychological counseling.

Athletics Member NJCAA. *Intercollegiate sports:* baseball M(s), basketball M(s)/W(s), cheerleading M(s)/W(s), soccer M(c)/W(c), softball W(s), volleyball W(s).

Costs (2009–10) *Tuition:* state resident $2376 full-time, $102 per credit hour part-time; nonresident $8316 full-time, $358 per credit hour part-time. *Required fees:* $414 full-time, $23 per credit hour part-time. *Payment plan:* installment. *Waivers:* senior citizens and employees or children of employees.

Financial Aid Of all full-time matriculated undergraduates who enrolled in 2008, 132 Federal Work-Study jobs (averaging $2567).

Applying *Options:* electronic application, early admission. *Application fee:* $40. *Application deadlines:* rolling (freshmen), rolling (transfers).

Freshman Application Contact Ms. Kathy Thompson, Salt Lake Community College, Salt Lake City, UT 84130. *Phone:* 801-957-4485. *E-mail:* kathy.thompson@slcc.edu.

SNOW COLLEGE

Ephraim, Utah **www.snow.edu/**

- **State-supported** 2-year, founded 1888, part of Utah System of Higher Education
- **Rural** 50-acre campus
- **Endowment** $6.2 million
- **Coed,** 4,368 undergraduate students, 61% full-time, 54% women, 46% men

Undergraduates 2,666 full-time, 1,702 part-time. Students come from 34 states and territories, 12 other countries, 9% are from out of state, 0.8% African American, 2% Asian American or Pacific Islander, 3% Hispanic American, 2% Native American, 3% international, 1% transferred in. *Retention:* 52% of 2008 full-time freshmen returned.

Freshmen *Admission:* 2,440 applied, 2,440 admitted, 1,224 enrolled. *Average high school GPA:* 3.3. *Test scores:* ACT scores over 18: 73%; ACT scores over 24: 22%; ACT scores over 30: 2%.

Faculty *Total:* 258, 44% full-time, 6% with terminal degrees. *Student/faculty ratio:* 18:1.

Majors Accounting; administrative assistant and secretarial science; agricultural business and management; agriculture; animal sciences; art; automobile/automotive mechanics technology; biology/biological sciences; botany/plant biology; building/construction finishing, management, and inspection related; business administration and management; business teacher education; chemistry; child development; computer science; construction engineering technology; criminal justice/law enforcement administration; dance; dramatic/theater arts; economics; education; elementary education; family and community services; family and consumer sciences/human sciences; farm and ranch management; foods, nutrition, and wellness; forestry; French; geography; geology/earth science; history; humanities; information science/studies; Japanese; kindergarten/preschool education; liberal arts and sciences/liberal studies; mass communication/media; mathematics; music; music history, literature, and theory; music teacher education; philosophy; physical education teaching and coaching; physical sciences; physics; political science and government; pre-engineering; range science and management; science teacher education; sociology; soil science and agronomy; Spanish; trade and industrial teacher education; voice and opera; zoology/animal biology.

Academics *Calendar:* semesters. *Degree:* certificates, diplomas, and associate. *Special study options:* academic remediation for entering students, adult/continuing education programs, advanced placement credit, cooperative education, English as a second language, external degree program, honors programs, independent study, part-time degree program, services for LD students, summer session for credit.

Library Lucy Phillips Library with 31,911 titles, 1,870 audiovisual materials, an OPAC, a Web page.

Student Life *Housing Options:* coed. Campus housing is university owned. *Activities and Organizations:* drama/theater group, student-run newspaper, radio station, choral group, Phi Beta Lambda, Latter-Day Saints Singers, International Student Society, BAAD Club (Alcohol and Drug Prevention), Dead Cats Society (Life Science Club). *Campus security:* 24-hour emergency response devices and patrols, student patrols, late-night transport/escort service. *Student services:* health clinic, personal/psychological counseling.

Athletics Member NJCAA. *Intercollegiate sports:* basketball M(s)/W(s), football M(s), softball W(s), volleyball W(s). *Intramural sports:* badminton M/W, basketball M/W, bowling M/W, football M/W, golf M/W, lacrosse M/W, racquetball M/W, soccer M/W, softball M/W, tennis M/W, ultimate Frisbee M/W, volleyball M/W, water polo M/W, wrestling M.

Standardized Tests *Recommended:* SAT or ACT (for admission).

Costs (2010–11) *Tuition:* state resident $2152 full-time, $140 per credit hour part-time; nonresident $7848 full-time, $500 per credit hour part-time. Full-time tuition and fees vary according to course load. Part-time tuition and fees vary according to course load. *Required fees:* $390 full-time, $25 per credit hour part-time. *Room and board:* $4000. Room and board charges vary according to board plan, housing facility, and location. *Payment plan:* installment. *Waivers:* employees or children of employees.

Financial Aid Of all full-time matriculated undergraduates who enrolled in 2008, 302 Federal Work-Study jobs (averaging $1017).

Applying *Options:* electronic application, early admission. *Application fee:* $30. *Required:* high school transcript. *Notification:* continuous (freshmen), continuous (transfers).

Freshman Application Contact Ms. Lorie Parry, Admissions Advisor, Snow College, 150 East College Avenue, Ephraim, UT 84627. *Phone:* 435-283-7144. *Fax:* 435-283-7157. *E-mail:* snowcollege@snow.edu.

UTAH CAREER COLLEGE

West Jordan, Utah **www.utahcollege.edu/**

Freshman Application Contact Ms. Karma Cooper, Director of Admissions, Utah Career College, 1902 West 7800 South, West Jordan, UT 84088. *Phone:* 801-304-4224 Ext. 158. *Toll-free phone:* 866-304-4224. *Fax:* 801-304-4229. *E-mail:* kcooper@utahcollege.edu.

UTAH CAREER COLLEGE–LAYTON CAMPUS

Layton, Utah **www.utahcollege.edu/**

Admissions Office Contact Utah Career College–Layton Campus, 869 West Hill Field Road, Layton, UT 84041.

VERMONT

COMMUNITY COLLEGE OF VERMONT

Montpelier, Vermont **www.ccv.edu/**

- **State-supported** 2-year, founded 1970, part of Vermont State Colleges System
- **Rural** campus
- **Coed,** 6,299 undergraduate students, 20% full-time, 69% women, 31% men

Undergraduates 1,283 full-time, 5,016 part-time. Students come from 18 states and territories, 3% are from out of state, 2% African American, 1% Asian American or Pacific Islander, 2% Hispanic American, 0.9% Native American, 0.3% international, 135% transferred in.

Freshmen *Admission:* 856 applied, 856 admitted, 799 enrolled.

Faculty *Total:* 698, 12% with terminal degrees. *Student/faculty ratio:* 13:1.

Majors Accounting; administrative assistant and secretarial science; art; business administration and management; CAD/CADD drafting/design technology; child development; community organization and advocacy; computer and information sciences; computer science; computer systems networking and telecommunications; criminal justice/law enforcement administration; data entry/microcomputer applications; developmental and child psychology; digital communication and media/multimedia; early childhood education; education; environmental science; graphic design; hospitality administration; human services; industrial technology; information technology; liberal arts and sciences/liberal studies; massage therapy; social sciences; teacher assistant/aide.

Academics *Calendar:* semesters. *Degree:* certificates, diplomas, and associate. *Special study options:* academic remediation for entering students, accelerated degree program, adult/continuing education programs, advanced placement credit, cooperative education, distance learning, double majors, English as a second language, external degree program, independent study, internships, part-time degree program, services for LD students, student-designed majors, study abroad, summer session for credit.

Library Hartness Library plus 1 other with 57,000 titles, 27,000 serial subscriptions, 5,000 audiovisual materials, an OPAC, a Web page.

Student Life *Housing:* college housing not available.

Costs (2010–11) *Tuition:* state resident $6150 full-time, $205 per credit hour part-time; nonresident $12,300 full-time, $410 per credit hour part-time. *Required fees:* $150 full-time, $50 per term part-time. *Payment plan:* installment. *Waivers:* employees or children of employees.

Financial Aid Of all full-time matriculated undergraduates who enrolled in 2008, 84 Federal Work-Study jobs (averaging $2000).

Community College of Vermont (continued)

Applying *Options:* electronic application. *Application deadlines:* rolling (freshmen), rolling (out-of-state freshmen), rolling (transfers). *Notification:* continuous (freshmen), continuous (out-of-state freshmen), continuous (transfers).

Freshman Application Contact Community College of Vermont, PO Box 489, Montpelier, VT 05601. *Phone:* 802-654-0505.

LANDMARK COLLEGE

Putney, Vermont **www.landmark.edu/**

- **Independent** 2-year, founded 1983
- **Small-town** 125-acre campus
- **Endowment** $9.9 million
- **Coed,** 498 undergraduate students, 100% full-time, 28% women, 72% men

Undergraduates 498 full-time. Students come from 36 states and territories, 11 other countries, 94% are from out of state, 5% African American, 1% Asian American or Pacific Islander, 5% Hispanic American, 4% international, 17% transferred in, 95% live on campus.

Freshmen *Admission:* 330 applied, 241 admitted, 146 enrolled.

Faculty *Total:* 88, 98% full-time, 11% with terminal degrees. *Student/faculty ratio:* 6:1.

Majors Business administration and management; business/commerce; general studies; liberal arts and sciences/liberal studies.

Academics *Calendar:* semesters. *Degree:* associate. *Special study options:* academic remediation for entering students, advanced placement credit, services for LD students, study abroad, summer session for credit.

Library Landmark College Library with 32,786 titles, 165 serial subscriptions, 1,535 audiovisual materials, an OPAC, a Web page.

Student Life *Housing:* on-campus residence required for freshman year. *Options:* coed, disabled students. Campus housing is university owned. Freshman campus housing is guaranteed. *Activities and Organizations:* drama/theater group, student-run newspaper, radio station, choral group, Student Government Association, Campus Activities Board, Phi Theta Kappa Honor Society, Equestrian Club, PBL Business Club. *Campus security:* 24-hour emergency response devices and patrols, controlled dormitory access. *Student services:* health clinic, personal/psychological counseling, women's center.

Athletics *Intercollegiate sports:* baseball M(c), basketball M(c)/W(c), cross-country running M(c)/W(c), equestrian sports M/W, rock climbing M(c)/W(c), soccer M/W, softball W(c). *Intramural sports:* badminton M(c)/W(c), basketball M(c)/W(c), fencing M(c)/W(c), skiing (cross-country) M(c)/W(c), tennis M(c)/W(c), volleyball M(c)/W(c), weight lifting M(c)/W(c).

Standardized Tests *Required:* Wechsler Adult Intelligence Scale III and Nelson Denny Reading Test (for admission).

Costs (2010–11) *Comprehensive fee:* $56,500 includes full-time tuition ($47,500), mandatory fees ($500), and room and board ($8500). *Room and board:* Room and board charges vary according to board plan and housing facility. *Payment plan:* installment. *Waivers:* employees or children of employees.

Financial Aid Of all full-time matriculated undergraduates who enrolled in 2009, 80 Federal Work-Study jobs (averaging $1000). 5 state and other part-time jobs (averaging $1000).

Applying *Options:* electronic application, deferred entrance. *Application fee:* $75. *Required:* essay or personal statement, high school transcript, 2 letters of recommendation, interview, diagnosis of LD and/or ADHD and cognitive testing. *Application deadlines:* rolling (freshmen), rolling (transfers). *Notification:* continuous (freshmen), continuous (transfers).

Freshman Application Contact Admissions Main Desk, Landmark College, 1 River Road South, Putney, VT 05346. *Phone:* 802-387-6718. *Fax:* 802-387-6868. *E-mail:* admissions@landmark.edu.

▶See page 458 for the College Close-Up.

NEW ENGLAND CULINARY INSTITUTE

Montpelier, Vermont **www.neci.edu/**

Freshman Application Contact Jan Knutsen, Vice President of Enrollment, New England Culinary Institute, 250 Main Street, Montpelier, VT 05602. *Toll-free phone:* 877-223-6324. *Fax:* 802-225-3280. *E-mail:* janknutsen@neci.edu.

NEW ENGLAND CULINARY INSTITUTE AT ESSEX

Essex Junction, Vermont **www.neci.edu/**

Freshman Application Contact Sherri Gilmore, Director of Admissions, New England Culinary Institute at Essex, 48 1/2 Park Street, Essex Junction, VT 05452. *Phone:* 802-223-6324. *Fax:* 802-225-3280. *E-mail:* sherrigilmore@neci.edu.

VIRGINIA

ACT COLLEGE

Arlington, Virginia **www.healthtraining.com/**

Freshman Application Contact Admissions Office, ACT College, 1100 Wilson Boulevard, Suite M780, Arlington, VA 22209-2297.

ADVANCED TECHNOLOGY INSTITUTE

Virginia Beach, Virginia **www.auto.edu/**

Freshman Application Contact Admissions Office, Advanced Technology Institute, 5700 Southern Boulevard, Suite 100, Virginia Beach, VA 23462. *Phone:* 757-490-1241.

AVIATION INSTITUTE OF MAINTENANCE–MANASSAS

Manassas, Virginia **www.aviationmaintenance.edu/aviation-washington-dc.asp**

Freshman Application Contact Washington, DC School Director, Aviation Institute of Maintenance–Manassas, 9821 Godwin Drive, Manassas, VA 20110. *Phone:* 703-257-5515. *Toll-free phone:* 877-604-2121. *Fax:* 703-257-5523. *E-mail:* directoramm@tidetech.com.

AVIATION INSTITUTE OF MAINTENANCE–VIRGINIA BEACH

Virginia Beach, Virginia **www.aviationmaintenance.edu/aviation-norfolk.asp**

Freshman Application Contact Virginia Beach School Director, Aviation Institute of Maintenance–Virginia Beach, 1429 Miller Store Road, Virginia Beach, VA 23455. *Phone:* 757-363-2121. *Toll-free phone:* 888-349-5387. *Fax:* 757-363-2044. *E-mail:* directoramn@tidetech.com.

BLUE RIDGE COMMUNITY COLLEGE

Weyers Cave, Virginia **www.brcc.edu/**

Freshman Application Contact Ms. Mary Wayland, Dean of Admissions and Records, Blue Ridge Community College, PO Box 80, Weyers Cave, VA 24486-0080. *Phone:* 540-453-2332. *E-mail:* waylandm@brcc.edu.

Bryant & Stratton College - Richmond Campus

Richmond, Virginia **www.bryantstratton.edu/**

- **Proprietary** primarily 2-year, founded 1952, part of Bryant and Stratton Business Institute, Inc
- **Suburban** campus
- **Coed,** 572 undergraduate students, 49% full-time, 82% women, 18% men

Undergraduates 280 full-time, 292 part-time. Students come from 1 other state, 85% African American, 0.7% Asian American or Pacific Islander, 2% Hispanic American, 0.2% Native American, 7% transferred in.

Freshmen *Admission:* 76 admitted, 76 enrolled.

Faculty *Total:* 49, 29% full-time, 16% with terminal degrees. *Student/faculty ratio:* 10:1.

Majors Accounting; administrative assistant and secretarial science; business administration and management; business/commerce; computer and information systems security; criminal justice/law enforcement administration; executive assistant/executive secretary; health services administration; human resources management and services related; legal administrative assistant/secretary; legal assistant/paralegal; medical/clinical assistant; system, networking, and LAN/WAN management.

Academics *Calendar:* semesters. *Degrees:* associate and bachelor's. *Special study options:* academic remediation for entering students, adult/continuing education programs, advanced placement credit, distance learning, double majors, independent study, internships, part-time degree program, summer session for credit.

Library Bryant and Stratton Library with 3,176 titles, 84 serial subscriptions.

Student Life *Housing:* college housing not available. *Activities and Organizations:* Phi Beta Lambda, Alpha Beta Gamma, Student Council, Medical Assisting Club, Paralegal Club. *Campus security:* late-night transport/escort service.

Standardized Tests *Required:* TABE, CPAt (for admission). *Recommended:* SAT or ACT (for admission).

Applying *Options:* deferred entrance. *Required:* high school transcript, interview, entrance evaluation and placement evaluation. *Application deadlines:* rolling (freshmen), rolling (transfers).

Freshman Application Contact Mr. David K. Mayle, Director of Admissions, Bryant & Stratton College - Richmond Campus, 8141 Hull Street Road, Richmond, VA 23235-6411. *Phone:* 804-745-2444. *Fax:* 804-745-6884. *E-mail:* tlawson@bryanstratton.edu.

Bryant & Stratton College - Virginia Beach

Virginia Beach, Virginia **www.bryantstratton.edu/**

- **Proprietary** primarily 2-year, founded 1952, part of Bryant and Stratton Business Institute, Inc.
- **Suburban** campus
- **Coed,** 595 undergraduate students, 45% full-time, 77% women, 23% men

Undergraduates 267 full-time, 328 part-time. Students come from 2 states and territories, 1% are from out of state, 63% African American, 2% Asian American or Pacific Islander, 6% Hispanic American, 1% Native American, 10% transferred in.

Freshmen *Admission:* 259 applied, 227 admitted, 139 enrolled.

Faculty *Total:* 60, 33% full-time, 25% with terminal degrees. *Student/faculty ratio:* 12:1.

Majors Accounting; administrative assistant and secretarial science; business administration and management; business administration, management and operations related; computer and information sciences; computer and information systems security; criminal justice/law enforcement administration; executive assistant/executive secretary; financial planning and services; health services administration; human resources management; legal assistant/paralegal; medical/clinical assistant; system, networking, and LAN/WAN management.

Academics *Calendar:* semesters. *Degrees:* associate and bachelor's. *Special study options:* academic remediation for entering students, adult/continuing education programs, advanced placement credit, double majors, independent study, internships, part-time degree program, services for LD students, summer session for credit.

Library Campus Library with 8,700 titles, 124 serial subscriptions, 447 audiovisual materials, an OPAC, a Web page.

Student Life *Housing:* college housing not available. *Activities and Organizations:* student-run newspaper. *Campus security:* 24-hour emergency response devices, late-night transport/escort service.

Standardized Tests *Required:* CPAt (for admission).

Costs (2009–10) *One-time required fee:* $135. *Tuition:* $14,670 full-time, $489 per credit hour part-time.

Financial Aid Of all full-time matriculated undergraduates who enrolled in 2008, 30 Federal Work-Study jobs (averaging $5000).

Applying *Options:* electronic application. *Application fee:* $35. *Required:* essay or personal statement, high school transcript, interview. *Application deadlines:* rolling (freshmen), rolling (transfers).

Freshman Application Contact Bryant & Stratton College - Virginia Beach, 301 Centre Pointe Drive, Virginia Beach, VA 23462-4417. *Phone:* 757-499-7900 Ext. 173.

Central Virginia Community College

Lynchburg, Virginia **www.cvcc.vccs.edu/**

Freshman Application Contact Ms. Judy Wilhelm, Admissions, Central Virginia Community College, 3506 Wards Road, Lynchburg, VA 24502-2498. *Phone:* 434-832-7633. *Toll-free phone:* 800-562-3060. *Fax:* 434-832-7793.

Centura College

Chesapeake, Virginia **www.centuracollege.com/**

Admissions Office Contact Centura College, 932 Ventures Way, Chesapeake, VA 23320.

Centura College

Newport News, Virginia **www.centuracollege.edu/**

Admissions Office Contact Centura College, 616 Denbigh Boulevard, Newport News, VA 23608.

Centura College

Norfolk, Virginia **www.centuracollege.edu/**

Admissions Office Contact Centura College, 7020 North Military Highway, Norfolk, VA 23518.

Centura College

Richmond, Virginia **www.centuracollege.edu/**

Admissions Office Contact Centura College, 7001 West Broad Street, Richmond, VA 23294.

Centura College

Richmond, Virginia **www.centuracollege.edu/**

Freshman Application Contact Admissions Office, Centura College, 7914 Midlothian Turnpike, Richmond, VA 23235-5230. *E-mail:* directorbtr@tidetech.com.

Centura College

Virginia Beach, Virginia **www.centuracollege.edu/**

Admissions Office Contact Centura College, 2697 Dean Drive, Suite 100, Virginia Beach, VA 23452. *Toll-free phone:* 877-604-2121.

Dabney S. Lancaster Community College

Clifton Forge, Virginia **www.dslcc.edu/**

- **State-supported** 2-year, founded 1964, part of Virginia Community College System
- **Rural** 117-acre campus
- **Endowment** $3.3 million
- **Coed,** 1,453 undergraduate students

Undergraduates Students come from 5 states and territories, 4% are from out of state, 5% African American, 0.5% Asian American or Pacific Islander, 0.7% Hispanic American, 0.3% Native American.

Faculty *Total:* 95, 22% full-time. *Student/faculty ratio:* 15:1.

Majors Administrative assistant and secretarial science; biological and physical sciences; business administration and management; computer programming; criminal justice/law enforcement administration; data processing and data processing technology; drafting and design technology; drafting/design engineering technologies related; education; electrical, electronic and communications engineering technology; forestry technology; information science/studies; legal administrative assistant/secretary; liberal arts and sciences/liberal studies; medical administrative assistant and medical secretary; nursing (registered nurse training); wood science and wood products/pulp and paper technology.

Academics *Calendar:* semesters. *Degree:* certificates, diplomas, and associate. *Special study options:* academic remediation for entering students, adult/continuing education programs, advanced placement credit, cooperative education, distance learning, honors programs, independent study, internships, part-time degree program, study abroad, summer session for credit.

Library Scott Hall plus 1 other with 37,716 titles, 376 serial subscriptions, an OPAC.

Student Life *Housing:* college housing not available. *Activities and Organizations:* drama/theater group. *Campus security:* 24-hour emergency response devices. *Student services:* personal/psychological counseling.

Athletics *Intercollegiate sports:* basketball M. *Intramural sports:* basketball M/W, bowling M/W, equestrian sports M/W, football M/W, golf M/W, skiing (downhill) M/W, soccer M/W, tennis M/W, volleyball M/W.

Costs (2010–11) *Tuition:* state resident $2268 full-time, $95 per credit hour part-time; nonresident $6398 full-time, $267 per credit hour part-time. Full-time tuition and fees vary according to reciprocity agreements. Part-time tuition and fees vary according to reciprocity agreements. *Required fees:* $173 full-time. *Waivers:* senior citizens.

Applying *Options:* early admission, deferred entrance. *Recommended:* interview. *Application deadlines:* rolling (freshmen), rolling (transfers). *Notification:* continuous (freshmen), continuous (transfers).

Freshman Application Contact Ms. Kathy Nicely, Registration Specialist, Dabney S. Lancaster Community College, 1000 Dabney Drive, PO Box 1000, Clifton Forge, VA 24422. *Phone:* 540-863-2815. *E-mail:* knicely@dslcc.edu.

Danville Community College

Danville, Virginia **www.dcc.vccs.edu/**

Director of Admissions Mr. Peter Castiglione, Director of Student Development and Enrollment Management, Danville Community College, 1008 South Main Street, Danville, VA 24541-4088. *Phone:* 434-797-8490. *Toll-free phone:* 800-560-4291.

Eastern Shore Community College

Melfa, Virginia **www.es.vccs.edu/**

- **State-supported** 2-year, founded 1971, part of Virginia Community College System
- **Rural** 117-acre campus with easy access to Hampton Roads/ Virginia Beach Norfolk
- **Coed,** 1,332 undergraduate students, 17% full-time, 67% women, 33% men

Undergraduates 229 full-time, 1,103 part-time. Students come from 3 states and territories, 2% are from out of state, 36% African American, 1% Asian American or Pacific Islander, 3% Hispanic American, 0.7% Native American.

Faculty *Total:* 57, 32% full-time, 7% with terminal degrees. *Student/faculty ratio:* 13:1.

Majors Administrative assistant and secretarial science; biological and physical sciences; business administration and management; computer and information sciences and support services related; computer/information technology services administration related; education; electrical, electronic and communications engineering technology; liberal arts and sciences/liberal studies; nursing (registered nurse training).

Academics *Calendar:* semesters. *Degree:* certificates and associate. *Special study options:* academic remediation for entering students, adult/continuing education programs, distance learning, English as a second language, honors programs, off-campus study, part-time degree program, services for LD students, summer session for credit.

Library Learning Resources Center plus 1 other with 25,000 titles, 102 serial subscriptions, an OPAC, a Web page.

Student Life *Housing:* college housing not available. *Activities and Organizations:* All Christians Together in Service (ACTS), Phi Theta Kappa, Phi Beta Lambda, The Electronics Club. *Campus security:* night security guard. *Student services:* personal/psychological counseling.

Standardized Tests *Required:* COMPASS (for admission).

Costs (2009–10) *Tuition:* state resident $2468 full-time, $87 per credit hour part-time; nonresident $7372 full-time, $259 per credit hour part-time. Full-time tuition and fees vary according to course load. Part-time tuition and fees vary according to course load. *Required fees:* $225 full-time, $8 per credit hour part-time. *Payment plan:* installment. *Waivers:* senior citizens.

Financial Aid Of all full-time matriculated undergraduates who enrolled in 2008, 11 Federal Work-Study jobs.

Applying *Options:* electronic application. *Required:* high school transcript, high school diploma. *Application deadlines:* rolling (freshmen), rolling (transfers). *Notification:* continuous (freshmen), continuous (transfers).

Freshman Application Contact P. Bryan Smith, Dean of Student Services, Eastern Shore Community College, 29300 Lankford Highway, Melfa, VA 23410. *Phone:* 757-789-1732. *Toll-free phone:* 877-871-8455. *Fax:* 757-789-1737. *E-mail:* bsmith@es.vccs.edu.

ECPI Technical College

Richmond, Virginia **www.ecpitech.edu/**

Freshman Application Contact Director, ECPI Technical College, 800 Moorefield Park Drive, Richmond, VA 23236. *Phone:* 804-330-5533. *Toll-free phone:* 800-986-1200. *Fax:* 804-330-5577. *E-mail:* agerard@ecpi.edu.

Everest College

Arlington, Virginia **www.everest.edu/**

Freshman Application Contact Director of Admissions, Everest College, 801 North Quincy Street, Arlington, VA 22203. *Phone:* 703-248-8887. *Fax:* 703-351-2202.

Germanna Community College

Locust Grove, Virginia **www.gcc.vccs.edu/**

- **State-supported** 2-year, founded 1970, part of Virginia Community College System
- **Suburban** 100-acre campus with easy access to Washington, DC
- **Coed,** 7,035 undergraduate students, 33% full-time, 63% women, 37% men

Undergraduates 2,296 full-time, 4,739 part-time. 15% African American, 3% Asian American or Pacific Islander, 5% Hispanic American, 0.5% Native American, 0.2% international.

Freshmen *Admission:* 1,338 applied, 1,338 admitted, 1,122 enrolled.

Faculty *Total:* 372, 19% full-time. *Student/faculty ratio:* 19:1.

Majors Biological and physical sciences; business administration and management; criminal justice/police science; dental hygiene; education; general studies; information technology; liberal arts and sciences/liberal studies; nursing (registered nurse training).

Academics *Calendar:* semesters. *Degree:* certificates and associate. *Special study options:* academic remediation for entering students, advanced placement credit, distance learning, double majors, English as a second language, independent study, off-campus study, part-time degree program, services for LD students, study abroad, summer session for credit.

Library Locust Grove Campus Library plus 2 others with 124,808 titles, 208 serial subscriptions, 2,382 audiovisual materials, an OPAC, a Web page.

Student Life *Housing:* college housing not available. *Activities and Organizations:* drama/theater group, Student Nurses Association, Student Government

Association, Phi Theta Kappa. *Campus security:* 24-hour patrols. *Student services:* personal/psychological counseling.

Athletics *Intramural sports:* archery M/W, basketball M/W, volleyball M/W.

Costs (2009–10) *Tuition:* state resident $2879 full-time, $95 per credit hour part-time; nonresident $8312 full-time, $277 per credit hour part-time. Full-time tuition and fees vary according to course load. Part-time tuition and fees vary according to course load. *Payment plans:* installment, deferred payment. *Waivers:* senior citizens.

Financial Aid Of all full-time matriculated undergraduates who enrolled in 2008, 31 Federal Work-Study jobs (averaging $1212). 14 state and other part-time jobs (averaging $1667).

Applying *Options:* electronic application, early admission. *Required for some:* high school transcript. *Application deadlines:* rolling (freshmen), rolling (transfers). *Notification:* continuous (freshmen), continuous (transfers).

Freshman Application Contact Ms. Rita Dunston, Registrar, Germanna Community College, 10000 Germanna Point Drive, Fredericksburg, VA 22408. *Phone:* 540-891-3020. *Fax:* 540-891-3092.

ITT Technical Institute

Chantilly, Virginia

www.itt-tech.edu/

- **Proprietary** primarily 2-year, founded 2002, part of ITT Educational Services, Inc.
- **Coed**

Majors Business administration and management; CAD/CADD drafting/design technology; computer and information systems security; computer engineering technology; computer software and media applications related; computer software engineering; computer software technology; construction management; criminal justice/law enforcement administration; design and visual communications; electrical, electronic and communications engineering technology; legal assistant/paralegal; system, networking, and LAN/WAN management; web/multimedia management and webmaster; web page, digital/multimedia and information resources design.

Academics *Calendar:* quarters. *Degrees:* associate and bachelor's.

Student Life *Housing:* college housing not available.

Freshman Application Contact Director of Recruitment, ITT Technical Institute, 14420 Albemarle Point Place, Chantilly, VA 20151. *Phone:* 703-263-2541. *Toll-free phone:* 888-895-8324.

ITT Technical Institute

Norfolk, Virginia

www.itt-tech.edu/

- **Proprietary** primarily 2-year, founded 1988, part of ITT Educational Services, Inc.
- **Suburban** campus
- **Coed**

Majors Animation, interactive technology, video graphics and special effects; business administration and management; CAD/CADD drafting/design technology; computer and information systems security; computer engineering technology; computer software and media applications related; computer software engineering; computer software technology; construction management; criminal justice/law enforcement administration; design and visual communications; electrical, electronic and communications engineering technology; legal assistant/paralegal; nursing (registered nurse training); system, networking, and LAN/WAN management; web/multimedia management and webmaster; web page, digital/multimedia and information resources design.

Academics *Calendar:* quarters. *Degrees:* associate and bachelor's.

Student Life *Housing:* college housing not available.

Financial Aid Of all full-time matriculated undergraduates who enrolled in 2008, 3 Federal Work-Study jobs (averaging $5000).

Freshman Application Contact Director of Recruitment, ITT Technical Institute, 863 Glenrock Road, Suite 100, Norfolk, VA 23502*3701. *Phone:* 757-466-1260. *Toll-free phone:* 888-253-8324.

ITT Technical Institute

Richmond, Virginia

www.itt-tech.edu/

- **Proprietary** primarily 2-year, founded 1999, part of ITT Educational Services, Inc.
- **Coed**

Majors Animation, interactive technology, video graphics and special effects; business administration and management; CAD/CADD drafting/design technology; computer and information systems security; computer engineering technology; computer software and media applications related; computer software engineering; computer software technology; construction management; criminal justice/law enforcement administration; design and visual communications; electrical, electronic and communications engineering technology; legal assistant/paralegal; system, networking, and LAN/WAN management; web/multimedia management and webmaster; web page, digital/multimedia and information resources design.

Academics *Calendar:* quarters. *Degrees:* associate and bachelor's.

Student Life *Housing:* college housing not available.

Freshman Application Contact Director of Recruitment, ITT Technical Institute, 300 Gateway Centre Parkway, Richmond, VA 23235. *Phone:* 804-330-4992. *Toll-free phone:* 888-330-4888.

ITT Technical Institute

Salem, Virginia

www.itt-tech.edu/

- **Proprietary** primarily 2-year
- **Coed**

Majors CAD/CADD drafting/design technology; computer and information systems security; computer engineering technology; construction management; criminal justice/law enforcement administration; electrical, electronic and communications engineering technology; legal assistant/paralegal; system, networking, and LAN/WAN management.

Academics *Degrees:* associate and bachelor's.

Freshman Application Contact Director of Recruitment, ITT Technical Institute, 2159 Apperson Drive, Salem, VA 24153. *Phone:* 540-989-2500. *Toll-free phone:* 877-208-6132.

ITT Technical Institute

Springfield, Virginia

www.itt-tech.edu/

- **Proprietary** primarily 2-year, founded 2002, part of ITT Educational Services, Inc.
- **Coed**

Majors Animation, interactive technology, video graphics and special effects; business administration and management; CAD/CADD drafting/design technology; computer and information systems security; computer engineering technology; computer software and media applications related; computer software engineering; computer software technology; construction management; criminal justice/law enforcement administration; design and visual communications; electrical, electronic and communications engineering technology; legal assistant/paralegal; system, networking, and LAN/WAN management; web/multimedia management and webmaster; web page, digital/multimedia and information resources design.

Academics *Calendar:* quarters. *Degrees:* associate and bachelor's.

Student Life *Housing:* college housing not available.

Freshman Application Contact Director of Recruitment, ITT Technical Institute, 7300 Boston Boulevard, Springfield, VA 22153. *Phone:* 703-440-9535. *Toll-free phone:* 866-817-8324.

John Tyler Community College

Chester, Virginia

www.jtcc.edu/

- **State-supported** 2-year, founded 1967, part of Virginia Community College System
- **Suburban** 160-acre campus with easy access to Richmond
- **Endowment** $1.5 million
- **Coed,** 9,692 undergraduate students, 29% full-time, 59% women, 41% men

Undergraduates 2,773 full-time, 6,919 part-time. Students come from 7 states and territories, 3 other countries, 1% are from out of state, 26% African American, 3% Asian American or Pacific Islander, 3% Hispanic American, 0.7% Native American, 0.2% international, 32% transferred in.

Freshmen *Admission:* 2,929 applied, 2,929 admitted, 1,319 enrolled.

Faculty *Total:* 400, 19% full-time, 10% with terminal degrees. *Student/faculty ratio:* 20:1.

Majors Administrative assistant and secretarial science; architectural engineering technology; business/commerce; electrical, electronics and communications

John Tyler Community College (continued)

engineering; engineering technology; funeral service and mortuary science; human services; liberal arts and sciences/liberal studies; management information systems; mechanical engineering/mechanical technology; nursing (registered nurse training); quality control and safety technologies related.

Academics *Calendar:* semesters. *Degree:* certificates and associate. *Special study options:* academic remediation for entering students, adult/continuing education programs, advanced placement credit, distance learning, external degree program, honors programs, off-campus study, part-time degree program, services for LD students, study abroad, summer session for credit. *ROTC:* Army (c).

Library John Tyler Community College Learning Resource and Technology Center with 49,393 titles, 179 serial subscriptions, an OPAC, a Web page.

Student Life *Housing:* college housing not available. *Activities and Organizations:* drama/theater group, choral group, Phi Theta Kappa -TauRho, Phi Theta Kappa-BOO, Art Club, Elements OF Life Club, Funeral Services Club. *Campus security:* 24-hour emergency response devices and patrols.

Costs (2009–10) *Tuition:* state resident $2225 full-time, $93 per credit hour part-time; nonresident $6595 full-time, $275 per credit hour part-time. Full-time tuition and fees vary according to course load. Part-time tuition and fees vary according to course load. *Required fees:* $50 full-time, $25 per term part-time. *Payment plan:* installment. *Waivers:* senior citizens.

Applying *Options:* early admission, deferred entrance. *Recommended:* high school transcript. *Application deadline:* rolling (freshmen). *Notification:* continuous (freshmen).

Freshman Application Contact Ms. Joy James, Director of Admission, John Tyler Community College, 13101 Jefferson Davis Highway, Chester, VA 23831. *Phone:* 804-796-4150. *Toll-free phone:* 800-552-3490.

J. Sargeant Reynolds Community College

Richmond, Virginia **www.reynolds.edu/**

- **State-supported** 2-year, founded 1972, part of Virginia Community College System
- **Suburban** 207-acre campus
- **Coed,** 12,740 undergraduate students

Undergraduates 33% African American, 4% Asian American or Pacific Islander, 3% Hispanic American, 0.6% Native American.

Majors Administrative assistant and secretarial science; agricultural business and management; biological and physical sciences; business administration and management; business/commerce; clinical/medical laboratory technology; computer and information sciences; dental laboratory technology; electrical and electronic engineering technologies related; emergency medical technology (EMT paramedic); engineering; engineering technologies related; industrial technology; liberal arts and sciences/liberal studies; management information systems; mental and social health services and allied professions related; nursing (registered nurse training); occupational therapist assistant; optometric technician; public administration and social service professions related; respiratory care therapy; security and protective services related; social sciences; special education; vehicle maintenance and repair technologies related; visual and performing arts related.

Academics *Calendar:* semesters. *Degree:* certificates and associate. *Special study options:* academic remediation for entering students, adult/continuing education programs, advanced placement credit, distance learning, English as a second language, independent study, internships, off-campus study, part-time degree program, services for LD students, summer session for credit.

Library J. Sargeant Reynolds Community College Library plus 3 others with 101,858 titles, 45,875 serial subscriptions, 2,483 audiovisual materials, an OPAC, a Web page.

Student Life *Housing:* college housing not available. *Activities and Organizations:* drama/theater group, choral group. *Campus security:* 24-hour emergency response devices and patrols, late-night transport/escort service, security during open hours. *Student services:* personal/psychological counseling.

Costs (2010–11) *Tuition:* state resident $3000 full-time, $100 per credit hour part-time; nonresident $8463 full-time, $282 per credit hour part-time. Full-time tuition and fees vary according to course load. Part-time tuition and fees vary according to course load. *Payment plan:* installment. *Waivers:* senior citizens.

Financial Aid Of all full-time matriculated undergraduates who enrolled in 2008, 11,688 applied for aid, 9,261 were judged to have need. 60 Federal Work-Study jobs (averaging $2500). In 2008, 109 non-need-based awards were made. *Average percent of need met:* 47%. *Average financial aid package:* $6800. *Average need-based loan:* $2475. *Average need-based gift aid:* $3300. *Average non-need-based aid:* $885. *Average indebtedness upon graduation:* $3624.

Applying *Options:* electronic application. *Required:* high school transcript. *Required for some:* interview. *Application deadlines:* rolling (freshmen), rolling (transfers). *Notification:* continuous (freshmen), continuous (transfers).

Freshman Application Contact Ms. Karen Pettis-Walden, Director of Admissions and Records, J. Sargeant Reynolds Community College, PO Box 85622, Richmond, VA 23285-5622. *Phone:* 804-523-5029. *Fax:* 804-371-3650. *E-mail:* kpettis-walden@reynolds.edu.

Lord Fairfax Community College

Middletown, Virginia **www.lfcc.edu/**

Freshman Application Contact Ms. Cynthia Bambara, Vice President of Student Success, Lord Fairfax Community College, 173 Skirmisher Lane, Middletown, VA 22645. *Phone:* 540-868-7105. *Toll-free phone:* 800-906-5322 Ext. 7107. *Fax:* 540-868-7005. *E-mail:* lfsmitt@lfcc.edu.

Medical Careers Institute

Newport News, Virginia **www.medical.edu/**

Freshman Application Contact Admissions Office, Medical Careers Institute, 1001 Omni Boulevard, Suite 200, Newport News, VA 23606.

Medical Careers Institute

Richmond, Virginia **www.careers.edu/**

Freshman Application Contact Admissions Office, Medical Careers Institute, 800 Moorefield Park Drive, Suite 302, Richmond, VA 23236-3659. *Phone:* 804-521-0400.

Medical Careers Institute

Virginia Beach, Virginia **www.medical.edu/**

Freshman Application Contact Admissions Office, Medical Careers Institute, 5501 Greenwich Road, #100, Virginia Beach, VA 23462.

Mountain Empire Community College

Big Stone Gap, Virginia **www.mecc.edu/**

- **State-supported** 2-year, founded 1972, part of Virginia Community College System
- **Rural** campus with easy access to Tri-Cities TN/VA MSA
- **Coed,** 3,383 undergraduate students, 43% full-time, 61% women, 39% men

Undergraduates 1,471 full-time, 1,912 part-time. Students come from 9 states and territories, 3% are from out of state, 2% African American, 0.3% Asian American or Pacific Islander, 0.3% Hispanic American, 0.3% Native American. *Retention:* 51% of 2008 full-time freshmen returned.

Faculty *Total:* 189, 22% full-time.

Majors Accounting; accounting related; administrative assistant and secretarial science; architectural engineering technology; business administration and management; business administration, management and operations related; business operations support and secretarial services related; CAD/CADD drafting/design technology; corrections; criminal justice/law enforcement administration; electrical and electronic engineering technologies related; electrical, electronic and communications engineering technology; emergency medical technology (EMT paramedic); environmental control technologies related; industrial production technologies related; industrial technology; legal assistant/paralegal; liberal arts and sciences/liberal studies; marketing/marketing management; mechanical engineering technologies related; natural resources/conservation; nursing (registered nurse training); respiratory care therapy; security and protective services related.

Academics *Calendar:* semesters. *Degree:* certificates and associate. *Special study options:* academic remediation for entering students, adult/continuing education programs, advanced placement credit, cooperative education, distance learning, double majors, external degree program, internships, part-time degree program, student-designed majors, summer session for credit.

Library Wampler Library with 43,674 titles, 148 serial subscriptions, an OPAC, a Web page.

Student Life *Housing:* college housing not available. *Activities and Organizations:* drama/theater group, Phi Theta Kappa, Healing Hands, Rho Nu (SNAV), Students in Free Enterprise (SIFE), Merits. *Campus security:* 24-hour emergency response devices and patrols. *Student services:* personal/psychological counseling.

Athletics *Intramural sports:* basketball M/W, football M/W, volleyball M/W.

Costs (2009–10) *Tuition:* state resident $2297 full-time, $96 per credit hour part-time; nonresident $6667 full-time, $228 per credit hour part-time.

Financial Aid Of all full-time matriculated undergraduates who enrolled in 2008, 150 Federal Work-Study jobs (averaging $1200). 30 state and other part-time jobs (averaging $650).

Applying *Options:* electronic application, early admission, deferred entrance. *Required:* high school transcript. *Required for some:* minimum 2 GPA. *Application deadlines:* rolling (freshmen), rolling (transfers). *Notification:* continuous (freshmen), continuous (transfers).

Freshman Application Contact Mountain Empire Community College, 3441 Mountain Empire Road, Big Stone Gap, VA 24219. *Phone:* 276-523-2400 Ext. 219.

NATIONAL COLLEGE

Bluefield, Virginia **www.national-college.edu/**

Freshman Application Contact National College, 100 Logan Street, Bluefield, VA 24605. *Phone:* 276-326-3621. *Toll-free phone:* 800-664-1886.

NATIONAL COLLEGE

Charlottesville, Virginia **www.national-college.edu/**

Director of Admissions Kimberly Moore, Campus Director, National College, 1819 Emmet Street, Charlottesville, VA 22903. *Phone:* 434-295-0136. *Toll-free phone:* 800-664-1886. *Fax:* 434-979-8061.

NATIONAL COLLEGE

Danville, Virginia **www.national-college.edu/**

Freshman Application Contact Admissions Office, National College, 336 Old Riverside Drive, Danville, VA 24540. *Phone:* 434-793-6822. *Toll-free phone:* 800-664-1886.

NATIONAL COLLEGE

Harrisonburg, Virginia **www.national-college.edu/**

Director of Admissions Jack Evey, Campus Director, National College, 1515 Country club Road, Harrisonburg, VA 22802. *Phone:* 540-432-0943. *Toll-free phone:* 800-664-1886.

NATIONAL COLLEGE

Lynchburg, Virginia **www.national-college.edu/**

Freshman Application Contact Admissions Representative, National College, 104 Candlewood Court, Lynchburg, VA 24502. *Phone:* 804-239-3500. *Toll-free phone:* 800-664-1886.

NATIONAL COLLEGE

Martinsville, Virginia **www.national-college.edu/**

Director of Admissions Mr. John Scott, Campus Director, National College, 10 Church Street, PO Box 232, Martinsville, VA 24114. *Phone:* 276-632-5621. *Toll-free phone:* 800-664-1886 (in-state); 800-664-1866 (out-of-state).

NATIONAL COLLEGE

Salem, Virginia **www.national-college.edu/**

Freshman Application Contact Director of Admissions, National College, 1813 East Main Street, Salem, VA 24153. *Phone:* 540-986-1800. *Toll-free phone:* 800-664-1886. *Fax:* 540-444-4198.

NEW RIVER COMMUNITY COLLEGE

Dublin, Virginia **www.nr.cc.va.us/**

Freshman Application Contact Ms. Margaret G. Taylor, Director of Student Services, New River Community College, PO Box 1127, 5251 College Drive, Dublin, VA 24084. *Phone:* 540-674-3600. *Fax:* 540-674-3644. *E-mail:* nrtaylm@nr.edu.

NORTHERN VIRGINIA COMMUNITY COLLEGE

Annandale, Virginia **www.nvcc.edu/**

- **State-supported** 2-year, founded 1965, part of Virginia Community College System
- **Suburban** 435-acre campus with easy access to Washington, DC
- **Coed**

Academics *Calendar:* semesters. *Degree:* certificates and associate. *Special study options:* academic remediation for entering students, adult/continuing education programs, advanced placement credit, cooperative education, distance learning, double majors, English as a second language, external degree program, honors programs, part-time degree program, services for LD students, study abroad, summer session for credit.

Student Life *Campus security:* 24-hour emergency response devices, campus police.

Applying *Options:* early admission, deferred entrance. *Required for some:* high school transcript.

Director of Admissions Dr. Max L. Bassett, Dean of Academic and Student Services, Northern Virginia Community College, 4001 Wakefield Chapel Road, Annandale, VA 22003-3796. *Phone:* 703-323-3195.

PATRICK HENRY COMMUNITY COLLEGE

Martinsville, Virginia **www.ph.vccs.edu/**

- **State-supported** 2-year, founded 1962, part of Virginia Community College System
- **Rural** 137-acre campus
- **Coed,** 3,501 undergraduate students, 100% full-time, 61% women, 39% men

Undergraduates 3,501 full-time. Students come from 4 states and territories, 25% African American, 0.4% Asian American or Pacific Islander, 2% Hispanic American, 0.1% Native American, 0.4% international. *Retention:* 49% of 2008 full-time freshmen returned.

Faculty *Total:* 149, 33% full-time.

Majors Accounting; administrative assistant and secretarial science; biological and physical sciences; business administration and management; computer programming; computer programming related; computer systems networking and telecommunications; data entry/microcomputer applications related; data processing and data processing technology; electrical, electronic and communications engineering technology; engineering technology; industrial technology; information technology; liberal arts and sciences/liberal studies; nursing (registered nurse training).

Academics *Calendar:* semesters. *Degree:* associate. *Special study options:* academic remediation for entering students, adult/continuing education programs, advanced placement credit, cooperative education, distance learning, independent study, internships, part-time degree program, services for LD students, summer session for credit.

Library Lester Library with 26,160 titles, 259 serial subscriptions, an OPAC, a Web page.

Student Life *Housing:* college housing not available. *Activities and Organizations:* drama/theater group, Student Government Association, Student Support

Patrick Henry Community College (continued)

Services, Phi Theta Kappa, Gospel Choir, Black Student Association. *Campus security:* 24-hour emergency response devices and patrols, late-night transport/escort service.

Athletics Member NJCAA. *Intramural sports:* baseball M/W, basketball M/W, cheerleading W, soccer M, table tennis M/W, tennis M/W, volleyball M/W, weight lifting M/W.

Financial Aid Of all full-time matriculated undergraduates who enrolled in 2008, 41 Federal Work-Study jobs (averaging $2000).

Applying *Options:* electronic application, early admission, deferred entrance. *Required:* high school transcript. *Application deadlines:* rolling (freshmen), rolling (transfers). *Notification:* continuous (freshmen), continuous (transfers).

Freshman Application Contact Mr. Travis Tisdale, Coordinator, Admissions and Records, Patrick Henry Community College, PO Box 5311, 645 Patriot Avenue, Martinsville, VA 24115. *Phone:* 276-656-0311. *Toll-free phone:* 800-232-7997. *Fax:* 276-656-0352.

Paul D. Camp Community College

Franklin, Virginia **www.pc.vccs.edu/**

Freshman Application Contact Mr. Joe Edenfield, Director of Admissions and Records, Paul D. Camp Community College, PO Box 737, 100 North College Drive, Franklin, VA 23851-0737. *Phone:* 757-569-6744. *E-mail:* jedenfield@pc.vccs.edu.

Piedmont Virginia Community College

Charlottesville, Virginia **www.pvcc.edu/**

Freshman Application Contact Ms. Mary Lee Walsh, Dean of Student Services, Piedmont Virginia Community College, 501 College Drive, Charlottesville, VA 22902-7589. *Phone:* 434-961-6540. *Fax:* 434-961-5425. *E-mail:* mwalsh@pvcc.edu.

Rappahannock Community College

Glenns, Virginia **www.rappahannock.edu/**

- **State-related** 2-year, founded 1970, part of Virginia Community College System
- **Rural** 217-acre campus
- **Coed,** 3,406 undergraduate students, 25% full-time, 63% women, 37% men

Undergraduates 837 full-time, 2,569 part-time. 20% African American, 1% Asian American or Pacific Islander, 2% Hispanic American, 0.6% Native American.

Freshmen *Admission:* 317 enrolled.

Majors Accounting; administrative assistant and secretarial science; biological and physical sciences; business administration and management; criminal justice/police science; engineering technology; information science/studies; liberal arts and sciences/liberal studies; nursing (registered nurse training).

Academics *Calendar:* semesters. *Degree:* certificates, diplomas, and associate. *Special study options:* academic remediation for entering students, adult/continuing education programs, distance learning, internships, off-campus study, part-time degree program, summer session for credit.

Library The College Library with 46,000 titles, 85 serial subscriptions, an OPAC.

Student Life *Housing:* college housing not available. *Activities and Organizations:* student-run newspaper, Phi Theta Kappa, Culture Club, Poetry Club, student government. *Campus security:* 24-hour emergency response devices. *Student services:* personal/psychological counseling, women's center.

Athletics *Intramural sports:* baseball M, table tennis M/W, tennis M/W, volleyball M/W.

Financial Aid Of all full-time matriculated undergraduates who enrolled in 2008, 40 Federal Work-Study jobs (averaging $1015).

Applying *Options:* early admission. *Application deadlines:* rolling (freshmen), rolling (transfers). *Notification:* continuous (freshmen), continuous (transfers).

Freshman Application Contact Ms. Wilnet Willis, Admissions and Records Officer, Rappahannock Community College, Glenns Campus, 12745 College Drive, Glenns, VA 23149-2616. *Phone:* 804-758-6742. *Toll-free phone:* 800-836-9381.

Richard Bland College of The College of William and Mary

Petersburg, Virginia **www.rbc.edu/**

- **State-supported** 2-year, founded 1961, administratively affiliated with College of William and Mary
- **Rural** 712-acre campus with easy access to Richmond
- **Coed**

Undergraduates 1,038 full-time, 596 part-time. Students come from 5 states and territories, 2 other countries, 1% are from out of state, 6% transferred in. *Retention:* 59% of 2008 full-time freshmen returned.

Faculty *Student/faculty ratio:* 25:1.

Academics *Calendar:* semesters. *Degree:* associate. *Special study options:* academic remediation for entering students, accelerated degree program, advanced placement credit, part-time degree program, services for LD students, summer session for credit. *ROTC:* Army (c).

Student Life *Campus security:* 24-hour emergency response devices and patrols, controlled dormitory access, full-time dedicated Campus Police Force.

Standardized Tests *Recommended:* SAT or ACT (for admission).

Costs (2009–10) *Tuition:* state resident $3102 full-time, $102 per credit hour part-time; nonresident $11,830 full-time, $465 per credit hour part-time. Full-time tuition and fees vary according to program. Part-time tuition and fees vary according to program. Contact school for availability and cost of single, double, or quad occupancy rooms. *Required fees:* $1010 full-time, $12 per credit hour part-time. *Room and board:* room only: $8240. *Payment plans:* installment, deferred payment.

Financial Aid Of all full-time matriculated undergraduates who enrolled in 2008, 10 Federal Work-Study jobs (averaging $2000).

Applying *Options:* electronic application. *Application fee:* $20. *Required:* essay or personal statement, high school transcript, minimum 2 GPA, in-state residency form. *Required for some:* interview.

Freshman Application Contact Office of Admissions, Richard Bland College of The College of William and Mary, 11301 Johnson Road, Petersburg, VA 23805-7100. *Phone:* 804-862-6249.

Southside Virginia Community College

Alberta, Virginia **www.southside.edu/**

- **State-supported** 2-year, founded 1970, part of Virginia Community College System
- **Rural** 207-acre campus
- **Endowment** $527,455
- **Coed,** 4,686 undergraduate students, 29% full-time, 65% women, 35% men

Undergraduates 1,359 full-time, 3,327 part-time. Students come from 3 states and territories, 2 other countries, 1% are from out of state, 46% African American, 0.7% Asian American or Pacific Islander, 0.5% Hispanic American, 0.2% Native American.

Freshmen *Admission:* 470 applied, 470 admitted, 380 enrolled.

Faculty *Total:* 295, 24% full-time, 6% with terminal degrees. *Student/faculty ratio:* 17:1.

Majors Administrative assistant and secretarial science; biological and physical sciences; business administration and management; criminal justice/law enforcement administration; education; electrical, electronic and communications engineering technology; emergency care attendant (EMT ambulance); fire science; general studies; human services; information science/studies; information technology; liberal arts and sciences/liberal studies; nursing (registered nurse training); respiratory care therapy.

Academics *Calendar:* semesters. *Degree:* certificates, diplomas, and associate. *Special study options:* academic remediation for entering students, advanced placement credit, distance learning, honors programs, off-campus study, part-time degree program, services for LD students, study abroad, summer session for credit. *ROTC:* Army (c).

Library Julian M. Howell Library plus 1 other with 27,691 titles, 164 serial subscriptions, 1,307 audiovisual materials, an OPAC, a Web page.

Student Life *Housing:* college housing not available. *Activities and Organizations:* choral group, Student Forum, Phi Theta Kappa, Phi Beta Lambda, Alpha Delta Omega.

Athletics *Intramural sports:* baseball M(c), basketball M(c), cheerleading M(c)/W(c), softball M(c)/W(c), table tennis M(c)/W(c), tennis M(c)/W(c), volleyball M/W.

Applying *Options:* electronic application, deferred entrance. *Required:* high school transcript, interview. *Application deadlines:* rolling (freshmen), rolling (transfers). *Notification:* continuous (freshmen), continuous (transfers).

Freshman Application Contact Mr. Brent Richey, Dean of Enrollment Management, Southside Virginia Community College, 109 Campus Drive, Alberta, VA 23821. *Phone:* 434-949-1012. *Fax:* 434-949-7863. *E-mail:* rhina.jones@sv.vccs.edu.

SOUTHWEST VIRGINIA COMMUNITY COLLEGE

Richlands, Virginia **www.sw.edu/**

- **State-supported** 2-year, founded 1968, part of Virginia Community College System
- **Rural** 100-acre campus
- **Endowment** $8.3 million
- **Coed,** 3,855 undergraduate students, 43% full-time, 55% women, 45% men

Undergraduates 1,648 full-time, 2,207 part-time. Students come from 5 states and territories, 1% are from out of state, 3% African American, 0.5% Asian American or Pacific Islander, 2% Hispanic American, 0.3% Native American, 4% transferred in. *Retention:* 56% of 2008 full-time freshmen returned.

Freshmen *Admission:* 675 enrolled.

Faculty *Total:* 256, 21% full-time. *Student/faculty ratio:* 20:1.

Majors Accounting; accounting related; administrative assistant and secretarial science; business administration and management; business administration, management and operations related; business operations support and secretarial services related; child-care provision; computer and information sciences; criminal justice/law enforcement administration; criminal justice/police science; education; electrical, electronic and communications engineering technology; emergency medical technology (EMT paramedic); engineering; human services; industrial radiologic technology; industrial technology; information science/studies; land use planning and management; liberal arts and sciences and humanities related; liberal arts and sciences/liberal studies; mental and social health services and allied professions related; mining technology; music; nursing (registered nurse training); radiologic technology/science; respiratory care therapy.

Academics *Calendar:* semesters. *Degree:* certificates, diplomas, and associate. *Special study options:* academic remediation for entering students, adult/continuing education programs, advanced placement credit, distance learning, double majors, honors programs, internships, part-time degree program, summer session for credit.

Library Southwest Virginia Community College Library with 110,000 titles, 950 serial subscriptions, 800 audiovisual materials, an OPAC, a Web page.

Student Life *Housing:* college housing not available. *Activities and Organizations:* choral group, Phi Theta Kappa, Phi Beta Lambda, Intervoice, Helping Minds Club, Project ACHEIVE. *Campus security:* 24-hour emergency response devices and patrols, student patrols, heavily saturated camera system. *Student services:* personal/psychological counseling.

Athletics *Intramural sports:* basketball M, racquetball M/W, volleyball M/W.

Standardized Tests *Required:* ASSET or COMPASS (for admission).

Costs (2010–11) *Tuition:* state resident $2424 full-time, $103 per credit hour part-time; nonresident $7226 full-time, $301 per credit hour part-time. *Required fees:* $192 full-time, $7 per credit hour part-time. *Waivers:* senior citizens.

Financial Aid Of all full-time matriculated undergraduates who enrolled in 2008, 150 Federal Work-Study jobs (averaging $1140).

Applying *Options:* electronic application, early admission, deferred entrance. *Required:* high school transcript, interview. *Application deadlines:* rolling (freshmen), rolling (transfers).

Freshman Application Contact Mr. Jim Farris, Director of Admissions, Records, and Counseling, Southwest Virginia Community College, Box SVCC, Richlands, VA 24641. *Phone:* 276-964-7300. *Toll-free phone:* 800-822-7822. *Fax:* 276-964-7716.

TESST COLLEGE OF TECHNOLOGY

Alexandria, Virginia **www.tesst.com/**

Director of Admissions Mr. Bob Somers, Director, TESST College of Technology, 6315 Bren Mar Drive, Alexandria, VA 22312-6342. *Phone:* 703-548-4800. *Toll-free phone:* 800-833-0209. *Fax:* 703-683-2765. *E-mail:* tesstal@erols.com.

THOMAS NELSON COMMUNITY COLLEGE

Hampton, Virginia **www.tncc.edu/**

- **State-supported** 2-year, founded 1968, part of Virginia Community College System
- **Suburban** 85-acre campus with easy access to Virginia Beach
- **Coed,** 10,606 undergraduate students

Faculty *Student/faculty ratio:* 22:1.

Majors Accounting; accounting related; administrative assistant and secretarial science; automobile/automotive mechanics technology; biological and physical sciences; business administration and management; CAD/CADD drafting/design technology; commercial and advertising art; computer and information sciences; computer science; criminal justice/law enforcement administration; criminal justice/police science; design and visual communications; drafting and design technology; emergency medical technology (EMT paramedic); engineering; fire science; general studies; heating, air conditioning, ventilation and refrigeration maintenance technology; humanities; industrial electronics technology; industrial technology; kindergarten/preschool education; legal assistant/paralegal; mechanical engineering/mechanical technology; mechanical engineering technologies related; nursing (registered nurse training); photography; public administration; social sciences; visual and performing arts related.

Academics *Calendar:* semesters. *Degree:* certificates, diplomas, and associate. *Special study options:* academic remediation for entering students, accelerated degree program, adult/continuing education programs, advanced placement credit, cooperative education, distance learning, English as a second language, external degree program, honors programs, internships, off-campus study, part-time degree program, services for LD students, summer session for credit.

Library Thomas Nelson Community College Library with 56,143 titles, 19,421 serial subscriptions, 546 audiovisual materials, an OPAC, a Web page.

Student Life *Activities and Organizations:* drama/theater group, choral group, Phi Theta Kappa, Future Nurses Association, International Club, Student Government Association, Health Care Advocates. *Campus security:* 24-hour emergency response devices and patrols, late-night transport/escort service. *Student services:* personal/psychological counseling.

Athletics *Intramural sports:* baseball M, basketball M/W.

Costs (2009–10) *Tuition:* state resident $2616 full-time, $87 per credit hour part-time; nonresident $7779 full-time, $259 per credit hour part-time. *Required fees:* $186 full-time, $6 per credit hour part-time, $11 per term part-time. *Waivers:* senior citizens and employees or children of employees.

Financial Aid Of all full-time matriculated undergraduates who enrolled in 2008, 110 Federal Work-Study jobs (averaging $3000).

Applying *Options:* electronic application, early admission, deferred entrance. *Required for some:* interview. *Recommended:* high school transcript. *Application deadlines:* rolling (freshmen), rolling (transfers). *Notification:* continuous (freshmen), continuous (transfers).

Freshman Application Contact Ms. Jerri Newson, Admissions Office Manager, Thomas Nelson Community College, PO Box 9407, 99 Thomas Nelson Drive, Hampton, VA 23670. *Phone:* 757-825-2800. *Fax:* 757-825-2763. *E-mail:* admissions@tncc.edu.

TIDEWATER COMMUNITY COLLEGE

Norfolk, Virginia **www.tcc.edu/**

- **State-supported** 2-year, founded 1968, part of Virginia Community College System
- **Suburban** 520-acre campus
- **Endowment** $7.1 million
- **Coed,** 30,447 undergraduate students, 40% full-time, 61% women, 39% men

Undergraduates 12,101 full-time, 18,346 part-time. Students come from 53 states and territories, 10% are from out of state, 33% African American, 6% Asian American or Pacific Islander, 5% Hispanic American, 0.7% Native American.

Faculty *Total:* 1,219, 27% full-time. *Student/faculty ratio:* 29:1.

Majors Accounting; administrative assistant and secretarial science; advertising; automobile/automotive mechanics technology; biological and physical sciences; business administration and management; civil engineering; commercial and advertising art; computer programming; drafting and design technology; education; electrical, electronic and communications engineering technology; engineering; finance; fine/studio arts; graphic design; horticultural science; information technology; interior design; kindergarten/preschool education; legal assistant/paralegal; liberal arts and sciences/liberal studies; marketing/marketing management; music; nursing (registered nurse training); real estate.

Tidewater Community College (continued)

Academics *Calendar:* semesters. *Degree:* certificates, diplomas, and associate. *Special study options:* academic remediation for entering students, accelerated degree program, adult/continuing education programs, advanced placement credit, cooperative education, distance learning, English as a second language, honors programs, independent study, internships, off-campus study, part-time degree program, services for LD students, summer session for credit.

Library Main Library plus 5 others with 147,126 titles, 913 serial subscriptions, an OPAC, a Web page.

Student Life *Housing:* college housing not available. *Activities and Organizations:* drama/theater group, student-run newspaper. *Campus security:* 24-hour patrols. *Student services:* personal/psychological counseling, women's center.

Athletics *Intramural sports:* basketball M/W, soccer M, softball W, tennis M/W, volleyball W.

Costs (2010–11) *Tuition:* state resident $2268 full-time, $95 per credit hour part-time; nonresident $6398 full-time, $267 per credit hour part-time. *Required fees:* $510 full-time, $36 per credit hour part-time. *Payment plan:* installment. *Waivers:* senior citizens.

Financial Aid Of all full-time matriculated undergraduates who enrolled in 2008, 64 Federal Work-Study jobs (averaging $2000).

Applying *Options:* early admission, deferred entrance. *Application deadlines:* rolling (freshmen), rolling (transfers). *Notification:* continuous (freshmen), continuous (transfers).

Freshman Application Contact Kellie Sorey PhD, Registrar, Tidewater Community College, 7000 College Drive, Portsmouth, VA 23703. *Phone:* 757-822-1900. *E-mail:* CentralRecords@tcc.edu.

VIRGINIA HIGHLANDS COMMUNITY COLLEGE

Abingdon, Virginia **www.vhcc.edu/**

Freshman Application Contact Karen Cheers, Acting Director of Admissions, Records, and Financial Aid, Virginia Highlands Community College, PO Box 828, 100 VHCC Drive Abingdon, Abingdon, VA 24210. *Phone:* 276-739-2490. *Toll-free phone:* 877-207-6115. *E-mail:* kcheers@vhcc.edu.

VIRGINIA WESTERN COMMUNITY COLLEGE

Roanoke, Virginia **www.virginiawestern.edu/**

Freshman Application Contact Admissions Office, Virginia Western Community College, 3095 Colonial Avenue, Roanoke, VA 24038. *Phone:* 540-857-7231.

WYTHEVILLE COMMUNITY COLLEGE

Wytheville, Virginia **www.wcc.vccs.edu/**

Director of Admissions Ms. Sabrina Terry, Registrar, Wytheville Community College, 1000 East Main Street, Wytheville, VA 24382-3308. *Phone:* 276-223-4755. *Toll-free phone:* 800-468-1195. *E-mail:* wcdixxs@wcc.vccs.edu.

WASHINGTON

APOLLO COLLEGE

Spokane, Washington **www.apollocollege.com/**

- **Proprietary** 2-year, founded 1976
- **Coed**

Academics *Degree:* associate.

Director of Admissions Deanna Baker, Campus Director, Apollo College, 10102 East Knox, Suite 200, Spokane, WA 99206. *Phone:* 509-532-8888. *Fax:* 509-533-5983.

THE ART INSTITUTE OF SEATTLE

Seattle, Washington **www.artinstitutes.edu/seattle/**

- **Proprietary** primarily 2-year, founded 1982, part of Education Management Corporation
- **Urban** campus
- **Coed**

Majors Animation, interactive technology, video graphics and special effects; baking and pastry arts; cinematography and film/video production; culinary arts; fashion/apparel design; fashion merchandising; graphic design; industrial design; interior design; photography; recording arts technology; restaurant, culinary, and catering management; web page, digital/multimedia and information resources design.

Academics *Calendar:* quarters. *Degrees:* diplomas, associate, and bachelor's.

Costs (2009–10) *Tuition:* Tuition cost varies by program. Prospective students should contact the school for current tuition costs. Other charges include a starting kit for all first-quarter students. Kits vary in price, depending on the program of study.

Freshman Application Contact The Art Institute of Seattle, 2323 Elliott Avenue, Seattle, WA 98121-1622. *Phone:* 206-448-6600. *Toll-free phone:* 800-275-2471.

►**See page 400 for the College Close-Up.**

BATES TECHNICAL COLLEGE

Tacoma, Washington **www.bates.ctc.edu/**

- **State-supported** 2-year, part of Washington State Board for Community and Technical Colleges
- **Urban** campus with easy access to Seattle
- **Coed**

Academics *Calendar:* quarters. *Degree:* certificates, diplomas, and associate.

Student Life *Campus security:* 24-hour emergency response devices, on-campus weekday security to 10 pm.

Financial Aid Of all full-time matriculated undergraduates who enrolled in 2008, 15 Federal Work-Study jobs (averaging $3500). 35 state and other part-time jobs (averaging $3500).

Applying *Application fee:* $56.

Director of Admissions Director of Admissions, Bates Technical College, 1101 South Yakima Avenue, Tacoma, WA 98405. *Phone:* 253-680-7000. *Toll-free phone:* 800-562-7099. *E-mail:* registration@bates.ctc.edu.

BELLEVUE COLLEGE

Bellevue, Washington **www.bcc.ctc.edu/**

- **State-supported** primarily 2-year, founded 1966, part of Washington State Board for Community and Technical Colleges
- **Suburban** 96-acre campus with easy access to Seattle
- **Coed**

Academics *Calendar:* quarters. *Degrees:* certificates, associate, and bachelor's. *Special study options:* academic remediation for entering students, advanced placement credit, cooperative education, distance learning, English as a second language, honors programs, independent study, internships, part-time degree program, services for LD students, summer session for credit.

Financial Aid Of all full-time matriculated undergraduates who enrolled in 2008, 65 Federal Work-Study jobs (averaging $3400). 43 state and other part-time jobs (averaging $3000).

Applying *Options:* electronic application. *Application fee:* $28.

Freshman Application Contact Morenika Jacobs, Associate Dean of Enrollment Services, Bellevue College, 3000 Landerholm Circle SE, Bellerne, WA 98007. *Phone:* 425-564-2205. *Fax:* 425-564-4065.

BELLINGHAM TECHNICAL COLLEGE

Bellingham, Washington **www.btc.ctc.edu/**

Freshman Application Contact Ms. Erin Runestrand, Coordinator, Admissions, Bellingham Technical College, 3028 Lindbergh Avenue, Bellingham, WA 98225-1599. *Phone:* 360-752-8324. *Fax:* 360-676-2798. *E-mail:* beltcadm@beltc.ctc.edu.

Big Bend Community College

Moses Lake, Washington www.bigbend.edu/

Freshman Application Contact Ms. Candis Lacher, Dean of Enrollment Services, Big Bend Community College, 7662 Chanute Street, Moses Lake, WA 98837. *Phone:* 509-793-2061. *Fax:* 509-782-6243. *E-mail:* admissions@bigbend.edu.

Cascadia Community College

Bothell, Washington www.cascadia.ctc.edu/

- **State-supported** 2-year, founded 1999
- **Suburban** 128-acre campus
- **Coed,** 3,250 undergraduate students, 45% full-time, 52% women, 48% men

Undergraduates 1,467 full-time, 1,783 part-time. Students come from 4 states and territories, 7 other countries, 1% are from out of state, 2% African American, 9% Asian American or Pacific Islander, 3% Hispanic American, 0.4% Native American, 10% transferred in.

Freshmen *Admission:* 704 enrolled.

Faculty *Total:* 123, 26% full-time. *Student/faculty ratio:* 26:1.

Majors Liberal arts and sciences and humanities related; liberal arts and sciences/liberal studies; science technologies related.

Academics *Calendar:* quarters. *Degree:* certificates and associate. *Special study options:* academic remediation for entering students, accelerated degree program, adult/continuing education programs, advanced placement credit, cooperative education, distance learning, English as a second language, independent study, internships, off-campus study, part-time degree program, services for LD students, study abroad, summer session for credit.

Library UWB/CCC Campus Library with 73,749 titles, 850 serial subscriptions, 6,100 audiovisual materials, an OPAC, a Web page.

Student Life *Housing:* college housing not available. *Campus security:* 24-hour emergency response devices, late-night transport/escort service.

Costs (2009–10) *Tuition:* state resident $2925 full-time, $81 per credit hour part-time; nonresident $8145 full-time, $253 per credit hour part-time. *Required fees:* $150 full-time, $50 per term part-time. *Waivers:* senior citizens and employees or children of employees.

Applying *Options:* electronic application. *Application deadlines:* rolling (freshmen), rolling (out-of-state freshmen), rolling (transfers). *Notification:* continuous (freshmen), continuous (out-of-state freshmen), continuous (transfers).

Freshman Application Contact Ms. Erin Blakeney, Dean for Student Success, Cascadia Community College, 18345 Campus Way, NE, Bothell, WA 98011. *Phone:* 425-352-8000. *Fax:* 425-352-8137. *E-mail:* admissions@cascadia.ctc.edu.

Centralia College

Centralia, Washington www.centralia.edu/

Freshman Application Contact Mr. Scott Copeland, Director of Enrollment Services and College Registrar, Centralia College, 600 West Locust, Centralia, WA 98531. *Phone:* 360-736-9391 Ext. 682. *Fax:* 360-330-7503. *E-mail:* admissions@centralia.edu.

Clark College

Vancouver, Washington www.clark.edu/

- **State-supported** 2-year, founded 1933, part of Washington State Board for Community and Technical Colleges
- **Urban** 101-acre campus with easy access to Portland
- **Endowment** $44.0 million
- **Coed,** 12,646 undergraduate students, 49% full-time, 58% women, 42% men

Undergraduates 6,181 full-time, 6,465 part-time. Students come from 9 states and territories, 24 other countries, 3% are from out of state, 3% African American, 5% Asian American or Pacific Islander, 5% Hispanic American, 1% Native American, 4% international.

Freshmen *Admission:* 1,484 enrolled.

Faculty *Total:* 778, 33% full-time, 10% with terminal degrees. *Student/faculty ratio:* 19:1.

Majors Accounting technology and bookkeeping; applied horticulture; automobile/automotive mechanics technology; baking and pastry arts; business administration and management; business automation/technology/data entry; computer programming; computer systems networking and telecommunications; construction engineering technology; culinary arts; data entry/microcomputer applications; dental hygiene; diesel mechanics technology; early childhood education; electrical, electronic and communications engineering technology; emergency medical technology (EMT paramedic); executive assistant/executive secretary; graphic communications; human resources management; landscaping and groundskeeping; legal administrative assistant/secretary; legal assistant/paralegal; liberal arts and sciences/liberal studies; machine tool technology; manufacturing technology; medical administrative assistant and medical secretary; medical/clinical assistant; nursing (registered nurse training); radiologic technology/science; retailing; selling skills and sales; sport and fitness administration/management; substance abuse/addiction counseling; survey technology; telecommunications technology; web/multimedia management and webmaster; welding technology.

Academics *Calendar:* quarters. *Degree:* certificates, diplomas, and associate. *Special study options:* academic remediation for entering students, accelerated degree program, adult/continuing education programs, advanced placement credit, cooperative education, distance learning, English as a second language, independent study, internships, part-time degree program, services for LD students, study abroad, summer session for credit. *ROTC:* Army (c), Air Force (c).

Library Lewis D. Cannell Library with 67,991 titles, 20,823 serial subscriptions, 2,701 audiovisual materials, an OPAC, a Web page.

Student Life *Housing:* college housing not available. *Activities and Organizations:* drama/theater group, student-run newspaper, choral group, Engineering Club, History Club, International Club, Multicultural Student Union, Queer Penguins and Allies. *Campus security:* 24-hour patrols, late-night transport/escort service, security staff during hours of operation. *Student services:* health clinic, personal/psychological counseling, legal services.

Athletics *Intercollegiate sports:* baseball M, basketball M(s)/W(s), cross-country running M(s)/W(s), fencing M(c)/W(c), soccer M(s)/W(s), softball W, track and field M(s)/W(s), volleyball W(s). *Intramural sports:* basketball M/W, fencing M/W, soccer M/W, softball M/W, volleyball M/W.

Costs (2009–10) *Tuition:* state resident $3175 full-time, $87 per credit hour part-time; nonresident $8395 full-time, $259 per credit hour part-time. Full-time tuition and fees vary according to course load and reciprocity agreements. Part-time tuition and fees vary according to course load and reciprocity agreements. *Payment plan:* installment. *Waivers:* senior citizens and employees or children of employees.

Financial Aid Of all full-time matriculated undergraduates who enrolled in 2008, 170 Federal Work-Study jobs (averaging $1900). 164 state and other part-time jobs (averaging $2150).

Applying *Options:* electronic application, early admission, deferred entrance. *Application fee:* $20. *Required for some:* high school transcript, interview. *Application deadlines:* 7/30 (freshmen), 7/30 (transfers). *Notification:* continuous (freshmen), continuous (transfers).

Freshman Application Contact Ms. Sheryl Anderson, Director of Admissions, Clark College, 1800 East McLoughlin Boulevard, Vancover, WA 98663. *Phone:* 360-992-2308. *Fax:* 360-992-2867. *E-mail:* sanderson@clark.edu.

Clover Park Technical College

Lakewood, Washington www.cptc.edu/

- **State-supported** 2-year, founded 1942, part of Washington State Community and Technical College System
- **Coed**

Academics *Degree:* certificates and associate. *Special study options:* academic remediation for entering students, accelerated degree program, cooperative education, distance learning, English as a second language, internships, part-time degree program, services for LD students.

Student Life *Campus security:* 24-hour patrols, late-night transport/escort service.

Applying *Options:* electronic application. *Application fee:* $41. *Required for some:* high school transcript, interview.

Director of Admissions Ms. Judy Richardson, Registrar, Clover Park Technical College, 4500 Steilacoom Boulevard Southwest, Lakewood, WA 98499. *Phone:* 253-589-5570.

Columbia Basin College

Pasco, Washington www.columbiabasin.edu/

Freshman Application Contact Ms. Donna Korstad, Program Support Supervisor, Enrollment Management, Columbia Basin College, 2600 North 20th Avenue, Pasco, WA 99301. *Phone:* 509-547-0511 Ext. 2250.

Edmonds Community College

Lynnwood, Washington **www.edcc.edu/**

Freshman Application Contact Ms. Nancy Froemming, Enrollment Services Office Manager, Edmonds Community College, 20000 68th Avenue West, Lynnwood, WA 98036-5999. *Phone:* 425-640-1853. *Fax:* 425-640-1159. *E-mail:* nanci.froemming@edcc.edu.

Everest College

Vancouver, Washington **www.everest.edu/**

Director of Admissions Ms. Renee Schiffhauer, Director of Admissions, Everest College, 120 Northeast 136th Avenue, Suite 300, Vancouver, WA 98684. *Phone:* 360-254-3282. *Fax:* 360-254-3035. *E-mail:* rschiffhauer@cci.edu.

Everett Community College

Everett, Washington **www.everettcc.edu/**

- **State-supported** 2-year, founded 1941, part of Washington State Board for Community and Technical Colleges
- **Suburban** 22-acre campus with easy access to Seattle
- **Coed,** 7,562 undergraduate students, 49% full-time, 57% women, 43% men

Undergraduates 3,707 full-time, 3,855 part-time. Students come from 24 other countries, 3% are from out of state, 3% African American, 7% Asian American or Pacific Islander, 5% Hispanic American, 2% Native American, 0.9% international, 3% transferred in. *Retention:* 46% of 2008 full-time freshmen returned.

Freshmen *Admission:* 708 enrolled.

Faculty *Total:* 369, 37% full-time. *Student/faculty ratio:* 24:1.

Majors Accounting; administrative assistant and secretarial science; anthropology; atmospheric sciences and meteorology; avionics maintenance technology; biology/biological sciences; botany/plant biology; business administration and management; business/commerce; CAD/CADD drafting/design technology; chemistry; computer science; corrections; cosmetology; creative writing; criminal justice/law enforcement administration; criminal justice/police science; data processing and data processing technology; dramatic/theater arts; early childhood education; education; engineering; engineering technology; English; entrepreneurship; environmental studies; fire science; foreign languages and literatures; geology/earth science; graphic design; history; humanities; human nutrition; information technology; international/global studies; journalism; liberal arts and sciences/liberal studies; manufacturing technology; mathematics; medical/clinical assistant; music; nursing (registered nurse training); oceanography (chemical and physical); philosophy; photography; physical education teaching and coaching; physics; political science and government; psychology; sociology; speech and rhetoric; web page, digital/multimedia and information resources design; welding technology.

Academics *Calendar:* quarters. *Degree:* certificates, diplomas, and associate. *Special study options:* academic remediation for entering students, adult/continuing education programs, advanced placement credit, cooperative education, distance learning, English as a second language, independent study, internships, part-time degree program, services for LD students, study abroad, summer session for credit.

Library John Terrey Library/Media Center with an OPAC, a Web page.

Student Life *Housing:* college housing not available. *Activities and Organizations:* drama/theater group, student-run newspaper, choral group, United Native American Council, Nippon Friendship Club, Student Nurses Association, International Students Club, Math, Engineering and Science Student Organization. *Campus security:* 24-hour emergency response devices and patrols, late-night transport/escort service. *Student services:* personal/psychological counseling, women's center.

Athletics Member NJCAA. *Intercollegiate sports:* baseball M(s), basketball M(s)/W(s), cross-country running M(s)/W(s), soccer M(s)/W(s), softball W(s), volleyball W(s). *Intramural sports:* basketball M/W, bowling M/W, crew M(c)/W(c), football M/W, golf M/W, soccer M/W, softball M/W, tennis M/W, volleyball M/W, weight lifting M/W.

Standardized Tests *Required:* ACT ASSET, ACT COMPASS (for admission).

Financial Aid Of all full-time matriculated undergraduates who enrolled in 2008, 152 Federal Work-Study jobs (averaging $3000). 48 state and other part-time jobs (averaging $3000).

Applying *Options:* electronic application, early admission, deferred entrance. *Recommended:* high school transcript. *Application deadlines:* rolling (freshmen), rolling (transfers). *Notification:* continuous (freshmen), continuous (transfers).

Freshman Application Contact Ms. Linda Baca, Entry Services Manager, Everett Community College, 2000 Tower Street, Everett, WA 98201-1352. *Phone:* 425-388-9219. *Fax:* 425-388-9173. *E-mail:* admissions@everettcc.edu.

Grays Harbor College

Aberdeen, Washington **www.ghc.ctc.edu/**

- **State-supported** 2-year, founded 1930, part of Washington State Board for Community and Technical Colleges
- **Small-town** 125-acre campus
- **Endowment** $8.3 million
- **Coed**

Undergraduates 1,183 full-time, 1,147 part-time. 1% African American, 2% Asian American or Pacific Islander, 5% Hispanic American, 5% Native American, 0.1% international. *Retention:* 60% of 2008 full-time freshmen returned.

Faculty *Student/faculty ratio:* 16:1.

Academics *Calendar:* quarters. *Degree:* certificates, diplomas, and associate. *Special study options:* academic remediation for entering students, accelerated degree program, adult/continuing education programs, advanced placement credit, cooperative education, distance learning, double majors, English as a second language, external degree program, honors programs, independent study, internships, part-time degree program, services for LD students, study abroad, summer session for credit.

Student Life *Campus security:* 24-hour emergency response devices, late-night transport/escort service.

Costs (2009–10) *Tuition:* state resident $2913 full-time, $81 per credit hour part-time; nonresident $8133 full-time, $253 per credit hour part-time. *Required fees:* $225 full-time, $6 per credit hour part-time.

Applying *Options:* electronic application, early admission. *Recommended:* high school transcript.

Freshman Application Contact Ms. Brenda Dell, Admissions Officer, Grays Harbor College, 1620 Edward P. Smith Drive, Aberdeen, WA 98520-7599. *Phone:* 360-532-9020 Ext. 4026. *Toll-free phone:* 800-562-4830.

Green River Community College

Auburn, Washington **www.greenriver.edu/**

- **State-supported** 2-year, founded 1965, part of Washington State Board for Community and Technical Colleges
- **Small-town** 168-acre campus with easy access to Seattle
- **Coed,** 9,114 undergraduate students, 55% full-time, 55% women, 45% men

Undergraduates 5,056 full-time, 4,058 part-time. Students come from 41 other countries, 5% African American, 7% Asian American or Pacific Islander, 5% Hispanic American, 0.9% Native American, 10% international. *Retention:* 61% of 2008 full-time freshmen returned.

Freshmen *Admission:* 920 enrolled.

Faculty *Total:* 436, 31% full-time. *Student/faculty ratio:* 23:1.

Majors Accounting technology and bookkeeping; airline pilot and flight crew; air traffic control; autobody/collision and repair technology; automobile/automotive mechanics technology; aviation/airway management; business/commerce; carpentry; computer and information systems security; computer systems networking and telecommunications; criminal justice/police science; data entry/microcomputer applications; drafting and design technology; early childhood education; forensic science and technology; forestry technology; geography related; legal administrative assistant/secretary; liberal arts and sciences/liberal studies; machine tool technology; marketing/marketing management; medical administrative assistant and medical secretary; nursing (licensed practical/vocational nurse training); occupational therapist assistant; office management; parks, recreation, and leisure related; physical sciences; physical therapist assistant; teacher assistant/aide; welding technology.

Academics *Calendar:* quarters. *Degree:* certificates, diplomas, and associate. *Special study options:* academic remediation for entering students, adult/continuing education programs, advanced placement credit, cooperative education, distance learning, English as a second language, internships, off-campus study, part-time degree program, services for LD students, study abroad, summer session for credit.

Library Holman Library with 32,500 titles, 2,100 serial subscriptions, 4,471 audiovisual materials, an OPAC, a Web page.

Student Life *Activities and Organizations:* drama/theater group, student-run newspaper, radio station, choral group. *Campus security:* 24-hour emergency response devices and patrols, student patrols, late-night transport/escort service. *Student services:* health clinic, personal/psychological counseling, women's center.

Athletics Member NJCAA. *Intercollegiate sports:* baseball M(s), basketball M(s)/W(s), golf M(s)/W(s), soccer W(s), softball W(s), tennis M(s)/W(s), volleyball W(s). *Intramural sports:* badminton M/W, basketball M/W, football M/W, tennis M/W, volleyball M/W, weight lifting M/W.

Costs (2010–11) *Tuition:* state resident $2925 full-time, $81 per credit hour part-time; nonresident $3345 full-time, $94 per credit hour part-time. Full-time tuition and fees vary according to course load. Part-time tuition and fees vary according to course load. *Required fees:* $398 full-time, $12 per credit hour part-time, $120 per credit hour part-time. *Payment plan:* installment. *Waivers:* senior citizens and employees or children of employees.

Financial Aid Of all full-time matriculated undergraduates who enrolled in 2008, 137 Federal Work-Study jobs (averaging $2224). 186 state and other part-time jobs (averaging $1164).

Applying *Options:* electronic application, early admission, deferred entrance. *Required for some:* high school transcript. *Application deadlines:* rolling (freshmen), rolling (transfers). *Notification:* continuous (freshmen), continuous (transfers).

Freshman Application Contact Ms. Peggy Morgan, Program Support Supervisor, Green River Community College, 12401 Southeast 320th Street, Auburn, WA 98092-3699. *Phone:* 253-833-9111. *Fax:* 253-288-3454.

HIGHLINE COMMUNITY COLLEGE

Des Moines, Washington **www.highline.edu/**

- **State-supported** 2-year, founded 1961, part of Washington State Board for Community and Technical Colleges
- **Suburban** 81-acre campus with easy access to Seattle
- **Endowment** $1.4 million
- **Coed,** 6,725 undergraduate students, 55% full-time, 60% women, 40% men

Undergraduates 3,722 full-time, 3,003 part-time. Students come from 6 states and territories, 50 other countries, 1% are from out of state, 10% African American, 16% Asian American or Pacific Islander, 6% Hispanic American, 0.9% Native American, 6% international, 49% transferred in. *Retention:* 59% of 2008 full-time freshmen returned.

Freshmen *Admission:* 4,424 applied, 4,424 admitted, 674 enrolled.

Faculty *Total:* 360, 40% full-time, 23% with terminal degrees. *Student/faculty ratio:* 22:1.

Majors Accounting; administrative assistant and secretarial science; art; behavioral sciences; biological and physical sciences; business administration and management; clinical/medical laboratory science and allied professions related; computer engineering technology; computer programming; computer systems networking and telecommunications; computer typography and composition equipment operation; criminal justice/law enforcement administration; criminal justice/police science; data entry/microcomputer applications related; dental hygiene; drafting and design technology; education; engineering; engineering technology; English; graphic and printing equipment operation/production; hotel/motel administration; humanities; human services; industrial technology; interior design; international business/trade/commerce; journalism; kindergarten/preschool education; legal administrative assistant/secretary; legal assistant/paralegal; library science; marine technology; mathematics; medical/clinical assistant; music; natural sciences; nursing (registered nurse training); plastics engineering technology; pre-engineering; psychology; respiratory care therapy; Romance languages; social sciences; tourism and travel services management; transportation and materials moving related; web page, digital/multimedia and information resources design.

Academics *Calendar:* quarters. *Degree:* certificates, diplomas, and associate. *Special study options:* academic remediation for entering students, advanced placement credit, cooperative education, distance learning, English as a second language, freshman honors college, honors programs, independent study, internships, off-campus study, part-time degree program, services for LD students, student-designed majors, study abroad, summer session for credit. *ROTC:* Army (c), Air Force (c).

Library Highline Community College Library with 57,678 titles, 585 serial subscriptions, an OPAC, a Web page.

Student Life *Housing:* college housing not available. *Activities and Organizations:* drama/theater group, student-run newspaper, choral group, Black Student Union, Pacific Islander Club, Friends of Bosnia, United Latino Association, Muslim Student Association. *Campus security:* 24-hour emergency response devices and patrols, late-night transport/escort service. *Student services:* personal/psychological counseling, women's center.

Athletics Member NJCAA. *Intercollegiate sports:* basketball M(s)/W(s), cross-country running M(s)/W(s), soccer M(s)/W(s), softball W(s), track and field M(s)/W(s), volleyball W(s), wrestling M(s).

Costs (2010–11) *Tuition:* $87 per credit part-time; state resident $3135 full-time, $105 per credit part-time; nonresident $3771 full-time, $259 per credit part-time. Full-time tuition and fees vary according to course load. Part-time tuition and fees vary according to course load. *Required fees:* $75 full-time. *Payment plan:* installment. *Waivers:* employees or children of employees.

Applying *Options:* electronic application. *Application fee:* $26. *Application deadlines:* rolling (freshmen), rolling (transfers).

Freshman Application Contact Ms. Laura Westergard, Director of Admissions, Highline Community College, PO Box 98000, 2400 South 240th Street, Des Moines, WA 98198-9800. *Phone:* 206-878-3710 Ext. 9800.

ITT TECHNICAL INSTITUTE

Everett, Washington **www.itt-tech.edu/**

- **Proprietary** primarily 2-year, part of ITT Educational Services, Inc.
- **Coed**

Majors Animation, interactive technology, video graphics and special effects; CAD/CADD drafting/design technology; computer and information systems security; computer engineering technology; computer software and media applications related; computer software engineering; computer software technology; construction management; criminal justice/law enforcement administration; design and visual communications; electrical, electronic and communications engineering technology; legal assistant/paralegal; system, networking, and LAN/WAN management; web/multimedia management and webmaster; web page, digital/multimedia and information resources design.

Academics *Degrees:* associate and bachelor's.

Freshman Application Contact Director of Recruitment, ITT Technical Institute, 1615 75th Street SW, Everett, WA 98203. *Phone:* 425-583-0200. *Toll-free phone:* 800-272-3791.

ITT TECHNICAL INSTITUTE

Seattle, Washington **www.itt-tech.edu/**

- **Proprietary** primarily 2-year, founded 1932, part of ITT Educational Services, Inc.
- **Urban** campus
- **Coed**

Majors Animation, interactive technology, video graphics and special effects; CAD/CADD drafting/design technology; computer and information systems security; computer engineering technology; computer software and media applications related; computer software engineering; computer software technology; construction management; criminal justice/law enforcement administration; design and visual communications; electrical, electronic and communications engineering technology; legal assistant/paralegal; system, networking, and LAN/WAN management; web/multimedia management and webmaster; web page, digital/multimedia and information resources design.

Academics *Calendar:* quarters. *Degrees:* associate and bachelor's.

Student Life *Housing:* college housing not available.

Freshman Application Contact Director of Recruitment, ITT Technical Institute, 12720 Gateway Drive, Suite 100, Seattle, WA 98168-3334. *Phone:* 206-244-3300. *Toll-free phone:* 800-422-2029.

ITT TECHNICAL INSTITUTE

Spokane Valley, Washington **www.itt-tech.edu/**

- **Proprietary** primarily 2-year, founded 1985, part of ITT Educational Services, Inc.
- **Suburban** campus
- **Coed**

Majors Animation, interactive technology, video graphics and special effects; CAD/CADD drafting/design technology; computer and information systems security; computer software engineering; computer software technology; construction management; criminal justice/law enforcement administration; design and visual communications; electrical, electronic and communications engineering technology; legal assistant/paralegal; system, networking, and LAN/WAN management; web/multimedia management and webmaster; web page, digital/multimedia and information resources design.

Academics *Calendar:* quarters. *Degrees:* associate and bachelor's.

ITT Technical Institute (continued)

Student Life *Housing:* college housing not available.

Freshman Application Contact Director of Recruitment, ITT Technical Institute, 13518 East Indiana Avenue, Spokane Valley, WA 99216. *Phone:* 509-926-2900. *Toll-free phone:* 800-777-8324.

LAKE WASHINGTON TECHNICAL COLLEGE

Kirkland, Washington **www.lwtc.edu/**

- **State-supported** 2-year, founded 1949, part of Washington State Board for Community and Technical Colleges
- **Suburban** 57-acre campus with easy access to Seattle
- **Coed**

Academics *Calendar:* quarters. *Degree:* certificates and associate. *Special study options:* academic remediation for entering students, advanced placement credit, cooperative education, English as a second language, internships, services for LD students, summer session for credit.

Student Life *Campus security:* 24-hour emergency response devices, late-night transport/escort service, parking lot security, security cameras.

Costs (2009–10) *Tuition:* state resident $88 per credit part-time; nonresident $260 per credit part-time.

Financial Aid Of all full-time matriculated undergraduates who enrolled in 2008, 21 Federal Work-Study jobs (averaging $3321). 61 state and other part-time jobs (averaging $3091).

Applying *Options:* early admission. *Required for some:* high school transcript.

Freshman Application Contact Shawn Miller, Registrar Enrollment Services, Lake Washington Technical College, 11605 132nd Avenue NE, Kirkland, WA 98034-8506. *Phone:* 425-739-8104. *E-mail:* info@lwtc.edu.

LOWER COLUMBIA COLLEGE

Longview, Washington **www.lcc.ctc.edu/**

- **State-supported** 2-year, founded 1934, part of Washington State Board for Community and Technical Colleges
- **Small-town** 39-acre campus with easy access to Portland
- **Endowment** $6.8 million
- **Coed,** 4,245 undergraduate students, 47% full-time, 66% women, 34% men

Undergraduates 2,012 full-time, 2,233 part-time. Students come from 10 states and territories, 1 other country, 8% are from out of state, 12% transferred in. *Retention:* 51% of 2008 full-time freshmen returned.

Freshmen *Admission:* 258 enrolled.

Faculty *Total:* 213, 35% full-time. *Student/faculty ratio:* 24:1.

Majors Accounting; accounting technology and bookkeeping; administrative assistant and secretarial science; automobile/automotive mechanics technology; business administration and management; criminal justice/law enforcement administration; data entry/microcomputer applications; diesel mechanics technology; early childhood education; fire science; industrial mechanics and maintenance technology; instrumentation technology; legal administrative assistant/secretary; liberal arts and sciences/liberal studies; machine tool technology; medical administrative assistant and medical secretary; medical/clinical assistant; music related; nursing (registered nurse training); substance abuse/addiction counseling; welding technology; wood science and wood products/pulp and paper technology.

Academics *Calendar:* quarters. *Degree:* certificates, diplomas, and associate. *Special study options:* academic remediation for entering students, adult/continuing education programs, cooperative education, distance learning, English as a second language, honors programs, internships, part-time degree program, services for LD students, student-designed majors, study abroad, summer session for credit.

Library Alan Thompson Library plus 1 other with 40,674 titles, 2,774 serial subscriptions, an OPAC, a Web page.

Student Life *Housing:* college housing not available. *Activities and Organizations:* drama/theater group, choral group, Multicultural Students Club, Drama Club, Symphonic Band, Forensic, Concert Choir. *Campus security:* 24-hour emergency response devices and patrols. *Student services:* personal/psychological counseling.

Athletics *Intercollegiate sports:* baseball M(s), basketball M(s)/W(s), volleyball W(s).

Costs (2010–11) *One-time required fee:* $16. *Tuition:* state resident $3145 full-time, $81 per credit part-time; nonresident $3670 full-time, $104 per credit part-time. Full-time tuition and fees vary according to course load and reciprocity agreements. Part-time tuition and fees vary according to course load and reciprocity agreements. *Required fees:* $290 full-time, $7 per credit part-time, $7 per credit part-time. *Payment plans:* installment, deferred payment. *Waivers:* senior citizens and employees or children of employees.

Financial Aid Of all full-time matriculated undergraduates who enrolled in 2008, 440 Federal Work-Study jobs (averaging $708). 447 state and other part-time jobs (averaging $2415).

Applying *Options:* electronic application. *Application fee:* $14. *Recommended:* high school transcript. *Application deadlines:* rolling (freshmen), rolling (transfers). *Notification:* continuous (freshmen).

Freshman Application Contact Ms. Mary Harding, Vice President for Student Success, Lower Columbia College, 1600 Maple Street, Longview, WA 98632. *Phone:* 360-442-2300. *Fax:* 360-442-2379. *E-mail:* registration@lowercolumbia.edu.

NORTH SEATTLE COMMUNITY COLLEGE

Seattle, Washington **www.northseattle.edu/**

Freshman Application Contact Ms. Betsy Abts, Registrar, North Seattle Community College, 9600 College Way North, Seattle, WA 98103-3599. *Phone:* 206-527-3663. *Fax:* 206-527-3671. *E-mail:* arrc@sccd.ctc.edu.

NORTHWEST AVIATION COLLEGE

Auburn, Washington **www.afsnac.com/**

Freshman Application Contact Mr. Shawn Pratt, Assistant Director of Education, Northwest Aviation College, 506 23rd, NE, Auburn, WA 98002. *Phone:* 253-854-4960. *Toll-free phone:* 800-246-4960. *Fax:* 253-931-0768. *E-mail:* spratt@afsmac.com.

NORTHWEST INDIAN COLLEGE

Bellingham, Washington **www.nwic.edu/**

Freshman Application Contact Admissions, Northwest Indian College, 2522 Kwina Road, Bellingham, WA 98226. *Phone:* 360-676-2772 Ext. 4269. *Toll-free phone:* 866-676-2772 Ext. 4264. *Fax:* 360-392-4333. *E-mail:* cbogby@nwic.edu.

NORTHWEST SCHOOL OF WOODEN BOATBUILDING

Port Hadlock, Washington **www.nwboatschool.org/**

Director of Admissions Student Services Coordinator, Northwest School of Wooden Boatbuilding, 42 North Water Street, Port Hadlock, WA 98339. *Phone:* 360-385-4948. *Fax:* 360-385-5089. *E-mail:* info@nwboatschool.org.

OLYMPIC COLLEGE

Bremerton, Washington **www.olympic.edu/**

- **State-supported** primarily 2-year, founded 1946, part of Washington State Board for Community and Technical Colleges
- **Suburban** 33-acre campus with easy access to Seattle
- **Endowment** $6.8 million
- **Coed,** 7,536 undergraduate students, 52% full-time, 56% women, 44% men

Undergraduates 3,930 full-time, 3,606 part-time. Students come from 5 states and territories, 3% African American, 6% Asian American or Pacific Islander, 5% Hispanic American, 1% Native American, 0.5% international, 14% transferred in.

Freshmen *Admission:* 7,536 applied, 7,536 admitted, 734 enrolled.

Faculty *Total:* 498, 23% full-time. *Student/faculty ratio:* 21:1.

Majors Accounting technology and bookkeeping; administrative assistant and secretarial science; aesthetician/esthetician and skin care; animation, interactive technology, video graphics and special effects; automobile/automotive mechanics technology; barbering; business administration and management; CAD/CADD drafting/design technology; child-care and support services management; communication and journalism related; computer and information sciences and support services related; computer and information sciences related; computer and information systems security; computer graphics; computer programming; computer programming related; computer software and media applications related; computer systems networking and telecommunications; corrections and criminal justice related; cosmetology; cosmetology, barber/styling, and nail instruction; criminal justice/law enforcement administration; criminal justice/police science; culinary arts; culinary arts related; customer service support/call center/teleservice operation; digital communication and media/multimedia; drafting and design technology; early childhood education; electrical, electronic and communications engineering technology; engineering; fire science; fire services administration; health professions related; hospitality administration; industrial technology; information science/studies; information technology; legal administrative assistant/secretary; liberal arts and sciences/liberal studies; marine maintenance and ship repair technology; medical/clinical assistant; medical reception; nail technician and manicurist; natural resources/conservation; nursing assistant/aide and patient care assistant; nursing (licensed practical/vocational nurse training); nursing (registered nurse training); office management; phlebotomy; photographic and film/video technology; physical sciences; recording arts technology; special education (early childhood); substance abuse/addiction counseling; system administration; system, networking, and LAN/WAN management; web/multimedia management and webmaster; welding technology; youth services.

Academics *Calendar:* quarters. *Degrees:* certificates, diplomas, associate, and bachelor's. *Special study options:* academic remediation for entering students, adult/continuing education programs, advanced placement credit, cooperative education, distance learning, English as a second language, honors programs, independent study, off-campus study, part-time degree program, services for LD students, summer session for credit.

Library Haselwood Library with 60,000 titles, 541 serial subscriptions, an OPAC, a Web page.

Student Life *Housing:* college housing not available. *Activities and Organizations:* drama/theater group, student-run newspaper, choral group, Phi Theta Kappa, Aware, Oceans (Nursing), ASOC, ASAD. *Campus security:* 24-hour emergency response devices and patrols, student patrols, late-night transport/escort service. *Student services:* personal/psychological counseling, women's center.

Athletics *Intercollegiate sports:* baseball M(s), basketball M(s)/W(s), cross-country running M/W, golf M/W, soccer M(s)/W(s), softball W(s), volleyball W(s). *Intramural sports:* basketball M/W, volleyball M/W.

Costs (2009–10) *Tuition:* state resident $2925 full-time, $81 per quarter hour part-time; nonresident $3315 full-time, $94 per credit part-time. Full-time tuition and fees vary according to course level, course load, and degree level. Part-time tuition and fees vary according to course level, course load, and degree level. *Required fees:* $240 full-time, $5 per credit part-time, $61 per term part-time. *Payment plan:* installment. *Waivers:* senior citizens.

Financial Aid Of all full-time matriculated undergraduates who enrolled in 2008, 105 Federal Work-Study jobs (averaging $2380). 31 state and other part-time jobs (averaging $2880).

Applying *Options:* electronic application, early admission, deferred entrance. *Required for some:* high school transcript. *Application deadlines:* rolling (freshmen), rolling (transfers). *Notification:* continuous (freshmen), continuous (transfers).

Freshman Application Contact Ms. Jennifer Fyllingness, Director of Admissions and Outreach, Olympic College, 1600 Chester Avenue, Bremerton, WA 98337-1699. *Phone:* 360-475-7128. *Toll-free phone:* 800-259-6718. *Fax:* 360-475-7202. *E-mail:* jfyllingness@olympic.edu.

Peninsula College

Port Angeles, Washington **www.pc.ctc.edu/**

- **State-supported** primarily 2-year, founded 1961, part of Washington State Community and Technical Colleges
- **Small-town** 75-acre campus
- **Coed**

Undergraduates 1,835 full-time, 1,941 part-time. 0.6% African American, 2% Asian American or Pacific Islander, 5% Hispanic American, 3% Native American, 5% international.

Faculty *Student/faculty ratio:* 18:1.

Academics *Calendar:* quarters. *Degrees:* certificates, associate, and bachelor's. *Special study options:* academic remediation for entering students, adult/continuing education programs, advanced placement credit, distance learning, English as a second language, honors programs, internships, part-time degree program, services for LD students, summer session for credit.

Student Life *Campus security:* 8-hour patrols by trained security personnel.

Costs (2009–10) *Tuition:* state resident $3012 full-time, $81 per credit hour part-time; nonresident $3402 full-time, $94 per credit hour part-time. Full-time tuition and fees vary according to course load. Part-time tuition and fees vary according to course load. *Required fees:* $87 full-time, $87 per year part-time.

Financial Aid Of all full-time matriculated undergraduates who enrolled in 2008, 30 Federal Work-Study jobs (averaging $3600). 25 state and other part-time jobs (averaging $3600).

Applying *Required for some:* high school transcript.

Freshman Application Contact Ms. Pauline Marvin, Peninsula College, 1502 East Lauridsen Boulevard, Port Angeles, WA 98362-2779. *Phone:* 360-417-6596. *Fax:* 360-457-8100. *E-mail:* admissions@pcadmin.ctc.edu.

Pierce College at Puyallup

Puyallup, Washington **www.pierce.ctc.edu/**

Director of Admissions Ms. Cindy Burbank, Director of Admissions, Pierce College at Puyallup, 1601 39th Avenue Southeast, Puyallup, WA 98374-2222. *Phone:* 253-964-6686.

Pima Medical Institute

Seattle, Washington **www.pmi.edu/**

- **Proprietary** 2-year, founded 1989, part of Vocational Training Institutes, Inc.
- **Urban** campus
- **Coed**

Academics *Calendar:* modular. *Degree:* certificates and associate.

Standardized Tests *Required:* Wonderlic aptitude test (for admission).

Applying *Required:* interview. *Required for some:* high school transcript.

Freshman Application Contact Admissions Office, Pima Medical Institute, 1627 Eastlake Avenue East, Seattle, WA 98102. *Phone:* 206-322-6100. *Toll-free phone:* 888-898-9048.

Renton Technical College

Renton, Washington **www.rtc.edu/**

Director of Admissions Becky Riverman, Vice President for Student Services, Renton Technical College, 3000 Fourth Street, NE, Renton, WA 98056. *Phone:* 425-235-2463.

Seattle Central Community College

Seattle, Washington **www.seattlecentral.edu/**

Freshman Application Contact Admissions Office, Seattle Central Community College, 1701 Broadway, Seattle, WA 98122-2400. *Phone:* 206-587-5450.

Shoreline Community College

Shoreline, Washington **www.shore.ctc.edu/**

Director of Admissions Mr. Chris Linebarger, Director, Recruiting and Enrollment Services, Shoreline Community College, 16101 Greenwood Avenue North, Seattle, WA 98133. *Phone:* 206-546-4581.

Skagit Valley College

Mount Vernon, Washington **www.skagit.edu/**

Freshman Application Contact Ms. Karen Marie Bade, Admissions and Recruitment Coordinator, Skagit Valley College, 2405 College Way, Mount Vernon, WA 98273-5899. *Phone:* 360-416-7620. *E-mail:* karenmarie.bade@skagit.edu.

South Puget Sound Community College

Olympia, Washington www.spscc.ctc.edu/

- **State-supported** 2-year, founded 1970, part of Washington State Board for Community and Technical Colleges
- **Suburban** 102-acre campus with easy access to Seattle
- **Coed,** 5,617 undergraduate students, 54% full-time, 60% women, 40% men

Undergraduates 3,014 full-time, 2,603 part-time. Students come from 11 states and territories, 10 other countries, 2% are from out of state, 2% African American, 5% Asian American or Pacific Islander, 5% Hispanic American, 1% Native American, 2% international, 3% transferred in. *Retention:* 56% of 2008 full-time freshmen returned.

Freshmen *Admission:* 411 applied, 411 admitted, 411 enrolled.

Faculty *Total:* 351, 27% full-time, 6% with terminal degrees. *Student/faculty ratio:* 22:1.

Majors Accounting; administrative assistant and secretarial science; automobile/automotive mechanics technology; business administration and management; computer and information sciences; computer programming; culinary arts; data processing and data processing technology; dental assisting; drafting and design technology; fire science; food technology and processing; horticultural science; information science/studies; kindergarten/preschool education; legal administrative assistant/secretary; legal assistant/paralegal; liberal arts and sciences/liberal studies; medical administrative assistant and medical secretary; medical/clinical assistant; nursing (licensed practical/vocational nurse training); nursing (registered nurse training); welding technology.

Academics *Calendar:* quarters. *Degree:* certificates, diplomas, and associate. *Special study options:* academic remediation for entering students, adult/continuing education programs, advanced placement credit, cooperative education, English as a second language, internships, part-time degree program, services for LD students, study abroad, summer session for credit. *ROTC:* Army (c).

Library Media Center plus 1 other with 70,879 titles, 8,656 serial subscriptions, 6,573 audiovisual materials, an OPAC, a Web page.

Student Life *Housing:* college housing not available. *Activities and Organizations:* drama/theater group, student-run newspaper, Welding Club, Geology Club, Forensic Club, Christian Club, Building Revolution by Increasing Community Knowledge (BRICK). *Campus security:* 24-hour emergency response devices and patrols, late-night transport/escort service. *Student services:* personal/psychological counseling.

Athletics *Intercollegiate sports:* basketball M(s)/W(s), soccer M(s), softball W(s).

Costs (2010–11) *Tuition:* state resident $2913 full-time, $84 per credit hour part-time; nonresident $3390 full-time, $102 per credit hour part-time. Full-time tuition and fees vary according to course load. Part-time tuition and fees vary according to course load. *Required fees:* $113 full-time. *Payment plan:* installment.

Financial Aid Of all full-time matriculated undergraduates who enrolled in 2008, 42 Federal Work-Study jobs (averaging $3150). 14 state and other part-time jobs (averaging $4400). *Financial aid deadline:* 6/29.

Applying *Options:* electronic application, early admission, deferred entrance. *Application deadlines:* rolling (freshmen), rolling (transfers). *Notification:* continuous (freshmen), continuous (transfers).

Freshman Application Contact Ms. Lyn Sharp, South Puget Sound Community College, 2011 Mottman Road, SW, Olympia, WA 98512. *Phone:* 360-754-7711 Ext. 5237. *E-mail:* lsharp@spcc.ctc.edu.

South Seattle Community College

Seattle, Washington southseattle.edu/

Director of Admissions Ms. Kim Manderbach, Dean of Student Services/Registration, South Seattle Community College, 6000 16th Avenue, SW, Seattle, WA 98106-1499. *Phone:* 206-764-5378. *Fax:* 206-764-7947. *E-mail:* kimmanderb@sccd.ctc.edu.

Spokane Community College

Spokane, Washington www.scc.spokane.edu/

Freshman Application Contact Ms. Brenda Burns, Researcher, District Institutional Research, Spokane Community College, North 1810 Greene Street, Spokane, WA 99217-5399. *Phone:* 509-434-5242. *Toll-free phone:* 800-248-5644. *Fax:* 509-434-5249. *E-mail:* mlee@ccs.spokane.edu.

Spokane Falls Community College

Spokane, Washington www.spokanefalls.edu/

Freshman Application Contact Admissions Office, Spokane Falls Community College, 3410 West Fort George Wright Drive, Spokane, WA 99224-5288. *Phone:* 509-533-3401. *Toll-free phone:* 888-509-7944. *Fax:* 509-533-3852.

Tacoma Community College

Tacoma, Washington www.tacomacc.edu/

Freshman Application Contact Enrollment Services, Tacoma Community College, 6501 South 19th Street, Tacoma, WA 98466. *Phone:* 253-566-5325. *Fax:* 253-566-6034.

Walla Walla Community College

Walla Walla, Washington www.wwcc.edu/home/

Freshman Application Contact Walla Walla Community College, 500 Tausick Way, Walla Walla, WA 99362-9267. *Phone:* 509-522-2500. *Toll-free phone:* 877-992-9922.

Wenatchee Valley College

Wenatchee, Washington www.wvc.edu/

- **State and locally supported** 2-year, founded 1939, part of Washington State Board for Community and Technical Colleges
- **Rural** 56-acre campus
- **Endowment** $358,000
- **Coed**

Undergraduates 2,095 full-time, 1,409 part-time. Students come from 6 other countries, 0.3% African American, 1% Asian American or Pacific Islander, 20% Hispanic American, 3% Native American, 0.3% international. *Retention:* 51% of 2008 full-time freshmen returned.

Academics *Calendar:* quarters. *Degree:* certificates, diplomas, and associate. *Special study options:* academic remediation for entering students, adult/continuing education programs, advanced placement credit, cooperative education, distance learning, English as a second language, external degree program, honors programs, independent study, part-time degree program, services for LD students, summer session for credit.

Student Life *Campus security:* evening and late night security patrols.

Applying *Options:* electronic application, early admission, deferred entrance. *Application fee:* $25. *Required for some:* high school transcript.

Freshman Application Contact Ms. Cecilia Escobedo, Registrar/Admissions Coordinator, Wenatchee Valley College, 1300 Fifth Street, Wenatchee, WA 98801-1799. *Phone:* 509-682-6836. *E-mail:* cescobedo@wvc.edu.

Whatcom Community College

Bellingham, Washington www.whatcom.ctc.edu/

Freshman Application Contact Entry and Advising Center, Whatcom Community College, 237 West Kellogg Road, Bellingham, WA 98226. *Phone:* 360-676-2170. *Fax:* 360-676-2171. *E-mail:* admit@whatcom.ctc.edu.

Yakima Valley Community College

Yakima, Washington www.yvcc.edu/

Freshman Application Contact Denise Anderson, Registrar and Director for Enrollment Services, Yakima Valley Community College, PO Box 22520, Yakima, WA 98907-2520. *Phone:* 509-574-4702. *Fax:* 509-574-6879. *E-mail:* admis@yvcc.edu.

WEST VIRGINIA

BLUE RIDGE COMMUNITY AND TECHNICAL COLLEGE

Martinsburg, West Virginia www.blueridgectc.edu/

- **State-supported** 2-year, founded 1974
- **Small-town** campus
- **Coed,** 3,422 undergraduate students, 27% full-time, 59% women, 41% men

Undergraduates 922 full-time, 2,500 part-time. 6% are from out of state, 0.3% transferred in. *Retention:* 55% of 2008 full-time freshmen returned.

Freshmen *Admission:* 402 enrolled. *Test scores:* SAT verbal scores over 500: 45%; ACT scores over 18: 34%; SAT verbal scores over 600: 10%; ACT scores over 24: 1%.

Faculty *Total:* 106, 32% full-time. *Student/faculty ratio:* 29:1.

Majors Automobile/automotive mechanics technology; business, management, and marketing related; criminal justice/safety; culinary arts; design and visual communications; electromechanical technology; emergency medical technology (EMT paramedic); fashion merchandising; fire science; general studies; heating, air conditioning, ventilation and refrigeration maintenance technology; information technology; legal assistant/paralegal; office occupations and clerical services; quality control and safety technologies related.

Academics *Degree:* certificates and associate. *Special study options:* academic remediation for entering students, accelerated degree program, adult/continuing education programs, advanced placement credit, double majors, English as a second language, independent study, internships, part-time degree program, services for LD students.

Student Life *Activities and Organizations:* national fraternities. *Campus security:* late-night transport/escort service.

Standardized Tests *Recommended:* SAT and SAT Subject Tests or ACT (for admission).

Costs (2010–11) *Tuition:* state resident $3072 full-time, $128 per credit hour part-time; nonresident $5520 full-time, $230 per credit hour part-time. Full-time tuition and fees vary according to course load and program. Part-time tuition and fees vary according to course load and program. *Waivers:* senior citizens and employees or children of employees.

Applying *Options:* deferred entrance. *Application fee:* $25. *Required:* high school transcript. *Required for some:* interview.

Freshman Application Contact Brenda K. Neal, Director of Access, Blue Ridge Community and Technical College, 400 West Stephen Street, Martinsburg, WV 25401. *Phone:* 304-260-4380 Ext. 2109. *Fax:* 304-260-4376. *E-mail:* bneal@blueridgectc.edu.

COMMUNITY & TECHNICAL COLLEGE AT WEST VIRGINIA UNIVERSITY INSTITUTE OF TECHNOLOGY

Montgomery, West Virginia ctc.wvutech.edu/

- **County-supported** 2-year
- **Coed**

Academics *Degree:* certificates and associate.

Director of Admissions Ms. Lisa Graham, Director of Admissions, Community & Technical College at West Virginia University Institute of Technology, Box 10, Old Main, Montgomery, WV 25136. *Phone:* 304-442-3167. *Toll-free phone:* 888-554-8324.

EASTERN WEST VIRGINIA COMMUNITY AND TECHNICAL COLLEGE

Moorefield, West Virginia www.eastern.wvnet.edu/

Freshman Application Contact Ms. Sharon Bungard, Dean for Learner Support Services, Eastern West Virginia Community and Technical College, 1929 State Road 55, Moorefield, WV 26836. *Phone:* 304-434-8000. *Toll-free phone:* 877-982-2322. *Fax:* 304-434-7001.

EVEREST INSTITUTE

Cross Lanes, West Virginia www.everest.edu/

Freshman Application Contact Director of Admissions, Everest Institute, 5514 Big Tyler Road, Cross Lanes, WV 25313. *Phone:* 304-776-6290. *Toll-free phone:* 888-741-4271. *Fax:* 304-776-6262.

HUNTINGTON JUNIOR COLLEGE

Huntington, West Virginia www.huntingtonjuniorcollege.com/

- **Proprietary** 2-year, founded 1936
- **Urban** campus
- **Coed**

Academics *Calendar:* quarters. *Degree:* associate. *Special study options:* academic remediation for entering students, part-time degree program, services for LD students, summer session for credit.

Applying *Required:* high school transcript.

Director of Admissions Mr. James Garrett, Educational Services Director, Huntington Junior College, 900 Fifth Avenue, Huntington, WV 25701-2004. *Phone:* 304-697-7550.

ITT TECHNICAL INSTITUTE

Huntington, West Virginia www.itt-tech.edu/

- **Proprietary** 2-year, part of ITT Educational Services, Inc.
- **Coed**

Majors CAD/CADD drafting/design technology; computer engineering technology; computer software technology; criminal justice/law enforcement administration; design and visual communications; legal assistant/paralegal; system, networking, and LAN/WAN management.

Academics *Calendar:* quarters. *Degree:* associate.

Freshman Application Contact Director of Recruitment, ITT Technical Institute, 5183 US Route 60, Building 1, Suite 40, Huntington, WV 25705. *Phone:* 304-733-8700. *Toll-free phone:* 800-224-4695.

KANAWHA VALLEY COMMUNITY AND TECHNICAL COLLEGE

Institute, West Virginia www.wvsctc.edu/

Freshman Application Contact Mr. Bryce Casto, Vice President Student Affairs, Kanawha Valley Community and Technical College, PO Box 1000, Institute, WV 25112-1000. *Phone:* 304-766-3140. *Toll-free phone:* 800-987-2112. *Fax:* 304-766-4158. *E-mail:* castosb@wvstateu.edu.

MOUNTAIN STATE COLLEGE

Parkersburg, West Virginia www.msc.edu/

- **Proprietary** 2-year, founded 1888
- **Small-town** campus
- **Coed,** 166 undergraduate students, 100% full-time, 83% women, 17% men

Undergraduates 166 full-time. Students come from 2 states and territories, 1% African American, 0.6% Asian American or Pacific Islander, 0.6% Hispanic American, 4% transferred in. *Retention:* 70% of 2008 full-time freshmen returned.

Freshmen *Admission:* 27 enrolled.

Faculty *Total:* 11, 64% full-time, 36% with terminal degrees. *Student/faculty ratio:* 17:1.

Majors Accounting and business/management; administrative assistant and secretarial science; computer and information sciences; legal assistant/paralegal; medical/clinical assistant; medical transcription; substance abuse/addiction counseling.

Academics *Calendar:* quarters. *Degree:* diplomas and associate. *Special study options:* distance learning, double majors, honors programs, independent study, internships, part-time degree program.

Mountain State College (continued)

Library Mountain State College Library with an OPAC.
Student Life *Housing:* college housing not available. *Student services:* personal/psychological counseling.
Standardized Tests *Required:* CPAt (for admission).
Applying *Required:* interview.
Freshman Application Contact Ms. Judith Sutton, President, Mountain State College, 1508 Spring Street, Parkersburg, WV 26101-3993. *Phone:* 304-485-5487. *Toll-free phone:* 800-841-0201. *Fax:* 304-485-3524. *E-mail:* jsutton@msc.edu.

MOUNTWEST COMMUNITY & TECHNICAL COLLEGE

Huntington, West Virginia **www.mctc.edu/**

- **County-supported** 2-year, part of Community and Technical College System of West Virginia
- **Urban** 70-acre campus
- **Endowment** $27,466
- **Coed**

Undergraduates 1,400 full-time, 1,134 part-time. Students come from 26 states and territories, 5 other countries, 16% are from out of state, 7% African American, 0.6% Asian American or Pacific Islander, 0.9% Hispanic American, 0.4% Native American, 0.2% international, 9% transferred in. *Retention:* 43% of 2008 full-time freshmen returned.
Faculty *Student/faculty ratio:* 21:1.
Academics *Calendar:* semesters. *Degree:* certificates and associate. *Special study options:* academic remediation for entering students, accelerated degree program, cooperative education, distance learning, double majors, English as a second language, independent study, internships, off-campus study, part-time degree program, services for LD students, summer session for credit. *ROTC:* Army (b).
Student Life *Campus security:* 24-hour emergency response devices and patrols, controlled dormitory access.
Costs (2009–10) *Tuition:* state resident $2856 full-time, $119 per credit hour part-time; nonresident $8160 full-time, $340 per credit hour part-time. Full-time tuition and fees vary according to reciprocity agreements. Part-time tuition and fees vary according to reciprocity agreements. *Room and board:* $7556; room only: $4474. Room and board charges vary according to board plan and housing facility.
Applying *Options:* electronic application, deferred entrance. *Application fee:* $30. *Required:* high school transcript, minimum 2 GPA.
Freshman Application Contact Dr. Tammy Johnson, Admissions Director, Mountwest Community & Technical College, 1 John Marshall Drive, Huntington, WV 25755. *Phone:* 304-696-3160. *Toll-free phone:* 800-642-3499. *Fax:* 304-696-3135. *E-mail:* admissions@marshall.edu.

►**See page 466 for the College Close-Up.**

NEW RIVER COMMUNITY AND TECHNICAL COLLEGE

Beckley, West Virginia **www.newriver.edu/**

- **County-supported** 2-year, founded 2003
- **Coed**

Academics *Degree:* certificates and associate.
Director of Admissions Mr. Michael Palm, Director of Student Services, New River Community and Technical College, 101 Church Street, Lewisburg, WV 24901. *Phone:* 304-647-6564.

PIERPONT COMMUNITY & TECHNICAL COLLEGE OF FAIRMONT STATE UNIVERSITY

Fairmont, West Virginia **www.fairmontstate.edu/**

Freshman Application Contact Mr. Steve Leadman, Director of Admissions and Recruiting, Pierpont Community & Technical College of Fairmont State University, 1201 Locust Avenue, Fairmont, WV 26554. *Phone:* 304-367-4892. *Toll-free phone:* 800-641-5678. *Fax:* 304-367-4789.

POTOMAC STATE COLLEGE OF WEST VIRGINIA UNIVERSITY

Keyser, West Virginia **www.potomacstatecollege.edu/**

- **State-supported** primarily 2-year, founded 1901, part of West Virginia Higher Education Policy Commission
- **Small-town** 18-acre campus
- **Coed,** 1,810 undergraduate students, 74% full-time, 53% women, 47% men

Undergraduates 1,344 full-time, 466 part-time. Students come from 19 states and territories, 2 other countries, 29% are from out of state, 13% African American, 0.7% Asian American or Pacific Islander, 3% Hispanic American, 0.2% Native American, 0.1% international, 3% transferred in. *Retention:* 50% of 2008 full-time freshmen returned.
Freshmen *Admission:* 1,006 admitted, 723 enrolled. *Average high school GPA:* 2.78. *Test scores:* SAT verbal scores over 500: 16%; SAT math scores over 500: 17%; ACT scores over 18: 60%; SAT verbal scores over 600: 3%; SAT math scores over 600: 5%; ACT scores over 24: 10%; ACT scores over 30: 1%.
Faculty *Total:* 87, 47% full-time, 18% with terminal degrees. *Student/faculty ratio:* 27:1.
Majors Accounting; administrative assistant and secretarial science; agricultural business and management; agricultural economics; agricultural mechanization; agricultural teacher education; agriculture; agriculture and agriculture operations related; agronomy and crop science; animal sciences; biological and physical sciences; biology/biological sciences; business administration and management; business/managerial economics; chemistry; civil engineering technology; computer and information sciences related; computer engineering technology; computer programming; computer programming (specific applications); computer science; computer systems networking and telecommunications; criminal justice/safety; data processing and data processing technology; economics; education; electrical, electronic and communications engineering technology; elementary education; engineering; English; forestry; forestry technology; geology/earth science; history; horticultural science; hospitality administration; information technology; journalism; kindergarten/preschool education; liberal arts and sciences/liberal studies; mathematics; mechanical engineering/mechanical technology; medical administrative assistant and medical secretary; parks, recreation and leisure facilities management; physical education teaching and coaching; political science and government; pre-engineering; psychology; social work; sociology; system administration; wildlife and wildlands science and management; wood science and wood products/pulp and paper technology.
Academics *Calendar:* semesters. *Degrees:* certificates, associate, and bachelor's. *Special study options:* academic remediation for entering students, adult/continuing education programs, advanced placement credit, distance learning, double majors, honors programs, independent study, internships, part-time degree program, services for LD students, study abroad, summer session for credit.
Library Mary F. Shipper Library with 44,197 titles, 304 serial subscriptions, 23,395 audiovisual materials, an OPAC, a Web page.
Student Life *Housing:* on-campus residence required through sophomore year. *Options:* coed. Campus housing is university owned. Freshman applicants given priority for college housing. *Activities and Organizations:* drama/theater group, student-run newspaper, choral group, Circle K, Agriculture and Forestry Club, Business Club, Community Chorus. *Campus security:* 24-hour patrols, late-night transport/escort service, controlled dormitory access. *Student services:* health clinic, personal/psychological counseling.
Athletics Member NJCAA. *Intercollegiate sports:* baseball M(s), basketball M(s)/W(s), golf M(s)/W(s), soccer M/W, softball W(s), volleyball W(s). *Intramural sports:* basketball M/W, football M/W, volleyball M/W.
Standardized Tests *Required for some:* SAT or ACT (for admission).
Financial Aid Of all full-time matriculated undergraduates who enrolled in 2008, 70 Federal Work-Study jobs (averaging $1300).
Applying *Options:* electronic application, early admission. *Required:* high school transcript. *Application deadlines:* rolling (freshmen), rolling (transfers).
Freshman Application Contact Ms. Beth Little, Director of Enrollment Services, Potomac State College of West Virginia University, One Grand Central Business Center, Suite 2090, Keyser, WV 26726. *Phone:* 304-788-6820. *Toll-free phone:* 800-262-7332 Ext. 6820. *Fax:* 304-788-6939. *E-mail:* go2psc@mail.wvu.edu.

SOUTHERN WEST VIRGINIA COMMUNITY AND TECHNICAL COLLEGE

Mount Gay, West Virginia **southernwv.edu/**

Freshman Application Contact Mr. Roy Simmons, Registrar, Southern West Virginia Community and Technical College, PO Box 2900, Mt. Gay, WV 25637. *Phone:* 304-792-7160 Ext. 120. *Fax:* 304-792-7096. *E-mail:* admissions@southern.wvnet.edu.

Valley College of Technology

Martinsburg, West Virginia www.vct.edu/

Freshman Application Contact Ms. Gail Kennedy, Admissions Director, Valley College of Technology, 287 Aikens Center, Martinsburg, WV 25404. *Phone:* 304-263-0878. *Fax:* 304-263-2413. *E-mail:* gkennedy@vct.edu.

West Virginia Business College

Nutter Fort, West Virginia www.wvbc.edu/

Director of Admissions Robert Wright, Campus Director, West Virginia Business College, 116 Pennsylvania Avenue, Nutter Fort, WV 26301. *Phone:* 304-624-7695. *E-mail:* info@wvbc.edu.

West Virginia Business College

Wheeling, West Virginia www.wvbc.edu/

Freshman Application Contact Ms. Karen D. Shaw, Director, West Virginia Business College, 1052 Main Street, Wheeling, WV 26003. *Phone:* 304-232-0361. *Fax:* 304-232-0363. *E-mail:* wvbcwheeling@stratuswave.net.

West Virginia Junior College

Bridgeport, West Virginia www.wvjc.com/

Freshman Application Contact Admissions Office, West Virginia Junior College, 176 Thompson Drive, Bridgeport, WV 26330. *Phone:* 304-842-4007. *Toll-free phone:* 800-470-5627. *E-mail:* admissions@wvjcinfo.net.

West Virginia Junior College

Charleston, West Virginia www.wvjc.com/

Freshman Application Contact West Virginia Junior College, 1000 Virginia Street East, Charleston, WV 25301-2817. *Phone:* 304-345-2820. *Toll-free phone:* 800-924-5208.

West Virginia Junior College

Morgantown, West Virginia www.wvjc.com/

Freshman Application Contact Admissions Office, West Virginia Junior College, 148 Willey Street, Morgantown, WV 26505-5521. *Phone:* 304-296-8282.

West Virginia Northern Community College

Wheeling, West Virginia www.wvncc.edu/

- **State-supported** 2-year, founded 1972
- **Small-town** campus with easy access to Pittsburgh
- **Endowment** $700,706
- **Coed,** 3,150 undergraduate students, 50% full-time, 67% women, 33% men

Undergraduates 1,590 full-time, 1,560 part-time. Students come from 7 states and territories, 21% are from out of state, 3% African American, 0.4% Asian American or Pacific Islander, 0.6% Hispanic American, 0.4% Native American, 12% transferred in. *Retention:* 57% of 2008 full-time freshmen returned.

Freshmen *Admission:* 1,019 applied, 544 admitted, 540 enrolled. *Average high school GPA:* 2.6. *Test scores:* SAT verbal scores over 500: 28%; SAT math scores over 500: 11%; ACT scores over 18: 60%; SAT verbal scores over 600: 6%; SAT math scores over 600: 6%; ACT scores over 24: 7%.

Faculty *Total:* 223, 28% full-time, 22% with terminal degrees. *Student/faculty ratio:* 14:1.

Majors Accounting technology and bookkeeping; administrative assistant and secretarial science; computer programming; criminal justice/police science; health information/medical records technology; heating, air conditioning, ventilation and refrigeration maintenance technology; hospitality administration; liberal arts and sciences/liberal studies; nursing (registered nurse training); social work.

Academics *Calendar:* semesters. *Degree:* certificates and associate. *Special study options:* academic remediation for entering students, accelerated degree program, adult/continuing education programs, advanced placement credit, distance learning, double majors, honors programs, internships, part-time degree program, student-designed majors, summer session for credit.

Library Wheeling B and O Campus Library plus 2 others with 36,650 titles, 188 serial subscriptions, 3,495 audiovisual materials, an OPAC, a Web page.

Student Life *Housing:* college housing not available. *Activities and Organizations:* student-run newspaper. *Campus security:* security personnel during evening and night classes. *Student services:* personal/psychological counseling.

Athletics *Intramural sports:* basketball M/W, bowling M/W, softball M/W, volleyball M/W.

Standardized Tests *Recommended:* SAT or ACT (for admission).

Costs (2009–10) *Tuition:* state resident $1968 full-time, $82 per credit hour part-time; nonresident $6870 full-time, $270 per credit hour part-time. Full-time tuition and fees vary according to course load and program. Part-time tuition and fees vary according to course load and program. *Required fees:* $390 full-time, $15 per credit hour part-time, $15 per term part-time. *Payment plan:* installment. *Waivers:* adult students, senior citizens, and employees or children of employees.

Applying *Options:* electronic application, early admission, deferred entrance. *Required for some:* high school transcript. *Application deadlines:* rolling (freshmen), rolling (transfers).

Freshman Application Contact Mr. Richard McCray, Assistant Director of Admissions, West Virginia Northern Community College, 1704 Market Street, Wheeling, WV 26003-3699. *Phone:* 304-214-8838. *E-mail:* rmccray@northern.wvnet.edu.

West Virginia University at Parkersburg

Parkersburg, West Virginia www.wvup.edu/

Freshman Application Contact Ms. Violet Mosser, Senior Admissions Counselor, West Virginia University at Parkersburg, 300 Campus Drive, Parkersburg, WV 26101. *Phone:* 304-424-8223 Ext. 223. *Toll-free phone:* 800-WVA-WVUP. *Fax:* 304-424-8332. *E-mail:* violet.mosser@mail.wvu.edu.

WISCONSIN

Blackhawk Technical College

Janesville, Wisconsin www.blackhawk.edu/

- **District-supported** 2-year, founded 1968, part of Wisconsin Technical College System
- **Rural** 84-acre campus
- **Coed**

Academics *Calendar:* semesters. *Degree:* associate. *Special study options:* academic remediation for entering students, accelerated degree program, adult/continuing education programs, advanced placement credit, cooperative education, distance learning, English as a second language, external degree program, independent study, internships, part-time degree program, services for LD students, student-designed majors, summer session for credit.

Financial Aid Of all full-time matriculated undergraduates who enrolled in 2008, 33 Federal Work-Study jobs (averaging $1150).

Applying *Options:* electronic application. *Application fee:* $30. *Required:* high school transcript.

Director of Admissions Ms. Barbara Erlandson, Student Services Manager, Blackhawk Technical College, PO Box 5009, Janesville, WI 53547-5009. *Phone:* 608-757-7713. *Toll-free phone:* 800-472-0024.

BRYANT & STRATTON COLLEGE

Milwaukee, Wisconsin **www.bryantstratton.edu/**

- **Proprietary** primarily 2-year, founded 1863, part of Bryant and Stratton College, Inc.
- **Urban** campus
- **Coed,** 828 undergraduate students, 56% full-time, 84% women, 16% men

Undergraduates 460 full-time, 368 part-time. Students come from 1 other state, 91% African American, 1% Asian American or Pacific Islander, 4% Hispanic American, 33% transferred in. *Retention:* 70% of 2008 full-time freshmen returned.

Freshmen *Admission:* 433 applied, 387 admitted, 385 enrolled.

Faculty *Total:* 102, 19% full-time. *Student/faculty ratio:* 13:1.

Majors Accounting; administrative assistant and secretarial science; business/commerce; commercial and advertising art; computer and information systems security; criminal justice/law enforcement administration; design and visual communications; financial planning and services; human resources management and services related; legal assistant/paralegal; medical/clinical assistant; system, networking, and LAN/WAN management.

Academics *Calendar:* semesters. *Degrees:* associate and bachelor's. *Special study options:* academic remediation for entering students, adult/continuing education programs, advanced placement credit, cooperative education, distance learning, double majors, independent study, internships, part-time degree program, summer session for credit.

Library Bryant and Stratton College Library with 120 serial subscriptions, 100 audiovisual materials.

Student Life *Housing:* college housing not available. *Activities and Organizations:* student-run newspaper, Phi Beta Lambda, Association of Information Technology Professionals, Allied Health Association, Institute of Management Accountants, Student Advisory Board. *Campus security:* 24-hour emergency response devices and patrols.

Standardized Tests *Required:* CPAt; Accuplacer (for admission). *Recommended:* SAT or ACT (for admission).

Applying *Options:* electronic application. *Required:* high school transcript, interview, entrance and placement evaluations. *Application deadlines:* rolling (freshmen), rolling (transfers). *Notification:* continuous (freshmen), continuous (transfers).

Freshman Application Contact Ms. Kristin Weiss, Director of Admissions, Bryant & Stratton College, 310 West Wisconsin Avenue, Milwaukee, WI 53203-2214. *Phone:* 414-276-5200.

CHIPPEWA VALLEY TECHNICAL COLLEGE

Eau Claire, Wisconsin **www.cvtc.edu/**

Director of Admissions Mr. Timothy Shepardson, Director of Admissions, Chippewa Valley Technical College, 620 West Clairemont Avenue, Eau Claire, WI 54701-6162. *Phone:* 715-833-6245. *Toll-free phone:* 800-547-2882.

COLLEGE OF MENOMINEE NATION

Keshena, Wisconsin **www.menominee.edu/**

Director of Admissions Ms. Cynthia Norton, Admissions Representative, College of Menominee Nation, PO Box 1179, Keshena, WI 54135. *Phone:* 715-799-5600 Ext. 3053. *Toll-free phone:* 800-567-2344.

FOX VALLEY TECHNICAL COLLEGE

Appleton, Wisconsin **www.fvtc.edu/**

- **State and locally supported** 2-year, founded 1967, part of Wisconsin Technical College System
- **Suburban** 100-acre campus
- **Endowment** $1.4 million
- **Coed,** 10,244 undergraduate students, 30% full-time, 49% women, 51% men

Undergraduates 3,080 full-time, 7,164 part-time. Students come from 13 states and territories, 16 other countries, 0.9% are from out of state, 1% African American, 3% Asian American or Pacific Islander, 3% Hispanic American, 1% Native American, 0.3% international.

Freshmen *Admission:* 1,067 enrolled.

Faculty *Total:* 867, 34% full-time. *Student/faculty ratio:* 13:1.

Majors Accounting; administrative assistant and secretarial science; agricultural business and management; airline pilot and flight crew; automobile/automotive mechanics technology; business administration and management; child development; commercial and advertising art; computer programming; computer typography and composition equipment operation; consumer merchandising/retailing management; criminal justice/law enforcement administration; criminal justice/police science; culinary arts; drafting and design technology; drafting/design engineering technologies related; electrical, electronic and communications engineering technology; finance; fire science; fishing and fisheries sciences and management; forestry technology; graphic and printing equipment operation/production; hospitality administration; industrial technology; insurance; interior design; legal administrative assistant/secretary; marketing/marketing management; mechanical engineering/mechanical technology; natural resources/conservation; nursing (registered nurse training); occupational therapy; special products marketing; welding technology; wood science and wood products/pulp and paper technology.

Academics *Calendar:* semesters. *Degree:* certificates, diplomas, and associate. *Special study options:* academic remediation for entering students, accelerated degree program, advanced placement credit, cooperative education, distance learning, double majors, English as a second language, independent study, internships, off-campus study, part-time degree program, services for LD students, student-designed majors, summer session for credit.

Library William M. Sirek Educational Resource Center plus 1 other with 43,307 titles, 185 serial subscriptions, 7,836 audiovisual materials, an OPAC, a Web page.

Student Life *Housing:* college housing not available. *Activities and Organizations:* student-run newspaper, Student Government Association, Phi Theta Kappa, Culinary Arts, Student Nurses, Post Secondary Agribusiness. *Campus security:* late-night transport/escort service, 16-hour patrols by trained security personnel. *Student services:* health clinic, personal/psychological counseling.

Athletics *Intercollegiate sports:* basketball M/W, volleyball M/W. *Intramural sports:* archery M/W, basketball M/W, football M/W, soccer M/W, softball M/W, table tennis M/W, volleyball M/W, weight lifting M/W.

Costs (2010–11) *Tuition:* state resident $3042 full-time; nonresident $4563 full-time. *Payment plan:* installment.

Financial Aid Of all full-time matriculated undergraduates who enrolled in 2008, 86 Federal Work-Study jobs (averaging $3200).

Applying *Options:* electronic application, early admission, deferred entrance. *Application fee:* $30. *Required:* high school transcript. *Application deadlines:* rolling (freshmen), rolling (transfers).

Freshman Application Contact Admissions Center, Fox Valley Technical College, 1825 North Bluemound Drive, PO Box 2277, Appleton, WI 54912-2277. *Phone:* 920-735-5643. *Toll-free phone:* 800-735-3882. *Fax:* 920-735-2582.

GATEWAY TECHNICAL COLLEGE

Kenosha, Wisconsin **www.gtc.edu/**

Freshman Application Contact Ms. Susan Roberts, Director, Admissions and Testing, Gateway Technical College, 3520 30th Avenue, Kenosha, WI 53144-1690. *Phone:* 262-564-3224. *Toll-free phone:* 800-247-7122. *Fax:* 262-564-2301. *E-mail:* admissions@gtc.edu.

ITT TECHNICAL INSTITUTE

Green Bay, Wisconsin **www.itt-tech.edu/**

- **Proprietary** primarily 2-year, founded 2000, part of ITT Educational Services, Inc.
- **Coed**

Majors Animation, interactive technology, video graphics and special effects; business administration and management; CAD/CADD drafting/design technology; computer and information systems security; computer engineering technology; computer software and media applications related; computer software engineering; computer software technology; construction management; criminal justice/law enforcement administration; design and visual communications; electrical, electronic and communications engineering technology; legal assistant/paralegal; system, networking, and LAN/WAN management; web page, digital/multimedia and information resources design.

Academics *Calendar:* quarters. *Degrees:* associate and bachelor's.

Student Life *Housing:* college housing not available.
Freshman Application Contact Director of Recruitment, ITT Technical Institute, 470 Security Boulevard, Green Bay, WI 54313. *Phone:* 920-662-9000. *Toll-free phone:* 888-884-3626. *Fax:* 920-662-9384.

ITT Technical Institute

Greenfield, Wisconsin **www.itt-tech.edu/**

- **Proprietary** primarily 2-year, founded 1968, part of ITT Educational Services, Inc.
- **Suburban** campus
- **Coed**

Majors Animation, interactive technology, video graphics and special effects; business administration and management; CAD/CADD drafting/design technology; computer and information systems security; computer engineering technology; computer software and media applications related; computer software engineering; computer software technology; construction management; criminal justice/law enforcement administration; design and visual communications; electrical, electronic and communications engineering technology; legal assistant/paralegal; system, networking, and LAN/WAN management; web page, digital/multimedia and information resources design.
Academics *Calendar:* quarters. *Degrees:* associate and bachelor's.
Student Life *Housing:* college housing not available.
Freshman Application Contact Director of Recruitment, ITT Technical Institute, 6300 West Layton Avenue, Greenfield, WI 53220-4612. *Phone:* 414-282-9494.

ITT Technical Institute

Madison, Wisconsin **www.itt-tech.edu/**

- **Proprietary** primarily 2-year, part of ITT Educational Services, Inc.
- **Coed**

Majors CAD/CADD drafting/design technology; computer and information systems security; computer engineering technology; computer software engineering; computer software technology; construction management; criminal justice/law enforcement administration; electrical, electronic and communications engineering technology; legal assistant/paralegal; system, networking, and LAN/WAN management.
Academics *Degrees:* associate and bachelor's.
Freshman Application Contact Director of Recruitment, ITT Technical Institute, 2450 Rimrock Road, Suite 100, Madison, WI 53713. *Phone:* 608-288-6301. *Toll-free phone:* 877-628-5960.

Lac Courte Oreilles Ojibwa Community College

Hayward, Wisconsin **www.lco.edu/**

- **Federally supported** 2-year, founded 1982
- **Rural** 2-acre campus
- **Endowment** $2.3 million
- **Coed,** 561 undergraduate students, 61% full-time, 68% women, 32% men

Undergraduates 341 full-time, 220 part-time. 0.4% African American, 0.7% Hispanic American, 75% Native American, 6% transferred in.
Freshmen *Admission:* 135 applied, 135 admitted, 135 enrolled.
Faculty *Total:* 70, 21% full-time, 1% with terminal degrees. *Student/faculty ratio:* 15:1.
Majors Accounting; administrative assistant and secretarial science; agriculture; American Indian/Native American studies; biological and biomedical sciences related; business administration and management; carpentry; computer systems analysis; early childhood education; hospitality and recreation marketing; liberal arts and sciences/liberal studies; medical/clinical assistant; medical office management; medical transcription; natural resources management and policy; nursing (registered nurse training); sales, distribution and marketing; social work; solar energy technology; substance abuse/addiction counseling.
Academics *Calendar:* semesters. *Degree:* certificates and associate. *Special study options:* academic remediation for entering students, adult/continuing education programs, distance learning, double majors, external degree program, honors programs, independent study, internships, part-time degree program, services for LD students.
Library Lac Courte Oreilles Ojibwa Community College Library with 25,267 titles, 82 serial subscriptions, 4,193 audiovisual materials, an OPAC, a Web page.
Student Life *Housing:* college housing not available. *Activities and Organizations:* drama/theater group, Student Association, AISES, Drama Club, Student Ambassadors. *Campus security:* 24-hour emergency response devices.
Athletics *Intramural sports:* basketball M, softball W, volleyball M/W, weight lifting M/W.
Standardized Tests *Required:* ACT COMPASS (for admission).
Costs (2010–11) *One-time required fee:* $10. *Tuition:* state resident $3360 full-time, $140 per credit part-time; nonresident $3360 full-time, $140 per credit part-time. Full-time tuition and fees vary according to class time, course level, course load, degree level, location, program, reciprocity agreements, and student level. Part-time tuition and fees vary according to class time, course level, course load, degree level, location, program, reciprocity agreements, and student level. *Required fees:* $30 full-time, $140 per credit part-time, $140 per credit part-time. *Payment plan:* installment. *Waivers:* senior citizens and employees or children of employees.
Financial Aid Of all full-time matriculated undergraduates who enrolled in 2008, 15 Federal Work-Study jobs (averaging $1400).
Applying *Options:* early admission. *Application fee:* $10. *Required:* high school transcript. *Application deadlines:* rolling (freshmen), rolling (transfers).
Freshman Application Contact Ms. Annette Wiggins, Registrar, Lac Courte Oreilles Ojibwa Community College, 13466 West Trepania Road, Hayward, WI 54843-2181. *Phone:* 715-634-4790 Ext. 104. *Toll-free phone:* 888-526-6221.

Lakeshore Technical College

Cleveland, Wisconsin **www.gotoltc.com/**

Freshman Application Contact Lakeshore Technical College, 1290 North Avenue, Cleveland, WI 53015. *Phone:* 920-693-1339. *Toll-free phone:* 888-GO TO LTC. *Fax:* 920-693-3561.

Madison Area Technical College

Madison, Wisconsin **www.matcmadison.edu/matc/**

Director of Admissions Ms. Maureen Menendez, Interim Admissions Administrator, Madison Area Technical College, 3550 Anderson Street, Madison, WI 53704-2599. *Phone:* 608-246-6212. *Toll-free phone:* 800-322-6282.

Madison Media Institute

Madison, Wisconsin **www.madisonmedia.edu/**

Freshman Application Contact Mr. Chris K. Hutchings, President/Director, Madison Media Institute, 2702 Agriculture Drive, Madison, WI 53718. *Phone:* 608-237-8301. *Toll-free phone:* 800-236-4997.

Mid-State Technical College

Wisconsin Rapids, Wisconsin **www.mstc.edu/**

Freshman Application Contact Ms. Carole Prochnow, Admissions Assistant, Mid-State Technical College, 500 32nd Street North, Wisconsin Rapids, WI 54494-5599. *Phone:* 715-422-5444. *Toll-free phone:* 888-575-6782.

Milwaukee Area Technical College

Milwaukee, Wisconsin **www.matc.edu/**

- **District-supported** 2-year, founded 1912, part of Wisconsin Technical College System
- **Urban** campus
- **Coed,** 20,215 undergraduate students, 35% full-time, 55% women, 45% men

Undergraduates 7,048 full-time, 13,167 part-time. Students come from 16 states and territories, 50 other countries, 1% are from out of state, 16% transferred in. *Retention:* 47% of 2008 full-time freshmen returned.

Milwaukee Area Technical College (continued)

Freshmen *Admission:* 13,086 applied, 6,712 admitted, 2,232 enrolled.

Faculty *Total:* 1,351, 43% full-time, 7% with terminal degrees. *Student/faculty ratio:* 14:1.

Majors Accounting; administrative assistant and secretarial science; allied health and medical assisting services related; allied health diagnostic, intervention, and treatment professions related; anesthesiologist assistant; apparel and accessories marketing; architectural engineering technology; automobile/automotive mechanics technology; banking and financial support services; biomedical technology; business administration and management; business administration, management and operations related; business, management, and marketing related; cardiovascular technology; chemical technology; civil engineering technology; clinical/medical laboratory technology; commercial and advertising art; commercial photography; computer and information systems security; computer graphics; computer/information technology services administration related; computer programming (specific applications); computer programming (vendor/product certification); computer systems analysis; computer systems networking and telecommunications; computer technology/computer systems technology; criminal justice/police science; culinary arts; dental hygiene; dietetic technician; early childhood education; e-commerce; education; electrical, electronic and communications engineering technology; engineering related; engineering technologies related; fire science; funeral service and mortuary science; graphic communications; graphic communications related; graphic design; health and medical administrative services related; health professions related; heating, air conditioning and refrigeration technology; hotel/motel administration; industrial technology; interdisciplinary studies; interior design; landscaping and groundskeeping; legal administrative assistant/secretary; legal assistant/paralegal; liberal arts and sciences/liberal studies; logistics and materials management; machine tool technology; manufacturing technology; marketing/marketing management; materials engineering; mechanical drafting and CAD/CADD; mechanical engineering/mechanical technology; medical administrative assistant and medical secretary; medical radiologic technology; mental and social health services and allied professions related; music; nursing (licensed practical/vocational nurse training); nursing (registered nurse training); occupational therapy; operations management; opticianry; physical therapy; plastics engineering technology; radio and television broadcasting technology; real estate; respiratory care therapy; restaurant, culinary, and catering management; sign language interpretation and translation; surgical technology; tourism and travel services marketing; water quality and wastewater treatment management and recycling technology; welding technology.

Academics *Calendar:* semesters. *Degree:* certificates, diplomas, and associate. *Special study options:* academic remediation for entering students, accelerated degree program, adult/continuing education programs, advanced placement credit, cooperative education, distance learning, double majors, English as a second language, external degree program, freshman honors college, honors programs, independent study, internships, off-campus study, part-time degree program, services for LD students, student-designed majors, study abroad, summer session for credit.

Library William F. Rasche Library plus 4 others with 90,000 titles, 17,000 serial subscriptions, 3,500 audiovisual materials, an OPAC, a Web page.

Student Life *Housing:* college housing not available. *Activities and Organizations:* student-run newspaper, television station, choral group, Student Senate, MATC Times, Ethnic Organizations - Latino Students, Black Student Union, Native American, and Asian Student groups, Black Engineers Organization, Future Hospitality Managers of America. *Campus security:* 24-hour emergency response devices and patrols, student patrols, late-night transport/escort service. *Student services:* personal/psychological counseling, women's center, legal services.

Athletics Member NJCAA. *Intercollegiate sports:* baseball M, basketball M/W, golf M/W, soccer M, volleyball W. *Intramural sports:* badminton M/W, baseball M, basketball M, bowling M/W, soccer M/W, table tennis M/W, tennis M/W, volleyball M/W.

Standardized Tests *Required:* ACCUPLACER (for admission).

Costs (2010–11) *Tuition:* state resident $3042 full-time, $113 per credit hour part-time; nonresident $7292 full-time, $164 per credit hour part-time. Full-time tuition and fees vary according to course level and degree level. Part-time tuition and fees vary according to course level and degree level. *Required fees:* $395 full-time. *Payment plans:* installment, deferred payment. *Waivers:* minority students and senior citizens.

Financial Aid Of all full-time matriculated undergraduates who enrolled in 2008, 300 Federal Work-Study jobs (averaging $3900).

Applying *Options:* electronic application. *Application fee:* $30. *Required:* high school transcript. *Application deadlines:* rolling (freshmen), rolling (transfers). *Notification:* continuous until 8/20 (freshmen), continuous until 8/20 (transfers).

Freshman Application Contact Sarah Adams, Director, Enrollment Services, Milwaukee Area Technical College, 700 West State Street, Milwaukee, WI 53233. *Phone:* 414-297-6595. *Fax:* 414-297-7800. *E-mail:* adamss4@matc.edu.

Moraine Park Technical College

Fond du Lac, Wisconsin **www.morainepark.edu/**

- **District-supported** 2-year, founded 1967, part of Wisconsin Technical College System
- **Small-town** 40-acre campus with easy access to Milwaukee
- **Coed,** 8,466 undergraduate students, 20% full-time, 57% women, 43% men

Undergraduates 1,691 full-time, 6,775 part-time. 1% African American, 0.9% Asian American or Pacific Islander, 3% Hispanic American, 0.7% Native American.

Freshmen *Admission:* 479 enrolled.

Faculty *Total:* 405, 38% full-time. *Student/faculty ratio:* 14:1.

Majors Accounting; accounting technology and bookkeeping; administrative assistant and secretarial science; automobile/automotive mechanics technology; automotive engineering technology; building/construction finishing, management, and inspection related; business administration and management; childcare provision; chiropractic assistant; clinical/medical laboratory technology; computer and information sciences and support services related; computer programming related; computer systems networking and telecommunications; corrections; court reporting; early childhood education; electrician; emergency medical technology (EMT paramedic); food preparation; graphic communications; graphic design; hair styling and hair design; health information/medical records technology; heating, air conditioning and refrigeration technology; heating, air conditioning, ventilation and refrigeration maintenance technology; hotel/motel administration; industrial mechanics and maintenance technology; industrial production technologies related; industrial technology; legal administrative assistant/secretary; legal assistant/paralegal; lineworker; machine shop technology; marketing/marketing management; mechanical drafting and CAD/CADD; mechanical engineering technologies related; medical/clinical assistant; medical office assistant; medical radiologic technology; medical transcription; merchandising, sales, and marketing operations related (general); multi/interdisciplinary studies related; nursing assistant/aide and patient care assistant; nursing (licensed practical/vocational nurse training); nursing (registered nurse training); nursing related; office occupations and clerical services; operations management; pharmacy technician; respiratory care therapy; restaurant, culinary, and catering management; structural engineering; substance abuse/addiction counseling; surgical technology; teacher assistant/aide; veterinary/animal health technology; water quality and wastewater treatment management and recycling technology; web page, digital/multimedia and information resources design; welding technology.

Academics *Calendar:* semesters. *Degree:* certificates, diplomas, and associate. *Special study options:* academic remediation for entering students, accelerated degree program, adult/continuing education programs, advanced placement credit, distance learning, English as a second language, external degree program, independent study, internships, part-time degree program, services for LD students, summer session for credit.

Library Moraine Park Technical College Library/Learning Resource Center with 41,737 titles, 280 serial subscriptions, 11,438 audiovisual materials, an OPAC, a Web page.

Student Life *Housing:* college housing not available. *Campus security:* 24-hour emergency response devices. *Student services:* personal/psychological counseling.

Standardized Tests *Required:* ACT, ACCUPLACER OR COMPASS (for admission). *Required for some:* ACT (for admission).

Applying *Options:* electronic application, deferred entrance. *Application fee:* $30. *Required:* high school transcript, placement test. *Required for some:* interview. *Application deadlines:* rolling (freshmen), rolling (out-of-state freshmen), rolling (transfers). *Notification:* continuous (freshmen), continuous (out-of-state freshmen), continuous (transfers).

Freshman Application Contact Ms. Karen Jarvis, Student Services, Moraine Park Technical College, 235 North National Avenue, PO Box 1940, Fond du Lac, WI 54936-1940. *Phone:* 920-924-3200. *Toll-free phone:* 800-472-4554. *Fax:* 920-924-3421. *E-mail:* kjarvis@morainepark.edu.

Nicolet Area Technical College

Rhinelander, Wisconsin **www.nicoletcollege.edu/**

- **State and locally supported** 2-year, founded 1968, part of Wisconsin Technical College System
- **Rural** 280-acre campus
- **Coed,** 1,600 undergraduate students

Undergraduates Students come from 8 states and territories, 4 other countries, 1% are from out of state.

Faculty *Total:* 100. *Student/faculty ratio:* 16:1.

Majors Accounting; administrative assistant and secretarial science; automobile/automotive mechanics technology; business administration and management; child development; computer and information sciences; computer science; criminal justice/police science; culinary arts; data processing and data processing technology; hotel/motel administration; kindergarten/preschool education; liberal arts and sciences/liberal studies; machine tool technology; marketing/marketing management; medical administrative assistant and medical secretary; nursing (registered nurse training); physical therapist assistant; real estate; survey technology; welding technology.

Academics *Calendar:* semesters. *Degree:* certificates, diplomas, and associate. *Special study options:* academic remediation for entering students, adult/continuing education programs, advanced placement credit, cooperative education, distance learning, double majors, English as a second language, independent study, internships, part-time degree program, services for LD students, study abroad, summer session for credit.

Library Richard Brown Library with 38,369 titles, 598 serial subscriptions, an OPAC, a Web page.

Student Life *Housing:* college housing not available. *Activities and Organizations:* drama/theater group, student-run newspaper. *Campus security:* 24-hour emergency response devices, student patrols. *Student services:* personal/psychological counseling.

Athletics Member NJCAA. *Intercollegiate sports:* golf M/W. *Intramural sports:* skiing (cross-country) M/W, skiing (downhill) M/W, soccer M/W, volleyball M/W, weight lifting M/W.

Standardized Tests *Recommended:* ACT (for admission).

Applying *Options:* electronic application, early admission. *Application fee:* $30. *Required:* high school transcript, Accuplacer Testing or ACT. *Application deadlines:* rolling (freshmen), rolling (transfers). *Notification:* continuous (freshmen), continuous (transfers).

Freshman Application Contact Ms. Susan Kordula, Director of Admissions, Nicolet Area Technical College, Box 518, Rhinelander, WI 54501-0518. *Phone:* 715-365-4451. *Toll-free phone:* 800-544-3039 Ext. 4451. *E-mail:* inquire@nicoletcollege.edu.

NORTHCENTRAL TECHNICAL COLLEGE

Wausau, Wisconsin **www.ntc.edu/**

- **District-supported** 2-year, founded 1912, part of Wisconsin Technical College System
- **Rural** 96-acre campus
- **Coed**

Academics *Calendar:* semesters. *Degree:* certificates, diplomas, and associate. *Special study options:* academic remediation for entering students, adult/continuing education programs, advanced placement credit, distance learning, double majors, English as a second language, independent study, internships, part-time degree program, services for LD students, student-designed majors, summer session for credit.

Student Life *Campus security:* 24-hour emergency response devices, late-night transport/escort service.

Financial Aid Of all full-time matriculated undergraduates who enrolled in 2008, 366 Federal Work-Study jobs (averaging $2000).

Applying *Options:* electronic application, early admission, deferred entrance. *Application fee:* $30. *Required:* high school transcript. *Required for some:* interview.

Director of Admissions Ms. Carolyn Michalski, Team Leader, Student Services, Northcentral Technical College, 1000 West Campus Drive, Wausau, WI 54401-1899. *Phone:* 715-675-3331 Ext. 4285.

NORTHEAST WISCONSIN TECHNICAL COLLEGE

Green Bay, Wisconsin **www.nwtc.edu/**

- **State and locally supported** 2-year, founded 1913, part of Wisconsin Technical College System
- **Suburban** 192-acre campus
- **Coed**

Academics *Calendar:* semesters. *Degree:* certificates, diplomas, and associate. *Special study options:* academic remediation for entering students, accelerated degree program, adult/continuing education programs, advanced placement credit, distance learning, English as a second language, part-time degree program, services for LD students, student-designed majors, summer session for credit.

Student Life *Campus security:* 24-hour emergency response devices, late-night transport/escort service.

Financial Aid Of all full-time matriculated undergraduates who enrolled in 2008, 84 Federal Work-Study jobs (averaging $2542).

Applying *Options:* early admission. *Application fee:* $30. *Required for some:* high school transcript.

Freshman Application Contact Ms. Heather Hill, Director of Admission, Northeast Wisconsin Technical College, 2740 West Mason Street, PO Box 19042, Green Bay, WI 54307-9042. *Phone:* 920-498-5612. *Toll-free phone:* 800-498-5444 (in-state); 800-422-6982 (out-of-state). *Fax:* 920-498-6882. *E-mail:* heather.hill@nwtc.edu.

RASMUSSEN COLLEGE GREEN BAY

Green Bay, Wisconsin **www.rasmussen.edu/**

Admissions Office Contact Rasmussen College Green Bay, 940 South Taylor Street, Suite 100, Green Bay, WI 54303. *Toll-free phone:* 888-201-9144.

SOUTHWEST WISCONSIN TECHNICAL COLLEGE

Fennimore, Wisconsin **www.swtc.edu/**

- **State and locally supported** 2-year, founded 1967, part of Wisconsin Technical College System
- **Rural** 53-acre campus
- **Coed,** 3,409 undergraduate students, 25% full-time, 56% women, 44% men

Undergraduates 852 full-time, 2,557 part-time. Students come from 5 states and territories, 4% African American, 0.6% Asian American or Pacific Islander, 0.7% Hispanic American, 0.9% Native American, 1% transferred in, 3% live on campus. *Retention:* 71% of 2008 full-time freshmen returned.

Freshmen *Admission:* 500 applied, 500 admitted, 500 enrolled.

Faculty *Total:* 112, 84% full-time. *Student/faculty ratio:* 18:1.

Majors Accounting; administrative assistant and secretarial science; agricultural/farm supplies retailing and wholesaling; computer and information sciences and support services related; computer graphics; computer programming; computer systems networking and telecommunications; criminal justice/police science; direct entry midwifery; early childhood education; electromechanical technology; finance; marketing/marketing management; mechanical drafting and CAD/CADD; mental and social health services and allied professions related; multi/interdisciplinary studies related; nursing (registered nurse training); operations management; parks, recreation and leisure facilities management; restaurant, culinary, and catering management.

Academics *Calendar:* semesters. *Degree:* certificates, diplomas, and associate. *Special study options:* academic remediation for entering students, advanced placement credit, distance learning, double majors, English as a second language, independent study, internships, off campus study, part-time degree program, services for LD students, student-designed majors, summer session for credit.

Library Southwest Technical College Library with 28,000 titles, 400 serial subscriptions, 5,600 audiovisual materials, an OPAC, a Web page.

Student Life *Housing Options:* coed. Campus housing is provided by a third party. *Activities and Organizations:* Student Senate, Student Ambassadors, Phi Theta Kappa. *Campus security:* 24-hour emergency response devices. *Student services:* personal/psychological counseling.

Athletics Member NJCAA. *Intercollegiate sports:* golf M/W. *Intramural sports:* basketball M/W, volleyball M/W.

Standardized Tests *Required for some:* TABE and the HESI (nursing students only) for admissions decisions.

Costs (2010–11) *Tuition:* state resident $3042 full-time, $101 per credit part-time; nonresident $4563 full-time, $152 per credit part-time. Full-time tuition and fees vary according to course load, degree level, program, and reciprocity agreements. Part-time tuition and fees vary according to course load, degree level, program, and reciprocity agreements. *Required fees:* $278 full-time. *Room and board:* $6137; room only: $3000. Room and board charges vary according to housing facility. *Payment plans:* installment, deferred payment. *Waivers:* senior citizens.

Applying *Options:* electronic application, early admission. *Application fee:* $30. *Required:* high school transcript, interview. *Application deadlines:* rolling (freshmen), rolling (out-of-state freshmen), rolling (transfers). *Notification:* continuous (freshmen), continuous (out-of-state freshmen), continuous (transfers).

Freshman Application Contact Student Services, Southwest Wisconsin Technical College, 1800 Bronson Boulevard, Fennimore, WI 53813. *Phone:* 608-822-2354. *Toll-free phone:* 800-362-3322. *Fax:* 608-822-6019. *E-mail:* student-services@swtc.edu.

UNIVERSITY OF WISCONSIN–BARABOO/ SAUK COUNTY

Baraboo, Wisconsin www.baraboo.uwc.edu/

Freshman Application Contact Ms. Jan Gerlach, Assistant Director of Student Services, University of Wisconsin–Baraboo/Sauk County, 1006 Connie Road, Baraboo, WI 53913-1015. *Phone:* 608-355-5270. *E-mail:* booinfo@uwc.edu.

UNIVERSITY OF WISCONSIN–BARRON COUNTY

Rice Lake, Wisconsin www.barron.uwc.edu/

Freshman Application Contact Assistant Dean for Student Services, University of Wisconsin–Barron County, 1800 College Drive, Rice Lake, WI 54868. *Phone:* 715-234-8024. *Fax:* 715-234-8024.

UNIVERSITY OF WISCONSIN– FOND DU LAC

Fond du Lac, Wisconsin www.fdl.uwc.edu/

- **State-supported** 2-year, founded 1968, part of University of Wisconsin System
- **Small-town** 182-acre campus with easy access to Milwaukee
- **Coed,** 779 undergraduate students, 65% full-time, 52% women, 48% men

Undergraduates 506 full-time, 273 part-time. Students come from 3 states and territories, 1% are from out of state, 1% African American, 2% Asian American or Pacific Islander, 2% Hispanic American, 0.5% Native American, 4% transferred in. *Retention:* 58% of 2008 full-time freshmen returned.

Freshmen *Admission:* 381 applied, 325 admitted, 275 enrolled. *Average high school GPA:* 2.5. *Test scores:* ACT scores over 18: 93%; ACT scores over 24: 20%; ACT scores over 30: 1%.

Faculty *Total:* 37, 54% full-time, 78% with terminal degrees. *Student/faculty ratio:* 19:1.

Majors Liberal arts and sciences/liberal studies.

Academics *Calendar:* semesters. *Degree:* associate. *Special study options:* academic remediation for entering students, accelerated degree program, adult/continuing education programs, advanced placement credit, cooperative education, distance learning, independent study, off-campus study, part-time degree program, services for LD students, study abroad, summer session for credit.

Library 41,891 titles, 160 serial subscriptions.

Student Life *Housing:* college housing not available. *Activities and Organizations:* drama/theater group, student-run newspaper, choral group, student government, Campus Ambassadors, Multicultural Club, chorus, band. *Campus security:* 24-hour emergency response devices. *Student services:* personal/psychological counseling.

Athletics Member NJCAA. *Intercollegiate sports:* basketball M/W, golf M/W, soccer M/W, tennis M/W, volleyball W. *Intramural sports:* basketball M/W, bowling M/W, golf M/W, volleyball M/W.

Standardized Tests *Required:* SAT or ACT (for admission).

Costs (2009–10) *Tuition:* state resident $4268 full-time, $178 per credit part-time; nonresident $11,578 full-time, $482 per credit part-time. Full-time tuition and fees vary according to reciprocity agreements. Part-time tuition and fees vary according to reciprocity agreements. *Required fees:* $163 full-time, $14 per credit part-time. *Payment plan:* installment.

Financial Aid Of all full-time matriculated undergraduates who enrolled in 2008, 30 Federal Work-Study jobs (averaging $2100).

Applying *Options:* electronic application. *Application fee:* $35. *Required:* high school transcript. *Application deadlines:* rolling (freshmen), rolling (out-of-state freshmen), rolling (transfers).

Freshman Application Contact University of Wisconsin–Fond du Lac, 400 University Drive, Fond du Lac, WI 54935-2950. *Phone:* 920-929-1122.

UNIVERSITY OF WISCONSIN– FOX VALLEY

Menasha, Wisconsin www.uwfoxvalley.uwc.edu/

- **State-supported** 2-year, founded 1933, part of University of Wisconsin System
- **Urban** 33-acre campus
- **Coed,** 1,747 undergraduate students, 56% full-time, 51% women, 49% men

Undergraduates 987 full-time, 760 part-time. Students come from 3 states and territories, 4 other countries, 1% are from out of state, 0.6% African American, 4% Asian American or Pacific Islander, 2% Hispanic American, 0.6% Native American.

Freshmen *Admission:* 1,116 enrolled. *Average high school GPA:* 2.5.

Faculty *Total:* 84, 37% full-time.

Majors Liberal arts and sciences/liberal studies.

Academics *Calendar:* semesters. *Degree:* certificates and associate. *Special study options:* academic remediation for entering students, adult/continuing education programs, advanced placement credit, cooperative education, distance learning, honors programs, independent study, off-campus study, part-time degree program, services for LD students, study abroad, summer session for credit.

Library 29,000 titles, 230 serial subscriptions, an OPAC, a Web page.

Student Life *Housing:* college housing not available. *Activities and Organizations:* drama/theater group, student-run newspaper, radio and television station, choral group, Business Club, Education Club, Earth Science Club, Computer Science Club, Political Science Club. *Campus security:* late-night transport/escort service. *Student services:* personal/psychological counseling.

Athletics Member NJCAA. *Intercollegiate sports:* basketball M/W, golf M/W, soccer M/W, tennis M/W, volleyball M/W. *Intramural sports:* basketball M/W, volleyball M/W, wrestling M.

Standardized Tests *Required:* ACT (for admission).

Costs (2010–11) *Tuition:* state resident $4506 full-time; nonresident $11,500 full-time. Full-time tuition and fees vary according to course load and reciprocity agreements. Part-time tuition and fees vary according to course load and reciprocity agreements. *Payment plans:* installment, deferred payment. *Waivers:* minority students and senior citizens.

Financial Aid Of all full-time matriculated undergraduates who enrolled in 2008, 66 Federal Work-Study jobs (averaging $2100).

Applying *Options:* electronic application, early admission. *Application fee:* $35. *Required:* essay or personal statement, high school transcript. *Application deadlines:* rolling (freshmen), rolling (out-of-state freshmen), rolling (transfers). *Notification:* continuous (freshmen), continuous (transfers).

Freshman Application Contact University of Wisconsin–Fox Valley, 1478 Midway Road, Menasha, WI 54952. *Phone:* 920-832-2620. *Toll-free phone:* 888-INFOUWC.

UNIVERSITY OF WISCONSIN– MANITOWOC

Manitowoc, Wisconsin www.manitowoc.uwc.edu/

Freshman Application Contact Dr. Christopher Lewis, Assistant Campus Dean for Student Services, University of Wisconsin–Manitowoc, 705 Viebahn Street, Manitowoc, WI 54220-6699. *Phone:* 920-683-4707. *Fax:* 920-683-4776. *E-mail:* christopher.lewis@uwc.edu.

UNIVERSITY OF WISCONSIN– MARATHON COUNTY

Wausau, Wisconsin www.uwmc.uwc.edu/

Freshman Application Contact Dr. Nolan Beck, Director of Student Services, University of Wisconsin–Marathon County, 518 South Seventh Avenue, Wausau, WI 54401-5396. *Phone:* 715-261-6238. *Toll-free phone:* 888-367-8962. *Fax:* 715-848-3568.

University of Wisconsin–Marinette

Marinette, Wisconsin **www.uwc.edu/**

Freshman Application Contact Ms. Cynthia M. Bailey, Assistant Campus Dean for Student Services, University of Wisconsin–Marinette, 750 West Bay Shore, Marinette, WI 54143-4299. *Phone:* 715-735-4301. *E-mail:* cynthia.bailey@uwc.edu.

University of Wisconsin–Marshfield/Wood County

Marshfield, Wisconsin **marshfield.uwc.edu/**

Freshman Application Contact Mr. Jeff Meece, Director of Student Services, University of Wisconsin–Marshfield/Wood County, 2000 West Fifth Street, Marshfield, WI 54449. *Phone:* 715-389-6500. *Fax:* 715-384-1718.

University of Wisconsin–Richland

Richland Center, Wisconsin **richland.uwc.edu/**

- **State-supported** 2-year, founded 1967, part of University of Wisconsin System
- **Rural** 135-acre campus
- **Coed,** 495 undergraduate students, 67% full-time, 56% women, 44% men

Undergraduates 331 full-time, 164 part-time. 3% African American, 2% Asian American or Pacific Islander, 0.6% Hispanic American, 0.4% Native American, 4% international. *Retention:* 55% of 2008 full-time freshmen returned.

Freshmen *Admission:* 495 enrolled.

Faculty *Total:* 31, 48% full-time, 55% with terminal degrees. *Student/faculty ratio:* 17:1.

Majors Biological and physical sciences; liberal arts and sciences/liberal studies.

Academics *Calendar:* semesters. *Degree:* associate. *Special study options:* academic remediation for entering students, adult/continuing education programs, advanced placement credit, distance learning, external degree program, independent study, off-campus study, part-time degree program, services for LD students, study abroad, summer session for credit.

Library Miller Memorial Library with 40,000 titles, 200 serial subscriptions, an OPAC, a Web page.

Student Life *Housing Options:* coed. Campus housing is provided by a third party. *Activities and Organizations:* drama/theater group, Student Senate, International Club, Campus Ambassadors, Educators of the Future-Student WEA, Biology Club. *Student services:* personal/psychological counseling.

Athletics *Intercollegiate sports:* basketball M/W, volleyball W. *Intramural sports:* badminton M/W, basketball M/W, football M/W, golf M/W, racquetball M/W, swimming and diving M/W, table tennis M/W, tennis M/W, volleyball M/W.

Standardized Tests *Required:* SAT or ACT (for admission). *Recommended:* ACT (for admission).

Costs (2009–10) *Tuition:* state resident $4747 full-time, $198 per credit part-time; nonresident $11,731 full-time, $489 per credit part-time. Full-time tuition and fees vary according to reciprocity agreements. Part-time tuition and fees vary according to reciprocity agreements. *Room and board:* room only: $3200. Room and board charges vary according to board plan. *Payment plan:* installment. *Waivers:* senior citizens.

Applying *Options:* electronic application. *Application fee:* $44. *Required:* high school transcript. *Required for some:* interview. *Application deadline:* rolling (freshmen). *Notification:* continuous until 9/1 (freshmen), continuous until 9/1 (transfers).

Freshman Application Contact Mr. John D. Poole, Assistant Campus Dean, University of Wisconsin–Richland, 1200 Highway 14 West, Richland Center, WI 53581. *Phone:* 608-647-8422. *Fax:* 608-647-2275. *E-mail:* john.poole@uwc.edu.

University of Wisconsin–Rock County

Janesville, Wisconsin **rock.uwc.edu/**

Freshman Application Contact University of Wisconsin–Rock County, 2909 Kellogg Avenue, Janesville, WI 53456. *Phone:* 608-758-6523. *Toll-free phone:* 888-INFO-UWC.

University of Wisconsin–Sheboygan

Sheboygan, Wisconsin **www.sheboygan.uwc.edu/**

Director of Admissions Assistant Campus Dean for Student Services, University of Wisconsin–Sheboygan, One University Drive, Sheboygan, WI 53081-4789. *Phone:* 920-459-6633.

University of Wisconsin–Washington County

West Bend, Wisconsin **www.washington.uwc.edu/**

Freshman Application Contact Mr. Dan Cebrario, Associate Director of Student Services, University of Wisconsin–Washington County, Student Services Office, 400 University Drive, West Bend, WI 53095. *Phone:* 262-335-5201. *Fax:* 262-335-5220. *E-mail:* dan.cibrario@uwc.edu.

University of Wisconsin–Waukesha

Waukesha, Wisconsin **www.waukesha.uwc.edu/**

- **State-supported** 2-year, founded 1966, part of University of Wisconsin System
- **Suburban** 86-acre campus with easy access to Milwaukee
- **Coed,** 2,087 undergraduate students, 56% full-time, 47% women, 53% men

Undergraduates 1,161 full-time, 926 part-time. 1% are from out of state, 3% African American, 2% Asian American or Pacific Islander, 3% Hispanic American, 0.4% Native American, 0.2% international, 8% transferred in.

Freshmen *Admission:* 1,343 enrolled.

Faculty *Total:* 84, 68% full-time, 48% with terminal degrees. *Student/faculty ratio:* 25:1.

Majors Liberal arts and sciences/liberal studies.

Academics *Calendar:* semesters. *Degree:* associate. *Special study options:* academic remediation for entering students, advanced placement credit, honors programs, internships, off-campus study, part-time degree program, services for LD students, study abroad, summer session for credit.

Library University of Wisconsin-Waukesha Library plus 1 other with 61,000 titles, 300 serial subscriptions.

Student Life *Housing:* college housing not available. *Activities and Organizations:* drama/theater group, student-run newspaper, choral group, student government, Student Activities Committee, Campus Crusade, Phi Theta Kappa, Circle K. *Campus security:* late-night transport/escort service, part-time patrols by trained security personnel. *Student services:* personal/psychological counseling.

Athletics Member NJCAA. *Intercollegiate sports:* basketball M/W, golf M/W, soccer M/W, tennis M/W, volleyball W. *Intramural sports:* basketball M, bowling M/W, football M/W, skiing (downhill) M/W, table tennis M/W, volleyball M(c).

Standardized Tests *Required:* SAT or ACT (for admission).

Costs (2010–11) *Tuition:* state resident $4556 full-time, $191 per credit hour part-time; nonresident $11,544 full-time, $482 per credit hour part-time. Full-time tuition and fees vary according to course load and reciprocity agreements. Part-time tuition and fees vary according to course load and reciprocity agreements. *Payment plan:* installment. *Waivers:* senior citizens.

Financial Aid Of all full-time matriculated undergraduates who enrolled in 2008, 49 Federal Work-Study jobs (averaging $2100).

Applying *Options:* electronic application, early admission, deferred entrance. *Application fee:* $44. *Required:* high school transcript. *Recommended:* interview, admission interview may be recommended. *Application deadline:* rolling (freshmen). *Notification:* continuous (freshmen).

Freshman Application Contact Ms. Deb Kusick, Admissions Specialist, University of Wisconsin–Waukesha, 1500 North University Drive, Waukesha, WI 53188. *Phone:* 262-521-5200. *Fax:* 262-521-5530. *E-mail:* deborah.kusick@uwc.edu.

Waukesha County Technical College

Pewaukee, Wisconsin **www.wctc.edu/**

- **State and locally supported** 2-year, founded 1923, part of Wisconsin Technical College System
- **Suburban** 137-acre campus with easy access to Milwaukee
- **Coed,** 7,606 undergraduate students, 28% full-time, 52% women, 48% men

Undergraduates 2,128 full-time, 5,478 part-time. Students come from 13 states and territories.

Freshmen *Admission:* 814 enrolled.

Faculty *Total:* 894, 21% full-time.

Majors Accounting; administrative assistant and secretarial science; architectural drafting and CAD/CADD; autobody/collision and repair technology; automobile/automotive mechanics technology; computer and information sciences and support services related; computer installation and repair technology; computer programming; computer systems analysis; computer systems networking and telecommunications; criminal justice/police science; dental hygiene; early childhood education; electrical, electronic and communications engineering technology; electrical/electronics drafting and CAD/CADD; electromechanical and instrumentation and maintenance technologies related; financial planning and services; fire protection and safety technology; graphic communications; graphic design; hospitality administration; interior design; manufacturing technology; marketing/marketing management; mechanical drafting and CAD/CADD; mental and social health services and allied professions related; multi/interdisciplinary studies related; nursing (registered nurse training); operations management; restaurant, culinary, and catering management; retailing; surgical technology; teacher assistant/aide; telecommunications technology.

Academics *Calendar:* semesters. *Degree:* certificates, diplomas, and associate. *Special study options:* academic remediation for entering students, adult/continuing education programs, advanced placement credit, cooperative education, distance learning, English as a second language, part-time degree program, services for LD students, student-designed majors, summer session for credit.

Student Life *Housing:* college housing not available. *Campus security:* patrols by police officers 8 am to 10 pm. *Student services:* health clinic.

Costs (2009–10) *Tuition:* state resident $3042 full-time, $101 per credit hour part-time; nonresident $18,206 full-time, $607 per credit hour part-time. Full-time tuition and fees vary according to program. Part-time tuition and fees vary according to program. *Required fees:* $303 full-time, $10 per credit hour part-time. *Payment plans:* installment, deferred payment. *Waivers:* senior citizens.

Financial Aid Of all full-time matriculated undergraduates who enrolled in 2009, 42 Federal Work-Study jobs (averaging $2500). 107 state and other part-time jobs (averaging $2000).

Applying *Application fee:* $30. *Required:* high school transcript. *Required for some:* interview. *Application deadlines:* rolling (freshmen), rolling (transfers).

Freshman Application Contact Waukesha County Technical College, 800 Main Street, Pewaukee, WI 53072-4601. *Phone:* 262-691-5464. *Toll-free phone:* 888-892-WCTC.

Western Technical College

La Crosse, Wisconsin **www.westerntc.edu/**

Freshman Application Contact Ms. Jane Wells, Manager of Admissions, Registration and Records, Western Technical College, PO Box 908, La Crosse, WI 54602-0908. *Phone:* 608-785-9158. *Toll-free phone:* 800-322-9982 (in-state); 800-248-9982 (out-of-state). *Fax:* 608-785-9094. *E-mail:* mildes@wwtc.edu.

Wisconsin Indianhead Technical College

Shell Lake, Wisconsin **www.witc.edu/**

- **District-supported** 2-year, founded 1912, part of Wisconsin Technical College System
- **Urban** 113-acre campus
- **Endowment** $1.9 million
- **Coed,** 4,118 undergraduate students, 42% full-time, 60% women, 40% men

Undergraduates 1,718 full-time, 2,400 part-time. Students come from 4 states and territories, 8% are from out of state, 0.7% African American, 0.8% Asian American or Pacific Islander, 0.4% Hispanic American, 3% Native American. *Retention:* 70% of 2008 full-time freshmen returned.

Freshmen *Admission:* 967 enrolled.

Faculty *Total:* 436, 34% full-time. *Student/faculty ratio:* 10:1.

Majors Accounting; administrative assistant and secretarial science; architectural engineering technology; business administration and management; computer installation and repair technology; computer systems networking and telecommunications; corrections; criminal justice/police science; early childhood education; emergency medical technology (EMT paramedic); finance; heating, air conditioning and refrigeration technology; marketing/marketing management; mechanical drafting and CAD/CADD; medical administrative assistant and medical secretary; multi/interdisciplinary studies related; nursing (registered nurse training); occupational therapist assistant; operations management; retailing; web page, digital/multimedia and information resources design.

Academics *Calendar:* semesters. *Degree:* certificates, diplomas, and associate.

Student Life *Housing:* college housing not available. *Student services:* health clinic.

Costs (2009–10) *Tuition:* state resident $3388 full-time. Full-time tuition and fees vary according to course level, course load, degree level, program, and reciprocity agreements. Part-time tuition and fees vary according to course level, course load, degree level, program, and reciprocity agreements. *Payment plan:* installment.

Applying *Options:* electronic application. *Application fee:* $30. *Application deadline:* rolling (freshmen).

Freshman Application Contact Mr. Steve Bitzer, Vice President, Student Affairs and Campus Administrator, Wisconsin Indianhead Technical College, 505 Pine Ridge Drive, Shell Lake, WI 54871. *Phone:* 715-468-2815 Ext. 3149. *Toll-free phone:* 800-243-9482. *Fax:* 715-468-2819. *E-mail:* Steve.Bitzer@witc.edu.

WYOMING

Casper College

Casper, Wyoming **www.caspercollege.edu/**

- **State and locally supported** 2-year, founded 1945, part of Wyoming Community College Commission
- **Small-town** 200-acre campus
- **Coed,** 4,478 undergraduate students, 46% full-time, 57% women, 43% men

Undergraduates 2,078 full-time, 2,400 part-time. Students come from 38 states and territories, 21 other countries, 12% are from out of state, 1% African American, 0.6% Asian American or Pacific Islander, 4% Hispanic American, 0.8% Native American, 1% international, 3% transferred in, 15% live on campus. *Retention:* 60% of 2008 full-time freshmen returned.

Freshmen *Admission:* 1,160 applied, 1,160 admitted, 750 enrolled. *Average high school GPA:* 3. *Test scores:* SAT verbal scores over 500: 36%; SAT math scores over 500: 28%; SAT writing scores over 500: 18%; ACT scores over 18: 74%; SAT math scores over 600: 11%; ACT scores over 24: 18%; ACT scores over 30: 1%.

Faculty *Total:* 257, 60% full-time, 21% with terminal degrees. *Student/faculty ratio:* 15:1.

Majors Accounting; accounting technology and bookkeeping; acting; administrative assistant and secretarial science; agricultural business and management; agriculture; airline pilot and flight crew; animal sciences; anthropology; art; art teacher education; athletic training; autobody/collision and repair technology; automobile/automotive mechanics technology; biology/biological sciences; business administration and management; chemistry; clinical laboratory science/medical technology; communication/speech communication and rhetoric; computer programming; construction engineering technology; construction management; criminal justice/law enforcement administration; dance; diesel mechanics technology; drafting and design technology; economics; electrical, electronic and communications engineering technology; elementary education; emergency medical technology (EMT paramedic); engineering; English; entrepreneurship; environmental science; fine/studio arts; fire science; foreign languages and literatures; forensic science and technology; general studies; geography related; geology/earth science; graphic design; health aide; history; hospitality administration; industrial mechanics and maintenance technology; information technology; international relations and affairs; kindergarten/preschool education; legal assistant/paralegal; liberal arts and sciences/liberal studies; machine tool technology; management information systems; manufacturing technology; marketing/marketing management; mathematics; mining technology; museum studies; music; music performance; music teacher education; nursing (registered nurse training); nutrition sciences; occupational therapist assistant; pharmacy technician; phlebotomy; photography; physical education teaching and coaching; physics; political science and government; pre-law studies; premedical studies; pre-pharmacy studies; pre-veterinary studies; psychology; radiologic technology/science; range science and management; respiratory care therapy; retailing; robotics technology; social studies teacher education; social work; sociology; statistics related; substance abuse/addiction counseling; teacher assistant/aide; technology/industrial arts teacher education; theater design and technology; water quality and wastewater treatment management and recycling technology; web page, digital/multimedia and information resources design; welding technology; wildlife and wildlands science and management; women's studies.

Academics *Calendar:* semesters. *Degree:* certificates and associate. *Special study options:* academic remediation for entering students, accelerated degree program, advanced placement credit, cooperative education, distance learning, English as a second language, honors programs, independent study, internships, off-campus study, part-time degree program, services for LD students, summer session for credit.

Library Goodstein Library with 124,000 titles, 385 serial subscriptions, an OPAC, a Web page.

Student Life *Housing Options:* coed. Campus housing is university owned. *Activities and Organizations:* drama/theater group, student-run newspaper, choral group, Student Senate, Student Activities Board, Agriculture Club, Theater Club, Phi Theta Kappa. *Campus security:* 24-hour patrols, late-night transport/escort service. *Student services:* health clinic, personal/psychological counseling.

Athletics Member NJCAA. *Intercollegiate sports:* basketball M(s)/W(s), cheerleading M/W, equestrian sports M/W, volleyball W(s). *Intramural sports:* basketball M/W, bowling M/W, football M/W, golf M/W, racquetball M/W, soccer M/W, softball M/W, tennis M/W.

Costs (2009–10) *Tuition:* state resident $1632 full-time, $68 per credit hour part-time; nonresident $4896 full-time, $204 per credit hour part-time. Part-time tuition and fees vary according to course load. *Required fees:* $216 full-time, $9 per credit hour part-time. *Room and board:* $4160. Room and board charges vary according to board plan and housing facility. *Payment plan:* installment. *Waivers:* senior citizens and employees or children of employees.

Financial Aid Of all full-time matriculated undergraduates who enrolled in 2008, 80 Federal Work-Study jobs (averaging $2000).

Applying *Options:* electronic application, early admission. *Required:* high school transcript. *Notification:* continuous until 8/15 (freshmen), continuous until 8/15 (transfers).

Freshman Application Contact Mrs. Kyla Foltz, Admissions Coordinator, Casper College, 125 College Drive, Casper, WY 82601. *Phone:* 307-268-2111. *Toll-free phone:* 800-442-2963. *Fax:* 307-268-2611. *E-mail:* kfoltz@caspercollege.edu.

CENTRAL WYOMING COLLEGE

Riverton, Wyoming **www.cwc.edu/**

- **State and locally supported** 2-year, founded 1966, part of Wyoming Community College Commission
- **Small-town** 200-acre campus
- **Endowment** $7.6 million
- **Coed,** 2,158 undergraduate students, 43% full-time, 59% women, 41% men

Undergraduates 934 full-time, 1,224 part-time. Students come from 46 states and territories, 18 other countries, 14% are from out of state, 0.5% African American, 0.4% Asian American or Pacific Islander, 4% Hispanic American, 13% Native American, 1% international, 8% transferred in, 10% live on campus. *Retention:* 52% of 2008 full-time freshmen returned.

Freshmen *Admission:* 572 applied, 572 admitted, 465 enrolled. *Average high school GPA:* 2.97. *Test scores:* SAT math scores over 500: 47%; ACT scores over 18: 71%; SAT math scores over 600: 14%; ACT scores over 24: 19%; SAT math scores over 700: 7%; ACT scores over 30: 1%.

Faculty *Total:* 238, 58% full-time, 28% with terminal degrees. *Student/faculty ratio:* 8:1.

Majors Accounting; accounting technology and bookkeeping; acting; administrative assistant and secretarial science; agricultural and domestic animals services related; agricultural business and management; American Indian/Native American studies; area studies related; art; athletic training; automobile/automotive mechanics technology; biology/biological sciences; business administration and management; business automation/technology/data entry; business/commerce; carpentry; child-care and support services management; commercial photography; computer science; computer technology/computer systems technology; criminal justice/law enforcement administration; culinary arts; customer service support/call center/teleservice operation; dental assisting; dramatic/theater arts; early childhood education; elementary education; emergency medical technology (EMT paramedic); engineering; English; environmental/environmental health engineering; environmental science; equestrian studies; fire science; general studies; geology/earth science; graphic design; health services/allied health/health sciences; hotel/motel administration; international/global studies; manufacturing engineering; mathematics; medical office assistant; music; nursing (registered nurse training); occupational safety and health technology; office occupations and clerical services; parks, recreation and leisure; parks, recreation and leisure facilities management; physical sciences; pre-law studies; psychology; radio and television; range science and management; rehabilitation and therapeutic professions related; secondary education; security and protective services related; selling skills and sales; social sciences; teacher assistant/aide; theater design and technology; welding technology.

Academics *Calendar:* semesters. *Degree:* certificates, diplomas, and associate. *Special study options:* academic remediation for entering students, adult/continuing education programs, advanced placement credit, cooperative education, distance learning, double majors, English as a second language, honors programs, independent study, off-campus study, part-time degree program, services for LD students, summer session for credit.

Library Central Wyoming College Library with 54,974 titles, 2,940 serial subscriptions, 1,450 audiovisual materials, an OPAC, a Web page.

Student Life *Housing Options:* coed. Campus housing is university owned. *Activities and Organizations:* drama/theater group, student-run radio and television station, choral group, Multi-Cultural Club, La Vida Nueva Club, Fellowship of College Christians, Quality Leaders, Science Club. *Campus security:* 24-hour emergency response devices, late-night transport/escort service, controlled dormitory access. *Student services:* personal/psychological counseling.

Athletics Member NJCAA. *Intercollegiate sports:* basketball M(s)/W(s), equestrian sports M(s)/W(s), volleyball W(s). *Intramural sports:* badminton M/W, basketball M/W, football M/W, rock climbing M/W, skiing (cross-country) M/W, skiing (downhill) M/W, soccer M/W, softball M/W, swimming and diving M/W, table tennis M/W, tennis M/W, ultimate Frisbee M/W, volleyball M/W, weight lifting M/W.

Costs (2010–11) *Tuition:* state resident $1632 full-time, $68 per credit part-time; nonresident $4896 full-time, $204 per credit part-time. Full-time tuition and fees vary according to course load, program, and reciprocity agreements. Part-time tuition and fees vary according to course load, program, and reciprocity agreements. *Required fees:* $504 full-time, $21 per credit part-time. *Room and board:* $4085; room only: $1985. Room and board charges vary according to board plan and housing facility. *Payment plans:* installment, deferred payment. *Waivers:* senior citizens and employees or children of employees.

Financial Aid Of all full-time matriculated undergraduates who enrolled in 2009, 608 applied for aid, 484 were judged to have need. 96 Federal Work-Study jobs (averaging $2123). *Financial aid deadline:* 6/30.

Applying *Options:* electronic application, early admission, deferred entrance. *Recommended:* high school transcript. *Application deadlines:* rolling (freshmen), rolling (out-of-state freshmen), rolling (transfers).

Freshman Application Contact Mrs. Brenda Barlow, Admissions Assistant, Central Wyoming College, 2660 Peck Avenue, Riverton, WY 82501-2273. *Phone:* 307-855-2119. *Toll-free phone:* 800-735-8418 Ext. 2119. *Fax:* 307-855-2093. *E-mail:* admit@cwc.edu.

EASTERN WYOMING COLLEGE

Torrington, Wyoming **www.ewc.wy.edu/**

- **State and locally supported** 2-year, founded 1948, part of Wyoming Community College Commission
- **Rural** 40-acre campus
- **Coed,** 1,391 undergraduate students, 45% full-time, 61% women, 39% men

Undergraduates 624 full-time, 767 part-time. 0.7% African American, 2% Hispanic American, 0.7% international.

Freshmen *Admission:* 232 enrolled.

Faculty *Total:* 100, 47% full-time. *Student/faculty ratio:* 14:1.

Majors Accounting; administrative assistant and secretarial science; agribusiness; agricultural economics; agricultural teacher education; agriculture; animal sciences; art; biology/biological sciences; business administration and management; business teacher education; communication/speech communication and rhetoric; computer systems networking and telecommunications; construction trades; corrections administration; cosmetology; criminal justice/law enforcement administration; criminal justice/police science; criminal justice/safety; early childhood education; economics; elementary education; English; environmental biology; farm and ranch management; foreign languages and literatures; general studies; health/medical preparatory programs related; history; liberal arts and sciences/liberal studies; mathematics; mathematics teacher education; music; music teacher education; office management; physical education teaching and coaching; political science and government; pre-dentistry studies; premedical studies; pre-pharmacy studies; pre-veterinary studies; psy-

Eastern Wyoming College (continued)

chology; range science and management; secondary education; sociology; statistics; veterinary/animal health technology; welding technology; wildlife and wildlands science and management.

Academics *Calendar:* semesters. *Degree:* certificates, diplomas, and associate. *Special study options:* academic remediation for entering students, accelerated degree program, adult/continuing education programs, advanced placement credit, cooperative education, distance learning, English as a second language, honors programs, independent study, internships, part-time degree program, services for LD students, student-designed majors, summer session for credit.

Library Eastern Wyoming College Library with an OPAC, a Web page.

Student Life *Housing Options:* coed, men-only, women-only. Campus housing is university owned. *Activities and Organizations:* drama/theater group, student-run newspaper, choral group, Criminal Justice Club, Veterinary Technology Club, Student Senate, Music Club, Rodeo Club. *Campus security:* 24-hour emergency response devices, controlled dormitory access. *Student services:* personal/psychological counseling.

Athletics Member NJCAA.

Costs (2010–11) *Tuition:* state resident $1632 full-time, $68 per credit hour part-time; nonresident $4896 full-time, $204 per credit hour part-time. Full-time tuition and fees vary according to location. Part-time tuition and fees vary according to location. *Required fees:* $384 full-time, $16 per credit hour part-time. *Room and board:* $3806; room only: $1704. Room and board charges vary according to housing facility. *Payment plan:* installment. *Waivers:* senior citizens and employees or children of employees.

Financial Aid Of all full-time matriculated undergraduates who enrolled in 2008, 100 Federal Work-Study jobs (averaging $700). 60 state and other part-time jobs (averaging $700).

Applying *Options:* electronic application, early admission. *Recommended:* high school transcript. *Application deadlines:* rolling (freshmen), rolling (transfers).

Freshman Application Contact Dr. Rex Cogdill, Vice President for Students Services, Eastern Wyoming College, 3200 West C Street, Torrington, WY 82240. *Phone:* 307-532-8257. *Toll-free phone:* 800-658-3195. *Fax:* 307-532-8222. *E-mail:* rex.cogdill@ewc.wy.edu.

LARAMIE COUNTY COMMUNITY COLLEGE

Cheyenne, Wyoming **www.lccc.wy.edu/**

- **State-supported** 2-year, founded 1968, part of Wyoming Community College Commission
- **Small-town** 271-acre campus
- **Endowment** $12.1 million
- **Coed,** 4,905 undergraduate students, 43% full-time, 60% women, 40% men

Undergraduates 2,121 full-time, 2,784 part-time. Students come from 41 states and territories, 8 other countries, 13% are from out of state, 2% African American, 0.3% Asian American or Pacific Islander, 8% Hispanic American, 0.9% Native American, 1% international, 5% transferred in, 4% live on campus. *Retention:* 48% of 2008 full-time freshmen returned.

Freshmen *Admission:* 1,427 applied, 1,427 admitted, 418 enrolled. *Average high school GPA:* 2.99. *Test scores:* ACT scores over 18: 76%; ACT scores over 24: 16%.

Faculty *Total:* 325, 4% with terminal degrees. *Student/faculty ratio:* 18:1.

Majors Accounting; agribusiness; agricultural business technology; agricultural production; agriculture; anthropology; art; autobody/collision and repair technology; automobile/automotive mechanics technology; biological and physical sciences; biology/biological sciences; business administration and management; business/commerce; chemistry; communication/speech communication and rhetoric; computer and information sciences; computer programming; computer programming (vendor/product certification); computer science; computer systems analysis; construction trades; construction trades related; corrections; criminal justice/law enforcement administration; dental hygiene; diagnostic medical sonography and ultrasound technology; diesel mechanics technology; digital communication and media/multimedia; drafting and design technology; dramatic/theater arts; early childhood education; economics; education; education (specific levels and methods) related; energy management and systems technology; engineering; English; entrepreneurship; equestrian studies; health/medical preparatory programs related; history; humanities; human services; information technology; legal assistant/paralegal; mass communication/media; mathematics; multi/interdisciplinary studies related; music; nursing (registered nurse training); philosophy; physical education teaching and coaching; physical therapist assistant; political science and government; pre-dentistry studies; pre-law studies; premedical studies; pre-pharmacy studies; pre-veterinary studies; psychology; public administration; radiologic technology/science; religious studies; security and protective services related; social sciences; sociology; Spanish; surgical technology; web page, digital/multimedia and information resources design; wildlife and wildlands science and management.

Academics *Calendar:* semesters. *Degree:* certificates and associate. *Special study options:* academic remediation for entering students, adult/continuing education programs, advanced placement credit, cooperative education, distance learning, double majors, English as a second language, honors programs, independent study, internships, off-campus study, part-time degree program, services for LD students, summer session for credit. *ROTC:* Air Force (c).

Library Ludden Library plus 1 other with 56,356 titles, 220 serial subscriptions, 5,907 audiovisual materials, an OPAC, a Web page.

Student Life *Housing Options:* coed. Campus housing is university owned. *Activities and Organizations:* drama/theater group, student-run newspaper, choral group. *Campus security:* 24-hour emergency response devices and patrols, late-night transport/escort service, controlled dormitory access. *Student services:* personal/psychological counseling.

Athletics Member NJCAA. *Intercollegiate sports:* basketball M(s), cheerleading M(s)/W(s), equestrian sports M(s)/W(s), soccer M(s)/W(s), volleyball W(s). *Intramural sports:* basketball M/W, equestrian sports M/W, golf M/W, racquetball M/W, rock climbing M/W, skiing (cross-country) M/W, soccer M/W, table tennis M/W, ultimate Frisbee M/W, volleyball M/W.

Costs (2010–11) *One-time required fee:* $20. *Tuition:* state resident $1632 full-time, $68 per credit hour part-time; nonresident $4896 full-time, $204 per credit hour part-time. Part-time tuition and fees vary according to course load. *Required fees:* $840 full-time, $35 per credit hour part-time. *Room and board:* $7140; room only: $4527. Room and board charges vary according to board plan and housing facility. *Payment plan:* installment. *Waivers:* senior citizens and employees or children of employees.

Applying *Options:* electronic application, early admission. *Application fee:* $20. *Required for some:* high school transcript, interview. *Application deadlines:* rolling (freshmen), rolling (out-of-state freshmen), rolling (transfers). *Notification:* continuous (freshmen), continuous (out-of-state freshmen), continuous (transfers).

Freshman Application Contact Ms. Holly Allison, Director of Admissions, Laramie County Community College, 1400 East College Drive, Cheyenne, WY 82007. *Phone:* 307-778-1117. *Toll-free phone:* 800-522-2993 Ext. 1357. *Fax:* 307-778-1360. *E-mail:* learnmore@lccc.wy.edu.

NORTHWEST COLLEGE

Powell, Wyoming **www.northwestcollege.edu/**

- **State and locally supported** 2-year, founded 1946, part of Wyoming Community College Commission
- **Rural** 124-acre campus
- **Endowment** $6.7 million
- **Coed,** 2,099 undergraduate students, 64% full-time, 58% women, 42% men

Undergraduates 1,348 full-time, 751 part-time. Students come from 39 states and territories, 18 other countries, 27% are from out of state, 0.6% African American, 2% Asian American or Pacific Islander, 7% Hispanic American, 2% Native American, 3% international. *Retention:* 58% of 2008 full-time freshmen returned.

Freshmen *Admission:* 560 enrolled.

Faculty *Total:* 152, 53% full-time. *Student/faculty ratio:* 15:1.

Majors Accounting; administrative assistant and secretarial science; agribusiness; agricultural business and management; agricultural communication/journalism; agricultural production; agricultural teacher education; animal sciences; anthropology; archeology; art; athletic training; biology/biological sciences; broadcast journalism; business administration and management; business/commerce; CAD/CADD drafting/design technology; chemistry; cinematography and film/video production; commercial and advertising art; commercial photography; communication/speech communication and rhetoric; criminal justice/law enforcement administration; criminal justice/safety; crop production; desktop publishing and digital imaging design; ecology, evolution, systematics and population biology related; electrician; elementary education; engineering; English; equestrian studies; farm and ranch management; French; general studies; graphic and printing equipment operation/production; health and physical education; health/medical preparatory programs related; health services/allied health/health sciences; history; journalism; kindergarten/preschool education; liberal arts and sciences/liberal studies; mathematics; music; natural resources management and policy; nursing (registered nurse training); nursing related; occupational safety and health technology; parks, recreation and leisure; photography; physics; playwriting and screenwriting; political science and government; pre-pharmacy studies; psychology; radio and television; radio, television, and digital communication related; range science and management; secondary education; social sciences; sociology; Spanish; veterinary/animal health technology; visual and performing arts related; welding technology.

Academics *Calendar:* semesters. *Degree:* certificates and associate. *Special study options:* academic remediation for entering students, adult/continuing

education programs, advanced placement credit, cooperative education, distance learning, double majors, English as a second language, external degree program, independent study, internships, part-time degree program, services for LD students, study abroad, summer session for credit.

Library John Taggart Hinckley Library plus 1 other with 50,100 titles, 27,652 serial subscriptions, 2,515 audiovisual materials, an OPAC, a Web page.

Student Life *Housing:* on-campus residence required for freshman year. *Options:* coed, women-only. Campus housing is university owned. Freshman campus housing is guaranteed. *Activities and Organizations:* drama/theater group, student-run newspaper, radio and television station, choral group. *Campus security:* 24-hour emergency response devices and patrols, late-night transport/escort service, controlled dormitory access. *Student services:* health clinic, personal/psychological counseling.

Athletics Member NJCAA. *Intercollegiate sports:* basketball M(s)/W(s), equestrian sports M(s)/W(s), soccer M(s)/W(s), volleyball W(s), wrestling M(s). *Intramural sports:* basketball M/W, football M/W, golf M/W, racquetball M/W, softball M/W, tennis M/W, volleyball M/W.

Standardized Tests *Required for some:* SAT or ACT (for admission), ACT COMPASS.

Costs (2009–10) *Tuition:* state resident $2235 full-time, $89 per credit hour part-time; nonresident $5499 full-time, $225 per credit hour part-time. Full-time tuition and fees vary according to course load, location, program, and reciprocity agreements. Part-time tuition and fees vary according to location, program, and reciprocity agreements. *Room and board:* $3916; room only: $1730. Room and board charges vary according to board plan and housing facility. *Payment plan:* installment. *Waivers:* children of alumni, senior citizens, and employees or children of employees.

Financial Aid Of all full-time matriculated undergraduates who enrolled in 2008, 115 Federal Work-Study jobs (averaging $2700). 215 state and other part-time jobs (averaging $2700).

Applying *Options:* electronic application. *Required:* high school transcript. *Required for some:* minimum 2 GPA. *Recommended:* minimum 2 GPA. *Application deadlines:* rolling (freshmen), rolling (out-of-state freshmen), rolling (transfers). *Notification:* continuous (freshmen), continuous (out-of-state freshmen), continuous (transfers).

Freshman Application Contact Mr. West Hernandez, Admissions Manager, Northwest College, 231 West Sixth Street, Powell, WY 82435. *Phone:* 307-754-6103. *Toll-free phone:* 800-560-4692. *E-mail:* west.hernandez@northwestcollege.edu.

SHERIDAN COLLEGE

Sheridan, Wyoming **www.sheridan.edu/**

- **State and locally supported** 2-year, founded 1948, part of Wyoming Community College Commission
- **Small-town** 124-acre campus
- **Endowment** $10.2 million
- **Coed,** 3,930 undergraduate students, 36% full-time, 49% women, 51% men

Undergraduates 1,422 full-time, 2,508 part-time. Students come from 37 states and territories, 10 other countries, 12% are from out of state, 0.9% African American, 0.8% Asian American or Pacific Islander, 4% Hispanic American, 1% Native American, 0.6% international, 9% transferred in, 11% live on campus.

Freshmen *Admission:* 674 admitted, 503 enrolled.

Faculty *Total:* 176, 52% full-time, 7% with terminal degrees. *Student/faculty ratio:* 18:1.

Majors Administrative assistant and secretarial science; agricultural business and management; agriculture; agriculture and agriculture operations related; art; biological and physical sciences; biology/biological sciences; business/commerce; CAD/CADD drafting/design technology; communication and journalism related; computer and information sciences; construction trades; criminal justice/safety; culinary arts; dental hygiene; diesel mechanics technology; dramatic/theater arts; early childhood education; electrical and electronic engineering technologies related; elementary education; engineering; engineering technologies related; English; foreign languages and literatures; general studies; health and physical education; history; horticultural science; hospitality administration; information science/studies; machine tool technology; massage therapy; mathematics; multi/interdisciplinary studies related; music; nursing (registered nurse training); precision production related; psychology; range science and management; secondary education; social sciences; survey technology; teacher assistant/aide; turf and turfgrass management; web/multimedia management and webmaster; welding technology.

Academics *Calendar:* semesters. *Degree:* certificates and associate. *Special study options:* academic remediation for entering students, advanced placement credit, cooperative education, distance learning, double majors, English as a second language, independent study, internships, off-campus study, part-time degree program, services for LD students, summer session for credit.

Library Griffith Memorial Library plus 1 other with 36,574 titles, 108 serial subscriptions, 2,884 audiovisual materials, an OPAC, a Web page.

Student Life *Housing Options:* coed, women-only, disabled students. Campus housing is university owned. *Activities and Organizations:* drama/theater group, student-run newspaper, choral group, student government, Phi Theta Kappa, Art Club, Nursing Club, Police Science Club. *Campus security:* 24-hour emergency response devices, student patrols, controlled dormitory access, night patrols by certified officers. *Student services:* personal/psychological counseling, legal services.

Athletics Member NJCAA. *Intercollegiate sports:* basketball M(s)/W(s), cross-country running M(s)/W(s), volleyball W(s). *Intramural sports:* basketball M/W, bowling M/W, soccer M/W, softball M/W, table tennis M/W, tennis M/W, ultimate Frisbee M/W, volleyball M/W.

Costs (2010–11) *Tuition:* state resident $1632 full-time, $68 per credit hour part-time; nonresident $4896 full-time, $204 per credit hour part-time. Full-time tuition and fees vary according to course load, location, program, and reciprocity agreements. Part-time tuition and fees vary according to course load, location, program, and reciprocity agreements. *Required fees:* $552 full-time, $23 per credit hour part-time. *Room and board:* $4600. Room and board charges vary according to board plan, housing facility, and location. *Payment plans:* installment, deferred payment. *Waivers:* senior citizens and employees or children of employees.

Financial Aid Of all full-time matriculated undergraduates who enrolled in 2008, 92 Federal Work-Study jobs (averaging $1798).

Applying *Options:* electronic application, early admission, deferred entrance. *Required for some:* high school transcript. *Recommended:* high school transcript. *Application deadlines:* rolling (freshmen), rolling (transfers). *Notification:* continuous (freshmen), continuous (transfers).

Freshman Application Contact Mr. Zane Garstad, Director of Enrollment Services, Sheridan College, PO Box 1500, Sheridan, WY 82801-1500. *Phone:* 307-674-6446 Ext. 2002. *Toll-free phone:* 800-913-9139 Ext. 2002. *Fax:* 307-674-7205. *E-mail:* admissions@sheridan.edu.

WESTERN WYOMING COMMUNITY COLLEGE

Rock Springs, Wyoming **www.wwcc.wy.edu/**

- **State and locally supported** 2-year, founded 1959
- **Small-town** 342-acre campus
- **Endowment** $9.3 million
- **Coed,** 4,120 undergraduate students, 30% full-time, 47% women, 53% men

Undergraduates 1,242 full-time, 2,878 part-time. 11% live on campus.

Freshmen *Admission:* 589 enrolled. *Test scores:* ACT scores over 18: 90%; ACT scores over 24: 10%.

Faculty *Total:* 218, 33% full-time. *Student/faculty ratio:* 18:1.

Majors Accounting; administrative assistant and secretarial science; anthropology; archeology; art; automobile/automotive mechanics technology; biological and physical sciences; biology/biological sciences; business administration and management; chemistry; communication/speech communication and rhetoric; computer and information sciences; computer programming (specific applications); computer science; criminal justice/law enforcement administration; criminology; dance; data entry/microcomputer applications; data processing and data processing technology; diesel mechanics technology; dramatic/theater arts; early childhood education; economics; education; education (multiple levels); electrical, electronic and communications engineering technology; electrical/electronics equipment installation and repair; electrician; elementary education; engineering technology; English; environmental science; forestry; general studies; geology/earth science; health/medical preparatory programs related; health services/allied health/health sciences; heavy equipment maintenance technology; history; humanities; human services; industrial electronics technology; industrial mechanics and maintenance technology; information science/studies; information technology; instrumentation technology; international relations and affairs; journalism; kinesiology and exercise science; legal administrative assistant/secretary; liberal arts and sciences/liberal studies; marketing/marketing management; mathematics; mechanics and repair; medical administrative assistant and medical secretary; medical/clinical assistant; medical office assistant; medical office computer specialist; mining technology; music; nursing assistant/aide and patient care assistant; nursing (licensed practical/vocational nurse training); photography; political science and government; pre-dentistry studies; pre-engineering; pre-law studies; premedical studies; prenursing studies; pre-pharmacy studies; pre-veterinary studies; psychology; secondary education; social sciences; social work; sociology; Spanish; theater design and technology; visual and performing arts; web/multimedia management and webmaster; web page, digital/multimedia and information resources design; welding technology; wildlife and wildlands science and management; word processing.

Academics *Calendar:* semesters. *Degree:* certificates, diplomas, and associate. *Special study options:* academic remediation for entering students, adult/continuing education programs, advanced placement credit, cooperative education,

Western Wyoming Community College (continued)

distance learning, double majors, English as a second language, honors programs, independent study, internships, part-time degree program, services for LD students, summer session for credit.

Library Hay Library with 146,229 titles, 14,072 serial subscriptions, 4,467 audiovisual materials, an OPAC, a Web page.

Student Life *Housing Options:* coed, disabled students. Campus housing is university owned. *Activities and Organizations:* drama/theater group, student-run newspaper, radio station, choral group, marching band, Phi Theta Kappa, Students Without Borders (international club), Residence Hall Association, Associated Student Government, LDSSA. *Campus security:* 24-hour emergency response devices and patrols, late-night transport/escort service, controlled dormitory access, patrols by trained security personnel from 4 pm to 8 am, 24-hour patrols on weekends and holidays. *Student services:* personal/psychological counseling.

Athletics Member NJCAA. *Intercollegiate sports:* basketball M(s)/W(s), cheerleading M(s)/W(s), soccer M(s)(c)/W(s)(c), volleyball W(s), wrestling M(s). *Intramural sports:* badminton M/W, basketball M/W, bowling M/W, football M/W, rock climbing M/W, skiing (downhill) M/W, soccer M/W, softball M/W, table tennis M/W, tennis M/W, ultimate Frisbee M/W, volleyball M/W, water polo M/W.

Costs (2010–11) *Tuition:* $84 per credit hour part-time; state resident $1994 full-time, $118 per credit hour part-time; nonresident $5258 full-time, $220 per credit hour part-time. Full-time tuition and fees vary according to reciprocity agreements. Part-time tuition and fees vary according to course load and reciprocity agreements. *Room and board:* $3837; room only: $2072. Room and board charges vary according to board plan and housing facility. *Payment plan:* installment. *Waivers:* children of alumni, senior citizens, and employees or children of employees.

Financial Aid Of all full-time matriculated undergraduates who enrolled in 2008, 20 Federal Work-Study jobs (averaging $1500).

Applying *Options:* electronic application, early admission, deferred entrance. *Required:* high school transcript. *Application deadlines:* rolling (freshmen), rolling (transfers).

Freshman Application Contact Director of AdmissionsDirector of Admissions, Western Wyoming Community College, PO Box 428, 2500 College Drive, Rock Springs, WY 82902-0428. *Phone:* 307-382-1647382-1647. *Toll-free phone:* 800-226-1181. *Fax:* 307-382-1636382-1636. *E-mail:* admissions@wwcc.wy.eduadmissions@wwcc.wy.edu.

WyoTech

Laramie, Wyoming **www.wyotech.com/**

Director of Admissions Director of Admissions, WyoTech, 4373 North Third Street, Laramie, WY 82072-9519. *Phone:* 307-742-3776. *Toll-free phone:* 800-521-7158. *Fax:* 307-721-4854.

CANADA

Southern Alberta Institute of Technology

Calgary, Alberta, Canada **www.sait.ca/**

- **Province-supported** primarily 2-year, founded 1916
- **Urban** 96-acre campus
- **Coed,** 7,672 undergraduate students, 91% full-time, 42% women, 58% men

Undergraduates 6,954 full-time, 718 part-time.

Faculty *Total:* 962.

Majors Business administration and management; business administration, management and operations related; geography related; information science/studies; petroleum engineering.

Academics *Calendar:* trimesters. *Degrees:* certificates, diplomas, associate, and bachelor's. *Special study options:* cooperative education, distance learning, independent study, internships, off-campus study, services for LD students.

Library SAIT Library with 135,000 titles, 100 serial subscriptions, an OPAC, a Web page.

Student Life *Housing Options:* coed, disabled students. Campus housing is university owned. *Activities and Organizations:* drama/theater group, student-run newspaper, radio and television station, SAIT Petroleum Society, Business Student's Association, Global Passport, Environmental Technology Students Organization, Civil Engineering Technology Concrete Toboggan. *Campus security:* 24-hour emergency response devices and patrols, late-night transport/escort service. *Student services:* health clinic, personal/psychological counseling.

Athletics *Intercollegiate sports:* basketball M(s)/W(s), cross-country running M/W, ice hockey M(s)/W(s), soccer M(s)/W(s), volleyball M(s)/W(s). *Intramural sports:* basketball M/W, football M/W, ice hockey M/W, soccer M/W, softball M/W, volleyball M/W.

Applying *Options:* electronic application, early admission, early decision. *Application fee:* $50 Canadian dollars. *Required:* high school transcript. *Required for some:* essay or personal statement, interview. *Application deadlines:* rolling (freshmen), rolling (out-of-state freshmen), rolling (transfers). *Early decision deadline:* rolling.

Freshman Application Contact Southern Alberta Institute of Technology, 1301-16 Avenue, NW, Calgary, AB T2N 3W2, Canada. *Phone:* 403-284-8857. *Toll-free phone:* 877-284-SAIT.

INTERNATIONAL

MARSHALL ISLANDS

COLLEGE OF THE MARSHALL ISLANDS

Majuro, Marshall Islands **www.cmi.edu/**

Freshman Application Contact Ms. Rosita Capelle, Director of Admissions and Records, College of the Marshall Islands, PO Box 1258, Majuro 96960, Marshall Islands. *Phone:* 692-625-6823. *Fax:* 692-625-7203. *E-mail:* cmiadmissions@cmi.edu.

MEXICO

WESTHILL UNIVERSITY

Sante Fe, Mexico **www.westhill.edu.mx/**

Freshman Application Contact Admissions, Westhill University, 56 Domingo Garcia Ramos, Zona Escolar, Prados de la Montana I, Sante Fe, Mexico. *Phone:* 52-55 5292-2377.

PALAU

PALAU COMMUNITY COLLEGE

Koror, Palau **www.palau.edu/**

Freshman Application Contact Ms. Dahlia Katosang, Director of Admissions and Financial Aid, Palau Community College, PO Box 9, Koror, PW 96940-0009, Palau. *Phone:* 680-488-2471 Ext. 233. *Fax:* 680-488-4468. *E-mail:* dahliapcc@palaunet.com.

College

CLOSE-UPS

ARGOSY UNIVERSITY, TWIN CITIES
College of Health Sciences
EAGAN, MINNESOTA

ARGOSY UNIVERSITY.

Argosy University is an institution of higher education offering a variety of degree programs that focus on the human side of success alongside professional competence. For students looking for a more personal approach to education, Argosy University may just be the answer. Drawing upon over thirty years of history, Argosy University has developed a curriculum that focuses on interpersonal skills and practical experience alongside academic learning. Argosy's programs are taught by practicing professionals who bring real-world experience into the classroom. Students graduate with both a solid foundation of knowledge and the power to put it to work. To accommodate busy working adults, many programs at Argosy University have a flexible structure with both on-campus and online learning, and evening, weekend, and daytime classes. There are financial aid options available for students who qualify.

Argosy University is a private institution of higher education dedicated to providing quality professional education programs at the doctoral, master's, bachelor's, and associate degree levels as well as continuing education to individuals who seek to enhance their professional and personal lives. The University emphasizes programs in the behavioral sciences (psychology and counseling), business, education, and the health-care professions. A limited number of preprofessional programs and general education offerings are provided to permit students to prepare for entry into these professional fields. The programs of Argosy University are designed to instill the knowledge, skills, and ethical values of professional practice and to foster values of social responsibility in a supportive, learning-centered environment of mutual respect and professional excellence.

With nineteen campuses nationwide, Argosy University provides students with a network of resources found at larger universities, including a career resources office, an academic resources center, and extensive information access for research.

The University's innovative programs feature dynamic, relevant, and practical curricula delivered in flexible class formats. Students enjoy scheduling options that make it easier to fit school into their busy lives. They can choose from day and evening courses, on campus or online. Many students find a combination of both to be an ideal way of continuing their education while meeting family and professional demands.

Most students are full-time working professionals who live within driving distance of the campus. The University does not offer or operate student housing.

Argosy University is accredited by The Higher Learning Commission of the North Central Association and is a member of the North Central Association, 30 North LaSalle Street, Suite 2400, Chicago, Illinois 60602; phone: 800-621-7440 (toll-free); Web site: http://ncahlc.org.

The Associate of Applied Science in diagnostic medical sonography degree program is accredited by the Commission on Accreditation of Allied Health Education Programs upon recommendation of the Joint Review Committee on Education in Diagnostic Medical Sonography (JRC-DMS). Commission on Accreditation of Allied Health Education Programs, 1361 Park Street, Clearwater, Florida 33756; phone: 727-210-2350; Web site: http://www.caahep.org. The program has been placed on probationary accreditation as of September 19, 2008.

The echocardiography concentration in the Associate of Applied Science in diagnostic medical sonography degree program is accredited by the Commission on Accreditation of Allied Health education Programs upon the recommendation of the Joint Review Committee on Education in Diagnostic Medical Sonography (JRC-DMS). Commission on Accreditation of Allied Health Education Programs, 1361 Park Street, Clearwater, Florida 33756; phone: 727-210-2350; Web site: http://www.caahep.org.

The Associate of Applied Science in histotechnology degree program is accredited by the National Accrediting Agency for Clinical Laboratory Sciences, 8410 West Bryn Mawr, Suite 670, Chicago, Illinois 60631; phone: 773-714-8880.

The Associate of Applied Science in medical assisting degree program is accredited by the Commission on Allied Health Education Programs upon the recommendation of the Curriculum Review Board of the American Association of Medical Assistants Endowment (AAMAE), 1361 Park Street, Clearwater, Florida 33756; phone: 727-210-2350; Web site: http://www.caahep.org.

The Associate of Applied Science in radiologic technology degree program is accredited by the Joint Review Committee on Education in Radiologic Technology, 20 North Wacker Drive, Suite 2850, Chicago, Illinois 60606-3182; phone: 312-704-5300.

The Associate of Applied Science in veterinary technology degree program is accredited through the American Veterinary Medical Association (AVMA) Committee on Veterinary Technician Education and Activities (CVTEA), 1931 North Meachum Road, Suite 100, Schaumburg, Illinois 60173; phone: 847-925-8070.

The Associate of Science in medical laboratory technology degree program is accredited by the National Accrediting Agency for Clinical Laboratory Sciences, 8410 West Bryn Mawr, Suite 670, Chicago, Illinois 60631; phone: 773-714-8880.

The Associate of Science in dental hygiene degree program is accredited by the Commission on Dental Accreditation, 211 East Chicago Avenue, Chicago, Illinois 60611; phone: 312-440-4653. The commission is a specialized accrediting body recognized by the United States Department of Education.

The Associate of Science in radiation therapy degree program is accredited by the Joint Review Committee on Education in Radiologic Technology, 20 North Wacker Drive, Suite 2850, Chicago, Illinois 60606-3182; phone: 312-704-5300; Web site: http://www.jrcert.org.

Academic Programs

The College of Health Sciences at Argosy University, Twin Cities, offers the Associate of Applied Science (A.A.S.) degree in diagnostic medical sonography, histotechnology, medical assisting, radiation therapy, radiologic technology, and veterinary technology and the Associate of Science (A.S.) degree in dental hygiene, medical laboratory technology, and radiation therapy. Typically, associate degree programs are completed in one to two years.

The A.A.S. in diagnostic medical sonography degree program is designed to prepare students to develop the best possible technical skills in sonography to work under the direction of a doctor using ultrasound imaging techniques for purposes of diagnosis. Students must choose a concentration in general sonography, echocardiography, or vascular technology.

The A.A.S. in histotechnology degree program is designed to prepare students to provide health-care services and demonstrate the utmost respect and concern for the well-being of the patients they serve. Histotechnicians prepare tissue specimens for examination and diagnosis by pathologists.

The A.A.S. in medical assisting degree program is designed to train students to be multiskilled allied health-care professionals. Postgraduate professional responsibilities include patient care, laboratory testing, limited X-ray, office management, and assisting the physician.

The A.A.S. in radiologic technology degree program is designed to prepare students to become skilled professionals who are qualified to perform imaging examinations and accompanying responsibilities at the request of physicians who are qualified to prescribe and/or perform radiologic procedures.

The A.A.S. in veterinary technology degree program is designed to prepare students to work as health-care professionals who professionally interact with veterinarians, other technicians, and animal owners. Veterinary technicians provide critical and ongoing assistance in the care of all types of animals.

The A.S. in dental hygiene degree program is designed to prepare students to provide effective and professional preventive dental services under the supervision of the dentist. The integrated curriculum provides opportunities to acquire assessment skills, cognitive skills, and technical skills.

The A.S. in medical laboratory technology degree program is designed to prepare students to perform extensive laboratory testing procedures. The program also emphasizes interaction with pathologists, technologists, other medical personnel, and patients in a professional and ethical manner.

The A.S. in radiation therapy degree program is designed to prepare students with the knowledge and technical skills required to assist cancer patients. Students have the opportunity to learn to prepare patients for radiation treatment, position patients under a linear accelerator, and administer prescribed doses of ionizing radiation to specific parts of the body.

Costs

Tuition varies by program. Students should contact Argosy University's Twin Cities location for tuition information.

Financial Aid

Financial aid options are available to students who qualify. Argosy University offers access to federal and state aid programs, merit-based awards, grants, loans, and a work-study program. As a first step, students should complete the Free Application for Federal Student Aid (FAFSA). Prospective students can apply online at http://www.fafsa.ed.gov or at the campus. To receive consideration for financial aid and ensure timely receipt of funds, it is best to submit an application promptly.

Faculty

The Argosy University faculty is composed of working professionals who are committed to student success. Members bring real-world experience and practice innovations to the academic setting. Argosy's diverse faculty is widely recognized for contributions to the field. Most hold doctoral degrees. They provide a substantive education that combines comprehensive knowledge with critical skills and practical workplace relevance. Above all, faculty members of the College of Health Sciences are committed to their students' personal and professional development.

Student Activities

Argosy University, Twin Cities, offers unique opportunities for student involvement beyond individual programs of study. Most faculty committees include a student representative. In addition, a student group meets with faculty members and administrators regularly to discuss pertinent campus-related issues.

Facilities and Resources

Argosy University libraries provide curriculum support and educational resources, including current text materials, diagnostic training documents, reference materials and databases, journals and dissertations, and major and current titles in program areas. The University provides an online public-access catalog of library resources throughout the Argosy University system. Students enjoy full remote access to their campus library database, enabling them to study and conduct research at home. Academic databases offer dissertation abstracts, academic journals, and professional periodicals. All library computers are Internet accessible. Software applications include Word, Excel, PowerPoint, SPSS, and various test-scoring programs.

Location

Argosy University's Twin Cities location offers academics in a supportive environment. The campus is nestled in a parklike suburban setting within 10 miles of the airport and the Mall of America. Students enjoy the convenience of nearby shops, restaurants, and housing and easy freeway access. The neighboring Eagan Community Center offers many amenities, including walking paths, a fitness center, meeting rooms, and an outdoor amphitheater. The Twin Cities of Minneapolis and St. Paul have been rated by popular magazines as one of the most livable metropolitan areas in the country. With a population of 2.5 million, the area offers an abundance of recreational activities. Year-round outdoor activities; nationally acclaimed venues for theater, art, and music; and professional sports teams attract residents and visitors alike. The Minneapolis–St. Paul metropolitan area offers a diversified economic base fueled by a broad array of companies. Among the numerous publicly traded companies headquartered in the area are Target, UnitedHealth Group, 3M, General Mills, and U.S. Bancorp.

Admission Requirements

Students who have successfully completed a program of secondary education or the equivalent (GED) are eligible for admission to the health sciences programs. Entrance requirements include either an ACT composite score of 18 or above, a combined math and verbal SAT score of 960 or above, a passing score on the Argosy University Entrance Exam, or a minimum TOEFL score of 550 (paper version), 213 (computer version), or 79 (Internet version) for all applicants whose native language is not English or who have not graduated from an institution in which English is the language of instruction.

All applicants must include a completed application form; proof of high school graduation or successful completion of the GED test; official postsecondary transcripts; SAT, ACT, Argosy University exam, or TOEFL scores; and the nonrefundable application fee. Additional materials are required prior to matriculation. Some programs have additional application requirements. An admissions representative can provide further detailed information.

Application and Information

Argosy University, Twin Cities, accepts students on a rolling admissions basis year-round, depending on availability of required courses. Applications for admission are available online or by contacting the campus, using the information listed in this description.

Argosy University, Twin Cities
1515 Central Parkway
Eagan, Minnesota 55121
Phone: 651-846-2882
888-844-2004 (toll-free)
E-mail: auadmissions@argosy.edu
Web site: http://www.argosy.edu/twincities

THE ART INSTITUTE OF NEW YORK CITY

NEW YORK, NEW YORK

The Art Institute of New York City prepares students to pursue entry-level employment in the creative arts. Students learn through programs of study that reflect the needs of a changing job market. Courses are taught by faculty members who have knowledge and experience in their fields of expertise. The school offers six associate degree programs.

Individualized job search assistance is available to help students with resume writing, networking, and keeping aware of what employers are looking for in job candidates.

The Art Institute of New York City is accredited by the Accrediting Council for Independent Colleges and Schools (ACICS) to award associate degrees. ACICS is listed as a nationally recognized accrediting agency by the United States Department of Education and is recognized by the Council for Higher Education Accreditation. ACICS can be contacted at 750 First Street NE, Suite 980, Washington, D.C. 20002; phone: 202-336-6780.

The Art Institute of New York City has received permission to operate from the State of New York Board of Regents, State Education Department, 89 Washington Avenue, 5 North Mezzanine, Albany, New York 12234; phone: 518-474-2593.

Academic Programs

The Art Institute of New York City offers associate degree programs in art and design technology (with concentrations in interior design and video production), digital filmmaking, fashion design, graphic design, and Web design and interactive media. Each academic program is offered on a year-round basis, allowing students to continue to work uninterrupted toward their degrees.

Costs

Tuition costs vary by program. Prospective students should contact the school for current tuition costs. Other charges include a starting kit for all first-quarter students. Kits vary in price, depending on the program of study.

Financial Aid

Financial aid is available for those who qualify. Students who require financial assistance should first complete and submit a Free Application for Federal Student Aid (FAFSA) and meet with a financial aid officer.

Faculty

Faculty members at The Art Institute of New York City are professionals, many of whom have experience in their respective fields. There are full-time and part-time faculty members at the school.

Student Body Profile

Students come to The Art Institute of New York City from throughout the United States and abroad. The student population includes recent high school graduates, transfer students, and those who have left a previous employment situation to study and train for a new career. Students are creative, competitive, and open to new ideas. They place great value on an education that prepares them for an exciting entry-level position in the arts.

Student Activities

There are several events for students throughout the year that celebrate culture, health, and holidays. The Student Activities Office also provides shape-up and wellness programs for students, along with The Art Institute of New York City Celebrates Women program. Students are offered many opportunities to volunteer throughout the year. Culinary students work at various events throughout the city as well as open-house programs at the school.

Facilities and Resources

The Art Institute of New York City is located in the SoHo/Tribeca district of New York City. The school contains computer labs, drawing studios, a student bookstore, and an art gallery.

Location

Manhattan is a hub of contemporary style, and New York City provides a wealth of opportunities for students to explore their creative side. Broadway plays, art museums, music halls, and professional sports teams are just some of the many entertainment options available to students who make the Big Apple their home.

Admission Requirements

Applicants must complete an application form and write a 150-word essay to apply for admission to The Art Institute of New York City. A personal interview with an admissions representative is required. Applicants must provide official high school transcripts, proof of successful completion of the General Educational Development (GED) test, or transcripts from any college previously attended. There is a $50 application fee.

For the most recent information regarding admission requirements, please refer to the current academic catalog.

Application and Information

To obtain an application or make arrangements for an interview or tour of the school, prospective students should contact:

The Art Institute of New York City
11 Beach Street
New York, New York 10013
Phone: 212-226-5500
800-654-2433 (toll-free)
Fax: 212-966-0706
Web site: http://www.artinstitutes.edu/newyork

The Art Institute of Atlanta; The Art Institute of Atlanta–Decatur[1]; The Art Institute of Austin[2]; The Art Institute of California–Hollywood; The Art Institute of California–Inland Empire; The Art Institute of California–Los Angeles; The Art Institute of California–Orange County; The Art Institute of California–Sacramento; The Art Institute of California–San Diego; The Art Institute of California–San Francisco; The Art Institute of California–Sunnyvale; The Art Institute of Charleston[1]; The Art Institute of Charlotte; The Art Institute of Colorado; The Art Institute of Dallas; The Art Institute of Fort Lauderdale; The Art Institute of Fort Worth[3]; The Art Institute of Houston; The Art Institute of Houston–North[2]; The Art Institute of Indianapolis[4]; The Art Institute of Jacksonville[5]; The Art Institute of Las Vegas; The Art Institute of Michigan; The Art Institute of New York City; The Art Institute of Ohio–Cincinnati[6]; The Art Institute of Philadelphia; The Art Institute of Phoenix; The Art Institute of Pittsburgh; The Art Institute of Portland; The Art Institute of Raleigh–Durham; The Art Institute of Salt Lake City; The Art Institute of San Antonio[2];The Art Institute of Seattle; The Art Institute of Tampa[5]; The Art Institute of Tennessee–Nashville[1,7]; The Art Institute of Tucson; The Art Institute of Vancouver; The Art Institute of Virginia Beach[1,8]; The Art Institute of Washington[1,8]; The Art Institute of Washington–Northern Virginia[1,8]; The Art Institute of York–Pennsylvania; The Art Institutes International–Kansas City; The Art Institutes International Minnesota; The Illinois Institute of Art–Chicago; The Illinois Institute of Art–Schaumburg; Miami International University of Art & Design; The New England Institute of Art.

[1]A branch of The Art Institute of Atlanta
[2]A branch of The Art Institute of Houston
[3]A branch of The Art Institute of Dallas
[4]The Art Institute of Indianapolis is regulated by the Indiana Commission on Proprietary Education, 302 West Washington Street, Room E201, Indianapolis, Indiana 46204, AC-0080
[5]A branch of Miami International University of Art & Design
[6]The Art Institute of Ohio–Cincinnati, 8845 Governors Hill Drive, Suite 100, Cincinnati, Ohio 45249-3317, OH Reg. #04-01-1698B
[7]The Art Institute of Tennessee–Nashville is authorized for operation as a postsecondary educational institution by the Tennessee Higher Education Commission.
[8]Certified by the State Council of Higher Education to operate in Virginia

THE ART INSTITUTE OF SEATTLE

SEATTLE, WASHINGTON

The Art Institute of Seattle provides programs that prepare graduates to pursue entry-level employment in the creative arts. Programs are developed with and taught by experienced educators. The Art Institute of Seattle has a proud history both as a part of the Seattle community and as a contributor to the Northwest's creative industries.

The Art Institute of Seattle offers twelve associate degree programs and twelve bachelor's degree programs.

The Career Services Department works with students to refine their presentations to potential employers. The department also helps provide student advisers with insight into each student's specialized skills and interests. Specific career advising occurs during the last two quarters of a student's education. Interviewing techniques and resume-writing skills are developed, and students receive portfolio advising from faculty members.

The Student Affairs Department offers a variety of services to students to help them make the most of their educational experience. These services include both school-sponsored and independent housing options.

The Art Institute of Seattle is accredited by the Northwest Commission on Colleges and Universities (NWCCU), an institutional accrediting body recognized by the United States Department of Education.

The Art Institute of Seattle is licensed under Chapter 28c.10RCW; inquiries or complaints regarding this or any other private vocational school may be made to the Workforce Training and Education Coordinating Board, 128 10th Avenue SW, P.O. Box 43105, Olympia, Washington 98504-3105; phone: 360-753-5662.

The Associate of Applied Arts in culinary arts degree program is accredited by the Accrediting Commission of the American Culinary Federation Education Foundation.

Academic Programs

Associate degrees are available in animation art and design, audio production, baking and pastry, culinary arts, fashion design, fashion marketing, graphic design, industrial design technology, interior design, photography, video production, and Web design and interactive media.

Bachelor's degree programs are available in audio design technology, culinary arts management, digital filmmaking and video production, fashion design, fashion marketing, game art and design, graphic design, industrial design, interior design, media arts and animation, photography, and Web design and interactive media.

The Art Institute of Seattle operates on a year-round, quarterly basis. Each quarter totals eleven weeks. Bachelor's degree programs are twelve quarters in length.

Costs

Tuition costs vary by program. Prospective students should contact the school for current tuition costs. Other charges include a starting kit for all first-quarter students. Kits vary in price, depending on the program of study.

Financial Aid

Financial aid is available for those who qualify. Students who require financial assistance should first complete and submit a Free Application for Federal Student Aid (FAFSA) and meet with a financial aid officer.

Faculty

Faculty members at The Art Institute of Seattle are experienced professionals, many of whom bring real-world knowledge into the classroom. There are full-time and part-time faculty members.

Student Body Profile

Students come to The Art Institute of Seattle from throughout the United States and abroad. The student population includes recent high school graduates, transfer students, and those who have left a previous employment situation to study and train for a new career. Students are creative, competitive, and open to new ideas. They place great value on an education that prepares them for an exciting entry-level position in the arts.

Student Activities

The Art Institute of Seattle places high importance on student life, both inside and outside the classroom. The school provides an environment that encourages involvement in a wide variety of activities, including clubs and organizations, community service opportunities, and various committees designed to enhance the quality of student life. Numerous all-school programs and events are planned throughout the year to meet students' needs.

Facilities and Resources

The Art Institute of Seattle is an urban campus that comprises three facilities. The school houses classrooms, audio and video studios, a student store, student lounges, copy centers, a gallery, a woodshop, a sculpture room, fashion display windows, a resource center, a technology center, and culinary facilities. The Art Institute of Seattle is also home to a public student-run restaurant.

Location

The Art Institute of Seattle is located in the city's Belltown district. Founded by Native Americans and traders, the city has retained respect for its different cultures and customs. People from all over the world come to study, work, and live in this city, known for its friendly people and beautiful natural surroundings.

World-class companies, such as Microsoft, Boeing, Starbucks, Amazon.com, and Nordstrom, make their global headquarters in Seattle. As a gateway to the Pacific Rim, Seattle is a crossroads where creativity, technology, and business meet.

Admission Requirements

A student seeking admission to The Art Institute of Seattle is required to interview with an admissions representative (in person or over the phone). Applicants are required to have a high school diploma or a General Educational Development (GED) certificate and to submit an admissions application and an essay describing how an education at The Art Institute of Seattle may help the student to achieve career goals. For advanced placement, additional information, including college transcripts, letters of recommendation, or portfolio work, may be required. Students may apply for admission online.

The Art Institute of Seattle follows a rolling admissions schedule. Students are encouraged to apply for their chosen quarter early so that they may take advantage of orientation activities. There is a $50 application fee.

For the most recent information regarding admission requirements, please refer to the current academic catalog.

Application and Information

To obtain an application, make arrangements for an interview, or tour the school, prospective students should contact:

The Art Institute of Seattle
2323 Elliott Avenue
Seattle, Washington 98121-1642
Phone: 206-448-6600
800-275-2471 (toll-free)
Fax: 206-269-0275
Web site: http://www.artinstitutes.edu/seattle

The Art Institute of Atlanta; The Art Institute of Atlanta–Decatur[1]; The Art Institute of Austin[2]; The Art Institute of California–Hollywood; The Art Institute of California–Inland Empire; The Art Institute of California–Los Angeles; The Art Institute of California–Orange County; The Art Institute of California–Sacramento; The Art Institute of California–San Diego; The Art Institute of California–San Francisco; The Art Institute of California–Sunnyvale; The Art Institute of Charleston[1]; The Art Institute of Charlotte; The Art Institute of Colorado; The Art Institute of Dallas; The Art Institute of Fort Lauderdale; The Art Institute of Fort Worth[3]; The Art Institute of Houston; The Art Institute of Houston–North[2]; The Art Institute of Indianapolis[4]; The Art Institute of Jacksonville[5]; The Art Institute of Las Vegas; The Art Institute of Michigan; The Art Institute of New York City; The Art Institute of Ohio–Cincinnati[6]; The Art Institute of Philadelphia; The Art Institute of Phoenix; The Art Institute of Pittsburgh; The Art Institute of Portland; The Art Institute of Raleigh–Durham; The Art Institute of Salt Lake City; The Art Institute of San Antonio[2];The Art Institute of Seattle; The Art Institute of Tampa[5]; The Art Institute of Tennessee–Nashville[1,7]; The Art Institute of Tucson; The Art Institute of Vancouver; The Art Institute of Virginia Beach[1,8]; The Art Institute of Washington[1,8]; The Art Institute of Washington–Northern Virginia[1,8]; The Art Institute of York–Pennsylvania; The Art Institutes International–Kansas City; The Art Institutes International Minnesota; The Illinois Institute of Art–Chicago; The Illinois Institute of Art–Schaumburg; Miami International University of Art & Design; The New England Institute of Art.

[1]A branch of The Art Institute of Atlanta
[2]A branch of The Art Institute of Houston
[3]A branch of The Art Institute of Dallas
[4]The Art Institute of Indianapolis is regulated by the Indiana Commission on Proprietary Education, 302 West Washington Street, Room E201, Indianapolis, Indiana 46204, AC-0080
[5]A branch of Miami International University of Art & Design
[6]The Art Institute of Ohio–Cincinnati, 8845 Governors Hill Drive, Suite 100, Cincinnati, Ohio 45249-3317, OH Reg. #04-01-1698B
[7]The Art Institute of Tennessee–Nashville is authorized for operation as a postsecondary educational institution by the Tennessee Higher Education Commission.
[8]Certified by the State Council of Higher Education to operate in Virginia

BAY STATE COLLEGE

BOSTON, MASSACHUSETTS

The College and Its Mission

Founded in 1946, Bay State College is a private, independent, coeducational institution located in Boston's historic Back Bay. Since its founding, Bay State College has been preparing graduates for outstanding careers and continued education.

Bay State College is a small, private college focused on passionate students who want to turn their interests into a rewarding career. The College offers associate and bachelor's degrees in a number of rewarding fields. Everyone at Bay State—from admissions counselors and professors to the career services team—helps to assist, guide, and advise students, from the moment they apply and throughout their careers. Located in Boston's Back Bay, the College offers the city of Boston as a campus, small classes, and one-on-one attention. For students seeking a career in one of the professions offered by Bay State, a degree program at the College could be a strong first step on their career path.

The College offers associate degrees and bachelor's degrees. The educational experience offered through the variety of programs prepares students to excel in the careers of their choice. Personalized attention is the cornerstone of a Bay State College education. Through the transformative power of its core values of quality, respect, and support, Bay State College has been able to assist students with setting and achieving goals that prepare them for careers and continued education.

Recognizing that one of the most important aspects of college is life outside the classroom, the Office of Student Affairs seeks to provide services from orientation through graduation and beyond. Special events throughout the year include a fashion show and a host of events produced by the Entertainment Management Association. Students also enjoy professional sports teams such as the Boston Celtics and Boston Red Sox.

Bay State College's campus experience can be whatever the student chooses it to be. It's not the typical college campus—its residence halls are actually brownstones along Boston's trendy Commonwealth Avenue and Bay State's quad could be Boston Common, the banks of the Charles River by the Esplanade, or Copley Square. That's the advantage of being located in in Boston's Back Bay, which is also the safest neighborhood in the city. Campus activities can also be as varied as the students' interests. Students can relax at a favorite coffee shop, bike along the Charles River, ice skate on the Frog Pond, check out the city's nightlife, or take in a baseball game at Fenway Park.

Bay State College is accredited by the New England Association of Schools and Colleges, is authorized to award the Associate in Science, Associate in Applied Science, and three Bachelor of Science degrees by the Commonwealth of Massachusetts. Bay State is a member of several professional educational associations. Its medical assisting program is accredited by the Accrediting Bureau of Health Education Schools (ABHES). The physical therapist assistant program is accredited by the Commission on Accreditation in Physical Therapy Education (CAPTE) of the American Physical Therapy Association (APTA).

Academic Programs

Bay State College operates on a semester calendar. The fall semester runs from early September to late December. The spring semester runs from late January until mid-May. A satellite campus is located in Middleborough, Massachusetts.

Bachelor's degrees are offered in entertainment management, fashion merchandising, and management.

Associate degrees are offered in business administration, criminal justice, early childhood education, entertainment management (with a concentration in audio production), fashion design, fashion merchandising, health studies, marketing, medical assisting, nursing, physical therapist assistant studies, retail business management, and hospitality management.

Bay State College also offers courses to working adults in its Evening Division. The courses are offered in eight-week sessions and allow more flexibility for students who must balance work and family commitments while pursuing their education.

Bay State College continually reviews, enhances, and adds new programs to help graduates remain industry-current in their respective fields.

Off-Campus Programs

Many students cite Bay State's internship program as a turning point for them. Bay State internships allow students to gain hands-on experience and spend time working in their chosen fields. These valuable opportunities can give students an advantage when they apply for positions after they have completed school.

Bay State's Boston location allows the College to offer internships at many well-known companies and organizations. Students are able to apply what they've learned in the classroom and do meaningful work in their field of study. In addition, they build working relationships with people in their chosen profession. For more information on internships, prospective students may contact Tom Corrigan, Director of Career Services, at 617-217-9000.

Costs

Tuition for 2010–11 for full-time students is $20,880, based on 30 credits per year ($696 per credit). However, many students choose to take 24 credits, which is also considered full-time enrollment, bringing the cost to $16,704 per year. Evening students pay $257 per credit. Room and board are $11,800 per year, the application fee is $40, a student services fee is $375, and the student activity fee is $50. The cost of books and additional fees vary by major. A residence hall security deposit of $200 and a technology fee of $250 are required of all resident students.

The fall tuition payment due date is July 1; the spring tuition payment is due December 1.

Financial Aid

Each student works with a personal advocate to thoroughly explain financial options and guide them through the financial aid application process. Many options are available: aid, grants and scholarships, federal programs, and private loans. Bay State College's Financial Aid Department and tuition planners can help students determine what aid may apply. Approximately 85 percent of students receive some form of financial assistance. Bay State College requires a completed Free Application for Federal Student Aid (FAFSA) form and signed federal tax forms. The College's institutional financial aid priority deadline is March 15. Financial aid is granted on a rolling basis.

Faculty

There are 72 faculty members, many holding advanced degrees and several holding doctoral degrees. The student-faculty ratio is 20:1.

Student Body Profile

There are approximately 1,100 students in degree programs in both the Day and Evening Divisions.

Student Activities

Bay State College students participate in a multitude of activities offered by the College through existing student organizations. Students also have the opportunity to create clubs and organizations that meet their interests. Existing organizations include the Student Government Association, Entertainment Management Association,

Justice Society, the Criminal Justice Society, DEX, and the Early Childhood Education Club. Students also produce an annual talent show as well as an annual fashion show that showcases the original designs of the students in the College's fashion design program. A literary magazine is also published annually and features the work of students throughout the College.

Facilities and Resources

Advisement/Counseling: Trained staff members assist students in selecting courses and programs of study to satisfy their educational objectives. A counseling center is available to provide mental and physical health referrals to all Bay State College students in need of such services. Referral networks are extensive, within a wide range of geographic areas, and provide access to a variety of public and private health agencies.

Specialized Services: The Office of Academic Development at Bay State College is designed to meet and support the various academic needs of the student body and serve as a resource for supplemental instruction, academic plans, learning accommodations, and other types of support. The Office of Academic Development operates on the belief that all students can achieve success in their courses by accessing support services and creating individual academic plans.

The Center for Learning and Academic Success (CLAS) at Bay State College is a key component available to help students achieve academic success. Students come to CLAS to get support in specific subject areas as well as study skills such as note-taking, reading comprehension, writing research papers, time management, and coping with exam anxiety. They utilize CLAS to develop study plans and strategies that positively impact their grades in all subjects. Students can also take advantage of the tutoring and seminars CLAS offers. CLAS's goal is to ensure that students are provided with exceptional academic support in all areas of study.

Career Planning/Placement: For many college students, the transition from student life to professional life is filled with questions and uncharted realities. But Bay State College's Career Services Department offers students their own personal career advancement team. The Career Services Department can help students learn to write a resume and cover letter, use social networks, practice interviewing skills, find the right job opportunity, and learn other career-related functions. Bay State College even provides each student with a Professionalism Grade, which lets future employers know they have what it takes to start contributing on day one. The Career Services Department at Bay State College is determined to see each student succeed and offers valuable instruction that will serve students throughout their professional careers.

Library and Audiovisual Services: The library is staffed with trained librarians who are available to guide students in their research process. The library's resources include 7,500 books, eighty-five periodical subscriptions, and a dramatically increased reach through its online library resource databases that include ProQuest, InfoTrac, and LexisNexis. In addition, the library provides computer access and study space for students. The library catalog and databases are accessible from any Internet-ready terminal.

First-Year Experience: The First-Year Experience (FYE) is a 1-credit course that is required of all first-year students and takes place during the first three days that students are on campus. FYE combines social activities with an academic syllabus that is designed to ease the transition into the college experience. Through FYE, students have the opportunity to connect with their academic advisers as well as with other students in their academic programs. At the conclusion of FYE, students are on the road to mapping out their personal action plan for success. The plan, designed by students, guided by academic advisers, and revisited each semester, helps students set, monitor, and achieve academic and life goals. It also builds the preparation for lifelong accomplishment.

Location

Located in the historic city of Boston, Massachusetts, and surrounded by dozens of colleges and universities, Bay State College is an ideal setting in which to pursue a college degree. Tree-lined streets around the school are mirrored in the skyscrapers of the Back Bay. The College is located within walking distance of several major league sport franchises, concert halls, museums, the Freedom Train, Boston Symphony Hall, the Boston Public Library, and the Boston Public Garden. World-class shopping and major cultural and sporting events help make college life an experience that students will always remember. The College is accessible by the MBTA and commuter rail and bus, and is near Boston Logan International Airport.

Admission Requirements

An applicant to Bay State College must be a high school graduate, a current high school student working toward graduation, or a recipient of a GED certificate. The Office of Admissions requires that applicants to the associate degree programs have a minimum of a 2.0 GPA (on a 4.0 scale); if available, applicants may submit SAT and/or ACT scores. Applicants to bachelor's degree programs must have a minimum 2.3 GPA (on a 4.0 scale) and must also submit SAT or ACT scores.

International applicants must also submit high school transcripts translated to English with an explanation of the grading system, financial documentation, and a minimum TOEFL score of 500 on the paper-based exam or 173 on the computer-based exam if English is not their native language.

The physical therapist assistant studies program requires a minimum 2.7 GPA (on a 4.0 scale) and the Evening Division has different or additional admission requirements. For more information about these programs, interested students should visit the Web site at http://www.baystate.edu.

A personal interview is required for all prospective students—parents are encouraged to attend. Applicants must receive the recommendation of a Bay State College Admissions Officer.

Application and Information

Applications are accepted on a rolling basis. A $40 fee is required at the time of application.

Students are responsible for arranging for their official high school transcripts, test scores, and letters of recommendation to be submitted to Bay State College.

The Bay State College Admissions Office notifies applicants of a decision within one week of receipt of the transcript and other required documents. When a student is accepted to Bay State College, there is a $100 nonrefundable tuition deposit required to ensure a place in the class; the deposit is credited toward the tuition fee. Deposits are due within thirty days of acceptance. Once a student is accepted, a Bay State College representative creates a personalized financial plan that provides payment options for a Bay State College education.

Applications should be submitted to:

Admissions Office
Bay State College
122 Commonwealth Avenue
Boston, Massachusetts 02116
Phone: 800-81-LEARN (53276)
Fax: 617-249-0400 (eFax)
E-mail: admissions@baystate.edu
Web site: http://www.baystate.edu

BROWN MACKIE COLLEGE–AKRON

AKRON, OHIO

The College and Its Mission

Brown Mackie College–Akron is one of over twenty locations in the Brown Mackie College family of schools (http://www.brownmackie.edu), which is dedicated to providing educational programs that prepare students to pursue entry-level positions in a competitive, rapidly-changing workplace. Brown Mackie College schools offer bachelor's degree, associate degree, certificate, and diploma programs in health sciences, business, information technology, legal studies, and design to over 19,000 students in the Midwest, Southeast, Southwest, and Western United States.

The College was founded in Cincinnati, Ohio, in February 1927, as a traditional business college. In March 1980, the College added a branch campus in Akron, Ohio. The College outgrew this space and relocated to its current address in January 2007.

Brown Mackie College–Akron is accredited by the Accrediting Council for Independent Colleges and Schools (ACICS) to award associate degrees and diplomas. ACICS is listed as a nationally recognized accrediting agency by the United States Department of Education and is recognized by the Council for Higher Education Accreditation. ACICS can be contacted at 750 First Street NE, Suite 980, Washington, D.C. 20002-4241; phone: 202-336-6780.

Brown Mackie College–Akron is licensed by the Ohio State Board of Career Colleges and Schools, 35 East Gay Street, Suite 403, Columbus, Ohio 43215 (Ohio registration #03-09-1685T).

The Brown Mackie College–Akron Associate of Applied Science degree in medical assisting is accredited by the Commission on Accreditation of Allied Health Education Programs (http://www.caahep.org) upon recommendation of the Curriculum Review Board of the American Association of Medical Assistants Endowment (AAMAE).

The occupational therapy assistant studies program has applied for accreditation by the Accreditation Council for Occupational Therapy Education (ACOTE) of the American Occupational Therapy Association (AOTA), located at 4720 Montgomery Lane, P.O. Box 31220, Bethesda, Maryland 20824; phone: 301-652-AOTA.

The practical nursing diploma program is accredited by the Ohio Board of Nursing (OBN), 17 South High Street, Suite 400, Columbus, Ohio 43215-7410; phone: 330-722-7670.

The College is a nonresidential, smoke-free institution.

Academic Programs

Brown Mackie College–Akron provides higher education to traditional and nontraditional students through associate degree and diploma programs that can assist them in enhancing their career opportunities, broadening their perspectives through appropriate general education courses, thinking independently and critically, and improving problem-solving abilities.

Each College quarter comprises twelve weeks. Associate degree programs require a minimum of eight quarters to complete. Programs are offered on a year-round basis, providing students with the ability to work uninterrupted toward their degree. The College offers all programs in a unique One Course a Month format. This schedule allows students to focus studies on only one course for four weeks and has proven convenient for students with multiple obligations such as jobs and family.

Associate Degree Programs: The Associate of Applied Business degree is awarded in accounting technology, business management, criminal justice, office management, and paralegal studies. The Associate of Applied Science degree is awarded in database technology, early childhood education, health-care administration, information technology, medical assisting, occupational therapy assistant studies, pharmacy technology, surgical technology, and veterinary technology.

Diploma Programs: The College also offers diploma programs in accounting, business, computer software applications, criminal justice, medical assistant studies, medical coding and billing, paralegal assistant studies, and practical nursing.

Costs

Tuition for the 2010–11 academic year is $266 per credit hour for all programs except the practical nursing program, which is $325 per credit hour and the surgical technology program, which is $310 per credit hour. Tuition for certain courses in the occupational therapy assistant studies program is $365 per credit hour, with fees of $15 per credit hour. The cost of textbooks and other instructional materials varies by program.

Financial Aid

Financial aid is available to those who qualify. The College maintains a full-time staff of financial aid professionals to assist qualified students in obtaining financial assistance. The College participates in several student aid programs. Forms of financial aid available through federal resources include the Federal Pell Grant Program, Federal Supplemental Educational Opportunity Grant (FSEOG) Program, Federal Work-Study Program, Federal Perkins Loan Program, Federal Stafford Student Loan Program (subsidized and unsubsidized), and the Federal PLUS Loan Program. Through the Ohio Instructional Grant (OIG) program, Ohio residents enrolled in a degree program may receive an award to apply to their tuition costs. The amount of the award varies according to family income and other determining factors. Eligible students may also apply for veterans' educational benefits. Students with physical or mental disabilities that are a handicap to employment may be eligible for training services through the state Agency for Vocational Rehabilitation. For further information, students should contact the College's Student Financial Services Office.

Each year, the College makes available scholarships of up to $1000 each to qualifying seniors from area high schools. Only one scholarship is awarded per high school. In order to qualify, a senior must be graduating from a participating high school, have maintained a cumulative grade point average of at least 2.0, and submitted a brief essay. The student's extracurricular activities and community service are also considered. These scholarships are available only to students enrolling in one of the College's degree programs. Students awarded the scholarship must enroll at Brown Mackie College–Akron between June and September immediately following their high school graduation. Applications for these scholarships can be obtained from the guidance departments of participating high schools. These applications must be completed and returned to the College by March 31.

Faculty

There are 25 full-time and 61 part-time faculty members. The student-faculty ratio is 17:1.

Facilities and Resources

Brown Mackie College–Akron provides media presentation rooms for special instructional needs, libraries that provide instructional resources and academic support for both faculty members and students, and qualified and experienced faculty members who are committed to the academic and technical preparation of their students. The College is nonresidential; students who are unable to commute daily from their homes may request assistance from the Office of Admissions in locating off-campus housing. The College is accessible by public transportation and provides ample parking, available at no charge.

Location

The College is located at 755 White Pond Drive in Akron, Ohio. For added convenience, the College also operates a downtown learning site at 388 South Main Street in Akron.

Admission Requirements

Each applicant for admission is assigned an Assistant Director of Admissions who directs the applicant through the steps of the admissions process, providing information on curriculum, policies, procedures, and services and assisting the applicant in setting necessary appointments and interviews.

To qualify for admission, each applicant must provide documentation of graduation from an accredited high school or from a state-approved secondary education curriculum or provide official documentation of high school graduation equivalency. All transcripts become the property of the College. Admission to the College is based upon the applicant meeting the stated requirements, a review of the applicant's previous education records, and a review of the applicant's career interests. If previous academic records indicate that the College's education and training programs would not benefit the applicant, the College reserves the right to advise the applicant not to enroll. Special requirements for enrollment into certain programs are discussed in the descriptions of those programs.

For the most recent information regarding admission requirements, please refer to the current academic catalog.

Application and Information

Applicants must complete and submit an application form along with documentation of graduation from an accredited high school or state-approved secondary education curriculum, or applicants must provide official documentation of high school graduation equivalency. For additional information, prospective students should contact:

Senior Director of Admissions
Brown Mackie College–Akron
755 White Pond Drive
Akron, Ohio 44320
Phone: 330-869-3600
Fax: 330-869-3650
E-mail: bmcakadm@brownmackie.edu
Web site: http://www.brownmackie.edu/Akron

BROWN MACKIE COLLEGE–ALBUQUERQUE

ALBUQUERQUE, NEW MEXICO

The College and Its Mission

Brown Mackie College–Albuquerque is one of over twenty locations in the Brown Mackie College family of schools (http://www.brownmackie.edu), which is dedicated to providing educational programs that prepare students to pursue entry-level positions in a competitive, rapidly-changing workplace. Brown Mackie College schools offer bachelor's degree, associate degree, and diploma programs in health sciences, business, information technology, legal studies, and design to over 19,000 students in the Midwest, Southeast, Southwest, and Western United States.

Brown Mackie College–Albuquerque was founded in 2010 as a branch of Brown Mackie College–Tucson, Arizona.

Brown Mackie College–Albuquerque is accredited by the Accrediting Council for Independent Colleges and Schools (ACICS) to award bachelor's degrees, associate degrees, and certificates. ACICS is listed as a nationally recognized accrediting agency by the United States Department of Education and is recognized by the Council for Higher Education Accreditation. ACICS can be contacted at 750 First Street NE, Suite 980, Washington, D.C. 20002; phone: 202-336-6780.

This institution is licensed by the New Mexico Higher Education Department, 2048 Galisteo Street, Santa Fe, New Mexico 87505-2100; phone: 505-476-8400.

Academic Programs

Brown Mackie College–Albuquerque provides higher education to traditional and nontraditional students through associate degree and diploma programs that can assist them in enhancing their career opportunities, broadening their perspectives through appropriate general education courses, thinking independently and critically, and improving problem-solving abilities.

Each College quarter comprises twelve weeks. Bachelor's degree programs require a minimum of sixteen quarters to complete. Associate degree programs require a minimum of eight quarters to complete. Programs are offered on a year-round basis, providing students with the ability to work uninterrupted toward their degrees. The College offers all programs in a unique One Course a Month format. This schedule allows students to focus studies on only one course for four weeks and has proven convenient for students with multiple obligations such as jobs and family.

Bachelor's Degree Programs: The Bachelor of Science degree is awarded in business administration, criminal justice, health-care management, and legal studies.

Associate Degree Programs: The Associate of Applied Science degree is awarded in accounting technology, architectural design and drafting technology, business management, criminal justice, health-care administration, information technology, medical assisting, occupational therapy assistant studies, paralegal studies, pharmacy technology, surgical technology, and veterinary technology.

Diploma Programs: The College also offers diploma programs in accounting, business, criminal justice, medical assistant studies, and paralegal assistant studies.

Costs

Tuition in the 2010–11 academic year for most bachelor's and associate degree programs is $266 per credit hour; fees are $15 per credit hour. Textbooks and other instructional expenses vary by program.

Financial Aid

Financial aid is available for those who qualify. The College maintains a full-time staff of financial aid professionals to assist qualified students in obtaining the financial assistance they require to meet their educational expenses. Available resources include federal and state aid, student loans from private lenders, and Federal Work-Study opportunities, both on and off College premises.

Each year, the College makes available scholarships of up to $1000 each to qualifying seniors from area high schools. No more than one scholarship is awarded per high school. In order to qualify, a senior must be graduating from a participating high school, have maintained a cumulative grade point average of at least 2.0, and submitted a brief essay. The student's extracurricular activities and community service are also considered. These scholarships are available only to students enrolling in one of the College's degree programs. Students awarded the scholarship must enroll at Brown Mackie College–Albuquerque between June and September immediately following their high school graduation. Applications for these scholarships can be obtained from the guidance departments of participating high schools. These applications must be completed and returned to the College by March 31.

Faculty

Experienced faculty members provide academic support and are committed to the academic and technical preparation of their students. The College has both full-time and part-time instructors, with a typical student-faculty ratio of 13:1. Each student is assigned a faculty adviser.

Facilities and Resources

A modern facility, Brown Mackie College–Albuquerque offers approximately 35,000 square feet of tastefully appointed classrooms, laboratories, and office space designed to the specifications of the College for its business, medical, and technical programs. Instructional equipment is comparable to current technology used in business and industry. Well-equipped classrooms for special instructional needs offer multimedia capabilities with surround sound and overhead projectors accessible through computer, DVD, or VHS. Internet access and instructional resources are available at the College's library, and wireless Internet access throughout the campus.

Location

Brown Mackie College–Albuquerque is conveniently located at 10500 Copper Avenue NE in Albuquerque, New Mexico. The College has a generous parking area and is also easily accessible by public transportation.

Admission Requirements

Each applicant for admission is assigned an Assistant Director of Admissions who directs the applicant through the steps of the admissions process. They provide information on curriculum, policies, procedures, and services and assist the applicant in setting up necessary appointments and interviews.

To qualify for admission, each applicant must provide documentation of graduation from an accredited high school, or from a state-approved secondary education curriculum, or provide official documentation of high school graduation equivalency. All transcripts become the property of the College. Admission to the College is based on the applicant meeting the stated requirements, a review of the applicant's previous educational records, and a review of the applicant's career interests. If previous academic records indicate the College's education and training programs would not benefit the applicant, the College reserves the right to advise the applicant not to enroll. Special requirements for enrollment into certain programs are discussed in the descriptions of those programs.

For the most recent information regarding admission requirements, please refer to the current academic catalog.

Application and Information

Applicants must complete and submit an application form, along with documentation of graduation from an accredited high school or state-approved secondary education curriculum or official documentation of high school graduation equivalency.

For additional information, prospective students should contact:

Senior Director of Admissions
Brown Mackie College–Albuquerque
10500 Copper Avenue NE
Albuquerque, New Mexico 87123
Phone: 505-559-5200
877-271-3488 (toll-free)
Fax: 505-559-5222
E-mail: bmcalbadm@brownmackie.edu
Web site: http://www.brownmackie.edu/Albuquerque

BROWN MACKIE COLLEGE–ATLANTA

ATLANTA, GEORGIA

The College and Its Mission

Brown Mackie College–Atlanta is one of over twenty locations in the Brown Mackie College family of schools (http://www.brownmackie.edu), which is dedicated to providing educational programs that prepare students to pursue entry-level positions in a competitive, rapidly-changing workplace. Brown Mackie College schools offer bachelor's degree, associate degree, certificate, and diploma programs in health sciences, business, information technology, legal studies, and design to over 19,000 students in the Midwest, Southeast, Southwest, and Western United States.

Brown Mackie College–Atlanta is accredited by the Accrediting Council for Independent Colleges and Schools (ACICS) to award associate degrees, diplomas, and certificates. ACICS is listed as a nationally recognized accrediting agency by the United States Department of Education and is recognized by the Council for Higher Education Accreditation. ACICS can be contacted at 750 First Street NE, Suite 980, Washington, D.C. 20002; phone: 202-336-6780.

The occupational therapy assistant studies program is accredited by the Accreditation Council for Occupational Therapy Education (ACOTE) of the American Occupational Therapy Association (AOTA), located at 4720 Montgomery Lane, P.O. Box 31220, Bethesda, Maryland 20824; phone: 301-652-AOTA.

The Brown Mackie College–Atlanta Associate of Applied Science in surgical technology program is accredited by the Accrediting Bureau of Health Education Schools (http://www.abhes.org).

The College is a nonresidential, smoke-free institution.

Academic Programs

Brown Mackie College–Atlanta provides higher education to traditional and nontraditional students through associate degree and diploma programs that can assist students in enhancing their career opportunities, broadening their perspectives through appropriate general education courses, thinking independently and critically, and improving problem-solving abilities. The College strives to develop within its students the desire for lifelong and continued education.

Each College quarter comprises twelve weeks. Associate degree programs require a minimum of eight quarters to complete. Programs are offered on a year-round basis, providing students with the ability to work uninterrupted toward their degrees. The College offers all programs in a unique One Course a Month format. This schedule allows students to focus studies on only one course for four weeks and has proven convenient for students with multiple obligations such as jobs and family.

Associate Degree Programs The Associate of Applied Business degree is awarded in accounting technology, business management, criminal justice, and paralegal studies. The Associate of Applied Science degree is awarded in early childhood education, health-care administration, medical assisting, occupational therapy assistant studies, pharmacy technology, and surgical technology.

Diploma Programs The College also offers diploma programs in accounting, business, criminal justice, medical assistant studies, and paralegal assistant studies.

Costs

Tuition for the 2010–11 academic year is $314 per credit hour. The tuition for occupational therapy assistant studies program-specific courses is $365 per credit hour. The tuition for the surgical technology program is $310 per credit hour. The cost of textbooks and other instructional materials varies by program.

Financial Aid

Financial aid is available to those who qualify. The College maintains a full-time staff of financial aid professionals to assist qualified students in obtaining financial assistance. The College participates in several student aid programs. Forms of financial aid available through federal resources include the Federal Pell Grant Program, Federal Supplemental Educational Opportunity Grant (FSEOG) Program, Federal Work-Study Program, Federal Perkins Loan Program, Federal Stafford Student Loan Program (subsidized and unsubsidized), and the Federal PLUS Loan Program. Eligible students may also apply for state awards and veterans' educational benefits. Students with physical or mental disabilities that are a handicap to employment may be eligible for training services through the state Agency for Vocational Rehabilitation. For further information, students should contact the College's Student Financial Services Office.

Faculty

There are 4 full-time and 5 part-time faculty members. The average student-faculty ratio is 19:1. Each student has a faculty and student adviser.

Facilities and Resources

The College comprises administrative offices, faculty and student lounges, a reception area, and spacious classrooms and laboratories. Instructional equipment includes personal computers, LANs, printers, and transcribers. The library provides support for the academic programs through volumes covering a broad range of subjects, as well as through Internet access. Vehicle parking is provided for both students and staff members.

Location

Brown Mackie College–Atlanta is located at 4370 Peachtree Road NE in Atlanta, Georgia. The school also operates a learning site at 6600 Peachtree Dunwoody Road NE, 600 Embassy Row, Suite 130 in Atlanta, which is easily accessible from I-285 and the MARTA Sandy Springs rail station.

Admission Requirements

Each applicant for admission is assigned an Assistant Director of Admissions who directs the applicant through the steps of the admissions process, providing information on curriculum, policies, procedures, and services and assisting the applicant in setting necessary appointments and interviews.

To qualify for admission, each applicant must provide documentation of graduation from an accredited high school or from a state-approved secondary education curriculum or provide official documentation of high school graduation equivalency. All transcripts become the property of the College. Admission to the College is based upon the applicant meeting the stated requirements, a review of the applicant's previous education records, and a review of the applicant's career interests. If previous academic records indicate that the College's education and training programs would not benefit the applicant, the College reserves the right to advise the applicant not to enroll. Special requirements for enrollment into certain programs are discussed in the descriptions of those programs.

For the most recent information regarding admission requirements, please refer to the current academic catalog.

Application and Information

Applicants must complete and submit an application form along with documentation of graduation from an accredited high school or state-approved secondary education curriculum, or applicants must provide official documentation of high school graduation equivalency.

For additional information, prospective students should contact:

Director of Admissions
Brown Mackie College–Atlanta
4370 Peachtree Road NE
Atlanta, Georgia 30319
Phone: 404-799-4500
877-479-8419 (toll-free)
Fax: 404-799-4522
E-mail: bmcatadm@brownmackie.edu
Web site: http://www.brownmackie.edu/Atlanta

BROWN MACKIE COLLEGE–BOISE

BOISE, IDAHO

The College and Its Mission

Brown Mackie College–Boise is one of over twenty locations in the Brown Mackie College family of schools (http://www.brownmackie.edu), which is dedicated to providing educational programs that prepare students to pursue entry-level positions in a competitive, rapidly-changing workplace. Brown Mackie College schools offer bachelor's degree, associate degree, certificate, and diploma programs in health sciences, business, information technology, legal studies, and design to over 19,000 students in the Midwest, Southeast, Southwest, and Western United States.

Brown Mackie College–Boise was founded in 2008 as a branch of Brown Mackie College–South Bend, Indiana. Brown Mackie College–Boise is accredited by the Accrediting Council for Independent Colleges and Schools (ACICS) to award bachelor's degrees, associate degrees, and diplomas. ACICS is listed as a nationally recognized accrediting agency by the United States Department of Education and is recognized by the Council for Higher Education Accreditation. ACICS can be contacted at 750 First Street NE, Suite 980, Washington, D.C. 20002-4241; phone: 202-336-6780.

The Brown Mackie College–Boise Associate of Science degree in surgical technology has applied for accreditation by the Commission on Accreditation of Allied Health Education Programs (http://www.caahep.org).

The occupational therapy assistant studies program has applied for accreditation by the Accreditation Council for Occupational Therapy Education (ACOTE) of the American Occupational Therapy Association (AOTA), located at 4720 Montgomery Lane, P.O. Box 31220, Bethesda, Maryland 20824; phone: 301-652-AOTA.

The veterinarian technology program has applied for accreditation by the American Veterinary Medical Association (http://www.avma.org)

Academic Programs

Brown Mackie College–Boise provides higher education to traditional and nontraditional students through bachelor's degree, associate degree, and diploma programs that can assist in enhancing their career opportunities, broadening their perspectives through appropriate general education courses, thinking independently and critically, and improving problem-solving abilities.

Each College quarter comprises twelve weeks. Bachelor's degree programs require a minimum of sixteen quarters to complete. Associate degree programs require a minimum of eight quarters to complete. Programs are offered on a year-round basis, providing students with the ability to work uninterrupted toward completion of their programs. The College offers all programs in a unique One Course a Month format. This schedule allows students to focus studies on only one course for four weeks and has proven convenient for students with multiple obligations such as jobs and family.

Bachelor's Degree Programs: The Bachelor of Science degree is awarded in business administration, criminal justice, health-care management, and legal studies.

Associate Degree Programs: The Associate of Science degree is awarded in accounting technology, bioscience laboratory technology, business management, criminal justice, health-care administration, information technology, medical assisting, paralegal studies, and surgical technology.

The Associate of Applied Science degree is awarded in architectural design and drafting technology, occupational therapy assistant studies, and veterinary technology.

Diploma Programs: The College offers diploma programs in accounting, business, criminal justice, medical assistant studies, dental assisting, and paralegal studies.

Costs

Tuition for the 2010–11 academic year is $275 per credit hour for all programs, with a $15 per credit general fee applied to instructional costs for activities and services. The cost of textbooks and other instructional materials varies by program. Tuition for certain occupational therapy assistant studies courses is $365 per credit hour with a $15 per credit hour general fee applied to instructional costs for activities and services. Tuition for certain surgical technology courses is $310 per credit hour with a $15 per credit hour general fee applied to instructional costs for activities.

Financial Aid

Financial aid is available to those who qualify. The College maintains a full-time staff of financial aid professionals to assist qualified students in obtaining financial assistance. The College participates in several student aid programs. Forms of financial aid available through federal resources include the Federal Pell Grant Program, Federal Supplemental Educational Opportunity Grant (FSEOG) Program, Federal Work-Study Program, Federal Perkins Loan Program, Federal Stafford Student Loan Program (subsidized and unsubsidized), and the Federal PLUS Loan Program.

Each year, the College makes available President's Scholarships of up to $1000 each to qualifying seniors from area high schools. No more than one scholarship is awarded per high school. In order to qualify, a senior must be graduating from a participating high school, have maintained a cumulative grade point average of at least 2.0, and submitted a brief essay. The student's extracurricular activities and community service are also considered. The President's Scholarship is available only to students enrolling in one of the College's degree programs. Students awarded the scholarship must enroll at Brown Mackie College–Boise between June and September immediately following their high school graduation. Applications for these scholarships can be obtained from the guidance departments of participating high schools. These applications must be completed and returned to the College by March 31.

Faculty

There are 27 full-time and 30 part-time faculty members at the College. The average student-faculty ratio is 18:1. Each student is assigned a program director as an adviser.

Facilities and Resources

Brown Mackie College–Boise provides media presentation rooms for special instructional needs, libraries that provide instructional resources and academic support for both faculty members and students, and qualified and experienced faculty members who are committed to the academic and technical preparation of their students.

The College is nonresidential; students who are unable to commute daily from their homes may request assistance from the Office of Admissions in locating off-campus housing. The College is accessible by public transportation and provides ample parking at no cost.

Location

Brown Mackie College–Boise is conveniently located at 9050 West Overland Road in Boise, Idaho. The College has a generous parking area and is also easily accessible by public transportation.

Admission Requirements

Each applicant for admission is assigned an Assistant Director of Admissions who directs the applicant through the steps of the admissions process, providing information on curriculum, policies, procedures, and services and assisting the applicant in setting necessary appointments and interviews.

To qualify for admission, each applicant must provide documentation of graduation from an accredited high school or from a state-approved secondary education curriculum or provide official documentation of high school graduation equivalency. All transcripts become the property of the College.

Admission to the College is based upon the applicant meeting the stated requirements, a review of the applicant's previous education records, and a review of the applicant's career interests. If previous academic records indicate that the College's education and training programs would not benefit the applicant, the College reserves the right to advise the applicant not to enroll. Special requirements for enrollment into certain programs are discussed in the descriptions of those programs.

In addition to the College's general admission requirements, applicants enrolling in the occupational therapy assistant studies program must document one of the following: a high school cumulative grade point average of at least 2.5 or a score on the GED examination of at least 557 (57 if taken on or before January 15, 2002). Applicants enrolling in the occupational therapy assistant studies associate degree program must complete an academic readiness assessment and obtain minimum scores in reading, writing, and mathematics that demonstrate the ability to be successful in the program. In the event that applicants do not demonstrate proficiency in any of these areas, they will be enrolled in transitional studies courses. Following the successful completion of these courses, academic readiness will be reevaluated to determine if the program is an appropriate choice for the student. The student may attempt this second academic readiness assessment only once, and only after successfully completing all transitional studies course(s) indicated as required by the initial academic readiness assessment. If the applicant does not successfully obtain the minimum scores in reading, writing, and mathematics, the student will not be allowed to continue with the occupational therapy assistant studies program, but can be considered for another program of study at Brown Mackie College–Boise.

For the most recent information regarding admission requirements, please refer to the current academic catalog.

Application and Information

Applicants must complete and submit an application form, along with documentation of graduation from an accredited high school or state-approved secondary education curriculum or provide official documentation of high school graduation equivalency.

For additional information, prospective students should contact:

Brown Mackie College–Boise
9050 West Overland Road
Boise, Idaho 83709

Phone: 208-321-8800
888-810-9286 (toll-free)
Fax: 208-375-3249
E-mail: bmcboiadm@brownmackie.edu
Web site: http://www.brownmackie.edu/Boise

BROWN MACKIE COLLEGE–CINCINNATI

CINCINNATI, OHIO

The College and Its Mission

Brown Mackie College–Cincinnati is one of over twenty locations in the Brown Mackie College family of schools (http://www.brownmackie.edu), which is dedicated to providing educational programs that prepare students to pursue entry-level positions in a competitive, rapidly-changing workplace. Brown Mackie College schools offer bachelor's degree, associate degree, certificate, and diploma programs in health sciences, business, information technology, legal studies, and design to over 19,000 students in the Midwest, Southeast, Southwest, and Western United States.

The College was founded in February 1927 as Southern Ohio Business College. In 1978, the College's main location was relocated from downtown Cincinnati to the Bond Hill–Roselawn area and in 1995 to its current location at 1011 Glendale-Milford Road in the community of Woodlawn.

Brown Mackie College–Cincinnati is accredited by the Accrediting Council for Independent Colleges and Schools (ACICS) to award associate degrees, diplomas, and certificates. ACICS is listed as a nationally recognized accrediting agency by the United States Department of Education and is recognized by the Council for Higher Education Accreditation. ACICS can be contacted at 750 First Street NE, Suite 980, Washington, D.C. 20002-4241; phone: 202-336-6780.

The Brown Mackie College–Cincinnati Associate of Applied Science degree in medical assisting is accredited by the Commission on Accreditation of Allied Health Education Programs (http://www.caahep.org), upon the recommendation of the curriculum Review board of the American Association of Medical Assistants endowment (AAMEA).

(Ohio registration #03-09-1686T).

The College is nonresidential and smoke free.

Academic Programs

Brown Mackie College–Cincinnati provides higher education to traditional and nontraditional students through associate degree, diploma, and certificate programs that can assist them in enhancing their career opportunities, broadening their perspectives through appropriate general education courses, thinking independently and critically, and improving problem-solving abilities. The College strives to develop within its students the desire for lifelong and continued education.

Each College quarter comprises twelve weeks. Associate degree programs require a minimum of eight quarters to complete. Programs are offered on a year-round basis, providing students with the ability to work uninterrupted toward their degrees. The College offers all programs in a unique One Course a Month format. This schedule allows students to focus studies on only one course for four weeks and has proven convenient for students with multiple obligations such as jobs and family.

Associate Degree Programs: The Associate of Applied Business degree is awarded in accounting technology, business management, computer networking and applications, criminal justice, information technology, office management, and paralegal studies. The Associate of Applied Science degree is awarded in architectural design and drafting technology, audio/video production, biomedical equipment technology, early childhood education, health-care administration, medical assisting, pharmacy technology, surgical technology, and veterinary technology.

Diploma Programs: The College offers diploma programs in accounting, audio/video technician studies, business, criminal justice, medical assistant studies, office applications specialist studies, paralegal assistant studies, and practical nursing.

Certificate Program: The College offers a certificate program in computer networking.

Costs

Tuition for the 2010–11 academic year is $266 per credit hour, with the exception of the practical nursing program at $325 per credit hour, the surgical technology program at $310 per credit hour, and Microsoft Certified Systems Engineer (MCSE) courses at $300 per credit hour plus a $25 per credit hour technology fee. Textbooks and other instructional materials vary by program.

Financial Aid

Financial aid is available to those who qualify. The College maintains a full-time staff of financial aid professionals to assist qualified students in obtaining financial assistance. The College participates in several student aid programs. Forms of financial aid available to qualified students through federal resources include the Federal Pell Grant Program, Federal Supplemental Educational Opportunity Grant (FSEOG) Program, Federal Work-Study Program, Federal Perkins Loan Program, Federal Stafford Student Loan Program (subsidized and unsubsidized), and the Federal PLUS Loan Program. Eligible students may apply for state awards, such as veterans' educational benefits. Students with physical or mental disabilities that are a handicap to employment may be eligible for training services through the state Agency for Vocational Rehabilitation. For further information, students should contact the College's Student Financial Services Office.

Each year, the College makes available President's Scholarships of up to $1000 each to qualifying seniors from area high schools. No more than one scholarship is awarded per high school. In order to qualify, a senior must be graduating from a participating high school, have maintained a cumulative grade point average of at least 2.0, and submitted a brief essay. The student's extracurricular activities and community service are also considered. The President's Scholarship is available only to students enrolling in one of the College's degree programs. Students awarded the scholarship must enroll at Brown Mackie College–Cincinnati between June and September immediately following their high school graduation. Applications for these scholarships can be obtained from the guidance departments of participating high schools. These applications must be completed and returned to the College by March 31.

The Education Foundation was established in 2000 to offer scholarship support to students interested in continuing their education at one of the postsecondary, career-focused schools in the EDMC system. The number and amount of the awards can vary depending on the funds available. Scholarship applications are considered every quarter. At Brown Mackie College–Cincinnati, applicants must be currently enrolled in an associate's degree program and in their fourth quarter or higher (but no further than their second-to-last quarter) at the time of application. Awards are made based on academic performance and potential, as well as financial need.

Faculty

There are 40 full-time and 90 part-time faculty members. The average student-faculty ratio is 20:1. Each student has a faculty and student adviser.

Academic Facilities

Brown Mackie College–Cincinnati consists of more than 57,000 square feet of classroom, laboratory, and office space at the main campus and more than 28,000 square feet at the learning site. Both sites are designed to specifications of the College for its business, computer, medical, and creative programs.

Location

Brown Mackie College–Cincinnati is located in the Woodlawn section of Cincinnati, Ohio. The College is accessible by public transportation and provides parking at no cost. For added convenience, the College also holds classes at the Norwood Learning Site at 4805 Montgomery Road in Norwood, Ohio.

Admission Requirements

Each applicant for admission is assigned an Assistant Director of Admissions, who directs the applicant through the steps of the admissions process, providing information on curriculum, policies, procedures, and services and assisting the applicant in setting necessary appointments and interviews.

To qualify for admission, each applicant must provide documentation of graduation from an accredited high school or from a state-approved secondary education curriculum or provide official documentation of high school graduation equivalency. All transcripts become the property of the College. Admission to the College is based on the applicant meeting the stated requirements, a review of the applicant's previous educational records, and a review of the applicant's career interests. If previous academic records indicate that the College's education and training programs would not benefit the applicant, the College reserves the right to advise the applicant not to enroll. Special requirements for enrollment into certain programs are discussed in the descriptions of those programs.

For the most recent information regarding admission requirements, please refer to the current academic catalog.

Application and Information

Applicants must complete and submit an application form, along with documentation of graduation from an accredited high school or state-approved secondary education curriculum or official documentation of high school graduation equivalency.

For additional information, prospective students should contact:

Senior Director of Admissions
Brown Mackie College–Cincinnati
1011 Glendale-Milford Road
Cincinnati, Ohio 45215
Phone: 512-771-2424
800-888-1445 (toll-free)
Fax: 513-771-3413
E-mail: bmcciadm@brownmackie.edu
Web site: http://www.brownmackie.edu/Cincinnati

BROWN MACKIE COLLEGE–FINDLAY

FINDLAY, OHIO

The College and Its Mission

Brown Mackie College–Findlay is one of over twenty locations in the Brown Mackie College family of schools (http://www.brownmackie.edu), which is dedicated to providing educational programs that prepare students to pursue entry-level positions in a competitive, rapidly-changing workplace. Brown Mackie College schools offer bachelor's degree, associate degree, certificate, and diploma programs in health sciences, business, information technology, legal studies, and design to over 19,000 students in the Midwest, Southeast, Southwest, and Western United States.

Brown Mackie College–Findlay was founded in 1926 by William H. Stautzenberger to provide solid business education at a reasonable cost. In 1960, the College was acquired by George R. Hawes, who served as its president until 1969. The College changed its name from Southern Ohio College–Findlay in 2001 to AEC Southern Ohio College; it was changed again to Brown Mackie College–Findlay in November 2004.

Brown Mackie College–Findlay is accredited by the Accrediting Council for Independent Colleges and Schools (ACICS) to award associate degrees and diplomas. ACICS is listed as a nationally recognized accrediting agency by the United States Department of Education and is recognized by the Council for Higher Education Accreditation. ACICS can be contacted at 750 First Street NE, Suite 980, Washington, D.C. 20002; phone: 202-336-6780.

The practical nursing program is approved by the Ohio Board of Nursing, 17 South High Street, Suite 400, Columbus, Ohio 43215-3413; phone: 614-466-3947.

The surgical technology program is accredited by the Commission on Accreditation of Allied Health Education Programs (CAAHEP), located at 1361 Park Street, Clearwater, Florida 33756; phone: 727-210-2350.

The occupational therapy assistant studies program has applied for accreditation by the Accreditation Council for Occupational Therapy Education (ACOTE) of the American Occupational Therapy Association (AOTA), located at 4720 Montgomery Lane, P.O. Box 31220, Bethesda, Maryland 20824; phone: 301-652-AOTA.

(Ohio registration #0309-1687T).

Brown Mackie College–Findlay is a nonresidential, smoke-free institution. Although the College does not offer residential housing, students who are unable to commute daily from their homes may request assistance from the Admissions Office in locating housing. Ample parking is available at no additional cost.

Academic Programs

Brown Mackie College–Findlay provides higher education to traditional and nontraditional students through associate degree and diploma programs that can assist them in enhancing their career opportunities, broadening their perspectives through appropriate general education courses, thinking independently and critically, and improving problem-solving abilities. The College strives to develop within its students the desire for lifelong and continued education.

Each College quarter comprises twelve weeks. Associate degree programs require a minimum of eight quarters to complete. Programs are offered on a year-round basis, providing students with the ability to work uninterrupted toward completion of their programs. The College offers all programs in a unique One Course a Month format. This schedule allows students to focus studies on only one course for four weeks and has proven convenient for students with multiple obligations such as jobs and family.

Associate Degree Programs: The Associate of Applied Business degree is awarded in accounting technology, business management, criminal justice, office management, and paralegal studies. The Associate of Applied Science degree is awarded in early childhood education, health-care administration, medical assisting, occupational therapy assistant studies, pharmacy technology, surgical technology, and veterinary technology.

Diploma Programs: In addition to the associate degree programs, the College offers diploma programs in business, computer software applications, criminal justice, medical assistant studies, medical transcription, paralegal assistant studies, and practical nursing.

Costs

Tuition for programs in the 2010–11 academic year is $266 per credit hour, with the exceptions of the practical nursing diploma program, which is $325 per credit hour; occupational therapy assistant studies program, which is $365 per credit hour; and surgical technology program, which is $310 per credit hour. The length of the program determines total cost. Textbooks and other instructional materials vary by program.

Financial Aid

Financial aid is available to those who qualify. The College maintains a full-time staff of financial aid professionals to assist qualified students in obtaining financial assistance. The College participates in several student aid programs. Forms of financial aid available through federal resources include the Federal Pell Grant Program, Federal Supplemental Educational Opportunity Grant (FSEOG) Program, Federal Work-Study Program, Federal Perkins Loan Program, Federal Stafford Student Loan Program (subsidized and unsubsidized), and the Federal PLUS Loan Program. Eligible students may apply for state awards, such as the Ohio Instructional Grant (OIG), and veterans' educational benefits. Students with physical or mental disabilities that are a handicap to employment may be eligible for training services through the state Agency for Vocational Rehabilitation. For further information, students should contact the College's Student Financial Services Office.

Each year, the College makes available President's Scholarships of up to $1000 each to qualifying seniors from area high schools. No more than one scholarship is awarded per high school. In order to qualify, a senior must be graduating from a participating high school, have maintained a cumulative grade point average of at least 2.0, and submitted a brief essay. The student's extracurricular activities and community service are also considered. The President's Scholarship is available only to students enrolling in one of the College's degree programs. Students awarded the scholarship must enroll at Brown Mackie College–Findlay between June and September immediately following their high school graduation. Applications for these scholarships can be obtained from the guidance departments of participating high schools. These applications must be completed and returned to the College by March 31.

Faculty

There are 27 full-time and 90 part-time adjunct instructors at the College. The average student-faculty ratio is 14:1. Each student is assigned a faculty adviser.

Academic Facilities

The College has approximately 50,000 square feet of academic classrooms, laboratories, and offices. The facility includes seven networked computer labs, a criminal justice lab, a surgical technology lab, a pharmacy technology lab, two veterinary technology labs, four nursing labs, and a medical assisting lab. The labs provide students with hands-on opportunities to apply knowledge and skills learned in the classroom.

Location

Located at 1700 Fostoria Avenue, Suite 100, in Findlay, Ohio, the College is easily accessible from Interstate 75.

Admission Requirements

Each applicant for admission is assigned an Assistant Director of Admissions, who directs the applicant through the steps of the admissions process, providing information on curriculum, policies, procedures, and services and assisting the applicant in setting necessary appointments and interviews.

To qualify for admission, each applicant must provide documentation of graduation from an accredited high school or from a state-approved secondary education curriculum or provide official documentation of high school graduation equivalency. All transcripts become the property of the College. Admission to the College is based upon the applicant meeting the stated requirements, a review of the applicant's previous educational records, and a review of the applicant's career interests. If previous academic records indicate that the College's education and training programs would not benefit the applicant, the College reserves the right to advise the applicant not to enroll. Special requirements for enrollment into certain programs are discussed in the descriptions of those programs.

For the most recent information regarding admission requirements, please refer to the current academic catalog.

Application and Information

Applicants must complete and submit an application form, along with documentation of graduation from an accredited high school or state-approved secondary education curriculum or official documentation of high school graduation equivalency.

For additional information, prospective students should contact:

Director of Admissions
Brown Mackie College–Findlay
1700 Fostoria Avenue, Suite 100
Findlay, Ohio 45840
Phone: 419-423-2211
800-842-3687 (toll-free)
Fax: 419-423-0725
E-mail: bmcfiadm@brownmackie.edu
Web site: http://www.brownmackie.edu/Findlay

BROWN MACKIE COLLEGE–FORT WAYNE

FORT WAYNE, INDIANA

The College and Its Mission

Brown Mackie College–Fort Wayne is one of over twenty locations in the Brown Mackie College family of schools (http://www.brownmackie.edu), which is dedicated to providing educational programs that prepare students to pursue entry-level positions in a competitive, rapidly-changing workplace. Brown Mackie College schools offer bachelor's degree, associate degree, certificate, and diploma programs in health sciences, business, information technology, legal studies, and design to over 19,000 students in the Midwest, Southeast, Southwest, and Western United States.

In 1992, the school, currently known as Brown Mackie College–South Bend, added a branch campus in Fort Wayne, Indiana. In 2004, Michiana College's Fort Wayne location changed its name to Brown Mackie College–Fort Wayne.

Brown Mackie College–Fort Wayne is accredited by the Accrediting Council for Independent Colleges and Schools (ACICS) to award bachelor's degrees, associate degrees, and certificates. ACICS is listed as a nationally recognized accrediting agency by the United States Department of Education and is recognized by the Council for Higher Education Accreditation. ACICS can be contacted at 750 First Street NE, Suite 980, Washington, D.C. 20002-4241; phone: 202-336-6780.

The Brown Mackie College–Fort Wayne medical assisting program is accredited by the Commission on Accreditation of Allied Health Education Programs (http://www.caahep.org) upon the recommendation of the Curriculum Review Board of the American Association of Medical Assistants Endowment (AAMAE).

Brown Mackie College–Fort Wayne is regulated by the Indiana Commission on Proprietary Education, 302 West Washington Street, Indianapolis, Indiana 46204; phone: 317-232-1320 or 800-227-5695 (toll-free). (Indiana advertising code: AC-0109).

The occupational therapy assistant studies program is accredited by the Accreditation Council for Occupational Therapy Education (ACOTE) of the American Occupational Therapy Association (AOTA), located at 4720 Montgomery Lane, P.O. Box 31220, Bethesda, Maryland 20824; phone: 301-652-AOTA.

Accreditation for the physical therapy assistant studies program is pending from the Commission on Accreditation in Physical Therapy Education (CAPTE).

Academic Programs

Brown Mackie College–Fort Wayne provides higher education to traditional and nontraditional students through bachelor's degree, associate degree, diploma, and certificate programs that can assist them in enhancing their career opportunities, broadening their perspectives through appropriate general education courses, thinking independently and critically, and improving problem-solving abilities. The College strives to develop within its students the desire for lifelong and continued education.

Each College quarter comprises twelve weeks. Bachelor's degree programs require a minimum of sixteen quarters to complete. Associate degree programs require a minimum of eight quarters to complete. Programs are offered on a year-round basis, providing students with the ability to work uninterrupted toward their degrees. The College offers all programs in a unique One Course a Month format. This schedule allows students to focus studies on only one course for four weeks and has proven convenient for students with multiple obligations such as jobs and family.

Bachelor's Degree Programs: The Bachelor of Science degree is awarded in business administration, criminal justice, health-care management, and legal studies.

Associate Degree Programs: The Associate of Science degree is awarded in accounting technology, business management, computer software technology, criminal justice, health-care administration, medical assisting, office management, paralegal studies, and surgical technology. The Associate of Applied Science degree is awarded in biomedical equipment technology, dietetics technology, health and fitness training, occupational therapy assistant studies, and physical therapist assistant studies.

Diploma Program: The College offers a diploma program in practical nursing.

Certificate Programs: The College offers certificate programs in accounting, business, computer software applications, criminal justice, medical assistant studies, and paralegal assistant studies.

Costs

Tuition in the 2010–11 academic year for all programs except practical nursing and occupational therapy assistant studies is $266 per credit hour, fees are $15 per credit hour. For the practical nursing program, tuition is $325 per credit hour, fees are $25 per credit hour. For certain courses in the occupational therapy assistant and the physical therapist assistant studies program, tuition is $365 per credit hour, fees are $15 per credit hour. For certain courses in the surgical technology program, tuition is $310 per credit hour, fees are $15 per credit hour. The cost of textbooks and other instructional materials varies by program.

Financial Aid

Financial aid is available to those who qualify. The College maintains a full-time staff of financial aid professionals to assist qualified students in obtaining the financial assistance they require to meet their educational expenses. Available resources include federal and state aid, student loans from private lenders, and Federal Work-Study opportunities, both on and off college premises. Federal assistance programs are administered through the U.S. Department of Education, Office of Student Financial Assistance. Any U.S. citizen, national, or person in the United States, other than temporary residents, who is enrolled or accepted for enrollment may apply for these programs.

Each year, the College makes available scholarships of up to $1000 each to qualifying seniors from area high schools. No more than one scholarship is awarded per high school. In order to qualify, a senior must be graduating from a participating high school, be maintaining a cumulative grade point average of at least 2.0, and submit a brief essay. The student's extracurricular activities and community service are also considered. These scholarships are available only to students enrolling in one of the College's degree programs. Students awarded the scholarship must enroll at Brown Mackie College–Fort Wayne between June and September immediately following their high school graduation. Applications for these scholarships can be obtained from the guidance departments of participating high schools. These applications must be completed and returned to the College by March 31.

Faculty

The College has 27 full-time and 65 part-time instructors, with a student-faculty ratio of 15:1. Each student is assigned a faculty adviser.

Facilities and Resources

In 2005, the campus relocated to a 50,000 square foot facility at 3000 East Coliseum Boulevard. Record enrollment allowed the institution to triple in size in less than a year. The three-story building offers a professional environment for study. Five classrooms are outfitted as "classrooms of the future," with an instructor workstation, full multimedia capabilities, a surround sound system, and projection screen that can be accessed by computer, DVD, or VHS equipment. The Brown Mackie College–Fort Wayne facility includes medical labs, computer labs, and occupational and physical therapy labs, as well as a library and bookstore. The labs provide students with hands-on opportunities to apply knowledge and skills learned in the classroom. Students are welcome to use the labs when those facilities are not in use for scheduled classes.

The College is nonresidential and smoke free.

Location

Brown Mackie College–Fort Wayne is located at 3000 East Coliseum Boulevard in Fort Wayne, Indiana. The College is accessible by public transportation and provides ample parking at no cost. For added convenience, the College also operates a learning site at 2135 South Hannah Drive in Fort Wayne.

Admission Requirements

Each applicant for admission is assigned an Assistant Director of Admissions, who directs the applicant through the steps of the admissions process, providing information on curriculum, policies, procedures, and services and assisting the applicant in setting necessary appointments and interviews.

To qualify for admission, each applicant must provide documentation of graduation from an accredited high school or from a state-approved secondary education curriculum or provide official documentation of high school graduation equivalency. All transcripts become the property of the College. Admission to the College is based on the applicant meeting the stated requirements, a review of the applicant's previous educational records, and a review of the applicant's career interests. If previous academic records indicate the College's education and training programs would not benefit the applicant, the College reserves the right to advise the applicant not to enroll. Special requirements for enrollment into certain programs are discussed in the descriptions of those programs.

In addition to the College's general admission requirements, applicants enrolling in the practical nursing program must document the following, which must be completed and a record of proof must appear in the student's file prior to the start of the Nursing Fundamentals course. No student will be admitted to a clinical agency unless all paperwork is completed. The paperwork is a requirement of all contracted agencies. This paperwork includes records of (1) a complete physical, current to within six months of admission; (2) a two-step Mantoux test that is kept current throughout schooling; (3) a hepatitis B vaccination or signed refusal; (4) up-to-date immunizations, including tetanus and rubella; (5) a record of current CPR certification that is maintained throughout the student's clinical experience; and (6) hospitalization insurance or a signed waiver.

For the most recent information regarding admission requirements, please refer to the current academic catalog.

Application and Information

Applicants must complete and submit an application form along with documentation of graduation from an accredited high school or state-approved secondary education curriculum, or official documentation of high school graduation equivalency.

For additional information, prospective students should contact:

Director of Admissions
Brown Mackie College–Fort Wayne
3000 East Coliseum Boulevard
Fort Wayne, Indiana 46805
Phone: 260-484-4400
866-433-2289 (toll-free)
Fax: 260-484-2678
E-mail: bmcfwaadm@brownmackie.edu
Web site: http://www.brownmackie.edu/FortWayne

BROWN MACKIE COLLEGE–GREENVILLE

GREENVILLE, SOUTH CAROLINA

The College and Its Mission

Brown Mackie College–Greenville is one of over twenty locations in the Brown Mackie College family of schools (http://www.brownmackie.edu), which is dedicated to providing educational programs that prepare students to pursue entry-level positions in a competitive, rapidly-changing workplace. Brown Mackie College schools offer bachelor's degree, associate degree, and diploma programs in health sciences, business, information technology, legal studies, and design to over 19,000 students in the Midwest, Southeast, Southwest, and Western United States.

Brown Mackie College–Greenville was founded in 2009 as a branch of Brown Mackie College–Tucson, Arizona.

Brown Mackie College–Greenville is accredited by the Accrediting Council for Independent Colleges and Schools (ACICS) to award bachelor's degrees, associate degrees, and certificates. ACICS is listed as a nationally recognized accrediting agency by the United States Department of Education and is recognized by the Council for Higher Education Accreditation. ACICS can be contacted at 750 First Street NE, Suite 980, Washington, D.C. 20002; phone: 202-336-6780.

This institution is licensed by the South Carolina Commission on Higher Education, 1333 Main Street, Suite 200, Columbia, South Carolina 29201.

Academic Programs

Brown Mackie College–Greenville provides higher education to traditional and nontraditional students through associate degree and diploma programs that can assist them in enhancing their career opportunities, broadening their perspectives through appropriate general education courses, thinking independently and critically, and improving problem-solving abilities.

Each College quarter comprises twelve weeks. Bachelor's degree programs require a minimum of sixteen quarters to complete. Associate degree programs require a minimum of eight quarters to complete. Programs are offered on a year-round basis, providing students with the ability to work uninterrupted toward their degrees. The College offers all programs in a unique One Course a Month format. This schedule allows students to focus studies on only one course for four weeks and has proven convenient for students with multiple obligations such as jobs and family.

Bachelor's Degree Programs: The Bachelor of Science degree is awarded in business administration, criminal justice, health-care management, and legal studies.

Associate Degree Programs: The Associate of Applied Science degree is awarded in accounting technology, business management, criminal justice, health-care administration, information technology, medical assisting, office management, paralegal studies, and surgical technology.

Certificate Programs: The College also offers certificate programs in accounting, business, criminal justice, medical assistant studies, and paralegal assistant studies.

Costs

Tuition in the 2010–11 academic year for most bachelor's and associate degree programs is $260 per credit hour; fees are $15 per credit hour. Tuition for the surgical technology program is $310 per credit hour with fees of $15 per credit hour. Textbooks and other instructional expenses vary by program.

Financial Aid

Financial aid is available for those who qualify. The College maintains a full-time staff of financial aid professionals to assist qualified students in obtaining the financial assistance they require to meet their educational expenses. Available resources include federal and state aid, student loans from private lenders, and Federal Work-Study opportunities, both on and off college premises.

Each year, the College makes available scholarships of up to $1000 each to qualifying seniors from area high schools. No more than one scholarship is awarded per high school. In order to qualify, a senior must be graduating from a participating high school, have maintained a cumulative grade point average of at least 2.0, and submitted a brief essay. The student's extracurricular activities and community service are also considered. These scholarships are available only to students enrolling in one of the College's degree programs. Students awarded the scholarship must enroll at Brown Mackie College–Greenville between June and September immediately following their high school graduation. Applications for these scholarships can be obtained from the guidance departments of participating high schools. These applications must be completed and returned to the College by March 31.

Faculty

Experienced faculty members provide academic support and are committed to the academic and technical preparation of their students. The college has 8 full-time and 20 part-time instructors, with a student-faculty ratio of 24:1. Each student is assigned a faculty adviser.

Facilities and Resources

A modern facility, Brown Mackie College–Greenville offers approximately 25,000 square feet of tastefully appointed classrooms, laboratories, and office space designed to the specifications of the College for its business, medical, and technical programs. Instructional equipment is comparable to current technology used in business and industry today. Modern classrooms for special instructional needs offer multimedia capabilities with surround sound and overhead projectors accessible through computer, DVD, or VHS. Internet access and instructional resources are available at the College's library.

Location

Brown Mackie College–Greenville is conveniently located at Two Liberty Square, 75 Beattie Place, Suite 100, in Greenville, South Carolina. The College has a generous parking area and is also easily accessible by public transportation.

Admission Requirements

Each applicant for admission is assigned an Assistant Director of Admissions who directs the applicant through the steps of the admissions process. They provide information on curriculum, policies, procedures, and services and assist the applicant in setting up necessary appointments and interviews.

To qualify for admission, each applicant must provide documentation of graduation from an accredited high school, or from a state-approved secondary education curriculum, or provide official documentation of high school graduation equivalency. All transcripts become the property of the College. Admission to the College is based on the applicant meeting the stated requirements, a review of the applicant's previous educational records, and a review of the applicant's career interests. If previous academic records indicate the College's education and training programs would not benefit the applicant, the College reserves the right to advise the applicant not to enroll. Special requirements for enrollment into certain programs are discussed in the descriptions of those programs.

For the most recent information regarding admission requirements, please refer to the current academic catalog.

Application and Information

Applicants must complete and submit an application form, along with documentation of graduation from an accredited high school or state-approved secondary education curriculum or official documentation of high school graduation equivalency.

For additional information, prospective students should contact:

Senior Director of Admissions
Brown Mackie College–Greenville
Two Liberty Square
75 Beattie Place, Suite 100
Greenville, South Carolina 29601
Phone: 864-239-5300
877-479-8465 (toll-free)
Fax: 864-232-4094
E-mail: bmcgrweb@brownmackie.edu
Web site: http://www.brownmackie.edu/Greenville

BROWN MACKIE COLLEGE–HOPKINSVILLE

HOPKINSVILLE, KENTUCKY

The College and Its Mission

Brown Mackie College–Hopkinsville is one of over twenty locations in the Brown Mackie College family of schools (http://www.brownmackie.edu), which is dedicated to providing educational programs that prepare students to pursue entry-level positions in a competitive, rapidly-changing workplace. Brown Mackie College schools offer bachelor's degree, associate degree, certificate, and diploma programs in health sciences, business, information technology, legal studies, and design to over 19,000 students in the Midwest, Southeast, Southwest, and Western United States.

Brown Mackie College–Hopkinsville is accredited by the Accrediting Council for Independent Colleges and Schools (ACICS) to award associate degrees and diplomas. ACICS is listed as a nationally recognized accrediting agency by the United States Department of Education and is recognized by the Council for Higher Education Accreditation. ACICS may be contacted at 750 First Street NE, Suite 980, Washington, D.C. 20002-4241; phone: 202-336-6780.

The occupational therapy assistant studies program is accredited by the Accreditation Council for Occupational Therapy Education (ACOTE) of the American Occupational Therapy Association (AOTA), located at 4720 Montgomery Lane, P.O. Box 31220, Bethesda, Maryland 20824; phone: 301-652-AOTA.

The College is a nonresidential, smoke-free institution.

Academic Programs

Brown Mackie College–Hopkinsville provides higher education to traditional and nontraditional students through associate degree and diploma programs that can assist them in enhancing their career opportunities, broadening their perspectives through appropriate general education courses, thinking independently and critically, and improving problem-solving abilities.

Each College quarter comprises ten to twelve weeks. Programs are offered on a year-round basis, providing students with the ability to work uninterrupted toward their degrees. The College offers all programs in a unique One Course a Month format. This schedule allows students to focus studies on only one course for four weeks and has proven convenient for students with multiple obligations such as jobs and family.

Associate Degree Programs: Associate degree programs require a minimum of eight quarters to complete. The Associate of Applied Business degree is awarded in accounting technology, business management, computer programming and applications, computer software technology, criminal justice, and paralegal studies. The Associate of Applied Science degree is awarded in medical assisting, medical office management, and occupational therapy assistant studies.

Diploma Programs: The College also offers diploma programs in accounting, business, computer software applications, criminal justice, medical assistant studies, medical coding and billing for health care, and paralegal assistant studies.

Costs

Tuition is $266 per credit hour. A general fee of $15 per credit hour is charged and applied to the cost of institutional activities and services. For the occupational therapy assistant program, tuition is $266 per credit hour for general courses and $365 per credit hour for program-specific courses. The cost of textbooks and other instructional materials varies by program.

Financial Aid

Financial aid is available to those who qualify. The College maintains a full-time staff of financial aid professionals to assist qualified students in obtaining the financial assistance they require to meet their educational expenses. The College participates in several student aid programs. Forms of financial aid available through federal resources include Federal Pell Grants, Federal Supplemental Educational Opportunity Grants (FSEOG), the Federal Work-Study Program, Federal Perkins Loans, Federal Stafford Student Loans (subsidized and unsubsidized), and the Federal PLUS Program. Students may apply for the College Access Program (CAP) Grant Program and the Kentucky Education Excellence Award (KEES), a scholarship program based on their final high school grade point average. Eligible students may also apply for veterans' educational benefits. Students with physical or mental disabilities that are a handicap to employment may be eligible for training services through the State Vocational Rehabilitation Agency. For further information, students should contact the College's Student Financial Services Office.

Each year, the College makes available President's Scholarships of up to $1000 each to qualifying seniors from area high schools. No more than one scholarship is awarded per high school. In order to qualify, a senior must be graduating from a participating high school, have maintained a cumulative grade point average of at least 2.0, and submitted a brief essay. The student's extracurricular activities and community service are also considered. The President's Scholarship is available only to students enrolling in one of the College's degree programs. Students awarded the scholarship must enroll at Brown Mackie College–Hopkinsville between June and September immediately following their high school graduation. Applications for these scholarships can be obtained from the guidance departments of participating high schools. These applications must be completed and returned to the College by March 31.

Faculty

There are 5 full-time and 15 part-time faculty members. The student-faculty ratio is 15:1.

Facilities and Resources

Brown Mackie College–Hopkinsville occupies a spacious building that has been specifically designed to provide a comfortable and effective environment for learning. The facility comprises approximately 11,250 square feet, including sixteen classrooms, two medical laboratories, three computer laboratories, an academic resource center, administrative and faculty offices, a bookstore, and a student lounge. Computer equipment for hands-on learning includes three networked laboratories. Medical equipment includes monocular and binocular microscopes, electrocardiograph, autoclave, centrifuge, and other equipment appropriate to hands-on laboratory and clinical instruction. Convenient parking is available to all students.

Location

The College is conveniently located at 4001 Fort Campbell Boulevard in Hopkinsville, Kentucky.

Admission Requirements

Each applicant for admission is assigned an Assistant Director of Admissions who directs the applicant through the steps of the admissions process, providing information on curriculum, policies, procedures, and services and assisting the applicant in setting necessary appointments and interviews.

To qualify for admission, each applicant must provide documentation of graduation from an accredited high school or from a state-approved secondary education curriculum or provide official documentation of high school graduation equivalency. All transcripts become the property of the College. Admission to the College is based upon the applicant meeting the stated requirements, a review of the applicant's previous education records, and a review of the applicant's career interests. If previous academic records indicate that the College's education and training programs would not benefit the applicant, the College reserves the right to advise the applicant not to enroll. Special requirements for enrollment into certain programs are discussed in the descriptions of those programs.

For the most recent information regarding admission requirements, please refer to the current academic catalog.

Application and Information

Applicants must complete and submit an application form, along with documentation of graduation from an accredited high school or state-approved secondary education curriculum or provide official documentation of high school graduation equivalency. For additional information, prospective students should contact:

Director of Admissions
Brown Mackie College–Hopkinsville
4001 Fort Campbell Boulevard
Hopkinsville, Kentucky 42240
Phone: 270-886-1302
800-359-4753 (toll-free)
Fax: 270-886-3544
E-mail: bmchoadm@brownmackie.edu
Web site: http://www.brownmackie.edu/Hopkinsville

BROWN MACKIE COLLEGE–INDIANAPOLIS

INDIANAPOLIS, INDIANA

The College and Its Mission

Brown Mackie College–Indianapolis is one of over twenty locations in the Brown Mackie College family of schools (http://www.brownmackie.edu), which is dedicated to providing educational programs that prepare students to pursue entry-level positions in a competitive, rapidly-changing workplace. Brown Mackie College schools offer bachelor's degree, associate degree, certificate, and diploma programs in health sciences, business, information technology, legal studies, and design to over 19,000 students in the Midwest, Southeast, Southwest, and Western United States.

Brown Mackie College–Indianapolis was founded in 2007 as a branch of Brown Mackie College–Findlay, Ohio.

Brown Mackie College–Indianapolis is accredited by the Accrediting Council for Independent Colleges and Schools (ACICS) to award bachelor's degrees, associate degrees, diplomas, and certificates. ACICS is listed as a national recognized accrediting agency by the United States Department of Education and is recognized by the Council for Higher Education Accreditation. ACICS can be contacted at 750 First Street NE, Suite 980, Washington, D.C. 20002; phone: 202-336-6780.

The occupational therapy assistant studies program is accredited by the Accreditation Council for Occupational Therapy Education (ACOTE) of the American Occupational Therapy Association (AOTA), located at 4720 Montgomery Lane, P.O. Box 31220, Bethesda, Maryland 20824; phone: 301-652-AOTA.

Brown Mackie College–Indianapolis is regulated by the Indiana Commission on Proprietary Education, 302 West Washington Street, Indianapolis, Indiana 46204; phone: 317-232-1320 or 800-227-5695 (toll-free). (Indiana advertising code: AC-0078).

Academic Programs

Brown Mackie College–Indianapolis provides higher education to traditional and nontraditional students through bachelor's degree, associate degree, diploma, and certificate programs that can assist them in enhancing their career opportunities, broadening their perspectives through appropriate general education courses, thinking independently and critically, and improving problem-solving abilities. The College strives to develop within its students the desire for lifelong and continued education.

Each College quarter comprises twelve weeks. Bachelor's degree programs require a minimum of sixteen quarters to complete. Associate degree programs require a minimum of eight quarters to complete. Programs are offered on a year-round basis, providing students with the ability to work uninterrupted toward their degrees. The College offers all programs in a unique One Course a Month format. This schedule allows students to focus studies on only one course for four weeks and has proven convenient for students with multiple obligations such as jobs and family.

Bachelor's Degree Programs: The Bachelor of Science degree is awarded in business administration, criminal justice, and legal studies.

Associate Degree Programs: The Associate of Science degree is awarded in business management, criminal justice, health-care administration, medical assisting, and paralegal studies. The Associate of Applied Science degree is awarded in occupational therapy assistant studies.

Diploma Program: The College offers a diploma program in practical nursing.

Certificate Programs: The College offers certificate programs in business and medical assistant studies.

Costs

Tuition for most programs in the 2010–11 academic year is $283 per credit hour with a $15 per credit hour general fee. Tuition for the practical nursing diploma program is $325 per credit hour with a $25 per credit hour general fee applied to instructional costs for activities and services. For certain occupational therapy assistant courses the tuition is $283 per credit hour for general courses and $365 per credit hour for program-specific courses; general fees are $15 per credit hour.

Financial Aid

Financial aid is available to those who qualify. The College maintains a full-time staff of financial aid professionals to assist qualified students in obtaining the financial assistance they require to meet their educational expenses. Available resources include federal and state aid, student loans from private lenders, and Federal Work-Study opportunities, both on and off college premises. Federal assistance programs are administered through the U.S. Department of Education, Office of Student Financial Assistance. Any U.S. citizen, national, or person in the United States for other than temporary reasons who is enrolled or accepted for enrollment may apply for these programs.

Each year, the College makes available scholarships of up to $1000 each to qualifying seniors from area high schools. No more than one scholarship is awarded per high school. In order to qualify, a senior must be graduating from a participating high school, have maintained a cumulative grade point average of at least 2.0, and submitted a brief essay. The student's extracurricular activities and community service are also considered. These scholarships are available only to students enrolling in one of the College's degree programs. Students awarded the scholarship must enroll at Brown Mackie College–Indianapolis between June and September immediately following their high school graduation. Applications for these scholarships can be obtained from the guidance departments of participating high schools. These applications must be completed and returned to the College by March 31.

Faculty

The College has 8 full-time and 24 part-time instructors, with a student-faculty ratio of 25:1. Faculty members provide tutoring and additional academic services to students as needed.

Facilities and Resources

Opened in January 2008, this modern facility offers more than 22,000 square feet of tastefully decorated classrooms, laboratories, and office space designed to the specifications of the College for its business, medical, and technical programs. Instructional equipment is comparable to industry-current technology used in business today. Modern classrooms for special instructional needs offer multimedia capabilities with surround sound and overhead projectors accessible through computer, DVD, or VHS. Internet access and instructional resources are available at the College's library. Experienced faculty members provide academic support and are committed to the academic and technical preparation of their students.

Location

Brown Mackie College–Indianapolis is located at 1200 North Meridian Street, Indianapolis, Indiana. The College is accessible by public transportation and provides ample parking at no cost.

Admission Requirements

Each applicant for admission is assigned an Assistant Director of Admissions, who directs the applicant through the steps of the admissions process, providing information on curriculum, policies, procedures, and services and assisting the applicant in setting necessary appointments and interviews.

To qualify for admission, each applicant must provide documentation of graduation from an accredited high school or from a state-approved secondary education curriculum or provide official documentation of high school graduation equivalency. All transcripts become the property of the College. Admission to the College is based on the applicant meeting the stated requirements, a review of the applicant's previous educational records, and a review of the applicant's career interests. If previous academic records indicate the College's education and training programs would not benefit the applicant, the College reserves the right to advise the applicant not to enroll. Special requirements for enrollment into certain programs are discussed in the descriptions of those programs.

For the most recent information regarding admission requirements, please refer to the current academic catalog.

Application and Information

Applicants must complete and submit an application form, along with documentation of graduation from an accredited high school or state-approved secondary education curriculum or official documentation of high school graduation equivalency.

For additional information, prospective students should contact:

Director of Admissions
Brown Mackie College–Indianapolis
1200 North Meridian Street, Suite 100
Indianapolis, Indiana 46204
Phone: 317-554-8301
866-255-0279 (toll-free)
Fax: 317-632-4557
E-mail: bmcindadm@brownmackie.edu
Web site: http://www.brownmackie.edu/Indianapolis

BROWN MACKIE COLLEGE–KANSAS CITY

LENEXA, KANSAS

The College and Its Mission

Brown Mackie College–Kansas City is one of over twenty locations in the Brown Mackie College family of schools (http://www.brownmackie.edu), which is dedicated to providing educational programs that prepare students to pursue entry-level positions in a competitive, rapidly-changing workplace. Brown Mackie College schools offer bachelor's degree, associate degree, certificate, and diploma programs in health sciences, business, information technology, legal studies, and design to over 19,000 students in the Midwest, Southeast, Southwest, and Western United States.

The College was originally founded in Salina, Kansas, in July 1892 as the Kansas Wesleyan School of Business. In 1938, the College was incorporated as the Brown Mackie School of Business under the ownership of former Kansas Wesleyan instructors Perry E. Brown and A. B. Mackie. It became Brown Mackie College in January 1975.

Brown Mackie College–Kansas City is accredited by the Higher Learning Commission and is a member of the North Central Association, 30 North LaSalle Street, Suite 2400, Chicago, Illinois 60602; phone: 800-621-7440; Web site: http://www.ncahlc.org.

Brown Mackie College–Kansas City is authorized to grant the Associate of Applied Science degree by the Kansas Board of Regents, 1000 Southwest Jackson Street, Suite 520, Topeka, Kansas 66612-1368.

The occupational therapy assistant program has applied for accreditation by the Accreditation Council for Occupational Therapy Education (ACOTE) of the American Occupational Therapy Association (AOTA), located at 4720 Montgomery Lane, P.O. Box 31220, Bethesda, Maryland 20824; phone: 301-652-AOTA.

The veterinary technology program has applied for accreditation by the American Veterinary Medical Association, located at 1931 North Meacham Road, Suite 100, Schaumburg, Illinois 60173; phone: 800-248-2862 (toll-free).

Brown Mackie College–Kansas City is nonresidential, smoke free, and provides ample parking at no additional cost.

Academic Programs

Brown Mackie College–Kansas City provides higher education to traditional and nontraditional students through associate degree, diploma, and certificate programs that can assist them in enhancing their career opportunities, broadening their perspectives through appropriate general education courses, thinking independently and critically, and improving problem-solving abilities. The College strives to develop within its students the desire for lifelong and continued education.

In most programs, students can participate in day or evening classes, which begin every month. Programs are offered on a year-round basis, providing students with the ability to work uninterrupted toward completion of their programs. The College offers all programs in a unique One Course a Month format. This schedule allows students to focus studies on only one course for four weeks and has proven convenient for students with multiple obligations such as jobs and family.

Associate Degree Programs: The Associate of Applied Science degree is awarded in accounting technology, architectural design and drafting technology, business management, computer-aided design and drafting technology, criminal justice, health and fitness training, health-care administration, medical assisting, nursing, occupational therapy assistant studies, office management, paralegal studies, and veterinary technology.

Diploma Programs: The College also offers diploma programs in accounting, business, computer-aided design and drafting technician studies, computer software applications, criminal justice, fitness trainer studies, medical assistant studies, medical coding and billing, and paralegal assistant studies.

Certificate Program: A certificate program is offered in practical nursing.

Costs

Tuition for programs in the 2010–11 academic year is $266 per credit hour ($325 for nursing programs). Tuition for the health and fitness training program is $275 per credit hour with fees of $15 per credit hour. Tuition for certain courses in the occupational therapy assistant studies program is $365 per credit hour with fees of $15 per credit hour. The cost of textbooks and other instructional materials varies by program.

Financial Aid

Financial aid is available to those who qualify. The College maintains a full-time staff of financial aid professionals to assist qualified students in obtaining financial assistance. The College participates in several student aid programs. Forms of financial aid available to qualified students through federal resources include Federal Pell Grants, Federal Supplemental Educational Opportunity Grants (FSEOG), Academic Competitiveness Grant, Federal Work-Study Program, Federal Perkins Loans, Federal Stafford Student Loans (subsidized and unsubsidized), Federal Direct Loans (subsidized and unsubsidized), and the Federal PLUS Program. Eligible students may apply for veterans' educational benefits. Students with physical or mental disabilities that are a handicap to employment may be eligible for training services through the state Vocational Rehabilitation Agency. For further information, students should contact the College's Student Financial Services Office.

Each year, the College makes available President's Scholarships of up to $1000 each to qualifying seniors from area high schools. No more than one scholarship is awarded per high school. In order to qualify, a senior must be graduating from a participating high school, have maintained a cumulative grade point average of at least 2.0, and submitted a brief essay. The student's extracurricular activities and community service are also considered. The President's Scholarship is available only to students enrolling in one of the College's degree programs. Students awarded the scholarship must enroll at Brown Mackie College–Kansas City between June and September immediately following their high school graduation. Applications for these scholarships can be obtained from the guidance departments of participating high schools. These applications must be completed and returned to the College by March 31.

Faculty

There are 23 full-time faculty members and 25 adjunct faculty members. The average class student-instructor ratio is 14:1.

Facilities and Resources

In addition to classrooms and computer labs, the College maintains a library of curriculum-related resources, technical and general education materials, academic and professional periodicals, and audiovisual resources. Internet access also is available for research. The College has a bookstore that stocks texts, courseware, and other educational supplies required for courses and a variety of personal, recreational, and gift items, including apparel, supplies, and general merchandise incorporating the College logo. Hours are posted at the bookstore entrance.

Location

Brown Mackie College–Kansas City is located at 9705 Lenexa Drive in Lenexa, Kansas, just off Interstate 35 at 95th Street in Johnson County. The Olathe course site is located at 450 North Rogers Road, Suite 175, in Olathe, Kansas, just off Interstate 35 and Santa Fe Street in Johnson County.

Admission Requirements

Each applicant for admission is assigned an Assistant Director of Admissions, who directs the applicant through the steps of the admissions process, providing information on curriculum, policies, procedures, and services and assisting the applicant in setting necessary appointments and interviews.

To qualify for admission, each applicant must provide documentation of graduation from an accredited high school or from a state-approved secondary education curriculum or provide official documentation of high school graduation equivalency. All transcripts become the property of the College. Admission to the College is based upon the applicant meeting the stated requirements, a review of the applicant's previous education records, and a review of the applicant's career interests. If previous academic records indicate that the College's education and training programs would not benefit the applicant, the College reserves the right to advise the applicant not to enroll. Special requirements for enrollment into certain programs are discussed in the descriptions of those programs.

For the most recent information regarding admission requirements, please refer to the current academic catalog.

Application and Information

Applicants must complete and submit an application form, along with documentation of graduation from an accredited high school or state-approved secondary education curriculum or official documentation of high school graduation equivalency. For additional information, prospective students should contact:

Director of Admissions
Brown Mackie College–Kansas City
9705 Lenexa Drive
Lenexa, Kansas 66215
Phone: 913-768-1900
800-635-9101 (toll-freeFax:
Fax: 913-495-9555
E-mail: bmckcadm@brownmackie.edu
Web site: http://www.brownmackie.edu/KansasCity

BROWN MACKIE COLLEGE–LOUISVILLE

LOUISVILLE, KENTUCKY

The College and Its Mission

Brown Mackie College–Louisville is one of over twenty locations in the Brown Mackie College family of schools (http://www.brownmackie.edu), which is dedicated to providing educational programs that prepare students to pursue entry-level positions in a competitive, rapidly-changing workplace. Brown Mackie College schools offer bachelor's degree, associate degree, certificate, and diploma programs in health sciences, business, information technology, legal studies, and design to over 19,000 students in the Midwest, Southeast, Southwest, and Western United States.

Brown Mackie College–Louisville opened in 1972 as RETS Institute of Technology. The first RETS school was founded in 1935 in Detroit in response to the rapid growth of radio broadcasting and the need for qualified radio technicians. The RETS Institute changed its name to Brown Mackie College–Louisville in 2004.

Brown Mackie College–Louisville is accredited by the Accrediting Council for Independent Colleges and Schools (ACICS) to award associate degrees, diplomas, and certificates. ACICS is listed as a nationally recognized accrediting agency by the United States Department of Education and is recognized by the Council for Higher Education Accreditation. ACICS can be contacted at 750 First Street NE, Suite 980, Washington, D.C. 20002-4241; phone: 202-336-6780.

Brown Mackie College–Louisville is approved under Chapter 31 of the Kentucky Revised Statues for the offering of all programs by the Kentucky State Board for Proprietary Education, P.O. Box 456, Frankfort, Kentucky 40602; phone: 502-564-4233.

The Brown Mackie College–Louisville's Associate of Applied Science degree in surgical technology is accredited by the Accrediting Bureau of Health Education Schools, 7777 Leesburg Pike, Suite 314N, Falls Church, Virginia 22043; phone: 703-917-9503.

The occupational therapy assistant studies program has applied for accreditation by the Accreditation Council for Occupational Therapy Education (ACOTE) of the American Occupational Therapy Association (AOTA), located at 4720 Montgomery Lane, P.O. Box 31220, Bethesda, Maryland 20824; phone: 301-652-AOTA.

The College is a nonresidential, smoke-free institution and provides ample parking at no additional cost.

Academic Programs

Brown Mackie College–Louisville provides higher education to traditional and nontraditional students through associate degree, diploma, and certificate programs that can assist them in enhancing their career opportunities, broadening their perspectives through appropriate general education courses, thinking independently and critically, and improving problem-solving abilities.

Each College quarter comprises twelve weeks. Bachelor's degree programs require a minimum of 16 quarters to complete and associate degree programs require a minimum of eight quarters to complete. Programs are offered on a year-round basis, providing students with the ability to work uninterrupted toward their degrees. The College offers all programs in a unique One Course a Month format. This schedule allows students to focus studies on only one course for four weeks and has proven convenient for students with multiple obligations such as jobs and family.

Bachelor's Degree Programs: The Bachelor of Science degree is awarded in business administration, criminal justice, health-care management, and legal studies.

Associate Degree Programs: The Associate of Applied Business degree is awarded in accounting technology, business management, computer networking and applications, criminal justice, and paralegal studies. The Associate of Applied Science degree is awarded in biomedical equipment technology, early childhood education, electronics, graphic design, health-care administration, medical assisting, occupational therapy assistant studies, pharmacy technology, surgical technology, and veterinary technician studies.

Diploma Program: The College offers a diploma program in practical nursing.

Certificate Program: The College offers a certificate program in computer networking.

Costs

Tuition for programs in the 2010–11 academic year is $266 per credit hour, with some exceptions. Tuition for the practical nursing diploma program is $365 per credit hour, the surgical technology program is $310 per credit hour, the occupational therapy assistant studies program is $325 per credit hour, and computer networking courses are $300 per credit hour. The length of the program determines total cost. The cost of textbooks and other instructional materials varies by program.

Financial Aid

Financial aid is available to those who qualify. The College maintains a full-time staff of financial aid professionals to assist qualified students in obtaining financial assistance. The College participates in several student aid programs. Forms of financial aid available to qualified students through federal resources include the Federal Pell Grant Program, Federal Supplemental Educational Opportunity Grant (FSEOG) Program, Federal Work-Study Program, Federal Perkins Loan Program, Federal Stafford Student Loan Program (subsidized and unsubsidized), and the Federal PLUS Loan Program. Students may apply for state-based award programs, such as the College Access Program (CAP) Grant Program and the Kentucky Educational Excellence Award (KEES). Eligible students may also apply for veterans' benefits. Students with physical or mental disabilities that are a handicap to employment may be eligible for training services through the state Agency for Vocational Rehabilitation. For further information, students should contact the College's Student Financial Services Office.

Each year, the College makes available President's Scholarships of up to $1000 each to qualifying seniors from area high schools. No more than one scholarship is awarded per high school. In order to qualify, a senior must be graduating from a participating high school, have maintained a cumulative grade point average of at least 2.0, and submitted a brief essay. The student's extracurricular activities and community service are also considered. The President's Scholarship is available only to students enrolling in one of the College's degree programs. Students awarded the scholarship must enroll at Brown Mackie College–Louisville between June and September immediately following their high school graduation. Applications for these scholarships can be obtained from the guidance departments of participating high schools. These applications must be completed and returned to the College by March 31.

Faculty

There are 20 full-time and over 40 part-time faculty members at the College. The average student-faculty ratio is 20:1.

Facilities and Resources

Brown Mackie College–Louisville has more than 42,000 square feet of multipurpose classrooms, including networked computer laboratories, electronics laboratories, veterinary technology labs, a resource center, and offices for administrative personnel as well as for student services such as admissions, student financial services, and career-services assistance. In May 2009, an additional 6,000 square feet was opened at the Louisville location. Included in this build-out are an occupational therapy lab, a criminal justice lab, additional classrooms, and faculty space.

Location

The College is at 3605 Fern Valley Road, Louisville, Kentucky, conveniently located at the intersection of Fern Valley and Preston Highway.

Admission Requirements

Each applicant for admission is assigned an Assistant Director of Admissions who directs the applicant through the steps of the admissions process, providing information on curriculum, policies, procedures, and services and assisting the applicant in setting necessary appointments and interviews.

To qualify for admission, each applicant must provide documentation of graduation from an accredited high school or completion of a state-approved secondary education curriculum or provide official documentation of high school graduation equivalency. All transcripts become the property of the College. Admission to the College is based on the applicant meeting the above requirements, a review of the applicant's previous educational records, and a review of the applicant's career interests. If previous academic records indicate that the College's education and training programs would not benefit the applicant, the College reserves the right to advise the applicant not to enroll. Special requirements for enrollment into certain programs are discussed in the descriptions of those programs.

For the most recent information regarding admission requirements, please refer to the current academic catalog.

Application and Information

Applicants must complete and submit an application form along with documentation of graduation from an accredited high school or completion of state-approved secondary education curriculum or provide official documentation of high school graduation equivalency. For additional information, prospective students should contact:

Director of Admissions
Brown Mackie College–Louisville
3605 Fern Valley Road
Louisville, Kentucky 40219
Phone: 502-968-7191
800-999-7387 (toll-free)
Fax: 502-357-9956
E-mail: bmcloadm@brownmackie.edu
Web site: http://www.brownmackie.edu/Louisville

BROWN MACKIE COLLEGE–MERRILLVILLE

MERRILLVILLE, INDIANA

BROWN MACKIE COLLEGE
MERRILLVILLE™

The College and Its Mission

Brown Mackie College–Merrillville is one of over twenty locations in the Brown Mackie College family of schools (http://www.brownmackie.edu), which is dedicated to providing educational programs that prepare students to pursue entry-level positions in a competitive, rapidly-changing workplace. Brown Mackie College schools offer bachelor's degree, associate degree, certificate, and diploma programs in health sciences, business, information technology, legal studies, and design to over 19,000 students in the Midwest, Southeast, Southwest, and Western United States.

Founded in 1890 by A. N. Hirons as LaPorte Business College in LaPorte, Indiana, the institution later became known as Commonwealth Business College. In 1919, ownership was transferred to Grace and J. J. Moore, who successfully operated the College under the name of Reese School of Business for several decades. In 1975, the College came under the ownership of Steven C. Smith as Commonwealth Business College. A second location, now known as Brown Mackie College–Merrillville, was opened in 1984, in Merrillville, Indiana. The College changed ownership again in September 2003 and the College name was changed to Brown Mackie College–Merrillville in November 2004.

Brown Mackie College–Merrillville is accredited by the Accrediting Council for Independent Colleges and Schools (ACICS) to award bachelor's degrees, associate degrees, certificates, and diplomas. ACICS is listed as a nationally recognized accrediting agency by the United States Department of Education and is recognized by the Council for Higher Education Accreditation. ACICS can be contacted at 750 First Street NE, Suite 980, Washington, D.C. 20002; phone: 202-336-6780.

Brown Mackie College–Merrillville is licensed and regulated by the Indiana Commission on Proprietary Education, 302 West Washington Street, Indianapolis, Indiana 46204; phone: 317-232-1320 or 800-227-5695 (toll-free). (Indiana advertising code: AC-0138.)

Brown Mackie College–Merrillville's Associate of Science degree in medical assisting is accredited by the Accrediting Bureau of Health Education Schools (ABHES), 7777 Leesburg Pike, Suite 214 North, Falls Church, Virginia 22043; phone: 703-917-9503.

Brown Mackie College–Merrillville's Associate of Science degree in surgical technology is accredited by the Commission on Accreditation of Allied Health Education Programs (http://www.caahep.org) upon the recommendation of the Accreditation Review Committee on Education in Surgical Technology.

The occupational therapy assistant program is accredited by the Accreditation Council for Occupational Therapy Education (ACOTE) of the American Occupational Therapy Association (AOTA), located at 4720 Montgomery Lane, P.O. Box 31220, Bethesda, Maryland 20824; phone: 301-652-AOTA.

The College is a nonresidential, smoke-free institution.

Academic Programs

Brown Mackie College–Merrillville provides higher education to traditional and nontraditional students through bachelor's degree, associate degree, and certificate programs that can assist them in enhancing their career opportunities, broadening their perspectives through appropriate general education courses, thinking independently and critically, and improving problem-solving abilities. The College strives to develop within its students the desire for lifelong and continued education.

Each College quarter comprises twelve weeks. Bachelor's degree programs require a minimum of sixteen quarters to complete. Associate degree programs require a minimum of eight quarters to complete. Programs are offered on a year-round basis, providing students with the ability to work uninterrupted toward their degrees. The College offers all programs in a unique One Course a Month format. This schedule allows students to focus studies on only one course for four weeks and has proven convenient for students with multiple obligations such as jobs and family.

Bachelor's Degree Programs: The Bachelor of Science degree is awarded in business administration, criminal justice, health-care management, and legal studies.

Associate Degree Programs: The Associate of Science degree is awarded in accounting technology, administration in gerontology, business management, computer software technology, criminal justice, medical assisting studies, medical office management, paralegal studies, and surgical technology. The Associate of Applied Science degree is awarded in health and fitness training, and occupational therapy assistant studies.

Diploma Program: The College offers a diploma program in practical nursing.

Certificate Programs: The College offers certificate programs in accounting, business, computer software applications, criminal justice, fitness trainer studies, medical assistant studies, and paralegal assistant studies.

Costs

Tuition for programs in the 2010–11 academic year is $266 per credit hour and fees are $15 per credit hour, with the exception of the practical nursing diploma program, which is $325 per credit hour with fees of $25 per credit hour; and the surgical technology program, which is $310 per credit hour with fees of $15 per credit hour. For certain courses in the occupational therapy assistant studies program the tuition is $365 per credit hour and fees are $15 per credit hour. The length of the program determines total cost. Textbook fees vary according to program.

Financial Aid

Financial aid is available to those who qualify. The College maintains a full-time staff of financial aid professionals to assist qualified students in obtaining financial assistance. The College participates in several student aid programs. Forms of financial aid available through federal resources include the Federal Pell Grant Program, Federal Supplemental Educational Opportunity Grant (FSEOG) Program, Federal Work-Study Program, Federal Perkins Loan Program, Federal Stafford Student Loan Program (subsidized and unsubsidized), and the Federal PLUS Loan Program. Eligible students may apply for Indiana state awards, such as the Higher Education Award and Twenty-First Century Scholarships for high school students, the Core 40 awards, and veteran's educational benefits. Students with physical or mental disabilities that are a handicap to employment may be eligible for training services through the state's Bureau of Vocational Rehabilitation. For further information, students should contact the College's Student Financial Services Office.

Each year, the College makes available scholarships of up to $1000 each to qualifying seniors from area high schools. No more than one scholarship is awarded per high school. In order to qualify, a senior must be graduating from a participating high school, have maintained a cumulative grade point average of at least 2.0, and submitted a brief essay. The student's extracurricular activities and community service are also considered. These scholarships are available only to students enrolling in one of the College's degree programs. Students awarded the scholarship must enroll at Brown Mackie College–Merrillville between June and September immediately following their high school graduation. Applications for these scholarships can be obtained from the guidance departments of participating high schools. These applications must be completed and returned to the College by March 31.

Faculty

There are approximately 30 full-time and 25 part-time faculty members at the College, practitioners in their fields of expertise. The average student-faculty ratio is 17:1.

Facilities and Resources

Occupying 26,000 square feet, Brown Mackie College–Merrillville was opened to students in October 1998, in the Twin Towers complex of Merrillville. The College comprises several instructional rooms, including five computer labs with networked computers and four medical laboratories. The administrative offices, college library, and student lounge are all easily accessible to students. The College bookstore stocks texts, courseware, and other educational supplies required for courses at the College. Students can also find a variety of personal, recreational, and gift items, including apparel, supplies, and general merchandise incorporating the College logo. Hours are posted at the bookstore entrance.

Location

Brown Mackie College–Merrillville is conveniently located at 1000 East 80th Place, Merrillville, in northwest Indiana. The College is housed in the Twin Towers business complex, just west of the intersection of U.S. Route 30 and Interstate 65. A spacious parking lot provides ample parking at no additional cost.

Admission Requirements

Each applicant for admission is assigned an Assistant Director of Admissions who directs the applicant through the steps of the admissions process, providing information on curriculum, policies, procedures, and services and assisting the applicant in setting necessary appointments and interviews.

To qualify for admission, each applicant must provide documentation of graduation from an accredited high school or completion of a state-approved secondary education curriculum or provide official documentation of high school graduation equivalency. All transcripts become the property of the College.

In addition to the College's general admission requirements, applicants enrolling in the practical nursing program must document the following, which must be completed and a record of proof must appear in the student's file prior to the start of the Nursing Fundamentals course. No student will be admitted to a clinical agency unless all paperwork is completed. The paperwork is a requirement of all contracted agencies. This paperwork includes records of (1) a complete physical, current to within six months of admission; (2) a two-step Mantoux test that is kept current throughout schooling; (3) a hepatitis B vaccination or signed refusal; (4) up-to-date immunizations, including tetanus and rubella; (5) a record of current CPR certification that is maintained throughout the student's clinical experience; and (6) hospitalization insurance or a signed waiver.

For the most recent information regarding Admission Requirements, please refer to the current academic catalog.

Application and Information

Applicants must complete and submit an application form along with documentation of graduation from an accredited high school or state-approved secondary education curriculum, or applicants must provide official documentation of high school graduation equivalency.

For additional information, prospective students should contact:

Director of Admissions
Brown Mackie College–Merrillville
1000 East 80th Place, Suite 101N
Merrillville, Indiana 46410
Phone: 219-769-3321
800-258-3321 (toll-free)
Fax: 219-738-1076
E-mail: bmcmeadm@brownmackie.edu
Web site: http://www.brownmackie.edu/Merrillville

BROWN MACKIE COLLEGE–MIAMI

MIAMI, FLORIDA

The College and Its Mission

Brown Mackie College–Miami is one of over twenty locations in the Brown Mackie College family of schools (http://www.brownmackie.edu), which is dedicated to providing educational programs that prepare students to pursue entry-level positions in a competitive, rapidly-changing workplace. Brown Mackie College schools offer bachelor's degree, associate degree, certificate, and diploma programs in health sciences, business, information technology, legal studies, and design to over 19,000 students in the Midwest, Southeast, Southwest, and Western United States.

Brown Mackie College–Miami is accredited by the Accrediting Council for Independent Colleges and Schools (ACICS) to award bachelor's and associate degrees. ACICS is listed as a nationally recognized accrediting agency by the United States Department of Education and is recognized by the Council for Higher Education Accreditation. ACICS can be contacted at 750 First Street NE, Suite 980, Washington, D.C. 20002; phone: 202-336-6780.

The College is a nonresidential, smoke-free institution.

Academic Programs

Brown Mackie College–Miami provides higher education to traditional and nontraditional students through bachelor's degree and associate degree programs that can assist them in enhancing their career opportunities, broadening their perspectives through appropriate general education courses, thinking independently and critically, and improving problem-solving abilities. The College strives to develop within its students the desire for lifelong and continued education.

Each College quarter comprises twelve weeks. Associate degree programs require a minimum of eight quarters to complete. Programs are offered on a year-round basis, providing students with the ability to work uninterrupted toward their degree. The College offers all programs in a unique One Course a Month format. This schedule allows students to focus studies on only one course for four weeks and has proven convenient for students with multiple obligations such as jobs and family.

Bachelor's Degree Programs: The Bachelor of Science degree is awarded in business administration, criminal justice, and health-care management.

Associate Degree Programs: The Associate of Science degree is awarded in accounting technology, business management, criminal justice, early childhood education, health-care administration, information technology, medical assisting, and paralegal studies.

Costs

Tuition in the 2010–11 academic year for all programs is $336 per credit hour; fees are $15 per credit hour. The costs for textbooks and other instructional materials varies by program.

Financial Aid

Financial aid is available to those who qualify. The College maintains a full-time staff of financial aid professionals to assist qualified students in obtaining financial assistance. The College participates in several student aid programs. Forms of financial aid available to qualified students through federal resources include the Federal Pell Grant Program, Federal Supplemental Educational Opportunity Grant (FSEOG) Program, Federal Work-Study Program, Federal Perkins Loan Program, Federal Stafford Student Loan Program (subsidized and unsubsidized), Federal PLUS loan program, and Florida State grant program. Eligible students may apply for veterans' educational benefits. Students with physical or mental disabilities that are a handicap to employment may be eligible for training services through the state Agency for Vocational Rehabilitation. For further information, students should contact the College's Student Financial Services Office.

Each year, the College makes available President's Scholarships of up to $1000 each to qualifying seniors from area high schools. No more than one scholarship is awarded per high school. In order to qualify, a senior must be graduating from a participating high school, have maintained a cumulative grade point average of at least 2.0, and submitted a brief essay. The student's extracurricular activities and community service are also considered. The President's Scholarship is available only to students enrolling in one of the College's degree programs. Students awarded the scholarship must enroll at Brown Mackie College–Miami between June and September immediately following their high school graduation. Applications for these scholarships can be obtained from the financial aid departments of participating high schools. These applications must be completed and returned to the College by March 31.

Faculty

There are 15 full-time and 27 adjunct faculty members at the College. The average student-faculty ratio is 20:1.

Facilities and Resources

The College recently relocated its main campus to a larger facility. Hands-on experiences are available in the College's many labs, including a criminal justice lab featuring facial recognition software and a multitude of forensic equipment. The computer networking lab has eight computer classrooms and offers students a modern and professional environment for study. Every student has access to the technology, tools, and facilities needed to complete projects in each subject area. Students are able to use the labs when they are not being used for scheduled classes. The new location features a comfortable student lounge as well as an on-site eatery available during all class shifts. The College bookstore offers retail items including college gear as well as textbooks and kits specific to programs of study.

Location

Brown Mackie College–Miami is conveniently located at One Herald Plaza in Miami, Florida. The College recently moved its main campus from Biscayne Boulevard to 50,000 square feet on the top floor of the Miami Herald Building, which sits on beautiful Biscayne Bay and offers a clear view of Miami's famous South Beach. The location is near the OMNI Metro Mover and bus stop, with access to Metro Rail and Florida's regional Tri-Rail system; ample parking is also available.

Admission Requirements

Each applicant for admission is assigned an Assistant Director of Admissions, who directs the applicant through the steps of the admissions process, providing information on curriculum, policies, procedures, and services and assisting the applicant in setting necessary appointments and interviews.

To qualify for admission, applicants must be a graduate of a public or private high school or a correspondence school or education center that is accredited by an agency that is recognized by the U.S. or State of Florida Department of Education, or any of its approved agents. As part of the admissions process applicants must sign a document attesting to graduation or completion and containing the information to obtain verification of such. Verification must be obtained within the first term. All transcripts become the property of the College. Admission to the College is based on the applicant meeting the stated requirements, a review of the applicant's previous educational records, and a review of the applicant's career interests. If previous academic records indicate the College's education and training programs would not benefit the applicant, the College reserves the right to advise the applicant not to enroll. Special requirements for enrollment into certain programs are discussed in the descriptions of those programs.

Students are given an assessment of academic skills during the first two weeks of class. Although the results of this assessment do not determine eligibility for admission, they provide the College with a means of determining the need for academic support as well as a means by which the College can evaluate the effectiveness of its educational programs. All new students are required to complete this assessment.

For the most recent information regarding admission requirements, please refer to the current academic catalog.

Application and Information

Applicants must complete and submit an application form.

For additional information, prospective students should contact:

Director of Admissions
Brown Mackie College–Miami
One Herald Plaza
Miami, Florida 33132-1418
Phone: 305-341-6600
866-505-0335 (toll-free)
Fax: 305-373-8814
E-mail: bmmiadm@brownmackie.edu
Web site: http://www.brownmackie.edu/Miami

BROWN MACKIE COLLEGE–MICHIGAN CITY

MICHIGAN CITY, INDIANA

The College and Its Mission

Brown Mackie College–Michigan City is one of over twenty locations in the Brown Mackie College family of schools (http://www.brownmackie.edu), which is dedicated to providing educational programs that prepare students to pursue entry-level positions in a competitive, rapidly-changing workplace. Brown Mackie College schools offer bachelor's degree, associate degree, certificate, and diploma programs in health sciences, business, information technology, legal studies, and design to over 19,000 students in the Midwest, Southeast, Southwest, and Western United States.

Founded in 1890 by A. N. Hirons as LaPorte Business College in LaPorte, Indiana, the institution later became known as Commonwealth Business College. In 1919, ownership was transferred to Grace and J. J. Moore, who successfully operated the College under the name of Reese School of Business for several decades. In 1975, the College came under the ownership of Steven C. Smith as Commonwealth Business College. In 1997, the College relocated to its present site in Michigan City, Indiana.

Brown Mackie College–Michigan City is accredited by the Accrediting Council for Independent Colleges and Schools (ACICS) to award bachelor's degrees, associate degrees, and certificates. ACICS is listed as a nationally recognized accrediting agency by the United States Department of Education and is recognized by the Council for Higher Education Accreditation. ACICS can be contacted at 750 First Street NE, Suite 980, Washington, D.C. 20002; phone: 202-336-6780.

The Brown Mackie College–Michigan City's Associate of Science degree in medical assisting is accredited by the Commission on Accreditation of Allied Health Education Programs (hppt://www.caahep.org) upon the recommendation of the Curriculum Review Board of the American Association of Medical Assistants Endowment (AAMAE).

The Brown Mackie College–Michigan City's Associate of Science degree in surgical technology is accredited by the Commission on Accreditation of Allied Health Education Programs (hppt://www.caahep.org) upon the recommendation of the Curriculum Review Board of the American Association of Medical Assistants Endowment (AAMAE).

The Associate of Applied Science in veterinary technology program at Brown Mackie College–Michigan City is accredited by the AVMA as a program for educating veterinary technicians.

This institution is regulated by the Indiana Commission of Proprietary Education, 302 West Washington Street, Room E201, Indianapolis, Indiana 46204; phone: 317-232-1320 or 800-227-5695 (toll-free). (Indiana advertising code: AC-0138.)

The campus is nonresidential; public transportation is available and there is no additional charge for parking. The College is a smoke-free environment.

Academic Programs

Brown Mackie College–Michigan City provides higher education to traditional and nontraditional students through bachelor's degree, associate degree, and certificate programs that can assist them in enhancing their career opportunities, broadening their perspectives through appropriate general education courses, thinking independently and critically, and improving problem-solving abilities. The College strives to develop within its students the desire for lifelong and continued education.

Each College quarter comprises twelve weeks. Bachelor's degree programs require a minimum of sixteen quarters to complete. Associate degree programs require a minimum of eight quarters to complete. Programs are offered on a year-round basis, providing students with the ability to work uninterrupted toward their degrees. The College offers all programs in a unique One Course a Month format. This schedule allows students to focus studies on only one course for four weeks and has proven convenient for students with multiple obligations such as jobs and family.

Bachelor's Degree Programs: The Bachelor of Science degree is awarded in business administration, criminal justice, health-care management, and legal studies.

Associate Degree Programs: The Associate of Science degree is awarded in accounting technology, business management, computer software technology, criminal justice, early childhood education, health and therapeutic massage, health-care administration, medical assisting, medical office management, paralegal studies, surgical technology, and veterinary technology.

Certificate Programs: The College offers certificate programs in accounting, business, computer software applications, criminal justice, medical assistant studies, medical coding and billing, and paralegal assistant studies.

Costs

Tuition in the 2010–11 academic year is $266 per credit hour with general fees of $15 per credit hour. For the surgical technology program, the tuition is $310 per credit hour; fees are $15 per credit hour. The cost of textbooks and other instructional materials varies according to the program.

Financial Aid

Financial aid is available to those who qualify. The College maintains a full-time staff of financial aid professionals to assist qualified students in obtaining financial assistance. The College participates in several student aid programs. Forms of financial aid available to qualified students through federal resources include the Federal Pell Grant Program, Federal Supplemental Educational Opportunity Grant (FSEOG) Program, Federal Work-Study Program, Federal Stafford Student Loan Program (subsidized and unsubsidized), and Federal PLUS loan program. Eligible students may apply for Indiana state awards, such as the Higher Education Award and Twenty-First Century

Scholarships for high school students, the Core 40 awards, and veteran's educational benefits. Students with physical or mental disabilities that are a handicap to employment may be eligible for training services through the state's Bureau of Vocational Rehabilitation. For further information, students should contact the College's Student Financial Services Office.

Each year, the College makes available scholarships of up to $1000 each to qualifying seniors from area high schools. No more than one scholarship is awarded per high school. In order to qualify, a senior must be graduating from a participating high school, have maintained a cumulative grade point average of at least 2.0, and submitted a brief essay. The student's extracurricular activities and community service are also considered. These scholarships are available only to students enrolling in one of the College's degree programs. Students awarded the scholarship must enroll at Brown Mackie College–Michigan City between June and September immediately following their high school graduation. Applications for these scholarships can be obtained from the guidance departments of participating high schools. These applications must be completed and returned to the College by March 31.

Faculty

The College has 9 full-time and 31 part-time faculty members. The average student-faculty ratio is 13:1. Each student is assigned a faculty adviser.

Facilities and Resources

The College offers a modern, professional environment for study, and includes attractive classrooms, administration offices, and a bookstore. The library and classrooms offer multimedia capabilities through overhead projectors with surround-sound audio systems, DVD/CD/VCR players, and Internet access. Five of the classrooms are equipped with networked computer systems, while two medical laboratories contain newly acquired medical equipment and instructional tools. The labs provide students with hands-on opportunities to apply skills learned in the classroom. Students are welcome to use those facilities when not in use for scheduled classes.

Location

Brown Mackie College–Michigan City is conveniently located in northwest Indiana, at 325 East U.S. Highway 20, Michigan City, 1 mile north of Interstate 94, near the intersection of routes 20 and 421. Public transportation is available. Additional parking spaces were added in 2002, providing students and employees with ample parking at no additional charge.

Admission Requirements

Each applicant for admission is assigned an Assistant Director of Admissions, who directs the applicant through the steps of the admissions process, providing information on curriculum, policies, procedures, and services; and assisting the applicant in setting necessary appointments and interviews.

To qualify for admission, each applicant must provide documentation of graduation from an accredited high school or from a state-approved secondary education curriculum or provide official documentation of high school graduation equivalency. All transcripts become the property of the College.

As part of the admission process, students are given an assessment of academic skills. Although the results of this assessment do not determine eligibility for admission, they provide the College with a means of determining the need for academic support, as well as a means by which the College can evaluate the effectiveness of its educational programs. All new students are required to complete this assessment, which is re-administered at the end of the student's program so results may be compared with those of the initial administration.

For the most recent information regarding admission requirements, please refer to the current academic catalog.

Application and Information

Applicants must complete and submit an application form along with documentation of graduation from an accredited high school or state-approved secondary education curriculum, or applicants must provide official documentation of high school graduation equivalency.

For additional information, prospective students should contact:

Director of Admissions
Brown Mackie College–Michigan City
325 East U.S. Highway 20
Michigan City, Indiana 46360
Phone: 219-877-3100
800-519-2416 (toll-free)
Fax: 219-877-3110
E-mail: bmcmcadm@brownmackie.edu
Web site: http://www.brownmackie.edu/MichiganCity

BROWN MACKIE COLLEGE–NORTH CANTON

NORTH CANTON, OHIO

The College and Its Mission

Brown Mackie College–North Canton is one of over twenty locations in the Brown Mackie College family of schools (http://www.brownmackie.edu), which is dedicated to providing educational programs that prepare students to pursue entry-level positions in a competitive, rapidly-changing workplace. Brown Mackie College schools offer bachelor's degree, associate degree, certificate, and diploma programs in health sciences, business, information technology, legal studies, and design to over 19,000 students in the Midwest, Southeast, Southwest, and Western United States.

Brown Mackie College–North Canton opened its classroom doors in January 1984 as National Electronics Institute (NEI). In July 1985, the school was purchased by Electronics Technology Institute of Cleveland and became a branch facility. The name was changed to Electronic Technology Institute. When Electronic Technical Institute of Cleveland was granted the right to confer the bachelor's degree, it changed its name to ETI Technical College. In May 1995, the assets of ETI Technical College of Canton were purchased by Career Options Inc., an Ohio corporation. In June 2002, the College came under the ownership of Southern Ohio College LLC, and the College's name then changed to AEC Southern Ohio College. The name of the College was changed to Brown Mackie College in November 2004. In June 2007, Brown Mackie College of North Canton moved into its new facility at 4300 Munson Street in Canton.

Brown Mackie College–North Canton is accredited by the Accrediting Council for Independent Colleges and Schools (ACICS) to award associate degrees and diplomas. ACICS is listed as a nationally recognized accrediting agency by the United States Department of Education and is recognized by the Council for Higher Education Accreditation. ACICS may be contacted at 750 First Street NE, Suite 980, Washington, D.C. 20002-4241; phone: 202-336-6780.

The Associate of Applied Science in surgical technology program is accredited by the Accrediting Bureau of Health Education Schools.

Ohio registration #03-09-1688T.

The College is a nonresidential, smoke-free institution.

Academic Programs

Brown Mackie College–North Canton provides higher education to traditional and nontraditional students through associate degree and diploma programs that can assist them in enhancing their career opportunities, broadening their perspectives through appropriate general education courses, thinking independently and critically, and improving problem-solving abilities. The College strives to develop within its students the desire for lifelong and continued education.

Each College quarter comprises twelve weeks. Programs are offered on a year-round basis, providing students with the ability to work uninterrupted toward the completion of their programs. The College offers all programs in a unique One Course a Month format. This schedule allows students to focus studies on only one course for four weeks and has proven convenient for students with multiple obligations such as jobs and family.

Associate Degree Programs: Associate degree programs require a minimum of eight quarters to complete. The Associate of Applied Business degree is awarded in accounting technology, business management, computer networking and applications, criminal justice, and paralegal studies. The Associate of Applied Science degree is awarded in computer-aided design and drafting technology, health-care administration, medical assisting, pharmacy technology, surgical technology, and veterinary technology.

Diploma Programs: The College offers diploma programs in accounting, business, computer-aided design and drafting technician studies, criminal justice, medical assistant studies, paralegal assistant studies, and practical nursing.

Costs

Tuition for most programs in the 2010–11 academic year is $266 per credit hour, with general fees of $15 per credit hour. Tuition for practical nursing is $325 per credit hour, with general fees of $25 per credit hour; surgical technology is $310 per credit hour, with general fees of $25 per credit hour; and the six core classes for computer networking and applications are $300 per credit hour with general fees of $25 per credit hour. Textbooks and other instructional materials vary by program.

Financial Aid

Financial aid is available to those who qualify. The College maintains a full-time staff of financial aid professionals to assist qualified students in obtaining financial assistance. The College participates in several student aid programs. Forms of financial aid available through federal resources include Federal Pell Grants, Federal Supplemental Educational Opportunity Grants (FSEOG), the Federal Work-Study Program, Federal Perkins Loans, Federal Stafford Student Loans (subsidized and unsubsidized), the Federal PLUS Program, and veterans' educational benefits. Eligible students may apply for state awards such as the Ohio College Opportunity Grant (OCOG). Students with physical or mental disabilities that are a handicap may be eligible for training services through the state Vocational Rehabilitation Agency. For further information, students should contact the College's Student Financial Services Office.

Each year, the College makes available President's Scholarships of up to $1000 each to qualifying seniors from area high schools. No more than one scholarship is awarded per high school. In order to qualify, a senior must be graduating from a participating high school, have maintained a cumulative grade point average of at least 2.0, and submitted a brief essay. The student's extracurricular activities and community service are also considered. The President's Scholarship is available only to students enrolling in one of the College's degree programs. Students who receive the scholarship must enroll at Brown Mackie College–North Canton between June and September immediately following their high school graduation. Applications for these scholarships can be obtained from the guidance departments of participating high schools. These applications must be completed and returned to the College by March 31.

Faculty

Currently, there are 22 full-time and 68 part-time faculty members. The average student-faculty ratio is 20:1. The College has seven program chairs who have advanced degrees and real-world experience in each of the fields of study offered by the college. In addition to program chairs, the academic affairs department of the College has two librarians and two academic advisors who are available to the students during school hours.

Facilities and Resources

In addition to classrooms and computer labs, the College maintains a library of curriculum-related resources, technical and general education materials, academic and professional periodicals, and audiovisual resources. Internet access also is available for research.

Location

Brown Mackie College–North Canton is located at 4300 Munson Street, NW in Canton, Ohio.

Admission Requirements

Each applicant for admission is assigned an Assistant Director of Admissions, who directs the applicant through the steps of the admissions process, providing information on curriculum, policies, procedures, and services and assisting the applicant in setting necessary appointments and interviews. To qualify for admission, each applicant must provide documentation of graduation from an accredited high school or from a state-approved secondary education curriculum or provide official documentation of high school graduation equivalency. All transcripts become the property of the College. Admission to the College is based upon the applicant meeting the above requirements, a review of the applicant's previous educational records, and a review of the applicant's career interests. If previous academic records indicate that the College's education and training programs would not benefit the applicant, the College reserves the right to advise the applicant not to enroll. Special requirements for enrollment into certain programs are discussed in the descriptions of those programs.

Application and Information

Applicants must complete and submit an application form, along with documentation of graduation from an accredited high school or state-approved secondary education curriculum or official documentation of high school graduation equivalency. For further information, prospective students should contact:

Director of Admissions
Brown Mackie College–North Canton
4300 Munson Street NW
Canton, Ohio 44718-3674
Phone: 330-494-1214
Fax: 330-494-8112
E-mail: bmcncadm@brownmackie.edu
Web site: http://www.brownmackie.edu/NorthCanton

BROWN MACKIE COLLEGE–NORTHERN KENTUCKY

FORT MITCHELL, KENTUCKY

BROWN MACKIE COLLEGE
NORTHERN KENTUCKY™

The College and Its Mission

Brown Mackie College–Northern Kentucky is one of over twenty locations in the Brown Mackie College family of schools (http://www.brownmackie.edu), which is dedicated to providing educational programs that prepare students to pursue entry-level positions in a competitive, rapidly-changing workplace. Brown Mackie College schools offer bachelor's degree, associate degree, certificate, and diploma programs in health sciences, business, information technology, legal studies, and design to over 19,000 students in the Midwest, Southeast, Southwest, and Western United States.

The College was founded in Cincinnati, Ohio, in February 1927 as a traditional business college. In May 1981, the College opened a branch location in northern Kentucky, which moved in 1986 to its current location in Fort Mitchell.

Brown Mackie College–Northern Kentucky is accredited by the Accrediting Council for Independent Colleges and Schools (ACICS) to award bachelor's degrees, associate degrees, certificates, and diplomas. ACICS is listed as a nationally recognized accrediting agency by the United States Department of Education and is recognized by the Council for Higher Education Accreditation. ACICS may be contacted at 750 First Street NE, Suite 980, Washington, D.C. 20002-4241; phone: 202-336-6780.

The occupational therapy assistant studies program has applied for accreditation by the Accreditation Council for Occupational Therapy Education (ACOTE) of the American Occupational Therapy Association (AOTA), located at 4720 Montgomery Lane, P.O. Box 31220, Bethesda, Maryland 20824; phone: 301-652-AOTA.

Ohio registration #03-09-1686T.

The College is a nonresidential, smoke-free institution.

Academic Programs

Brown Mackie College–Northern Kentucky provides higher education to traditional and nontraditional students through associate degree and diploma programs that can assist them in enhancing their career opportunities, broadening their perspectives through appropriate general education courses, thinking independently and critically, and improving problem-solving abilities.

Each College quarter comprises twelve weeks. Programs are offered on a year-round basis, providing students with the ability to work uninterrupted toward their degrees. The College offers all programs in a unique One Course a Month format. This schedule allows students to focus studies on only one course for four weeks and has proven convenient for students with multiple obligations such as jobs and family.

Associate Degree Programs: Associate degree programs require a minimum of eight quarters to complete. The Associate of Applied Business degree is awarded in accounting technology, business management, computer software technology, criminal justice, health-care administration, information technology, and paralegal studies. The Associate of Applied Science degree is awarded in computer-aided design and drafting technology, medical assisting, occupational therapy assistant studies, pharmacy technology, and surgical technology.

Diploma Programs: The College offers diploma programs in accounting, business, medical assistant studies, and practical nursing.

Costs

Tuition for the 2010–11 academic year is $266 per credit hour and general fees are $15 per credit hour, with some exceptions. The practical nursing program tuition is $325 per credit hour and general fees are $25 per credit hour. The surgical technology tuition is $310 per credit hour. Tuition for the occupational therapy assistant program is $266 per credit hour for general courses and $365 per credit hour for program-specific courses. Textbooks and other instructional materials vary by program.

Financial Aid

Financial aid is available to those who qualify. The College maintains a full-time staff of financial aid professionals to assist qualified students in obtaining financial assistance. The College participates in several student aid programs. Forms of financial aid available through federal resources include Federal Pell Grants, Federal Supplemental Educational Opportunity Grants (FSEOG), Federal Work-Study Program awards, Federal Perkins Loans, Federal Stafford Student Loans (subsidized and unsubsidized), and Federal PLUS loans. Eligible students may apply for veterans' educational benefits. Students with physical or mental disabilities that are a handicap to employment may be eligible for training services through the state Vocational Rehabilitation Agency. For further information, students should contact the College's Student Financial Services Office.

Each year, the College makes available President's Scholarships of up to $1000 each to qualifying seniors from area high schools. No more than one scholarship is awarded per high school. In order to qualify, a senior must be graduating from a participating high school, have maintained a cumulative grade point average of at least 2.0, and submitted a brief essay. The student's extracurricular activities and community service are also considered. The President's Scholarship is available only to students enrolling in one of the College's degree programs. Students who receive the scholarship must enroll at Brown Mackie College–Northern Kentucky between June and September immediately following their high school graduation. Applications for these scholarships can be obtained from the guidance departments of participating high schools. These applications must be completed and returned to the College by March 31.

Faculty

There are 11 full-time and 20 part-time faculty members. The student-faculty ratio is 15:1.

Facilities and Resources

Brown Mackie College–Northern Kentucky provides media presentation rooms for special instructional needs and a library that provides instructional resources and academic support for both faculty members and students. The College is nonresidential. It is accessible by public transportation and provides ample parking at no cost.

Location

The College is located at 309 Buttermilk Pike in Fort Mitchell, Kentucky.

Admission Requirements

Each applicant for admission is assigned an Assistant Director of Admissions, who directs the applicant through the steps of the admissions process, providing information on curriculum, policies, procedures, and services and assisting the applicant in setting necessary appointments and interviews. To qualify for admission, each applicant must provide documentation of graduation from an accredited high school or from a state-approved secondary education curriculum or provide official documentation of high school graduation equivalency. All transcripts become the property of the College. Admission to the College is based upon the applicant meeting the above requirements, a review of the applicant's previous education records, and a review of the applicant's career interests. If previous academic records indicate that the College's education and training programs would not benefit the applicant, the College reserves the right to advise the applicant not to enroll. Special requirements for enrollment into certain programs are discussed in the descriptions of those programs.

For the most recent information regarding admission requirements, please refer to the current academic catalog.

Application and Information

Applicants must complete and submit an application form, along with documentation of graduation from an accredited high school or state-approved secondary education curriculum or official documentation of high school graduation equivalency. For additional information, prospective students should contact:

Director of Admissions
Brown Mackie College–Northern Kentucky
309 Buttermilk Pike
Fort Mitchell, Kentucky 41017
Phone: 859-341-5627
800-888-1445 (toll-free)
Fax: 859-341-6483
E-mail: bmcnkadm@brownmackie.edu
Web site: http://www.brownmackie.edu/NorthernKentucky

BROWN MACKIE COLLEGE–PHOENIX

PHOENIX, ARIZONA

The College and Its Mission

Brown Mackie College–Phoenix is one of over twenty locations in the Brown Mackie College family of schools (http://www.brownmackie.edu), which is dedicated to providing educational programs that prepare students to pursue entry-level positions in a competitive, rapidly-changing workplace. Brown Mackie College schools offer bachelor's degree, associate degree, certificate, and diploma programs in health sciences, business, information technology, legal studies, and design to over 19,000 students in the Midwest, Southeast, Southwest, and Western United States.

Brown Mackie College–Phoenix was founded in 2009 as a branch of Brown Mackie College–Tucson, Arizona.

Brown Mackie College–Phoenix is accredited by the Accrediting Council for Independent Colleges and Schools (ACICS) to award bachelor's degrees, associate degrees, and diplomas. ACICS is listed as a nationally recognized accrediting agency by the United States Department of Education and is recognized by the Council for Higher Education Accreditation. ACICS can be contacted at 750 First Street NE, Suite 980, Washington, D.C. 20002; phone: 202-336-6780.

The occupational therapy assistant program has applied for accreditation by the Accreditation Council for Occupational Therapy Education (ACOTE) of the American Occupational Therapy Association (AOTA), located at 4720 Montgomery Lane, P.O. Box 31220, Bethesda, Maryland 20824; phone: 301-652-AOTA.

This institution is licensed by the Arizona State Board for Private Postsecondary Education, 1400 West Washington Street, Room 260, Phoenix, Arizona 85007; phone: 620-543-5709.

The College is a nonresidential, smoke-free institution.

Academic Programs

Brown Mackie College–Phoenix provides higher education to traditional and nontraditional students through bachelor's degree, associate degree, and diploma programs that can assist them in enhancing their career opportunities, broadening their perspectives through appropriate general education courses, thinking independently and critically, and improving problem-solving abilities.

Each College quarter comprises twelve weeks. Associate degree programs require a minimum of eight quarters to complete. Programs are offered on a year-round basis, providing students with the ability to work uninterrupted toward the completion of their programs. The College offers all programs in a unique One Course a Month format. This schedule allows students to focus studies on only one course for four weeks and has proven convenient for students with multiple obligations such as jobs and family.

Bachelor's Degree Programs: The Bachelor of Science degree is awarded in business administration, criminal justice, health-care management, and legal studies.

Associate Degree Programs: The Associate of Science degree is awarded in accounting technology, business management, criminal justice, health-care administration, information technology, medical assisting, paralegal studies, and surgical technology. The Associate of Applied Science degree is awarded in occupational therapy assistant studies.

Costs

Tuition for the 2010–11 academic year is $250 per credit hour, with a $15 per credit hour general fee applied to instructional costs for activities and services. For the surgical technology program, the tuition is $275 per credit hour with a $15 per credit hour general fee. Tuition for certain courses in the occupational therapy assistant studies program is $350 per credit hour with a $15 per credit hour general fee. Costs for textbooks and other instructional materials vary by program.

Financial Aid

Financial aid is available to those who qualify. The College maintains a full-time staff of financial aid professionals to assist qualified students in obtaining financial assistance. The College participates in several student aid programs. Forms of financial aid available to those who qualify through federal resources include the Federal Pell Grant Program, Federal Supplemental Educational Opportunity Grant (FSEOG) Program, Federal Work-Study Program, Federal Perkins Loan Program, Federal Stafford Student Loan Program (subsidized and unsubsidized), and the Federal PLUS Loan Program. For further information, students should contact the College's Student Financial Services Office.

Each year, the College makes available scholarships of up to $1000 each to qualifying seniors from area high schools. Only one scholarship is awarded per high school. In order to qualify, a senior must be graduating from a participating high school, have maintained a cumulative grade point average of at least 2.0, and submitted a brief essay. The student's extracurricular activities and community service are also considered. The scholarship is available only to students enrolling in one of the College's degree programs. Students awarded the scholarship must enroll at Brown Mackie College–Phoenix between June and September immediately following their high school graduation. Applications for these scholarships can be obtained from the guidance departments of participating high schools. These applications must be completed and returned to the College by March 31.

Faculty

Experienced faculty members provide academic support and are committed to the academic and technical preparation of their students. The College has both full- and part-time faculty members. The average student-faculty ratio is 12:1. Each student is assigned a program director as an adviser.

Facilities and Resources

Brown Mackie College–Phoenix occupies a beautiful facility with a variety of classrooms including computer labs housing industry-current technology. High-speed access to the Internet and other online resources are available for students and faculty. Multimedia classrooms are equipped with overhead projectors, TVs and DVD/VCR players, computers, and sound systems.

Location

Brown Mackie College–Phoenix is conveniently located at 13430 North Black Canyon Highway, Phoenix, Arizona. The College has a generous parking area and is also easily accessible by public transportation.

Admission Requirements

Each applicant for admission is assigned an Assistant Director of Admissions who directs the applicant through the steps of the admissions process, providing information on curriculum, policies, procedures, and services and assisting the applicant in setting necessary appointments and interviews.

To qualify for admission, each applicant must provide documentation of graduation from an accredited high school or from a state-approved secondary education curriculum or provide official documentation of high school graduation equivalency. All transcripts become the property of the College.

Application and Information

Applicants must complete and submit an application form along with documentation of graduation from an accredited high school or state-approved secondary education curriculum, or applicants must provide official documentation of high school graduation equivalency.

For additional information, prospective students should contact:

Director of Admissions
Brown Mackie College–Phoenix
13430 N. Black Canyon Highway
Phoenix, Arizona 85029
Phone: 602-337-3044
866-824-4793 (toll-free)
Fax: 480-375-2450
E-mail: bmcpxadm@brownmackie.edu
Web site: http://www.brownmackie.edu/Phoenix

BROWN MACKIE COLLEGE–QUAD CITIES

MOLINE, ILLINOIS

The College and Its Mission

Brown Mackie College–Quad Cities is one of over twenty locations in the Brown Mackie College family of schools (http://www.brownmackie.edu), which is dedicated to providing educational programs that prepare students to pursue entry-level positions in a competitive, rapidly-changing workplace. Brown Mackie College schools offer bachelor's degree, associate degree, certificate, and diploma programs in health sciences, business, information technology, legal studies, and design to over 19,000 students in the Midwest, Southeast, Southwest, and Western United States.

Founded in 1890 by A. N. Hirons as LaPorte Business College in LaPorte, Indiana, the institution later became known as Commonwealth Business College. In 1919, ownership was transferred to Grace and J. J. Moore, who successfully operated the College for almost thirty years. Following World War II, Harley and Stephanie Reese operated the College under the name of Reese School of Business for several decades.

In 1975, the College came under the ownership of Steven C. Smith as Commonwealth Business College. A second location, now known as Brown Mackie College–Merrillville, was opened in 1984 in Merrillville, Indiana, and a third location was opened a year later in Davenport, Iowa. In 1987, the Davenport location relocated to its present site in Moline, Illinois. In September 2003, the College changed ownership again and the College's name was changed to Brown Mackie College–Moline in November 2004.

Brown Mackie College–Quad Cities is accredited by the Accrediting Council for Independent Colleges and Schools (ACICS) to award associate degrees, diplomas, and certificates. ACICS is listed as a nationally recognized accrediting agency by the United States Department of Education and is recognized by the Council for Higher Education Accreditation. ACICS can be contacted at 750 First Street NE, Suite 980, Washington, D.C. 20002; 202-336-6780.

The College is a nonresidential, smoke-free institution.

Academic Programs

Brown Mackie College–Quad Cities provides higher education to traditional and nontraditional students through associate degree and diploma programs that can assist them in enhancing their career opportunities, broadening their perspectives through appropriate general education courses, thinking independently and critically, and improving problem-solving abilities. The College strives to develop within its students the desire for lifelong and continued education.

Each College quarter comprises twelve weeks. Programs are offered on a year-round basis, providing students with the ability to work uninterrupted toward the completion of their programs. The College offers all programs in a unique One Course a Month format. This schedule allows students to focus studies on only one course for four weeks and has proven convenient for students with multiple obligations such as jobs and family.

Associate Degree Programs: The Associate of Applied Science degree is awarded in accounting technology, business management, and medical assisting.

Diploma Programs: The College offers diploma programs in accounting, business, medical assistant studies, medical office management, and paralegal assistant studies.

Costs

Tuition for the 2010–11 academic year is $266 per credit hour; fees are $15 per credit hour. Textbook costs vary by program.

Financial Aid

Financial aid is available to those who qualify. The College maintains a full-time staff of financial aid professionals to assist qualified students in obtaining the financial assistance they require to meet their educational expenses. The College participates in several student aid programs. Forms of financial aid available through federal resources include the Federal Pell Grant Program, Federal Supplemental Educational Opportunity Grant (FSEOG) Program, Federal Work-Study Program, Federal Perkins Loan Program, Federal Stafford Student Loan Program (subsidized and unsubsidized), and Federal PLUS loan program. Eligible students may apply for veterans' educational benefits. Students with physical or mental disabilities that are a handicap to employment may be eligible for training services through the state Agency for Vocational Rehabilitation. For further information, students should contact the College's Student Financial Services Office.

Each year, the College makes available scholarships of up to $1000 each to qualifying seniors from area high schools. Only one scholarship is awarded per high school. In order to qualify, a senior must be graduating from a participating high school, have maintained a cumulative grade point average of at least 2.0, and submitted a brief essay. The student's extracurricular activities and community service are also considered. These scholarships are available only to students enrolling in one of the College's diploma programs. Students awarded the scholarship must enroll at Brown Mackie College–Quad Cities between June and September immediately following their high school graduation. Applications for these scholarships can be obtained from the guidance departments of participating high schools. These applications must be completed and returned to the College by March 31.

Faculty

Brown Mackie College–Quad Cities has 2 full-time and 12 regular adjunct faculty members, with an average student-faculty ratio of 9:1.

Facilities and Resources

The College maintains a library of curriculum-related resources. Technical and general education materials, academic and professional periodicals, and audiovisual resources are available to both students and faculty members. Students have borrowing privileges at several local libraries. Internet access is available for research.

Location

Brown Mackie College–Quad Cities is located at 1527 47th Avenue in Moline, Illinois. The College is easily accessible by public transportation, and ample parking is available at no cost.

Admission Requirements

Each applicant for admission is assigned an Assistant Director of Admissions, who directs the applicant through the steps of the admissions process, providing information on curriculum, policies, procedures, and services and assisting the applicant in setting necessary appointments and interviews.

To qualify for admission, each applicant must provide documentation of graduation from an accredited high school or from a state-approved secondary education curriculum or provide official documentation of high school graduation equivalency. All transcripts become the property of the College. Admission to the College is based on the applicant meeting the above requirements, a review of the applicant's previous education records, and a review of the applicant's career interests. If previous academic records indicate that the College's education and training programs would not benefit the applicant, the College reserves the right to advise the applicant not to enroll. Special requirements for enrollment into certain programs are discussed in the descriptions of those programs.

Application and Information

Applicants must complete and submit an application form along with documentation of graduation from an accredited high school or state-approved secondary education curriculum, or applicants must provide official documentation of high school graduation equivalency. For further information, prospective students should contact:

Director of Admissions
Brown Mackie College–Quad Cities
1527 47th Avenue
Moline, Illinois 61265
Phone: 309-762-2100
Fax: 309-762-2374
E-mail: bmcmoadm@brownmackie.edu
Web site: http://www.brownmackie.edu/Quad-Cities

BROWN MACKIE COLLEGE–ST. LOUIS

FENTON, MISSOURI

The College and Its Mission

Brown Mackie College–St. Louis is one of over twenty locations in the Brown Mackie College family of schools (http://www.brownmackie.edu), which is dedicated to providing educational programs that prepare students to pursue entry-level positions in a competitive, rapidly-changing workplace. Brown Mackie College schools offer bachelor's degree, associate degree, and diploma programs in health sciences, business, information technology, legal studies, and design to over 19,000 students in the Midwest, Southeast, Southwest, and Western United States.

Brown Mackie College–St. Louis was founded in 2010 as a branch of Brown Mackie College–Tucson, Arizona.

Brown Mackie College–St. Louis is accredited by the Accrediting Council for Independent Colleges and Schools (ACICS) to award bachelor's degrees, associate degrees, and diplomas. ACICS is listed as a nationally recognized accrediting agency by the United States Department of Education and is recognized by the Council for Higher Education Accreditation. ACICS can be contacted at 750 First Street NE, Suite 980, Washington, D.C. 20002; phone: 202-336-6780.

This institution is approved to operate by the Missouri Department of Higher Education, 3515 Amazonas Drive, Jefferson City, Missouri 65109-5717; phone: 573-751-2361.

Academic Programs

Each College quarter comprises twelve weeks. Bachelor's degree programs require a minimum of sixteen quarters to complete. Associate degree programs require a minimum of eight quarters to complete. Programs are offered on a year-round basis, providing students with the ability to work uninterrupted toward their degrees. The College offers all programs in a unique One Course a Month format. This schedule allows students to focus studies on only one course for four weeks and has proven convenient for students with multiple obligations such as jobs and family.

Bachelor's Degree Programs: The Bachelor of Science degree is awarded in business administration, criminal justice, health-care management, and legal studies.

Associate Degree Programs: The Associate of Applied Science degree is awarded in accounting technology, architectural design and drafting technology, business management, criminal justice, health-care administration, information technology, medical assisting, office management, paralegal studies, pharmacy technology, and surgical technology.

Diploma Programs: The College also offers diploma programs in accounting, business, criminal justice, medical assistant studies, and paralegal assistant studies.

Costs

Tuition in the 2010–11 academic year for most bachelor's and associate degree programs is $260 per credit hour; fees are $15 per credit hour. Tuition for the surgical technology program is $310 per credit hour with fees of $15 per credit hour. Textbooks and other instructional expenses vary by program.

Financial Aid

Financial aid is available for those who qualify. The College maintains a full-time staff of financial aid professionals to assist qualified students in obtaining the financial assistance they require to meet their educational expenses. Available resources include federal and state aid, student loans from private lenders, and Federal Work-Study opportunities, both on and off college premises.

Faculty

Experienced faculty members provide academic support and are committed to the academic and technical preparation of their students. The college has both full- and part-time instructors, with a competitive student-faculty ratio. Each student is assigned a faculty adviser.

Facilities and Resources

A modern facility, Brown Mackie College–St. Louis offers tastefully appointed classrooms, laboratories, and office space designed to the specifications of the College for its business, medical, and technical programs. Instructional equipment is comparable to current technology used in business and industry today. Modern classrooms for special instructional needs offer multimedia capabilities with surround sound and overhead projectors accessible through computer, DVD, or VHS. Internet access and instructional resources are available at the College's library.

Location

Brown Mackie College–St. Louis is conveniently located at #2 Soccer Park Road in Fenton, Missouri. The College has a generous parking area and is also easily accessible by public transportation.

Admission Requirements

Each applicant for admission is assigned an Assistant Director of Admissions who directs the applicant through the steps of the admissions process. They provide information on curriculum, policies, procedures, and services and assist the applicant in setting up necessary appointments and interviews.

To qualify for admission, each applicant must provide documentation of graduation from an accredited high school, or from a state-approved secondary education curriculum, or provide official documentation of high school graduation equivalency. All transcripts become the property of the College. Admission to the College is based on the applicant meeting the stated requirements, a review of the applicant's previous educational records, and a review of the applicant's career interests. If previous academic records indicate the College's education and training programs would not benefit the applicant, the College reserves the right to advise the applicant not to enroll. Special requirements for enrollment into certain programs are discussed in the descriptions of those programs.

For the most recent information regarding admission requirements, please refer to the current academic catalog.

Application and Information

Applicants must complete and submit an application form, along with documentation of graduation from an accredited high school or state-approved secondary education curriculum or official documentation of high school graduation equivalency.

For additional information, prospective students should contact:

Senior Director of Admissions
Brown Mackie College–St. Louis
#2 Soccer Park Road
Fenton, Missouri 63026
Phone: 636-651-3290
888-874-4375 (toll-free)
Fax: 636-651-3349
E-mail: bmcstladm@brownmackie.edu
Web site: http://www.brownmackie.edu/St-Louis

BROWN MACKIE COLLEGE–SALINA

SALINA, KANSAS

The College and Its Mission

Brown Mackie College–Salina is one of over twenty locations in the Brown Mackie College family of schools (http://www.brownmackie.edu), which is dedicated to providing educational programs that prepare students to pursue entry-level positions in a competitive, rapidly-changing workplace. Brown Mackie College schools offer bachelor's degree, associate degree, certificate, and diploma programs in health sciences, business, information technology, legal studies, and design to over 19,000 students in the Midwest, Southeast, Southwest, and Western United States.

The College was originally founded in July 1892 as the Kansas Wesleyan School of Business. In 1938, the College was incorporated as the Brown Mackie School of Business under the ownership of former Kansas Wesleyan instructors Perry E. Brown and A. B. Mackie; it became Brown Mackie College in January 1975.

Brown Mackie College–Salina is accredited by the Higher Learning Commission and is a member of the North Central Association, 30 North LaSalle Street, Suite 2400, Chicago, Illinois 60602-2504; Web site: http://www.ncahlc.org.

The occupational therapy assistant studies program has applied for accreditation by the Accreditation Council for Occupational Therapy Education (ACOTE) of the American Occupational Therapy Association (AOTA), located at 4720 Montgomery Lane, P.O. Box 31220, Bethesda, Maryland 20824; phone: 301-652-AOTA.

Brown Mackie College–Salina is approved and authorized to grant the Associate of Applied Science (AAS) degree by the Kansas Board of Regents, 1000 Southwest Jackson Street, Suite 520, Topeka, Kansas 66612-1368.

Academic Programs

Brown Mackie College–Salina provides higher education to traditional and nontraditional students through associate degree, diploma, and certificate programs that can assist them in enhancing their career opportunities, broadening their perspectives through appropriate general education courses, thinking independently and critically, and improving problem-solving abilities. The College strives to develop within its students the desire for lifelong and continued education.

In most programs, students can participate in day or evening classes, which begin every month. Programs are offered on a year-round basis, providing students with the ability to work uninterrupted toward completion of their programs. The College offers all programs in a unique One Course a Month format. This schedule allows students to focus studies on only one course for four weeks and has proven convenient for students with multiple obligations such as jobs and family.

Associate Degree Programs: The Associate of Applied Science degree is awarded in accounting technology, architectural design and drafting technology, business management, computer-aided design and drafting technology, computer networking and applications, criminal justice, health and fitness training, health-care administration, medical assisting, nursing, occupational therapy assistant studies, office management, and paralegal studies. An associate degree in general studies is also offered to create a greater level of flexibility for students who may be unsure of their career choice, who want a more generalized education, or who want to transfer to a baccalaureate program.

Diploma Programs: The College also offers diploma programs in accounting, business, computer-aided design and drafting technician studies, computer software applications, criminal justice, fitness trainer studies, medical assistant studies, and paralegal assistant studies.

Certificate Programs: Certificate programs are offered in computer networking and practical nursing.

Costs

Tuition is $266 per credit hour and general fees are $15 per credit hour, with some exceptions. Tuition for computer networking is $266 per credit hour for general courses and $300 per credit hour for program-specific courses. Courses in the nursing programs are $325 per credit hour and general fees are $25 per credit hour. Tuition for certain courses in the occupational therapy assistant studies program is $365 per credit hour and fees are $15 per credit hour. Textbooks and other instructional materials vary by program.

Financial Aid

Financial aid is available to those who qualify. The College maintains a full-time staff of financial aid professionals to assist qualified students in obtaining financial assistance. The College participates in several student aid programs. Forms of financial aid that are available through federal resources include Federal Pell Grants, Federal Supplemental Educational Opportunity Grants (FSEOG), Academic Competitiveness Grant, Federal Work-Study Program awards, Federal Perkins Loans, Federal Stafford Student Loans (subsidized and unsubsidized), and Federal PLUS loans. Eligible students may apply for veterans' educational benefits. Students with physical or mental disabilities that are a handicap to employment may be eligible for training services through the state Vocational Rehabilitation Agency. For further information, students should contact the College's Student Financial Services Office.

Each year, the College makes available President's Scholarships of up to $1000 each to qualifying seniors from area high schools. No more than one scholarship is awarded per high school. In order to qualify, a senior must be graduating from a participating high school, have maintained a cumulative grade point average of at least 2.0, and submitted a brief essay. The student's extracurricular activities and community service are also considered. The President's Scholarship is available only to students enrolling in one of the College's degree programs. Students awarded the scholarship must enroll at Brown Mackie College–Salina between June and September immediately following their high school graduation. Applications for these scholarships can be obtained from the guidance departments of participating high schools. These applications must be completed and returned to the College by March 31.

The Merit Scholarship is a College-sponsored scholarship that may be awarded to students who demonstrate exceptional academic ability. To qualify for a Merit Scholarship, an applicant or student must have scored 21 or higher on the ACT or 900 or higher on the SAT. The maximum amount awarded by this scholarship to any student is $500.

Athletic scholarships may be awarded to students who participate in athletic programs that are sponsored by the College. Current sports are men's baseball, men's and women's basketball, and women's fast-pitch softball. Maximum awards for any applicant or student are determined by the College President. Further information is available from the Athletic Office. Recipients of athletic scholarships must achieve a cumulative grade point average of at least 2.0 by their graduation. Recipients who fail to maintain full-time status or the required grade point average forfeit their awards.

Faculty

There are 19 full-time and 19 adjunct faculty members. The average student-instructor ratio is 15:1.

Facilities and Resources

In addition to classrooms and computer labs, the College maintains a library of curriculum-related resources, technical and general education materials, academic and professional periodicals, and audiovisual resources. Internet access is also available for research. The College has a bookstore that stocks texts, courseware, and other educational supplies that are required for courses and a variety of personal, recreational, and gift items, including apparel, supplies, and general merchandise incorporating the College logo. Hours are posted at the bookstore entrance.

Location

Brown Mackie College–Salina is located at 2106 South Ninth Street in Salina, Kansas.

Admission Requirements

Each applicant for admission is assigned an Assistant Director of Admissions, who directs the applicant through the steps of the admissions process, providing information on curriculum, policies, procedures, and services and assisting the applicant in setting necessary appointments and interviews.

To qualify for admission, each applicant must provide documentation of graduation from an accredited high school or from a state-approved secondary education curriculum or provide official documentation of high school graduation equivalency. All transcripts become the property of the College. Admission to the College is based upon the applicant meeting the above requirements, a review of the applicant's previous education records, and a review of the applicant's career interests. If previous academic records indicate that the College's education and training programs would not benefit the applicant, the College reserves the right to advise the applicant not to enroll. Special requirements for enrollment into certain programs are discussed in the descriptions of those programs.

For the most recent information regarding admissions requirements, please refer to the most current academic catalog.

Application and Information

Applicants must complete and submit an application form, along with documentation of graduation from an accredited high school or state-approved secondary education curriculum or official documentation of high school graduation equivalency. For additional information, prospective students should contact:

Director of Admissions
Brown Mackie College–Salina
2106 South Ninth Street
Salina, Kansas 67401
Phone: 785-825-5422
800-365-0433 (toll-free)
Fax: 785-827-7623
E-mail: bmcsaadm@brownmackie.edu
Web site: http://www.brownmackie.edu/Salina

BROWN MACKIE COLLEGE–SOUTH BEND

SOUTH BEND, INDIANA

The College and Its Mission

Brown Mackie College–South Bend is one of over twenty locations in the Brown Mackie College family of schools (http://www.brownmackie.edu), which is dedicated to providing educational programs that prepare students to pursue entry-level positions in a competitive, rapidly-changing workplace. Brown Mackie College schools offer bachelor's degree, associate degree, certificate, and diploma programs in health sciences, business, information technology, legal studies, and design to over 19,000 students in the Midwest, Southeast, Southwest, and Western United States.

The College is one of the oldest institutions of its kind in the country. Established in 1882 as the South Bend Commercial College, the school later changed its name to Michiana College. In 1930, the school was incorporated under the laws of the state of Indiana and was authorized to confer associate degrees and certificates in business. The College relocated to its current location on East Jefferson Boulevard in 1987.

Brown Mackie College–South Bend is accredited by the Accrediting Council for Independent Colleges and Schools (ACICS) to award bachelor's degrees, associate degrees, diplomas, and certificates. ACICS is listed as a nationally recognized accrediting agency by the United States Department of Education and is recognized by the Council for Higher Education Accreditation. ACICS can be contacted at 750 First Street NE, Suite 980, Washington, D.C. 20002; phone: 202-336-6780.

The Brown Mackie College–South Bend Associate of Science degree in medical assisting is accredited by the Commission on Accreditation of Allied Health Education Programs (http://www.caahep.org), upon recommendation of the Curriculum Review Board of the American Association of Medical Assistants Endowment (AAMAE).

The occupational therapy assistant studies program is accredited by the Accreditation Council for Occupational Therapy Education (ACOTE) of the American Occupational Therapy Association (AOTA), located at 4720 Montgomery Lane, P.O. Box 31220, Bethesda, Maryland 20824; phone: 301-652-AOTA.

The Brown Mackie College–South Bend Associate of Applied Science degree in physical therapist assistant studies is accredited by the Commission on Accreditation in Physical Therapy Education (CAPTE) of the American Physical Therapy Association (APTA), 1111 North Fairfax Street, Alexandria, Virginia 22314; phone: 703-706-3241.

The Brown Mackie College–South Bend practical nursing program is accredited by the Indiana State Board of Nursing, 402 West Washington Street, Room W066, Indianapolis, Indiana 46204; phone: 317-234-2043.

Brown Mackie College–South Bend is licensed and regulated by the Indiana Commission on Proprietary Education, 302 West Washington Street, Indianapolis, Indiana 46204; phone: 317-232-1320 or 800-227-5695 (toll-free). (Indiana advertising code: AC-0110.)

The College is a nonresidential, smoke-free institution.

Academic Programs

Brown Mackie College–South Bend provides higher education to traditional and nontraditional students through bachelor's degree, associate degree, certificate, and diploma programs that can assist them in enhancing their career opportunities, broadening their perspectives through appropriate general education courses, thinking independently and critically, and improving problem-solving abilities. The College strives to develop within its students the desire for lifelong and continued education.

Each College quarter comprises twelve weeks. Bachelor's degree programs require a minimum of sixteen quarters to complete. Associate degree programs require a minimum of eight quarters to complete. Programs are offered on a year-round basis, providing students with the ability to work uninterrupted toward their degrees. The College offers all programs in a unique One Course a Month format. This schedule allows students to focus studies on only one course for four weeks and has proven convenient for students with multiple obligations such as jobs and family.

Bachelor's Degree Programs: The Bachelor of Science degree is awarded in business administration, criminal justice, health-care management, and legal studies.

Associate Degree Programs: The Associate of Science degree is awarded in accounting technology, business management, computer software technology, criminal justice, early childhood education, health and therapeutic massage, health-care administration, information technology, medical assisting, paralegal studies, and veterinary technology. The Associate of Applied Science degree is awarded in occupational therapy assistant studies and physical therapist assistant studies.

Diploma Program: The College offers a diploma program in practical nursing.

Certificate Programs: The College offers certificate programs in accounting, business, computer software applications, criminal justice, medical assistant studies, and paralegal assistant studies.

Costs

Tuition for most programs in the 2010–11 academic year is $266 per credit hour, with a $15 per credit hour general fee applied to instructional costs for activities and services. Tuition for all courses in the practical nursing program is $325 per credit hour, with a $25 per credit hour general fee. Tuition for certain courses in the physical therapist assistant studies program is $365 per credit hour. Tuition for certain courses in the occupational therapy assistant studies program is $365 per credit hour. The cost of textbooks and other instructional materials varies by program.

Financial Aid

Financial aid is available to those who qualify. The College maintains a full-time staff of financial aid professionals to assist qualified students in obtaining financial assistance. The College participates in several student aid programs. Forms of financial aid available through federal resources include the Federal Pell Grant Program, Federal Supplemental Educational Opportunity

Grant (FSEOG) Program, Federal Work-Study Program, Federal Perkins Loan Program, Federal Stafford Student Loan Program (subsidized and unsubsidized), and the Federal PLUS Loan Program.

Eligible students may apply for Indiana state awards, such as the Frank O'Bannon Grant Program (formerly the Indiana Higher Education Grant) and Twenty-First Century Scholars Program for high school students, the Core 40 awards, and veteran's educational benefits. Students with physical or mental disabilities that are a handicap to employment may be eligible for training services through the state's Bureau of Vocational Rehabilitation. For further information, students should contact the College's Student Financial Services Office.

Each year, the College makes available scholarships of up to $1000 each to qualifying seniors from area high schools. No more than one scholarship is awarded per high school. In order to qualify, a senior must be graduating from a participating high school, have maintained a cumulative grade point average of at least 2.0, and submitted a brief essay. The student's extracurricular activities and community service are also considered. These scholarships are available only to students enrolling in one of the College's degree programs. Students awarded the scholarship must enroll at Brown Mackie College–South Bend between June and September immediately following their high school graduation. Applications for these scholarships can be obtained from the guidance departments of participating high schools. These applications must be completed and returned to the College by March 31.

Faculty

There are 19 full-time and 24 part-time faculty members at the College. The average student-faculty ratio is 12:1. Each student is assigned a program director as an adviser.

Facilities and Resources

Brown Mackie College–South Bend's four-story facility comprises 31,000 square feet of classrooms. The building offers a modern, professional environment for study. Five classrooms are outfitted as "classrooms of the future," with an instructor workstation and multimedia capabilities including a surround-sound system and projection screen that can be accessed by computer, DVD, or VHS equipment. The facility also includes medical, computer, and occupational and physical therapy labs, as well as a library and bookstore. The labs provide students with hands-on opportunities to apply knowledge and skills learned in the classroom. Students are welcome to use the labs when those facilities are not in use for scheduled classes.

Location

Brown Mackie College–South Bend is conveniently located in new, larger facilities at 3454 Douglas Road in South Bend, Indiana. The College is accessible by public transportation; a generous parking area is available at no additional charge. The College also operates a learning site at 2930 South Nappanee Street in Elkhart, Indiana.

Admission Requirements

Each applicant for admission is assigned an Assistant Director of Admissions, who directs the applicant through the steps of the admissions process, providing information on curriculum, policies, procedures, and services and assisting the applicant in setting necessary appointments and interviews. To qualify for admission, each applicant must provide documentation of graduation from an accredited high school, or from a state-approved secondary education curriculum, or provide official documentation of high school graduation equivalency. All transcripts become the property of the College.

As part of the admission process, students are given an assessment of academic skills. Although the results of this assessment do not determine eligibility for admission, they provide the College with a means of determining the need for academic support as well as a means by which the College can evaluate the effectiveness of its educational programs. All new students are required to complete this assessment, which is readministered at the end of the student's program so results may be compared with those of the initial administration.

In addition to the College's general admission requirements, applicants enrolling in the occupational therapy assistant studies or physical therapist assistant studies programs must document one of the following: a high school cumulative grade point average of at least 2.5, a score on the GED examination of at least 557 (57 if taken before January 15, 2002), or completion of 12 quarter-credit hours or 8 semester-credit hours of collegiate course work with a grade point average of at least 2.5. Credit hours may not include Professional Development (CF 1100), the Brown Mackie College–South Bend course. Students entering either program must also have completed a biology course with a grade of at least a C (or an average of at least 2.0 on a 4.0 scale).

In addition to the College's general admission requirements, applicants enrolling in the practical nursing program must document the following: fulfillment of Brown Mackie College–South Bend general requirements; complete physical (must be current to within six months of admission); two-step Mantoux TB skin test (must be current throughout schooling); hepatitis B vaccination or signed refusal; up-to-date immunizations, including tetanus and rubella; record of current CPR certification (certification must be current throughout the clinical experience through health-care provider certification or the American Heart Association); and hospitalization insurance or a signed waiver.

For the most recent information regarding admission requirements, please refer to the current academic catalog.

Application and Information

Applicants must complete and submit an application form along with documentation of graduation from an accredited high school or state-approved secondary education curriculum or official documentation of high school graduation equivalency.

For additional information, prospective students should contact:

Director of Admissions
Brown Mackie College–South Bend
3454 Douglas Road
South Bend, Indiana 46635

Phone: 574-237-0774
800-743-2447 (toll-free)
Fax: 574-237-3585
E-mail: bmcsbadm@brownmackie.edu
Web site: http://www.brownmackie.edu/SouthBend

BROWN MACKIE COLLEGE–TUCSON

TUCSON, ARIZONA

The College and Its Mission

Brown Mackie College–Tucson is one of over twenty locations in the Brown Mackie College family of schools (http://www.brownmackie.edu), which is dedicated to providing educational programs that prepare students to pursue entry-level positions in a competitive, rapidly changing workplace. Brown Mackie College schools offer bachelor's degree, associate degree, and diploma programs in health sciences, business, information technology, legal studies, and design to over 19,000 students in the Midwest, Southeast, Southwest, and Western United States.

Brown Mackie College was originally founded and approved by the board of trustees of Kansas Wesleyan College in Salina, Kansas on July 30, 1892. In 1938, the College was incorporated as The Brown Mackie School of Business under the ownership of Perry E. Brown and A. B. Mackie, former instructors at Kansas Wesleyan University in Salina, Kansas. Their last names formed the name of Brown Mackie. By January 1975, with improvements in curricula and higher degree-granting status, The Brown Mackie School of Business became Brown Mackie College.

Brown Mackie College entered Arizona in 2007, when it purchased a school that had been previously established in the Tucson area. That school was converted into what is now known as Brown Mackie College–Tucson and has a strong history with the community. The timeline of Brown Mackie College–Tucson started in 1972, when Rockland West Corporation first formed a partnership with Lamson Business College. At that time the school was a career college which offered only short-term programs focusing on computer training and secretarial skills. In 1994, the College became accredited as a junior college and began offering associate degrees in academic subjects. The mission was then modified to include the goal of instilling in graduates an appreciation for lifelong learning through the general education courses which became a part of every program.

In 1996, the College applied for and received status as a senior college by the Accrediting Council for Independent Colleges and Schools. This gave the school the ability to offer course work leading to a Bachelor of Science degree in business administration. Since then the program offerings for bachelor and associate degrees have expanded.

In 1986, the campus moved to the location where it remains today. During 2008, two of the College's three buildings were remodeled which resulted in updated classrooms; networked computer laboratories; new medical, surgical technology, and forensics laboratories; a larger library; offices for student services such as academics, admissions, and student financial services; and a college store. In 2009, the third building was also remodeled, providing newer classrooms and a new career services department.

Brown Mackie College–Tucson is accredited by the Accrediting Council for Independent Colleges and Schools (ACICS) to award bachelor's degrees, associate degrees, and certificates. ACICS is listed as a nationally recognized accrediting agency by the United States Department of Education and is recognized by the Council for Higher Education Accreditation. ACICS can be contacted at 750 First Street NE, Suite 980, Washington, D.C. 20002; phone: 202-336-6780.

The Brown Mackie College–Tucson Associate of Science in surgical technology program is accredited by the Accrediting Bureau of Health Education Schools.

The occupational therapy assistant studies program is accredited by the Accreditation Council for Occupational Therapy Education (ACOTE) of the American Occupational Therapy Association (AOTA), located at 4720 Montgomery Lane, P.O. Box 31220, Bethesda, Maryland 20824-1220; phone: 301-652-AOTA.

This institution is authorized by the Arizona State Board for Private Postsecondary Education, 1400 West Washington Street, Room 260, Phoenix, Arizona 85007; phone: 620-543-5709.

Academic Programs

Each College quarter comprises twelve weeks. Bachelor's degree programs require a minimum of sixteen quarters to complete. Associate degree programs require a minimum of eight quarters to complete. Programs are offered on a year-round basis, providing students with the ability to work uninterrupted toward their degrees. The College offers all programs in a unique One Course a Month format. This schedule allows students to focus studies on only one course for four weeks and has proven convenient for students with multiple obligations such as jobs and family.

Bachelor's Degree Programs: The Bachelor of Science degree is awarded in accounting, business administration, criminal justice, health-care management, information technology, and legal studies.

Associate Degree Programs: The Associate of Science degree is awarded in accounting technology, business management, computer networking and security, criminal justice, early childhood education, health-care administration, information technology, medical assisting, paralegal studies, and surgical technology. The Associate of Applied Science degree is awarded in biomedical equipment technology, health and fitness training, and occupational therapy assistant studies.

Diploma Program: The College offers a diploma program in fitness trainer studies.

Costs

Tuition in the 2010–11 academic year for most bachelor's and associate degree programs is $294 per credit hour; fees are $15 per credit hour. Tuition for the surgical technology program is $310 per credit hour with fees of $15 per credit hour. Tuition for certain courses in the occupational therapy assistant program is $365 per credit hour with fees of $15 per credit hour. Textbooks and other instructional expenses vary by program.

Financial Aid

Financial aid is available for those who qualify. The College maintains a full-time staff of financial aid professionals to assist qualified students in obtaining the financial assistance they require to meet their educational expenses. Available resources include federal and state aid, student loans from private lenders, and Federal Work-Study opportunities, both on and off college premises.

Each year, the College makes available scholarships of up to $1000 each to qualifying seniors from area high schools. No more than one scholarship is awarded per high school. In order to qualify, a senior must be graduating from a participating high school, have maintained a cumulative grade point average of at least 2.0, and submitted a brief, essay. The student's extracurricular activities and community service are also considered. These scholarships are available only to students enrolling in one of the College's degree programs. Students awarded the scholarship must enroll at Brown Mackie College–Tucson between June and September immediately following their high school graduation. Applications for these scholarships can be obtained from the guidance departments of participating high schools. These applications must be completed and returned to the College by March 31.

Faculty

Experienced faculty members provide academic support and are committed to the academic and technical preparation of their students. The College has 15 full-time and 35 part-time instructors, with a student-faculty ratio of 12:1. Each student is assigned a faculty adviser.

Facilities and Resources

A modern facility, Brown Mackie College–Tucson offers approximately 30,000 square feet of tastefully appointed classrooms, laboratories, and office space designed to the specifications of the College for its business, medical, and technical programs. Instructional equipment is comparable to current technology used in business and industry today. Modern classrooms for special instructional needs offer multimedia capabilities with surround sound and overhead projectors accessible through computer, DVD, or VHS. Internet access and instructional resources are available at the College's library.

Location

Brown Mackie College–Tucson is conveniently located at 4585 East Speedway Boulevard in Tucson, Arizona. The College has a generous parking area and is also easily accessible by public transportation.

Admission Requirements

Each applicant for admission is assigned an Assistant Director of Admissions who directs the applicant through the steps of the admissions process. They provide information on curriculum, policies, procedures, and services and assist the applicant in setting up necessary appointments and interviews.

To qualify for admission, each applicant must provide documentation of graduation from an accredited high school, or from a state-approved secondary education curriculum, or provide official documentation of high school graduation equivalency. All transcripts become the property of the College. Admission to the College is based on the applicant meeting the stated requirements, a review of the applicant's previous educational records, and a review of the applicant's career interests. If previous academic records indicate the College's education and training programs would not benefit the applicant, the College reserves the right to advise the applicant not to enroll. Special requirements for enrollment into certain programs are discussed in the descriptions of those programs.

For the most recent information regarding admission requirements, please refer to the current academic catalog.

Application and Information

Applicants must complete and submit an application form, along with documentation of graduation from an accredited high school or state-approved secondary education curriculum or official documentation of high school graduation equivalency.

For additional information, prospective students should contact:

Senior Director of Admissions
Brown Mackie College–Tucson
4585 East Speedway Boulevard, Suite 204
Tucson, Arizona 85712
Phone: 520-319-3300
Fax: 520-325-0108
E-mail: bmctuadm@brownmackie.edu
Web site: http://www.brownmackie.edu/Tucson

BROWN MACKIE COLLEGE–TULSA

TULSA, OKLAHOMA

The College and Its Mission

Brown Mackie College–Tulsa is one of over twenty locations in the Brown Mackie College family of schools (http://www.brownmackie.edu), which is dedicated to providing educational programs that prepare students to pursue entry-level positions in a competitive, rapidly-changing workplace. Brown Mackie College schools offer bachelor's degree, associate degree, certificate, and diploma programs in health sciences, business, information technology, legal studies, and design to over 19,000 students in the Midwest, Southeast, Southwest, and Western United States.

Brown Mackie College–Tulsa was founded in 2008 as a branch of Brown Mackie College–South Bend, Indiana.

Brown Mackie College–Tulsa is accredited by the Accrediting Council for Independent Colleges and Schools (ACICS) to award bachelor's degrees, associate degrees, and diplomas. ACICS is listed as a nationally recognized accrediting agency by the United States Department of Education and is recognized by the Council for Higher Education Accreditation. ACICS can be contacted at 750 First Street NE, Suite 980, Washington, D.C. 20002; phone: 202-336-6780.

The occupational therapy assistant studies program is accredited by the Accreditation Council for Occupational Therapy Education (ACOTE) of the American Occupational Therapy Association (AOTA), located at 4720 Montgomery Lane, P.O. Box 31220, Bethesda, Maryland 20824; phone: 301-652-AOTA.

Brown Mackie College–Tulsa is licensed by the Oklahoma Board of Private Vocational Schools (OBPVS), 3700 North Classen Boulevard, Suite 250, Oklahoma City, Oklahoma 73118; phone: 405-528-3370.

The College is a nonresidential, smoke-free institution.

Academic Programs

Brown Mackie College–Tulsa provides higher education to traditional and nontraditional students through bachelor's degree, associate degree, and diploma programs that can assist students in enhancing their career opportunities, broadening their perspectives through appropriate general education courses, thinking independently and critically, and improving problem-solving abilities.

Each College quarter comprises twelve weeks. Bachelor's degree programs require a minimum of sixteen quarters to complete. Associate degree programs require a minimum of eight quarters to complete. Programs are offered on a year-round basis, providing students with the ability to work uninterrupted toward completion of their programs. The College offers all programs in a unique One Course a Month format. This schedule allows students to focus studies on only one course for four weeks and has proven convenient for students with multiple obligations such as jobs and family.

Bachelor's Degree Programs: The Bachelor of Science degree is awarded in business administration, criminal justice, health-care management, and legal studies.

Associate Degree Programs: The Associate of Applied Business degree is awarded in accounting technology, business management, criminal justice, health-care administration, information technology, medical assisting, occupational therapy assistant studies, office management, paralegal studies, and surgical technology.

Diploma Programs: The College offers diploma programs in accounting, business, criminal justice, medical assistant studies, and paralegal assistant studies.

Costs

Tuition for programs in the 2010–11 academic year is $250 per credit hour, with a $15 per credit hour general fee applied to instructional costs for activities and services. Tuition for the occupational therapy program courses is $365 per credit hour with a $15 per credit hour general fee. Tuition for the surgical technology program courses is $310 per credit hour with a $15 per credit hour general fee. The cost of textbooks and other instructional materials varies by program.

Financial Aid

Financial aid is available to those who qualify. The College maintains a full-time staff of financial aid professionals to assist qualified students in obtaining financial assistance. The College participates in several student aid programs. Forms of financial aid available through federal resources include the Federal Pell Grant Program, Federal Supplemental Educational Opportunity Grant (FSEOG) Program, Federal Work-Study Program, Federal Perkins Loan Program, Federal Stafford Student Loan Program (subsidized and unsubsidized), and the Federal PLUS Loan Program.

Facilities and Resources

Opened in 2008, this modern facility offers more than 25,000 square feet of tastefully decorated classrooms, laboratories, and office space designed to specifications of the College for its business, medical, and technical programs. Instructional equipment is comparable to industry-current technology used in business today. Modern classrooms for special instructional needs offer multimedia capabilities with surround sound and overhead projectors accessible through computer, DVD, or VHS. Internet access and instructional resources are available at the College's library. Experienced faculty members provide academic support and are committed to the academic and technical preparation of their students.

Location

Brown Mackie College–Tulsa is conveniently located at 4608 South Garnett Road, Suite 110 in Tulsa, Oklahoma. The College has a generous parking area and is also easily accessible by public transportation.

Admission Requirements

Each applicant for admission is assigned an Assistant Director of Admissions who directs the applicant through the steps of the admissions process, providing information on curriculum, policies, procedures, and services and assisting the applicant in setting necessary appointments and interviews.

To qualify for admission, applicants must be a graduate of a public or private high school or a correspondence school or education center that is accredited by an agency that is recognized by the U.S. or State of Oklahoma Department of Education or any of its approved agents. As part of the admissions process applicants must sign a document attesting to graduation or completion and containing the information to obtain verification of such. Verification must be obtained within the first term (90 days) or the student will be withdrawn from the institution following established guidelines for withdrawn students noted in the catalog. Title IV aid will not be dispersed until verification of graduation or completion has been received by the College.

All transcripts or other documentation related to graduation or completion becomes the property of the College. Admission to the College is based upon the applicant meeting the above requirements, a review of the applicant's previous educational records, and a review of the applicant's career interests. If previous academic records indicate that the College's education and training programs would not benefit the applicant, the College reserves the right to advise the applicant not to enroll. Special requirements for enrollment into certain programs are discussed in the descriptions of those programs. It is the responsibility of the applicant to ensure that the College receives all required documentation, and all records provided become the property of the College. No action upon an application for admission will proceed without the required documentation.

Students are given an assessment of academic skills. Although the results of this assessment do not determine eligibility for admission, they provide the College with a means of determining the need for academic support.

For the most recent information regarding admission requirements, please refer to the current academic catalog.

Application and Information

Applicants must complete and submit an application form along with documentation of graduation from an accredited high school or state-approved secondary education curriculum, or applicants must provide official documentation of high school graduation equivalency.

For additional information, prospective students should contact:

Senior Director of Admissions
Brown Mackie College–Tulsa
4608 South Garnett
Tulsa, Oklahoma 74146

Phone: 918-628-3700
888-794-8411 (toll-free)
Fax: 918-828-9083
E-mail: bmctuladm@brownmackie.edu
Web site: http://www.brownmackie.edu/Tulsa

FASHION INSTITUTE OF TECHNOLOGY
State University of New York

NEW YORK, NEW YORK

The College and Its Mission

The Fashion Institute of Technology (FIT) is New York's celebrated urban college for creative and business talent. A selective State University of New York (SUNY) college of art and design, business, and technology, FIT is a creative mix of innovative achievers, original thinkers, and industry pioneers. FIT balances a real-world-based curriculum and hands-on instruction with a rigorous liberal arts foundation. The college marries design and business, supports individual creativity in a collaborative environment, and encourages faculty members to match teaching expertise with professional experience. It offers a complete college experience with a vibrant student and residential life.

With an extraordinary location at the center of New York City—world capital of the arts, business, and media—FIT maintains close ties with the design, fashion, advertising, communications, and international commerce industries it serves. Academic departments consult with advisory boards of noted experts in their fields to ensure that the curriculum and classroom technology remain current with evolving industry practices. The college's faculty of successful professionals brings experience to the classroom, while field trips, guest lectures, and sponsored competitions introduce students to the opportunities and challenges of their disciplines.

FIT's mission is to produce well-rounded graduates—doers and thinkers who raise the professional bar to become the next generation of business pacesetters and creative icons.

All full-time, matriculated students are eligible for FIT housing. Four residence halls house approximately 2,300 in fully furnished single-, double-, triple-, and quad-occupancy rooms. Each residence hall has lounges and laundry facilities; the George and Mariana Kaufman Residence Hall also provides an on-site fitness center. Students have the option of either traditional (meal plan included) or apartment-style accommodations. Counselors and student staff live in the halls, helping students adjust to college life and living in New York City.

FIT is accredited by the Middle States Association of Colleges and Schools, the National Association of Schools of Art and Design, and the Council for Interior Design Accreditation.

Academic Programs

FIT serves approximately 10,000 full-time, part-time, and evening/weekend students from the metropolitan area, New York State, across the country, and around the world, offering more than forty programs leading to the A.A.S., B.F.A., B.S., M.A., and M.P.S. degrees. Each undergraduate program includes a core of traditional liberal arts courses, providing students with a global perspective, critical-thinking skills, and the ability to communicate effectively. All degree programs are designed to prepare students for creative and business careers—the college's Career Services, which offers lifetime placement, reports a graduate employment rate of 90 percent—and to provide them with the prerequisite studies so they may go on to baccalaureate, master's, or doctoral degrees.

All students complete a two-year A.A.S. program in their major area of study and the liberal arts. They may then choose to either go on to a related, two-year B.F.A. or B.S. program or begin their careers with their A.A.S. degree, which qualifies them for entry positions in a range of creative and/or business professions. *Community College Week* has ranked FIT first in the nation for awarding A.A.S. degrees in communications, journalism, and related programs and seventh in the nation for awarding A.A.S. degrees in business, management, marketing, and related support services.

Associate Degree Programs: For the A.A.S. degree, FIT offers eleven majors through its School of Art and Design and four through its Jay and Patty Baker School of Business and Technology. The fifteen A.A.S. degree programs are accessories design*, advertising and marketing communications*, communication design*, fashion design*, fashion merchandising management* (with an online option), fine arts (with a career-exploration component), illustration, interior design, jewelry design*, menswear, photography, production management: fashion and related industries, textile development and marketing*, textile/surface design*, and visual presentation and exhibition design. Programs with an asterisk (*) are also available in a one-year format for students with acceptable transferable credits.

Bachelor's Degree Programs: Most A.A.S. graduates opt to pursue a related, two-year baccalaureate-level program of study at the college. FIT offers twenty-three baccalaureate programs—thirteen B.F.A. programs through the School of Art and Design, nine B.S. programs through the Baker School of Business and Technology, and one B.S. program through the School of Liberal Arts. The thirteen B.F.A. degree programs are accessories design and fabrication, advertising design, computer animation and interactive media, fabric styling, fashion design (with specializations in children's wear, fashion design, intimate apparel, and knitting), fine arts, graphic design, illustration, interior design, packaging design, photography and the digital image, textile/surface design, and toy design. The ten B.S. programs are advertising and marketing communications, cosmetics and fragrance marketing, direct and interactive marketing, fashion merchandising management, home products development, international trade and marketing for the fashion industries, production management: fashion and related industries, technical design, textile development and marketing, and visual art management.

Liberal Arts Minor: The School of Liberal Arts offers FIT students the opportunity to minor in a variety of liberal arts areas in two forms: traditional subject-based minors and interdisciplinary minors unique to the FIT liberal arts curriculum. Selected minors include film and media, economics, Latin American studies, and sustainability.

Evening/Weekend Programs: FIT's School of Continuing Education and Professional Studies provides evening and weekend credit and noncredit classes to students and working professionals interested in pursuing a degree or certificate or furthering their knowledge of a particular industry, while balancing the demands of career or family. There are nine degree programs available through evening/weekend study: advertising and marketing communications (A.A.S. and B.S.), communication design (A.A.S.), fashion design (A.A.S.), fashion merchandising management (A.A.S. and B.S.), graphic design (B.F.A.), illustration (B.F.A.), and international trade and marketing for the fashion industries (B.S.).

Honors Program: The Presidential Scholars honors program, available to academically exceptional students in all majors, offers special courses, projects, colloquia, and off-campus trips that broaden horizons and stimulate discourse. Presidential Scholars receive priority course registration and an annual merit stipend.

Internships: Internships are a required element of most programs and are available to all matriculated students. More than one third of internships result in job offers from the sponsoring organization; past sponsors include American Eagle, Bloomingdale's, Calvin Klein, Estée Lauder, Fairchild Publications, MTV, and Saatchi & Saatchi.

Precollege Programs: Precollege programs (Saturday and Sunday/Summer Live) are available to high school students during the fall, spring, and summer. More than sixty courses provide the chance to learn in an innovative environment, develop art and design portfolios, explore the business and technological sides of a wide range of creative careers, and discover natural talents and abilities. Courses for middle school students are also available in the summer.

Off-Campus Programs

The study-abroad experience lets students immerse themselves in diverse cultures and prepares them to live and work in a global community. Australia, China, England, France, and Mexico are some of the countries where FIT semester study-abroad courses are offered. Students can also study abroad in Italy for a semester, or a full academic year, concentrating in fashion design or fashion merchandising management.

Costs

As a SUNY college, FIT offers affordable tuition for both New York State residents and nonresidents. The 2009–10 associate-level tuition per semester for in-state residents was $1857; for nonresidents, $5571. Baccalaureate-level tuition per semester was $2584 for in-state residents, $6302 for nonresidents. Per-semester housing costs were $5435–$5590 for traditional residence hall accommodations with mandatory meal plan and $4580–$8325 for apartment-style accommodations. Meal plans ranged from $1510 to $1940 per semester. Textbook costs and other nominal fees, such as locker rental or laboratory use, vary per program. All costs are subject to change.

Financial Aid

FIT offers scholarships, grants, loans, and work-study employment for students with financial need. Nearly all full-time, matriculated undergraduate students who complete the financial aid application process receive some type of assistance. The college directly administers its own institutional grants and scholarships, which are provided by The Educational Foundation for the Fashion Industries.

College-administered funding includes Federal Pell Grants, Federal Perkins Loans, Federal Supplemental Educational Opportunity Grants, Federal Work-Study Program awards, and the Federal Family Educational Loan Program, which includes student and parent loans. New York State residents who meet eligibility guidelines may also receive Tuition Assistance Program (TAP) and/or Educational Opportunity Program (EOP) grants. Financial aid applicants must file the Free Application for Federal Student Aid (FAFSA) and should also apply to all available outside sources of aid. Other documentation may be requested by the Financial Aid Office. Applications for financial aid should be completed prior to February 15 for fall admission or prior to November 1 for spring admission.

Faculty

FIT's faculty is drawn from top professionals in academia, art, design, communications, and business, providing a curriculum rich in real-world experience and traditional educational values. Student-instructor interaction is encouraged, with a maximum class size of 25, and courses are structured to foster participation, independent thinking, and self-expression.

Student Body Profile

Fall 2009 enrollment was 10,413 with 8,195 students enrolled in degree programs. Forty-eight percent of degree-seeking students are enrolled in the School of Art and Design; 49 percent are in the Baker School of Business and Technology. The average age of the student population is 23. Forty-two percent of FIT's students are New York City residents, 23 percent are New York State (non–New York City) residents, and 35 percent are out-of-state residents or international. The ethnic/racial makeup of the student body is approximately 14.3 percent Asian/Pacific Islander, 10.7 percent black/non-Hispanic, 15.3 percent Hispanic, and 59.4 percent white/non-Hispanic, and 0.2 percent American Indian. There are 818 international students.

Student Activities

Participation in campus life is encouraged, and the college is home to more than sixty clubs, societies, athletic teams, major-related organizations, and hobby groups. Each organization is open to all students who have paid their activity fee.

Student Government: The Student Council, the governing body of the Student Association, grants all students the privileges and responsibilities of citizens in a self-governing college community. Faculty committees often include student representatives, and the president of the student government sits on FIT's Board of Trustees.

Athletics: FIT has intercollegiate teams in basketball, cross-country, half marathon, outdoor track, dance, table tennis, tennis, swimming and diving, and volleyball. In 2009, FIT's women's volleyball team achieved a 14-0 record in regular-season play, a top-ten Division III ranking, and Region XV Player and Coach of the Year honors. Athletics and Recreation offers group fitness classes at no extra cost to students. Classes include cardio sculpting, boxing, and yoga. Intramural sports allow students to participate in team and individual sports.

Events: Concerts, dances, field trips, films, flea markets, and other events are planned by the Student Association and Programming Board and various clubs. Student-run publications include a campus newspaper, a literary and art magazine, and the FIT yearbook.

Facilities and Resources

FIT's campus provides its students with classrooms, laboratories, and studios that reflect the most advanced educational and industry practices. The Fred P. Pomerantz Art and Design Center houses drawing, painting, photography, printmaking, and sculpture studios; display and exhibit design rooms; a model-making workshop; and a graphics printing service bureau. The Peter G. Scotese Computer-Aided Design and Communications facility provides the latest technology in computer graphics, photography, and the design of advertising, fashion, interiors, textiles, and toys. Other facilities include a professionally equipped fragrance-development laboratory, cutting and sewing labs, a design/research lighting laboratory, knitting lab, broadcasting studio, multimedia foreign languages laboratory, and twenty-three computer labs containing Mac and PC workstations in addition to several other labs with computers reserved for students in specific programs.

The Museum at FIT, New York City's only museum dedicated to fashion, contains one of the most important collections of fashion and textiles in the world. The museum operates year-round, and its exhibitions are free and open to the public. The Gladys Marcus Library provides more than 300,000 volumes of print, nonprint, and electronic materials. The periodicals collection includes over 500 current subscriptions, with a specialization in international design and trade publications; online resources include more than 90 searchable databases.

The David Dubinsky Student Center offers lounges, a game room, a student radio station, the Style Shop (a student-run boutique), a dining hall, student government and club offices, a comprehensive health center, two gyms, a dance studio, weight room, and counseling center.

Location

Occupying an entire block in Manhattan's Chelsea neighborhood, FIT makes extensive use of the city's creative, commercial, and cultural resources, providing students unrivaled internship opportunities and professional connections. A wide range of cultural and entertainment options are available within a short walk of the campus, as is convenient access to several subway and bus routes and the city's major rail and bus transportation hubs.

Admission Requirements

Applicants for admission must be either candidates for or recipients of a high school diploma or a General Educational Development (GED) certificate. Admission is based on class rank, strength and performance in college-preparatory course work, and the student essay. A portfolio evaluation is required for art and design majors. Specific portfolio requirements are explained on FIT's Web site. SAT and ACT scores are required for placement in math and English classes and they are required for students applying to the Presidential Scholars honors program. Letters of recommendation are not required.

Transfer students must submit official transcripts for credit evaluation. Students may qualify for the one-year A.A.S. option if they hold a bachelor's degree or if they have a minimum of 30 transferable credits from a regionally accredited institution, including 24 credits equivalent to FIT's liberal arts requirements, and at least one semester of physical education.

Students seeking admission to a B.F.A. or B.S. program must hold an A.A.S. degree from FIT or an equivalent college degree and must meet the prerequisites for the specific major. Further requirements may include an interview with a departmental committee, review of academic standing, and portfolio review for applicants to B.F.A. programs. Any student who applies for baccalaureate-level transfer to FIT from a four-year program must have completed a minimum of 60 credits, including the requisite art or technical courses and the liberal arts requirements.

Application and Information

Students wishing to visit FIT are encouraged to attend a group information session. The visit schedule is available online at http://www.fitnyc.edu/visitfit. Candidates may apply online at http://www.fitnyc.edu/admissions. More information is available by contacting:

Admissions
Fashion Institute of Technology
227 West 27th Street
New York, New York 10001-5992

Phone: 212-217-3760
800-GO-TO-FIT (toll-free)
E-mail: fitinfo@fitnyc.edu
Web site: http://www.fitnyc.edu

FIDM/FASHION INSTITUTE OF DESIGN & MERCHANDISING

LOS ANGELES, CALIFORNIA

The Institute and Its Mission

FIDM/Fashion Institute of Design & Merchandising provides a dynamic and exciting community of learning in the fashion, graphics, interior design, digital media, and entertainment industries. Students can launch into one of thousands of exciting careers in as little as two years. FIDM offers Associate of Arts (A.A.), A.A. professional designation, A.A. advanced study, and Bachelor of Science degree programs.

FIDM offers a highly focused education that prepares students for the professional world. Students can choose from twenty specialized creative business and design majors. With a database of over 10,000 employer contacts and more than 1000 job postings each month, FIDM offers students and graduates ongoing career opportunities within the industries it serves. Since its inception, FIDM has graduated over 40,000 students in its forty-year history.

FIDM is accredited by the Accrediting Commission for Community and Junior Colleges of the Western Association of Schools and Colleges (WASC) and the National Association of Schools of Art and Design (NASAD).

Academic Programs

FIDM operates on a four-quarter academic calendar. Students can choose from twenty specialized creative business and design majors. New students may begin their studies at the start of any quarter throughout the year. A two-year Associate of Arts degree requires completion of 90 units. Advanced study programs are available to students who have previously completed an A.A. degree from FIDM. Professional designation programs are offered for students who want to enhance their previous education from another college or are interested in transferring to FIDM.

Bachelor of Science Degree Program: The Bachelor of Science in business management program prepares students who have received an A.A. degree from FIDM to enter the global industries of fashion, interior design, and entertainment.

Associate Degree Programs: FIDM offers Associate of Arts degrees in apparel industry management, beauty industry merchandising and marketing, digital media, fashion design, fashion knitwear design, graphic design, interior design, jewelry design, merchandise marketing (fashion merchandising or product development), textile design, and visual communications. All of these programs offer the highly specialized curriculum of a specific major combined with a core general education/liberal arts foundation.

Associate of Arts Advanced Study Programs: These programs develop specialized expertise in the student's unique area of study. They are open to students who possess extensive prior academic and professional experience within the discipline area. These areas include advanced fashion design, interior design specialties, film and TV costume design, footwear design, international manufacturing and product development, theater costume design, and visual communications. Completion requirements for these programs are 45 units. Some classes are offered online.

Transfer Arrangements: FIDM accepts course work from other accredited colleges if there is an equivalent course at FIDM and the grade is a C or better. FIDM courses at the 100, 200, and 300 levels are certified by FIDM to be baccalaureate level. FIDM maintains articulation agreements with selected colleges with the intent of enhancing a student's transfer opportunities. Academic counselors assist students interested in transferring to other institutions to attain a four-year degree. Students from other regionally accredited college programs have the opportunity to complement their previous college education by enrolling in FIDM's professional designation programs. FIDM offers professional designation programs in apparel industry management, beauty industry management, digital media, graphic design, interior design, jewelry design, merchandise marketing (or product development), textile design, and visual communications. Requirements for completion range from 45 to 66 units, depending on the field of study.

Internship and Co-op Programs: Internships are available within each of the various majors. Paid and volunteer positions provide work experience for students to gain practical application of classroom skills.

Special Programs and Services: FIDM's eLearning program ensures that a student's educational experience can take place anywhere in the world. The online courses are designed to replicate the experience of classes on campus. Students in the eLearning program are granted the same quality education as students on campus and have immediate access to valuable campus resources, including the FIDM library, career advisers, and instructors.

In response to student needs, FIDM has established an evening program in addition to the regular daytime courses. The program has been designed to accommodate the time requirements of working students. The entire evening program for the Associate of Arts degree can be completed in 2½ years.

FIDM offers English as a second language (ESL) for students requiring English development to complete their major field of study. The program is concurrent and within FIDM's existing college-level course work. These classes focus on the special needs of students in the areas of oral communication, reading comprehension, and English composition.

Community Programs: Community service programs are offered both independently and in cooperation with various community groups. General studies course credit may be awarded to participating students. Each FIDM campus identifies community projects that allow students to support local service agencies.

Off-Campus Programs

FIDM provides the opportunity for students to participate in academic study tours in Europe, Asia, and New York. These tours are specifically designed to broaden and enhance the specialized education offered at the Institute. Study tour participants may earn academic credit under faculty-supervised directed studies. Exchange programs are also available with Esmod, Paris; Instituto Artictico dell' Abbigliamento Marangoni, Milan; Accademia Internazionale d'Alta Mode e d'Arte del Costume Koefia, Rome; St. Martins School of Art, London; College of Distributive Trades, London; and Janette Klein Design School, Mexico City.

Credit for Nontraditional Learning Experiences

The Institute may give credit for demonstrated proficiency in areas related to college-level courses. Sources used to determine proficiency are the College-Level Examination Program (CLEP) and Credit for Academically Relevant Experience (CARE), an Institute-sponsored program.

Costs

For the 2009–10 academic year, tuition and fees started at $24,000, depending on the major selected by the student. Textbooks and supplies started at $2500 per year, depending on the major. First-year application fees start at $225 for California residents and range up to $525 for international students.

Financial Aid

There are several sources of financial funding available to the student, including federal financial aid and education loan programs, California state aid programs, institutional loan programs, and FIDM awards and scholarships. The FIDM Student Financial Services office and FIDM admissions advisers work with students and parents to help them find funding for an FIDM education.

Faculty

FIDM faculty members are selected as specialists in their fields. Many are actively employed in their respective fields of expertise. They bring daily exposure to their industry into the classroom for the benefit of the students. In pursuit of the best faculty members, consideration is given to both academic excellence as well as practical experience. FIDM has a 16:1 student-instructor ratio.

Student Body Profile

FIDM's ethnically and culturally diverse student body is one of the attractions to the Institute. Fifteen percent of the current student body are international students from more than thirty different countries. Twenty percent of the students are more than 25 years of age. More than 90 percent find career positions within one year of graduation.

Student Activities

The Student Activities Committee plans and coordinates social activities, cultural events, and community projects, including the ASID Student Chapter, International Club, Delta Epsilon Chi (DEX), Association of Manufacturing Students, Honor Society, and the Alumni Association. The students also produce their own trend newsletter, *The Mode.*

Facilities and Resources

Advisement/Counseling: Department chairs and other trained staff members assist students in selecting the correct sequence of courses to allow each student to complete degree requirements. The counseling department provides personal guidance and referral to outside counseling services as well as matching peer tutors to specific students' needs. Individual Development and Education Assistance (IDEA) centers at each campus provide students with additional educational assistance to supplement classroom instruction. Services are available in the areas of writing, mathematics, computer competency, study skills, research skills, and reading comprehension.

Career Planning/Placement Offices: Career planning and job placement are among the most important services offered by the Institute. Career assistance includes job search techniques, preparation for employment interviews, resume preparation, and job adjustment assistance. Services provided by the center include undergraduate placement, graduate placement, alumni placement, internships, and industry work/study programs. FIDM's full-time career services department and advisers provide support to help current students and graduates move toward their career goals. Employers post over 16,000 jobs a year on FIDM's Alumni Job Search site, available 24/7. Career advisers connect students to internships and directly to people in the industry. FIDM also offers job fairs, portfolio days, and networking days to allow students to meet alumni and industry leaders face-to-face.

Alumni Association: Students can expand their network instantly upon graduation. There are more than 40,000 FIDM grads and each of them is automatically granted a free lifetime membership in the Alumni Association, which keeps them connected while providing up-to the minute alumni news and industry information. FIDM alumni chapter events are held in thirty-five locations around the United States, Europe, and Asia.

Library and Audiovisual Services FIDM's library goes beyond the traditional sources of information. The library houses a print and electronic collection of over 2.5 million titles encompassing all subject areas, with an emphasis on fashion, interior design, retailing, and costume. The library subscribes to over 160 international and national periodicals which offer the latest information on art, design, graphics, fashion, beauty, business, and current trends. The FIDM library also features an international video library, subscriptions to major predictive services, interior design workrooms, textile samples, a trimmings/findings collection, and access to the Internet. FIDM's Costume Museum houses more than 4,500 garments from the seventeenth century to present day. The collection includes items from the California Historical Society (First Families), the Hollywood Collection, and the Rudi Gernreich Collection.

State-of-the-art computer labs support and enhance the educational programs of the Institute. Specialized labs offer computerized cutting and marking, graphic and textile design, word processing, and database management.

Location

Established in 1969, FIDM is a private college that is proud to enroll more than 7,500 students a year. The main campus is in the heart of downtown Los Angeles near the famed California Mart and Garment District. This campus is adjacent to the beautiful Grand Hope Park. There are additional California branch campuses located in San Francisco, San Diego, and Orange County.

Admission Requirements

The Institute provides educational opportunities to high school graduates or applicants that meet the Institute's Ability to Benefit (ATB) criteria to pursue a two-year Associate of Arts degree. In order to qualify for the professional designation programs students must meet the general education core requirements or have a U.S. accredited degree. All applicants must have an initial interview with an admissions representative. In addition, students must submit references and specific portfolio projects if applicable to the chosen major. The Institute is on the approved list of the U.S. Department of Justice for nonimmigrant students and is authorized to issue Certificates of Eligibility (Form I-20).

Application and Information

Applications are accepted on an ongoing basis. All prospective students should contact:

Director of Admissions
FIDM/Fashion Institute of Design & Merchandising
919 South Grand Avenue
Los Angeles, California 90015
Phone: 800-624-1200 (toll-free)
Fax: 213-624-4799
Web site: http://www.fidm.edu

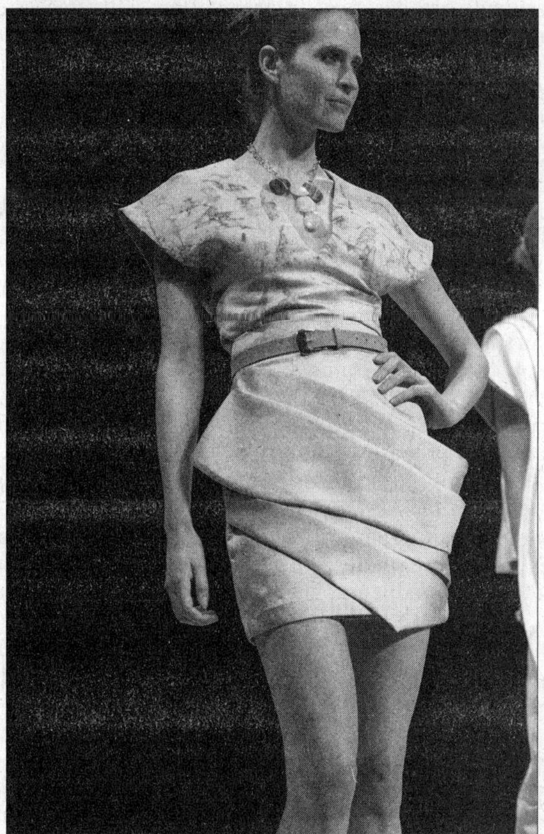

FIDM Debut Show. Student designer: Kapasa Musonda.

HESSER COLLEGE

MANCHESTER, NEW HAMPSHIRE

The College and Its Mission

The primary purpose of Hesser College is to provide a high-quality education that is personalized and employment oriented. Hesser College's innovative approach to higher education provides students with increased flexibility. After two years of college, students can earn an associate degree and are prepared to enter the workplace, or, if they prefer, students can continue on in one of Hesser College's bachelor's degree programs.

Hesser College was established in 1900 as Hesser Business College, a private, nonsectarian college. Since 1972, Hesser College has expanded and enriched its curriculum in keeping with its tradition of providing an affordable career education of high quality.

Hesser College is accredited by the New England Association of Schools and Colleges. Students who choose Hesser College receive a high-quality education.

Academic Programs

The primary goal of the curricula is to prepare students for success in specific career areas. The general education requirements are designed to provide the skills necessary for career growth and lifelong learning. Internships, practicums, and opportunities for part-time work experience are available in all majors. An education from Hesser College provides a solid career foundation. The College's goal is quite simple: to prepare people for careers and career advancement.

Many of the Hesser College programs are for the career-minded student who wants to concentrate on the skills required to be successful in the workplace. Seventy-five percent of the courses that students take are directly related to their career choices. Upon completion of the associate degree program, a student may pursue a four-year degree by enrolling in one of Hesser's bachelor's degree programs.

Associate Degree Programs: Hesser offers a wide range of programs that prepare students for high-demand careers. They include accounting, business administration, communications and public relations, criminal justice, early childhood education, graphic design, interior design, liberal studies, medical assistant studies, paralegal studies, physical therapist assistant studies, psychology, and radio and video production and broadcasting.

Bachelor's Degree Programs: Hesser College offers bachelor's degree programs in accounting, business administration, criminal justice, and psychology.

Off-Campus Programs

The College offers opportunities for cooperative education and externships in most of its academic programs. The early childhood education program includes practicums and supervised fieldwork in the freshman and senior years, utilizing a variety of child-care facilities. In addition, the curricula of several programs incorporate short-term study trips to such places as Walt Disney World and Washington, D.C.

Costs

Costs vary by program. Interested students should contact Hesser College for more information.

Financial Aid

Hesser College offers financial assistance to students who qualify. Many students receive some form of aid. Scholarships are awarded each year to students based on academic and financial standing. Hesser College also offers loans and grants.

Faculty

The faculty members of Hesser College consistently receive high student evaluations for their interest in each student's success and for the high quality of their teaching. The majority of the faculty members have completed programs of advanced study, many hold doctoral degrees, and all have practical experience in business or other career fields.

Student Body Profile

Most students work in the afternoons, evenings, or weekends while attending Hesser. The men and women currently enrolled represent several states and more than fifteen countries. A large part of the student population is from the New England region.

Student Activities

Hesser College offers intercollegiate sports teams in men's and women's basketball, soccer, and volleyball; men's baseball; and women's softball. The basketball and volleyball teams have consistently been a major power in the Northern New England Small College Conference. Students also participate in a number of intramural sports programs. Extracurricular activities are varied and include social activities, clubs, trips, and programs in the residence halls.

Facilities and Resources

The College includes dormitories for many students. A wide range of resources are located on campus. Academic advising is coordinated through department chairpersons and the Center for Teaching, Learning, and Assessment. The size of the College allows for individual attention to the financial and career counseling needs of each student.

The academic facilities include five computer labs, a Mac-based graphic design lab, medical assistant labs, a physical therapist assistant lab, and a radio/video production lab. Hesser College's library contains more than 30,000 titles. The Center for Teaching, Learning, and Assessment provides special tutoring and programs in study skills, reading, writing, math, and computer skills.

Hesser College has also developed a number of learning assistance programs to help students succeed in their studies. Tutoring and special classes are provided by the faculty throughout each semester. In addition, several departments offer honor programs and special opportunities for independent study. The College also sponsors an active chapter of the national honor society Phi Theta Kappa, which promotes scholarship and service to the College and the community.

Location

Hesser College is located in Manchester, New Hampshire. With a population of more than 100,000, Manchester is a medium-sized city that offers many cultural, historical, and social events. Hesser College's central location provides easy access to entertainment, shopping, and a variety of part-time jobs and academic work experiences.

Manchester was recently named by *Money* magazine as the number one small city in the northeast United States. In addition, Manchester was recently named as one of the best cities in the United States for business. According to *U.S. News & World Report*, Manchester is "at the hub of things" in the fast-growing, high-technology, financial, and information-oriented businesses of southern New Hampshire. Manchester has been called the "Gateway to Northern New England," and several major carriers serve the Manchester Airport. Manchester is within 1 hour of Boston, and the mountains and major ski resorts are within 1–2 hours of Hesser's campus.

Admission Requirements

Hesser College has a rolling admissions policy. Students may apply for admission at any time.

Advisers are available to talk with students about their education and career goals, and interested students should contact Hesser College for more information.

Application and Information

Applicants must submit an application form with a $10 nonrefundable fee. Applications are reviewed on a first-come, first-served basis and normally take seven to fourteen days to be fully reviewed upon receipt of all required information.

Requests for additional information and application forms should be addressed to:

Director of Admissions
Hesser College
3 Sundial Avenue
Manchester, New Hampshire 03103
Phone: 800-994-8412 Dept. 266 (toll-free)
Web site: http://www.hesser.edu/

Students at Hesser College's main campus.

LANDMARK COLLEGE

PUTNEY, VERMONT

The College and Its Mission

Landmark College is one of only two accredited colleges in the country designed exclusively for students of average to superior intellectual potential with LD or AD/HD or other specific learning disabilities. Life-changing experiences are commonplace at Landmark College.

Landmark's beautiful campus offers all the resources students expect at a high-quality college, including an athletics center, a student center, a dining facility, a café, residence halls, and a Center for Academic Support. The College has also invested substantially in technology and offers a wireless network in all of its classrooms, along with LAN, telephone, and cable connections in all of the residence rooms. Notebook computers are required and are used in nearly every class session. The College's programs extensively integrate assistive technologies, such as Dragon Naturally Speaking, Read and Write Gold text-to-speech software, and Inspiration.

Landmark's faculty and staff members make it unique. The College's more than 80 full-time faculty members are all highly experienced in serving students with learning disabilities and attention deficit disorders. More than 100 staff members provide an array of support services that are unusually comprehensive for a student population of more than 490 students.

Academic Programs

Students can earn an associate degree in business administration, business studies, general studies, or liberal arts. Landmark College builds strong literacy, organizational, study, and other skills—positioning students to successfully pursue a baccalaureate or advanced degree and to be successful in their professional careers. More than 80 percent of Landmark College graduates go on to colleges or universities that grant four-year degrees.

With more than 80 faculty members and slightly more than 490 students, Landmark College's small classes and personalized instruction provide a uniquely challenging, yet supportive, academic program. Students at Landmark College learn how to learn.

The College's diverse curriculum includes English, communications, the humanities, math, science, foreign language, theater, video, music, art, physical education, and other classes taught in a multimodal, multimedia environment that is highly interactive. There is no "back of the room" in a Landmark College classroom, and all students participate in class discussions while building strong academic skills.

Landmark College has articulation agreements with a number of other colleges. These colleges have agreed to admit Landmark College graduates as juniors and transfer their credits if they attain a specific grade point average upon graduation from Landmark.

Through a carefully sequenced, integrated curriculum, students develop the confidence and independence needed to meet the demands of college work. When students graduate with an associate degree from Landmark College, they are ready to succeed in a four-year college, a technical or professional program, or the workforce.

Off-Campus Programs

The Landmark Study Abroad Program has developed programs with students' diverse learning styles in mind. Landmark College's faculty members design and teach experiential courses in their specific disciplines that fulfill Landmark core requirements while helping students gain confidence and independence in new academic structures. College faculty members accompany students abroad, providing them with the Landmark College academic experience in an international setting. The College offers summer credit programs in England, Ireland, Italy, and Spain; in January, a two-week program in Costa Rica is offered.

Costs

Landmark College's tuition for the 2009–10 academic year was $45,300. Room and board costs were $8100. Single rooms or suites are available at an added cost of between $1000 and $1500. A damage deposit of $300 is required.

Since admission to Landmark College requires a diagnosis of a learning disability or attention deficit disorder, in most cases, the entire cost of a Landmark College education may be tax deductible as a medical expense. For more information, parents are advised to consult a tax attorney.

Financial Aid

Landmark College participates in all major federal and state financial aid programs, including the Federal Pell Grant, Federal Family Education Loans, and work-study. Institutional scholarships are available. To apply for financial assistance, students should submit the Free Application for Federal Student Aid (FAFSA), the Landmark College Financial Aid Application, and federal tax returns.

Faculty

With the College's low student-faculty ratio, Landmark College faculty members are unusually accessible to students. There are more than 80 full-time faculty members, who provide classroom teaching, professional advising, and office hours to students. In addition, faculty members provide individualized instruction throughout the day and into the evening at the Charles Drake Center for Academic Support. Landmark College does not typically employ adjunct faculty members or student teaching assistants. Regular faculty members deliver all instruction and advising. Their depth of experience in serving students with learning differences ensures that students receive the individualized education that is most appropriate to their learning style.

Student Body Profile

Landmark College students come from thirty-eight states, two U.S. territories, and ten other countries. Approximately two thirds of the student body are men. Ninety-five percent of all students are residential students living on campus in one of twelve residence facilities. Representatives of multicultural groups make up approximately 14 percent of Landmark College students.

Student Activities

Landmark College closely integrates academics and student life. Academic deans, advisers, and faculty members work closely with student life deans and directors to provide a comprehensive program that serves the whole student. The goal is not simply to support academic success but also to guide and challenge students in their personal and social development. Each student has access to a comprehensive support team, including an academic adviser, classroom instructors, and a resident dean; an extensive program of athletics, adventure education, and activities; and a highly trained and experienced counseling department.

For a college its size, Landmark College has an extraordinary range of student-development resources, providing general educational, social, and recreational opportunities. Clubs at Landmark are active. In the past, they have included the Running Club, Monday Night Art, the Multicultural Awareness Club, the Gay/Lesbian/Bisexual/Transgender Alliance, the Mountain Biking Club, the Jazz Ensemble, *Impressions Literary Magazine,* the Coffee House Writers Group, the International Club, the Small Business Management Club, Choral Singing, the Weight Lifting Group, and the Spirituality Group.

Outdoor programs provide students with a diverse range of outdoor and experiential learning opportunities, including wilderness first-aid training, a ropes course, rock-climbing instruction, an indoor climbing wall, and a full inventory of camping equipment, cross-country skis, snowshoes, and mountain bikes. The College has an active intercollegiate and intramural athletics program that is supported by a well-equipped athletics center that opened in 2001.

Facilities and Resources

Landmark College's residence halls, academic buildings, athletics center, and student center provide a rich array of resources and educational, recreational, and social opportunities. The traditional brick campus, which was designed by noted architect Edward Durell Stone in the 1960s and entirely renovated beginning in the mid-1980s, includes such amenities as a 400-seat theater, an NCAA regulation basketball court, an exercise pool, three fitness centers, a tennis court, science laboratories, an infirmary, a Center for Academic Support, a bookstore, a café, a game room, an indoor climbing wall, and a ropes course.

Location

Located in scenic southeastern Vermont, Landmark College overlooks the Connecticut River Valley, with sweeping views of the mountains and valleys of southern Vermont and northern Massachusetts. Wilderness areas, national forests, ski areas, lakes and streams, and other natural attractions abound. Nearby Brattleboro, Vermont, and the five-college region in the Amherst, Massachusetts, area offer opportunities for culture, the arts, fine dining, and more. Putney is a picturesque Vermont village with several shops, stores, restaurants, a bakery/coffeehouse, a bookstore, and other resources.

The College is located just off Exit 4 on Interstate 91. The most convenient airport is Bradley International Airport in Hartford, Connecticut, which is about 1½ hours away by car. Metropolitan areas within a 4-hour driving radius include Boston, New York, and Providence.

Admission Requirements

Applicants to Landmark College must have a diagnosis of dyslexia, attention deficit disorder, or another specific learning disability. Diagnostic testing within the last three years is required, along with a diagnosis of a learning disability or AD/HD. One of the Wechsler Scales (WAIS-III or WISC-III) administered within three years of application is required. Scores and subtest scores and their analysis are required to be submitted as well. Alternately, the Woodcock Johnson Cognitive Assessment may be substituted if administered within three years of application. Other criteria for admission include average to superior intellectual potential and high motivation to undertake the program.

The College offers rolling admission and enrolls students for fall and spring semesters. Students may begin in August (for the fall semester) or January (for the spring semester). The College offers credit-bearing courses each summer in addition to programs for students from other colleges, high school students, and students entering other colleges in the fall.

Application and Information

For more information, students should contact:

Office of Admissions
Landmark College
River Road South
Putney, Vermont 05346-0820
Phone: 802-387-6718
Fax: 802-387-6868
E-mail: admissions@landmark.edu
Web site: http://www.landmark.edu

Students on the campus of Landmark College.

MANOR COLLEGE

JENKINTOWN, PENNSYLVANIA

The College and Its Mission

Manor College is a private, coed Catholic college founded in 1947 by the Ukrainian Sisters of Saint Basil the Great. The College is characterized by its dedication to the education, growth, and self-actualization of the whole person through its personalized and nurturing atmosphere. Upon graduation, 40 percent of Manor's students are employed in their chosen fields; the remaining 60 percent of students transfer to four-year institutions to earn baccalaureate degrees.

There are approximately 952 full- and part-time students enrolled at Manor. Extracurricular activities include honor societies, men's and women's intercollegiate soccer and basketball, and women's volleyball, as well as the yearbook and special interest and cultural clubs. Manor provides free counseling and tutoring services through an on-campus learning center. Trained counselors are available to assist students on an individual and confidential basis for academic, career, and personal concerns. Upon entering Manor, students are assigned an academic adviser, who provides guidance and support throughout their Manor experience. Transfer counseling is available for students interested in pursuing a four-year degree.

The College's 35-acre campus includes a modern three-story dormitory, a library/administration building, and an academic building that also houses the bookstore, the dining hall, an auditorium/gymnasium, and a student lounge. The Ukrainian Heritage Studies Center and the Manor Dental Health Center are also located on the campus grounds. Manor is accredited by the Middle States Association of Colleges and Schools.

Academic Programs

Manor offers career-oriented, two-year associate degrees as well as transfer programs for the purpose of pursuing a bachelor's degree. Internships provide theory with practice, enhancing employment opportunities. The liberal arts core ensures a common breadth of knowledge along with mobility and future advancement. Manor College offers ten programs with twenty majors/concentrations leading to associate degrees and transfer programs through its three divisions: Liberal Arts, Allied Health/Science/Mathematics, and Business.

The Liberal Arts Division offers **Associate in Arts** degrees in early childhood education, liberal arts, and psychology. In addition, the Liberal Arts Division provides a liberal arts transfer major as well as an elementary education transfer major, an early child-care major, and a concentration in communications.

The Allied Health/Science/Mathematics Division offers **Associate in Science** degrees in dental hygiene, expanded functions dental assisting, and veterinary technology. This division also includes allied health and science transfer programs for students who seek preprofessional programs in biotechnology, chiropractic, cytotechnology, general sciences, medical technology, nursing, occupational therapy, pharmacy, physical therapy, radiologic science, and veterinary animal science.

The Business Division offers **Associate in Science** degrees in accounting, business administration, business administration/international business, business administration/management, business administration/marketing, information systems and technology, and paralegal studies. There are three certificate programs. There is a certificate program in paralegal studies for students who have a bachelor's degree, a legal nurse consultant certificate, and an expanded functions dental assisting certificate. Manor also offers selected courses through two modes of distance learning: online Web-based learning and teleconferencing.

The Office of Continuing Education serves adult learners by providing educational options for those who want to attend college on a part-time basis. The office also supports the needs of the community and business and industry by offering noncredit classes and workshops, as well as on- and off-site corporate training programs, throughout the year. Approved as an authorized provider by the International Association for Continuing Education and Training, the office also grants continuing education units (CEUs) for selected professional development courses each semester.

Off-Campus Programs

Externships are incorporated into various academic studies programs. Students earn credits as they gain practical experience under the supervision of professionals in a specific field of study. Externships are offered in the career-oriented programs of study and in some transfer programs. Manor's affiliation with several area hospitals, as well as Manor College's on-campus Dental Health Center, enables the allied health program student to fulfill clinical requirements at these sites. Students in other programs serve externships in law offices, courtrooms, day-care centers, businesses, and veterinary facilities. Manor has dual admissions, 2+2, and 2+3 articulation agreements with major allied health universities, hospitals, and local universities.

Credit for Nontraditional Learning Experiences

Manor College awards credit by examination for college-level learning through the College-Level Examination Program (CLEP). Manor administers exemption tests for courses not available through CLEP. Adults may also receive college credit for military experience and education through the Army/American Council on Education Registry Transcript System (AARTS), by submitting a transcript to Manor for evaluation of credits, and by requesting assessment of previous life and job experiences through nontraditional means.

Costs

Tuition for the 2009–10 academic year was $12,226 for full-time studies. Part-time study was $265 per credit hour. Students in certain allied health programs pay an additional $596 per year. On-campus room and board were available for men and women and cost $5972 per year. There was an additional $800 fee for a private room.

Financial Aid

Manor College offers need-based financial aid to eligible applicants in the form of grants, loans, and campus employment. Scholarships are awarded on the basis of academic promise. Approximately 85 percent of Manor's students receive some form of financial aid. Federally funded sources include the Federal Pell Grant, Federal Supplemental Educational Opportunity Grant, Federal Perkins Loan, Federal Stafford Student Loan, Federal PLUS loan, and Federal Work-Study Program. State-funded programs offered are the PHEAA State Grant and State Work-Study programs. The institutionally funded sources are the Manor Grant and the Resident Grant. Scholarships available for attendance at Manor include the following: Manor Presidential Scholarship; Joseph and Rose Wawriw Scholarships; Henry Lewandowski Memorial Scholarship; Elizabeth A. Stahlecker Memorial Scholarship; Mary Wolchonsky Scholarship; John Woloschuk Memorial Scholarship; Lorraine Osinski Keating Memorial Scholarship; Yuri and Jaroslava Rybak Scholarship; Dr. and Mrs. Volodymyr and Lydia Bazarko Scholarship; Heritage Foundation Scholarship of First Securities Federal Savings Bank; Father Chlystun Scholarship; Sesok Family Memorial Scholarship; Eileen Freedman Memorial Scholarship; Manor Allied Health, Science, and Math Division Scholarship; Business Division Scholarship; Liberal Arts Division Scholarship; Basilian Scholarships; Scholar Athlete Award; St. Basil Academy Scholarship; Wasyl and

Jozefa Soroka Scholarships; and International Scholarships. Scholarship eligibility requirements vary; details are available from the Admissions Office.

Faculty

There are 24 full-time and 100 part-time faculty members at Manor. Forty-seven percent of the faculty members have master's degrees and 35 percent possess doctorates in their field. Faculty members spend three fourths of their time teaching and the remainder counseling and advising students. The overall faculty-student ratio is 1:13. Small class size allows for personal attention in an environment conducive to learning.

Student Body Profile

Of the approximately 952 full- and part-time students enrolled at Manor, 223 entered the College as full-time freshman students in fall 2009. Twenty percent of the recent freshman class lived in the on-campus residence hall. Twenty-nine percent of the recent freshman class were members of minority groups, including international students from Albania, Ecuador, Guatemala, Haiti, India, Korea, Pakistan, Philippines, Sierra Leone, Russia, Ukraine, and Uzbekistan.

Student Activities

Manor encourages students to develop leadership skills through active participation in all aspects of College life. A variety of options for extracurricular participation fall under the umbrella of Manor's student life department, including the Student Senate, athletic teams, and clubs. The Student Senate forms an important part of the College community. The Senate, representing the student population, responds to student interests and concerns and acts as a liaison between the administration and the student body. Other extracurricular activities include intercollegiate men's and women's basketball and soccer, and women's volleyball. Manor's sports teams compete in the National Junior College Athletic Association. Additional extracurricular activities include the honor societies, intramural sports, the yearbook, and various special interest and cultural clubs. Student services is also responsible for the campus ministry, the counseling center, the residence hall, and the on-campus security force.

Facilities and Resources

The Academic Building (also called Mother of Perpetual Help Hall) includes classrooms, lecture rooms, laboratories, the chapel, and the Offices of Student Services, Campus Ministry, and Counseling. The Academic Building is equipped with up-to-date facilities, including biology, chemistry, and clinical laboratories, as well as modern IBM-compatible microsystems network labs. The Learning Center provides professional and student tutors in all College subjects and conducts workshops in study and research skills. Courses in English as a second language are also offered at the center.

The Basileiad Library has the capacity for 60,000 books, journals, multimedia materials, and periodicals. The library offers study areas, a multimedia room, a special collections and rare book archive, and computer access. The current library collection contains 50,000 volumes, including a special law collection and a Ukrainian Language collection.

An on-campus community Manor Dental Health Center was established in 1979 as an adjunct to the Expanded Functions Dental Assisting (EFDA) Program. Located on the lower level of St. Josaphat Hall, the center provides students enrolled in the EFDA Program or the Dental Hygiene Program at Manor with training under the direct supervision of faculty dentists. Currently, more than 2,500 patients receive care, including the following services: general dentistry, oral hygiene, orthodontics, prosthodontics, endodontics, and cosmetic dentistry. Because Manor Dental Health Center is a teaching facility, the fees charged for services are lower than those charged by private practitioners. Community residents are welcome as patients.

The Ukrainian Heritage Studies Center, located on the campus, preserves and promotes Ukrainian heritage, arts, and culture through four areas: academic programs, a museum collection, a library, and archives. Special events, exhibits, workshops, and seminars are offered throughout the year. The center is open to the public for tours and educational presentations by appointment.

Location

Manor is located in Jenkintown, Pennsylvania, 15 miles north of Center City Philadelphia. Manor is accessible via public transportation and is located near the Pennsylvania Turnpike, Route 611, U.S. 1, and Route 232. Centers of cultural and historic interest are found in nearby Philadelphia, Valley Forge, and beautiful Bucks County. Manor's suburban campus is within walking distance of a large shopping mall, medical offices, and a township park.

Admission Requirements

Manor is open to qualified applicants of all races, creeds, and national origins. Candidates are required to have a high school diploma or its equivalent. Admission is based on the applicant's scholastic record, test scores, and interviews. The application procedure involves submission of a completed application form, a high school transcript, SAT or ACT scores (required for students less than 21 years old), an interview, and an essay. Transfer students must submit transcripts of all college work completed. International students must also submit results of the Test of English as a Foreign Language (TOEFL) or, for the Liberal Arts/ESL program, must have completed two years of English language study at the high school or college level in their native country.

Application and Information

Manor has a rolling admission policy. Students may apply for admission in either the fall or the spring semester. Interested students are invited to visit the campus and meet with the admissions staff, faculty members, program directors, and students. Open houses, career days and nights, and classroom visits are scheduled throughout the year. The Admissions Office is open Monday through Friday, 8:30 a.m. to 6 p.m. (Saturday hours are by appointment). Admissions staff members can schedule visits and answer questions concerning admission, careers, programs, special features, and student life. For application forms, program-of-study bulletins, and catalogs, students should write to:

I. Jerry Czenstuch
Vice President of Enrollment Management
Manor College
700 Fox Chase Road
Jenkintown, Pennsylvania 19046
Phone: 215-884-2216
E-mail: ftadmiss@manor.edu
Web site: http://www.manor.edu

Manor College students relax between classes on the steps outside Mother of Perpetual Help Hall.

MIAMI DADE COLLEGE

MIAMI, FLORIDA

The College and Its Mission

Miami Dade College's mission is to change lives through the opportunity of education. As democracy's college, MDC provides high-quality teaching and learning experiences that are accessible and affordable to meet the needs of its diverse students and prepare them to be responsible global citizens and successful lifelong learners. The College embraces its responsibility to serve as an economic, cultural, and civic beacon in its community.

Miami Dade College (MDC) is recognized as one of the most outstanding colleges in the nation. With more than 170,000 credit and noncredit students, MDC has the largest undergraduate enrollment in the United States. Accredited by the Southern Association of Colleges and Schools, MDC works in partnership with its dynamic, multicultural community to place learners' needs at the center of its decision-making process.

Academic Programs

Miami Dade College offers seven bachelor's degree programs in addition to Associate in Arts, Associate in Science, and Associate in Applied Science degrees in more than 300 areas.

MDC's Bachelor of Science degree in education is designed to prepare students to become teachers and pass state professional certification exams in the areas of exceptional student education (K–12), secondary mathematics (6–12), and secondary science education (6–12), with concentrations in biology, chemistry, earth and space science, and physics. For more details on the specifics of MDC's seven bachelor's degrees, in addition to its Associate in Arts, Associate in Science, and Associate in Applied Science degrees in more than 300 areas, prospective students should visit https://sisvsr.mdc.edu/ps/sheet.aspx.

MDC's School of Justice offers a Bachelor of Applied Science (B.A.S.) degree in public safety management, with concentrations in basic police academy, basic corrections academy, corrections, crime scene investigation, emergency management, field internship, law enforcement, probation and parole, security/loss prevention, and criminal justice.

The B.A.S. degree with a major in film, television, and digital production is designed to offer the South Florida workforce a highly skilled applicant pool to fulfill job demands. It also provides an affordable opportunity for students completing either an Associate of Science or an Associate of Arts degree to seamlessly continue and complete a baccalaureate degree. Graduates of this program develop the abilities and skills needed to succeed in the film and television industry.

The B.A.S. degree with a major in health science and an option in physician assistant studies (concentration) incorporates A.A. and A.S. lower-division course work. Students complete course work in basic sciences, general studies, clinical medicine, history, physical examination techniques, and surgical, clinical, and practice management skills. Students have the opportunity to develop discipline-specific medical skills and to expand their knowledge by participating in structured clinical experiences under the supervision of physician assistants and physicians.

The B.A.S. degree in supervision and management provides an opportunity for students completing an associate degree to seamlessly complete a bachelor's degree. Graduates of this program have the abilities and skills needed to succeed as managers or supervisors in the dynamic and global business environment.

The bachelor's degree in electronics engineering technology is designed to prepare students for such entry-level engineering positions as electronics engineers, test engineers, project engineers, electronics manufacturing engineers, electronics systems engineers, electronics hardware engineers, technical support engineers, quality control engineers, reliability engineers, field engineers, processing engineers, and sales engineers.

The Bachelor of Science in Nursing (B.S.N.) is designed for licensed RNs with an A.S. degree in nursing from a regionally accredited program who want to attain the next level of education in order to provide global professional nursing in all clinical practice settings or be eligible for advanced nursing leadership, management, staff education, and practice positions in a multicultural society.

MDC also offers Associate in Arts (A.A.), Associate in Science (A.S.), and Associate in Applied Science (A.A.S.) degrees in more than 300 areas, in addition to College Credit Certificate programs, Advanced Technical Certificate programs, Career Technical Certificate programs, and supplemental courses to prepare students to enter the job market or upgrade skills. These programs vary in length. Program areas include, but are not limited to, business, computers, aviation, hospitality and travel, criminal justice, fire science, health sciences, nursing, public service, entertainment, and other occupational program areas. For more detailed information, visit https://sisvsr.mdc.edu/ps/sheet.aspx.

The **Honors College** at Miami Dade College provides a rigorous and comprehensive curriculum in a supportive environment where goal-oriented, academically gifted students explore new ideas, discuss global and environmental issues, engage in intellectual collaborations with experienced faculty members, and participate in study, travel, and culturally enriching experiences. Graduates of the Honors College transfer to some of the nation's finest schools including NYU, Stanford, and Yale. In response to industry demands, the Honors College's dual language program, located at MDC's InterAmerican campus, ensures that students are able to write, read, and speak at the college level in both Spanish and English. In the program, some courses are taught entirely in English and some entirely in Spanish; colloquia and leadership courses are taught in Spanish.

Distance Education Through the Virtual College, high-quality online academic and vocational programs are offered to meet the needs of nontraditional students outside of the South Florida area as well as students who find it difficult to attend classes. An array of Web-based instructional activities engages students in interactive and collaborative learning and covers the established competencies. Visit the Virtual College at http://virtual.mdc.edu for more information.

Transfer Arrangements A statewide articulation agreement among all Florida institutions of higher education ensures that any student who is awarded the Associate in Arts degree at Miami Dade College is guaranteed admission to a state university in Florida. In addition, MDC has established articulation agreements with seventy prestigious colleges and universities across the country including Michigan State, Smith, and the University of Wisconsin. Top graduates of MDC have been accepted at prominent institutions including Columbia, Georgetown, and Harvard, to name a few.

Internship and Co-op Programs Miami Dade College is committed to giving students a competitive edge in the marketplace. Through its co-op and internship programs, students are given the opportunity to work with professionals in the field, obtaining valuable real-life employment skills while earning college credit, work experience, and/or compensation.

Special Programs and Services New World School of the Arts (NWSA) is a unique educational partnership of Miami-Dade County Public Schools, Miami Dade College, and the University of Florida. Through its sponsoring institutions, NWSA awards high school diplomas, A.A. degrees, and Bachelor of Music and Bachelor of Fine Arts degrees. Students are admitted through audition or portfolio presentation. Other special programs include academic remediation for entering students, English as a second language, services for disabled students (including learning disabled), study abroad, and advanced placement.

Miami Dade College provides students the opportunity to obtain Continuing Education Units (CEUs) for certain courses. Transcripts designating CEUs are provided.

Off-Campus Programs

Study-abroad programs are available in nearly twenty-eight countries around the world. Faculty-led study-abroad programs are also available.

Credit for Learning Experiences

The College may award credit for demonstrated proficiency in areas related to college-level courses. Sources used to determine such proficiency are the College-Level Examination Program (CLEP), the Advanced Placement Program, the ACT Proficiency Examination Program, the International Baccalaureate Program, the Defense Activity for Non-Traditional Educational Support, the United States Armed Forces Institute, the Institutional Credit by Exam, and internal MDC procedures.

Costs

For the 2009–10 academic year, tuition was $86.19 per college credit hour for Florida residents; it was $312.58 per college credit hour for nonresidents. Textbooks and supplies for full-time students were estimated at $1500. Although housing is not available on campus, there are numerous and varied housing options near each of the College's eight campuses.

Financial Aid

Financial aid is determined by federal, state, and institutional guidelines and is offered to students in packages that may consist of grants, loans, and employment, as well as merit-based scholarships to qualified students.

Assistance includes Federal Pell Grants, Federal Supplemental Educational Opportunity Grants, the Florida Student Assistance Grant, the Florida Bright Futures Scholarship, the Federal Work-Study Program, the Florida Work Experience Program (FWEP), Federal Perkins Loans, Federal Stafford Student Loans, and Federal PLUS loans.

In addition, the College offers Foundation and Institutional Grants, short-term tuition loans, employment, and funding for the purchase of special equipment for disabled students. More information on all types of financial aid and scholarships can be found at http://www.mdc.edu/financial_aid/.

Faculty

MDC employs 2,097 faculty members, 688 full-time and 2,255 part-time.

Student Body Profile

Of the 80,000 credit students enrolled at Miami Dade College annually, almost 2,500 are international. Eighty-two percent of students with an A.A. degree continue their education at a four-year college. The average age of students is 26; 30 percent of MDC credit students are in the "traditional" college age group of 18 to 20 years. Sixty-two percent attend on a part-time basis, and 60 percent are women. The student body is ethnically and culturally diverse. For more information regarding admission and services for international students, prospective students should visit the Web site at http://www.mdc.edu/internationalstudents.

Student Activities

More than 100 organizations offer opportunities for students to participate in student government, publications, music ensembles, drama productions (in English and Spanish), religious activities, service and political clubs, professional organizations, and honor societies.

Intercollegiate and intramural athletics are an integral part of the overall educational process and play an important role at Miami Dade College, which is a member of NJCAA and competes at the Division I level. Intercollegiate teams include women's basketball, softball, and volleyball, and men's baseball and basketball. Sports facilities include wellness centers, swimming pools, and a track, along with racquetball, tennis, and handball courts.

Academic Facilities

Library and Media Services The campus libraries have a combined collection of more than 360,000 books and 3,824 periodicals. There are approximately 31,000 audiovisual materials; online databases are also available. Access to these databases is available 24 hours a day, seven days a week from any computer with an Internet connection.

Computers for student use are available in computer labs, learning resource centers, science labs, classrooms, and in the libraries. The Center for Digital Education and *Converge* magazine recently recognized Miami Dade College as one of the most tech-advanced community colleges in the nation.

Each campus has a Career Services Center designed to help students with their career development and employment opportunities and to provide information on transfer options. Career Services sponsors career and college fairs and employer programs and supplies students with lists of available jobs, internships, and cooperative opportunities.

The College is a leader in working proactively to assist students with disabilities. Each campus has a ground-floor ACCESS office to provide guidance and technological accommodations. Computers equipped with voice synthesizer programs are available, as are note-takers to help physically challenged students. Sign-language interpreters are available for deaf and hearing-impaired students.

Location

Eight campuses and numerous outreach centers are located throughout the greater Miami area. The region offers a rich variety of exciting multicultural, athletic, and intellectual activities and year-round sunshine. Opportunities abound to explore unique settings, such as Miami Beach's historic Art Deco District and Miami's colorful Little Havana or nearby Everglades National Park.

Admission Requirements

Miami Dade has an open-door admission policy. The College provides educational opportunities to all high school graduates, including those who have a state high school equivalency diploma, and to transfer students from other colleges and universities.

In addition to the College's application for admission and the $20 application fee, students must request that official transcripts from high school, college, university, or other postsecondary educational institutions be sent directly to the College's Office of Admissions. High school equivalency diploma or certificate holders must provide the original document and score report or an exact copy. Prospective students should note that the College will return the original copies to the student. Florida residents must complete a Florida residency statement.

While not required for admission, SAT, ACT, or TOEFL scores may be submitted. If so, they should be sent directly to the Office of Admissions by the testing board. Students not presenting test scores are tested for placement purposes upon acceptance.

Application and Information

Applications are accepted on an ongoing basis. All prospective students should contact:

Admissions Office
Miami Dade College
300 NE Second Avenue
Miami, Florida 33132
Phone: 305-237-8888
Web site: http://www.mdc.edu

MOHAWK VALLEY COMMUNITY COLLEGE

UTICA AND ROME, NEW YORK

The College and Its Mission

Mission: Mohawk Valley Community College promotes student success and community involvement through a commitment to excellence and a spirit of service.

Vision: To transform lives by creating an innovative learning environment that meets the needs of the rapidly changing communities.

Statement of purpose: As a diverse institution with a global view, the College provides opportunities for affordable education, with support from Oneida County and the State of New York, and offers career, transfer, and transitional education and programs for personal and cultural enrichment; and supports community and economic development.

The College was founded in 1946 as the New York State Institute of Applied Arts and Sciences at Utica. One of five postsecondary institutions established on an experimental basis after World War II, the public institute offered programs leading to technical and semiprofessional employment in business and industry. After name changes in the 1950s, redefining its mission, the College moved to its current 80-acre campus location in Utica in 1960. In 1961, the College was renamed Mohawk Valley Community College. Today, the College offers a full range of academic programs.

The College is accredited by the Middle States Association of Colleges and Schools. Individual program accreditations are as follows: airframe and power plant technology by the Federal Aviation Administration (FAA); civil, electrical, and mechanical engineering technology and surveying technology by the Commission for Technology Accreditation of the Accreditation Board for Engineering and Technology, Inc. (ABET); nursing by the National League for Nursing Accrediting Commission (NLNAC); and respiratory care by the Commission on Accreditation of Allied Health Education Programs, in cooperation with the Committee on Accreditation for Respiratory Care.

Academic Programs

The College has been authorized to offer the following degrees and certificates: Associate in Arts (A.A.) degree, Associate in Science (A.S.) degree, Associate in Applied Science (A.A.S.) degree, Associate in Occupational Studies (A.O.S.) degree, and the MVCC Certificate.

The structure of academic programming at MVCC has two main purposes. Certificate, A.O.S., and A.A.S. programs emphasize the development of employable skills through a combination of classroom and laboratory instruction. Some programs also include internship experiences. A.A. and A.S. programs provide students with the liberal arts, science, mathematics, business, engineering, or computer course work necessary for transfer into the junior year of a preprofessional program at a four-year public or private college or university upon the completion of their associate degree.

The minimum number of credits needed to earn an associate degree is 62. The maximum credits required for a degree differ by program and degree type.

Opportunities for specialization include the honors program, independent study, internships, study abroad, and ROTC (Army and Air Force).

The College operates on a semester calendar. Fall classes begin before Labor Day and end before Christmas. Spring classes begin in mid-January and end in mid-May. The airframe and power plant certificate program follows a slightly different calendar, with opportunities for enrollment in August, December, and April.

Career and transfer programs are available. Majors offered include accounting (A.A.S.); administrative assistant (A.A.S.); air conditioning technology (A.O.S.); building management and maintenance (A.A.S.); business administration (A.S.); business management (A.A.S.); chemical dependency practitioner (A.A.S.); chemical technology (A.A.S.); civil engineering technology (A.A.S.); computer-aided drafting (A.O.S.); computer information systems (A.A.S.); computer science (A.S.); criminal justice (A.A.S.); culinary arts management (A.O.S.), also with baking and pastry emphasis; data processing, programming and systems (A.A.S.); digital animation (A.A.S.); educational sign language interpretation (A.A.S.); electrical engineering technology (A.A.S.); electrical service technician (A.O.S.), with options in electrical maintenance and fiber optics; emergency medical services/paramedic (A.A.S.); engineering science (A.S.); environmental analysis–chemical technology (A.A.S.); financial services management (A.A.S.); fine arts (A.S.); fire protection technology (A.A.S., available to graduates of the Utica Fire Academy only); general studies (A.S.); general studies–childhood education (A.S., joint admission with the State University of New York (SUNY) College at Oneonta); graphic arts technology (A.A.S.); graphic design (A.A.S.); hotel technology–meeting services management (A.A.S.); human services (A.A.S.); illustration (A.A.S.); individual studies (A.A., A.A.S., A.S., and A.O.S.); international studies (A.A.); liberal arts–adolescence education (teacher transfer) (A.S.); liberal arts–childhood education (teacher transfer) (A.S.); liberal arts–humanities and social science (A.A.); liberal arts–psychology (A.S.); liberal arts–public policy (A.S.); liberal arts–theater (A.A.); manufacturing technology (A.O.S.); mathematics (A.S.); mechanical engineering technology (A.A.S.); mechanical technology–aircraft maintenance (A.A.S., requires an FAA-approved airframe and power plant license to enroll); media marketing and management (A.A.S.); medical assisting (A.A.S.); nursing (A.A.S.); nutrition and dietetics (A.S.); photography (A.A.S.); pre–environmental science (A.S.); programming and systems (A.A.S.); radiologic technology (A.S., transfer in only with appropriate radiology credentials); recreation and leisure services (A.A.S.); respiratory care (A.A.S.); restaurant management (A.A.S.); school facilities management (A.A.S., online); science (A.S.), with emphasis areas in biology, chemistry, physical education, physics, and sports medicine; semiconductor manufacturing technology (A.A.S.); surveying technology (A.A.S.); telecommunications technology–Verizon Next Step (A.A.S.); Web development and information design (A.A.S.); and welding technology (A.O.S.).

Certificate programs include administrative assistant; airframe and power plant technology; allied health care: medical claims management; carpentry and masonry; chef training; CNC machinist technology; coaching; computer-aided drafting; cybersecurity (online);electronic technician; English as a second language; finance; graphic communication; heating and air conditioning; individual studies: business and industry; industrial and commercial electricity; insurance; machinist technology; managerial accounting; media marketing and management; medical assistant; photography; refrigeration; school facilities management (online); small business management; supervisory management; surgical technician; surveying; transportation management (online); and welding.

A jointly registered degree program with SUNY College at Oneonta offers applicants the opportunity to complete a bachelor's degree in childhood education (grades 1–6) at MVCC.

Credit for Nontraditional Learning Experiences

MVCC offers adult students the opportunity to earn credits through the CLEP examination, MVCC-administered examinations, life experience, and course work completed in a noncollegiate setting. The accumulated credit earned cannot exceed 75 percent of the student's degree program.

Costs

Tuition for New York State residents is $1675 per semester for full-time students and $120 per credit hour for part-time students; for out-of-state and international students, it is $3350 per semester for full-time students and $240 per credit hour for part-time students. The student activity fee is $105 per semester for full-time students and $5 per credit hour for part-time students, and the technology fee is $100 per semester full-time and $35 per semester part-time. Books and supplies range from $300 to $500 per semester, depending on the student's major. Residence hall occupants must purchase one of the available room and board packages each semester. Costs range from $3315 to $4575 per semester, depending on room type and meal plan chosen. The residence hall technology fee is $100 per semester for Internet and phone access. The residence hall social fee is $10 per semester. The residence hall orientation fee is $40 and covers new-resident orientation programming and meals.

Financial Aid

One of MVCC's major objectives is to make college affordable for all. Approximately 90 percent of MVCC students receive some form of state or federal financial aid. The College offers a comprehensive financial assistance program of scholarships, loans, and grants. Most of the financial assistance received by MVCC students is need based. Non–need-based scholarships include the Presidential Scholarship Program for the top 10 percent of Oneida County (the College's sponsoring county) graduates, two similar Exceptional Student Scholarships for those not from Oneida County, and the Sodexo/MVCC Meal Plan Scholarships, which consider exceptional citizenship. Students eligible for non–need-based scholarships are expected to apply for state and federal financial assistance as applicable.

Faculty

The full-time faculty members number 149, and the part-time faculty members number 130. Approximately 8 percent of all faculty members have doctoral degrees. The student-faculty ratio is approximately 21:1.

Student Body Profile

MVCC enrolls approximately 5,400 students each year. Enrollment is divided between the main campus in Utica, New York, and the branch campus in Rome, New York, with approximately 80 percent of the student population enrolled on the main campus.

The College is designed to be predominantly commuter based; 85 percent of the students live within 60 miles of the campus in central New York State. The College has added an additional residence hall on the main campus in Utica, increasing housing capacity to approximately 505 students.

The international student population is currently 80 students. Nineteen different countries are represented on campus.

The average age of students is about 22, with approximately 35 percent of the population being over the age of 25. Approximately 52 percent of the enrolled students are women. The racial/ethnic makeup of the campus is currently 80 percent white, non-Hispanic; 7 percent black, non-Hispanic; 1 percent American Indian/Alaskan native; 1 percent Asian/Pacific Islander; and 3 percent Hispanic. Of the total student body, 8 percent chose not to identify with any of the listed groups.

Enrolling students typically exhibit a 75 percent grade average in high school and a rank in the top 50 percent of their high school class.

Student Activities

The Student Activities program offers a wide variety of experiences for students through clubs, Student Congress, and other activities. On each campus, the staff assists students with the planning of events and programs. There are seventeen professional, curriculum-related clubs. In addition, there are thirty service/interest clubs that provide students with the opportunity to participate in a wide range of social, cultural, theatrical, athletic, and international activities to broaden their experiences.

MVCC participates in Division III of the National Junior College Athletic Association. Men's teams include baseball, basketball, bowling, cross-country, golf, ice hockey, indoor track, lacrosse, soccer, tennis, and track and field. Women's teams include basketball, bowling, cross-country, golf, indoor track, lacrosse, softball, soccer, tennis, track and field, and volleyball.

Throughout the last decade, MVCC's athletic teams have an impressive record, winning more than 70 percent of their contests.

Facilities and Resources

The main campus in Utica is composed of three residence halls; the Alumni College Center, which includes dining facilities, a bookstore, and the health center; the Gymnasium; the Academic Building; the Science and Technology building; the Information Technology and Performing Arts Conference Center (open computer labs and a handicap-accessible, state-of-the-art theater), and Payne Hall (library, administrative offices, and a comprehensive Student Services Center).

The branch campus in Rome consists of the Rome Academic Building, including a bookstore and dining room facilities for the hospitality programs, and the John D. Plumley Science and Technology Complex that includes a library, classrooms, and labs.

The goal of MVCC's libraries is to link students to the information they need. With more than 86,000 volumes and over 500 periodical titles, MVCC offers a comprehensive collection to support the College's curricula; library holdings also include popular best-sellers and feature film collections. MVCC students as well as faculty and staff members may request materials outside the collection through the College's comprehensive interlibrary loan service. The online resources include catalogs and periodical indexes with full-text articles. Coin-operated photocopiers and microfilm reader/printers are also available.

Academic tutoring is available at no cost to students in the Learning Centers on both campuses. The centers offer instructional support in mathematics, writing, reading, study skills, life sciences, and computer and social sciences.

Location

The main campus is in Utica, New York, a small city of 60,000 people. The branch campus in Rome, New York, is located in a community of 30,000 people. The small-city atmosphere, coupled with a wide range of cultural activities, museums, access to the Adirondack Mountains, good public transportation, and sports venues, provides an excellent location for student growth and development.

Admission Requirements

The College is an open-admission, full-opportunity college. The College does not require applicants to complete standardized admissions tests such as the ACT or SAT.

Application and Information

Students can apply in a variety of ways. MVCC provides its own admission application (print and online versions); no processing fee is required. It is available from the Admissions Office or from selected high schools in central New York State. MVCC applications can be accessed on the College's Web site at www.mvcc.edu/apply. MVCC also participates in the SUNY application process. Students can use the SUNY application—hard copy or online version; SUNY processing fees apply.

For further information, interested students should contact:

Admissions Office
Mohawk Valley Community College
1101 Sherman Drive
Utica, New York 13501

Phone: 315-792-5354
Fax: 315-792-5527
E-mail: admissions@mvcc.edu (domestic)
International.admissions@mvcc.edu (international)
Web site: http://www.mvcc.edu

MOUNTWEST COMMUNITY & TECHNICAL COLLEGE

HUNTINGTON, WEST VIRGINIA

The College and Its Mission

Mountwest Community & Technical College (MCTC) is a public institution with contract services provided by Marshall University. The College provides open access to education and training for a diverse population and assists students and employers to meet regional and global workforce demands. The College fulfills its educational mission through developmental, career and technical, university transfer, and general education; professional and personal development; lifelong learning; and workforce training programs and services.

The College was founded in 1975 as a separate college within Marshall University to better serve students by bringing together many of the two-year associate degree programs under one college. Classes began in fall 1975 with a wide range of programs. From the outset, the College's mission has been to provide two-year associate degrees as well as continuing education and community service. In 1991, the College's name was changed to Marshall Community and Technical College to better reflect the technical nature of many of the programs offered. On October 30, 2003, MCTC became accredited as an independent institution by the Higher Learning Commission, North Central Association of Colleges and Schools.

On July 1, 2008, MCTC became a free-standing institution with contract services provided by Marshall University. In April 2010, the school's name was officially changed to Mountwest Community & Technical College.

MCTC's campus has been rated by APB News as one of the safest campuses in the nation. In addition to being a safe environment, the campus offers a wealth of resources, services, and organizations to enhance students' academic, social, spiritual, professional, and personal growth.

Academic Programs

The College offers associate degrees, one-year certificate programs, and noncredit courses. Associate degrees are available in accounting, administrative assistant technology (with a focus in executive, legal, medical, or medical transcription), agricultural science, air conditioning/refrigeration, animation and game developer studies, automotive technology, banking and finance, biomedical/electronics technology, building and construction, business administration, call center supervision, child development specialist studies, clinical assistant studies, culinary arts, dental laboratory technology, early childhood education, electronics technology, firefighter studies, general building construction, general/transfer studies, geospatial studies, graphic design/graphic communications, health information technology, hotel/lodging management, industrial management, interior design, law enforcement, legal assistant studies, machinist technology, management, maritime training, massage therapy, medical assistant studies, mine inspection, network systems (administration, development, or security), occupational development, painting and allied trades, paramedic science, physical therapist assistant studies, police science, program developer studies, public library technology, radiologic technology, respiratory therapy, social work assistant studies, Web developer studies, and welding.

In addition, the Board of Governors Associate in Applied Science Degree is designed to assist adult learners to meet occupational goals and employment requirements, establish professional credentials, or achieve personal goals. This provides Mountwest Community & Technical College a mechanism to deliver educational programs to nontraditional students desiring to complete their postsecondary education.

Students can pursue a certificate in accounting and bookkeeping, agricultural science, certified coding specialist, CISCO Certified Network Associate (CCNA), clinical assistant, culinary arts, dental laboratory technology, graphic design/graphic communications, machinist technology, maritime training, medical transcription, Microsoft Certified Systems Engineer (MCSE), paramedic science, police science, or public library technology. Specific information, including program requirements, can be found at http://www.mctc.edu/academics/programs.

For students who are unsure what their major should be, there is an undecided major that they can follow for up to one semester. A student must declare a major as soon as possible because each two-year program has specific degree requirements.

The Department of Continuing and Corporate Education of Mountwest Community & Technical College is committed to growth and expansion, while maintaining dedication to quality training and service delivery. Today's workforce education providers must cope with continual change in economic conditions, government mandates, and community needs. It is the vision of the department to focus on becoming the provider of choice for delivering high-quality education and training that advances the economic and workforce development of the service district. A list of all the department has to offer is available at http://www.marshall.edu/ctc/www/programs/professional_personal_development.shtml.

The Cooking and Culinary Institute also offers several noncredit options, which can be found at http://www.marshall.edu/ctc/cci/classes.asp.

Off-Campus Programs

Students should contact the Office of Off-Campus Programs at 304-696-3016 for more information.

Credit for Nontraditional Learning Experiences

The faculty at Mountwest Community & Technical College believes that what students know is more important than how it is learned. If students can demonstrate or document knowledge and skills reasonably comparable to Mountwest Community & Technical College courses, equal credit may be awarded. Credit may be awarded by examination, through accepted standards, or for knowledge and skills.

Costs

Tuition for West Virginia students is $119.25 per credit hour, or $2856 for two semesters of full-time study. Nonresidents pay $340 per credit hour, or $8142 for two semesters of full-time study. Fees are additional. Room and board are available from Marshall University for a cost of around $6800 per year; for housing only, students pay about $4000 a year.

Financial Aid

Students have three main types of financial aid options—grants and scholarships, which do not have to be repaid; work-study programs, which are employment opportunities based upon a student's financial need; and loans, which must be repaid upon graduation or when dropping below half-time enrollment.

To apply for need-based financial aid, a student must complete the Free Application for Federal Student Aid (FAFSA), available from the Marshall University Office of Student Financial Assistance, high school guidance counselors, or public libraries or online at http://www.fafsa.ed.gov. A student should mail or electronically submit the FAFSA as soon after January 1 as possible to receive consideration for programs with limited funding. The application deadline for the West Virginia Higher Education Grant Program is March 1.

Incoming freshmen and transfer students are automatically considered for scholarship assistance based upon their admission records. Transfer students must have a minimum cumulative transfer GPA of 3.5 and a minimum ACT composite score of 25. The award amount for a transfer student is $1000 for the academic year. Scholarships are listed in detail at http://www.mctc.edu/admissions/financial_aid_and_scholarships.

Faculty

MCTC has 142 faculty members, 29 percent of whom are full-time. The student-faculty ratio is 22:1.

Student Body Profile

Of the 2,476 students enrolled at MCTC, 42 percent are women, and 10 percent are transfer students. Nearly 10 percent of the student body is African American; 0.7 percent is Asian American or Pacific Islander; another 0.7 percent is Hispanic American; 0.5 percent is Native American; and 0.2 percent is from one of three other countries.

Student Activities

The Student Recreation Center will be 121,000 square feet and will house swimming pools, a running track, group exercise rooms, basketball courts, a climbing wall, and racquetball courts. The facility also will be equipped with a wide range of exercise equipment, including treadmills, step machines, and weight machines.

MCTC students who are enrolled for a minimum of 12 credit hours each semester can live in Marshall University dorms. Interested students should contact Residence Services at 800-438-5391.

Academic Facilities

The College currently is housed in three buildings on the Marshall campus. The John Deaver Drinko Library, located on the western side of campus beside Old Main, opened in 1998 and is named for John Deaver Drinko, a Marshall graduate, philanthropist, and strong supporter of higher education. The facility melds a full range of traditional library services with state-of-the-art computer and advanced technological education facilities that include multimedia training and presentation rooms, workstations, distance education, and computer carrels. There is a twenty-four-hour reading room/computer lab with computer consultation stations and assistive technology. The library's collection includes books, bound periodicals, and a wide variety of media and Internet-accessible electronic materials. The Drinko Library has study rooms, conference collaboration rooms, and an auditorium and houses the Offices of Information Technology, University Libraries, Instructional Technology, University Computing Services, and Telecommunications.

The Academic Skills Center, located in Mountwest Community & Technical College building Room 138, is operated by a director and a highly qualified staff of math and English instructors offering tutorial assistance to individuals and study groups. In addition to working with teachers, students have available to them computers and videos to assist in building academic skills and in refreshing existing skills.

Location

The MCTC campus is in Huntington, West Virginia, on the western edge of the state. Tucked between West Virginia mountains and the mighty Ohio River, MCTC lies about 100 miles south of Columbus, Ohio. The average temperature in Huntington is around 55°F. Each year, the area gets a total of around 26 inches of snowfall.

Admission Requirements

MCTC has an open enrollment policy. All students must submit a completed admission application and the application fee. All transcripts must be on file by the end of the first semester for registration in subsequent terms. Proof of measles, mumps, and rubella immunization must be submitted by the end of the first semester. Students do not have to have ACT/SAT scores to be admitted. Students who have completed college credit from another institution or who wish to transfer from another college at Marshall may request to have their academic record and courses evaluated.

Application and Information

Applications are processed on a rolling basis.

Sonja Cantrell, Director of Admissions and Recruitment
Mountwest Community and Technical College
One John Marshall Drive
Huntington, West Virginia 25755
Phone: 304-696-6282
866-676-5533 (toll-free)
Fax: 304-696-7104
E-mail: cotrone@mctc.edu
Web site: http://www.mctc.edu

PENNSYLVANIA COLLEGE OF TECHNOLOGY

An Affiliate of Penn State

WILLIAMSPORT, PENNSYLVANIA

Pennsylvania College of Technology
PENNSTATE

The College and Its Mission

Pennsylvania College of Technology (Penn College) is a special mission affiliate of Penn State, committed to applied technology education. The College has a national reputation for the high quality and diversity of its "degrees that work" in traditional and advanced technology majors. Partnerships with industry leaders, including Honda, Ford, and Caterpillar, provide students unique opportunities to advance their careers.

Excellent placement rates exceed 95 percent annually (100 percent in some majors). Among the keys to graduate success are Penn College's emphasis on small classes, personal attention, and hands-on experience using the latest technology. Student projects reflect real working situations. A number of campus buildings were designed and constructed by students—including a conference center, a Victorian guest house, an athletic field house, and a rustic retreat used for professional gatherings—and are maintained by students. The facilities stand as testimony to the quality of a Penn College education. State-of-the-art classrooms and laboratories on the ultramodern campus located in Williamsport, Pennsylvania, reflect the expectations of the modern workforce.

Academic Programs

Associate Degree Majors: **Associate degrees (A.A.S., A.A.A., or A.A.)** are offered in accounting; advertising art; architectural technology; automated manufacturing technology; automotive service sales and marketing; automotive technology (including Ford ASSET and Honda PACT industry-sponsored majors); aviation technology; baking and pastry arts; building construction technology; building construction technology/masonry; business management; civil engineering technology; collision repair technology; computer-aided drafting technology; culinary arts technology; dental hygiene; diesel technology; early childhood education; electric power generation technology; electrical technology; electromechanical maintenance technology; electronics and computer engineering technology (emphases in communications and fiber optics, nanofabrication technology, and robotics and automation); emergency medical services; forest technology; general studies; graphic communications technology; health arts; health arts/practical nursing; health information technology; heating, ventilation, and air conditioning (HVAC) technology; heavy construction equipment technology (emphases in Caterpillar equipment industry-sponsored, operator, and technician); hospitality management; human services; individual studies; information technology (emphases in network administration, network technology, technical support technology, and Web and applications technology); landscape/nursery technology/turfgrass management; legal assistant/paralegal; machine tool technology; mass media communication; nursing; occupational therapy assistant studies; ornamental horticulture (emphases in landscape technology and plant production); physical fitness specialist studies; plastics and polymer technology; radiography; renewable energy technologies; studio arts; surgical technology; surveying technology; and welding technology.

Bachelor's Degree Majors: Many associate degree graduates choose to continue their education with unique **Bachelor of Science (B.S.) degrees** that focus on applied technology in traditional and emerging career fields. Majors include accounting; applied health studies; applied human services; automotive technology management; aviation maintenance technology; building automation technology; building science and sustainable design (concentrations in architectural technology and building construction technology); business administration (concentrations in banking and finance, human resource management, management, marketing, and small business and entrepreneurship); civil engineering technology; computer-aided product design; construction management; culinary arts and systems; dental hygiene (concentrations in health policy and administration and special-population care); electronics and computer engineering technology; graphic communications management; graphic design; health information management; heating, ventilation, and air conditioning (HVAC) technology; industrial and human factors design; information technology (concentrations in IT security specialist, network specialist, and Web and applications development); legal assistant/paralegal studies; manufacturing engineering technology; nursing; physician assistant; plastics and polymer engineering technology; residential construction technology and management; technology management; Web design and multimedia; and welding and fabrication engineering technology.

Certificate Majors: Certificates are offered in automotive service technician, aviation maintenance technician, collision repair technician, construction carpentry, diesel technician, electrical occupations, health information coding specialist, machinist general, nurse/health-care paralegal, paramedic technician, plumbing, practical nursing, and welding.

Off-Campus Programs

Internships give students the opportunity to gain workforce experience. Penn College students have worked throughout Pennsylvania, the United States, and the world.

Costs

Tuition and related fees are based on a per-credit charge. Pennsylvania residents attending Penn College in 2009–10 paid approximately $21,530 per year, and out-of-state students paid approximately $24,680 per year. These estimated costs were based on tuition and fees for an average of 15 credits per semester, plus estimated expenses for housing, meals, books, and supplies. Rates vary according to specific choices for classes, housing, and meal plans.

On-campus housing offers apartment-style and lodge-style living options. On-campus housing is alcohol-free, drug-free, noise-controlled, and secure. Students are offered a variety of meal plans, which are accepted in the College's dining facilities, including the main dining hall, an all-you-can-eat buffet, a gourmet restaurant, a convenience store, snack bars, and a café.

Financial Aid

Approximately 4 out of 5 Penn College students receive some form of financial assistance. Types of aid available include Federal Pell Grants, Pennsylvania Higher Education Assistance Agency Grants, Federal Supplemental Educational Opportunity Grants, Federal Work-Study Program awards, Federal Stafford Student Loans, Federal PLUS loans, veterans' benefits, and Bureau of Vocational Rehabilitation benefits. A deferred-payment plan allows students to spread their tuition cost over two payments each semester. Penn College offers academic, need-based, and technical scholarships to qualified students. For detailed information on scholarships, students should contact the Financial Aid Office or visit the Web at www.pct.edu/finaid.

Faculty

Penn College's faculty members (308 full-time and 199 part-time) provide individual attention that students need to be successful in the classroom and the workplace. Faculty members are experienced in their fields. Each year, Penn College recognizes excellence among the faculty members through distinguished faculty award programs. Small class sizes (fewer than 20 students in most classes) promote student success. Advisory committees of faculty members and business and industry leaders work together to ensure that programs meet current workplace needs.

Student Body Profile

More than 6,400 students attend Penn College. More than 5,000 additional men and women take part in noncredit classes, including customized business and industry courses offered through Workforce Development and Continuing Education.

Student Activities

Penn College is a place where future technicians and designers mingle easily with chefs, health-care personnel, and business students. It is a place where students actually construct campus buildings, cater important campus functions, compute strategies for engineering technology problems, and care for children in an on-campus day-care center. The magnificent Campus Center provides an opportunity to eat, shop, work out, and spend time with friends. A modern fitness center, College Store, convenience store, TV lounge, video rental and game room, and all-you-can-eat restaurant are among the features of the Campus Center. Impressive cultural activities are available both on the main campus and at Penn College's Community Arts Center, a restored 1920s-era theater in downtown Williamsport. Student ticket rates are available for performances that include Broadway shows, opera, ballet, symphony orchestras, and popular entertainers.

The Student Government Association (SGA) and Wildcat Events Board (WEB) represent the student body in matters related to College policy and activities. Participation offers students the opportunity to develop leadership skills while contributing to the well-being of the College and the student body. In addition, Greek Life (4 fraternities and 2 sororities) more than fifty student organizations, including the Residence Hall Association that represents all on-campus student residents, offer opportunities for organized campus activity and leadership experiences.

Most Penn College Wildcat sports teams compete regionally in the Penn State University Athletic Conference (PSUAC) and nationally in the United States Collegiate Athletic Association (USCAA). Varsity sports include archery, baseball, basketball, bowling, cross-country, dance team, golf, soccer, softball, team tennis, and volleyball.

Facilities and Resources

The hands-on experience offered at Penn College creates a need for a variety of special academic facilities. Campus computers are very accessible. Wireless zones and networked on-campus residences make study across the campus very convenient. Besides extensive, accessible computer labs, the main campus has an automated manufacturing center, plastics manufacturing center, printing and publishing facility, dental hygiene clinic, automotive repair center, machine shop, welding shop, building technologies center, architectural studio, computer-aided drafting labs, broadcast studio, video production studio, modern science laboratories, fine-dining restaurant, campus guest house, aviation and avionics instructional facility located at the regional airport, greenhouses, working sawmill, diesel center, and heavy-equipment training site.

Library Services: The Madigan Library on the main campus is open every day during the academic semesters and offers an impressive selection of print and electronic resources. Services available include a professional reference staff, a well-developed instructional program, reciprocal borrowing with regional libraries, interlibrary loans, and paper and electronic reserves. The library also houses fourteen study areas, two computer laboratories, a 100-seat open computer lab complex, a café, and the art gallery.

Location

Penn College is located in north-central Pennsylvania. The main campus is in Williamsport, a city known around the world as the home of the Little League Baseball World Series. Penn College also offers classes at three other locations: the Advanced Automotive Technology Center at Wahoo Drive Industrial Park in Williamsport, the Aviation Center at the Williamsport Regional Airport in Montoursville, and the Earth Science Center, 10 miles south of Williamsport near Allenwood. Noncredit classes are offered from locations in Williamsport and Wellsboro.

Admission Requirements

Penn College offers educational opportunities to anyone who has the interest, desire, and ability to pursue advanced study. Due to the wide variety of majors, admission criteria vary according to the major. At a minimum, applicants must have a high school diploma or its equivalent. Some majors are restricted to persons who meet certain academic skill levels and prerequisites, have attained certain levels of academic achievement, and have earned an acceptable score on the SAT or ACT. Questions regarding the admission standards for specific majors should be directed to the Admissions Office. To ensure that applicants have the entry-level skills needed for success in college majors, all students are required to take placement examinations, which are used to assess skills in math, English, and reading. The College provides opportunities for students to develop the basic skills necessary for enrollment in associate degree and certificate majors when the placement tests indicate that such help is needed. International students whose native language is not English are required to take the TOEFL, submit an affidavit of support, and comply with test regulations of the Immigration and Naturalization Service, along with meeting all other admission requirements. The College offers equal opportunity for admission without regard to age, race, color, creed, sex, national origin, disability, veteran status, or political affiliation.

Penn College offers opportunities for students to transfer the following course credits: credit earned at other institutions, college credit earned before high school graduation, service credit, DANTES credit, and credit earned through the College-Level Examination Program (CLEP).

Application and Information

Viewbooks, financial aid information, and other informative brochures, along with applications for admission, are available from the Admissions Office. Prospective students and their families should contact the Admissions Office to arrange a personal interview or campus tour. Fall and spring open-house events are held annually.

All inquiries should be addressed to:

Admissions Office, DIF 119
Pennsylvania College of Technology
One College Avenue
Williamsport, Pennsylvania 17701-5799

Phone: 570-327-4761
800-367-9222 (toll-free)
E-mail: pctinfo@pct.edu
Web site: http://www.pct.edu/peter2

Banners representing each of the eight academic schools at Penn College adorn lampposts leading from the main entrance to the heart of the campus.

STATE UNIVERSITY OF NEW YORK COLLEGE OF ENVIRONMENTAL SCIENCE AND FORESTRY, THE RANGER SCHOOL

WANAKENA, NEW YORK

The College and Its Mission

The forest technology and land surveying technology programs are offered through the State University of New York College of Environmental Science and Forestry (ESF) at The Ranger School campus. Throughout its history, the College has focused on the environmental issues of the time in each of its three mission areas: instruction, research, and public service. The College is dedicated to educating future scientists and managers who, through specialized skills, will be able to use a holistic approach to solving the environmental and resource problems facing society.

More than 3,200 students have graduated from the program over the past ninety-five years, including more than 180 women since 1974. Established in 1912 with the gift of 1,800 acres of land in the Adirondack Mountains, the ESF forest technology program is the oldest in the nation. The Ranger School's managed forest includes both hardwood and coniferous trees and is bounded on two sides by the New York State Forest Preserve. It is also adjacent to several acres of virgin timber in the Adirondack Forest preserve.

The main campus building houses the central academic, dining, and recreational facilities. Dormitory wings are located on either side of the main campus building. Dorm rooms are designed to accommodate 1 or 2 people. All second-year students live on campus, with the exception of married students accompanied by their families. These students should arrange for rental accommodations well before the start of the academic year.

A $6-million renovation and expansion of The Ranger School was completed in 2003. This project included renovations and an addition to the main campus building, a new dining hall, distance learning classrooms, additional residence hall facilities, and a new student recreational area.

Academic Programs

Associate Degree Programs: Students who complete the program earn an **Associate in Applied Science (A.A.S.)** degree in forest technology or land surveying technology.

Both degree programs at The Ranger School are 1+1 programs, meaning they require 30 credit hours of course work in general studies to fulfill the program's freshman liberal arts requirements. Students who are considering later transfer to a four-year program should follow the suggestions for freshman-year selections outlined in the ESF catalog. The 30 credits taken in the freshman year may be taken at the College's Syracuse campus or any other accredited college a student chooses to attend. These are followed by an additional 48 credit hours at the Wanakena campus in the second year of the program. The sophomore year takes place at The Ranger School, where time is equally divided between classroom and laboratory work and experience in the field. Fieldwork is a large component of the curriculum. Students take several short field trips during the second year of study, at no additional expense to them. These trips enhance courses in dendrology, silviculture, forest management, recreation, wildlife, ecology, and surveying. On weekends and evenings, students devote much of their time to studying, but there is time for recreation as well, when students can take advantage of the College's beautiful setting in the Adirondacks.

Transfer Arrangements: Counseling is available for students interested in pursuing a four-year degree on the main campus in Syracuse. Students should contact the ESF admissions office.

Costs

The cost of the first year varies according to the institution attended. Estimated tuition and fees for the 2008–09 academic year at the Wanakena campus total $5675 for residents of New York State and $11,935 for out-of-state residents. Room and board at the Wanakena campus are $9270, and the estimated cost of books, personal expenses, and travel is $3250. (Books and supplies are sold on campus.)

Financial Aid

More than 80 percent of Ranger School students receive some form of financial aid, including grants and scholarships, low-interest loans, and student employment. All students are encouraged to apply for financial aid by completing the Free Application for Federal Student Aid.

Faculty

Five full-time faculty members and 1 part-time instructor teach at the Wanakena campus. The student-faculty ratio is approximately 10:1. Students have ready access to faculty members for consultations. Faculty members are housed on campus, and faculty offices are located near student living quarters. There is close contact between students and faculty members in the classroom and at fieldwork sites.

Student Body Profile

Ninety percent of all students complete the forest technology or land surveying technology program. About 50 percent go on to careers as forest technicians or aides with private companies or government agencies; some 30 percent become surveyors. Many graduates of the forest technology or land surveying technology program go on to receive Bachelor of Science and even graduate-level degrees at ESF's main campus in Syracuse or at other colleges and universities.

Student Activities

Students have a variety of activities available to them at the Wanakena campus. Many recreational activities are readily available, including hiking, camping, canoeing, cross-country skiing, and ice-skating. Students are assigned a canoe for their use during the year. Each class forms a student government, which plans a number of class activities. A new recreational facility is available for student use. Students at The Ranger

School follow the ESF code of student conduct and follow the house rules of the Wanakena campus.

Location

The 2,800-acre campus is situated on the banks of the Oswegatchie River near the Adirondack Mountain hamlet of Wanakena, approximately 65 miles east of Watertown, New York, and 35 miles west of Tupper Lake on New York State's Route 3. At the Wanakena campus, social and recreational activities utilize the area's year-round opportunities for outdoor enjoyment. An excellent hospital, located in Star Lake, New York, serves the community.

Admission Requirements

Students may apply to ESF for admission to The Ranger School's programs during their senior year in high school for guaranteed transfer admission or during their freshman year of college for transfer admission. Prospective students should consult the current catalog for specific information concerning the application process. ESF cooperates with more than fifty colleges in cooperative transfer programs. Acceptance to The Ranger School is contingent upon satisfactory completion of first-year courses. While in high school, applicants should successfully complete a college-preparatory program with an emphasis in mathematics and science. Electives in such areas as computer applications and mechanical drawing are recommended. Transfer students are considered on the basis of college course work and interest in the program. In addition to academic requirements, applicants must be able to meet the physical requirements of the Ranger School program and must submit a full medical report. Parents of applicants under 18 years old should be aware of the field nature of the program and its rigorous study-work regimen.

Application and Information

The Ranger School accepts students for fall admission only. Fall admission decisions are made beginning around the middle of January and continue on a rolling basis until the class is filled. Application forms for New York State residents are available at all high schools in the state and at all colleges in the state university system. Out-of-state students should request application forms from the Office of Undergraduate Admissions. Prospective students who wish to visit the 2,800-acre campus can do so by contacting the Director, New York State Ranger School, Wanakena, New York 13695-0106 (phone: 315-848-2566 or fax: 315-848-3249).

The Admissions Office at the Syracuse campus also serves as the Admissions Office for The Ranger School. Students may request an application or information about course or college selection for the freshman year from the Office of Undergraduate Admissions.

Office of Undergraduate Admissions
106 Bray Hall
State University of New York College of Environmental Science and Forestry
1 Forestry Drive
Syracuse, New York 13210-2779
Phone: 315-470-6600
Fax: 315-470-6933
E-mail: esfinfo@esf.edu
Web site: http://rangerschool.esf.edu

VALLEY FORGE MILITARY COLLEGE

WAYNE, PENNSYLVANIA

The College and Its Mission

Valley Forge Military College – The Military College of Pennsylvania™ (VFMC) is a private, coeducational residential college that offers the freshman and sophomore years of college. The primary mission of the College is to prepare students for transfer to competitive four-year colleges and universities. Established in 1935, the College has a long tradition of fostering personal growth through a comprehensive system built on the five cornerstones that make Valley Forge unique: academic excellence, character development, leadership, personal motivation, and physical development for all students regardless of race, creed, or national origin. The diverse student body represents more than nineteen states and four countries. The College has an excellent transfer record, with 95 percent of cadets accepted to their first- or second-choice schools. More than 63 percent were admitted to the top-tier schools in the country.

Valley Forge Military College is the only college in the northeastern United States that offers qualified freshmen the opportunity to participate in an Early Commissioning Program, leading to a commission as a second lieutenant in the U.S. Army Reserves or Army National Guard at the end of their sophomore year. The U.S. Air Force Academy, the U.S. Coast Guard Academy, the U.S. Military Academy, and the U.S. Naval Academy have all sponsored cadets through their Foundation Scholarship Programs and other programs to attend Valley Forge Military College.

In October 2007, the Pennsylvania House of Representatives adopted a resolution introduced by state Rep. Bryan Lentz, designating Valley Forge Military College as the official military college of the commonwealth of Pennsylvania. For nearly two years, Valley Forge Military College has used the trademarked tagline "The Military College of Pennsylvania™," and now the designation is official. This in no way will change the name of the school; it will remain Valley Forge Military College. This resolution sets in stone what many local citizens, family members, and alumni already know—Valley Forge provides elite military education and training for future leaders in every aspect of society and is in a class of its own.

The College is accredited by the Middle States Association of Colleges and Schools and is approved by the Pennsylvania State Council of Education and the Commission on Higher Education of the Pennsylvania State Department of Education. The College is a member of the National Association of Independent Colleges and Universities, the Association of Independent Colleges/Universities of Pennsylvania, the Pennsylvania Association of Two-Year Colleges, and the Association of Military Colleges and Schools in the United States.

Academic Programs

All students are required to complete an academic program of 60 credits, including a core program of approximately 45 credits designed to establish the essential competencies that are necessary for continued intellectual development and to facilitate the transfer process. Included in the core program are one semester of computer science, two semesters of English, one semester of literature, two semesters of mathematics, one semester of science, and one semester of Western civilization. Qualified cadets must also complete a minimum of two semesters of military science. To satisfy the requirement for the associate degree, cadets must complete at least 15 additional credits in courses related to their selected area of concentration. Associate degrees are awarded upon satisfactory completion of the degree requirements with a quality point average of 2.0 or higher.

Associate Degree Programs: Valley Forge Military College offers concentrations in business, criminal justice, general studies, leadership, and liberal arts, leading to an Associate of Arts degree, as well as concentrations in general studies, life sciences, physical sciences, and pre-engineering, leading to an Associate of Science degree.

Transfer Arrangements: Transfer of academic credits and completion of the baccalaureate degree are facilitated by established relationships with a number of outstanding colleges and universities, including articulation agreements with the neighboring institutions of Cabrini College, Eastern University, and Rosemont College.

Credit for Nontraditional Learning Experiences

Valley Forge Military College may give credit for demonstrated proficiency in areas related to college-level courses. Sources used to determine such proficiency are the College-Level Examination Program (CLEP), Advanced Placement (AP) examinations, Defense Activity for Nontraditional Education Support (DANTES), and the Office of Education Credit and Credentials of the American Council on Education (ACE). All such requests must be approved by the Office of the Dean.

Costs

The annual charge for 2009–10 was $36,890. This charge included haircuts, maintenance, room and board, tuition, uniforms, and other fees. Optional expenses may include fee-based courses, such as aviation, driver's education, membership in the cavalry troop or artillery battery, or scuba. A fee is charged for Health Center confinement over 24 hours' duration. For information on the payment plan, students should contact the Business Office.

Financial Aid

The College offers a combination of merit- and need-based scholarships and grants as well as endowed scholarships based on donor specifications to help VFMC cadets finance their education. The academic scholarships reward incoming and returning cadets for demonstrated academic excellence. Performance scholarships are awarded to eligible cadets who participate in the athletic teams, band, or choir. To qualify for federal, state, and VFMC grants, students must file the Free Application for Federal Student Aid (FAFSA) by the published priority deadlines. In addition, qualified cadets in the advanced ROTC commissioning program are eligible for two-year, full-tuition scholarships. These scholarships are supplemented by assistance for room and board provided by the College. The FAFSA is also required for ROTC scholarship applications.

Valley Forge Military College offers federal student aid to eligible cadets in the form of Federal Pell Grants, Federal Supplemental Educational Opportunity Grants (FSEOG), Federal Work-Study (FWS) Program positions, Federal Stafford Student Loans, and Parent Loans for Undergraduate Students (PLUS) through the Federal Family Education Loan Program. Applicants must file the FAFSA and the VFMC financial aid application for consideration for all student aid.

Faculty

There are 12 full-time and 11 part-time faculty members holding the academic rank of assistant professor, associate professor, instructor, or professor. These faculty members are selected for their professional ability and strong personal leadership qualities; 50 percent of the full-time staff members hold doctorates in their field. Faculty members perform additional duties as advisers and athletic coaches of extracurricular activities. The Military Science Department has 5 active-duty Army officers and 4 noncommissioned officers assigned as full-time faculty members for the ROTC program. The faculty-student ratio is approximately 1:12. Classes are small, and the classroom atmosphere contributes to a harmonious relationship between faculty members and the students.

Student Body Profile

The military structure of Valley Forge provides extraordinary opportunities for cadets to develop and exercise leadership abilities. The Corps of Cadets is a self-administering body organized in nine company units along military lines, with a cadet officer and noncommissioned officer organization for cadet control and administration. The College's cadets are appointed to major command positions in the Corps. The First Captain is generally a sophomore in the College. Cadet leadership and positive peer pressure within this structured setting result in a unique camaraderie among cadets. Cadets, through their student representatives, cooperate with the administration in enforcing regulations regarding student conduct. A Student Advisory Council represents the cadets in the school administration. The Dean's Council meets regularly to discuss aspects of academic life.

Student Activities

The proximity to many colleges and universities ensures a full schedule of local college-oriented events in addition to Valley Forge's own activities. Cadets are encouraged to become involved in community-service activities. The scholarship-supported Regimental Band has performed for U.S. presidents, royalty, and countless military and social events. The Regimental Chorus has performed at the Capitol Building in Washington, D.C.; New York's Carnegie Hall; and the Philadelphia Academy of Music. In addition, eligible students can participate in VFMC honor societies: Alpha Beta Gamma, Lambda Alpha Epsilon, or Phi Theta Kappa. Other available activities include Black Student Union, business and political clubs, flight training, French Club, participation in the local Radnor Fire Company, and Rotoract.

Sports: Athletics and physical well-being are important elements in a Valley Forge education. The aim of the program is to develop alertness, all-around fitness, character, competitive spirit, courage, esprit de corps, leadership, and genuine desire for physical and mental achievement. For students aspiring to compete at the Division I-A or Division I-AA level, Valley Forge's residential college football and basketball programs offer a distinctive opportunity that combines a strong academic transfer program with a highly successful athletic program that has habitually placed players at the national level. Continuing a legacy that began with its high school program, in only eight years, the College has placed 40 players on national-level teams in basketball and football. In the last seven years, the Valley Forge wrestling program has also produced 3 National Champions and 7 All-Americans in the National Collegiate Wrestling Association. Students may also compete at the collegiate level in men's and women's cross-country, men's and women's track and field, lacrosse, soccer, women's basketball, women's softball, women's volleyball, and tennis. Club and interscholastic teams are available in golf, and riflery.

Facilities and Resources

Campus buildings are equipped to meet student needs. A fiber-optic, Internet-capable computer network connects all campus classrooms, dormitory rooms, laboratories, and the library. All rooms are computer accessible and provide access to CadetNET, the institutional local area network. This network provides access to the library and the Internet. College classrooms are located in two buildings and contain biology, chemistry, and physics laboratories. A computer laboratory supports the computer science curriculum and student requirements through a local area network.

Library and Audiovisual Services: The May H. Baker Memorial Library is a learning resource center for independent study and research. The library has more than 100,000 volumes and audiovisual materials, microfilm, and periodicals and houses the Cadet Achievement Center. It provides online database access, membership in the Tri-State Library Consortium, and computer links to ACCESS Pennsylvania and other databases to support the College requirements.

Location

Valley Forge Military College is situated on a beautifully landscaped 120-acre campus in the Main Line community of Wayne, 15 miles west of Philadelphia and close to Valley Forge National Historic Park. Ample opportunities exist for cadets to enjoy cultural and entertainment resources and activities in the Philadelphia area.

Admission Requirements

Admission to the College is based upon review of an applicant's SAT or ACT scores, high school transcript, recommendations from a guidance counselor, and personal interview. Students may be accepted for midyear admission. Minimum requirements for admission on a nonprobation status are a high school diploma or equivalency diploma with a minimum 2.0 average, rank in the upper half of the class, and minimum combined SAT score of 850 or ACT score of 17. The College reviews the new SAT standards and scores on a case-by-case basis. An international student for whom English is a second language must have a minimum score of 550 on the paper-based version of the Test of English as a Foreign Language (TOEFL). Up to 20 percent of an entering class may be admitted on a conditional or probationary status, and individual entrance requirements may be waived by the Dean of the College for students who display a sincere commitment to pursuing a college degree.

Application and Information

Valley Forge Military College follows a program of rolling admissions. Applicants are notified of the admission decision as soon as their files are complete. A nonrefundable registration fee of $25 is required of all applicants.

For application forms and further information, students should contact:

College Admissions Officer
Valley Forge Military College
1001 Eagle Road
Wayne, Pennsylvania 19087
Phone: 800-234-VFMC (toll-free)
E-mail: admissions@vfmac.edu
Web site: http://www.vfmac.edu

On the campus of Valley Forge Military College.

Appendix

2009–10 Changes in Institutions

Following is an alphabetical listing of institutions that have recently closed, merged with other institutions, or changed their name or status. In the case of a name change, the former name appears first, followed by the new name.

Abraham Baldwin Agricultural College (Tifton, GA): now classified as 4-year college.

Allen County Community College (Iola, KS): name changed to Allen Community College.

Allied Medical and Technical Careers (Forty Fort, PA): name changed to Fortis Institute.

American Academy of Dramatic Arts/Hollywood (Hollywood, CA): name changed to American Academy of Dramatic Arts.

Andover College (South Portland, ME): name changed to Kaplan University.

Apollo College–Tucson (Tucson, AZ): name changed to Apollo College–Tucson, Inc..

Appalachian Technical College (Jasper, GA): merged into a single entry for Chattahoochee Technical College (Marietta, GA .

ATI Career Training Center (Miami, FL): no longer degree granting.

Austin Business College (Austin, TX): closed.

Australasian College of Health Sciences (Portland, OR): name changed to American College of Healthcare Sciences.

Beta Tech (Richmond, VA): name changed to Centura College.

Bluegrass Community and Technical College–Cooper Campus (Lexington, KY): name changed to Bluegrass Community and Technical College.

Bohecker's Business College (Ravenna, OH): name changed to Fortis College–Ravenna.

Border Institute of Technology (El Paso, TX): closed.

Briarwood College (Southington, CT): now classified as 4-year college.

Brooks College (Long Beach, CA): closed.

Brooks College (Sunnyvale, CA): closed.

Broward Community College (Fort Lauderdale, FL): name changed to Broward College.

Brown Mackie College–Moline (Moline, IL): name changed to Brown Mackie College–Quad Cities.

Central Florida College (Winter Park, FL): name changed to Fortis College.

Chattanooga State Technical Community College (Chattanooga, TN): name changed to Chattanooga State Community College.

Cincinnati College of Mortuary Science (Cincinnati, OH): now classified as 4-year college.

Cisco Junior College (Cisco, TX): name changed to Cisco College.

Coleman College (San Marcos, CA): name changed to Coleman University.

College of Art Advertising (Cincinnati, OH): closed.

College of Coastal Georgia (Brunswick, GA): now classified as 4-year college.

Columbia College (Yauco, PR): now classified as 4-year college.

The Columbus Culinary Institute (Columbus, OH): name changed to Columbus Culinary Institute at Bradford School.

The Cooking and Hospitality Institute of Chicago (Chicago, IL): name changed to Le Cordon Bleu College of Culinary Arts in Chicago.

Coosa Valley Technical College (Rome, GA): name changed to Georgia Northwestern Technical College.

The Creative Center (Omaha, NE): name changed to Creative Center.

Crownpoint Institute of Technology (Crownpoint, NM): name changed to Navajo Technical College.

Culinary Institute of Virginia (Norfolk, VA): now classified as 4-year college.

Draughons Junior College (Bowling Green, KY): name changed to Daymar College.

Draughons Junior College (Clarksville, TN): now classified as 4-year college.

Draughons Junior College (Nashville, TN): name changed to Daymar Institute.

ECPI College of Technology (Virginia Beach, VA): now classified as 4-year college.

ECPI Technical College (Roanoke, VA): now classified as 4-year college.

Enterprise-Ozark Community College (Enterprise, AL): name changed to Enterprise State Community College.

Fisher College (Boston, MA): now classified as 4-year college.

Florida Community College at Jacksonville (Jacksonville, FL): name changed to Florida State College at Jacksonville.

Florida Culinary Institute (West Palm Beach, FL): now classified as 4-year college.

Florida National College (Hialeah, FL): now classified as 4-year college.

Foundation College (San Diego, CA): closed.

Gibbs College (Norwalk, CT): closed.

Gibbs College (Boston, MA): closed.

Gibbs College (Livingston, NJ): closed.

Globe College (Oakdale, MN): now classified as 4-year college.

Hallmark Institute of Technology (San Antonio, TX): name changed to Hallmark College of Technology.

Hawaii Business College (Honolulu, HI): closed.

Heritage College (Las Vegas, NV): name changed to Kaplan College–Las Vegas Campus.

Heritage College of Hair Design (Oklahoma City, OK): name changed to Heritage College.

Herzing College (Atlanta, GA): now classified as 4-year college.

Herzing College (Madison, WI): now classified as 4-year college.

Hesser College, Concord Campus (Concord, NH): name changed to Hesser College, Concord.

Hesser College, Manchester Campus (Manchester, NH): name changed to Hesser College, Manchester.

Hesser College, Nashua Campus (Nashua, NH): name changed to Hesser College, Nashua.

Hesser College, Portsmouth Campus (Portsmouth, NH): name changed to Hesser College, Portsmouth.

Hesser College, Salem Campus (Salem, NH): name changed to Hesser College, Salem.

Hickey College (St. Louis, MO): now classified as 4-year college.

Holy Cross College (Notre Dame, IN): now classified as 4-year college.

IIA College (Mesa, AZ): now classified as 4-year college.

IIA College (Phoenix, AZ): now classified as 4-year college.

IIA College (Tucson, AZ): now classified as 4-year college.

IIA College (Albuquerque, NM): now classified as 4-year college.

Indiana Business College (Anderson, IN): name changed to Harrison College.

Indiana Business College (Columbus, IN): name changed to Harrison College.

Indiana Business College (Evansville, IN): name changed to Harrison College.

Indiana Business College (Fort Wayne, IN): name changed to Harrison College.

Indiana Business College (Indianapolis, IN): name changed to Harrison College.

Indiana Business College (Indianapolis, IN): name changed to Harrison College.

Indiana Business College (Lafayette, IN): name changed to Harrison College.

Indiana Business College (Marion, IN): closed.

Indiana Business College (Muncie, IN): name changed to Harrison College.

Indiana Business College (Terre Haute, IN): name changed to Harrison College.

Indiana Business College–Medical (Indianapolis, IN): name changed to Harrison College.

Indian River Community College (Fort Pierce, FL): name changed to Indian River State College.

Information Computer Systems Institute (Allentown, PA): name changed to Pennsylvania School of Business.

Interboro Institute (New York, NY): closed.

International Academy of Design & Technology (Pittsburgh, PA): closed.

International Business College (Fort Wayne, IN): now classified as 4-year college.

International College of Hospitality Management (Suffield, CT): name changed to Lincoln College of New England.

International Junior College (Santurce, PR): closed.

Ivy Tech Community College–Whitewater (Richmond, IN): name changed to Ivy Tech Community College–Richmond.

Jefferson Community College (Steubenville, OH): name changed to Eastern Gateway Community College.

Katharine Gibbs School (Melville, NY): closed.

Katharine Gibbs School (New York, NY): closed.

Katharine Gibbs School (Norristown, PA): closed.

Kent State University, Ashtabula Campus (Ashtabula, OH): name changed to Kent State University at Ashtabula.

Kent State University, East Liverpool Campus (East Liverpool, OH): name changed to Kent State University at East Liverpool.

Kent State University, Geauga Campus (Burton, OH): name changed to Kent State University at Geauga.

Kent State University, Salem Campus (Salem, OH): name changed to Kent State University at Salem.

Kent State University, Trumbull Campus (Warren, OH): name changed to Kent State University at Trumbull.

Kent State University, Tuscarawas Campus (New Philadelphia, OH): name changed to Kent State University at Tuscarawas.

Las Vegas College (Las Vegas, NV): merged into Everest College (Henderson, NV).

Lehigh Valley College (Center Valley, PA): closed.

Lewis College of Business (Detroit, MI): no longer accredited by agency recognized by USDE or CHEA.

Louisville Technical Institute (Louisville, KY): name changed to Sullivan College of Technology and Design.

Manatee Community College (Bradenton, FL): name changed to State College of Florida Manatee-Sarasota.

Maria College (Albany, NY): now classified as 4-year college.

Marshall Community and Technical College (Huntington, WV): name changed to Mountwest Community & Technical College.

Marymount College, Palos Verdes, California (Rancho Palos Verdes, CA): now classified as 4-year college.

Metropolitan Community College (Gretna, LA): closed.

Minnesota State Community and Technical College–Fergus Falls (Fergus Falls, MN): name changed to Minnesota State Community and Technical College.

Minot State University–Bottineau Campus (Bottineau, ND): name changed to Dakota College at Bottineau.

National College (Bayamón, PR): now classified as 4-year college.

National Polytechnic College of Engineering and Oceaneering (Wilmington, CA): name changed to National Polytechnic College of Science.

New England College of Finance (Boston, MA): now classified as 4-year college.

New Hampshire Community Technical College, Berlin/Laconia (Berlin, NH): name changed to White Mountains Community College.

New Hampshire Community Technical College, Nashua/Claremont (Nashua, NH): name changed to Nashua Community College.

Northampton County Area Community College (Bethlehem, PA): name changed to Northampton Community College.

Northland Community and Technical College–East Grand Forks (East Grand Forks, MN): merged into a single entry for Northland Community and Technical College–Thief River Falls (Thief River Falls, MN) by request from the institution.

North Metro Technical College (Acworth, GA): merged into a single entry for Chattahoochee Technical College (Marietta, GA) .

Northrop Rice Aviation Institute of Technology (Inglewood, CA): name changed to Crimson Technical College.

Northwestern Technical College (Rock Springs, GA): merged into a single entry for Georgia Northwestern Technical College (Rome, GA).

Ohio Institute of Photography and Technology (Dayton, OH): name changed to Kaplan College, Dayton Campus.

Okaloosa-Walton College (Niceville, FL): name changed to Northwest Florida State College.

Oklahoma State University, Okmulgee (Okmulgee, OK): name changed to Oklahoma State University Institute of Technology.

Palm Beach Community College (Lake Worth, FL): name changed to Palm Beach State College.

Pierce College (Puyallup, WA): name changed to Pierce College at Puyallup.

Pioneer Pacific College (Wilsonville, OR): now classified as 4-year college.

Platt College San Diego (San Diego, CA): now classified as 4-year college.

Polk Community College (Winter Haven, FL): name changed to Polk State College.

Quality College of Culinary Careers (Fresno, CA): closed.

Queen of the Holy Rosary College (Mission San Jose, CA): no longer accredited by agency recognized by USDE or CHEA.

Redstone College–Los Angeles (Inglewood, CA): closed.

RETS Tech Center (Centerville, OH): name changed to Fortis College.

St. Petersburg College (St. Petersburg, FL): now classified as 4-year college.

Saint Vincent Catholic Medical Centers School of Nursing (Fresh Meadows, NY): name changed to St. Paul's School of Nursing.

Santa Fe Community College (Gainesville, FL): now classified as 4-year college.

School of Urban Missions–New Orleans (New Orleans, LA): name changed to School of Urban Missions.

Schuylkill Institute of Business and Technology (Pottsville, PA): closed.

Seminole Community College (Sanford, FL): name changed to Seminole State College of Florida.

Sheridan College–Sheridan and Gillette (Sheridan, WY): name changed to Sheridan College.

Sonoma College (Petaluma, CA): closed.

Sonoma College (San Francisco, CA): closed.

South College (Knoxville, TN): now classified as 4-year college.

Southeastern Business College (Chillicothe, OH): name changed to Daymar College.

Southeastern Business College (Jackson, OH): name changed to Daymar College.

Southeastern Business College (Lancaster, OH): name changed to Daymar College.

Southeastern Business College (New Boston, OH): name changed to Daymar College.

Southeastern Career Institute (Dallas, TX): name changed to Kaplan College, Dallas.

Southeastern Community College, North Campus (West Burlington, IA): name changed to Southeastern Community College.

Southeastern Community College, South Campus (Keokuk, IA): merged into a single entry for Southeastern Community College (West Burlington, IA) by request from the institution

Southern California Institute of Technology (Anaheim, CA): now classified as 4-year college.

Southwest Florida College (Fort Myers, FL): now classified as 4-year college.

Stevens-Henager College (West Haven, UT): now classified as 4-year college.

Swainsboro Technical College (Swainsboro, GA): merged into a single entry for Southeastern Technical College (Vidalia, GA).

Technology Education College (Columbus, OH): closed.

Tidewater Tech (Virginia Beach, VA): name changed to Centura College.

TransPacific Hawaii College (Honolulu, HI): closed.

Triangle Tech, Inc.–Greensburg School (Greensburg, PA): name changed to Triangle Tech–Greensburg School.

Vet Tech Institute at International Business College, Fort Wayne (Fort Wayne, IN): name changed to Vet Tech Institute at International Business College.

Vet Tech Institute at International Business College, Indianapolis (Indianapolis, IN): name changed to Vet Tech Institute at International Business College.

Vet Tech Institute Houston (Houston, TX): name changed to Vet Tech Institute of Houston.

Villa Maria College of Buffalo (Buffalo, NY): now classified as 4-year college.

Virginia College at Huntsville (Huntsville, AL): now classified as 4-year college.

Wentworth Military Academy and Junior College (Lexington, MO): name changed to Wentworth Military Academy and College.

West Central Technical College (Waco, GA): merged into a single entry for West Georgia Technical College (Waco, GA).

Western Nevada Community College (Carson City, NV): name changed to Western Nevada College.

West Virginia State Community and Technical College (Institute, WV): name changed to Kanawha Valley Community and Technical College.

Westwood College–Anaheim (Anaheim, CA): now classified as 4-year college.

Westwood College–Atlanta Midtown (Atlanta, GA): now classified as 4-year college.

Westwood College–Chicago Loop Campus (Chicago, IL): now classified as 4-year college.

Westwood College–Chicago O'Hare Airport (Schiller Park, IL): now classified as 4-year college.

Westwood College–Chicago River Oaks (Calumet City, IL): now classified as 4-year college.

Westwood College–Dallas (Dallas, TX): now classified as 4-year college.

Westwood College–Denver North (Denver, CO): now classified as 4-year college.

Westwood College–Denver South (Denver, CO): now classified as 4-year college.

Westwood College–Fort Worth (Euless, TX): now classified as 4-year college.

Westwood College–Inland Empire (Upland, CA): now classified as 4-year college.

Westwood College–Los Angeles (Los Angeles, CA): now classified as 4-year college.

Westwood College–South Bay Campus (Torrance, CA): now classified as 4-year college.

Winner Institute of Arts & Sciences (Transfer, PA): closed.

Young Harris College (Young Harris, GA): now classified as 4-year college.

Indexes

Associate Degree Programs at Two-Year Colleges

Accounting
Albany Tech Coll (GA)
Alexandria Tech Coll (MN)
Allan Hancock Coll (CA)
Allen Comm Coll (KS)
Alpena Comm Coll (MI)
Alvin Comm Coll (TX)
Amarillo Coll (TX)
Anne Arundel Comm Coll (MD)
Anoka-Ramsey Comm Coll (MN)
Anoka-Ramsey Comm Coll, Cambridge Campus (MN)
Athens Tech Coll (GA)
Atlanta Tech Coll (GA)
Augusta Tech Coll (GA)
Austin Comm Coll (TX)
Bainbridge Coll (GA)
Bakersfield Coll (CA)
Barton County Comm Coll (KS)
Beaufort County Comm Coll (NC)
Berkeley City Coll (CA)
Black Hawk Coll, Moline (IL)
Bronx Comm Coll of the City U of New York (NY)
Brown Mackie Coll–Tucson (AZ)
Bryant & Stratton Coll, Eastlake (OH)
Bryant & Stratton Coll, Parma (OH)
Bryant & Stratton Coll (WI)
Bryant & Stratton Coll - Albany Campus (NY)
Bryant & Stratton Coll - Amherst Campus (NY)
Bryant & Stratton Coll - Buffalo Campus (NY)
Bryant & Stratton Coll - Greece Campus (NY)
Bryant & Stratton Coll - Henrietta Campus (NY)
Bryant & Stratton Coll - North Campus (NY)
Bryant & Stratton Coll - Richmond Campus (VA)
Bryant & Stratton Coll - Southtowns Campus (NY)
Bryant & Stratton Coll - Syracuse Campus (NY)
Bryant & Stratton Coll - Virginia Beach (VA)
Bucks County Comm Coll (PA)
Bunker Hill Comm Coll (MA)
Burlington County Coll (NJ)
Cambridge Career Coll (CA)
Carroll Comm Coll (MD)
Casper Coll (WY)
Central Arizona Coll (AZ)
Central Carolina Comm Coll (NC)
Central Carolina Tech Coll (SC)
Central Comm Coll–Columbus Campus (NE)
Central Comm Coll–Grand Island Campus (NE)
Central Comm Coll–Hastings Campus (NE)
Central Georgia Tech Coll (GA)
Central Lakes Coll (MN)
Central New Mexico Comm Coll (NM)
Central Ohio Tech Coll (OH)
Central Oregon Comm Coll (OR)
Central Piedmont Comm Coll (NC)
Central Wyoming Coll (WY)
Century Coll (MN)
Chattahoochee Tech Coll (GA)
Chattanooga State Comm Coll (TN)
Chipola Coll (FL)
Cincinnati State Tech and Comm Coll (OH)
City Colls of Chicago, Malcolm X College (IL)
City Colls of Chicago, Richard J. Daley College (IL)
Clackamas Comm Coll (OR)
Clarendon Coll (TX)
Clovis Comm Coll (NM)
Coll of DuPage (IL)
Coll of Southern Maryland (MD)
Coll of the Canyons (CA)
Columbus Tech Coll (GA)
Comm Coll of Philadelphia (PA)
Comm Coll of Rhode Island (RI)
Comm Coll of Vermont (VT)
Consolidated School of Business, Lancaster (PA)
Corning Comm Coll (NY)
Cowley County Comm Coll and Area Vocational–Tech School (KS)
Cumberland County Coll (NJ)
Cuyahoga Comm Coll (OH)
Cuyamaca Coll (CA)
Dakota Coll at Bottineau (ND)
Darton Coll (GA)
Davis Coll (OH)
Daytona State Coll (FL)
DeKalb Tech Coll (GA)
Delaware Tech & Comm Coll, Jack F. Owens Campus (DE)
Delaware Tech & Comm Coll, Stanton/Wilmington Campus (DE)
Delaware Tech & Comm Coll, Terry Campus (DE)
Del Mar Coll (TX)
Delta Coll (MI)
Des Moines Area Comm Coll (IA)
Eastern Wyoming Coll (WY)
Eastfield Coll (TX)
East Los Angeles Coll (CA)
Edison State Comm Coll (OH)
El Centro Coll (TX)
Elgin Comm Coll (IL)
El Paso Comm Coll (TX)
Essex County Coll (NJ)
Everett Comm Coll (WA)
Fayetteville Tech Comm Coll (NC)
Finger Lakes Comm Coll (NY)
Fiorello H. LaGuardia Comm Coll of the City U of New York (NY)
Flathead Valley Comm Coll (MT)
Flint River Tech Coll (GA)
Folsom Lake Coll (CA)
Forrest Jr Coll (SC)
Fox Valley Tech Coll (WI)
Frederick Comm Coll (MD)
Fulton-Montgomery Comm Coll (NY)
Gateway Comm Coll (CT)
Genesee Comm Coll (NY)
Georgia Highlands Coll (GA)
Georgia Northwestern Tech Coll (GA)
Glendale Comm Coll (AZ)
Golden West Coll (CA)
Greenfield Comm Coll (MA)
Griffin Tech Coll (GA)
Gwinnett Tech Coll (GA)
Harford Comm Coll (MD)
Harrison Coll, Anderson (IN)
Harrison Coll, Columbus (IN)
Harrison Coll, Elkhart (IN)
Harrison Coll, Evansville (IN)
Harrison Coll, Fort Wayne (IN)
Harrison Coll, Indianapolis (IN)
Harrison Coll, Lafayette (IN)
Harrison Coll, Muncie (IN)
Harrison Coll, Terre Haute (IN)
Harrison Coll (OH)
Hawkeye Comm Coll (IA)
Hesser Coll, Manchester (NH)
Highland Comm Coll (IL)
Highline Comm Coll (WA)
Housatonic Comm Coll (CT)
Houston Comm Coll System (TX)
Howard Coll (TX)
Howard Comm Coll (MD)
Illinois Eastern Comm Colls, Olney Central College (IL)
Illinois Valley Comm Coll (IL)
Indian River State Coll (FL)
Inver Hills Comm Coll (MN)
Iowa Lakes Comm Coll (IA)
Itasca Comm Coll (MN)
Ivy Tech Comm Coll–Lafayette (IN)
James Sprunt Comm Coll (NC)
Jamestown Business Coll (NY)
Jamestown Comm Coll (NY)
Jefferson Comm Coll (NY)
J. F. Drake State Tech Coll (AL)
Johnston Comm Coll (NC)
John Wood Comm Coll (IL)
Kankakee Comm Coll (IL)
Kaplan Career Inst, Harrisburg (PA)
Kaplan Career Inst, ICM Campus (PA)
Kaplan Coll, Merrillville Campus (IN)
Kaplan U, South Portland (ME)
Kaplan U, Cedar Rapids (IA)
Kaplan U, Hagerstown Campus (MD)
Kaplan U, Lincoln (NE)
Kaplan U, Omaha (NE)
Kaskaskia Coll (IL)
Kauai Comm Coll (HI)
Kellogg Comm Coll (MI)
Kent State U at Ashtabula (OH)
Kent State U at East Liverpool (OH)
Kent State U at Tuscarawas (OH)
Kilian Comm Coll (SD)
Kingsborough Comm Coll of the City U of New York (NY)
Kirkwood Comm Coll (IA)
Lac Courte Oreilles Ojibwa Comm Coll (WI)
Lackawanna Coll (PA)
Lakeland Comm Coll (OH)
Lake Michigan Coll (MI)
Lake Region State Coll (ND)
Lanier Tech Coll (GA)
Lansing Comm Coll (MI)
Laramie County Comm Coll (WY)
Lawson State Comm Coll (AL)
LDS Business Coll (UT)
Leeward Comm Coll (HI)
Lewis and Clark Comm Coll (IL)
Linn-Benton Comm Coll (OR)
Lonestar Coll–Cy-Fair (TX)
Lonestar Coll–Kingwood (TX)
Lonestar Coll–North Harris (TX)
Lonestar Coll–Tomball (TX)
Long Island Business Inst (NY)
Lon Morris Coll (TX)
Los Angeles Harbor Coll (CA)
Lower Columbia Coll (WA)
Luna Comm Coll (NM)
Macomb Comm Coll (MI)
Manchester Comm Coll (CT)
Marion Tech Coll (OH)
Massasoit Comm Coll (MA)
Mendocino Coll (CA)
Mercer County Comm Coll (NJ)
Metropolitan Comm Coll (NE)
Metropolitan Comm Coll–Business & Technology Campus (MO)
Metropolitan Comm Coll–Longview (MO)
Metropolitan Comm Coll–Maple Woods (MO)
Metropolitan Comm Coll–Penn Valley (MO)
Middle Georgia Tech Coll (GA)
Middlesex Comm Coll (CT)
Midlands Tech Coll (SC)
Milwaukee Area Tech Coll (WI)
Minnesota State Coll–Southeast Tech (MN)
Minnesota State Comm and Tech Coll (MN)
Minnesota West Comm and Tech Coll (MN)
Missouri State U–West Plains (MO)
Mitchell Tech Inst (SD)
Mohave Comm Coll (AZ)
Montana State U–Great Falls Coll of Technology (MT)
Montcalm Comm Coll (MI)
Montgomery Comm Coll (NC)
Montgomery County Comm Coll (PA)
Moraine Park Tech Coll (WI)
Moultrie Tech Coll (GA)
Mountain Empire Comm Coll (VA)
Muskegon Comm Coll (MI)
Nassau Comm Coll (NY)
New Mexico State U–Carlsbad (NM)
Niagara County Comm Coll (NY)
Nicolet Area Tech Coll (WI)
Northeast Comm Coll (NE)
Northeastern Jr Coll (CO)
Northeast Iowa Comm Coll (IA)
North Hennepin Comm Coll (MN)
North Iowa Area Comm Coll (IA)
North Lake Coll (TX)
Northland Comm and Tech Coll–Thief River Falls (MN)
NorthWest Arkansas Comm Coll (AR)
Northwest Coll (WY)
Northwestern Connecticut Comm Coll (CT)
Northwest Florida State Coll (FL)
Northwest-Shoals Comm Coll (AL)
Northwest Tech Coll (MN)
Ocean County Coll (NJ)
Odessa Coll (TX)
Ogeechee Tech Coll (GA)
Oklahoma City Comm Coll (OK)
Oklahoma State U, Oklahoma City (OK)
Olean Business Inst (NY)
Orangeburg-Calhoun Tech Coll (SC)
Orange Coast Coll (CA)
Ouachita Tech Coll (AR)
Palm Beach State Coll (FL)
Paradise Valley Comm Coll (AZ)
Pasadena City Coll (CA)
Patrick Henry Comm Coll (VA)
Pennsylvania Highlands Comm Coll (PA)
Phoenix Coll (AZ)
Piedmont Comm Coll (NC)
Pima Comm Coll (AZ)
Potomac State Coll of West Virginia U (WV)
Quinsigamond Comm Coll (MA)
Randolph Comm Coll (NC)
Rappahannock Comm Coll (VA)
Raritan Valley Comm Coll (NJ)
Reedley Coll (CA)
Rockingham Comm Coll (NC)
Rockland Comm Coll (NY)
Saint Charles Comm Coll (MO)
St. Cloud Tech Coll (MN)
Saint Paul Coll–A Comm & Tech College (MN)
St. Philip's Coll (TX)
Sandersville Tech Coll (GA)
Sandhills Comm Coll (NC)
San Diego City Coll (CA)
San Diego Mesa Coll (CA)
San Jacinto Coll District (TX)
Savannah Tech Coll (GA)
Scottsdale Comm Coll (AZ)
Seminole State Coll (OK)
Seminole State Coll of Florida (FL)
Shawnee Comm Coll (IL)
Sierra Coll (CA)
Sisseton-Wahpeton Comm Coll (SD)
Snow Coll (UT)
Solex Coll (IL)
Southeastern Comm Coll (IA)
Southeastern Tech Coll (GA)
Southeast Tech Inst (SD)
South Georgia Coll (GA)
South Georgia Tech Coll (GA)
South Plains Coll (TX)
South Puget Sound Comm Coll (WA)
South Suburban Coll (IL)
Southwest Georgia Tech Coll (GA)
Southwest Mississippi Comm Coll (MS)
Southwest Virginia Comm Coll (VA)
Southwest Wisconsin Tech Coll (WI)
Spartanburg Comm Coll (SC)
Spencerian Coll (KY)
Springfield Tech Comm Coll (MA)
Stark State Coll of Technology (OH)
State Coll of Florida Manatee-Sarasota (FL)
State Fair Comm Coll (MO)
State U of New York Coll of Technology at Alfred (NY)
Suffolk County Comm Coll (NY)
Tarrant County Coll District (TX)
Terra State Comm Coll (OH)
Thomas Nelson Comm Coll (VA)
Three Rivers Comm Coll (CT)
Three Rivers Comm Coll (MO)
Tidewater Comm Coll (VA)
Tri-County Comm Coll (NC)
Trident Tech Coll (SC)

Trinity Valley Comm Coll (TX)
Triton Coll (IL)
Tunxis Comm Coll (CT)
Umpqua Comm Coll (OR)
U of Alaska Anchorage, Matanuska-Susitna Coll (AK)
U of Cincinnati Clermont Coll (OH)
U of Pittsburgh at Titusville (PA)
Valdosta Tech Coll (GA)
Victoria Coll (TX)
Vincennes U Jasper Campus (IN)
Waukesha County Tech Coll (WI)
Westchester Comm Coll (NY)
Western Wyoming Comm Coll (WY)
West Georgia Tech Coll (GA)
West Kentucky Comm and Tech Coll (KY)
West Shore Comm Coll (MI)
White Mountains Comm Coll (NH)
Wilson Comm Coll (NC)
Wisconsin Indianhead Tech Coll (WI)
Yavapai Coll (AZ)
York County Comm Coll (ME)

Accounting and Business/Management
Antonelli Coll (OH)
Bradford School (OH)
Bradford School (PA)
Cambridge Career Coll (CA)
Camden County Coll (NJ)
Des Moines Area Comm Coll (IA)
Fox Coll (IL)
Harrisburg Area Comm Coll (PA)
International Business Coll, Indianapolis (IN)
LDS Business Coll (UT)
Lonestar Coll–Montgomery (TX)
Minneapolis Business Coll (MN)
Mountain State Coll (WV)
Oakland Comm Coll (MI)
Spencerian Coll (KY)
Wood Tobe–Coburn School (NY)

Accounting and Computer Science
Glendale Comm Coll (AZ)
State Fair Comm Coll (MO)

Accounting and Finance
Jackson Comm Coll (MI)
Massasoit Comm Coll (MA)

Accounting Related
Davis Coll (OH)
Mountain Empire Comm Coll (VA)
Raritan Valley Comm Coll (NJ)
Southwest Virginia Comm Coll (VA)
Thomas Nelson Comm Coll (VA)

Accounting Technology and Bookkeeping
Alamance Comm Coll (NC)
Allegany Coll of Maryland (MD)
Anoka-Ramsey Comm Coll (MN)
Anoka-Ramsey Comm Coll, Cambridge Campus (MN)
Antonelli Coll, Hattiesburg (MS)
Antonelli Coll, Jackson (MS)
Austin Comm Coll (TX)
Black Hawk Coll, Moline (IL)
Bowling Green State U–Firelands Coll (OH)
Broome Comm Coll (NY)
Brown Mackie Coll–Akron (OH)
Brown Mackie Coll–Albuquerque (NM)
Brown Mackie Coll–Atlanta (GA)
Brown Mackie Coll–Boise (ID)
Brown Mackie Coll–Cincinnati (OH)
Brown Mackie Coll–Findlay (OH)
Brown Mackie Coll–Fort Wayne (IN)
Brown Mackie Coll–Greenville (SC)
Brown Mackie Coll–Hopkinsville (KY)
Brown Mackie Coll–Kansas City (KS)
Brown Mackie Coll–Louisville (KY)
Brown Mackie Coll–Merrillville (IN)
Brown Mackie Coll–Miami (FL)
Brown Mackie Coll–Michigan City (IN)
Brown Mackie Coll–North Canton (OH)
Brown Mackie Coll–Northern Kentucky (KY)
Brown Mackie Coll–Phoenix (AZ)
Brown Mackie Coll–Quad Cities (IL)
Brown Mackie Coll–St. Louis (MO)
Brown Mackie Coll–Salina (KS)
Brown Mackie Coll–South Bend (IN)
Brown Mackie Coll–Tucson (AZ)
Brown Mackie Coll–Tulsa (OK)
Cape Fear Comm Coll (NC)
Casper Coll (WY)
Catawba Valley Comm Coll (NC)
Cecil Coll (MD)
Central Wyoming Coll (WY)
Century Coll (MN)
Chattanooga State Comm Coll (TN)
Clark Coll (WA)
Coll of Lake County (IL)
Coll of Southern Maryland (MD)
Comm Coll of Allegheny County (PA)
The Comm Coll of Baltimore County (MD)
Cuyamaca Coll (CA)
Dakota Coll at Bottineau (ND)
Danville Area Comm Coll (IL)
Delaware County Comm Coll (PA)
Del Mar Coll (TX)
Des Moines Area Comm Coll (IA)
East Central Coll (MO)
Essex County Coll (NJ)
Everest Inst (NY)
Fiorello H. LaGuardia Comm Coll of the City U of New York (NY)
Front Range Comm Coll (CO)
Gadsden State Comm Coll (AL)
Gateway Comm and Tech Coll (KY)
Glendale Comm Coll (AZ)
Goodwin Coll (CT)
Green River Comm Coll (WA)
Guilford Tech Comm Coll (NC)
Harford Comm Coll (MD)
Harrisburg Area Comm Coll (PA)
H. Councill Trenholm State Tech Coll (AL)
Hillsborough Comm Coll (FL)
Holyoke Comm Coll (MA)
Inst of Business & Medical Careers (CO)
Iowa Lakes Comm Coll (IA)
ITT Tech Inst, Norwood (OH)
ITT Tech Inst, Strongsville (OH)
ITT Tech Inst, Austin (TX)
ITT Tech Inst, Richardson (TX)
ITT Tech Inst, San Antonio (TX)
Ivy Tech Comm Coll–Bloomington (IN)
Ivy Tech Comm Coll–Central Indiana (IN)
Ivy Tech Comm Coll–Columbus (IN)
Ivy Tech Comm Coll–East Central (IN)
Ivy Tech Comm Coll–Kokomo (IN)
Ivy Tech Comm Coll–Lafayette (IN)
Ivy Tech Comm Coll–North Central (IN)
Ivy Tech Comm Coll–Northeast (IN)
Ivy Tech Comm Coll–Northwest (IN)
Ivy Tech Comm Coll–Richmond (IN)
Ivy Tech Comm Coll–Southeast (IN)
Ivy Tech Comm Coll–Southern Indiana (IN)
Ivy Tech Comm Coll–Southwest (IN)
Ivy Tech Comm Coll–Wabash Valley (IN)
Jefferson Comm Coll (NY)
Jefferson State Comm Coll (AL)
Johnston Comm Coll (NC)
John Wood Comm Coll (IL)
Kalamazoo Valley Comm Coll (MI)
Kennebec Valley Comm Coll (ME)
Kent State U at Geauga (OH)
Kent State U at Trumbull (OH)
Kilgore Coll (TX)
Lackawanna Coll (PA)
Lake Region State Coll (ND)
LDS Business Coll (UT)
Lehigh Carbon Comm Coll (PA)
Louisiana Tech Coll (LA)
Lower Columbia Coll (WA)
Lurleen B. Wallace Comm Coll (AL)
Metropolitan Comm Coll–Blue River (MO)
Metropolitan Comm Coll–Business & Technology Campus (MO)
Miami Dade Coll (FL)
Minneapolis Comm and Tech Coll (MN)
Minnesota State Coll–Southeast Tech (MN)
Mohawk Valley Comm Coll (NY)
Montana State U–Great Falls Coll of Technology (MT)
Montgomery Coll (MD)
Montgomery County Comm Coll (PA)
Moraine Park Tech Coll (WI)
Nassau Comm Coll (NY)
Northampton Comm Coll (PA)
North Iowa Area Comm Coll (IA)
Northland Pioneer Coll (AZ)
Northwestern Coll (IL)
Oakland Comm Coll (MI)
Olympic Coll (WA)
Owens Comm Coll, Toledo (OH)
Paradise Valley Comm Coll (AZ)
Pasadena City Coll (CA)
Pennsylvania Coll of Technology (PA)
Pensacola Jr Coll (FL)
Pikes Peak Comm Coll (CO)
Plaza Coll (NY)
Polk State Coll (FL)
Pueblo Comm Coll (CO)
Randolph Comm Coll (NC)
Raritan Valley Comm Coll (NJ)
Saint Charles Comm Coll (MO)
Salt Lake Comm Coll (UT)
San Juan Coll (NM)
Southern State Comm Coll (OH)
South Suburban Coll (IL)
Southwestern Comm Coll (IA)
Southwestern Indian Polytechnic Inst (NM)
Southwestern Michigan Coll (MI)
Stanly Comm Coll (NC)
Tallahassee Comm Coll (FL)
Tompkins Cortland Comm Coll (NY)
Ulster County Comm Coll (NY)
Union County Coll (NJ)
The U of Montana–Helena Coll of Technology (MT)
Wayne Comm Coll (NC)
Westmoreland County Comm Coll (PA)
West Virginia Northern Comm Coll (WV)
Wor-Wic Comm Coll (MD)

Acting
Casper Coll (WY)
Central Wyoming Coll (WY)
KD Studio (TX)
Northampton Comm Coll (PA)

Administrative Assistant and Secretarial Science
Alexandria Tech Coll (MN)
Allan Hancock Coll (CA)
Allegany Coll of Maryland (MD)
Allen Comm Coll (KS)
Alpena Comm Coll (MI)
Altamaha Tech Coll (GA)
Alvin Comm Coll (TX)
Amarillo Coll (TX)
Anne Arundel Comm Coll (MD)
Antelope Valley Coll (CA)
Antonelli Coll, Hattiesburg (MS)
Arizona Western Coll (AZ)
Athens Tech Coll (GA)
Augusta Tech Coll (GA)
Austin Comm Coll (TX)
Bainbridge Coll (GA)
Bakersfield Coll (CA)
Barton County Comm Coll (KS)
Beaufort County Comm Coll (NC)
Bevill State Comm Coll (AL)
Black Hawk Coll, Moline (IL)
Bladen Comm Coll (NC)
Bronx Comm Coll of the City U of New York (NY)
Bryant & Stratton Coll, Eastlake (OH)
Bryant & Stratton Coll, Parma (OH)
Bryant & Stratton Coll (WI)
Bryant & Stratton Coll - Albany Campus (NY)
Bryant & Stratton Coll - Amherst Campus (NY)
Bryant & Stratton Coll - Buffalo Campus (NY)
Bryant & Stratton Coll - Greece Campus (NY)
Bryant & Stratton Coll - Henrietta Campus (NY)
Bryant & Stratton Coll - North Campus (NY)
Bryant & Stratton Coll - Richmond Campus (VA)
Bryant & Stratton Coll - Southtowns Campus (NY)
Bryant & Stratton Coll - Syracuse Campus (NY)
Bryant & Stratton Coll - Virginia Beach (VA)
Camden County Coll (NJ)
Carroll Comm Coll (MD)
Carteret Comm Coll (NC)
Casper Coll (WY)
Central Arizona Coll (AZ)
Central Carolina Comm Coll (NC)
Central Carolina Tech Coll (SC)
Central Comm Coll–Columbus Campus (NE)
Central Comm Coll–Grand Island Campus (NE)
Central Comm Coll–Hastings Campus (NE)
Central Georgia Tech Coll (GA)
Central Lakes Coll (MN)
Central New Mexico Comm Coll (NM)
Central Oregon Comm Coll (OR)
Central Piedmont Comm Coll (NC)
Central Texas Coll (TX)
Central Wyoming Coll (WY)
Century Coll (MN)
Chattahoochee Tech Coll (GA)
Chattanooga State Comm Coll (TN)
Cincinnati State Tech and Comm Coll (OH)
City Colls of Chicago, Malcolm X College (IL)
Clackamas Comm Coll (OR)
Cleveland State Comm Coll (TN)
Clovis Comm Coll (NM)
Colby Comm Coll (KS)
Coll of DuPage (IL)
Coll of Lake County (IL)
Coll of the Canyons (CA)
Collin County Comm Coll District (TX)
Columbus Tech Coll (GA)
Comm Coll of Allegheny County (PA)
The Comm Coll of Baltimore County (MD)
Comm Coll of Rhode Island (RI)
Comm Coll of Vermont (VT)
Corning Comm Coll (NY)
County Coll of Morris (NJ)
Cowley County Comm Coll and Area Vocational–Tech School (KS)
Crowder Coll (MO)
Cumberland County Coll (NJ)
Cuyahoga Comm Coll (OH)
Dabney S. Lancaster Comm Coll (VA)
Dakota Coll at Bottineau (ND)
Darton Coll (GA)
Davis Coll (OH)
Daytona State Coll (FL)
DeKalb Tech Coll (GA)
Del Mar Coll (TX)
Delta Coll (MI)
Denmark Tech Coll (SC)
East Central Tech Coll (GA)
Eastern Shore Comm Coll (VA)
Eastern Wyoming Coll (WY)
East Los Angeles Coll (CA)
Edison State Comm Coll (OH)
Elaine P. Nunez Comm Coll (LA)
Elgin Comm Coll (IL)
El Paso Comm Coll (TX)
Erie Comm Coll (NY)
Essex County Coll (NJ)
Everest Inst (NY)
Everett Comm Coll (WA)
Finger Lakes Comm Coll (NY)
Fiorello H. LaGuardia Comm Coll of the City U of New York (NY)
Flathead Valley Comm Coll (MT)
Flint River Tech Coll (GA)
Fox Coll (IL)
Fox Valley Tech Coll (WI)
Fulton-Montgomery Comm Coll (NY)
Gadsden State Comm Coll (AL)
Genesee Comm Coll (NY)
Glendale Comm Coll (AZ)
Golden West Coll (CA)
Grand Rapids Comm Coll (MI)
Greenfield Comm Coll (MA)
Griffin Tech Coll (GA)
Gwinnett Tech Coll (GA)
Harford Comm Coll (MD)
Harrisburg Area Comm Coll (PA)
Harrison Coll, Anderson (IN)
Harrison Coll, Columbus (IN)
Harrison Coll, Elkhart (IN)
Harrison Coll, Evansville (IN)
Harrison Coll, Fort Wayne (IN)
Harrison Coll, Indianapolis (IN)
Harrison Coll, Lafayette (IN)
Harrison Coll, Muncie (IN)
Harrison Coll, Terre Haute (IN)
Harrison Coll (OH)
H. Councill Trenholm State Tech Coll (AL)
Highland Comm Coll (IL)
Highline Comm Coll (WA)
Holyoke Comm Coll (MA)
Hopkinsville Comm Coll (KY)
Housatonic Comm Coll (CT)
Howard Coll (TX)
Howard Comm Coll (MD)
Hutchinson Comm Coll and Area Vocational School (KS)
Illinois Eastern Comm Colls, Frontier Community College (IL)
Illinois Eastern Comm Colls, Olney Central College (IL)
Illinois Eastern Comm Colls, Wabash Valley College (IL)
Illinois Valley Comm Coll (IL)
Indian River State Coll (FL)
Iowa Lakes Comm Coll (IA)
Jackson Comm Coll (MI)
James Sprunt Comm Coll (NC)
Jamestown Business Coll (NY)
Jefferson State Comm Coll (AL)
J. F. Drake State Tech Coll (AL)
Johnston Comm Coll (NC)
John Tyler Comm Coll (VA)
John Wood Comm Coll (IL)
J. Sargeant Reynolds Comm Coll (VA)
Kankakee Comm Coll (IL)
Kaplan U, South Portland (ME)
Kaplan U, Hagerstown Campus (MD)
Kauai Comm Coll (HI)
Kellogg Comm Coll (MI)
Kent State U at Ashtabula (OH)
Kent State U at Salem (OH)
Kent State U at Tuscarawas (OH)
Kingsborough Comm Coll of the City U of New York (NY)
Kirkwood Comm Coll (IA)
Kirtland Comm Coll (MI)
Lac Courte Oreilles Ojibwa Comm Coll (WI)
Lackawanna Coll (PA)
Lakeland Comm Coll (OH)
Lake Michigan Coll (MI)
Lake Region State Coll (ND)
Lanier Tech Coll (GA)
Lansing Comm Coll (MI)
Lawson State Comm Coll (AL)
LDS Business Coll (UT)
Leeward Comm Coll (HI)
Lewis and Clark Comm Coll (IL)
Lincoln Land Comm Coll (IL)
Linn-Benton Comm Coll (OR)
Lonestar Coll–Kingwood (TX)
Lonestar Coll–Montgomery (TX)
Lonestar Coll–North Harris (TX)
Lonestar Coll–Tomball (TX)
Los Angeles Harbor Coll (CA)

Louisiana Tech Coll (LA)
Lower Columbia Coll (WA)
Luna Comm Coll (NM)
Lurleen B. Wallace Comm Coll (AL)
Macomb Comm Coll (MI)
Manchester Comm Coll (CT)
Marion Tech Coll (OH)
Massasoit Comm Coll (MA)
Mendocino Coll (CA)
Mercer County Comm Coll (NJ)
Meridian Comm Coll (MS)
Mesabi Range Comm and Tech Coll (MN)
Metropolitan Comm Coll (NE)
Metropolitan Comm Coll–Blue River (MO)
Metropolitan Comm Coll–Longview (MO)
Metropolitan Comm Coll–Maple Woods (MO)
Metropolitan Comm Coll–Penn Valley (MO)
Miami Dade Coll (FL)
Middle Georgia Tech Coll (GA)
Middlesex Comm Coll (CT)
Midlands Tech Coll (SC)
Mid-Plains Comm Coll, North Platte (NE)
Milwaukee Area Tech Coll (WI)
Minneapolis Comm and Tech Coll (MN)
Minnesota State Coll–Southeast Tech (MN)
Minnesota State Comm and Tech Coll (MN)
Minnesota West Comm and Tech Coll (MN)
Mitchell Tech Inst (SD)
Mohawk Valley Comm Coll (NY)
Montcalm Comm Coll (MI)
Montgomery Comm Coll (NC)
Montgomery County Comm Coll (PA)
Moraine Park Tech Coll (WI)
Moraine Valley Comm Coll (IL)
Moultrie Tech Coll (GA)
Mountain Empire Comm Coll (VA)
Mountain State Coll (WV)
Mt. San Jacinto Coll (CA)
Murray State Coll (OK)
Muskegon Comm Coll (MI)
Nassau Comm Coll (NY)
New Mexico State U–Carlsbad (NM)
Newport Business Inst, Williamsport (PA)
Niagara County Comm Coll (NY)
Nicolet Area Tech Coll (WI)
Northampton Comm Coll (PA)
North Central Texas Coll (TX)
Northeast Comm Coll (NE)
Northeast Iowa Comm Coll (IA)
North Georgia Tech Coll (GA)
North Idaho Coll (ID)
North Iowa Area Comm Coll (IA)
North Lake Coll (TX)
Northland Comm and Tech Coll–Thief River Falls (MN)
Northland Pioneer Coll (AZ)
NorthWest Arkansas Comm Coll (AR)
Northwest Coll (WY)
Northwestern Coll (IL)
Northwestern Connecticut Comm Coll (CT)
Northwest Florida State Coll (FL)
Northwest-Shoals Comm Coll (AL)
Northwest Tech Coll (MN)
Ocean County Coll (NJ)
Odessa Coll (TX)
Ogeechee Tech Coll (GA)
Okefenokee Tech Coll (GA)
Olean Business Inst (NY)
Olympic Coll (WA)
Orangeburg-Calhoun Tech Coll (SC)
Orange Coast Coll (CA)
Otero Jr Coll (CO)
Ouachita Tech Coll (AR)
Palm Beach State Coll (FL)
Paradise Valley Comm Coll (AZ)
Pasadena City Coll (CA)
Patrick Henry Comm Coll (VA)
Pennsylvania Coll of Technology (PA)
Phoenix Coll (AZ)
Pima Comm Coll (AZ)
Plaza Coll (NY)
Potomac State Coll of West Virginia U (WV)
Pulaski Tech Coll (AR)
Quinsigamond Comm Coll (MA)
Randolph Comm Coll (NC)
Rappahannock Comm Coll (VA)
Raritan Valley Comm Coll (NJ)
Reedley Coll (CA)
Reid State Tech Coll (AL)
Rockingham Comm Coll (NC)
Rockland Comm Coll (NY)
Saint Charles Comm Coll (MO)
Saint Paul Coll–A Comm & Tech College (MN)
St. Philip's Coll (TX)
Sandersville Tech Coll (GA)
Sandhills Comm Coll (NC)
San Diego City Coll (CA)
San Diego Mesa Coll (CA)
San Jacinto Coll District (TX)
San Juan Coll (NM)
Savannah Tech Coll (GA)
Scottsdale Comm Coll (AZ)
Seminole State Coll (OK)
Seminole State Coll of Florida (FL)
Shawnee Comm Coll (IL)
Sheridan Coll (WY)
Sierra Coll (CA)
Snow Coll (UT)
Southeastern Comm Coll (IA)
Southeastern Tech Coll (GA)
Southeast Kentucky Comm and Tech Coll (KY)
Southern Union State Comm Coll (AL)
South Georgia Coll (GA)
South Georgia Tech Coll (GA)
South Plains Coll (TX)
South Puget Sound Comm Coll (WA)
Southside Virginia Comm Coll (VA)
Southwest Georgia Tech Coll (GA)
Southwest Mississippi Comm Coll (MS)
Southwest Virginia Comm Coll (VA)
Southwest Wisconsin Tech Coll (WI)
Spartanburg Comm Coll (SC)
Springfield Tech Comm Coll (MA)
Stark State Coll of Technology (OH)
State Coll of Florida Manatee-Sarasota (FL)
Tallahassee Comm Coll (FL)
Tarrant County Coll District (TX)
Temple Coll (TX)
Thomas Nelson Comm Coll (VA)
Three Rivers Comm Coll (CT)
Three Rivers Comm Coll (MO)
Tidewater Comm Coll (VA)
Tompkins Cortland Comm Coll (NY)
Trident Tech Coll (SC)
Tunxis Comm Coll (CT)
Umpqua Comm Coll (OR)
Union County Coll (NJ)
U of Alaska Anchorage, Matanuska-Susitna Coll (AK)
Valdosta Tech Coll (GA)
Victoria Coll (TX)
Victor Valley Coll (CA)
Vincennes U Jasper Campus (IN)
Walters State Comm Coll (TN)
Waukesha County Tech Coll (WI)
Westchester Comm Coll (NY)
Western Wyoming Comm Coll (WY)
West Georgia Tech Coll (GA)
West Virginia Northern Comm Coll (WV)
White Mountains Comm Coll (NH)
Wilson Comm Coll (NC)
Wisconsin Indianhead Tech Coll (WI)
Wor-Wic Comm Coll (MD)
Yavapai Coll (AZ)

Adult Development and Aging
Albany Tech Coll (GA)
Central Georgia Tech Coll (GA)
Comm Coll of Rhode Island (RI)
Dakota Coll at Bottineau (ND)
El Paso Comm Coll (TX)
Fiorello H. LaGuardia Comm Coll of the City U of New York (NY)
Glendale Comm Coll (AZ)
Mt. San Jacinto Coll (CA)

Advertising
Central Piedmont Comm Coll (NC)
Dakota Coll at Bottineau (ND)
Edison State Comm Coll (OH)
Fashion Inst of Technology (NY)
Mohawk Valley Comm Coll (NY)
Muskegon Comm Coll (MI)
Rockland Comm Coll (NY)
St. Cloud Tech Coll (MN)
South Plains Coll (TX)
Southwest Mississippi Comm Coll (MS)
State Coll of Florida Manatee-Sarasota (FL)
Tidewater Comm Coll (VA)

Aeronautical/Aerospace Engineering Technology
Cincinnati State Tech and Comm Coll (OH)
Cumberland County Coll (NJ)
Delaware Tech & Comm Coll, Jack F. Owens Campus (DE)
Pennsylvania Coll of Technology (PA)
Spartan Coll of Aeronautics and Technology (OK)

Aeronautics/Aviation/Aerospace Science and Technology
Alvin Comm Coll (TX)
The Comm Coll of Baltimore County (MD)
Miami Dade Coll (FL)
Montana State U–Great Falls Coll of Technology (MT)
Northland Comm and Tech Coll–Thief River Falls (MN)
Orange Coast Coll (CA)
U of Cincinnati Clermont Coll (OH)

Aerospace, Aeronautical and Astronautical Engineering
Allan Hancock Coll (CA)
Kilgore Coll (TX)
San Jacinto Coll District (TX)

Aesthetician/Esthetician and Skin Care
Olympic Coll (WA)
Saint Paul Coll–A Comm & Tech College (MN)

African American/Black Studies
Bronx Comm Coll of the City U of New York (NY)
Nassau Comm Coll (NY)
Pasadena City Coll (CA)
San Diego City Coll (CA)
San Diego Mesa Coll (CA)
State Coll of Florida Manatee-Sarasota (FL)

Agribusiness
Allan Hancock Coll (CA)
Burlington County Coll (NJ)
Clarendon Coll (TX)
Colby Comm Coll (KS)
Crowder Coll (MO)
Eastern Arizona Coll (AZ)
Eastern Wyoming Coll (WY)
Harrisburg Area Comm Coll (PA)
Iowa Lakes Comm Coll (IA)
James Sprunt Comm Coll (NC)
Laramie County Comm Coll (WY)
Northeast Comm Coll (NE)
Northeast Iowa Comm Coll (IA)
Northwest Coll (WY)
Ogeechee Tech Coll (GA)
The Ohio State U Ag Tech Inst (OH)
Southwestern Comm Coll (IA)
State Fair Comm Coll (MO)
Wayne Comm Coll (NC)
Yavapai Coll (AZ)

Agricultural and Domestic Animals Services Related
Central Wyoming Coll (WY)

Agricultural and Food Products Processing
Northeast Iowa Comm Coll (IA)

Agricultural Business and Management
Arizona Western Coll (AZ)
Bakersfield Coll (CA)
Barton County Comm Coll (KS)
Black Hawk Coll, Moline (IL)
Casper Coll (WY)
Central Arizona Coll (AZ)
Central Comm Coll–Columbus Campus (NE)
Central Comm Coll–Hastings Campus (NE)
Central Wyoming Coll (WY)
Colby Comm Coll (KS)
County Coll of Morris (NJ)
Danville Area Comm Coll (IL)
Delaware Tech & Comm Coll, Jack F. Owens Campus (DE)
Delaware Tech & Comm Coll, Stanton/Wilmington Campus (DE)
Delaware Tech & Comm Coll, Terry Campus (DE)
Fox Valley Tech Coll (WI)
Highland Comm Coll (IL)
Illinois Eastern Comm Colls, Wabash Valley College (IL)
Illinois Valley Comm Coll (IL)
Indian River State Coll (FL)
Iowa Lakes Comm Coll (IA)
Jefferson State Comm Coll (AL)
John Wood Comm Coll (IL)
J. Sargeant Reynolds Comm Coll (VA)
Kirkwood Comm Coll (IA)
Lake Region State Coll (ND)
Linn-Benton Comm Coll (OR)
Lonestar Coll–Cy-Fair (TX)
Mitchell Tech Inst (SD)
Nebraska Coll of Tech Agriculture (NE)
Northeastern Jr Coll (CO)
Northwest Coll (WY)
The Ohio State U Ag Tech Inst (OH)
Otero Jr Coll (CO)
Owens Comm Coll, Toledo (OH)
Potomac State Coll of West Virginia U (WV)
Reedley Coll (CA)
San Juan Coll (NM)
Santa Rosa Jr Coll (CA)
Shawnee Comm Coll (IL)
Sheridan Coll (WY)
Snow Coll (UT)
Southeastern Comm Coll (IA)
South Georgia Coll (GA)
State U of New York Coll of Technology at Alfred (NY)
Terra State Comm Coll (OH)
Three Rivers Comm Coll (MO)
Walters State Comm Coll (TN)
Yavapai Coll (AZ)

Agricultural Business and Management Related
Iowa Lakes Comm Coll (IA)
Penn State Beaver (PA)
Penn State Brandywine (PA)
Penn State DuBois (PA)
Penn State Fayette, The Eberly Campus (PA)
Penn State Greater Allegheny (PA)
Penn State Hazleton (PA)
Penn State Lehigh Valley (PA)
Penn State Mont Alto (PA)
Penn State New Kensington (PA)
Penn State Schuylkill (PA)
Penn State Shenango (PA)
Penn State Wilkes-Barre (PA)
Penn State Worthington Scranton (PA)
Penn State York (PA)

Agricultural Business Technology
Blue Ridge Comm Coll (NC)
Iowa Lakes Comm Coll (IA)
Laramie County Comm Coll (WY)
The Ohio State U Ag Tech Inst (OH)

Agricultural Communication/Journalism
Northwest Coll (WY)
The Ohio State U Ag Tech Inst (OH)

Agricultural Economics
Clarendon Coll (TX)
Eastern Wyoming Coll (WY)
Iowa Lakes Comm Coll (IA)
Northeastern Jr Coll (CO)
The Ohio State U Ag Tech Inst (OH)
Potomac State Coll of West Virginia U (WV)
South Plains Coll (TX)

Agricultural/Farm Supplies Retailing and Wholesaling
Des Moines Area Comm Coll (IA)
Hawkeye Comm Coll (IA)
Iowa Lakes Comm Coll (IA)
Kirkwood Comm Coll (IA)
Southwest Wisconsin Tech Coll (WI)

Agricultural Mechanics and Equipment Technology
Black Hawk Coll, Moline (IL)
Central Arizona Coll (AZ)
Iowa Lakes Comm Coll (IA)
Northeast Comm Coll (NE)
Rend Lake Coll (IL)

Agricultural Mechanization
Highland Comm Coll (IL)
Hutchinson Comm Coll and Area Vocational School (KS)
Iowa Lakes Comm Coll (IA)
Metropolitan Comm Coll–Longview (MO)
North Central Texas Coll (TX)
Northeast Comm Coll (NE)
Northeastern Jr Coll (CO)
The Ohio State U Ag Tech Inst (OH)
Owens Comm Coll, Toledo (OH)
Paris Jr Coll (TX)
Potomac State Coll of West Virginia U (WV)
Rend Lake Coll (IL)
Santa Rosa Jr Coll (CA)
Southwest Georgia Tech Coll (GA)
Three Rivers Comm Coll (MO)

Agricultural Mechanization Related
Reedley Coll (CA)

Agricultural Power Machinery Operation
Guilford Tech Comm Coll (NC)
Hawkeye Comm Coll (IA)
Iowa Lakes Comm Coll (IA)
Kirkwood Comm Coll (IA)
Northeast Iowa Comm Coll (IA)
The Ohio State U Ag Tech Inst (OH)

Agricultural Production
Allen Comm Coll (KS)
Black Hawk Coll, Moline (IL)
Delaware Tech & Comm Coll, Jack F. Owens Campus (DE)
Hopkinsville Comm Coll (KY)
Illinois Eastern Comm Colls, Wabash Valley College (IL)
Iowa Lakes Comm Coll (IA)
John Wood Comm Coll (IL)
Kirkwood Comm Coll (IA)
Laramie County Comm Coll (WY)
Lincoln Land Comm Coll (IL)
Mitchell Tech Inst (SD)
Nebraska Coll of Tech Agriculture (NE)
Northeast Iowa Comm Coll (IA)
North Iowa Area Comm Coll (IA)
Northwest Coll (WY)
Rend Lake Coll (IL)
Southern State Comm Coll (OH)
Wayne Comm Coll (NC)

Agricultural Production Related
Iowa Lakes Comm Coll (IA)

Agricultural Teacher Education
Colby Comm Coll (KS)
Eastern Wyoming Coll (WY)
Iowa Lakes Comm Coll (IA)
Linn-Benton Comm Coll (OR)
Murray State Coll (OK)
Northeastern Jr Coll (CO)
Northwest Coll (WY)
The Ohio State U Ag Tech Inst (OH)
Potomac State Coll of West Virginia U (WV)
South Georgia Coll (GA)
Trinity Valley Comm Coll (TX)
Victor Valley Coll (CA)

Agriculture
Arizona Western Coll (AZ)
Arkansas State U–Beebe (AR)
Bainbridge Coll (GA)
Bakersfield Coll (CA)
Barton County Comm Coll (KS)
Casper Coll (WY)
Central Arizona Coll (AZ)
Central New Mexico Comm Coll (NM)
Central Texas Coll (TX)
Chipola Coll (FL)
Clarendon Coll (TX)
Cowley County Comm Coll and Area Vocational–Tech School (KS)
Crowder Coll (MO)
Dakota Coll at Bottineau (ND)
Darton Coll (GA)
Eastern Arizona Coll (AZ)
Eastern Wyoming Coll (WY)
Georgia Highlands Coll (GA)
Howard Coll (TX)
Hutchinson Comm Coll and Area Vocational School (KS)
Illinois Valley Comm Coll (IL)
Iowa Lakes Comm Coll (IA)
Jackson State Comm Coll (TN)
Kankakee Comm Coll (IL)
Kilgore Coll (TX)
Kirkwood Comm Coll (IA)
Lac Courte Oreilles Ojibwa Comm Coll (WI)
Laramie County Comm Coll (WY)
Linn-Benton Comm Coll (OR)
Macomb Comm Coll (MI)
Mendocino Coll (CA)
Miami Dade Coll (FL)
Missouri State U–West Plains (MO)
Murray State Coll (OK)
Northeast Comm Coll (NE)
Northeastern Jr Coll (CO)
North Idaho Coll (ID)
Northland Pioneer Coll (AZ)
Odessa Coll (TX)
Owensboro Comm and Tech Coll (KY)
Potomac State Coll of West Virginia U (WV)
Reedley Coll (CA)
Santa Rosa Jr Coll (CA)
Shawnee Comm Coll (IL)
Sheridan Coll (WY)
Sierra Coll (CA)
Snow Coll (UT)
South Georgia Coll (GA)
South Plains Coll (TX)
State U of New York Coll of Technology at Alfred (NY)
Umpqua Comm Coll (OR)
Yavapai Coll (AZ)

Agriculture and Agriculture Operations Related
Northeast Comm Coll (NE)
Potomac State Coll of West Virginia U (WV)
Sheridan Coll (WY)

Agronomy and Crop Science
Chipola Coll (FL)
Colby Comm Coll (KS)
Iowa Lakes Comm Coll (IA)
Northeast Comm Coll (NE)
Northeastern Jr Coll (CO)
The Ohio State U Ag Tech Inst (OH)
Potomac State Coll of West Virginia U (WV)
Shawnee Comm Coll (IL)
Southeastern Comm Coll (IA)
Southern Maine Comm Coll (ME)
South Plains Coll (TX)

Aircraft Powerplant Technology
Antelope Valley Coll (CA)
Central Texas Coll (TX)
Hallmark Inst of Aeronautics (TX)
Linn State Tech Coll (MO)
Louisiana Tech Coll (LA)
Minneapolis Comm and Tech Coll (MN)
Pennsylvania Coll of Technology (PA)
Pima Comm Coll (AZ)
Pulaski Tech Coll (AR)
St. Philip's Coll (TX)
Somerset Comm Coll (KY)

Airframe Mechanics and Aircraft Maintenance Technology
Amarillo Coll (TX)
Antelope Valley Coll (CA)
Hallmark Inst of Aeronautics (TX)
Ivy Tech Comm Coll–Wabash Valley (IN)
Linn State Tech Coll (MO)
Middle Georgia Tech Coll (GA)
Minneapolis Comm and Tech Coll (MN)
Mohawk Valley Comm Coll (NY)
Oklahoma City Comm Coll (OK)
St. Philip's Coll (TX)
Trident Tech Coll (SC)
The U of Montana–Helena Coll of Technology (MT)

Airline Flight Attendant
Mercer County Comm Coll (NJ)

Airline Pilot and Flight Crew
Casper Coll (WY)
Central Oregon Comm Coll (OR)
Central Texas Coll (TX)
Comm Coll of Allegheny County (PA)
County Coll of Morris (NJ)
Fox Valley Tech Coll (WI)
Green River Comm Coll (WA)
Guilford Tech Comm Coll (NC)
Indian River State Coll (FL)
Iowa Lakes Comm Coll (IA)
Jackson Comm Coll (MI)
Jamestown Comm Coll (NY)
Lansing Comm Coll (MI)
Lehigh Carbon Comm Coll (PA)
Mercer County Comm Coll (NJ)
Miami Dade Coll (FL)
Montana State U–Great Falls Coll of Technology (MT)
Orange Coast Coll (CA)
Palm Beach State Coll (FL)
Pulaski Tech Coll (AR)
Salt Lake Comm Coll (UT)
San Jacinto Coll District (TX)
San Juan Coll (NM)
Spartan Coll of Aeronautics and Technology (OK)

Air Traffic Control
Green River Comm Coll (WA)
Miami Dade Coll (FL)
Minneapolis Comm and Tech Coll (MN)

Air Transportation Related
Lehigh Carbon Comm Coll (PA)

Allied Health and Medical Assisting Services Related
Antonelli Coll, Hattiesburg (MS)
Cincinnati State Tech and Comm Coll (OH)
Everest Inst (NY)
Milwaukee Area Tech Coll (WI)
Mount Wachusett Comm Coll (MA)
Ocean County Coll (NJ)
Pennsylvania Inst of Technology (PA)
Plaza Coll (NY)

Allied Health Diagnostic, Intervention, and Treatment Professions Related
Catawba Valley Comm Coll (NC)
Harcum Coll (PA)
Ivy Tech Comm Coll–Wabash Valley (IN)
Kent State U at Salem (OH)
Milwaukee Area Tech Coll (WI)
Minneapolis Comm and Tech Coll (MN)
Pennsylvania Coll of Technology (PA)
Union County Coll (NJ)

Alternative and Complementary Medical Support Services Related
Anoka-Ramsey Comm Coll (MN)
Anoka-Ramsey Comm Coll, Cambridge Campus (MN)
Mount Wachusett Comm Coll (MA)

Alternative and Complementary Medicine Related
Quinsigamond Comm Coll (MA)

American Government and Politics
Oklahoma City Comm Coll (OK)
State Coll of Florida Manatee-Sarasota (FL)

American Indian/Native American Studies
Central Wyoming Coll (WY)
Itasca Comm Coll (MN)
Lac Courte Oreilles Ojibwa Comm Coll (WI)
North Idaho Coll (ID)
Pima Comm Coll (AZ)
Sisseton-Wahpeton Comm Coll (SD)

American Sign Language (ASL)
Burlington County Coll (NJ)
Oklahoma State U, Oklahoma City (OK)
Sierra Coll (CA)

American Studies
Anne Arundel Comm Coll (MD)
Bucks County Comm Coll (PA)
Greenfield Comm Coll (MA)
Miami Dade Coll (FL)
State Coll of Florida Manatee-Sarasota (FL)

Anatomy
Northeastern Jr Coll (CO)

Anesthesiologist Assistant
Milwaukee Area Tech Coll (WI)

Animal Health
Front Range Comm Coll (CO)

Animal/Livestock Husbandry and Production
Hawkeye Comm Coll (IA)
Hopkinsville Comm Coll (KY)
Iowa Lakes Comm Coll (IA)
Jefferson Comm Coll (NY)
John Wood Comm Coll (IL)
North Central Texas Coll (TX)
The Ohio State U Ag Tech Inst (OH)
Sierra Coll (CA)

Animal Sciences
Alamance Comm Coll (NC)
Arkansas State U–Beebe (AR)
Bakersfield Coll (CA)
Casper Coll (WY)
Eastern Wyoming Coll (WY)
Harcum Coll (PA)
Iowa Lakes Comm Coll (IA)
James Sprunt Comm Coll (NC)
Linn-Benton Comm Coll (OR)
Murray State Coll (OK)
Niagara County Comm Coll (NY)
Northeast Comm Coll (NE)
Northeastern Jr Coll (CO)
Northwest Coll (WY)
The Ohio State U Ag Tech Inst (OH)
Potomac State Coll of West Virginia U (WV)
Reedley Coll (CA)
Santa Rosa Jr Coll (CA)
Shawnee Comm Coll (IL)
Snow Coll (UT)
South Georgia Coll (GA)
State U of New York Coll of Technology at Alfred (NY)
Trinity Valley Comm Coll (TX)

Animal Sciences Related
Pensacola Jr Coll (FL)

Animation, Interactive Technology, Video Graphics and Special Effects
The Art Inst of Seattle (WA)
Austin Comm Coll (TX)
Burlington County Coll (NJ)
Coll of the Canyons (CA)
Collin County Comm Coll District (TX)
Delaware County Comm Coll (PA)
Elgin Comm Coll (IL)
Finger Lakes Comm Coll (NY)
Front Range Comm Coll (CO)
Houston Comm Coll System (TX)
Kalamazoo Valley Comm Coll (MI)
Kent State U at Tuscarawas (OH)
Lehigh Carbon Comm Coll (PA)
Lonestar Coll–Montgomery (TX)
Lonestar Coll–North Harris (TX)
Lonestar Coll–Tomball (TX)
Montgomery Coll (MD)
Olympic Coll (WA)
Pasadena City Coll (CA)
Pikes Peak Comm Coll (CO)
Pima Comm Coll (AZ)
Pueblo Comm Coll (CO)
Raritan Valley Comm Coll (NJ)
Red Rocks Comm Coll (CO)
Saint Paul Coll–A Comm & Tech College (MN)
Southeast Tech Inst (SD)
Springfield Tech Comm Coll (MA)
State U of New York Coll of Technology at Alfred (NY)
Sullivan Coll of Technology and Design (KY)
Terra State Comm Coll (OH)
Union County Coll (NJ)

Anthropology
Austin Comm Coll (TX)
Bakersfield Coll (CA)
Barton County Comm Coll (KS)
Casper Coll (WY)
Darton Coll (GA)
Delaware County Comm Coll (PA)
Eastern Arizona Coll (AZ)
East Los Angeles Coll (CA)
Everett Comm Coll (WA)
Gainesville State Coll (GA)
Indian River State Coll (FL)
Laramie County Comm Coll (WY)
Lonestar Coll–Cy-Fair (TX)
Lonestar Coll–Montgomery (TX)
Lonestar Coll–North Harris (TX)
Miami Dade Coll (FL)
Muskegon Comm Coll (MI)
North Idaho Coll (ID)
Northwest Coll (WY)
Orange Coast Coll (CA)
Pasadena City Coll (CA)
Pima Comm Coll (AZ)
San Diego City Coll (CA)
Santa Rosa Jr Coll (CA)
Triton Coll (IL)
Umpqua Comm Coll (OR)
Western Wyoming Comm Coll (WY)

Apparel and Accessories Marketing
Des Moines Area Comm Coll (IA)
El Centro Coll (TX)
FIDM/The Fashion Inst of Design & Merchandising, Los Angeles Campus (CA)
FIDM/The Fashion Inst of Design & Merchandising, San Diego Campus (CA)
FIDM/The Fashion Inst of Design & Merchandising, San Francisco Campus (CA)
Kirkwood Comm Coll (IA)
Milwaukee Area Tech Coll (WI)

Apparel and Textile Manufacturing
Fashion Inst of Technology (NY)
Sierra Coll (CA)

Apparel and Textile Marketing Management
Sierra Coll (CA)

Apparel and Textiles
Antelope Valley Coll (CA)
Fashion Inst of Technology (NY)
FIDM/The Fashion Inst of Design & Merchandising, Los Angeles Campus (CA)
FIDM/The Fashion Inst of Design & Merchandising, San Francisco Campus (CA)
Indian River State Coll (FL)
Northland Pioneer Coll (AZ)
Palm Beach State Coll (FL)

Appliance Installation and Repair Technology
Mitchell Tech Inst (SD)

Applied Art
Allan Hancock Coll (CA)
Anne Arundel Comm Coll (MD)
Central Piedmont Comm Coll (NC)
Del Mar Coll (TX)
Howard Comm Coll (MD)
Iowa Lakes Comm Coll (IA)
Kingsborough Comm Coll of the City U of New York (NY)
Lon Morris Coll (TX)
Muskegon Comm Coll (MI)
Odessa Coll (TX)
Oklahoma City Comm Coll (OK)
Pennsylvania Coll of Technology (PA)
Rockland Comm Coll (NY)
Tunxis Comm Coll (CT)
Westchester Comm Coll (NY)

Applied Horticulture
Alamance Comm Coll (NC)
Black Hawk Coll, Moline (IL)
Blue Ridge Comm Coll (NC)
Catawba Valley Comm Coll (NC)
Central Comm Coll–Hastings Campus (NE)
Central Lakes Coll (MN)
Clackamas Comm Coll (OR)
Clark Coll (WA)
Comm Coll of Allegheny County (PA)
The Comm Coll of Baltimore County (MD)
Dakota Coll at Bottineau (ND)
Delaware Tech & Comm Coll, Jack F. Owens Campus (DE)
Fayetteville Tech Comm Coll (NC)
Front Range Comm Coll (CO)
Harford Comm Coll (MD)
Hawkeye Comm Coll (IA)
Houston Comm Coll System (TX)
John Wood Comm Coll (IL)
Kankakee Comm Coll (IL)
Kent State U at Geauga (OH)
Kent State U at Salem (OH)
Montgomery Coll (MD)
Nebraska Coll of Tech Agriculture (NE)
Northeast Comm Coll (NE)
Pennsylvania Coll of Technology (PA)
Rend Lake Coll (IL)
Sierra Coll (CA)
Southeast Tech Inst (SD)
Southern Maine Comm Coll (ME)
Spartanburg Comm Coll (SC)
State Fair Comm Coll (MO)
Westmoreland County Comm Coll (PA)

Applied Horticulture/Horticultural Business Services Related
Cincinnati State Tech and Comm Coll (OH)
Dakota Coll at Bottineau (ND)
Des Moines Area Comm Coll (IA)
Kirkwood Comm Coll (IA)
Northeast Comm Coll (NE)
Pennsylvania Coll of Technology (PA)

Applied Mathematics
Muskegon Comm Coll (MI)
Northeastern Jr Coll (CO)
South Georgia Coll (GA)

Aquaculture
Hillsborough Comm Coll (FL)
Yavapai Coll (AZ)

Archeology
Northwest Coll (WY)
Western Wyoming Comm Coll (WY)

Architectural Drafting and CAD/CADD
Brown Mackie Coll–Albuquerque (NM)
Carroll Comm Coll (MD)
Central New Mexico Comm Coll (NM)
Clackamas Comm Coll (OR)
Coll of Lake County (IL)
Coll of the Canyons (CA)
Comm Coll of Allegheny County (PA)
The Comm Coll of Baltimore County (MD)
Des Moines Area Comm Coll (IA)
Glendale Comm Coll (AZ)
Hawkeye Comm Coll (IA)
Hennepin Tech Coll (MN)
Indian River State Coll (FL)
Island Drafting and Tech Inst (NY)
Kaskaskia Coll (IL)
Kirkwood Comm Coll (IA)
Lincoln Land Comm Coll (IL)
Macomb Comm Coll (MI)
Miami Dade Coll (FL)
Minnesota State Comm and Tech Coll (MN)
Mitchell Tech Inst (SD)
Montgomery Coll (MD)

Montgomery County Comm Coll (PA)
New Mexico State U–Carlsbad (NM)
Northeast Comm Coll (NE)
Northwest Tech Inst (MN)
Owens Comm Coll, Toledo (OH)
Pima Comm Coll (AZ)
Rend Lake Coll (IL)
St. Cloud Tech Coll (MN)
Sierra Coll (CA)
Southern Maine Comm Coll (ME)
South Suburban Coll (IL)
Sullivan Coll of Technology and Design (KY)
Triangle Tech, Inc.–Erie School (PA)
Triton Coll (IL)
Waukesha County Tech Coll (WI)
Westmoreland County Comm Coll (PA)
Westwood Coll–Houston South Campus (TX)
Yavapai Coll (AZ)

Architectural Engineering Technology
Allan Hancock Coll (CA)
Amarillo Coll (TX)
Anne Arundel Comm Coll (MD)
Bakersfield Coll (CA)
Cape Fear Comm Coll (NC)
Catawba Valley Comm Coll (NC)
Central Piedmont Comm Coll (NC)
Cincinnati State Tech and Comm Coll (OH)
City Colls of Chicago, Richard J. Daley College (IL)
Comm Coll of Philadelphia (PA)
Daytona State Coll (FL)
Delaware County Comm Coll (PA)
Delaware Tech & Comm Coll, Jack F. Owens Campus (DE)
Delaware Tech & Comm Coll, Stanton/Wilmington Campus (DE)
Delaware Tech & Comm Coll, Terry Campus (DE)
Del Mar Coll (TX)
Delta Coll (MI)
East Los Angeles Coll (CA)
Erie Comm Coll, South Campus (NY)
Essex County Coll (NJ)
Fayetteville Tech Comm Coll (NC)
Finger Lakes Comm Coll (NY)
Front Range Comm Coll (CO)
Golden West Coll (CA)
Grand Rapids Comm Coll (MI)
Guilford Tech Comm Coll (NC)
Harrisburg Area Comm Coll (PA)
Hillsborough Comm Coll (FL)
Honolulu Comm Coll (HI)
John Tyler Comm Coll (VA)
Lansing Comm Coll (MI)
Los Angeles Harbor Coll (CA)
Massasoit Comm Coll (MA)
Mercer County Comm Coll (NJ)
Metropolitan Comm Coll (NE)
Miami Dade Coll (FL)
Midlands Tech Coll (SC)
Milwaukee Area Tech Coll (WI)
Mountain Empire Comm Coll (VA)
Northampton Comm Coll (PA)
Northland Comm and Tech Coll–Thief River Falls (MN)
Oakland Comm Coll (MI)
Oklahoma State U, Oklahoma City (OK)
Orange Coast Coll (CA)
Owens Comm Coll, Toledo (OH)
Penn State Fayette, The Eberly Campus (PA)
Penn State Worthington Scranton (PA)
Pennsylvania Coll of Technology (PA)
Pennsylvania Inst of Technology (PA)
Phoenix Coll (AZ)
Pikes Peak Comm Coll (CO)
Salt Lake Comm Coll (UT)
Sandhills Comm Coll (NC)
San Diego Mesa Coll (CA)
Seminole State Coll of Florida (FL)
Southeast Tech Inst (SD)
Southern Maine Comm Coll (ME)
Springfield Tech Comm Coll (MA)
Stark State Coll of Technology (OH)
State U of New York Coll of Technology at Alfred (NY)
Sullivan Coll of Technology and Design (KY)
Tarrant County Coll District (TX)
Terra State Comm Coll (OH)
Three Rivers Comm Coll (CT)
U of Alaska Anchorage, Matanuska-Susitna Coll (AK)
Wisconsin Indianhead Tech Coll (WI)

Architecture
Allen Comm Coll (KS)
Barton County Comm Coll (KS)
Clarendon Coll (TX)
Harrisburg Area Comm Coll (PA)
Howard Comm Coll (MD)
Kilgore Coll (TX)
Lonestar Coll–Cy-Fair (TX)
Lonestar Coll–Kingwood (TX)
Lonestar Coll–Montgomery (TX)
Lonestar Coll–North Harris (TX)
Pasadena City Coll (CA)
San Diego Mesa Coll (CA)
Santa Rosa Jr Coll (CA)

Architecture Related
Santa Rosa Jr Coll (CA)
Sullivan Coll of Technology and Design (KY)

Area, Ethnic, Cultural, and Gender Studies Related
New Mexico State U–Carlsbad (NM)

Area Studies Related
Central Wyoming Coll (WY)
Oklahoma City Comm Coll (OK)

Army ROTC/Military Science
Georgia Military Coll (GA)

Art
Allan Hancock Coll (CA)
Allen Comm Coll (KS)
Alvin Comm Coll (TX)
Amarillo Coll (TX)
Anne Arundel Comm Coll (MD)
Arizona Western Coll (AZ)
Austin Comm Coll (TX)
Bainbridge Coll (GA)
Bakersfield Coll (CA)
Barton County Comm Coll (KS)
Berkeley City Coll (CA)
Bronx Comm Coll of the City U of New York (NY)
Bucks County Comm Coll (PA)
Bunker Hill Comm Coll (MA)
Burlington County Coll (NJ)
Carroll Comm Coll (MD)
Casper Coll (WY)
Central New Mexico Comm Coll (NM)
Central Oregon Comm Coll (OR)
Central Piedmont Comm Coll (NC)
Central Wyoming Coll (WY)
Chipola Coll (FL)
City Colls of Chicago, Malcolm X College (IL)
Clarendon Coll (TX)
Coll of Lake County (IL)
Coll of the Canyons (CA)
Comm Coll of Allegheny County (PA)
Comm Coll of Philadelphia (PA)
Comm Coll of Rhode Island (RI)
Comm Coll of Vermont (VT)
Cowley County Comm Coll and Area Vocational–Tech School (KS)
Crowder Coll (MO)
Darton Coll (GA)
Del Mar Coll (TX)
Delta Coll (MI)
Douglas Education Center (PA)
Eastern Arizona Coll (AZ)
Eastern Wyoming Coll (WY)
East Los Angeles Coll (CA)
Edison State Comm Coll (OH)
Essex County Coll (NJ)
Folsom Lake Coll (CA)
Frederick Comm Coll (MD)
Fulton-Montgomery Comm Coll (NY)
Georgia Highlands Coll (GA)
Golden West Coll (CA)
Grand Rapids Comm Coll (MI)
Greenfield Comm Coll (MA)
Harrisburg Area Comm Coll (PA)
Highland Comm Coll (IL)
Highline Comm Coll (WA)
Holyoke Comm Coll (MA)
Housatonic Comm Coll (CT)
Howard Coll (TX)
Howard Comm Coll (MD)
Iowa Lakes Comm Coll (IA)
Kilgore Coll (TX)
Kingsborough Comm Coll of the City U of New York (NY)
Kirtland Comm Coll (MI)
Lake Michigan Coll (MI)
Lansing Comm Coll (MI)
Laramie County Comm Coll (WY)
Lehigh Carbon Comm Coll (PA)
Lewis and Clark Comm Coll (IL)
Lincoln Land Comm Coll (IL)
Linn-Benton Comm Coll (OR)
Lonestar Coll–Cy-Fair (TX)
Lonestar Coll–Kingwood (TX)
Lonestar Coll–Montgomery (TX)
Lonestar Coll–North Harris (TX)
Lonestar Coll–Tomball (TX)
Lon Morris Coll (TX)
Mendocino Coll (CA)
Mercer County Comm Coll (NJ)
Miami Dade Coll (FL)
Mohave Comm Coll (AZ)
Mohawk Valley Comm Coll (NY)
Montgomery Coll (MD)
Montgomery County Comm Coll (PA)
Mt. San Jacinto Coll (CA)
Mount Wachusett Comm Coll (MA)
Murray State Coll (OK)
Muskegon Comm Coll (MI)
Nassau Comm Coll (NY)
Northeast Comm Coll (NE)
Northeastern Jr Coll (CO)
North Idaho Coll (ID)
Northwest Coll (WY)
Northwestern Connecticut Comm Coll (CT)
Northwest Florida State Coll (FL)
Odessa Coll (TX)
Oklahoma City Comm Coll (OK)
Oklahoma State U, Oklahoma City (OK)
Orange Coast Coll (CA)
Palm Beach State Coll (FL)
Paris Jr Coll (TX)
Pasadena City Coll (CA)
Phoenix Coll (AZ)
Quinsigamond Comm Coll (MA)
Red Rocks Comm Coll (CO)
Reedley Coll (CA)
Rockland Comm Coll (NY)
St. Philip's Coll (TX)
Sandhills Comm Coll (NC)
San Diego City Coll (CA)
San Diego Mesa Coll (CA)
San Jacinto Coll District (TX)
Santa Rosa Jr Coll (CA)
Seminole State Coll (OK)
Sheridan Coll (WY)
Sierra Coll (CA)
Snow Coll (UT)
South Plains Coll (TX)
State Coll of Florida Manatee-Sarasota (FL)
Suffolk County Comm Coll (NY)
Temple Coll (TX)
Trinity Valley Comm Coll (TX)
Triton Coll (IL)
Tunxis Comm Coll (CT)
Umpqua Comm Coll (OR)
Victor Valley Coll (CA)
Walters State Comm Coll (TN)
Western Wyoming Comm Coll (WY)

Art History, Criticism and Conservation
Iowa Lakes Comm Coll (IA)
Lon Morris Coll (TX)
Mercer County Comm Coll (NJ)
Muskegon Comm Coll (MI)
Palm Beach State Coll (FL)
Pasadena City Coll (CA)
Santa Rosa Jr Coll (CA)
State Coll of Florida Manatee-Sarasota (FL)
Terra State Comm Coll (OH)
Umpqua Comm Coll (OR)

Artificial Intelligence and Robotics
Metropolitan Comm Coll–Business & Technology Campus (MO)
San Diego City Coll (CA)
Southeastern Comm Coll (IA)
Sullivan Coll of Technology and Design (KY)

Arts Management
Dean Coll (MA)

Art Teacher Education
Bakersfield Coll (CA)
Casper Coll (WY)
Darton Coll (GA)
Del Mar Coll (TX)
Eastern Arizona Coll (AZ)
Indian River State Coll (FL)
Iowa Lakes Comm Coll (IA)
Lon Morris Coll (TX)
Muskegon Comm Coll (MI)
Northeastern Jr Coll (CO)
Sandhills Comm Coll (NC)
Umpqua Comm Coll (OR)

Asian American Studies
Pasadena City Coll (CA)

Asian Studies
East Los Angeles Coll (CA)
Miami Dade Coll (FL)
State Coll of Florida Manatee-Sarasota (FL)

Astronomy
Anne Arundel Comm Coll (MD)
Iowa Lakes Comm Coll (IA)
Lonestar Coll–Kingwood (TX)
Lonestar Coll–Montgomery (TX)
North Idaho Coll (ID)
State Coll of Florida Manatee-Sarasota (FL)

Athletic Training
Allen Comm Coll (KS)
Barton County Comm Coll (KS)
Brown Mackie Coll–Fort Wayne (IN)
Brown Mackie Coll–Kansas City (KS)
Brown Mackie Coll–Salina (KS)
Brown Mackie Coll–Tucson (AZ)
Casper Coll (WY)
Central Wyoming Coll (WY)
Coll of the Canyons (CA)
Comm Coll of Allegheny County (PA)
Dean Coll (MA)
Iowa Lakes Comm Coll (IA)
Lake Michigan Coll (MI)
Meridian Comm Coll (MS)
Northampton Comm Coll (PA)
North Idaho Coll (ID)
Northwest Coll (WY)
Odessa Coll (TX)
Orange Coast Coll (CA)
Saint Paul Coll–A Comm & Tech College (MN)

Atmospheric Sciences and Meteorology
Diablo Valley Coll (CA)
Everett Comm Coll (WA)
Northwest Florida State Coll (FL)

Audio Engineering
Collin County Comm Coll District (TX)
South Plains Coll (TX)

Audiology and Speech-Language Pathology
Miami Dade Coll (FL)
Pasadena City Coll (CA)

Audiovisual Communications Technologies Related
Brown Mackie Coll–Cincinnati (OH)
Lonestar Coll–Montgomery (TX)

Autobody/Collision and Repair Technology
Antelope Valley Coll (CA)
Black Hawk Coll, Moline (IL)
Casper Coll (WY)
Central Comm Coll–Hastings Campus (NE)
Century Coll (MN)
Clackamas Comm Coll (OR)
The Comm Coll of Baltimore County (MD)
Corning Comm Coll (NY)
Des Moines Area Comm Coll (IA)
Eastfield Coll (TX)
Erie Comm Coll, South Campus (NY)
Green River Comm Coll (WA)
Hawkeye Comm Coll (IA)
H. Councill Trenholm State Tech Coll (AL)
Highland Comm Coll (IL)
Hutchinson Comm Coll and Area Vocational School (KS)
Illinois Eastern Comm Colls, Olney Central College (IL)
Iowa Lakes Comm Coll (IA)
Kaskaskia Coll (IL)
Kauai Comm Coll (HI)
Kilgore Coll (TX)
Laramie County Comm Coll (WY)
Linn State Tech Coll (MO)
Luna Comm Coll (NM)
Manhattan Area Tech Coll (KS)
Mid-Plains Comm Coll, North Platte (NE)
Minnesota State Comm and Tech Coll (MN)
Montana State U–Great Falls Coll of Technology (MT)
Northeast Comm Coll (NE)
Northland Comm and Tech Coll–Thief River Falls (MN)
Pennsylvania Coll of Technology (PA)
Pikes Peak Comm Coll (CO)
Pueblo Comm Coll (CO)
St. Cloud Tech Coll (MN)
Saint Paul Coll–A Comm & Tech College (MN)
St. Philip's Coll (TX)
Salt Lake Comm Coll (UT)
San Jacinto Coll District (TX)
San Juan Coll (NM)
Southeast Tech Inst (SD)
Southern Union State Comm Coll (AL)
Southwestern Comm Coll (IA)
Stanly Comm Coll (NC)
State U of New York Coll of Technology at Alfred (NY)
U of Arkansas Comm Coll at Morrilton (AR)
Waukesha County Tech Coll (WI)

Automobile/Automotive Mechanics Technology
Alamance Comm Coll (NC)
Allan Hancock Coll (CA)
Allegany Coll of Maryland (MD)
Alpena Comm Coll (MI)
Amarillo Coll (TX)
Antelope Valley Coll (CA)
Arizona Western Coll (AZ)
Austin Comm Coll (TX)
Bainbridge Coll (GA)
Bakersfield Coll (CA)
Barton County Comm Coll (KS)
Beaufort County Comm Coll (NC)
Black Hawk Coll, Moline (IL)
Blue Ridge Comm and Tech Coll (WV)
Blue Ridge Comm Coll (NC)
Cape Fear Comm Coll (NC)
Casper Coll (WY)
Catawba Valley Comm Coll (NC)
Central Arizona Coll (AZ)
Central Carolina Comm Coll (NC)
Central Comm Coll–Columbus Campus (NE)
Central Comm Coll–Grand Island Campus (NE)
Central Comm Coll–Hastings Campus (NE)
Central Oregon Comm Coll (OR)
Central Piedmont Comm Coll (NC)
Central Texas Coll (TX)
Central Wyoming Coll (WY)
Century Coll (MN)
Chattahoochee Tech Coll (GA)
Clackamas Comm Coll (OR)
Clark Coll (WA)
Clovis Comm Coll (NM)
Coll of DuPage (IL)
Coll of Lake County (IL)
Coll of the Canyons (CA)
Columbus Tech Coll (GA)
The Comm Coll of Baltimore County (MD)
Comm Coll of Philadelphia (PA)
Corning Comm Coll (NY)
Cossatot Comm Coll of the U of Arkansas (AR)
Cowley County Comm Coll and Area Vocational–Tech School (KS)

Cuyahoga Comm Coll (OH)
Cuyamaca Coll (CA)
Danville Area Comm Coll (IL)
Daytona State Coll (FL)
DeKalb Tech Coll (GA)
Delaware County Comm Coll (PA)
Delaware Tech & Comm Coll, Jack F. Owens Campus (DE)
Delaware Tech & Comm Coll, Stanton/Wilmington Campus (DE)
Del Mar Coll (TX)
Delta Coll (MI)
Denmark Tech Coll (SC)
Des Moines Area Comm Coll (IA)
East Central Coll (MO)
Eastern Arizona Coll (AZ)
Eastfield Coll (TX)
East Los Angeles Coll (CA)
Elgin Comm Coll (IL)
El Paso Comm Coll (TX)
Erie Comm Coll, South Campus (NY)
Fayetteville Tech Comm Coll (NC)
Fox Valley Tech Coll (WI)
Front Range Comm Coll (CO)
Fulton-Montgomery Comm Coll (NY)
Gateway Comm Coll (CT)
Georgia Highlands Coll (GA)
Glendale Comm Coll (AZ)
Golden West Coll (CA)
Grand Rapids Comm Coll (MI)
Green River Comm Coll (WA)
Griffin Tech Coll (GA)
Guilford Tech Comm Coll (NC)
Gwinnett Tech Coll (GA)
Harrisburg Area Comm Coll (PA)
Hawkeye Comm Coll (IA)
Hennepin Tech Coll (MN)
Highland Comm Coll (IL)
Honolulu Comm Coll (HI)
Houston Comm Coll System (TX)
Howard Coll (TX)
Hutchinson Comm Coll and Area Vocational School (KS)
Illinois Eastern Comm Colls, Frontier Community College (IL)
Illinois Eastern Comm Colls, Olney Central College (IL)
Illinois Valley Comm Coll (IL)
Indian River State Coll (FL)
Iowa Lakes Comm Coll (IA)
Ivy Tech Comm Coll–Central Indiana (IN)
Ivy Tech Comm Coll–Columbus (IN)
Ivy Tech Comm Coll–East Central (IN)
Ivy Tech Comm Coll–Kokomo (IN)
Ivy Tech Comm Coll–Lafayette (IN)
Ivy Tech Comm Coll–North Central (IN)
Ivy Tech Comm Coll–Northeast (IN)
Ivy Tech Comm Coll–Northwest (IN)
Ivy Tech Comm Coll–Richmond (IN)
Ivy Tech Comm Coll–Southern Indiana (IN)
Ivy Tech Comm Coll–Southwest (IN)
Ivy Tech Comm Coll–Wabash Valley (IN)
Jackson Comm Coll (MI)
Kalamazoo Valley Comm Coll (MI)
Kankakee Comm Coll (IL)
Kaskaskia Coll (IL)
Kauai Comm Coll (HI)
Kent State U at Trumbull (OH)
Kilgore Coll (TX)
Kirkwood Comm Coll (IA)
Kirtland Comm Coll (MI)
Lake Region State Coll (ND)
Lansing Comm Coll (MI)
Laramie County Comm Coll (WY)
Leeward Comm Coll (HI)
Lewis and Clark Comm Coll (IL)
Lincoln Land Comm Coll (IL)
Linn-Benton Comm Coll (OR)
Linn State Tech Coll (MO)
Lonestar Coll–Montgomery (TX)
Lonestar Coll–North Harris (TX)
Los Angeles Harbor Coll (CA)
Louisiana Tech Coll (LA)
Lower Columbia Coll (WA)
Macomb Comm Coll (MI)
Manhattan Area Tech Coll (KS)
Mendocino Coll (CA)
Metropolitan Comm Coll (NE)
Metropolitan Comm Coll–Longview (MO)
Midlands Tech Coll (SC)
Mid-Plains Comm Coll, North Platte (NE)
Milwaukee Area Tech Coll (WI)
Minnesota State Coll–Southeast Tech (MN)
Mohave Comm Coll (AZ)
Montgomery Coll (MD)
Moraine Park Tech Coll (WI)
Moraine Valley Comm Coll (IL)
Mt. San Jacinto Coll (CA)
Mount Wachusett Comm Coll (MA)
Muskegon Comm Coll (MI)
Nicolet Area Tech Coll (WI)
Northampton Comm Coll (PA)
North Central Texas Coll (TX)
Northeast Comm Coll (NE)
Northeastern Jr Coll (CO)
Northeast Iowa Comm Coll (IA)
North Idaho Coll (ID)
North Iowa Area Comm Coll (IA)
Northland Comm and Tech Coll–Thief River Falls (MN)
Northwest Florida State Coll (FL)
Northwest Tech Coll (MN)
Odessa Coll (TX)
Ogeechee Tech Coll (GA)
Oklahoma City Comm Coll (OK)
Oklahoma Tech Coll (OK)
Olympic Coll (WA)
Orangeburg-Calhoun Tech Coll (SC)
Otero Jr Coll (CO)
Ouachita Tech Coll (AR)
Pasadena City Coll (CA)
Pensacola Jr Coll (FL)
Pikes Peak Comm Coll (CO)
Pima Comm Coll (AZ)
Pueblo Comm Coll (CO)
Quinsigamond Comm Coll (MA)
Randolph Comm Coll (NC)
Reedley Coll (CA)
Rend Lake Coll (IL)
Rockland Comm Coll (NY)
Rogue Comm Coll (OR)
St. Cloud Tech Coll (MN)
Saint Paul Coll–A Comm & Tech College (MN)
St. Philip's Coll (TX)
Sandhills Comm Coll (NC)
San Diego City Coll (CA)
San Jacinto Coll District (TX)
San Juan Coll (NM)
Santa Rosa Jr Coll (CA)
Savannah Tech Coll (GA)
Seminole State Coll of Florida (FL)
Shawnee Comm Coll (IL)
Sierra Coll (CA)
Snow Coll (UT)
Southeastern Comm Coll (IA)
Southeast Tech Inst (SD)
Southern Maine Comm Coll (ME)
Southern Union State Comm Coll (AL)
South Plains Coll (TX)
South Puget Sound Comm Coll (WA)
Southwestern Comm Coll (IA)
Southwestern Michigan Coll (MI)
Southwest Mississippi Comm Coll (MS)
Spartanburg Comm Coll (SC)
Stark State Coll of Technology (OH)
State Fair Comm Coll (MO)
State U of New York Coll of Technology at Alfred (NY)
Suffolk County Comm Coll (NY)
Tarrant County Coll District (TX)
Thomas Nelson Comm Coll (VA)
Tidewater Comm Coll (VA)
Tri-County Comm Coll (NC)
Trident Tech Coll (SC)
Trinity Valley Comm Coll (TX)
Triton Coll (IL)
Umpqua Comm Coll (OR)
U of Arkansas Comm Coll at Morrilton (AR)
The U of Montana–Helena Coll of Technology (MT)
Victor Valley Coll (CA)
Waukesha County Tech Coll (WI)
Wayne Comm Coll (NC)
Western Wyoming Comm Coll (WY)
West Georgia Tech Coll (GA)
White Mountains Comm Coll (NH)
WyoTech, Fremont (CA)
Yavapai Coll (AZ)

Automotive Engineering Technology
Burlington County Coll (NJ)
Camden County Coll (NJ)
Central New Mexico Comm Coll (NM)
Cincinnati State Tech and Comm Coll (OH)
Comm Coll of Allegheny County (PA)
Corning Comm Coll (NY)
H. Councill Trenholm State Tech Coll (AL)
Macomb Comm Coll (MI)
Mercer County Comm Coll (NJ)
Minnesota State Comm and Tech Coll (MN)
Montgomery County Comm Coll (PA)
Moraine Park Tech Coll (WI)
Owens Comm Coll, Toledo (OH)
Raritan Valley Comm Coll (NJ)
San Jacinto Coll District (TX)
Springfield Tech Comm Coll (MA)
Terra State Comm Coll (OH)
WyoTech, Fremont (CA)

Aviation/Airway Management
Comm Coll of Allegheny County (PA)
Green River Comm Coll (WA)
Iowa Lakes Comm Coll (IA)
Lonestar Coll–North Harris (TX)
Mercer County Comm Coll (NJ)
Miami Dade Coll (FL)
Northland Comm and Tech Coll–Thief River Falls (MN)

Avionics Maintenance Technology
Antelope Valley Coll (CA)
Cuyahoga Comm Coll (OH)
Delta Coll (MI)
Everett Comm Coll (WA)
Gateway Comm Coll (CT)
Guilford Tech Comm Coll (NC)
Honolulu Comm Coll (HI)
Housatonic Comm Coll (CT)
Kankakee Comm Coll (IL)
Lake Region State Coll (ND)
Lansing Comm Coll (MI)
Metropolitan Comm Coll–Maple Woods (MO)
Minnesota State Coll–Southeast Tech (MN)
Northland Comm and Tech Coll–Thief River Falls (MN)
Northwest Florida State Coll (FL)
Oklahoma City Comm Coll (OK)
Orange Coast Coll (CA)
Redstone Coll–Denver (CO)
Reedley Coll (CA)
Salt Lake Comm Coll (UT)
Tarrant County Coll District (TX)
Three Rivers Comm Coll (CT)
Wayne Comm Coll (NC)

Baking and Pastry Arts
The Art Inst of Seattle (WA)
Clark Coll (WA)
Coll of DuPage (IL)
El Centro Coll (TX)
Elgin Comm Coll (IL)
Harrison Coll, Indianapolis (IN)
Montgomery County Comm Coll (PA)
Pennsylvania Coll of Technology (PA)
The Restaurant School at Walnut Hill Coll (PA)
State U of New York Coll of Technology at Alfred (NY)
Westmoreland County Comm Coll (PA)

Banking and Financial Support Services
Alamance Comm Coll (NC)
Alexandria Tech Coll (MN)
Allen Comm Coll (KS)
Austin Comm Coll (TX)
Barton County Comm Coll (KS)
Black Hawk Coll, Moline (IL)
Camden County Coll (NJ)
Catawba Valley Comm Coll (NC)
Central Georgia Tech Coll (GA)
Central New Mexico Comm Coll (NM)
Comm Coll of Allegheny County (PA)
The Comm Coll of Baltimore County (MD)
Comm Coll of Rhode Island (RI)
Delaware Tech & Comm Coll, Stanton/Wilmington Campus (DE)
Fayetteville Tech Comm Coll (NC)
Harrisburg Area Comm Coll (PA)
Harrison Coll, Anderson (IN)
Harrison Coll, Columbus (IN)
Harrison Coll, Lafayette (IN)
Houston Comm Coll System (TX)
Indian River State Coll (FL)
Jefferson State Comm Coll (AL)
Lackawanna Coll (PA)
Lanier Tech Coll (GA)
Milwaukee Area Tech Coll (WI)
Mohawk Valley Comm Coll (NY)
Northeast Comm Coll (NE)
Ogeechee Tech Coll (GA)
Pennsylvania Coll of Technology (PA)
Pennsylvania Highlands Comm Coll (PA)
St. Cloud Tech Coll (MN)
San Juan Coll (NM)
Seminole State Coll of Florida (FL)
Southeast Tech Inst (SD)
Terra State Comm Coll (OH)
Valdosta Tech Coll (GA)
Westmoreland County Comm Coll (PA)

Barbering
Oklahoma Tech Coll (OK)
Olympic Coll (WA)

Behavioral Sciences
Amarillo Coll (TX)
Anne Arundel Comm Coll (MD)
Clarendon Coll (TX)
Fulton-Montgomery Comm Coll (NY)
Glendale Comm Coll (AZ)
Greenfield Comm Coll (MA)
Highline Comm Coll (WA)
Howard Coll (TX)
Iowa Lakes Comm Coll (IA)
Miami Dade Coll (FL)
Northwestern Connecticut Comm Coll (CT)
Orange Coast Coll (CA)
Phoenix Coll (AZ)
San Diego City Coll (CA)
Santa Rosa Jr Coll (CA)
Seminole State Coll (OK)
Umpqua Comm Coll (OR)
Vincennes U Jasper Campus (IN)

Biblical Studies
Amarillo Coll (TX)
Lon Morris Coll (TX)
San Jacinto Coll District (TX)
School of Urban Missions (CA)

Bilingual and Multilingual Education
Clovis Comm Coll (NM)
Delaware Tech & Comm Coll, Terry Campus (DE)

Biochemistry
Pasadena City Coll (CA)

Bioethics/Medical Ethics
Pasadena City Coll (CA)

Biological and Biomedical Sciences Related
Darton Coll (GA)
Lac Courte Oreilles Ojibwa Comm Coll (WI)
Northeast Comm Coll (NE)

Biological and Physical Sciences
Anne Arundel Comm Coll (MD)
Arizona Western Coll (AZ)
Bowling Green State U–Firelands Coll (OH)
Burlington County Coll (NJ)
Central Oregon Comm Coll (OR)
Chipola Coll (FL)
Coll of DuPage (IL)
Coll of Lake County (IL)
The Comm Coll of Baltimore County (MD)
Comm Coll of Rhode Island (RI)
Corning Comm Coll (NY)
Cuyamaca Coll (CA)
Dabney S. Lancaster Comm Coll (VA)
Delaware County Comm Coll (PA)
Eastern Shore Comm Coll (VA)
Elgin Comm Coll (IL)
Finger Lakes Comm Coll (NY)
Fulton-Montgomery Comm Coll (NY)
Georgia Highlands Coll (GA)
Georgia Military Coll (GA)
Germanna Comm Coll (VA)
Golden West Coll (CA)
Greenfield Comm Coll (MA)
Highland Comm Coll (IL)
Highline Comm Coll (WA)
Howard Comm Coll (MD)
Illinois Eastern Comm Colls, Frontier Community College (IL)
Illinois Eastern Comm Colls, Lincoln Trail College (IL)
Illinois Eastern Comm Colls, Olney Central College (IL)
Illinois Eastern Comm Colls, Wabash Valley College (IL)
Illinois Valley Comm Coll (IL)
Iowa Lakes Comm Coll (IA)
John Wood Comm Coll (IL)
J. Sargeant Reynolds Comm Coll (VA)
Kankakee Comm Coll (IL)
Kaskaskia Coll (IL)
Kilgore Coll (TX)
Kirtland Comm Coll (MI)
Lansing Comm Coll (MI)
Laramie County Comm Coll (WY)
Lewis and Clark Comm Coll (IL)
Lincoln Land Comm Coll (IL)
Linn-Benton Comm Coll (OR)
Metropolitan Comm Coll–Longview (MO)
Metropolitan Comm Coll–Maple Woods (MO)
Metropolitan Comm Coll–Penn Valley (MO)
Middlesex Comm Coll (CT)
Moraine Valley Comm Coll (IL)
Mt. San Jacinto Coll (CA)
Murray State Coll (OK)
Niagara County Comm Coll (NY)
North Central Texas Coll (TX)
Northeastern Jr Coll (CO)
North Idaho Coll (ID)
Northland Pioneer Coll (AZ)
Northwest Florida State Coll (FL)
Otero Jr Coll (CO)
Paris Jr Coll (TX)
Pasadena City Coll (CA)
Patrick Henry Comm Coll (VA)
Penn State Beaver (PA)
Penn State DuBois (PA)
Penn State Fayette, The Eberly Campus (PA)
Penn State Greater Allegheny (PA)
Penn State New Kensington (PA)
Penn State Schuylkill (PA)
Penn State Shenango (PA)
Potomac State Coll of West Virginia U (WV)
Rappahannock Comm Coll (VA)
Rend Lake Coll (IL)
Rockland Comm Coll (NY)
Sandhills Comm Coll (NC)
Shawnee Comm Coll (IL)
Sheridan Coll (WY)
Sierra Coll (CA)
South Georgia Coll (GA)
South Plains Coll (TX)
Southside Virginia Comm Coll (VA)
South Suburban Coll (IL)
Southwest Mississippi Comm Coll (MS)
State U of New York Coll of Technology at Alfred (NY)
Suffolk County Comm Coll (NY)
Terra State Comm Coll (OH)
Thomas Nelson Comm Coll (VA)
Tidewater Comm Coll (VA)
Trident Tech Coll (SC)
Triton Coll (IL)
Umpqua Comm Coll (OR)

U of Wisconsin–Richland (WI)
Victor Valley Coll (CA)
Wayne Comm Coll (NC)
Western Wyoming Comm Coll (WY)
Wor-Wic Comm Coll (MD)

Biology/Biological Sciences
Allan Hancock Coll (CA)
Allen Comm Coll (KS)
Alpena Comm Coll (MI)
Alvin Comm Coll (TX)
Amarillo Coll (TX)
Anne Arundel Comm Coll (MD)
Anoka-Ramsey Comm Coll (MN)
Anoka-Ramsey Comm Coll, Cambridge Campus (MN)
Antelope Valley Coll (CA)
Arizona Western Coll (AZ)
Austin Comm Coll (TX)
Bainbridge Coll (GA)
Bakersfield Coll (CA)
Barton County Comm Coll (KS)
Bronx Comm Coll of the City U of New York (NY)
Bucks County Comm Coll (PA)
Bunker Hill Comm Coll (MA)
Burlington County Coll (NJ)
Casper Coll (WY)
Cecil Coll (MD)
Central Oregon Comm Coll (OR)
Central Piedmont Comm Coll (NC)
Central Texas Coll (TX)
Central Wyoming Coll (WY)
Clarendon Coll (TX)
Coll of the Canyons (CA)
Comm Coll of Allegheny County (PA)
Cowley County Comm Coll and Area Vocational–Tech School (KS)
Crowder Coll (MO)
Dakota Coll at Bottineau (ND)
Darton Coll (GA)
Delaware Tech & Comm Coll, Jack F. Owens Campus (DE)
Delaware Tech & Comm Coll, Stanton/Wilmington Campus (DE)
Del Mar Coll (TX)
Eastern Arizona Coll (AZ)
Eastern Wyoming Coll (WY)
East Los Angeles Coll (CA)
Essex County Coll (NJ)
Everett Comm Coll (WA)
Finger Lakes Comm Coll (NY)
Folsom Lake Coll (CA)
Frederick Comm Coll (MD)
Fulton-Montgomery Comm Coll (NY)
Gainesville State Coll (GA)
Georgia Military Coll (GA)
Golden West Coll (CA)
Harrisburg Area Comm Coll (PA)
Howard Coll (TX)
Hutchinson Comm Coll and Area Vocational School (KS)
Indian River State Coll (FL)
Inver Hills Comm Coll (MN)
Iowa Lakes Comm Coll (IA)
Kingsborough Comm Coll of the City U of New York (NY)
Lackawanna Coll (PA)
Lake Michigan Coll (MI)
Lansing Comm Coll (MI)
Laramie County Comm Coll (WY)
Lawson State Comm Coll (AL)
Lehigh Carbon Comm Coll (PA)
Linn-Benton Comm Coll (OR)
Lonestar Coll–Cy-Fair (TX)
Lonestar Coll–Kingwood (TX)
Lonestar Coll–Montgomery (TX)
Lonestar Coll–North Harris (TX)
Lonestar Coll–Tomball (TX)
Lon Morris Coll (TX)
Los Angeles Harbor Coll (CA)
Macomb Comm Coll (MI)
Mendocino Coll (CA)
Mercer County Comm Coll (NJ)
Metropolitan Comm Coll–Longview (MO)
Metropolitan Comm Coll–Maple Woods (MO)
Metropolitan Comm Coll–Penn Valley (MO)
Miami Dade Coll (FL)
Minneapolis Comm and Tech Coll (MN)
Minnesota State Comm and Tech Coll (MN)
Montgomery County Comm Coll (PA)
Northampton Comm Coll (PA)
Northeast Comm Coll (NE)
Northeastern Jr Coll (CO)
North Hennepin Comm Coll (MN)
North Idaho Coll (ID)
Northwest Coll (WY)
Northwestern Connecticut Comm Coll (CT)
Northwest Florida State Coll (FL)
Odessa Coll (TX)
Oklahoma City Comm Coll (OK)
Orange Coast Coll (CA)
Otero Jr Coll (CO)
Palm Beach State Coll (FL)
Pasadena City Coll (CA)
Pennsylvania Coll of Technology (PA)
Potomac State Coll of West Virginia U (WV)
Red Rocks Comm Coll (CO)
Reedley Coll (CA)
Saint Charles Comm Coll (MO)
St. Philip's Coll (TX)
Salt Lake Comm Coll (UT)
San Diego City Coll (CA)
San Diego Mesa Coll (CA)
San Jacinto Coll District (TX)
San Juan Coll (NM)
Santa Rosa Jr Coll (CA)
Seminole State Coll (OK)
Sheridan Coll (WY)
Sierra Coll (CA)
Snow Coll (UT)
South Georgia Coll (GA)
South Plains Coll (TX)
Southwest Mississippi Comm Coll (MS)
Springfield Tech Comm Coll (MA)
State Coll of Florida Manatee-Sarasota (FL)
Suffolk County Comm Coll (NY)
Terra State Comm Coll (OH)
Trinity Valley Comm Coll (TX)
Triton Coll (IL)
Umpqua Comm Coll (OR)
U of Cincinnati Clermont Coll (OH)
Victor Valley Coll (CA)
Western Wyoming Comm Coll (WY)

Biology/Biotechnology Laboratory Technician
Anoka-Ramsey Comm Coll (MN)
Anoka-Ramsey Comm Coll, Cambridge Campus (MN)
Athens Tech Coll (GA)
Austin Comm Coll (TX)
Berkeley City Coll (CA)
Camden County Coll (NJ)
Collin County Comm Coll District (TX)
County Coll of Morris (NJ)
Delaware Tech & Comm Coll, Jack F. Owens Campus (DE)
Delaware Tech & Comm Coll, Stanton/Wilmington Campus (DE)
East Central Coll (MO)
Fayetteville Tech Comm Coll (NC)
Finger Lakes Comm Coll (NY)
Guilford Tech Comm Coll (NC)
Houston Comm Coll System (TX)
Kennebec Valley Comm Coll (ME)
Lansing Comm Coll (MI)
Lonestar Coll–Montgomery (TX)
Mercer County Comm Coll (NJ)
Middlesex Comm Coll (CT)
Montgomery Coll (MD)
Muskegon Comm Coll (MI)
The Ohio State U Ag Tech Inst (OH)
Randolph Comm Coll (NC)
Salt Lake Comm Coll (UT)
Temple Coll (TX)
Westmoreland County Comm Coll (PA)

Biology Teacher Education
State Coll of Florida Manatee-Sarasota (FL)
Ulster County Comm Coll (NY)

Biomedical Technology
Brown Mackie Coll–Cincinnati (OH)
Brown Mackie Coll–Fort Wayne (IN)
Brown Mackie Coll–Louisville (KY)
Brown Mackie Coll–Tucson (AZ)
Chattahoochee Tech Coll (GA)
Cincinnati State Tech and Comm Coll (OH)
Delaware County Comm Coll (PA)
Delaware Tech & Comm Coll, Terry Campus (DE)
Des Moines Area Comm Coll (IA)
Gateway Comm Coll (CT)
Hillsborough Comm Coll (FL)
Howard Comm Coll (MD)
Miami Dade Coll (FL)
Milwaukee Area Tech Coll (WI)
Muskegon Comm Coll (MI)
North Arkansas Coll (AR)
Oklahoma City Comm Coll (OK)
Owens Comm Coll, Toledo (OH)
Penn State DuBois (PA)
Penn State Fayette, The Eberly Campus (PA)
Penn State Hazleton (PA)
Penn State New Kensington (PA)
Penn State Schuylkill (PA)
Penn State Shenango (PA)
Penn State York (PA)
Pennsylvania Coll of Technology (PA)
Saint Paul Coll–A Comm & Tech College (MN)
St. Philip's Coll (TX)
Southeastern Comm Coll (IA)
Southeast Tech Inst (SD)
Stanly Comm Coll (NC)
Stark State Coll of Technology (OH)

Biotechnology
Alamance Comm Coll (NC)
Augusta Tech Coll (GA)
Bladen Comm Coll (NC)
Burlington County Coll (NJ)
Central New Mexico Comm Coll (NM)
Comm Coll of Rhode Island (RI)
El Centro Coll (TX)
Glendale Comm Coll (AZ)
Hillsborough Comm Coll (FL)
Howard Comm Coll (MD)
Hutchinson Comm Coll and Area Vocational School (KS)
Ivy Tech Comm Coll–Central Indiana (IN)
Ivy Tech Comm Coll–Lafayette (IN)
Ivy Tech Comm Coll–North Central (IN)
Kirkwood Comm Coll (IA)
Lackawanna Coll (PA)
Lakeland Comm Coll (OH)
Lehigh Carbon Comm Coll (PA)
Miami Dade Coll (FL)
Minneapolis Comm and Tech Coll (MN)
Montgomery County Comm Coll (PA)
Mount Wachusett Comm Coll (MA)
Northampton Comm Coll (PA)
Oklahoma City Comm Coll (OK)
Raritan Valley Comm Coll (NJ)
Red Rocks Comm Coll (CO)
San Jacinto Coll District (TX)
Southern Maine Comm Coll (ME)
Springfield Tech Comm Coll (MA)
Tompkins Cortland Comm Coll (NY)

Boilermaking
Ivy Tech Comm Coll–Southwest (IN)

Botany/Plant Biology
Anne Arundel Comm Coll (MD)
Everett Comm Coll (WA)
Iowa Lakes Comm Coll (IA)
Lon Morris Coll (TX)
North Idaho Coll (ID)
Palm Beach State Coll (FL)
Snow Coll (UT)
Southern Maine Comm Coll (ME)

Broadcast Journalism
Amarillo Coll (TX)
Anne Arundel Comm Coll (MD)
Arizona Western Coll (AZ)
Bakersfield Coll (CA)
Colby Comm Coll (KS)
Finger Lakes Comm Coll (NY)
Iowa Lakes Comm Coll (IA)
Kingsborough Comm Coll of the City U of New York (NY)
Lansing Comm Coll (MI)
Meridian Comm Coll (MS)
Middlesex Comm Coll (CT)
Northwest Coll (WY)
Ocean County Coll (NJ)
Oklahoma City Comm Coll (OK)
Pasadena City Coll (CA)
Pennsylvania Coll of Technology (PA)

Building/Construction Finishing, Management, and Inspection Related
Central New Mexico Comm Coll (NM)
Coll of Southern Maryland (MD)
The Comm Coll of Baltimore County (MD)
Cumberland County Coll (NJ)
Delta Coll (MI)
Fayetteville Tech Comm Coll (NC)
Frederick Comm Coll (MD)
Gwinnett Tech Coll (GA)
Inver Hills Comm Coll (MN)
Ivy Tech Comm Coll–Northwest (IN)
Manhattan Area Tech Coll (KS)
Mid-Plains Comm Coll, North Platte (NE)
Mohave Comm Coll (AZ)
Montgomery Coll (MD)
Moraine Park Tech Coll (WI)
Northeast Comm Coll (NE)
Palm Beach State Coll (FL)
Pikes Peak Comm Coll (CO)
St. Philip's Coll (TX)
Salt Lake Comm Coll (UT)
Seminole State Coll of Florida (FL)
Snow Coll (UT)
Southeast Tech Inst (SD)
Springfield Tech Comm Coll (MA)
Victor Valley Coll (CA)

Building/Construction Site Management
Coll of the Canyons (CA)
The Comm Coll of Baltimore County (MD)
Hillsborough Comm Coll (FL)
Metropolitan Comm Coll–Business & Technology Campus (MO)
Minnesota State Comm and Tech Coll (MN)
North Hennepin Comm Coll (MN)
The Ohio State U Ag Tech Inst (OH)
Saint Paul Coll–A Comm & Tech College (MN)
State Fair Comm Coll (MO)

Building/Home/Construction Inspection
The Comm Coll of Baltimore County (MD)
Harrisburg Area Comm Coll (PA)
Inver Hills Comm Coll (MN)
North Hennepin Comm Coll (MN)
Oklahoma State U, Oklahoma City (OK)
Orange Coast Coll (CA)
Pasadena City Coll (CA)
South Suburban Coll (IL)

Building/Property Maintenance and Management
Cape Fear Comm Coll (NC)
Century Coll (MN)
Coll of DuPage (IL)
Comm Coll of Allegheny County (PA)
Delaware County Comm Coll (PA)
Del Mar Coll (TX)
Erie Comm Coll (NY)
Guilford Tech Comm Coll (NC)
Illinois Eastern Comm Colls, Lincoln Trail College (IL)
Ivy Tech Comm Coll–Bloomington (IN)
Ivy Tech Comm Coll–Central Indiana (IN)
Ivy Tech Comm Coll–Columbus (IN)
Ivy Tech Comm Coll–East Central (IN)
Ivy Tech Comm Coll–Kokomo (IN)
Ivy Tech Comm Coll–Lafayette (IN)
Ivy Tech Comm Coll–North Central (IN)
Ivy Tech Comm Coll–Northeast (IN)
Ivy Tech Comm Coll–Northwest (IN)
Ivy Tech Comm Coll–Richmond (IN)
Ivy Tech Comm Coll–Southern Indiana (IN)
Ivy Tech Comm Coll–Southwest (IN)
Ivy Tech Comm Coll–Wabash Valley (IN)
Mohawk Valley Comm Coll (NY)
New Mexico State U–Carlsbad (NM)
Northland Pioneer Coll (AZ)
Piedmont Comm Coll (NC)
Pima Comm Coll (AZ)

Business Administration and Management
Alamance Comm Coll (NC)
Alexandria Tech Coll (MN)
Allan Hancock Coll (CA)
Allegany Coll of Maryland (MD)
Allen Comm Coll (KS)
Alpena Comm Coll (MI)
Alvin Comm Coll (TX)
Amarillo Coll (TX)
Anne Arundel Comm Coll (MD)
Anoka-Ramsey Comm Coll (MN)
Anoka-Ramsey Comm Coll, Cambridge Campus (MN)
Antelope Valley Coll (CA)
Arizona Western Coll (AZ)
Arkansas State U–Beebe (AR)
Augusta Tech Coll (GA)
Austin Comm Coll (TX)
Bainbridge Coll (GA)
Bakersfield Coll (CA)
Barton County Comm Coll (KS)
Beaufort County Comm Coll (NC)
Berkeley City Coll (CA)
Berkshire Comm Coll (MA)
Bladen Comm Coll (NC)
Blue Ridge Comm Coll (NC)
Bradford School (OH)
Bradford School (PA)
Bronx Comm Coll of the City U of New York (NY)
Broome Comm Coll (NY)
Brown Mackie Coll–Akron (OH)
Brown Mackie Coll–Albuquerque (NM)
Brown Mackie Coll–Atlanta (GA)
Brown Mackie Coll–Boise (ID)
Brown Mackie Coll–Cincinnati (OH)
Brown Mackie Coll–Findlay (OH)
Brown Mackie Coll–Fort Wayne (IN)
Brown Mackie Coll–Greenville (SC)
Brown Mackie Coll–Hopkinsville (KY)
Brown Mackie Coll–Indianapolis (IN)
Brown Mackie Coll–Kansas City (KS)
Brown Mackie Coll–Louisville (KY)
Brown Mackie Coll–Merrillville (IN)
Brown Mackie Coll–Miami (FL)
Brown Mackie Coll–Michigan City (IN)
Brown Mackie Coll–North Canton (OH)
Brown Mackie Coll–Northern Kentucky (KY)
Brown Mackie Coll–Phoenix (AZ)
Brown Mackie Coll–Quad Cities (IL)
Brown Mackie Coll–St. Louis (MO)
Brown Mackie Coll–Salina (KS)
Brown Mackie Coll–South Bend (IN)
Brown Mackie Coll–Tucson (AZ)
Brown Mackie Coll–Tulsa (OK)
Bryant & Stratton Coll, Eastlake (OH)
Bryant & Stratton Coll - Henrietta Campus (NY)
Bryant & Stratton Coll - North Campus (NY)
Bucks County Comm Coll (PA)
Bunker Hill Comm Coll (MA)
Burlington County Coll (NJ)
Camden County Coll (NJ)
Cape Fear Comm Coll (NC)
Career Coll of Northern Nevada (NV)
Carroll Comm Coll (MD)

Carteret Comm Coll (NC)
Casper Coll (WY)
Catawba Valley Comm Coll (NC)
Cecil Coll (MD)
Central Carolina Comm Coll (NC)
Central Carolina Tech Coll (SC)
Central Comm Coll–Columbus Campus (NE)
Central Comm Coll–Grand Island Campus (NE)
Central Comm Coll–Hastings Campus (NE)
Central Georgia Tech Coll (GA)
Central Lakes Coll (MN)
Central New Mexico Comm Coll (NM)
Central Ohio Tech Coll (OH)
Central Oregon Comm Coll (OR)
Central Piedmont Comm Coll (NC)
Central Texas Coll (TX)
Central Wyoming Coll (WY)
Century Coll (MN)
Chattahoochee Tech Coll (GA)
Chipola Coll (FL)
Cincinnati State Tech and Comm Coll (OH)
City Colls of Chicago, Richard J. Daley College (IL)
Clarendon Coll (TX)
Clark Coll (WA)
Cleveland State Comm Coll (TN)
Clovis Comm Coll (NM)
Colby Comm Coll (KS)
Coll of DuPage (IL)
Coll of Lake County (IL)
Coll of Southern Maryland (MD)
Coll of the Canyons (CA)
Collin County Comm Coll District (TX)
Comm Coll of Allegheny County (PA)
The Comm Coll of Baltimore County (MD)
Comm Coll of Philadelphia (PA)
Comm Coll of Rhode Island (RI)
Comm Coll of Vermont (VT)
Consolidated School of Business, Lancaster (PA)
Corning Comm Coll (NY)
Cossatot Comm Coll of the U of Arkansas (AR)
County Coll of Morris (NJ)
Cowley County Comm Coll and Area Vocational–Tech School (KS)
Crowder Coll (MO)
Cumberland County Coll (NJ)
Cuyahoga Comm Coll (OH)
Cuyamaca Coll (CA)
Dabney S. Lancaster Comm Coll (VA)
Dakota Coll at Bottineau (ND)
Darton Coll (GA)
Davis Coll (OH)
Daytona State Coll (FL)
Dean Coll (MA)
Delaware County Comm Coll (PA)
Delaware Tech & Comm Coll, Stanton/Wilmington Campus (DE)
Delaware Tech & Comm Coll, Terry Campus (DE)
Del Mar Coll (TX)
Delta Coll (MI)
Denmark Tech Coll (SC)
Des Moines Area Comm Coll (IA)
Douglas Education Center (PA)
Eastern Arizona Coll (AZ)
Eastern Shore Comm Coll (VA)
Eastern Wyoming Coll (WY)
Eastfield Coll (TX)
East Los Angeles Coll (CA)
Edison State Comm Coll (OH)
El Centro Coll (TX)
Elgin Comm Coll (IL)
El Paso Comm Coll (TX)
Erie Comm Coll (NY)
Erie Comm Coll, North Campus (NY)
Erie Comm Coll, South Campus (NY)
Essex County Coll (NJ)
Everest Inst (NY)
Everett Comm Coll (WA)
Fayetteville Tech Comm Coll (NC)
Finger Lakes Comm Coll (NY)
Fiorello H. LaGuardia Comm Coll of the City U of New York (NY)
Flathead Valley Comm Coll (MT)
Folsom Lake Coll (CA)
Forrest Jr Coll (SC)
Fox Coll (IL)
Fox Valley Tech Coll (WI)
Frederick Comm Coll (MD)
Fulton-Montgomery Comm Coll (NY)
Gainesville State Coll (GA)
Gateway Comm and Tech Coll (KY)
Gateway Comm Coll (CT)
Genesee Comm Coll (NY)
Georgia Highlands Coll (GA)
Georgia Military Coll (GA)
Germanna Comm Coll (VA)
Golden West Coll (CA)
Goodwin Coll (CT)
Grand Rapids Comm Coll (MI)
Greenfield Comm Coll (MA)
Griffin Tech Coll (GA)
Guilford Tech Comm Coll (NC)
Gwinnett Tech Coll (GA)
Harcum Coll (PA)
Harford Comm Coll (MD)
Harrisburg Area Comm Coll (PA)
Harrison Coll, Anderson (IN)
Harrison Coll, Columbus (IN)
Harrison Coll, Elkhart (IN)
Harrison Coll, Evansville (IN)
Harrison Coll, Fort Wayne (IN)
Harrison Coll, Indianapolis (IN)
Harrison Coll, Lafayette (IN)
Harrison Coll, Muncie (IN)
Harrison Coll, Terre Haute (IN)
Harrison Coll (OH)
Hazard Comm and Tech Coll (KY)
Hesser Coll, Manchester (NH)
Highland Comm Coll (IL)
Highline Comm Coll (WA)
Hillsborough Comm Coll (FL)
Holyoke Comm Coll (MA)
Hopkinsville Comm Coll (KY)
Housatonic Comm Coll (CT)
Houston Comm Coll System (TX)
Howard Coll (TX)
Howard Comm Coll (MD)
Illinois Eastern Comm Colls, Wabash Valley College (IL)
Illinois Valley Comm Coll (IL)
Indian River State Coll (FL)
Inst of Business & Medical Careers (CO)
International Business Coll, Indianapolis (IN)
Inver Hills Comm Coll (MN)
Iowa Lakes Comm Coll (IA)
Itasca Comm Coll (MN)
ITT Tech Inst, Canton (MI)
ITT Tech Inst, Swartz Creek (MI)
ITT Tech Inst, Troy (MI)
ITT Tech Inst, Wyoming (MI)
ITT Tech Inst, Dayton (OH)
ITT Tech Inst, Maumee (OH)
ITT Tech Inst, Norwood (OH)
ITT Tech Inst, Strongsville (OH)
ITT Tech Inst, Warrensville Heights (OH)
ITT Tech Inst, Youngstown (OH)
ITT Tech Inst, Greenfield (WI)
Ivy Tech Comm Coll–Bloomington (IN)
Ivy Tech Comm Coll–Central Indiana (IN)
Ivy Tech Comm Coll–Columbus (IN)
Ivy Tech Comm Coll–East Central (IN)
Ivy Tech Comm Coll–Kokomo (IN)
Ivy Tech Comm Coll–Lafayette (IN)
Ivy Tech Comm Coll–North Central (IN)
Ivy Tech Comm Coll–Northeast (IN)
Ivy Tech Comm Coll–Northwest (IN)
Ivy Tech Comm Coll–Richmond (IN)
Ivy Tech Comm Coll–Southeast (IN)
Ivy Tech Comm Coll–Southern Indiana (IN)
Ivy Tech Comm Coll–Southwest (IN)
Ivy Tech Comm Coll–Wabash Valley (IN)
Jackson Comm Coll (MI)
Jackson State Comm Coll (TN)
James Sprunt Comm Coll (NC)
Jamestown Business Coll (NY)
Jamestown Comm Coll (NY)
Jefferson Comm Coll (NY)
Johnston Comm Coll (NC)
John Wood Comm Coll (IL)
J. Sargeant Reynolds Comm Coll (VA)
Kalamazoo Valley Comm Coll (MI)
Kaplan Career Inst, Harrisburg (PA)
Kaplan Career Inst, ICM Campus (PA)
Kaplan Coll, Denver Campus (CO)
Kaplan U, South Portland (ME)
Kaplan U, Cedar Rapids (IA)
Kaplan U, Hagerstown Campus (MD)
Kaplan U, Lincoln (NE)
Kaplan U, Omaha (NE)
Kellogg Comm Coll (MI)
Kent State U at Ashtabula (OH)
Kent State U at East Liverpool (OH)
Kent State U at Geauga (OH)
Kent State U at Trumbull (OH)
Kent State U at Tuscarawas (OH)
Kilgore Coll (TX)
Kilian Comm Coll (SD)
Kingsborough Comm Coll of the City U of New York (NY)
Kirkwood Comm Coll (IA)
Kirtland Comm Coll (MI)
Lac Courte Oreilles Ojibwa Comm Coll (WI)
Lackawanna Coll (PA)
Lakeland Comm Coll (OH)
Lake Michigan Coll (MI)
Lake Region State Coll (ND)
Lake-Sumter Comm Coll (FL)
Lamson Coll (AZ)
Landmark Coll (VT)
Lansing Comm Coll (MI)
Laramie County Comm Coll (WY)
Lawson State Comm Coll (AL)
LDS Business Coll (UT)
Leeward Comm Coll (HI)
Lehigh Carbon Comm Coll (PA)
Lewis and Clark Comm Coll (IL)
Lincoln Land Comm Coll (IL)
Linn-Benton Comm Coll (OR)
Lonestar Coll–Cy-Fair (TX)
Lonestar Coll–Kingwood (TX)
Lonestar Coll–Montgomery (TX)
Lonestar Coll–North Harris (TX)
Long Island Business Inst (NY)
Lon Morris Coll (TX)
Los Angeles Harbor Coll (CA)
Lower Columbia Coll (WA)
Luna Comm Coll (NM)
Macomb Comm Coll (MI)
Manchester Comm Coll (CT)
Marion Tech Coll (OH)
Massasoit Comm Coll (MA)
Mendocino Coll (CA)
Mercer County Comm Coll (NJ)
Metropolitan Comm Coll (NE)
Metropolitan Comm Coll–Blue River (MO)
Metropolitan Comm Coll–Business & Technology Campus (MO)
Metropolitan Comm Coll–Longview (MO)
Metropolitan Comm Coll–Maple Woods (MO)
Metropolitan Comm Coll–Penn Valley (MO)
Miami Dade Coll (FL)
Middle Georgia Coll (GA)
Middlesex Comm Coll (CT)
Midlands Tech Coll (SC)
Mid-Plains Comm Coll, North Platte (NE)
Milwaukee Area Tech Coll (WI)
Minneapolis Business Coll (MN)
Minneapolis Comm and Tech Coll (MN)
Minnesota State Coll–Southeast Tech (MN)
Minnesota State Comm and Tech Coll (MN)
Missouri State U–West Plains (MO)
Mohave Comm Coll (AZ)
Mohawk Valley Comm Coll (NY)
Montana State U–Great Falls Coll of Technology (MT)
Montcalm Comm Coll (MI)
Montgomery Comm Coll (NC)
Montgomery County Comm Coll (PA)
Moraine Park Tech Coll (WI)
Moraine Valley Comm Coll (IL)
Mountain Empire Comm Coll (VA)
Mt. San Jacinto Coll (CA)
Murray State Coll (OK)
Muskegon Comm Coll (MI)
Nassau Comm Coll (NY)
Newport Business Inst, Williamsport (PA)
Niagara County Comm Coll (NY)
Nicolet Area Tech Coll (WI)
Northampton Comm Coll (PA)
North Central Texas Coll (TX)
Northeast Comm Coll (NE)
Northeastern Jr Coll (CO)
Northeast Iowa Comm Coll (IA)
North Hennepin Comm Coll (MN)
North Idaho Coll (ID)
North Iowa Area Comm Coll (IA)
North Lake Coll (TX)
Northland Comm and Tech Coll–Thief River Falls (MN)
Northland Pioneer Coll (AZ)
NorthWest Arkansas Comm Coll (AR)
Northwest Coll (WY)
Northwestern Coll (IL)
Northwestern Connecticut Comm Coll (CT)
Northwest Florida State Coll (FL)
Northwest Tech Coll (MN)
Oakland Comm Coll (MI)
Ocean County Coll (NJ)
Odessa Coll (TX)
Oklahoma City Comm Coll (OK)
Oklahoma State U, Oklahoma City (OK)
Olean Business Inst (NY)
Olympic Coll (WA)
Orange Coast Coll (CA)
Otero Jr Coll (CO)
Ouachita Tech Coll (AR)
Owensboro Comm and Tech Coll (KY)
Palm Beach State Coll (FL)
Paradise Valley Comm Coll (AZ)
Paris Jr Coll (TX)
Pasadena City Coll (CA)
Pasco-Hernando Comm Coll (FL)
Patrick Henry Comm Coll (VA)
Pennsylvania Inst of Technology (PA)
Pensacola Jr Coll (FL)
Phoenix Coll (AZ)
Piedmont Comm Coll (NC)
Pikes Peak Comm Coll (CO)
Pima Comm Coll (AZ)
Plaza Coll (NY)
Polk State Coll (FL)
Potomac State Coll of West Virginia U (WV)
Pueblo Comm Coll (CO)
Quinsigamond Comm Coll (MA)
Randolph Comm Coll (NC)
Rappahannock Comm Coll (VA)
Raritan Valley Comm Coll (NJ)
Red Rocks Comm Coll (CO)
Rio Salado Coll (AZ)
Rockingham Comm Coll (NC)
Rockland Comm Coll (NY)
Rogue Comm Coll (OR)
Saint Charles Comm Coll (MO)
St. Cloud Tech Coll (MN)
Saint Paul Coll–A Comm & Tech College (MN)
St. Philip's Coll (TX)
Salt Lake Comm Coll (UT)
Sandhills Comm Coll (NC)
San Diego City Coll (CA)
San Diego Mesa Coll (CA)
San Jacinto Coll District (TX)
San Juan Coll (NM)
Santa Rosa Jr Coll (CA)
Scottsdale Comm Coll (AZ)
Seminole State Coll (OK)
Seminole State Coll of Florida (FL)
Shawnee Comm Coll (IL)
Sierra Coll (CA)
Sisseton-Wahpeton Comm Coll (SD)
Snow Coll (UT)
Somerset Comm Coll (KY)
Southeastern Comm Coll (IA)
Southeast Kentucky Comm and Tech Coll (KY)
Southeast Tech Inst (SD)
Southern Alberta Inst of Technology (AB, Canada)
Southern Maine Comm Coll (ME)
South Georgia Coll (GA)
South Plains Coll (TX)
South Puget Sound Comm Coll (WA)
Southside Virginia Comm Coll (VA)
Southwestern Comm Coll (IA)
Southwestern Indian Polytechnic Inst (NM)
Southwestern Michigan Coll (MI)
Southwest Mississippi Comm Coll (MS)
Southwest Virginia Comm Coll (VA)
Spartanburg Comm Coll (SC)
Spencerian Coll (KY)
Springfield Tech Comm Coll (MA)
Stanly Comm Coll (NC)
Stark State Coll of Technology (OH)
State Coll of Florida Manatee-Sarasota (FL)
State Fair Comm Coll (MO)
State U of New York Coll of Technology at Alfred (NY)
Suffolk County Comm Coll (NY)
Tallahassee Comm Coll (FL)
Tarrant County Coll District (TX)
Temple Coll (TX)
Terra State Comm Coll (OH)
Thomas Nelson Comm Coll (VA)
Three Rivers Comm Coll (CT)
Three Rivers Comm Coll (MO)
Tidewater Comm Coll (VA)
Tohono O'odham Comm Coll (AZ)
Tompkins Cortland Comm Coll (NY)
Tri-County Comm Coll (NC)
Trident Tech Coll (SC)
Trinity Valley Comm Coll (TX)
Triton Coll (IL)
Tunxis Comm Coll (CT)
Ulster County Comm Coll (NY)
Umpqua Comm Coll (OR)
Union County Coll (NJ)
U of Alaska Anchorage, Kenai Peninsula Coll (AK)
U of Alaska Anchorage, Matanuska-Susitna Coll (AK)
U of Cincinnati Clermont Coll (OH)
U of South Carolina Lancaster (SC)
Victoria Coll (TX)
Victor Valley Coll (CA)
Vincennes U Jasper Campus (IN)
Volunteer State Comm Coll (TN)
Walters State Comm Coll (TN)
Wayne Comm Coll (NC)
Westchester Comm Coll (NY)
Western Wyoming Comm Coll (WY)
West Kentucky Comm and Tech Coll (KY)
Westmoreland County Comm Coll (PA)
White Mountains Comm Coll (NH)
Wilson Comm Coll (NC)
Wisconsin Indianhead Tech Coll (WI)
Wood Tobe–Coburn School (NY)
Wor-Wic Comm Coll (MD)
Yavapai Coll (AZ)
York County Comm Coll (ME)

Business Administration, Management and Operations Related

Bryant & Stratton Coll - Buffalo Campus (NY)
Bryant & Stratton Coll - Greece Campus (NY)
Bryant & Stratton Coll - Henrietta Campus (NY)
Bryant & Stratton Coll - Southtowns Campus (NY)
Bryant & Stratton Coll - Virginia Beach (VA)
Cecil Coll (MD)

Comm Care Coll (OK)
The Comm Coll of Baltimore County (MD)
Fayetteville Tech Comm Coll (NC)
Harrison Coll, Muncie (IN)
Harrison Coll, Terre Haute (IN)
Kaplan Coll, Panorama City Campus (CA)
Lackawanna Coll (PA)
Leech Lake Tribal Coll (MN)
Massasoit Comm Coll (MA)
Milwaukee Area Tech Coll (WI)
Mountain Empire Comm Coll (VA)
Southern Alberta Inst of Technology (AB, Canada)
Southwest Virginia Comm Coll (VA)

Business and Personal/Financial Services Marketing
Hutchinson Comm Coll and Area Vocational School (KS)
North Central Texas Coll (TX)
Northland Pioneer Coll (AZ)
Union County Coll (NJ)

Business Automation/ Technology/Data Entry
Alpena Comm Coll (MI)
Antonelli Coll, Hattiesburg (MS)
Antonelli Coll, Jackson (MS)
Arkansas State U–Mountain Home (AR)
Berkshire Comm Coll (MA)
Black Hawk Coll, Moline (IL)
Central Wyoming Coll (WY)
Chattanooga State Comm Coll (TN)
Clark Coll (WA)
Clovis Comm Coll (NM)
Coll of Lake County (IL)
Collin County Comm Coll District (TX)
Comm Coll of Allegheny County (PA)
Crowder Coll (MO)
Dakota Coll at Bottineau (ND)
Danville Area Comm Coll (IL)
Delaware Tech & Comm Coll, Jack F. Owens Campus (DE)
Delaware Tech & Comm Coll, Stanton/Wilmington Campus (DE)
Delaware Tech & Comm Coll, Terry Campus (DE)
El Centro Coll (TX)
El Paso Comm Coll (TX)
Glendale Comm Coll (AZ)
Houston Comm Coll System (TX)
Illinois Eastern Comm Colls, Frontier Community College (IL)
Illinois Eastern Comm Colls, Lincoln Trail College (IL)
Illinois Eastern Comm Colls, Olney Central College (IL)
Illinois Eastern Comm Colls, Wabash Valley College (IL)
Illinois Valley Comm Coll (IL)
Iowa Lakes Comm Coll (IA)
Ivy Tech Comm Coll–Bloomington (IN)
Ivy Tech Comm Coll–Central Indiana (IN)
Ivy Tech Comm Coll–Columbus (IN)
Ivy Tech Comm Coll–East Central (IN)
Ivy Tech Comm Coll–Kokomo (IN)
Ivy Tech Comm Coll–Lafayette (IN)
Ivy Tech Comm Coll–North Central (IN)
Ivy Tech Comm Coll–Northeast (IN)
Ivy Tech Comm Coll–Northwest (IN)
Ivy Tech Comm Coll–Richmond (IN)
Ivy Tech Comm Coll–Southeast (IN)
Ivy Tech Comm Coll–Southern Indiana (IN)
Ivy Tech Comm Coll–Southwest (IN)
Kaskaskia Coll (IL)
Lincoln Land Comm Coll (IL)
Macomb Comm Coll (MI)
Massasoit Comm Coll (MA)
Minneapolis Comm and Tech Coll (MN)
Minnesota State Comm and Tech Coll (MN)
Northeast Iowa Comm Coll (IA)
Northland Pioneer Coll (AZ)
Oakland Comm Coll (MI)
Panola Coll (TX)
Paradise Valley Comm Coll (AZ)
Pasadena City Coll (CA)
Pennsylvania Coll of Technology (PA)
San Jacinto Coll District (TX)
Southwestern Indian Polytechnic Inst (NM)
The U of Montana–Helena Coll of Technology (MT)

Business/Commerce
Allen Comm Coll (KS)
Anoka-Ramsey Comm Coll (MN)
Anoka-Ramsey Comm Coll, Cambridge Campus (MN)
Antelope Valley Coll (CA)
Austin Comm Coll (TX)
Berkeley City Coll (CA)
Berkshire Comm Coll (MA)
Bryant & Stratton Coll, Parma (OH)
Bryant & Stratton Coll (WI)
Bryant & Stratton Coll - Albany Campus (NY)
Bryant & Stratton Coll - Amherst Campus (NY)
Bryant & Stratton Coll - Buffalo Campus (NY)
Bryant & Stratton Coll - Greece Campus (NY)
Bryant & Stratton Coll - Henrietta Campus (NY)
Bryant & Stratton Coll - Richmond Campus (VA)
Bryant & Stratton Coll - Southtowns Campus (NY)
Bryant & Stratton Coll - Syracuse Campus (NY)
Cecil Coll (MD)
Central Arizona Coll (AZ)
Central Wyoming Coll (WY)
Coll of Southern Maryland (MD)
The Comm Coll of Baltimore County (MD)
Comm Coll of Rhode Island (RI)
Cuyamaca Coll (CA)
DeKalb Tech Coll (GA)
Delaware Tech & Comm Coll, Jack F. Owens Campus (DE)
Delaware Tech & Comm Coll, Stanton/Wilmington Campus (DE)
Delaware Tech & Comm Coll, Terry Campus (DE)
Del Mar Coll (TX)
Eastfield Coll (TX)
Elaine P. Nunez Comm Coll (LA)
El Centro Coll (TX)
El Paso Comm Coll (TX)
Everett Comm Coll (WA)
Glendale Comm Coll (AZ)
Goodwin Coll (CT)
Green River Comm Coll (WA)
Harford Comm Coll (MD)
Harrisburg Area Comm Coll (PA)
Howard Coll (TX)
Hutchinson Comm Coll and Area Vocational School (KS)
Jefferson State Comm Coll (AL)
John Tyler Comm Coll (VA)
John Wood Comm Coll (IL)
J. Sargeant Reynolds Comm Coll (VA)
Kankakee Comm Coll (IL)
Kaskaskia Coll (IL)
Kent State U at Salem (OH)
Kilgore Coll (TX)
Lackawanna Coll (PA)
Landmark Coll (VT)
Laramie County Comm Coll (WY)
Macomb Comm Coll (MI)
Mesabi Range Comm and Tech Coll (MN)
Metropolitan Comm Coll–Business & Technology Campus (MO)
Midlands Tech Coll (SC)
Missouri State U–West Plains (MO)
Montgomery Coll (MD)
Montgomery County Comm Coll (PA)
Moraine Valley Comm Coll (IL)
New Mexico State U–Carlsbad (NM)
Northampton Comm Coll (PA)
North Arkansas Coll (AR)
Northland Pioneer Coll (AZ)
Northwest Coll (WY)
Ocean County Coll (NJ)
Orangeburg-Calhoun Tech Coll (SC)
Owens Comm Coll, Toledo (OH)
Paradise Valley Comm Coll (AZ)
Penn State Beaver (PA)
Penn State Brandywine (PA)
Penn State DuBois (PA)
Penn State Fayette, The Eberly Campus (PA)
Penn State Greater Allegheny (PA)
Penn State Hazleton (PA)
Penn State Lehigh Valley (PA)
Penn State Mont Alto (PA)
Penn State New Kensington (PA)
Penn State Schuylkill (PA)
Penn State Shenango (PA)
Penn State Wilkes-Barre (PA)
Penn State Worthington Scranton (PA)
Penn State York (PA)
Quinsigamond Comm Coll (MA)
Raritan Valley Comm Coll (NJ)
Reedley Coll (CA)
Rogue Comm Coll (OR)
San Jacinto Coll District (TX)
Sheridan Coll (WY)
Sierra Coll (CA)
Southern State Comm Coll (OH)
Southern Union State Comm Coll (AL)
Southwestern Indian Polytechnic Inst (NM)
Springfield Tech Comm Coll (MA)
State Coll of Florida Manatee-Sarasota (FL)
Terra State Comm Coll (OH)
Union County Coll (NJ)
U of Arkansas Comm Coll at Morrilton (AR)
U of Cincinnati Clermont Coll (OH)
U of Pittsburgh at Titusville (PA)
Victor Valley Coll (CA)
Wor-Wic Comm Coll (MD)

Business/Corporate Communications
Cecil Coll (MD)
Houston Comm Coll System (TX)
Montgomery County Comm Coll (PA)

Business Machine Repair
Central Piedmont Comm Coll (NC)
Comm Coll of Allegheny County (PA)
Del Mar Coll (TX)
Iowa Lakes Comm Coll (IA)
Minnesota State Coll–Southeast Tech (MN)
Muskegon Comm Coll (MI)
Southern Maine Comm Coll (ME)

Business, Management, and Marketing Related
Blue Ridge Comm and Tech Coll (WV)
Cincinnati State Tech and Comm Coll (OH)
County Coll of Morris (NJ)
East Central Coll (MO)
Eastern Arizona Coll (AZ)
Heart of Georgia Tech Coll (GA)
Kankakee Comm Coll (IL)
Miller-Motte Tech Coll (SC)
Milwaukee Area Tech Coll (WI)
Sandhills Comm Coll (NC)
Tompkins Cortland Comm Coll (NY)

Business/Managerial Economics
Anne Arundel Comm Coll (MD)
Potomac State Coll of West Virginia U (WV)
South Georgia Coll (GA)
State Coll of Florida Manatee-Sarasota (FL)

Business Operations Support and Secretarial Services Related
Bowling Green State U–Firelands Coll (OH)
East Central Coll (MO)
Eastern Arizona Coll (AZ)
Mountain Empire Comm Coll (VA)
Northeast Comm Coll (NE)
Pulaski Tech Coll (AR)
Southwest Virginia Comm Coll (VA)

Business Teacher Education
Allen Comm Coll (KS)
Amarillo Coll (TX)
Bainbridge Coll (GA)
Bronx Comm Coll of the City U of New York (NY)
Darton Coll (GA)
Eastern Arizona Coll (AZ)
Eastern Wyoming Coll (WY)
Essex County Coll (NJ)
Iowa Lakes Comm Coll (IA)
Lawson State Comm Coll (AL)
Murray State Coll (OK)
Northeastern Jr Coll (CO)
North Idaho Coll (ID)
Paris Jr Coll (TX)
Snow Coll (UT)
South Georgia Coll (GA)
Southwest Mississippi Comm Coll (MS)
Trinity Valley Comm Coll (TX)
Vincennes U Jasper Campus (IN)

Cabinetmaking and Millwork
Central Georgia Tech Coll (GA)
Ivy Tech Comm Coll–Bloomington (IN)
Ivy Tech Comm Coll–Central Indiana (IN)
Ivy Tech Comm Coll–Columbus (IN)
Ivy Tech Comm Coll–East Central (IN)
Ivy Tech Comm Coll–Kokomo (IN)
Ivy Tech Comm Coll–Lafayette (IN)
Ivy Tech Comm Coll–North Central (IN)
Ivy Tech Comm Coll–Northeast (IN)
Ivy Tech Comm Coll–Northwest (IN)
Ivy Tech Comm Coll–Richmond (IN)
Ivy Tech Comm Coll–Southern Indiana (IN)
Ivy Tech Comm Coll–Southwest (IN)
Ivy Tech Comm Coll–Wabash Valley (IN)
Macomb Comm Coll (MI)
Minneapolis Comm and Tech Coll (MN)
Pennsylvania Coll of Technology (PA)
Sierra Coll (CA)

CAD/CADD Drafting/ Design Technology
Brown Mackie Coll–Kansas City (KS)
Brown Mackie Coll–North Canton (OH)
Brown Mackie Coll–Northern Kentucky (KY)
Brown Mackie Coll–Salina (KS)
Central Oregon Comm Coll (OR)
Century Coll (MN)
Clackamas Comm Coll (OR)
Comm Coll of Vermont (VT)
Danville Area Comm Coll (IL)
Delaware County Comm Coll (PA)
Delaware Tech & Comm Coll, Stanton/Wilmington Campus (DE)
Elgin Comm Coll (IL)
Erie Comm Coll, South Campus (NY)
Everett Comm Coll (WA)
Front Range Comm Coll (CO)
Gateway Comm and Tech Coll (KY)
Glendale Comm Coll (AZ)
Harford Comm Coll (MD)
Illinois Valley Comm Coll (IL)
ITT Tech Inst, Bessemer (AL)
ITT Tech Inst, Madison (AL)
ITT Tech Inst, Mobile (AL)
ITT Tech Inst, Phoenix (AZ)
ITT Tech Inst, Tucson (AZ)
ITT Tech Inst (AR)
ITT Tech Inst, Anaheim (CA)
ITT Tech Inst, Lathrop (CA)
ITT Tech Inst, Oxnard (CA)
ITT Tech Inst, Rancho Cordova (CA)
ITT Tech Inst, San Bernardino (CA)
ITT Tech Inst, San Diego (CA)
ITT Tech Inst, San Dimas (CA)
ITT Tech Inst, Sylmar (CA)
ITT Tech Inst, Torrance (CA)
ITT Tech Inst, Aurora (CO)
ITT Tech Inst, Thornton (CO)
ITT Tech Inst, Fort Lauderdale (FL)
ITT Tech Inst, Fort Myers (FL)
ITT Tech Inst, Jacksonville (FL)
ITT Tech Inst, Lake Mary (FL)
ITT Tech Inst, Miami (FL)
ITT Tech Inst, Pinellas Park (FL)
ITT Tech Inst, Tallahassee (FL)
ITT Tech Inst, Tampa (FL)
ITT Tech Inst, Atlanta (GA)
ITT Tech Inst, Duluth (GA)
ITT Tech Inst, Kennesaw (GA)
ITT Tech Inst (ID)
ITT Tech Inst, Burr Ridge (IL)
ITT Tech Inst, Mount Prospect (IL)
ITT Tech Inst, Orland Park (IL)
ITT Tech Inst, Fort Wayne (IN)
ITT Tech Inst, Indianapolis (IN)
ITT Tech Inst, Merrillville (IN)
ITT Tech Inst, Newburgh (IN)
ITT Tech Inst, Cedar Rapids (IA)
ITT Tech Inst, Clive (IA)
ITT Tech Inst, Louisville (KY)
ITT Tech Inst, Baton Rouge (LA)
ITT Tech Inst, St. Rose (LA)
ITT Tech Inst (MD)
ITT Tech Inst, Norwood (MA)
ITT Tech Inst, Woburn (MA)
ITT Tech Inst, Canton (MI)
ITT Tech Inst, Swartz Creek (MI)
ITT Tech Inst, Troy (MI)
ITT Tech Inst, Wyoming (MI)
ITT Tech Inst (MN)
ITT Tech Inst, Arnold (MO)
ITT Tech Inst, Earth City (MO)
ITT Tech Inst, Kansas City (MO)
ITT Tech Inst (NE)
ITT Tech Inst (NV)
ITT Tech Inst (NM)
ITT Tech Inst, Albany (NY)
ITT Tech Inst, Getzville (NY)
ITT Tech Inst, Liverpool (NY)
ITT Tech Inst, Akron (OH)
ITT Tech Inst, Columbus (OH)
ITT Tech Inst, Dayton (OH)
ITT Tech Inst, Hilliard (OH)
ITT Tech Inst, Maumee (OH)
ITT Tech Inst, Norwood (OH)
ITT Tech Inst, Strongsville (OH)
ITT Tech Inst, Warrensville Heights (OH)
ITT Tech Inst, Youngstown (OH)
ITT Tech Inst, Tulsa (OK)
ITT Tech Inst (OR)
ITT Tech Inst, Bensalem (PA)
ITT Tech Inst, Dunmore (PA)
ITT Tech Inst, Harrisburg (PA)
ITT Tech Inst, King of Prussia (PA)
ITT Tech Inst, Pittsburgh (PA)
ITT Tech Inst, Tarentum (PA)
ITT Tech Inst, Columbia (SC)
ITT Tech Inst, Greenville (SC)
ITT Tech Inst, Chattanooga (TN)
ITT Tech Inst, Cordova (TN)
ITT Tech Inst, Johnson City (TN)
ITT Tech Inst, Knoxville (TN)
ITT Tech Inst, Nashville (TN)
ITT Tech Inst, Arlington (TX)
ITT Tech Inst, Austin (TX)
ITT Tech Inst, DeSoto (TX)
ITT Tech Inst, Houston (TX)
ITT Tech Inst, Houston (TX)
ITT Tech Inst, Richardson (TX)
ITT Tech Inst, San Antonio (TX)
ITT Tech Inst, Webster (TX)
ITT Tech Inst (UT)
ITT Tech Inst, Chantilly (VA)
ITT Tech Inst, Norfolk (VA)

ITT Tech Inst, Richmond (VA)
ITT Tech Inst, Salem (VA)
ITT Tech Inst, Springfield (VA)
ITT Tech Inst, Everett (WA)
ITT Tech Inst, Seattle (WA)
ITT Tech Inst, Spokane Valley (WA)
ITT Tech Inst (WV)
ITT Tech Inst, Green Bay (WI)
ITT Tech Inst, Greenfield (WI)
ITT Tech Inst, Madison (WI)
Kalamazoo Valley Comm Coll (MI)
Lewis and Clark Comm Coll (IL)
Lonestar Coll–Montgomery (TX)
Lonestar Coll–North Harris (TX)
Montgomery County Comm Coll (PA)
Mountain Empire Comm Coll (VA)
Northampton Comm Coll (PA)
Northwest Coll (WY)
Northwest Tech Inst (MN)
Olympic Coll (WA)
Pikes Peak Comm Coll (CO)
St. Philip's Coll (TX)
Sheridan Coll (WY)
South Suburban Coll (IL)
State Fair Comm Coll (MO)
State U of New York Coll of Technology at Alfred (NY)
Sullivan Coll of Technology and Design (KY)
Thomas Nelson Comm Coll (VA)
Triton Coll (IL)

Cardiopulmonary Technology
Lackawanna Coll (PA)

Cardiovascular Technology
Augusta Tech Coll (GA)
Bunker Hill Comm Coll (MA)
Central Georgia Tech Coll (GA)
Chattanooga State Comm Coll (TN)
Darton Coll (GA)
Delaware Tech & Comm Coll, Stanton/Wilmington Campus (DE)
El Centro Coll (TX)
Harrisburg Area Comm Coll (PA)
Houston Comm Coll System (TX)
Howard Comm Coll (MD)
Kirtland Comm Coll (MI)
Milwaukee Area Tech Coll (WI)
Northland Comm and Tech Coll–Thief River Falls (MN)
Orange Coast Coll (CA)
Polk State Coll (FL)
St. Cloud Tech Coll (MN)
Southeast Tech Inst (SD)
Southern Maine Comm Coll (ME)
Spencerian Coll (KY)

Carpentry
Alamance Comm Coll (NC)
Alexandria Tech Coll (MN)
Austin Comm Coll (TX)
Bakersfield Coll (CA)
Black Hawk Coll, Moline (IL)
Central Georgia Tech Coll (GA)
Central Wyoming Coll (WY)
Comm Coll of Allegheny County (PA)
Delta Coll (MI)
Elaine P. Nunez Comm Coll (LA)
Flathead Valley Comm Coll (MT)
Fulton-Montgomery Comm Coll (NY)
Gateway Comm and Tech Coll (KY)
Green River Comm Coll (WA)
Hennepin Tech Coll (MN)
Honolulu Comm Coll (HI)
Hutchinson Comm Coll and Area Vocational School (KS)
Illinois Valley Comm Coll (IL)
Indian River State Coll (FL)
Iowa Lakes Comm Coll (IA)
Ivy Tech Comm Coll–Central Indiana (IN)
Ivy Tech Comm Coll–East Central (IN)
Ivy Tech Comm Coll–Lafayette (IN)
Ivy Tech Comm Coll–North Central (IN)
Ivy Tech Comm Coll–Northwest (IN)
Ivy Tech Comm Coll–Southern Indiana (IN)
Ivy Tech Comm Coll–Southwest (IN)
Ivy Tech Comm Coll–Wabash Valley (IN)
Kaskaskia Coll (IL)
Kauai Comm Coll (HI)
Kirtland Comm Coll (MI)
Lac Courte Oreilles Ojibwa Comm Coll (WI)
Lansing Comm Coll (MI)
Metropolitan Comm Coll–Business & Technology Campus (MO)
Minnesota State Coll–Southeast Tech (MN)
Minnesota State Comm and Tech Coll (MN)
Mitchell Tech Inst (SD)
Montana State U–Great Falls Coll of Technology (MT)
New Mexico State U–Carlsbad (NM)
North Idaho Coll (ID)
North Iowa Area Comm Coll (IA)
North Lake Coll (TX)
Northland Comm and Tech Coll–Thief River Falls (MN)
Northland Pioneer Coll (AZ)
Oakland Comm Coll (MI)
Pennsylvania Coll of Technology (PA)
St. Cloud Tech Coll (MN)
San Diego City Coll (CA)
San Juan Coll (NM)
Southern Maine Comm Coll (ME)
South Plains Coll (TX)
Southwestern Comm Coll (IA)
Southwest Mississippi Comm Coll (MS)
State U of New York Coll of Technology at Alfred (NY)
Triangle Tech–Greensburg School (PA)
Triangle Tech Inc–Bethlehem (PA)
Triangle Tech, Inc.–DuBois School (PA)
Triangle Tech, Inc.–Erie School (PA)
Triangle Tech, Inc.–Sunbury School (PA)
The U of Montana–Helena Coll of Technology (MT)

Cartography
Alexandria Tech Coll (MN)
Austin Comm Coll (TX)
Houston Comm Coll System (TX)
Southwestern Indian Polytechnic Inst (NM)
White Mountains Comm Coll (NH)

Ceramic Arts and Ceramics
Iowa Lakes Comm Coll (IA)
Mercer County Comm Coll (NJ)
Montgomery Comm Coll (NC)
Oakland Comm Coll (MI)
Palm Beach State Coll (FL)

Chemical Engineering
Alpena Comm Coll (MI)
Burlington County Coll (NJ)
Delta Coll (MI)
Itasca Comm Coll (MN)
Kilgore Coll (TX)
Lansing Comm Coll (MI)
Muskegon Comm Coll (MI)
Pasadena City Coll (CA)
Westchester Comm Coll (NY)

Chemical Technology
Alvin Comm Coll (TX)
Amarillo Coll (TX)
Cape Fear Comm Coll (NC)
Cincinnati State Tech and Comm Coll (OH)
Coll of Lake County (IL)
Comm Coll of Allegheny County (PA)
Comm Coll of Philadelphia (PA)
Comm Coll of Rhode Island (RI)
Corning Comm Coll (NY)
County Coll of Morris (NJ)
Delaware Tech & Comm Coll, Stanton/Wilmington Campus (DE)
Del Mar Coll (TX)
Essex County Coll (NJ)
Guilford Tech Comm Coll (NC)
Houston Comm Coll System (TX)
ITI Tech Coll (LA)
Kalamazoo Valley Comm Coll (MI)
Kellogg Comm Coll (MI)
Lehigh Carbon Comm Coll (PA)
Milwaukee Area Tech Coll (WI)
Mohawk Valley Comm Coll (NY)
Niagara County Comm Coll (NY)
Northampton Comm Coll (PA)
Raritan Valley Comm Coll (NJ)
Saint Paul Coll–A Comm & Tech College (MN)
San Jacinto Coll District (TX)
Westmoreland County Comm Coll (PA)

Chemistry
Allan Hancock Coll (CA)
Allen Comm Coll (KS)
Alpena Comm Coll (MI)
Amarillo Coll (TX)
Anne Arundel Comm Coll (MD)
Arizona Western Coll (AZ)
Austin Comm Coll (TX)
Bainbridge Coll (GA)
Bakersfield Coll (CA)
Barton County Comm Coll (KS)
Bronx Comm Coll of the City U of New York (NY)
Bucks County Comm Coll (PA)
Bunker Hill Comm Coll (MA)
Burlington County Coll (NJ)
Casper Coll (WY)
Central Texas Coll (TX)
Clarendon Coll (TX)
Comm Coll of Allegheny County (PA)
Cowley County Comm Coll and Area Vocational–Tech School (KS)
Cuyamaca Coll (CA)
Dakota Coll at Bottineau (ND)
Darton Coll (GA)
Del Mar Coll (TX)
Eastern Arizona Coll (AZ)
East Los Angeles Coll (CA)
Essex County Coll (NJ)
Everett Comm Coll (WA)
Finger Lakes Comm Coll (NY)
Frederick Comm Coll (MD)
Gainesville State Coll (GA)
Harrisburg Area Comm Coll (PA)
Highland Comm Coll (IL)
Howard Coll (TX)
Indian River State Coll (FL)
Iowa Lakes Comm Coll (IA)
Kilgore Coll (TX)
Kingsborough Comm Coll of the City U of New York (NY)
Lake Michigan Coll (MI)
Lansing Comm Coll (MI)
Laramie County Comm Coll (WY)
Lawson State Comm Coll (AL)
Linn-Benton Comm Coll (OR)
Lonestar Coll–Cy-Fair (TX)
Lonestar Coll–Kingwood (TX)
Lonestar Coll–Montgomery (TX)
Lonestar Coll–North Harris (TX)
Lonestar Coll–Tomball (TX)
Lon Morris Coll (TX)
Macomb Comm Coll (MI)
Mendocino Coll (CA)
Mercer County Comm Coll (NJ)
Metropolitan Comm Coll–Longview (MO)
Metropolitan Comm Coll–Maple Woods (MO)
Metropolitan Comm Coll–Penn Valley (MO)
Miami Dade Coll (FL)
Minneapolis Comm and Tech Coll (MN)
Murray State Coll (OK)
Northampton Comm Coll (PA)
Northeast Comm Coll (NE)
North Hennepin Comm Coll (MN)
North Idaho Coll (ID)
Northwest Coll (WY)
Northwest Florida State Coll (FL)
Odessa Coll (TX)
Oklahoma City Comm Coll (OK)
Orange Coast Coll (CA)
Palm Beach State Coll (FL)
Pasadena City Coll (CA)
Potomac State Coll of West Virginia U (WV)
Red Rocks Comm Coll (CO)
Saint Charles Comm Coll (MO)
St. Philip's Coll (TX)
Salt Lake Comm Coll (UT)
San Diego Mesa Coll (CA)
San Jacinto Coll District (TX)
San Juan Coll (NM)
Santa Rosa Jr Coll (CA)
Sierra Coll (CA)
Snow Coll (UT)
South Georgia Coll (GA)
South Plains Coll (TX)
Southwest Mississippi Comm Coll (MS)
Springfield Tech Comm Coll (MA)
State Coll of Florida Manatee-Sarasota (FL)
Suffolk County Comm Coll (NY)
Terra State Comm Coll (OH)
Trinity Valley Comm Coll (TX)
Triton Coll (IL)
Umpqua Comm Coll (OR)
Union County Coll (NJ)
U of Cincinnati Clermont Coll (OH)
Western Wyoming Comm Coll (WY)

Chemistry Teacher Education
The Comm Coll of Baltimore County (MD)
Harford Comm Coll (MD)
Howard Coll (TX)
Montgomery Coll (MD)
State Coll of Florida Manatee-Sarasota (FL)
Ulster County Comm Coll (NY)

Child-Care and Support Services Management
Alexandria Tech Coll (MN)
Antelope Valley Coll (CA)
Barton County Comm Coll (KS)
Bevill State Comm Coll (AL)
Blue Ridge Comm Coll (NC)
Broome Comm Coll (NY)
Carroll Comm Coll (MD)
Cecil Coll (MD)
Central Carolina Tech Coll (SC)
Central Comm Coll–Columbus Campus (NE)
Central Comm Coll–Hastings Campus (NE)
Central Georgia Tech Coll (GA)
Central Lakes Coll (MN)
Central New Mexico Comm Coll (NM)
Central Oregon Comm Coll (OR)
Central Texas Coll (TX)
Central Wyoming Coll (WY)
Clackamas Comm Coll (OR)
Colby Comm Coll (KS)
Coll of DuPage (IL)
Coll of Southern Maryland (MD)
The Comm Coll of Baltimore County (MD)
Cowley County Comm Coll and Area Vocational–Tech School (KS)
Dakota Coll at Bottineau (ND)
East Central Coll (MO)
Eastfield Coll (TX)
El Paso Comm Coll (TX)
Erie Comm Coll (NY)
Flathead Valley Comm Coll (MT)
Forrest Jr Coll (SC)
Front Range Comm Coll (CO)
Gadsden State Comm Coll (AL)
Glendale Comm Coll (AZ)
Harford Comm Coll (MD)
H. Councill Trenholm State Tech Coll (AL)
Highland Comm Coll (IL)
Hillsborough Comm Coll (FL)
Holyoke Comm Coll (MA)
Hopkinsville Comm Coll (KY)
Hutchinson Comm Coll and Area Vocational School (KS)
Ivy Tech Comm Coll–Bloomington (IN)
Ivy Tech Comm Coll–Central Indiana (IN)
Ivy Tech Comm Coll–Columbus (IN)
Ivy Tech Comm Coll–East Central (IN)
Ivy Tech Comm Coll–Kokomo (IN)
Ivy Tech Comm Coll–Lafayette (IN)
Ivy Tech Comm Coll–North Central (IN)
Ivy Tech Comm Coll–Northeast (IN)
Ivy Tech Comm Coll–Northwest (IN)
Ivy Tech Comm Coll–Richmond (IN)
Ivy Tech Comm Coll–Southeast (IN)
Ivy Tech Comm Coll–Southern Indiana (IN)
Ivy Tech Comm Coll–Southwest (IN)
Ivy Tech Comm Coll–Wabash Valley (IN)
Jefferson Comm Coll (NY)
Jefferson State Comm Coll (AL)
Kaplan U, South Portland (ME)
Kilgore Coll (TX)
Lake Region State Coll (ND)
Linn-Benton Comm Coll (OR)
Lurleen B. Wallace Comm Coll (AL)
Macomb Comm Coll (MI)
Massasoit Comm Coll (MA)
Minneapolis Comm and Tech Coll (MN)
Missouri State U–West Plains (MO)
Montcalm Comm Coll (MI)
Montgomery Comm Coll (NC)
Montgomery County Comm Coll (PA)
Mount Wachusett Comm Coll (MA)
Northland Pioneer Coll (AZ)
Northwest Tech Coll (MN)
Oakland Comm Coll (MI)
Ocean County Coll (NJ)
Olympic Coll (WA)
Orange Coast Coll (CA)
Ouachita Tech Coll (AR)
Pennsylvania Coll of Technology (PA)
Piedmont Comm Coll (NC)
Reedley Coll (CA)
Rogue Comm Coll (OR)
Saint Charles Comm Coll (MO)
St. Cloud Tech Coll (MN)
Saint Paul Coll–A Comm & Tech College (MN)
Southeast Tech Inst (SD)
Southern Union State Comm Coll (AL)
Stanly Comm Coll (NC)
State Fair Comm Coll (MO)
Tompkins Cortland Comm Coll (NY)
Victor Valley Coll (CA)
Wor-Wic Comm Coll (MD)

Child Care Provider
Somerset Comm Coll (KY)

Child-Care Provision
Alexandria Tech Coll (MN)
Black Hawk Coll, Moline (IL)
Bladen Comm Coll (NC)
Cincinnati State Tech and Comm Coll (OH)
City Colls of Chicago, Malcolm X College (IL)
Coll of DuPage (IL)
Coll of Lake County (IL)
Collin County Comm Coll District (TX)
Comm Coll of Allegheny County (PA)
The Comm Coll of Baltimore County (MD)
Corning Comm Coll (NY)
Dakota Coll at Bottineau (ND)
Danville Area Comm Coll (IL)
Des Moines Area Comm Coll (IA)
Eastern Arizona Coll (AZ)
Elaine P. Nunez Comm Coll (LA)
Elgin Comm Coll (IL)
Harcum Coll (PA)
Hawkeye Comm Coll (IA)
Hazard Comm and Tech Coll (KY)
Highland Comm Coll (IL)
Hopkinsville Comm Coll (KY)
Illinois Valley Comm Coll (IL)
Iowa Lakes Comm Coll (IA)
Kaskaskia Coll (IL)
Kilgore Coll (TX)
Kirkwood Comm Coll (IA)
Lakeland Comm Coll (OH)
Lake Region State Coll (ND)
Lake-Sumter Comm Coll (FL)
Lewis and Clark Comm Coll (IL)
Lincoln Land Comm Coll (IL)
Louisiana Tech Coll (LA)
Massasoit Comm Coll (MA)
Metropolitan Comm Coll–Penn Valley (MO)
Midlands Tech Coll (SC)
Montcalm Comm Coll (MI)
Montgomery Coll (MD)
Moraine Park Tech Coll (WI)
Moraine Valley Comm Coll (IL)

Northland Comm and Tech Coll–Thief River Falls (MN)
Northland Pioneer Coll (AZ)
Orange Coast Coll (CA)
Pennsylvania Coll of Technology (PA)
Pensacola Jr Coll (FL)
Raritan Valley Comm Coll (NJ)
Rend Lake Coll (IL)
San Diego Mesa Coll (CA)
San Juan Coll (NM)
Southeast Tech Inst (SD)
South Suburban Coll (IL)
Southwest Virginia Comm Coll (VA)
Trident Tech Coll (SC)
Triton Coll (IL)
Westchester Comm Coll (NY)
Westmoreland County Comm Coll (PA)

Child Development
Albany Tech Coll (GA)
Allen Comm Coll (KS)
Altamaha Tech Coll (GA)
Alvin Comm Coll (TX)
Amarillo Coll (TX)
Antelope Valley Coll (CA)
Athens Tech Coll (GA)
Atlanta Tech Coll (GA)
Augusta Tech Coll (GA)
Austin Comm Coll (TX)
Bakersfield Coll (CA)
Black Hawk Coll, Moline (IL)
Bronx Comm Coll of the City U of New York (NY)
Central Arizona Coll (AZ)
Central Comm Coll–Grand Island Campus (NE)
Central Comm Coll–Hastings Campus (NE)
Central Georgia Tech Coll (GA)
Central Piedmont Comm Coll (NC)
Chattahoochee Tech Coll (GA)
Chattanooga State Comm Coll (TN)
City Colls of Chicago, Richard J. Daley College (IL)
Cleveland State Comm Coll (TN)
Colby Comm Coll (KS)
Coll of DuPage (IL)
Coll of the Canyons (CA)
Collin County Comm Coll District (TX)
Columbus Tech Coll (GA)
Comm Coll of Allegheny County (PA)
Comm Coll of Vermont (VT)
Cowley County Comm Coll and Area Vocational–Tech School (KS)
Cuyamaca Coll (CA)
Daytona State Coll (FL)
Del Mar Coll (TX)
Delta Coll (MI)
East Central Tech Coll (GA)
East Los Angeles Coll (CA)
Edison State Comm Coll (OH)
El Paso Comm Coll (TX)
Flint River Tech Coll (GA)
Fox Valley Tech Coll (WI)
Frederick Comm Coll (MD)
Georgia Northwestern Tech Coll (GA)
Griffin Tech Coll (GA)
Heart of Georgia Tech Coll (GA)
Hennepin Tech Coll (MN)
Highland Comm Coll (IL)
Housatonic Comm Coll (CT)
Houston Comm Coll System (TX)
Howard Coll (TX)
Howard Comm Coll (MD)
Illinois Eastern Comm Colls, Wabash Valley College (IL)
Illinois Valley Comm Coll (IL)
Indian River State Coll (FL)
Iowa Lakes Comm Coll (IA)
Ivy Tech Comm Coll–Central Indiana (IN)
Jackson State Comm Coll (TN)
Jefferson Comm Coll (NY)
Kankakee Comm Coll (IL)
Kennebec Valley Comm Coll (ME)
Lanier Tech Coll (GA)
Lansing Comm Coll (MI)
Lincoln Land Comm Coll (IL)
Mendocino Coll (CA)
Metropolitan Comm Coll (NE)
Miami Dade Coll (FL)
Middle Georgia Tech Coll (GA)
Minnesota State Coll–Southeast Tech (MN)
Moultrie Tech Coll (GA)
Mt. San Jacinto Coll (CA)
Mount Wachusett Comm Coll (MA)
Murray State Coll (OK)
Muskegon Comm Coll (MI)
Nicolet Area Tech Coll (WI)
Northeastern Jr Coll (CO)
Northland Comm and Tech Coll–Thief River Falls (MN)
Northland Pioneer Coll (AZ)
Northwestern Connecticut Comm Coll (CT)
Northwest Florida State Coll (FL)
Northwest-Shoals Comm Coll (AL)
Odessa Coll (TX)
Ogeechee Tech Coll (GA)
Okefenokee Tech Coll (GA)
Oklahoma City Comm Coll (OK)
Otero Jr Coll (CO)
Pasadena City Coll (CA)
Pikes Peak Comm Coll (CO)
Polk State Coll (FL)
Pueblo Comm Coll (CO)
Pulaski Tech Coll (AR)
Rogue Comm Coll (OR)
Saint Charles Comm Coll (MO)
Sandersville Tech Coll (GA)
Sandhills Comm Coll (NC)
San Jacinto Coll District (TX)
Santa Rosa Jr Coll (CA)
Savannah Tech Coll (GA)
Seminole State Coll of Florida (FL)
Shawnee Comm Coll (IL)
Sierra Coll (CA)
Snow Coll (UT)
Southeastern Comm Coll (IA)
Southeastern Tech Coll (GA)
Southern Maine Comm Coll (ME)
South Georgia Tech Coll (GA)
South Plains Coll (TX)
Southwest Georgia Tech Coll (GA)
Stark State Coll of Technology (OH)
State Coll of Florida Manatee-Sarasota (FL)
Suffolk County Comm Coll (NY)
Tohono O'odham Comm Coll (AZ)
Trinity Valley Comm Coll (TX)
Umpqua Comm Coll (OR)
U of Arkansas Comm Coll at Morrilton (AR)
Valdosta Tech Coll (GA)
Victor Valley Coll (CA)
Volunteer State Comm Coll (TN)
Walters State Comm Coll (TN)
Westchester Comm Coll (NY)
West Georgia Tech Coll (GA)

Chinese
Austin Comm Coll (TX)

Chiropractic Assistant
Barton County Comm Coll (KS)
Iowa Lakes Comm Coll (IA)
Moraine Park Tech Coll (WI)

Cinematography and Film/Video Production
Anne Arundel Comm Coll (MD)
Antelope Valley Coll (CA)
The Art Inst of New York City (NY)
The Art Inst of Ohio–Cincinnati (OH)
The Art Inst of Seattle (WA)
Bucks County Comm Coll (PA)
Camden County Coll (NJ)
Cape Fear Comm Coll (NC)
Cincinnati State Tech and Comm Coll (OH)
Coll of DuPage (IL)
Coll of the Canyons (CA)
El Paso Comm Coll (TX)
Glendale Comm Coll (AZ)
Hillsborough Comm Coll (FL)
Houston Comm Coll System (TX)
Lansing Comm Coll (MI)
Minneapolis Comm and Tech Coll (MN)
Northwest Coll (WY)
Orange Coast Coll (CA)
Pasadena City Coll (CA)
Pensacola Jr Coll (FL)
Piedmont Comm Coll (NC)
Raritan Valley Comm Coll (NJ)
Red Rocks Comm Coll (CO)
Southern Maine Comm Coll (ME)

Civil Drafting and CAD/CADD
Comm Coll of Allegheny County (PA)
Delaware Tech & Comm Coll, Stanton/Wilmington Campus (DE)
Southwestern Comm Coll (IA)

Civil Engineering
Fiorello H. LaGuardia Comm Coll of the City U of New York (NY)
Itasca Comm Coll (MN)
Kilgore Coll (TX)
Pasadena City Coll (CA)
Saint Charles Comm Coll (MO)
Santa Rosa Jr Coll (CA)
Tidewater Comm Coll (VA)

Civil Engineering Technology
Allan Hancock Coll (CA)
Broome Comm Coll (NY)
Central Arizona Coll (AZ)
Central Carolina Tech Coll (SC)
Central Piedmont Comm Coll (NC)
Chattahoochee Tech Coll (GA)
Chattanooga State Comm Coll (TN)
Cincinnati State Tech and Comm Coll (OH)
Coll of Lake County (IL)
Comm Coll of Allegheny County (PA)
The Comm Coll of Baltimore County (MD)
Delaware Tech & Comm Coll, Jack F. Owens Campus (DE)
Delaware Tech & Comm Coll, Terry Campus (DE)
Des Moines Area Comm Coll (IA)
Eastern Arizona Coll (AZ)
East Los Angeles Coll (CA)
Erie Comm Coll, North Campus (NY)
Essex County Coll (NJ)
Fayetteville Tech Comm Coll (NC)
Gadsden State Comm Coll (AL)
Guilford Tech Comm Coll (NC)
Harrisburg Area Comm Coll (PA)
Hawkeye Comm Coll (IA)
Indian River State Coll (FL)
Lakeland Comm Coll (OH)
Lansing Comm Coll (MI)
Linn-Benton Comm Coll (OR)
Linn State Tech Coll (MO)
Macomb Comm Coll (MI)
Mercer County Comm Coll (NJ)
Metropolitan Comm Coll (NE)
Miami Dade Coll (FL)
Midlands Tech Coll (SC)
Milwaukee Area Tech Coll (WI)
Minnesota State Comm and Tech Coll (MN)
Mohawk Valley Comm Coll (NY)
Moultrie Tech Coll (GA)
Nassau Comm Coll (NY)
Ocean County Coll (NJ)
Oklahoma State U, Oklahoma City (OK)
Pensacola Jr Coll (FL)
Phoenix Coll (AZ)
Potomac State Coll of West Virginia U (WV)
Quinsigamond Comm Coll (MA)
St. Cloud Tech Coll (MN)
Sandhills Comm Coll (NC)
Seminole State Coll of Florida (FL)
Southeast Tech Inst (SD)
Springfield Tech Comm Coll (MA)
Stark State Coll of Technology (OH)
State Coll of Florida Manatee-Sarasota (FL)
Suffolk County Comm Coll (NY)
Tallahassee Comm Coll (FL)
Three Rivers Comm Coll (CT)
Trident Tech Coll (SC)
Umpqua Comm Coll (OR)
Union County Coll (NJ)
Westchester Comm Coll (NY)

Classics and Languages, Literatures And Linguistics
Pasadena City Coll (CA)

Clinical Laboratory Science/Medical Technology
Amarillo Coll (TX)
Anne Arundel Comm Coll (MD)
Athens Tech Coll (GA)
Casper Coll (WY)
Central Piedmont Comm Coll (NC)
Chipola Coll (FL)
City Colls of Chicago, Richard J. Daley College (IL)
Cuyahoga Comm Coll (OH)
Darton Coll (GA)
Del Mar Coll (TX)
Georgia Highlands Coll (GA)
Harrison Coll, Indianapolis (IN)
Howard Comm Coll (MD)
Lansing Comm Coll (MI)
Lawson State Comm Coll (AL)
Northeastern Jr Coll (CO)
North Idaho Coll (ID)
Northwest Florida State Coll (FL)
Orange Coast Coll (CA)
Phoenix Coll (AZ)
San Jacinto Coll District (TX)
Spencerian Coll (KY)
Tarrant County Coll District (TX)
Westchester Comm Coll (NY)

Clinical/Medical Laboratory Assistant
Allegany Coll of Maryland (MD)
Delaware Tech & Comm Coll, Jack F. Owens Campus (DE)
Louisiana Tech Coll (LA)
Minnesota State Comm and Tech Coll (MN)
Somerset Comm Coll (KY)

Clinical/Medical Laboratory Science and Allied Professions Related
Highline Comm Coll (WA)
Houston Comm Coll System (TX)
Pima Comm Coll (AZ)
Southeast Tech Inst (SD)

Clinical/Medical Laboratory Technology
Alamance Comm Coll (NC)
Alexandria Tech Coll (MN)
Allegany Coll of Maryland (MD)
Arkansas State U–Beebe (AR)
Austin Comm Coll (TX)
Barton County Comm Coll (KS)
Beaufort County Comm Coll (NC)
Bronx Comm Coll of the City U of New York (NY)
Broome Comm Coll (NY)
Camden County Coll (NJ)
Central Georgia Tech Coll (GA)
Central New Mexico Comm Coll (NM)
Central Piedmont Comm Coll (NC)
Central Texas Coll (TX)
Cincinnati State Tech and Comm Coll (OH)
City Colls of Chicago, Malcolm X College (IL)
Coll of Southern Maryland (MD)
Comm Coll of Allegheny County (PA)
The Comm Coll of Baltimore County (MD)
Comm Coll of Philadelphia (PA)
Comm Coll of Rhode Island (RI)
DeKalb Tech Coll (GA)
Del Mar Coll (TX)
Des Moines Area Comm Coll (IA)
Edison State Comm Coll (OH)
El Centro Coll (TX)
Elgin Comm Coll (IL)
El Paso Comm Coll (TX)
Erie Comm Coll, North Campus (NY)
Gadsden State Comm Coll (AL)
Genesee Comm Coll (NY)
Georgia Perimeter Coll (GA)
Harcum Coll (PA)
Harrisburg Area Comm Coll (PA)
Hawkeye Comm Coll (IA)
Housatonic Comm Coll (CT)
Houston Comm Coll System (TX)
Indian River State Coll (FL)
Ivy Tech Comm Coll–North Central (IN)
Ivy Tech Comm Coll–Wabash Valley (IN)
Jackson State Comm Coll (TN)
Jamestown Comm Coll (NY)
Jefferson State Comm Coll (AL)
John Wood Comm Coll (IL)
J. Sargeant Reynolds Comm Coll (VA)
Kankakee Comm Coll (IL)
Kellogg Comm Coll (MI)
Kilgore Coll (TX)
Lakeland Comm Coll (OH)
Manchester Comm Coll (CT)
Marion Tech Coll (OH)
Mercer County Comm Coll (NJ)
Meridian Comm Coll (MS)
Miami Dade Coll (FL)
Midlands Tech Coll (SC)
Mid-Plains Comm Coll, North Platte (NE)
Milwaukee Area Tech Coll (WI)
Minnesota State Comm and Tech Coll (MN)
Minnesota West Comm and Tech Coll (MN)
Mitchell Tech Inst (SD)
Montgomery County Comm Coll (PA)
Moraine Park Tech Coll (WI)
Mount Wachusett Comm Coll (MA)
Nassau Comm Coll (NY)
North Arkansas Coll (AR)
Northeast Iowa Comm Coll (IA)
North Hennepin Comm Coll (MN)
North Iowa Area Comm Coll (IA)
Ocean County Coll (NJ)
Odessa Coll (TX)
The Ohio State U Ag Tech Inst (OH)
Okefenokee Tech Coll (GA)
Orangeburg-Calhoun Tech Coll (SC)
Penn State Hazleton (PA)
Penn State Schuylkill (PA)
Phoenix Coll (AZ)
Pima Comm Coll (AZ)
Rend Lake Coll (IL)
Saint Paul Coll–A Comm & Tech College (MN)
St. Philip's Coll (TX)
Salt Lake Comm Coll (UT)
Sandhills Comm Coll (NC)
San Diego Mesa Coll (CA)
San Jacinto Coll District (TX)
San Juan Coll (NM)
Seminole State Coll (OK)
Southeast Kentucky Comm and Tech Coll (KY)
Southeast Tech Inst (SD)
Spartanburg Comm Coll (SC)
Springfield Tech Comm Coll (MA)
Stark State Coll of Technology (OH)
Tarrant County Coll District (TX)
Three Rivers Comm Coll (MO)
Trident Tech Coll (SC)
Victoria Coll (TX)
Volunteer State Comm Coll (TN)
Westchester Comm Coll (NY)

Clinical/Medical Social Work
Central Comm Coll–Grand Island Campus (NE)
Central Comm Coll–Hastings Campus (NE)
Piedmont Comm Coll (NC)
Pima Comm Coll (AZ)
Wayne Comm Coll (NC)

Clinical Nutrition
Central Arizona Coll (AZ)

Commercial and Advertising Art
Alamance Comm Coll (NC)
Alexandria Tech Coll (MN)
Allan Hancock Coll (CA)
Amarillo Coll (TX)
Antonelli Coll, Jackson (MS)
Antonelli Coll (OH)
Austin Comm Coll (TX)
Bryant & Stratton Coll (WI)
Bryant & Stratton Coll - Amherst Campus (NY)
Bryant & Stratton Coll - Henrietta Campus (NY)
Bucks County Comm Coll (PA)
Burlington County Coll (NJ)
Carroll Comm Coll (MD)
Catawba Valley Comm Coll (NC)
Central Comm Coll–Columbus Campus (NE)
Central Comm Coll–Hastings Campus (NE)
Central Lakes Coll (MN)
Central Piedmont Comm Coll (NC)
Central Texas Coll (TX)
Chattanooga State Comm Coll (TN)
Cincinnati State Tech and Comm Coll (OH)

Clovis Comm Coll (NM)
Coll of DuPage (IL)
Collin County Comm Coll District (TX)
Comm Coll of Allegheny County (PA)
The Comm Coll of Baltimore County (MD)
Cuyahoga Comm Coll (OH)
Cuyamaca Coll (CA)
Davis Coll (OH)
Delaware County Comm Coll (PA)
Delaware Tech & Comm Coll, Terry Campus (DE)
Des Moines Area Comm Coll (IA)
East Central Coll (MO)
Eastern Arizona Coll (AZ)
Edison State Comm Coll (OH)
El Paso Comm Coll (TX)
Fashion Inst of Technology (NY)
Fayetteville Tech Comm Coll (NC)
FIDM/The Fashion Inst of Design & Merchandising, Los Angeles Campus (CA)
FIDM/The Fashion Inst of Design & Merchandising, San Diego Campus (CA)
FIDM/The Fashion Inst of Design & Merchandising, San Francisco Campus (CA)
Finger Lakes Comm Coll (NY)
Fox Valley Tech Coll (WI)
Fulton-Montgomery Comm Coll (NY)
Glendale Comm Coll (AZ)
Golden West Coll (CA)
Greenfield Comm Coll (MA)
Guilford Tech Comm Coll (NC)
Highland Comm Coll (IL)
Honolulu Comm Coll (HI)
Housatonic Comm Coll (CT)
Iowa Lakes Comm Coll (IA)
James Sprunt Comm Coll (NC)
J. F. Drake State Tech Coll (AL)
Johnston Comm Coll (NC)
Kilgore Coll (TX)
Kingsborough Comm Coll of the City U of New York (NY)
Lakeland Comm Coll (OH)
Lake-Sumter Comm Coll (FL)
Lansing Comm Coll (MI)
Leeward Comm Coll (HI)
Lehigh Carbon Comm Coll (PA)
Linn-Benton Comm Coll (OR)
Macomb Comm Coll (MI)
Manchester Comm Coll (CT)
Mercer County Comm Coll (NJ)
Metropolitan Comm Coll (NE)
Metropolitan Comm Coll–Penn Valley (MO)
Miami Dade Coll (FL)
Middlesex Comm Coll (CT)
Midlands Tech Coll (SC)
Mid-Plains Comm Coll, North Platte (NE)
Milwaukee Area Tech Coll (WI)
Mohawk Valley Comm Coll (NY)
Montgomery Coll (MD)
Montgomery County Comm Coll (PA)
Muskegon Comm Coll (MI)
Nassau Comm Coll (NY)
North Idaho Coll (ID)
NorthWest Arkansas Comm Coll (AR)
Northwest Coll (WY)
Northwestern Connecticut Comm Coll (CT)
Northwest Florida State Coll (FL)
Ocean County Coll (NJ)
Oklahoma City Comm Coll (OK)
Orange Coast Coll (CA)
Owens Comm Coll, Toledo (OH)
Palm Beach State Coll (FL)
Paradise Valley Comm Coll (AZ)
Pensacola Jr Coll (FL)
Quinsigamond Comm Coll (MA)
Randolph Comm Coll (NC)
Reedley Coll (CA)
Rockland Comm Coll (NY)
San Diego City Coll (CA)
San Jacinto Coll District (TX)
San Juan Coll (NM)
Southeast Tech Inst (SD)
South Plains Coll (TX)
Springfield Tech Comm Coll (MA)
State Coll of Florida Manatee-Sarasota (FL)
Terra State Comm Coll (OH)
Thomas Nelson Comm Coll (VA)
Tidewater Comm Coll (VA)
Tompkins Cortland Comm Coll (NY)
Trident Tech Coll (SC)
Tunxis Comm Coll (CT)
Ulster County Comm Coll (NY)
U of Arkansas Comm Coll at Morrilton (AR)
Virginia Marti Coll of Art and Design (OH)
Yavapai Coll (AZ)

Commercial Photography
Austin Comm Coll (TX)
Cecil Coll (MD)
Central Wyoming Coll (WY)
The Comm Coll of Baltimore County (MD)
Fashion Inst of Technology (NY)
Fiorello H. LaGuardia Comm Coll of the City U of New York (NY)
Harford Comm Coll (MD)
Hawkeye Comm Coll (IA)
Houston Comm Coll System (TX)
Kilgore Coll (TX)
Milwaukee Area Tech Coll (WI)
Minneapolis Comm and Tech Coll (MN)
Mohawk Valley Comm Coll (NY)
Montgomery Coll (MD)
Northwest Coll (WY)
Randolph Comm Coll (NC)
Sierra Coll (CA)
Springfield Tech Comm Coll (MA)

Communication and Journalism Related
Delaware County Comm Coll (PA)
Folsom Lake Coll (CA)
Gadsden State Comm Coll (AL)
Iowa Lakes Comm Coll (IA)
Olympic Coll (WA)
Sheridan Coll (WY)

Communication and Media Related
Raritan Valley Comm Coll (NJ)

Communication Disorders
Red Rocks Comm Coll (CO)

Communication Disorders Sciences and Services Related
Burlington County Coll (NJ)

Communication/ Speech Communication and Rhetoric
Barton County Comm Coll (KS)
Broome Comm Coll (NY)
Bunker Hill Comm Coll (MA)
Casper Coll (WY)
Central Oregon Comm Coll (OR)
Collin County Comm Coll District (TX)
Dean Coll (MA)
Delaware County Comm Coll (PA)
Eastern Wyoming Coll (WY)
Eastfield Coll (TX)
Edison State Comm Coll (OH)
El Paso Comm Coll (TX)
Erie Comm Coll, South Campus (NY)
Fiorello H. LaGuardia Comm Coll of the City U of New York (NY)
Hesser Coll, Manchester (NH)
Howard Coll (TX)
Hutchinson Comm Coll and Area Vocational School (KS)
Jamestown Comm Coll (NY)
Lackawanna Coll (PA)
Laramie County Comm Coll (WY)
Lehigh Carbon Comm Coll (PA)
Lonestar Coll–Cy-Fair (TX)
Macomb Comm Coll (MI)
Manchester Comm Coll (CT)
Montgomery Coll (MD)
Montgomery County Comm Coll (PA)
Nassau Comm Coll (NY)
Northampton Comm Coll (PA)
Northwest Coll (WY)
Pasadena City Coll (CA)
Red Rocks Comm Coll (CO)
Salt Lake Comm Coll (UT)
San Jacinto Coll District (TX)
San Juan Coll (NM)
Tompkins Cortland Comm Coll (NY)
Triton Coll (IL)
Ulster County Comm Coll (NY)
Western Wyoming Comm Coll (WY)

Communications Systems Installation and Repair Technology
Broome Comm Coll (NY)
Coll of DuPage (IL)
Des Moines Area Comm Coll (IA)
Erie Comm Coll, South Campus (NY)
Louisiana Tech Coll (LA)
Mohawk Valley Comm Coll (NY)
Suffolk County Comm Coll (NY)

Communications Technologies and Support Services Related
Bowling Green State U–Firelands Coll (OH)
Comm Coll of Allegheny County (PA)
East Central Coll (MO)
Harford Comm Coll (MD)
Mitchell Tech Inst (SD)
Montgomery Coll (MD)
Montgomery County Comm Coll (PA)
Ocean County Coll (NJ)
Springfield Tech Comm Coll (MA)

Communications Technology
Allegany Coll of Maryland (MD)
Anne Arundel Comm Coll (MD)
Athens Tech Coll (GA)
Coll of DuPage (IL)
Daytona State Coll (FL)
Essex County Coll (NJ)
Hutchinson Comm Coll and Area Vocational School (KS)
Kent State U at Tuscarawas (OH)
Lackawanna Coll (PA)
North Lake Coll (TX)
Northwestern Connecticut Comm Coll (CT)
Ocean County Coll (NJ)
Orange Coast Coll (CA)
Owens Comm Coll, Toledo (OH)
Pueblo Comm Coll (CO)
Southern Maine Comm Coll (ME)

Community Health Services Counseling
Comm Coll of Allegheny County (PA)
Erie Comm Coll (NY)
Kingsborough Comm Coll of the City U of New York (NY)
Oakland Comm Coll (MI)
State Coll of Florida Manatee-Sarasota (FL)

Community Organization and Advocacy
Berkshire Comm Coll (MA)
Chattanooga State Comm Coll (TN)
Clackamas Comm Coll (OR)
Cleveland State Comm Coll (TN)
Comm Coll of Vermont (VT)
Del Mar Coll (TX)
Honolulu Comm Coll (HI)
Kirkwood Comm Coll (IA)
Mercer County Comm Coll (NJ)
Mohawk Valley Comm Coll (NY)
Quinsigamond Comm Coll (MA)
Tompkins Cortland Comm Coll (NY)
Ulster County Comm Coll (NY)
Volunteer State Comm Coll (TN)
Westchester Comm Coll (NY)

Comparative Literature
Iowa Lakes Comm Coll (IA)
Lincoln Land Comm Coll (IL)
Miami Dade Coll (FL)
Oklahoma City Comm Coll (OK)
Otero Jr Coll (CO)
Palm Beach State Coll (FL)

Computer and Information Sciences
Albany Tech Coll (GA)
Alexandria Tech Coll (MN)
Alpena Comm Coll (MI)
Antelope Valley Coll (CA)
Antonelli Coll (OH)
Austin Comm Coll (TX)
Berkeley City Coll (CA)
Berkshire Comm Coll (MA)
Bevill State Comm Coll (AL)
Broome Comm Coll (NY)
Bryant & Stratton Coll - Amherst Campus (NY)
Bryant & Stratton Coll - Buffalo Campus (NY)
Bryant & Stratton Coll - Greece Campus (NY)
Bryant & Stratton Coll - Henrietta Campus (NY)
Bryant & Stratton Coll - Southtowns Campus (NY)
Bryant & Stratton Coll - Virginia Beach (VA)
Bucks County Comm Coll (PA)
Career Coll of Northern Nevada (NV)
Carroll Comm Coll (MD)
Cecil Coll (MD)
Central Arizona Coll (AZ)
Central Comm Coll–Columbus Campus (NE)
Central Comm Coll–Grand Island Campus (NE)
Central Comm Coll–Hastings Campus (NE)
Central Texas Coll (TX)
Century Coll (MN)
Cincinnati State Tech and Comm Coll (OH)
Clarendon Coll (TX)
Clovis Comm Coll (NM)
Colby Comm Coll (KS)
Coll of Southern Maryland (MD)
Collin County Comm Coll District (TX)
The Comm Coll of Baltimore County (MD)
Comm Coll of Rhode Island (RI)
Comm Coll of Vermont (VT)
Corning Comm Coll (NY)
Cowley County Comm Coll and Area Vocational–Tech School (KS)
Cumberland County Coll (NJ)
Dakota Coll at Bottineau (ND)
Darton Coll (GA)
Delaware County Comm Coll (PA)
Delaware Tech & Comm Coll, Jack F. Owens Campus (DE)
Delaware Tech & Comm Coll, Stanton/Wilmington Campus (DE)
Delaware Tech & Comm Coll, Terry Campus (DE)
Denmark Tech Coll (SC)
Edison State Comm Coll (OH)
El Paso Comm Coll (TX)
Erie Comm Coll, North Campus (NY)
Finger Lakes Comm Coll (NY)
Folsom Lake Coll (CA)
Gadsden State Comm Coll (AL)
Glendale Comm Coll (AZ)
Goodwin Coll (CT)
Harford Comm Coll (MD)
Harrisburg Area Comm Coll (PA)
Harrison Coll, Indianapolis (IN)
Hawkeye Comm Coll (IA)
Hazard Comm and Tech Coll (KY)
H. Councill Trenholm State Tech Coll (AL)
Hopkinsville Comm Coll (KY)
Howard Coll (TX)
Hutchinson Comm Coll and Area Vocational School (KS)
ITT Tech Inst, Indianapolis (IN)
Ivy Tech Comm Coll–Bloomington (IN)
Ivy Tech Comm Coll–Central Indiana (IN)
Ivy Tech Comm Coll–Columbus (IN)
Ivy Tech Comm Coll–East Central (IN)
Ivy Tech Comm Coll–Kokomo (IN)
Ivy Tech Comm Coll–Lafayette (IN)
Ivy Tech Comm Coll–North Central (IN)
Ivy Tech Comm Coll–Northeast (IN)
Ivy Tech Comm Coll–Northwest (IN)
Ivy Tech Comm Coll–Richmond (IN)
Ivy Tech Comm Coll–Southeast (IN)
Ivy Tech Comm Coll–Southern Indiana (IN)
Ivy Tech Comm Coll–Southwest (IN)
Ivy Tech Comm Coll–Wabash Valley (IN)
Jamestown Business Coll (NY)
Jamestown Comm Coll (NY)
Jefferson Comm Coll (NY)
Jefferson State Comm Coll (AL)
J. Sargeant Reynolds Comm Coll (VA)
Kaplan U, Lincoln (NE)
Kaplan U, Omaha (NE)
Kilgore Coll (TX)
Kingsborough Comm Coll of the City U of New York (NY)
Lackawanna Coll (PA)
Lake Michigan Coll (MI)
Lake Region State Coll (ND)
Laramie County Comm Coll (WY)
Linn-Benton Comm Coll (OR)
Lonestar Coll–Cy-Fair (TX)
Lonestar Coll–Kingwood (TX)
Lonestar Coll–North Harris (TX)
Lonestar Coll–Tomball (TX)
Lurleen B. Wallace Comm Coll (AL)
Massasoit Comm Coll (MA)
Metropolitan Comm Coll–Business & Technology Campus (MO)
Mid-Plains Comm Coll, North Platte (NE)
Miller-Motte Tech Coll (SC)
Mitchell Tech Inst (SD)
Mohawk Valley Comm Coll (NY)
Montgomery Coll (MD)
Montgomery County Comm Coll (PA)
Mountain State Coll (WV)
Mount Wachusett Comm Coll (MA)
Nassau Comm Coll (NY)
Nicolet Area Tech Coll (WI)
North Arkansas Coll (AR)
Northeast Comm Coll (NE)
Northland Pioneer Coll (AZ)
Northwest-Shoals Comm Coll (AL)
Ocean County Coll (NJ)
Odessa Coll (TX)
Olean Business Inst (NY)
Ouachita Tech Coll (AR)
Owensboro Comm and Tech Coll (KY)
Penn State Schuylkill (PA)
Pennsylvania Coll of Technology (PA)
Pennsylvania Highlands Comm Coll (PA)
Phoenix Coll (AZ)
Reedley Coll (CA)
Salt Lake Comm Coll (UT)
San Diego Mesa Coll (CA)
San Jacinto Coll District (TX)
Sheridan Coll (WY)
Somerset Comm Coll (KY)
Southern Union State Comm Coll (AL)
South Georgia Coll (GA)
South Puget Sound Comm Coll (WA)
Southwest Virginia Comm Coll (VA)
Spartanburg Comm Coll (SC)
State Coll of Florida Manatee-Sarasota (FL)
Sullivan Coll of Technology and Design (KY)
Tallahassee Comm Coll (FL)
Temple Coll (TX)
Terra State Comm Coll (OH)
Thomas Nelson Comm Coll (VA)
Tompkins Cortland Comm Coll (NY)
Triton Coll (IL)
Ulster County Comm Coll (NY)
U of Cincinnati Clermont Coll (OH)
Victor Valley Coll (CA)
Westchester Comm Coll (NY)
Western Wyoming Comm Coll (WY)
West Kentucky Comm and Tech Coll (KY)
White Mountains Comm Coll (NH)
Wor-Wic Comm Coll (MD)

Computer and Information Sciences And Support Services Related
Anne Arundel Comm Coll (MD)
Blue Ridge Comm Coll (NC)
Bowling Green State U–Firelands Coll (OH)

Bunker Hill Comm Coll (MA)
CHI Inst, Broomall Campus (PA)
Dakota Coll at Bottineau (ND)
Darton Coll (GA)
Del Mar Coll (TX)
Des Moines Area Comm Coll (IA)
Eastern Shore Comm Coll (VA)
Elaine P. Nunez Comm Coll (LA)
Fiorello H. LaGuardia Comm Coll of the City U of New York (NY)
Harrison Coll, Muncie (IN)
Highland Comm Coll (IL)
Inver Hills Comm Coll (MN)
Island Drafting and Tech Inst (NY)
Jackson Comm Coll (MI)
Jefferson Comm Coll (NY)
Kirkwood Comm Coll (IA)
LDS Business Coll (UT)
Linn-Benton Comm Coll (OR)
Massasoit Comm Coll (MA)
Metropolitan Comm Coll–Business & Technology Campus (MO)
Midlands Tech Coll (SC)
Mitchell Tech Inst (SD)
Mohawk Valley Comm Coll (NY)
Moraine Park Tech Coll (WI)
North Central Texas Coll (TX)
Northeast Comm Coll (NE)
North Idaho Coll (ID)
Northland Comm and Tech Coll–Thief River Falls (MN)
Northwestern Coll (IL)
Oakland Comm Coll (MI)
Olean Business Inst (NY)
Olympic Coll (WA)
Palm Beach State Coll (FL)
Pennsylvania Coll of Technology (PA)
Pennsylvania Highlands Comm Coll (PA)
Raritan Valley Comm Coll (NJ)
Rio Salado Coll (AZ)
Saint Charles Comm Coll (MO)
Seminole State Coll of Florida (FL)
Sierra Coll (CA)
Southeast Tech Inst (SD)
Southwest Wisconsin Tech Coll (WI)
Stanly Comm Coll (NC)
Stark State Coll of Technology (OH)
Suffolk County Comm Coll (NY)
Sullivan Coll of Technology and Design (KY)
Three Rivers Comm Coll (MO)
Tompkins Cortland Comm Coll (NY)
Ulster County Comm Coll (NY)
Union County Coll (NJ)
Waukesha County Tech Coll (WI)
Westchester Comm Coll (NY)

Computer and Information Sciences Related

Anne Arundel Comm Coll (MD)
Berkeley City Coll (CA)
Bucks County Comm Coll (PA)
Central Oregon Comm Coll (OR)
Chipola Coll (FL)
Colby Comm Coll (KS)
Corning Comm Coll (NY)
Daytona State Coll (FL)
Del Mar Coll (TX)
Eastfield Coll (TX)
Gateway Comm Coll (CT)
Genesee Comm Coll (NY)
Highland Comm Coll (IL)
Howard Coll (TX)
Howard Comm Coll (MD)
Iowa Lakes Comm Coll (IA)
Jamestown Comm Coll (NY)
Kaplan Coll, Panorama City Campus (CA)
Kaplan U, Cedar Rapids (IA)
Kent State U at East Liverpool (OH)
Lake-Sumter Comm Coll (FL)
Lawson State Comm Coll (AL)
Massasoit Comm Coll (MA)
Metropolitan Comm Coll–Blue River (MO)
Metropolitan Comm Coll–Business & Technology Campus (MO)
Metropolitan Comm Coll–Longview (MO)
Metropolitan Comm Coll–Maple Woods (MO)
Metropolitan Comm Coll–Penn Valley (MO)
Middle Georgia Coll (GA)
Missouri State U–West Plains (MO)
Mohave Comm Coll (AZ)
Nassau Comm Coll (NY)
North Idaho Coll (ID)
Northland Comm and Tech Coll–Thief River Falls (MN)
Olympic Coll (WA)
Pensacola Jr Coll (FL)
Potomac State Coll of West Virginia U (WV)
Rio Salado Coll (AZ)
Rockland Comm Coll (NY)
Seminole State Coll of Florida (FL)
Stark State Coll of Technology (OH)
State Coll of Florida Manatee-Sarasota (FL)
Three Rivers Comm Coll (MO)
Walters State Comm Coll (TN)
Westchester Comm Coll (NY)

Computer and Information Systems Security

Alexandria Tech Coll (MN)
Berkeley City Coll (CA)
Brown Mackie Coll–Tucson (AZ)
Bryant & Stratton Coll, Eastlake (OH)
Bryant & Stratton Coll, Parma (OH)
Bryant & Stratton Coll (WI)
Bryant & Stratton Coll - Albany Campus (NY)
Bryant & Stratton Coll - Amherst Campus (NY)
Bryant & Stratton Coll - Buffalo Campus (NY)
Bryant & Stratton Coll - Greece Campus (NY)
Bryant & Stratton Coll - Henrietta Campus (NY)
Bryant & Stratton Coll - North Campus (NY)
Bryant & Stratton Coll - Richmond Campus (VA)
Bryant & Stratton Coll - Virginia Beach (VA)
Century Coll (MN)
Chattahoochee Tech Coll (GA)
Chattanooga State Comm Coll (TN)
Collin County Comm Coll District (TX)
Cowley County Comm Coll and Area Vocational–Tech School (KS)
Delta Coll (MI)
Edison State Comm Coll (OH)
El Centro Coll (TX)
Fayetteville Tech Comm Coll (NC)
Flint River Tech Coll (GA)
Glendale Comm Coll (AZ)
Green River Comm Coll (WA)
Griffin Tech Coll (GA)
Harford Comm Coll (MD)
Harrisburg Area Comm Coll (PA)
Island Drafting and Tech Inst (NY)
Jamestown Comm Coll (NY)
Kaplan U, Hagerstown Campus (MD)
Lanier Tech Coll (GA)
Lehigh Carbon Comm Coll (PA)
Lonestar Coll–Montgomery (TX)
Metropolitan Comm Coll–Business & Technology Campus (MO)
Milwaukee Area Tech Coll (WI)
Minneapolis Comm and Tech Coll (MN)
Minnesota State Comm and Tech Coll (MN)
Montgomery Coll (MD)
Moraine Valley Comm Coll (IL)
Northampton Comm Coll (PA)
Northwestern Coll (IL)
Oakland Comm Coll (MI)
Olympic Coll (WA)
St. Philip's Coll (TX)
San Jacinto Coll District (TX)
Seminole State Coll of Florida (FL)
Southeast Tech Inst (SD)
Springfield Tech Comm Coll (MA)
Sullivan Coll of Technology and Design (KY)
Valdosta Tech Coll (GA)
Westchester Comm Coll (NY)
Westmoreland County Comm Coll (PA)

Computer Engineering

Itasca Comm Coll (MN)

Computer Engineering Related

Columbus Tech Coll (GA)
Daytona State Coll (FL)
Gateway Comm Coll (CT)
Itasca Comm Coll (MN)
Middle Georgia Coll (GA)
Northwest Florida State Coll (FL)
Sandhills Comm Coll (NC)
Seminole State Coll of Florida (FL)
Stark State Coll of Technology (OH)

Computer Engineering Technologies Related

Pennsylvania Coll of Technology (PA)

Computer Engineering Technology

Allan Hancock Coll (CA)
Allegany Coll of Maryland (MD)
Alvin Comm Coll (TX)
Amarillo Coll (TX)
Anne Arundel Comm Coll (MD)
Bowling Green State U–Firelands Coll (OH)
Broome Comm Coll (NY)
Bucks County Comm Coll (PA)
Carteret Comm Coll (NC)
Catawba Valley Comm Coll (NC)
Central Piedmont Comm Coll (NC)
CHI Inst, Franklin Mills Campus (PA)
Cincinnati State Tech and Comm Coll (OH)
Comm Coll of Allegheny County (PA)
Comm Coll of Rhode Island (RI)
Cuyahoga Comm Coll (OH)
DeKalb Tech Coll (GA)
Delaware Tech & Comm Coll, Stanton/Wilmington Campus (DE)
Delaware Tech & Comm Coll, Terry Campus (DE)
Des Moines Area Comm Coll (IA)
Eastfield Coll (TX)
East Los Angeles Coll (CA)
Edison State Comm Coll (OH)
Elaine P. Nunez Comm Coll (LA)
Fiorello H. LaGuardia Comm Coll of the City U of New York (NY)
Flathead Valley Comm Coll (MT)
Frederick Comm Coll (MD)
Fulton-Montgomery Comm Coll (NY)
Gateway Comm Coll (CT)
Genesee Comm Coll (NY)
Grand Rapids Comm Coll (MI)
Highline Comm Coll (WA)
Houston Comm Coll System (TX)
Indian River State Coll (FL)
ITT Tech Inst, Bessemer (AL)
ITT Tech Inst, Madison (AL)
ITT Tech Inst, Mobile (AL)
ITT Tech Inst, Phoenix (AZ)
ITT Tech Inst (AR)
ITT Tech Inst, Lathrop (CA)
ITT Tech Inst, Oxnard (CA)
ITT Tech Inst, Rancho Cordova (CA)
ITT Tech Inst, San Bernardino (CA)
ITT Tech Inst, San Diego (CA)
ITT Tech Inst, San Dimas (CA)
ITT Tech Inst, Sylmar (CA)
ITT Tech Inst, Torrance (CA)
ITT Tech Inst, Aurora (CO)
ITT Tech Inst, Fort Lauderdale (FL)
ITT Tech Inst, Fort Myers (FL)
ITT Tech Inst, Jacksonville (FL)
ITT Tech Inst, Lake Mary (FL)
ITT Tech Inst, Miami (FL)
ITT Tech Inst, Pinellas Park (FL)
ITT Tech Inst, Tallahassee (FL)
ITT Tech Inst, Tampa (FL)
ITT Tech Inst, Atlanta (GA)
ITT Tech Inst, Duluth (GA)
ITT Tech Inst, Kennesaw (GA)
ITT Tech Inst (ID)
ITT Tech Inst, Burr Ridge (IL)
ITT Tech Inst, Orland Park (IL)
ITT Tech Inst, Fort Wayne (IN)
ITT Tech Inst, Indianapolis (IN)
ITT Tech Inst, Merrillville (IN)
ITT Tech Inst, Newburgh (IN)
ITT Tech Inst, Cedar Rapids (IA)
ITT Tech Inst, Clive (IA)
ITT Tech Inst, Louisville (KY)
ITT Tech Inst, Baton Rouge (LA)
ITT Tech Inst, St. Rose (LA)
ITT Tech Inst (MD)
ITT Tech Inst, Woburn (MA)
ITT Tech Inst, Canton (MI)
ITT Tech Inst, Swartz Creek (MI)
ITT Tech Inst, Troy (MI)
ITT Tech Inst, Wyoming (MI)
ITT Tech Inst (MN)
ITT Tech Inst, Arnold (MO)
ITT Tech Inst, Earth City (MO)
ITT Tech Inst, Kansas City (MO)
ITT Tech Inst (NE)
ITT Tech Inst (NV)
ITT Tech Inst (NM)
ITT Tech Inst, Albany (NY)
ITT Tech Inst, Getzville (NY)
ITT Tech Inst, Liverpool (NY)
ITT Tech Inst, Charlotte (NC)
ITT Tech Inst, High Point (NC)
ITT Tech Inst, Morrisville (NC)
ITT Tech Inst, Akron (OH)
ITT Tech Inst, Columbus (OH)
ITT Tech Inst, Dayton (OH)
ITT Tech Inst, Hilliard (OH)
ITT Tech Inst, Maumee (OH)
ITT Tech Inst, Norwood (OH)
ITT Tech Inst, Strongsville (OH)
ITT Tech Inst, Warrensville Heights (OH)
ITT Tech Inst, Youngstown (OH)
ITT Tech Inst, Tulsa (OK)
ITT Tech Inst (OR)
ITT Tech Inst, Bensalem (PA)
ITT Tech Inst, Dunmore (PA)
ITT Tech Inst, Harrisburg (PA)
ITT Tech Inst, Pittsburgh (PA)
ITT Tech Inst, Tarentum (PA)
ITT Tech Inst, Columbia (SC)
ITT Tech Inst, Greenville (SC)
ITT Tech Inst, Chattanooga (TN)
ITT Tech Inst, Johnson City (TN)
ITT Tech Inst, Knoxville (TN)
ITT Tech Inst, Nashville (TN)
ITT Tech Inst, Austin (TX)
ITT Tech Inst, DeSoto (TX)
ITT Tech Inst, Houston (TX)
ITT Tech Inst, Richardson (TX)
ITT Tech Inst, Webster (TX)
ITT Tech Inst (UT)
ITT Tech Inst, Chantilly (VA)
ITT Tech Inst, Norfolk (VA)
ITT Tech Inst, Richmond (VA)
ITT Tech Inst, Salem (VA)
ITT Tech Inst, Springfield (VA)
ITT Tech Inst, Everett (WA)
ITT Tech Inst, Seattle (WA)
ITT Tech Inst (WV)
ITT Tech Inst, Green Bay (WI)
ITT Tech Inst, Greenfield (WI)
ITT Tech Inst, Madison (WI)
Jamestown Comm Coll (NY)
Kellogg Comm Coll (MI)
Kent State U at Ashtabula (OH)
Kent State U at East Liverpool (OH)
Kent State U at Trumbull (OH)
Kent State U at Tuscarawas (OH)
Lakeland Comm Coll (OH)
Lansing Comm Coll (MI)
Lehigh Carbon Comm Coll (PA)
Lonestar Coll–Kingwood (TX)
Los Angeles Harbor Coll (CA)
Meridian Comm Coll (MS)
Miami Dade Coll (FL)
Minnesota State Coll–Southeast Tech (MN)
Minnesota State Comm and Tech Coll (MN)
North Central Texas Coll (TX)
Northeastern Jr Coll (CO)
Northwestern Connecticut Comm Coll (CT)
Oklahoma City Comm Coll (OK)
Orange Coast Coll (CA)
Owens Comm Coll, Toledo (OH)
Paris Jr Coll (TX)
Penn State New Kensington (PA)
Potomac State Coll of West Virginia U (WV)
Quinsigamond Comm Coll (MA)
Sandhills Comm Coll (NC)
San Diego City Coll (CA)
Seminole State Coll of Florida (FL)
Southeast Kentucky Comm and Tech Coll (KY)
Southern Maine Comm Coll (ME)
South Plains Coll (TX)
Springfield Tech Comm Coll (MA)
State Coll of Florida Manatee-Sarasota (FL)
Sullivan Coll of Technology and Design (KY)
Three Rivers Comm Coll (CT)
Three Rivers Comm Coll (MO)
Trident Tech Coll (SC)
Umpqua Comm Coll (OR)
Westmoreland County Comm Coll (PA)
White Mountains Comm Coll (NH)

Computer Graphics

Antelope Valley Coll (CA)
Berkeley City Coll (CA)
Burlington County Coll (NJ)
Carroll Comm Coll (MD)
Corning Comm Coll (NY)
Cowley County Comm Coll and Area Vocational–Tech School (KS)
Creative Center (NE)
Daytona State Coll (FL)
Edison State Comm Coll (OH)
Gateway Comm Coll (CT)
Genesee Comm Coll (NY)
Glendale Comm Coll (AZ)
Howard Comm Coll (MD)
Iowa Lakes Comm Coll (IA)
Kellogg Comm Coll (MI)
Lansing Comm Coll (MI)
Lewis and Clark Comm Coll (IL)
Lonestar Coll–Kingwood (TX)
Mercer County Comm Coll (NJ)
Meridian Comm Coll (MS)
Mesabi Range Comm and Tech Coll (MN)
Metropolitan Comm Coll–Business & Technology Campus (MO)
Miami Dade Coll (FL)
Milwaukee Area Tech Coll (WI)
Missouri State U–West Plains (MO)
Mount Wachusett Comm Coll (MA)
Nassau Comm Coll (NY)
North Central Texas Coll (TX)
Northland Comm and Tech Coll–Thief River Falls (MN)
Northland Pioneer Coll (AZ)
Northwestern Connecticut Comm Coll (CT)
Olympic Coll (WA)
Orange Coast Coll (CA)
Phoenix Coll (AZ)
Quinsigamond Comm Coll (MA)
Rockland Comm Coll (NY)
Saint Paul Coll–A Comm & Tech College (MN)
Seminole State Coll of Florida (FL)
Southwest Wisconsin Tech Coll (WI)
State Coll of Florida Manatee-Sarasota (FL)
Sullivan Coll of Technology and Design (KY)
Tallahassee Comm Coll (FL)
Trident Tech Coll (SC)

Computer Hardware Engineering
Eastfield Coll (TX)
Seminole State Coll of Florida (FL)
Stanly Comm Coll (NC)
Stark State Coll of Technology (OH)
State U of New York Coll of Technology at Alfred (NY)
Sullivan Coll of Technology and Design (KY)

Computer Hardware Technology
Comm Coll of Rhode Island (RI)
Oakland Comm Coll (MI)
Sullivan Coll of Technology and Design (KY)

Computer/Information Technology Services Administration Related
Alpena Comm Coll (MI)
Barton County Comm Coll (KS)
Bucks County Comm Coll (PA)
Central Carolina Comm Coll (NC)
Cleveland Inst of Electronics (OH)
Corning Comm Coll (NY)
Daytona State Coll (FL)
Eastern Shore Comm Coll (VA)
Eastfield Coll (TX)
El Centro Coll (TX)
ETI Tech Coll of Niles (OH)
Flathead Valley Comm Coll (MT)
Hillsborough Comm Coll (FL)
Howard Comm Coll (MD)
Iowa Lakes Comm Coll (IA)
Jefferson Comm Coll (NY)
Kent State U at Trumbull (OH)
Kirkwood Comm Coll (IA)
Mesabi Range Comm and Tech Coll (MN)
Metropolitan Comm Coll–Business & Technology Campus (MO)
Middle Georgia Coll (GA)
Milwaukee Area Tech Coll (WI)
Mitchell Tech Inst (SD)
North Central Texas Coll (TX)
Oakland Comm Coll (MI)
Owensboro Comm and Tech Coll (KY)
Pasadena City Coll (CA)
Pennsylvania Coll of Technology (PA)
Pennsylvania Highlands Comm Coll (PA)
Pueblo Comm Coll (CO)
Rockland Comm Coll (NY)
Sandhills Comm Coll (NC)
Seminole State Coll of Florida (FL)
Southeast Kentucky Comm and Tech Coll (KY)
Southeast Tech Inst (SD)
Stanly Comm Coll (NC)
Stark State Coll of Technology (OH)
Trident Tech Coll (SC)
York County Comm Coll (ME)

Computer Installation and Repair Technology
Coll of DuPage (IL)
Coll of Lake County (IL)
Darton Coll (GA)
Fiorello H. LaGuardia Comm Coll of the City U of New York (NY)
Forrest Jr Coll (SC)
Harrisburg Area Comm Coll (PA)
Kilgore Coll (TX)
Louisiana Tech Coll (LA)
Midlands Tech Coll (SC)
Montcalm Comm Coll (MI)
Northampton Comm Coll (PA)
Northland Pioneer Coll (AZ)
Paradise Valley Comm Coll (AZ)
Sierra Coll (CA)
Southeast Tech Inst (SD)
State U of New York Coll of Technology at Alfred (NY)
Sullivan Coll of Technology and Design (KY)
Waukesha County Tech Coll (WI)
Wisconsin Indianhead Tech Coll (WI)

Computer Programming
Alexandria Tech Coll (MN)
Altamaha Tech Coll (GA)
Alvin Comm Coll (TX)
Amarillo Coll (TX)
Anne Arundel Comm Coll (MD)
Antelope Valley Coll (CA)
Athens Tech Coll (GA)
Atlanta Tech Coll (GA)
Augusta Tech Coll (GA)
Austin Comm Coll (TX)
Beaufort County Comm Coll (NC)
Black Hawk Coll, Moline (IL)
Bladen Comm Coll (NC)
Blue Ridge Comm Coll (NC)
Bowling Green State U–Firelands Coll (OH)
Bradford School (OH)
Bradford School (PA)
Brown Mackie Coll–Hopkinsville (KY)
Bucks County Comm Coll (PA)
Bunker Hill Comm Coll (MA)
Casper Coll (WY)
Catawba Valley Comm Coll (NC)
Cecil Coll (MD)
Central Carolina Comm Coll (NC)
Central Georgia Tech Coll (GA)
Central Ohio Tech Coll (OH)
Central Piedmont Comm Coll (NC)
Central Texas Coll (TX)
Chattahoochee Tech Coll (GA)
CHI Inst, Broomall Campus (PA)
Cincinnati State Tech and Comm Coll (OH)
Clark Coll (WA)
Coll of Southern Maryland (MD)
Collin County Comm Coll District (TX)
Comm Coll of Rhode Island (RI)
Corning Comm Coll (NY)
Dabney S. Lancaster Comm Coll (VA)
Danville Area Comm Coll (IL)
Daytona State Coll (FL)
DeKalb Tech Coll (GA)
Del Mar Coll (TX)
Eastfield Coll (TX)
East Los Angeles Coll (CA)
Edison State Comm Coll (OH)
El Centro Coll (TX)
El Paso Comm Coll (TX)
Essex County Coll (NJ)
Fayetteville Tech Comm Coll (NC)
Fiorello H. LaGuardia Comm Coll of the City U of New York (NY)
Fox Valley Tech Coll (WI)
Georgia Highlands Coll (GA)
Georgia Northwestern Tech Coll (GA)
Grand Rapids Comm Coll (MI)
Greenfield Comm Coll (MA)
Griffin Tech Coll (GA)
Guilford Tech Comm Coll (NC)
Gwinnett Tech Coll (GA)
Hennepin Tech Coll (MN)
Highline Comm Coll (WA)
Houston Comm Coll System (TX)
Howard Coll (TX)
Illinois Valley Comm Coll (IL)
Indian River State Coll (FL)
International Business Coll, Indianapolis (IN)
Iowa Lakes Comm Coll (IA)
Johnston Comm Coll (NC)
Kalamazoo Valley Comm Coll (MI)
Kaplan Coll, Merrillville Campus (IN)
Kellogg Comm Coll (MI)
Kilgore Coll (TX)
Lanier Tech Coll (GA)
Lansing Comm Coll (MI)
Laramie County Comm Coll (WY)
Lehigh Carbon Comm Coll (PA)
Lewis and Clark Comm Coll (IL)
Linn State Tech Coll (MO)
Lonestar Coll–Montgomery (TX)
Lonestar Coll–Tomball (TX)
Macomb Comm Coll (MI)
Massasoit Comm Coll (MA)
Metropolitan Comm Coll (NE)
Metropolitan Comm Coll–Business & Technology Campus (MO)
Metropolitan Comm Coll–Longview (MO)
Metropolitan Comm Coll–Maple Woods (MO)
Miami Dade Coll (FL)
Middlesex Comm Coll (CT)
Minneapolis Business Coll (MN)
Minneapolis Comm and Tech Coll (MN)
Minnesota State Coll–Southeast Tech (MN)
Minnesota State Comm and Tech Coll (MN)
Mohawk Valley Comm Coll (NY)
Montgomery County Comm Coll (PA)
Northampton Comm Coll (PA)
North Central Texas Coll (TX)
Northeast Comm Coll (NE)
North Idaho Coll (ID)
North Lake Coll (TX)
NorthWest Arkansas Comm Coll (AR)
Northwestern Coll (IL)
Northwestern Connecticut Comm Coll (CT)
Northwest Florida State Coll (FL)
Northwest-Shoals Comm Coll (AL)
Oakland Comm Coll (MI)
Ocean County Coll (NJ)
Olympic Coll (WA)
Orange Coast Coll (CA)
Palm Beach State Coll (FL)
Patrick Henry Comm Coll (VA)
Pennsylvania Highlands Comm Coll (PA)
Potomac State Coll of West Virginia U (WV)
Quinsigamond Comm Coll (MA)
Rockland Comm Coll (NY)
Saint Charles Comm Coll (MO)
St. Cloud Tech Coll (MN)
Saint Paul Coll–A Comm & Tech College (MN)
Sandhills Comm Coll (NC)
San Jacinto Coll District (TX)
Seminole State Coll of Florida (FL)
Sierra Coll (CA)
Southeastern Comm Coll (IA)
Southeast Tech Inst (SD)
South Georgia Coll (GA)
South Plains Coll (TX)
South Puget Sound Comm Coll (WA)
Southwestern Michigan Coll (MI)
Southwest Wisconsin Tech Coll (WI)
Stark State Coll of Technology (OH)
State Coll of Florida Manatee-Sarasota (FL)
Suffolk County Comm Coll (NY)
Tallahassee Comm Coll (FL)
Tarrant County Coll District (TX)
Temple Coll (TX)
Terra State Comm Coll (OH)
Three Rivers Comm Coll (CT)
Tidewater Comm Coll (VA)
The U of Montana–Helena Coll of Technology (MT)
Valdosta Tech Coll (GA)
Victoria Coll (TX)
Vincennes U Jasper Campus (IN)
Waukesha County Tech Coll (WI)
Westmoreland County Comm Coll (PA)
West Virginia Northern Comm Coll (WV)
Wilson Comm Coll (NC)
Wood Tobe–Coburn School (NY)

Computer Programming Related
Blue Ridge Comm Coll (NC)
Bucks County Comm Coll (PA)
Central Texas Coll (TX)
Corning Comm Coll (NY)
Del Mar Coll (TX)
Eastfield Coll (TX)
Mesabi Range Comm and Tech Coll (MN)
Metropolitan Comm Coll–Business & Technology Campus (MO)
Moraine Park Tech Coll (WI)
North Central Texas Coll (TX)
Olympic Coll (WA)
Orangeburg-Calhoun Tech Coll (SC)
Pasco-Hernando Comm Coll (FL)
Patrick Henry Comm Coll (VA)
Pennsylvania Highlands Comm Coll (PA)
Rio Salado Coll (AZ)
Rockland Comm Coll (NY)
Saint Charles Comm Coll (MO)
San Diego Mesa Coll (CA)
Seminole State Coll of Florida (FL)
Southeast Tech Inst (SD)
Southwest Mississippi Comm Coll (MS)
Stanly Comm Coll (NC)
Stark State Coll of Technology (OH)
State Coll of Florida Manatee-Sarasota (FL)
Vincennes U Jasper Campus (IN)

Computer Programming (Specific Applications)
Barton County Comm Coll (KS)
Bladen Comm Coll (NC)
Brown Mackie Coll–Hopkinsville (KY)
Bucks County Comm Coll (PA)
Bunker Hill Comm Coll (MA)
Cecil Coll (MD)
Central Carolina Comm Coll (NC)
Central Comm Coll–Columbus Campus (NE)
Central Comm Coll–Grand Island Campus (NE)
Central Comm Coll–Hastings Campus (NE)
Central Piedmont Comm Coll (NC)
Central Texas Coll (TX)
Cincinnati State Tech and Comm Coll (OH)
City Colls of Chicago, Malcolm X College (IL)
Clackamas Comm Coll (OR)
Coll of DuPage (IL)
Coll of Lake County (IL)
Comm Coll of Rhode Island (RI)
Cowley County Comm Coll and Area Vocational–Tech School (KS)
Danville Area Comm Coll (IL)
Daytona State Coll (FL)
Delaware County Comm Coll (PA)
Del Mar Coll (TX)
Des Moines Area Comm Coll (IA)
Essex County Coll (NJ)
ETI Tech Coll of Niles (OH)
Harford Comm Coll (MD)
Highland Comm Coll (IL)
Hillsborough Comm Coll (FL)
Holyoke Comm Coll (MA)
Houston Comm Coll System (TX)
Inver Hills Comm Coll (MN)
Kaplan Coll, Northwest Indianapolis Campus (IN)
Kellogg Comm Coll (MI)
Kent State U at Salem (OH)
Kirkwood Comm Coll (IA)
Lakeland Comm Coll (OH)
Lake Region State Coll (ND)
Lincoln Land Comm Coll (IL)
Linn-Benton Comm Coll (OR)
Louisiana Tech Coll (LA)
Macomb Comm Coll (MI)
Mesabi Range Comm and Tech Coll (MN)
Metropolitan Comm Coll–Business & Technology Campus (MO)
Milwaukee Area Tech Coll (WI)
Missouri State U–West Plains (MO)
Mohave Comm Coll (AZ)
North Central Texas Coll (TX)
Northeast Comm Coll (NE)
Northeast Iowa Comm Coll (IA)
Northwest Florida State Coll (FL)
Orange Coast Coll (CA)
Owens Comm Coll, Toledo (OH)
Palm Beach State Coll (FL)
Pasco-Hernando Comm Coll (FL)
Pennsylvania Coll of Technology (PA)
Pennsylvania Highlands Comm Coll (PA)
Pensacola Jr Coll (FL)
Piedmont Comm Coll (NC)
Potomac State Coll of West Virginia U (WV)
Quinsigamond Comm Coll (MA)
Rockland Comm Coll (NY)
Saint Charles Comm Coll (MO)
St. Cloud Tech Coll (MN)
Sandhills Comm Coll (NC)
San Diego Mesa Coll (CA)
Seminole State Coll of Florida (FL)
Southern State Comm Coll (OH)
Springfield Tech Comm Coll (MA)
Stanly Comm Coll (NC)
Stark State Coll of Technology (OH)
State Fair Comm Coll (MO)
Tallahassee Comm Coll (FL)
Trident Tech Coll (SC)
Victor Valley Coll (CA)
Western Wyoming Comm Coll (WY)

Computer Programming (Vendor/Product Certification)
Arkansas State U–Beebe (AR)
Central Texas Coll (TX)
Del Mar Coll (TX)
ETI Tech Coll of Niles (OH)
Inver Hills Comm Coll (MN)
Lake Region State Coll (ND)
Laramie County Comm Coll (WY)
Luna Comm Coll (NM)
Marion Tech Coll (OH)
Metropolitan Comm Coll–Business & Technology Campus (MO)
Milwaukee Area Tech Coll (WI)
North Central Texas Coll (TX)
Paradise Valley Comm Coll (AZ)
Raritan Valley Comm Coll (NJ)
Seminole State Coll of Florida (FL)
Stark State Coll of Technology (OH)
Sullivan Coll of Technology and Design (KY)

Computer Science
Allan Hancock Coll (CA)
Allen Comm Coll (KS)
Amarillo Coll (TX)
Anne Arundel Comm Coll (MD)
Anoka-Ramsey Comm Coll (MN)
Anoka-Ramsey Comm Coll, Cambridge Campus (MN)
Arizona Western Coll (AZ)
Bakersfield Coll (CA)
Barton County Comm Coll (KS)
Bronx Comm Coll of the City U of New York (NY)
Bucks County Comm Coll (PA)
Bunker Hill Comm Coll (MA)
Burlington County Coll (NJ)
Central Arizona Coll (AZ)
Central Oregon Comm Coll (OR)
Central Piedmont Comm Coll (NC)
Central Wyoming Coll (WY)
Century Coll (MN)
Chipola Coll (FL)
Coll of the Canyons (CA)
Comm Coll of Philadelphia (PA)
Comm Coll of Vermont (VT)
Corning Comm Coll (NY)
Cowley County Comm Coll and Area Vocational–Tech School (KS)
Darton Coll (GA)
Daytona State Coll (FL)
Del Mar Coll (TX)
Delta Coll (MI)
Edison State Comm Coll (OH)
El Centro Coll (TX)
Essex County Coll (NJ)
Everett Comm Coll (WA)
Finger Lakes Comm Coll (NY)
Fiorello H. LaGuardia Comm Coll of the City U of New York (NY)
Frederick Comm Coll (MD)
Fulton-Montgomery Comm Coll (NY)
Gainesville State Coll (GA)
Grand Rapids Comm Coll (MI)
Gwinnett Tech Coll (GA)
Harrisburg Area Comm Coll (PA)
Highland Comm Coll (IL)
Howard Coll (TX)
Howard Comm Coll (MD)
Indian River State Coll (FL)
Iowa Lakes Comm Coll (IA)
Jackson State Comm Coll (TN)
Jamestown Comm Coll (NY)
Jefferson Comm Coll (NY)

Kingsborough Comm Coll of the City U of New York (NY)
Lake Region State Coll (ND)
Lake-Sumter Comm Coll (FL)
Lanier Tech Coll (GA)
Laramie County Comm Coll (WY)
Leeward Comm Coll (HI)
Lonestar Coll–Cy-Fair (TX)
Lonestar Coll–Kingwood (TX)
Lonestar Coll–North Harris (TX)
Lonestar Coll–Tomball (TX)
Lon Morris Coll (TX)
Mercer County Comm Coll (NJ)
Metropolitan Comm Coll–Blue River (MO)
Metropolitan Comm Coll–Business & Technology Campus (MO)
Metropolitan Comm Coll–Longview (MO)
Metropolitan Comm Coll–Maple Woods (MO)
Metropolitan Comm Coll–Penn Valley (MO)
Miami Dade Coll (FL)
Middle Georgia Coll (GA)
Mohave Comm Coll (AZ)
Murray State Coll (OK)
Nassau Comm Coll (NY)
Niagara County Comm Coll (NY)
Nicolet Area Tech Coll (WI)
Northampton Comm Coll (PA)
North Central Texas Coll (TX)
Northeast Comm Coll (NE)
Northeastern Jr Coll (CO)
North Hennepin Comm Coll (MN)
North Idaho Coll (ID)
Northland Comm and Tech Coll–Thief River Falls (MN)
Northwestern Connecticut Comm Coll (CT)
Northwest Florida State Coll (FL)
Northwest-Shoals Comm Coll (AL)
Odessa Coll (TX)
Oklahoma City Comm Coll (OK)
Palm Beach State Coll (FL)
Pasadena City Coll (CA)
Potomac State Coll of West Virginia U (WV)
Red Rocks Comm Coll (CO)
Rio Salado Coll (AZ)
Saint Charles Comm Coll (MO)
Saint Paul Coll–A Comm & Tech College (MN)
Salt Lake Comm Coll (UT)
San Diego Mesa Coll (CA)
San Jacinto Coll District (TX)
San Juan Coll (NM)
Santa Rosa Jr Coll (CA)
Seminole State Coll (OK)
Snow Coll (UT)
South Georgia Coll (GA)
South Plains Coll (TX)
Southwest Mississippi Comm Coll (MS)
Springfield Tech Comm Coll (MA)
State U of New York Coll of Technology at Alfred (NY)
Suffolk County Comm Coll (NY)
Tarrant County Coll District (TX)
Temple Coll (TX)
Thomas Nelson Comm Coll (VA)
Trinity Valley Comm Coll (TX)
Triton Coll (IL)
Umpqua Comm Coll (OR)
Union County Coll (NJ)
Victor Valley Coll (CA)
Walters State Comm Coll (TN)
Westchester Comm Coll (NY)
Western Wyoming Comm Coll (WY)

Computer Software and Media Applications Related

Berkeley City Coll (CA)
Carteret Comm Coll (NC)
ETI Tech Coll of Niles (OH)
Genesee Comm Coll (NY)
ITT Tech Inst, Bessemer (AL)
ITT Tech Inst (AR)
ITT Tech Inst, San Bernardino (CA)
ITT Tech Inst, Fort Lauderdale (FL)
ITT Tech Inst, Fort Myers (FL)
ITT Tech Inst, Jacksonville (FL)
ITT Tech Inst, Lake Mary (FL)
ITT Tech Inst, Miami (FL)
ITT Tech Inst, Pinellas Park (FL)
ITT Tech Inst, Tallahassee (FL)
ITT Tech Inst, Tampa (FL)
ITT Tech Inst, Fort Wayne (IN)
ITT Tech Inst, Indianapolis (IN)
ITT Tech Inst, Newburgh (IN)
ITT Tech Inst, Louisville (KY)
ITT Tech Inst, Baton Rouge (LA)
ITT Tech Inst, St. Rose (LA)
ITT Tech Inst (MD)
ITT Tech Inst, Woburn (MA)
ITT Tech Inst, Canton (MI)
ITT Tech Inst, Swartz Creek (MI)
ITT Tech Inst, Troy (MI)
ITT Tech Inst, Wyoming (MI)
ITT Tech Inst (MN)
ITT Tech Inst, Arnold (MO)
ITT Tech Inst, Earth City (MO)
ITT Tech Inst (NE)
ITT Tech Inst (NV)
ITT Tech Inst (NM)
ITT Tech Inst, Albany (NY)
ITT Tech Inst, Getzville (NY)
ITT Tech Inst, Liverpool (NY)
ITT Tech Inst, Dayton (OH)
ITT Tech Inst, Norwood (OH)
ITT Tech Inst, Strongsville (OH)
ITT Tech Inst, Youngstown (OH)
ITT Tech Inst (OR)
ITT Tech Inst, Harrisburg (PA)
ITT Tech Inst, Pittsburgh (PA)
ITT Tech Inst, Tarentum (PA)
ITT Tech Inst, Columbia (SC)
ITT Tech Inst, Greenville (SC)
ITT Tech Inst, Knoxville (TN)
ITT Tech Inst, Nashville (TN)
ITT Tech Inst, Arlington (TX)
ITT Tech Inst, Austin (TX)
ITT Tech Inst, Richardson (TX)
ITT Tech Inst (UT)
ITT Tech Inst, Chantilly (VA)
ITT Tech Inst, Norfolk (VA)
ITT Tech Inst, Richmond (VA)
ITT Tech Inst, Springfield (VA)
ITT Tech Inst, Everett (WA)
ITT Tech Inst, Seattle (WA)
ITT Tech Inst, Green Bay (WI)
ITT Tech Inst, Greenfield (WI)
Kaplan Coll, Northwest Indianapolis Campus (IN)
Kellogg Comm Coll (MI)
Marion Tech Coll (OH)
Mesabi Range Comm and Tech Coll (MN)
Metropolitan Comm Coll–Business & Technology Campus (MO)
Mitchell Tech Inst (SD)
Northland Comm and Tech Coll–Thief River Falls (MN)
Northwestern Coll (IL)
Olympic Coll (WA)
San Diego Mesa Coll (CA)
Seminole State Coll of Florida (FL)
Stark State Coll of Technology (OH)

Computer Software Engineering

Cleveland Inst of Electronics (OH)
ETI Tech Coll of Niles (OH)
Seminole State Coll of Florida (FL)
Southeast Tech Inst (SD)
Stark State Coll of Technology (OH)

Computer Software Technology

Brown Mackie Coll–Fort Wayne (IN)
Brown Mackie Coll–Hopkinsville (KY)
Brown Mackie Coll–Merrillville (IN)
Brown Mackie Coll–Michigan City (IN)
Brown Mackie Coll–Northern Kentucky (KY)
Brown Mackie Coll–South Bend (IN)
Iowa Lakes Comm Coll (IA)
ITT Tech Inst, Bessemer (AL)
ITT Tech Inst, Madison (AL)
ITT Tech Inst, Mobile (AL)
ITT Tech Inst, Phoenix (AZ)
ITT Tech Inst, Tucson (AZ)
ITT Tech Inst, Thornton (CO)
ITT Tech Inst, Fort Lauderdale (FL)
ITT Tech Inst, Jacksonville (FL)
ITT Tech Inst, Lake Mary (FL)
ITT Tech Inst, Pinellas Park (FL)
ITT Tech Inst, Tampa (FL)
ITT Tech Inst, Fort Wayne (IN)
ITT Tech Inst, Indianapolis (IN)
ITT Tech Inst, Newburgh (IN)
ITT Tech Inst, Louisville (KY)
ITT Tech Inst, Baton Rouge (LA)
ITT Tech Inst, St. Rose (LA)
ITT Tech Inst, Canton (MI)
ITT Tech Inst, Swartz Creek (MI)
ITT Tech Inst, Troy (MI)
ITT Tech Inst, Wyoming (MI)
ITT Tech Inst (MN)
ITT Tech Inst, Arnold (MO)
ITT Tech Inst, Earth City (MO)
ITT Tech Inst, Kansas City (MO)
ITT Tech Inst (NV)
ITT Tech Inst, Columbus (OH)
ITT Tech Inst, Hilliard (OH)
ITT Tech Inst, Warrensville Heights (OH)
ITT Tech Inst, Tulsa (OK)
ITT Tech Inst (OR)
ITT Tech Inst, Nashville (TN)
ITT Tech Inst, Arlington (TX)
ITT Tech Inst, Austin (TX)
ITT Tech Inst, Houston (TX)
ITT Tech Inst, Houston (TX)
ITT Tech Inst, Richardson (TX)
ITT Tech Inst, San Antonio (TX)
ITT Tech Inst, Webster (TX)
ITT Tech Inst (UT)
ITT Tech Inst, Chantilly (VA)
ITT Tech Inst, Norfolk (VA)
ITT Tech Inst, Richmond (VA)
ITT Tech Inst, Springfield (VA)
ITT Tech Inst, Everett (WA)
ITT Tech Inst, Seattle (WA)
ITT Tech Inst, Spokane Valley (WA)
ITT Tech Inst (WV)
ITT Tech Inst, Green Bay (WI)
ITT Tech Inst, Greenfield (WI)
ITT Tech Inst, Madison (WI)
Lonestar Coll–Montgomery (TX)
Miami Dade Coll (FL)
Rogue Comm Coll (OR)

Computer Systems Analysis

Amarillo Coll (TX)
Blue Ridge Comm Coll (NC)
Central New Mexico Comm Coll (NM)
Glendale Comm Coll (AZ)
Guilford Tech Comm Coll (NC)
Hillsborough Comm Coll (FL)
Hutchinson Comm Coll and Area Vocational School (KS)
James Sprunt Comm Coll (NC)
Kalamazoo Valley Comm Coll (MI)
Lac Courte Oreilles Ojibwa Comm Coll (WI)
Lakeland Comm Coll (OH)
Laramie County Comm Coll (WY)
Lehigh Carbon Comm Coll (PA)
Louisiana Tech Coll (LA)
Metropolitan Comm Coll–Business & Technology Campus (MO)
Milwaukee Area Tech Coll (WI)
Oakland Comm Coll (MI)
Pensacola Jr Coll (FL)
Pima Comm Coll (AZ)
Quinsigamond Comm Coll (MA)
Tohono O'odham Comm Coll (AZ)
Waukesha County Tech Coll (WI)
Wayne Comm Coll (NC)
Wor-Wic Comm Coll (MD)

Computer Systems Networking and Telecommunications

Alexandria Tech Coll (MN)
Allen Comm Coll (KS)
Alpena Comm Coll (MI)
Altamaha Tech Coll (GA)
Anoka-Ramsey Comm Coll (MN)
Anoka-Ramsey Comm Coll, Cambridge Campus (MN)
Antonelli Coll, Jackson (MS)
Antonelli Coll (OH)
Arkansas State U–Beebe (AR)
Athens Tech Coll (GA)
Augusta Tech Coll (GA)
Austin Comm Coll (TX)
Barton County Comm Coll (KS)
Bowling Green State U–Firelands Coll (OH)
Brown Mackie Coll–Cincinnati (OH)
Brown Mackie Coll–Louisville (KY)
Brown Mackie Coll–North Canton (OH)
Brown Mackie Coll–Salina (KS)
Bunker Hill Comm Coll (MA)
Cape Fear Comm Coll (NC)
Carteret Comm Coll (NC)
Catawba Valley Comm Coll (NC)
Central Carolina Comm Coll (NC)
Central Georgia Tech Coll (GA)
Central Lakes Coll (MN)
Central Oregon Comm Coll (OR)
Century Coll (MN)
Chattahoochee Tech Coll (GA)
Clackamas Comm Coll (OR)
Clark Coll (WA)
Coll of Lake County (IL)
Coll of the Canyons (CA)
Collin County Comm Coll District (TX)
Columbus Tech Coll (GA)
Comm Coll of Allegheny County (PA)
The Comm Coll of Baltimore County (MD)
Comm Coll of Rhode Island (RI)
Comm Coll of Vermont (VT)
Corning Comm Coll (NY)
Crowder Coll (MO)
Cumberland County Coll (NJ)
Danville Area Comm Coll (IL)
Davis Coll (OH)
Daytona State Coll (FL)
DeKalb Tech Coll (GA)
Delaware County Comm Coll (PA)
Delaware Tech & Comm Coll, Stanton/Wilmington Campus (DE)
Delaware Tech & Comm Coll, Terry Campus (DE)
Del Mar Coll (TX)
East Central Coll (MO)
East Central Tech Coll (GA)
Eastern Wyoming Coll (WY)
Eastfield Coll (TX)
Edison State Comm Coll (OH)
Elgin Comm Coll (IL)
Flint River Tech Coll (GA)
Glendale Comm Coll (AZ)
Green River Comm Coll (WA)
Griffin Tech Coll (GA)
Guilford Tech Comm Coll (NC)
Gwinnett Tech Coll (GA)
Harrisburg Area Comm Coll (PA)
Harrison Coll, Indianapolis (IN)
Hawkeye Comm Coll (IA)
Hennepin Tech Coll (MN)
Highline Comm Coll (WA)
Houston Comm Coll System (TX)
Howard Comm Coll (MD)
Illinois Valley Comm Coll (IL)
Inver Hills Comm Coll (MN)
Iowa Lakes Comm Coll (IA)
Island Drafting and Tech Inst (NY)
Kaplan Coll, Merrillville Campus (IN)
Kilgore Coll (TX)
Lakeland Comm Coll (OH)
Lake Region State Coll (ND)
Lanier Tech Coll (GA)
Lehigh Carbon Comm Coll (PA)
Lewis and Clark Comm Coll (IL)
Lincoln Land Comm Coll (IL)
Linn State Tech Coll (MO)
Lonestar Coll–Montgomery (TX)
Louisiana Tech Coll (LA)
Manhattan Area Tech Coll (KS)
Marion Tech Coll (OH)
Mercer County Comm Coll (NJ)
Mesabi Range Comm and Tech Coll (MN)
Metropolitan Comm Coll–Business & Technology Campus (MO)
Middle Georgia Tech Coll (GA)
Midlands Tech Coll (SC)
Milwaukee Area Tech Coll (WI)
Minneapolis Comm and Tech Coll (MN)
Minnesota State Coll–Southeast Tech (MN)
Minnesota State Comm and Tech Coll (MN)
Mitchell Tech Inst (SD)
Montana State U–Great Falls Coll of Technology (MT)
Montgomery County Comm Coll (PA)
Moraine Park Tech Coll (WI)
Moultrie Tech Coll (GA)
Nassau Comm Coll (NY)
Northampton Comm Coll (PA)
North Georgia Tech Coll (GA)
Northland Pioneer Coll (AZ)
Northwest Florida State Coll (FL)
Odessa Coll (TX)
Ogeechee Tech Coll (GA)
Okefenokee Tech Coll (GA)
Olympic Coll (WA)
Paradise Valley Comm Coll (AZ)
Pasco-Hernando Comm Coll (FL)
Patrick Henry Comm Coll (VA)
Piedmont Comm Coll (NC)
Pima Comm Coll (AZ)
Potomac State Coll of West Virginia U (WV)
Randolph Comm Coll (NC)
Raritan Valley Comm Coll (NJ)
Rockland Comm Coll (NY)
Saint Charles Comm Coll (MO)
St. Cloud Tech Coll (MN)
Saint Paul Coll–A Comm & Tech College (MN)
St. Philip's Coll (TX)
Sandersville Tech Coll (GA)
Savannah Tech Coll (GA)
Seminole State Coll of Florida (FL)
Sierra Coll (CA)
Southeastern Tech Coll (GA)
Southeast Tech Inst (SD)
South Georgia Tech Coll (GA)
Southwestern Comm Coll (IA)
Southwestern Michigan Coll (MI)
Southwest Georgia Tech Coll (GA)
Southwest Mississippi Comm Coll (MS)
Southwest Wisconsin Tech Coll (WI)
Stanly Comm Coll (NC)
Stark State Coll of Technology (OH)
State Fair Comm Coll (MO)
Sullivan Coll of Technology and Design (KY)
Tallahassee Comm Coll (FL)
Terra State Comm Coll (OH)
TESST Coll of Technology, Baltimore (MD)
TESST Coll of Technology, Beltsville (MD)
Trident Tech Coll (SC)
Triton Coll (IL)
Valdosta Tech Coll (GA)
Victoria Coll (TX)
Vincennes U Jasper Campus (IN)
Waukesha County Tech Coll (WI)
Westchester Comm Coll (NY)
West Georgia Tech Coll (GA)
Westmoreland County Comm Coll (PA)

Wisconsin Indianhead Tech Coll (WI)
York County Comm Coll (ME)

Computer Technology/Computer Systems Technology
Alexandria Tech Coll (MN)
Arkansas State U–Beebe (AR)
Cape Fear Comm Coll (NC)
Central Lakes Coll (MN)
Central Wyoming Coll (WY)
Century Coll (MN)
Clackamas Comm Coll (OR)
Comm Coll of Allegheny County (PA)
The Comm Coll of Baltimore County (MD)
Corning Comm Coll (NY)
Dakota Coll at Bottineau (ND)
Delaware County Comm Coll (PA)
Delaware Tech & Comm Coll, Jack F. Owens Campus (DE)
Delaware Tech & Comm Coll, Terry Campus (DE)
Edison State Comm Coll (OH)
Erie Comm Coll, South Campus (NY)
Forrest Jr Coll (SC)
Harrison Coll, Indianapolis (IN)
Harrison Coll, Muncie (IN)
Hillsborough Comm Coll (FL)
Island Drafting and Tech Inst (NY)
ITI Tech Coll (LA)
Kaplan Coll, Merrillville Campus (IN)
Kent State U at Trumbull (OH)
Lakeland Comm Coll (OH)
Manhattan Area Tech Coll (KS)
Miami Dade Coll (FL)
Milwaukee Area Tech Coll (WI)
Minnesota State Comm and Tech Coll (MN)
Mitchell Tech Inst (SD)
Montgomery Coll (MD)
Mount Wachusett Comm Coll (MA)
Oakland Comm Coll (MI)
Okefenokee Tech Coll (GA)
Pasadena City Coll (CA)
Pasco-Hernando Comm Coll (FL)
Pennsylvania Coll of Technology (PA)
Pulaski Tech Coll (AR)
Quinsigamond Comm Coll (MA)
Rend Lake Coll (IL)
St. Philip's Coll (TX)
Southeast Tech Inst (SD)
Southern State Comm Coll (OH)
Stanly Comm Coll (NC)
Sullivan Coll of Technology and Design (KY)
U of Arkansas Comm Coll at Morrilton (AR)
U of Cincinnati Clermont Coll (OH)

Computer Typography and Composition Equipment Operation
Clovis Comm Coll (NM)
Coll of DuPage (IL)
Cuyahoga Comm Coll (OH)
Del Mar Coll (TX)
Fox Valley Tech Coll (WI)
Fulton-Montgomery Comm Coll (NY)
Gateway Comm Coll (CT)
Highline Comm Coll (WA)
Housatonic Comm Coll (CT)
Indian River State Coll (FL)
Lansing Comm Coll (MI)
Lonestar Coll–Kingwood (TX)
Metropolitan Comm Coll–Longview (MO)
Minnesota State Coll–Southeast Tech (MN)
Orange Coast Coll (CA)
Paradise Valley Comm Coll (AZ)
Paris Jr Coll (TX)
U of Cincinnati Clermont Coll (OH)

Concrete Finishing
Black Hawk Coll, Moline (IL)

Conservation Biology
Central Lakes Coll (MN)

Construction Engineering Technology
Antelope Valley Coll (CA)
Burlington County Coll (NJ)
Casper Coll (WY)
Central Comm Coll–Hastings Campus (NE)
Clark Coll (WA)
Coll of Lake County (IL)
Comm Coll of Allegheny County (PA)
Comm Coll of Philadelphia (PA)
Crowder Coll (MO)
Delta Coll (MI)
Fulton-Montgomery Comm Coll (NY)
Harrisburg Area Comm Coll (PA)
Houston Comm Coll System (TX)
Iowa Lakes Comm Coll (IA)
Jefferson State Comm Coll (AL)
Lansing Comm Coll (MI)
Lehigh Carbon Comm Coll (PA)
Macomb Comm Coll (MI)
Metropolitan Comm Coll (NE)
Miami Dade Coll (FL)
Midlands Tech Coll (SC)
Mid-Plains Comm Coll, North Platte (NE)
North Lake Coll (TX)
Northwest Florida State Coll (FL)
Ocean County Coll (NJ)
Odessa Coll (TX)
The Ohio State U Ag Tech Inst (OH)
Oklahoma State U, Oklahoma City (OK)
Orange Coast Coll (CA)
Pennsylvania Highlands Comm Coll (PA)
Pensacola Jr Coll (FL)
Phoenix Coll (AZ)
Raritan Valley Comm Coll (NJ)
Rogue Comm Coll (OR)
St. Philip's Coll (TX)
San Diego Mesa Coll (CA)
San Jacinto Coll District (TX)
Seminole State Coll of Florida (FL)
Snow Coll (UT)
Southeastern Comm Coll (IA)
Southern Maine Comm Coll (ME)
South Suburban Coll (IL)
Southwest Mississippi Comm Coll (MS)
State Coll of Florida Manatee-Sarasota (FL)
State U of New York Coll of Technology at Alfred (NY)
Suffolk County Comm Coll (NY)
Tallahassee Comm Coll (FL)
Tarrant County Coll District (TX)
Three Rivers Comm Coll (MO)
Victor Valley Coll (CA)
Yavapai Coll (AZ)

Construction/Heavy Equipment/Earthmoving Equipment Operation
Central Arizona Coll (AZ)
Ivy Tech Comm Coll–Southwest (IN)
Ivy Tech Comm Coll–Wabash Valley (IN)

Construction Management
Casper Coll (WY)
Delaware County Comm Coll (PA)
Delaware Tech & Comm Coll, Jack F. Owens Campus (DE)
Delaware Tech & Comm Coll, Stanton/Wilmington Campus (DE)
Delaware Tech & Comm Coll, Terry Campus (DE)
Erie Comm Coll, North Campus (NY)
Iowa Lakes Comm Coll (IA)
Kankakee Comm Coll (IL)
Lehigh Carbon Comm Coll (PA)
Northampton Comm Coll (PA)
North Hennepin Comm Coll (MN)
Oakland Comm Coll (MI)
The Ohio State U Ag Tech Inst (OH)
Oklahoma State U, Oklahoma City (OK)
Redstone Coll–Denver (CO)
Rogue Comm Coll (OR)
Triton Coll (IL)
Westwood Coll–Houston South Campus (TX)

Construction Trades
Clackamas Comm Coll (OR)
Delta Coll (MI)
East Central Coll (MO)
Eastern Wyoming Coll (WY)
Harrisburg Area Comm Coll (PA)
Iowa Lakes Comm Coll (IA)
ITT Tech Inst, Indianapolis (IN)
Ivy Tech Comm Coll–East Central (IN)
Ivy Tech Comm Coll–Northeast (IN)
Ivy Tech Comm Coll–Northwest (IN)
Ivy Tech Comm Coll–Richmond (IN)
Kirkwood Comm Coll (IA)
Laramie County Comm Coll (WY)
Northeast Iowa Comm Coll (IA)
Ogeechee Tech Coll (GA)
Oklahoma State U, Oklahoma City (OK)
Pasadena City Coll (CA)
Rogue Comm Coll (OR)
Sheridan Coll (WY)
Sierra Coll (CA)
Southern Maine Comm Coll (ME)
Triangle Tech–Greensburg School (PA)

Construction Trades Related
Central New Mexico Comm Coll (NM)
Comm Coll of Allegheny County (PA)
East Central Coll (MO)
Ivy Tech Comm Coll–East Central (IN)
Ivy Tech Comm Coll–Kokomo (IN)
Ivy Tech Comm Coll–Northeast (IN)
Ivy Tech Comm Coll–Richmond (IN)
Jackson Comm Coll (MI)
Laramie County Comm Coll (WY)
Mitchell Tech Inst (SD)
Pulaski Tech Coll (AR)
Tompkins Cortland Comm Coll (NY)

Consumer Merchandising/ Retailing Management
Anne Arundel Comm Coll (MD)
Bucks County Comm Coll (PA)
Central Piedmont Comm Coll (NC)
Del Mar Coll (TX)
Delta Coll (MI)
FIDM/The Fashion Inst of Design & Merchandising, Los Angeles Campus (CA)
FIDM/The Fashion Inst of Design & Merchandising, San Diego Campus (CA)
FIDM/The Fashion Inst of Design & Merchandising, San Francisco Campus (CA)
Fox Valley Tech Coll (WI)
Gateway Comm Coll (CT)
Golden West Coll (CA)
Harcum Coll (PA)
Howard Comm Coll (MD)
Indian River State Coll (FL)
Iowa Lakes Comm Coll (IA)
Lansing Comm Coll (MI)
Leeward Comm Coll (HI)
Minnesota State Coll–Southeast Tech (MN)
Niagara County Comm Coll (NY)
Northland Comm and Tech Coll–Thief River Falls (MN)
Pennsylvania Highlands Comm Coll (PA)
Quinsigamond Comm Coll (MA)
South Plains Coll (TX)
Stark State Coll of Technology (OH)
Suffolk County Comm Coll (NY)
Tarrant County Coll District (TX)
Three Rivers Comm Coll (CT)
Westchester Comm Coll (NY)

Consumer Services and Advocacy
Rio Salado Coll (AZ)
San Diego City Coll (CA)

Cooking and Related Culinary Arts
Central Oregon Comm Coll (OR)
Iowa Lakes Comm Coll (IA)
Miami Dade Coll (FL)
Pikes Peak Comm Coll (CO)

Corrections
Alpena Comm Coll (MI)
Alvin Comm Coll (TX)
Amarillo Coll (TX)
Anne Arundel Comm Coll (MD)
Antelope Valley Coll (CA)
Austin Comm Coll (TX)
Bakersfield Coll (CA)
Barton County Comm Coll (KS)
Broome Comm Coll (NY)
Bucks County Comm Coll (PA)
Central Arizona Coll (AZ)
Clackamas Comm Coll (OR)
Clovis Comm Coll (NM)
Coll of DuPage (IL)
Comm Coll of Allegheny County (PA)
Danville Area Comm Coll (IL)
Delta Coll (MI)
Eastern Arizona Coll (AZ)
El Paso Comm Coll (TX)
Everett Comm Coll (WA)
Grand Rapids Comm Coll (MI)
Illinois Eastern Comm Colls, Frontier Community College (IL)
Illinois Eastern Comm Colls, Lincoln Trail College (IL)
Illinois Eastern Comm Colls, Olney Central College (IL)
Illinois Eastern Comm Colls, Wabash Valley College (IL)
Illinois Valley Comm Coll (IL)
Indian River State Coll (FL)
Iowa Lakes Comm Coll (IA)
Jackson Comm Coll (MI)
Kaplan Coll, Sacramento Campus (CA)
Kellogg Comm Coll (MI)
Kilgore Coll (TX)
Kirkwood Comm Coll (IA)
Kirtland Comm Coll (MI)
Lakeland Comm Coll (OH)
Lake Michigan Coll (MI)
Lansing Comm Coll (MI)
Laramie County Comm Coll (WY)
Mercer County Comm Coll (NJ)
Metropolitan Comm Coll–Longview (MO)
Metropolitan Comm Coll–Penn Valley (MO)
Minnesota State Comm and Tech Coll (MN)
Montcalm Comm Coll (MI)
Moraine Park Tech Coll (WI)
Mountain Empire Comm Coll (VA)
Mount Wachusett Comm Coll (MA)
Northeast Comm Coll (NE)
Northeastern Jr Coll (CO)
Northland Pioneer Coll (AZ)
Oakland Comm Coll (MI)
Owens Comm Coll, Toledo (OH)
Phoenix Coll (AZ)
Polk State Coll (FL)
Raritan Valley Comm Coll (NJ)
Sierra Coll (CA)
Southern State Comm Coll (OH)
Three Rivers Comm Coll (CT)
Trinity Valley Comm Coll (TX)
Tunxis Comm Coll (CT)
Westchester Comm Coll (NY)
West Shore Comm Coll (MI)
Wisconsin Indianhead Tech Coll (WI)

Corrections Administration
Eastern Wyoming Coll (WY)

Corrections and Criminal Justice Related
Albany Tech Coll (GA)
Catawba Valley Comm Coll (NC)
Central Arizona Coll (AZ)
Corning Comm Coll (NY)
El Paso Comm Coll (TX)
Everest Inst (NY)
Fayetteville Tech Comm Coll (NC)
Kaplan Career Inst, Harrisburg (PA)
Olympic Coll (WA)
Raritan Valley Comm Coll (NJ)
Reedley Coll (CA)

Cosmetology
Allan Hancock Coll (CA)
Bakersfield Coll (CA)
Bladen Comm Coll (NC)
Blue Ridge Comm Coll (NC)
Central New Mexico Comm Coll (NM)
Central Texas Coll (TX)
Century Coll (MN)
Clovis Comm Coll (NM)
Cowley County Comm Coll and Area Vocational–Tech School (KS)
Del Mar Coll (TX)
Delta Coll (MI)
Douglas Education Center (PA)
Eastern Wyoming Coll (WY)
Everett Comm Coll (WA)
Golden West Coll (CA)
Guilford Tech Comm Coll (NC)
Honolulu Comm Coll (HI)
Houston Comm Coll System (TX)
Howard Coll (TX)
Indian River State Coll (FL)
James Sprunt Comm Coll (NC)
Kirtland Comm Coll (MI)
Lonestar Coll–Kingwood (TX)
Lonestar Coll–North Harris (TX)
Minnesota State Coll–Southeast Tech (MN)
Minnesota State Comm and Tech Coll (MN)
Montcalm Comm Coll (MI)
Northeastern Jr Coll (CO)
Northeast Iowa Comm Coll (IA)
Northland Comm and Tech Coll–Thief River Falls (MN)
Northland Pioneer Coll (AZ)
Oakland Comm Coll (MI)
Odessa Coll (TX)
Olympic Coll (WA)
Paris Jr Coll (TX)
Pasadena City Coll (CA)
Pueblo Comm Coll (CO)
Randolph Comm Coll (NC)
Saint Paul Coll–A Comm & Tech College (MN)
Salt Lake Comm Coll (UT)
Sandhills Comm Coll (NC)
San Diego City Coll (CA)
San Jacinto Coll District (TX)
San Juan Coll (NM)
Shawnee Comm Coll (IL)
Southeastern Comm Coll (IA)
Southern Union State Comm Coll (AL)
South Plains Coll (TX)
Southwest Mississippi Comm Coll (MS)
Springfield Tech Comm Coll (MA)
Stanly Comm Coll (NC)
Trinity Valley Comm Coll (TX)
Umpqua Comm Coll (OR)

Cosmetology and Personal Grooming Arts Related
Allegany Coll of Maryland (MD)
Comm Coll of Allegheny County (PA)

Cosmetology, Barber/ Styling, and Nail Instruction
Olympic Coll (WA)
Pasadena City Coll (CA)

Counseling Psychology
Kilian Comm Coll (SD)

Counselor Education/ School Counseling and Guidance
East Los Angeles Coll (CA)

Court Reporting
Alvin Comm Coll (TX)
Bryant & Stratton Coll - Southtowns Campus (NY)
Chattanooga State Comm Coll (TN)
Comm Coll of Allegheny County (PA)
The Comm Coll of Baltimore County (MD)
Cuyahoga Comm Coll (OH)
Del Mar Coll (TX)
El Paso Comm Coll (TX)
Gadsden State Comm Coll (AL)
Harrisburg Area Comm Coll (PA)
Houston Comm Coll System (TX)
Kaplan Coll, Panorama City Campus (CA)
Kilgore Coll (TX)
Lansing Comm Coll (MI)
Long Island Business Inst (NY)
Miami Dade Coll (FL)
Midlands Tech Coll (SC)
Moraine Park Tech Coll (WI)
Northland Pioneer Coll (AZ)
Oakland Comm Coll (MI)
Pennsylvania Highlands Comm Coll (PA)
San Diego City Coll (CA)
South Suburban Coll (IL)

Stark State Coll of Technology (OH)
State U of New York Coll of Technology at Alfred (NY)
West Kentucky Comm and Tech Coll (KY)

Crafts, Folk Art and Artisanry
Harrisburg Area Comm Coll (PA)
Hazard Comm and Tech Coll (KY)

Creative Writing
Berkeley City Coll (CA)
Everett Comm Coll (WA)
Kirtland Comm Coll (MI)
South Georgia Coll (GA)
Tompkins Cortland Comm Coll (NY)

Criminalistics and Criminal Science
Central Lakes Coll (MN)
Century Coll (MN)
Harrisburg Area Comm Coll (PA)
Oakland Comm Coll (MI)

Criminal Justice/Law Enforcement Administration
Allen Comm Coll (KS)
Amarillo Coll (TX)
Anne Arundel Comm Coll (MD)
Antelope Valley Coll (CA)
Arizona Western Coll (AZ)
Arkansas State U–Mountain Home (AR)
Athens Tech Coll (GA)
Bainbridge Coll (GA)
Bakersfield Coll (CA)
Beaufort County Comm Coll (NC)
Black Hawk Coll, Moline (IL)
Blue Cliff Coll–Shreveport (LA)
Brown Mackie Coll–Akron (OH)
Brown Mackie Coll–Albuquerque (NM)
Brown Mackie Coll–Atlanta (GA)
Brown Mackie Coll–Boise (ID)
Brown Mackie Coll–Cincinnati (OH)
Brown Mackie Coll–Findlay (OH)
Brown Mackie Coll–Fort Wayne (IN)
Brown Mackie Coll–Greenville (SC)
Brown Mackie Coll–Hopkinsville (KY)
Brown Mackie Coll–Indianapolis (IN)
Brown Mackie Coll–Kansas City (KS)
Brown Mackie Coll–Louisville (KY)
Brown Mackie Coll–Merrillville (IN)
Brown Mackie Coll–Miami (FL)
Brown Mackie Coll–Michigan City (IN)
Brown Mackie Coll–North Canton (OH)
Brown Mackie Coll–Northern Kentucky (KY)
Brown Mackie Coll–Phoenix (AZ)
Brown Mackie Coll–St. Louis (MO)
Brown Mackie Coll–Salina (KS)
Brown Mackie Coll–South Bend (IN)
Brown Mackie Coll–Tucson (AZ)
Brown Mackie Coll–Tulsa (OK)
Bryant & Stratton Coll, Parma (OH)
Bryant & Stratton Coll (WI)
Bryant & Stratton Coll - Albany Campus (NY)
Bryant & Stratton Coll - Buffalo Campus (NY)
Bryant & Stratton Coll - Greece Campus (NY)
Bryant & Stratton Coll - Henrietta Campus (NY)
Bryant & Stratton Coll - Richmond Campus (VA)
Bryant & Stratton Coll - Southtowns Campus (NY)
Bryant & Stratton Coll - Virginia Beach (VA)
Bucks County Comm Coll (PA)
Bunker Hill Comm Coll (MA)
Camden County Coll (NJ)
Carteret Comm Coll (NC)
Casper Coll (WY)
Central Arizona Coll (AZ)
Central Carolina Comm Coll (NC)
Central Ohio Tech Coll (OH)
Central Piedmont Comm Coll (NC)
Central Wyoming Coll (WY)
CHI Inst, Franklin Mills Campus (PA)
Colby Comm Coll (KS)
Coll of DuPage (IL)
Coll of Southern Maryland (MD)
Coll of the Canyons (CA)
Comm Coll of Philadelphia (PA)
Comm Coll of Vermont (VT)
Corning Comm Coll (NY)
Cossatot Comm Coll of the U of Arkansas (AR)
Cowley County Comm Coll and Area Vocational–Tech School (KS)
Dabney S. Lancaster Comm Coll (VA)
Darton Coll (GA)
Daytona State Coll (FL)
Dean Coll (MA)
Delaware Tech & Comm Coll, Jack F. Owens Campus (DE)
Delaware Tech & Comm Coll, Stanton/Wilmington Campus (DE)
Delaware Tech & Comm Coll, Terry Campus (DE)
Del Mar Coll (TX)
Delta Coll (MI)
Denmark Tech Coll (SC)
Des Moines Area Comm Coll (IA)
Eastern Arizona Coll (AZ)
Eastern Wyoming Coll (WY)
East Los Angeles Coll (CA)
Erie Comm Coll (NY)
Essex County Coll (NJ)
Everett Comm Coll (WA)
Finger Lakes Comm Coll (NY)
Flathead Valley Comm Coll (MT)
Folsom Lake Coll (CA)
Fox Valley Tech Coll (WI)
Frederick Comm Coll (MD)
Fulton-Montgomery Comm Coll (NY)
Gainesville State Coll (GA)
Gateway Comm and Tech Coll (KY)
Genesee Comm Coll (NY)
Georgia Military Coll (GA)
Golden West Coll (CA)
Grand Rapids Comm Coll (MI)
Greenfield Comm Coll (MA)
Harcum Coll (PA)
Harrisburg Area Comm Coll (PA)
Harrison Coll, Anderson (IN)
Harrison Coll, Elkhart (IN)
Harrison Coll (OH)
Hesser Coll, Manchester (NH)
Highline Comm Coll (WA)
Hillsborough Comm Coll (FL)
Hopkinsville Comm Coll (KY)
Housatonic Comm Coll (CT)
Howard Coll (TX)
Howard Comm Coll (MD)
Illinois Valley Comm Coll (IL)
Indian River State Coll (FL)
Iowa Lakes Comm Coll (IA)
ITT Tech Inst, Madison (AL)
ITT Tech Inst, Mobile (AL)
ITT Tech Inst (AR)
ITT Tech Inst, Anaheim (CA)
ITT Tech Inst, Lathrop (CA)
ITT Tech Inst, Oxnard (CA)
ITT Tech Inst, Rancho Cordova (CA)
ITT Tech Inst, San Bernardino (CA)
ITT Tech Inst, San Diego (CA)
ITT Tech Inst, San Dimas (CA)
ITT Tech Inst, Sylmar (CA)
ITT Tech Inst, Torrance (CA)
ITT Tech Inst, Aurora (CO)
ITT Tech Inst, Thornton (CO)
ITT Tech Inst, Fort Lauderdale (FL)
ITT Tech Inst, Fort Myers (FL)
ITT Tech Inst, Jacksonville (FL)
ITT Tech Inst, Lake Mary (FL)
ITT Tech Inst, Miami (FL)
ITT Tech Inst, Pinellas Park (FL)
ITT Tech Inst, Tallahassee (FL)
ITT Tech Inst, Tampa (FL)
ITT Tech Inst, Atlanta (GA)
ITT Tech Inst, Duluth (GA)
ITT Tech Inst, Kennesaw (GA)
ITT Tech Inst (ID)
ITT Tech Inst, Fort Wayne (IN)
ITT Tech Inst, Merrillville (IN)
ITT Tech Inst, Newburgh (IN)
ITT Tech Inst, Louisville (KY)
ITT Tech Inst, Baton Rouge (LA)
ITT Tech Inst, St. Rose (LA)
ITT Tech Inst, Canton (MI)
ITT Tech Inst, Swartz Creek (MI)
ITT Tech Inst, Troy (MI)
ITT Tech Inst, Wyoming (MI)
ITT Tech Inst (MN)
ITT Tech Inst, Arnold (MO)
ITT Tech Inst, Earth City (MO)
ITT Tech Inst, Kansas City (MO)
ITT Tech Inst (NE)
ITT Tech Inst (NV)
ITT Tech Inst (NM)
ITT Tech Inst, Columbus (OH)
ITT Tech Inst, Dayton (OH)
ITT Tech Inst, Hilliard (OH)
ITT Tech Inst, Maumee (OH)
ITT Tech Inst, Norwood (OH)
ITT Tech Inst, Strongsville (OH)
ITT Tech Inst, Warrensville Heights (OH)
ITT Tech Inst, Youngstown (OH)
ITT Tech Inst, Tulsa (OK)
ITT Tech Inst (OR)
ITT Tech Inst, Dunmore (PA)
ITT Tech Inst, King of Prussia (PA)
ITT Tech Inst, Pittsburgh (PA)
ITT Tech Inst, Tarentum (PA)
ITT Tech Inst, Columbia (SC)
ITT Tech Inst, Greenville (SC)
ITT Tech Inst, Chattanooga (TN)
ITT Tech Inst, Cordova (TN)
ITT Tech Inst, Knoxville (TN)
ITT Tech Inst, Nashville (TN)
ITT Tech Inst (UT)
ITT Tech Inst, Chantilly (VA)
ITT Tech Inst, Norfolk (VA)
ITT Tech Inst, Richmond (VA)
ITT Tech Inst, Salem (VA)
ITT Tech Inst, Springfield (VA)
ITT Tech Inst, Everett (WA)
ITT Tech Inst, Seattle (WA)
ITT Tech Inst, Spokane Valley (WA)
ITT Tech Inst (WV)
ITT Tech Inst, Green Bay (WI)
ITT Tech Inst, Greenfield (WI)
ITT Tech Inst, Madison (WI)
Jackson Comm Coll (MI)
Jefferson Comm Coll (NY)
Kankakee Comm Coll (IL)
Kaplan Career Inst, ICM Campus (PA)
Kaplan Career Inst, Nashville Campus (TN)
Kaplan Coll, Dayton Campus (OH)
Kaplan U, South Portland (ME)
Kaplan U, Cedar Rapids (IA)
Kaplan U, Hagerstown Campus (MD)
Kaplan U, Lincoln (NE)
Kaplan U, Omaha (NE)
Kaskaskia Coll (IL)
Kent State U at East Liverpool (OH)
Kilgore Coll (TX)
Kilian Comm Coll (SD)
Kirtland Comm Coll (MI)
Lake Michigan Coll (MI)
Lake-Sumter Comm Coll (FL)
Lansing Comm Coll (MI)
Laramie County Comm Coll (WY)
Lawson State Comm Coll (AL)
Lehigh Carbon Comm Coll (PA)
Lewis and Clark Comm Coll (IL)
Lonestar Coll–Cy-Fair (TX)
Lonestar Coll–Kingwood (TX)
Lonestar Coll–Montgomery (TX)
Lonestar Coll–North Harris (TX)
Lonestar Coll–Tomball (TX)
Lower Columbia Coll (WA)
Macomb Comm Coll (MI)
Manchester Comm Coll (CT)
Mendocino Coll (CA)
Metropolitan Comm Coll–Longview (MO)
Metropolitan Comm Coll–Maple Woods (MO)
Metropolitan Comm Coll–Penn Valley (MO)
Miami Dade Coll (FL)
Miller-Motte Tech Coll (SC)
Missouri State U–West Plains (MO)
Mohawk Valley Comm Coll (NY)
Montcalm Comm Coll (MI)
Mountain Empire Comm Coll (VA)
Mount Wachusett Comm Coll (MA)
Muskegon Comm Coll (MI)
Nassau Comm Coll (NY)
New Mexico State U–Carlsbad (NM)
Niagara County Comm Coll (NY)
North Arkansas Coll (AR)
North Central Texas Coll (TX)
North Hennepin Comm Coll (MN)
North Idaho Coll (ID)
Northland Comm and Tech Coll–Thief River Falls (MN)
NorthWest Arkansas Comm Coll (AR)
Northwest Coll (WY)
Northwestern Coll (IL)
Northwestern Connecticut Comm Coll (CT)
Northwest Florida State Coll (FL)
Northwest-Shoals Comm Coll (AL)
Odessa Coll (TX)
Olympic Coll (WA)
Owens Comm Coll, Toledo (OH)
Palm Beach State Coll (FL)
Pasadena City Coll (CA)
Pasco-Hernando Comm Coll (FL)
Pensacola Jr Coll (FL)
Piedmont Comm Coll (NC)
Pikes Peak Comm Coll (CO)
Polk State Coll (FL)
Pueblo Comm Coll (CO)
Quinsigamond Comm Coll (MA)
Raritan Valley Comm Coll (NJ)
Red Rocks Comm Coll (CO)
Rockland Comm Coll (NY)
Rogue Comm Coll (OR)
Saint Charles Comm Coll (MO)
St. Philip's Coll (TX)
Salt Lake Comm Coll (UT)
Sandhills Comm Coll (NC)
Santa Rosa Jr Coll (CA)
Scottsdale Comm Coll (AZ)
Seminole State Coll of Florida (FL)
Snow Coll (UT)
Somerset Comm Coll (KY)
Southeastern Comm Coll (IA)
Southern Maine Comm Coll (ME)
Southern State Comm Coll (OH)
South Georgia Coll (GA)
South Plains Coll (TX)
Southside Virginia Comm Coll (VA)
Southwest Virginia Comm Coll (VA)
Spartanburg Methodist Coll (SC)
Suffolk County Comm Coll (NY)
Tallahassee Comm Coll (FL)
Tarrant County Coll District (TX)
Temple Coll (TX)
TESST Coll of Technology, Baltimore (MD)
Thomas Nelson Comm Coll (VA)
Three Rivers Comm Coll (CT)
Three Rivers Comm Coll (MO)
Tompkins Cortland Comm Coll (NY)
Trident Tech Coll (SC)
Trinity Valley Comm Coll (TX)
Triton Coll (IL)
Tunxis Comm Coll (CT)
Ulster County Comm Coll (NY)
Umpqua Comm Coll (OR)
U of Arkansas Comm Coll at Morrilton (AR)
U of South Carolina Lancaster (SC)
Walters State Comm Coll (TN)
Western Wyoming Comm Coll (WY)
West Kentucky Comm and Tech Coll (KY)
Wilson Comm Coll (NC)
York County Comm Coll (ME)

Criminal Justice/Police Science
Alexandria Tech Coll (MN)
Allan Hancock Coll (CA)
Allegany Coll of Maryland (MD)
Alpena Comm Coll (MI)
Alvin Comm Coll (TX)
Amarillo Coll (TX)
Anne Arundel Comm Coll (MD)
Antelope Valley Coll (CA)
Arizona Western Coll (AZ)
Austin Comm Coll (TX)
Bakersfield Coll (CA)
Barton County Comm Coll (KS)
Beaufort County Comm Coll (NC)
Black Hawk Coll, Moline (IL)
Bladen Comm Coll (NC)
Broome Comm Coll (NY)
Bucks County Comm Coll (PA)
Burlington County Coll (NJ)
Cape Fear Comm Coll (NC)
Carroll Comm Coll (MD)
Cecil Coll (MD)
Central Lakes Coll (MN)
Central Ohio Tech Coll (OH)
Central Piedmont Comm Coll (NC)
Central Texas Coll (TX)
Century Coll (MN)
Cincinnati State Tech and Comm Coll (OH)
City Colls of Chicago, Richard J. Daley College (IL)
Clackamas Comm Coll (OR)
Cleveland State Comm Coll (TN)
Clovis Comm Coll (NM)
Coll of DuPage (IL)
Coll of Lake County (IL)
Collin County Comm Coll District (TX)
Comm Coll of Allegheny County (PA)
The Comm Coll of Baltimore County (MD)
Comm Coll of Rhode Island (RI)
County Coll of Morris (NJ)
Cowley County Comm Coll and Area Vocational–Tech School (KS)
Cumberland County Coll (NJ)
Cuyahoga Comm Coll (OH)
Danville Area Comm Coll (IL)
Daytona State Coll (FL)
Dean Coll (MA)
Delaware County Comm Coll (PA)
Delaware Tech & Comm Coll, Jack F. Owens Campus (DE)
Delaware Tech & Comm Coll, Stanton/Wilmington Campus (DE)
Delaware Tech & Comm Coll, Terry Campus (DE)
Del Mar Coll (TX)
Delta Coll (MI)
East Central Coll (MO)
Eastern Arizona Coll (AZ)
Eastern Wyoming Coll (WY)
East Los Angeles Coll (CA)
Edison State Comm Coll (OH)
Elgin Comm Coll (IL)
El Paso Comm Coll (TX)
Erie Comm Coll (NY)
Erie Comm Coll, North Campus (NY)
Erie Comm Coll, South Campus (NY)
Essex County Coll (NJ)
Everett Comm Coll (WA)
Finger Lakes Comm Coll (NY)
Fox Valley Tech Coll (WI)
Gadsden State Comm Coll (AL)
Georgia Highlands Coll (GA)
Germanna Comm Coll (VA)
Glendale Comm Coll (AZ)
Golden West Coll (CA)
Grand Rapids Comm Coll (MI)
Green River Comm Coll (WA)
Harford Comm Coll (MD)
Harrisburg Area Comm Coll (PA)
Hawkeye Comm Coll (IA)
Highline Comm Coll (WA)
Honolulu Comm Coll (HI)
Hopkinsville Comm Coll (KY)

Houston Comm Coll System (TX)
Howard Coll (TX)
Hutchinson Comm Coll and Area Vocational School (KS)
Illinois Eastern Comm Colls, Olney Central College (IL)
Illinois Valley Comm Coll (IL)
Indian River State Coll (FL)
Inver Hills Comm Coll (MN)
Iowa Lakes Comm Coll (IA)
James Sprunt Comm Coll (NC)
Jamestown Comm Coll (NY)
Jefferson State Comm Coll (AL)
Johnston Comm Coll (NC)
John Wood Comm Coll (IL)
Kalamazoo Valley Comm Coll (MI)
Kellogg Comm Coll (MI)
Kent State U at Ashtabula (OH)
Kent State U at Tuscarawas (OH)
Kirkwood Comm Coll (IA)
Lakeland Comm Coll (OH)
Lake Region State Coll (ND)
Lansing Comm Coll (MI)
Lawson State Comm Coll (AL)
Lincoln Land Comm Coll (IL)
Linn-Benton Comm Coll (OR)
Los Angeles Harbor Coll (CA)
Macomb Comm Coll (MI)
Massasoit Comm Coll (MA)
Mendocino Coll (CA)
Mercer County Comm Coll (NJ)
Metropolitan Comm Coll (NE)
Metropolitan Comm Coll–Blue River (MO)
Metropolitan Comm Coll–Longview (MO)
Metropolitan Comm Coll–Maple Woods (MO)
Metropolitan Comm Coll–Penn Valley (MO)
Miami Dade Coll (FL)
Middle Georgia Coll (GA)
Milwaukee Area Tech Coll (WI)
Minneapolis Comm and Tech Coll (MN)
Missouri State U–West Plains (MO)
Mohave Comm Coll (AZ)
Montgomery Coll (MD)
Montgomery Comm Coll (NC)
Montgomery County Comm Coll (PA)
Moraine Valley Comm Coll (IL)
Mt. San Jacinto Coll (CA)
Nicolet Area Tech Coll (WI)
North Central Texas Coll (TX)
Northeast Comm Coll (NE)
Northeastern Jr Coll (CO)
North Hennepin Comm Coll (MN)
North Idaho Coll (ID)
North Iowa Area Comm Coll (IA)
Northland Comm and Tech Coll–Thief River Falls (MN)
Northwestern Connecticut Comm Coll (CT)
Northwest Florida State Coll (FL)
Northwest-Shoals Comm Coll (AL)
Oakland Comm Coll (MI)
Ocean County Coll (NJ)
Odessa Coll (TX)
Okefenokee Tech Coll (GA)
Oklahoma State U, Oklahoma City (OK)
Olympic Coll (WA)
Owensboro Comm and Tech Coll (KY)
Owens Comm Coll, Toledo (OH)
Palm Beach State Coll (FL)
Phoenix Coll (AZ)
Pima Comm Coll (AZ)
Quinsigamond Comm Coll (MA)
Randolph Comm Coll (NC)
Rappahannock Comm Coll (VA)
Raritan Valley Comm Coll (NJ)
Reedley Coll (CA)
Rend Lake Coll (IL)
Rockingham Comm Coll (NC)
Rogue Comm Coll (OR)
Sandhills Comm Coll (NC)
San Jacinto Coll District (TX)
San Juan Coll (NM)
Seminole State Coll (OK)
Shawnee Comm Coll (IL)
Sierra Coll (CA)
Southeast Kentucky Comm and Tech Coll (KY)
Southeast Tech Inst (SD)
Southern Maine Comm Coll (ME)
South Plains Coll (TX)
Southwest Virginia Comm Coll (VA)
Southwest Wisconsin Tech Coll (WI)
Springfield Tech Comm Coll (MA)
Stanly Comm Coll (NC)
State Fair Comm Coll (MO)
Suffolk County Comm Coll (NY)
Temple Coll (TX)
Terra State Comm Coll (OH)
TESST Coll of Technology, Beltsville (MD)
Thomas Nelson Comm Coll (VA)
Three Rivers Comm Coll (MO)
Trinity Valley Comm Coll (TX)
Union County Coll (NJ)
Victoria Coll (TX)
Victor Valley Coll (CA)
Vincennes U Jasper Campus (IN)
Volunteer State Comm Coll (TN)
Waukesha County Tech Coll (WI)
Wayne Comm Coll (NC)
West Shore Comm Coll (MI)
West Virginia Northern Comm Coll (WV)
Wisconsin Indianhead Tech Coll (WI)
Wor-Wic Comm Coll (MD)
Yavapai Coll (AZ)

Criminal Justice/Safety

Alamance Comm Coll (NC)
Altamaha Tech Coll (GA)
Arkansas State U–Mountain Home (AR)
Augusta Tech Coll (GA)
Berkshire Comm Coll (MA)
Blue Ridge Comm and Tech Coll (WV)
Bowling Green State U–Firelands Coll (OH)
Catawba Valley Comm Coll (NC)
Central Carolina Tech Coll (SC)
Central Comm Coll–Columbus Campus (NE)
Central Comm Coll–Grand Island Campus (NE)
Central Comm Coll–Hastings Campus (NE)
Central Georgia Tech Coll (GA)
Central Lakes Coll (MN)
Central New Mexico Comm Coll (NM)
Central Texas Coll (TX)
Century Coll (MN)
Chattahoochee Tech Coll (GA)
DeKalb Tech Coll (GA)
East Central Tech Coll (GA)
Eastern Wyoming Coll (WY)
Eastfield Coll (TX)
El Paso Comm Coll (TX)
Fayetteville Tech Comm Coll (NC)
Flint River Tech Coll (GA)
Georgia Highlands Coll (GA)
Georgia Northwestern Tech Coll (GA)
Glendale Comm Coll (AZ)
Griffin Tech Coll (GA)
Guilford Tech Comm Coll (NC)
Harrison Coll, Evansville (IN)
Harrison Coll, Fort Wayne (IN)
Harrison Coll, Indianapolis (IN)
Harrison Coll, Muncie (IN)
Heart of Georgia Tech Coll (GA)
Holyoke Comm Coll (MA)
Howard Coll (TX)
Inver Hills Comm Coll (MN)
Ivy Tech Comm Coll–Bloomington (IN)
Ivy Tech Comm Coll–Central Indiana (IN)
Ivy Tech Comm Coll–East Central (IN)
Ivy Tech Comm Coll–Kokomo (IN)
Ivy Tech Comm Coll–North Central (IN)
Ivy Tech Comm Coll–Northwest (IN)
Ivy Tech Comm Coll–Southwest (IN)
Ivy Tech Comm Coll–Wabash Valley (IN)
Jamestown Comm Coll (NY)
Kaplan Coll, Denver Campus (CO)
Kaplan Coll, Modesto Campus (CA)
Kellogg Comm Coll (MI)
Kent State U at Trumbull (OH)
Lackawanna Coll (PA)
Lanier Tech Coll (GA)
Lehigh Carbon Comm Coll (PA)
Linn-Benton Comm Coll (OR)
Louisiana Tech Coll (LA)
Luna Comm Coll (NM)
Midlands Tech Coll (SC)
Minneapolis Comm and Tech Coll (MN)
Minnesota State Comm and Tech Coll (MN)
Moultrie Tech Coll (GA)
Mount Wachusett Comm Coll (MA)
Nassau Comm Coll (NY)
New Mexico State U Carlsbad (NM)
Northampton Comm Coll (PA)
North Georgia Tech Coll (GA)
North Hennepin Comm Coll (MN)
NorthWest Arkansas Comm Coll (AR)
Northwest Coll (WY)
Orangeburg-Calhoun Tech Coll (SC)
Paradise Valley Comm Coll (AZ)
Phoenix Coll (AZ)
Pima Comm Coll (AZ)
Potomac State Coll of West Virginia U (WV)
Randolph Comm Coll (NC)
San Juan Coll (NM)
Savannah Tech Coll (GA)
Sheridan Coll (WY)
Southeastern Tech Coll (GA)
South Georgia Tech Coll (GA)
South Suburban Coll (IL)
Southwest Georgia Tech Coll (GA)
State Coll of Florida Manatee-Sarasota (FL)
U of Cincinnati Clermont Coll (OH)
Valdosta Tech Coll (GA)
West Georgia Tech Coll (GA)
Westmoreland County Comm Coll (PA)
York County Comm Coll (ME)

Criminology

Genesee Comm Coll (NY)
North Iowa Area Comm Coll (IA)
Northland Comm and Tech Coll–Thief River Falls (MN)
South Georgia Coll (GA)
Western Wyoming Comm Coll (WY)

Crop Production

Barton County Comm Coll (KS)
Black Hawk Coll, Moline (IL)
Iowa Lakes Comm Coll (IA)
Northeast Comm Coll (NE)
Northeast Iowa Comm Coll (IA)
Northwest Coll (WY)
The Ohio State U Ag Tech Inst (OH)

Culinary Arts

Alamance Comm Coll (NC)
Albany Tech Coll (GA)
Allegany Coll of Maryland (MD)
The Art Inst of Ohio–Cincinnati (OH)
The Art Inst of Seattle (WA)
Atlanta Tech Coll (GA)
Augusta Tech Coll (GA)
Austin Comm Coll (TX)
Bakersfield Coll (CA)
Black Hawk Coll, Moline (IL)
Blue Ridge Comm and Tech Coll (WV)
Bradford School (OH)
Bucks County Comm Coll (PA)
Bunker Hill Comm Coll (MA)
Cape Fear Comm Coll (NC)
Central New Mexico Comm Coll (NM)
Central Ohio Tech Coll (OH)
Central Piedmont Comm Coll (NC)
Central Wyoming Coll (WY)
Chattahoochee Tech Coll (GA)
Cincinnati State Tech and Comm Coll (OH)
Clark Coll (WA)
Coll of DuPage (IL)
Collin County Comm Coll District (TX)
Columbus Culinary Inst at Bradford School (OH)
Comm Coll of Allegheny County (PA)
Comm Coll of Philadelphia (PA)
Daytona State Coll (FL)
Delaware Tech & Comm Coll, Stanton/Wilmington Campus (DE)
Delaware Tech & Comm Coll, Terry Campus (DE)
Del Mar Coll (TX)
Des Moines Area Comm Coll (IA)
East Central Coll (MO)
Elaine P. Nunez Comm Coll (LA)
El Centro Coll (TX)
Elgin Comm Coll (IL)
El Paso Comm Coll (TX)
Erie Comm Coll (NY)
Erie Comm Coll, North Campus (NY)
Fayetteville Tech Comm Coll (NC)
Flathead Valley Comm Coll (MT)
Fox Valley Tech Coll (WI)
Grand Rapids Comm Coll (MI)
Guilford Tech Comm Coll (NC)
Harrisburg Area Comm Coll (PA)
Harrison Coll, Indianapolis (IN)
H. Councill Trenholm State Tech Coll (AL)
Houston Comm Coll System (TX)
Illinois Eastern Comm Colls, Lincoln Trail College (IL)
Indian River State Coll (FL)
Kaskaskia Coll (IL)
Kauai Comm Coll (HI)
Kirkwood Comm Coll (IA)
Linn-Benton Comm Coll (OR)
Louisiana Tech Coll (LA)
Luna Comm Coll (NM)
Macomb Comm Coll (MI)
Massasoit Comm Coll (MA)
Mercer County Comm Coll (NJ)
Metropolitan Comm Coll (NE)
Milwaukee Area Tech Coll (WI)
Minneapolis Comm and Tech Coll (MN)
Mitchell Tech Inst (SD)
Mohave Comm Coll (AZ)
Montgomery County Comm Coll (PA)
Niagara County Comm Coll (NY)
Nicolet Area Tech Coll (WI)
Northampton Comm Coll (PA)
Northeast Comm Coll (NE)
North Georgia Tech Coll (GA)
North Idaho Coll (ID)
NorthWest Arkansas Comm Coll (AR)
Oakland Comm Coll (MI)
Odessa Coll (TX)
Ogeechee Tech Coll (GA)
Olympic Coll (WA)
Orange Coast Coll (CA)
Pulaski Tech Coll (AR)
Rend Lake Coll (IL)
The Restaurant School at Walnut Hill Coll (PA)
Rockland Comm Coll (NY)
Saint Paul Coll–A Comm & Tech College (MN)
St. Philip's Coll (TX)
Salt Lake Comm Coll (UT)
Sandhills Comm Coll (NC)
San Jacinto Coll District (TX)
Santa Rosa Jr Coll (CA)
Savannah Tech Coll (GA)
Scottsdale Comm Coll (AZ)
Sheridan Coll (WY)
Southern Maine Comm Coll (ME)
South Georgia Tech Coll (GA)
South Puget Sound Comm Coll (WA)
State U of New York Coll of Technology at Alfred (NY)
Suffolk County Comm Coll (NY)
Trident Tech Coll (SC)
Triton Coll (IL)
Westchester Comm Coll (NY)
West Kentucky Comm and Tech Coll (KY)
Westmoreland County Comm Coll (PA)
White Mountains Comm Coll (NH)
York County Comm Coll (ME)

Culinary Arts Related

Iowa Lakes Comm Coll (IA)
Lehigh Carbon Comm Coll (PA)
Linn-Benton Comm Coll (OR)
Olympic Coll (WA)

Customer Service Management

Alexandria Tech Coll (MN)
Catawba Valley Comm Coll (NC)
Central Oregon Comm Coll (OR)
Comm Coll of Rhode Island (RI)
Delaware Tech & Comm Coll, Stanton/Wilmington Campus (DE)

Customer Service Support/Call Center/Teleservice Operation

Central Wyoming Coll (WY)
Delaware Tech & Comm Coll, Jack F. Owens Campus (DE)
Delaware Tech & Comm Coll, Stanton/Wilmington Campus (DE)
Olympic Coll (WA)
Union County Coll (NJ)

Cytotechnology

Barton County Comm Coll (KS)

Dairy Husbandry and Production

Linn-Benton Comm Coll (OR)
Northeast Iowa Comm Coll (IA)
The Ohio State U Ag Tech Inst (OH)

Dairy Science

Northeast Comm Coll (NE)
The Ohio State U Ag Tech Inst (OH)

Dance

Allan Hancock Coll (CA)
Austin Comm Coll (TX)
Barton County Comm Coll (KS)
Casper Coll (WY)
Central Piedmont Comm Coll (NC)
Darton Coll (GA)
Dean Coll (MA)
Kilgore Coll (TX)
Lansing Comm Coll (MI)
Lonestar Coll–Cy-Fair (TX)
Lonestar Coll–North Harris (TX)
Lonestar Coll–Tomball (TX)
Lon Morris Coll (TX)
Mercer County Comm Coll (NJ)
Miami Dade Coll (FL)
Mt. San Jacinto Coll (CA)
Nassau Comm Coll (NY)
Orange Coast Coll (CA)
Pasadena City Coll (CA)
Raritan Valley Comm Coll (NJ)
Santa Rosa Jr Coll (CA)
Snow Coll (UT)
Trinity Valley Comm Coll (TX)
Westchester Comm Coll (NY)
Western Wyoming Comm Coll (WY)

Data Entry/Microcomputer Applications

Anne Arundel Comm Coll (MD)
Bunker Hill Comm Coll (MA)
Clark Coll (WA)
Comm Coll of Vermont (VT)
Delaware County Comm Coll (PA)
Del Mar Coll (TX)
Eastern Arizona Coll (AZ)
Eastfield Coll (TX)
Elgin Comm Coll (IL)
ETI Tech Coll of Niles (OH)
Fiorello H. LaGuardia Comm Coll of the City U of New York (NY)
Gateway Comm Coll (CT)
Glendale Comm Coll (AZ)
Green River Comm Coll (WA)
Howard Comm Coll (MD)
Iowa Lakes Comm Coll (IA)
Lower Columbia Coll (WA)
Metropolitan Comm Coll–Business & Technology Campus (MO)
Mitchell Tech Inst (SD)
Montgomery Coll (MD)
Northland Comm and Tech Coll–Thief River Falls (MN)

Northwest Florida State Coll (FL)
Owensboro Comm and Tech Coll (KY)
Rio Salado Coll (AZ)
St. Philip's Coll (TX)
Seminole State Coll of Florida (FL)
Sierra Coll (CA)
Stark State Coll of Technology (OH)
Three Rivers Comm Coll (MO)
Western Wyoming Comm Coll (WY)

Data Entry/Microcomputer Applications Related
Berkeley City Coll (CA)
Camden County Coll (NJ)
Coll of DuPage (IL)
ETI Tech Coll of Niles (OH)
Highline Comm Coll (WA)
Kellogg Comm Coll (MI)
Metropolitan Comm Coll–Business & Technology Campus (MO)
Northland Comm and Tech Coll–Thief River Falls (MN)
Orange Coast Coll (CA)
Pasadena City Coll (CA)
Patrick Henry Comm Coll (VA)
San Diego Mesa Coll (CA)
Seminole State Coll of Florida (FL)
Stark State Coll of Technology (OH)
Three Rivers Comm Coll (MO)
West Shore Comm Coll (MI)

Data Modeling/ Warehousing and Database Administration
Brown Mackie Coll–Akron (OH)
Brown Mackie Coll–Cincinnati (OH)
Kaplan Career Inst, ICM Campus (PA)
Metropolitan Comm Coll–Business & Technology Campus (MO)
Northland Comm and Tech Coll–Thief River Falls (MN)
Northland Pioneer Coll (AZ)
Seminole State Coll of Florida (FL)

Data Processing and Data Processing Technology
Allen Comm Coll (KS)
Alpena Comm Coll (MI)
Anne Arundel Comm Coll (MD)
Antelope Valley Coll (CA)
Bainbridge Coll (GA)
Bakersfield Coll (CA)
Bronx Comm Coll of the City U of New York (NY)
Broome Comm Coll (NY)
Bryant & Stratton Coll, Eastlake (OH)
Bucks County Comm Coll (PA)
Career Coll of Northern Nevada (NV)
Cecil Coll (MD)
Central Carolina Tech Coll (SC)
Central Comm Coll–Grand Island Campus (NE)
Central New Mexico Comm Coll (NM)
Central Ohio Tech Coll (OH)
Central Piedmont Comm Coll (NC)
Central Texas Coll (TX)
Dabney S. Lancaster Comm Coll (VA)
Davis Coll (OH)
Eastfield Coll (TX)
East Los Angeles Coll (CA)
Edison State Comm Coll (OH)
El Centro Coll (TX)
Essex County Coll (NJ)
Everest Inst (NY)
Everett Comm Coll (WA)
Finger Lakes Comm Coll (NY)
Frederick Comm Coll (MD)
Fulton-Montgomery Comm Coll (NY)
Gateway Comm Coll (CT)
Highland Comm Coll (IL)
Housatonic Comm Coll (CT)
Illinois Valley Comm Coll (IL)
Iowa Lakes Comm Coll (IA)
Jackson Comm Coll (MI)
Kaplan Coll, Hammond Campus (IN)
Kaplan Coll, Merrillville Campus (IN)
Kaplan U, Hagerstown Campus (MD)
Kingsborough Comm Coll of the City U of New York (NY)
Los Angeles Harbor Coll (CA)
Louisiana Tech Coll (LA)
Mendocino Coll (CA)
Metropolitan Comm Coll–Business & Technology Campus (MO)
Metropolitan Comm Coll–Longview (MO)
Metropolitan Comm Coll–Maple Woods (MO)
Metropolitan Comm Coll–Penn Valley (MO)
Miami Dade Coll (FL)
Middle Georgia Coll (GA)
Midlands Tech Coll (SC)
Montcalm Comm Coll (MI)
Muskegon Comm Coll (MI)
Nassau Comm Coll (NY)
Nicolet Area Tech Coll (WI)
North Central Texas Coll (TX)
North Lake Coll (TX)
NorthWest Arkansas Comm Coll (AR)
Oakland Comm Coll (MI)
Odessa Coll (TX)
Orange Coast Coll (CA)
Otero Jr Coll (CO)
Palm Beach State Coll (FL)
Patrick Henry Comm Coll (VA)
Phoenix Coll (AZ)
Polk State Coll (FL)
Potomac State Coll of West Virginia U (WV)
Quinsigamond Comm Coll (MA)
Raritan Valley Comm Coll (NJ)
Rockland Comm Coll (NY)
San Diego City Coll (CA)
San Juan Coll (NM)
Seminole State Coll of Florida (FL)
Southeast Kentucky Comm and Tech Coll (KY)
South Plains Coll (TX)
South Puget Sound Comm Coll (WA)
Southwestern Indian Polytechnic Inst (NM)
Spartanburg Comm Coll (SC)
Springfield Tech Comm Coll (MA)
Suffolk County Comm Coll (NY)
Tallahassee Comm Coll (FL)
Temple Coll (TX)
Terra State Comm Coll (OH)
Three Rivers Comm Coll (CT)
Trinity Valley Comm Coll (TX)
Tunxis Comm Coll (CT)
U of Cincinnati Clermont Coll (OH)
Westchester Comm Coll (NY)
Western Wyoming Comm Coll (WY)
West Shore Comm Coll (MI)

Dental Assisting
Allan Hancock Coll (CA)
Athens Tech Coll (GA)
Bradford School (PA)
Camden County Coll (NJ)
Central Comm Coll–Hastings Campus (NE)
Central Oregon Comm Coll (OR)
Central Wyoming Coll (WY)
Century Coll (MN)
Chattanooga State Comm Coll (TN)
Comm Care Coll (OK)
Delta Coll (MI)
El Paso Comm Coll (TX)
Essex County Coll (NJ)
Harcum Coll (PA)
H. Councill Trenholm State Tech Coll (AL)
Hennepin Tech Coll (MN)
International Business Coll, Indianapolis (IN)
Kirkwood Comm Coll (IA)
Lake Michigan Coll (MI)
Luna Comm Coll (NM)
Massasoit Comm Coll (MA)
Midlands Tech Coll (SC)
Mid-Plains Comm Coll, North Platte (NE)
Minneapolis Comm and Tech Coll (MN)
Minnesota State Comm and Tech Coll (MN)
Mohave Comm Coll (AZ)
Montana State U–Great Falls Coll of Technology (MT)
Pasadena City Coll (CA)
Pikes Peak Comm Coll (CO)
Pueblo Comm Coll (CO)
Raritan Valley Comm Coll (NJ)
Reedley Coll (CA)
St. Cloud Tech Coll (MN)
San Diego Mesa Coll (CA)
South Puget Sound Comm Coll (WA)

Dental Hygiene
Allegany Coll of Maryland (MD)
Amarillo Coll (TX)
Argosy U, Twin Cities (MN)
Athens Tech Coll (GA)
Atlanta Tech Coll (GA)
Austin Comm Coll (TX)
Bakersfield Coll (CA)
Barton County Comm Coll (KS)
Broome Comm Coll (NY)
Burlington County Coll (NJ)
Camden County Coll (NJ)
Cape Fear Comm Coll (NC)
Catawba Valley Comm Coll (NC)
Central Comm Coll–Hastings Campus (NE)
Central Georgia Tech Coll (GA)
Central Piedmont Comm Coll (NC)
Century Coll (MN)
Chattanooga State Comm Coll (TN)
Clark Coll (WA)
Colby Comm Coll (KS)
Coll of DuPage (IL)
Coll of Lake County (IL)
Collin County Comm Coll District (TX)
Columbus Tech Coll (GA)
The Comm Coll of Baltimore County (MD)
Comm Coll of Philadelphia (PA)
Comm Coll of Rhode Island (RI)
Darton Coll (GA)
Daytona State Coll (FL)
Delaware Tech & Comm Coll, Stanton/Wilmington Campus (DE)
Del Mar Coll (TX)
Delta Coll (MI)
Des Moines Area Comm Coll (IA)
El Paso Comm Coll (TX)
Erie Comm Coll, North Campus (NY)
Essex County Coll (NJ)
Fayetteville Tech Comm Coll (NC)
Georgia Highlands Coll (GA)
Georgia Perimeter Coll (GA)
Germanna Comm Coll (VA)
Grand Rapids Comm Coll (MI)
Guilford Tech Comm Coll (NC)
Harcum Coll (PA)
Harrisburg Area Comm Coll (PA)
Hawkeye Comm Coll (IA)
Highline Comm Coll (WA)
Hillsborough Comm Coll (FL)
Howard Coll (TX)
Indian River State Coll (FL)
Kalamazoo Valley Comm Coll (MI)
Kellogg Comm Coll (MI)
Kirkwood Comm Coll (IA)
Lakeland Comm Coll (OH)
Lansing Comm Coll (MI)
Laramie County Comm Coll (WY)
Lewis and Clark Comm Coll (IL)
Lonestar Coll–Kingwood (TX)
Meridian Comm Coll (MS)
Miami Dade Coll (FL)
Middle Georgia Tech Coll (GA)
Midlands Tech Coll (SC)
Milwaukee Area Tech Coll (WI)
Minnesota State Comm and Tech Coll (MN)
Mohave Comm Coll (AZ)
Montana State U–Great Falls Coll of Technology (MT)
Montgomery County Comm Coll (PA)
Mount Wachusett Comm Coll (MA)
Northampton Comm Coll (PA)
Oakland Comm Coll (MI)
Ogeechee Tech Coll (GA)
Orange Coast Coll (CA)
Owens Comm Coll, Toledo (OH)
Palm Beach State Coll (FL)
Pasadena City Coll (CA)
Pasco-Hernando Comm Coll (FL)
Pensacola Jr Coll (FL)
Phoenix Coll (AZ)
Pima Comm Coll (AZ)
Pueblo Comm Coll (CO)
Quinsigamond Comm Coll (MA)
Raritan Valley Comm Coll (NJ)
Rio Salado Coll (AZ)
St. Cloud Tech Coll (MN)
Salt Lake Comm Coll (UT)
San Juan Coll (NM)
Santa Rosa Jr Coll (CA)
Sheridan Coll (WY)
Southeastern Tech Coll (GA)
Springfield Tech Comm Coll (MA)
Stark State Coll of Technology (OH)
State Fair Comm Coll (MO)
Tallahassee Comm Coll (FL)
Tarrant County Coll District (TX)
Temple Coll (TX)
Trident Tech Coll (SC)
Tunxis Comm Coll (CT)
Union County Coll (NJ)
Waukesha County Tech Coll (WI)
Wayne Comm Coll (NC)
Westmoreland County Comm Coll (PA)

Dental Laboratory Technology
Erie Comm Coll, South Campus (NY)
J. Sargeant Reynolds Comm Coll (VA)
Kirkwood Comm Coll (IA)
Pasadena City Coll (CA)
Pima Comm Coll (AZ)

Dental Services and Allied Professions Related
Pennsylvania Coll of Technology (PA)
Quinsigamond Comm Coll (MA)

Design and Applied Arts Related
County Coll of Morris (NJ)
Mohawk Valley Comm Coll (NY)
Niagara County Comm Coll (NY)
Raritan Valley Comm Coll (NJ)

Design and Visual Communications
Black Hawk Coll, Moline (IL)
Blue Ridge Comm and Tech Coll (WV)
Bryant & Stratton Coll (WI)
Bryant & Stratton Coll - Amherst Campus (NY)
Bryant & Stratton Coll - Henrietta Campus (NY)
Bunker Hill Comm Coll (MA)
Coll of DuPage (IL)
Creative Center (NE)
Douglas Education Center (PA)
Edison State Comm Coll (OH)
Elgin Comm Coll (IL)
FIDM/The Fashion Inst of Design & Merchandising, Los Angeles Campus (CA)
FIDM/The Fashion Inst of Design & Merchandising, San Diego Campus (CA)
FIDM/The Fashion Inst of Design & Merchandising, San Francisco Campus (CA)
Harford Comm Coll (MD)
Harrisburg Area Comm Coll (PA)
ITT Tech Inst, Bessemer (AL)
ITT Tech Inst, Madison (AL)
ITT Tech Inst, Mobile (AL)
ITT Tech Inst, Phoenix (AZ)
ITT Tech Inst, Tucson (AZ)
ITT Tech Inst (AR)
ITT Tech Inst, Anaheim (CA)
ITT Tech Inst, Lathrop (CA)
ITT Tech Inst, Oxnard (CA)
ITT Tech Inst, Rancho Cordova (CA)
ITT Tech Inst, San Bernardino (CA)
ITT Tech Inst, San Diego (CA)
ITT Tech Inst, San Dimas (CA)
ITT Tech Inst, Sylmar (CA)
ITT Tech Inst, Torrance (CA)
ITT Tech Inst, Aurora (CO)
ITT Tech Inst, Thornton (CO)
ITT Tech Inst, Fort Lauderdale (FL)
ITT Tech Inst, Jacksonville (FL)
ITT Tech Inst, Lake Mary (FL)
ITT Tech Inst, Miami (FL)
ITT Tech Inst, Pinellas Park (FL)
ITT Tech Inst, Tallahassee (FL)
ITT Tech Inst, Tampa (FL)
ITT Tech Inst, Atlanta (GA)
ITT Tech Inst, Duluth (GA)
ITT Tech Inst, Kennesaw (GA)
ITT Tech Inst (ID)
ITT Tech Inst, Burr Ridge (IL)
ITT Tech Inst, Mount Prospect (IL)
ITT Tech Inst, Orland Park (IL)
ITT Tech Inst, Fort Wayne (IN)
ITT Tech Inst, Indianapolis (IN)
ITT Tech Inst, Newburgh (IN)
ITT Tech Inst, Louisville (KY)
ITT Tech Inst, Baton Rouge (LA)
ITT Tech Inst, St. Rose (LA)
ITT Tech Inst, Canton (MI)
ITT Tech Inst, Swartz Creek (MI)
ITT Tech Inst, Troy (MI)
ITT Tech Inst, Wyoming (MI)
ITT Tech Inst (MN)
ITT Tech Inst, Arnold (MO)
ITT Tech Inst, Earth City (MO)
ITT Tech Inst, Kansas City (MO)
ITT Tech Inst (NE)
ITT Tech Inst (NV)
ITT Tech Inst (NM)
ITT Tech Inst, Columbus (OH)
ITT Tech Inst, Dayton (OH)
ITT Tech Inst, Hilliard (OH)
ITT Tech Inst, Maumee (OH)
ITT Tech Inst, Norwood (OH)
ITT Tech Inst, Strongsville (OH)
ITT Tech Inst, Warrensville Heights (OH)
ITT Tech Inst, Youngstown (OH)
ITT Tech Inst, Tulsa (OK)
ITT Tech Inst (OR)
ITT Tech Inst, Columbia (SC)
ITT Tech Inst, Greenville (SC)
ITT Tech Inst, Chattanooga (TN)
ITT Tech Inst, Cordova (TN)
ITT Tech Inst, Knoxville (TN)
ITT Tech Inst, Nashville (TN)
ITT Tech Inst (UT)
ITT Tech Inst, Chantilly (VA)
ITT Tech Inst, Norfolk (VA)
ITT Tech Inst, Richmond (VA)
ITT Tech Inst, Springfield (VA)
ITT Tech Inst, Everett (WA)
ITT Tech Inst, Seattle (WA)
ITT Tech Inst, Spokane Valley (WA)
ITT Tech Inst (WV)
ITT Tech Inst, Green Bay (WI)
ITT Tech Inst, Greenfield (WI)
Ivy Tech Comm Coll–Central Indiana (IN)
Ivy Tech Comm Coll–Columbus (IN)
Ivy Tech Comm Coll–North Central (IN)
Ivy Tech Comm Coll–Southern Indiana (IN)
Ivy Tech Comm Coll–Southwest (IN)
Ivy Tech Comm Coll–Wabash Valley (IN)
Lonestar Coll–Cy-Fair (TX)
Lonestar Coll–Kingwood (TX)
Lonestar Coll–Montgomery (TX)
Lonestar Coll–North Harris (TX)
Minneapolis Comm and Tech Coll (MN)
Mt. San Jacinto Coll (CA)
Nassau Comm Coll (NY)
Oklahoma City Comm Coll (OK)
Pima Comm Coll (AZ)
Salt Lake Comm Coll (UT)
Southeastern Tech Coll (GA)
Thomas Nelson Comm Coll (VA)
Triton Coll (IL)

Desktop Publishing and Digital Imaging Design
Camden County Coll (NJ)
Central Ohio Tech Coll (OH)
Coll of DuPage (IL)

Des Moines Area Comm Coll (IA)
Hennepin Tech Coll (MN)
Houston Comm Coll System (TX)
Howard Coll (TX)
Iowa Lakes Comm Coll (IA)
Linn-Benton Comm Coll (OR)
Louisiana Tech Coll (LA)
Northeast Iowa Comm Coll (IA)
Northwest Coll (WY)
Northwestern Coll (IL)
Pasadena City Coll (CA)
Southeast Tech Inst (SD)
Sullivan Coll of Technology and Design (KY)
Terra State Comm Coll (OH)
Umpqua Comm Coll (OR)

Developmental and Child Psychology

Arizona Western Coll (AZ)
Bakersfield Coll (CA)
Central Lakes Coll (MN)
Comm Coll of Vermont (VT)
East Los Angeles Coll (CA)
Fulton-Montgomery Comm Coll (NY)
Iowa Lakes Comm Coll (IA)
Lansing Comm Coll (MI)
Los Angeles Harbor Coll (CA)
Mendocino Coll (CA)
Muskegon Comm Coll (MI)
North Idaho Coll (ID)
Rockland Comm Coll (NY)
San Diego City Coll (CA)
South Plains Coll (TX)
Tarrant County Coll District (TX)
Trinity Valley Comm Coll (TX)

Diagnostic Medical Sonography and Ultrasound Technology

Argosy U, Twin Cities (MN)
Athens Tech Coll (GA)
Austin Comm Coll (TX)
Cape Fear Comm Coll (NC)
Central New Mexico Comm Coll (NM)
Central Ohio Tech Coll (OH)
Chattanooga State Comm Coll (TN)
Cincinnati State Tech and Comm Coll (OH)
Columbus Tech Coll (GA)
Comm Coll of Allegheny County (PA)
The Comm Coll of Baltimore County (MD)
Comm Coll of Rhode Island (RI)
Darton Coll (GA)
Delaware Tech & Comm Coll, Jack F. Owens Campus (DE)
Delaware Tech & Comm Coll, Stanton/Wilmington Campus (DE)
Del Mar Coll (TX)
Delta Coll (MI)
El Centro Coll (TX)
El Paso Comm Coll (TX)
Harrisburg Area Comm Coll (PA)
H. Councill Trenholm State Tech Coll (AL)
Hillsborough Comm Coll (FL)
Jackson Comm Coll (MI)
Kennebec Valley Comm Coll (ME)
Lackawanna Coll (PA)
Lake Michigan Coll (MI)
Lansing Comm Coll (MI)
Laramie County Comm Coll (WY)
Lonestar Coll–Cy-Fair (TX)
Miami Dade Coll (FL)
Montgomery Coll (MD)
Mt. San Jacinto Coll (CA)
Northampton Comm Coll (PA)
Oakland Comm Coll (MI)
Owensboro Comm and Tech Coll (KY)
Owens Comm Coll, Toledo (OH)
Pensacola Jr Coll (FL)
Polk State Coll (FL)
Pueblo Comm Coll (CO)
St. Cloud Tech Coll (MN)
Southeast Tech Inst (SD)
Springfield Tech Comm Coll (MA)
Temple Coll (TX)
Triton Coll (IL)
Union County Coll (NJ)
West Kentucky Comm and Tech Coll (KY)

Diesel Mechanics Technology

Alexandria Tech Coll (MN)
Black Hawk Coll, Moline (IL)
Casper Coll (WY)
Central Arizona Coll (AZ)
Central Comm Coll–Hastings Campus (NE)
Central Lakes Coll (MN)
Clark Coll (WA)
The Comm Coll of Baltimore County (MD)
Des Moines Area Comm Coll (IA)
Hawkeye Comm Coll (IA)
Illinois Eastern Comm Colls, Wabash Valley College (IL)
Johnston Comm Coll (NC)
Kilgore Coll (TX)
Kirkwood Comm Coll (IA)
Lake Region State Coll (ND)
Laramie County Comm Coll (WY)
Linn-Benton Comm Coll (OR)
Lower Columbia Coll (WA)
Massasoit Comm Coll (MA)
Mid-Plains Comm Coll, North Platte (NE)
Minnesota State Comm and Tech Coll (MN)
Northeast Comm Coll (NE)
Oklahoma Tech Coll (OK)
Pennsylvania Coll of Technology (PA)
Raritan Valley Comm Coll (NJ)
Rogue Comm Coll (OR)
St. Philip's Coll (TX)
Salt Lake Comm Coll (UT)
San Jacinto Coll District (TX)
San Juan Coll (NM)
Santa Rosa Jr Coll (CA)
Sheridan Coll (WY)
Southeast Tech Inst (SD)
Southwest Mississippi Comm Coll (MS)
The U of Montana–Helena Coll of Technology (MT)
Western Wyoming Comm Coll (WY)
White Mountains Comm Coll (NH)

Dietetics

Allan Hancock Coll (CA)
Bakersfield Coll (CA)
Camden County Coll (NJ)
Central Arizona Coll (AZ)
Central Oregon Comm Coll (OR)
Cincinnati State Tech and Comm Coll (OH)
El Paso Comm Coll (TX)
Fiorello H. LaGuardia Comm Coll of the City U of New York (NY)
Gateway Comm Coll (CT)
Harrisburg Area Comm Coll (PA)
Lawson State Comm Coll (AL)
Miami Dade Coll (FL)
Northwest Florida State Coll (FL)
Orange Coast Coll (CA)
Owens Comm Coll, Toledo (OH)
Pasadena City Coll (CA)
Pensacola Jr Coll (FL)
Rockland Comm Coll (NY)
Southern Maine Comm Coll (ME)
South Plains Coll (TX)
State Coll of Florida Manatee-Sarasota (FL)
Suffolk County Comm Coll (NY)
Tarrant County Coll District (TX)
Westchester Comm Coll (NY)

Dietetics and Clinical Nutrition Services Related

Cowley County Comm Coll and Area Vocational–Tech School (KS)
Harrisburg Area Comm Coll (PA)

Dietetic Technician

Brown Mackie Coll–Fort Wayne (IN)
Fiorello H. LaGuardia Comm Coll of the City U of New York (NY)
Miami Dade Coll (FL)
Milwaukee Area Tech Coll (WI)
Southern Maine Comm Coll (ME)
Westmoreland County Comm Coll (PA)

Dietitian Assistant

Barton County Comm Coll (KS)
City Colls of Chicago, Malcolm X College (IL)
Comm Coll of Allegheny County (PA)
Erie Comm Coll, North Campus (NY)
Front Range Comm Coll (CO)
Hillsborough Comm Coll (FL)
Pennsylvania Coll of Technology (PA)
San Jacinto Coll District (TX)

Digital Communication and Media/Multimedia

Century Coll (MN)
Clackamas Comm Coll (OR)
Coll of the Canyons (CA)
Comm Coll of Vermont (VT)
Delaware Tech & Comm Coll, Terry Campus (DE)
Finger Lakes Comm Coll (NY)
Kaplan Career Inst, Harrisburg (PA)
Laramie County Comm Coll (WY)
Minneapolis Comm and Tech Coll (MN)
Mt. San Jacinto Coll (CA)
New Mexico State U–Carlsbad (NM)
Olympic Coll (WA)
Pasadena City Coll (CA)
Raritan Valley Comm Coll (NJ)
Sierra Coll (CA)
Southern Maine Comm Coll (ME)
Sullivan Coll of Technology and Design (KY)
U of Alaska Anchorage, Kenai Peninsula Coll (AK)
Virginia Marti Coll of Art and Design (OH)

Direct Entry Midwifery

Southwest Wisconsin Tech Coll (WI)

Divinity/Ministry

Lon Morris Coll (TX)
Northwest Florida State Coll (FL)

Drafting and Design Technology

Albany Tech Coll (GA)
Allen Comm Coll (KS)
Alpena Comm Coll (MI)
Alvin Comm Coll (TX)
Amarillo Coll (TX)
Antelope Valley Coll (CA)
Arizona Western Coll (AZ)
Arkansas State U–Beebe (AR)
Austin Comm Coll (TX)
Bainbridge Coll (GA)
Bakersfield Coll (CA)
Beaufort County Comm Coll (NC)
Bevill State Comm Coll (AL)
Burlington County Coll (NJ)
Camden County Coll (NJ)
Casper Coll (WY)
Central Carolina Comm Coll (NC)
Central Comm Coll–Columbus Campus (NE)
Central Comm Coll–Grand Island Campus (NE)
Central Comm Coll–Hastings Campus (NE)
Central Georgia Tech Coll (GA)
Central Ohio Tech Coll (OH)
Central Oregon Comm Coll (OR)
Central Piedmont Comm Coll (NC)
Central Texas Coll (TX)
Chattahoochee Tech Coll (GA)
Chattanooga State Comm Coll (TN)
Clackamas Comm Coll (OR)
Coll of DuPage (IL)
Collin County Comm Coll District (TX)
Columbus Tech Coll (GA)
Comm Coll of Allegheny County (PA)
The Comm Coll of Baltimore County (MD)
Comm Coll of Philadelphia (PA)
Corning Comm Coll (NY)
Cowley County Comm Coll and Area Vocational–Tech School (KS)
Crowder Coll (MO)
Cuyamaca Coll (CA)
Dabney S. Lancaster Comm Coll (VA)
Daytona State Coll (FL)
DeKalb Tech Coll (GA)
Delaware Tech & Comm Coll, Jack F. Owens Campus (DE)
Delaware Tech & Comm Coll, Stanton/Wilmington Campus (DE)
Delaware Tech & Comm Coll, Terry Campus (DE)
Del Mar Coll (TX)
Delta Coll (MI)
East Central Coll (MO)
Eastern Arizona Coll (AZ)
Eastfield Coll (TX)
East Los Angeles Coll (CA)
Edison State Comm Coll (OH)
El Paso Comm Coll (TX)
Finger Lakes Comm Coll (NY)
Fox Valley Tech Coll (WI)
Frederick Comm Coll (MD)
Gadsden State Comm Coll (AL)
Genesee Comm Coll (NY)
Golden West Coll (CA)
Grand Rapids Comm Coll (MI)
Green River Comm Coll (WA)
Griffin Tech Coll (GA)
Gwinnett Tech Coll (GA)
H. Councill Trenholm State Tech Coll (AL)
Highland Comm Coll (IL)
Highline Comm Coll (WA)
Honolulu Comm Coll (HI)
Houston Comm Coll System (TX)
Howard Coll (TX)
Hutchinson Comm Coll and Area Vocational School (KS)
Illinois Valley Comm Coll (IL)
Indian River State Coll (FL)
ITI Tech Coll (LA)
ITT Tech Inst, Arlington (TX)
Ivy Tech Comm Coll–Central Indiana (IN)
Ivy Tech Comm Coll–Columbus (IN)
Ivy Tech Comm Coll–Kokomo (IN)
Ivy Tech Comm Coll–Lafayette (IN)
Ivy Tech Comm Coll–Northeast (IN)
Ivy Tech Comm Coll–Northwest (IN)
J. F. Drake State Tech Coll (AL)
Kankakee Comm Coll (IL)
Kaplan Career Inst, Harrisburg (PA)
Kellogg Comm Coll (MI)
Kilgore Coll (TX)
Kirtland Comm Coll (MI)
Lake Michigan Coll (MI)
Lanier Tech Coll (GA)
Lansing Comm Coll (MI)
Laramie County Comm Coll (WY)
Lawson State Comm Coll (AL)
Leeward Comm Coll (HI)
Lehigh Carbon Comm Coll (PA)
Linn-Benton Comm Coll (OR)
Linn State Tech Coll (MO)
Lonestar Coll–North Harris (TX)
Los Angeles Harbor Coll (CA)
Louisiana Tech Coll (LA)
Luna Comm Coll (NM)
Lurleen B. Wallace Comm Coll (AL)
Macomb Comm Coll (MI)
Manhattan Area Tech Coll (KS)
Marion Tech Coll (OH)
Meridian Comm Coll (MS)
Metropolitan Comm Coll (NE)
Metropolitan Comm Coll–Business & Technology Campus (MO)
Miami Dade Coll (FL)
Middle Georgia Tech Coll (GA)
Minnesota State Coll–Southeast Tech (MN)
Mitchell Tech Inst (SD)
Mohave Comm Coll (AZ)
Mohawk Valley Comm Coll (NY)
Montana State U–Great Falls Coll of Technology (MT)
Montcalm Comm Coll (MI)
Mt. San Jacinto Coll (CA)
Murray State Coll (OK)
Muskegon Comm Coll (MI)
Niagara County Comm Coll (NY)
North Central Texas Coll (TX)
North Idaho Coll (ID)
Northland Comm and Tech Coll–Thief River Falls (MN)
Northland Pioneer Coll (AZ)
NorthWest Arkansas Comm Coll (AR)
Northwest Florida State Coll (FL)
Northwest-Shoals Comm Coll (AL)
Oakland Comm Coll (MI)
Odessa Coll (TX)
Oklahoma City Comm Coll (OK)
Oklahoma State U, Oklahoma City (OK)
Olympic Coll (WA)
Orange Coast Coll (CA)
Palm Beach State Coll (FL)
Paris Jr Coll (TX)
Pasadena City Coll (CA)
Pasco-Hernando Comm Coll (FL)
Pennsylvania Coll of Technology (PA)
Pensacola Jr Coll (FL)
Phoenix Coll (AZ)
Pulaski Tech Coll (AR)
Rend Lake Coll (IL)
Rockland Comm Coll (NY)
Saint Charles Comm Coll (MO)
Salt Lake Comm Coll (UT)
San Diego City Coll (CA)
San Jacinto Coll District (TX)
San Juan Coll (NM)
Seminole State Coll of Florida (FL)
Southeastern Comm Coll (IA)
Southern Maine Comm Coll (ME)
Southern State Comm Coll (OH)
South Georgia Tech Coll (GA)
South Plains Coll (TX)
South Puget Sound Comm Coll (WA)
Southwestern Michigan Coll (MI)
Spartanburg Comm Coll (SC)
Stark State Coll of Technology (OH)
State Coll of Florida Manatee-Sarasota (FL)
State U of New York Coll of Technology at Alfred (NY)
Suffolk County Comm Coll (NY)
Sullivan Coll of Technology and Design (KY)
Tarrant County Coll District (TX)
Temple Coll (TX)
Thomas Nelson Comm Coll (VA)
Three Rivers Comm Coll (CT)
Tidewater Comm Coll (VA)
Triangle Tech–Greensburg School (PA)
Triangle Tech, Inc.–DuBois School (PA)
Trinity Valley Comm Coll (TX)
U of Arkansas Comm Coll at Morrilton (AR)
Valdosta Tech Coll (GA)
Victoria Coll (TX)
Vincennes U Jasper Campus (IN)
York County Comm Coll (ME)

Drafting/Design Engineering Technologies Related

Bowling Green State U–Firelands Coll (OH)
Coll of DuPage (IL)
Comm Coll of Allegheny County (PA)
Cuyamaca Coll (CA)
Dabney S. Lancaster Comm Coll (VA)
Delta Coll (MI)
Fox Valley Tech Coll (WI)
Hennepin Tech Coll (MN)
Illinois Valley Comm Coll (IL)
Kennebec Valley Comm Coll (ME)
Lansing Comm Coll (MI)
Lehigh Carbon Comm Coll (PA)
Lonestar Coll–Montgomery (TX)
Macomb Comm Coll (MI)
Minnesota State Coll–Southeast Tech (MN)
Niagara County Comm Coll (NY)
Pennsylvania Coll of Technology (PA)
Phoenix Coll (AZ)
State U of New York Coll of Technology at Alfred (NY)
Sullivan Coll of Technology and Design (KY)
Ulster County Comm Coll (NY)

Drama and Dance Teacher Education

Darton Coll (GA)
Howard Coll (TX)

Dramatic/Theater Arts

Allen Comm Coll (KS)
Alvin Comm Coll (TX)
Amarillo Coll (TX)
American Academy of Dramatic Arts (CA)
American Academy of Dramatic Arts (NY)
Anoka-Ramsey Comm Coll (MN)
Anoka-Ramsey Comm Coll, Cambridge Campus (MN)
Arizona Western Coll (AZ)
Austin Comm Coll (TX)
Bainbridge Coll (GA)
Bakersfield Coll (CA)
Barton County Comm Coll (KS)

Bucks County Comm Coll (PA)
Bunker Hill Comm Coll (MA)
Burlington County Coll (NJ)
Central Wyoming Coll (WY)
Clarendon Coll (TX)
Coll of the Canyons (CA)
Comm Coll of Allegheny County (PA)
Comm Coll of Rhode Island (RI)
Cowley County Comm Coll and Area Vocational–Tech School (KS)
Crowder Coll (MO)
Darton Coll (GA)
Dean Coll (MA)
Del Mar Coll (TX)
Eastern Arizona Coll (AZ)
East Los Angeles Coll (CA)
Edison State Comm Coll (OH)
Everett Comm Coll (WA)
Finger Lakes Comm Coll (NY)
Fulton-Montgomery Comm Coll (NY)
Gainesville State Coll (GA)
Genesee Comm Coll (NY)
Harrisburg Area Comm Coll (PA)
Highland Comm Coll (IL)
Howard Coll (TX)
Howard Comm Coll (MD)
Indian River State Coll (FL)
Kilgore Coll (TX)
Kingsborough Comm Coll of the City U of New York (NY)
Lake Michigan Coll (MI)
Lansing Comm Coll (MI)
Laramie County Comm Coll (WY)
Linn-Benton Comm Coll (OR)
Lonestar Coll–Cy-Fair (TX)
Lonestar Coll–Kingwood (TX)
Lonestar Coll–Montgomery (TX)
Lonestar Coll–North Harris (TX)
Lonestar Coll–Tomball (TX)
Lon Morris Coll (TX)
Manchester Comm Coll (CT)
Massasoit Comm Coll (MA)
Mendocino Coll (CA)
Mercer County Comm Coll (NJ)
Miami Dade Coll (FL)
Minneapolis Comm and Tech Coll (MN)
Mohawk Valley Comm Coll (NY)
Mt. San Jacinto Coll (CA)
Nassau Comm Coll (NY)
Niagara County Comm Coll (NY)
Northeast Comm Coll (NE)
Northeastern Jr Coll (CO)
North Idaho Coll (ID)
Oakland Comm Coll (MI)
Oklahoma City Comm Coll (OK)
Orange Coast Coll (CA)
Otero Jr Coll (CO)
Palm Beach State Coll (FL)
Pasadena City Coll (CA)
Red Rocks Comm Coll (CO)
Rockland Comm Coll (NY)
Saint Charles Comm Coll (MO)
St. Philip's Coll (TX)
San Diego City Coll (CA)
San Jacinto Coll District (TX)
San Juan Coll (NM)
Santa Rosa Jr Coll (CA)
Scottsdale Comm Coll (AZ)
Sheridan Coll (WY)
Snow Coll (UT)
South Georgia Coll (GA)
State Coll of Florida Manatee-Sarasota (FL)
Suffolk County Comm Coll (NY)
Three Rivers Comm Coll (CT)
Trinity Valley Comm Coll (TX)
Ulster County Comm Coll (NY)
Umpqua Comm Coll (OR)
Victor Valley Coll (CA)
Western Wyoming Comm Coll (WY)

Dramatic/Theater Arts and Stagecraft Related
St. Philip's Coll (TX)

Drawing
Cuyamaca Coll (CA)
Iowa Lakes Comm Coll (IA)
Lon Morris Coll (TX)
Northeastern Jr Coll (CO)

Early Childhood Education
Austin Comm Coll (TX)
Barton County Comm Coll (KS)
Black Hawk Coll, Moline (IL)
Blue Ridge Comm Coll (NC)
Brown Mackie Coll–Akron (OH)
Brown Mackie Coll–Atlanta (GA)
Brown Mackie Coll–Cincinnati (OH)
Brown Mackie Coll–Findlay (OH)
Brown Mackie Coll–Louisville (KY)
Brown Mackie Coll–Miami (FL)
Brown Mackie Coll–Michigan City (IN)
Brown Mackie Coll–South Bend (IN)
Brown Mackie Coll–Tucson (AZ)
Bunker Hill Comm Coll (MA)
Cape Fear Comm Coll (NC)
Central Oregon Comm Coll (OR)
Central Wyoming Coll (WY)
Clark Coll (WA)
Coll of Southern Maryland (MD)
Collin County Comm Coll District (TX)
Comm Care Coll (OK)
The Comm Coll of Baltimore County (MD)
Comm Coll of Rhode Island (RI)
Comm Coll of Vermont (VT)
Cossatot Comm Coll of the U of Arkansas (AR)
Davis Coll (OH)
Dean Coll (MA)
Delaware County Comm Coll (PA)
Delaware Tech & Comm Coll, Jack F. Owens Campus (DE)
Delaware Tech & Comm Coll, Stanton/Wilmington Campus (DE)
Delaware Tech & Comm Coll, Terry Campus (DE)
Eastern Wyoming Coll (WY)
Everett Comm Coll (WA)
Fayetteville Tech Comm Coll (NC)
Finger Lakes Comm Coll (NY)
Folsom Lake Coll (CA)
Front Range Comm Coll (CO)
Gainesville State Coll (GA)
Gateway Comm and Tech Coll (KY)
Georgia Military Coll (GA)
Glendale Comm Coll (AZ)
Goodwin Coll (CT)
Green River Comm Coll (WA)
Guilford Tech Comm Coll (NC)
Harford Comm Coll (MD)
Harrisburg Area Comm Coll (PA)
Hesser Coll, Manchester (NH)
Hopkinsville Comm Coll (KY)
Illinois Valley Comm Coll (IL)
Iowa Lakes Comm Coll (IA)
Ivy Tech Comm Coll–Bloomington (IN)
Ivy Tech Comm Coll–Central Indiana (IN)
Ivy Tech Comm Coll–Columbus (IN)
Ivy Tech Comm Coll–East Central (IN)
Ivy Tech Comm Coll–Kokomo (IN)
Ivy Tech Comm Coll–Lafayette (IN)
Ivy Tech Comm Coll–North Central (IN)
Ivy Tech Comm Coll–Northeast (IN)
Ivy Tech Comm Coll–Northwest (IN)
Ivy Tech Comm Coll–Richmond (IN)
Ivy Tech Comm Coll–Southeast (IN)
Ivy Tech Comm Coll–Southern Indiana (IN)
Ivy Tech Comm Coll–Southwest (IN)
Ivy Tech Comm Coll–Wabash Valley (IN)
Jackson Comm Coll (MI)
Jamestown Comm Coll (NY)
Jefferson Comm Coll (NY)
Johnston Comm Coll (NC)
John Wood Comm Coll (IL)
Kent State U at Tuscarawas (OH)
Kingsborough Comm Coll of the City U of New York (NY)
Lac Courte Oreilles Ojibwa Comm Coll (WI)
Lackawanna Coll (PA)
Lake Michigan Coll (MI)
Laramie County Comm Coll (WY)
Leech Lake Tribal Coll (MN)
Lehigh Carbon Comm Coll (PA)
Lower Columbia Coll (WA)
Milwaukee Area Tech Coll (WI)
Montgomery Coll (MD)
Moraine Park Tech Coll (WI)
New Mexico State U–Carlsbad (NM)
Northampton Comm Coll (PA)
Northeast Comm Coll (NE)
North Iowa Area Comm Coll (IA)
Northland Pioneer Coll (AZ)
NorthWest Arkansas Comm Coll (AR)
Oklahoma State U, Oklahoma City (OK)
Olympic Coll (WA)
Owens Comm Coll, Toledo (OH)
Paradise Valley Comm Coll (AZ)
Pennsylvania Coll of Technology (PA)
Pima Comm Coll (AZ)
Randolph Comm Coll (NC)
St. Philip's Coll (TX)
Sheridan Coll (WY)
Southern Maine Comm Coll (ME)
Southwestern Indian Polytechnic Inst (NM)
Southwestern Michigan Coll (MI)
Southwest Mississippi Comm Coll (MS)
Southwest Wisconsin Tech Coll (WI)
Springfield Tech Comm Coll (MA)
Tohono O'odham Comm Coll (AZ)
Tompkins Cortland Comm Coll (NY)
Tri-County Comm Coll (NC)
Triton Coll (IL)
U of Alaska Anchorage, Kenai Peninsula Coll (AK)
Waukesha County Tech Coll (WI)
Western Wyoming Comm Coll (WY)
Westmoreland County Comm Coll (PA)
Wisconsin Indianhead Tech Coll (WI)
Wor-Wic Comm Coll (MD)

Ecology
Iowa Lakes Comm Coll (IA)

Ecology, Evolution, Systematics and Population Biology Related
Northwest Coll (WY)

E-Commerce
Augusta Tech Coll (GA)
Catawba Valley Comm Coll (NC)
Central Georgia Tech Coll (GA)
Delaware County Comm Coll (PA)
Delaware Tech & Comm Coll, Jack F. Owens Campus (DE)
Delaware Tech & Comm Coll, Terry Campus (DE)
Del Mar Coll (TX)
Eastfield Coll (TX)
Fayetteville Tech Comm Coll (NC)
Finger Lakes Comm Coll (NY)
Kalamazoo Valley Comm Coll (MI)
Milwaukee Area Tech Coll (WI)
Pasco-Hernando Comm Coll (FL)
Piedmont Comm Coll (NC)
Rend Lake Coll (IL)
St. Philip's Coll (TX)
Valdosta Tech Coll (GA)

Economics
Allen Comm Coll (KS)
Anne Arundel Comm Coll (MD)
Austin Comm Coll (TX)
Bakersfield Coll (CA)
Barton County Comm Coll (KS)
Casper Coll (WY)
Clarendon Coll (TX)
Darton Coll (GA)
Eastern Wyoming Coll (WY)
Georgia Highlands Coll (GA)
Indian River State Coll (FL)
Iowa Lakes Comm Coll (IA)
Laramie County Comm Coll (WY)
Linn-Benton Comm Coll (OR)
Lonestar Coll–Cy-Fair (TX)
Lonestar Coll–Kingwood (TX)
Lonestar Coll–Montgomery (TX)
Lonestar Coll–North Harris (TX)
Lonestar Coll–Tomball (TX)
Miami Dade Coll (FL)
Muskegon Comm Coll (MI)
Northeastern Jr Coll (CO)
Oklahoma State U, Oklahoma City (OK)
Orange Coast Coll (CA)
Palm Beach State Coll (FL)
Pasadena City Coll (CA)
Potomac State Coll of West Virginia U (WV)
Red Rocks Comm Coll (CO)
Saint Charles Comm Coll (MO)
St. Philip's Coll (TX)
Salt Lake Comm Coll (UT)
Santa Rosa Jr Coll (CA)
Snow Coll (UT)
South Georgia Coll (GA)
State Coll of Florida Manatee-Sarasota (FL)
Terra State Comm Coll (OH)
Triton Coll (IL)
Umpqua Comm Coll (OR)
Western Wyoming Comm Coll (WY)

Education
Anne Arundel Comm Coll (MD)
Arizona Western Coll (AZ)
Bainbridge Coll (GA)
Bucks County Comm Coll (PA)
Bunker Hill Comm Coll (MA)
Burlington County Coll (NJ)
Camden County Coll (NJ)
Cecil Coll (MD)
Central Oregon Comm Coll (OR)
Chattanooga State Comm Coll (TN)
Chipola Coll (FL)
Clarendon Coll (TX)
Coll of Southern Maryland (MD)
The Comm Coll of Baltimore County (MD)
Comm Coll of Philadelphia (PA)
Comm Coll of Vermont (VT)
Cowley County Comm Coll and Area Vocational–Tech School (KS)
Crowder Coll (MO)
Cumberland County Coll (NJ)
Dabney S. Lancaster Comm Coll (VA)
Dakota Coll at Bottineau (ND)
Del Mar Coll (TX)
East Central Coll (MO)
Eastern Shore Comm Coll (VA)
Eastfield Coll (TX)
Edison State Comm Coll (OH)
Elaine P. Nunez Comm Coll (LA)
Everett Comm Coll (WA)
Folsom Lake Coll (CA)
Frederick Comm Coll (MD)
Genesee Comm Coll (NY)
Georgia Military Coll (GA)
Germanna Comm Coll (VA)
Greenfield Comm Coll (MA)
Harford Comm Coll (MD)
Highland Comm Coll (IL)
Highline Comm Coll (WA)
Howard Coll (TX)
Hutchinson Comm Coll and Area Vocational School (KS)
Illinois Valley Comm Coll (IL)
Indian River State Coll (FL)
Inver Hills Comm Coll (MN)
Iowa Lakes Comm Coll (IA)
Itasca Comm Coll (MN)
Jackson State Comm Coll (TN)
Kent State U at Salem (OH)
Kingsborough Comm Coll of the City U of New York (NY)
Kirkwood Comm Coll (IA)
Lackawanna Coll (PA)
Lansing Comm Coll (MI)
Laramie County Comm Coll (WY)
Lehigh Carbon Comm Coll (PA)
Linn-Benton Comm Coll (OR)
Lonestar Coll–Cy-Fair (TX)
Lonestar Coll–Kingwood (TX)
Lonestar Coll–Montgomery (TX)
Lonestar Coll–North Harris (TX)
Lonestar Coll–Tomball (TX)
Lon Morris Coll (TX)
Luna Comm Coll (NM)
Miami Dade Coll (FL)
Milwaukee Area Tech Coll (WI)
Mohave Comm Coll (AZ)
Montana State U–Great Falls Coll of Technology (MT)
Muskegon Comm Coll (MI)
New Mexico State U–Carlsbad (NM)
Northeast Comm Coll (NE)
Northeastern Jr Coll (CO)
North Idaho Coll (ID)
North Iowa Area Comm Coll (IA)
NorthWest Arkansas Comm Coll (AR)
Northwest Florida State Coll (FL)
Odessa Coll (TX)
Owens Comm Coll, Toledo (OH)
Palm Beach State Coll (FL)
Paris Jr Coll (TX)
Pensacola Jr Coll (FL)
Potomac State Coll of West Virginia U (WV)
Saint Charles Comm Coll (MO)
St. Philip's Coll (TX)
San Juan Coll (NM)
Snow Coll (UT)
South Georgia Coll (GA)
South Plains Coll (TX)
Southside Virginia Comm Coll (VA)
Southwest Mississippi Comm Coll (MS)
Southwest Virginia Comm Coll (VA)
Terra State Comm Coll (OH)
Three Rivers Comm Coll (MO)
Tidewater Comm Coll (VA)
Trinity Valley Comm Coll (TX)
Triton Coll (IL)
Umpqua Comm Coll (OR)
Vincennes U Jasper Campus (IN)
Volunteer State Comm Coll (TN)
Walters State Comm Coll (TN)
Western Wyoming Comm Coll (WY)
Wor-Wic Comm Coll (MD)

Educational/Instructional Media Design
Collin County Comm Coll District (TX)
Hutchinson Comm Coll and Area Vocational School (KS)
Ivy Tech Comm Coll–North Central (IN)
Pikes Peak Comm Coll (CO)
Tarrant County Coll District (TX)
Triton Coll (IL)

Educational Leadership and Administration
Glendale Comm Coll (AZ)

Education (Multiple Levels)
Carroll Comm Coll (MD)
Century Coll (MN)
Delaware County Comm Coll (PA)
Delaware Tech & Comm Coll, Jack F. Owens Campus (DE)
Delaware Tech & Comm Coll, Stanton/Wilmington Campus (DE)
Delaware Tech & Comm Coll, Terry Campus (DE)
Itasca Comm Coll (MN)
Kirtland Comm Coll (MI)
Minneapolis Comm and Tech Coll (MN)
North Arkansas Coll (AR)
Raritan Valley Comm Coll (NJ)
San Jacinto Coll District (TX)
U of Arkansas Comm Coll at Morrilton (AR)
Vincennes U Jasper Campus (IN)
Westchester Comm Coll (NY)
Western Wyoming Comm Coll (WY)

Education Related
Corning Comm Coll (NY)
East Central Coll (MO)
Guilford Tech Comm Coll (NC)

Howard Coll (TX)
Miami Dade Coll (FL)
Yavapai Coll (AZ)

Education (Specific Levels and Methods) Related
Comm Coll of Allegheny County (PA)
Laramie County Comm Coll (WY)

Education (Specific Subject Areas) Related
Comm Coll of Allegheny County (PA)
Pennsylvania Coll of Technology (PA)
Saint Charles Comm Coll (MO)
State Fair Comm Coll (MO)

Electrical and Electronic Engineering Technologies Related
Albany Tech Coll (GA)
Cincinnati State Tech and Comm Coll (OH)
J. Sargeant Reynolds Comm Coll (VA)
Lake Region State Coll (ND)
Miami Dade Coll (FL)
Minnesota State Comm and Tech Coll (MN)
Mitchell Tech Inst (SD)
Mohawk Valley Comm Coll (NY)
Mountain Empire Comm Coll (VA)
Pasadena City Coll (CA)
Pennsylvania Coll of Technology (PA)
Randolph Comm Coll (NC)
San Juan Coll (NM)
Sheridan Coll (WY)
Springfield Tech Comm Coll (MA)
Sullivan Coll of Technology and Design (KY)
Terra State Comm Coll (OH)

Electrical and Power Transmission Installation
Clackamas Comm Coll (OR)
Delaware County Comm Coll (PA)
Ivy Tech Comm Coll–Columbus (IN)
Mitchell Tech Inst (SD)
Oklahoma State U, Oklahoma City (OK)
Orange Coast Coll (CA)
Piedmont Comm Coll (NC)
Rogue Comm Coll (OR)
St. Cloud Tech Coll (MN)
San Jacinto Coll District (TX)

Electrical and Power Transmission Installation Related
Manhattan Area Tech Coll (KS)
Pennsylvania Coll of Technology (PA)

Electrical, Electronic and Communications Engineering Technology
Alamance Comm Coll (NC)
Allan Hancock Coll (CA)
Allen Comm Coll (KS)
Alvin Comm Coll (TX)
Amarillo Coll (TX)
Anne Arundel Comm Coll (MD)
Antelope Valley Coll (CA)
Arizona Western Coll (AZ)
Arkansas State U–Beebe (AR)
Athens Tech Coll (GA)
Augusta Tech Coll (GA)
Austin Comm Coll (TX)
Bainbridge Coll (GA)
Bakersfield Coll (CA)
Beaufort County Comm Coll (NC)
Berkshire Comm Coll (MA)
Bladen Comm Coll (NC)
Blue Ridge Comm Coll (NC)
Bowling Green State U–Firelands Coll (OH)
Bronx Comm Coll of the City U of New York (NY)
Broome Comm Coll (NY)
Brown Mackie Coll–Cincinnati (OH)
Brown Mackie Coll–Louisville (KY)
Bryant & Stratton Coll, Eastlake (OH)
Burlington County Coll (NJ)
Camden County Coll (NJ)
Cape Fear Comm Coll (NC)
Career Coll of Northern Nevada (NV)
Casper Coll (WY)
Catawba Valley Comm Coll (NC)
Central Carolina Comm Coll (NC)
Central Comm Coll–Columbus Campus (NE)
Central Comm Coll–Grand Island Campus (NE)
Central Comm Coll–Hastings Campus (NE)
Central Georgia Tech Coll (GA)
Central New Mexico Comm Coll (NM)
Central Ohio Tech Coll (OH)
Central Oregon Comm Coll (OR)
Central Piedmont Comm Coll (NC)
Central Texas Coll (TX)
Chattahoochee Tech Coll (GA)
Chattanooga State Comm Coll (TN)
Cincinnati State Tech and Comm Coll (OH)
City Colls of Chicago, Richard J. Daley College (IL)
Clackamas Comm Coll (OR)
Clark Coll (WA)
Cleveland Inst of Electronics (OH)
Coll of DuPage (IL)
Coll of Lake County (IL)
Collin County Comm Coll District (TX)
Columbus Tech Coll (GA)
Comm Coll of Allegheny County (PA)
The Comm Coll of Baltimore County (MD)
Comm Coll of Rhode Island (RI)
Corning Comm Coll (NY)
County Coll of Morris (NJ)
Crowder Coll (MO)
Dabney S. Lancaster Comm Coll (VA)
Daytona State Coll (FL)
DeKalb Tech Coll (GA)
Delaware County Comm Coll (PA)
Delaware Tech & Comm Coll, Jack F. Owens Campus (DE)
Delaware Tech & Comm Coll, Stanton/Wilmington Campus (DE)
Delaware Tech & Comm Coll, Terry Campus (DE)
Del Mar Coll (TX)
Des Moines Area Comm Coll (IA)
Eastern Shore Comm Coll (VA)
Eastfield Coll (TX)
East Los Angeles Coll (CA)
Edison State Comm Coll (OH)
Elaine P. Nunez Comm Coll (LA)
Elgin Comm Coll (IL)
El Paso Comm Coll (TX)
Erie Comm Coll, North Campus (NY)
Essex County Coll (NJ)
ETI Tech Coll of Niles (OH)
Fayetteville Tech Comm Coll (NC)
Flint River Tech Coll (GA)
Fox Valley Tech Coll (WI)
Frederick Comm Coll (MD)
Front Range Comm Coll (CO)
Fulton-Montgomery Comm Coll (NY)
Gadsden State Comm Coll (AL)
Gateway Comm Coll (CT)
Genesee Comm Coll (NY)
Georgia Highlands Coll (GA)
Golden West Coll (CA)
Grand Rapids Comm Coll (MI)
Griffin Tech Coll (GA)
Guilford Tech Comm Coll (NC)
Gwinnett Tech Coll (GA)
Harrisburg Area Comm Coll (PA)
Hawkeye Comm Coll (IA)
Heart of Georgia Tech Coll (GA)
Hennepin Tech Coll (MN)
Highland Comm Coll (IL)
Hillsborough Comm Coll (FL)
Honolulu Comm Coll (HI)
Hopkinsville Comm Coll (KY)
Howard Comm Coll (MD)
Illinois Eastern Comm Colls, Wabash Valley College (IL)
Illinois Valley Comm Coll (IL)
Indian River State Coll (FL)
Island Drafting and Tech Inst (NY)
ITI Tech Coll (LA)
Ivy Tech Comm Coll–Bloomington (IN)
Ivy Tech Comm Coll–Central Indiana (IN)
Ivy Tech Comm Coll–Columbus (IN)
Ivy Tech Comm Coll–East Central (IN)
Ivy Tech Comm Coll–Kokomo (IN)
Ivy Tech Comm Coll–Lafayette (IN)
Ivy Tech Comm Coll–North Central (IN)
Ivy Tech Comm Coll–Northeast (IN)
Ivy Tech Comm Coll–Northwest (IN)
Ivy Tech Comm Coll–Richmond (IN)
Ivy Tech Comm Coll–Southeast (IN)
Ivy Tech Comm Coll–Southern Indiana (IN)
Ivy Tech Comm Coll–Southwest (IN)
Ivy Tech Comm Coll–Wabash Valley (IN)
Jackson Comm Coll (MI)
Jamestown Comm Coll (NY)
J. F. Drake State Tech Coll (AL)
Johnston Comm Coll (NC)
John Wood Comm Coll (IL)
Kalamazoo Valley Comm Coll (MI)
Kankakee Comm Coll (IL)
Kaskaskia Coll (IL)
Kauai Comm Coll (HI)
Kennebec Valley Comm Coll (ME)
Kent State U at Ashtabula (OH)
Kent State U at Trumbull (OH)
Kent State U at Tuscarawas (OH)
Kilgore Coll (TX)
Kirkwood Comm Coll (IA)
Kirtland Comm Coll (MI)
Lakeland Comm Coll (OH)
Lanier Tech Coll (GA)
Lansing Comm Coll (MI)
Lawson State Comm Coll (AL)
Lehigh Carbon Comm Coll (PA)
Lincoln Land Comm Coll (IL)
Linn State Tech Coll (MO)
Lonestar Coll–Cy-Fair (TX)
Lonestar Coll–North Harris (TX)
Los Angeles Harbor Coll (CA)
Luna Comm Coll (NM)
Macomb Comm Coll (MI)
Marion Tech Coll (OH)
Massasoit Comm Coll (MA)
Mercer County Comm Coll (NJ)
Meridian Comm Coll (MS)
Metropolitan Comm Coll (NE)
Metropolitan Comm Coll–Business & Technology Campus (MO)
Miami Dade Coll (FL)
Midlands Tech Coll (SC)
Milwaukee Area Tech Coll (WI)
Minnesota State Coll–Southeast Tech (MN)
Minnesota State Comm and Tech Coll (MN)
Mitchell Tech Inst (SD)
Mohawk Valley Comm Coll (NY)
Montcalm Comm Coll (MI)
Montgomery County Comm Coll (PA)
Moultrie Tech Coll (GA)
Mountain Empire Comm Coll (VA)
Murray State Coll (OK)
Muskegon Comm Coll (MI)
New Mexico State U–Carlsbad (NM)
Niagara County Comm Coll (NY)
Northampton Comm Coll (PA)
North Arkansas Coll (AR)
North Central Texas Coll (TX)
Northeast Iowa Comm Coll (IA)
North Idaho Coll (ID)
North Iowa Area Comm Coll (IA)
North Lake Coll (TX)
Northland Comm and Tech Coll–Thief River Falls (MN)
Northland Pioneer Coll (AZ)
NorthWest Arkansas Comm Coll (AR)
Northwestern Connecticut Comm Coll (CT)
Northwest Florida State Coll (FL)
Northwest-Shoals Comm Coll (AL)
Oakland Comm Coll (MI)
Ocean County Coll (NJ)
Odessa Coll (TX)
Oklahoma City Comm Coll (OK)
Oklahoma State U, Oklahoma City (OK)
Olympic Coll (WA)
Orangeburg-Calhoun Tech Coll (SC)
Orange Coast Coll (CA)
Owensboro Comm and Tech Coll (KY)
Owens Comm Coll, Toledo (OH)
Palm Beach State Coll (FL)
Paris Jr Coll (TX)
Patrick Henry Comm Coll (VA)
Penn State Brandywine (PA)
Penn State DuBois (PA)
Penn State Fayette, The Eberly Campus (PA)
Penn State Hazleton (PA)
Penn State New Kensington (PA)
Penn State Schuylkill (PA)
Penn State Shenango (PA)
Penn State Wilkes-Barre (PA)
Penn State Worthington Scranton (PA)
Penn State York (PA)
Pennsylvania Highlands Comm Coll (PA)
Pennsylvania Inst of Technology (PA)
Pensacola Jr Coll (FL)
Pikes Peak Comm Coll (CO)
Pima Comm Coll (AZ)
Potomac State Coll of West Virginia U (WV)
Pueblo Comm Coll (CO)
Quinsigamond Comm Coll (MA)
Reid State Tech Coll (AL)
Rend Lake Coll (IL)
Rockland Comm Coll (NY)
Rogue Comm Coll (OR)
St. Cloud Tech Coll (MN)
Saint Paul Coll–A Comm & Tech College (MN)
Salt Lake Comm Coll (UT)
San Diego City Coll (CA)
San Jacinto Coll District (TX)
Santa Rosa Jr Coll (CA)
Savannah Tech Coll (GA)
Scottsdale Comm Coll (AZ)
Seminole State Coll of Florida (FL)
Shawnee Comm Coll (IL)
Sisseton-Wahpeton Comm Coll (SD)
Southeastern Comm Coll (IA)
Southeastern Tech Coll (GA)
Southeast Tech Inst (SD)
Southern Maine Comm Coll (ME)
Southern Union State Comm Coll (AL)
South Georgia Tech Coll (GA)
South Plains Coll (TX)
Southside Virginia Comm Coll (VA)
South Suburban Coll (IL)
Southwestern Michigan Coll (MI)
Southwest Mississippi Comm Coll (MS)
Southwest Virginia Comm Coll (VA)
Spartanburg Comm Coll (SC)
Springfield Tech Comm Coll (MA)
Stanly Comm Coll (NC)
State Coll of Florida Manatee-Sarasota (FL)
Suffolk County Comm Coll (NY)
Sullivan Coll of Technology and Design (KY)
Tarrant County Coll District (TX)
Terra State Comm Coll (OH)
TESST Coll of Technology, Baltimore (MD)
TESST Coll of Technology, Beltsville (MD)
Three Rivers Comm Coll (CT)
Tidewater Comm Coll (VA)
Tompkins Cortland Comm Coll (NY)
Triangle Tech, Inc.–DuBois School (PA)
Tri-County Comm Coll (NC)
Trident Tech Coll (SC)
Umpqua Comm Coll (OR)
U of Alaska Anchorage, Matanuska-Susitna Coll (AK)
Victoria Coll (TX)
Victor Valley Coll (CA)
Waukesha County Tech Coll (WI)
Wayne Comm Coll (NC)
Westchester Comm Coll (NY)
Western Wyoming Comm Coll (WY)
West Georgia Tech Coll (GA)
Westmoreland County Comm Coll (PA)
West Shore Comm Coll (MI)
Wilson Comm Coll (NC)
Wor-Wic Comm Coll (MD)

Electrical, Electronics and Communications Engineering
Allen Comm Coll (KS)
Fiorello H. LaGuardia Comm Coll of the City U of New York (NY)
John Tyler Comm Coll (VA)
Lake Region State Coll (ND)
Pasadena City Coll (CA)
State U of New York Coll of Technology at Alfred (NY)

Electrical/Electronics Drafting and Cad/Cadd
Central New Mexico Comm Coll (NM)
Collin County Comm Coll District (TX)
Eastfield Coll (TX)
Waukesha County Tech Coll (WI)

Electrical/Electronics Equipment Installation and Repair
Cape Fear Comm Coll (NC)
Coll of DuPage (IL)
Collin County Comm Coll District (TX)
Diablo Valley Coll (CA)
Hutchinson Comm Coll and Area Vocational School (KS)
Lake Region State Coll (ND)
Linn State Tech Coll (MO)
Macomb Comm Coll (MI)
Mesabi Range Comm and Tech Coll (MN)
Orange Coast Coll (CA)
St. Philip's Coll (TX)
Sierra Coll (CA)
Southeast Tech Inst (SD)
State U of New York Coll of Technology at Alfred (NY)
Sullivan Coll of Technology and Design (KY)
Triangle Tech–Greensburg School (PA)
Western Wyoming Comm Coll (WY)

Electrical/Electronics Maintenance and Repair Technology Related
Bunker Hill Comm Coll (MA)
Kennebec Valley Comm Coll (ME)
Mohawk Valley Comm Coll (NY)
Sullivan Coll of Technology and Design (KY)
Triangle Tech–Greensburg School (PA)

Electrician
Bevill State Comm Coll (AL)
Black Hawk Coll, Moline (IL)
Chattanooga State Comm Coll (TN)
Coll of Lake County (IL)
Coll of Southern Maryland (MD)
Delta Coll (MI)
Fayetteville Tech Comm Coll (NC)
Flathead Valley Comm Coll (MT)
Guilford Tech Comm Coll (NC)
Harrisburg Area Comm Coll (PA)
H. Councill Trenholm State Tech Coll (AL)
Illinois Valley Comm Coll (IL)
Ivy Tech Comm Coll–Bloomington (IN)
Ivy Tech Comm Coll–Central Indiana (IN)
Ivy Tech Comm Coll–East Central (IN)
Ivy Tech Comm Coll–Kokomo (IN)
Ivy Tech Comm Coll–Lafayette (IN)
Ivy Tech Comm Coll–North Central (IN)
Ivy Tech Comm Coll–Northeast (IN)
Ivy Tech Comm Coll–Northwest (IN)
Ivy Tech Comm Coll–Richmond (IN)
Ivy Tech Comm Coll–Southern Indiana (IN)
Ivy Tech Comm Coll–Southwest (IN)
Ivy Tech Comm Coll–Wabash Valley (IN)
John Wood Comm Coll (IL)
Kennebec Valley Comm Coll (ME)
Linn State Tech Coll (MO)

Lurleen B. Wallace Comm Coll (AL)
Mitchell Tech Inst (SD)
Moraine Park Tech Coll (WI)
Northampton Comm Coll (PA)
Northeast Comm Coll (NE)
Northeast Iowa Comm Coll (IA)
Northland Pioneer Coll (AZ)
Northwest Coll (WY)
Oakland Comm Coll (MI)
Pennsylvania Coll of Technology (PA)
Piedmont Comm Coll (NC)
Randolph Comm Coll (NC)
Rend Lake Coll (IL)
Triangle Tech Inc–Bethlehem (PA)
Triangle Tech, Inc.–Erie School (PA)
Triangle Tech, Inc.–Sunbury School (PA)
Western Wyoming Comm Coll (WY)
West Kentucky Comm and Tech Coll (KY)

Electrocardiograph Technology
Argosy U, Twin Cities (MN)
Delaware Tech & Comm Coll, Stanton/Wilmington Campus (DE)
Oklahoma State U, Oklahoma City (OK)

Electromechanical and Instrumentation And Maintenance Technologies Related
Cape Fear Comm Coll (NC)
Catawba Valley Comm Coll (NC)
Cowley County Comm Coll and Area Vocational–Tech School (KS)
Piedmont Comm Coll (NC)
Randolph Comm Coll (NC)
Sullivan Coll of Technology and Design (KY)
Waukesha County Tech Coll (WI)

Electromechanical Technology
Blue Ridge Comm and Tech Coll (WV)
Blue Ridge Comm Coll (NC)
Camden County Coll (NJ)
Central Comm Coll–Columbus Campus (NE)
Central Ohio Tech Coll (OH)
Central Piedmont Comm Coll (NC)
Cincinnati State Tech and Comm Coll (OH)
Clovis Comm Coll (NM)
Coll of DuPage (IL)
DeKalb Tech Coll (GA)
Delaware Tech & Comm Coll, Terry Campus (DE)
Edison State Comm Coll (OH)
Guilford Tech Comm Coll (NC)
Lansing Comm Coll (MI)
Los Angeles Harbor Coll (CA)
Macomb Comm Coll (MI)
Mitchell Tech Inst (SD)
Montgomery County Comm Coll (PA)
Muskegon Comm Coll (MI)
Northampton Comm Coll (PA)
Northeast Comm Coll (NE)
Oakland Comm Coll (MI)
Owens Comm Coll, Toledo (OH)
Pulaski Tech Coll (AR)
Quinsigamond Comm Coll (MA)
Rockingham Comm Coll (NC)
St. Philip's Coll (TX)
Southeast Tech Inst (SD)
Southwest Wisconsin Tech Coll (WI)
Springfield Tech Comm Coll (MA)
State U of New York Coll of Technology at Alfred (NY)
Tarrant County Coll District (TX)
Union County Coll (NJ)
Wayne Comm Coll (NC)

Electroneurodiagnostic/ Electroencephalographic Technology
Black Hawk Coll, Moline (IL)
Comm Coll of Allegheny County (PA)
Harcum Coll (PA)
Harford Comm Coll (MD)
Kirkwood Comm Coll (IA)
Minneapolis Comm and Tech Coll (MN)
Niagara County Comm Coll (NY)

Elementary and Middle School Administration/ Principalship
Jamestown Comm Coll (NY)

Elementary Education
Allen Comm Coll (KS)
Alpena Comm Coll (MI)
Amarillo Coll (TX)
Anne Arundel Comm Coll (MD)
Bainbridge Coll (GA)
Barton County Comm Coll (KS)
Casper Coll (WY)
Cecil Coll (MD)
Central Arizona Coll (AZ)
Central New Mexico Comm Coll (NM)
Central Wyoming Coll (WY)
City Colls of Chicago, Malcolm X College (IL)
Clarendon Coll (TX)
Coll of Southern Maryland (MD)
The Comm Coll of Baltimore County (MD)
Corning Comm Coll (NY)
Cowley County Comm Coll and Area Vocational–Tech School (KS)
Crowder Coll (MO)
Cuyamaca Coll (CA)
Delaware Tech & Comm Coll, Jack F. Owens Campus (DE)
Delaware Tech & Comm Coll, Stanton/Wilmington Campus (DE)
Delaware Tech & Comm Coll, Terry Campus (DE)
Del Mar Coll (TX)
Eastern Arizona Coll (AZ)
Eastern Wyoming Coll (WY)
Essex County Coll (NJ)
Fayetteville Tech Comm Coll (NC)
Frederick Comm Coll (MD)
Fulton-Montgomery Comm Coll (NY)
Gainesville State Coll (GA)
Genesee Comm Coll (NY)
Harford Comm Coll (MD)
Harrisburg Area Comm Coll (PA)
Howard Coll (TX)
Howard Comm Coll (MD)
Illinois Valley Comm Coll (IL)
Iowa Lakes Comm Coll (IA)
Kalamazoo Valley Comm Coll (MI)
Kankakee Comm Coll (IL)
Kellogg Comm Coll (MI)
Kilgore Coll (TX)
Kingsborough Comm Coll of the City U of New York (NY)
Lake Michigan Coll (MI)
Lansing Comm Coll (MI)
Linn-Benton Comm Coll (OR)
Lon Morris Coll (TX)
Miami Dade Coll (FL)
Mohawk Valley Comm Coll (NY)
Montgomery Coll (MD)
Montgomery County Comm Coll (PA)
Murray State Coll (OK)
Muskegon Comm Coll (MI)
Northeast Comm Coll (NE)
Northeastern Jr Coll (CO)
North Idaho Coll (ID)
Northland Pioneer Coll (AZ)
Northwest Coll (WY)
Northwest Florida State Coll (FL)
Otero Jr Coll (CO)
Palm Beach State Coll (FL)
Paradise Valley Comm Coll (AZ)
Paris Jr Coll (TX)
Piedmont Comm Coll (NC)
Pima Comm Coll (AZ)
Potomac State Coll of West Virginia U (WV)
Red Rocks Comm Coll (CO)
San Jacinto Coll District (TX)
San Juan Coll (NM)
Seminole State Coll (OK)
Sheridan Coll (WY)
Snow Coll (UT)
South Georgia Coll (GA)
Southwest Mississippi Comm Coll (MS)
Springfield Tech Comm Coll (MA)
Three Rivers Comm Coll (MO)
Trinity Valley Comm Coll (TX)
Umpqua Comm Coll (OR)
U of Cincinnati Clermont Coll (OH)
Vincennes U Jasper Campus (IN)
Western Wyoming Comm Coll (WY)
Wor-Wic Comm Coll (MD)

Emergency Care Attendant (EMT Ambulance)
Barton County Comm Coll (KS)
Carroll Comm Coll (MD)
Delaware Tech & Comm Coll, Stanton/Wilmington Campus (DE)
Iowa Lakes Comm Coll (IA)
Southside Virginia Comm Coll (VA)

Emergency Medical Technology (EMT Paramedic)
Allen Comm Coll (KS)
Alvin Comm Coll (TX)
Amarillo Coll (TX)
Anne Arundel Comm Coll (MD)
Arkansas State U–Mountain Home (AR)
Athens Tech Coll (GA)
Augusta Tech Coll (GA)
Austin Comm Coll (TX)
Bakersfield Coll (CA)
Barton County Comm Coll (KS)
Bevill State Comm Coll (AL)
Black Hawk Coll, Moline (IL)
Blue Ridge Comm and Tech Coll (WV)
Broome Comm Coll (NY)
Camden County Coll (NJ)
Casper Coll (WY)
Catawba Valley Comm Coll (NC)
Cecil Coll (MD)
Central Arizona Coll (AZ)
Central Ohio Tech Coll (OH)
Central Oregon Comm Coll (OR)
Central Texas Coll (TX)
Central Wyoming Coll (WY)
Century Coll (MN)
Cincinnati State Tech and Comm Coll (OH)
City Colls of Chicago, Malcolm X College (IL)
Clackamas Comm Coll (OR)
Clark Coll (WA)
Coll of DuPage (IL)
Coll of Southern Maryland (MD)
Collin County Comm Coll District (TX)
Columbus Tech Coll (GA)
The Comm Coll of Baltimore County (MD)
Corning Comm Coll (NY)
Cowley County Comm Coll and Area Vocational–Tech School (KS)
Darton Coll (GA)
Daytona State Coll (FL)
Delaware County Comm Coll (PA)
Delaware Tech & Comm Coll, Jack F. Owens Campus (DE)
Delaware Tech & Comm Coll, Stanton/Wilmington Campus (DE)
Delaware Tech & Comm Coll, Terry Campus (DE)
Del Mar Coll (TX)
Delta Coll (MI)
East Central Coll (MO)
Eastern Arizona Coll (AZ)
East Los Angeles Coll (CA)
Elaine P. Nunez Comm Coll (LA)
El Centro Coll (TX)
Elgin Comm Coll (IL)
El Paso Comm Coll (TX)
Erie Comm Coll, South Campus (NY)
Essex County Coll (NJ)
Fayetteville Tech Comm Coll (NC)
Finger Lakes Comm Coll (NY)
Fiorello H. LaGuardia Comm Coll of the City U of New York (NY)
Flathead Valley Comm Coll (MT)
Frederick Comm Coll (MD)
Front Range Comm Coll (CO)
Gadsden State Comm Coll (AL)
Georgia Highlands Coll (GA)
Glendale Comm Coll (AZ)
Goodwin Coll (CT)
Griffin Tech Coll (GA)
Guilford Tech Comm Coll (NC)
Gwinnett Tech Coll (GA)
Harrisburg Area Comm Coll (PA)
H. Councill Trenholm State Tech Coll (AL)
Hillsborough Comm Coll (FL)
Houston Comm Coll System (TX)
Howard Comm Coll (MD)
Hutchinson Comm Coll and Area Vocational School (KS)
Indian River State Coll (FL)
Inver Hills Comm Coll (MN)
Ivy Tech Comm Coll–Bloomington (IN)
Ivy Tech Comm Coll–Kokomo (IN)
Ivy Tech Comm Coll–North Central (IN)
Ivy Tech Comm Coll–Southwest (IN)
Ivy Tech Comm Coll–Wabash Valley (IN)
Jackson Comm Coll (MI)
Jefferson Comm Coll (NY)
Jefferson State Comm Coll (AL)
John Wood Comm Coll (IL)
J. Sargeant Reynolds Comm Coll (VA)
Kalamazoo Valley Comm Coll (MI)
Kankakee Comm Coll (IL)
Kaskaskia Coll (IL)
Kellogg Comm Coll (MI)
Kennebec Valley Comm Coll (ME)
Kent State U at Geauga (OH)
Kilgore Coll (TX)
Kirkwood Comm Coll (IA)
Lackawanna Coll (PA)
Lake Michigan Coll (MI)
Lake-Sumter Comm Coll (FL)
Lansing Comm Coll (MI)
Lonestar Coll–Cy-Fair (TX)
Lonestar Coll–Montgomery (TX)
Lonestar Coll–North Harris (TX)
Lurleen B. Wallace Comm Coll (AL)
Macomb Comm Coll (MI)
Meridian Comm Coll (MS)
Metropolitan Comm Coll–Penn Valley (MO)
Miami Dade Coll (FL)
Minnesota State Coll–Southeast Tech (MN)
Mohave Comm Coll (AZ)
Mohawk Valley Comm Coll (NY)
Montana State U–Great Falls Coll of Technology (MT)
Montcalm Comm Coll (MI)
Moraine Park Tech Coll (WI)
Mountain Empire Comm Coll (VA)
North Arkansas Coll (AR)
North Central Texas Coll (TX)
Northeast Comm Coll (NE)
Northeastern Jr Coll (CO)
Northeast Iowa Comm Coll (IA)
North Iowa Area Comm Coll (IA)
Northland Comm and Tech Coll–Thief River Falls (MN)
Northland Pioneer Coll (AZ)
NorthWest Arkansas Comm Coll (AR)
Oakland Comm Coll (MI)
Odessa Coll (TX)
Oklahoma City Comm Coll (OK)
Oklahoma State U, Oklahoma City (OK)
Orange Coast Coll (CA)
Paradise Valley Comm Coll (AZ)
Paris Jr Coll (TX)
Pasco-Hernando Comm Coll (FL)
Pennsylvania Coll of Technology (PA)
Pensacola Jr Coll (FL)
Phoenix Coll (AZ)
Pikes Peak Comm Coll (CO)
Pima Comm Coll (AZ)
Polk State Coll (FL)
Pueblo Comm Coll (CO)
Quinsigamond Comm Coll (MA)
Rend Lake Coll (IL)
Rockland Comm Coll (NY)
Rogue Comm Coll (OR)
Saint Charles Comm Coll (MO)
St. Cloud Tech Coll (MN)
San Diego City Coll (CA)
San Jacinto Coll District (TX)
San Juan Coll (NM)
Santa Rosa Jr Coll (CA)
Scottsdale Comm Coll (AZ)
Seminole State Coll of Florida (FL)
Southeastern Comm Coll (IA)
Southern Maine Comm Coll (ME)
Southern State Comm Coll (OH)
Southern Union State Comm Coll (AL)
Southwestern Michigan Coll (MI)
Southwest Mississippi Comm Coll (MS)
Southwest Virginia Comm Coll (VA)
Tallahassee Comm Coll (FL)
Tarrant County Coll District (TX)
Temple Coll (TX)
Thomas Nelson Comm Coll (VA)
Trinity Valley Comm Coll (TX)
Triton Coll (IL)
Umpqua Comm Coll (OR)
U of Alaska Anchorage, Kenai Peninsula Coll (AK)
U of Alaska Anchorage, Matanuska-Susitna Coll (AK)
U of Cincinnati Clermont Coll (OH)
Victoria Coll (TX)
Westchester Comm Coll (NY)
West Shore Comm Coll (MI)
Wisconsin Indianhead Tech Coll (WI)
Wor-Wic Comm Coll (MD)

Energy Management and Systems Technology
Alexandria Tech Coll (MN)
Century Coll (MN)
Comm Coll of Allegheny County (PA)
Glendale Comm Coll (AZ)
Iowa Lakes Comm Coll (IA)
Lakeland Comm Coll (OH)
Laramie County Comm Coll (WY)
Macomb Comm Coll (MI)
Northeast Comm Coll (NE)
Pueblo Comm Coll (CO)

Engineering
Allan Hancock Coll (CA)
Allen Comm Coll (KS)
Amarillo Coll (TX)
Anoka-Ramsey Comm Coll (MN)
Anoka-Ramsey Comm Coll, Cambridge Campus (MN)
Antelope Valley Coll (CA)
Austin Comm Coll (TX)
Bakersfield Coll (CA)
Berkshire Comm Coll (MA)
Bucks County Comm Coll (PA)
Burlington County Coll (NJ)
Casper Coll (WY)
Central Lakes Coll (MN)
Central New Mexico Comm Coll (NM)
Central Oregon Comm Coll (OR)
Central Texas Coll (TX)
Central Wyoming Coll (WY)
Century Coll (MN)
Clarendon Coll (TX)
Coll of DuPage (IL)
Coll of Lake County (IL)
Coll of Southern Maryland (MD)
Coll of the Canyons (CA)
The Comm Coll of Baltimore County (MD)
Comm Coll of Philadelphia (PA)
Comm Coll of Rhode Island (RI)
Danville Area Comm Coll (IL)
Delaware County Comm Coll (PA)
East Central Coll (MO)
East Los Angeles Coll (CA)
Elgin Comm Coll (IL)
El Paso Comm Coll (TX)
Erie Comm Coll, North Campus (NY)
Everett Comm Coll (WA)
Frederick Comm Coll (MD)
Georgia Military Coll (GA)
Harford Comm Coll (MD)
Harrisburg Area Comm Coll (PA)
Highland Comm Coll (IL)
Highline Comm Coll (WA)
Holyoke Comm Coll (MA)
Howard Comm Coll (MD)
Hutchinson Comm Coll and Area Vocational School (KS)
Illinois Valley Comm Coll (IL)
Indian River State Coll (FL)
Iowa Lakes Comm Coll (IA)
Itasca Comm Coll (MN)
Jamestown Comm Coll (NY)
J. Sargeant Reynolds Comm Coll (VA)
Kalamazoo Valley Comm Coll (MI)
Kankakee Comm Coll (IL)
Kellogg Comm Coll (MI)

Lansing Comm Coll (MI)
Laramie County Comm Coll (WY)
Lehigh Carbon Comm Coll (PA)
Lewis and Clark Comm Coll (IL)
Linn-Benton Comm Coll (OR)
Lonestar Coll–Cy-Fair (TX)
Lonestar Coll–Kingwood (TX)
Lonestar Coll–Montgomery (TX)
Lonestar Coll–North Harris (TX)
Lonestar Coll–Tomball (TX)
Metropolitan Comm Coll–Business & Technology Campus (MO)
Metropolitan Comm Coll–Longview (MO)
Metropolitan Comm Coll–Penn Valley (MO)
Miami Dade Coll (FL)
Missouri State U–West Plains (MO)
Mohawk Valley Comm Coll (NY)
Montgomery Coll (MD)
Murray State Coll (OK)
Nassau Comm Coll (NY)
New Mexico State U–Carlsbad (NM)
Northampton Comm Coll (PA)
Northeast Comm Coll (NE)
North Hennepin Comm Coll (MN)
North Idaho Coll (ID)
Northwest Coll (WY)
Northwestern Connecticut Comm Coll (CT)
Northwest Florida State Coll (FL)
Oakland Comm Coll (MI)
Ocean County Coll (NJ)
Olympic Coll (WA)
Orange Coast Coll (CA)
Paris Jr Coll (TX)
Potomac State Coll of West Virginia U (WV)
Red Rocks Comm Coll (CO)
Rend Lake Coll (IL)
Saint Charles Comm Coll (MO)
Salt Lake Comm Coll (UT)
San Diego Mesa Coll (CA)
San Jacinto Coll District (TX)
San Juan Coll (NM)
Sheridan Coll (WY)
Sierra Coll (CA)
South Plains Coll (TX)
Southwestern Indian Polytechnic Inst (NM)
Southwest Mississippi Comm Coll (MS)
Southwest Virginia Comm Coll (VA)
Springfield Tech Comm Coll (MA)
State Coll of Florida Manatee-Sarasota (FL)
Suffolk County Comm Coll (NY)
Tallahassee Comm Coll (FL)
Terra State Comm Coll (OH)
Thomas Nelson Comm Coll (VA)
Three Rivers Comm Coll (CT)
Tidewater Comm Coll (VA)
Tompkins Cortland Comm Coll (NY)
Tunxis Comm Coll (CT)
Ulster County Comm Coll (NY)
Umpqua Comm Coll (OR)
Union County Coll (NJ)

Engineering/Industrial Management
Delaware Tech & Comm Coll, Stanton/Wilmington Campus (DE)

Engineering Mechanics
San Jacinto Coll District (TX)

Engineering Related
Itasca Comm Coll (MN)
Macomb Comm Coll (MI)
Miami Dade Coll (FL)
Milwaukee Area Tech Coll (WI)
Southeastern Comm Coll (IA)
Southern Maine Comm Coll (ME)

Engineering-Related Technologies
Metropolitan Comm Coll–Business & Technology Campus (MO)

Engineering Science
Broome Comm Coll (NY)
Camden County Coll (NJ)
County Coll of Morris (NJ)
Finger Lakes Comm Coll (NY)
Fiorello H. LaGuardia Comm Coll of the City U of New York (NY)
Fulton-Montgomery Comm Coll (NY)
Genesee Comm Coll (NY)
Greenfield Comm Coll (MA)
Highland Comm Coll (IL)
Itasca Comm Coll (MN)
Jefferson Comm Coll (NY)
Kingsborough Comm Coll of the City U of New York (NY)
Manchester Comm Coll (CT)
Mercer County Comm Coll (NJ)
Middlesex Comm Coll (CT)
Montgomery County Comm Coll (PA)
Pennsylvania Coll of Technology (PA)
Raritan Valley Comm Coll (NJ)
State U of New York Coll of Technology at Alfred (NY)
Suffolk County Comm Coll (NY)
Three Rivers Comm Coll (CT)
Westchester Comm Coll (NY)

Engineering Technologies Related
Bowling Green State U–Firelands Coll (OH)
Burlington County Coll (NJ)
Coll of Southern Maryland (MD)
Comm Coll of Allegheny County (PA)
The Comm Coll of Baltimore County (MD)
Harford Comm Coll (MD)
Harrisburg Area Comm Coll (PA)
J. Sargeant Reynolds Comm Coll (VA)
Milwaukee Area Tech Coll (WI)
Mitchell Tech Inst (SD)
Montgomery County Comm Coll (PA)
Raritan Valley Comm Coll (NJ)
Sheridan Coll (WY)
Southern Maine Comm Coll (ME)
Sullivan Coll of Technology and Design (KY)
Wor-Wic Comm Coll (MD)

Engineering Technology
Allan Hancock Coll (CA)
Allen Comm Coll (KS)
Anne Arundel Comm Coll (MD)
Antelope Valley Coll (CA)
Arizona Western Coll (AZ)
Barton County Comm Coll (KS)
Central Piedmont Comm Coll (NC)
Chattanooga State Comm Coll (TN)
Collin County Comm Coll District (TX)
Comm Coll of Philadelphia (PA)
Cowley County Comm Coll and Area Vocational–Tech School (KS)
Cuyahoga Comm Coll (OH)
Darton Coll (GA)
DeKalb Tech Coll (GA)
Delta Coll (MI)
Denmark Tech Coll (SC)
Edison State Comm Coll (OH)
Everett Comm Coll (WA)
Gainesville State Coll (GA)
Gateway Comm and Tech Coll (KY)
Gateway Comm Coll (CT)
Golden West Coll (CA)
Highland Comm Coll (IL)
Highline Comm Coll (WA)
Hillsborough Comm Coll (FL)
Honolulu Comm Coll (HI)
Hopkinsville Comm Coll (KY)
Indian River State Coll (FL)
Itasca Comm Coll (MN)
Jefferson State Comm Coll (AL)
John Tyler Comm Coll (VA)
Kalamazoo Valley Comm Coll (MI)
Kent State U at Ashtabula (OH)
Kent State U at Tuscarawas (OH)
Lansing Comm Coll (MI)
Los Angeles Harbor Coll (CA)
Marion Tech Coll (OH)
Miami Dade Coll (FL)
Middlesex Comm Coll (CT)
Midlands Tech Coll (SC)
Murray State Coll (OK)
Muskegon Comm Coll (MI)
North Central Texas Coll (TX)
Oklahoma State U, Oklahoma City (OK)
Pasadena City Coll (CA)
Patrick Henry Comm Coll (VA)
Pennsylvania Inst of Technology (PA)
Pueblo Comm Coll (CO)
Rappahannock Comm Coll (VA)
Salt Lake Comm Coll (UT)
San Diego City Coll (CA)
Somerset Comm Coll (KY)
Spartanburg Comm Coll (SC)
Sullivan Coll of Technology and Design (KY)
Three Rivers Comm Coll (CT)
Three Rivers Comm Coll (MO)
Trident Tech Coll (SC)
Tunxis Comm Coll (CT)
Westchester Comm Coll (NY)
Western Wyoming Comm Coll (WY)

Engine Machinist
Northwest Tech Coll (MN)
Tri-County Comm Coll (NC)

English
Allan Hancock Coll (CA)
Alpena Comm Coll (MI)
Amarillo Coll (TX)
Anne Arundel Comm Coll (MD)
Arizona Western Coll (AZ)
Austin Comm Coll (TX)
Bainbridge Coll (GA)
Bakersfield Coll (CA)
Barton County Comm Coll (KS)
Berkeley City Coll (CA)
Bunker Hill Comm Coll (MA)
Burlington County Coll (NJ)
Casper Coll (WY)
Central Wyoming Coll (WY)
Clarendon Coll (TX)
Coll of the Canyons (CA)
Comm Coll of Allegheny County (PA)
Cuyamaca Coll (CA)
Darton Coll (GA)
Del Mar Coll (TX)
Diablo Valley Coll (CA)
Eastern Arizona Coll (AZ)
Eastern Wyoming Coll (WY)
East Los Angeles Coll (CA)
Everett Comm Coll (WA)
Folsom Lake Coll (CA)
Frederick Comm Coll (MD)
Fulton-Montgomery Comm Coll (NY)
Gainesville State Coll (GA)
Georgia Highlands Coll (GA)
Highline Comm Coll (WA)
Howard Coll (TX)
Hutchinson Comm Coll and Area Vocational School (KS)
Illinois Valley Comm Coll (IL)
Indian River State Coll (FL)
Iowa Lakes Comm Coll (IA)
Kilgore Coll (TX)
Lake Michigan Coll (MI)
Lansing Comm Coll (MI)
Laramie County Comm Coll (WY)
Lawson State Comm Coll (AL)
Linn-Benton Comm Coll (OR)
Lonestar Coll–Cy-Fair (TX)
Lonestar Coll–Kingwood (TX)
Lonestar Coll–Montgomery (TX)
Lonestar Coll–North Harris (TX)
Lonestar Coll–Tomball (TX)
Lon Morris Coll (TX)
Mendocino Coll (CA)
Miami Dade Coll (FL)
Mohave Comm Coll (AZ)
Murray State Coll (OK)
Northeast Comm Coll (NE)
Northeastern Jr Coll (CO)
North Idaho Coll (ID)
Northwest Coll (WY)
Northwestern Connecticut Comm Coll (CT)
Odessa Coll (TX)
Orange Coast Coll (CA)
Palm Beach State Coll (FL)
Potomac State Coll of West Virginia U (WV)
Raritan Valley Comm Coll (NJ)
Red Rocks Comm Coll (CO)
Reedley Coll (CA)
Saint Charles Comm Coll (MO)
St. Philip's Coll (TX)
Salt Lake Comm Coll (UT)
San Diego City Coll (CA)
San Diego Mesa Coll (CA)
San Jacinto Coll District (TX)
San Juan Coll (NM)
Santa Rosa Jr Coll (CA)
Seminole State Coll (OK)
Sheridan Coll (WY)
Sierra Coll (CA)
South Georgia Coll (GA)
Southwest Mississippi Comm Coll (MS)
State Coll of Florida Manatee-Sarasota (FL)
Suffolk County Comm Coll (NY)
Terra State Comm Coll (OH)
Trinity Valley Comm Coll (TX)
Triton Coll (IL)
Umpqua Comm Coll (OR)
Western Wyoming Comm Coll (WY)

English Composition
Allen Comm Coll (KS)
Austin Comm Coll (TX)
Berkeley City Coll (CA)

English/Language Arts Teacher Education
Darton Coll (GA)
Montgomery Coll (MD)
State Coll of Florida Manatee-Sarasota (FL)

Entrepreneurial and Small Business Related
Dakota Coll at Bottineau (ND)
Northland Pioneer Coll (AZ)

Entrepreneurship
Casper Coll (WY)
Central Ohio Tech Coll (OH)
Cincinnati State Tech and Comm Coll (OH)
Comm Coll of Allegheny County (PA)
Cowley County Comm Coll and Area Vocational–Tech School (KS)
Cuyamaca Coll (CA)
Delaware County Comm Coll (PA)
Delaware Tech & Comm Coll, Jack F. Owens Campus (DE)
Delaware Tech & Comm Coll, Terry Campus (DE)
Delta Coll (MI)
Eastern Arizona Coll (AZ)
Elgin Comm Coll (IL)
Everett Comm Coll (WA)
Glendale Comm Coll (AZ)
Goodwin Coll (CT)
Harcum Coll (PA)
Laramie County Comm Coll (WY)
LDS Business Coll (UT)
Missouri State U–West Plains (MO)
Mohawk Valley Comm Coll (NY)
Montcalm Comm Coll (MI)
Nassau Comm Coll (NY)
Northeast Comm Coll (NE)
North Iowa Area Comm Coll (IA)
Northland Comm and Tech Coll–Thief River Falls (MN)
Oakland Comm Coll (MI)
Pasadena City Coll (CA)
Randolph Comm Coll (NC)
Reedley Coll (CA)
Saint Paul Coll–A Comm & Tech College (MN)
Salt Lake Comm Coll (UT)
Springfield Tech Comm Coll (MA)
State U of New York Coll of Technology at Alfred (NY)

Environmental Biology
Eastern Wyoming Coll (WY)

Environmental Control Technologies Related
Central Carolina Tech Coll (SC)
Hillsborough Comm Coll (FL)
Holyoke Comm Coll (MA)
Mountain Empire Comm Coll (VA)
Pennsylvania Coll of Technology (PA)

Environmental Design/Architecture
Iowa Lakes Comm Coll (IA)
Scottsdale Comm Coll (AZ)

Environmental Education
Iowa Lakes Comm Coll (IA)

Environmental Engineering Technology
Allan Hancock Coll (CA)
Austin Comm Coll (TX)
Bakersfield Coll (CA)
Black Hawk Coll, Moline (IL)
Central Piedmont Comm Coll (NC)
Chattanooga State Comm Coll (TN)
Cincinnati State Tech and Comm Coll (OH)
Coll of Southern Maryland (MD)
Collin County Comm Coll District (TX)
Comm Coll of Allegheny County (PA)
The Comm Coll of Baltimore County (MD)
Crowder Coll (MO)
Cuyamaca Coll (CA)
Dakota Coll at Bottineau (ND)
Delta Coll (MI)
El Paso Comm Coll (TX)
Georgia Northwestern Tech Coll (GA)
Harford Comm Coll (MD)
Iowa Lakes Comm Coll (IA)
Kent State U at Trumbull (OH)
Metropolitan Comm Coll–Business & Technology Campus (MO)
Miami Dade Coll (FL)
Owens Comm Coll, Toledo (OH)
Pennsylvania Highlands Comm Coll (PA)
Pima Comm Coll (AZ)
Pulaski Tech Coll (AR)
Salt Lake Comm Coll (UT)
San Diego City Coll (CA)
San Jacinto Coll District (TX)
Southern Maine Comm Coll (ME)
Three Rivers Comm Coll (CT)

Environmental/Environmental Health Engineering
Central New Mexico Comm Coll (NM)
Central Wyoming Coll (WY)

Environmental Health
Amarillo Coll (TX)
Chattanooga State Comm Coll (TN)
Crowder Coll (MO)
North Idaho Coll (ID)

Environmental Science
Anoka-Ramsey Comm Coll (MN)
Anoka-Ramsey Comm Coll, Cambridge Campus (MN)
Blue Ridge Comm Coll (NC)
Burlington County Coll (NJ)
Casper Coll (WY)
Central Wyoming Coll (WY)
Clarendon Coll (TX)
Comm Coll of Vermont (VT)
Harrisburg Area Comm Coll (PA)
Lake Michigan Coll (MI)
Montgomery County Comm Coll (PA)
NorthWest Arkansas Comm Coll (AR)
Ocean County Coll (NJ)
The Ohio State U Ag Tech Inst (OH)
Pasadena City Coll (CA)
St. Philip's Coll (TX)
Western Wyoming Comm Coll (WY)

Environmental Studies
Anne Arundel Comm Coll (MD)
Arizona Western Coll (AZ)
Berkshire Comm Coll (MA)
Bucks County Comm Coll (PA)
Central Texas Coll (TX)
Darton Coll (GA)
East Los Angeles Coll (CA)
Everett Comm Coll (WA)
Finger Lakes Comm Coll (NY)
Fulton-Montgomery Comm Coll (NY)
Harrisburg Area Comm Coll (PA)
Housatonic Comm Coll (CT)
Howard Comm Coll (MD)
Iowa Lakes Comm Coll (IA)
Itasca Comm Coll (MN)
Kent State U at Ashtabula (OH)
Kent State U at Tuscarawas (OH)
Lackawanna Coll (PA)
Middlesex Comm Coll (CT)
Minnesota State Comm and Tech Coll (MN)
Mount Wachusett Comm Coll (MA)

Santa Rosa Jr Coll (CA)
Stark State Coll of Technology (OH)
State U of New York Coll of Technology at Alfred (NY)
White Mountains Comm Coll (NH)

Equestrian Studies
Allen Comm Coll (KS)
Black Hawk Coll, Moline (IL)
Central Texas Coll (TX)
Central Wyoming Coll (WY)
Laramie County Comm Coll (WY)
Murray State Coll (OK)
North Central Texas Coll (TX)
Northeastern Jr Coll (CO)
Northwest Coll (WY)
The Ohio State U Ag Tech Inst (OH)
Scottsdale Comm Coll (AZ)
Sierra Coll (CA)
Yavapai Coll (AZ)

Ethnic, Cultural Minority, and Gender Studies Related
Santa Rosa Jr Coll (CA)

European Studies
Anne Arundel Comm Coll (MD)
Pasadena City Coll (CA)

European Studies (Central and Eastern)
State Coll of Florida Manatee-Sarasota (FL)

Executive Assistant/ Executive Secretary
Alamance Comm Coll (NC)
Blue Ridge Comm Coll (NC)
Broome Comm Coll (NY)
Cape Fear Comm Coll (NC)
Central New Mexico Comm Coll (NM)
Cincinnati State Tech and Comm Coll (OH)
Clark Coll (WA)
Clovis Comm Coll (NM)
Crowder Coll (MO)
Dakota Coll at Bottineau (ND)
Danville Area Comm Coll (IL)
Delta Coll (MI)
Eastfield Coll (TX)
Edison State Comm Coll (OH)
El Centro Coll (TX)
Elgin Comm Coll (IL)
Hawkeye Comm Coll (IA)
Hillsborough Comm Coll (FL)
Hopkinsville Comm Coll (KY)
Ivy Tech Comm Coll–Bloomington (IN)
Ivy Tech Comm Coll–Central Indiana (IN)
Ivy Tech Comm Coll–Columbus (IN)
Ivy Tech Comm Coll–East Central (IN)
Ivy Tech Comm Coll–Kokomo (IN)
Ivy Tech Comm Coll–Lafayette (IN)
Ivy Tech Comm Coll–North Central (IN)
Ivy Tech Comm Coll–Northeast (IN)
Ivy Tech Comm Coll–Northwest (IN)
Ivy Tech Comm Coll–Richmond (IN)
Ivy Tech Comm Coll–Southeast (IN)
Ivy Tech Comm Coll–Southern Indiana (IN)
Ivy Tech Comm Coll–Southwest (IN)
Ivy Tech Comm Coll–Wabash Valley (IN)
Jackson Comm Coll (MI)
John Wood Comm Coll (IL)
Kalamazoo Valley Comm Coll (MI)
Kaskaskia Coll (IL)
Kellogg Comm Coll (MI)
Kennebec Valley Comm Coll (ME)
Kilgore Coll (TX)
Lake Region State Coll (ND)
LDS Business Coll (UT)
Lehigh Carbon Comm Coll (PA)
Montcalm Comm Coll (MI)
Owensboro Comm and Tech Coll (KY)
Owens Comm Coll, Toledo (OH)
Pensacola Jr Coll (FL)
Quinsigamond Comm Coll (MA)
St. Cloud Tech Coll (MN)
Somerset Comm Coll (KY)
Southern State Comm Coll (OH)
South Suburban Coll (IL)
Southwestern Michigan Coll (MI)
Stanly Comm Coll (NC)
Terra State Comm Coll (OH)
The U of Montana–Helena Coll of Technology (MT)
Wayne Comm Coll (NC)
Westmoreland County Comm Coll (PA)

Facilities Planning and Management
Comm Coll of Philadelphia (PA)
Lonestar Coll–Kingwood (TX)

Family and Community Services
Bowling Green State U–Firelands Coll (OH)
Glendale Comm Coll (AZ)
Snow Coll (UT)

Family and Consumer Economics Related
Allan Hancock Coll (CA)
Arizona Western Coll (AZ)
Bakersfield Coll (CA)
Orange Coast Coll (CA)

Family and Consumer Sciences/Home Economics Teacher Education
Antelope Valley Coll (CA)
Northwest Florida State Coll (FL)
State Coll of Florida Manatee-Sarasota (FL)

Family and Consumer Sciences/Human Sciences
Allen Comm Coll (KS)
Bainbridge Coll (GA)
East Los Angeles Coll (CA)
Greenfield Comm Coll (MA)
Hutchinson Comm Coll and Area Vocational School (KS)
Indian River State Coll (FL)
Iowa Lakes Comm Coll (IA)
Linn-Benton Comm Coll (OR)
Metropolitan Comm Coll–Penn Valley (MO)
Northeastern Jr Coll (CO)
North Iowa Area Comm Coll (IA)
Orange Coast Coll (CA)
Palm Beach State Coll (FL)
Phoenix Coll (AZ)
Snow Coll (UT)

Farm and Ranch Management
Alexandria Tech Coll (MN)
Allen Comm Coll (KS)
Central Texas Coll (TX)
Clarendon Coll (TX)
Colby Comm Coll (KS)
Crowder Coll (MO)
Eastern Wyoming Coll (WY)
Hutchinson Comm Coll and Area Vocational School (KS)
Iowa Lakes Comm Coll (IA)
Mitchell Tech Inst (SD)
North Central Texas Coll (TX)
Northeast Comm Coll (NE)
Northeastern Jr Coll (CO)
Northland Comm and Tech Coll–Thief River Falls (MN)
Northwest Coll (WY)
Snow Coll (UT)
Trinity Valley Comm Coll (TX)

Fashion and Fabric Consulting
Coll of DuPage (IL)
Santa Rosa Jr Coll (CA)

Fashion/Apparel Design
Allan Hancock Coll (CA)
The Art Inst of New York City (NY)
The Art Inst of Seattle (WA)
Burlington County Coll (NJ)
Coll of DuPage (IL)
El Centro Coll (TX)
El Paso Comm Coll (TX)
Fashion Careers Coll (CA)
Fashion Inst of Technology (NY)
FIDM/The Fashion Inst of Design & Merchandising, Los Angeles Campus (CA)
FIDM/The Fashion Inst of Design & Merchandising, San Diego Campus (CA)
FIDM/The Fashion Inst of Design & Merchandising, San Francisco Campus (CA)
Harcum Coll (PA)
Honolulu Comm Coll (HI)
Houston Comm Coll System (TX)
Lehigh Carbon Comm Coll (PA)
Metropolitan Comm Coll–Penn Valley (MO)
Nassau Comm Coll (NY)
Palm Beach State Coll (FL)
Pasadena City Coll (CA)
Phoenix Coll (AZ)
San Diego Mesa Coll (CA)
Santa Rosa Jr Coll (CA)
Virginia Marti Coll of Art and Design (OH)
Wade Coll (TX)
Wood Tobe–Coburn School (NY)

Fashion Merchandising
Alexandria Tech Coll (MN)
The Art Inst of Ohio–Cincinnati (OH)
The Art Inst of Seattle (WA)
Blue Ridge Comm and Tech Coll (WV)
Central Piedmont Comm Coll (NC)
Coll of DuPage (IL)
Davis Coll (OH)
Fashion Careers Coll (CA)
Fashion Inst of Technology (NY)
FIDM/The Fashion Inst of Design & Merchandising, Los Angeles Campus (CA)
FIDM/The Fashion Inst of Design & Merchandising, San Diego Campus (CA)
FIDM/The Fashion Inst of Design & Merchandising, San Francisco Campus (CA)
Gateway Comm Coll (CT)
Genesee Comm Coll (NY)
Grand Rapids Comm Coll (MI)
Harcum Coll (PA)
Harrison Coll, Indianapolis (IN)
Houston Comm Coll System (TX)
Howard Comm Coll (MD)
Indian River State Coll (FL)
Iowa Lakes Comm Coll (IA)
Kaplan Career Inst, ICM Campus (PA)
Kilgore Coll (TX)
Kingsborough Comm Coll of the City U of New York (NY)
Lake Region State Coll (ND)
Metropolitan Comm Coll–Penn Valley (MO)
Middle Georgia Coll (GA)
Minnesota State Comm and Tech Coll (MN)
Nassau Comm Coll (NY)
Northeastern Jr Coll (CO)
Northwest Florida State Coll (FL)
Orange Coast Coll (CA)
Palm Beach State Coll (FL)
Pasadena City Coll (CA)
San Diego City Coll (CA)
San Diego Mesa Coll (CA)
San Jacinto Coll District (TX)
Santa Rosa Jr Coll (CA)
Scottsdale Comm Coll (AZ)
South Plains Coll (TX)
Southwest Mississippi Comm Coll (MS)
Tarrant County Coll District (TX)
Trinity Valley Comm Coll (TX)
Tunxis Comm Coll (CT)
Virginia Marti Coll of Art and Design (OH)
Wood Tobe–Coburn School (NY)

Fashion Modeling
Fashion Inst of Technology (NY)

Fiber, Textile and Weaving Arts
Antelope Valley Coll (CA)
Mendocino Coll (CA)

Film/Cinema Studies
Allan Hancock Coll (CA)
Douglas Education Center (PA)
Lansing Comm Coll (MI)
Orange Coast Coll (CA)
San Jacinto Coll District (TX)
Tallahassee Comm Coll (FL)
Yavapai Coll (AZ)

Film/Video and Photographic Arts Related
Westchester Comm Coll (NY)

Finance
Bakersfield Coll (CA)
Black Hawk Coll, Moline (IL)
Bunker Hill Comm Coll (MA)
Central Piedmont Comm Coll (NC)
Chattanooga State Comm Coll (TN)
Chipola Coll (FL)
Clarendon Coll (TX)
Clovis Comm Coll (NM)
Comm Coll of Philadelphia (PA)
Cuyahoga Comm Coll (OH)
Del Mar Coll (TX)
East Los Angeles Coll (CA)
Folsom Lake Coll (CA)
Fox Valley Tech Coll (WI)
Frederick Comm Coll (MD)
Fulton-Montgomery Comm Coll (NY)
Harrison Coll, Elkhart (IN)
Harrison Coll, Evansville (IN)
Harrison Coll, Fort Wayne (IN)
Harrison Coll, Indianapolis (IN)
Harrison Coll, Muncie (IN)
Harrison Coll, Terre Haute (IN)
Harrison Coll (OH)
Howard Coll (TX)
Indian River State Coll (FL)
Iowa Lakes Comm Coll (IA)
Kent State U at Ashtabula (OH)
Kirkwood Comm Coll (IA)
Lansing Comm Coll (MI)
Lonestar Coll–Cy-Fair (TX)
Lonestar Coll–Kingwood (TX)
Lonestar Coll–Montgomery (TX)
Lonestar Coll–North Harris (TX)
Lonestar Coll–Tomball (TX)
Macomb Comm Coll (MI)
Marion Tech Coll (OH)
Mendocino Coll (CA)
Miami Dade Coll (FL)
Muskegon Comm Coll (MI)
North Hennepin Comm Coll (MN)
NorthWest Arkansas Comm Coll (AR)
Northwest Florida State Coll (FL)
Oklahoma City Comm Coll (OK)
Palm Beach State Coll (FL)
Phoenix Coll (AZ)
Polk State Coll (FL)
Rockland Comm Coll (NY)
Salt Lake Comm Coll (UT)
San Diego City Coll (CA)
Scottsdale Comm Coll (AZ)
Seminole State Coll of Florida (FL)
Southeast Tech Inst (SD)
South Georgia Coll (GA)
Southwest Mississippi Comm Coll (MS)
Southwest Wisconsin Tech Coll (WI)
Springfield Tech Comm Coll (MA)
Stark State Coll of Technology (OH)
State Coll of Florida Manatee-Sarasota (FL)
State U of New York Coll of Technology at Alfred (NY)
Tallahassee Comm Coll (FL)
Tidewater Comm Coll (VA)
Trinity Valley Comm Coll (TX)
Vincennes U Jasper Campus (IN)
Westchester Comm Coll (NY)
Wisconsin Indianhead Tech Coll (WI)

Finance and Financial Management Services Related
Northeast Comm Coll (NE)

Financial Planning and Services
Barton County Comm Coll (KS)
Broome Comm Coll (NY)
Howard Comm Coll (MD)
Minnesota State Comm and Tech Coll (MN)
Pasadena City Coll (CA)
Raritan Valley Comm Coll (NJ)
Triton Coll (IL)
Waukesha County Tech Coll (WI)

Fine Arts Related
Reedley Coll (CA)
Yavapai Coll (AZ)

Fine/Studio Arts
Amarillo Coll (TX)
Anoka-Ramsey Comm Coll (MN)
Anoka-Ramsey Comm Coll, Cambridge Campus (MN)
Berkeley City Coll (CA)
Camden County Coll (NJ)
Casper Coll (WY)
Clovis Comm Coll (NM)
Corning Comm Coll (NY)
County Coll of Morris (NJ)
Cumberland County Coll (NJ)
Delaware County Comm Coll (PA)
Del Mar Coll (TX)
Elgin Comm Coll (IL)
Fashion Inst of Technology (NY)
Finger Lakes Comm Coll (NY)
Fulton-Montgomery Comm Coll (NY)
Inver Hills Comm Coll (MN)
Iowa Lakes Comm Coll (IA)
Jamestown Comm Coll (NY)
Kankakee Comm Coll (IL)
Lansing Comm Coll (MI)
Lon Morris Coll (TX)
Manchester Comm Coll (CT)
Massasoit Comm Coll (MA)
Middlesex Comm Coll (CT)
Minneapolis Comm and Tech Coll (MN)
Niagara County Comm Coll (NY)
Northampton Comm Coll (PA)
Northeastern Jr Coll (CO)
North Hennepin Comm Coll (MN)
Oklahoma City Comm Coll (OK)
Paradise Valley Comm Coll (AZ)
Pennsylvania Coll of Technology (PA)
Raritan Valley Comm Coll (NJ)
Rend Lake Coll (IL)
Rockland Comm Coll (NY)
Sandhills Comm Coll (NC)
South Suburban Coll (IL)
Springfield Tech Comm Coll (MA)
State Coll of Florida Manatee-Sarasota (FL)
Terra State Comm Coll (OH)
Tidewater Comm Coll (VA)
Triton Coll (IL)
Westchester Comm Coll (NY)

Fire Protection and Safety Technology
Antelope Valley Coll (CA)
Austin Comm Coll (TX)
Bunker Hill Comm Coll (MA)
Camden County Coll (NJ)
Catawba Valley Comm Coll (NC)
Central New Mexico Comm Coll (NM)
Coll of Lake County (IL)
Coll of Southern Maryland (MD)
Collin County Comm Coll District (TX)
Comm Coll of Allegheny County (PA)
The Comm Coll of Baltimore County (MD)
County Coll of Morris (NJ)
Delaware County Comm Coll (PA)
Delaware Tech & Comm Coll, Stanton/Wilmington Campus (DE)
Del Mar Coll (TX)
Des Moines Area Comm Coll (IA)
El Paso Comm Coll (TX)
Fayetteville Tech Comm Coll (NC)
Georgia Perimeter Coll (GA)
Guilford Tech Comm Coll (NC)
Hillsborough Comm Coll (FL)
Houston Comm Coll System (TX)
Jefferson Comm Coll (NY)
John Wood Comm Coll (IL)
Kellogg Comm Coll (MI)
Kirkwood Comm Coll (IA)
Lakeland Comm Coll (OH)
Lincoln Land Comm Coll (IL)
Macomb Comm Coll (MI)
Montgomery Coll (MD)
Montgomery County Comm Coll (PA)
Mount Wachusett Comm Coll (MA)
Northland Comm and Tech Coll–Thief River Falls (MN)
Ocean County Coll (NJ)
Oklahoma State U, Oklahoma City (OK)
Owens Comm Coll, Toledo (OH)
Pasadena City Coll (CA)

Pensacola Jr Coll (FL)
Pikes Peak Comm Coll (CO)
Rogue Comm Coll (OR)
San Jacinto Coll District (TX)
San Juan Coll (NM)
Union County Coll (NJ)
Victor Valley Coll (CA)
Waukesha County Tech Coll (WI)
Westmoreland County Comm Coll (PA)

Fire Protection Related
Central Arizona Coll (AZ)
Erie Comm Coll (NY)
Fayetteville Tech Comm Coll (NC)
San Jacinto Coll District (TX)

Fire Science
Allan Hancock Coll (CA)
Amarillo Coll (TX)
Arizona Western Coll (AZ)
Augusta Tech Coll (GA)
Bakersfield Coll (CA)
Barton County Comm Coll (KS)
Berkshire Comm Coll (MA)
Blue Ridge Comm and Tech Coll (WV)
Broome Comm Coll (NY)
Burlington County Coll (NJ)
Casper Coll (WY)
Cecil Coll (MD)
Central Ohio Tech Coll (OH)
Central Oregon Comm Coll (OR)
Central Piedmont Comm Coll (NC)
Central Wyoming Coll (WY)
Chattahoochee Tech Coll (GA)
Chattanooga State Comm Coll (TN)
Cincinnati State Tech and Comm Coll (OH)
Clackamas Comm Coll (OR)
Coll of DuPage (IL)
Coll of Southern Maryland (MD)
Coll of the Canyons (CA)
Collin County Comm Coll District (TX)
Comm Coll of Philadelphia (PA)
Comm Coll of Rhode Island (RI)
Corning Comm Coll (NY)
Crowder Coll (MO)
Cuyahoga Comm Coll (OH)
Danville Area Comm Coll (IL)
Daytona State Coll (FL)
Delaware Tech & Comm Coll, Stanton/Wilmington Campus (DE)
Del Mar Coll (TX)
Delta Coll (MI)
East Central Coll (MO)
East Los Angeles Coll (CA)
Elgin Comm Coll (IL)
Essex County Coll (NJ)
Everett Comm Coll (WA)
Fox Valley Tech Coll (WI)
Frederick Comm Coll (MD)
Gateway Comm and Tech Coll (KY)
Gateway Comm Coll (CT)
Georgia Military Coll (GA)
Georgia Northwestern Tech Coll (GA)
Glendale Comm Coll (AZ)
Greenfield Comm Coll (MA)
Harrisburg Area Comm Coll (PA)
Hennepin Tech Coll (MN)
Honolulu Comm Coll (HI)
Hutchinson Comm Coll and Area Vocational School (KS)
Indian River State Coll (FL)
Jamestown Comm Coll (NY)
Kalamazoo Valley Comm Coll (MI)
Kirkwood Comm Coll (IA)
Lake-Sumter Comm Coll (FL)
Lanier Tech Coll (GA)
Lansing Comm Coll (MI)
Lewis and Clark Comm Coll (IL)
Lonestar Coll–Cy-Fair (TX)
Lonestar Coll–Montgomery (TX)
Los Angeles Harbor Coll (CA)
Lower Columbia Coll (WA)
Massasoit Comm Coll (MA)
Mercer County Comm Coll (NJ)
Meridian Comm Coll (MS)
Metropolitan Comm Coll–Blue River (MO)
Miami Dade Coll (FL)
Mid-Plains Comm Coll, North Platte (NE)
Milwaukee Area Tech Coll (WI)
Missouri State U–West Plains (MO)
Mohave Comm Coll (AZ)
Montana State U–Great Falls Coll of Technology (MT)
Moraine Valley Comm Coll (IL)
Mt. San Jacinto Coll (CA)
Northampton Comm Coll (PA)
Northeast Iowa Comm Coll (IA)
Northland Pioneer Coll (AZ)
Oakland Comm Coll (MI)
Odessa Coll (TX)
Oklahoma State U, Oklahoma City (OK)
Olympic Coll (WA)
Owensboro Comm and Tech Coll (KY)
Palm Beach State Coll (FL)
Paradise Valley Comm Coll (AZ)
Phoenix Coll (AZ)
Pima Comm Coll (AZ)
Polk State Coll (FL)
Pueblo Comm Coll (CO)
Quinsigamond Comm Coll (MA)
Rockland Comm Coll (NY)
Rogue Comm Coll (OR)
Saint Charles Comm Coll (MO)
San Jacinto Coll District (TX)
San Juan Coll (NM)
Santa Rosa Jr Coll (CA)
Savannah Tech Coll (GA)
Scottsdale Comm Coll (AZ)
Seminole State Coll of Florida (FL)
Sierra Coll (CA)
Southern Maine Comm Coll (ME)
South Plains Coll (TX)
South Puget Sound Comm Coll (WA)
Southside Virginia Comm Coll (VA)
Springfield Tech Comm Coll (MA)
Stark State Coll of Technology (OH)
State Coll of Florida Manatee-Sarasota (FL)
Tarrant County Coll District (TX)
Thomas Nelson Comm Coll (VA)
Three Rivers Comm Coll (CT)
Triton Coll (IL)
Umpqua Comm Coll (OR)
The U of Montana–Helena Coll of Technology (MT)
Valdosta Tech Coll (GA)
Victor Valley Coll (CA)
Volunteer State Comm Coll (TN)
West Georgia Tech Coll (GA)
West Kentucky Comm and Tech Coll (KY)
Westmoreland County Comm Coll (PA)
Wilson Comm Coll (NC)
Yavapai Coll (AZ)

Fire Services Administration
Delaware Tech & Comm Coll, Stanton/Wilmington Campus (DE)
Erie Comm Coll, South Campus (NY)
Jefferson State Comm Coll (AL)
Kirtland Comm Coll (MI)
Minnesota State Comm and Tech Coll (MN)
Mohawk Valley Comm Coll (NY)
Northampton Comm Coll (PA)
North Iowa Area Comm Coll (IA)
NorthWest Arkansas Comm Coll (AR)
Olympic Coll (WA)
Quinsigamond Comm Coll (MA)

Fishing and Fisheries Sciences And Management
Central Oregon Comm Coll (OR)
Dakota Coll at Bottineau (ND)
Finger Lakes Comm Coll (NY)
Fox Valley Tech Coll (WI)
Iowa Lakes Comm Coll (IA)
Itasca Comm Coll (MN)
North Idaho Coll (ID)

Flight Instruction
Iowa Lakes Comm Coll (IA)

Floriculture/Floristry Management
Dakota Coll at Bottineau (ND)
Danville Area Comm Coll (IL)
Illinois Valley Comm Coll (IL)
The Ohio State U Ag Tech Inst (OH)
Santa Rosa Jr Coll (CA)
Westmoreland County Comm Coll (PA)

Food Preparation
Iowa Lakes Comm Coll (IA)
Moraine Park Tech Coll (WI)
San Jacinto Coll District (TX)

Foods and Nutrition Related
Iowa Lakes Comm Coll (IA)
San Diego Mesa Coll (CA)

Food Science
Central Piedmont Comm Coll (NC)
Greenfield Comm Coll (MA)
Lonestar Coll–Cy-Fair (TX)
Miami Dade Coll (FL)
Missouri State U–West Plains (MO)
Orange Coast Coll (CA)

Food Service and Dining Room Management
Iowa Lakes Comm Coll (IA)
Pasadena City Coll (CA)

Food Service Systems Administration
Burlington County Coll (NJ)
Comm Coll of Allegheny County (PA)
Harrisburg Area Comm Coll (PA)
Mohawk Valley Comm Coll (NY)
Northeast Comm Coll (NE)
San Jacinto Coll District (TX)

Foods, Nutrition, and Wellness
Antelope Valley Coll (CA)
Bakersfield Coll (CA)
Chattanooga State Comm Coll (TN)
Glendale Comm Coll (AZ)
Indian River State Coll (FL)
Leech Lake Tribal Coll (MN)
Northwest Florida State Coll (FL)
Orange Coast Coll (CA)
Palm Beach State Coll (FL)
San Diego Mesa Coll (CA)
Snow Coll (UT)

Food Technology and Processing
Anne Arundel Comm Coll (MD)
Central Piedmont Comm Coll (NC)
Honolulu Comm Coll (HI)
Leeward Comm Coll (HI)
Orange Coast Coll (CA)
Owens Comm Coll, Toledo (OH)
Southern Maine Comm Coll (ME)
South Puget Sound Comm Coll (WA)
Stark State Coll of Technology (OH)
Tarrant County Coll District (TX)
Victor Valley Coll (CA)
Westchester Comm Coll (NY)

Foreign Languages and Literatures
Austin Comm Coll (TX)
Casper Coll (WY)
Central Oregon Comm Coll (OR)
Comm Coll of Allegheny County (PA)
Darton Coll (GA)
Eastern Arizona Coll (AZ)
Eastern Wyoming Coll (WY)
Everett Comm Coll (WA)
Gainesville State Coll (GA)
Georgia Highlands Coll (GA)
Hutchinson Comm Coll and Area Vocational School (KS)
Iowa Lakes Comm Coll (IA)
Lake Michigan Coll (MI)
Linn-Benton Comm Coll (OR)
Lonestar Coll–Cy-Fair (TX)
Lonestar Coll–Kingwood (TX)
Lonestar Coll–Montgomery (TX)
Lonestar Coll–North Harris (TX)
Lonestar Coll–Tomball (TX)
Oklahoma City Comm Coll (OK)
Reedley Coll (CA)
Saint Charles Comm Coll (MO)
San Jacinto Coll District (TX)
San Juan Coll (NM)
Sheridan Coll (WY)

Foreign Language Teacher Education
Howard Coll (TX)
State Coll of Florida Manatee-Sarasota (FL)

Forensic Science and Technology
Arkansas State U–Mountain Home (AR)
Carroll Comm Coll (MD)
Casper Coll (WY)
Catawba Valley Comm Coll (NC)
Central Ohio Tech Coll (OH)
Comm Coll of Philadelphia (PA)
Cossatot Comm Coll of the U of Arkansas (AR)
Cowley County Comm Coll and Area Vocational–Tech School (KS)
Darton Coll (GA)
Fayetteville Tech Comm Coll (NC)
Green River Comm Coll (WA)
Illinois Valley Comm Coll (IL)
Macomb Comm Coll (MI)
Minnesota State Comm and Tech Coll (MN)
North Arkansas Coll (AR)
Tompkins Cortland Comm Coll (NY)
Tunxis Comm Coll (CT)
U of Arkansas Comm Coll at Morrilton (AR)

Forest/Forest Resources Management
Allegany Coll of Maryland (MD)

Forestry
Allen Comm Coll (KS)
Bainbridge Coll (GA)
Bakersfield Coll (CA)
Barton County Comm Coll (KS)
Central Oregon Comm Coll (OR)
Darton Coll (GA)
Eastern Arizona Coll (AZ)
Gainesville State Coll (GA)
Georgia Highlands Coll (GA)
Grand Rapids Comm Coll (MI)
Indian River State Coll (FL)
Iowa Lakes Comm Coll (IA)
Itasca Comm Coll (MN)
Jamestown Comm Coll (NY)
Kilgore Coll (TX)
Miami Dade Coll (FL)
North Idaho Coll (ID)
Potomac State Coll of West Virginia U (WV)
Sierra Coll (CA)
Snow Coll (UT)
Umpqua Comm Coll (OR)
Western Wyoming Comm Coll (WY)

Forestry Technology
Albany Tech Coll (GA)
Central Oregon Comm Coll (OR)
Dabney S. Lancaster Comm Coll (VA)
Fox Valley Tech Coll (WI)
Green River Comm Coll (WA)
Itasca Comm Coll (MN)
Jefferson Comm Coll (NY)
Louisiana Tech Coll (LA)
Lurleen B. Wallace Comm Coll (AL)
Montgomery Comm Coll (NC)
Ogeechee Tech Coll (GA)
Okefenokee Tech Coll (GA)
Penn State Mont Alto (PA)
Pennsylvania Coll of Technology (PA)
Pensacola Jr Coll (FL)
Potomac State Coll of West Virginia U (WV)
Wayne Comm Coll (NC)

French
Austin Comm Coll (TX)
Bakersfield Coll (CA)
Coll of the Canyons (CA)
East Los Angeles Coll (CA)
Indian River State Coll (FL)
Mendocino Coll (CA)
Miami Dade Coll (FL)
North Idaho Coll (ID)
Northwest Coll (WY)
Orange Coast Coll (CA)
Red Rocks Comm Coll (CO)
Saint Charles Comm Coll (MO)
San Diego Mesa Coll (CA)
Snow Coll (UT)
South Georgia Coll (GA)
State Coll of Florida Manatee-Sarasota (FL)
Triton Coll (IL)

Funeral Service and Mortuary Science
Allen Comm Coll (KS)
Amarillo Coll (TX)
Arkansas State U–Mountain Home (AR)
Barton County Comm Coll (KS)
Catawba Valley Comm Coll (NC)
City Colls of Chicago, Malcolm X College (IL)
Commonwealth Inst of Funeral Service (TX)
The Comm Coll of Baltimore County (MD)
Des Moines Area Comm Coll (IA)
Fayetteville Tech Comm Coll (NC)
Fiorello H. LaGuardia Comm Coll of the City U of New York (NY)
Ivy Tech Comm Coll–Northwest (IN)
Jefferson State Comm Coll (AL)
John Tyler Comm Coll (VA)
Mercer County Comm Coll (NJ)
Miami Dade Coll (FL)
Milwaukee Area Tech Coll (WI)
Nassau Comm Coll (NY)
Northampton Comm Coll (PA)
North Iowa Area Comm Coll (IA)
Ogeechee Tech Coll (GA)
Pittsburgh Inst of Mortuary Science, Incorporated (PA)
Randolph Comm Coll (NC)

Furniture Design and Manufacturing
Catawba Valley Comm Coll (NC)
Vincennes U Jasper Campus (IN)

General Studies
Alexandria Tech Coll (MN)
Allen Comm Coll (KS)
Alpena Comm Coll (MI)
Amarillo Coll (TX)
Arkansas State U–Beebe (AR)
Austin Comm Coll (TX)
Barton County Comm Coll (KS)
Berkeley City Coll (CA)
Bevill State Comm Coll (AL)
Black Hawk Coll, Moline (IL)
Bladen Comm Coll (NC)
Blue Ridge Comm and Tech Coll (WV)
Blue Ridge Comm Coll (NC)
Brown Mackie Coll–Salina (KS)
Bunker Hill Comm Coll (MA)
Carroll Comm Coll (MD)
Casper Coll (WY)
Catawba Valley Comm Coll (NC)
Cecil Coll (MD)
Central Arizona Coll (AZ)
Central New Mexico Comm Coll (NM)
Central Wyoming Coll (WY)
Chattanooga State Comm Coll (TN)
Cincinnati State Tech and Comm Coll (OH)
City Colls of Chicago, Malcolm X College (IL)
Clackamas Comm Coll (OR)
Clarendon Coll (TX)
Cleveland State Comm Coll (TN)
Collin County Comm Coll District (TX)
Comm Coll of Allegheny County (PA)
Comm Coll of Rhode Island (RI)
Corning Comm Coll (NY)
Cossatot Comm Coll of the U of Arkansas (AR)
Crowder Coll (MO)
Cuyamaca Coll (CA)
Dakota Coll at Bottineau (ND)
Danville Area Comm Coll (IL)
Darton Coll (GA)
Delaware County Comm Coll (PA)
East Central Coll (MO)
Eastern Wyoming Coll (WY)
Elaine P. Nunez Comm Coll (LA)

Elgin Comm Coll (IL)
El Paso Comm Coll (TX)
Estrella Mountain Comm Coll (AZ)
Frederick Comm Coll (MD)
Front Range Comm Coll (CO)
Gadsden State Comm Coll (AL)
Gainesville State Coll (GA)
Gateway Comm and Tech Coll (KY)
Georgia Military Coll (GA)
Germanna Comm Coll (VA)
Guilford Tech Comm Coll (NC)
Harcum Coll (PA)
Harrisburg Area Comm Coll (PA)
Highland Comm Coll (IL)
Howard Coll (TX)
Howard Comm Coll (MD)
Illinois Eastern Comm Colls, Frontier Community College (IL)
Illinois Eastern Comm Colls, Lincoln Trail College (IL)
Illinois Eastern Comm Colls, Olney Central College (IL)
Illinois Eastern Comm Colls, Wabash Valley College (IL)
Illinois Valley Comm Coll (IL)
Iowa Lakes Comm Coll (IA)
Itasca Comm Coll (MN)
Ivy Tech Comm Coll–Bloomington (IN)
Ivy Tech Comm Coll–Central Indiana (IN)
Ivy Tech Comm Coll–Columbus (IN)
Ivy Tech Comm Coll–East Central (IN)
Ivy Tech Comm Coll–Kokomo (IN)
Ivy Tech Comm Coll–Lafayette (IN)
Ivy Tech Comm Coll–North Central (IN)
Ivy Tech Comm Coll–Northeast (IN)
Ivy Tech Comm Coll–Northwest (IN)
Ivy Tech Comm Coll–Richmond (IN)
Ivy Tech Comm Coll–Southeast (IN)
Ivy Tech Comm Coll–Southern Indiana (IN)
Ivy Tech Comm Coll–Southwest (IN)
Ivy Tech Comm Coll–Wabash Valley (IN)
Jackson Comm Coll (MI)
Jackson State Comm Coll (TN)
Jefferson State Comm Coll (AL)
John Wood Comm Coll (IL)
Kalamazoo Valley Comm Coll (MI)
Kankakee Comm Coll (IL)
Kaskaskia Coll (IL)
Kellogg Comm Coll (MI)
Kilgore Coll (TX)
Kirtland Comm Coll (MI)
Lackawanna Coll (PA)
Lake Michigan Coll (MI)
Landmark Coll (VT)
LDS Business Coll (UT)
Lehigh Carbon Comm Coll (PA)
Lewis and Clark Comm Coll (IL)
Lincoln Land Comm Coll (IL)
Luna Comm Coll (NM)
Lurleen B. Wallace Comm Coll (AL)
Macomb Comm Coll (MI)
Manchester Comm Coll (CT)
Miami Dade Coll (FL)
Missouri State U–West Plains (MO)
Montcalm Comm Coll (MI)
Mount Wachusett Comm Coll (MA)
Nassau Comm Coll (NY)
New Mexico State U–Carlsbad (NM)
Niagara County Comm Coll (NY)
Northampton Comm Coll (PA)
North Arkansas Coll (AR)
Northeast Comm Coll (NE)
Northland Pioneer Coll (AZ)
Northwest Coll (WY)
Northwest-Shoals Comm Coll (AL)
Oakland Comm Coll (MI)
Ocean County Coll (NJ)
Oklahoma State U, Oklahoma City (OK)
Oregon Coast Comm Coll (OR)
Owens Comm Coll, Toledo (OH)
Panola Coll (TX)
Paradise Valley Comm Coll (AZ)
Pennsylvania Coll of Technology (PA)
Pennsylvania Highlands Comm Coll (PA)
Piedmont Comm Coll (NC)
Pikes Peak Comm Coll (CO)
Pima Comm Coll (AZ)
Pueblo Comm Coll (CO)
Quinsigamond Comm Coll (MA)
Red Rocks Comm Coll (CO)
Reedley Coll (CA)
Rogue Comm Coll (OR)
Saint Charles Comm Coll (MO)
Salt Lake Comm Coll (UT)
San Jacinto Coll District (TX)
San Juan Coll (NM)
Sheridan Coll (WY)
Sierra Coll (CA)
Southern Maine Comm Coll (ME)
Southern Union State Comm Coll (AL)
Southside Virginia Comm Coll (VA)
Springfield Tech Comm Coll (MA)
Terra State Comm Coll (OH)
Thomas Nelson Comm Coll (VA)
U of Arkansas Comm Coll at Morrilton (AR)
U of Cincinnati Clermont Coll (OH)
The U of Montana–Helena Coll of Technology (MT)
Volunteer State Comm Coll (TN)
Western Wyoming Comm Coll (WY)
White Mountains Comm Coll (NH)
Wilson Comm Coll (NC)
York County Comm Coll (ME)

Geography
Allen Comm Coll (KS)
Austin Comm Coll (TX)
Bakersfield Coll (CA)
The Comm Coll of Baltimore County (MD)
Darton Coll (GA)
Del Mar Coll (TX)
Diablo Valley Coll (CA)
East Los Angeles Coll (CA)
Gainesville State Coll (GA)
Holyoke Comm Coll (MA)
Itasca Comm Coll (MN)
Lake Michigan Coll (MI)
Lansing Comm Coll (MI)
Lonestar Coll–Cy-Fair (TX)
Lonestar Coll–Kingwood (TX)
Lonestar Coll–North Harris (TX)
Lonestar Coll–Tomball (TX)
Montgomery Coll (MD)
North Iowa Area Comm Coll (IA)
Orange Coast Coll (CA)
Pennsylvania Highlands Comm Coll (PA)
San Diego Mesa Coll (CA)
Snow Coll (UT)
Triton Coll (IL)

Geography Related
Casper Coll (WY)
Green River Comm Coll (WA)
Mt. San Jacinto Coll (CA)
Southern Alberta Inst of Technology (AB, Canada)

Geological and Earth Sciences/Geosciences Related
Burlington County Coll (NJ)

Geology/Earth Science
Amarillo Coll (TX)
Arizona Western Coll (AZ)
Austin Comm Coll (TX)
Bakersfield Coll (CA)
Barton County Comm Coll (KS)
Casper Coll (WY)
Central Texas Coll (TX)
Central Wyoming Coll (WY)
Del Mar Coll (TX)
Eastern Arizona Coll (AZ)
East Los Angeles Coll (CA)
Everett Comm Coll (WA)
Folsom Lake Coll (CA)
Gainesville State Coll (GA)
Georgia Highlands Coll (GA)
Grand Rapids Comm Coll (MI)
Highland Comm Coll (IL)
Iowa Lakes Comm Coll (IA)
Kilgore Coll (TX)
Lake Michigan Coll (MI)
Lansing Comm Coll (MI)
Lonestar Coll–Cy-Fair (TX)
Lonestar Coll–Kingwood (TX)
Lonestar Coll–Montgomery (TX)
Lonestar Coll–North Harris (TX)
Lonestar Coll–Tomball (TX)
Miami Dade Coll (FL)
North Idaho Coll (ID)
Odessa Coll (TX)
Orange Coast Coll (CA)
Potomac State Coll of West Virginia U (WV)
Red Rocks Comm Coll (CO)
St. Philip's Coll (TX)
Salt Lake Comm Coll (UT)
San Jacinto Coll District (TX)
San Juan Coll (NM)
Sierra Coll (CA)
Snow Coll (UT)
Trinity Valley Comm Coll (TX)
Triton Coll (IL)
Western Wyoming Comm Coll (WY)

German
Austin Comm Coll (TX)
Bakersfield Coll (CA)
Miami Dade Coll (FL)
North Idaho Coll (ID)
Orange Coast Coll (CA)
Red Rocks Comm Coll (CO)
South Georgia Coll (GA)
State Coll of Florida Manatee-Sarasota (FL)

Gerontology
Brown Mackie Coll–Merrillville (IN)
Fiorello H. LaGuardia Comm Coll of the City U of New York (NY)
Gateway Comm Coll (CT)
Genesee Comm Coll (NY)
Lansing Comm Coll (MI)
Midlands Tech Coll (SC)
Sandhills Comm Coll (NC)

Glazier
Metropolitan Comm Coll–Business & Technology Campus (MO)

Graphic and Printing Equipment Operation/Production
Burlington County Coll (NJ)
Central Comm Coll–Hastings Campus (NE)
Central Piedmont Comm Coll (NC)
Central Texas Coll (TX)
Coll of DuPage (IL)
The Comm Coll of Baltimore County (MD)
Eastfield Coll (TX)
Erie Comm Coll, South Campus (NY)
Fox Valley Tech Coll (WI)
Fulton-Montgomery Comm Coll (NY)
Golden West Coll (CA)
H. Councill Trenholm State Tech Coll (AL)
Highline Comm Coll (WA)
Houston Comm Coll System (TX)
Iowa Lakes Comm Coll (IA)
Macomb Comm Coll (MI)
Metropolitan Comm Coll (NE)
Montgomery Coll (MD)
Northwest Coll (WY)
Pasadena City Coll (CA)
San Diego City Coll (CA)
San Jacinto Coll District (TX)
Southwestern Michigan Coll (MI)
Sullivan Coll of Technology and Design (KY)
Tarrant County Coll District (TX)

Graphic Communications
Clark Coll (WA)
Hawkeye Comm Coll (IA)
Iowa Lakes Comm Coll (IA)
Kirkwood Comm Coll (IA)
Milwaukee Area Tech Coll (WI)
Moraine Park Tech Coll (WI)
Piedmont Comm Coll (NC)
Sullivan Coll of Technology and Design (KY)
Waukesha County Tech Coll (WI)

Graphic Communications Related
Linn-Benton Comm Coll (OR)
Milwaukee Area Tech Coll (WI)
Sullivan Coll of Technology and Design (KY)

Graphic Design
Antonelli Coll (OH)
The Art Inst of New York City (NY)
The Art Inst of Ohio–Cincinnati (OH)
The Art Inst of Seattle (WA)
The Art Inst of York–Pennsylvania (PA)
Barton County Comm Coll (KS)
Bradford School (OH)
Bradford School (PA)
Brown Mackie Coll–Louisville (KY)
Bryant & Stratton Coll - Amherst Campus (NY)
Bryant & Stratton Coll - Henrietta Campus (NY)
Bryant & Stratton Coll - North Campus (NY)
Burlington County Coll (NJ)
Casper Coll (WY)
Cecil Coll (MD)
Central Wyoming Coll (WY)
CHI Inst, Franklin Mills Campus (PA)
Coll of the Canyons (CA)
Comm Coll of Vermont (VT)
County Coll of Morris (NJ)
Davis Coll (OH)
Douglas Education Center (PA)
Elgin Comm Coll (IL)
Everett Comm Coll (WA)
Flathead Valley Comm Coll (MT)
Fox Coll (IL)
Glendale Comm Coll (AZ)
Harrisburg Area Comm Coll (PA)
Hesser Coll, Manchester (NH)
Highland Comm Coll (IL)
Illinois Valley Comm Coll (IL)
International Business Coll, Indianapolis (IN)
Iowa Lakes Comm Coll (IA)
Ivy Tech Comm Coll–Southwest (IN)
Jackson Comm Coll (MI)
Kalamazoo Valley Comm Coll (MI)
Kankakee Comm Coll (IL)
Kaplan Coll, Dayton Campus (OH)
Kirtland Comm Coll (MI)
Lake Michigan Coll (MI)
Massasoit Comm Coll (MA)
Milwaukee Area Tech Coll (WI)
Minneapolis Business Coll (MN)
Minnesota State Comm and Tech Coll (MN)
Montana State U–Great Falls Coll of Technology (MT)
Moraine Park Tech Coll (WI)
Moraine Valley Comm Coll (IL)
Northampton Comm Coll (PA)
Northeast Comm Coll (NE)
North Hennepin Comm Coll (MN)
Oakland Comm Coll (MI)
Pasadena City Coll (CA)
Red Rocks Comm Coll (CO)
Rend Lake Coll (IL)
Salt Lake Comm Coll (UT)
Santa Rosa Jr Coll (CA)
Sierra Coll (CA)
Springfield Tech Comm Coll (MA)
Sullivan Coll of Technology and Design (KY)
Tidewater Comm Coll (VA)
Wade Coll (TX)
Waukesha County Tech Coll (WI)
Westwood Coll–Houston South Campus (TX)
Wood Tobe–Coburn School (NY)
Yavapai Coll (AZ)

Greenhouse Management
Century Coll (MN)
Comm Coll of Allegheny County (PA)
Dakota Coll at Bottineau (ND)
The Ohio State U Ag Tech Inst (OH)

Gunsmithing
Colorado School of Trades (CO)
Yavapai Coll (AZ)

Hair Styling and Hair Design
Moraine Park Tech Coll (WI)
Pueblo Comm Coll (CO)

Hazardous Materials Management and Waste Technology
Barton County Comm Coll (KS)
Odessa Coll (TX)
Sierra Coll (CA)

Health Aide
Allen Comm Coll (KS)
Casper Coll (WY)
Central Arizona Coll (AZ)
Northeast Comm Coll (NE)

Health Aides/Attendants/Orderlies Related
Barton County Comm Coll (KS)
Moraine Valley Comm Coll (IL)

Health and Medical Administrative Services Related
Barton County Comm Coll (KS)
The Comm Coll of Baltimore County (MD)
Cumberland County Coll (NJ)
Milwaukee Area Tech Coll (WI)
Northeast Comm Coll (NE)
Pima Comm Coll (AZ)
Westmoreland County Comm Coll (PA)

Health and Physical Education
Alexandria Tech Coll (MN)
Allen Comm Coll (KS)
Antelope Valley Coll (CA)
Austin Comm Coll (TX)
Central Oregon Comm Coll (OR)
Clovis Comm Coll (NM)
Coll of the Canyons (CA)
Comm Care Coll (OK)
Comm Coll of Allegheny County (PA)
Corning Comm Coll (NY)
Dakota Coll at Bottineau (ND)
Darton Coll (GA)
Eastern Arizona Coll (AZ)
Holyoke Comm Coll (MA)
Houston Comm Coll System (TX)
Howard Coll (TX)
Iowa Lakes Comm Coll (IA)
Jamestown Comm Coll (NY)
John Wood Comm Coll (IL)
Lake Michigan Coll (MI)
Lawson State Comm Coll (AL)
Mt. San Jacinto Coll (CA)
Northeast Comm Coll (NE)
Northwest Coll (WY)
Raritan Valley Comm Coll (NJ)
Reedley Coll (CA)
San Jacinto Coll District (TX)
San Juan Coll (NM)
Sheridan Coll (WY)
Sierra Coll (CA)
Triton Coll (IL)

Health and Physical Education Related
Coll of Southern Maryland (MD)
Kingsborough Comm Coll of the City U of New York (NY)
Pennsylvania Coll of Technology (PA)
Santa Rosa Jr Coll (CA)

Health/Health-Care Administration
Brown Mackie Coll–Akron (OH)
Brown Mackie Coll–Atlanta (GA)
Brown Mackie Coll–Boise (ID)
Brown Mackie Coll–Cincinnati (OH)
Brown Mackie Coll–Findlay (OH)
Brown Mackie Coll–Fort Wayne (IN)
Brown Mackie Coll–Greenville (SC)
Brown Mackie Coll–Indianapolis (IN)
Brown Mackie Coll–Kansas City (KS)
Brown Mackie Coll–Louisville (KY)
Brown Mackie Coll–Miami (FL)
Brown Mackie Coll–Michigan City (IN)
Brown Mackie Coll–North Canton (OH)
Brown Mackie Coll–Northern Kentucky (KY)
Brown Mackie Coll–St. Louis (MO)
Brown Mackie Coll–Salina (KS)
Brown Mackie Coll–South Bend (IN)
Brown Mackie Coll–Tucson (AZ)
Central Piedmont Comm Coll (NC)
Coll of DuPage (IL)
Comm Care Coll (OK)
Consolidated School of Business, Lancaster (PA)
Des Moines Area Comm Coll (IA)
Essex County Coll (NJ)
Harrisburg Area Comm Coll (PA)
Inver Hills Comm Coll (MN)

Iowa Lakes Comm Coll (IA)
North Idaho Coll (ID)
Oakland Comm Coll (MI)
Oklahoma State U, Oklahoma City (OK)
Owens Comm Coll, Toledo (OH)
Pennsylvania Highlands Comm Coll (PA)
Pensacola Jr Coll (FL)
South Plains Coll (TX)
State Coll of Florida Manatee-Sarasota (FL)
Terra State Comm Coll (OH)

Health Information/ Medical Records Administration
Amarillo Coll (TX)
Barton County Comm Coll (KS)
Black Hawk Coll, Moline (IL)
Bowling Green State U–Firelands Coll (OH)
Bunker Hill Comm Coll (MA)
Camden County Coll (NJ)
Central New Mexico Comm Coll (NM)
Central Piedmont Comm Coll (NC)
Coll of DuPage (IL)
Comm Coll of Philadelphia (PA)
Darton Coll (GA)
Daytona State Coll (FL)
East Los Angeles Coll (CA)
Edison State Comm Coll (OH)
Elaine P. Nunez Comm Coll (LA)
El Centro Coll (TX)
El Paso Comm Coll (TX)
Howard Coll (TX)
Illinois Eastern Comm Colls, Lincoln Trail College (IL)
Indian River State Coll (FL)
Kaplan U, Hagerstown Campus (MD)
Lake-Sumter Comm Coll (FL)
LDS Business Coll (UT)
Meridian Comm Coll (MS)
Metropolitan Comm Coll–Penn Valley (MO)
Miami Dade Coll (FL)
Montana State U–Great Falls Coll of Technology (MT)
North Central Texas Coll (TX)
Northland Pioneer Coll (AZ)
Oklahoma City Comm Coll (OK)
Pennsylvania Coll of Technology (PA)
Pensacola Jr Coll (FL)
Phoenix Coll (AZ)
Polk State Coll (FL)
Rockland Comm Coll (NY)
Saint Charles Comm Coll (MO)
San Diego Mesa Coll (CA)
South Plains Coll (TX)
Stark State Coll of Technology (OH)
State U of New York Coll of Technology at Alfred (NY)
Tarrant County Coll District (TX)
Terra State Comm Coll (OH)

Health Information/ Medical Records Technology
Atlanta Tech Coll (GA)
Austin Comm Coll (TX)
Black Hawk Coll, Moline (IL)
Broome Comm Coll (NY)
Burlington County Coll (NJ)
Carroll Comm Coll (MD)
Catawba Valley Comm Coll (NC)
Central Comm Coll–Hastings Campus (NE)
Central Oregon Comm Coll (OR)
Chattanooga State Comm Coll (TN)
Cincinnati State Tech and Comm Coll (OH)
Coll of DuPage (IL)
Collin County Comm Coll District (TX)
Columbus Tech Coll (GA)
Comm Coll of Allegheny County (PA)
The Comm Coll of Baltimore County (MD)
Danville Area Comm Coll (IL)
Darton Coll (GA)
Del Mar Coll (TX)
Erie Comm Coll, North Campus (NY)
Fayetteville Tech Comm Coll (NC)
Front Range Comm Coll (CO)
Harrisburg Area Comm Coll (PA)
Harrison Coll, Anderson (IN)
Harrison Coll, Columbus (IN)
Harrison Coll, Indianapolis (IN)
Harrison Coll, Lafayette (IN)
Harrison Coll, Muncie (IN)
Heart of Georgia Tech Coll (GA)
Highland Comm Coll (IL)
Houston Comm Coll System (TX)
Howard Coll (TX)
Hutchinson Comm Coll and Area Vocational School (KS)
ITT Tech Inst, Anaheim (CA)
ITT Tech Inst, Oxnard (CA)
ITT Tech Inst, San Bernardino (CA)
ITT Tech Inst, San Dimas (CA)
ITT Tech Inst, Sylmar (CA)
ITT Tech Inst, Torrance (CA)
ITT Tech Inst, Fort Lauderdale (FL)
ITT Tech Inst, Lake Mary (FL)
ITT Tech Inst, Miami (FL)
ITT Tech Inst, Tampa (FL)
ITT Tech Inst (ID)
ITT Tech Inst, Indianapolis (IN)
ITT Tech Inst (NM)
Kennebec Valley Comm Coll (ME)
Kirkwood Comm Coll (IA)
Lehigh Carbon Comm Coll (PA)
Lonestar Coll–Cy-Fair (TX)
Lonestar Coll–Kingwood (TX)
Lonestar Coll–Montgomery (TX)
Lonestar Coll–North Harris (TX)
Lonestar Coll–Tomball (TX)
Midlands Tech Coll (SC)
Minnesota State Comm and Tech Coll (MN)
Montana State U–Great Falls Coll of Technology (MT)
Montgomery Coll (MD)
Moraine Park Tech Coll (WI)
Moraine Valley Comm Coll (IL)
Northeast Iowa Comm Coll (IA)
Northwestern Coll (IL)
Ogeechee Tech Coll (GA)
Owens Comm Coll, Toledo (OH)
Panola Coll (TX)
Pennsylvania Coll of Technology (PA)
Randolph Comm Coll (NC)
Raritan Valley Comm Coll (NJ)
Rend Lake Coll (IL)
Saint Charles Comm Coll (MO)
St. Cloud Tech Coll (MN)
Saint Paul Coll–A Comm & Tech College (MN)
St. Philip's Coll (TX)
San Jacinto Coll District (TX)
San Juan Coll (NM)
Southern Union State Comm Coll (AL)
Southwestern Michigan Coll (MI)
Southwest Mississippi Comm Coll (MS)
State Fair Comm Coll (MO)
Tallahassee Comm Coll (FL)
Terra State Comm Coll (OH)
Volunteer State Comm Coll (TN)
West Georgia Tech Coll (GA)
West Virginia Northern Comm Coll (WV)

Health/Medical Physics
Chattanooga State Comm Coll (TN)

Health/Medical Preparatory Programs Related
Arkansas State U–Beebe (AR)
Darton Coll (GA)
Eastern Arizona Coll (AZ)
Eastern Wyoming Coll (WY)
Laramie County Comm Coll (WY)
Miami Dade Coll (FL)
Northeast Comm Coll (NE)
Northwest Coll (WY)
Western Wyoming Comm Coll (WY)

Health Occupations Teacher Education
Howard Coll (TX)

Health Professions Related
Allegany Coll of Maryland (MD)
Arizona Western Coll (AZ)
Berkshire Comm Coll (MA)
Bowling Green State U–Firelands Coll (OH)
Bucks County Comm Coll (PA)
Carroll Comm Coll (MD)
Cincinnati State Tech and Comm Coll (OH)
Comm Coll of Allegheny County (PA)
Comm Coll of Philadelphia (PA)
Essex County Coll (NJ)
Gateway Comm and Tech Coll (KY)
Genesee Comm Coll (NY)
Harcum Coll (PA)
Lakeland Comm Coll (OH)
Lake Michigan Coll (MI)
Lanier Tech Coll (GA)
Mendocino Coll (CA)
Mercer County Comm Coll (NJ)
Miami Dade Coll (FL)
Midlands Tech Coll (SC)
Milwaukee Area Tech Coll (WI)
Murray State Coll (OK)
Nassau Comm Coll (NY)
Northeastern Jr Coll (CO)
Northwestern Connecticut Comm Coll (CT)
Oakland Comm Coll (MI)
Ocean County Coll (NJ)
Olympic Coll (WA)
Orange Coast Coll (CA)
Phillips Beth Israel School of Nursing (NY)
Piedmont Comm Coll (NC)
Salt Lake Comm Coll (UT)
Southwest Mississippi Comm Coll (MS)
Terra State Comm Coll (OH)
Volunteer State Comm Coll (TN)
Waycross Coll (GA)

Health Services Administration
Brown Mackie Coll–Phoenix (AZ)
Brown Mackie Coll–Tulsa (OK)
Harrisburg Area Comm Coll (PA)

Health Services/Allied Health/Health Sciences
Burlington County Coll (NJ)
Camden County Coll (NJ)
Catawba Valley Comm Coll (NC)
Cecil Coll (MD)
Central Wyoming Coll (WY)
Clarendon Coll (TX)
Dakota Coll at Bottineau (ND)
Delaware County Comm Coll (PA)
Georgia Military Coll (GA)
Northwest Coll (WY)
Pennsylvania Coll of Technology (PA)
Raritan Valley Comm Coll (NJ)
Volunteer State Comm Coll (TN)
Western Wyoming Comm Coll (WY)

Health Teacher Education
Anne Arundel Comm Coll (MD)
Austin Comm Coll (TX)
Bainbridge Coll (GA)
Bucks County Comm Coll (PA)
Del Mar Coll (TX)
Fulton-Montgomery Comm Coll (NY)
Howard Comm Coll (MD)
Kilgore Coll (TX)
Palm Beach State Coll (FL)
South Georgia Coll (GA)
State Coll of Florida Manatee-Sarasota (FL)
Umpqua Comm Coll (OR)

Health Unit Coordinator/Ward Clerk
Comm Coll of Allegheny County (PA)
Southeast Tech Inst (SD)

Health Unit Management/Ward Supervision
Delaware County Comm Coll (PA)

Heating, Air Conditioning and Refrigeration Technology
Alamance Comm Coll (NC)
Austin Comm Coll (TX)
Bevill State Comm Coll (AL)
Cincinnati State Tech and Comm Coll (OH)
DeKalb Tech Coll (GA)
Delaware County Comm Coll (PA)
Delaware Tech & Comm Coll, Stanton/Wilmington Campus (DE)
Delta Coll (MI)
Front Range Comm Coll (CO)
Gadsden State Comm Coll (AL)
Griffin Tech Coll (GA)
H. Councill Trenholm State Tech Coll (AL)
Jackson Comm Coll (MI)
Kalamazoo Valley Comm Coll (MI)
Macomb Comm Coll (MI)
Manhattan Area Tech Coll (KS)
Massasoit Comm Coll (MA)
Mercer County Comm Coll (NJ)
Miami Dade Coll (FL)
Milwaukee Area Tech Coll (WI)
Minnesota State Comm and Tech Coll (MN)
Mitchell Tech Inst (SD)
Mohawk Valley Comm Coll (NY)
Moraine Park Tech Coll (WI)
New Mexico State U–Carlsbad (NM)
North Georgia Tech Coll (GA)
Oakland Comm Coll (MI)
Pennsylvania Highlands Comm Coll (PA)
Raritan Valley Comm Coll (NJ)
Savannah Tech Coll (GA)
South Georgia Tech Coll (GA)
Springfield Tech Comm Coll (MA)
State U of New York Coll of Technology at Alfred (NY)
Sullivan Coll of Technology and Design (KY)
Terra State Comm Coll (OH)
Triangle Tech–Greensburg School (PA)
Wisconsin Indianhead Tech Coll (WI)

Heating, Air Conditioning, Ventilation and Refrigeration Maintenance Technology
Amarillo Coll (TX)
Antelope Valley Coll (CA)
Arizona Western Coll (AZ)
Black Hawk Coll, Moline (IL)
Blue Ridge Comm and Tech Coll (WV)
Central Comm Coll–Grand Island Campus (NE)
Central Comm Coll–Hastings Campus (NE)
Central Texas Coll (TX)
Century Coll (MN)
Clovis Comm Coll (NM)
Coll of DuPage (IL)
Coll of Lake County (IL)
Comm Coll of Allegheny County (PA)
The Comm Coll of Baltimore County (MD)
Delaware County Comm Coll (PA)
Delaware Tech & Comm Coll, Jack F. Owens Campus (DE)
Delta Coll (MI)
Des Moines Area Comm Coll (IA)
East Central Coll (MO)
Eastfield Coll (TX)
Elaine P. Nunez Comm Coll (LA)
Elgin Comm Coll (IL)
El Paso Comm Coll (TX)
Fayetteville Tech Comm Coll (NC)
Grand Rapids Comm Coll (MI)
Guilford Tech Comm Coll (NC)
Harrisburg Area Comm Coll (PA)
Honolulu Comm Coll (HI)
Indian River State Coll (FL)
Ivy Tech Comm Coll–Bloomington (IN)
Ivy Tech Comm Coll–Central Indiana (IN)
Ivy Tech Comm Coll–Columbus (IN)
Ivy Tech Comm Coll–East Central (IN)
Ivy Tech Comm Coll–Kokomo (IN)
Ivy Tech Comm Coll–Lafayette (IN)
Ivy Tech Comm Coll–North Central (IN)
Ivy Tech Comm Coll–Northeast (IN)
Ivy Tech Comm Coll–Northwest (IN)
Ivy Tech Comm Coll–Richmond (IN)
Ivy Tech Comm Coll–Southern Indiana (IN)
Ivy Tech Comm Coll–Southwest (IN)
Ivy Tech Comm Coll–Wabash Valley (IN)
Johnston Comm Coll (NC)
Kankakee Comm Coll (IL)
Kellogg Comm Coll (MI)
Kilgore Coll (TX)
Kirtland Comm Coll (MI)
Lansing Comm Coll (MI)
Lehigh Carbon Comm Coll (PA)
Linn State Tech Coll (MO)
Lonestar Coll–Montgomery (TX)
Lonestar Coll–North Harris (TX)
Macomb Comm Coll (MI)
Metropolitan Comm Coll (NE)
Miami Dade Coll (FL)
Midlands Tech Coll (SC)
Mid-Plains Comm Coll, North Platte (NE)
Minneapolis Comm and Tech Coll (MN)
Minnesota State Coll–Southeast Tech (MN)
Minnesota West Comm and Tech Coll (MN)
Mitchell Tech Inst (SD)
Mohave Comm Coll (AZ)
Moraine Park Tech Coll (WI)
Moraine Valley Comm Coll (IL)
Northampton Comm Coll (PA)
Northeast Comm Coll (NE)
North Idaho Coll (ID)
North Iowa Area Comm Coll (IA)
North Lake Coll (TX)
Northland Comm and Tech Coll–Thief River Falls (MN)
Northwest Florida State Coll (FL)
Odessa Coll (TX)
Orange Coast Coll (CA)
Paris Jr Coll (TX)
Pulaski Tech Coll (AR)
St. Cloud Tech Coll (MN)
St. Philip's Coll (TX)
Salt Lake Comm Coll (UT)
San Jacinto Coll District (TX)
Southeast Tech Inst (SD)
Southern Maine Comm Coll (ME)
Southern Union State Comm Coll (AL)
South Plains Coll (TX)
Southwest Mississippi Comm Coll (MS)
Spartanburg Comm Coll (SC)
State U of New York Coll of Technology at Alfred (NY)
Tarrant County Coll District (TX)
Thomas Nelson Comm Coll (VA)
Triangle Tech–Greensburg School (PA)
Trinity Valley Comm Coll (TX)
Triton Coll (IL)
U of Alaska Anchorage, Matanuska-Susitna Coll (AK)
U of Arkansas Comm Coll at Morrilton (AR)
Westmoreland County Comm Coll (PA)
West Virginia Northern Comm Coll (WV)

Heavy Equipment Maintenance Technology
Allan Hancock Coll (CA)
Amarillo Coll (TX)
Beaufort County Comm Coll (NC)
Del Mar Coll (TX)
Highland Comm Coll (IL)
Lansing Comm Coll (MI)
Linn State Tech Coll (MO)
Metropolitan Comm Coll (NE)
Metropolitan Comm Coll–Longview (MO)
North Idaho Coll (ID)
The Ohio State U Ag Tech Inst (OH)
Pennsylvania Coll of Technology (PA)
Rend Lake Coll (IL)
State U of New York Coll of Technology at Alfred (NY)
Western Wyoming Comm Coll (WY)

Heavy/Industrial Equipment Maintenance Technologies Related
Blue Ridge Comm Coll (NC)

East Central Coll (MO)
Pennsylvania Coll of Technology (PA)
State U of New York Coll of Technology at Alfred (NY)

Hispanic American, Puerto Rican, and Mexican American/ Chicano Studies
Collin County Comm Coll District (TX)
East Los Angeles Coll (CA)
Pasadena City Coll (CA)
San Diego City Coll (CA)
San Diego Mesa Coll (CA)

Histologic Technician
Comm Coll of Rhode Island (RI)
Darton Coll (GA)
Goodwin Coll (CT)
Houston Comm Coll System (TX)
Miami Dade Coll (FL)
Pima Comm Coll (AZ)
Volunteer State Comm Coll (TN)

Histologic Technology/ Histotechnologist
Argosy U, Twin Cities (MN)
Delaware Tech & Comm Coll, Stanton/Wilmington Campus (DE)
Harcum Coll (PA)
North Hennepin Comm Coll (MN)
Oakland Comm Coll (MI)

Historic Preservation and Conservation
Bucks County Comm Coll (PA)

History
Allen Comm Coll (KS)
Amarillo Coll (TX)
Austin Comm Coll (TX)
Bainbridge Coll (GA)
Bakersfield Coll (CA)
Barton County Comm Coll (KS)
Bronx Comm Coll of the City U of New York (NY)
Bunker Hill Comm Coll (MA)
Burlington County Coll (NJ)
Casper Coll (WY)
Clarendon Coll (TX)
Cuyamaca Coll (CA)
Dakota Coll at Bottineau (ND)
Darton Coll (GA)
Del Mar Coll (TX)
Eastern Arizona Coll (AZ)
Eastern Wyoming Coll (WY)
East Los Angeles Coll (CA)
Everett Comm Coll (WA)
Fulton-Montgomery Comm Coll (NY)
Gainesville State Coll (GA)
Georgia Highlands Coll (GA)
Georgia Military Coll (GA)
Highland Comm Coll (IL)
Howard Coll (TX)
Indian River State Coll (FL)
Iowa Lakes Comm Coll (IA)
Lake Michigan Coll (MI)
Laramie County Comm Coll (WY)
Lawson State Comm Coll (AL)
Lonestar Coll–Cy-Fair (TX)
Lonestar Coll–Kingwood (TX)
Lonestar Coll–Montgomery (TX)
Lonestar Coll–North Harris (TX)
Lonestar Coll–Tomball (TX)
Lon Morris Coll (TX)
Miami Dade Coll (FL)
Mohave Comm Coll (AZ)
Murray State Coll (OK)
Northeastern Jr Coll (CO)
North Hennepin Comm Coll (MN)
North Idaho Coll (ID)
Northwest Coll (WY)
Odessa Coll (TX)
Oklahoma City Comm Coll (OK)
Oklahoma State U, Oklahoma City (OK)
Orange Coast Coll (CA)
Otero Jr Coll (CO)
Palm Beach State Coll (FL)
Pasadena City Coll (CA)
Potomac State Coll of West Virginia U (WV)
Red Rocks Comm Coll (CO)
Saint Charles Comm Coll (MO)
St. Philip's Coll (TX)
Salt Lake Comm Coll (UT)
San Jacinto Coll District (TX)
San Juan Coll (NM)
Santa Rosa Jr Coll (CA)
Sheridan Coll (WY)
Snow Coll (UT)
South Georgia Coll (GA)
Southwest Mississippi Comm Coll (MS)
State Coll of Florida Manatee-Sarasota (FL)
Terra State Comm Coll (OH)
Trinity Valley Comm Coll (TX)
Triton Coll (IL)
Umpqua Comm Coll (OR)
Western Wyoming Comm Coll (WY)

History Teacher Education
Darton Coll (GA)
Howard Coll (TX)

Home Furnishings and Equipment Installation
Triton Coll (IL)

Home Health Aide/ Home Attendant
Allen Comm Coll (KS)
Barton County Comm Coll (KS)

Homeopathic Medicine
Minneapolis Comm and Tech Coll (MN)

Horse Husbandry/ Equine Science and Management
Black Hawk Coll, Moline (IL)
Cecil Coll (MD)
Clarendon Coll (TX)
Colby Comm Coll (KS)
Kirkwood Comm Coll (IA)
Linn-Benton Comm Coll (OR)
The Ohio State U Ag Tech Inst (OH)
Santa Rosa Jr Coll (CA)
Yavapai Coll (AZ)

Horticultural Science
Anne Arundel Comm Coll (MD)
Bakersfield Coll (CA)
Black Hawk Coll, Moline (IL)
Central Lakes Coll (MN)
Central Piedmont Comm Coll (NC)
Century Coll (MN)
Chattahoochee Tech Coll (GA)
City Colls of Chicago, Richard J. Daley College (IL)
Columbus Tech Coll (GA)
Cumberland County Coll (NJ)
Dakota Coll at Bottineau (ND)
Georgia Highlands Coll (GA)
Griffin Tech Coll (GA)
Gwinnett Tech Coll (GA)
Kankakee Comm Coll (IL)
Lansing Comm Coll (MI)
Lehigh Carbon Comm Coll (PA)
Linn-Benton Comm Coll (OR)
Meridian Comm Coll (MS)
Miami Dade Coll (FL)
Missouri State U–West Plains (MO)
North Georgia Tech Coll (GA)
The Ohio State U Ag Tech Inst (OH)
Oklahoma State U, Oklahoma City (OK)
Orange Coast Coll (CA)
Potomac State Coll of West Virginia U (WV)
Reedley Coll (CA)
Shawnee Comm Coll (IL)
Sheridan Coll (WY)
Southeast Tech Inst (SD)
Southern Maine Comm Coll (ME)
South Georgia Tech Coll (GA)
South Puget Sound Comm Coll (WA)
Spartanburg Comm Coll (SC)
Tarrant County Coll District (TX)
Tidewater Comm Coll (VA)
Trident Tech Coll (SC)
Trinity Valley Comm Coll (TX)
Victor Valley Coll (CA)

Hospital and Health-Care Facilities Administration
Allen Comm Coll (KS)
Central Comm Coll–Columbus Campus (NE)
Central Comm Coll–Grand Island Campus (NE)
Central Comm Coll–Hastings Campus (NE)
City Colls of Chicago, Malcolm X College (IL)
Coll of DuPage (IL)
State Coll of Florida Manatee-Sarasota (FL)

Hospitality Administration
Alexandria Tech Coll (MN)
Allegany Coll of Maryland (MD)
Arizona Western Coll (AZ)
Austin Comm Coll (TX)
Berkshire Comm Coll (MA)
Bucks County Comm Coll (PA)
Bunker Hill Comm Coll (MA)
Burlington County Coll (NJ)
Casper Coll (WY)
Central Comm Coll–Hastings Campus (NE)
Central New Mexico Comm Coll (NM)
Central Piedmont Comm Coll (NC)
Coll of DuPage (IL)
Coll of Southern Maryland (MD)
Coll of the Canyons (CA)
Collin County Comm Coll District (TX)
Comm Coll of Vermont (VT)
Daytona State Coll (FL)
Des Moines Area Comm Coll (IA)
Fox Valley Tech Coll (WI)
Front Range Comm Coll (CO)
Harrisburg Area Comm Coll (PA)
Hillsborough Comm Coll (FL)
Iowa Lakes Comm Coll (IA)
Ivy Tech Comm Coll–East Central (IN)
Ivy Tech Comm Coll–North Central (IN)
Ivy Tech Comm Coll–Northeast (IN)
Ivy Tech Comm Coll–Northwest (IN)
Jefferson Comm Coll (NY)
Jefferson State Comm Coll (AL)
Kauai Comm Coll (HI)
Kirkwood Comm Coll (IA)
Lakeland Comm Coll (OH)
Lake Michigan Coll (MI)
Lansing Comm Coll (MI)
Lonestar Coll–North Harris (TX)
Massasoit Comm Coll (MA)
Miami Dade Coll (FL)
Muskegon Comm Coll (MI)
Niagara County Comm Coll (NY)
North Idaho Coll (ID)
Olympic Coll (WA)
Pasadena City Coll (CA)
Pennsylvania Coll of Technology (PA)
Pennsylvania Highlands Comm Coll (PA)
Pensacola Jr Coll (FL)
Pima Comm Coll (AZ)
Potomac State Coll of West Virginia U (WV)
Pulaski Tech Coll (AR)
Quinsigamond Comm Coll (MA)
Reedley Coll (CA)
Rockland Comm Coll (NY)
Saint Paul Coll–A Comm & Tech College (MN)
San Diego City Coll (CA)
Scottsdale Comm Coll (AZ)
Sheridan Coll (WY)
Sisseton-Wahpeton Comm Coll (SD)
Southern Maine Comm Coll (ME)
Terra State Comm Coll (OH)
Three Rivers Comm Coll (CT)
Waukesha County Tech Coll (WI)
West Virginia Northern Comm Coll (WV)
Wor-Wic Comm Coll (MD)

Hospitality Administration Related
Arizona Western Coll (AZ)
Corning Comm Coll (NY)
Holyoke Comm Coll (MA)
Ivy Tech Comm Coll–Central Indiana (IN)
Ivy Tech Comm Coll–East Central (IN)
Ivy Tech Comm Coll–Northeast (IN)
Penn State Beaver (PA)
Raritan Valley Comm Coll (NJ)

Hospitality and Recreation Marketing
County Coll of Morris (NJ)
Dakota Coll at Bottineau (ND)
Flathead Valley Comm Coll (MT)
Lac Courte Oreilles Ojibwa Comm Coll (WI)
Montgomery County Comm Coll (PA)
Muskegon Comm Coll (MI)
Pueblo Comm Coll (CO)
San Diego Mesa Coll (CA)
San Jacinto Coll District (TX)

Hotel/Motel Administration
Albany Tech Coll (GA)
Anne Arundel Comm Coll (MD)
Athens Tech Coll (GA)
Atlanta Tech Coll (GA)
Bakersfield Coll (CA)
Broome Comm Coll (NY)
Bryant & Stratton Coll - Syracuse Campus (NY)
Bucks County Comm Coll (PA)
Bunker Hill Comm Coll (MA)
Cape Fear Comm Coll (NC)
Central Arizona Coll (AZ)
Central Comm Coll–Hastings Campus (NE)
Central Georgia Tech Coll (GA)
Central Oregon Comm Coll (OR)
Central Piedmont Comm Coll (NC)
Central Texas Coll (TX)
Central Wyoming Coll (WY)
Cincinnati State Tech and Comm Coll (OH)
Coll of DuPage (IL)
Coll of the Canyons (CA)
Comm Coll of Allegheny County (PA)
The Comm Coll of Baltimore County (MD)
Comm Coll of Philadelphia (PA)
Cowley County Comm Coll and Area Vocational–Tech School (KS)
Daytona State Coll (FL)
Delaware County Comm Coll (PA)
Delaware Tech & Comm Coll, Stanton/Wilmington Campus (DE)
Delaware Tech & Comm Coll, Terry Campus (DE)
Del Mar Coll (TX)
Elgin Comm Coll (IL)
El Paso Comm Coll (TX)
Essex County Coll (NJ)
Fayetteville Tech Comm Coll (NC)
Finger Lakes Comm Coll (NY)
Gateway Comm Coll (CT)
Genesee Comm Coll (NY)
Georgia Highlands Coll (GA)
Guilford Tech Comm Coll (NC)
Gwinnett Tech Coll (GA)
Harrisburg Area Comm Coll (PA)
Highline Comm Coll (WA)
Houston Comm Coll System (TX)
Indian River State Coll (FL)
Iowa Lakes Comm Coll (IA)
John Wood Comm Coll (IL)
Lansing Comm Coll (MI)
Lehigh Carbon Comm Coll (PA)
Lincoln Land Comm Coll (IL)
Louisiana Tech Coll (LA)
Manchester Comm Coll (CT)
Mercer County Comm Coll (NJ)
Meridian Comm Coll (MS)
Milwaukee Area Tech Coll (WI)
Mohawk Valley Comm Coll (NY)
Montgomery Coll (MD)
Moraine Park Tech Coll (WI)
Muskegon Comm Coll (MI)
Nassau Comm Coll (NY)
Nicolet Area Tech Coll (WI)
Northampton Comm Coll (PA)
Northwest Florida State Coll (FL)
Oakland Comm Coll (MI)
Ogeechee Tech Coll (GA)
Orange Coast Coll (CA)
Palm Beach State Coll (FL)
Pasadena City Coll (CA)
Quinsigamond Comm Coll (MA)
The Restaurant School at Walnut Hill Coll (PA)
St. Philip's Coll (TX)
Sandhills Comm Coll (NC)
San Diego Mesa Coll (CA)
Savannah Tech Coll (GA)
Scottsdale Comm Coll (AZ)
Southern Maine Comm Coll (ME)
Three Rivers Comm Coll (CT)
Tompkins Cortland Comm Coll (NY)
Trident Tech Coll (SC)
Triton Coll (IL)
Union County Coll (NJ)

Housing and Human Environments
Orange Coast Coll (CA)
Sullivan Coll of Technology and Design (KY)

Housing and Human Environments Related
Comm Coll of Allegheny County (PA)

Human Development and Family Studies
Georgia Military Coll (GA)
Orange Coast Coll (CA)
Penn State Brandywine (PA)
Penn State DuBois (PA)
Penn State Fayette, The Eberly Campus (PA)
Penn State Mont Alto (PA)
Penn State New Kensington (PA)
Penn State Schuylkill (PA)
Penn State Shenango (PA)
Penn State Worthington Scranton (PA)
Penn State York (PA)
Rogue Comm Coll (OR)
Salt Lake Comm Coll (UT)

Human Development and Family Studies Related
Albany Tech Coll (GA)
Comm Coll of Allegheny County (PA)
Glendale Comm Coll (AZ)

Humanities
Allen Comm Coll (KS)
Anne Arundel Comm Coll (MD)
Blue Ridge Comm Coll (NC)
Bowling Green State U–Firelands Coll (OH)
Bucks County Comm Coll (PA)
Central Oregon Comm Coll (OR)
City Colls of Chicago, Richard J. Daley College (IL)
Coll of the Canyons (CA)
Comm Coll of Allegheny County (PA)
Corning Comm Coll (NY)
Dakota Coll at Bottineau (ND)
Diablo Valley Coll (CA)
Erie Comm Coll (NY)
Erie Comm Coll, North Campus (NY)
Erie Comm Coll, South Campus (NY)
Everett Comm Coll (WA)
Finger Lakes Comm Coll (NY)
Fulton-Montgomery Comm Coll (NY)
Golden West Coll (CA)
Greenfield Comm Coll (MA)
Highline Comm Coll (WA)
Housatonic Comm Coll (CT)
Indian River State Coll (FL)
Iowa Lakes Comm Coll (IA)
Jamestown Comm Coll (NY)
Jefferson Comm Coll (NY)
Lackawanna Coll (PA)
Lake Michigan Coll (MI)
Laramie County Comm Coll (WY)
Lehigh Carbon Comm Coll (PA)
Lonestar Coll–Cy-Fair (TX)
Lonestar Coll–Kingwood (TX)
Lonestar Coll–Montgomery (TX)
Lonestar Coll–Tomball (TX)
Lon Morris Coll (TX)
Mercer County Comm Coll (NJ)
Miami Dade Coll (FL)
Mohawk Valley Comm Coll (NY)
Montgomery County Comm Coll (PA)
Mt. San Jacinto Coll (CA)
Niagara County Comm Coll (NY)
Northeastern Jr Coll (CO)
Northwest Florida State Coll (FL)
Oklahoma City Comm Coll (OK)
Oklahoma State U, Oklahoma City (OK)
Orange Coast Coll (CA)
Otero Jr Coll (CO)
Pasadena City Coll (CA)
Red Rocks Comm Coll (CO)
Salt Lake Comm Coll (UT)
Santa Rosa Jr Coll (CA)
Snow Coll (UT)
South Georgia Coll (GA)
Southwest Mississippi Comm Coll (MS)
State Coll of Florida Manatee-Sarasota (FL)

State U of New York Coll of Technology at Alfred (NY)
Suffolk County Comm Coll (NY)
Terra State Comm Coll (OH)
Thomas Nelson Comm Coll (VA)
Tompkins Cortland Comm Coll (NY)
Umpqua Comm Coll (OR)
Victor Valley Coll (CA)
Westchester Comm Coll (NY)
Western Wyoming Comm Coll (WY)

Human Nutrition
Everett Comm Coll (WA)

Human Resources Development
Alexandria Tech Coll (MN)

Human Resources Management
Anoka-Ramsey Comm Coll (MN)
Anoka-Ramsey Comm Coll, Cambridge Campus (MN)
Barton County Comm Coll (KS)
Bryant & Stratton Coll, Eastlake (OH)
Bryant & Stratton Coll - Amherst Campus (NY)
Bryant & Stratton Coll - Buffalo Campus (NY)
Bryant & Stratton Coll - Greece Campus (NY)
Bryant & Stratton Coll - Henrietta Campus (NY)
Bryant & Stratton Coll - North Campus (NY)
Bryant & Stratton Coll - Southtowns Campus (NY)
Bryant & Stratton Coll - Virginia Beach (VA)
Clark Coll (WA)
Comm Coll of Allegheny County (PA)
The Comm Coll of Baltimore County (MD)
Delaware Tech & Comm Coll, Terry Campus (DE)
Edison State Comm Coll (OH)
Fayetteville Tech Comm Coll (NC)
Guilford Tech Comm Coll (NC)
Harrison Coll, Anderson (IN)
Harrison Coll, Indianapolis (IN)
Harrison Coll, Lafayette (IN)
Harrison Coll, Muncie (IN)
Harrison Coll, Terre Haute (IN)
Harrison Coll (OH)
Lansing Comm Coll (MI)
Lehigh Carbon Comm Coll (PA)
Minnesota State Comm and Tech Coll (MN)
Moraine Valley Comm Coll (IL)
Northwest Florida State Coll (FL)
Rockingham Comm Coll (NC)
Saint Paul Coll–A Comm & Tech College (MN)
Triton Coll (IL)
Umpqua Comm Coll (OR)
Westmoreland County Comm Coll (PA)

Human Resources Management and Services Related
Barton County Comm Coll (KS)
Bryant & Stratton Coll, Parma (OH)
Bryant & Stratton Coll (WI)
Bryant & Stratton Coll - Albany Campus (NY)
Bryant & Stratton Coll - Amherst Campus (NY)
Bryant & Stratton Coll - Buffalo Campus (NY)
Bryant & Stratton Coll - Greece Campus (NY)
Bryant & Stratton Coll - Henrietta Campus (NY)
Bryant & Stratton Coll - Richmond Campus (VA)
Bryant & Stratton Coll - Southtowns Campus (NY)
Bryant & Stratton Coll - Syracuse Campus (NY)
Iowa Lakes Comm Coll (IA)

Human Services
Alexandria Tech Coll (MN)
Allan Hancock Coll (CA)
Anne Arundel Comm Coll (MD)
Arizona Western Coll (AZ)
Austin Comm Coll (TX)
Bakersfield Coll (CA)
Berkshire Comm Coll (MA)
Bowling Green State U–Firelands Coll (OH)
Bronx Comm Coll of the City U of New York (NY)
Bunker Hill Comm Coll (MA)
Burlington County Coll (NJ)
Carroll Comm Coll (MD)
Central Ohio Tech Coll (OH)
Central Piedmont Comm Coll (NC)
Century Coll (MN)
Coll of DuPage (IL)
Comm Coll of Philadelphia (PA)
Comm Coll of Vermont (VT)
Corning Comm Coll (NY)
Daytona State Coll (FL)
Delaware County Comm Coll (PA)
Delaware Tech & Comm Coll, Jack F. Owens Campus (DE)
Delaware Tech & Comm Coll, Stanton/Wilmington Campus (DE)
Delaware Tech & Comm Coll, Terry Campus (DE)
Denmark Tech Coll (SC)
Edison State Comm Coll (OH)
Essex County Coll (NJ)
Finger Lakes Comm Coll (NY)
Fiorello H. LaGuardia Comm Coll of the City U of New York (NY)
Flathead Valley Comm Coll (MT)
Folsom Lake Coll (CA)
Frederick Comm Coll (MD)
Fulton-Montgomery Comm Coll (NY)
Gateway Comm Coll (CT)
Genesee Comm Coll (NY)
Georgia Highlands Coll (GA)
Goodwin Coll (CT)
Greenfield Comm Coll (MA)
Harcum Coll (PA)
Harrisburg Area Comm Coll (PA)
Highland Comm Coll (IL)
Highline Comm Coll (WA)
Honolulu Comm Coll (HI)
Hopkinsville Comm Coll (KY)
Housatonic Comm Coll (CT)
Indian River State Coll (FL)
Inver Hills Comm Coll (MN)
Itasca Comm Coll (MN)
Ivy Tech Comm Coll–Bloomington (IN)
Ivy Tech Comm Coll–Central Indiana (IN)
Ivy Tech Comm Coll–Columbus (IN)
Ivy Tech Comm Coll–East Central (IN)
Ivy Tech Comm Coll–Kokomo (IN)
Ivy Tech Comm Coll–Lafayette (IN)
Ivy Tech Comm Coll–North Central (IN)
Ivy Tech Comm Coll–Northeast (IN)
Ivy Tech Comm Coll–Northwest (IN)
Ivy Tech Comm Coll–Richmond (IN)
Ivy Tech Comm Coll–Southeast (IN)
Ivy Tech Comm Coll–Southern Indiana (IN)
Ivy Tech Comm Coll–Southwest (IN)
Ivy Tech Comm Coll–Wabash Valley (IN)
Jamestown Comm Coll (NY)
Jefferson Comm Coll (NY)
John Tyler Comm Coll (VA)
Kellogg Comm Coll (MI)
Kent State U at Ashtabula (OH)
Kingsborough Comm Coll of the City U of New York (NY)
Lackawanna Coll (PA)
Lansing Comm Coll (MI)
Laramie County Comm Coll (WY)
Leeward Comm Coll (HI)
Lehigh Carbon Comm Coll (PA)
Lonestar Coll–Montgomery (TX)
Lonestar Coll–North Harris (TX)
Manchester Comm Coll (CT)
Marion Tech Coll (OH)
Massasoit Comm Coll (MA)
Mendocino Coll (CA)
Mesabi Range Comm and Tech Coll (MN)
Metropolitan Comm Coll (NE)
Metropolitan Comm Coll–Longview (MO)
Miami Dade Coll (FL)
Middlesex Comm Coll (CT)
Minneapolis Comm and Tech Coll (MN)
Mount Wachusett Comm Coll (MA)
New Mexico State U–Carlsbad (NM)
Niagara County Comm Coll (NY)
North Idaho Coll (ID)
Northwestern Connecticut Comm Coll (CT)
Odessa Coll (TX)
Oklahoma State U, Oklahoma City (OK)
Owensboro Comm and Tech Coll (KY)
Pasco-Hernando Comm Coll (FL)
Pennsylvania Highlands Comm Coll (PA)
Quinsigamond Comm Coll (MA)
Rockland Comm Coll (NY)
Sandhills Comm Coll (NC)
San Juan Coll (NM)
Santa Rosa Jr Coll (CA)
Shawnee Comm Coll (IL)
Southern State Comm Coll (OH)
Southside Virginia Comm Coll (VA)
Southwest Virginia Comm Coll (VA)
Stanly Comm Coll (NC)
Stark State Coll of Technology (OH)
State U of New York Coll of Technology at Alfred (NY)
Suffolk County Comm Coll (NY)
Three Rivers Comm Coll (CT)
Tohono O'odham Comm Coll (AZ)
Trident Tech Coll (SC)
Tunxis Comm Coll (CT)
U of Alaska Anchorage, Kenai Peninsula Coll (AK)
U of Alaska Anchorage, Matanuska-Susitna Coll (AK)
U of Pittsburgh at Titusville (PA)
Western Wyoming Comm Coll (WY)
Westmoreland County Comm Coll (PA)
White Mountains Comm Coll (NH)

Hydraulics and Fluid Power Technology
Alexandria Tech Coll (MN)
The Comm Coll of Baltimore County (MD)
Hennepin Tech Coll (MN)
The Ohio State U Ag Tech Inst (OH)

Hydrology and Water Resources Science
Indian River State Coll (FL)
Iowa Lakes Comm Coll (IA)
Three Rivers Comm Coll (CT)

Illustration
Creative Center (NE)
Douglas Education Center (PA)
Fashion Inst of Technology (NY)
Kalamazoo Valley Comm Coll (MI)
Oklahoma State U, Oklahoma City (OK)

Industrial Arts
Allen Comm Coll (KS)
Bakersfield Coll (CA)
Chattanooga State Comm Coll (TN)
Cleveland State Comm Coll (TN)
Delta Coll (MI)
Honolulu Comm Coll (HI)
Howard Coll (TX)
Jackson State Comm Coll (TN)
Luna Comm Coll (NM)
Muskegon Comm Coll (MI)
Ouachita Tech Coll (AR)
San Diego City Coll (CA)
Volunteer State Comm Coll (TN)

Industrial Design
The Art Inst of Seattle (WA)
Kirtland Comm Coll (MI)
Orange Coast Coll (CA)

Industrial Electronics Technology
Bevill State Comm Coll (AL)
Central Carolina Tech Coll (SC)
Central Lakes Coll (MN)
Coll of DuPage (IL)
Danville Area Comm Coll (IL)
Des Moines Area Comm Coll (IA)
H. Councill Trenholm State Tech Coll (AL)
John Wood Comm Coll (IL)
Kirkwood Comm Coll (IA)
Lackawanna Coll (PA)
Lehigh Carbon Comm Coll (PA)
Louisiana Tech Coll (LA)
Lurleen B. Wallace Comm Coll (AL)
Midlands Tech Coll (SC)
Mitchell Tech Inst (SD)
Moraine Valley Comm Coll (IL)
New Mexico State U–Carlsbad (NM)
Northampton Comm Coll (PA)
North Iowa Area Comm Coll (IA)
Northland Comm and Tech Coll–Thief River Falls (MN)
Northwest-Shoals Comm Coll (AL)
Pasadena City Coll (CA)
Pennsylvania Coll of Technology (PA)
Pima Comm Coll (AZ)
Randolph Comm Coll (NC)
Sierra Coll (CA)
Southern Union State Comm Coll (AL)
Spartanburg Comm Coll (SC)
Sullivan Coll of Technology and Design (KY)
Thomas Nelson Comm Coll (VA)
Western Wyoming Comm Coll (WY)

Industrial Engineering
Catawba Valley Comm Coll (NC)
Central Lakes Coll (MN)
Clackamas Comm Coll (OR)
Manchester Comm Coll (CT)
Randolph Comm Coll (NC)

Industrial Mechanics and Maintenance Technology
Alexandria Tech Coll (MN)
Arkansas State U–Beebe (AR)
Casper Coll (WY)
Coll of Lake County (IL)
Danville Area Comm Coll (IL)
Delaware County Comm Coll (PA)
Des Moines Area Comm Coll (IA)
Gadsden State Comm Coll (AL)
Harrisburg Area Comm Coll (PA)
H. Councill Trenholm State Tech Coll (AL)
Illinois Eastern Comm Colls, Olney Central College (IL)
Ivy Tech Comm Coll–East Central (IN)
John Wood Comm Coll (IL)
Kaskaskia Coll (IL)
Kennebec Valley Comm Coll (ME)
Lower Columbia Coll (WA)
Macomb Comm Coll (MI)
Midlands Tech Coll (SC)
Moraine Park Tech Coll (WI)
North Central Texas Coll (TX)
Northeast Comm Coll (NE)
Northland Pioneer Coll (AZ)
Northwest-Shoals Comm Coll (AL)
Pennsylvania Coll of Technology (PA)
Rend Lake Coll (IL)
San Juan Coll (NM)
Somerset Comm Coll (KY)
Southern Union State Comm Coll (AL)
Southwestern Michigan Coll (MI)
Sullivan Coll of Technology and Design (KY)
Western Wyoming Comm Coll (WY)
Westmoreland County Comm Coll (PA)

Industrial Production Technologies Related
Barton County Comm Coll (KS)
Broome Comm Coll (NY)
Camden County Coll (NJ)
Essex County Coll (NJ)
Guilford Tech Comm Coll (NC)
Howard Coll (TX)
Ivy Tech Comm Coll–Central Indiana (IN)
Ivy Tech Comm Coll–East Central (IN)
Ivy Tech Comm Coll–Lafayette (IN)
Ivy Tech Comm Coll–North Central (IN)
Ivy Tech Comm Coll–Northeast (IN)
Ivy Tech Comm Coll–Richmond (IN)
Ivy Tech Comm Coll–Southwest (IN)
Ivy Tech Comm Coll–Wabash Valley (IN)
Louisiana Tech Coll (LA)
Mohawk Valley Comm Coll (NY)
Moraine Park Tech Coll (WI)
Mountain Empire Comm Coll (VA)
Pima Comm Coll (AZ)
Southwestern Michigan Coll (MI)

Industrial Radiologic Technology
Amarillo Coll (TX)
Anne Arundel Comm Coll (MD)
Bakersfield Coll (CA)
Carteret Comm Coll (NC)
Comm Coll of Philadelphia (PA)
Cowley County Comm Coll and Area Vocational–Tech School (KS)
Cuyahoga Comm Coll (OH)
Daytona State Coll (FL)
Del Mar Coll (TX)
Delta Coll (MI)
Gateway Comm Coll (CT)
Indian River State Coll (FL)
Kankakee Comm Coll (IL)
Middlesex Comm Coll (CT)
Odessa Coll (TX)
Orange Coast Coll (CA)
Palm Beach State Coll (FL)
Salt Lake Comm Coll (UT)
San Diego Mesa Coll (CA)
Southeastern Comm Coll (IA)
Southern Maine Comm Coll (ME)
South Plains Coll (TX)
Southwest Virginia Comm Coll (VA)
Tarrant County Coll District (TX)

Industrial Technology
Albany Tech Coll (GA)
Alexandria Tech Coll (MN)
Allen Comm Coll (KS)
Anne Arundel Comm Coll (MD)
Bakersfield Coll (CA)
Bladen Comm Coll (NC)
Bowling Green State U–Firelands Coll (OH)
Central Arizona Coll (AZ)
Central Comm Coll–Columbus Campus (NE)
Central Comm Coll–Grand Island Campus (NE)
Central Comm Coll–Hastings Campus (NE)
Central Georgia Tech Coll (GA)
Central Oregon Comm Coll (OR)
Central Piedmont Comm Coll (NC)
Chattanooga State Comm Coll (TN)
Clackamas Comm Coll (OR)
Cleveland State Comm Coll (TN)
Coll of DuPage (IL)
Columbus Tech Coll (GA)
Comm Coll of Allegheny County (PA)
The Comm Coll of Baltimore County (MD)
Comm Coll of Vermont (VT)
Corning Comm Coll (NY)
Crowder Coll (MO)
Cumberland County Coll (NJ)
Daytona State Coll (FL)
DeKalb Tech Coll (GA)
Edison State Comm Coll (OH)
Elaine P. Nunez Comm Coll (LA)
Erie Comm Coll, North Campus (NY)
Erie Comm Coll, South Campus (NY)
Fox Valley Tech Coll (WI)
Gateway Comm and Tech Coll (KY)
Gateway Comm Coll (CT)
Grand Rapids Comm Coll (MI)
Greenfield Comm Coll (MA)
Griffin Tech Coll (GA)
Highline Comm Coll (WA)
Hopkinsville Comm Coll (KY)
Illinois Eastern Comm Colls, Wabash Valley College (IL)
Illinois Valley Comm Coll (IL)
Ivy Tech Comm Coll–Bloomington (IN)
Ivy Tech Comm Coll–Central Indiana (IN)
Ivy Tech Comm Coll–Columbus (IN)
Ivy Tech Comm Coll–East Central (IN)
Ivy Tech Comm Coll–Kokomo (IN)

Ivy Tech Comm Coll–Lafayette (IN)
Ivy Tech Comm Coll–North Central (IN)
Ivy Tech Comm Coll–Northeast (IN)
Ivy Tech Comm Coll–Northwest (IN)
Ivy Tech Comm Coll–Richmond (IN)
Ivy Tech Comm Coll–Southeast (IN)
Ivy Tech Comm Coll–Southern Indiana (IN)
Ivy Tech Comm Coll–Southwest (IN)
Ivy Tech Comm Coll–Wabash Valley (IN)
Jackson State Comm Coll (TN)
J. Sargeant Reynolds Comm Coll (VA)
Kellogg Comm Coll (MI)
Kent State U at Ashtabula (OH)
Kent State U at Geauga (OH)
Kent State U at Salem (OH)
Kent State U at Trumbull (OH)
Kent State U at Tuscarawas (OH)
Kirtland Comm Coll (MI)
Lackawanna Coll (PA)
Lake Michigan Coll (MI)
Lanier Tech Coll (GA)
Lansing Comm Coll (MI)
Linn-Benton Comm Coll (OR)
Lonestar Coll–Cy-Fair (TX)
Macomb Comm Coll (MI)
Manchester Comm Coll (CT)
Marion Tech Coll (OH)
Miami Dade Coll (FL)
Milwaukee Area Tech Coll (WI)
Minnesota State Coll–Southeast Tech (MN)
Missouri State U–West Plains (MO)
Montcalm Comm Coll (MI)
Moraine Park Tech Coll (WI)
Mountain Empire Comm Coll (VA)
Muskegon Comm Coll (MI)
North Georgia Tech Coll (GA)
Northland Pioneer Coll (AZ)
Northwest Tech Coll (MN)
Oakland Comm Coll (MI)
The Ohio State U Ag Tech Inst (OH)
Olympic Coll (WA)
Ouachita Tech Coll (AR)
Owens Comm Coll, Toledo (OH)
Panola Coll (TX)
Patrick Henry Comm Coll (VA)
Penn State York (PA)
Pennsylvania Highlands Comm Coll (PA)
Piedmont Comm Coll (NC)
Pima Comm Coll (AZ)
Pulaski Tech Coll (AR)
Randolph Comm Coll (NC)
Rogue Comm Coll (OR)
Saint Charles Comm Coll (MO)
Saint Paul Coll–A Comm & Tech College (MN)
San Diego City Coll (CA)
San Juan Coll (NM)
Savannah Tech Coll (GA)
Seminole State Coll of Florida (FL)
Southeast Tech Inst (SD)
South Georgia Tech Coll (GA)
Southwest Virginia Comm Coll (VA)
Stanly Comm Coll (NC)
Stark State Coll of Technology (OH)
Thomas Nelson Comm Coll (VA)
Three Rivers Comm Coll (CT)
Three Rivers Comm Coll (MO)
Trident Tech Coll (SC)
Victoria Coll (TX)
Vincennes U Jasper Campus (IN)
West Georgia Tech Coll (GA)
Wilson Comm Coll (NC)

Information Science/ Studies

Alamance Comm Coll (NC)
Allan Hancock Coll (CA)
Allen Comm Coll (KS)
Alpena Comm Coll (MI)
Altamaha Tech Coll (GA)
Amarillo Coll (TX)
Anne Arundel Comm Coll (MD)
Arizona Western Coll (AZ)
Arkansas State U–Mountain Home (AR)
Athens Tech Coll (GA)
Augusta Tech Coll (GA)
Bainbridge Coll (GA)
Bakersfield Coll (CA)
Barton County Comm Coll (KS)
Beaufort County Comm Coll (NC)
Blue Ridge Comm Coll (NC)
Broome Comm Coll (NY)
Bucks County Comm Coll (PA)
Cecil Coll (MD)
Central Carolina Comm Coll (NC)
Central Georgia Tech Coll (GA)
Central New Mexico Comm Coll (NM)
Chattahoochee Tech Coll (GA)
Cincinnati State Tech and Comm Coll (OH)
Columbus Tech Coll (GA)
Cuyamaca Coll (CA)
Dabney S. Lancaster Comm Coll (VA)
Dakota Coll at Bottineau (ND)
DeKalb Tech Coll (GA)
Del Mar Coll (TX)
East Central Tech Coll (GA)
Eastern Arizona Coll (AZ)
Elaine P. Nunez Comm Coll (LA)
El Centro Coll (TX)
Essex County Coll (NJ)
Fayetteville Tech Comm Coll (NC)
Fiorello H. LaGuardia Comm Coll of the City U of New York (NY)
Flint River Tech Coll (GA)
Fulton-Montgomery Comm Coll (NY)
Genesee Comm Coll (NY)
Georgia Highlands Coll (GA)
Georgia Northwestern Tech Coll (GA)
Greenfield Comm Coll (MA)
Guilford Tech Comm Coll (NC)
Gwinnett Tech Coll (GA)
Howard Comm Coll (MD)
Indian River State Coll (FL)
J. F. Drake State Tech Coll (AL)
Kankakee Comm Coll (IL)
Kaplan U, Hagerstown Campus (MD)
Kirtland Comm Coll (MI)
Lanier Tech Coll (GA)
Lansing Comm Coll (MI)
Lawson State Comm Coll (AL)
Lehigh Carbon Comm Coll (PA)
Lonestar Coll–Kingwood (TX)
Lonestar Coll–North Harris (TX)
Los Angeles Harbor Coll (CA)
Manchester Comm Coll (CT)
Mendocino Coll (CA)
Metropolitan Comm Coll–Blue River (MO)
Metropolitan Comm Coll–Business & Technology Campus (MO)
Miami Dade Coll (FL)
Middle Georgia Coll (GA)
Middle Georgia Tech Coll (GA)
Mitchell Tech Inst (SD)
Montgomery County Comm Coll (PA)
Moultrie Tech Coll (GA)
Murray State Coll (OK)
Muskegon Comm Coll (MI)
Niagara County Comm Coll (NY)
North Central Texas Coll (TX)
North Lake Coll (TX)
Northland Pioneer Coll (AZ)
Northwestern Connecticut Comm Coll (CT)
Northwest-Shoals Comm Coll (AL)
Ocean County Coll (NJ)
Odessa Coll (TX)
Ogeechee Tech Coll (GA)
Okefenokee Tech Coll (GA)
Oklahoma State U, Oklahoma City (OK)
Olympic Coll (WA)
Orange Coast Coll (CA)
Panola Coll (TX)
Paris Jr Coll (TX)
Penn State DuBois (PA)
Penn State Hazleton (PA)
Penn State Lehigh Valley (PA)
Penn State New Kensington (PA)
Penn State Schuylkill (PA)
Phoenix Coll (AZ)
Polk State Coll (FL)
Quinsigamond Comm Coll (MA)
Rappahannock Comm Coll (VA)
Reedley Coll (CA)
Rio Salado Coll (AZ)
Salt Lake Comm Coll (UT)
Sandersville Tech Coll (GA)
Sandhills Comm Coll (NC)
San Juan Coll (NM)
Scottsdale Comm Coll (AZ)
Seminole State Coll of Florida (FL)
Shawnee Comm Coll (IL)
Sheridan Coll (WY)
Sisseton-Wahpeton Comm Coll (SD)
Snow Coll (UT)
Southeastern Comm Coll (IA)
Southeastern Tech Coll (GA)
Southern Alberta Inst of Technology (AB, Canada)
Southern Maine Comm Coll (ME)
South Georgia Coll (GA)
South Georgia Tech Coll (GA)
South Puget Sound Comm Coll (WA)
Southside Virginia Comm Coll (VA)
Southwest Georgia Tech Coll (GA)
Southwest Virginia Comm Coll (VA)
Stanly Comm Coll (NC)
State Coll of Florida Manatee-Sarasota (FL)
Suffolk County Comm Coll (NY)
Tompkins Cortland Comm Coll (NY)
Triton Coll (IL)
Tunxis Comm Coll (CT)
Union County Coll (NJ)
Victoria Coll (TX)
Victor Valley Coll (CA)
Westchester Comm Coll (NY)
Western Wyoming Comm Coll (WY)
West Georgia Tech Coll (GA)
Wilson Comm Coll (NC)
Yavapai Coll (AZ)

Information Technology

Antonelli Coll, Hattiesburg (MS)
Arkansas State U–Beebe (AR)
Atlanta Tech Coll (GA)
Bladen Comm Coll (NC)
Blue Ridge Comm and Tech Coll (WV)
Blue Ridge Comm Coll (NC)
Brown Mackie Coll–Akron (OH)
Brown Mackie Coll–Albuquerque (NM)
Brown Mackie Coll–Boise (ID)
Brown Mackie Coll–Cincinnati (OH)
Brown Mackie Coll–Greenville (SC)
Brown Mackie Coll–Miami (FL)
Brown Mackie Coll–Northern Kentucky (KY)
Brown Mackie Coll–Phoenix (AZ)
Brown Mackie Coll–St. Louis (MO)
Brown Mackie Coll–South Bend (IN)
Brown Mackie Coll–Tucson (AZ)
Brown Mackie Coll–Tulsa (OK)
Bryant & Stratton Coll, Eastlake (OH)
Bryant & Stratton Coll, Parma (OH)
Bryant & Stratton Coll - Albany Campus (NY)
Bryant & Stratton Coll - Amherst Campus (NY)
Bryant & Stratton Coll - Buffalo Campus (NY)
Bryant & Stratton Coll - Greece Campus (NY)
Bryant & Stratton Coll - Henrietta Campus (NY)
Bryant & Stratton Coll - North Campus (NY)
Bryant & Stratton Coll - Southtowns Campus (NY)
Bryant & Stratton Coll - Syracuse Campus (NY)
Bucks County Comm Coll (PA)
Burlington County Coll (NJ)
Carteret Comm Coll (NC)
Casper Coll (WY)
Catawba Valley Comm Coll (NC)
Cecil Coll (MD)
Central Carolina Comm Coll (NC)
Central Comm Coll–Columbus Campus (NE)
Central Comm Coll–Grand Island Campus (NE)
Central Comm Coll–Hastings Campus (NE)
Coll of Southern Maryland (MD)
Comm Coll of Vermont (VT)
Corning Comm Coll (NY)
Dakota Coll at Bottineau (ND)
Davis Coll (OH)
Daytona State Coll (FL)
Del Mar Coll (TX)
Delta Coll (MI)
Des Moines Area Comm Coll (IA)
Edison State Comm Coll (OH)
Erie Comm Coll (NY)
Erie Comm Coll, North Campus (NY)
Erie Comm Coll, South Campus (NY)
Everett Comm Coll (WA)
Fayetteville Tech Comm Coll (NC)
Frederick Comm Coll (MD)
Gateway Comm and Tech Coll (KY)
Georgia Military Coll (GA)
Germanna Comm Coll (VA)
Guilford Tech Comm Coll (NC)
Harrisburg Area Comm Coll (PA)
Harrison Coll, Evansville (IN)
Harrison Coll, Fort Wayne (IN)
Harrison Coll, Indianapolis (IN)
Harrison Coll, Muncie (IN)
Harrison Coll, Terre Haute (IN)
Highland Comm Coll (IL)
Howard Comm Coll (MD)
Illinois Valley Comm Coll (IL)
Iowa Lakes Comm Coll (IA)
ITI Tech Coll (LA)
Jamestown Comm Coll (NY)
Kent State U at Geauga (OH)
Kilian Comm Coll (SD)
Lake Region State Coll (ND)
Laramie County Comm Coll (WY)
LDS Business Coll (UT)
Lonestar Coll–Cy-Fair (TX)
Lonestar Coll–Montgomery (TX)
Marion Tech Coll (OH)
Mesabi Range Comm and Tech Coll (MN)
Metropolitan Comm Coll–Business & Technology Campus (MO)
Missouri State U–West Plains (MO)
Mohave Comm Coll (AZ)
Montana State U–Great Falls Coll of Technology (MT)
Mt. San Jacinto Coll (CA)
Northland Comm and Tech Coll–Thief River Falls (MN)
Northwest Florida State Coll (FL)
Oakland Comm Coll (MI)
Oklahoma State U, Oklahoma City (OK)
Olympic Coll (WA)
Owensboro Comm and Tech Coll (KY)
Owens Comm Coll, Toledo (OH)
Pasco-Hernando Comm Coll (FL)
Patrick Henry Comm Coll (VA)
Pennsylvania Coll of Technology (PA)
Piedmont Comm Coll (NC)
Potomac State Coll of West Virginia U (WV)
Randolph Comm Coll (NC)
Raritan Valley Comm Coll (NJ)
Rio Salado Coll (AZ)
Salt Lake Comm Coll (UT)
Savannah Tech Coll (GA)
Seminole State Coll of Florida (FL)
Sierra Coll (CA)
Southeast Kentucky Comm and Tech Coll (KY)
Southside Virginia Comm Coll (VA)
South Suburban Coll (IL)
Southwest Mississippi Comm Coll (MS)
Stark State Coll of Technology (OH)
Suffolk County Comm Coll (NY)
Sullivan Coll of Technology and Design (KY)
Three Rivers Comm Coll (MO)
Tidewater Comm Coll (VA)
Tri-County Comm Coll (NC)
Western Wyoming Comm Coll (WY)
West Shore Comm Coll (MI)
Westwood Coll–Houston South Campus (TX)

Institutional Food Workers

El Paso Comm Coll (TX)
Iowa Lakes Comm Coll (IA)
Pennsylvania Coll of Technology (PA)
San Jacinto Coll District (TX)

Instrumentation Technology

Amarillo Coll (TX)
Cape Fear Comm Coll (NC)
Central Carolina Comm Coll (NC)
The Comm Coll of Baltimore County (MD)
DeKalb Tech Coll (GA)
Houston Comm Coll System (TX)
ITI Tech Coll (LA)
Lakeland Comm Coll (OH)
Louisiana Tech Coll (LA)
Lower Columbia Coll (WA)
Mesabi Range Comm and Tech Coll (MN)
Moraine Valley Comm Coll (IL)
Nassau Comm Coll (NY)
Orangeburg-Calhoun Tech Coll (SC)
Pennsylvania Coll of Technology (PA)
St. Cloud Tech Coll (MN)
Salt Lake Comm Coll (UT)
San Jacinto Coll District (TX)
San Juan Coll (NM)
Southwestern Indian Polytechnic Inst (NM)
Spartan Coll of Aeronautics and Technology (OK)
Western Wyoming Comm Coll (WY)

Insurance

Central Piedmont Comm Coll (NC)
Comm Coll of Allegheny County (PA)
Davis Coll (OH)
Fox Valley Tech Coll (WI)
Nassau Comm Coll (NY)
Oklahoma City Comm Coll (OK)
San Diego City Coll (CA)
Trinity Valley Comm Coll (TX)

Intercultural/ Multicultural and Diversity Studies

Triton Coll (IL)

Interdisciplinary Studies

Bowling Green State U–Firelands Coll (OH)
Central Texas Coll (TX)
Del Mar Coll (TX)
Folsom Lake Coll (CA)
Kaplan U, Cedar Rapids (IA)
Kaplan U, Lincoln (NE)
Kaplan U, Omaha (NE)
Lonestar Coll–Cy-Fair (TX)
Lonestar Coll–Kingwood (TX)
Lonestar Coll–Montgomery (TX)
Lonestar Coll–North Harris (TX)
Lonestar Coll–Tomball (TX)
Milwaukee Area Tech Coll (WI)
Walters State Comm Coll (TN)

Interior Design

Alexandria Tech Coll (MN)
Allan Hancock Coll (CA)
Amarillo Coll (TX)
Antelope Valley Coll (CA)
Antonelli Coll, Hattiesburg (MS)
Antonelli Coll, Jackson (MS)
Antonelli Coll (OH)
The Art Inst of New York City (NY)
The Art Inst of Ohio–Cincinnati (OH)
The Art Inst of Seattle (WA)
The Art Inst of York–Pennsylvania (PA)
Bakersfield Coll (CA)
Black Hawk Coll, Moline (IL)
Cape Fear Comm Coll (NC)
Carteret Comm Coll (NC)
Central Piedmont Comm Coll (NC)
Century Coll (MN)
Coll of DuPage (IL)
Coll of the Canyons (CA)
Collin County Comm Coll District (TX)
Davis Coll (OH)
Daytona State Coll (FL)
Delaware Tech & Comm Coll, Terry Campus (DE)
Delta Coll (MI)
El Centro Coll (TX)
El Paso Comm Coll (TX)

Fashion Inst of Technology (NY)
FIDM/The Fashion Inst of Design & Merchandising, Los Angeles Campus (CA)
FIDM/The Fashion Inst of Design & Merchandising, San Diego Campus (CA)
FIDM/The Fashion Inst of Design & Merchandising, San Francisco Campus (CA)
Fox Valley Tech Coll (WI)
Front Range Comm Coll (CO)
Glendale Comm Coll (AZ)
Gwinnett Tech Coll (GA)
Harcum Coll (PA)
Harford Comm Coll (MD)
Hawkeye Comm Coll (IA)
Hesser Coll, Manchester (NH)
Highline Comm Coll (WA)
Houston Comm Coll System (TX)
Indian River State Coll (FL)
Ivy Tech Comm Coll–North Central (IN)
Ivy Tech Comm Coll–Southwest (IN)
Kaplan Coll, Sacramento Campus (CA)
Lanier Tech Coll (GA)
LDS Business Coll (UT)
Lehigh Carbon Comm Coll (PA)
Lonestar Coll–Kingwood (TX)
Metropolitan Comm Coll (NE)
Miami Dade Coll (FL)
Milwaukee Area Tech Coll (WI)
Montana State U–Great Falls Coll of Technology (MT)
Montgomery Coll (MD)
Nassau Comm Coll (NY)
Northampton Comm Coll (PA)
Northwest Florida State Coll (FL)
Oakland Comm Coll (MI)
Ogeechee Tech Coll (GA)
Orange Coast Coll (CA)
Palm Beach State Coll (FL)
Phoenix Coll (AZ)
Pikes Peak Comm Coll (CO)
Randolph Comm Coll (NC)
Raritan Valley Comm Coll (NJ)
San Diego City Coll (CA)
San Diego Mesa Coll (CA)
San Jacinto Coll District (TX)
Santa Rosa Jr Coll (CA)
Scottsdale Comm Coll (AZ)
Seminole State Coll of Florida (FL)
State U of New York Coll of Technology at Alfred (NY)
Suffolk County Comm Coll (NY)
Sullivan Coll of Technology and Design (KY)
Tidewater Comm Coll (VA)
Virginia Marti Coll of Art and Design (OH)
Wade Coll (TX)
Waukesha County Tech Coll (WI)

Intermedia/Multimedia
Coll of the Canyons (CA)
Middlesex Comm Coll (CT)
San Diego Mesa Coll (CA)

International Business/Trade/Commerce
Austin Comm Coll (TX)
Bunker Hill Comm Coll (MA)
Central New Mexico Comm Coll (NM)
Cincinnati State Tech and Comm Coll (OH)
Comm Coll of Philadelphia (PA)
El Paso Comm Coll (TX)
Frederick Comm Coll (MD)
Harcum Coll (PA)
Highline Comm Coll (WA)
Houston Comm Coll System (TX)
Lansing Comm Coll (MI)
Northeast Comm Coll (NE)
Oakland Comm Coll (MI)
Paradise Valley Comm Coll (AZ)
Pasadena City Coll (CA)
Raritan Valley Comm Coll (NJ)
San Jacinto Coll District (TX)
Stark State Coll of Technology (OH)
Tompkins Cortland Comm Coll (NY)
Triton Coll (IL)
Westchester Comm Coll (NY)

International Finance
Broome Comm Coll (NY)

International/Global Studies
Berkshire Comm Coll (MA)
Burlington County Coll (NJ)
Central Wyoming Coll (WY)
Century Coll (MN)
Everett Comm Coll (WA)
Kalamazoo Valley Comm Coll (MI)
Macomb Comm Coll (MI)
Pasadena City Coll (CA)
Salt Lake Comm Coll (UT)

International Marketing
Saint Paul Coll–A Comm & Tech College (MN)

International Relations and Affairs
Allan Hancock Coll (CA)
Bronx Comm Coll of the City U of New York (NY)
Casper Coll (WY)
Georgia Military Coll (GA)
Harrisburg Area Comm Coll (PA)
Miami Dade Coll (FL)
Pasadena City Coll (CA)
Salt Lake Comm Coll (UT)
Western Wyoming Comm Coll (WY)

Ironworking
Ivy Tech Comm Coll–Lafayette (IN)
Ivy Tech Comm Coll–North Central (IN)
Ivy Tech Comm Coll–Northeast (IN)
Ivy Tech Comm Coll–Northwest (IN)
Ivy Tech Comm Coll–Southwest (IN)
Ivy Tech Comm Coll–Wabash Valley (IN)

Italian
Miami Dade Coll (FL)
Triton Coll (IL)

Japanese
Austin Comm Coll (TX)
East Los Angeles Coll (CA)
Hawaii Tokai International Coll (HI)
Snow Coll (UT)

Japanese Studies
Hawaii Tokai International Coll (HI)

Jazz/Jazz Studies
Comm Coll of Rhode Island (RI)
Iowa Lakes Comm Coll (IA)
State Coll of Florida Manatee-Sarasota (FL)

Jewish/Judaic Studies
State Coll of Florida Manatee-Sarasota (FL)

Journalism
Allen Comm Coll (KS)
Amarillo Coll (TX)
Bainbridge Coll (GA)
Bakersfield Coll (CA)
Barton County Comm Coll (KS)
Bucks County Comm Coll (PA)
Burlington County Coll (NJ)
Central Texas Coll (TX)
Coll of the Canyons (CA)
Comm Coll of Allegheny County (PA)
Cowley County Comm Coll and Area Vocational–Tech School (KS)
Darton Coll (GA)
Delaware County Comm Coll (PA)
Del Mar Coll (TX)
East Los Angeles Coll (CA)
Everett Comm Coll (WA)
Gainesville State Coll (GA)
Georgia Highlands Coll (GA)
Golden West Coll (CA)
Highline Comm Coll (WA)
Housatonic Comm Coll (CT)
Illinois Valley Comm Coll (IL)
Indian River State Coll (FL)
Iowa Lakes Comm Coll (IA)
Kilgore Coll (TX)
Kingsborough Comm Coll of the City U of New York (NY)
Lansing Comm Coll (MI)
Lonestar Coll–North Harris (TX)
Manchester Comm Coll (CT)
Miami Dade Coll (FL)
Northampton Comm Coll (PA)
Northeast Comm Coll (NE)
Northeastern Jr Coll (CO)
North Idaho Coll (ID)
Northwest Coll (WY)
Ocean County Coll (NJ)
Orange Coast Coll (CA)
Palm Beach State Coll (FL)
Paradise Valley Comm Coll (AZ)
Pasadena City Coll (CA)
Potomac State Coll of West Virginia U (WV)
San Diego City Coll (CA)
San Jacinto Coll District (TX)
South Georgia Coll (GA)
South Plains Coll (TX)
State Coll of Florida Manatee-Sarasota (FL)
Suffolk County Comm Coll (NY)
Trinity Valley Comm Coll (TX)
Umpqua Comm Coll (OR)
Western Wyoming Comm Coll (WY)

Juvenile Corrections
Danville Area Comm Coll (IL)
Illinois Valley Comm Coll (IL)
Kaskaskia Coll (IL)
Linn-Benton Comm Coll (OR)
KINDERGARTEN/PRESCHOOL EDUCATION
Kindergarten/Preschool Education
Alamance Comm Coll (NC)
Allan Hancock Coll (CA)
Anne Arundel Comm Coll (MD)
Bainbridge Coll (GA)
Beaufort County Comm Coll (NC)
Bowling Green State U–Firelands Coll (OH)
Bucks County Comm Coll (PA)
Carroll Comm Coll (MD)
Casper Coll (WY)
Cecil Coll (MD)
Central Arizona Coll (AZ)
Central Carolina Comm Coll (NC)
Central Lakes Coll (MN)
Central Ohio Tech Coll (OH)
Central Piedmont Comm Coll (NC)
Cleveland State Comm Coll (TN)
Collin County Comm Coll District (TX)
Comm Coll of Philadelphia (PA)
Comm Coll of Rhode Island (RI)
County Coll of Morris (NJ)
Cuyahoga Comm Coll (OH)
Daytona State Coll (FL)
Delaware Tech & Comm Coll, Jack F. Owens Campus (DE)
Delaware Tech & Comm Coll, Stanton/Wilmington Campus (DE)
Delaware Tech & Comm Coll, Terry Campus (DE)
Del Mar Coll (TX)
Denmark Tech Coll (SC)
Edison State Comm Coll (OH)
Elaine P. Nunez Comm Coll (LA)
El Paso Comm Coll (TX)
Essex County Coll (NJ)
Finger Lakes Comm Coll (NY)
Frederick Comm Coll (MD)
Fulton-Montgomery Comm Coll (NY)
Gateway Comm Coll (CT)
Genesee Comm Coll (NY)
Georgia Highlands Coll (GA)
Georgia Military Coll (GA)
Greenfield Comm Coll (MA)
Highland Comm Coll (IL)
Highline Comm Coll (WA)
Honolulu Comm Coll (HI)
Howard Comm Coll (MD)
Indian River State Coll (FL)
Iowa Lakes Comm Coll (IA)
James Sprunt Comm Coll (NC)
Johnston Comm Coll (NC)
Kauai Comm Coll (HI)
Kent State U at Ashtabula (OH)
Lansing Comm Coll (MI)
Luna Comm Coll (NM)
Manchester Comm Coll (CT)
Mendocino Coll (CA)
Metropolitan Comm Coll (NE)
Metropolitan Comm Coll–Penn Valley (MO)
Miami Dade Coll (FL)
Minnesota State Coll–Southeast Tech (MN)
Minnesota State Comm and Tech Coll (MN)
Nassau Comm Coll (NY)
Nicolet Area Tech Coll (WI)
Northeastern Jr Coll (CO)
Northland Pioneer Coll (AZ)
Northwest Coll (WY)
Northwestern Connecticut Comm Coll (CT)
Northwest Florida State Coll (FL)
Odessa Coll (TX)
Orangeburg-Calhoun Tech Coll (SC)
Orange Coast Coll (CA)
Otero Jr Coll (CO)
Owensboro Comm and Tech Coll (KY)
Palm Beach State Coll (FL)
Potomac State Coll of West Virginia U (WV)
Quinsigamond Comm Coll (MA)
Raritan Valley Comm Coll (NJ)
Red Rocks Comm Coll (CO)
Sandhills Comm Coll (NC)
San Juan Coll (NM)
Scottsdale Comm Coll (AZ)
Sisseton-Wahpeton Comm Coll (SD)
Snow Coll (UT)
Southern Maine Comm Coll (ME)
Southern State Comm Coll (OH)
South Georgia Coll (GA)
South Puget Sound Comm Coll (WA)
State Coll of Florida Manatee-Sarasota (FL)
Suffolk County Comm Coll (NY)
Tallahassee Comm Coll (FL)
Terra State Comm Coll (OH)
Thomas Nelson Comm Coll (VA)
Three Rivers Comm Coll (CT)
Tidewater Comm Coll (VA)
Tompkins Cortland Comm Coll (NY)
Trinity Valley Comm Coll (TX)
Tunxis Comm Coll (CT)
Ulster County Comm Coll (NY)
Umpqua Comm Coll (OR)
U of Cincinnati Clermont Coll (OH)
Victor Valley Coll (CA)
White Mountains Comm Coll (NH)
Wilson Comm Coll (NC)
York County Comm Coll (ME)

Kinesiology and Exercise Science
Barton County Comm Coll (KS)
Carroll Comm Coll (MD)
Central Oregon Comm Coll (OR)
Clarendon Coll (TX)
County Coll of Morris (NJ)
Delaware Tech & Comm Coll, Stanton/Wilmington Campus (DE)
Elgin Comm Coll (IL)
Gainesville State Coll (GA)
Glendale Comm Coll (AZ)
Lewis and Clark Comm Coll (IL)
Lonestar Coll–Cy-Fair (TX)
Lonestar Coll–Kingwood (TX)
Lonestar Coll–Montgomery (TX)
Lonestar Coll–North Harris (TX)
Lonestar Coll–Tomball (TX)
North Lake Coll (TX)
Oakland Comm Coll (MI)
Orange Coast Coll (CA)
Paradise Valley Comm Coll (AZ)
Raritan Valley Comm Coll (NJ)
St. Philip's Coll (TX)
Salt Lake Comm Coll (UT)
South Georgia Coll (GA)
South Suburban Coll (IL)
Western Wyoming Comm Coll (WY)

Labor and Industrial Relations
The Comm Coll of Baltimore County (MD)
Kingsborough Comm Coll of the City U of New York (NY)
Lansing Comm Coll (MI)
San Diego City Coll (CA)

Landscape Architecture
Anne Arundel Comm Coll (MD)
Lansing Comm Coll (MI)
Oakland Comm Coll (MI)
San Diego Mesa Coll (CA)
Santa Rosa Jr Coll (CA)

Landscaping and Groundskeeping
Cape Fear Comm Coll (NC)
Century Coll (MN)
Cincinnati State Tech and Comm Coll (OH)
Clackamas Comm Coll (OR)
Clark Coll (WA)
Coll of DuPage (IL)
Coll of Lake County (IL)
Coll of the Canyons (CA)
Comm Coll of Allegheny County (PA)
Cuyamaca Coll (CA)
Dakota Coll at Bottineau (ND)
Danville Area Comm Coll (IL)
Harrisburg Area Comm Coll (PA)
Hillsborough Comm Coll (FL)
Illinois Valley Comm Coll (IL)
Iowa Lakes Comm Coll (IA)
Johnston Comm Coll (NC)
Kirkwood Comm Coll (IA)
Lincoln Land Comm Coll (IL)
Miami Dade Coll (FL)
Milwaukee Area Tech Coll (WI)
Northwest Tech Coll (MN)
Oakland Comm Coll (MI)
The Ohio State U Ag Tech Inst (OH)
Owens Comm Coll, Toledo (OH)
Pennsylvania Coll of Technology (PA)
Pensacola Jr Coll (FL)
Sandhills Comm Coll (NC)
Southern Maine Comm Coll (ME)
Springfield Tech Comm Coll (MA)

Land Use Planning and Management
Lonestar Coll–Montgomery (TX)
Southwest Virginia Comm Coll (VA)

Language Interpretation and Translation
Allen Comm Coll (KS)
Century Coll (MN)
Des Moines Area Comm Coll (IA)
Fayetteville Tech Comm Coll (NC)
Indian River State Coll (FL)
Lonestar Coll–Cy-Fair (TX)
Lonestar Coll–North Harris (TX)
Oklahoma State U, Oklahoma City (OK)
Pima Comm Coll (AZ)
Terra State Comm Coll (OH)
Union County Coll (NJ)
Wilson Comm Coll (NC)

Laser and Optical Technology
Amarillo Coll (TX)
Camden County Coll (NJ)
Central Carolina Comm Coll (NC)
Central New Mexico Comm Coll (NM)
Cincinnati State Tech and Comm Coll (OH)
Pennsylvania Coll of Technology (PA)
Springfield Tech Comm Coll (MA)
Three Rivers Comm Coll (CT)

Latin
Austin Comm Coll (TX)

Latin American Studies
Miami Dade Coll (FL)
Pasadena City Coll (CA)
San Diego City Coll (CA)
Santa Rosa Jr Coll (CA)
State Coll of Florida Manatee-Sarasota (FL)

Legal Administrative Assistant/Secretary
Alamance Comm Coll (NC)
Alexandria Tech Coll (MN)
Allan Hancock Coll (CA)
Alvin Comm Coll (TX)
Amarillo Coll (TX)
Antonelli Coll, Hattiesburg (MS)
Bakersfield Coll (CA)
Black Hawk Coll, Moline (IL)
Bradford School (OH)
Bradford School (PA)
Bryant & Stratton Coll, Parma (OH)
Bryant & Stratton Coll - Richmond Campus (VA)
Carteret Comm Coll (NC)
Central Arizona Coll (AZ)

Central Carolina Comm Coll (NC)
Central Lakes Coll (MN)
Central Piedmont Comm Coll (NC)
Chattanooga State Comm Coll (TN)
Clark Coll (WA)
Clovis Comm Coll (NM)
Coll of DuPage (IL)
Comm Coll of Allegheny County (PA)
Comm Coll of Rhode Island (RI)
Consolidated School of Business, Lancaster (PA)
Cowley County Comm Coll and Area Vocational–Tech School (KS)
Crowder Coll (MO)
Dabney S. Lancaster Comm Coll (VA)
DeKalb Tech Coll (GA)
Delaware Tech & Comm Coll, Jack F. Owens Campus (DE)
Delaware Tech & Comm Coll, Terry Campus (DE)
Del Mar Coll (TX)
Delta Coll (MI)
East Central Coll (MO)
Eastfield Coll (TX)
East Los Angeles Coll (CA)
Edison State Comm Coll (OH)
El Centro Coll (TX)
Elgin Comm Coll (IL)
Fiorello H. LaGuardia Comm Coll of the City U of New York (NY)
Forrest Jr Coll (SC)
Fox Valley Tech Coll (WI)
Frederick Comm Coll (MD)
Fulton-Montgomery Comm Coll (NY)
Gateway Comm Coll (CT)
Golden West Coll (CA)
Grand Rapids Comm Coll (MI)
Green River Comm Coll (WA)
Hennepin Tech Coll (MN)
Highline Comm Coll (WA)
Howard Comm Coll (MD)
Inst of Business & Medical Careers (CO)
International Business Coll, Indianapolis (IN)
Inver Hills Comm Coll (MN)
Iowa Lakes Comm Coll (IA)
Jamestown Business Coll (NY)
John Wood Comm Coll (IL)
Kaplan Career Inst, ICM Campus (PA)
Kaplan Coll, Merrillville Campus (IN)
Kaplan U, Hagerstown Campus (MD)
Kellogg Comm Coll (MI)
Kennebec Valley Comm Coll (ME)
Kent State U at Ashtabula (OH)
Kent State U at East Liverpool (OH)
Kirtland Comm Coll (MI)
Lake Michigan Coll (MI)
Lake Region State Coll (ND)
Lansing Comm Coll (MI)
Lawson State Comm Coll (AL)
LDS Business Coll (UT)
Lehigh Carbon Comm Coll (PA)
Lewis and Clark Comm Coll (IL)
Lincoln Land Comm Coll (IL)
Linn-Benton Comm Coll (OR)
Lonestar Coll–North Harris (TX)
Los Angeles Harbor Coll (CA)
Lower Columbia Coll (WA)
Manchester Comm Coll (CT)
Metropolitan Comm Coll (NE)
Metropolitan Comm Coll–Longview (MO)
Metropolitan Comm Coll–Maple Woods (MO)
Metropolitan Comm Coll–Penn Valley (MO)
Miami Dade Coll (FL)
Middlesex Comm Coll (CT)
Milwaukee Area Tech Coll (WI)
Minneapolis Business Coll (MN)
Minnesota State Coll–Southeast Tech (MN)
Minnesota State Comm and Tech Coll (MN)
Moraine Park Tech Coll (WI)
Muskegon Comm Coll (MI)
Nassau Comm Coll (NY)
Newport Business Inst, Williamsport (PA)
Northampton Comm Coll (PA)
North Central Texas Coll (TX)
Northeast Comm Coll (NE)
Northeastern Jr Coll (CO)
North Idaho Coll (ID)
North Lake Coll (TX)
Northland Comm and Tech Coll–Thief River Falls (MN)
Northland Pioneer Coll (AZ)
Odessa Coll (TX)
Olympic Coll (WA)
Orange Coast Coll (CA)
Otero Jr Coll (CO)
Ouachita Tech Coll (AR)
Palm Beach State Coll (FL)
Phoenix Coll (AZ)
St. Cloud Tech Coll (MN)
St. Philip's Coll (TX)
San Diego City Coll (CA)
San Diego Mesa Coll (CA)
Shawnee Comm Coll (IL)
South Plains Coll (TX)
South Puget Sound Comm Coll (WA)
Southwest Mississippi Comm Coll (MS)
Stanly Comm Coll (NC)
Stark State Coll of Technology (OH)
Tallahassee Comm Coll (FL)
Three Rivers Comm Coll (CT)
Trinity Valley Comm Coll (TX)
Tunxis Comm Coll (CT)
Umpqua Comm Coll (OR)
The U of Montana–Helena Coll of Technology (MT)
Vincennes U Jasper Campus (IN)
Western Wyoming Comm Coll (WY)
Yavapai Coll (AZ)

Legal Assistant/ Paralegal

Alexandria Tech Coll (MN)
Allegany Coll of Maryland (MD)
Alvin Comm Coll (TX)
Anne Arundel Comm Coll (MD)
Antonelli Coll, Jackson (MS)
Athens Tech Coll (GA)
Atlanta Tech Coll (GA)
Austin Comm Coll (TX)
Bevill State Comm Coll (AL)
Black Hawk Coll, Moline (IL)
Blue Ridge Comm and Tech Coll (WV)
Bradford School (OH)
Bradford School (PA)
Bronx Comm Coll of the City U of New York (NY)
Broome Comm Coll (NY)
Brown Mackie Coll–Akron (OH)
Brown Mackie Coll–Albuquerque (NM)
Brown Mackie Coll–Atlanta (GA)
Brown Mackie Coll–Boise (ID)
Brown Mackie Coll–Cincinnati (OH)
Brown Mackie Coll–Findlay (OH)
Brown Mackie Coll–Fort Wayne (IN)
Brown Mackie Coll–Greenville (SC)
Brown Mackie Coll–Hopkinsville (KY)
Brown Mackie Coll–Indianapolis (IN)
Brown Mackie Coll–Kansas City (KS)
Brown Mackie Coll–Louisville (KY)
Brown Mackie Coll–Merrillville (IN)
Brown Mackie Coll–Miami (FL)
Brown Mackie Coll–Michigan City (IN)
Brown Mackie Coll–North Canton (OH)
Brown Mackie Coll–Northern Kentucky (KY)
Brown Mackie Coll–Phoenix (AZ)
Brown Mackie Coll–St. Louis (MO)
Brown Mackie Coll–Salina (KS)
Brown Mackie Coll–South Bend (IN)
Brown Mackie Coll–Tucson (AZ)
Brown Mackie Coll–Tulsa (OK)
Bryant & Stratton Coll, Eastlake (OH)
Bryant & Stratton Coll (WI)
Bryant & Stratton Coll - Albany Campus (NY)
Bryant & Stratton Coll - Amherst Campus (NY)
Bryant & Stratton Coll - Henrietta Campus (NY)
Bryant & Stratton Coll - North Campus (NY)
Bryant & Stratton Coll - Richmond Campus (VA)
Bryant & Stratton Coll - Virginia Beach (VA)
Bucks County Comm Coll (PA)
Burlington County Coll (NJ)
Camden County Coll (NJ)
Cape Fear Comm Coll (NC)
Carteret Comm Coll (NC)
Casper Coll (WY)
Catawba Valley Comm Coll (NC)
Central Carolina Comm Coll (NC)
Central Carolina Tech Coll (SC)
Central Comm Coll–Grand Island Campus (NE)
Central Georgia Tech Coll (GA)
Central New Mexico Comm Coll (NM)
Central Piedmont Comm Coll (NC)
Central Texas Coll (TX)
Chattanooga State Comm Coll (TN)
Clark Coll (WA)
Clovis Comm Coll (NM)
Coll of Southern Maryland (MD)
Coll of the Canyons (CA)
Collin County Comm Coll District (TX)
Comm Coll of Allegheny County (PA)
The Comm Coll of Baltimore County (MD)
Comm Coll of Philadelphia (PA)
Comm Coll of Rhode Island (RI)
Cumberland County Coll (NJ)
Cuyahoga Comm Coll (OH)
Cuyamaca Coll (CA)
Daytona State Coll (FL)
DeKalb Tech Coll (GA)
Delaware County Comm Coll (PA)
Delta Coll (MI)
Des Moines Area Comm Coll (IA)
Edison State Comm Coll (OH)
Elaine P. Nunez Comm Coll (LA)
El Centro Coll (TX)
Elgin Comm Coll (IL)
El Paso Comm Coll (TX)
Erie Comm Coll (NY)
Essex County Coll (NJ)
ETI Tech Coll of Niles (OH)
Everest Inst (NY)
Fayetteville Tech Comm Coll (NC)
Finger Lakes Comm Coll (NY)
Fiorello H. LaGuardia Comm Coll of the City U of New York (NY)
Forrest Jr Coll (SC)
Frederick Comm Coll (MD)
Front Range Comm Coll (CO)
Gadsden State Comm Coll (AL)
Genesee Comm Coll (NY)
Georgia Highlands Coll (GA)
Georgia Military Coll (GA)
Georgia Northwestern Tech Coll (GA)
Griffin Tech Coll (GA)
Guilford Tech Comm Coll (NC)
Harford Comm Coll (MD)
Harrisburg Area Comm Coll (PA)
Hesser Coll, Manchester (NH)
Highline Comm Coll (WA)
Hillsborough Comm Coll (FL)
Houston Comm Coll System (TX)
Hutchinson Comm Coll and Area Vocational School (KS)
Indian River State Coll (FL)
Inst of Business & Medical Careers (CO)
International Business Coll, Indianapolis (IN)
Inver Hills Comm Coll (MN)
Iowa Lakes Comm Coll (IA)
ITT Tech Inst, Bessemer (AL)
ITT Tech Inst, Madison (AL)
ITT Tech Inst, Mobile (AL)
ITT Tech Inst, Phoenix (AZ)
ITT Tech Inst, Tucson (AZ)
ITT Tech Inst, Anaheim (CA)
ITT Tech Inst, Lathrop (CA)
ITT Tech Inst, Oxnard (CA)
ITT Tech Inst, Rancho Cordova (CA)
ITT Tech Inst, San Bernardino (CA)
ITT Tech Inst, San Diego (CA)
ITT Tech Inst, San Dimas (CA)
ITT Tech Inst, Sylmar (CA)
ITT Tech Inst, Torrance (CA)
ITT Tech Inst, Aurora (CO)
ITT Tech Inst, Thornton (CO)
ITT Tech Inst, Fort Lauderdale (FL)
ITT Tech Inst, Jacksonville (FL)
ITT Tech Inst, Lake Mary (FL)
ITT Tech Inst, Miami (FL)
ITT Tech Inst, Pinellas Park (FL)
ITT Tech Inst, Tampa (FL)
ITT Tech Inst (ID)
ITT Tech Inst, Fort Wayne (IN)
ITT Tech Inst, Indianapolis (IN)
ITT Tech Inst, Merrillville (IN)
ITT Tech Inst, Newburgh (IN)
ITT Tech Inst, Cedar Rapids (IA)
ITT Tech Inst, Louisville (KY)
ITT Tech Inst, Baton Rouge (LA)
ITT Tech Inst, St. Rose (LA)
ITT Tech Inst, Canton (MI)
ITT Tech Inst, Swartz Creek (MI)
ITT Tech Inst, Troy (MI)
ITT Tech Inst, Wyoming (MI)
ITT Tech Inst (MN)
ITT Tech Inst, Arnold (MO)
ITT Tech Inst, Earth City (MO)
ITT Tech Inst, Kansas City (MO)
ITT Tech Inst (NM)
ITT Tech Inst, Akron (OH)
ITT Tech Inst, Columbus (OH)
ITT Tech Inst, Dayton (OH)
ITT Tech Inst, Hilliard (OH)
ITT Tech Inst, Maumee (OH)
ITT Tech Inst, Norwood (OH)
ITT Tech Inst, Strongsville (OH)
ITT Tech Inst, Warrensville Heights (OH)
ITT Tech Inst, Youngstown (OH)
ITT Tech Inst, Tulsa (OK)
ITT Tech Inst (OR)
ITT Tech Inst, Cordova (TN)
ITT Tech Inst, Johnson City (TN)
ITT Tech Inst, Knoxville (TN)
ITT Tech Inst, Nashville (TN)
ITT Tech Inst, Arlington (TX)
ITT Tech Inst, Austin (TX)
ITT Tech Inst, DeSoto (TX)
ITT Tech Inst, Houston (TX)
ITT Tech Inst, Houston (TX)
ITT Tech Inst, Richardson (TX)
ITT Tech Inst, San Antonio (TX)
ITT Tech Inst, Webster (TX)
ITT Tech Inst (UT)
ITT Tech Inst, Chantilly (VA)
ITT Tech Inst, Norfolk (VA)
ITT Tech Inst, Richmond (VA)
ITT Tech Inst, Salem (VA)
ITT Tech Inst, Springfield (VA)
ITT Tech Inst, Everett (WA)
ITT Tech Inst, Seattle (WA)
ITT Tech Inst, Spokane Valley (WA)
ITT Tech Inst (WV)
ITT Tech Inst, Green Bay (WI)
ITT Tech Inst, Greenfield (WI)
ITT Tech Inst, Madison (WI)
Ivy Tech Comm Coll–Bloomington (IN)
Ivy Tech Comm Coll–Central Indiana (IN)
Ivy Tech Comm Coll–Columbus (IN)
Ivy Tech Comm Coll–East Central (IN)
Ivy Tech Comm Coll–Kokomo (IN)
Ivy Tech Comm Coll–Lafayette (IN)
Ivy Tech Comm Coll–North Central (IN)
Ivy Tech Comm Coll–Northeast (IN)
Ivy Tech Comm Coll–Northwest (IN)
Ivy Tech Comm Coll–Richmond (IN)
Ivy Tech Comm Coll–Southeast (IN)
Ivy Tech Comm Coll–Southern Indiana (IN)
Ivy Tech Comm Coll–Southwest (IN)
Ivy Tech Comm Coll–Wabash Valley (IN)
Jefferson Comm Coll (NY)
Johnston Comm Coll (NC)
Kankakee Comm Coll (IL)
Kaplan Career Inst, Nashville Campus (TN)
Kaplan Coll, Denver Campus (CO)
Kaplan Coll, Panorama City Campus (CA)
Kaplan Coll, Sacramento Campus (CA)
Kaplan U, South Portland (ME)
Kaplan U, Hagerstown Campus (MD)
Kaplan U, Lincoln (NE)
Kaplan U, Omaha (NE)
Kellogg Comm Coll (MI)
Kent State U at Trumbull (OH)
Kilgore Coll (TX)
Kirkwood Comm Coll (IA)
Lackawanna Coll (PA)
Lakeland Comm Coll (OH)
Lake Region State Coll (ND)
Lamson Coll (AZ)
Lansing Comm Coll (MI)
Laramie County Comm Coll (WY)
Lehigh Carbon Comm Coll (PA)
Lewis and Clark Comm Coll (IL)
Macomb Comm Coll (MI)
Manchester Comm Coll (CT)
Marion Tech Coll (OH)
Mercer County Comm Coll (NJ)
Metropolitan Comm Coll (NE)
Metropolitan Comm Coll–Penn Valley (MO)
Miami Dade Coll (FL)
Midlands Tech Coll (SC)
Miller-Motte Tech Coll (SC)
Milwaukee Area Tech Coll (WI)
Minneapolis Business Coll (MN)
Minnesota State Comm and Tech Coll (MN)
Missouri State U–West Plains (MO)
Mohave Comm Coll (AZ)
Montgomery Coll (MD)
Moraine Park Tech Coll (WI)
Mountain Empire Comm Coll (VA)
Mountain State Coll (WV)
Mt. San Jacinto Coll (CA)
Mount Wachusett Comm Coll (MA)
Nassau Comm Coll (NY)
Northampton Comm Coll (PA)
North Central Texas Coll (TX)
North Hennepin Comm Coll (MN)
North Idaho Coll (ID)
Northland Pioneer Coll (AZ)
NorthWest Arkansas Comm Coll (AR)
Northwestern Coll (IL)
Northwestern Connecticut Comm Coll (CT)
Northwest Florida State Coll (FL)
Oakland Comm Coll (MI)
Ocean County Coll (NJ)
Ogeechee Tech Coll (GA)
Olean Business Inst (NY)
Orangeburg-Calhoun Tech Coll (SC)
Ouachita Tech Coll (AR)
Pasadena City Coll (CA)
Pasco-Hernando Comm Coll (FL)
Pennsylvania Coll of Technology (PA)
Pensacola Jr Coll (FL)
Phoenix Coll (AZ)
Pikes Peak Comm Coll (CO)
Pima Comm Coll (AZ)
Raritan Valley Comm Coll (NJ)
Salt Lake Comm Coll (UT)
San Diego City Coll (CA)
San Jacinto Coll District (TX)
San Juan Coll (NM)
Seminole State Coll of Florida (FL)
South Georgia Tech Coll (GA)
South Puget Sound Comm Coll (WA)
South Suburban Coll (IL)
State Coll of Florida Manatee-Sarasota (FL)
Suffolk County Comm Coll (NY)
Tallahassee Comm Coll (FL)

Tarrant County Coll District (TX)
Thomas Nelson Comm Coll (VA)
Tidewater Comm Coll (VA)
Tompkins Cortland Comm Coll (NY)
Trident Tech Coll (SC)
Union County Coll (NJ)
U of Cincinnati Clermont Coll (OH)
Victoria Coll (TX)
Volunteer State Comm Coll (TN)
Westchester Comm Coll (NY)
Westmoreland County Comm Coll (PA)
Westwood Coll–Houston South Campus (TX)
Wilson Comm Coll (NC)
Yavapai Coll (AZ)

Legal Professions and Studies Related
Essex County Coll (NJ)
Northland Pioneer Coll (AZ)

Legal Studies
Alvin Comm Coll (TX)
Carroll Comm Coll (MD)
Del Mar Coll (TX)
Edison State Comm Coll (OH)
Harcum Coll (PA)
Harford Comm Coll (MD)
Iowa Lakes Comm Coll (IA)
Lonestar Coll–North Harris (TX)
Macomb Comm Coll (MI)
Metropolitan Comm Coll (NE)
Northwest Florida State Coll (FL)
Pasadena City Coll (CA)
Trident Tech Coll (SC)

Liberal Arts and Sciences And Humanities Related
Cascadia Comm Coll (WA)
Coll of Southern Maryland (MD)
The Comm Coll of Baltimore County (MD)
Dakota Coll at Bottineau (ND)
Elaine P. Nunez Comm Coll (LA)
Fayetteville Tech Comm Coll (NC)
Front Range Comm Coll (CO)
Guilford Tech Comm Coll (NC)
Harford Comm Coll (MD)
Holyoke Comm Coll (MA)
Iowa Lakes Comm Coll (IA)
Jamestown Comm Coll (NY)
Kennebec Valley Comm Coll (ME)
Mohawk Valley Comm Coll (NY)
Montana State U–Great Falls Coll of Technology (MT)
Montgomery Coll (MD)
Northampton Comm Coll (PA)
Pennsylvania Coll of Technology (PA)
Piedmont Comm Coll (NC)
Pueblo Comm Coll (CO)
Randolph Comm Coll (NC)
Southern Maine Comm Coll (ME)
Southwest Virginia Comm Coll (VA)
Wor-Wic Comm Coll (MD)

Liberal Arts and Sciences/Liberal Studies
Alamance Comm Coll (NC)
Allan Hancock Coll (CA)
Allegany Coll of Maryland (MD)
Alpena Comm Coll (MI)
Alvin Comm Coll (TX)
Amarillo Coll (TX)
Anne Arundel Comm Coll (MD)
Anoka-Ramsey Comm Coll (MN)
Anoka-Ramsey Comm Coll, Cambridge Campus (MN)
Antelope Valley Coll (CA)
Arkansas State U–Beebe (AR)
Arkansas State U–Mountain Home (AR)
Bainbridge Coll (GA)
Bakersfield Coll (CA)
Barton County Comm Coll (KS)
Beaufort County Comm Coll (NC)
Berkeley City Coll (CA)
Berkshire Comm Coll (MA)
Bevill State Comm Coll (AL)
Bladen Comm Coll (NC)
Blue Ridge Comm Coll (NC)
Bowling Green State U–Firelands Coll (OH)
Bronx Comm Coll of the City U of New York (NY)
Broome Comm Coll (NY)
Bucks County Comm Coll (PA)
Burlington County Coll (NJ)
Camden County Coll (NJ)
Cape Fear Comm Coll (NC)
Carroll Comm Coll (MD)
Carteret Comm Coll (NC)
Cascadia Comm Coll (WA)
Casper Coll (WY)
Catawba Valley Comm Coll (NC)
Cecil Coll (MD)
Central Arizona Coll (AZ)
Central Carolina Comm Coll (NC)
Central Carolina Tech Coll (SC)
Central Comm Coll–Columbus Campus (NE)
Central Comm Coll–Grand Island Campus (NE)
Central Comm Coll–Hastings Campus (NE)
Central Lakes Coll (MN)
Central New Mexico Comm Coll (NM)
Central Ohio Tech Coll (OH)
Central Oregon Comm Coll (OR)
Central Piedmont Comm Coll (NC)
Central Texas Coll (TX)
Century Coll (MN)
Chipola Coll (FL)
Cincinnati State Tech and Comm Coll (OH)
City Colls of Chicago, Malcolm X College (IL)
City Colls of Chicago, Richard J. Daley College (IL)
Clackamas Comm Coll (OR)
Clarendon Coll (TX)
Clark Coll (WA)
Cleveland State Comm Coll (TN)
Clovis Comm Coll (NM)
Coll of DuPage (IL)
Coll of Lake County (IL)
Coll of Southern Maryland (MD)
Coll of the Canyons (CA)
Collin County Comm Coll District (TX)
Comm Coll of Allegheny County (PA)
The Comm Coll of Baltimore County (MD)
Comm Coll of Philadelphia (PA)
Comm Coll of Rhode Island (RI)
Comm Coll of Vermont (VT)
Corning Comm Coll (NY)
Cossatot Comm Coll of the U of Arkansas (AR)
County Coll of Morris (NJ)
Cowley County Comm Coll and Area Vocational–Tech School (KS)
Crowder Coll (MO)
Cumberland County Coll (NJ)
Cuyahoga Comm Coll (OH)
Cuyamaca Coll (CA)
Dabney S. Lancaster Comm Coll (VA)
Dakota Coll at Bottineau (ND)
Dean Coll (MA)
Deep Springs Coll (CA)
Delaware County Comm Coll (PA)
Del Mar Coll (TX)
Delta Coll (MI)
Des Moines Area Comm Coll (IA)
Diablo Valley Coll (CA)
Donnelly Coll (KS)
Eastern Arizona Coll (AZ)
Eastern Shore Comm Coll (VA)
Eastern Wyoming Coll (WY)
Eastfield Coll (TX)
East Los Angeles Coll (CA)
Edison State Comm Coll (OH)
Elaine P. Nunez Comm Coll (LA)
Elgin Comm Coll (IL)
El Paso Comm Coll (TX)
Emory U, Oxford Coll (GA)
Erie Comm Coll (NY)
Erie Comm Coll, North Campus (NY)
Erie Comm Coll, South Campus (NY)
Essex County Coll (NJ)
Estrella Mountain Comm Coll (AZ)
Everett Comm Coll (WA)
Fayetteville Tech Comm Coll (NC)
Finger Lakes Comm Coll (NY)
Fiorello H. LaGuardia Comm Coll of the City U of New York (NY)
Flathead Valley Comm Coll (MT)
Folsom Lake Coll (CA)
Frederick Comm Coll (MD)
Front Range Comm Coll (CO)
Fulton-Montgomery Comm Coll (NY)
Gadsden State Comm Coll (AL)
Gateway Comm Coll (CT)
Genesee Comm Coll (NY)
Georgia Highlands Coll (GA)
Georgia Military Coll (GA)
Georgia Perimeter Coll (GA)
Germanna Comm Coll (VA)
Golden West Coll (CA)
Goodwin Coll (CT)
Grand Rapids Comm Coll (MI)
Greenfield Comm Coll (MA)
Green River Comm Coll (WA)
Guilford Tech Comm Coll (NC)
Harford Comm Coll (MD)
Hawaii Tokai International Coll (HI)
Hawkeye Comm Coll (IA)
Hazard Comm and Tech Coll (KY)
Hesser Coll, Manchester (NH)
Highland Comm Coll (IL)
Hillsborough Comm Coll (FL)
Holyoke Comm Coll (MA)
Honolulu Comm Coll (HI)
Hopkinsville Comm Coll (KY)
Housatonic Comm Coll (CT)
Howard Comm Coll (MD)
Hutchinson Comm Coll and Area Vocational School (KS)
Illinois Eastern Comm Colls, Frontier Community College (IL)
Illinois Eastern Comm Colls, Lincoln Trail College (IL)
Illinois Eastern Comm Colls, Olney Central College (IL)
Illinois Eastern Comm Colls, Wabash Valley College (IL)
Illinois Valley Comm Coll (IL)
Indian River State Coll (FL)
Inver Hills Comm Coll (MN)
Iowa Lakes Comm Coll (IA)
Itasca Comm Coll (MN)
Ivy Tech Comm Coll–Bloomington (IN)
Ivy Tech Comm Coll–Central Indiana (IN)
Ivy Tech Comm Coll–Columbus (IN)
Ivy Tech Comm Coll–East Central (IN)
Ivy Tech Comm Coll–Kokomo (IN)
Ivy Tech Comm Coll–Lafayette (IN)
Ivy Tech Comm Coll–North Central (IN)
Ivy Tech Comm Coll–Northeast (IN)
Ivy Tech Comm Coll–Northwest (IN)
Ivy Tech Comm Coll–Richmond (IN)
Ivy Tech Comm Coll–Southeast (IN)
Ivy Tech Comm Coll–Southern Indiana (IN)
Ivy Tech Comm Coll–Southwest (IN)
Ivy Tech Comm Coll–Wabash Valley (IN)
Jackson Comm Coll (MI)
Jackson State Comm Coll (TN)
James Sprunt Comm Coll (NC)
Jamestown Comm Coll (NY)
Jefferson State Comm Coll (AL)
Johnston Comm Coll (NC)
John Tyler Comm Coll (VA)
John Wood Comm Coll (IL)
J. Sargeant Reynolds Comm Coll (VA)
Kalamazoo Valley Comm Coll (MI)
Kaskaskia Coll (IL)
Kauai Comm Coll (HI)
Kellogg Comm Coll (MI)
Kennebec Valley Comm Coll (ME)
Kent State U at Ashtabula (OH)
Kent State U at East Liverpool (OH)
Kent State U at Geauga (OH)
Kent State U at Salem (OH)
Kent State U at Trumbull (OH)
Kent State U at Tuscarawas (OH)
Kilian Comm Coll (SD)
Kingsborough Comm Coll of the City U of New York (NY)
Kirkwood Comm Coll (IA)
Kirtland Comm Coll (MI)
Lac Courte Oreilles Ojibwa Comm Coll (WI)
Lackawanna Coll (PA)
Lakeland Comm Coll (OH)
Lake Michigan Coll (MI)
Lake Region State Coll (ND)
Lake-Sumter Comm Coll (FL)
Landmark Coll (VT)
Lansing Comm Coll (MI)
Lawson State Comm Coll (AL)
LDS Business Coll (UT)
Leech Lake Tribal Coll (MN)
Leeward Comm Coll (HI)
Lehigh Carbon Comm Coll (PA)
Lewis and Clark Comm Coll (IL)
Lincoln Land Comm Coll (IL)
Linn-Benton Comm Coll (OR)
Lonestar Coll–North Harris (TX)
Lon Morris Coll (TX)
Los Angeles Harbor Coll (CA)
Lower Columbia Coll (WA)
Luna Comm Coll (NM)
Lurleen B. Wallace Comm Coll (AL)
Macomb Comm Coll (MI)
Manchester Comm Coll (CT)
Massasoit Comm Coll (MA)
Mendocino Coll (CA)
Mercer County Comm Coll (NJ)
Mesabi Range Comm and Tech Coll (MN)
Metropolitan Comm Coll (NE)
Metropolitan Comm Coll–Blue River (MO)
Metropolitan Comm Coll–Business & Technology Campus (MO)
Metropolitan Comm Coll–Longview (MO)
Metropolitan Comm Coll–Maple Woods (MO)
Metropolitan Comm Coll–Penn Valley (MO)
Middle Georgia Coll (GA)
Middlesex Comm Coll (CT)
Midlands Tech Coll (SC)
Mid-Plains Comm Coll, North Platte (NE)
Milwaukee Area Tech Coll (WI)
Minneapolis Comm and Tech Coll (MN)
Minnesota State Comm and Tech Coll (MN)
Minnesota West Comm and Tech Coll (MN)
Mohave Comm Coll (AZ)
Mohawk Valley Comm Coll (NY)
Montcalm Comm Coll (MI)
Montgomery Coll (MD)
Montgomery Comm Coll (NC)
Montgomery County Comm Coll (PA)
Moraine Valley Comm Coll (IL)
Mountain Empire Comm Coll (VA)
Mt. San Jacinto Coll (CA)
Mount Wachusett Comm Coll (MA)
Murray State Coll (OK)
Muskegon Comm Coll (MI)
Nassau Comm Coll (NY)
Niagara County Comm Coll (NY)
Nicolet Area Tech Coll (WI)
Northampton Comm Coll (PA)
North Arkansas Coll (AR)
North Central Texas Coll (TX)
Northeast Comm Coll (NE)
Northeastern Jr Coll (CO)
Northeast Iowa Comm Coll (IA)
North Hennepin Comm Coll (MN)
North Idaho Coll (ID)
North Iowa Area Comm Coll (IA)
North Lake Coll (TX)
Northland Comm and Tech Coll–Thief River Falls (MN)
Northland Pioneer Coll (AZ)
NorthWest Arkansas Comm Coll (AR)
Northwest Coll (WY)
Northwestern Connecticut Comm Coll (CT)
Northwest Florida State Coll (FL)
Northwest-Shoals Comm Coll (AL)
Northwest Tech Coll (MN)
Oakland Comm Coll (MI)
Ocean County Coll (NJ)
Odessa Coll (TX)
Oklahoma City Comm Coll (OK)
Olympic Coll (WA)
Orangeburg-Calhoun Tech Coll (SC)
Orange Coast Coll (CA)
Oregon Coast Comm Coll (OR)
Otero Jr Coll (CO)
Ouachita Tech Coll (AR)
Owensboro Comm and Tech Coll (KY)
Palm Beach State Coll (FL)
Paradise Valley Comm Coll (AZ)
Paris Jr Coll (TX)
Pasadena City Coll (CA)
Pasco-Hernando Comm Coll (FL)
Patrick Henry Comm Coll (VA)
Penn State Beaver (PA)
Penn State Brandywine (PA)
Penn State DuBois (PA)
Penn State Fayette, The Eberly Campus (PA)
Penn State Greater Allegheny (PA)
Penn State Hazleton (PA)
Penn State Lehigh Valley (PA)
Penn State Mont Alto (PA)
Penn State New Kensington (PA)
Penn State Schuylkill (PA)
Penn State Shenango (PA)
Penn State Wilkes-Barre (PA)
Penn State Worthington Scranton (PA)
Penn State York (PA)
Pennsylvania Coll of Technology (PA)
Pennsylvania Highlands Comm Coll (PA)
Pensacola Jr Coll (FL)
Phoenix Coll (AZ)
Piedmont Comm Coll (NC)
Pikes Peak Comm Coll (CO)
Pima Comm Coll (AZ)
Polk State Coll (FL)
Potomac State Coll of West Virginia U (WV)
Pueblo Comm Coll (CO)
Pulaski Tech Coll (AR)
Quinsigamond Comm Coll (MA)
Randolph Comm Coll (NC)
Rappahannock Comm Coll (VA)
Raritan Valley Comm Coll (NJ)
Red Rocks Comm Coll (CO)
Reedley Coll (CA)
Rend Lake Coll (IL)
Rockingham Comm Coll (NC)
Rockland Comm Coll (NY)
Rogue Comm Coll (OR)
Saint Charles Comm Coll (MO)
Saint Paul Coll–A Comm & Tech College (MN)
St. Philip's Coll (TX)
Sandhills Comm Coll (NC)
San Diego City Coll (CA)
San Diego Mesa Coll (CA)
San Juan Coll (NM)
Seminole State Coll (OK)
Seminole State Coll of Florida (FL)
Shawnee Comm Coll (IL)
Sierra Coll (CA)
Sisseton-Wahpeton Comm Coll (SD)
Snow Coll (UT)
Somerset Comm Coll (KY)
Southeastern Comm Coll (IA)
Southeast Kentucky Comm and Tech Coll (KY)
Southern Maine Comm Coll (ME)
Southern State Comm Coll (OH)
Southern Union State Comm Coll (AL)
South Georgia Coll (GA)
South Plains Coll (TX)
South Puget Sound Comm Coll (WA)
Southside Virginia Comm Coll (VA)
South Suburban Coll (IL)
Southwestern Comm Coll (IA)
Southwestern Indian Polytechnic Inst (NM)
Southwestern Michigan Coll (MI)
Southwest Mississippi Comm Coll (MS)

Southwest Virginia Comm Coll (VA)
Spartanburg Comm Coll (SC)
Spartanburg Methodist Coll (SC)
Springfield Tech Comm Coll (MA)
State Coll of Florida Manatee-Sarasota (FL)
State Fair Comm Coll (MO)
State U of New York Coll of Technology at Alfred (NY)
Suffolk County Comm Coll (NY)
Tallahassee Comm Coll (FL)
Tarrant County Coll District (TX)
Temple Coll (TX)
Terra State Comm Coll (OH)
Three Rivers Comm Coll (CT)
Three Rivers Comm Coll (MO)
Tidewater Comm Coll (VA)
Tohono O'odham Comm Coll (AZ)
Tompkins Cortland Comm Coll (NY)
Tri-County Comm Coll (NC)
Trident Tech Coll (SC)
Trinity Valley Comm Coll (TX)
Triton Coll (IL)
Tunxis Comm Coll (CT)
Ulster County Comm Coll (NY)
Umpqua Comm Coll (OR)
Union County Coll (NJ)
U of Alaska Anchorage, Kenai Peninsula Coll (AK)
U of Alaska Anchorage, Matanuska-Susitna Coll (AK)
U of Arkansas Comm Coll at Morrilton (AR)
U of Cincinnati Clermont Coll (OH)
U of Pittsburgh at Titusville (PA)
U of South Carolina Lancaster (SC)
U of South Carolina Salkehatchie (SC)
U of Wisconsin–Fond du Lac (WI)
U of Wisconsin–Fox Valley (WI)
U of Wisconsin–Richland (WI)
U of Wisconsin–Waukesha (WI)
Victoria Coll (TX)
Victor Valley Coll (CA)
Vincennes U Jasper Campus (IN)
Volunteer State Comm Coll (TN)
Walters State Comm Coll (TN)
Waycross Coll (GA)
Wayne Comm Coll (NC)
Westchester Comm Coll (NY)
Western Wyoming Comm Coll (WY)
Westmoreland County Comm Coll (PA)
West Shore Comm Coll (MI)
West Virginia Northern Comm Coll (WV)
White Mountains Comm Coll (NH)
Wilson Comm Coll (NC)
Yavapai Coll (AZ)

Library Assistant
Clovis Comm Coll (NM)
Coll of DuPage (IL)
Coll of the Canyons (CA)
Georgia Perimeter Coll (GA)
Ivy Tech Comm Coll–Bloomington (IN)
Ivy Tech Comm Coll–Columbus (IN)
Ivy Tech Comm Coll–East Central (IN)
Ivy Tech Comm Coll–Kokomo (IN)
Ivy Tech Comm Coll–Lafayette (IN)
Ivy Tech Comm Coll–North Central (IN)
Ivy Tech Comm Coll–Northeast (IN)
Ivy Tech Comm Coll–Northwest (IN)
Ivy Tech Comm Coll–Richmond (IN)
Ivy Tech Comm Coll–Southeast (IN)
Ivy Tech Comm Coll–Southern Indiana (IN)
Ivy Tech Comm Coll–Southwest (IN)
Ivy Tech Comm Coll–Wabash Valley (IN)
Lewis and Clark Comm Coll (IL)
Minneapolis Comm and Tech Coll (MN)
Northeast Comm Coll (NE)
Northland Pioneer Coll (AZ)
Oakland Comm Coll (MI)
Pueblo Comm Coll (CO)

Library Science
Allen Comm Coll (KS)
Coll of DuPage (IL)
Highline Comm Coll (WA)
Indian River State Coll (FL)
Southwestern Comm Coll (IA)

Library Science Related
Pasadena City Coll (CA)

Lineworker
Coll of Southern Maryland (MD)
Harrisburg Area Comm Coll (PA)
Ivy Tech Comm Coll–Lafayette (IN)
Kennebec Valley Comm Coll (ME)
Linn State Tech Coll (MO)
Minnesota State Comm and Tech Coll (MN)
Mitchell Tech Inst (SD)
Moraine Park Tech Coll (WI)
Northeast Comm Coll (NE)
Raritan Valley Comm Coll (NJ)

Livestock Management
Barton County Comm Coll (KS)
Northeast Comm Coll (NE)
The Ohio State U Ag Tech Inst (OH)

Logistics and Materials Management
Athens Tech Coll (GA)
Barton County Comm Coll (KS)
Cecil Coll (MD)
Chattahoochee Tech Coll (GA)
Edison State Comm Coll (OH)
Georgia Military Coll (GA)
Guilford Tech Comm Coll (NC)
Houston Comm Coll System (TX)
Lehigh Carbon Comm Coll (PA)
Lonestar Coll–Cy-Fair (TX)
Milwaukee Area Tech Coll (WI)
Pima Comm Coll (AZ)
Randolph Comm Coll (NC)
Saint Paul Coll–A Comm & Tech College (MN)

Machine Shop Technology
Cape Fear Comm Coll (NC)
Coll of Lake County (IL)
Comm Coll of Allegheny County (PA)
Corning Comm Coll (NY)
Daytona State Coll (FL)
Eastern Arizona Coll (AZ)
Fayetteville Tech Comm Coll (NC)
Front Range Comm Coll (CO)
Guilford Tech Comm Coll (NC)
Illinois Eastern Comm Colls, Wabash Valley College (IL)
Ivy Tech Comm Coll–Central Indiana (IN)
Johnston Comm Coll (NC)
Metropolitan Comm Coll–Business & Technology Campus (MO)
Moraine Park Tech Coll (WI)
North Central Texas Coll (TX)
North Iowa Area Comm Coll (IA)
Orange Coast Coll (CA)
Pasadena City Coll (CA)
Pennsylvania Coll of Technology (PA)
Pima Comm Coll (AZ)
Pueblo Comm Coll (CO)
Randolph Comm Coll (NC)
San Juan Coll (NM)
Southeast Tech Inst (SD)
Southern Union State Comm Coll (AL)
West Kentucky Comm and Tech Coll (KY)
Westmoreland County Comm Coll (PA)

Machine Tool Technology
Alamance Comm Coll (NC)
Alexandria Tech Coll (MN)
Allan Hancock Coll (CA)
Altamaha Tech Coll (GA)
Amarillo Coll (TX)
Bakersfield Coll (CA)
Blue Ridge Comm Coll (NC)
Casper Coll (WY)
Central Comm Coll–Columbus Campus (NE)
Central Comm Coll–Hastings Campus (NE)
Central Lakes Coll (MN)
Central Piedmont Comm Coll (NC)
Clackamas Comm Coll (OR)
Clark Coll (WA)
Coll of DuPage (IL)
Columbus Tech Coll (GA)
Corning Comm Coll (NY)
Cowley County Comm Coll and Area Vocational–Tech School (KS)
DeKalb Tech Coll (GA)
Delaware County Comm Coll (PA)
Del Mar Coll (TX)
Delta Coll (MI)
Des Moines Area Comm Coll (IA)
East Central Coll (MO)
Elgin Comm Coll (IL)
El Paso Comm Coll (TX)
Green River Comm Coll (WA)
Gwinnett Tech Coll (GA)
Hawkeye Comm Coll (IA)
H. Councill Trenholm State Tech Coll (AL)
Heart of Georgia Tech Coll (GA)
Hennepin Tech Coll (MN)
Hutchinson Comm Coll and Area Vocational School (KS)
Ivy Tech Comm Coll–Bloomington (IN)
Ivy Tech Comm Coll–Central Indiana (IN)
Ivy Tech Comm Coll–Columbus (IN)
Ivy Tech Comm Coll–East Central (IN)
Ivy Tech Comm Coll–Kokomo (IN)
Ivy Tech Comm Coll–Lafayette (IN)
Ivy Tech Comm Coll–North Central (IN)
Ivy Tech Comm Coll–Northeast (IN)
Ivy Tech Comm Coll–Northwest (IN)
Ivy Tech Comm Coll–Richmond (IN)
Ivy Tech Comm Coll–Southern Indiana (IN)
Ivy Tech Comm Coll–Southwest (IN)
Ivy Tech Comm Coll–Wabash Valley (IN)
J. F. Drake State Tech Coll (AL)
Johnston Comm Coll (NC)
Kalamazoo Valley Comm Coll (MI)
Kankakee Comm Coll (IL)
Kellogg Comm Coll (MI)
Kennebec Valley Comm Coll (ME)
Kirkwood Comm Coll (IA)
Lake Michigan Coll (MI)
Lansing Comm Coll (MI)
Linn-Benton Comm Coll (OR)
Linn State Tech Coll (MO)
Lower Columbia Coll (WA)
Macomb Comm Coll (MI)
Meridian Comm Coll (MS)
Milwaukee Area Tech Coll (WI)
Minnesota State Coll–Southeast Tech (MN)
Muskegon Comm Coll (MI)
Nicolet Area Tech Coll (WI)
North Central Texas Coll (TX)
North Idaho Coll (ID)
North Iowa Area Comm Coll (IA)
Oakland Comm Coll (MI)
Odessa Coll (TX)
Orangeburg-Calhoun Tech Coll (SC)
Orange Coast Coll (CA)
Ouachita Tech Coll (AR)
Randolph Comm Coll (NC)
Reedley Coll (CA)
St. Cloud Tech Coll (MN)
San Diego City Coll (CA)
Sheridan Coll (WY)
Southeastern Comm Coll (IA)
Southeast Tech Inst (SD)
Southern Maine Comm Coll (ME)
South Plains Coll (TX)
Spartanburg Comm Coll (SC)
State Fair Comm Coll (MO)
State U of New York Coll of Technology at Alfred (NY)
Tarrant County Coll District (TX)
Trident Tech Coll (SC)
The U of Montana–Helena Coll of Technology (MT)
Valdosta Tech Coll (GA)
Wayne Comm Coll (NC)
Westmoreland County Comm Coll (PA)
West Shore Comm Coll (MI)

Management Information Systems
Allegany Coll of Maryland (MD)
Burlington County Coll (NJ)
Camden County Coll (NJ)
Career Coll of Northern Nevada (NV)
Carroll Comm Coll (MD)
Casper Coll (WY)
Cecil Coll (MD)
Central Oregon Comm Coll (OR)
Chattanooga State Comm Coll (TN)
Cincinnati State Tech and Comm Coll (OH)
Clovis Comm Coll (NM)
Comm Coll of Allegheny County (PA)
The Comm Coll of Baltimore County (MD)
Cossatot Comm Coll of the U of Arkansas (AR)
County Coll of Morris (NJ)
Delaware County Comm Coll (PA)
Delaware Tech & Comm Coll, Jack F. Owens Campus (DE)
Delaware Tech & Comm Coll, Stanton/Wilmington Campus (DE)
Delaware Tech & Comm Coll, Terry Campus (DE)
Del Mar Coll (TX)
Front Range Comm Coll (CO)
Gwinnett Tech Coll (GA)
Hillsborough Comm Coll (FL)
Jackson State Comm Coll (TN)
John Tyler Comm Coll (VA)
J. Sargeant Reynolds Comm Coll (VA)
Kaplan U, South Portland (ME)
Kennebec Valley Comm Coll (ME)
Kilgore Coll (TX)
Kirtland Comm Coll (MI)
Lackawanna Coll (PA)
Lakeland Comm Coll (OH)
Lake Region State Coll (ND)
Lansing Comm Coll (MI)
Linn State Tech Coll (MO)
Lonestar Coll–North Harris (TX)
Manchester Comm Coll (CT)
Manhattan Area Tech Coll (KS)
Mercer County Comm Coll (NJ)
Miami Dade Coll (FL)
Montcalm Comm Coll (MI)
Montgomery Comm Coll (NC)
Moraine Valley Comm Coll (IL)
Nassau Comm Coll (NY)
North Hennepin Comm Coll (MN)
Northland Pioneer Coll (AZ)
Northwestern Coll (IL)
Ouachita Tech Coll (AR)
Pikes Peak Comm Coll (CO)
Pulaski Tech Coll (AR)
Raritan Valley Comm Coll (NJ)
Saint Paul Coll–A Comm & Tech College (MN)
San Jacinto Coll District (TX)
Southeast Kentucky Comm and Tech Coll (KY)
Southern Maine Comm Coll (ME)
Tallahassee Comm Coll (FL)
Union County Coll (NJ)
U of Pittsburgh at Titusville (PA)
Victor Valley Coll (CA)
Vincennes U Jasper Campus (IN)

Management Information Systems and Services Related
Eastern Arizona Coll (AZ)
Harrisburg Area Comm Coll (PA)
Harrison Coll, Indianapolis (IN)
Harrison Coll, Muncie (IN)
Hillsborough Comm Coll (FL)
Metropolitan Comm Coll–Business & Technology Campus (MO)
Missouri State U–West Plains (MO)
Mohawk Valley Comm Coll (NY)
Montgomery Coll (MD)
Montgomery County Comm Coll (PA)
Northland Pioneer Coll (AZ)
Pensacola Jr Coll (FL)
Southwestern Indian Polytechnic Inst (NM)
Ulster County Comm Coll (NY)

Management Science
Delaware Tech & Comm Coll, Stanton/Wilmington Campus (DE)
Lonestar Coll–Cy-Fair (TX)
Pasadena City Coll (CA)
Phoenix Coll (AZ)
Reedley Coll (CA)

Manufacturing Engineering
Central Arizona Coll (AZ)
Central Wyoming Coll (WY)
Kent State U at Trumbull (OH)
Lake Michigan Coll (MI)
Penn State Fayette, The Eberly Campus (PA)
Penn State Greater Allegheny (PA)
Penn State Hazleton (PA)
Penn State Wilkes-Barre (PA)
Penn State York (PA)

Manufacturing Technology
Albany Tech Coll (GA)
Alexandria Tech Coll (MN)
Alpena Comm Coll (MI)
Altamaha Tech Coll (GA)
Black Hawk Coll, Moline (IL)
Casper Coll (WY)
Central New Mexico Comm Coll (NM)
Central Ohio Tech Coll (OH)
Central Oregon Comm Coll (OR)
Clackamas Comm Coll (OR)
Clark Coll (WA)
Coll of DuPage (IL)
Coll of the Canyons (CA)
Danville Area Comm Coll (IL)
Delaware Tech & Comm Coll, Stanton/Wilmington Campus (DE)
East Central Coll (MO)
Elgin Comm Coll (IL)
Everett Comm Coll (WA)
Flint River Tech Coll (GA)
Front Range Comm Coll (CO)
Gadsden State Comm Coll (AL)
Gateway Comm and Tech Coll (KY)
Griffin Tech Coll (GA)
Hawkeye Comm Coll (IA)
Houston Comm Coll System (TX)
Hutchinson Comm Coll and Area Vocational School (KS)
Illinois Eastern Comm Colls, Wabash Valley College (IL)
Jefferson State Comm Coll (AL)
Lehigh Carbon Comm Coll (PA)
Lewis and Clark Comm Coll (IL)
Linn State Tech Coll (MO)
Macomb Comm Coll (MI)
Milwaukee Area Tech Coll (WI)
Minnesota State Comm and Tech Coll (MN)
Northland Comm and Tech Coll–Thief River Falls (MN)
Northwest Tech Coll (MN)
Oakland Comm Coll (MI)
Owens Comm Coll, Toledo (OH)
Pensacola Jr Coll (FL)
Quinsigamond Comm Coll (MA)
Raritan Valley Comm Coll (NJ)
Rogue Comm Coll (OR)
Saint Paul Coll–A Comm & Tech College (MN)
Sierra Coll (CA)
South Georgia Tech Coll (GA)
Southwestern Indian Polytechnic Inst (NM)
State Fair Comm Coll (MO)
Terra State Comm Coll (OH)
Union County Coll (NJ)
Waukesha County Tech Coll (WI)
Westmoreland County Comm Coll (PA)

Marine Biology and Biological Oceanography
Oregon Coast Comm Coll (OR)
Southern Maine Comm Coll (ME)

Marine Maintenance and Ship Repair Technology
Alexandria Tech Coll (MN)
Cape Fear Comm Coll (NC)
Iowa Lakes Comm Coll (IA)

Minnesota State Comm and Tech Coll (MN)
Olympic Coll (WA)
State Fair Comm Coll (MO)

Marine Science/ Merchant Marine Officer
Anne Arundel Comm Coll (MD)
Indian River State Coll (FL)

Marine Technology
Cape Fear Comm Coll (NC)
Highline Comm Coll (WA)
Honolulu Comm Coll (HI)
Kingsborough Comm Coll of the City U of New York (NY)
North Idaho Coll (ID)
Orange Coast Coll (CA)

Marketing/Marketing Management
Albany Tech Coll (GA)
Alexandria Tech Coll (MN)
Allegany Coll of Maryland (MD)
Altamaha Tech Coll (GA)
Alvin Comm Coll (TX)
Anne Arundel Comm Coll (MD)
Anoka-Ramsey Comm Coll (MN)
Anoka-Ramsey Comm Coll, Cambridge Campus (MN)
Antelope Valley Coll (CA)
Arizona Western Coll (AZ)
Athens Tech Coll (GA)
Atlanta Tech Coll (GA)
Augusta Tech Coll (GA)
Austin Comm Coll (TX)
Bainbridge Coll (GA)
Bakersfield Coll (CA)
Barton County Comm Coll (KS)
Blue Ridge Comm Coll (NC)
Bronx Comm Coll of the City U of New York (NY)
Bucks County Comm Coll (PA)
Camden County Coll (NJ)
Casper Coll (WY)
Cecil Coll (MD)
Central Carolina Comm Coll (NC)
Central Comm Coll–Columbus Campus (NE)
Central Georgia Tech Coll (GA)
Central Lakes Coll (MN)
Central Oregon Comm Coll (OR)
Central Piedmont Comm Coll (NC)
Central Texas Coll (TX)
Century Coll (MN)
Chattahoochee Tech Coll (GA)
Cincinnati State Tech and Comm Coll (OH)
City Colls of Chicago, Richard J. Daley College (IL)
Clackamas Comm Coll (OR)
Clarendon Coll (TX)
Coll of DuPage (IL)
Comm Coll of Allegheny County (PA)
Comm Coll of Philadelphia (PA)
Comm Coll of Rhode Island (RI)
Cowley County Comm Coll and Area Vocational–Tech School (KS)
Cuyahoga Comm Coll (OH)
Dakota Coll at Bottineau (ND)
Davis Coll (OH)
DeKalb Tech Coll (GA)
Delaware Tech & Comm Coll, Jack F. Owens Campus (DE)
Delaware Tech & Comm Coll, Stanton/Wilmington Campus (DE)
Delaware Tech & Comm Coll, Terry Campus (DE)
Delta Coll (MI)
Des Moines Area Comm Coll (IA)
East Los Angeles Coll (CA)
Edison State Comm Coll (OH)
Elgin Comm Coll (IL)
Fayetteville Tech Comm Coll (NC)
Finger Lakes Comm Coll (NY)
Folsom Lake Coll (CA)
Fox Valley Tech Coll (WI)
Frederick Comm Coll (MD)
Genesee Comm Coll (NY)
Georgia Highlands Coll (GA)
Georgia Northwestern Tech Coll (GA)
Glendale Comm Coll (AZ)
Golden West Coll (CA)
Greenfield Comm Coll (MA)
Green River Comm Coll (WA)
Griffin Tech Coll (GA)
Gwinnett Tech Coll (GA)
Harrison Coll, Anderson (IN)
Harrison Coll, Columbus (IN)
Harrison Coll, Elkhart (IN)
Harrison Coll, Evansville (IN)
Harrison Coll, Fort Wayne (IN)
Harrison Coll, Indianapolis (IN)
Harrison Coll, Lafayette (IN)
Harrison Coll, Muncie (IN)
Harrison Coll, Terre Haute (IN)
Harrison Coll (OH)
Heart of Georgia Tech Coll (GA)
Highland Comm Coll (IL)
Houston Comm Coll System (TX)
Illinois Valley Comm Coll (IL)
Indian River State Coll (FL)
Iowa Lakes Comm Coll (IA)
Jackson Comm Coll (MI)
Jamestown Business Coll (NY)
Kalamazoo Valley Comm Coll (MI)
Kankakee Comm Coll (IL)
Kaplan U, Hagerstown Campus (MD)
Kennebec Valley Comm Coll (ME)
Kent State U at Ashtabula (OH)
Kingsborough Comm Coll of the City U of New York (NY)
Kirkwood Comm Coll (IA)
Lakeland Comm Coll (OH)
Lake Michigan Coll (MI)
Lanier Tech Coll (GA)
Lansing Comm Coll (MI)
Lonestar Coll–Cy-Fair (TX)
Lonestar Coll–Kingwood (TX)
Lonestar Coll–Montgomery (TX)
Lonestar Coll–North Harris (TX)
Lonestar Coll–Tomball (TX)
Macomb Comm Coll (MI)
Manchester Comm Coll (CT)
Marion Tech Coll (OH)
Meridian Comm Coll (MS)
Metropolitan Comm Coll–Longview (MO)
Metropolitan Comm Coll–Maple Woods (MO)
Metropolitan Comm Coll–Penn Valley (MO)
Miami Dade Coll (FL)
Middle Georgia Tech Coll (GA)
Middlesex Comm Coll (CT)
Milwaukee Area Tech Coll (WI)
Minnesota State Coll–Southeast Tech (MN)
Minnesota State Comm and Tech Coll (MN)
Moraine Park Tech Coll (WI)
Moultrie Tech Coll (GA)
Mountain Empire Comm Coll (VA)
Muskegon Comm Coll (MI)
Nassau Comm Coll (NY)
Nicolet Area Tech Coll (WI)
Northampton Comm Coll (PA)
Northeast Comm Coll (NE)
Northeastern Jr Coll (CO)
North Hennepin Comm Coll (MN)
Northland Comm and Tech Coll–Thief River Falls (MN)
Ogeechee Tech Coll (GA)
Orange Coast Coll (CA)
Ouachita Tech Coll (AR)
Palm Beach State Coll (FL)
Pasadena City Coll (CA)
Pasco-Hernando Comm Coll (FL)
Phoenix Coll (AZ)
Polk State Coll (FL)
Raritan Valley Comm Coll (NJ)
Rockland Comm Coll (NY)
Saint Charles Comm Coll (MO)
Salt Lake Comm Coll (UT)
San Diego City Coll (CA)
San Diego Mesa Coll (CA)
Savannah Tech Coll (GA)
Seminole State Coll of Florida (FL)
Southeastern Tech Coll (GA)
Southeast Tech Inst (SD)
South Georgia Tech Coll (GA)
South Plains Coll (TX)
Southwest Mississippi Comm Coll (MS)
Southwest Wisconsin Tech Coll (WI)
Spartanburg Comm Coll (SC)
Springfield Tech Comm Coll (MA)
Stark State Coll of Technology (OH)
State U of New York Coll of Technology at Alfred (NY)
Suffolk County Comm Coll (NY)
Tallahassee Comm Coll (FL)
Tarrant County Coll District (TX)
Terra State Comm Coll (OH)
Three Rivers Comm Coll (CT)
Three Rivers Comm Coll (MO)
Tidewater Comm Coll (VA)
Trident Tech Coll (SC)
Trinity Valley Comm Coll (TX)
Tunxis Comm Coll (CT)
Umpqua Comm Coll (OR)
Union County Coll (NJ)
Valdosta Tech Coll (GA)
Waukesha County Tech Coll (WI)
Westchester Comm Coll (NY)
Western Wyoming Comm Coll (WY)
West Georgia Tech Coll (GA)
Westmoreland County Comm Coll (PA)
West Shore Comm Coll (MI)
Wisconsin Indianhead Tech Coll (WI)

Marketing Related
Dakota Coll at Bottineau (ND)
Davis Coll (OH)

Marketing Research
Lake Region State Coll (ND)
San Diego Mesa Coll (CA)

Masonry
Alexandria Tech Coll (MN)
Front Range Comm Coll (CO)
Ivy Tech Comm Coll–Central Indiana (IN)
Ivy Tech Comm Coll–Columbus (IN)
Ivy Tech Comm Coll–East Central (IN)
Ivy Tech Comm Coll–Lafayette (IN)
Ivy Tech Comm Coll–North Central (IN)
Ivy Tech Comm Coll–Northeast (IN)
Ivy Tech Comm Coll–Northwest (IN)
Ivy Tech Comm Coll–Southern Indiana (IN)
Ivy Tech Comm Coll–Southwest (IN)
Ivy Tech Comm Coll–Wabash Valley (IN)
Metropolitan Comm Coll–Business & Technology Campus (MO)
Pennsylvania Coll of Technology (PA)
State U of New York Coll of Technology at Alfred (NY)

Massage Therapy
Antonelli Coll, Hattiesburg (MS)
Antonelli Coll, Jackson (MS)
Arizona Western Coll (AZ)
Blue Cliff Coll–Shreveport (LA)
Brown Mackie Coll–Michigan City (IN)
Brown Mackie Coll–South Bend (IN)
Camden County Coll (NJ)
Career Training Academy, Pittsburgh (PA)
Central Arizona Coll (AZ)
Central Oregon Comm Coll (OR)
Coll of DuPage (IL)
Coll of Southern Maryland (MD)
Comm Care Coll (OK)
Comm Coll of Rhode Island (RI)
Comm Coll of Vermont (VT)
Harford Comm Coll (MD)
Harrison Coll, Indianapolis (IN)
Illinois Valley Comm Coll (IL)
Inst of Business & Medical Careers (CO)
Iowa Lakes Comm Coll (IA)
Ivy Tech Comm Coll–Northeast (IN)
Kaplan Coll, Merrillville Campus (IN)
Kennebec Valley Comm Coll (ME)
Kirtland Comm Coll (MI)
Lewis and Clark Comm Coll (IL)
Miller-Motte Tech Coll (SC)
Northeast Iowa Comm Coll (IA)
Northland Comm and Tech Coll–Thief River Falls (MN)
Northland Pioneer Coll (AZ)
Northwestern Coll (IL)
Oakland Comm Coll (MI)
Owens Comm Coll, Toledo (OH)
Pima Comm Coll (AZ)
Saint Charles Comm Coll (MO)
Saint Paul Coll–A Comm & Tech College (MN)
Sheridan Coll (WY)
Southwest Mississippi Comm Coll (MS)
Spencerian Coll (KY)
Springfield Tech Comm Coll (MA)

Mass Communication/ Media
Amarillo Coll (TX)
Anne Arundel Comm Coll (MD)
Bucks County Comm Coll (PA)
Bunker Hill Comm Coll (MA)
Central Comm Coll–Hastings Campus (NE)
Chipola Coll (FL)
Clarendon Coll (TX)
Crowder Coll (MO)
Finger Lakes Comm Coll (NY)
Frederick Comm Coll (MD)
Fulton-Montgomery Comm Coll (NY)
Gainesville State Coll (GA)
Genesee Comm Coll (NY)
Georgia Military Coll (GA)
Grand Rapids Comm Coll (MI)
Greenfield Comm Coll (MA)
Harrisburg Area Comm Coll (PA)
Iowa Lakes Comm Coll (IA)
Lackawanna Coll (PA)
Lake Michigan Coll (MI)
Lansing Comm Coll (MI)
Laramie County Comm Coll (WY)
Lon Morris Coll (TX)
Massasoit Comm Coll (MA)
Mercer County Comm Coll (NJ)
Miami Dade Coll (FL)
Middlesex Comm Coll (CT)
Nassau Comm Coll (NY)
Niagara County Comm Coll (NY)
Northeast Comm Coll (NE)
North Idaho Coll (ID)
Northland Comm and Tech Coll–Thief River Falls (MN)
Oklahoma City Comm Coll (OK)
Orange Coast Coll (CA)
Palm Beach State Coll (FL)
Pennsylvania Coll of Technology (PA)
Phoenix Coll (AZ)
Red Rocks Comm Coll (CO)
Rockland Comm Coll (NY)
Salt Lake Comm Coll (UT)
Snow Coll (UT)
South Georgia Coll (GA)
South Plains Coll (TX)
State Coll of Florida Manatee-Sarasota (FL)
Westchester Comm Coll (NY)

Materials Engineering
Milwaukee Area Tech Coll (WI)

Materials Science
Kent State U at Ashtabula (OH)

Mathematics
Allen Comm Coll (KS)
Alpena Comm Coll (MI)
Alvin Comm Coll (TX)
Amarillo Coll (TX)
Anne Arundel Comm Coll (MD)
Antelope Valley Coll (CA)
Arizona Western Coll (AZ)
Austin Comm Coll (TX)
Bainbridge Coll (GA)
Bakersfield Coll (CA)
Barton County Comm Coll (KS)
Bronx Comm Coll of the City U of New York (NY)
Bucks County Comm Coll (PA)
Bunker Hill Comm Coll (MA)
Burlington County Coll (NJ)
Casper Coll (WY)
Cecil Coll (MD)
Central Oregon Comm Coll (OR)
Central Texas Coll (TX)
Central Wyoming Coll (WY)
Clarendon Coll (TX)
Clovis Comm Coll (NM)
Coll of the Canyons (CA)
Comm Coll of Allegheny County (PA)
Corning Comm Coll (NY)
Crowder Coll (MO)
Dakota Coll at Bottineau (ND)
Darton Coll (GA)
Del Mar Coll (TX)
Eastern Arizona Coll (AZ)
Eastern Wyoming Coll (WY)
East Los Angeles Coll (CA)
Essex County Coll (NJ)
Everett Comm Coll (WA)
Finger Lakes Comm Coll (NY)
Folsom Lake Coll (CA)
Frederick Comm Coll (MD)
Fulton-Montgomery Comm Coll (NY)
Gainesville State Coll (GA)
Genesee Comm Coll (NY)
Golden West Coll (CA)
Greenfield Comm Coll (MA)
Harrisburg Area Comm Coll (PA)
Highland Comm Coll (IL)
Highline Comm Coll (WA)
Housatonic Comm Coll (CT)
Howard Coll (TX)
Hutchinson Comm Coll and Area Vocational School (KS)
Indian River State Coll (FL)
Iowa Lakes Comm Coll (IA)
Jamestown Comm Coll (NY)
Jefferson Comm Coll (NY)
Kilgore Coll (TX)
Kingsborough Comm Coll of the City U of New York (NY)
Lake Michigan Coll (MI)
Lansing Comm Coll (MI)
Laramie County Comm Coll (WY)
Lawson State Comm Coll (AL)
Lehigh Carbon Comm Coll (PA)
Linn-Benton Comm Coll (OR)
Lonestar Coll–Cy-Fair (TX)
Lonestar Coll–Kingwood (TX)
Lonestar Coll–Montgomery (TX)
Lonestar Coll–North Harris (TX)
Lonestar Coll–Tomball (TX)
Lon Morris Coll (TX)
Macomb Comm Coll (MI)
Mendocino Coll (CA)
Mercer County Comm Coll (NJ)
Miami Dade Coll (FL)
Minneapolis Comm and Tech Coll (MN)
Mohave Comm Coll (AZ)
Montgomery County Comm Coll (PA)
Mt. San Jacinto Coll (CA)
Murray State Coll (OK)
Nassau Comm Coll (NY)
Niagara County Comm Coll (NY)
Northampton Comm Coll (PA)
Northeast Comm Coll (NE)
Northeastern Jr Coll (CO)
North Hennepin Comm Coll (MN)
North Idaho Coll (ID)
Northwest Coll (WY)
Northwestern Connecticut Comm Coll (CT)
Northwest Florida State Coll (FL)
Odessa Coll (TX)
Oklahoma City Comm Coll (OK)
Orange Coast Coll (CA)
Otero Jr Coll (CO)
Palm Beach State Coll (FL)
Paris Jr Coll (TX)
Pasadena City Coll (CA)
Potomac State Coll of West Virginia U (WV)
Red Rocks Comm Coll (CO)
Reedley Coll (CA)
Rockland Comm Coll (NY)
Saint Charles Comm Coll (MO)
St. Philip's Coll (TX)
Sandhills Comm Coll (NC)
San Diego City Coll (CA)
San Diego Mesa Coll (CA)
San Jacinto Coll District (TX)
San Juan Coll (NM)
Santa Rosa Jr Coll (CA)
Scottsdale Comm Coll (AZ)
Seminole State Coll (OK)
Sheridan Coll (WY)
Sierra Coll (CA)

Snow Coll (UT)
South Georgia Coll (GA)
Springfield Tech Comm Coll (MA)
Suffolk County Comm Coll (NY)
Terra State Comm Coll (OH)
Trinity Valley Comm Coll (TX)
Triton Coll (IL)
Umpqua Comm Coll (OR)
Victor Valley Coll (CA)
Western Wyoming Comm Coll (WY)

Mathematics and Computer Science
Crowder Coll (MO)
Dean Coll (MA)

Mathematics Teacher Education
Black Hawk Coll, Moline (IL)
The Comm Coll of Baltimore County (MD)
Darton Coll (GA)
Delaware Tech & Comm Coll, Jack F. Owens Campus (DE)
Delaware Tech & Comm Coll, Stanton/Wilmington Campus (DE)
Delaware Tech & Comm Coll, Terry Campus (DE)
Eastern Wyoming Coll (WY)
Frederick Comm Coll (MD)
Harford Comm Coll (MD)
Highland Comm Coll (IL)
Howard Coll (TX)
Kankakee Comm Coll (IL)
Kaskaskia Coll (IL)
Montgomery Coll (MD)
Moraine Valley Comm Coll (IL)
State Coll of Florida Manatee-Sarasota (FL)
Triton Coll (IL)
Ulster County Comm Coll (NY)

Mechanical Drafting and CAD/CADD
Alexandria Tech Coll (MN)
Central Carolina Tech Coll (SC)
Central Lakes Coll (MN)
Comm Coll of Allegheny County (PA)
Delaware Tech & Comm Coll, Jack F. Owens Campus (DE)
Des Moines Area Comm Coll (IA)
Edison State Comm Coll (OH)
Island Drafting and Tech Inst (NY)
John Wood Comm Coll (IL)
Kirkwood Comm Coll (IA)
Macomb Comm Coll (MI)
Midlands Tech Coll (SC)
Milwaukee Area Tech Coll (WI)
Minnesota State Comm and Tech Coll (MN)
Montgomery County Comm Coll (PA)
Moraine Park Tech Coll (WI)
Oakland Comm Coll (MI)
St. Cloud Tech Coll (MN)
Sierra Coll (CA)
Southwest Wisconsin Tech Coll (WI)
Spartanburg Comm Coll (SC)
Stanly Comm Coll (NC)
Sullivan Coll of Technology and Design (KY)
Triangle Tech–Greensburg School (PA)
Triangle Tech, Inc.–Erie School (PA)
Waukesha County Tech Coll (WI)
Westmoreland County Comm Coll (PA)
Wisconsin Indianhead Tech Coll (WI)

Mechanical Engineering
Fiorello H. LaGuardia Comm Coll of the City U of New York (NY)
Itasca Comm Coll (MN)
Kilgore Coll (TX)
Lehigh Carbon Comm Coll (PA)
Pasadena City Coll (CA)
Saint Charles Comm Coll (MO)

Mechanical Engineering/ Mechanical Technology
Alamance Comm Coll (NC)
Anne Arundel Comm Coll (MD)
Augusta Tech Coll (GA)
Beaufort County Comm Coll (NC)
Blue Ridge Comm Coll (NC)
Broome Comm Coll (NY)
Camden County Coll (NJ)
Cape Fear Comm Coll (NC)
Catawba Valley Comm Coll (NC)
Central Piedmont Comm Coll (NC)
Cincinnati State Tech and Comm Coll (OH)
Coll of Lake County (IL)
Columbus Tech Coll (GA)
The Comm Coll of Baltimore County (MD)
Comm Coll of Rhode Island (RI)
Corning Comm Coll (NY)
County Coll of Morris (NJ)
Danville Area Comm Coll (IL)
Delaware County Comm Coll (PA)
Delaware Tech & Comm Coll, Stanton/Wilmington Campus (DE)
Delta Coll (MI)
Edison State Comm Coll (OH)
Erie Comm Coll, North Campus (NY)
Finger Lakes Comm Coll (NY)
Fox Valley Tech Coll (WI)
Gadsden State Comm Coll (AL)
Gateway Comm Coll (CT)
Guilford Tech Comm Coll (NC)
Harrisburg Area Comm Coll (PA)
Highland Comm Coll (IL)
Illinois Eastern Comm Colls, Lincoln Trail College (IL)
Illinois Valley Comm Coll (IL)
Jamestown Comm Coll (NY)
John Tyler Comm Coll (VA)
Kalamazoo Valley Comm Coll (MI)
Kent State U at Ashtabula (OH)
Kent State U at Trumbull (OH)
Kent State U at Tuscarawas (OH)
Lakeland Comm Coll (OH)
Lansing Comm Coll (MI)
Lehigh Carbon Comm Coll (PA)
Macomb Comm Coll (MI)
Marion Tech Coll (OH)
Midlands Tech Coll (SC)
Milwaukee Area Tech Coll (WI)
Mohawk Valley Comm Coll (NY)
Montgomery County Comm Coll (PA)
Moraine Valley Comm Coll (IL)
Owens Comm Coll, Toledo (OH)
Penn State DuBois (PA)
Penn State Hazleton (PA)
Penn State New Kensington (PA)
Penn State Shenango (PA)
Penn State York (PA)
Pennsylvania Inst of Technology (PA)
Potomac State Coll of West Virginia U (WV)
Southeastern Comm Coll (IA)
Southeast Tech Inst (SD)
Spartanburg Comm Coll (SC)
Springfield Tech Comm Coll (MA)
Stark State Coll of Technology (OH)
State U of New York Coll of Technology at Alfred (NY)
Sullivan Coll of Technology and Design (KY)
Tarrant County Coll District (TX)
Terra State Comm Coll (OH)
Thomas Nelson Comm Coll (VA)
Three Rivers Comm Coll (CT)
Trident Tech Coll (SC)
Triton Coll (IL)
Union County Coll (NJ)
Wayne Comm Coll (NC)
Westchester Comm Coll (NY)
Westmoreland County Comm Coll (PA)
Wilson Comm Coll (NC)

Mechanical Engineering Technologies Related
Blue Ridge Comm Coll (NC)
Moraine Park Tech Coll (WI)
Mountain Empire Comm Coll (VA)
Pennsylvania Inst of Technology (PA)
Terra State Comm Coll (OH)
Thomas Nelson Comm Coll (VA)

Mechanic and Repair Technologies Related
Cincinnati State Tech and Comm Coll (OH)
Delta Coll (MI)
Ivy Tech Comm Coll–Bloomington (IN)
Ivy Tech Comm Coll–Columbus (IN)
Ivy Tech Comm Coll–Kokomo (IN)
Ivy Tech Comm Coll–Lafayette (IN)
Ivy Tech Comm Coll–North Central (IN)
Ivy Tech Comm Coll–Northwest (IN)
Ivy Tech Comm Coll–Southwest (IN)
Macomb Comm Coll (MI)
Pennsylvania Coll of Technology (PA)
State Fair Comm Coll (MO)
Triton Coll (IL)

Mechanics and Repair
Ivy Tech Comm Coll–Bloomington (IN)
Ivy Tech Comm Coll–Central Indiana (IN)
Ivy Tech Comm Coll–Columbus (IN)
Ivy Tech Comm Coll–Kokomo (IN)
Ivy Tech Comm Coll–Lafayette (IN)
Ivy Tech Comm Coll–North Central (IN)
Ivy Tech Comm Coll–Northeast (IN)
Ivy Tech Comm Coll–Northwest (IN)
Ivy Tech Comm Coll–Richmond (IN)
Ivy Tech Comm Coll–Southern Indiana (IN)
Ivy Tech Comm Coll–Southwest (IN)
Ivy Tech Comm Coll–Wabash Valley (IN)
Kalamazoo Valley Comm Coll (MI)
Oakland Comm Coll (MI)
Rogue Comm Coll (OR)
Western Wyoming Comm Coll (WY)

Medical Administrative Assistant and Medical Secretary
Alamance Comm Coll (NC)
Alexandria Tech Coll (MN)
Alvin Comm Coll (TX)
Amarillo Coll (TX)
Antelope Valley Coll (CA)
Barton County Comm Coll (KS)
Berkeley City Coll (CA)
Blue Cliff Coll–Shreveport (LA)
Bronx Comm Coll of the City U of New York (NY)
Bryant & Stratton Coll, Eastlake (OH)
Bryant & Stratton Coll, Parma (OH)
Bryant & Stratton Coll - Albany Campus (NY)
Bryant & Stratton Coll - Amherst Campus (NY)
Bryant & Stratton Coll - Buffalo Campus (NY)
Bryant & Stratton Coll - Greece Campus (NY)
Bryant & Stratton Coll - Henrietta Campus (NY)
Bryant & Stratton Coll - North Campus (NY)
Bryant & Stratton Coll - Southtowns Campus (NY)
Bryant & Stratton Coll - Syracuse Campus (NY)
Central Arizona Coll (AZ)
Central Carolina Comm Coll (NC)
Central Comm Coll–Hastings Campus (NE)
Central Lakes Coll (MN)
Central Piedmont Comm Coll (NC)
Central Texas Coll (TX)
Century Coll (MN)
City Colls of Chicago, Richard J. Daley College (IL)
Clark Coll (WA)
Clovis Comm Coll (NM)
Comm Coll of Allegheny County (PA)
The Comm Coll of Baltimore County (MD)
Comm Coll of Philadelphia (PA)
Comm Coll of Rhode Island (RI)
Consolidated School of Business, Lancaster (PA)
Crowder Coll (MO)
Dabney S. Lancaster Comm Coll (VA)
Dakota Coll at Bottineau (ND)
Danville Area Comm Coll (IL)
Davis Coll (OH)
Daytona State Coll (FL)
Del Mar Coll (TX)
Delta Coll (MI)
Des Moines Area Comm Coll (IA)
East Central Coll (MO)
East Los Angeles Coll (CA)
Edison State Comm Coll (OH)
Essex County Coll (NJ)
Flathead Valley Comm Coll (MT)
Frederick Comm Coll (MD)
Fulton-Montgomery Comm Coll (NY)
Gateway Comm Coll (CT)
Goodwin Coll (CT)
Grand Rapids Comm Coll (MI)
Green River Comm Coll (WA)
Hawkeye Comm Coll (IA)
Hazard Comm and Tech Coll (KY)
Hennepin Tech Coll (MN)
Howard Comm Coll (MD)
Illinois Eastern Comm Colls, Olney Central College (IL)
Indian River State Coll (FL)
Inst of Business & Medical Careers (CO)
Inver Hills Comm Coll (MN)
Iowa Lakes Comm Coll (IA)
Jamestown Business Coll (NY)
Johnston Comm Coll (NC)
John Wood Comm Coll (IL)
Kaplan Career Inst, ICM Campus (PA)
Kaplan Coll, Hammond Campus (IN)
Kaplan U, Hagerstown Campus (MD)
Kellogg Comm Coll (MI)
Kennebec Valley Comm Coll (ME)
Kirtland Comm Coll (MI)
Lackawanna Coll (PA)
Lake Michigan Coll (MI)
Lake Region State Coll (ND)
LDS Business Coll (UT)
Lewis and Clark Comm Coll (IL)
Linn-Benton Comm Coll (OR)
Los Angeles Harbor Coll (CA)
Lower Columbia Coll (WA)
Manchester Comm Coll (CT)
Marion Tech Coll (OH)
Metropolitan Comm Coll–Longview (MO)
Metropolitan Comm Coll–Maple Woods (MO)
Metropolitan Comm Coll–Penn Valley (MO)
Middlesex Comm Coll (CT)
Milwaukee Area Tech Coll (WI)
Minnesota State Coll–Southeast Tech (MN)
Minnesota State Comm and Tech Coll (MN)
Minnesota West Comm and Tech Coll (MN)
Mitchell Tech Inst (SD)
Montcalm Comm Coll (MI)
Muskegon Comm Coll (MI)
Nassau Comm Coll (NY)
Newport Business Inst, Williamsport (PA)
Nicolet Area Tech Coll (WI)
Northampton Comm Coll (PA)
Northeast Comm Coll (NE)
Northeastern Jr Coll (CO)
North Idaho Coll (ID)
Northland Comm and Tech Coll–Thief River Falls (MN)
Northwest Tech Coll (MN)
Orange Coast Coll (CA)
Otero Jr Coll (CO)
Ouachita Tech Coll (AR)
Pennsylvania Coll of Technology (PA)
Phoenix Coll (AZ)
Piedmont Comm Coll (NC)
Polk State Coll (FL)
Potomac State Coll of West Virginia U (WV)
Rockingham Comm Coll (NC)
St. Philip's Coll (TX)
Sandhills Comm Coll (NC)
San Jacinto Coll District (TX)
Scottsdale Comm Coll (AZ)
Shawnee Comm Coll (IL)
Somerset Comm Coll (KY)
South Plains Coll (TX)
South Puget Sound Comm Coll (WA)
Springfield Tech Comm Coll (MA)
Stanly Comm Coll (NC)
State Fair Comm Coll (MO)
Terra State Comm Coll (OH)
Trident Tech Coll (SC)
Tunxis Comm Coll (CT)
Umpqua Comm Coll (OR)
The U of Montana–Helena Coll of Technology (MT)
Vincennes U Jasper Campus (IN)
Wayne Comm Coll (NC)
Western Wyoming Comm Coll (WY)
Wisconsin Indianhead Tech Coll (WI)

Medical/Clinical Assistant
Alamance Comm Coll (NC)
Allan Hancock Coll (CA)
Anne Arundel Comm Coll (MD)
Antonelli Coll, Jackson (MS)
Argosy U, Twin Cities (MN)
Barton County Comm Coll (KS)
Bradford School (OH)
Bradford School (PA)
Broome Comm Coll (NY)
Brown Mackie Coll–Akron (OH)
Brown Mackie Coll–Albuquerque (NM)
Brown Mackie Coll–Atlanta (GA)
Brown Mackie Coll–Boise (ID)
Brown Mackie Coll–Cincinnati (OH)
Brown Mackie Coll–Findlay (OH)
Brown Mackie Coll–Fort Wayne (IN)
Brown Mackie Coll–Greenville (SC)
Brown Mackie Coll–Hopkinsville (KY)
Brown Mackie Coll–Indianapolis (IN)
Brown Mackie Coll–Kansas City (KS)
Brown Mackie Coll–Louisville (KY)
Brown Mackie Coll–Merrillville (IN)
Brown Mackie Coll–Miami (FL)
Brown Mackie Coll–Michigan City (IN)
Brown Mackie Coll–North Canton (OH)
Brown Mackie Coll–Northern Kentucky (KY)
Brown Mackie Coll–Phoenix (AZ)
Brown Mackie Coll–Quad Cities (IL)
Brown Mackie Coll–St. Louis (MO)
Brown Mackie Coll–Salina (KS)
Brown Mackie Coll–South Bend (IN)
Brown Mackie Coll–Tucson (AZ)
Brown Mackie Coll–Tulsa (OK)
Bryant & Stratton Coll, Eastlake (OH)
Bryant & Stratton Coll, Parma (OH)
Bryant & Stratton Coll (WI)
Bryant & Stratton Coll - Albany Campus (NY)
Bryant & Stratton Coll - Buffalo Campus (NY)
Bryant & Stratton Coll - Greece Campus (NY)
Bryant & Stratton Coll - Henrietta Campus (NY)
Bryant & Stratton Coll - North Campus (NY)
Bryant & Stratton Coll - Richmond Campus (VA)
Bryant & Stratton Coll - Southtowns Campus (NY)
Bryant & Stratton Coll - Syracuse Campus (NY)
Bryant & Stratton Coll - Virginia Beach (VA)
Bucks County Comm Coll (PA)
Career Coll of Northern Nevada (NV)
Career Training Academy, Pittsburgh (PA)
Carteret Comm Coll (NC)
Central Carolina Comm Coll (NC)
Central Comm Coll–Columbus Campus (NE)
Central Comm Coll–Grand Island Campus (NE)
Central Comm Coll–Hastings Campus (NE)
Central Oregon Comm Coll (OR)
Central Piedmont Comm Coll (NC)
Century Coll (MN)
CHI Inst, Broomall Campus (PA)
Cincinnati State Tech and Comm Coll (OH)
City Colls of Chicago, Malcolm X College (IL)
Clark Coll (WA)
Comm Care Coll (OK)

Comm Coll of Allegheny County (PA)
The Comm Coll of Baltimore County (MD)
Comm Coll of Philadelphia (PA)
Cossatot Comm Coll of the U of Arkansas (AR)
Dakota Coll at Bottineau (ND)
Davis Coll (OH)
DeKalb Tech Coll (GA)
Delaware County Comm Coll (PA)
Delaware Tech & Comm Coll, Jack F. Owens Campus (DE)
Delaware Tech & Comm Coll, Stanton/Wilmington Campus (DE)
Delaware Tech & Comm Coll, Terry Campus (DE)
Delta Coll (MI)
Des Moines Area Comm Coll (IA)
Douglas Education Center (PA)
East Los Angeles Coll (CA)
El Centro Coll (TX)
El Paso Comm Coll (TX)
ETI Tech Coll of Niles (OH)
Everett Comm Coll (WA)
Flathead Valley Comm Coll (MT)
Forrest Jr Coll (SC)
Fox Coll (IL)
Georgia Perimeter Coll (GA)
Goodwin Coll (CT)
Guilford Tech Comm Coll (NC)
Gwinnett Tech Coll (GA)
Harford Comm Coll (MD)
Harrisburg Area Comm Coll (PA)
Harrison Coll, Anderson (IN)
Harrison Coll, Columbus (IN)
Harrison Coll, Elkhart (IN)
Harrison Coll, Evansville (IN)
Harrison Coll, Fort Wayne (IN)
Harrison Coll, Indianapolis (IN)
Harrison Coll, Indianapolis (IN)
Harrison Coll, Lafayette (IN)
Harrison Coll, Muncie (IN)
Harrison Coll, Terre Haute (IN)
Harrison Coll (OH)
H. Councill Trenholm State Tech Coll (AL)
Hesser Coll, Manchester (NH)
Highland Comm Coll (IL)
Highline Comm Coll (WA)
Inst of Business & Medical Careers (CO)
International Business Coll, Indianapolis (IN)
Iowa Lakes Comm Coll (IA)
Ivy Tech Comm Coll–Central Indiana (IN)
Ivy Tech Comm Coll–Columbus (IN)
Ivy Tech Comm Coll–East Central (IN)
Ivy Tech Comm Coll–Kokomo (IN)
Ivy Tech Comm Coll–Lafayette (IN)
Ivy Tech Comm Coll–North Central (IN)
Ivy Tech Comm Coll–Northeast (IN)
Ivy Tech Comm Coll–Northwest (IN)
Ivy Tech Comm Coll–Richmond (IN)
Ivy Tech Comm Coll–Southeast (IN)
Ivy Tech Comm Coll–Southern Indiana (IN)
Ivy Tech Comm Coll–Southwest (IN)
Ivy Tech Comm Coll–Wabash Valley (IN)
Jackson Comm Coll (MI)
James Sprunt Comm Coll (NC)
Johnston Comm Coll (NC)
Kaplan Career Inst, Harrisburg (PA)
Kaplan Coll, Hammond Campus (IN)
Kaplan Coll, Merrillville Campus (IN)
Kaplan U, South Portland (ME)
Kaplan U, Cedar Rapids (IA)
Kaplan U, Hagerstown Campus (MD)
Kaplan U, Lincoln (NE)
Kaplan U, Omaha (NE)
Kennebec Valley Comm Coll (ME)
Kirkwood Comm Coll (IA)
Lac Courte Oreilles Ojibwa Comm Coll (WI)
Lansing Comm Coll (MI)
LDS Business Coll (UT)
Lehigh Carbon Comm Coll (PA)
Linn-Benton Comm Coll (OR)
Lower Columbia Coll (WA)
Macomb Comm Coll (MI)
Massasoit Comm Coll (MA)
Miami Dade Coll (FL)
Midlands Tech Coll (SC)
Miller-Motte Tech Coll (SC)
Minneapolis Business Coll (MN)
Minnesota West Comm and Tech Coll (MN)
Mitchell Tech Inst (SD)
Mohave Comm Coll (AZ)
Mohawk Valley Comm Coll (NY)
Montana State U–Great Falls Coll of Technology (MT)
Montgomery Comm Coll (NC)
Montgomery County Comm Coll (PA)
Moraine Park Tech Coll (WI)
Mountain State Coll (WV)
Mt. San Jacinto Coll (CA)
Mount Wachusett Comm Coll (MA)
Niagara County Comm Coll (NY)
North Iowa Area Comm Coll (IA)
Northwestern Coll (IL)
Northwestern Connecticut Comm Coll (CT)
Oakland Comm Coll (MI)
Ocean County Coll (NJ)
Olean Business Inst (NY)
Olympic Coll (WA)
Orange Coast Coll (CA)
Pasadena City Coll (CA)
Phoenix Coll (AZ)
Raritan Valley Comm Coll (NJ)
Salt Lake Comm Coll (UT)
San Diego Mesa Coll (CA)
San Jacinto Coll District (TX)
Southeastern Comm Coll (IA)
Southern Maine Comm Coll (ME)
Southern State Comm Coll (OH)
South Puget Sound Comm Coll (WA)
Southwestern Michigan Coll (MI)
Springfield Tech Comm Coll (MA)
Stanly Comm Coll (NC)
Stark State Coll of Technology (OH)
Terra State Comm Coll (OH)
Tri-County Comm Coll (NC)
Wayne Comm Coll (NC)
Western Wyoming Comm Coll (WY)
Wood Tobe–Coburn School (NY)

Medical/Health Management and Clinical Assistant
Owens Comm Coll, Toledo (OH)
Terra State Comm Coll (OH)

Medical Informatics
The Comm Coll of Baltimore County (MD)

Medical Insurance Coding
Alexandria Tech Coll (MN)
Antonelli Coll, Hattiesburg (MS)
Antonelli Coll, Jackson (MS)
Barton County Comm Coll (KS)
Career Training Academy, Pittsburgh (PA)
Comm Care Coll (OK)
Cowley County Comm Coll and Area Vocational–Tech School (KS)
Dakota Coll at Bottineau (ND)
Darton Coll (GA)
Everest Inst (NY)
Goodwin Coll (CT)
Harrison Coll, Anderson (IN)
Harrison Coll, Columbus (IN)
Harrison Coll, Evansville (IN)
Harrison Coll, Indianapolis (IN)
Harrison Coll, Lafayette (IN)
Northeast Comm Coll (NE)
Paris Jr Coll (TX)
Springfield Tech Comm Coll (MA)
Terra State Comm Coll (OH)

Medical Insurance/ Medical Billing
Goodwin Coll (CT)
Harrison Coll, Elkhart (IN)
Harrison Coll, Evansville (IN)
Harrison Coll, Fort Wayne (IN)
Harrison Coll, Terre Haute (IN)
Harrison Coll (OH)
Jackson Comm Coll (MI)
Montana State U–Great Falls Coll of Technology (MT)
Pasadena City Coll (CA)
Southwest Mississippi Comm Coll (MS)
Spencerian Coll (KY)

Medical Office Assistant
Alpena Comm Coll (MI)
Barton County Comm Coll (KS)
Central Wyoming Coll (WY)
Clovis Comm Coll (NM)
Dakota Coll at Bottineau (ND)
Front Range Comm Coll (CO)
Iowa Lakes Comm Coll (IA)
Jamestown Comm Coll (NY)
Kankakee Comm Coll (IL)
LDS Business Coll (UT)
Moraine Park Tech Coll (WI)
Pasadena City Coll (CA)
Quinsigamond Comm Coll (MA)
Saint Paul Coll–A Comm & Tech College (MN)
Terra State Comm Coll (OH)
Western Wyoming Comm Coll (WY)

Medical Office Computer Specialist
Iowa Lakes Comm Coll (IA)
Rogue Comm Coll (OR)
Western Wyoming Comm Coll (WY)

Medical Office Management
Beaufort County Comm Coll (NC)
Brown Mackie Coll–Hopkinsville (KY)
Brown Mackie Coll–Merrillville (IN)
Brown Mackie Coll–Michigan City (IN)
Cape Fear Comm Coll (NC)
Catawba Valley Comm Coll (NC)
Coll of Lake County (IL)
Columbus Tech Coll (GA)
Douglas Education Center (PA)
Elaine P. Nunez Comm Coll (LA)
Erie Comm Coll, North Campus (NY)
Fayetteville Tech Comm Coll (NC)
Forrest Jr Coll (SC)
Georgia Northwestern Tech Coll (GA)
Guilford Tech Comm Coll (NC)
Johnston Comm Coll (NC)
Kaplan Coll, Dayton Campus (OH)
Kilian Comm Coll (SD)
Lac Courte Oreilles Ojibwa Comm Coll (WI)
Long Island Business Inst (NY)
Pennsylvania Inst of Technology (PA)
Pikes Peak Comm Coll (CO)
Randolph Comm Coll (NC)
Spencerian Coll (KY)
Wayne Comm Coll (NC)

Medical Radiologic Technology
Albany Tech Coll (GA)
Allegany Coll of Maryland (MD)
Argosy U, Twin Cities (MN)
Athens Tech Coll (GA)
Augusta Tech Coll (GA)
Broome Comm Coll (NY)
Bunker Hill Comm Coll (MA)
Burlington County Coll (NJ)
Cape Fear Comm Coll (NC)
Carolinas Coll of Health Sciences (NC)
Catawba Valley Comm Coll (NC)
Central Georgia Tech Coll (GA)
Central New Mexico Comm Coll (NM)
Central Ohio Tech Coll (OH)
Central Texas Coll (TX)
Chattahoochee Tech Coll (GA)
Chattanooga State Comm Coll (TN)
City Colls of Chicago, Malcolm X College (IL)
Clovis Comm Coll (NM)
Coll of DuPage (IL)
Coll of Lake County (IL)
Columbus Tech Coll (GA)
Comm Coll of Allegheny County (PA)
The Comm Coll of Baltimore County (MD)
Cumberland County Coll (NJ)
Del Mar Coll (TX)
East Central Coll (MO)
El Centro Coll (TX)
El Paso Comm Coll (TX)
Erie Comm Coll (NY)
Essex County Coll (NJ)
Flathead Valley Comm Coll (MT)
Gadsden State Comm Coll (AL)
Griffin Tech Coll (GA)
Gwinnett Tech Coll (GA)
Harcum Coll (PA)
Hazard Comm and Tech Coll (KY)
Heart of Georgia Tech Coll (GA)
Hillsborough Comm Coll (FL)
Holyoke Comm Coll (MA)
Hutchinson Comm Coll and Area Vocational School (KS)
Illinois Eastern Comm Colls, Olney Central College (IL)
Ivy Tech Comm Coll–Central Indiana (IN)
Ivy Tech Comm Coll–Columbus (IN)
Ivy Tech Comm Coll–East Central (IN)
Ivy Tech Comm Coll–Wabash Valley (IN)
Jackson Comm Coll (MI)
Jackson State Comm Coll (TN)
Jefferson State Comm Coll (AL)
Johnston Comm Coll (NC)
John Wood Comm Coll (IL)
Kellogg Comm Coll (MI)
Kent State U at Salem (OH)
Kilgore Coll (TX)
Lakeland Comm Coll (OH)
Lake Michigan Coll (MI)
Lanier Tech Coll (GA)
Lansing Comm Coll (MI)
Lincoln Land Comm Coll (IL)
Lonestar Coll–Cy-Fair (TX)
Lonestar Coll–Montgomery (TX)
Mercer County Comm Coll (NJ)
Meridian Comm Coll (MS)
Middle Georgia Tech Coll (GA)
Midlands Tech Coll (SC)
Milwaukee Area Tech Coll (WI)
Mohawk Valley Comm Coll (NY)
Montana State U–Great Falls Coll of Technology (MT)
Montcalm Comm Coll (MI)
Montgomery Coll (MD)
Montgomery County Comm Coll (PA)
Moraine Park Tech Coll (WI)
Nassau Comm Coll (NY)
North Arkansas Coll (AR)
Northeast Comm Coll (NE)
Oakland Comm Coll (MI)
Orangeburg-Calhoun Tech Coll (SC)
Owensboro Comm and Tech Coll (KY)
Owens Comm Coll, Toledo (OH)
Penn State New Kensington (PA)
Penn State Schuylkill (PA)
Pennsylvania Coll of Technology (PA)
Pensacola Jr Coll (FL)
Pima Comm Coll (AZ)
Quinsigamond Comm Coll (MA)
St. Philip's Coll (TX)
Salt Lake Comm Coll (UT)
San Jacinto Coll District (TX)
Somerset Comm Coll (KY)
Southeastern Tech Coll (GA)
Southeast Kentucky Comm and Tech Coll (KY)
Southern Maine Comm Coll (ME)
Southern Union State Comm Coll (AL)
Southwest Georgia Tech Coll (GA)
Spartanburg Comm Coll (SC)
Spencerian Coll (KY)
Springfield Tech Comm Coll (MA)
State Coll of Florida Manatee-Sarasota (FL)
Union County Coll (NJ)
Valdosta Tech Coll (GA)
Volunteer State Comm Coll (TN)
West Georgia Tech Coll (GA)
Wor-Wic Comm Coll (MD)

Medical Reception
Alexandria Tech Coll (MN)
Iowa Lakes Comm Coll (IA)
Kaplan Coll, Merrillville Campus (IN)
Olympic Coll (WA)

Medical Staff Services Technology
Rend Lake Coll (IL)

Medical Transcription
Alexandria Tech Coll (MN)
Antonelli Coll, Hattiesburg (MS)
Antonelli Coll, Jackson (MS)
Barton County Comm Coll (KS)
Central Arizona Coll (AZ)
Collin County Comm Coll District (TX)
Cowley County Comm Coll and Area Vocational–Tech School (KS)
Dakota Coll at Bottineau (ND)
El Centro Coll (TX)
Elgin Comm Coll (IL)
Iowa Lakes Comm Coll (IA)
Jackson Comm Coll (MI)
Lac Courte Oreilles Ojibwa Comm Coll (WI)
LDS Business Coll (UT)
Montana State U–Great Falls Coll of Technology (MT)
Moraine Park Tech Coll (WI)
Mountain State Coll (WV)
New Mexico State U–Carlsbad (NM)
Northland Pioneer Coll (AZ)
Oakland Comm Coll (MI)
Saint Charles Comm Coll (MO)
Southwestern Comm Coll (IA)

Medication Aide
Barton County Comm Coll (KS)

Medium/Heavy Vehicle and Truck Technology
Edison State Comm Coll (OH)
Linn State Tech Coll (MO)
Northeast Comm Coll (NE)
Oakland Comm Coll (MI)
St. Cloud Tech Coll (MN)

Mental and Social Health Services And Allied Professions Related
Broome Comm Coll (NY)
Coll of Southern Maryland (MD)
Glendale Comm Coll (AZ)
J. Sargeant Reynolds Comm Coll (VA)
Kennebec Valley Comm Coll (ME)
Milwaukee Area Tech Coll (WI)
Southern Maine Comm Coll (ME)
Southwest Virginia Comm Coll (VA)
Southwest Wisconsin Tech Coll (WI)
Waukesha County Tech Coll (WI)

Mental Health Counseling
Comm Coll of Rhode Island (RI)

Mental Health/Rehabilitation
Alvin Comm Coll (TX)
Anne Arundel Comm Coll (MD)
Comm Coll of Philadelphia (PA)
Del Mar Coll (TX)
Fiorello H. LaGuardia Comm Coll of the City U of New York (NY)
Gateway Comm Coll (CT)
Housatonic Comm Coll (CT)
Kingsborough Comm Coll of the City U of New York (NY)
Lackawanna Coll (PA)
Macomb Comm Coll (MI)
Metropolitan Comm Coll (NE)
Middlesex Comm Coll (CT)
Sandhills Comm Coll (NC)
South Plains Coll (TX)
Tarrant County Coll District (TX)

Merchandising
Bradford School (PA)
Coll of DuPage (IL)
Cuyahoga Comm Coll (OH)
Delta Coll (MI)
North Central Texas Coll (TX)
Northeast Comm Coll (NE)

Merchandising, Sales, and Marketing Operations Related (General)
Broome Comm Coll (NY)
The Comm Coll of Baltimore County (MD)
Iowa Lakes Comm Coll (IA)
Minnesota State Comm and Tech Coll (MN)
Moraine Park Tech Coll (WI)
Southeast Tech Inst (SD)

Merchandising, Sales, and Marketing Operations Related (Specialized)
Wade Coll (TX)

Metal and Jewelry Arts
Fashion Inst of Technology (NY)
FIDM/The Fashion Inst of Design & Merchandising, Los Angeles Campus (CA)
Flathead Valley Comm Coll (MT)
Paris Jr Coll (TX)

Metallurgical Technology
Kilgore Coll (TX)
Linn-Benton Comm Coll (OR)
Lonestar Coll–Cy-Fair (TX)
Macomb Comm Coll (MI)
Murray State Coll (OK)
Penn State DuBois (PA)
Penn State Fayette, The Eberly Campus (PA)
Penn State Hazleton (PA)
Penn State New Kensington (PA)
Penn State Schuylkill (PA)
Penn State Shenango (PA)
Penn State Wilkes-Barre (PA)
Penn State York (PA)

Middle School Education
Arkansas State U–Mountain Home (AR)
Austin Comm Coll (TX)
Collin County Comm Coll District (TX)
Cossatot Comm Coll of the U of Arkansas (AR)
Darton Coll (GA)
Delaware Tech & Comm Coll, Jack F. Owens Campus (DE)
Delaware Tech & Comm Coll, Stanton/Wilmington Campus (DE)
Delaware Tech & Comm Coll, Terry Campus (DE)
El Paso Comm Coll (TX)
Gainesville State Coll (GA)
Howard Coll (TX)
Miami Dade Coll (FL)
Northampton Comm Coll (PA)
South Georgia Coll (GA)
U of Cincinnati Clermont Coll (OH)

Military Studies
Barton County Comm Coll (KS)

Military Technologies
Barton County Comm Coll (KS)
Pulaski Tech Coll (AR)

Mining Technology
Casper Coll (WY)
Eastern Arizona Coll (AZ)
Illinois Eastern Comm Colls, Wabash Valley College (IL)
Southwest Virginia Comm Coll (VA)
Western Wyoming Comm Coll (WY)

Modern Languages
Amarillo Coll (TX)
Barton County Comm Coll (KS)
Lon Morris Coll (TX)
Northwest Florida State Coll (FL)
Odessa Coll (TX)
Oklahoma City Comm Coll (OK)
Otero Jr Coll (CO)
San Diego City Coll (CA)

Montessori Teacher Education
Lehigh Carbon Comm Coll (PA)

Mortuary Science and Embalming
Lake Michigan Coll (MI)

Motorcycle Maintenance and Repair Technology
Iowa Lakes Comm Coll (IA)
Linn State Tech Coll (MO)

Multi/Interdisciplinary Studies Related
Anoka-Ramsey Comm Coll (MN)
Anoka-Ramsey Comm Coll, Cambridge Campus (MN)
Central Carolina Tech Coll (SC)
Coll of Southern Maryland (MD)
Coll of the Canyons (CA)
The Comm Coll of Baltimore County (MD)
Cossatot Comm Coll of the U of Arkansas (AR)
County Coll of Morris (NJ)
Eastfield Coll (TX)
El Paso Comm Coll (TX)
Harford Comm Coll (MD)
Hawkeye Comm Coll (IA)
Hazard Comm and Tech Coll (KY)
Hopkinsville Comm Coll (KY)
Kilgore Coll (TX)
Laramie County Comm Coll (WY)
Linn-Benton Comm Coll (OR)
Midlands Tech Coll (SC)
Moraine Park Tech Coll (WI)
New Mexico State U–Carlsbad (NM)
North Arkansas Coll (AR)
North Hennepin Comm Coll (MN)
Northwest-Shoals Comm Coll (AL)
Panola Coll (TX)
Pennsylvania Coll of Technology (PA)
Raritan Valley Comm Coll (NJ)
San Jacinto Coll District (TX)
Sheridan Coll (WY)
Somerset Comm Coll (KY)
Southern Union State Comm Coll (AL)
Southwest Wisconsin Tech Coll (WI)
Spartanburg Comm Coll (SC)
Triton Coll (IL)
U of Cincinnati Clermont Coll (OH)
Waukesha County Tech Coll (WI)
Wisconsin Indianhead Tech Coll (WI)

Museum Studies
Casper Coll (WY)
Northland Pioneer Coll (AZ)

Music
Allan Hancock Coll (CA)
Allen Comm Coll (KS)
Alvin Comm Coll (TX)
Amarillo Coll (TX)
Anne Arundel Comm Coll (MD)
Anoka-Ramsey Comm Coll (MN)
Anoka-Ramsey Comm Coll, Cambridge Campus (MN)
Antelope Valley Coll (CA)
Arizona Western Coll (AZ)
Austin Comm Coll (TX)
Bakersfield Coll (CA)
Barton County Comm Coll (KS)
Bronx Comm Coll of the City U of New York (NY)
Bucks County Comm Coll (PA)
Burlington County Coll (NJ)
Carroll Comm Coll (MD)
Casper Coll (WY)
Central Piedmont Comm Coll (NC)
Central Texas Coll (TX)
Central Wyoming Coll (WY)
Century Coll (MN)
City Colls of Chicago, Malcolm X College (IL)
Clarendon Coll (TX)
Coll of Lake County (IL)
Coll of the Canyons (CA)
Collin County Comm Coll District (TX)
Comm Coll of Allegheny County (PA)
Comm Coll of Philadelphia (PA)
Comm Coll of Rhode Island (RI)
County Coll of Morris (NJ)
Cowley County Comm Coll and Area Vocational–Tech School (KS)
Crowder Coll (MO)
Darton Coll (GA)
Del Mar Coll (TX)
Eastern Arizona Coll (AZ)
Eastern Wyoming Coll (WY)
Eastfield Coll (TX)
East Los Angeles Coll (CA)
Elgin Comm Coll (IL)
El Paso Comm Coll (TX)
Essex County Coll (NJ)
Everett Comm Coll (WA)
Finger Lakes Comm Coll (NY)
Gainesville State Coll (GA)
Glendale Comm Coll (AZ)
Golden West Coll (CA)
Grand Rapids Comm Coll (MI)
Harrisburg Area Comm Coll (PA)
Highline Comm Coll (WA)
Holyoke Comm Coll (MA)
Howard Coll (TX)
Howard Comm Coll (MD)
Illinois Eastern Comm Colls, Lincoln Trail College (IL)
Illinois Eastern Comm Colls, Olney Central College (IL)
Indian River State Coll (FL)
Iowa Lakes Comm Coll (IA)
Jamestown Comm Coll (NY)
Kilgore Coll (TX)
Kingsborough Comm Coll of the City U of New York (NY)
Lake Michigan Coll (MI)
Lansing Comm Coll (MI)
Laramie County Comm Coll (WY)
Lawson State Comm Coll (AL)
Lincoln Land Comm Coll (IL)
Lonestar Coll–Cy-Fair (TX)
Lonestar Coll–Kingwood (TX)
Lonestar Coll–Montgomery (TX)
Lonestar Coll–North Harris (TX)
Lonestar Coll–Tomball (TX)
Lon Morris Coll (TX)
Manchester Comm Coll (CT)
Mendocino Coll (CA)
Mercer County Comm Coll (NJ)
Miami Dade Coll (FL)
Milwaukee Area Tech Coll (WI)
Minnesota State Comm and Tech Coll (MN)
Mt. San Jacinto Coll (CA)
Niagara County Comm Coll (NY)
Northeastern Jr Coll (CO)
North Idaho Coll (ID)
Northwest Coll (WY)
Northwest Florida State Coll (FL)
Odessa Coll (TX)
Oklahoma City Comm Coll (OK)
Orange Coast Coll (CA)
Palm Beach State Coll (FL)
Pasadena City Coll (CA)
Pima Comm Coll (AZ)
Raritan Valley Comm Coll (NJ)
St. Philip's Coll (TX)
Salt Lake Comm Coll (UT)
Sandhills Comm Coll (NC)
San Diego City Coll (CA)
San Diego Mesa Coll (CA)
San Jacinto Coll District (TX)
Sheridan Coll (WY)
Sierra Coll (CA)
Snow Coll (UT)
South Plains Coll (TX)
Southwestern Comm Coll (IA)
Southwest Mississippi Comm Coll (MS)
Southwest Virginia Comm Coll (VA)
State Coll of Florida Manatee-Sarasota (FL)
Suffolk County Comm Coll (NY)
Terra State Comm Coll (OH)
Three Rivers Comm Coll (MO)
Tidewater Comm Coll (VA)
Trinity Valley Comm Coll (TX)
Triton Coll (IL)
Umpqua Comm Coll (OR)
Victor Valley Coll (CA)
Western Wyoming Comm Coll (WY)

Musical Instrument Fabrication and Repair
Minnesota State Coll–Southeast Tech (MN)
Orange Coast Coll (CA)

Music History, Literature, and Theory
Saint Charles Comm Coll (MO)
Snow Coll (UT)

Music Management and Merchandising
Austin Comm Coll (TX)
Collin County Comm Coll District (TX)
Glendale Comm Coll (AZ)
Harrisburg Area Comm Coll (PA)
Houston Comm Coll System (TX)
Mt. San Jacinto Coll (CA)
Northeast Comm Coll (NE)
Orange Coast Coll (CA)
Paradise Valley Comm Coll (AZ)
Terra State Comm Coll (OH)

Music Performance
Casper Coll (WY)
Houston Comm Coll System (TX)
Macomb Comm Coll (MI)
Miami Dade Coll (FL)
Nassau Comm Coll (NY)
Northeast Comm Coll (NE)
Oakland Comm Coll (MI)
Red Rocks Comm Coll (CO)
Reedley Coll (CA)
State Coll of Florida Manatee-Sarasota (FL)
Terra State Comm Coll (OH)

Music Related
KD Studio (TX)
Lower Columbia Coll (WA)
Terra State Comm Coll (OH)
Triton Coll (IL)

Music Teacher Education
Amarillo Coll (TX)
Casper Coll (WY)
Coll of Lake County (IL)
Darton Coll (GA)
Del Mar Coll (TX)
Eastern Wyoming Coll (WY)
Frederick Comm Coll (MD)
Highland Comm Coll (IL)
Howard Coll (TX)
Iowa Lakes Comm Coll (IA)
Miami Dade Coll (FL)
Northeast Comm Coll (NE)
Northeastern Jr Coll (CO)
North Idaho Coll (ID)
Sandhills Comm Coll (NC)
Snow Coll (UT)
Southwest Mississippi Comm Coll (MS)
State Coll of Florida Manatee-Sarasota (FL)
Umpqua Comm Coll (OR)

Music Theory and Composition
Houston Comm Coll System (TX)
Oakland Comm Coll (MI)
State Coll of Florida Manatee-Sarasota (FL)

Nail Technician and Manicurist
Century Coll (MN)
Clovis Comm Coll (NM)
Olympic Coll (WA)

Natural Resources and Conservation Related
Southwestern Indian Polytechnic Inst (NM)

Natural Resources/ Conservation
Central Lakes Coll (MN)
Central Oregon Comm Coll (OR)
Dakota Coll at Bottineau (ND)
Finger Lakes Comm Coll (NY)
Fox Valley Tech Coll (WI)
Fulton-Montgomery Comm Coll (NY)
Iowa Lakes Comm Coll (IA)
Itasca Comm Coll (MN)
Kirkwood Comm Coll (IA)
Mountain Empire Comm Coll (VA)
Murray State Coll (OK)
Niagara County Comm Coll (NY)
Olympic Coll (WA)
Santa Rosa Jr Coll (CA)
Tompkins Cortland Comm Coll (NY)
Ulster County Comm Coll (NY)

Natural Resources/ Conservation Related
Greenfield Comm Coll (MA)

Natural Resources Management
Finger Lakes Comm Coll (NY)
The Ohio State U Ag Tech Inst (OH)
Reedley Coll (CA)

Natural Resources Management and Policy
Central Carolina Tech Coll (SC)
Coll of Lake County (IL)
Finger Lakes Comm Coll (NY)
Greenfield Comm Coll (MA)
Hawkeye Comm Coll (IA)
Itasca Comm Coll (MN)
Lac Courte Oreilles Ojibwa Comm Coll (WI)
Northwest Coll (WY)
The Ohio State U Ag Tech Inst (OH)
Pikes Peak Comm Coll (CO)
Santa Rosa Jr Coll (CA)

Natural Sciences
Amarillo Coll (TX)
Golden West Coll (CA)
Highline Comm Coll (WA)
Iowa Lakes Comm Coll (IA)
Miami Dade Coll (FL)
Northeastern Jr Coll (CO)
Orange Coast Coll (CA)
Paradise Valley Comm Coll (AZ)
Sisseton-Wahpeton Comm Coll (SD)
Umpqua Comm Coll (OR)
U of Pittsburgh at Titusville (PA)
Victor Valley Coll (CA)

Nonprofit Management
Miami Dade Coll (FL)

Nuclear Engineering
Itasca Comm Coll (MN)

Nuclear Engineering Technology
Delaware Tech & Comm Coll, Jack F. Owens Campus (DE)
Delaware Tech & Comm Coll, Stanton/Wilmington Campus (DE)

Nuclear Medical Technology
Amarillo Coll (TX)
Bronx Comm Coll of the City U of New York (NY)
Coll of DuPage (IL)
Comm Coll of Allegheny County (PA)
Darton Coll (GA)
Delaware Tech & Comm Coll, Stanton/Wilmington Campus (DE)
Del Mar Coll (TX)
Fayetteville Tech Comm Coll (NC)
Frederick Comm Coll (MD)
Gateway Comm Coll (CT)
Harrisburg Area Comm Coll (PA)
Hillsborough Comm Coll (FL)
Houston Comm Coll System (TX)
Howard Comm Coll (MD)
Lakeland Comm Coll (OH)
Miami Dade Coll (FL)
Midlands Tech Coll (SC)
Oakland Comm Coll (MI)
Orange Coast Coll (CA)
Owens Comm Coll, Toledo (OH)
Southeast Tech Inst (SD)
Springfield Tech Comm Coll (MA)
Triton Coll (IL)
Union County Coll (NJ)

Nuclear/Nuclear Power Technology
Allen Comm Coll (KS)
Cape Fear Comm Coll (NC)
Georgia Military Coll (GA)
Lake Michigan Coll (MI)
Linn State Tech Coll (MO)
Terra State Comm Coll (OH)
Three Rivers Comm Coll (CT)

Nursing Administration
South Suburban Coll (IL)

Nursing Assistant/ Aide and Patient Care Assistant
Alexandria Tech Coll (MN)
Allen Comm Coll (KS)
Barton County Comm Coll (KS)
Century Coll (MN)
Comm Coll of Allegheny County (PA)
Elaine P. Nunez Comm Coll (LA)
Lake Region State Coll (ND)
Moraine Park Tech Coll (WI)
North Iowa Area Comm Coll (IA)
Olympic Coll (WA)
Paradise Valley Comm Coll (AZ)
Sandhills Comm Coll (NC)
Southwest Mississippi Comm Coll (MS)
Western Wyoming Comm Coll (WY)

Nursing (Licensed Practical/Vocational Nurse Training)
Alexandria Tech Coll (MN)
Allan Hancock Coll (CA)
Alpena Comm Coll (MI)
Amarillo Coll (TX)

Arizona Western Coll (AZ)
Athens Tech Coll (GA)
ATS Inst of Technology (OH)
Bainbridge Coll (GA)
Barton County Comm Coll (KS)
Brown Mackie Coll–Kansas City (KS)
Brown Mackie Coll–Salina (KS)
Carteret Comm Coll (NC)
Central Arizona Coll (AZ)
Central Comm Coll–Columbus Campus (NE)
Central Comm Coll–Grand Island Campus (NE)
Central Ohio Tech Coll (OH)
Central Oregon Comm Coll (OR)
Central Piedmont Comm Coll (NC)
Central Texas Coll (TX)
Colby Comm Coll (KS)
Coll of Southern Maryland (MD)
Comm Coll of Allegheny County (PA)
Comm Coll of Rhode Island (RI)
Dakota Coll at Bottineau (ND)
Darton Coll (GA)
Delaware Tech & Comm Coll, Jack F. Owens Campus (DE)
Delta Coll (MI)
Des Moines Area Comm Coll (IA)
El Centro Coll (TX)
Fiorello H. LaGuardia Comm Coll of the City U of New York (NY)
Flathead Valley Comm Coll (MT)
Glendale Comm Coll (AZ)
Grand Rapids Comm Coll (MI)
Green River Comm Coll (WA)
Howard Coll (TX)
Howard Comm Coll (MD)
Indian River State Coll (FL)
Itasca Comm Coll (MN)
Ivy Tech Comm Coll–Southeast (IN)
Jackson Comm Coll (MI)
Jefferson State Comm Coll (AL)
Kellogg Comm Coll (MI)
Kirtland Comm Coll (MI)
Lake Region State Coll (ND)
Lansing Comm Coll (MI)
Lehigh Carbon Comm Coll (PA)
Lonestar Coll–Kingwood (TX)
Manhattan Area Tech Coll (KS)
Metropolitan Comm Coll (NE)
Midlands Tech Coll (SC)
Mid-Plains Comm Coll, North Platte (NE)
Milwaukee Area Tech Coll (WI)
Minnesota State Coll–Southeast Tech (MN)
Minnesota State Comm and Tech Coll (MN)
Montana State U–Great Falls Coll of Technology (MT)
Moraine Park Tech Coll (WI)
Northeast Comm Coll (NE)
Northeastern Jr Coll (CO)
North Idaho Coll (ID)
North Iowa Area Comm Coll (IA)
Northland Comm and Tech Coll–Thief River Falls (MN)
Northland Pioneer Coll (AZ)
Northwest Tech Coll (MN)
Olympic Coll (WA)
Ouachita Tech Coll (AR)
Owens Comm Coll, Toledo (OH)
Pasadena City Coll (CA)
Pennsylvania Coll of Technology (PA)
Saint Charles Comm Coll (MO)
St. Cloud Tech Coll (MN)
Saint Paul Coll–A Comm & Tech College (MN)
Sandhills Comm Coll (NC)
San Diego City Coll (CA)
San Jacinto Coll District (TX)
Santa Rosa Jr Coll (CA)
Sierra Coll (CA)
Southeastern Comm Coll (IA)
Southeast Tech Inst (SD)
Southern Maine Comm Coll (ME)
South Plains Coll (TX)
South Puget Sound Comm Coll (WA)
Southwest Mississippi Comm Coll (MS)
Temple Coll (TX)
Trinity Valley Comm Coll (TX)
Union County Coll (NJ)
The U of Montana–Helena Coll of Technology (MT)
Western Wyoming Comm Coll (WY)
West Shore Comm Coll (MI)

Nursing (Registered Nurse Training)

Alamance Comm Coll (NC)
Alexandria Tech Coll (MN)
Allan Hancock Coll (CA)
Allegany Coll of Maryland (MD)
Alpena Comm Coll (MI)
Alvin Comm Coll (TX)
Amarillo Coll (TX)
Anne Arundel Comm Coll (MD)
Anoka-Ramsey Comm Coll (MN)
Anoka-Ramsey Comm Coll, Cambridge Campus (MN)
Antelope Valley Coll (CA)
Arizona Western Coll (AZ)
Arkansas State U–Beebe (AR)
Athens Tech Coll (GA)
Austin Comm Coll (TX)
Bainbridge Coll (GA)
Bakersfield Coll (CA)
Barton County Comm Coll (KS)
Beaufort County Comm Coll (NC)
Berkshire Comm Coll (MA)
Bevill State Comm Coll (AL)
Black Hawk Coll, Moline (IL)
Bladen Comm Coll (NC)
Blue Ridge Comm Coll (NC)
Bowling Green State U–Firelands Coll (OH)
Bronx Comm Coll of the City U of New York (NY)
Broome Comm Coll (NY)
Bryant & Stratton Coll, Eastlake (OH)
Bryant & Stratton Coll, Parma (OH)
Bucks County Comm Coll (PA)
Bunker Hill Comm Coll (MA)
Burlington County Coll (NJ)
Camden County Coll (NJ)
Cape Fear Comm Coll (NC)
Carolinas Coll of Health Sciences (NC)
Carroll Comm Coll (MD)
Casper Coll (WY)
Catawba Valley Comm Coll (NC)
Cecil Coll (MD)
Central Arizona Coll (AZ)
Central Carolina Comm Coll (NC)
Central Carolina Tech Coll (SC)
Central Comm Coll–Grand Island Campus (NE)
Central Lakes Coll (MN)
Central Maine Medical Center Coll of Nursing and Health Professions (ME)
Central New Mexico Comm Coll (NM)
Central Ohio Tech Coll (OH)
Central Oregon Comm Coll (OR)
Central Piedmont Comm Coll (NC)
Central Texas Coll (TX)
Central Wyoming Coll (WY)
Century Coll (MN)
Chattanooga State Comm Coll (TN)
Chipola Coll (FL)
Cincinnati State Tech and Comm Coll (OH)
City Colls of Chicago, Malcolm X College (IL)
City Colls of Chicago, Richard J. Daley College (IL)
Clackamas Comm Coll (OR)
Clarendon Coll (TX)
Clark Coll (WA)
Cleveland State Comm Coll (TN)
Clovis Comm Coll (NM)
Colby Comm Coll (KS)
Coll of DuPage (IL)
Coll of Lake County (IL)
Coll of Southern Maryland (MD)
Coll of the Canyons (CA)
Collin County Comm Coll District (TX)
Columbus Tech Coll (GA)
Comm Coll of Allegheny County (PA)
The Comm Coll of Baltimore County (MD)
Comm Coll of Philadelphia (PA)
Comm Coll of Rhode Island (RI)
Corning Comm Coll (NY)
County Coll of Morris (NJ)
Crouse Hospital School of Nursing (NY)
Crowder Coll (MO)
Cumberland County Coll (NJ)
Cuyahoga Comm Coll (OH)
Dabney S. Lancaster Comm Coll (VA)
Dakota Coll at Bottineau (ND)
Danville Area Comm Coll (IL)
Darton Coll (GA)
Daytona State Coll (FL)
Delaware County Comm Coll (PA)
Delaware Tech & Comm Coll, Jack F. Owens Campus (DE)
Delaware Tech & Comm Coll, Stanton/Wilmington Campus (DE)
Delaware Tech & Comm Coll, Terry Campus (DE)
Del Mar Coll (TX)
Delta Coll (MI)
Des Moines Area Comm Coll (IA)
East Central Coll (MO)
Eastern Arizona Coll (AZ)
Eastern Shore Comm Coll (VA)
East Los Angeles Coll (CA)
Edison State Comm Coll (OH)
El Centro Coll (TX)
Elgin Comm Coll (IL)
El Paso Comm Coll (TX)
Erie Comm Coll (NY)
Erie Comm Coll, North Campus (NY)
Essex County Coll (NJ)
Everett Comm Coll (WA)
Fayetteville Tech Comm Coll (NC)
Finger Lakes Comm Coll (NY)
Fiorello H. LaGuardia Comm Coll of the City U of New York (NY)
Fox Valley Tech Coll (WI)
Frederick Comm Coll (MD)
Front Range Comm Coll (CO)
Fulton-Montgomery Comm Coll (NY)
Gadsden State Comm Coll (AL)
Gateway Comm and Tech Coll (KY)
Gateway Comm Coll (CT)
Genesee Comm Coll (NY)
Georgia Highlands Coll (GA)
Georgia Perimeter Coll (GA)
Germanna Comm Coll (VA)
Glendale Comm Coll (AZ)
Golden West Coll (CA)
Goodwin Coll (CT)
Grand Rapids Comm Coll (MI)
Greenfield Comm Coll (MA)
Guilford Tech Comm Coll (NC)
Harcum Coll (PA)
Harford Comm Coll (MD)
Harrisburg Area Comm Coll (PA)
Harrison Coll, Indianapolis (IN)
Hawkeye Comm Coll (IA)
Hazard Comm and Tech Coll (KY)
Highland Comm Coll (IL)
Highline Comm Coll (WA)
Hillsborough Comm Coll (FL)
Holyoke Comm Coll (MA)
Hopkinsville Comm Coll (KY)
Housatonic Comm Coll (CT)
Houston Comm Coll System (TX)
Howard Coll (TX)
Howard Comm Coll (MD)
Hutchinson Comm Coll and Area Vocational School (KS)
Illinois Eastern Comm Colls, Frontier Community College (IL)
Illinois Eastern Comm Colls, Olney Central College (IL)
Illinois Valley Comm Coll (IL)
Indian River State Coll (FL)
Inver Hills Comm Coll (MN)
Iowa Lakes Comm Coll (IA)
ITT Tech Inst, Phoenix (AZ)
ITT Tech Inst, Tampa (FL)
ITT Tech Inst (ID)
ITT Tech Inst, Fort Wayne (IN)
ITT Tech Inst, Indianapolis (IN)
ITT Tech Inst, Newburgh (IN)
ITT Tech Inst, Canton (MI)
ITT Tech Inst, Earth City (MO)
ITT Tech Inst (NE)
ITT Tech Inst (NM)
ITT Tech Inst, Tulsa (OK)
ITT Tech Inst, Norfolk (VA)
Ivy Tech Comm Coll–Bloomington (IN)
Ivy Tech Comm Coll–Central Indiana (IN)
Ivy Tech Comm Coll–East Central (IN)
Ivy Tech Comm Coll–Lafayette (IN)
Ivy Tech Comm Coll–North Central (IN)
Ivy Tech Comm Coll–Northwest (IN)
Ivy Tech Comm Coll–Richmond (IN)
Ivy Tech Comm Coll–Southeast (IN)
Ivy Tech Comm Coll–Southern Indiana (IN)
Ivy Tech Comm Coll–Southwest (IN)
Ivy Tech Comm Coll–Wabash Valley (IN)
Jackson Comm Coll (MI)
Jackson State Comm Coll (TN)
James Sprunt Comm Coll (NC)
Jamestown Comm Coll (NY)
Jefferson Comm Coll (NY)
Jefferson State Comm Coll (AL)
Johnston Comm Coll (NC)
John Tyler Comm Coll (VA)
John Wood Comm Coll (IL)
J. Sargeant Reynolds Comm Coll (VA)
Kalamazoo Valley Comm Coll (MI)
Kankakee Comm Coll (IL)
Kaplan Coll, San Diego Campus (CA)
Kaskaskia Coll (IL)
Kauai Comm Coll (HI)
Kellogg Comm Coll (MI)
Kennebec Valley Comm Coll (ME)
Kent State U at Ashtabula (OH)
Kent State U at East Liverpool (OH)
Kent State U at Tuscarawas (OH)
Kilgore Coll (TX)
Kingsborough Comm Coll of the City U of New York (NY)
Kirkwood Comm Coll (IA)
Kirtland Comm Coll (MI)
Lac Courte Oreilles Ojibwa Comm Coll (WI)
Lakeland Comm Coll (OH)
Lake Michigan Coll (MI)
Lake-Sumter Comm Coll (FL)
Lansing Comm Coll (MI)
Laramie County Comm Coll (WY)
Lawson State Comm Coll (AL)
Lehigh Carbon Comm Coll (PA)
Lewis and Clark Comm Coll (IL)
Lincoln Land Comm Coll (IL)
Linn-Benton Comm Coll (OR)
Lonestar Coll–Cy-Fair (TX)
Lonestar Coll–Montgomery (TX)
Lonestar Coll–North Harris (TX)
Los Angeles Harbor Coll (CA)
Lower Columbia Coll (WA)
Luna Comm Coll (NM)
Lurleen B. Wallace Comm Coll (AL)
Macomb Comm Coll (MI)
Manhattan Area Tech Coll (KS)
Marion Tech Coll (OH)
Massasoit Comm Coll (MA)
Mercer County Comm Coll (NJ)
Meridian Comm Coll (MS)
Metropolitan Comm Coll (NE)
Metropolitan Comm Coll–Penn Valley (MO)
Miami Dade Coll (FL)
Middle Georgia Coll (GA)
Midlands Tech Coll (SC)
Mid-Plains Comm Coll, North Platte (NE)
Milwaukee Area Tech Coll (WI)
Minneapolis Comm and Tech Coll (MN)
Minnesota State Coll–Southeast Tech (MN)
Minnesota State Comm and Tech Coll (MN)
Missouri State U–West Plains (MO)
Mohave Comm Coll (AZ)
Mohawk Valley Comm Coll (NY)
Montcalm Comm Coll (MI)
Montgomery County Comm Coll (PA)
Moraine Park Tech Coll (WI)
Moraine Valley Comm Coll (IL)
Mountain Empire Comm Coll (VA)
Mt. San Jacinto Coll (CA)
Mount Wachusett Comm Coll (MA)
Murray State Coll (OK)
Muskegon Comm Coll (MI)
Nassau Comm Coll (NY)
New Mexico State U–Carlsbad (NM)
Niagara County Comm Coll (NY)
Nicolet Area Tech Coll (WI)
Northampton Comm Coll (PA)
North Arkansas Coll (AR)
North Central Texas Coll (TX)
Northeast Comm Coll (NE)
Northeastern Jr Coll (CO)
Northeast Iowa Comm Coll (IA)
North Hennepin Comm Coll (MN)
North Idaho Coll (ID)
North Iowa Area Comm Coll (IA)
Northland Comm and Tech Coll–Thief River Falls (MN)
Northland Pioneer Coll (AZ)
NorthWest Arkansas Comm Coll (AR)
Northwest Coll (WY)
Northwest Florida State Coll (FL)
Northwest-Shoals Comm Coll (AL)
Northwest Tech Coll (MN)
Oakland Comm Coll (MI)
Ocean County Coll (NJ)
Odessa Coll (TX)
Oklahoma City Comm Coll (OK)
Oklahoma State U, Oklahoma City (OK)
Olympic Coll (WA)
Orangeburg-Calhoun Tech Coll (SC)
Oregon Coast Comm Coll (OR)
Otero Jr Coll (CO)
Owensboro Comm and Tech Coll (KY)
Owens Comm Coll, Toledo (OH)
Palm Beach State Coll (FL)
Panola Coll (TX)
Paradise Valley Comm Coll (AZ)
Paris Jr Coll (TX)
Pasadena City Coll (CA)
Pasco-Hernando Comm Coll (FL)
Patrick Henry Comm Coll (VA)
Penn State Fayette, The Eberly Campus (PA)
Penn State Mont Alto (PA)
Penn State Worthington Scranton (PA)
Pensacola Jr Coll (FL)
Phillips Beth Israel School of Nursing (NY)
Phoenix Coll (AZ)
Piedmont Comm Coll (NC)
Pikes Peak Comm Coll (CO)
Pima Comm Coll (AZ)
Polk State Coll (FL)
Pueblo Comm Coll (CO)
Quinsigamond Comm Coll (MA)
Randolph Comm Coll (NC)
Rappahannock Comm Coll (VA)
Raritan Valley Comm Coll (NJ)
Rockingham Comm Coll (NC)
Rockland Comm Coll (NY)
Rogue Comm Coll (OR)
Saint Charles Comm Coll (MO)
St. Elizabeth Coll of Nursing (NY)
St. Joseph's Coll of Nursing (NY)
St. Luke's Coll (IA)
Salt Lake Comm Coll (UT)
Sandhills Comm Coll (NC)
San Diego City Coll (CA)
San Jacinto Coll District (TX)
San Juan Coll (NM)
Santa Rosa Jr Coll (CA)
Scottsdale Comm Coll (AZ)
Seminole State Coll (OK)
Seminole State Coll of Florida (FL)
Shawnee Comm Coll (IL)
Sheridan Coll (WY)
Sierra Coll (CA)
Sisseton-Wahpeton Comm Coll (SD)
Somerset Comm Coll (KY)
Southeastern Comm Coll (IA)

Southeast Kentucky Comm and Tech Coll (KY)
Southern Maine Comm Coll (ME)
Southern State Comm Coll (OH)
Southern Union State Comm Coll (AL)
South Georgia Coll (GA)
South Plains Coll (TX)
South Puget Sound Comm Coll (WA)
Southside Virginia Comm Coll (VA)
Southwestern Comm Coll (IA)
Southwestern Michigan Coll (MI)
Southwest Georgia Tech Coll (GA)
Southwest Mississippi Comm Coll (MS)
Southwest Virginia Comm Coll (VA)
Southwest Wisconsin Tech Coll (WI)
Spartanburg Comm Coll (SC)
Spencerian Coll (KY)
Springfield Tech Comm Coll (MA)
Stanly Comm Coll (NC)
Stark State Coll of Technology (OH)
State Coll of Florida Manatee-Sarasota (FL)
State Fair Comm Coll (MO)
State U of New York Coll of Technology at Alfred (NY)
Suffolk County Comm Coll (NY)
Tallahassee Comm Coll (FL)
Tarrant County Coll District (TX)
Temple Coll (TX)
Terra State Comm Coll (OH)
Thomas Nelson Comm Coll (VA)
Three Rivers Comm Coll (CT)
Three Rivers Comm Coll (MO)
Tidewater Comm Coll (VA)
Tompkins Cortland Comm Coll (NY)
Tri-County Comm Coll (NC)
Trident Tech Coll (SC)
Trinity Valley Comm Coll (TX)
Triton Coll (IL)
Ulster County Comm Coll (NY)
Umpqua Comm Coll (OR)
Union County Coll (NJ)
U of Arkansas Comm Coll at Morrilton (AR)
U of Pittsburgh at Titusville (PA)
U of South Carolina Lancaster (SC)
Victoria Coll (TX)
Victor Valley Coll (CA)
Walters State Comm Coll (TN)
Waukesha County Tech Coll (WI)
Wayne Comm Coll (NC)
Westchester Comm Coll (NY)
West Kentucky Comm and Tech Coll (KY)
Westmoreland County Comm Coll (PA)
West Shore Comm Coll (MI)
West Virginia Northern Comm Coll (WV)
White Mountains Comm Coll (NH)
Wilson Comm Coll (NC)
Wisconsin Indianhead Tech Coll (WI)
Wor-Wic Comm Coll (MD)
Yavapai Coll (AZ)

Nursing Related
Cincinnati State Tech and Comm Coll (OH)
Moraine Park Tech Coll (WI)
Northwest Coll (WY)
Southeast Tech Inst (SD)

Nutrition Sciences
Casper Coll (WY)
Mohawk Valley Comm Coll (NY)
Sisseton-Wahpeton Comm Coll (SD)

Occupational Health and Industrial Hygiene
Niagara County Comm Coll (NY)

Occupational Safety and Health Technology
Central Wyoming Coll (WY)
The Comm Coll of Baltimore County (MD)
Cuyamaca Coll (CA)
Del Mar Coll (TX)
Honolulu Comm Coll (HI)
Ivy Tech Comm Coll–Central Indiana (IN)
Ivy Tech Comm Coll–Northeast (IN)
Ivy Tech Comm Coll–Northwest (IN)
Ivy Tech Comm Coll–Wabash Valley (IN)
Kilgore Coll (TX)
Lanier Tech Coll (GA)
NorthWest Arkansas Comm Coll (AR)
Northwest Coll (WY)
Okefenokee Tech Coll (GA)
Oklahoma State U, Oklahoma City (OK)
Paradise Valley Comm Coll (AZ)
San Diego City Coll (CA)
San Jacinto Coll District (TX)
San Juan Coll (NM)
Southwest Mississippi Comm Coll (MS)
U of Alaska Anchorage, Kenai Peninsula Coll (AK)

Occupational Therapist Assistant
Allegany Coll of Maryland (MD)
Augusta Tech Coll (GA)
Austin Comm Coll (TX)
Brown Mackie Coll–Akron (OH)
Brown Mackie Coll–Albuquerque (NM)
Brown Mackie Coll–Atlanta (GA)
Brown Mackie Coll–Boise (ID)
Brown Mackie Coll–Findlay (OH)
Brown Mackie Coll–Fort Wayne (IN)
Brown Mackie Coll–Hopkinsville (KY)
Brown Mackie Coll–Indianapolis (IN)
Brown Mackie Coll–Kansas City (KS)
Brown Mackie Coll–Louisville (KY)
Brown Mackie Coll–Merrillville (IN)
Brown Mackie Coll–Northern Kentucky (KY)
Brown Mackie Coll–Phoenix (AZ)
Brown Mackie Coll–Salina (KS)
Brown Mackie Coll–South Bend (IN)
Brown Mackie Coll–Tucson (AZ)
Brown Mackie Coll–Tulsa (OK)
Cape Fear Comm Coll (NC)
Casper Coll (WY)
Cincinnati State Tech and Comm Coll (OH)
Coll of DuPage (IL)
Comm Coll of Allegheny County (PA)
Comm Coll of Rhode Island (RI)
Darton Coll (GA)
Daytona State Coll (FL)
Delaware Tech & Comm Coll, Jack F. Owens Campus (DE)
Delaware Tech & Comm Coll, Stanton/Wilmington Campus (DE)
Del Mar Coll (TX)
East Central Coll (MO)
Erie Comm Coll, North Campus (NY)
Fiorello H. LaGuardia Comm Coll of the City U of New York (NY)
Green River Comm Coll (WA)
Harcum Coll (PA)
H. Councill Trenholm State Tech Coll (AL)
Houston Comm Coll System (TX)
Ivy Tech Comm Coll–Central Indiana (IN)
Jamestown Comm Coll (NY)
J. Sargeant Reynolds Comm Coll (VA)
Kennebec Valley Comm Coll (ME)
Kilgore Coll (TX)
Kirkwood Comm Coll (IA)
Lehigh Carbon Comm Coll (PA)
Lewis and Clark Comm Coll (IL)
Lincoln Land Comm Coll (IL)
Macomb Comm Coll (MI)
Manchester Comm Coll (CT)
Middle Georgia Coll (GA)
Midlands Tech Coll (SC)
Northland Comm and Tech Coll–Thief River Falls (MN)
Oakland Comm Coll (MI)
Owens Comm Coll, Toledo (OH)
Panola Coll (TX)
Penn State DuBois (PA)
Penn State Mont Alto (PA)
Pennsylvania Coll of Technology (PA)
Polk State Coll (FL)
Pueblo Comm Coll (CO)
Pulaski Tech Coll (AR)
Quinsigamond Comm Coll (MA)
Rend Lake Coll (IL)
Saint Charles Comm Coll (MO)
St. Philip's Coll (TX)
Salt Lake Comm Coll (UT)
South Suburban Coll (IL)
Springfield Tech Comm Coll (MA)
Stanly Comm Coll (NC)
State Coll of Florida Manatee-Sarasota (FL)
State Fair Comm Coll (MO)
Wisconsin Indianhead Tech Coll (WI)

Occupational Therapy
Allegany Coll of Maryland (MD)
Amarillo Coll (TX)
Barton County Comm Coll (KS)
Coll of DuPage (IL)
The Comm Coll of Baltimore County (MD)
Fiorello H. LaGuardia Comm Coll of the City U of New York (NY)
Fox Valley Tech Coll (WI)
Georgia Highlands Coll (GA)
Kaplan Career Inst, ICM Campus (PA)
Kent State U at East Liverpool (OH)
Lonestar Coll–Kingwood (TX)
Lonestar Coll–Tomball (TX)
Metropolitan Comm Coll–Penn Valley (MO)
Milwaukee Area Tech Coll (WI)
North Central Texas Coll (TX)
Oklahoma City Comm Coll (OK)
Palm Beach State Coll (FL)
Pasadena City Coll (CA)
Quinsigamond Comm Coll (MA)
Rockland Comm Coll (NY)
Saint Charles Comm Coll (MO)
Stark State Coll of Technology (OH)
State Coll of Florida Manatee-Sarasota (FL)
Trident Tech Coll (SC)

Oceanography (Chemical and Physical)
Everett Comm Coll (WA)
Southern Maine Comm Coll (ME)

Office Management
Alexandria Tech Coll (MN)
Alpena Comm Coll (MI)
Berkeley City Coll (CA)
Brown Mackie Coll–Akron (OH)
Brown Mackie Coll–Boise (ID)
Brown Mackie Coll–Cincinnati (OH)
Brown Mackie Coll–Findlay (OH)
Brown Mackie Coll–Fort Wayne (IN)
Brown Mackie Coll–Greenville (SC)
Brown Mackie Coll–Kansas City (KS)
Brown Mackie Coll–St. Louis (MO)
Brown Mackie Coll–Salina (KS)
Brown Mackie Coll–Tulsa (OK)
Catawba Valley Comm Coll (NC)
Central Texas Coll (TX)
Cincinnati State Tech and Comm Coll (OH)
Clackamas Comm Coll (OR)
Coll of DuPage (IL)
Comm Coll of Allegheny County (PA)
Consolidated School of Business, Lancaster (PA)
Cuyamaca Coll (CA)
Dakota Coll at Bottineau (ND)
Delaware County Comm Coll (PA)
Delaware Tech & Comm Coll, Jack F. Owens Campus (DE)
Delaware Tech & Comm Coll, Stanton/Wilmington Campus (DE)
Delaware Tech & Comm Coll, Terry Campus (DE)
Delta Coll (MI)
Des Moines Area Comm Coll (IA)
Eastern Wyoming Coll (WY)
Erie Comm Coll (NY)
Erie Comm Coll, North Campus (NY)
Erie Comm Coll, South Campus (NY)
Fayetteville Tech Comm Coll (NC)
Forrest Jr Coll (SC)
Front Range Comm Coll (CO)
Glendale Comm Coll (AZ)
Green River Comm Coll (WA)
Guilford Tech Comm Coll (NC)
Howard Comm Coll (MD)
Iowa Lakes Comm Coll (IA)
Ivy Tech Comm Coll–Wabash Valley (IN)
Jefferson Comm Coll (NY)
Johnston Comm Coll (NC)
Lake Region State Coll (ND)
Lake-Sumter Comm Coll (FL)
Luna Comm Coll (NM)
Massasoit Comm Coll (MA)
Northeast Comm Coll (NE)
Olympic Coll (WA)
Piedmont Comm Coll (NC)
Randolph Comm Coll (NC)
Saint Charles Comm Coll (MO)
Saint Paul Coll–A Comm & Tech College (MN)
South Suburban Coll (IL)

Office Occupations and Clerical Services
Alamance Comm Coll (NC)
Alexandria Tech Coll (MN)
Blue Ridge Comm and Tech Coll (WV)
Central Wyoming Coll (WY)
Century Coll (MN)
Dakota Coll at Bottineau (ND)
Darton Coll (GA)
Del Mar Coll (TX)
Delta Coll (MI)
El Centro Coll (TX)
Gateway Comm and Tech Coll (KY)
Inst of Business & Medical Careers (CO)
Iowa Lakes Comm Coll (IA)
ITI Tech Coll (LA)
Jamestown Comm Coll (NY)
Lake Region State Coll (ND)
Lonestar Coll–Cy-Fair (TX)
Massasoit Comm Coll (MA)
Moraine Park Tech Coll (WI)
New Mexico State U–Carlsbad (NM)
Northeast Comm Coll (NE)
Pennsylvania Coll of Technology (PA)
Pennsylvania Inst of Technology (PA)
Reedley Coll (CA)
Southeast Tech Inst (SD)
The U of Montana–Helena Coll of Technology (MT)

Operations Management
Alexandria Tech Coll (MN)
Alpena Comm Coll (MI)
Bowling Green State U–Firelands Coll (OH)
Bunker Hill Comm Coll (MA)
Catawba Valley Comm Coll (NC)
Central Carolina Comm Coll (NC)
Chattanooga State Comm Coll (TN)
Clackamas Comm Coll (OR)
DeKalb Tech Coll (GA)
Fayetteville Tech Comm Coll (NC)
Hillsborough Comm Coll (FL)
Kilgore Coll (TX)
Lehigh Carbon Comm Coll (PA)
Macomb Comm Coll (MI)
Milwaukee Area Tech Coll (WI)
Moraine Park Tech Coll (WI)
Owens Comm Coll, Toledo (OH)
Pensacola Jr Coll (FL)
Southwest Wisconsin Tech Coll (WI)
Stark State Coll of Technology (OH)
Terra State Comm Coll (OH)
Waukesha County Tech Coll (WI)
Wisconsin Indianhead Tech Coll (WI)

Operations Research
Delaware Tech & Comm Coll, Stanton/Wilmington Campus (DE)

Ophthalmic Laboratory Technology
DeKalb Tech Coll (GA)
Middlesex Comm Coll (CT)

Ophthalmic Technology
Lakeland Comm Coll (OH)
Miami Dade Coll (FL)
Triton Coll (IL)
Volunteer State Comm Coll (TN)

Optical Sciences
Corning Comm Coll (NY)

Opticianry
Camden County Coll (NJ)
Comm Coll of Rhode Island (RI)
Cuyahoga Comm Coll (OH)
DeKalb Tech Coll (GA)
El Paso Comm Coll (TX)
Erie Comm Coll, North Campus (NY)
Essex County Coll (NJ)
Hillsborough Comm Coll (FL)
Holyoke Comm Coll (MA)
Milwaukee Area Tech Coll (WI)
Ogeechee Tech Coll (GA)
Raritan Valley Comm Coll (NJ)
Southwestern Indian Polytechnic Inst (NM)

Optometric Technician
Barton County Comm Coll (KS)
El Paso Comm Coll (TX)
Hillsborough Comm Coll (FL)
J. Sargeant Reynolds Comm Coll (VA)
Raritan Valley Comm Coll (NJ)
San Jacinto Coll District (TX)

Organizational Behavior
U of Cincinnati Clermont Coll (OH)

Ornamental Horticulture
Antelope Valley Coll (CA)
Bakersfield Coll (CA)
Bronx Comm Coll of the City U of New York (NY)
Clackamas Comm Coll (OR)
Coll of DuPage (IL)
Coll of Lake County (IL)
Comm Coll of Allegheny County (PA)
Cumberland County Coll (NJ)
Cuyamaca Coll (CA)
Dakota Coll at Bottineau (ND)
Finger Lakes Comm Coll (NY)
Golden West Coll (CA)
Gwinnett Tech Coll (GA)
Howard Coll (TX)
Mendocino Coll (CA)
Mercer County Comm Coll (NJ)
Metropolitan Comm Coll (NE)
Miami Dade Coll (FL)
Orange Coast Coll (CA)
Pennsylvania Coll of Technology (PA)
Triton Coll (IL)
Victor Valley Coll (CA)

Orthotics/Prosthetics
Century Coll (MN)

Painting
Cuyamaca Coll (CA)

Painting and Wall Covering
Ivy Tech Comm Coll–Central Indiana (IN)
Ivy Tech Comm Coll–East Central (IN)
Ivy Tech Comm Coll–Lafayette (IN)
Ivy Tech Comm Coll–North Central (IN)
Ivy Tech Comm Coll–Northeast (IN)
Ivy Tech Comm Coll–Northwest (IN)
Ivy Tech Comm Coll–Southwest (IN)
Ivy Tech Comm Coll–Wabash Valley (IN)

Parks, Recreation and Leisure
Allan Hancock Coll (CA)
Bakersfield Coll (CA)
Central New Mexico Comm Coll (NM)
Central Wyoming Coll (WY)
Coll of the Canyons (CA)
The Comm Coll of Baltimore County (MD)
Dakota Coll at Bottineau (ND)
Del Mar Coll (TX)
Greenfield Comm Coll (MA)

Iowa Lakes Comm Coll (IA)
Kingsborough Comm Coll of the City U of New York (NY)
Leeward Comm Coll (HI)
Miami Dade Coll (FL)
Minneapolis Comm and Tech Coll (MN)
Muskegon Comm Coll (MI)
Niagara County Comm Coll (NY)
Northwest Coll (WY)
Northwestern Connecticut Comm Coll (CT)
Red Rocks Comm Coll (CO)
San Diego City Coll (CA)
San Juan Coll (NM)
Sierra Coll (CA)
South Georgia Coll (GA)
Tallahassee Comm Coll (FL)

Parks, Recreation and Leisure Facilities Management
Allen Comm Coll (KS)
Augusta Tech Coll (GA)
Central Wyoming Coll (WY)
Chattahoochee Tech Coll (GA)
Dakota Coll at Bottineau (ND)
Erie Comm Coll, South Campus (NY)
Finger Lakes Comm Coll (NY)
Mohawk Valley Comm Coll (NY)
Moraine Valley Comm Coll (IL)
North Georgia Tech Coll (GA)
Northland Pioneer Coll (AZ)
Northwestern Connecticut Comm Coll (CT)
Potomac State Coll of West Virginia U (WV)
Southwest Wisconsin Tech Coll (WI)
Tompkins Cortland Comm Coll (NY)
Ulster County Comm Coll (NY)

Parks, Recreation, and Leisure Related
Cincinnati State Tech and Comm Coll (OH)
Dakota Coll at Bottineau (ND)
Green River Comm Coll (WA)
Tompkins Cortland Comm Coll (NY)

Pathologist Assistant
Lake Region State Coll (ND)

Peace Studies and Conflict Resolution
El Centro Coll (TX)

Perioperative/Operating Room and Surgical Nursing
Comm Coll of Allegheny County (PA)

Personal and Culinary Services Related
Mohave Comm Coll (AZ)

Petroleum Engineering
Kilgore Coll (TX)
Southern Alberta Inst of Technology (AB, Canada)

Petroleum Technology
Bakersfield Coll (CA)
Lackawanna Coll (PA)
South Plains Coll (TX)
Southwest Mississippi Comm Coll (MS)
U of Arkansas Comm Coll at Morrilton (AR)

Pharmacy
Barton County Comm Coll (KS)
Indian River State Coll (FL)
Iowa Lakes Comm Coll (IA)

Pharmacy Technician
Albany Tech Coll (GA)
Augusta Tech Coll (GA)
Barton County Comm Coll (KS)
Brown Mackie Coll–Akron (OH)
Brown Mackie Coll–Albuquerque (NM)
Brown Mackie Coll–Atlanta (GA)
Brown Mackie Coll–Cincinnati (OH)
Brown Mackie Coll–Findlay (OH)
Brown Mackie Coll–Louisville (KY)
Brown Mackie Coll–North Canton (OH)
Brown Mackie Coll–Northern Kentucky (KY)
Brown Mackie Coll–St. Louis (MO)
Casper Coll (WY)
Chattanooga State Comm Coll (TN)
Columbus Tech Coll (GA)
Comm Care Coll (OK)
Comm Coll of Allegheny County (PA)
El Paso Comm Coll (TX)
Griffin Tech Coll (GA)
Guilford Tech Comm Coll (NC)
Inst of Business & Medical Careers (CO)
Lonestar Coll–North Harris (TX)
Lonestar Coll–Tomball (TX)
Midlands Tech Coll (SC)
Minnesota State Comm and Tech Coll (MN)
Mohave Comm Coll (AZ)
Moraine Park Tech Coll (WI)
Northland Comm and Tech Coll–Thief River Falls (MN)
Oakland Comm Coll (MI)
Pima Comm Coll (AZ)
West Georgia Tech Coll (GA)

Philosophy
Allen Comm Coll (KS)
Austin Comm Coll (TX)
Bakersfield Coll (CA)
Barton County Comm Coll (KS)
Burlington County Coll (NJ)
Darton Coll (GA)
East Los Angeles Coll (CA)
Everett Comm Coll (WA)
Georgia Highlands Coll (GA)
Indian River State Coll (FL)
Iowa Lakes Comm Coll (IA)
Lake Michigan Coll (MI)
Lansing Comm Coll (MI)
Laramie County Comm Coll (WY)
Lonestar Coll–Cy-Fair (TX)
Lonestar Coll–Kingwood (TX)
Lonestar Coll–Montgomery (TX)
Lonestar Coll–North Harris (TX)
Lonestar Coll–Tomball (TX)
Lon Morris Coll (TX)
Miami Dade Coll (FL)
Oklahoma City Comm Coll (OK)
Orange Coast Coll (CA)
Palm Beach State Coll (FL)
Pasadena City Coll (CA)
Red Rocks Comm Coll (CO)
Saint Charles Comm Coll (MO)
St. Philip's Coll (TX)
San Jacinto Coll District (TX)
San Juan Coll (NM)
Santa Rosa Jr Coll (CA)
Sierra Coll (CA)
Snow Coll (UT)
State Coll of Florida Manatee-Sarasota (FL)
Triton Coll (IL)

Phlebotomy
Alexandria Tech Coll (MN)
Barton County Comm Coll (KS)
Casper Coll (WY)
Olympic Coll (WA)

Photographic and Film/Video Technology
Catawba Valley Comm Coll (NC)
Central Lakes Coll (MN)
Daytona State Coll (FL)
Fiorello H. LaGuardia Comm Coll of the City U of New York (NY)
Miami Dade Coll (FL)
Minneapolis Comm and Tech Coll (MN)
Oakland Comm Coll (MI)
Olympic Coll (WA)
Pensacola Jr Coll (FL)
Randolph Comm Coll (NC)
Salt Lake Comm Coll (UT)
Suffolk County Comm Coll (NY)
Westmoreland County Comm Coll (PA)

Photography
Allan Hancock Coll (CA)
Amarillo Coll (TX)
Anne Arundel Comm Coll (MD)
Antelope Valley Coll (CA)
Antonelli Coll (OH)
The Art Inst of Seattle (WA)
Bakersfield Coll (CA)
Carteret Comm Coll (NC)
Casper Coll (WY)
Cecil Coll (MD)
Coll of DuPage (IL)
Coll of the Canyons (CA)
Comm Coll of Philadelphia (PA)
County Coll of Morris (NJ)
Cuyahoga Comm Coll (OH)
Delaware Tech & Comm Coll, Terry Campus (DE)
East Los Angeles Coll (CA)
Everett Comm Coll (WA)
Greenfield Comm Coll (MA)
Gwinnett Tech Coll (GA)
Harrisburg Area Comm Coll (PA)
Hennepin Tech Coll (MN)
Howard Comm Coll (MD)
Iowa Lakes Comm Coll (IA)
Kaplan Coll, Dayton Campus (OH)
Lansing Comm Coll (MI)
Lonestar Coll–North Harris (TX)
Mercer County Comm Coll (NJ)
Metropolitan Comm Coll (NE)
Miami Dade Coll (FL)
Mt. San Jacinto Coll (CA)
Nassau Comm Coll (NY)
Northland Pioneer Coll (AZ)
Northwest Coll (WY)
Oakland Comm Coll (MI)
Odessa Coll (TX)
Orange Coast Coll (CA)
Palm Beach State Coll (FL)
Pasadena City Coll (CA)
Randolph Comm Coll (NC)
Rockland Comm Coll (NY)
San Diego City Coll (CA)
Scottsdale Comm Coll (AZ)
Thomas Nelson Comm Coll (VA)
Tompkins Cortland Comm Coll (NY)
Western Wyoming Comm Coll (WY)

Photojournalism
Pasadena City Coll (CA)
Randolph Comm Coll (NC)

Physical Anthropology
Cowley County Comm Coll and Area Vocational–Tech School (KS)

Physical Education Teaching and Coaching
Allan Hancock Coll (CA)
Alvin Comm Coll (TX)
Amarillo Coll (TX)
Anne Arundel Comm Coll (MD)
Arizona Western Coll (AZ)
Bakersfield Coll (CA)
Barton County Comm Coll (KS)
Bucks County Comm Coll (PA)
Casper Coll (WY)
Central Texas Coll (TX)
City Colls of Chicago, Malcolm X College (IL)
Clarendon Coll (TX)
Crowder Coll (MO)
Dean Coll (MA)
Del Mar Coll (TX)
Eastern Wyoming Coll (WY)
East Los Angeles Coll (CA)
Erie Comm Coll (NY)
Erie Comm Coll, North Campus (NY)
Erie Comm Coll, South Campus (NY)
Essex County Coll (NJ)
Everett Comm Coll (WA)
Finger Lakes Comm Coll (NY)
Frederick Comm Coll (MD)
Fulton-Montgomery Comm Coll (NY)
Genesee Comm Coll (NY)
Howard Coll (TX)
Indian River State Coll (FL)
Inver Hills Comm Coll (MN)
Iowa Lakes Comm Coll (IA)
Kilgore Coll (TX)
Lansing Comm Coll (MI)
Laramie County Comm Coll (WY)
Linn-Benton Comm Coll (OR)
Lonestar Coll–North Harris (TX)
Lon Morris Coll (TX)
Mendocino Coll (CA)
Miami Dade Coll (FL)
Montgomery County Comm Coll (PA)
Murray State Coll (OK)
Niagara County Comm Coll (NY)
Northeastern Jr Coll (CO)
North Hennepin Comm Coll (MN)
North Iowa Area Comm Coll (IA)
Northwest Florida State Coll (FL)
Odessa Coll (TX)
Orange Coast Coll (CA)
Palm Beach State Coll (FL)
Pasadena City Coll (CA)
Potomac State Coll of West Virginia U (WV)
Red Rocks Comm Coll (CO)
San Diego City Coll (CA)
San Diego Mesa Coll (CA)
Seminole State Coll (OK)
Snow Coll (UT)
South Plains Coll (TX)
Southwest Mississippi Comm Coll (MS)
State Coll of Florida Manatee-Sarasota (FL)
Trinity Valley Comm Coll (TX)
Umpqua Comm Coll (OR)

Physical Sciences
Alvin Comm Coll (TX)
Amarillo Coll (TX)
Antelope Valley Coll (CA)
Austin Comm Coll (TX)
Barton County Comm Coll (KS)
Cecil Coll (MD)
Central Oregon Comm Coll (OR)
Central Wyoming Coll (WY)
Clovis Comm Coll (NM)
Crowder Coll (MO)
Dakota Coll at Bottineau (ND)
Frederick Comm Coll (MD)
Fulton-Montgomery Comm Coll (NY)
Golden West Coll (CA)
Green River Comm Coll (WA)
Harrisburg Area Comm Coll (PA)
Highland Comm Coll (IL)
Howard Comm Coll (MD)
Hutchinson Comm Coll and Area Vocational School (KS)
Iowa Lakes Comm Coll (IA)
Jamestown Comm Coll (NY)
Kent State U at Geauga (OH)
Lake Michigan Coll (MI)
Lawson State Comm Coll (AL)
Lehigh Carbon Comm Coll (PA)
Linn-Benton Comm Coll (OR)
Mendocino Coll (CA)
Miami Dade Coll (FL)
Montgomery County Comm Coll (PA)
Northeastern Jr Coll (CO)
North Idaho Coll (ID)
Northwestern Connecticut Comm Coll (CT)
Olympic Coll (WA)
Palm Beach State Coll (FL)
Paradise Valley Comm Coll (AZ)
Pennsylvania Coll of Technology (PA)
Reedley Coll (CA)
Salt Lake Comm Coll (UT)
San Diego City Coll (CA)
San Diego Mesa Coll (CA)
San Jacinto Coll District (TX)
San Juan Coll (NM)
Seminole State Coll (OK)
Snow Coll (UT)
Southwest Mississippi Comm Coll (MS)
Trinity Valley Comm Coll (TX)
Umpqua Comm Coll (OR)
Victor Valley Coll (CA)

Physical Sciences Related
Dakota Coll at Bottineau (ND)
Folsom Lake Coll (CA)

Physical Therapist Assistant
Allegany Coll of Maryland (MD)
Anoka-Ramsey Comm Coll (MN)
Austin Comm Coll (TX)
Barton County Comm Coll (KS)
Berkshire Comm Coll (MA)
Black Hawk Coll, Moline (IL)
Broome Comm Coll (NY)
Brown Mackie Coll–Fort Wayne (IN)
Brown Mackie Coll–South Bend (IN)
Carroll Comm Coll (MD)
Chattanooga State Comm Coll (TN)
Colby Comm Coll (KS)
Coll of DuPage (IL)
Coll of Southern Maryland (MD)
Comm Coll of Allegheny County (PA)
Comm Coll of Rhode Island (RI)
Darton Coll (GA)
Delaware Tech & Comm Coll, Jack F. Owens Campus (DE)
Delaware Tech & Comm Coll, Stanton/Wilmington Campus (DE)
Delta Coll (MI)
Edison State Comm Coll (OH)
Elgin Comm Coll (IL)
El Paso Comm Coll (TX)
Essex County Coll (NJ)
Fayetteville Tech Comm Coll (NC)
Fiorello H. LaGuardia Comm Coll of the City U of New York (NY)
Fox Coll (IL)
Georgia Highlands Coll (GA)
Green River Comm Coll (WA)
Guilford Tech Comm Coll (NC)
Gwinnett Tech Coll (GA)
Harcum Coll (PA)
Hazard Comm and Tech Coll (KY)
Hesser Coll, Manchester (NH)
Houston Comm Coll System (TX)
Hutchinson Comm Coll and Area Vocational School (KS)
Indian River State Coll (FL)
Ivy Tech Comm Coll–East Central (IN)
Jackson State Comm Coll (TN)
Jefferson State Comm Coll (AL)
Kankakee Comm Coll (IL)
Kaskaskia Coll (IL)
Kellogg Comm Coll (MI)
Kennebec Valley Comm Coll (ME)
Kilgore Coll (TX)
Kingsborough Comm Coll of the City U of New York (NY)
Kirkwood Comm Coll (IA)
Laramie County Comm Coll (WY)
Lehigh Carbon Comm Coll (PA)
Lincoln Land Comm Coll (IL)
Linn State Tech Coll (MO)
Lonestar Coll–Montgomery (TX)
Macomb Comm Coll (MI)
Manchester Comm Coll (CT)
Marion Tech Coll (OH)
Mercer County Comm Coll (NJ)
Miami Dade Coll (FL)
Middle Georgia Coll (GA)
Midlands Tech Coll (SC)
Mohave Comm Coll (AZ)
Montana State U–Great Falls Coll of Technology (MT)
Montgomery Coll (MD)
Mount Wachusett Comm Coll (MA)
Nassau Comm Coll (NY)
Niagara County Comm Coll (NY)
Nicolet Area Tech Coll (WI)
Northeast Comm Coll (NE)
North Iowa Area Comm Coll (IA)
Northland Comm and Tech Coll–Thief River Falls (MN)
Owens Comm Coll, Toledo (OH)
Pasco-Hernando Comm Coll (FL)
Penn State DuBois (PA)
Penn State Hazleton (PA)
Penn State Mont Alto (PA)
Penn State Shenango (PA)
Pensacola Jr Coll (FL)
Polk State Coll (FL)
Pueblo Comm Coll (CO)
Randolph Comm Coll (NC)
St. Philip's Coll (TX)
Salt Lake Comm Coll (UT)
San Diego Mesa Coll (CA)
San Jacinto Coll District (TX)
San Juan Coll (NM)
Somerset Comm Coll (KY)
Southeast Kentucky Comm and Tech Coll (KY)
Springfield Tech Comm Coll (MA)
Stanly Comm Coll (NC)
State Coll of Florida Manatee-Sarasota (FL)
State Fair Comm Coll (MO)
Union County Coll (NJ)
U of Cincinnati Clermont Coll (OH)
U of Pittsburgh at Titusville (PA)
Volunteer State Comm Coll (TN)
West Kentucky Comm and Tech Coll (KY)

Physical Therapy
Allan Hancock Coll (CA)
Allen Comm Coll (KS)
Amarillo Coll (TX)
Athens Tech Coll (GA)

Barton County Comm Coll (KS)
Central Oregon Comm Coll (OR)
Central Piedmont Comm Coll (NC)
Clarendon Coll (TX)
Daytona State Coll (FL)
Essex County Coll (NJ)
Fiorello H. LaGuardia Comm Coll of the City U of New York (NY)
Genesee Comm Coll (NY)
Georgia Highlands Coll (GA)
Gwinnett Tech Coll (GA)
Housatonic Comm Coll (CT)
Indian River State Coll (FL)
Kent State U at Ashtabula (OH)
Kent State U at East Liverpool (OH)
Kilgore Coll (TX)
Kingsborough Comm Coll of the City U of New York (NY)
Lake Michigan Coll (MI)
Lawson State Comm Coll (AL)
Meridian Comm Coll (MS)
Metropolitan Comm Coll–Penn Valley (MO)
Milwaukee Area Tech Coll (WI)
Murray State Coll (OK)
NorthWest Arkansas Comm Coll (AR)
Odessa Coll (TX)
Oklahoma City Comm Coll (OK)
Palm Beach State Coll (FL)
Pasadena City Coll (CA)
Seminole State Coll of Florida (FL)
South Plains Coll (TX)
Stark State Coll of Technology (OH)
State Coll of Florida Manatee-Sarasota (FL)
Suffolk County Comm Coll (NY)
Tarrant County Coll District (TX)
Trident Tech Coll (SC)
Tunxis Comm Coll (CT)

Physician Assistant
Barton County Comm Coll (KS)
City Colls of Chicago, Malcolm X College (IL)
The Comm Coll of Baltimore County (MD)
Cuyahoga Comm Coll (OH)
Delta Coll (MI)
Georgia Highlands Coll (GA)
Lake Michigan Coll (MI)
Pasadena City Coll (CA)
State Coll of Florida Manatee-Sarasota (FL)

Physics
Allan Hancock Coll (CA)
Allen Comm Coll (KS)
Amarillo Coll (TX)
Arizona Western Coll (AZ)
Austin Comm Coll (TX)
Bakersfield Coll (CA)
Barton County Comm Coll (KS)
Bunker Hill Comm Coll (MA)
Burlington County Coll (NJ)
Casper Coll (WY)
Cecil Coll (MD)
Comm Coll of Allegheny County (PA)
Cuyamaca Coll (CA)
Darton Coll (GA)
Del Mar Coll (TX)
Eastern Arizona Coll (AZ)
Everett Comm Coll (WA)
Finger Lakes Comm Coll (NY)
Gainesville State Coll (GA)
Highland Comm Coll (IL)
Indian River State Coll (FL)
Kilgore Coll (TX)
Kingsborough Comm Coll of the City U of New York (NY)
Lake Michigan Coll (MI)
Linn-Benton Comm Coll (OR)
Lonestar Coll–Cy-Fair (TX)
Lonestar Coll–Kingwood (TX)
Lonestar Coll–Montgomery (TX)
Lonestar Coll–North Harris (TX)
Lonestar Coll–Tomball (TX)
Lon Morris Coll (TX)
Los Angeles Harbor Coll (CA)
Mercer County Comm Coll (NJ)
Miami Dade Coll (FL)
Northampton Comm Coll (PA)
Northeast Comm Coll (NE)
North Idaho Coll (ID)
Northwest Coll (WY)
Northwest Florida State Coll (FL)
Odessa Coll (TX)
Oklahoma City Comm Coll (OK)
Oklahoma State U, Oklahoma City (OK)
Orange Coast Coll (CA)
Pasadena City Coll (CA)
Red Rocks Comm Coll (CO)
Salt Lake Comm Coll (UT)
San Diego Mesa Coll (CA)
San Jacinto Coll District (TX)
San Juan Coll (NM)
Santa Rosa Jr Coll (CA)
Sierra Coll (CA)
Snow Coll (UT)
Springfield Tech Comm Coll (MA)
State Coll of Florida Manatee-Sarasota (FL)
Terra State Comm Coll (OH)
Triton Coll (IL)

Physics Teacher Education
The Comm Coll of Baltimore County (MD)
Howard Coll (TX)
Montgomery Coll (MD)
State Coll of Florida Manatee-Sarasota (FL)

Piano and Organ
Iowa Lakes Comm Coll (IA)
Lon Morris Coll (TX)

Pipefitting and Sprinkler Fitting
Bakersfield Coll (CA)
Black Hawk Coll, Moline (IL)
Delta Coll (MI)
Ivy Tech Comm Coll–Bloomington (IN)
Ivy Tech Comm Coll–Central Indiana (IN)
Ivy Tech Comm Coll–Columbus (IN)
Ivy Tech Comm Coll–East Central (IN)
Ivy Tech Comm Coll–Kokomo (IN)
Ivy Tech Comm Coll–Lafayette (IN)
Ivy Tech Comm Coll–North Central (IN)
Ivy Tech Comm Coll–Northeast (IN)
Ivy Tech Comm Coll–Northwest (IN)
Ivy Tech Comm Coll–Richmond (IN)
Ivy Tech Comm Coll–Southern Indiana (IN)
Ivy Tech Comm Coll–Southwest (IN)
Ivy Tech Comm Coll–Wabash Valley (IN)
Kellogg Comm Coll (MI)
Oakland Comm Coll (MI)
Southern Maine Comm Coll (ME)

Plant Nursery Management
Comm Coll of Allegheny County (PA)
Cuyamaca Coll (CA)
Miami Dade Coll (FL)
The Ohio State U Ag Tech Inst (OH)
Pennsylvania Coll of Technology (PA)

Plant Sciences
The Comm Coll of Baltimore County (MD)
Mercer County Comm Coll (NJ)
Reedley Coll (CA)
Rend Lake Coll (IL)

Plastics Engineering Technology
Cincinnati State Tech and Comm Coll (OH)
Coll of DuPage (IL)
Daytona State Coll (FL)
El Paso Comm Coll (TX)
Grand Rapids Comm Coll (MI)
Hennepin Tech Coll (MN)
Highline Comm Coll (WA)
Kellogg Comm Coll (MI)
Kent State U at Tuscarawas (OH)
Macomb Comm Coll (MI)
Milwaukee Area Tech Coll (WI)
Mount Wachusett Comm Coll (MA)
Terra State Comm Coll (OH)
West Georgia Tech Coll (GA)

Platemaking/Imaging
Pasadena City Coll (CA)
Pennsylvania Coll of Technology (PA)

Playwriting and Screenwriting
Minneapolis Comm and Tech Coll (MN)
Northwest Coll (WY)

Plumbing Technology
Macomb Comm Coll (MI)
Minnesota State Comm and Tech Coll (MN)
Minnesota West Comm and Tech Coll (MN)
Northeast Iowa Comm Coll (IA)
Northland Comm and Tech Coll–Thief River Falls (MN)
Pennsylvania Coll of Technology (PA)
St. Cloud Tech Coll (MN)
Southern Maine Comm Coll (ME)

Political Science and Government
Allen Comm Coll (KS)
Austin Comm Coll (TX)
Bainbridge Coll (GA)
Bakersfield Coll (CA)
Barton County Comm Coll (KS)
Casper Coll (WY)
Darton Coll (GA)
Del Mar Coll (TX)
Diablo Valley Coll (CA)
Eastern Arizona Coll (AZ)
Eastern Wyoming Coll (WY)
East Los Angeles Coll (CA)
Everett Comm Coll (WA)
Finger Lakes Comm Coll (NY)
Frederick Comm Coll (MD)
Gainesville State Coll (GA)
Georgia Highlands Coll (GA)
Highland Comm Coll (IL)
Indian River State Coll (FL)
Iowa Lakes Comm Coll (IA)
Lake Michigan Coll (MI)
Laramie County Comm Coll (WY)
Lawson State Comm Coll (AL)
Lonestar Coll–Cy-Fair (TX)
Lonestar Coll–Kingwood (TX)
Lonestar Coll–Montgomery (TX)
Lonestar Coll–North Harris (TX)
Lonestar Coll–Tomball (TX)
Lon Morris Coll (TX)
Miami Dade Coll (FL)
North Idaho Coll (ID)
North Iowa Area Comm Coll (IA)
Northwest Coll (WY)
Odessa Coll (TX)
Oklahoma City Comm Coll (OK)
Orange Coast Coll (CA)
Otero Jr Coll (CO)
Palm Beach State Coll (FL)
Pima Comm Coll (AZ)
Potomac State Coll of West Virginia U (WV)
Red Rocks Comm Coll (CO)
Saint Charles Comm Coll (MO)
St. Philip's Coll (TX)
Salt Lake Comm Coll (UT)
San Diego City Coll (CA)
Santa Rosa Jr Coll (CA)
Snow Coll (UT)
Trinity Valley Comm Coll (TX)
Triton Coll (IL)
Umpqua Comm Coll (OR)
Western Wyoming Comm Coll (WY)

Political Science and Government Related
Pasadena City Coll (CA)

Polymer/Plastics Engineering
Central Oregon Comm Coll (OR)

Portuguese
Miami Dade Coll (FL)

Postal Management
Allen Comm Coll (KS)
Central Piedmont Comm Coll (NC)
Metropolitan Comm Coll–Longview (MO)
San Diego City Coll (CA)
South Plains Coll (TX)
Tarrant County Coll District (TX)

Poultry Science
Crowder Coll (MO)
Delaware Tech & Comm Coll, Jack F. Owens Campus (DE)
Wayne Comm Coll (NC)

Precision Metal Working Related
Oakland Comm Coll (MI)
Reedley Coll (CA)

Precision Production Related
Lake Michigan Coll (MI)
Midlands Tech Coll (SC)
Saint Charles Comm Coll (MO)
Sheridan Coll (WY)
Waycross Coll (GA)

Precision Production Trades
Coll of DuPage (IL)
Midlands Tech Coll (SC)
Owensboro Comm and Tech Coll (KY)
Santa Rosa Jr Coll (CA)

Precision Systems Maintenance and Repair Technologies Related
Louisiana Tech Coll (LA)
Southwestern Michigan Coll (MI)

Pre-Dentistry Studies
Allen Comm Coll (KS)
Austin Comm Coll (TX)
Barton County Comm Coll (KS)
Clarendon Coll (TX)
Darton Coll (GA)
Eastern Wyoming Coll (WY)
Howard Comm Coll (MD)
Iowa Lakes Comm Coll (IA)
Kilgore Coll (TX)
Lake Michigan Coll (MI)
Laramie County Comm Coll (WY)
Northeast Comm Coll (NE)
Pasadena City Coll (CA)
St. Philip's Coll (TX)
Western Wyoming Comm Coll (WY)

Pre-Engineering
Alpena Comm Coll (MI)
Amarillo Coll (TX)
Barton County Comm Coll (KS)
Bowling Green State U–Firelands Coll (OH)
Bronx Comm Coll of the City U of New York (NY)
Chipola Coll (FL)
City Colls of Chicago, Richard J. Daley College (IL)
Comm Coll of Philadelphia (PA)
Corning Comm Coll (NY)
Cowley County Comm Coll and Area Vocational–Tech School (KS)
Crowder Coll (MO)
Darton Coll (GA)
Del Mar Coll (TX)
East Los Angeles Coll (CA)
Edison State Comm Coll (OH)
Essex County Coll (NJ)
Finger Lakes Comm Coll (NY)
Georgia Military Coll (GA)
Greenfield Comm Coll (MA)
Highland Comm Coll (IL)
Highline Comm Coll (WA)
Housatonic Comm Coll (CT)
Illinois Valley Comm Coll (IL)
Indian River State Coll (FL)
Iowa Lakes Comm Coll (IA)
Itasca Comm Coll (MN)
Lake Michigan Coll (MI)
Lansing Comm Coll (MI)
Lawson State Comm Coll (AL)
Lincoln Land Comm Coll (IL)
Linn-Benton Comm Coll (OR)
Lonestar Coll–North Harris (TX)
Lon Morris Coll (TX)
Los Angeles Harbor Coll (CA)
Macomb Comm Coll (MI)
Mesabi Range Comm and Tech Coll (MN)
Metropolitan Comm Coll (NE)
Metropolitan Comm Coll–Longview (MO)
Metropolitan Comm Coll–Maple Woods (MO)
Miami Dade Coll (FL)
Middlesex Comm Coll (CT)
Minnesota State Comm and Tech Coll (MN)
Murray State Coll (OK)
North Central Texas Coll (TX)
Northeast Comm Coll (NE)
Northeastern Jr Coll (CO)
North Hennepin Comm Coll (MN)
Northwestern Connecticut Comm Coll (CT)
Odessa Coll (TX)
Oklahoma City Comm Coll (OK)
Oklahoma State U, Oklahoma City (OK)
Otero Jr Coll (CO)
Palm Beach State Coll (FL)
Polk State Coll (FL)
Potomac State Coll of West Virginia U (WV)
Saint Charles Comm Coll (MO)
St. Philip's Coll (TX)
Sandhills Comm Coll (NC)
San Diego City Coll (CA)
Seminole State Coll (OK)
Snow Coll (UT)
South Plains Coll (TX)
Three Rivers Comm Coll (CT)
Trinity Valley Comm Coll (TX)
Umpqua Comm Coll (OR)
Western Wyoming Comm Coll (WY)

Pre-Law Studies
Allen Comm Coll (KS)
Barton County Comm Coll (KS)
Casper Coll (WY)
Central Oregon Comm Coll (OR)
Central Wyoming Coll (WY)
Clarendon Coll (TX)
Darton Coll (GA)
Eastern Arizona Coll (AZ)
Iowa Lakes Comm Coll (IA)
Kilgore Coll (TX)
Lake Michigan Coll (MI)
Laramie County Comm Coll (WY)
Lawson State Comm Coll (AL)
Northeast Comm Coll (NE)
St. Philip's Coll (TX)
U of Cincinnati Clermont Coll (OH)
Western Wyoming Comm Coll (WY)

Premedical Studies
Allen Comm Coll (KS)
Austin Comm Coll (TX)
Barton County Comm Coll (KS)
Casper Coll (WY)
Central Oregon Comm Coll (OR)
City Colls of Chicago, Malcolm X College (IL)
Clarendon Coll (TX)
Dakota Coll at Bottineau (ND)
Darton Coll (GA)
Eastern Arizona Coll (AZ)
Eastern Wyoming Coll (WY)
Gainesville State Coll (GA)
Howard Comm Coll (MD)
Iowa Lakes Comm Coll (IA)
Kilgore Coll (TX)
Lake Michigan Coll (MI)
Laramie County Comm Coll (WY)
Northeast Comm Coll (NE)
Pasadena City Coll (CA)
St. Philip's Coll (TX)
San Juan Coll (NM)
Western Wyoming Comm Coll (WY)

Prenursing Studies
Dakota Coll at Bottineau (ND)
Gainesville State Coll (GA)
Georgia Military Coll (GA)
Harcum Coll (PA)
Iowa Lakes Comm Coll (IA)
Northeast Comm Coll (NE)
Oklahoma State U, Oklahoma City (OK)
Randolph Comm Coll (NC)
St. Philip's Coll (TX)
Western Wyoming Comm Coll (WY)

Pre-Pharmacy Studies
Allen Comm Coll (KS)
Amarillo Coll (TX)
Austin Comm Coll (TX)
Casper Coll (WY)
Central Oregon Comm Coll (OR)
City Colls of Chicago, Malcolm X College (IL)
Darton Coll (GA)
Eastern Arizona Coll (AZ)
Eastern Wyoming Coll (WY)
Gainesville State Coll (GA)
Howard Comm Coll (MD)
Iowa Lakes Comm Coll (IA)
Kilgore Coll (TX)
Lake Michigan Coll (MI)
Laramie County Comm Coll (WY)
Northeast Comm Coll (NE)
Northwest Coll (WY)
Pasadena City Coll (CA)
St. Philip's Coll (TX)
Santa Rosa Jr Coll (CA)
State Coll of Florida Manatee-Sarasota (FL)
U of Cincinnati Clermont Coll (OH)
Western Wyoming Comm Coll (WY)

Pre-Veterinary Studies
Allen Comm Coll (KS)
Austin Comm Coll (TX)
Barton County Comm Coll (KS)
Casper Coll (WY)
Dakota Coll at Bottineau (ND)
Darton Coll (GA)

Eastern Wyoming Coll (WY)
Howard Comm Coll (MD)
Iowa Lakes Comm Coll (IA)
Kilgore Coll (TX)
Lake Michigan Coll (MI)
Laramie County Comm Coll (WY)
Northeast Comm Coll (NE)
Pasadena City Coll (CA)
Western Wyoming Comm Coll (WY)

Printing Press Operation
Iowa Lakes Comm Coll (IA)
Louisiana Tech Coll (LA)

Psychiatric/Mental Health Services Technology
Allegany Coll of Maryland (MD)
Comm Coll of Allegheny County (PA)
The Comm Coll of Baltimore County (MD)
Eastfield Coll (TX)
El Paso Comm Coll (TX)
Fiorello H. LaGuardia Comm Coll of the City U of New York (NY)
Guilford Tech Comm Coll (NC)
Harford Comm Coll (MD)
Hillsborough Comm Coll (FL)
Houston Comm Coll System (TX)
Ivy Tech Comm Coll–Bloomington (IN)
Ivy Tech Comm Coll–Central Indiana (IN)
Ivy Tech Comm Coll–Columbus (IN)
Ivy Tech Comm Coll–East Central (IN)
Ivy Tech Comm Coll–Kokomo (IN)
Ivy Tech Comm Coll–Lafayette (IN)
Ivy Tech Comm Coll–Northeast (IN)
Ivy Tech Comm Coll–Northwest (IN)
Ivy Tech Comm Coll–Richmond (IN)
Ivy Tech Comm Coll–Southeast (IN)
Ivy Tech Comm Coll–Southern Indiana (IN)
Ivy Tech Comm Coll–Southwest (IN)
Ivy Tech Comm Coll–Wabash Valley (IN)
Kingsborough Comm Coll of the City U of New York (NY)
Montgomery Coll (MD)
Montgomery County Comm Coll (PA)
Mount Wachusett Comm Coll (MA)
Pikes Peak Comm Coll (CO)
Wayne Comm Coll (NC)

Psychology
Allen Comm Coll (KS)
Amarillo Coll (TX)
Austin Comm Coll (TX)
Bainbridge Coll (GA)
Bakersfield Coll (CA)
Barton County Comm Coll (KS)
Bronx Comm Coll of the City U of New York (NY)
Bucks County Comm Coll (PA)
Bunker Hill Comm Coll (MA)
Burlington County Coll (NJ)
Carroll Comm Coll (MD)
Casper Coll (WY)
Central Wyoming Coll (WY)
Clarendon Coll (TX)
Clovis Comm Coll (NM)
Coll of the Canyons (CA)
Comm Coll of Allegheny County (PA)
Crowder Coll (MO)
Dakota Coll at Bottineau (ND)
Darton Coll (GA)
Delaware County Comm Coll (PA)
Del Mar Coll (TX)
Delta Coll (MI)
Diablo Valley Coll (CA)
Eastern Arizona Coll (AZ)
Eastern Wyoming Coll (WY)
East Los Angeles Coll (CA)
Everett Comm Coll (WA)
Finger Lakes Comm Coll (NY)
Folsom Lake Coll (CA)
Frederick Comm Coll (MD)
Fulton-Montgomery Comm Coll (NY)
Gainesville State Coll (GA)
Genesee Comm Coll (NY)
Georgia Highlands Coll (GA)
Georgia Military Coll (GA)
Harrisburg Area Comm Coll (PA)
Hesser Coll, Manchester (NH)
Highland Comm Coll (IL)
Highline Comm Coll (WA)
Howard Coll (TX)
Howard Comm Coll (MD)
Hutchinson Comm Coll and Area Vocational School (KS)
Indian River State Coll (FL)
Iowa Lakes Comm Coll (IA)
Itasca Comm Coll (MN)
John Wood Comm Coll (IL)
Kankakee Comm Coll (IL)
Kilgore Coll (TX)
Lake Michigan Coll (MI)
Laramie County Comm Coll (WY)
Lawson State Comm Coll (AL)
Lehigh Carbon Comm Coll (PA)
Lonestar Coll–Cy-Fair (TX)
Lonestar Coll–Kingwood (TX)
Lonestar Coll–Montgomery (TX)
Lonestar Coll–North Harris (TX)
Lon Morris Coll (TX)
Mendocino Coll (CA)
Miami Dade Coll (FL)
Mohave Comm Coll (AZ)
Northeast Comm Coll (NE)
Northeastern Jr Coll (CO)
North Idaho Coll (ID)
Northwest Coll (WY)
Odessa Coll (TX)
Oklahoma City Comm Coll (OK)
Oklahoma State U, Oklahoma City (OK)
Otero Jr Coll (CO)
Palm Beach State Coll (FL)
Pasadena City Coll (CA)
Potomac State Coll of West Virginia U (WV)
Red Rocks Comm Coll (CO)
Saint Charles Comm Coll (MO)
St. Philip's Coll (TX)
Salt Lake Comm Coll (UT)
San Diego City Coll (CA)
San Diego Mesa Coll (CA)
San Jacinto Coll District (TX)
San Juan Coll (NM)
Santa Rosa Jr Coll (CA)
Sheridan Coll (WY)
Sierra Coll (CA)
State Coll of Florida Manatee-Sarasota (FL)
Terra State Comm Coll (OH)
Trinity Valley Comm Coll (TX)
Triton Coll (IL)
Umpqua Comm Coll (OR)
U of Cincinnati Clermont Coll (OH)
Vincennes U Jasper Campus (IN)
Western Wyoming Comm Coll (WY)

Public Administration
Anne Arundel Comm Coll (MD)
Barton County Comm Coll (KS)
Central Texas Coll (TX)
The Comm Coll of Baltimore County (MD)
County Coll of Morris (NJ)
Del Mar Coll (TX)
East Los Angeles Coll (CA)
Fayetteville Tech Comm Coll (NC)
Housatonic Comm Coll (CT)
Houston Comm Coll System (TX)
Lansing Comm Coll (MI)
Laramie County Comm Coll (WY)
Miami Dade Coll (FL)
Middle Georgia Coll (GA)
Minneapolis Comm and Tech Coll (MN)
Mohawk Valley Comm Coll (NY)
Owens Comm Coll, Toledo (OH)
Rio Salado Coll (AZ)
San Jacinto Coll District (TX)
San Juan Coll (NM)
Scottsdale Comm Coll (AZ)
State Coll of Florida Manatee-Sarasota (FL)
Tallahassee Comm Coll (FL)
Thomas Nelson Comm Coll (VA)
Three Rivers Comm Coll (CT)
Westchester Comm Coll (NY)

Public Administration and Social Service Professions Related
Cleveland State Comm Coll (TN)
Erie Comm Coll, South Campus (NY)
J. Sargeant Reynolds Comm Coll (VA)
Oklahoma State U, Oklahoma City (OK)
Ulster County Comm Coll (NY)

Public Health Education and Promotion
Anoka-Ramsey Comm Coll (MN)
Anoka-Ramsey Comm Coll, Cambridge Campus (MN)
Delta Coll (MI)
Georgia Military Coll (GA)

Public Health Related
Salt Lake Comm Coll (UT)

Public Policy Analysis
Anne Arundel Comm Coll (MD)
Del Mar Coll (TX)
Pasadena City Coll (CA)

Public Relations/ Image Management
Amarillo Coll (TX)
Cecil Coll (MD)
Crowder Coll (MO)
Glendale Comm Coll (AZ)
Lansing Comm Coll (MI)

Publishing
Hennepin Tech Coll (MN)

Purchasing, Procurement/ Acquisitions and Contracts Management
Cincinnati State Tech and Comm Coll (OH)

Quality Control and Safety Technologies Related
Blue Ridge Comm and Tech Coll (WV)
Cuyahoga Comm Coll (OH)
Ivy Tech Comm Coll–Lafayette (IN)
Ivy Tech Comm Coll–Wabash Valley (IN)
John Tyler Comm Coll (VA)
Macomb Comm Coll (MI)

Quality Control Technology
Arkansas State U–Beebe (AR)
Austin Comm Coll (TX)
Broome Comm Coll (NY)
Central Carolina Comm Coll (NC)
Central Comm Coll–Columbus Campus (NE)
Comm Coll of Allegheny County (PA)
The Comm Coll of Baltimore County (MD)
Grand Rapids Comm Coll (MI)
Illinois Eastern Comm Colls, Frontier Community College (IL)
Illinois Eastern Comm Colls, Lincoln Trail College (IL)
Ivy Tech Comm Coll–Lafayette (IN)
Lakeland Comm Coll (OH)
Lansing Comm Coll (MI)
Macomb Comm Coll (MI)
Metropolitan Comm Coll–Business & Technology Campus (MO)
Northampton Comm Coll (PA)
Owens Comm Coll, Toledo (OH)
Pennsylvania Coll of Technology (PA)
Salt Lake Comm Coll (UT)
Spartan Coll of Aeronautics and Technology (OK)
Tarrant County Coll District (TX)

Radiation Protection/ Health Physics Technology
Lonestar Coll–Cy-Fair (TX)
Lonestar Coll–Montgomery (TX)
Spartanburg Comm Coll (SC)

Radio and Television
Alvin Comm Coll (TX)
Amarillo Coll (TX)
Austin Comm Coll (TX)
Bucks County Comm Coll (PA)
Central Carolina Comm Coll (NC)
Central Texas Coll (TX)
Central Wyoming Coll (WY)
Chattanooga State Comm Coll (TN)
Colby Comm Coll (KS)
Coll of the Canyons (CA)
Daytona State Coll (FL)
Del Mar Coll (TX)
Golden West Coll (CA)
Hesser Coll, Manchester (NH)
Illinois Eastern Comm Colls, Wabash Valley College (IL)
Iowa Lakes Comm Coll (IA)
Lansing Comm Coll (MI)
Lewis and Clark Comm Coll (IL)
Miami Dade Coll (FL)
Northwest Coll (WY)
Pasadena City Coll (CA)
Pima Comm Coll (AZ)
San Diego City Coll (CA)
State Coll of Florida Manatee-Sarasota (FL)

Radio and Television Broadcasting Technology
Central Comm Coll–Hastings Campus (NE)
The Comm Coll of Baltimore County (MD)
Delta Coll (MI)
Glendale Comm Coll (AZ)
Houston Comm Coll System (TX)
Iowa Lakes Comm Coll (IA)
Jefferson State Comm Coll (AL)
Kirkwood Comm Coll (IA)
Mercer County Comm Coll (NJ)
Miami Dade Coll (FL)
Milwaukee Area Tech Coll (WI)
Mount Wachusett Comm Coll (MA)
Northampton Comm Coll (PA)
Northeast Comm Coll (NE)
Oakland Comm Coll (MI)
Pasadena City Coll (CA)
Pikes Peak Comm Coll (CO)
Salt Lake Comm Coll (UT)
Springfield Tech Comm Coll (MA)
State Coll of Florida Manatee-Sarasota (FL)
Tompkins Cortland Comm Coll (NY)

Radiologic Technology/Science
Amarillo Coll (TX)
Argosy U, Twin Cities (MN)
Arizona Western Coll (AZ)
Austin Comm Coll (TX)
Barton County Comm Coll (KS)
Black Hawk Coll, Moline (IL)
Carolinas Coll of Health Sciences (NC)
Casper Coll (WY)
Central Maine Medical Center Coll of Nursing and Health Professions (ME)
Central Oregon Comm Coll (OR)
Century Coll (MN)
Clark Coll (WA)
Comm Coll of Rhode Island (RI)
County Coll of Morris (NJ)
Danville Area Comm Coll (IL)
Delaware Tech & Comm Coll, Jack F. Owens Campus (DE)
Delaware Tech & Comm Coll, Stanton/Wilmington Campus (DE)
Delta Coll (MI)
East Central Coll (MO)
El Centro Coll (TX)
Elgin Comm Coll (IL)
El Paso Comm Coll (TX)
Fayetteville Tech Comm Coll (NC)
Georgia Highlands Coll (GA)
Harrisburg Area Comm Coll (PA)
H. Councill Trenholm State Tech Coll (AL)
Houston Comm Coll System (TX)
Howard Coll (TX)
Kankakee Comm Coll (IL)
Kaskaskia Coll (IL)
Kennebec Valley Comm Coll (ME)
Kilgore Coll (TX)
Lake Michigan Coll (MI)
Laramie County Comm Coll (WY)
Marion Tech Coll (OH)
Massasoit Comm Coll (MA)
Miami Dade Coll (FL)
Minnesota State Comm and Tech Coll (MN)
Mitchell Tech Inst (SD)
Montana State U–Great Falls Coll of Technology (MT)
Moraine Valley Comm Coll (IL)
Niagara County Comm Coll (NY)
Northampton Comm Coll (PA)
Northeast Iowa Comm Coll (IA)
Northland Comm and Tech Coll–Thief River Falls (MN)
Oklahoma State U, Oklahoma City (OK)
Paris Jr Coll (TX)
Pasadena City Coll (CA)
Pasco-Hernando Comm Coll (FL)
Pennsylvania Coll of Technology (PA)
Pima Comm Coll (AZ)
Polk State Coll (FL)
Pueblo Comm Coll (CO)
Randolph Comm Coll (NC)
St. Luke's Coll (IA)
Sandhills Comm Coll (NC)
San Jacinto Coll District (TX)
Southern Maine Comm Coll (ME)
South Suburban Coll (IL)
Southwest Virginia Comm Coll (VA)
Spencerian Coll (KY)
State Coll of Florida Manatee-Sarasota (FL)
State Fair Comm Coll (MO)
Triton Coll (IL)
Westmoreland County Comm Coll (PA)

Radio, Television, and Digital Communication Related
Montgomery County Comm Coll (PA)
Northwest Coll (WY)

Range Science and Management
Casper Coll (WY)
Central Wyoming Coll (WY)
Eastern Wyoming Coll (WY)
Northwest Coll (WY)
Sheridan Coll (WY)
Snow Coll (UT)
Trinity Valley Comm Coll (TX)

Reading Teacher Education
Howard Coll (TX)

Real Estate
Amarillo Coll (TX)
Anne Arundel Comm Coll (MD)
Antelope Valley Coll (CA)
Austin Comm Coll (TX)
Bakersfield Coll (CA)
Camden County Coll (NJ)
Catawba Valley Comm Coll (NC)
Central Piedmont Comm Coll (NC)
Cincinnati State Tech and Comm Coll (OH)
Coll of DuPage (IL)
Coll of the Canyons (CA)
Collin County Comm Coll District (TX)
Comm Coll of Allegheny County (PA)
The Comm Coll of Baltimore County (MD)
Cuyahoga Comm Coll (OH)
Cuyamaca Coll (CA)
Del Mar Coll (TX)
East Los Angeles Coll (CA)
Edison State Comm Coll (OH)
El Paso Comm Coll (TX)
Folsom Lake Coll (CA)
Glendale Comm Coll (AZ)
Golden West Coll (CA)
Harrisburg Area Comm Coll (PA)
Houston Comm Coll System (TX)
Iowa Lakes Comm Coll (IA)
Kent State U at Ashtabula (OH)
Lansing Comm Coll (MI)
Los Angeles Harbor Coll (CA)
Mendocino Coll (CA)
Milwaukee Area Tech Coll (WI)
Montgomery County Comm Coll (PA)
Mt. San Jacinto Coll (CA)
Nassau Comm Coll (NY)
Nicolet Area Tech Coll (WI)
North Central Texas Coll (TX)
Northeast Comm Coll (NE)
North Lake Coll (TX)
Northwest Florida State Coll (FL)
Ocean County Coll (NJ)
Phoenix Coll (AZ)
San Diego City Coll (CA)
San Diego Mesa Coll (CA)
San Jacinto Coll District (TX)
Scottsdale Comm Coll (AZ)
Sierra Coll (CA)
Southern State Comm Coll (OH)

South Plains Coll (TX)
Terra State Comm Coll (OH)
Tidewater Comm Coll (VA)
Trinity Valley Comm Coll (TX)
Victor Valley Coll (CA)
Westmoreland County Comm Coll (PA)

Receptionist
Alexandria Tech Coll (MN)
Dakota Coll at Bottineau (ND)
Iowa Lakes Comm Coll (IA)

Recording Arts Technology
The Art Inst of Seattle (WA)
Comm Coll of Philadelphia (PA)
Finger Lakes Comm Coll (NY)
Glendale Comm Coll (AZ)
Guilford Tech Comm Coll (NC)
Lehigh Carbon Comm Coll (PA)
Miami Dade Coll (FL)
Minneapolis Comm and Tech Coll (MN)
Montgomery County Comm Coll (PA)
Northeast Comm Coll (NE)
Olympic Coll (WA)
Paradise Valley Comm Coll (AZ)
Springfield Tech Comm Coll (MA)

Rehabilitation and Therapeutic Professions Related
Central Wyoming Coll (WY)
Springfield Tech Comm Coll (MA)
Union County Coll (NJ)

Rehabilitation Therapy
Iowa Lakes Comm Coll (IA)
Nassau Comm Coll (NY)
Wayne Comm Coll (NC)

Religious Education
Lon Morris Coll (TX)

Religious Studies
Allen Comm Coll (KS)
Amarillo Coll (TX)
Barton County Comm Coll (KS)
Cowley County Comm Coll and Area Vocational–Tech School (KS)
Kilgore Coll (TX)
Lansing Comm Coll (MI)
Laramie County Comm Coll (WY)
Lonestar Coll–Cy-Fair (TX)
Lonestar Coll–Montgomery (TX)
Lonestar Coll–North Harris (TX)
Lonestar Coll–Tomball (TX)
Lon Morris Coll (TX)
Orange Coast Coll (CA)
Palm Beach State Coll (FL)
Pasadena City Coll (CA)
State Coll of Florida Manatee-Sarasota (FL)
Trinity Valley Comm Coll (TX)

Religious Studies Related
Spartanburg Methodist Coll (SC)

Resort Management
Lehigh Carbon Comm Coll (PA)

Respiratory Care Therapy
Allegany Coll of Maryland (MD)
Alvin Comm Coll (TX)
Amarillo Coll (TX)
Arkansas State U–Mountain Home (AR)
Athens Tech Coll (GA)
Augusta Tech Coll (GA)
Barton County Comm Coll (KS)
Berkshire Comm Coll (MA)
Bowling Green State U–Firelands Coll (OH)
Burlington County Coll (NJ)
Carteret Comm Coll (NC)
Casper Coll (WY)
Catawba Valley Comm Coll (NC)
Central New Mexico Comm Coll (NM)
Central Piedmont Comm Coll (NC)
Chattanooga State Comm Coll (TN)
Cincinnati State Tech and Comm Coll (OH)
City Colls of Chicago, Malcolm X College (IL)
Coll of DuPage (IL)
Collin County Comm Coll District (TX)
Comm Coll of Allegheny County (PA)
The Comm Coll of Baltimore County (MD)
Comm Coll of Philadelphia (PA)
Comm Coll of Rhode Island (RI)
County Coll of Morris (NJ)
Cumberland County Coll (NJ)
Cuyahoga Comm Coll (OH)
Darton Coll (GA)
Daytona State Coll (FL)
Delaware County Comm Coll (PA)
Del Mar Coll (TX)
Delta Coll (MI)
Des Moines Area Comm Coll (IA)
East Central Coll (MO)
East Los Angeles Coll (CA)
El Centro Coll (TX)
El Paso Comm Coll (TX)
Erie Comm Coll, North Campus (NY)
Essex County Coll (NJ)
Fayetteville Tech Comm Coll (NC)
Frederick Comm Coll (MD)
Genesee Comm Coll (NY)
Georgia Highlands Coll (GA)
Goodwin Coll (CT)
Gwinnett Tech Coll (GA)
Harrisburg Area Comm Coll (PA)
Hawkeye Comm Coll (IA)
Highline Comm Coll (WA)
Hillsborough Comm Coll (FL)
Houston Comm Coll System (TX)
Howard Coll (TX)
Hutchinson Comm Coll and Area Vocational School (KS)
Indian River State Coll (FL)
Ivy Tech Comm Coll–Central Indiana (IN)
Ivy Tech Comm Coll–Lafayette (IN)
Ivy Tech Comm Coll–Northeast (IN)
Ivy Tech Comm Coll–Northwest (IN)
Ivy Tech Comm Coll–Southern Indiana (IN)
Jackson State Comm Coll (TN)
J. Sargeant Reynolds Comm Coll (VA)
Kalamazoo Valley Comm Coll (MI)
Kankakee Comm Coll (IL)
Kaplan Coll, Phoenix Campus (AZ)
Kaskaskia Coll (IL)
Kennebec Valley Comm Coll (ME)
Kirkwood Comm Coll (IA)
Lakeland Comm Coll (OH)
Lansing Comm Coll (MI)
Lincoln Land Comm Coll (IL)
Lonestar Coll–Kingwood (TX)
Lonestar Coll–North Harris (TX)
Macomb Comm Coll (MI)
Manchester Comm Coll (CT)
Massasoit Comm Coll (MA)
Mercer County Comm Coll (NJ)
Meridian Comm Coll (MS)
Metropolitan Comm Coll (NE)
Metropolitan Comm Coll–Penn Valley (MO)
Miami Dade Coll (FL)
Midlands Tech Coll (SC)
Milwaukee Area Tech Coll (WI)
Mohawk Valley Comm Coll (NY)
Montana State U–Great Falls Coll of Technology (MT)
Moraine Park Tech Coll (WI)
Moraine Valley Comm Coll (IL)
Mountain Empire Comm Coll (VA)
Nassau Comm Coll (NY)
Northeast Iowa Comm Coll (IA)
Northland Comm and Tech Coll–Thief River Falls (MN)
NorthWest Arkansas Comm Coll (AR)
Oakland Comm Coll (MI)
Oklahoma City Comm Coll (OK)
Orangeburg-Calhoun Tech Coll (SC)
Orange Coast Coll (CA)
Pima Comm Coll (AZ)
Polk State Coll (FL)
Pueblo Comm Coll (CO)
Pulaski Tech Coll (AR)
Quinsigamond Comm Coll (MA)
Raritan Valley Comm Coll (NJ)
Rockingham Comm Coll (NC)
Rockland Comm Coll (NY)
St. Luke's Coll (IA)
Saint Paul Coll–A Comm & Tech College (MN)
St. Philip's Coll (TX)
Sandhills Comm Coll (NC)
San Jacinto Coll District (TX)
San Juan Coll (NM)
Seminole State Coll of Florida (FL)
Somerset Comm Coll (KY)
Southeastern Comm Coll (IA)
Southeast Kentucky Comm and Tech Coll (KY)
Southern Maine Comm Coll (ME)
Southern State Comm Coll (OH)
South Plains Coll (TX)
Southside Virginia Comm Coll (VA)
Southwest Georgia Tech Coll (GA)
Southwest Virginia Comm Coll (VA)
Spartanburg Comm Coll (SC)
Springfield Tech Comm Coll (MA)
Stanly Comm Coll (NC)
Stark State Coll of Technology (OH)
State Coll of Florida Manatee-Sarasota (FL)
Tallahassee Comm Coll (FL)
Tarrant County Coll District (TX)
Temple Coll (TX)
Trident Tech Coll (SC)
Triton Coll (IL)
Union County Coll (NJ)
U of Cincinnati Clermont Coll (OH)
Victoria Coll (TX)
Victor Valley Coll (CA)
Volunteer State Comm Coll (TN)
Westchester Comm Coll (NY)
West Kentucky Comm and Tech Coll (KY)

Respiratory Therapy Technician
Augusta Tech Coll (GA)
Columbus Tech Coll (GA)
Delaware Tech & Comm Coll, Jack F. Owens Campus (DE)
Delaware Tech & Comm Coll, Stanton/Wilmington Campus (DE)
Georgia Northwestern Tech Coll (GA)
Griffin Tech Coll (GA)
Heart of Georgia Tech Coll (GA)
Kaplan Coll, Modesto Campus (CA)
Louisiana Tech Coll (LA)
Miami Dade Coll (FL)
Missouri State U–West Plains (MO)
Okefenokee Tech Coll (GA)
Southeastern Tech Coll (GA)

Restaurant, Culinary, and Catering Management
Cincinnati State Tech and Comm Coll (OH)
City Colls of Chicago, Malcolm X College (IL)
Coll of DuPage (IL)
Coll of Lake County (IL)
Coll of the Canyons (CA)
Comm Coll of Allegheny County (PA)
The Comm Coll of Baltimore County (MD)
Cuyahoga Comm Coll (OH)
Delaware Tech & Comm Coll, Stanton/Wilmington Campus (DE)
Elgin Comm Coll (IL)
Erie Comm Coll, North Campus (NY)
Hillsborough Comm Coll (FL)
Iowa Lakes Comm Coll (IA)
John Wood Comm Coll (IL)
Kirkwood Comm Coll (IA)
Lakeland Comm Coll (OH)
Linn-Benton Comm Coll (OR)
Milwaukee Area Tech Coll (WI)
Mohawk Valley Comm Coll (NY)
Moraine Park Tech Coll (WI)
Moraine Valley Comm Coll (IL)
Northland Pioneer Coll (AZ)
Orange Coast Coll (CA)
Pensacola Jr Coll (FL)
Pima Comm Coll (AZ)
Raritan Valley Comm Coll (NJ)
Southwest Wisconsin Tech Coll (WI)
Waukesha County Tech Coll (WI)
Westmoreland County Comm Coll (PA)

Restaurant/Food Services Management
Burlington County Coll (NJ)
Fiorello H. LaGuardia Comm Coll of the City U of New York (NY)
Harrisburg Area Comm Coll (PA)
Hillsborough Comm Coll (FL)
Iowa Lakes Comm Coll (IA)
Lehigh Carbon Comm Coll (PA)
Northampton Comm Coll (PA)
Oakland Comm Coll (MI)
Owens Comm Coll, Toledo (OH)
Quinsigamond Comm Coll (MA)
The Restaurant School at Walnut Hill Coll (PA)
St. Philip's Coll (TX)
Triton Coll (IL)

Retailing
Alamance Comm Coll (NC)
Black Hawk Coll, Moline (IL)
Blue Ridge Comm Coll (NC)
Burlington County Coll (NJ)
Casper Coll (WY)
Central Oregon Comm Coll (OR)
Clackamas Comm Coll (OR)
Clark Coll (WA)
Coll of DuPage (IL)
Comm Coll of Allegheny County (PA)
Delaware County Comm Coll (PA)
Elgin Comm Coll (IL)
Fox Coll (IL)
Holyoke Comm Coll (MA)
Hutchinson Comm Coll and Area Vocational School (KS)
Iowa Lakes Comm Coll (IA)
Minnesota State Coll–Southeast Tech (MN)
Moraine Valley Comm Coll (IL)
Nassau Comm Coll (NY)
North Central Texas Coll (TX)
Orange Coast Coll (CA)
Pasadena City Coll (CA)
Waukesha County Tech Coll (WI)
Wayne Comm Coll (NC)
Wisconsin Indianhead Tech Coll (WI)

Robotics Technology
Casper Coll (WY)
Central Lakes Coll (MN)
Coll of DuPage (IL)
Comm Coll of Allegheny County (PA)
Daytona State Coll (FL)
Delaware County Comm Coll (PA)
Ivy Tech Comm Coll–Columbus (IN)
Ivy Tech Comm Coll–Lafayette (IN)
Ivy Tech Comm Coll–North Central (IN)
Ivy Tech Comm Coll–Northeast (IN)
Ivy Tech Comm Coll–Richmond (IN)
Ivy Tech Comm Coll–Southwest (IN)
Ivy Tech Comm Coll–Wabash Valley (IN)
Jefferson State Comm Coll (AL)
Lonestar Coll–Montgomery (TX)
Macomb Comm Coll (MI)
Oakland Comm Coll (MI)
Pennsylvania Coll of Technology (PA)
State U of New York Coll of Technology at Alfred (NY)
Sullivan Coll of Technology and Design (KY)
Terra State Comm Coll (OH)

Romance Languages
Highline Comm Coll (WA)

Russian
Austin Comm Coll (TX)

Russian Studies
State Coll of Florida Manatee-Sarasota (FL)

Sales, Distribution and Marketing
Burlington County Coll (NJ)
Central Carolina Tech Coll (SC)
Coll of DuPage (IL)
Coll of the Canyons (CA)
Collin County Comm Coll District (TX)
The Comm Coll of Baltimore County (MD)
Cuyahoga Comm Coll (OH)
Des Moines Area Comm Coll (IA)
Edison State Comm Coll (OH)
Gadsden State Comm Coll (AL)
Harrisburg Area Comm Coll (PA)
Hawkeye Comm Coll (IA)
Iowa Lakes Comm Coll (IA)
John Wood Comm Coll (IL)
Lac Courte Oreilles Ojibwa Comm Coll (WI)
Lake Region State Coll (ND)
Midlands Tech Coll (SC)
Montgomery County Comm Coll (PA)
North Central Texas Coll (TX)
Northeast Iowa Comm Coll (IA)
Northwest Tech Coll (MN)
Owens Comm Coll, Toledo (OH)
St. Cloud Tech Coll (MN)
Sierra Coll (CA)
Spartanburg Comm Coll (SC)

Salon/Beauty Salon Management
Oakland Comm Coll (MI)

Science Teacher Education
Darton Coll (GA)
Iowa Lakes Comm Coll (IA)
Miami Dade Coll (FL)
Moraine Valley Comm Coll (IL)
Sandhills Comm Coll (NC)
Snow Coll (UT)
State Coll of Florida Manatee-Sarasota (FL)
Ulster County Comm Coll (NY)

Science Technologies Related
Cascadia Comm Coll (WA)
Cincinnati State Tech and Comm Coll (OH)
Comm Coll of Allegheny County (PA)
The Comm Coll of Baltimore County (MD)
Dakota Coll at Bottineau (ND)
Delaware County Comm Coll (PA)
Delaware Tech & Comm Coll, Stanton/Wilmington Campus (DE)
Front Range Comm Coll (CO)
Harford Comm Coll (MD)
Jackson State Comm Coll (TN)
Pueblo Comm Coll (CO)
U of Cincinnati Clermont Coll (OH)
Victor Valley Coll (CA)

Sculpture
Mercer County Comm Coll (NJ)

Secondary Education
Allen Comm Coll (KS)
Alpena Comm Coll (MI)
Austin Comm Coll (TX)
Barton County Comm Coll (KS)
Central Wyoming Coll (WY)
City Colls of Chicago, Malcolm X College (IL)
Clarendon Coll (TX)
Collin County Comm Coll District (TX)
Eastern Arizona Coll (AZ)
Eastern Wyoming Coll (WY)
Essex County Coll (NJ)
Gainesville State Coll (GA)
Georgia Highlands Coll (GA)
Harrisburg Area Comm Coll (PA)
Howard Coll (TX)
Howard Comm Coll (MD)
Kankakee Comm Coll (IL)
Lake Michigan Coll (MI)
Mohawk Valley Comm Coll (NY)
Montgomery County Comm Coll (PA)
Northeast Comm Coll (NE)
North Iowa Area Comm Coll (IA)
Northwest Coll (WY)
Red Rocks Comm Coll (CO)
San Juan Coll (NM)
Sheridan Coll (WY)
Springfield Tech Comm Coll (MA)

U of Cincinnati Clermont Coll (OH)
Western Wyoming Comm Coll (WY)

Security and Loss Prevention
Cincinnati State Tech and Comm Coll (OH)
Delta Coll (MI)
Glendale Comm Coll (AZ)
Harford Comm Coll (MD)
Nassau Comm Coll (NY)

Security and Protective Services Related
Barton County Comm Coll (KS)
Central Wyoming Coll (WY)
Century Coll (MN)
El Paso Comm Coll (TX)
Georgia Military Coll (GA)
Glendale Comm Coll (AZ)
Goodwin Coll (CT)
J. Sargeant Reynolds Comm Coll (VA)
Lakeland Comm Coll (OH)
Laramie County Comm Coll (WY)
Miami Dade Coll (FL)
Montana State U–Great Falls Coll of Technology (MT)
Mountain Empire Comm Coll (VA)
NorthWest Arkansas Comm Coll (AR)
Pikes Peak Comm Coll (CO)
Pima Comm Coll (AZ)

Selling Skills and Sales
Alexandria Tech Coll (MN)
Central Wyoming Coll (WY)
Clark Coll (WA)
Coll of DuPage (IL)
Coll of Lake County (IL)
Cuyahoga Comm Coll (OH)
Illinois Valley Comm Coll (IL)
Iowa Lakes Comm Coll (IA)
Lincoln Land Comm Coll (IL)
Minnesota State Coll–Southeast Tech (MN)
Orange Coast Coll (CA)
Triton Coll (IL)

Sheet Metal Technology
Comm Coll of Allegheny County (PA)
Ivy Tech Comm Coll–Central Indiana (IN)
Ivy Tech Comm Coll–Lafayette (IN)
Ivy Tech Comm Coll–North Central (IN)
Ivy Tech Comm Coll–Northeast (IN)
Ivy Tech Comm Coll–Northwest (IN)
Ivy Tech Comm Coll–Southern Indiana (IN)
Ivy Tech Comm Coll–Southwest (IN)
Ivy Tech Comm Coll–Wabash Valley (IN)
Kellogg Comm Coll (MI)
Kirkwood Comm Coll (IA)
Macomb Comm Coll (MI)
Oakland Comm Coll (MI)
Terra State Comm Coll (OH)

Sign Language Interpretation and Translation
Austin Comm Coll (TX)
Black Hawk Coll, Moline (IL)
Blue Ridge Comm Coll (NC)
Burlington County Coll (NJ)
Camden County Coll (NJ)
Central Piedmont Comm Coll (NC)
Cincinnati State Tech and Comm Coll (OH)
Clovis Comm Coll (NM)
Coll of the Canyons (CA)
Collin County Comm Coll District (TX)
Comm Coll of Allegheny County (PA)
The Comm Coll of Baltimore County (MD)
Comm Coll of Philadelphia (PA)
Del Mar Coll (TX)
Eastfield Coll (TX)
El Paso Comm Coll (TX)
Front Range Comm Coll (CO)
Georgia Perimeter Coll (GA)
Golden West Coll (CA)
Houston Comm Coll System (TX)
Howard Coll (TX)
Kirkwood Comm Coll (IA)
Lakeland Comm Coll (OH)
Lake Region State Coll (ND)
Lansing Comm Coll (MI)
Miami Dade Coll (FL)
Milwaukee Area Tech Coll (WI)
Mohawk Valley Comm Coll (NY)
Montgomery Coll (MD)
Northwestern Connecticut Comm Coll (CT)
Oakland Comm Coll (MI)
Ocean County Coll (NJ)
Oklahoma State U, Oklahoma City (OK)
Pikes Peak Comm Coll (CO)
Pima Comm Coll (AZ)
Saint Paul Coll–A Comm & Tech College (MN)
Salt Lake Comm Coll (UT)
Suffolk County Comm Coll (NY)
Tarrant County Coll District (TX)
Union County Coll (NJ)
Wilson Comm Coll (NC)

Small Business Administration
Black Hawk Coll, Moline (IL)
Coll of the Canyons (CA)
Flathead Valley Comm Coll (MT)
Harrisburg Area Comm Coll (PA)
Iowa Lakes Comm Coll (IA)
Lake Region State Coll (ND)
Moraine Valley Comm Coll (IL)
North Hennepin Comm Coll (MN)
Northland Pioneer Coll (AZ)
Raritan Valley Comm Coll (NJ)
Sierra Coll (CA)
South Suburban Coll (IL)

Small Engine Mechanics and Repair Technology
Alexandria Tech Coll (MN)
Iowa Lakes Comm Coll (IA)
Kirtland Comm Coll (MI)

Social Psychology
Macomb Comm Coll (MI)
State Coll of Florida Manatee-Sarasota (FL)

Social Sciences
Allan Hancock Coll (CA)
Amarillo Coll (TX)
Anne Arundel Comm Coll (MD)
Arizona Western Coll (AZ)
Bowling Green State U–Firelands Coll (OH)
Bucks County Comm Coll (PA)
Burlington County Coll (NJ)
Central Oregon Comm Coll (OR)
Central Texas Coll (TX)
Central Wyoming Coll (WY)
Clarendon Coll (TX)
Coll of the Canyons (CA)
Comm Coll of Allegheny County (PA)
Comm Coll of Vermont (VT)
Corning Comm Coll (NY)
Dakota Coll at Bottineau (ND)
Essex County Coll (NJ)
Finger Lakes Comm Coll (NY)
Folsom Lake Coll (CA)
Fulton-Montgomery Comm Coll (NY)
Georgia Military Coll (GA)
Harrisburg Area Comm Coll (PA)
Highline Comm Coll (WA)
Housatonic Comm Coll (CT)
Howard Coll (TX)
Howard Comm Coll (MD)
Hutchinson Comm Coll and Area Vocational School (KS)
Indian River State Coll (FL)
Iowa Lakes Comm Coll (IA)
Jamestown Comm Coll (NY)
J. Sargeant Reynolds Comm Coll (VA)
Kilgore Coll (TX)
Laramie County Comm Coll (WY)
Lawson State Comm Coll (AL)
Lehigh Carbon Comm Coll (PA)
Lonestar Coll–Cy-Fair (TX)
Lonestar Coll–Kingwood (TX)
Lon Morris Coll (TX)
Mendocino Coll (CA)
Miami Dade Coll (FL)
Montgomery County Comm Coll (PA)
Mt. San Jacinto Coll (CA)
Niagara County Comm Coll (NY)
Northeast Comm Coll (NE)
Northeastern Jr Coll (CO)
North Idaho Coll (ID)
North Iowa Area Comm Coll (IA)
Northwest Coll (WY)
Northwestern Connecticut Comm Coll (CT)
Northwest Florida State Coll (FL)
Odessa Coll (TX)
Orange Coast Coll (CA)
Otero Jr Coll (CO)
Palm Beach State Coll (FL)
Reedley Coll (CA)
San Diego City Coll (CA)
San Diego Mesa Coll (CA)
San Jacinto Coll District (TX)
Santa Rosa Jr Coll (CA)
Seminole State Coll (OK)
Sheridan Coll (WY)
Sierra Coll (CA)
Southwest Mississippi Comm Coll (MS)
State Coll of Florida Manatee-Sarasota (FL)
State U of New York Coll of Technology at Alfred (NY)
Suffolk County Comm Coll (NY)
Terra State Comm Coll (OH)
Thomas Nelson Comm Coll (VA)
Umpqua Comm Coll (OR)
U of Cincinnati Clermont Coll (OH)
Victor Valley Coll (CA)
Vincennes U Jasper Campus (IN)
Westchester Comm Coll (NY)
Western Wyoming Comm Coll (WY)

Social Science Teacher Education
Howard Coll (TX)

Social Studies Teacher Education
Casper Coll (WY)
Howard Coll (TX)
State Coll of Florida Manatee-Sarasota (FL)
Ulster County Comm Coll (NY)

Social Work
Allen Comm Coll (KS)
Amarillo Coll (TX)
Austin Comm Coll (TX)
Barton County Comm Coll (KS)
Bucks County Comm Coll (PA)
Camden County Coll (NJ)
Casper Coll (WY)
Central Carolina Comm Coll (NC)
Central Piedmont Comm Coll (NC)
Chipola Coll (FL)
Clackamas Comm Coll (OR)
Coll of Lake County (IL)
Comm Coll of Allegheny County (PA)
Comm Coll of Rhode Island (RI)
Cowley County Comm Coll and Area Vocational–Tech School (KS)
Cumberland County Coll (NJ)
Darton Coll (GA)
Del Mar Coll (TX)
Eastfield Coll (TX)
East Los Angeles Coll (CA)
Edison State Comm Coll (OH)
Elgin Comm Coll (IL)
El Paso Comm Coll (TX)
Essex County Coll (NJ)
Gainesville State Coll (GA)
Harrisburg Area Comm Coll (PA)
Holyoke Comm Coll (MA)
Hopkinsville Comm Coll (KY)
Illinois Eastern Comm Colls, Wabash Valley College (IL)
Illinois Valley Comm Coll (IL)
Indian River State Coll (FL)
Iowa Lakes Comm Coll (IA)
Kellogg Comm Coll (MI)
Kilian Comm Coll (SD)
Lac Courte Oreilles Ojibwa Comm Coll (WI)
Lakeland Comm Coll (OH)
Lake Michigan Coll (MI)
Lansing Comm Coll (MI)
Lawson State Comm Coll (AL)
Lonestar Coll–Montgomery (TX)
Manchester Comm Coll (CT)
Marion Tech Coll (OH)
Miami Dade Coll (FL)
Northampton Comm Coll (PA)
Northeastern Jr Coll (CO)
Northeast Iowa Comm Coll (IA)
Northwest Florida State Coll (FL)
Ocean County Coll (NJ)
Owensboro Comm and Tech Coll (KY)
Palm Beach State Coll (FL)
Potomac State Coll of West Virginia U (WV)
Rogue Comm Coll (OR)
Saint Charles Comm Coll (MO)
St. Philip's Coll (TX)
Salt Lake Comm Coll (UT)
San Diego City Coll (CA)
San Juan Coll (NM)
Shawnee Comm Coll (IL)
South Plains Coll (TX)
South Suburban Coll (IL)
Southwestern Michigan Coll (MI)
State Coll of Florida Manatee-Sarasota (FL)
Terra State Comm Coll (OH)
Umpqua Comm Coll (OR)
U of Cincinnati Clermont Coll (OH)
Vincennes U Jasper Campus (IN)
Western Wyoming Comm Coll (WY)
West Georgia Tech Coll (GA)
West Virginia Northern Comm Coll (WV)

Social Work Related
Clarendon Coll (TX)
Kirkwood Comm Coll (IA)

Sociology
Allen Comm Coll (KS)
Austin Comm Coll (TX)
Bainbridge Coll (GA)
Bakersfield Coll (CA)
Barton County Comm Coll (KS)
Bunker Hill Comm Coll (MA)
Burlington County Coll (NJ)
Casper Coll (WY)
Clarendon Coll (TX)
Coll of the Canyons (CA)
Comm Coll of Allegheny County (PA)
Darton Coll (GA)
Delaware County Comm Coll (PA)
Del Mar Coll (TX)
Eastern Arizona Coll (AZ)
Eastern Wyoming Coll (WY)
East Los Angeles Coll (CA)
Everett Comm Coll (WA)
Finger Lakes Comm Coll (NY)
Gainesville State Coll (GA)
Georgia Highlands Coll (GA)
Highland Comm Coll (IL)
Howard Coll (TX)
Indian River State Coll (FL)
Iowa Lakes Comm Coll (IA)
John Wood Comm Coll (IL)
Lake Michigan Coll (MI)
Laramie County Comm Coll (WY)
Lawson State Comm Coll (AL)
Lonestar Coll–Cy-Fair (TX)
Lonestar Coll–Kingwood (TX)
Lonestar Coll–Montgomery (TX)
Lonestar Coll–North Harris (TX)
Lonestar Coll–Tomball (TX)
Lon Morris Coll (TX)
Miami Dade Coll (FL)
Mohave Comm Coll (AZ)
North Idaho Coll (ID)
North Iowa Area Comm Coll (IA)
Northwest Coll (WY)
Odessa Coll (TX)
Oklahoma City Comm Coll (OK)
Orange Coast Coll (CA)
Pasadena City Coll (CA)
Pima Comm Coll (AZ)
Potomac State Coll of West Virginia U (WV)
Red Rocks Comm Coll (CO)
Saint Charles Comm Coll (MO)
St. Philip's Coll (TX)
Salt Lake Comm Coll (UT)
San Diego City Coll (CA)
San Diego Mesa Coll (CA)
San Jacinto Coll District (TX)
Snow Coll (UT)
Trinity Valley Comm Coll (TX)
Triton Coll (IL)
Umpqua Comm Coll (OR)
Vincennes U Jasper Campus (IN)
Western Wyoming Comm Coll (WY)

Soil Science and Agronomy
Iowa Lakes Comm Coll (IA)
The Ohio State U Ag Tech Inst (OH)
Snow Coll (UT)

Solar Energy Technology
Century Coll (MN)
Comm Coll of Allegheny County (PA)
Lac Courte Oreilles Ojibwa Comm Coll (WI)
Pennsylvania Coll of Technology (PA)
San Juan Coll (NM)

Spanish
Allan Hancock Coll (CA)
Arizona Western Coll (AZ)
Austin Comm Coll (TX)
Bakersfield Coll (CA)
Berkeley City Coll (CA)
Coll of the Canyons (CA)
East Los Angeles Coll (CA)
Fiorello H. LaGuardia Comm Coll of the City U of New York (NY)
Howard Coll (TX)
Indian River State Coll (FL)
Iowa Lakes Comm Coll (IA)
Laramie County Comm Coll (WY)
Lon Morris Coll (TX)
Mendocino Coll (CA)
Miami Dade Coll (FL)
North Idaho Coll (ID)
Northwest Coll (WY)
Orange Coast Coll (CA)
Pasadena City Coll (CA)
Red Rocks Comm Coll (CO)
Saint Charles Comm Coll (MO)
St. Philip's Coll (TX)
San Diego Mesa Coll (CA)
Snow Coll (UT)
State Coll of Florida Manatee-Sarasota (FL)
Trinity Valley Comm Coll (TX)
Triton Coll (IL)
Western Wyoming Comm Coll (WY)

Spanish Language Teacher Education
The Comm Coll of Baltimore County (MD)
Frederick Comm Coll (MD)
Montgomery Coll (MD)
Ulster County Comm Coll (NY)

Special Education
Black Hawk Coll, Moline (IL)
The Comm Coll of Baltimore County (MD)
Comm Coll of Rhode Island (RI)
Darton Coll (GA)
Fayetteville Tech Comm Coll (NC)
Highland Comm Coll (IL)
Howard Coll (TX)
J. Sargeant Reynolds Comm Coll (VA)
Kankakee Comm Coll (IL)
Lehigh Carbon Comm Coll (PA)
Moraine Valley Comm Coll (IL)
Rend Lake Coll (IL)
San Juan Coll (NM)
U of Cincinnati Clermont Coll (OH)

Special Education (Early Childhood)
Blue Ridge Comm Coll (NC)
Coll of the Canyons (CA)
Itasca Comm Coll (MN)
Northland Pioneer Coll (AZ)
Olympic Coll (WA)

Special Education (Hearing Impaired)
Hillsborough Comm Coll (FL)

Special Products Marketing
Central Piedmont Comm Coll (NC)
Cuyamaca Coll (CA)
Del Mar Coll (TX)
El Centro Coll (TX)
Fox Valley Tech Coll (WI)
Gateway Comm Coll (CT)
Indian River State Coll (FL)
Lansing Comm Coll (MI)
Metropolitan Comm Coll–Penn Valley (MO)
Muskegon Comm Coll (MI)
Orange Coast Coll (CA)
Palm Beach State Coll (FL)
Phoenix Coll (AZ)
San Diego City Coll (CA)
Scottsdale Comm Coll (AZ)
Southern Maine Comm Coll (ME)
South Plains Coll (TX)
State Fair Comm Coll (MO)

Three Rivers Comm Coll (CT)

Speech and Rhetoric
Allen Comm Coll (KS)
Amarillo Coll (TX)
Austin Comm Coll (TX)
Bainbridge Coll (GA)
Bakersfield Coll (CA)
Clarendon Coll (TX)
Cuyamaca Coll (CA)
Darton Coll (GA)
Del Mar Coll (TX)
East Los Angeles Coll (CA)
Everett Comm Coll (WA)
Howard Coll (TX)
Indian River State Coll (FL)
Iowa Lakes Comm Coll (IA)
Kilgore Coll (TX)
Lansing Comm Coll (MI)
Linn-Benton Comm Coll (OR)
Lonestar Coll–Cy-Fair (TX)
Lonestar Coll–Kingwood (TX)
Lonestar Coll–Montgomery (TX)
Lonestar Coll–North Harris (TX)
Lonestar Coll–Tomball (TX)
Lon Morris Coll (TX)
Mendocino Coll (CA)
Northeast Comm Coll (NE)
Odessa Coll (TX)
Saint Charles Comm Coll (MO)
St. Philip's Coll (TX)
San Diego City Coll (CA)
San Diego Mesa Coll (CA)
San Jacinto Coll District (TX)
Sierra Coll (CA)
State Coll of Florida Manatee-Sarasota (FL)
Trinity Valley Comm Coll (TX)
Triton Coll (IL)

Speech-Language Pathology
Catawba Valley Comm Coll (NC)
Coll of DuPage (IL)
Fayetteville Tech Comm Coll (NC)

Speech Teacher Education
Darton Coll (GA)
Highland Comm Coll (IL)
Howard Coll (TX)

Sport and Fitness Administration/ Management
Barton County Comm Coll (KS)
Bucks County Comm Coll (PA)
Camden County Coll (NJ)
Central Oregon Comm Coll (OR)
Century Coll (MN)
Clark Coll (WA)
Dean Coll (MA)
Des Moines Area Comm Coll (IA)
Gainesville State Coll (GA)
Harcum Coll (PA)
Holyoke Comm Coll (MA)
Howard Comm Coll (MD)
Iowa Lakes Comm Coll (IA)
Kingsborough Comm Coll of the City U of New York (NY)
Lehigh Carbon Comm Coll (PA)
Niagara County Comm Coll (NY)
Northampton Comm Coll (PA)
North Iowa Area Comm Coll (IA)
Salt Lake Comm Coll (UT)
Springfield Tech Comm Coll (MA)
State U of New York Coll of Technology at Alfred (NY)
Tompkins Cortland Comm Coll (NY)

Statistics
Eastern Wyoming Coll (WY)
State Coll of Florida Manatee-Sarasota (FL)

Statistics Related
Casper Coll (WY)

Structural Engineering
Moraine Park Tech Coll (WI)

Substance Abuse/ Addiction Counseling
Alvin Comm Coll (TX)
Amarillo Coll (TX)
Austin Comm Coll (TX)
Broome Comm Coll (NY)
Camden County Coll (NJ)
Casper Coll (WY)
Central Oregon Comm Coll (OR)
Central Texas Coll (TX)
Century Coll (MN)
Clark Coll (WA)
Coll of DuPage (IL)
Coll of Lake County (IL)
Comm Coll of Allegheny County (PA)
The Comm Coll of Baltimore County (MD)
Comm Coll of Rhode Island (RI)
Corning Comm Coll (NY)
Delaware Tech & Comm Coll, Stanton/Wilmington Campus (DE)
Delaware Tech & Comm Coll, Terry Campus (DE)
Eastfield Coll (TX)
El Paso Comm Coll (TX)
Erie Comm Coll (NY)
Finger Lakes Comm Coll (NY)
Flathead Valley Comm Coll (MT)
Gadsden State Comm Coll (AL)
Gateway Comm Coll (CT)
Genesee Comm Coll (NY)
Guilford Tech Comm Coll (NC)
Harford Comm Coll (MD)
Housatonic Comm Coll (CT)
Howard Coll (TX)
Howard Comm Coll (MD)
Lac Courte Oreilles Ojibwa Comm Coll (WI)
Lower Columbia Coll (WA)
Mendocino Coll (CA)
Mesabi Range Comm and Tech Coll (MN)
Miami Dade Coll (FL)
Middlesex Comm Coll (CT)
Minneapolis Comm and Tech Coll (MN)
Mohave Comm Coll (AZ)
Mohawk Valley Comm Coll (NY)
Moraine Park Tech Coll (WI)
Moraine Valley Comm Coll (IL)
Mountain State Coll (WV)
Mt. San Jacinto Coll (CA)
Northwestern Connecticut Comm Coll (CT)
Odessa Coll (TX)
Oklahoma State U, Oklahoma City (OK)
Olympic Coll (WA)
Rio Salado Coll (AZ)
Sandhills Comm Coll (NC)
Sisseton-Wahpeton Comm Coll (SD)
Southeastern Comm Coll (IA)
Suffolk County Comm Coll (NY)
Three Rivers Comm Coll (CT)
Tompkins Cortland Comm Coll (NY)
Triton Coll (IL)
Tunxis Comm Coll (CT)
Westchester Comm Coll (NY)
Wor-Wic Comm Coll (MD)

Surgical Technology
Athens Tech Coll (GA)
Augusta Tech Coll (GA)
Austin Comm Coll (TX)
Blue Ridge Comm Coll (NC)
Brown Mackie Coll–Akron (OH)
Brown Mackie Coll–Atlanta (GA)
Brown Mackie Coll–Boise (ID)
Brown Mackie Coll–Cincinnati (OH)
Brown Mackie Coll–Findlay (OH)
Brown Mackie Coll–Fort Wayne (IN)
Brown Mackie Coll–Greenville (SC)
Brown Mackie Coll–Louisville (KY)
Brown Mackie Coll–Merrillville (IN)
Brown Mackie Coll–Michigan City (IN)
Brown Mackie Coll–North Canton (OH)
Brown Mackie Coll–Northern Kentucky (KY)
Brown Mackie Coll–Phoenix (AZ)
Brown Mackie Coll–St. Louis (MO)
Brown Mackie Coll–Tucson (AZ)
Brown Mackie Coll–Tulsa (OK)
Cape Fear Comm Coll (NC)
Central Carolina Tech Coll (SC)
Central Ohio Tech Coll (OH)
Cincinnati State Tech and Comm Coll (OH)
City Colls of Chicago, Malcolm X College (IL)
Coll of DuPage (IL)
Collin County Comm Coll District (TX)
Columbus Tech Coll (GA)
Comm Care Coll (OK)
Comm Coll of Allegheny County (PA)
Cuyahoga Comm Coll (OH)
DeKalb Tech Coll (GA)
Delaware County Comm Coll (PA)
Delta Coll (MI)
El Centro Coll (TX)
El Paso Comm Coll (TX)
Fayetteville Tech Comm Coll (NC)
Flathead Valley Comm Coll (MT)
Frederick Comm Coll (MD)
Georgia Northwestern Tech Coll (GA)
Griffin Tech Coll (GA)
Guilford Tech Comm Coll (NC)
Harrison Coll, Fort Wayne (IN)
Harrison Coll, Indianapolis (IN)
Iowa Lakes Comm Coll (IA)
Ivy Tech Comm Coll–Central Indiana (IN)
Ivy Tech Comm Coll–Columbus (IN)
Ivy Tech Comm Coll–East Central (IN)
Ivy Tech Comm Coll–Kokomo (IN)
Ivy Tech Comm Coll–Lafayette (IN)
Ivy Tech Comm Coll–Northwest (IN)
Ivy Tech Comm Coll–Southwest (IN)
Ivy Tech Comm Coll–Wabash Valley (IN)
Kalamazoo Valley Comm Coll (MI)
Kilgore Coll (TX)
Kirkwood Comm Coll (IA)
Kirtland Comm Coll (MI)
Lackawanna Coll (PA)
Lakeland Comm Coll (OH)
Lanier Tech Coll (GA)
Lansing Comm Coll (MI)
Laramie County Comm Coll (WY)
Louisiana Tech Coll (LA)
Macomb Comm Coll (MI)
Manchester Comm Coll (CT)
Metropolitan Comm Coll (NE)
Midlands Tech Coll (SC)
Miller-Motte Tech Coll (SC)
Milwaukee Area Tech Coll (WI)
Mohave Comm Coll (AZ)
Montana State U–Great Falls Coll of Technology (MT)
Montgomery Coll (MD)
Montgomery County Comm Coll (PA)
Moraine Park Tech Coll (WI)
Nassau Comm Coll (NY)
Niagara County Comm Coll (NY)
Northampton Comm Coll (PA)
North Arkansas Coll (AR)
Northeast Comm Coll (NE)
Northland Comm and Tech Coll–Thief River Falls (MN)
Oakland Comm Coll (MI)
Okefenokee Tech Coll (GA)
Oklahoma City Comm Coll (OK)
Owens Comm Coll, Toledo (OH)
Paris Jr Coll (TX)
Pennsylvania Coll of Technology (PA)
St. Cloud Tech Coll (MN)
Sandhills Comm Coll (NC)
San Jacinto Coll District (TX)
San Juan Coll (NM)
Savannah Tech Coll (GA)
Somerset Comm Coll (KY)
Southeast Tech Inst (SD)
Southern Maine Comm Coll (ME)
South Plains Coll (TX)
Southwest Georgia Tech Coll (GA)
Spencerian Coll (KY)
Springfield Tech Comm Coll (MA)
Tarrant County Coll District (TX)
Trinity Valley Comm Coll (TX)
U of Cincinnati Clermont Coll (OH)
Waukesha County Tech Coll (WI)
West Kentucky Comm and Tech Coll (KY)

Surveying Engineering
Comm Coll of Rhode Island (RI)
Des Moines Area Comm Coll (IA)
Kirkwood Comm Coll (IA)
Santa Rosa Jr Coll (CA)
State U of New York Coll of Technology at Alfred (NY)

Survey Technology
Austin Comm Coll (TX)
Bakersfield Coll (CA)
Central New Mexico Comm Coll (NM)
Central Piedmont Comm Coll (NC)
Cincinnati State Tech and Comm Coll (OH)
Clackamas Comm Coll (OR)
Clark Coll (WA)
Coll of the Canyons (CA)
Cuyamaca Coll (CA)
Delaware Tech & Comm Coll, Jack F. Owens Campus (DE)
Delaware Tech & Comm Coll, Stanton/Wilmington Campus (DE)
Fayetteville Tech Comm Coll (NC)
Flathead Valley Comm Coll (MT)
Guilford Tech Comm Coll (NC)
Indian River State Coll (FL)
Lansing Comm Coll (MI)
Louisiana Tech Coll (LA)
Macomb Comm Coll (MI)
Middle Georgia Coll (GA)
Mohawk Valley Comm Coll (NY)
Nicolet Area Tech Coll (WI)
Oklahoma State U, Oklahoma City (OK)
Owens Comm Coll, Toledo (OH)
Palm Beach State Coll (FL)
Penn State Wilkes-Barre (PA)
Pennsylvania Coll of Technology (PA)
Saint Paul Coll–A Comm & Tech College (MN)
Salt Lake Comm Coll (UT)
Sandhills Comm Coll (NC)
San Jacinto Coll District (TX)
San Juan Coll (NM)
Sheridan Coll (WY)
Stark State Coll of Technology (OH)
Triton Coll (IL)
U of Arkansas Comm Coll at Morrilton (AR)
White Mountains Comm Coll (NH)

System Administration
Anne Arundel Comm Coll (MD)
Central Comm Coll–Columbus Campus (NE)
Central Comm Coll–Grand Island Campus (NE)
Central Comm Coll–Hastings Campus (NE)
Century Coll (MN)
Dakota Coll at Bottineau (ND)
Davis Coll (OH)
Del Mar Coll (TX)
Eastfield Coll (TX)
Genesee Comm Coll (NY)
Houston Comm Coll System (TX)
Illinois Valley Comm Coll (IL)
Inver Hills Comm Coll (MN)
Iowa Lakes Comm Coll (IA)
Island Drafting and Tech Inst (NY)
Kirkwood Comm Coll (IA)
Linn-Benton Comm Coll (OR)
Louisiana Tech Coll (LA)
Metropolitan Comm Coll–Business & Technology Campus (MO)
Montana State U–Great Falls Coll of Technology (MT)
North Iowa Area Comm Coll (IA)
Northland Comm and Tech Coll–Thief River Falls (MN)
Olympic Coll (WA)
Owensboro Comm and Tech Coll (KY)
Palm Beach State Coll (FL)
Pennsylvania Coll of Technology (PA)
Pennsylvania Highlands Comm Coll (PA)
Potomac State Coll of West Virginia U (WV)
Rio Salado Coll (AZ)
Rockland Comm Coll (NY)
Seminole State Coll of Florida (FL)
Sierra Coll (CA)
Southwest Mississippi Comm Coll (MS)
Springfield Tech Comm Coll (MA)
Stanly Comm Coll (NC)
Sullivan Coll of Technology and Design (KY)
Tallahassee Comm Coll (FL)

System, Networking, and LAN/WAN Management
Blue Ridge Comm Coll (NC)
Bradford School (OH)
Bradford School (PA)
Bryant & Stratton Coll, Eastlake (OH)
Bryant & Stratton Coll, Parma (OH)
Bryant & Stratton Coll (WI)
Bryant & Stratton Coll - Albany Campus (NY)
Bryant & Stratton Coll - Amherst Campus (NY)
Bryant & Stratton Coll - Buffalo Campus (NY)
Bryant & Stratton Coll - Greece Campus (NY)
Bryant & Stratton Coll - Henrietta Campus (NY)
Bryant & Stratton Coll - North Campus (NY)
Bryant & Stratton Coll - Richmond Campus (VA)
Bryant & Stratton Coll - Virginia Beach (VA)
El Paso Comm Coll (TX)
Fayetteville Tech Comm Coll (NC)
Glendale Comm Coll (AZ)
Guilford Tech Comm Coll (NC)
International Business Coll, Indianapolis (IN)
Iowa Lakes Comm Coll (IA)
ITT Tech Inst, Bessemer (AL)
ITT Tech Inst, Madison (AL)
ITT Tech Inst, Mobile (AL)
ITT Tech Inst, Phoenix (AZ)
ITT Tech Inst, Tucson (AZ)
ITT Tech Inst (AR)
ITT Tech Inst, Anaheim (CA)
ITT Tech Inst, Lathrop (CA)
ITT Tech Inst, Oxnard (CA)
ITT Tech Inst, Rancho Cordova (CA)
ITT Tech Inst, San Bernardino (CA)
ITT Tech Inst, San Diego (CA)
ITT Tech Inst, San Dimas (CA)
ITT Tech Inst, Sylmar (CA)
ITT Tech Inst, Torrance (CA)
ITT Tech Inst, Aurora (CO)
ITT Tech Inst, Thornton (CO)
ITT Tech Inst, Fort Lauderdale (FL)
ITT Tech Inst, Fort Myers (FL)
ITT Tech Inst, Jacksonville (FL)
ITT Tech Inst, Lake Mary (FL)
ITT Tech Inst, Miami (FL)
ITT Tech Inst, Pinellas Park (FL)
ITT Tech Inst, Tallahassee (FL)
ITT Tech Inst, Tampa (FL)
ITT Tech Inst, Atlanta (GA)
ITT Tech Inst, Duluth (GA)
ITT Tech Inst, Kennesaw (GA)
ITT Tech Inst (ID)
ITT Tech Inst, Burr Ridge (IL)
ITT Tech Inst, Mount Prospect (IL)
ITT Tech Inst, Orland Park (IL)
ITT Tech Inst, Fort Wayne (IN)
ITT Tech Inst, Indianapolis (IN)
ITT Tech Inst, Merrillville (IN)
ITT Tech Inst, Newburgh (IN)
ITT Tech Inst, Cedar Rapids (IA)
ITT Tech Inst, Clive (IA)
ITT Tech Inst, Louisville (KY)
ITT Tech Inst, Baton Rouge (LA)
ITT Tech Inst, St. Rose (LA)
ITT Tech Inst (MD)
ITT Tech Inst, Norwood (MA)
ITT Tech Inst, Woburn (MA)
ITT Tech Inst, Canton (MI)
ITT Tech Inst, Swartz Creek (MI)
ITT Tech Inst, Troy (MI)
ITT Tech Inst, Wyoming (MI)
ITT Tech Inst (MN)
ITT Tech Inst, Arnold (MO)
ITT Tech Inst, Earth City (MO)

ITT Tech Inst, Kansas City (MO)
ITT Tech Inst (NE)
ITT Tech Inst (NV)
ITT Tech Inst (NM)
ITT Tech Inst, Albany (NY)
ITT Tech Inst, Getzville (NY)
ITT Tech Inst, Liverpool (NY)
ITT Tech Inst, Charlotte (NC)
ITT Tech Inst, High Point (NC)
ITT Tech Inst, Morrisville (NC)
ITT Tech Inst, Akron (OH)
ITT Tech Inst, Columbus (OH)
ITT Tech Inst, Dayton (OH)
ITT Tech Inst, Hilliard (OH)
ITT Tech Inst, Maumee (OH)
ITT Tech Inst, Norwood (OH)
ITT Tech Inst, Strongsville (OH)
ITT Tech Inst, Warrensville Heights (OH)
ITT Tech Inst, Youngstown (OH)
ITT Tech Inst, Tulsa (OK)
ITT Tech Inst (OR)
ITT Tech Inst, Bensalem (PA)
ITT Tech Inst, Dunmore (PA)
ITT Tech Inst, Harrisburg (PA)
ITT Tech Inst, King of Prussia (PA)
ITT Tech Inst, Pittsburgh (PA)
ITT Tech Inst, Tarentum (PA)
ITT Tech Inst, Columbia (SC)
ITT Tech Inst, Greenville (SC)
ITT Tech Inst, Chattanooga (TN)
ITT Tech Inst, Cordova (TN)
ITT Tech Inst, Johnson City (TN)
ITT Tech Inst, Knoxville (TN)
ITT Tech Inst, Nashville (TN)
ITT Tech Inst, Arlington (TX)
ITT Tech Inst, Austin (TX)
ITT Tech Inst, DeSoto (TX)
ITT Tech Inst, Houston (TX)
ITT Tech Inst, Houston (TX)
ITT Tech Inst, Richardson (TX)
ITT Tech Inst, San Antonio (TX)
ITT Tech Inst, Webster (TX)
ITT Tech Inst (UT)
ITT Tech Inst, Chantilly (VA)
ITT Tech Inst, Norfolk (VA)
ITT Tech Inst, Richmond (VA)
ITT Tech Inst, Salem (VA)
ITT Tech Inst, Springfield (VA)
ITT Tech Inst, Everett (WA)
ITT Tech Inst, Seattle (WA)
ITT Tech Inst, Spokane Valley (WA)
ITT Tech Inst (WV)
ITT Tech Inst, Green Bay (WI)
ITT Tech Inst, Greenfield (WI)
ITT Tech Inst, Madison (WI)
Kaplan Career Inst, Harrisburg (PA)
LDS Business Coll (UT)
Lonestar Coll–Montgomery (TX)
Lonestar Coll–Tomball (TX)
Metropolitan Comm Coll–Business & Technology Campus (MO)
Minneapolis Business Coll (MN)
Mitchell Tech Inst (SD)
Moraine Valley Comm Coll (IL)
Olympic Coll (WA)
St. Philip's Coll (TX)
San Jacinto Coll District (TX)
Southwestern Indian Polytechnic Inst (NM)
Temple Coll (TX)
Wood Tobe–Coburn School (NY)

Systems Engineering
Kent State U at Trumbull (OH)

Teacher Assistant/ Aide
Alamance Comm Coll (NC)
Antelope Valley Coll (CA)
Blue Ridge Comm Coll (NC)
Bucks County Comm Coll (PA)
Carteret Comm Coll (NC)
Casper Coll (WY)
Catawba Valley Comm Coll (NC)
Central Wyoming Coll (WY)
Century Coll (MN)
City Colls of Chicago, Malcolm X College (IL)
Clovis Comm Coll (NM)
Comm Coll of Vermont (VT)
Dakota Coll at Bottineau (ND)
Danville Area Comm Coll (IL)
East Central Coll (MO)
El Centro Coll (TX)
Fiorello H. LaGuardia Comm Coll of the City U of New York (NY)
Fulton-Montgomery Comm Coll (NY)
Goodwin Coll (CT)
Green River Comm Coll (WA)
Highland Comm Coll (IL)
Hopkinsville Comm Coll (KY)
Illinois Eastern Comm Colls, Lincoln Trail College (IL)
Illinois Valley Comm Coll (IL)
Indian River State Coll (FL)
Kankakee Comm Coll (IL)
Kaskaskia Coll (IL)
Kennebec Valley Comm Coll (ME)
Kingsborough Comm Coll of the City U of New York (NY)
Lake Region State Coll (ND)
Lansing Comm Coll (MI)
Lehigh Carbon Comm Coll (PA)
Linn-Benton Comm Coll (OR)
Manchester Comm Coll (CT)
Massasoit Comm Coll (MA)
Mercer County Comm Coll (NJ)
Miami Dade Coll (FL)
Montcalm Comm Coll (MI)
Montgomery County Comm Coll (PA)
Moraine Park Tech Coll (WI)
Moraine Valley Comm Coll (IL)
New Mexico State U–Carlsbad (NM)
Northampton Comm Coll (PA)
Northland Pioneer Coll (AZ)
Ocean County Coll (NJ)
Odessa Coll (TX)
Saint Charles Comm Coll (MO)
St. Cloud Tech Coll (MN)
St. Philip's Coll (TX)
Salt Lake Comm Coll (UT)
San Diego City Coll (CA)
Sheridan Coll (WY)
Somerset Comm Coll (KY)
Southwestern Michigan Coll (MI)
State Fair Comm Coll (MO)
Victor Valley Coll (CA)
Waukesha County Tech Coll (WI)

Teaching Assistants/ Aides Related
Northland Pioneer Coll (AZ)
Raritan Valley Comm Coll (NJ)
Terra State Comm Coll (OH)

Technical and Business Writing
Austin Comm Coll (TX)
Black Hawk Coll, Moline (IL)
Cincinnati State Tech and Comm Coll (OH)
Clovis Comm Coll (NM)
Coll of Lake County (IL)
Linn-Benton Comm Coll (OR)
Oklahoma State U, Oklahoma City (OK)
Three Rivers Comm Coll (CT)

Technical Teacher Education
Howard Coll (TX)
Lake Region State Coll (ND)
Louisiana Tech Coll (LA)
State Fair Comm Coll (MO)

Technology/Industrial Arts Teacher Education
Allen Comm Coll (KS)
Casper Coll (WY)
Central New Mexico Comm Coll (NM)
Cowley County Comm Coll and Area Vocational–Tech School (KS)
Eastern Arizona Coll (AZ)
Iowa Lakes Comm Coll (IA)
State Coll of Florida Manatee-Sarasota (FL)

Telecommunications Technology
Amarillo Coll (TX)
Anne Arundel Comm Coll (MD)
Central Carolina Comm Coll (NC)
Cincinnati State Tech and Comm Coll (OH)
Clark Coll (WA)
Collin County Comm Coll District (TX)
Comm Coll of Rhode Island (RI)
County Coll of Morris (NJ)
DeKalb Tech Coll (GA)
Delaware County Comm Coll (PA)
Erie Comm Coll, South Campus (NY)
Gadsden State Comm Coll (AL)
Guilford Tech Comm Coll (NC)
Howard Comm Coll (MD)
Illinois Eastern Comm Colls, Lincoln Trail College (IL)
Ivy Tech Comm Coll–North Central (IN)
Ivy Tech Comm Coll–Northwest (IN)
Kirkwood Comm Coll (IA)
Lansing Comm Coll (MI)
Marion Tech Coll (OH)
Massasoit Comm Coll (MA)
Meridian Comm Coll (MS)
Miami Dade Coll (FL)
Minnesota State Comm and Tech Coll (MN)
Mitchell Tech Inst (SD)
Penn State DuBois (PA)
Penn State Fayette, The Eberly Campus (PA)
Penn State Hazleton (PA)
Penn State New Kensington (PA)
Penn State Schuylkill (PA)
Penn State Shenango (PA)
Penn State Wilkes-Barre (PA)
Penn State York (PA)
Quinsigamond Comm Coll (MA)
Salt Lake Comm Coll (UT)
San Diego City Coll (CA)
Seminole State Coll of Florida (FL)
South Plains Coll (TX)
Spartan Coll of Aeronautics and Technology (OK)
Springfield Tech Comm Coll (MA)
Trident Tech Coll (SC)
Waukesha County Tech Coll (WI)

Theater Design and Technology
Carroll Comm Coll (MD)
Casper Coll (WY)
Central Wyoming Coll (WY)
Comm Coll of Rhode Island (RI)
Harford Comm Coll (MD)
Howard Comm Coll (MD)
Nassau Comm Coll (NY)
Pasadena City Coll (CA)
Raritan Valley Comm Coll (NJ)
Western Wyoming Comm Coll (WY)

Theology
Lon Morris Coll (TX)

Therapeutic Recreation
Austin Comm Coll (TX)
Comm Coll of Allegheny County (PA)
Northwestern Connecticut Comm Coll (CT)

Tool and Die Technology
Bevill State Comm Coll (AL)
Delta Coll (MI)
Des Moines Area Comm Coll (IA)
Gadsden State Comm Coll (AL)
Hawkeye Comm Coll (IA)
Ivy Tech Comm Coll–Bloomington (IN)
Ivy Tech Comm Coll–Central Indiana (IN)
Ivy Tech Comm Coll–Columbus (IN)
Ivy Tech Comm Coll–East Central (IN)
Ivy Tech Comm Coll–Kokomo (IN)
Ivy Tech Comm Coll–Lafayette (IN)
Ivy Tech Comm Coll–North Central (IN)
Ivy Tech Comm Coll–Northeast (IN)
Ivy Tech Comm Coll–Northwest (IN)
Ivy Tech Comm Coll–Richmond (IN)
Ivy Tech Comm Coll–Southern Indiana (IN)
Ivy Tech Comm Coll–Southwest (IN)
Ivy Tech Comm Coll Wabash Valley (IN)
Macomb Comm Coll (MI)
North Iowa Area Comm Coll (IA)
Oakland Comm Coll (MI)
Pennsylvania Coll of Technology (PA)
Wilson Comm Coll (NC)

Tourism and Travel Services Management
Albany Tech Coll (GA)
Amarillo Coll (TX)
Athens Tech Coll (GA)
Atlanta Tech Coll (GA)
Austin Comm Coll (TX)
Blue Ridge Comm Coll (NC)
Bradford School (OH)
Bradford School (PA)
Bryant & Stratton Coll - Syracuse Campus (NY)
Bunker Hill Comm Coll (MA)
Central Georgia Tech Coll (GA)
Central Piedmont Comm Coll (NC)
Coll of DuPage (IL)
Daytona State Coll (FL)
El Paso Comm Coll (TX)
Finger Lakes Comm Coll (NY)
Fiorello H. LaGuardia Comm Coll of the City U of New York (NY)
Fox Coll (IL)
Genesee Comm Coll (NY)
Gwinnett Tech Coll (GA)
Harrisburg Area Comm Coll (PA)
Highline Comm Coll (WA)
Houston Comm Coll System (TX)
International Business Coll, Indianapolis (IN)
Kaplan U, South Portland (ME)
Kingsborough Comm Coll of the City U of New York (NY)
Lakeland Comm Coll (OH)
Lansing Comm Coll (MI)
Miami Dade Coll (FL)
Minneapolis Business Coll (MN)
Moraine Valley Comm Coll (IL)
Ogeechee Tech Coll (GA)
Pennsylvania Coll of Technology (PA)
Phoenix Coll (AZ)
Quinsigamond Comm Coll (MA)
Rockland Comm Coll (NY)
San Diego City Coll (CA)
San Diego Mesa Coll (CA)
Savannah Tech Coll (GA)
Three Rivers Comm Coll (CT)
Westmoreland County Comm Coll (PA)
Wood Tobe–Coburn School (NY)

Tourism and Travel Services Marketing
Coll of DuPage (IL)
Milwaukee Area Tech Coll (WI)
Montgomery County Comm Coll (PA)
San Diego Mesa Coll (CA)

Tourism Promotion
Blue Ridge Comm Coll (NC)
Coll of DuPage (IL)
Comm Coll of Allegheny County (PA)
Pasadena City Coll (CA)

Trade and Industrial Teacher Education
Darton Coll (GA)
Del Mar Coll (TX)
East Los Angeles Coll (CA)
Glendale Comm Coll (AZ)
Howard Coll (TX)
Iowa Lakes Comm Coll (IA)
Kilgore Coll (TX)
Northeastern Jr Coll (CO)
Snow Coll (UT)
Southeastern Comm Coll (IA)
State Coll of Florida Manatee-Sarasota (FL)
Victor Valley Coll (CA)

Transportation and Materials Moving Related
Cecil Coll (MD)
Central Piedmont Comm Coll (NC)
City Colls of Chicago, Richard J. Daley College (IL)
Coll of DuPage (IL)
Highline Comm Coll (WA)
Mid-Plains Comm Coll, North Platte (NE)
Muskegon Comm Coll (MI)
Nassau Comm Coll (NY)
San Diego City Coll (CA)

Transportation Management
Cecil Coll (MD)
Del Mar Coll (TX)

Truck and Bus Driver/Commercial Vehicle Operation
Alexandria Tech Coll (MN)
Glendale Comm Coll (AZ)
Mohave Comm Coll (AZ)

Turf and Turfgrass Management
Catawba Valley Comm Coll (NC)
Cincinnati State Tech and Comm Coll (OH)
Coll of Lake County (IL)
Comm Coll of Allegheny County (PA)
Cuyamaca Coll (CA)
Dakota Coll at Bottineau (ND)
Danville Area Comm Coll (IL)
Delaware Tech & Comm Coll, Jack F. Owens Campus (DE)
Guilford Tech Comm Coll (NC)
Houston Comm Coll System (TX)
Iowa Lakes Comm Coll (IA)
Kirkwood Comm Coll (IA)
Linn State Tech Coll (MO)
Mt. San Jacinto Coll (CA)
North Georgia Tech Coll (GA)
Northland Pioneer Coll (AZ)
The Ohio State U Ag Tech Inst (OH)
Oklahoma State U, Oklahoma City (OK)
Pennsylvania Coll of Technology (PA)
Sandhills Comm Coll (NC)
Sheridan Coll (WY)
Southeast Tech Inst (SD)
Wayne Comm Coll (NC)
Westmoreland County Comm Coll (PA)

Urban Forestry
Dakota Coll at Bottineau (ND)

Urban Studies/Affairs
Comm Coll of Rhode Island (RI)
Pasadena City Coll (CA)
U of Cincinnati Clermont Coll (OH)

Vehicle and Vehicle Parts And Accessories Marketing
Central Comm Coll–Hastings Campus (NE)
Pennsylvania Coll of Technology (PA)

Vehicle Maintenance and Repair Technologies Related
Arkansas State U–Beebe (AR)
Central New Mexico Comm Coll (NM)
Guilford Tech Comm Coll (NC)
J. Sargeant Reynolds Comm Coll (VA)
Pennsylvania Coll of Technology (PA)
Victor Valley Coll (CA)

Vehicle/Petroleum Products Marketing
Central Comm Coll–Hastings Campus (NE)

Veterinary/Animal Health Technology
Argosy U, Twin Cities (MN)
Athens Tech Coll (GA)
Bradford School (OH)
Brown Mackie Coll–Akron (OH)
Brown Mackie Coll–Albuquerque (NM)
Brown Mackie Coll–Boise (ID)
Brown Mackie Coll–Cincinnati (OH)
Brown Mackie Coll–Findlay (OH)
Brown Mackie Coll–Kansas City (KS)
Brown Mackie Coll–Louisville (KY)
Brown Mackie Coll–Michigan City (IN)
Brown Mackie Coll–North Canton (OH)
Brown Mackie Coll–South Bend (IN)
Camden County Coll (NJ)
Central Carolina Comm Coll (NC)
Central Georgia Tech Coll (GA)
Central New Mexico Comm Coll (NM)
Chattanooga State Comm Coll (TN)

Colby Comm Coll (KS)
Comm Care Coll (OK)
The Comm Coll of Baltimore County (MD)
County Coll of Morris (NJ)
Cuyahoga Comm Coll (OH)
Delaware Tech & Comm Coll, Jack F. Owens Campus (DE)
Des Moines Area Comm Coll (IA)
Eastern Wyoming Coll (WY)
Fiorello H. LaGuardia Comm Coll of the City U of New York (NY)
Fox Coll (IL)
Front Range Comm Coll (CO)
Gwinnett Tech Coll (GA)
Harcum Coll (PA)
Harrison Coll, Indianapolis (IN)
Hillsborough Comm Coll (FL)
Holyoke Comm Coll (MA)
International Business Coll, Indianapolis (IN)
Jefferson State Comm Coll (AL)
Kaplan Coll, Phoenix Campus (AZ)
Kaskaskia Coll (IL)
Kent State U at Tuscarawas (OH)
Kirkwood Comm Coll (IA)
Lansing Comm Coll (MI)
Lehigh Carbon Comm Coll (PA)
Lonestar Coll–Tomball (TX)
Macomb Comm Coll (MI)
Metropolitan Comm Coll–Maple Woods (MO)
Moraine Park Tech Coll (WI)
Murray State Coll (OK)
Nebraska Coll of Tech Agriculture (NE)
Northampton Comm Coll (PA)
Northeast Comm Coll (NE)
Northwest Coll (WY)
Northwestern Connecticut Comm Coll (CT)
Oakland Comm Coll (MI)
Ogeechee Tech Coll (GA)
Oklahoma State U, Oklahoma City (OK)
Pima Comm Coll (AZ)
San Diego Mesa Coll (CA)
San Juan Coll (NM)
State U of New York Coll of Technology at Alfred (NY)
Trident Tech Coll (SC)
Ulster County Comm Coll (NY)
Vet Tech Inst (PA)
Vet Tech Inst at Bradford School (OH)
Vet Tech Inst at Fox Coll (IL)
Vet Tech Inst at Hickey Coll (MO)
Vet Tech Inst at International Business Coll, Fort Wayne (IN)
Vet Tech Inst at International Business Coll, Indianapolis (IN)
Vet Tech Inst of Houston (TX)

Violin, Viola, Guitar and Other Stringed Instruments

Minnesota State Coll–Southeast Tech (MN)

Visual and Performing Arts

Amarillo Coll (TX)
Berkshire Comm Coll (MA)
Bucks County Comm Coll (PA)
The Comm Coll of Baltimore County (MD)
Fiorello H. LaGuardia Comm Coll of the City U of New York (NY)
Harford Comm Coll (MD)
Harrisburg Area Comm Coll (PA)
Hutchinson Comm Coll and Area Vocational School (KS)
Lonestar Coll–Kingwood (TX)
Moraine Valley Comm Coll (IL)
Mt. San Jacinto Coll (CA)
Nassau Comm Coll (NY)
Paradise Valley Comm Coll (AZ)
Pima Comm Coll (AZ)
Sierra Coll (CA)
Ulster County Comm Coll (NY)
Western Wyoming Comm Coll (WY)

Visual and Performing Arts Related

Comm Coll of Allegheny County (PA)
J. Sargeant Reynolds Comm Coll (VA)
Kankakee Comm Coll (IL)
Northwest Coll (WY)
Thomas Nelson Comm Coll (VA)

Vocational Rehabilitation Counseling

State Coll of Florida Manatee-Sarasota (FL)

Voice and Opera

Alvin Comm Coll (TX)
Del Mar Coll (TX)
Iowa Lakes Comm Coll (IA)
Lansing Comm Coll (MI)
Lon Morris Coll (TX)
Oakland Comm Coll (MI)
Reedley Coll (CA)
Snow Coll (UT)

Watchmaking and Jewelrymaking

Austin Comm Coll (TX)
Minneapolis Comm and Tech Coll (MN)

Water Quality and Wastewater Treatment Management And Recycling Technology

Arizona Western Coll (AZ)
Blue Ridge Comm Coll (NC)
Casper Coll (WY)
Clackamas Comm Coll (OR)
Coll of the Canyons (CA)
The Comm Coll of Baltimore County (MD)
Delaware Tech & Comm Coll, Jack F. Owens Campus (DE)
Delta Coll (MI)
Kirkwood Comm Coll (IA)
Linn-Benton Comm Coll (OR)
Milwaukee Area Tech Coll (WI)
Moraine Park Tech Coll (WI)
Mt. San Jacinto Coll (CA)
Northwest-Shoals Comm Coll (AL)
Ogeechee Tech Coll (GA)
St. Cloud Tech Coll (MN)

Water, Wetlands, and Marine Resources Management

Iowa Lakes Comm Coll (IA)

Web/Multimedia Management and Webmaster

Antonelli Coll (OH)
Black Hawk Coll, Moline (IL)
Central Comm Coll–Columbus Campus (NE)
Central Comm Coll–Grand Island Campus (NE)
Central Comm Coll–Hastings Campus (NE)
Clackamas Comm Coll (OR)
Clark Coll (WA)
Clovis Comm Coll (NM)
Comm Coll of Rhode Island (RI)
Delaware County Comm Coll (PA)
Del Mar Coll (TX)
Delta Coll (MI)
Flathead Valley Comm Coll (MT)
Howard Coll (TX)
ITT Tech Inst, Bessemer (AL)
ITT Tech Inst, Tucson (AZ)
ITT Tech Inst, Thornton (CO)
ITT Tech Inst, Fort Lauderdale (FL)
ITT Tech Inst, Fort Myers (FL)
ITT Tech Inst, Jacksonville (FL)
ITT Tech Inst, Lake Mary (FL)
ITT Tech Inst, Miami (FL)
ITT Tech Inst, Pinellas Park (FL)
ITT Tech Inst, Tallahassee (FL)
ITT Tech Inst, Tampa (FL)
ITT Tech Inst (ID)
ITT Tech Inst, Indianapolis (IN)
ITT Tech Inst, Baton Rouge (LA)
ITT Tech Inst, St. Rose (LA)
ITT Tech Inst, Norwood (MA)
ITT Tech Inst, Woburn (MA)
ITT Tech Inst, Canton (MI)
ITT Tech Inst, Swartz Creek (MI)
ITT Tech Inst, Troy (MI)
ITT Tech Inst, Wyoming (MI)
ITT Tech Inst, Arnold (MO)
ITT Tech Inst (NV)
ITT Tech Inst (NM)
ITT Tech Inst, Albany (NY)
ITT Tech Inst, Getzville (NY)
ITT Tech Inst, Liverpool (NY)
ITT Tech Inst, Norwood (OH)
ITT Tech Inst, Strongsville (OH)
ITT Tech Inst, Youngstown (OH)
ITT Tech Inst (OR)
ITT Tech Inst, Tarentum (PA)
ITT Tech Inst, Columbia (SC)
ITT Tech Inst, Greenville (SC)
ITT Tech Inst (UT)
ITT Tech Inst, Chantilly (VA)
ITT Tech Inst, Norfolk (VA)
ITT Tech Inst, Richmond (VA)
ITT Tech Inst, Springfield (VA)
ITT Tech Inst, Everett (WA)
ITT Tech Inst, Seattle (WA)
ITT Tech Inst, Spokane Valley (WA)
Kalamazoo Valley Comm Coll (MI)
Kilgore Coll (TX)
Lonestar Coll–Montgomery (TX)
Metropolitan Comm Coll–Business & Technology Campus (MO)
Moraine Valley Comm Coll (IL)
Northland Comm and Tech Coll–Thief River Falls (MN)
Olympic Coll (WA)
Pennsylvania Highlands Comm Coll (PA)
Rio Salado Coll (AZ)
Saint Charles Comm Coll (MO)
Sandhills Comm Coll (NC)
Seminole State Coll of Florida (FL)
Sheridan Coll (WY)
Southwest Mississippi Comm Coll (MS)
Stanly Comm Coll (NC)
Stark State Coll of Technology (OH)
Temple Coll (TX)
Tompkins Cortland Comm Coll (NY)
Trident Tech Coll (SC)
Western Wyoming Comm Coll (WY)

Web Page, Digital/ Multimedia and Information Resources Design

Alexandria Tech Coll (MN)
The Art Inst of New York City (NY)
The Art Inst of Ohio–Cincinnati (OH)
The Art Inst of Seattle (WA)
Berkeley City Coll (CA)
Bryant & Stratton Coll - North Campus (NY)
Bunker Hill Comm Coll (MA)
Casper Coll (WY)
Cecil Coll (MD)
Central Georgia Tech Coll (GA)
Chattahoochee Tech Coll (GA)
Chattanooga State Comm Coll (TN)
Clovis Comm Coll (NM)
Collin County Comm Coll District (TX)
Columbus Tech Coll (GA)
County Coll of Morris (NJ)
Davis Coll (OH)
Delaware County Comm Coll (PA)
Del Mar Coll (TX)
Delta Coll (MI)
El Centro Coll (TX)
Elgin Comm Coll (IL)
Everett Comm Coll (WA)
Flint River Tech Coll (GA)
Georgia Northwestern Tech Coll (GA)
Glendale Comm Coll (AZ)
Griffin Tech Coll (GA)
Harrisburg Area Comm Coll (PA)
Hawkeye Comm Coll (IA)
Highland Comm Coll (IL)
Highline Comm Coll (WA)
ITT Tech Inst, Bessemer (AL)
ITT Tech Inst, Tucson (AZ)
ITT Tech Inst (AR)
ITT Tech Inst, Lathrop (CA)
ITT Tech Inst, Rancho Cordova (CA)
ITT Tech Inst, San Bernardino (CA)
ITT Tech Inst, San Diego (CA)
ITT Tech Inst, San Dimas (CA)
ITT Tech Inst, Sylmar (CA)
ITT Tech Inst, Torrance (CA)
ITT Tech Inst, Thornton (CO)
ITT Tech Inst, Fort Lauderdale (FL)
ITT Tech Inst, Jacksonville (FL)
ITT Tech Inst, Lake Mary (FL)
ITT Tech Inst, Miami (FL)
ITT Tech Inst, Tampa (FL)
ITT Tech Inst, Duluth (GA)
ITT Tech Inst, Kennesaw (GA)
ITT Tech Inst (ID)
ITT Tech Inst, Burr Ridge (IL)
ITT Tech Inst, Mount Prospect (IL)
ITT Tech Inst, Orland Park (IL)
ITT Tech Inst, Fort Wayne (IN)
ITT Tech Inst, Indianapolis (IN)
ITT Tech Inst, Newburgh (IN)
ITT Tech Inst, Louisville (KY)
ITT Tech Inst, St. Rose (LA)
ITT Tech Inst (MD)
ITT Tech Inst, Norwood (MA)
ITT Tech Inst, Woburn (MA)
ITT Tech Inst, Canton (MI)
ITT Tech Inst, Swartz Creek (MI)
ITT Tech Inst, Troy (MI)
ITT Tech Inst, Wyoming (MI)
ITT Tech Inst (MN)
ITT Tech Inst, Arnold (MO)
ITT Tech Inst, Earth City (MO)
ITT Tech Inst (NE)
ITT Tech Inst (NV)
ITT Tech Inst (NM)
ITT Tech Inst, Albany (NY)
ITT Tech Inst, Getzville (NY)
ITT Tech Inst, Liverpool (NY)
ITT Tech Inst, Charlotte (NC)
ITT Tech Inst, Dayton (OH)
ITT Tech Inst, Hilliard (OH)
ITT Tech Inst, Norwood (OH)
ITT Tech Inst, Strongsville (OH)
ITT Tech Inst, Warrensville Heights (OH)
ITT Tech Inst, Youngstown (OH)
ITT Tech Inst (OR)
ITT Tech Inst, Bensalem (PA)
ITT Tech Inst, Harrisburg (PA)
ITT Tech Inst, King of Prussia (PA)
ITT Tech Inst, Pittsburgh (PA)
ITT Tech Inst, Tarentum (PA)
ITT Tech Inst, Columbia (SC)
ITT Tech Inst, Greenville (SC)
ITT Tech Inst, Cordova (TN)
ITT Tech Inst, Knoxville (TN)
ITT Tech Inst, Nashville (TN)
ITT Tech Inst, Austin (TX)
ITT Tech Inst, Richardson (TX)
ITT Tech Inst, San Antonio (TX)
ITT Tech Inst (UT)
ITT Tech Inst, Chantilly (VA)
ITT Tech Inst, Norfolk (VA)
ITT Tech Inst, Richmond (VA)
ITT Tech Inst, Springfield (VA)
ITT Tech Inst, Everett (WA)
ITT Tech Inst, Seattle (WA)
ITT Tech Inst, Spokane Valley (WA)
ITT Tech Inst, Green Bay (WI)
ITT Tech Inst, Greenfield (WI)
Kalamazoo Valley Comm Coll (MI)
Kaplan Coll, Merrillville Campus (IN)
Kirkwood Comm Coll (IA)
Lanier Tech Coll (GA)
Laramie County Comm Coll (WY)
LDS Business Coll (UT)
Lehigh Carbon Comm Coll (PA)
Lewis and Clark Comm Coll (IL)
Lonestar Coll–Montgomery (TX)
Mesabi Range Comm and Tech Coll (MN)
Metropolitan Comm Coll–Business & Technology Campus (MO)
Middle Georgia Tech Coll (GA)
Minneapolis Comm and Tech Coll (MN)
Minnesota State Coll–Southeast Tech (MN)
Minnesota State Comm and Tech Coll (MN)
Montana State U–Great Falls Coll of Technology (MT)
Moraine Park Tech Coll (WI)
Moultrie Tech Coll (GA)
Mount Wachusett Comm Coll (MA)
Niagara County Comm Coll (NY)
Northampton Comm Coll (PA)
North Georgia Tech Coll (GA)
Northland Comm and Tech Coll–Thief River Falls (MN)
Northwestern Coll (IL)
Oklahoma State U, Oklahoma City (OK)
Palm Beach State Coll (FL)
Paradise Valley Comm Coll (AZ)
Pasco-Hernando Comm Coll (FL)
Pennsylvania Coll of Technology (PA)
Pennsylvania Inst of Technology (PA)
Pueblo Comm Coll (CO)
Quinsigamond Comm Coll (MA)
Raritan Valley Comm Coll (NJ)
Rio Salado Coll (AZ)
St. Cloud Tech Coll (MN)
Seminole State Coll of Florida (FL)
Sierra Coll (CA)
Southeastern Tech Coll (GA)
Southwestern Comm Coll (IA)
Springfield Tech Comm Coll (MA)
Stanly Comm Coll (NC)
Stark State Coll of Technology (OH)
State Fair Comm Coll (MO)
Sullivan Coll of Technology and Design (KY)
Terra State Comm Coll (OH)
Trident Tech Coll (SC)
Valdosta Tech Coll (GA)
Volunteer State Comm Coll (TN)
Western Wyoming Comm Coll (WY)
West Georgia Tech Coll (GA)
Westmoreland County Comm Coll (PA)
Wisconsin Indianhead Tech Coll (WI)
York County Comm Coll (ME)

Welding Technology

Alamance Comm Coll (NC)
Alexandria Tech Coll (MN)
Allan Hancock Coll (CA)
Antelope Valley Coll (CA)
Arizona Western Coll (AZ)
Austin Comm Coll (TX)
Bainbridge Coll (GA)
Bakersfield Coll (CA)
Beaufort County Comm Coll (NC)
Bladen Comm Coll (NC)
Blue Ridge Comm Coll (NC)
Casper Coll (WY)
Central Comm Coll–Columbus Campus (NE)
Central Comm Coll–Grand Island Campus (NE)
Central Comm Coll–Hastings Campus (NE)
Central Lakes Coll (MN)
Central Piedmont Comm Coll (NC)
Central Texas Coll (TX)
Central Wyoming Coll (WY)
Clackamas Comm Coll (OR)
Clark Coll (WA)
Coll of DuPage (IL)
Coll of the Canyons (CA)
Comm Coll of Allegheny County (PA)
Cowley County Comm Coll and Area Vocational–Tech School (KS)
Del Mar Coll (TX)
Delta Coll (MI)
East Central Coll (MO)
Eastern Arizona Coll (AZ)
Eastern Wyoming Coll (WY)
Edison State Comm Coll (OH)
Elaine P. Nunez Comm Coll (LA)
Elgin Comm Coll (IL)
Everett Comm Coll (WA)
Fox Valley Tech Coll (WI)
Front Range Comm Coll (CO)
Grand Rapids Comm Coll (MI)

Green River Comm Coll (WA)
Honolulu Comm Coll (HI)
Hutchinson Comm Coll and Area Vocational School (KS)
Iowa Lakes Comm Coll (IA)
Jamestown Comm Coll (NY)
Kalamazoo Valley Comm Coll (MI)
Kankakee Comm Coll (IL)
Kellogg Comm Coll (MI)
Kilgore Coll (TX)
Kirkwood Comm Coll (IA)
Kirtland Comm Coll (MI)
Lansing Comm Coll (MI)
Linn-Benton Comm Coll (OR)
Lonestar Coll–Cy-Fair (TX)
Lonestar Coll–Montgomery (TX)
Lonestar Coll–North Harris (TX)
Lower Columbia Coll (WA)
Macomb Comm Coll (MI)
Manhattan Area Tech Coll (KS)
Metropolitan Comm Coll (NE)
Mid-Plains Comm Coll, North Platte (NE)
Milwaukee Area Tech Coll (WI)
Minnesota State Coll–Southeast Tech (MN)
Mohave Comm Coll (AZ)
Montana State U–Great Falls Coll of Technology (MT)
Moraine Park Tech Coll (WI)
Muskegon Comm Coll (MI)
New Mexico State U–Carlsbad (NM)
Nicolet Area Tech Coll (WI)
North Central Texas Coll (TX)
Northeast Comm Coll (NE)
North Idaho Coll (ID)
North Iowa Area Comm Coll (IA)
Northland Comm and Tech Coll–Thief River Falls (MN)
Northland Pioneer Coll (AZ)
Northwest Coll (WY)
Northwest Florida State Coll (FL)
Northwest-Shoals Comm Coll (AL)
Oakland Comm Coll (MI)
Odessa Coll (TX)
Oklahoma Tech Coll (OK)
Olympic Coll (WA)
Orange Coast Coll (CA)
Owens Comm Coll, Toledo (OH)
Paris Jr Coll (TX)
Pasadena City Coll (CA)
Pikes Peak Comm Coll (CO)
Pima Comm Coll (AZ)
Pueblo Comm Coll (CO)
Reedley Coll (CA)
Rogue Comm Coll (OR)
St. Cloud Tech Coll (MN)
St. Philip's Coll (TX)
Salt Lake Comm Coll (UT)
San Diego City Coll (CA)
San Jacinto Coll District (TX)
San Juan Coll (NM)
Shawnee Comm Coll (IL)
Sheridan Coll (WY)
Southeastern Comm Coll (IA)
Southern Union State Comm Coll (AL)
South Plains Coll (TX)
South Puget Sound Comm Coll (WA)
Southwest Mississippi Comm Coll (MS)
State U of New York Coll of Technology at Alfred (NY)
Tarrant County Coll District (TX)
Terra State Comm Coll (OH)
Triangle Tech, Inc.–DuBois School (PA)
Triangle Tech, Inc.–Sunbury School (PA)
Tri-County Comm Coll (NC)
Trinity Valley Comm Coll (TX)
Triton Coll (IL)
The U of Montana–Helena Coll of Technology (MT)
Victor Valley Coll (CA)
Western Wyoming Comm Coll (WY)
Westmoreland County Comm Coll (PA)
West Shore Comm Coll (MI)

Well Drilling
Southwest Mississippi Comm Coll (MS)

Wildlife and Wildlands Science And Management
Barton County Comm Coll (KS)
Casper Coll (WY)
Dakota Coll at Bottineau (ND)
Eastern Wyoming Coll (WY)
Flathead Valley Comm Coll (MT)
Front Range Comm Coll (CO)
Iowa Lakes Comm Coll (IA)
Itasca Comm Coll (MN)
Laramie County Comm Coll (WY)
Murray State Coll (OK)
North Idaho Coll (ID)
Ogeechee Tech Coll (GA)
Penn State DuBois (PA)
Potomac State Coll of West Virginia U (WV)
Shawnee Comm Coll (IL)
Western Wyoming Comm Coll (WY)

Wildlife Biology
Eastern Arizona Coll (AZ)
Iowa Lakes Comm Coll (IA)
North Idaho Coll (ID)

Wind/Percussion Instruments
Iowa Lakes Comm Coll (IA)

Women's Studies
Casper Coll (WY)
Century Coll (MN)
Santa Rosa Jr Coll (CA)
Sierra Coll (CA)
State Coll of Florida Manatee-Sarasota (FL)
Suffolk County Comm Coll (NY)
Triton Coll (IL)

Wood Science and Wood Products/Pulp And Paper Technology
Allen Comm Coll (KS)
Bakersfield Coll (CA)
Dabney S. Lancaster Comm Coll (VA)
Fox Valley Tech Coll (WI)
Kennebec Valley Comm Coll (ME)
Lower Columbia Coll (WA)
Ogeechee Tech Coll (GA)
Potomac State Coll of West Virginia U (WV)

Woodworking
Bucks County Comm Coll (PA)

Woodworking Related
Harrisburg Area Comm Coll (PA)
Oakland Comm Coll (MI)

Word Processing
Corning Comm Coll (NY)
Del Mar Coll (TX)
Eastfield Coll (TX)
ETI Tech Coll of Niles (OH)
Flathead Valley Comm Coll (MT)
Gateway Comm Coll (CT)
Iowa Lakes Comm Coll (IA)
Kellogg Comm Coll (MI)
Metropolitan Comm Coll–Business & Technology Campus (MO)
New Mexico State U–Carlsbad (NM)
North Central Texas Coll (TX)
Northland Comm and Tech Coll–Thief River Falls (MN)
Northwest Florida State Coll (FL)
Orange Coast Coll (CA)
Owensboro Comm and Tech Coll (KY)
Palm Beach State Coll (FL)
Seminole State Coll of Florida (FL)
Stanly Comm Coll (NC)
Stark State Coll of Technology (OH)
Tallahassee Comm Coll (FL)
Three Rivers Comm Coll (MO)
Vincennes U Jasper Campus (IN)
Western Wyoming Comm Coll (WY)

Work and Family Studies
Antelope Valley Coll (CA)

Youth Services
Midlands Tech Coll (SC)
Olympic Coll (WA)

Zoology/Animal Biology
Dakota Coll at Bottineau (ND)
Northeastern Jr Coll (CO)
North Idaho Coll (ID)
Palm Beach State Coll (FL)
Snow Coll (UT)

Associate Degree Programs at Four-Year Colleges

Accounting
Abraham Baldwin Ag Coll (GA)
AIB Coll of Business (IA)
American Public U System (WV)
Baker Coll of Allen Park (MI)
Baker Coll of Auburn Hills (MI)
Baker Coll of Clinton Township (MI)
Baker Coll of Owosso (MI)
Brookline Coll, Phoenix (AZ)
Brookline Coll, Tempe (AZ)
Brookline Coll, Tucson (AZ)
Brookline Coll (NM)
Bryant & Stratton Coll - Wauwatosa Campus (WI)
Calumet Coll of Saint Joseph (IN)
Central Pennsylvania Coll (PA)
Coll of Mount St. Joseph (OH)
Coll of St. Joseph (VT)
Coll of Saint Mary (NE)
Coll of Staten Island of the City U of New York (NY)
Dakota Wesleyan U (SD)
Davenport U, Grand Rapids (MI)
DeVry U, Fremont (CA)
DeVry U, Pomona (CA)
DeVry U, Westminster (CO)
DeVry U, Miramar (FL)
DeVry U, Orlando (FL)
DeVry U, Decatur (GA)
DeVry U (MI)
DeVry U, Edina (MN)
DeVry U, Federal Way (WA)
DeVry U Online (IL)
ECPI Coll of Technology, Virginia Beach (VA)
ECPI Tech Coll, Roanoke (VA)
Elizabethtown Coll (PA)
Fairmont State U (WV)
Fisher Coll (MA)
Florida National Coll (FL)
Franciscan U of Steubenville (OH)
Franklin U (OH)
Goldey-Beacom Coll (DE)
Gwynedd-Mercy Coll (PA)
Hawai'i Pacific U (HI)
Husson U (ME)
Immaculata U (PA)
Indiana Tech (IN)
Indiana U of Pennsylvania (PA)
Indiana Wesleyan U (IN)
Inter American U of Puerto Rico, Aguadilla Campus (PR)
Inter American U of Puerto Rico, Arecibo Campus (PR)
Inter American U of Puerto Rico, Bayamón Campus (PR)
Inter American U of Puerto Rico, Fajardo Campus (PR)
Inter American U of Puerto Rico, Guayama Campus (PR)
Inter American U of Puerto Rico, Ponce Campus (PR)
Inter American U of Puerto Rico, San Germán Campus (PR)
Johnson & Wales U (CO)
Johnson & Wales U (FL)
Johnson & Wales U (RI)
Johnson & Wales U - Charlotte Campus (NC)
Johnson State Coll (VT)
Kaplan U, Davenport Campus (IA)
Kaplan U, Mason City Campus (IA)
Keiser U, Fort Lauderdale (FL)
Lake Superior State U (MI)
Lebanon Valley Coll (PA)
Liberty U (VA)
Lincoln Coll of New England, Southington (CT)
Manchester Coll (IN)
Maria Coll (NY)
Methodist U (NC)
Missouri Southern State U (MO)
Monroe Coll, Bronx (NY)
Mountain State U (WV)
Mount Aloysius Coll (PA)
Mount Marty Coll (SD)
Mount Olive Coll (NC)
Mount St. Mary's Coll (CA)
Muhlenberg Coll (PA)
New England Coll of Business (MA)
Oakwood U (AL)
Oklahoma Wesleyan U (OK)
Pioneer Pacific Coll, Clackamas (OR)
Pioneer Pacific Coll, Wilsonville (OR)
Pioneer Pacific Coll–Eugene/Springfield Branch (OR)
Point Park U (PA)
Post U (CT)
Potomac Coll (DC)
Regent U (VA)
Rogers State U (OK)
Saint Francis U (PA)
St. John's U (NY)
Saint Joseph's U (PA)
Shawnee State U (OH)
Southern Adventist U (TN)
Southern New Hampshire U (NH)
Southwest Minnesota State U (MN)
Stratford U, Woodbridge (VA)
Strayer U - Akron Campus (OH)
Strayer U - Alexandria Campus (VA)
Strayer U - Allentown Campus (PA)
Strayer U - Anne Arundel Campus (MD)
Strayer U - Arlington Campus (VA)
Strayer U - Augusta Campus (GA)
Strayer U - Baymeadows Campus (FL)
Strayer U - Birmingham Campus (AL)
Strayer U - Brickell Campus (FL)
Strayer U - Center City Campus (PA)
Strayer U - Central Austin Campus (TX)
Strayer U - Chamblee Campus (GA)
Strayer U - Charleston Campus (SC)
Strayer U - Chesapeake Campus (VA)
Strayer U - Chesterfield Campus (VA)
Strayer U - Christiana Campus (DE)
Strayer U - Cobb County Campus (GA)
Strayer U - Columbia Campus (SC)
Strayer U - Columbus Campus (OH)
Strayer U - Coral Springs Campus (FL)
Strayer U - Cranberry Woods Campus (PA)
Strayer U - Delaware County Campus (PA)
Strayer U - Doral Campus (FL)
Strayer U - Douglasville Campus (GA)
Strayer U - Fairview Park Campus (OH)
Strayer U - Florence Campus (KY)
Strayer U - Fort Lauderdale Campus (FL)
Strayer U - Fredericksburg Campus (VA)
Strayer U - Garner Campus (NC)
Strayer U - Greensboro Campus (NC)
Strayer U - Greenville Campus (SC)
Strayer U - Henrico Campus (VA)
Strayer U - Huntersville Campus (NC)
Strayer U - Huntsville Campus (AL)
Strayer U - King of Prussia Campus (PA)
Strayer U - Knoxville Campus (TN)
Strayer U - Lexington Campus (KY)
Strayer U - Lithonia Campus (GA)
Strayer U - Loudoun Campus (VA)
Strayer U - Louisville Campus (KY)
Strayer U - Lower Bucks County Campus (PA)
Strayer U - Maitland Campus (FL)
Strayer U - Manassas Campus (VA)
Strayer U - Mason Campus (OH)
Strayer U - Metairie Campus (LA)
Strayer U - Miramar Campus (FL)
Strayer U - Morrow Campus (GA)
Strayer U - Nashville Campus (TN)
Strayer U - Newport News Campus (VA)
Strayer U - North Charlotte Campus (NC)
Strayer U - North Raleigh Campus (NC)
Strayer U - Orlando East Campus (FL)
Strayer U - Owings Mills Campus (MD)
Strayer U - Palm Beach Gardens Campus (FL)
Strayer U - Penn Center West Campus (PA)
Strayer U - Prince George's Campus (MD)
Strayer U - Rockville Campus (MD)
Strayer U - Roswell Campus (GA)
Strayer U - RTP Campus (NC)
Strayer U - Salt Lake Campus (UT)
Strayer U - Sand Lake Campus (FL)
Strayer U - Savannah Campus (GA)
Strayer U - Shelby Oaks Campus (TN)
Strayer U - South Charlotte Campus (NC)
Strayer U - Takoma Park Campus (DC)
Strayer U - Tampa East Campus (FL)
Strayer U - Tampa Westshore Campus (FL)
Strayer U - Teays Valley Campus (WV)
Strayer U - Thousand Oaks Campus (TN)
Strayer U - Virginia Beach Campus (VA)
Strayer U - Washington Campus (DC)
Strayer U - White Marsh Campus (MD)
Strayer U - Woodbridge Campus (VA)
Sullivan U (KY)
Thiel Coll (PA)
Thomas More Coll (KY)
Tiffin U (OH)
Trine U (IN)
Union Coll (NE)
U of Alaska Anchorage (AK)
U of Cincinnati (OH)
U of Dubuque (IA)
The U of Findlay (OH)
U of Rio Grande (OH)
U of the Virgin Islands (VI)
The U of Toledo (OH)
The U of West Alabama (AL)
Utah Valley U (UT)
Walsh U (OH)
Webber International U (FL)
Wilson Coll (PA)
Youngstown State U (OH)

Accounting and Business/Management
Hickey Coll (MO)
Kansas State U (KS)

Accounting and Finance
Central Christian Coll of Kansas (KS)

Accounting Related
Franklin U (OH)
Montana State U Billings (MT)

Accounting Technology and Bookkeeping
Baker Coll of Flint (MI)
Cleary U (MI)
Daymar Inst, Clarksville (TN)
Ferris State U (MI)
Gannon U (PA)
Lewis-Clark State Coll (ID)
Mercy Coll (NY)
Miami U (OH)
Montana State U Billings (MT)
Montana Tech of The U of Montana (MT)
New York City Coll of Technology of the City U of New York (NY)
New York Inst of Technology (NY)
Peirce Coll (PA)
Pennsylvania Coll of Technology (PA)
St. Augustine Coll (IL)
Southwest Florida Coll, Fort Myers (FL)
State U of New York Coll of Technology at Canton (NY)
The U of Akron (OH)
U of Alaska Fairbanks (AK)
U of Rio Grande (OH)
Wright State U (OH)

Acting
Central Christian Coll of Kansas (KS)

Administrative Assistant and Secretarial Science
AIB Coll of Business (IA)
Alabama State U (AL)
Arkansas Tech U (AR)
Baker Coll of Auburn Hills (MI)
Baker Coll of Cadillac (MI)
Baker Coll of Clinton Township (MI)
Baker Coll of Jackson (MI)
Baker Coll of Muskegon (MI)
Baker Coll of Owosso (MI)
Ball State U (IN)
Baptist Bible Coll of Pennsylvania (PA)
Black Hills State U (SD)
Bryant & Stratton Coll, Cleveland (OH)
Campbellsville U (KY)
Central Pennsylvania Coll (PA)
Clayton State U (GA)
Columbia Coll, Caguas (PR)
Columbia Coll, Yauco (PR)
Dickinson State U (ND)
Dordt Coll (IA)
EDP Coll of Puerto Rico, Inc. (PR)
EDP Coll of Puerto Rico–San Sebastian (PR)
Fairmont State U (WV)
Faith Baptist Bible Coll and Theological Seminary (IA)
Florida National Coll (FL)
Fort Hays State U (KS)
Fort Valley State U (GA)
Free Will Baptist Bible Coll (TN)
Idaho State U (ID)
Inter American U of Puerto Rico, Bayamón Campus (PR)
Inter American U of Puerto Rico, San Germán Campus (PR)
Kuyper Coll (MI)
Lamar U (TX)
Lewis-Clark State Coll (ID)
Maranatha Baptist Bible Coll (WI)
Miami U (OH)
Montana State U Billings (MT)
Montana Tech of The U of Montana (MT)
Mountain State U (WV)
Murray State U (KY)
New York Inst of Technology (NY)
Northern Michigan U (MI)
Oakland City U (IN)
Oakwood U (AL)
Pennsylvania Coll of Technology (PA)
Rider U (NJ)
St. Augustine Coll (IL)
State U of New York Coll of Technology at Canton (NY)
Sul Ross State U (TX)
Tabor Coll (KS)
Universidad Adventista de las Antillas (PR)
The U of Akron (OH)
U of Alaska Southeast (AK)
U of Central Missouri (MO)
U of Cincinnati (OH)
U of Rio Grande (OH)
U of the District of Columbia (DC)
The U of Toledo (OH)
Washburn U (KS)
Wright State U (OH)

Adult and Continuing Education
Fisher Coll (MA)

Adult Development and Aging
Madonna U (MI)
The U of Toledo (OH)

Advertising
Academy of Art U (CA)
The Art Inst of California–San Diego (CA)
Fashion Inst of Technology (NY)
Inter American U of Puerto Rico, San Germán Campus (PR)
Johnson & Wales U (CO)
Johnson & Wales U (FL)
Johnson & Wales U (RI)
U of the District of Columbia (DC)
Xavier U (OH)

Aeronautical/Aerospace Engineering Technology
Pennsylvania Coll of Technology (PA)
Purdue U (IN)
Vaughn Coll of Aeronautics and Technology (NY)

Aeronautics/Aviation/Aerospace Science and Technology
Embry-Riddle Aeronautical U Worldwide (FL)

Indiana State U (IN)
Ohio U (OH)
Pacific Union Coll (CA)
Vaughn Coll of Aeronautics and Technology (NY)

Aesthetician/Esthetician and Skin Care
Lincoln Coll–Normal (IL)

Agribusiness
Morehead State U (KY)
Southern Arkansas U–Magnolia (AR)
Southwest Minnesota State U (MN)
Vermont Tech Coll (VT)

Agricultural and Domestic Animals Services Related
Sterling Coll (VT)

Agricultural and Food Products Processing
North Carolina State U (NC)

Agricultural and Horticultural Plant Breeding
Sterling Coll (VT)

Agricultural Business and Management
Abraham Baldwin Ag Coll (GA)
Coll of Coastal Georgia (GA)
Dickinson State U (ND)
North Carolina State U (NC)

Agricultural Business and Management Related
Penn State Abington (PA)
Penn State Altoona (PA)
Penn State Berks (PA)
Penn State Erie, The Behrend Coll (PA)
Penn State U Park (PA)

Agricultural Economics
Abraham Baldwin Ag Coll (GA)

Agricultural Production
Eastern New Mexico U (NM)
U of Arkansas at Monticello (AR)
U of Puerto Rico at Utuado (PR)
Western Kentucky U (KY)

Agriculture
Abraham Baldwin Ag Coll (GA)
Dalton State Coll (GA)
North Carolina State U (NC)
Oklahoma Panhandle State U (OK)
South Dakota State U (SD)
Southern Utah U (UT)
U of Delaware (DE)
Young Harris Coll (GA)

Aircraft Powerplant Technology
Clayton State U (GA)
Embry-Riddle Aeronautical U (FL)
Embry-Riddle Aeronautical U Worldwide (FL)
Idaho State U (ID)
Northern Michigan U (MI)
Pennsylvania Coll of Technology (PA)
U of Alaska Fairbanks (AK)

Airframe Mechanics and Aircraft Maintenance Technology
Kansas State U (KS)
Lewis U (IL)
Piedmont Baptist Coll and Graduate School (NC)
Thomas Edison State Coll (NJ)
U of Alaska Anchorage (AK)

Airline Pilot and Flight Crew
Baker Coll of Flint (MI)
Baker Coll of Muskegon (MI)
Central Christian Coll of Kansas (KS)
Kansas State U (KS)
Midland Coll (TX)
Santa Fe Coll (FL)
Southern Illinois U Carbondale (IL)
U of Alaska Anchorage (AK)
U of Alaska Fairbanks (AK)
U of Dubuque (IA)
Utah Valley U (UT)

Air Traffic Control
LeTourneau U (TX)
Thomas Edison State Coll (NJ)
U of Alaska Anchorage (AK)

Air Transportation Related
Thomas Edison State Coll (NJ)

Allied Health and Medical Assisting Services Related
Florida National Coll (FL)
Jones Coll, Jacksonville (FL)
Nebraska Methodist Coll (NE)
Thomas Edison State Coll (NJ)
Widener U (PA)

Allied Health Diagnostic, Intervention, and Treatment Professions Related
Cameron U (OK)
Gwynedd-Mercy Coll (PA)
Mercy Coll of Health Sciences (IA)
Pennsylvania Coll of Technology (PA)
Thomas Edison State Coll (NJ)

American Native/Native American Languages
Idaho State U (ID)
U of Alaska Fairbanks (AK)

American Sign Language (ASL)
Bethel Coll (IN)
Idaho State U (ID)
Madonna U (MI)

Ancient Near Eastern and Biblical Languages
Indiana Wesleyan U (IN)

Anesthesiologist Assistant
Thompson Rivers U (BC, Canada)

Animal/Livestock Husbandry and Production
Thompson Rivers U (BC, Canada)
U of Connecticut (CT)

Animal Sciences
Abraham Baldwin Ag Coll (GA)
Sul Ross State U (TX)
U of Connecticut (CT)
U of New Hampshire (NH)
U of Puerto Rico at Utuado (PR)

Animal Sciences Related
Santa Fe Coll (FL)

Animation, Interactive Technology, Video Graphics and Special Effects
Academy of Art U (CA)
Keiser U, Fort Lauderdale (FL)
National U (CA)
Platt Coll San Diego (CA)

Anthropology
Kwantlen Polytechnic U (BC, Canada)
Midland Coll (TX)

Apparel and Textile Manufacturing
Fashion Inst of Technology (NY)

Apparel and Textile Marketing Management
The Art Inst of Philadelphia (PA)
U of the Incarnate Word (TX)

Apparel and Textiles
Fashion Inst of Technology (NY)

Applied Art
Pennsylvania Coll of Technology (PA)
U of Maine at Presque Isle (ME)

Applied Horticulture
Farmingdale State Coll (NY)
Oakland City U (IN)
Pennsylvania Coll of Technology (PA)
Temple U (PA)
Thomas Edison State Coll (NJ)
U of Connecticut (CT)
U of Maine at Augusta (ME)
U of New Hampshire (NH)

Applied Horticulture/Horticultural Business Services Related
Pennsylvania Coll of Technology (PA)
U of Massachusetts Amherst (MA)

Archeology
Weber State U (UT)

Architectural Drafting and CAD/CADD
Baker Coll of Flint (MI)
Baker Coll of Muskegon (MI)
Clayton State U (GA)
Indiana U–Purdue U Indianapolis (IN)
New York City Coll of Technology of the City U of New York (NY)
Purdue U Calumet (IN)
Purdue U North Central (IN)
Thomas Edison State Coll (NJ)
The U of Toledo (OH)
Western Kentucky U (KY)
Westwood Coll–Anaheim (CA)
Westwood Coll–Annandale Campus (VA)
Westwood Coll–Arlington Ballston Campus (VA)
Westwood Coll–Atlanta Midtown (GA)
Westwood Coll–Atlanta Northlake (GA)
Westwood Coll–Chicago Loop Campus (IL)
Westwood Coll–Chicago O'Hare Airport (IL)
Westwood Coll–Dallas (TX)
Westwood Coll–Denver South (CO)
Westwood Coll–Fort Worth (TX)
Westwood Coll–Los Angeles (CA)
Westwood Coll–South Bay Campus (CA)

Architectural Engineering Technology
Baker Coll of Clinton Township (MI)
Baker Coll of Owosso (MI)
Baker Coll of Port Huron (MI)
Bluefield State Coll (WV)
Ferris State U (MI)
Indiana U–Purdue U Fort Wayne (IN)
Norfolk State U (VA)
Northern Kentucky U (KY)
Pennsylvania Coll of Technology (PA)
U of Alaska Anchorage (AK)
U of Cincinnati (OH)
U of the District of Columbia (DC)
Vermont Tech Coll (VT)
Wentworth Inst of Technology (MA)

Architectural Technology
Coll of Staten Island of the City U of New York (NY)
U of Maine at Augusta (ME)

Architecture Related
Abilene Christian U (TX)

Army Rotc/Military Science
Methodist U (NC)

Art
Abraham Baldwin Ag Coll (GA)
Central Christian Coll of Kansas (KS)
Coll of Coastal Georgia (GA)
Coll of Mount St. Joseph (OH)
Eastern New Mexico U (NM)
Felician Coll (NJ)
Hannibal-LaGrange Coll (MO)
Idaho State U (ID)
Indiana Wesleyan U (IN)
Kent State U at Stark (OH)
Keystone Coll (PA)
Lourdes Coll (OH)
Manchester Coll (IN)
Methodist U (NC)
Midland Coll (TX)
Mount Olive Coll (NC)
Rivier Coll (NH)
Shawnee State U (OH)
State U of New York Empire State Coll (NY)
Union Coll (NE)
U of Rio Grande (OH)
The U of Toledo (OH)
Young Harris Coll (GA)

Art History, Criticism and Conservation
John Cabot U (Italy)
Thomas More Coll (KY)

Artificial Intelligence and Robotics
Lamar U (TX)
U of Cincinnati (OH)

Art Teacher Education
Central Christian Coll of Kansas (KS)
Young Harris Coll (GA)

Athletic Training
Central Christian Coll of Kansas (KS)
Keiser U, Fort Lauderdale (FL)

Audio Engineering
Five Towns Coll (NY)

Autobody/Collision and Repair Technology
Idaho State U (ID)
Lewis-Clark State Coll (ID)
Montana State U Billings (MT)
Pennsylvania Coll of Technology (PA)
Utah Valley U (UT)
Weber State U (UT)

Automobile/Automotive Mechanics Technology
Baker Coll of Flint (MI)
Dixie State Coll of Utah (UT)
EDP Coll of Puerto Rico, Inc. (PR)
Ferris State U (MI)
Idaho State U (ID)
Lamar U (TX)
Lewis-Clark State Coll (ID)
Midland Coll (TX)
Montana State U Billings (MT)
Montana Tech of The U of Montana (MT)
Northern Michigan U (MI)
Oakland City U (IN)
Pittsburg State U (KS)
Santa Fe Coll (FL)
Southern Adventist U (TN)
Southern Utah U (UT)
State U of New York Coll of Technology at Canton (NY)
U of Alaska Anchorage (AK)
Utah Valley U (UT)
Westwood Coll–Denver North (CO)

Automotive Engineering Technology
Santa Fe Coll (FL)
Vermont Tech Coll (VT)

Aviation/Airway Management
Fairmont State U (WV)
Mountain State U (WV)
U of Alaska Anchorage (AK)
U of Dubuque (IA)
U of the District of Columbia (DC)
Vaughn Coll of Aeronautics and Technology (NY)

Avionics Maintenance Technology
Baker Coll of Flint (MI)
Excelsior Coll (NY)
Fairmont State U (WV)
U of Alaska Anchorage (AK)
U of the District of Columbia (DC)
Vaughn Coll of Aeronautics and Technology (NY)

Baking and Pastry Arts
The Art Inst of California–Inland Empire (CA)
The Art Inst of California–Los Angeles (CA)
The Art Inst of California–Orange County (CA)
The Art Inst of California–Sacramento (CA)
The Art Inst of California–San Diego (CA)
The Art Inst of California–San Francisco (CA)
The Art Inst of Colorado (CO)
The Art Inst of Dallas (TX)
The Art Inst of Fort Lauderdale (FL)
The Art Inst of Houston (TX)
The Art Inst of Indianapolis (IN)
The Art Inst of Las Vegas (NV)
The Art Inst of Phoenix (AZ)
The Art Inst of Pittsburgh (PA)
The Art Inst of Salt Lake City (UT)
The Art Inst of Tampa (FL)
The Art Inst of Tucson (AZ)
The Art Insts International–Kansas City (KS)
The Art Insts International Minnesota (MN)
The Culinary Inst of America (NY)
Florida Culinary Inst (FL)
Johnson & Wales U (CO)
Johnson & Wales U (FL)
Johnson & Wales U (RI)
Johnson & Wales U - Charlotte Campus (NC)
Keiser U, Fort Lauderdale (FL)
Kendall Coll (IL)
Monroe Coll, Bronx (NY)
Pennsylvania Coll of Technology (PA)
Southern New Hampshire U (NH)
Stratford U, Woodbridge (VA)

Banking and Financial Support Services
Brescia U (KY)
Globe Inst of Technology (NY)
Hilbert Coll (NY)
Pennsylvania Coll of Technology (PA)
St. Petersburg Coll (FL)
Utah Valley U (UT)
Washburn U (KS)

Behavioral Sciences
Felician Coll (NJ)
Granite State Coll (NH)
Lewis-Clark State Coll (ID)
Methodist U (NC)
Midland Coll (TX)
Oklahoma Wesleyan U (OK)
Utah Valley U (UT)

Biblical Studies
Appalachian Bible Coll (WV)
Atlanta Christian Coll (GA)
Barclay Coll (KS)
Bethel Coll (IN)
Beulah Heights U (GA)
Boston Baptist Coll (MA)
Calvary Bible Coll and Theological Seminary (MO)
Carolina Christian Coll (NC)
Central Christian Coll of Kansas (KS)
Cincinnati Christian U (OH)
Clear Creek Baptist Bible Coll (KY)
Coll of Biblical Studies–Houston (TX)
Columbia International U (SC)
Corban U (OR)
Covenant Coll (GA)
Dallas Baptist U (TX)
Davis Coll (NY)
Eastern Mennonite U (VA)
Ecclesia Coll (AR)
Faith Baptist Bible Coll and Theological Seminary (IA)
Free Will Baptist Bible Coll (TN)
Heritage Christian U (AL)
Hillsdale Free Will Baptist Coll (OK)
Houghton Coll (NY)
Howard Payne U (TX)
John Brown U (AR)
Kuyper Coll (MI)
Lincoln Christian U (IL)
Maple Springs Baptist Bible Coll and Seminary (MD)
Mid-Atlantic Christian U (NC)
Nazarene Bible Coll (CO)
New Life Theological Seminary (NC)
Oakwood U (AL)
Pacific Union Coll (CA)
Patten U (CA)
Piedmont Baptist Coll and Graduate School (NC)
Shasta Bible Coll (CA)
Simpson U (CA)
Somerset Christian Coll (NJ)
Southeastern Bible Coll (AL)
Southwestern Assemblies of God U (TX)
Trinity Coll of Florida (FL)
Tri-State Bible Coll (OH)
Valley Forge Christian Coll (PA)

Biological and Biomedical Sciences Related
Alderson-Broaddus Coll (WV)
Gwynedd-Mercy Coll (PA)
Roberts Wesleyan Coll (NY)

Biological and Physical Sciences
Abraham Baldwin Ag Coll (GA)
Central Christian Coll of Kansas (KS)
Dalton State Coll (GA)
Ferris State U (MI)
Free Will Baptist Bible Coll (TN)
Indiana U East (IN)
Jefferson Coll of Health Sciences (VA)
John Brown U (AR)
Mount Olive Coll (NC)
Ohio U–Zanesville (OH)
Penn State Altoona (PA)
State U of New York Empire State Coll (NY)
Trine U (IN)
U of Cincinnati (OH)
Valparaiso U (IN)
Young Harris Coll (GA)

Biology/Biological Sciences
Abraham Baldwin Ag Coll (GA)
Brewton-Parker Coll (GA)
Cleveland Chiropractic Coll–Los Angeles Campus (CA)

Coll of Coastal Georgia (GA)
Cumberland U (TN)
Dalton State Coll (GA)
East-West U (IL)
Felician Coll (NJ)
Free Will Baptist Bible Coll (TN)
Idaho State U (ID)
Indiana U Northwest (IN)
Indiana U–Purdue U Fort Wayne (IN)
Indiana U South Bend (IN)
Indiana Wesleyan U (IN)
Lourdes Coll (OH)
Methodist U (NC)
Midland Coll (TX)
Mount Olive Coll (NC)
Mount St. Mary's Coll (CA)
Oklahoma Wesleyan U (OK)
Pennsylvania Coll of Technology (PA)
Presentation Coll (SD)
Purdue U North Central (IN)
Rogers State U (OK)
Saint Joseph's U (PA)
Shawnee State U (OH)
Thomas Edison State Coll (NJ)
Thomas More Coll (KY)
U of Dubuque (IA)
U of New Hampshire at Manchester (NH)
U of Rio Grande (OH)
The U of Tampa (FL)
The U of Toledo (OH)
Utah Valley U (UT)
Wright State U (OH)
York Coll of Pennsylvania (PA)
Young Harris Coll (GA)

Biology/ Biotechnology Laboratory Technician
Santa Fe Coll (FL)
U of the District of Columbia (DC)
Weber State U (UT)

Biology Teacher Education
Central Christian Coll of Kansas (KS)

Biomedical Technology
Baker Coll of Flint (MI)
ECPI Coll of Technology, Virginia Beach (VA)
Indiana U–Purdue U Indianapolis (IN)
Penn State Altoona (PA)
Penn State Berks (PA)
Penn State Erie, The Behrend Coll (PA)
Pennsylvania Coll of Technology (PA)
Santa Fe Coll (FL)
Thomas Edison State Coll (NJ)

Biotechnology
Indiana U–Purdue U Indianapolis (IN)
Keiser U, Fort Lauderdale (FL)

Broadcast Journalism
Cornerstone U (MI)
Evangel U (MO)
Manchester Coll (IN)
Ohio U–Zanesville (OH)
Pennsylvania Coll of Technology (PA)

Building/Construction Finishing, Management, and Inspection Related
Baker Coll of Flint (MI)
John Brown U (AR)
Pratt Inst (NY)
Wentworth Inst of Technology (MA)

Building/Construction Site Management
Utah Valley U (UT)

Building/Home/ Construction Inspection
Utah Valley U (UT)

Building/Property Maintenance and Management
Park U (MO)
Southern Adventist U (TN)
State U of New York Coll of Technology at Canton (NY)
Utah Valley U (UT)

Business Administration and Management
Abraham Baldwin Ag Coll (GA)
AIB Coll of Business (IA)
Alabama State U (AL)
Alaska Pacific U (AK)
American International Coll (MA)
American Public U System (WV)
Amridge U (AL)
Anderson U (IN)
Atlanta Christian Coll (GA)
Austin Peay State U (TN)
Baker Coll of Allen Park (MI)
Baker Coll of Auburn Hills (MI)
Baker Coll of Flint (MI)
Baker Coll of Owosso (MI)
Ball State U (IN)
Bauder Coll (GA)
Benedictine Coll (KS)
Benedictine U (IL)
Bentley U (MA)
Bethel Coll (IN)
Brewton-Parker Coll (GA)
Brookline Coll, Phoenix (AZ)
Brookline Coll, Tempe (AZ)
Brookline Coll, Tucson (AZ)
Brookline Coll (NM)
Bryan Coll (TN)
Calumet Coll of Saint Joseph (IN)
Cameron U (OK)
Campbellsville U (KY)
Cazenovia Coll (NY)
Central Pennsylvania Coll (PA)
Chaminade U of Honolulu (HI)
Clarion U of Pennsylvania (PA)
Clearwater Christian Coll (FL)
Cleary U (MI)
Coll of Coastal Georgia (GA)
Coll of Mount St. Joseph (OH)
Coll of St. Joseph (VT)
Coll of Saint Mary (NE)
Columbia Coll, Caguas (PR)
Columbia Coll, Yauco (PR)
Columbia Southern U (AL)
Concord U (WV)
Corban U (OR)
Crown Coll (MN)
Dakota State U (SD)
Dakota Wesleyan U (SD)
Dallas Baptist U (TX)
Dalton State Coll (GA)
Davenport U, Grand Rapids (MI)
Daymar Inst, Clarksville (TN)
DeVry U, North Brunswick (NJ)
Dixie State Coll of Utah (UT)
East-West U (IL)
Edinboro U of Pennsylvania (PA)
EDP Coll of Puerto Rico, Inc. (PR)
EDP Coll of Puerto Rico–San Sebastian (PR)
Elizabethtown Coll (PA)
Excelsior Coll (NY)
Fairmont State U (WV)
Farmingdale State Coll (NY)
Faulkner U (AL)
Felician Coll (NJ)
Ferris State U (MI)
Fisher Coll (MA)
Five Towns Coll (NY)
Florida Inst of Technology (FL)
Florida National Coll (FL)
Franciscan U of Steubenville (OH)
Franklin U (OH)
Free Will Baptist Bible Coll (TN)
Friends U (KS)
Geneva Coll (PA)
Globe Inst of Technology (NY)
Goldey-Beacom Coll (DE)
Grace Bible Coll (MI)
Grantham U (MO)
Gwynedd-Mercy Coll (PA)
Hawai'i Pacific U (HI)
Herzing U (GA)
Huntington U (IN)
Husson U (ME)
Immaculata U (PA)
Indiana Tech (IN)
Indiana U of Pennsylvania (PA)
Indiana U–Purdue U Fort Wayne (IN)
Indiana Wesleyan U (IN)
Inter American U of Puerto Rico, Aguadilla Campus (PR)
Inter American U of Puerto Rico, Arecibo Campus (PR)
Inter American U of Puerto Rico, Bayamón Campus (PR)
Inter American U of Puerto Rico, Fajardo Campus (PR)
Inter American U of Puerto Rico, Guayama Campus (PR)
Inter American U of Puerto Rico, Ponce Campus (PR)
Inter American U of Puerto Rico, San Germán Campus (PR)
John Cabot U (Italy)
Johnson & Wales U (CO)
Johnson & Wales U (FL)
Johnson & Wales U (RI)
Johnson & Wales U - Charlotte Campus (NC)
Johnson State Coll (VT)
Jones Coll, Jacksonville (FL)
Jones International U (CO)
Kaplan U, Davenport Campus (IA)
Kaplan U, Mason City Campus (IA)
Keiser U, Fort Lauderdale (FL)
Kent State U (OH)
Kent State U at Stark (OH)
Keystone Coll (PA)
King's Coll (PA)
Lake Superior State U (MI)
Lebanon Valley Coll (PA)
Lincoln Coll of New England, Southington (CT)
Lincoln Memorial U (TN)
Lock Haven U of Pennsylvania (PA)
Long Island U, Brooklyn Campus (NY)
Madonna U (MI)
Manchester Coll (IN)
Maria Coll (NY)
Marietta Coll (OH)
Medaille Coll (NY)
Medgar Evers Coll of the City U of New York (NY)
Mercy Coll (NY)
Methodist U (NC)
Miami U Hamilton (OH)
MidAmerica Nazarene U (KS)
Midway Coll (KY)
Missouri Baptist U (MO)
Missouri Western State U (MO)
Montana State U Billings (MT)
Mount Aloysius Coll (PA)
Mount Marty Coll (SD)
Mount Olive Coll (NC)
Muhlenberg Coll (PA)
Newbury Coll (MA)
New England Coll of Business (MA)
Newman U (KS)
New Mexico Inst of Mining and Technology (NM)
Niagara U (NY)
Nichols Coll (MA)
Nyack Coll (NY)
Oakland City U (IN)
Ohio Dominican U (OH)
Oklahoma Panhandle State U (OK)
Oklahoma Wesleyan U (OK)
Patricia Stevens Coll (MO)
Peirce Coll (PA)
Pikeville Coll (KY)
Pioneer Pacific Coll, Clackamas (OR)
Pioneer Pacific Coll, Wilsonville (OR)
Pioneer Pacific Coll–Eugene/Springfield Branch (OR)
Point Park U (PA)
Pontifical Catholic U of Puerto Rico (PR)
Post U (CT)
Providence Coll (RI)
Regent U (VA)
Rider U (NJ)
Rivier Coll (NH)
Robert Morris U Illinois (IL)
Rogers State U (OK)
St. Augustine Coll (IL)
St. Francis Coll (NY)
Saint Francis U (PA)
St. John's U (NY)
Saint Joseph's U (PA)
St. Petersburg Coll (FL)
St. Thomas Aquinas Coll (NY)
Salve Regina U (RI)
Santa Fe Coll (FL)
Shawnee State U (OH)
Shaw U (NC)
Siena Heights U (MI)
Southern Adventist U (TN)
Southern California Inst of Technology (CA)
Southern New Hampshire U (NH)
Southern Vermont Coll (VT)
South U (AL)
South U, Royal Palm Beach (FL)
South U (GA)
South U, Columbia (SC)
Southwestern Assemblies of God U (TX)
Southwest Minnesota State U (MN)
State U of New York Coll of Technology at Canton (NY)
State U of New York Empire State Coll (NY)
Stratford U, Woodbridge (VA)
Strayer U - Akron Campus (OH)
Strayer U - Alexandria Campus (VA)
Strayer U - Allentown Campus (PA)
Strayer U - Anne Arundel Campus (MD)
Strayer U - Arlington Campus (VA)
Strayer U - Augusta Campus (GA)
Strayer U - Baymeadows Campus (FL)
Strayer U - Birmingham Campus (AL)
Strayer U - Brickell Campus (FL)
Strayer U - Center City Campus (PA)
Strayer U - Central Austin Campus (TX)
Strayer U - Chamblee Campus (GA)
Strayer U - Charleston Campus (SC)
Strayer U - Chesapeake Campus (VA)
Strayer U - Chesterfield Campus (VA)
Strayer U - Christiana Campus (DE)
Strayer U - Cobb County Campus (GA)
Strayer U - Columbia Campus (SC)
Strayer U - Columbus Campus (OH)
Strayer U - Coral Springs Campus (FL)
Strayer U - Cranberry Woods Campus (PA)
Strayer U - Delaware County Campus (PA)
Strayer U - Doral Campus (FL)
Strayer U - Douglasville Campus (GA)
Strayer U - Fairview Park Campus (OH)
Strayer U - Florence Campus (KY)
Strayer U - Fort Lauderdale Campus (FL)
Strayer U - Fredericksburg Campus (VA)
Strayer U - Garner Campus (NC)
Strayer U - Greensboro Campus (NC)
Strayer U - Greenville Campus (SC)
Strayer U - Henrico Campus (VA)
Strayer U - Huntersville Campus (NC)
Strayer U - Huntsville Campus (AL)
Strayer U - King of Prussia Campus (PA)
Strayer U - Knoxville Campus (TN)
Strayer U - Lexington Campus (KY)
Strayer U - Lithonia Campus (GA)
Strayer U - Loudoun Campus (VA)
Strayer U - Louisville Campus (KY)
Strayer U - Lower Bucks County Campus (PA)
Strayer U - Maitland Campus (FL)
Strayer U - Manassas Campus (VA)
Strayer U - Mason Campus (OH)
Strayer U - Metairie Campus (LA)
Strayer U - Miramar Campus (FL)
Strayer U - Morrow Campus (GA)
Strayer U - Nashville Campus (TN)
Strayer U - Newport News Campus (VA)
Strayer U - North Charlotte Campus (NC)
Strayer U - North Raleigh Campus (NC)
Strayer U - Orlando East Campus (FL)
Strayer U - Owings Mills Campus (MD)
Strayer U - Palm Beach Gardens Campus (FL)
Strayer U - Penn Center West Campus (PA)
Strayer U - Prince George's Campus (MD)
Strayer U - Rockville Campus (MD)
Strayer U - Roswell Campus (GA)
Strayer U - RTP Campus (NC)
Strayer U - Salt Lake Campus (UT)
Strayer U - Sand Lake Campus (FL)
Strayer U - Savannah Campus (GA)
Strayer U - Shelby Oaks Campus (TN)
Strayer U - South Charlotte Campus (NC)
Strayer U - Takoma Park Campus (DC)
Strayer U - Tampa East Campus (FL)
Strayer U - Tampa Westshore Campus (FL)
Strayer U - Teays Valley Campus (WV)
Strayer U - Thousand Oaks Campus (TN)
Strayer U - Virginia Beach Campus (VA)
Strayer U - Washington Campus (DC)
Strayer U - White Marsh Campus (MD)
Strayer U - Woodbridge Campus (VA)
Sullivan U (KY)
Taylor U (IN)
Thomas More Coll (KY)
Tiffin U (OH)
Trine U (IN)
Tulane U (LA)
Union Coll (NE)
Universidad Adventista de las Antillas (PR)
The U of Akron (OH)
U of Alaska Anchorage (AK)
U of Alaska Fairbanks (AK)
U of Alaska Southeast (AK)
U of Arkansas at Fort Smith (AR)
U of Cincinnati (OH)
U of Dubuque (IA)
The U of Findlay (OH)
U of Maine at Augusta (ME)
U of Maine at Fort Kent (ME)
The U of Montana Western (MT)
U of New Hampshire (NH)
U of New Hampshire at Manchester (NH)
U of Pennsylvania (PA)
U of Puerto Rico at Utuado (PR)
U of Rio Grande (OH)
The U of Scranton (PA)
The U of Tampa (FL)
U of the Incarnate Word (TX)
U of the Virgin Islands (VI)
The U of Toledo (OH)
Upper Iowa U (IA)
Utah Valley U (UT)
Vermont Tech Coll (VT)
Villa Maria Coll of Buffalo (NY)
Walsh U (OH)
Wayland Baptist U (TX)
Waynesburg U (PA)
Webber International U (FL)
Western International U (AZ)
Western Kentucky U (KY)
Westwood Coll–Dallas (TX)
Westwood Coll–Fort Worth (TX)
Westwood Coll–Los Angeles (CA)
Wilson Coll (PA)
Xavier U (OH)
York Coll of Pennsylvania (PA)
Young Harris Coll (GA)
Youngstown State U (OH)

Business Administration, Management and Operations Related
AIB Coll of Business (IA)
Daymar Inst, Clarksville (TN)
Embry-Riddle Aeronautical U Worldwide (FL)
Mountain State U (WV)
St. Augustine Coll (IL)

Business Automation/ Technology/Data Entry
Baker Coll of Clinton Township (MI)
Mercy Coll (NY)
Midland Coll (TX)
Montana State U Billings (MT)
Northern Michigan U (MI)
Pennsylvania Coll of Technology (PA)
U of Rio Grande (OH)
The U of Toledo (OH)
Utah Valley U (UT)

Business/Commerce
Adams State Coll (CO)
AIB Coll of Business (IA)
Alvernia U (PA)
Andrew Jackson U (AL)
Baker Coll of Flint (MI)
Brescia U (KY)
Bryant & Stratton Coll, Cleveland (OH)
Bryant & Stratton Coll - Wauwatosa Campus (WI)
Castleton State Coll (VT)
Coll of Staten Island of the City U of New York (NY)
Columbia Coll (MO)
Columbia Southern U (AL)
Cumberland U (TN)
Dalton State Coll (GA)
Delaware Valley Coll (PA)
Dixie State Coll of Utah (UT)
Eastern Nazarene Coll (MA)
Ferris State U (MI)
Fisher Coll (MA)
Franklin U (OH)

Gannon U (PA)
Glenville State Coll (WV)
Granite State Coll (NH)
Hillsdale Free Will Baptist Coll (OK)
Idaho State U (ID)
Indiana U East (IN)
Indiana U Kokomo (IN)
Indiana U Northwest (IN)
Indiana U South Bend (IN)
Indiana U Southeast (IN)
Keystone Coll (PA)
Limestone Coll (SC)
Lourdes Coll (OH)
Mayville State U (ND)
Metropolitan Coll of New York (NY)
Midland Coll (TX)
Midway Coll (KY)
Missouri Southern State U (MO)
Montana State U Billings (MT)
Mount Vernon Nazarene U (OH)
New York U (NY)
Northern Kentucky U (KY)
Northern Michigan U (MI)
Northwestern State U of Louisiana (LA)
Penn State Abington (PA)
Penn State Altoona (PA)
Penn State Berks (PA)
Penn State Erie, The Behrend Coll (PA)
Penn State Harrisburg (PA)
Penn State U Park (PA)
Saint Leo U (FL)
Saint Mary-of-the-Woods Coll (IN)
Southern Arkansas U–Magnolia (AR)
Southern Wesleyan U (SC)
Southwest Baptist U (MO)
Southwestern Assemblies of God U (TX)
Spalding U (KY)
Troy U (AL)
Tulane U (LA)
U of Bridgeport (CT)
The U of Montana Western (MT)
The U of Toledo (OH)
Youngstown State U (OH)

Business/Corporate Communications
Central Christian Coll of Kansas (KS)

Business Machine Repair
ECPI Coll of Technology, Virginia Beach (VA)
Lamar U (TX)
U of Alaska Anchorage (AK)

Business, Management, and Marketing Related
Indiana Tech (IN)
Presentation Coll (SD)
Purdue U North Central (IN)
Southwest Florida Coll, Fort Myers (FL)

Business/Managerial Economics
Central Christian Coll of Kansas (KS)

Business Operations Support and Secretarial Services Related
Thomas Edison State Coll (NJ)

Business Teacher Education
Central Christian Coll of Kansas (KS)

Cabinetmaking and Millwork
Pennsylvania Coll of Technology (PA)
Utah Valley U (UT)

CAD/CADD Drafting/Design Technology
The Art Insts International Minnesota (MN)
Ferris State U (MI)
Idaho State U (ID)
ITT Tech Inst, Tempe (AZ)
ITT Tech Inst, Clovis (CA)
ITT Tech Inst, Concord (CA)
ITT Tech Inst, Corona (CA)
ITT Tech Inst, South Bend (IN)
ITT Tech Inst (KS)
ITT Tech Inst, Lexington (KY)
ITT Tech Inst (MS)
ITT Tech Inst, Springfield (MO)
ITT Tech Inst, Oklahoma City (OK)
Johnson & Wales U (RI)
Keiser U, Fort Lauderdale (FL)
Montana Tech of The U of Montana (MT)
Northern Michigan U (MI)
Shawnee State U (OH)
Southwest Florida Coll, Fort Myers (FL)

Cardiovascular Technology
Gwynedd-Mercy Coll (PA)
Keiser U, Fort Lauderdale (FL)
Molloy Coll (NY)
Nebraska Methodist Coll (NE)
New York U (NY)
Santa Fe Coll (FL)
Thompson Rivers U (BC, Canada)
The U of Toledo (OH)

Carpentry
Bob Jones U (SC)
Idaho State U (ID)
Montana State U Billings (MT)
Montana Tech of The U of Montana (MT)
Pennsylvania Coll of Technology (PA)
Santa Fe Coll (FL)
Southern Utah U (UT)
Thompson Rivers U (BC, Canada)
U of Alaska Fairbanks (AK)

Cartography
The U of Akron (OH)

Chemical Engineering
Ball State U (IN)
U of New Haven (CT)
U of the District of Columbia (DC)

Chemical Technology
Ball State U (IN)
Excelsior Coll (NY)
Ferris State U (MI)
Indiana U–Purdue U Fort Wayne (IN)
Inter American U of Puerto Rico, Guayama Campus (PR)
Lawrence Technological U (MI)
Miami U (OH)
Millersville U of Pennsylvania (PA)
New York City Coll of Technology of the City U of New York (NY)
U of Puerto Rico at Humacao (PR)
The U of Toledo (OH)
Weber State U (UT)

Chemistry
Abraham Baldwin Ag Coll (GA)
Castleton State Coll (VT)
Coll of Coastal Georgia (GA)
Dalton State Coll (GA)
Idaho State U (ID)
Indiana Wesleyan U (IN)
Lake Superior State U (MI)
Lindsey Wilson Coll (KY)
Methodist U (NC)
Midland Coll (TX)
Ohio Dominican U (OH)
Oklahoma Wesleyan U (OK)
Presentation Coll (SD)
Purdue U North Central (IN)
Saint Joseph's U (PA)
Southern Arkansas U–Magnolia (AR)
Thomas More Coll (KY)
U of Rio Grande (OH)
The U of Tampa (FL)
U of the Incarnate Word (TX)
Utah Valley U (UT)
Wright State U (OH)
York Coll of Pennsylvania (PA)
Young Harris Coll (GA)

Chemistry Teacher Education
Central Christian Coll of Kansas (KS)

Child-Care and Support Services Management
Bob Jones U (SC)
Cameron U (OK)
Eastern New Mexico U (NM)
Ferris State U (MI)
Henderson State U (AR)
Idaho State U (ID)
Mount Vernon Nazarene U (OH)
Nicholls State U (LA)
Pennsylvania Coll of Technology (PA)
Post U (CT)
Purdue U Calumet (IN)
Southeast Missouri State U (MO)
Thomas Edison State Coll (NJ)
Thompson Rivers U (BC, Canada)
Weber State U (UT)
Youngstown State U (OH)

Child-Care Provision
Mayville State U (ND)
Midland Coll (TX)
Murray State U (KY)
Pacific Union Coll (CA)
Pennsylvania Coll of Technology (PA)
Saint Mary-of-the-Woods Coll (IN)
Santa Fe Coll (FL)
U of Louisiana at Monroe (LA)

Child Development
Abraham Baldwin Ag Coll (GA)
Alabama State U (AL)
Arkansas Tech U (AR)
Evangel U (MO)
Fairmont State U (WV)
Franciscan U of Steubenville (OH)
Grambling State U (LA)
Kuyper Coll (MI)
Lamar U (TX)
Lewis-Clark State Coll (ID)
Lincoln Coll of New England, Southington (CT)
Madonna U (MI)
Northern Michigan U (MI)
Ohio U (OH)
Southern Utah U (UT)
Trevecca Nazarene U (TN)
U of Cincinnati (OH)
U of the District of Columbia (DC)
Youngstown State U (OH)

Christian Studies
Crown Coll (MN)
Dallas Baptist U (TX)
Heritage Bible Coll (NC)
Oklahoma Baptist U (OK)
Regent U (VA)
Wayland Baptist U (TX)

Cinematography and Film/Video Production
Academy of Art U (CA)
The Art Inst of Atlanta (GA)
The Art Inst of California–Los Angeles (CA)
The Art Inst of Colorado (CO)
The Art Inst of Dallas (TX)
The Art Inst of Fort Lauderdale (FL)
The Art Inst of Philadelphia (PA)
The Art Inst of Pittsburgh (PA)
The Art Inst of Tennessee–Nashville (TN)
The Art Inst of Washington (VA)
Collins Coll: A School of Design and Technology (AZ)
Santa Fe Coll (FL)

Civil Engineering Technology
Bluefield State Coll (WV)
Fairmont State U (WV)
Ferris State U (MI)
Idaho State U (ID)
Indiana U–Purdue U Fort Wayne (IN)
Indiana U–Purdue U Indianapolis (IN)
Michigan Technological U (MI)
Montana Tech of The U of Montana (MT)
New York City Coll of Technology of the City U of New York (NY)
Point Park U (PA)
Purdue U Calumet (IN)
Purdue U North Central (IN)
State U of New York Coll of Technology at Canton (NY)
U of Cincinnati (OH)
U of Massachusetts Lowell (MA)
U of New Hampshire (NH)
U of Puerto Rico at Bayamón (PR)
U of the District of Columbia (DC)
The U of Toledo (OH)
Vermont Tech Coll (VT)
Youngstown State U (OH)

Clinical Laboratory Science/Medical Technology
Arkansas State U - Jonesboro (AR)
Dalton State Coll (GA)
Thomas Edison State Coll (NJ)
The U of Toledo (OH)
Young Harris Coll (GA)

Clinical/Medical Laboratory Assistant
U of Maine at Augusta (ME)

Clinical/Medical Laboratory Science and Allied Professions Related
Youngstown State U (OH)

Clinical/Medical Laboratory Technology
Baker Coll of Owosso (MI)
Coll of Coastal Georgia (GA)
Dalton State Coll (GA)
Fairmont State U (WV)
Farmingdale State Coll (NY)
Felician Coll (NJ)
Ferris State U (MI)
The George Washington U (DC)
Indiana U East (IN)
Indiana U Northwest (IN)
Marshall U (WV)
Mount Aloysius Coll (PA)
Northern Michigan U (MI)
Our Lady of the Lake Coll (LA)
St. Petersburg Coll (FL)
Shawnee State U (OH)
U of Alaska Anchorage (AK)
U of Cincinnati (OH)
U of Maine at Presque Isle (ME)
U of Rio Grande (OH)
The U of Texas at Brownsville (TX)
U of the District of Columbia (DC)
Youngstown State U (OH)

Commercial and Advertising Art
The Art Center Design Coll, Tucson (AZ)
Baker Coll of Auburn Hills (MI)
Baker Coll of Clinton Township (MI)
Baker Coll of Muskegon (MI)
Baker Coll of Owosso (MI)
Baker Coll of Port Huron (MI)
Central Pennsylvania Coll (PA)
Collins Coll: A School of Design and Technology (AZ)
Fairmont State U (WV)
Fashion Inst of Technology (NY)
Felician Coll (NJ)
Ferris State U (MI)
Indiana U–Purdue U Fort Wayne (IN)
International Academy of Design & Technology (IL)
Mercy Coll (NY)
Midland Coll (TX)
Mitchell Coll (CT)
Newbury Coll (MA)
New York City Coll of Technology of the City U of New York (NY)
Northern Michigan U (MI)
Northern State U (SD)
Oakwood U (AL)
Platt Coll San Diego (CA)
Pratt Inst (NY)
Robert Morris U Illinois (IL)
Santa Fe Coll (FL)
Suffolk U (MA)
U of New Haven (CT)
U of the District of Columbia (DC)
Utah Valley U (UT)
Villa Maria Coll of Buffalo (NY)
Virginia Intermont Coll (VA)

Commercial Photography
The Art Inst of Atlanta (GA)
The Art Inst of Washington (VA)
Fashion Inst of Technology (NY)
Harrington Coll of Design (IL)

Communication and Journalism Related
Keystone Coll (PA)
Madonna U (MI)
Tulane U (LA)
Valparaiso U (IN)

Communication and Media Related
AIB Coll of Business (IA)
Elizabethtown Coll (PA)
Keystone Coll (PA)

Communication/Speech Communication and Rhetoric
Albertus Magnus Coll (CT)
American Public U System (WV)
Andrew Jackson U (AL)
Baker Coll of Jackson (MI)
Central Pennsylvania Coll (PA)
Coll of Mount St. Joseph (OH)
Idaho State U (ID)
Indiana Wesleyan U (IN)
John Brown U (AR)
Keystone Coll (PA)
Lincoln Coll of New England, Southington (CT)
Madonna U (MI)
Presentation Coll (SD)
Saint Joseph's U (PA)
Thomas More Coll (KY)
Trine U (IN)
Tulane U (LA)
U of New Haven (CT)
U of Rio Grande (OH)
Utah Valley U (UT)
Wright State U (OH)

Communications Systems Installation and Repair Technology
Idaho State U (ID)
Thompson Rivers U (BC, Canada)

Communications Technologies and Support Services Related
Southern Adventist U (TN)

Communications Technology
East Stroudsburg U of Pennsylvania (PA)
ECPI Coll of Technology, Virginia Beach (VA)
ECPI Tech Coll, Roanoke (VA)
U of Puerto Rico at Humacao (PR)

Community Health and Preventive Medicine
Utah Valley U (UT)

Community Organization and Advocacy
Alabama State U (AL)
Fairmont State U (WV)
State U of New York Empire State Coll (NY)
Thomas Edison State Coll (NJ)
U of Alaska Fairbanks (AK)
The U of Findlay (OH)
U of New Hampshire (NH)

Community Psychology
Kwantlen Polytechnic U (BC, Canada)

Comparative Literature
John Cabot U (Italy)
Manchester Coll (IN)
Midland Coll (TX)

Computer and Information Sciences
Alvernia U (PA)
American Public U System (WV)
Baker Coll of Allen Park (MI)
Ball State U (IN)
Black Hills State U (SD)
Chaminade U of Honolulu (HI)
Coll of Mount St. Joseph (OH)
Coll of Saint Mary (NE)
Columbia Coll (MO)
Dalton State Coll (GA)
Daymar Inst, Clarksville (TN)
Delaware Valley Coll (PA)
ECPI Coll of Technology, Virginia Beach (VA)
ECPI Tech Coll, Roanoke (VA)
Edinboro U of Pennsylvania (PA)
Fisher Coll (MA)
Franklin U (OH)
Globe Inst of Technology (NY)
Herzing U (GA)
Herzing U (WI)
Indiana Wesleyan U (IN)
Inter American U of Puerto Rico, Fajardo Campus (PR)
Inter American U of Puerto Rico, Ponce Campus (PR)
Jones Coll, Jacksonville (FL)
Keene State Coll (NH)
King's Coll (PA)
Lewis-Clark State Coll (ID)
Midway Coll (KY)
Millersville U of Pennsylvania (PA)
Montana State U Billings (MT)
Pennsylvania Coll of Technology (PA)
Pontifical Catholic U of Puerto Rico (PR)
Rogers State U (OK)
St. Augustine Coll (IL)
St. John's U (NY)
Southern New Hampshire U (NH)
Troy U (AL)
Tulane U (LA)
U of Alaska Anchorage (AK)
U of Arkansas at Fort Smith (AR)
U of Cincinnati (OH)
U of Maine at Augusta (ME)
The U of Tampa (FL)
Utah Valley U (UT)
Webber International U (FL)

Computer and Information Sciences And Support Services Related
Cleary U (MI)
Florida National Coll (FL)
Inter American U of Puerto Rico, Guayama Campus (PR)

Montana State U Billings (MT)
Pennsylvania Coll of Technology (PA)
Utah Valley U (UT)

Computer and Information Sciences Related
ECPI Tech Coll, Roanoke (VA)
Limestone Coll (SC)
Lindsey Wilson Coll (KY)
Madonna U (MI)
Sacred Heart U (CT)
Washburn U (KS)

Computer and Information Systems Security
Bryant & Stratton Coll, Cleveland (OH)
ECPI Tech Coll, Roanoke (VA)
Florida National Coll (FL)
Peirce Coll (PA)
St. John's U (NY)
Stratford U, Woodbridge (VA)

Computer Engineering
The U of Scranton (PA)

Computer Engineering Related
Thompson Rivers U (BC, Canada)

Computer Engineering Technologies Related
Pennsylvania Coll of Technology (PA)
Thomas Edison State Coll (NJ)

Computer Engineering Technology
Abraham Baldwin Ag Coll (GA)
Baker Coll of Owosso (MI)
Dalton State Coll (GA)
ECPI Coll of Technology, Virginia Beach (VA)
ECPI Tech Coll, Roanoke (VA)
Grantham U (MO)
Indiana U–Purdue U Indianapolis (IN)
ITT Tech Inst, Clovis (CA)
ITT Tech Inst, Concord (CA)
ITT Tech Inst, Corona (CA)
ITT Tech Inst, South Bend (IN)
ITT Tech Inst (KS)
ITT Tech Inst, Lexington (KY)
ITT Tech Inst (MS)
ITT Tech Inst, Springfield (MO)
ITT Tech Inst, Charlotte (NC)
ITT Tech Inst, Oklahoma City (OK)
Johnson & Wales U (RI)
Lake Superior State U (MI)
Oakland City U (IN)
Oregon Inst of Technology (OR)
St. Petersburg Coll (FL)
U of Cincinnati (OH)
U of Hartford (CT)
U of the District of Columbia (DC)
Vermont Tech Coll (VT)
Weber State U (UT)

Computer Graphics
Academy of Art U (CA)
Baker Coll of Cadillac (MI)
Florida National Coll (FL)
Indiana Tech (IN)
International Academy of Design & Technology (IL)
Johnson & Wales U (RI)
Keiser U, Fort Lauderdale (FL)
Mountain State U (WV)
Platt Coll San Diego (CA)
Thompson Rivers U (BC, Canada)
U of Advancing Technology (AZ)

Computer/Information Technology Services Administration Related
Dalton State Coll (GA)
Johnson & Wales U (RI)
Keystone Coll (PA)
Limestone Coll (SC)
Maria Coll (NY)
Mercy Coll (NY)
Pennsylvania Coll of Technology (PA)
St. Petersburg Coll (FL)
Santa Fe Coll (FL)

Computer Installation and Repair Technology
Dalton State Coll (GA)
Inter American U of Puerto Rico, Bayamón Campus (PR)
Inter American U of Puerto Rico, Fajardo Campus (PR)
Thompson Rivers U (BC, Canada)
U of Alaska Fairbanks (AK)

Computer Programming
Baker Coll of Muskegon (MI)
Baker Coll of Owosso (MI)
Baker Coll of Port Huron (MI)
Black Hills State U (SD)
Castleton State Coll (VT)
Coll of Staten Island of the City U of New York (NY)
Dakota State U (SD)
Delaware Valley Coll (PA)
ECPI Coll of Technology, Virginia Beach (VA)
EDP Coll of Puerto Rico, Inc. (PR)
EDP Coll of Puerto Rico–San Sebastian (PR)
Farmingdale State Coll (NY)
Florida National Coll (FL)
Gwynedd-Mercy Coll (PA)
Hickey Coll (MO)
Indiana U East (IN)
Indiana U South Bend (IN)
Indiana U Southeast (IN)
Johnson & Wales U (RI)
Keiser U, Fort Lauderdale (FL)
Kent State U (OH)
Keystone Coll (PA)
Limestone Coll (SC)
Medgar Evers Coll of the City U of New York (NY)
Missouri Southern State U (MO)
Oakland City U (IN)
Oregon Inst of Technology (OR)
Purdue U Calumet (IN)
Saint Francis U (PA)
Santa Fe Coll (FL)
Southwest Florida Coll, Fort Myers (FL)
U of Advancing Technology (AZ)
U of Arkansas at Little Rock (AR)
U of Cincinnati (OH)
The U of Toledo (OH)
Youngstown State U (OH)

Computer Programming Related
American Public U System (WV)
Florida National Coll (FL)
Herzing U (WI)

Computer Programming (Specific Applications)
Florida National Coll (FL)
Idaho State U (ID)
Indiana U East (IN)
Indiana U Southeast (IN)
Kent State U (OH)
Midland Coll (TX)
Pennsylvania Coll of Technology (PA)
Pontifical Catholic U of Puerto Rico (PR)
The U of Toledo (OH)

Computer Programming (Vendor/Product Certification)
Peirce Coll (PA)

Computer Science
Abraham Baldwin Ag Coll (GA)
Alderson-Broaddus Coll (WV)
Baker Coll of Allen Park (MI)
Baker Coll of Owosso (MI)
Bethel Coll (IN)
Black Hills State U (SD)
Calumet Coll of Saint Joseph (IN)
Central Christian Coll of Kansas (KS)
Central Pennsylvania Coll (PA)
Coll of Coastal Georgia (GA)
Creighton U (NE)
Dalton State Coll (GA)
ECPI Coll of Technology, Virginia Beach (VA)
ECPI Tech Coll, Roanoke (VA)
Farmingdale State Coll (NY)
Felician Coll (NJ)
Florida National Coll (FL)
Grantham U (MO)
Hawai'i Pacific U (HI)
Inter American U of Puerto Rico, Aguadilla Campus (PR)
Inter American U of Puerto Rico, Arecibo Campus (PR)
Inter American U of Puerto Rico, Bayamón Campus (PR)
Inter American U of Puerto Rico, Ponce Campus (PR)
John Cabot U (Italy)
Lincoln U (MO)
Madonna U (MI)
Manchester Coll (IN)
Methodist U (NC)
Monroe Coll, Bronx (NY)
Monroe Coll, New Rochelle (NY)
Mountain State U (WV)
New England Coll of Business (MA)
New York City Coll of Technology of the City U of New York (NY)
Oakland City U (IN)
Rivier Coll (NH)
Southern California Inst of Technology (CA)
Southwest Baptist U (MO)
Tabor Coll (KS)
Thomas Edison State Coll (NJ)
Universidad Adventista de las Antillas (PR)
U of Dubuque (IA)
The U of Findlay (OH)
U of Maine at Fort Kent (ME)
U of New Haven (CT)
U of Rio Grande (OH)
U of the Virgin Islands (VI)
Utah Valley U (UT)
Walsh U (OH)
Waynesburg U (PA)
Young Harris Coll (GA)

Computer Software and Media Applications Related
Academy of Art U (CA)
AIB Coll of Business (IA)
Platt Coll San Diego (CA)

Computer Software Engineering
Vermont Tech Coll (VT)

Computer Software Technology
Grantham U (MO)
ITT Tech Inst, Tempe (AZ)
ITT Tech Inst, Clovis (CA)
ITT Tech Inst, Concord (CA)
ITT Tech Inst, South Bend (IN)
ITT Tech Inst (KS)
ITT Tech Inst, Lexington (KY)
ITT Tech Inst (MS)
ITT Tech Inst, Springfield (MO)
ITT Tech Inst, Oklahoma City (OK)

Computer Systems Analysis
Davenport U, Grand Rapids (MI)
DeVry U, North Brunswick (NJ)
Santa Fe Coll (FL)
The U of Akron (OH)
The U of Toledo (OH)

Computer Systems Networking and Telecommunications
Baker Coll of Allen Park (MI)
Baker Coll of Flint (MI)
Clayton State U (GA)
Daymar Inst, Clarksville (TN)
DeVry Coll of New York (NY)
DeVry U, Phoenix (AZ)
DeVry U, Fremont (CA)
DeVry U, Long Beach (CA)
DeVry U, Pomona (CA)
DeVry U, Sherman Oaks (CA)
DeVry U, Westminster (CO)
DeVry U, Miramar (FL)
DeVry U, Orlando (FL)
DeVry U, Alpharetta (GA)
DeVry U, Decatur (GA)
DeVry U, Addison (IL)
DeVry U, Chicago (IL)
DeVry U, Tinley Park (IL)
DeVry U, Indianapolis (IN)
DeVry U (KY)
DeVry U (MI)
DeVry U, Edina (MN)
DeVry U, Kansas City (MO)
DeVry U (NV)
DeVry U, North Brunswick (NJ)
DeVry U, Charlotte (NC)
DeVry U, Columbus (OH)
DeVry U (OK)
DeVry U (OR)
DeVry U, Fort Washington (PA)
DeVry U, Memphis (TN)
DeVry U, Houston (TX)
DeVry U, Irving (TX)
DeVry U (UT)
DeVry U, Arlington (VA)
DeVry U, Federal Way (WA)
DeVry U Online (IL)
Florida National Coll (FL)
Herzing U (WI)
Idaho State U (ID)
Indiana Tech (IN)
Inter American U of Puerto Rico, Aguadilla Campus (PR)
Montana Tech of The U of Montana (MT)
Pioneer Pacific Coll–Eugene/Springfield Branch (OR)
Robert Morris U Illinois (IL)
The U of Akron (OH)

Computer Teacher Education
Baker Coll of Flint (MI)
Central Christian Coll of Kansas (KS)

Computer Technology/Computer Systems Technology
Collins Coll: A School of Design and Technology (AZ)
Dalton State Coll (GA)
ECPI Tech Coll, Roanoke (VA)
Miami U Hamilton (OH)
New York City Coll of Technology of the City U of New York (NY)
Pennsylvania Coll of Technology (PA)
Southeast Missouri State U (MO)
Thompson Rivers U (BC, Canada)

Computer Typography and Composition Equipment Operation
Baker Coll of Auburn Hills (MI)
Baker Coll of Cadillac (MI)
Baker Coll of Clinton Township (MI)
Baker Coll of Flint (MI)
Baker Coll of Jackson (MI)
Calumet Coll of Saint Joseph (IN)
ECPI Coll of Technology, Virginia Beach (VA)
ECPI Tech Coll, Roanoke (VA)
The U of Toledo (OH)

Construction Engineering Technology
Baker Coll of Owosso (MI)
Coll of Staten Island of the City U of New York (NY)
Fairmont State U (WV)
Ferris State U (MI)
Lake Superior State U (MI)
Lawrence Technological U (MI)
New York City Coll of Technology of the City U of New York (NY)
Santa Fe Coll (FL)
State U of New York Coll of Technology at Canton (NY)
The U of Akron (OH)
U of Cincinnati (OH)
The U of Toledo (OH)
Vermont Tech Coll (VT)
Wright State U (OH)

Construction Management
U of Alaska Fairbanks (AK)
Vermont Tech Coll (VT)
Westwood Coll–Dallas (TX)
Westwood Coll–Fort Worth (TX)

Construction Trades
Northern Michigan U (MI)
U of Alaska Southeast (AK)
Utah Valley U (UT)

Construction Trades Related
John Brown U (AR)
Utah Valley U (UT)

Consumer Economics
U of Alaska Southeast (AK)

Consumer Merchandising/Retailing Management
Baker Coll of Owosso (MI)
Fairmont State U (WV)
Johnson & Wales U (RI)
Madonna U (MI)
Newbury Coll (MA)
The U of Toledo (OH)

Cooking and Related Culinary Arts
Hickey Coll (MO)
Kendall Coll (IL)

Corrections
Baker Coll of Muskegon (MI)
Lake Superior State U (MI)
Lamar U (TX)
Mount Aloysius Coll (PA)
U of the District of Columbia (DC)
The U of Toledo (OH)
Washburn U (KS)
Xavier U (OH)

Corrections Administration
John Jay Coll of Criminal Justice of the City U of New York (NY)

Corrections and Criminal Justice Related
Florida Inst of Technology (FL)
Inter American U of Puerto Rico, Fajardo Campus (PR)

Cosmetology
Bob Jones U (SC)
Lamar U (TX)
Lincoln Coll–Normal (IL)

Counseling Psychology
Atlanta Christian Coll (GA)

Court Reporting
AIB Coll of Business (IA)
U of Cincinnati (OH)

Crafts, Folk Art and Artisanry
Northern Michigan U (MI)

Creative Writing
Bethel Coll (IN)
Manchester Coll (IN)
U of Maine at Presque Isle (ME)
The U of Tampa (FL)

Criminalistics and Criminal Science
Keiser U, Fort Lauderdale (FL)

Criminal Justice/Law Enforcement Administration
Abraham Baldwin Ag Coll (GA)
Anderson U (IN)
Arkansas State U - Jonesboro (AR)
Bemidji State U (MN)
Brookline Coll, Phoenix (AZ)
Brookline Coll, Tempe (AZ)
Brookline Coll, Tucson (AZ)
Brookline Coll (NM)
Bryant & Stratton Coll, Cleveland (OH)
Bryant & Stratton Coll - Wauwatosa Campus (WI)
Calumet Coll of Saint Joseph (IN)
Campbellsville U (KY)
Castleton State Coll (VT)
Central Christian Coll of Kansas (KS)
Coll of Coastal Georgia (GA)
Coll of St. Joseph (VT)
Columbia Coll (MO)
Dakota Wesleyan U (SD)
Dalton State Coll (GA)
ECPI Coll of Technology, Virginia Beach (VA)
Farmingdale State Coll (NY)
Faulkner U (AL)
Fisher Coll (MA)
Fort Valley State U (GA)
Glenville State Coll (WV)
Grantham U (MO)
Hannibal-LaGrange Coll (MO)
Hawai'i Pacific U (HI)
Indiana Tech (IN)
ITT Tech Inst, Tempe (AZ)
ITT Tech Inst, Clovis (CA)
ITT Tech Inst, Concord (CA)
ITT Tech Inst, South Bend (IN)
ITT Tech Inst (KS)
ITT Tech Inst, Lexington (KY)
ITT Tech Inst (MS)
ITT Tech Inst, Springfield (MO)
ITT Tech Inst, Oklahoma City (OK)
Johnson & Wales U (CO)
Johnson & Wales U (FL)
Johnson & Wales U (RI)
Kaplan U, Mason City Campus (IA)
Keiser U, Fort Lauderdale (FL)
Lake Superior State U (MI)
Lincoln Coll of New England, Southington (CT)
Lincoln U (MO)
Lock Haven U of Pennsylvania (PA)
Mansfield U of Pennsylvania (PA)
Methodist U (NC)
Monroe Coll, Bronx (NY)
Northern Michigan U (MI)
Pioneer Pacific Coll, Clackamas (OR)
Pioneer Pacific Coll–Eugene/Springfield Branch (OR)
Point Park U (PA)
Regent U (VA)
Reinhardt U (GA)
St. John's U (NY)
St. Petersburg Coll (FL)
Santa Fe Coll (FL)

Southern Utah U (UT)
Southern Vermont Coll (VT)
Strayer U - Alexandria Campus (VA)
Strayer U - Allentown Campus (PA)
Strayer U - Arlington Campus (VA)
Strayer U - Augusta Campus (GA)
Strayer U - Baymeadows Campus (FL)
Strayer U - Birmingham Campus (AL)
Strayer U - Brickell Campus (FL)
Strayer U - Center City Campus (PA)
Strayer U - Central Austin Campus (TX)
Strayer U - Chamblee Campus (GA)
Strayer U - Charleston Campus (SC)
Strayer U - Chesapeake Campus (VA)
Strayer U - Chesterfield Campus (VA)
Strayer U - Christiana Campus (DE)
Strayer U - Cobb County Campus (GA)
Strayer U - Columbia Campus (SC)
Strayer U - Coral Springs Campus (FL)
Strayer U - Cranberry Woods Campus (PA)
Strayer U - Delaware County Campus (PA)
Strayer U - Doral Campus (FL)
Strayer U - Douglasville Campus (GA)
Strayer U - Florence Campus (KY)
Strayer U - Fort Lauderdale Campus (FL)
Strayer U - Fredericksburg Campus (VA)
Strayer U - Garner Campus (NC)
Strayer U - Greensboro Campus (NC)
Strayer U - Greenville Campus (SC)
Strayer U - Henrico Campus (VA)
Strayer U - Huntersville Campus (NC)
Strayer U - Huntsville Campus (AL)
Strayer U - King of Prussia Campus (PA)
Strayer U - Knoxville Campus (TN)
Strayer U - Lexington Campus (KY)
Strayer U - Lithonia Campus (GA)
Strayer U - Loudoun Campus (VA)
Strayer U - Louisville Campus (KY)
Strayer U - Lower Bucks County Campus (PA)
Strayer U - Maitland Campus (FL)
Strayer U - Manassas Campus (VA)
Strayer U - Metairie Campus (LA)
Strayer U - Miramar Campus (FL)
Strayer U - Morrow Campus (GA)
Strayer U - Nashville Campus (TN)
Strayer U - Newport News Campus (VA)
Strayer U - North Charlotte Campus (NC)
Strayer U - North Raleigh Campus (NC)
Strayer U - Orlando East Campus (FL)
Strayer U - Palm Beach Gardens Campus (FL)
Strayer U - Penn Center West Campus (PA)
Strayer U - Roswell Campus (GA)
Strayer U - RTP Campus (NC)
Strayer U - Salt Lake Campus (UT)
Strayer U - Sand Lake Campus (FL)
Strayer U - Savannah Campus (GA)
Strayer U - Shelby Oaks Campus (TN)
Strayer U - South Charlotte Campus (NC)
Strayer U - Takoma Park Campus (DC)
Strayer U - Tampa East Campus (FL)
Strayer U - Tampa Westshore Campus (FL)
Strayer U - Teays Valley Campus (WV)
Strayer U - Thousand Oaks Campus (TN)
Strayer U - Virginia Beach Campus (VA)
Strayer U - Washington Campus (DC)
Strayer U - Woodbridge Campus (VA)
Suffolk U (MA)
Thomas Edison State Coll (NJ)
Tiffin U (OH)
Trine U (IN)
U of Arkansas at Fort Smith (AR)
U of Arkansas at Monticello (AR)
U of Arkansas at Pine Bluff (AR)
U of Cincinnati (OH)
The U of Findlay (OH)
U of Maine at Fort Kent (ME)
U of Maine at Presque Isle (ME)
Utah Valley U (UT)
Washburn U (KS)
Wayland Baptist U (TX)
York Coll of Pennsylvania (PA)
Young Harris Coll (GA)

Criminal Justice/ Police Science
Abraham Baldwin Ag Coll (GA)
Arkansas State U - Jonesboro (AR)
Armstrong Atlantic State U (GA)
Cameron U (OK)
Dalton State Coll (GA)
Fairmont State U (WV)
Ferris State U (MI)
Grambling State U (LA)
Husson U (ME)
Idaho State U (ID)
John Jay Coll of Criminal Justice of the City U of New York (NY)
Lake Superior State U (MI)
Miami U (OH)
Midland Coll (TX)
Missouri Southern State U (MO)
Monroe Coll, Bronx (NY)
Monroe Coll, New Rochelle (NY)
Northern Kentucky U (KY)
Northwestern State U of Louisiana (LA)
Pioneer Pacific Coll, Wilsonville (OR)
Rogers State U (OK)
Southeastern Louisiana U (LA)
Southern U and A&M Coll (LA)
State U of New York Coll of Technology at Canton (NY)
The U of Akron (OH)
U of Arkansas at Little Rock (AR)
U of Arkansas at Pine Bluff (AR)
U of Cincinnati (OH)
U of Louisiana at Monroe (LA)
U of New Haven (CT)
U of the District of Columbia (DC)
U of the Virgin Islands (VI)
The U of Toledo (OH)
Washburn U (KS)

Criminal Justice/ Safety
Amridge U (AL)
Andrew Jackson U (AL)
Arkansas Tech U (AR)
Ball State U (IN)
Bauder Coll (GA)
Bethel Coll (IN)
Cazenovia Coll (NY)
Central Christian Coll of Kansas (KS)
Central Pennsylvania Coll (PA)
Columbia Southern U (AL)
Columbus State U (GA)
Dixie State Coll of Utah (UT)
Eastern Nazarene Coll (MA)
Edinboro U of Pennsylvania (PA)
Fisher Coll (MA)
Gannon U (PA)
Grantham U (MO)
Husson U (ME)
Idaho State U (ID)
Indiana U East (IN)
Indiana U Kokomo (IN)
Indiana U Northwest (IN)
Indiana U–Purdue U Indianapolis (IN)
Indiana U South Bend (IN)
Indiana Wesleyan U (IN)
Kaplan U, Davenport Campus (IA)
Keystone Coll (PA)
King's Coll (PA)
Lourdes Coll (OH)
Madonna U (MI)
Manchester Coll (IN)
Missouri Western State U (MO)
Mountain State U (WV)
New Mexico State U (NM)
Northern Michigan U (MI)
Penn State Altoona (PA)
Pikeville Coll (KY)
St. Francis Coll (NY)
Shaw U (NC)
Southern Arkansas U–Magnolia (AR)
Southwest Florida Coll, Fort Myers (FL)
Sullivan U (KY)
Thomas Edison State Coll (NJ)
Thomas More Coll (KY)
U of Maine at Augusta (ME)
The U of Scranton (PA)
Xavier U (OH)
Youngstown State U (OH)

Criminology
Chaminade U of Honolulu (HI)
Dalton State Coll (GA)
Elizabethtown Coll (PA)
Faulkner U (AL)
Indiana U of Pennsylvania (PA)
Kwantlen Polytechnic U (BC, Canada)
Saint Joseph's U (PA)
U of the District of Columbia (DC)

Crop Production
U of Massachusetts Amherst (MA)

Culinary Arts
The Art Inst of Atlanta (GA)
The Art Inst of Austin (TX)
The Art Inst of California–Hollywood (CA)
The Art Inst of California–Inland Empire (CA)
The Art Inst of California–Los Angeles (CA)
The Art Inst of California–Orange County (CA)
The Art Inst of California–Sacramento (CA)
The Art Inst of California–San Diego (CA)
The Art Inst of California–San Francisco (CA)
The Art Inst of California–Sunnyvale (CA)
The Art Inst of Charleston (SC)
The Art Inst of Charlotte (NC)
The Art Inst of Colorado (CO)
The Art Inst of Dallas (TX)
The Art Inst of Fort Lauderdale (FL)
The Art Inst of Houston (TX)
The Art Inst of Indianapolis (IN)
The Art Inst of Jacksonville (FL)
The Art Inst of Las Vegas (NV)
The Art Inst of Michigan (MI)
The Art Inst of Philadelphia (PA)
The Art Inst of Phoenix (AZ)
The Art Inst of Pittsburgh (PA)
The Art Inst of Portland (OR)
The Art Inst of Raleigh-Durham (NC)
The Art Inst of Salt Lake City (UT)
The Art Inst of San Antonio (TX)
The Art Inst of Tampa (FL)
The Art Inst of Tennessee–Nashville (TN)
The Art Inst of Tucson (AZ)
The Art Inst of Vrigina Beach (VA)
The Art Inst of Washington (VA)
The Art Insts International–Kansas City (KS)
The Art Insts International Minnesota (MN)
Baker Coll of Muskegon (MI)
Bob Jones U (SC)
The Culinary Inst of America (NY)
Culinary Inst of Virginia (VA)
ECPI Coll of Technology, Virginia Beach (VA)
Florida Culinary Inst (FL)
Hickey Coll (MO)
Idaho State U (ID)
The Illinois Inst of Art–Chicago (IL)
Johnson & Wales U (CO)
Johnson & Wales U (FL)
Johnson & Wales U (RI)
Johnson & Wales U - Charlotte Campus (NC)
Keiser U, Fort Lauderdale (FL)
Kendall Coll (IL)
Keystone Coll (PA)
Monroe Coll, Bronx (NY)
Mountain State U (WV)
Newbury Coll (MA)
Nicholls State U (LA)
Oakland City U (IN)
Robert Morris U Illinois (IL)
St. Augustine Coll (IL)
Southern New Hampshire U (NH)
Stratford U, Woodbridge (VA)
Sullivan U (KY)
The U of Akron (OH)
U of Alaska Anchorage (AK)
U of Alaska Fairbanks (AK)
Utah Valley U (UT)

Culinary Arts Related
Delaware Valley Coll (PA)
Keystone Coll (PA)
New York Inst of Technology (NY)

Dairy Science
Vermont Tech Coll (VT)

Dance
Utah Valley U (UT)

Data Entry/Microcomputer Applications
Baker Coll of Allen Park (MI)
ECPI Tech Coll, Roanoke (VA)
Florida National Coll (FL)
The U of Akron (OH)

Data Entry/Microcomputer Applications Related
AIB Coll of Business (IA)
Baker Coll of Allen Park (MI)
Florida National Coll (FL)

Data Modeling/ Warehousing and Database Administration
Midland Coll (TX)

Data Processing and Data Processing Technology
Baker Coll of Auburn Hills (MI)
Baker Coll of Cadillac (MI)
Baker Coll of Clinton Township (MI)
Baker Coll of Flint (MI)
Baker Coll of Jackson (MI)
Baker Coll of Muskegon (MI)
Baker Coll of Owosso (MI)
Baker Coll of Port Huron (MI)
Campbellsville U (KY)
Dordt Coll (IA)
ECPI Coll of Technology, Virginia Beach (VA)
Farmingdale State Coll (NY)
Florida National Coll (FL)
Lamar U (TX)
Miami U (OH)
Montana State U Billings (MT)
Mount Vernon Nazarene U (OH)
New York City Coll of Technology of the City U of New York (NY)
New York Inst of Technology (NY)
Northern State U (SD)
Pace U (NY)
Peirce Coll (PA)
U of Cincinnati (OH)
The U of Toledo (OH)
Utah Valley U (UT)
Western Kentucky U (KY)
Wright State U (OH)
Youngstown State U (OH)

Dental Assisting
ECPI Coll of Technology, Virginia Beach (VA)
Lincoln Coll of New England, Southington (CT)
Thomas Edison State Coll (NJ)
U of Alaska Anchorage (AK)
U of Alaska Fairbanks (AK)
U of Southern Indiana (IN)

Dental Hygiene
Argosy U, Twin Cities (MN)
Armstrong Atlantic State U (GA)
Baker Coll of Port Huron (MI)
Coll of Coastal Georgia (GA)
Dalton State Coll (GA)
Dixie State Coll of Utah (UT)
Farmingdale State Coll (NY)
Ferris State U (MI)
Florida National Coll (FL)
Indiana U Northwest (IN)
Indiana U–Purdue U Fort Wayne (IN)
Indiana U–Purdue U Indianapolis (IN)
Indiana U South Bend (IN)
Lamar U (TX)
Missouri Southern State U (MO)
Mount Ida Coll (MA)
New York City Coll of Technology of the City U of New York (NY)
New York U (NY)
St. Petersburg Coll (FL)
Santa Fe Coll (FL)
Shawnee State U (OH)
Southern Adventist U (TN)
State U of New York Coll of Technology at Canton (NY)
Thomas Edison State Coll (NJ)
U of Alaska Anchorage (AK)
U of Alaska Fairbanks (AK)
U of Arkansas at Fort Smith (AR)
U of Bridgeport (CT)
U of Maine at Augusta (ME)
U of New England (ME)
U of New Haven (CT)
Utah Valley U (UT)
Vermont Tech Coll (VT)
Western Kentucky U (KY)
West Liberty U (WV)
Wichita State U (KS)
Youngstown State U (OH)

Dental Laboratory Technology
Idaho State U (ID)
Indiana U–Purdue U Fort Wayne (IN)
Louisiana State U Health Sciences Center (LA)
New York City Coll of Technology of the City U of New York (NY)

Dental Services and Allied Professions Related
Pennsylvania Coll of Technology (PA)
Valdosta State U (GA)

Design and Visual Communications
Academy of Art U (CA)
Collins Coll: A School of Design and Technology (AZ)
ITT Tech Inst, Tempe (AZ)
ITT Tech Inst, Clovis (CA)
ITT Tech Inst, Concord (CA)
ITT Tech Inst, South Bend (IN)
ITT Tech Inst (KS)
ITT Tech Inst, Lexington (KY)
ITT Tech Inst (MS)
ITT Tech Inst, Oklahoma City (OK)
Utah Valley U (UT)

Desktop Publishing and Digital Imaging Design
Academy of Art U (CA)
Ferris State U (MI)
Thompson Rivers U (BC, Canada)

Developmental and Child Psychology
Midland Coll (TX)

Diagnostic Medical Sonography and Ultrasound Technology
Argosy U, Twin Cities (MN)
Arkansas State U - Jonesboro (AR)
Baker Coll of Auburn Hills (MI)
Baker Coll of Owosso (MI)
Baker Coll of Port Huron (MI)
Ferris State U (MI)
Florida National Coll (FL)
Keiser U, Fort Lauderdale (FL)
Keystone Coll (PA)
Lincoln U (CA)
Mercy Coll of Health Sciences (IA)
Mountain State U (WV)
Nebraska Methodist Coll (NE)
St. Catherine U (MN)
Santa Fe Coll (FL)
The U of Texas at Brownsville (TX)

Diesel Mechanics Technology
Idaho State U (ID)
Lewis-Clark State Coll (ID)
Montana State U Billings (MT)
Pennsylvania Coll of Technology (PA)
U of Alaska Anchorage (AK)
Utah Valley U (UT)
Vermont Tech Coll (VT)
Weber State U (UT)

Dietetics
Life U (GA)
Lincoln Coll of New England, Southington (CT)
Oakwood U (AL)

Dietetic Technician
Youngstown State U (OH)

Dietitian Assistant
Penn State U Park (PA)
Pennsylvania Coll of Technology (PA)
Youngstown State U (OH)

Digital Communication and Media/Multimedia
Academy of Art U (CA)
Corcoran Coll of Art and Design (DC)

Indiana U–Purdue U Indianapolis (IN)
Jones International U (CO)
Platt Coll San Diego (CA)
Vaughn Coll of Aeronautics and Technology (NY)

Divinity/Ministry
Amridge U (AL)
Atlantic Union Coll (MA)
Carson-Newman Coll (TN)
Christian Life Coll (IL)
Clear Creek Baptist Bible Coll (KY)
Faith Baptist Bible Coll and Theological Seminary (IA)
Great Lakes Christian Coll (MI)
Mount Olive Coll (NC)
Providence Coll (RI)
Southeastern Baptist Theological Seminary (NC)
Victory U (TN)

Drafting and Design Technology
The Art Inst of Las Vegas (NV)
Baker Coll of Auburn Hills (MI)
Baker Coll of Clinton Township (MI)
Baker Coll of Owosso (MI)
Baker Coll of Port Huron (MI)
Black Hills State U (SD)
Dalton State Coll (GA)
Fairmont State U (WV)
Herzing U (WI)
Indiana U East (IN)
Kentucky State U (KY)
Lamar U (TX)
LeTourneau U (TX)
Lewis-Clark State Coll (ID)
Lincoln U (MO)
Midland Coll (TX)
Montana State U Billings (MT)
Montana Tech of The U of Montana (MT)
Murray State U (KY)
Pennsylvania Coll of Technology (PA)
Robert Morris U Illinois (IL)
St. Petersburg Coll (FL)
Southern Utah U (UT)
Thompson Rivers U (BC, Canada)
The U of Akron (OH)
U of Alaska Anchorage (AK)
U of Arkansas at Fort Smith (AR)
U of Cincinnati (OH)
U of Rio Grande (OH)
The U of Toledo (OH)
Utah State U (UT)
Utah Valley U (UT)
Washburn U (KS)
Weber State U (UT)
Wright State U (OH)
Youngstown State U (OH)

Drafting/Design Engineering Technologies Related
Pennsylvania Coll of Technology (PA)
Thomas Edison State Coll (NJ)

Drama and Dance Teacher Education
Central Christian Coll of Kansas (KS)

Dramatic/Theater Arts
Adams State Coll (CO)
Brigham Young U–Hawaii (HI)
Methodist U (NC)
Thomas More Coll (KY)
Utah Valley U (UT)
Young Harris Coll (GA)

Dramatic/Theater Arts and Stagecraft Related
Utah Valley U (UT)

Drawing
Midland Coll (TX)
Pratt Inst (NY)

Early Childhood Education
Adams State Coll (CO)
American Public U System (WV)
Baker Coll of Allen Park (MI)
Baker Coll of Jackson (MI)
Baptist Bible Coll of Pennsylvania (PA)
Bethel Coll (IN)
Coll of Saint Mary (NE)
Davis Coll (NY)
Dixie State Coll of Utah (UT)
Eastern Nazarene Coll (MA)
Gannon U (PA)
Granite State Coll (NH)
Great Lakes Christian Coll (MI)
Indiana U–Purdue U Fort Wayne (IN)
Indiana U–Purdue U Indianapolis (IN)
Indiana U South Bend (IN)
Keystone Coll (PA)
Lake Superior State U (MI)
Lincoln U (MO)
Lindsey Wilson Coll (KY)
Mitchell Coll (CT)
Nova Southeastern U (FL)
Oakland City U (IN)
Pennsylvania Coll of Technology (PA)
Point Park U (PA)
Presentation Coll (SD)
St. Augustine Coll (IL)
St. Petersburg Coll (FL)
Shasta Bible Coll (CA)
Southwestern Assemblies of God U (TX)
Southwest Florida Coll, Fort Myers (FL)
State U of New York Coll of Technology at Canton (NY)
Sullivan U (KY)
Taylor U (IN)
Texas Coll (TX)
Thompson Rivers U (BC, Canada)
U of Alaska Fairbanks (AK)
U of Arkansas at Fort Smith (AR)
U of Cincinnati (OH)
U of Great Falls (MT)
U of Southern Indiana (IN)
Utah Valley U (UT)
Valley Forge Christian Coll (PA)
Washburn U (KS)
Washington Adventist U (MD)

E-Commerce
Daymar Inst, Clarksville (TN)
Inter American U of Puerto Rico, Aguadilla Campus (PR)

Economics
Central Christian Coll of Kansas (KS)
Dalton State Coll (GA)
Hawai'i Pacific U (HI)
John Cabot U (Italy)
Methodist U (NC)
Midland Coll (TX)
State U of New York Empire State Coll (NY)
Strayer U - Akron Campus (OH)
Strayer U - Alexandria Campus (VA)
Strayer U - Allentown Campus (PA)
Strayer U - Anne Arundel Campus (MD)
Strayer U - Arlington Campus (VA)
Strayer U - Augusta Campus (GA)
Strayer U - Baymeadows Campus (FL)
Strayer U - Birmingham Campus (AL)
Strayer U - Brickell Campus (FL)
Strayer U - Center City Campus (PA)
Strayer U - Central Austin Campus (TX)
Strayer U - Chamblee Campus (GA)
Strayer U - Charleston Campus (SC)
Strayer U - Chesapeake Campus (VA)
Strayer U - Chesterfield Campus (VA)
Strayer U - Christiana Campus (DE)
Strayer U - Cobb County Campus (GA)
Strayer U - Columbia Campus (SC)
Strayer U - Columbus Campus (OH)
Strayer U - Coral Springs Campus (FL)
Strayer U - Cranberry Woods Campus (PA)
Strayer U - Delaware County Campus (PA)
Strayer U - Doral Campus (FL)
Strayer U - Douglasville Campus (GA)
Strayer U - Fairview Park Campus (OH)
Strayer U - Florence Campus (KY)
Strayer U - Fort Lauderdale Campus (FL)
Strayer U - Fredericksburg Campus (VA)
Strayer U - Garner Campus (NC)
Strayer U - Greensboro Campus (NC)
Strayer U - Greenville Campus (SC)
Strayer U - Henrico Campus (VA)
Strayer U - Huntersville Campus (NC)
Strayer U - Huntsville Campus (AL)
Strayer U - King of Prussia Campus (PA)
Strayer U - Knoxville Campus (TN)
Strayer U - Lexington Campus (KY)
Strayer U - Lithonia Campus (GA)
Strayer U - Loudoun Campus (VA)
Strayer U - Louisville Campus (KY)
Strayer U - Lower Bucks County Campus (PA)
Strayer U - Maitland Campus (FL)
Strayer U - Manassas Campus (VA)
Strayer U - Mason Campus (OH)
Strayer U - Metairie Campus (LA)
Strayer U - Miramar Campus (FL)
Strayer U - Morrow Campus (GA)
Strayer U - Nashville Campus (TN)
Strayer U - Newport News Campus (VA)
Strayer U - North Charlotte Campus (NC)
Strayer U - North Raleigh Campus (NC)
Strayer U - Orlando East Campus (FL)
Strayer U - Owings Mills Campus (MD)
Strayer U - Palm Beach Gardens Campus (FL)
Strayer U - Penn Center West Campus (PA)
Strayer U - Prince George's Campus (MD)
Strayer U - Rockville Campus (MD)
Strayer U - Roswell Campus (GA)
Strayer U - RTP Campus (NC)
Strayer U - Salt Lake Campus (UT)
Strayer U - Sand Lake Campus (FL)
Strayer U - Savannah Campus (GA)
Strayer U - Shelby Oaks Campus (TN)
Strayer U - South Charlotte Campus (NC)
Strayer U - Takoma Park Campus (DC)
Strayer U - Tampa East Campus (FL)
Strayer U - Tampa Westshore Campus (FL)
Strayer U - Teays Valley Campus (WV)
Strayer U - Thousand Oaks Campus (TN)
Strayer U - Virginia Beach Campus (VA)
Strayer U - Washington Campus (DC)
Strayer U - White Marsh Campus (MD)
Strayer U - Woodbridge Campus (VA)
Thomas More Coll (KY)
The U of Tampa (FL)

Education
Abraham Baldwin Ag Coll (GA)
Alabama State U (AL)
Baker Coll of Auburn Hills (MI)
Baker Coll of Cadillac (MI)
Central Baptist Coll (AR)
Cincinnati Christian U (OH)
Cumberland U (TN)
Dalton State Coll (GA)
Florida National Coll (FL)
Kent State U (OH)
Lamar U (TX)
Montana State U Billings (MT)
National U (CA)
Pontifical Catholic U of Puerto Rico (PR)
Saint Francis U (PA)
Southwestern Assemblies of God U (TX)
State U of New York Empire State Coll (NY)
Truett-McConnell Coll (GA)
U of Puerto Rico at Utuado (PR)
Villa Maria Coll of Buffalo (NY)
Young Harris Coll (GA)

Education (Multiple Levels)
Coll of Coastal Georgia (GA)
Keystone Coll (PA)
St. Cloud State U (MN)

Education Related
The U of Akron (OH)
Wayland Baptist U (TX)

Education (Specific Subject Areas) Related
Pennsylvania Coll of Technology (PA)

Electrical and Electronic Engineering Technologies Related
Inter American U of Puerto Rico, Aguadilla Campus (PR)
Lawrence Technological U (MI)
Miami U Hamilton (OH)
Pennsylvania Coll of Technology (PA)
Point Park U (PA)
Rochester Inst of Technology (NY)
Thomas Edison State Coll (NJ)
Vaughn Coll of Aeronautics and Technology (NY)
Youngstown State U (OH)

Electrical and Power Transmission Installation Related
Pennsylvania Coll of Technology (PA)

Electrical, Electronic and Communications Engineering Technology
Baker Coll of Cadillac (MI)
Baker Coll of Owosso (MI)
Bluefield State Coll (WV)
Bryant & Stratton Coll, Cleveland (OH)
Cameron U (OK)
Columbia Coll, Caguas (PR)
Dalton State Coll (GA)
DeVry Coll of New York (NY)
DeVry U, Phoenix (AZ)
DeVry U, Fremont (CA)
DeVry U, Long Beach (CA)
DeVry U, Pomona (CA)
DeVry U, Sherman Oaks (CA)
DeVry U, Westminster (CO)
DeVry U, Miramar (FL)
DeVry U, Orlando (FL)
DeVry U, Alpharetta (GA)
DeVry U, Decatur (GA)
DeVry U, Addison (IL)
DeVry U, Chicago (IL)
DeVry U, Tinley Park (IL)
DeVry U, Indianapolis (IN)
DeVry U, Edina (MN)
DeVry U, Kansas City (MO)
DeVry U (NV)
DeVry U, North Brunswick (NJ)
DeVry U, Charlotte (NC)
DeVry U, Columbus (OH)
DeVry U, Fort Washington (PA)
DeVry U, Houston (TX)
DeVry U, Irving (TX)
DeVry U, Federal Way (WA)
DeVry U Online (IL)
ECPI Coll of Technology, Virginia Beach (VA)
ECPI Tech Coll, Roanoke (VA)
Fairmont State U (WV)
Fort Valley State U (GA)
Grantham U (MO)
Hamilton Tech Coll (IA)
Herzing U (GA)
Herzing U (WI)
Idaho State U (ID)
Indiana State U (IN)
Indiana U–Purdue U Fort Wayne (IN)
Indiana U–Purdue U Indianapolis (IN)
Indiana U South Bend (IN)
Johnson & Wales U (RI)
Kentucky State U (KY)
Lake Superior State U (MI)
Lamar U (TX)
Lawrence Technological U (MI)
Michigan Technological U (MI)
Midland Coll (TX)
New York City Coll of Technology of the City U of New York (NY)
Northern Michigan U (MI)
Northwestern State U of Louisiana (LA)
Oregon Inst of Technology (OR)
Penn State Altoona (PA)
Penn State Berks (PA)
Penn State Erie, The Behrend Coll (PA)
Pittsburg State U (KS)
Purdue U Calumet (IN)
Purdue U North Central (IN)
Southern Utah U (UT)
State U of New York Coll of Technology at Canton (NY)
Thomas Edison State Coll (NJ)
The U of Akron (OH)
U of Alaska Anchorage (AK)
U of Arkansas at Little Rock (AR)
U of Cincinnati (OH)
U of Hartford (CT)
U of Massachusetts Lowell (MA)
U of Puerto Rico at Humacao (PR)
U of the District of Columbia (DC)
The U of Toledo (OH)
Utah Valley U (UT)
Vermont Tech Coll (VT)
Wright State U (OH)
Youngstown State U (OH)

Electrical, Electronics and Communications Engineering
Fairfield U (CT)
Southern California Inst of Technology (CA)
Thompson Rivers U (BC, Canada)

Electrical/Electronics Equipment Installation and Repair
Lewis-Clark State Coll (ID)
Thompson Rivers U (BC, Canada)
U of Arkansas at Fort Smith (AR)

Electrician
Pennsylvania Coll of Technology (PA)
Santa Fe Coll (FL)
Thompson Rivers U (BC, Canada)

Electrocardiograph Technology
Argosy U, Twin Cities (MN)

Electromechanical Technology
ECPI Coll of Technology, Virginia Beach (VA)
ECPI Tech Coll, Roanoke (VA)
Idaho State U (ID)
John Brown U (AR)
Michigan Technological U (MI)
New York City Coll of Technology of the City U of New York (NY)
Northern Michigan U (MI)
Purdue U Calumet (IN)
Shawnee State U (OH)
Utah Valley U (UT)
Wright State U (OH)

Electroneurodiagnostic/ Electroencephalographic Technology
DeVry U, North Brunswick (NJ)

Elementary Education
Abraham Baldwin Ag Coll (GA)
Adams State Coll (CO)
Alaska Pacific U (AK)
Central Christian Coll of Kansas (KS)
Dalton State Coll (GA)
Ferris State U (MI)
Hillsdale Free Will Baptist Coll (OK)
Indiana U East (IN)
Mountain State U (WV)
Mount St. Mary's Coll (CA)
New Mexico Highlands U (NM)
Rogers State U (OK)
Wilson Coll (PA)

Emergency Medical Technology (EMT Paramedic)
Baker Coll of Cadillac (MI)
Baker Coll of Clinton Township (MI)
Baker Coll of Muskegon (MI)
Creighton U (NE)
Dixie State Coll of Utah (UT)
EDP Coll of Puerto Rico, Inc. (PR)
EDP Coll of Puerto Rico–San Sebastian (PR)
Idaho State U (ID)
Indiana U–Purdue U Indianapolis (IN)
Indiana U South Bend (IN)
Jefferson Coll of Health Sciences (VA)
Mercy Coll of Health Sciences (IA)
Midland Coll (TX)
Missouri Western State U (MO)
Montana State U Billings (MT)
Mountain State U (WV)
Our Lady of the Lake Coll (LA)
Pennsylvania Coll of Technology (PA)
Rogers State U (OK)
St. Petersburg Coll (FL)
Santa Fe Coll (FL)
Shawnee State U (OH)
Southwest Baptist U (MO)
Spalding U (KY)
U of Alaska Anchorage (AK)
U of Pittsburgh at Johnstown (PA)
The U of Texas at Brownsville (TX)
The U of Toledo (OH)
Weber State U (UT)
Western Kentucky U (KY)
Youngstown State U (OH)

Energy Management and Systems Technology
Baker Coll of Flint (MI)
Idaho State U (ID)
Montana State U Billings (MT)

U of Cincinnati (OH)
U of Rio Grande (OH)

Engineering
Brescia U (KY)
Central Christian Coll of Kansas (KS)
Coll of Staten Island of the City U of New York (NY)
Dixie State Coll of Utah (UT)
Ferris State U (MI)
Geneva Coll (PA)
Lake Superior State U (MI)
Lindsey Wilson Coll (KY)
Mountain State U (WV)
Southern Adventist U (TN)
State U of New York Coll of Technology at Canton (NY)
Thompson Rivers U (BC, Canada)
Union Coll (NE)
Utah Valley U (UT)
Washington Adventist U (MD)

Engineering Related
McNally Smith Coll of Music (MN)

Engineering-Related Technologies
U of Alaska Southeast (AK)

Engineering Science
Merrimack Coll (MA)
Pennsylvania Coll of Technology (PA)
Rochester Inst of Technology (NY)
U of Cincinnati (OH)
U of Pittsburgh at Bradford (PA)

Engineering Technologies Related
Arkansas State U - Jonesboro (AR)
Cameron U (OK)
Keene State Coll (NH)
McNally Smith Coll of Music (MN)
Missouri Southern State U (MO)
Rogers State U (OK)
State U of New York Maritime Coll (NY)
U of Puerto Rico at Bayamón (PR)
Utah Valley U (UT)

Engineering Technology
Brescia U (KY)
ECPI Coll of Technology, Virginia Beach (VA)
ECPI Tech Coll, Roanoke (VA)
Excelsior Coll (NY)
Fairmont State U (WV)
John Brown U (AR)
Kansas State U (KS)
Lake Superior State U (MI)
McNeese State U (LA)
Miami U (OH)
Michigan Technological U (MI)
St. Cloud State U (MN)
St. Petersburg Coll (FL)
U of Alaska Anchorage (AK)
Youngstown State U (OH)

English
Abraham Baldwin Ag Coll (GA)
Calumet Coll of Saint Joseph (IN)
Coll of Coastal Georgia (GA)
Dalton State Coll (GA)
Felician Coll (NJ)
Hannibal-LaGrange Coll (MO)
Hillsdale Free Will Baptist Coll (OK)
Idaho State U (ID)
Indiana U–Purdue U Fort Wayne (IN)
Indiana Wesleyan U (IN)
Kwantlen Polytechnic U (BC, Canada)
Lourdes Coll (OH)
Madonna U (MI)
Manchester Coll (IN)
Methodist U (NC)
Midland Coll (TX)
Presentation Coll (SD)
Saint Joseph's U (PA)
Southwestern Assemblies of God U (TX)
Thomas More Coll (KY)
U of Dubuque (IA)
The U of Tampa (FL)
Utah Valley U (UT)
Xavier U (OH)
Young Harris Coll (GA)

English Composition
Kwantlen Polytechnic U (BC, Canada)

English Language and Literature Related
Presentation Coll (SD)

English/Language Arts Teacher Education
John Brown U (AR)

Entrepreneurship
Baker Coll of Flint (MI)
Central Pennsylvania Coll (PA)
Johnson & Wales U (CO)
Peirce Coll (PA)
U of the District of Columbia (DC)

Environmental Control Technologies Related
Montana Tech of The U of Montana (MT)
Pennsylvania Coll of Technology (PA)
Utah Valley U (UT)

Environmental Engineering Technology
Baker Coll of Flint (MI)
Baker Coll of Owosso (MI)
Baker Coll of Port Huron (MI)
New York City Coll of Technology of the City U of New York (NY)
U of Cincinnati (OH)
U of the District of Columbia (DC)
The U of Toledo (OH)

Environmental Science
Thomas Edison State Coll (NJ)

Environmental Studies
Central Christian Coll of Kansas (KS)
Columbia Coll (MO)
Dickinson State U (ND)
Mountain State U (WV)
Southern Vermont Coll (VT)
U of Cincinnati (OH)
U of Dubuque (IA)
The U of Findlay (OH)
The U of Toledo (OH)

Equestrian Studies
Centenary Coll (NJ)
Johnson & Wales U (RI)
Midway Coll (KY)
Post U (CT)
Saint Mary-of-the-Woods Coll (IN)
The U of Findlay (OH)
U of Massachusetts Amherst (MA)
The U of Montana Western (MT)

Executive Assistant/ Executive Secretary
Baker Coll of Allen Park (MI)
Baker Coll of Flint (MI)
Davenport U, Grand Rapids (MI)
Murray State U (KY)
Santa Fe Coll (FL)
Thompson Rivers U (BC, Canada)
U of Arkansas at Fort Smith (AR)
Western Kentucky U (KY)

Family and Community Services
Baker Coll of Flint (MI)
Central Christian Coll of Kansas (KS)

Family and Consumer Economics Related
Dalton State Coll (GA)
Fairmont State U (WV)

Family and Consumer Sciences/Human Sciences
Abraham Baldwin Ag Coll (GA)
Mount Vernon Nazarene U (OH)
U of Alaska Anchorage (AK)

Farm and Ranch Management
Abraham Baldwin Ag Coll (GA)
Johnson & Wales U (RI)

Fashion/Apparel Design
Academy of Art U (CA)
The Art Inst of California–Hollywood (CA)
The Art Inst of California–San Francisco (CA)
The Art Inst of Dallas (TX)
The Art Inst of Fort Lauderdale (FL)
The Art Inst of Philadelphia (PA)
The Art Inst of Portland (OR)
Bauder Coll (GA)
EDP Coll of Puerto Rico, Inc. (PR)
Fashion Inst of Technology (NY)
Fisher Coll (MA)
International Academy of Design & Technology (IL)
Keiser U, Fort Lauderdale (FL)
Miami International U of Art & Design (FL)
Parsons The New School for Design (NY)
Pontifical Catholic U of Puerto Rico (PR)

Fashion Merchandising
Abraham Baldwin Ag Coll (GA)
The Art Inst of California–Hollywood (CA)
The Art Inst of California–San Francisco (CA)
The Art Inst of Charlotte (NC)
The Art Inst of Michigan (MI)
The Art Inst of Raleigh-Durham (NC)
Bauder Coll (GA)
Fairmont State U (WV)
Fashion Inst of Technology (NY)
Fisher Coll (MA)
The Illinois Inst of Art–Chicago (IL)
International Academy of Design & Technology (IL)
Johnson & Wales U (CO)
Johnson & Wales U (FL)
Johnson & Wales U (RI)
Johnson & Wales U - Charlotte Campus (NC)
Keiser U, Fort Lauderdale (FL)
LIM Coll (NY)
Lincoln Coll of New England, Southington (CT)
Miami International U of Art & Design (FL)
New York City Coll of Technology of the City U of New York (NY)
Parsons The New School for Design (NY)
Patricia Stevens Coll (MO)
Southern New Hampshire U (NH)
U of Bridgeport (CT)
U of the District of Columbia (DC)
Weber State U (UT)

Fashion Modeling
Fashion Inst of Technology (NY)

Film/Cinema Studies
Burlington Coll (VT)

Film/Video and Photographic Arts Related
Northern Michigan U (MI)

Finance
AIB Coll of Business (IA)
Central Christian Coll of Kansas (KS)
Fairmont State U (WV)
Franklin U (OH)
Hawai'i Pacific U (HI)
Indiana Wesleyan U (IN)
Methodist U (NC)
New England Coll of Business (MA)
Saint Joseph's U (PA)
U of Cincinnati (OH)
The U of Findlay (OH)
Walsh U (OH)
Youngstown State U (OH)

Financial Planning and Services
U of Maine at Augusta (ME)

Fine Arts Related
Saint Francis U (PA)

Fine/Studio Arts
Academy of Art U (CA)
Adams State Coll (CO)
Corcoran Coll of Art and Design (DC)
Fashion Inst of Technology (NY)
Keystone Coll (PA)
Lindsey Wilson Coll (KY)
Madonna U (MI)
Manchester Coll (IN)
Midland Coll (TX)
New Mexico State U (NM)
Pennsylvania Coll of Technology (PA)
Pratt Inst (NY)
Thomas More Coll (KY)
U of Maine at Augusta (ME)
U of New Hampshire at Manchester (NH)
Villa Maria Coll of Buffalo (NY)
York Coll of Pennsylvania (PA)

Fire Protection and Safety Technology
Jefferson Coll of Health Sciences (VA)
Montana State U Billings (MT)
Santa Fe Coll (FL)
Thomas Edison State Coll (NJ)
The U of Akron (OH)
U of Nebraska–Lincoln (NE)
U of New Haven (CT)
The U of Toledo (OH)

Fire Protection Related
American Public U System (WV)
The U of Akron (OH)

Fire Science
American Public U System (WV)
Idaho State U (ID)
Keiser U, Fort Lauderdale (FL)
Lake Superior State U (MI)
Lamar U (TX)
Lewis-Clark State Coll (ID)
Madonna U (MI)
Midland Coll (TX)
Mountain State U (WV)
Providence Coll (RI)
St. Petersburg Coll (FL)
Santa Fe Coll (FL)
U of Alaska Anchorage (AK)
U of Alaska Fairbanks (AK)
U of Cincinnati (OH)
Utah Valley U (UT)
Vermont Tech Coll (VT)

Fire Services Administration
Columbia Coll (MO)
Columbia Southern U (AL)
Midland Coll (TX)

Fishing and Fisheries Sciences And Management
Abraham Baldwin Ag Coll (GA)

Food Preparation
Keystone Coll (PA)

Food Science
Lamar U (TX)
U of Puerto Rico at Utuado (PR)

Food Service and Dining Room Management
Johnson & Wales U (FL)
Johnson & Wales U - Charlotte Campus (NC)

Food Service Systems Administration
Inter American U of Puerto Rico, Aguadilla Campus (PR)
Murray State U (KY)
Northern Michigan U (MI)
U of New Hampshire (NH)
U of New Haven (CT)

Foods, Nutrition, and Wellness
Huntington Coll of Health Sciences (TN)
Madonna U (MI)
Southern Adventist U (TN)
U of Maine at Presque Isle (ME)

Food Technology and Processing
Arkansas State U - Jonesboro (AR)
U of the District of Columbia (DC)
Washburn U (KS)

Foreign Languages and Literatures
Coll of Coastal Georgia (GA)
Dalton State Coll (GA)
Midland Coll (TX)
Southwestern Assemblies of God U (TX)
The U of Tampa (FL)

Foreign Languages Related
U of Alaska Fairbanks (AK)

Forensic Science and Technology
Arkansas State U - Jonesboro (AR)
St. Petersburg Coll (FL)
U of Arkansas at Fort Smith (AR)
U of Arkansas at Monticello (AR)

Forestry
Abraham Baldwin Ag Coll (GA)
Coll of Coastal Georgia (GA)
Dalton State Coll (GA)
Keystone Coll (PA)
Thomas Edison State Coll (NJ)
U of Alaska Fairbanks (AK)
U of Maine at Fort Kent (ME)

Forestry Technology
Abraham Baldwin Ag Coll (GA)
Glenville State Coll (WV)
Keystone Coll (PA)
Michigan Technological U (MI)
Pennsylvania Coll of Technology (PA)
State U of New York Coll of Technology at Canton (NY)
U of Maine at Fort Kent (ME)
U of New Hampshire (NH)

French
Idaho State U (ID)
Indiana U–Purdue U Fort Wayne (IN)
Methodist U (NC)
Midland Coll (TX)
Thomas More Coll (KY)
The U of Tampa (FL)
Xavier U (OH)
Young Harris Coll (GA)

Funeral Service and Mortuary Science
Cincinnati Coll of Mortuary Science (OH)
Ferris State U (MI)
Lincoln Coll of New England, Southington (CT)
Mount Ida Coll (MA)
Point Park U (PA)
St. Petersburg Coll (FL)
State U of New York Coll of Technology at Canton (NY)

General Studies
AIB Coll of Business (IA)
Alderson-Broaddus Coll (WV)
Alverno Coll (WI)
American Public U System (WV)
Anderson U (IN)
Arkansas State U - Jonesboro (AR)
Arkansas Tech U (AR)
Asbury U (KY)
Atlanta Christian Coll (GA)
Averett U (VA)
Baptist Bible Coll of Pennsylvania (PA)
Barclay Coll (KS)
Belhaven U (MS)
Black Hills State U (SD)
Bob Jones U (SC)
Brewton-Parker Coll (GA)
Burlington Coll (VT)
Calumet Coll of Saint Joseph (IN)
Castleton State Coll (VT)
Central Baptist Coll (AR)
Chaminade U of Honolulu (HI)
City U of Seattle (WA)
Clearwater Christian Coll (FL)
Coll of Mount St. Joseph (OH)
Columbia Coll (MO)
Columbia Southern U (AL)
Concordia U (CA)
Concordia U, St. Paul (MN)
Concordia U Texas (TX)
Dakota State U (SD)
Dalton State Coll (GA)
Eastern Connecticut State U (CT)
Eastern Mennonite U (VA)
Ferris State U (MI)
Fisher Coll (MA)
Fort Hays State U (KS)
Franciscan U of Steubenville (OH)
Friends U (KS)
Great Lakes Christian Coll (MI)
Hillsdale Free Will Baptist Coll (OK)
Idaho State U (ID)
Indiana Tech (IN)
Indiana U East (IN)
Indiana U Kokomo (IN)
Indiana U Northwest (IN)
Indiana U of Pennsylvania (PA)
Indiana U–Purdue U Fort Wayne (IN)
Indiana U–Purdue U Indianapolis (IN)
Indiana U South Bend (IN)
Indiana U Southeast (IN)
Indiana Wesleyan U (IN)
Johnson State Coll (VT)
Keene State Coll (NH)
LaGrange Coll (GA)
La Salle U (PA)
Lawrence Technological U (MI)
Lebanon Valley Coll (PA)
Lincoln Coll of New England, Southington (CT)
Louisiana Tech U (LA)
McNeese State U (LA)
Mercy Coll of Northwest Ohio (OH)
Miami U (OH)
Miami U Hamilton (OH)
Mid-Continent U (KY)
Monmouth U (NJ)
Montana State U Billings (MT)
Morehead State U (KY)
Mount Aloysius Coll (PA)
Mount Marty Coll (SD)
Mount Vernon Nazarene U (OH)
Newbury Coll (MA)
New Mexico Inst of Mining and Technology (NM)
Nicholls State U (LA)
Northern Michigan U (MI)
Northwest Christian U (OR)
Northwestern State U of Louisiana (LA)
Northwest U (WA)
Nyack Coll (NY)

Oak Hills Christian Coll (MN)
Ohio Dominican U (OH)
The Ohio State U at Lima (OH)
Oklahoma Panhandle State U (OK)
Our Lady of the Lake Coll (LA)
Pennsylvania Coll of Technology (PA)
Presentation Coll (SD)
Regent U (VA)
St. Augustine Coll (IL)
Shawnee State U (OH)
Siena Heights U (MI)
Silver Lake Coll (WI)
Simpson U (CA)
South Dakota School of Mines and Technology (SD)
South Dakota State U (SD)
Southeastern Louisiana U (LA)
Southern Adventist U (TN)
Southern Arkansas U–Magnolia (AR)
Southern Wesleyan U (SC)
Southwest Baptist U (MO)
Southwestern Assemblies of God U (TX)
Strayer U - Alexandria Campus (VA)
Strayer U - Allentown Campus (PA)
Strayer U - Anne Arundel Campus (MD)
Strayer U - Arlington Campus (VA)
Strayer U - Augusta Campus (GA)
Strayer U - Baymeadows Campus (FL)
Strayer U - Birmingham Campus (AL)
Strayer U - Brickell Campus (FL)
Strayer U - Center City Campus (PA)
Strayer U - Central Austin Campus (TX)
Strayer U - Chamblee Campus (GA)
Strayer U - Charleston Campus (SC)
Strayer U - Chesapeake Campus (VA)
Strayer U - Chesterfield Campus (VA)
Strayer U - Christiana Campus (DE)
Strayer U - Cobb County Campus (GA)
Strayer U - Columbia Campus (SC)
Strayer U - Coral Springs Campus (FL)
Strayer U - Cranberry Woods Campus (PA)
Strayer U - Delaware County Campus (PA)
Strayer U - Doral Campus (FL)
Strayer U - Douglasville Campus (GA)
Strayer U - Florence Campus (KY)
Strayer U - Fort Lauderdale Campus (FL)
Strayer U - Fredericksburg Campus (VA)
Strayer U - Garner Campus (NC)
Strayer U - Greensboro Campus (NC)
Strayer U - Greenville Campus (SC)
Strayer U - Henrico Campus (VA)
Strayer U - Huntersville Campus (NC)
Strayer U - Huntsville Campus (AL)
Strayer U - King of Prussia Campus (PA)
Strayer U - Knoxville Campus (TN)
Strayer U - Lexington Campus (KY)
Strayer U - Lithonia Campus (GA)
Strayer U - Loudoun Campus (VA)
Strayer U - Louisville Campus (KY)
Strayer U - Lower Bucks County Campus (PA)
Strayer U - Maitland Campus (FL)
Strayer U - Manassas Campus (VA)
Strayer U - Metairie Campus (LA)
Strayer U - Miramar Campus (FL)
Strayer U - Morrow Campus (GA)
Strayer U - Nashville Campus (TN)
Strayer U - Newport News Campus (VA)
Strayer U - North Charlotte Campus (NC)
Strayer U - North Raleigh Campus (NC)
Strayer U - Orlando East Campus (FL)
Strayer U - Owings Mills Campus (MD)
Strayer U - Palm Beach Gardens Campus (FL)
Strayer U - Penn Center West Campus (PA)
Strayer U - Prince George's Campus (MD)
Strayer U - Rockville Campus (MD)
Strayer U - Roswell Campus (GA)
Strayer U - RTP Campus (NC)
Strayer U - Salt Lake Campus (UT)
Strayer U - Sand Lake Campus (FL)
Strayer U - Savannah Campus (GA)
Strayer U - Shelby Oaks Campus (TN)
Strayer U - South Charlotte Campus (NC)
Strayer U - Takoma Park Campus (DC)
Strayer U - Tampa East Campus (FL)
Strayer U - Tampa Westshore Campus (FL)
Strayer U - Teays Valley Campus (WV)
Strayer U - Thousand Oaks Campus (TN)
Strayer U - Virginia Beach Campus (VA)
Strayer U - Washington Campus (DC)
Strayer U - White Marsh Campus (MD)
Strayer U - Woodbridge Campus (VA)
Temple U (PA)
Texas Coll (TX)
Thompson Rivers U (BC, Canada)
Tiffin U (OH)
Trevecca Nazarene U (TN)
Trinity Coll of Florida (FL)
Truett-McConnell Coll (GA)
U of Alaska Fairbanks (AK)
U of Alaska Southeast (AK)
U of Arkansas at Fort Smith (AR)
U of Arkansas at Little Rock (AR)
U of Bridgeport (CT)
U of La Verne (CA)
U of Louisiana at Monroe (LA)
U of Maine at Fort Kent (ME)
U of Mobile (AL)
The U of Montana Western (MT)
U of New Haven (CT)
U of North Florida (FL)
U of Rio Grande (OH)
The U of Toledo (OH)
U of Wisconsin–Superior (WI)
Utah State U (UT)
Utah Valley U (UT)
Viterbo U (WI)
Western Kentucky U (KY)
Widener U (PA)
York Coll of Pennsylvania (PA)

Geography
Dalton State Coll (GA)
Kwantlen Polytechnic U (BC, Canada)
Wright State U (OH)

Geography Related
Adams State Coll (CO)

Geological and Earth Sciences/Geosciences Related
Kwantlen Polytechnic U (BC, Canada)
Utah Valley U (UT)

Geology/Earth Science
Coll of Coastal Georgia (GA)
Dalton State Coll (GA)
Idaho State U (ID)
Midland Coll (TX)
Young Harris Coll (GA)

German
Idaho State U (ID)
Indiana U–Purdue U Fort Wayne (IN)
Methodist U (NC)
Midland Coll (TX)
Xavier U (OH)

Gerontology
Madonna U (MI)
Manchester Coll (IN)
Ohio Dominican U (OH)
Siena Heights U (MI)
Thomas Edison State Coll (NJ)
Thomas More Coll (KY)
The U of Toledo (OH)

Graphic and Printing Equipment Operation/Production
Chowan U (NC)
Fairmont State U (WV)
Idaho State U (ID)
Lewis-Clark State Coll (ID)

Graphic Design
Academy of Art U (CA)
The Art Inst of Atlanta (GA)
The Art Inst of Atlanta–Decatur (GA)
The Art Inst of Austin (TX)
The Art Inst of California–Hollywood (CA)
The Art Inst of California–Inland Empire (CA)
The Art Inst of California–Los Angeles (CA)
The Art Inst of California–Orange County (CA)
The Art Inst of California–Sacramento (CA)
The Art Inst of California–San Diego (CA)
The Art Inst of California–San Francisco (CA)
The Art Inst of California–Sunnyvale (CA)
The Art Inst of Charleston (SC)
The Art Inst of Charlotte (NC)
The Art Inst of Colorado (CO)
The Art Inst of Dallas (TX)
The Art Inst of Fort Lauderdale (FL)
The Art Inst of Fort Worth (TX)
The Art Inst of Houston (TX)
The Art Inst of Houston - North (TX)
The Art Inst of Indianapolis (IN)
The Art Inst of Jacksonville (FL)
The Art Inst of Michigan (MI)
The Art Inst of Philadelphia (PA)
The Art Inst of Phoenix (AZ)
The Art Inst of Pittsburgh (PA)
The Art Inst of Portland (OR)
The Art Inst of Raleigh-Durham (NC)
The Art Inst of Salt Lake City (UT)
The Art Inst of San Antonio (TX)
The Art Inst of Tampa (FL)
The Art Inst of Tennessee–Nashville (TN)
The Art Inst of Tucson (AZ)
The Art Inst of Virginia Beach (VA)
The Art Inst of Washington (VA)
The Art Inst of Washington–Northern Virginia (VA)
The Art Insts International–Kansas City (KS)
The Art Insts International Minnesota (MN)
Bauder Coll (GA)
Bryant & Stratton Coll - Wauwatosa Campus (WI)
Coll of Mount St. Joseph (OH)
Collins Coll: A School of Design and Technology (AZ)
Corcoran Coll of Art and Design (DC)
Ferris State U (MI)
Hickey Coll (MO)
The Illinois Inst of Art–Chicago (IL)
The Illinois Inst of Art–Schaumburg (IL)
Keystone Coll (PA)
Madonna U (MI)
Mountain State U (WV)
Parsons The New School for Design (NY)
Platt Coll San Diego (CA)
Pratt Inst (NY)
Southern Adventist U (TN)
South U, Columbia (SC)
Southwest Florida Coll, Fort Myers (FL)
Thompson Rivers U (BC, Canada)
Union Coll (NE)
U of Arkansas at Fort Smith (AR)
Villa Maria Coll of Buffalo (NY)
Westwood Coll–Anaheim (CA)
Westwood Coll–Annandale Campus (VA)
Westwood Coll–Arlington Ballston Campus (VA)
Westwood Coll–Atlanta Midtown (GA)
Westwood Coll–Chicago Du Page (IL)
Westwood Coll–Chicago Loop Campus (IL)
Westwood Coll–Chicago O'Hare Airport (IL)
Westwood Coll–Chicago River Oaks (IL)
Westwood Coll–Fort Worth (TX)
Westwood Coll–Inland Empire (CA)
Westwood Coll–Los Angeles (CA)
Westwood Coll–Online Campus (CO)

Hazardous Materials Information Systems Technology
American Public U System (WV)

Health and Medical Administrative Services Related
Kent State U (OH)

Health and Physical Education
Central Christian Coll of Kansas (KS)
Coll of Coastal Georgia (GA)
Mount Vernon Nazarene U (OH)
Robert Morris U Illinois (IL)
Utah Valley U (UT)

Health and Physical Education Related
Pennsylvania Coll of Technology (PA)
Thomas Edison State Coll (NJ)

Health/Health-Care Administration
Baker Coll of Auburn Hills (MI)
Baker Coll of Flint (MI)
Brookline Coll, Phoenix (AZ)
Brookline Coll, Tempe (AZ)
Brookline Coll, Tucson (AZ)
Brookline Coll (NM)
ECPI Coll of Technology, Virginia Beach (VA)
ECPI Tech Coll, Roanoke (VA)
Methodist U (NC)
Park U (MO)
Pioneer Pacific Coll, Clackamas (OR)
Pioneer Pacific Coll, Wilsonville (OR)
Pioneer Pacific Coll–Eugene/Springfield Branch (OR)
The U of Scranton (PA)
Washburn U (KS)

Health Information/Medical Records Administration
Baker Coll of Auburn Hills (MI)
Baker Coll of Cadillac (MI)
Baker Coll of Clinton Township (MI)
Baker Coll of Flint (MI)
Baker Coll of Jackson (MI)
Baker Coll of Port Huron (MI)
Boise State U (ID)
Charles Drew U of Medicine and Science (CA)
Dalton State Coll (GA)
Daymar Inst, Clarksville (TN)
ECPI Coll of Technology, Virginia Beach (VA)
ECPI Tech Coll, Roanoke (VA)
Fairmont State U (WV)
Inter American U of Puerto Rico, San Germán Campus (PR)
Keiser U, Fort Lauderdale (FL)
Lincoln Coll of New England, Southington (CT)
Montana State U Billings (MT)
Park U (MO)
Pennsylvania Coll of Technology (PA)
St. Petersburg Coll (FL)
Santa Fe Coll (FL)
Universidad Adventista de las Antillas (PR)
U of Cincinnati (OH)

Health Information/Medical Records Technology
Baker Coll of Flint (MI)
Baker Coll of Jackson (MI)
Charles Drew U of Medicine and Science (CA)
Dakota State U (SD)
Davenport U, Grand Rapids (MI)
DeVry U, Long Beach (CA)
DeVry U, Pomona (CA)
DeVry U, Sherman Oaks (CA)
DeVry U, Alpharetta (GA)
DeVry U, Decatur (GA)
DeVry U, Chicago (IL)
DeVry U, North Brunswick (NJ)
DeVry U, Columbus (OH)
DeVry U, Fort Washington (PA)
DeVry U, Houston (TX)
DeVry U, Irving (TX)
DeVry U Online (IL)
Ferris State U (MI)
Fisher Coll (MA)
Gwynedd-Mercy Coll (PA)
Hodges U (FL)
Idaho State U (ID)
Indiana U Northwest (IN)
Indiana U Southeast (IN)
Louisiana Tech U (LA)
Mercy Coll of Northwest Ohio (OH)
Midland Coll (TX)
Missouri Western State U (MO)
Molloy Coll (NY)
Northern Michigan U (MI)
Pennsylvania Coll of Technology (PA)
St. Catherine U (MN)
Santa Fe Coll (FL)
Southwest Florida Coll, Fort Myers (FL)
Washburn U (KS)
Weber State U (UT)
Western Kentucky U (KY)

Health/Medical Preparatory Programs Related
Ohio Valley U (WV)
Union Coll (NE)

Health Professions Related
Arkansas Tech U (AR)
Fisher Coll (MA)
Lock Haven U of Pennsylvania (PA)
National U (CA)
Newman U (KS)
New York U (NY)
Northwest U (WA)
Point Park U (PA)
Presentation Coll (SD)
South U (AL)
Thomas Edison State Coll (NJ)
Thompson Rivers U (BC, Canada)
Union Coll (NE)
U of Alaska Southeast (AK)
U of Hartford (CT)
Villa Maria Coll of Buffalo (NY)

Health Services Administration
Keiser U, Fort Lauderdale (FL)

Health Services/Allied Health/Health Sciences
Fisher Coll (MA)
Florida National Coll (FL)
Howard Payne U (TX)
Immaculata U (PA)
Lindsey Wilson Coll (KY)
Pennsylvania Coll of Technology (PA)
U of Hartford (CT)

Health Teacher Education
Central Christian Coll of Kansas (KS)
Young Harris Coll (GA)

Heating, Air Conditioning and Refrigeration Technology
Ferris State U (MI)
Northern Michigan U (MI)
Oakland City U (IN)
State U of New York Coll of Technology at Canton (NY)
U of Cincinnati (OH)
Utah Valley U (UT)

Heating, Air Conditioning, Ventilation and Refrigeration Maintenance Technology
Lamar U (TX)
Lewis-Clark State Coll (ID)
Midland Coll (TX)
Montana State U Billings (MT)
Oakland City U (IN)
Santa Fe Coll (FL)
U of Alaska Anchorage (AK)
U of Cincinnati (OH)
Utah Valley U (UT)

Heavy Equipment Maintenance Technology
Ferris State U (MI)
Pennsylvania Coll of Technology (PA)
U of Alaska Anchorage (AK)

Heavy/Industrial Equipment Maintenance Technologies Related
Pennsylvania Coll of Technology (PA)

Histologic Technician
Indiana U–Purdue U Indianapolis (IN)
Keiser U, Fort Lauderdale (FL)
Northern Michigan U (MI)
The U of Akron (OH)

Histologic Technology/Histotechnologist
Argosy U, Twin Cities (MN)
Tarleton State U (TX)

History
Abraham Baldwin Ag Coll (GA)
American Public U System (WV)
Central Christian Coll of Kansas (KS)
Coll of Coastal Georgia (GA)
Dalton State Coll (GA)
Felician Coll (NJ)
Idaho State U (ID)
Indiana U–Purdue U Fort Wayne (IN)
Indiana Wesleyan U (IN)
John Brown U (AR)
Kwantlen Polytechnic U (BC, Canada)
Lindsey Wilson Coll (KY)
Lourdes Coll (OH)
Methodist U (NC)
Midland Coll (TX)
Regent U (VA)
Rogers State U (OK)
State U of New York Empire State Coll (NY)
Thomas More Coll (KY)
U of Rio Grande (OH)
The U of Tampa (FL)
Utah Valley U (UT)
Wright State U (OH)
Xavier U (OH)
Young Harris Coll (GA)

History Related
American Public U System (WV)

History Teacher Education
Central Christian Coll of Kansas (KS)

Horticultural Science
Abraham Baldwin Ag Coll (GA)
Andrews U (MI)
U of Connecticut (CT)
U of Puerto Rico at Utuado (PR)

Hospitality Administration
American Public U System (WV)
Baker Coll of Flint (MI)
Baker Coll of Owosso (MI)
Florida National Coll (FL)
The Illinois Inst of Art–Chicago (IL)
Johnson & Wales U (FL)
Kaplan U, Davenport Campus (IA)
Lewis-Clark State Coll (ID)
Lexington Coll (IL)
Monroe Coll, Bronx (NY)
Monroe Coll, New Rochelle (NY)
Pennsylvania Coll of Technology (PA)
St. Petersburg Coll (FL)
The U of Akron (OH)
U of the District of Columbia (DC)
Utah Valley U (UT)
Webber International U (FL)
Western Kentucky U (KY)
Young Harris Coll (GA)
Youngstown State U (OH)

Hospitality Administration Related
Penn State Berks (PA)
Penn State U Park (PA)
Purdue U (IN)
Purdue U Calumet (IN)

Hospitality and Recreation Marketing
AIB Coll of Business (IA)
Johnson & Wales U (RI)
Thompson Rivers U (BC, Canada)

Hotel/Motel Administration
Baker Coll of Muskegon (MI)
Baker Coll of Owosso (MI)
Baker Coll of Port Huron (MI)
Inter American U of Puerto Rico, Fajardo Campus (PR)
Johnson & Wales U (FL)
Johnson & Wales U (RI)
Johnson & Wales U - Charlotte Campus (NC)
Stratford U, Woodbridge (VA)
Thompson Rivers U (BC, Canada)
The U of Akron (OH)
U of the Virgin Islands (VI)

Human Development and Family Studies
Amridge U (AL)
Penn State Abington (PA)
Penn State Altoona (PA)
Penn State Berks (PA)
Penn State Erie, The Behrend Coll (PA)
Penn State U Park (PA)
State U of New York Empire State Coll (NY)
Syracuse U (NY)

Human Development and Family Studies Related
The U of Toledo (OH)
Utah State U (UT)

Humanities
Abraham Baldwin Ag Coll (GA)
Coll of the Humanities and Sciences, Harrison Middleton U (AZ)
Faulkner U (AL)
Felician Coll (NJ)
Fisher Coll (MA)
Holy Apostles Coll and Seminary (CT)
Indiana U South Bend (IN)
John Cabot U (Italy)
Michigan Technological U (MI)
Newbury Coll (MA)
Ohio U (OH)
Shawnee State U (OH)
State U of New York Empire State Coll (NY)
Thomas More Coll (KY)
U of Alaska Southeast (AK)
U of Cincinnati (OH)
The U of Findlay (OH)
U of Puerto Rico at Bayamón (PR)
Utah Valley U (UT)
Valparaiso U (IN)
Washburn U (KS)

Human Resources Development
Park U (MO)

Human Resources Management
Alvernia U (PA)
Baker Coll of Owosso (MI)
Central Christian Coll of Kansas (KS)
King's Coll (PA)
Montana State U Billings (MT)
Mountain State U (WV)
Peirce Coll (PA)
Regent U (VA)
U of Alaska Fairbanks (AK)
The U of Findlay (OH)

Human Resources Management and Services Related
American Public U System (WV)
Bryant & Stratton Coll, Cleveland (OH)
Bryant & Stratton Coll - Wauwatosa Campus (WI)

Human Services
Baker Coll of Clinton Township (MI)
Baker Coll of Flint (MI)
Baker Coll of Muskegon (MI)
Beacon Coll (FL)
Bethel Coll (IN)
Brescia U (KY)
Cazenovia Coll (NY)
Coll of St. Joseph (VT)
Columbia Coll (MO)
Edinboro U of Pennsylvania (PA)
Elizabethtown Coll (PA)
Indiana U East (IN)
Kendall Coll (IL)
Mercy Coll (NY)
Mount Vernon Nazarene U (OH)
New York City Coll of Technology of the City U of New York (NY)
Southern Vermont Coll (VT)
State U of New York Empire State Coll (NY)
Thomas Edison State Coll (NJ)
U of Alaska Anchorage (AK)
U of Cincinnati (OH)
U of Great Falls (MT)
U of Maine at Augusta (ME)
U of Maine at Fort Kent (ME)
The U of Scranton (PA)
Walsh U (OH)
Wayland Baptist U (TX)

Hydrology and Water Resources Science
Lake Superior State U (MI)
U of the District of Columbia (DC)

Illustration
Academy of Art U (CA)
Fashion Inst of Technology (NY)
Pratt Inst (NY)

Industrial Arts
Austin Peay State U (TN)
Dalton State Coll (GA)
U of Cincinnati (OH)
Weber State U (UT)

Industrial Design
Academy of Art U (CA)
The Art Inst of Pittsburgh (PA)
Northern Michigan U (MI)
Oakland City U (IN)

Industrial Electronics Technology
Dalton State Coll (GA)
EDP Coll of Puerto Rico, Inc. (PR)
Ferris State U (MI)
Lewis-Clark State Coll (ID)
Pennsylvania Coll of Technology (PA)
Thompson Rivers U (BC, Canada)

Industrial Engineering
Indiana Tech (IN)
The U of Toledo (OH)

Industrial Mechanics and Maintenance Technology
Dalton State Coll (GA)
Northern Michigan U (MI)
Pennsylvania Coll of Technology (PA)
U of Arkansas at Monticello (AR)

Industrial Production Technologies Related
Austin Peay State U (TN)
Ferris State U (MI)
U of Alaska Fairbanks (AK)

Industrial Radiologic Technology
Baker Coll of Owosso (MI)
The George Washington U (DC)
Lamar U (TX)
Our Lady of the Lake Coll (LA)
U of Cincinnati (OH)
U of the District of Columbia (DC)
Widener U (PA)

Industrial Technology
Arkansas Tech U (AR)
Baker Coll of Muskegon (MI)
Dalton State Coll (GA)
Edinboro U of Pennsylvania (PA)
Fairmont State U (WV)
Indiana U–Purdue U Fort Wayne (IN)
Kansas State U (KS)
Kent State U (OH)
Millersville U of Pennsylvania (PA)
Morehead State U (KY)
Oklahoma Panhandle State U (OK)
Purdue U Calumet (IN)
Purdue U North Central (IN)
St. Petersburg Coll (FL)
Southeastern Louisiana U (LA)
Southern Arkansas U–Magnolia (AR)
Trine U (IN)
U of Arkansas at Pine Bluff (AR)
U of Cincinnati (OH)
U of Puerto Rico at Bayamón (PR)
U of Rio Grande (OH)
The U of Toledo (OH)
Washburn U (KS)
Wright State U (OH)

Information Science/Studies
Baker Coll of Clinton Township (MI)
Baker Coll of Owosso (MI)
Beacon Coll (FL)
Calumet Coll of Saint Joseph (IN)
Campbellsville U (KY)
Dalton State Coll (GA)
ECPI Coll of Technology, Virginia Beach (VA)
ECPI Tech Coll, Roanoke (VA)
Elizabethtown Coll (PA)
Fairmont State U (WV)
Farmingdale State Coll (NY)
Faulkner U (AL)
Goldey-Beacom Coll (DE)
Grantham U (MO)
Herzing U (GA)
Husson U (ME)
Immaculata U (PA)
Indiana U–Purdue U Fort Wayne (IN)
Johnson State Coll (VT)
Mansfield U of Pennsylvania (PA)
Mount Olive Coll (NC)
Newman U (KS)
New York City Coll of Technology of the City U of New York (NY)
Oakland City U (IN)
Oakwood U (AL)
Oklahoma Wesleyan U (OK)
Pace U (NY)
Penn State Abington (PA)
Penn State Altoona (PA)
Penn State Berks (PA)
Penn State Erie, The Behrend Coll (PA)
Penn State U Park (PA)
Pioneer Pacific Coll, Wilsonville (OR)
Rivier Coll (NH)
Saint Joseph's U (PA)
Southern Utah U (UT)
Southwestern Adventist U (TX)
State U of New York Coll of Technology at Canton (NY)
Tulane U (LA)
Union Coll (NE)
U of Alaska Anchorage (AK)
U of Cincinnati (OH)
U of Pittsburgh at Bradford (PA)
The U of Scranton (PA)
The U of Toledo (OH)

Information Technology
AIB Coll of Business (IA)
Arkansas Tech U (AR)
Bryant & Stratton Coll, Cleveland (OH)
Cameron U (OK)
Collins Coll: A School of Design and Technology (AZ)
Ferris State U (MI)
Franklin U (OH)
International Academy of Design & Technology (IL)
Kaplan U, Davenport Campus (IA)
Kaplan U, Mason City Campus (IA)
Keiser U, Fort Lauderdale (FL)
Keystone Coll (PA)
McNeese State U (LA)
Mercy Coll (NY)
Monroe Coll, Bronx (NY)
Pennsylvania Coll of Technology (PA)
Point Park U (PA)
Pontifical Catholic U of Puerto Rico (PR)
Regent U (VA)
South U (AL)
South U, Royal Palm Beach (FL)
South U (GA)
South U, Columbia (SC)
Sullivan U (KY)
Thomas More Coll (KY)
Tiffin U (OH)
Trevecca Nazarene U (TN)
U of Massachusetts Lowell (MA)
Vermont Tech Coll (VT)
Westwood Coll–Annandale Campus (VA)
Westwood Coll–Arlington Ballston Campus (VA)
Westwood Coll–Atlanta Midtown (GA)
Westwood Coll–Atlanta Northlake (GA)
Westwood Coll–Chicago Du Page (IL)
Westwood Coll–Chicago Loop Campus (IL)
Westwood Coll–Chicago O'Hare Airport (IL)
Westwood Coll–Chicago River Oaks (IL)
Westwood Coll–Dallas (TX)
Westwood Coll–Denver North (CO)
Westwood Coll–Fort Worth (TX)
Westwood Coll–Inland Empire (CA)
Westwood Coll–Los Angeles (CA)
Westwood Coll–Online Campus (CO)
Youngstown State U (OH)

Institutional Food Workers
Fairmont State U (WV)
Kendall Coll (IL)
Pennsylvania Coll of Technology (PA)

Instrumentation Technology
Idaho State U (ID)
Pennsylvania Coll of Technology (PA)
U of Puerto Rico at Bayamón (PR)

Insurance
U of Cincinnati (OH)

Intercultural/Multicultural and Diversity Studies
Immaculata U (PA)

Interdisciplinary Studies
Kansas State U (KS)
Kaplan U, Davenport Campus (IA)
Kaplan U, Mason City Campus (IA)
Lesley U (MA)
State U of New York Empire State Coll (NY)
Suffolk U (MA)
Tabor Coll (KS)

Interior Architecture
U of New Haven (CT)
Villa Maria Coll of Buffalo (NY)

Interior Design
Academy of Art U (CA)
The Art Inst of Charlotte (NC)
The Art Inst of Colorado (CO)
The Art Inst of Dallas (TX)
The Art Inst of Fort Lauderdale (FL)
The Art Inst of Philadelphia (PA)
The Art Inst of Pittsburgh (PA)
The Art Insts International Minnesota (MN)
Baker Coll of Allen Park (MI)
Baker Coll of Auburn Hills (MI)
Baker Coll of Clinton Township (MI)
Baker Coll of Muskegon (MI)
Baker Coll of Owosso (MI)
Baker Coll of Port Huron (MI)
Bauder Coll (GA)
Chaminade U of Honolulu (HI)
Coll of Mount St. Joseph (OH)
Fairmont State U (WV)
Fashion Inst of Technology (NY)
Harrington Coll of Design (IL)
Indiana U–Purdue U Fort Wayne (IN)
Interior Designers Inst (CA)
International Academy of Design & Technology (IL)
New York School of Interior Design (NY)
Parsons The New School for Design (NY)
Patricia Stevens Coll (MO)
Robert Morris U Illinois (IL)
Southern Utah U (UT)
Southwest Florida Coll, Fort Myers (FL)
Weber State U (UT)

Intermedia/Multimedia
The Art Inst of Atlanta (GA)
International Academy of Design & Technology (IL)
Platt Coll San Diego (CA)

International Business/Trade/Commerce
Potomac Coll (DC)
Regent U (VA)
Utah Valley U (UT)
Young Harris Coll (GA)

International/Global Studies
Thomas More Coll (KY)

International Relations and Affairs
American Public U System (WV)
John Cabot U (Italy)

Italian Studies
John Cabot U (Italy)

Japanese
Idaho State U (ID)

Jazz/Jazz Studies
Five Towns Coll (NY)
Villa Maria Coll of Buffalo (NY)

Journalism
Abraham Baldwin Ag Coll (GA)
Dalton State Coll (GA)
Indiana U Southeast (IN)
Madonna U (MI)
Manchester Coll (IN)
Midland Coll (TX)
Young Harris Coll (GA)

Journalism Related
Adams State Coll (CO)

Kindergarten/Preschool Education
Abraham Baldwin Ag Coll (GA)
Atlantic Union Coll (MA)
Baker Coll of Clinton Township (MI)
Baker Coll of Muskegon (MI)
Baker Coll of Owosso (MI)
Central Christian Coll of Kansas (KS)
Eastern Nazarene Coll (MA)
Fisher Coll (MA)
Indiana U–Purdue U Indianapolis (IN)
Keystone Coll (PA)
Manchester Coll (IN)
Maranatha Baptist Bible Coll (WI)
Maria Coll (NY)
Miami U (OH)
Mid-Atlantic Christian U (NC)
Mount Aloysius Coll (PA)
Mount St. Mary's Coll (CA)
Pacific Union Coll (CA)
Patten U (CA)
Piedmont Baptist Coll and Graduate School (NC)
Rivier Coll (NH)
U of Great Falls (MT)
The U of Montana Western (MT)

U of Rio Grande (OH)
Villa Maria Coll of Buffalo (NY)
Western Kentucky U (KY)
Wilmington U (DE)

Kinesiology and Exercise Science
Central Christian Coll of Kansas (KS)
Manchester Coll (IN)
Thomas More Coll (KY)

Labor and Industrial Relations
Indiana U Kokomo (IN)
Indiana U–Purdue U Indianapolis (IN)
Indiana U Southeast (IN)
Rider U (NJ)
State U of New York Empire State Coll (NY)
Youngstown State U (OH)

Labor Studies
Indiana U Kokomo (IN)
Indiana U Northwest (IN)
Indiana U–Purdue U Fort Wayne (IN)
Indiana U South Bend (IN)

Landscape Architecture
Keystone Coll (PA)

Landscaping and Groundskeeping
Abraham Baldwin Ag Coll (GA)
Farmingdale State Coll (NY)
North Carolina State U (NC)
Pennsylvania Coll of Technology (PA)
U of Massachusetts Amherst (MA)
Vermont Tech Coll (VT)

Laser and Optical Technology
Idaho State U (ID)
Pennsylvania Coll of Technology (PA)

Latin
Idaho State U (ID)

Legal Administrative Assistant/Secretary
Baker Coll of Auburn Hills (MI)
Baker Coll of Clinton Township (MI)
Baker Coll of Flint (MI)
Baker Coll of Jackson (MI)
Baker Coll of Muskegon (MI)
Baker Coll of Owosso (MI)
Baker Coll of Port Huron (MI)
Bryant & Stratton Coll, Cleveland (OH)
Clarion U of Pennsylvania (PA)
Dordt Coll (IA)
Florida National Coll (FL)
Hickey Coll (MO)
Lamar U (TX)
Lewis-Clark State Coll (ID)
Lincoln Coll of New England, Southington (CT)
Pacific Union Coll (CA)
Shawnee State U (OH)
Sullivan U (KY)
U of Cincinnati (OH)
U of Rio Grande (OH)
U of the District of Columbia (DC)
The U of Toledo (OH)
Washburn U (KS)
Wright State U (OH)
Youngstown State U (OH)

Legal Assistant/Paralegal
American Public U System (WV)
Brookline Coll, Phoenix (AZ)
Brookline Coll, Tempe (AZ)
Brookline Coll, Tucson (AZ)
Brookline Coll (NM)
Bryant & Stratton Coll, Cleveland (OH)
Bryant & Stratton Coll - Wauwatosa Campus (WI)
Central Pennsylvania Coll (PA)
Coll of Mount St. Joseph (OH)
Coll of Saint Mary (NE)
Davenport U, Grand Rapids (MI)
Daymar Inst, Clarksville (TN)
Faulkner U (AL)
Ferris State U (MI)
Fisher Coll (MA)
Florida National Coll (FL)
Gannon U (PA)
Grambling State U (LA)
Hickey Coll (MO)
Hodges U (FL)
Husson U (ME)
Idaho State U (ID)
ITT Tech Inst, Tempe (AZ)
ITT Tech Inst, Clovis (CA)
ITT Tech Inst, Concord (CA)
ITT Tech Inst, Corona (CA)
ITT Tech Inst, South Bend (IN)
ITT Tech Inst (KS)
ITT Tech Inst, Lexington (KY)
ITT Tech Inst (MS)
ITT Tech Inst, Springfield (MO)
Johnson & Wales U (RI)
Jones Coll, Jacksonville (FL)
Kaplan U, Davenport Campus (IA)
Kaplan U, Mason City Campus (IA)
Keiser U, Fort Lauderdale (FL)
Lake Superior State U (MI)
Lewis-Clark State Coll (ID)
Lincoln Coll of New England, Southington (CT)
Madonna U (MI)
Maria Coll (NY)
McNeese State U (LA)
Midland Coll (TX)
Missouri Western State U (MO)
Mountain State U (WV)
Mount Aloysius Coll (PA)
Newman U (KS)
New York City Coll of Technology of the City U of New York (NY)
Patricia Stevens Coll (MO)
Peirce Coll (PA)
Pennsylvania Coll of Technology (PA)
Pioneer Pacific Coll, Clackamas (OR)
Pioneer Pacific Coll, Wilsonville (OR)
Post U (CT)
Robert Morris U Illinois (IL)
Rogers State U (OK)
Saint Mary-of-the-Woods Coll (IN)
St. Petersburg Coll (FL)
Santa Fe Coll (FL)
Shawnee State U (OH)
South U (AL)
South U, Royal Palm Beach (FL)
South U (GA)
South U, Columbia (SC)
South U, Virginia Beach (VA)
Southwest Florida Coll, Fort Myers (FL)
Suffolk U (MA)
Sullivan U (KY)
Thomas Edison State Coll (NJ)
Tulane U (LA)
The U of Akron (OH)
U of Alaska Anchorage (AK)
U of Alaska Fairbanks (AK)
U of Arkansas at Fort Smith (AR)
U of Cincinnati (OH)
U of Great Falls (MT)
U of Hartford (CT)
U of Louisville (KY)
The U of Toledo (OH)
Utah Valley U (UT)
Western Kentucky U (KY)
Westwood Coll–Anaheim (CA)
Westwood Coll–Dallas (TX)
Westwood Coll–Fort Worth (TX)
Westwood Coll–Inland Empire (CA)
Westwood Coll–Los Angeles (CA)
Westwood Coll–Online Campus (CO)
Westwood Coll–South Bay Campus (CA)
Widener U (PA)

Legal Professions and Studies Related
Florida National Coll (FL)

Legal Studies
Central Christian Coll of Kansas (KS)
Florida National Coll (FL)
Lake Superior State U (MI)
Maria Coll (NY)
Post U (CT)
St. John's U (NY)
Saint Joseph's U (PA)
U of Alaska Southeast (AK)
U of Hartford (CT)
U of New Haven (CT)

Liberal Arts and Sciences And Humanities Related
Adams State Coll (CO)
Ball State U (IN)
Concordia U (CA)
Crown Coll (MN)
Ferris State U (MI)
Indiana U East (IN)
Indiana U Kokomo (IN)
Indiana U South Bend (IN)
Indiana U Southeast (IN)
Mount Aloysius Coll (PA)
New York U (NY)
Pennsylvania Coll of Technology (PA)
Sacred Heart U (CT)
Southern New Hampshire U (NH)
Taylor U (IN)
U of Hartford (CT)
U of Wisconsin–Green Bay (WI)
U of Wisconsin–La Crosse (WI)
Walsh U (OH)

Liberal Arts and Sciences/Liberal Studies
Abraham Baldwin Ag Coll (GA)
Adams State Coll (CO)
Adelphi U (NY)
Alabama State U (AL)
Alverno Coll (WI)
American International Coll (MA)
Aquinas Coll (MI)
Aquinas Coll (TN)
Arkansas State U - Jonesboro (AR)
Armstrong Atlantic State U (GA)
Ashland U (OH)
Austin Peay State U (TN)
Ball State U (IN)
Bard Coll (NY)
Bard Coll at Simon's Rock (MA)
Beacon Coll (FL)
Bemidji State U (MN)
Bethany U (CA)
Bethel Coll (IN)
Bethel U (MN)
Brescia U (KY)
Briar Cliff U (IA)
Bryan Coll (TN)
Bryn Athyn Coll of the New Church (PA)
Butler U (IN)
Calumet Coll of Saint Joseph (IN)
Cazenovia Coll (NY)
Centenary Coll (NJ)
Charter Oak State Coll (CT)
Christendom Coll (VA)
Clarion U of Pennsylvania (PA)
Clarke Coll (IA)
Clayton State U (GA)
Coll of Coastal Georgia (GA)
Coll of St. Joseph (VT)
Coll of Staten Island of the City U of New York (NY)
Columbia Coll (MO)
Columbus State U (GA)
Concordia U Texas (TX)
Cumberland U (TN)
Dakota Wesleyan U (SD)
Dallas Baptist U (TX)
Dickinson State U (ND)
Dixie State Coll of Utah (UT)
Dominican Coll (NY)
East-West U (IL)
Ecclesia Coll (AR)
Edgewood Coll (WI)
Edinboro U of Pennsylvania (PA)
Emmanuel Coll (GA)
Emory U (GA)
Endicott Coll (MA)
Excelsior Coll (NY)
Fairfield U (CT)
Fairleigh Dickinson U, Metropolitan Campus (NJ)
Fairmont State U (WV)
Farmingdale State Coll (NY)
Faulkner U (AL)
Felician Coll (NJ)
Ferris State U (MI)
Fisher Coll (MA)
Five Towns Coll (NY)
Florida A&M U (FL)
Florida Atlantic U (FL)
Florida Coll (FL)
Florida Inst of Technology (FL)
Florida National Coll (FL)
Florida State U (FL)
Franklin Coll Switzerland (Switzerland)
Gannon U (PA)
Glenville State Coll (WV)
Grace Bible Coll (MI)
Grand View U (IA)
Granite State Coll (NH)
Gwynedd-Mercy Coll (PA)
Hilbert Coll (NY)
Houghton Coll (NY)
Indiana State U (IN)
Indiana U Kokomo (IN)
Indiana U–Purdue U Indianapolis (IN)
John Brown U (AR)
Johnson State Coll (VT)
John Wesley Coll (NC)
Kent State U (OH)
Kent State U at Stark (OH)
Kentucky State U (KY)
Keystone Coll (PA)
Kuyper Coll (MI)
LaGrange Coll (GA)
Lake Superior State U (MI)
Lewis-Clark State Coll (ID)
Limestone Coll (SC)
Lincoln Coll–Normal (IL)
Long Island U, Brooklyn Campus (NY)
Lourdes Coll (OH)
Maria Coll (NY)
Marian U (IN)
Marymount Coll, Palos Verdes, California (CA)
Medaille Coll (NY)
Medgar Evers Coll of the City U of New York (NY)
Mercy Coll (NY)
Merrimack Coll (MA)
Methodist U (NC)
MidAmerica Nazarene U (KS)
Midland Coll (TX)
Midwestern State U (TX)
Minnesota State U Mankato (MN)
Minnesota State U Moorhead (MN)
Missouri Southern State U (MO)
Mitchell Coll (CT)
Molloy Coll (NY)
Montana State U Billings (MT)
Mountain State U (WV)
Mount Aloysius Coll (PA)
Mount Marty Coll (SD)
Mount Olive Coll (NC)
Mount St. Mary's Coll (CA)
Neumann U (PA)
New England Coll (NH)
Newman U (KS)
New Saint Andrews Coll (ID)
New York City Coll of Technology of the City U of New York (NY)
New York U (NY)
Niagara U (NY)
Northern Kentucky U (KY)
Northern Michigan U (MI)
Northern State U (SD)
Northwestern Coll (MN)
Nyack Coll (NY)
Oakland City U (IN)
The Ohio State U at Marion (OH)
The Ohio State U–Mansfield Campus (OH)
The Ohio State U–Newark Campus (OH)
Ohio U (OH)
Ohio Valley U (WV)
Oklahoma Wesleyan U (OK)
Oregon Inst of Technology (OR)
Pace U (NY)
Patten U (CA)
Penn State Abington (PA)
Penn State Altoona (PA)
Penn State Berks (PA)
Penn State Erie, The Behrend Coll (PA)
Penn State Harrisburg (PA)
Penn State U Park (PA)
Pennsylvania Coll of Technology (PA)
Post U (CT)
Providence Coll (RI)
Reinhardt U (GA)
Rider U (NJ)
Rivier Coll (NH)
Rochester Coll (MI)
Rocky Mountain Coll (MT)
Rogers State U (OK)
St. Augustine Coll (IL)
St. Catherine U (MN)
St. Cloud State U (MN)
St. Francis Coll (NY)
St. John's U (NY)
Saint Joseph's U (PA)
Saint Leo U (FL)
St. Louis Christian Coll (MO)
Saint Mary-of-the-Woods Coll (IN)
St. Petersburg Coll (FL)
St. Thomas Aquinas Coll (NY)
Salve Regina U (RI)
Santa Fe Coll (FL)
Schreiner U (TX)
Southeastern Baptist Theological Seminary (NC)
Southern Polytechnic State U (GA)
Southern Vermont Coll (VT)
Spring Arbor U (MI)
State U of New York Coll of Technology at Canton (NY)
Stephens Coll (MO)
Suffolk U (MA)
Tabor Coll (KS)
Thiel Coll (PA)
Thomas More Coll (KY)
Thompson Rivers U (BC, Canada)
Trine U (IN)
Troy U (AL)
Truett-McConnell Coll (GA)
The U of Akron (OH)
U of Alaska Fairbanks (AK)
U of Alaska Southeast (AK)
U of Arkansas at Fort Smith (AR)
U of Arkansas at Monticello (AR)
U of Central Florida (FL)
U of Cincinnati (OH)
U of Delaware (DE)
U of Hartford (CT)
U of La Verne (CA)
U of Maine at Augusta (ME)
U of Maine at Fort Kent (ME)
U of Maine at Presque Isle (ME)
The U of Montana Western (MT)
U of New Hampshire at Manchester (NH)
U of North Florida (FL)
U of Pittsburgh at Bradford (PA)
U of Saint Mary (KS)
U of South Florida (FL)
U of the Incarnate Word (TX)
The U of Toledo (OH)
U of West Florida (FL)
U of Wisconsin–Eau Claire (WI)
U of Wisconsin–Oshkosh (WI)
U of Wisconsin–Platteville (WI)
U of Wisconsin–Stevens Point (WI)
U of Wisconsin–Superior (WI)
U of Wisconsin–Whitewater (WI)
Upper Iowa U (IA)
Valdosta State U (GA)
Villa Maria Coll of Buffalo (NY)
Virginia U of Lynchburg (VA)
Washburn U (KS)
Waynesburg U (PA)
Western Connecticut State U (CT)
Western New England Coll (MA)
Western Oregon U (OR)
Wichita State U (KS)
Wilson Coll (PA)
Xavier U (OH)
York Coll (NE)
Young Harris Coll (GA)
Youngstown State U (OH)

Library Assistant
U of Maine at Augusta (ME)

Lineworker
Utah Valley U (UT)

Linguistics
Oklahoma Wesleyan U (OK)

Logistics and Materials Management
Park U (MO)
Sullivan U (KY)
The U of Akron (OH)
The U of Toledo (OH)

Machine Shop Technology
Dalton State Coll (GA)
Missouri Southern State U (MO)
Pennsylvania Coll of Technology (PA)

Machine Tool Technology
Boise State U (ID)
Idaho State U (ID)
Lamar U (TX)
Northern Michigan U (MI)
Weber State U (UT)

Management Information Systems
Amridge U (AL)
Arkansas State U - Jonesboro (AR)
Columbia Coll, Caguas (PR)
Columbia Coll, Yauco (PR)
Globe Inst of Technology (NY)
Hilbert Coll (NY)
Husson U (ME)
Inter American U of Puerto Rico, Bayamón Campus (PR)
Johnson State Coll (VT)
Lake Superior State U (MI)
Liberty U (VA)
Lindsey Wilson Coll (KY)
Lock Haven U of Pennsylvania (PA)
Miami U Hamilton (OH)
Morehead State U (KY)
New England Coll of Business (MA)
Peirce Coll (PA)
Potomac Coll (DC)
St. Augustine Coll (IL)
Saint Joseph's U (PA)
Shawnee State U (OH)
Strayer U - Akron Campus (OH)
Strayer U - Alexandria Campus (VA)
Strayer U - Allentown Campus (PA)
Strayer U - Anne Arundel Campus (MD)
Strayer U - Arlington Campus (VA)
Strayer U - Augusta Campus (GA)
Strayer U - Baymeadows Campus (FL)
Strayer U - Birmingham Campus (AL)
Strayer U - Brickell Campus (FL)

Strayer U - Center City Campus (PA)
Strayer U - Central Austin Campus (TX)
Strayer U - Chamblee Campus (GA)
Strayer U - Charleston Campus (SC)
Strayer U - Chesapeake Campus (VA)
Strayer U - Chesterfield Campus (VA)
Strayer U - Christiana Campus (DE)
Strayer U - Cobb County Campus (GA)
Strayer U - Columbia Campus (SC)
Strayer U - Columbus Campus (OH)
Strayer U - Coral Springs Campus (FL)
Strayer U - Cranberry Woods Campus (PA)
Strayer U - Delaware County Campus (PA)
Strayer U - Doral Campus (FL)
Strayer U - Douglasville Campus (GA)
Strayer U - Fairview Park Campus (OH)
Strayer U - Florence Campus (KY)
Strayer U - Fort Lauderdale Campus (FL)
Strayer U - Fredericksburg Campus (VA)
Strayer U - Garner Campus (NC)
Strayer U - Greensboro Campus (NC)
Strayer U - Greenville Campus (SC)
Strayer U - Henrico Campus (VA)
Strayer U - Huntersville Campus (NC)
Strayer U - Huntsville Campus (AL)
Strayer U - King of Prussia Campus (PA)
Strayer U - Knoxville Campus (TN)
Strayer U - Lexington Campus (KY)
Strayer U - Lithonia Campus (GA)
Strayer U - Loudoun Campus (VA)
Strayer U - Louisville Campus (KY)
Strayer U - Lower Bucks County Campus (PA)
Strayer U - Maitland Campus (FL)
Strayer U - Manassas Campus (VA)
Strayer U - Mason Campus (OH)
Strayer U - Metairie Campus (LA)
Strayer U - Miramar Campus (FL)
Strayer U - Morrow Campus (GA)
Strayer U - Nashville Campus (TN)
Strayer U - Newport News Campus (VA)
Strayer U - North Charlotte Campus (NC)
Strayer U - North Raleigh Campus (NC)
Strayer U - Orlando East Campus (FL)
Strayer U - Owings Mills Campus (MD)
Strayer U - Palm Beach Gardens Campus (FL)
Strayer U - Penn Center West Campus (PA)
Strayer U - Prince George's Campus (MD)
Strayer U - Rockville Campus (MD)
Strayer U - Roswell Campus (GA)
Strayer U - RTP Campus (NC)
Strayer U - Salt Lake Campus (UT)
Strayer U - Sand Lake Campus (FL)
Strayer U - Savannah Campus (GA)
Strayer U - Shelby Oaks Campus (TN)
Strayer U - South Charlotte Campus (NC)
Strayer U - Takoma Park Campus (DC)
Strayer U - Tampa East Campus (FL)
Strayer U - Tampa Westshore Campus (FL)
Strayer U - Teays Valley Campus (WV)
Strayer U - Thousand Oaks Campus (TN)
Strayer U - Virginia Beach Campus (VA)
Strayer U - Washington Campus (DC)
Strayer U - White Marsh Campus (MD)
Strayer U - Woodbridge Campus (VA)
Thiel Coll (PA)
Wilson Coll (PA)
Wright State U (OH)

Management Information Systems and Services Related
Indiana U–Purdue U Indianapolis (IN)
Mount Aloysius Coll (PA)
Purdue U North Central (IN)
Santa Fe Coll (FL)

Management Science
Hawai'i Pacific U (HI)
U of Massachusetts Lowell (MA)

Manufacturing Technology
Excelsior Coll (NY)
Lawrence Technological U (MI)
Lewis-Clark State Coll (ID)
Missouri Western State U (MO)
Morehead State U (KY)
Thomas Edison State Coll (NJ)
Thompson Rivers U (BC, Canada)
The U of Akron (OH)
Western Kentucky U (KY)

Marine Science/ Merchant Marine Officer
U of the District of Columbia (DC)

Marketing/Marketing Management
Abraham Baldwin Ag Coll (GA)
AIB Coll of Business (IA)
Baker Coll of Allen Park (MI)
Baker Coll of Auburn Hills (MI)
Baker Coll of Cadillac (MI)
Baker Coll of Clinton Township (MI)
Baker Coll of Owosso (MI)
Central Christian Coll of Kansas (KS)
Central Pennsylvania Coll (PA)
Dalton State Coll (GA)
Davenport U, Grand Rapids (MI)
Hawai'i Pacific U (HI)
Idaho State U (ID)
Johnson & Wales U (CO)
Johnson & Wales U (FL)
Johnson & Wales U (RI)
Miami U (OH)
Miami U Hamilton (OH)
Mount St. Mary's Coll (CA)
New England Coll of Business (MA)
New York City Coll of Technology of the City U of New York (NY)
Peirce Coll (PA)
Pioneer Pacific Coll, Clackamas (OR)
Pioneer Pacific Coll–Eugene/Springfield Branch (OR)
Post U (CT)
Regent U (VA)
Saint Joseph's U (PA)
St. Petersburg Coll (FL)
Southern New Hampshire U (NH)
Southwest Minnesota State U (MN)
Strayer U - Akron Campus (OH)
Strayer U - Alexandria Campus (VA)
Strayer U - Allentown Campus (PA)
Strayer U - Anne Arundel Campus (MD)
Strayer U - Arlington Campus (VA)
Strayer U - Augusta Campus (GA)
Strayer U - Baymeadows Campus (FL)
Strayer U - Birmingham Campus (AL)
Strayer U - Brickell Campus (FL)
Strayer U - Center City Campus (PA)
Strayer U - Central Austin Campus (TX)
Strayer U - Chamblee Campus (GA)
Strayer U - Charleston Campus (SC)
Strayer U - Chesapeake Campus (VA)
Strayer U - Chesterfield Campus (VA)
Strayer U - Christiana Campus (DE)
Strayer U - Cobb County Campus (GA)
Strayer U - Columbia Campus (SC)
Strayer U - Columbus Campus (OH)
Strayer U - Coral Springs Campus (FL)
Strayer U - Cranberry Woods Campus (PA)
Strayer U - Delaware County Campus (PA)
Strayer U - Doral Campus (FL)
Strayer U - Douglasville Campus (GA)
Strayer U - Fairview Park Campus (OH)
Strayer U - Florence Campus (KY)
Strayer U - Fort Lauderdale Campus (FL)
Strayer U - Fredericksburg Campus (VA)
Strayer U - Garner Campus (NC)
Strayer U - Greensboro Campus (NC)
Strayer U - Greenville Campus (SC)
Strayer U - Henrico Campus (VA)
Strayer U - Huntersville Campus (NC)
Strayer U - Huntsville Campus (AL)
Strayer U - King of Prussia Campus (PA)
Strayer U - Knoxville Campus (TN)
Strayer U - Lexington Campus (KY)
Strayer U - Lithonia Campus (GA)
Strayer U - Loudoun Campus (VA)
Strayer U - Louisville Campus (KY)
Strayer U - Lower Bucks County Campus (PA)
Strayer U - Maitland Campus (FL)
Strayer U - Manassas Campus (VA)
Strayer U - Mason Campus (OH)
Strayer U - Miramar Campus (FL)
Strayer U - Morrow Campus (GA)
Strayer U - Nashville Campus (TN)
Strayer U - Newport News Campus (VA)
Strayer U - North Charlotte Campus (NC)
Strayer U - North Raleigh Campus (NC)
Strayer U - Orlando East Campus (FL)
Strayer U - Owings Mills Campus (MD)
Strayer U - Palm Beach Gardens Campus (FL)
Strayer U - Penn Center West Campus (PA)
Strayer U - Prince George's Campus (MD)
Strayer U - Rockville Campus (MD)
Strayer U - Roswell Campus (GA)
Strayer U - RTP Campus (NC)
Strayer U - Salt Lake Campus (UT)
Strayer U - Sand Lake Campus (FL)
Strayer U - Savannah Campus (GA)
Strayer U - Shelby Oaks Campus (TN)
Strayer U - South Charlotte Campus (NC)
Strayer U - Takoma Park Campus (DC)
Strayer U - Tampa East Campus (FL)
Strayer U - Tampa Westshore Campus (FL)
Strayer U - Teays Valley Campus (WV)
Strayer U - Thousand Oaks Campus (TN)
Strayer U - Virginia Beach Campus (VA)
Strayer U - Washington Campus (DC)
Strayer U - White Marsh Campus (MD)
Strayer U - Woodbridge Campus (VA)
Sullivan U (KY)
Tulane U (LA)
The U of Akron (OH)
U of Cincinnati (OH)
Walsh U (OH)
Webber International U (FL)
Wright State U (OH)
Youngstown State U (OH)

Masonry
Pennsylvania Coll of Technology (PA)

Massage Therapy
ECPI Coll of Technology, Virginia Beach (VA)
Idaho State U (ID)
Keiser U, Fort Lauderdale (FL)

Mass Communication/ Media
Black Hills State U (SD)
Inter American U of Puerto Rico, Bayamón Campus (PR)
John Cabot U (Italy)
Methodist U (NC)
Midland Coll (TX)
Pennsylvania Coll of Technology (PA)
Southern Adventist U (TN)
Southwestern Assemblies of God U (TX)
U of Dubuque (IA)
U of Rio Grande (OH)
York Coll of Pennsylvania (PA)

Mathematics
Abraham Baldwin Ag Coll (GA)
Central Christian Coll of Kansas (KS)
Coll of Coastal Georgia (GA)
Creighton U (NE)
Dalton State Coll (GA)
Felician Coll (NJ)
Hawai'i Pacific U (HI)
Idaho State U (ID)
Indiana U–Purdue U Fort Wayne (IN)
Indiana Wesleyan U (IN)
Methodist U (NC)
Midland Coll (TX)
Purdue U North Central (IN)
State U of New York Empire State Coll (NY)
Thomas Edison State Coll (NJ)
Thomas More Coll (KY)
Trine U (IN)
U of Great Falls (MT)
U of Rio Grande (OH)
The U of Tampa (FL)
Utah Valley U (UT)
Young Harris Coll (GA)

Mathematics and Computer Science
Immaculata U (PA)

Mathematics Teacher Education
Central Christian Coll of Kansas (KS)

Mechanical Drafting and CAD/CADD
Baker Coll of Flint (MI)
Cameron U (OK)
Indiana U–Purdue U Indianapolis (IN)
New York City Coll of Technology of the City U of New York (NY)
Purdue U Calumet (IN)

Mechanical Engineering
Fairfield U (CT)
U of New Haven (CT)

Mechanical Engineering/ Mechanical Technology
Baker Coll of Flint (MI)
Bluefield State Coll (WV)
ECPI Coll of Technology, Virginia Beach (VA)
ECPI Tech Coll, Roanoke (VA)
Fairmont State U (WV)
Farmingdale State Coll (NY)
Ferris State U (MI)
Idaho State U (ID)
Indiana U–Purdue U Fort Wayne (IN)
Lake Superior State U (MI)
Lawrence Technological U (MI)
Miami U (OH)
Miami U Hamilton (OH)
Michigan Technological U (MI)
Murray State U (KY)
New York City Coll of Technology of the City U of New York (NY)
Penn State Altoona (PA)
Penn State Berks (PA)
Penn State Erie, The Behrend Coll (PA)
Point Park U (PA)
State U of New York Coll of Technology at Canton (NY)
Thomas Edison State Coll (NJ)
The U of Akron (OH)
U of Arkansas at Little Rock (AR)
U of Cincinnati (OH)
U of Massachusetts Lowell (MA)
U of Rio Grande (OH)
U of the District of Columbia (DC)
The U of Toledo (OH)
Vermont Tech Coll (VT)
Youngstown State U (OH)

Mechanical Engineering Technologies Related
Indiana U–Purdue U Indianapolis (IN)
Purdue U Calumet (IN)
Purdue U North Central (IN)
Thomas Edison State Coll (NJ)

Mechanic and Repair Technologies Related
Pennsylvania Coll of Technology (PA)
Thomas Edison State Coll (NJ)

Mechanics and Repair
Idaho State U (ID)
Lewis-Clark State Coll (ID)
Utah Valley U (UT)

Medical Administrative Assistant and Medical Secretary
Baker Coll of Auburn Hills (MI)
Baker Coll of Cadillac (MI)
Baker Coll of Clinton Township (MI)
Baker Coll of Flint (MI)
Baker Coll of Jackson (MI)
Baker Coll of Muskegon (MI)
Baker Coll of Owosso (MI)
Baker Coll of Port Huron (MI)
Boise State U (ID)
Dickinson State U (ND)
ECPI Coll of Technology, Virginia Beach (VA)
ECPI Tech Coll, Roanoke (VA)
Florida National Coll (FL)
Lamar U (TX)
Lincoln Coll of New England, Southington (CT)
Monroe Coll, Bronx (NY)
Monroe Coll, New Rochelle (NY)
Montana State U Billings (MT)
Mountain State U (WV)
Northern Michigan U (MI)
Pacific Union Coll (CA)
Pennsylvania Coll of Technology (PA)
Universidad Adventista de las Antillas (PR)
U of Rio Grande (OH)
Wright State U (OH)

Medical/Clinical Assistant
Argosy U, Twin Cities (MN)
Arkansas Tech U (AR)
Baker Coll of Allen Park (MI)
Baker Coll of Auburn Hills (MI)
Baker Coll of Cadillac (MI)
Baker Coll of Clinton Township (MI)
Baker Coll of Flint (MI)
Baker Coll of Jackson (MI)
Baker Coll of Muskegon (MI)
Baker Coll of Owosso (MI)
Baker Coll of Port Huron (MI)
Bauder Coll (GA)
Central Pennsylvania Coll (PA)
Clayton State U (GA)
Davenport U, Grand Rapids (MI)
Daymar Inst, Clarksville (TN)
ECPI Tech Coll, Roanoke (VA)
Florida National Coll (FL)
Hodges U (FL)
Idaho State U (ID)
Kaplan U, Davenport Campus (IA)
Kaplan U, Mason City Campus (IA)
Keiser U, Fort Lauderdale (FL)
Lincoln Coll of New England, Southington (CT)
Mercy Coll of Health Sciences (IA)
Monroe Coll, Bronx (NY)
Montana State U Billings (MT)
Montana Tech of The U of Montana (MT)
Mountain State U (WV)
Mount Aloysius Coll (PA)
Palmer Coll of Chiropractic (IA)
Pioneer Pacific Coll, Clackamas (OR)
Pioneer Pacific Coll, Wilsonville (OR)
Pioneer Pacific Coll–Eugene/Springfield Branch (OR)
Presentation Coll (SD)
Robert Morris U Illinois (IL)
South U (AL)
South U (GA)
South U, Columbia (SC)
Southwest Florida Coll, Fort Myers (FL)
The U of Akron (OH)
U of Alaska Anchorage (AK)
U of Alaska Fairbanks (AK)
The U of Toledo (OH)
Westwood Coll–Atlanta Midtown (GA)
Westwood Coll–Atlanta Northlake (GA)
Westwood Coll–Denver North (CO)

Westwood Coll–Denver South (CO)
Youngstown State U (OH)

Medical/Health Management and Clinical Assistant
Lewis-Clark State Coll (ID)
Stratford U, Woodbridge (VA)

Medical Informatics
Idaho State U (ID)
Montana Tech of The U of Montana (MT)

Medical Insurance Coding
Baker Coll of Allen Park (MI)
Stratford U, Woodbridge (VA)

Medical Insurance/ Medical Billing
Baker Coll of Allen Park (MI)

Medical Office Assistant
Bryant & Stratton Coll - Wauwatosa Campus (WI)
Lewis-Clark State Coll (ID)
Mercy Coll of Health Sciences (IA)

Medical Office Computer Specialist
Baker Coll of Allen Park (MI)

Medical Office Management
Dalton State Coll (GA)
Hickey Coll (MO)
Kaplan U, Davenport Campus (IA)
Presentation Coll (SD)
Sullivan U (KY)
The U of Akron (OH)

Medical Radiologic Technology
Argosy U, Twin Cities (MN)
Arkansas State U - Jonesboro (AR)
Ball State U (IN)
Bluefield State Coll (WV)
Charles Drew U of Medicine and Science (CA)
Coll of Coastal Georgia (GA)
Ferris State U (MI)
Gannon U (PA)
Idaho State U (ID)
Indiana U–Purdue U Indianapolis (IN)
Indiana U South Bend (IN)
Inter American U of Puerto Rico, Ponce Campus (PR)
Inter American U of Puerto Rico, San Germán Campus (PR)
Keiser U, Fort Lauderdale (FL)
Keystone Coll (PA)
La Roche Coll (PA)
Mercy Coll of Health Sciences (IA)
Mercy Coll of Northwest Ohio (OH)
Midland Coll (TX)
Missouri Southern State U (MO)
Morehead State U (KY)
Mount Aloysius Coll (PA)
Newman U (KS)
New York City Coll of Technology of the City U of New York (NY)
Northern Kentucky U (KY)
Pennsylvania Coll of Technology (PA)
St. Catherine U (MN)
Santa Fe Coll (FL)
Shawnee State U (OH)
Southern Vermont Coll (VT)
Thomas Edison State Coll (NJ)
The U of Akron (OH)
U of New Mexico (NM)

Medical Transcription
Baker Coll of Flint (MI)
Baker Coll of Jackson (MI)
Dalton State Coll (GA)
Kaplan U, Davenport Campus (IA)
Mercyhurst Coll (PA)

Mental and Social Health Services And Allied Professions Related
U of Alaska Fairbanks (AK)
U of Maine at Augusta (ME)

Mental Health/Rehabilitation
Felician Coll (NJ)
Lake Superior State U (MI)
The U of Toledo (OH)

Merchandising
The Art Inst of Philadelphia (PA)
The U of Akron (OH)

Metal and Jewelry Arts
Fashion Inst of Technology (NY)

Metallurgical Technology
Penn State Altoona (PA)
Penn State Berks (PA)
Penn State Erie, The Behrend Coll (PA)

Meteorology
Western Kentucky U (KY)

Middle School Education
Dalton State Coll (GA)

Military Studies
Hawai'i Pacific U (HI)

Military Technologies
Central Baptist Coll (AR)
Murray State U (KY)
Thomas Edison State Coll (NJ)

Mining Technology
Mountain State U (WV)

Missionary Studies and Missiology
Central Christian Coll of Kansas (KS)
Faith Baptist Bible Coll and Theological Seminary (IA)
Hillsdale Free Will Baptist Coll (OK)
New Life Theological Seminary (NC)

Modern Languages
Midland Coll (TX)

Multi/Interdisciplinary Studies Related
Arkansas Tech U (AR)
Cameron U (OK)
Grantham U (MO)
Miami U (OH)
Montana Tech of The U of Montana (MT)
Ohio U (OH)
Pennsylvania Coll of Technology (PA)
Providence Coll (RI)
U of Alaska Fairbanks (AK)
U of Arkansas at Monticello (AR)
The U of Montana Western (MT)
The U of Toledo (OH)
Utah Valley U (UT)

Music
Abraham Baldwin Ag Coll (GA)
Alverno Coll (WI)
Central Baptist Coll (AR)
Central Christian Coll of Kansas (KS)
Chowan U (NC)
Clayton State U (GA)
Crown Coll (MN)
Five Towns Coll (NY)
Hannibal-LaGrange Coll (MO)
Hillsdale Free Will Baptist Coll (OK)
Indiana Wesleyan U (IN)
Kwantlen Polytechnic U (BC, Canada)
Methodist U (NC)
Midland Coll (TX)
Mount Olive Coll (NC)
Mount Vernon Nazarene U (OH)
Pacific Union Coll (CA)
St. Petersburg Coll (FL)
Shawnee State U (OH)
Southwestern Assemblies of God U (TX)
Thomas More Coll (KY)
U of Maine at Augusta (ME)
U of Rio Grande (OH)
Utah Valley U (UT)
Villa Maria Coll of Buffalo (NY)
York Coll of Pennsylvania (PA)
Young Harris Coll (GA)

Music History, Literature, and Theory
Central Christian Coll of Kansas (KS)

Music Management and Merchandising
Five Towns Coll (NY)
McNally Smith Coll of Music (MN)
Villa Maria Coll of Buffalo (NY)

Music Performance
Central Christian Coll of Kansas (KS)
McNally Smith Coll of Music (MN)

Music Related
Academy of Art U (CA)
Young Harris Coll (GA)

Music Teacher Education
Central Christian Coll of Kansas (KS)
Midland Coll (TX)
Union Coll (NE)
Young Harris Coll (GA)

Music Theory and Composition
Kwantlen Polytechnic U (BC, Canada)

Nail Technician and Manicurist
Lincoln Coll–Normal (IL)

Natural Resources/ Conservation
State U of New York Coll of Environmental Science and Forestry (NY)
U of Alaska Southeast (AK)

Natural Resources Management and Policy
Lake Superior State U (MI)
U of Alaska Fairbanks (AK)

Natural Sciences
Alderson-Broaddus Coll (WV)
Central Christian Coll of Kansas (KS)
Felician Coll (NJ)
Indiana U East (IN)
Lourdes Coll (OH)
Madonna U (MI)
Roberts Wesleyan Coll (NY)
St. Petersburg Coll (FL)
Shawnee State U (OH)
U of Alaska Fairbanks (AK)
U of Cincinnati (OH)
U of Puerto Rico at Utuado (PR)
The U of Toledo (OH)
Washburn U (KS)
Young Harris Coll (GA)

Nuclear Engineering Technology
Arkansas Tech U (AR)
Thomas Edison State Coll (NJ)

Nuclear Medical Technology
Ball State U (IN)
Central Pennsylvania Coll (PA)
Dalton State Coll (GA)
Ferris State U (MI)
The George Washington U (DC)
Keiser U, Fort Lauderdale (FL)
Molloy Coll (NY)
Santa Fe Coll (FL)
Thomas Edison State Coll (NJ)
The U of Findlay (OH)

Nuclear/Nuclear Power Technology
Excelsior Coll (NY)

Nursing Assistant/ Aide and Patient Care Assistant
Central Christian Coll of Kansas (KS)

Nursing (Licensed Practical/Vocational Nurse Training)
Campbellsville U (KY)
Central Christian Coll of Kansas (KS)
Dickinson State U (ND)
ECPI Coll of Technology, Virginia Beach (VA)
ECPI Tech Coll, Roanoke (VA)
Inter American U of Puerto Rico, Arecibo Campus (PR)
Inter American U of Puerto Rico, Ponce Campus (PR)
Lamar U (TX)
Lewis-Clark State Coll (ID)
Maria Coll (NY)
Medgar Evers Coll of the City U of New York (NY)
Monroe Coll, Bronx (NY)
Montana State U Billings (MT)
Pennsylvania Coll of Technology (PA)
Thompson Rivers U (BC, Canada)
The U of Texas at Brownsville (TX)
U of the District of Columbia (DC)
Virginia State U (VA)

Nursing (Registered Nurse Training)
Abraham Baldwin Ag Coll (GA)
Alcorn State U (MS)
Angelo State U (TX)
Aquinas Coll (TN)
Arkansas State U - Jonesboro (AR)
Atlantic Union Coll (MA)
Baker Coll of Auburn Hills (MI)
Baker Coll of Clinton Township (MI)
Baker Coll of Flint (MI)
Baker Coll of Muskegon (MI)
Baker Coll of Owosso (MI)
Ball State U (IN)
Bethel Coll (IN)
Bluefield State Coll (WV)
Boise State U (ID)
Brookline Coll, Phoenix (AZ)
Bryant & Stratton Coll - Wauwatosa Campus (WI)
Castleton State Coll (VT)
Central Christian Coll of Kansas (KS)
Clarion U of Pennsylvania (PA)
Coll of Coastal Georgia (GA)
Coll of Saint Mary (NE)
Coll of Staten Island of the City U of New York (NY)
Columbia Coll (MO)
Columbia Coll, Caguas (PR)
Columbia Coll, Yauco (PR)
Dalton State Coll (GA)
Dixie State Coll of Utah (UT)
ECPI Coll of Technology, Virginia Beach (VA)
Excelsior Coll (NY)
Fairmont State U (WV)
Farmingdale State Coll (NY)
Felician Coll (NJ)
Ferris State U (MI)
Freed-Hardeman U (TN)
Gardner-Webb U (NC)
Gwynedd-Mercy Coll (PA)
Hannibal-LaGrange Coll (MO)
Idaho State U (ID)
Indiana U East (IN)
Indiana U Kokomo (IN)
Indiana U Northwest (IN)
Indiana U–Purdue U Indianapolis (IN)
Inter American U of Puerto Rico, Aguadilla Campus (PR)
Inter American U of Puerto Rico, Guayama Campus (PR)
Inter American U of Puerto Rico, Ponce Campus (PR)
Inter American U of Puerto Rico, San Germán Campus (PR)
ITT Tech Inst, South Bend (IN)
ITT Tech Inst, Oklahoma City (OK)
Jefferson Coll of Health Sciences (VA)
Keiser U, Fort Lauderdale (FL)
Kent State U (OH)
Kentucky State U (KY)
Lamar U (TX)
La Roche Coll (PA)
Lincoln Memorial U (TN)
Lincoln U (MO)
Lock Haven U of Pennsylvania (PA)
Louisiana Tech U (LA)
Maria Coll (NY)
Marshall U (WV)
McNeese State U (LA)
Mercy Coll of Health Sciences (IA)
Mercy Coll of Northwest Ohio (OH)
Miami U (OH)
Midland Coll (TX)
Midway Coll (KY)
Mississippi U for Women (MS)
Montana State U Billings (MT)
Montana Tech of The U of Montana (MT)
Morehead State U (KY)
Mount Aloysius Coll (PA)
Mount St. Mary's Coll (CA)
New York City Coll of Technology of the City U of New York (NY)
Norfolk State U (VA)
Northern Kentucky U (KY)
North Georgia Coll & State U (GA)
Northwestern State U of Louisiana (LA)
Oakwood U (AL)
Ohio U (OH)
Our Lady of the Lake Coll (LA)
Pacific Union Coll (CA)
Park U (MO)
Penn State Altoona (PA)
Penn State Berks (PA)
Penn State Erie, The Behrend Coll (PA)
Penn State U Park (PA)
Pikeville Coll (KY)
Presentation Coll (SD)
Purdue U North Central (IN)
Queens U of Charlotte (NC)
Regis Coll (MA)
Reinhardt U (GA)
Rivier Coll (NH)
Robert Morris U Illinois (IL)
Rogers State U (OK)
St. Petersburg Coll (FL)
Santa Fe Coll (FL)
Shawnee State U (OH)
Southern Adventist U (TN)
Southern Arkansas U–Magnolia (AR)
Southern Vermont Coll (VT)
Southwest Baptist U (MO)
State U of New York Coll of Technology at Canton (NY)
Sul Ross State U (TX)
Troy U (AL)
Universidad Adventista de las Antillas (PR)
U of Alaska Anchorage (AK)
U of Arkansas at Fort Smith (AR)
U of Arkansas at Little Rock (AR)
U of Arkansas at Monticello (AR)
U of Charleston (WV)
U of Cincinnati (OH)
U of Guam (GU)
U of Maine at Augusta (ME)
U of Mobile (AL)
U of New England (ME)
U of Pittsburgh at Bradford (PA)
U of Rio Grande (OH)
The U of South Dakota (SD)
U of the Virgin Islands (VI)
The U of Toledo (OH)
The U of West Alabama (AL)
Utah Valley U (UT)
Vermont Tech Coll (VT)
Warner Pacific Coll (OR)
Western Kentucky U (KY)
Young Harris Coll (GA)

Nursing Related
Alverno Coll (WI)
Columbia Coll, Yauco (PR)
EDP Coll of Puerto Rico–San Sebastian (PR)
Ferris State U (MI)
Madonna U (MI)
Mount Aloysius Coll (PA)
Saint Mary's Coll of California (CA)
Simpson U (CA)

Nursing Science
National U (CA)

Occupational Safety and Health Technology
Columbia Southern U (AL)
Indiana U Southeast (IN)
Lamar U (TX)
U of Cincinnati (OH)
U of New Haven (CT)
Wright State U (OH)

Occupational Therapist Assistant
Baker Coll of Muskegon (MI)
Clarion U of Pennsylvania (PA)
Inter American U of Puerto Rico, Ponce Campus (PR)
Jefferson Coll of Health Sciences (VA)
Keiser U, Fort Lauderdale (FL)
Lincoln Coll of New England, Southington (CT)
Maria Coll (NY)
Mercy Coll (NY)
Mountain State U (WV)
Newman U (KS)
Penn State Berks (PA)
Pennsylvania Coll of Technology (PA)
St. Catherine U (MN)
U of Louisiana at Monroe (LA)
U of Puerto Rico at Humacao (PR)
U of Southern Indiana (IN)

Occupational Therapy
Coll of Coastal Georgia (GA)
Dalton State Coll (GA)
Keystone Coll (PA)
Oakwood U (AL)
Shawnee State U (OH)
Southern Adventist U (TN)

Ocean Engineering
Keiser U, Fort Lauderdale (FL)

Office Management
Baker Coll of Jackson (MI)
Dakota State U (SD)
Dalton State Coll (GA)
Emmanuel Coll (GA)
Inter American U of Puerto Rico, Aguadilla Campus (PR)
Inter American U of Puerto Rico, Arecibo Campus (PR)
Inter American U of Puerto Rico, Fajardo Campus (PR)
Inter American U of Puerto Rico, Guayama Campus (PR)
Inter American U of Puerto Rico, Ponce Campus (PR)
Lake Superior State U (MI)
Mercyhurst Coll (PA)
Miami U (OH)

Mount Vernon Nazarene U (OH)
Park U (MO)
Shawnee State U (OH)
Sullivan U (KY)
Thompson Rivers U (BC, Canada)
Washburn U (KS)

Office Occupations and Clerical Services
Bob Jones U (SC)
Pennsylvania Coll of Technology (PA)
Pontifical Catholic U of Puerto Rico (PR)
U of Puerto Rico at Bayamón (PR)
U of Puerto Rico at Humacao (PR)
U of Puerto Rico, Cayey U Coll (PR)
Wright State U (OH)

Operations Management
Indiana U–Purdue U Fort Wayne (IN)
Indiana U–Purdue U Indianapolis (IN)
Purdue U North Central (IN)

Ophthalmic Laboratory Technology
Rochester Inst of Technology (NY)

Optical Sciences
Indiana U of Pennsylvania (PA)

Opticianry
New York City Coll of Technology of the City U of New York (NY)

Optometric Technician
Inter American U of Puerto Rico, Ponce Campus (PR)
St. Cloud State U (MN)

Organizational Behavior
Hawai'i Pacific U (HI)
Regent U (VA)

Organizational Communication
Creighton U (NE)

Ornamental Horticulture
Abraham Baldwin Ag Coll (GA)
Farmingdale State Coll (NY)
Ferris State U (MI)
Pennsylvania Coll of Technology (PA)
Vermont Tech Coll (VT)

Orthotics/Prosthetics
Baker Coll of Flint (MI)

Painting
Keystone Coll (PA)
Pratt Inst (NY)

Parks, Recreation and Leisure
Johnson & Wales U (RI)
Johnson & Wales U - Charlotte Campus (NC)
Mount Olive Coll (NC)
St. Petersburg Coll (FL)
Thomas Edison State Coll (NJ)
U of Maine at Presque Isle (ME)
Young Harris Coll (GA)

Parks, Recreation and Leisure Facilities Management
Coll of Coastal Georgia (GA)
Indiana Tech (IN)
Johnson & Wales U (RI)
Johnson & Wales U - Charlotte Campus (NC)
Keiser U, Fort Lauderdale (FL)
Webber International U (FL)

Parks, Recreation, and Leisure Related
Indiana U Southeast (IN)

Pastoral Counseling and Specialized Ministries Related
Brescia U (KY)

Pastoral Studies/ Counseling
Central Christian Coll of Kansas (KS)
Indiana Wesleyan U (IN)
Marian U (IN)
Oakwood U (AL)

Perfusion Technology
Thompson Rivers U (BC, Canada)

Petroleum Technology
Montana State U Billings (MT)
Nicholls State U (LA)
U of Alaska Anchorage (AK)

Pharmacy, Pharmaceutical Sciences, and Administration Related
EDP Coll of Puerto Rico–San Sebastian (PR)

Pharmacy Technician
Abraham Baldwin Ag Coll (GA)
Baker Coll of Flint (MI)
Baker Coll of Jackson (MI)
Baker Coll of Muskegon (MI)
Charles Drew U of Medicine and Science (CA)
Daymar Inst, Clarksville (TN)
Inter American U of Puerto Rico, Aguadilla Campus (PR)
Madonna U (MI)
Robert Morris U Illinois (IL)
Stratford U, Woodbridge (VA)

Philosophy
Coll of Coastal Georgia (GA)
Dalton State Coll (GA)
Felician Coll (NJ)
Holy Apostles Coll and Seminary (CT)
Kwantlen Polytechnic U (BC, Canada)
Methodist U (NC)
Thomas More Coll (KY)
The U of Tampa (FL)
Utah Valley U (UT)

Phlebotomy
Stratford U, Woodbridge (VA)

Photographic and Film/Video Technology
St. John's U (NY)
Villa Maria Coll of Buffalo (NY)

Photography
Academy of Art U (CA)
Albertus Magnus Coll (CT)
The Art Inst of California–Hollywood (CA)
The Art Inst of California–Orange County (CA)
The Art Inst of Colorado (CO)
The Art Inst of Dallas (TX)
The Art Inst of Fort Lauderdale (FL)
The Art Inst of Indianapolis (IN)
The Art Inst of Philadelphia (PA)
The Art Inst of Pittsburgh (PA)
Central Christian Coll of Kansas (KS)
Corcoran Coll of Art and Design (DC)
Keystone Coll (PA)
The New England Inst of Art (MA)
Pacific Union Coll (CA)
St. Petersburg Coll (FL)
U of Maine at Augusta (ME)

Physical Education Teaching and Coaching
Abraham Baldwin Ag Coll (GA)
Central Christian Coll of Kansas (KS)
Hillsdale Free Will Baptist Coll (OK)
Methodist U (NC)
Midland Coll (TX)
U of Rio Grande (OH)

Physical Sciences
Abraham Baldwin Ag Coll (GA)
Hillsdale Free Will Baptist Coll (OK)
Pennsylvania Coll of Technology (PA)
Roberts Wesleyan Coll (NY)
U of the District of Columbia (DC)
Utah Valley U (UT)

Physical Therapist Assistant
Arkansas State U - Jonesboro (AR)
Arkansas Tech U (AR)
Baker Coll of Flint (MI)
Baker Coll of Muskegon (MI)
Central Pennsylvania Coll (PA)
Dixie State Coll of Utah (UT)
ECPI Coll of Technology, Virginia Beach (VA)
Idaho State U (ID)
Inter American U of Puerto Rico, Ponce Campus (PR)
Jefferson Coll of Health Sciences (VA)
Keiser U, Fort Lauderdale (FL)
Louisiana Coll (LA)
Maria Coll (NY)
Mercy Coll of Health Sciences (IA)
Mercyhurst Coll (PA)
Missouri Western State U (MO)
Mountain State U (WV)
Mount Aloysius Coll (PA)
Nebraska Methodist Coll (NE)
Our Lady of the Lake Coll (LA)
St. Catherine U (MN)
St. Petersburg Coll (FL)
Southern Illinois U Carbondale (IL)
South U (AL)
South U, Royal Palm Beach (FL)
South U, Tampa (FL)
South U (GA)
State U of New York Coll of Technology at Canton (NY)
U of Evansville (IN)
U of Indianapolis (IN)
U of Puerto Rico at Humacao (PR)
Villa Maria Coll of Buffalo (NY)
Washburn U (KS)

Physical Therapy
Clarkson Coll (NE)
Coll of Coastal Georgia (GA)
Dalton State Coll (GA)
EDP Coll of Puerto Rico–San Sebastian (PR)
Fairmont State U (WV)
Oakwood U (AL)
Shawnee State U (OH)
Southern Adventist U (TN)
U of Cincinnati (OH)
Young Harris Coll (GA)

Physician Assistant
Central Christian Coll of Kansas (KS)
Coll of Coastal Georgia (GA)
Dalton State Coll (GA)
Southern Adventist U (TN)

Physics
Coll of Coastal Georgia (GA)
Dalton State Coll (GA)
Idaho State U (ID)
Midland Coll (TX)
Purdue U North Central (IN)
Rogers State U (OK)
Thomas More Coll (KY)
U of the Virgin Islands (VI)
Utah Valley U (UT)
York Coll of Pennsylvania (PA)
Young Harris Coll (GA)

Piano and Organ
Kwantlen Polytechnic U (BC, Canada)

Pipefitting and Sprinkler Fitting
Thompson Rivers U (BC, Canada)

Plant Nursery Management
Pennsylvania Coll of Technology (PA)

Plant Protection and Integrated Pest Management
North Carolina State U (NC)
U of Puerto Rico at Utuado (PR)

Plastics Engineering Technology
Ferris State U (MI)
Penn State Erie, The Behrend Coll (PA)
Santa Fe Coll (FL)
Shawnee State U (OH)

Platemaking/Imaging
Pennsylvania Coll of Technology (PA)

Plumbing Technology
Pennsylvania Coll of Technology (PA)
Santa Fe Coll (FL)
Thompson Rivers U (BC, Canada)

Political Science and Government
Abraham Baldwin Ag Coll (GA)
Adams State Coll (CO)
Coll of Coastal Georgia (GA)
Dalton State Coll (GA)
Idaho State U (ID)
Indiana U–Purdue U Fort Wayne (IN)
Indiana Wesleyan U (IN)
John Cabot U (Italy)
Kwantlen Polytechnic U (BC, Canada)
Methodist U (NC)
Midland Coll (TX)
Mount St. Mary's Coll (CA)
Thomas More Coll (KY)
The U of Scranton (PA)
The U of Tampa (FL)
The U of Toledo (OH)
Xavier U (OH)
York Coll of Pennsylvania (PA)
Young Harris Coll (GA)

Poultry Science
Abraham Baldwin Ag Coll (GA)

Precision Metal Working Related
Montana Tech of The U of Montana (MT)

Pre-Dentistry Studies
Coll of Coastal Georgia (GA)
Concordia U Wisconsin (WI)

Pre-Engineering
Abraham Baldwin Ag Coll (GA)
Coll of Coastal Georgia (GA)
Fort Valley State U (GA)
Lincoln U (MO)
Methodist U (NC)
Midland Coll (TX)
Newman U (KS)
Niagara U (NY)
Northern State U (SD)
Shawnee State U (OH)
Siena Heights U (MI)
Southern Utah U (UT)
Young Harris Coll (GA)

Pre-Law Studies
Calumet Coll of Saint Joseph (IN)
Central Christian Coll of Kansas (KS)
Ferris State U (MI)
Immaculata U (PA)
Northern Kentucky U (KY)
Peirce Coll (PA)
Thomas More Coll (KY)

Premedical Studies
Coll of Coastal Georgia (GA)
Concordia U Wisconsin (WI)

Prenursing Studies
Concordia U Wisconsin (WI)
Keystone Coll (PA)
Reinhardt U (GA)
Tabor Coll (KS)

Pre-Pharmacy Studies
Coll of Coastal Georgia (GA)
Dalton State Coll (GA)
Emmanuel Coll (GA)
Ferris State U (MI)
Keystone Coll (PA)
Madonna U (MI)
Thompson Rivers U (BC, Canada)

Pre-Theology/Pre-Ministerial Studies
Eastern Mennonite U (VA)
Manchester Coll (IN)
Nazarene Bible Coll (CO)

Pre-Veterinary Studies
Coll of Coastal Georgia (GA)
Shawnee State U (OH)

Printmaking
Keystone Coll (PA)

Psychiatric/Mental Health Services Technology
Lake Superior State U (MI)
The U of Toledo (OH)

Psychoanalysis and Psychotherapy
St. Cloud State U (MN)

Psychology
Abraham Baldwin Ag Coll (GA)
Central Christian Coll of Kansas (KS)
Coll of Coastal Georgia (GA)
Dalton State Coll (GA)
Eastern New Mexico U (NM)
Felician Coll (NJ)
Ferris State U (MI)
Fisher Coll (MA)
Hillsdale Free Will Baptist Coll (OK)
Indiana U–Purdue U Fort Wayne (IN)
Kwantlen Polytechnic U (BC, Canada)
Liberty U (VA)
Marian U (IN)
Methodist U (NC)
Midland Coll (TX)
Montana State U Billings (MT)
Mount Olive Coll (NC)
Muhlenberg Coll (PA)
Regent U (VA)
Siena Heights U (MI)
Southwestern Assemblies of God U (TX)
Thomas More Coll (KY)
U of Rio Grande (OH)
The U of Tampa (FL)
Utah Valley U (UT)
Wright State U (OH)
Xavier U (OH)
Young Harris Coll (GA)

Psychology Related
Mountain State U (WV)

Psychology Teacher Education
Central Christian Coll of Kansas (KS)

Public Administration
Indiana U Northwest (IN)
Indiana U–Purdue U Indianapolis (IN)
Point Park U (PA)
U of Maine at Augusta (ME)

Public Administration and Social Service Professions Related
The U of Akron (OH)

Public Health
American Public U System (WV)
U of Alaska Fairbanks (AK)

Public Relations, Advertising, and Applied Communication Related
John Brown U (AR)
Keystone Coll (PA)

Public Relations/ Image Management
John Brown U (AR)
Johnson & Wales U - Charlotte Campus (NC)
Xavier U (OH)

Purchasing, Procurement/ Acquisitions and Contracts Management
Mercyhurst Coll (PA)
Miami U Hamilton (OH)
Saint Joseph's U (PA)
Strayer U - Akron Campus (OH)
Strayer U - Alexandria Campus (VA)
Strayer U - Allentown Campus (PA)
Strayer U - Anne Arundel Campus (MD)
Strayer U - Arlington Campus (VA)
Strayer U - Augusta Campus (GA)
Strayer U - Baymeadows Campus (FL)
Strayer U - Birmingham Campus (AL)
Strayer U - Brickell Campus (FL)
Strayer U - Center City Campus (PA)
Strayer U - Central Austin Campus (TX)
Strayer U - Chamblee Campus (GA)
Strayer U - Charleston Campus (SC)
Strayer U - Chesapeake Campus (VA)
Strayer U - Chesterfield Campus (VA)
Strayer U - Christiana Campus (DE)
Strayer U - Cobb County Campus (GA)
Strayer U - Columbia Campus (SC)
Strayer U - Columbus Campus (OH)
Strayer U - Coral Springs Campus (FL)
Strayer U - Cranberry Woods Campus (PA)
Strayer U - Delaware County Campus (PA)
Strayer U - Doral Campus (FL)
Strayer U - Douglasville Campus (GA)
Strayer U - Fairview Park Campus (OH)
Strayer U - Florence Campus (KY)
Strayer U - Fort Lauderdale Campus (FL)
Strayer U - Fredericksburg Campus (VA)
Strayer U - Greenville Campus (SC)
Strayer U - Henrico Campus (VA)
Strayer U - Huntsville Campus (AL)
Strayer U - King of Prussia Campus (PA)
Strayer U - Knoxville Campus (TN)
Strayer U - Lexington Campus (KY)
Strayer U - Lithonia Campus (GA)
Strayer U - Loudoun Campus (VA)
Strayer U - Louisville Campus (KY)
Strayer U - Lower Bucks County Campus (PA)
Strayer U - Maitland Campus (FL)
Strayer U - Manassas Campus (VA)
Strayer U - Mason Campus (OH)

Strayer U - Miramar Campus (FL)
Strayer U - Morrow Campus (GA)
Strayer U - Nashville Campus (TN)
Strayer U - Newport News Campus (VA)
Strayer U - Orlando East Campus (FL)
Strayer U - Owings Mills Campus (MD)
Strayer U - Palm Beach Gardens Campus (FL)
Strayer U - Penn Center West Campus (PA)
Strayer U - Prince George's Campus (MD)
Strayer U - Rockville Campus (MD)
Strayer U - Roswell Campus (GA)
Strayer U - Salt Lake Campus (UT)
Strayer U - Sand Lake Campus (FL)
Strayer U - Savannah Campus (GA)
Strayer U - Shelby Oaks Campus (TN)
Strayer U - Takoma Park Campus (DC)
Strayer U - Tampa East Campus (FL)
Strayer U - Tampa Westshore Campus (FL)
Strayer U - Teays Valley Campus (WV)
Strayer U - Thousand Oaks Campus (TN)
Strayer U - Virginia Beach Campus (VA)
Strayer U - Washington Campus (DC)
Strayer U - White Marsh Campus (MD)
Strayer U - Woodbridge Campus (VA)

Quality Control and Safety Technologies Related
Lamar U (TX)
Madonna U (MI)
Rochester Inst of Technology (NY)
U of Cincinnati (OH)

Quality Control Technology
Baker Coll of Cadillac (MI)
Baker Coll of Flint (MI)
Baker Coll of Muskegon (MI)
Pennsylvania Coll of Technology (PA)
U of Cincinnati (OH)

Radiation Protection/ Health Physics Technology
Indiana U Northwest (IN)
Thomas Edison State Coll (NJ)

Radio and Television
The Art Inst of Fort Lauderdale (FL)
Indiana U–Purdue U Indianapolis (IN)
Keystone Coll (PA)
Lawrence Technological U (MI)
Newbury Coll (MA)
Northwestern Coll (MN)
Ohio U–Zanesville (OH)
Xavier U (OH)

Radio and Television Broadcasting Technology
Lincoln Coll of New England, Southington (CT)
The New England Inst of Art (MA)
New York Inst of Technology (NY)
Southern Adventist U (TN)

Radiologic Technology/Science
Allen Coll (IA)
Argosy U, Twin Cities (MN)
Baker Coll of Clinton Township (MI)
Baker Coll of Muskegon (MI)
Champlain Coll (VT)
Clarkson Coll (NE)
Coll of St. Joseph (VT)
Dalton State Coll (GA)
Dixie State Coll of Utah (UT)
Fairleigh Dickinson U, Metropolitan Campus (NJ)
Florida National Coll (FL)
Fort Hays State U (KS)
Holy Family U (PA)
Indiana U East (IN)
Indiana U Kokomo (IN)
Indiana U Northwest (IN)
Indiana U–Purdue U Fort Wayne (IN)
Indiana U–Purdue U Indianapolis (IN)
Indiana U South Bend (IN)
Indiana U Southeast (IN)
Keystone Coll (PA)
Lewis-Clark State Coll (ID)
Mansfield U of Pennsylvania (PA)
Midland Coll (TX)
Midwestern State U (TX)
Montana Tech of The U of Montana (MT)
Mountain State U (WV)
Nebraska Methodist Coll (NE)
Newman U (KS)
Northern Michigan U (MI)
Pennsylvania Coll of Technology (PA)
Presentation Coll (SD)
Regis Coll (MA)
St. Petersburg Coll (FL)
U of Arkansas at Fort Smith (AR)
U of Rio Grande (OH)
The U of Texas at Brownsville (TX)
Washburn U (KS)
Widener U (PA)

Radio, Television, and Digital Communication Related
Keystone Coll (PA)
Madonna U (MI)

Real Estate
American Public U System (WV)
Fairmont State U (WV)
Lamar U (TX)
Miami U (OH)
Miami U Hamilton (OH)
Saint Francis U (PA)
U of Cincinnati (OH)

Receptionist
Baker Coll of Allen Park (MI)

Recording Arts Technology
The New England Inst of Art (MA)

Religious Education
Apex School of Theology (NC)
Calvary Bible Coll and Theological Seminary (MO)
Cincinnati Christian U (OH)
Heritage Bible Coll (NC)
Hillsdale Free Will Baptist Coll (OK)
Houghton Coll (NY)
Indiana Wesleyan U (IN)
Kuyper Coll (MI)
Methodist U (NC)
Nazarene Bible Coll (CO)
Oakland City U (IN)
Piedmont Baptist Coll and Graduate School (NC)

Religious/Sacred Music
Central Christian Coll of Kansas (KS)
Cincinnati Christian U (OH)
Dallas Baptist U (TX)
Hillsdale Free Will Baptist Coll (OK)
Immaculata U (PA)
Indiana Wesleyan U (IN)
Mount Vernon Nazarene U (OH)
Nazarene Bible Coll (CO)

Religious Studies
Atlantic Union Coll (MA)
Brewton-Parker Coll (GA)
Calumet Coll of Saint Joseph (IN)
Central Christian Coll of Kansas (KS)
Felician Coll (NJ)
Global U (MO)
Grace Bible Coll (MI)
Griggs U (MD)
Holy Apostles Coll and Seminary (CT)
Huntington U (IN)
Kentucky Mountain Bible Coll (KY)
Liberty U (VA)
Lourdes Coll (OH)
Madonna U (MI)
Manchester Coll (IN)
Maranatha Baptist Bible Coll (WI)
Missouri Baptist U (MO)
Mount Marty Coll (SD)
Mount Olive Coll (NC)
Mount Vernon Nazarene U (OH)
Northwest U (WA)
Oakwood U (AL)
Presentation Coll (SD)
Shaw U (NC)
Southern Adventist U (TN)
Thomas More Coll (KY)
The U of Findlay (OH)
Young Harris Coll (GA)

Resort Management
Thompson Rivers U (BC, Canada)

Respiratory Care Therapy
Cameron U (OK)
Coll of Coastal Georgia (GA)
Dakota State U (SD)
Dalton State Coll (GA)
Dixie State Coll of Utah (UT)
Ferris State U (MI)
Gannon U (PA)
Gwynedd-Mercy Coll (PA)
Hannibal-LaGrange Coll (MO)
Idaho State U (ID)
Indiana U Northwest (IN)
Indiana U–Purdue U Indianapolis (IN)
Jefferson Coll of Health Sciences (VA)
Lamar U (TX)
Mansfield U of Pennsylvania (PA)
Midland Coll (TX)
Molloy Coll (NY)
Morehead State U (KY)
Nebraska Methodist Coll (NE)
Newman U (KS)
Northern Kentucky U (KY)
St. Augustine Coll (IL)
St. Petersburg Coll (FL)
Santa Fe Coll (FL)
Shawnee State U (OH)
Shenandoah U (VA)
Southern Adventist U (TN)
Thomas Edison State Coll (NJ)
Universidad Adventista de las Antillas (PR)
The U of Akron (OH)
U of Arkansas at Fort Smith (AR)
U of Pittsburgh at Johnstown (PA)
U of Southern Indiana (IN)
The U of Texas at Brownsville (TX)
U of the District of Columbia (DC)
The U of Toledo (OH)
Vermont Tech Coll (VT)
Washburn U (KS)
York Coll of Pennsylvania (PA)

Respiratory Therapy Technician
Northern Michigan U (MI)
Thompson Rivers U (BC, Canada)

Restaurant, Culinary, and Catering Management
Arkansas Tech U (AR)
The Art Inst of Atlanta (GA)
The Art Inst of Charleston (SC)
The Art Inst of Dallas (TX)
The Art Inst of Houston (TX)
The Art Inst of Tampa (FL)
The Art Inst of Washington (VA)
Bob Jones U (SC)
Ferris State U (MI)
Florida Culinary Inst (FL)
Johnson & Wales U (FL)
Johnson & Wales U (RI)
Johnson & Wales U - Charlotte Campus (NC)
Keystone Coll (PA)

Restaurant/Food Services Management
Johnson & Wales U (CO)
The U of Akron (OH)

Retailing
Johnson & Wales U (RI)
Patricia Stevens Coll (MO)

Robotics Technology
Indiana U–Purdue U Indianapolis (IN)
Pennsylvania Coll of Technology (PA)
Purdue U (IN)
U of Rio Grande (OH)

Romance Languages Related
Merrimack Coll (MA)

Russian
Idaho State U (ID)

Sales and Marketing/ Marketing And Distribution Teacher Education
Central Christian Coll of Kansas (KS)

Sales, Distribution and Marketing
Baker Coll of Flint (MI)
Baker Coll of Jackson (MI)
Clayton State U (GA)
Dalton State Coll (GA)
Johnson & Wales U (RI)
Johnson & Wales U - Charlotte Campus (NC)
Pioneer Pacific Coll, Wilsonville (OR)
St. Cloud State U (MN)
Thompson Rivers U (BC, Canada)
The U of Findlay (OH)

Science Teacher Education
Central Christian Coll of Kansas (KS)
U of Cincinnati (OH)

Science Technologies Related
Madonna U (MI)
Maria Coll (NY)
Ohio Valley U (WV)
U of Alaska Fairbanks (AK)

Sculpture
Keystone Coll (PA)

Secondary Education
Central Christian Coll of Kansas (KS)
Dalton State Coll (GA)
Ferris State U (MI)
Mountain State U (WV)
Rogers State U (OK)
Utah Valley U (UT)

Securities Services Administration
Herzing U (GA)

Security and Loss Prevention
John Jay Coll of Criminal Justice of the City U of New York (NY)
Potomac Coll (DC)

Security and Protective Services Related
Idaho State U (ID)
Keiser U, Fort Lauderdale (FL)
St. Petersburg Coll (FL)
Thomas Edison State Coll (NJ)

Selling Skills and Sales
Inter American U of Puerto Rico, San Germán Campus (PR)
The U of Akron (OH)

Sheet Metal Technology
Montana State U Billings (MT)

Sign Language Interpretation and Translation
Bethel Coll (IN)
Cincinnati Christian U (OH)
Fairmont State U (WV)
Mount Aloysius Coll (PA)
St. Catherine U (MN)
St. Petersburg Coll (FL)
U of Arkansas at Little Rock (AR)
U of Louisville (KY)

Small Business Administration
Lewis-Clark State Coll (ID)
The U of Akron (OH)

Social Psychology
Central Christian Coll of Kansas (KS)
Kwantlen Polytechnic U (BC, Canada)

Social Sciences
Abraham Baldwin Ag Coll (GA)
Campbellsville U (KY)
Central Christian Coll of Kansas (KS)
Faulkner U (AL)
Felician Coll (NJ)
Fisher Coll (MA)
Hillsdale Free Will Baptist Coll (OK)
Holy Apostles Coll and Seminary (CT)
Indiana Wesleyan U (IN)
Kwantlen Polytechnic U (BC, Canada)
Long Island U, Brooklyn Campus (NY)
Newbury Coll (MA)
Ohio U–Zanesville (OH)
Shawnee State U (OH)
Southwestern Assemblies of God U (TX)
State U of New York Empire State Coll (NY)
Trine U (IN)
U of Cincinnati (OH)
The U of Findlay (OH)
U of Maine at Augusta (ME)
U of Puerto Rico at Utuado (PR)
U of Southern Indiana (IN)
The U of Toledo (OH)
Valparaiso U (IN)
Wayland Baptist U (TX)

Social Sciences Related
Concordia U Texas (TX)

Social Science Teacher Education
Central Christian Coll of Kansas (KS)

Social Studies Teacher Education
Central Christian Coll of Kansas (KS)

Social Work
Abraham Baldwin Ag Coll (GA)
Central Christian Coll of Kansas (KS)
Dalton State Coll (GA)
Elizabethtown Coll (PA)
Ferris State U (MI)
Indiana U East (IN)
Methodist U (NC)
Northern State U (SD)
Suffolk U (MA)
U of Cincinnati (OH)
U of Rio Grande (OH)
The U of Toledo (OH)
Wright State U (OH)
Youngstown State U (OH)

Social Work Related
The U of Akron (OH)

Sociology
Abraham Baldwin Ag Coll (GA)
Central Christian Coll of Kansas (KS)
Coll of Coastal Georgia (GA)
Dalton State Coll (GA)
Felician Coll (NJ)
Grand View U (IA)
Indiana U Northwest (IN)
Kwantlen Polytechnic U (BC, Canada)
Lourdes Coll (OH)
Marymount Manhattan Coll (NY)
Methodist U (NC)
Midland Coll (TX)
Montana State U Billings (MT)
Newbury Coll (MA)
Penn State U Park (PA)
Saint Joseph's U (PA)
Thomas More Coll (KY)
U of Dubuque (IA)
U of Rio Grande (OH)
The U of Scranton (PA)
The U of Tampa (FL)
Wright State U (OH)
Xavier U (OH)
Young Harris Coll (GA)

Solar Energy Technology
Pennsylvania Coll of Technology (PA)

Spanish
Idaho State U (ID)
Indiana U–Purdue U Fort Wayne (IN)
Methodist U (NC)
Midland Coll (TX)
Thomas More Coll (KY)
Xavier U (OH)
Young Harris Coll (GA)

Special Education
Edinboro U of Pennsylvania (PA)
Montana State U Billings (MT)

Special Education Related
Minot State U (ND)

Special Products Marketing
Johnson & Wales U (FL)
Johnson & Wales U (RI)
Lamar U (TX)
Newbury Coll (MA)

Speech and Rhetoric
Abraham Baldwin Ag Coll (GA)
Dalton State Coll (GA)
Ferris State U (MI)
Midland Coll (TX)

Speech-Language Pathology
Baker Coll of Muskegon (MI)
Southern Adventist U (TN)

Speech Teacher Education
Central Christian Coll of Kansas (KS)

Sport and Fitness Administration/ Management
Central Christian Coll of Kansas (KS)
Keiser U, Fort Lauderdale (FL)
Lake Superior State U (MI)
Mount Vernon Nazarene U (OH)
Thompson Rivers U (BC, Canada)

Student Counseling and Personnel Services Related
Samford U (AL)

Substance Abuse/ Addiction Counseling
Charles Drew U of Medicine and Science (CA)
Indiana Wesleyan U (IN)
Keene State Coll (NH)
Midland Coll (TX)
Newman U (KS)
St. Augustine Coll (IL)
St. Petersburg Coll (FL)
The U of Akron (OH)
U of Great Falls (MT)
The U of Toledo (OH)
Washburn U (KS)

Surgical Technology
Baker Coll of Clinton Township (MI)
Baker Coll of Flint (MI)
Baker Coll of Jackson (MI)
Baker Coll of Muskegon (MI)
Keiser U, Fort Lauderdale (FL)
Mercy Coll of Health Sciences (IA)
Montana State U Billings (MT)

Mount Aloysius Coll (PA)
Nebraska Methodist Coll (NE)
Northern Michigan U (MI)
Our Lady of the Lake Coll (LA)
Pennsylvania Coll of Technology (PA)
Presentation Coll (SD)
Robert Morris U Illinois (IL)
Southwest Florida Coll, Fort Myers (FL)
The U of Akron (OH)
U of Arkansas at Fort Smith (AR)
U of Pittsburgh at Johnstown (PA)
Washburn U (KS)

Survey Technology
Ferris State U (MI)
Glenville State Coll (WV)
Pennsylvania Coll of Technology (PA)
Thomas Edison State Coll (NJ)
The U of Akron (OH)
U of Alaska Anchorage (AK)
U of Arkansas at Monticello (AR)
Westwood Coll–Denver North (CO)

System Administration
Florida National Coll (FL)
Midland Coll (TX)
Peirce Coll (PA)
Pennsylvania Coll of Technology (PA)
Santa Fe Coll (FL)
Thompson Rivers U (BC, Canada)

System, Networking, and LAN/WAN Management
Baker Coll of Auburn Hills (MI)
Bryant & Stratton Coll, Cleveland (OH)
Dakota State U (SD)
Herzing U (GA)
Hickey Coll (MO)
ITT Tech Inst, Tempe (AZ)
ITT Tech Inst, Clovis (CA)
ITT Tech Inst, Concord (CA)
ITT Tech Inst, Corona (CA)
ITT Tech Inst, South Bend (IN)
ITT Tech Inst (KS)
ITT Tech Inst, Lexington (KY)
ITT Tech Inst (MS)
ITT Tech Inst, Springfield (MO)
ITT Tech Inst, Charlotte (NC)
ITT Tech Inst, Oklahoma City (OK)
Midland Coll (TX)
Southwest Florida Coll, Fort Myers (FL)
Thompson Rivers U (BC, Canada)

Teacher Assistant/Aide
Alabama State U (AL)
Alverno Coll (WI)
Dordt Coll (IA)
Eastern Mennonite U (VA)
Johnson Bible Coll (TN)
Lamar U (TX)
Tiffin U (OH)
U of Alaska Fairbanks (AK)
The U of Montana Western (MT)
Valparaiso U (IN)

Teaching Assistants/Aides Related
Trevecca Nazarene U (TN)

Technical and Business Writing
Florida National Coll (FL)
Murray State U (KY)

Technical Teacher Education
New York Inst of Technology (NY)
Western Kentucky U (KY)

Technology/Industrial Arts Teacher Education
Alaska Pacific U (AK)
EDP Coll of Puerto Rico, Inc. (PR)

Telecommunications Technology
ECPI Coll of Technology, Virginia Beach (VA)
ECPI Tech Coll, Roanoke (VA)
Inter American U of Puerto Rico, Bayamón Campus (PR)
Pace U (NY)
St. John's U (NY)

Theater Design and Technology
Johnson State Coll (VT)
U of Rio Grande (OH)

Theology
Appalachian Bible Coll (WV)
Briar Cliff U (IA)
Central Christian Coll of Kansas (KS)
Creighton U (NE)
Franciscan U of Steubenville (OH)
Griggs U (MD)
Marian U (IN)
Missouri Baptist U (MO)
Ohio Dominican U (OH)
Piedmont Baptist Coll and Graduate School (NC)
Sacred Heart Major Seminary (MI)
William Jessup U (CA)
Xavier U (OH)

Therapeutic Recreation
U of Southern Maine (ME)

Tool and Die Technology
Ferris State U (MI)
Pennsylvania Coll of Technology (PA)

Tourism and Travel Services Management
AIB Coll of Business (IA)
Baker Coll of Flint (MI)
Baker Coll of Muskegon (MI)
Black Hills State U (SD)
Fisher Coll (MA)
Florida National Coll (FL)
Johnson & Wales U (FL)
Johnson & Wales U (RI)
Newbury Coll (MA)
Patricia Stevens Coll (MO)
Pennsylvania Coll of Technology (PA)
Sullivan U (KY)
The U of Akron (OH)
The U of Montana Western (MT)

Tourism and Travel Services Marketing
AIB Coll of Business (IA)
Johnson & Wales U (RI)

Tourism Promotion
AIB Coll of Business (IA)
Florida National Coll (FL)
St. Cloud State U (MN)
Thompson Rivers U (BC, Canada)

Trade and Industrial Teacher Education
Cincinnati Christian U (OH)

Transportation and Materials Moving Related
Baker Coll of Flint (MI)
U of Cincinnati (OH)
The U of Toledo (OH)

Turf and Turfgrass Management
North Carolina State U (NC)
Pennsylvania Coll of Technology (PA)
U of Massachusetts Amherst (MA)

Urban Studies/Affairs
Beulah Heights U (GA)

Vehicle and Vehicle Parts And Accessories Marketing
Pennsylvania Coll of Technology (PA)

Vehicle/Equipment Operation
Baker Coll of Flint (MI)

Vehicle Maintenance and Repair Technologies Related
Pennsylvania Coll of Technology (PA)

Veterinary/Animal Health Technology
Argosy U, Twin Cities (MN)
Baker Coll of Cadillac (MI)
Baker Coll of Jackson (MI)
Baker Coll of Muskegon (MI)
Baker Coll of Port Huron (MI)
Fairmont State U (WV)
Fort Valley State U (GA)
Hickey Coll (MO)
Lincoln Memorial U (TN)
Medaille Coll (NY)
Midland Coll (TX)
Morehead State U (KY)
Mount Ida Coll (MA)
Northwestern State U of Louisiana (LA)
Purdue U (IN)
St. Petersburg Coll (FL)
State U of New York Coll of Technology at Canton (NY)
Sul Ross State U (TX)
Thomas Edison State Coll (NJ)
Thompson Rivers U (BC, Canada)
U of Maine at Augusta (ME)
Vermont Tech Coll (VT)

Violin, Viola, Guitar and Other Stringed Instruments
Five Towns Coll (NY)
Kwantlen Polytechnic U (BC, Canada)

Visual and Performing Arts Related
Alverno Coll (WI)

Voice and Opera
Five Towns Coll (NY)
Kwantlen Polytechnic U (BC, Canada)

Water Quality and Wastewater Treatment Management And Recycling Technology
Lake Superior State U (MI)
U of the District of Columbia (DC)
Wright State U (OH)

Water, Wetlands, and Marine Resources Management
Keystone Coll (PA)

Web/Multimedia Management and Webmaster
American Public U System (WV)
ITT Tech Inst, Tempe (AZ)
Lewis-Clark State Coll (ID)
Montana Tech of The U of Montana (MT)
Mountain State U (WV)
Pioneer Pacific Coll, Wilsonville (OR)
Platt Coll San Diego (CA)
St. Petersburg Coll (FL)

Web Page, Digital/Multimedia and Information Resources Design
Academy of Art U (CA)
The Art Inst of Atlanta (GA)
The Art Inst of Atlanta–Decatur (GA)
The Art Inst of Austin (TX)
The Art Inst of California–Hollywood (CA)
The Art Inst of California–Los Angeles (CA)
The Art Inst of California–Orange County (CA)
The Art Inst of California–Sacramento (CA)
The Art Inst of California–San Francisco (CA)
The Art Inst of California–Sunnyvale (CA)
The Art Inst of Charleston (SC)
The Art Inst of Charlotte (NC)
The Art Inst of Colorado (CO)
The Art Inst of Fort Lauderdale (FL)
The Art Inst of Fort Worth (TX)
The Art Inst of Houston (TX)
The Art Inst of Jacksonville (FL)
The Art Inst of Michigan (MI)
The Art Inst of Philadelphia (PA)
The Art Inst of Pittsburgh (PA)
The Art Inst of Raleigh-Durham (NC)
The Art Inst of San Antonio (TX)
The Art Inst of Tampa (FL)
The Art Inst of Tennessee–Nashville (TN)
The Art Inst of Vrigina Beach (VA)
The Art Inst of Washington (VA)
The Art Inst of Washington–Northern Virginia (VA)
The Art Insts International Minnesota (MN)
Baker Coll of Allen Park (MI)
DeVry U, Phoenix (AZ)
DeVry U, Fremont (CA)
DeVry U, Long Beach (CA)
DeVry U, Pomona (CA)
DeVry U, Sherman Oaks (CA)
DeVry U, Westminster (CO)
DeVry U, Miramar (FL)
DeVry U, Orlando (FL)
DeVry U, Alpharetta (GA)
DeVry U, Decatur (GA)
DeVry U, Addison (IL)
DeVry U, Chicago (IL)
DeVry U, Tinley Park (IL)
DeVry U, Indianapolis (IN)
DeVry U (KY)
DeVry U (MI)
DeVry U, Edina (MN)
DeVry U, Kansas City (MO)
DeVry U (NV)
DeVry U, Columbus (OH)
DeVry U (OK)
DeVry U (OR)
DeVry U, Fort Washington (PA)
DeVry U, Houston (TX)
DeVry U, Irving (TX)
DeVry U (UT)
DeVry U, Arlington (VA)
DeVry U, Federal Way (WA)
DeVry U Online (IL)
Florida National Coll (FL)
Idaho State U (ID)
The Illinois Inst of Art–Schaumburg (IL)
Indiana Tech (IN)
ITT Tech Inst, Tempe (AZ)
ITT Tech Inst, Lexington (KY)
Keiser U, Fort Lauderdale (FL)
Pennsylvania Coll of Technology (PA)
Platt Coll San Diego (CA)
St. Petersburg Coll (FL)
Southwest Florida Coll, Fort Myers (FL)
Stratford U, Woodbridge (VA)
Thomas More Coll (KY)
Thompson Rivers U (BC, Canada)
Utah Valley U (UT)

Welding Technology
Excelsior Coll (NY)
Ferris State U (MI)
Idaho State U (ID)
Lamar U (TX)
Lewis-Clark State Coll (ID)
Midland Coll (TX)
Oakland City U (IN)
U of Alaska Anchorage (AK)
The U of Toledo (OH)
Utah Valley U (UT)

Wildlife and Wildlands Science And Management
Abraham Baldwin Ag Coll (GA)
Keystone Coll (PA)
Mountain State U (WV)

Wildlife Biology
Central Christian Coll of Kansas (KS)
Keystone Coll (PA)

Wind/Percussion Instruments
Five Towns Coll (NY)

Women's Studies
Fisher Coll (MA)
Indiana U–Purdue U Fort Wayne (IN)
Nazarene Bible Coll (CO)

Wood Science and Wood Products/Pulp And Paper Technology
U of Arkansas at Monticello (AR)

Woodworking
Burlington Coll (VT)

Word Processing
Baker Coll of Allen Park (MI)
Florida National Coll (FL)

Youth Ministry
Brescia U (KY)
Central Christian Coll of Kansas (KS)
Mount Vernon Nazarene U (OH)

Zoology/Animal Biology
Central Christian Coll of Kansas (KS)

Alphabetical Listing of Two-Year Colleges

In this index, the page locations of profiles are printed in regular type, **Display ads** in *italics*, and **Close-Ups** in **bold type.**

Academy of Court Reporting, Akron (OH) 278
Academy of Court Reporting, Cleveland (OH) 278
The Academy of Health Care Professions (TX) 341
ACT College, Arlington (VA) 364
Adirondack Community College (NY) 244
Advanced Technology Institute (VA) 364
Aiken Technical College (SC) 329
Aims Community College (CO) 101
Alabama Southern Community College (AL) 55
Alamance Community College (NC) 264
Albany Technical College (GA) 124
Alexandria Technical College (MN) 204
Allan Hancock College (CA) 74
Allegany College of Maryland (MD) 185
Allen Community College (KS) 168
Allied College (MO) 218
Alpena Community College (MI) 196
Altamaha Technical College (GA) 124
Alvin Community College (TX) 341
Amarillo College (TX) 342
American Academy McAllister Institute of Funeral Service (NY) 245
American Academy of Dramatic Arts (CA) 75
American Academy of Dramatic Arts (NY) 245
American Career College, Anaheim (CA) 75
American Career College, Los Angeles (CA) 75
American Career College, Ontario (CA) 75
American College of Healthcare Sciences (OR) 299
American College of Technology (MO) 218
American River College (CA) 75
American Samoa Community College (AS) 61
Ancilla College (IN) 151
Andrew College (GA) 124
Angelina College (TX) 342
Angley College (FL) 111
Anne Arundel Community College (MD) 185
Anoka-Ramsey Community College (MN) 205
Anoka-Ramsey Community College, Cambridge Campus (MN) 205
Anoka Technical College (MN) 206
Antelope Valley College (CA) 75
Anthem College Aurora (CO) 101
Antonelli College, Hattiesburg (MS) 215
Antonelli College, Jackson (MS) 216
Antonelli College (OH) 278
Antonelli Institute (PA) 303
Apollo College (WA) 372
Apollo College–Boise (ID) 137
Apollo College–Phoenix (AZ) 61
Apollo College–Portland (OR) 299
Apollo College–Tri-City, Inc. (AZ) 61
Apollo College–Tucson, Inc. (AZ) 62
Apollo College–Westside, Inc. (AZ) 62
Applied Professional Training, Inc. (CA) 76
Arapahoe Community College (CO) 101
Argosy University, Twin Cities (MN) 206, **396**
Arizona Automotive Institute (AZ) 62
Arizona College of Allied Health (AZ) 62
Arizona Western College (AZ) 62
Arkansas Northeastern College (AR) 70
Arkansas State University–Beebe (AR) 70
Arkansas State University–Mountain Home (AR) 70
Arkansas State University–Newport (AR) 70
The Art Institute of Cincinnati (OH) 279
The Art Institute of New York City (NY) 245, **398**
The Art Institute of Ohio–Cincinnati (OH) 279
The Art Institute of Seattle (WA) 372, **400**
The Art Institute of York–Pennsylvania (PA) 303
ASA Institute, The College of Advanced Technology (NY) 245
Asheville-Buncombe Technical Community College (NC) 264
Ashland Community and Technical College (KY) 173
Asnuntuck Community College (CT) 107
Assumption College for Sisters (NJ) 235
ATA Career Education (KY) 173
Athens Technical College (GA) 124
ATI Career Training Center, Fort Lauderdale (FL) 112
ATI Career Training Center, Oakland Park (FL) 112
ATI College of Health (FL) 112
ATI Technical Training Center (TX) 342
Atlanta Metropolitan College (GA) 125
Atlanta Technical College (GA) 125
Atlantic Cape Community College (NJ) 236
ATS Institute of Technology (OH) 279
Augusta Technical College (GA) 125
Austin Community College (TX) 342
Aviation & Electronic Schools of America (CA) 76
Aviation Institute of Maintenance–Indianapolis, Indianapolis (IN) 152
Aviation Institute of Maintenance–Kansas City (MO) 218
Aviation Institute of Maintenance–Manassas (VA) 364
Aviation Institute of Maintenance–Virginia Beach (VA) 364
Bainbridge College (GA) 125
Bakersfield College (CA) 76
Baltimore City Community College (MD) 185
Baltimore International College (MD) 186
Barstow College (CA) 76
Barton County Community College (KS) 168
Bates Technical College (WA) 372
Baton Rouge Community College (LA) 179
Baton Rouge School of Computers (LA) 179
Bay de Noc Community College (MI) 196
Bay Mills Community College (MI) 196
Bay State College (MA) 190, **402**
Beal College (ME) 182
Beaufort County Community College (NC) 264
Beckfield College (KY) 173
Bellevue College (WA) 372
Bellingham Technical College (WA) 372
Belmont Technical College (OH) 279
Bel–Rea Institute of Animal Technology (CO) 101
Benjamin Franklin Institute of Technology (MA) 190
Bergen Community College (NJ) 236
Berkeley City College (CA) 76
Berkeley College, Woodland Park (NJ) 236
Berkeley College–New York City Campus (NY) 245
Berkeley College–Westchester Campus (NY) 245
Berkshire Community College (MA) 191
Berks Technical Institute (PA) 303
Bevill State Community College (AL) 55
Bidwell Training Center (PA) 303
Big Bend Community College (WA) 373
Big Sandy Community and Technical College (KY) 174
Bishop State Community College (AL) 55
Bismarck State College (ND) 276
Blackfeet Community College (MT) 227
Black Hawk College, Moline (IL) 138
Blackhawk Technical College (WI) 381
Black River Technical College (AR) 70
Bladen Community College (NC) 265
Blinn College (TX) 343
Blue Cliff College–Lafayette (LA) 179
Blue Cliff College–Shreveport (LA) 179
Bluegrass Community and Technical College (KY) 174
Blue Mountain Community College (OR) 299
Blue Ridge Community and Technical College (WV) 379
Blue Ridge Community College (NC) 265
Blue Ridge Community College (VA) 364
Borough of Manhattan Community College of the City University of New York (NY) 245
Bossier Parish Community College (LA) 180
Boulder College of Massage Therapy (CO) 101
Bowling Green State University–Firelands College (OH) 279
Bowling Green Technical College (KY) 174
Bradford School (OH) 280
Bradford School (PA) 303
Bramson ORT College (NY) 246
Brazosport College (TX) 343
Brevard Community College (FL) 112
Brigham Young University–Idaho (ID) 137
Bristol Community College (MA) 191
Bronx Community College of the City University of New York (NY) 246
Brookdale Community College (NJ) 236
Brookhaven College (TX) 343
Broome Community College (NY) 246
Broward College (FL) 112
Brown College (MN) 206
Brown Mackie College–Akron (OH) 280, **404**
Brown Mackie College–Albuquerque (NM) 240, **406**
Brown Mackie College–Atlanta (GA) 126, **408**
Brown Mackie College–Boise (ID) 137, **410**
Brown Mackie College–Cincinnati (OH) 280, **412**
Brown Mackie College–Findlay (OH) 280, **414**
Brown Mackie College–Fort Wayne (IN) 152, **416**
Brown Mackie College–Greenville (SC) 329, **418**
Brown Mackie College–Hopkinsville (KY) 174, **420**
Brown Mackie College–Indianapolis (IN) 152, **422**
Brown Mackie College–Kansas City (KS) 169, **424**
Brown Mackie College–Louisville (KY) 174, **426**
Brown Mackie College–Merrillville (IN) 152, **428**
Brown Mackie College–Miami (FL) 112, **430**
Brown Mackie College–Michigan City (IN) 152, **432**
Brown Mackie College–North Canton (OH) 280, **434**
Brown Mackie College–Northern Kentucky (KY) 174, **436**
Brown Mackie College–Phoenix (AZ) 62, **438**
Brown Mackie College–Quad Cities (IL) 138, **440**
Brown Mackie College–St. Louis (MO) 218, **442**
Brown Mackie College–Salina (KS) 169, **444**
Brown Mackie College–South Bend (IN) 152, **446**
Brown Mackie College–Tucson (AZ) 62, **448**
Brown Mackie College–Tulsa (OK) 295, **450**
Brunswick Community College (NC) 265
Bryan College (CA) 76
Bryant & Stratton College, Eastlake (OH) 280
Bryant & Stratton College, Parma (OH) 281
Bryant & Stratton College (WI) 382
Bryant & Stratton College - Albany Campus (NY) 246
Bryant & Stratton College - Amherst Campus (NY) 247
Bryant & Stratton College - Buffalo Campus (NY) 247
Bryant & Stratton College - Greece Campus (NY) 247
Bryant & Stratton College - Henrietta Campus (NY) 248
Bryant & Stratton College - North Campus (NY) 248
Bryant & Stratton College - Richmond Campus (VA) 365
Bryant & Stratton College - Southtowns Campus (NY) 248
Bryant & Stratton College - Syracuse Campus (NY) 249
Bryant & Stratton College - Virginia Beach (VA) 365
The Bryman School of Arizona (AZ) 63
Bucks County Community College (PA) 303
Bunker Hill Community College (MA) 191
Burlington County College (NJ) 236
Business Informatics Center, Inc. (NY) 249
Butler Community College (KS) 169
Butler County Community College (PA) 304
Butte College (CA) 77
Cabrillo College (CA) 77
Caldwell Community College and Technical Institute (NC) 265
Calhoun Community College (AL) 55
California Culinary Academy (CA) 77
California School of Culinary Arts (CA) 77
Cambria-Rowe Business College, Indiana (PA) 304
Cambria-Rowe Business College, Johnstown (PA) 304
Cambridge Career College (CA) 77
Camden County College (NJ) 236
Camelot College (LA) 180
Cameron College (LA) 180
Cankdeska Cikana Community College (ND) 277
Cañada College (CA) 77
Cape Cod Community College (MA) 191
Cape Fear Community College (NC) 266
Capital Community College (CT) 107
Career College of Northern Nevada (NV) 233
Career Technical College (LA) 180
Career Training Academy, Monroeville (PA) 304
Career Training Academy, New Kensington (PA) 304
Career Training Academy, Pittsburgh (PA) 304
Carl Albert State College (OK) 295
Carl Sandburg College (IL) 138
Carolinas College of Health Sciences (NC) 266
Carroll Community College (MD) 186
Carteret Community College (NC) 266
Cascadia Community College (WA) 373
Casper College (WY) 388
Catawba Valley Community College (NC) 267
Cayuga County Community College (NY) 249
Cecil College (MD) 186
Cedar Valley College (TX) 343
Center for Advanced Legal Studies (TX) 343
Central Alabama Community College (AL) 55
Central Arizona College (AZ) 63
Central Carolina Community College (NC) 267
Central Carolina Technical College (SC) 330
Central Community College–Columbus Campus (NE) 229
Central Community College–Grand Island Campus (NE) 229
Central Community College–Hastings Campus (NE) 230
Central Florida Community College (FL) 112

Central Florida Institute (FL) 112
Central Georgia Technical College (GA) 126
Centralia College (WA) 373
Central Lakes College (MN) 206
Central Maine Community College (ME) 182
Central Maine Medical Center College of Nursing and Health Professions (ME) 183
Central New Mexico Community College (NM) 240
Central Ohio Technical College (OH) 281
Central Oregon Community College (OR) 299
Central Piedmont Community College (NC) 267
Central Texas College (TX) 343
Central Virginia Community College (VA) 365
Central Wyoming College (WY) 389
Centro de Estudios Multidisciplinarios (PR) 328
Centura College, Chesapeake (VA) 365
Centura College, Newport News (VA) 365
Centura College, Norfolk (VA) 365
Centura College, Richmond (VA) 365
Centura College, Richmond (VA) 365
Centura College, Virginia Beach (VA) 365
Centura Institute (FL) 112
Century College (MN) 206
Cerritos College (CA) 77
Cerro Coso Community College (CA) 77
Chabot College (CA) 77
Chaffey College (CA) 78
Chandler-Gilbert Community College (AZ) 63
Charter College (AK) 60
Chatfield College (OH) 281
Chattahoochee Technical College (GA) 126
Chattahoochee Valley Community College (AL) 55
Chattanooga College–Medical, Dental and Technical Careers (TN) 336
Chattanooga State Community College (TN) 336
Chemeketa Community College (OR) 300
Chesapeake College (MD) 186
Chief Dull Knife College (MT) 227
CHI Institute, Broomall Campus (PA) 304
CHI Institute, Franklin Mills Campus (PA) 304
Chipola College (FL) 112
Chippewa Valley Technical College (WI) 382
The Christ College of Nursing and Health Sciences (OH) 281
Cincinnati State Technical and Community College (OH) 281
Cisco College (TX) 344
Citrus College (CA) 78
City College, Casselberry (FL) 113
City College, Fort Lauderdale (FL) 113
City College, Gainesville (FL) 113
City College, Miami (FL) 113
City College of San Francisco (CA) 78
City Colleges of Chicago, Harold Washington College (IL) 139
City Colleges of Chicago, Harry S. Truman College (IL) 139
City Colleges of Chicago, Kennedy-King College (IL) 139
City Colleges of Chicago, Malcolm X College (IL) 139
City Colleges of Chicago, Olive-Harvey College (IL) 139
City Colleges of Chicago, Richard J. Daley College (IL) 139
City Colleges of Chicago, Wilbur Wright College (IL) 140
Clackamas Community College (OR) 300
Clarendon College (TX) 344
Clark College (WA) 373
Clark State Community College (OH) 282
Clary Sage College (OK) 295
Clatsop Community College (OR) 300
Cleveland Community College (NC) 268
Cleveland Institute of Electronics (OH) 282
Cleveland State Community College (TN) 337
Clinton Community College (IA) 162
Clinton Community College (NY) 249
Clinton Junior College (SC) 330
Cloud County Community College (KS) 169
Clover Park Technical College (WA) 373
Clovis Community College (NM) 241
Coahoma Community College (MS) 216
Coastal Bend College (TX) 344
Coastal Carolina Community College (NC) 268
Coastline Community College (CA) 78
Cochise College, Sierra Vista (AZ) 63
Cochran School of Nursing (NY) 249
Coconino Community College (AZ) 63
Coffeyville Community College (KS) 169
Colby Community College (KS) 170
Colegio Universitario de San Juan, San Juan (PR) 328
Coleman University, San Marcos (CA) 78
CollegeAmerica–Colorado Springs (CO) 101
CollegeAmerica–Denver (CO) 101
CollegeAmerica–Flagstaff (AZ) 63
CollegeAmerica–Fort Collins (CO) 101
College of Alameda (CA) 78
College of Business and Technology (FL) 113
College of Court Reporting (IN) 152
College of DuPage (IL) 140
College of Eastern Utah (UT) 361
College of Lake County (IL) 140
College of Marin (CA) 78
College of Menominee Nation (WI) 382
College of Micronesia–FSM (FM, Micronesia) 204
The College of Office Technology (IL) 141
College of San Mateo (CA) 78
College of Southern Idaho (ID) 137
College of Southern Maryland (MD) 186
College of Southern Nevada (NV) 233
College of The Albemarle (NC) 268
College of the Canyons (CA) 78
College of the Desert (CA) 79
College of the Mainland (TX) 344
College of the Marshall Islands (Marshall Islands) 393
College of the Redwoods (CA) 79
College of the Sequoias (CA) 79
College of the Siskiyous (CA) 79
The College of Westchester (NY) 249
Collin County Community College District (TX) 344
Colorado Mountain College (CO) 101
Colorado Mountain College, Alpine Campus (CO) 101
Colorado Mountain College, Timberline Campus (CO) 102
Colorado Northwestern Community College (CO) 102
Colorado School of Healing Arts (CO) 102
Colorado School of Trades (CO) 102
Columbia Basin College (WA) 373
Columbia College (CA) 79
Columbia Gorge Community College (OR) 300
Columbia-Greene Community College (NY) 249
Columbia State Community College (TN) 337
Columbus Culinary Institute at Bradford School (OH) 282
Columbus State Community College (OH) 282
Columbus Technical College (GA) 126
Commonwealth Institute of Funeral Service (TX) 345
Commonwealth Technical Institute (PA) 304
Community & Technical College at West Virginia University Institute of Technology (WV) 379
Community Care College (OK) 295
Community Christian College (CA) 80
Community College of Allegheny County (PA) 304
Community College of Aurora (CO) 102
The Community College of Baltimore County (MD) 187
Community College of Beaver County (PA) 305
Community College of Denver (CO) 102
Community College of Philadelphia (PA) 305
Community College of Rhode Island (RI) 329
Community College of the Air Force (AL) 55
Community College of Vermont (VT) 363
Computer Career Center (TX) 345
Concorde Career College (CA) 80
Concorde Career College (TN) 337
Concorde Career Institute, North Hollywood (CA) 80
Concorde Career Institute (MO) 218
Connors State College (OK) 296
Consolidated School of Business, Lancaster (PA) 305
Consolidated School of Business, York (PA) 306
Contra Costa College (CA) 80
Copiah-Lincoln Community College (MS) 216
Copiah-Lincoln Community College–Natchez Campus (MS) 216
Copper Mountain College (CA) 80
Corning Community College (NY) 249
Cossatot Community College of the University of Arkansas (AR) 71
Cosumnes River College, Sacramento (CA) 80
Cottey College (MO) 219
County College of Morris (NJ) 237
Court Reporting Institute of Dallas (TX) 345
Court Reporting Institute of Houston (TX) 345
Cowley County Community College and Area Vocational–Technical School (KS) 170
Crafton Hills College (CA) 80
Craven Community College (NC) 268
Creative Center (NE) 230
Crimson Technical College (CA) 80
Crouse Hospital School of Nursing (NY) 250
Crowder College (MO) 219
Crowley's Ridge College (AR) 71
Cuesta College (CA) 80
Culinary Institute Alain & Marie LeNotre (TX) 345
Culinary Institute of St. Louis at Hickey College (MO) 219
Cumberland County College (NJ) 237
Cuyahoga Community College (OH) 282
Cuyamaca College (CA) 80
Cypress College (CA) 80
Dabney S. Lancaster Community College (VA) 366
Dakota College at Bottineau (ND) 277
Dakota County Technical College (MN) 207
Dallas Institute of Funeral Service (TX) 345
Danville Area Community College (IL) 141
Danville Community College (VA) 366
Darton College (GA) 126
Davidson County Community College (NC) 268
Davis College (OH) 283
Dawson Community College (MT) 227
Daymar College, Bellevue (KY) 174
Daymar College, Bowling Green (KY) 174
Daymar College, Louisville (KY) 175
Daymar College, Owensboro (KY) 175
Daymar College, Paducah (KY) 175
Daymar College, Chillicothe (OH) 283
Daymar College, Jackson (OH) 283
Daymar College, Lancaster (OH) 283
Daymar College, New Boston (OH) 283
Daymar Institute, Nashville (TN) 337
Daytona State College (FL) 113
Dean College (MA) 192
Dean Institute of Technology (PA) 306
De Anza College (CA) 81
Deep Springs College (CA) 81
DeKalb Technical College (GA) 127
Delaware College of Art and Design (DE) 110
Delaware County Community College (PA) 306
Delaware Technical & Community College, Jack F. Owens Campus (DE) 110
Delaware Technical & Community College, Stanton/Wilmington Campus (DE) 111
Delaware Technical & Community College, Terry Campus (DE) 111
Delgado Community College (LA) 180
Del Mar College (TX) 345
Delta College (MI) 197
Delta College of Arts and Technology (LA) 180
Delta School of Business & Technology (LA) 180
Denmark Technical College (SC) 330
Denver Academy of Court Reporting (CO) 102
Denver Automotive and Diesel College (CO) 102
Des Moines Area Community College (IA) 162
Diablo Valley College (CA) 81
Diné College (AZ) 63
Dodge City Community College (KS) 171
Doña Ana Branch Community College (NM) 241
Donnelly College (KS) 171
Dorothea Hopfer School of Nursing at The Mount Vernon Hospital (NY) 250
Douglas Education Center (PA) 306
DuBois Business College (PA) 307
Duluth Business University (MN) 207
Dunwoody College of Technology (MN) 207
Durham Technical Community College (NC) 268
Dutchess Community College (NY) 250
Dyersburg State Community College (TN) 337
East Arkansas Community College (AR) 71
East Central College (MO) 219
East Central Community College (MS) 216
East Central Technical College (GA) 127
Eastern Arizona College (AZ) 64
Eastern Gateway Community College (OH) 283
Eastern Idaho Technical College (ID) 137
Eastern Maine Community College (ME) 183
Eastern New Mexico University–Roswell (NM) 241
Eastern Oklahoma State College (OK) 296
Eastern Shore Community College (VA) 366
Eastern West Virginia Community and Technical College (WV) 379
Eastern Wyoming College (WY) 389
Eastfield College (TX) 346
East Georgia College (GA) 127
East Los Angeles College (CA) 81
East Mississippi Community College (MS) 216
ECPI Technical College (NC) 268
ECPI Technical College, Richmond (VA) 366
Edgecombe Community College (NC) 269
Edison State College (FL) 114
Edison State Community College (OH) 283
Edmonds Community College (WA) 374
Elaine P. Nunez Community College (LA) 180
El Camino College (CA) 82
El Centro College (TX) 346
Elgin Community College (IL) 141
Elizabethtown Community and Technical College, Elizabethtown (KY) 175
Ellis Hospital School of Nursing (NY) 250
Ellsworth Community College (IA) 162
Elmira Business Institute (NY) 250
El Paso Community College (TX) 347
Emory University, Oxford College (GA) 127
Empire College (CA) 82
Enterprise State Community College (AL) 55
Erie Business Center, Main (PA) 307
Erie Business Center, South (PA) 307
Erie Community College (NY) 250
Erie Community College, North Campus (NY) 251
Erie Community College, South Campus (NY) 251
Erie Institute of Technology, Erie (PA) 307
Essex County College (NJ) 237
Estrella Mountain Community College (AZ) 64
ETI Technical College of Niles (OH) 284
Eugenio María de Hostos Community College of the City University of New York (NY) 252
Everest College, Phoenix (AZ) 64
Everest College, City of Industry (CA) 82
Everest College, Ontario (CA) 82
Everest College, Rancho Cucamonga (CA) 82
Everest College, Aurora (CO) 102
Everest College, Colorado Springs (CO) 102
Everest College, Denver (CO) 103
Everest College, Springfield (MO) 220
Everest College (NV) 233
Everest College (OR) 300
Everest College, Arlington (TX) 347
Everest College, Dallas (TX) 347
Everest College, Fort Worth (TX) 347
Everest College (UT) 362
Everest College (VA) 366
Everest College (WA) 374
Everest Institute (CA) 82
Everest Institute, Fort Lauderdale (FL) 114
Everest Institute, Hialeah (FL) 114
Everest Institute, Miami (FL) 114
Everest Institute, Miami (FL) 114
Everest Institute (GA) 128
Everest Institute (NY) 252
Everest Institute (OH) 284
Everest Institute (PA) 307
Everest Institute (WV) 379
Everest University, Orange Park (FL) 114
Everett Community College (WA) 374
Evergreen Valley College (CA) 82
Fashion Careers College (CA) 82
Fashion Institute of Technology (NY) 252, **452**
Fayetteville Technical Community College (NC) 269
Feather River College (CA) 82
FIDM/The Fashion Institute of Design & Merchandising, Los Angeles Campus (CA) 82, **454**
FIDM/The Fashion Institute of Design & Merchandising, Orange County Campus (CA) 83
FIDM/The Fashion Institute of Design & Merchandising, San Diego Campus (CA) 83

FIDM/The Fashion Institute of Design & Merchandising, San Francisco Campus (CA) 83
FINE Mortuary College, LLC (MA) 192
Finger Lakes Community College (NY) 252
Fiorello H. LaGuardia Community College of the City University of New York (NY) 253
Flathead Valley Community College (MT) 227
Flint Hills Technical College (KS) 171
Flint River Technical College (GA) 128
Florence-Darlington Technical College (SC) 330
Florida Career College (FL) 114
Florida College of Natural Health, Bradenton (FL) 114
Florida College of Natural Health, Maitland (FL) 114
Florida College of Natural Health, Miami (FL) 114
Florida College of Natural Health, Pompano Beach (FL) 114
Florida Keys Community College (FL) 115
The Florida School of Midwifery (FL) 115
Florida State College at Jacksonville (FL) 115
Florida Technical College, Auburndale (FL) 115
Florida Technical College, DeLand (FL) 115
Florida Technical College, Jacksonville (FL) 115
Florida Technical College, Orlando (FL) 115
Folsom Lake College (CA) 84
Fond du Lac Tribal and Community College (MN) 207
Foothill College (CA) 84
Forrest Junior College (SC) 330
Forsyth Technical Community College (NC) 269
Fort Belknap College (MT) 228
Fort Berthold Community College (ND) 277
Fortis College (FL) 115
Fortis College (OH) 284
Fortis College–Ravenna (OH) 284
Fortis Institute (PA) 307
Fort Peck Community College (MT) 228
Fort Scott Community College (KS) 171
Fountainhead College of Technology (TN) 337
Fox College (IL) 142
Fox Valley Technical College (WI) 382
Frank Phillips College (TX) 347
Frederick Community College (MD) 187
Fresno City College (CA) 84
Front Range Community College (CO) 103
Fullerton College (CA) 84
Fulton-Montgomery Community College (NY) 253
Gadsden State Community College (AL) 56
Gainesville State College (GA) 128
Gallipolis Career College (OH) 285
Galveston College (TX) 348
Gamla College (NY) 254
Garden City Community College (KS) 171
Garrett College (MD) 188
Gaston College (NC) 269
Gateway Community and Technical College (KY) 175
GateWay Community College (AZ) 64
Gateway Community College (CT) 107
Gateway Technical College (WI) 382
Gavilan College (CA) 84
Gem City College (IL) 142
Genesee Community College (NY) 254
George Corley Wallace State Community College (AL) 56
George C. Wallace Community College (AL) 56
Georgia Highlands College (GA) 128
Georgia Military College (GA) 129
Georgia Northwestern Technical College (GA) 129
Georgia Perimeter College (GA) 129
Germanna Community College (VA) 366
Glendale Community College (AZ) 64
Glendale Community College (CA) 84
Glen Oaks Community College (MI) 197
Gloucester County College (NJ) 238
Gogebic Community College (MI) 197
Golden West College (CA) 84
Good Samaritan College of Nursing and Health Science (OH) 285
Goodwin College (CT) 107
Gordon College (GA) 130
Grand Rapids Community College (MI) 197
Grays Harbor College (WA) 374
Grayson County College (TX) 348
Great Basin College (NV) 234
Great Bay Community College (NH) 234
Greenfield Community College (MA) 192
Green River Community College (WA) 374
Greenville Technical College (SC) 331
Gretna Career College (LA) 181
Griffin Technical College (GA) 130
Grossmont College (CA) 84
Guam Community College (GU) 135
Guilford Technical Community College (NC) 269
Gulf Coast College (FL) 115
Gulf Coast Community College (FL) 115
Gupton-Jones College of Funeral Service (GA) 130
Gwinnett Technical College (GA) 130
Hagerstown Community College (MD) 188
Halifax Community College (NC) 270
Hallmark College of Technology (TX) 348
Hallmark Institute of Aeronautics (TX) 348
Harcum College (PA) 307
Harford Community College (MD) 188
Harper College (IL) 142
Harrisburg Area Community College (PA) 307
Harrison College, Anderson (IN) 152
Harrison College, Columbus (IN) 153
Harrison College, Elkhart (IN) 153
Harrison College, Evansville (IN) 153
Harrison College, Fort Wayne (IN) 153
Harrison College, Indianapolis (IN) 153
Harrison College, Indianapolis (IN) 154
Harrison College, Indianapolis (IN) 154
Harrison College, Lafayette (IN) 154
Harrison College, Muncie (IN) 154
Harrison College, Terre Haute (IN) 155
Harrison College (OH) 285
Hartnell College (CA) 84
Hawaii Community College (HI) 135
Hawaii Tokai International College (HI) 135
Hawkeye Community College (IA) 162
Haywood Community College (NC) 270
Hazard Community and Technical College (KY) 175
H. Councill Trenholm State Technical College (AL) 56
Heald College–Concord, Concord (CA) 85
Heald College–Fresno (CA) 85
Heald College–Hayward (CA) 85
Heald College–Honolulu (HI) 135
Heald College–Portland (OR) 300
Heald College–Rancho Cordova (CA) 85
Heald College–Roseville (CA) 85
Heald College–Salinas (CA) 85
Heald College–San Francisco (CA) 85
Heald College–San Jose (CA) 85
Heald College–Stockton (CA) 85
Heartland Community College (IL) 142
Heart of Georgia Technical College (GA) 130
Helene Fuld College of Nursing of North General Hospital (NY) 254
Henderson Community College (KY) 175
Hennepin Technical College (MN) 207
Henry Ford Community College (MI) 198
Heritage College (CO) 103
Heritage College (MO) 220
Heritage College (OK) 296
Herkimer County Community College (NY) 254
Herzing College (AL) 57
Herzing College, Winter Park (FL) 116
Herzing College (LA) 181
Herzing College (MN) 208
Hesser College, Concord (NH) 234
Hesser College, Manchester (NH) 234, **456**
Hesser College, Nashua (NH) 235
Hesser College, Portsmouth (NH) 235
Hesser College, Salem (NH) 235
Hesston College (KS) 171
Hibbing Community College (MN) 208
Highland Community College (IL) 142
Highland Community College (KS) 171
Highline Community College (WA) 375
High-Tech Institute (AZ) 65
High-Tech Institute (CA) 85
High-Tech Institute (FL) 116
High-Tech Institute (GA) 130
High-Tech Institute (MN) 208
High-Tech Institute (MO) 220
High-Tech Institute (NV) 234
High-Tech Institute, Memphis (TN) 337
High-Tech Institute, Nashville (TN) 338
Hill College of the Hill Junior College District (TX) 348
Hillsborough Community College (FL) 116
Hinds Community College (MS) 216
Hocking College (OH) 285
Holmes Community College (MS) 216
Holyoke Community College (MA) 192
Hondros College (OH) 285
Honolulu Community College (HI) 135
Hopkinsville Community College (KY) 176
Horry-Georgetown Technical College (SC) 331
Housatonic Community College (CT) 108
Houston Community College System (TX) 348
Howard College (TX) 349
Howard Community College (MD) 188
Hudson County Community College (NJ) 238
Hudson Valley Community College (NY) 254
Huertas Junior College (PR) 328
Humacao Community College (PR) 328
Huntington Junior College (WV) 379
Hussian School of Art (PA) 308
Hutchinson Community College and Area Vocational School (KS) 171
IHM Health Studies Center (MO) 220
Ilisagvik College (AK) 60
Illinois Central College (IL) 143
Illinois Eastern Community Colleges, Frontier Community College (IL) 143
Illinois Eastern Community Colleges, Lincoln Trail College (IL) 143
Illinois Eastern Community Colleges, Olney Central College (IL) 143
Illinois Eastern Community Colleges, Wabash Valley College (IL) 144
Illinois Valley Community College (IL) 144
Imperial Valley College (CA) 85
Independence Community College (KS) 172
Indian Hills Community College (IA) 163
Indian River State College (FL) 116
Institute of American Indian Arts (NM) 241
Institute of Business & Medical Careers (CO) 103
Institute of Design and Construction (NY) 254
Instituto Comercial de Puerto Rico Junior College (PR) 328
IntelliTec College, Colorado Springs (CO) 103
IntelliTec College, Grand Junction (CO) 103
IntelliTec Medical Institute (CO) 103
Interactive College of Technology (GA) 131
International Business College, Indianapolis (IN) 155
International College of Broadcasting (OH) 285
Inver Hills Community College (MN) 208
Iowa Central Community College (IA) 163
Iowa Lakes Community College (IA) 163
Iowa Western Community College (IA) 164
Irvine Valley College (CA) 85
Island Drafting and Technical Institute (NY) 255
Isothermal Community College (NC) 270
Itasca Community College (MN) 208
Itawamba Community College (MS) 217
ITI Technical College (LA) 181
ITT Technical Institute, Bessemer (AL) 57
ITT Technical Institute, Madison (AL) 57
ITT Technical Institute, Mobile (AL) 57
ITT Technical Institute, Phoenix (AZ) 65
ITT Technical Institute, Tucson (AZ) 65
ITT Technical Institute (AR) 71
ITT Technical Institute, Anaheim (CA) 85
ITT Technical Institute, Lathrop (CA) 86
ITT Technical Institute, Oxnard (CA) 86
ITT Technical Institute, Rancho Cordova (CA) 86
ITT Technical Institute, San Bernardino (CA) 86
ITT Technical Institute, San Diego (CA) 86
ITT Technical Institute, San Dimas (CA) 86
ITT Technical Institute, Sylmar (CA) 86
ITT Technical Institute, Torrance (CA) 87
ITT Technical Institute, Aurora (CO) 104
ITT Technical Institute, Thornton (CO) 104
ITT Technical Institute, Fort Lauderdale (FL) 117
ITT Technical Institute, Fort Myers (FL) 117
ITT Technical Institute, Jacksonville (FL) 117
ITT Technical Institute, Lake Mary (FL) 117
ITT Technical Institute, Miami (FL) 117
ITT Technical Institute, Pinellas Park (FL) 117
ITT Technical Institute, Tallahassee (FL) 118
ITT Technical Institute, Tampa (FL) 118
ITT Technical Institute, Atlanta (GA) 131
ITT Technical Institute, Duluth (GA) 131
ITT Technical Institute, Kennesaw (GA) 131
ITT Technical Institute (ID) 137
ITT Technical Institute, Burr Ridge (IL) 144
ITT Technical Institute, Mount Prospect (IL) 144
ITT Technical Institute, Orland Park (IL) 145
ITT Technical Institute, Fort Wayne (IN) 155
ITT Technical Institute, Indianapolis (IN) 155
ITT Technical Institute, Merrillville (IN) 155
ITT Technical Institute, Newburgh (IN) 155
ITT Technical Institute, Cedar Rapids (IA) 164
ITT Technical Institute, Clive (IA) 164
ITT Technical Institute, Louisville (KY) 176
ITT Technical Institute, Baton Rouge (LA) 181
ITT Technical Institute, St. Rose (LA) 181
ITT Technical Institute (MD) 189
ITT Technical Institute, Norwood (MA) 193
ITT Technical Institute, Woburn (MA) 193
ITT Technical Institute, Canton (MI) 198
ITT Technical Institute, Swartz Creek (MI) 198
ITT Technical Institute, Troy (MI) 198
ITT Technical Institute, Wyoming (MI) 198
ITT Technical Institute (MN) 209
ITT Technical Institute, Arnold (MO) 220
ITT Technical Institute, Earth City (MO) 220
ITT Technical Institute, Kansas City (MO) 220
ITT Technical Institute (NE) 230
ITT Technical Institute (NV) 234
ITT Technical Institute (NM) 242
ITT Technical Institute, Albany (NY) 255
ITT Technical Institute, Getzville (NY) 255
ITT Technical Institute, Liverpool (NY) 255
ITT Technical Institute, Charlotte (NC) 270
ITT Technical Institute, High Point (NC) 270
ITT Technical Institute, Morrisville (NC) 270
ITT Technical Institute, Akron (OH) 285
ITT Technical Institute, Columbus (OH) 285
ITT Technical Institute, Dayton (OH) 285
ITT Technical Institute, Hilliard (OH) 285
ITT Technical Institute, Maumee (OH) 286
ITT Technical Institute, Norwood (OH) 286
ITT Technical Institute, Strongsville (OH) 286
ITT Technical Institute, Warrensville Heights (OH) 286
ITT Technical Institute, Youngstown (OH) 286
ITT Technical Institute, Tulsa (OK) 296
ITT Technical Institute (OR) 300
ITT Technical Institute, Bensalem (PA) 308
ITT Technical Institute, Dunmore (PA) 308
ITT Technical Institute, Harrisburg (PA) 308
ITT Technical Institute, King of Prussia (PA) 308
ITT Technical Institute, Pittsburgh (PA) 309
ITT Technical Institute, Tarentum (PA) 309
ITT Technical Institute, Columbia (SC) 331
ITT Technical Institute, Greenville (SC) 331
ITT Technical Institute, Chattanooga (TN) 338
ITT Technical Institute, Cordova (TN) 338
ITT Technical Institute, Johnson City (TN) 338
ITT Technical Institute, Knoxville (TN) 338
ITT Technical Institute, Nashville (TN) 338
ITT Technical Institute, Arlington (TX) 349
ITT Technical Institute, Austin (TX) 349
ITT Technical Institute, DeSoto (TX) 350
ITT Technical Institute, Houston (TX) 350
ITT Technical Institute, Houston (TX) 350
ITT Technical Institute, Richardson (TX) 350
ITT Technical Institute, San Antonio (TX) 350
ITT Technical Institute, Webster (TX) 350
ITT Technical Institute (UT) 362
ITT Technical Institute, Chantilly (VA) 367
ITT Technical Institute, Norfolk (VA) 367
ITT Technical Institute, Richmond (VA) 367
ITT Technical Institute, Salem (VA) 367
ITT Technical Institute, Springfield (VA) 367
ITT Technical Institute, Everett (WA) 375
ITT Technical Institute, Seattle (WA) 375

ITT Technical Institute, Spokane Valley (WA) 375
ITT Technical Institute (WV) 379
ITT Technical Institute, Green Bay (WI) 382
ITT Technical Institute, Greenfield (WI) 383
ITT Technical Institute, Madison (WI) 383
Ivy Tech Community College–Bloomington (IN) 155
Ivy Tech Community College–Central Indiana (IN) 156
Ivy Tech Community College–Columbus (IN) 156
Ivy Tech Community College–East Central (IN) 157
Ivy Tech Community College–Kokomo (IN) 157
Ivy Tech Community College–Lafayette (IN) 157
Ivy Tech Community College–North Central (IN) 158
Ivy Tech Community College–Northeast (IN) 158
Ivy Tech Community College–Northwest (IN) 158
Ivy Tech Community College–Richmond (IN) 159
Ivy Tech Community College–Southeast (IN) 159
Ivy Tech Community College–Southern Indiana (IN) 159
Ivy Tech Community College–Southwest (IN) 160
Ivy Tech Community College–Wabash Valley (IN) 160
Jackson Community College (MI) 198
Jackson State Community College (TN) 338
Jacksonville College (TX) 350
James A. Rhodes State College (OH) 286
James H. Faulkner State Community College (AL) 57
James Sprunt Community College (NC) 271
Jamestown Business College (NY) 255
Jamestown Community College (NY) 255
Jefferson College (MO) 220
Jefferson Community and Technical College (KY) 176
Jefferson Community College (NY) 256
Jefferson Davis Community College (AL) 57
Jefferson State Community College (AL) 57
J. F. Drake State Technical College (AL) 58
JNA Institute of Culinary Arts (PA) 309
John A. Gupton College (TN) 339
John A. Logan College (IL) 145
Johnson College (PA) 309
Johnson County Community College (KS) 172
Johnston Community College (NC) 271
John Tyler Community College (VA) 367
John Wood Community College (IL) 145
Joliet Junior College (IL) 145
Jones County Junior College (MS) 217
J. Sargeant Reynolds Community College (VA) 368
Kalamazoo Valley Community College (MI) 199
Kanawha Valley Community and Technical College (WV) 379
Kankakee Community College (IL) 145
Kansas City Kansas Community College (KS) 172
Kapiolani Community College (HI) 136
Kaplan Career Institute, Harrisburg (PA) 309
Kaplan Career Institute, ICM Campus (PA) 309
Kaplan Career Institute, Nashville Campus (TN) 339
Kaplan College, Arlington (TX) 350
Kaplan College, Bakersfield Campus (CA) 87
Kaplan College, Chula Vista Campus (CA) 87
Kaplan College, Cincinnati Campus (OH) 286
Kaplan College, Columbus Campus (OH) 286
Kaplan College, Dallas (TX) 351
Kaplan College, Dayton Campus (OH) 287
Kaplan College, Denver Campus (CO) 104
Kaplan College, Fresno Campus (CA) 87
Kaplan College, Hammond Campus (IN) 160
Kaplan College–Las Vegas Campus, Las Vegas (NV) 234
Kaplan College, Merrillville Campus (IN) 161
Kaplan College, Modesto Campus (CA) 87
Kaplan College, Northwest Indianapolis Campus (IN) 161
Kaplan College, Palm Springs Campus (CA) 87
Kaplan College, Panorama City Campus (CA) 87
Kaplan College, Pembroke Pines (FL) 118
Kaplan College, Phoenix Campus (AZ) 65
Kaplan College, Riverside Campus (CA) 87
Kaplan College, Sacramento Campus (CA) 87
Kaplan College, San Diego Campus (CA) 88
Kaplan College, Stockton Campus (CA) 88
Kaplan College, Vista Campus (CA) 88
Kaplan University, Lewiston (ME) 183
Kaplan University, South Portland (ME) 183
Kaplan University, Cedar Falls (IA) 164
Kaplan University, Cedar Rapids (IA) 164
Kaplan University, Council Bluffs (IA) 164
Kaplan University, Des Moines (IA) 165
Kaplan University, Hagerstown Campus (MD) 189
Kaplan University, Lincoln (NE) 231
Kaplan University, Omaha (NE) 231
Kaskaskia College (IL) 146
Kauai Community College (HI) 136
KD Studio (TX) 351
Keiser Career College–Greenacres (FL) 118
Kellogg Community College (MI) 199
Kennebec Valley Community College (ME) 183
Kent State University at Ashtabula (OH) 287
Kent State University at East Liverpool (OH) 287
Kent State University at Geauga (OH) 287
Kent State University at Salem (OH) 288
Kent State University at Trumbull (OH) 288
Kent State University at Tuscarawas (OH) 288
Keweenaw Bay Ojibwa Community College (MI) 200
Key College (FL) 118
Keystone Technical Institute (PA) 309
Kilgore College (TX) 351
Kilian Community College (SD) 334
Kingsborough Community College of the City University of New York (NY) 256
King's College (NC) 271
Kirkwood Community College (IA) 165
Kirtland Community College (MI) 200
Kishwaukee College (IL) 146
Klamath Community College (OR) 301
Labette Community College (KS) 172
Labouré College (MA) 193
Lac Courte Oreilles Ojibwa Community College (WI) 383
Lackawanna College (PA) 309
Lake Area Technical Institute (SD) 335
Lake City Community College (FL) 118
Lake Land College (IL) 146
Lakeland Community College (OH) 289
Lake Michigan College (MI) 200
Lake Region State College (ND) 277
Lakeshore Technical College (WI) 383
Lakes Region Community College (NH) 235
Lake-Sumter Community College (FL) 118
Lake Superior College (MN) 209
Lake Tahoe Community College (CA) 88
Lake Washington Technical College (WA) 376
Lamar Community College (CO) 104
Lamar Institute of Technology (TX) 351
Lamar State College–Orange (TX) 351
Lamar State College–Port Arthur (TX) 351
Lamson College (AZ) 65
Lancaster General College of Nursing & Health Sciences (PA) 310
Landmark College (VT) 364, **458**
Lane Community College (OR) 301
Laney College (CA) 88
Lanier Technical College (GA) 131
Lansdale School of Business (PA) 310
Lansing Community College (MI) 201
Laramie County Community College (WY) 390
Laredo Community College (TX) 351
Las Positas College (CA) 88
Lassen Community College District (CA) 88
Laurel Business Institute (PA) 310
Laurel Technical Institute, Meadville (PA) 310
Laurel Technical Institute, Sharon (PA) 310
Lawson State Community College (AL) 58
LDS Business College (UT) 362
Le Cordon Bleu College of Culinary Arts (MN) 209
Le Cordon Bleu College of Culinary Arts, Atlanta (GA) 131
Le Cordon Bleu College of Culinary Arts in Chicago (IL) 146
Le Cordon Bleu College of Culinary Arts, Las Vegas (NV) 234
Le Cordon Bleu College of Culinary Arts, Miami (FL) 119
Leech Lake Tribal College (MN) 209
Lee College (TX) 352
Leeward Community College (HI) 136
Lehigh Carbon Community College (PA) 310
Lenoir Community College (NC) 271
Lewis and Clark Community College (IL) 146
Lincoln College (IL) 147
Lincoln College of New England, Suffield (CT) 108
Lincoln College of Technology (FL) 119
Lincoln Land Community College (IL) 147
Lincoln Technical Institute (IN) 161
Lincoln Technical Institute, Allentown (PA) 311
Lincoln Technical Institute, Philadelphia (PA) 311
Lincoln Technical Institute, Plymouth Meeting (PA) 311
Linn-Benton Community College (OR) 301
Linn State Technical College (MO) 221
Little Big Horn College (MT) 228
Little Priest Tribal College (NE) 231
Lonestar College–Cy-Fair (TX) 352
Lonestar College–Kingwood (TX) 352
Lonestar College–Montgomery (TX) 352
Lonestar College–North Harris (TX) 353
Lonestar College–Tomball (TX) 353
Long Beach City College (CA) 88
Long Island Business Institute (NY) 257
Long Island College Hospital School of Nursing (NY) 257
Lon Morris College (TX) 354
Lorain County Community College (OH) 289
Lord Fairfax Community College (VA) 368
Los Angeles City College (CA) 88, *89*
Los Angeles County College of Nursing and Allied Health (CA) 88
Los Angeles Harbor College (CA) 88
Los Angeles Mission College (CA) 90
Los Angeles Pierce College (CA) 90
Los Angeles Southwest College (CA) 90
Los Angeles Trade-Technical College (CA) 90
Los Angeles Valley College (CA) 90
Los Medanos College (CA) 90
Louisburg College (NC) 271
Louisiana State University at Alexandria (LA) 181
Louisiana State University at Eunice (LA) 181
Louisiana Technical College (LA) 181
Louisiana Technical College–Florida Parishes Campus (LA) 182
Louisiana Technical College–Northeast Louisiana Campus (LA) 182
Louisiana Technical College–Young Memorial Campus (LA) 182
Lower Columbia College (WA) 376
Luna Community College (NM) 242
Lurleen B. Wallace Community College (AL) 58
Luzerne County Community College (PA) 311
MacCormac College (IL) 147
Macomb Community College (MI) 201
Madison Area Technical College (WI) 383
Madison Media Institute (WI) 383
Madisonville Community College (KY) 176
Manchester Community College (CT) 108
Manchester Community College (NH) 235
Manhattan Area Technical College (KS) 172
Manor College (PA) 311, **460**
Marian Court College (MA) 193
Marion Military Institute (AL) 59
Marion Technical College (OH) 289
Marshalltown Community College (IA) 165
Martin Community College (NC) 271
Massachusetts Bay Community College (MA) 193
Massasoit Community College (MA) 193
Maui Community College (HI) 136
Mayland Community College (NC) 271
Maysville Community and Technical College, Maysville (KY) 176
Maysville Community and Technical College, Morehead (KY) 176
McCann School of Business & Technology, Pottsville (PA) 311
McDowell Technical Community College (NC) 272
McHenry County College (IL) 147
McLennan Community College (TX) 354
Medical Careers Institute, Newport News (VA) 368
Medical Careers Institute, Richmond (VA) 368
Medical Careers Institute, Virginia Beach (VA) 368
MedVance Institute (FL) 119
MedVance Institute (LA) 182
MedVance Institute (TN) 339
Memorial Hospital School of Nursing (NY) 257
Mendocino College (CA) 90
Merced College (CA) 90
Mercer County Community College (NJ) 238
Mercyhurst North East, North East (PA) 311
Meridian Community College (MS) 217
Merritt College (CA) 90
Mesabi Range Community and Technical College (MN) 209
Mesa Community College (AZ) 66
Mesalands Community College (NM) 242
Metro Business College, Cape Girardeau (MO) 221
Metro Business College, Jefferson City (MO) 221
Metro Business College, Rolla (MO) 221
Metropolitan Career Center (PA) 311
Metropolitan Community College (NE) 231
Metropolitan Community College–Blue River (MO) 221
Metropolitan Community College–Business & Technology Campus (MO) 222
Metropolitan Community College–Longview (MO) 222
Metropolitan Community College–Maple Woods (MO) 222
Metropolitan Community College–Penn Valley (MO) 223
Miami Dade College (FL) 119, **462**
Miami–Jacobs College (OH) 290
Miami University–Middletown Campus (OH) 290
Mid-America Baptist Theological Seminary (TN) 339
Mid-America College of Funeral Service (IN) 161
Middle Georgia College (GA) 131
Middle Georgia Technical College (GA) 132
Middlesex Community College (CT) 108
Middlesex Community College (MA) 194
Middlesex County College (NJ) 238
Midlands Technical College (SC) 331
Mid Michigan Community College (MI) 202
Mid-Plains Community College, North Platte (NE) 231
Mid-South Community College (AR) 71
Mid-State Technical College (WI) 383
Midwest Institute, Earth City (MO) 223
Midwest Institute, Kirkwood (MO) 223
Mildred Elley School (NY) 257
Miles Community College (MT) 228
Miller-Motte Technical College (SC) 332
Miller-Motte Technical College, Clarksville (TN) 339
Milwaukee Area Technical College (WI) 383
Mineral Area College (MO) 223
Minneapolis Business College (MN) 209
Minneapolis Community and Technical College (MN) 210
Minnesota School of Business–Brooklyn Center (MN) 210
Minnesota School of Business–Plymouth (MN) 210
Minnesota School of Business–Richfield (MN) 210
Minnesota School of Business–St. Cloud (MN) 210
Minnesota School of Business–Shakopee (MN) 210
Minnesota State College–Southeast Technical (MN) 210
Minnesota State Community and Technical College (MN) 211
Minnesota West Community and Technical College (MN) 211
MiraCosta College (CA) *91*
Mission College (CA) 91
Mississippi Delta Community College (MS) 217
Mississippi Gulf Coast Community College (MS) 217
Missouri College (MO) 223
Missouri State University–West Plains (MO) 223
Mitchell Community College (NC) 272
Mitchell Technical Institute (SD) 335
Moberly Area Community College (MO) 224
Modesto Junior College (CA) 91
Mohave Community College (AZ) 66
Mohawk Valley Community College (NY) 257, **464**
Monroe Community College (NY) 258
Monroe County Community College (MI) 202
Montana State University–Great Falls College of Technology (MT) 228
Montcalm Community College (MI) 202
Monterey Peninsula College (CA) 91
Montgomery College (MD) 189
Montgomery Community College (NC) 272
Montgomery County Community College (PA) 311
Moorpark College (CA) 92
Moraine Park Technical College (WI) 384
Moraine Valley Community College (IL) 147
Morgan Community College (CO) 104
Morrison Institute of Technology (IL) 148
Morton College (IL) 148
Motlow State Community College (TN) 339
Mott Community College (MI) 202
Moultrie Technical College (GA) 132
Mountain Empire Community College (VA) 368
Mountain State College (WV) 379

Mountain View College (TX) 354
Mt. Hood Community College (OR) 301
Mt. San Antonio College (CA) 92
Mt. San Jacinto College (CA) 92
Mount Wachusett Community College (MA) 194
Mountwest Community & Technical College (WV) 380, **466**
MTI College of Business & Technology (CA) 92
Murray State College (OK) 296
Muscatine Community College (IA) 165
Muskegon Community College (MI) 202
Myotherapy Institute (NE) 232
Napa Valley College (CA) 92
Nash Community College (NC) 272
Nashua Community College (NH) 235
Nashville Auto Diesel College (TN) 339
Nashville State Technical Community College (TN) 339
Nassau Community College (NY) 258
National American University (KS) 173
National American University, Bloomington (MN) 212
National American University, Brooklyn Center (MN) 212
National American University, Rio Rancho (NM) 242
National American University, Ellsworth AFB (SD) 335
National College, Danville (KY) 177
National College, Florence (KY) 177
National College, Lexington (KY) 177
National College, Louisville (KY) 177
National College, Pikeville (KY) 177
National College, Richmond (KY) 177
National College, Bristol (TN) 339
National College, Knoxville (TN) 340
National College, Nashville (TN) 340
National College, Bluefield (VA) 369
National College, Charlottesville (VA) 369
National College, Danville (VA) 369
National College, Harrisonburg (VA) 369
National College, Lynchburg (VA) 369
National College, Martinsville (VA) 369
National College, Salem (VA) 369
National Park Community College (AR) 71
National Polytechnic College of Science (CA) 92
Naugatuck Valley Community College (CT) 109
Navajo Technical College (NM) 242
Navarro College (TX) 354
Nebraska College of Technical Agriculture (NE) 232
Nebraska Indian Community College (NE) 232
Neosho County Community College (KS) 173
New Castle School of Trades (PA) 312
New England Culinary Institute (VT) 364
New England Culinary Institute at Essex (VT) 364
New England Institute of Technology (RI) 329
New Hampshire Technical Institute (NH) 235
New Mexico Junior College (NM) 242
New Mexico Military Institute (NM) 242
New Mexico State University–Alamogordo (NM) 242
New Mexico State University–Carlsbad (NM) 242
New Mexico State University–Grants (NM) 243
Newport Business Institute, Lower Burrell (PA) 312
Newport Business Institute, Williamsport (PA) 312
New River Community and Technical College (WV) 380
New River Community College (VA) 369
New York Career Institute (NY) 258
New York College of Health Professions (NY) 258
New York Film Academy (CA) 92
NHTI, Concord's Community College (NH) 235
Niagara County Community College (NY) 258
Nicolet Area Technical College (WI) 384
Normandale Community College (MN) 212
Northampton Community College (PA) 312
North Arkansas College (AR) 71
North Central Industrial Technical Education Center (PA) 313
North Central Institute (TN) 340
North Central Kansas Technical College (KS) 173
North Central Michigan College (MI) 203
North Central Missouri College (MO) 224
North Central State College (OH) 290
Northcentral Technical College (WI) 385
North Central Texas College (TX) 354
North Country Community College (NY) 259
North Dakota State College of Science (ND) 278
Northeast Alabama Community College (AL) 59
Northeast Community College (NE) 232
Northeastern Junior College (CO) 104
Northeastern Oklahoma Agricultural and Mechanical College (OK) 296
Northeastern Technical College (SC) 332
Northeast Iowa Community College (IA) 166
Northeast Kansas Technical Center of Highland Community College (KS) 173
Northeast Mississippi Community College (MS) 217
Northeast State Technical Community College (TN) 340
Northeast Texas Community College (TX) 355
Northeast Wisconsin Technical College (WI) 385
Northern Essex Community College (MA) 194
Northern Maine Community College (ME) 184
Northern Marianas College (MP) 278
Northern New Mexico College (NM) 243
Northern Oklahoma College (OK) 296
Northern Virginia Community College (VA) 369
North Florida Community College (FL) 119
North Georgia Technical College (GA) 132
North Hennepin Community College (MN) 212
North Idaho College (ID) 137
North Iowa Area Community College (IA) 166
North Lake College (TX) 355
Northland Community and Technical College–Thief River Falls (MN) 212
Northland Pioneer College (AZ) 66
North Seattle Community College (WA) 376
North Shore Community College (MA) 194
NorthWest Arkansas Community College (AR) 72
Northwest Aviation College (WA) 376
Northwest College (WY) 390
Northwestern College (IL) 148
Northwestern Connecticut Community College (CT) 109
Northwestern Michigan College (MI) 203
Northwest Florida State College (FL) 119
Northwest Indian College (WA) 376
Northwest Iowa Community College (IA) 166
Northwest Kansas Technical College (KS) 173
Northwest Mississippi Community College (MS) 217
Northwest School of Wooden Boatbuilding (WA) 376
Northwest-Shoals Community College (AL) 59
Northwest State Community College (OH) 290
Northwest Technical College (MN) 213
Northwest Technical Institute (MN) 213
Northwest Vista College (TX) 355
Norwalk Community College (CT) 109
Nossi College of Art (TN) 340
Oakbridge Academy of Arts (PA) 313
Oakland Community College (MI) 203
Oakton Community College (IL) 148
Ocean County College (NJ) 238
Odessa College (TX) 355
Ogeechee Technical College (GA) 132
Ohio Business College, Lorain (OH) 290
Ohio Business College, Sandusky (OH) 290
Ohio College of Massotherapy (OH) 290
The Ohio State University Agricultural Technical Institute (OH) 291
Ohio Technical College (OH) 291
Ohio Valley College of Technology (OH) 291
Ohlone College (CA) 92
Okefenokee Technical College (GA) 132
Oklahoma City Community College (OK) 297
Oklahoma State University Institute of Technology (OK) 297
Oklahoma State University, Oklahoma City (OK) 297
Oklahoma Technical College (OK) 297
Olean Business Institute (NY) 259
Olympic College (WA) 376
Onondaga Community College (NY) 259
Orangeburg-Calhoun Technical College (SC) 332
Orange Coast College (CA) 93
Orange County Community College (NY) 259
Oregon Coast Community College (OR) 301
Orlando Culinary Academy (FL) 120
Orleans Technical Institute (PA) 313
Otero Junior College (CO) 105
Ouachita Technical College (AR) 72
Owensboro Community and Technical College (KY) 177
Owens Community College, Toledo (OH) 291
Oxnard College (CA) 93
Ozarka College (AR) 72
Ozarks Technical Community College (MO) 224
Pace Institute (PA) 313
Palau Community College (Palau) 393
Palm Beach State College (FL) 120
Palo Alto College (TX) 356
Palomar College (CA) 93
Palo Verde College (CA) 93
Pamlico Community College (NC) 272
Panola College (TX) 356
Paradise Valley Community College (AZ) 66
The Paralegal Institute, Inc. (AZ) 67
Paris Junior College (TX) 356
Parkland College (IL) 148
Pasadena City College (CA) 93
Pasco-Hernando Community College (FL) 120
Passaic County Community College (NJ) 239
Patrick Henry Community College (VA) 369
Paul D. Camp Community College (VA) 370
Pearl River Community College (MS) 218
Pellissippi State Technical Community College (TN) 340
Peninsula College (WA) 377
Penn Commercial Business and Technical School (PA) 313
Pennco Tech (PA) 313
Penn Foster Career School (PA) 313
Penn State Beaver (PA) 313
Penn State Brandywine (PA) 314
Penn State DuBois (PA) 315
Penn State Fayette, The Eberly Campus (PA) 315
Penn State Greater Allegheny (PA) 316
Penn State Hazleton (PA) 317
Penn State Lehigh Valley (PA) 317
Penn State Mont Alto (PA) 318
Penn State New Kensington (PA) 318
Penn State Schuylkill (PA) 319
Penn State Shenango (PA) 320
Penn State Wilkes-Barre (PA) 320
Penn State Worthington Scranton (PA) 321
Penn State York (PA) 321
Pennsylvania College of Technology (PA) 322, **468**
Pennsylvania Culinary Institute (PA) 323
Pennsylvania Highlands Community College (PA) 323
Pennsylvania Institute of Technology (PA) 323
Pennsylvania School of Business (PA) 324
Pensacola Junior College (FL) 121
Phillips Beth Israel School of Nursing (NY) 259
Phillips Community College of the University of Arkansas (AR) 73
Phoenix College (AZ) 67
Piedmont Community College (NC) 272
Piedmont Technical College (SC) 332
Piedmont Virginia Community College (VA) 370
Pierce College at Puyallup (WA) 377
Pierpont Community & Technical College of Fairmont State University (WV) 380
Pikes Peak Community College (CO) 105
Pima Community College (AZ) 67
Pima Medical Institute, Mesa (AZ) 68
Pima Medical Institute, Tucson (AZ) 68
Pima Medical Institute (CA) 94
Pima Medical Institute, Denver (CO) 105
Pima Medical Institute (NV) 234
Pima Medical Institute (NM) 243
Pima Medical Institute (WA) 377
Pine Technical College (MN) 213
Pinnacle Career Institute (MO) 224
Pitt Community College (NC) 273
Pittsburgh Institute of Aeronautics (PA) 324
Pittsburgh Institute of Mortuary Science, Incorporated (PA) 324
Pittsburgh Technical Institute, Oakdale (PA) 324
The PJA School (PA) 324
Platt College, Cerritos (CA) 94
Platt College, Huntington Beach (CA) 94
Platt College, Ontario (CA) 94
Platt College (CO) 105
Platt College, Moore (OK) 298
Platt College, Oklahoma City (OK) 298
Platt College, Tulsa (OK) 298
Platt College–Los Angeles (CA) 94
Plaza College (NY) 259
Polk State College (FL) 121
Porterville College (CA) 94
Portland Community College (OR) 301
Potomac State College of West Virginia University (WV) 380
Prairie State College (IL) 148
Pratt Community College (KS) 173
Prince George's Community College (MD) 190
Prince Institute of Professional Studies (AL) 59
Professional Golfers Career College (CA) 95
Professional Skills Institute (OH) 292
Provo College (UT) 362
Pueblo Community College (CO) 106
Puerto Rico Technical Junior College, San Juan (PR) 328
Pulaski Technical College (AR) 73
Queensborough Community College of the City University of New York (NY) 260
Quincy College (MA) 195
Quinebaug Valley Community College (CT) 109
Quinsigamond Community College (MA) 195
Rainy River Community College (MN) 213
Ramírez College of Business and Technology (PR) 329
Randolph Community College (NC) 273
Ranger College (TX) 356
Ranken Technical College (MO) 224
Rappahannock Community College (VA) 370
Raritan Valley Community College (NJ) 239
Rasmussen College Aurora (IL) 149
Rasmussen College Bismarck (ND) 278
Rasmussen College Brooklyn Park (MN) 213
Rasmussen College Eagan (MN) 214
Rasmussen College Eden Prairie (MN) 214
Rasmussen College Fargo (ND) 278
Rasmussen College Fort Myers (FL) 122
Rasmussen College Green Bay (WI) 385
Rasmussen College Lake Elmo/Woodbury (MN) 214
Rasmussen College Mankato (MN) 214
Rasmussen College Moorhead (MN) 214
Rasmussen College Ocala (FL) 122
Rasmussen College Pasco County (FL) 122
Rasmussen College Rockford, Illinois (IL) 149
Rasmussen College St. Cloud (MN) 214
Reading Area Community College (PA) 324
Redlands Community College (OK) 298
Red Rocks Community College (CO) 106
Redstone College–Denver (CO) 106
Reedley College (CA) 95
The Refrigeration School (AZ) 68
Reid State Technical College (AL) 59
Remington College–Baton Rouge Campus (LA) 182
Remington College–Cleveland Campus (OH) 292
Remington College–Cleveland West Campus (OH) 292
Remington College–Colorado Springs Campus (CO) 106
Remington College–Dallas Campus (TX) 356
Remington College–Fort Worth Campus (TX) 356
Remington College–Honolulu Campus (HI) 137
Remington College–Houston Campus (TX) 356
Remington College–Houston Southeast (TX) 357
Remington College–Lafayette Campus (LA) 182
Remington College–Largo Campus (FL) 122
Remington College–Little Rock Campus (AR) 73
Remington College–Memphis Campus (TN) 340
Remington College–Mobile Campus (AL) 60
Remington College–Nashville Campus (TN) 340
Remington College–North Houston Campus (TX) 357
Remington College–Shreveport (LA) 182
Remington College–Tampa Campus (FL) 122
Rend Lake College (IL) 149
Renton Technical College (WA) 377
The Restaurant School at Walnut Hill College (PA) 324
Richard Bland College of The College of William and Mary (VA) 370
Richland College (TX) 357
Richland Community College (IL) 149
Richmond Community College (NC) 273
Rich Mountain Community College (AR) 73
Ridgewater College (MN) 214
Rio Hondo College (CA) 95
Rio Salado College (AZ) 68
Riverland Community College (MN) 214
River Parishes Community College (LA) 182
Riverside Community College District (CA) 95
River Valley Community College (NH) 235

Roane State Community College (TN) 340
Roanoke-Chowan Community College (NC) 273
Robeson Community College (NC) 274
Rochester Community and Technical College (MN) 214
Rockford Business College (IL) 149
Rockingham Community College (NC) 274
Rockland Community College (NY) 260
Rock Valley College (IL) 149
Rogue Community College (OR) 302
Rosedale Bible College (OH) 292
Rosedale Technical Institute (PA) 324
Rose State College (OK) 298
Rowan-Cabarrus Community College (NC) 274
Roxbury Community College (MA) 195
Sacramento City College (CA) 95
Saddleback College (CA) 95
Sage College (CA) 95
Saginaw Chippewa Tribal College (MI) 203
St. Catharine College (KY) 177
Saint Charles Community College (MO) 224
St. Clair County Community College (MI) 203
St. Cloud Technical College (MN) 214
St. Elizabeth College of Nursing (NY) 260
St. Johns River Community College (FL) 122
St. Joseph's College of Nursing (NY) 260
St. Louis College of Health Careers (MO) 225
St. Louis Community College at Florissant Valley (MO) 225
St. Louis Community College at Forest Park (MO) 225
St. Louis Community College at Meramec (MO) 225
St. Luke's College (IA) 166
Saint Paul College–A Community & Technical College (MN) 215
St. Paul's School of Nursing (NY) 261
St. Philip's College (TX) 357
St. Vincent's College (CT) 109
Salem Community College (NJ) 239
Salish Kootenai College (MT) 229
Salt Lake Community College (UT) 362
The Salvation Army College for Officer Training at Crestmont (CA) 95
Samaritan Hospital School of Nursing (NY) 261
Sampson Community College (NC) 274
San Antonio College (TX) 357
San Bernardino Valley College (CA) 95
Sandersville Technical College (GA) 133
Sandhills Community College (NC) 274
San Diego City College (CA) 95
San Diego Golf Academy (CA) 96
San Diego Mesa College (CA) 96
San Diego Miramar College (CA) 96
Sanford-Brown College, Fenton (MO) 225
Sanford-Brown College, Hazelwood (MO) 225
Sanford-Brown College, St. Peters (MO) 225
Sanford-Brown Institute, Fort Lauderdale (FL) 122
Sanford-Brown Institute, Jacksonville (FL) 122
Sanford-Brown Institute, Tampa (FL) 122
Sanford-Brown Institute–Monroeville (PA) 325
Sanford-Brown Institute–Pittsburgh (PA) 325
San Jacinto College District (TX) 357
San Joaquin Delta College (CA) 97
San Joaquin Valley College, Bakersfield (CA) 97
San Joaquin Valley College, Visalia (CA) 97
San Joaquin Valley College–Fresno Aviation Campus (CA) 97
San Joaquin Valley College–Online (CA) 97
San Jose City College (CA) 97
San Juan College (NM) 243
Santa Ana College (CA) 97
Santa Barbara City College (CA) 97
Santa Fe Community College (NM) 244
Santa Monica College (CA) 97
Santa Rosa Junior College (CA) 98
Santiago Canyon College (CA) 98
Sauk Valley Community College (IL) 149
Savannah River College (GA) 133
Savannah Technical College (GA) 133
Schenectady County Community College (NY) 261
Schoolcraft College (MI) 203
School of Advertising Art (OH) 292
School of Communication Arts (NC) 275
School of Urban Missions (CA) 98
Scott Community College (IA) 167
Scottsdale Community College (AZ) 68
Scottsdale Culinary Institute (AZ) 69
Seattle Central Community College (WA) 377
Seminole State College (OK) 298
Seminole State College of Florida (FL) 122
Sessions College for Professional Design (AZ) 69
Seward County Community College (KS) 173
Shasta College (CA) 98
Shawnee Community College (IL) 150
Shelton State Community College (AL) 60
Sheridan College (WY) 391
Shoreline Community College (WA) 377
Sierra College (CA) 98
Simmons Institute of Funeral Service (NY) 261
Sinclair Community College (OH) 292
Sisseton-Wahpeton Community College (SD) 335
Sitting Bull College (ND) 278
Skagit Valley College (WA) 377
Skyline College (CA) 99
Snead State Community College (AL) 60
Snow College (UT) 363
Solano Community College (CA) 99
Solex College (IL) 150
Somerset Community College (KY) 177
South Arkansas Community College (AR) 73
South Central College (MN) 215
South Coast College (CA) 99
South College–Asheville (NC) 275
Southeast Arkansas College (AR) 73
Southeast Community College, Beatrice Campus (NE) 233
Southeast Community College, Lincoln Campus (NE) 233
Southeast Community College, Milford Campus (NE) 233
Southeastern Community College (IA) 167
Southeastern Community College (NC) 275
Southeastern Illinois College (IL) 150
Southeastern Technical College (GA) 133
Southeast Kentucky Community and Technical College (KY) 178
Southeast Missouri Hospital College of Nursing and Health Sciences (MO) 225
Southeast Technical Institute (SD) 335
Southern Alberta Institute of Technology (AB, Canada) 392
Southern Arkansas University Tech (AR) 73
Southern Maine Community College (ME) 184
Southern State Community College (OH) 292
Southern Union State Community College (AL) 60
Southern University at Shreveport (LA) 182
Southern West Virginia Community and Technical College (WV) 380
South Florida Community College (FL) 123
South Georgia College (GA) 133
South Georgia Technical College (GA) 134
South Hills School of Business & Technology, Altoona (PA) 325
South Hills School of Business & Technology, State College (PA) 325
South Mountain Community College (AZ) 69
South Piedmont Community College (NC) 275
South Plains College (TX) 358
South Puget Sound Community College (WA) 378
South Seattle Community College (WA) 378
Southside Virginia Community College (VA) 370
South Suburban College (IL) 150
South Texas College (TX) 358
Southwestern College (CA) 99
Southwestern College of Business (KY) 178
Southwestern College of Business, Cincinnati (OH) 292
Southwestern College of Business, Cincinnati (OH) 292
Southwestern College of Business, Dayton (OH) 293
Southwestern College of Business, Franklin (OH) 293
Southwestern Community College (IA) 167
Southwestern Community College (NC) 275
Southwestern Illinois College (IL) 150
Southwestern Indian Polytechnic Institute (NM) 244
Southwestern Michigan College (MI) 203
Southwestern Oklahoma State University at Sayre (OK) 298
Southwestern Oregon Community College (OR) 302
Southwest Florida College, Tampa (FL) 123
Southwest Georgia Technical College (GA) 134
Southwest Institute of Healing Arts (AZ) 69
Southwest Institute of Technology (TX) 358
Southwest Mississippi Community College (MS) 218
Southwest Tennessee Community College (TN) 340
Southwest Texas Junior College (TX) 358
Southwest Virginia Community College (VA) 371
Southwest Wisconsin Technical College (WI) 385
Spartanburg Community College (SC) 332
Spartanburg Methodist College (SC) 333
Spartan College of Aeronautics and Technology (OK) 298
Spencerian College (KY) 178
Spencerian College–Lexington (KY) 178
Spokane Community College (WA) 378
Spokane Falls Community College (WA) 378
Spoon River College (IL) 151
Springfield College in Illinois (IL) 151
Springfield Technical Community College (MA) 195
Stanbridge College (CA) 99
Stanly Community College (NC) 275
Stark State College of Technology (OH) 293
State College of Florida Manatee-Sarasota (FL) 123
State Fair Community College (MO) 226
State University of New York College of Environmental Science & Forestry, Ranger School (NY) 261, **470**
State University of New York College of Technology at Alfred (NY) 261
Stautzenberger College (OH) 293
Stone Child College (MT) 229
Suffolk County Community College (NY) 262
Sullivan College of Technology and Design (KY) 178
Sullivan County Community College (NY) 262
Surry Community College (NC) 275
Sussex County Community College (NJ) 239
Tacoma Community College (WA) 378
Taft College (CA) 99
Tallahassee Community College (FL) 123
Tarrant County College District (TX) 358
Taylor Business Institute (IL) 151
Taylor Business Institute (NY) 262
TCI–The College of Technology (NY) 262
Technical College of the Lowcountry (SC) 333
Temple College (TX) 359
Terra State Community College (OH) 293
TESST College of Technology, Baltimore (MD) 190
TESST College of Technology, Beltsville (MD) 190
TESST College of Technology, Towson (MD) 190
TESST College of Technology (VA) 371
Texarkana College (TX) 359
Texas Culinary Academy (TX) 359
Texas Southmost College (TX) 359
Texas State Technical College Harlingen (TX) 359
Texas State Technical College–Marshall (TX) 359
Texas State Technical College Waco (TX) 360
Texas State Technical College West Texas (TX) 360
Thaddeus Stevens College of Technology (PA) 325
Thomas Nelson Community College (VA) 371
Three Rivers Community College (CT) 109
Three Rivers Community College (MO) 226
Tidewater Community College (VA) 371
Tillamook Bay Community College (OR) 302
Tohono O'odham Community College (AZ) 69
Tompkins Cortland Community College (NY) 262
Treasure Valley Community College (OR) 302
Triangle Tech–Greensburg School (PA) 325
Triangle Tech Inc–Bethlehem (PA) 325
Triangle Tech, Inc.–DuBois School (PA) 325
Triangle Tech, Inc.–Erie School (PA) 326
Triangle Tech, Inc.–Pittsburgh School (PA) 326
Triangle Tech, Inc.–Sunbury School (PA) 326
Tri-County Community College (NC) 275
Tri-County Technical College (SC) 333
Trident Technical College (SC) 333
Trinidad State Junior College (CO) 107
Trinity Valley Community College (TX) 360
Tri-State Business Institute (PA) 326
Triton College (IL) 151
Trocaire College (NY) 263
Truckee Meadows Community College (NV) 234
Trumbull Business College (OH) 294
Tulsa Community College (OK) 298
Tulsa Welding School (OK) 299
Tunxis Community College (CT) 110
Turtle Mountain Community College (ND) 278
Tyler Junior College (TX) 360
Ulster County Community College (NY) 263
Umpqua Community College (OR) 302
Union County College (NJ) 240
United Tribes Technical College (ND) 278
Universal Technical Institute (AZ) 69
Universal Technical Institute (TX) 360
Universidad Central del Caribe (PR) 329
The University of Akron–Wayne College (OH) 294
University of Alaska Anchorage, Kenai Peninsula College (AK) 60
University of Alaska Anchorage, Kodiak College (AK) 61
University of Alaska Anchorage, Matanuska-Susitna College (AK) 61
University of Alaska, Prince William Sound Community College (AK) 61
University of Alaska Southeast, Ketchikan Campus (AK) 61
University of Alaska Southeast, Sitka Campus (AK) 61
University of Arkansas Community College at Batesville (AR) 74
University of Arkansas Community College at Hope (AR) 74
University of Arkansas Community College at Morrilton (AR) 74
University of Cincinnati Clermont College (OH) 294
University of Cincinnati Raymond Walters College (OH) 294
The University of Montana–Helena College of Technology (MT) 229
University of New Mexico–Gallup (NM) 244
University of New Mexico–Los Alamos Branch (NM) 244
University of New Mexico–Taos (NM) 244
University of New Mexico–Valencia Campus (NM) 244
University of Northwestern Ohio (OH) 294
University of Pittsburgh at Titusville (PA) 326
University of Puerto Rico at Carolina (PR) 329
University of South Carolina Lancaster (SC) 333
University of South Carolina Salkehatchie (SC) 334
University of South Carolina Sumter (SC) 334
University of South Carolina Union (SC) 334
University of Wisconsin–Baraboo/Sauk County (WI) 386
University of Wisconsin–Barron County (WI) 386
University of Wisconsin–Fond du Lac (WI) 386
University of Wisconsin–Fox Valley (WI) 386
University of Wisconsin–Manitowoc (WI) 386
University of Wisconsin–Marathon County (WI) 386
University of Wisconsin–Marinette (WI) 387
University of Wisconsin–Marshfield/Wood County (WI) 387
University of Wisconsin–Richland (WI) 387
University of Wisconsin–Rock County (WI) 387
University of Wisconsin–Sheboygan (WI) 387
University of Wisconsin–Washington County (WI) 387
University of Wisconsin–Waukesha (WI) 387
Urban College of Boston (MA) 196
Utah Career College (UT) 363
Utah Career College–Layton Campus (UT) 363
Utica School of Commerce (NY) 263
Valdosta Technical College (GA) 134
Valencia Community College (FL) 124
Valley College of Technology, Martinsburg (WV) 381
Valley Forge Military College (PA) 327, **472**
Vance-Granville Community College (NC) 276
Vatterott College (IA) 168
Vatterott College, Kansas City (MO) 226
Vatterott College, O'Fallon (MO) 226
Vatterott College, St. Ann (MO) 226
Vatterott College, St. Joseph (MO) 226
Vatterott College, St. Louis (MO) 227
Vatterott College, Springfield (MO) 227
Vatterott College, Omaha (NE) 233
Vatterott College (OH) 294
Vatterott College, Oklahoma City (OK) 299
Vatterott College, Tulsa (OK) 299
Vatterott College (TN) 340
Ventura College (CA) 99
Vermilion Community College (MN) 215
Vernon College (TX) 360
Vet Tech Institute (PA) 327
Vet Tech Institute at Bradford School (OH) 294
Vet Tech Institute at Fox College (IL) 151
Vet Tech Institute at Hickey College (MO) 227

Vet Tech Institute at International Business College, Fort Wayne (IN) 161
Vet Tech Institute at International Business College, Indianapolis (IN) 161
Vet Tech Institute of Houston (TX) 360
Victoria College (TX) 360
Victor Valley College (CA) 99
Vincennes University (IN) 161
Vincennes University Jasper Campus (IN) 161
Virginia College at Austin (TX) 361
Virginia College at Jackson (MS) 218
Virginia Highlands Community College (VA) 372
Virginia Marti College of Art and Design (OH) 295
Virginia Western Community College (VA) 372
Volunteer State Community College (TN) 340
Wade College (TX) 361
Wake Technical Community College (NC) 276
Wallace State Community College (AL) 60
Walla Walla Community College (WA) 378
Walters State Community College (TN) 341
Warren County Community College (NJ) 240
Washington County Community College (ME) 184
Washington State Community College (OH) 295
Washtenaw Community College (MI) 204
Waubonsee Community College (IL) 151
Waukesha County Technical College (WI) 388
Waycross College (GA) 134
Wayne Community College (NC) 276
Wayne County Community College District (MI) 204
Weatherford College (TX) 361
Wenatchee Valley College (WA) 378
Wentworth Military Academy and College (MO) 227
Westchester Community College (NY) 263
Western Career College, Emeryville (CA) 100
Western Career College, Fremont (CA) 100
Western Career College, Pleasant Hill (CA) 100
Western Career College, Sacramento (CA) 100
Western Career College, San Jose (CA) 100
Western Career College, San Leandro (CA) 100
Western Career College, Walnut Creek (CA) 100
Western Culinary Institute (OR) 303
Western Dakota Technical Institute (SD) 336
Western Iowa Tech Community College (IA) 168
Western Nebraska Community College (NE) 233
Western Nevada College (NV) 234
Western Oklahoma State College (OK) 299
Western Piedmont Community College (NC) 276
Western Technical College, El Paso (TX) 361
Western Technical College, El Paso (TX) 361
Western Technical College (WI) 388
Western Texas College (TX) 361
Western Wyoming Community College (WY) 391
West Georgia Technical College (GA) 134
West Hills Community College (CA) 100
Westhill University (Mexico) 393
West Kentucky Community and Technical College (KY) 179
West Los Angeles College (CA) 100
Westmoreland County Community College (PA) 327
West Shore Community College (MI) 204
West Valley College (CA) 100
West Virginia Business College, Nutter Fort (WV) 381
West Virginia Business College, Wheeling (WV) 381
West Virginia Junior College, Bridgeport (WV) 381
West Virginia Junior College, Charleston (WV) 381
West Virginia Junior College, Morgantown (WV) 381
West Virginia Northern Community College (WV) 381
West Virginia University at Parkersburg (WV) 381
Westwood College–Houston South Campus (TX) 361
Wharton County Junior College (TX) 361
Whatcom Community College (WA) 378
White Mountains Community College (NH) 235
Wichita Area Technical College (KS) 173
Wilkes Community College (NC) 276
Williamsburg Technical College (SC) 334
The Williamson Free School of Mechanical Trades (PA) 328
Williston State College (ND) 278
Wilson Community College (NC) 276
Windward Community College (HI) 137
Wisconsin Indianhead Technical College (WI) 388
Woodland Community College (CA) 100
Wood Tobe–Coburn School (NY) 264
Worsham College of Mortuary Science (IL) 151
Wor-Wic Community College (MD) 190
Wright State University, Lake Campus (OH) 295
WyoTech, Fremont (CA) 100
WyoTech, West Sacramento (CA) 101
WyoTech (PA) 328
WyoTech (WY) 392
Wytheville Community College (VA) 372
Yakima Valley Community College (WA) 378
Yavapai College (AZ) 69
York County Community College (ME) 184
York Technical College (SC) 334
Yorktowne Business Institute (PA) 328
YTI Career Institute–York (PA) 328
Yuba College (CA) 101
Zane State College (OH) 295